International Directory of
COMPANY HISTORIES

International Directory of
COMPANY
HISTORIES

VOLUME 106

Editors

Derek Jacques and Paula Kepos

ST. JAMES PRESS
A part of Gale, Cengage Learning

GALE
CENGAGE Learning

Detroit • New York • San Francisco • New Haven, Conn • Waterville, Maine • London

GALE
CENGAGE Learning

International Directory of Company Histories, Volume 106

Dereck Jacques and Paula Kepos, Editors

Project Editor: Miranda H. Ferrara

Editorial: Virgil Burton, Donna Craft, Louise Gagné, Peggy Geeseman, Julie Gough, Sonya Hill, Keith Jones, Lynn Pearce, Laura Peterson, Holly Selden, Justine Ventimiglia

Production Technology Specialist: Mike Weaver

Imaging and Multimedia: John Watkins

Composition and Electronic Prepress: Gary Leach, Evi Seoud

Manufacturing: Rhonda Dover

Product Manager: Jenai Drouillard

For product information and technology assistance, contact us at **Gale Customer Support, 1-800-877-4253.**
For permission to use material from this text or product, submit all requests online at **www.cengage.com/permissions.**
Further permissions questions can be emailed to **permissionrequest@cengage.com**

Gale
27500 Drake Rd.
Farmington Hills, MI, 48331-3535

LIBRARY OF CONGRESS CATALOG NUMBER 89-190943
ISBN-13: 978-1-55862-640-9
ISBN-10: 1-55862-640-9

This title is also available as an e-book
ISBN-13: 978-1-55862-769-7 ISBN-10: 1-55862-769-3
Contact your Gale, a part of Cengage Learning sales representative for ordering information.

BRITISH LIBRARY CATALOGUING IN PUBLICATION DATA
International directory of company histories, Vol. 106
Dereck Jacques and Paula Kepos
33.87409

Contents

Preface vii
Notes on Contributors ix
List of Abbreviations xi

Absa Group Ltd. 1
Acadia Realty Trust 6
Adobe Systems Inc. 11
Affymetrix Inc. 18
Alliant Energy Corporation 25
Alpha Natural Resources Inc. 30
Amedisys, Inc. 34
Anadarko Petroleum
    Corporation 38
Andretti Green Racing 44
Atlas Van Lines Inc. 49
Banner Corporation 54
Bernard L. Madoff Investment
    Securities LLC 58
Bidvest Group Ltd. 63
Brightpoint Inc. 68
Brocade Communications Systems
    Inc. 75
Bulgari S.p.A. 82
Cadence Financial Corporation 88
Calumet Specialty Products Partners,
    L.P. 93
CAMAC International
    Corporation 97
Centex Corporation 100

Chicago Symphony Orchestra 105
Chicken of the Sea
    International 110
ChildFund International 114
Concur Technologies, Inc. 118
Conexant Systems Inc. 123
CryptoLogic Limited 129
D.A. Davidson & Company 133
Dannon Company, Inc. 138
Digital Angel Corporation 143
Disney/ABC Television Group 149
DLA Piper 155
Dollar General Corporation 159
DreamWorks Animation
    SKG, Inc. 163
DW II Distribution Co. LLC 168
EOG Resources 174
Exxaro Resources Ltd. 178
EZchip Semiconductor Ltd. 182
Fiserv, Inc. 186
Four Seasons Hotels Limited 191
Fyffes PLC 196
Gianni Versace S.p.A. 202
Globe Newspaper Company Inc. . .208
The Habitat Company LLC 213
Habitat for Humanity International,
    Inc. 218
Harley-Davidson, Inc. 223

Hittite Microwave
  Corporation 229
Hologic, Inc. 233
ICU Medical, Inc. 237
Interactive Intelligence Inc. 243
Jacobs Engineering Group Inc. ...248
The Jim Henson Company 255
John F. Kennedy Center for the
  Performing Arts 260
KBR Inc. 264
Key Technology Inc. 271
Lambda Legal Defense and Education
  Fund, Inc. 276
Las Vegas Sands Corp. 281
LodgeNet Interactive
  Corporation 285
Man Group PLC 290
Moen Inc. 295
Mozilla Foundation 299
MTN Group Ltd. 304
Museum of Modern Art 308
Namco Bandai Holdings Inc. 313
National Council of La Raza 320
NSTAR 324
Olympus Corporation 332
Oplink Communications, Inc. 337
Otto Group 342
People's United Financial Inc. 349
Perry Ellis International Inc. 353
Peter Pan Bus Lines Inc. 359
The Phillies 364
Piedmont Investment Advisors,
  LLC 369

Plantronics, Inc. 373
Plum Creek Timber
  Company, Inc. 378
Quest Diagnostics Inc. 383
Random House Inc. 388
Raycom Media, Inc. 399
Regions Financial Corporation 403
Republic Engineered Products
  Inc. 408
Research in Motion Limited 415
Rockwell Collins 423
Rosneft 428
SENTEL Corporation 432
Southern Sun Hotel Interest
  (Pty) Ltd. 435
Sport Supply Group, Inc. 440
Starent Networks Corp. 446
Sterling Financial Corporation 451
Tecmo Koei Holdings
  Company Ltd. 456
Telkom S.A. Ltd. 460
3Com Corporation 462
Trustmark Corporation 473
Ubisoft Entertainment S.A. 477
Vodacom Group Pty. Ltd. 481
Webster Financial Corporation ...486
Westwood One Inc. 490
Wintrust Financial Corporation ...497
Wipro Limited 502
WWRD Holdings Limited 508

Cumulative Index to Companies 517
Index to Industries 605
Geographic Index 675

Preface

The St. James Press series *The International Directory of Company Histories* (*IDCH*) is intended for reference use by students, business people, librarians, historians, economists, investors, job candidates, and others who seek to learn more about the historical development of the world's most important companies. To date, *IDCH* has covered more than 10,435 companies in 106 volumes.

INCLUSION CRITERIA

Most companies chosen for inclusion in *IDCH* have achieved a minimum of US$25 million in annual sales and are leading influences in their industries or geographical locations. Companies may be publicly held, private, or nonprofit. State-owned companies that are important in their industries and that may operate much like public or private companies also are included. Wholly owned subsidiaries and divisions are profiled if they meet the requirements for inclusion. Entries on companies that have had major changes since they were last profiled may be selected for updating.

The *IDCH* series highlights 25% private and nonprofit companies, and features updated entries on approximately 35 companies per volume.

ENTRY FORMAT

Each entry begins with the company's legal name; the address of its headquarters; its telephone, toll-free, and fax numbers; and its web site. A statement of public, private, state, or parent ownership follows. A company with a legal name in both English and the language of its headquarters country is listed by the English name, with the native-language name in parentheses.

The company's founding or earliest incorporation date, the number of employees, and the most recent available sales figures follow. Sales figures are given in local currencies with equivalents in U.S. dollars. For some private companies, sales figures are estimates and indicated by the abbreviation *est*. The entry lists the exchanges on which the company's stock is traded and its ticker symbol, as well as the company's NAICS codes.

Entries generally contain a *Company Perspectives* box which provides a short summary of the company's mission, goals, and ideals; a *Key Dates* box highlighting milestones in the company's history; lists of *Principal Subsidiaries*, *Principal Divisions*, *Principal Operating Units*, *Principal Competitors*; and articles for *Further Reading*.

American spelling is used throughout *IDCH*, and the word "billion" is used in its U.S. sense of one thousand million.

SOURCES

Entries have been compiled from publicly accessible sources both in print and on the Internet such as general and academic periodicals, books, and annual reports, as well as material supplied by the companies themselves.

CUMULATIVE INDEXES

IDCH contains three indexes: the **Cumulative Index to Companies**, which provides an alphabetical index to companies profiled in the *IDCH* series, the **Index to Industries**, which allows researchers to locate companies by their principal industry, and the **Geographic Index**, which lists companies alphabetically by the country of their headquarters. The indexes are cumulative and specific instructions for using them are found immediately preceding each index.

SPECIAL TO THIS VOLUME

This volume of *IDCH* contains an entry on Bernard L. Madoff Inverment Securities LLC, the company at the center of the largest investment fraud case in hitory.

SUGGESTIONS WELCOME

Comments and suggestions from users of *IDCH* on any aspect of the product as well as suggestions for companies to be included or updated are cordially invited. Please write:

The Editor
International Directory of Company Histories
St. James Press
Gale, Cengage Learning
27500 Drake Rd.
Farmington Hills, Michigan 48331-3535

St. James Press does not endorse any of the companies or products mentioned in this series. Companies appearing in the *International Directory of Company Histories* were selected without reference to their wishes and have in no way endorsed their entries.

Notes on Contributors

Stephen V. Beitel
Writer and copyeditor based in East Amherst, New York.

Joyce Helena Brusin
Writer and essayist; contributor to the *Encyclopedia of World Governments*.

Melanie Bush
Journalist and teacher in upstate New York.

Melissa Doak
Writer and editor based in Ithaca, New York.

Robert Jacobson
Writer, musician, and communications consultant based in Madison, Wisconsin.

Brenda Kubiac
Business writer and researcher; contributor to *Notable Hispanic American Women*, *Women in World History*, *American Men and Women of Science*, *Contemporary Black Biography*, *Encyclopedia of Emerging Industries*, and *Encyclopedia of American Industries*.

R. Anthony Kugler
Writer and researcher in Madison, Wisconsin; contributor to *Gale Encyclopedia of World History: Governments*, *Contemporary Black Biography*, and *Literature Online*; holder of a doctorate in classics and author of a chapter for *Greek Romans and Roman Greeks* (2002).

Judson MacLaury
Retired historian of the U.S. Department of Labor; author of *To Advance Their Opportunities* (2008) and of numerous articles, reviews, and encyclopedia entries.

Doris Maxfield
Michigan-based editorial services professional specializing in reference works, textbooks, and nonprofit grants.

Stephen Meyer
Writer and editor based in Missoula, Montana.

Margaret L. Moser
Writer based in New York City; licensed attorney, former COO of boutique financial consulting firm, and onetime actor and director.

Marie O'Sullivan
Researcher, writer, and editor based in Ireland; expertise includes international education, student mobility, and globalization; editor and writer for the IIEPassport Study Abroad Directories.

Ann E. Robertson
Washington, D.C.–based writer and editor of economic policy studies.

Diane E. Telgen
Writer based in Michigan; author of *Defining Moments: Brown vs. Board of Education* (2005) and contributor to numerous reference series, including *The Industrial Revolution in America* and *Biography Today*.

Gillian Wolf
Writer and teacher living in Skokie, Illinois.

List of Abbreviations

¥ Japanese yen
£ United Kingdom pound
$ United States dollar

A

AB Aktiebolag (Finland, Sweden)
AB Oy Aktiebolag Osakeyhtiot (Finland)
A.E. Anonimos Eteria (Greece)
AED Emirati dirham
AG Aktiengesellschaft (Austria, Germany, Switzerland, Liechtenstein)
aG auf Gegenseitigkeit (Austria, Germany)
A.m.b.a. Andelsselskab med begraenset ansvar (Denmark)
A.O. Anonim Ortaklari/Ortakligi (Turkey)
ApS Amparteselskab (Denmark)
ARS Argentine peso
A.S. Anonim Sirketi (Turkey)
A/S Aksjeselskap (Norway)
A/S Aktieselskab (Denmark, Sweden)
Ay Avoinyhtio (Finland)
ATS Austrian shilling
AUD Australian dollar
ApS Amparteselskab (Denmark)
Ay Avoinyhtio (Finland)

B

B.A. Buttengewone Aansprakeiijkheid (Netherlands)
BEF Belgian franc

BHD Bahraini dinar
Bhd. Berhad (Malaysia, Brunei)
BND Brunei dollar
BRL Brazilian real
B.V. Besloten Vennootschap (Belgium, Netherlands)

C

C.A. Compania Anonima (Ecuador, Venezuela)
CAD Canadian dollar
C. de R.L. Compania de Responsabilidad Limitada (Spain)
CEO Chief Executive Officer
CFO Chief Financial Officer
CHF Swiss franc
Cia. Companhia (Brazil, Portugal)
Cia. Compania (Latin America [except Brazil], Spain)
Cia. Compagnia (Italy)
Cie. Compagnie (Belgium, France, Luxembourg, Netherlands)
CIO Chief Information Officer
CLP Chilean peso
CNY Chinese yuan
Co. Company
COO Chief Operating Officer
Coop. Cooperative
COP Colombian peso
Corp. Corporation
C. por A. Compania por Acciones (Dominican Republic)
CPT Cuideachta Phoibi Theoranta

(Republic of Ireland)
CRL Companhia a Responsabilidao Limitida (Portugal, Spain)
C.V. Commanditaire Vennootschap (Netherlands, Belgium)
CZK Czech koruna

D

D&B Dunn & Bradstreet
DEM German deutsche mark
Div. Division (United States)
DKK Danish krone
DM Deutsche Mark (W. Germany to 1990; unified Germany to 2002
DZD Algerian dinar

E

EC Exempt Company (Arab countries)
Edms. Bpk. Eiendoms Beperk (South Africa)
EEK Estonian Kroon
eG eingetragene Genossenschaft (Germany)
EGMBH Eingetragene Genossenschaft mit beschraenkter Haftung (Austria, Germany)
EGP Egyptian pound
Ek For Ekonomisk Forening (Sweden)
EP Empresa Portuguesa (Portugal)
E.P.E. Etema Pemorismenis Evthynis (Greece)

ESOP Employee Stock Options and Ownership
ESP Spanish peseta
Et(s). Etablissement(s) (Belgium, France, Luxembourg)
eV eingetragener Verein (Germany)
EUR euro

F

FIM Finnish markka
FRF French franc

G

G.I.E. Groupement d'Interet Economique (France)
gGmbH gemeinnutzige Gesellschaft mit beschraenkter Haftung (Austria, Germany, Switzerland)
G.I.E. Groupement d'Interet Economique (France)
GmbH Gesellschaft mit beschraenkter Haftung (Austria, Germany, Switzerland)
GRD Greek drachma
GWA Gewerbte Amt (Austria, Germany)

H

HB Handelsbolag (Sweden)
HF Hlutafelag (Iceland)
HKD Hong Kong dollar
HUF Hungarian forint

I

IDR Indonesian rupiah
IEP Irish pound
ILS new Israeli shekel
Inc. Incorporated (United States, Canada)
INR Indian rupee
IPO Initial Public Offering
I/S Interesentselskap (Norway)
I/S Interessentselskab (Denmark)
ISK Icelandic krona
ITL Italian lira

J

JMD Jamaican dollar
JOD Jordanian dinar

K

KB Kommanditbolag (Sweden)
KES Kenyan schilling
Kft Korlatolt Felelossegu Tarsasag (Hungary)

KG Kommanditgesellschaft (Austria, Germany, Switzerland)
KGaA Kommanditgesellschaft auf Aktien (Austria, Germany, Switzerland)
KK Kabushiki Kaisha (Japan)
KPW North Korean won
KRW South Korean won
K/S Kommanditselskab (Denmark)
K/S Kommandittselskap (Norway)
KWD Kuwaiti dinar
Ky Kommandiitiyhtio (Finland)

L

LBO Leveraged Buyout
Lda. Limitada (Spain)
L.L.C. Limited Liability Company (Arab countries, Egypt, Greece, United States)
L.L.P. Limited Liability Partnership (United States)
L.P. Limited Partnership (Canada, South Africa, United Kingdom, United States)
Ltd. Limited
Ltda. Limitada (Brazil, Portugal)
Ltee. Limitee (Canada, France)
LUF Luxembourg franc

M

mbH mit beschraenkter Haftung (Austria, Germany)
Mij. Maatschappij (Netherlands)
MUR Mauritian rupee
MXN Mexican peso
MYR Malaysian ringgit

N

N.A. National Association (United States)
NGN Nigerian naira
NLG Netherlands guilder
NOK Norwegian krone
N.V. Naamloze Vennootschap (Belgium, Netherlands)
NZD New Zealand dollar

O

OAO Otkrytoe Aktsionernoe Obshchestve (Russia)
OHG Offene Handelsgesellschaft (Austria, Germany, Switzerland)
OMR Omani rial
OOO Obschestvo s Ogranichennoi

Otvetstvennostiu (Russia)
OOUR Osnova Organizacija Udruzenog Rada (Yugoslavia)
Oy Osakeyhtî (Finland)

P

P.C. Private Corp. (United States)
PEN Peruvian Nuevo Sol
PHP Philippine peso
PKR Pakistani rupee
P/L Part Lag (Norway)
PLC Public Limited Co. (United Kingdom, Ireland)
P.L.L.C. Professional Limited Liability Corporation (United States)
PLN Polish zloty
P.T. Perusahaan/Perseroan Terbatas (Indonesia)
PTE Portuguese escudo
Pte. Private (Singapore)
Pty. Proprietary (Australia, South Africa, United Kingdom)
Pvt. Private (India, Zimbabwe)
PVBA Personen Vennootschap met Beperkte Aansprakelijkheid (Belgium)
PYG Paraguay guarani

Q

QAR Qatar riyal

R

REIT Real Estate Investment Trust
RMB Chinese renminbi
Rt Reszvenytarsasag (Hungary)
RUB Russian ruble

S

S.A. Société Anonyme (Arab countries, Belgium, France, Jordan, Luxembourg, Switzerland)
S.A. Sociedad Anónima (Latin America [except Brazil], Spain, Mexico)
S.A. Sociedades Anônimas (Brazil, Portugal)
SAA Societe Anonyme Arabienne (Arab countries)
S.A.B. de C.V. Sociedad Anónima Bursátil de Capital Variable (Mexico)
S.A.C. Sociedad Anonima Comercial (Latin America [except Brazil])

S.A.C.I. Sociedad Anonima Comercial e Industrial (Latin America [except Brazil])

S.A.C.I.y.F. Sociedad Anonima Comercial e Industrial y Financiera (Latin America [except Brazil])

S.A. de C.V. Sociedad Anonima de Capital Variable (Mexico)

SAK Societe Anonyme Kuweitienne (Arab countries)

SAL Societe Anonyme Libanaise (Arab countries)

SAO Societe Anonyme Omanienne (Arab countries)

SAQ Societe Anonyme Qatarienne (Arab countries)

SAR Saudi riyal

S.A.R.L. Sociedade Anonima de Responsabilidade Limitada (Brazil, Portugal)

S.A.R.L. Société à Responsabilité Limitée (France, Belgium, Luxembourg)

S.A.S. Societá in Accomandita Semplice (Italy)

S.A.S. Societe Anonyme Syrienne (Arab countries)

S.C. Societe en Commandite (Belgium, France, Luxembourg)

S.C.A. Societe Cooperativa Agricole (France, Italy, Luxembourg)

S.C.I. Sociedad Cooperativa Ilimitada (Spain)

S.C.L. Sociedad Cooperativa Limitada (Spain)

S.C.R.L. Societe Cooperative a Responsabilite Limitee (Belgium)

Sdn. Bhd. Sendirian Berhad (Malaysia)

SEK Swedish krona

SGD Singapore dollar

S.L. Sociedad Limitada (Latin America [except Brazil], Portugal, Spain)

S/L Salgslag (Norway)

S.N.C. Société en Nom Collectif (France)

Soc. Sociedad (Latin America [except Brazil], Spain)

Soc. Sociedade (Brazil, Portugal)

Soc. Societa (Italy)

S.p.A. Società per Azioni (Italy)

Sp. z.o.o. Spólka z ograniczona odpowiedzialnoscia (Poland)

S.R.L. Sociedad de Responsabilidad Limitada (Spain, Mexico, Latin America [except Brazil])

S.R.L. Società a Responsabilità Limitata (Italy)

S.R.O. Spolecnost s Rucenim Omezenym (Czechoslovakia

S.S.K. Sherkate Sahami Khass (Iran)

Ste. Societe (France, Belgium, Luxembourg, Switzerland)

Ste. Cve. Societe Cooperative (Belgium)

S.V. Samemwerkende Vennootschap (Belgium)

S.Z.R.L. Societe Zairoise a Responsabilite Limitee (Zaire)

T

THB Thai baht

TND Tunisian dinar

TRL Turkish lira

TWD new Taiwan dollar

U

U.A. Uitgesloten Aansporakeiijkheid (Netherlands)

u.p.a. utan personligt ansvar (Sweden)

V

VAG Verein der Arbeitgeber (Austria, Germany)

VEB Venezuelan bolivar

VERTR Vertriebs (Austria, Germany)

VND Vietnamese dong

V.O.f. Vennootschap onder firma (Netherlands)

VVAG Versicherungsverein auf Gegenseitigkeit (Austria, Germany)

W–Z

WA Wettelika Aansprakalikhaed (Netherlands)

WLL With Limited Liability (Bahrain, Kuwait, Qatar, Saudi Arabia)

YK Yugen Kaisha (Japan)

ZAO Zakrytoe Aktsionernoe Obshchestve (Russia)

ZAR South African rand

ZMK Zambian kwacha

ZWD Zimbabwean dollar

Absa Group Ltd.

Third Floor, Absa Towers East
170 Main Street
Johannesburg, 2001
South Africa
Telephone: (+27 11) 350-4000
Fax: (+27 11) 350-4009
Web site: http://www.absa.co.za/absacoza

Public Company
Founded: 1991
Employees: 37,828
Total Assets: $78.3 billion (2008)
Stock Exchanges: Johannesburg
Ticker Symbol: ASA
NAICS: 522110 Commercial Banking; 522298 All Other Nondepository Credit Intermediation; 524113 Direct Life Insurance Carriers; 524114 Direct Health and Medical Insurance Carriers; 524126 Direct Property and Casualty Insurance Carriers

■ ■ ■

Absa Group Ltd., known until 1977 as the Amalgamated Banks of South Africa, is one of the largest financial services companies operating in South Africa. A subsidiary of Barclay's Bank, Absa has expanded from retail and commercial banking to a full-service model that includes investment banking and insurance. Absa has also expanded geographically, purchasing banks in Mozambique and Tanzania.

NEW ERA BRINGS BANK MERGERS

The story of Absa Group Ltd. began in the mid-1980s, when international demonstrations against the South Africa's apartheid regime swelled to a crescendo that could not be ignored. Nevertheless, the nationalist government did not choose to dismantle apartheid, so that South Africans of all races could share in the country's abundant wealth and opportunities. Instead, it dug its heels in. Refusing to be ignored on this crucial issue, the United States and several other countries instituted economic sanctions against the stubborn apartheid regime. The effects were felt in every aspect of South African life: Essential items such as computers and crude oil were no longer shipped to South African ports; huge companies such as Exxon and Eastman-Kodak closed their South African operations and took their business elsewhere; and travel to and from South Africa became tedious, because the country's airline now had to follow circuitous routes to avoid hostile airspace over Africa. On the reverse track, South African goods such as fruit and produce, once welcomed in the markets of Europe and North America, were now barred. Even South African athletes were excluded from taking part in international events.

All this inevitably took its toll on the banking industry. As just one example, at the end of 1985, the Chase Manhattan Bank decided not to roll over its short-term loans to South Africa. The following year banks in the United States and in other countries then increased the pressure even further by actually forbidding any further bank loans to South Africa.

COMPANY PERSPECTIVES

Absa's stated goal is to maintain a competitive leadership in the African banking field by constantly improving its service to reach a level that ensures customer loyalty. Another explicitly stated goal is to reduce unnecessary risk in three important ways: by diversifying its interests to include bank assurance, by using the most efficient and accurate technology available, and by looking for growth opportunities outside of South Africa.

To continue doing business, many of South Africa's financial institutions had to face two new facts of life. The first was that the days of apartheid were numbered. Soon, there would be a whole new market of clients of all races, with differing ranges of banking needs. The banks realized that they needed to revamp their customer service by training their employees on how to deal with the cultural and financial differences among their future clients.

The second issue, a considerable lack of banking choices for consumers, had been acknowledged in 1988 by the South African government, which had compensated for this by allowing building societies to act as banks. This, in turn, created an oversupply. As a result, even though the sanctions were steadily crumbling, South African banks understood that intense competition between them would do nothing but weaken all of them. As a result, several of these banks decided to merge to form financial powerhouses.

In March 1991 UBS Holdings, a prominent building society, merged with Sage Financial Services and the Allied and Volkskas banking groups to form Amalgamated Banks of South Africa (Absa), a financial institution that had a formidable combined asset base of over $16 billion. There were now four banks in the lineup, and each was operating independently and catering to its own clients. Incredibly, these four banks all operated with separate computer and checking systems and client lists.

In January 1992 Piet Badenhorst, the chief executive officer (CEO) of Absa, expanded the group further by acquiring the Bankorp Group, the fourth-largest group in the country, for $1.2 billion. Included in the deal were the Bankorp subsidiaries TrustBank, Senbank, and Bankfin. This acquisition, which extended Absa's asset base even further to exceed ZAR 83 billion,

increased the number of bank branches to 470 and expanded its installment and leasing sales to the point that one out of three South African mortgages was held by Absa.

This rosy picture did not make the new acquisition a perfect one. Bankorp came complete with a huge amount of debt dating back to 1985, when the start of sanctions had spurred it to expand so rapidly that it had outgrown its cash reserves. The South African Reserve Bank had obligingly granted a loan of about ZAR 300 million to Bankorp in 1985. The reserve bank granted another loan in 1990 and a third in 1991 and agreed to transfer this help to Absa when Bankorp was purchased. In spite of this debt, Badenhorst was still pleased with the purchase. "The result," he told Lucien Vallun of *Forbes* in 1992, "has been the creation of a very sophisticated and market-oriented banking sector, which compares favorably with the best elsewhere in the world."

In 1998 the lifeboat loans given to Bankorp came under scrutiny by an anticorruption task force headed by Judge Willem Heath. The investigation centered on whether the Reserve Bank had the legal authority to grant Bankorp an ultra-low interest lifeboat loan, and whether Bankorp used the government funds appropriately. It was alleged that Bankorp had taken the loans at 1 percent interest and invested the funds in government securities with a 16 percent interest rate, turning a tidy profit. Absa, which had inherited all Bankorp liabilities as well as assets, denied that there had been any impropriety. In November 1999 investigators dropped the charges, stating that although they had sufficient evidence to go after Absa for the loan profits, they declined to do so out of fear that litigation would destabilize the South African banking system.

ELECTIONS BRING NEW OPPORTUNITIES

The mood in South Africa was upbeat because the country was beginning to plan for the free elections that would bring victory to Nelson Mandela's party, the African National Congress, in 1994. With this colossal change, Absa knew that there would be numerous opportunities to expand its client base.

Absa was also looking beyond its borders for new opportunities to expand and grow. In 1997 a chance presented itself when the Tanzanian government decided to privatize the country's largest bank, National Bank of Commerce. In a deal that would take three years to finalize, Absa took a 70 percent stake in the National Bank of Commerce and the Tanzanian government retained the remaining 30 percent. As requested by

KEY DATES

1991: Amalgamated Banks of South Africa (Absa) is formed through the merging of UBS Holdings, Sage Financial Services, Volkskas Group, and the Allied Group.

1992: Acquisition of Bankorp Group, which includes Trustbank, Senbank, and Bankfin for $1.2 billion.

1997: Amalgamated Banks of South Africa changes name to Absa.

1998: Member banks are consolidated under the Absa name and brand; United, Volkskas, Allied, and TrustBank brands are discontinued.

1998: Acquires 70% stake in Tanzania's National Bank of Commerce.

2002: Acquires Mozambique's Banco Austral.

2005: Barclays acquires a controlling interest in Absa.

Tanzania, Absa immediately took control of operations by restructuring all of the bank's 35 branches.

REBRANDING

The following year brought changes in a different direction. Previously, the banks had been operating independently, under the banner of Amalgamated Banks of South Africa. Each had its own corporate identity and client base. Nevertheless, Absa's top management noted in 1998 that even though the banks were operating at profitable levels, there was zero brand recognition among all these clients. Dismayed, Absa decided to change this by reinventing Absa as a bank for all South Africans.

First came a new logo, an artistically designed "A" to denote a new beginning for Absa. By making it bright red, Absa believed it was a way to symbolize freshness and youthfulness. Then came free Internet access and e-mail to attract young, computer-literate clients. New mini-ads began to appearing on television to update clients on events at Absa branches during the past 24 hours, such as people opening checking accounts, using e-mail, or trying other financial services. The bank added another innovation: an internal bank television channel that gave advice to employees on proper dress and how to interact with clients. These communication techniques were also reinforced with special employee packs, each holding a CD with Absa information on it, a letter from the CEO, and a special

edition of *Abacus*, the bank's internal newsletter.

Next, Absa turned its attention to the needs of its ever-growing client base. Through its Absa Foundation, the bank began sponsoring sporting events and creating scholarships for the underprivileged. Job creation, education, and health improvement, especially with regard to the human immunodeficiency virus and the acquired immunodeficiency syndrome, also became points of focus. Furthermore, the bank supported athletes by sponsoring sports scholarships and young artists via the Atelier Awards.

This whole scheme melded into a strategy of protecting the overall brand first, then targeting specific markets. All these efforts were aimed at one important target, which soon became reality: Absa became known as the bank that helped people's dreams come true. The rebranding campaign bore handsome fruit: In 2001 not only did most South Africans instantly recognize Absa but the bank also scored as the top banking brand in a *Johannesburg Sunday Times* survey.

ENTER NALLIE BOSMAN

This was not the only newsworthy event of that year. In January 2001 there was a change in the top management, when Executive Director Jean Brown had to retire early because of ill health.

Into the breach stepped Nallie Bosman, who assumed the post of Absa Group managing director. Bosman had been with Absa from its very beginning, having been a Volkskas staff member since his graduation from high school in 1963. His first job was at the branch bank in Cradock, a town in the sheep-farming and wool-producing area of the Eastern Cape Province. He was in a career that had definite prospects for advancement, for in that part of the country, where drought was a major dasher of dreams and plans, the bank was an ever-important friend to its clients.

As it happened, most of the Cradock Volkskas clients that Bosman served were conservative and stalwart supporters of apartheid. By 1994, when the African National Congress came to power, he was an educated and sophisticated banker, one who understood that Cradock-type clients occupied only one space on a long list of potential customers, all of whose financial needs differed according to language, cultural preferences, and heritage. Realizing the significance of these delicate issues, he encouraged the bank to offer its products to as broad an audience as possible, make all comers welcome, and offer them the best service available. In 1996 he oversaw the opening of the first Absa branch bank in Dobsonville, a middle-class black suburb of Soweto. There, the bank placed its first black female branch manager, Innocentia Nkomo, who knew the neighborhood population well enough to recognize anyone needing a bank account. As a result, taxi drivers in business for themselves became a marketing target, as did others with tiny self-owned businesses such as fruit stalls and hairdressing salons.

Bosman's innovative thinking proved to be extremely profitable. By the time he retired in August 2004, Absa was the largest consumer lender in the country. The return on shareholders' funds had increased by 24.6 percent, and its earnings were almost ZAR 4.45 billion. The Absa Group was offering personal banking as well as commercial banking, plus wholesale banking to its own subsidiaries: Absa Corporate and Merchant Bank and Abvest Trading and Investment Holdings Ltd. Its international lineup had also increased. Besides its African holdings, it had offices in Singapore; London, England; and Hamburg, Germany. Bosman, however, was modest about his achievements; he attributed all this success to low interest rates and a housing market boom.

By the time Bosman's successor, 41-year-old Steve F. Booysen, took the Absa helm in August 2004, the bank had 6.3 million clients, 670 branches, and 4,600 automated teller machines (ATMs) and was the leader in the mortgage market. Of all the banks in South Africa, it was also top in its service to its black customers.

BARCLAYS BANK BUYS ABSA

All of this success caught the attention of Barclays Bank, headquartered in London. Once a formidable banking force in South Africa, Barclays had been forced to leave South Africa in 1986 by vociferous pro-sanctions activism in South Africa and customer boycotts overseas. Now seeing the marketing potential in the new South African climate, Barclays wanted to return. In July 2005 it paid £2.9 billion (ZAR 30 billion) in return for a controlling interest of about 60 percent in Absa.

Several sweeping changes resulted from the deal. First, the agreement stipulated that Barclays's South African operations would be run by Absa and that Absa would keep its own name. Second, Absa's financial year would end on December 31 instead of on March 31, so that Absa could be consolidated with other Barclays banks in its financial statements. Third, Barclays consolidated all of Absa's activities under just three headings: African Operations, Financial Services, and All Other Activities, which included investor relations and real estate operations. Fourth, a brand-new executive team was established for the company. This team would consist of 17 members who covered important areas of company operations such as human resources,

implementation, and corporate and merchant banking. The goal here was to boost Absa's share of the credit card market and enhance its corporate banking capabilities.

ISLAMIC BANKING ARRIVES

March 2006 saw another important change: the introduction of Islamic banking. This method of banking requires extensive training for personnel because it is all done under a strict adherence to the sharia, the Islamic code of law. Included in this type of banking are a year-end audit, an internal review, and supervision by a governance committee. Another feature concerns an Absa Islamic checking account, which uses both ATM and debit card convenience but makes no provision for overdraft protection. An Absa Islamic savings account, using all convenient means of operation, pays an annual profit-sharing fee instead of interest.

The addition of Islamic banking led to a 464 percent increase in clients within one year. Absa's staff, however, was so well trained in sharia banking techniques that only a 29 percent increase in the number of employees was necessary to cope with this rising demand. As of mid 2009, this service was still available only in South Africa, but Absa had plans to extend it into other African markets.

BOOYSEN RETIRES

At the end of 2008, when Absa's earnings had grown 5.3 percent, representing earnings of ZAR 9.9 billion, Booysen announced his own retirement, noting that the bank's strategy of earnings diversification, prudent risk management, and cost-cutting had proved successful. Nevertheless, he also noted that a decline in the international economic climate, high local interest rates, and rising levels of household debt were putting a brake on progress. Those problems would be handled by Maria Ramos, Booysen's successor, who took over in March 2009.

Gillian Wolf

PRINCIPAL SUBSIDIARIES

Absa Corporate and Business Bank; Absa Insurance Company Ltd.; Absa Trust Ltd.; Absa Investment Management Services Pty. Ltd.; Absa Development Company Holdings Pty. Ltd.; Banco Comercial Angelano (Angola; 50%); Barclays Bank Mozambique, S.A. (80%); National Bank of Commerce (Tanzania; 55%).

PRINCIPAL COMPETITORS

Standard Bank; Nedbank; First National Bank.

FURTHER READING

"Absa Group: Group Chief Executive Nallie Bosman," *Banker*, January 5, 2004.

"Absa Warns of Even Harder Times Ahead," Africa News Service, April 23, 2009.

"Absa's Allure; Banking in South Africa," *Economist*, April 30, 2005.

"Banks' Ranks Thin," *London: Euromoney*, September 1993.

"Barclays Back in South Africa after Raising Offer for Absa," *Independent* (London), May 9, 2005.

"Barclays Eyes Deals to Achieve 'Top 5' Goal," Reuters, October 11, 2005.

"Bosman Has More Tricks up His Sleeve," News 24.com, November 25, 2001.

"The Eagle Circles: Banking in South Africa," *Economist*, October 2, 2004.

Faure, Ray, "Bosman Leaves Absa with a Bang," Fin24.com, May 31, 2004, http://www.fin24.com/articles/default/display_article.aspx?Nav=ns&ArticleID=1518-24_1535397.

Feder, Barnaby J., "Businesses Avoid South Africa Ties," *New York Times*, July 24, 1991, p. A1.

Gunnion, Stephen, "Barclays Swoops into Absa Hot Seat," *Business Day*, July 28, 2005.

Hamlyn, Michael, "Land Bank: Apartheid to Blame," Fin24.com, September 4, 2007, http://www.fin24.com/articles/default/display_article.aspx?ArticleId=1518-24_2176932.

Holmes, Steven A., "Transition in Africa: Officials in U.S. Are Moving for a Removal of Sanctions," *New York Times*, September 25, 1993.

Irwin, Ron, "Absa Bank Gaining Interest," Brandchannel.com, February 18, 2002.

John, Ongeri, and Justin Arenstein, "Absa Continues Restructuring Tanzanian Bank Despite Union Opposition," African Eye News Service, May 10, 2000.

Maunya, Morice, "Absa Buys Tanzanian Bank," Africa News Service, August 2, 1999.

"Nallie Bosman, CEO, Absa Bank," Africa News Service, June 5, 2003.

O'Grady, Kevin, "With a History Like This, What Do You Expect?" *Business Day Weekender Edition*, November 4, 2006.

Pirikisi, Maxwell, ed., "Absa Gears Up for Africa," *Economist*, October 20, 2000.

Potgieter, Carina, "Banking Giant Re-defines Its Communication Mandate," *Communication World*, June 1, 1996, p. 49.

Reece, Damian, "Steve Booysen, Chief Executive of ABSA: Holder of the Key to Barclays African Deal," *Independent* (London), November 6, 2004.

Rose, Rob, "ABSA: Job Done?" *Financial Mail*, February 20, 2009.

———. "How Steve Booysens Changed ABSA," *Leader*, February 27, 2009.

Theobald, Stuart, "Measure by Measure," *Financial Mail*, May 23, 2003, p. 26.

"Tough Times Ahead for Ramos at Absa," Africa News Service, February 11, 2009.

Vallun, Lucien, "ABSA." *Forbes*, May 25, 1992, p. 16.

Walker, Julie, "Bosman an Expert in the Art of Name-Dropping," *Sunday Times: Business Times*, May 24, 1998.

Acadia Realty Trust

1311 Mamaroneck Avenue, Suite 260
White Plains, New York 10605
U.S.A.
Telephone: (914) 288-8100
Toll Free: (800) 227-5570
Fax: (914) 428-2760
Web site: http://www.acadiarealty.com/

Public Company
Founded: 1960 as Mark Development Group
Employees: 135
Total Assets: $1.29 billion (2008)
Stock Exchanges: New York
Ticker Symbol: AKR
NAISC: 531120 Lessors of Nonresidential Buildings
(except Miniwarehouses)

■ ■ ■

Headquartered in White Plains, New York, Acadia Realty Trust is a real estate investment trust (REIT) that specializes in neighborhood and community shopping centers anchored by discounters, supermarkets, and drugstores. The company owns a portfolio of several dozen commercial properties located in 16 states, chiefly in the northeastern United States, totaling about 8 million square feet of floor space, and also participates in joint ventures with other investors. Its tenants include well-known retail brands such as A&P, Albertson's, Best Buy, Borders, CVS, Home Depot, JCPenney, Kroger, Macy's, Payless ShoeSource, Restoration Hardware, Safeway, Sears, T.J. Maxx, Walgreens, and Wal-Mart.

Through a strategy of slow but steady expansion centering on purchasing undervalued retail properties, many of them in underserved urban and suburban areas, Acadia has become a leading retail REIT in its core regions. Even though the company is relatively small when compared to some of its competitors, it stands out for its geographic focus on the Northeast Corridor and its commitment to working in difficult settings such as New York City and other large urban centers.

MARK DEVELOPMENT GROUP
FOUNDED: 1960

Founded in 1960 by Marvin L. Slomowitz, Mark Development Group developed and purchased shopping centers in the mid-Atlantic and southeastern regions of the United States. Slomowitz was the principal shareholder of the company and served as chairman of the board, chief executive officer (CEO), and president. By 1993 the company owned 31 retail properties. That year, Mark Development Group transformed itself into an equity real estate development trust called Mark Centers Trust, registered in Maryland and keeping its headquarters in Kingston, Pennsylvania. The company was one of several dozen private real estate investment firms in the United States to convert itself into a REIT in 1993 and 1994, taking advantage of liberalized regulations that allowed these businesses to develop and administer their own properties instead of relying on third-party management firms. Going public and issuing stock enabled these companies to raise capital much more readily in a depressed real estate market and purchase valuable properties at low prices.

COMPANY PERSPECTIVES

Acadia is well-positioned to take advantage of profitable opportunities for growth. Its strengths include an experienced management team with a proven track record, a portfolio of high-quality retail properties, and the financial stability and resources to enhance existing assets while selectively making new investments.

However, Mark Centers Trust encountered setbacks in the prospering but volatile retail REIT sector. A series of tenant bankruptcies starting in 1996 forced the company to find and install new tenants for the vacated spaces. The company thus accumulated substantial debt, which reached $183.9 million by the end of 1997. This heavy debt load hindered the company from updating its properties to attract coveted anchor tenants. Its stock price, which had been $19.50 per share at its initial public offering in 1993, steadily declined, falling to under $9 per share by the end of 1997.

Mark Centers Trust also faced lawsuits filed in state and federal court by Jack Wertheimer, who had briefly served as the company's president in 1994. The lawsuits alleged that Wertheimer had been wrongfully terminated and accused Slomowitz and the board of trustees of securities fraud. While many of the charges were dismissed, Acadia Realty Trust, the successor company, reached a $2.9 million settlement with Wertheimer in 1998.

A TIMELY MERGER: 1998

In 1997 Mark Centers Trust hired Bear Stearns to advise it on how it could continue to expand in this difficult situation. Bear Stearns helped bring the company together with RD Capital Inc., a private real estate investment company led by Ross Dworman and Kenneth Bernstein, with its headquarters in New York City. RD Capital saw an ideal opportunity to jump into the public real estate market through a merger with a struggling REIT such as Mark Centers Trust.

In April 1998 Mark Centers Trust agreed to a reverse merger, in which RD Capital's management would assume control of the firm, to be renamed Acadia Realty Trust; that August shareholders formally approved the deal. To give the merger more credibility with institutional investors, Rothschild Realty committed $17 million through its Five Arrows Real Estate Securities funds. RD Capital received a total of $100 million from investors and contributed its own portfolio of 12 retail malls and five multifamily residential units, valued at around $280 million. Postmerger, the company owned 56 properties totaling about 11 million square feet with a market capitalization of around $600 million, more than double the previous amount.

Acadia took the form of an umbrella partnership REIT, in which the investors received shares in the umbrella partnership, which owned the company's assets. The company issued to RD Capital both common shares and operating partnership units (a device designed to shelter the principals from capital gains taxes) at a designated share value of $7.50. These operating partnership units could be exchanged one-to-one for common shares, giving RD Capital 72 percent effective ownership of the company.

Dworman became the chairman of the board and the CEO of Acadia, and Bernstein became the president. Slomowitz remained a member of the board of trustees after the merger, but then resigned in December 1999. Bernstein took over the position of CEO in 2000. In 2002 Dworman resigned from his position as chairman of the board and became a trustee, leaving Bernstein as the company's clear leader.

NEW NAME, NEW DIRECTIONS: 1998–2003

Acadia emerged into the industry limelight only to suffer through a severe decline in the REIT sector. Its stock price hovered around $5 in late 1998 and 1999, and the company struggled to raise capital. Many investors turned their backs on REITs because they were obsessed with the high-flying dot-com stocks and feared that the conventional retail shopping sector would suffer from the rise of Internet shopping.

Bernstein described Acadia to *Commercial Property News* in 1999 as having a "contrarian philosophy," which the company followed in developing a strategy based on short-term consolidation and selective long-term growth. During the next few years, Acadia sold both its residential units and its shopping centers that were underperforming or that management considered to be too concentrated in a single retailer, especially struggling discounters such as Kmart and Ames. This consolidation culminated in April 2002, when the company sold a set of 17 properties for $52.7 million to the Lightstone Group. Acadia planned to use the proceeds from these sales to purchase other shopping centers, particularly ones anchored by supermarkets. The company had thus reduced its holdings to 35 properties with about 7 million square feet.

Frustrated that the company's low stock values were failing to reflect the value of its underlying assets, in

KEY DATES

1960: Marvin L. Slomowitz founds Mark Development Group.

1993: Mark Centers Trust is created as a Maryland real estate investment trust to continue the business of Mark Development Group; Mark Centers Trust goes public with an initial public offering.

1998: Mark Centers Trust agrees to a merger with RD Capital Inc.; the company name is changed to Acadia Realty Trust.

2001: The company creates its first Acadia Strategic Development Fund.

2003: Acadia moves its headquarters to White Plains, New York.

2004: Company begins the Retailer Controlled Property Venture and the New York Urban/ Infill Redevelopment Program.

2001 Acadia sought unsuccessfully for a merger or acquisition, and even solicited a bid to sell its core portfolio, which it rejected as too low. Acadia then created three joint ventures with four of its institutional shareholders: the Acadia Strategic Opportunity Fund, LP, in 2001; the Acadia Strategic Opportunity Fund II, LLC, in 2004; and the Acadia Strategic Opportunity Fund III, LLC, in 2007. This type of joint venture financing partially insulated Acadia from the effects of stock price swings and allowed the company to avoid relying on its credit line to finance projects and thus accumulating too much debt. Each of the first two funds were launched with $300 million in equity and the third fund with $503 million; through leverage, the company could use this capital to purchase property valued up to three or more times higher.

In 2003 the company transferred its headquarters from Port Washington on Long Island to White Plains in Westchester County, New York, to obtain a larger office space that was closer to where many employees and managers lived. The additional office space also allowed the company to hire more employees so that it could handle expanded property holdings.

TWO NEW VENTURES
CONTINUED GROWTH: 2004–09

By 2004 Acadia management was becoming convinced that retail real estate prices were becoming inflated, so it decided to shift is focus on acquiring value-added properties. This decision led to the development of two major programs that would reshape its industry profile. The Retailer Controlled Property (RCP) Venture, in which Acadia participated with its partners Lubert-Adler Management Inc. and Klaff Realty LP, was designed to acquire properties throughout the country from distressed or bankrupt retailers. The RCP Venture was part of a consortium that purchased in September 2004 the Mervyn's Department Store chain from Target Corporation, acquiring 265 stores for $1.2 billion. In 2006 and 2007 the venture helped purchase hundreds of stores from Albertson's, one of the leading grocery chains in the United States; Cub Food, a small supermarket chain in the Midwest; Marsh, a midwestern supermarket chain; Skopko, a regional department store chain in the Midwest and Northwest; and Rex Stores, an electronics retailer.

The New York Urban/Infill Redevelopment Program, a joint venture of Acadia and P/A Associates, LLC, was created to purchase and redevelop office and retail properties in and around New York City, particularly in areas underserved by leading retailers. Acadia believed that its expertise in local real estate conditions gave it an edge in this difficult retail market. As Bernstein explained it to Marianne Nardone of *Real Estate Finance and Investment*, "People get intimidated by doing business in New York, and they trade in a different style [than the rest of the country]." The company anticipated that urban consumers would welcome convenient nearby access to major retailers and that high population density and street traffic would drive high sales in spite of the low average incomes in the surrounding areas. The joint venture would also take advantage of rents that were typically much lower per square foot than in lower Manhattan or many suburban locations.

The partners' first acquisitions were a 16-acre tract of land in Pelham Manor in Westchester County, where it intended to build a new shopping center, and an existing retail building on Fordham Road in the Bronx, the most important retail corridor in that borough. Construction of the Pelham Manor center was mostly complete by early 2009, with BJ's Wholesale Club as the intended anchor tenant. The renovation and enlargement of the Fordham Road building began in March 2007. By early 2009 the retail space was almost completely leased, with Best Buy, Sears, and Walgreens as the anchor tenants. This project also included the construction of a 14-story office building next to the original building. Several other projects were planned and constructed across New York City in subsequent years, and the company moved to acquire and develop properties in other large cities such as Philadelphia, Pennsylvania, and Chicago, Illinois.

Acadia entered another property management field by including self-storage facilities with several of its urban redevelopment projects and acquiring 11 self-storage centers from Storage Post in 2008. Company management determined that self-storage was compatible with shopping centers and had a high growth potential.

Meanwhile, Acadia continued to sell off properties to help raise capital, particularly ones located away from its core region in the Northeast. Bernstein stated to Lynn Novelli of *Real Estate Portfolio*, "We have chosen to remain relatively small, which means that we can quickly push the needle that much more and maintain a very healthy balance sheet while supercharging shareholder returns." Wall Street seemed to approve of Acadia's strategy, because its share prices substantially outperformed REIT stock indexes throughout this period. Acadia stock reached a new peak of $29 in October 2007 and retained most of its value for the next year, even during the mounting real estate crisis. However, prices plunged in late 2008 and early 2009 to under $10 per share before recovering somewhat later that year.

LOOKING CAUTIOUSLY TOWARD THE FUTURE

In spite of the economic downturn that began in 2007, Acadia remained optimistic that it could continue to grow and even prosper by taking advantage of opportunities to acquire distressed properties at especially low prices. Company management believed that its relatively conservative investment strategy and low debt-to-total market capitalization ratio would help it weather financial storms. Industry analysts regarded the company as fairly well placed for the future because it derived the bulk of its income from stable long-term leases and kept plenty of capital in reserve for investment.

Acadia concentrated its activities on shopping-center management, a sector that features restricted competition and high economic barriers to entry—particularly in the urban Northeast. Falling consumer spending threatened the revenues of large retailers, leading to the continuing danger of bankruptcies and the loss of anchor tenants, as the company had experienced with Circuit City in early 2009. However, Acadia's focus was on certain types of stores, such as supermarkets, drugstores, and discounters, that sold products that

consumers needed and seemed less likely to cut back or stop spending on during hard economic times.

Stephen V. Beitel

PRINCIPAL SUBSIDIARIES

Acadia Strategic Opportunity Fund I, LP; Acadia Strategic Opportunity Fund II, LLC; Acadia Strategic Opportunity Fund III, LLC; Acadia-P/A Holding Company I, LLC; Acadia-P/A Holding Company II LLC; Acadia Realty Acquisition I; Acadia Realty Acquisition II; Acadia Realty Acquisition III.

PRINCIPAL COMPETITORS

Developers Diversified Realty Corporation; General Growth Properties Inc.; Glimcher Realty Trust; Kimco Realty Corporation; Ramco-Gershenson Properties Trust; Vornado Realty Trust.

FURTHER READING

"Acadia Realty Trust—History," *Datamonitor Company Profiles*, January 22, 2004.

"Acadia Realty Trust Resolves Litigation Exposure," *PR Newswire*, December 31, 1998.

"Acadia Steers away from Single-Tenant Concentrations," *Real Estate Finance and Investment*, October 21, 2002, p. 6.

Anastasi, Nick, "Acadia Bolts from LI to White Plains," *Long Island Business News*, July 4, 2003.

Bergsman, Steve, "Fire Sale," *Retail Traffic*, May 1, 2004.

Bindrim, Kira, "Major Renovation Draws Big Tenant," *Crain's New York Business*, April 16, 2007, p. 16.

"BJ's Wholesale Club to Anchor Pelham Manor Shopping Plaza," *Business Wire*, September 19, 2008.

Brenner, Elsa, "Laying the Groundwork for the Big-Box Retailers," *New York Times*, October 27, 2004, p. C6.

"Company Interview: Kenneth F. Bernstein, Acadia Realty Trust (AKR)," *Wall Street Transcript*, January 3, 2005, p. 34.

"Company Interview: Kenneth F. Bernstein, Acadia Realty Trust (AKR)," *Wall Street Transcript*, November 7, 2005, p. 25.

Fitzgerald, Therese, "Acadia Makes Changes in Corporate Governance; Dworman Steps Aside," *Commercial Property News*, July 7, 2003.

"Five Arrows Backs East Group, Helps Acadia/Mark Centers Merge," *Commercial Property News*, January 1, 1999.

Golden, John, "Acadia Acquires Cortlandt Center," *Westchester County Business Journal*, February 9, 2009, p. 10.

Kalinoski, Gail, "Acadia Acquires Self-Storage Portfolio for $175M," *Commercial Property News*, March 6, 2008.

"Lightstone Rapidly Expands Portfolio with Retail Acquisition ($300M More Planned)," *Real Estate Finance and Investment*, May 13, 2002, p. 7.

"Marvin L. Slomowitz Resigns from Acadia Realty Trust's Board," *PR Newswire*, February 17, 2000.

Mayfield, Lisa Pritchard, "REITs Feel Lucky," *National Real Estate Investor*, February 28, 2000, p. 110.

Mullaney, John A., *REITs: Building Profits with Real Estate Investment Trusts*, New York: Wiley, 1998.

Nardone, Marianne, "Acadia Realty Targeting Bronx Retail Opportunities," *Real Estate Finance and Investment*, November 15, 2004.

Novelli, Lynn, "Acadia's Winning Game Plan," *Real Estate Portfolio*, January–February 2006.

Pappas, Lorna, "Kenneth Bernstein: Anchors away with Acadia Realty Trust," *Real Estate Portfolio*, January–February 2007.

Philippidis, Alex, "REIT Eyes Expansion with Move to County," *Westchester County Business Journal*, June 30, 2003, p. 2.

Siwolop, Sana, "A Bronx Retailing Hub Is Getting Offices, Too," *New York Times*, July 11, 2007, p. C7.

Adobe Systems Inc.

345 Park Avenue
San Jose, California 95110-2704
U.S.A.
Telephone: (408) 536-6000
Fax: (408) 537-6000
Web site: http://www.adobe.com

Public Company
Incorporated: 1983
Employees: 7,544 (worldwide)
Sales: $3.58 billion (2008)
Stock Exchanges: NASDAQ
Ticker Symbol: ADBE
NAICS: 51121 Software Publishers; 334611 Software Reproducing; 541511 Custom Computer Programming Services

■ ■ ■

Adobe Systems Inc. is a leading developer of desktop publishing, creative business solutions, and mobile device software. Sales of three of the company's software products—Photoshop, Illustrator, and PageMaker—account for about 50 percent of Adobe's sales. Adobe also developed and distributes, free of charge, Acrobat Reader, which allows Internet users to view and print portable document format files. The company has investments in about 20 technology companies and is involved in two venture capital partnerships. Adobe sells print technology to original equipment manufacturers; the company's PostScript page description language became the industry standard for the imaging and print-ing of electronic documents. Adobe also offers Creative Solutions software and continues to capitalize on the growth of digital photography and film by innovating in the area of photo and film editing.

SPARKING THE DESKTOP PUBLISHING REVOLUTION IN THE 1980S

Adobe was founded in 1982 by John Warnock and Charles Geschke, both former employees of Xerox Corporation's Research Center in Palo Alto, California. At Xerox, Warnock conducted interactive graphics research, while Geschke directed computer science and graphics research as the manager of the company's Imaging Sciences Laboratory. In an interview with Genevieve Leone of the *San Jose Business Journal* in 1989, Warnock recalled that he and Geschke were frustrated at Xerox "because of the difficulty in getting our products out of the research stage." Believing in the profitability of an independent venture, they left Xerox to establish their own business, which they named after a creek that ran by their homes in Los Altos, California.

Shortly after it was launched, Adobe introduced PostScript, a powerful computer language that essentially described to a printer or other output device the appearance of an electronic page, including the placement of characters, lines, or images. The introduction of PostScript proved integral to the desktop publishing revolution. With a personal computer (PC) and a laser printer equipped with PostScript, users could produce polished, professional-looking documents with high-quality graphics. Martha Groves of the *Los Angeles*

COMPANY PERSPECTIVES

Adobe's mission is to be the premier provider of products and services in the information age for professional publishing solutions, business publishing solutions, document solutions, and digital imaging solutions in the company's addressed market segments while: achieving and maintaining an above-average return on investment for shareholders measured in terms of return on equity, earnings per share, revenue growth, and operating profit; maintaining or achieving the number one or two position in addressed market segments in terms of market share, customer satisfaction, revenue generation, product margin, product functionality, and technological leadership; treating all employees with respect and rewarding both group and individual performance that exceeds commitments and expectations; being a good corporate citizen in the local and national locations where the company produces, sells, and services its products.

Times stated in 1989 that Adobe's PostScript "made desktop publishing possible by enabling laser printers, typesetting equipment and other such devices to produce pages integrating text and graphics." Advertising agencies, in particular, soon found the new technology indispensable.

Realizing the wealth of potential uses for the Post-Script language, Adobe marketed and licensed PostScript to manufacturers of computers, printers, imagesetters, and film recorders. In 1985 Apple Computer Inc., the maker of the Macintosh computer, incorporated Post-Script for its LaserWriter printer. Shortly thereafter, Apple invested in a 19 percent stake in Adobe, which had reported revenues of $1.7 million the year before. Adobe's rapid growth led to an increase in staff from 27 in 1985 to 54 by 1986.

More than 5,000 PostScript applications were developed and made available for every operating system and hardware configuration. In 1986 Adobe signed an agreement to supply Texas Instruments Inc. with the software for two of its laser printers, producing the first PostScript-equipped printers made for use with IBM-compatible PCs. In addition, PostScript soon became available for use with minicomputers and mainframes, and it remained the only page description language available for multiple-computer environments, such as corporate office networks. Independent software vendors marketed products that used PostScript to render images

and text onto film, slides, and screens, for less money than traditional typesetting methods incurred. Used by corporations, professional publishers, and the U.S. government, PostScript rapidly became one of the most ubiquitous computer languages worldwide.

To supplement the PostScript language system, Adobe introduced a software technology known as Type 1, which provided digital type fonts that could be printed at any resolution. Vendors soon began developing different Type 1 typefaces until there were more than 15,000, including Japanese and Cyrillic character sets. By the end of 1986 Adobe reported sales of $16 million and an income of $3.6 million. During this time, the company went public and began expanding its customer base to include IBM and Digital Equipment Corporation.

The strategy of marketing and licensing technology to original equipment manufacturers such as Apple became the cornerstone of Adobe's success. In 1986 Apple accounted for 80 percent of Adobe's sales, and the other 20 percent consisted of retail sales, an area into which Adobe moved the following year.

NEW TYPES OF SOFTWARE PROGRAMS LAUNCHED

In 1987 the company introduced Adobe Illustrator, a design and illustration software program. Enabling users to create high-quality line drawings, Illustrator became popular among graphic designers, desktop publishers, and technical illustrators. The company also released the Adobe Type Library, which contained a large selection of type fonts, many of which were original typefaces Adobe had created especially for the electronic medium. The Type Library eventually became the most widely used collection in the industry.

As graphics became more widely used in business communications, Adobe was poised to offer new technologies. The company's introduction of a new version of Illustrator was designed for use with Microsoft's Windows program, offered PC users an array of graphics tools, and helped pave the way for other PostScript language-based graphics packages. By 1988 many industries and universities had adopted the Illustrator standard. Moreover, the Type Library, with 300 typefaces, had become the world's largest collection of typefaces for PCs.

Having successfully marketed its technology to both Macintosh and IBM, Adobe tackled a new project: developing Illustrator and the Type Library for the NeXT computer system. Once this was accomplished, the NeXT computer system became the first to implement a new Adobe technology: Display PostScript. This adaptation of the original PostScript was unique in that

KEY DATES

1982: John Warnock and Charles Geschke form Adobe Systems Inc.
1986: Adobe goes public.
1987: Adobe releases Adobe Illustrator.
1990: Adobe acquires BluePoint Technologies.
1991: John Warnock and Charles Geschke receive the *MacUser* magazine's John J. Anderson Distinguished Service Award.
1992: Adobe acquires OCR Systems.
1994: Adobe acquires Aldus, the developer of Page-Maker software.
1996: Adobe releases PhotoDeluxe and PageMill.
1999: Adobe introduces InDesign, a professional publishing software package; sales surpass $1 billion for the first time.
2000: *Fortune* names Adobe as one of the 100 best companies to work for in the United States; Bruce R. Chizen is appointed the chief executive officer (CEO).
2005: Adobe acquires Macromedia Inc.
2007: Shantanu Narayen is appointed CEO.
2009: Adobe is named the 11th best company to work for by *Fortune*.

it communicated directly with the computer's screen, rather than through the printer. Representing a breakthrough in the long struggle for what computer buffs called WYSIWYG (What You See Is What You Get), Display PostScript ensured users that images on the screen would be replicated exactly on paper through the printer. Display PostScript also allowed users to manipulate graphics on the screen; rotating, scaling, and skewing could all be performed to suit the user's needs. IBM and Digital Equipment Corporation soon followed NeXT's lead by licensing Display PostScript for their desktop systems.

In 1988 more than 25 PostScript printers and typesetters were on the market and 20 computer corporations had signed PostScript licensing agreements with Adobe. The company's revenues for 1988 were an impressive $83.5 million, representing a 112 percent increase over revenues of $39.3 million the year before. Moreover, the net income for 1988 increased 137 percent, reaching $21 million. During this time, Apple Computer remained the company's biggest customer, accounting for 33 percent of Adobe's revenues. By the following year, Adobe's staff had increased to 300. As one of the fastest growing software developers, Adobe sought to maintain its position in the industry and foil any potential competitors. Toward this end, Adobe kept its typeface strategies confidential, while it continued to expand into new areas.

At the 1989 Mac World Exposition in San Francisco, California, Adobe introduced two new applications. Adobe Streamline software permitted users to reproduce hardcopy graphics onscreen, converting bit-mapped images into high-quality PostScript artwork. The second product, Collectors Edition II, could be used to set patterns. Adobe eventually adapted these technologies for IBM and IBM-compatible computers that used the Windows program.

Next on Adobe's agenda was international expansion. The company signed an agreement with Canon Inc. of Japan, under which Canon had full licensing rights to Adobe PostScript. As the world's leading manufacturer of laser printers, Canon could bring the PostScript technology to international and multinational customers. To enhance its Type Library, Adobe signed agreements that permitted several companies to develop downloadable typefaces based on Adobe's proprietary technology.

Adobe ended the 1980s on a high note; revenues in 1989 were more than $121 million, and its net income reached $33.7 million. That same year the company introduced Adobe Type Manager. This program used Adobe's outline fonts to generate scalable characters on screen, giving users greater flexibility and better WYSIWYG. The Type Manager also represented an expansion of the Type Library to 420 typefaces.

Also during this time, Adobe announced that it had acquired all rights to a software program called Photo-Shop, an image editing application. PhotoShop, which was designed especially for artists and desktop publishers, was slated for market in conjunction with the Apple Macintosh. Designed to work with type, line art, and other images, PhotoShop provided users with a complete toolbox for editing, creating, and manipulating images. Other unique PhotoShop features included color correction, retouching, and color separation capabilities.

CONTINUED GROWTH IN THE EARLY 1990S

By the end of the 1980s, the incredible boom in the computer business was showing signs of subsiding. In an interview with Martha Groves, Warnock suggested that "if you think you have a formula for success, you'd better figure out how to change it from year to year." Coming up with fresh formulas to ensure continued success was Adobe's focus as the company entered the 1990s. One of its strategies involved developing software that could operate platform-independent, allowing documents to be worked on and sent over many different computers and networks. In other words, Adobe envisioned a world in which a document could be produced on an IBM PC, for example, and sent directly to a Macintosh.

On the way to realizing this goal, Adobe continued to set the pace for technological developments in the industry. In 1990 Adobe received what was believed to be the first copyright registration for a typeface program. The ITC Garamond font program was registered with the U.S. Copyright Office, a move that suggested that typeface programs could be considered creative works of authorship.

By this time, the Adobe Type Library had burgeoned from the original 12 type families to 134. The down loadable typefaces were available for both IBM and Macintosh PCs. The Type Manager, Adobe's scalable-font technology, was made available for IBM PCs and was compatible with UNIX, DOS, and OS/2 systems. Adobe launched PostScript Level 2, which enhanced the PostScript language with new features, such as improved forms handling, color support, and pattern manipulation, making PostScript a more practical and convenient language. One important feature of Level 2 was its use of data compression to reduce transmission times and save disk space by reducing the size of PostScript files on disk. Level 2 also boasted new screening and half-toning technology, better memory, and better printer support features, allowing users to specify color choices and receive those colors in their output.

Late in 1990 Adobe acquired BluePoint Technologies, a leading creator of chips for rendering type. Adobe also signed a new agreement with Apple Computer to work jointly on developing new products using Adobe's PostScript software and Apple's printer technology. Moreover, Adobe announced the creation of Adobe Illustrator for the NeXT system, providing NeXT users with the same powerful design and illustration tool used by owners of Macintosh and IBM PCs.

Adobe's revenues continued to soar. In 1990 the company hit a new record of $168.7 million in revenues, with a net income of $40 million. The following year Adobe announced that it was developing a new type technology, multiple master typefaces, which would allow users to control the weight, width, visual scale, and style of a single typeface to produce endless variations.

Furthering its strategy of providing numerous licensing agreements throughout the early 1990s, Adobe

signed contracts with Lotus Development Corporation, Eastman Kodak, Tektronix Inc., and others. Besides its updated version of PhotoShop, Adobe was also responsible for another breakthrough in printing technology with the development of the Adobe Type 1 Coprocessor. The new device could render text 25 times faster than the fastest existing printers.

The company celebrated another year of record earnings in 1991. Revenues increased 36 percent to $229.7 million, and income shot up 29 percent to $51.6 million. Warnock and Geschke received the *MacUser* magazine's John J. Anderson Distinguished Service Award for "enduring achievement in the Macintosh industry."

Adobe's efforts to create a universal standard for viewing complex documents continued in 1992. That same year the company marked its 10th anniversary and branched out into new ventures. Adobe signed an agreement with Hayden, a division of Prentice Hall Computer Publishing, to create Adobe Press, a joint publishing venture for developing books about graphic arts, Adobe computer applications, and advanced technologies.

During this period, competition in the industry intensified, and Adobe sought new ways to maintain its lead in the industry. Adobe Carousel was the company's first foray into electronic transmission of newspapers, magazines, and other print media. Carousel would allow these materials to be displayed on screen complete with pictures, color, and multiple typefaces.

In June 1992 Geschke was kidnapped. Although he was eventually returned safely and began granting interviews two months after the incident, he refused to discuss details of the abduction. In an interview with *San Jose Business Journal*'s Jonathan Weisman, Geschke discussed Adobe's plans for the future. Maintaining that the company was beginning "a long journey down a digital highway," Geschke revealed that its primary mission was to make text, pictures, video, and, perhaps, sound computer-readable. Toward that end, Adobe acquired OCR Systems, an optical character recognition company that turned scanned documents into manipulatable text.

With the introduction of Adobe Premiere 3.0 for Macintosh in 1993, Adobe entered the fields of video and multimedia. The software enabled users to perform desktop video editing formerly achieved only with expensive equipment. Adobe Premiere featured nonlinear editing, graphics, and special effects.

In 1993 Adobe realized its goal of enabling incompatible computer systems to communicate. Adobe Acrobat software was designed to turn computers into information distributors that would allow Macintosh users to view a document in its original form, with formatting and graphics intact, even if the document had been created on an IBM. Analysts hailed Acrobat as a tool that could facilitate electronic distribution of everything from interoffice memos to training manuals to magazines. Adobe's revenues for the year rose to $313.4 million, up from $265.9 million in 1992, and its net income was reported at $57 million.

CHALLENGES AND DIVERSIFICATION IN THE MID- TO LATE 1990S

Adobe solidified its position in the desktop publishing market in 1994 when it acquired Aldus, the maker of the industry-leading PageMaker desktop publishing software. Adobe and Aldus had worked together previously, and Adobe's font software was used in PageMaker. That same year Adobe introduced After Effects, a program geared toward multimedia and film production efforts. After Effects provided tools for producing two-dimensional animation, as well as special effects and motion compositing. Adobe reported revenues of $676 million for fiscal 1994, up from $580 million the previous year.

In the mid-1990s Adobe continued to grow through acquisitions and worked to strengthen its position in the volatile software industry. The acquisition of Frame Technology Corporation, the developer of Frame-Maker publishing software, in 1995 proved to be an unfortunate purchase; after integrating Frame into the Adobe family of operations, Frame's sales declined heavily. Industry observers attributed the drop to Adobe's decision to close down Frame's technical support division. Also in 1995 Adobe bought Ceneca Communications, which developed tools for creating Web pages. The following year Adobe made additional acquisitions, including Ares Software, for $15.5 million, and the research and development efforts of Swell Software, for $6 million. The research project, however, was discontinued soon after the purchase. Also in 1996 Adobe spun off its pre-press division to Luminous Corporation for $43.6 million and moved its headquarters from Mountain View to downtown San Jose. The following year Adobe divested its investment in Netscape Communications Corporation and separately acquired three software companies, spending a total of $8.5 million.

On the software front, Adobe released PhotoDeluxe and PageMill in 1996. PhotoDeluxe, the first of its category, allowed consumers to manipulate and edit photographs on their computers. PageMill included tools for easily creating Web pages. In 1997 Adobe released upgrades of PageMaker, Illustrator, and FrameMaker. These releases, coupled with increased demand for Photoshop, PhotoDeluxe, and Acrobat products, led to total revenues of $912 million for fiscal 1997, up from $787 million the previous year. In addition, the company's balance of software revenues shifted from predominantly Macintosh-based software to Windows-based software.

Not everything was rosy at Adobe headquarters, however, and 1998 proved to be the most grueling in the company's history. In 1997 Hewlett-Packard chose to stop licensing PostScript from Adobe when it developed its own clone version of the software. By the following year Adobe was feeling the effects of Hewlett-Packard's decision, and its licensing sales suffered. The decline in Macintosh software sales hurt Adobe as well, and competitors such as Microsoft Corporation took away precious market share. In addition, because of the economic recession in Asia, sales in Japan, one of Adobe's stronger markets, fell about 40 percent. Adobe's stock price fell as well, hitting a low that was less than half of its value. Industry observers noted that Adobe had not kept up with the pace of software introductions. As Scott Thurm of the *Wall Street Journal* reported in 1998, "In fast-moving industries, the quest for perfection can get in the way of cranking out good-enough products." Adobe's methodical approach to developing software had hindered its growth and success. Adobe had also grown its workforce too enthusiastically, anticipating demand that failed to materialize.

In August 1998 Adobe indicated that third-quarter revenues would not meet expectations. For the nine months ended August 28, 1998, sales reached $101 million, down from $179 million for the same period in 1997. The company also announced a major restructuring that was designed to streamline operations and increase profitability. The firm planned to eliminate 12 percent of its workforce, about 300 people, including several top executives, and to concentrate more heavily on corporations and businesses, which represented a wider and more profitable niche than Adobe's traditional audience of designers and graphic artists. Just as Adobe announced its intentions, it received a hostile takeover bid from the competitor Quark Inc., the developer of the leading QuarkXPress professional publishing software. Adobe successfully fended off Quark's attempt and embarked on its restructuring journey. Despite the company's trials, Warnock shrugged off Adobe's financial problems. "I don't think Adobe's struggling," Warnock told Lee Pender of the *Computer Reseller News.* "We're not a company that's in a turnaround situation. What we are is a company that was letting expenses get out of line."

The year 1999 proved to be busy for Adobe. Adobe sold two noncore operations as part of its reorganization tactic: Adobe Enterprise Publishing Services Inc., which offered services related to Adobe Acrobat products, and Image Club Graphics, which produced and marketed graphics products and typefaces. In addition, because Adobe wished to enhance its reputation as a provider of tools for Internet and Web applications, the company acquired GoLive Systems, which developed Web design software. Thanks in part to marketing efforts, an increasing number of consumers began to use existing Adobe products Photoshop and Illustrator to design Web pages. Adobe Acrobat, which had failed to catch on in the mid-1990s, was quickly becoming a ubiquitous presence on the Web in the late 1990s.

Adobe released a number of products in 1999, including a new version of Photoshop, GoLive, Press-Ready, ActiveShare, and InDesign. InDesign was Adobe's first offering in the high-end professional publishing segment, a segment dominated by Quark products. Called by many "Quark Killer," InDesign quickly created the largest backlog ever experienced by Adobe for a new product. In September 1999 Adobe reported record revenues of $260.9 million for the third quarter. Profit reached $72 million, up greatly compared with a loss of $6.1 million for the third quarter of 1998. Adobe's stock price more than tripled during the year. Bear, Stearns & Co. analyst Robert Fagin told the *Wall Street Journal*'s Don Clark, "It's staggering.... In the space of one year, the company has been able to put together a true turnaround."

For the fiscal year ended December 3, 1999, Adobe reported revenues of more than $1 billion, the first time in the company's history that sales exceeded $1 billion. In January 2000 Adobe was named one of the 100 best companies to work for in the United States by *Fortune*. The company had successfully carried out its restructuring efforts and appeared ready to tackle new challenges. As Adobe approached a new era, it planned to increase profitability and continue developing cutting-edge technological solutions for publishers, graphic and Web designers, and businesses. Geschke, who announced plans to retire effective March 2000, stated in a prepared statement, "Adobe enters the next millennium in its strongest position ever—in terms of the strength of its management team, its leadership market position, and the quality of its products."

ENGAGING WITH INFORMATION IN THE 21ST CENTURY

In 2000 Bruce R. Chizen was appointed chief executive officer (CEO) of Adobe Systems. Chizen joined the senior management team at Adobe in 1994, when Aldus

was acquired by Adobe. He spent six years in management at Adobe, including senior vice president and general manager of the Consumer Products Division.

Under Chizen's leadership Adobe continued to grow in its visibility and omnipresence in daily computer interactions. Adobe refined its strategy of reaching five key audiences: creative professionals (graphic and Web designers and photographers), knowledge workers (professionals who collaborate around information sharing), enterprise users (computer professionals and corporate executives), high-end users (photography and digital video hobbyists), and application developers (mobile device manufacturers and print and Internet developers). By reaching each audience with unique product lines, Adobe was able to diversify its offerings enough to dominate a larger segment of the computer software and development market.

With Chizen at the helm, Adobe's profits continued to rise. Between 2000 and 2006 Adobe's revenues increased by 70 percent, and its stock increased 40 percent in value despite tough economic times. As Chizen noted in an interview with Juston Jones of the *New York Times* in 2006, "Adobe is everywhere." Adobe created newspaper fonts, magazine layouts, graphics for everything from soda cans to billboards, graphics for global positioning system software, and eventually software for smartphones.

In 2005 Adobe and Macromedia Inc. merged in a $3.4 billion deal, one of the largest ever in the software industry. The merger brought significant new capabilities to Adobe, and in January 2006 a new engagement platform was unveiled that married technology from Adobe Reader with Macromedia's Flash Player. This new technology proved invaluable in moving into the mobile device market.

In 2007, with the company in good health both financially and strategically and poised for continued growth, Chizen stepped aside. Shantanu Narayen was appointed CEO, after distinguishing himself by coleading the merger with Macromedia. Narayen joined Adobe in 1998, serving as a key product researcher and developer before he became a vice president.

Adobe launched its first Flash-based Web phone software in 2009. The Hero smartphone, developed in partnership with HTC Designs, was scheduled to become available in Europe, Asia, and the United States by the end of the year. That same year it was named the 11th best company to work for by *Fortune*.

In the next decade, Adobe hoped to continue to innovate and hold its leadership role in the software market. It planned to make Adobe software build off of itself, so each that application worked with increasing numbers of Adobe applications.

Marinell James
Updated, Mariko Fujinaka; Robert Jacobson

PRINCIPAL SUBSIDIARIES

Adobe Systems Pty. Ltd. (Australia); Adobe Systems Europe Ltd. (UK); Adobe Systems Co. Ltd. (Japan).

PRINCIPAL COMPETITORS

Quark Inc.; Corel Corporation; Microsoft Corporation.

FURTHER READING

"Adobe Crumbles," *BusinessWeek*, February 12, 2001, p. 44.

"Adobe Earnings Top Estimates Again; Cost-Cutting and Strong Web Demand Credited," *Seattle Post-Intelligencer*, December 18, 1999, p. B4.

"Adobe Posts 41% Gain," *New York Times*, June 17, 2008, p. C4.

"Adobe Systems Reports Record Revenue and Operating Profit for Both Fourth Quarter and Fiscal Year 1999" (press release), San Jose, CA: Adobe Systems Inc., December 16, 1999, http://www.adobe.com/aboutadobe/pressroom/pressreleases/pdfs/199912/19991216.adbeq4.pdf.

Clark, Don, "Adobe Systems Beat Estimates for 3rd Quarter," *Wall Street Journal*, September 17, 1999, p. B11.

Collins, LaVon, "Adobe and IBM Sign Joint Marketing Agreement," *Business Wire*, November 16, 1988.

Darrow, Barbara, "Adobe Comes out Swinging—What a Difference a Year Makes," *Computer Reseller News*, September 27, 1999, p. 190.

Downing, David, "Adobe Sets New Direction in Digital Type," *Business Wire*, March 5, 1991.

"Flash Comes to Android," *Linux Gram*, June 29, 2009.

Goldman, James S., "Will Steve Jobs Buy Apple's Former Stake in Adobe Systems?" *San Jose Business Journal*, July 10, 1989, p. 1.

Groves, Martha, "Adobe: Redesigning the Future," *Los Angeles Times*, April 30, 1989, p. B9.

Hansen, Brenda, "Adobe Announces Adobe Illustrator for the IBM Personal Computer," *Business Wire*, September 14, 1988.

Jones, Juston, "Adobe Reaches Far and Wide," *New York Times*, August 5, 2006, p. C3.

Lacy, Sarah, "A Flashy New Adobe," *BusinessWeek*, February 13, 2006, p. 52.

Leone, Genevieve, "High-Flying Adobe Succeeds in Holding off Clone Products," *San Jose Business Journal*, January 23, 1989, p. 4.

Pender, Lee, "John Warnock: Adobe—The Developer Must Meet the New Challenges of Today's Publishing World," *Computer Reseller News*, November 9, 1998, p. 133.

Privett, Cyndi, "Adobe Supplies Software for New Laser Printers," *San Jose Business Journal*, May 26, 1986, p. 15.

Prosser, Linda, "Adobe Previews PostScript Level 2," *Business Wire*, June 4, 1990.

Rensbarger, Fran, "Have Desk, Will Publish," *Washington Business Journal*, March 9, 1987, p. 9.

Rodriguez, Karen, "Adobe Plots Rebound around Business, Corporate Market," *San Jose Business Journal*, September 28, 1998, p. 6.

Thurm, Scott, "Quark Tries to Catch a Fallen High-Tech Star," *Wall Street Journal*, August 27, 1998, p. B1.

Van Horn, Royal, "Technology—Adobe Acrobat Mysteries," *Phi Delta Kappan*, November 2001, p. 186.

Weber, Jonathan, "Adobe Software Could Start New Era in Computer Communication," *Los Angeles Times*, June 15, 1993, p. D1.

Weisman, Jonathan, "Adobe's Hopes Riding on Carousel," *San Jose Business Journal*, August 24, 1992, p. 1.

Wildstrom, Stephen H., "Photoshop's Little Online Brother," *BusinessWeek*, April 28, 2008, p. 128.

Young, Margaret, "Adobe Expands Retail Role with Two Distribution Pacts," *San Jose Business Journal*, October 19, 1987, p. 11.

Affymetrix Inc.

3420 Central Expressway
Santa Clara, California 95051
U.S.A.
Telephone: (408) 731-5000
Toll Free: (888) 362-2447
Fax: (408) 731-5380
Web site: http://www.affymetrix.com

Public Company
Founded: 1991
Incorporated: 1992; reincorporated, 1998
Employees: 1,128
Sales: $410.30 million (2008)
Stock Exchanges: NASDAQ
Ticker Symbol: AFFX
NAICS: 334516 Analytical Laboratory Instrument Manufacturing; 541710 Research and Development in the Physical Sciences and Engineering Sciences

∎ ∎ ∎

Treatments for a wide range of diseases can be improved and made more effective as scientists improve their understanding of human DNA and the valuable information it offers. Affymetrix Inc. develops, manufactures, and sells products used in genetic analysis in the life sciences and clinical health care markets. Markets for Affymetrix products include all aspects of molecular biology research, including genetic analysis; drug research and development; toxicogenomics (the study of how genes respond to environmental stress and toxic substances); and pharmacogenetics (the study of

how genes influence responses to drug treatment). Affymetrix provides DNA probe arrays, scanners, other instruments, and software to process probe arrays and analyze and manage genomic or genetic information.

Headquartered in Santa Clara, California, Affymetrix is considered a pioneer and consistent leader in its field. It maintains manufacturing facilities in Cleveland, Ohio, and Singapore. Affymetrix has sales and distribution operations in place across Europe and Asia, as well as in the United States.

PIONEERING STUDIES

Uruguayan-born research scientist and biotech entrepreneur Alejandro Zaffaroni founded Affymax, a pharmaceutical research company and the one-time parent company of Affymetrix, in 1988. As a young man of 28 years, Zaffaroni had been instrumental in the successful launch in Mexico of Syntex, a birth control company. In 1968 he founded his first company, ALZA, which produced the first drug delivery systems, such as skin patches, slow-release capsules, and small, implantable pumps. With Affymax, as with his other companies, Zaffaroni chose to concentrate his efforts on developing sets of scientific tools rather than a few select products.

In 1989 Zaffaroni recruited Stephen P. A. Fodor, a postdoctoral fellow in chemistry at the University of California, Berkeley, to join the research team at Affymax and lead a developing project exploring how to put computer chip technology to use for research on the human genome (a person's DNA). Fodor and fellow biochemist and author Lubert Stryer began to report on

COMPANY PERSPECTIVES

■

Our mission is to revolutionize how the world benefits from genetic information. We are continually expanding our presence in genetic analysis by broadening our product portfolio, making genetic products more accessible, and introducing next-generation technologies. Affymetrix contributed significantly to the formation of today's genetic analysis markets, and we will continue to drive the genomics revolution with a single-minded vision: to help all individuals benefit from understanding their own DNA.

their teamwork in leading scientific journals, including the journal *Science* in 1991. That year Affymetrix was formed as a subsidiary of Affymax. Potential applications for its developing "bio-chip" research included clinical medicine, bio-medical research, agriculture, forensic investigations, and environmental testing.

The research team's success prompted Zaffaroni to sell the subsidiary Affymetrix as a spin-off company in 1992. Fodor became the Affymetrix founding president. His research teams published additional articles describing their work in the journals *Nature* and the *Proceedings of the National Academy of Sciences*. Team members were recognized with various awards for their work from the early 1990s onward, including the Newcomb-Cleveland Award from the American Association for Advancement of Science in 1992, the Intellectual Property Owners Association's Distinguished Inventor Award in 1993, and the Newcomb-Cleveland Award again in 2008. In 1994 team efforts to combine computer technology with DNA research resulted in the introduction of the original GeneChip brand array by Affymetrix. The first of its kind introduced to the market, the GeneChip array became the centerpiece of Affymetrix technology. In keeping with Zaffaroni's vision of developing sets of scientific tools rather than just a few select products, Affymetrix developed instrument systems to accompany the GeneChip brand. These included machines to deliver the tissue sample to the chip and scanners to read and analyze the results.

GENECHIP ARRAYS

GeneChip arrays, also called biochips and DNA arrays, resembled the microprocessing chips used in computers, but instead of transistors, they contained microscopic

grids designed to grip and analyze DNA. When test samples, such as a drop of blood, were washed over the chip, each microscopic square on the approximately half-inch sliver of glass selected and united with one particular gene in the sample. A specially designed scanner read the chip's reaction to the test sample and interpreted the results. Biochip technology and its accompanying software allowed technicians to analyze sections of genetic information and identify variations from the normal or expected. These variations could then be targeted for gene-based therapies or drugs. Among its many possible implications, GeneChip technology had the potential to radically change how genetically acquired conditions were understood, prevented, and treated. Use of biochips such as GeneChip arrays became standard practice for large-scale genomics studies in academia and private industry. The use of these chips allowed hundreds of thousands of genetic assays to be performed rapidly and accurately.

The introduction of GeneChip arrays allowed Affymetrix to expand its collaborative efforts with research firms and drug development companies. Affymetrix and Incyte Genomics Inc. expanded their previous collaboration and entered into a gene expression database joint venture. Each company pledged to handle its own development costs and to share equally in profits and in ownership of any intellectual property that emerged from the venture.

In addition to its collaborative efforts, Affymetrix continued to supply increasing numbers of medical research and pharmaceutical companies with its GeneChip technology. By 1999 more than 80 major companies, including Glaxo Wellcome and Pfizer, were using Affymetrix biochips in their research.

GENE WARS AND ALLIANCES

The success of Affymetrix GeneChip technology within the highly competitive world of genomic research led to episodes of corporate intrigue and civil litigation. In one particularly dramatic instance in 1999, FBI agents served search warrants at the Bay Area offices of Affymetrix rival Roche Bioscience and seized computer disk drives. FBI agents also appeared that day at the home of a former Roche employee who, with a colleague, was preparing to publish a paper on how to bypass some perceived shortcomings of Affymetrix software. The agents confiscated software and demanded to know if the former Roche employee had stolen computer code belonging to Affymetrix. In the end these incidents did not adversely affect the former employee's career nor prevent Affymetrix from having a long-term relationship with Roche. They illustrated, however, the importance placed on trade secrets and proprietary information in a

KEY DATES

1968: Alejandro Zaffaroni establishes his first company, drug delivery firm ALZA.

1988: Zaffaroni founds Affymax, predecessor of Affymetrix.

1991: Zaffaroni forms Affymetrix as a subsidiary of Affymax.

1992: Successful research on DNA probes prompts Zaffaroni to sell Affymetrix as a spin-off company of Affymax.

1994: Affymetrix introduces the first GeneChip brand array to the market; Affymetrix and Incyte Genomics Inc. enter into joint venture.

1995: President Bill Clinton awards Zaffaroni the National Medal of Technology.

1998: Zaffaroni receives Lifetime Achievement Award from the University of California at Berkeley Entrepreneurs Forum.

1999: Oxford Gene Technology Ltd. launches legal proceedings against Affymetrix.

2000: Affymetrix acquires Genetic MicroSystems Inc.; Affymetrix contracts with Cystic Fibrosis Foundation to design custom DNA array; Affymetrix acquires Neomorphic Inc. and creates the spin-off company Perlegen Sciences Inc. to absorb it.

2001: Affymetrix and Oxford Gene Technology Ltd. settle patent case; flaws are revealed in GeneChip Murine Genome U74 Set.

2002: Affymetrix establishes wholly owned Japanese subsidiary.

2003: Affymetrix introduces the FoodExpert-ID Array.

2004: Affymetrix introduces the 179 Nimble Express Array.

2005: Affymetrix acquires collaborator ParAllele Bioscience Inc.

2006: Chemical Heritage Foundation and Biotechnology Industry Organization awards Zaffaroni the 8th Annual Biotechnology Heritage Award; President George W. Bush presents Affymetrix researcher Lubert Stryer with National Medal of Science.

2007: Affymetrix launches Collaborations for Cancer Research Program; Affymetrix partners with NuGEN Technologies Inc. to market NuGEN products.

2008: Affymetrix completes acquisition of Panomics Inc.; *Fast Company* magazine selects Affymetrix as one of the 50 most innovative companies in the world.

2009: San Francisco Business Times names Affymetrix "One of the Best Places to Work in the Bay Area." *Entrepreneur* magazine selects Affymetrix as one of its Top 100 Companies to Watch.

growing industry that offered both potential profit and improved quality of life.

In December 1999 the British company Oxford Gene Technology Ltd. (OGT) launched legal proceedings in the English High Court of Justice to revoke two British DNA micro-array patents held by Affymetrix. The Oxford-based, privately held company contended that the two patents held by Affymetrix were unjustifiably broad and had been acquired from a third company, Beckman-Coulter, that had obtained a license to the chip technology from Oxford University in 1998. OGT contended that Beckman-Coulter had no right to sell the license to Affymetrix. Affymetrix declared its decision to defend its patents.

The English High Court of Justice ruled in April 2000 that because Beckman-Coulter had not developed the technology licensed to it, as stipulated in the original agreement with Oxford University, it had no right to sell the technology's license to Affymetrix. Later in 2000 the legal battle moved to the United States, where OGT sued Affymetrix for infringement of its U.S. patents.

Most of Affymetrix's associations with other companies, however, were not adversarial. In the years after the introduction of the GeneChip array and associated product lines, Affymetrix established numerous clinical research partnerships with notable academic research centers, as well as prominent pharmaceutical and biotechnology companies. Some partnerships allowed broad access to Affymetrix GeneChip arrays, instrumentation, and software for use in research and development activities. In 2000 those entering into such research partnerships with Affymetrix included Proctor and Gamble, Merck, and Novartis Pharmaceuticals.

ACQUISITIONS AND OPPORTUNITIES FOR GROWTH

In February 2000 Affymetrix acquired Genetic Micro-Systems Inc., a privately owned Massachusetts-based instrumentation company specializing in DNA array technology, including the use of ink-jet printing technology to manufacture less expensive biochips. Also in early 2000 Affymetrix introduced two sequence-specific micro-arrays that could provide highly efficient measurement and analysis of specific gene expression. The GeneChip Human Cancer G110 array allowed researchers to simultaneously measure more than 1,700 specially chosen genes linked to human cancers. The ability to measure changes in gene expression under various conditions allowed researchers to understand the function of these select genes and their relevance to the development of disease. The GeneChip Yeast Genome S98 array, also introduced in 2000, permitted single-array-based analysis of the entire yeast genome, an important biological model for laboratory research.

Affymetrix entered into its first collaboration with a nonprofit organization when it agreed to custom design a DNA array for the Cystic Fibrosis Foundation in August 2000. The array would be based on the *Pseudomonas aeruginosa* bacterium, the most common cause of potentially chronic or fatal respiratory infections in individuals with cystic fibrosis. The custom arrays were intended for use by nonprofit and commercial cystic fibrosis researchers. The Cystic Fibrosis Foundation's president and CEO, Robert Beall, said his foundation chose Affymetrix for its knowledge of the technology and its willingness to work quickly.

In October 2000 Affymetrix acquired Neomorphic Inc., a privately held computational genomics company located in Berkeley, California, with whom it had been collaborating on genome annotation projects. Annotation identifies genes and other regulatory regions within genomic sequences. "We realized that there was eminently greater benefit to both as a single company," said Neomorphic Inc. cofounder and chief technical officer David Kulp, as quoted by Brendan Doherty in the *San Francisco Business Times*. The 1.4 million shares of Neomorphic stock acquired by Affymetrix were valued at approximately $70 million.

Affymetrix created a spin-off company, Perlegen Sciences Inc., to absorb Neomorphic. Neomorphic computational technology was integrated with Affymetrix data, producing tools to help interpret laboratory findings. The company used Affymetrix DNA probe arrays to perform multiple whole genome scans. Whole genome scans could spot genetic variations responsible for disease, as well as variations that predicted how an individual might respond to a particular drug. The information obtained from these scans helped drug companies improve safety and efficacy of their products, and to optimize clinical trials.

In March 2001 flaws traceable to ambiguities in a public genome database were revealed in the GeneChip Murine Genome U74 Set, an array of thousands of known sequences of mouse genes. Flaws were revealed in 25 percent of probes in the set's arrays A and B and in 60 percent of probes in array C. The sets were being used in a wide variety of medical research experiments, including ones on aging, neurodegenerative diseases, gene therapy, and human behavior. Once revealed, the flaws set some research back for months and halted the progress of other work. It raised questions about the reliability of emerging genetic research technology and the publicly available genome databases on which it is based. In response, Affymetrix sent masks to screen out the faulty probes so that research could resume. It also set in motion plans to replace the faulty sets within three months.

Some Affymetrix collaborative partnerships with leading institutions and companies were narrowly focused on specific issues. In July 2001 deCODE Genetics Inc. and Affymetrix agreed to collaborate on the development of DNA-based tests to determine the responsiveness of individual patients to treatments for common diseases.

LITIGATION SETTLEMENTS

During 2001 Affymetrix settled three significant patent-related court cases with rival biotech firms. In March it settled all its litigation regarding GeneChip patents and licensing with OGT, an aforementioned dispute that had begun in late 1999. Details of the settlement between Affymetrix and OGT were not made public, but both companies declared they wanted to put the litigation behind them in order to concentrate on their respective businesses. Oxford University professor Edward Southern, whose foundational work on Gene-Chip technology helped lead to the patents in question, declared, as quoted by Andrew Pollack in the *New York Times*, that "it is essential for genomic research that these matters have been resolved and that O.G.T. can concentrate on its main objectives of developing its own technology and business and licensing others to do the same."

In September 2001 Affymetrix and Hyseq Inc. settled all existing patent litigation between them, which had begun in 1997. The two companies dismissed all lawsuits pending in U.S. district court and agreed to acknowledge validity and enforceability of patents named in the lawsuits. The terms of the settlement granted Affymetrix access to a commercial license for Hyseq patents related to DNA arrays. Hyseq gained internal use license to certain Affymetrix intellectual property for its pharmaceutical business. In addition, Hyseq and Affymetrix formed and funded a joint venture, N-Mer Inc., which would use gene sequencing technology from Hyseq and the Affymetrix GeneChip technology platform to develop high density micro-array products. Affymetrix was named N-Mer's sole array and systems supplier, as well as the exclusive agent for distribution of N-Mer products.

Affymetrix and Incyte Genomics Inc. began as partners in a gene-expression database joint venture in 1996. In December 2001 they settled all existing patent infringement litigation that had ensued. At issue were micro-array patents held by Affymetrix and RNA amplification patents held by Incyte. The two companies agreed to cross licenses under their respective intellectual property portfolios.

RAPID GROWTH

The growing use of GeneChip technology in academic and private industry research around the world allowed Affymetrix to expand its presence globally. To meet growing Japanese demand for its GeneChip brand products, Affymetrix established a wholly owned subsidiary, Affymetrix Japan, in September 2002 to manage direct sales, marketing, and technical support from headquarters in Tokyo.

In 2003 Affymetrix added to the agriculture applications of its technology when it introduced its FoodExpert-ID Array. The tool allowed scientists to genetically identify the presence or absence of 33 species of animal in any food product. A year later Affymetrix introduced its 179 NimbleExpress Array, specifically designed for use in microbiological and infectious disease research. It could be applied to everything from the study of costly agricultural pathogens to life-threatening human diseases.

In October 2005 Affymetrix acquired a former collaborator and supplier of assays used in genetic research, the privately held South San Francisco company ParAllele Bioscience Inc. The value of the all-stock acquisition deal was estimated at $120 million. According to Fodor, founding president of Affymetrix, the acquisition "would accelerate discovery and product development in a wide variety of areas, from basic research to the clinic," as quoted by DrugResearcher.

RECOGNITION AND MORE GROWTH

In 2006 the Chemical Heritage Foundation and the Biotechnology Industry Organization awarded Affyme-

trix founder Zaffaroni the 8th Annual Biotechnology Heritage Award in recognition of his scientific contributions, particularly in the area of drug delivery. That same year President George W. Bush presented Affymetrix pioneer researcher Stryer with the National Medal of Science, citing among other accomplishments his work on the development of high density micro-arrays for genetic analysis.

As recognition of its contributions to genetic research increased, Affymetrix sought additional opportunities for collaboration and expansion. In 2007 it acquired USB Corporation, a privately held developer and manufacturer of biochemical and molecular biology products. Also in 2007 Affymetrix announced plans to partner with biotechnology developer NuGEN Technologies Inc. to market the NuGEN WT-Ovation FFPE System, which allowed GeneChip studies on previously unusable formalin-fixed, paraffin-embedded tissue samples acquired from laboratories conducting large-scale clinical studies.

A busy year, 2007 also saw Affymetrix launch the Collaborations in Cancer Research Program, a joint effort with 30 individual cancer researchers at universities, research institutes, and medical centers across Europe. Initially limited to European researchers, the program expanded to researchers in North America in 2008 and Japan. It provided financial support and GeneChip brand products to researchers working on detailed genetic profiles of certain cancers. If successful, the program could yield micro-arrays useful for early screening or diagnosis of patients suspected of having these types of cancers.

In 2008 Affymetrix completed its acquisition of the privately held life sciences company Panomics Inc., which manufactured products to measure molecular events, such as intracellular pathway analysis, cell signaling, and gene expression profiling. In July of that year, for a cash purchase price of $25 million, Affymetrix acquired the privately held, San Francisco-based start-up True Materials Inc., a developer of digitally encoded microparticle technology that used a minimal amount of sample material and decreased test processing time.

Fodor transferred his CEO responsibilities to Kevin King on January 1, 2009. Previously president of the company, King also became a member of the board of directors at that time. King had joined the company in January 2007 with a mission to help refocus its life sciences business. He rebuilt the executive leadership team, defined the company's longer-term growth strategy, and strengthened its market position by successfully launching the SNP Array 6.0 ahead of schedule.

POPULAR IN THE PRESS

Three major business publications singled Affymetrix out for special recognition during 2008 and 2009. In March 2008 *Fast Company* magazine selected Affymetrix as one of the 50 most innovative companies in the world, citing its work on the relationship between genetics and drug metabolism. Affymetrix was the only life sciences company selected for the honor.

In a 2009 annual survey conducted by the *San Francisco Business Times*, Affymetrix employees at the company's headquarters in Santa Clara voted their employer "One of the Best Places to Work in the Bay Area." In addition to the effectiveness they perceived in their managers and coworkers, employees commented on the close and trusting relationships they enjoyed with their coworkers and their own overall job satisfaction. Furthermore, that year *Entrepreneur* magazine selected Affymetrix as one of the Top 100 Companies to Watch and noted its resilient use of "brainpower, determination and good timing" in challenging economic times, as noted in *Wireless News*.

By 2009 Affymetrix was focused on developing products that other companies and scientists use in cancer diagnosis, as well as the diagnosis of metabolic, infectious, and cardiovascular diseases. Affymetrix expected that use of its GeneChip assays would continue to improve disease detection, prognosis, and treatment selection, and improve overall treatment efficiency and effectiveness. For example, genetic mutations known to correlate with specific diseases could be monitored, and biologically relevant markers for drug response could be identified in individual patients. Adverse drug reactions could be reduced by comparing the patient's DNA with the drug's profile using the company's DMET Plus Premier Pack, which contained a panel that enabled scientists to study a wide range of known relevant genetic markers. To further increase its research capabilities, Affymetrix continued to establish clinical research partnerships with notable academic research centers as well as prominent pharmaceutical and biotechnology companies. These included Sysmex; F. Hoffmann-La Roche Ltd. (Roche); bioMerieux Inc.; Veridex LLC; and CapitalBio in China.

Joyce Helena Brusin

PRINCIPAL SUBSIDIARIES

USB Corporation; Panomics Inc; Affymetrix Japan KK; Affymetrix UK Ltd; Affymetrix Singapore Pte Ltd; True Materials Inc.; ParAllele BioScience Inc; Anatrace Inc; Neomorphic Inc; Genetic Microsystems Inc.

PRINCIPAL COMPETITORS

Caliper Life Sciences Inc.; Illumina Inc.; Luminex Corporation; CombiMatrix Corporation; Qiagen NV; Agilent Technologies Inc.; Life Technologies.

FURTHER READING

"Affymetrix Acquires ParAllele BioScience," DrugResearcher, June 1, 2005, http://www.drugresearcher.com/Research-management/Affymetrix-acquires-ParAllele-BioScience.

"Affymetrix and Hyseq Resolve Dispute," *New York Times*, October 26, 2001, p. C5.

"Affymetrix Announces New Cost-Effective Product for Standardizing Drug Metabolism Studies," *Chemical Business Newsbase*, November 11, 2008.

"Affymetrix Chosen as One of the Top Places to Work in the Bay Area," Reuters, April 30, 2009, http://www.reuters.com/article/pressRelease/idUS288790+30-Apr-2009+BW20090430.

"Affymetrix Completes Acquisition of Panomics," *Chemical Business Newsbase*, December 8, 2008.

"Affymetrix Earns 'Innovative Company' Honors," *Wireless News*, March 12, 2008.

"Affymetrix, Inc. (NMS: AFFX)," Mergent Online, http://www.mergentonline.com.

"Affymetrix Launches Comprehensive Array," *Analytic Separations News*, December 2004.

"Affymetrix Tapped as One of the Top Places to Work in the Bay Area," *Washington Post*, May 6, 2009.

Ananthaswamy, Anil, "Technical Hitch Trips Up Gene Revolutionaries," *New Scientist*, March 17, 2001, p. 12.

"Biotech's Father William (Alejandro Zaffaroni)," *Economist*, June 26, 1999.

"Cincinnati Children's Hospital Deploying Affymetrix Technology," *Wireless News*, December 14, 2008.

Doherty, Brendan, "Biotech Number Cruncher Neomorphic Fetches $70M," *San Francisco Business Times*, October 6, 2000, p. 8.

"Entrepreneur Magazine Taps Affymetrix as One of Top 100 Companies to Watch," *Wireless News*, June 2, 2009.

Firn, David. "Oxford Gene Wins Key Point in Affymetrix Fight: Pharmaceuticals Legal Battle Will Now Move to U.S.," *Financial Times*, April 8, 2000, p. 16.

———, "UK: Oxford Gene to Bring Action," *Financial Times*, December 16, 1999, p. 28.

Fodor S. P., J. L. Read, M. C. Pirrung, L. Stryer, A. T. Lu, and D. Solas, "Light-Directed Spatially Addressable Parallel Chemical Synthesis," *Science*, February 15, 1991, pp. 767–73.

Fodor, Stephen P. A., Richard P. Rava, Xiaohua C. Huang, Ann C. Pease, Christopher P. Holmes, and Cynthia L. Adams, "Multiplexed Biochemical Assays with Biological Chips," *Nature*, August 5, 1993.

"The Great DNA Chip Derby," *Business Week*, October 25, 1999, p. 90.

Hoover, Ken, "Gene-on-a-Chip Work Pays Off: Affymetrix Grows Rapidly, Teams Up with China Firm," *Investor's Business Daily*, May 2, 2005.

Kher, Unmesh, "The Workhorse of Genomic Medicine," *Time*, January 15, 2001, p. 62.

Lamb, Celia, "Affymetrix Gets Cystic Fibrosis Contract," *Sacramento Business Journal*, September 8, 2000, p.17.

Leuty, Ron, "QB3 Garage Startup Snapped Up for $25M," *San Francisco Business Times*, August 8, 2008.

Marcial, Gene G., "Affymetrix: A Lab Boost," *Business Week*, April 25, 2005, p. 132.

Moukheiber, Gina, "Chip+DNA=Hype," *Forbes*, June 15, 1998, p. 126.

———, "Gene Bully," *Forbes*, July 9, 2001, p. 74.

Nash, Jim, "Affymax N.V. Will Sell Off One of Its Subsidiaries," *Business Journal*, August 30, 1993, p. 1.

"NOVEL: Affymetrix Introduces GeneChip Probe Arrays," *High Tech Separations News*, February 2000.

Osborne, Randall, "Affymetrix, Incyte Make Peace; Will Deals Replace Bitter Fight?" *Bioworld Financial Watch* December 31, 2001, p. 1.

Pollack, Andrew. "Two Biotech Companies Settle Gene-Chip Case," *New York Times*, March 26, 2001, p. C6.

Stipp, David, "Gene Chip Breakthrough," *Fortune*, March 31, 1997.

"2006 Biotechnology Heritage Award Given," *Pharmaceutical Technology*, May 2006.

"U.S. Biotech Leader Affymetrix Sets Up Sales Unit in Japan," *AsiaPulse News*, September 4, 2002, p. 2611.

Alliant Energy Corporation

4902 North Biltmore Lane
P.O. Box 77007
Madison, Wisconsin 53718-2148
U.S.A.
Telephone: (608) 458-3311
Toll Free: (800) 255-4268
Fax: (608) 458-0100
Web site: http://www.alliantenergy.com

Public Company
Incorporated: 1981 as WPL Holdings, Inc.
Employees: 5,179 (2009)
Sales: $3.44 billion (2009)
Stock Exchanges: NYSE
Ticker Symbol: LNT
NAICS: 221112 Fossil Fuel Electric Power Generation; 221119 Other Electric Power Generation; 221121 Electric Bulk Power Transmission and Control; 221122 Electric Power Distribution; 221210 Natural Gas Distribution

■ ■ ■

Alliant Energy Corporation provides electricity and natural gas to nearly 1.5 million customers in Wisconsin, Iowa, and Minnesota. Based in Madison, Wisconsin, its holdings include coal-fired power stations, transmission lines, gas pipelines, wind farms, and energy-related consulting businesses. Founded in 1981 as WPL Holdings, Inc., its roots extend back to the early decades of the twentieth century, when Wisconsin Power and Light Company, Interstate Power Company, and IES Industries, Inc., which were to form the backbone of Alliant Energy, were established as independent utilities.

EARLY GROWTH

The history of Alliant, which follows that of the U.S. utility industry, is largely one of mergers and consolidations. In the early 1900s, electricity was supplied by small, localized utilities, many of which were dependent on the electric-railway lines then found in most cities and towns. Those lines rapidly disappeared as automobiles gained popularity, and many utilities found themselves on the verge of bankruptcy. The result was consolidation opportunities for the industry's stronger players, including the Eastern Wisconsin Electric Company (EWEC), which was also known as Eastern Wisconsin Power Company. Seven years after its founding in 1917, EWEC arranged a merger with five other utilities in the region (Middle Wisconsin Power Company, Mineral Point Public Service Company, Janesville Electric Company, Wisconsin Utilities Company, and Wisconsin Power, Light & Heat Company). The new entity would be known as the Wisconsin Power and Light Company (WPL). As of 2009, 85 years after its founding, WPL remained a fixture in the state as one of Alliant's main subsidiaries.

Within a year of WPL's incorporation in 1924, two other utilities were established in the neighboring state of Iowa. One was Dubuque-based Interstate Power Company (IPC) with operations throughout the eastern half of the state. IPC also had operations in southern Minnesota and western Wisconsin. Areas to the south

COMPANY PERSPECTIVES

Alliant Energy Corporation is committed to providing safe, reliable, affordable, and environmentally responsible energy for current and future generations. Our core values are safety, ethics, environment, diversity, and efficiency.

and west of IPC's territory were the domain of the Iowa Railway and Light Corporation, which later became known as IES Industries, Inc.

All three companies struggled through the Depression of the 1930s, as power consumption by factories and other large enterprises declined sharply. This drop was partially offset by the rapid electrification of rural areas, a development strongly encouraged by the U.S. government. It was not until World War II, however, that the companies' balance sheets became strong enough to support a major expansion of generating capacity. WPL, in particular, grew rapidly between 1945 and 1960, building three new coal-fired plants and expanding a fourth. That period also brought significant growth in natural-gas operations, as new pipelines from Texas reduced transportation costs.

ADAPTATIONS TO CHANGES IN THE MARKETPLACE

A foreshadowing of the companies' later union under Alliant came in December of 1953, when IPC sold WPL its properties in Wisconsin. As IPC refocused its efforts on its core territories west of the Mississippi, WPL worked to integrate the new acquisitions, an effort that required significant infrastructure investments. Demand for power continued to increase for both companies. That pressure, coupled with a growing concern over air pollution and rising fossil-fuel prices, prompted new interest in alternate energy sources. The most prominent alternative at the time was nuclear power, and utilities throughout the region would devote considerable resources in the 1960s and early 1970s to the development of nuclear plants. Iowa's only nuclear facility, the Duane Arnold Energy Center in Palo, would be completed by IES in 1974. In Wisconsin, meanwhile, WPL joined the Wisconsin Public Service Corporation and MGE Energy, Inc., in building the 556-megawatt Kewaunee Power Station, also completed in 1974. By that time, however, public opposition to nuclear power had begun to grow, and WPL's plans to

expand its nuclear capacity further had been shelved by 1980.

Energy demand in the Midwest, as well as across the country, rose steadily through the 1980s. A variety of disparate factors contributed to this growth, including the closure of 1970s-era conservation programs, population increases, suburban development, and the rise in the use of computers and other personal electronics. Significant changes in the way state governments as well as the federal government regulated utilities also occurred in the 1970s, particularly with regard to liability and antitrust issues. James Underkofler, then the president of WPL, would adapt to those changes with a thorough reorganization of the company's structure. The central feature of the new framework was a holding company, WPL Holdings (WPLH), Inc., which Underkofler and his board established in 1981 to serve as Wisconsin Power and Light's corporate parent. Final approval for the change, however, would not come from regulators until 1988.

The mid-1980s and early 1990s were a time of increasing competition across the utility industry. In response to that challenge, many companies diversified their holdings through acquisitions, particularly in the fields of energy-related engineering and consulting. In 1983, for example, WPLH purchased RMT, Inc., a Wisconsin consulting firm dedicated, according to its Web site, to finding "balanced solutions for complex energy and environmental problems." While RMT was well established by that time, other investments by WPLH and its Iowa peers were directed toward "start-up" enterprises. In 1988, for example, IES joined two other companies to provide the initial capital for a venture called Microfuel Corporation. While that particular investment was not a success, others proved more profitable. RMT, in particular, would grow steadily as a unit of WPLH, adding hundreds of employees and opening several overseas branches.

RESTRUCTURING AND RENEWABLE ENERGY

In 1998, 10 years after regulators had approved the structure of WPLH, the company underwent another major administrative overhaul through merger. Like many other utilities, WPLH felt two conflicting pressures. One was from shareholders demanding revenue growth and the other from state regulators and the public who were generally opposed to the rate hikes that easily would have provided that growth. Company management believed the simplest solution to that quandary was to expand its service area. By adding more customers, the company could theoretically increase its revenues without raising rates. However, because every

KEY DATES

1917: Eastern Wisconsin Electric Company is incorporated.

1924: Eastern Wisconsin Electric Company merges with five other utilities to form Wisconsin Power and Light Company.

1925: IES Utilities, Inc., is incorporated as Iowa Railway and Light Corporation; Interstate Power Company is incorporated in Dubuque, Iowa.

1953: Interstate Power Company sells its Wisconsin operations to Wisconsin Power and Light Company.

1981: WPL Holdings, Inc., is incorporated as a holding company for Wisconsin Power and Light Company.

1983: WPL Holdings, Inc., purchases RMT, Inc., a consulting firm specializing in environmental issues.

1998: WPL Holdings, Inc., merges with Interstate Power Company and IES Industries, Inc., to form Alliant Energy Corporation.

2002: IES Utilities, Inc., the primary subsidiary of IES Industries, Inc., merges with Interstate Power Company to form Interstate Power and Light Company in an internal reorganization.

2008: Commercial operations begin at Alliant's first wind-power facility, Cedar Ridge Wind Farm in Fond du Lac County, Wisconsin.

square mile of the Midwest was already covered by a utility, the only way to expand was to find a partner.

WPLH found two such partners in IES and ICP. In an unusual three-way merger, the companies were joined into a single entity called Alliant Energy Corporation. The headquarters of the new company would be in the Wisconsin capital of Madison, a city that ironically was served by competitor MGE Energy, Inc. (better known as Madison Gas and Electric). The merger was accompanied by several internal restructurings as the new company streamlined its operations. These changes took several years to complete and resulted in a four-part organizational structure. The first division was Wisconsin Power and Light. The second was a new entity called Interstate Power and Light Company that was formed in 2002 when Alliant merged the utility

operations of IES with IPC. The third division, Alliant Energy Corporate Services, Inc., was incorporated in 1997 as the administrative arm of the company. The last division, Alliant Energy Resources, LLC, was established as a corporation but was converted into a limited-liability company in 2008. Alliant Energy Resources was responsible for all of Alliant's non-utility businesses, including RMT; Industrial Energy Applications (IEA), which designed, developed, and operated on-site power systems for factories and other industrial clients; Alliant Energy Transportation, which oversaw a variety of rail, barge, and trucking resources, many focused on the shipment of coal; and WindConnect, a leading developer of wind resources.

The rise of WindConnect in the early 2000s signaled a significant shift in the company's long-term plans. As fossil-fuel prices rose and concern grew over the carbon emissions of coal-fired power plants, Alliant and its competitors faced considerable public pressure to move toward renewable energy sources. While the company has also invested in solar and geothermal facilities, the bulk of its efforts in renewable energy have been focused on wind, largely for geographical reasons. With some of the best wind resources in the world, wind turbines were being built rapidly for use in the upper Midwest, many clustered in so-called wind farms. While WindConnect has generally functioned as a consultancy, offering its design and installation services to a variety of utilities and other businesses, it has also played a major role in developing wind resources for its parent company. Alliant's first project of this sort, Cedar Ridge Wind Farm in Fond du Lac County, Wisconsin, began commercial operations in December 2008. At least two more wind projects were in development, including Whispering Willow Wind Farm in Franklin County, Iowa, and Bent Tree Wind Farm in Freeborn County, Minnesota. In its annual report for 2008, Alliant noted that both Whispering Willow and Bent Tree would be roughly three times as large as the 68-megawatt facility at Cedar Ridge. The company expects that Bent Tree eventually will support enough turbines to generate 400 megawatts of electricity a year, an amount sufficient to power 100,000 homes.

A RECESSION'S IMPACT

Alliant's wind farms and other new projects were expensive. While the company's balance sheet remained relatively strong, raising the capital necessary to complete the projects proved challenging amid the global economic recession that began in 2008. As demand for finished products plummeted, factories across the region closed, sharply reducing the demand for gas and electricity. Like many of its peers, Alliant had relatively few options for alleviating the effect of that decline on its capital and its bottom line. As a regulated utility, it could not raise its rates without the explicit approval of state regulators, whose primary mission has been to protect the interests of citizens, not utilities. Given that mandate, most regulators were understandably reluctant to raise rates at a time when consumers and small businesses were struggling. Alliant had to turn, therefore, to the nation's credit markets, but they also were affected by the slowdown. Loans quickly became more difficult and more expensive to obtain, a shift that contributed to a marked decline in the company's net income. After earning $425.3 million in 2007, Alliant made just $288 million the following year, a drop of 32 percent.

Alliant's stock price declined as well, from $40.69 as of December 31, 2007 to $29.18 by December 31, 2008. Although that represented a sharp drop, it was significantly better than the S&P 500 Index, a widely followed measure of the stock market's performance as a whole. The picture changed, however, when the company was measured against its peers. When compared with an industry-specific benchmark, the S&P Utilities Index, Alliant stock was a slacker in 2008, trailing by 12 percent.

FLOODING IN 2008

While there were many reasons for the drop in value, one important factor was undoubtedly the effect flooding in Wisconsin and Iowa had on the company. In June 2008, rivers overflowed throughout the region and, in at least one case (Lake Delton, Wisconsin), breached an earthen dam. Homes, businesses, and hundreds of thousands of acres of cropland in the heart of Alliant's territory were devastated. The worst damage occurred in and around Cedar Rapids, Iowa, the largest city serviced by the company. More than 900 employees were evacuated, and many of Alliant's offices and industrial facilities were inundated by the Cedar River, which rose to a level not seen in several centuries. The company would later estimate its losses at more than $200 million. However, Alliant took pride in the speed with which it restored service in the wake of the disaster, restoring power to most customers within a week. Alliant's efforts in this area would be recognized by the Edison Electric Institute (EEI), which presented the company with a 2008 Emergency Recovery Award. In Alliant's 2008 annual report, EEI President Thomas R. Kuhn said that Alliant's IPL subsidiary, the unit most affected by the flooding, "did not miss one beat in restoring power to its customers." He went on to say, "The company's ac-

complishments are a testament to the unrelenting drive our industry exhibits year-in and year-out in restoring power after devastating natural disasters."

Repairs would continue for months at several Alliant facilities, especially at Cedar Rapids' Prairie Creek Generating Station, where partial operations did not resume until January 2009. The temporary loss of generating capacity at Prairie Creek and other damaged plants exacerbated the effects the ongoing economic recession was having on the company's financial health. The closure of the enormous General Motors facility in Janesville, Wisconsin, in December 2008 was another major setback. As the demand for gas and electricity continued to fall throughout the region, Alliant moved aggressively to cut costs, principally through staffing cuts. Thomas Content reported in the *Milwaukee Journal Sentinel* in May 2009 that Alliant had laid off 15 workers and mandated one-week furloughs for all employees not represented by a union. The company also suspended its program to match 401(K) retirement contributions for the rest of the year. Bill Harvey, chairman and chief executive, told Content that the moves were expected to save between $16.5 and $22 million.

ECONOMIC AND ENVIRONMENTAL CHALLENGES

Arguably the biggest challenge for Alliant in the summer of 2009, however, was an increasingly uncertain and potentially burdensome regulatory environment. As providers of two commodities essential to public and private life, gas-and-electric utilities like Alliant have always been heavily regulated. Beginning in the second half of the twentieth century, however, government involvement grew considerably as public concern increased over the pollution generated by power plants. Like most utilities in the Midwest, Alliant has long produced the bulk of its electricity by burning coal, a fuel widely criticized for its role in air and water pollution, and which has been cited as a cause of global climate change. While pollution-control technologies have improved significantly over the years, the basic issue of environmental damage has continued to affect Alliant's public image and day-to-day operations. In November 2008, for example, the Wisconsin Public Service Commission rejected Alliant's application to build a new coal-fired generating plant at an existing facility in Cassville. In a press release, the commission specifically cited "uncertainty over the costs of complying with future possible carbon dioxide regulations" as a major factor in its decision. Emissions of carbon dioxide have been identified as one of the primary causes of climate change. Alliant responded with apparent equanimity, noting in its annual report that it "respect[ed]" the decision and was "resolved to move forward."

In contrast to the Wisconsin regulators, the federal government under the administration of U.S. President George W. Bush (2001–09) generally took a laissez-faire approach to utilities. That attitude was expected to end during the administration of President Barack Obama, who had identified climate change as a priority. Within months of entering office, Obama and his Congressional allies had introduced legislation aimed at reducing carbon-dioxide emissions, principally through a so-called "cap-and-trade" system. Under the plan, utilities and other industrial facilities would have to purchase credits to cover their carbon emissions. Because any unused credits could be sold or traded, a utility would have a strong financial incentive to reduce emissions. Critics of the plan, however, have argued that its impact on global climate change would be far less noticeable than its effect on electricity rates throughout the country. As debate in Congress continued in the mid-2009, the bill's passage was by no means assured. Amid that uncertainty, Alliant seemed to be hedging its bets, rapidly increasing its involvement in wind and other alternative energies, but continuing to rely heavily on coal. As the company's annual report stated, "When and how carbon emissions will be regulated remains anyone's guess."

R. Anthony Kugler

PRINCIPAL SUBSIDIARIES

Interstate Power and Light Company; Wisconsin Power and Light Company; RMT, Inc.; Industrial Energy Ap-plications; Alliant Energy Transportation; WindConnect; Alliant Energy Resources, LLC; Alliant Energy Corporate Services, Inc.; Alliant Energy Investments Inc.

PRINCIPAL COMPETITORS

MGE Energy, Inc.; Wisconsin Energy Corporation; Xcel Energy, Inc; MidAmerican Energy Company.

FURTHER READING

"Alliant Energy to Sell Some Units and Cut Dividend," *New York Times*, November 23, 2002, p. C4.

Beck, Bill, *Transforming the Heartland: The History of Wisconsin Power & Light Company*, Madison, WI: Wisconsin Power & Light Co., 1990.

"Compilation of Investor-Owned Utility Transactions—Mergers and Major Acquisitions," APPANet.org.

Content, Thomas, "Alliant Turns to Layoffs, Other Cost Cutting," *Milwaukee Journal Sentinel*, May 1, 2009.

———, "Recession Darkens Madison Utility's View for '10," *Milwaukee Journal Sentinel*, July 29, 2009.

"EEI Emergency Response Award Winners—2008," EEI.org.

Johnston, David Cay, "Company News: Alliant Energy Is Told to Pay $18.5 Million in Taxes," *New York Times*, November 15, 2003, p. C5.

"PSC Rejects Wisconsin Power and Light's Proposed Coal Power Plant" (press release), Public Service Commission of Wisconsin, November 11, 2008.

The First Fifty Years: A History of Interstate Power Company, Dubuque, IA: Interstate Power Company, 1975.

"Wis PSC's Approval Is First Step for Wind Farm in Minn," Associated Press, July 9, 2009.

Alpha Natural Resources Inc.

One Alpha Place
P.O. Box 2345
Abingdon, Virginia 24212
U.S.A.
Telephone: (276) 619-4410
Toll Free: (866) 322-5742
Fax: (276) 619-4410
Web site: http://www.alphanr.com

Public Company
Founded: 2002
Employees: 3,779
Sales: $2.55 billion (2008)
Stock Exchanges: New York
Ticker Symbol: ANR
NAISC: 212111 Bituminous Coal and Lignite Surface Mining; 212112 Bituminous Coal Underground Mining

■ ■ ■

Alpha Natural Resources Inc. is a coal producer located in the Appalachian coal region in the eastern United States. The company produces both metallurgical coal, used to make coke, a key ingredient in steel production, and steam coal, used as fuel for electricity generation by large utilities and factories. The company is made up of 8 regional business units and maintains 33 underground mines, 24 strip mines, and 11 coal preparation plants. The company also purchases and resells coal mined by other companies. In 2009 Alpha was poised for a merger with Foundation Coal Holdings Inc. This merger would make Alpha a major player in the industry as the third-largest coal producer in the United States.

AN ACQUISITION STRATEGY

Alpha Natural Resources Inc. was formed in 2002 when the private equity firm First Reserve Corporation acquired most of the Virginia coal operations of Pittston Coal Company. The following year the new company acquired Coastal Coal Company's mining operations in Kentucky, West Virginia, and Virginia, and the U.S. coal operations of American Metals and Coal International Inc. In November 2003 Alpha acquired the Pennsylvania coal operations of Mears Enterprises. The new company focused on mining high-quality coal that commanded the highest revenues. Most of its coal was produced in underground mines, whereas 20 percent was produced in surface mines.

Mike Quillen, the president and chief executive officer of Alpha, pointed out to Brian Salgado in *Exploration + Processing* that the management team had been in the coal business for over 30 years, giving the company the advantage of experience despite its youth. "We've been in the business for three decades," he explained. "So we're always strategizing about what actions to take if the market goes one direction or another, because we've been there before." Quillen expressed optimism about the future of the coal industry. Although labor shortages and regulatory issues kept coal production down, other factors indicated that the demand for coal would continue to rise, "both through rising worldwide steel production and America's

COMPANY PERSPECTIVES

■

Alpha Natural Resources Inc. and its subsidiaries are a leading Central Appalachian coal producer with significant operations in Northern Appalachia. Our reserves primarily consist of high BTU, low sulfur steam coal that is currently in high demand in U.S. coal markets and metallurgical coal that is currently in high demand in both U.S. and international coal markets.

We produce, process and sell steam and metallurgical coal from eight regional business units supported by 30 active underground mines, 20 active surface mines and 10 coal preparation plants located throughout Virginia, West Virginia, Kentucky and Pennsylvania.

insatiable appetite for electricity, 50 percent of which is produced by coal-fired power plants."

GOING PUBLIC AND CONTINUED GROWTH

Investors greeted Alpha's 2005 initial public offering with enthusiasm, given burgeoning worldwide energy demands. During its first day of trading, the stock price jumped from $19 a share to $21.92 a share. Within a few days, the stock price reached $25.34. By November Alpha was trading at $27 a share. Alpha management continued its acquisitions strategy, while keeping its eye on small coal producers in Appalachia. In October 2005 the company completed its acquisition of Nicewonder Coal Group for $316.2 million in cash and stock. This acquisition increased Alpha's coal output by about 20 percent. That same year the company also embarked on a program of internal expansion, aiming to open seven new mines by the end of 2007. In 2006 it acquired two surface and two underground mines owned by Progress Fuels Corporation, located in eastern Kentucky, for $23 million, and announced plans to develop a mine in the company's new coal reserves by 2008. In 2008 it acquired Mingo Logan–Ben Creek, a mine complex near Alpha's mining operations in West Virginia, from Arch Coal for $40 million.

In July 2008 Cleveland-Cliffs Inc., the largest producer of iron-ore pellets in North America, announced that it would buy Alpha Natural Resources for $10 billion to attain Alpha's metallurgical coal used in steelmaking. Alpha shareholders would be paid in Cleveland-Cliffs stock and in cash at a rate about a third higher than Alpha's stock price.

However, on November 18 the two companies called off their impending merger. This announcement drastically decreased the stock in both companies. Cleveland-Cliffs's stock closed at $16.51 on November 19, down from $121.95 on June 30, before the merger was announced. Alpha's stock closed at $18.32 on November 19, down from $119.30 on July 16, one day before the merger had been announced. The companies cited the economic downturn and uncertainty in the steel industry as the reason for the merger's collapse. In fact, the hedge fund Harbinger Capital Partners LLP, a shareholder in Cleveland-Cliffs, had opposed the deal. Harbinger held an 18 percent share in the company and attempted to increase its stake to 33 percent, which would allow it to cancel the deal single-handedly. Even though it failed to increase its stake in the company, Harbinger's opposition made it unlikely that the merger would gain approval from the required two-thirds of Cleveland-Cliffs shareholders. As the analyst Jorge Beristain told Mick Bowen of *American Metal Market* in November 2008, "This deal was a casualty of the financial crisis, and clearly investors don't have the appetite."

Nevertheless, Alpha posted a soaring income of $165.5 million in 2008, compared with only $27.7 million in 2007. However, the company posted a net loss in the last quarter of 2008, and it subsequently announced several cost-saving measures, including the closure of the Whitetail Kittanning mine complex in Preston County, West Virginia.

IMPACT OF THE GLOBAL RECESSION

Alpha nonetheless faced tough times in 2009, mainly because of tightening supplies of coal. Under the administration of Barack Obama, the U.S. Environmental Protection Agency began restricting permits for surface mining in the eastern United States and scrutinizing lax environmental regulations put in place by the administration of George W. Bush. Labor shortages were also a constant problem. Recruiting workers, especially in underground mines, was a continual challenge because potential workers remained wary of potentially fatal mine accidents. For example, one miner was killed in October 2005 at Whitetail Kittanning Mine in Newburg, West Virginia, a subsidiary of Alpha, when a wall collapsed. In another example; two workers were killed in a mine collapse in January 2007 at Brooks Run Mining Company, another subsidiary of Alpha. The Obama administration stepped up enforcement of safety regulations in 2009; as a result,

KEY DATES

2002: Alpha Natural Resources Inc. is formed.
2003: Alpha acquires Coastal Coal Company, the U.S. coal production operations of American Metals and Coal International Inc. and Mears Enterprises Inc.
2004: Alpha acquires Moravian Run Reclamation Co. Inc.
2005: Alpha is listed on the New York Stock Exchange; it acquires the Nicewonder Coal Group.
2006: Alpha acquires the coal mining operations of Progress Fuels Corporation.
2008: Alpha acquires Mingo Logan–Ben Creek coal mining assets from Arch Coal Inc.
2009: Alpha announces the pending acquisition of Foundation Coal Holdings Inc.

mines were shut down and coal production was restricted by as much as 10 percent.

Despite these pressures and the worldwide economic slowdown, Alpha announced an increase of 60.8 percent in first quarter earnings over the first quarter in 2008. This earnings jump occurred despite lower production and sales because of larger profit margins. The sale price for coal in that quarter was on average 25 percent higher than the price had been the year before.

In May 2009 Alpha announced that it would buy Foundation Coal Holdings Inc. for about $1.5 billion in stock; stockholders in both companies would vote on the proposal in special meetings on July 31, 2009. The merger would make Alpha the third-largest coal producer in the United States, with 59 coal mines and 14 coal-preparation plants and with the capacity to produce more than 91 million tons of coal a year. Alpha sought to acquire Foundation to spread out the risk from more pending stringent environmental regulations. Foundation owned mines in Wyoming and Montana, where surface mining faced less opposition than it did in the eastern United States, where Alpha currently operated. In addition, the merger would diversify Alpha's coal production, allowing it to produce more steam coal. Alpha was the largest metallurgical coal producer in the country. Metallurgical coal, which was used to produce steel, could be highly profitable; however, demand for metallurgical coal rose and fell due to economic factors. By contrast, demand for steam coal, which was used to produce electricity, remained relatively constant. Quillen told Bowen in May 2009 that the merger "gives us a hedge against the highly profitable but somewhat erratic metallurgical steel business because of the consistency of the steam coal market."

In spite of the economic recession, Alpha Natural Resources remained strong. In 2009 more than half of the electricity in the United States was generated from coal, and demand for coal worldwide was high. The United States held 25 percent of the world's coal reserves, and Europe and China imported U.S. coal to make steel and generate electricity. Many analysts projected that demand for coal in China, India, and the United States will rise by 50 percent by 2030; if these predictions held up, Alpha may grow even larger in the coming decades. In addition, the proposed merger with Foundation allowed the company to, in effect, hedge its bets. Although it made its greatest profit from the production of high-quality metallurgical coal, the demand for steam coal, which was produced by Foundation, was recession-proof. As a *Wall Street Journal* headline proclaimed in 2005, Alpha was one coal company that was likely to "stay hot."

Melissa J. Doak

PRINCIPAL SUBSIDIARIES

Alpha Coal Sales Co. LLC; Alpha Natural Resources Capital Corporation; Alpha Terminal Company LLC; Cobra Natural Resources LLC; Esperanza Coal Co. LLC; Maxxim Rebuild Co. LLC; Maxxum Carbon Resources LLC; AMFIRE LLC; McDowell-Wyoming Coal Company LLC; Palladian Holdings LLC; Premium Energy LLC.

PRINCIPLE OPERATING UNITS

Paramont; Dickenson-Russell; Kingwood; Brooks Run North; Brooks Run South; AMFIRE; Enterprise; Callaway/Cobra.

PRINCIPAL COMPETITORS

Peabody Energy Corporation; Arch Coal Inc.; CONSOL Energy Inc.; Massey Energy Corporation.

FURTHER READING

"Alpha Earnings Jump 60.8% in 1st Qtr. Despite Output Dip," *American Metal Market*, May 12, 2009, p. 6.
"Alpha Natural Resources to Acquire Mining Operations, 73 Million Tons of Coal Reserves from Progress Fuels," *PR*

Newswire, April 6, 2006.

"Alpha Natural Resources Completes Acquisition of Nicewonder Coal Group, Syndication of Credit Facilities," *PR Newswire*, October 26, 2005.

"Alpha Natural Resources Completes Mingo Logan Acquisition," *PR Newswire*, June 29, 2007.

"Alpha Natural Resources and Foundation Coal Holdings Announce Expiration of HSR Waiting Period for Proposed Merger," *PR Newswire*, June 22, 2009.

"Alpha Natural Resources Reports 60 Percent Improvement in Net Income for First Quarter," *PR Newswire*, May 6, 2009.

"Alpha's Coal Glows Hot," *BusinessWeek*, August 22, 2005, p. 138.

"Alpha Upbeat on Coal as Quarterly Income Up," *American Metal Market*, November 4, 2005, p. 5.

"Arch Coal Divests Mining Complex in Central Appalachia to Alpha," *Coal Age (1996)*, July 2007, p. 6.

Benoit, David, "Holders Back Cleveland-Cliffs," *Wall Street Journal*, October 4, 2008, p. B6.

Bowen, Mick, "Alpha Creates Buffer in Met Coal Mart with Foundation Buy," *American Metal Market*, May 13, 2009, p. 6.

———, "Cliffs' Alpha Buy Seen Killed by Differing Views," *American Metal Market*, November 20, 2008, pp. 1, 6.

———, "Downturn Puts Cliffs-Alpha Plan on Ice," *American Metal Market*, November 19, 2008, p. 6.

"Cliffs and Alpha End Merger Plan," *New York Times*, November 17, 2008.

"Coal Producer Buys a Rival for $1.4 Billion in Stock," Associated Press, May 12, 2009.

"Corporate News: Cleveland-Cliffs Again Urges 'No,'" *Wall Street Journal*, September 9, 2008, p. B3.

Crofts, Dale, "Cleveland-Cliffs to Buy Alpha Natural for $10 Billion," Bloomberg.com, July 16, 2008.

"El Paso Closes Asset Sales," *Oil Daily*, February 5, 2003.

Gladder, Paul, "Coal Attracts Private-Equity Groups—With $1 Billion Purchase, Blackstone Leads Investors Buying U.S. Mining Assets," *Wall Street Journal*, May 25, 2004, p. A2.

"Harbinger Opposes Cleveland-Cliffs Deal," *Wall Street Journal*, July 18, 2008, p. B5.

Maher, Kris, "Coal Price May Fall Despite Tight Supply," *Wall Street Journal*, September 24, 2008, p. C8.

———, "Coal Stocks Stay Hot Thanks to Steel Markets, Power Plants," *Wall Street Journal*, May 6, 2005, p. C3.

———, "Corporate News: Coal Merger Ends Hiatus of Mine Deals," *Wall Street Journal*, May 13, 2009, p. B2.

———, "Corporate News: Resource Deals Continue—Cleveland-Cliffs Is to Buy Alpha for Coal Reserves," *Wall Street Journal*, July 17, 2008, p. B2.

———, "U.S. News: Appalachia Is a Bright Spot as Coal Country Seeks Workers," *Wall Street Journal*, November 22, 2008, p. A3.

"Mine Collapse Kills 2 Workers in West Virginia," *New York Times*, January 14, 2007.

"New Stock Listings," *Wall Street Journal*, February 22, 2005, p. C7.

Pollack, Lauren, "Cliffs, Alpha Natural Quit Deal," *Wall Street Journal*, November 18, 2008, p. B7.

Riley, Anne, "Alpha Income Soars in 'Outstanding Year'," *American Metal Market*, February 6, 2009, p. 9.

Salgado, Brian, "Pooling Its Resources: Alpha Natural Resources Inc. May Be Only a Few Years Old, but the Firms That Merged to Form the Company Have Plenty of Experience," *Exploration + Processing*, Fall 2005, pp. 62–64.

"Stock Alert Newsletter Alerts Alpha Natural Resources," M2 Presswire, February 18, 2005.

Amedisys, Inc.

5959 South Sherwood Forest Boulevard
Baton Rouge, Louisiana 70816-6038
U.S.A.
Telephone: (225) 292-2031
Fax: (225) 229-8163
Web site: http://www.amedisys.com/

Public Company
Founded: 1982
Incorporated: 1982 (Louisiana); 1994 (Delaware)
Employees: 14,800
Revenues: $1.19 billion (2008)
Stock Exchanges: NASDAQ
Ticker Symbol: AMED
NAICS: 621610 Home Health Care Services; 561310
　　Employment Placement Services

■ ■ ■

Baton Rouge-based Amedisys, Inc., was founded in 1982 as a nurse staffing service. Experimenting throughout its first 15 years with diverse aspects of health care, by 1998 and facing a financial crisis, Borne was betting the bank on home health care. The gamble paid off, with the following decade seeing exponential growth. In 2006 the company's net service revenue was $541.1 million; by 2008 it was $1.19 billion, an increase of 119.4 percent in two years. In 2008 Amedisys acquired TLC Health Services, giving the company an additional 92 home health agencies and 11 hospice agencies. By 2009 Amedisys was the second-largest provider of home health care in the nation, operating 480 Medicare-certified home health agencies and 48 Medicare-certified hospice agencies in 38 states and the District of Columbia and Puerto Rico.

DIVERSE BEGINNINGS: MID-1990S

William F. Borne began Analytical Medical Enterprises, the parent company of Amedisys, when he was laid off from his job at a hospital. Subsidiaries included a catering business, a frozen Cajun food company, and a seafood processing plant, as well as Amerinurse, a traveling nurse service, and Nursing Enterprises, a consulting business. In the process of taking the company public in 1994, Borne sold the subsidiaries not related to health.

Borne then set his sights on expanding into the outpatient surgery business. In 1995 Amedisys merged with Surgical Care Centers of Texas. In the following years it constructed several free-standing outpatient surgery centers in Louisiana and Texas. In 1997 Amedisys broke ground for the East Houston Surgery Center, its third free-standing outpatient surgery center. The center was a cooperative effort between Houston-area surgeons and Amedisys; the center was majority owned by surgeons and physicians, and Amedisys would manage it. That same year, Amedisys began trading on the NASDAQ.

More successes followed. In 1997 Amedisys was awarded a contract to provide home health care services for the Veterans' Administration program in Louisiana. At the same time, the company ventured into alternate-site infusion therapy. Infusion therapy is the intravenous administration of medication and nutrition to patients with a wide range of health conditions, including

COMPANY PERSPECTIVES

■

We believe in the future of home care and know that by providing the highest quality of care for patients, constantly improving efficiencies and remaining on the cutting edge of technology and innovation, we will continue to be the leading provider of home health care and hospice services.

cancer, HIV, and other disorders. Expansion of the company's home health care business continued as well.

TROUBLED TIMES: LATE 1990S

Amedisys, however, faced a crisis in 1998. That year Medicare announced changes to its payment system. Previously the only limits on Medicare payments were per beneficiary caps, a system that rewarded agencies that continued to provide services to chronically ill patients up to their individual limit. By 2000 a new system had been ushered in that set a limit for each patient depending on the person's condition. It favored medical treatment for acute conditions or crises in chronic cases, generally involving specific medical therapies to help a patient recover from an injury or illness. The interim system, retroactive for six months and in effect from 1998 to 2000, slashed Amedisys's revenue by half. The company had to return $17 million in revenues and had millions of dollars of unpaid bills. Borne joked with writer Luisa Kroll in *Forbes*, "I wouldn't stop at red lights because I was afraid I'd get dragged out of my car."

Borne decided to focus Amedisys solely on home health care, a sector he believed would grow exponentially as the aging U.S. population and exploding health care costs would make home care an attractive alterative to institutionally based care. He acquired the home health care operations of Columbia/HCA Corporation in Alabama, Georgia, North Carolina, Oklahoma, Louisiana, and Tennessee. However, the huge acquisition coupled with the Medicare changes caused Amedisys to become cash-strapped. To make matters worse, during the Medicare transition, Amedisys overstated earnings and faced two class-action suits as a result, as well as a significant drop in the value of its stock. By the end of 1998 Amedisys announced a net loss of $24.9 million, or $8.14 per share. The company's future looked dim indeed. Borne was reported by Smiley Anders in the *Baton Rouge Advocate*

as saying that he did not declare bankruptcy at that time because he could not pay the legal fees.

Instead of declaring bankruptcy, the company restructured. It divested itself of all divisions except for home health care, immediately jettisoning its staffing and patient care division, its durable medical equipment division, and its software information division. By mid-1999 the company also intended to divest itself of its six ambulatory surgery centers and its infusion therapy division in order to become solely focused on home health care. At the same time, its net tangible assets dropped below the requirements of the NASDAQ, and it began trading on the OTC Bulletin Board, used to list companies considered financially risky.

A SUCCESS STORY: EARLY 2000S

The restructuring, however, paid dividends. In 2001 Amedisys won a contract to provide managed home health care to patients of United Healthcare of Alabama and United Healthcare of Georgia. In September of that year the company sold its last outpatient surgery center. In a *PR Newswire* report for September 17, 2001, Borne was quoted as saying, "All of our resources are now solely devoted to home health care nursing, and we expect to participate fully in the anticipated growth of the home nursing industry in coming years." With the company's restructuring complete, Amedisys common stock was reapproved for listing on the NASDAQ. In a *PR Newswire* report on March 25, 2002, Borne was quoted as saying, "It has been a relentless journey to get to our Nasdaq destination, one which began the day we were de-listed.... Our next objective is to return to the Nasdaq National Market prior to year end." Just seven months later, Amedisys stock was approved for re-listing on the NASDAQ.

Borne credited a positive corporate culture with much of the company's success. The CEO met with every new employee of the company, even those who worked for companies that Amedisys acquired. In addition, the company stressed the quality of care its employees give their homebound patients. Tom Guarisco in the *Greater Baton Rouge Business Report* quoted Borne as saying, "It's a privilege to treat people in their homes." Stock analysts have noted that the company's commitment both to its employees and to developing quality disease management protocols help keep the company on top. Borne told Guarisco, "A happy, confident and motivated nurse will help patients achieve better outcomes than an unhappy, unengaged employee who follows the same clinical protocol."

By 2004 the company had debuted on the *Forbes* list of Best Small Companies in America at number four; Borne himself was named Entrepreneur of the

KEY DATES

1982: William F. Borne founds Amedisys and becomes chairman and CEO.

1994: Company is reincorporated in Delaware and is publicly traded for the first time.

1998: Medicare restructures payment systems; Amedisys buys portion of Columbia/HCA Corporation's operations.

2001: Company sells last outpatient surgery center and becomes focused solely on home nursing.

2004: Amedisys debuts at number four on the *Forbes* list of Best Small Companies in America.

2007: Amedisys acquires IntegriCare, operating home health care and hospice agencies in nine states.

2008: Amedisys acquires TLC Health Care Services, consisting of 92 home health agencies and 11 hospice agencies in 22 states and the District of Columbia.

2009: Amedisys acquires hospices in South Carolina and Mississippi.

Year. In 2006 Amedisys ranked seventh on *Fortune*'s 100 Fastest-Growing Companies list. Amedisys continued to pursue a growth strategy of acquisitions, large and small, as well as organic growth reflecting increases in the aging population. Borne also began to acquire hospice care companies, believing hospice care is a natural extension of Amedisys services. In 2005 Amedisys increased its size by 50 percent, and in 2006 the company raised $200 million for acquisitions.

Borne set his sights on becoming a national player in home health care when in 2007 Amedisys acquired IntegriCare, which included 19 home health agencies and 11 hospice agencies. At this point Amedisys had operations in eight states outside the southeastern United States. In 2008 Amedisys acquired TLC Health Care Services, Inc.; with 92 home health agencies and 11 hospice agencies located in 22 states and the District of Columbia, TLC was the company's largest acquisition ever. Amedisys continued to acquire new agencies in 2009, announcing in January the purchase of three home health agencies and one hospice agency in Arkansas, the purchase of two home health agencies in Yuma, Arizona, in February, and the purchase of a home health and hospice agency in Baltimore, Maryland, in March, the company's first acquisition in that state.

The market for home health care would continue to grow as the baby boomer generation began to become Medicare eligible in 2011; the number of Americans age 65 or older and Medicare eligible was projected by the Census Bureau to grow from 40.2 million in 2010 to 63.9 million in 2025 and to 88.5 million by 2050. The economic recession of the early 2000s had negligible effect on Amedisys, with the company announcing in July 2009 that second-quarter revenue had increased 20.9 percent over the second quarter of 2008. The outlook for Amedisys could hardly be brighter.

Melissa J. Doak

PRINCIPAL SUBSIDIARIES

Accumed Holding Corp.; Adventa Hospice, Inc.; Arnica Therapy Services, L.L.C.; Brookside Home Health, LLC; Comprehensive Home Healthcare, Inc.; Emerald Care, Inc.; Family Home Health Care, Inc.; Home Health of Alexandria, Inc.; Horizons Hospice Care, Inc.; Housecall, Inc.; TLC Health Care Services, Inc.

PRINCIPAL COMPETITORS

Gentiva Health Services, Inc.

FURTHER READING

Alexander, Kelly King, "Building on a Winning Prescription," *Greater Baton Rouge Business Report*, April 1, 1990, p. 42.

———, "Nursing an IPO," *Greater Baton Rouge Business Report*, May 19, 1992, p. 26.

"Amedisys Acquires Hospice Agencies in South Carolina and Mississippi" (press release), Baton Rouge, LA: Amedisys, Inc., August 3, 2009.

"Amedisys Acquires Two Home Health Agencies in Arizona" (press release), Baton Rouge, LA: Amedisys, Inc., February 3, 2009.

"Amedisys, a Healthy Investment" (pamphlet), Baton Rouge, LA: Amedisys, Inc., May 2009, http://www.amedisys.com/pdf/investorpresentation_050109.pdf.

"Amedisys CEO Borne Bent on More Growth: Acquisition Spree Turns Home Health Care Firm into National Contender," *Investor's Business Daily*, February 19, 2008, p. A9.

"Amedisys Common Stock Approved for Listing on Nasdaq Stock Market," *PR Newswire*, March 25, 2002, p. LAM09725032002.

"Amedisys, Inc. Announces the Sale of Two Surgery Centers," *PR Newswire*, August 31, 1999, p. 8615.

"Amedisys, Inc. Announces Trading Symbol Change," *PR Newswire*, September 30, 1998, p. 456.

"Amedisys, Inc. Awarded VA Home Health Care Contract," *PR Newswire*, November 17, 1997.

"Amedisys, Inc. Begins Trading on Nasdaq National Market," *PR Newswire*, June 3, 1997.

"Amedisys, Inc. Secures $28 Million Line of Credit, Acquires Texas Ambulatory Surgery Center and Sells DME Division," *PR Newswire*, December 30, 1998, p. 554.

"Amedisys Reports Second Quarter Revenue and Earnings" (press release), Baton Rouge, LA: Amedisys, Inc., July 28, 2009.

"Amedisys Sees Growth in New Year," *Wall Street Journal*, January 7, 2009.

"Amedisys Sells Infusion Operations to Park Pharmacy Corporation," *PR Newswire*, August 14, 2000, p. 5897.

"Amedisys Sells Interest in Surgery Center for $1.65 Million," *PR Newswire*, January 3, 2001, p. 5630.

"Amedisys Sells Outpatient Surgery Center; Divestiture Strategy for Non-Core Assets Now Complete," *PR Newswire*, September 17, 2001, p. 1968.

"Amedisys Signs Managed Care Contracts to Cover 650,000 Georgia and Alabama Residents," *PR Newswire*, April 30, 2001.

"Amedisys Signs Purchase Agreement for Maryland Home Health and Hospice Agencies" (press release), Baton Rouge, LA: Amedisys, Inc., March 12, 2009.

"Amedisys Signs Purchase Agreement for Three Home Health Agencies and One Hospice Agency" (press release), Baton Rouge, LA: Amedisys, Inc., January 27, 2009.

"Amedisys to Sell Staffing Sub," *Mergers & Acquisitions Report*, August 24, 1998.

Anders, Smiley, "When Opportunity Knocks: Borne's Home-Health Giant Amedisys Riding High, but Road Has Been Rough," *Baton Rouge Advocate*, May 22, 2005, p. 1-I.

Benesh, Peter, "Home-Care Provider Nurses Itself Back to Health; Amedisys," *Investor's Business Daily*, April 12, 2004, p. A9.

Catton, Grant, "Highly-Acquisitive Amedisys Seeks Private Financing for Latest Buy," *Private Placement Letter*, March 3, 2008.

Clark, Steve, "B.R.'s Economic Giant," *Greater Baton Rouge Business Report*, April 21, 2009, p. 20.

"Company News; Colombia/HCA to Sell Some Home Care Operations," *New York Times*, June 3, 1998, p. D4.

Courreges, Patrick, "Major Shake-Up for Home Health," *Greater Baton Rouge Business Report*, November 21, 2000, p. 27.

Gautreau, Chris, "In Need of a Transfusion?" *Greater Baton Rouge Business Report*, November 10, 1998, p. 20.

———, "Suit Says Investors Deceived: Legal Woes Mount against Amedisys," *Baton Rouge Advocate*, August 23, 2001, p. 1-D.

Griggs, Ted, "Uncertain Effect: Medicare Changes Might Hurt or Help Local Health-Care Companies," *Baton Rouge Advocate*, July 22, 2007, p. 1.

Guarisco, Tom, "Resuscitated and Ready," *Greater Baton Rouge Business Report*, January 6, 2004, p. 17.

———, "2005 Business Awards: Amedisys: Free Reading for Life," *Greater Baton Rouge Business Report*, March 29, 2005, p. A15.

"Home-Care Demand Benefits Amedisys," *Baton Rouge Advocate*, May 4, 2005, p. 3-C.

"Home Healthcare Co. Gears Up for Expansion," *Corporate Financing Week*, December 25, 2006.

"Houston Physicians and Amedisys, Inc. Begin Construction of East Houston Surgery Center," *PR Newswire*, May 8, 1997.

Hundley, Kris, "Columbia/HCA to Sell Home Health Units in 11 States," *Knight Ridder/Tribune Business News*, June 3, 1998, p. A4.

"Immunology First Alternate-Site Infusion Therapy Office Opened," *Disease Weekly Plus*, January 19, 1998.

Kroll, Luisa, "At Death's Door," *Forbes*, November 1, 2004, p. 140.

Mero, Jenny, "The Joy of Growth," *Fortune*, September 18, 2006, p. 138.

Shinkle, Kirk, "Amedisys' CEO Keeps Firm Growing by Swimming Upstream," *Investor's Business Daily*, December 16, 2004, p. A4.

Square, Jonathan, "Catching Up: Bill Borne," *Greater Baton Rouge Business Report*, March 28, 2006, p. 13.

"United States: Target—Home Care Plus Inc," *Mergers & Acquisitions Report*, July 3, 1995.

Anadarko Petroleum Corporation

———■———

1201 Lake Robbins Drive
The Woodlands, Texas 77380-1046
U.S.A.
Telephone: (832) 636-1000
Toll Free: (800) 800-1101
Fax: (832) 636-8220
Web site: http://www.anadarko.com

Public Company
Incorporated: 1959 as Anadarko Production Company
Employees: 4,300 (2008)
Sales: $15.72 billion (2008)
Stock Exchanges: New York
Ticker Symbol: APC
NAICS: 211111 Crude Petroleum and Natural Gas
    Extraction; 213111 Drilling Oil and Gas Wells

■ ■ ■

Anadarko Petroleum Corporation is among the largest independent oil and natural gas exploration and production companies in the United States. The company's North American operations include drilling facilities in Wyoming, the Great Plains, and the Gulf of Mexico. Although a majority of the company's reserves are in North America, since the early 1990s it has developed a substantial overseas presence, establishing operations in Algeria, the Red Sea, and Peru. Between its domestic and international holdings, by 2009 the company owned total proven reserves of more than 2.4 billion barrels of oil equivalent (BOE).

DOMESTIC GROWTH AND EXPANSION: 1959-70

Anadarko was created in 1959 as a wholly owned subsidiary of Panhandle Eastern Pipe Line Company. At that time, Federal Power Commission (FPC) rules placed lower price limits on gas produced from properties owned by pipeline companies than on gas produced from independently owned properties. Panhandle owned a substantial amount of gas-producing property, located primarily in the Anadarko Basin, a gas-rich region covering parts of the Texas and Oklahoma panhandles and southwestern Kansas. Since regulations prevented Panhandle from charging the market price for the gas it produced, the company sought ways to skirt these price ceilings. Efforts in the courtroom failed, leaving the creation of a wholly owned subsidiary for gas exploration and production as the only option. Anadarko Production Company was officially incorporated in June 1959, with Panhandle owning all of its stock. Headquarters for the new company were established in Liberal, Kansas; Frederick Robinson was named chairperson, and Robert Harkins became company president.

Since properties developed by Anadarko were not subject to FPC pipeline pricing regulations, all of Panhandle's undeveloped properties were transferred to its new subsidiary. Although its gas properties that were already developed remained under FPC jurisdiction, Panhandle's oil-producing properties were not subject to the same pricing rules. Therefore, they were transferred to Anadarko as well. By the end of 1959, Anadarko had drilled 17 wells in the Anadarko Basin, 14 of which were development wells, all of which were producers.

COMPANY PERSPECTIVES

At Anadarko, we are committed to maintaining a balance between protecting our environment, public health and our communities while producing the energy we all need. Energy is fundamental to human existence. It is nearly as important as clean air, water and affordable food. We take our responsibility very seriously to deliver resources to our energy-hungry world, and we hold true to our core values of integrity and trust, servant leadership and open communication in all of our business activities.

One of the three exploratory wells was also a producer. Before its first full year of operation had ended, Anadarko had spent $2.5 million on exploration and had purchased 27 producing gas wells in the Texas panhandle.

Anadarko signed its first major long-term contract in 1960, a 20-year agreement with Pioneer Natural Gas Company to provide gas from the Red Cave formation in the Texas panhandle to several communities in the area. The following year, the company built an 84-mile pipeline in Kansas. The pipeline carried gas from the Spivey Grabs Field in Kingman and Harper counties to the Skelly Oil Refinery in El Dorado. Anadarko continued to grow quickly over the next few years, mainly by exploiting its rich properties on its home turf, the Anadarko Basin. Between 1962 and 1964, the company doubled its sales of natural gas, from 27 billion cubic feet to 53 billion. Its oil sales doubled over the same period, from 911,000 to 1.8 million barrels.

By the mid-1960s, Anadarko's future growth clearly depended on expansion outside the Anadarko Basin. Toward this end, in August 1965, the company purchased Ambassador Oil Corporation of Fort Worth, Texas, for $12 million. In purchasing Ambassador, Anadarko acquired assets that included undeveloped leases and proven oil and gas reserves totaling about 600,000 acres, located in 19 states and Canada. Most of Ambassador's personnel were retained, and because of its more central location, Ambassador's Fort Worth offices were designated as Anadarko's new headquarters. While this transfer was taking place, Anadarko President Harkins died, and Richard O'Shields was named to replace him.

In 1968 O'Shields was promoted to executive vice-president of parent Panhandle Eastern, and R. C. Dixon succeeded him as Anadarko's top officer. Although the bulk of its operations were still taking place in the Ana-

darko Basin, the company was quite active in other places, particularly Alberta, Canada, where it was participating in seven oil wells near the Bantry West Field. This Alberta development program also included the acquisition of producing properties with 1.4 million barrels of estimated reserves. By 1969, 12 percent of parent company Panhandle's net income was being generated by Anadarko.

THE SEARCH FOR NEW RESERVES: 1970-80

Anadarko's involvement in offshore exploration began in 1970. That year, the company acquired a one-eighth working interest in drilling rights to nine property blocks in the Gulf of Mexico. In 1971 Robert Stephens succeeded Dixon as Anadarko's president, and under Stephens, the company placed increasing emphasis on offshore operations, developing its own methods for collecting and analyzing geological and geophysical information used to evaluate potential offshore drilling leases. Of the Gulf of Mexico properties in which Anadarko had working interests, 24 blocks showed oil or gas in exploratory drilling between 1971 and 1976, and 10 of them proved commercially productive.

In 1972 Panhandle created Pan Eastern Exploration Company, a new wholly owned subsidiary. All of Panhandle's remaining producing properties were transferred to Pan Eastern, which was to be operated by Anadarko. Pan Eastern spent $29 million on leases and drilling in its first year of existence and produced 116 billion cubic feet of gas from its Anadarko Basin reserves. Pan Eastern became part of Anadarko in 1981 and was eventually renamed APX Corporation in 1987. Anadarko's headquarters were moved from Fort Worth to Houston in 1974. Two years later, when Stephens left the company, his replacement was Robert Allison Jr., a petroleum engineer whom Stephens had brought on board as vice-president of operations.

Anadarko closed its second decade of operation by breaking the $100 million revenue barrier for the first time in 1978. By 1979 the company was contributing about 30 percent of Panhandle's net income. About that time, Anadarko sought to expand its activities in the Gulf of Mexico, as higher gas prices resulting from the passage of the Gas Policy Act of 1978 created a major boom in gas exploration. Anadarko joined this expansion by entering a farm-in arrangement with Amoco Corporation, in which Anadarko was to operate a project until a discovery was made. After the discovery, Amoco would have the option of re-entering the project as a half-interest partner. Located on Matagorda Island, the block (Matagorda 623) became a producer in early 1980. The group, consisting of Anadarko, Amoco, and

KEY DATES

1959: Anadarko Production Company is formed as a subsidiary of Panhandle Eastern Pipe Line Company.

1960: Anadarko enters into 20-year agreement with the Pioneer Natural Gas Company.

1965: The company acquires Ambassador Oil Corporation and moves its headquarters to Fort Worth, Texas.

1985: Anadarko Petroleum Corporation is formed as an independent company.

1993: Anadarko discovers oil in Algeria.

2000: Anadarko acquires Union Pacific Resources.

2001: Anadarko acquires Berkley Petroleum Corporation.

2003: The company names James T. Hackett CEO.

2006: Anadarko acquires rivals Kerr-McGee and Western Gas for roughly $23 billion

Champlin Petroleum Company (to whom Anadarko had sold 25 percent of its deal with Amoco), then bid on a neighboring block that geophysical testing had shown to be promising. In 1982 the first well at Matagorda 622 was completed, and the block was found to have huge gas reserves. The Matagorda 622/623 blocks taken together represented a huge find for Anadarko, and the discovery sparked new interest in the Gulf of Mexico among many wildcat drillers.

THE 1980S: FORMATION OF ANADARKO PETROLEUM COMPANY

During this time, the company's onshore projects continued to operate successfully as well. A producing natural gas and oillike condensate discovery well, wholly owned and operated by Anadarko, was completed in San Patricio County, Texas, in 1982. By the mid-1980s, Anadarko was clearly the most important subsidiary of Panhandle, accounting for 37 percent of Panhandle's 1984 profit while contributing only 11 percent of its revenue. Panhandle management recognized that the price of its stock was not reflecting the true value of the company, given the impressive results being turned in by Anadarko. As a result, management decided to spin Anadarko off to Panhandle's stockholders, in order to discourage potential takeover attempts. Anadarko Petroleum Corporation was created in 1985, and all of

Anadarko Production Company's oil and gas assets were handed over to the new company.

However, one major obstacle prevented the spin-off from taking place immediately. In 1975 Panhandle had entered a 20-year contract with Sonatrach, Algeria's national energy company, to import liquefied natural gas from that country during the gas shortages of that period. By the time Algeria began shipping the gas in 1982, however, conditions in the United States had changed, and there was no longer a market for the wildly overpriced Algerian gas. Panhandle suspended deliveries, leading to an international squabble between the two companies, during which Panhandle could not spin off any assets, including Anadarko. In 1986 when Panhandle received word that a takeover attempt by a Texas investment group was imminent, attention to the Sonatrach negotiations was heightened, and the dispute was settled, with Sonatrach receiving six million shares of Panhandle stock and $300 million in cash. Anadarko then became an independent company.

Although the spin-off was essentially a friendly one, it was not entirely without conflict. Late in 1986, Anadarko sued its former parent over contracts the company considered unfair. Under the terms of the contracts, Anadarko sold gas to Panhandle at below-market prices, an agreement made when Anadarko's board was still dominated by Panhandle officials. The Federal Energy Regulatory Commission eventually freed Anadarko from those agreements. For 1986, its first year as an independent company, Anadarko had net income of $10.1 million on revenue of $205.7 million.

By 1987 Anadarko had natural gas reserves of 1.7 trillion cubic feet, of which only 200 to 250 million cubic feet per day were being produced. In order to make better use of its reserves, in February of that year, the company launched a program of infill drilling at its Hugoton Field property in southwestern Kansas. Infill drilling involved the addition of a second well at an existing unit capable of tapping deeper gas reserves. Infill gas could be sold at a higher price than gas produced by the original well at a site. By early 1989 the company had drilled 146 infill wells. In addition to beefing up its exploration activities, Anadarko grew through acquisition during its first few years on its own. Among its purchases were certain oil-producing properties in western Texas from Parker & Parsley Development Partners, a regional energy company. By 1989 the company's revenue had grown to $361 million.

GLOBAL EXPANSION IN THE EARLY 1990S

Ground was broken in Houston in 1991 for Anadarko Towers, the company's new headquarters building and the first major commercial office building started in that city in over five years. Anadarko's revenue slipped to $336.6 million in 1991, but rebounded slightly to $375 million the following year. However, the company's earnings dropped further, sinking to $27 million, half that reported in 1990. In early 1993 Anadarko became the first foreign-owned company to discover oil in Algeria. The company had initially entered that country in 1989, the first year it was opened to foreign investment. Along with two European partners in the venture, Anadarko maintained drilling rights to a 5.1 million-acre area in the Sahara Desert. Anadarko's interest in the venture was 50 percent. Sonatrach, Algeria's national oil and gas enterprise, in turn retained over 10 percent ownership of Anadarko's common stock.

Later in 1993, Anadarko teamed up with Amoco and Phillips Petroleum in discovering a huge shallow-water oil field in the Gulf of Mexico. The field, called Mahogany, was thought to hold at least 100 million barrels of oil, 37.5 percent of which was owned by Anadarko. For fiscal 1993, Anadarko reported record-high net income of $117 million on revenue of $476 million. For the 12th consecutive year, the company more than matched its production volumes of oil and gas with new proved reserves. Anadarko increased its exploration activities in the Gulf in early 1994. Hoping to repeat the success of Mahogany, the company paid $98 million for 26 different Gulf properties in a U.S. Minerals Management Service lease sale that April. Like Mahogany, the properties were nearly all "sub-salt plays," or potential finds located under salt formations. Anadarko also announced further oil discoveries in the deserts of Algeria, and development of those properties was accelerated.

In the short period since its spin-off from Panhandle Eastern, Anadarko's rate of success at wildcat drilling was remarkable. Its wealth of natural gas reserves in the Hugoton Basin also gave the company a great deal of control over its production, a huge advantage in an industry susceptible to market fluctuations. Anadarko was expected to become an even larger force among independent energy companies, if its discoveries of oil and gas in the Gulf of Mexico and Algeria continued into the late 1990s.

NEW OPPORTUNITIES AT HOME AND ABROAD: 1995-2002

Anadarko's Algerian operations began to reap significant dividends by 1995, when new discoveries increased the company's total reserves in the region to approximately one billion barrels. In addition to these proven reserves, the company's overall success rate in the country, where six of its nine wells had struck oil, made the prospect of

future discoveries seem extremely promising. Although the company expected lingering political unrest in Algeria to hamper its operations to some extent, it still hoped to be producing in excess of 30,000 barrels of crude per day within a year after obtaining its exploitation license.

Buoyed by its success in North Africa, Anadarko began exploring other overseas opportunities during the mid-1990s, most notably in the Red Sea. In the fall of 1995 the company entered into a production agreement with the Energy Ministry in Eritrea, in East Africa. With an initial investment of $28.5 million, the company planned to utilize the same computer technology used to analyze salt structures in the Gulf of Mexico to explore similar deposits in the Red Sea, where Eritrea's offshore reserves were still largely untapped. The company expanded its international operations even further the following year, when it entered into an agreement with Perupetro, the state oil company of Peru, to begin preliminary exploration of the country's Ucayali Basin.

However, Anadarko's overseas expansion efforts hit a snag in the late 1990s, when a steep decline in oil and natural gas prices took a significant bite out of Anadarko's revenues. The company's earnings fell by nearly 80 percent for the first quarter of 1998, with overall sales declining by 14 percent. Seeking to salvage something from the drop in prices, Anadarko began to look into expansion opportunities closer to home. In March 1998 the company acquired several new oil fields in Oklahoma from the Occidental Petroleum Corporation. With the cost of reserves down to $6 a barrel, the company was able to make the acquisition for only $120 million, while the addition of these new operations doubled the company's oil reserves in the Anadarko Basin.

The company began to experience a turnaround in July 1998, when it uncovered a reserve of more than 140 million barrels of oil in the Gulf of Mexico. In addition to being Anadarko's largest discovery in nearly two decades, the success also granted some much needed legitimacy to the company's subsalt exploration technology, paving the way for future discoveries in the Gulf and in the Red Sea. In order to sustain such ambitious expansion, however, the company needed to bolster its operations. To this end, in April 2000 Anadarko announced its intention to acquire the Union Pacific Resources Group. The deal, worth more than $4.4 billion, promised to make the combined entity the largest oil and gas company in North America. In February 2001 the company further increased its presence in the Canadian oil market with the acquisition of Berkley Petroleum in Alberta for $777 million. In July of that year the company also acquired Gulfstream Resources Canada for $137 million. The latter deal gave Anadarko three offshore drilling sites off the coast of Qatar, with proven reserves of more than 70 million barrels of oil. Perhaps most significantly, the deal represented Anadarko's first substantial foray into the Middle East.

Anadarko suffered a setback in January 2002, when an internal accounting error resulted in the announcement of a net loss of $1.35 billion for the third quarter of 2001, substantially higher than the previously expected loss of $270 million. However, the loss did not prevent the company from pursuing further opportunities for growth, and by October 2002 it was able to invest more than $200 million to acquire two substantial oil fields in Wyoming, a state where potential reserves were estimated to exceed 500 million barrels. With this latest acquisition, Anadarko's position as the largest independent oil producer in the United States seemed more secure than ever.

A RESHUFFLING OF ASSETS: 2003-09

The year 2003 marked the beginning of a period of transition at Anadarko. In March CEO John Seitz suddenly resigned, after holding the position for only 14 months. During Seitz's brief tenure, Anadarko's stock market value dropped several percentage points, at a time when soaring fuel prices and increased global demand were delivering significant dividends to other leading oil and gas firms. Some industry analysts attributed Anadarko's sluggish performance to its string of acquisitions, claiming that the company had overextended itself with its ambitious growth strategy. To make matters worse, in the months following Seitz's resignation Anadarko lost other key executives, notably Bill Sullivan, the company's executive vice-president of exploration and production. In summer 2003 Seitz's replacement, former CEO and long-time board chairman Robert Allison Jr. implemented a number of measures designed to stabilize Anadarko's financial health, cutting 400 jobs and closing two of the company's Texas facilities.

In the face of this upheaval, Anadarko found itself the subject of takeover rumors. Potential suitors included some of the largest oil and gas conglomerates in the world, among them the Italian firm Eni S.p.A., which held preliminary discussions with the company about a possible merger. In spite of all the speculation, however, most experts considered Anadarko an unattractive investment. For one, too many of the company's proven reserves were located in the United States, at a time when most oil and gas companies were eyeing more lucrative opportunities overseas. At the same time,

Anadarko's debt, which had reached $5 billion, also represented a major obstacle to a possible purchase. Furthermore, the company showed little interest in losing its independence and remained intent on finding its own solution to its financial downturn. In order to restore investor confidence in the company, Anadarko made another leadership change in December 2003, naming James T. Hackett, former president and COO of Devon Energy Corp., as its new CEO.

Under Hackett's leadership, Anadarko embarked on a major restructuring program, selling several of its properties in Western Canada and the Gulf of Mexico. By the end of 2004, the company had unloaded $3.5 billion worth of its reserves, while paying off roughly $1.4 billion of debt. By streamlining its holdings, Anadarko was able to redirect its efforts toward existing operations with a high potential for growth. By 2005, the company had increased its exploration budget to between $3.1 and $3.3 billion, with the aim of expanding production by between 5 percent and 9 percent annually over the next four years.

With its financial health restored, Anadarko once again became the subject of acquisition rumors, as analysts saw the company as an appealing target for a larger company seeking growth. It subsequently came as a shock when Anadarko made two major acquisitions of its own, purchasing two of its long-time rivals, Kerr-McGee and Western Gas, for a total sum between $22 billion and $24 billion, according to various estimates. Between the two acquisitions, Anadarko increased its proven reserves by over a billion barrels of oil equivalent. In order to pay for the new properties, however, the company was forced to unload several of its existing holdings. In September 2006 it sold its Canadian subsidiary, Anadarko Canada Corporation, to Canadian Natural Resources Limited, in a deal worth $4.2 billion; two months later, the company reached a $900 million agreement to sell two of its properties in the Gulf of Mexico to Norway's Statoil. A series of new deals followed in 2007, including the sale of 28 oil fields in West Texas for roughly $1 billion. Still, these sales did not completely defray the costs of the company's acquisitions, leaving some industry experts concerned about Anadarko's long-term prospects.

By mid-2007, however, Anadarko's existing assets began to pay some unforeseen dividends. In June 2007 the company struck oil off the coast of Ghana; the discovery was expected to yield between 300 and 600 millions barrels of oil, more than double what had been originally predicted. The company made another major discovery in December 2007, when it uncovered an oil reserve of roughly 100 million barrels in its West Tonga site in the Gulf of Mexico. While the precipitous drop in oil prices in the last months of 2008 had a negative impact on the industry as a whole, Anadarko managed to maintain its growth through the early part of 2009; indeed, reports showed a rise in production of 3 percent in the first quarter of the year, combined with a 5 percent decline in costs. Clearly, Anadarko's aggressive restructuring was proving to be beneficial to the company's long-term health.

Robert R. Jacobson
Updated, Erin Brown; Stephen Meyer

PRINCIPAL SUBSIDIARIES

Anadarko E&P Company LP; Anadarko Energy Services Company; Anadarko Holding Company; Anadarko Land Corporation; Anadarko Midkiff/ Chaney Dell LLC; Anadarko Offshore Holding Company LLC.; Anadarko West Texas LLC; Howell Petroleum Corporation; Kerr-McGee Corporation; Kerr-McGee (Nevada) LLC; Kerr-McGee Oil & Gas Corporation; Kerr-McGee Oil & Gas Onshore LP; Kerr-McGee Onshore Holding LLC; Kerr-McGee Shared Services Company LLC; Kerr-McGee Worldwide Corporation; KM Investment Corporation; Lance Oil & Gas Company Inc.; Mountain Gas Resources LLC; Resources Holdings Inc.; Upland Industries Corporation; Western Gas Resources Inc.; WGR Asset Holding Company LLC; WHL Inc.; Anadarko Algeria Company LLC (UK); Anadarko Global Funding II Ltd. (Bahamas); Anadarko Worldwide Holdings CV (Netherlands); KM BM-C-Seven Ltd. (Bahamas); Kerr-McGee China Petroleum LTD. (Bahamas).

PRINCIPAL COMPETITORS

Apache Corporation; BP p.l.c. (UK); Chevron Corporation; ConocoPhillips; Eni S.p.A. (Italy); Exxon Mobile Corporation; Hess Corporation; Marathon Oil Corporation; Occidental Petroleum Corporation; Valero Energy Corporation.

FURTHER READING

Antosh, Nelson, "Anadarko Ups Estimate of Reserves in Algeria," *Houston Chronicle*, March 9, 1995, Business Section, p. 1.

Barker, Robert, "Anadarko Isn't Cooking with Gas," *Business Week*, July 7, 2003, p. 106.

Burrough, Bryan, "Panhandle Eastern Considering Spinoff or Sale of Unit as Anti-Takeover Move," *Wall Street Journal*, August 19, 1985, p. 5.

Byrne, Harlan S., "Anadarko Petroleum," *Barron's*, December 18, 1989, p. 56.

Davis, Michael, "Anadarko Set to Buy UP Resources; $4.43 Billion Deal Would Unite Firms," *Houston Chronicle*, April 4, 2000, Business Section, p. 1.

Durgin, Hillary, "Anadarko Buys More Oklahoma Properties," *Houston Chronicle*, March 12, 1998.

Frazier, Steve, "Anadarko Sues Panhandle Eastern over Gas Contracts," *Wall Street Journal*, November 25, 1986, p. 18.

Ivanovich, David, "Anadarko Pays $98 Million for Gulf of Mexico Blocks," *Journal of Commerce*, April 4, 1994, p. 5B.

———, "Oil Discovery Is a First for Anadarko in Algeria," *Journal of Commerce*, February 22, 1993, p. B6.

Mack, Toni, "Elephants, Anyone?" *Forbes*, April 11, 1994, p. 71.

———, "Of Sharks and Albatrosses," *Forbes*, September 23, 1985, pp. 114-15.

Marcial, Gene G., "A Slick Play in Energy," *Business Week*, December 27, 1993, p. 88.

Salpukas, Agis, "Anadarko Planning to Drill in Red Sea Salt Formations," *New York Times*, September 29, 1995, p. D2.

Shook, Barbara, and Jeff Gosmano, "Anadarko Multi-Million Buying Spree Good Offense and Defense," *Natural Gas Week*, June 26, 2006.

Smith, Richard M., "'Too Nice to Get Ahead?' The CEO of Anadarko Petroleum Proves Otherwise," *Newsweek*, March 24, 2008, p. E15.

Stuart, Lettice, "New Office Tower Project Is Houston's First in 5 Years," *New York Times*, February 20, 1991, p. D20.

Taylor, Gary, "Anadarko Grows with Revamped Portfolio; after Pruning Assets, CEO Maps a Comeback for US Upstream Laggard," *Platts Oilgram News*, June 23, 2005, p. 1.

"Thirty Years of History," Houston: Anadarko Petroleum Corporation, 1989.

Thomas, Paulette, "Anadarko to Post Third-Quarter Profit, Faces Choices on Drilling, Acquisitions," *Wall Street Journal*, September 8, 1987, p. 16.

Andretti Green Racing

7615 Zionsville Road
Indianapolis, Indiana 46268
U.S.A.
Telephone: (317) 872-2700
Fax: (317) 872-2600
Web site: http://www.andrettigreen.com/

Private Company
Founded: 2002
Incorporated: 2002
Employees: 100 (est.)
NAICS: 711219 Automobile Racing Teams

■ ■ ■

Andretti Green Racing (AGR) is one of the premier teams competing in the Indy Racing League (IRL), the U.S. circuit that features open-wheel race cars. Since their first season of competition in 2003, AGR drivers have won three series championships, in 2004, 2005, and 2007. In the latter two seasons they also won the Indianapolis 500, which is considered to be the most famous event in racing. In its first six years of operation, Andretti Green was the most successful team on the IRL circuit, winning 34 of 97 events with at least one driver in the top five in 90 races. The company has also claimed victories on the Indy Lights and American Le Mans circuits and in 2008 signed an agreement to manage Team USA in the A1 Grand Prix World Cup of Motorsport. AGR has also branched out into racing event management, establishing Andretti Green Promotions to manage the Honda Grand Prix of St. Petersburg

(Florida), the first street-course race on the IRL circuit. In 2009 AGR's subsidiary Andretti Green Canada assumed management of the Honda Indy Toronto, another street-race on the IRL circuit. With an IRL-series high of four cars and some of the circuit's most popular drivers, AGR is poised to remain successful in the highly competitive sport of motor racing.

ORIGINS IN THE CART CIRCUIT

Andretti Green has deep roots in U.S. open-wheel racing. Chairman Michael Andretti is the winningest driver in the history of the Championship Auto Racing Teams (CART) series, which was the premier open-wheel car racing circuit in the United States from 1979 to 2002. Michael Andretti won a record 42 career races over his 18 full seasons in CART and won the series title in 1991. That season he won eight races, tying a single-season record held by seven-time Indy Car series champ A. J. Foyt. Andretti's 6,702 career Indy Car-laps-led is second only to his father, racing legend Mario Andretti. When Michael Andretti decided to retire from full-time racing after the 2002 season, he moved into team management. He bought a controlling stake in Team Green Racing, which had managed his Team Motorola car in 2001 and 2002.

Team Green had its own history of success on the Indy Car circuit. The company was founded as Forsythe-Green Racing by Australian Barry Green and American Gerry Forsythe in 1994; Barry Green's brother Kim joined as team manager. The following year Forsythe left and the company was renamed Team Green. Kim Green served as manager for driver Jacques

COMPANY PERSPECTIVES

Andretti Green has been taking care of business on the racetrack. But more importantly, Andretti Green, which showcases a group of over 50 sponsor partners that total more than $300 billion in annual revenues, has been taking care of "business"—the business of providing an effective marketing platform from which those partners can flourish. Andretti Green is about the business of racing and it is a company that takes its business seriously. Three owners, six race car drivers and more than 100 dedicated employees drive Andretti Green's initiatives to a higher level.

Villeneuve's car that year, which won the 1995 CART series title. When Michael Andretti bought out Barry Green, Kim Green became CEO of the newly named Andretti Green Racing, Inc. They were joined by a third partner, president and COO Kevin Savoree, who brought accounting and contracts experience to the team.

Although Andretti was one of the most recognizable names on the CART circuit, he did not promise to remain with the league when he announced the deal forming AGR. He hoped AGR might retain Team Green's drivers but would not commit to the number of cars that the new firm would manage. Dan Gelston in *USA Today* reported that Andretti said, "I don't have anything solid." He went on to say, "It is going to come down to the sponsors. But I would like to do Indianapolis, that is a race I really want." The Indianapolis 500 was sanctioned by the Indy Racing League (IRL) circuit, although CART drivers sometimes crossed over to compete in this prestigious event. Andretti himself had never won Indy as a driver, although he had come close, leading over 430 laps during his career.

MOVING TO THE INDY RACING LEAGUE

Andretti Green's announcement that they would start their first season in the IRL was an important development in American open-wheel racing. Formed by the president of Indianapolis Motor Speedway, the IRL had split from CART in 1996, and at first they attracted few of the top-rank racing teams in the sport. The Indianapolis 500 proved too strong an attraction, however, and by 2000 many CART teams were crossing

over to compete in the IRL. After two CART events were cancelled in 2001, leading one racetrack to file a lawsuit, one top team and two engine manufacturers switched to the IRL. The departure of Michael Andretti, one of the best known (and one of the few U.S.) names on the circuit, was another nail in CART's coffin. By late 2003 CART had declared bankruptcy, rebranding itself as the Champ Car World Series, and in 2008 its assets were merged with the IRL. Andretti Green had picked the winning side in this rivalry, demonstrating an insight into what sponsors and fans wanted that would serve them well in establishing their team.

AGR started their inaugural season in 2003 with three drivers: Scotsman Dario Franchitti, who had finished as high as second in CART's champ car series with Team Green; Brazilian Tony Kanaan, a former Indy development league champion; and Dan Wheldon, a promising young driver from England. The season started well, with Kanaan winning the pole position in the first two races and finishing first at the Phoenix race. After Franchitti was injured in a motorcycle accident, American Bryan Herta drove his car for the rest of the year, winning his third start at the Kansas Indy 300. As the season went on, teams using another manufacturer's engines outperformed them. Kanaan finished the season fourth overall, Wheldon finished eleventh, and Herta finished thirteenth. Wheldon was named Rookie of the Year, and the team was determined to improve their overall win total for the 2004 season.

Although most IRL teams only field two cars to race the entire season, Herta's success led AGR to expand to four cars for 2004. "We're not going into this season with any different thoughts or mindset than last season," CEO Kim Green told Tim Haddock in the *Los Angeles Daily News*. "It's going to be very competitive and a lot of hard work, and we're going to have our work cut out for us to try to win the championship. But we're capable of getting it done." AGR put in a lot of work with Honda, their engine manufacturer, to get the most out of their cars. Driver Bryan Herta added, "We learned a lot about the aerodynamic changes and also about the new engines. Honda has done a great job in its development of the 3.0-liter engine. That is one of the great things about Andretti Green Racing; we have very good partners who provide us with the best equipment and give us a chance to win every time we go out on the track."

In 2004 AGR's drivers proved the team had the formula for success, winning 8 of 16 races. Kanaan and Wheldon finished the season in first and second place overall, and the other two drivers finished in the top ten. "I take my hat off to [Andretti] with the job they've done," rival team owner Roger Penske told John Sturbin

KEY DATES

1994: Forsythe-Green Racing is founded by Barry Green and Gerry Forsythe.

1995: Forsythe leaves; company is renamed Team Green and wins Championship Auto Racing Teams (CART) series title with driver Jacques Villeneuve.

2002: Former CART driver Michael Andretti buys controlling interest of Team Green; with partners Kim Green and Kevin Savoree, Andretti renames company Andretti Green Racing, Inc. (AGR).

2003: AGR joins Indy Racing League (IRL) circuit.

2004: AGR wins IRL series title with driver Tony Kanaan; Andretti Green Promotions is created; company organizes first IRL street-course race in St. Petersburg, Florida.

2005: AGR wins Indianapolis 500 and IRL series title with driver Dan Wheldon.

2007: Company wins Indianapolis 500 and IRL series title with driver Dario Franchitti.

2008: Joint AGR-AFS Racing team wins Firestone Indy Lights title with driver Raphael Matos; Andretti Green Toronto, a subsidiary of Andretti Green Canada, is created to manage Honda Indy Toronto race; Andretti Green A1GP is created to manage U.S. team in A1GP racing series.

in the *Fort Worth Star-Telegram*. "These [AGR drivers] are seasoned. These guys, it's not a driving school. These are four guys that can win the race." Not only did Kanaan win three individual races and set an IRL record with 15 consecutive top-five finishes, but he also became the first driver in any major U.S. racing series to finish every lap of every race during the season.

BUILDING SUCCESS ON AND OFF THE TRACK

AGR took the same four drivers into 2005, hoping to continue their winning ways. The incredible success the team enjoyed could not have been predicted. Dan Wheldon won four of the first five races, including the Indianapolis 500, and finished the season with a record six total victories, claiming the overall series title. Kanaan and Franchitti finished second and fourth overall, claiming two races each, and seventh-place

finisher Herta also earned a race victory of his own. In total, AGR drivers won 11 of the 17 races held in 2005.

The team's drivers swept the top four positions at the Honda Grand Prix of St. Petersburg. The race was also notable as the first event sponsored by Andretti Green Promotions, which was a subsidiary created in 2004 to manage and promote events on the IRL circuit. The St. Petersburg, Florida, event was the first IRL race to be conducted on city streets instead of a racing oval. In succeeding years the race drew record crowds, resulting in the city extending their agreement with Andretti Green Promotions through 2013.

The 2006 season brought major changes for Andretti Green. First, Honda became the only engine provider for the circuit, putting the competitors on a level playing field. Second, driver Dan Wheldon left for a rival team and was replaced by Marco Andretti, the 19-year-old son of owner Michael Andretti. The younger Andretti had won three races in the IRL Infiniti Pro Series, a developmental circuit, and soon provided some of the only highlights of AGR's 2006 season. He finished second in his first Indianapolis 500, less than seven-tenths of a second behind the winner, and just ahead of his father, who came out of retirement to race with his son. Later in the year Marco Andretti became the youngest racer ever to win an IRL event, finishing first at the Indy Grand Prix of Sonoma. Overall, however, the 2006 season was disappointing, with only two victories and the four AGR drivers finishing sixth, seventh, eighth, and eleventh in the final standings. Although Marco Andretti was named Rookie of the Year, co-owner Kim Green told Dave Kallmann in the *Milwaukee Sentinel-Journal* that "[n]ot one person on the team at Andretti Green is happy right now, because we expect to win races and know we're good enough to win races."

ADDING STAR POWER TO THE TRACK

AGR made additional changes before the 2007 season. The most interesting occurred when Danica Patrick joined the team. Patrick was a talented female racer who had been 2005 IRL Rookie of the Year and whose good looks had made her a nationally recognized figure. Driver Bryan Herta shifted to the American Le Mans Series (ALMS), a series for both manufacturer prototypes and production-based cars that included endurance events in the spirit of France's famous 24 Hours of Le Mans. In their first ALMS event, the 12 Hours of Sebring, the Andretti Green team of Herta, Franchitti, and Kanaan won their LMP2 (Le Mans Prototype 2) division and barely lost the overall race to an LMP1 car with a larger engine. That proved to be their only victory of the season, however, and the team finished fifth in the series standings for 2007.

The team hoped to have better results in the IRL's 2007 season despite their subpar showing the previous year. As driver Kanaan explained to A. J. Perez in *USA Today*, "We dominated the series for two years in a row. We knew we may have a year [2006] that wasn't all that wonderful, but we didn't beat ourselves up over it. We used it as a tool to become stronger." AGR drivers performed well, with Kanaan winning the third race of the season and Franchitti winning a rain-shortened Indianapolis 500. Patrick had the best finishes of her career, placing third twice and placing second at the Detroit Indy Grand Prix, and Kanaan won five races overall, but it was Franchitti who captured the series championship on the last lap of the last race. Kanaan finished third, while Patrick posted a career-best seventh place, and Marco Andretti took eleventh place.

Franchitti's decision to leave IRL for NASCAR in 2008 meant more changes for the Andretti Green team. AGR picked up Japanese driver Hideki Mutoh, who had won races in the Indy Pro Series developmental league, for their fourth car. The IRL itself reported an increase in teams, as the Champ Car Series (formerly CART) finally merged with the IRL. There were a few changes in qualifying rules, but AGR still hoped to continue their success on the track. The first races of the season were promising, with a different AGR driver finishing in the top three each time, and Patrick won the Indy Japan 300 to become the first woman to win a major U.S. open-wheel race.

Intense competition meant podium finishes were harder to come by, however, and Kanaan was the only other AGR driver to win a race in 2008. After a race in Edmonton where the top AGR driver finished ninth, management called a meeting. "We just didn't perform as a team, and we want to make sure everybody is working together," team owner Michael Andretti told Bruce Martin in an article for SI.com, "I'm most upset about our results. We weren't good all weekend and we have to work together more. We have to get it back on track again." At the end of the season, however, all four AGR drivers had finished in the top 10 final standings: Kanaan was third, Patrick finished with a career-best sixth, Marco Andretti was seventh, and Mutoh was tenth, earning Rookie of the Year honors.

EXPANDING THE BUSINESS

AGR had better success in 2008 with their program in the Firestone Indy Lights series, the developmental racing league sponsored by the IRL. Andretti Green had formed a partnership with California-based AFS Racing

in 2007 to field two teams, and their drivers finished the season third and sixth overall. In 2008 they captured the series title with Brazilian driver Raphael Matos, who won three races en route to the title. Team member Arie Luyendyk Jr. also won a race and placed fourth overall. The AGR-AFS Racing team appeared ready for a successful 2009 season based on the combined five victories and seven additional podium finishes of AGR-AFS drivers J. R. Hildebrand and Sebastian Saavedra, who led the overall series after 9 of the 14 races of the season were completed.

Although Andretti Green had two wins and finished fourth overall in the 2008 American Le Mans Series, they did not participate in the program in 2009. Instead, they assumed responsibility for the United States's entry in the A1GP series, a Formula One–style series billed as the "World Cup of Motorsport" because each team represented a country. "This is a great opportunity to put our guys in a really difficult series racing on road courses, as well as from the team side in getting our Andretti Green brand out there on a solid, international platform," Michael Andretti told John Oreovicz in a special report for ESPN.com. "This is a great, great way to do it." AGR's Marco Andretti drove most of the races for the 2008–09 season, finishing on the podium once and leading Team USA to an eleventh place finish overall. Although adjusting to a new car and learning new courses were challenging, the driver told Oreovicz the effort was well worth it. "The competition is unbelievable over there and the field is so tight, it's going to help when we come back to IndyCar on the road courses," he said, adding, "There are no negatives, and it's the best possible scenario for the offseason."

AGR's competition was stronger than ever in the 2009 IRL season. The team had no wins in the first 11 races, although each driver had at least one top five finish and Patrick placed third at the Indianapolis 500, the best finish ever for a woman at the "Greatest Spectacle in Racing." Although AGR was no longer a dominant force in racing, Chairman Michael Andretti still predicted a good future for the company. In 2009 AGR's promotions arm successfully added a second IRL race, the Honda Indy Toronto, which would be managed by their subsidiary, Andretti Green Canada/ Toronto, which had been created the year before. The IRL itself was in solid financial shape, with good prospects for attracting more fans, even in an economic recession. AGR was considered to be well positioned to make the most of the various aspects of the racing business. "We've branched out," Andretti told Michael Smith in *SportsBusiness Journal*, "but it's important to stay within racing because that's our expertise. As long as we do that, we'll be OK."

Diane E. Telgen

PRINCIPAL SUBSIDIARIES

Andretti Green A1 Team USA, LLC; Andretti Green Canada Inc. (includes Andretti Green Toronto); Andretti Green Promotions, LLC.

PRINCIPAL COMPETITORS

Newman/Haas/Lanigan Racing; Panther Racing; Penske Racing, Inc.; Target Chip Ganassi Racing.

FURTHER READING

Brassfield, Mike, "City a Grand Prix Winner," *St. Petersburg Times*, April 6, 2009.

Brudenell, Mike, "Spirited Franchitti Is Deserving IRL Champion," *Detroit Free Press*, September 11, 2007.

Gelston, Dan, "Andretti May Move New Team to IRL," *USA Today Online*, July 23, 2002.

Haddock, Tim, "Andretti Green a Winning Machine," *Daily News* (Los Angeles), May 8, 2004, p.SC4.

———, "Andretti Green Racing Expects to Win," *Daily News* (Los Angeles), June 7, 2003.

———, "Team Green Will Try Four Drivers," *Daily News* (Los Angeles), February 28, 2004, p. SC5.

———, "What a Season for Andretti Green," *Daily News* (Los Angeles), August 20, 2005, p. SC2.

Hinton, Ed, "Move to Andretti Keeps Patrick in IRL." *South Florida Sun-Sentinel*, July 26, 2006.

Kallmann, Dave, "Andretti Green Searches for First Victory of Indy Season," *Milwaukee Journal Sentinel*, July 21, 2006.

Martin, Bruce, "AGR Holds Private Meeting after Danica, Marco Collide during Race," SI.com, July 27, 2008, http://sportsillustrated.cnn.com/2008/writers/bruce_martin/07/26/danica.andretti.meeting/.

Nelson, Jim, "IRL: Andretti Team Aids Tornado, Flood Relief," *Waterloo Courier* (Waterloo, IA), June 22, 2008.

Oreovicz, John, "Andretti Green Racing Takes Place on International Stage," ESPN: Open-Wheel, December 2, 2008, http://sports.espn.go.com/espn/print?id=3739183&type=story.

Pappone, Jeff, "Acura's Showing Proves Team a Quick Study," *Globe & Mail* (Toronto), March 22, 2007, p. G18.

Perez, A. J., "Andretti Green Likes Road," *USA Today*, March 28, 2007, p. 9C.

———, "Indy-car Racers Give Le Mans a Go," *USA Today*, March 14, 2007, p. 7C.

Ryan, Nate, "Finally, Victory Is Hers," *USA Today*, April 21, 2008, p. 1C.

Smith, Michael, "Andretti Has Eye on Regaining Market Share," *SportsBusiness Journal*, May 18, 2009, p. 19.

Struby, Tim, "Fast Friends," *ESPN the Magazine*, October 24, 2005.

Sturbin, John, "Michael Andretti Primed for First Title," *Fort Worth Star-Telegram*, May 29, 2004.

Atlas Van Lines Inc.

1212 St. George Road
Evansville, Indiana 47711-2364
U.S.A.
Telephone: (812) 424-2222
Toll Free: (800) 638-9797
Fax: (812) 421-7128
Web site: http://www.atlasworldgroup.com

Wholly Owned Subsidiary of Atlas World Group Inc.
Incorporated: 1948
Employees: 400
Sales: $370 million (2008 est.)
NAICS: 484121 General Freight Trucking, Long-Distance, Truckload; 484210 Van Lines, Moving and Storage Services

■ ■ ■

Atlas Van Lines Inc. is the second-largest moving company in the United States. Founded in 1948, the company became a wholly owned subsidiary of the Atlas World Group in 1994. Atlas Van Lines is divided into two principal segments. The company's Relocation Services Group, which focuses primarily on corporate clients, represents its core business and offers relocation services throughout the United States and Canada. The Specialized Transportation Group is dedicated to transporting high-value shipments, such as art exhibitions or commercial inventories. The vast bulk of the company's business is conducted through independent agents, who operate trucking and moving companies using the Atlas name. Atlas Van Lines is the largest

subsidiary of the Atlas World Group. As of 2008 the company had approximately 400 employees and annual operating revenues of $370 million.

EMERGENCE OF A NATIONWIDE MOVER: 1940S AND 1950S

As they had for the past decade, members of the Independent Movers' & Warehousemen's Association gathered together in 1947 for their annual convention to discuss topics of mutual interest. Long-distance movers from across the country had made the journey to the convention site in French Lick, Indiana, to be among their peers and discuss the nuances of the household goods moving industry. Over the course of the previous half century, the household goods moving industry had evolved from the entrepreneurial efforts of commercial freight operators who supplemented their paychecks by helping people move from one residence to another. Horse-drawn wagons that hauled coal, ice, groceries, and other goods were used in their off-hours to move furniture, clothes, and other household goods, marking the beginning of moving such objects as a commercial enterprise. Eventually, some of these part-time enterprises developed into full-time businesses.

Soon the business of transporting household goods depended on wagons and then motor-powered trucks operating exclusively as moving-company carriers. As the 20th century unfolded and the decades passed, a host of small, locally operating moving companies were organized across the country, collectively forming what was then called the transfer and storage industry. Moving companies were governed by a federally empowered

COMPANY PERSPECTIVES

At Atlas, we respond to unique customer needs with a time-proven commitment to integrity, quality and solutions. These are the values that made Atlas a world leader in moving and logistics. Now these values are the foundation for a full range of business solutions in global relocation, benefits, recruiting, logistics and travel. Our values are the promises we make to you.

regulatory body, the Interstate Commerce Commission, and were represented by their own national association, the Independent Movers' & Warehousemen's Association Inc. Despite having a national association and being governed by a regulatory commission, the companies comprising the household goods moving industry were relatively weak and confined to a limited service area, which tended to place a ceiling on their financial growth.

For several years prior to the 1947 convention, some members of the Independent Movers' & Warehousemen's Association had discussed removing this barrier to their growth by establishing a national operating organization. At French Lick talk turned to action, and a small group of movers began mapping plans to create a national operating organization. The following year, in 1948, 33 movers banded together in a cooperative effort to realize their common goal, creating a new long-distance moving company named Atlas Van-Lines Inc.

Incorporated on May 19, the newly created, agent-owned company made its first move toward acquiring operating authority throughout the country two weeks later, when its directors purchased operating authority for direct service within 36 states and the District of Columbia. With head offices in Chicago, Atlas Van-Lines began its inaugural year of operation with the ability to direct service throughout the eastern half of the United States. For the next three decades the company would strive to secure operating authority throughout the rest of the country, an objective that would propel its growth and dictate its acquisitive strategy, eventually creating one of the nation's largest companies in the household goods moving industry.

The company derived much of its business during its quest for nationwide operating authority from military personnel moving from one location to another, the most itinerant segment of the country's population during the cold-war era. This constant source of business helped Atlas Van-Lines record $365,000 in sales after its first year of operation, a total that would climb to $1 million the following year. From the outset, the company's directors implemented a recruiting program to attract more agents, hoping to increase the company's ranks and, in turn, drive its annual sales total upward. In order to gain access to additional regions in the country, the company's annual revenue volume needed to grow, which it did during the early and mid-1950s, climbing to roughly $5 million by 1957.

STEADY GROWTH IN THE 1960S AND 1970S

At this point, Atlas Van-Lines was making enough money to finance another acquisition and continue the pursuit of its goal to obtain operating authority in the 48 contiguous states. With the acquisition of Howard Van Lines in 1958, which was renamed Atlas Van Service, Atlas Van-Lines gained access to Utah, Nevada, Arizona, New Mexico, and California, extending the company's service territory from coast to coast. On the heels of this acquisition, the company moved its corporate headquarters in 1960 from Chicago to Evansville, Indiana, where the directors of Atlas Van-Lines would orchestrate the geographic expansion of the agent-owned company into the 1990s.

At the time of the move from Chicago to Evansville, annual sales were discouragingly stagnant, hovering around $8 million for the preceding three years. In order to boost revenues for the continued expansion of the company, Atlas implemented a public relations campaign, the highlight of which was a *New York Times* article in 1962 that described Atlas Van-Lines' revival of Evansville's economy. Two years later the company took further steps to draw public attention to Atlas Van-Lines: the company's board of directors voted to double from 1 percent to 2 percent the advertising and sales development fund deduction taken from agents' settlement accounts, thereby enabling the company to expand its advertising program to include national print media.

Although the acquisition of Howard Van Lines in 1958 had extended Atlas Van-Lines' service territory from coast to coast, areas within the United States still remained where the company maintained no operations, particularly in the Rocky Mountain region and in the Pacific Northwest. During the early 1960s, while advertising efforts were increased to cover the entire country, the company's directors set their sights on obtaining operating authority in those regions where Atlas Van-Lines held no operating authority. In 1962 the company purchased the authority owned by Golden

KEY DATES

1948: Atlas Van-Lines Inc. is formed.
1958: Atlas acquires Howard Van Lines.
1960: The company relocates its headquarters from Chicago, Illinois, to Evansville, Indiana.
1962: Atlas enters into an agreement with Golden Van Lines, begins operating in the Rocky Mountain West region.
1980: Atlas Van Lines goes public.
1984: Atlas is acquired by Wesray Transportation Inc. for $71.6 million.
1988: Atlas terminates merger with Wesray, regains independence.
1994: Atlas World Group Inc., a holding company, is formed by Atlas shareholders; Atlas Van Lines becomes principal subsidiary.
2004: Atlas Van Lines founder O. H. Frisbie dies at the age of 98.
2009: Atlas Van Lines introduces the Kenworth T370, the company's first hybrid truck.

Van Lines of Colorado, giving it the opportunity to add new agents from the independent moving companies located in Idaho, Montana, Utah, and Wyoming. In 1964 Atlas Van-Lines acquired various interstate operating authorities by purchasing three companies that added Washington, Oregon, part of Idaho, and part of North Dakota to the company's growing map of regions served by Atlas Van-Lines vehicles.

Much had been achieved during the 1960s toward extending Atlas Van-Lines' geographic coverage across the United States, but the company also established an international presence during the decade, beginning with its acquisition of Torrance, California-based International Sea Van Inc. in 1959. Through this subsidiary, Atlas Van-Lines began shipping household goods overseas, then in 1960 began shipping to international markets through the air, giving the company two conduits for its service to foreign markets.

Late in the decade, the directors of Atlas Van-Lines made another pivotal move when they organized and hosted an industry forum for corporate traffic and transportation managers. Held in 1967, the Forum, which became an annual event, focused on tailoring moving services for relocating corporate clientele, a small but burgeoning market that 20 years later would provide the bulk of the company's business. Since its formation, Atlas Van-Lines had subsisted primarily on

relocating military personnel, a market that would continue to drive the company's growth as it entered the 1970s. However, during the 1980s and 1990s, moving employees of major corporations would overtake military relocations as government defense spending waned. Eventually, corporate relocations would account for roughly two-thirds of Atlas Van-Lines' business. By addressing this new market in 1967, Atlas tapped an essential source of future revenue, gaining an early lead on its competition as the company entered the 1970s.

In 1974 the day arrived when Atlas Van Lines (the company dropped the hyphen from its name in 1971) could finally boast that its authority extended throughout the contiguous United States. On September 13, the company achieved its goal after 26 years of pursuing operating authority throughout the contiguous 48 states. Hawaii and Alaska were added to the company's service territory in 1976 and 1981 respectively, making Atlas Van Lines one of the few genuine national moving companies in the country.

DEREGULATION AND THE CHANGING FACE OF THE MOVING INDUSTRY: 1980–95

Atlas Van Lines achieved its long-sought-after goal of blanketing the country with its moving vans a few short years before the household goods moving industry was dramatically reshaped by federal deregulation. Until 1980 the Interstate Commerce Commission wielded extensive control over moving companies like Atlas, dictating whether a moving company could go into business, what goods it could haul, where it could operate, and how much it could charge for its services. When the federal government deregulated the household goods moving industry through the Motor Carrier Act of 1980, the industry underwent radical and sudden changes. The number of moving companies in the country nearly doubled during a four-year span, jumping from 18,045 in 1980 to 30,481 in 1984, an increase that greatly intensified competition and sent service prices cascading downward.

The inaugural year of deregulation also marked the beginning of a new era at Atlas Van Lines. Since its inception in 1948, the company had been privately owned and tightly held by its agents, who had watched over its development from a fledgling enterprise into the sixth-largest moving company in the United States. In search of capital to finance further expansion, however, the agents decided to offer Atlas Van Lines stock to the public in 1980.

Four years after going public, the company became the object of a hostile takeover. Contrans Acquisitions

Inc., a Canadian company led by a former Atlas Van Lines president, announced its intention to purchase control of Atlas Van Lines in May 1984. The hostile takeover attempt came as a shock to Atlas directors, forcing them to act quickly if they were to keep Contrans from gaining control. The potential takeover by Contrans was avoided in October 1984 when Wesray Transportation Inc., an affiliate of Wesray Group, purchased Atlas Van Lines for $71.6 million, thereby thwarting Contrans' unsolicited advances toward Atlas Van Lines.

Forced into the arms of Wesray, Atlas Van Lines now found itself owned by another company after 36 years of independence. The transition was difficult for Atlas directors, agents, and employees, who struggled with Wesray's focus on the profitability of the company rather than the service and support it provided. Exacerbated by contrary operating philosophies, the relationship between Wesray and Atlas soured, formally ending four years after it began, when Atlas Van Lines agents purchased the company in a leveraged buyout.

Returned to independence and private ownership during its 40th anniversary year, Atlas Van Lines attempted to put the troubled years of the 1980s behind it. The dramatic changes in the household goods moving industry engendered by deregulation had proven to be a formidable challenge to many moving companies across the country, but Atlas Van Lines, despite its difficult years in the middle of the decade, had emerged from the first 10 years of deregulation buoyed by encouraging success. Transportation and handling of trade show exhibits and sophisticated electronic equipment had developed into a promising business that complemented the company's mainstay business of relocating corporate clientele, giving Atlas Van Lines the means with which to build a strong business for the future.

Financially, however, the company's performance was discouragingly lackluster, a problem the directors of Atlas Van Lines hoped to solve as the company entered the 1990s. Despite an economic recession during the early 1990s, Atlas recorded stable financial growth, becoming the fifth-largest moving company in the country early in the decade. Annual revenue jumped from $217.5 million in 1992 to nearly $295 million in 1994, the year shareholders agreed to establish a new holding company, Atlas World Group Inc., for Atlas Van Lines and its seven subsidiaries.

Encouraged by the success recorded during the first half of the decade, Atlas Van Lines exited the mid-1990s firmly positioned as a leader in the household goods moving industry. In 1995 the company recorded its fifth consecutive year of record earnings, a feat that harkened back to the robust growth registered during the 1960s and 1970s and fueled hoped for success in the future.

COMPETITION IN THE INFORMATION AGE: 1996–2009

By the mid-1990s, competition within the moving industry had become especially fierce, as traditional nationwide carriers continued to see large portions of their market share devoured by smaller regional relocation companies. Within this atmosphere of heightened opposition, further consolidation became inevitable. In April 1995, another long-standing independent firm, Mayflower Transit, was acquired by UniGroup Inc. for $90 million. At the time, Mayflower was the fourth-largest household mover in the country and a long-time rival of Atlas Van Lines.

In the face of this persistent challenge, Atlas Van Lines continued to seek innovative ways to win new customers. In 1996 the company became the first nationwide moving company to establish an Internet presence. The Web site gave the company's agents the ability to conduct a number of key business functions online, such as generating quotes and processing orders. Perhaps most significantly, the Web-based system empowered agents to track the status of shipments via satellite technology. This capability allowed company representatives to dispatch new assignments to truck drivers more efficiently, while also enabling them to provide more accurate delivery estimates to customers. By implementing these improvements, the company reasoned, it would be able to provide more reliable and efficient service to its clients.

The company's technological leap was well timed. In the midst of the tense competitive landscape, the moving business continued to grow during the late 1990s. As the company's own research revealed, the year 1997 witnessed a dramatic increase in relocations throughout the United States, with the number of moves rising by more than 55 percent over the year before. Atlas remained an industry leader throughout this growth period. By the time of its 50th anniversary in 1998, Atlas Van Lines ranked fourth among the nation's top moving companies, and third in the lucrative household relocation segment. In June 1999 the company undertook a massive renovation of its Evansville plant, adding 20,000 square feet of additional space and hiring 50 new employees. That same year, the company was named Employer of the Year by the Indiana Private Industry Council. As it entered the 21st century, Atlas continued to place a high premium on technological advancement. Beginning in February 2001, the company's corporate and specialty relocation clients were able to track their own shipments on the Atlas Web site.

The relocation business suffered a steep decline in late 2001, largely because of the economic downturn that followed the terrorist attacks against the United States on September 11. In spite of this industry-wide slump, Atlas Van Lines continued to see steady growth. According to a study conducted by the American Moving and Storage Association, Atlas was one of only two national moving companies to experience increased earnings during the late 1990s and early 2000s. Indeed, between 1996 and 2002, Atlas was the industry leader with a growth rate of 54 percent; by 2004 the company's overall fleet had grown to nearly 1,700 trucks, 4,180 trailers, and 2,900 tractors. In the midst of this brisk growth, Atlas Van lines suffered a sad loss in October 2004, when its founder and former president O. H. Frisbie died at the age of 98.

Throughout the second half of the decade, Atlas Van Lines remained among the industry leaders in the area of technological innovation. In 2007, as part of the company's larger goal of managing all of its records and transactions digitally, Atlas began maintaining its inventory in electronic format. Over time, the company eventually hoped to provide all of its drivers with computers, allowing them to keep records and obtain customer signatures without using paper. In April 2009 Atlas Van Lines unveiled its first hybrid truck, the diesel-electric Kenworth T370, at a ceremony in Evansville. In the face of mounting fuel costs and concerns about the long-term effects of carbon emissions on the environment, the company's shift toward more fuel-efficient, cleaner vehicles was considered a promising one.

Jeffrey L. Covell
Updated, Stephen Meyer

PRINCIPAL DIVISIONS

Relocation Services Group; Specialized Transportation Group.

PRINCIPAL COMPETITORS

SIRVA Inc.; UniGroup Inc.

FURTHER READING

"Atlas Founder O. H. Frisbie, 98," *Traffic World*, October 11, 2004, p. 33.

"Atlas Soars in Customer Poll," *Evansville Press*, September 29, 1994, p. 18.

"Atlas Stockholders Agree to Form Holding Company," *Evansville Courier*, September 22, 1994, p. C6.

Atlas Van Lines, *Atlas Van Lines: Moving On*, Phoenix: Heritage, 1994.

"Atlas World Posts Record Profits 5th Straight Year," *Evansville Press*, March 8, 1995, p. 20.

Kroeger, Mark, "From the Home Office in Evansville, Here's the List," *Sunday Courier*, January 2, 1994, p. E1.

Mather, Joan, "Technology Helps Carriers Streamline Operations," *Tradeshow Week*, May 13, 2002, p. 11.

Mcguffie, Deborah, "Keeps on Moving," *Fleet Owner*, March 1, 2004.

Muller, E. J., "Encouraging Carriers to Go for the Gold," *Distribution*, August 1992, pp. 82-88.

Nguyen, Terrence, "Atlas Van Lines Goes Paperless," *Fleet Owner*, September 21, 2006.

"Relocation: Things Companies Pay For," *Inc.*, January 1993, p. 42.

Sword, Doug, "Gee Whiz!" *Indiana Business Magazine*, February 1992, pp. 11-15.

Banner Corporation

10 South First Avenue
P.O. Box 907
Walla Walla, Washington 99362-0265
U.S.A.
Telephone: (509) 527-3636
Toll Free: (800) 272-9933
Fax: (509) 526-8898
Web site: http://www.bannerbank.com

Public Company
Founded: 1890 as National Building Loan & Trust Association
Employees: 1,140
Total Assets: $4.6 billion (2009)
Stock Exchanges: NASDAQ
Ticker Symbol: BANR
NAICS: 551111 Offices of Bank Holding Companies

■ ■ ■

Banner Corporation is based in Walla Walla, Washington, and is a holding company for Banner Bank. Banner is also the holding company of Islanders Bank, which maintains three branch offices in Washington's San Juan Islands. Throughout the 1960s Banner Bank went through a period of expansion until it had 86 branch offices and 12 loan production offices in Washington, Oregon, and Idaho. The company offers traditional retail banking products, as well as business, consumer, agricultural loans, and investing advice. Construction and land loans represent about one-third of the company's loan portfolio, and commercial real estate loans make up about one-quarter provided by its subsidiary, Community Financial Corporation.

EARLY ORIGINS AND HISTORY

The National Building Loan & Trust Association was founded in 1890, but the name was soon changed to Interstate Building Loan & Trust Association in 1893 and then to Interstate Savings & Loan in 1924. A decade later, the bank became First Federal Savings & Loan Association of Walla Walla. The company's first acquisition came in 1982, when it bought Home Federal in Yakima, Washington. In 1989 First Federal Savings & Loan Association of Walla Walla became First Federal Savings Bank of Washington, and in 1991 it changed its name to First Savings Bank of Washington.

In October 1995 the holding company First Washington Bancorp was established when First Savings Bank of Washington became a publicly traded establishment. Shortly thereafter, it began acquiring banks with the purchase of Inland Empire Bank in 1996 and Towne Bank in 1998, followed by a pair of acquisitions in 1999: Whatcom State Bank and Seaport Citizens Bank. Whatcom State Bank was set up as a division of First Savings Bank of Washington to strengthen First Savings' presence in the cities of Bellingham, Ferndale, Lynden, Blaine, and Point Roberts.

CHANGE IN FOCUS

During the mid-1990s thrift institutions (such as savings-and-loan associations and mutual savings banks) were finding that their bottom lines could be improved

COMPANY PERSPECTIVES

∎

Banner Bank is a dynamic full-service Northwest financial institution, operating safely and profitably within a framework of shared integrity. Working as a team, we will deliver superior products and services to our valued customers. We will emphasize strong customer relationships and a high level of community involvement. We will provide a culture which attracts, empowers, rewards and provides growth opportunities for employees. Our success will build long-term shareholder value.

by switching to commercial state charters. The most significant advantage of commercial banks, when compared to thrift institutions, was the ability to offer more types of financial products and services and being able to charge for them. According to Peter Neurath of *Puget Sound Business Journal*, these extra fees enabled "a commercial bank [to have] more opportunities to bolster the revenues of the company."

Thus, in 2000 First Washington Bancorp reorganized its subsidiaries into two state-chartered commercial banks. First Savings Bank, Whatcom State Bank, Seaport Citizens Bank, and Towne Bank were merged into one Washington-chartered commercial bank, and Inland Empire Bank continued as an Oregon-chartered commercial bank. At that time, the company's subsidiaries operated a total of 37 branch offices and six loan offices in Washington, Oregon, and Idaho. Converting from a thrift institution to a commercial bank was a smooth transition for First Washington Bancorp because it was considered "more banklike" following the two commercial banks (Inland Empire Bank and Towne Bank) that were merged into the thrift bank, as reported by Joe Nabbefeld in *Puget Sound Business Journal*. Also, many thrift institutions used consolidation of their existing financial institutions as a means to balance their extra capital. For First Washington Bancorp, the merger would save about $1 million a year.

In late 2000 the holding company First Washington Bancorp officially changed its name to Banner Corporation. At the same time, its branch offices took on the name Banner Bank. Gary Sirmon, the president and chief executive officer (CEO) of the holding company, told *Business Journal–Portland*'s Robert Goldfield, "We chose a name that would set us apart and capture our corporate goals—focusing on the company's growth across several states throughout the

Northwest and supporting our position as a leader in our expanding markets." In addition, Inland Empire Bank became Banner Bank Oregon, which maintained six branch locations.

TROUBLING YEARS

Despite these successful changes, Banner came under the media spotlight with a check-kiting scheme that was conducted by its former senior vice president, Rory O'Flaherty. Besides having its reputation tarnished, this scandal bruised Banner's credit image and led to the loss of millions of dollars.

With the help of lower interest rates through Banner's subsidiary, Community Financial Corporation, which it had purchased in 2000, mortgage loan sales climbed 82 percent, from $2.5 million in 2000 to $4.6 million in 2001. Even though loan sales were up, the company's technological expenditures to get all of its banks onto one central data processing system cost Banner $1.4 million. Additional cost factors were incurred as a direct result of the check-kiting scheme to the tune of $11.9 million for 2001. In spite of these expenditures, Banner was the fifth-largest bank in the state of Washington based on assets. According to the Federal Deposit Insurance Corporation, in 2001 the national average efficiency ratio for banking institutions similar to that of Banner was 55.75 percent, whereas Banner's stood at 70.01 percent, up from a reported 59.65 percent before "centralizing the various data processing systems left over from earlier acquisitions," wrote Katie Kuehner-Hebert of *American Banker* in March 2002.

In 2002 Sirmon stepped down as president and CEO and was replaced by D. Michael Jones, who had considerable banking experience, especially when it came to established banks. Having served as president and CEO of Source Capital Corp.; president of West One Bancorp of Boise, Idaho, with total assets of $9 billion; and president of Old National Bancorp of Spokane, Jones was expected to get Banner back on track. The first two items on Jones's agenda were to get Banner's balance sheet on track and to decrease the bank's growth. "When a lot of community banks grow up, staff will wear eight to 10 hats for a while," the financial analyst James Bradshaw told Kuehner-Hebert, adding that "oftentimes scandals like [the check-kiting scheme] end up falling through the cracks." At the close of 2002, a sluggish economy in the Puget Sound region was evident when Banner reported a $1.6 million loss in the fourth quarter of 2002, compared to a net gain of $3.7 million for the same period in 2001.

KEY DATES

1890: The National Building Loan & Trust Association is founded.
1893: Name is changed to Interstate Building Loan & Trust Association.
1924: New name, Interstate Savings & Loan, is adopted.
1934: Name is changed to First Federal Savings & Loan Association of Walla Walla.
1982: First Federal Savings & Loan acquires Home Federal of Yakima, Washington.
1989: Name is changed to First Federal Savings Bank of Washington.
1991: Name is changed to First Savings Bank of Washington.
1995: The holding company First Washington Bancorp is established.
1996: Inland Empire Bank is purchased by First Savings Bank of Washington.
1998: First Savings Bank of Washington acquires Towne Bank.
1999: Whatcom State Bank and Seaport Citizens Bank are acquired by First Savings Bank of Washington.
2000: The holding company First Washington Bancorp changes its name to Banner Corporation.
2007: Banner purchases F&M Bank, San Juan Financial Holdings Company, and NCW Community Bank.

EXPANSION RESUMED

With the company's tarnished image behind it, Banner was poised to resume growing its total number of banks. In mid-2004 it picked up four of 15 properties shed by former competitor Pacific Northwest Bank, which was acquired by Wells Fargo & Co. in 2003, thus growing its deposits and market presence in the Puget Sound area. According to Eric Engleman and Jeanne Lang Jones of *Puget Sound Business Journal*, Lloyd Baker, the chief financial officer of Banner Bank, said, "This is a critical market for us [because Puget Sound] is the most highly populated area in the Pacific Northwest with the most significant business activity." Later that year the company branched out into Portland, Oregon, and Boise and Twin Falls, Idaho. The total number of branch locations in the Puget Sound region numbered 13, and there were plans to expand further with future

construction—Banner was definitely leaving its mark in Washington as its mainstay.

In 2007 Banner purchased F&M Bank of Spokane, Washington. According to a Banner press release, Jones explained "when the prospect of this transaction arose, we viewed it as an excellent opportunity to fully serve the fourth largest metropolitan area in the Pacific Northwest which has important ties to our other three markets of emphasis, the Puget Sound Region, greater Portland and greater Boise."

That same year Banner completed the acquisition of San Juan Financial Holdings Company (SJFHC), the holding company of Islanders Bank. SJFHC was merged into Banner Corporation, and Islanders Bank continued to operate as a separate subsidiary of Banner Corporation. It also absorbed NCW Community Bank of central Washington in 2007. NCW added $90 million in assets and $81 million in loans under Banner's umbrella. With Banner's goals reached, acquisition activity was expected to slow down with only three additional branches expected to come online in 2008.

THE MELTDOWN OF FINANCIAL INSTITUTIONS

Although 2007 was considered a good year for the banking business, 2008 witnessed plunging interest rates, a weakening housing market, falling home prices, rising foreclosures, and increasing unemployment—all of which cut into financial institutions' profit margins and resulted in significant write-downs. Not surprising, the rising number of mortgages over 30 days past due were on the rise, forcing banks to tighten their purse strings.

Faced with a financial crisis that affected most financial institutions, Banner included, the federal government put in place the Emergency Economic Stabilization Act (EESA) in October 2008. Under the EESA, financial institutions could apply for funding to offset their losses and keep them running. In November 2008 Banner participated in the Troubled Asset Relief Program (TARP) and received $124 million in TARP funds. Banner put $50 million of these funds into its Great Northwest Home Rush program, which offered a 30-year mortgage that had a fixed-rate of less than 4 percent with a 20 percent down payment. Within a three-week period beginning in March 2009 the bank completed 60 mortgage loan applications. Given the response to this program, the bank planned to extend a comparable program to the other markets that it served.

The volatility that the capital and credit markets experienced in 2008 was anticipated to reach unprecedented levels in 2009. Competition in the industry was expected to intensify as a result of the increasing consolidation of financial services companies in connection with the market conditions. In addition, market turmoil and a tightening of credit in mid-2009 led to an increased level of commercial and consumer delinquencies, a lack of consumer confidence, increased market volatility, and widespread reduction of overall business activity for Banner and for other financial institutions.

Brenda Kubiac

PRINCIPAL SUBSIDIARIES

Banner Bank; Islanders Bank.

PRINCIPAL COMPETITORS

Sterling Financial Corp.; Umpqua Holdings Corp.

FURTHER READING

"Bank Plans to Expand in Spokane," *Pacific Builder and Engineer*, December 4, 2006, p. 14.

"Banner Buying F&M Bank for $98.8M," *Puget Sound Business Journal*, December 12, 2006.

"Banner Buying Wenatchee Bank for $18.5M," *Puget Sound Business Journal*, June 28, 2007.

Banner Corporation, "Banner Corporation Signs Definitive Agreement to Acquire F&M Bank of Spokane, Washington" (press release), December 12, 2006, http://www.bannerbank.com/AboutUs/NewsRoom/ArchivedNewsReleases/Releases2006/Documents/BANR_Acquisition_FM.pdf.

Engleman, Eric, and Jeanne Lang Jones, "Banner Blows Westward," *Puget Sound Business Journal*, July 2, 2004.

Goldfield, Robert, "A Banner Name," *Business Journal–Portland*, November 17, 2000, p. 16.

Hillis, David, "In Brief: Four Bankers Agree to Quit Business," *American Banker*, June 13, 2003, p. 20.

Kuehner-Hebert, Katie, "New CEO for a Wash. Bank That Grew Fast, Fell Faster," *American Banker*, March 27, 2002, p. 1.

———, "Urban 'Renewal' in Northwest," *American Banker*, July 9, 2004, p. 1.

McGeer, Bonnie, "Putting Tarp Funds to Work with Mortgage Promotions," *American Banker*, April 28, 2009, p. 6A.

Nabbefeld, Joe, "First Washington Turning Its Three Banks into One," *Puget Sound Business Journal*, November 19, 1999.

Neurath, Peter, "Banner Acquisition Raises Profile—and Questions," *Puget Sound Business Journal*, October 5, 2001, p. 12.

———, "Commercial Conversion Gives Banks More Options," *Puget Sound Business Journal*, April 30, 2001.

Reosti, John, "Bad Loans Pushed Banner to 4Q Loss," *American Banker*, February 7, 2003, p. 5.

Steadham, Edward, telephone interview, May 7, 2009.

"Walla Walla Bank Completes Purchase of Bellingham Institution," *Puget Sound Business Journal*, January 4, 1999.

Bernard L. Madoff Investment Securities LLC

885 Third Avenue
New York, New York 10022
U.S.A.
Toll Free: (888) 727-8695 (trustee)
Web site: http://www.madofftrustee.com/ (trustee)

Private Company
Founded: 1960
Employees: 250 (2008 est.)
Sales: $28.7 million (2008 est.)
NAICS: 523120 Securities Brokerage; 523920 Portfolio Management

■ ■ ■

Bernard L. Madoff Investment Securities LLC (BLMIS) was a stock trading and investment firm established in 1960 by Bernard L. Madoff. It grew to become a major stock trader and a leader in the adoption of technology in the securities industry. Madoff supplemented the apparently legitimate trading business with an investment operation that became a Ponzi scheme in the late 1980s or early 1990s. It was exposed in 2008, at which time it was estimated that its investors lost an estimated $65 billion. Madoff was arrested and the firm went into bankruptcy. He was convicted of fraud and sentenced to 150 years in federal prison.

FOUNDED AS STOCK TRADER IN 1960

Bernard L. Madoff was born in Queens, New York, in 1938 to Ralph and Sylvia Madoff. Ralph Madoff was a plumber turned stockbroker, and for a time he operated a small brokerage firm registered in his wife's name. Bernard Madoff went to Rockaway High School in Queens, where he was an average student, and he graduated from Hofstra University in 1960 with a major in political science. He married Ruth Alpern, also of Queens, in November 1959. They had two sons, Mark and Andrew, both born in the mid-1960s. Madoff's wife and sons eventually joined the firm, along with his brother Peter.

Madoff founded BLMIS with initial capital of $5,000, which he claimed to have saved working summers and part time as a lifeguard and installer of lawn sprinklers. On March 26, 1960, BLMIS registered with the Securities and Exchange Commission (SEC) as a broker-dealer making inter-dealer markets in corporation securities over the counter and trading securities for its own account. Madoff held the title of chairman of the company throughout its history.

In order to break into the relatively closed world of stock trading without possessing a seat on the New York Stock Exchange (NYSE), Madoff started off as a market maker trading over-the-counter stocks (stocks issued by small companies that are not listed on the NYSE). Market makers are firms that buy and sell stocks at published prices, thereby creating a "market" for the stocks. Like other market makers, BLMIS used the National Quotation Bureau's published "pink sheet" stock listings and made its money on the difference between the bid (buy) and ask (sell) prices for stocks. Ruth Madoff's father, an accountant, helped the fledgling company by referring his clients and their friends and families.

COMPANY PERSPECTIVES

Madoff Securities' superior service is made possible by a sophisticated dealing staff backed by the securities industry's most advanced technology. It is underpinned by the personal commitment of founder Bernard L. Madoff, his brother Peter B. Madoff, who is the senior managing director and head of trading, and Madoff Securities' team of 250 employees. Their dedication to providing the best prices and the fastest execution has enabled the firm to become a leader in the U.S. "third market."

BLMIS later employed two interrelated trading techniques that greatly expanded its market share: trading NYSE stocks off the trading floor and paying other brokers to send orders its way. The firm took advantage of NYSE Rule 390 (since rescinded), which barred registered traders from trading listed stocks away from the NYSE floor. This allowed non-NYSE member firms, such as BLMIS, to directly execute orders for NYSE stocks with retail brokers (representing small investors) in the over-the-counter market. BLMIS took full advantage of this "third market" opportunity and amplified the resulting volume by paying other brokers a small fee, typically one cent per share, to send orders to it. This practice, known as "payment for order flow," was legal as long as the broker informed clients beforehand. These techniques helped to swell BLMIS trading volume to as much as 10 percent of daily NYSE trades.

TECHNOLOGY INNOVATOR IN THE 1970S

Deregulation of the stock market under the Securities Acts Amendments of 1975 vastly increased stock trading volumes by allowing brokers to slash trading fees. This ushered in discount brokerages and allowed a wave of small investors into the market. To handle the increased business and reduce costs, BLMIS developed and applied computerized operations. Peter Madoff, who had joined the firm in 1965, led the effort. BLMIS became one of the first traders to automate the reading of stock quotations from market networks. It also became one of the first to use plasma flat panel monitors, installing 30 IBM displays in its offices in 1987. It developed software to match the best bid and ask prices nationally and instantly execute orders of 5,000 shares or less. This freed the firm's agents to personally negotiate more

profitable large orders. In 1975 BLMIS helped to design and finance the automation of the Cincinnati Stock Exchange (CSE), which became the first completely computerized exchange. BLMIS listed its market quotes on the CSE and traded large volumes of securities there. BLMIS also developed computer modeling to allow it to hedge positions taken. In 1997 it introduced "time slicing," a computer-aided technique that allowed customers to spread the execution of orders across the span of an entire day or within a specified period. This technique was designed to eliminate the micromanagement necessary to execute orders, lessen client vulnerability to price swings, and allow opportunities for price improvement.

BLMIS also developed several special service programs. In 1992 it established a fully equipped and staffed disaster recovery facility near New York City's LaGuardia Airport. Duplicating all of the features of the headquarters in Manhattan, this facility was designed to receive and transact all orders and handle the clearing and settlement process. To reassure clients in the wake of the September 11, 2001, attacks on the World Trade Center, BLMIS created a Business Continuity Plan (BCP) in 2004. This was intended to enable a rapid resumption of operations following a catastrophic disruption at the firm's primary location. The BCP detailed how the firm would meet obligations to clients in the case of a disruption.

Through its innovative practices, BLMIS grew rapidly. In the 1980s it had achieved a market share of 5 percent of the NYSE volume. By 2000 it was one of the top three market makers on Wall Street and had a net worth of $300 million. The firm moved into three floors of the prestigious Lipstick Building in midtown Manhattan.

This success could not have been achieved without the explosive growth taking place in the securities industry itself. Daily NYSE volume swelled from four million shares per day in 1960 to more than one billion shares by the 2000s. BLMIS helped bring about such growth through extensive involvement in the industry. It actively promoted increased use of technology and greater access to the markets by small investors, breaking the monopoly of the decades-old system of human traders on an exchange floor. Madoff took a leadership position in the National Association of Securities Dealers (NASD). In 1971, under urging from Madoff and others, NASD established the National Association of Securities Dealers Automated Quotations (NASDAQ), an electronic exchange that used a computer system based on the automated trading system developed by BLMIS. The NASDAQ quickly developed the highest hourly volume of trading of any market in the world.

KEY DATES

1960: Bernard L. Madoff Investment Securities (BLMIS) founded as stock trading firm by Bernard L. Madoff.

1971: Madoff takes lead in establishing the NASDAQ.

1975: BLMIS computerizes the Cincinnati Stock Exchange.

1990: Madoff chairs NASDAQ Board of Governors.

1992: BLMIS disaster recovery facility established.

2000: BLMIS becomes one of the top three Wall Street market makers; net worth reaches $300 million.

2008: Madoff arrested on fraud charges after Ponzi scheme revealed; BLMIS goes into bankruptcy.

2009: Madoff convicted in federal court and sentenced to 150 years in prison.

Madoff was appointed to NASDAQ's Board of Governors and chaired it in 1990. His sons Mark and Andrew served on NASDAQ committees. Madoff also sat on the board of directors of the Securities Industry Association, and Peter Madoff served on the board of a successor organization, the Securities Industry and Financial Markets Association (SIFMA). Peter's daughter, Shana Madoff, who was the BLMIS compliance attorney and the wife of SEC official Eric Swanson, served in SIFMA's legal division. In doing good for the securities industry, the Madoffs were also doing well for BLMIS. In 2008 it was the sixth-largest market maker on Wall Street.

DEVELOPED FRAUDULENT INVESTMENT BUSINESS: 1990S

Possibly as early as 1962, BLMIS branched out from stock trading and began to invest money for clients. The operation developed into a hedge fund, which is a managed investment partnership employing sophisticated strategies to achieve a high rate of return. Because hedge funds cater to wealthy, presumably experienced investors, they are largely unregulated by the SEC, and the investment manager has great latitude. As his reputation in the financial world grew, Madoff leveraged his "brand" to develop an exclusive investment clientele of wealthy individuals and managers of large investment funds. He did not make extravagant claims of spectacular gains, unlike other hedge funds. He

promised and produced an unspectacular but remarkably steady 1 percent per month in returns, through both bull (up) and bear (down) markets.

Madoff's stated investment method involved portfolios of S&P100 stocks, related stock indexes, and the "split strike conversion strategy." An investment tool designed to minimize market losses and guarantee moderate returns, the split strike strategy normally produces gains in up markets and losses in down markets. Madoff, however, reported only seven down months.

BLMIS investment operations had turned into a fraudulent Ponzi scheme by the late 1980s or early 1990s. A Ponzi, or pyramid scheme, is an illegal investment scheme in which money from later investors is used to pay returns to earlier investors. Named after Charles Ponzi, an Italian immigrant to the United States who engaged in large-scale fraud through such a method in the 1920s, Ponzi schemes often collapse when new investments are not sufficient to cover the payments due, as was the case with BLMIS. Madoff concealed the fraud by providing clients with false trading reports and sending the SEC falsified audits and account statements. Some in the financial community had become skeptical of Madoff's investment program and raised questions with the SEC.

EVADED REGULATORS, 2000–07

Over the years the SEC had made a few investigations into BLMIS operations. During the 1960s and 1970s the firm was cited for minor violations of SEC trading regulations. In 1992 the SEC, acting on a tip, investigated the investment firm Avellino and Bienes (A&B), which was a feeder fund into Madoff's investment operations. A&B was reporting unusually high and steady returns. The SEC ordered the firm liquidated on a technicality: A&B had not registered its securities under the Securities Act of 1933. BLMIS was unaffected. In 2000 the SEC cited BLMIS's stock-trading operation for violations of the limit order protection rule: in order to maximize their own profits, BLMIS was preventing clients from receiving the best price for a security. This citation had no impact on the Ponzi scheme.

Suspicions about Madoff's stock trading practices led the SEC to investigate charges of "front-running" in 2004 and 2005. Front-running by a stock dealer is the illegal practice of taking advantage of advance knowledge that a client is about to place a large, potentially market-changing order. The dealer then buys or sells ahead of the order. The SEC broadened the inquiry to include the BLMIS investment operation in

2005. It raised questions about whether the firm should be registered with the SEC as an investment adviser. Madoff used his familiarity with SEC's rules to convince it to drop both aspects of the investigation.

Given that Madoff was running a Ponzi scheme, it was not surprising that BLMIS did not use a major accounting firm. Instead it used the obscure firm of Friehling and Horowitz, which employed only one certified accountant, David Friehling. (After the Ponzi scheme was revealed, David Friehling was arrested for falsely certifying that he had audited BLMIS statements.) The use of a questionable accounting firm was but one of 29 suspicious "red flags" that investment analyst Harry Markopolos, working for Rampart Investment Management, turned up in 2005 when he was asked by his employer to try to figure out how BLMIS was producing its high reported returns on investment. Markopolos analyzed stock market activities but could not account for the returns that BLMIS claimed from the split strike conversion strategy. Markopolos, who had been suspicious of Madoff and had informed the SEC about this beginning in 1999, sent his 29 red flags to them. In response the SEC reopened its investigations and cited BLMIS for minor registration violations, but found no evidence of fraud.

In 2007 the Financial Industry Regulatory Authority (FINRA), successor to the NASD, conducted a routine examination of BLMIS's books and found a few irregularities. However, FINRA was only responsible for examining stock trading and did not pursue questions that BLMIS's conduct raised about its investments.

Madoff relied on his high stature in the financial community and on wealthy contacts to attract clients, largely through word of mouth. He cultivated a mystique by revealing little about his operations but producing steady and attractive gains in both up and down markets. As recounted by Peter Sander in *Madoff: Corruption, Deceit, and the Making of the World's Most Notorious Ponzi Scheme*, Madoff cryptically told one investor: "I make money when the markets go up. I make money when the markets go down." Because of the nature of hedge funds, only the very wealthy could participate, which guaranteed Madoff a flow of substantial investments. In an interesting twist, he often refused to accept clients and would put them off for a while. This only added to the mystique and whetted the appetites of his potential clients.

FRAUD SCHEME REVEALED IN 2008

While the investment fund initially relied on individual investors, often in Madoff's social group, he also sought investment by large investment funds and cultivated ties with their directors to send money his way. These feeder funds brought in the bulk of the investment money. Madoff rewarded the fund directors with large fees. They did not always inform their investors that Madoff was managing their funds.

For years, whenever investors wanted to withdraw their principal and earnings, Madoff redeemed immediately, though only in full (he did not allow investors to remove only part of their principal and earnings), drawing on funds invested by other clients to pay out the investor's nonexistent "profits." That was the nature of the Ponzi scheme; there were no actual earnings. This worked well as long as the stock market trends were upward, as they generally were from the late 1980s until 2007–08. When the market collapsed in the fall of 2008, Madoff began to have difficulty meeting calls for redemptions.

When he received a redemption request for $7 billion, he was unable to meet it. Madoff now knew the Ponzi scheme was finished. With his two sons acting as intermediaries, he agreed to surrender to federal authorities. On December 11, 2008, he was charged under federal civil and criminal complaints with securities fraud and placed under house arrest. Bail was set at $10 million. He admitted to defrauding investors of $50 billion. In February 2009 the SEC banned Madoff from the securities industry for life.

BLMIS was placed under a court-appointed trustee, and bankruptcy proceedings were initiated. The trustee, New York attorney Irving H. Picard, was given the task of liquidating BLMIS. The stock trading operation was sold to Castor Pollux Securities LLC for $25.5 million in 2009. The trustee also began reclaiming lost funds and ruling on victims' claims for restitution. As of July 1, 2009, the trustee had secured just over $1 billion for the victims.

AFTERMATH: RESTITUTION AND IMPRISONMENT

At a hearing on March 12, 2009, Madoff pled guilty to an 11-count federal criminal information, which included securities fraud, money laundering, theft, and embezzlement. Federal prosecutors estimated that he had defrauded investors of $64.8 billion. At the hearing, Madoff admitted that he operated a Ponzi scheme through the investment advisory side of BLMIS. He admitted that he knew what he was doing was criminal. In his plea allocution, he stated that he told prospective clients that he would invest their money in shares of common stock, options, and other securities and would return profit and principal in full whenever requested. In fact, he admitted, no securities were ever purchased.

Instead, he deposited the funds in an account at Chase Manhattan Bank. Madoff described how he moved funds between this account and other BLMIS accounts in an attempt to conceal the fraud. He attempted to shield his wife and other family members, who were heavily involved with the legitimate operations of BLMIS, from any connection to the Ponzi scheme. He steadfastly, if implausibly, maintained that he conducted the entire fraud himself.

On June 29, 2009, Madoff was sentenced to the maximum possible term of 150 years in prison without parole. Separately, a federal judge held him liable for up to $170 billion in restitution to victims of the fraud. These ranged from such huge feeder funds as Fairfield Sentry (lost $7.5 billion), Tremont Group Holdings ($3.3 billion), and Kingate Management ($2.8 billion), to thousands of individual investors, large and small. In some cases fund managers aided and abetted the fraud. In June 2009 the SEC filed civil fraud charges against both Cohmad Securities Corp. and investor Stanley Chais for passing client funds to Madoff and helping conceal the Ponzi scheme. Considered particularly reprehensible on Madoff's part was his defrauding of charitable organizations such as the Shapiro Family Foundation ($90 million), Hadassah ($90 million), and Holocaust-survivor Elie Wiesel's Foundation for Humanity ($15.2 million). Federal investigators pursued possible prosecutions of Madoff family members and others but had not brought any charges by July 2009. The fate of most of the estimated $64.8 billion in investments and attributed earnings that were lost was unknown. On July 14, 2009, Madoff arrived at the Butner Federal Correctional Complex in North Carolina to serve out his sentence.

Judson MacLaury

PRINCIPAL SUBSIDIARIES

Madoff Securities International Ltd., London.

PRINCIPAL COMPETITORS

The Bear Stearns Companies Inc. (collapsed, 2008); The Charles Schwab Corporation; The Goldman Sachs Group, Inc.; Lehman Brothers Holdings Inc. (entered bankruptcy, 2008); Morgan Stanley.

FURTHER READING

"Bernard L. Madoff," *New York Times* [collection of articles], 2009, http://topics.nytimes.com/top/reference/timestopics/people/m/bernard_l_madoff/index.html?s=oldest&.

Bernard L. Madoff, Plea Allocution, March 15, 2009, http://online.wsj.com/public/resources/documents/20090315madoffall.pdf.

Chernow, Ron, "Madoff and His Models, the Pioneers of the Swindle," *New Yorker*, March 23, 2009.

Franklin, Nancy, "The Dolor Of Money," *New Yorker*, March 23, 2009.

"Madoff Begins 150-Year Prison Sentence," *Los Angles Times*, July 15, 2009.

Picard, Irving H., Trustee for the Liquidation of Bernard L. Madoff Investment Securities LLC, "Interim Report," Period of Dec. 11, 2008 to June 30, 2009,"July 9, 2009, http://www.madofftrustee.com/press/TrusteeInterimReport_090709.pdf.

Sander, Peter, *Madoff: Corruption, Deceit, and the Making of the World's Most Notorious Ponzi Scheme*. Guilford, CT: The Lyons Press, 2009.

Strober, Deborah and Gerald, *Catastrophe: The Story of Bernard L. Madoff, the Man Who Swindled the World*. Beverly Hills, CA: Phoenix Books, 2009.

Bidvest Group Ltd.

Bidvest House
18 Crescent Drive
Melrose Arch
Johannesburg, 2196
South Africa
Telephone: (+27 11) 772-8700
Fax: (+27 11) 772-8970
Web site: http://www.bidvest.com

Public Company
Founded: 1988
Employees: 106,225
Sales: ZAR 110.5 million (2008)
Stock Exchanges: Johannesburg
Ticker Symbol: BVT
NAICS: 311812 Commercial Bakeries; 424490 Other Grocery and Related Products Merchant Wholesalers; 441110 New Car Dealers; 453210 Office Supplies and Stationery Stores; 488510 Freight Transportation Arrangement; 561210 Facilities Support Services

■ ■ ■

Bidvest Group Ltd. is a distribution, manufacturing, and service company that operates in Africa, Australia, Europe, and New Zealand. Nine divisions make up the company, and each is concerned with a major area of its interests. For example, Bidserv handles domestic and industrial cleaning services, interior and exterior landscaping, travel services and aviation, and all facets of banking. Bidvest's chief executive officer is Brian Joffe, who is based in Johannesburg.

EARLY YEARS

A chartered accountant by training, Brian Joffe worked in corporate finance, first as a consultant for Standard Merchant Bank's corporate finance division and then as the group managing director for W&A Investment Corporation Ltd., before he decided to open his own company. In November 1988, using a ZAR 8 million cash shell, he listed Bidvest on the Johannesburg Stock Exchange for the first time.

Joffe's first acquisition, shortly after Bidvest's own debut, was a food company. Well known throughout South Africa, Walter A. Chipkin Pty. Ltd. was a major supplier to the hotel and hospitality industry, offering everything from crockery and barware to dried fruit, canned foods, wine, and supplies for bakeries. The Chipkin acquisition was followed shortly thereafter by the purchase of Seaworld, a supplier of frozen foods. Together, these two companies created the nucleus of the Bidfood division.

These two acquisitions also set the stage for what would become a Joffe acquisition hallmark: namely, buying companies that supply merchandise which is always in demand. This principle was firmly in place when the African Commerce Developing Company (Afcom) joined the Bidvest lineup. Afcom's products, such as packing tape, shrink-wrap, strapping materials, labels, carton closers, and the devices that run them, were used in nearly every industry. These products seemed to be worlds apart from Joffe's original acquisitions, but the

COMPANY PERSPECTIVES

In a big business environment we run our company with the determination and commitment evident in a small business heart. We believe in empowering people, building relationships and improving lives. Entrepreneurship, incentivisation, decentralised management and communication are the keys. We subscribe to a philosophy of transparency, accountability, integrity, excellence and innovation in all our business dealings. We turn ordinary companies into extraordinary performers, delivering strong and consistent shareholder returns in the process. But most importantly, we understand that people create wealth, and that companies only report it.

underlying objective—stellar service tailored to the needs of each customer—formed the beating heart of both product ranges.

BROADENING HORIZONS

In 1991 Joffe expanded the range of his acquisitions with the purchase of Steiner Group, a company that focused on hygiene products and services for public washrooms, hotels, airports, and other away-from-home venues. When Steiner was combined with the 1993 acquisition of Prestige Cleaning, the two companies formed the Bidserv division.

That same year Bidvest established the Bidfreight division, whose first member was Safcor Panalpina. This 100-year-old company specialized in "supply chain management"—using a network of interconnected companies that took the customer through each phase of the freight process, from packaging, to pickup, to cross-country shipping, to delivery. Safcor was a first for Bidvest in other ways. It was the first acquisition with international roots, a sign that the days of apartheid-induced economic sanctions, which had been in place since 1986, were coming to an end.

That said, the company's first truly international step took it not to Europe, but to Australia, where Joffe bought a 50.1 percent share of the conglomerate Manettas Ltd. in 1995. Manettas had three divisions: fresh and frozen foods, commercial hospitality supplies (e.g., cutlery, tableware, glassware, and their attendant services), and paper supplies. Courtesy of Manettas, now known as Bidvest Australia, 29 Australian business units

joined Bidvest, along with 13 business units across New Zealand.

A company like this did not come cheap. Joffe, however, who was well known to have an aversion to debt, had raised $300 million the year before by means of an off-shore rights issue to finance this purchase.

CONSISTENT STRATEGY

In all these cases, as well as in the hundreds of acquisitions that have followed them, Joffe's strategy remained consistent. Even though there were few exceptions, such as Manettas, he preferred to buy each company in its entirety, rather than choosing to be a significant shareholder. "We only want to have one entry point into Bidvest," he told Marcia Klein of the South African *Times*. "There are no minorities and no conflicts of interest. We are all working towards one common goal."

He focused mostly on acquiring poorly managed companies that had the potential for improvement, to enhance cash flow, and to create jobs. A good example of this strategy was in 1997, when he acquired Waltons, a stationery and office supply company based in Capetown, South Africa. Despite the company being weighed down by massive debt, Joffe paid ZAR 1 billion for Waltons—the first time he had ever spent so much on an acquisition. Like the other Bidvest companies, Waltons conducted its business with decentralized management that allowed it to function and make relevant decisions without interference from Bidvest headquarters. This hands-off strategy notwithstanding, Waltons, like all other Bidvest subsidiaries, knew that there was plenty of strategic advice available from the corporate management and that financial backup would be offered if needed.

Joffe believed this was the best type of business plan for a developing economy such as the postapartheid one in South Africa, because it allowed each company to create jobs that were tailored to its individual needs. This plan also offered the prospect of advancement for motivated employees who remained mindful of the performance reviews marking their progress at six-month intervals. Employees in each company who were truly determined and hardworking received further acknowledgment of their efforts, in the form of bonuses, stock options, and deferred bonus payments.

COMPANY AWARDS

For both employer and employee, this was a win-win strategy that earned Bidvest some highly respected awards. In 1996 it was voted as one of South Africa's top 100 companies by the influential *Sunday Times Busi-*

KEY DATES

■

1988: Brian Joffe founds Bidvest; the company acquires Walter A. Chipkin and Seaworld.
1991: Bidvest acquires Steiner Group.
1993: Safcor Panalpina is acquired, which leads to the start-up of Bidfreight; the company acquires Prestige Cleaning Services and groups it with Steiner to establish Bidserv.
1995: Bidvest acquires Manettas Ltd. and renames it Bidvest Australia.
1996: Bidvest is voted as one of South Africa's top 100 companies by the *Sunday Times Business Times's* annual survey.
2003: Dinatla buys a 15 percent stake in Bidvest; the Bidvest Academy begins training managerial employees.
2007: The Bidvest Graduate Academy is opened.
2008: Bidvest's annual revenue tops ZAR 100 billion.

ness *Times's* annual survey. Ciaran Ryan of the *Sunday Times Business Times* noted that within six years Bidvest expanded to oversee five major subdivisions. One of these, Bidfreight, was working in tandem with Safcon, another acquisition that offered Bidvest freight customers the option of overnight courier services. In 1996 this division alone provided 22 percent of Bidvest's operating income, which was ZAR 450 million.

Another division showing the same world-class performance was Bidserv, whose core business, Steiner Group, provided washroom products such as soaps and paper goods, in addition to cleaning services and textile rentals. By 1996 it had been joined by Prestige Cleaning Service and Prestige Pest Control. Combined, these Bidserv companies provided 17 percent of the 1996 annual income, while the Bidfood division's piece of the pie equaled a healthy 15 percent.

This dazzling array of seemingly unrelated products and services attracted many comments from business analysts, who suggested that Bidvest's acquisitions seemed to lack a single focus. Joffe, however, was unperturbed by their comments. "There is a theme which runs through each of the businesses in the Bidvest group," he told Ryan. "All the businesses are in the service, distribution and trading fields. ... We have been able to add value by bundling several companies together."

The truth of this sentiment came to the fore in February 2000, when Bidvest bought Island View Storage for ZAR 206 million. This acquisition, added to the Safcor lineup, broadened the Bidfreight line by providing container and handling logistics. Joffe's wisdom showed up in Bidvest's annual revenues, which reached ZAR 26.4 billion. The company was also given a place on the *Financial Mail's* list of "Top Companies."

BLACK ECONOMIC EMPOWERMENT

During the 1990s the political climate of the country had changed radically. By 1996 the African National Congress was firmly in power and the legacy of apartheid was slowly being dismantled. No longer were black South Africans restricted to jobs at the bottom of the economic pyramid—they were now able to compete with whites in any sphere they chose. Nevertheless, this did nothing to make the majority of black South Africans any wealthier than they had been during apartheid. The reason was obvious: Almost all of them had received a deliberately inferior education, which made job advancement difficult if not impossible. This led, in turn, to a lack of experience at the managerial level, so that black employees were unable to compete with their white rivals, who thus enjoyed an almost entirely undisturbed advancement track, even though they represented only 10 percent of the country's population.

The South African government was determined to change this by making the economic climate of the country more representative of the country's rainbow heritage. In 2003 the Broad-Based Black Economic Empowerment Act was passed to make sure that black ownership of existing businesses increased, that a certain number of jobs in each industrial setting were occupied by nonwhite employees, and that training and opportunities were provided for ambitious and diligent nonwhite workers.

Wholeheartedly agreeing with this strategy, Bidvest had begun to institute its own black empowerment initiative in 1996, when it awarded a 10 percent stake to two black-owned South African companies. Five percent went to Women Investment Portfolio Holdings Pty. Ltd., a company that provided both stock-broking services and hedge fund and asset management. The other 5 percent went to Worldwide African Investment Holdings Pty. Ltd., a company that focused on energy sources throughout sub-Saharan Africa.

As such, by the time the act was passed in 2003, Joffe had been planning the company's transformation for several years. That same year, he welcomed Dinatla, which paid about ZAR 2.2 billion for a 15 percent stake of Bidvest. Entirely black owned, Dinatla counted among its members the Shanduka Group, which was headed by Matamela Cyril Ramaphosa. In 2004 Ramaphosa became the nonexecutive chairman of Bidvest.

Working in tandem, Bidvest and Dinatla developed the Bidvest Charter, which was unveiled in November 2003. This was the company's stated commitment to black economic empowerment, by which it set targets for the following five to 10 years in areas that were specifically mentioned by the act, such as providing preferential procurement, guaranteeing black-owned companies a share of service and manufacturing contracts, and offering equity sharing, skills development, and enterprise development. Each Bidvest company was able to follow these requirements according to its own needs and economic goals.

THE BIDVEST ACADEMY

Parts of this charter were publicized earlier in the year. For example, in May the company announced the creation of the Bidvest Academy, which would provide training in leadership and other management skills for promising young executives. This training course proved so successful that the Bidvest Graduate Academy was added in 2007 to extend this vital education.

Like most aspects of Bidvest strategy, the academy was precisely tailored to its goals. Each member of its student body was handpicked by his or her peers and managers as a promising future leader. Once accepted, students were expected to complete individual projects as well as team efforts lasting six months. The results were then presented to Joffe and other Bidvest executives, who readily adopted any profitable ideas that were offered.

Even though the academy was aimed at higher-level Bidvest employees, others lower in the hierarchy also had an opportunity to improve themselves. They were offered the chance to increase their basic educational and life skills via the Adult Basic Education Training program that was offered within each company.

2005 AND BEYOND

In 2004 Bidvest acquired McCarthy Motor Holdings for ZAR 980 million. As the second largest motor company in South Africa, McCarthy formed the nucleus of Bid Auto division, where it offered both new and secondhand cars.

By the end of 2005 Bidvest's revenues stood at ZAR 62.8 billion, and its lineup consisted of nine divisions. Among these divisions was Bidvest Europe, which consisted of subsidiary companies in Belgium, the Netherlands, the United Kingdom, and the United Arab Emirates that supplied food and other products for the hospitality industry.

One of these subsidiary companies was 3663 First for Foodservice, a British company that Bidvest acquired in 1999 for £125 million. Ten years later 3663 (the numbers spell the word *food* on a telephone keypad) held the Royal Warrant, meaning that it supplied fresh and frozen foods to the queen's household. Its other customers included military bases, prisons, police stations, and upscale hotels and restaurants.

As is the case with all Bidvest companies, 3663 incorporated the highest standards of corporate responsibility into its business plan. The company prided itself on using produce from local farmers wherever possible, and it followed the precepts of other environmentally conscientious businesses by recycling paper and plastic. By the end of 2008, 3663's revenue was nearly 10 times its purchase price. According to the company's 2008 annual report, its income for the year topped £1 billion.

By June 2008, the end of Bidvest's financial year, revenues for the entire company stood at ZAR 110.5 billion. The company's nine company divisions consisted of Bidfreight, which handled all shipping and transport services, and Bidserv, which provided outsourced services ranging from laundry and landscaping to security, aviation, travel, and banking. Bidvest Europe and Bidvest Asia Pacific, which included Bidvest Australia, Bidvest New Zealand, and the Angliss Group, were foodservice distributors. Bidfood, which consisted of Caterplus and other foodservice, was based in South Africa. Bid Industrial and Commercial Products consisted of companies that handled electrical appliances, office stationery, and furniture; Bidpaper produced and distributed paper products all over southern Africa; Bidvest Namibia presided over Bidvest's fishing and other interests in Namibia; and Bid Auto listed companies that produced automobile-related products. Presiding over all these divisions was Bidvest Corporate, which provided guidance in implementing the company's decentralized way of doing business and ensured that employees were secure in both their training and their paycheck.

Gillian Wolf

PRINCIPAL SUBSIDIARIES

Bidfreight; Bidserv; Bidvest Europe; Bidvest Asia Pacific; Bidfood; Bid Industrial and Commercial Products; Bidpaper Plus; Bidvest Namibia; Bid Auto.

PRINCIPAL COMPETITORS

Compass Group; Sodexo; DHL.

FURTHER READING

Klein, Marcia, "Joffe Might Be Low on Profile, but He's High on Performance," *Times* (South Africa), November 7, 2007.

McNulty, Andrew, "Hope and Caution," *Financial Mail*, March 13, 2009.

Mokopanele, Thabang, "Deal Boosts Bidvest BEE Profile," Fin24.com, July 9, 2003, http://www.fin24.com/articles/ default/display_article.aspx?ArticleId=1518-24_1385144.

Newmarch, Jocelyn, "Bidvest Goes Banking," *Mail Guardian Online*, August 13, 2007.

Ryan, Ciaran, "Sustaining a Breakneck Pace of Growth with Zero Debt," *Sunday Times Business Times*, 1996.

Theunissen, Garth, "Bidvest Takes the Cake," *Finweek 24*, 2007.

"Time's Top 100 People," *Time*, June 16, 2009.

"Top 100 Africans of 2001," Africa Almanac, 2004, http:// www.africaalmanac.com/top100africans.html.

Brightpoint Inc.

7635 Interactive Way, Suite 200
Indianapolis, Indiana 46278
U.S.A.
Toll Free: (800) 952-2355
Fax: (317) 707-2512
Web site: http://www.brightpoint.com

Public Company
Incorporated: 1989 as Wholesale Cellular USA
Employees: 3,000
Sales: $4.64 billion (2008)
Stock Exchanges: NASDAQ
Ticker Symbol: CELL
NAISC: 423690 Other Electronic Parts and Equipment
    Merchant Wholesalers

∎ ∎ ∎

Brightpoint Inc. is one of the world's largest distributors of cell phones, cell phone accessories, and other wireless devices. It acts as a middleman between many of the biggest wireless providers, cell phone manufacturers, and cell-phone end-users. In 2006 Steve Kaelble noted in *Indiana Business Magazine* that Brightpoint touches one out of every five wireless devices in the United States. Besides its core distribution operations, the company offers customized logistics services to companies involved in every phase of the wireless industry. These services include inventory management, same-day shipment, product training, cell phone programming, and custom packaging, or "kitting." Brightpoint has operation centers and/or sales offices across the globe, including sites in Australia, Austria, Belgium, Colombia, Denmark, Finland, France, Germany, India, Italy, the Netherlands, New Zealand, Norway, the Philippines, Poland, Portugal, Russia, Singapore, Slovakia, Spain, Sweden, Switzerland, the United Arab Emirates, and the United States. All told, its 25,000 customers include agents, dealers, chain stores, resellers, exporters, direct marketers, expediters, and cellular service providers. Brightpoint was named one of the United States' Most Admired Companies by *Fortune* magazine in both 2007 and 2009.

THE BIRTH OF AN INDUSTRY: 1984–89

The first test to determine the commercial feasibility of cellular communication technology was conducted in 1962, 15 years after AT&T's Bell Laboratories introduced the idea of cellular transmission of radio communications signals. In 1970 the Federal Communications Commission (FCC) set aside radio frequencies for "land mobile communications," and by 1977 it had announced the construction of two cellular development systems in Baltimore, Maryland/Washington, D.C., and Chicago, Illinois. As the U.S. cellular phone industry began to emerge in the 1980s, the FCC decided to authorize only two cell phone service carriers for each urban market, a decision that helped keep the average monthly cost for cell phone service well above that of conventional phone lines for several years. Nevertheless, by 1985 roughly 300,000 U.S. cell phone subscribers were using cell phones throughout the United States.

COMPANY PERSPECTIVES

Our customers are some of the most successful organizations in wireless. We're proud of our role in their success, and are deeply committed to expanding our customers' growth. At the center of Brightpoint's commitment are Brightpoint people, some of the sharpest thinkers in wireless. We are innovators, collaborators and exceptional performers, all made evident by the facts: millions of wireless devices handled annually and more than 25,000 B2B customers supported globally. We understand that when we do more, our customers can do more. With every device shipped, we are delivering on a promise to our customers: your success is our business.

In 1986 a young entrepreneur named Robert J. Laikin established a travel agency in Indianapolis, Indiana, to cater to the corporate customers he had acquired through his first business enterprise, Tickets Up Front, a ticket agency for corporate clients. When Arnie Goldberg, a salesman for a communications firm, brought in an early model cell phone, Laikin became intrigued by the technology and agreed to buy one for his on-the-road business calls. He also invited Goldberg to contact him if he ever wanted to go into the business of selling phones. Two weeks later Goldberg took Laikin up on his offer, and a short while later Laikin, Goldberg, and their partners bought a 50 percent share in Century Car Phones (later renamed Century Cellular Network Inc.). By charging customers as much as $500 less per unit than his competitors, Goldberg began signing up new accounts in droves, and Century was soon expanding its monthly cell phone orders from 100 to 1,000. By 1987 the number of cellular phone subscribers in the United States had grown to 1 million, and the average monthly cell phone subscription had dropped to a modest $50. Century rode the wave and was Indiana's leading cellular retailer by 1988.

As the boom in cellular service grew, cell phone manufacturers struggled to keep up with demand, and retailers in small markets, such as Century, found themselves wait-listed while the big urban markets were supplied. Dismayed by the practice, Laikin decided to establish his own low-cost cell phone supplier to buy Century's phones inexpensively through bulk purchases from manufacturers. In partnership with Daniel Koerselman, a salesman for a car phone accessory firm,

Laikin founded Wholesale Cellular USA in 1989. When the nation's cellular service carriers began reducing the commissions they paid local retailers such as Century, Laikin focused more of his attention and energy on Wholesale rather than on Century to increase his chances for success in the cellular industry.

GROWTH OF WHOLESALE: 1989–93

Laikin's strategy for growing Wholesale Cellular read like a primer on successful business startups: The company's Midwest location capitalized on a trend in the cell phone manufacturing industry, where firms were now beginning to look for new markets outside the major urban areas. Wholesale was strategically positioned to supply cell phones not only to Century but also to agents in several midwestern states. Laikin also promptly paid manufacturers for all orders and was rewarded with first priority whenever manufacturers had to dole out cell phones during periods of short supply. Finally, Laikin kept Wholesale's costs to a minimum. With little real capital or collateral and a desk piled high with banks' loan rejections, Laikin was forced to operate with a low overhead and minimal inventory. To keep Wholesale's cash flow strong and steady, he made sure customers received their phones right away. Within a year of its birth, Wholesale had ceased to be merely a vehicle for Century's growth and was amassing sales of $12 million.

As the wireless industry expanded, the cellular service providers began reducing the number of operations they involved themselves in to concentrate on selling "minutes of use" rather than on storing and, more often than not, essentially giving away expensive handsets to attract customers, who often discontinued service after only a few months. Hundreds of small third-party distributors such as Wholesale began to occupy a larger segment of the middle market between the buying public and the cellular service carriers and phone manufacturers. Besides buying the cell phones from the manufacturers, these small, low-capital, usually privately owned distributors began to take on the "hardware" functions of the cellular service carriers. They maintained and managed their phone equipment inventory, programmed the cell phones for the individual markets they were destined to be used in, executed the delivery of the cell phone to customers, and sometimes activated the customers' cell phone signal. As the price of cell phones dropped and the number of subscribers grew, competition among the industry's scattered distributors heated up, and low-cost firms such as Wholesale could grab larger wedges of market share by buying phones in enormous volume, thereby undercutting their competitors' prices. The wireless distribution

KEY DATES

1986: Robert J. Laikin and his partners buy a 50 percent share in Century Car Phones.

1989: Laikin and Daniel Koerselman establish Wholesale Cellular USA to serve as a low-cost cell phone supplier for Century's phones.

1994: Wholesale goes public with an initial public offering of common stock that raises $13.5 million.

1995: Wholesale Cellular USA is renamed Brightpoint Inc.; Brightpoint acquires Technology Resources International Ltd. to establish Brightpoint International Ltd. in Manchester, England; *Forbes* magazine ranks Brightpoint among the top three "Best Small Companies in America."

1996: Brightpoint begins marketing a line of cell phone accessories called Brightlink; acquires Allied Communications Inc.; acquires Hatadicorp Pty. Ltd. of Sydney, Australia, to form Brightpoint Australia Pty. Ltd.

1997: Brightpoint's market value is over $1 billion.

1998: Brightpoint and the American International Group Inc. (AIG) create a scheme to hide Brightpoint's losses by exaggerating its earnings.

2003: The U.S. Securities and Exchange Commission charges AIG and Brightpoint with committing fraud; Brightpoint pays a $450,000 civil fine.

2007: Brightpoint purchases Dangaard Telecom of Denmark; Laikin receives a Stevie Award from the American Business Awards for best turnaround executive; Brightpoint is named by *Fortune* as one of the "Most Admired Companies" in the United States.

2009: *Fortune* names Brightpoint as one of the "Most Admired Companies" in the United States.

industry began to consolidate rapidly, a trend that was only exacerbated when, in an economizing move, the cellular service carriers cut the number of suppliers with which they worked. In an industry driven by rapid technological change, cutthroat competition, constantly falling prices, and hairline profit margins, only the distributors with the best management, the most financial resources, and the greatest flexibility stood any chance of surviving.

Wholesale Cellular was quickly establishing itself as that kind of company. By 1991 it had 500 customers and sales of $32 million. By 1992 the number of cell phone users in the United States had grown from zero only nine years before to 10 million, and no fewer than 1,500 cellular systems were up and running across the country. With the adoption of wireless technology growing faster than virtually any previous technology—including color television, videocassette recorders, and personal computers—at least one industry analyst anointed wireless technology "the product of the century." In 1992 Wholesale's sales leaped 50 percent to $48 million and then in 1993 another 60 percent to $77 million. As profits broke the $2 million mark, Laikin stepped down as president of Century in February 1993 to enter the potentially gargantuan international wireless market by launching a Wholesale presence in Brazil.

"PEOPLE DON'T LIKE WIRES": 1994–95

With net sales closing in on $169 million, Laikin took Wholesale public in April 1994 with an initial public offering (IPO) of common stock that raised $13.5 million. Like most IPOs, the decision to yield part ownership to public shareholders was driven by Laikin's desperate need for capital to keep his five-year-old juggernaut rolling. He used part of the year's cash influx for the continuation of Wholesale's international expansion. The Chilean market was opened up in January, followed by Argentina in July, Columbia and Mexico in November, and Israel in December. In October Wholesale established an office and warehouse facility in Miami, Florida, to serve its burgeoning Latin American customers. Moreover, Laikin was also pursuing a joint venture with the Indian information technology giant Pertech Computers Ltd. to distribute cellular equipment to the vast Indian middle class. In less than two years in the global marketplace, Wholesale's international business had grown to 10 percent of total sales.

Since Wholesale's inception, Laikin had been working double time to juggle the company's growing operations while visiting potential foreign markets and anticipating the latest developments in the wireless industry and cell phone technology. "I wanted to delegate," Laikin told the *Indianapolis Business Journal*, "I just had no time to delegate." On a friend's recommendation, he began exploring the possibility of bringing J. Mark Howell, the chief accountant of the automobile auction firm Adesa Corporation, on board to manage Wholesale's finances. In July 1994 Howell was named executive vice president in charge of Wholesale's financial operations, administration, information services, and human resources.

By 1994 Wholesale's market-winning strategy had become clear. The cellular service providers who made up the bulk of its customers paid Wholesale a flat dollar amount for each phone sold, and Wholesale negotiated directly for distribution rights with roughly 45 phone manufacturers—virtually all the major brands—to guarantee inventories of cell phone products, which were selected on the basis of quality, price, customer demand, product availability, and brand recognition. Wholesale's staff placed daily orders for equipment with the manufacturers, who then shipped them directly to Wholesale's warehouses in Indianapolis and Miami, where Wholesale's proprietary order fulfillment system shipped them in bulk to large buyers or singly to individual customers. By carefully avoiding dependence on any single supplier and by offering phones for every cellular transmission standard, Laikin could essentially eliminate the risk of being stuck with a product suddenly out of favor in the marketplace. Moreover, by resisting a contractual obligation to a single manufacturer (such as Cellstar's relationship with Motorola), Wholesale could market itself to manufacturers, service providers, and end users alike as a truly independent supplier.

Wholesale also expanded its order fulfillment services to encompass not only traditional product handling and warehousing but also custom phone labeling, branding, and packaging; phone warranty and repair services; and overnight "just-in-time" delivery. Laikin's quip that the cell phone industry's growth was being driven in part by the simple fact that "people don't like wires" was proven true when truly portable "walk-and-talk" cell phones began to become as common as the traditional car-mounted mobile phone. A whole new range of accessories became available for the new nonautomotive cell phone market, from antennas and carrying cases to batteries, rechargers, and hands-free kits, and all were integrated into Wholesale's distribution system. Because such accessories could normally be priced for a much greater profit margin than cell phones, Wholesale gained a welcome jolt of income, and by 1994 accessories were accounting for 12 percent of company sales.

In 1995 Wholesale announced a five-year agreement with the cellular service provider BellSouth Cellular Corporation and HSN Direct, the infomercial division of Home Shopping Network Inc., to sell cellular phones and service. Under the plan, HSN Direct would initially produce 30-minute infomercials marketing BellSouth's "Mobile America" cellular service and products through an 800 number, with Wholesale fulfilling the orders.

Wholesale also formed the joint venture Wholesale Cellular Latina in 1995 with Garrido, the German consumer electronics distributor, to distribute cell phones and accessories in Argentina, Bolivia, Chile, Ecuador, Paraguay, Peru, and Uruguay while expanding its warehousing facilities in Miami to absorb the additional traffic. As midyear sales showed Wholesale on a course to break the $269 million mark for the year, Laikin announced that a new $4 million headquarters, warehouse, and distribution complex would be constructed in Indianapolis, a few miles from its existing site.

BECOMING BRIGHTPOINT INC.: 1995–97

As Wholesale's business continued to expand far beyond phone distribution, Laikin began to search for a new name to reflect the company's growing scope and potential. In September 1995 Wholesale Cellular USA was officially renamed Brightpoint Inc. because, as Howell explained, "we wanted a name that was not limiting in any way. We're just trying to get away from the perception of the company being a box-moving distributor." By August Brightpoint had agreed to form a joint venture with India's Pertech Computers to begin distributing cell phones, pagers, and accessories in India in late 1995 and early 1996.

As Brightpoint expanded, it accumulated debt and a pressing need for additional growth capital. In October 1995 Laikin made a second stock offering to the public for about $34 million, which resulted in increased equity of $59 million and the necessary means to pay down its debt, fund the move to its new 90,000-square-foot office and distribution facility, and install a new management information system. In November it established a presence in mainland China and Hong Kong and expanded its Miami facility further. In December Brightpoint entered the Philippine, Malaysian, Singapore, and Taiwan markets for the first time. As the year drew to a close, Brightpoint announced the acquisition of the British firm Technology Resources International Ltd., which became part of a new operation, Brightpoint International Ltd. Headquartered in Manchester, England, it would conduct all of Brightpoint's sales and marketing activities outside of North and South America.

Meanwhile, the cellular phone industry was changing almost as rapidly as Brightpoint's efforts to keep up with it. New lightweight phone designs and the introduction of a new generation of digital cellular technology called PCS (personal cellular service) were beginning to fuel a booming phone replacement market as consumers began to substitute their older phones for the latest technology. New battery-less plug-in phones and long-life lithium ion batteries were giving Brightpoint new products to add to its line of accessories, and as cell phone service and equipment prices fell, consumer demand for new phone styles, colors, features, and accessories continued to increase. By the end of 1995 Brightpoint's sales had surpassed $260 million, and international customers in 35 countries were now accounting for 27 percent of its sales. Of Brightpoint's 6,000 customers, Nokia, BellSouth Cellular Corporation, Motorola, and AT&T Wireless Services were now accounting for 58 percent of its product purchases. On the strength of Brightpoint's 91 percent return on equity, *Forbes* magazine ranked it among the top three "Best Small Companies in America" in 1995.

The year 1996 was Brightpoint's best ever. Distributors were handling 30 percent of the cell phones and accessories being sold by the industry, with the remaining 70 percent shipped by the phone manufacturer to the service carrier or directly to retail stores such as Radio Shack and Office Depot. Laikin wanted a piece of the retail pie, so he announced in March that Brightpoint would be performing the repackaging and preprogramming of the "Cellular to Go" phone products marketed by U.S. Communications Inc. in mass retail outlets such as Target, Kmart, and CompUSA. Brightpoint also announced that its own branded line of cell phone accessories named Brightlink would be sold in mass market retail outlets around the United States. Moreover, in 1996 Brightpoint agreed to provide the inventory management, order fulfillment, and packaging and telemarketing services for the new joint venture named Wireless LLC formed with the paging service provider Metrocall Inc. and the wireless developer America Unplugged of South Carolina. Finally, in late 1996 Brightpoint expanded its participation in the "Cellular to Go" venture by adding the Michigan chain Meijer Inc. to its growing list of retail customers.

The year's biggest move, however, was the acquisition of Allied Communications Inc., the fourth largest cell phone distributor in the United States and one of Brightpoint's sharpest competitors. In exchange for $42 million of Brightpoint stock, Allied added $150 million in sales to Brightpoint's kitty and vastly expanded its U.S. and Latin American presence. Howell explained that the acquisition—which transformed Brightpoint from the third largest to the second largest U.S. cell phone distributor—gave the company more "purchasing

power and financial stability, as well as more infrastructure." It also fit neatly with Brightpoint's new focus on retail sales, which had been Allied's specialty. Of the hundreds of distributors that once crowded the wireless equipment distribution market, only five remained.

The feverish growth continued as the year wore on. Brightpoint secured a beachhead in the new PCS digital cellular technology standard by becoming the sole distributor of PCS phone equipment for BellSouth Mobility DCS in three southern states and won a contract with Omnipoint Communications Inc., the fifth largest PCS operator in the United States, to provide phone packaging, inventory management, and order fulfillment services for Omnipoint's market of 40 million potential PCS customers. Finally, Brightpoint further consolidated its international strategy by acquiring the distributor Hatadicorp Ltd. of Sydney, Australia, to form Brightpoint Australia Ltd. and increasing its ownership of Brightpoint International Ltd. to 100 percent.

INTO THE NEW CENTURY

By 1997 Brightpoint's market value was over $1 billion, more than 30 times what the company was worth when it went public just three years earlier. Brightpoint was the fastest growing distributor of cellular products and was poised to overtake the industry leader Cellstar Corp. within a couple years. In addition, the company was making rapid strides in offering a more robust set of middleman services to its clients, including assembling, programming, and financing cell phones for customers, services that offered better profit margins than straight wholesaling. Big players in the wireless industry, including Iridium, Nextel, and Bell South, began farming out most of their back-office operations to Brightpoint.

Soon, however, the company began to hit some speed bumps. Brightpoint had been acquiring other companies so quickly that it was becoming harder and harder to integrate them efficiently. Furthermore, the company had taken on so much debt that investors began to fear that Brightpoint would be unable to meet its bond obligations, which totaled about $150 million. The company's stock plummeted in value. The situation became so serious that the company resorted to some unfortunate tactics to hide the magnitude of its losses. In 1998 Brightpoint executives worked out a scheme with the insurance giant American International Group Inc. (AIG) that amounted to sending money on a round trip "disguised" as insurance, thereby allowing Brightpoint to exaggerate its earnings. The U.S. Securities and Exchange Commission uncovered the misdeeds, and the company ended up paying a $450,000 civil penalty without admitting any wrongdoing in 2003.

Brightpoint lost $53 million in 2001 and was on pace to lose a similar amount in 2002. Determined to weather the storm, Laikin implored investors to stay the course and hold onto their shares and bonds. However, the company's value on paper continue to shrink, and bonds were trading at half of their original price. It looked as if bankruptcy was a real possibility.

Gradually, Laikin and Brightpoint regained their footing. The company implemented a number of cost-cutting measures and pulled out of several of the countries in which it had been doing business. By 2003 a new, leaner Brightpoint was once again turning a profit, and investors who had kept faith in the company were rewarded for their loyalty. The company was virtually debt-free by 2006, and an individual who had invested $1,000 when Brightpoint went public 12 years earlier would now be holding stock worth $13,000.

Brightpoint's 2007 purchase of Dangaard Telecom of Denmark—the largest cell phone distributor in Europe—made it the world leader in wireless phone distribution and logistics. That same year the American Business Awards honored Laikin as the best turnaround executive for his revival of Brightpoint's fortunes.

As the global economy sagged in 2008 and the first half of 2009, with sales of wireless devices shrinking everywhere, Brightpoint, like so many companies, was forced to cut jobs and seek other ways to contain costs. Laikin remained upbeat, however, convinced that the growing popularity of smart phones, which can perform many of the tasks usually done by personal computers, would soon lead Brightpoint and the rest of the wireless industry into a new era of prosperity.

Paul S. Bodine
Updated, Bob Jacobson

PRINCIPAL SUBSIDIARIES

Brightpoint Australia; Brightpoint Austria; Brightpoint Belgium; Brightpoint Denmark; Brightpoint Dubai; Brightpoint Finland; Brightpoint Hong Kong; Brightpoint India; Brightpoint Latin America; Brightpoint North America; Brightpoint Singapore.

PRINCIPAL COMPETITORS

Brightstar Corp.; Ingram Micro Inc.; Tessco Technologies Inc.

FURTHER READING

"Agreement Signed to Buy Allied Communications Inc.," *Wall Street Journal*, January 24, 1996, p. A6.

Andrews, Greg, "Laikin Makes the Right Calls," *Indianapolis Business Journal*, February 19, 1996, p. 11A.

"Brightpoint, Inc." (stock report), Baltimore, MD: Legg Mason Wood Walker, July 11, 1996.

"Brightpoint, Inc." (stock report), Boston, MA: Cowen and Co., November 16, 1995.

"Brightpoint, Inc." (stock reports), Cleveland, OH: McDonald and Company Securities Inc., July 2, 1996, and November 14, 1996.

"Brightpoint, Inc." (stock report), Dallas, TX: Rauscher Pierce Refnes Inc., March 7, 1996.

"Brightpoint, Inc." (stock report), Indianapolis, IN: NatCity Investments Inc., March 29, 1996.

"Brightpoint, Inc." (stock report), Milwaukee, MN: Cleary Gull Reiland & McDevitt Inc., November 18, 1996.

Dinnen, S. P., "Analysts Expect a Lot from Brightpoint," *Indianapolis Star/News*, October 28, 1996.

Galarza, Pablo, "Brightpoint: Cell Phone Peddler," *Financial World*, January 30, 1996, pp. 22–23.

"Great Lakes Review: Brightpoint, Inc." (stock report), San Francisco, CA: Hancock Institutional Equity Services, January 4, 1996.

Heiken, Norman, "Dietrich, Laikin Bring Home Big Recognition," *Indianapolis Business Journal*, January 1, 1995, p. 10A.

Kaelble, Steve, "Brightpoint: It's Not a Household Name but the Global Distributor Touches One of Every Five Wireless Devices in U.S. and 42 Million Worldwide," *Indiana Business Magazine*, March 1, 2006, p. 6.

"LJR Great Lakes Review: Brightpoint, Inc." (stock report), Cleveland, OH: Lynch, Jones and Ryan, November 4, 1996.

Maurer, Mickey, "A Story We All Should Heed," *Indianapolis Business Journal*, February 11, 2008, p. 10.

O'Malley, Chris, "Ringing Up Fewer Sales," *Indianapolis Business Journal*, March 2, 2009, p. 3.

"Omnipoint Communications Inc. Selects Brightpoint, Inc. for PCS Equipment Distribution," *PR Newswire*, September 17, 1996.

Perrone, Ellen, "Cell Firm Makes Overseas Push," *Indianapolis Business Journal*, December 25, 1995, p. 8A.

"Research Reports: Brightpoint, Inc.," *Barron's*, January 29, 1996, p. 53.

"Research Reports: Brightpoint, Inc.," *Barron's*, February 19, 1996, p. 50.

Schneider, A. J., "Brightpoint Offering Fueled by Fast Growth," *Indianapolis Business Journal*, January 1, 1995, p. 13A.

———, "Wholesale Reaches 'Bright Point' in History," *Indianapolis Business Journal*, September 11, 1995, p. 4.

Schnitzler, Peter, "Brightpoint Boss Psyched about Smart Phones," *Indianapolis Business Journal*, September 22, 2008, p. 8A.

———, "Deals Give Brightpoint World Lead in Wireless Logistics," *Indianapolis Business Journal*, August 13, 2007, p. 5.

————, "Ringing Up Big Returns," *Indianapolis Business Journal*, December 19, 2005, p. 3.

Silberg, Lurie, "A Wider Reach in Cellular," *HFN*, April 29, 1996, pp. 71, 75.

Taub, Stephen, "For AIG, What Goes Around Comes Around," CFO, September 12, 2003, http://www.cfo.com/article.cfm/3010399.

Upbin, Bruce, "Bright Vision," *Forbes*, January 11, 1999, p. 198.

"Wireless: Brightpoint, Inc. Announces India Wireless Product Venture," *Cambridge Telecom Report*, 1995.

"Wireless Telecommunications Distribution and Value-Added Services Industry" (stock report), New York, NY: Sands Brothers and Co. Ltd., September 19, 1996.

Brocade Communications Systems Inc.

1745 Technology Drive
San Jose, California 95110-1310
U.S.A.
Telephone: (408) 333-8000
Fax: (408) 333-8101
Web site: http://www.brocade.com

Public Company
Founded: 1995
Incorporated: 1995; reincorporated, 1999
Employees: 2,834
Sales: $1.47 billion (2008)
Stock Exchanges: NASDAQ
Ticker Symbol: BRCD
NAICS: 334119 Other Computer Peripheral Equipment
Manufacturing

∎ ∎ ∎

Brocade Communications Systems Inc., based in San Jose, California, helps companies manage and preserve their business information by providing mechanisms for data storage, data backup, and disaster recovery. Offering storage networking products, software, and services, Brocade is also the world's largest maker of switches used in computer data-storage systems. The company markets and sells its products through distribution partners, equipment manufacturers, other distributors, and directly to end-user customers.

Brocade offers its file and data management solutions in the form of integrated suites of applications that manage and distribute files and data across a variety of environments for its customers. In doing so, Brocade also provides professional and support services to help clients with their projects while also assisting them in the design, implementation, management, and operation of their data centers. As part of a broader offering, Brocade, in addition to its products, offers support services directly to end-user customers or through its partner organizations.

EARLY YEARS

"Fibre channel" is a technology used for speeding data between computers. Brocade was founded in 1995 as one of a handful of U.S. companies developing and manufacturing fibre channel switches that allowed users of storage area networks, sometimes known as SANs, to link computer and video feeds and, within a matter of seconds, direct the feeds to work stations in a variety of locations. Companies faced with the task of storing, managing, administering, and providing access to ever-increasing amounts of data found that implementing SANs helped them manage data growth while reducing the costs associated with data storage and retrieval. Brocade's switches connected servers with storage devices through these storage area networks.

In January 1997 Brocade began selling its fibre channel switches and products to computer manufacturers and related companies. In March of that year Brocade unveiled its SilkWorm line of SAN-related products by introducing the SilkWorm fibre channel switch. By the end of 1997 Brocade had raised $21 million in private financing to pay for increased research and development efforts and company expansion. The

COMPANY PERSPECTIVES

Brocade is an industry leader in data center networking solutions and services that enable organizations to manage their most vital information assets. It's no wonder that Global 500 companies rely on Brocade technology to keep their businesses running around the clock. Brocade has pioneered the technologies that enable highly reliable and secure data center connectivity. Today most of the world's data flows through Brocade equipment and data center networks built on Brocade technology.

money, provided by northern California venture capital firms, reflected the expectation that the market for fibre channel switches would increase exponentially.

In May 1999 Brocade made an initial public offering (IPO) of 3.3 million shares of its stock. A month later the company introduced improvements to its Silk-Worm line of fibre channel switches and signed a contract with International Business Machines Corp. (IBM) to include the new products as part of IBM's storage area network solutions. According to Peter Tarrant, Brocade's vice president of marketing and business development, the new switches were easier to install and service and would lower the total cost of owning a storage solution. Analysts predicted that IBM's inclusion of the fibre channel switches with its mainframe systems would help propel the growth of storage area networks and help drive the industry standard. In further product improvements, Brocade in March 2000 introduced the Remote Switch, a software add-on to its SilkWorm family of products that would enable information technology (IT) departments to expand storage area networks across unlimited distances.

FOREIGN EXPANSION BEGINS

In June 2000 Brocade announced plans to join with Japanese storage system manufacturer Fujitsu Ltd. to develop software for the integrated management of storage area networks. Their development agenda included software for monitoring network devices and packages for remote system management and data backup. Brocade expanded its operations into the Canadian telecommunications market by opening an office in Toronto in October of that year.

Several months later, in May 2001, Brocade launched operations in Japan. James LaLonde, Brocade's

vice president for the Asia and Pacific region, was quoted by *AsiaPulse News* in 2001 as saying that "Brocade products have been sold in Japan for several years.... By opening operations in Japan, Brocade will be able to offer even greater support to our customers and partners and will help the entire region grow its IT infrastructure."

Brocade expanded its operations into the Chinese market by opening an office in Beijing in October 2001. China's increasing demand for storage networks was driven by increasing internet usage and an increasingly competitive environment among data-intensive businesses, such as government agencies, telecommunication companies, financial firms, utility companies, and manufacturers. Brocade's reach into China included establishing a SAN technology laboratory, as well as a scholarship program at Qinghua University. Brocade also offered training programs on the use of SAN technology and related market opportunities to information technology professionals in major Chinese cities. By the fall of 2001, in addition to the new offices in Canada, Japan, and Beijing, Brocade had opened other operations in the Asia and Pacific region, including ones in Singapore, Hong Kong, Seoul, and Sydney. Other foreign offices were located in Switzerland, the United Kingdom, France, and Germany.

While expansion dominated 2001's activities, setbacks occurred that year as well. In August a class action lawsuit was filed by some Brocade shareholders regarding the company's initial public offering of stock in 1999. The complaint alleged that the prospectus issued with the offering was materially false and misleading because it failed to mention alleged agreements the company had made with other potential shareholders regarding obtaining shares in the original IPO and purchasing future shares at predetermined prices.

CEO REYES EXPLAINS PRIORITIES

Brocade's CEO, Gregory L. Reyes, ended 2001 with an *Investor's Business Daily* interview with Brian Deagon discussing the importance his company placed on its customers' return on investment. "Our products are fully backward compatible," he noted, "so you don't have to replace your prior investments." Reyes also noted the increased desire by businesses worldwide, following the terrorist attacks against the United States on September 11, 2001, to move and save data to a remote location site to allow not only data backup and restoration but also business continuance.

Reyes also stressed the reluctance of Brocade to skimp on research and development in the troubled economic times that were to follow September 11. "It

KEY DATES

■

1995: Brocade Communications Systems Inc. is founded.

1997: Brocade introduces SilkWorm brand fibre channel switches.

1999: Brocade makes IPO of 3.3 million shares.

2000: SAN software is added to SilkWorm family of products; international expansion begins.

2001: Class action lawsuit is filed by shareholders who acquired Brocade shares during the company's IPO.

2002: Storage networking company McData files patent infringement lawsuit against Brocade; Internet networking giant Cisco Systems Inc. enters storage-switching market.

2003: Brocade acquires software-maker Rhapsody Networks; storage networking company Vixel files patent infringement lawsuit against Brocade.

2004: Brocade and Vixel parent company Emulex reach litigation standstill agreement.

2005: Brocade CEO Gregory L. Reyes resigns; Brocade announces it will restate income earned in 2001–04; shareholders file class action lawsuit alleging misleading financial statements.

2007: Brocade acquires rival McData Corporation; trial begins for Reyes and former Brocade vice president Stephanie Jensen in stock options-related case; Reyes and Jensen are convicted of charges; Brocade agrees to pay $7 million penalty to settle charges of stock-option backdating fraud.

2008: Reyes and Jensen are sentenced to prison time and fined; Brocade agrees to settle shareholder class action lawsuit originally filed in May 2005.

2009: IBM agrees to rebrand select Brocade products and sell them to mutual corporate customers; Reyes's conviction is overturned and a new trial is ordered.

would be easy, given the current economic environment, to scale back R&D," Reyes told Deagon. "But we're using it as an opportunity to pull ahead. We invested 20% of revenue, or $100 million, into R&D this past year. That's 50% more than our next closest competitor."

In January 2002 Brocade announced a comprehensive SAN education program to support expansion of storage area network technology into the Chinese market. The initiative, titled SAN*Ed, offered in-depth, hands-on educational opportunities as well as scholarships to Chinese information technology professionals through Brocade's new alliance with Jiao Tong University in Shanghai, one of China's leading educational institutions.

The next couple of months focused on legal affairs. In February McData Corporation, a storage networking company, filed a patent infringement lawsuit against Brocade, alleging that the company's use of technology to help prevent data bottlenecks in computer networks was in violation of patents granted to McData in May of 2001. In more favorable news for Brocade, in March 2002 a New York federal court threw out a class action lawsuit filed against Brocade by some of its shareholders regarding its handling of shares during its initial public offering.

By April 2002 expansion and partnerships were again the focus, with Brocade announcing its joint initiative with the Indian Institute of Science to explore research and educational opportunities for the Indian SAN industry. The joint initiative called for Brocade to set up and equip a SAN laboratory to foster the development of Indian SAN expertise. The Institute of Science would conduct seminars for local informational technology professionals. In June Brocade announced it was engaging in several joint initiatives with Nortel Networks. These included accelerating deployment of optical SAN solutions to their mutual customers worldwide, as well as making available three jointly developed SAN applications that would enable companies to inter-network their storage access networks across metropolitan area networks (MAN) and wide area networks (WAN).

CISCO IN THE RUNNING

In August 2002 Cisco Systems Inc. entered the market for storage switching products with the introduction of a new line of switches intended to compete with those manufactured by both Brocade and McData, companies that were at that time dominating the market. Brocade responded to the Cisco challenge by increasing its efforts in the high-end market while slashing prices of low-end products to compete with McData. It also acquired software maker Rhapsody Networks in order to increase the number of features available on its switches. Following Cisco's entry into the market, Brocade initially lost some market share. In the end, however, price reductions of low-end products fueled more demand for storage switches because small and mid-size businesses found it more affordable to install storage area networks.

Brocade joined with the Indian state-owned company National Informatics Centre in July 2003 to establish a company-owned Centre of Excellence. The organization received regular technology updates for dissemination to Indian companies, as well as assistance from Brocade engineers in deployment and transfer of SAN technology. Brocade provided assistance in architectural designs and analyzed returns-on-investment for its major SAN deployments in India.

Information management and technology company EMC began collaborating with Brocade in July 2004 to bring to market a pre-configured, entry-level networked storage solution capable of meeting the increasing data management requirements of small and medium-sized businesses.

Legal issues still followed Brocade. Storage networking company Vixel, which would later become a subsidiary of Emulex, had filed a patent infringement lawsuit against Brocade in June 2003. The suit alleged patent infringement through the unauthorized manufacture, use, and sale of various SAN switching products, including features of Brocade's SilkWorm fabric switch. Emulex and Brocade reached a three-year "litigation standstill agreement" in October 2004. Both dismissed without prejudice the claims and counterclaims of the patent infringement lawsuit originated by Vixel in 2003. In November of that year Emulex and Brocade expanded their multi-year strategic partnership to simplify deployment of SAN capability to small and medium-sized businesses.

STOCK OPTIONS CONTROVERSY

Brocade Chairman and CEO Reyes stepped down from his post on January 31, 2005, the same day that Brocade announced it would restate its earnings for 2001 through 2004. The company board named Brocade's vice president of worldwide sales, Michael Klayko, as Reyes' replacement. Reyes remained on Brocade's board of directors and would serve as a company adviser.

The earnings restatements resulted from an investigation into the company's process for granting stock options and possibly backdating some of them. Employees and executives of a company frequently receive stock options as a form of noncash compensation. Stock options allow those possessing them to buy shares in the company at a later date, usually at the price for which the shares were trading on the day the options were granted. Stock options are a commonly used employee recruiting and retention tool. If

unused, they eventually expire. Backdating a stock option involves reporting the grant date (or "strike" date) to be prior to the date the option was actually granted. This is usually done to ensure as high a stock value as possible. Leading companies in competitive fields, such as information technology, may experience trouble recruiting and retaining the best talent available. Potentially valuable stock options may help a job candidate decide between competing companies.

Backdating stock options is not itself illegal, as long as the grants are disclosed to shareholders. Neglecting to disclose and record the stock option date accurately, however, can hide actual compensation expenses from shareholders and regulators. The practice can allow companies to misrepresent their financial health by allowing them to appear more profitable than they actually are. Concern over increased backdating of stock options led the Securities and Exchange Commission (SEC) and the U.S. Department of Justice to investigate approximately 200 companies, including Brocade, for the practice.

In restating its earnings, Brocade admitted to incorrectly accounting for some stock options. In the restatements, the company's losses for fiscal year 2003 increased from $136 to $147 million and for fiscal year 2004 from $2 million to $32 million. For fiscal year 2002, however, profits increased from $60 million to $126 million. Brocade stated that none of the adjustments affected historical revenues, cash positions, or non-stock option-related operating expenses. The company emphasized that its core business remained strong.

On May 16, 2005, Brocade revealed that because of its improper accounting of stock option expenses it had become the target of a government probe. The company announced it was cooperating fully with a joint investigation by the Department of Justice and the SEC. Also in May, a class action lawsuit was filed by shareholders who had bought, converted, exchanged, or otherwise acquired stock in Brocade between February 21, 2001, and May 15, 2005. It named the company, along with certain key officers and directors, as defendants. The shareholders charged that between these dates the company had released materially false and misleading financial statements to the investing public.

FURTHER EXPANSION

In early 2006, as a response to declining revenue and resignations of key personnel, Brocade began diversifying its business model from an all-hardware product line and support vendor to a model that would encompass a greater mix of switches, software, and services. Brocade planned to develop the new products through internal research and existing partnerships and said the bulk of the products would support its Tapestry brand switch platform. By March Brocade acquired NuView Inc., a six-year-old Houston-based provider of network-attached storage management for a purchase price of $60 million. NuView software products were to be offered as part of the Tapestry suite of software.

The following year brought more—and larger—acquisitions. In January 2007 Brocade acquired Colorado-based rival McData Corporation for a purchase price of $973 million. Analysts expected the merger to create a company better suited to challenging the entrance of corporate giant Cisco Systems into the market for data-storage switches. That month, Brocade also acquired Silverback Systems, Inc., a privately held network acceleration technologies provider. Silverback products improved the speed and performance of storage traffic in networked storage environments.

Also in early 2007 Brocade announced the availability of a software-only version of its Tapestry Wide Area File Services (WAFS) solution. The product provided high speed access to files across wide area networks, such as those found in organizations with branch offices and other widely distributed locations. Brocade continued its upswing when in February TechTarget awarded its annual Storage Product of the Year award to Brocade's SAN platform, the 48000 Director. "This is an important validation of years of feedback from our customers and partners," Bryan Young, Brocade's director of enterprise business, was quoted as saying in *eWeek*. "The Brocade 48000 allows business owners to deploy a single, highly available platform in the most complex, mission-critical open systems and mainframe environments."

Brocade joined Cadence Design Systems to underwrite the 20th annual Tech Challenge for Bay Area youth in March. The 2007 competition, administered by San Jose's Tech Museum of Innovation, assigned teams to design, build, and operate an unmanned vehicle for use on the surface of Mars. Brocade CEO Klayko said the program "augments classroom instruction with a real world experience that we believe helps inspire the innovators of tomorrow," as quoted by *Wireless News*.

In May 2007 Brocade joined the Microsoft Interop Vendor Alliance, a community of software and hardware vendors working together to enhance interoperability of their products with Microsoft systems. Brocade joined the alliance to help ensure that its products and technologies could perform optimally in its customers' multi-vendor environments.

STOCK-OPTION BACKDATING TRIALS

By the summer of 2007 Brocade had to shift its attention back to legal woes. On June 4 the company agreed to pay a $7 million penalty to settle charges of stock-option backdating fraud brought in the SEC civil action. On June 19 Reyes went on trial in San Francisco federal court on charges of securities fraud and conspiracy. Observers considered the case to be a test of how much federal prosecutors could punish companies that backdated employee and executive stock options and as a consequence allegedly misrepresented the company's profitability.

The trial of Brocade CEO Reyes was the first courtroom test of the federal government's ability to associate securities fraud with the practice of option backdating. Prosecutors contended that Reyes, together with former Brocade vice president for human resources, Stephanie Jensen, had altered the minutes of board meetings, job offer letters, and other documents to make it appear that employees were granted stock options at earlier dates than they actually were—dates when the price of Brocade shares was lower.

The SEC also filed a civil case against the two Brocade executives, in which they also named former Brocade CFO Antonio Canova. (Canova was not named in the criminal case.) In addition, the SEC filed a separate civil case against former Brocade CFO Michael J. Byrd, who had served the company from 1999 to 2001. At a San Francisco press conference on the day charges were announced, SEC Chairman Christopher Cox declared the practice of backdating options to be "poisonous," and declared that the SEC was determined to bring it to an end nationwide.

In August 2007 a federal jury convicted Reyes of 10 counts of securities fraud. In January 2008 he was sentenced to 21 months in prison and fined $15 million. In handing down his sentence, the federal judge remarked on the potential of backdating schemes to harm public trust in the accounting of public companies. Four months later, in December 2007, a federal jury in San Francisco convicted Jensen on charges of conspiracy and falsifying records. She was sentenced the following March to four months in prison and fined $1.25 million. In June 2008 Brocade agreed to settle a stock options-related class action lawsuit originally filed by shareholders in May 2005. Some relief on the matter came to Brocade in August 2009, when the conviction of Reyes was overturned by a federal court of appeals on the grounds of misconduct by prosecutors, and a new trial was ordered. Jensen's conviction, however, was upheld, although resentencing was ordered.

In spite of the court trouble, Brocade continued its corporate growth. During the last six months of 2008 the company completed the acquisition of its former competitor Foundry Networks Inc. The acquisition, for a cost of $16.50 per Foundry share, or approximately $2.6 billion, expanded the Brocade product line, customer reach, and sales channels. The deal combined Foundry's specialty in enterprise Ethernet LANs with Brocade's manufacturing of fibre channel storage network switches.

THE FUTURE

In May 2008 Brocade purchased three parcels of land in San Jose on which it planned to build a new corporate headquarters building. The new structure was expected to house up to 2,200 employees. In efforts to bolster further growth, in April 2009 Brocade strengthened its IBM partnership. IBM agreed to rebrand Ethernet switching and routing products manufactured by Brocade as IBM products and sell them to mutual corporate customers. The agreement included switches and routers made by Foundry Networks, the Brocade subsidiary acquired in late 2008. IBM already sold some Brocade equipment and accounted for at least 10 percent of Brocade's sales.

Network management vendors such as Brocade can expect growth in data processing by businesses and organizations worldwide to continue increasing demand for servers, storage arrays, and the infrastructure needed to support these devices. Network management products, such as the ones manufactured by Brocade, enable businesses and other enterprises to extract more value from their networks by increasing productivity and protecting data.

Joyce Helena Brusin

PRINCIPAL SUBSIDIARIES

Foundry Networks Inc.; Strategic Business Systems Inc.; McData Corporation; Silverback Systems Inc.; NuView Inc.

PRINCIPAL COMPETITORS

EMC Corporation; NetApp Inc.; Qualstar Corporation; Overland Storage Inc.; Dot Hill Systems Corporation; Data Domain Inc.; Quantum Corporation; Cisco Systems Inc.; QLogic Corporation; Emulex.

FURTHER READING

Barlas, Pete, "Brocade Raises $21M for Expansion, R&D." *Business Journal*, December 15, 1997, p. 6.

"Brocade Accounting Probed," *eWeek*, May 16, 2005.

"Brocade Accused of Sparking Price War," *MicroScope*, November 15, 2004, p. 1.

"Brocade Aims to Broaden Business Model," *RETHINK IT*, March 2006, p. 11.

"Brocade and Cadence Sign On as Key Sponsors of the Tech Museum of Innovation's Tech Challenge," *Wireless News*, March 17, 2007.

"Brocade Buys NuView for $60M," *Computerworld*, March 13, 2006, p. 12.

"Brocade Buys NuView, Rolls Out New Offerings," *eWeek*, March 6, 2006.

"Brocade Class Action Suit Dismissed," *Client Server News*, March 11, 2002.

"Brocade Communications Sets Up Joint Indian R&D venture," *AsiaPulse News*, April 5, 2002, p. 665.

"Brocade Communications Systems and Nortel Networks Announced Several Joint Initiatives," *InfoStor*, June 2002, p. 6.

"Brocade Communications Systems, Inc.," *Japan-U.S. Business Report*, June 2000, p. 18.

"Brocade Communications Systems, Inc. (NMS: BRCD)," Mergent Online, http://www.mergentonline.com.

"Brocade Communications Systems Opens Office in Beijing," *AsiaPulse News*, October 12, 2001, p. 803.

"Brocade Continues Expansion in China," *AsiaPulse News*, January 30, 2002, p. 409.

"Brocade, India's NIC Join Hands to Set Up Centre of Excellence," *AsiaPulse News*, July 14, 2003, p. 1616.

"Brocade Is Collaborating with EMC to Bring to Market a Pre-configured, Entry-level, Networked Storage Solution," *InfoStor*, July 2004, p. 6.

"Brocade, Jaycor Networks Dive into Fibre Channel," *PC Week*, March 24, 1997, p. 104.

"Brocade Opens Operations in Japan," *AsiaPulse News*, May 23, 2001, p. 72.

"Brocade's Secure Storage Platform Gets a Gold," *eWeek*, February 9, 2007.

"Brocade Settles Suit over Timing of Options," *New York Times*, June 3, 2008, p. C7.

"Brocade Signs on to Microsoft Interop Vendor Alliance," *Wireless News*, May 21, 2007.

"Brocade Spreads Out the SAN," *PC Week*, March 27, 2000, p. 73.

"Brocade to Buy Network Firm," *New York Times*, July 22, 2008, p. C2.

"Brocade to Pay $7M SEC Penalty," *Computerworld*, June 4, 2007, p. 6.

"Brocade to Use Incentives as Competition Toughens," *MicroScope*, December 6, 2004, p. 20.

Burrows, Peter, and Lorraine Woellert, "A Smaller Options Scandal? The Campaign to Lock Up Accused Backdaters Is Moving Slowly. Here's How a Key Case Is Playing Out," *BusinessWeek*, March 5, 2007, p. 28.

"Collared; Corporate Crime in America," *Economist*, August 11, 2007, p. 54.

"Conviction in Backdating Case," *New York Times*, December 6, 2007, p. C6.

Darlin, Damon, and Eric Dash, "2 Are Charged in Criminal Case on Stock Options," *New York Times*, July 21, 2006, p. A1.

"Data Storage Provider Says S.E.C. Raises Level of Inquiry," *New York Times*, June 11, 2005, p. C2.

Deagon, Brian, "Brocade Strives to Stay Ahead of the Curve in Storage Trends," *Investor's Business Daily*, December 20, 2001, p. A8.

de la Merced, Michael J., "Ex-Brocade Chief's Backdating Conviction Overturned," DealBook, *New York Times*, August 18, 2009, http://dealbook.blogs.nytimes.com/2009/08/18/brocade-chiefs-backdating-conviction-is-overturned/.

"Emulex, Brocade Smoke Peace Pipe," *Client Server News*, October 4, 2004.

"Equity Offerings Scheduled for Week," *New York Times*, May 24, 1999.

"Ex-Finance Chief Accused of Options Fraud," *New York Times*, August 18, 2007, p. C8.

Fillion, Roger, "Brocade, McData Deal Nears Close, Shareholders Expected to OK Purchase Today," *Rocky Mountain News*, January 25, 2007, p. 6.

"First Backdating Conviction Brings Prison Term and $15 million Fine," *New York Times*, January 17, 2008, p. C2.

"Former Brocade Official Sentenced in Backdating Case," *New York Times*, March 20, 2008, p. C11.

Garvey, Martin J., "Brocade's New Switches—Silkworm Line Offers Improved Detection Capabilities and Compatibility," *Information Week*, June 28, 1999, p. 89.

"The Great Green Collision," *Software World*, September 2008, p. 20.

"IBM, Brocade Boost Ties as Cisco Rivalry Heats Up," *PC Magazine Online*, April 28, 2009.

Kalinoski, Gail, "Brocade Buys San Jose Land for New HQ in $223M deal," *Commercial Property News*, May 29, 2008.

Krane, Jim, "Brocade Buys Silverback Systems," *America's Intelligence Wire*, January 9, 2007.

Lawson, Stephen, "Brocade Takes Aim at Cisco with $3B Foundry Deal," *Computerworld*, July 28, 2008, p. 6.

Lee, Henry K., "More Legal Woes Beset Brocade," *San Francisco Chronicle*, August 18, 2007, p. C1.

Lozano, Juan A., "Brocade, Foundry Agree to Revised Buyout Terms," *America's Intelligence Wire*, November 8, 2008.

"McData Receives Decision on Motion for Preliminary Injunction," *AsiaPulse News*, December 10, 2002, p. 4313.

Mearian, Lucas, "Struggling Brocade Plans Extreme Makeover," *Computerworld*, February 6, 2006, p. 8.

"Network Management Vendors Managing Well," *Investor's Business Daily*, July 17, 2009, p. A4.

Norris, Floyd, "Options Brought Riches and Now Big Trouble," *New York Times*, July 25, 2006, p. C1.

"Nortel, Brocade Get Optical Together," *Net Economy*, May 14, 2002.

Rao, Raga, "Brocade CEO Quits; Income Restated for Several Years," *Client Server News*, January 31, 2005, p. 11.

"Schiffrin & Barroway, LLP Announces Class Periods for Shareholder Lawsuits against Several Companies who Recently Issued IPOs—BRCD, IISX, LQID, OMNY," *PrimeZone Media Network*, August 16, 2001.

Simpson, Dave, "Brocade to Acquire Rhapsody," *InfoStor*, December 2002, p. 8.

"Software Improves Enterprise-wide File Data Access," *Product News Network*, January 23, 2007.

"Solution Providers See Potential in Storage Area Networks," *New Straits Times*, December 13, 2001.

Southworth, Natalie, "Silicon Valley Whiz Kid Ventures North," *Globe & Mail*, October 4, 2000, p. B5.

Stone, Amey, "Storage Network Rivals Crank It Up," *BusinessWeek*, October 30, 2003.

"Technology Briefing Hardware: Brocade Loss Caused by Job-cut Costs," *New York Times*, February 13, 2003, p. C6.

"Technology Briefing Hardware: Request for Injunction against Brocade Is Denied," *New York Times*, December 10, 2002, p. C12.

"Trial Starts for Former Chief in Options-Backdating Case," *New York Times*, June 19, 2007, p. C2.

"Vixel Sues Brocade," *Client Server News*, June 2, 2003.

Bulgari S.p.A.

Lungotevere Marzio, 11
Roma, 00187
Italy
Telephone: (+39 06) 688-101
Fax: (+33 06) 688-10401
Web site: www.bulgari.com

Public Company
Founded: 1884
Employees: 3,675
Sales: $1.52 billion (2008)
Stock Exchanges: Milan
Ticker Symbol: BULG
NAICS: 334518 Watch, Clock, and Part Manufacturing; 339911 Jewelry (including Precious Metal) Manufacturing; 423940 Jewelry, Watch, Precious Stone, and Precious Metal Merchant Wholesalers; 448310 Jewelry Stores, Precious

■ ■ ■

Bulgari S.p.A. is one of the world's leading manufacturers and marketers of luxury goods. From its traditional emphasis on the highest-quality jewelry and watches, the company has expanded into perfumes, silk scarves, and eyewear. Bulgari sells its fine wares via 259 company-owned stores as well as thousands of perfumeries, department stores, and duty free outlets. Although the company went public in 1995, brothers Paolo and Nicola Bulgari, grandsons of the founder, continued to share a controlling share of its equity along with their

nephew, Francesco Trapani, who has served as chief executive officer since 1987.

COMPANY ORIGINS STRETCH BACK TO 19TH-CENTURY GREECE

Company founder Sotirio Boulgaris was born in 1857, the lone heir to an apparently long line of itinerant Greek silversmiths. Fleeing the violence and banditry endemic to mainland Greece at the time, Sotirio and his parents moved to Corfu, where they established a shop in the late 1870s. The young metalworker soon sought to find his own way in the world and in 1880 settled in Rome, Italy. After operating a short-lived partnership, Sotirio founded a variety store featuring silver belts, buckles, bracelets, and buttons as well as tableware and antiques in 1884. By the turn of the century the enterprising businessman would have established outlets in St. Moritz, San Remo, Naples, Bellagio, and Sorrento. He romanized the family name to Bulgari, and in 1880 bestowed that name on his bride, Eleni. The couple had two sons, Costantino and Giorgio, in 1889 and 1890, respectively.

Around the turn of the century Sotirio sold his budding chain of shops in order to concentrate on a single jewelry and silver business. In 1905 he purchased a shop at no. 10 Via Condotti in Rome, a location that would remain the Bulgari headquarters for the duration of the 20th century and into the 21st century. The new outlet offered a more upscale selection of goods ranging from embossed and engraved silver serving pieces to decorative ceramics as well as gold and silver jewelry,

COMPANY PERSPECTIVES

■

For over a century, Bulgari has been setting the pace for Italian style in jewellery. A forward-looking, creative spirit which never ceases to draw inspiration from the timeless beauty of Greek and Roman art, while giving it a distinctive contemporary touch. Greek like its founder, Sotirio Bulgari—and Roman like the culture he embraced.

The finest expression for style and beauty.

often set with gemstones. Over the course of the first two decades of the 20th century, Bulgari gradually took on a more cosmopolitan air. Giorgio and Costantino had their first involvement in the family business during this period. By the time the Bulgaris resumed business after the interruptions of World War I, the company had completed its shift from an emphasis on silver to pricier bejeweled pieces.

THE SECOND GENERATION TAKES THE HELM IN 1930S

After Sotirio died in 1932, his sons undertook an extravagant remodeling of both the interior and the exterior of the Via Condotti store and formally changed the company logo to BVLGARI, an application of the traditional Roman alphabet. The ITL2 million project took two years and featured the pink and beige Italian marble that would become the worldwide hallmark of the firm's retail outlets. Giorgio's global gem-sourcing travels exposed him to the latest fashions in the then-Paris-based jewelry industry, while Costantino's penchant for collecting ancient silver wares would later be a source of inspiration for the company's adaptation of classical themes.

Having latched on to style trends emanating from Paris, Bulgari continued to follow the lead of what was then the world's jewelry capital throughout the first half of the century. In the 1920s Bulgari embraced Art Deco themes. In the 1930s the company concentrated on diamonds set in platinum. Wartime restrictions and a general climate of austerity were reflected in a dearth of jewelry designs of the 1940s. When the company did produce a piece, it often featured yellow gold and few or no precious jewels. Though highly regarded for their craftsmanship, the Bulgari brothers continued to follow, rather than set, trends after World War II. In the prosperous years of the immediate postwar era, the

jewelry house produced lavish settings of diamonds, emeralds, sapphires, and rubies in platinum. Floral motifs, many featuring *en tremblant* settings that moved with the wearer, were especially popular during this period.

The store's marble-decked facade would be the backdrop of many paparazzi photos in the postwar era, as celebrities from around the world were drawn to the Bulgari shop. The expanding clientele—which prior to the 1960s included Italian nobility; South American political figure Evita Perón; American businessmen like Nelson Rockefeller and Woolworth's founder Samuel Henry Kress; and U.S. Ambassador to Italy Clare Boothe Luce—reflected Bulgari's growing stature among the world's high-class jewelry houses.

BVLGARI STYLE EMERGES IN 1960S

In the 1960s Italian jewelers in general and the Bulgari brothers in particular began to break away from France's fashion dictates to establish their own recognizable styles. The Bulgari mode of design that emerged over the ensuing decade departed from the French in several respects. In place of large, faceted diamond centerpieces, Bulgari began to substitute colored gemstones in a smooth, domed cut known in the industry as "cabochon." Diamonds—often brilliant cut and/or pavé set—became the supporting actors in these color plays. When choosing its stones, the jewelry house shunned the traditional emerald-ruby-sapphire trio and instead began to choose gem-stones based more on their artistic contribution to the piece than their financial contribution. Smooth outlines and highly stylized forms in yellow gold would complete the Bulgari look. In their 1990 essay on the firm for *The Master Jewelers*, Charles M. Newton and Omar Torres aptly noted that "the symmetry and proportions of Bulgari products are based more upon art and architecture than on nature—a factor which distinguishes the Bulgari jewel from that of the French masters."

The family's third generation, represented by Giorgio's three sons Paolo, Gianni, and Nicola, took the helm in 1967. Eldest son Gianni earned a law degree and favored a playboy lifestyle, complete with a stint as a race car driver, but was soon drawn into the family business and served as chief executive into the early 1980s. Paolo, the artist of the trio, has been called "one of the world's foremost jewelers." *The Master Jewelers* noted that "one of his greatest talents is his ability to translate his understanding of his family's traditions into recognizably Bulgari jewels while continually moving forward with new and exciting forms and ideas." Though Nicola, the youngest, has been characterized as

KEY DATES

∎

1884: Greek jeweler Sotirio Boulgaris opens first shop in via Sistina, Rome, manufacturing and retailing silver; romanizes family name to Bulgari.

1905: With help of his sons, Costantino and Giorgio, Sotirio moves the shop to via Condotti.

1910: Bulgari names the store The Old Curiosity Shop after Charles Dickens's novel in order to attract English and American tourists.

1932: Sotirio Bulgari dies; his sons change the company name to Bulgari; company produces jewelry based on popular Parisian designs.

1950: Bulgari begins to create a look based on Greek and Roman classicism; over the next two decades all stores are redesigned with the pink and beige marble that came to represent the brand's retail image; Bulgari experiences tremendous growth.

1967: Giorgio's three sons, Paolo, Gianni, and Nicola, take over the business.

1970: Bulgari begins to expand into the international arena by opening stores in New York, Paris, Geneva, and Monte Carlo.

1985: Company's growth stalls, perhaps as a result of disagreements between the three brothers; Gianni resigns post as CEO.

1987: Paolo and Nicola become chairman and vice-chairman, respectively, and appoint their nephew, Francesco Trapani, as CEO.

1990: Trapani throughout the decade opens two dozen new retail outlets, including in the Middle East, Australia, Asia, and countries of the former Soviet Union.

1995: Bulgari S.p.A. is listed on the Milan and London stock exchanges.

2001: Company creates Bulgari Hotels & Resorts, a joint venture with Mariott International.

2008: Bulgari posts a loss of EUR 29.3 ($38.3) million caused by the worldwide drop in demand for luxury goods.

2009: As part of its 125th anniversary Bulgari partners with Save the Children to raise money for education in developing countries.

the businessman of the family, he was also responsible for an important design contribution. An avid collector of ancient coins, in the late 1960s he revived their use in jewelry, dubbing them *gemme nummarie*, or "coin gems." Bulgari's most popular treatment featured coins set in heavy, open-linked, yellow gold chains, but the firm also produced rings, earrings, bracelets, and even tableware and gift items on this theme. The juxtaposition of patinated coins and highly polished precious metals would become a Bulgari hallmark.

INTERNATIONAL EXPANSION IN 1970S

The brothers established their first international outlet in 1970 in New York's Pierre Hotel on Fifth Avenue. By the end of the decade they had launched locations in Geneva, Monte Carlo, and even Paris. Bulgari's jewelry designs of this decade were strongly influenced by the exhibitions of the treasures of Tutankhamen's ancient Egyptian treasures. Indian motifs, particularly the "boten" (leaf), were also prevalent in the 1970s. The company's purchase of a collection of carved Indian jewels, which were remounted to create new treasures, was a key to this in-house trend.

Though the company had made and sold pocket, lapel, and wrist watches throughout its history, Bulgari did not introduce a major collection of timepieces until the late 1970s. The simple lines of the BVLGARI-BVLGARI wristwatch, which featured a black face encircled by a gold band, would become the company's most-recognized and highest-selling watch. Another important design was Bulgari's snake watch, which evolved from the jewel-encrusted, Art Deco snake of the 1920s (its hinged head concealed a watch face) into a highly stylized coil bracelet set with an exposed face.

The 1970s were a period of great success for the company, a time when Bulgari enhanced its ranking among the world's greatest jewelers through innovative designs. The firm's patronage grew accordingly, expanding to include celebrities like Sophia Loren, Audrey Hepburn, Kirk Douglas, and perhaps the house's best-known client, Elizabeth Taylor. Royalty from around the world shopped at the company's showcases. Perhaps most tellingly, lesser jewelers began to copy Bulgari designs. At the end of the decade, outside observers pegged the company's annual sales at $50 million.

BULGARI IN THE 1980S

Bulgari's growth came to a halt in the early 1980s. According to published estimates, annual revenues remained at the $50 million level through 1985, and the company did not open a single new retail outlet during the first half of the decade. Some sources blamed squabbling among the three brothers, and indeed, eldest Gianni resigned the chief executive office in 1985. Two years later Nicola and Paolo bought out their brother's one-third stake and prohibited him from using the Bulgari trademark. (Giorgio went on to chair global footwear giant Fila S.p.A.) In the meantime, they had asked a nephew, Francesco Trapani, to revitalize the business. The new CEO, who had first joined the company in 1981, guided an aggressive strategy for growth, opening new retail outlets in Milan (1986), Tokyo (1987), Hong Kong, Osaka, Singapore, and London (all 1988). Before the decade was out, the company had also launched new stores, in Munich and New York. Returning to Sotirio's old summer haunt, St. Moritz, Bulgari opened a store there in 1990. Trapani also hired new designers, boosted advertising, and reacquired some franchised stores during this period of rapid growth.

Though the company remained firmly ensconced in the high end of the jewelry market, designs from the 1980s on were noteworthy for their increased "wearability" and the development of design themes. Before he departed the company, Gianni Bulgari reflected on this strategic shift, asserting that Bulgari was attempting to change its image from a company for only the very wealthy to one offering quality products to those of discerning taste. This concept formed a strategy that allowed Bulgari to expand its potential audience while maintaining the highest quality of design and execution.

The jewelry house introduced the first of several collections based on modular designs in 1982. "Parentesi" (parenthesis) featured several bracket-shaped elements arranged in a pattern. The individual elements could be combined in a seemingly infinite variety of ways to form rings, bracelets, watches, necklaces, and earrings. Bulgari made more or less expensive pieces of jewelry based on this design by executing the parts in more or less valuable materials ranging from polished steel and coral at the low end to fine gemstones and gold or platinum at the upper end. The point, however, was not necessarily to manufacture less expensive pieces—price tags averaged $3,000 and ranged up to $1 million in the mid-1990s—but to make fine jewelry that could be worn from day into night.

Trapani reflected on the strategy in a 1996 article for fashion magazine *WWD*, commenting, "We are becoming a jeweler that sells products for everyday use, not just special occasions. This is what has been driving our growth." Periodic launches may also have introduced an element of planned obsolescence, as evinced by the parade of thematic collections that followed. In the 1980s these included "Doppio Cuore"

(double heart, 1983), "Boules" (beads, 1986), "Gancio" (hook, 1987), and "Alveare" (beehive, 1988). These strategies succeeded in tripling Bulgari's sales in the latter years of the decade, reaching an estimated $150 million by 1989.

DIVERSIFICATION INTO OTHER LUXURY GOODS AND SERVICES IN 1990S

The firm continued to launch collections of modular jewelry in the early 1990s, introducing "Saetta" (thunderbolt) and "Spiga" (ear of wheat) in 1990; "Naturalia," which featured stylized fish and birds, in 1991; "Celtica," based on ancient Celtic motifs, and "Doppio Passo" (classical ballet) in 1993; "Chandra" (Sanskrit for moon) in 1994; and "Trika" (braid) in 1996. These patterns were virtually instant status symbols, highly recognized as Bulgari pieces.

Though Bulgari had long emphasized jewelry and watches, it had from the outset sold other goods, including silver tableware and giftware. In the early 1990s CEO Trapani followed the lead of other major luxury goods companies that had parlayed their well-recognized and highly respected brand names into highly profitable growth vehicles. It was not a foolproof process; Trapani had to take care that he did not devalue the venerable Bulgari cachet while seeking a wider clientele. After two years of research and development, the company launched its first fragrance, Eau Parfumée, a unisex scent based on green tea. BVLGARI pour Femme followed in 1994 and BVLGARI pour Homme in 1995. By the end of 1996 perfume was contributing 14 percent of annual sales and generating an estimated $40 million (IFL63 billion). Bulgari launched silk scarves and neckties in 1996. That same year, the firm licensed its trademark to fellow Italian firm Luxottica for use on a line of sunglasses and optical frames. A collection of Bulgari leather goods, including handbags and other accessories, was slated for 1997.

New store openings increased Bulgari's retail concentration in Europe (including the countries of the former Soviet Union), the United States, and Asia, and broadened its geographic reach to include the Middle East and Australia. From 1990 to 1996 the company added more than two dozen new shops. Trapani confidently forecast that the company would increase its distribution points to 70 company-owned boutiques, 300 independent watch retailers, and 5,000 perfume sales outlets by the end of the 20th century.

Bulgari's sales increased from ITL154.3 billion in 1991 to ITL448.8 billion ($268.9 million) in 1996, while after-tax net grew from ITL6.9 billion to ITL57.7

billion ($34.6 million). The company went public on the Milan exchange in July 1995, selling out a 32.1 percent stake in only two days. Its stock performance reflected the rapid expansion of its bottom line. Shares rose from an offering price of ITL8,600 ($5.32) to ITL36,000 ($21.44) in mid-1997 before a four-for-one stock split that June. CEO Trapani was by this time the unquestioned leader of Bulgari. Beginning in 1996, at just 38 years old, the astute strategist was rewarded for his service to the family company with a significant stake in its equity.

Trapani proved to be an able forecaster. The firm continued to do spectacularly well throughout the late 1990s into the mid 2000s, opening new retail stores in far-flung locations such as Egypt, Kuwait, and Bali. Trapani would be responsible for Bulgari's expansion to 259 stores between 1984 and 2009, and a 150 percent increase in revenue between the years 1997 and 2003.

In 2001 the company began a joint venture with Marriott International called Bulgari Hotels & Resorts. In the partnership Bulgari was in charge of the hotels' design, while elements such as service and marketing were contributed by Marriott's Ritz-Carlton luxury division. This partnership resulted in the opening of two hotels, the first in Milan in 2004 and the second in Bali in 2006. "The real impact of the hotel," said Trapani, speaking of the Bulgari Hotel Spa in Milan, as quoted by Tracie Rozhon in a 2007 *New York Times* article, "is to promote the brand." Unlike rivals such as Armani and Versace, Bulgari did not license its name in opening its hotels. "We did not want to be just an investor," said Trapani. "We own 65 percent, and the Ritz-Carlton owns 35 percent. In this role, we not only control the image and design, we decide what kind of services to offer." In 2007 Bulgari also opened two restaurants in Tokyo, one in a particularly spectacular location on the top four floors of the Bulgari Ginza Tower.

The company, however, has stayed true to its origins, with the production and retail of high-quality silver jewelry and accessories remaining the basis for the business. "Our clients can ask us to make virtually anything for them in silver," Nicola Bulgari told *Architectural Digest* in 2009. "We've made scale models of yachts and even buildings—as well as one very fine roulette wheel! We've worked closely for generations with the same family of silversmiths here, so they are now well used to unusual requests. Nothing pleases them more than to have to design a whole new dinner service in silver or create some unusual centerpiece for an elegantly laid table."

RECESSION AND DECREASED LUXURY SALES

The collapse of Wall Street in 2008, however, lessened demand for silver roulette wheels and elegant dinner services. That year Bulgari's sales and stock ratings went into a freefall. The company saw sales rise only two percent in the third quarter of 2008, reflecting a global drop in demand for luxury items. The company posted a loss of EUR 29.3 ($38.3) million for the first quarter of 2009. "Customers are purchasing less. Trade has been difficult in 2009," Trapani was quoted as saying in the *Guardian* in March 2009.

Bulgari's profits for 2008 dropped 45 percent, a number comparable to the losses suffered by competitors: Sales of high-end jewelry worldwide were so low that by early 2009 diamond group De Beers, which controlled 40 percent of the global diamond trade, had ceased production in Botswana, where most diamonds in the world originate. Bulgari implemented broad cost-cutting measures to weather the economic downturn, such as shuttering low-performing stores, negotiating with landlords on existing leases, eliminating jobs, limiting production, and pressing its suppliers for discounts on raw materials such as gems and precious metals.

According to Andrew Roberts in *WWD*, Trapani stated that "management was working on reducing investments and keeping the inventory at cash neutral levels [in 2009] and cash free in 2010." Trapani continued, "Facing equally challenging situations in the past, Bulgari has always been able to evolve, becoming one of the main players in the worldwide luxury market." Celebrating its 125th anniversary, in 2009 Bulgari partnered with Save the Children to raise money for education in developing countries.

April Dougal Gasbarre
Updated, Melanie Bush

PRINCIPAL SUBSIDIARIES

Bulgari Gioielli S.p.A.; Bulgari Italia S.p.A.; Bulgari Parfums Italia S.p.A.; Bulgari Portugal Acessorios de Luxo Lda; Bulgari Netherlands B.V.; Bulgari International Corporation (BIC) N.V.; Bulgari (Luxembourg) S.A.; Bulgari Milan Hotel Leasing Company S.r.l.; Crova S.p.A.

PRINCIPAL COMPETITORS

Cartier; LVMH; Tiffany & Co.

FURTHER READING

Barry, Colleen, "Bulgari Faces Difficult Turnaround," *America's Intelligence Wire*, May 22, 2009.

Bentley, Logan, "Rome's Gianni Bulgari Hangs the Right Stuff around the World's Richest Necks," *People*, May 8, 1981, p. 104.

Boye, Bryan, "Watch Him Grow: Bulgari CEO Francesco Trapani Has an Eye toward Broadening the Reach of His Family-Run Luxury Business," *Daily News Record*, July 14, 2000.

Conti, Samantha, "Bulgari Slates Major Expansion," *WWD*, September 26, 1995, p. 9.

Forden, Sara Gay, "Bulgari's World-Class Plans," *WWD*, August 16, 1993, pp. 8–9.

"Gianni Bought Out of Bulgari," *WWD*, January 15, 1988, p. 7.

Hessen, Wendy, "Bulgari's West Coast Barrage," *WWD*, October 7, 1996, p. 16.

Mascetti, Daniela, and Amanda Triossi, *Bulgari*, New York: Abbeville Press, 1996.

Newton, Charles M., and Omar Torres, *The Master Jewelers*, New York: H. N. Abrams, 1990.

Newman, Jill, "Bulgari: Going All Out in New York," *WWD*, November 3, 1989, p. 14.

Peppiatt, Michael, "Bulgari at 125," *Architectural Digest*, August 2009.

Roberts, Andrew, "Bulgari Cutting Jobs, Closing Stores," *WWD*, March 12, 2009, p. 3.

———, "Bulgari Posts $38.3M Loss in 1st Quarter," *WWD*, May 13, 2009, p. 14.

Rozhon, Tracie, "From Handbags to Hotels, Bulgari Is Remodeling Itself," *New York Times*, April 7, 2007, p. C1.

Schwartz, Nelson, "Luxury Brands Face Slowing Economies," *New York Times*, December 8, 2008.

Seckler, Valerie, "Bulgari: Luxe Goes Public," *WWD*, February 26, 1996, pp. 20–22.

Torcellini, Carolyn, "Peacemaker," *Forbes*, March 5, 1990, p. 154.

Warhol, Andy, "Nicola Bulgari: Wearable Wealth," *Interview*, November 1980, pp. 62–63.

Weissmann, Arnie, "Marriott, Bulgari Partnership to Open First Hotel," *Travel Weekly*, February 23, 2004, p. 16.

Wray, Richard, "Global Recession Drags on Luxury Jeweller Bulgari," *Guardian* (London), March 12, 2009.

CADENCE
FINANCIAL
CORPORATION

Cadence Financial Corporation

301 East Main Street
Starkville, Mississippi 39759
U.S.A.
Telephone: (662) 343-1341
Toll Free: (800) 636-7622
Fax: (662) 324-4257
Web site: http://www.cadencebanking.com

Public Company
Founded: 1984
Employees: 484
Sales: $139.6 million (2009 est.)
Total Assets: $1.98 billion
Stock Exchanges: NASDAQ
Ticker Symbol: CADE
NAICS: 522110 Commercial Banking 551111 Offices
of Bank Holding Companies

∎ ∎ ∎

Cadence Financial Corporation is a financial holding company serving the southern United States with over 100 years of experience, providing full financial services, including banking, trust services, mortgage services, insurance, and investment products. Cadence Financial Corporation's assets consist mostly of its investment in Cadence Bank N.A., a regional banking corporation that serves the needs of business, agricultural, government, educational, and individual customers at more than 35 locations in Alabama, Florida, Georgia, Mississippi, and Tennessee. The company also has three wholly owned insurance and financial service subsidiar-

ies: Galloway-Chandler-McKinney Insurance Agency, Inc. (GCM), which offers property and casualty insurance, title insurance, life insurance annuities, and other commercial lines; NBC Service Corporation; and NBC Insurance Services of Alabama, Inc.

EARLY DAYS

Cadence Financial Corporation, formerly known as National Bank of Commerce (NBC) Capital Corporation, traces its roots to Starkville, Mississippi, where the People's Bank was founded in 1885. Starkville, in north central Mississippi, is a town of 22,000 residents and home to Mississippi State University, the largest university in the state.

In 1965 Lewis F. Mallory Jr. became head of People's Bank and continued to serve through the first decade of the twenty-first century as chairman and chief executive officer of People's successor, Cadence Financial Corporation. In the late 1960s the People's Bank board and executives, including Mallory, made a strategic decision to expand and create a regional institution that could serve north central Mississippi and the surrounding area.

MERGERS IN THE 1970S AND 1990S

A series of mergers between People's Bank and other Mississippi banks helped create what eventually became the National Bank of Commerce (NBC) and NBC Capital Corporation. In 1972 Maben Home Bank merged with People's Bank. First National Bank of Monroe County, with branches in Aberdeen, Amory,

COMPANY PERSPECTIVES

Cadence Financial Corporation is a customer driven organization with a strong commitment to strategic planning and implementation. Cadence believes in growth through offering a complete range of financial services to its market and by acquiring additional customers. Cadence Financial Corporation is committed to improving its service quality and sales performance.

and Hamilton, merged with People's Bank in March 1974. In October 1974 the National Bank of Commerce, with branches in Columbus, Brooksville, and Artesia, Mississippi, merged with People's Bank, after which People's Bank became known as the National Bank of Commerce (NBC) of Mississippi. NBC became the lead bank in the financial holding company NBC Capital Corporation formed in 1984.

NBC Capital Corporation completed additional significant mergers with other Mississippi and regional banks in the 1990s. Like the earlier mergers, they enabled NBC Capital Corporation to further diversify its sources of income. In 1992 Bank of Philadelphia (Mississippi) merged with NBC Capital Corporation. In 1994 NBC Capital Corporation entered the out-of-state market for the first time when it acquired First State Bank, which had branches in Tuscaloosa and Northport, Alabama. First National Bank, with branches in West Point, Mississippi and Tuscaloosa, Alabama, merged with NBC Capital Corporation in 1998. The following year NBC Capital Corporation acquired First Federal Bank for Savings in Columbus, Mississippi.

The mergers brought new efficiencies to bank operations. In 1997, in the midst of these mergers, NBC Capital Corporation instituted the Teller Management System in its 23 Cadence Bank branches to track transactions by teller and by hour. The program was intended to help the company avoid understaffing and overstaffing by identifying peak times for teller demand and calculating each teller's cost per transaction based on salaries and benefits. The goals of the program were to generate 25 teller transactions per teller hour and cut teller transaction costs in half. "These peak transaction times stay pretty consistent from month to month," according to NBC Senior Vice-President for Operations Jim Leftwich in an interview in *US Banker*. "With this system and the information it gives us, we are able to staff properly at all times."

NBC Capital Corporation's series of mergers also diversified the products it could offer. By 2003 NBC Capital Corporation was able to offer mortgage lending, personal trusts, employee benefit plans, and investment management trusts. The company also offered retail non-deposit investments, which included annuities and various securities and mutual funds. "All of those things…were strategically pursued to enable the company to diversify its sources of income and we've had considerable success in doing this," said Lewis Mallory in an interview with the *Mississippi Business Journal* in 2003. "We wanted it to be a national bank," added Mallory. "When I started with the bank, it was a $6-million dollar bank. I remember we had a goal of getting to $100 million, then $500 million and then $1 billion. Now we're looking to go to the next billion. In 1965, we certainly didn't envision anything like this."

CONTINUED ACQUISITIONS IN THE FIRST DECADE OF THE 21ST CENTURY

In 2002 NBC Capital Corporation CEO Lewis Mallory was elected to serve a three-year term on the Board of Directors of the Federal Reserve Bank of St. Louis. In this position, Mallory joined eight other corporate and banking leaders familiar with economic and credit conditions in the 8th Federal Reserve Bank district, encompassing all of Arkansas and portions of Mississippi, Louisiana, Illinois, Indiana, Kentucky, Tennessee, and Missouri.

In March 2004 NBC Capital Corporation announced it had completed the acquisition of Enterprise Bancshares of Memphis, Tennessee, for $53.1 million, which included $47.1 million in cash and $6 million in options. Enterprise Bancshares kept its name, charter, all 100 employees, and board of directors as part of the acquisition. The privately held company was the parent of Enterprise National Bank. The acquisition gave NBC Capital Corporation its first presence in the Memphis area, from which it could expand into DeSoto County and other parts of western Tennessee. At the time of the acquisition, Memphis-area household incomes, population, and residential property values were increasing significantly faster than those in NBC Capital Corporation's primary market of east central Mississippi and western Alabama.

INITIAL PUBLIC OFFERING AND NAME CHANGE

In May 2006 NBC Capital Corporation offered 2.4 million shares of common stock for sale in an initial public offering (IPO). The money raised would be spent

KEY DATES

1885: People's Bank is founded in Starkville, Mississippi.

1965: Lewis F. Mallory Jr. becomes chairman and chief executive officer of People's Bank.

1974: People's Bank is renamed National Bank of Commerce (NBC) of Mississippi after several mergers and acquisitions.

1984: NBC Capital Corporation, a financial holding company, is formed.

1997: NBC Capital Corporation initiates use of the Teller Management System in its banks.

2002: Company CEO and Chairman Lewis Mallory is elected to three-year term on the Board of Directors of the Federal Reserve Bank of St. Louis.

2006: NBC Capital Corporation offers 2.4 million shares for sale in initial public offering; name is changed to Cadence Financial Corporation; Cadence common shares are delisted from the AMEX and listed on the NASDAQ.

2007: Cadence Financial Corporation announces record increase in loans in 2006; President and CEO Lewis F. Mallory Jr. presides over opening bell of the NASDAQ on July 30.

2009: Shareholders approve participation in the U.S. Treasury Department's Capital Purchase Program.

on out-of-state expansion, especially on acquisitions in Florida and Georgia that were scheduled to be completed later in the year.

NBC Capital Corporation changed its name to Cadence Financial Corporation in June 2006 to rebrand and reposition itself for expansion into additional markets, as well as to appeal to young, progressive, and affluent customers. The name was chosen to suggest the company's ability to keep pace and rhythm with expanding customer needs. Following the name change, Cadence Financial acquired SunCoast Bancorp, Inc., of Sarasota, Florida, marking Cadence's entry into the Florida market. SunCoast bank branches would become branches of Cadence. Approximately half of the $35.5 million acquisition was paid in cash and half in shares of Cadence common stock. Cadence issued 922,000 shares as part of the transaction.

The end of 2006 included another acquisition and a shift in trading of company shares. In November Cadence entered the Georgia market with the acquisition of Seasons Bancshares, Inc., of Blairsville, Georgia. The all-cash transaction was valued at approximately $16.9 million. In an interview with the *Mississippi Journal* Lewis Mallory said, "The acquisition provides Cadence with access to a strong market in the northeast corridor of Atlanta, one of the fastest-growing areas in the state." In December 2006 Cadence's shares were delisted from the American Stock Exchange (AMEX) and were moved to the NASDAQ. Lewis Mallory remarked in an interview with the *Mississippi Business Journal* that he expected the move to "improve the visibility of our stock, enhance trading liquidity in our shares, and provide Cadence with greater exposure to institutional investors." To celebrate Cadence's move to the NASDAQ, Lewis Mallory presided over the NASDAQ's opening bell on July 30, 2007.

Cadence reported a record number of loans for 2006, increasing "42% to a record $1.2 billion, up from $851 million in 2005," according to Lewis Mallory in an interview with the *Mississippi Business Journal*. Mallory credited the acquisitions of SunCoast Bancorp in Florida and Seasons Bancshares in Georgia for a significant portion of the increase. "Our existing operations accounted for about 44% of the loan growth and the two acquisitions accounted for 56% of new loans added in 2006."

PARTICIPATION IN THE CAPITAL PURCHASE PROGRAM

Cadence received preliminary approval in December 2008 from the U.S. Treasury Department to participate in the Capital Purchase Program, a federal initiative through the Troubled Asset Relief Program (TARP) to assist financial institutions. Participation had been encouraged by the Treasury Department to supply banks with funds that could provide additional credit to various segments of the economy. The Cadence board of directors had recommended participation in the program, which would allow Cadence "to raise Tier One capital at a time when traditional capital markets are essentially closed to banks," according to Lewis Mallory in an interview in the *Mississippi Business Journal*. In January 2009 Cadence shareholders overwhelmingly approved the company's participation in the Capital Purchase Program and authorized the sale of $44 million in preferred stock to enable the company to participate.

In a discussion of the authorization Mallory told the *Mississippi Business Journal* that Cadence was well-capitalized, and the funding provided by the Capital

Purchase Program would fortify the bank's Tier One capital base. Tier One capital is the metric that regulators use to judge a bank's financial stability. "We believe a strong capital base will be important to Cadence if the economy remains weak for an extended period of time. We also expect the new capital will provide increased resources to support future loan growth as the economy improves," remarked Mallory. Sale of the preferred stock to the Treasury Department was completed within the month.

MANAGING LOSSES AT THE END OF THE FIRST DECADE OF THE 2000S

Losses began to mount for Cadence at the end of 2008. The bank reported a net loss of $2.7 million for the fourth quarter of 2008, adding to the net loss of $3.4 million for the year ended December 31, 2008. Mallory acknowledged in a February 2009 interview in the *Mississippi Business Journal*, "Cadence's loss for the fourth quarter and year was due to increases in our loss provision in the second half of 2008 that reflected the economic recession, increased unemployment, and the continued weakness in the real estate markets we serve" In 2008 approximately 76 percent of Cadence's loan portfolio was in real estate. Cadence took what chairman Mallory called "an aggressive stance" in accounting for problem loans in the company's portfolio, including increasing the company's provision for loan losses to $10.6 million in the fourth quarter of 2008, up from $2.9 million in the fourth quarter of 2007. "We believe these steps are an important part of our strategy to minimize future losses in light of the continued softness in our markets," he said in an interview with the *Mississippi Business Journal*. "The U.S. and global economies are facing real challenges," added Mallory. "The earnings and credit portfolios of many banks are reflecting these challenges."

Cadence took additional steps in early 2009 to reduce its exposure to real estate loans across its franchise and achieved a decrease in loans for speculative residential construction, land development, and lots to builders, in addition to lower balances on commercial real estate loans. The bank reported that these higher risk loan categories were down $91.7 million since the second quarter of 2008, but losses continued.

In March 2009, in spite of continued losses for Cadence, Lewis Mallory was chosen by his banking and corporate colleagues at the Federal Reserve Bank of St. Louis to represent their district on the 12-member Federal Advisory Council. The council, made up of representatives from the banking industry, consults with

and advises the Federal Reserve Board of Governors on all matters within its jurisdiction.

Cadence Financial Corporation announced a loss of $17.6 million for the first quarter of 2009. "Cadence's first quarter loss was disappointing and reflects the impact of the economy on real estate based loans where we have experienced the majority of our losses," remarked Lewis Mallory in an interview with Cadence's hometown newspaper, the *Starkville Daily News*. Mallory reassured shareholders that Cadence Financial Corporation remained well-capitalized and that it had retained the highest regulatory ranking for banks. According to Mallory in the same interview, "We remain focused on managing the bank through this tough economy and expect Cadence to continue as a leading bank in the markets we serve." Cadence management attributed a large share of the reported losses for the first quarter to circumstances in the Middle Tennessee market, which had a high concentration of large construction and development loans.

On May 12, 2009, Cadence Financial Corporation reported losses for the first quarter of the year totaling $84.5 million. The additional first-quarter losses resulted from a mandatory write-down of goodwill, which was driven by deterioration in the general economy, related decline in the price of Cadence Financial Corporation stock, and the concurrent transaction values paid for banks comparable to Cadence Bank. "Cadence's first quarter write-down of goodwill has no effect on our financial condition or our regulatory capital position," said Lewis Mallory in the *Starkville Daily News*, adding that "Cadence remains a well-capitalized bank."

For the second quarter of 2009, ending on June 30, Cadence posted a net loss of $14.7 million. The company increased its provision for loan losses to $23 million from $3.3 million a year before.

In late July 2009 Cadence announced an offering of common and preferred stock, which was intended to raise between $80 million and $90 million in capital. "Our balance sheet already contains capital that meets the publicly stated regulatory requirements for a well-capitalized bank," according to Lewis Mallory in the *Starkville Daily News*. He went on to say, "What we're talking about doing is putting additional capital on top of that, so there should be no doubt as to the strength of Cadence's balance sheet."

Joyce Helena Brusin

PRINCIPAL SUBSIDIARIES

Cadence Bank N.A.; Galloway-Chandler-McKinney Insurance Agency, Inc.; NBC Service Corporation; NBC Insurance Services.

PRINCIPAL COMPETITORS

Bancorp South, Inc.; Trustmark Corporation; First M & F Corporation; Renasant Corporation; First Horizon National Corporation; Pinnacle Financial Partners, Inc.; Peoples Financial Corporation; Hancock Holding Company.

FURTHER READING

"Cadence Completes Merger," *Mississippi Business Journal*, August 28, 2006.

"Cadence Financial Corporation (CADE) Chairman and Chief Executive Officer to Ring the NASDAQ Stock Market Opening Bell," *PrimeZone Media Network*, July 30, 2007.

"Cadence Financial Closes $44 Million Preferred Stock Sale to U.S. Treasury Department," *Investment Weekly News*, January 31, 2009, p. 101.

"Cadence Financial Corporation Reports Second Quarter Results," *Business Wire*, July 23, 2009.

"Cadence Hurt by Real Estate Loans," *Mississippi Business Journal*, February 9, 2009, p. 26.

"Cadence Moves to NASDAQ," *Mississippi Business Journal*, January 8, 2007, p. 7.

"Cadence Opts for Treasury Aid," *Mississippi Business Journal*, December 22, 2008, p. 21.

"Cadence Sees Record Loans," *Mississippi Business Journal*, February 5, 2007, p. 10.

"Cadence Sells Shares to Treasury," *Mississippi Business Journal*, January 19, 2009, p. 24.

Flaum, David, "NBC Capital Enters Memphis, Tenn., Market with Enterprise Bancshares Purchase," *Commercial Appeal* (Memphis, TN), December 12, 2003.

Kirkland, Elizabeth, "Starkville-based NBC Looking to the Next Billion," *Mississippi Business Journal*, March 10, 2003, p. 35.

"Launch Brochure for Branding Campaign," *ARA Bank Marketing*, May 2007, p. 6.

Marshall, Jeffrey, "It Sounds Almost Too Simple to Be True," *US Banker*, January 1997, p. 41.

Mullins, Luke, "NBC of Miss. to Raise $47M," *American Banker*, May 5, 2006, p. 4.

"National Bank of Commerce (People to Watch)," *Mississippi Business Journal*, January 14, 2002, p. 7.

"NBC Capital Corporation Signs Definitive Agreement to Acquire Seasons Bancshares, Inc. of Blairsville, GA," *Business Wire*, March 21, 2006.

"NBC Capital Corporation Signs Definitive Agreement to Acquire SunCoast Bancorp., Inc. of Sarasota, FL," *Business Wire*, March 16, 2006.

Northway, Wally, "Cadence Moves to NASDAQ." *Mississippi Business Journal*, January 8, 2007.

Osuri, Laura Thompson, "NBC Capital Changes Name of Lead Unit," *American Banker*, October 12, 2005, p. 20.

"Seasons Merger Reworked," *Mississippi Business Journal*, October 9, 2006, p. 8.

"Shareholders Approve Issuance (Strictly Business)," *Mississippi Business Journal*, January 5, 2009, p. 20.

Sims, Paul, "Cadence Financial Corp Posts $84.5 Loss for Quarter," *Starkville Daily News*, May 12, 2009.

———, "Losses on Loans Result in $14.7M Drop for Cadence," *Starkville Daily News*, July 24, 2009.

———, "Mallory: Nationalizing a Temporary Idea," *Starkville Daily News*, March 2, 2009.

———, "Preliminary Report: Cadence to Show $17.6M Loss," *Starkville Daily News*, April 22, 2009.

Calumet Specialty Products, L.P.

Calumet Specialty Products Partners, L.P.

2780 Waterfront Parkway East Drive, Suite 200
Indianapolis, Indiana 46241
U.S.A.
Telephone: (317) 328-5660
Toll Free: (800) 437-3188
Fax: (317) 328-2359
Web site: http://www.calumetspecialty.com/

Public Company
Founded: 1919
Employees: 640
Sales: $2.49 billion (2008)
Stock Exchanges: NASDAQ
Ticker Symbol: CLMT
NAICS: 211112 Liquid Hydrocarbons Recovered from Oil and Gas Field Gases; 324110 Petroleum Refineries; 325110 Acyclic Hydrocarbons (e.g., butane, ethylene, propene) (except Acetylene) Made from Refined Petroleum or Liquid Hydrocarbons

∎ ∎ ∎

Calumet Specialty Products Partners, L.P., is a diversified company specializing in the processing and sale of hydrocarbons and other crude oil products. The company is divided into two core businesses: petroleum-based specialty products and fuel. Calumet's specialty products division accounts for the bulk of its operating revenue and produces base oils for use in everything from tires and car wax to cosmetics and chewing gum. For decades, the company's core business revolved around naphthenic oils, but following a major restructuring in the early 1990s the company has diversified its operation to include the manufacturing of paraffinic-based oil products. Since the early 2000s, the company has also experienced rapid growth in its fuel production business, selling petroleum for use in automobiles, diesel trucks, and jet airplanes. Headquartered in Indianapolis, Calumet operated oil refineries in Louisiana, Texas, and Pennsylvania, and employed roughly 640 people as of 2009.

FROM THE OIL FIELDS OF LOUISIANA TO THE CHICAGO SUBURBS: 1916–80

Relatively little is known about the early years of Calumet. The original incarnation of the company dates to 1916, with the formation of the Red River Oil Company. In the beginning, the company purchased crude oil from various suppliers in northwest Louisiana and transported it to a refinery outside of Chicago. In 1919 the company was reformed as the Calumet Refining Company, establishing new headquarters in Burnham, Illinois. At this time, the company dealt exclusively in naphthenics, a type of mineral oil known for its high solubility and low wax content. For many years, Calumet products were used primarily in lubricants and medicinal white oils.

Calumet continued to ship oil from Louisiana to the Chicago area for the next several decades. By the early 1950s, however, the company had begun to realize that this aspect of its business was too costly and inefficient to remain viable. In 1953, to reduce the time and expense related to transportation, Calumet built a new

KEY DATES

1916: Red River Oil Company is formed.
1919: Red River Oil becomes the Calumet Refining Company; headquarters is moved to Burnham, Illinois.
1953: Princeton, Louisiana, refinery is built.
1990: Calumet is acquired by The Heritage Group and is renamed Calumet Lubricants Company.
2005: Company announces IPO, becomes Calumet Specialty Products Partners, L.P.
2008: Calumet acquires Penreco for $267 million.

refinery in Princeton, Louisiana, not far from the area where it acquired its crude oil. By the middle of the decade, the bulk of Calumet's refinery operations were based in Princeton, while its Burnham plant continued to handle the final distillation process for its specialty products.

By the time of the oil crisis from late 1973 through early 1975, industry analysts became worried that naphthenics shortages would cause problems for producers in the long-term. As a major producer of naphthenic oils, Calumet was undoubtedly concerned about the future of its core business.

REGULATION AND THE NAPHTHENICS INDUSTRY: THE 1980S

However, by the early 1980s the naphthenics industry was experiencing significant overcapacity in spite of the grim predictions that had been made in the previous decade. Nationwide, naphthenics manufacturers were producing the equivalent of roughly 66,500 barrels of product a day. However, demand had hit a plateau of approximately 45,000 barrels a day. This surplus forced Calumet into an intense battle for market share with its competitors.

This strain on the company was exacerbated further in 1985 when the Occupational Safety and Health Administration (OSHA) announced the implementation of more strict regulations concerning the labeling and marketing of a range of oil-based products. The government's concern stemmed from scientific findings that showed that certain distillation methods had the potential to render oils carcinogenic. Under the updated regulations, makers of naphthenic and paraffinic oils would be required to put warning labels on their products indicating that they had been proven to cause cancer in animals.

The announcement hit naphthenics producers especially hard, since naphthenic oils had a greater tendency to possess carcinogenic properties. In order to address these concerns, the company announced its intention to retrofit its distillation facilities to comply with the new standards. Nevertheless, the cost of the necessary upgrades, which were estimated to be between $20 and $25 million, caused Calumet to consider the regulations potentially disastrous. In a July 17, 1985, article published in *Chemical Week*, Calumet's vice-president of research and development was quoted as saying that the law could deliver a "death blow" to the company.

By early 1987 the company had installed a new hydrotreating unit, which was designed to remove harmful sulfur from its oil products, at its Princeton refinery with a cost of roughly $27 million. Nonetheless, a downturn in the naphthenics industry during the late 1980s proved too much of a burden for the beleaguered company, and in mid-1989 Calumet's board of directors voted to sell the company. By February 1990 the company was forced to file for Chapter 11 bankruptcy protection.

BANKRUPTCY, RESTRUCTURING, AND A FRESH START: 1990–2000

For most of 1990 Calumet's future remained uncertain. A solution to the company's financial struggles finally came in November of that year when the Heritage Group, a holding company based in Indianapolis, acquired Calumet for $21.5 million. Owned by the Fehsenfeld family, the Heritage Group created a new corporate subsidiary, Calumet Lubricants Company, as a limited partnership. Under the terms of the takeover, Fred Fehsenfeld Jr. became chairman of the new company, and F. William Grube, a former executive vice president of Rock Island Refinery, was named the company's president and CEO.

Company headquarters were moved to Indianapolis, and the newly-reconfigured Calumet began to restore the company's profitability. One key aspect of the company's new business strategy was diversification. During the 1990s Calumet added paraffinic oils to its product line and built a second refinery in Cotton Valley, Louisiana. In early 2000 the company purchased another refinery in Rouseville, Pennsylvania, from Pennzoil Quaker State. By March of that year, the company had converted the Rouseville facility into a specialty wax division to manufacture microcrystalline waxes for use in the painting and cosmetics industries.

CONTINUED GROWTH: 2001–05

As the first decade of the new century began, Calumet continued to explore ways to expand its core business. In 2001 the company acquired a second refinery from Pennzoil Quaker State in Shreveport, Louisiana. Over the next three years, Calumet devoted close to $40 million to upgrading the Shreveport refinery's capacity to allow the company to begin refining fuel products. In 2004 as the refurbishing of the Shreveport refinery neared completion, Calumet established a new division dedicated to the production of gasoline, jet fuel, and diesel. The company completed the transformation of the Shreveport refinery in February 2005.

By the time the refinery upgrades were complete, Calumet's Shreveport facility was producing roughly 42,000 barrels of oil per day. The refinery was dedicated primarily to production of waxes and lubricants, while also producing a variety of fuels. Meanwhile, the refinery at Princeton was producing an additional 10,000 barrels a day, and the Cotton Valley refinery accounted for approximately 13,500 barrels a day. This increased capacity, combined with a steady expansion of the company's product line, played a key role in helping the company remain profitable. Earnings for the first half of 2005 were $526.7 million, of which $18.6 million was profit.

GOING PUBLIC

In October 2005 Calumet Lubricants Co., L.P., filed papers with the SEC announcing a planned initial public offering (IPO). Less than 25 percent of the company actually would go on sale to outside investors, and the Fehsenfelds would maintain majority control of the company, as well as the exclusive right to name the board of directors. However, analysts regarded the move as well-timed, particularly since the company's Louisiana facilities had managed to elude the devastation of Hurricanes Katrina and Rita, allowing it to avoid any significant interruptions in its operations. Investor interest in oil trading was extremely high during this time. Meanwhile, Calumet's sales for 2005 topped $1.3 billion, with roughly 70 percent of the company's total earnings coming from its specialty oils and the remaining 30 percent from its fuel business. Overall specialty oil sales during the final quarter of the year were approximately 24,266 barrels a day, compared to 21,607 for the same period in 2004. The company's fuel oil production resulted in an even more substantial jump, while fourth-quarter production in 2004 totaled only 2,094 barrels a day, the company reported an increase in production to 27,007 for the final quarter of 2005.

Calumet's IPO took place on January 25, 2006, with the company garnering $144 million for the 6,450,000 shares of common stock sold on the NASDAQ. Calumet stock was particularly enticing to investors because of the company's generous dividend policy. According to the company's SEC filing, Calumet promised an annual return of 8 percent, substantially higher than that offered by its competitors. With the IPO, the company's name was officially changed to Calumet Specialty Products, L.P.

In the first several months of 2006, Calumet reported a 40 percent increase in sales. The earnings increase was driven by rising fuel prices, as well as by the increased capacity of the company's three Louisiana refineries, which were producing more than 65,000 barrels of oil per day. At the same time, several industry giants, notably Shell Oil, were in the process of divesting their specialty oil products divisions, creating unique opportunities for Calumet to expand its market presence. The company reported unprecedented growth from 2004 to 2006. According to a report published in the *Indianapolis Business Journal* on September 17, 2007, Calumet was the fastest-growing company in greater Indianapolis during that time, with sales more than doubling from $539.6 million to $1.6 billion two years later.

CHALLENGES: 2006–09

The company suffered a slight drop in earnings in 2007 as sales reached $1.64 billion, down 0.2 percent over 2006 figures. Profits took a more sizable hit over the same period, with the company registering a net gain of $82.9 million in 2007, down 13.3 percent from the prior year. The company also experienced a dramatic shift in the respective values of its core business segments during this time frame. Between 2006 and 2007 Calumet's specialty petroleum products reported a decrease in earnings of roughly $46 million; over the same period, while the fuel products line experienced an increase in earnings of $43.2 million. By the end of 2007 approximately 36.4 percent of the company's gross earnings came from its fuel products division.

In 2007 the company once again invested in massive improvements to its Shreveport plant, which resulted in a 40 percent increase in production capacity, from 42,000 to 57,000 barrels a day. However, the volatility of oil markets, combined with delays and cost increases associated with the Shreveport upgrades, created a significant financial strain on Calumet. By February 2008 estimated costs to get the plant up and running had risen to $300 million. As CEO William Grube told analysts that month, for each day that the Shreveport facility was not in operation, Calumet was losing $700,000. Skyrocketing crude oil costs added to the company's economic woes during this period, with the price of a barrel of oil passing the $100 mark in February 2008. The price of the company's stock took an even more significant hit during this time, dropping from a peak of nearly $55 a share in the spring of 2007 to only $14 a share less than a year later.

Undeterred by these setbacks, in January 2008 Calumet made another bold move when it purchased Penreco, a producer of specialty oils, from the Conoco-Phillips Company for $267 million. With the acquisition, Calumet acquired Penreco's refineries in Karns City, Pennsylvania, and Dickinson, Texas. Although the combined production capacity of the two facilities was only 6,800 barrels of oil a day, it nonetheless represented a substantial boost to Calumet's core business.

Once devoted exclusively to the manufacturing and sale of naphthenic oils, by 2009 Calumet was selling 250 different specialty oil products. The company's offerings at the end of the first decade of the 2000s included paraffinic base oils, as well as asphalt and other oil by-products. Calumet's fuel business also was growing rapidly during this period. Overall, Calumet was selling its products to more than 800 companies, including such corporate titans as ExxonMobil and Goodyear. The company had five refineries in three states, as well as a distribution center based in its original hometown of Burnham, Indiana. Furthermore, by the end of the decade Calumet had grown to 640 employees, up from 375 in 2006. In spite of the unstable economic climate during the latter part of the decade, Calumet appeared

to be settling into its role as a diversified specialty oil products company.

Stephen Meyer

PRINCIPAL SUBSIDIARIES

Calumet Lubricants Co.; Calumet Penreco LLC.

PRINCIPAL COMPETITORS

Alon USA Energy Inc.; AmeriGas Partners, L.P.; CVR Energy Inc.; Ergon Inc.; Farmland Industries, Inc.; Frontier Oil Corp.; Holly Corp.; Koch Industries, Inc.; Marathon Petroleum Company LLC; National Cooperative Refinery Association; Valero Energy Corporation.

FURTHER READING

Agoos, Alice, with Lisa Lazorko Abercauph, "An OSHA Rule Rattles Naphthenics," *Chemical Week*, July 17, 1985, p. 44.

Andrews, Greg, "Locally Based Oil Refiner Sees Boom Times Vanish," *Indianapolis Business Journal*, May 5, 2008, p. 4.

Calumet Specialty Products Partners, L.P., "Calumet Specialty Products Partners, L.P. Closes on Acquisition of Penreco," *PR Newswire*, January 4, 2008.

Calumet Specialty Products Partners, L.P., "Calumet Specialty Products Partners, L.P. Reports Fourth Quarter and Full Year 2005 Earnings," *PR Newswire*, February 23, 2006.

Murphy, Tom, "Trying to Strike Oil in Public Markets," *Indianapolis Business Journal*, October 17, 2005, p. 1.

O'Malley, Chris, "Refiner Enjoys Oil Boom: Calumet Specialty Products Sees Stock Price Take Off," *Indianapolis Business Journal*, May 8, 2006, p. 3.

CAMAC International Corporation

Four Oaks Place
1330 Post Oak Boulevard, Suite 2200
Houston, Texas 77056
U.S.A.
Telephone: (713) 965-5100
Fax: (713) 965-5128
Web site: http://www.camac.com

Private Company
Founded: 1986 as Cameroon-American Corporation
Employees: 300
Sales: $2.43 billion (2008)
NAICS: 211111 Crude Petroleum and Natural Gas Extraction

■ ■ ■

CAMAC International Corporation is an integrated oil and gas company that has been instrumental in opening up Nigeria and other African nations for oil exploration. Headed by Kase L. Lawal, a Nigerian immigrant, CA-MAC was the first company to obtain drilling rights in oil-rich West Africa. By partnering with industry giants, such as Houston-based Conoco, Lawal was able to get the needed financing to do exploratory drilling. The company partnered with other energy giants over the years, opened subsidiaries in Nigeria, South Africa, London, and Colombia, and integrated the production of oil and gas with the refining and trading of energy products, a move that resulted in phenomenal revenue growth. The company is the second-largest African-American business in the United States and is listed among the top 400 *Forbes* companies in the nation.

AN IMMIGRANT FROM NIGERIA

Kase L. Lawal, the chief executive officer of CAMAC, was born in Nigeria, but he dreamed of moving to the United States. He worked hard to get accepted into an American university, and in 1971 he arrived in the United States at the age of 17 to attend Fort Valley State College in Georgia, a historically African-American institution. He later transferred to Texas Southern University, another historically African-American institution, where he earned a degree in chemical engineering. He then went to work for Shell Oil at an oil refinery, work that convinced him that he wanted to continue his education and wear a business suit rather than a hard hat. Lawal earned his master of finance and marketing from Prairie View A&M University in Texas. In the subsequent decade, Lawal worked first as a chemist and then as an executive in several oil and finance companies.

Before long, Lawal decided to strike out on his own. In 1986 he founded the Cameroon-American Corporation, later known as CAMAC International Corporation, as an international trade operation. That same year he partnered with tobacco and cigarette manufacturing entrepreneurs from Cameroon. Lawal's company served as the middleman, in that it purchased tobacco in the United States and sold it to the cigarette manufacturers in Cameroon.

Lawal began to accumulate impressive knowledge of the political and legal climates in Nigeria, Cameroon,

COMPANY PERSPECTIVES

CAMAC International's mission is to be a leading independent provider of crude oil, natural gas and electric power around the world. CAMAC and its affiliated group of companies are linked under the CAMAC umbrella by a shared vision of entrepreneurial excellence and achievement. With a thorough analysis of business investments, CAMAC maximizes opportunities while also stimulating economic development and encouraging empowerment in the communities where we operate.

and other parts of the world. In 1989 he had a chance meeting with the Nigerian foreign minister Rilwanu Lukman, later the secretary-general of the Organization of Petroleum Exporting Countries. His political and business acumen helped him to use this meeting as a stepping stone to securing the drilling rights to explore parts of Nigeria for oil. He then had to find capital for the venture. He approached major oil companies in the United States and in Europe with little success. Undeterred, Lawal borrowed a country club membership card from a friend and began hanging around the country club, hoping to meet up with golf-playing oil industry executives. A chance meeting with a Conoco executive led to the first of many partnerships.

PARTNERSHIPS KEY TO SUCCESS

Lawal's search for capital to finance oil exploration highlighted the key to his success: he had little capital to start, but he contributed his political and cultural knowledge and connections to the partnerships, and the oil industry giants provided the financing. His partnership with Conoco in 1991 would be the first of many and would eventually result in the production of more than 20,000 barrels of oil per day. Lawal later partnered with Chevron, British Petroleum, and Statoil. CAMAC acquired the rights to exploratory drilling, and the large oil industry leaders paid to drill the exploratory well. The companies then split any profits.

CAMAC eventually expanded to provide both upstream and downstream services. Upstream services included the production of oil and gas, including exploratory drilling, whereas downstream services included the refining and selling of products. The addition of a sales force fueled impressive growth in the company after 2000; revenues grew by 757 percent in

two years, from $114.3 million in 1999 to $979.5 million in 2001. CAMAC's nearly billion-dollar revenues earned the company the top spot on *Black Enterprise*'s "Industrial/Service 100" list in 2002.

COMMUNITY GIVING

Lawal engaged in several philanthropic efforts, both privately and as the chief executive officer of CAMAC. In 2005 Lawal was one of a group of investors who acquired a 21 percent interest in Unity National Bank, the only African-Amerian–owned federally chartered bank in Texas. Lawal, who served as the bank's vice chairman, stated that he intended the bank to extend credit to African-American businesses and communities as an economic development tool. He told Alan Hughes and Tennille M. Robinson of *Black Enterprise*, "It wasn't really for profit, because it takes time to make money in banking. I can drill more wells, and hopefully I can hit one to make more money than being in the heavily regulated industry that is banking." Instead, Lawal's expansion into the financial sector reflected his commitment to helping empower the African-American community.

The company also donated to universities in an effort to encourage other Africans and African-Americans to enter business and engineering. In 2003 Lawal established a $1 million endowment at Texas Southern University to develop the Kase and Eileen Lawal International Development Center within the business school. In 2009 he pledged $1 million over 10 years to fund the CAMAC International Corporation endowment at the university, which would fund the establishment of the Lawal Center for Global Trade and provide student scholarships.

Lawal viewed his 2008 decision to list CAMAC's Nigerian subsidiary company, Allied Energy, on the Nigerian Stock Exchange as a way to empower Nigeria's people. Twenty percent of the available shares were earmarked for the Niger Delta region, and CAMAC was expected to retain a 65 percent to 70 percent interest in the subsidiary after its initial public offering. Shares were expected to begin trading in the fourth quarter of 2009, pending approval by the U.S. Securities and Exchange Commission. Furthermore, Lawal told *Black Enterprise*'s Alan Hughes that as the economy improved after the recession that began in 2008, he expected to list CAMAC on the U.S. stock exchange as well.

RECORD PROFITS IN 2008

The price of crude oil reached $150 a barrel in 2008, pushing CAMAC's revenue to a record $2.4 billion, up 50 percent from the year before and marking the first time the company's revenues had surpassed $2 billion.

KEY DATES

1986: Kase L. Lawal founds Cameroon-American Corporation, which later becomes known as CAMAC International Corporation.

1991: CAMAC partners with Conoco to jointly operate an exploratory drill off the coast of Nigeria.

2002: CAMAC becomes the largest African-American–owned U.S. company.

2006: CAMAC is selected as the *Black Enterprise* Company of the Year.

2008: Gross revenues exceed $2 billion for the first time; Kase L. Lawal seeks approval to list Allied Energy on the Nigerian Stock Exchange.

CAMAC remained at number two on *Black Enterprise*'s list of the nation's 100 largest African-American–owned businesses in 2009, a position it had occupied since 2004. However, the economic slowdown in late 2008 and 2009 led crude oil prices to drop to one-third of what they had been at their height. Lawal predicted that his company's profits would not suffer much. He invested in hiring talented geoscientists and expanding the company's research and development program, believing the effort would translate into greater profits down the road.

CAMAC grew exponentially in the first decade of the 21st century, and observers believed the company was poised to continue its rapid growth. Lawal's connections to Nigeria and his political and business acumen—as well as his dogged perseverance and a little bit of luck—translated into the emergence of a very successful energy corporation.

Melissa Doak

PRINCIPAL SUBSIDIARIES

Allied Energy Corporation; Allied Energy PLC (Nigeria); Allied Energy Colombia; South African Trading Company (Great Britain); CAMAC International Nigeria Ltd.; CAMAC International Ltd. (Nigeria); South African Oil Company; Allied School Bus Service (South Africa).

PRINCIPAL COMPETITORS

Exxon Mobil Corporation; Hess Corporation; Occidental Petroleum Corporation.

FURTHER READING

"America's Largest Private Companies," *Forbes*, November 27, 2006, p. 196.

Buggs, Shannon, "Chronicle 100 Private Companies—The Other Nine at the Top: No. 9: CAMAC International Corp.," *Houston Chronicle*, May 17, 2009, p. 15.

"CAMAC CEO and Chairman Dr. Kase Lawal Presents the First Installment of a One Million Dollar Pledge for the CAMAC Endowment at Texas Southern University" (press release), Houston, TX: CAMAC International Corporation, January 28, 2009, http://www.camac.com/newsroom/CAMAC_Establishes_Endowment_at_TSU.pdf.

Chappell, Kevin, "Kase Lawal: From Nigeria to Houston to History," *Ebony*, January 2006, pp. 74–78.

"Former Houston Mayor Leads Business Group's Acquisition of Local Bank Shares," GlobeNewswire, July 6, 2005.

Hughes, Alan, "A New Leader Emerges," *Black Enterprise*, June 2002, p. 127.

———, "CAMAC Going Public," *Black Enterprise*, November 2008, p. 30.

Hughes, Alan, and Tennille M. Robinson, "Black Gold: Kase Lawal's Business Prowess, Along with a Spike in Oil Prices, Is Fueling CAMAC International's Rise to the Nation's Second-Largest Black Business," *Black Enterprise*, June 2006, pp. 128–134.

"Industrial/Service Companies," *Black Enterprise*, June 2003, pp. 117–121.

"Industrial/Service Companies," *Black Enterprise*, June 2004, pp. 118–126.

"Industrial/Service Companies," *Black Enterprise*, June 2005, pp. 113–120.

"Industrial/Service Companies," *Black Enterprise*, June 2007, pp. 115–126.

"Industrial/Service Companies," *Black Enterprise*, June 2008, pp. 108–114.

"Industrial/Service Companies," *Black Enterprise*, June 2009, pp. 98–104.

Lynch, David J., "From Nigeria to Texas Oilman," *USA Today*, January 8, 2007.

Morgan, Barry, "Setting an Example in Historic African Listing," *Upstream*, November 7, 2008, p. 56.

"The Next Generation of Titans," *Black Enterprise*, May 2003, p. 120.

Centex®

Centex Corporation

2728 North Harwood
Dallas, Texas 75201-1516
U.S.A.
Telephone: (214) 981-5000
Fax: (214) 981-6855
Web site: http://www.centexhomes.com

Public Company
Incorporated: 1950 as Centex Construction Company
Employees: 2,463
Sales: $3.83 billion (2008)
Stock Exchanges: New York London
Ticker Symbol: CTX
NAICS: 236117 New Housing Operative Builders

■ ■ ■

Centex Corporation is one of the most successful diversified building companies in the United States, with products and services ranging from new home construction, manufactured housing, and industrial construction to mortgage lending, pest control, and construction contracting. Centex has protected itself from the cyclical nature of building construction not only through diversification but also through geographical expansion. By 2009 Centex had built homes for more than 500,000 households nationally and was the fourth-largest homebuilder in the United States. That year Centex announced its intent to merge with Pulte Homes, creating the largest homebuilder in the United States.

EARLY HISTORY

The company got its start just after World War II, a time characterized in the United States by growth and consumerism. In 1945 Texas native Tom Lively "scraped together $500 and drew up his 5 feet 6 inches to talk business with Ira Rupley, a successful Dallas land developer," as a 1956 *Newsweek* article related. A young entrepreneur, Lively had "left his home town of White-write, Texas, in 1937, and for years had scraped along selling clothing and hardware and 'a little of this and that' before settling on real estate."

Rupley, who had made his name in home construction, entered into partnership with Lively on a still-unnamed building company. They began "modestly enough with a scattering of single and double houses around Dallas," noted *Newsweek*. In 1949 they undertook their first major project, a subdivision of 300 houses that sold for $6,500 each. The success of the subdivision led to the 1950 formation of the Centex Construction Company.

For its first few years, the company concentrated its building efforts exclusively in Texas. However, by the mid-1950s Centex was ready to expand. One of the company's early projects was also an historic one. Centex built Elk Grove Village near Chicago, America's first master-planned community. This was the forerunner of modern master-planned areas, and boasted some 7,000 homes, all built by Centex, by the 1990s.

COMPANY PERSPECTIVES

Our mission at Centex is simple: Build the best. The best homes. The best neighborhoods. The best communities. The best company. In our efforts to build the best, we're always looking for a better way. A better way to build our homes, a better way to serve our customers. More than any other home builder, we believe Centex knows how to address the most basic needs for home and life.

DIVERSIFICATION AND EXPANSION: 1960S–70S

By 1960 Centex Construction Company had produced some 25,000 residences in several states. The company began expanding its operations to include the production of housing materials. Centex opened a cement manufacturing business with facilities in Texas and Nevada, then bought out a Dallas contractor, J. W. Bateson, which had specialized in commercial buildings. Reflecting its new diversification, the company changed its name during the 1960s to Centex Corporation.

In 1969 Centex went public, selling 500,000 shares of common stock. By this time the builder's net worth stood at about $10 million, with gross revenues of almost $100 million. As Centex moved into the 1970s, it increased its scope of operations. The company acquired two leading builders, one in Chicago, the other Dallas-based Fox & Jacobs, then the largest builder of single-family homes in the Southwest. Fox & Jacobs's strategy for producing affordable housing seemed to be working. A 1976 *Fortune* article noted that the Centex subsidiary was able to "turn over its $1 million inventory of building materials 15 times a year. The extraordinarily fast turnover is the key to the company's ability to hold down prices and still keep profit margins healthy on houses in a wide variety of sizes." Expansion continued as Centex acquired Frank J. Rooney Inc., Florida's largest general contractor.

The 1970s became a peak time for building, and as need dictated, Centex expanded its cement business in Texas and became a partner in another cement plant in Illinois. Centex also opened an oil-and-gas plant that would come to be named Cenergy. However, for all its diversification efforts, Centex was still primarily associated with one region of the United States. Explained William Barrett in a 1990 *Forbes* article, "In fiscal 1979, 72 percent of the company's ... homes were built in Texas, a dangerously high concentration. Centex execu-

tives started cutting back there and expanding elsewhere before the economic bust set in, but not nearly fast enough." Per-share profits subsequently fell 59 percent, from $3.44 for the fiscal year ending March 1981 to $1.41 the following fiscal year.

BEYOND TEXAS IN THE 1980S

A crash in Texas construction followed the plummet in oil prices in 1986 and the subsequent failure of a number of Texas savings and loans. Although Centex was affected, its home construction in other parts of the United States kept the company afloat. However, the company owned $76 million worth of land that it was not practical to develop in the collapsed Texas market. In 1987 Centex established a new subsidiary, Centex Development Company, to oversee the land. The same year, Centex invested in further diversification, moving into medical facility construction with the subsidiary Centex-Rodgers Construction.

A rebound of sorts began by the late 1980s, with Centex's homes numbering more than 100,000. That decade saw the company increase its market from eight cities to 35 (by 1992 that number would rise to 39) through a combination of new business launches and acquisitions. One particularly key acquisition was that of the John Crosland Company, a major name in the Carolinas.

At the same time, Centex was also trimming and consolidating its forces to build a stronger organization. The oil-and-gas subsidiary Cenergy, for example, was spun off as a separate company in 1984; this divestment more firmly planted Centex in the construction business.

ENTERING THE MORTGAGE INDUSTRY

By the early 1990s, Centex operated several subsidiaries, all aimed at supporting the building business. One offshoot was Centex Mortgage Banking, which by 1985 had changed its name to CTX Mortgage Company and had expanded into all of the builder's major markets. Its purpose was to establish home prices and facilitate mortgages for Centex customers. According to company history, CTX initiated title and insurance operations, thus clearing the way to develop real estate as well as build on it. That development subsidiary made its debut in 1987 as Centex Development Company. By fiscal 1992, CTX Mortgage Co. had cleared $2.5 billion in home loans.

Centex banking interests did not end there, however. The corporation ran its own savings and loan institution, Texas Trust Savings Bank, FSB. The smaller

KEY DATES

1950: Centex Construction Company incorporated.
1969: Company goes public.
1979: 72 percent of Centex's homes in Texas.
1987: Centex Development Corporation incorporated.
1996: Centex diversifies into pest control and security systems.
2006: Centex begins selling off non-essential subsidiaries.
2009: Announces merger with Pulte Inc.

interest provided just 1 percent of Centex's total 1992 revenues, with the bulk of incoming money (53 percent) coming from the building and mortgage banking subsidiaries. Contracting and construction services were also a big part of Centex's subsidiary interests. With Centex Cement Enterprises, which later changed its name to Centex Construction Products, the company had the ability to produce and deliver not only cement but also ready-mix concrete and gypsum boarding.

It was the homes themselves, however, that brought Centex into the public eye. A typical Centex home was somewhat unique; a staff of three in-house architects would trek to different building sites around the United States to determine just the kind of residence that would fit the development best. With the architects designing upward of 300 home concepts each year, there were plenty of options from which to choose. Thus, a "typical" Centex home could span from 900 to over 5,000 square feet, and cost from as little as $50,000 to as much as $1.1 million. (The higher-end projects were sold under the name Centex Custom Homes.)

RISING TO THE TOP

Though its primary focus was on residential homes, Centex had a hand in the development of some public buildings. Contracts for 1992 included Veterans Administration medical centers in Detroit and Indianapolis; hospital expansions in San Diego and Miami; a wastewater treatment plant in Hot Springs, Arkansas; and even a Wal-Mart store in Paducah, Kentucky. Other high-profile Centex projects included Cinderella's Castle, EPCOT Center's Land Pavilion, and the Grand Floridian Beach Resort, all built for Disney World in Orlando, Florida.

The company's success was attributed in part to the team-building attitude demonstrated by its top

managers. Indeed, "in an industry famous for its flamboyant, ego-driven characters, CEO Larry Hirsch and his crew are quiet, low-key types who keep pretty much to themselves," reported Barrett. When CEO successor William J. Gillian was introduced, a *New York Times* article quoted a securities analyst as remarking, "One of the beauties of Centex is that they are decentralized. The company has demonstrated its ability to grow and to build its markets without running into the control problems that have plagued others." Centex described its business plan as based on a "3-D" strategy: diversify, decentralize, and differentiate.

Whatever the strategy, it resulted in top scores for Centex. A *Builder* survey of America's top 100 building manufacturers ranked by closings rated Centex number one in 1992. Its unit output (9,184) easily outdistanced second-place, Michigan-based Pulte Homes (6,493). As *Builder* reported, Centex also posted a 29 percent increase in closings over 1991, as well as a 10 percent increase in gross revenues covering the same period.

SUCCEEDING THROUGH HOUSING DOWNTURN: EARLY 1990S

Although the home building industry suffered a downturn in the early 1990s, conditions had begun to improve. While hardly recession-proof, Centex took advantage of the times. Then-CEO Larry Hirsch even remarked to *Forbes*, "I think a national recession would be a tremendous opportunity for Centex." As *Forbes* writer Barrett explained, Hirsch meant that a recession would "drive down the cost of land and interest rates—the bread of life for home builders—and would almost certainly weed out some smaller, highly leveraged competitors."

These predictions proved correct. By late 1992, with a slow recovery in the works, housing interest rates dropped to new lows and sales began to take flight. "Wall Street has started to appreciate home builders as manufacturers of a basic consumer product," a securities analyst told *Builder*. Centex benefited, posting 1992 revenues of $2.3 billion, with the high margins attributed to improvements in both the home-building and mortgage banking areas. (The company claimed the distinction of never having reported either a quarterly or an annual loss since becoming a public company.)

For all Centex's success in Texas, Florida, and other areas, one important region proved difficult for the company to penetrate. The company had entered highly competitive Southern California several years before, but the area proved "a tough market to crack," as Centex president Tim Eller told *Builder*. Eller noted, however, that the shaky economy gave the company "an opening we needed. We expect to increase our volumes there significantly."

Centex Construction Products benefited from an increase in demand for cement, aggregate, concrete, and wallboard in the mid-1990s. Its revenues nearly doubled in 1994. That year Centex took the subsidiary public, although it retained 56 percent of the stock after the initial public offering. In a somewhat unusual set-up for an IPO, Centex Corporation not only retained all of the offering proceeds, it left Centex Construction with an increased debt load. With the company's strong cash flow, the increased debt was not seen as a problem by analysts.

Although rising interest rates had slowed new home construction and had affected the company's mortgage banking subsidiary in the early 1990s, Centex enjoyed a leap in net income in 1993, from $35 million in 1992 to $61 million. In 1994 net income had risen to $85 million on revenues of $3.2 billion.

DIVERSIFYING INTO RELATED INDUSTRY SEGMENTS

In the mid-1990s the company made several changes in its stable of subsidiaries. In 1994 Centex sold its remaining savings and loans operations. The same year, it began a joint venture that would build assisted living centers for Alzheimer's sufferers, as well as luxury homes in the United Kingdom. In 1995 the company purchased Vista Properties Inc., a $115 million acquisition that provided 3,500 acres of land in seven states to Centex for residential, commercial, and industrial development.

Centex diversified into two new industries in 1996: pest control, with the purchase of Environmental Safety Systems, and security systems, with the purchase of portions of Advanced Protection Systems. Although both acquisitions moved Centex into new areas, the company tied them into its traditional business by selling the services to its new home buyers.

Centex's expansion and diversification continued into the late 1990s. In 1998 the company purchased 80 percent of Cavco Industries, a maker and retailer of manufactured housing based in Phoenix. Cavco homes generally were priced between $60,000 and $110,000 and sold in the western United States. The $75 million deal gave Centex entry into an area of housing construction that chairman Bill Gillian characterized in *Builder* as "a profitable business with a high return on revenue and assets." Centex followed up on its move into this new industry in 1998 by purchasing AAA Homes, a retailer of manufactured homes with approximately 260

retail outlets in the United States, Japan, and Canada. Centex also planned on using the manufactured housing in its own developments rather than selling them solely to customers with their own land.

Expanding on the idea of selling housing-related products, such as security systems, to its home buyers, Centex opened two retail stores that sold a variety of products for use in the home. Dubbed Life Solutions, the stores offered products ranging from walking shoes to medical devices to foot massagers, and services ranging from delivery and installation to gift wrapping to notary service. The stores opened in suburbs of Chicago and Washington, D.C., and enjoyed very good sales their first year, according to Mike Albright, chairman and CEO of Centex Life Solutions.

REVENUES INCREASED BY HOME CONSTRUCTION BRANDS

Although Centex had diversified into several new industries in the 1990s, it remained primarily a home construction company. In 1998 it purchased Wayne Homes, a construction company that specialized in building on land owned by the homebuyer rather than a speculative developer. In 1999 Centex began selling lower-priced homes under the brand name Fox & Jacobs. At $90,000 to $134,000, the homes were targeted at first-time home buyers, although the company also saw interest from empty-nesters. In addition, the company planned to purchase the suburban operating assets of Chicago-based Sundance Homes. Centex's revenues and net income rose steadily throughout the mid- to late 1990s. By 1998 the company was earning $145 million on revenues of $3.98 billion.

In 2000 Centex posted the highest quarterly earnings in company history. Conventional homes were up 31 percent, and home building was up 29 percent overall. The average conventional home price was just over $191,000. In 2002 Timothy Eller, the president of Centex Homes, was named the new chief executive officer of Centex.

Over the next several years, Centex continued on a positive path; however the U.S. housing market began to spiral downward later in the decade. Centex was hit particularly hard. In less than a decade, company earnings fell from their highest levels ever to nearly rock bottom.

SURVIVING THE COLLAPSE OF THE HOUSING MARKET: 2006–09

In 2006, beginning with a British homebuilding unit that it sold for $290 million, Centex began selling some of its subsidiary companies in an attempt to shore up its finances. It also began a strategic review of its subprime home equity lending business and looked for other ways to weather the housing crisis. It began offering Centex Energy Advantage homes to capitalize on the eco-friendly building movement. Energy Advantage homes were 22 percent more energy efficient than a typical new home and profited from the growing demand for entry-level energy-efficient homes.

Despite these efforts, Centex stock continued to plummet over the next several years as the U.S. housing market melted down even further. For the last quarter of 2008, Centex posted a $976 million net loss. In the first quarter of 2009, Centex announced its intention to merge with Pulte Corporation. The combined company would become the nation's largest homebuilder.

While Pulte did not escape the effects of the housing downturn either, posting a $338 million net loss in the last quarter of 2008, it offered new possibilities to Centex. The combined new company would cover a broader segment of the housing market. Centex's strengths with first-time homebuyers and at the lower end of the market would be complemented by Pulte's niche with second homes and buyers looking to step up from their current housing. Through the merger, approved by the boards of both companies in 2009, Centex and Pulte anticipated a quicker recovery from the housing crisis.

Susan Salter
Updated, Susan Windisch Brown; Robert Jacobson

PRINCIPAL SUBSIDIARIES

Centex Real Estate Corp.

PRINCIPAL COMPETITORS

D. R. Horton Inc.; Lennar Corporation.

FURTHER READING

Barrett, William P., "A Tremendous Opportunity," *Forbes*, May 28, 1990, pp. 72-76.

"Builder 100," *Builder*, May 1993, p. 172.

"Centex Climbs in Chicago Market," *Professional Builder*, March 1999, p. 48.

"Centex Reports Record Fourth Quarter Results; Company Marks Fourth Consecutive Record Year," *Business Wire*, April 27, 2000, p. 0228.

"Centex Earns $85 Million in Quarter Due to One-time Tax Benefit," *Dallas Morning News*, August 4, 2009.

"Centex Energy Advantage Homes Use ENERGY STAR® Qualified Appliances from Whirlpool Corporation," April 29, 2009.

"Centex Enters Manufactured Arena," *Builder*, January 1998, pp. 15-17.

Cochran, Thomas N., "Offerings in the Offing: Centex Construction Products," *Barron's*, March 28, 1994, p. 50.

"How a Texas Outfit Builds a Good Cheap House," *Fortune*, April 1976, p. 164.

Hylton, Richard D., "Home Building Is Good for Some," *New York Times*, April 27, 1990.

"Lively's the Name," *Newsweek*, March 26, 1956.

Maynard, Roberta, "Centex Goes Retail," *Builder*, May 1998, p. 40.

"New Operating Chief Is Selected at Centex," *New York Times*, January 8, 1990.

O'Malley, Sharon, "Centex Goes Back to Basics," *Builder*, January/February 1999, p. 10.

"Pulte and Centex Merger to Create Nation's Largest Homebuilder," *Electrical Wholesaling*, May 1, 2009.

"Pulte Homes and Centex Set Meeting Date for Shareholder Vote on Merger," *Business Wire*, July 17, 2009.

"Pulte Homes Buys Centex In Stock Deal Of $1.3 Billion," *New York Times*, April 9, 2009, p. B6.

Wotapka, Dawn, "Pulte Buys Centex, Tries Branding Strategy," *Wall Street Journal,*, August 19, 2009.

Chicago Symphony Orchestra

Symphony Center
220 South Michigan Avenue, 8th Floor
Chicago, Illinois 60604-2559
U.S.A.
Telephone: (312) 294-3000
Toll Free: (800) 223-7114
Fax: (312) 294-3329
Web site: http://www.cso.org

Nonprofit Company
Founded: 1891
Employees: Not available
Sales: Not available
NAICS: 711130 Musical Groups and Artists

■ ■ ■

Together with the Cleveland Orchestra, Philadelphia Orchestra, Boston Symphony Orchestra, and New York Philharmonic, the Chicago Symphony Orchestra (CSO) is widely regarded as one of the United States' most famous orchestras. The CSO has 107 musicians, who perform 150 events per year. The orchestra routinely welcomes cellist Yo-Yo Ma, soprano Renée Fleming, violinist Itzhak Perlman, and other classical music stars, as well as young artists, as performers at Orchestra Hall or at the orchestra's summer home, Ravinia Park.

As a nonprofit institution, the CSO has two partners-in-music: the Chicago Symphony Chorus and the Civic Orchestra, which is made up of musicians in training. In 2008 the Institute for Learning, Access and Training was formed by the CSO to bring musical performance and appreciation to young people in Illinois and beyond.

19TH-CENTURY ORIGINS

The CSO's origins date back to 1890, when Chicago could look back on 50 years as the fastest-growing city in the United States. The city had a booming economy, a fledgling art institute, and a university preparing to welcome its first students. At the time, however, the cultural community lacked an orchestra, so businessman Charles Fay persuaded seasoned conductor Theodore Thomas to come to Chicago and start the Chicago Orchestra.

In December 1890 Fay and Thomas tapped some of Chicago's business leaders to form the Orchestral Association whose goal was to organize an orchestra for the city. The association got off to a brisk start by giving Thomas a three-year contract as music director at a generous salary of $15,000 per year. Thomas was given the responsibility of choosing both the best music and the best 86 musicians he could find anywhere. He was allowed to set pay schedules for the 28-week, 108-concert season, which at $30 a week was considered generous for the time. Musicians were paid $6 for each additional concert played. Subscription ticket prices ranged from $10 to $30 for evening concerts and $10 to $20 for matinees, with boxes seating five people priced at $200 for evenings and $150 for matinees.

The first concert took place on October 17, 1891, at the city's beautiful Auditorium Theater. The program was substantial, featuring the overture to Richard Wag-

COMPANY PERSPECTIVES

The central mission of the Chicago Symphony Orchestra Association is to present classical music through the Chicago Symphony Orchestra to Chicago, national and international audiences. The mission is supported by four mutually reinforcing elements: artistic excellence; audience development; education, and financial stability.

ner's *Faust* and Ludwig van Beethoven's Fifth Symphony before intermission, which was followed by Pyotr Tchaikovsky's First Piano Concerto and the overture of Antonín Dvořák's *Husitska*. The concert, the ambitious program, and especially the piano soloist—who was not a Chicagoan—were highly criticized by the musically unsophisticated audience. Thomas's conducting was also considered to be "too safe and conventional." The displeasure with Thomas continued, particularly because his music choices were often too heavy for the developing audience. There were also problems with the acoustics in the Auditorium Theater. A large number of seats often remained empty unless a great soloist was featured. Wealthy subscribers who were supporting the developing orchestra were offended, and they stayed away from the concerts.

Despite these difficulties, Thomas introduced audiences to the music of Wagner and Richard Strauss, and such historic composers as Henry Purcell and Jean-Philippe Rameau. Thomas, however, had a tendency to insist on providing what he thought audiences should hear, which included soaring Beethoven symphonies played on hot summer afternoons.

LEARNING CURVE

The director quickly learned from the mistakes made in the first season and adjusted the selection of music and musicians to appeal to the CSO's audience. The pianist Ignacy Jan Paderewski played to sold-out houses, but the second season finished with a deficit of more than $53,000. The Orchestral Association's efforts to remedy the situation by increasing the number of associate members of their organization was only partly successful.

In April 1896, in the midst of an economic downturn, the orchestra agreed unenthusiastically to play for its own fund-raiser, a costume ball. The publication of the prior year's donations was

instrumental in raising the subscription level from $38,767 in 1895 to $57,000 in 1896.

The orchestra went on tour to Boston and New York in January 1897. Thomas had toured with the orchestra before, usually eliciting grumbles about an orchestra in need of refinement and a conductor in need of warmth. Applause was generous during this tour but the trip was destined to be remembered for a serious train accident east of Buffalo, New York. Although no one was hurt, many irreplaceable instruments were destroyed.

By 1898 the CSO's reputation had improved but ticket sales remained low. A fund-raising dinner in November of that year added $47,500 to previous contributions, bringing the total amount received in donations from 1890 to 1898 to more than $255,000.

A CHICAGO LANDMARK IS BORN

As the 19th century drew to a close, the CSO still did not have a permanent home. In February 1903 fundraising for this purpose began with a letter in the newspapers from the Orchestral Association trustees explaining the need for an orchestral hall. The letter announced a fund-raising goal of $750,000, $450,000 of which was needed for the lot on Michigan Avenue and an additional $300,000 to build a hall that would seat 2,500 people. Personal letters of appeal were sent to subscribers, and Thomas gave press interviews and speeches. By March 1904, $650,000 had been raised and the trustees were confident that the rest would be raised over the following year.

The building that would house the CSO was designed by Daniel Burnham, the architect who had designed Burnham Park, the beautiful stretch of green park that lines miles of the Chicago shore of Lake Michigan. Burnham kept his façade simple but designed the interior according to the acoustic requirements outlined by Thomas. "Walls and ceiling should be connected by a continuous curve which will allow the sound waves to move unhindered," according to Thomas's instructions, as quoted in the *Memoirs of Theodore Thomas* by Rose Fay Thomas.

The hall that came to enchant millions of concertgoers opened its doors for the first performance of the CSO on December 14, 1904. The evening was a triumph, but Thomas, the man who had inspired it, had caught a cold that became pneumonia and died three weeks later.

FREDERICK STOCK, THE INNOVATOR: 1904–42

Thomas was succeeded by Frederick Stock, a young German musician Thomas had brought to the CSO to

KEY DATES

∎

1891: Chicago Symphony Orchestra (CSO) is founded with Theodore Thomas as first director.

1916: Orchestra makes its first recording under director Frederick Stock.

1953: Fritz Reiner takes over as music director.

1957: Chicago Symphony Chorus is established.

1969: Sir Georg Solti becomes music director.

1971: CSO makes its first European tour.

1991: Daniel Barenboim is named music director.

2006: Barenboim is succeeded by principal conductor Bernard Haitink.

2008: CSO announces Riccardo Muti will become music director in 2010; Institute for Learning, Access and Training is launched as an educational arm of the CSO.

strengthen the viola section. Stock had displayed leadership qualities that resulted in the younger man becoming Thomas's assistant conductor in 1899. Stock stepped into the role of music director after Thomas's death. The young German instituted many firsts for the orchestra, including a pension fund for musicians, concerts at Ravinia Park in 1905, and a recording in 1916 that featured the "Incidental Music" from Felix Mendelssohn's *A Midsummer Night's Dream*.

In 1919 Stock started to hold youth auditions and organized the Civic Orchestra to train musicians. Stock's audiences were slightly more sophisticated, and as a lover of modern music, he introduced them to the works of Gustav Mahler and Igor Stravinsky, whose Symphony in C he would later commission for the orchestra's 50th anniversary. Audiences and CSO supporters felt great sorrow when Stock died following a heart attack in 1942.

CONDUCTOR TURNOVERS: 1943–53

The following decade proved to be an unstable time for the CSO. It began with Belgian-born Désiré Defauw as director. He was considered charming initially and was welcomed at a luncheon for sustaining members held at Chicago's historic Palmer House Hotel on April 16, 1943. Defauw described the CSO as "a Stradivarius," enchanting luncheon guests, who were persuaded to add liberally to the CSO's coffers, which reached about $39,000 out of a targeted $50,000.

Nevertheless, Defauw's remark about the quality of the orchestra came back to haunt him, because it supplied ammunition to the *Chicago Tribune*'s music critic, Claudia Cassidy. Defauw's first concert had not impressed Cassidy, who described it in her review on April 18, 1943, as "music the orchestra could have played in their sleep." She continued a stinging commentary, writing, "Mr. Defauw has described our orchestra as a Stradivarius. ... Such an instrument is useless without a master hand to give it life." Her scathing review was an unfortunate prophecy of things to come because Defauw was gone as soon as his contract expired.

The next conductor fared no better than Defauw. Although Artur Rodziński was a prominent conductor who had led such orchestras as the Cleveland Orchestra and the New York Philharmonic, he was not in agreement with the behind-the-scenes management of the orchestra. He was summarily fired after a year.

Rafael Kubelík, the next director, lasted through his three-year contract but alienated conservative Chicago music lovers by insisting on programs of modern music. Kubelík earned Cassidy's kiss of death—"mediocrity." Nevertheless, thanks to improvements in recording technology, Kubelík left a worthwhile legacy of an unforgettable recording of the CSO's performance of Modest Petrovich Mussorgsky's *Pictures at an Exhibition*, which was paired with Bedřich Smetana's *Má vlast*.

THE LEGENDARY FRITZ REINER

By the early 1950s it was obvious that it was time for someone to take charge. Fritz Reiner, who was named director in the fall of 1953, was exceedingly well known as a martinet. At Reiner's first rehearsal he fired a musician, telling him, "I don't accept that kind of playing in my orchestra," as quoted in the biography *Fritz Reiner* by Philip Hart. Paying strict attention to sound, to phrasing, and especially to interpretation, he added polish to the CSO. In addition, Reiner founded the Chicago Symphony Chorus in 1957, which he placed under the direction of Margaret Hillis, while keeping a strict eye on its progress. Under Reiner the CSO made many spectacular recordings for RCA Victor at the dawn of the stereo era, including Strauss's *Ein Heldenleben* and works by Mahler. Many critics consider these recordings to continue to be the finest interpretations of the music.

Not everything was rosy, however, even with Reiner. As Hart noted in his biography, when Reiner arrived in 1953 the Orchestral Association boasted assets of more than $8 million. A large proportion of this came from the building, whose office space and rehearsal studios made it essentially rent free. This made the Orchestral Association one of the most affluent in the country. Nonetheless, fund-raising remained a necessity, and Reiner's cooperation was required. The director's intense desire for privacy, however, kept him from the public contact necessary for fund-raising. The result was that only about 1,600 contributors to the orchestra remained, leaving the trustees to rely on endowments to offset the ticket sales, which, although they covered more than half the orchestra's expenses, needed supplementing.

When Reiner left Chicago in 1962, he was succeeded by Jean Martinon, who had a tough act to follow and left after five years. The financial issues remained, however, and became public in 1968 when the CSO's trustees went to the business community for help. According to *Chicago Tribune* reporter William Clark, the Orchestral Association was seeking $500,000 per year for the following five years, an increase from the $85,000 requested a season earlier. The association asked for an additional $525,000 from trustees, the Women's Board, and subscribers. Another urgent new goal was the capital fund drive for $10 million. Operating expenses for the 1967-68 season were recorded at $700,000.

In addition to the financial deficit, discord among members of the association's administration was reported. There was also a lack of cohesion in the orchestra itself. The CSO needed a firm, new hand at the end of the 1960s.

MUSICAL MAGIC WITH SIR GEORG SOLTI: 1969–91

The CSO found the needed leadership when Sir Georg Solti walked onto the podium in 1969. Like Reiner, Solti was a disciple of the Hungarian musical tradition. He always described his arrival in Chicago as "love at first sight," and the romance never ended. His first concert, a Thanksgiving offering on November 28, 1969, galvanized music critic Thomas Willis who said, "Georg Solti began his tenure as the eighth musical director in a festive and highly auspicious manner which should give cause for joy to everyone concerned for the ensemble's future."

In contrast to Reiner, who had suffered from heart trouble and therefore did not undertake strenuous overseas tours, Solti toured enthusiastically with the CSO, enhancing their reputation wherever they played. In 1971 Chicago Mayor Richard Daley gave the CSO $100,000 toward expenses for a successful tour of 10 European cities. When the orchestra returned to Chicago at the end of the tour, they were welcomed with a ticker-tape parade.

Concert tickets were difficult to buy unless they were purchased in advance of a performance, and it was not easy to find seats in the covered pavilion when the orchestra played at its summer home, Ravinia Park. It was always easy, however, to choose a recording of one or more of the CSO's vast repertoire of classical music, ranging from Baroque composers such as Joseph Haydn, to an entire cycle of nine Beethoven symphonies, to Dvořák and Wagner operas, to such modern classical music icons as Strauss and Stravinsky. This success brought handsome rewards to the CSO, to Solti, and to the orchestra's recording company, Decca Records. Solti won a total of 31 Grammy Awards, and there was a satisfying increase to the orchestra's financial statement. According to *Time* magazine, annual donations rose from $425,919 in 1968 to $1,607,846 in 1972, when the Orchestral Association achieved its corporate goal of $500,000. The endowment fund also increased, reaching $7 million.

Although Solti retired in 1991, he came back often. He died in 1997 at age 84, just before he was due to direct his 1,000th performance with his beloved CSO.

THE BARENBOIM YEARS: 1991–2006

Solti was succeeded by Daniel Barenboim, who was to stay in the post until 2006. This was not Barenboim's first experience with the CSO. Beginning in 1970 he had conducted the orchestra several times, and had started his career as conductor-designate in 1989. He had also played with the CSO as one of the world's most famous pianists.

In his 2002 autobiography *A Life in Music*, Barenboim remarked on the difficulty of following a legend such as Solti. Barenboim not only wanted to preserve the clarity and sound that had made the CSO famous but he also wanted to put his own stamp on it. The desire for originality won. He moved the players from their accustomed seating plans and used his own interpretations for orchestral scores. Barenboim also took the CSO on 21 international tours, on which they delighted audiences. Full houses were a feature of concerts led by Barenboim, who adapted to the style of almost any artist, providing a steady and reassuring presence when his soloist seemed inexperienced or nervous.

By the 1990s Orchestra Hall needed extensive renovation to meet modern acoustical standards, both for live concerts and for the recording sessions that often took place simultaneously. The trustees approved renovations in 1993, setting aside $110 million for the purpose. Symphony Center opened in October 1997, featuring a rotunda, expanded rehearsal space, and cutting-edge acoustics.

An individual to the last, Barenboim left Chicago in 2006 and moved to Berlin, Germany. His extensive recordings, including operas, symphonies, concertos, and chamber works, rank with the finest ever produced, whether he is featured as a conductor, a pianist or, as is often the case, conducting from the keyboard. He was succeeded at the CSO by Bernard Haitink as principal conductor.

MOVING FORWARD IN THE 21ST CENTURY

In 2008 the CSO announced that Haitink would be succeeded by Riccardo Muti, who would become the music director in 2010. For the fiscal year ended June 30, 2008, overall ticket sales topped $20 million, the association raised $19.6 million, there was a surplus of $232,000, and overall revenues reached $61.5 million. The CSO reported more than 31,000 subscribers, and more than half a million music lovers attended concerts.

Gillian Wolf

PRINCIPAL DIVISIONS

Civic Orchestra of Chicago; Chicago Symphony Chorus.

FURTHER READING

Barenboim, Daniel, *A Life in Music*, New York: Arcade, 2002.

Cassidy, Claudia, "Désiré Defauw Assumes Baton of Symphony: Makes Debut at Second Rate Concert," *Chicago Tribune*, April 18, 1943.

Clark, William, "Help from Business Asked by Symphony," *Chicago Tribune*, February 20, 1969.

Furlong, William Barry, *Season with Solti: A Year in the Life of the Chicago Symphony*, New York: Macmillan, 1974.

Hart, Philip, *Fritz Reiner: A Biography*, Evanston, IL: Northwestern University Press, 1994.

Schabas, Ezra, *Theodore Thomas: America's Conductor and Builder of Orchestras, 1835–1905*, Urbana: University of Illinois Press, 1989.

"Solti and Chicago: A Musical Romance," *Time*, May 7, 1973.

Thomas, Rose Fay, *Memoirs of Theodore Thomas*, New York: Moffat, Yard, 1911.

Willis, Thomas, "A Festive Beginning for Solti," *Chicago Tribune*, November 28, 1969, p. B5.

Chicken of the Sea International

9330 Scranton Road, Suite 500
San Diego, California 92121-7706
U.S.A.
Telephone: (619) 558-9662
Fax: (858) 597-4782
Web site: http://www.chickenofthesea.com

Wholly Owned Subsidiary of Thai Union International, Inc.
Founded: 1914 as Van Camp Seafood Company, Inc.
Employees: 360
Sales: $400 million (2005 est.)
NAICS: 311711 Seafood Canning

■ ■ ■

Chicken of the Sea International is one of the world's leading canned seafood companies. The company specializes in tuna products but also markets more than a dozen other varieties of fish and shellfish products, including canned salmon, crabmeat, shrimp, mackerel, and oysters.

VAN CAMP SEAFOOD, 1914–75

Van Camp Seafood Company was founded in 1914 when Frank Van Camp and his son, Gilbert, bought the California Tunny Canning Company to can albacore. The company attained widespread recognition in the late 1950s with the creation of the famous commercial jingle: "Ask any mermaid you happen to see, what's the best tuna? Chicken of the Sea." The mermaid the company adopted as its mascot at that time became a food industry icon, along with the Pillsbury Doughboy and the Green Giant. In 1963 Van Camp was sold to Missouri-based Ralston Purina, known primarily as a producer of processed foods, pet food, and livestock and poultry feeds.

Tuna processing begins on the boat, where fresh-caught tuna is frozen in brine at temperatures as low as 10 degrees Fahrenheit. Once at the cannery, the tuna is thawed, which takes one to two hours. Next it is butchered and gutted, with the entrails ground up to make organic fertilizer. The butchered fish is steam cooked and then cooled. In the packing room the head, tail, fins, skin, and bones are removed, as is the red meat. The red meat is used to manufacture pet food, while the bony parts are ground up to make fish meal, animal feed, and fertilizer. What remains is a loin, or large, dressed piece of tuna, and flakes of tuna that have come off in the cleaning process. They are packed by an automatic filling machine into cans. The loin portions are used to pack chunk, or solid, tuna, while the flakes are used for lower grades of canned tuna. Salt and water or oil are added to the can. The can is sealed with lids in a vacuum process, then washed. The tuna is pasteurized and the can is heated with steam to kill bacteria, giving the can a shelf life of about five years. Finally, the cooled can is labeled and shipped.

During the three decades following World War II, southern California was the world center for tuna, albacore, and bluefin processing and canning. By 1975 the U.S. Tuna Foundation, Van Camp Seafood, Bumble Bee Seafoods, Pan Pacific Fisheries, Mitsubishi Foods, and others maintained as many as 16 bustling canneries

COMPANY PERSPECTIVES

Chicken of the Sea is focused on promoting health, nutrition and convenience, and is dedicated to providing consumers with affordable shelf-stable seafood products that taste great and help improve health.

Providing consumers these three values—health, nutrition and convenience—are the company's hallmarks and standards by which Chicken of the Sea ensures confidence among consumers.

employing more than 10,000 workers, while tuna sandwiches, tuna salads, and tuna casseroles had become commonplace throughout the United States. By 1976 Van Camp Seafood was operating canneries in San Diego and Terminal Island, California; American Samoa (in the South Pacific); and Ponce, Puerto Rico.

LEAVING THE WEST COAST, 1980S

In 1984 Ralston Purina closed Van Camp's San Diego facilities, moving its operations to American Samoa to access a less expensive labor pool and one of the richest fishing grounds in the world. Ralston Purina also moved Van Camp's main offices to St. Louis, Missouri. Four years later a group of private investors from Indonesia, called P. T. Mantrust Corporation, purchased Van Camp from Ralston Purina in a highly leveraged transaction. The new owners planned to ally their fishing fleet and canning operation in Indonesia with Van Camp's American Samoa cannery and brand name for a fully integrated approach to supplying canned tuna to the United States. However, P. T. Mantrust experienced cash flow difficulties due to high interest rates in Indonesia and its highly leveraged financing, and the company's primary creditor, the Prudential Life Insurance Company of America, became the majority owner of Van Camp's.

BOYCOTT FOR DOLPHINS, EARLY 1990S

In April 1990 the tuna industry was faced with a growing consumer boycott of canned tuna products when the public was made aware that more than 100,000 dolphins died each year when they were caught by purse-seine methods, in which fishermen cast a large net around a school of tuna and then pull it taut like the drawstring of a purse. In response, the three largest sell-

ers of canned tuna in the United States resolved that they would no longer sell tuna caught by methods harmful to dolphins. Star-Kist, the world's largest tuna canner at the time, led the way, followed by the two other major canners, Bumble Bee Seafoods and Van Camp Seafood. In October of that year, Van Camp Seafood moved its corporate headquarters and 115-member staff from St. Louis back to its home city of San Diego.

By the mid-1990s most tuna operations in the United States had been shuttered. In 1995 Pan Pacific Fisheries filed for bankruptcy, leaving nearly 700 people without jobs and closing the last full-service tuna processing plant in the continental United States. However, in 1996 Tri-Marine International bought the former Pan Pacific Fisheries plant, reopening the cannery in June of that year under the name Tri-Union Seafoods and putting a U.S. canning facility back in business. Tri-Union rehired nearly 300 of the former Pan Pacific workers, and another 400 workers were hired a few months later when the renovations were completed. Meanwhile, the consumer research group Leo J. Shapiro & Associates listed the Chicken of the Sea brand name as one of the top 10 consumer brands of packaged goods in the United States.

NEW OWNERS, NEW NAME, LATE 1990S

In October 1997, Tri-Union Seafoods purchased Van Camp for $97 million. Van Camp's name was changed to Chicken of the Sea International, in part to help avoid confusion with the St. Louis-based Van de Kamp's. Although best known for their pork and beans, Van de Kamp's also manufactured a line of frozen breaded fish sticks. Chicken of the Sea International, under its new leadership, began aggressive marketing of its products in retail, food service, and club stores. The company also began a campaign to increase sales of its non-tuna canned products, such as shrimp, crab, clams, oysters, and sardines, which made up only 20 percent of the business. The new owners allowed the Chicken of the Sea main offices to remain in San Diego.

By 1998 the company was the Port of San Diego's largest container customer, importing more than 700,000 cases of canned-food products every month and sorting them at Chicken of the Sea's 100,000-square-foot central warehouse. The company was looking beyond its main markets in the United States and Israel to the Pacific Rim for expansion.

At the same time, the tuna industry as a whole began to acknowledge the need for advertising to promote tuna products, which had suffered a worldwide

KEY DATES

1914: Frank Van Camp and son Gilbert buy the California Tunny Canning Company, which cans albacore tuna.

1950s: Company develops the famous Chicken of the Sea jingle: "Ask any mermaid you happen to see, what's the best tuna? Chicken of the Sea."

1963: Van Camp Seafood is sold to Ralston Purina.

1984: Ralston Purina closes Van Camp's San Diego facilities, moving all canning operations to American Samoa.

1988: P. T. Mantrust, an Indonesian private investment group, buys Van Camp from Ralston Purina.

1990: Tuna industry suffers global downturn as consumers become aware of the huge number of dolphins accidentally killed by tuna fisheries.

1997: Van Camp is purchased by a group of Thai companies under the name Tri-Union Seafoods; Tri-Union changes Van Camp's name to Chicken of the Sea.

2009: Chicken of the Sea announces the return of tuna canning to the United States, in Lyons, Georgia.

sales downturn. Chicken of the Sea responded by investing $7 million in a series of new television commercials, the company's first in seven years. The first spot, which appeared in time for the year-end holidays, promoted "Chicken of the Sea-son," a recipe for tuna dip, and a free snowman mold with every purchase. The national ads featured the "Ask any mermaid" jingle, which, according to Don George, senior vice president of marketing, as quoted in *Brandweek*, "still has a lot of equity with consumers," Chicken of the Sea ended that year ranking third in the canned tuna category after StarKist and Bumble Bee, which also mounted invigorated ad campaigns.

The company increased its processing capacity, allowing Chicken of the Sea to become a strategic partner to other companies by offering private label brands to selected customers as well as offering complete canned seafood selections (both branded and private label) to retail, foodservice, club store, mass merchandiser, and pharmaceutical trade customers. Chicken of the Sea also

produced high grade, "gourmet-quality" canned cat food for U.S. and export markets.

NEW PRODUCTS, NEW MEDIA, 2000S

In 2000 two of the three investment partners in Tri-Union Seafoods, Tri-Marine International and Edmund Gann, sold their 50 percent interest in Chicken of the Sea to the third partner, Thai Union International, for $38.5 million, making Thai Union the sole owner of Chicken of the Sea. In 2001 the company closed the last fish cannery based in the United States, located on Terminal Island in Los Angeles harbor, citing labor costs. In 2002 sales stood at $445 million. The following year Chicken of the Sea acquired Empress International, an importer of frozen shrimp and other shellfish, with annual sales of $260 million.

In the popular media Chicken of the Sea received an unexpected publicity boost in 2003 when Jessica Simpson and Nick Lachey had a dialogue about the product on the MTV show *Newlyweds: Nick and Jessica*. In the show, Jessica claims to be unaware that Chicken of the Sea is actually not chicken, but tuna. Nick, incredulous, sets her straight. This exchange received so much media attention that Don George parlayed it into a publicity extravaganza by inviting Simpson to appear at the company's annual sales meeting, where Simpson sang the Chicken of the Sea theme song "Ask Any Mermaid" and autographed tuna cans for employees. George then widely distributed videos of this sales meeting, which were aired by 750 prime time stations and 10 national TV shows. The company claims that video of this event reached 38 million viewers.

In 2006 Thai Union formed a new division, Chicken of the Sea Frozen Foods, intended to promote sales of premium frozen seafood products. This division expanded rapidly, increasing the brand's visibility with consumers as well as its distribution capabilities to the food service and retail industries.

The years 2002 to 2008 were notable for Chicken of the Sea due to the wide array of new products the company brought onto the consumer market. The year 2002 saw the introduction of boneless and skinless salmon in 7-ounce pouches, which Chicken of the Sea was the first company to produce. In 2004 the company announced smoked Pacific salmon, a wood-smoked filet sold in a ready-to-eat pouch. The year 2006 saw the debut of 2.8-ounce peel-and-eat cups of chunk tuna and salmon, in response to consumer demand for portion-controlled single meals. In 2007 the company began to offer several new varieties of Italian-style tuna and salmon, and in 2008 it introduced Healthy Selections tuna pouches. Also that year, the company partnered with an organization called Feeding America to distribute seafood to charities and educate the public about seafood's health benefits.

In 2009 the company mounted another TV-based publicity campaign partnering with the NBC program "Celebrity Apprentice." Contestants were asked to complete one of three marketing tasks: 1) Create a new product concept; 2) Design a promotion for Chicken of the Sea's Healthy Selections or its pink salmon, albacore, and light tuna cups; or 3) Outline a viral campaign to be carried out on a social network. The contest was won by a California advertising student named Benjamin Hernandez, who created a character called Tommy Tuna. In a 90-second promotional video, Tommy Tuna shares important facts about Chicken of the Sea products with people he encounters at supermarkets or on the street. Chicken of the Sea's senior vice president of sales and marketing, John Sawyer, said Hernandez' entry was chosen because it "creatively communicated our key attributes, including health, nutrition, convenience and the importance of eating seafood twice a week." A spokesperson for Chicken of the Sea maintains that this was the most-viewed episode of the season.

In May 2009 Chicken of the Sea made the announcement that it would bring tuna canning back to the United States by opening a canning plant in Lyons, Georgia. The company planned to spend $20 million to open the new facility by October 2009 and create 200 new jobs.

Daryl F. Mallett
Updated, *Melanie Bush*

PRINCIPAL OPERATING UNITS

Chicken of the Sea International; Chicken of the Sea Frozen Foods.

PRINCIPAL COMPETITORS

StarKist Foods Inc.; Bumble Bee Seafoods, L.L.C.

FURTHER READING

"Chicken of the Sea to Open Ga. Plant," *Atlanta Business Chronicle*, May 4, 2009.

Green, Frank, "Global Factors Shrivel San Diego's Tuna-Processing Business," *Knight-Ridder/Tribune Business News*, August 2, 1994.

Siedsma, Andrea, "Chicken of the Sea Rises from the Depths," *San Diego Business Journal*, October 20, 1997, p. 1.

Stevens-Huffman, Leslie, "Food & Beverage Tunaround Artist," *Smart Business San Diego*, November 2006.

Thompson, Stephanie, "Chicken of the Sea Returns to TV," *Brandweek*, June 1, 1998, p. 6.

"Thai Companies to Buy Chicken of the Sea," *New York Times*, July 17, 1992, p. C3(N)/D3(L).

"Tri-Union Adds VP Position," *Supermarket News*, January 20, 1997, p. 48.

"Tuna without the Guilt: Canners Aim to Make the Seas Safer for Cetaceans," *Time*, April 23, 1990, p. 63.

Utumporn, Pichayaporn, "Thai Exporters Ride Tide," *Asian Wall Street Journal*, February 9, 1998, p. 20.

"Van Camp Becomes Chicken of the Sea," *Nation's Restaurant News*, August 25, 1997, p. 43.

"Van Camp Moves Its Staff Back to San Diego," *San Diego Business Journal*, October 1, 1990, p. 16.

"Van Camp Unveils Corporate Restructuring," *Nation's Restaurant News*, December 21, 1992, p. 90.

Wong, Art, "Tuna Cannery Makes Comeback on Southern California's Terminal Island," *Knight-Ridder/Tribune Business News*, July 29, 1996, p. 7290274.

ChildFund International

2821 Emerywood Parkway
Richmond, Virginia 23294
U.S.A.
Telephone: (804) 756-2700
Toll Free: (800) 776-6767
Web site: http://www.childfund.org/

Nonprofit Company
Founded: 1938
Employees: 610 in United States; approximately 1,500 worldwide
Revenues: $137 million

∎ ∎ ∎

ChildFund International is an international child development organization that provides food, clothing, medical care, and educational opportunities to deprived, excluded, and vulnerable children of all races and creeds. It seeks to address the root causes of poverty, improve nutrition and sanitation, generate family income, and enhance early childhood development. ChildFund International provides emergency response and assistance in case of natural disasters and seeks to alleviate any exploitation of children, for example, as child soldiers. Previously known as the Christian Children's Fund, ChildFund International accomplishes its work using the donations of individual sponsors who maintain personal contact with the child or children they are sponsoring. It works with affiliated organizations around the world and is a member of the NGO Committee on UNICEF.

THE EARLY YEARS

In 1938 J. Calvitt Clarke—a Presbyterian minister who had assisted other aid organizations during and after World War I—wanted to find a way to help feed and house Chinese children who had been orphaned during China's war with Japan, which had begun in 1937. Clarke began by launching a fund-raising appeal from his hometown of Richmond, Virginia. The first donations he received, $2,000 and $13,000 each, allowed support of a school and an orphanage. Clarke believed that the most effective way to continue securing funding would be to have each U.S. contributor sponsor a single orphaned child in China. This successful effort eventually grew into the China Children's Fund (CCF). By 1945 more than $372,000 in donations was reaching China annually.

At the end of World War II, the CCF expanded its outreach and humanitarian efforts beyond China to assist children in other Asian countries. By 1946 the CCF was supporting children in Burma and the Philippines. Missionaries affiliated with the CCF continued expansion efforts into northern China, Korea, Japan, Malaysia, Borneo, India, and Indonesia. Following the success of these efforts, the CCF turned its attention to children vulnerable to disease and poverty in postwar Europe, beginning with children in Belgium, Finland, France, Germany, Italy, Spain, and several other European countries.

Beginning in the 1950s children living in poverty in Syria, Lebanon, and the Palestine began receiving assistance from the CCF. To better reflect its growing international reach, the China Children's Fund changed

COMPANY PERSPECTIVES

∎

ChildFund International is one of the most respected child development organizations in the world. We are a non-sectarian charitable organization dedicated to serving the needs of children worldwide. Our work is inspired and driven by the potential inherent in children; the potential not only to survive, but to thrive and become leaders capable of bringing positive change. We focus on childhood as the one window of opportunity to physical, cognitive, psychological, emotional, and social development. We work to reduce the roots of poverty by working directly with local communities, where we implement child development, child protection, and emergency response and assistance programs. In each community we serve, we make a 12- to 15-year commitment to children living there. ChildFund International works in 31 countries, including the United States, and assists approximately 15.2 million children and their family members, regardless of race, creed, or gender. Our mission is to promote societies where individuals and institutions participate in valuing, protecting, and advancing the worth and the rights of children.

its name to the Christian Children's Fund in 1951. The first CCF international affiliate, the Christian Children's Fund of Canada, was established in 1960.

THE CCF IN THE 1950S AND 1960S

During the 1950s and 1960s the CCF's annual budget grew to $4.5 million, and it served children in more than 50 countries. In 1960 the CCF broadened its activities to include family assistance and community and early childhood development programs. This expansion was prompted in part by Korean authorities who expressed concern that parents were abandoning their children to the care of CCF orphanages, where they received superior care and educational opportunities. In response to these concerns, the CCF established Family Helper projects and Community Adviser programs to assist families in their own homes and communities. The CCF began to regard poverty to be as great an enemy to the well-being of children as war. Work with Family Helper projects and Community Adviser programs continued when the CCF began assisting children in Latin America.

By 1967 the CCF had gained on-the-ground experience in 56 countries. Based on this experience, it began implementing an important policy change. Whenever possible the CCF would use local personnel to develop and lead programs in their community. This policy used the expertise of local people and their greater familiarity with traditional customs and the challenges faced by children in their community.

THE CCF IN THE 1970S AND 1980S

Several developments in the 1970s signaled the CCF's intention to broaden its efforts and increase its visibility. The CCF left Europe and the Middle East, but expanded its activities to Africa, where it began work with children in Nairobi, Kenya. The CCF's African efforts expanded to countries throughout the continent, and included emergency responses to famine and drought.

During this period the CCF adopted an official Code of Fund-raising Ethics that exemplified its strict adherence to principles of honesty, accountability, integrity, and financial stewardship. This code was still in effect as of mid-2009. Throughout the 1970s and 1980s the CCF gradually stopped including Christian education or religious teachings in its program efforts. However, it continued its established practice of welcoming people of all faiths as sponsored children, parents, donors, and employees.

By the mid-1980s the CCF sponsored more than 325,000 children worldwide. Affiliated organizations were established in Denmark, Germany, Great Britain, and Australia. In 1987 the CCF received the Presidential End Hunger Award from the U.S. Agency for International Development.

THE CCF IN THE 1990S

To address the needs of children in particularly desperate circumstances during times of civil unrest, war, and natural disaster, the CCF created the ChildAlert program in the 1990s. This special fund was set aside to allow emergency response teams to offer children immediate assistance and to provide opportunities for long-term psychosocial recovery.

As the CCF's outreach and visibility increased, its administrators wanted to find a way to be more accountable to their donors, as well as give the communities where they were active a tool to assess how well the CCF's programs were working and whether they were having a positive impact. In 1995 the CCF began work on an evaluation system that would help it accomplish both of these goals. The Annual Impact Evaluation

KEY DATES

1938: The China Children's Fund is founded by J. Calvitt Clarke to assist children displaced and orphaned by China's war with Japan.

1945: The China Children's Fund expands its efforts to other Asian countries and parts of Europe following the end of World War II.

1951: The China Children's Fund changes its name to the Christian Children's Fund (CCF).

1960: The Christian Children's Fund of Canada is established.

1960: The CCF establishes Family Helper projects and Community Adviser programs.

1987: The CCF receives the Presidential End Hunger Award from the U.S. Agency for International Development.

1995: The CCF develops the Annual Impact Evaluation System to assess impact and effectiveness of programs.

1999: The CCF establishes Child Centered Spaces to offer children opportunities for recovery and healing following trauma, war, or natural disaster.

2000: The CCF establishes the Grants Unit to focus on seeking grant funding.

2002: The CCF institutes study tours for donors to visit countries where CCF is active.

2009: The CCF changes its name to ChildFund International.

System emerged out of discussions among program managers, CCF administrators, representatives of sponsored services, and other interested parties. Using information collected by program staff and volunteers in the communities where the CCF was active, the system measured impacts rather than activities and gauged each program's effect on children in terms of broadly defined health and education outcomes. It tracked progress made on indicators such as infant and childhood mortality, management of respiratory and other infections, sanitation practices, and adult literacy. The system did not prescribe any strategies for programs, nor did it limit the kinds of programs a community could use to promote child welfare. However, communities could use the information to set priorities, allocate resources, and take follow-up actions.

In 1999 the CCF established the Child Centered Spaces program. The program allows children affected by war the opportunity to recover, learn, play, and heal in peaceful surroundings. The program sought to restore children's hope for the future and facilitate a return to "normal" in an uncertain world. The first Child Centered Space was established in East Timor following civil strife and widespread destruction.

THE CCF IN THE 21ST CENTURY

In 2000 the CCF established the Grants Unit to seek out grant funding that could help it expand its efforts on behalf of children, families, and communities. By 2009 grant funding to the CCF had increased sevenfold.

Between 2001 and 2002 the CCF put together an exhibit of over 100 special toys made by sponsored children. The exhibit originated with a visit by the CCF President John F. Schultz to Kenya, where five-year-old Thomas Akimat Ekirua presented him with the gift of a sailboat made from a scrap of sandal and a plastic bag. At the suggestion of Schultz, CCF workers from Africa, Latin America, and Asia sent examples of toys children had made from normally discarded materials. Schultz believed that examples of such toys might make the lives of children in developing countries more understandable to others. The children used materials such as pesticide cans; oil barrels; scraps of wire, wood, and cloth; bottle caps; and plastic bags. With these they produced a wide assortment of toys, including toy motorbikes, airplanes, and cars; soccer balls and baseballs; and musical instruments. The collection, titled "Not Sold in Stores," was shown at the headquarters of the United Nations in New York and at the National Geographic Explorers Hall in Washington, D.C.

In 2002 the CCF began organizing two to three study tours a year to countries and communities where it was active. Open to current and prospective donors, the 7- to 12-day tours provided an opportunity for donors to meet firsthand with their sponsored child, with whom they had developed a relationship through letter writing. The majority of time, however, was devoted to learning about the specific country's culture, history, music, and customs.

In July 2009 the CCF officially changed its name to ChildFund International. The change coincided with the CCF's 70th anniversary and efforts to broaden its appeal and outreach. Along with the name change, ChildFund International increased its visibility worldwide by offering blogs and participating in social networking sites. According to Mark Hrywna of the *NonProfit Times*, Cheri Dahl, the vice president for international communication and fund-raising, said, "We want to engage people in many different ways. Right now it's a communications strategy, to keep people informed about the work we're doing."

The name change also coincided with efforts to emphasize programs that reflected the CCF's three-stage approach to aiding healthy child development. Each stage represented one part of a child's journey from birth to young adulthood: (1) develop healthy and secure infants; (2) develop educated and confident children; and (3) develop skilled and involved youth. Joe Macenka of the *Richmond Times-Dispatch* noted that Anne Lynam Goddard, the president and chief executive officer of ChildFund International, said in a press release, "Our strategy allows children to get healthy, to get smart and to change their world."

The name change also allowed ChildFund International to be recognized as one of 12 affiliated organizations around the world known as the ChildFund Alliance. Each affiliated organization grew and developed along with ChildFund International, adopted its model, and adhered to its rigorous standards in program governance, fund-raising, and financial management. The alliance provided a global presence that could help address the challenges that children will face in the 21st century, including global pandemics, ongoing regional conflicts, escalating poverty, and major natural disasters. The other members of the ChildFund Alliance were Barnfonden (Sweden), BORNEfonden (Denmark), CCF Kinderhilfswerk (Germany), ChildFund Australia, ChildFund Ireland, ChildFund Japan, ChildFund New Zealand, Christian Children's Fund of Canada, ChildFund Korea, Taiwan Fund for Children and Families, and Un Enfant Par La Main (France). The U.S.-based ChildFund International was active in 31 countries, whereas the combined membership of the ChildFund Alliance was able to coordinate activities and pool resources in 55 countries.

Joyce Helena Brusin

PRINCIPAL COMPETITORS

Help the Helpless; Foundation of American Compassionate Samaritans; Children International; Love a Child Inc.; Kids Alive International; Love without Boundaries; Christian Foundation for Children and Aging; World Vision Inc.; Compassion International; Save the Children Inc.; Child Aid.

FURTHER READING

Banda, Joseph, "Children's Christian Fund Empowering Women and Youth," *Times of Zambia*, March 20, 2007.

Banks, Adelle M., "Christian Children's Fund Drops 'Christian' from Name." *Christianity Today,* May 2009.

"Changed Its Name to ChildFund International," *Christianity Today*, July 2009, p. 17.

"Children's Charity Group Will Monitor Spending," *New York Times*, December 14, 1998.

"Dr. Calvitt Clarke; Led Children's Fund," *New York Times*, July 18, 1970, p. 19.

Hailey, Foster, "Korean Orphans Display Talents," *New York Times*, June 18, 1955, p. 19.

Hrywna, Mark, "The Name Game: Is This Really What We Do?" *NonProfit Times*, June 15, 2009.

Janss, Edmund W., *Yankee Si: The Story of Dr. J. Calvitt Clarke and His 36,000 Children*, New York: Morrow, 1961.

Macenka, Joe, "Henrico-Based Children's Charity Changes Name," *Richmond Times-Dispatch* (Richmond, VA), April 25, 2009.

Roha, Ronaleen H., and Bertha Kainen, "Sponsoring a Child," *Changing Times*, January 1990, p. 76.

"Sailing Away on Imagination: Around the World, Children Make Their Own Fun," *National Geographic*, December 2001.

"Toys Not Sold in Stores," *UN Chronicle*, September 1, 2002.

Wessells, Michael, *Child Soldiers: From Violence to Protection*, Cambridge, MA: Harvard University Press, 2006.

Concur Technologies, Inc.

18400 NE Union Hill Road
Redmond, Washington 98052
U.S.A.
Telephone: (425) 702-8808
Toll Free: (800) 401-8412
Fax: (425) 702-8828
Web site: http://www.concur.com

Public Company
Founded: 1993 as Moorea Software Corp.
Incorporated: 1998 as Concur Technologies, Inc.
Employees: 932
Sales: $215.49 million (2008)
Stock Exchanges: NASDAQ
Ticker Symbol: CNQR
NAICS: 511210 Software Publishers

■ ■ ■

Concur Technologies, Inc., based in Redmond, Washington, is one of the world's leading manufacturers of software designed to help organizations manage employee travel and entertainment expenses. Concur has more than 8,000 clients representing a wide range of businesses, including such prominent multinational corporations as Bombardier, Ericsson, JCPenney, Texas Instruments, Unisys, and Wolters-Kluwer. The company operates in more than 90 countries and has offices in Great Britain, Germany, France, Belgium, Czech Republic, Australia, Canada, Hong Kong, and Singapore. By specializing in a profitable and expanding niche, the company has thrived while competing with much larger, comprehensive software producers.

FOUNDING: 1993

In 1993 a group of software industry veterans led by Michael Hilton and Rajeev Singh established Moorea Software Corp. The founders aimed to develop software applications that would simplify and automate reporting expenses and would help companies control and reduce their business travel expenses. Hilton and Singh suspected there must be considerable demand for such software among business travelers who dreaded having to complete long series of complicated forms to submit their expense reports.

Leading company investor and future CEO Steve Singh would estimate a few years later that the market for travel expense processing in the United States alone was $2.5 billion per year. Many large organizations relied on cumbersome paper-based accounting systems, leaving them unable to track and process expense reports quickly and efficiently, potentially losing a lot of money. No other software publisher had tried to produce comprehensive travel reporting software, in part because there were so many different kinds of forms and in part because the demand for such a product had been underestimated.

FIRST PRODUCTS AND INITIAL SUCCESS: 1994–97

By October 1994, when the company introduced "QuickXpense" software, Moorea had been renamed

COMPANY PERSPECTIVES

Our core purpose is: Innovate to drive costs out of business. We feel that everyone at Concur can make a difference. As we work together to maintain our leadership position as developers of Employee Spend Management solutions, we emphasize these values: Passion for and responsibility to the customer; Hire, develop, and reward great people; Leadership through innovation in everything we do; Passion for what you do and a drive to improve; Relentless commitment to win; Personal and corporate integrity.

Portable Software Corp. At almost the same time, the company received $2 million from Brentwood Associates, a leading high-tech venture capital firm. In a software market dominated by such giant firms as Microsoft and Oracle, Portable Software stood out by providing an array of specialized forms targeting specific industries and by offering to customize its product for free for any Fortune 1000 customer. Portable Software had only a few dozen employees and was unable to afford a direct sales force, so management hoped that employees would pick up its software in retail stores for use in their companies, causing increased demand for larger-scale solutions. Reviews in computer-oriented publications lauded the software, and the company's business was off and running.

The following year Portable Software received an additional $3 million in venture capital. The company developed an advanced version of "QuickXpense" in collaboration with GE Capital that allowed users to automatically enter charge card transactions into their expense reports. Portable Software quickly reached deals with other leading credit card issuers to integrate their transaction data into expense reports.

In early 1996 the company began to shift its marketing focus toward large corporate clients and started to develop applications for corporate intranets and the Internet, as well as for stand-alone computers. Michael Hilton became vice-president of development and was replaced as CEO by Steve Singh. Later that year, Portable Software launched "Xpense Management Solution" (XMS), a set of five applications designed for corporate client/servers. Within less than a year, the company would announce that more than 20 Fortune 1000 firms had agreed to use its technology. Organizations using this software could not only eliminate paper

forms, but also could track expenses for particular vendors and would be able to use the information to negotiate better deals for travel services and discourage employees from spending on nonpreferred vendors.

In early 1997 Portable Software established a branch office in London, England. The company was working with European customers to design products for the European market that could instantaneously convert numerous national currencies and meet E.U. regulations. Later that year, Portable Software received an additional $7.5 million of venture capital. In addition, Portable Software made deals with SABRE Business Travel Solutions and Internet Travel Network to integrate their travel booking systems into the XMS platform, which promised to further streamline expense reporting by enabling employees to book travel reservations as well as keep track of travel expenses on the same system.

A NEW NAME AND A MOVE TO PUBLIC MARKET: 1998–99

American Express stopped trying to develop its own expense reporting software and joined with Portable Software to promote XMS in 1998. XMS was incorporated into the American Express Roundtrip Services package. Company management soon decided to offer stock, taking advantage of the company's rising industry profile to raise money to finance further expansion. The initial public offering (IPO) would also cover the company's mounting losses, which had soared from $5.5 million in 1997 to about $13 million in the first eight months of 1998. That August, the company purchased 7Software, known for the "CompanyStore" corporate procurement software package. At around the same time, Portable Software changed its name again, becoming Concur Technologies, Inc.

That December, the newly renamed company launched an IPO on the NASDAQ, issuing over 3.5 million shares of stock at $12.50 per share, raising $44.6 million. By late February 1999 the share price had more than doubled, reaching more than $30. In April, Concur, along with some of its stockholders, was making another offering of 3.1 million shares at $43.50 per share. Later that month, the share price topped out at $59.25. Concur was one of dozens of aggressively growing young firms that rode the crest of the late 1990s high-tech stock boom, although company balance sheets often showed losses.

Concur targeted the burgeoning business-to-business e-commerce market, which already dwarfed business-to-consumer commerce. The company's "EmployeeDesktop 5.0" combined the functions of XMS

KEY DATES

1993: Moorea Software Corp. is incorporated in Washington.
1994: Company name changes to Portable Software Inc.; "QuickXpense" is introduced.
1998: Portable Software is renamed Concur Technologies, Inc.; company makes initial public offering on the NASDAQ.
2002: Concur purchases leading competitor Captura.
2006: Concur acquires Outtask, Inc., and its popular "Cliqbook" product line.
2008: Concur and American Express sign a mutual marketing agreement.

and "CompanyStore" in a portal through which employees could handle every step in the purchasing cycle, as well as access other company documents, services, and Internet applications. The software also was designed to be compatible with corporate applications from large providers, such as Oracle, PeopleSoft, and SAP. In June 1999 the company strengthened its offerings in this market with the acquisition of Seeker Software, which published corporate human resources applications. Another company initiative was a reverse auction site that targeted corporate procurement staff, who could use the site to list wanted goods and services and solicit bids from suppliers. The company's workforce had grown to around 500, and CEO Singh announced the intention to add 400 more employees.

Concur's software solutions were attracting a swelling rank of big-name clients, such as Texaco, Lucent Technologies, American Airlines, AT&T, the Hearst Corporation, AlliedSignal, and Knight Ridder. By September 1999 the company estimated that its products were installed on more than 1.8 million desktop computers.

In October 1999 the company renamed its product line under the Concur brand: XMS became "Concur Expense," "EmployeeDesktop" became "eWorkplace. com," "CompanyStore" became "Concur Procurement," and "The Seeker Workplace" became "Concur Human Resource." Concur introduced a version of "eWorkplace. com" that was an outsourced Internet product available by monthly subscription. It was tailored for small and medium-sized enterprises that could not afford to purchase and install the full suite.

FINANCIAL CRISIS: 2000–01

Early in 2000 Concur announced the upcoming launch of Concur Business Advantage, an e-commerce trading network designed for small and mid-sized businesses. Nortel Networks and Safeco committed $35 million to Concur to help support this network in exchange for large equity stakes in the company. Concur and its partners contracted with leading equipment and travel suppliers to make their products and services available on the network at deep discounts that small organizations could not have negotiated on their own.

However, financial problems were threatening to undermine Concur's ambitions. Companies reeling from the collapse of the dot.com boom were cutting back on software spending, and anticipation of the Year 2000 (Y2K) crisis had also diverted many potential clients' attention. The company was continuing to lose money, and as it repeatedly failed to meet earnings targets, its share prices plunged in late 1999 and the first half of 2000 before dropping to a low of $0.28 in December. Instead of hiring hundreds of new employees, Concur had to lay off part of its workforce in June 2000, including some of its key managers, fueling rumors that the company would be put up for sale.

Concur responded by no longer offering procurement software and spinning off its human resources unit, which it would sell in April 2001 to MBH Solutions, Inc. The company also decided to shift from a conventional licensing model toward an application service provider (ASP) model. Under this model, instead of receiving the full price of the product up front, the company would receive steady monthly payments from customers. This plan would reduce the company's revenues in the short term, but was expected to provide a more steady income stream in the long run. Concur's main strength was its large cash reserves.

A STRONG RECOVERY: 2002–07

Concur quickly started a financial recovery, exceeding projected performance beginning in the second half of 2000 and continuing every year through 2008. Although the company continued to report losses, those losses steadily diminished, and in the third quarter of fiscal year 2003 Concur was able to report a profit. The company's net revenues steadily increased from $39.73 million in fiscal year 2001 to $71.83 million in fiscal year 2005 and to $215.49 million in fiscal year 2008. Share prices would rise steadily throughout most of the decade, reaching a high of $50 in September 2008 before declining modestly over the following year.

Steve Singh told the *Puget Sound Business Journal* in June 2001, "Right now, our competitors like Captura and Extensity don't have the buying power to acquire us. But over the next five years, I think we'll see consolidation in the payroll space." Concur was successful in maintaining its independence amid industry consolidation and the following year purchased Bellevue, Washington-based Captura for cash and stock at an estimated value of between $12.5 million and $14.9 million, respectively, which was a bargain based on the capital originally invested.

Concur continued to refine its existing product line and introduce other new applications. In 2002 the company presented a platform designed for mobile devices like cell phones and Palm Pilots. In 2004 Concur launched the Concur Benchmarking Service, which enabled customers to measure their travel expenses against typical market prices as well as against their competitors' spending. The following year, Concur introduced "Cognos ReportNet," an application that streamlined the process of creating financial reports. Concur Audit Service was launched in 2006 to help customers certify that receipts comply with organizational standards and regulatory requirements.

In January 2006 the company purchased Outtask, Inc., producer of "Cliqbook," the industry-leading travel booking tool. The company purchased Gelco Information Network, its strongest remaining competitor in travel expense software, in 2007. In 2008 Concur combined "Cliqbook" technology with its own expense management software to create "Concur Travel & Expense," the first application that could handle travel bookings and expenses from start to finish. Concur has maintained this brand name in its "Concur Cliqbook Travel" application.

BRIGHT PROSPECTS FOR THE FUTURE

In July 2008 Concur and American Express reached a seven-year reciprocal marketing agreement in which Concur would encourage its customers to use American Express Corporate Cards, and American Express would market Concur's applications to its customers. In return, American Express received a 13 percent stake in the company.

By 2009 the company estimated that its products managed approximately $35 billion in travel and entertainment expenses every year. In the first half of 2009 Concur's revenues continued to grow and the company was reporting healthy profits, unlike many of its competitors. Stock analysts and industry observers were generally optimistic about the company's future under CEO and chairman of the board Steve Singh, president and chief operating officer Rajeev Singh, and

chief financial officer John Adair, the same management team that had guided it throughout the decade. In spite of the global economic crisis, Concur was expected to benefit from the need of many organizations to reduce costs wherever possible.

Stephen V. Beitel

PRINCIPAL SUBSIDIARIES

Concur Technologies (UK) Ltd.; Concur Technologies (Australia) Pty. Limited; Concur Technologies (Hong Kong) Ltd.; Concur Czech (s.r.o.); Concur (Germany) GmbH; Captura Software, Inc.; Captura Software International, Ltd.; Outtask LLC; H-G Holdings, Inc.; H-G Intermediate Holdings, Inc.; Gelco Information Network, Inc.; Gelco Information Network GSD, Inc.; Gelco Information Network Canada, Inc.; Gelco Expense Management Limited

PRINCIPAL COMPETITORS

Compuware Corporation; Oracle Corporation; SAP Aktiengesellschaft

FURTHER READING

"American Express and Concur Enter into Exclusive Alliance to Offer Corporate Clients T&E Expense Management Services," *Business Wire*, July 29, 2008.

"American Express Switch a Huge Deal for Portable Software," *Newsbytes*, January 13, 1998.

"Audit Service Validates and Verifies Client Expense Receipts," *Product News Network*, October 18, 2006.

Baker, M. Sharon, "Portable Software Gets $7.5 Million for Sales Push," *Puget Sound Business Journal*, July 26, 1996, p. 3.

———, "Portable Software Lands $2 Million for Rollout," *Puget Sound Business Journal*, October 28, 1994, p. 13.

"BancBoston Robertson Stephens Underwrites Concur Technologies Initial Public Offering," *PR Newswire*, February 25, 1999.

Berst, Jesse, "A Clever Way to Create a Competitive Barrier," *PC Week*, September 12, 1994, p. 117.

Boehmer, Jay, "Tool to Benchmark Expense," *Business Travel News*, August 2, 2004, p. 4.

———, "Concur Acquires Outtask," *Business Travel News*, February 6, 2006, p. 1.

"Concur, Nortel Networks, SAFECO, and Microsoft Join Forces to Deliver World's Largest eCommerce Trading Network for the Small and Middle Business Market," *M2 Presswire*, February 24, 2000.

"Concur Re-Launches EmployeeDesktop as Concur eWorkplace," *Business Wire*, October 5, 1999.

"Concur Technologies, Inc. Announces Completion of Follow-On Public Offering," *Business Wire*, April 16, 1999.

"Concur Technologies Announces a New Operating Plan," *PR Newswire*, June 8, 2000.

"Concur Technologies Introduces World's First On-Demand Report Authoring Solution for Corporate Expense Management," *PR Newswire*, December 21, 2005.

"Corum Assists Concur Technologies with Strategic Divestiture," *PR Newswire*, April 13, 2001.

Duryee, Tricia, "Kirkland, Wash., Expense-Management Firm Sells at Loss for Investors," *Knight Ridder/Tribune Business News*, August 1, 2002.

Ernst, Steve, "Concur Stumbles but Has Cash to Fall Back On," *Puget Sound Business Journal*, July 28, 2000, p. 9.

———, "Concur Technologies Set for Push In e-Commerce," *Puget Sound Business Journal*, September 24, 1999, p. 4.

"Expense Software Downloads Credit Card Data," *Newsbytes*, September 28, 1995.

"Internet Travel Network, Portable Software Enter Alliance," *Business Wire*, July 28, 1997.

Karpinski, Richard, "Concur Broadens Its Electronic Service Offerings," *InformationWeek*, October 18, 1999, p. 150.

McNulty, Mary Ann, "Vendors Ready T&E Web Product," *Business Travel News*, September 8, 1997, p. 14.

Meisner, Jeff, "Buyouts May Lie Ahead in Enterprise Software," *Puget Sound Business Journal*, June 22, 2001, p. 6.

"Portable Software Acquires a Procurement Software Leader; Changes Company Name to Concur Technologies," *Business Wire*, August 3, 1998.

"Portable Software First to Deliver Integrated Travel Booking Data in T&E Expense Management Solution," *Business Wire*, May 20, 1997.

"Portable Software Corp. Announces Global Expansion," *Business Wire*, February 10, 1997.

"Portable Software Signs On Over 20 New Fortune 1000 Companies," *Business Wire*, March 26, 1997.

Tartakoff, Joseph, "American Express Takes a Stake in Redmond's Concur," *Seattle Post-Intelligencer*, July 30, 2008, p. D1.

Woods, Lynn, "E-reimbursement Will Save Big," *Business Travel News*, November 27, 2000, p. 38.

Conexant Systems Inc.

4000 Macarthur Boulevard
Newport Beach, California 92660-2558
U.S.A.
Telephone: (949) 483-4600
Toll Free: (888) 855-4562
Fax: (949) 483-4078
Web site: http://www.conexant.com

Public Company
Incorporated: 1999
Employees: 1,279 (2008)
Sales: $502.66 million (2008)
Stock Exchanges: NASDAQ
Ticker Symbol: CNXT
NAICS: 334413 Semiconductor and Related Device
Manufacturing

■ ■ ■

Conexant Systems Inc. began as a unit of Rockwell International that made semiconductors, or chips, beginning in the 1960s. Although not its largest division, Rockwell Semiconductor Systems (RSS) was Rockwell International's fastest-growing business in the 1990s until demand for chips dropped off in 1996, when the industry went through a period of excess supplies. In 1998 Rockwell International decided to spin off RSS to its shareholders in a tax-free stock exchange in an effort to improve its profits and make its semiconductor business more competitive. The new company, Conexant Systems Inc., began business in January 1999 with $1.2 billion in revenues and a workforce of about 6,300.

Conexant quickly returned to profitability by focusing exclusively on developing semiconductors for the communications market. However, a decade later the company's annual revenues had dropped to $502.7 million due to economic conditions and management decisions.

INNOVATIVE PRODUCTS FROM ROCKWELL'S SEMICONDUCTOR DIVISION: 1960S–90S

The business unit of Rockwell International that later became its Microelectronics Division developed 4800bps/9600bps 1C modems during the 1960s. In 1968 the company entered the commercial modem business when the first modem market was fax machines. In 1971 it developed the first 4800bps LST modems. The Rockwell International Microelectronics Division was created in 1971 to fuel the development of microprocessor technology and computer products. In 1977 it was renamed the Electronic Devices Division and became the largest producer of the R6502 microprocessor. In 1978 it began shipping high-speed OEM (original equipment manufacturer) modems (4800bps and 9600bps) to facsimile (fax) manufacturers.

The division was renamed Semiconductor Products Division in 1982. During the 1980s it introduced a series of OEM fax, data, and very large scale integration (VLSI) modems and in 1985 began its fax-modem chipset business that would subsequently dominate the industry. It also helped create the analog modem market for desktop computers. In 1988 the Semiconductor Products Division opened a European Design Center in Sophia Antipolis, France.

COMPANY PERSPECTIVES

Conexant Systems Inc. is a leading provider of solutions for imaging, video, audio, and Internet connectivity applications, and holds leadership positions in the major segments it addresses. Conexant Systems Inc. is committed to the preservation of the environment and to the health and safety of our employees. Conexant Systems Inc. pledges to provide continually improving product and service performance to our customers.

In 1990 the division was renamed the Digital Communications Division, with headquarters in Newport Beach, California, as part of Rockwell International's reorganization of its semiconductor and communications business. It opened a design center in Tokyo, Japan, and introduced the world's first integrated, low-speed data and fax modem as well as the first high-speed, single-device fax modem operating at 14,400bps transmission.

The division continued to introduce innovative data and fax modem products throughout the decade. In 1993 the division became Rockwell International's Telecommunications business unit as part of the firm's reorganization of its digital communications and switching systems business. In 1994 its wafer fabrication plant in Newport Beach completed a $200 million facility expansion.

MULTIMEDIA AND WIRELESS COMMUNICATIONS PRODUCTS IN THE MID-1990S

In 1995 the division was renamed Rockwell Semiconductor Systems (RSS) and focused on multimedia and wireless communications. Another $200 million expansion of the Newport Beach fabrication facility was begun. During the year RSS introduced several new products, including the industry's first single-package 28.8Kbps modem-chip family integrating speakerphone/data/fax/telephone answering machine functions. RSS was not Rockwell International's largest business, but it was the fastest growing. It dominated the fax modem market, selling 80 percent of the chips used in fax machines. From 1992 through 1995 RSS enjoyed a compound annual growth rate of about 35 percent.

In 1996 RSS opened a semiconductor systems design center in Israel. Early in the year it broke ground for a new wafer fabrication facility in Colorado Springs on land that it had acquired from United Technologies. The plant was scheduled to open in mid-1997. In addition to its plant in Newport Beach, Rockwell had another chipmaking plant in Newbury Park, California. Later in the year Rockwell announced that it would delay the opening of the Colorado Springs plant until early 1998. The delay reflected a change in the overall semiconductor industry, which was experiencing a slump in demand that made it less expensive for Rockwell to purchase wafers rather than make its own. Chip manufacturers with excess capacity were selling wafers at significant discounts in the face of a falloff in demand.

Later in 1996 parent company Rockwell International sold its military and aerospace business to Boeing Co. in a deal valued at $3.2 billion. Boeing assumed $2.17 billion in debt and other Rockwell liabilities and gave Rockwell shareholders about $860 million in Boeing stock. The deal would leave Rockwell virtually debt-free and in a position to expand through acquisitions. Rockwell International would keep its four commercial electronics and automation businesses. At the time of the sale, semiconductors accounted for about 16 percent of Rockwell's revenues. The semiconductor division planned to focus on higher margin products and not concentrate on commodity semiconductors. These products included personal communications chipsets for sale to OEMs, global positioning system (GPS) receivers, and wireless systems devices.

About this same time Rockwell acquired chipmaker Brooktree Corp. for $275 million in stock. The acquisition of Brooktree, a San Diego-based firm with 575 employees and operations in Colorado and Texas as well as San Diego, gave RSS the technology to expand its high-speed digital communications and multimedia product lines.

56K MODEM TECHNOLOGY THE FOCUS IN 1996–97

In 1996 RSS and Lucent Technologies agreed to make their 56Kbps modem chipsets interoperable, even though industry standards had not yet been determined. RSS introduced several new products, including new modem technology enabling Internet connections at rates up to 56Kbps across standard phone lines. RSS also introduced the first in a family of 56Kbps digital modem devices for central-site equipment at the fall 1996 Comdex industry trade show and exhibition. Rockwell was proposing 56Kbps as the new industry standard for Internet modems, a speed nearly twice that of most high-end modems available at the time.

KEY DATES

■

1971: The Rockwell International Microelectronics Division is created to fuel the development of microprocessor technology and computer products.

1977: The division is renamed the Electronic Devices Division and becomes the largest producer of the R6502 microprocessor.

1990: The division becomes the Digital Communications Division, with headquarters in Newport Beach, California.

1995: The division is renamed Rockwell Semiconductor Systems and focuses on multimedia and wireless communications.

1999: Rockwell International spins off Rockwell Semiconductor Systems as a public company, Conexant Systems Inc.

2004: The company merges with Globespan Virata and acquires Paxonet Communications.

2009: The company sells its Broadband Access division to focus on core strengths in imaging and audio technologies.

RSS planned to begin volume production of the 56Kbps chipsets in the first quarter of 1997, but a problem discovered by Motorola in field tests delayed full production until April. By May, Rockwell was shipping a million units per month. Rockwell's primary competitor was U.S. Robotics, which had signed major Internet service providers (ISPs) America Online and CompuServe (later merged into AOL), while Rockwell had received commitments from hundreds of smaller ISPs. U.S. Robotics was subsequently acquired by 3Com Corp. Rockwell and 3Com used different standards, and their modems could only talk to each other at speeds up to 33.6Kbps.

Toward the end of 1997 RSS introduced a new high-speed modem technology called consumer digital subscriber line (CDSL). CDSL was designed to ease the transition for consumers from analog modems to higher speed digital formats. CDSL technology would enable modem manufacturers to combine DSL and traditional modem technology in a single device. The CDSL chips were expected to be ready for shipment to OEMs in the spring of 1998. As part of its CDSL initiative, RSS entered into a joint development agreement with Orckit Communications for high bit rate DSL products (HDSL) and with Northern Telecom (Nortel) to make

Rockwell's CDSL format interoperable with Nortel's similar one-megabyte modem system. At the same time, RSS announced its first chipset to support high-speed cable modems, which were considered the primary competition for xDSL lines in the consumer market. The company also reached a tentative agreement with 3Com Corp. to produce 56Kbps modems using a common standard before the end of 1997.

A NEW CORPORATE IDENTITY: 1998–2000

In mid-1998 Rockwell International Corp. announced that it would spin off Rockwell Semiconductor Systems as a separate company, which would subsequently be called Conexant Systems Inc., by the end of 1998. For fiscal 1998 RSS was expected to show an operating loss, due in part to a weak PC modem market and a work stoppage at its Newport Beach facility. Parent company Rockwell International's quarterly results were also well below analysts' expectations, and the company planned to cut 3,800 jobs from its workforce after spinning off RSS to its shareholders. RSS had about 7,000 employees and would have about $1.3 billion in revenues for fiscal 1998.

Before the spin-off was completed, RSS laid off 700 employees, about 10 percent of its workforce, and closed its wafer fabrication plant in Colorado Springs. For fiscal 1998, ending September 30, RSS posted a loss of $275 million, including charges of about $90 million to close its Colorado Springs facility and reduce its workforce. The semiconductor industry was going through a period of weak demand and faced a worldwide glut of semiconductors.

In its first formal filing regarding the spin-off, RSS estimated that it had 70 percent of the worldwide market for fax chips and was the largest maker of modem chips. Approximately 45 percent of its revenues came from Asia, which was going through a financial crisis. The company had experienced 18 months of declining sales as weak demand and excess inventories buffeted the semiconductor sector.

In January 1999 Conexant Systems Inc. was launched as an independent entity after Rockwell International Corp. completed the spin-off of Rockwell Semiconductor Systems to shareholders. Dwight Decker, president of RSS, would continue as chairman and CEO of Conexant. Conexant's stock began trading on the NASDAQ on January 4 at $17 to $18 a share. Conexant began operations with nearly 6,300 employees and annual revenues of about $1.2 billion.

Conexant would continue to share some resources with Rockwell International, including the Rockwell

Science Center, where technologies such as gallium arsenide chips and complementary metal-oxide semiconductor (CMOS) imaging technology were invented. Conexant would provide some funding for the lab, which employed 280 researchers, and share in technology research focused on the communications market. Rockwell International also would remain a customer for Conexant's avionics and automotive products.

In March 1999 Conexant announced that it had developed a single chip for cable modems that could handle digital data, audio, and video signals, functions that were currently being performed by four to six chips. The same month Conexant also unveiled its interactive digital television (DTV) set-top box (STB) platform. With its strategy firmly focused on semiconductors for the communications market, Conexant returned to profitability ahead of schedule in its second quarter ending March 30, 1999, with net income of $7.6 million on revenue of $316.9 million. Its third quarter results exceeded analysts' expectations. Conexant was the largest semiconductor company in the world focused exclusively on communications semiconductors, and it had the broadest product portfolio of communications products of any similar company. It had achieved twice the market share of its nearest competitor in 56K modems. The company's wireless communications and network access divisions were growing faster than expected. In addition, the personal computing division was experiencing a reversal of declining demand for PC modems. In July 1999 Conexant became part of the NASDAQ 100 Index. Later in the year Conexant announced a two-for-one stock split.

GROWTH THROUGH ACQUISITIONS: 1999–2000

Before the end of 1999 Conexant announced plans to acquire smaller technology firms over the next several months. Rival chip makers Intel Corp. and Broadcom Corp. had recently acquired communication-technology companies as demand fueled by Internet communications exploded. In August, Conexant invested $10 million in Entridia Corp., a privately held start-up that designed chips that route voice, video, and data transmissions from a server to a workplace computer. In December it acquired Maker Communications Inc. of Framingham, Massachusetts, for $942.8 million in stock. The company developed software that enabled engineers to create semiconductors for Internet communications. Conexant also opened a design center in Portland, Oregon, to attract talent in the area known as Silicon Forest.

At the end of 1999 Broadcom and Conexant both announced competing versions of a tuner chip to replace the bulky channel-switching device in cable boxes and televisions. An inexpensive tuner chip would make such multiple functions as Internet access over a television screen and picture-in-picture more commonplace. Conexant also was seeking industry certification for its cable modem, which failed the first test. Broadcom was considered the industry leader in cable modems.

At the start of 2000 Conexant acquired British chip maker Microcosm Communications Ltd. for about $128 million in stock. The acquisition of the high-volume chip producer was expected to boost revenue in Conexant's fiber-optic networking business. In acquiring smaller firms, Conexant was focusing on companies that already had products and were generating revenue.

In January 2000 Conexant was chosen to replace Consolidated Natural Gas Co. in the Standard & Poor's 500 Index. The company's stock rose 18 percent in one day. At the end of February, though, it dropped about 16 percent in one day when an investment banker downgraded the stock from "strong buy" to "buy." In early March analysts were concerned about one of Conexant's major customers, Lucent Technologies, and the possibility Conexant had been designed out of some of Lucent's next-generation products. One analyst estimated Lucent accounted for 6 percent of Conexant's revenues and as much as 10 percent of its profits. Conexant was also facing new competition from companies such as RF Micro Devices in the power amplifier business for cell phones, which accounted for 12 percent of Conexant's revenues. On the positive side, analysts noted that Conexant seemed to be making a successful transition from its older analog modem business to digital technology and cable. After initial problems getting its cable modem design certified, Conexant received industry certification in July 2000 for a single-chip cable modem that would allow consumers to purchase PCs with always-on, high-speed cable modems.

In April 2000 Conexant acquired Philsar Semiconductor Inc. of Ottawa, Canada, for stock worth from $166.5 million to $186 million. Philsar designed chips that enabled wireless devices to connect to one another and change functions quickly. Another acquisition involved Illinois-based Applied Telecom Inc., a supplier of telecommunications software and hardware. The following month Conexant bought Sierra Imaging Inc. for about $43.6 million in stock. Sierra made software and semiconductors for digital cameras.

In June 2000 Conexant acquired high-speed network chip maker HotRail Inc. for about $394 million in stock. The acquisition strengthened Conexant's network offerings. The acquired technology would enable the company to deliver complete systems for next-generation Internet infrastructure, including high-speed routers, Internet protocol and Ethernet switches, and optical networking equipment.

Conexant continued its acquisitions in July with the purchase of two companies. One was NetPlane Systems of Dedham, Massachusetts, which developed software for network control and other functions. The technology would facilitate Conexant's entry into network switching and complemented the HotRail acquisition. Conexant acquired NetPlane for 2.4 million shares of stock valued at about $120 million. The second company was Novanet Semiconductor, a designer of high-speed physical layer networking solutions based in Israel. Conexant acquired Novanet for 2.7 million shares of stock valued at about $140 million. Both companies became part of Conexant's Network Access division.

LOSSES LEAD TO DOWNSIZING: 2001–09

Facing an inevitable decline in its core dial-up PC modem business, Conexant's acquisition strategy was designed to strengthen its Network Access and Wireless divisions. Entering the 21st century, Conexant was facing a host of new competitors, particularly in the developing areas of wireless and broadband technologies. The company's goal, however, was to be the number one communications semiconductor company.

In an effort to remain competitive Conexant management used mergers and partnerships to bolster its market positions. In 2001 its global positioning system business merged with SiRF Technology. In 2002, through a partnership with the Carlyle Group, Conexant created Jazz Semiconductor; its wireless communications business's merger with Alpha Industries created Skyworks Solutions; and its digital imaging business's merger with Zing Network created Pictos Technologies. Conexant spun off its Internet infrastructure subsidiary, Mindspeed Technologies, in 2003. The year 2004 brought a merger with Globespan Virata (for $969.5 million) and the acquisition of Paxonet Communications. Although an unprofitable company, Globespan Virata expanded Conexant's market reach into chips for home computer networks.

Besides confronting changes in the high-tech industry, Conexant also had to deal with cleaning up chemical spills dating back to when it was a unit of Rockwell International. The Environmental Protection Agency declared its Parker Ford, Pennsylvania, location a Superfund site (a high-priority hazardous waste site). The company expected to spend $3 million on remediations in 2004. Conexant also faced a class action lawsuit

in 2004 by investors who believed they had been duped. Some blamed CEO Dwight Decker for concentrating on acquisitions and mergers instead of operations. Post-merger, Globespan Virata CEO Armando Geday briefly took over the Conexant CEO spot, but resigned in late 2004, opening the way for Decker to once again take the helm.

Once worth $20 billion, Conexant's market value plummeted to $680 million by 2005. Between 2005 and 2006, the company closed operating sites and notified 385 employees of their involuntary termination. Management's goal for the first quarter of 2005 was to cut $6 million in operating expenses. The business's core value had plummeted from $20 billion during the technology boom to $680 million by 2005, and it was seeking to lure investors. The company's chief products were chips for modems, fax machines, and home networking devices.

After Conexant lost $840 million over three years, the board of directors hired Daniel Artusi in 2007 to take over as CEO and chairman from Decker. Artusi, whose experience included stints at various chip makers, would be replaced in 2008 by board member D. Scott Mercer. In 2007 Conexant Systems closed several facilities and reduced its workforce even further. Some 140 workers received layoff notices when the company discontinued development of LAN chips. However, it planned to continue to putting wireless LAN technology into products and support its wireless customers. The company also sold its investment in Jazz Semiconductor. Planning to discontinue investments in standalone wireless networking solutions and other product areas, Conexant Systems sold part of its Broadband Media Processing business to NXP for $110 million in April 2008. In June the company affected a 1-for-10 reverse stock split.

Although industry conditions and a downturn in the U.S. economy created ongoing challenges for Conexant, a boost came in 2009 when the company's CX20562 speakers on a chip (SPoC) audio solution won EDN's 19th Annual Innovation Award in the Application Specific Standard Product category. The device supports high-definition audio and voice applications in PCs, docking systems, and peripherals. Also in 2009 the company continued restructuring operations by divesting its Broadband Access product lines. The $54 million cash transaction sold Conexant products used for DSL network connectivity and passive optical network applications to Ikanos Communications Inc. Conexant's new structure focused exclusively on imaging, audio, video, and embedded-modem applications, and the company optimistically looked forward to product development and further acquisitions in these technology segments.

David P. Bianco
Updated, Doris Maxfield

PRINCIPAL DIVISIONS

Imaging; PC Media.

PRINCIPAL COMPETITORS

Advanced Micro Devices Inc.; California Micro Devices Corporation; Intel Corporation; Micron Technology Inc.; RF Micro Devices Inc.; Texas Instruments Inc.; TranSwitch Corporation; Zarlink Semiconductor Inc.

FURTHER READING

Berry, Kate, "Newport Beach, Calif., Communications-Chip Maker Buys British Firm," *Knight-Ridder/Tribune Business News*, January 7, 2000.

Bradley, Gale, "Done Deal! It's Now Boeing North American," *Electronic News (1991)*, December 9, 1996, p. 56.

Brinton, James B., "Reborn Rockwell Rolls Toward 2000," *Electronic Business Today*, December 1996, p. 45.

Brown, Peter, "The Race for STB Dominance," *Electronic News (1991)*, March 22, 1999, p. 20.

Campbell, Ronald, "Rockwell Picks Up Speed, Saying Bug in Its Modems Has Been Fixed," *Knight-Ridder/Tribune Business News*, April 10, 1997.

——, "Rockwell Semiconductor Faces Restructuring Pains," *Knight-Ridder/Tribune Business News*, September 15, 1998.

——, "War of Two Modem Technologies Rages at 56,000 Bits per Second," *Knight-Ridder/Tribune Business News*, August 13, 1997.

Cassell, Jonathan, "CEO Maps Conexant's Course," *Electronic News (1991)*, April 5, 1999, p. 10.

Chmielewski, Dawn C., "California's Broadcom and Conexant Make Separate Buyout Deals," *Knight-Ridder/Tribune Business News*, May 23, 2000.

"Conexant a Nasdaq Choice," *Electronic News (1991)*, July 19, 1999, p. 6.

"Conexant Buys Sierra Imaging," *Electronic News (1991)*, May 29, 2000, p. 4.

"Conexant Names New CEO," *Wireless News*, April 16, 2008.

"Conexant Stock Split," *Electronic News (1991)*, September 20, 1999, p. 6.

"Conexant Supplies New Imaging Solution for Advanced Multifunction Printers," *Wireless News*, January 2, 2009.

"Conexant Systems Inc.," *Microwaves & RF*, January 2009, p. 48.

"Conexant Takes Its First Steps," *Electronic News (1991)*, January 11, 1999, p. 14.

"Conexant to Beat Analysts," *Electronic News (1991)*, June 14, 1999, p. 6.

Doan, Amy, "56Kbps Modems Arrive without Standards," *InfoWorld*, November 25, 1996, p. 47.

Dunn, Darrell, "Conexant Proceeds With Plan to Split Into Three," *EBN*, June 3, 2002, p. 8.

Farnsworth, Chris, "California's Broadcom, Conexant Brace for Cable-TV Computer-Chip Battle," *Knight-Ridder/Tribune Business News*, December 7, 1999.

——, "Chip Manufacturer Expands Into New Irvine, Calif., Office," *Knight-Ridder/Tribune Business News*, December 2, 1999.

——, "New Products Intensify Rivalry Between California Tuner-Chip Makers," *Knight-Ridder/Tribune Business News*, December 6, 1999.

——, "Orange County, Calif.-Based Communications-Chip Maker Buys Canadian Firm," *Knight-Ridder/Tribune Business News*, April 12, 2000.

——, "Orange County, Calif., Chip Maker Spends $394 Million for Network Firm," *Knight-Ridder/Tribune Business News*, June 27, 2000.

Haber, Carol, "Conexant Challenge: Modem, Wireless," *Electronic News (1991)*, May 1, 2000, p. 56.

——, "Conexant Shares Socked," *Electronic News (1991)*, March 6, 2000, p. 42.

——, "Wireless Winners in Acquisition Mode," *Electronic News (1991)*, February 21, 2000, p. 36.

Humphry, Sara, "56K bps Across Regular Phone Lines?" *PC Week*, September 23, 1996, p. N14.

Lavilla, Stacy, "Rockwell Nabs Brooktree to Bolster Chip Holdings," *PC Week*, July 8, 1996, p. 10.

Mateyaschuk, Jennifer, "Rockwell to Spin Off Semiconductor Unit," *InformationWeek*, July 6, 1998, p. 12.

——, "Conexant Rolls STB Chipsets," *Electronic News (1991)*, May 22, 2000, p. 50.

Niccolai, James, "Modem Companies Rush to Get on 56Kbps Uplink Bandwagon," *InfoWorld*, September 23, 1996, p. 49.

Roberts, Bill, "Spinning-off to Profits," *Electronic Business*, August 1999, p. 50.

"Rockwell, 3Com Make a Pact," *Computerworld*, December 8, 1997, p. 8.

Salamone, Salvatore, "New Flavors of DSL Just Keep Coming," *InternetWeek*, November 10, 1997, p. 41.

Schaff, William, "Conexant Is Worth a Premium," *InformationWeek*, July 3, 2000, p. 146.

Simons, Andrew, "Chipmaking Companies Burdened by Seeping Problems," *Los Angeles Business Journal*, March 21, 2005, p. 20.

"Technology Briefing Hardware: Conexant to Buy Globespan Virata," *New York Times*, November 4, 2003, p. C7.

"Then vs. Now," *Los Angeles Business Journal*, March 28, 2005, p. 37.

——, "Rockwell Launches High-Speed Modem Technology for Home User," *Electronic News (1991)*, November 3, 1997, p. 14.

Wallace, Bob, "56K Modems on Deck," *Computerworld*, September 16, 1996, p. 1.

Young, Pebby, "Roller-coaster Ride for Conexant: Can the Communications Chip Maker Stage a Comeback? *Electronic Business*, March 2005, p. 22.

CryptoLogic Limited

Marine House, 3rd floor
Clanwilliam Place
Dublin, 2
Ireland
Telephone: (416) 545-1455
Fax: (416) 545-1454
Web site: http://www.cryptologic.com/

Public Company
Founded: 1995
Incorporated: 1996
Employees: 276
Sales: $61.53 million (2008)
Stock Exchanges: NASDAQ Toronto London
Ticker Symbol: CRYP (NASDAQ); CRY (Toronto); CRP (London)
NAICS: 541511 Custom Computer Programming Services; 511210 Games, Computer Software, Publishing

■ ■ ■

One of the first companies to develop software for the online gaming industry, CryptoLogic Limited has grown since its founding in 1995 to become one of the world's leading providers of software and gaming systems to online casino operators and Internet gaming companies. It has created the software to run more than 280 casino games, including poker, slots, and other table games, which it licenses to respected gaming providers worldwide. By combining its gaming software with e-commerce software, the company achieved immediate success and remains one of the giants in the gaming software field.

EXCEPTIONAL GROWTH IN EARLY YEARS

Brothers Andrew and Mark Rivkin founded CryptoLogic in 1995, working in their parents' basement. The company was incorporated in Canada the following year, focusing on the development of electronic commerce (e-commerce) software. After spending months searching for investors, the founders realized they could profitably combine e-commerce and online gaming. This pairing landed them the seed money to develop their gaming software. In 1996 the Rivkins and Chief Technical Officer Anatoly Plotkin rolled out the first version of their gaming package, which included *Blackjack*, *Roulette*, *Caribbean Poker*, *Video Poker*, *Slots*, and a Sports Book. By 1998, just three years after CryptoLogic was founded, the company was outperforming forecasts. This success was repeated in subsequent years. According to Max Drayman of *WINNERonline*, "The response was instantaneous: real players gambling real dollars had money dropping into CryptoLogic's bank account from day one."

In 1999 CryptoLogic purchased Gamesmania, an electronic magazine and video game site. The company announced that, "The acquisition of Gamesmania is part of CryptoLogic's strategy of adding to growth through acquisition and increasing its presence in the entertainment/media segment of the Internet." The same year, CryptoLogic licensed its gaming software to William Hill, the second largest sports book in the

COMPANY PERSPECTIVES

As a TSX, NASDAQ and London Stock Exchange-listed company, CryptoLogic adheres to the world's highest standards for corporate governance. We were one of the very first e-gaming companies to go public. As a result, we have a long, proud track record of transparency and disclosure. We are one of very few companies with gaming software that is certified to strict standards similar to land-based gaming, and we strongly advocate regulation as the best way to protect players and the integrity of the Internet gaming industry.

United Kingdom. In licensing agreements, CryptoLogic provided the gaming sites in exchange for a licensing fee and a percentage of the profits. By 2000, when the company was listed on the NASDAQ, licensees included not only William Hill, but also The Sand of the Caribbean, InterCasino, eBet Online (based in Australia), Kiwi Casino (based in New Zealand), and Casino Sur (based in Argentina).

In December 2000 CryptoLogic announced that the founders of the company, Andrew Rivkin and Mark Rivkin, would step aside as Chief Executive Officer and Chief Operating Officer, respectively. Jean Noelting became the company's new president and CEO on January 8, 2001. The Rivkins remained directors of the company.

Noelting oversaw the expansion of the company into Internet poker as CryptoLogic announced the establishment of interactive poker rooms in May 2001. These interactive rooms allowed far-flung competitors to face each other at virtual poker tables, gambling real money. The first license holder was LasVegasFromHome.com. CEO Noelting said, "Poker is the most popular card game in the world—and for CryptoLogic, it's a huge untapped segment of the Internet gaming market." In 2001 CryptoLogic also introduced online bingo and acquired WinnerOnLine, a gaming content provider that served as a portal for Internet gamblers.

DIFFICULTIES DUE TO U.S. GAMING REGULATIONS

From its beginnings, Cryptologic kept a sharp eye on the legal status of Internet gaming in the United States, which was the largest market in the world. Although Internet gambling was considered illegal in the United States under the Interstate Wire Act of 1961, which criminalized using telephone lines for placing sports bets, for the first 10 years of CryptoLogic's existence, the law was rarely enforced. Beginning in 1995, Congress repeatedly considered legislation to specifically prohibit online gambling, but none of the laws passed. In 2001, following passage of a law in Nevada to allow Internet gaming within a regulated environment, CryptoLogic hired a U.S. lawyer to advise the company as it entered the Nevada market. At the same time, the company embarked on a strategy to diversify its operations globally.

CryptoLogic experienced upheaval in 2002. Exceptional growth in the first five years of the company's existence had earned it the number one ranking in the PROFIT 100, Canada's ranking of high-growth companies. However, some U.S. banks, under pressure from state law enforcement authorities, had started to disallow credit card transactions at online gambling sites, which resulted in a significant decline in revenues. However, the diversification strategy helped soften the blow to the company's finances. In July 2002 Noelting left CryptoLogic, and Lewis Rose was appointed interim CEO. That appointment was made permanent in March 2003. Also in 2003 the company was listed on the London Stock Exchange.

CryptoLogic continued to develop new gaming products, which helped it remain successful even as its growth slowed. In 2005 the company signed an agreement with Marvel Entertainment to use Marvel superheroes in its gaming software. The same year, the company launched a game based on the popular *Bejeweled* matching game. These games became some of the company's most popular.

In 2006 the U.S. Congress passed the Unlawful Internet Gambling Enforcement Act, which prohibited banks from processing payments to online gaming sites. CryptoLogic announced it would no longer license its software to companies that accepted bets from residents in the United States, which at the time accounted for 30 percent of its business. The value of CryptoLogic shares plunged 18 percent on the NASDAQ. In 2007, when asked about the challenges to Internet gaming in the United States, newly appointed CEO Javaid Aziz told *Canadian Business Online*, "The U.S. Challenge has opened up new doors in Europe, where operators see new opportunities for growth; and in Asia, with a huge population, growing Internet access and a long tradition of gaming, the possibilities are even greater. While we'll keep an eye on what's going on in North America, our bets have been firmly on Europe and Asia for several years." As a result of favorable regulations in the United

KEY DATES

1995: Brothers Andrew and Mark Rivkin found CryptoLogic.

1996: Company is initially offered on the Canadian Dealing Network; InterCasino is launched, one of the first play-for-money Internet casinos.

1998: CryptoLogic begins trading on the Toronto Stock Exchange.

1999: CryptoLogic signs U.K. gaming operation William Hill.

2000: CryptoLogic begins trading on the NASDAQ.

2002: Company introduces online poker and bingo.

2003: CryptoLogic begins trading on the London Stock Exchange.

2005: Online games based on *Bejeweled* and Marvel superheroes are launched.

2006: U.S. Congress passes Unlawful Internet Gambling Enforcement Act.

2007: Company reincorporates and moves headquarters from Canada to Dublin, Ireland.

Kingdom and unfavorable laws in North America, the company reincorporated under the laws of Guernsey, under a new parent company, CryptoLogic Limited, and moved its headquarters from Toronto to Dublin in June 2007.

RESPONSE TO DECLINE IN PROFITS DURING GLOBAL RECESSION

CryptoLogic shares took a big hit during the worldwide recession that began in 2008 as revenue dropped 16.8 percent from the year before. In May CryptoLogic announced that Javaid Aziz had resigned after less than a year as CEO. A public fight between Aziz and CryptoLogic's board ensued, with Aziz attempting to influence the direction of the company by buying 10 percent of the shares and then requesting a seat on the company's board of directors in an effort to set his own recovery plan in motion. In February 2009 the board refused Aziz's request for a special meeting of CryptoLogic shareholders to present his proposals for consideration.

The company accused Aziz of violating the terms of his severance contract, as well as of "inappropriate conduct" during his time as CEO. CryptoLogic then publicly released threatening e-mails that Aziz had sent the company chairman. The company sought the release of EUR 1.543 being held in escrow until April 30, 2009, that would be paid to Aziz should another change in control of the company occur before that date. New CEO Brian Hadfield issued a press release stating that, "While we regret being forced to take this step, CryptoLogic made substantial payments and commitments to Mr. Aziz in negotiating his severance, and we believe that his failure to adhere to his obligations has been damaging to the company and its shareholders."

In the meantime, CryptoLogic responded to the economic crisis by implementing a cost savings plan and a growth strategy. CEO Hadfield merged CryptoLogic's online poker operations with the operations of online gaming company Boss Media in an effort to get out of the business of running online gaming sites and back to the company's roots of developing gaming web sites for other companies. Eleven new companies were signed in 2008.

By mid-2009 CryptoLogic seemed to be on the road to a comeback. In June 2009 Victor Chandler Group, one of the world's top gaming companies, licensed at least 10 CryptoLogic games in a multi-year contract. The same month, the leading Irish online gaming company licensed nine CryptoLogic slot games and Sportingbet.com licensed 10 online slot games. According to Hadfield, "This is an excellent example of CryptoLogic's 'build-once-license-often' business strategy in action—and a sign of the continued demand for our games among the world's top operators." The expansion of CryptoLogic's partnership with 888.com, one of the largest online gaming sites in the world, in July 2009 was also promising. By the end of the year, 888.com would introduce five new CryptoLogic games to its online casinos, bringing its total to eight CryptoLogic games.

Despite these deals, it remained uncertain whether CryptoLogic could recover in 2009. Earnings had declined from $11.4 million in the fourth quarter of 2008 to $10.1 million in the first quarter of 2009. However, CryptoLogic had earned *Gambling Online Magazine*'s Top Casino Software Award, the industry's top honor, for the fourth consecutive year, attesting to the continued high quality of its gaming software. Also in 2009 CryptoLogic had extended its licensing agreement with Marvel through 2013. The company had 12 licensees around the world and was pursuing a strategy of marketing their software to key markets in Europe and Asia. In addition, the company held minority interests in several Asian game developers. While expanding into Asia posed some problems, including limited payment forms to support Internet gambling in the region and potential legal issues, Asia represented a huge potential market for CryptoLogic's software. CryptoLogic appeared to be on the path to phenomenal success in the second decade of the 2000s.

Melissa Doak

PRINCIPAL SUBSIDIARIES

Hilbeck Trading Limited (Cyprus); CryptoLogic Callco ULC (Canada); CryptoLogic Exchange Corporation (Canada); CryptoLogic Inc. (Canada); A.L.I. Online Inc. (Canada); WagerLogic Limited (Cyprus); Gaming Portals Limited; WagerLogic (Ireland) Limited; Wager-Logic Malta Software Limited; WagerLogic Malta Holdings Limited; WagerLogic Malta Casino Limited; WagerLogic Malta Poker Limited; Ecash Direct UK Limited; Adsdotcom Limited (UK).

PRINCIPAL COMPETITORS

Interactive Systems Worldwide Inc.; GTECH G2; International Game Technology.

FURTHER READING

"6 Questions: One-on-One with Javaid Aziz, President & CEO, CryptoLogic," *Canadian Business* Online, June 20, 2007, http://www.canadianbusiness.com/innovation/article.jsp?content=20070620_110252_5348.

"10 Amazing True Stories of Canada's Fastest-Growing Companies," *Profit*, June 2003, p. 93.

"Australia's Ebet to License Online Software to CryptoLogic," *AsiaPulse News*, July 13, 2000, p. 330.

Cordeiro, Anjali, "Ameristar Casinos, Pacific Sunwear Advance; Optimal Group Falls," *Wall Street Journal*, October 3, 2006, p. C5.

"CryptoLogic Acquires Leading Online Gaming Portal—WinnerOnLine," *Business Wire*, October 1, 2001, p. 1423.

"CryptoLogic Appoints New CEO; Javaid Aziz Brings 30 Years of Technology Management, Having Served as Chief Executive of IBM UK," *Internet Wire*, April 2, 2007.

"CryptoLogic Approved to List on Nasdaq," *Business Wire*, March 3, 2000, p. 1154.

"CryptoLogic CEO Javaid Aziz Has Resigned Less Than a Year after Taking Over Leadership of the Software, Games, and Systems Giant," *IGWB: International Gaming & Wagering Business*, May 2008, p. 19.

"CryptoLogic Confirms Lewis Rose as President & CEO," *Canadian Corporate News*, March 7, 2003, p. 1008066.

"CryptoLogic Engages Leading U.S. Expert to Advance Entry into Nevada & Other Key Internet Gaming Markets," *Business Wire*, November 5, 2001, p. 446.

"CryptoLogic Extends Relationship with Marvel," *Canadian Corporate News*, June 22, 2009.

"CryptoLogic Inc. Announces Acquisition of Gamesmania Internet Magazine," *Market Wire*, January 6, 1999, p. 1380.

"CryptoLogic Inc. Earns #1 Ranking in Profit 100," *Market Wire*, May 22, 2002.

"CryptoLogic Issues Statement Regarding Former CEO Filing," *Internet Wire*, December 23, 2008.

"CryptoLogic Licenses Top Internet Casino Games to Sportingbet.com," *Canadian Corporate News*, June 11, 2009.

"CryptoLogic Lists in London, Launches New 'Headhunter' Game," *Dow Jones International News*, June 14, 2007.

"CryptoLogic Praises UK Decision to Embrace Internet Gaming," *Canadian Corporate News*, March 11, 2001, p. 1008068.

"CryptoLogic Releases Gaming Software Version 2.2," *Business Wire*, August 25, 1997, p. 8251290.

"CryptoLogic Reports Failure of Proposed U.S. Internet Gaming Legislation," *Business Wire*, October 21, 1998, p. 0447.

Drayman, Max, "The Big Four Gambling Software Providers," WINNERonline.com, September 18, 2000, http://www.winneronline.com/articles/september2000/big4_cryptologic.htm.

"888.com to Launch Five More CryptoLogic Games in 2009," Dublin, Ireland: CryptoLogic Limited, July 7, 2009 (press release).

"Ex-CEO in Breach of Contractual Obligations to CryptoLogic; Company Seeks Return of EUR 1.543 Million," *Internet Wire*, February 23, 2009.

"First Internet Casino Licensed in Argentina Goes Live with CryptoLogic Software," *Business Wire*, October 2, 2000, p. 2577.

Gray, John, "Texas Fold 'Em: New U.S. Laws against Online Gambling Have Dealt the Online Casino Industry—and Investors—a Bad Hand," *Canadian Business Online*, October 9, 2006, http://www.canadianbusiness.com/managing/strategy/article.jsp?content=20061009_81089_81089.

"Kiwi Casino to Use CryptoLogic Gaming Software," *Business Wire*, August 3, 2000, p. 228.

Lyall, Ian, "CryptoLogic Is a Recovery Plan in the Making," *Daily Mail*, February 7, 2009.

MacDonald, Peter, "Dreamers with an Edge," *Profit*, June 2002, p. 21.

Moulds, Josephine, "Cryptologic Denies Former Chief Executive Javaid Aziz a Seat on the Board," Telegraph.co.uk, December 24, 2008, http://www.telegraph.co.uk/finance/newsbysector/mediatechnologyandtelecoms/3933516/Cryptologic-denies-former-chief-executive-Javaid-Aziz-a-seat-on-the-board.html.

"Paddy Power Games Adds CryptoLogic as a New Supplier," *Canadian Corporate News*, June 15, 2009.

Shiffman, Kim, "Lewis Rose," *Profit*, May 2005, p. 10.

Yuk, Pan Kwan, "CryptoLogic Dispute Erupts," *Financial Times*, February 25, 2009, p. 21.

D.A. Davidson & Co.
Davidson Investment Advisors
Davidson Trust Co.
Davidson Fixed Income Management
Davidson Travel

D.A. Davidson & Company

8 Third Street, North
Great Falls, Montana 59401
U.S.A.
Telephone: (406) 727-4200
Toll Free: (800) 332-5915
Fax: (406) 782-2687
Web site: http://www.dadavidson.com

Wholly Owned Subsidiary of Davidson Companies
Founded: 1935 as E.J. Gibson Inc.
Employees: 300
Assets under Management: $18 billion (2008)
NAICS: 523120 Securities Brokerage

■ ■ ■

An employee-owned company and a wholly owned subsidiary of Davidson Companies, D.A. Davidson & Company is the largest full-service investment firm based in the northwestern United States. It provides financial services to individual investors and corporate clients nationwide, with an emphasis on the West and Midwest. D.A. Davidson's regional origins remain important to its mission and its stated commitment to guidance, loyalty, and trust.

Key individuals mark the history of D.A. Davidson & Company. Chief among them are the company namesake David Adams Davidson and his son Ian B. Davidson. As they presided over the company, they never abandoned their core belief that earning the trust of clients and providing superior service to them would allow a financial services company to succeed in an

unlikely location through good economic times and bad. David and Ian Davidson also shared a belief in finding and retaining the best financial professionals and support staff they could find.

BEGINNINGS

The brokerage firm of E.J. Gibson Inc. opened its first and only branch office in Great Falls, Montana, in 1935. David Adams Davidson, a Montana banker, served as its director. The challenge of opening a retail stock brokerage in the midst of the Great Depression was considerable. E.J. Gibson faced an additional challenge because the only other stock brokerage in Great Falls had closed in bankruptcy amid scandal and rumors of fraud and stock manipulation. Disillusioned investors and local residents were distrustful and suspicious of anything having to do with the stock market or investing. Davidson was confident that he could overcome these obstacles and ensure the success of the firm if he could just win the trust of his clients. He was determined to make their welfare his first priority in all his business dealings.

In 1937 E. J. Gibson renamed his company Gibson Associates and made the firm a member of the Chicago Board of Trade. This membership enabled Gibson Associates and later D.A. Davidson to buy and sell contracts in commodities such as wheat, corn, gold, and silver. In 1941 Davidson and his family purchased all the stock in Gibson Associates. Davidson became president and his brothers Harry and Charles served as directors. In its earliest years, D.A. Davidson concentrated on the continued survival and healthy vi-

COMPANY PERSPECTIVES

■

When David Adams Davidson joined a tiny Montana brokerage in 1935, he was planting seeds that would grow into a family of financial services firms. Today, we at Davidson Companies are proud to maintain our local roots and regional focus while expanding to serve clients across the West and beyond. We're proud to be known for our exceptional service, strong ethics and deep sense of responsibility to our communities.

At Davidson Companies, we believe our unwavering commitment to you, our clients, differentiates us from the crowd. We listen to you. Only by listening, and working closely with you, can we find the best financial solutions for you. That personal touch is what makes us uniquely capable of being your financial partners.

ability of the company. No one expressed interest or placed a priority on expansion beyond the comfortable surroundings of Great Falls.

IAN B. DAVIDSON'S MASTER'S THESIS

Possibly the most formative document in the company's history was the thesis written by Ian B. Davidson in fulfillment of his master's degree in business administration from the University of California, Berkeley, in 1956. Titled "The Potential of a Small, Single-Office Investment Firm," it outlined in detail how to develop and grow a successful securities organization in a predominantly rural area of the nation, such as Montana.

Ian determined that the success and prosperity of such a firm depended on its ability to establish itself as a leader in some particular niche of the market. The more Ian studied his family firm, Gibson Associates, the more convinced he became that providing highly personal and superior customer service at a competitive price could provide just such a niche. As the company developed through the years, this remained its dominant goal.

Ian's thesis also stressed the importance of scrutinizing and maintaining efficient and effective operating procedures, thereby making sure clients received the best service possible for the price they paid. His third recommendation called for small investment firms whose operations were limited to particular geographical areas

or specific market segments to obtain membership in a regional stock exchange. This provided a lower-cost and satisfactory alternative to membership in a national stock exchange.

Ian also researched and discussed how a growing investment firm in Great Falls might expand its reach beyond that small city. He examined the demographics and income levels within the state. Based on this information, he determined that the capital city of Helena offered the best expansion opportunities for a firm offering complete financial services.

IAN B. DAVIDSON JOINS THE FIRM

In 1958 Ian B. Davidson joined Gibson Associates as the firm's third employee. He began putting his thesis to the test in 1959, the same year the firm was renamed D.A. Davidson & Company in honor of his father, its earliest director and first president. That year the firm made its first move beyond Great Falls, as Ian's thesis suggested, by opening a branch office in Helena. Also in 1959 the firm applied for membership in the Pacific Coast Stock Exchange, with trading floors in San Francisco and Los Angeles, California.

If D.A. Davidson clients were to prosper, they had to be able to select the best products and investments at the right time to meet their particular needs. As part of its commitment to financial literacy, D.A. Davidson began offering in 1964 investment seminars in communities where it had branch offices. Sponsored by the firm's local financial consultants and intended for both current investors and potential clients, the seminars discussed the latest company research, as well as the options available for individual investors to increase their financial security.

NEW LEADERSHIP

During the next several years, D.A. Davidson continued to grow. When Ian B. Davidson assumed the roles of chairman, president, and chief executive officer in 1970 following his father's death, he took charge of a solidly established Montana business with branch offices in four of the state's five major cities. Knowing the methods by which D.A. Davidson had prospered and grown, Ian retained the company's core values of honesty, industry, and fair dealing. He also continued finding the best-qualified people. To retain them, he made them partners in the company and shared the profits with them as the firm prospered.

Among other changes, the firm reexamined its ability to buy and sell contracts in commodities. The volatile nature of the commodities market was not in step with the generally conservative nature of D.A.

KEY DATES

1935: The brokerage firm E.J. Gibson Inc. opens office in Great Falls, Montana; David Adams Davidson oversees the office.

1937: E.J. Gibson Inc. changes its name to Gibson Associates; the company becomes a member of the Chicago Board of Trade.

1941: David Adams Davidson and his family purchase all the stock of Gibson Associates.

1958: Ian B. Davidson, son of David Adams Davidson, joins Gibson Associates as its third employee.

1959: Gibson Associates joins the Pacific Coast Stock Exchange as a corporate member; Gibson Associates is renamed D.A. Davidson & Company; its first branch office opens in Helena, Montana.

1970: David Adams Davidson dies and Ian B. Davidson becomes chairman, chief executive officer (CEO), and president.

1974: D.A. Davidson gives up its Chicago Board of Trade membership, ending company involvement in commodities investing.

1975: D.A. Davidson acquires Financial Aims Corporation.

1980: D.A. Davidson opens first out-of-state branch office in Williston, North Dakota.

1985: D.A. Davidson is selected for its first Specialist Post at the Pacific Stock Exchange in San Francisco.

1986: D.A. Davidson is named by *Changing Times* as one of seven leading regional investment firms in the United States; the financial services holding company DADCO is formed.

1987: Ian B. Davidson is named to the board of governors of the Pacific Stock Exchange.

1998: D.A. Davidson acquires Jensen Securities in Portland, Oregon.

2000: The holding company DADCO is renamed Davidson Companies.

2004: D.A. Davidson establishes the Davidson 99 Regional Stock Index.

Davidson's investment philosophy. As a result, the firm gave up its membership in the Chicago Board of Trade and ceased trading in commodities in 1974.

D.A. Davidson's entrance onto the national stage began in 1980, when Allan Sloan of *Forbes* magazine profiled the company. Sloan described D.A. Davidson & Company as the "Merrill Lynch of Montana" and "a quintessential regional brokerage firm."

MORE GROWTH AND DIVERSIFICATION: 1980S AND 1990S

In 1986 the company became a subsidiary of the financial services holding company DADCO (later named Davidson Companies), which also included Davidson Investment Advisors, a professional money management firm; Davidson Trust Company, a wealth management and trust operation; Davidson Fixed Income Management, a registered investment adviser providing fixed income services; and Davidson Travel, a full-service travel agency.

Two pivotal events for D.A. Davidson happened in 1987. First, Ian B. Davidson was elected to the board of governors of the Pacific Stock Exchange, the first of several increasingly visible regional and national leadership positions that he would assume in the brokerage industry. The second was the development of the public television program *Wall Street in the Rockies*. Produced in conjunction with Montana State University and aired quarterly, the program was modeled on the popular nationwide program *Wall Street Week* and featured a panel of four financial and business experts. It aired throughout the northern Rockies and earned the company excellent recognition in its broadcast area.

In 1995 the company began recognizing its associates for their community involvement and service. From the very beginning, company officers and executives had set an example and encouraged all D.A. Davidson personnel to be active in their communities. The Bragg Lewis Knutson Community Service Award, established in memory of three company executives killed in a plane crash in 1994, was awarded annually to the company associate who best exemplified the ideal of community service. D.A. Davidson associates from throughout the Northwest have received the award.

To bolster its research capabilities, D.A. Davidson acquired Jensen Securities of Portland, Oregon, in 1998. Jensen Securities was a leading research firm that specialized in companies located in the Pacific Northwest, and its expertise in research was a good match for one of D.A. Davidson's founding beliefs, in that intensive and extensive research was essential for success. The conservative investment philosophy evident at the firm emphasized fundamental research, which focused on a given company's underlying values, rather than technical research, which focused on momentary trends in the overall market. Both types of research were important, but D.A. Davidson analysts believed fundamental research was likely to predict future performance of a company more reliably over a long period of time. In subsequent years trained analysts continued to provide the backbone of D.A. Davidson's research efforts. The firm retained its in-house research department, but it also maintained strong research relationships with companies such as Donaldson, Lufkin, and Jenrette, one of the top investment-banking firms in the United States.

DAVIDSON 99 REGIONAL STOCK INDEX

D.A. Davidson had long believed that just as its clients shared a conservative investment philosophy, they also shared a common interest in companies they viewed as local or regional. The creation of the Davidson 99 Regional Stock Index reflected this belief.

Founded on January 1, 2004, the index included 99 of the most important publicly traded companies with headquarters or a major presence in seven northwestern and Rocky Mountain states: Colorado, Idaho, Montana, Oregon, Utah, Washington, and Wyoming. The index was intended to serve as an economic indicator of emerging regional economic trends that national stock indices might overlook. Stocks were selected based on market capitalization, importance within their sectors, and importance in the states where they were headquartered or active. All 10 major market sectors (energy, materials, industrials, consumer discretionary, consumer staples, health care, financial, information technology, telecommunication services, and utilities) were represented in the index. The index was published daily at http://www.dadavidson.com.

The Davidson 99 Regional Stock Index was not managed or sold. D.A. Davidson made a market in some of the component stocks, which was noted on the descriptions for those companies. Since its inception in 2004 the index had outperformed both the Dow Jones Industrial Average and the Standard and Poor's 500. According to an April 2009 article by *Business Wire*, Fred Dickson, the senior vice president and chief market strategist for D.A. Davidson, attributed this to "the broad diversification of the economy in the Pacific Northwest and Rocky Mountain regions, which were hurt less by the credit crisis and housing slowdown than other major regions of the country that are more heavily weighted in the major market indices."

CONTINUED GROWTH

Since that first Helena branch office opened in 1959, the number of D.A. Davidson branch offices continued to grow. By 2009 over 300 D.A. Davidson financial consultants served clients in eight states.

The concern that D.A. Davidson displayed for its rural and small-town clients established it as a company concerned for the financial welfare of individual investors. Its activities in larger metropolitan areas likewise established its ability to compete and prosper in urban metropolitan markets. D.A. Davidson kept its investing philosophy in line with the generally conservative nature of its original Montana investors. According to a May 2009 article by John Harrington of the *Independent Record*, D.A. Davidson "doesn't deal in commodities; trades very few options; and penny stocks are frowned upon." Instead, it focused on traditional blue chip stocks and other more conservative investment options. Although located in an unlikely place to build and maintain a financial services company, D.A. Davidson sought to distinguish itself through customer service. The firm made a special effort to retain good employees because it believed they were essential to maintaining customer satisfaction. In 2001 the company historian William G. Preston wrote in *The Lengthening Shadow: The Story of D. A. Davidson & Company and the Davidson Companies* that the firm's leadership style "inspires people, in whatever capacity they serve."

In 2008 D.A. Davidson began donating 3.5 percent of pre-tax earnings to civic and charitable organizations in education, arts and culture, and human services. Its educational contributions targeted programs that promote financial literacy and an understanding of the nation's economic system. Its contributions to arts and cultural organizations focused on building an understanding of different cultures and fostering art appreciation among young people. Its human services contributions stressed programs that promote self-sufficiency, strengthen families, foster economic independence, and provide for children's welfare.

THE FUTURE

"Gibson Associates has potential that is not being realized," wrote Ian B. Davidson in his master's thesis in 1956. "If the firm were to increase its present staff, adopt an aggressive sales policy, place more emphasis on non-listed securities and take advantage of regional stock exchange membership opportunities, it would show a great deal of improvement in its present status." Ian saw his vision for a solidly established and highly reputable investment services firm realized. It had gained the industry recognition he sought as a "different" kind of securities firm, capable of delivering a complete line of financial services while maintaining a distinctive personal relationship with each of its clients. Whether managing large trust accounts or paying the bills of beneficiaries who were unable to handle their own financial affairs, the firm that David Adams Davidson first directed still put the welfare and needs of its individual clients first in 2009.

Joyce Helena Brusin

PRINCIPAL COMPETITORS

Edward D. Jones and Company, L. P.; Merrill Lynch & Company Inc.; Charles Schwab; Raymond James Financial Inc.; Morgan Stanley Smith Barney.

FURTHER READING

"Davidson 99 Regional Stock Index® Performance Still Higher Than Broad Indices since Inception, down for Quarter," *Business Wire*, April 1, 2009.

Harrington, John, "Helena Branch of D.A. Davidson Marks 50th Year," *Independent Record* (Helena, MT), May 4, 2009.

Preston, William G., *The Lengthening Shadow: The Story of D. A. Davidson & Company and the Davidson Companies*, Great Falls, MT: Davidson Companies, 2001.

Sloan, Allan, "Making It Big in Big Sky Country," *Forbes*, October 27, 1980, p. 124.

Solomon, Jolie, "West of Wall Street: Having a New York Address Means Much Less in the Securities Industry," *Newsweek*, May 24, 1993.

Stern, Richard L., "D. A. Davidson: Just Plain Folks," *Forbes*, November 14, 1988, p. 210.

———, "When Wall Street Sneezes, Middle America Laughs," *Forbes*, March 19, 1990, p. 36.

"Students Invest Using Firm's Money," KING 5 News (Seattle, WA), May 20, 2009, http://www.king5.com/education/stories/NW_052009EDB-students-investing-KC.22dffa0f.html.

Dannon Company, Inc.

100 Hillside Avenue
White Plains, New York 10603
U.S.A.
Telephone: (914) 872-8400
Toll Free: (877) 326-6668
Fax: (914) 872-1565
Web site: http://www.dannon.com

Wholly Owned Subsidiary of Groupe Danone
Incorporated: 1942 as Dannon Milk Products Inc.
Employees: 1,200
Sales: $1 billion (2008 est.)
NAISC: 311511 Yogurt (except Frozen) Manufacturing; 424430 Yogurt Merchant Wholesalers; 424430 Dairy Products (except Canned, Dried) Merchant Wholesalers

■ ■ ■

Dannon Company, Inc., popularized yogurt in the United States in the 1950s and has remained one of the nation's leading producers of yogurt. Originally marketed as a no-frills health food, Dannon yogurt has also achieved success with its fruit-filled and sweetened varieties. The brand is sold throughout the United States by an expansive network of food brokers.

THE BIRTH OF A BRAND: IMPORTING DANNON TO THE UNITED STATES IN THE 1940S

Yogurt has long been a staple in the diet of Balkan and Near East peasants. A product formed from milk into the consistency of custard by fermentation in the open air, it was popularized in western Europe soon after 1900 by Elie Metchnikoff, a Nobel laureate who attributed the long life of Bulgarians to one of the two bacteria that converted milk into yogurt. Even though Metchnikoff's hypothesis was never proven by further investigation, it was still considered a nutritious, vitamin-rich food. It could be eaten by the estimated 50 million Americans who had difficulty in digesting milk, and studies suggested that it could aid in the prevention of gastrointestinal infections.

By virtue of his position as director of the Pasteur Institute in Paris, Metchnikoff conferred credibility on yogurt as a health food. Its consumption spread to western Europe, especially France (where even in the 1980s eight times as much yogurt was being eaten per person as in the United States). The Spanish businessman Isaac Carasso obtained cultures from Bulgaria and the Pasteur Institute, and in 1919 he started manufacturing yogurt in Barcelona, Spain, for sale through pharmacies. As his business expanded, he established a French branch in the 1920s. His son Daniel, for whom he named the product Danone, directed the French operation.

Daniel Carasso came to the United States in 1942 with Joe Metzger, a Swiss-born Spanish businessman, and Metzger's son Juan. They purchased a small yogurt factory in New York City and continued production using the family formula but changing the name from Danone to Dannon. At first, Dannon Milk Products turned out only 200 half-pint glass jars a day of the obscure product for small numbers of ethnic Turks, Arabs, Greeks, and, in Juan's words, "health-food

COMPANY PERSPECTIVES

∎

The Dannon Company, Inc., prides itself on consistently delivering high-quality, wholesome products and responding to consumer needs with nutritious, innovative new products and flavors.

To this end, Dannon established the Dannon Institute, an independent, nonprofit organization that creates and supports programs that explore and reinforce the relationship between nutrition and better health.

fanatics." Juan Metzger, who washed out the returnable jars every day, later recalled in an interview with Barbara Rowes of *People Weekly*, "We only sold $20 worth a day, but even then we were the bigger of the two companies in the business."

To publicize yogurt, Dannon's founders hired an advertising firm. Samples were distributed in quality restaurants, airports, and places where international travelers congregated. Soon, radio comedians were poking fun at the product. In one week the Metzgers counted 24 jokes about yogurt on the air, mostly ridiculing its claims to foster longevity.

Even though the U.S. public of the 1940s seemed to find yogurt's exotic name and origin hilarious, it was slow to accept the product. In that era "health food" was generally regarded as a preoccupation of wacky cultists, based largely in southern California. Moreover, the tart flavor of yogurt was not to the liking of the U.S. public. Around 1950, however, Dannon found the key to wider acceptance by adding a layer of strawberry preserves to the bottom of the container. The company slogan changed from "Doctors recommend it" to "A wonderful snack ... a delicious dessert." A low-fat yogurt was introduced later to soothe the qualms of weight-conscious customers.

EXPANDING POPULARITY AND GROWTH: THE 1950S AND 1960S

Before long a fleet of 55 leased trucks was supplying virtually every New York supermarket and delicatessen with Dannon yogurt. Celebrities such as Bernard Baruch, Danny Kaye, Adlai E. Stevenson, Judy Holliday, and Kim Novak admitted to liking it. Waxed cups replaced the glass jars. Dannon moved from the Bronx in 1952 to a larger facility in Long Island City, Queens.

By 1959 Dannon had yogurt in six flavors. It was also producing one-half to three-quarters of the yogurt made in the United States and was generating annual sales of about $3 million. That same year the company was acquired by the Chicago-based Beatrice Foods Company for between $3 million and $3.5 million in stock.

By 1967 Dannon came in 10 varieties. The company was selling about 30 percent of the 100 million half-pint cups of yogurt being purchased annually in the United States. Automation had dramatically increased production, but the basic method of making yogurt continued almost unchanged: bacteria converted the sugar in pasteurized low-fat milk, causing it to thicken and become yogurt. Shipping depots had been established in Boston, Massachusetts; Detroit, Michigan; Philadelphia, Pennsylvania; and Washington, D.C., because Dannon, which claimed to be the first company to achieve national distribution for perishable foods, would not trust delivery of its product to anyone else.

BUILDING A NATIONWIDE BRAND CONSCIOUSNESS: THE 1970S AND 1980S

To broaden its customer base, Dannon added rock 'n' roll shows to its radio outlets and distributed "Go Yogurt" buttons to schoolchildren. An airplane-borne streamer spread the message "Yannon Dogurt—oops Dannon Yogurt" to crowds at Brooklyn's Coney Island. Dannon later shot the first U.S. television commercial made in the Soviet Union. It featured an 89-year-old native of the Caucasian republic of Georgia eating Dannon yogurt while a background voice said, "And this pleased his mother very much. She was 114."

By 1981 U.S. yogurt sales had reached 1.3 billion containers a year, with Dannon accounting for one-third. It had plants in California, Florida, New Jersey, Ohio, and Texas, as well as in New York City. The number of flavors had grown to 15, including apricot, Dutch apple, boysenberry, and coffee, although strawberry remained the most popular. Frozen yogurt and a premixed yogurt called Melange had also been successfully introduced.

In 1981 Dannon was acquired by BSN-Gervais-Danone, a Paris-based company that partly stemmed from the original Carasso yogurt venture and had grown into one of France's largest conglomerates. BSN paid a hefty $84.3 million in cash for the company, which earned about $3.7 million on sales of about $130 million in 1981, but a BSN spokesman told *Advertising Age*'s Janet Neiman, "To buy back the name we own around the world, all over Europe, in South America and Japan, is something we were prepared to pay for."

KEY DATES

1942: Dannon begins yogurt production in the United States.

1950: Dannon launches its first fruit-filled yogurt product.

1952: Joe Metzger becomes the president of Dannon Milk Products Inc.

1959: Beatrice Foods Company acquires Dannon Milk Products Inc.

1981: Dannon is acquired by the French conglomerate BSN-Gervais-Danone.

1992: Dannon begins marketing Sprinkl'ins, a yogurt and candy product.

1999: The company begins selling Actimel, a probiotic yogurt drink, in health food and specialty food stores.

2005: Dannon launches its popular probiotic yogurt Activia.

2009: Daniel Carasso, the Dannon founder, dies at the age of 103.

By 1985 the U.S. yogurt market had grown to about $1 billion, but Dannon's share had fallen to about 21 percent. For three years the company's advertisements had been urging the public to "Get a Dannon body," but now it was adding new, richer yogurt products to stay ahead of the competition, which now consisted of 125 other brands. Between 1984 and 1985 the company brought to market a French-style yogurt called Dannon Extra Smooth, another French-style breakfast yogurt with nuts and raisins, and the extra-fruity Dannon Supreme, a dessert yogurt with higher fat content and more sugar.

These new products, aided by a doubling of the advertising budget to $12 million in 1985, lifted Dannon's market share to 26 percent in 1986. For the first time the company began advertising on network television and doing trade promotion, as well as consumer advertising, to make sure it received enough shelf space in supermarkets. Minipacks of six cups were introduced in 1985. By Dannon's silver anniversary in 1992, the company was selling 2 million cups a day in dozens of varieties and flavors.

PRODUCT DIVERSIFICATION IN THE 1990S

The consumption of yogurt dropped in 1989 and recovered only marginally in the following years. To stimulate sales, Dannon in 1992 began test marketing Sprinkl'ins, a yogurt for children filled with fruit, sugar, and mix-in candy bits. An employee at Grey Advertising, Dannon's agency, told Kim Foltz of the *New York Times*, "Yogurt hasn't been very kid-friendly in the past because the taste was too sour. This is a way of creating a new generation of yogurt eaters." Games and puzzles were printed on the inside of the package that held four small cups of Sprinkl'ins.

Nutritionists had nothing good to say about Sprinkl'ins; one compared it to junk food because of its high sugar content. Children, however, responded enthusiastically. Introduced nationally in 1993, Sprinkl'ins had sales of $43.9 million that year. The following year the company introduced Dannon Danimals, a new yogurt line decorated with pictures of wild elephants and bears. Dannon promised to donate 1.5 percent of the sale price to the National Wildlife Federation.

At the same time Dannon was increasing the sugar content in its product line, it was running print ads encouraging people to substitute yogurt for oil, sour cream, milk, or eggs in preparing food. These ads included recipes for lower-calorie versions of desserts such as brownies. It was also testing a sour cream alternative and was considering expansion of its own branded yogurt cheese into other areas.

Dannon introduced no fewer than 23 new products in 1994 and 11 more in the first part of 1995. Its share of the $1.6 billion U.S. market for refrigerated spoonable yogurt reached 37 percent in early 1995. In April of that year the company won two Edison Awards for product innovation: a silver for its new Pure Indulgence frozen yogurt and a bronze for Sprinkl'ins. Grey Advertising won an award from the Advertising Research Foundation for a campaign that, according to the foundation's president, "clearly moved the needle on sales." The campaign, introduced in July 1994 with the theme "Taste Why It's Dannon," showed spots with scenes such as a woman watching the fattening treats on a dessert cart transformed into their Dannon Light counterparts.

Among the new 1994–95 products were Tropifruta, aimed at the Hispanic market; Dannon Light dessert flavors such as créme caramel and banana cream pie; and Double Delights, which combined fruit toppings with Bavarian cream or cheesecake yogurt. "For years it was 'health, health, health,' with consumers," Dannon marketing executive Robert Wallach told *Brandweek*'s Betsy Spethmann. "Now they're swinging back to moderation, looking to balance taste with health."

In 1994, 89.32 percent of the Dannon Company was owned by Groupe Danone, the new name adopted by what had been BSN-Gervais-Danone. That same year Dannon's corporate headquarters moved from White Plains to Tarrytown, New York. The streamlined manufacturing system consisted of a production plant in Minster, Ohio, and another in Fort Worth, Texas. The research and development center in Minster scrutinized freshly made yogurt for quality, developed new products, and selected and studied the bacteria used in making yogurt for optimum taste and texture. Dannon's distribution network carefully timed delivery to store shelves for optimal freshness and quality.

Dannon's dominance of the U.S. yogurt industry continued for most of the 1990s. In 1996 the company still controlled more than 36 percent of yogurt sales. Its strong sales during the latter part of the decade coincided with a surge in yogurt consumption nationwide, as the industry as a whole saw revenues increase from roughly $600 million in 1996 to nearly $1.8 billion in 1999. As consumer demand for yogurt increased, however, Dannon found itself battling a host of emerging rivals. Prominent among these was General Mills, maker of Yoplait and Colombo yogurt products, which began to make inroads into Dannon's market share with a new line of yogurt products aimed at children. Among the most popular of Yoplait's innovative offerings was Go-Gurt, a flavored yogurt snack packaged in a portable tube. By mid-1999 Dannon's share of the market had dropped nearly 7 percent, whereas General Mills saw its share rise by 19 percent.

To contend with this challenge, Dannon set out to explore new ways to bolster its presence in the lucrative children's market. In early 2000 the company launched Danimals Drinkables, a liquid version of its popular yogurt treat. Later that year it introduced a new line of Sprinkl'ins called the Mystery Surprise. The company strengthened its marketing effort for these new products by tripling the advertising budget for its children's yogurt line to $12 million. In spite of these efforts, General Mills continued to infiltrate Dannon's core market. By 2000 Dannon had lost its status as America's premiere brand of yogurt, with 1999 sales reaching $537 million, compared to $629 million for General Mills. As Dannon saw its market position slide, it began to consider a different direction for its core business.

FOCUSING ON THE HEALTHY FOOD NICHE: THE PROBIOTICS TREND OF THE 21ST CENTURY

Intent on recapturing its number-one ranking, Dannon developed several new yogurt offerings during the first years of the new century. In early 2001 it launched Light 'n Fit, a retooled version of its Dannon Light line of products; two years later it introduced Frusion, a yogurt smoothie drink. As U.S. demand for healthier food options began to rise, Dannon shifted its attention toward capturing this emerging market. In particular, the company hoped to capitalize on growing interest in probiotics, live microorganisms found in certain foods and dietary supplements, which have been alleged to offer a wide range of health benefits. Dannon had actually introduced its first probiotic product, the yogurt drink Actimel, in 1999, although at the time it was aimed at the relatively small health food niche. By 2004 the company began to sell Actimel nationwide under a new name, DanActive, using an aggressive marketing push to promote the drink's benefits to the immune system. A year later Dannon launched Activia, a probiotic yogurt that supposedly aided with digestion.

A number of commentators noted that marketing products with 10 times the live bacteria of traditional yogurt presented a unique challenge to Dannon. However, with consumer interest in probiotic food steadily increasing, the company's gamble seemed to promise large dividends over the long term. The company further established its position as a leader in the expanding probiotic market by sponsoring a number of health and fitness programs during these years. In October 2006 Dannon helped organize the Snack Healthy, Work Smart program, which was designed to encourage healthy snack choices among working women. That same month the company introduced the Dannon Next Generation Nutrition Grants, an education campaign promoting good dietary habits among school children.

In the last years of the decade, it remained to be seen whether the benefits promised by probiotic foods would lead to increased consumer demand for Dannon's healthier line of products. Early trends seemed to support the company's strategy as sales of Activia topped $130 million in 2006. However, not all consumers were pleased with the company's advertising blitz. In January 2008 a group of plaintiffs in California filed a class-action lawsuit against the company, insisting that its claims for the health benefits of its probiotic products were unsupported by scientific data. A year later the company entered into settlement discussions with the plaintiffs. More significantly, the company suffered a personal loss in the midst of these legal issues when Daniel Carasso died in May 2009. He was 103 years old.

Robert Halasz
Updated, Stephen Meyer

PRINCIPAL COMPETITORS

General Mills Inc.; Kraft Foods Inc.; HP Hood LLC.

FURTHER READING

"Dannon Fattens Up on Nothing but Yogurt," *BusinessWeek*, September 9, 1967, pp. 82, 84, 86, 89.

"Dannon Yogurt: Its Cups Overfloweth," *Nation's Business*, March 1981, p. 89.

Fannin, Rebecca, "Dannon's Culture Coup," *Marketing & Media Decisions*, November 1986, pp. 59–60, 64–65.

Foltz, Kim, "Dannon's Bet: Yogurt 'Just for Kids,'" *New York Times*, May 1, 1992, p. C1.

Grimes, William, "Daniel Carasso, 103, a Pioneer of Yogurt," *New York Times*, May 21, 2009, p. 12.

Neiman, Janet, "Dannon Buyer Eyes U.S.," *Advertising Age*, June 29, 1981, pp. 1, 80.

Pollack, Judann, "General Mills Lays Claim to Victory over Dannon," *Advertising Age*, July 5, 1999, p. 3.

Rowes, Barbara, "This Yogurt King Has Turned a Sour-Tasting Snack into a Sweet Story of Success," *People Weekly*, November 10, 1980, pp. 121–122.

Rubenstein, Carin, "The Culture Competition," *New York Times*, March 23, 2003, p. L3.

Spethmann, Betsy, "Dannon: Kudos on Taste," *Brandweek*, May 15, 1995, pp. 18, 20.

Stewart-Gordon, James, "Yogurt's March from Fad to Fashion," *Reader's Digest*, December 1968, pp. 158–162.

Digital Angel Corporation

490 Villaume Avenue
South Saint Paul, Minnesota 55075
U.S.A.
Telephone: (651) 552-6301
Web site: http://www.digitalangel.com

Public Company
Founded: 1988 as Applied Cellular Technology
Incorporated: 1993
Employees: 364
Sales: $78.2 million (2008)
Stock Exchanges: NASDAQ
Ticker Symbol: DIGA
NAISC: 334290 Other Communication Equipment Manufacturing; 423430 Computer and Computer Peripheral Equipment and Software Merchant Wholesalers; 541512 Computer Systems Design Services

■ ■ ■

Digital Angel Corporation is an advanced technology company in the field of animal identification and emergency identification solutions. Digital Angel's products are used around the world in applications such as pet identification using its patented implantable microchip; livestock identification and tracking using visual and radio frequency identification (RFID) ear tags; and global positioning systems (GPS) search and rescue beacons for use on aircraft, ships, and boats and by adventure enthusiasts. Its brands in the animal identification segment include Destron Fearing livestock

visual and RFID ear tags, with related scanners and other equipment and support, and Digital Angel's patented Bio-Thermo temperature-sensing technology. Additionally, Digital Angel's implantable RFID microchips for companion pets are distributed to veterinarians in the United States through Intervet/Schering-Plough Animal Health under the Schering-Plough's Home Again brand. The emergency identification segment, which is based in the United Kingdom, produces GPS emergency locator beacons for military, commercial, and recreational markets. The military product, known as SARBE (Search and Rescue Beacon Equipment), has been a world-leading supplier to defense departments around the world since World War II. Commercial (marine and aviation) and recreational markets are served by the McMurdo range of products.

THE BIRTH OF THE DIGITAL ANGEL

The company was founded in 1988 as Applied Cellular Technology by Richard J. Sullivan. Originally a computer sales business, the company was incorporated in 1993 and went public in 1994. Sullivan was a savvy entrepreneur who quickly turned his attention to wireless communications technologies. Through a series of acquisitions—more than 60 in eight years—Sullivan positioned his company as a one-stop shop for integrated communications packages. Serving as the chief executive officer (CEO) and chairman, Sullivan maintained offices in Missouri and New Hampshire when, in 1996, he moved the entire operation to Palm Beach, Florida. Sullivan rarely used cash in his dealings and instead relied on the company's stock as his primary

143

COMPANY PERSPECTIVES

Digital Angel has manufactured RFID microchips for millions of pets throughout the world, providing them with unalterable and permanent identification should they become lost or stolen. Similarly, Digital Angel has pioneered RFID solutions to help farmers, ranchers, sale barns and other livestock producers to identify and track animals in efforts to ensure the health and safety of the world's food supply.

Digital Angel has also established a core competency and leadership position in the high tech industry through the development of GPS search and rescue beacons that integrate geosynchronous communications for use by the military and the private sector to track aircraft, ships and other high value assets. This is a growing area for the Company and one poised to experience substantial growth in the coming years.

In short, Digital Angel's products are used in innumerous ways around the world to safeguard those things we value most: our food supply, our natural resources and environment, and the well-being of those we love.

currency. Some of his acquisitions appeared overly ambitious and ill-suited for the company's business plan. For example, purchases included companies that traded in auto accessories, auto parts, and commercial heating and air conditioning, which resulted in erratic share price fluctuations. Filings with the U.S. Securities and Exchange Commission (SEC) indicated that the company's strategy changed on an annual basis, with business segments going from seven, to five, then three, and eventually one: the technology development business.

In June 1999 Applied Cellular Technology Inc. announced the merger of two Canadian acquisitions, Contour Telecom Management Inc. and TigerTel Services Ltd., to form TigerTel Inc., giving Applied Cellular 70 percent ownership in this new entity. In July 1999 Applied Cellular Technology changed its corporate name to Applied Digital Solutions Inc. (ADS), and in November it sold TigerTel Inc. to AT&T Canada Inc. for $47 million. One month later, ADS acquired the patent rights to develop a GPS transceiver implant dubbed the "Digital Angel." Peter Zhou, a leading

scientist in the field of electronic detecting systems, was hired in January 2000 to oversee the development of the technology at DigitalAngel.net Inc., a wholly owned subsidiary of the company. That same year the company won the prestigious Technology Pioneers award from the World Economic Forum, which is given to companies that are "involved in the development of life-changing technology innovation and have potential for long-term impact on business and society."

ADS envisioned the Digital Angel as a beneficial device in a variety of areas, including health care and patient monitoring, e-commerce security, and law enforcement. Other potential applications included tracking pets, wildlife, and livestock; locating lost property or mailed packages; and managing the food supply chain. Once implanted in a person's body, the Digital Angel would be powered electromechanically through muscle movement and activated either by the wearer or by an external monitoring facility. While location technology had its obvious attraction in certain conditions, such as adult care facilities with Alzheimer's patients or parents of autistic children, it did raise questions of an ethical nature regarding privacy issues. Richard Smith, a privacy policy expert at the Privacy Foundation in Denver, voiced his concerns to Bob Brewin of *Computerworld*, "Someone could buy a pet tracker, throw it in their spouse's car and find out where they have been." Others raised issues of a more serious nature, suggesting that repressive government regimes may abuse the technology by tracking the general population. According to *Computerworld*, Zhou dismissed his detractors by stating, "An inventor is not responsible for evil uses of his products. No one blames the atom bomb on Einstein."

UNVEILING THE DIGITAL ANGEL

When ADS announced in March 2000 its plans to acquire Destron Fearing Corporation, a leader in the field of animal identification since 1945, ADS's share rose by nearly $1.00 to $16.125 and Destron Fearing's soared by $3.00 to $7.688. In September 2000 the strategic merger between Digital Angel.net Inc. and Destron Fearing Corporation was complete, and Destron Fearing's CEO, Randolph K. Geissler, was named chairman and CEO of Digital Angel.net. Within weeks, Schering-Plough, the distributor of Destron microchips, placed a follow-up order for the Digital Angel.net microchips for the U.S. companion animal market. This resupply not only had a positive impact on sales growth but also served as further testimony to the importance of this merger. The following month, ADS unveiled its Digital Angel before more than 300 invited guests at Cipriani 42nd Street in New York City.

KEY DATES

■

1988: Applied Cellular Technology is founded by Richard J. Sullivan.

1999: Applied Cellular Technology changes its name to Applied Digital Solutions Inc. (ADS).

2000: Peter Zhou is appointed to oversee the development of the human implantable microchip; ADS acquires Destron Fearing Corporation.

2001: The first generation of Digital Angel wristwatches goes on display at TechShow 2001.

2002: ADS completes a major restructuring to form the publicly held company Digital Angel Corporation.

2003: The U.S. Food and Drug Administration approves the Bio-Thermo microchip.

2004: Digital Angel sells Medical Advisory Systems Inc. to MedAire Inc.

2006: Digital Angel is awarded U.S. patents for its Bio-Thermo chip and syringe-implantable glucose-monitoring radio frequency identification microchip.

2007: ADS is merged into Digital Angel; Digital Angel acquires McMurdo.

2008: Digital Angel acquires Geissler Technologies.

In stark contrast to the Renaissance-inspired backdrop, Zhou presented the highlight of the evening: a demonstration of the futuristic technology. As an ADS engineer roamed the streets of New York, his location and movements were tracked via GPS, relayed to the Internet, and displayed on a large screen before the captivated audience. To give the group of distinguished guests, government officials, potential investors, and members of the press a taste of the Digital Angel's medical monitoring capabilities, the engineer's pulse and body temperature for the last two weeks were visible on a second screen.

However, the controversy over subdermal implantation of microchips in humans prevailed, and ADS soon removed all references to human implantation from its Web site. Instead, the company turned its attention to externally worn devices, and the first generation of its Digital Angel wristwatch with full location and biomonitoring functionality went on display at Tech-Show 2001 at the Harvard Business School. Referring to the wristwatch in *Business Wire* in January 2001, Mer-

cedes Walton, the president and chief operating officer (COO) of ADS said, "Demand from consumers, businesses and non-profit organizations is fueling increasing interest for our product." With a McKinsey & Company report estimating that there would be a $70 billion market in the United States for wireless monitoring devices by 2005, ADS was eager to jump on the bandwagon. In February 2001 ADS opened its e-Business Practice Inc. headquarters at the University Research Park in Riverside, California. The facility served as the hub for the development, marketing, and distribution of Digital Angel products and services, including a new line of external devices and pet-protection applications. With a staggering 14,315 percent growth in revenues over the preceding four years, ADS was recognized as a leading, single-source provider of e-business solutions and was ranked in the top tier of Deloitte & Touche's "Technology Fast 500."

In March 2001 Digital Angel.net purchased 16.6 percent interest in Medical Advisory Systems Inc. (MAS). This transaction, which also included adding Walton to the MAS board of directors, gave Digital Angel access to a secure 24/7 physician-staffed medical call center for use by its customers and end-patients. Commenting on the move in February 2001 for *Business Wire*, Walton stated, "The completion of this transaction allows us to further our strategy to define the Digital Angel 'product' as a combination of device and service." In addition, MAS provided health care to ships at sea and other remote areas through a worldwide telecommunications network, and ADS saw this new interrelationship as an opportunity to expand into key geographic markets.

In early June 2001 ADS announced that it had begun the first production run of its Digital Angel devices. Delivery and beta testing were scheduled for mid-July with a group of participants selected from several thousand preregistered subscribers. The beta testing was expected to last 90 days, during which the test group would provide crucial input based on real-life situations. Soon after this announcement, Digital Angel was named one of four "Cool Products" in *Fortune*'s "Cool List 2001." This accolade, coupled with the "Best of Show" award at the Internet World Wireless Show earlier that year, seemed affirmation that the Digital Angel was emerging as a technological force in the global arena.

The company at large, however, was experiencing its fair share of difficulties. According to Ed Duggan of the *South Florida Business Journal* in September 2001, "The troubled company has suffered sizable losses over the past few years, recently has been cautioned on a possible delisting from Nasdaq, and has said that it is out of compliance with its line of credit." Duggan also noted that Walton had resigned as CEO "to pursue other opportunities" and that Sullivan would serve as president and CEO until a new president was selected.

LEAN AND FOCUSED

This announcement was lost as the nation reeled from the terrorist attacks against the United States on September 11, 2001. Even though Digital Angel was still in testing mode, ADS recognized its duty to offer free units to the New York Fire Department and the U.S. Department of Transportation to aid in their search and rescue efforts. In the wake of the terrorist attacks, Americans turned their attention from issues of privacy to those of safety and homeland security. Now more than ever before, tracking devices were in the public's consciousness. According to Anika Myers of the *Miami Daily Business Review*, the California Department of Corrections entered into an agreement with ADS to establish a parolee monitoring pilot program in Los Angeles Country.

By the end of February 2002 ADS had completed a corporate restructuring that included selling seven business units, closing 20 others, and reducing the workforce from more than 1,600 to less than 400. Under this plan, Digitalangel.net Inc., e-Business Practice Inc., Destron Fearing Corporation, MAS, and the London-based Signature Industries (a satellite communications company) were merged to form the publicly held company Digital Angel Corporation. The company also created another wholly owned subsidiary called Advanced Power Solutions Inc. to develop and market Thermo Life, a thermoelectric generator powered by body heat. "We have completely transformed this company," Sullivan said in a statement to the *Business Wire* in February 2002. "The restructuring creates a leaner, more focused and agile organization." The restructuring generated $11 million, which ADS used to reduce its debt owed to IBM Credit Corp. The company expected to be cash-flow positive by 2002, providing it executed a new debt restructuring agreement with IBM Credit Corp.

By April 2002, with Scott R. Silverman in place as the new president, ADS was once again publicizing VeriChip, the implantable microchip. No bigger than a grain of rice, the device was touted as a replacement for medical tags whereby health professionals could obtain vital information, such as the pacemaker model or drug allergies, in emergency situations. ADS maintained that because the chips would only contain identification codes that would refer to a medical database and not medical details the VeriChip would not need approval by the U.S. Food and Drug Administration (FDA). Ac-

cording to the *Palm Beach Post*'s Deborah Circelli, things took a downturn in May, when the FDA opened an investigation into the VeriChip, which the company had already implanted in eight people. In addition, financial woes continued to plague the beleaguered company. With mounting operating losses, the resignation of two auditors over a dispute involving how to record a one-time $14.3 million expense, and a lawsuit filed by disgruntled shareholders, Sullivan said to Beatrice E. Garcia of the *Miami Herald* in May 2002, "Let's be perfectly frank, Applied Digital has been through hell in the past two years."

Changing tack, by mid-summer Digital Angel Corporation was promoting a unit the size of a matchbook that could be clipped onto a belt or incorporated into a watch or collar. The new device combined "assisted-GPS technology with GSM or CDMA wireless protocols, making it usable worldwide," a company official said to Paul Dykewicz of *Satellite News*. Shortly thereafter, Digital Angel Corporation signed a ten-year agreement with Angel Guardian in Mexico to distribute the product—a deal that had the potential to bring in $18 million over five years. Besides targeting Latin America, the company was also focusing its marketing efforts on Asia and Europe.

In October 2002 the FDA ruled that the VeriChip did not need to be regulated if its use was restricted to security, financial, and personal identification. However, if used for diagnosis or treatment of injury or illness, the chip would come under FDA regulation. Buoyed by this news, ADS planned on marketing the product in the United States. Beverly Enterprises Inc, the largest nursing home chain in the country, soon came onboard by signing a three-year contract with Digital Angel Corporation to sell its equipment to its customers. However, there was a major concern about this technology: Unless a hospital or emergency-care center had the scanner that was needed to read the information, the implanted chips were useless. By February 2003 Garcia reported in the *Miami Herald* that the only scanners were in "Applied Digital's hands." This was closely followed by the news that Sullivan had left Applied Digital, although he remained as one of the largest shareholders with 20 percent of the stake.

NEW DIRECTION

At the same time, Digital Angel Corporation got the boost it needed when the FDA approved its Bio-Thermo chip, a temperature-sensing chip for pets, livestock, and wildlife. In June 2003 Digital Angel Corporation ceased retail orders and restricted sales to business partners. Randolph K. Geissler, the CEO of Digital Angel, took up the reins as CEO of the company's Animal Applications and Information/ Medical Divisions, and Kevin McLaughlin, the president and COO of ADS, assumed the position of interim CEO for Digital Angel. The London-based Signature Industries announced the launch of its latest GPS Emergency Location Transmitter, its new Search and Rescue Beacon Equipment (SARBE), and an agreement with China Link Company Ltd. to market the SARBE equipment in China. In October 2003 Digital Angel signed a contract with the U.S. Department of Agriculture to supply 300,000 electronic tracking devices to monitor and isolate diseased livestock. When the first case of mad cow disease in the United States was announced, Digital Angel's stock doubled, peaking at $5 per share. The following month Digital Angel signed an agreement with OuterLink Corporation, a satellite tracking and mobile satellite communications systems company, and appointed the company's CEO, Van Chu, as Digital's new CEO. In January 2004, when the acquisition was completed, Chu was replaced by Kevin N. McGrath, who soon secured a contract with Petroleum Helicopters to equip its entire fleet with OuterLink's CP-2 Satcom System. Predicting that the company would be in the black by year end, McGrath was feeling optimistic. "The company made a bunch of big bets," he said to Alina Tugend of the *New York Times*. "It's not that they shouldn't have made them, but they shouldn't have made as many."

In an effort to streamline its activities, Digital Angel sold MAS to MedAire Inc. in April 2004. Later that year the European Parliament and the Council of the European Union passed an initiative mandating that all pets traveling into and between EU member countries must be microchipped. On the heels of this announcement, Digital Angel won a $600,000 contract from the Portuguese Ministry of Agriculture for its dog-identification program, and the Bio-Thermo chip was launched in the United Kingdom. Through 2005 Digital Angel was showing increased revenues across the company. The following year the U.S. Patent and Trademark Office granted Digital Angel patents for its Bio-Thermo chip and syringe-implantable RFID microchip that measured glucose levels in diabetics. The chip would be marketed and distributed by what was now its sister company, VeriChip Corporation. In 2007 Digital Angel signed a multiyear distribution agreement with Schering-Plough Home Again LLC and completed its acquisition of McMurdo. In December 2007 Digital Angel Corporation merged with Applied Digital Solutions Inc., and Joseph J. Grillo was selected as the new CEO to lead the combined company.

Within two weeks of the merger, Digital Angel acquired Geissler Technologies, which was incorporated into Destron Fearing. The acquisition brought back a founder, Raymond Geissler, who resumed the position as president of the animal identification segment. In April 2008 the company received a further boost when McMurdo's *FAST*FIND personal locator beacon was approved by the Federal Communications Commission for sale in the United States.

In a further effort to cut costs, the company implemented another restructuring program aimed at its animal identification business, which included relocating its corporate office from Florida to Minnesota, reducing staff numbers, outsourcing some manufacturing, and moving part of its operation overseas. With fewer than 1,000 customers agreeing to be implanted with the human RFID microchip and years of costly clinical trials ahead, Digital Angel also made the decision in November 2008 to sell all of its shares in VeriChip Corporation to R&R Consulting Partners, a company that was now controlled by Silverman.

According to *Business Wire*, Grillo stated in a letter to shareholders in January 2009, "Looking ahead, we still believe that our two core businesses operate in markets that are relatively recession-resistant, and we see opportunities to increase market share both organically and through the introduction of new products."

Marie O'Sullivan

PRINCIPAL SUBSIDIARIES

Destron Fearing; Signature Industries Ltd.

PRINCIPAL DIVISIONS

McMurdo.

PRINCIPAL COMPETITORS

Allflex USA Inc.; American Medical Alert Corp.; GTX Corp.; Location Based Technologies; LoJack Corporation; Trimble Navigation Ltd.; WebTech Wireless.

FURTHER READING

"Applied Digital Solutions Completes Far-Reaching Corporate Restructuring with Sale or Closure of 27 Business Units," *Business Wire*, February 19, 2002.

"Applied Digital Solutions' Wholly Owned Subsidiary Digital Angel Corporation Completes Acquisition of 16.6% Interest in Medical Advisory Systems, Inc.," *Business Wire*, February 27, 2001.

Brewin, Bob, "Digital Angel to Watch Over Patients," *Computerworld*, January 1, 2001, p. 8.

Chea, Terence, "Digital Angel Exiting Applied Digital? Did Company Fail to Verify VeriChip Risks?" *America's Intel-*

ligence Wire, October 21, 2004.

Circelli, Deborah, "'Chipping' Away at Their Problems: Applied Digital Solutions Inc. Continues to Move Forward with Its Implantable VeriChip Despite Regulatory and Business Setbacks," *Palm Beach Post*, October 27, 2002, p. 1F.

"Digital Angel Focuses on Identification," *Feedstuffs*, October 31, 2005, p. 6.

"Digital Angel Wristwatch to Be Unveiled at Tech Show 2001 at Harvard Business School," *Business Wire*, January 18, 2001.

Duggan, Ed, "From Pet Tracking to Helping People," *South Florida Business Journal*, April 20, 2001, p. 53.

———, "Stock of Digital Angel's Parent Falls to Earth," *South Florida Business Journal*, April 20, 2001, p. 1.

———, "Walton Out at Applied Digital," *South Florida Business Journal*, September 20, 2001, p. 14.

Dykewicz, Paul, "Spotlight: Digital Angel Touches Consumers with GPS-Based Location Devices," *Satellite News*, July 22, 2002.

Feder, Barnaby J., "Deal to Simplify Business of Implantable Identity Chips," *New York Times*, August 10, 2007.

Forster, Julie, "Mad Cow Scare May Boost St. Paul-based Animal Chip Seller," *Saint Paul Pioneer Press* (Saint Paul, MN), December 27, 2003.

Garcia, Beatrice E., "Despite Potential, Applied Digital Solutions Faces Tough Road," *Miami Herald*, July 29, 2003.

———, "Palm Beach, Fla., Microchip Maker Must Raise Money Quickly," *Miami Herald*, February 24, 2003.

———, "Palm Beach Fla.-based Firm Struggles Despite Implantable Chip's Sizzle," *Miami Herald*, May 29, 2002.

Lee, Jennifer, "Implantable Chip Headed for Market," *New York Times*, April 5, 2002, p. C3.

"Letter to Digital Angel Stockholders from CEO Joseph J. Grillo," *Business Wire*, January 5, 2009.

Martin, Darla, "Riverside, Calif., Internet-Based Tracking Company Changes Strategy," *Business Press* (Ontario, CA), June 2, 2003.

Miller, Dale, "Electronic Data Analysis Flings Open Doors," *National Hog Farmer*, August 15, 2005.

Mooney, Elizabeth, "Digital Angel to Provide Doctors with Real-Time Wireless Patient Data," *RCR Wireless News*, November 6, 2000, p. 42.

Myers, Anika, "Applied Digital Spins off Subsidiary for Merger," *Miami Daily Business Review*, November 7, 2001, p. A5.

Phelps, David, "Digital Angel's Microchips Help Tracking," *Star Tribune* (Minneapolis, MN), December 27, 2003, p. 1D.

Powell, Jay, "Animal Trackers," *Star Tribune* (Minneapolis, MN), September 4, 2004, p. 1D.

Price, Dave, "IBM's Dispute with Florida Firm Threatens Digital Angel," *Finance and Commerce Daily Newspaper, MN*, March 12, 2003.

Sullivan, Laurie, "RFID Goes to the Dogs in Portugal," *Information Week*, July 23, 2004.

Suzukamo, Leslie Brooks, "New Chip Can Tell If Fido Has Fever: Digital Angel Wins Patent for Temperature Sensor," *Saint Paul Pioneer Press* (Saint Paul, MN), April 12, 2006.

"Technology Pioneers Programme," World Economic Forum, 2009, http://www.weforum.org/en/Communities/Technology%20Pioneers/index.htm.

Tugend, Alina, "Sensing Opportunity in Mad Cow Worries," *New York Times*, February 26, 2004, p. C7.

Useem, Jerry, "Digital Angel," *Fortune*, June 25, 2001, p. 166.

Wallace, David J., "Wearing Your Vital Signs on Your Wrist," *New York Times*, February 22, 2001, p. G3.

Warmack, Lena, "St. Paul, Minn.-based Firm's Device Allows Government to Track Sick Livestock," *Saint Paul Pioneer Press* (Saint Paul, MN), October 8, 2003.

Disney/ABC Television Group

———■———

500 South Buena Vista Street
Burbank, California 91521-4581
U.S.A.
Telephone: (818) 260-8766
Web site: http://www.disneyabctv.com/

Wholly Owned Subsidiary of Walt Disney Company
Founded: 1943 as American Broadcasting Company
Employees: 15,000
Sales: $6.38 million (2007)
NAICS: 515120 Television Broadcasting; 511110 Newspaper Publishers; 511120 Periodical Publishers; 515112 Radio Stations

■ ■ ■

Disney/ABC Television Group, owned by the Walt Disney Company, is a conglomeration of worldwide news, sports, and entertainment television operations. Disney/ABC creates programming that it distributes via broadcast, cable, wireless, and Internet, which it controls. It also produces content for other media outlets. In addition, Disney/ABC has a book publishing unit.

FCC RULING SPAWNS NEW NETWORK

Of three major networks in the United States, ABC is the youngest. The first broadcasting company in the United States was the National Broadcasting Company (NBC), founded by the Radio Corporation of America (RCA) in 1926. By 1928 NBC had grown so large that

RCA divided the company into two networks, the red and the blue, and it is in the blue network that ABC's origins lie. The Federal Communications Commission (FCC), worried by the monopolistic tendencies in the broadcasting industry, decided in 1941 that no single company could own more than one network and ordered NBC to divest itself of one of its two networks. Accordingly, in 1943 NBC sold the less profitable blue network to Edward J. Noble, who had made his fortune as the head of Life Savers Inc. Noble dubbed his network the American Broadcasting Company (ABC).

At first ABC was only a radio broadcaster. NBC and Columbia Broadcasting System (CBS) had been involved in experimental television production and transmission for over a decade by the time ABC was created, and the new network found the transition to television difficult. It was not until 1953, when ABC merged with United Paramount Theatres Inc., that ABC emerged as a third network of full stature.

NETWORK MERGES WITH STUDIO

United Paramount Theatres had been the movie theater arm of Paramount Pictures until the company was forced by antitrust legislation to divest itself of its theater chain. In the merger, Leonard H. Goldenson, Paramount's president, became president of the new American Broadcasting–Paramount Theatres Inc. (AB-PT), the owner of 708 movie theaters, a radio network with 355 affiliates, a television network with 14 affiliates, and television and radio stations in five major cities.

COMPANY PERSPECTIVES

The success of ABC and its owned stations is driven by high-quality creative content, with much of that content produced by the Company's in-house television studio. ABC Studios develops and produces programming for network, cable, Web, video-on-demand, mobile and broadband platforms for the Company and other outlets.

More important, the merger brought ABC cash. Goldenson's first major expenditure as head of AB-PT went to Walt Disney. In return for a $4.5 million loan from the network to complete the construction of Disneyland, Disney agreed to provide a television show for ABC. This deal was the first time that a movie company produced a show for a television network. AB-PT also acquired a 35 percent interest in the amusement park, presaging later purchases of similar parks.

The broadcasting division of AB-PT expanded its television programming that same year from 21 to 35 hours per week. Besides producing popular shows, such as *The Adventures of Ozzie and Harriet, Make Room for Daddy*, and *The Lone Ranger*, the network introduced two innovative dramatic series in 1954: *The U.S. Steel Hour* and *Kraft Television Theatre*. ABC also broadcast 186 hours of the hearings involving the U.S. Army and Senator Joseph R. McCarthy. The network was able to broadcast the interrogations live without preempting any of its own programs because ABC did not have a regular daytime schedule.

In 1955 Warner Brothers, a major motion picture studio, agreed to begin producing shows for the network, eventually providing ABC with *Lawman, Maverick, Colt .45*, and others. Meanwhile, Disney studios provided the program *The Mickey Mouse Club Show. The Lawrence Welk Show* debuted in 1955. Lasting until 1982, the show became one of ABC's longest-running primetime series ever.

By 1957 the broadcasting division of AB-PT had passed the theater division as the largest revenue producer for the company—in part because the theater division had, by government order, been reduced to a chain of 537 theaters.

ABC ENTERS NEW MARKETS

Meanwhile, Am-Par Records, founded in 1954, released its first record to sell a million copies in 1957: "A Rose and a Baby Ruth" by the singer George Hamilton. That same year Am-Par asked Dick Clark, a Philadelphia disc jockey, to come to AB-PT to help promote its records. Clark proposed that he host a television show devoted to music appreciation for teenagers; *American Bandstand* was on the air until 1987.

By the end of the 1950s ABC had entered regular daytime programming. The company also entered another field by buying stock in the Prairie Farmer Publishing Company to gain full ownership of WLS radio station in Chicago, Illinois. Soon afterward, prompted by the tremendous success of Disneyland, AB-PT also bought the Weeki Wachee Spring, a 600-acre scenic attraction near Tampa, Florida.

The 1960s brought important changes to ABC. Everett H. Erlick joined the company in 1961 after leaving the advertising firm of Young & Rubicam. He would play a major role in shaping the network in the coming decades, remaining with ABC for more than 25 years.

In 1961 AB-PT expanded Am-Par Records through the acquisition of the Westminster classical music label (Beverly Sills was among its artists) and the introduction of the Impulse jazz label (Duke Ellington was its major star).

ABC had entered sports broadcasting in 1960, when it won the television rights to National Collegiate Athletic Association college football and basketball games. ABC Sports was founded in 1961 and made a groundbreaking contribution that Thanksgiving during its broadcast of the Texas–Texas A&M football game when it offered television viewers their first instant replay. Three years later ABC Sports began its long association with the Olympic Games when it covered the Winter Games from Innsbruck, Austria. Even though ABC ranked third, well behind CBS and NBC, the network was number one in the sports-broadcasting business.

ABC WORKS TO STAY AFLOAT

By the middle of the decade, ABC had started looking for financing to cover the massive costs of conversion to color broadcasting (which had been in limited use since 1962) and help it bid competitively for feature-film packages. In 1965 the company announced plans to merge with International Telephone and Telegraph Inc. (ITT), a company with enormous financial resources. The FCC approved the merger and hopes were high at ABC (its name was shortened that year to American Broadcasting Companies). However, the U.S. Department of Justice's (DOJ) antitrust division appealed the approval, delaying the merger so long that ITT finally exercised its right to opt out of the deal. However, ITT

KEY DATES

∎

1943: Complying with a 1941 Federal Communications Commission decision, National Broadcasting Company (NBC) sells its blue network to Edward J. Noble, who calls the new entity the American Broadcasting Company (ABC).

1953: A merger with United Paramount Theatres creates American Broadcasting–Paramount Theatres Inc. (AB-PT), which is listed on the New York Stock Exchange, and raises ABC to full stature as a third television network; the network expands programming with programs that will eventually become classics.

1954: AB-PT forms Am-Par Records.

1961: Newly founded ABC Sports introduces instant replay during a college football game.

1975: Fred Silverman joins ABC and begins to guide the company's rise to first place in primetime ratings.

1977: ABC broadcasts *Roots*, the first television miniseries.

1979: Special daily reports on Americans held hostage in Iran leads to creation of *Nightline* news program.

1985: Capital Cities Communications Inc. buys ABC, which is third in ratings but more profitable that Columbia Broadcasting System and NBC; the combined operation is called Capital Cities/ABC Inc.

1993: ABC begins putting violence advisories on programs.

1996: Walt Disney Company renames the company ABC Inc. after buying it; ABC is no longer listed separately on the New York Stock Exchange.

1999: Walt Disney Company merges its television production and network operations to form ABC Entertainment Television Group.

2006: ABC allows viewers to access free downloads from its Web site and paid downloads through iTunes of its popular programs.

2009: A company reorganization creates the Disney/ABC Television Group; ABC and ABC Studios become part of ABC Entertainment division.

did loan ABC $25 million to help the network convert to color broadcasting; within a year the entire primetime schedule was in color.

After the ITT deal fell through, the eccentric billionaire Howard Hughes attempted to gain control of ABC through a tender offer for 43 percent of the company's stock. The management at ABC fought against Hughes until he dropped his bid two weeks after his initial proposal.

In 1968 ABC was divided into three separate divisions, each to provide the ABC television network with programming: entertainment, news, and sports. The other two networks followed ABC's lead in this restructuring.

The 1960s were a trying time for ABC. Despite an influx of financial support, the network lost more than $120 million between 1961 and 1971. The company was sustained during this time primarily by revenues from its theater chain, its record company, and the television stations that it owned. Radio broadcasting also contributed to its survival—in fact, the network had 500 affiliate radio stations by the end of the decade. Like the television network, ABC organized its radio network into several divisions: American contemporary, American information, American entertainment, and American FM networks.

DECISIONS AFFECT ABC

In 1971 the FCC limited the number of hours of primetime programming a network could schedule. This rule proved to be a blessing for ABC because the network had been unable to fill the time. During the following year the network became profitable for the first time in a decade. Revenues passed the $800 million mark and net earnings were over $35 million. However, just as things were looking up, in 1972 the DOJ filed an antitrust suit against all three networks. The suit aimed to bar the networks from carrying network-produced entertainment programs, including feature films, and charged the networks with monopolizing primetime television entertainment programming. ABC claimed that documents from the White House, the DOJ, and the Watergate prosecution would prove that the government's antitrust suit was intended to suppress the three networks, presumably in retaliation for press "harassment" of President Richard M. Nixon. Although the suit was dismissed without prejudice in November 1974, the matter was not fully resolved until six years later.

In the meantime, ABC was engaged in the further divestiture of its movie theaters and an expansion of its record business. Anchor Records was established in 1973 to develop European talent for the company.

ABC ENTERS FIRST PLACE

One of the most famous mass-media programmers in the United States joined ABC in 1975. ABC tempted Fred Silverman away from CBS with an offer of a $300,000 salary, a $1 million life insurance policy, stock options, and homes on both coasts of the United States. ABC's stock rose two points on the day he joined the network. Under Silverman's guidance, ABC introduced such hits as *Laverne and Shirley* and *The Love Boat* and expanded its soap operas to hour-length features that were not afraid to touch controversial topics, greatly boosting ABC's daytime ratings.

Within a year, ABC had moved into first place in primetime ratings. That same year the network created a stir by offering Barbara Walters, then the cohost of NBC's *Today Show*, a $5 million contract to coanchor *ABC Evening News*. Walters accepted and became the first full-time female news anchor on any network. Shortly thereafter, the show flopped. Roone Arledge, the former head of ABC Sports who was now head of ABC News, moved in to salvage things. He changed the format of *ABC Evening News*, renaming it *ABC World News Tonight* and using three anchormen, in London, Washington, and Chicago, connected by satellite. By the following year ABC had surpassed CBS as the world's largest advertising medium, and within another year ABC also led in daytime programming.

In 1978 Silverman was lured from ABC by NBC, not quite three years after he was hired. Silverman's tenure, although brief, benefited the company tremendously. Between 1975 and 1978 broadcasting profits rose from $82 million to $311 million. His departure marked the beginning of a period of streamlining for ABC as the company sold its theaters and record business to concentrate on broadcasting and publishing (it retained its farming journals).

During the Iranian hostage crisis in 1979, ABC aired daily special reports on their condition after the local 10pm/11pm news. These reports were so popular that when the hostage crisis ended, ABC continued to broadcast a special news report in the same time slot, and *Nightline* was born.

ABC FACES CHALLENGES

ABC's fortunes soon changed. Scandal clouded the success of the popular *Charlie's Angels* when in 1980 a reporter for the *New York Times* uncovered numerous accounting oddities in connection with the show, the show's producers, and Elton H. Rule, the president of ABC. Some of these oddities, based on informal oral understandings, ran into the millions of dollars. This scandal was followed by an agreement to a consent decree in connection with the antitrust suit the DOJ

had brought in the early 1970s, in which ABC agreed to place ceilings on the number of shows it produced in-house for network broadcast and to give actors, producers, and writers involved in its primetime schedule greater freedom to leave ABC for other networks. It was a poor start to the 1980s.

By the middle of the decade ABC had once again fallen behind both CBS and NBC in ratings. Despite this poor showing, ABC was more profitable than either of the other two networks. This led, as many had predicted, to ABC's takeover.

CAPITAL CITIES BUYS ABC

In 1985 Capital Cities Communications Inc., a communications company with one-quarter of ABC's sales, bought ABC for $3.5 billion. The name of the combined operation was changed to Capital Cities/ABC Inc. The business community reacted quite favorably to the announcement: both ABC's and Capital Cities' stock rose as soon as the deal was announced.

Capital Cities owned seven television stations and 12 radio stations and had annual sales of slightly less than $1 billion before the takeover. In addition, the company controlled several publishing interests, including the *Kansas City Star* and a few medical journals—a mix that reproduced ABC's on a smaller scale. Capital Cities had long held a reputation for being extremely efficient and many at ABC feared for their jobs. Thomas S. Murphy and Daniel Burke, the chairman and president of Capital Cities, respectively, placed Frederick S. Pierce in charge of ABC. Pierce had been second to Goldenson for several years before the takeover.

THE INDUSTRY UNDERGOES CHANGE

The broadcast industry went through a period of rapid change in the second half of the 1980s as competition from cable television and videocassette recorders reduced network viewing audiences. By 1986 ABC was in last place among the three networks and recorded a substantial loss that year. To cut costs, the company trimmed the budget of its nonprogramming-related expenditures. In addition, the company lowered the amount it paid affiliates to carry its programs by about 4 percent and announced that it would not pay any clearance fees for special events such as miniseries and the Academy Awards. This move touched off a struggle between the network and its affiliate stations, which became less inclined to grant clearances for shows with poor ratings. This tension continued even when ABC's ratings edged past CBS's to take second place in 1987. However, the network still trailed far behind NBC.

In the late 1980s ABC's epic miniseries programs, once a network strength, lost the viewing public. *Amerika*, aired in 1987, led the week's ratings, but was hardly a smash success. A year later *War and Remembrance* lost $20 million for the network. ABC had pioneered the miniseries in 1977 with *Roots*, but the appeal of the format seemed to have waned.

ABC's coverage of the 1988 Olympic Games gave the network a big ratings boost, but resulted in a $65 million loss. By contrast, ABC's news division was doing well late in the decade with *ABC World News Tonight*, *20/20*, and *Nightline*. In addition, while the network struggled to cope with a changing industry, ABC's owned-and-operated stations did very well on an individual basis.

ABC SEEKS TO IMPROVE ITS BOTTOM LINE

The company expanded into new markets with the purchase of Mariner Newspapers in 1989 and Harcourt Brace Jovanovich's farm publications in 1991. The latter expanded Capital Cities' Farm Progress subsidiary. ABC also extended cable and television services globally when it set up Ultra Entertainment.

In the early 1990s ABC introduced TGIF, a Friday-night lineup of family friendly shows intended to get people to stay home and watch television together. It was reintroduced in 2003 after the company lost $500 million the previous year.

Along with three other television networks, ABC began issuing content advisories in 1993 for its programs. The following year Capital Cities/ABC, the Washington Post Co., and Oracle Corporation teamed up to offer news-on-demand to computer users. That same year the company joined with the National Association of Broadcasters, CBS, and NBC to create a new program ratings system.

ABC IS BOUGHT BY DISNEY

A whirlwind deal—negotiated and struck in just eight days in 1995—transferred ownership of Capital Cities/ABC to the Walt Disney Company for $19 billion in cash and stock. Renamed ABC Inc., the company launched ABCNews.com in 1997 to provide continuous news, sports, and information via the Internet.

In 1999 the Walt Disney Company merged its television production studios with the ABC television network to form ABC Entertainment Television Group. That television season would find ABC first place in the seasonal ratings. The game show *Who Wants to Be a Millionaire* was the network's centerpiece program.

However, a scheme to build on the show's popularity fell flat when viewers became bored after watching it several nights a week. The show, which brought in 66 percent of the company's profits in 2000, dropped 20 percent the next year in both ratings and ad revenues.

ABC's early attempts at reality programming were weak alternatives to CBS's *Survivor*. That changed when the network began airing *Extreme Makeover: Home Edition* and *Dancing with the Stars*. These programs, along with a few very popular comedies and dramas, such as *According to Jim* and *Boston Legal*, drew regular audiences but were not large enough to put the network in first place again.

With the introduction of *Desperate Housewives* and *Lost* in 2004 and the popularity of its main reality shows, ABC eventually reached second place. However, by 2007 the network was again in third position.

As the economic recession that began in 2008 extended into the following year, Disney/ABC Television Group was forced to lay off employees. It also merged its entertainment and studios units into ABC Entertainment Group. The company continued to distribute content and license content for distribution through a variety of broadcast, DVD, wireless, and electronic media. Its vendors included Netflix and Verizon via VCAST video.

Updated, Doris Maxfield

PRINCIPAL DIVISIONS

ABC Entertainment Group (includes ABC Entertainment and ABC Studios); Disney/ABC Domestic Television; Disney/ABC/ESPN Television.

PRINCIPAL OPERATING UNITS

ABC Television Network (includes ABC Daytime, ABC Entertainment, and ABC News divisions); Disney Channels Worldwide; Radio Disney Network; Disney XD; ABC Family; Walt Disney Animation; Hyperion Publishing.

PRINCIPAL COMPETITORS

CBS; NBC; FOX Broadcasting; Warner Bros.

FURTHER READING

"ABC Entertainment Group Formed, Stephen McPherson to Oversee," *Mediaweek*, January 26, 2009, p. 5.

Adalian, Josef, and Michael Schneider, "Mouse Meltdown: ABC Shuffles Its Exec Deck amid Continued Misfires," *Daily Variety*, April 21, 2004, p. 1.

Atkinson, Claire, "Make Her Happy: Give Her a Problem," *Broadcasting & Cable*, January 26, 2009, p. 8.

Carter, Bill, "Disney to Join Operations of Studio and ABC Units," *New York Times*, July 9, 1999.

Consoli, John, "Straight Shooter: On the Verge of Unveiling His Second Fall Season, ABC Entertainment President Steve McPherson Is Focusing on Comedy and Strong Drama Characters," *Mediaweek*, May 15, 2006, p. 18.

"Desperate for *Lost*? Watch Free Streams on ABC.com," *Online Reporter*, April 15, 2006, p. 1.

"Disney, ABC to Merge International TV Units," *Globe & Mail* (Toronto, Canada), June 26, 1996, p. B9.

"Disney/ABC Television Group and ESPN Extend Agreement with Verizon to Offer Entertainment, Kids, Sports and News Programming," *PR Newswire*, January 26, 2009.

McClellan, Steve, "Disney/ABC: $19 Billion Done Deal," *Broadcasting & Cable*, February 12, 1996, p. 9.

"Netflix Announces Agreement with Disney-ABC Television Group to Stream Several Hit ABC Series," *PR Newswire*, August 3, 2009.

Qinlan, Sterling, *Inside ABC: American Broadcasting Company's Rise to Power*, New York: Hastings House, 1979.

Schlosser, Joe, "A Mouse In-house," *Broadcasting & Cable*, November 29, 1999, p. 22.

Steinberg, Brian, "Reruns Go from Déjà Vu to New: Networks Keep Viewer Attention by Adding Extra Features to Rerun Episodes," *Advertising Age*, March 10, 2008, p. 10.

"Worst to First—Hits Give ABC Surprise Lead in New Season," *New York Post*, October 5, 2004, p. 33.

DLA Piper

500 Eighth Street NW
Washington, D.C. 20004
U.S.A.
Telephone: (202) 779-4000
Fax: (202) 779-5000
Web site: http://www.dlapiper.com

Private Company
Founded: 2005
Employees: 3,700
Sales: $902.70 million (2008)
NAICS: 541110 Offices of Lawyers

∎ ∎ ∎

DLA Piper was formed in 2005 when three law firms merged: Maryland-based Piper Rudnick, California-based Gray Cary Ware & Freidenrich, and the British firm DLA. The CEOs of Piper Rudnick, Francis B. Burch Jr. and Lee I. Miller, and the CEO of DLA, Nigel Knowles, became joint CEOs of the new firm, called DLA Piper Rudnick Gray Cary. The merging of the companies, whose roots dated to 1853, made it one of the world's largest law firms, and it continued to expand in subsequent years. Shortening its name to DLA Piper in 2006, the company by 2009 had 67 offices in 29 countries, including more than 20 offices in the United States and more than 25 offices in continental Europe, 8 offices in Britain, 7 offices in the Middle East, and 6 offices in Asia. In 2008 *American Lawyer* ranked DLA Piper U.S. 15th in the world and DLA Piper International 16th in the world in terms of gross revenue. Had the two divisions been treated as one firm in the Global 100 list, the firm would have been ranked fourth, with $2.21 billion in combined revenue that year.

INTERNATIONAL MERGER

From the outset DLA Piper functioned much like two different law firms, although under the same brand name. Two sets of partners controlled two different financial entities, one in the United States and one based in Britain and encompassing offices throughout the rest of the world. In 2007 DLA Piper International and DLA Piper U.S. would agree to a set of proposals that would improve integration between the two entities. However, the two entities did not become financially integrated or share profits, despite the creation of a bonus pool that would be used to reward referral of work between the two parts of the firm.

Despite these divisions, the 2005 merger led to phenomenal growth. Several new offices were opened in the first 10 months after the merger, including ones in Frankfurt, Germany; Tbilisi, Georgia; Kiev, Ukraine; Beijing, Tokyo; and Raleigh, North Carolina.

The quick international growth drew criticism. Some critics saw the relentless international expansion as imprudent, claiming the firm did not take the time to ensure the proper personnel were in place. For example, DLA Piper International attempted to penetrate the huge Chinese market by opening an office in Beijing in December 2005. Writer Richard Lloyd stated in the November 2008 issue of *American Lawyer*, "It was a classic DLA move—opportunistic, quickly executed, and

COMPANY PERSPECTIVES

At DLA Piper, "Everything Matters" is our commitment to understanding all our clients' needs—business, managerial and personal—and acting accordingly. This does not mean that we focus on issues that aren't significant. Rather, we focus on providing practical and innovative legal solutions that help our clients succeed, while striving to deliver a consistent experience of working with DLA Piper across our practices, around the world and in every legal matter we undertake.

Equally important, Everything Matters speaks to our commitment to our communities and our people.

with seemingly more thought for getting the deal done than whether the attorneys were the right fit." In fact the head of the Chinese office, Jingzhou Tao, objected to the DLA Piper International's interference in the Chinese office, calling the law firm "colonial." He eventually was fired and replaced by an American lawyer, despite protests of many of the staff there. As Lloyd noted, "The firm ... does not appear built to bear the strain of assimilating a constant stream of laterals."

INVESTIGATION OF DRUG USE IN MAJOR LEAGUE BASEBALL

DLA Piper U.S. remained most widely known in the United States for its role in the investigation into the use of performance-enhancing drugs in Major League Baseball. In 2006 George J. Mitchell, the chairman of DLA Piper and a former U.S. senator, was named by baseball commissioner Allan H. Selig to conduct an independent investigation into the use of steroids and other illegal performance-enhancing drugs in baseball. DLA Piper lawyers assisted Mitchell in the investigation. Relying on hundreds of hours of interviews with 700 people and 135,000 digital and hardcopy documents, Mitchell's 2007 report outlined a "steroids era" that, beginning in the 1980s, affected all of the baseball clubs and ensnared many of its players. Mitchell contended, "Widespread use by players of such substances unfairly disadvantages the honest athletes who refuse to use them and raises questions about the validity of baseball records."

The report outlined baseball's inadequate early response to the use of performance-enhancing drugs and made a series of recommendations. The random drug testing program begun in 2002 effectively curtailed the use of steroids, but it is also blamed for spurring the use of human growth hormone, which is undetectable through urine testing. Mitchell's recommendations included improving Major League Baseball's ability to investigate drug abuse allegations by creating a separate Department of Investigations; the implementation of a comprehensive education program about the health risks of performance-enhancing drugs; and implementation of a state-of-the-art drug program that would include an independent program administrator, random drug testing, transparent practices, and enhanced accountability.

The most controversial part of the report was Mitchell's identification of dozens of former or current Major League players who were alleged to have used performance-enhancing drugs during their careers. Mitchell argued these players should not be punished but instead that baseball should move forward. He wrote, "I urge the Commissioner to forego imposing discipline on players for past violations of baseball's rules on performance enhancing substances, including the players named in this report, except in those cases where he determines that the conduct is so serious that discipline is necessary to maintain the integrity of the game."

Mitchell's report immediately came under criticism. Some criticized Mitchell for naming names without giving players the opportunity to defend themselves. *USA Today* quoted a Los Angeles defense attorney who stated: "This is not a legal document. He included a lot of innuendo that would not stand up in a court of law." Mitchell and DLA lawyers were also faulted for doing little investigation of their own. Of the 91 players named in the report, 88 of them were identified by U.S. Department of Justice prosecutors and other press reports; only three were uncovered by the work of the DLA Piper lawyers.

SOCIAL RESPONSIBILITY

Aside from its involvement with Major League Baseball, DLA Piper has made a firm commitment to reducing the firm's environmental impact as well as donating time and services to nonprofit organizations in the communities they served. For example, the firm attempted to reduce the company's carbon footprint by reducing the amount of air travel, requiring staff to meet basic criteria for travel and also experimenting with video conferencing.

DLA Piper also engaged in pro bono work from its beginning, creating New Perimeter, an international nonprofit organization established to support important projects and initiatives around the world. Each year

KEY DATES

2005: Merger of U.S. firms Piper Rudnick and Gray Cary Ware & Freidenrich with British firm DLA forms DLA Piper Rudnick Gray Cary.

2006: George J. Mitchell begins investigation into steroid use in baseball; firm shortens its name to DLA Piper.

2007: Proposals to improve integration of DLA Piper International and DLA Piper U.S. are implemented; Mitchell's report to the commissioner of baseball is released.

2008: DLA Piper office opens in Qatar; Francis B. Burch Jr. steps down as CEO and becomes global chairman.

DLA Piper lawyers donated 13,000 hours to New Perimeter. By 2009 the projects would include support of Addis Ababa Law School in Ethiopia, the Zimbabwean Women's Rights Project, and the Prince of Wales Rainforest Project; support of a climate change project in Africa and law reform in Kosovo; and identification of impediments to investment in cities in Africa.

DLA lawyers have donated their time to other causes as well. For example, in 2005 the firm represented 6,000 foster children in Nebraska who, in a civil rights lawsuit, charged the state of Nebraska with failing to provide safe and proper care for its foster children. In 2007 DLA partners Berl Bernhard and James Pickup created the Middle East Investment Initiative (MEII), a nonprofit organization that aimed to revitalize the economy of the West Bank by making loans to small and medium-size businesses. These loans would be guaranteed not through traditional collateral but through the independent Palestinian Investment Fund, allowing a broader range of business people to access capital.

In 2007 the firm donated 150,000 hours of pro bono and corporate social responsibility work. In December of that year DLA Piper U.S. received the Robert F. Mullen Pro Bono Award from the Lawyers' Committee for Civil Rights Under Law to honor the firm's work with the committee. In 2008 and 2009 DLA Piper would work with the Lawyers' Committee for Civil Rights and the Mississippi Center for Justice to provide legal assistance for Mississippi residents whose homes were damaged or destroyed by Hurricane Katrina. By June 30, 2009, these efforts had helped residents access more than $1.4 million in government homeowner grants for defraying costs of repairing their homes.

RECESSION OF 2007 AND 2009

Compared with other international law firms, DLA Piper fared relatively well during the global recession that began in 2007. The firm cut fairly few jobs and hired 96 partners over the course of the year, particularly in real estate. In fact, many DLA partners focused on helping U.S. developers pursue international opportunities during the slowdown. The financial services sector was one area of the firm's business, and the firm faced a tough year in 2009 as a result. However, the company also served other sectors that prospered during the slowdown. In February 2009 joint CEO Knowles told London's *Independent:* "By being so big, we enjoy a diversification of sector and geography that other firms don't. When one part of the business is suffering, another is doing well." The company, in fact, saw an increase in business due to the restructuring of companies and regulatory problems.

Nearing the end of 2009, DLA Piper seemed poised to weather the economic slowdown and resume its phenomenal growth. The firm remained focused on its goal of becoming a successful global corporate law firm, with branches all over the world and the ability to respond to the needs of businesses, wherever they are. International expansion remained a central strategy for growth, even in the face of the recession. CEO Lee Miller told Lynne Marek in the *National Law Journal* that the firm sought expansion into the Persian Gulf region in order to capitalize on its oil wealth and booming real estate market, and in October 2008 the firm opened a new office in Doha, Qatar, making it the only international law firm with an office in that country. Nonetheless, as Richard Lloyd noted in *American Lawyer*, the firm faced challenges arising from its unique division between the U.S. branch and the international branch. However, Lloyd wrote, CEO Knowles's "bet that DLA Piper International had to go global to thrive still looks like it might pay off."

Melissa Doak

PRINCIPAL DIVISIONS

DLA Piper International; DLA Piper U.S.

PRINCIPAL COMPETITORS

Baker & McKenzie; Cooley Godward Kronish; Holland & Knight; Jones Day; Saul Ewing LLP; Skadden, Arps; Wilson Sonsini.

FURTHER READING

"About the Poster," *American Lawyer*, October 2008, pp. 163–72.

Baldas, Tresa, "Foster Care Suit Gets Help from a Global Firm," *National Law Journal*, October 3, 2005.

"The Bigger the Better? Law Firms," *Economist*, December 11, 2005, p. 60.

Blum, Ronald, "Baseball Drug Results to Be Announced," *USA Today*, December 12, 2007.

Braverman, Paul, "Five Years Later: Piper Marbury and Rudnick & Wolfe Made a Merger of Equals Work. Now They're Poised to Join with 1,800-Lawyer DLA, one of the British Behemoths. Can They Pull It Off Again?" *American Lawyer*, July 2004, pp. 84–89, 170.

————, "Shut Out: George Mitchell and His Team at DLA Piper Lavished Two Years, 25 Lawyers, and Millions of Dollars on Its Steroids Investigation. Was There Any Real Hope They Would Succeed?" *American Lawyer*, March 2008, pp. 105–11.

Chen, Vivia, "The Great Brawl of China: Two Feuding Partners Leave the Firm's Beijing Office," *American Lawyer*, February 2008, p. 22.

"DLA and Piper Rudnick Merge," *European Venture Capital Journal*, February 2005, p. 63.

"The DLA Dilemma," *American Lawyer*, May 2006, p. 135.

"DLA Piper Celebrates Opening of Office in Qatar," Al Bawaba, October 23, 2008, http://albawaba.com/en/main/237151/&searchWords=dla percent20piper.

"Eleven Firms Break the Billion-Dollar Mark," *American Lawyer*, May 2007, pp. 161–65.

Evans, Simon, "If the City Is a Law unto Itself, It Needs Lawyers More Than Ever," *Independent on Sunday*, February 22, 2009, p. 82.

Gemson, Christine, "Top Law Firms Able to Limit the Damage," *Financial Times*, October 27, 2008, p. 4.

Heintz, Francesca, "Banking on the West Bank: A DLA Project Seeks to Revitalize the Troubled Region's Economy by Providing Loans to Small and Midsize Businesses," *American Lawyer*, July 2008, pp. 115–16.

Hogarth, Marie-Anne, "DLA Piper Challenges Concepts of Law Firm Growth," *National Law Journal*, October 24, 2005.

Jones, Ashby, "Law Firms Willing to Pay to Work for Nothing," *Wall Street Journal*, June 19, 2007, p. B1.

Jones, Leigh, "DLA Piper Fulfills a National Move with Atlanta," *National Law Journal*, May 1, 2006.

Koppel, Nathan, "Corporate News: Some Law Firms Hire in Slump—Staff Expansions Focus on Specialty Practice Areas and Geographic Diversity," *Wall Street Journal*, October 9, 2008, p. B2.

"Lawyers' Committee for Civil Rights Honors Outstanding Lawyers, Law Firms, and Clients," *U.S. Newswire*, December 6, 2007.

Lloyd, Richard, "Putting It Together: DLA Piper's American and International Units Share a Name, a Brand, and—the Firm Says—a Vision. But They Still Don't Share Profits. Is the Firm a Harbinger, or Just Poorly Integrated?" *American Lawyer*, November 2008, pp. 90–93, 102.

Marek, Lynne, "DLA Piper Gets Ready to Shorten Its Name," *National Law Journal*, August 14, 2006.

————, "DLA Wants 'Global Real Estate' Practice," *National Law Journal*, August 27, 2007.

Mitchell, George J., *Report to the Commissioner of Baseball of an Independent Investigation into the Illegal Use of Steroids and Other Performance Enhancing Substances by Players in Major League Baseball*, New York, NY: Office of the Commissioner of Baseball, December 13, 2007, http://files.mlb.com/mitchrpt.pdf.

"A Model for Peace & Tolerance," *APS Review Downstream Trends*, June 2, 2008.

Nightengale, Bob. "Lawyers Met with Hundreds in Probe," *USA Today*, December 14, 2007, p. C10.

Perez, A. J., "Mitchell Report Built on a Shaky Legal Foundation," *USA Today* online, December 14, 2007, http://www.usatoday.com/sports/baseball/2007-12-13-Mitchell-Report-legal_N.htm/.

Qualters, Sheri, "Real Estate Practices Go Abroad," *National Law Journal*, July 7, 2008.

Willman, John, "Law Firms Have Solid Local Roots and Global Ambitions," *Financial Times*, March 12, 2008, p. 4.

Wilson, Duff, and Michael S. Schmitt, "Steroid Report Cites 'Collective Failure,'" *New York Times*, December 13, 2007.

Dollar General Corporation

100 Mission Ridge
Goodlettsville, Tennessee 37072-2171
U.S.A.
Telephone: (615) 855-4000
Fax: (615) 855-5252
Web site: http://www.dollargeneral.com

Private Company
Founded: 1956
Employees: 72,500
Sales: $10.50 billion (2008)
NAICS: 452990 All Other General Merchandise Stores; 442299 All Other Home Furnishings Stores; 448140 Family Clothing Stores

■ ■ ■

Dollar General Corporation is the leading dollar store chain in the United States. J. L. Turner & Son originated the dollar store concept, opening the first Dollar General store in Springfield, Kentucky, in 1956. The chain inspired dozens of imitators through the decades. The company changed its name to Dollar General in the 1960s and grew exponentially through the following decades. By 2009 Dollar General was ranked 259 in the Fortune 500 and 29 in *Forbes*'s list of America's Largest Private Companies. Nearly 8,500 stores located in 35 states, primarily in the eastern and southeastern United States, sell the majority of their products at $10 or less, and one-fourth of their products for $1 or less. The stores sell basic, everyday items at low prices, targeting low- and middle-income residents of small towns. The company has historically been among the fastest-growing retailers in the United States.

J. L. TURNER & SON

Dollar General traces its beginnings to the opening of J. L. Turner & Son, a dry goods wholesaling operation in Scottsville, Kentucky, begun by J. L. Turner and his son, Cal Turner Sr., in 1939. Within a few years the father and son team had entered the retail trade when they found themselves with a large quantity of women's underwear. In 1956 J. L. Turner & Son opened the first Dollar General Store in Springfield, Kentucky. The new store sold everything for under a dollar. This innovative retail concept led the company into a period of rapid expansion. By 1966 there were 255 Dollar General stores operating throughout the southeastern United States.

The 1960s were a time of big changes for J. L. Turner & Son. In 1968 the company changed its name to Dollar General and went public. In the same year Cal Turner Jr. joined the company. In 1977 Cal Jr. took over the reins of the company from his father when he was named president and CEO. Cal Jr. oversaw the acquisition of other retail chains in the following years. In 1983 Dollar General acquired the 280 stores of the P. N. Hirsch chain. Two years later the company took over the 203 stores of the Eagle Family Discount chain. The exponential growth forced the company to open an additional distribution center in Homerville, Georgia, to keep up with the growing demands of the rapidly multiplying stores. However, the company stretched itself too thin with such rapid expansion, and in 1987

COMPANY PERSPECTIVES

Through decades of change, Dollar General's approach to business has remained the same. Our mission has been brought to life through the positive attitudes shared by our employees and the satisfaction of our customers. Our Mission: Serving Others. For Customers ... A Better Life. For Shareholders ... A Superior Return. For Employees ... Respect and Opportunity.

its stock price plummeted by almost 85 percent. In 1988 Cal Jr. turned away from the acquisitions strategy, ousting his brother Steve, who had spearheaded that plan, and replacing many other top executives.

Thereafter Dollar General's growth was powered by internal rather than external expansion. The company focused on opening stores in small towns where giant discounters such as Wal-Mart had not penetrated. Stores in metropolitan areas tended to be located in low-income neighborhoods where giant retailers avoided. By 1995 more than 2,000 Dollar General stores were operating, and several new distribution centers had opened to keep up with demand. In 1998 the company ceased advertising because most of its stores were located in small towns with fewer than 20,000 residents. Instead it relied on direct mailings to announce the openings of new stores and simple word-of-mouth. The following year, Dollar General was listed in the Fortune 500 for the first time.

Scandal rocked the company in April 2001 when the Securities and Exchange Commission launched an investigation into what the company called "accounting irregularities" that had inflated reported earnings. Dollar General asserted that it had made errors in accounting for expenses, taxes, and leases on properties, leading to the earnings overstatement. The scandal led Cal Jr. to step down the following year. In the meantime, the company restated its financial results for the years 1998, 1999 and 2000, cutting net income for that period by one-third, including the $99 million price tag for settling shareholder lawsuits. In April 2003 David Perdue was named the company's new chairman and CEO. In April 2005 the company paid a $10 million civil penalty to resolve the investigation.

RECESSION GOOD FOR BUSINESS

Despite the ongoing investigation, Dollar General saw a boom in the early 21st century. Discount retailers in general saw business boom, partially because of the economic recession following the 2001 terrorist attacks against the United States but also because these modern five-and-dimes began to broaden their appeal past their traditional low-income clientele. The number of dollar stores in operation around the country tripled between 1994 and 2004. Americans demanded low prices for everyday household goods and visited dollar stores to find these bargains.

Dollar General embarked on a strategy to expand its customer base. It remodeled some of its stores, eliminating front-end clutter and moving away from its traditional "no frills" décor in order to attract better-heeled customers. Dollar General reported to the *Wall Street Journal* in 2004 that households with incomes higher than $50,000 were its fastest-growing customers, increasing by 27 percent between 2001 and 2004. In fact, a 2005 survey noted that almost three out of four households had shopped at a dollar store in the past six months. In addition, the company introduced Dollar General Market stores, which were larger retail outlets that included more food items, including refrigerated and frozen items as well as fresh produce. Including these food items allowed the retailer to begin to accept food stamps.

By 2005, however, it was clear to many observers that Dollar General's reliance on its traditional business model would not translate into the same phenomenal success in the 21st century that it had achieved in the 20th. Sales slumped in 2006 and 2007. Analysts blamed a variety of factors for the company's troubles, including a change in product offerings to favor low-margin items such as food rather than higher-margin items such as apparel; poor inventory management, including "packing away" seasonal items for sale the following year rather than lowering the prices to clear them out of inventory; poor choice of products, especially apparel, to sell in its stores; high employee turnover rates; and high shrinkage, or inventory loss, through theft or other means. Observers noted that the chain had opened too many new stores, overextending its reach and driving down sales. In 2001 same-store sales had risen 7 percent, while in 2005 same-store sales rose only 2 percent. Rapid store expansion without conducting adequate market research hurt the chain.

BUYOUT AND NEW OPPORTUNITIES

After Dollar General reported another quarter of dismal sales in July 2007, Kohlberg Kravis & Roberts (KKR), a private equity firm, offered Dollar General shareholders a buyout at $22 per share, 31 percent more per share

KEY DATES

1939: J. L. Turner and his son Cal Turner Sr. open a dry goods wholesaling store in Scottsville, Kentucky.

1945: J. L. Turner & Son enter the retail trade.

1956: The first Dollar General Store opens in Springfield, Kentucky.

1966: Dollar General Stores number 255.

1968: J. L. Turner & Son goes public and changes name to Dollar General.

1977: Cal Turner Jr. is named president and CEO; company acquires United Dollar Stores.

1983: Company acquires P. N. Hirsch stores.

1985: Company acquires Eagle Family Discount chain.

1990: Nearly 1,400 Dollar General stores are operating.

1995: Over 2,000 Dollar General stores are operating.

1999: Dollar General is listed on the Fortune 500 for the first time.

2001: Company announces accounting irregularities, leading to a stock plunge.

2002: Cal Turner Jr. steps down as president and CEO.

2003: David Perdue becomes chairman and CEO.

2005: Securities and Exchange Commission investigation is resolved with a $10 million civil penalty.

2007: Company is bought by Kohlberg Kravis & Roberts, GS Capital Partners, and Citi Private Equity and becomes private.

2008: Richard Dreiling is named CEO.

than the March 9 share value of $16.78. Analysts noted that KKR had moved to buy the company just as Dollar General likely hit bottom, having recently invested in information systems, store efficiency projects, and better transportation and distribution systems that would soon begin paying dividends. Shareholders approved the deal, and KKR took Dollar General private. As Mike Troy in *Retailing Today* noted, "Dollar General shareholders may be receiving a premium, but it is KKR that appears to be getting the dollar store deal."

KKR in fact moved at an opportune time. The global recession beginning in 2008 benefited discount retailers across the board as shoppers sought to buy staples for less money. The merger took place in July 2007 and CEO David Perdue resigned at that time. The following January, Richard Dreiling was named CEO and implemented a strategy to close poorly performing stores and change the firm's inventory strategies to improve Dollar General's sales. In the fourth quarter of 2008 Dollar General sales increased 11.2 percent over the year before. Sales in 2008 as a whole were up 10.1 percent. As quoted by *Bank Loan Report* that year, Dreiling stated: "Our sales increases ... offer further evidence that customers continue to trust and rely on Dollar General. While we believe that we may be benefiting somewhat from current economic conditions, we are confident that our recently implemented operating priorities are accelerating our progress." In 2008, at the height of the downturn, the chain opened 207 new stores, remodeled 404 stores, and closed 39 stores.

The company's strategy for future growth included attracting customers to the store by improving customer service and carrying a greater variety of consumables. However, it also wanted to drive the average customer's purchase to over its $10 average in 2008 by focusing on non-consumable products, including expanding its product offerings to include more private-label offerings, especially in over-the-counter medications. The company also announced its intention to carry more home goods and apparel.

Dollar General also targeted low-income shoppers with the introduction of a prepaid and reloadable Discover card that could be used at all of Dollar General's stores and other chain stores and online outlets that accept the Discover card. Shoppers could buy a card at any Dollar General store for $5.95 and reload the card for $2.95, with a monthly maintenance fee of $2.95. This initiative was designed to help low-income shoppers who carried no credit cards or "maxed-out" credit cards and who previously did all business on a cash-only basis.

It appeared that KKR's gamble paid off. Dollar General reported that its first quarter 2009 profits were $83 million, up from only $5.9 million in the first quarter of 2008, prompting Jonathan Birchall in the *Financial Times* to call Dollar General "one of the success stories of the U.S. recession." While all bargain retailers benefited from the recession, Dollar General boomed more than most. Dollar General's first quarter sales were up 15.7 percent. In contrast, rivals Family Dollar and Dollar Tree were up only 6.4 percent and 9.2 percent, respectively. Dollar General planned to open 450 new stores and create up to 4,000 new jobs in 2009. Dollar General ranked second only to Walgreen's in the number of new stores slated to open between 2009 and 2011.

Melissa Doak

PRINCIPAL COMPETITORS

Wal-Mart Stores, Inc.; Dollar Tree, Inc.; Family Dollar Stores, Inc.; 99¢ Only Stores; Fred's, Inc.

FURTHER READING

Birchall, Jonathan, "Recession-Hit Shoppers Lift Sales 13 percent at Dollar General," *Financial Times*, June 3, 2009, p. 16.

Corral, Cecile B., "Perdue Tuning Up Dollar General," *Home Textiles Today*, January 30, 2006, p. 6.

"Dollar General Eyes Home Goods Growth," Home Textiles Today, February 23, 2009, p. 2.

"Dollar General Plans to Create up to 4,000 Jobs," *Business Wire*, April 1, 2009.

"Dollar General Posts a Record First Quarter," *Home Textiles Today*, June 8, 2009, p. 16.

"Dollar General Posts 1Q 2009 Financial Results," *Wireless News*, June 6, 2009.

"Dollar General's Debt Inches Closer to a Dollar," *Bank Loan Report*, September 8, 2008, pp. 1, 5.

"Dollar Sells for Billions," *Shopping Centers Today*, May 2007, p. 146–47.

"A Fresh Start for Dollar General (Annual Report)," *MMR*, May 5, 2008, p. 103.

Howell, Debbie, "Dollar General Beats Rivals but Posts Mixed Results," *Retailing Today*, June 12, 2006, pp. 5, 50.

———, "Dollar General Builds Brand in Increasingly Tough Market," *Retailing Today*, June 13, 2005, pp. 6, 73.

———, "Dollar Store Past Paved with $1B Success Stories," *Retailing Today*, September 26, 2005, pp. 12, 14.

———, "Push into Grocery Helps Dollar General Regain Edge," *Retailing Today*, September 26, 2005, pp. 12, 14.

Hudson, Kris, "Dollar General Lags Behind Rival—Family Dollar Makes Successful Approach into Urban Markets," *Wall Street Journal*, March 26, 2007, p. B5.

———, "KKR Spots Cash in Dollar General's Till—Private Equity Displays More Taste for Returns Than Growth in Retail," *Wall Street Journal*, March 13, 2007, p. A10.

———, "Making Sense of 'Dollar Stores'—Declining Sales and Competition from Big Retailers Lead Some to Think Growth Has Hit a Peak," *Wall Street Journal*, September 21, 2005, p. C1.

"I'd Buy That for a Dollar: KKR Likes Dollar General," *Bank Loan Report*, March 19, 2007, pp. 1, 5, 12.

Johnsen, Michael, "Vasos Joins Dollar General Team, Focuses on Nonconsumables," *Drug Store News*, December 8, 2008, p. 6.

Mammarella, James, "Dollar General Ready to Attack Soft Goods," *Home Textiles Today*, April 6, 2009, p. 17.

Murphy, Samantha, "Filling the Plastic Gap: Dollar General Offers Customers Prepaid Reloadable-Card Option," *Chain Store Age*, February 2009, pp. 56–57.

Orgel, David, "When Fast-Growing Retailers Decide to Hit the Brakes," *Supermarket News*, April 7, 2008.

"Perdue Chickens Out on KKR as Firm Acquires Dollar General," *Retailing Today*, July 16, 2007, p. 4.

Popovec, Jennifer, "Bright Spots: Amid Retailer Closings and Bankruptcies, Value-Oriented Chains Shine," *Retail Traffic*, May 2009, pp. 51–54.

Springer, Jon, "Dollar General CEO Sets New Path for Growth," *Supermarket News*, April 7, 2008.

Troy, Mike, "DG Shareholders See Extreme Value in KKR Offer," *Retailing Today*, April 9, 2007, pp. 4, 45.

Zimmerman, Ann, "Cents and Sensibility—Behind the Dollar-Store Boom: A Nation of Bargain Hunters—Not Only for Poorer Families, Chains Outpace Wal-Mart; New Threat to Retailers—A $50 Gift Amid $1 Cereals," *Wall Street Journal*, December 13, 2004, p. A1.

DreamWorks Animation SKG, Inc.

1000 Flower Street
Glendale, California 91201
U.S.A.
Telephone: (818) 695-5000
Fax: (818) 695-9944
Web site: http://www.dreamworksanimation.com/

Public Company
Founded: 2004
Incorporated: 2004
Employees: 1,700
Revenues: $650.1 million (2008)
Stock Exchanges: NASDAQ
Ticker Symbol: DWA
NAICS: 512110 Motion Picture and Video Production and Distribution; 512191 Motion Picture Animation, Post-Production

∎ ∎ ∎

DreamWorks Animation SKG, Inc., is among the industry leaders in the production of animated feature films. Originally part of DreamWorks SKG, Dream-Works Animation SKG, Inc., was spun off in 2004 as part of an initial public offering (IPO) that raised more than $800 million. Since releasing its first animated feature, *Antz,* in 1998, the company has enjoyed a series of critical and commercial successes, among them the *Shrek* movies, *Madagascar, Over the Hedge,* and *Kung-Fu Panda.* In March 2009 the studio made its first foray

into the emerging field of 3-D movie technology with the debut of *Monsters vs. Aliens.*

BREAKING AWAY FROM THE PACK: 1994–2000

The origins of DreamWorks Animation date back to 1994, when entertainment titans Steven Spielberg, Jeffrey Katzenberg, and David Geffen joined forces to form the multimedia movie studio DreamWorks SKG. From the beginning, one of the studio's primary business objectives was the production of feature-length animated films. To pursue this aim, the company created the wholly-owned subsidiary DreamWorks Animation. From the beginning, the animation division was led by Katzenberg, who had established a reputation for producing hit animated movies while working as an executive for Walt Disney during the 1980s.

After several years of anticipation, DreamWorks Animation released its first full-length cartoon feature, *Antz,* in October 1998. With Woody Allen and Sharon Stone supplying the voices for the lead roles, *Antz* was the second computer-animated feature in history, after Pixar's 1995 blockbuster *Toy Story. Antz,* which cost DreamWorks $105 million to produce, went on to earn $171.8 million in theaters. DreamWorks Animation's second cartoon feature, *The Prince of Egypt,* was released in December 1998. Aimed at older children and adults, the film grossed $218.5 million nationwide. With these successes under its belt, the new animation company was quickly emerging as the strongest member of the DreamWorks SKG team.

COMPANY PERSPECTIVES

DreamWorks Animation SKG is devoted to producing high-quality family entertainment through the use of computer-generated (CG) animation. With world-class creative talent and technological capabilities, our goal is to release two CG animated feature films a year that deliver great stories, breathtaking visual imagery and a sensibility that appeals to both children and adults.

In 2004, DreamWorks Animation SKG became the first animation company to produce and distribute two CG animated features in a single year, including Shrek 2, the third highest-grossing movie of all time.

With each film, we strive to tell great stories that are fun and comedic, told with a level of sophistication and irreverence that appeals to the broadest audience possible and captures the imaginations of all people regardless of age.

Our management is one of the most experienced and dynamic teams in the entertainment industry, overseeing a stellar collection of artistic and technical leaders from a wide range of backgrounds in film and animation production, computer graphics and information technology. Many of them have been with the company since its inception."

THE BIRTH OF A GREEN EMPIRE: 2001-04

A key moment in the company's history came in 2001, with the release of the movie *Shrek*. Based on William Steig's children's book about a green ogre, the film enjoyed phenomenal success. Released in theaters in mid-May, the film grossed roughly $112 million by the end of the month. DreamWorks did not hesitate to capitalize on the movie's runaway success, and less than two weeks after *Shrek* opened, DreamWorks announced plans to produce a *Shrek* sequel. By February 2002 the company had persuaded all three of the movie's principal actors—Mike Myers, Cameron Diaz, and Eddie Murphy—to commit to the next movie.

The original *Shrek* garnered box office revenues of more than $267 million in the United States alone. Video sales of the movie were a major source of additional revenue, with more than 42 million units sold by 2004. Months before *Shrek 2* appeared in theaters,

the studio announced plans to produce *Shrek 3*. When *Shrek 2* opened in theaters in May 2004, it became an instant blockbuster, and by July it had become the most lucrative animated feature in history with domestic revenues of $425 million and a total gross of $735.6 worldwide. With a video release of the sequel scheduled for later that year, the company had every reason to be confident about its long term future.

DREAMWORKS ANIMATION GOES PUBLIC: 2004-05

The decision to spin off the company's animation business was driven by a number of factors. For one, many of the original investors in DreamWorks SKG, notably Paul Allen, who had a $500 million stake in the company, had lost patience with the company's inability to be consistently profitable. A high-profile IPO that revolved around the company's most lucrative operating unit offered DreamWorks SKG its best opportunity to compensate its early backers.

Nonetheless, many analysts cautioned against excessive optimism surrounding a DreamWorks Animation IPO. In spite of the continuing popularity of the Shrek franchise, an IPO presented significant risks to investors. In spite of its successes, DreamWorks Animation was a costly venture, and even successful movies often cost the company money. After enjoying a modest profit in 2001 that was largely a result of the revenues generated by *Shrek*, DreamWorks Animation had posted substantial losses in 2002 and 2003. While 2004 promised to be another big year for the company, the ability to sustain steady growth was dependent on its ability to create more breakaway movie franchises.

Many industry observers were also concerned by the relative newness of computer-generated (CG) films, cautioning that enthusiasm for the technology would gradually fade. Even DreamWorks SKG acknowledged that CG technology had not proven that it had long-term staying power among moviegoers. In papers filed with the Securities and Exchange Commission on July 21, 2004, the company warned that it could not guarantee that "new animated filmmaking techniques, an increase in the number of CG animated films or the resurgence in popularity of older animated filmmaking techniques, will not adversely impact the popularity of CG films."

Meanwhile, the *Shrek* franchise continued to deliver huge dividends to the company. By August 2004 DreamWorks was ranked fourth in box office earnings among major studios for the year with sales of $644 million, ahead of Disney, which was ranked fifth with revenues of $618 million. Many in Hollywood

KEY DATES

1994: DreamWorks SKG is formed by Steven Spielberg, Jeffrey Katzenberg, and David Geffen.

1998: *Antz* and *The Prince of Egypt*, the company's first major animated productions, premiere in theaters.

2001: *Shrek* is released in U.S. theaters, earning $267 million nationwide.

2004: *Shrek 2* sets record with $425 million in U.S. box office earnings; DreamWorks SKG spins off animation division in highly-anticipated IPO, creating DreamWorks Animation SKG, Inc.

2009: DreamWorks Animation releases *Monsters vs. Aliens*, the studio's first feature produced in 3-D.

considered Disney's apparent slump as an ideal moment for a DreamWorks IPO. The timing of the company going public was scheduled to coincide with the opening of its next animated feature, *A Shark Tale*, which was scheduled for release in theaters in October 2004.

DreamWorks Animation went public on October 27, 2004, earning $812 million its first day on the market. By the end of its second day of trading, DreamWorks Animation was valued at $4.15 billion, catapulting it into the same realm as Pixar, which had a market value of $4.56 billion. Meanwhile, *A Shark Tale* had grossed over $138 million by month's end. In December 2004 the company's stock value was nearly $42 a share. With the much-anticipated release of the company's next animated feature, *Madagascar*, scheduled for May 2005, DreamWorks Animation appeared to be on a roll.

AN UNLIKELY COLLABORATION, CONTINUED UNCERTAINTY: 2005–07

The year 2005 proved to difficult for DreamWorks Animation, as the company's earnings for DVD sales of *Shrek 2* fell far short of projections, angering investors. In addition, the company had failed to produce a second animation release that year. In order to compensate for this shortfall in its production schedule, DreamWorks struck a $45 million deal with British animators Aardman to release a second animated feature, *Wallace and Gromit: The Curse of the Were-Rabbit*, later that year. The two companies had collaborated successfully on the animated film *Chicken Run* in 2000.

While *Wallace and Gromit: The Curse of the Were-Rabbit* helped the studio meet its pledge to produce two cartoon features a year, it fell far short of the performance level expected of a DreamWorks title. By December 2005 the movie had earned only $55 million from U.S. box offices, compared to $120 million in overseas revenues. Even after winning an Oscar for best animated feature at the March 2006 Academy Awards, the film had grossed only $184 million worldwide, well below the studio's expectations, and DVD sales also fared poorly. In the end, the movie delivered a $25 million loss to DreamWorks Animation.

By late 2005 the company had determined that it needed to hire someone to help manage its finances. In December, Katzenberg hired Lewis Coleman to serve as the company's new president. While Coleman had virtually no history in the movie business, his experience as an executive with banking giants Wells Fargo and Bank of America promised to deliver some much-needed fiscal expertise to the struggling animation company.

Around this time, DreamWorks Animation finally began to report increased earnings, based largely on the global box office receipts of *Madagascar*, which totaled $533 million for the year. The company's next high-profile feature, *Over the Hedge*, appeared in 2006, but the movie failed to achieve the same popularity as its predecessor, earning only $327 million worldwide. In October 2006 investor Paul Allen demanded that the company announce another public stock offering, suggesting that it coincide with the November release of its third collaboration with Aardman, *Flushed Away*.

Although praised by critics, *Flushed Away* was ultimately a disappointment at the box office, forcing the studio to write off a loss of more than $100 million. In the aftermath of another failed collaboration, DreamWorks Animation and Aardman cut ties in 2007. In the eyes of many industry insiders, the larger problem confronting DreamWorks Animation concerned the sheer number of cartoon features being shown in theaters. In 2006 and 2007 Hollywood studios were scheduled to release approximately 30 animated features, the most on record.

Once again an irascible green ogre came to the company's rescue. Released nationwide on May 18, 2007, *Shrek 3* shattered the franchise's own record for an opening weekend, taking in $122 million while showing in 4,122 theaters. The film's performance dwarfed the receipts of that weekend's second-highest grossing film, *Spider-Man 3*, which earned less than $30 million. By early August, DreamWorks Animation was reporting a sharp rise in profits.

THE RISE OF 3-D ANIMATION: 2008-09

Meanwhile, company head Jeffrey Katzenberg had his eyes squarely set on the company's future projects. At trade shows and in interviews, the CEO boldly predicted that 3-D technology would represent the next great age of filmmaking for animated as well as live-action features. As Katzenberg recounted to reporters, his personal 3-D conversion experience had come in 2004 when he screened a 3-D IMAX version of Robert Zemeckis's *The Polar Express*, the first feature-length animated film to be produced with the new technology.

Katzenberg was immediately sold on the potential of the new technology to revolutionize Hollywood and swiftly began hatching plans to forge a new direction for DreamWorks Animation. As he attempted to sell the concept to the public, Katzenberg continually insisted that the 3-D technology of the 2004 was a far cry from its previous incarnations. By the spring of 2008 Katzenberg had begun exploring the possibility a deal with Italian eyewear manufacturer Luxoticca to make designer 3-D glasses.

The company scored another major success in its traditional animation line with the June 2008 release of *Kung-Fu Panda*. The movie earned $60 million on its opening weekend and generated $630 million overall by the fall. Roughly two-thirds of these revenues came from overseas markets. The company's two animated offerings, *Kung-Fu Panda* and *Madagascar: Return 2 Africa*, earned $1.2 billion worldwide, an increase of more than 10 percent over the studio's earnings for its 2007 theatrical releases. In late 2008 *Shrek: The Musical* opened on Broadway, eventually earning $21.7 million and winning a Tony award for best costume design in a musical.

The economic downturn that began in 2008 forced the company to scale back expectations for its premiere 3-D feature, *Monsters vs. Aliens*, scheduled for March 2009. While Katzenberg had originally anticipated the existence of more than 4,000 3-D theaters by the time of the movie's release, by December 2008 there were only 1,500 such theaters ready to show the film with the new technology. Nevertheless, Katzenberg remained upbeat, asserting that the latest incarnation of 3-D moviemaking would be as revolutionary as the introduction of sound and color films during the 1920s and 1930s. Katzenberg confidently projected that by the middle of the second decade of the 2000s, all Hollywood movies would be released in 3-D. Speaking to

Peter Howell in December 2008, he was quoted in the *Toronto Star*, "There is that old cliché that a picture is worth a thousand words. Well, a 3D picture is worth 3,000 words."

Unfortunately, the company's InTru 3D technology was not inexpensive, adding an additional $15 million onto each film. Nonetheless, company executives considered the figure to be relatively small compared to a typical $150 million production budget and expected to recoup the additional expense fairly quickly by passing the increased price directly to the consumer. With 3-D films anticipated to cost an additional $5 per ticket, however, some analysts suggested that the extra cost to consumers posed a potential pitfall to the new strategy.

Monsters vs. Aliens debuted on March 27, 2009, and earned roughly $58.2 million during its opening weekend. While the movie was released in 7,000 theaters nationwide, only 2,100 of those theaters screened the movie in 3-D. Nevertheless, 3-D showings accounted for 56 percent of the movie's box office, signifying the new technology's widespread appeal. By April the film had grossed more than $110 million in the domestic box office. Later that month, the movie earned an additional $33.3 million with its international premiere. As with the domestic audience, the 3-D version of the film consistently outperformed the two-dimensional version.

At around this time, DreamWorks Animation also began seeking other ways of capitalizing on its successful cartoon franchises. Driven by the continued decline in DVD sales, the company explored deals to create amusement park rides at theme parks in Singapore and Dubai, as well as a stage adaptation of *Kung-Fu Panda* inspired by Cirque du Soleil. Meanwhile, in May 2009 Katzenberg announced the studio's intention to increase its production schedule to accommodate five new 3-D releases over a two-year span with a goal to cut overall production costs by 10 percent.

Moving into the second decade of the 2000s, the studio was expected to produce 3-D sequels of *Shrek* and *Kung-Fu Panda*, in addition to several new releases, including *Oobermind* and *The Guardians*. While it remained to be seen whether or not the new technology would have the same watershed impact that talkies and Technicolor had caused during earlier ages in Hollywood, it was clear that DreamWorks Animation was planning for the future.

Stephen Meyer

PRINCIPAL SUBSIDIARIES

DreamWorks Animation Home Entertainment, L.L.C.

PRINCIPAL COMPETITORS

Aardsman Animations Ltd. (UK); Blue Sky Studios, Inc.; Pixar Animation Studios Inc.; Sony Pictures Animation; The Walt Disney Company.

FURTHER READING

Barnes, Brooks, "DreamWorks Aims to Charm Reluctant Investors," *New York Times*, February 8, 2009, p. 1.

———, "3-D Helps Propel 'Monsters' Success," *New York Times,* March 29, 2009, p. 2.

Bray, Hiawatha, "DreamWorks Chief Says Crisis Is Slowing Switch to Digital 3-D," *Boston Globe*, December 16, 2008, p. B5.

Cohen, David S., "Sony's Cartoon Unit Faces Uphill Battle," *Variety*, September 6, 2007, p. A12.

Debruge, Peter, "DreamWorks Animates Its Output," *Variety*, May 27, 2009, p. 1.

DiOrio, Carl, "D'Works Toons IPO," *Variety*, February 11, 2004, p. 1.

Fritz, Ben, "DreamWorks Reworks Plans," *Variety*, October 31, 2006, p. 1.

———, "D'Works Will Rely on Animal Instinct," *Variety*, September 14, 2005, p. 1.

———, "CGI Toons: Is There More 'Shrek' Green?" *Variety*, October 31, 2004, p. 6.

Furman, Phyllis, "Plunging Profits Hit DreamWorks," *Daily News* (New York), July 12, 2005, p. 48.

Hayes, Dade, "'Shrek' Adds Green to DreamWorks," *Daily Variety*, October 30, 2007, p. 5.

Holson, Laura, "Investor Pushes DreamWorks to Sell Shares in Offering," *New York Times*, October 12, 2006, p. 5.

Hoyle, Ben, "Switch to 3-D Will Be One in the Eye for Film Pirates," *Times* (London), June 28, 2007, p. 31.

Kolesnikov-Jessop, Sonia, "Film Studios Are Looking to 3-D to Revive the Industry the Way Sound and Color Once Did," *Newsweek*, January 19, 2009.

Litterick, David, "Curse of Wallace & Gromit Hits DreamWorks," *Daily Telegraph* (London), November 12, 2005, p. 30.

Sabbagh, Dan, "Wallace & Gromit Film Is a DreamWorks Loser," *Times* (London), March 11, 2006, p. 64.

Syre, Steven, "Betting on Shrek," *Boston Globe*, July 22, 2004, p. C1.

Turner, Henry, "3-D for the New Age," *Daily Variety*, October 12, 2007, p. B2.

Verrier, Richard, "DreamWorks Cranks Up Its Film Production Line," *Los Angeles Times*, May 29, 2009, p. 3.

Williamson, Kevin, "Shape of Things to Come: 3D and How It Will Change Movies as We Know Them (for Real This Time)," *Toronto Sun*, January 4, 2009, p. E6.

DW II Distribution Co. LLC

1000 Flower Street
Glendale, California 91201
U.S.A.
Telephone: (818) 733-7000
Fax: (818) 695-7574
Web site: http://www.dreamworks.com

Private Company
Incorporated: 1994 as DreamWorks SKG
NAICS: 512110 Motion Picture and Video Production
and Distribution

■ ■ ■

DW II Distribution Co. LLC, more commonly known as DreamWorks SKG Studios, is a motion picture company led by renowned producer and director Steven Spielberg with financial backing from Indian film entrepreneur Anil Ambani. The company is a continuation of DreamWorks SKG, which was founded in 1994 with great fanfare by Spielberg, former Disney chairman Jeffrey Katzenberg, and record executive David Geffen. While the company had notable successes, including Academy Awards for Best Picture for *American Beauty*, *Gladiator*, and *A Beautiful Mind*, financial stability remained elusive. DreamWorks was acquired by Paramount Pictures in 2005, became independent again in 2008, and announced a deal for significant financial backing from Ambani's company, Reliance Big Entertainment, in 2009.

THREE ENTERTAINMENT MOGULS UNITE

The "S," "K," and "G" in DreamWorks SKG are the first letters of the last names of the company's founders. Spielberg is responsible for some of the most successful films in history as director of *Jaws* (1975), *Close Encounters of the Third Kind* (1977), *Raiders of the Lost Ark* (1981), *E.T., The Extra-Terrestrial* (1982), *Jurassic Park* (1993), *Schindler's List* (1993), *Twister* (1996), and *Saving Private Ryan* (1998). He was also a producer or executive producer of dozens of other blockbuster live-action and animated films, including *Back to the Future* (1985), *Who Framed Roger Rabbit* (1988), *An American Tail: Fievel Goes West* (1991), *Men in Black* (1997), and *Deep Impact* (1998). Spielberg has also worked in network, cable, and syndicated television.

Before co-founding DreamWorks, Katzenberg made a name for himself as an executive in the entertainment business, most notably as chairman of The Walt Disney Studios from 1984 to 1994. He was responsible for the production, marketing, and distribution of all Disney filmed entertainment, which included motion pictures, television, cable, syndication, home video, and interactive entertainment. Under his direction, Disney's studios created some of its most successful films, including *Good Morning Vietnam*, *Pretty Woman*, *The Little Mermaid*, *Beauty and the Beast* (the first animated feature to be nominated for the Best Picture Oscar), *Aladdin*, and *The Lion King* (the highest domestic grossing animated film of all time at $313 million). Citing differences with fellow Disney executive Michael Eisner, Katzenberg left the Magic Kingdom and almost immediately joined Spielberg and Geffen to found DreamWorks. The departure

KEY DATES

∎

1994: Steven Spielberg, Jeffrey Katzenberg, and David Geffen found DreamWorks SKG.

1995: Company joins with Microsoft to create DreamWorks Interactive.

1996: Company forms special-effects venture PDI/DreamWorks.

1997: *The Peacemaker* debuts as DreamWorks' first feature film.

1998: *Saving Private Ryan* and *The Prince of Egypt* become the company's first major successes.

2000: DreamWorks Interactive is sold to Electronic Arts; DreamWorks purchases a majority stake in PDI.

2001: Computer-animated feature film *Shrek* puts company's animation on par with Disney's.

2004: Company spins off DreamWorks Animation.

2005: DreamWorks SKG is purchased by Paramount Pictures for $1.6 billion.

2008: DreamWorks SKG leaves Paramount, once again becoming an independent film studio.

2009: DreamWorks SKG strikes $325 million financing deal with Bollywood mogul Anil Ambani.

would later prove to be an unclean break, as Katzenberg found himself to be in a long, high-profile battle to cash in on a bonus that he maintained Disney owed him.

By the time Geffen helped found DreamWorks, he was already head of his own empire in the music business. Geffen Records was one of the largest record labels in the industry, the crowning achievement of his three decades in the corporate rock world. He is credited with guiding the careers of 1970s big-name acts including Crosby, Stills, Nash, and Young; Jackson Browne; and the Eagles. When he founded Geffen Records in 1980, he was able to immediately sign Elton John, Donna Summer, and Neil Young, the first in a notable list of artists, which later also included Guns N' Roses, Aerosmith, Cher, Sonic Youth, and Nirvana.

A SHAKY START: 1994-97

Spielberg, Katzenberg, and Geffen headed the company's core businesses: live-action movies, animated movies, and music, respectively. With $2 billion in start-up capital and a host of impressive high-tech partnerships, DreamWorks was one of the most exciting companies to watch from the outset. By 1995 Microsoft had invested $30 million in DreamWorks to co-develop interactive games, spawning a new division, Dream-Works Interactive. Paul Allen, the co-founder of Microsoft, showed even greater interest, investing about $500 million for a stake in the new company.

In 1997 DreamWorks released its first movie, *The Peacemaker*, with George Clooney and Nicole Kidman, but it was not a success, earning only $12 million during its opening weekend. A string of more successful movies followed: *Mouse Hunt* (with Nathan Lane), *Amistad* (with Morgan Freeman and Anthony Hopkins), *Small Soldiers* (with the voice of Tommy Lee Jones), *Paulie* (with Gena Rowlands, Cheech Marin, and Buddy Hackett), and *Deep Impact* (with Robert Duvall and Morgan Freeman). In animated films, DreamWorks joined with PDI in 1996 to co-produce original computer-generated feature films, including *Antz*, which was completed in 1998 just weeks ahead of Disney's own insect-themed animation film, *A Bug's Life*. Katzenberg also landed for DreamWorks the rights to *Chicken Run*, a promising clay animation project that was in development by Oscar-winning Aaardman Animations. The film was a hit upon its release in 2000.

DreamWorks's music subsidiary was originally named DreamWorks SKG Music, with DreamWorks Records and SKG Records as separate labels—the first for soundtracks and specialty recordings and the second for individual recording artists and bands. The first artist signed to SKG Records was George Michael, whose 1996 album turned out to be much less successful than expected. A subsequent release by the indie rock band Morphine was a critical success but not the breakout hit the company hoped for.

In addition to movies and music, DreamWorks explored other entertainment outlets. DreamWorks TV turned out its first shows for ABC, *High Incident* and *Champs*, followed by the high-profile *Ink* for CBS, starring Ted Danson, which lasted one full season. That same year DreamWorks debuted *Spin City* for ABC, starring Michael J. Fox, which became DreamWorks' most successful television show.

In April 1996 DreamWorks, Sega, and Universal founded Sega Game Works, a chain of electronic game centers in Seattle; Las Vegas; Ontario, California; and other cities. It was no surprise that Spielberg would get into the game business, being an avid gamer himself. With cutting-edge games, a club-like atmosphere, and slick merchandising, the chain was well received. DreamWorks' biggest-selling game that year was *Goosebumps: Escape from Horrorland*, an animated adventure game based on the R. L. Stine children's books and TV series.

A TURNING POINT: 1998

DreamWorks began to outgrow its shaky start and turn out critically acclaimed, successful films. *Deep Impact* was released in early 1998 and was DreamWorks' highest-grossing film, at an impressive $350.9 million worldwide, which was split with co-producer Paramount Pictures. Later that year *Saving Private Ryan* became the year's highest grossing film (at $216 million) and was awarded several Oscars, including Best Picture and Best Director for Spielberg. Even though the opening weekend sales for *Antz* were about half that of the Disney film, the DreamWorks project, headed by Katzenberg, was the first of many to seriously challenge Disney's position as head of the animation kingdom. Not only did *Antz* open in theaters weeks before Disney's *A Bug's Life*, but it also managed to make $70 million, making it the most successful non-Disney animated film to date.

Released during the holiday season, *The Prince of Egypt* proved to be a success as well. It was Dream-Works' first animated film that was created completely in house. To help promote the movie, DreamWorks made a unique deal with Wal-Mart in which the retailer would sell special gift packs that included commemorative tickets (good at any theater in the country), a collectors' edition book, a limited edition lithograph, and a collectors' edition CD set. Even *Small Soldiers* earned the studio approximately $10 million dollars, despite its disappointing $46 million gross. DreamWorks finished the year with the highest average gross per film of all the major studios. The company's total box office gross for the year reached a high of $473 million.

CHAOS AMID CONTINUED SUCCESS: 1999

Spielberg, Katzenberg, and Geffen had been planning for years to build a state-of-the-art studio to serve as the central home for the company, which was scattered all over the Los Angeles area. By November 1998 they had purchased about 47 acres of land just west of Los Angeles for $20 million, which was to be the focal point for a larger 1,100-acre development for high-tech companies, new housing, and a man-made lake. The development project was projected to create at least 50,000 new jobs, inspiring local government to pledge tens of millions of dollars in tax breaks.

The proposed studio would have been the first new studio built in the Los Angeles area in 70 years. However, the Wetlands Action Network, Southwest Center, and Cal-PIRG filed a lawsuit against Dream-Works, citing concerns about the studio's plans to develop on the last significant wetland in the Los Angeles basin. The protestors also arranged sit-ins and demonstrations at movie premieres, proving to be a significant problem for DreamWorks. Later in 1999, DreamWorks pulled out of the development project for what they claimed were financial reasons. DreamWorks has since remained a decentralized network of facilities around Los Angeles.

Despite the company's inability to find a new home, 1999 proved to be another good year for Dream-Works, with Oscar-winning Best Picture of 1999, *American Beauty* (with Kevin Spacey), *Galaxy Quest* (with Tim Allen), *Forces of Nature* (with Sandra Bullock and Ben Affleck), *The Haunting* (with Liam Neeson), and *What Lies Beneath* (with Harrison Ford and Michelle Pfeifer). The home video rental release of *Saving Private Ryan*, released mid-year, became 1999's most successful rental release. Still riding high on the wave of the war film's success, DreamWorks secured a deal with NBC to launch the animated *Semper Fi*, which would draw on resources used in making *Saving Private Ryan*, including Spielberg as executive producer. DreamWorks closed its television animation unit, however, looking instead to possible partnerships with Fox and Nickelodeon for future animated shows.

The company celebrated its fifth anniversary in October 1999, looking back at an impressive series of projects, including 14 feature films, several television shows, and more than 40 record releases. That same month, DreamWorks joined forces with Imagine Entertainment to create the Internet entertainment company Pop.com. Funded by Paul Allen's Vulcan Ventures, Inc., the ambitious partnership was set up to develop a Web site that would produce and broadcast original Internet-only programming. The site was intended to offer a mix of live action and animation shorts, video on demand, live events, and non-linear interactive features and games. However, the site folded 11 months later, amid the dot-com shakeout and failed attempts to sell the site to Atom Films or to merge it with iFilm.

FILMS REMAIN PRIORITY

In early 2000 DreamWorks moved to refocus its efforts on live-action and animated films. DreamWorks Interactive was sold to Electronic Arts, a company that was on its way to becoming the leader in Internet-based gaming. DreamWorks then purchased a majority stake in special effects and animation leader PDI. The company also stepped up its television program development efforts to include two new half-hour shows—one called *The Job*, starring Denis Leary, and the other called *Freaks and Geeks*. Also in the television line-up were the 10-part miniseries *Band of Brothers* and the 20-hour *Taken* for the Sci-Fi Channel. The Emmy award-winning *Spin City* continued to be a success, even after Michael J. Fox left and was replaced by Charlie Sheen. The show entered syndication in the fall, having brought in an estimated $2.5 to $3 million per segment. According to Katzenberg and Fox executive Dan Mc-Dermott, it was enough to cover the division's operating costs and ensure profitability.

In an effort to jumpstart another of DreamWorks' non-film ventures, this time the music division, Dream-Works Records began offering a new service whereby unsigned musicians could submit their music clips to the label via the Web site. Geffen's part of the Dream-Works empire could have used the extra momentum. Despite having an impressive array of critically ac-claimed artists signed to the label, DreamWorks Records had not managed to generate impressive record sales. In 1999 the label had only three albums that earned industry distinctions for sales. One artist, Papa Roach, made the top-10 charts in 2000. However, the label's head of new media, Jed Simon, insisted, "The rest of the industry is more of a singles-driven business. We still believe in artist development and feel that ultimately will be the winning strategy."

By mid-2000, DreamWorks managed to top its 1998 total gross of $473 million with $475 million. This was also a year distinguished by five Oscar awards and $336 million for *American Beauty*, strong box office debuts for *Gladiator* ($32.7 million) and the clay anima-tion film *Chicken Run* ($17.5 million), $67 million from *Road Trip*, and a $30 million opening weekend for *What Lies Beneath*. Three of DreamWorks' films appear-ing in 2000 grossed more than $100 million for the year: *American Beauty*, *Gladiator*, and *Chicken Run*.

Despite Spielberg's personal zeal for gaming, DreamWorks shed its stake in the GameWorks business, focusing on its core film strengths. In another strategic move, DreamWorks secured a five-year extension on its distribution deal with Universal Studios. The pact granted Universal the enviable international distribution rights to live action and animated DreamWorks features and worldwide home video, as well as music distribu-tion rights. "This is an extremely important and significant milestone for DreamWorks," Katzenberg said. "With this deal we have very much secured Dream-Works' future capital needs for the next two to three years in what is going to be a difficult, demanding and turbulent debt marketplace." Days after the lucrative deal, DreamWorks struck another one with Turner Broadcasting Systems. The precedent-setting theatrical output deal, combined with an earlier 1998 syndication agreement between the two companies, gave TBS access to nearly all of DreamWorks' titles released from 1997

to 2007 and rights to titles as far out as 2015. In exchange, DreamWorks would get $350 to $450 mil-lion, depending on the final box office revenue.

In March *Gladiator* won Oscars for Best Picture, Best Actor (Russell Crowe), and in three other categories. By the end of the summer of 2001, Dream-Works SKG's new animated feature film *Shrek* reached an estimated $261 million gross, dwarfing all other releases earlier in the year, including Disney's animated movie *Atlantis* and DreamWorks' co-production with Warner Brothers Studios *A.I.* The Oscar-worthy *Shrek* firmly established DreamWorks' position as a major force in the feature animation business.

A SERIES OF UPHEAVALS: 2002-09

As DreamWorks struggled to find its footing in the new century, it was becoming increasingly clear that the company's ambitious, diversified business model might be ill-suited to the reality of Hollywood. The company's Internet business ultimately failed to gain traction after the dot-com bubble burst in the early part of the decade, and the majority of its television shows failed to attract large audiences. In 2003 the company sold its music division to Universal for $100 million. The company's strongest division remained DreamWorks Animation, which was bringing in significant earnings throughout these years largely on the strength of its *Shrek* franchise.

In the face of the company's inability to achieve consistent profitability, many of its original investors were beginning to search for the exits. Leading the exodus was Paul Allen, who was becoming anxious about recouping the $600 million he had poured into the company. By mid-2004, DreamWorks SKG recognized that the best way to save the core company might be to spin off its most lucrative business, Dream-Works Animation. The IPO took place on October 27, 2004, and earned $812 million. Jeffrey Katzenberg took control of the new entity as its CEO. Spielberg and Geffen became shareholders, each with substantial vot-ing power.

Soon after selling its animation division, the founders of DreamWorks began to have doubts about the original company's future. Industry analysts began to speculate that Spielberg in particular had become frustrated with the complexities of trying to run a studio and wanted to devote more time to directing and producing. By mid-2005 rumors were surfacing that DreamWorks SKG was poised for a major takeover, with NBC Universal and Viacom's subsidiary Paramount Pictures emerging as the most likely suitors. In December of that year, after several months of conjecture, DreamWorks SKG was purchased by Paramount for $1.6 billion. The following March, Paramount sold the DreamWorks film library to billionaire George Soros for $900 million.

At first the merger seemed like a good fit for both companies. DreamWorks would achieve some level of financial stability, while Paramount head Brad Grey would gain control over Spielberg's popular film projects. Unfortunately, the marriage between Dream-Works and Paramount was short-lived. Spielberg was reported to be especially unhappy with the new parent company's management style, complaining to his associates that Paramount frequently claimed credit for projects primarily produced by DreamWorks. Based on the relative performance of the two companies' films, Spielberg had good reason to resent his new bosses. Of Paramount's eight theatrical releases in 2007, the top four in box office revenues were all DreamWorks productions. Indeed, the discrepancy was striking: while Spielberg's top film, *Transformers*, had earned $224 million by late July of that year, Paramount's top earner was *Shooter* at $47 million.

By late 2008 it was clear that the new business partnership was doomed. Under the terms of the original merger, DreamWorks had the option to leave Paramount after three years; in October 2008 it opted to do so. David Geffen declined to join the latest incarnation of DreamWorks, leaving Spielberg as the only one of the founders to remain actively involved with the company. By mid-2009, rumors were circulating that DreamWorks might be open to another takeover. In July of that year, Spielberg reached a financing agreement with Indian film entrepreneur Anil Ambani. Under the terms of the deal, the billionaire paid $325 million into the company's total operating budget of $825 million. As analysts noted, the deal represented the first significant collaboration between Hollywood and Bollywood production forces. Writing about the deal in the *Times* (London) on July 16, 2009, Rhys Blakely quoted Spielberg as saying: "This opens a new door to our future."

Heidi Wrightsman
Updated, Stephen Meyer

PRINCIPAL COMPETITORS

Carsey-Werner, LLC; Fox Entertainment Group, Inc.; Lions Gate Entertainment Corp.; Lucasfilm Ltd.; Metro-Goldwyn-Mayer Inc.; Sony Corporation; Universal Studios, Inc.; Paramount Pictures Corporation.

FURTHER READING

Adalian, Josef, "D'Works TV Gets Busy," *Daily Variety*, January 10, 2000, p. 1.

Bart, Peter, "Amblin along with the Three Faces of Steve," *Variety*, August 18, 1997.

Blakely, Rhys, "When Holly met Bolly: Indian Tycoon Backs New Films from Spielberg," *Times* (London), July 16, 2009, p. 47.

Cieply, Michael, "DreamWorks Wins Financing for Its Films," *New York Times*, August 17, 2009.

Cox, Dan, "D'Works Feat of Clay," *Variety*, December 4, 1997, p. 1.

Diorio, Carl, and Cathy Dunkley, "Dream Dollars: U Extends Distribution Pact for Five Years," *Daily Variety*, April 17, 2001, pp. 1.

"DreamWorks Forces Theaters' Hands," *Mr. Showbiz*, March 24, 1999, http://www.mrshowbiz.com.

"DreamWorks' *Princely* Deal," *Mr. Showbiz*, October 30, 1998, http://www.mrshowbiz.com.

"DreamWorks Sheds GameWorks," *Los Angeles Business Journal*, February 12, 2001.

"DreamWorks Television Launches Olympic Web Site," *Business Wire*, July 18, 1996, http://businesswire.com.

Duke, Paul, "D'Works: What Lies Beneath?" *Variety*, July 24, 2000, p. 1.

Duke, Paul, and Carl Diorio, "Dream Quirks: Biz Plan Seems Iffy," *Variety*, July 26, 2000, p. 1.

Dunphy, Laura, "Struggling Record Label at DreamWorks Turns to Net," *Los Angeles Business Journal*, July 3, 2000.

Errico, Marcus, "DreamWorks Scraps Dream Studio," *E! Online News*, July 1, 1999, http://www.eonline.com.

Farmer, Melanie Austria, "Electronic Arts to Buy DreamWorks, Microsoft Venture," *CNET News.com*, February 24, 2000, http://www.cnet.com.

Fleming, Michael, "D'Works' 'Semper Fi' Hits the Beach at NBC," *Daily Variety*, September 30, 1999, p. 1.

Fritz, Ben, and Nicole LaPorte, "D'Works on a High after IPO Kickoff," *Daily Variety*, October 29, 2004, p. 1.

Gelmis, Joseph, "The Game Plan for DreamWorks," *Newsday*, September 24, 1997, p. C04.

Gennusa, Chris, "DreamWorks at 5: Still Pushing Ahead—After Growing Pains, It's a Mini-Major," *Hollywood Reporter*, October 21, 1999.

"Gladiator Axes Scream 3 Record," *Mr. Showbiz*, May 9, 2000, http://www.mrshowbiz.com.

"Gladiator Wins the Crowd," *Mr. Showbiz*, May 7, 2000, http://www.mrshowbiz.com.

Grove, Martin, "Looking Back at Summer's Hits and Misses," *Hollywood Reporter*, August 31, 2001.

Grover, Ronald, "What Burst Pop.com's Bubble?" *BusinessWeek Online*, September 25, 2000, http://www.businessweek.com.

Harlow, John, "How the DVD Saved Hollywood," *Sunday Times (London)*, August 19, 2001.

Hindes, Andrew, "'Antz Colony' Cranks It Up: DreamWorks Becoming a Success," *Variety*, October 19, 1998.

Holson, Laura M., and Sharon Waxman, "Is a DreamWorks IPO in the Works?" *International Herald Tribune*, May 17, 2004, p. 9.

"Interview with Steve Hickner, Co-Director, *The Prince of Egypt*," *VFXPro*, December 18, 1998, http://www.vfxpro.com.

"Katzenberg Settlement Revealed," *Mr. Showbiz*, July 8, 1999, http://www.mrshowbiz.com.

Kurutz, Steve, "AMG Biography: David Geffen," *All Music Guide*, October 1, 2001, http://www.allmusic.com.

McConville, Jim, "DreamWorks Pics to Turner: TBS Will Pay Up to $450 million in Precedent-Setting Deal," *Hollywood Reporter*, April 25, 2001.

"Mo Ostin, Lenny Waronker & Michael Ostin Named to Head DreamWorks SKG Music," *PR Newswire*, October 5, 1995, http://prnewswire.com.

Natale, Richard, and Jack Matthews, "DreamWorks on Cloud 9 with 'Shrek,' Studio Becomes Disney's Peer," *Daily News (New York)*, June 19, 2001, p. 37.

"Production to Begin in September on 'Taken,' 20-Hour Miniseries Event from Sci-Fi Channel, Steven Spielberg, and DreamWorks Television," *Business Wire*, July 12, 2001, http://busi-nesswire.com.

Rice, Lynette, "D'Works Closes Animated TV Unit, Feature Division Absorbs Direct-to-Video Arm in Retooling," *Hollywood Reporter*, March 9, 1999.

Rich, Laura, "Mickey Mouse's Worst Nightmare," *Industry Standard Magazine*, May 14, 2001.

Robischon, Noah, "Intelligence Community: A Guide to the "A.I." Web game—Its Creators Tell EW.com All You Need to Know About Playing the Hot New Cyber-Mystery," *Entertainment Weekly's EW.com*, July 2, 2001, http://www.ew.com/ew.

Sandler, Adam, "D'Works Takes Double Dose of Morphine," *Variety*, December 19, 1996.

Smith, Sean, "DreamWorks Sale—Why the Dream Didn't Work," *Newsweek*, December 19, 2005, p. 10.

"*Spin City* Wins Time Period in Adults 18–34 and Retains 96 percent of Adults 18–49 Audience from Lead-In, According to Fast National Ratings Information Provided By Nielsen Media Research," *PR Newswire*, November 30, 2000, http://www.prnewswire.com.

Spring, Greg, "DreamWorks Down, But Not Out of TV, Eyes Next Big Thing," *Electronic Media*, June 16, 1997, p. 3.

"Steven Spielberg Sets First DreamWorks Project," *Mr. Showbiz*, November 7, 1996, http://www.mrshowbiz.com.

"Steven Spielberg's *Saving Private Ryan* Becomes No. 1 Rental Title of All Time: American Audiences Respond to Award-Winning WWII Drama during Memorial Day Weekend," *Business Wire*, June 4, 1999, http://businesswire.com.

Waller, Don, "Diskery Slow to Get Rolling," *Variety*, July 24, 2000, pp. 69.

Wapshott, Nicholas, "End of a Dream," *Sunday Telegraph* (London), August 14, 2005, p. 5.

"Woody Migrates to DreamWorks," *Mr. Showbiz*, March 30, 2000, http://www.mrshowbiz.go.com.

EOG Resources

1111 Bagby, Sky Lobby 2
Houston, Texas 77002
U.S.A.
Telephone: (713) 651-7000
Toll Free: (877) 363-EOGR
Fax: (713) 651-6995
Web site: http://www.eogresources

Public Company
Founded: 1987 as Enron Oil & Gas Company
Employees: 2,100
Sales: $7.13 billion (2008)
Stock Exchanges: New York
Ticker Symbol: EOG
NAICS: 211111 Crude Petroleum and Natural Gas Extraction; 213112 Support Activities for Oil and Gas Operations

■ ■ ■

EOG Resources is one of the largest independent oil and natural gas companies in the United States. While many energy exploration companies expand production by acquiring new land holdings, EOG uses advanced technology—such as horizontal drilling, simulation models, three-dimensional seismic data, and redesigned drill bits—to explore its existing holdings for new oil and natural gas deposits. EOG Resources is popular with investors because its high-tech exploration processes considerably reduce the capital risks inherent in energy exploration and extraction.

EARLY DEVELOPMENT AS AN ENRON SUBSIDIARY: 1987–99

EOG Resources is one of the few survivors of the Enron Corporation's collapse in 2001. Enron Oil & Gas Company began as a subsidiary of Enron Corporation in 1987. Two years later the company made an initial public offering of 16 percent of its stock on the New York Stock Exchange with Enron remaining the majority stakeholder in the company.

Enron Oil & Gas Company steadily expanded operations throughout the 1990s, signing production-sharing agreements with the government of Trinidad and Tobago, the Indian National Oil Company, the Indian Oil & Natural Gas Corporation, and China National Petroleum. Each deal yielded productive, profitable arrangements that allowed Enron access to resources in different regions of the world. In Trinidad, Enron Oil & Gas developed three new fields in the South East Coast Consortium Block, previously held by three companies owned by the government. The company was allowed to explore a nearby block in a subsequent 1995 deal and in 1996 signed a product-sharing contract with the government. In India, Enron Oil & Gas Company became the operator of three offshore blocks near Bombay and secured 30 percent interest in these projects. In China, Enron Oil & Gas held a 100 percent interest in the Chuan Zhong Block in Sichuan, as well as serving as operator. These foreign holdings played an important role in the company's 1999 exit from Enron.

During the late 1990s, the management of Enron Corporation opted to stress commodity market opera-

COMPANY PERSPECTIVES

Our growing expertise in the application of horizontal drilling and completion technology to develop crude oil reservoirs sets EOG apart, giving us a competitive edge with plays such as the North Dakota Bakken and the Fort Worth Barnett Shale Combo. We will continue to focus on this advantage as we look for opportunities to replicate this success in other crude oil reservoirs.

tions over pipelines and oil rigs and began to divest itself of hard-asset divisions, including Enron Oil & Gas Company. As Enron Corporation sought buyers, two Enron Oil & Gas executives devised a strategy whereby the company could buy out Enron Corporation's share itself. Led by Forrest Hoglund, the retired chairman of Enron Oil & Gas, and Mark G. Papa, its president, CEO, and director, the company utilized Enron Oil & Gas energy assets in India and China and added another $600 million in cash to seal the deal for about $1.46 billion. The transfer was completed in August 1999. By 2006 the company was valued at $15 billion.

LEAVING ENRON BEHIND: 1999–2002

In its first year of independence, EOG expanded both east and west. The company opened its ninth division office, in Pittsburgh, Pennsylvania, with plans to explore the potential holdings of the Appalachian Basin. EOG also signed an innovative marketing deal with the California firm Calpine, under which the daily price of natural gas would be indexed to the price of electricity.

Barely two years after EOG became independent, its former parent corporation filed for bankruptcy on December 2, 2001, leaving unpaid debts of $31.8 billion. At the time, Enron Corporation owned 11.5 million shares of EOG. In November 2002 a bankruptcy court allowed the sale of the shares to a broker, providing the proceeds were placed in escrow. EOG purchased one million shares from the broker.

EOG's Trinidad operations expanded in 2002 when natural gas was discovered in Parula and two new blocks opened to exploration. The company also started operations at a new CNC Ammonia plant on the island. EOG also supplied feedstock to the M5000 Methanol Plant in Trinidad, as well as to the Atlantic Liquified Natural Gas Train 4 in 2005.

EXPLORATION IN CANADA PROVES PROFITABLE: 2003–08

Canadian holdings dramatically expanded in 2003, when EOG acquired properties in southeastern Alberta from Husky Energy. The most lucrative holdings, however, were thought to be in the Muskwa Shale site in British Columbia.

The Muskwa discovery was the product of a new strategy pioneered by EOG. In May 2005 Barbara Shook reported in *Natural Gas Week* that CEO Mark Papa believed it was time for the industry to consider "weird" gas, defined as resources extracted from difficult environments, such as tight sand, dense shale, and coalbed methane structures. Many of these sites had been considered too expensive to develop, but with new efficient technologies and rising prices, the cost becomes affordable. "After about three years of covert operations in the northern wilds of Canada," vice-president of exploration Loren Leiker revealed in *Natural Gas Week* in 2008, "we're finally ready to talk about our BC shale play." Papa told *Natural Gas Week* that EOG is leading a "major sea change" in the industry "caused by the technical improvements in horizontal drilling and also the associated well completion portions of that." The technique was pioneered at the Barnett Shale project, near Fort Worth, and later applied to holdings in Mississippi, Texas, and Colorado. The new methods also allowed EOG to deplete a well in only eight years, compared with the typical 12 years. Horizontal drilling involves boring several thousand feet into the ground and then turning right or left for further exploration. The horizontal offshoots can be done at multiple depths, creating "stacked layers." Thus thousands of feet of subsurface can be explored using just one borehole. Horizontal drilling made up only 22 percent of EOG's explorations in 2005, but was expected to jump to 60 percent in 2009. Based on three new horizontal wells, EOG predicted net reserves of 6 trillion cubic feet of gas.

The Barnett Shale project was potentially the most lucrative, with estimates of 4.5 to 6.7 trillion cubic feet equivalent. At an industry conference in September 2007 EOG vice-president Lindell Looger announced, "We're getting fantastic rates of return on the Barnett. This is the premier gas asset in North America, we believe, and we've got a big chunk of it."

While Barnett yields natural gas, EOG was also using innovative techniques to extract crude oil from the Bakken Shale project, a deposit running from Montana to North Dakota and Saskatchewan. The U.S. Geological Survey estimated that 4.3 billion barrels of oil could be pumped out of Bakken. EOG also started to develop the Marcellus Shale deposit in Pennsylvania. As

KEY DATES

1985: InterNorth and Houston Natural Gas companies merge, forming Enron Corporation.

1987: Enron Oil & Gas Company is launched as a subsidiary of the Enron Corporation.

1989: Enron Oil & Gas Company is taken public through an initial public offering on the New York Stock Exchange.

1997: Enron Oil & Gas signs a 30-year production-sharing contract with China National Petroleum.

1999: The company changes its name to EOG Resources Inc. and separates from Enron Corporation.

2003: The company makes the largest acquisition in its history, purchasing a huge block of natural gas properties in Alberta, Canada, for an estimated $320 million.

2007: EOG Resources is named one of *Fortune*'s "100 Best Companies to Work For."

2009: EOG announces the discovery of crude oil in its Waskada Field, Manitoba.

of 2009 EOG Resources was exploring six main sites in North America: British Columbia Horn River Basin, Fort Worth Barnett Shale Combo, Haynesville Shale, Marcellus Shale, North Dakota Bakken Core, and North Dakota Bakken Lite.

In addition to North American sites, EOG moved to reclaim some of its former holdings in China. In late 2007 ConocoPhillips sold the Chuan Zhong natural gas block to EOG, which had sold the same block as part of its 1999 buyout from Enron Corporation.

HARD ASSETS, SOLID GROWTH

At the end of 2008, EOG Resources estimated its net proved natural gas reserves as 7,339 billion cubic feet and estimated net proved crude oil, condensate, and natural gas liquids reserves at 225 million barrels. Approximately 71 percent of the firm's reserves on a natural gas equivalent basis were in the United States, 15 percent in Canada, and 14 percent in Trinidad. The final 1 percent was distributed in China and the North Sea. EOG had nine independent business units in the United States, as well as subsidiary operations in Canada, Trinidad, and the United Kingdom

EOG weathered economic and energy slumps thanks to its commitment to conservative growth. Papa won praise for his adept management of the company, which he had directed since 1998. In a 2007 press release, he restated the company's commitment to "organic production growth, managing costs, and maintaining a strong balance sheet." Papa's cautious approach had won over many fund investors, including Energy Ventures Group, Davis New York Venture Fund, and Calvert Social Investment Equity Fund. As explained in the company's 2008 annual report, "We grow EOG organically through the drillbit rather than buying high priced reserves through large acquisitions and mergers. This concentration has enabled us to develop a low cost, first-mover advantage in establishing a foothold in new natural gas and crude oil resource lays that are amenable to horizontal drilling." EOG finished 2008 with the second-best stock performance within the Standard & Poor's 500 Oil and Gas Exploration and Production Average. Its five- and 10-year return to stockholders as of December 31, 2008, were 188 percent and 672 percent, respectively.

Ann E. Robertson

PRINCIPAL SUBSIDIARIES

EOG Resources Canada Inc.; EOG Resources International; EOG Resources United Kingdom Ltd.; EOGR Trinidad Ltd.

PRINCIPAL COMPETITORS

Anadarko Petroleum Corp.; Apache Corp.; Canadian Superior Energy Inc.; Noble Energy Inc.; Pioneer Natural Resources Company; XTO Energy.

FURTHER READING

Casselman, Ben, "Oil Squeeze," *Wall Street Journal*, May 29, 2008, p. A8.

Couturier, Greg, "EOG Resources Head Says Firm Growing Organically, Avoids Debt," *Natural Gas Week*, September 17, 2007, pp. 4-5.

Darbonne, Nissa, "Breaking into the Barnett," *Oil and Gas Investor*, April 2006, pp. 48-61.

"EOG Unveils British Columbia's Prolific Muskwa Shale Gas Play," *Natural Gas Week*, March 3, 2008, pp. 3-4.

Gold, Russell, "Gas Find Shows Shale's Promise," *Wall Street Journal*, November 30, 2006, p. C2.

———, "Gas Producers Rush to Pennsylvania," *Wall Street Journal*, April 2, 2008, p. A2.

———, "There May Still Be Ways to Ride Energy Wave," *Wall Street Journal*, August 26, 2005, p. C1.

Kelly, Andrew, "EOG Bullish for Long Term, Steps up Hedging," *Natural Gas Week*, November 10, 2003, p. 9.

McLean, Bethany and Peter Elkind, *Smartest Guys in the Room: The Amazing Rise and Scandalous Fall of Enron*. New York: Portfolio, 2003, 466 p.

Palmeri, Christopher, "Old Flame," *Forbes*, December 13, 1999, p. 114.

Piller, Dan, "Enron Did EOG a Favor by Selling It," *Fort Worth Star-Telegram*, January 26, 2006.

Serwer, Andy, "All's Well at the Other Enron," *Fortune*, July 5, 2006.

Shook, Barbara, "EOG Bets Future on 'Weird' Gas Plays Once Eschewed, Now Prized," *Natural Gas Week*, May 16, 2005, pp. 3-4.

Snow, Nick, "EOG, Others Stress Their Balance Sheets Are Not Like Enron's," *Oil and Gas Investor*, April 2002, pp. 36-37.

Taylor, Bertie, "EOG's Papa: LNG Essential to U.S., but Competition to Be Tough," *Oil and Gast Investor*, November 2005, p. 21.

POWERING POSSIBILITY

Exxaro Resources Ltd.

Exxaro Corporate Center
Roger Dyason Road
Pretoria West, 0183
South Africa
Telephone: (+27 12) 307-5000
Fax: (+27 12) 323-3400
Web site: http://www.exxaro.com

Public Company
Founded: 2006
Employees: 10,135
Sales: ZAR 13.8 billion (2008)
Stock Exchanges: Johannesburg
Ticker Symbol: EXX
NAICS: 212111 Bituminous Coal and Lignite Surface
   Mining; 212112 Bituminous Coal Underground
   Mining; 212210 Iron Ore Mining; 212231 Lead
   Ore and Zinc Ore Mining

■ ■ ■

Exxaro Resources Ltd. has been in existence since 2006.
By 2008, however, it boasted revenues of ZAR 13.8 billion and had 15 mines, ties with operations in China
and Australia, and an employee list that showed the
entire rainbow palette of South Africa. This great
achievement, only a few years in the making, shows how
the mining industry of South Africa has transformed
itself from an economic sector that was once a bulwark
of apartheid to one that brings opportunities for
advancement to all the country's previously
disadvantaged people.

RIGHTING THE WRONGS OF
APARTHEID

Exxaro's existence was still far in the future in 1994
when the African National Congress swept away the
memories of apartheid by winning the country's first
democratic elections. Absolute equality for all was the
stated goal. Nevertheless, it did not take long for these
hopes to fade; by 2001 black South Africans were still
earning only a 3 percent share of modern industry
profits, even though they made up 90 percent of the
country's population.

In an attempt to bring this inequality to an end,
the South African government passed in 2003 the
Broad-Based Black Economic Empowerment (BBBEE)
Act, which attacked the problem on several fronts. First,
the act mandated management training to improve the
performance of inexperienced employees. Next, it specified that a healthy percentage of ownership must pass
into the hands of previously disadvantaged people. Only
in these ways, the government believed, could it heal the
wounds of apartheid, increase job potential for previously disadvantaged people, and see to it that the
economy represented South Africa's full population
range.

Besides these guarantees of black participation in
South Africa's bounty, the BBBEE mandated that each
of the country's most influential economic sectors had
to create its own charter, so that its goals could be
shaped to meet its own industrial needs. The mining
industry charter, which was established in 2002 by the
Department of Minerals and Energy, specified two
broad types of objectives: those that partly overlapped

COMPANY PERSPECTIVES

The Exxaro brand is built on a strong vision— Everything we do and deliver today will allow others to realise their vision tomorrow. At Exxaro, we look beyond the current commodities and operations and see the impact we have on people and the planet. This way of thinking is what drives our essence of "defining possibility." We believe in the power of people and their ability to explore and shift boundaries which lead to success.

the act, such as black management and control, and those that were tailored specifically to day-to-day mining industry operations, such as strategies for developing rural and mining communities. Other aspects of the charter concerned black participation in resources development, employment equity, improvement in housing and living conditions, and nondiscrimination against migrant labor, which had previously been a problem among black South Africans desperate to protect their meager turf. Constantinus J. Fauconnier, the first chief executive officer (CEO) of Exxaro Resources, and Babita Mathur-Helm made the charter's purpose clear in the article "Black Economic Empowerment in the South African Mining Industry: A Case Study of Exxaro Limited." They declared that "the objective of the Mining Industry Charter was to achieve 26 percent ownership of the previously disadvantaged people in the mining companies by 2012."

THE SPIN-OFF OF KUMBA RESOURCES

These changes had yet to occur in 2001, when Iscor, the country's largest steel producer, spun off its subsidiary Kumba Resources Ltd., which would later become Exxaro's parent company. Because Kumba's interests were based in mining iron ore, coal, mineral sands, and base metals, news of this change grabbed the attention of the mining giant Anglo American PLC, which quickly moved to acquire Kumba to broaden its list of mining interests.

The transaction was complete by the end of 2003, and Anglo American had added a 35 percent interest in Kumba Resources to its already impressive lineup. Anticipating a respectable amount of interest from stock market buyers, Anglo American was surprised to see the buying fervor exceed its expectations—in fact, it eventually found itself the owner of 66 percent of Kumba

Resources. Justifying this increase in ownership was not easy because it had made a promise to the South African government to keep its interest in Kumba well under 50 percent. For this reason, both Anglo American and Kumba Resources decided in 2005 that a split was necessary. A deciding factor was Kumba's iron ore operations, which Anglo American wanted to keep. In addition, given that both companies had an interest in mineral sands, coal, and base metals, there was a definite possibility that a conflict of interest would eventually arise. As such, Kumba was split into Kumba Iron Ore, still wholly owned by Anglo American, and Kumba Resources.

EXXARO RESOURCES BORN

This transaction was extremely complicated because it required careful navigation between the BBBEE on the one hand and the mining industry charter guidelines on the other hand. Nevertheless, both Anglo American and Kumba Resources were determined to ensure that historically disadvantaged South Africans would receive the management and ownership opportunities to which they were entitled, so they decided to include the black-owned Eyesizwe Coal Ltd., a successful six-year-old coal and energy company.

As the CEO of Kumba Resources, Fauconnier was well acquainted with Sipho A. Nkosi, the CEO of Eyesizwe. Together, the two worked out the formation of Black Economic Empowerment Holdco (BEE Holdco), an umbrella company that encompassed several black interest groups and that became a subsidiary of Eyesizwe SPV, the holding company for Eyesizwe Coal. Like Eyesizwe Coal, BEE Holdco was completely owned by blacks.

In 2006 the agreement between the three companies blossomed into reality, and Kumba Iron Ore Ltd. was listed separately on the Johannesburg Stock Exchange as a subsidiary of Anglo American. Because the names of the two companies were so similar, Kumba Resources was renamed Exxaro Resources Ltd. According to Fauconnier, the ownership stakes were divided in the following manner: Anglo American, the original owner of Kumba Resources, was to own 19 percent of Exxaro, and 53 percent was to belong to BEE Holdco, a percentage that included an 11 percent stake for the South African Women in Mining Association, which was a group member of BEE Holdco.

In November 2006 Exxaro Resources, a ZAR 16 billion company with interests in coal, mineral, sands, base metals, industrial minerals, and iron ore, was listed on the Johannesburg Stock Exchange for the first time. At the helm was Fauconnier, who had taken this position for a year.

```
┌─────────────────────────────────────────┐
│                                           │
│              KEY DATES                    │
│                   ■                       │
├───────────────────────────────────────────┤
│  2006:  Exxaro Resources Ltd. is founded. │
│  2007:  Exxaro and Eskom sign a 40-year   │
│         coal supply contract.             │
│  2008:  Exxaro acquires Namakwa Sands, a  │
│         mine supplying heavy minerals,    │
│         and a 26 percent stake in Black   │
│         Mountain Mining, a supplier of    │
│         zinc, lead, and copper.           │
│                                           │
└───────────────────────────────────────────┘
```

EXXARO'S FIRST YEAR

Exxaro's first annual report, which was issued for 2006, listed the lineup of the company's operating interests as follows. First came its seven coal mines: Grootegeluk and Leeuwpan, both open-pit mines, plus the underground mines Arnot, Matla, North Block Complex, New Clydesdale, and Tshikondeni. Second came the company's mineral sands operations, which were split evenly between South Africa-based KZN Sands and an overseas operation called Australia Sands, while the company's zinc mining operations, Rosh Pinah, in Namibia provided raw materials for the Zincor refinery in Gauteng, South Africa. This operation, one of the few integrated zinc mining and refining operations in the world, shared Exxaro's lineup with the Chifeng Smelter in China. This considerable list of operations was completed by FerroAlloys, a manufacturer of ferrosilicons, and by the Glen Douglas Dolomite Quarry, a provider of products for steel works.

All these operations proved their worth in a very short time. When Exxaro Resources released its group financial results at the end of June 2007 for what was essentially its first seven months in existence, it showed satisfactory revenues of ZAR 4.85 billion, of which ZAR 839 million represented attributable earnings. By the end of the financial year, revenues had grown to reach ZAR 10.16 billion.

THE DEAL WITH ESKOM

In Afrikaans, the name "Grootegeluk" means "great good fortune," and it was an aptly named mine for Exxaro. Grootegeluk proved its worth in 2007 when it was chosen to provide the coal for Medupi, a new power station that was owned by South Africa's state-owned Eskom. Signed in March 2007, the agreement specified that Grootegeluk would supply 7.3 million tons of coal per year to the Medupi Power Station for the next 40 years.

Other events in 2007 for Exxaro concerned the retirement of Fauconnier, who intended to continue transforming South Africa's mining industry to comply with the mining industry charter. He was replaced by Nkosi.

As president of the Chamber of Mines and a veteran in both marketing and mining, the highly experienced Nkosi found himself with several challenges during his first year in office. First, there was the problem of safety. There had been four fatal accidents in Exxaro's mines during the year, New Clydesdale Mine had been briefly shut down due to concern about its underground safety pillars, and Leeuwpan had required extensive repairs for safety reasons. Dissatisfied with this distressing list of problems, Nkosi ordered that 9 of Exxaro's 12 mines achieve health, safety, and environmental certification by the end of 2007 and that the remaining three mines achieve this same status by the end of the following year.

Another of Nkosi's ongoing woes was a long list of vacant positions at Exxaro. In keeping with both the mining industry charter of 2002 and the Generic Scorecard issued by the Department of Trade and Industry (DTI) in 2004, Exxaro made every effort to fill management positions with black workers to reach the target of 26 percent black ownership by 2012.

This was not, however, an easy task. Nkosi explained to Brendan Ryan of *Finweek* that there were two reasons for the large number of vacancies not only in Exxaro but also in many South African companies. The first was employee poaching. To save money on their training programs, companies who were short of skilled employees lured them away from other companies. Second, because there were only a certain number of top management jobs available, it was hard to achieve equality in the workplace without removing opportunities from others who were already trained and experienced. Passed over or even discreetly forced out, these highly qualified employees left the country to look for better opportunities. *Harvard International Review*'s Natasia Kovacevic noted that between 1994 and 2001 the percentage of businesses seeing a significant "brain drain" rose from 2 percent to 33 percent. By 2003, when the BBBEE was passed and a quota system was established, guaranteeing a number of positions for South Africans of color at every level, there were few workers left who were qualified to train their replacements.

THREE BIG LINEUP CHANGES

In spite of the safety and employment issues, Exxaro continued to see progress in 2008. The big item on its agenda was the acquisition of Namakwa Sands, a heavy minerals mining business based on South Africa's Western Cape Province coast, near Saldanha Bay. Acquired from Anglo American, Namakwa Sands cost ZAR 2 billion and was bought to position Exxaro as one of the world's premier producers of high-grade titanium dioxide feedstock. At the same time, the company bought a 26 percent interest in Black Mountain Mining Ltd. in Northern Cape Province and applied for a conversion in its mining rights. A producer of zinc concentrate that supplied Exxaro's Zincor refinery in Gauteng, Black Mountain cost the company ZAR 180 million.

In June 2008 Exxaro saw a reduction in its stake of the Rosh Pinah Mine, a supplier of zinc concentrate situated in Namibia. Even though Exxaro continued to manage the mine, its stake decreased from 93.9 percent to 50.04 percent, with the remaining 49.96 percent belonging to Namibian shareholders.

CORPORATE RESPONSIBILITY

Employment and literacy issues, as mandated by the DTI, also received attention during 2008. To make sure students were up to course standards when they entered their professional studies programs, Exxaro began sponsoring 12 disadvantaged students per year for a 12-month bridging course at the University of Pretoria. All of its employees received biannual performance reviews, so that training and development could be provided in areas where they were needed. In addition, the company offered university scholarships and made skills training and formal education available in disadvantaged communities close to its operations.

All of these improvements had handsome dividends. As 2008 came to an end, Exxaro reported a consolidated revenue of ZAR 13.8 billion, representing a 36 percent increase from its 2007 revenues.

Gillian Wolf

PRINCIPAL SUBSIDIARIES

AlloyStream Pty. Ltd.; Exxaro Base Metals Pty. Ltd.; Exxaro FerroAlloys Pty. Ltd.; Exxaro Base Metals and Industrial Minerals Holdings Pty. Ltd.; Exxaro Sands Pty. Ltd.

PRINCIPAL COMPETITORS

BHP Billiton; Bisichi Mining PLC; Xstrata PLC.

FURTHER READING

Anglo American PLC, "REG-Anglo American PLC Offer for Kumba Resources" (press release), October 31, 2003, http://www.angloamerican.co.uk/aa/investors/rns/rnsitem?id=1067610803nRNSe5527R&t=popup.

Bond, Patrick, "The New Apartheid," *New Internationalist*, April 2003.

Eskom, "Eskom Suspends Load Shedding" (press release), May 5, 2008, http://www.eskom.co.za.

Exxaro Resources Ltd., "Exxaro and Eskom Agree on Coal Contract for New Power Station" (press release), March 29, 2007, http://www.exxaro.com/content/media/newsReleasesNews.asp?Current_ID=204.

———, "Exxaro Resources Reviewed Group Financial Results and Physical Information for the Six-Month Period Ended 30 June 2007" (press release), August 16, 2007, http://www.exxaro.com/content/media/newsReleasesNews.asp?Current_ID=189.

Fauconnier, Constantinus J., and Babita Mathur-Helm, "Black Economic Empowerment in the South African Mining Industry: A Case Study of Exxaro Limited," *South African Journal of Business Management*, 2008.

Kovacevic, Natasia, "Righting Wrongs: Affirmative Action in South Africa," *Harvard International Review*, Spring 2007.

"Kumba in SA's Biggest BEE Deal," Southafrica.info, October 14, 2005, http://www.southafrica.info/business/trends/empowerment/kumba-131005.htm.

Kumba Resources Ltd., "Kumba Circular to Shareholders Released" (press release), October 9, 2006, http://www.kumba.co.za/pr_091006.php.

Prinsloo, Loni, "Increased Namibian Ownership of Rosh Pinah Mine," *Mining Weekly*, August 15, 2008.

"Questions for Baum," Africa News Service, July 27, 2006.

Ryan, Brendan, "Exxaro Sets Out 2012 Coal Strategy," *Miningmx*, November 2, 2006.

———, "Too Many Positions Vacant," *Finweek*, April 10, 2008.

"SA's Largest Empowerment Deal Unveiled," *South Africa: The Good News*, October 13, 2005.

Van der Merwe, Christy, "Exxaro Pays R2 Billion for Namakwa Sands Operation," *Mining Weekly*, October 1, 2009.

"Way to BEE; Business in South Africa," *Economist*, December 23, 2006.

EZchip Semiconductor Ltd.

1 Hatamar Street
P.O. Box 527
Yokneam, 20692
Israel
Telephone: (+972 4) 959-6644
Fax: (+972 4) 959-4177
Web site: http://www.ezchip.com/

Public Company
Founded: 1990
Employees: 97
Sales: $8.7 million (2008)
Stock Exchanges: NASDAQ Global Tel Aviv
Ticker Symbol: EZCH
NAICS: 334413 Semiconductor and Related Device Manufacturing

■ ■ ■

EZchip Semiconductor Ltd. traces its origins to 1999 when EZchip Technologies was founded as a subsidiary of Israel-based firm LanOptics Ltd. Eli Fruchter, a cofounder of LanOptics, became president and CEO of EZchip. The company set out to create software-based Ethernet chips for use in local area network (LAN) switches. The software-based chips would improve the quality of service in local networks and make it easy to upgrade LAN switches to the newest features and technologies. The NP-1, EZchip's first-generation product, was the first processor that could transfer information at 10-gigabits per second (Gbps), which attracted the attention of industry analysts. The company was not profitable for several years when it spent large amounts of money on research and development. However, the research guaranteed that EZchip would remain at the forefront of network processing technology. By 2009 EZchip, although still a relatively small company, had become extremely competitive in a market typically dominated by huge corporations.

FASTER, BETTER, CHEAPER

EZchip founders initially gambled that they could create a product that was substantially faster and more efficient than the competition, while also being less expensive. The company sought to make new, faster networking processors by breaking down networking tasks and using a different, optimized processor for each task. This innovative approach to processing allowed information to be transferred at a never before reached speed of 10 Gbps. Because EZchip provided on one chip what other companies required several chips to do, the cost was significantly less as well. These high-speed processors could provide Internet access to a neighborhood or even an entire city, as opposed to lower speed processors that might service only a building or a street.

From the start EZchip faced delays in getting its products to market. Although EZchip announced that its first product would be available in April 2001, the company had difficulties producing its new technology until signing a deal with IBM in late 2000. The deal involved IBM producing the NP-1 network processors in exchange for a 5 percent stake in EZchip. The following year, EZchip established a North American headquarters in San Jose, California. Three years after its

COMPANY PERSPECTIVES

EZchip Technologies is a fabless semiconductor company that provides Ethernet network processors. EZchip provides its customers with solutions that scale from 1-Gigabit to 100-Gigabits per second with a common architecture and software across all products. EZchip's network processors provide the flexibility and integration that enable triple-play data, voice, and video services in systems that make up the new Carrier Ethernet networks. Flexibility and integration make EZchip's solutions ideal for building systems for a wide range of applications in telecom networks, data centers and enterprise backbones. EZchip Technologies was formed as a spin-off in 1999 and is fully-owned by EZchip Semiconductor (formerly LanOptics Ltd.). EZchip Semiconductor is a public company traded on NASDAQ Global Market and the Tel Aviv Stock Exchange (symbol EZCH).

founding in 2002 EZchip announced that it had actual customers for the high-speed network processor. Analysts said those eight customers constituted a large number given that few networks were capable of handling the 10 Gbps systems. EZchip's first product finally shipped in April 2002. At that time, EZchip and its parent company, LanOptics, had been operating at a loss for several quarters.

Things began to turn around in August 2002 when ZTE, China's largest public telecom equipment manufacturer, announced it would use EZchip's NP-1 in its next generation metro switch. The following month, *Communications Systems Design* named EZchip as one of the rising stars in the industry. Meanwhile, the company continued to work on advancing its core technology by increasing the number of processors in the NP-1 to boost performance. The company posted revenues for the first time in 2002, as parent company LanOptics discontinued all other operations and became solely focused on its EZchip subsidiary.

INDUSTRY RECOGNITION

In March 2003 EZchip won the 2002 Microprocessor Report Analysts' Choice Award for the NP-1 processor. Because processing and classifying were integrated on one chip, the NP-1 was significantly less expensive, required less power, and was smaller than other networking alternatives. Editor-in-chief Peter Glaskow-

sky of the *Microprocessor Report* said, "The NP-1 is one of the fastest NPUs [network processing units] on the market and offers a high degree of integration with is on-chip search engines and multiple standards-based interfaces. Of all the NPUs available during 2002, we believe the NP-1 offers the best overall package of current capabilities and future potential." The NP-1 was an attractive alternative to competing products.

Not resting on its laurels, EZchip continued to spend huge amounts of money on research and development. By 2003 EZchip was rolling out prototypes of its next generation chip, the NP-2 network processor. This network processor remained a 10 Gbps network processor with combined search engine block, but its capabilities also included traffic management, security processing, and TCP processing. Fruchter explained the advantages of the NP-2 in *Business Wire* on June 23, 2003, "With NP-1 and NP-1c we integrated the first two of the five key processing components onto a single chip, enabling our customers to reduce their system chip count, power and cost by as much as 80%. NP-2 adds the three remaining building blocks to address high-end applications that require all five processing elements." The company declared that a single NP-2 could replace the 20 to 50 chips typically used in LAN switches and routers.

By the end of 2004 EZchip was on solid financial ground. Revenues had nearly tripled, increasing from $1.76 million in 2003 to $4.75 million in 2004. The company had 44 customers at the time, with the NP-2 chip slated to be available to sample the following year. Nevertheless, some analysts wondered if EZchip was equal to its reputation. Tech journalist Gitit Pincas pointed out that EZchip's products had been continually delayed and the rhetoric surrounding their introductions overblown. He wrote in *Israel Business Arena*, "EZchip really does quite a bit of promising, so far without fulfilling any of the promise." Schlomo Greenberg, also commenting in *Israel Business Arena*, wrote in 2005, "Leaving Intel far behind? That's just a bit too arrogant. EZchip has been around for awhile, and if Intel were the least bit worried about being left behind, it would surely be acquiring the company for $200 million." Revenue growth slowed in 2005, with net operating loss that increased from $8.4 million in 2004 to $10.1 million in 2005.

STILL GROWING

Revenues grew 44.8 percent from $5.85 million in 2005 to $8.47 million in 2006. Net operating loss, however, had increased to $12.32 million. In 2006 LanOptics

KEY DATES

1999: EZchip Technologies is created as a subsidiary of LanOptics Ltd.
2002: NP-1 becomes available; China's ZTE Corporation announces it will use the NP-1 in its next generation metro switch.
2003: NP-1 wins 2002 Microprocessor Report Analysts' Choice Award.
2005: NP-2 begins shipping to customers.
2008: Samples of NP-3 are shipped to customers; LanOptics changes its corporate name to EZchip Semiconductor Ltd.

increased its shares in EZchip from 60 percent to 78 percent, with the goal of acquiring 100 percent of the company over the next several years.

Even before samples of its third generation product, the NP-3, shipped in July 2008, EZchip announced the development of the NP-4, a single-chip, 100-gigabit network processor that included integrated traffic management. In May 2008 the company announced that its NP-4 network processor would support enhanced transport of video applications, which would speed video downloads from the Internet. CEO Fruchter told *Israel Business Arena*, "Today, when you open a video file on a computer, it takes ages for it to appear, and sometimes it stops and then carries on loading. If that were to happen while switching channels on the television, we wouldn't stand for it. ... The quality of the experience on the Internet should be no less than on cable, and that is how it will be." The company promised that kind of quality when the fourth generation NP-4 is finished.

In January 2008 LanOptics completed its acquisition of all equity in EZchip and changed its corporate name to EZchip Semiconductor Ltd. Fruchter stated, "The new company name better reflects our corporate mission—to make EZchip the leading network processor vendor." In 2008 EZchip seemed finally to be achieving expected results despite the global economic recession. Annual revenues were up 72 percent over 2007, reaching $33.6 million. First quarter 2009 revenues were up 42 percent over first quarter 2008 revenues. However, summer 2009 brought sobering, potentially disastrous news for the company. Among its customers, EZchip counted two of the big-three producers of routers, Juniper, which accounted for over half of EZchip's business, and Cisco. EZchip stock plummeted

in July 2009 when news leaked that Juniper did not intend to move to the next generation of EZchip processors, instead developing a processor in-house. Even though EZchip had been able to weather the recession, it remained to be seen whether EZchip could recover from the loss of its major customer.

Melissa Doak

PRINCIPAL SUBSIDIARIES

EZchip Technologies Ltd. (Israel); EZchip Inc.

PRINCIPAL COMPETITORS

Bay Microsystems, Inc.; Broadcom Corporation; Xelerated Inc.

FURTHER READING

Bursky, Dave, "Task-Optimized Architecture Lets Network Processor Handle 10-Gbit/s Wire-Speed Applications," *Electronic Design*, October 30, 2000, p. 40.

Cohen, Shlomi, "It Gets Tougher for EZchip," *Israel Business Arena*, July 7, 2009.

———, "Not Such Hard Times for EZchip," *Israel Business Arena*, December 16, 2008.

———, "When a Fall Is Not a Collapse," *Israel Business Arena*, May 12, 2009.

"EZchip Announces New Ethernet Network Processors for Access Market," *PR Newswire*, October 11, 2007.

"EZchip Announces the NP-4, a Single-Chip 100-Gigabit Network Processor with Integrated Traffic Manager," *PR Newswire*, May 30, 2007.

"EZchip Establishes North American Headquarters in Silicon Valley," *Business Wire*, July 9, 2001, p. 2384.

"EZchip's NP-1 Wins Prestigious Microprocessor Report Analysts' Choice Award for Best Network Processor," *Business Wire*, March 4, 2003, p. 5341.

"EZchip NP-4 Network Processor to Support Transport of Video Applications," *Wireless News*, May 16, 2008.

"EZchip Technologies and IBM Sign Network Processor Technology Deal," *Business Wire*, November 1, 2000, p. 2049.

"EZchip Technologies Unveils the NP-Process; Single Chip, Full Duplex, 10-Gigabit NPU with Integrated Co-Processors," *Business Wire*, June 23, 2003.

Freeman, Tyson, "EZchip Gets Not-So-Easy $24.5M," *Daily Deal*, December 17, 2002.

Greenberg, Shlomo, "EZchip—Silence Is Golden," *Israel Business Arena*, March 29, 2005.

Gwennap, Linley, "Execute or Be Executed," *Electronic Engineering Times*, May 6, 2002, p. 39.

Habib, Shiri, "Our Market Will Reach $250 Million in 2008–2009, and We'll Have a Sizeable Chunk," *Israel Business Arena*, May 2, 2007.

Hesseldahl, Arik, "EZchip Eyes Next-Gen NPUs," *Electronic News* , February 21, 2000, p. 18.

Keenan, Robert, "Startups Take Next Step at NPU Confab—Networking Chips, Content Processor Ready to Role at Net Processor Conference," *Electronic Engineering Times*, June 23, 2003, p. 37.

Keenan, Robert, and Loring Wirbel, "EZchip, AMCC Expected to Detail Plans at NPU Conference—Chip Vendors Move to Upgrade Net Processors," *Electronic Engineering Times*, October 21, 2002, p. 37.

"LanOptics Announces 2002 Fourth Quarter and Year End Results," *Business Wire*, March 21, 2003, p. 5135.

"LanOptics Announces 2004 Fourth Quarter and Year End Results," *Business Wire*, February 17, 2005.

"LanOptics Announces 2005 Fourth Quarter and Year End Results," *Business Wire*, February 22, 2006.

"LanOptics Announces 2006 Fourth Quarter and Year End Results," *Business Wire*, February 13, 2007.

"LanOptics Changes Its Corporate Name to EZchip Semiconductor," *PR Newswire*, July 30, 2008.

"LanOptics Loses $251,000 from Continuing Operations in Q2," *Asia Africa Intelligence Wire*, July 29, 2002.

"LanOptics Seeks Investment for New Chip Business," *Network Briefing*, July 28, 1999.

"LanOptics to Complete Acquisition of Substantially All of EZchip's Equity," *PR Newswire*, January 3, 2008.

Mannion, Patrick, "20 Companies That Will Shape the Future," *Communications Systems Design*, September 1, 2002, p. 18.

Mathew, Jayant, "EZchip Muscles Past NPU Field," *Electronic News*, July 24, 2000, p. 22.

Matsumoto, Craig, "Startup's 10-Gbit/s Net CPU Uses New Processing Twist," *Electronic Engineering Times*, April 3, 2000, p. 1.

Morrison, Gale, "EZchip Lines Up 8 Customers: Samples Going Out in March from IBM's 0.18-Micron Process," *Electronic News*, January 7, 2002, pp. 1, 4.

Ovadia, Avishay, "EZchip Unveils Second Generation Processor," *Israel Business Arena*, October 22, 2002.

Pincas, Gitit, "LanOptics Completes Full Acquisition of EZchip," *Israel Business Arena*, January 6, 2008.

Pincas, Gitit, and Ofer Levi, "EZchip CEO: $75M in Revenue by 2008 Possible," *Israel Business Arena*, March 29, 2005.

Shohet, Dan, "LanOptics Is Dead, Long Live EZchip," *Israel Business Arena*, July 10, 2008.

Wong, William, "Second-Generation NPU Doubles Performance," *Electronic Design*, December 9, 2002, p. 38.

"ZTE Corporation Selects the NP-1 from EZchip Technologies to Power Next Generation Metro Switch," *Business Wire*, August 1, 2002, p. 2089.

Fiserv, Inc.

225 Fiserv Drive
Brookfield, Wisconsin 53008-0979
U.S.A.
Telephone: (262) 879-5000
Toll Free: (800) 872-7882
Fax: (262) 879-5013
Web site: http://www.fiserv.com

Public Company
Founded: 1984
Incorporated: 1992
Employees: 25,000
Sales: $3.92 billion (2009 est.)
Stock Exchanges: NASDAQ
Ticker Symbol: FISV
NAICS: 518210 Automated Data Processing Services

■ ■ ■

Wisconsin-based Fiserv, Inc., is a global leader in the field of financial processing. Founded in 1984, the company has grown rapidly, largely through acquisitions. As of 2009, more than 16,000 financial institutions worldwide relied on Fiserv products to facilitate online banking, ATM transactions, and other basic technology-based resources in the financial services industry.

FISERV'S PREDECESSORS

Fiserv was started by data-processing entrepreneurs George Dalton and Leslie Muma. Realizing that lasting success in their field required a national network of clients and a wide variety of products, the two merged Sunshine State Systems of Tampa and First Data Processing of Milwaukee to form Fiserv. Dalton became the new company's CEO. Although peers described him as a visionary, he attributed much of his success to careful planning and hard work. As he recalled to the *Business Journal of Milwaukee* in 1993, one of his first jobs had been at a Kroger grocery store. Between the ages of 14 and 16 he advanced from stock boy to butcher to journeyman, outpacing his peers. "I worked nights, weekends, and during the summers," he remembered. Meanwhile, he had also "[fallen] in love with data processing." Following several years of military service, he entered Northwestern University in 1947. He remained there only a few semesters, however, dropping out to accept a position with Bell & Howell Co.'s data-processing department, which was then called the tabulating department.

Dalton's three years at Bell & Howell were marked by his quick mastery of the firm's systems and procedures. Despite a lack of banking knowledge, his enthusiasm helped him land a position as the head of Marine Bank's data-processing division. After 12 years there, he became the head of Midland National Bank's data-processing department in 1965. Midland wanted Dalton to run the division as a separate profit center, which was a new concept at the time. Under that mandate, he quickly led the department into non-banking areas, particularly retail, and established a healthy contracting business. When First Bank Systems, Inc., acquired Midland in 1977, it was not sure how to treat Dalton's unique operation. Five years later, it

COMPANY PERSPECTIVES

Our enhanced market approach and vibrant new identity are reflective of the significant change occurring within the financial services industry. We have the expertise, resources and scale to lead this transformation. Fiserv provides processing technology solutions for more financial institutions than anyone in the world. That scale, combined with our market-leading products and services, uniquely positions us to lead the development of next-generation solutions that will transform the way financial services are delivered.

would spin the unit off as a subsidiary called First Data Processing, Inc., with Dalton at the helm.

Having gained an in-depth understanding of the fledgling industry, Dalton was ready to branch out on his own by the late 1970s. His ally would be Leslie Muma of the Freedom Savings and Loan Association in Tampa, Florida. The two had become friends in the 1970s when Dalton was looking for fellow data-processing executives to share software-development costs. By pooling their resources, Dalton reasoned, banks could reduce data-processing bills as much as 60 percent.

Although he was only in his mid-30s when he and Dalton began working together, Muma had considerable experience in data processing. A math major as an undergraduate, he later obtained a master's degree in business administration from the University of South Florida. After working for several years as a data-processing consultant at an accounting firm, he joined Freedom Savings and Loan in 1971. The following year, the bank established a data-processing subsidiary, Sunshine State Systems, and named Muma its president.

FOUNDING OF FISERV: 1984

By 1984 the subsidiaries headed by Dalton and Muma were serving more than 100 clients and generating annual revenues in excess of $22 million. Frustrated by their inability to get an existing corporation to merge the two businesses, they decided to do it themselves. With venture-capital backing, they merged Sunshine and First Data into a single entity called Fiserv. In return for their involvement, the financiers took 89 percent of the new venture's equity. "Eleven percent of something is worth more than 100 percent of nothing," noted Dalton in an April 1992 issue of *Forbes*.

Dalton and Muma's business plan was rooted in their long-held belief that increased efficiency was possible through economies of scale. Up to that time, most corporations had run their own data-processing operations, creating their own software and managing their own systems at enormous expense. Fiserv could reduce these costs significantly by using essentially the same software and systems for every client. The partners planned to build their customer base quickly by acquiring regional processing firms similar to Fiserv but smaller in size.

To finance its acquisitions, Fiserv made an initial public offering (IPO) on the NASDAQ on September 25, 1986. Although this strategy reduced the founders' ownership interest to only 2 percent each, it allowed them to avoid the heavy debts that burdened many new enterprises. As CEO, Dalton searched for businesses to purchase, while Muma, the firm's president, focused on developing an efficient, customer-oriented operation that could smoothly integrate new acquisitions and the clients that accompanied them.

RAPID GROWTH THROUGH ACQUISITIONS: 1984-89

Fiserv's success in acquisitions soon paid off. Between 1984 and 1989 it bought 16 companies, boosting annual sales more than 3,000 percent to $700 million. In the same period, Fiserv's work force swelled from 300 to 2,300. By the beginning of the 1990s the company was processing data in 36 states for 800 financial institutions and had begun to expand overseas, with clients in Europe, Australia, and Canada.

The company's rapid growth was partially a result of changes in the U.S. financial markets. As a result of the Tax Reform Act of 1986, an easing of interstate banking regulations, and other factors, prospective Fiserv customers were increasingly anxious to reduce costs through centralized automated data processing. In addition, the company benefited from careful management. Fiserv showed extreme caution, for example, when it purchased new companies, such as in 1992, it purchased only 6 of the 600 acquisition candidates it considered. Besides examining a candidate's information systems, financial condition, and customer base, Dalton carefully contemplated the quality of its employees. To retain them, he encouraged a high degree of autonomy in day-to-day operations.

Muma and other members of Fiserv's operations team complemented Dalton's prudent growth strategy by focusing on customer service. "Fiserv is very professional, very current, and up-to-date on all the new advances," a client told the *Business Journal of Milwaukee*

KEY DATES

■

1984: Fiserv is formed by the merger of Sunshine State Systems of Tampa and First Data Processing of Milwaukee.

1986: Fiserv goes public on the NASDAQ.

1988: Fiserv acquires Minnesota On-Line, Inc., entering the credit union services business.

1993: Fiserv acquires Basis Information Technologies, Inc.

1999: George Dalton retires and Leslie Muma becomes CEO.

2002: Company serves more clients than any other provider of financial-services processing in North America.

2005: Fiserv Global Services is established to expand company's presence worldwide; Jeffery W. Yabuki succeeds Muma as CEO.

2007: Company makes largest acquisition to date, buying CheckFree Corporation, valued at $4.2 billion.

2009: Company launches a major re-branding effort.

in 1989. "They are extremely responsive to our concerns." That responsiveness was especially apparent in the company's willingness to adapt to a client's unique needs. Unlike many of its competitors, for example, Fiserv did not push its new customers to utilize its software. Instead, the company adjusted its services to work with the institution's existing systems.

Although other competitors, such as Fidelity National Information Services, Inc., had a broader customer base than Fiserv, the latter's more focused approach was deliberate. Of the industry's leaders, only Fiserv concentrated solely on financial institutions. "It's the best managed company of its kind because it's got a clear focus on what its business actually is," noted analyst Paul Shain in the *Business Journal of Milwaukee* in 1992. "It's a simple strategy of offering banks more sophisticated financial services and better customer service than they could otherwise afford."

A GROWING CLIENT BASE: THE EARLY 1990S

Fiserv's strategy continued to benefit shareholders during the early 1990s, as growth in revenues and client base accelerated. In 1990 and 1991 alone, it made 15

acquisitions, including a Citicorp data-processing division for $49 million, which added 400 clients, many of them major institutions. Although Fiserv had initially focused on small and mid-size institutions, by the early 1990s it had several clients with assets of more than $1 billion. By 1991 Fiserv was serving more than 1,400 banks, savings and loans, and credit unions of all sizes. In addition, its sales had risen to $281 million and profits were $18.3 million.

Meanwhile Fiserv also had shifted its operational focus from modems that connected its mainframes to its clients' systems. In the early 1990s the company began taking over data-processing departments, hiring the existing staff and operating entirely on-site. This strategy helped the company build its customer base to more than 5,400 in 1992, while its workforce swelled to 4,800. At the same time, sales grew to $332 million.

Fiserv continued to grow aggressively in 1993. Two data-processing businesses owned by Mellon Bank were among acquisitions early in that year. Most of the 200 clients gained in those acquisitions had assets of more than $300 million, and were worth an estimated $70 million per year in revenue. Most notable during 1993, however, was the company's purchase of Basis Information Technologies, Inc., which added 1,000 new workers to Fiserv's payroll. The company finished the year with record growth, as sales rose an impressive 38 percent. In the annual report that followed, Dalton and Muma reflected on the company's rise. "With the dedication and hard work of Fiserv people, we have grown this organization from two data processing centers in Milwaukee and Tampa employing less than 300 professionals to a company with locations in 61 cities. ... We've built a strong foundation on which to base our future."

Although both founders were approaching retirement age, their energy and enthusiasm remained high. To prepare for his 12-hour workday, for example, Muma jogged six miles. He had been an avid runner since the age of 32, when he began competing in marathons to overcome a smoking habit. Dalton, meanwhile, filled his free hours by cruising on his motorcycle. By their own admission, however, both men remained workaholics. "We don't bowl on Saturdays," Muma told *Forbes* in 1992. "We come to work."

STEADY GROWTH THROUGH THE LATE 1990S

Steady growth continued for the rest of the decade as downsizing, consolidation, and cost-cutting prompted banks to hand over back-office functions to external providers. Bankers were beginning to "view their business not as transaction processing, but as information management and distribution," according to consultant James Wells in *ABA Banking* in 1996. "The third party performs processing, but channels the information back to the bank, so that the information becomes the primary currency." By the end of 1995 Fiserv was providing processing services to more than 3,000 financial institutions and had annual profits of almost $64 million. The following year, the company won a 10-year contract to handle back-office processing for two leading Canadian banks in a deal worth no less than $1.6 billion.

Between 1996 and 1998 Fiserv increased its annual sales from roughly $900 million to more than $1 billion as its customer base grew to 5,000. The company's basic strategy of carefully selecting and integrating acquisitions, allowing a large degree of autonomy, and focusing on customer service, remained consistent. Company policy included surveying clients twice a year for feedback and tying the compensation of business-unit directors to customer satisfaction. At the same time, however, Fiserv was branching out into other areas of the financial-processing sector. Six of the company's 10 acquisitions in 1997, for example, were related to the brokerage industry, including a retail brokerage and a manufacturer of software that enabled customers to enter trade orders via the Internet or touch-tone phone. Fiserv also acquired businesses that provided marketing, seminar, and training materials for the financial industry. The following year it added two software developers, one focused on insurance administration and the other on auto leasing. Fiserv acquired 11 new businesses in 1998, bringing its total number of acquisitions since 1984 to 73.

Fiserv's diversification into other businesses in the late 1990s was part of a new cross-selling strategy. In an effort to reduce the need for acquisitions, new products were introduced and marketed to existing clients. An online product for banks, for example, allowed customers access to their bank-branded insurance accounts from the bank's home page. A similar but more comprehensive service called ePrime@Fiserv, which was launched in 1999, bundled online banking, bill payment, investment and insurance products, cash-management automation, back-office processing, and core-account processing into one solution. Fiserv also introduced TheLendingSite.com, which provided the technological backbone for Internet-based lending, including loan approval and credit card authorization. To complement its new strategy, Fiserv implemented a major branding effort that included a national television campaign and a new corporate slogan ("Where money and technology meet"). The company's Web site was launched about the same time.

Although Fiserv had a presence in 60 countries by late 1999, management recognized the continued potential for overseas growth. International expansion appeared particularly attractive given the changing nature of the domestic industry. While U.S. growth rates remained at a healthy average of about 20 percent annually, bank mergers were drying up the pool of potential customers. Meanwhile, the privatization of banks in foreign countries, along with the European Union's conversion to a single currency in 1999, had opened doors for data-processing companies. In emerging markets like Mexico, Brazil, and Argentina, projected growth for financial services providers was estimated to be between 30 and 35 percent per year.

THE 2000S: CONTINUED GROWTH AND NEW CHALLENGES

After 15 years as CEO, Dalton retired in 1999. Muma, his replacement, continued the strategy of rapid growth through acquisitions. For example, in 2001 Fiserv bought Remarketing Services of America, Inc., a specialist in auto-lease management and home mortgages; EPSIIA Corporation, a pioneer in electronic-document delivery for the financial industry; Catapult Technology Limited, a London-based developer of banking technology; and the item-processing operations of Metavante Corporation and the Federal Home Loan Bank of Pittsburgh. By 2002 these purchases had given Fiserv the distinction of serving more clients than any other financial-services processor in North America. Growth in Europe and Asia, meanwhile, was even more robust, especially following the 2005 launch of Fiserv Global Services, an IT subsidiary based in India and Costa Rica.

Following Muma's retirement in 2005, his successor, Jeffrey W. Yabuki, moved quickly to strengthen the company's brand. He did so in part by shedding businesses outside its primary strength in banking and financial processing. For example, in 2007 he supervised the sale of several insurance subsidiaries, including a unit that processed health insurance claims and a business that specialized in the management of personal trusts and retirement accounts. At the same time, he worked to enhance the company's banking products, notably through the acquisition of the online bill processor CheckFree Corporation. That deal, which closed in December 2007, was valued at $4.2 billion, and was Fiserv's largest acquisition through mid-2009.

By 2008 Fiserv's annual revenues were approaching $5 billion, nearly 10 times what it had earned 15 years earlier. Challenges were increasingly apparent, however. Many of these were rooted in the pronounced economic downturn that began with the collapse of the sub-prime mortgage market in 2007. Banks sharply reduced their spending as their profits declined. While Fiserv felt the impact of these cutbacks, its strong balance sheet helped shield it from the worst effects. Other challenges appeared as well, especially in the legal arena, where the company faced several significant lawsuits. Fiserv, like most major corporations, had significant resources set aside to handle such lawsuits, which had the potential to lessen the threat of such proceedings to the company's finances. In this respect, the most serious allegations were those made by Diana B. Henriques of the *New York Times* in 2009. In July of that year, Henriques noted that the company faced several lawsuits arising from three separate investment frauds, including the notorious one perpetrated by Bernard L. Madoff, who had been convicted of fraud in June. "According to interviews and court records," Henriques wrote, Madoff, Louis J. Pearlman, and Daniel Heath "all told their victims to use various units of Fiserv" to service their investments. She concluded, "At a minimum, this coincidence would appear to be a mystery worthy of investigation by regulators." Fiserv, which had sold its investment support business in 2008, vigorously denied wrongdoing.

In March 2009 the company announced a rebranding effort that would "reflect an enhanced market approach and new energy," according to the 2008 Annual Report. The rebranding included a new logo and gave all of the company's acquisitions the Fiserv name. By the summer of 2009 the Fiserv Web site claimed that the company had become "the world's largest service provider to banks, credit unions, and lending institutions." While it was not certain that the company would be able to sustain the rapid growth that had characterized its first 25 years, its continued prominence in the financial industry seemed assured.

Dave Mote
Updated, Carrie Rothburd; R. Anthony Kugler

PRINCIPAL SUBSIDIARIES

Fiserv Global Services; Fiserv Clearing Network; Financial Institution Services; Depository Institution Services; Card Services; CheckFree.

PRINCIPAL COMPETITORS

Fidelity National Information Services, Inc.; Electronic Data Systems an HP Company; Deluxe Corporation; Affiliated Computer Services, Inc.

FURTHER READING

"$4.2 Billion Deal for Bank Concern," Associated Press, August 3, 2007.

Banker, John, "Big Competitors Can't Keep Pace with Fiserv," *Business Journal of Milwaukee*, August 7, 1993, p. 7.

Barret, Victoria, "Surviving a Credit Crunch," *Forbes*, April 27, 2009.

Burton, Jonathan, "Customers Come First," MarketWatch.com.

Barthel, Matt, "Fiserv's Strategy for Rapid Growth," *American Banker*, August 27, 1993.

Causey, James E., "Fiserv, Dalton Setting Torrid Pace," *Milwaukee Journal Sentinel*, February 25, 1998, p. 1.

———, "New CEO to Keep Fiserv Growing," *Milwaukee Journal Sentinel*, March 29, 1999, p. 1.

———, "World Now the Arena for Local Data Processing Firms," *Milwaukee Journal Sentinel*, August 10, 1998, p. 12.

"The CEOs of Wisconsin: George Dalton," *Business Journal of Milwaukee*, March 27, 1993, sec. 3, p. 15.

Cone, Edward, "Buy and Build—Fiserv's Two-Track Strategy Fuels 20 Percent Annual Growth," *Information Week*, October 5, 1998.

Dires, Michael, "Shades of CEO: Heart and Soul—How Who They Are Plays a Role in How They Lead: George Dalton," *Business Journal of Milwaukee*, March 27, 1993, sec. 3, p. 8.

———, "Hot Shots—Wisconsin's Best-Performing Public Companies: Fiserv Inc.," *Business Journal of Milwaukee*, July 31, 1993, sec. 3, p. 12.

Elliot, Suzanne, "Fiserv Plans Move to Cheaper Offices for Ex-Mellon Subs," *Pittsburgh Business Times & Journal*, August 16, 1993, p. 1.

"Fiserv, Inc. and Mellon Bank Corp. Announce Agreement for Sale of Two Mellon Outsourcing Businesses for Bank Processing and Related Services," *Business Wire*, August 2, 1993.

Henriques, Diana B., "Questions for a Custodian after Scams Hit I.R.A.'s," *New York Times*, July 25, 2009, p. B1.

Higgins, Terry, "Fiserv Inc.," *Business Journal of Milwaukee*, July 25, 1992, sec. 3, p. 12.

"Lawsuit Filed over Possible Overtime Violations by Fiserv; Filed by Stember Feinstein Doyle & Payne," *Business Wire*, January 22, 2009.

O'Heney, Sheila, "Outsourcing Is Hotter Than Ever," *ABA Banking Journal*, May 1996, p. 44.

Palmeri, Christopher, "We Don't Bowl on Saturdays," *Forbes*, April 27, 1992, p. 104.

Snell, Ned, "Fiserv Inc.," *Datamation*, June 15, 1993, p. 120.

Weier, Anita, "Muma's Marathon Pace Keeps Fiserv on Growth Track," *Business Journal of Milwaukee*, November 20, 1989, sec. 1, p. 10.

Willoughby, Jack, "Fiserv Is Largely Immune to Banking's Plagues," *Barron's*, March 23, 2009.

Four Seasons Hotels Limited

■

1165 Leslie Street
Toronto, Ontario M3C 2K8
Canada
Telephone: (416) 449-1750
Fax: (416) 441-4374
Web site: http://www.fourseasons.com

Private Company
Founded: 1961
Employees: 32,800
Revenues: US$253.40 million (2006)
NAISC: 72111 Hotels (except Casino Hotels) & Motels

■ ■ ■

Four Seasons Hotels Limited is one of the world's leading hotel management companies specializing in luxury hotel, resort, and residential properties. The company manages over 70 hotels and resorts in North, South, and Central America, Europe, Asia, the Middle East, Australia, and the Caribbean, with others properties projected to be added. The company owns its own hotels, principally under the Four Seasons name, as well as some others, including the Ritz-Carlton in Chicago, Illinois, and the Beverly Wilshire in Beverly Hills, California. About half the company's earnings come from management fees and half from properties it owns directly.

HUMBLE BEGINNINGS

Four Seasons was founded by Isadore "Issy" Sharp. Sharp's father, Max, emigrated from Poland to Palestine in 1920, where he helped build one of the first kibbutzim. Relocating to Toronto, Canada, five years later, Max worked for a few years as a journeyman plasterer; he married and began a family that would include his son Issy and three daughters. Drawing on his home renovation experience, Max soon began purchasing houses, repairing and decorating them, and then selling them at a profit. Issy Sharp had lived in 15 houses by the time he was 16 years old.

Sharp attended Toronto's Ryerson Polytechnical Institute and won high marks in architecture while distinguishing himself in athletics. After graduating, he worked alongside his father building small apartment buildings and houses. Determined to build a hotel on his own, Sharp struggled for five years to find the money to fulfill his dream. Unable to convince banks and venture capitalists that his hotel would succeed, Sharp finally turned to his brother-in-law, Eddie Creed, the owner of a high fashion emporium in Toronto, and Creed's best friend, Murray Koffler, the founder and chair of the Shoppers Drug Mart chain. These two men contributed $150,000 each to Sharp's project.

Still requiring over $700,000 in capital, Sharp approached one of his father's business acquaintances, Cecil Forsyth, who managed the mortgage department at Great West Life Insurance Company. Sharp's plan was to raise the rest of the necessary funds through a mortgage. Skeptical of Sharp's business acumen, Forsyth initially refused the application. However, he eventually yielded to Sharp's persistent requests, agreeing to provide the rest of the money.

Sharp's hotel cost nearly $1.5 million to build and featured 126 rooms that would garner premium

COMPANY PERSPECTIVES

■

We have chosen to specialise within the hospitality industry by offering only experiences of exceptional quality. Our objective is to be recognised as the company that manages the finest hotels, resorts and residence clubs wherever we locate.

We create properties of enduring value using superior design and finishes, and support them with a deeply instilled ethic of personal service. Doing so allows Four Seasons to satisfy the needs and tastes of our discriminating customers, and to maintain our position as the world's premier luxury hospitality company.

prices. Opening on the first day of spring in 1961, the Four Seasons Motor Hotel was an immediate success. Despite the hotel's location in a downtown Toronto area known for its prostitutes and indigent population, patrons were attracted to the structure's casual but upscale atmosphere and to its innovative inner courtyard surrounding a swimming pool. Soon, the employees of the Canadian Broadcast System, which was located across the street, adopted the hotel as their after work watering hole, signaling the beginning of the hotel's celebrity association.

From the time the Four Seasons opened for business, Sharp created a climate that fostered professionalism and devotion among his employees. He initiated a profit-sharing plan, scheduled two "stress breaks" every day, and paid his front desk clerks twice the average rate, asserting their importance in providing the public with its first impression of the hotel. One of the more notable examples of employee dedication involved Roy Dyment, a bellboy at Four Seasons since 1967. Dyment discovered that a dignitary had left his briefcase behind during checkout, and he felt responsible because he hadn't placed the briefcase in the limousine trunk. When the worried guest phoned from Washington, D.C., stating that the material in the briefcase was essential for an upcoming meeting, Dyment purchased a plane ticket at his own expense and personally delivered the briefcase.

Sharp's second venture in the hotel business proved even riskier than his first. Opened in 1963, Toronto's Inn on the Park was built on 17 acres in a desolate area north of the city, where the only nearby business was a large garbage dump. Short $1 million before the start of

construction, Sharp again approached Forsyth for a loan. Impressed by Sharp's instant success with the motor hotel, Forsyth did not hesitate in providing the money. Despite its location, Sharp's second hotel was also successful, and the area he had chosen for the 569-room resort hotel quickly grew into a sprawling corporate suburbia.

GROWTH ABROAD IN THE 1970S

Next, Sharp sought to establish a hotel overlooking London's historic Hyde Park. In doing so, he ignored market research indicating that a new luxury hotel in that location would have trouble competing with established first-class hotels, such as the Dorchester, Claridge, and Savoy. Sharp opened his 227-room Inn on the Park in 1970. Despite its higher rates and the overcrowded market, the Inn on the Park enjoyed a 95 percent occupancy rate and became one of the most profitable hotels in the world. Its small size, luxurious appointments, and impeccable service were all elements that had become Sharp's personal trademark.

In the early 1970s Sharp began developing hotels in smaller, less urban areas. He opened an inn in Belleville, Ontario, whose population was 35,000, and spent a year operating a resort in Nassau. Shortly thereafter, he built a luxury condo hotel in Israel that was marginally profitable but experienced difficulties maintaining staff, owing largely to the Israeli draft for military service. Plans for hotel projects in Europe were postponed due to disagreements with potential partners from Paris and Athens. When construction finally started on a hotel in Rome, workers kept uncovering Roman artifacts, and preservationists were able to block further construction on the site. Hoping to develop residential and office buildings in both Canada and Florida, Sharp was continually thwarted by civic officials, who placed restrictions on commercial development.

Undismayed by his setbacks, Sharp approached the Sheraton division of ITT Corporation in 1972 and proposed a joint Four Seasons–Sheraton partnership. The result was the Toronto Four Seasons Sheraton, a 1,450-room establishment whose first year of operation was plagued by cost overruns, disagreements with city building inspectors, and a singles event that resulted in a temporary suspension of the hotel's liquor license. Even though Sharp was hired as assistant manager of the property, he had no real authority to make decisions. In 1976 he sold his 49 percent interest for $18.5 million and decided to return to what he did best: developing and operating midsized hotels that catered to the luxury market.

That same year Sharp began his first U.S. property management contract with The Clift, an elegant but ag-

KEY DATES

1961: The Four Seasons Motor Hotel is built in Toronto, Canada, by Max and Isadore "Issy" Sharp.

1963: Issy Sharp builds the Inn on the Park in Toronto.

1969: Four Seasons begins publicly issuing shares.

1970: The Inn on the Park in London is built by Four Seasons.

1972: A Four Seasons–Sheraton partnership is formed, which results in the building of the Toronto Four Seasons Sheraton.

1976: Four Seasons begins its first U.S. property management contract with The Clift in San Francisco, California.

1977: After suffering from decreasing share prices, Four Seasons becomes a private company.

1985: Four Seasons becomes a publicly trade company for a second time.

1992: Four Seasons acquires Regent International Hotels Ltd.

1994: Saudi Prince Al-Walid bin Talal bin Abd al-Aziz Al Saud becomes a major stockholder.

1997: Four Seasons is listed on the New York Stock Exchange.

1998: Four Seasons is named one of the "100 Best Companies to Work For" by *Fortune*.

2004: *Fortune* selects Four Seasons to be in its Hall of Fame.

2006: Four Seasons receives *Fortune*'s Great Place to Work Respect Award; the Four Seasons Centre for the Performing Arts becomes the home of the Canadian Opera Company and the National Ballet of Canada.

2007: Four Seasons establishes a partnership with Bill Gates, thereby enabling it to become a private corporation.

ing hotel in San Francisco, California. He also opened the Four Seasons Hotel in Vancouver, Canada, and one year later he won a bidding war to manage the new Ritz-Carlton in Chicago. In 1978 Sharp bought a property from Hyatt Hotels in Toronto and remodeled it to suit the Four Seasons style. This Four Seasons hotel offered service to the wealthy, who frequented Yorkville, Toronto's most exclusive shopping district. In 1979 the Four Seasons Hotel Washington, D.C., began opera-

tions, and a short time later Sharp opened the first of several hotel and resort properties in Texas. One of Sharp's most successful moves came in 1981, when he took over the management of The Pierre, a landmark hotel in New York City frequently cited as one of the best in the city. With a multimillion dollar renovation, The Pierre developed into a showcase of Four Seasons' style and service.

FINANCIAL UPS AND DOWNS IN THE 1980S

Many hoteliers, Sharp included, followed Conrad Hilton's strategy of managing properties rather than owning them. Between 1980 and 1985 Four Seasons opened hotels with a value of over $500 million at a cost of only $15 million. Nevertheless, Four Seasons also owned many properties, and in the early 1980s Sharp initiated an expensive renovation drive of the hotels in which Four Seasons was owner or part-owner. By 1982 the hotel chain had approximated $116 million in long-term debt.

To lessen this debt, Four Seasons began selling its assets. Between 1980 and 1985 nearly $31.2 million worth of assets were sold, including equity in Montreal, Toronto, and San Francisco. Nevertheless, Four Seasons continued to manage these hotels under long-term contracts. When Sharp, Creed, and Koffler, the three original investors, created a new company to manage nonhotel assets, such as development property and a laundry facility, another $22 million in debt was eliminated. The company's final tactic was to apply $30 million of an initial $60 million raised from a stock offering to reducing the remainder of the debt. Through these three moves, Four Seasons' debt-equity ratio was reduced to a comfortable 1:1 ratio by 1986.

When Four Seasons first publicly issued shares in the company in 1969, stock shares climbed as high as $22. However, after the erratic management and declining profits of the early and mid-1970s, Four Seasons stock had plummeted to only $4 per share by 1977. Sharp and his partners then decided that it was in their best interest to turn Four Seasons into a private company. In 1985, when they decided to take Four Seasons public again, Creed and Koffler retained a combined 8 percent stake in the company but sold $8.5 million worth of stock. Sharp agreed to the public offering on the condition that a class of "multiple voting shares" be created for him. As a result of this arrangement, Sharp tightened his grip on Four Seasons; while the public had one vote for each share, Sharp's multiple voting shares carried 12 votes for each share. With a 29 percent share of Four Seasons equity and 83 percent of the votes, Sharp planned to thwart any takeover threat in the future.

RAPID GROWTH INTO THE 1990S

During the late 1980s Four Seasons began examining the world's financial centers, such as Tokyo, Paris, and Frankfurt, for future development sites. Expansion proceeded slowly as Sharp wanted only premium locations and refused to settle for less. However, from 1988 onward the acquisition, development, and building of properties was rapid.

By 1992, with the acquisition of Regent International Hotels Ltd., a leading operator of luxury hotels in Asia and Australia, Sharp had created the largest network of luxury hotels in the world. Together, Four Seasons and Regent International Hotels owned and operated 45 medium-sized luxury properties and resorts in 19 countries around the world. In 1992 and 1993 Four Seasons opened hotels in Bali, Milan, and London. New construction and development was ongoing in Singapore, New York, Mexico City, Paris, Berlin, Jakarta, and Prague, and resort properties were under development in Hawaii and California.

With a one-to-one employee-guest ratio, gourmet cuisine, and sumptuous decor resulting in accolades from diverse publications such as *Consumer Reports*, *Mobil Travel Guide*, and *Condé Nast Traveller*, Sharp nevertheless strove to improve his properties. His goal was to transform the name Four Seasons into a common name for high-quality hotels, and, during the early 1990s, he believed this goal was well within his reach.

Nevertheless, the company was plagued by debt, leading almost to paralysis in the mid-1990s. A downturn that plagued the hotel industry between 1990 and 1992 made the company turn more to management at that time because it was both more profitable and more stable in the long run than owning hotels. As a way of opening the door to a successful management contract, the chain typically bought a small equity stake in hotels it hoped to manager. However, because of its debt burden, the company was kept from bidding on some of the hotels it wanted to control. By 1994 it had 15 contracts under negotiation, and a company analyst expected Four Seasons to win just five of them.

Four Seasons was rescued by an outside investor, Saudi Prince Al-Walid bin Talal bin Abd al-Aziz Al Saud. He bought up 25 percent of the company's stock in 1994 and set aside C$100 million to fund further expansion of the chain. Al-Walid was an international investor who had previously bailed out Euro Disney SCA, the floundering French Disneyland. The prince was reportedly impressed with the Four Seasons brand

and service and wanted to provide financial backing for long-term growth. With Al-Walid's deep pockets, the company was able to complete its bids on management properties, and soon Four Seasons began building and buying worldwide.

Another development was the teaming up with Carlson Hospitality Worldwide, a Minnesota-based hotel management company, in 1996. Carlson was known for its formidable development of midpriced hotels and restaurants. It had brokered deals for more than 1,000 hotels and restaurants around the globe, which it managed through franchise and partnership agreements. Four Seasons entered a joint agreement with Carlson to develop its Regent brand of hotels. Four Seasons ran only nine Regents, which were revered in Asia, although there was only one in North America, in Beverly Hills. The company wanted to expand the brand, so it turned to Carlson to manage this project. That same year Moody's upgraded Four Seasons' debt, which indicated that the company was clearly on the mend.

By 1997 *BusinessWeek* declared that the company had never been healthier. Sales and profits were on the rise, and Four Seasons planned to run almost 20 more hotels over the next few years. It was also listed on the New York Stock Exchange. Al-Walid had helped the company get into lucrative Middle Eastern markets, and the chain also angled for properties in Paris, Las Vegas, and Caracas. Moreover, the luxury hotel industry in general had picked up remarkably from its early-1990s slump, and occupancy rates at some prime Four Seasons hotels were running better than 90 percent. The company continued to impress clients with its dedication to service, and stories abounded of employees going the limit to please. The chain was preferred by many famous people, from rock stars to politicians. While a sudden economic downturn in Asia in 1998 sent Four Seasons' Asian earnings way down, its hotels in the rest of the world seemed in fine condition, with average revenues per room rising significantly. The company was profitable and prospering despite the shock to its Asian markets. As an innovator in the hospitality industry, Four Seasons opened a resort in the Maldives, where guests could dive and cruise the islands on a private vessel. Guests of the resort praised staff for saving lives and seeing to their needs when a tsunami hit in 2005.

CORPORATE VALUES

Four Seasons' long-term goals centered on building its reputation worldwide through dedication to customer service. This was an area in which Four Seasons had always excelled, and one that also translated into a favorable corporate environment. In 1998 *Fortune* magazine named Four Seasons one of the "100 Best Companies to Work For," a designation the company would repeatedly earn during the first decade of the 21st century. *Fortune* put Four Seasons into its Hall of Fame in 2004 and presented it with the Great Place to Work Respect Award in 2006.

Corporate values extended to the company's commitment "to enrich and contribute positively to the global community." Support for cancer research and environmental sustainability were two particular areas of interest to the company. Hotel Hampshire implemented an extensive recycling program, the Four Seasons Resort Costa Rica donated organic food waste to a farmer to feed his animals, and the Tented Camp Golden Triangle provided a refuge for elephants rescued from the streets of Thailand. In 2006 the new Four Seasons Centre for the Performing Arts became the home of the Canadian Opera Company and the National Ballet of Canada.

TRANSITIONS IN THE 21ST CENTURY

As the 21st century began, Four Seasons extended its brand to include Four Seasons Private Residences (villas and penthouses priced from $750,000), Four Seasons Residence Clubs, and Four Seasons Ocean Residences. The latter were spacious private homes on a cruise liner scheduled to stop at ports around the globe. Four Seasons residential properties provided owners and guests with the same luxuries as at the company's hotels. By 2001 every Four Seasons resort offered full spa services.

The company continued to expand operations abroad, adding a hotel in Cairo, a resort at Sharm El Sheikh, and resorts in South America. In 2002 it entered the Chinese market by opening the Four Seasons Hotel Shanghai. However, a global recession and the after effects of the September 11, 2001, terrorist attacks against the United States reduced travel. Sales fell 5 percent and net income decreased more than 75 percent in 2002. Even though earnings continued to decline the next year, the company did not drop rates or cancel expansion plans. In 2003 Four Seasons Jackson Hole became the company's first mountain resort. The following year the company opened a resort on the Danube River in Hungary.

The company's focus on service and quality garnered it kudos. In 2006 the *Robb Report* included Four Seasons among 20 of "the most exclusive brands of all time." The Zagat Survey of Top U.S. Hotels, Resorts, and Spas ranked the chain first in 2007 and 2008. Also in 2008, 23 of the company's hotels and resorts received

the 2009 Diamond Award from the American Automobile Association. In addition, *Condé Nast Traveller* included 16 of the company's properties on its reader-elected "Top 100 List" and ranked the Tented Camp Golden Triangle as the world's top hotel. In 2008 *Fortune* called Four Seasons Hotel Mumbai one of the "10 Best New Business Hotels of the World."

These kudos came in even as the company transitioned into a private corporation in 2007. Already a majority shareholder, Al-Walid partnered with Microsoft founder Bill Gates to purchase a 90 percent stake for $3.8 billion through their respective holding companies—Kingdom Hotels International and Cascade Investment LLC. Sharp, who saw the transaction as the means to take the company he built in new directions, and his family, through Triples Holdings Ltd., retained a 10 percent share and operating involvement in the company.

Thomas Derdak
Updated, A. Woodward; Doris Maxfield

FURTHER READING

Byrne, Harlan S., "The Secret: Service," *Barren's*, May 11, 1998, pp. 20–22.

Church, Elizabeth, and Jacquie McNish, "Four Seasons Strikes Deal to Go Private: Gates, Saudi Prince to Buy 90% Stake of Hotel Chain; Sharp Retains 10%," *Globe & Mail* (Toronto, Canada), November 7, 2006, p. B1.

"Four Seasons Agrees to $3.8 Billion Offer," *International Herald Tribune*, February 13, 2007, p. 9.

Gale, Derek, "Fours Seasons Goes to Sea," *Hotels*, April 1, 2008, p. 18.

Greenberg, Larry M., and Peter Truell, "Saudi Investor Seeks to Buy 25% of Four Seasons," *Wall Street Journal*, September 28, 1994, p. A14.

"Issy: Quality Innkeeper—Quality Gentleman," *Report on Business Magazine*, June 1986, p. 612.

Iverson, Doug, "Minnesota-Based Carlson Hospitality Worldwide Strikes Luxurious Deal," Knight-Ridder/Tribune Business News, December 4, 1996.

Kummer, Corby, et al., "Does Isadore Sharp Run the Best Hotels Anywhere?" *Connoisseur*, February 1990, pp. 72–76.

"Nine Openings in 12 Months for Four Seasons Hotels & Resorts," *Middle East and North Africa Business Report*, December 10, 2008.

Olive, David, "Puttin' on the Ritz," *Report on Business Magazine*, June 1986, pp. 28–35.

Selwitz, Robert, "Four Seasons Stays on Course," *Hotel and Motel Management*, July 21, 2003, p. 3.

Sharp, Isadorc, *Four Seasons: The Story of a Business Philosophy*, New York: Portfolio, 2009.

Weber, Joseph, "The Whirlwind at the Four Seasons," *BusinessWeek*, October 13, 1997, p. 82.

Fyffes PLC

29 North Anne Street
Dublin, 7
Ireland
Telephone: (+353 1) 887-2700
Fax: (+353 1) 887-2755
Web site: http://www.fyffes.com

Public Company
Founded: 1888 as E. W. Fyffe Son and Co.
Employees: 4,800
Sales: €758.23 million ($1,069.1 billion) (2008)
Stock Exchanges: Dublin London
Ticker Symbol: FFY
NAICS: 111336 Fruit and Tree Nut Combination Farming; 424480 Fresh Fruit and Vegetable Merchant Wholesalers

■ ■ ■

Fyffes PLC (the Group) is a leading international importer and distributor of tropical fruit. Fyffes, which began importing bananas during the late 1880s, boasts the oldest fruit brand in the world, dating back to 1929. Production, procurement, shipping, ripening, distribution, and marketing of bananas, pineapples, and melons are the Group's main activities. Along with its Dublin headquarters, Fyffes has operations in Europe, the United States, and Central and South America. Their operations included five ripening centers in Ireland and the United Kingdom, and a Florida-based melon distribution center. Total Produce PLC, which was created by the Fyffes general produce and distribution de-

merger, as well as Fyffes' existing companies, are responsible for the distribution of the tropical produce throughout Europe. Most of the fruit is procured and shipped from Central and South America, where the Group and its joint ventures own or lease more than 11,000 hectares of land. Fyffes supplies Europe with approximately 36 million cases of bananas each year, and the Group's Turbana joint venture distributes about 13 million cases in North America. Pineapples account for eight million cases of the Group's product, and in winter another eight million cases of melons are shipped to North America and Europe. The bananas, which are available loose or prepacked, are obrained from countries such as Costa Rica, Guatemala, and Colombia. Fyffes' well-known Gold Pineapple also comes from Costa Rica, as well as Ecuador, Panama, and Guatemala. The range of melons, which includes such varieties as Charentais, Galia, and Piel de Sapo, come mainly from Brazil and Costa Rica. Fyffes attributes its long standing to the quality of its produce and the Group's superior level of service.

BANANA IMPORTING IN THE 19TH CENTURY

The predecessor companies to Fyffes PLC both had their roots in the 19th century. Edward Wathen Fyffe was one of the first to bring commercial shipments of bananas to the United Kingdom in the 1880s. Fyffe had discovered the fruit while living in the Canary Islands, where he had accompanied his wife during her convalescence from tuberculosis. Fyffe decided that England was ripe for the exotic fruit and began commercial imports of bananas in 1888 through his

COMPANY PERSPECTIVES

Fyffes' principal objectives are: To increase the Group's revenues and earnings based on the growing worldwide demand for fresh produce. To continually find better ways to work with its suppliers, increase efficiency and meet its customers' needs. To maximise the returns earned by shareholders on their investment. To provide interesting and fulfilling careers for its people.

company, E.W. Fyffe Son and Co. About 10 years later, Fyffe joined his company with another London-based greengrocery supplier, Hudson Brothers, forming Fyffe Hudson & Co. Limited.

Fyffe Hudson continued to build up imports of bananas from British colonial islands. At the turn of the century, the company took a step to solve one of the largest difficulties in transporting bananas: how to prevent them from ripening during the voyage itself. A breakthrough in the banana industry came when it was discovered that maintaining bananas below a certain temperature inhibited the ripening process. Fyffe Hudson commissioned a ship outfitted with a cooling system developed by J & E Hall, and the company's first refrigerated vessel, the *Port Morant*, completed its maiden voyage between Avonmouth, England, and Kingston, Jamaica, in 1901.

That same year, Fyffe Hudson, which had been operating from a location in eastern England, merged with the Liverpool-based Elder Dempster and Company, adding that company's port in western England. The merger, which created the company Elders and Fyffes Limited, secured operations in England's two major ports serving shipping between the United Kingdom and its island colonies. The company went public, continuing to add to its fleet of ships and becoming a major importer in the English market.

Meanwhile, in Ireland, the other half of the future Fyffes PLC was making a name for itself. The McCann family's involvement with fruit began during the 1890s, when Charles McCann began packing apples in stone barrels for shipment to Canada. By 1902 McCann had raised enough funds to open his own greengrocer's store in Dundalk, Ireland. At the same time, McCann began a relationship with the newly merged Elders and Fyffes company, becoming the first to sell the English company's bananas on the Irish market. While running a retail store, McCann also developed a significant

wholesale business, becoming one of the principal distributors of fruits and vegetables in County Armagh.

CHALLENGED BY A COMPETITIVE MARKET: MID-20TH CENTURY

In 1913 the United Fruit Company, later known as United Brands and then Chiquita Brands International, bought a controlling share of Elders and Fyffes' stock. The U.S. company quickly acquired the rest of Elders and Fyffes, establishing itself as the leading banana importer in the United Kingdom. Elders and Fyffes continued to operate under its own name, and in 1929 scored a marketing coup when it became the first company to place its own label on its fruit. The famed "blue label" soon became synonymous with bananas in the United Kingdom and inspired similar labeling practices across the world's fruits segments.

With the clout of its parent company behind it, Elders and Fyffes was able to build up its banana business to the extent that it had gained a de facto monopoly of banana imports to the United Kingdom. After the disruption of its business caused by World War II, Elders and Fyffes made the world's newsreels with its resumption of banana deliveries in 1945.

By the 1950s Elders and Fyffes began to face increasing competition in its home markets. Among its new competitors was Geest Horticultural Products, which in the early 1950s decided to challenge Fyffes by launching banana-growing operations in the Windward Islands. Geest succeeded in signing supply agreements with a number of supermarket groups in the United Kingdom, and it steadily imposed itself on the banana imports scene. By the mid-1960s, Elders and Fyffes had been forced to relinquish nearly half of the United Kingdom's banana market to Geest.

PARTNERSHIPS AND OPERATIONS GROWTH: 1960S

Elders and Fyffes were also seeing challenges from the Irish market. In 1956 Neil McCann, who had extended his father's Dundalk business into the Dublin market, while adding banana ripening and distribution to its wholesale activities, joined with a number of other Irish wholesalers to form United Fruit Importers Limited, based in Dublin. Two years later, McCann joined with another group of wholesalers to form Torney Brothers & McCann Limited, which extended both companies' distribution and storage facilities in the Dublin area and expanded the two companies' distribution reach throughout Ireland.

KEY DATES

1888: Edward Fyffe begins commercial imports of bananas to the United Kingdom.

1897: Fyffe forms Fyffe Hudson & Co. Limited.

1901: The company merges with Elder Dempster and Company to form Elders and Fyffes.

1902: Charles McCann opens fruit and vegetable store in Dundalk.

1913: United Fruit Company acquires Elders and Fyffes.

1929: Fyffes introduces "blue label," establishing brand identity for bananas.

1956: United Fruit Importers Limited is formed.

1958: Torney Brothers & McCann is formed.

1965: Banana Importers of Ireland is created.

1968: Torney Brothers & McCann merges with United Fruit Importers Limited to form Fruit Importers of Ireland Limited (FII).

1969: Elders and Fyffes becomes Fyffes Group Limited.

1981: FII goes public.

1986: FII acquires Fyffes.

1990: Company name is changed to Fyffes PLC.

1996: Fyffes acquires banana business from Geest PLC.

2002: Fyffes acquires 70 percent of Hortim International sro and 80 percent of Internationale Fruchtimport Gesellschaft Weichert & Co. KG.

2003: Chairman Neil McCann retires and is succeeded by his son Carl McCann.

2005: Fyffes loses its lawsuit against DCC PLC.

2006: Fyffes demerges its general produce and distribution business to form Total Produce PLC.

In the mid-1960s, Torney Brothers & McCann and a number of other banana importers, ripeners, and distributors in the region (including Charles McCann Limited of Dundalk and Red Diamond Limited of Cork) set up their own banana supply company, Banana Importers of Ireland (BII). The new company, founded in 1965, further undermined Elders and Fyffes' market share in Ireland as BII offered direct shipments to Ireland's ports, cutting the costs of bananas for BII's group of ripeners and distributors.

If Elders and Fyffes saw its overall market share shrinking, it was comforted by seeing that market undergo a strong expansion as consumer demand for bananas raised the fruit to one of the most popular in the U.K. market. Nonetheless, the company saw fit to diversify its operations in the early 1960s. The purchase of Midlands-based produce distributor George Jackson & Co. in 1964 extended Elders and Fyffes' range of business and reduced its reliance on bananas for the first time. Four years later, Elders and Fyffes bought George Monro Limited, which added further fresh fruit and vegetable distribution. The purchase led Elders and Fyffes to change its name to Fyffes Group Limited in 1969.

By then, Neil McCann had assumed leadership of Torney Brothers & McCann operations and steered the combination of that business with United Fruit Importers Limited. The merger of the two wholesalers groups created Fruit Importers of Ireland Limited (FII) in 1968. Under Neil McCann, FII began to consolidate much of the fruit import market in Ireland, before turning to the greater U.K. market during the 1980s.

FRUIT IMPORTERS OF IRELAND: 1970S–80S

Among FII's first acquisitions was that of Connolly Shaw Limited, which brought that company's importer rights to the Jaffa (Israel) and Cape and Outspan (both South Africa) fruit brands. The company extended its penetration into southern Ireland with the acquisition of Southern Fruit Suppliers Limited, based in Waterford, Ireland, in 1971. The following year, the company acquired Shell & Byrne Limited, adding that company's supplier relationship to the Five Star grocery chain, as well as its imports of apples and onions from the United States.

In 1973 FII completed two more significant acquisitions, adding the Kilkenny area to its operations with the purchase of Philip Lenehan Limited, then boosting its banana business with the purchase of Red Diamond Limited. A number of other acquisitions followed through the 1970s, including Munster Fruit and Produce Limited in 1974, extending the company into the Kerry and West Cork areas. In 1977 FII's subsidiary McCann Nurseries, which grew apples and tomatoes, formed the Green Ace Produce Group to pack and sell apples and tomatoes in the European market.

Neil V. McCann succeeded his father as CEO in 1979 and accelerated FII's growth. In 1980 FII merged operations with those of subsidiary Charles McCann Limited under a new holding company, known as FII Limited. The following year, the company sold 25 percent of its shares to an outside investor group, Development Capital Corporation (DCC), setting the gears in motion for the company's public offering, completed in February 1981, on the Dublin stock exchange.

The public offering gave FII the capital to begin a series of acquisitions through the 1980s that helped it grow into one of the 10 largest public companies in Ireland. Among the company's acquisitions for the decade were those of Uniplumo Limited, adding, in 1981, the importing, cultivation, and distribution, including retail operations, of house plants to the company's portfolio; the 1983 acquisition of Frank E. Benner, which added that Northern Ireland company's flowers, fruits, and vegetables trade; the acquisition of Daniel P. Hale & Co., based in Belfast, in 1984; and the acquisitions of Kinsealy Farms Limited and 50 percent of Gillespie & Co. in 1985.

FII's biggest score of the decade came in 1986 when it agreed to acquire the Fyffes operation from United Brands. The deal marked FII's first overseas acquisition, transforming it into one of the premier fruit distribution groups in the United Kingdom. The transformed group also changed its name, becoming FII-Fyffes. The company renamed itself again, as Fyffes PLC, in 1990.

INTERNATIONAL FOCUS IN 1990S

The company maintained its acquisition pace through the end of the 1980s and into the 1990s. Fyffes added Jack Dolan Limited and Sunpak Mayfield Fresh Produce Limited in 1988, Bernard Dempsey & Co. and J. Langan & Sons in 1989, and J. Grey & Son in 1990. Whereas these acquisitions remained centered primarily on the Irish and English markets, in the early 1990s, Fyffes turned its sights on building a position for itself throughout Europe. The company added Erobanancanarias S.A., based in Spain, and Brdr. Lemcke A.S. of Denmark in 1993, followed by Velleman & Tas B.V. of The Netherlands, J.A. Kahl GmbH of Germany, Sofiprim S.A. of France, and Jamaica Banana Holdings Limited, all in 1994.

Not all of the company's acquisition attempts were successful. In 1992 Fyffes made an offer to buy rival Del Monte for an estimated $500 million, an acquisition that would have catapulted the company to the top of the world's fruit distribution market. That offer was turned aside by Del Monte. Soon after, Fyffes itself became the object of a takeover offer from another rival, Dole. Fyffes rejected this offer. Instead, with the war chest it had built up for the Del Monte acquisition attempt, Fyffes went shopping again. After picking up a new string of companies in 1995, including Angel Rey of Spain, International Fruit Company of The

Netherlands, and J.W. Swithenbank Limited, the company joined with the newly formed Windward Isle Banana Company to acquire Geest's banana operations in 1996. This acquisition helped boost Fyffes into the world's top five fruit distribution companies, giving it two-thirds of the U.K. banana market, and a top share across Europe as well.

Neil V. McCann began to eye retirement, naming his eldest son, Carl P. McCann, as Fyffes' vice-chairman and younger son, David V. McCann, as chief executive officer. The younger generation continued the diversification moves of their father, as Fyffes sought to reduce its reliance on bananas. This was seen as especially important given increasing pressure from the United States to end a system of preferential tariffs that all but excluded so-called dollar bananas, grown in Latin America, from the European market in favor of the more expensive bananas from the smaller plantations on the former European islands and colonies. The dispute, which later erupted into threats of an all-out trade war at the end of the decade, encouraged Fyffes to boost its distribution activities in other fresh fruit and vegetable markets, while the company broadened its sourcing to include a good share of dollar bananas as well. Among the company's moves was the acquisition of a 50 percent share of South Africa's Capespan Holdings International, giving Fyffes a strong share of the fresh fruits market.

FACING CHALLENGES IN THE 21ST CENTURY

At the turn of the century, Fyffes turned toward the Internet, launching two Web sites, worldoffruit.com, offering a business-to-business portal for fruit transactions and information, which went online in mid-2000, and ingredientsnet.com, a joint venture with the Glanbia Group, offering similar business-to-business services to the food ingredients market. As more and more of the world's sourcing activity turned to the Internet, Fyffes' moves were seen as giving the company a strong position in the top ranks of the world's fresh fruit and vegetables distributors. After its initial launch, more than 200 traders had registered on worldoffruit.com, and Fyffes confidently opened sales offices across Europe, and was planning to do the same in the United States. By June 2000, due to a weak banana market caused by currency fluctuations, and losses at its South African fruit subsidiary and its e-commerce ventures, the company was experiencing losses of more than 50 percent in its interim profits. By the end of that year, in an effort to cut costs, the Group closed one if its U.K. ripening centers, while Geest closed two others. By January of 2001 it became apparent that the Group would not be able to raise the capital needed to develop worldoffruit.com, and all investment in the venture was ceased. This was followed in July 2001 with Fyffes and Glanbia deciding to suspend the ingredientsnet.com operation. Further adding to the company's financial woes was the revelation that a Mafia-run banana-smuggling ring had created the extra volume in 2000, causing a price decrease when an increase was needed. According to Carl McCann in the *Financial Times*, the prior trading year was "the worldwide banana industry's toughest."

By September 2001 the Group reorganized its shipping operation by disposing of three refrigerated ships and a general cargo business. Further cost cuts were made by selling JA Kahl in Munich, and its 50 percent interest in Sofiprim SA (France). These measures, coupled with a European Union (EU) directive that set banana quotas through 2006, put the Group back on the path of profitability. By June 30, 2002, the Group was reporting pre-tax profits of €32.5 million. In August 2002 Fyffes bought 70 percent of Hortim International sro based in the Czech Republic, and followed this acquisition in December 2002 with the purchase of 80 percent of Germany's Internationale Fruchtimport Gesellschaft Weichert & Co. KG. While the company continued on its acquisition trail, it was embroiled in a legal battle with DCC PLC, accusing the company of insider trading. DCC's CEO was James F. Flavin, a Fyffes director, and early in 2000 the company had sold its 10.2 percent share of Fyffes. Fyffes contended that this was because Flavin was privy to internal financial reports that projected difficult times ahead.

In December 2003 Neil McCann retired as chairman with his son, Carl, succeeding him, while Neil retained his position as director. By May 2004 Fyffes had acquired 60 percent of Everfresh, one of Sweden's leading fresh produce company's, with a view of purchasing the remaining 40 percent by 2007. While the Group's profits continued to grow, it was still immersed in litigation with DCC. During the January 2005 court proceedings, it was revealed that both Fyffes and DCC had sought legal advice as to whether DCC's sale of its shares would raise questions of insider trading nearly two years before the transaction took place. In March 2005 as the euro strengthened against the dollar, the Group was reporting profits that exceeded expectations. This positive announcement was offset by the fact that Fyffes had spent $5.25 million on legal costs the previous year, and the DCC lawsuit was expected to continue for several months. The Group's profits were further affected when the EU implemented a new import tariff that would not only lift the existing quota restrictions, but would also cost Fyffes an estimated €40 million per year. In September 2005, in a strategic move, Fyffes entered into an agreement with Uniban SA for a 50 percent ownership of Turbana Corporation, a leading provider of bananas and plaintains in the United States, making Fyffes the fifth-largest supplier of bananas in the country.

In November 2005, after a career that spanned 55 years in the business, Neil McCann retired as director. The following month, Fyffes lost its lawsuit against DCC, with Justice Mary Laffoy ruling that Flavin "was not in possession of price-sensitive information" and that the sale was not unlawful. The decision could have cost the Group dearly but Fyffes continued to forge ahead, acquiring 60 percent of Nolem in January 2006, a leading Brazilian melon exporter, and spinning off its property company, Blackrock International Land PLC, in May 2006.

The new EU directives, combined with higher costs, were cutting substantially into the Group's profits, and in December 2006 Fyffes made the strategic decision to demerge its general produce and distribution business to form Total Produce PLC. Following the demerger, Carl McCann retired as chairman of Fyffes, and David McCann stepped down as CEO, with Jimmy Tolan succeeding him until his resignation in April 2008. By mid-2009, under the leadership of chairman David McCann and chief operating officer Coen Bos, Fyffes was projecting year-end earnings before interest and tax (EBIT) of €16 to €20 million, and held steadfast to the Group's commitment of developing the business both organically and through acquisitions.

M. L. Cohen
Updated, Marie O'Sullivan

PRINCIPAL SUBSIDIARIES

Fyffes Atlantic Shipping Limited; Fyffes Bananas (Swords) Limited; Fyffes International; Fyffes International Holdings Limited; Fyffes Tropical Ireland Limited; Ananas Export Company SA (Costa Rica); FII Holdings Limited (UK); Fyffes Caribbean Limited (Jersey); Fyffes Group Limited (UK); Fyffes Inc. (U.S.A.); Fyffes International Fruit Traders Limited (Jersey); Fyffes Investment Limited (Jersey); Fyffes Treasury Services Limited (Jersey); Fyffes Tropical Produce LLC (USA); Fyffes Windward Holdings Limited (Jersey); Banana Importers of Ireland Limited (95%); Internationale Fruchtimport Gesellschaft Weichert & Co. KG (Germany; 80%); Fyffes Fruit Procurement Limited (76%); Hortim International sro (Czech Republic; 70%); Everfresh (Sweden; 60%); Nolem (Brazil; 60%); Sol Marketing Company Inc (U.S.A.; 60%); Capespan Holdings International (South Africa; 50%); Turbana Corporation (U.S.A.; 50%).

PRINCIPAL COMPETITORS

Chiquita Brands International Inc.; Dole Food Company Inc.; Fresh Del Monte Produce Inc.

FURTHER READING

Barker, Thorold, "Fyffes Freezes Investment in Internet Venture," *Financial Times*, January 19, 2001, p. 21.

Blackwell, David Harold, "Fyffes Tripped by Weak Banana Market," *Financial Times*, June 20, 2000, p. 34.

———, "Price Rises and Cost Cuts Help Fyffes Recover," *Financial Times*, February 28, 2002, p. 27.

Boyle, Pat, "New EU Banana Tarriff to Cost Fyffes 40m a Year," *Europe Intelligence Wire*, November 29, 2005.

Brown, John Murray, "Mafia Racket behind Fyffes Fall," *Financial Times*, March 22, 2001, p. 22.

Davies, Peter N., *Fyffes and the Banana: Musa Sapientum*. London: Athlone Press, 1990.

Fottrell, Quentin, "Fyffes Reputation at Stake in Action against DCC," *FWN Select*, December 20, 2004.

"Fyffes Defies Costs to Report Sales up 9.6%," *Grocer*, March 14, 2009, p. 34.

"Fyffes PLC—Demerger of General Produce," *Europe Intelligence Wire*, September 7, 2006.

"Fyffes PLC—Retirement of Director," *Europe Intelligence Wire*, February 28, 2007.

Grose, Thomas K., "Two Sides of the Banana Split," *USA Today*, March 3, 1999, p. 3B.

"Investors in Fyffes Back Plan to Split into Two," *Europe Intelligence Wire*, December 6, 2006.

Lavery, Brian, "Ex-Director Sued on Trading," *New York Times*, February 20, 2002.

———, "Trade Feud on Bananas Not as Clear as It Looks," *New York Times*, February 7, 2001.

O'Laughlin, Ann, "Flavin Did Deal in Firm's Shares but Not Illegally, High Court Judge Rules," *Europe Intelligence Wire*, December 22, 2005.

Payne, Doug, "Fyffes Enjoys Fruits of Growth," *European*, January 1, 1996, p. 28.

Roddam, Tony, "Fyffes Marches through Banana War Flak," *Reuters*, June 14, 1999.

Smith, Kevin, "Fyffes Eyes Big Slice of Web Fresh Produce Trade," *Reuters*, January 13, 2000.

Gianni Versace S.p.A.

Via Manzoni, 38
Milan, 20121
Italy
Telephone: (+39 02) 76 09 31
Toll Free: (888) 721-7219
Fax: (+39 02) 76 00 41 22
Web site: http://www.versace.it

Private Company
Founded: 1978
Employees: 1,500 (2004 est.)
Sales: EUR 336.3 million (2008)
NAICS: 315233 Women's and Girls' Cut and Sew Dress Manufacturing; 315222 Men's and Boys' Cut and Sew Suit, Coat, and Overcoat Manufacturing; 315223 Men's and Boys' Cut and Sew Shirt (except Work Shirt) Manufacturing; 315224 Men's and Boys' Cut And Sew Trouser, Slack, and Jean Manufacturing; 315228 Men's and Boys' Cut and Sew Other Outerwear Manufacturing; 315231 Women's and Girls' Cut and Sew Lingerie, Loungewear, and Nightwear Manufacturing; 315234 Women's and Girls' Cut and Sew Suit, Coat, Tailored Jacket, and Skirt Manufacturing; 315291 Infants' Cut and Sew Apparel Manufacturing; 315292 Fur and Leather Apparel Manufacturing; 315999 Other Apparel Accessories and Other Apparel Manufacturing; 721110 Hotels, Resort, without Casinos

Headquartered in Milan, Gianni Versace S.p.A. is second only to rival house Giorgio Armani among Italy's fashion designers. The company's diverse offerings, which include lingerie, umbrellas, makeup, hosiery, shoes, watches, jewelry, and fragrances, enable people to swathe themselves in Versace from head to toe. Clients can even surround themselves with furnishings from the Home Signature line of decor. Lines within the Versace group include Versace Jeans Couture, Versace Sport, and the Versace Home Collection. By the late 1990s the Versace fashion empire stretched from the design table to manufacturing sites to the sales counter, distributing its products through more than 300 boutiques and 2,000 affiliated stores.

The privately held business was within months of going public when on July 15, 1997, its founder and namesake, award-winning Italian fashion designer Gianni Versace, was gunned down in front of his Miami Beach, Florida, mansion. The 50-year-old's untimely death threatened to unravel his company. However, for virtually all of its 20 years in business, the apparel house has been a family affair. Gianni's older brother, Santo, managed the finances, while younger sister Donatella oversaw advertising, accessories, and her own line within the group. In the wake of the family tragedy, Donatella assumed the role of chief designer, helping transport the Versace legacy into the 21st century. While the company struggled financially for several years after its namesake's death, by 2007 it had restored itself to profitability, thanks in large part to the efforts of its new CEO, Giancarlo Di Risio.

COMPANY PERSPECTIVES

■

According to Donatella Versace: The woman I have in mind when designing is one whose individuality and inner confidence shines on the outside. She is also sophisticated, sexy, smart and dynamic. The contemporary woman is not afraid to be a woman. She can still be powerful by maintaining her femininity and sensuality.

The Versace man is charismatic, with an inner confidence which reflects on the outside. The Versace man seduces with his personality, attitude and carriage. True personality comes from within. My clothes are merely the choice of a woman or a man who wants to be seen and discovered.

LATE 1970S FOUNDATION

Born in southern Italy in 1946, Gianni Versace was the son of an appliance salesman and a seamstress. His mother, Francesca, fashioned gowns for the region's elite. Gianni is said to have started down the road to high fashion when, as a boy, he made little dolls and puppets from the snippets of fabric that littered the floor of her studio. After studying architecture, Gianni stayed in his hometown of Reggio Calabria through the 1960s, first apprenticing with his mother and later running two separate boutiques showcasing his men's and women's fashions.

In 1972 Ezio Nicosia, owner of Florentine Flowers of Lucca, invited Gianni to move to Milan and design a knitwear collection for fall and winter. The 25-year-old's designs were so successful that he earned a Volkswagen convertible as a bonus to his regular fee. In the years to come Versace contracted with De Parisini of Santa Margherita, Callaghan, Alma, and Genny Group for their ready-to-wear lines. Versace created the Complice collection for Genny before striking out on his own in 1977 and presenting his first signature collection the following spring. His brightly colored, sexy styles for women generated sales of ITL20 billion ($11 million) that first year. Versace opened his first Milanese boutique and brought out his first menswear collection in 1978.

Older brother Santo was with him from the beginning, having moved to Milan in 1976. An accountant, Santo put his business administration degree to good use as managing director and chairman of Gianni Versace S.p.A. Younger sister Donatella started out

coordinating accessories with Gianni's designs, and she quickly moved into advertising and promotion. Perhaps most importantly, she served as what Gianni called his "inspiring muse." The three siblings shared ownership of the apparel firm, albeit not evenly; Gianni held 45 percent, Santo held 35 percent, and Donatella held 20 percent.

SHOWMANSHIP DRIVES DESIGN HOUSE IN 1980S

Versace cultivated symbiotic relationships with the arts and artists, especially in the areas of theater, popular music, and dance. These ties would prove mutually beneficial. Versace fashioned the costumes and clothing that kept the famous looking chic, and his clients served as walking billboards for the designer's wares. Versace forged especially close ties to the Teatro alia Scala. This "sideline" was reflected in his fashion collections, which took on a theatricality of their own. His circle of celebrity friends/clients widened in step with his design prowess. Richard Avedon photographed his collections. Andy Warhol painted his portrait. Later, Sylvester Stallone and Madonna modeled for his advertisements.

Versace's own paradoxical tastes were reflected in his designs. He told Amy M. Spindler in an interview for the *New York Times* just before his death, "Contrasts [are] the key to all my creations." He designed costumes for Elton John's rock concerts, as well as for ballets produced by Maurice Béjart. His famous female fans ranged from punkish Courtney Love to impeccably chic Diana, Princess of Wales. He was called a "rock 'n' rolling exhibitionist," "vividly committed to the hedonism of late 20th-century culture," but he was also known as a devoted brother and uncle. These disparities found expression in designs that always featured some element of "intentional imperfection": draped gowns of metal mesh, leopard-print baby-doll dresses, asymmetrical necklines and hemlines, and lace/metal combinations. Other Versace trademarks would emerge over the course of the 1980s, including colorful silk prints, high heels, baroque themes, leather, and overt sexuality.

The designer's fall/winter women's collection earned Versace his first major award, the first of four career L'Occhio d'Oros, in 1982. With his creative reputation firmly in place, Versace moved quickly to capitalize on his brand equity. Like fashion icons before him, Versace realized that while most women could not afford a $15,000 signature dress, many could afford a distinctively printed silk scarf or a watch with his Medusa-head logo. The designer started his diversifica-

KEY DATES

■

1946: Gianni Versace is born in Milan, Italy.

1955: Versace's younger sister, Donatella, is born.

1972: Gianni Versace designs first knitwear collection for Ezio Nicosia, proprietor of Florentine Flowers of Lucca.

1978: Gianni Versace opens first store in Milan.

1981: Versace opens first U.S. store in Coconut Grove, Florida.

1982: Versace wins first L'Occhio d'Oros award for his fall/winter women's collection.

1985: Versace introduces his Istante line, designed in collaboration with Donatella.

1991: Versace launches Versace Jeans Couture.

1997: Gianni Versace is murdered by Andrew Cunanan on July 15.

2000: Company opens first luxury hotel, Palazzo Versace, on Australia's Gold Coast.

2003: Donatella Versace becomes vice-chair of the company.

2004: Donatella's daughter, Allegra Beck, turns 18, inheriting 50 percent stake in the company.

2007: Francesca Versace launches debut collection, Francesca V, at Paris Fashion Week.

tion with fragrances. Accessories, most produced from Versace designs by licensees, ran the gamut from socks to umbrellas, sunglasses, jewelry, and watches. Versace was also quick to make international forays, establishing company-owned and franchised boutiques in Europe and Asia in the early 1980s. By the mid-1990s, 25 percent of sales would come from Asia.

March 1985 saw the introduction of Versace's first Istante collection, a ready-to-wear line of "conservative-chic" clothing designed by Gianni with help from longtime companion Antonio D'Amico and sister Donatella. Istante was organized not only as a separate brand but also a distinct subsidiary of the Versace group, Istante Vesa s.r.l. In 1989 Versace introduced Atelier Versace, a haute couture line featuring custom-made fashions costing tens of thousands of dollars. The Versus line, also launched in 1989, was Donatella's venue. Its ready-to-wear garments were targeted at a younger, trendier audience. By the mid-1990s Versus would generate 10 percent of corporate sales.

By 1989 Gianni Versace S.p.A.'s annual revenues totaled ITL58 billion, with net income of ITL7.6

billion. At this time, the Versace brand was generating ITL520 billion at wholesale.

RAPID DIVERSIFICATION PACES 1990S EXPANSION

The family business stepped up the pace of growth through brand extension—known in fashion parlance as "product pyramiding"—in the 1990s. In 1991 the company introduced Versatile, a line of designer clothes for full-figured women that included leopard catsuits, pleated miniskirts, and bejeweled bustiers in bright colors. That same year, Versace brought out Versace Jeans Couture, a casual line of clothing headlined by $200 jeans. A line of Home Signature tableware, bath and bed linens, lamps, carpets, and more was launched in 1993. The company diversified into the highly competitive realm of color cosmetics with the European introduction of Versace Make-up in 1997. It was a rapid but well-considered expansion that was careful not to oversaturate, and possibly diminish, the brand's aura of exclusivity and cachet.

Analysts praised the company's managerial and manufacturing agility. John Roussant in *Business Week* noted that "the Versaces typically made decisions with lightning speed—a key competitive advantage in an industry where styles and fads change overnight." Over the years, Versace also accumulated controlling interests in 10 of its manufacturing licensees, a factor that enabled the company to seize the initiative when a product proved particularly popular. Weekly sales reports kept the family troika up-to-date on their company's hottest items.

Geographic as well as product diversification proved vital to Versace's expansion. In 1994 Europe was still the company's largest market, accounting for half of annual revenues. Although the company had established its initial U.S. boutique in Coconut Grove, Florida, in 1981, North America generated less than 20 percent of sales in 1994. That year, Gianni and Santo announced their intent to make the United States Versace's primary export market and a generator of at least 30 percent of annual sales. Santo Versace told Sara Gay Forden in *WWD* that "the U.S. is our leading priority right now. It has to become our biggest export market." The strategy for achieving this goal included the establishment of a U.S. distribution subsidiary and the launch of a nine-story boutique in a landmark New York City building on Fifth Avenue.

Sales more than doubled, from ITL221 billion in 1990 to ITL510 billion in 1994, while net income mushroomed from ITLI4.2 billion to ITL39.7 billion. In 1994 the Versace brand generated nearly ITLI.2 trillion at wholesale.

Versace planned a mid-decade initial public offering to finance continued growth. Preparations for this were traced to 1986, when Versace opened his books to the public and hired an accounting firm to audit the records. In the spring of 1997 Gianni told Roussant in *BusinessWeek*, "I'd like people to be as crazy for my shares as they are for my clothes." Finance man Santo concurred, telling John Forden in *WWD* that the siblings sought to "give this group a life that is autonomous from that of its founders. A company that goes public is like a company that automatically acquires a second and third generation. It is a commitment to carry Versace beyond its founders." Versace bypassed the Milan stock market, instead seeking a listing on the New York Stock Exchange. In May 1997 Gianni Versace SpA spun off ITL150 billion ($86.9 million) worth of family property, including lavish homes and artwork, to a private company known as Ordersystem.

The company, however, had some troubling issues to overcome before winning the confidence of the investment community. In May 1997 Santo Versace was found guilty of bribing tax officials, a conviction that the Versace chairman predictably appealed. Then there were the persistent and steadfastly renounced rumors that the company had links to organized crime. Versace's European boutiques suffered six burglaries in just four months in 1996, losing L500 million ($320,000) worth of merchandise. Although none of these issues, perceived or real, were devastating, the Versaces sought to remove any encumbrances to its initial stock valuation.

FOUNDER'S MURDER BRINGS UNEXPECTED TRANSITION

All involved with Versace realized a public stock offering had the potential to serve as a turning point for the company that could shift its impressive growth into high gear. However, no one could have predicted the transition forced by spree killer Andrew Cunanan, who shot Gianni Versace twice in the head at point blank range on the morning of July 15, 1997.

More than one critic noted that Versace "was killed at his peak, a time when his continual retooling of his inventions had produced his best work ever." Trade magazine *Daily News Record* asserted that "fashion has lost one of its brightest superstars at the height of his career." *Time* magazine's John Greenwald concurred that "at his death, the designer was at the height of his powers." Barely a month before his murder, Gianni Versace had introduced what the *Daily News Record* called "one of the strongest collections in years." News of Versace's death spurred a run on the more than 2,000 boutiques and department stores worldwide that carried

his branded goods. Clients new and old, however, soon found that the designer's demise would not necessarily doom his company.

Although many design houses have died along with their founders, fashion analysts cited several attributes that would help the Versace group outlive its namesake. Foremost were the well-known brand and Medusa-head logo, embodying a core identity from which new product lines could continue to evolve. In addition, while Gianni Versace had been personally responsible for the creation of the signature lines that generated 45 percent of his company's profits, he had assembled his international team of design assistants headed by sister Donatella. Furthermore, Donatella had taken on increased responsibilities for several years in the mid-1990s, when Gianni was diagnosed with cancer of the lymph nodes. His 1996 recovery made his murder all the more tragic. A statement released by the family shortly after Versace's death asserted that "the indomitable spirit, the amazing vitality and the faith in creativity that makes Gianni Versace so important to everyone is something that we are completely committed to and most capable of continuing."

Preparations for the 1998 initial public offering continued. Just days before his murder, Gianni had hired investment banking house Morgan Stanley to underwrite the $350 million stock offering. That September, his surviving siblings moved to consolidate three directly controlled subsidiaries—Istante Vesa SRL, manufacturing arm Alias SpA, and boutique chain Modifin SA—into Gianni Versace SpA.

Gianni Versace left de facto control of his global enterprise in the hands of his sister Donatella by bequeathing his stake in the company to her 11-year-old daughter, Allegra Beck. Donatella presented her first emotion-charged signature collection in October 1997 to a crowd of supportive designers, Hollywood celebrities, and rock stars. Trade magazine *WWD* cheered her designs of rubber, leather, silk, and beads with the headline, "Bravo, Donatella!"

FAMILY DRAMA WITH A NEW LOOK

While the Versace family continued to explore ways to take the company public in the late 1990s, they remained adamant about retaining control of the day-to-day operations of the business. In February 1999, Donatella declared her intention to sell only a minority percentage of the business, telling a reporter for the London *Times* that she had no interest in "putting the whole company on the market." Many analysts saw tremendous growth potential in an initial public offering (IPO), predicting that the company's value could reach up to three times its annual revenues if it went public. Analysts also anticipated, however, that the family's insistence on retaining a majority stake might prove a deterrent to many investors. In any case, both the Versace family and industry insiders viewed an IPO as a long-term proposition.

Meanwhile, as the family worked to redefine its business for the 21st century, the legacy of Gianni Versace continued to loom large. Two highly publicized books exploring the fashion icon's murder were published in 1999: Gary Indiana's *Three-Month Fever: The Andrew Cunanan Story*, and Maureen Orth's *Vulgar Favors: Andrew Cunanan, Gianni Versace, and the Largest Failed Manhunt in U.S. History*. An unauthorized biography, Christopher Mason's *Undressed: A Biography of Gianni Versace* was also scheduled to appear that year. The work reportedly offered an unflattering glimpse into Versace's private life, depicting him as a vain, untrustworthy, and power-hungry man. Displeased with Mason's portrait of their late brother, Versace family members swiftly threatened legal action against the book's publisher, Little, Brown, claiming the book was libelous. Little, Brown withdrew the book from publication, and Mason's biography never actually made it into print.

Not all of the media attention surrounding the deceased designer was unwelcome. In October 2002 a major retrospective of Versace's career, "Versace at the V&A," opened at the Victoria & Albert Museum in London. Reviewing the show's opening for the *Daily Telegraph* on October 17, 2002, Hilary Alexander praised the enduring appeal of Gianni Versace's "life-long romance with luxury and sexuality in fashion," while noting his "contribution to the phenomenon of the supermodel and the cult of celebrity dressing." As some commentators noted, the extravagance—or, as the designer's detractors called it, vulgarity—on display at the exhibition offered a stark contrast to the direction the Versace brand had taken under Donatella's leadership. Since the late 1990s fashion journalists had noted a difference in the Versace look, seeing in Donatella's designs a more refined, understated quality that seemed to mark a dramatic shift away from her brother's trademark excessiveness.

By 2003 this attitude of restraint had begun to dictate the family's approach to other areas of its business. In January 2003, when the company began promoting its new spring-summer haute couture collection in Paris, it unexpectedly cancelled its traditional runway show, choosing instead to unveil the new line on mannequins and with video presentations. Many industry insiders viewed this sudden turn toward

moderation as a sign of the company's mounting financial woes. Versace lost close to EUR 6 million in 2002; by the end of 2003, the company was more than $140 million in debt. The company's fortunes had fallen precipitously since its heyday in the 1990s, with annual revenues plummeting by $300 million in the years following its founder's death. In the face of these struggles, the Versace family once again considered selling a stake in the company to outside investors.

The year 2004 proved to be a defining year in the post-Gianni history of the company. On June 30, Donatella's daughter, Allegra, turned 18 years old, inheriting half of the company and raising widespread speculation about the future direction of the label. Less than two months later it was revealed that Donatella had been addicted to cocaine for the past several years. After an intervention led by singer and longtime family friend Elton John, the designer agreed to enter rehab treatment. In the midst of this upheaval, the company appointed Giancarlo Di Risio, former head of Fendi, to serve as the new CEO. The move was significant as it represented the first time in Versace's history that someone outside the family had been put in charge of the company's finances. Di Risio immediately set out to streamline the company's operations, dropping its Versus label and other unprofitable assets, while focusing greater attention on marketing its lucrative accessories line. Di Risio also expanded the company's hotel interests, entering into a pact with the Australian firm Sunland Group Ltd. in 2006 to develop 15 new resorts worldwide.

Under Di Risio's stewardship, the company was restored to solvency. Versace enjoyed profits of EUR 19.1 million in 2006, while earnings rose an additional 30 percent in 2007. That year, Santo Versace's daughter Francesca made her debut as a designer. When her debut collection, Francesca V, opened at the Fall 2007 Paris Fashion Week, many journalists speculated that she would soon become the new creative force behind the company's fashion line. Writing in the *Guardian* on September 24, 2007, Hadley Freeman anticipated the company's "complete rejuvenation" with the premier of Francesca's new line, while William Langley declared Francesca the "heir apparent" to the Versace brand in the September 30 edition of the London *Telegraph*. Several commentators predicted that Francesca would soon take over Donatella's design responsibilities at the company.

In the midst of these changes, Versace continued to pursue new markets for its unique brand. In April 2008 the company opened a resort in Dubai. Dubbed Palazzo Versace, it was the first hotel in the world to feature an air-conditioned beach. The rumors suggesting that the Versace family had outgrown its trademark penchant for luxury and excess would seem to have been exaggerated. By 2009 the company was in the midst of a massive, and costly, restructuring, renovating many of its existing boutiques and opening new locations worldwide, notably in Asia. In June of that year Giancarlo Di Risio resigned, and the company hired a new CEO, Gian Giacomo Ferraris. As the decade drew to a close, it remained to be seen whether or not Ferraris would succeed in imposing the same level of fiscal discipline as his predecessor.

April Dougal Gasbarre
Updated, Stephen Meyer

PRINCIPAL COMPETITORS

Christian Dior SA (France); Dolce & Gabbana Srl; Giorgio Armani S.p.A.; Gucci Group NV (Netherlands); Hermès International (France); Prada SpA Group; Valentino Fashion Group S.p.A.

FURTHER READING

Bellafante, Ginia, "La Dolce Vita: Gianni Versace Sold the World a Fantasy of Unrestrained Opulence," *Time*, July 28, 1997, pp. 36-42.

Bounds, Wendy, and Beth Burkstrand, "Shoppers Pay Respects to Versace at Cash Registers across Country," *Wall Street Journal*, July 17, 1997, p. B1.

"Bravo Donatella!" *WWD*, October 10, 1997, pp. 1-3.

Collins, Lauren, "Viva Donatella! What It Takes to Carry on the Versace Legacy," *New Yorker*, September 24, 2007, pp. 153-63.

Conti, Samantha, "Versace Wills His Stake to Niece," *WWD*, September 18, 1997, p. 8.

Costin, Glynis, "Remembering Gianni," *Los Angeles Magazine*, September 1997, pp. 78-83.

Daspin, Eileen, "Breaking the Rules," *WWD*, March 11, 1992, p. S30.

DeCarlo, Frank, "Legacy of a Celebrity Designer," *Newsweek*, July 28, 1997, p. 40.

Foley, Bridget, "Donatella's First Collection," *WWD*, October 1, 1997, pp. 1-2.

Forden, Sara Gay, "Versace Going Forward with IPO Preparations," *WWD*, August 14, 1997, p. 13.

———, "Versace Sets Sights on Wall Street," *WWD*, February 23, 1994, p. 18.

———, "Very Versace: Making America No. 1," *WWD*, November 1, 1994, p. 15.

Givhan, Robin, "Donatella Versace's Liberating Restraint," *Washington Post*, March 6, 1999, p. C1.

Greenwald, John, "Will His Fashion Empire Survive?" *Time*, July 28, 1997, p. 42.

Horyn, Cathy, "A New Half-Owner for Versace, and She's Almost 18," *New York Times*, June 15, 2004, p. B8.

Kaplan, Don, "Versace's Flagship Boutique Opens Today," *Daily News Record*, August 26, 1996, p. 6.

Luscombe, Belinda, "Little Sister, Big Success," *Time*, October 20, 1997, p. 119.

Martin, Richard, *Versace*, New York: Vendôme Press, 1997.

Morgan, Edel, "Why Palazzo Versace? Because You're Worth It," *Irish Times*, April 17, 2008, p. 13.

Pener, Degen, "Murder in Miami," *Entertainment Weekly*, July 25, 1997, pp. 6-7.

Phillips, Andrew, "Versace's Strange Murder," *Maclean's*, July 28, 1997, p. 25.

Roussant, John, "After Versace: Can a Fashion Empire Survive the Slaying of Its Creative Soul?" *BusinessWeek*, July 28, 1997.

Socha, Miles, "Carrying On after the Death of a Designer," *Daily News Record*, September 19, 1997, p. 6.

———, "The Versace Legacy: Bold and Baroque," *Daily News Record*, July 16, 1997, p. 1.

Spindler, Amy M., "Versace's Errors Showed Him a Way," *New York Times*, August 5, 1997, p. B9.

Steinhauer, Jennifer, "His Good Label Lives after Him," *New York Times*, July 19, 1997, pp. 31, 33.

Versace, Donatella, "Versace's Russian Revolution," *Times* (London), January 16, 2008, p. 8.

Versace, Gianni, *South Beach Stories*, Milano: Leonardo Arte, 1993.

Walsh, Sharon, "Versace Empire's Fate Up to Family," *Washington Post*, July 17, 1997, p. C3.

Webb, Iain R., "Renaissance Man," *Independent* (London), March 23, 2006, p. 40.

Globe Newspaper Company Inc.

135 Morrissey Boulevard
Boston, Massachusetts 02125
U.S.A.
Telephone: (617) 929-2000
Web site: http://www.bostonglobe.com

Wholly Owned Subsidiary of New York Times Company
Founded: 1872
Employees: 2,394 (New England Media Group)
Sales: $524 million (New England Media Group) (2008)
Stock Exchanges: New York Stock Exchange
Ticker Symbol: NYT
NAISC: 511110 Newspaper Publishers (Primary); 454390 Other Direct Selling Establishments; 424920 Book, Periodical, and Newspaper Merchant Wholesalers

■ ■ ■

The Globe Newspaper Company Inc., better known as the *Boston Globe* or simply the *Globe*, is the best-selling paper in New England and one of the premier newspapers in the United States. Owned by the New York Times Company, it makes up the largest component of the parent company's New England Media Group. The *Globe* has long been known for its first-rate reporting and is the recipient of 20 Pulitzer Prizes. It also owns Boston.com, the most frequently visited regional news Web site in the nation. However, for all its accolades and success, the challenges in the early 21st century, predominately the Internet and the global economic crisis, threaten the paper's (and the entire industry's) continued existence. It had lost $50 million in 2008 and was projected to be $85 million in the red in 2009. The innovation of the *Globe*'s management, the patience of its struggling parent company, and a substantial amount of luck would be necessary to offer a practical hope for its future.

FOUNDED IN 1872

The *Boston Globe* was founded in 1872 by six Boston businessmen with a combined investment of $150,000. The leader of these investors, and the only one who remained with the paper, was Eben Jordan, who also established the Jordan Marsh retail store, which eventually became a part of Macy's. The first issue of the *Globe* was published on March 4 and cost four cents, but the onset of the Panic of 1873 (an economic depression) rendered it almost instantly an economic failure. Jordan thus cast about for someone to counteract the paper's reverses and settled on Charles H. Taylor, a young Civil War veteran who had packed a great deal into his 27 years.

Born in Charlestown, Massachusetts, in July 1846, Taylor went to work in a Boston printing office at the age of 15. He fought and was wounded in the Civil War as a 16-year-old soldier, and was working as a typesetter back in Boston by the time he was 18. At 19, he became a newspaper reporter for the *Daily Evening Traveller* (Boston) and a correspondent for the *New York Tribune*. Three years later, he was hired as the private secretary to Massachusetts Governor William Claflin, and he was elected to the state legislature in 1872. The

COMPANY PERSPECTIVES

■

Our Vision: We seek to inform, to explore, to entertain, to contribute creatively to the commonwealth. To grow and prosper. To extend our franchise in the written word. To capture new growth in Greater Boston and beyond, while still serving our core. To excel in all ways that this region can excel.

Our Purpose: To be the indispensable source of trusted relevant and authoritative news and information for all our readers, thereby helping them meet the challenges in their lives.

To set a thoughtful agenda of issues that require attention in the communities we serve.

To provide a lively forum for a variety of viewpoints.

To build and sustain a readership that is large enough to respond powerfully en masse and yet targeted enough to support geographic and subject interests.

To create a vibrant marketplace for our advertisers, providing them with the most effective means of reaching consumers.

same year, he became the founding publisher of the magazine *American Homes*, but its promising start was destroyed by fire. When Jordan approached him for the second time in 1873 about running the failing *Globe*, Taylor accepted the position. It was the beginning of a dynasty that would last more than 125 years.

When Taylor signed on with the *Globe* in August 1873, the paper had lost $100,000 and was accumulating an additional deficit at the rate of $1,200 per week. Those losses had risen to $300,000 by 1877 and all the original investors, except Jordan, had abandoned the enterprise. However, that same year Taylor turned the dire situation around in three bold strokes. First, he lowered the price from four cents to two. Second, he invoked a strict impartiality rule, requiring the news to be reported in a politically nonpartisan manner. Third, and most notably, he restructured the paper's content to include information of interest to everyone from stock market quotations to household topics to sports coverage to humor. It was a shrewd and winning combination, as evidenced by a remarkable jump in circulation from 8,000 to 30,000 within just three weeks of the

changes. He went on to add a Sunday edition in October and an evening edition early in 1878, thereby ensuring that the *Globe*'s newfound prosperity would last for years to come.

PATH TO PRESTIGE

The *Globe*'s early success was based on innovation and forward thinking. For example, it was once known as the "maid's paper" because of its even-handed treatment of Boston's much-abused Irish immigrants and its routine upbraiding of the wealthy Brahmin establishment. By the 1960s, however, it was not even considered the best of the six newspapers in a town largely viewed as a journalistic desert. Its editorial voice had become wishy-washy, with the lead daily editorial quaintly signed "Uncle Dudley," and its front page sported advertisements. However, all that changed under the pioneering editorial direction of Thomas Winship.

Winship came into the newspaper business naturally, as his grandfather, A. E. Winship, had been the editor of the *Boston Traveller* and his father, Lawrence, served in the same position for the *Globe*. Thomas Winship began his career as a combat correspondent during World War II and then went to work at the *Washington Post*, first writing obituaries and later as a reporter. After an interlude as press secretary for Senator Leverett Saltonstall, he returned to the *Post* for several years before taking a job with the *Globe* as its Washington correspondent. By 1958 he was back in Boston to become the metropolitan editor of the *Globe*. His father was the paper's editor at the time, and the son went on to be named managing editor under him. Then in 1965 Thomas Winship took the reins from his father to become editor of the paper.

Attired in his trademark bowtie and red suspenders, Winship lost no time in placing his own stamp on the *Globe*. Front page ads and Uncle Dudley were banished. Coverage of sports, science, and the arts was expanded, while dogged investigative reporting and strong editorial positions became the paper's hallmarks. The *Globe* won its first Pulitzer Prize (for investigating the credentials of the federal judge nominee Francis X. Morrissey) just one year after Winship became the editor. The *Globe* was the second major newspaper to speak out for the United States' withdrawal from Vietnam and the third to publish the Pentagon Papers. Its exhaustive and balanced coverage of the divisive school busing issue earned it another Pulitzer in 1975 (the paper won a total of 12 under Winship's watch). Mary McGrory of the *Washington Post* noted that Winship "transformed the newspaper into a thunderous liberal voice of New England." He also brought it to regional dominance and national

KEY DATES

◼

1872: The *Boston Globe* is founded by Eben Jordan and five other Boston businessmen.

1873: Charles H. Taylor is hired and soon becomes the first of five generations of Taylors to serve as the *Globe*'s publisher.

1877: The paper is revamped and the first Sunday edition is published.

1965: Thomas Winship succeeds his father, Lawrence, as editor.

1966: The *Globe* wins its first Pulitzer Prize.

1973: The paper goes public as a subsidiary and principal property of Affiliated Publications.

1993: Affiliated Publications is purchased by the New York Times Company for a record $1.1 billion.

1995: Boston.com is launched.

1999: The era of the Taylor family ends with the naming of Richard H. Gilman as publisher.

2003: The *Globe* picks up its 17th Pulitzer Prize for exposure of sexual abuse scandal within the Roman Catholic Church.

2009: The newspaper industry at large continues to falter, and the *Globe* faces possible extinction.

prominence as circulation rose 40 percent to 520,000 daily and 792,786 on Sunday during his tenure.

Winship's *Globe* was distinctive for its demanding, yet nurturing, culture. He referred to his young, eager reporters as "my city-room Weathermen," a reference to the radical group of the 1960s, and he was famous for mentoring new writers. He was aided in cultivating such an atmosphere by the notably low-key Taylors, who still served as publishers (both William Davis Taylor and William O. Taylor served during Winship's time). Giving each employee a turkey for Christmas, for example, was a long-standing tradition, as were fruit baskets for those who were ill. The *Globe* personnel of that period were, in short, a rather close-knit family whose members received a great deal of individual attention.

When Winship retired in 1984, another era had already begun. The paper had become a public company in 1973 when it became a subsidiary and principal property of the newly-created Affiliated Publications. The *Evening Globe* had ceased publication in 1979, ending a 100-year run, and the raucous competition from five other newspapers had been reduced to one: the *Boston Herald*, which the press mogul Rupert Murdoch

had purchased in 1982. However, the *Globe* remained prosperous, being $40 million in the black when Winship stepped down, and was firmly established as one of the finest newspapers in the nation.

CHANGING TIMES

Throughout its 20 years of operation, Affiliated Publications had expanded to include interests such as television and radio stations and magazines, and the *Globe* had retained its popularity and prestige. The advent of the 1990s, however, brought the Taylor family a concern outside the scope of mere profitability. The trusts that controlled the voting power over Affiliated Publications were due to expire in 1996, making the sale of the company a near certainty and a potentially divisive bidding war a definite possibility. To avoid the latter scenario, the Taylors sought a buyer themselves and found one in the New York Times Company.

The *New York Times*, like the *Globe*, had been run by the same family for generations—in its case, the Sulzbergers. Unsurprisingly, the two great publishing dynasties had known one another for some time. So it was only natural that they should form an alliance when the need arose. That alliance took place on October 1, 1993, when the New York Times Company acquired Affiliated Publications for $1.1 billion—the largest buyout in newspaper history. The merger created the fifth largest newspaper company in the United States, with a combined daily circulation of 2.5 million and $2.2 billion in annual revenue. The deal also ensured the *Globe* editorial autonomy for at least five years, thus preserving the Taylor's control for the time being. All in all, the arrangement was widely viewed as a positive move for both parties.

The 1990s brought new challenges for the newspaper industry in general. The most important of these was the increasing influence and accessibility of the Internet, which had begun to make inroads into the traditional domains of print products. The *Globe* addressed this situation in 1995 by launching Boston.com, a Web site that eventually became the most used regional newspaper site in the United States. However, the Internet's impact on the newspaper business was destined to become greater still in the next century. The end of the decade also saw transition more specific and personal to the *Globe* and its staff when Benjamin B. Taylor was replaced in 1999 by Richard H. Gilman as the paper's publisher, thus ending five generations of Taylor leadership.

Despite the many crucial changes of the 1990s, the *Globe* continued to perform well financially and professionally. Its daily circulation remained around 500,000 and Sunday's circulation held steady at approximately 800,000, just as they had been in Winship's time. Three more Pulitzer Prizes were won in 1995, 1996, and 1997, bringing the total to 15. In 1999 the *Worcester Telegram & Gazette* was purchased by the New York Times Company to create (with the *Globe* and Boston.com) the New England Media Group. There was controversy as well, most notably plagiarism scandals involving two different reporters in 1998. Regardless, the *Globe* was still indisputably the dominant paper in its region and one of the top-ranked in the country. Troubled times, however, lay ahead.

INDUSTRY IN CRISIS

In the early years of the 21st century, the *Globe*'s reputation and viability continued to thrive. Its newsroom was staffed by 550 people in 2000, making it one of the largest in the country, and it continued to produce award-winning journalism. The paper picked up two more Pulitzers in 2001 and 2003. The latter was for a series of articles, published beginning in January 2002, that exposed a long-term pattern of sexual abuse within the Roman Catholic Church and the cover-up that was maintained by church officials. The resulting firestorm culminated with the resignation of Cardinal Bernard Law and a comprehensive set of changes enacted within the church. Hailed as an example of great journalism that which truly affects people's lives and makes the world a better place, it was also a fine illustration of the expense involved in getting first-rate investigative reporting into print. Thomas F. Mulvoy, Jr., of the *Dorchester Reporter* quoted some remarks of Martin Baron, the *Globe* editor, on the subject from an address to students at the University of Oregon: "It required eight months of reporting and major litigation before a single word appeared in print. Another year of reporting by a team of eight staffers resulted in the publication of some 1,000 stories. The overall cost of this effort was probably more than $1 million in staff salaries, and tens of thousands of dollars in legal costs." However, the time of newspapers' ability to subsidize such efforts while remaining profitable was on the wane.

By 2008 circulation and revenue had suffered deep declines throughout the newspaper industry. The Internet was largely responsible for both phenomena because people were increasingly receiving their news online and were thus less likely to subscribe to physical papers. In addition, Web sites, such as Craigslist, were offering free classified advertising, which made potential advertisers disinclined to pay for the service. For example, in March 18 of the top 20 newspapers posted circulation declines for the previous six-month period. While visits to and advertising on newspaper Web sites had risen during the same time, it was not enough to offset the drop in print advertising revenues. Exacerbated by the global economic downturn that began in 2007, the overall picture in 2009 was even worse, resulting in lay-offs, wage reductions, and unpaid furloughs at major papers, such as the *Miami Herald* and the *Cleveland Plain Dealer,* and the outright closure of smaller dailies, such as the *Rocky Mountain News* and the *Seattle Post-Intelligencer*. The newspaper business was in trouble, and the *Boston Globe* was at particular risk.

The *Globe* had an operating loss of $50 million in 2008 and a projected loss of $85 million in 2009. Advertising revenue in 2008 for the New England Media Group (mainly consisting of the *Globe*) had fallen 33.7 percent from its 2004 level, compared to 21.5 percent for the entire industry. Weekday circulation in 2009 was down to 302,638, a 33.1 percent drop from 2004. Wages had been frozen for many employees and the newsroom count had been trimmed to 330, but the paper continued to lose money. In April 2009 the situation had become so serious that the New York Times Company, which was experiencing losses of its own, threatened to close the paper, but last-minute concessions from its unions to save $20 million a year allowed it to remain in operation, at least for the short term. Prospects for the long term, however, still looked bleak.

The survival of the *Globe* depended on a variety of circumstances, including the creativity of its management, the forbearance of its parent company, and an improvement in the overall economic climate. Its reporting continued to win awards, including three more Pulitzers in 2005, 2007, and 2008, and it was still the number one paper in the seventh largest media market in the United States. Its online audience was up to 5.2 million unique visitors per month in 2008, an increase of 21 percent from the previous year. These statistics rendered Boston.com the most used Web site of its kind in the country and suggested the possibility of only having an online publication, as other newspapers, such as the *Christian Science Monitor*, had done. There were also rumors of a potential sale, although the New York Times Company could not hope to recoup but a fraction of its record 1993 investment. Another cost-cutting possibility was a reduction in the number of days the paper would be published. In sum, a major shift was almost guaranteed. Even more certain, however, was that the absence of the venerable *Boston Globe* would leave an irreparable hole in the fabric of the newspaper industry.

Margaret L. Moser

PRINCIPAL SUBSIDIARIES

Retail Sales Inc.; Globe Direct; Boston.com.

PRINCIPAL COMPETITORS

Boston Herald; Yahoo! News; CNN.com; Craigslist.

FURTHER READING

Bernstein, Theodore M., "Newspaper Story," *New York Times*, February 27, 1972, p. BR35.

"Big Papers' Circulation Falls," Boston.com, April 29, 2008, http://www.boston.com/business/articles/2008/04/29/big_papers_circulation_falls/.

"Boston Globe," Omniglot, 2009, http://www.omniglot.com/onlineinfo/bost/the-boston-globe.html.

"Boston Globe March Ad Revenue Plunges," *Boston Business Journal*, April 17, 2008.

"Boston Globe's Drawn-out Death," *Europe Intelligence Wire*, April 7, 2009.

"Boston Globe Wins Pulitzer Prize," *News Hour*, April 8, 2003, http://www.pbs.org/newshour/media/media_watch/jan-june03/pulitzerglobe_4-8.html.

Butterfield, Fox, "The Globe's Own Family Is a Story Unto Itself," *New York Times*, June 13, 1993.

"Charles H. Taylor, Boston Editor, Dies," *New York Times*, June 23, 1921, p. 14.

Cohan, Peter, "How to Save the Boston Globe," *Boston Globe*, April 5, 2009.

"Company Overview," *BusinessWeek*, 2009, http://investing.businessweek.com/research/stocks/private/snapshot.asp?privcapId=7755943.

Criner, Kathleen, and Jane Wilson, "On the Cutting Edge," *Editor & Publisher*, November 25, 1995, p. 5.

Garneau, George, "Shareholders OK New York Times, Boston Globe Deal," *Editor & Publisher*, October 2, 1993, p. 21.

Henry, William A., III, "Twilight and Dawn on the Globe," *Time*, November 5, 1984, p. 78.

Kelly, James, and Robert Ajemian, "A Matter of Newsroom Style," *Time*, March 31, 1986, p. 59.

Liebman, Hanna, "New York Times Co. Buys Boston Globe for $1.1B in Biggest-Ever Newspaper Buy," *MediaWeek*, June 14, 1993, p. 3.

Lyons, Louis M., *Newspaper Story: One Hundred Years of the Boston Globe*, Cambridge, MA: Belknap Press of the Harvard University Press, 1971.

Marks, Alexandra, and Bridget Huber, "Boston Globe Avoids Shutdown—at Least for Now," *Christian Science Monitor*, May 4, 2009, http://www.csmonitor.com/2009/0505/p02s01-ussc.html.

Martin, Douglas, "Thomas Winship, Ex-editor of Boston Globe, Dies at 81," *New York Times*, March 15, 2002.

McGrory, Mary, "The Crusader Who Put the Boston Globe on the Map," *Washington Post*, March 15, 2002, p. C1.

Mulvoy, Thomas F., Jr., "Can the Globe Survive Online Only? Outlook Is Dicey," *Dorchester Reporter*, April 8, 2009.

O'Brien, Sinead, "For Barnicle, One Controversy Too Many," *American Journalism Review*, September 1998.

Pérez-Peña, Richard, "After Months of Tension, Globe Votes on Cuts," *New York Times*, June 7, 2009.

———, "Deal Reached to Keep Boston Globe in Print," *New York Times*, May 6, 2009.

Saba, Jennifer, "'Boston Globe' Revenue off 37%," Fitz & Jen, April 9, 2009, http://www.fitzandjen.com/2009/04/boston-globe-revenue-off-37.html.

"Two Major Boston Globe Unions Agree to Cuts," Boston.com, May 27, 2009, http://www.boston.com/news/local/massachusetts/articles/2009/05/27/two_major_boston_globe_unions_agree_to_cuts/.

THE HABITAT COMPANY
Management Makes The Difference®

The Habitat Company LLC

350 West Hubbard Street
Chicago, Illinois 60654
U.S.A.
Telephone: (312) 527-5400
Fax: (312) 527-7440
Web site: http://www.habitat.com/

Private Company
Founded: 1971
Incorporated: 1971
Employees: 1,000
Sales: More than $200 million (2008 est.)
NAICS: 531210 Offices of Real Estate Agents and Brokers; 531311 Residential Property Managers; 531390 Other Activities Related to Real Estate

■ ■ ■

The Habitat Company LLC is one of the largest property managers and real estate developers in the American Midwest. A private real estate firm that manages more than 20,000 residential apartments, condominiums, and townhomes, Habitat also manages commercial and recreational properties. The company offers asset and property management for many types of housing, including rental and condominium units, public housing, and housing for seniors and students. Habitat has also developed or redeveloped 17,000 new units of housing ranging from market-rate units to public housing. In its role as a developer of public housing, the company focuses on developing and managing properties that offer both market-priced apartments and low-income units located within a single building or development.

The company lists its core values as mutual respect, honesty and integrity, open communication and teamwork, accountability, and high customer and employee satisfaction. An employee-owned company, Habitat staffs property managers, lawyers, accountants, and architects. The company considers itself equally responsible to residents, owners, and investors, a triangulated loyalty that has been at times difficult to maintain yet is the cornerstone of the company's ethos. Habitat has won numerous accolades and awards from all segments of the housing industry government-run programs to luxury condo developments and is a major force in midwestern real estate. The company's unusual spectrum of commitments seems to be working, Habitat manages more than $2.5 billion worth of property and has annual revenues of more than $200 million.

EARLY SUCCESS IN HOUSING

Habitat's founder, Daniel E. Levin, has been the company's chairman since its inception. A graduate of the law school at the University of Chicago, Levin had been a developer of real estate in Chicago and other parts of the United States since 1957 and is considered to be responsible for the bulk of Habitat's programs and methods. "No development is only an investment in real estate," reads a statement by Levin that appears on the company's promotional materials. "It is also an investment in the future of the community and the lives of the people who live and work there."

COMPANY PERSPECTIVES

Our mission is to be the innovative leader in the development and management of a broad range of housing and real estate-related facilities and services. Guided by our Core Values and with a firm belief that our people make the difference, we strive for excellence every day.

When we founded The Habitat Company in 1971, we challenged ourselves to create a real estate company with the character and quality that would successfully meet the needs of Chicago's diverse communities, while also meeting the long-term financial objectives of our investors.

We look forward to continuing to meet the challenges we set with the single principle that guides each Habitat employee and has become an integral part of each endeavor—"Management Makes The Difference."

In its most public role in the housing industry, Habitat has developed and redeveloped more than 17,000 residential units in and around Chicago. This kind of development is the foundation of the company, which was founded following Levin's spectacular success in the early 1960s developing Chicago's Southland Commons, a 28-acre urban renewal, mixed-income project. Having established its commitment to the city, Habitat in 1987 was appointed "receiver" (or, granted authority) for all new family public housing for the Chicago Housing Authority (CHA). With the CHA, the company would develop 5,500 mixed-income units and constructed over 2,000 "scattered-site" (economically and racially integrated) units located in neighborhoods all around Chicago.

Habitat also developed numerous luxury properties throughout the 1970s and 1980s. Two examples of upscale properties built in the 1970s included Newberry Plaza and Elm Street Plaza. Newberry Plaza, built in 1973, was notable for being the first townhome-style development in which the residences were built above the structure's pedestal—above street level. At the time, Newberry Plaza was the sixth-tallest residential building in the world and the tallest building in the north part of Chicago. In 1976 the company built Elm Street Plaza, a luxury high-rise set in a historic brownstone neighborhood in Chicago. The building included amenities like sundecks and heated pools, and it offered, according to

company materials, an upscale resident the chance to "define urban living in your own way." In the 1980s, when the CHA began demolishing the city's housing projects, residents on public assistance, especially those from the notoriously troubled Cabrini Houses, another Habitat-managed property, were allowed to move into Elm Street Plaza in a move that was considered another example of Habitat's commitment to mixed-income housing.

PROMINENT LEADERSHIP

The highest-profile executive at Habitat for many years was Valerie Jarrett. A lawyer with a background in city government, Jarrett joined Habitat as an executive vice-president in 1995 and would be appointed CEO in 2007. Jarrett left the company in February 2009 to become the White House senior adviser to President Barack Obama, where her many job titles included Assistant to the President for Intergovernmental Relations, public liaison, and chair of the White House Council on Women and Girls.

Jarrett was Chicago public-housing royalty. Her grandfather was Robert Taylor, the first chairman of the CHA, a post he held from 1943 to 1950. "He believed in what we're doing today, which is why I do this," Jarrett told the *Chicago Tribune* in July 2008. She was speaking of Taylor's belief that mixed-income populations should be integrated in community developments, preferably low-rise buildings situated within existing neighborhoods. Taylor actually resigned his post over this issue, and the CHA went on to build dozens of isolated high-rise complexes, one of which they named after him.

The Robert Taylor Homes were built in 1962, after Taylor's death, and housed as many as 27,000 people in 28 16-story buildings. The complex had a long history of crime and other gang activity and eventually would be demolished by the city in 2008. Legends South, a low-rise, mixed-income community of exactly the type Taylor had envisioned was planned to replace it. Habitat was slated to direct the development.

Jarrett told *Affordable Housing Finance*, referencing an earlier legal decision mandating desegregation of city housing. "The court order requires that we build sustainable communities that are economically integrated and that will lead to racial integration as well. That's how my grandfather's vision will be realized."

LONG INVOLVEMENT WITH CHICAGO PUBLIC HOUSING

Robert Taylor Homes/Legends South was part of the Plan for Transformation, an enormous endeavor launched by the CHA in 2000 to redevelop 25,000

KEY DATES

1971: The Habitat Company is founded by Daniel Levin.

1973: Wheaton Center, Newberry Plaza, and Lincoln Park Terrace properties are opened.

1976: Elm Street Plaza property is opened.

1980: Columbus Plaza and Huron Plaza are opened; Lincoln Park Terrace is converted to condominiums.

1983: 530 Lakeshore Drive and Pines of Edgewater Phases I and II properties are opened.

1987: The Habitat Company is appointed receiver of the Scattered Site Housing Program for the Chicago Housing Authority.

1991: Cityfront Place property is opened.

1994: Habitat acquires Heritage House for Section 42 rehabilitation.

1998: South Commons property is converted to condominiums.

2000: Chicago's Plan for Transformation is inaugurated.

2001: Habitat has more than 23,000 units under its management.

2004: Habitat receives $74 million in federal grants to demolish and revitalize "severely distressed public housing."

2007: Valerie Jarrett is appointed CEO.

2008: Habitat is named program manager by the Detroit Housing Commission to redevelop public housing units.

units of Chicago's public housing. The Habitat Company was appointed by the CHA to help plan the projects and manage spending. The effort was an example of Habitat's long and complicated involvement with public housing in Chicago, with the company being the most visible for-profit company to play a role in the city's efforts to build quality housing for low-income people.

In 1987 a U.S. district court judge appointed Habitat as CHA's receiver, generally to oversee the agency's projects and specifically to rectify charges that the CHA was practicing segregation of low-income African-American families. The agency had been taken to court over this issue in 1966 by Dorothy Gautreaux and other residents of CHA public housing. In 1981 the resulting Gautreaux consent decree stated that the U.S. Department of Housing and Urban Development

(HUD) would situate public housing families—most of them African American—in areas that were either less than 30 percent African American or in neighborhoods experiencing "revitalization," so that African Americans would not be excluded from newly improving neighborhoods.

Habitat, however, has been criticized for perpetuating the very problems it was charged to improve. In 1998 Habitat blocked an agreement between residents and the CHA regarding redevelopment of the enormous Cabrini Green public housing project in Chicago. The agreement would have designated residents as "co-developers," giving them a vote and veto power in important decisions. Residents wanted to ensure that the number of low-income units stayed the same or increased during redevelopment and accused Habitat of plans to eliminate a large number of such units. Levin stated that, as the court's appointed receiver, Habitat was mandated to build desegregated communities. "We were required by the court to do a job," Levin told Brian Rogal in the *Chicago Reporter*, "and this is what we perceive as doing the job." He said the residents' plan actually violated the Gautreaux decision by including too many low-income units, thus leading to segregation. In May 1999 the Cabrini Green conflict would become moot when HUD took CHA out of receivership and shifted responsibility to Mayor Richard Daley. Chicago then enacted one of the most dramatic episodes in public housing history by demolishing 17,000 low-income apartments, primarily in high-rise developments including Cabrini Green.

Immediately following the announcement of the Plan for Transformation in 2000, which was directed by Habitat in conjunction with the CHA and other developers—and which essentially sought to attract middle-income residents to public housing sites and thereby integrate the communities—Habitat announced its calculations of what ratios were optimal for long-term success. The new numbers would limit the proportion of low-income housing that would still exist in those developments to one-third of the total. The ratio was not popular with everyone. "If you had more than a third, the sky would fall. Heaven and earth would not move [Habitat and the CHA] from that position," complained Richard Wheelock, as quoted by Jason Grotto and Laurie Cohen in the *Chicago Tribune*. Wheelock was an attorney for the Legal Assistance Foundation, an agency that would sue the CHA over this issue in 2004. In defense of Habitat's strategy, Jarrett was quoted by Grotto and Cohen as saying: "We looked for balance, with the goal being a healthy community and we were extremely cognizant and mindful of not wanting to recreate horizontally what [the Daley administration] had torn down vertically."

CRITICISM CONTINUED

Habitat has also been accused of maintaining tight control of the Cabrini Green redevelopment and of other projects in order to maximize company profit. In his 1999 story in the *Chicago Reporter*, Brian Rogal reported that Habitat's management of the Cabrini Green project would net the company roughly $3.8 million. Rogal also reported that Habitat's total payouts from HUD for CHA-related projects had at that time reached $17.3 million. Habitat later received a tremendous amount of federal funding from HUD in 2004 and 2005 as well. Over those two years, the company was reported to have received $74 million in federal grants, most of it earmarked for the demolition and redevelopment of public housing.

Habitat's success record in creating the socio-economically integrated housing it espouses was also mixed. According to Rogal in 1999, 53 percent of the scattered-site housing created by Habitat for African-American residents had been in neighborhoods with populations that were at least 60 percent Latino (rather than white). Furthermore, many black residents of demolished housing projects, such as Cabrini Green, were dissatisfied with Habitat's involvement in their communities. "Habitat is trying to eat up everything in this area, and wants no partnership with the residents," Rogal quoted Gwendolyn Merritt, then vice-president of It's Time for a Change Resident Management Corp., which managed 15 Cabrini buildings before their demolition.

Habitat has stood by its development strategies, defending the Plan for Transformation and in particular its own focus on integrating residents of varying incomes. "Progress has been dramatic and consistent," Jarrett told Andre F. Shashaty in *Affordable Housing Finance* in 2008. Habitat believed that its ratios create an ideal model for urban communities in which all parties—owners, investors, and residents—will "have a place at the table." Jarrett pointed out the lower rates of foreclosure occurring in redeveloped public housing, and she stated that all measures of community stability, including crime rates, rising incomes, and school performance, prove the efficacy of mixed-income housing. According to CHA CEO Lewis A. Jordan, as quoted by Shashaty, Habitat is doing an exceptional job: "The developments are doing exactly what they were intended to do: integrating families, improving lives, and generating renewal in the surrounding communities."

Habitat's association with the CHA continued, but has lessened over time. As of 2009 Habitat managed 12 mixed-income programs in Chicago funded by grants and other public housing funds.

Also by 2009 Habitat had expanded into the Detroit housing market. The company was appointed program manager by the Detroit Housing Commission in 2008 to manage the redevelopment of three public housing complexes with more than 1,300 units. Habitat also managed market-rate buildings in Detroit: the apartment and condo units of Lafayette Pavilion and Lafayette Towers, both designed by architect Mies van der Rohe, that offered upscale amenities, city views of downtown Detroit, and riverfront access. True to form, controversy followed Habitat as community residents and business leaders stopped the company from demolishing a local shopping mall called the Shops at Lafayette Park, also designed by van der Rohe, during Habitat's early involvement with the site.

FOCUSED ON DEVELOPMENT
AND MANAGEMENT

Despite the political hullabaloo involved in city housing, Habitat in 2009 continued to focus on its primary business of private property development and management. The company offers various services to developers, owners, and renters, including asset management, property management, and corporate apartment rentals. Habitat offers asset management services, such as research and analysis of a client's investment goals. In addition, the company will monitor supply-and-demand in the client's markets and submarkets and try to maximize profit by selling or repositioning assets. Habitat also promises to optimize the day-to-day performance of properties under its management and offers long-term strategic capital investment.

The company considers property management the backbone of the company, and, according to company materials, it strives to provide a maximal return on its investors' monies through "asset appreciation, capital reinvestments, and value enhancement." As incentives to property owners and developers to use Habitat as their management provider, the company offers such benefits as bulk purchasing power, a natural gas program, emergency planning, engineering and architectural assistance, real estate tax reduction coordination, health club and fitness center management and services, refinancing services, and construction services. As property managers, Habitat also offers special services to tenants, such as a 30-day guarantee allowing a tenant to cancel a lease agreement up to 30 days after moving in; a move-in maintenance coupon providing help with moving boxes or setting up furniture; a building transfer program allowing residents to move from one Habitat-managed building to another with no lease-breakage fees; and several other perks.

As of mid-2009 Habitat also managed more than 500 corporate apartment rentals in and around Chicago under the name "Corporate Suites." These units are intended for business travelers staying a minimum of 30 days in the area. The company has won numerous awards for this division, including nine CAMME (Chicagoland Apartment Marketing and Management Excellence) Awards in the category of best furnished apartments in Chicago.

Melanie Bush

PRINCIPAL COMPETITORS

Brinshore Development LLC.

FURTHER READING

Gallun, Alby, "Habitat Promotes Veteran to CEO," *Chicago Real Estate Daily*, February 5, 2009.

Grotto, Jason, and Laurie Cohen, "Obama Adviser Shapes City Housing Policy," *Chicago Tribune*, July 5, 2008.

Kaneya, Rui, and Danielle Gordon, "Finding Sites for New Public Housing No Easy Task," *Chicago Reporter*, March 1998.

Kantor, Jodi, "The New Team: Valerie Jarrett," *New York Times*, November 5, 2008.

Rogal, Brian, "The Habitat Company: Private Firm Keeps Tight Grip on Public Housing," *Chicago Reporter*, November 1999.

Shashaty, Andre F., "Valerie Jarrett's Struggle," *Affordable Housing Finance*, November 2008.

Habitat for Humanity International, Inc.

121 Habitat Street
Americus, Georgia 31709-3498
U.S.A.
Telephone: (229) 924-6935
Toll Free: (800) 422-4828
Fax: (229) 928-8811
Web site: http://www.habitat.org

Nonprofit Company
Founded: 1976
Employees: 1,072
Operating Revenues: $1.5 billion (2007 est.)
NAICS: 233210 Single Family Housing Construction;
813219 Other Grantmaking and Giving Services

■ ■ ■

Habitat for Humanity International, Inc. (HFHI), is a world service organization providing affordable homes with interest-free mortgages to families in need. Founded by Millard and Linda Fuller, HFHI seeks to eliminate homelessness from the world and make decent housing a matter of conscience and action. A prodigious list of sponsors and volunteers (including such luminaries as Jimmy Carter, Jerry Falwell, Louis Gossett Jr., Jack Kemp, Newt Gingrich, and Oprah Winfrey) have transformed many homeless families into proud homeowners and lifelong Habitat volunteers.

FROM LESS TO MORE: 1920S–50S

Millard Fuller was born in Chambers County in eastern Alabama, the son of poor sharecroppers. His mother died when he was three years old, and he was raised by his father. Religion was a big part of Fuller family life, with Millard's father working as the deacon of the local church in addition to his duties as farmer, grocer, and parent. From a very young age, Millard worked alongside his father in their country store, contributing to the family's income. He raised pigs, trapped minnows, and, as he grew older, sought various ways to earn money, from trading used cars to selling fireworks. He put himself through college at Auburn University, where he was the youngest director of the Junior Achievement program in the nation. He then attended the University of Alabama Law School.

As an aspiring young businessman, Fuller allied himself with another like-minded law student, Morris Dees, who also wanted to become a successful entrepreneur. Through hard work and with acuity beyond their years, the two young men established a number of business enterprises, eventually buying real estate and renovating apartments with help from Millard's father, who mortgaged the family farm to give his son funds. In his last year of law school, Fuller married his sweetheart, Linda.

After passing the bar, Fuller and Dees set out to make money. Among their endeavors was publishing regional and specialty cookbooks (*Favorite Recipes of American Home Economics Teachers, Favorite Recipes of New England, Favorite Recipes of the Deep South, Favorite Recipes of the Lions Clubs: A Lion in the Kitchen,* and many more), in which they had discovered a very lucrative market. The two also founded a law firm in Montgomery, Alabama, and quickly earned a good reputation and had growing client base. Before his 30th

COMPANY PERSPECTIVES

Habitat for Humanity International brings families and communities in need together with volunteers and resources to build decent, affordable housing.

birthday, Millard Fuller was a successful attorney and self-made millionaire.

FROM MORE TO LESS: LATE 1960S–70S

As many before him had learned, Fuller found that money could not buy happiness. He became obsessed with making more and more money, which left little time for Linda and the children, who had all the trappings of wealth but virtually no husband or father. Fuller was so busy that he and Linda eventually conducted church services in their living room, because it was more convenient and less time-consuming. Fuller's chronic absences endangered his marriage, and Linda flew to New York City with the children for marriage counseling. Fuller, in deteriorating health, was not ready to give up on his family and followed them to New York. "I could visualize myself as a lonely person with no family and a pile of money. That's cold comfort," Fuller later told Kelly Starling of *Ebony* magazine in 1997.

In a cab ride after a counseling session, Fuller realized that the root of his marital problems was money, and he decided to get rid of it all. Linda was in complete agreement, although some family members and friends tried to dissuade them. Undeterred, Fuller sold his half of the Montgomery law firm, as well as his stake in the publishing company. The Fullers sold their belongings and then gave more than $1 million to various Christian charities and educational funds. They prepared to live out their faith by doing God's work.

On a trip to Atlanta, Fuller met Clarence Jordan, who ran an interracial Christian commune called Koinonia Farm near Americus, Georgia. Although many in Sumpter County, Georgia, considered Koinonia Farm to be a radical, cult-like movement, the Fullers found the community comforting and moved in with their four children. There, near the end of the 1960s, Millard, Linda, Clarence, and others decided to build affordable housing in the area for lower income families. One of the earliest recipients of their homebuilding plan was Joseph "Bo" Johnson, who had saved his money to buy a parcel of land with hopes of building a home for his

family. He achieved the first part of his dream and became a property owner, but had nothing left to build even the simplest house. Fuller met Johnson and wanted to help; he was also a firm believer in the Biblical tenet that one should not earn interest or make a profit from the less fortunate. "You know it's interesting that the world's three great monotheistic religions—Islam, Judaism and Christianity—all teach in their Scriptures not to charge interest to the poor. But in the Western world we've largely taken that Scriptural idea and turned it upside down," Fuller explained to William Olcott of *Fund Raising Management* in October 1994. "We give the prime lending rate to the richest people and charge the highest interest to the poorest."

After completing Johnson's house and several others in Sumpter County, the Fuller family moved to Zaire (now the Democratic Republic of the Congo) in 1973 with volunteers from the Disciples of Christ Christian Church to construct housing. The home-building project was a success, just as it had been in Georgia, and the Fullers returned to the United States after three years with a more formalized plan to provide housing for those in need. By instituting a "biblical" finance plan (according to the "economics of Jesus"), the Fullers and a group of dedicated volunteers would build low-cost houses with interest-free financing everywhere, eradicating substandard housing. The organization formed in 1976 to oversee and carry out these aspirations was called Habitat for Humanity.

THE ECONOMICS OF JESUS: 1980S

After Habitat had been in the business of building homes for a few years, Fuller wrote about his vision. The resulting 192-page *Love in the Mortar Joints: The Story of Habitat for Humanity*, published by New Win Publishing in August 1980, brought notice to the growing organization. Habitat gained still greater notice in the group's eighth year, when Fuller persuaded a fellow Baptist church member, former U.S. president and avid carpenter Jimmy Carter, and his wife, Rosalynn, to join the effort. They soon set up the Jimmy Carter Work Project, in which they traveled to a new location every year to construct housing. The Carters' involvement was a tremendous boon for the organization, raising awareness of HFHI's mission and methods. Carter called Fuller "an inspiration," and the feeling was mutual.

Fuller's second book, *No More Shacks! The Daring Vision of Habitat for Humanity*, was published in July 1986, followed in 1990 by a treatise called *Restrictive Housing Regulation Increases Problems* and a collaboration with Linda titled *The Excitement Is Building: How Habitat for Humanity Is Putting Roofs over Heads and*

KEY DATES

1976: Nonprofit is founded by Millard and Linda Fuller.
1981: Habitat constructs its 10,000th home.
1983: Habitat completes its 20,000th home.
1984: Former U.S. president Jimmy Carter joins Habitat.
1994: Fullers receive the Harry S. Truman Public Service Award.
1996: Millard Fuller receives the Presidential Medal of Freedom.
1997: Habitat builds its 60,000th home, operates in 54 countries, and is the fourth-largest home builder in the world.
1999: Millard Fuller is named one of the most influential home builders in the 20th century by *Builder* magazine.
2000: Habitat, operating in 65 countries, builds its 100,000th home.
2004: Habitat reaches its goal of building in 100 countries.
2005: Habitat constructs its 200,000th home, providing shelter for one million people; Fuller is fired by Habitat board of directors.
2008: Habitat is named the 14th largest home builder in the United States.
2009: Millard Fuller dies at 74.

Hope in Hearts. Fuller's writings served not only as a means to spread the word about Habitat, but had also become a valuable source of funds. In 1992 he published the first of a series of gift books, *A Christmas Housewarming*, with a foreword by Carter.

In the early 1990s Habitat-built homes generally cost between $35,000 and $42,000 to construct in the United States (or as little as $500 in undeveloped countries), usually on donated or bargain-priced land parcels. Local businesses often provided basic building materials free of charge. Fuller's volunteers, from all religious backgrounds, worked tirelessly together toward their goal. As Fuller explained to D'Arcy Jenish of *Maclean's* magazine in August 1993, "We use the philosophy of the hammer. We may disagree with one another theologically or philosophically, but we can all wield the hammer as an expression of love." Although Habitat was clearly a Christian organization, Fuller stressed, "We are non-denominational and non-doctrinal. We welcome support from whoever wants to

give it and we do in fact have support from a broad segment of this country."

For their part, potential homeowners were required to lend a hand in the construction of their own homes as well as those of others, investing between 200 and 500 hours of what Habitat referred to as "sweat equity." In addition, future owners provided a small down payment, which HFHI pooled in a revolving fund and put toward the building of more homes.

ONWARD CHRISTIAN SOLDIERS: 1993–97

By 1993 HFHI was constructing an average of two dozen homes per day. The fact that Habitat had already built 20,000 homes in 40 countries simply was not enough. Fuller focused his entrepreneurial drive on expanding the reach of HFHI, which was already the 17th largest home builder in the United States according to *Builder* magazine, but Fuller wanted Habitat to rise to the top slot within three years. He hoped that HFHI would construct more than 45,000 houses annually, which came to more than 123 homes every day.

Accolades for Habitat came in 1994 when the Direct Marketing Association (DMA) named the organization the Non-Profit Organization of the Year. The Fullers later received the Harry S. Truman Public Service Award. By the end of the year, HFHI had constructed more than 40,000 homes in all 50 U.S. states and in 41 countries worldwide, and the organization and its affiliates had brought in more than $145 million in support and contributions. Habitat also managed a mailing list of more than one million names, which grew with increased exposure, such as when Fuller was named Builder of the Year by *Professional Builder* magazine in 1995. Later that year HFHI issued its second gift book, *Home for the Holidays: Stories and Art Created for the Benefit of Habitat for Humanity*.

Linda Fuller, meanwhile, in addition to building homes and getting women around the world involved in Habitat with WATCH (Women Accepting the Challenge of Housing), had begun a publishing project of her own. In 1993 she debuted the first in a series of cookbooks called *Partners in the Kitchen*, with *From Our House to Yours*, followed by *Home Sweet Habitat* (1995) and *Simple, Decent Cooking* (1997). The cookbooks were a successful fundraising tool for the organization, selling more than 100,000 copies. Millard Fuller also had continued to write, publishing *The Theology of the Hammer* (1994), *A Simple, Decent Place to Live: The Building Realization of Habitat for Humanity* (1995), and *Bokotola* (1997).

By 1997 Habitat had become the fourth-largest home builder in the world and was the nation's number one nonprofit home builder. There were 60,000 HFHI homes in 54 countries, with two-fifths of the organization's construction projects taking place outside the United States. Working with the Tucson Urban League and a grant from the National Urban Consortium, HFHI began constructing homes of the future using straw bales, replacing up to 13 percent of traditional wood building materials. Straw, it seems, has incredible insulating powers, and the Habitat homes with a straw component cost residents as much as 75 percent less to heat and cool. While Habitat did accept grants from a number of groups, including the federal government (including the previous year's $25 million grant from the Department of Housing and Urban Development), as a rule HFHI did not receive government funds, preferring to remain autonomous and also to maintain the separation of church and state. However, the 1996 federal grant marked 20 years of good deeds for Habitat, and Fuller was recognized by President Bill Clinton with the Presidential Medal of Freedom (the highest civilian award in the country). Clinton called HFHI "the most successful continuous community service project in the history of the United States."

DISASTER RELIEF: 1998–2000

Although not a disaster relief organization like the Red Cross, Habitat became involved in such operations in the late 1990s. After a tornado in Alabama and devastation caused by two hurricanes (Georges in September and Mitch in October 1998), HFHI sought donations to help victims of the catastrophes. Hoping to raise some $2 million in funds after Hurricane Mitch hit Central America, HFHI was buoyed by donations totaling $6 million and immediately began building homes for the many left homeless by the deadly storm. To better respond to natural disasters and coordinate volunteer efforts, Habitat created a Disaster Response Office.

Habitat-built homes had withstood other natural disasters such as Hurricane Andrew, the Los Angeles earthquake, and flooding in southern Georgia. When asked why these houses had survived when others had not, Fuller said that he believed God was keeping an eye on these homes because they had been built out of love and on a firm foundation of faith. While he was quick to point out, "I don't believe that only bad things happen to bad people and only good things happen to good people," his pride in Habitat's work was evident. "I was down there right after the hurricane and it did look like our houses were built after the hurricane," he told *Fund Raising Management's* Olcott. "It was amazing."

By the end of the 20th century, Habitat had built or renovated nearly 80,000 homes around the globe and made a profound difference in the lives of the more than 400,000 people who lived in them. Fuller was the recipient of the Jefferson Award from the American Institute of Public Service for his work on behalf of the disadvantaged, while *Builder* magazine named him one of the 20th century's most influential home builders. With nearly 1.3 million worldwide donors in 1999, and funds raised from its publishing ventures (including Fuller's new tome, *More Than Houses: How Habitat for Humanity Is Transforming Lives and Neighborhoods*), Habitat brought in more than $121.1 million in support for 1999. The next year, Jerome P. Raggett's exhaustive study of the ecumenical organization, *Habitat for Humanity: Building Private Homes, Building Public Religion*, was published by Temple University Press.

2001–09: EXPANSION, SCANDAL, AND CHANGE

HFHI continued to expand in the new century, with more houses being built in more countries each year than the year prior. HFHI expanded its nine regional U.S. offices to accommodate more than 1,600 affiliates nationally and partnered with the National Alliance for the Mentally Ill to build affordable homes for individuals with chronic mental illness. HFHI also expanded its prison program, in which inmates voluntarily helped build HFHI homes in exchange for learning valuable building skills.

In 2005 scandal erupted when Fuller, who had been battling allegations that he sexually harassed a female employee on a business trip, was fired by the Board of Directors. The allegations were dismissed; however, according to the board, Fuller's outspoken comments about the case were disrupting the work of the charity. As reported by Jennifer C. Berkshire in *Chronicle of Philanthropy* in April 2008, Fuller proffered an alternative explanation for the firing, noting a growing rift between himself and the board about the direction of the organization. Fuller was intent on expanding HFHI's role as a missionary organization, establishing offices in every country and building as many homes as possible, but the board wanted to focus on building the strength of HFHI as a business, closing less successful branches and keeping closer tabs on the branding of Habitat.

Later in 2005 Fuller founded a rival charity, Building Habitat. HFHI sued because the name was so similar, and ultimately Fuller's new charity was renamed the Fuller Center for Housing. Over the next few years, the new charity quickly grew to have chapters in more than 25 countries.

Fuller was replaced in late 2005 with Jonathan Reckford, who had a diverse background as a pastor, chief executive officer of a homebuilding ministry in Georgia, and president of several Best Buy stores. Habitat continued to prosper despite hard economic times nationally. The organization capitalized on the green renovation movement and opened a chain of stores, Habitat ReStores, which collected donated building supplies, such as flooring, cabinetry, lighting and appliances left over from construction jobs, and sold them to the general public at a 50 to 75 percent discount from retail prices. All proceeds went toward the building of new Habitat homes. HFHI also bolstered its corporate partnerships and individual donations, focusing on securing gifts of $100,000 or more. Thrivent Financial for Lutherans, Capital One, Aimco, Whirlpool, and other companies made significant investments and donations of building materials. In the fiscal year ending in June 2007, HFHI estimated that its activities generated approximately $1.5 billion in revenue, including $700 million in contributions, gifts, and grants; $400 million in sales of homes; and $300 million in other types of support.

In 2009 Millard Fuller passed away at the age of 74. As the founder of HFHI, his legacy includes housing more than a million needy individuals and creating a hugely successful nonprofit with billions of dollars in donations and homes across the world. Said former President Jimmy Carter, "he was an inspiration to me, other members of our family, and an untold number of volunteers who worked side by side under his leadership."

Nelson Rhodes
Updated, Robert Jacobson

FURTHER READING

Baggett, Jerome P., *Habitat for Humanity: Building Private Homes, Building Public Religion*, Chicago: Temple University Press, 2000, 360 p.

Berkshire, Jennifer C., "A Parting of Ways," *Chronicle of Philanthropy*, April 3, 2008.

Fuller, Millard, *Bokotola*, Clinton, N.J.: New Win, 1997, 176 p.

———, *More Than Houses: How Habitat for Humanity Is Transforming Lives and Neighborhoods*, Nashville: Word Books, 1999.

———, *A Simple, Decent Place to Live: The Building Realization of Habitat for Humanity*, Nashville: Word Books, 1995.

———, *The Theology of the Hammer*, Macon, Ga.: Smyth & Helwys, 1994.

Fuller, Millard, and Linda Fuller, *The Excitement Is Building: How Habitat for Humanity Is Putting Roofs over Heads and Hope in Hearts*, Nashville: Word Books, 1990.

Fuller, Millard, and Diane Scott, *Love in the Mortar Joints: The Story of Habitat for Humanity*, Clinton, N.J.: New Win, 1980, 192 p.

———, and Diane Scott, *No More Shacks! The Daring Vision of Habitat for Humanity*, Nashville: Word Books, 1986, 220p.

Gaillard, Frye, *If I Were a Carpenter: Twenty Years of Habitat for Humanity*, Winston-Salem, N.C.: John F. Blair, 1996, 182 p.

Home for the Holidays: Stories and Art Created for the Benefit of Habitat for Humanity, Atlanta: Peachtree Publishers Ltd., 1995.

Home, Laura, "Building Straw Houses on a Firm Foundation: Habitat for Humanity Goes Low-Tech with Big Results," *Christianity Today*, February 3, 1997, p. 56.

Jenish, D'Arcy, "Carter the Carpenter," *Maclean's*, August 2, 1993, p. 38.

Martin, Douglas, "Millard Fuller, 74, Who Founded Habitat for Humanity, Is Dead," *New York Times*, Feb 4, 2009, p. A28.

Maudlin, Michael G., "God's Contractor (Habitat for Humanity's Millard Fuller)," *Christianity Today*, June 14, 1999, p. 44.

"Millard Fuller," *International Bulletin of Missionary Research*, April 2009, p. 75.

Olcott, William, "The Theology of the Hammer," *Fund Raising Management*, October 1994, p. 6.

O'Sullivan, Orla, "Blessed Are the Poor; Habitat Considers Its Home-building a Higher Calling," *ABA Banking Journal*, August 1997, p. 57.

Pope, Tom, "Spending More in a Down Economy," *The Nonprofit Times*, April 1, 2009, p. 1.

Purks, James, *Habitat for Humanity: Building Around the World*, Americus, Ga.: Habitat for Humanity International, 1991.

Rogers, Patrick, "Fire Fighters: Their Dream House Destroyed by Arson, a Family Gets Help from Determined Volunteer Builders," *People Weekly*, September 16, 1996, p. 191.

Starling, Kelly, "Habitat for Humanity: Interracial Organization Builds Houses and Dreams," *Ebony*, November 1997, p. 200.

Stelton, Gene, ed., *A Christmas Housewarming*, Atlanta: Peachtree Publishers, 1992, 206 p.

Thanks, Mom! A Collection of Stories and Artwork to Benefit Habitat for Humanity, Atlanta: Peachtree Publishers Ltd., 1999, 148 p.

Harley-Davidson, Inc.

3700 West Juneau Avenue
P.O. Box 653
Milwaukee, Wisconsin 53201-0653
U.S.A.
Telephone: (414) 343-4680
Toll Free: (877) 437-8625
Web site: http://www.harley-davidson.com

Public Company
Founded: 1903
Incorporated: 1907 as Harley-Davidson Motor Company; reincorporated 1981 as Harley-Davidson, Inc.
Employees: 9,200
Sales: $5.59 billion (2008)
Stock Exchanges: New York
Ticker Symbol: HOG
NAICS: 336991 Motorcycle, Bicycle, and Parts Manufacturing; 551112 Offices of Other Holding Companies

■ ■ ■

The largest motorcycle manufacturer in the United States, Harley-Davidson, Inc., has been designing heavyweight machines for bike enthusiasts for more than a century. It is well known for the loyalty its vehicles have inspired in generations of riders.

EARLY ORIGINS

The first Harley-Davidson motorcycle was built in Milwaukee, Wisconsin, still the location of the company's headquarters, about 1902. After William S. Harley and Arthur Davidson, working in a small shed, developed the bike and its three-horsepower engine, two of Davidson's brothers, William and Walter, joined the enterprise. The machine went through many refinements until 1903, when the men established the Harley-Davidson Motor Company and produced three units for sale.

Over the next several years both demand and production grew at a healthy rate, and in 1907 the founders formally incorporated the company and launched its first major advertising campaign. Two years later they introduced a revolutionary V-twin engine. A company standard for decades, the V-twin produced the low, deep rumble that would become identified as Harley-Davidson's signature sound. It also enabled riders to reach 60 miles per hour, a speed previously believed impossible. Such capabilities served to set the company's motorcycles apart from a crowded field; by 1911 there were at least 150 motorcycle manufacturers in the country.

GROWTH AND MILITARY DEMAND

The onset of World War I was a boon for Harley-Davidson. The motorcycle, already in wide use by the police, was increasingly adopted by the U.S. military, which would purchase no less than 20,000 Harley-Davidson motorcycles during the war. The company's durable, easily maintained machines proved especially useful along the Mexican border, a remote area then under threat from the forces of Mexican revolutionary Pancho Villa. Harsh field conditions prompted numer-

COMPANY PERSPECTIVES

■

We fulfill dreams through the experience of motorcycling, by providing to motorcyclists and to the general public an expanded line of motorcycles and branded products and services in selected market segments.

ous improvements. Upon resuming normal production at the end of the war, Harley-Davidson began incorporating those changes, including a distinctive "teardrop" gas tank and a front brake, into its new models. The innovations attracted widespread notice, particularly on the rapidly growing racing circuit. In 1921, a rider on a Harley-Davidson won the first race involving average speeds of more than 100 miles per hour.

Automobile maker Henry Ford's introduction of the assembly line, meanwhile, had a profound effect on the motorcycle industry. As cars became more affordable, workers and trades people, in particular, began switching to the larger vehicles. Those who remained loyal to motorcycles did so, increasingly, simply because they enjoyed riding. Significant markets remained, nevertheless, in the military, the police, and the U.S. Postal Service, and it was those "official" uses that enabled the company to survive the Great Depression. A strong network of local dealers and decent sales abroad also helped, as did the collapse of weaker competitors. By the 1940s Harley-Davidson and the Indian Motocycle Company were the only domestic manufacturers still in existence.

Military procurement during World War II proved as helpful to Harley-Davidson as it had been during World War I. In 1941 the company turned its entire manufacturing effort toward the military, shipping nearly 100,000 machines overseas. Its efforts earned several Army-Navy "E" awards, an honor bestowed upon companies that excelled at wartime production. Soldiers returning from service remembered the vehicles fondly, and the healthy postwar economy meant that many had money to spend on recreation. To meet burgeoning demand, the company purchased additional manufacturing capacity in 1947.

THE "SUPERBIKE" ERA: 1950S AND 1960S

With the shutdown of the Indian Motocycle Company in 1953, Harley-Davidson became the sole American

motorcycle manufacturer, a distinction it would hold for the next 46 years. Continuing to prove itself a design innovator, the company introduced its Sportster model in 1957, heralding the era of the all-powerful, throaty "superbikes." A motorcycle subculture had meanwhile emerged, one that society as a whole often struggled to understand. A pivotal moment came in 1953, with the release of the Marlon Brando film *The Wild One*, which depicted biker gangs on Harley-Davidsons as lawless renegades. The stereotype that grew out of this image remained a powerful one for many years, and the company had to adjust its marketing repeatedly to dispel it.

In 1965 Harley-Davidson's two founding families decided to offer shares to the public. That decision enabled the American Machine and Foundry Co. (AMF), a leisure-equipment manufacturer, to purchase the company four years later. The deal proved, at least initially, to be a good one for Harley-Davidson, which was then experiencing its first competition since Indian's closure. The financial resources and stability that AMF provided helped the company compete with Japanese motorcycle manufacturers, who had begun exporting their vehicles around the world.

PROBLEMS AND CORRECTIVE MEASURES: THE 1970S AND 1980S

Demand for motorcycles continued to grow through the early 1970s, and, in an effort to keep up, the company opened an assembly plant in York, Pennsylvania, in 1974. While engines would still be made in the Milwaukee facilities, the bikes themselves would be assembled in the new factory. Under Vaughn Beals, who became the company's head in 1975, Harley implemented a number of manufacturing improvements, which were becoming increasingly necessary as production grew. Those efforts added more than a thousand dollars to the cost of each bike, however, and the profit line suffered as a result. To compensate, AMF management began to agitate for greater production and greater sales, with the result that quality began to decline. As production standards dropped, there were chronic shortages of parts, and as many as 30 percent of the company's machines emerged from the assembly line in an incomplete state. Extra manpower was required to finish these machines, a task that sometimes fell to dealers.

These production problems, combined with strong competition from Japan, reduced sales dramatically. In 1969 Harley-Davidson had enjoyed an 80 percent share of the U.S. market for super-heavyweight machines—bikes with engines over 850 cubic centimeters (cc). Ten years later, just when Japan's Honda Motor Co. was

KEY DATES

1903: William S. Harley and Arthur Davidson sell their first motorcycle in Milwaukee, Wisconsin.
1907: Harley-Davidson Motor Company is incorporated.
1912: Company begins exporting motorcycles abroad.
1953: With the closure of competitor Indian Motorcycle Company, Harley-Davidson becomes the only U.S. motorcycle maker, a distinction it would retain until 1999.
1969: Company merges with the American Machine and Foundry Co. (AMF).
1981: Senior executives buy the company back from AMF and reincorporate it under the name Harley-Davidson, Inc.
1987: Company is listed on the New York Stock Exchange.
1998: Company completes its purchase of the Buell Motorcycle Company.
1998: Company opens a factory in Manaus, Brazil, its first facility outside the United States.
2003: More than 250,000 people gather in Wisconsin to celebrate the company's centennial.
2006: First dealership is established in mainland China.
2008: Harley-Davidson Museum opens in Milwaukee.

opening a plant in Marysville, Ohio, that share had dropped sharply to 20 percent. While there were still some riders who insisted on a Harley-Davidson, newcomers to the motorcycle market opted increasingly for Japanese affordability and dependability. In the face of these problems, AMF began to lose interest in keeping Harley-Davidson afloat. To save the company, Beals and twelve other executives organized a leveraged management buyout. With the financial support of Citicorp, the management team succeeded in taking control from AMF on June 16, 1981, at a cost of $81.5 million. As part of the restructuring process, the company was reincorporated under the name Harley-Davidson, Inc.

Harley-Davidson's turnaround strategy called for improving quality through new management techniques, many of which their competitors had pioneered. After a

visit to Honda's Marysville plant in 1981, Beals recalled to *Fortune*, he realized that the company was "being wiped out by the Japanese because they were better managers. It wasn't robotics, or culture, or morning calisthenics and company songs—it was professional managers who understood their business and paid attention to detail." To improve its ability to compete, Harley-Davidson quickly implemented three new principles: worker involvement, "as-needed" materials management, and improved control of shop-floor operations. At the York factory, the company grouped employees in a plant-wide network to ensure their input in improving the manufacturing process. It also implemented a materials-management plan called MAN (Material as Needed) and introduced a statistical system to improve quality. Once statistical parameters were established, workers were able to chart the quality of the machines they produced and to introduce improvements where warranted.

SUCCESS WITH REVITALIZATION

The competition, meanwhile, was moving aggressively. When the recession of the early 1980s depressed demand for heavyweight bikes, Japanese manufacturers swamped the U.S. market with surplus inventory, driving prices down even farther. In 1982, however, the company won an antidumping judgment from the International Trade Commission (ITC). In accordance with that decision, U.S. President Ronald Reagan imposed temporary tariffs on heavyweight models imported from Japan. The new tariffs would give Harley-Davidson an opportunity to fulfill its revitalization plans. As the company's market share began to increase, so, too, did its profits. Harley-Davidson had lost $25 million in 1982, but it rebounded into the black in 1983 before posting $2.9 million in profits on sales of $294 million in 1984. Though Japanese bike makers were able to elude some of the tariffs by building more machines in the United States, by 1986 Harley-Davidson's share of the U.S. super-heavyweight market had crept back up to 33.3 percent, far ahead of Honda, its closest competitor.

It was also in this period that Harley-Davidson began several major marketing campaigns. The most prominent of these was the Harley Owners Group (HOG), a fan club established by the company in 1983. By the end of the 1980s membership in HOG had grown to 100,000 members. Several years later the company developed the SuperRide promotion, designed to attract upscale buyers. A series of SuperRide television commercials invited viewers to try out a new bike at one of 600 dealers nationwide. More than 40,000 people responded. Though immediate results did not cover the promotion's $3 million price tag, the effort did result in increased sales over the next several years.

FINANCIAL SETBACKS

Although Harley-Davidson was making progress, it suffered another setback in 1984. Citicorp, nervous that the industry was headed back into a recession, informed Harley-Davidson that in future years they would no longer provide over-advances—money over and above the conservative lending limits set as part of the company's business plan. Taking this as an indication that Citicorp wanted out of its arrangement with the company, Beals and Richard Teerlink, then the company's finance officer, began searching for another lender. Once word concerning Citicorp's plans got out, however, other banks showed little interest in making the commitment. By October 1985 Beals and his management team had contacted the investment firm Dean Witter Reynolds in order to begin Chapter 11 bankruptcy proceedings.

Before those plans were finalized, Heller Financial Corporation agreed to supply Harley-Davidson with $49 million to buy out Citicorp's stake in the business. While Citicorp would lose more than $18 million on its investment, Heller's faith in Harley-Davidson paid off handsomely. The company's market share climbed steadily, and profits for 1986 topped $4.3 million on sales of $295 million. That year Harley-Davidson went public again, offering two million shares of stock, first on the American Stock Exchange and then, in 1987, on the New York Stock Exchange.

As a result of its reviving fortunes, the company asked for the removal of the import tariffs in 1987, a year earlier than scheduled. That request was granted. Even so, Harley-Davidson's share of the super-heavyweight market continued to climb, reaching 62 percent by 1990. A serious economic downturn was looming, however, and Teerlink, who had by that time become the company's CEO, warned in the company's 1990 annual report that "maintaining Harley-Davidson's growth through a recessionary period will be a difficult, but not impossible task. We could easily exploit our worldwide motorcycle popularity for quick profits, a near-fatal mistake we made in the 1970s, but we are committed to a corporate vision that discourages short-term thinking."

THE 1990S AND 2000S: OPTIMISM AMID SERIOUS CHALLENGES

The early 1990s brought some minor setbacks, most of which involved the company's efforts to diversify into other product lines. Its 1986 purchase of the Holiday Rambler Corporation (HRC) was particularly problematic, as HRC's large recreational vehicles proved to be too far outside Harley-Davidson's expertise. After several years of disappointing sales, HRC was sold in 1996. Harley-Davidson's rising stock price, meanwhile, rewarded savvy investors, though the company's balance sheet was not perfect. Of particular concern to some investors was a decline in gross margin, due in part to the costs of a new Kansas City plant. While officials warned that further costs associated with plant openings and refurbishings would have to be absorbed, the company expressed confidence that its international sales and a new subsidiary, the Buell Motorcycle Company, would sustain profits into the 2000s. Buell, a small producer of handmade "sports bikes," was purchased by Harley-Davidson in 1998.

The early 2000s were a period of optimism and confidence. Earnings were strong, and the Harley-Davidson name remained one of the best-known brands in the world. The company's 100th anniversary celebration in 2003 would draw an extraordinary crowd of more than 250,000 fans to downtown Milwaukee. Politicians from both major parties, meanwhile, pointed to Harley-Davidson as proof that it was still possible for an American manufacturer to thrive amid the intense pressures of globalization.

Problems, however, were increasingly apparent. One of the most basic was rooted in the nation's rapidly changing demographics. For decades, Harley-Davidson had focused its marketing efforts on so-called "boomers"—those born in the "baby-boom" years between the end of World War II and, roughly, the early 1960s. That focus proved astute in the late 1980s and 1990s, when middle-aged boomers, then at the height of their careers, saw a new Harley-Davidson as an easy way to recapture some of the joy and freedom of their youth. By 2009, however, the picture had changed dramatically, and the company was struggling to keep pace. Many boomers had retired, and millions more were doing so every year. That change generally brought a sharp drop in household income, particularly after the stock market's sharp decline in 2008 decimated IRAs and other retirement accounts. The cost of the company's motorcycles, however, remained high, often exceeding the price of a new car. As retirees struggled with rising health care costs, mortgages, and other daily expenses, a new Harley-Davidson seemed increasingly out of reach. Sales and profits declined accordingly. In July 2009 the company announced dismal results for the quarter that ended on June 28 of that year. Compared with the corresponding quarter of 2008, its motorcycle sales had dropped 30 percent worldwide and 35 percent in the United States. Profits, meanwhile, were down 91 percent.

In the past, the company had often responded to sales drops by extending credit to customers on notably generous terms. While that policy often improved sales dramatically, it would do lasting damage to the company's financial position. Thousands of the customers who bought Harley-Davidsons on easy terms in the 1990s and 2000s would have difficulty paying off the loans as the economy worsened. With the collapse of the sub-prime mortgage market in 2008, the company's credit troubles were immense. While many current customers were defaulting on their obligations to Harley-Davidson Financial Services (HDFS), the company's financing subsidiary, potential customers often faced difficulties even getting a loan, as the nation's banks increasingly viewed HDFS, and motorcycle loans generally, as a poor risk. Unable to obtain funds itself, HDFS found that its traditional ability to contribute to sales growth was severely restricted.

As of the summer of 2009 the company had taken some steps to improve the situation. It has continued to expand aggressively overseas, particularly in emerging markets, an area many economists said was poised to outpace the U.S. economy for years to come. One of the centerpieces of this expansion was a factory in Manaus, Brazil. At the time of its opening in 1998, it was the company's first and only overseas production facility. Eight years later Harley-Davidson would establish its first dealership in China, one of the fastest-growing markets in the world. The company's domestic efforts, meanwhile, were increasingly devoted to the expansion of its customer base, with several new bike designs and accessories introduced specifically to appeal to women, a small but growing segment of the motorcycle-riding public. It has also tried to enhance its considerable nostalgic appeal as an icon of American design and manufacturing. In 2008, for example, it opened a 130,000-square-foot museum in Milwaukee. "A variety of exhibits," noted the company's Web.site, "tell the stories of the extraordinary people, products, history and culture of Harley-Davidson."

Perhaps the most dramatic sign of the company's efforts to revitalize itself, however, came in the form of layoffs. In July 2009 the business media reported that the company had announced plans to lay off more than 1,000 workers, or roughly 10 percent of its workforce. These cuts were in addition to the loss of about 1,450 jobs earlier in the year. While acknowledging the painful consequences of the layoffs for workers and their families, company executives argued that they were absolutely necessary for Harley-Davidson's survival. CEO Jim Ziemer told Susanna Hamner in the *New York*

Times that the company was determined to adapt to a rapidly changing world. "We have to be quicker, more responsive to what our customers want. And we will."

Etan Vlessing
Updated, Christine Ferran; R. Anthony Kugler

PRINCIPAL SUBSIDIARIES

Harley-Davidson Motor Company; Harley-Davidson Financial Services, Inc.; Buell Motorcycle Company; MV Agusta Group.

PRINCIPAL COMPETITORS

Kawasaki Motors Corp.; Yamaha Motor Corporation; Ducati Motor Holding S.p.A.; Suzuki Motor Corporation; Honda Motor Co., Ltd.

FURTHER READING

Barrett, Rick, "Harley Plans to Cut Another 1,000 Jobs: Company Also Plans Production Shutdowns at Several of its Plants," *Milwaukee Journal Sentinel*, July 17, 2009.

Davidson, Willie G., *100 Years of Harley-Davidson*, Boston: Bulfinch Press, 2002.

"Economy Watch," *Wisconsin State Journal*, July 17, 2009, p. B8.

"From 1903 Until Now," Harley-Davidson.com.

Gallun, Alby, "Manufacturers Expect Growth to Moderate in '98," *Business Journal Serving Greater Milwaukee*, January 9, 1998.

Goldberg, Steven T., and Nancy Stover, "12 Stocks That Keep Growing & Growing & Growing," *Kiplinger's Personal Finance Magazine*, May 1998, p. 66.

Hamner, Susanna, "Harley, You're Not Getting Any Younger," *New York Times*, March 21, 2009, p. BU1.

Holmstrom, Darwin, *The Harley-Davidson Century*, Osceola, WI: MBI, 2002.

"How Harley Beat Back the Japanese," *Fortune*, September 25, 1989.

Jelter, Jim, "Headed the Way of Indian?" MarketWatch.com, July 16, 2009.

Krauss, Clifford, "Harley Woos Female Bikers," *New York Times*, July 25, 2007.

"Maintaining Excellence through Change," *Target*, Spring 1989.

Reid, Peter, *Well Made in America: Lessons from Harley-Davidson on Being the Best*, New York: McGraw Hill, 1990.

"Riding the Road to Recovery at Harley-Davidson," Labor-Management Cooperation Brief No. 15, Washington, D.C.: U.S. Department of Labor, April 1988.

Roth, Stephen, "New Harley Plant Spotlights Training and Empowerment," *Kansas City Business Journal*, January 9–15, 1998.

Stuart, Devan, "Shop's Clothing Sales Ride Motorcycle's Popularity," *Jacksonville Business Journal*, January 16, 1998.

"The Success of Harley-Davidson: 89 Years in the Making," Milwaukee: Harley-Davidson, Inc., 1992.

Teerlink, Rich, and Lee Ozley, *More Than a Motorcycle: The Leadership Journey at Harley-Davidson*, Boston: Harvard Business School Press, 2000.

"Top 100 Places to Work," *Dealernews*, March 1998, p. 47.

Wagner, Herbert, *At the Creation: Myth, Reality, and the Origin of the Harley-Davidson Motorcycle, 1901-1909*, Madison, WI: Wisconsin Historical Society Press, 2003.

"Welcome," Harley-Davidson Museum, Harley-Davidson.com.

"Why Milwaukee Won't Die," *Cycle*, June 1987.

Yates, Brock W., *Outlaw Machine: Harley-Davidson and the Search for the American Soul*, Boston: Little, Brown, 1999.

Hittite Microwave Corporation

20 Alpha Road
Chelmsford, Massachusetts 01824-4123
U.S.A.
Telephone: (978) 250-3343
Fax: (978) 250-3373
Web site: http://www.hittite.com

Public Company
Founded: 1985
Employees: 332
Sales: $180.3 million (2008)
Stock Exchanges: NASDAQ
Ticker Symbol: HITT
NAICS: 334413 Semiconductor and Related Device Manufacturing; 334310 Audio and Video Equipment Manufacturing; 334515 Instrument Manufacturing for Measuring and Testing Electricity and Electrical Signals

∎ ∎ ∎

Hittite Microwave Corporation designs and develops integrated circuits, modules, subsystems, and instrumentation for what the company calls "technically demanding" radio-frequency, microwave, and millimeter-wave applications. Industry classifications served by Hittite are the automotive, broadband, cellular infrastructure, fiber-optic, military, space, and test and measurement electronics markets. To meet end-market demand and remain competitive, the company invests heavily in research and development to bring new products to market. Hittite's product line includes more than 750 products that span 20 various product lines with operations in the United States, France, Germany, Malaysia, South Korea, Taiwan, Thailand, and the United Kingdom. In addition, it has engineering design centers located in Colorado Springs, Colorado; Ottawa, Canada; and Istanbul, Turkey. As of 2009 the company held more than 32 patents and had published many industry-specific papers.

EARLY HISTORY

Originally from Turkey, Yalcin Ayasli founded Hittite Microwave Corporation in Chelmsford, Massachusetts, in 1985 to manufacture "high-performance integrated circuits for communications systems," according to Bob Sanders of the *New Hampshire Business Review*. Between 1985 and 1993 the U.S. government funded Hittite's research in and development of radio-frequency integrated circuits and monolithic microwave integrated circuits, largely for military and other government-related programs, such as radar applications and communications systems.

By 1993 the company had shifted its focus to develop and produce its own integrated circuits, modules, and subsystems for the commercial market. Through the mid- to late 1990s it continued to expand on its core design while supplying a variety of different industries. Hittite's engineers collaborated with its customers to develop and launch custom products specific to their business needs. Following the release of its first published catalog of more than 50 products, a sales force was put in place to promote its diverse line of products.

COMPANY PERSPECTIVES

Hittite Microwave Corporation is committed to:

• Being a supplier of products of the highest quality.

• Advancing state-of-the-art technology to support our products

• Enhancing our competitive position with superior products.

Hittite's Quality Policy Recognizes Responsibilities for Every Individual to:

   • Take the initiative to promote quality.

   • Create an environment where the highest quality standards are maintained.

   • Participate in continuous improvement practices.

In an effort to increase its global market presence, Hittite opened its first international office, Hittite Microwave Europe Ltd., in Berkshire, England, in July 2001. The following January Hittite Microwave Deutschland was opened in Rosenheim, Germany. Later that year, Hittite Microwave Asia Ltd. was established in Seoul, South Korea.

Closer to home, Hittite acquired Mythos Electronics Company Ltd. in October 2003. The following year the company relocated from Woburn, Massachusetts, to Chelmsford. In August 2005 it acquired a majority of Q-Dot Inc., a research and development subsidiary of Simtek Corporation, which was based in Colorado Springs, Colorado. The acquisition of Q-Dot strengthened Hittite's design ability in the areas of direct digital synthesis, analog-to-digital and digital-to-analog converters, and digital drivers and receivers. Also in 2005 the company opened a design center in Istanbul.

HITTITE SHINES ON WALL STREET

The *Boston Business Journal* stated in July 2005, "[Hittite] has increased revenue 13 straight years and has generated annual profits since 1986." The journal also noted that "at the end of [2004], the company had $25 million in cash, virtually no long-term debt and $55 million in total assets." By 2005 Hittite's product catalog had expanded to include 340 standard products. The company's decision early on to expand into the

international market further bolstered its bottom line, which led to record sales of $62 million in 2004, nearly a 50 percent increase compared to 2003 year-end results. Consequently, it came as no surprise when Hittite announced in July 2005 an initial public offering (IPO) of 2.7 million shares of common stock at $17 per share. By the end of the first day, the shares had climbed to $19.46.

According to Matthew Littlewood of the PricewaterhouseCoopers accounting firm, "You want companies with sustainable business models, that are going to continue to grow rapidly after the IPO," as reported by Robert Gavin of the *Boston Globe*. Hittite was a good example, in that it nearly doubled the value of its stock after its initial inception. The company reported a 56 percent increase in revenues and a 132 percent increase in profits for 2006. Besides being boosted by its IPO, Hittite was also benefiting from a thriving economic business climate in Massachusetts and a large pool of investors who were looking to make a profit.

Hittite's success had a lot to do with the person who was placed at the forefront of the company: Stephen G. Daly, who became president in January 2004 and chief executive officer in December 2004. One year later, in December 2005, he succeeded Ayasli as chairman. According to a company press release, Ayasli said of Daly, "His performance as President and Chief Executive Officer has been outstanding. We have great confidence in his ability to successfully lead the company and continue its growth into the future."

GROWTH IN A GLOBAL MARKET

In January 2006 Hittite announced in a press release that it had received ISO/TS 16949:2002 certification "for the design, manufacture, and sale of plastic-encapsulated analog and mixed-signal ICs [integrated circuits] for RF [radio-frequency], microwave and millimeterwave applications for the automotive industry." It explained that an "ISO/TS 16949 is a Quality Management System which specifies automotive industry quality and manufacturing standards that are more stringent then ISO 9001:2000 requirements." This new level of certification was another reason why the company continued to receive high marks throughout the industries it served. To sustain future growth, Hittite began hiring new staff throughout its organization in 2006, especially in the area of engineering.

By mid-2006 Hittite's global market presence had reached approximately 2,300 customers, such as Motorola, Boeing, Cisco Systems, and the National Aeronautics and Space Administration. "Wall Street seems to have underestimated Hittite since its initial

KEY DATES

1985: Hittite is founded by Yalcin Ayasli.

1996: Company publishes its first product catalog containing 50 products.

2001: Hittite opens its first international office in Berkshire, England.

2002: Company opens two more offices in Rosenheim, Germany, and in Seoul, Korea.

2003: Hittite opens an office in Shanghai; it acquires Mythos Electronics Company Ltd.

2004: Hittite relocates to Chelmsford, Massachusetts.

2005: Stephen G. Daly becomes the chairman of the board, succeeding Ayasli; Hittite acquires a majority of Q-Dot Inc.'s assets; it becomes a publicly traded company on NASDAQ.

2006: Hittite receives its ISO/TS 16949 certification.

2007: Hittite is named one of "200 Best Small Companies" by *Forbes*.

stock offering," Jack Hough noted in *SmartMoney* in August 2006. "Over the past four quarters the company has topped analysts' earnings estimates four times by an average of 30%." Thus, early estimates had Hittite sales on target to reach $32.4 million, up 71 percent compared to 2005. The company reported that 90 products would be brought to market in 2006, exceeding the 80 products introduced in 2005.

EXPANSION AND NEW PRODUCTS

The company rounded out 2006 with the opening of a design center in Ottawa, Ontario, in December, which further strengthened its commitment toward growth, expansion, and new product development. "These engineers have worked together for many years and have a track record of success," Daly noted in a company press release in December 2006. He further stated, "They bring to us a complementary design capability and will immediately contribute to our product expansion plan."

Hittite continued to thrive in 2007 with more than 2,500 customers. One area that was leading growth within the industry was mobile communication services, and Hittite was at the forefront of the newest technologies with advances in analog and digital communication products. The company bolstered revenues of $36.3 mil-

lion for the first quarter of 2007, up 30.4 percent from 2006. By the end of 2007 Hittite had launched three new product lines. Once again, it outperformed analysts' forecasts. Some industry watchers viewed Hittite's overall success as a result of its ability to minimize its manufacturing expenditures, while still being able to consistently bring new products and product lines to market.

In 2007 Hittite was 12th in *Forbes*'s "200 Best Small Companies." That same year it reported revenues of $156.4 million and a net income of $51.2 million. In late 2007 Hittite entered into a agreement with Northrop Grumman's Space Technology division to be the global supplier of the Velocium line of products. In exchange, Hittite would gain "access to Northrop Grumman's advanced semiconductor process technology for new Hittite products," as reported in an October 2007 press release by the company.

FROM GROWTH TO RECESSION

Between January and March 2008 Hittite's sales slowed, as its customers began to feel the effects of the global economic recession that started in 2007. Undeterred, Daly told the *Boston Globe*, "For 2008, we will remain focused on growing our revenue by further penetrating our target markets and continuing to invest in research and new product development." In short, Hittite would continue conducting business as usual until the economic conditions improved. That was exactly what the company did when it launched its 17th product line, which included 12 new products, during the first quarter of 2008. The overall industry may have been affected by the global recession, but Hittite was still seeing its revenues increase. It reported that its first-quarter sales in 2008 totaled $43.3 million, up 19.2 percent compared to the same period in 2007.

Nevertheless, as the global recession continued through 2008, Hittite felt its effects firsthand. During the first quarter of 2009, the company reported revenues of $38.2 million, down 11.8 percent compared to $43.3 million a year earlier. "It was a challenging quarter, six of our eight markets experienced sequential declines in demand, offset by two markets with growth," noted Daly in an April 2009 press release by the company. He added, "We maintain a long term perspective on our business and we are confident our investments in new products and technologies are the foundation for future growth. In 2009 we will focus on expanding sales beyond our current 3,000 customers."

Despite being weakened by the economic recession, Hittite was not without new product offerings. By mid-2009 its vast array of products had become more extensive. In addition, the company's products were readily available through any of its 16 global field sales offices, its Web site, and its distributor, Future Electronics, thereby making it easy to conduct business with its ever-growing customer base.

Brenda Kubiac

PRINCIPAL COMPETITORS

Analog Devices Inc.; Avago Technologies; M/A-Com.

FURTHER READING

Gavin, Robert, "Going Public Has Gotten Better in Massachusetts: IPO Growth in '05 Nearly Doubled," *Boston Globe*, May 16, 2006.

"Hittite Forecast below Expectations," *Boston Globe*, February 15, 2008.

"Hittite IPO Could Bode Well for Telecom Pickup," *CompoundSemi News*, August 4, 2005.

Hittite Microwave Corporation, "Hittite Microwave Achieves Automotive Quality Management System Certification" (press release), January 5, 2006, http://www.hittite.com/press_releases/index.html/view/229.

————, "Hittite Microwave Corporation and Northrop Grumman's Space Technology Sector Enter into Strategic Agreement" (press release), October 18, 2007, http://www.hittite.com/press_releases/index.html/view/346.

————, "Hittite Microwave Corporation Opens Design Center in Ottawa, Ontario" (press release), December 20, 2006, http://www.hittite.com/press_releases/index.html/view/283.

————, "Hittite Microwave Corporation Reports Financial Results for the First Quarter of 2009" (press release), April 23, 2009.

————, "Hittite Microwave Corporation Reports Financial Results for the Fourth Quarter of 2007" (press release), February 14, 2008, http://www.hittite.com/press_releases/index.html/view/374.

————, "Hittite Microwave Promotes Stephen G. Daly to Chairman" (press release), December 15, 2005, http://www.hittite.com/press_releases/index.html/view/226.

"Hittite Microwave Corporation (HITT): Stock Quote & Company Profile," *BusinessWeek*, June 16, 2009.

"Hittite to Raise $77M in IPO," *Boston Business Journal*, July 22, 2005.

"Hot Growth Special Report 2006: Hittite Microwave (HITT)," *BusinessWeek*, April 28, 2006.

Hough, Jack, "Love Hertz," *SmartMoney*, August 14, 2006.

Sanders, Bob, "Following the Money: Who Were the Big N.H. Contributors in the '08 election?" *New Hampshire Business Review*, December 5, 2008.

"Stephen G. Daly," *Forbes*, April 23, 2009.

"The 200 Best Small Companies: #12 Hittite Microwave," *Forbes*, October 8, 2008.

The Women's Health Company

Hologic, Inc.

35 Crosby Drive
Bedford, Massachusetts 01730
U.S.A.
Telephone: (781) 999-7300
Fax: (781) 280-0669
Web site: http://www.hologic.com

Public Company
Founded: 1985
Incorporated: 1985 (Massachusetts); 1990 (Delaware)
Employees: 3,933
Sales: $1.67 billion (2008)
Stock Exchanges: NASDAQ
Ticker Symbol: HOLX
NAICS: 334517 Irradiation Apparatus Manufacturing

∎ ∎ ∎

Hologic, Inc., maker of diagnostic imaging and surgical systems, has made its name by being at the cutting edge of technological developments in women's health care. Jay Stein and David Ellenbogen founded the company in 1985 with the intent to develop a more accurate machine for osteoporosis screening. Their first machine, the DXA, was sold in 1987, just in time to ride the wave of increased demand for bone scanners after the first nonhormonal drug treatment for osteoporosis came on the market. The company continued to be at the forefront of bone scanning technology in the 1990s, but key acquisitions late in the decade led the company in another direction after 2000, when research and development began to focus on breast cancer detection.

Hologic developed the first direct digital mammography system, introduced in 2002. They continued to introduce products to help diagnose and treat women's health. By 2009 Hologic led the burgeoning digital mammography market in the United States, a position gained by their massive investment in research and development and commitment to ongoing technological innovation.

EARLY START IN OSTEOPOROSIS SCREENING

Hologic was incorporated in Massachusetts in 1985, but the company considers its true founding date to be 1986, when work began on its revolutionary bone scanner. Jay A. Stein and S. David Ellenbogen had recently sold their first company, Diagnostic Technology, Inc. A chance meeting at a local research firm led Stein to consider the technology being used to detect osteoporosis, a serious loss of bone tissue particularly common in postmenopausal women. The founders believed it was imperative to find a better way to detect, measure, and treat the disease, because severe fractures could result and sometimes, especially in the case of hip fracture, lead to death. At that time, several drugs to treat osteoporosis were undergoing clinical trials, but bone density assessment machines were imprecise and expensive. Stein and Ellenbogen focused their efforts on developing a machine using x-rays that could quickly and precisely scan a patient with very low radiation exposure. By 1987 the new bone scanner, the DXA, was approved by the Food and Drug Administration (FDA), and the company sold its first machine.

COMPANY PERSPECTIVES

∎

Making a difference in the lives of women everywhere.

In 1990 Hologic reincorporated in Delaware and made its first public offering on the NASDAQ. The company set itself on a pathway to growth, focusing on the health care needs of women and constantly investing in research and the development of ever more accurate products and new technologies. By 1994 Hologic began selling their DXA machines worldwide. When Medicare began to cover bone density measurements, Hologic's product was even more in demand.

Business took off even more strongly in 1995, when the osteoporosis drug Fosamax gained FDA approval and came on the market. Fosamax was the first nonhormonal drug that could slow down bone loss in women with osteoporosis. The availability of an appropriate treatment fed the need for accurate bone density scanners that could diagnose osteoporosis as well as follow the progress of women on the new class of drugs. The sales of the DXA system doubled from $56.6 million in 1995 to $91.6 million in 1996.

EXPANSION INTO BREAST HEALTH

Hologic expanded into other arenas in women's health when they acquired at a steep cost the U.S. operations of Trex Medical Corporation in 1990. The acquisition gave Hologic a new line of mammography and breast biopsy systems. To pay for the acquisition, Hologic closed its conventional x-ray facilities. The Trex acquisition immediately made Hologic a leader in the conventional mammography market and led Hologic to a new focus on breast health. In 1995 Hologic bought the ultrasound bone scanner business of Walter Magnetic Group and that of Sophia Medical Systems. The same year, they also bought FluroScan Imaging Systems, a company specializing in x-ray equipment.

When sales of the DXA system slowed in the late 1990s, Hologic executives recognized the need to diversify and began to expand their product offerings to include detection and treatment of breast cancer. In 1999 Hologic acquired Direct Radiography, a maker of x-ray equipment that had developed a direct-to-digital imaging system, a purchase that they would soon use to develop direct-to-digital mammography machines. After restructuring in the early 2000s, Hologic resumed its strategy for growth in 2005 by acquiring Fischer

Imaging's SenoScan digital mammography machine and the MammoTest sterotactic breast biopsy system.

Again, the company's acquisitions and research and development of new products came at a fortuitous time. In 2005 the results of a four-year National Cancer Institute study on digital mammography were released, showing that digital mammography was better than film mammography in screening women with dense breast tissue for breast cancer. By 2006 the company's top-of-the-line digital mammography machine, Selenia, had captured more than 50 percent of the digital mammography market. The National Cancer Institute study spurred the transition from film to digital mammography machine, leaving the company poised for exponential growth.

The company also branched into other areas of breast cancer care. Hologic introduced a new system in 2002 for treating local breast cancer, called the MammoSite device. This device used a balloon catheter that is inserted into the breast at the site of a surgically removed breast tumor. The device delivers radiation from inside the body over five days, targeting the area where the tumor is most likely to recur and reducing the exposure of healthy tissue to radiation. A follow-up of 1,400 early stage breast cancer patients who had lumpectomies, rather than mastectomies, found that the treatment system resulted in low recurrence rates and had good cosmetic results.

In their effort to be at the forefront of breast cancer detection technologies, Hologic acquired R2 Technology, Inc., in 2006, the same year it bought AEG Elektrofotografie GmbH and Suros Surgical Systems, Inc. R2 Technology had developed a computer-aided detection system (CAD). CAD works by flagging suspicious areas on digital mammograms, basically acting as a second set of eyes for the radiologist. Hologic then had the rights to the best-selling CAD system. However, the National Cancer Institute and the American Cancer Society found in a study released in 2007 that CAD systems found no more cancers but led to more invasive extra testing and biopsies than did mammograms read by radiologists without the assistance of CAD. Hologic announced the next year that a study done in a large imaging practice in North Carolina found that CAD resulted in an 11 percent increase in sensitivity with only a 4 percent increase recall rate. The jury remained out on whether or not CAD helped or hurt efforts to detect breast cancer early.

A MARKET LEADER

In 2007 Hologic acquired women's health care company Cytyc Corp. Hologic CEO Jack Cumming said in a

KEY DATES

1985: Hologic incorporates in Massachusetts.
1986: Development of x-ray bone density scanners begins.
1987: DXA bone densitometer receives FDA clearance.
1990: Hologic incorporates in Delaware; company is listed on the NASDAQ.
1995: Company acquires technologies to analyze bone density from WalkerSonix and Sopha Medical.
1996: Company merges with FluroScan Imaging Systems, Inc.
1999: Company acquires Direct Radiography Corporation.
2000: Company acquires U.S. operations of Trex-Medical Corporation.
2005: Company acquires Fischer Imaging Corporation's mammography business and products.
2006: AEG Elektrofotografie GmbH, R2 Technology, Inc., and Suros Surgical Systems, Inc., are acquired.
2007: BioLucent, Inc., is acquired; company merges with Cytyc Corporation, and Cytyc becomes a subsidiary of Hologic.
2008: Third Wave Technologies, Inc., is acquired.

statement about the merger that appears on the company's Web site, "By combining our companies' complementary, best-in-class products and technologies, we expect to drive enhanced growth and value creation." The acquisition brought Hologic into the arena of treatment of menorrhagia, or excessive menstrual bleeding, with less invasive surgery than traditional methods. Hologic also acquired Cytyc's Pap-smear tests for cervical cancer. Some observers speculated that while the price tag for Cytyc was large—because more than 90 percent of gynecologists used Cytyc products—association alone would boost sales of Hologic's other products. Cytyc became a wholly owned subsidiary of the company with the completion of the purchase.

In 2008 Hologic acquired the medical technologies company Third Wave Technologies, Inc., an acquisition that almost doubled the size of Hologic as well as put the company deeply in debt. Third Wave was proprietor of a variety of medical tests used to diagnose and follow cystic fibrosis, hepatitis C, and cardiovascular problems.

Hologic's main interest in Third Wave, however, was in two tests to detect the human papillomavirus (known to cause cervical cancer and genital warts) that Third Wave had recently submitted to the FDA for approval. Growth in the use of these tests had exceeded 40 percent annually since 2003, leading Hologic to move to grab a share of the burgeoning market in this arena of women's health care. In March 2009 the FDA approved the screening tests and they went on the market.

In the meantime, Hologic continued to work on advancing breast cancer detection technologies. Under development was a 3-D mammography machine expected to be ready in 2009. The process, called tomosynthesis, would take pictures of the breast from several different angles, providing doctors with around 100 images of each breast, rather than the two available with current technology. However, the company announced in June 2009 that it would delay asking the FDA for approval of the system to complete additional clinical studies, leading to a decline in Hologic stock prices.

Despite the delay in the new mammogram machine, Hologic remained at the forefront of breast cancer screening and diagnosis. With its unfailing commitment to technological advancement in the field of women's health care, Hologic has competed against much larger companies and grabbed the market share of many different technology areas of women's health. Hologic had demonstrated for more than two decades that it knew how to stay at the forefront of developing technologies in women's health care.

Melissa J. Doak

PRINCIPAL SUBSIDIARIES

AEG Photoconductor Corporation; BioLucent, LLC; Cytyc Corporation; Direct Radiography Corp.; R2 Technology, Inc.; Suros Surgical Systems, Inc.; Third Wave Technologies, Inc.

PRINCIPAL COMPETITORS

GE Healthcare; Siemens Healthcare; Philips Healthcare.

FURTHER READING

"Advanced Image Enhancement (AIE) Announces Licensing Agreement with Hologic," *Biotech Business Week,* July 30, 2007, p. 202.

Armstrong, David, "Study Shows Flaw in Mammography Tool—Popular Computer-Aided Method Yields More False Positive Than Less-Expensive Approach; Risk of Unnecessary Procedures," *Wall Street Journal,* April 5, 2007, p. D1.

"Clinical Trial Research; SeqWright's Clinical Trial Support Contributes to the Approval of Two HPV Diagnostic Systems," *Women's Health Weekly*, April 23, 2009.

"Company News; Hologic Agrees to Merge with Fluoroscan," *New York Times*, July 20, 1996, p. 41.

"Company News; Trex Medical Will Be Bought by Hologic for $55 Million," *New York Times*, August 16, 2000, p. C4.

"Computer-Aided Detection in Screening Mammography Enhances Performance of a Single Reader," *Drug Week*, February 29, 2008, p. 116.

"Cost Cuts Called Key to Hologic's Success," *Boston Globe*, February 4, 2009, p. B9.

"Despite Slowdown, Hologic Sees More Profit," *Boston Globe*, January 13, 2009, p. B7.

"FDA Back Two Hologic Tests for Cancer," *Boston Globe*, March 14, 2009, p. B7.

Forelle, Charles, "Deal Creates Health Giant—Hologic to Buy Cytyc to Establish a Force in Women's Care," *Wall Street Journal*, May 21, 2007, p. A10.

"Goldman Shops $500M TLB for Hologic," *Bank Loan Report*, June 30, 2008, p. 3.

Hill, Sidney Jr., "Wielding the Right Tools," *Manufacturing Business Technology*, October 2003, pp. 18–20.

"Hologic Announces Sale of Gestiva," *Drug Week*, February 8, 2008, p. 2056.

"Hologic Buys Third Wave for $580 Million," *Medical Technology & Devices Week*, June 16, 2008.

"Hologic Falls on Delay of New Product," *Boston Globe*, May 10, 2009, p. 6.

"Hologic Jumps after Receiving FDA OK," *Boston Globe*, September 13, 2008, p. A13.

"Hologic May Steal the Show, Analyst Says," *Boston Globe*, November 25, 2008, p. B9.

"Hologic to Acquire BioLucent, Inc.," *Biotech Business Week*, July 9, 2007, p. 433.

"Hologic to Enter Molecular Diagnostics with Third Wave Buy," G-2 Reports, July 2008, http://www.g2reports.com/issues/DTTR/2008_7/1617076-1.html.

Johnson, Carolyn Y., "Hologic to Buy Cytyc in $6.2b Life Science Deal—Goal Is to Create a Powerhouse in Women's Health," *Boston Globe*, May 21, 2007, p. E1.

Kingsbury, Kevin, and Shara Tibken, "Business Technology: Hologic Agrees to Acquire Third Wave," *Wall Street Journal*, June 10, 2008, p. B4.

Rusli, Evelyn M., "Hologic's Expensive Match-Up," Forbes. com, May 21, 2007, http://www.forbes.com/2007/05/21/hologic-cytyc-cancer-markets-equity-cx_er_0521markets03.html.

"SeqWright's Clinical Trial Support Contributes to the Approval of Two HPV Diagnostic Systems," *Biotech Business Week*, April 20, 2009, p. 1678.

Stuart, Mary, "In Women's Health, Hologic Stays Ahead of the Curve," *In Vivo*, February 2007.

"U.S. Breast Disease Diagnostic and Therapeutic Devices Market Poised to Grow to Over $2.7 Billion by 2010," *Drug Week*, September 28, 2007, p. 144.

Vincini, Frank, et al., "Three-Year Analysis of Treatment Efficacy, Cosmesis, and Toxicity by the American Society of Breast Surgeons MammoSite Breast Brachytherapy Registry Trial in Patients Treated with Accelerated Partial Breast Irradiation," *Cancer*, vol. 112, issue 4, pp. 758–766.

Wallack, Todd, "Long Courtship Put Hologic on Cusp of Acquiring Cytyc Deal Would Create One of State's Largest Life Sciences Companies," *Boston Globe*, October 15, 2007, p. G1.

———, "New Dimension in Detection Hologic Expects Its 3-D Mammography to be Ready in 2009," *Boston Globe*, June 2, 2008, p. B5.

———, "Passion Helps Bind Hologic and Cytyc: Merger Created One of the Largest Women's Health Companies," *Boston Globe*, May 18, 2008, p. G8.

Weisman, Robert, "Hologic to Delay U.S. Launch of 3D X-Ray System," *Boston Globe*, May 6, 2009, p. 5.

ICU Medical, Inc.

951 Calle Amanecer
San Clemente, California 92673-6212
U.S.A.
Telephone: (949) 366-2183
Toll Free: (800) 824-7890
Fax: (949) 366-8368
Web site: http://www.icumed.com

Public Company
Incorporated: 1984
Employees: 1,696
Sales: $188.1 million (2009 est.)
Stock Exchanges: NASDAQ
Ticker Symbol: ICUI
NAICS: 339111 Laboratory Apparatus and Furniture Manufacturing; 339112 Surgical and Medical Instrument Manufacturing

■ ■ ■

ICU Medical, Inc., develops, manufactures, and sells disposable medical connection systems for use in intravenous therapy (I.V.) applications. The company also manufactures such critical care devices as catheters, angiography kits, and cardiac monitoring systems. In addition, the company produces custom-designed intravenous therapy systems. ICU Medical devices are designed to protect health care workers from suffering an accidental puncture of the skin with unsterilized or contaminated needles, avoiding the subsequent risk of exposure to such infectious diseases as HIV and Hepatitis B and C. They are also designed to protect patients from catheter related bloodstream infections.

ICU Medical sells its devices primarily to distributors and related medical product manufacturers throughout the United States and around the world, including intravenous therapy product manufacturers and independent distributors, as well as selling directly to end users.

ORIGINS: 1984

ICU Medical, Inc., was founded in 1984 by a practicing internist, Dr. George Lopez, after he lost a patient to an accidental disconnection of an intravenous (I.V.) therapy system. Dr. Lopez believed that there must be a better way of securing I.V. lines. ICU introduced its first products for this purpose that year: the Click Lock and the Piggy Lock. These provided a locking mechanism for I.V. systems and protected health care workers from accidental needlesticks. These products became the models on which all of ICU's subsequent protected-needle and intravenous (I.V.) therapy products were based.

Early attempts to secure capital for the fledgling business proved perilous. In 1989 ICU claimed that the financial strategies of a San Francisco-based brokerage house forced the company into involuntary Chapter 11 bankruptcy proceedings in order to facilitate a takeover of ICU and its patents. The brokerage house, which had been hired to locate investment capital for ICU, denied the allegations. ICU went on to earn $804,000 in the first eight months of 1989, and the company remained profitable thereafter.

COMPANY PERSPECTIVES

ICU Medical, Inc., is a leader in the development, manufacture, and sale of proprietary, disposable medical connection systems for use in vascular therapy applications. In the years since our founding, ICU has compiled an impressive list of landmark products. We remain solely focused on developing and manufacturing products that protect healthcare workers from accidental needlesticks and exposure to infectious diseases, as well as products that maintain the integrity of patient intravenous therapy (I.V.) systems and protect patients from catheter-related bloodstream infections. We are a leader in the production of custom I.V. systems and we incorporate our proprietary products into many of those customized systems. We are also a significant manufacturer of critical care medical devices, including catheters, angiography kits, and cardiac monitoring systems.

In 1992 ICU introduced a successor to the Click Lock and the Piggy Lock. The CLAVE NeedleFree Connector, a one-piece, needle-less intravenous connection device, was the first needle-free connector ever marketed. The CLAVE eventually became ICU's best-selling product and the number one connector sold worldwide. The CLAVE was designed to eliminate needles from certain applications in acute care hospitals, home health care settings, out-patient surgery centers, nursing homes, convalescent facilities, physician's offices, medical clinics, and emergency centers. Emergency medications and intravenous fluids could be administered through the CLAVE using a standard syringe and no hypodermic needle. In fact, the passive technology of the CLAVE did not even accept a needle. Because the CLAVE was self-sealing, the chance of spilling blood or medicinal fluids was significantly reduced. It also functioned as a closed microbiological system, which helped prevent contamination that could lead to patient bloodstream infections.

GROWTH AND INCREASED VISIBILITY: 1990–99

In April 1993 ICU Medical filed a complaint for patent infringement against Baxter Healthcare Corporation and Becton Dickinson and Company. The lawsuit alleged that marketing of certain Baxter products labeled "Inter-link" and "Needle Lock" infringed on ICU's proprietary methods.

In September 1993 ICU signed a distribution agreement with California-based McGaw, Inc., to distribute CLAVE products. McGaw was a leading supplier of intravenous therapy products and services to hospitals and other health care providers.

In the mid-1990s ICU began to expand through internal growth and decided to substantially increase its manufacture, distribution, and marketing of custom intravenous therapy sets. In 1995 it created Budget Medical Products (BMP) as a subsidiary to distribute ICU's custom intravenous therapy sets. BMP would supply the low-end market with safe medical connector products.

Also in 1995 ICU introduced the 102 device, the first one-way or two-way drug delivery system. The company followed the 102 device with the introduction of the 1to2 Valve, which could also function as a one-way or two-way drug delivery system, in November 1998. This set-up provided the safety of an automatic one-way valve, but a push of the button would allow for aspiration, or two-way function, when necessary.

In 1999 ICU launched the Setfinder.com Web site to distribute standard intravenous therapy sets directly to health care providers. Meanwhile, the company significantly expanded its existing supply and distribution agreement with Abbott Laboratories through 2009. The agreement named ICU as Abbott's preferred supplier for all needle-free technology. It anticipated substantial increases in sales volume and subsequent reductions in price as a result of increased sales.

CHANGES IN THE EARLY 21ST CENTURY

In November of 2000 U.S. President Bill Clinton signed the Needlestick Safety and Prevention Act, which was to be administered by the Occupational Safety and Health Administration. The law mandated hospitals and other health care facilities to use needle-less intravenous systems, such as ICU's CLAVE Connector, to protect health care workers from accidental needlesticks that could transmit blood-borne diseases. ICU founder George Lopez, M.D., anticipated that the new law would accelerate sales of ICU needleless systems, adding that "ICU Medical long ago recognized the danger of needlesticks and has pioneered the development of needleless and needle-safe systems since its founding in 1984."

In February 2001 Abbott Laboratories and ICU Medical announced a new promotion and distribution agreement. Under the eight-year agreement, ICU would

KEY DATES

1984: Dr. George Lopez founds ICU Medical, Incorporated; the Click Lock and the Piggy Lock are introduced.

1989: ICU files for involuntary Chapter 11 bankruptcy protection.

1993: ICU introduces Clave; ICU files a complaint for patent infringement against Baxter Healthcare Corporation and Becton Dickinson and Company.

1995: Budget Medical Products (BMP) is created as a subsidiary to distribute custom intravenous therapy sets.

1999: ICU introduces the 102 drug delivery system and the 1to2 valve; Setfinder.com Web site is launched.

2001: ICU sues B. Braun Medical, Inc., alleging contract violations; company agrees to manufacture all new custom intravenous therapy sets for sale through Abbott Laboratories Hospital Products Division.

2002: Suit between ICU and B. Braun Medical, Inc., is settled and contract expires.

2003: ICU begins acquisition of manufacturing facility in Verona, Italy.

2005: ICU signs a strategic manufacturing, commercialization, and development agreement with Hospira, Inc., for Hospira's critical care product line and acquires Hospira's Salt Lake City, Utah, manufacturing facility, related capital equipment, and inventory, moving manufacturing facilities to Salt Lake City.

2006: ICU launches the TEGO Connection, and Orbit 90 diabetes set.

2007: ICU begins marketing Genie device; CFO Frank O'Brien receives Legacy Award for Lifetime Achievement from California Society of Certified Public Accountants.

2009: ICU acquires Hospira, Inc.'s critical care product line.

manufacture custom intravenous therapy sets for sale through Abbott's Hospital Products Division. The two companies would jointly promote the products under the name SetSource.

A year later, in February 2002, Abbott Laboratories and ICU expanded their supply and distribution agree-ment for CLAVE products. The new contract contained assurances of substantial increases in sales volume, along with price reductions based on increased sales and market conditions.

In November 2002 ICU completed its acquisition of Connecticut-based Bio-Plexus, Inc., whose principal products were blood collection needles that were marketed under the name PUNCTUR-GUARD. The collection needles were designed to eliminate exposure to needlesticks and potentially contaminated blood products. ICU planned to increase sales and bring expenses in line with sales volume to improve Bio-Plexus's previously troubled finances.

ICU terminated its contract with B. Braun Medical, Inc., for sale of CLAVE products in November 2002. The end of the contract ended the litigation that ICU had begun in June 2001 claiming Braun had violated the terms of its contract.

In January 2004 ICU and Abbott Laboratories amended their marketing and distribution agreements to give Abbott sole distribution rights for ICU products outside the United States through its Hospital Products Division. Effective through 2014, the agreement would be supported by ICU in part through the acquisition of a manufacturing facility in Verona, Italy.

In June of 2004 ICU filed a patent infringement against Alaris Medical Systems, Inc., a California-based medical products company. The suit asserted that Alaris' manufacture and sale of its SmartSite and SmartSite Plus Needle-Free Valves and Systems infringed on patents held by ICU.

DIVERSIFICATION

By December 2004 ICU had decided to branch out after years of relying on the CLAVE as its primary product. In 2004 the CLAVE accounted for 76 percent of ICU sales. Chief Financial Officer Francis (Frank) O'Brien said ICU planned to spur growth with a mix of internal research and development combined with outside acquisitions. ICU quadrupled spending on research in the third quarter of 2004 to about 11 percent of sales, or $1.8 million.

An outside acquisition in 2005 provided further diversification and growth when ICU entered a strategic manufacturing, commercialization, and development agreement with the recently formed hospital products company Hospira, Inc. Hospira had been spun off from Abbott Laboratories as its critical care product line that included such devices as catheters and cardiac monitoring systems. In addition, ICU acquired Hospira's Salt Lake City, Utah, manufacturing facility, related capital equipment, and inventory. ICU instituted cost saving measures, including relocation of its manufacturing facilities from San Clemente, California, to Salt Lake City. However, corporate headquarters of ICU remained in San Clemente. Some lower-cost assembly operations were later outsourced from Utah to facilities in Ensenada, Mexico.

CUSTOMIZED APPROACHES TO MEDICAL CONNECTION SYSTEMS

In 2006 ICU began to explore how its line of customized intravenous therapy kits, some of which had been in production since 1995, might help the company diversify. Individually designed using proprietary software, built-to-order I.V. kits met particular or specialized needs, especially for oncology and pediatric medical specialties. Specialized health care facilities also offered a market for customized I.V. therapy kits. For example, the variety of customized I.V. therapy kits used at a nursing home differed from the assortment needed by a children's hospital.

Fiscal analysts noted that ICU's larger competitors had no interest in the specialized small orders to which ICU could cater. They also noted that customization offered a niche for ICU to exploit. Company founder Dr. George Lopez had long stated his belief that success could be found by entering small markets where no one was fulfilling needs rather than attempting to compete in larger markets with stiffer competition.

In 2006 ICU launched the TEGO Hemodialysis Connector, a catheter protection device designed for use in hemodialysis treatments. The connector's closed system protected the catheter from contamination and patients from bloodstream infections that could require hospitalization. ICU's Orbit 90 diabetes infusion set, which links insulin pumps to the diabetes patients who require them was also introduced in 2006.

In 2007 ICU began marketing the Genie Closed Vial Access Device, which helped protect health care workers from the adverse reproductive and health effects of handling powerful chemotherapy drugs. The Genie was designed to prevent the release of hazardous vapors and liquids as health care workers prepared the drugs for use.

RECOGNITION AND GROWTH

In November 2007 the California Society of Certified Public Accountants presented ICU CFO Frank O'Brien with the Legacy Award in recognition of lifetime achievement. The award recognizes individuals who have tutored and mentored others in the accounting profes-

sion and who exemplify the integrity of the profession. O'Brien served as Chief Financial Officer at ICU in 1996 until April 2008.

In 2008 Health Robotics, a global leader in the preparation, compounding, and dispensing of intravenous chemotherapy drugs, announced that it had collaborated with ICU to integrate the CLAVE Needle-Free Connector into its CytoCare hazardous drug compounding and dispensing process. The successful collaboration decreased the workload of compounding pharmacy technicians while protecting nursing and other medical personnel from the dangers of unnecessary exposure to chemotherapy drugs.

Also in 2008 Premier, Inc., one of the nation's largest health care purchasing networks, entered a five-year agreement to market ICU products. Premier made bulk purchases of the health and surgical items it distributed, allowing hospitals and clinics to exercise additional purchasing power. The agreement with Premier allowed ICU access to 2,000 hospitals and 50,000 other health care sites that it had been unable to reach because they only bought supplies through group purchasing arrangements. According to Dr. Lopez, "We can now go into the 40 percent of U.S. hospitals that were not available to us."

In late 2008 ICU announced plans to build a manufacturing plant in Slovakia that, along with the company's existing plant in Italy, would help ICU improve response time to European demand for its products. Rather than wait for delivery from Mexico or the United States, European customers would receive purchases within 48 to 72 hours. In an effort to further expand its European sales, ICU announced its plans to increase its European direct-sales force to 100 people.

In the summer of 2009 ICU completed the acquisition of the commercial rights and physical assets of the critical care product line produced by Hospira, Inc. The acquisition, which carried a price tag of approximately $35 million in cash, created a long-term growth opportunity for ICU. "We have been manufacturing the majority of Hospira's critical care offerings for over four years," remarked ICU founder, Dr. George Lopez. "This transaction will enable us to completely control worldwide commercial responsibility for the critical care products including sales, marketing, customer contracting, and distribution."

By the beginning of 2009 the ICU product line boasted nine products, including the CLAVE Needle-Free Connector, the Lopez Enteral Valve, the CLC2000 Positive Pressure Connector, and the TEGO Connector. The financial publication *Investor's Business Daily* noted in its profile of ICU in late 2008 that doctors and hospitals continued to use these products to care for patients regardless of economic conditions. "We're not affected by consumer consumption," noted Dr. Lopez. "We're a pretty recession-proof company."

In the late summer of 2009 ICU and the privately held infusion therapy company Medegen, Inc., reached an agreement to end patent infringement litigation that had been initiated by Medegen.

THE FUTURE

In an annual report, Dr. Lopez predicted significant momentum for the company as it moved into the second decade of the 2000s. "We continued to place a high priority on controlling costs and improving manufacturing efficiencies at our factories." Lopez went on to say that the company's "solid financial condition provides the proper resources for our growth initiatives going forward, including the continued development of new products, strengthening our sales and marketing team, and funding ongoing improvements at our manufacturing facilities."

Joyce Helena Brusin

PRINCIPAL SUBSIDIARIES

Budget Medical Products (BMP); Bio-Plexus, Inc.

PRINCIPAL COMPETITORS

Tyco International Ltd.; Cardinal Healthcare; Baxter Healthcare Corporation; B. Braun Medical, Inc.; Becton Dickinson; Fresenius; Edwards Lifesciences; Merit Medical.

FURTHER READING

Benesh, Peter, "ICU Medical, Inc. San Clemente, California Device Maker Focuses on Niches Where There's No Competition," *Investor's Business Daily*, November 10, 2008.

"Catheter Protection Device Helps Prevent Infections," *Product News Network*, September 13, 2006.

"Court Denies Request for Preliminary Injunction against Alaris Medical Systems," *Biotech Business Week*, September 6, 2004.

"B. Braun Medical, Inc. Agrees to Contract Settlement with Supplier ICU Medical," *Business Wire*, November 14, 2002.

Fantin, Linda, "Hospira to Be Shuttered," *Salt Lake Tribune*, March 2, 2005.

Halperin, Alex, "Intensive Focus Bolsters ICU," *Business Week Online*, September 22, 2006.

"ICU Gets FDA Approval to Begin Marketing Genie Device," *Orange County Register*, June 8, 2007.

"ICU Medical Announces Amendments to Abbott Agreement," *Biotech Business Week*, February 9, 2004.

"ICU Medical Announces Court Order in Patent Infringement Lawsuit," *Pharma Business Week*, July 19, 2004.

"ICU Medical Buys Critical Care Product Line from Hospira," *Medical Product Outsourcing*, July–August 2009.

"ICU Medical, Inc. and Health Robotics Announce Compatibility of CytoCare™ Robot and CLAVE® Needle-Free Connector to Enable Safer Hazardous Drug Handling," *Blood Weekly*, January 1, 2009.

"ICU Medical, Inc. Announces Agreement with Abbott Laboratories," *PR Newswire*, February 28, 2001.

"ICU Medical, Inc. Announces Amendments to Marketing and Distribution Agreements with Abbott Laboratories," *Asia Africa Intelligence Wire*, January 15, 2004.

"ICU Medical, Inc. Announces Expansion of Agreement with Abbott Laboratories," *Reuters Significant Developments*, June 27, 2002.

"ICU Medical, Inc. Announces Termination of Contract with B. Braun," *Reuters Significant Developments*, November 20, 2002.

"ICU Medical, Inc. Completes Acquisition of Interest in Bio-Plexus, Inc.," *PR Newswire*, November 1, 2002.

"ICU Medical, Inc. Enters First-ever Agreement with Leading Healthcare Purchasing Network, Premier, Inc.," *PrimeZone Media Network*, August 13, 2008.

"ICU Medical, Inc. Expands Contract with Abbott Laboratories," *PR Newswire*, January 15, 1999.

"ICU Medical, Inc. Files Complaint for Patent Infringement against Baxter," *Business Wire*, April 12, 1993.

"ICU Medical, Inc. Files Patent Infringement Lawsuit against Alaris Medical Systems, Inc.," *PR Newswire*, June 17, 2004.

"ICU Medical, Inc.—History," *Datamonitor Company Profiles*, January 23, 2004.

"ICU Medical, Inc. Notifies B. Braun Medical, Inc. That Contract Will Not Be Extended." *PR Newswire*, July 3, 2002.

"ICU Medical, Inc. Reports President Signs Federal Needlestick Safety and Prevention Act," *PR Newswire*, November 7, 2000.

"ICU Medical, Inc. to Acquire Hospira's Critical Care Product Line," *PR Newswire*, July 9, 2009.

"ICU Medical, Inc. and Health Robotics Announce Compatibility of CytoCare™ Robot and CLAVE® Needle-Free Connector to Enable Safer Hazardous Drug Handling," *Blood Weekly*, January 1, 2009.

"ICU Medical's Clave Needleless IV System to Be Distributed by McGaw, Inc.," *Business Wire*, September 15, 1993.

Lau, Gloria, "ICU Medical, Inc., San Clemente, California; An Inexpensive Device Brings Hope and Profit," *Investor's Business Daily*, June 21, 2001.

———, "ICU Medical, Inc. San Clemente, California; As Prices Move Lower, Volume Moves Higher," *Investor's Business Daily*, October 10, 2002.

Lee, Jason, "ICU Moving Production to Utah Site," *Plastics News*, August 1, 2005.

O'Hara, Kristy J., "Dr. George 'Doc' Lopez," *Smart Business* (Orange County), December 2006.

Rauber, Chris, "Brokerage Blamed by Irvine Firm That Filed Chapter 11," *San Francisco Business Times*, August 13, 1990.

Reed, Vita, "Company to Broaden by Buying, Investing," *San Diego Business Journal*, December 6, 2004.

Stewart, Colin, "Inventor Aims to Protect Nurses from Drugs," *Orange County Register*, June 30, 2006.

———, "Top CEOs Earn Their Keep," *Orange County Register*, June 30, 2006.

INTERACTIVE INTELLIGENCE
Deliberately Innovative

Interactive Intelligence Inc.

7601 Interactive Way
Indianapolis, Indiana 46278
U.S.A.
Telephone: (317) 872-3000
Toll Free: (800) 267-1364
Fax: (317) 872-3000
Web site: http://www.inin.com

Public Company
Founded: 1994 as Humanoid Software
Employees: 600
Sales: $121.41 million (2008)
Stock Exchanges: NASDAQ
Ticker Symbol: ININ
NAISC: 511210 Software Publishers

■ ■ ■

In just 15 years, the Indianapolis-based software firm Interactive Intelligence Inc. has become a leader in the field of business communications services. The firm started with a simple idea: provide a variety of services, from phone to fax to e-mail to data management, in a single system. By emphasizing integrated services that rely on software and session initiation protocol (SIP) rather than on different pieces of hardware, Interactive Intelligence has simplified business communications for a growing number of customers, including those in service industries such as banking, insurance, retail, health care, higher education, and government. As an indication of its success, it was named one of the "Top 50 Hot Growth Companies" by *BusinessWeek* and the

"100 Fastest Growing Small Companies in America" by *Fortune Small Business* in 2008.

BUILDING AN IDEA FROM SCRATCH

Interactive Intelligence was the third software company to be founded by Donald E. Brown, who wrote his first software program while still a student at Indiana University. He developed that program to help car dealerships calculate loan payments, while simultaneously earning his medical degree and a master's in computer science in the early 1980s. He and his marketing partner, Joe Adams, sold that first company to Electronic Data Systems, a division of General Motors, in 1987 for $1.2 million. With that payoff, Brown and Adams founded a second company, Software Artistry, which developed help-desk software for businesses. Brown left the company in October 1994, just before it went public, to seek new challenges. Soon after, he started Humanoid Software with John R. Gibbs; they soon changed the name of their fledgling company to Interactive Intelligence Inc.

Brown and Gibbs decided to focus their new company on developing integrated communications software that used Internet protocol (IP) technologies. The idea was inspired by Brown's own unsatisfactory experiences with call centers that transferred him from one operator to another and had him repeat his information each time. "It's just a byproduct of the organization you're dealing with having this cobbled together, balkanized communications system," Brown told Kevin Harlin of *Investor's Business Daily*. "They can get your call across, but they can't get any data over."

COMPANY PERSPECTIVES

While our business solutions equip more than 1,000 organizations in 30 countries, Interactive Intelligence isn't your typical company. For one thing, our headquarters are in Indianapolis, Indiana, no on the East or West Coast. And like the day we started in 1994, we still don't believe in suits and dresses and appearances. Instead, we coantinur to rely on the imaginations of our people and encourage their creativity and teamwork.

Interactive Intelligence sought to provide alternative solutions to these patchwork systems. The wealth Brown had earned from his earlier companies—his share of Software Artistry was over $20 million—allowed him to keep Interactive Intelligence's focus on product development and revenue growth rather than on profitability. He and his engineers worked on creating a program that would allow businesses to coordinate all their communications using their existing Windows operating system, thus avoiding the need for separate communications servers and software. "The consultants told us we were nuts," Brown told Bill Beck of *Indiana Business Magazine*. "They said the big companies can't do that. But that was enough to convince us to take this on."

Growing the staff from less than a dozen to almost a hundred, Interactive Intelligence had its first product ready in 1997. Called the Enterprise Interaction Center (EIC), this software program integrated the various communication programs that a business might use, from e-mail to fax to telephone, and let a single call-service person coordinate them all from a Windows desktop. If a client had a dedicated telephone network (a private branch exchange), the software integrated it with the user's computer systems. Interactive Intelligence realized there was lots of competition for its product, but it hoped that by providing an all-in-one service it would gain a share of the growing business communications market.

GOING PUBLIC

Within two years Interactive Intelligence had secured several large clients, including Ameritech Corporation, Toshiba America Consumer Products, and Deutsche Telekom, and was prepared to take the company public. In September 1999 its initial public offering (IPO) raised $31.5 million on share prices that doubled on the

first day. The company used part of these funds to pay off some of its debt and the remainder was invested in more research and development.

After its successful IPO, Interactive Intelligence continued adding functionality to its EIC program by including scheduling and teleconferencing capabilities. It signed several global agreements, moving into Asia by partnering with vendors in the Philippines and Japan and establishing a foothold in Europe with Deutsche Telekom. It also signed agreements with providers of communications servers, including Unisys Corporation in 2000 and Cisco Systems in 2001, to package its software with specific hardware.

Interactive Intelligence was making progress in its product lines as well. In 2000 it introduced Communité, a program that allowed voice-mail and fax messages to be delivered to a user's e-mail address or have e-mails translated to voice mail using text-to-speech software. The program was designed to be used in conjunction with common communications programs such as Microsoft's Outlook, Web browsers, and personal digital assistants. By using the open architecture of a Lightweight Directory Access Protocol system, it could customize the product for companies of any size, from a few dozen to thousands of users. Because the price of the software could be prohibitive for smaller companies, in 2000 Interactive Intelligence created a new subsidiary, Interactive Portal, to lease the EIC software and make it available via the Internet. This arrangement allowed it to bring in smaller clients, including those who traveled a lot and those with home offices.

SURVIVING THE DOT-COM BUBBLE

Interactive Intelligence was pleasing customers with its new products, but it was not having the same success with shareholders. Its stock had reached as high as $50 a share in 2000, but by the middle of 2001 it had dropped below its IPO price of $13. The drop was reflective of a general fall in technology stocks caused by the bursting of the dot-com bubble between 2000 and 2001. Speculators had run up the value of many stocks related to technology and the Internet, regardless of whether they were good or bad investments; when the bubble burst, the entire NASDAQ, the technology-oriented stock index on which Interactive Intelligence was listed, lost more than half its value.

When Interactive Intelligence posted more losses than expected in the second quarter of 2001, it was forced to lay off 10 percent of its workforce. However, the firm's leaders stressed that the company was healthy and had growing revenue. As executive vice president,

KEY DATES

1994: Humanoid Software is founded by Donald E. Brown and John R. Gibbs; the company's name is changed to Interactive Intelligence Inc.

1997: Interactive Intelligence releases Enterprise Interaction Center (EIC), the first integrated voice/data communication software suite to run on Windows.

1999: Interactive Intelligence offers a successful initial public offering and is listed on NASDAQ.

2000: Interactive Intelligence spins off Interactive Portal, a subsidiary designed to provide access to EIC software over the Internet.

2002: Interactive Intelligence releases the first communications application based entirely on the session initiation protocol, now the standard for Internet telephony.

2004: Interactive Intelligence spins off Vonexus, a subsidiary designed to distribute EIC as an entirely Microsoft-based product; the company also creates the first all-Microsoft IP private branch exchange.

2006: Interactive Intelligence releases its workforce management module to enhance the contact software suite.

2008: Interactive Intelligence is named one of the "Top 50 Hot Growth Companies" by *BusinessWeek* and one of the "100 Fastest Growing Small Companies in America" by *Fortune Small Business*.

Gibbs told Peter Schnitzler of the *Indianapolis Business Journal* in July 2001, "We have new products coming out. We're growing, and our long-term plans have not been diminished. We've simply had a little hiccup due to economic conditions." Interactive Intelligence had to enact more employee cuts in April 2002, but by the fall the company was recognized by the consulting firm Deloitte & Touche as one of the country's 150 fastest growing technology companies. Its revenues grew to over $50 million in 2001, and it had doubled its investment in research and development. As Brown told Jack Naudi of the *Indianapolis Star*, "It's one thing to be a survivor, but if you haven't invested in technology … there isn't a means for growth at the other end."

As before, it was research and development that helped the company make progress. In previous years, its sales growth had been slowed because companies had to have a special circuit board to connect their telephone lines to their computer servers. Because these boards could cost as much as $10,000, it put Interactive Intelligence's software out of reach of smaller firms. Brown steered the company toward developing voice over Internet protocol (VoIP) standards that would work with SIP, a signaling protocol. "We felt we had seen the future when we saw the SIP standard, and we decided to make a big bet," Brown told Schnitzler in September 2006. "You talk about betting the future of the company. That's what we did." The bet paid off when the software giant Microsoft adopted the SIP standard in 2001. Interactive Intelligence brought out its first SIP-based product in 2002 and eventually landed Microsoft as a client.

GROWING SERVICES AND CUSTOMERS

The company kept moving forward with the introduction of its Customer Interaction Center (CIC), a collection of applications for call centers that uses interactive voice response technology to help integrate a company's communications. These communications could include phone interactions and callbacks, Web chats, and e-mail, and the program could be used alone or integrated with other software programs. With the Communité program as part of the collection, clients could not only coordinate communications all in one place, whether via phone, desktop, or the Web, but also create rules based on call origin to automatically route certain callers to the appropriate outlet. In 2004 Interactive Intelligence partnered with Onyx, a customer relationship management solutions firm, to provide coordinated services, and the following year it signed an agreement with the United Kingdom-based CallScripter to offer script service with the CIC software.

As Interactive Intelligence kept adding to the services its software could offer, it also kept refining how the software was delivered, so that customers could have more choices as to how their system was configured. By making the most of voice processing software, Interactive Intelligence allowed its customers to forego purchases of specialized communications hardware. In moving to an entirely SIP-based directory protocol, it gave customers the option of hosting all their communications on a single server. In 2004 Interactive Intelligence created a new subsidiary, Vonexus, specifically to sell its products to smaller businesses. The version sold by Vonexus was completely based on a Microsoft operating system, meaning it could provide customers with IP communications without requiring any specialized hardware.

The innovations were paying off for Interactive Intelligence. In 2004 it posted its first full year of positive operating results, with over $51 million in total revenues for the year. By April 2006 sales had climbed by more than 20 percent over the previous year, largely due to the widespread acceptance of VoIP systems for providing telephone services. Later that year, the company opened regional offices in Irvine, California, and Herndon, Virginia. "We're maybe a little tentative about declaring victory," Brown told *Indianapolis Star*'s Erika D. Smith. "But it's beginning to feel like the old days [before the tech bubble burst]." An independent test of the company's software in the spring of 2006 demonstrated that the software could handle 5,000 users and a million calls a day, proving that Interactive Intelligence could serve larger clients. By 2007 international sales accounted for almost 30 percent of the company's revenue. It was also merging into the portable market by designing its software to link into cell phones, laptops, and other portable computing devices.

A UNIQUE CORPORATE CULTURE

Even though many technology firms are based on the West Coast, Interactive Intelligence found it easy to maintain and grow a staff in the heartland of the Midwest. Part of this was due to its relaxed corporate structure. "What I try to do is set up an environment where there really is not a defined hierarchy," Brown told Katie Culbertson of the *Indiana Business Journal*. "We don't have an organizational chart. We don't want to think in terms of different people having different levels of worth to a company based upon some arbitrary classification. At least so far we've pretty successfully avoided any sort of caste system that you find in almost any other professionally run company our size."

The firm also offers several amenities to keep its employees, who regularly work more than 50 hours a week, feeling relaxed, positive, and inspired. Besides offering flex time and a casual dress code, Interactive Intelligence's Indianapolis headquarters offers rooms where employees can exercise, play foosball, or even take a quick nap. The comfortable, encouraging atmosphere led the Indiana Chamber of Commerce to name Interactive Intelligence one of the state's best firms to work for in 2009. "We have a lot of fun," Brown told Beck. "We do this for the intellectual challenge. We see ourselves as a bunch of Hoosier farm kids taking on the big multinationals and kicking their asses. We don't have any big problem attracting people … if you've got a good idea, you can make it fly here just as easy as anywhere else."

EXPANDING FOR THE FUTURE

In 2006 Interactive Intelligence branched out once again by adding the Interaction Optimizer, a workforce management feature, to its CIC software package. The module was designed to provide real-time data about calls and feedback to help supervisors manage their agents' assignments. It used historical data about calls to help predict future volumes of calls; it then coordinated that information with schedule changes, time off requests, and needed skills to help managers arrange personnel schedules to optimize productivity and lower costs. Another CIC upgrade was scheduled for 2009 that would use software to identify when a competitor is mentioned or when a customer is getting frustrated, then notify a supervisor to jump in on the call. "There was no use thinking about these things, because they couldn't be done before," Brown told Harlin. "But now that you have voice as data, and you can act upon it with computer software."

Even though the economic downturn that began in 2008 affected the company's stock price, Brown was confident about Interactive Intelligence's future. "We're not losing business to competitors, but instead seeing delays in purchases, even sometimes when we have verbal approvals, because of our more cautious buying environment," he told Schnitzler in August 2008. "Our products are still being well-received." As of 2009 the company had no debt and had millions of dollars invested in research and development.

"I can't emphasize enough the extent to which the success of this company is not due to me," Brown told Beck, noting that many scientists and programmers had contributed to the company from the beginning. Nevertheless, Brown, who served as the chief executive officer, president, and chairman of the board, has been recognized as a big part of the firm's success. The next step for the company was to further develop its management software and sell it not just to call centers, but to any office environment that needs to match tasks with workers and monitor their progress and productivity. The company remained confident it would succeed in that task. As Interactive Intelligence board member Mark E. Hill, another software entrepreneur, told Schnitzler in August 2008, "Don is quite a visionary, and very much understands the industry. He's transforming the company, like all great companies have to do over time."

Diane E. Telgen

PRINCIPAL SUBSIDIARIES

Interactive Portal; Vonexus.

PRINCIPAL COMPETITORS

Alcatel-Lucent; Aspect Software Inc.; Avaya Inc.; Nortel Networks.

FURTHER READING

Beck, Bill, "The Genius of Dr. Brown," *Indiana Business Magazine*, January 2000, p. 8.

Culbertson, Katie, "The Renaissance Man," *Indianapolis Business Journal*, April 27, 1998, p. 1A.

Harlin, Kevin, "Interactive Intelligence Inc., Indianapolis, Indiana; Software Maker Reduces the Hassle on Customer Service Calls," *Investor's Business Daily*, November 12, 2007, p. A5.

Heikens, Norm, "Indianapolis Software Firm Announces Losses, Lays off Workers," *Indianapolis Star*, July 10, 2001.

"Interactive Intelligence Subsidiary to Sell All-Software IP PBX," *CommWeb*, July 8, 2004.

Sharp, Jo Ellen Meyers, "Tech Firm Offers Naps to Workers," *Indianapolis Business Journal*, June 16, 2003, p. 21.

Naudi, Jack, "Indianapolis Software Company Ranked on List of Elite Technology Firms," *Indianapolis Star*, October 28, 2002.

Pleasant, Blair, "Interacting with Interactive Intelligence," *CommWeb*, November 4, 2003.

Pletz, John, "Brown's New Venture Takes Off," *Indianapolis Business Journal*, January 12, 1998, p. 1.

————, "Interactive Files for IPO," *Indianapolis Business Journal*, June 7, 1999, p. 3.

Pugh, Lori, "Interactive Intelligence Rides the IPO Wave," *Indianapolis Business Journal*, September 27, 1999, p. 6.

————, "New Tech Start-up Spun Off," *Indianapolis Business Journal*, January 24, 2000, p. 3.

Schnitzler, Peter, "Interactive Intelligence Pledges Profit This Year," *Indianapolis Business Journal*, July 30, 2001, p. 13.

————, "Interactive Looking Past Stock Slump: Software-Maker Positions Itself to Outlast Listless Economic Conditions," *Indianapolis Business Journal*, August 11, 2008, p. 3.

————, "Tech Darling Once Again: Persistence Pays for Interactive Intelligence," *Indianapolis Business Journal*, September 4, 2006, p. 1A.

Smith, Erika D., "VoIP Sales Propel Tech Firm's Earnings," *Indianapolis Star*, April 27, 2006.

Woods, David, "Indianapolis Firm's Software Helps Family, Friends Connect with Troops Overseas," *Indianapolis Star*, January 4, 2005.

Jacobs Engineering Group Inc.

———■———

1111 South Arroyo Parkway
Pasadena, California 91109-7084
U.S.A.
Telephone: (626) 578-3500
Fax: (626) 568-7144
Web site: http://www.jacobs.com/

Public Company
Founded: 1947 as Jacobs Engineering Company
Incorporated: 1987
Employees: 43,700
Sales: $11.25 billion (2008)
Stock Exchanges: NYSE
Ticker Symbol: JEC
NAICS: 237990 Other Heavy and Civil Engineering Construction; 561110 Office Administrative Services; 561720 Janitorial Services

■ ■ ■

Jacobs Engineering Group Inc. is one of the world's largest and most diverse providers of technical, professional, and construction services to industrial, commercial, and government clients worldwide. The company provides a broad spectrum of services, including scientific and specialty consulting, operations and maintenance, and engineering and construction. Jacobs Engineering's successful growth is largely accredited to its relationship-based approach to business. More than 90 percent of its business can be attributed to longstanding customers in such fields as oil and gas explora-

tion, production, and refining; programs for various national governments; pharmaceuticals and biotechnology; chemicals and polymers; buildings (healthcare, education, civic, governmental, and others); infrastructure; technology and manufacturing; consumer products; and pulp and paper. As of 2009, the company had offices in 27 countries in North America, Europe, Asia, the Middle East, and Australia.

COMPANY ORIGINS

Of Lebanese descent, Joseph J. Jacobs viewed his own entrepreneurial success in the context of the traditional emphasis among the Lebanese on commerce and self-reliance. Jacobs grew up in Brooklyn, New York, the son of a notions peddler who became wealthy during World War I by selling straight razors. When the safety razor was subsequently invented, the Jacobs family fortune declined, and young Joseph Jacobs was forced to scramble for extra dollars wherever he could. With strong encouragement from his mother, Jacobs stayed in school, eventually graduating in 1937 from the Polytechnic Institute of Brooklyn with a degree in engineering.

Unable to find steady work in the midst of the Great Depression, Jacobs began teaching at Polytechnic while working on advanced degrees. In 1942 he earned a doctorate in chemical engineering and took a position as senior chemical engineer at Merck & Company in Rahway, New Jersey, where he was involved in the development of vitamin processing and the manufacture of DDT and penicillin. Strongly influenced by the

COMPANY PERSPECTIVES

Quality for Jacobs means fulfilling client needs. Every client has unique needs which demand fulfillment for their business success. We at Jacobs are focused on understanding these unique needs and translating them into our project delivery and execution process with the goal of contributing significantly to our clients' success.

On the back of each Jacobs employee's business card–from our engineers to our construction crews to our CEO—it states that one of our primary purposes is "to strive for flawless execution of my work and to deliver superior value to everyone."

This is more than just a mission statement; it is the way we do business. To achieve the highest level of quality possible, we strive to exceed our clients' expectations. Our goal is to delight our customers and our intent is to build customer loyalty.

Jacobs. Let us exceed your expectations.

Lebanese tradition of being in business for oneself, Jacobs started his own business in 1947, following a stint at Chemurgic Corporation in Richmond, California. Founding the Jacobs Engineering Company as both a consulting agency and a manufacturers' representative for makers of large-scale equipment in the processing industry, Jacobs relocated the firm to Pasadena in anticipation of the phenomenal growth that would soon occur in southern California.

Because of a potential conflict of interest between his role as consultant and his work as a broker, Jacobs took pains to advise his clients of his dual professions and to maintain the highest possible standards of integrity with both groups of business associates. Regarding honesty as one of the basic tenets of his business philosophy, Jacobs told the Newcomen Society in 1980, "Play it straight, deal with honesty and integrity, and you'll get your share. My Lebanese heritage... is never really very far from me."

At first, the sales work expanded more quickly than the consulting end of the business, and by 1954 Jacobs had added four more men to handle sales while he and his associate Stan Krugman concentrated on design consultation. Among their initial consulting clients were such companies as Eston Chemical, Southwest Potash Company (later AMAX Inc.), and Kaiser Aluminum &

Chemical, for which Jacobs Engineering provided varied services, including feasibility studies, the analysis of proposed new processes, and the development of flowsheets.

LARGER CONTRACTS IN THE 1950S AND 1960S

In 1956 Jacobs Engineering landed its largest contract to date. Kaiser Aluminum, wishing to build a new and quite large alumina plant for which its own in-house engineers lacked the requisite technological experience, asked Jacobs Engineering to assume design responsibilities for the project. Although this was new territory and represented a somewhat daunting venture, Jacobs Engineering did the job, hiring an extra 20 designers to help with the complex project, and Kaiser built it as specified and to the satisfaction of everyone involved. Moreover, a decade later when Kaiser wanted to expand the plant threefold, they called in Jacobs Engineering to come up with the additional designs. In 1960 Jacobs Engineering won another important contract from Southwest Potash for the design and construction of a potash flotation plant. Until this point in the company's history, Jacobs Engineering had not taken on any construction work, regarding the industry as unprofessional. However, the job for Southwest Potash dispelled that idea for Joseph Jacobs, and his company then offered a full range of both engineering and construction services.

A near disaster in 1962 illustrated the qualities that enabled Jacobs Engineering to grow from a tiny local outfit to one of international importance. The company built another plant for Southwest Potash in Vicksburg, Mississippi, which was equipped with a novel process for making potassium nitrate. When the plant developed serious problems shortly after start-up, Jacobs and a team of his top engineers moved to Vicksburg for six months so that the problems could be corrected as quickly as possible. After months of intensive repair work, the plant proved to be of sound design, fulfilling the needs of Southwest Potash and adding to Jacobs Engineering's growing reputation for going the extra distance to achieve its clients' full satisfaction. It was a demonstration of commitment and agility that few of the larger companies in the field could have matched, and on such quality performances Jacobs Engineering based its growth.

Parlaying its reputation for hard work and integrity into a period of sustained growth during the 1960s, Jacobs Engineering snatched smaller contracts away from the industry's larger competitors and convinced

KEY DATES

1947: Joseph J. Jacobs founds the Jacobs Engineering Company.

1956: Jacobs Engineering Company is hired by Kaiser Aluminum to engineer a chemical plant in Louisiana.

1960: Jacobs expands to 150 employees when it wins a contract to design and build a potash flotation plant.

1970: Jacobs Engineering goes public.

1974: The company merges with the Pace Companies.

1987: Jacobs Engineering buys out Robert E. McKee Corporation.

1992: Noel Watson assumes the positions of CEO & president.

1999: The company completes a merger with Sverdrup Corp.; Jacobs Engineering Group named the "Most Admired E&C Company" by *Fortune* magazine.

2002: Craig Martin promoted to president of the company.

2004: After the death of founder Joseph J. Jacobs, Noel Watson is elected chairman of the board.

2007: Company acquires Carter & Burgess; is awarded the "Nunn-Perry Award."

2009: Jacobs's Engineering, Science, and Technical Services (ESTS) Group awarded the "Dwight D. Eisenhower Award for Excellence."

important potential customers of their capabilities. By 1967 Jacobs Engineering had opened offices throughout the country, encouraging each to emulate the main office's entrepreneurial bent and willingness to take risks and assume responsibility. Joseph Jacobs's hope was that each of the branch offices would duplicate the parent company's own strengths, and by and large they were able to do so. By 1970 Jacobs Engineering had grown to the point where it was advantageous to take the company public. Primarily as a way of rewarding employees with stock options, Jacobs Engineering went public; however, the founder's family maintained control of approximately 40 percent of the stock, and the company tried to retain the atmosphere of a family-run business.

CONTINUED EXPANSION IN THE 1970S

Sales in 1972 reached $70 million, and Jacobs Engineering began to pursue international as well as domestic contracts. As early as 1964, Jacobs Engineering had been interested in a projected potash recovery plant to be built by Jordan on the Dead Sea. Trading on the experience gained in working for Southwest Potash, Jacobs Engineering was selected to prepare a technical evaluation of the project and, after a decade-long hiatus due to the Arab-Israeli war of 1967, eventually signed a contract to design and build a $450 million plant for the Jordanian government. According to *Business Week*, Joseph Jacobs, speaking fluent Arabic, was instrumental in landing this huge job. The project was handled by Jacobs Engineering's international division based in Dublin, Ireland, which subcontracted much of the heavy construction work to a British company. Because Jacobs Engineering handled the assignment without a hitch, it was asked upon completion in the late 1970s to operate the plant as well.

Merging with the Pace Companies of Houston, Texas, in 1974, Jacobs Engineering recorded skyrocketing sales of $250 million in fiscal 1977, quadrupling that of five years earlier. The Pace Companies brought to Jacobs Engineering a strong presence in the Gulf Coast industries of petroleum refining and petrochemicals, which remained staple ingredients of Jacobs Engineering's revenue mix thereafter. With the addition of Pace and its resounding success in the Middle East, Jacobs (which changed its name to Jacobs Engineering Group) set its sights on bigger game, hoping one day to rival industry leaders such as Fluor and Bechtel.

Believing that his company had become too large to remain under his personal guidance, Joseph Jacobs made several attempts in the late 1970s to delegate executive authority along the lines favored by his much larger competitors. In 1976 Jacobs hired the first of a series of company presidents and later added a string of executive vice-presidents intended to help the firm pursue further large international contracts like the Jordanian potash project. Jacobs's "concern with management may be coming just in time," wrote *Business Week*, a sentiment shared by those who believed that a single entrepreneur could not handle the administration of a mature corporation.

Subsequent events proved that thinking wrong, at least in the case of Jacobs Engineering. As Joseph Jacobs reduced his involvement in the day-to-day management, the company went after ever larger contracts just as the country plunged into the severe recession of 1982–83. Profits shrank and then disappeared in a small but steady wave of red ink, while revenues fell by an astonishing 50 percent to about $200 million in 1984. The cause of this disaster was twofold. The sudden infusion of extra management saddled the company with a high overhead; worse yet, the enlarged executive staff naturally sought to justify its existence by a corresponding increase in revenues. Jacobs Engineering found itself bidding on so-called fixed-price contracts, as opposed to cost-reimbursable jobs favored by Joseph Jacobs. In the weak economic conditions, competition was brutal for the available fixed-price contracts, which typically included the gigantic engineering projects now pursued by Jacobs Engineering. Thus, Jacobs Engineering was awarded a smaller number of larger-than-average contracts yielding little if any profit.

SCALING BACK IN THE 1980S

Distressed by swollen overhead costs and managerial complacency, in 1985 Joseph Jacobs came "roaring back from retirement," as *Forbes* put it, to save his once gleaming creation. The chairman fired almost half of the company's 2,300 employees, including 8 of 14 vice-presidents, and generally returned the company to its old-fashioned methods of the previous three decades, a time when "we made all our decisions standing in the hall," as Jacobs told *ENR* magazine. Starting with a fresh determination not to bid on fixed-price contracts regardless of their appeal, Jacobs Engineering ceded the biggest projects to its bigger rivals, concentrating instead on medium-sized process plants and specialty construction, such as a research and development center for Lockheed Missiles and Space Company in Austin, Texas, a $65 million project, and an addition to the Community Hospital of San Gabriel, California, costing about $20 million. In particular, Jacobs Engineering began lobbying for the many projects suddenly available in the area of environmental safety and clean-up, which typically require a high level of technical competence but not necessarily a contractor of great size. In other words, Joseph Jacobs left to his competitors the battle for mere revenue dollar volume and restored his company's emphasis on what he called the "net return on brain-power," a ratio based on the amount of profit divided by number of employees to measure the profitable productivity per each of his highly skilled engineers.

The results of this program were astonishing. Between 1987 and 1991 Jacobs Engineering returned an industry best 22.4 percent on shareholders equity while also managing to increase sales by an average of 37 percent annually, which also topped the industry by a wide margin—all this without incurring any long-term debt. Annual reports in the early 1990s revealed that the company had literally zero debt; according to a 1992

Forbes index of leading engineering firms which listed the median debt to capital ratio as 25 percent, with several companies reporting figures well over 40 percent, Jacobs Engineering's ratio was given as 0.0 percent.

In the early 1990s Jacobs Engineering Group enjoyed a balanced sales mix, having long since shed its former dependence on the petroleum industry. Again, with the emphasis on smaller, high-tech, higher margin contracts, Jacobs Engineering provided a broad variety of engineering services. From its earlier work in the minerals, fertilizers, and petrochemical segments, Jacobs Engineering had diversified into the areas of pharmaceuticals, biotechnology, and sterile facilities, along with the previously mentioned opportunities in environmental protection projects. The company was the third largest domestic hazardous waste contractor, with 25 percent of its professional staff dedicated to environmentally driven projects. A 1987 buyout of Robert E. McKee Corporation (formerly the construction arm of Santa Fe Southern Pacific Corporation) gave the company added strength in the construction end of its business.

In 1992 Jacobs stepped down as CEO, and Noel Watson, an employee at Jacobs Engineering for 32 years, replaced him at the head of the company. Watson focused the company on two of its most profitable and growing segments: government-financed environmental cleanup jobs and facilities engineering for the biopharmaceutical industry. In 1993, 10 percent of Jacobs's annual revenue came from government contracts, but those contracts generated 20 percent of the company's pretax profits. Jacobs pursued this area in the mid-1990s with several government projects. In a joint venture with industry leader Fluor, Jacobs was awarded a contract in 1993 to clean up former uranium production facilities in Fernold, Ohio. The $2.2 billion contract was expected to generate as much as $40 million in profit for Jacobs. The company was also developing clean-up plans with the U.S. Navy for several sites in the southwestern United States and with the Department of Energy for a weapons plant in Colorado. With clean-ups at military bases and weapons sites on the rise, Jacobs anticipated its environmental division would grow 20 to 30 percent a year throughout the 1990s.

EXPANSION IN THE 1990S

Watson also targeted the biotech industry for further investment. As the young biotech industry matured during the 1990s, Jacobs Engineering wanted to be in the position to build the specialized plants they would need for product development. To that end, Jacobs purchased Triad Technologies and Sigel Group in the early 1990s, two companies that expanded Jacobs's expertise in designing and constructing biotechnology facilities.

Once again aiming to compete with the industry leaders, Jacobs needed a stronger presence internationally. With foreign contracts accounting for only 16 percent of Jacobs's annual revenues in 1992, Jacobs lagged far behind the overseas activity of rivals Foster Wheeler, Fluor, and Bechtel. To narrow the gap, Jacobs purchased the U.K. companies H&G Process Contracting and H&G Contractors in 1993. Humphreys & Glasgow, as the companies were collectively known, were among Europe's most widely recognized contractors.

By 1993 the company had fully recovered from the hard years of the mid-1980s. Not only did the company earn $6.5 million on revenues of $26.6 million in fiscal 1992, but it also held a record backlog of $1.8 billion in contracted business.

Some of that profitability went toward funding further acquisitions. In 1994 Jacobs bought CRS Sirrine Engineers and CRSS Constructors for $38 million. The purchase moved Jacobs Engineering into design and construction for the paper and semiconductor industries. Although the company paused to catch its breath in 1995 and make headway on its backlog, in 1996 Jacobs's acquisitions spree continued. That year it further expanded its presence in Europe by purchasing 49 percent of Serete Group, an engineering company that primarily served the government sector and specialized in communications. In 1997 Jacobs formed a joint venture with Stone & Webster that would also extend its reach internationally. Named Stone & Webster/Humphreys & Glasgow Ltd., the venture would design and construct power plants in India. The same year, Jacobs purchased CPR Engineering and incorporated the specialist in paper plant engineering as a division.

As Jacobs Engineering grew in size, it maintained an impressive performance record. In 1997 it boasted a five-year return on capital of nearly 16 percent, and it beat out its rivals in terms of sales growth: a five-year average of 12.4 percent. For fiscal year 1998, the company reported record revenues of $2.1 billion and record net income of $54 million. The company expected a continued rise in revenues and income based on its backlog of $3.33 billion.

In 1999 Jacobs Engineering completed a merger with Sverdrup Corp., positioning itself as the premier full-service consulting firm in the engineering, architecture, construction and maintenance fields. As reported in *Business Wire*, Watson said, "Together, we would immediately emerge as a national leader in three very important and expanding markets: public sector buildings, civil engineering and infrastructure, and

federal sector operations and maintenance." Two months later, the company re-organized Sverdrup's business and management units, replacing Kraig Kreikemeier, president of Sverdrup facilities, with Warren Dean of CRSS, and renamed the facility Sverdrup CRSS. By September, the Sverdrup subsidiary landed a $12.6 million information technology task order contract from the U.S. Special Operations Command to provide local area network and automated information systems support to numerous sites throughout the country.

The company garnered further attention through its community development programs. Founded by Joseph Jacobs in 1988, the Jacobs Center for NonProfit Innovation implemented ways to strengthen underinvested neighborhoods through entrepreneurial opportunities, training workshops, and creative investments. In June 1999 the foundation undertook a $56 million development project for the residents of San Diego's Diamond Business Improvement District. At the end of its fiscal year ending September 30, 1999, the company again announced record net earnings in excess of $65 million. In that same year, *Fortune* named the Jacobs Engineering Group the "Most Admired E&C Company."

ACQUISITIONS AND SUCCESSES POST-2000

The company's rapid growth required improved and expanded facilities. Early in 2000, shortly after converting its Philadelphia office, the company broke ground on a 300,000 square-foot, 18-acre site in Houston's Oak Park at Westchase. According to Pete Kelly, vice-president of operations in Houston, this new facility would accommodate 3,000 employees. Jacobs also increased its presence in the global market through the acquisition of Stork NV's engineering and construction business. The combination of Jacobs and Stork operations in Europe created the continent's largest and most diverse engineering and construction group, while Jacobs's Asian presence was further supplemented by Stork's operations in Malaysia and Thailand. Within weeks of this acquisition, the company announced that it had signed an alliance agreement with Novartis, a global leader in healthcare, to provide engineering, architecture, and other services for Novartis's investments in India, Europe, and the United States. In April 2000, in a move to strengthen its position in Europe's pharmaceutical industry, Jacobs acquired Chemint, an engineering design and consulting services firm headquartered in Milan, Italy.

In February 2001 recognizing the company as the best qualified firm to oversee the architecture and engineering of the National Airspace System, the Federal Aviation Administration awarded Jacobs a $404 million contract to provide a broad range of design and construction services. In the last quarter of 2001 the company established a presence in Canada through the acquisition of McDermott Engineers & Constructors Limited, an engineering, construction, and maintenance services firm in the petrochemical, chemical, petroleum refining, and upstream oil and gas industries. The diversity of its customers continued to be one of the company's key strengths, with Jacobs's earnings growing between 14 percent and 19 percent for five consecutive years.

In a little more than three years, the company had more than doubled in size, and Noel Watson decided it was time to separate the positions of CEO and president. In July 2002, with Watson staying on as CEO, Craig Martin, Jacobs's executive vice-president of global sales and a 30-year veteran of the technical professional service business, was promoted to the position of president. While other companies were struggling in a weakening economy, Jacobs continued to thrive and, at the end of fiscal year 2003, boasted record net earnings of $128 million. For a second time, Jacobs Engineering Group was named the "Most Admired E&C Company" by *Fortune.*

By 2004 the company had more than 35,000 employees and revenues of nearly $5 billion. In a move to enhance its capabilities in the airport and aviation sector, Jacobs acquired Leigh Fisher Associates, a leading international airport consulting firm. Other acquisitions that year included Babtie Group Ltd., which expanded the company's international presence in the infrastructure market, and 34 percent of Fortum's Neste Engineering Oy, a leading energy company based in Finland. On October 23, 2004, at the age of 88, Joseph J. Jacobs passed away, leaving as his legacy one of the world's largest and most profitable engineering and construction companies. The board of directors elected Noel Watson to succeed Jacobs as chairman of the board.

As oil prices surged and market demand increased, Jacobs's revenues soared, with the company getting new energy-related contracts on a weekly basis. Of its $4.6 billion in revenues in 2005, approximately one-third was attributed to the fuel market. In 2006, with Craig Martin now at the helm as CEO, the company acquired the multidisciplinary engineering firm, Techna West Engineering Limited in Edmonton, Canada. This was followed by the acquisition of W.H. Linder & Associates Inc., an upstream/offshore engineering firm. In July 2006 the company stunned investors and competitors when it reported a staggering 38 percent increase in its third-quarter earnings. It came as no surprise when *Forbes* named the Jacobs Engineering Group one of "America's Best Big Companies" and again designated it

the "Most Admired Company in the E&C Industry."

By 2007 the company boasted more than 45,000 employees with revenues approaching $8 billion. The company continued to expand, and other high profile acquisitions included Edwards and Kelcey Inc., John F. Brown Company, and Carter & Burgess. Within the context of this success, the company continued to give back to the community. In April 2007, in recognition of its contributions to the Calgary community in Alberta, Canada, Jacobs received two awards from the United Way, the "Engineering Challenge Award" and the "Campaign Volunteer Spirit Award." In that same year, the company was also awarded the prestigious "Nunn-Perry Award" from the Department of Defense.

By the end of the 2008 fiscal year, the company reported record net earnings of $420.7 million, and was showing no signs of slowing down. Its multi-million dollar purchase of LES Engineering in the United Kingdom combined the company with Jacobs's operation in Immingham, creating a formidable presence in the United Kingdom and Europe. The company's stellar record continued, and in May 2009 its Engineering, Science, and Technical Services (ESTS) Group at NASA Marshall Space Flight Center was awarded the Dwight D. Eisenhower Award for Excellence. By mid-2009, the company's revenues exceeded $11 billion, proving its diversified business model was, indeed, a key to success.

Jonathan Martin
Updated, Susan Windisch Brown; Marie O'Sullivan

PRINCIPAL SUBSIDIARIES

Jacobs Carter Burgess; Jacobs Technology Inc.; Jacobs U.K. Limited.

PRINCIPAL COMPETITORS

Bechtel Corporation; Fluor Corporation; Foster Wheeler Inc.

FURTHER READING

Barnett, Chris, "Managing by Instinct," *Nation's Business,* December 1985.

Berry, Kate, "Jacobs Engineering Case Puts Past Contracts under Scrutiny," *Los Angeles Business Journal,* March 29, 2004, p. 3.

Cook, Lynn J., "Another Building Rises in Busy Hub," *Houston Business Journal,* February 4, 2000, p. 1.

Elliott, Alan R. "How to Engineer a Recession-Proof Strategy," *Investor's Business Daily,* August 26, 2002, p. A8.

Fine, Howard, "Strength in Capital Spending Gives Boost to Jacobs Shares," *Los Angeles Business Journal,* February 20,

2006, p. 35.

"Jacobs Buys Santa Fe's McKee," *ENR*, July 30, 1987.

"Jacobs Completes Agreement with Stork," *Business Wire*, February 16, 2000, p. 502.

"Jacobs Engineering Enters Merger Talks with Sverdrup Corp.," *Wall Street Journal*, November 6, 1998, p. A8.

"Jacobs Engineering Group Inc. and Sverdrup Corporation in Merger Talks," *Business Wire*, November 6, 1998, p. 323.

"Jacobs Engineering Group Reduces Expenses and Improves Productivity with WebEx Real-Time Web Meetings," *Business Wire*, March 15, 2001, p. 2129.

"Jacobs Engineering's Goal: Quintupling by 1986," *ENR*, August 13, 1981.

"Jacobs Eyes Smaller Jobs," *ENR*, December 2, 1982.

"Jacobs Giant Merger Brings Firms Together," *Europe Intelligence Wire*, August 27, 2008.

Jacobs, Joseph J., *Anatomy of an Entrepreneur: Family, Culture and Ethics*. New York: ICS Press, 1991.

———, *Jacobs Engineering Group Inc.: A Story of Pride, Reputation and Integrity*. New York: Newcomen Society in North America, 1980.

———, *The Compassionate Conservative: Assuming Responsibility and Respecting Human Dignity*. New York: ICS Press, 1999.

"Jacobs Selected as Best Qualified Firm for $404 Million FAA Contract," *Business Wire*, February 7, 2001, p. 93.

"A Loner Relaxes His Grip," *Business Week*, November 21, 1977.

Lubove, Seth, "Thank You, Jack Welch," *Forbes*, January 13, 1997, pp. 102–03.

Manning, Margie, "Jacobs Shakes Up Sverdrup," *St. Louis Business Journal*, March 22, 1999, p. A1.

Myerhoff, Matt, "Striking It Rich: Jacobs Engineering Benefits from High Oil Prices," *Los Angeles Business Journal*, June 6, 2005, p. 10.

Poole, Claire, "Faster, Better, Cheaper," *Forbes*, January 6, 1992.

"Potash Project Taps Dead Sea Salts," *ENR*, May 28, 1981.

Reid, Paul, "Independents Create New Benefit Model," *Drug Topics*, January 8, 2007, p. 28.

Scharf, Stewart, "A Sturdy Blueprint at Jacobs Engineering," *Business Week Online*, February 4, 2003.

Shinkle, Kirk, "With Public Tills Fatter, This Firm Takes a Bite," *Investor's Business Daily*, July 11, 2001, p. A8.

Taylor, John H., "After the Pink Slips," *Forbes*, August 2, 1993, p. 51.

Toth, Simone, "Neighbors Elated: Progress Comes to the Diamond Business District," *San Diego Business Journal*, June 14, 1999, p. 16.

Watkins, Steve, "Keeping Jacobs' Engineers Busy," *Investor's Business Daily*, July 9, 2007, p. A5.

The Jim Henson Company

1416 North La Brea Avenue
Charlie Chaplin Studios
Hollywood, California 90028
U.S.A.
Telephone: (323) 802-1500
Fax: (323) 802-1825
Web site: http://www.henson.com

Private Company
Incorporated: 1958 as Jim Henson Productions
Employees: 75
Sales: $110 million (2007 est.)
NAICS: 7812 Motion Picture & Video Production; 3944 Games, Toys, & Children's Vehicles; 2731 Book Publishing & Printing; 511130 Book Publishers

∎ ∎ ∎

The Jim Henson Company is a leading producer of films, live stage shows, television programming, and gaming content for family audiences. Products are based on its innovative puppetry, animatronics, and digital animation. The company also has a recording studio and acquires independent films produced around the world. The Henson Company has received more than 50 Emmy Awards and 9 Grammy Awards. Founded by puppeteer Jim Henson in 1955, the company has managed to maintain the highest standards of critical and artistic excellence while becoming a major financial success in the industry. The company experienced a crisis when Jim Henson died suddenly in 1990 at age 53, leaving the business to his five children. In 2000 the siblings sold the company to EM.TV, a German concern, from which they repurchased it in 2003.

COMPANY ORIGINS IN THE 1950S

Jim Henson combined extreme simplicity in puppet design with sophisticated comedy inspired by the vaudeville and radio performers he had admired in his youth. Many of his creations were little more than socks with eyes, and yet, through subtle manipulation and strong voicing he created characters that have become essential emblems of late 20th-century American culture. Born in Mississippi in 1936, Henson began experimenting with puppets as a child and had his first paying job as a puppeteer in 1954 at a local television station in Washington, DC, before he had finished college. One year later he formed a partnership with Jane Nebel, whom he later married, and the team produced a series of five-minute puppet shows for television entitled *Sam and Friends*. *Sam and Friends* introduced audiences to Kermit the Frog, the character that would later become most closely associated with Henson himself, as throughout his career Henson always provided Kermit's voice. By 1956 the Muppets had appeared on national network television on *The Steve Allen Show*. Henson and Nebel's work on *Sam and Friends* earned them their first Emmy Award for local television in 1958.

In 1963 the Hensons, along with scriptwriter Jerry Juhl, who had joined the team in 1961, moved their headquarters to New York City, where they were joined by master puppet builder Don Sahlin and versatile

COMPANY PERSPECTIVES

Making the world a better place by inspiring people to celebrate life is the company's mission.

performer Frank Oz. Oz was to become the voice behind many of the most famous Muppet characters, including Miss Piggy, the prima donna love match to the indomitable Kermit. In 1966 the Muppets had their first of many appearances on the *Ed Sullivan Show*, the premier avenue to stardom for variety acts during the period.

NATIONAL EXPOSURE IN THE 1970S

After a decade of steadily increasing critical success and popular recognition, the Muppets became part of a larger phenomenon in 1969, when they were featured as an integral part of the Children's Television Network's groundbreaking educational series *Sesame Street*. The Muppets' connection with *Sesame Street* assured their enduring popularity and salability for licensing purposes. Parents felt good about their children watching *Sesame Street*, which stressed education, while the timeless humor of the Muppets appealed to the parents themselves; parents and children became equally attached to the lovable characters. One year after the premiere of *Sesame Street*, the Jim Henson creation Big Bird appeared on the cover of *Time* magazine, marking both the meteoric rise of the educational television series and the recognition of the Muppets as cultural icons.

The unusual appeal of the Muppets to both children and adult members of their audience led to a prime-time Muppet venture in the mid-1970s entitled the *Muppet Show*. Aside from Kermit the Frog, all of the characters on the *Muppet Show* were fresh creations, distinct from their *Sesame Street* brethren. The first 24 episodes of the *Muppet Show* were produced at ATV studios in England and sold mostly to independent stations in the United States, including five wholly owned CBS affiliates. Despite its outsider position in the industry and its unusual status as a prime-time family series with puppets, the show became an enormous hit, winning an Emmy Award for variety and comedy series in 1978 and drawing the top talent of the period as guest stars. In the same year a record album based on music from the *Muppet Show* went platinum and won a Grammy Award for best recording for children.

Although Jim Henson's success depended on simplicity, subtlety, and a fine sense of classic comedy, the production of Muppet films, television series, and stage shows became increasingly high-tech. Eventually the Muppets became associated with both the simple green puppet that was Kermit the Frog as well as the cutting edge in electronically manipulated puppetry called animatronics. Animatronics is a generic term for puppet manipulation whereby the facial features of the puppet are manipulated by remote control by someone who is not necessarily in physical contact with the puppet. This technique allowed Henson to create enormous puppets which were manipulated by a team of technicians, some of whom moved the puppet's body physically while others electronically moved the eyes, ears, mouth, and so on. In order to create an effective illusion, the team members would all be in contact through headsets. This technology was particularly effective for traveling stage shows, such as *Muppet Treasure Island* and *Muppet Babies Onstage*, in which larger puppets were needed to be visible and effective in large theaters.

The fact that Jim Henson's team was on the cutting edge of techno-puppetry meant that its services were in demand for collaborations with other production companies. Under the trademark Jim Henson's Creature Shop, Jim Henson Productions sold its creative technology to a wide variety of other producers, such as film director George Lucas and his special effects company Industrial Light and Magic, which created the fantastical characters featured in the *Star Wars* series of films in the late 1970s.

BRANCHING OUT INTO FEATURE FILMS IN THE 1980S

The success of the *Muppet Show* on television prompted Jim Henson Productions to try its hand at a feature film, *The Muppet Movie*, which premiered in London in 1979. Although audience response to *The Muppet Movie* was less effusive than it had been to the same cast of characters on the small screen, the film did well enough to ensure a sequel, *The Great Muppet Caper*, released in 1981.

The *Muppet Show* went off the air in 1980 after 120 shows, but another film based on the show, *The Muppets Take Manhattan*, was produced in 1984, and the familiar cast of characters was maintained for other projects on both the large and small screen. Moreover, the company produced other features with new characters; fantasy films *The Dark Crystal* and *Labyrinth*, starring David Bowie, both of which were directed by Jim Henson, were produced in the mid-1980s. *Fraggle Rock* followed the *Muppet Show* as Henson's next major

KEY DATES

1958: Jim Henson founds and incorporates company as Muppets, Inc.

1969: *Sesame Street* debuts on television with Muppets characters.

1979: Jim Henson starts up the Creature Shop to produce special effects for films.

1989: Company enters partnership with Disney.

1990: Jim Henson dies of pneumonia at 53.

1993: *Kermit and Friends: Are We There Yet?* book and tape set receives Parents' Choice award for records.

1995: Environmental Protection Agency 25th Anniversary Earth Day honors Jim Henson Productions' characters for their ability to communicate environmental messages.

1998: Company is renamed The Jim Henson Company; Jim Henson honored as one of Time magazine's 100 Most Influential Artists and Entertainers of the Century.

2000: EM.TV & Merchandising of Germany acquires the company for $680 million.

2003: Jim Henson's five children buy back the company for $89 million.

2004: The Henson Company sells the Muppets and "Bear in the Big Blue House" properties to Walt Disney Co.

2005: Company wins awards for its restoration of the Charlie Chaplin lot.

television venture in 1983, but it never achieved an equivalent broad-based audience appeal. Nevertheless, the company produced 96 episodes before closing *Fraggle Rock* in 1986, when the show began a lucrative run in syndication.

In 1989 Jim Henson Productions entered into a partnership with Disney. In a deal negotiated by Jim Henson and Disney chief Michael Eisner, Disney acquired Henson Associates Inc., giving Disney the right to use the Muppet characters at its theme parks and on its cable network. Kermit the Frog would later appear in the inaugural special for The Disney Channel, and Big Bird marched in the celebratory parade. Disney also agreed to co-produce future projects with Jim Henson Productions. Unfortunately, Henson himself did not live to see the fruit of this deal; he died suddenly of streptococcal pneumonia in 1990, shortly before the release of another feature film, *The Witches*, based on a book by children's author Roald Dahl. Henson's last project was

the creation of *Jim Henson's Muppet Vision 3-D*, a featured attraction at the Walt Disney World Resort in Florida.

CONTINUED EXPANSION IN THE 1990S

The death of Jim Henson Productions' founder, president, and primary creative force came at a point in the company's history when its future had seemed brighter than ever. Jim Henson's son Brian Henson was appointed president in 1991. Brian Henson had been trained as a puppeteer by his father and had worked on *The Great Muppet Caper*, *The Muppets Take Manhattan*, and *Labyrinth*, as well as on puppet animation projects with other producers. His directorial debut came in 1992, only one year after being appointed president of the company, with *A Muppet Christmas Carol*, starring Michael Caine.

In 1993 Jim Henson's Creature Shop began research into refining its animatronic technique to create as high a degree of verisimilitude as possible. Rather than creating only fantastic or comic puppets, the company attempted to create absolutely realistic animals with human characteristics. Following two years of research, new techniques were developed and used to create talking animals with human emotions for the film *Babe*, produced by Universal Pictures. *Babe*, the story of a pig and his barnyard friends, was an enormous critical and box-office success, winning the 1996 Oscar for visual effects. Moreover, the success of *Babe* led to a deluge of films using the new animatronic technology, including Disney's *101 Dalmatians* and *George of the Jungle*. Jim Henson's Creature Shop's animatronic technology was equally in demand for television advertising and was eventually used to create 30-second spots for such brands as Carling, Smirnoff, Honda, Mercedes, and Weet-abix, among others.

The growth of the company led to the creation of several subdivisions and productive relationships with other corporations in the 1990s. Jim Henson Video and Jim Henson Records were launched in 1993, while the Muppet Press published more than 400 different children's book titles. Jim Henson Productions joined forces with Starwave Corporation in 1994 to create a series of educational games on CD-ROM, and as a result of this collaborative venture Jim Henson Interactive was established as a separate division. Jim Henson Productions and Sony Pictures Entertainment agreed to co-produce motion pictures, leading to the creation of Jim Henson Pictures in 1995. Stephanie Allain was named the first president of production at Jim Henson Pictures. The first feature to result from her tenure was *Buddy*, starring Rene Russo, in 1997. Also during this time, Jim Henson Interactive entered into an exclusive agreement with Microsoft to produce interactive programming for MSN, the third-largest online network worldwide.

Muppet toys, clothing, toiletries, and an array of other merchandise were created under more than 75 different licensing deals in the late 1990s, making Jim Henson Productions a major player worldwide. Kermit Hollywood boutiques were opened in the late 1990s to promote Muppet products at leading department stores, while Jim Henson Productions signed an exclusive licensing deal with Galoob Toys to produce toys based on Muppet characters in 1998.

Margaret Loesch was named president of Jim Henson Television Group in 1998. Due to the diversity of Jim Henson Productions' operations and its growing list of divisions and subsidiaries, the company changed its name to The Jim Henson Company in 1998. In 2000 the company moved to a location that embodied creative history, the Charlie Chaplin Studios in Hollywood, which was designated a historic cultural monument by the the Los Angeles Cultural Heritage Board. Chaplin opened the studios in 1918; later owners filmed television programs and produced records there. Lisa Henson told *Los Angeles Business Journal* writer Elizabeth Hayes, "It's not your typical corporate space, but it's ideal for the Muppets." The company won a Hollywood Entertainment Museum Legacy Award and a Hollywood Heritage Award for its sensitive renovation of the Chaplin lot in 2005.

OWNERSHIP CHANGES, AND CHANGES

The Henson siblings hoped to find a partner to underwrite costs, but they instead found a buyer for the Jim Henson Company in 2000. German company EM.TV & Merchandising acquired the company for $680 million. The sale included the rights to Sesame Street characters, which the new owner quickly sold to Sesame Workshop while retaining the rights to the popular Kermit the Frog, Miss Piggy, and Fozzie Bear characters. EM.TV also sold the company's rights in the Odyssey, Noggin, and Kermit cable channels. Under the deal the Hensons continued to run the Henson Company as a division of EM.TV.

Soon after the company announced in 2003 that it was producing a film about a creature who makes the desires of five siblings come true, the five Henson siblings successfully bought back the Jim Henson Company from EM.TV. Reportedly, their $89 million bid was accepted over higher offers by Walt Disney Co., a consortium backed by Sony Pictures Entertainment,

and others. Their acquisition brought the Muppets, the Muppet Babies, the Fraggles, the Hoobs, Farscape, and Bear in the Big Blue House—as well as the marketing of thousands of licensed products associated with these characters—back into family ownership. At the time of the buyback, the company's principal operations included Henson Television, Jim Henson Pictures, Jim Henson Interactive, Jim Henson Home Entertainment, the Henson Recording Studio, and Jim Henson's Creature Shop.

After reacquiring the company, the family decided to reduce its size and focus on producing creative films, television programs, and other entertainment and partner with fiscally sound companies for distribution and branding. Virtual puppetry and computer animation were at the core of this strategy. Henson Interactive teamed up with JHI in 2001 to use previously created content in new ways. The Muppets became central characters in PlayStation escapades and in games at MuppetWorld.com. Using the Henson Digital Performance System enabled Activision, Inc., to expeditiously create lifelike character animations for its military video games in 2004. Rapper Kanye West's 2008 Glow in the Dark concert tour featured a robot and puppets from the Creature Shop as part of a spectacular that also included holograms and a light show.

Virtual puppetry and computer animation aside, soft puppets remained part of the business through the Jim Henson Company's involvement as an outside producer of *Sesame Street* and a production agreement with Disney, owner of the Muppets and Bear in the Big Blue House characters since 2004. The deal with Walt Disney Co. included film and television libraries, copyrights and trademarks, and distribution and licensing rights for the characters. The Henson children's sale of the properties to Disney finalized their father's wish to give his characters a lasting home with a quality-conscious company.

As of 2009, Brian and Lisa Henson served as co-chairmen and CEOs. Brian Henson was in charge of corporate structure and digital technology, and Lisa Henson, a former president of Columbia Pictures, oversaw production and television development.

Donald C. McManus
Updated, Doris Maxfield

PRINCIPAL DIVISIONS

Jim Henson Company: Discoveries; Jim Henson's Creature Shop; Henson Recording Studios; Henson Alternative; The HUB.

FURTHER READING

Andrews, Andrew L., "For EM.TV, A Muppet Mission Accomplished," *New York Times*, February 28, 2000.

Farrow, Boyd, "Business and Media: It's Time to Play the Music, It's Time to Sell the Rights: The Muppet Masters Clan Are Back in Control—for Now," *Observer* (London), May 25, 2003.

Finch, Christopher, *Jim Henson the Works: The Art, the Magic, the Imagination*, New York: Random House, 1993.

Grala, Alyson, "Creature Creations," *License!*, July 2004.

Hayes, Elizabeth, "Henson Moving to Historical Charlie Chaplin Studios," *Los Angeles Business Journal*, February 21, 2000.

"Henson Heirs Buy Back Muppets for $78M," *New York Post*, May 8, 2003.

"Henson Siblings to Acquire The Jim Henson Co.," *Home Accents Today*, June 2003.

Hopkins, Nic, and Jack Malvern, "UK Home of the Muppets Faces Closure over Tax," *Times* (London), June 4, 2005.

"Jim Henson 40th Anniversary," special issue, *Variety*, December 11, 1995.

Miller, S., "Empire of the Imagination," *Variety*, December 11, 1995, pp. 55–56.

Olson, Catherine Applefeld, "Play the Music, Light the Lights: The Muppets Celebrate 25 Years," *Billboard*, August 3, 2002.

Richmond, Ray, "Creature Feature: Building on a 50-Year Legacy, the Jim Henson Co.'s Future Is a Powerful Blend of Traditional Puppeteering and Technology," *Hollywood Reporter*, September 20, 2005.

———, "Sibling Revelry: Jim Henson's Son and Daughter Maintain Their Father's Vision while Leading His Company into the Future," *Hollywood Reporter*, September 20, 2005.

Sheats, M., "Pulling Strings," *Variety*, December 11, 1995, p. 68.

Stalter, K., "Gone Digital," *Variety*, December 11, 1995, p. 74.

Swanson, Tim, "For a Muppet, It's All About Performance," *Variety*, January 22, 2001.

Yanover, N. S., "The Selling of the Green," *Variety*, December 11, 1995, p. 70.

John F. Kennedy Center for the Performing Arts

2700 F Street NW
Washington, D.C. 20566-0002
U.S.A.
Telephone: (202) 467-4600
Toll Free: (800) 444-1324
Fax: (202) 416-8676
Web site: http://www.kennedy-center.org

Nonprofit Company
Founded: 1958 (opened, 1971)
Employees: 700
Total Assets: $24.31 million (2007 est.)
NAICS: 711110 Theater Companies and Dinner Theaters; 711120 Dance Companies; 711130 Musical Groups and Artists

■ ■ ■

A massive edifice situated on 17 acres on the banks of the Potomac River in Washington, D.C., the John F. Kennedy Center for the Performing Arts is the largest cultural facility of its kind. Home to both the National Symphony Orchestra (NSO) and the Suzanne Farrell Ballet, its myriad of highly regarded programs draw some of the most venerable names in the artistic community to its staff. The Center presents music, dance, and theater across a broad spectrum of genres, as well as festivals, community outreach, educational programs, and media broadcasting. Additionally, the Center sponsors three prestigious annual awards: the Kennedy Center Mark Twain Prize for American Humor, the

Marion Anderson Award, and the Kennedy Center Honors. It attracts more than three million visitors from around the world each year and offers in excess of 2,000 performances annually.

The Center was designated by Congress in 1964 as a living memorial to U.S. President John F. Kennedy, who was assassinated the year before. The Center is committed to fulfilling Kennedy's vision of the arts as being a "contribution to the human spirit." This commitment is as apparent in the 21st century as it was when the Center opened its doors to the public in 1971.

ORIGINS IN 1958

The National Cultural Center that later became the Kennedy Center was conceived in 1958, when President Dwight D. Eisenhower signed bipartisan legislation authorizing its construction. The facility was to have a broad artistic mandate and a mission that contained an educational component, and it was defined as a self-sustaining, privately funded operation. A tremendous fundraising campaign was promptly launched and was enthusiastically spearheaded by longtime supporter of the arts John F. Kennedy upon his ascension to the presidency in 1961. Kennedy's strong backing of the endeavor was crucial to its eventual success in many ways, but perhaps the most significant of his contributions was appointing Roger Lacey Stevens as the Center's chairman.

Born in Detroit on March 12, 1910, Stevens faced the onset of the Great Depression as a young adult, when he was forced to forgo a Harvard education in

COMPANY PERSPECTIVES

"I am certain that after the dust of centuries has passed over our cities, we too, will be remembered not for our victories or defeats in battle or in politics, but for our contribution to the human spirit." (President John F. Kennedy)

As always, the Center continues its efforts to fulfill President Kennedy's vision by producing and presenting an unmatched variety of theater and musicals, dance and ballet, orchestral, chamber, jazz, popular, and folk music, and multi-media performances for all ages. Every year, the institution that bears President Kennedy's name brings his dream to fruition, touching the lives of millions of people through thousands of performances by the greatest artists from across America and around the world. The Center also nurtures new works and young artists, serving the nation as a leader in arts education and creating broadcasts, tours, and outreach programs.

favor of a more affordable one at the University of Michigan because of his father's financial troubles. It was a disappointment he felt keenly. By 1930 he had dropped out of college and started working on the Ford assembly line, where he acquired an appreciation for labor unions and liberal politics. In 1934 his life and fortunes were forever altered when he took up real estate as a trade. He proved to have a knack for it, amassing his first small fortune before he was 30 years old and continuing on to such legendary deals as the purchase and sale of the Empire State Building.

In the 1950s and 1960s Stevens turned his considerable energies toward Broadway, where he became the larger-than-life producer of more than 200 productions, including *West Side Story*, *Bus Stop*, *Cat on a Hot Tin Roof*, and *A Man for All Seasons*, as well as an influential proponent of the early work of such notable playwrights as Jean Kerr and Harold Pinter. Also committed to public service, he served as chairman of the Democratic Party's finance committee in 1956 and eventually became the first chair of the National Council on the Arts (later known as the National Endowment for the Arts). Stevens had, in short, a taste for risk, an eye for talent, and a gift for generating money. It made sense, then, that Stevens was approached by Kennedy in 1961 to help get his pet project started.

REALIZATION OF THE DREAM

Even with Stevens at the helm, the fundraising efforts moved slowly at first, and at one point Stevens was prompted to offer his resignation, which the president was wise enough to refuse. Washington, D.C., was largely considered a cultural wasteland at the time, which may have accounted for the initial sluggishness of the drive. Then, tragedy struck on November 22, 1963, when a sniper's bullet killed Kennedy in Dallas, Texas. That terrible loss was unexpectedly translated into something of a boon for the Center. In 1964 Congress renamed it in Kennedy's honor and designated it as a "living memorial" to the slain president. As a result, the project had a wider scope and appeal to prospective donors. Further, the new designation was accompanied by $23 million in federal funds to assist in construction. In addition, Congress had created a unique marriage of public and private funding through which the Center received annual federal money to pay for building maintenance and operation. The Center remained self-sustaining in that its artistic and educational programs were paid for via ticket sales and donations. With the project thus buoyed by increased visibility and the ensuing accelerated private gifts, as well as federal assistance, ground was broken later that year and construction on the Kennedy Center was begun.

Despite the newfound energy surrounding the project, more than $30 million in private contributions were necessary to bring it to fruition, which took time. Stevens persevered in his typical low-key manner though, notably aided by the Friends of the Kennedy Center volunteers, who traveled the nation to win private support. More than 40 countries lent their assistance as well, offering money, building materials, and artwork to the endeavor. Finally, the many years of persistence paid off on September 8, 1971, when the Kennedy Center opened its doors to the public for the first time.

Designed by Edward Durell Stone, the Center was an imposing rectangular structure covered with Italian Carrara marble and housing 1.5 million square feet of usable floor space. It had three operating theaters when it debuted (that number eventually grew to nine), and its grand foyer was one of the most extensive rooms in the world—75 feet longer than the entire height of the Washington Monument. Appropriately, a seven-foot high, 3,000-pound bronze bust of Kennedy (by American sculptor Robert Berks) was displayed in the grand foyer. Also fittingly, one of the theaters bore Eisenhower's name. The Center was, in short, an impressive edifice that most found suitable to its lofty calling.

KEY DATES

1958: President Dwight D. Eisenhower signs the National Cultural Center Act.

1961: Roger L. Stevens is appointed chairman of the National Cultural Center.

1964: Center is designated a living memorial to President John F. Kennedy after his assassination in November 1963.

1971: Facility opens as the John F. Kennedy Center for the Performing Arts on September 8.

1986: The National Symphony Orchestra becomes officially affiliated with the Center.

1988: Stevens ends his storied tenure as chairman.

1994: Billy Taylor becomes artistic director for jazz.

1998: Stevens dies.

2001: The Suzanne Farrell Ballet is founded as the Center's own ballet company.

2008: Christoph Eschenbach is named sixth music director of the National Symphony Orchestra, beginning with the 2010–11 season.

The opening night gala performance featured the world premier of *Mass*, a work commissioned to honor Kennedy by renowned composer and conductor Leonard Bernstein. It was an unmitigated triumph, which was aptly demonstrated by the audience response—a 30-minute standing ovation. Critics hailed the event and welcomed the capital's bid to become a cultural force in the United States. That goal was destined to come to pass over time, but those who had been instrumental in getting the Center built undoubtedly saw that September evening in 1971 as the moment when a long-held dream became reality.

CULTURAL JEWEL

Stevens stayed on as chairman until 1988, and under his direction the Kennedy Center attained an enviable reputation as one of the finest cultural institutions in the United States. He made the Center a showcase for important homegrown talent, presenting new works by writers such as Tennessee Williams, Arthur Miller, and Tom Stoppard, choreographers such as Agnes DeMille and Jerome Robbins, and composers such as Aaron Copland and John Cage. He also ensured that the Center made its mark as an international venue by hosting the American debuts of distinguished foreign performers, including the Bolshoi and La Scala Opera companies and the Ballet Nacional de Cuba. Indeed, by the time of

his retirement in 1988, Stevens's 27 years of leadership had shaped the Center permanently. He was honored with the Presidential Medal of Freedom the year he stepped down, and he died 10 years later at the age of 87. His biography on the Kennedy Center Web site succinctly sums up the legendary figure with his own words: "The Stevens angle is this: whatever I get involved in happens."

Among the countless major events that occurred during Stevens's tenure, the formal adoption of the National Symphony Orchestra (NSO) in 1986 was surely one of the most noteworthy. Officially founded in 1931 by well-known cellist Hans Kindler, the symphony began as a part-time, ad hoc outfit that played 24 concerts per year in Washington's DAR Constitution Hall. Musicians, who were often imported from out of town, were paid $40 per week during the five-month season. The lot of the players was only marginally improved under the leadership of Howard Mitchell from 1949 to 1969; the orchestra remained a part-time operation, but its reputation was enhanced by its overseas tours in 1959 and 1967.

In 1970, however, the NSO came into its own under the direction of Antal Dorati, who transformed it into a disciplined, full-time organization and oversaw its move into the new Kennedy Center in 1971. Dorati was replaced by Mstislav Leopoldovich Rostropovich in 1978. His 17-year reign was controversial and especially hampered by acoustic shortcomings in the concert hall. Rostropovich, however, was well respected for his musicality, and it was during his tenure that the NSO was formally incorporated into the Kennedy Center as its artistic affiliate. The orchestra had been performing at the Center for years, but acknowledgement of the facility as its official home was a professional boon to all concerned. The NSO continued to gain stature under the baton of Leonard Slatkin, who supervised the badly needed acoustical improvements in the concert hall and thereby delivered the finest sound the orchestra had demonstrated to that date. Slatkin left for the Detroit Symphony Orchestra at the end of 2008, leaving the NSO with a worthy principal conductor, Ivan Fischer, but no music director. That gap was to be filled by Christoph Eschenbach in 2010. Eschenbach was also hired to become the first music director of the Kennedy Center overall. By 2010 the NSO was to be made up of 100 musicians, playing 175 concerts each year, with an operating budget of more than $30 million, a far cry from the ragtag band it had once been. Despite its increasing success and the key association with the Center, a truly first-class reputation continued to elude the symphony early in the 21st century. It was hoped that Eschenbach, fresh from the leadership of the Philadelphia Orchestra (one of the country's so-called

"Big Five" symphonies, along with those of New York, Boston, Chicago, and Cleveland), would bring the NSO to the next level.

As the Kennedy Center's fortunes and artistic standing grew greater, so did its ability to attract top-notch talent and expand its programs. Eminent ballerina Suzanne Farrell, for instance, became affiliated with the Center via its Education Department in 1993, and in 2001 she formed its in-house ballet company, the Suzanne Farrell Ballet. Farrell had spent most of her impressive performing career as the muse of the legendary George Balanchine at the New York City Ballet and was a recipient of the National Medal of Arts (2003), so the cachet that she lent the Center was unmistakable. Another example was jazz giant Dr. Billy Taylor, who was also a National Medal of Arts winner (1992) and who joined the center as its artistic director for jazz in 1994. Taylor had landed his first job in 1944 in New York City. He proceeded to play piano with such musical greats as Dizzy Gillespie, Charlie Parker, and Miles Davis, as well as establish himself as a preeminent jazz educator and advocate. Innovations at the Center under his watch included the launch of the annual Mary Lou Williams Women in Jazz Festival in 1995 and the KC Jazz Club in 2002.

Less prominent artists also made an impact on the Center. James A. Johnson, who served as the organization's fourth chairman from May 1996 until May 2004, instituted the Performing Arts for Everyone community outreach program, an initiative designed to increase the visibility of low-priced and free Center events. A major component of that program was the Millennium Stage, which Johnson also founded and endowed. The stage offered a free performance 365 days a year at 6 p.m., broadcast live via the Internet.

Through the vision of its founders, the ongoing ingenuity of those that followed, and the diligence of countless volunteers and professionals, the Kennedy Center greeted the 21st century as a thriving institution that remained true to its commitment to the arts. By that time, the facility held, in addition to its theaters, two public restaurants, nine special-event rooms, and five public galleries. Visitors from every state and more than 20 countries passed through its portals every year, and more than 2,000 performances were presented annually. It sponsored three prestigious annual awards and produced programming for television, radio, and

the Internet. The Center's education programs, including lectures, open rehearsals, master classes, competitions, and workshops, reached more than 7 million people across the United States and had become blueprints for use in communities all over the country. It was, in short, a spectacular success and the living legacy that it was intended to be. As the late Rhode Island Democratic senator Claiborne Pell was quoted by Eric Pace in the *New York Times* back in 1998 as saying, "It's changed Washington from a cultural outpost into a cultural center—what a capital center should be."

Margaret L. Moser

FURTHER READING

Gamarekian, Barbara, "A Cultural Trailblazer to Seek New Path at 77," *New York Times*, January 12, 1988.

Geracimos, Ann, "Key Decision for Billy Taylor; Renowned Pianist, 83, Reduces Schedule; KenCen Role Remains," *Washington Times*, March 31, 2005, p. B05.

"John F. Kennedy Center for the Performing Arts," *Business Week* online, http://investing.businessweek.com/research/stocks/private/snapshot.asp?privcapId=4279962.

Midgette, Anne, "Christoph Eschenbach to Lead National Symphony," *Washington Post*, September 26, 2008, p. A01.

"New Post for Stevens," *New York Times*, March 9, 1988.

Oestreich, James R., "Slatkin New Director of National Symphony," *New York Times*, March 29, 1994.

Pace, Eric, "Roger L. Stevens, Real Estate Magnate, Producer and Fund-Raiser, Is Dead at 87," *New York Times*, February 4, 1998.

Page, Tim, "NSO Picks Fischer as Interim Maestro," *Washington Post*, April 13, 2007.

———, "The NSO: 75 and Counting Its Blessings," *Washington Post*, September 4, 2005.

Peterson, Eric, "John F. Kennedy Center for the Performing Arts National Memorial," How Stuff Works, http://adventure.howstuffworks.com/kennedy-center-for-the-performing-arts-national-memorial.htm.

"Presidential Honor," *Jet*, September 14, 1992, p. 54.

Stewart, Zan, "Giant among Giants; At 84, Dr. Billy Taylor will Receive Master Award in South Orange," *Star-Ledger (Newark, NJ)*, October 14, 2005, p. 24.

Stryker, Mark, "World-Class Maestro Heading to the Detroit Symphony Orchestra," *Detroit Free Press*, October 8, 2007.

"Suzanne Farrell," Florida State University, http://www.fsu.edu/profiles/farrell/.

KBR Inc.

601 Jefferson Street
Houston, Texas 77002
U.S.A.
Telephone: (713) 753-2000
Web site: http://www.kbr.com

Public Company
Founded: 1901
Incorporated: 2006
Employees: 57,000
Sales: $11.58 million (2008)
Stock Exchanges: New York
Ticker Symbol: KBR
NAISC: 237990 Other Heavy and Civil Engineering Construction; 236210 Industrial Building Construction; 541330 Engineering Services

■ ■ ■

KBR Inc. is a leading global engineering, construction, and services company supporting the energy, hydrocarbon, government services, and civil infrastructure sectors. The company is a leader in many of the growing end-markets it serves, particularly in gas monetization, having designed and constructed, alone or with joint venture partners, more than half of the world's operating liquefied natural gas (LNG) production capacity over the past 30 years. KBR provides services to a diverse customer base, including national and international oil and gas companies, independent refiners, petrochemical producers, fertilizer producers, and domestic and foreign governments. The company offers a wide range of services through its upstream, downstream, technology, services, government and infrastructure, and ventures business segments.

BROWN & ROOT'S ORIGINS

The humble beginning of KBR Inc. dates back to the early 1900s with the inception of two small and independent companies: Brown & Root and M.W. Kellogg. Nearly a century later they were merged to form KBR Inc., a global leader in the fields of engineering and construction, with more than 50,000 employees worldwide.

In 1919, with the financial backing of his brother-in-law Dan Root, Herman Brown founded a road building company. Mortgaging wagons and mules, and in considerable debt, he landed the company's first job in Freestone, Texas. This led to other road building work and, three years into the business, Brown & Root won contracts to rebuild four bridges in central Texas that had been destroyed by floods. One of the bridges posed a rather complex issue because it required underwater blasting to set its piers. Even though Herman had no experience in this area, his younger brother, George, had a degree in mining from the Colorado School of Mines and was ready to rise to the challenge. Through the 1920s the brothers successfully completed the bridge reconstructions, opened an office in Houston, Texas, and spent the remainder of the decade expanding their business largely through the procurement of building contracts awarded by the state of Texas.

Their contrasting personalities were a recipe for success. Herman was inclined to work on the jobsites

COMPANY PERSPECTIVES

■

KBR's core values are at the forefront of our daily business. Incorporating these core values in our daily work, and making them an integral part of our culture, is key to our future success. Our values solidify who we are and what we believe.

- Uncompromising commitment to health, safety and environment
- An open relationship with our employees based on mutual trust, respect and success
- Transparency, accountability and discipline in our business
- Best in class risk awareness
- Integrity in all we do
- Financial responsibility to our stakeholders

alongside his employees, whereas George's charming personality made him well suited to function as Brown & Root's salesman, a role in which he demonstrated sharp negotiating skills and methods of persuasion. George's technical expertise combined with Herman's entrepreneurial ambition resulted in a partnership that would last more than 40 years and result in the creation of one of the world's largest construction and engineering firms.

In 1929, the same year as the stock market crash that sent the nation into the Great Depression, Dan Root, who was instrumental in starting up the company 10 years earlier, suffered an untimely death. George and Herman made the decision to purchase Root's interest in the company and to incorporate as Brown & Root Inc. The Depression brought with it a significant slowdown in state-funded construction projects, so the brothers were forced to pursue other work, including garbage collection in Houston. However, this downturn was short lived when, in 1934, Brown & Root secured a road construction contract in Roanoke, Louisiana, for Humble Oil Company.

Another significant development occurred in 1936, when Brown & Root was awarded the construction contract for the Marshall Ford Dam, later renamed the Mansfield Dam. Measuring one mile wide and standing 25 stories high, the dam was the largest structure of its kind in Texas, and it marked the company's entry into heavy construction and the power industry. Lasting five years and using 2 million tons of concrete, the comple-

tion of this contract proved that the company was capable of taking on the world's largest construction projects. Other large federally funded contracts followed, including construction of the $90 million Corpus Christi Naval Air Station. In 1941 the U.S. Navy approached the company to build four submarine chasers, a contract valued at $640,000 per vessel. With no previous experience in shipbuilding, the brothers once again rose to the occasion and formed the Brown Shipbuilding Company. By the end of World War II the company had constructed a fleet for the U.S. Navy for a production total worth $500 million.

BROWN & ROOT'S POSTWAR EXPANSION

Emerging from the war as a major U.S. construction company, Brown & Root continued to secure a broad range of projects. The company's first overseas contract came in 1946, when it was selected as a managing partner for the reconstruction of Guam. That same year Brown & Root took on its first major engineering project for Diamond Alkali and was awarded a paper mill construction contract from Southland Paper in Lufkin, Texas. The following year, in a pivotal move for the company, Kerr-McGee awarded Brown & Root the contract to build the world's first commercial out-of-sight-of-land oil drilling platform.

Throughout the 1950s the company focused its attention on increasing its international presence. In 1951 Brown & Root established an office in Edmonton, Alberta, for the construction of a petrochemical and synthetic fiber plant. In the years that followed, building projects included a series of gas injection plants on Lake Maracaibo in Venezuela, the Bhumiphol Dam in Thailand, and the Tantangara Dam and Tunnel for the Snowy Mountains Hydroelectric Authority in Australia. By the close of the decade, the company opened an office in London to position itself for gas and oil exploration contracts in the North Sea.

On the domestic front, Brown & Root continued to diversify its operations. The company built a major petrochemical facility for the Celanese Corporation, constructed a polyethylene plant for Union Carbide, and added Ciba Geigy and DuPont to its list of clients. By the 1960s the company had gained a stellar reputation and was awarded two major projects. The first, in 1960, was sponsored by the National Science Foundation and involved the deepest offshore drilling ever attempted. Dubbed Project Mohole, the objective was to drill in 14,000 feet of water and penetrate 21,000 feet below the earth's crust. The following year, Brown &

KEY DATES

1901: Morris W. Kellogg opens a pipe fabrication business in New York City.

1905: M.W. Kellogg is incorporated and expanded to include power plant construction and power plant component fabrication.

1916: M.W. Kellogg moves into oil refining technology.

1919: Herman Brown founds Brown & Root in Texas.

1929: Brown & Root is incorporated.

1936: Brown & Root is awarded a construction contract for Marshall Ford Dam.

1941: Brown Shipbuilding Company is formed.

1943: M.W. Kellogg assists in the design of the Oak Ridge Gaseous Diffusion Plant.

1944: Pullman Inc. acquires M.W. Kellogg.

1951: Brown & Root establishes an office in Edmonton, Alberta, for the construction of a petrochemical and synthetic fiber plant.

1959: Brown & Root establishes an office in London.

1962: Halliburton Company acquires Brown & Root.

1970: M.W. Kellogg's headquarters are moved from New York City to Houston, Texas.

1975: M.W. Kellogg's research and development facilities move from New Jersey to Houston, Texas.

1976: M.W. Kellogg is renamed Pullman Kellogg.

1980: Wheelabrator-Frye acquires Pullman Kellogg and restores the M.W. Kellogg name.

1988: Dresser Industries acquires M.W. Kellogg.

1998: Halliburton acquires Dresser and combines M.W. Kellogg and Brown & Root to form Kellogg Brown & Root Inc. (KBR).

2004: KBR is awarded the Australian Construction Achievement Award for the construction of the Alice Springs to Darwin rail link.

2007: Halliburton spins off KBR Inc.

Root secured the National Aeronautics and Space Administration contract as architect-engineer for the Manned Spacecraft Center in Houston.

At this same time, Herman Brown's health had seriously deteriorated and, out of concern of the company's future, Brown & Root's executives made the decision to sell a controlling interest in the company. In November 1962, shortly after Herman's death, Halliburton Company, an oilfield services company, paid Brown & Root $32.6 million for approximately 95 percent of the company and acquired the remaining 5 percent in June 1963. George Brown served on Halliburton's board of directors and continued as Brown & Root's president and chief executive officer (CEO) for another year. By 1966 the establishment of the London office paid off when Brown & Root laid the first marine pipeline in the North Sea. Additional successes followed, including projects such as the completion of the world's first 48-inch offshore pipeline in Kuwait in 1968 and the design and construction of Chah Bahar Naval Port for the Iranian Imperial Navy in 1975.

In January 1977 the company announced that its documents pertaining to offshore oil platform activities had been subpoenaed by a federal grand jury to investigate possible antitrust charges. In December 1978 Brown & Root pleaded no contest and paid $90 million to settle related civil claims. In a separate lawsuit filed in 1981, the owners of the South Texas Nuclear Project alleged that Brown & Root were in breach of contract, resulting in a $750 million settlement paid by Brown & Root in 1985. However, these legal embattlements did not distract Brown & Root from its ongoing construction and engineering projects. During this period the company completed the Eisenhower Tunnel at Loveland Pass, Colorado, the world's first guyed tower platform in the Gulf of Mexico, and a military base for the U.S. Navy and Air Force on the island of Diego Garcia in the Indian Ocean.

In the early 1990s Brown & Root completed its first major project off the shore of China and assisted with Kuwait's reconstruction after the first Gulf War. Numerous opportunities for oil and gas development in eastern Europe presented themselves and, to this end, the company strengthened its position in the area by forming Brown & Root Skoda in the Czech Republic. In the late 1990s the company continued to excel at large-scale construction and engineering projects, but its relationship with Halliburton would pose its own set of challenges.

M.W. KELLOGG'S ORIGINS

In 1901 Morris W. Kellogg opened a pipe fabrication business in New York City. Within four years M.W. Kellogg was incorporated and had expanded to include power plant construction and power plant component fabrication. With the onset of World War I, the control of the oil supply was tantamount and, by 1916, Kellogg had moved into refining technology. By the 1920s Kellogg had established a research laboratory, expanded his petroleum refining and petrochemical processing facilities, and had emerged onto the international scene. The 1930s was a period of rapid growth for petroleum refining, and Kellogg's catalytic reforming process was a significant breakthrough. Known as hydroforming, the process was a major source of toluene for the production of TNT during World War II. In 1943 M.W. Kellogg assisted in the design of the Oak Ridge Gaseous Diffusion Plant, which was part of the Manhattan Project, and was acquired by Pullman Inc. the next year.

In the 1960s, now a division of Pullman Inc., M.W. Kellogg was awarded the Kirkpatrick Chemical Engineering Award for its advances in ammonia production technology, an integral component of fertilizer production and other industrial uses. In 1970 the company headquarters moved from New York City to Houston, with the New Jersey-based research and development facilities following in 1975. The following year the company was renamed Pullman Kellogg and became the first American company to receive contracts from the People's Republic of China. The focus of its activities during this period was on ethylene, fertilizer, and liquid petroleum gas. Wheelabrator-Frye acquired Pullman Inc. in 1980, and the M.W. Kellogg name was restored the following year. The next few years saw a variety of mergers and acquisitions when, in 1988, Dresser Industries, a provider of integrated services and project management for the oil and gas industry, acquired Kellogg. The company's reputation was now firmly established as a leader in the fields of ethylene technology, LNG production, and millisecond furnaces.

Through a series of acquisitions, Halliburton had grown significantly. One of these was the purchase of Dresser in 1998 for $7.7 billion, which combined Dresser's engineering subsidiary, M.W. Kellogg, with Halliburton's construction subsidiary, Brown & Root, to form Kellogg Brown & Root Inc (KBR).

THE NEW KBR

The merger created one of the world's largest oil services firms, and the new KBR was an immediate success. Operating under the Halliburton name, the company had three main business segments: Energy Services Group; Engineering and Construction Group; and Equipment Group. This positioned the company as a major contender for a host of contracts, such as a $1.5 billion contract to expand the Petronas LNG Complex in Bintulu, Malaysia. As KBR continued to focus its attention on growing the business, the parent company began to experience a number of problems related to asbestos claims and investigations into its accounting practices.

Since 1976 there had been 474,500 claims against the firm for its use of asbestos in certain products and by 2001 Halliburton faced an onslaught of new claims. In 2001 a Baltimore, Maryland, jury awarded a group of plaintiffs $30 million, which sent the company's stock plummeting. The following year Halliburton put the issue to rest by paying $4.2 billion to settle all outstanding claims, thus shielding the company from future asbestos litigation.

That same year the U.S. Securities and Exchange Commission (SEC) began an investigation into Halliburton's accounting practices. In 1998 the company changed how it booked revenue related to cost overruns on billion-dollar contracts. While the change itself was legal, the firm neglected to report it to shareholders and the SEC for over a year. By making the change, Halliburton was able to meet earnings expectations for 1998—the year of the Dresser merger. The SEC began its investigation in May, forcing Halliburton to hand over nearly 200,000 accounting documents to prove that it had not inflated cost overrun claims. The investigation came to a close and Halliburton eventually settled the case with shareholders for $6 million. As part of its asbestos settlement, Halliburton placed KBR under bankruptcy protection in 2003. The filing did not include KBR's military and government services business.

At the same time, the faltering economy, falling oil prices, and a slowdown in North American gas production contributed to an estimated loss of $984 million, compared to a net profit of $809 million in 2001. These losses and those brought on by litigation prompted Halliburton to restructure itself in 2002. Under the direction of David J. Lesar, who was named chairman and CEO in 2000, the company realigned its businesses into two major groups: Halliburton Energy Services Group and KBR, the engineering and construction group.

In 2001, through a competitive bidding process, KBR was awarded a Logistics Civil Augmentation Program contract known as Logcap III to provide logistical support to U.S. forces in Iraq. In 2003 the U.S. Army Corps of Engineers (USACE) contracted KBR to contain Iraqi oil well fires and restore oil facilities and infrastructure, but the company soon came under fire for its role in the country. According to Paula Dwyer and Frederik Balfour of *BusinessWeek*, critics claimed in April 2003 that "deals worth billions of dollars were being handed out in a secretive process that unfairly excluded foreign competitors." To add to the outcry, Halliburton disclosed that approximately 9 percent of its revenues and pre-tax operating profits for the second quarter of 2003 resulted from work in Iraq, most of which stemmed from Logcap III. In an effort to quell this public relations disaster, the USACE launched a competitive bidding process in June 2003.

BusinessWeek's Anthony Bianco and Stephanie Anderson Forest noted in September 2003, "The company's high-profile success in winning contracts, coupled with its intimate ties to the White House, has aroused suspicions that it is a beneficiary of political favoritism." However, the U.S. military has always relied heavily on private military companies (PMCs), and KBR had a proven track record of providing superlative military support in some of the world's most remote and politically dangerous regions, including Afghanistan, Kosovo, Georgia, Uzbekistan, and Bosnia and Herzegovina. "It is no exaggeration to say that wherever the U.S. military goes, so goes Brown & Root," said Peter W. Singer, author of *Corporate Warriors: The Rise of the Privatized Military Industry*.

In March 2004 the highest accolade for construction achievement in Australia, the Australian Construction Achievement Award, was awarded to the Alice Springs to Darwin rail link (ADrail) Joint Venture. KBR was a major partner in ADrail and the major shareholder in Asia Pacific Transport, the consortium appointed to finance, design, construct, maintain, and operate the line. Completed five months ahead of schedule, the $1 billion project involved the laying of 1,420 kilometers of track that linked all of Australia's mainland cities, resulting in the longest single-gauge railway in the world. This was a much needed boost for the company because KBR was facing criticism from the Pentagon and the U.S. Department of Justice for quality of work issues and billing and pricing matters.

Halliburton's second quarter results for 2004 revealed that work performed in Iraq totaled $1.7 billion, or approximately one-third of the company's revenues for that quarter, and that KBR's revenues were up 68 percent from the previous year. These profits came with a high price, however, as 43 of its workers had been killed in Iraq and Kuwait. Furthermore, the Pentagon auditors determined that Halliburton had failed to account for 43 percent of the $4.18 billion that KBR had charged for feeding and housing troops in these countries. This was followed by the disclosure that the SEC had opened an investigation involving KBR executives suspected of bribing Nigerian officials in the construction of a gas complex. By October 2004 it was revealed that, despite reports that KBR had been showing increased profitability from its work in the Middle East, the company had actually lost money in seven of its last 10 quarters. Investors and analysts began to speculate that Halliburton would eventually divest KBR. In January 2005 Lesar confirmed that Halliburton planned to spin off KBR.

KBR BECOMES AN INDEPENDENT COMPANY

In April 2006 KBR filed a registration statement with the SEC for a planned initial public offering (IPO) of $550 million in common stock, most of which was to pay down Halliburton's debt. After the IPO in November 2006, KBR's shares rose sharply from the offering price of $17 to close at $20.75. By April 2007 KBR had completed its separation from Halliburton and could now focus its attention on expanding as an independent company. A major gas development project management contract in the United Arab Emirates awarded in May and the founding of KBR Nigeria in Lagos in June appeared to be early indications that the company was moving in a positive direction. On the domestic front, in conjunction with the U.S. Department of Energy, Southern Company, and the Orlando Utilities Commission, KBR began construction on a new coal-based generating station, which was part of President George W. Bush's Clean Coal Power Initiative.

In March 2008 KBR announced that it had completed construction on facilities for the Coalition Forces on the Iraqi Transfer Platforms in the Persian Gulf two months ahead of schedule. The company, however, was once again rocked by scandal when it was disclosed that the mother of a U.S. soldier electrocuted in Iraq in January had filed a lawsuit against KBR, the contractor in charge of inspecting the wiring at the base where Sergeant Ryan Maseth had died. By September of that year, with the death toll caused by possible electrocutions now at 18, the Pentagon's inspector general issued a subpoena to KBR as part of an investigation into electrical work at U.S. bases. In January 2009 Peter Spiegel of the *Los Angeles Times* indicated that an army investigation called the electrocution of Sergeant Maseth a "negligent homicide" caused by KBR and two of its supervisors. Robin Acton of the *Pittsburgh Tribune-Review* noted that Heather L. Brown, KBR's director of corporate communications, stated in an e-mail that the company "maintains that its activities in Iraq did not play a role in Maseth's death." According to a KBR press release, William C. Brodie, KBR's interim president of government and infrastructure, issued the statement: "The military had directed KBR to perform only limited maintenance on Staff Sergeant Maseth's building, which was a pre-existing, Iraqi-constructed building. KBR did not wire the building." In a further blow to the company's reputation, in February 2009 KBR pleaded guilty to federal charges that it paid $180 million in bribes to Nigerian officials between 1994 and 2004 to secure $6 billion in contracts.

By mid-2009 KBR's outlook was turning more positive. In June 2009 Exxon Mobil awarded the Eos Joint Venture, a major LNG joint venture project in Australia, to WorleyParsons and KBR. That same month, Granherne Inc., a KBR subsidiary that specialized in onshore, offshore, and deepwater gas developments, was selected by StatoilHydro ASA to participate in a conceptual study of its Gullfaks 2030 project. The company received a further boost when it was given two awards at the 2009 Greater New Orleans Industrial Educational Council Contractor's Safety Excellence Awards event. In July 2009, in regards to a civil case that alleged that KBR was liable for its activities in Iraq under the Logcap contract, a federal court ruled that "the military, not civilian contractors, decides and directs the activities of contractors in battlefield situations." This was a significant development not only for KBR but also for other civilian contractors that provide services and conduct operations during wartime under the direction of the military. Clearly, KBR was leaving the worst behind as it continued on its mission to provide safe, high-quality, and cost-effective service throughout the world.

Jeffrey L. Covell
Updated, Christina M. Stansell; Marie O'Sullivan

PRINCIPAL SUBSIDIARIES

BITC LLC; Granherne Inc.; HBR NL Holdings LLC; KBR Group Holdings LLC; KBR Holdings LLC; Kellogg Brown & Root Holding B.V. (Netherlands); Kellogg Brown & Root Holdings Ltd. (England and Wales); Kellogg Brown & Root Holdings Ltd. (England and Wales); Kellogg Brown & Root Ltd. (England and Wales); Kellogg Brown & Root LLC; Kellogg Brown & Root Netherlands B.V. (Netherlands); Kellogg Brown & Root Services Inc.

PRINCIPAL COMPETITORS

AMEC; Bechtel Corporation; CH2M Hill Companies Ltd.; Chicago Bridge and Iron Co. N.V.; Chiyoda; Dyn-Corp International; Fluor Corporation; Foster Wheeler; Jacobs Engineering Group Inc.; The Shaw Group Inc.; Technip; URS Corporation; WorleyParsons Ltd.

FURTHER READING

Acton, Robin, "Shaler Soldier's Death in Iraq Deemed Criminal," *Pittsburgh Tribune-Review*, January 23, 2003.

Barnett, Chris, "Hazardous Duty," *Journal of Commerce*, June 13, 2005, p. 30.

Bianco, Anthony, and Stephanie Anderson Forest, "Outsourcing War," *BusinessWeek*, September 15, 2003.

Dillon, Robert, "Halliburton, US Draw Fire for Overhead Expenses in Iraq," *Oil Daily*, October 26, 2006.

Dinesh, Manimoli, "Bush: Halliburton Must Repay Overcharges," *Oil Daily*, December 15, 2003.

———, "Pentagon Awards Halliburton Unit Contract for Iraqi Oil Fields," *Oil Daily*, March 26, 2003.

———, "US May Strip KBR of Iraq Fuel Contract," *Oil Daily*, November 6, 2003.

Dwyer, Paula, and Frederik Balfour, "Iraq Deals: Who Got What—and Why," *BusinessWeek*, April 25, 2003.

Feeney, Sheila Anne, "A 'Wild West' Environment?" *Workforce Management*, June 1, 2004, p. 38.

Forest, Stephanie Anderson, "A Thorn in Halliburton's Side," *BusinessWeek*, September 23, 2004.

Husari, Ruba, "Oil Flows at Kirkuk as KBR Begins Damage Assessment," *Energy Intelligence Briefing*, May 1, 2003, p. 1.

Ismail, Norrazak Hj, and Thomas Roy Stuart, "The Train 7 Fire at Petronas' LNG Complex, Bintulu, Malaysia," *LNG Journal*, July–August 2005, p. 12.

"KBR Employee Killed in Iraq; Oil Output on Target," *Oil Daily*, August 6, 2003.

"KBR's Editorial Submission to the New York Times in Response to the May 23 'KBR Does It Again' Editorial" (press release), Houston, TX: KBR Inc., May 23, 2009, http://www.kbr.com/news/press_releases/2009/05/29/KBRs-Editorial-Submission-to-the-New-York-Times-in-response-to-the-May-23-KBR-Does-it-Again-Editiorial.aspx.

Kelly, Andrew, "Iraq Bidders May Be Left with Slim Pickings," *Oil Daily*, August 12, 2003.

———, "KBR Executive Defends Iraq Policy," *Oil Daily*, September 26, 2003.

Kelly, Deb, "Former Nigerian Presidents Named in US Bribery Investigation," *Oil Daily*, March 31, 2009.

Mack, Toni, "A Piece of the Action," *Forbes*, August 1, 1997, p. 60.

Meyers, Robert A., *Handbook of Petrochemicals Production Processes*, New York: McGraw-Hill, 2004.

Mitchell, Greg, "Soldier Electrocuted in Iraq: Who Is to Blame?" *Editor & Publisher*, March 20, 2008.

National Academy of Engineering, *Memorial Tributes*, Washington, D.C.: National Academies Press, 1979, pp. 148–150.

Richards, Catherine, "Not Just War Paint and Weaponry," *MEED Middle East Economic Digest*, August 29, 2003.

Risen, James, "Controversial Contractor's Iraq Work Is Split Up," *New York Times*, May 24, 2008.

Schwartz, Nelson D., "Why Halliburton Isn't Cleaning Up," *Fortune*, January 26, 2004.

Sikora, Martin, "Halliburton Shakes up KBR for Possible Disposal," *Mergers & Acquisitions: The Dealmaker's Journal*, November 1, 2004.

Singer, Peter W., *Corporate Warriors: The Rise of the Privatized Military Industry*, Ithaca, NY: Cornell University Press, 2003.

Sissell, Kara, "Halliburton's KBR Unit Files for Chapter 11," *Chemical Week*, December 24, 2003, p. 9.

Spiegel, Peter, "Army Investigator Said Green Beret's Death Was 'Negligent Homicide' by KBR," *Los Angeles Times*, January 23, 2009.

Terry, Larry, "Kellogg B&R-Exxon: Final Score," *Chemical Week*, March 24, 1999, p. 48.

Thomas, Cathy Booth, "Fear and Loathing on Iraqi Roads," *Time*, June 7, 2004, p. 40.

U.S. Department of Energy, "Construction Begins on First-of-Its-Kind Advanced Clean Coal Electric Generating Facility," press release, September 10, 2007, http://www.energy.gov/news/5474.htm.

U.S. Securities and Exchange Commission, "SEC Charges KBR and Halliburton for FCPA Violations," press release, February 11, 2009.

"You Don't Have to be Mad to Work Here: Doing Business in Dangerous Places," *The Economist*, August 14, 2004, p. 53.

Zagorin, Adam, and Timothy J. Burger, "Beyond the Call of Duty: A Whistle-Blower Objected to the Government's Halliburton Deals," *Time*, November 1, 2004, p. 64.

Key Technology Inc.

150 Avery Street
Walla Walla, Washington 99362-1668
U.S.A.
Telephone: (509) 529-2161
Fax: (509) 527-1331
Web site: http://www.key.net

Public Company
Founded: 1948
Incorporated: 1982 as Key Technology, Inc.
Employees: 612
Sales: $134.09 million (2009 est.)
Stock Exchanges: NASDAQ
Ticker Symbol: KTEC
NAICS: 333294 Food Product Machinery Manufacturing; 333314 Optical Instrument and Lens Manufacturing

■ ■ ■

Key Technology Inc., based in Walla Walla, Washington, offers products and services that have revolutionized the canned, frozen, and fresh food industries. The company engineers and produces conveyor belts, sorters, washers, and other machinery that ensure the safety and uniformity of food products, including vegetables such as potatoes or corn and such snacks as potato chips. Key Technology also supplies sorting equipment for over-the-counter medications, and tobacco and wood products, using a company-based and free-agent sales force to continue increasing orders. At the end of the first decade of the 2000s, the company had six subsidiaries located in Redmond, Oregon; Australia; Shanghai, China; Mexico; and the Netherlands.

EARLY YEARS: 1948 INVENTION STARTS SUCCESS

The business that would evolve into an internationally recognized company began just as World War II was drawing to a close. Key Technology was originally known as the Umatilla Processing Plant, which was opened to can pea crops for farmers around Milton-Freewater, Oregon. Before the era of automated machinery, this was a time-consuming series of pre-canning activities, including handpicking the pea vines, loading them onto trucks, and bringing them to the cannery for processing. It was no wonder that the plant's owners, Claude and Lloyd Key, began to look for ways to make the process faster and more efficient.

The Keys' first invention was a mechanical fork that has since been lost. Their next innovation, 1948's Key Pak Bed, started them on the road to manufacturing efficient machinery by compacting pea vines to allow more of them to be carried on each truck. The Key Pak Bed reduced the costs of operation by cutting the numbers of trucks and drivers needed to get the peas to the processing plant. Farmers in the area were enthusiastic about the Key Pak compactor. It was so successful that in 1948 the Keys leased a small packing shed, hired 12 workers, and formed a company called the Key Equipment Company.

Customers were equally pleased when the Keys introduced the Froth Flotation Cleaner in 1951, which streamlined the conveyor-belt cleaning and sorting

COMPANY PERSPECTIVES

We design, manufacture and market process automation systems for food and other industries. This technology integrates automated optical inspection systems, specialized conveyor systems, and processing/preparation systems, as well as research, development, and world-class engineering. Our served markets range from fruit, vegetables, potatoes, snacks, cereals, and meat, to tobacco, pet food, plastics, and pharmaceutical/nutraceutical manufacturing.

process. Large teams of pickers had always been stationed at intervals, inspecting the long streams of peas and picking out stems and debris as the vegetables traveled slowly past them. In an effort to get the job done more quickly, the pickers sometimes discarded perfect peas, a mistake traditionally seen as wasteful but unavoidable.

The Froth Flotation Cleaner ended the waste. Instead of human eyesight and hands, it used bubbles that stuck to lighter debris and floated it away from the heavier peas as they sank to the bottom of the machine's tank. The Froth Flotation Cleaner not only reduced the number of workers necessary but also reduced waste. Customers were so enthusiastic about this cleaner that they ordered it without hesitation. A 1951 letter from the Utah Canning Company declared that two of the Froth Flotation Cleaners had reduced Utah Canning's per-shift workforce from 42 to 18, demonstrating the savings and greater efficiency provided by Key Equipment's machines.

By the early 1960s, Key Equipment was capable of processing corn and lima beans in addition to the peas, and processors all over the United States were buying their machinery. The Key sales force was energetic and hardworking and present at every trade show and convention of food processors. Orders to the factory came quickly following the shows and conventions, and each customer's machinery was manufactured in time to handle all processing operations at harvest time.

KEY GOES INTERNATIONAL: THE 1960S

Froth Flotation Cleaners rapidly became familiar pieces of machinery not only in U.S. processing plants but also in Canada and Australia. In 1962 the company received recognition for growth in exports when it received President John F. Kennedy's prestigious "E" Award, which was presented to companies that had demonstrated outstanding efforts to promote U.S. exports.

By the late 1960s the original executives were reaching retirement age. On May 31, 1968, the Key brothers sold the company to Applied Magnetics Corporation, a company making magnetic heads for the emerging international computer industry. The sale was well timed to add expansion opportunities. In addition, the company's agricultural machinery was soon being exported to Poland.

The number of Key products continued to grow in the United States as well. One of them, the Key Oscillating Air Kooler, was introduced in 1973 and was designed to reduce the time for blanching, a process used to prepare vegetables for freezing. Blanching involves dropping the produce into boiling water for a very short time and then rapidly plunging it into icy-cold water to stop the cooking process. The Air Kooler, an oscillating device, was able to reduce the cooling time to 45 seconds, and added evaporation increased the time even more. Handling up to six tons of food per hour, the Air Kooler made it possible to send loads of vegetables through the canning process much faster than ever before, thus increasing production levels.

CHANGES: 1970S AND 1980S

In 1975 Key Equipment merged with Electro Sonic Control, another Applied Magnetics subsidiary that had been purchased in 1971. The new company, called Key Electro Sonic in an effort to preserve the identity of both businesses, was able to use computer-based technology to manufacture electronic controls for the food processors. This vastly increased the speed of food processing and added 120 employees to the company.

Nevertheless, despite reaching company goals, Applied Magnetics Corporation of California announced plans to sell Key Electro Sonic in 1982. The deal was completed in February 1983, with Key Electro Sonic purchased by its own management executives, including Harold Frank, formerly the head of Applied Magnetics, who became chairman of the new Key Technology, Inc.; Tom Madsen, who became chief executive officer; and Gordon Wicher, who would hold various vice-presidential positions, including global operations, until he retired in 2008.

TECHNOLOGICAL INNOVATIONS IN MACHINERY

The new company became private but the public noticed a subtle shift in the company's underlying philosophy. Key was no longer concerned only with

KEY DATES

■

1948: Key Equipment Company is cofounded by brothers Claude and Lloyd Key with 12 employees; company introduces Key Pak Bed to compact pea vines, allowing more tonnage truckload.

1951: Company introduces Froth Flotation Cleaners, which substantially cuts the number of shift workers needed to pick out debris.

1962: Key is presented with President John F. Kennedy's "E" Award in recognition of exports.

1968: Key brothers sell the company to Applied Magnetics Corporation.

1973: Company introduces Oscillating Air Kooler, which can cool about six tons of vegetables per hour while saving water.

1982: Automatic Defect Removal system is introduced to remove defective pieces from french fries.

1995: Key introduces the Tegra Optical Sorter, which uses color, shape, and size to remove defects from produce with puffs of air.

1996: Netherlands-based Superior B.V. is acquired.

2000: Key makes several acquisitions, including Advanced Machine Vision Corporation and Farmco Inc.

2005: Pharmaceutical business unit Symetix launches automated inspection for capsules, tablets, and softgels.

2006: Shanghai, China, facility is opened.

solving customers' unique problems, they were also concerned with noting new trends in the food-processing market and rising to the challenge of meeting them.

The most obvious new trend was the french fry, which was quickly becoming the most popular vegetable in the United States. Taking advantage of this swelling market niche, the company unveiled the Key Automatic Defect Removal (ADR) system, a new optical inspection device that had been introduced in 1982 and was destined to become a Key Technology staple. The ADR device carries two cameras that scan a passing bed of potatoes for defects which are automatically removed. A slightly streamlined model appeared in 1983. An immediate success, the ADR system fulfilled Key

Technology's underlying goal of increased efficiency with fewer workers, resulting in financial savings. In 1985 the company installed its first ADR system at the McCain Foods plant in France. McCain, which had processing plants in several countries, ordered a total of four of these systems.

In 1987 Key Technology took the ADR concept a little further with the Opti-Sort automatic potato chip defect removal system, which was an engineering design destined to become a mainstay for Hostess Food Products of Canada, a premier manufacturer of snack foods. The two main functions expected of this system were to enhance product quality by removing any defects in size or color, and to pay for itself by cutting down on the need for manual labor. Hostess reported that both goals were met by doing the work of at least 35 people and by its compatibility with existing machinery.

In 1990 Key introduced the Iso-Flo "S" conveyor, which was capable of transporting fragile products such as potato chips without breaking them. Another innovation, the Iso-Flo Smooth Cycle, eliminated extra vibration when handling these delicate products. These innovations brought the company further into the cereal and snack industries, because those brittle foods could be packed by these machines without fear of demolition.

KEY TECHNOLOGY GOES PUBLIC: 1993

In 1993 Key Technology Inc. made an initial public offering (IPO) of 1.3 million shares of common stock on the NASDAQ at $9 per share. The company planned to use the money raised from the IPO to acquire companies with technology, products, or desirable market segments.

By this time, the company had divided its products into three broad areas: automatic inspection systems, conveyor systems, and the after-market parts connected with both. Their year-end bottom line showed an increase from $31.135 million in net sales for automated inspection systems, conveying systems, parts, and service in 1994, to $42.653 million in 1995, and to $54.341 million by the end of the company's fiscal year in September 1996.

In 1994 the company acquired AgriVision Engineering, Inc., a California company, which brought with it two excellent new machines. The first, a channel sorter called the AVS-5000, was initially intended for use with almonds, using both shape and length to produce uniform amounts of nuts while removing their shells and other debris, but the company also used it for other dry products such as beans and seeds. The second piece of innovative equipment, the AVS-300, was designed to test the ripeness of olives.

By the time the European Union was formed in 1993, Key Technology had an extremely well-developed European network for a region that expected high quality. Determined to maintain world-class standards in manufacturing and service, the company began to get International Standards Organization (ISO) certification in 1995, knowing that it would take two years but realizing it would give them an edge over their competitors. In addition, management was determined to meet and surpass Key's own high standards of operation, whether they applied to fire codes or sanitation and reliability.

NEW IDEAS IN THE 1990S

Key Technology had not neglected its original lineup of innovative equipment for the food-processing industry. By 1995 the company had introduced two new offerings. One was a streamlined next generation of the ADR system. Incorporating cameras so highly efficient that they could detect defects no more than 1-16th of an inch in size, these cameras could be customized to any client's purpose and were available in color or in black and white. Nevertheless, although the ADR could handle many different vegetables, its technology was still used mainly for french fries, processing 26,000 pounds per hour when operating at full capacity.

The second automated inspection system sorter introduced in 1995 was the Tegra Optical Sorter, designed specifically to provide Key Technology access to new markets, such as those connected with green beans, leafy vegetables, peppers, and even tobacco. The great advantage of the Tegra Optical Sorter was that it recognized differences in shape as well as in size and color, so it could differentiate between a green bean and its stem. The system also incorporated technology that gave it access to its owner's entire computer system, thus improving production scheduling.

A variation of the Tegra system was included with the 1996 acquisition of the I-300 product line from the Imaging Division of Oncor, Inc. The I-300 was a patented optical inspection device that included cameras to identify defects in pills or softgels for such products as Benadryl. More than 50 of these types of systems were in use at the time, which resulted in the company being involved in a lawsuit in relation to the use of the I-300. For five years after the acquisition of the I-300, Key was allowed to sell it to only one particular customer.

By 1996 Key products included a second sophisticated conveyor system that came with the acquisition of Netherlands-based Suplusco Holdings,

B.V., and its subsidiary, Superior B.V. The acquisition cost $3.1 million and encompassed a conveyor system that allowed spiral elevation. Significantly, Superior brought with it a European base, enabling faster servicing of all European customers.

A second highly successful product in 1996 was the Turbo-Flo Hydrostatic Blancher/Cooker, which allowed for complete processing of vegetables. One satisfied customer was Reser's Fine Foods of Beaverton, Oregon, which bought four units. Reser's, $200 million delicatessen food company was able to process 15,000 pounds of potatoes per hour with the largest Turbo-Flo, which was significant for Reser's repertoire of 51 potato salads, saving labor and energy costs.

GROWTH AND ACQUISITIONS

By the mid-1990s Key Technology had almost 500 employees and was outgrowing its facility, even though an additional sales and service office had been opened in Beaver Dam, Wisconsin, for the convenience of its growing list of Tegra customers. To allow for expansion, in July 1996 the company leased a second facility from the Port of Walla Walla, Washington, adding 88,000 square feet of manufacturing space, so that they could move their AgriVision division from its original Woodland, California, home to this space. Because their operations were expanding anyway, they took the opportunity to separate their two major product lines into two distinct operations: Specialized Conveying Systems under Wicher, who had been with the company for many years, and Automated Inspection Systems, which was headed by Scott Mathews.

Foreign and export sales accounted for 28 percent of sales in 1994, dropped slightly to 27 percent the following year, and then jumped to 34 percent in 1996. The increase was attributed to the success of the Tegra. By the end of 1996 Key had shipped a total of 76 Tegra units, 18 of which were being used for green bean applications in the Midwest.

On April 25, 2000, Key Technology announced the acquisition of Advanced Machine Vision Corporation (AMVC), a holding company with two subsidiaries—SRC Vision B.V., a company with facilities in Oregon as well as in the Netherlands, and Oregon-based Ventek. Despite two subsidiaries, AMVC had financial challenges, having lost $1.6 million in the first quarter of 2000. Nevertheless, AMVC, with its SRC Vision subsidiary, was considered to be a valuable addition. SRC Vision provided expansion opportunities in the design and manufacture of machine vision systems for the food-processing, plastics, and tobacco industries, while Ventek provided the same for the wood pulp and paneling industries. With this merger, Key Technology expected to save at least $4 million to $5 million on costs of operation, principally by moving SRC Vision's manufacturing activities to Walla Walla. The 50 people who lost their jobs complimented Key Technology on the way they had handled the transition. Layoff dates had been given well in advance to allow those being laid off to make plans for retraining; severance packages were generous; and training courses for outplacement were made widely available. Total sales figures, however, dropped slightly from $68.028 million in 1999 to $67.634 million for 2000.

By the end of 2000 Key Technology had four main subsidiaries: U.S.-based Key Technology FSC, handling foreign sales; Key Holdings USA LLC; Key Technology AMVC LLC, with facilities in the United States and the Netherlands; and Ventec Inc. In Europe, Key' operations were conducted by Key Technology B.V., which was formed by the merger of KEY/Superior B.V. and SRC Vision B.V.

In 2005 the settlement terms of the Oncor pharmaceutical sorter lawsuit expired, leaving Key Technology open to start a business unit called Symetix. Removing broken or imperfect pills and softgels from medication packs became much more precise, owing to the introduction of Vantyx, a considerably streamlined inspection system. The advantage of Vantyx was the ability to use it alone or have it custom-built with up to six simultaneously working cameras to combine with other machinery, such as blister-packaging machines, for a smooth, complete operation.

INTERNATIONAL ARENAS

Key Technology expand further into the international arena in 2006, opening a full-service office in Shanghai to serve the company's Chinese market. Business in China had been brisk for some 10 years, especially for tobacco sorters. Key planned to target the growing Chinese preference for a Western diet that was convenient to prepare. By 2008 Key discovered that while the time had been ripe for opening the new office, tobacco sorters continued to be their best-selling product, helping to increase overall order volume 166 percent over that of 2007, their first full year of operation.

Key continued to establish its presence in Europe in 2007, installing one of the ADR systems at Hoff Norske Potetindustrier, the largest potato processor in Norway. The Norwegian company had initially hesitated because of limited space, but Key quickly manufactured a suitable unit, and Hoff Norske joined other Key Technol-

ogy customers who reported improvements in both yield and quality of their french fries.

In the United States, longtime customer McCain Foods, a producer of french fries and many other frozen foods, continued to be a steady customer. From 2006 through 2008, McCain represented a large segment of Key's food-processing and inspection equipment sale, with 17 percent in 2006, 9 percent in 2007, and 14 percent in 2008. Snack-food manufacturer Frito-Lay was not far behind, with 13 percent of total sales.

Overall net sales figures remained healthy, increasing from $84.84 million in 2006 to $107.54 million in 2007, and reaching $134.07 million in 2008. The innovative company continued to prove that the Key brothers' original goals were accurate for the long term.

Gillian Wolf

PRINCIPAL SUBSIDIARIES

Key Holdings USA LLC; Key Technology Australia Pty Ltd.; Productos Key Mexicana S. de R.L. de C.V.; Key Technology (Shanghai) Trading Co., Ltd.; Key Technology Asia-Pacific Pte. Ltd.; Key Technology AMVC LLC.

PRINCIPAL COMPETITORS

Pentair Inc.; Fanuc Ltd.; KLA–Tencor Corp.; Lam Research; Novellus Systems Inc.; Heat & Control, Inc.

FURTHER READING

Downhill, Shari, "SRC Vision Ceases Medford Production," *Medford Mail Tribune* (Medford, OR), January 1, 2001.

A History of Innovation ... A Vision for the Future: Celebrating 50 Years of Service, Walla Walla, WA: Key Technology, Inc., 1998.

"Key Technology Completes Merger with Advanced Machine Vision Corporation," *Business Wire*, July 12, 2000.

"Key Technology Opens Office in Shanghai to Provide World-Class Service and Support to Chinese Customers" (press release), Walla Walla, WA: Key Technology, Inc., June 13, 2006.

"Norwegian Potato Processor Turns to ADRFirst™ Solution to Increase Yields and Maximize Product Quality" (press release), Walla Walla, WA: Key Technology, Inc., October 1, 2008.

"Sorter Offers Automated Inspection of Frozen Potato Products," *Product News Network*, June 29, 2009.

"Steam Blancher Increases Throughput 300%" *Prepared Foods*, November 1996.

"SYMETIX™ Introduces Vantyx® Inspection System for Solid Dose Pharmaceuticals," *Pharmaceutical Online*, October 4, 2005.

Lambda Legal Defense and Education Fund, Inc.

120 Wall Street, Suite 1500
New York, New York 10005-3904
U.S.A.
Telephone: (212) 809-8585
Fax: (212) 809-0055
Web site: http://www.lambdalegal.org

Nonprofit Company
Founded: 1971
Incorporated: 1973
Employees: 100
Sales: Not available
NAICS: 813311 Civil Liberties/Human Rights Advocacy; 541110 Offices of Lawyers

∎ ∎ ∎

The Lambda Legal Defense and Education Fund, Inc., is the oldest and largest legal organization dedicated to the civil rights of lesbians, gay men, bisexuals, transgender (LGBT) people, as well as those with HIV (human immunodeficiency virus). Founded in the wake of the Stonewall Rebellion of 1969 and the ensuing flurry of emerging gay activism of the early 1970s, Lambda Legal experienced its first legal battle by winning the right to its own existence in 1973. The organization began an epic struggle to secure fundamental rights for the LGBT community and quickly became remarkably successful. Lambda started out when the word "gay" used in a homosexual context could not be printed in most newspapers. Thirty-six years later, same-sex marriage was allowed in six states, with more likely to be on the horizon. There were major disappointments as well,

such as the 2008 voter referendum in California that effectively overturned the California Supreme Court's approval of same-sex marriage. Nevertheless, public, judicial, and legislative opinion appeared to be becoming increasingly tolerant moving into the second decade of the 2000s. Lambda Legal also continued to thrive, as it grew from several volunteers in a New York City apartment in 1973 to a staff of approximately 100 with offices in five locations by 2009.

INCORPORATED IN 1973

Few people were willing to be openly identified as homosexuals in 1969. Although the tumultuous 1960s were marked by rising activism and notable progress on behalf of African Americans, women, and other minorities, gays and lesbians remained out of sight on the fringes of society. Their reticence was understandable, as homosexual sex was a crime in every state except Illinois and there were no federal, state, or local laws that protected them from discrimination.

All this began to change, however, in the small hours of June 28, 1969, when a routine police raid on a gay bar called the Stonewall Inn in New York City's Greenwich Village prompted a series of protests and marked an awakening within the gay community. The following year, the Stonewall uprising was commemorated by New York's first annual Gay Pride Parade and a new civil rights movement came into play.

One of the groups created in direct response to the Stonewall uprising was the Gay Liberation Front (GLF), which in turn produced the Gay Activists Alliance of New York (GAA) in 1969. The GAA offshoot solely

COMPANY PERSPECTIVES

Lambda Legal is a national organization committed to achieving full recognition of the civil rights of lesbians, gay men, bisexuals, transgender people and those with HIV through impact litigation, education and public policy work.

At Lambda Legal, we imagine a different world—a world of full equality for LGBT people and people living with HIV—and we work to create that world every day. We pursue impact litigation, education and advocacy to make the case for equality in state and federal court, the Supreme Court and in the court of public opinion.

Lambda Legal's work ultimately benefits all people, for it helps to fashion a society that is truly diverse and tolerant. Our mission to combat discrimination based on sexual orientation, gender identity and HIV status in this country has become an intrinsic part of the struggle for civil rights.

focused on gay and lesbian rights as opposed to the broader scope of the GLF, which worked alongside black and women's liberation groups. A young lawyer named Bill Thom had been volunteering his expertise to the GAA when it occurred to him that an organization dedicated to gay and lesbian legal issues would be a welcome addition to the movement. Following the examples of such groups as the Native American and Puerto Rican Legal Defense and Education Funds, Thom founded Lambda Legal. Achieving legal recognition as a nonprofit organization proved to be problematic though, and *In re Thom* became Lambda's first case.

In his application for incorporation, Thom used the exact wording of the existing Puerto Rican Legal Defense and Education Fund's paperwork, with the exception of changing the beneficiaries from "Puerto Ricans" to "lesbians and gay men." That alteration made all the difference to the court, however, which demonstrated its views on the gay community by denying the application on the grounds that Lambda was neither "benevolent nor charitable." Thom then spent nearly two years embroiled in litigation that eventually culminated at the Court of Appeals, New York State's highest court. The Lambda Legal Defense and Education Fund was finally officially incorporated on October 18, 1973.

The significance of the choice of the lower case Greek letter lambda (λ) is something of a mystery. The symbol had been adopted by the GAA in 1970 and quickly became a relatively safe and unobtrusive means of identification within the gay community, but the reason was lost when the GAA's records and headquarters were destroyed in an arson fire. Speculation on the matter has ranged from the letter "l" representing liberation to the ancient Spartan belief that it meant unity to various theories stemming from its use in chemistry and physics to denote energy in equations. Whatever the original intent, however, it has been in use since being declared the international symbol for gay and lesbian rights at the International Gay Rights Congress in Edinburgh, Scotland, in 1974.

ORGANIZATIONAL GROWTH

Lambda Legal began operations from Thom's New York apartment with just a couple of volunteers. Litigation and education were the dual goals and, even on a shoestring budget, the original volunteers envisioned action on a national scale. Cases were chosen carefully, with an eye toward the best possible facts and the potential for building legal precedent. Early courtroom victories included forcing the University of New Hampshire to give equal standing to gay student groups in 1974, helping a lesbian foster mother retain custody of her foster children in 1977, and gaining reinstatement for a college professor who was fired for being gay in 1978.

Lambda gained new sophistication as an entity with the hiring of its first managing attorney, Abby Rubenfeld, in 1982 and Thomas Stoddard as executive director in 1986. It also won more widespread recognition as a formidable legal force with such cases as *Berg v. Clayton* (1981) in which it won an honorable discharge and financial settlement for a gay Annapolis graduate, *People v. West 12 Tenants Corp* (1983), the first AIDS-discrimination suit filed and won in the United States, and *Gay Veterans Association, Inc. v. The American Legion* (1985) in which gay veterans gained the right to march in the New York Veterans' Day Parade. Such successes were dimmed, however in 1986, when the GLBT community suffered a major defeat with the U.S. Supreme Court's ruling that upheld Georgia's sodomy law in *Bowers v. Hardwick*.

Despite the disappointment of *Hardwick*, the Lambda organization continued to thrive. It opened its first regional office in 1990 in Los Angeles, California, and had 22 employees by 1992. A second regional office, the first of its kind in the Midwest, was opened in Chicago, Illinois, in 1993, and a third, which was

KEY DATES

1973: New York courts allow Lambda Legal to incorporate as a nonprofit organization.

1981: U.S. Supreme Court upholds Lambda Legal's victory against sodomy law in New York.

1983: Lambda Legal joins with the New York attorney general's office in filing the first AIDS-discrimination challenge in the United States.

1990: First regional office opens in Los Angeles.

1993: Regional office opens in Chicago.

1997: Regional office opens in Atlanta.

2002: Regional office opens in Dallas.

2003: Lambda Legal scores landmark victory in the U.S. Supreme Court in *Lawrence v. Texas*, which struck down all sodomy laws in the United States.

2009: Iowa Supreme Court hands down unanimous decision to allow same-sex marriage in a historic win for Lambda.

opened in Atlanta, Georgia, in 1997, broke barriers in the South. The 1990s were also a time of internal change, as Stoddard resigned because of illness and was replaced by Kenneth M. Cathcart as executive director in 1992. Stoddard had watched Lambda grow from 6 to 22 staff members during his tenure and oversaw the nonprofit's many advances. He authored a seminal 1986 bill protecting New York City homosexuals against discrimination in housing, employment, and public accommodations and was an important national spokesperson for civil liberties in general. Stoddard died of AIDS at the age of 48 in February 1997.

Under Cathcart's direction, Lambda continued to grow. A fourth regional office was opened in Dallas, Texas, in June 2002, and the organization's overall staff reached approximately 100 by 2009. Groundbreaking legal victories continued to mount as well, including one that required New York City to provide identical benefits to domestic partners and married people (*Lesbian and Gay Teachers Association v. New York City Board of Education*, 1993) and another that gave recognition to LGBT students' first amendment right to be "out" at school (*Henkle v. Gregory*, 2001). Lambda Legal had become the most influential legal advocate for LGBT rights in the United States and its success was directly mirrored by the civil rights and lifestyle advances within the community it served.

LITIGATION IN THE 21ST CENTURY

Although Lambda Legal prevailed in many pioneering cases throughout the years, its U.S. Supreme Court victory in *Lawrence v. Texas* in 2003 was widely considered its *tour de force*. The case began on September 17, 1998, when Tyron Gardner and John G. Lawrence were arrested for having consensual adult sex in Lawrence's apartment. Lambda signed on to represent the defendants and specifically challenged the Texas "Homosexual Conduct Law." At the time, Texas was one of 13 states with sodomy laws and one of four in which the prohibition applied only to gays and lesbians. A three-judge panel of a Texas appellate court overturned Gardner and Lawrence's convictions, but the full court upheld them. When the state's highest court declined to hear the case, the U.S. Supreme Court agreed to take it on. On June 26, 2003, the U.S. Supreme Court handed down a historic decision, reversing its own ruling in *Hardwick* and eliminating all remaining sodomy laws in the United States.

The ramifications of *Lawrence* were not only immediate and far-reaching, but also as simple as they were complex. The most direct impact was on gay people living in the 13 states where they had been released from the threat of arrest and prosecution. While such prosecutions were rare, the stigma and burden of being classified as a criminal were a day-to-day reminder of the vulnerability of members of the LGBT community as well as their status under the law. In addition, *Lawrence* had much broader implications as its decriminalization of gays and lesbians negated the legal rationale allowed by *Hardwick* to treat them differently than heterosexuals in many other contexts. Thus, by finding a constitutional right to personal liberty for *all* people in the conduct of their personal lives, the Court had opened the door for equal consideration of the LGBT community in such matters as employment, adoption, child custody, and marriage. Finally, *Lawrence* sent a powerful message about the changing mores of the time. First, the Court, including Justice Anthony Kennedy, who wrote the majority opinion, was mainly composed of Republican-nominated justices. Second, while it took nearly 60 years for the Court to overturn its 1896 decision in *Plessy v. Ferguson* and rule that racial segregation was unconstitutional, only 17 years separated *Hardwick* and *Lawrence*. To Lambda Legal and its supporters, this was positive and exhilarating progress. To political and social conservatives, however, it was appalling.

The most divisive gay civil rights issue of the 21st century was same-sex marriage. While a few states recognized civil unions or domestic partnerships between same-sex couples—the first of which was Vermont in 2000—same-sex marriage had long been a hot-button topic on both sides of the political aisle. This was aptly illustrated by the passage of the "Defense of Marriage Act," a law declaring that if any state legalized same-sex marriage, other states did not have to recognize that marriage despite the Constitution's "full faith and credit" clause, by the U.S. Congress in 1996. Nonetheless, starting with Massachusetts in 2004, same-sex marriage became a reality in California, Connecticut, Iowa, Maine, New Hampshire, and Vermont. California, however, became a prime example of the kind of battleground the issue had become by 2008.

Through the efforts of Lambda Legal and others that began in 2004, the California Supreme Court followed Massachusetts's lead by finding a ban on same-sex marriage was unconstitutional (*In Re Marriage Cases*, 2008). The ruling took effect in June and 18,000 gay and lesbian couples were married in the ensuing months. Meanwhile, conservatives mounted a counterattack that placed a ballot initiative known as "Proposition 8" on the November ballot, imposing a constitutional amendment defining marriage as a union between a man and a woman. It was a tightly contested vote, but the referendum passed by a 52 percent to 48 percent margin, outlawing same-sex marriage in California and handing a stunning blow to the LGBT community.

However, Lambda Legal scored a resounding and surprising victory for same-sex marriage in 2009 when the Republican-dominated Iowa Supreme Court unanimously held in *Varnum v. Brien* that barring same-sex marriage violated the equal protection clause of the state's constitution. Beyond the obvious implications for Iowa's gay and lesbian community, the ruling significantly indicated that the issue was no longer limited to the liberal confines of the East and West Coasts, but also resonated with the denizens of the more conservative Midwest.

It is difficult to overestimate the impact that Lambda Legal has had on both the LGBT community and U.S. society in general. In just 36 years, the organization's efforts helped move a marginalized faction of the country out of hiding and into an era of acceptance and dignity. Resistance continued, however, and despite recognition of same-sex marriage in six states, the number of states that passed bans through ballot initiatives increased. Much work remained before Lambda Legal could achieve its goal of full equality for all. Nevertheless, the tide had begun to turn more rapidly in the 21st century, partially because of a generational changing of the guard. By 2009, for example, Pew Research Center polling indicated that 32 percent of the population continued to oppose gays and

lesbians openly serving in the military, down significantly from 45 percent in 1994. In addition, a *New York Times*/CBS News poll in 2009 found that 57 percent of people under 40 years old supported same-sex marriage, while only 31 percent of those over age 40 approved. A cultural shift was clearly occurring, and there was no reason to expect that it would reverse itself.

Much work remained for Lambda Legal's goals to fully become realized, and strident opposition to those efforts had by no means disappeared, but it was abundantly clear that the organization would persevere. According to "Arc of History," a Lambda article published on January 24, 2008, "We have invoked the principles of the Constitution and will continue to do so in our search for greater freedom for LGBT people and people with HIV. We have seen history move toward justice, but we know it does not move on its own—we need to lead it."

Margaret L. Moser

FURTHER READING

Chen, Vivia, "Iowa Fight for Gay Marriage Was the Case of a Lifetime," *Recorder*, July 2, 2009.

Dahir, Mubarak, "In the Service of Justice," *Advocate*, December 19, 2000, p. 16.

Davey, Monica, "Iowa Court Voids Gay Marriage Ban," *New York Times*, April 3, 2009.

Dunlap, David W., "Thomas Stoddard, 48, Dies; An Advocate of Gay Rights," *New York Times*, February 14, 1997.

Goodnough, Abby, and Anahad O'Connor, "Vermont Overrides Veto, Allows Same-Sex Marriage," *Houston Chronicle*, April 8, 2009, p. 6.

Lauck, Scott, "Lawyer Outlines Strategy in Iowa Gay Marriage Case to KC Legal Group," *Missouri Lawyers Media*, July 9, 2009.

Lochhead, Carolyn, "High Court Ruling Likely to Usher in New Era for Gays," *San Francisco Chronicle*, June 29, 2003, p. A4.

Martin, Douglas, "Tyron Garner, 39, Plaintiff in Pivotal Sodomy Case, Dies," *New York Times*, September 14, 2006.

Moskowitz, Eric, and Martin Finucane, "N.H. Becomes Sixth State Where Gays Can Marry," *Boston Globe*, June 3, 2009.

Nagourney, Adam, "Political Shifts on Gay Rights Lag Behind Culture," *New York Times*, June 28, 2009.

Rich, Frank, "40 Years Later, Still Second-Class Americans," *New York Times*, June 28, 2009.

"Stonewall Rebellion," *New York Times*, April 10, 2009.

"University of Illinois at Chicago Gender Historian Cited in Supreme Court AntiSodomy Decision," *Europe Intelligence Wire*, July 1, 2003.

Washington, Chris McGreal, "California Ban on Gay Marriage Upheld but the Battle Goes On," *Guardian* (London), May 27, 2009, p. 17.

Wetzstein, Cheryl, "California High Court Explains Its Decision, Gay Marriage Ban Lawfully Established," *Washington Times*, May 28, 2009, p. A18.

Las Vegas Sands Corp.

3355 Las Vegas Boulevard South, Room 1A
Las Vegas, Nevada 89109-8931
U.S.A.
Telephone: (702) 414-1000
Toll Free: (877) 883-6423
Fax: (702) 414-4884
Web site: http://www.lasvegassands.com

Public Company
Incorporated: 1988 as Las Vegas Sands, Inc.
Employees: 28,500
Sales: $4.39 billion (2008)
Stock Exchanges: New York
Ticker Symbol: LVS
NAICS: 721120 Casino Hotels

■ ■ ■

The Las Vegas Sands Corp. (LVS) is one of the largest casino operators in the world, with properties in Las Vegas, Macao, Singapore, and Bethlehem, Pennsylvania. The centerpiece of LVS's empire is the Venetian Hotel and Casino, which opened in 1999 on the site of the former Sands Hotel in Las Vegas. Other properties in Las Vegas include the Palazzo Resort and Casino and the Sands Expo Center; properties in Macao include the Sands Macao, Venetian Macao, and Four Seasons Macao. All told, LVS's properties contain almost 11,000 rooms of hotel space, more than a million square feet of gaming space, and over 3 million square feet of convention center and meeting space.

A ROCKY BEGINNING: 1988–91

The Sands Hotel was a Vegas institution for 44 years. In its heyday it was the center of entertainment in Las Vegas, featuring some of show business's biggest names, most notably Frank Sinatra and the "Rat Pack" (as Sinatra, Dean Martin, Sammy Davis Jr. and Peter Lawford were known). In 1988 Sheldon G. Adelson's company, The Interface Group (TIG), incorporated Las Vegas Sands, Inc., (LVSI) for the purpose of buying and operating the Sands Hotel. Adelson was an entrepreneur who made a name for himself as creator of COMDEX, the world's premier computer trade show, held in Las Vegas, which grew in size and prestige exponentially during the 1990s. COMDEX was produced by TIG, a 21-employee trade show company that Adelson and his partners built into a vertically integrated organization that owned its own travel agency and airline.

However, convention-goers often found it difficult to find available hotel rooms in Las Vegas. "COMDEX and (similar) shows were bringing a lot of people into there who didn't gamble," said Harold Vogel, then a vice-president at Merrill Lynch Capital Markets. Hotel-casino owners were therefore reluctant to set rooms aside for convention guests. In addition, Adelson explained, "If we generate the passengers and carry them to their destinations, it only makes sense to own the destination, too. It gives us quality control over the product we sell to the customer." In order to provide their conventioneers a full service experience, TIG would need a hotel.

Adelson first attempted to buy the Dunes Hotel, but was outbid. Kirk Kerkorian, whose MGM Grand

COMPANY PERSPECTIVES

The Company's primary business objective is to provide a premium destination casino resort experience in order to drive superior returns on invested capital and to increase asset value. To achieve this objective, the Company operates a "must-see" destination resort at a premier location at the heart of the Strip; captures premium room rates through a differentiated superior all-suites product; drives hotel occupancy and casino utilization through the link to the Expo Center and the Congress Center; caters to a higher-budget customer mix by offering a unique combination of assets and facilities; leverages the Casino Resort's premium co-branding strategy to drive revenues; and targets premium gaming customers.

had purchased the Sands and the Desert Inn Hotels in 1987 from the heirs of Howard Hughes, was selling the Sands and the 58.7 acres of undeveloped land around it. In April 1988 LVSI agreed to purchase the property for $110 million; the Nevada Gaming Control Board approved the sale in February 1989. Adelson appointed Henri Lewin, a former Hilton executive, as the hotel's president.

Lewin was a colorful figure, and his style clashed with Adelson's, often publicly. Gaming revenues at the Sands were disappointing, and 10 months after he was appointed president of the Sands, Lewin was fired from his job. He later sued LVSI and settled out of court. Management of the hotel was handed to a team headed by Al Benedict, a former executive at MGM Grand. Benedict's team resigned seven months later, and Steve Norton was appointed interim president of the Sands.

LVSI added the 575,000-square-foot Sands Expo and Convention Center, the largest privately-owned convention center in the country, to the hotel. The plan was to add another tower to the hotel, almost doubling its capacity. The initial architect for the expansion project was Nikita Zukov, who was fired four months into the job by LVSI for failing to develop the project on budget. He later sued for breach of contract and won a $1.3 million award. During the trial, Henri Lewin testified for Zukov, blasting Adelson and his management style. The convention facility opened and was making money, but the old Sands, with 750 rooms, could not compete with the mega-resorts that were

sprouting around it, especially the gilded Mirage that had opened across the street.

In 1991 Adelson assumed leadership of the hotel, and in the ensuing years the convention center nearly doubled in size to 1.15 million square feet. The casino area expanded as well. The new rooms, however, were never added, and despite a $20 million refurbishment, the hotel, in the words of one Mirage guest, still looked "seedy." Under Adelson's watch, the Sands Hotel continued to lose money, even as the rival Mirage scored huge profits.

THE SANDS GIVES WAY TO THE VENETIAN

In 1995 TIG sold its Trade Show division to Japan's Softbank. Adelson used the proceeds from the $800 million cash sale to buy out his partners in LVSI, becoming sole owner of the company. William P. Weidner became LVSI's president and COO. Adelson had expressed his interest in opening a mega-resort, and in early 1996 the news broke that the famed Sands Hotel would be closed and demolished to make room for a new themed resort.

The Sands Hotel closed on June 30, 1996, and was imploded on November 26 of that same year. On April 14, 1997, the Venetian Resort Hotel Casino broke ground. The hotel was based on the theme of Renaissance Venice, including a reproduction of the Grand Canal in the shopping area. Two historians checked the accuracy of details during the hotel's construction. The Venetian opened on May 3, 1999, having cost $1.5 billion. With 500,000 square feet of retail space and suites averaging 700 square feet, the Venetian, as Peter Szecsodi wrote in the *Gambler* magazine in 2002, "raised the bar of expectation of what is considered a world-class mega-resort."

The Venetian hotel was run by Venetian Casino Resort, LLC, with Robert Goldstein as president and COO, but it was wholly owned and managed by LVSI. The property was physically connected to the Sands Expo and Convention Center, making the entire complex one of the largest hotel and meeting centers in the United States. In 2001 and 2002, the Venetian was featured in *Condé Nast Traveler* magazine's "Gold List of the World's Best Places to Stay." The hotel catered to both gamblers and business travelers to drive revenues. In the first quarter of 2002, the Venetian was one of only three Las Vegas hotels that showed increased cash flow compared with the same quarter the previous year.

In early 2002 the company was heading into global and virtual expansion. In February 2002 Galaxy Casino, Inc., a joint venture between Venetian Casino Resort, LLC, and investors based in Macao and Hong Kong, had been granted a provisional concession for a Macao

KEY DATES

■

1987: Financier Kirk Kerkorian's MGM Grand buys the Las Vegas Sands and Desert Inn hotels from the Summa Corporation.

1988: The Interface Group (TIG) agrees to purchase the Sands Hotel from Kerkorian for $110 million and forms Las Vegas Sands, Inc. (LVSI), to run the property.

1989: LVSI completes the purchase of the Sands Hotel and Casino from MGM Grand, Henri Lewin is named hotel president.

1990: Lewin is fired; Al Benedict assumes leadership of the hotel, resigns in August.

1991: LVSI Chairman Sheldon G. Adelson takes over management of the hotel.

1995: TIG sells its Trade Show division to Japan's Softbank; Adelson buys out his partners' share in LVSI.

1996: The Sands Hotel is closed and imploded; construction begins on the Casino Resort.

1997: Ground is broken for the Venetian Resort Hotel Casino.

1999: The Venetian opens under the management of Venetian Casino Resort, LLC; Robert Goldstein is president and COO.

2001: The Venetian is named one on *Condé Nast Traveler* magazine's "Gold List of the World's Best Places to Stay" for the second consecutive year.

2004: Sands Macao opens in the People's Republic of China; Las Vegas Sands Corp. (LVS) has initial public offering on the New York Stock Exchange.

2007: Macao Venetian Casino Resort opens.

2009: Sands Casino Resort Bethlehem opens; construction on St. Regis luxury condominiums addition to Venetian Palazzo is stalled.

gaming license. Macao, a small territory that had been controlled by Portugal for over 400 years, reverted back to China in 1999 but was allowed to retain its capitalist system for the following 50 years. The Macao gaming market was closed to competition for decades. Galaxy Casino and Stephen Wynn's Wynn Resorts (Macao) Ltd. were the first outside gaming companies to be granted concessions in Macao.

LVSI GOES PUBLIC AND INTERNATIONAL

In Las Vegas, 2003 room occupancy at the Venetian dropped, but overall profits soared as a result of increased sales at the Grand Canal retail shops. An increased emphasis on the restaurants in the Venetian also helped sales. In 2003 Thomas Keller opened Bouchon Restaurant at the Venetian. Over the next several years, the hotel would continue to open restaurants backed by more celebrity chefs, including Mario Batali and Emeril Lagasse. In addition, 1,000 luxury suites were also opened at the Venetian in 2003.

In anticipation of the company's initial public offering and continued expansion both in Las Vegas and abroad, LVSI sold its Grand Canal shops to General Growth Properties in April 2004. The deal was worth $766 million and included a promised sale of future retail space in the planned Palazzo Casino Resort, which would potentially bring the total sale price to nearly $1.5 billion.

The Sands Macao, the first Las Vegas-style casino in China, opened the following month. LVSI's intention was to replicate its Las Vegas model of maintaining a critical mass of real estate with gaming, restaurants, and a successful hotel and convention center within a short distance of each other. The Sands Macao was essentially the first step in Adelson's plan to reproduce the Las Vegas strip in another country.

In December 2004, with the memory of tens of thousands of Chinese crowding outside of the Sands Macao at its grand opening still fresh in the minds of American investors, Adelson took the company public. The IPO raised more than $690 million for the Las Vegas Sands Corp. (LVS), a new entity established for the IPO. LVSI, now known as Las Vegas Sands LLC, became a wholly owned subsidiary of the publicly traded LVS.

By 2007 LVS had a number of projects underway in Macao, including a new Venetian resort. In August 2007 the flagship Venetian Macao opened with 3,000 suites and boasting enough room to park 90 Boeing 747s at its convention center. The new resort housed more than 30 restaurants and nearly 400 shops.

By mid-2007 Adelson, the son of a Boston cab driver, was the third-richest man in the United States, estimated to be making more than $23 million dollars per day. The Venetian properties in Macao and Las Vegas, combined with the business model that combined fine dining, hotels, convention centers, and gaming, seemed to be nearly flawless. However, by the end of 2007 the world economy was on a downward trend. Although the company was turning a profit, the results were not as dramatic at its Macao resort as at its Las Vegas counterpart. A number of investors pulled out of the Asian enterprise, and construction costs in China were not offset by the casino's profits. Despite gains in revenue in late 2007, net income fell nearly 70 percent.

LVS forged ahead with large building projects in spite of diminishing revenues over the ensuing years. The Palazzo Resort Hotel Casino opened next door to the Venetian in Las Vegas on New Year's Eve, 2007. The Palazzo, proclaimed to be the world's largest "green" building, more than doubled LVS's hotel capacity in Las Vegas. In 2009 the Sands Casino Resort in Bethlehem, Pennsylvania, opened as a full-service resort and casino. The Pennsylvania Sands boasted the first Emeril Lagasse restaurant in the Northeast. A 300-room luxury hotel was expected to open in late 2009. Other LVS projects in development as of August 2009 were the Marina Bay Sands resort in Singapore and three more hotel/casinos in Macao. Poor economic conditions had suspended development of the St. Regis, a luxury condominium addition to the Venetian/Palazzo/Sands Expo complex in Las Vegas. The company was also pursuing a Hong Kong IPO to pay for the Macao developments.

Adi R. Ferrara
Updated, Robert Jacobson

PRINCIPAL SUBSIDIARIES

Las Vegas Sands, LLC; Venetian Casino Resort, LLC.; Marina Bay Sands Pte. Ltd.; Venetian Macau Limited; Venetian Cotai Limited.

PRINCIPAL COMPETITORS

Mandalay Resort Group; MGM Mirage; Park Place Entertainment; Harrah's Entertainment; Galaxy Casino S.A.

FURTHER READING

Bates, Warren, "Hotel's History Full of Legends, Mystique, Wild Weekends," *Las Vegas Review-Journal*, May 17, 1996, p.2A.

Berke, Jonathan, "Las Vegas Sands Cashes in on IPO," *Daily Deal*, December 16, 2004.

Bradsher, Keith, "Macao, Famously Seedy, Now Bets on Vegas Plush," *New York Times*, May 25, 2004, p.C1.

Carton, Barbara, "Needham Firm Wins Rights to Sands; Nevada Board Rejects Three Proposed Partners," *Boston Globe*, February 10, 1989, p. 21.

Coleman, Zach, "U.S. Regulators Are Expected to Scrutinize Macau Proposal—Venetian Awaits Nod from Nevada Authorities," *Wall Street Journal*, March 25, 2002, p. A12.

Harris, Kathryn, "Kerkorian to Sell Sands Hotel for $110 Million," *Los Angeles Times*, April 26, 1988, HOME magazine, p. 2.

"Hotel and Gaming Mogul Chases Bill Gates for 'Richest American' Tag," *InformationWeek*, January 16, 2007.

"Investors Leave Las Vegas Sands," *BusinessWeek*, February 7, 2007, http://www.businessweek.com/investor/content/feb2007/pi20070206_287364.htm.

Kanigher, Steve, "Resort Owner Has Much at Stake in Latest Gaming Industry Venture," *Las Vegas Sun*, April 29, 1999.

Nicholson, Chris V., "Adelson Considers IPO for Sands' Macao Assets," Dealbook, *New York Times*, July 8, 2009, http://dealbook.blogs.nytimes.com/2009/07/08/adelson-eyes-ipo-for-sands-macao-assets/.

"Occupancy Slips at Venetian, While Room Rates Increase," *Tradeshow Week*, June 2, 2003, p. 4.

Patterson, Gregory A., "Taking a Gamble on Las Vegas: Dynamic Interface Owner Pushes Charter Company into the Big Time," *Boston Globe*, May 8, 1988, p. Al.

Rivlin, Gary, "When Third Place on the Rich List Just Isn't Enough," *New York Times*, January 17, 2008, p. Al.

Stein, Joel, "Less Vegas," *Time*, August 24, 2009, p. 29.

Strow, David, "Adelson in Net Gaming Pact," *Las Vegas Sun*, April 1, 2002.

Stutz, Howard, "Adelson to Take Over Sands Operation," *Las Vegas Review-Journal*, April 30, 1991, p. 6E.

Szecsodi, Peter, "Where Fantasies Come True," *Gambler Magazine*, May 31, 2002.

"A Unique Approach: Las Vegas Sands Corp. Looks beyond the Traditional Approach to Casino Gaming," *U.S. Business Review*, July 2005, p. 18.

"Venetian Posts Increase in Cash Flow for First Quarter," Associated Press Newswires, April 24, 2002.

Wimberly, Rachel, "Public Companies Took Steep Drops in '08," *Tradeshow Week*, February 23, 2009, p. 3.

———, "Q2 Earnings Mixed for Casinos," *Tradeshow Week*, August 13, 2007.

LodgeNet
connect | inform | entertain

LodgeNet Interactive Corporation

3900 West Innovation Street
Sioux Falls, South Dakota 57107-7002
U.S.A.
Telephone: (605) 988-1000
Toll Free: (888) 563-4363
Fax: (605) 988-1511
Web site: http://www.lodgenet.com

Public Company
Founded: 1980 as Satellite Movie Company
Incorporated: 1983
Employees: 1,202
Sales: $533.88 million (2008)
Stock Exchanges: NASDAQ
Ticker Symbol: LNET
NAICS: 517910 Communication Services, Not Elsewhere Classified

■ ■ ■

LodgeNet Interactive Corporation is a leading provider of wired and wireless media marketing and connectivity technology to hospitality, healthcare, and other guest-based businesses in more than 20 countries worldwide. LodgeNet's network-based video-on-demand, sports and television programming, and broadband Internet are available at more than 10,000 hotel properties. In addition, it provides high-definition content. The company services such properties as DoubleTree Hotels, Fairmont Hotels and Resorts, Hilton, Hyatt, InterContinental, Loews Hotels, Marriott, Omni Hotels, Radisson, Ritz-Carlton, Westin Hotels and Resorts, and Wyndham Hotels and Resorts. LodgeNet also serves healthcare facilities throughout the United States with patient education and entertainment networks, clinical systems integration, and other applications. Healthcare customers include Brigham and Women's Hospital, MD Anderson Cancer Center, the University of Chicago Northshore Hospital, and Kaiser Oakland/Sunnyside.

FOUNDED AS SATELLITE MOVIE COMPANY IN 1980

LodgeNet Interactive Corporation was founded in 1980 by Tim C. Flynn as Satellite Movie Company. The company's initial business was providing satellite television systems to hotels and motels, including satellite earth stations, master antennae, and on-property signal distribution systems, plus programming and related marketing support materials. Programming sources included such services as ESPN, Cable News Network (CNN), Showtime, The Movie Channel, and national stations WTBS and WGN.

Satellite Movie Company, which was originally incorporated in South Dakota in February 1983, began offering pay-per-view (PPV) movie systems to the lodging industry in 1986. The company's initial PPV offering was a scheduled system, offering newer movies than those available on cable, broadcast at preset times over the guest-room television system.

DEVELOPED ON-DEMAND SERVICES IN EARLY 1990S

In September 1991 the company adopted the name LodgeNet Entertainment Corporation to reflect the

COMPANY PERSPECTIVES

LodgeNet Interactive envisions, designs, delivers and manages compelling interactive experiences that keep customers of guest-based businesses connected, informed and entertained.

We are experts at integrating and implementing consumer-facing media and connectivity technology, and are the leading provider of media and connectivity solutions to the industries we serve.

evolution of its services from satellite-based programming to a broader network distribution model. This move anticipated the introduction of the LodgeNet Guest Scheduled video-on-demand service in 1992, the company's initial interactive service. A significant advancement in guest room entertainment services, the Guest Scheduled video-on-demand system generated more movie buys and revenue because it responded instantly to the guest's order rather than requiring patrons to wait for a scheduled broadcast. Revenue also expanded because the on-demand service offered a greatly increased selection of movies. Finally, the technology that enabled Guest Scheduled video (two-way digital communication between each guest room and LodgeNet) also opened the door to additional interactive services.

In March 1993 the company, in a joint venture with NTN Communications of Carlsbad, California, began testing interactive television in approximately 5,000 hotel guest rooms over a period of five months. The full capability was demonstrated in late 1993 with the introduction by LodgeNet of network-based Super Nintendo Entertainment System (NES) video games for the guest room, which proved to be exceedingly popular with hotels and guests and, by mid-1999, was installed in more than 530,000 LodgeNet guest rooms. Subsequently, LodgeNet introduced additional interactive services, including guest satisfaction surveys, interactive hotel directories, interactive property tours, room service menu displays, Internet site promotions, and interactive check-out transactions with guest room printers.

The company incorporated in Delaware during 1993 via a merger as a successor to Satellite Movie Company. In October of that year the company went public, offering some 4.5 million shares in its initial public offering and bringing in $56.48 million in proceeds, which were used to redeem outstanding

preferred stock, reduce bank debt, and provide working capital.

FORMED STRATEGIC PARTNERSHIPS IN MID-1990S

In 1994 LodgeNet partnered with Sony Corporation, which made a series of Trinitron televisions compatible with LodgeNet's interactive systems. Meanwhile, competitors Spectradyne and COMSAT Video Enterprises were not idle. Dallas-based Spectradyne formed an alliance with Electronic Data Systems (EDS), to use compressed digital video to program scheduled movies to hotel rooms, calling their offering "SpectraVision"; and Bethesda, Maryland-based COMSAT Video Enterprises, a subsidiary of COMSAT Corp., allied with Silicon Graphics and Bell Atlantic to target two segments of the lodging business: traditional satellite programming combining channels free to the guest with for-pay movies and live special events and On Command Video, a paid entertainment and information system. Smaller competitors also were offering movies in hotel rooms. Peoria, Illinois-based SVI Systems offered movies with its Instant Entertainment or Super Video Cinema programs, but its technology relied on portable videocassette players rather than telecommunications equipment. Early in 1995, Santa Clara, California-based 4th Network began working on an interactive shopping and guest services system. Total revenue for LodgeNet in 1995 reached $63.2 million.

In January 1996 LodgeNet forged an agreement with PRIMESTAR Partners L.P., making LodgeNet the exclusive provider of PRIMESTAR products and services to the lodging industry. PRIMESTAR agreed to provide LodgeNet with access to its digital satellite technology, and the Philadelphia-based company featured more than 1.6 million sites installed throughout the United States. PRIMESTAR by LodgeNet (PbL) was formed as a division of LodgeNet to handle the alliance and, almost immediately, hotel owners and operators seized upon the programming, customer service, and low per-room cost offered by PbL. By the end of 1998, PRIMESTAR by LodgeNet was serving nearly 380,000 rooms with free-to-guest programming.

Also that month, the company formed ResNet Communications Inc. to extend its b-Local Area Network (LAN) system architecture and operational expertise into apartments, condominiums, and townhouses, which make up the multiple dwelling unit (MDU) market. In October, TCI Satellite MDU Inc., an affiliate of Tele-Communications Inc. (TCI), agreed to invest up to $40 million in ResNet in exchange for up to a 36.99 percent interest in ResNet and agreed to provide ResNet with long-term access to the digital DBS

KEY DATES

1980: Tim C. Flynn founds the Satellite Movie Company to deliver basic and premium satellite-delivered television programming.

1991: The company adopts the name LodgeNet Entertainment Corporation to reflect the evolution of its services from satellite-based programming to a broader network distribution model.

1993: The company becomes a publicly traded company on NASDAQ.

1998: LodgeNet Entertainment acquires Connect Group Corporation to provide plug-and-play high-speed Internet access to hotel guest rooms.

2008: The company's new name, LodgeNet Interactive Corporation, demonstrates the business's growth beyond entertainment provision into media advertising and connectivity technology.

signals provided by TCI Satellite for the MDU market on a nationwide basis via the PRIMESTAR satellite signal. Approximately $5.4 million in cash was paid to LodgeNet, with the remainder of the $34.6 million to be provided in the form of available financing.

By April 1996 the company had more than 200,000 hotel rooms set up to play Super NES games via its interactive network. Total revenue for the year reached $97.72 million, with a net loss of $3.25 million.

EXPANDING MARKETS IN 1997

Prior to 1997 the company focused its marketing efforts on hotels with at least 150 rooms, which comprised 38 percent of the lodging industry's 3.5 million rooms. In 1997 the company, in an effort to target an area of the industry not as saturated with competitors, began to market to locations with fewer than 150 rooms. June 1997 found the company announcing a strategic alliance with SkyMall Inc. to deliver a video version of the latter company's in-flight airline catalog. The service allowed hotel guests to browse and shop from an interactive video catalog in their room. Taking advantage of its market position as a leader in in-room entertainment, LodgeNet introduced advertising "banners" on its video screens in hotel rooms, similar to Internet-based ad banners, which provided a significant new revenue source for the company.

International sales efforts for the company expanded in 1997, with LodgeNet signing agreements with Panama-based Five Star Entertainment Inc. to introduce LodgeNet's services to Central America. Five Star began installing systems in Panama and testing markets in Belize, Costa Rica, Guatemala, El Salvador, Honduras, and Nicaragua. In addition, the company inked deals with TCI Net Vision for the Venezuelan market, Roombar S.A. in the Dominican Republic, and InfoAsia for the Indonesian, Philippine, Thai, Singaporan, and Malaysian markets.

The company added approximately 100,000 rooms to its guest pay base in 1997, bringing the total to 511,000, as well as 126,000 new rooms equipped with NES. The company's core lodging business was bolstered in 1997 by contract renewals and such new clients as Carefree Resorts and Prime Hospitality, as well as the addition of several high-profile ownership/ management companies to its corporate roster. The company's Canadian branch did well also, installing interactive systems in more than 125 hotel properties throughout that country, including Delta Hotels and Resorts, ITT Sheraton Canada, Centennial Hotels, Coast Hotels Limited, Westmont Hospitality Group, and Canadian Niagara Hotels Inc., as well as numerous independent properties. However, while total revenue that year reached $135.7 million, a 38.9 percent growth over the previous year, net losses continued to mount, reaching $25.41 million for the year.

RESTRUCTURING AND RELOCATION IN 1998

In May 1998 the company moved into a new headquarters location on West Innovation Street in Sioux Falls, South Dakota, and in July, Scott C. Petersen was promoted from executive vice-president and chief operating officer to president and chief executive officer, replacing Flynn, who became chairman of the board. By this time, LodgeNet was the second largest provider of interactive entertainment and information services to the lodging industry.

In June the company acquired Connect Group Corporation in a stock swap. The acquisition gave the company the ability to deliver a comprehensive, cost-effective solution to enable plug-and-play high-speed Internet access for hotel guest rooms and meeting spaces as well as the technology to allow guests with laptop computers to connect to the Internet from their rooms at more than 50 times the speed of conventional modems.

In November 1998 the company completed the merger of its subsidiary ResNet with Interactive Cable Systems Inc. and Shared Technologies Communications Corporation, to form Global Interactive Communications Corporation, a company designed to provide video, voice, and Internet services to the MDU market. At start-up, the new company (owned 30 percent by LodgeNet) had in excess of 650 properties and 55,000 subscribers in 28 states from coast to coast. The new Richardson, Texas-based company also featured customer service and field operations in Tampa, Florida, and construction and warehousing activities in Sioux Falls, South Dakota.

Also in 1998, LodgeNet signed agreements with the Red Roof chain and Carefree Resorts. The company added approximately 84,000 rooms to its guest pay base in 1998, bringing the total to 596,806. Still, while revenue continued to climb, net losses mounted as well, with the company bringing in a total $146.48 million, while losing $39.91 million in 1998.

INTERNET CONNECTIVITY THE FOCUS IN 1999

In March 1999 LodgeNet entered an agreement with AT&T, the world's premier provider of voice and data communications and the nation's largest direct Internet service provider, to provide high-speed Internet access to hotels across the country. With the world's largest, most powerful long distance network and the largest wireless network in North America, AT&T would supply high-speed Internet access to guest rooms equipped with On-Line by LodgeNet. The service also would supply the hotels themselves with connectivity to their meeting rooms, back offices, and public areas. Wingate Inns International Inc. announced in January that it would be the first hotel chain to deploy LodgeNet's services with Internet connectivity to some 23,000 rooms nationwide that year. By this time, partners in PRIME-STAR included TS AT, Time Warner Entertainment, Comcast Corporation, Cox Communications, Media-One, and GE Americom.

The company's primary focus at the end of the 20th century was on the North American hotel, motel, and resort market, and by mid-1999 LodgeNet served some 700,000 rooms at more than 4,500 lodging properties in the United States, Canada, Japan, South Korea, Brazil, Panama, Venezuela, and Peru.

EVOLVING BUSINESS IN THE 21ST CENTURY

As the 21st century got underway, LodgeNet was installing high-speed Internet lines in hotel rooms in an attempt to spur revenues. The new century saw a change in leadership, with Flynn assuming the role of chairman emeritus in 2000, and Peterson heading the board as chairman. In 2004 the company expanded its guest subscription programming to include sports and fitness content and added the Disney Channel to its on-demand lineup. Also in 2004, LodgeNet Entertainment partnered with McKesson to provide access to on-demand entertainment and interactive connectivity through Horizon PatientVision systems. Relying on its SigNETure platform, LodgeNet started offering high-definition programming to hotels around the same time. (By 2008 LG Electronics would be integrating LodgeNet and On Command interactive terminals into flat-panel HDTVs built for hotels.) In addition, with content from online movie distributor Movielink, the company started the Entertainment 2GoSM service in 2005 which let hotel guests download movies onto a laptop.

After years of perpetual losses, including $7 million in 2005, LodgeNet Entertainment earned $1.8 million in 2006. In February 2006 the company signed an agreement with GlobeCast WorldTV to offer hotels served by LodgeNet the international television and radio channels broadcast by the satellite television provider. The channels represented 41 countries and 33 languages. Late in 2006 some one million hotel rooms worldwide had television, on-demand movies, and Internet access provided by the company. LodgeNet also began installing interactive television systems in hospitals that allowed patients to select a movie or video game, make requests, and view patient education content.

In early 2007, the company finalized the purchase of StayOnline Inc. for $15 million. The acquisition quintupled LodgeNet's provision of broadband to hotel rooms in the United States. The same year, LodgeNet bought On Command from Liberty Media Corp. The acquisition, for $380 million in cash and stock, noted analyst Marla Backer in *Europe Intelligence Wire*, should "provide several benefits to LodgeNet including speeding up new product deployment and development, and expanding the opportunity to offer bundled video television/high-speed Internet access with its recent acquisition of Stay Online." More than 800,000 hotel rooms in North America had On Command interactive media services, and the business owned 80 percent of The Hotel Networks, which distributed satellite television programming to rooms in the United States.

RENAMED AND REORGANIZED IN 2008–09

In 2008 the company renamed itself LodgeNet Interactive Corporation to reflect its growth beyond entertainment provision into media advertising and connectivity technology. Later in the year, the company restructured its business into Hospitality and Healthcare divisions, while keeping The Hotel Networks a wholly owned media marketing subsidiary. LodgeNet Chairman and CEO Scott C. Petersen told *Marketing Weekly News*, "This new organizational structure will enhance our ability to deliver innovative new solutions to our current and prospective customers more quickly and effectively." The Hotel Networks subsidiary offers measurable results to advertiser-supported content directed toward business travelers. It delivers ten premium channels. The Hospitality unit announced in 2009 new offerings that included HD movies, independent films, more live sports programming, and other content, as well as on-demand access to Disney-ABC Television shows. Also in 2009, DirecTV selected LodgeNet Professional Solutions to provide technical assistance with its HDTV systems in hotels. As of 2008, the Healthcare division had installed the LodgeNetRX Interactive Patient Television System in more than 35 hospitals. The system integrates entertainment options, quality measures, patient education content, and clinical systems.

LodgeNet Interactive's services in 2009 encompassed digital video, broadband Internet connectivity, professional, and media marketing solutions for the hospitality, healthcare, and other guest-based businesses. The company was among the Top 10 multiple system operators in the U.S. and Canadian markets. Its first quarter revenues totaled $51.6 million.

Daryl F. Mallett
Updated, Doris Maxfield

PRINCIPAL SUBSIDIARIES

The Hotel Networks.

PRINCIPAL DIVISIONS

Hospitality; LodgeNet Healthcare.

PRINCIPAL COMPETITORS

Cox Communications Inc.; DIRECTV Group Inc.; Wayport Inc.

FURTHER READING

"AT&T and LodgeNet to Provide Hotels and Guests with High-Speed 'Plug and Play' Internet Access," *PR Newswire*, March 10, 1999, p. 2382.

"AT&T Inks Net Access Deal with LodgeNet," *Content Factory*, March 11, 1999, p. 1008069u3464.

Biddle, RiShawn, "Gloom Service," *Forbes*, January 24, 2000, p. 140.

"Daniel Brooking," *Television Digest*, February 17, 1997, p. 19.

"GlobeCast WorldTV and LodgeNet Join Forces to Expand In-Room Hotel Entertainment Network," *Wireless News*, February 24, 2006.

"Hospital Services Now Rivaling Those Found in Hotels," *America's Intelligence Wire*, August 6, 2006.

"Hotel Room Interactive TV," *Television Digest*, March 29, 1993, p. 18.

"Internet Inn," *PC Magazine*, May 27, 1997, p. 9.

Kerschbaumer, Ken, "High Def-inn-ition: The New Luxury Hotel Amenity: HD on a Flat-screen TV," *Broadcasting & Cable*, July 4, 2005, p. 12.

"Large Cap News: Current Research on LodgeNet Entertainment Corp.," *Europe Intelligence Wire*, March 27, 2007.

"LodgeNet Establishes Hospitality-Specific Division," *Hotels*, November 1, 2008.

"LodgeNet Expands Content, Selection," *Travel & Leisure Close-Up*, February 2, 2009.

"LodgeNet Interactive Corporation: Cutting-Edge Services and Solutions Keep Hoteliers Ahead of the Curve on Guest Expectations," *Hotels*, September 1, 2008.

"LodgeNet Posts First Yearly Profit," *AFX Asia (Focus)*, February 8, 2007.

"LodgeNet Realigns Its Business into Three Operating Divisions," *Marketing Weekly News*, September 13, 2008.

"LodgeNet Reorganizes, Changes Name," *Hotels*, February 1, 2008.

"LodgeNet to Buy On Command," *America's Intelligence Wire*, December 14, 2006.

McConville, Jim, "TCI Takes Stake in LodgeNet; Will Invest $40 Million in DTH Service to Apartments," *Broadcasting & Cable*, October 28, 1996, p. 86.

"Rising Demand for Interactive Patient Television Systems Drives LodgeNet Healthcare Sales Growth," *Women's Health Weekly*, October 30, 2008, p. 592.

Veilleux, C Thomas, "Primestar's Extending Its Service," *HFN*, January 15, 1996, p. 191.

Waxier, Caroline, "Movie Blues," *Forbes*, June 16, 1997, p. 270.

Weinstein, Jeff, "Will Guests Have Time to Sleep, Too?" *Hotels*, February 1995, p. 46.

Whitford, Marty, "High-Speed Access Gains Ground," *Hotel & Motel Management*, February 15, 1999, p. 3.

"Wireless Verticals: McKesson and LodgeNet Introduce Horizon PatientVision," *Wireless News*, July 12, 2004.

Wolff, Carlo, "A Garden of Digital Delights," *Lodging Hospitality*, December 1994, p. 87.

Worcester, Barbara A., "Saying Good-Bye to Industry Giants," *Hotel & Motel Management*, April 20, 1998, p. 26.

ManGroupplc

Man Group PLC

Sugar Quay, Lower Thames Street
London, EC3R 6DU
United Kingdom
Telephone: (+44 20) 7144-1000
Fax: (+44 20) 7144 1923
Web site: http://www.mangroupplc.com

Public Company
Founded: 1783
Incorporated: 2000
Employees: 1,700
Funds Under Management: $46.8 billion (2009)
Stock Exchanges: London
Ticker Symbol: EMG
NAICS: 523930 Investment Advice

■ ■ ■

Man Group PLC, headquartered in London, England, is one of the world's most prominent international financial services and investment advising firms. Man Group maintains offices in 13 countries and serves individual and institutional clients in some 80 countries around the world. After two centuries as a leading commodities broker, the company in the 1980s shifted its focus to investment management, becoming a pioneer and global leader in hedge funds. By 2009 the company was responsible for investments valued at over $40 billion.

A LONG HERITAGE OF INTERNATIONAL BUSINESS

In 1783 James Man, a cooper (barrel maker) in London, established a business trading rum and sugar, which were lucrative tropical commodities. The firm's first major success was winning the exclusive rights to supply rum to the Royal Navy, an arrangement the company maintained until 1970. The business later branched out into trading other popular consumer products such as coffee and cocoa. Man's descendents continued to operate the company; in 1860 his grandsons, Edward Desborough Man and Fredrick Man, renamed the company using their initials: ED & F Man.

During the 19th century, commodity trading in Britain developed from a business conducted informally in coffeehouses into a sophisticated industry housed in formal exchanges where brokers used hedging contracts to manage risk and protect themselves against price swings on the market. London was the center of the world sugar trade, and the London Futures Market became the center of sugar commodities trading as well.

In spite of long interruptions in commodities trading during and after the two world wars, Man retained its position as one of the world's leading commodities brokers. Trading and processing of sugar, cocoa, and coffee remained the core of its business; it also branched out into molasses, alcohol, nuts, and spices. In addition, it traded base metals and crude oil. Its trading activities sometimes involved the company in international politics, as it brokered sugar imports to the Soviet Union and later Russia, and sugar exports from Cuba. In 1994 Man would still handle about 15 percent of the

COMPANY PERSPECTIVES

Man is a uniquely three dimensional business in terms of the institutional and private investor balance that we have, the geography of our investors and the fact that we offer access to a wide range of underlying investment management styles.

Our capital, scale and resources give us the flexibility to create product for whatever type of investor in whatever format they want wherever they want it. In my view, that is an absolutely unique expertise.

The hedge fund industry continues to evolve both in terms of scale and scope, but the fundamental proposition of the hedge fund community remains constant. That is, to provide positive investment returns across market cycles and to diversify investors' portfolios. At Man our strengths in terms of capital, track record and access to underlying managers means that we are better placed than most to achieve this.

worldwide open market trade for sugar, and about 20 percent of the cocoa trade. The company had started a ship brokerage division in 1983, ED & F Man Shipping Ltd., which later started operating its own ships.

FROM COMMODITIES TRADING, TO COMMODITIES FUTURES, TO FINANCIAL SERVICES

In the 1970s and early 1980s commodity exchanges began developing futures contracts, financial instruments that served market traders and investors seeking to make money by betting for or against future trends in commodity prices. Futures trading began at the Chicago Board of Trade in 1973; futures trading exchanges soon opened in New York and London. Man became drawn into futures trading through serving as a broker to some of these investors and through its own desire to protect itself against price swings. It set up a series of futures trading companies specializing in particular industries, which it combined in 1985 into two units serving the United Kingdom and the United States through offices in London, New York, and Chicago. In 1990 the company acquired GNP Commodities, which had been banned from trading futures in the United States because some of its brokers had cheated clients. Four years later Man bought another American commodities broker, Geldermann Inc., from ConAgra.

From futures trading, Man decided to enter investment management, particularly "alternative" financial services such as hedge funds and managed futures. Hedge funds, developed in the 1950s and 1960s, were devised to protect investors against market swings, offering investors a seemingly optimal combination of security and relatively high returns. Hedge funds marketed their services only to small numbers of wealthy individuals so that they could operate outside the regulations of regular financial markets. In return for their expertise, hedge fund owners could charge high commissions and fees; for example, Man's funds would charge annual fees of up to 3 percent of the value of clients' investments, and 20 percent of earned profits.

Man entered the investment services industry in 1983, purchasing 50 percent of Mint Investment Management Co., a U.S.-based commodity fund management firm. The original fund partners continued to maintain their computerized trading system and authorize trades, which Man employees then executed. Through Mint, Man became the first fund manager to introduce "capital guaranteed funds," which promised to keep investors' principal intact for a stated time period while still promising high potential returns. Man would create many more such funds, which would become the bedrock of its asset management business.

Man aimed to deploy its skill in commodities trading to create distinctive commodities and futures-based hedge fund vehicles with superior performance. Its next step in doing this was to acquire a majority of the hedge fund company AHL in 1989; it acquired the rest of the company in 1994 for a total of only $34 million. AHL became one of Man's chief fund management units, specializing in managed futures. Like with Mint, AHL's trading strategies were based on a complex computerized trading system known as a black-box system; the transactions were spectacularly successful, reporting an average annual rate of return of 17.9 percent from 1990 through 2006. Man relied on a network of investment advisers, bank officers, and other financial professionals to publicize and distribute its funds. By 1994 Man's futures funds were worth over $1 billion.

Man rode the tremendous expansion of managed futures and hedge funds in the 1990s and early 2000s, much of it driven by institutions such as pension funds, foundations, and universities. In 1995 it created a new fund named AHL Alpha; designed to cater to institutions, AHL Alpha offered a somewhat more conservative investing strategy than Man's existing funds. In 1996 Man introduced its Man-IP 220 fund, the first capital guaranteed fund that employed two different fund managers, intended to ensure more regular returns.

KEY DATES

1783: James Man founds a sugar brokerage firm in London.
1869: The company changes its name to ED & F Man.
1983: Man enters the investment management field.
1994: Man stock is floated on the London Stock Exchange
2000: Man spins off its agricultural commodities unit, incorporates, and changes its name to Man Group PLC.
2007: Man Group sells most of its brokerage unit, devoting itself solely to asset management.

From the United Kingdom, Man sought to expand its asset management business abroad, starting in the relatively liberal financial markets of the Netherlands, where it started its first futures fund in 1988. In 1990 the company established a Switzerland office, where it based its investment products division. Man became a member of the French futures exchange Matif in 1994 and opened a Paris office not long afterwards. Other international offices were established in Hong Kong; Dubai; Montevideo, Uruguay; Sydney, Australia; Singapore; Tokyo; and Toronto.

TRANSFORMATION TO A PUBLIC COMPANY AND THE END OF AN ERA

Man had remained a partnership until the early 1970s, when it converted into a private company, with all of its stock held by senior management and employees. In 1994 the company offered a small portion of its stock on the London Stock Exchange. The stock's early performance was disappointing, attributed in part to investors' and analysts' unease with a company involved in disparate lines of business whose performance fluctuated.

Meanwhile, Man continued to expand its commodities business, purchasing and selling numerous agricultural products companies and units throughout the 1980s and 1990s. However, while Man remained an industry leader, the company's days in the commodities trade were numbered. In the late 1990s the sugar trade was buffeted by financial crises in Russia, Brazil, and the Far East. Market prices plunged, and with them the profits of Man's agricultural products units. The company was now relying on its flourishing financial services business to bolster its profits. Although Man's share prices had been steadily rising, management feared that exposure to the volatile commodities trades would continue to drag its performance down.

In March 2000 the company sold its agricultural products division to a group of its managers, who contributed £60.2 million in stock and assumed £508.8 million in debt. The new owners converted this division into a private company, which kept the name ED & F Man, while the rest of the company renamed itself Man Group PLC.

PURSUING NEW MARKETS

Man next set its sights on introducing its asset management services to clients in the United States. Remarkably, the company had become one of the world's largest hedge fund managers while almost completely avoiding the U.S. market, which accounted for some 80 percent of worldwide hedge fund investment. Company executive John Kelly explained to *Investment News* in January 2002 that Man had deliberately avoided the United States out of fear that it would overextend itself because this market was indeed so vast. Man Group prepared to formally enter the U.S. market by completing its purchase of Glenwood Capital Investments LLC in 2000 and establishing a U.S. division the following year. The company, however, waited to offer its first U.S.-based hedge funds until after it had carefully built up a network of agents and hired specialized staff to deal with American securities regulation. Despite extensive marketing in the United States, as of March 2009 Man Group estimated that only 7 percent of its managed funds by value was held by investors in North and South America, compared with 56 percent in Europe, 32 percent in the Asia-Pacific region, and 5 percent in the Middle East. Its most promising and rapidly growing markets were in East Asia, particularly Japan and the People's Republic of China.

Starting in 2000, a series of takeovers added more fund brands to Man's portfolio, starting with the Glenwood companies. Two years later it purchased Switzerland-based RMF Investment Group. In 2003 Man Group obtained a 25 percent interest in BlueCrest Capital Management Ltd., and in 2008 it purchased a 50 percent stake in the U.S. firm Orr Hill Partners LLC and a 25 percent share of Nephilia Capital Partners Ltd. The company also created a new unit named Pemba Capital Partners, focusing on European credit investments. These takeovers, savvy investment strategies, and a continuing influx of client money caused the value of Man Group's managed funds to soar, from $4.7 billion at the end of fiscal year 1999–2000 to a peak of $74.6 billion eight years later.

In July 2007 Man Group spun off its brokerage unit, renamed MF Global, issuing more than 80 percent of its stock on the New York Stock Exchange and distributing the proceeds to its shareholders. The company agreed to sell off its remaining stock in this company in August 2009, thus completing its transformation into a dedicated financial services firm.

In the first decade of the 21st century, Man Group began to pursue a series of environmental initiatives, which it regarded as inherently good for both global ecology and its public reputation. The pursuit also provided ripe opportunities for profit in swiftly expanding and poorly understood markets. The company officially became carbon-neutral in April 2007 through measures such as installing a new, highly efficient energy-producing facility for its London headquarters and purchasing carbon credits from community development projects in Africa. The company created a funds management unit in 2006 called Man Environmental Capital Opportunities (Man ECO) dedicated to ecologically related investments.

ECONOMIC CRISIS: CHALLENGES AND RENEWED OPPORTUNITY

Amid the global financial crisis starting in the second half of 2008, hedge fund assets shrank sharply. Man Group's share prices plunged by more than 50 percent in fiscal year 2008–09. Management could take comfort in the continuing strong performance of the AHL fund, which rose 7.7 percent in that same year, compared with a 15 percent loss for the HFRI Fund Weighted Composite Index (measuring the average return for hedge funds) and much deeper losses for leading stock indexes. Man's other leading funds suffered losses, but they were much lower losses than many competing funds. AHL's funds, still heavily based in futures, benefited from the relative strength of futures amid the credit crunch. However, as nervous clients cashed in their investments and Man Group was compelled to deleverage some of its hedge funds, the company's total funds under management fell in one year from $74.6 billion to $46.8 billion. These troubles convinced the company to announce in March 2009 that it would reorganize and combine many of its hedge fund divisions, while AHL would maintain its autonomy and distinctive identity.

Hedge funds faced renewed scrutiny of their ability to operate in relative secrecy, with calls in the United States and other important markets to impose tighter regulations on these organizations amid charges that hedge funds shared much of the responsibility for the global economic crisis that continued into 2009. Man Group management, however, suggested that economic turmoil and closer regulation provided renewed opportunities for intelligent investment strategies and industry consolidation that would favor the largest fund managers, opportunities that it intended to manage to its benefit.

Stephen V. Beitel

PRINCIPAL SUBSIDIARIES

BlueCrest Capital Management Limited (25%); E D & F Man Limited; Glenwood Capital Investments LLC (USA); Man Group Holdings Limited; Man Investments AG (Switzerland); Man Investments Finance Limited; Man Investments Holdings Limited; Man Investments Limited; Man Ultraviolet Limited; RMF Investment Management (Switzerland).

PRINCIPAL COMPETITORS

Invesco Ltd.; Soros Fund Management LLC; UBS AG.

FURTHER READING

Abbott, Susan, "Funds with a Guarantee: Gimmick or True Value?" *Futures* (Cedar Falls, IA), January 1990, p. 52F.

Allan, Caroline, "ED&F Man Funds Unit to Refocus on Institutions," *Reuters News*, July 18, 1995.

Benjamin, Jeff, "London Hedge Fund Group Crossing the Pond Gingerly," *Investment News*, January 14, 2002, p. 14.

———, "One on One with John Kelly of Man Investments Inc.," *Investment News*, May 2, 2005, p. 27.

Cameron, Doug, "Exotic Species Seeks to Emerge from the Margins with Wider Appeal: Doug Cameron Reports on the Changing Fortune of Man Group as It Stands on the Brink of Membership of the FTSE 100," *Financial Times*, June 14, 2001, p. 24.

Durr, Barbara, "ED&F Man to Take Over Chicago Brokerage," *Financial Times*, July 30, 1990, p. 18.

Foley, Stephen, "Man Group to Buy Swiss Rival RMF for Pounds 570m," *Independent* (London), May 24, 2002, p. 23.

Gowers, Andrew, "Commodities: Man Group Reorganises/ Leading Commodity Company to Reorganise Futures Trading Operations," *Financial Times*, June 7, 1985, p. 38.

Guthrie, Jonathan, "ED & F Man's Sugar Division Plunges into Red," *Financial Times*, November 13, 1998, p. 13.

Hays, Steve, "ED & F Man Extends Dutch Futures Bridgehead," *Reuters News*, October 10, 1994.

Jenkins, Alan C., *The House of Man*, London: Rainbird Publishing, 1989.

"Man Announces Strategic Partnership with Nephila Capital in the Insurance-Linked Securities Sector," Canada NewsWire, June 6, 2008.

Mathieson, Clyde, "ED&F Man Reveals Plan to Sell Agriculture Arm," *Times* (London), November 5, 1999, p. 39.

Reed, Stanley, "The Might of Man Group; It Just Might Be the World's Largest Hedge Fund—And Smart Management and a Diversified Business Model Indicate Continued Muscle," BusinessWeek, May 4, 2007, http://www.businessweek.com/ globalbiz/content/apr2007/gb20070430_273521.htm.

Szala, Ginger, "Making a Mint: How a Scientist, Statistician and Businessman Mixed," *Futures* (Cedar Falls, IA), March 1989, p. 80.

Timmons, Heather, "A London Hedge Fund That Opts for Engineers, Not M.B.A.'s," *New York Times*, August 18, 2006, p. C7.

Buy it for looks. Buy it for life.®

Moen Inc.

25300 Al Moen Drive
North Olmsted, Ohio 44070
U.S.A.
Telephone: (440) 962-2000
Toll Free: (800) 289-6636
Fax: (440) 962-2770
Web site: http://www.moen.com/

Wholly Owned Subsidiary of Fortune Brands Inc.
Founded: 1947
Employees: 3,000
Sales: $850 million (2008 est.)
NAICS: 332998 Plumbing Fixtures Metal, Manufacturing; 423720 Sanitary Ware, Enameled Iron

∎ ∎ ∎

As one of the world's largest manufacturers of faucets, sinks, and other plumbing products, Moen Inc. is a leading manufacturer of single-handle faucets, the top seller to the wholesale market, and the leading brand of faucets in the North American faucet market. Known for quality and style, Moen's faucets have been referred to as the "Cadillacs" of the industry. The firm is the leading subsidiary of Fortune Brands Inc., a conglomerate with interests in distilled spirits, golf, and home hardware products.

MOEN, THE EARLY YEARS:
1940–60

The firm and its products were named for Alfred Moen, the inventor of the single-handle faucet. Trained as a mechanical engineer at the University of Washington, Moen was inspired to create the device after scalding his hands under a conventional two-handled faucet in the late 1930s. His first design was a double-valve faucet with a cam that controlled the mixture of hot and cold water from the two valves. In consultation with a major faucet manufacturer, however, the inventor became convinced that the cam design was inappropriate, so he went back to the drawing board. Throughout the early 1940s Moen spent his spare time refining a cylindrical design with a piston action. He solicited several manufacturers to produce the faucet without success, and then World War II had begun. Brass was rationed, so it was impossible to produce his faucet.

During the war Moen designed tools for a military shipyard plant in Seattle, Washington. After the war, he went back searching for a backer, and he eventually convinced Ravenna Metal Products Corporation in Seattle to manufacture his unique faucet idea. The company sold its first single-handle mixing faucet in San Francisco, California, in late 1947 for about $12. Moen's faucet was later named one of the 100 best-designed mass-produced products of modern times, and Moen was nominated to the U.S. Patent Office's Inventors' Hall of Fame. Over the course of his career, Moen obtained more than 75 patents in a variety of areas.

Ravenna Metal Products was acquired and absorbed by Chicago's Standard Screw Co. in 1956 and moved to Elyria, Ohio, a suburb of Cleveland. Standard Screw had sought a retail product to complement its lines of fasteners, precision parts, and automotive valves. For the

COMPANY PERSPECTIVES

Timeless designs. Styles unlike anything else. Faucets and fixtures that are livable and enduring. These are just some of the reasons that Moen Incorporated is the number one brand of faucet in North America. But, Moen does more than make faucets. It's also a major supplier of stylish kitchen sinks and innovative bath accessories.

Moen is part of Fortune Brands' Home and Hardware group—a leading consumer brands company that includes leading cabinetry, door and lock manufacturers.

next three decades, Moen operated as a division of Standard Screw.

MOEN CONTINUED TO REINVENT ITSELF: 1960S AND 1970S

Moen's sales increased steadily with the help of its new parent and through its own continuous innovation. By 1960 single-handle faucets (of which Moen was not the only manufacturer) accounted for about 5 percent of the total faucet market. Moen catapulted to the lead of the single-handle segment during the 1960s on the strength of new faucet styles and technological innovations. Alfred Moen, who continued to lead the company's Engineering Department until 1982, was responsible for many of the innovations that drove this growth. These innovations included the replaceable cartridge, a patented, washerless device that served as the basis of the manufacturer's lifetime limited warranty against leaks and drips. Company publications touted the mechanism, which featured a self-contained assembly with no moving parts, as "the standard in performance by which other faucet systems are measured." Over the course of his career, Alfred Moen patented other key products in the company line, including the Flo Control Aerator, the Moentrol (a system to control shower pressure), the Swing'N Spray faucet with a sprayer head, a push button diverter, and a tub spout diverter.

By 1970, when Standard Screw was renamed Stanadyne Inc., the Moen Division had grown to become the company's most important operation. Stanadyne's sales had increased from $49.1 million to more than $120 million over the course of the previous decade.

MOEN BECAME A MAJOR PLAYER WITHIN ITS INDUSTRY: 1980S AND 1990S

During the 1970s and early 1980s Moen grew from a niche player among faucet manufacturers to the number-two marketer, behind Masco Corporation and its Delta, Epic, and Peerless brands. Despite competition from inexpensive Asian imports, the American faucet market enjoyed double digit growth beginning in 1986.

During the late 1980s Moen experienced a corresponding double-digit growth in sales, which caught the attention of the investment community; in March 1988 Stanadyne was acquired through a leveraged buyout by the New York investment firm of Forstmann, Little & Co. The new owner made Moen Stanadyne's primary focus by selling most of its other operating divisions, and Stanadyne assumed the name of its best-selling product in October 1989, becoming Moen Inc. In 1990, following the conclusion of the U.S.-Canada Free Trade Agreement, Moen merged its U.S. and Canadian operations. That same year Forstmann, Little sold Moen to MasterBrand Industries Inc. for $982 million.

MasterBrand appeared to be committed to Moen for the long term by supporting it with a $50 million infusion of capital. The money was spent on research and development, new manufacturing equipment, and facilities. During the early 1990s Moen shifted its sales focus from wholesale to include retail in response to economic and marketplace imperatives, which included an economic recession and a corresponding decline in new housing construction, as well as growth in the home improvement market and the development of new home improvement retail outlets such as Home Depot, Builders Square, and Lowe's. The faucet maker assimilated several of MasterBrand's plumbing-related subsidiaries, expanded its product line, and launched aggressive new sales and marketing strategies.

This shift required a transformation of many of the manufacturer's processes. For example, Moen had to develop attractive packaging, speedier delivery, bar coding, and nationwide service. As a result, the company revamped its distribution, transportation, customer service, industrial engineering, information systems, and warehouse operations. The overhaul benefited Moen in many respects, not the least of which was improved productivity through automation.

During the late 1980s and early 1990s Moen's product line diversified in both form and in function. Moen's faucets ranged from traditional cross-handled designs to sleek contemporary looks. Sinks made of Moenstone, "a high-tech, high-strength color-impregnated composite material," came in a wide variety of

KEY DATES

1947: Alfred Moen partners with Ravenna Metal Products Corporation to sell the first single-handle faucet.

1956: Ravenna Metal Products Corporation is acquired by Standard Screw.

1970: Standard Screw is renamed Standyne with Moen as its largest division.

1988: Stanadyne is acquired by Forstmann, Little & Co.

1989: Standyne becomes Moen Inc.

1990: Moen is acquired by MasterBrand Industries Inc., the operating company of American Brands.

1997: American Brands becomes Fortune Brands.

2001: Alfred Moen passes away.

2007: David B. Lingafelter becomes the president and chief executive officer of Moen.

fashion colors and bowl configurations. The company also added specially designed faucets for bars and laundry facilities, as well as accessories such as liquid soap dispensers and massage showerheads. The One-Touch faucet, a combination faucet and sprayer, and Riser spout, which lifted 10 inches above the sink, combined practicality and fashion for the kitchen. The Monti-cello Collection of lavatory faucets, introduced in 1993, became the company's most successful product introduction.

Between 1990 and 1994 Moen's sales nearly doubled. As it approached the turn of the 21st century, Moen counted competitive pricing, a strong reputation for quality, and good brand recognition among its strengths. Bruce A. Carbonari, the president and chief executive officer (CEO) of Moen, pegged future growth on international sales by focusing corporate efforts on joint ventures in Asia, the Middle East, Mexico, and Central and South America. By the end of 1994 Moen had captured 1 percent of the competitive Japanese plumbing market. Carbonari expected increasing international sales to push his company over the $1 billion mark by 2000.

In 1997 American Brands became Fortune Brands, and Moen became the largest company within Fortune Brands. Known for its modern elegance, Moen continued to push the boundaries of traditional design.

MOEN IN THE 21ST CENTURY

Alfred Moen, who had continued to run the company's research and development department until his retirement in 1982, died in 2001 at the age of 86. Moen had never held an ownership stake in the corporation, but he left an indelible imprint on the company that bears his name—and on the modern image of the American kitchen sink.

In 2006 Moen promoted David B. Lingafelter to president of United States Businesses. Lingafelter joined Moen in 1990 and served in a variety of capacities over the years, including manager of retail service, senior production manager, and director of marketing. He enjoyed an expanded role as the single voice for all of Moen's U.S.-based operations. Just a year later, Lingafelter succeeded Richard E. Posey as the president and CEO of Moen Inc.

Moving forward through the first decade of the new century, Moen continued to innovate and expand. The company stayed at the cutting edge of consumer desires by conducting extensive market research. A 2006 study by Moen found that while most consumers think they shower for 20 minutes or longer, they actually only shower for 10 minutes. It also confirmed that many consumers wanted eco-friendly products without compromising on the force of the shower stream.

Despite innovation, the tough economic recession that began in 2008 hit Moen's sales hard. Stock values for Fortune Brands dropped by 41 percent in 2008. As construction of single family homes fell by nearly 50 percent in the United States in 2008, the sales of Moen kitchen faucets fell by single-digit percentages as well. Despite the economic downturn, Moen poised itself to add India to the growing list of countries it supplied, including China and Canada.

Entering 2009, Moen remained the number-one faucet in the United States. That same year Moen introduced a new line of eco-friendly showerheads and kitchen faucets. This new line of products was sleek, sported the signature Moen look, and also featured a newly patented water-saving technology. According to a July 2009 company press release, Kevin Campbell, the director of marketing, said, "While homeowners are concerned about saving water, the thought of waiting at the kitchen sink to fill a pot or pitcher is not very appealing."

Moen continued to set the industry standard for design and innovation. The company planned to continue expanding its eco-friendly options to ensure that it remained at the forefront of the U.S. market, while continuing to expand its offerings in other parts of the world.

April Dougal Gasbarre
Updated, Robert Jacobson

PRINCIPAL SUBSIDIARIES

Moen Inc. (Canada); Moen Japan K.K.; Moen de Mexico; HCG-Moen Corporation (Taiwan).

PRINCIPAL COMPETITORS

Masco; Black & Decker; Kohler; American Standard.

FURTHER READING

"Available at the Home Depot, Moen's New Lindley Eco-Performance Faucet Offers First Water-Saving Option for the Kitchen" (press release), North Olmsted, OH: Moen Inc., July 20, 2009, http://www.moen.com/pressroom/pressRelease.cfm?release=4201.

"Big Picture," *Daily Herald* (Arlington Heights, IL), June 14, 2002, p. 1.

Canedy, Dana, "Kitchen Sink, Too," *Plain Dealer*, August 17, 1994, p. 1C.

"Cutting Edge Style, Technology Mark Faucet Lines," *Professional Builder*, December 2000, p. 115.

"Elyria Firm Will Be Acquired," *Plain Dealer*, July 21, 1990, p. 8C.

Gooley, Toby B., "Moen Catches the Retail Wave," *Traffic Management*, October 1994, p. 40.

Honan, William H., "Alfred Moen, 84, Whose Hands Found Need for a New Faucet," *New York Times*, April 21, 2001, p. A13.

Lans, Maxine S., "Protecting Your Product's Shape," *Marketing News*, March 14, 1994, p. 12.

Marsh, Simon, "Standard Screw Finds Diversification Rewarding," *Investment Dealers Digest*, March 31, 1969, p. 47.

"Net Income Falls 94% for Fortune Brands," Reuters, May 2, 2009, p. B2.

"New Collection of Eco-Performance Showerheads," *Environmental Design & Construction*, July 2009, p. 14.

"New Moen Executive Sees Opportunities Overseas," *Plain Dealer*, December 6, 1994, p. 1C.

Phillips, Lisa, "Faucet Sales Spout after Years in a Sink," *Advertising Age*, March 24, 1986, p. 34.

"Posey Retires from Moen," *Reeves Journal*, May 2007, p. 25.

Sabath, Donald, "Stanadyne Renames Itself," *Plain Dealer*, October 4, 1989, p. 1C.

There's Only One Al Moen, Elyria, OH: Moen Inc., 1993.

Mozilla Foundation

650 Castro Street, Suite 300
Mountain View, California 94041-2021
U.S.A.
Web site: www.mozilla.org/foundation

Nonprofit Company
Founded: 2003
Employees: 175
Total Assets: $75 million (2007)
NAICS: 511210 Software Publishers

■ ■ ■

Publisher of the popular Firefox Web browser, the Mozilla Foundation is one of the most unique software companies in the world. A tax-exempt nonprofit company, the Foundation supports and guides the development of open-source computer code—software that is freely distributed, with the explicit intent that volunteers and amateur programmers are welcome to modify and improve upon Mozilla's code. With the support of this open-source community, Firefox has become one of the most popular software brands on the planet, downloaded more than a billion times as of August 2009.

COMMERCIAL BEGINNINGS

Mozilla's origins lie with Mosaic Communications, later renamed Netscape Communications, a company founded by computer industry executive James H. Clark and 24-year-old programmer Marc Andreessen in 1994.

The company recruited members of the team that developed one of the first Internet browsers, Mosaic, at the University of Illinois. Their task was to develop an improved browser that would become a "killer application" on the Internet.

The firm's product, the Netscape Navigator, was a near-immediate sensation. Netscape offered its browser as a free download for noncommercial use, and the company made money by designing Web servers optimized for Netscape's browser technology, which they sold to companies who wanted to establish an online presence. By mid-1995 Navigator was well on its way to dominating the browser market, and Netscape's initial public offering was about to kick off the dot.com boom.

Competition, however, lurked around the corner. Microsoft had licensed the Mosaic browser technology, packaging it with the Windows 95 operating system under the name of Internet Explorer (IE). While Navigator initially enjoyed technological advantages over IE, Microsoft leveraged its dominance of the personal computer operating system market to cut into Netscape's market share. Netscape, in turn, accused Microsoft of anticompetitive practices and of using its influence with computer manufacturers to ensure that IE was the only browser preloaded on new computers.

As a reaction to the competition from Microsoft, Netscape began adding features to its product. In 1997 Netscape began promoting Netscape Communicator, a suite of applications that included the Web browser but also contained an e-mail program, an address book, a calendar, and an HTML editor, among other functions. The critical reception for Communicator was tepid. Mi-

COMPANY PERSPECTIVES

What is Mozilla? We're a global community of thousands who sincerely believe in the power of technology to enrich people's lives. We're a public benefit organization dedicated not to making money but to improving the way people everywhere experience the Internet. And we're an open source software project whose code has been used as a platform for some of the Internet's most innovative projects. The common thread that runs throughout Mozilla is our belief that, as the most significant social and technological development of our time, the Internet is a public resource that must remain open and accessible to all. With this in mind, our efforts are ultimately driven by our mission of encouraging choice, innovation and opportunity online. To achieve these goals, we use a highly transparent, collaborative process that brings together thousands of dedicated volunteers and corporate contributors from around the world with a small staff of employees to coordinate the creation of products like the Firefox web browser. This process is supported by the non-profit Mozilla Foundation and its subsidiaries, especially the Mozilla Corporation.

crosoft's assault on Netscape's share of the browser market continued unabated.

THE BIRTH OF MOZILLA

On March 31, 1998, Netscape made its source code for Communicator—essentially, the blueprint of its technology—available to the public so that anyone could use or modify it for free. From that momentous day forward, Netscape's software would be developed using a community-based open-source model, with volunteers and Netscape employees collaborating to improve the product. The name of this development project was "Mozilla."

The move marked a change in Netscape's business model, which would focus on its Web portal, now called NetCenter. Mozilla would develop the technology used in future versions of Communicator, which Netscape would release in order to drive traffic to the NetCenter Web site.

The match between Mozilla and Netscape was not perfect. It took time for the development community to come together to support Mozilla, and much of Communicator's code had to be scrapped before development could begin in earnest. Mozilla eventually developed a following among amateur and professional computer programmers alike. Collectively known as "the community," they served as an unpaid army of volunteer programmers, debuggers, and product testers. The group grew to more than 1,000 approved code generators, and thousands more would test the new software versions that were released every night. One of the hallmarks of Mozilla's open-source programming code became the ability to easily customize the browser. Members of the community found it easy to modify the programming, and with open access to the code, they could built their own plug-in applications. However, when the Mozilla-based Communicator 5.0 was released in November 2000 the program was panned by critics as slow and buggy.

At the same time, the Mozilla project began to take on a life of its own. Netscape's original vision was that Mozilla would only develop technology for Netscape, not release or market to the public its own branded software. After the release of Communicator 5.0, however, there was a clamor in the community for Mozilla to release its own version of Communicator. This version, called Mozilla Suite 1.0, was released to the public in the summer of 2002. It was much better received than Communicator 5.0.

INDEPENDENCE

AOL Time Warner, which bought Netscape in 1999, sued Microsoft in 2002, alleging antitrust violations on the IE/Netscape issue. A federal court had ruled in 2000 that Microsoft violated antitrust laws in its implementation of IE, so AOL's case was very strong. The parties reached a settlement in May 2003, which would prove to be the end of Netscape and a new beginning for Mozilla. Under the terms of the settlement, Microsoft paid AOL $750 million and gave AOL a royalty-free license to IE and other Microsoft Web technologies for seven years. With this deal, AOL no longer had need for its own browser and began to shut down the Netscape subsidiary. Mozilla became independent in July 2003, with AOL pledging $2 million in start-up funds. Mitch Kapor, author of the Lotus 1-2-3 software, chipped in $300,000 as well.

Under the name Mozilla Foundation, the company's unique philosophy and largely volunteer workforce made it a flexible, readily adaptable rival to Microsoft and IE. Mozilla's number of paid staff was surprisingly small. Several staff from the Netscape project at AOL moved to the new organization, includ-

KEY DATES

1998: Netscape creates Mozilla.org, a project to issue an open-source version of its Netscape Communicator browser.

1999: AOL buys Netscape Communications Corporation and pledges to continue the Mozilla project.

2000: Netscape 6.0 is released according to Mozilla's open-source guidelines.

2002: Mozilla Suite 1.0, precursor of Firefox, is released.

2003: Mozilla project splits from Netscape Communications, now an AOL division; Mozilla decides to separate Firefox and Thunderbird; nonprofit Mozilla Foundation is established.

2004: Mozilla Europe and Mozilla Japan are created; Firefox 1.0 is released; Thunderbird 1.0 is released.

2005: Mozilla Foundation creates Mozilla Corporation; Mozilla China opens; 100 millionth Firefox download is recorded.

2007: United Nations International Telecommunications Union presents Mozilla with its annual World Information Society Award.

2008: John Lilly replaces W. Mitchell Baker as CEO of Mozilla Corporation; Baker becomes chairperson; Mozilla Messaging created to focus on Thunderbird; Firefox sets Guinness World Record when 8 million people download version 3.0 in a 24-hour period.

2009: On July 31, Firefox is downloaded for the billionth time.

ing legal counsel W. Mitchell Baker, who became president of the new Foundation.

Away from AOL, the Mozilla Foundation unraveled the Communicator application suite, choosing to focus instead on two key products: Firefox, a lean and flexible Internet browser, and Thunderbird, an e-mail program. Firefox, initially named Phoenix, was popular with programmers and users alike due to its stability, capacity for customization, and innovative tabbed browsing. Whether changing the visual display by applying unique "skins," adding applets to block pop-up ads, deterring spammers and viruses, and rarely crashing, Firefox cultivated a very loyal following. When Firefox 1.0 released, some 10,000 fans donated the $250,000

needed to buy a two-page ad in the December 16, 2004, edition of the *New York Times*. The ad listed each donor by name.

Firefox tapped into a waiting market of people seeking an alternative to IE. An *InformationWeek* poll shortly after the browser's initial release found that 57 percent of surveyed companies had advised their employees to adopt Firefox; Penn State University issued the same recommendation for its 80,000 students. The company's underdog reputation has led to frequent comparisons between Mozilla and Godzilla (Microsoft).

Open-source programming allowed users to modify the Firefox architecture, but the company emphasized that it has not relinquished ownership of the Mozilla brand. "While there is considerable freedom to redistribute and modify our software and source code," according to the company's Web site, those actions cannot "incorporate our branding.... What this means is that distributing any modified versions of the branded software we release requires our permission and, in most cases, a distribution agreement between your organization and Mozilla." To facilitate this process, the company offered a "Rebranding Worksheet," available at http://wiki.mozilla.org/Firefox_Rebranding:Worksheet.

Unlike many firms, Mozilla encouraged users to find flaws, programming glitches, and security vulnerabilities in its products. It prided itself on quickly providing software patches to resolve issues and sought to set a standard of openness for the industry. In 2004 the company announced it would pay $500 to any individual reporting a new security bug. According to an August 30, 2004, *Wall Street Journal* article, in 2003 Microsoft waited 10 months before informing its users of an IE security gap.

REALIZING PROFITS

As the Firefox browser gained market share and became an increasingly valuable asset in its own right, company officials decided to leverage Firefox to provide a funding stream to support the broader Mozilla Foundation goal of expanding the open-source community. On August 3, 2005, the Mozilla Foundation created a separate, wholly owned, for-profit subsidiary—Mozilla Corporation—to pursue code development, marketing, and distribution of Firefox, Thunderbird, and related products from other sources, while not compromising the nonprofit character of the Foundation. At the time, 36 employees transferred to the new entity, while the Foundation was left with only three. By early 2008 the Firefox combined operation had 150 full-time employees.

Baker was named CEO of the new Mozilla Corporation. Her long focus on encouraging the spread of Firefox applications made her shift to the for-profit arm a logical move. Succeeding Baker as head of the Mozilla Foundation was Frank Hecker, who had extensive experience with Firefox and open-source computing; he had been part of the team developing the open code for Netscape Communicator in the 1990s.

The primary source of revenue for the corporation has been selling "real estate" on the browser home page; search engine firms would pay licensing fees to Mozilla in return for prominent placement on the Firefox browser interface. Some 88 percent of Mozilla's revenue began coming from one such deal with search engine giant Google, which was scheduled to run through November 2011.

In January 2008 the Mozilla Corporation's executive leadership changed, with chief operating officer John Lilly becoming chief executive officer. Former CEO Baker shifted to become chairman and day-to-day top executive. While Lilly began focusing on products, technology, and the operations of the corporation, Baker concentrated on interoperability, public programs, and implementing the Manifesto. Before joining Mozilla, Lilly had worked at a number of software developers, including Apple, Sun Microsystems, and Trilogy.

In February 2008 Mozilla Foundation formally created Mozilla Messaging to focus on developing the Thunderbird e-mail platform beyond its 5 million users. Briefly known as MailCo, Mozilla Messaging was headed by David Ascher, formerly of Active State Software. The new initiative sought to build on the open-source model to integrate additional features into e-mail, such as a calendar program and better search capabilities.

It was speculated, however, that Thunderbird may be a harder sell than the company's popular Firefox. A writer for *InformationWeek* in February 2008 noted that there was no existing e-mail platform that dominated the market as much as Microsoft Explorer had in the early days of Firefox. "In the absence of the marauding Microsoft of the mid-1990s, Thunderbird is likely to have a hard time inspiring its legions with the evangelical zeal that made Firefox such a success. The desktop e-mail client market may still be dominated by Microsoft, but it isn't frozen in time the way the browser market was when Firefox debuted." Furthermore, with messaging increasingly shifting from e-mail on computers to instant messages on mobile devices, user demand was differing from what Mozilla Messaging with Thunderbird intended to offer. The lack of interoperability between mobile device manufacturers and service providers as of 2008 further complicated efforts to introduce a common platform.

CATCHING UP TO MICROSOFT

As of 2009 the Mozilla brand had made a significant dent in Microsoft's hold on browser software. One advantage has come from customization; specifically, encouraging local variations of Firefox allowed for the quick global adoption of new releases. Firefox 3.0, for example, was available in 40 languages. Firefox 2.0 had released in 37 languages. Meanwhile, Microsoft's updated version of IE was released in English only, and it later expanded to just 8 languages. Consequently, Firefox gained a larger share outside of the United States: 28 percent in Europe and 35 percent in Germany.

When the Mozilla project began, Microsoft's IE was the browser of about 95 percent of Internet users. However by early 2009, Firefox controlled about 20 percent of the browser market, with more than 180 million users. Thanks also to the entry of other browsers such as Google Chrome and Apple Safari, Microsoft's share of the market dropped to 68 percent. On July 31, 2009, Firefox was downloaded for the one billionth time.

Mozilla was challenging Microsoft on other fronts as well. In 2009 the European Commission turned its attention to Microsoft's dominance in the Internet software sector. Like the earlier antitrust lawsuit in the United States, Europe wanted IE separated from Windows to allow rival browsers fair access to Windows users. Seeing the lawsuit as a way to expand its presence, Mozilla has sought to present its own perspective to the Commission. In February 2009 Mozilla's Baker offered her company's expertise to the Commission, writing in her blog, "The success of Mozilla and Firefox does not indicate a healthy marketplace for competitive products. Mozilla is a non-profit organization; a worldwide movement of people who strive to build the Internet we want to live in. I am convinced that we could not have been, and will not be, successful except as a public benefit organization living outside the commercial motivations. And I certainly hope that neither the EU nor any other government expects to maintain a healthy Internet ecosystem based on non-profits stepping in to correct market deficiencies."

Ann E. Robertson

PRINCIPAL SUBSIDIARIES

Mozilla Corporation; Mozilla Messaging; Mozilla Europe; Mozilla Japan; Mozilla China.

PRINCIPAL COMPETITORS

Microsoft Corporation; Apple Inc.

FURTHER READING

Athavaley, Anjali, "Mozilla Creates Unit to Promote Firefox," *Washington Post*, August 4, 2005, p. D5.

Baker, W. Mitchell, "The European Commission and Microsoft," Lizard Wrangling, February 6, 2009, http://blog.lizardwrangler.com/2009/02/06/the-european-commission-and-microsoft/.

Bove, Tony, *Just Say No to Microsoft: How to Ditch Microsoft and Why It's Not as Hard as You Think*, San Francisco: No Starch Press, 2005.

Claburn, Thomas, "Microsoft Nearly Killed Browser Competition, Mozilla's Baker Charges," *Information Week,* February 9, 2009.

Cohen, Noam, "Will Success, or All That Money from Google, Spoil Firefox?" *New York Times*, November 12, 2007, p. C1.

Cusumano, Michael A. and David B. Yoffie, *Competing on Internet Time: Lessons from Netscape and Its Battle with Microsoft*, New York: Free Press, 1998.

Espiner, Tom, "Mozilla Ready to Add IM to Thunderbird Stable?" ZDNet Australia, February 20, 2008, http://www.zdnet.com.au/news/software/soa/Mozilla-ready-to-add-IM-to-Thunderbird-stable-/0,130061733,339286101,00.htm.

Fildes, Jonathan, "Final Goodbye for Early Web Icon," BBC News, February 29, 2008.

"Firefox Ad Boosts Downloads," *InformationWeek*, December 22, 2004.

"Firefox Expects More in China," SinoCast, LLC China IT Watch, November 13, 2007, eNet.com.cn.

Fried, Ian, and Jim Hu, "Microsoft to Pay AOL $750 Million," CNET News, May 29, 2003, http://news.cnet.com/Microsoft-to-pay-AOL-750-million/2100-1032_3-1011296.html.

Granneman, Scott, *Don't Click on the Blue E!: Switching to Firefox*, Sebastopol, CA: O'Reilly Media, 2005.

Guth, Robert A. and David Bank, "Tech's Unlikely Comebacks," *Wall Street Journal*, August 30, 2004, p. B1.

Hamm, Steve, "The Gnat Nipping at Microsoft," *Business Week*, January 24, 2005, p. 78.

Kellner, Mark A., "Firefox Maker Assists Europe's Attack on Microsoft," *Washington Times*, February 11, 2009.

Kushner, David, "The Firefox Kid," IEEE Spectrum, November 2006, http://www.spectrum.ieee.org/computing/software/the-firefox-kid.

Lamb, Gregory M., "A Rising Star Even Microsoft Can't Snuff Out," *Christian Science Monitor*, February 3, 2005, p. 14.

Lashinsky, Adam, "Remembering Netscape: The Birth of the Web," *Fortune*, July 25, 2005.

Livingston, Jessica, *Founders at Work: Stories of Startups' Early Days*, New York: Springer Verlag, 2008.

Markoff, John, "Mozilla Names New Chief, but Reaffirms Open-Source Commitment," *New York Times*, January 8, 2008, p. C4

McHugh, Josh, "The Firefox Explosion," *Wired*, February 2005.

"Mozilla Charts an Independent Course," *eWeek*, October 13, 2003.

"Mozilla Forms E-mail Technology Company to Develop Thunderbird," *InformationWeek*, September 18, 2007.

"Mozilla Offers Rewards for Security Bugs," *InformationWeek*, August 3, 2004.

"Mozilla's Firefox Makes Formal Debut Today," *InformationWeek*, November 9, 2004.

"Mozilla's New CEO, John Lilly Steps Up to the Task," *InformationWeek*, January 16, 2008.

Ross, Blake, *Firefox for Dummies*, Hoboken, NJ: For Dummies, 2006.

Rupley, Sebastian, "Beyond the Browser Wars," *PC Magazine*, July 2002, p. 24.

Streitfeld, David, "An Awkward Anniversary," *Washington Post*, March 17, 2000, p. E1.

Stross, Randall, "The Fox Is in Microsoft's Henhouse (and Salivating)," *New York Times*, December 19, 2004, p. C5.

"Thunderbird Gets a New Home at Mozilla Messaging," *InformationWeek*, February 19, 2008.

Wagner, Mitch, "AOL Spins Off Mozilla Ownership to Independent Foundation," *Internet Week*, July 17, 2003.

MTN Group Ltd.

—•—

Innovation Centre, 216 14th Avenue
Fairlands, Johannesburg, Gauteng 2195
South Africa
Telephone: (+27 011) 912-3000
Fax: (+27 011) 912 4093
Web site: http://www.mtn.co.za

Public Company
Founded: 1994
Employees: 16,452
Sales: ZAR 102.5 billion ($12.5 billion) (2008)
Stock Exchanges: Johannesburg
Ticker Symbol: MTN
NAICS: 517110 Wired Telecommunications Carriers;
517212 Cellular and Other Wireless Telecommunications

■ ■ ■

The MTN Group Ltd. is a leading provider of cellular telecommunications equipment and services in 21 countries in Africa and the Middle East. The company divides its operations into three major sections in order to make management and strategy easier. The first of these covers South and East Africa. Included in this list are: MTN South Africa, MTN Swaziland, MTN Zambia, MTN Uganda, MTN Rwanda, and Mascom Botswana. West and Central African operations encompass nine subsidiaries; MTN Nigeria, MTN Cameroon, MTN Congo-Brazzaville, MTN Cote d'Ivoire, MTN Benin, MTN Ghana, MTN Guinea Bissau, MTN Guinea Conakry, and Lonestar Liberia. The third major section shows the company's footprint in the Middle East, where the name is seen in seven subsidiaries: MTN Irancell, MTN Afghanistan, MTN Cyprus, MTN Sudan, MTN Syria, MTN Yemen, and MTN International Carrier Services. All these subsidiaries, plus MTN customers in South Africa, make for a subscriber list reaching 90.7 million.

ORIGINS IN 1994

MTN's origins stretch back to November 23, 1994, when a new company was incorporated under the name Investment Facility Company Two Five Six. It was not destined to operate under this unwieldy name for long: On June 22, 1995, its name became M-Cell (Pty) Ltd. Just three weeks later M-Cell became a public company and was listed on the Johannesburg Stock Exchange in August 1995 under the name M-Cell Ltd. This time, the name stuck for a while longer, identifying the company until 2002 when it was changed again.

During its few short months as a private company, M-Cell received its first global systems for mobile (GSM) communications license, which was almost an industry first, because only one other company, Telkom South Africa, had thus far received this privilege. Being a parastatal (government-owned company) on the verge of privatization, Telkom was a formidable competitor; it would soon be given an official five-year monopoly on Internet access, through the nonnegotiable channel of the Telecommunications Act of 1996. If M-Cell wished to offer its own customers the benefits of Internet access, then this monopoly would require it to pay to use Telkom infrastructure.

COMPANY PERSPECTIVES

◼

MTN's vision is to be the emerging markets' leading telecommunications provider. Our strategy is built on three pillars: consolidation and diversification; leveraging our footprint and intellectual capacity; and convergence and operational evolution.

MTN EXPANDS INTO AFRICA

Mindful of this operating expense, M-Cell spent only a few years providing cell phone service in South Africa before eyeing opportunities to expand beyond the country's borders. Its first big break came in 1996, when the Ugandan government offered a 50 percent partnership with a phone company. This exciting prospect carried with it the challenge of providing 89,000 landlines and payphones in more than 150 towns and villages, all within five years.

M-Cell easily won the Ugandan deal, but it had to wait until 1998 before the actual enterprise began. The extra few months proved an advantage, however, because M-Cell was able to use fiber-optic technology, thereby adding such conveniences as fax, e-mail, and essential broadband services to its new Ugandan subscribers.

Other customers in Africa were also eager to use M-Cell services. In 1998 MTN Swaziland added 33,000 subscribers to MTN's list, and MTN Rwanda brought in 39,000 subscribers. MTN Cameroon, which joined M-Cell in 2001, brought in another 100,000 subscribers. In fact, 2001 turned out to be an excellent year all around, with MTN subscriber numbers swelling by another 327,000 when the company opened its office in Nigeria. Though this last acquisition cost the company $285 million, plus more than $1.8 billion that had to be spent on infrastructure to bring service to Nigeria's 223 towns and 10,000 villages, it did not make a huge dent in M-Cell's bottom line.

COMPANY CHANGES

Expansion characterized 2001, and changes characterized 2002. The first change was the installation of Cyril Ramaphosa as chairman. Ramaphosa had a great deal of experience with large-scale company management and came to MTN from serving as chairman of Johnnic Holdings, South Africa's largest black-owned company. Ramaphosa took the place of Phuthuma Nhleko, who became CEO.

Working smoothly together, the two men began to make changes in strategy. First, a name change occurred.

Henceforth, the company would be known as MTN, rather than M-Cell, a move intended to unify under one brand name the MTN subsidiaries swelling across Africa. Their next move was to divide the company into three divisions: MTN South Africa; MTN International, presiding over 14 African countries; and Strategic Investments, focusing on broadening the range of services, notably by the use of the newly established Orbicom, Africa's largest satellite signal distributor. Establishment of the Strategic Investments subdivision cost ZAR 12.3 million but proved to be a wise investment; the streamlined and broadened services generated 22 percent more subscribers in 2002, reaching 4.7 million, and swelling revenue to ZAR 12.4 billion.

By 2003 even larger changes were appearing on the horizon. The South African Government assessed the living standards of most nonwhite South Africans, noting that the majority of them were no better off than they had been during the apartheid era. Widespread joblessness and crime affected the townships where most black South Africans lived, and segregation persisted not necessarily because of race but because of class differences and distribution of wealth. The government sought positive change and a healthy economy that would allow all citizens equal opportunity.

BROAD-BASED BLACK ECONOMIC EMPOWERMENT INITIATIVES

New legislation was needed to facilitate economic growth and increased prosperity. The Broad Based Black Economic Empowerment (BBBEE) Act of 2003 was designed to ensure that black South Africans would have the chance to own, manage, and advance in business, rights formerly enjoyed only by white citizens. The act mandated new rules for businesses. First, black South Africans were to be directly empowered through ownership and control of enterprises and assets, and numbers of black managers at senior level were to increase. Second, indirect empowerment was to be achieved by giving preference to black-owned businesses in the procurement of goods and services, and inexperienced black entrepreneurs were to be encouraged and helped in setting up new enterprises. The act also stipulated that corporations had social responsibilities, including the obligation to focus on ways of improving the lives of disadvantaged black South Africans. The government also issued a scorecard that rated businesses on their effectiveness in complying with these requirements.

Fortunately, black empowerment issues were nothing new to MTN. Ramaphosa, who had taken his place as chairman of the board just one year earlier, was a lawyer by profession, a highly effective negotiator, and a onetime activist so skilled that he successfully led South

KEY DATES

■

1994: M-Cell is incorporated in South Africa under the name Investment Facility Company Two Six Five.

1995: M-Cell becomes a public company.

1998: M-Cell is expanded into Africa.

2002: M-Cell becomes MTN Group.

2006: Investcom is acquired for ZAR 33.5 billion ($5.53 billion).

2009: MTN introduces MTN Zone.

Africa's powerful National Union of Mineworkers to a crippling gold mining industry strike during the apartheid era. Later he helped to end apartheid peacefully, avoiding the violence people elsewhere in the world anticipated. Ramaphosa's lifelong experience prepared him to handle calmly the events that soon followed.

In 2003 black-owned Johnnic Holdings, with whom Ramaphosa was formerly associated, decided to sell half of the 62.5 percent stake it held in MTN so it could focus instead on hotel and casino management. MTN's black economic empowerment (BEE) equity ownership ratings for the scorecard now came from the Alpine Trust, a consortium jointly owned by the MTN management and the private investment arm MI Group of Najib Mikati, the former Lebanese prime minister. The shift to Alpine Trust was good for MLN, because Alpine Trust already had a strategy in place to help blacks progress economically. In 2002 Alpine Trust had established a company called Newshelf 664, which held 13.1 percent of MTN. Designed to last six years, this arrangement was specifically set up for the benefit of MTN's South African employees, who were encouraged to take part in a share distribution on the basis of length of employment in the company plus eligible seniority in the company's African operations.

MTN was not content to leave its BEE requirements at that. In 2005 MTN spent ZAR 750 million, compared with ZAR 650 million the year before, satisfying the preferential procurement requirement by buying its phones' subscriber identity module (SIM) cards, office stationery, and interconnection services from black-owned companies. In another move, MTN made sure to help improve the ratings of suppliers with weak credentials by linking them to companies from which they could obtain goods and services.

FURTHER EXPANSION

Even with all these empowerment innovations, the business of expanding business went on. In June 2005 MTN acquired the existing Telecel operation in Zambia, with 80,000 subscribers. An even bigger deal for MTN was a 51 percent stake in the recently privatized Loteny Telecom, known to its 800,000 Cote d'Ivoire subscribers as Telecel Cote d'Ivoire. Other new operations included a new office in Tehran, Iran; in Botswana, where MTN garnered 46 percent of the market; and also in Congo Brazzaville, where it was the first cell-phone service in the area. These new acquisitions were a fitting way to celebrate the company's 10 years on the Johannesburg Stock Exchange. Revenues for the year totaled ZAR 27.2 billion, and subscribers reached 23.2 million.

The company's growth speeded up even more in 2006. Early in May MTN spent ZAR 33.5 billion ($5.53 billion) acquiring the entire issued share capital of Investcom LLC, a company listed on both the London and Dubai stock exchanges. Investcom, like the Alpine Trust, had connections with Lebanon's former prime minister Mikati, who had cofounded the company in 1982. Since then, its telecommunications operations had expanded considerably, advancing across Ghana, Syria, Yemen, Benin, Liberia, Cyprus, Guinea-Bissau, Sudan, Afghanistan and Guinea Republic. Considerable experience and expertise lay behind the rise of Investcom, and MTN was pleased to have access to both. According to MTN CEO Phuthuma Nhleko, in the short months between its July acquisition and the end of the year, Investcom brought MTN $5.9 billion, or 12 percent to the company's total revenue, which reached ZAR 51.59 billion for the year. By December 2006 subscribers numbered in excess of 40 million.

This deal changed the structure of MTN again. By 2007 MTN Holdings still held the entire company, operating through two main subsidiaries—MTN South Africa, with three subsidiary companies, and MTN International, with 11 subsidiaries. Joining them now was the newly renamed MTN Dubai, with 11 subsidiaries, including a Mediterranean one called Mednet.

CORPORATE SOCIAL RESPONSIBILITY

While MTN's business interests were expanding steadily, the company continued to attend to its corporate responsibility to help less fortunate communities. In 2007 it formed a link with the Grameen Foundation, a social agency founded in Bangladesh in 1997 specifically for the purpose of providing information and "microloans" to people trying to rise out of extreme poverty. The foundation, now based in Kampala, had reached the rural poor through the Google search engine. Since

2004 the Grameen Foundation had been using Google technology to operate its Application Laboratory (AppLab) in Kampala, and it had recently added a system featuring village phone operators for those who did not have their own phones. By 2009 the system was fully operational. Thanks to the Grameen Foundation, MTN, and Google, such initiatives as the Farmer's Friend provided agricultural advice and weather forecasts; Health Tips provided reproductive health information; Clinic Finder helped locate nearby health clinics; and Google Trader matched buyers and sellers of agricultural services, so that they could broaden their marketing networks.

Also in 2007 the company launched its Y'ello Care program, which provided employees everywhere with opportunities to volunteer, an endeavor that MTN believed brings people together and encouraged them to trust each other. The company has also given each subsidiary a chance to pick a project that would benefit the people in its area. Some volunteers helped disadvantaged children with schoolwork, while other volunteers worked in hospitals or did painting projects and neighborhood cleanups. In Cyprus during 2007 the project of choice was a huge children's party, with clowns, face-painting, and food. Proceeds from this event went to a nearby charity that helped children with various kinds of cancer. Although the Y'ello Care Program was not a factor in company profits, in 2007 it added an extra gloss to a year that was golden for profits. Total revenue was ZAR 73.1 billion, with the South and East Africa region contributing ZAR 31.45 billion, West and Central Africa adding ZAR 31.12 billion, and ZAR 10.78 billion coming from the Middle East and North Africa. The list of subscribers had risen to a total of 61.4 million.

In 2008 MTN announced a new empowerment deal to transfer 30 percent of ownership to black South Africans. As stipulated in 2002, the Newshelf 664 arrangement was scheduled to unwind on December 22, 2008, with the dividend of MTN shares declared to the Alpine beneficiaries. In February 2009 this unbundling was the cause of much unhappiness among MTN employees. Alpine Trust had reportedly, without explanation, reduced the amount of money from the shares; Paul Jenkins, chairman of the Alpine Trust, corroborated this information with reporter Zweli Mokgata in *Business Times*. Of the 309 million shares originally purchased, 65.5 million had been used to pay for administrative costs. This left 243.5 million shares, out of which the funders received 209 million to pay off a refinancing debt, leaving just 34 million for distribution.

The disappointing distribution of shares aside, MTN's business matters remained on track. By 2008

MTN found its core network outdated and unable to cope with the soaring increase in subscribers. To improve its service, 98 percent of is network infrastructure was replaced with Internet Protocol fiber-based transmission. Another innovation, launched in 2009, was the creation of the MTN Zone, which encouraged South African subscribers to make their calls during times when traffic was low, and MTN charged them lower rates for doing so. The company ended the 2008 financial year with 90.7 million subscribers worldwide, and revenues of ZAR 102.5 billion ($12.5 billion).

Gillian Wolf

PRINCIPAL SUBSIDIARIES

MTN South Africa; MTN International; MTN Dubai; Blue Label Telecoms Limited; Celcom Group Limited; Huge Group Limited; Skype Technologies SA; Telkom SA; Vodafone Group PLC.

PRINCIPAL COMPETITORS

Orascom Telecom; Celtel.

FURTHER READING

"Bharti's Proposed Acquisition of MTN Runs into Pre-Condition Hurdle," domain-b.com, May 9, 2008, http://www.domain-b.com/companies/companies_b/Bharti_Tele-Ventures/20080509_acquisition.html.

Griffith, Dylan, "South Africa's Newest Magnate," *Age*, February 7, 2003.

Masango, Gugulakhe, "MTN's Procurement from BEE Firms Rises to R750 million," *Business Report*, February 9, 2005.

Mokgata, Zweli, "MTN's Employees Share Woes," *Business Times*, February 9, 2009.

"MTN Acquires Investcom," Light Reading, May 3, 2006, http://www.lightreading.com/document.asp?doc_id=93997.

"MTN Group—Announcement Relating to the Distribution by Newshelf 664 (Proprietary) Limited of MTN Group Limited Shares as a Dividend in Specie to the Beneficiaries of the Alpine Trust" (press release), Johannesburg: MTN Group Limited, December 15, 2008.

"MTN Group to Acquire Controlling Stakes in Cote d'Ivoire and Zambia," PR Newswire, June 22, 2005, http://www.prnewswire.co.uk/cgi/news/release?id=148728.

"MTN in New Empowerment Deal," MediaClubSouthAfrica.com, December 17, 2008, http://www.mediaclubsouthafrica.com/index.php?option=com_content&view=article&id=888:mtn171208&catid=45:economy_news&Itemid=114.

"MTN Opens Office in Iran," *Engineering News*, April 29, 2005.

"MTN Uganda Partners with Google, Grameen Foundation to launch Mobile Information Services," My Broadband News, June 30, 2009, http://mybroadband.co.za/news/Cellular/8599.html.

Museum of Modern Art

11 West 53 Street
New York, New York 10019
U.S.A.
Telephone: (212) 708-9400
Fax: (212) 708-9691
Web site: http://www.moma.org

Nonprofit Company
Founded: 1929
Employees: 825
Sales: $35.11 million (admissions and memberships) (2008)
NAICS: 712110 Museums

∎ ∎ ∎

With Alfred H. Barr Jr. as its first director, the Museum of Modern Art (MoMA) was founded in 1929 as a place to showcase the work of contemporary artists. Barr, who wanted to give New York City the "greatest museum of modern art in the world," may have influenced popular attitudes toward modern art more than anyone else in the twentieth century. He emphasized that the museum needed to stay current, constantly in a "metabolic ... state of renewal," and for decades Barr and the first trustees of MoMA showcased work that had broken sharply with tradition.

While MoMA is no longer at the cutting edge of all that is new in the art world, it has certainly fulfilled its founders' vision of greatness, having almost single-handedly defined what constitutes "modern" art. As Robert Hughes wrote in *Time* in May 1984, "There is

no fonder acronym in art than MoMA.... One cannot imagine New York City, or modernism itself, without it. More than any other museum in the world, MoMA is identified with its subject and defines its history." Jonathan Jones agreed, writing in the *Guardian* in 2000, "This museum has championed the modern movements from surrealism to pop ... and made modernism distinctively American."

Its founders' pioneering vision of art as encompassing not only painting and sculpture, but also drawing, photography, architecture, film, and industrial design extended the museum's influence still further. By 2009 MoMA held the most comprehensive collection of modern art in the world, including more than 150,000 paintings, sculptures, drawings, prints, photographs, and architectural models and drawings; 22,000 films and 4 million film stills; and archival materials including 300,000 books and periodicals and files on more than 70,000 artists. Along the way MoMA not only became the arbiter of greatness in 20th-century art but also reached into everyday life, shaping public taste for consumer goods.

FOUNDING, 1929–39

In the 1920s, three wealthy collectors of contemporary art, Lillie P. Bliss, Mary Quinn Sullivan, and Abby Aldrich Rockefeller, envisioned a museum that would be devoted exclusively to modern art, which at that time was shunned by traditional museums. Bliss, Sullivan, and Rockefeller, however, appreciated the genius of such artists as Paul Cézanne, Vincent van Gogh, Henri Matisse, Claude Monet, Georgia O'Keefe, and Pablo Pic-

COMPANY PERSPECTIVES

Founded in 1929 as an educational institution, The Museum of Modern Art is dedicated to being the foremost museum of modern art in the world.

Through the leadership of its Trustees and staff, The Museum of Modern Art manifests this commitment by establishing, preserving, and documenting a permanent collection of the highest order that reflects the vitality, complexity and unfolding patterns of modern and contemporary art; by presenting exhibitions and educational programs of unparalleled significance; by sustaining a library, archives, and conservation laboratory that are recognized as international centers of research; and by supporting scholarship and publications of preeminent intellectual merit.

Central to The Museum of Modern Art's mission is the encouragement of an ever-deeper understanding and enjoyment of modern and contemporary art by the diverse local, national, and international audiences that it serves.

asso, among others. They turned to A. Conger Goodyear, an art collector who had been forced to resign as president of the board of Albright Art Gallery in Buffalo, New York, when he purchased a work by Picasso for the museum. These four and three other trustees founded the Museum of Modern Art.

Barr had a visionary plan to include both the fine and applied arts. Departments included not only Painting and Sculpture, Drawings, and Prints and Illustrated Books, but also Architecture and Design, Film and Video, and Photography. He said, "The Plan was radical ... because it proposed an active and serious concern with the practical, commercial and popular arts as well as with the so-called 'fine' arts." Although the trustees were skeptical, telling him that they were primarily interested in painting and sculpture, Barr pressed on, constantly enlarging the scope of MoMA's exhibitions and collections.

The museum, which originally had a permanent collection of fewer than ten pieces, made do with exhibitions on loan for its first ten years. Its first exhibition, titled *Cézanne, Gauguin, Seurat, van Gogh*, opened ten days after the 1929 stock market crash but nevertheless attracted impressive crowds. The staging of the

exhibit was radical in that paintings were hung on neutral-colored walls, at approximately eye level and some distance from once another, and were arranged in a logical sequence. Before this time, paintings displayed in museums had been grouped close together, often on brightly colored or paneled walls, with little regard for thematic or chronological organization. Barr's exhibition techniques quickly became standard practice in 20th-century museums.

MoMA's second exhibition, *Painting by Nineteen Living Americans*, attracted fewer visitors, but Barr, at first cautious, became bolder in his selections. In 1936 MoMA put on two landmark exhibitions: *Cubism and Abstract Art: Painting, Sculpture, Constructions, Photography, Architecture, Industrial Art, Theater, Films, Posters, Typography* and *Fantastic Art, Dada, Surrealism*. In 1937 the museum mounted *Photography: 1839–1937*, the first comprehensive photography exhibition ever staged in the United States. A film library was established in 1935, and by 1939 MoMA could boast the largest library devoted to modern art in the United States.

During this period, MoMA began to stage shows featuring modern architecture and industrial design, including *Machine Art* in 1934 and *Useful Household Objects under Five Dollars* in 1938, which was the first in a series. With *Useful Household Objects*, MoMA set out to educate the public about modern visual culture, and in the process, directly affected not only consumer decisions by the entire manufacturing process. Low-priced, mass-produced household objects were arranged in a style much like that of a store; prices and manufacturers were listed on the exhibition labels, and many museum-goers then sought them out for purchase. Mary Anne Staniszewski wrote in her book *The Power of Display: A History of Exhibition Installations at the Museum of Modern Art*, "The show's success was secured by ... presenting modern culture as modest, down-home, democratic housewares.... *Useful Objects* was a very American manifestation of the international avant-garde's agenda to redesign the modern world."

MOMA'S CHANGING CHARACTER, 1939–68

In its early years MoMA acquired pieces mainly through bequests from patrons, and Barr did not have funds to purchase works until 1936. Soon after, the museum's growing collection necessitated a new building, which opened in May 1939. A visionary structure at the time, the six-story building designed by Philip Goodwin and Edward Durell Stone used an experimental glass called Thermolux to let in filtered sunlight and had a cantilevered roof with large "portholes" in it. As *Interior Design*

KEY DATES

■

1929: The Museum of Modern Art is founded in New York City.

1937: *Photography: 1839–1937* is the first comprehensive photography exhibition ever staged in the United States.

1938: *Useful Household Objects* exhibitions begin.

1939: MoMA moves into its permanent building in Midtown Manhattan.

1949: René d'Harnoncourt becomes MoMA's director.

1950: *What Is Good Design?* exhibitions begin.

1951: MoMA building is renovated and expanded.

1964: MoMA building is again renovated and expanded.

1984: Renovation doubles exhibition space in museum.

2002: MoMA relocates to temporary building in Long Island City, Queens, during museum renovation.

2004: Museum of Modern Art reopens in Midtown Manhattan.

noted in July 1989, "The 1939 Goodwin/Stone building introduced a fundamentally new kind of museum architecture. Its loft-like galleries incorporated such innovative details as track lighting, movable partitions and white walls that eventually became standard for displaying art."

Despite disruptions caused by World War II, MoMA's collection grew rapidly during the 1940s. Among the masterpieces acquired during this period were Vincent van Gogh's *Starry Night* and Henri Matisse's *Piano Lesson* and *The Red Studio*. At the same time, patriotism engendered by the war shifted the museum's focus from European to American artists, and MoMA began to acquire works by Abstract Expressionist painters, including Jackson Pollock. In 1940 the museum received Abby Aldrich Rockefeller's entire print collection. The Department of Photography was established, and between 1940 and 1943 MoMA's photography collection grew from 229 photographs to more than two thousand. Early exhibitions focused on the war effort, including the widely praised 1942 *Road to Victory*, which combined photography with patriotic poetry and texts.

In addition to the *Useful Objects* series, MoMA staged exhibitions on lamps, textiles, and other house wares, including a series of five exhibitions in 1950

titled *What Is Good Design?* As Roberta Smith wrote in the *New York Times* in June 2009, " With these astutely coordinated efforts, the Modern promulgated not the High Modernism of Picasso and Braque, et al., but the modernism of everyday life." The *What Is Good Design?* exhibitions consolidated MoMA's position as a shaper of consumer tastes.

Between 1949 and 1968, when René d'Harnoncourt served as MoMA's director, the museum expanded dramatically. He created a new International Program, dedicated to making American art better known around the world. An international exhibit, *The New American Painting*, shown in eight countries in 1958 and 1959, brought widespread recognition to American avant-garde artists. Exhibitions at MoMA drew massive crowds. Architect Philip Johnson created expansions to the building in 1951 and 1964 to contain the expanding permanent collections.

"GUARDIAN OF A CLOSING EPOCH"

The founders of MoMA had intended the museum to continually exhibit the newest, most exciting, cutting-edge art. In their vision, most works in the museum's collection would eventually be sold or transferred to other museums in order to buy new art. However, this policy changed in ensuring decades. In 1953 the board announced that the museum would no longer, as A. Conger Goodyear had put it two decades before, have "the same permanence that a river has." Instead, the chairman of the board announced that the Museum would make its collections permanent, setting aside special galleries in which to exhibit these works. This change in policy precipitated a bit of an identity crisis, as MoMA became, in the words of Robert Hughes, "more preoccupied with being the guardian of a closing epoch" than being the champion of the avante-garde.

By the 1970s, MoMA's success had created new challenges. Millions of people now visited the museum each year. New museums opening around the world looked to MoMA for guidance and as a source for loaned exhibitions. The museum had also become too large to be supported solely by wealthy patrons. Government and corporate grants began to figure more heavily into MoMA's budgets, which meant that the museum was now more accountable to outside forces, perhaps tending to make MoMA more conservative than it had been in the past.

The policy of maintaining permanent collections led the museum to quickly outgrow its space. Architect Cesar Pelli designed a renovation and addition, including a 44-story tower of luxury condominiums in the airspace above the museum as a way to earn needed funds. The newly renovated MoMA reopened with twice the amount of exhibition space in 1984, as well as significantly expanded space for circulation, conservation, storage, and museum offices. Each department now had its own gallery space for displaying permanent collections and exhibitions on loan.

MoMA inaugurated the new space by putting on its first large survey of contemporary art since 1970, titled *An International Survey Exhibition at the Modern since 1970.* The show was, in part, a response to criticism that the museum had lost its founders' commitment to contemporary art. Kynaston McShine, the senior curator of painting and sculpture, told Michael Brenson of the *New York Times*, "The show is a sign of hope … that contemporary art is being taken as seriously as it should be, a sign that the museum will restore the balance between contemporary art and art history that is part of what makes the place unique."

However, within a decade, MoMA needed to expand once again, because the museum's space constraints limited MoMA's ability to display new art. MoMA raised the needed funds by issuing $257 million in long-term revenue bonds and temporarily relocated to a building in Long Island City in Queens. Architect Yoshio Taniguchi was selected to handle the expansion, which included 630,000 feet of new and redesigned space, including a new building devoted solely to education and research, an expanded library and archives, and an enlarged sculpture garden. The renovated museum, which opened in 2004, won accolades. The building itself, noted the *Economist* in November of that year, "is in the service of beauty," including abundant natural light, views of Manhattan, and minimalist, soaring atriums.

However, critics remained divided over whether MoMA could regain its avant-garde spirit. *The Economist* noted, "The Museum of Modern Art is back, taking risks like the teenager it was several buildings ago," and, in fact, the first, most accessible floor was dedicated to contemporary work. However, Michael Kimmelman of the *New York Times* wrote in November 2004, "The Modern is clearly still not sure what to make of the art of the last 30 or 40 years…. Innumerable institutions not wielding its clout but not freighted with its history have come along and outflanked it." Nevertheless, the institution's continuing influence cannot be overstated. As Richard Lacayo noted in October 2004 in *Time*, "What it anoints as central to the story of modern art is hugely influential among scholars, col-

lectors and other museums. And what MoMA minimizes must struggle a bit to be taken seriously."

Melissa J. Doak

PRINCIPAL COMPETITORS

San Francisco Museum of Modern Art; Modern Art Museum of Fort Worth; Whitney Museum of American Art; Museum of Contemporary Art, Los Angeles; Massachusetts Museum of Contemporary Art; The Art Institute of Chicago.

FURTHER READING

Bartolucci, Marisa, "Eyes Wide Open," *Architecture*, February 2000, pp. 47–49.

Bee, Harriet Schoenholz, and Michelle Elligott, *Art in Our Time: A Chronicle of the Museum of Modern Art*, New York: Museum of Modern Art, 2004.

Brenson, Michael, "A Living Artists Show at the Modern Museum," *New York Times*, April 21, 1984.

"Bring on the New: Museum of Modern Art," *Economist*, November 20, 2004, p. 85.

Dietsch, Deborah K., "Museum Imports," *Architecture*, June 1997, p. 13.

Dixon, John Morris, "Monumental MoMA: Yoshio Taniguchi's Expansion of New York City's Museum of Modern Art Reinterprets Its Implicit Character at Enlarged Scale," *Architecture*, February 2005, pp. 40–49.

Fredericksen, Eric, "Sign of the Times: With Its Magnum Opus under Construction in Manhattan, the Museum of Modern Art's Temporary Home in Queens Suggests that Less Can Indeed Be More," *Architecture*, September 2002, pp. 66–71.

Glancey, Jonathan, "Cool, Calm and Collected: New York's Museum of Modern Art Is Back in Business," *New Statesman*, November 29, 2004, pp. 34–35.

Hughes, Robert, "Revelation on 53rd Street," *Time*, May 14, 1984, p. 98.

Hunter, Sam, *The Museum of Modern Art, New York: The History and the Collection*, New York: H. N. Abrams and the Museum of Modern Art, New York, 1984.

Jones, Jonathan, "A Picasso's Place Is Beside the Temporary Café," *Guardian*, August 29, 2000, p. 12.

Kantor, Sybil Gordon, *Alfred H. Barr, Jr. and the Intellectual Origins of the Museum of Modern Art*, Cambridge: MIT Press, 2002.

Kim, Sheila, "MoMA's Big Move," *Interior Design*, June 2002, p. 43.

Kimmelman, Michael, "Racing to Keep up with the Newest," *New York Times*, November 19, 2004.

Kramer, Louise, "Putting More Store in Commercial Efforts; Cultural Groups Add Income with Gift Shops, Web Sites, Other Ventures," *Crain's New York Business*, March 27, 2000, p. 39.

Lacayo, Richard, "The Bigger Picture Show: An Expanded Museum of Modern Art Prepares to Reopen in Manhattan. How Will It Change the Way We Look at Art?" *Time*, October 11, 2004, p. 86.

McKaig, Ryan, "N.Y.C.'s MoMA Selling $257M for Expansion," *Bond Buyer*, December 5, 2001, p. 44.

"Modern Architecture Is Back," *Economist*, April 19, 1997, pp. 83–84.

"Modern Museum Closing until May," *New York Times*, December 26, 1983, p. C11.

Museum of Modern Art, *Imagining the Future of the Museum of Modern Art*, New York: H. N. Abrams and the Museum of Modern Art, New York, 1998.

"New York's Museum of Modern Art Celebrates 50 Years in the Goodwin/Stone Building," *Interior Design*, July 1989, p. 38.

"Organization Case Study—MoMA Relocation Focuses on Community Commitment," *PR Week*, October 21, 2002, p. 10.

Ouroussoff, Nicholai, "Art Fuses with Urbanity in a Redesign of the Modern," *New York Times*, November 15, 2004.

Portillo, Michael, "Shock and Awe," *New Statesman*, November 29, 2004, pp. 36–37.

Russell, John, "The Old Modern's Farewell: A Show of Its Best Drawings," *New York Times*, October 28, 1983.

Sanger, Elizabeth, "New York's Museum of Modern Art Reaches New Level of Sticker Shock," *Newsday*, September 23, 2004.

Sloan, Carole, "MoMA Brings Design Store to SoHo," *Home Textiles Today*, March 26, 2001, pp. 2, 81.

Smith, Roberta, "The Ordinary as Object of Desire," *New York Times*, June 4, 2009.

Souccar, Miriam Kreinin, "MoMA Reinvents Itself, but Some Feel Left Out," *Crain's New York Business*, June 6, 2005, p. A22.

Staniszewski, Mary Anne, *The Power of Display: A History of Exhibition Installations at the Museum of Modern Art*, Cambridge: MIT Press, 1998, 400 p.

Vogel, Carol, "More than Child's Play: Making over the Modern; Curators Look for New Ways to Present Art in an Expanded Museum," *New York Times*, June 9, 2004.

Namco Bandai Holdings Inc.

4-5-15, Higashi-Shinagawa, Shinagawa-ku,
Tokyo, 140-8590
Japan
Telephone: (+81) 3-3847-5005
Fax: (+81) 3-3847-5067
Web site: http://www.bandainamco.co.jp

Public Company
Founded: 1950
Employees: 1,113
Sales: $995.40 (2008)
Stock Exchanges: Tokyo
Ticker Symbol: First Section, 7832
NAICS: 339932 Game, Toy, and Children's Vehicle
   Manufacturing

■ ■ ■

Namco Bandai Holdings Inc. is one of the largest entertainment companies in the world. The company is best known for products derived from popular television and comic book characters, video games, and experiential amusements. These range from action figures and their accessories to video game software, clothing, and candy. The firm has also had success with such faddish toys as the digital "pets" Tamagotchi and Digimon; selling toys in vending machines; and providing digital content online and through cell phones. Other Namco Bandai units make animated television programs and movies; design and manufacture amusement machines and amusement centers; make stationery; and sell, lease, and manage real estate properties. Based in Japan, where it is the leading toy maker, Namco Bandai distributes its products worldwide.

BEGINNINGS IN TOY BUSINESS AFTER WORLD WAR II

Bandai's roots date to post–World War II Japan, where Naoharu Yamashina, a war veteran who had lost an eye in combat, was struggling to make a living. The son of a rice retailer, Yamashina had studied business in high school, and after the war he began working for a textile wholesaler in Kanazawa run by his wife's brother. Business was slow, and when a neighbor told him of the potential for success in toy sales, Yamashina convinced his employer to send him to Tokyo to try this new field. Putting in long hours there with his wife, he gradually built up a small toy-distribution business.

In 1950 Yamashina took control of the toy distributorship and renamed it Bandai, which was derived from the Chinese phrase for "things that are eternal." At this time the firm was mainly selling celluloid and metallic toys, along with rubber swimming rings.

Deciding to add an original product to its lineup, in September of 1950 Bandai introduced the Rhythm Ball, a beach ball with a bell inside. The Rhythm Ball initially suffered from a high rate of defects, but its quality was improved and the company soon added such other products as the metal B-26 Night Plane. In March 1951 Bandai began to export inexpensive toys, including metal cars and planes, to the United States and other foreign markets. The growing company built a new

COMPANY PERSPECTIVES

Our mission is to provide "Dreams, Fun and Inspiration" to people around the world through entertainment, and our vision is to become "The Leading Innovator in Global Entertainment." Discovering how we can entertain and inspire customers is the starting point of realizing our vision, and this initiative comes from the commitment and determination of each individual employee. We believe that we can bolster the value of the Group by identifying its unique and superior human resources and by boosting the contribution made by our employees. We are firmly committed to making the BANDAI NAMCO Group into "a group focusing on human resource management, particularly on entertainment and imagination."

shipping and warehousing facility in the spring of 1953, and in the summer added research and development, product inspection, and transportation departments.

In early 1955 Bandai established a manufacturing facility, the Waraku Works, and during the summer began construction of a new Tokyo headquarters and introduced a new "BC" logo. The fall of 1955 saw the firm offer its first product guarantee for the Toyopet Crown model car. Bandai highlighted this in television commercials that began airing in 1958, which used the phrase, "The Red Box means a BC-guaranteed toy." The following year a Cars of the World model line was launched, and the company's logo was redesigned to stress its emphasis on quality. In the early 1960s Bandai began to establish direct overseas sales and opened an office in New York.

CHARACTER-BASED TOYS DEBUT IN 1963

In 1963 Bandai introduced its first toy based on a children's television character, the action figure Astroboy. The firm would go on to refine a strategy of helping to fund a new program's development and then sponsoring its episodes as they were broadcast, running ads for derivative products that might include action figures, toy vehicles, and costumes. Beginning in 1966 Bandai found success with toys based on Ultraman, a giant, caped, metal-skinned hero who fired laser beams and battled monsters. The live-action program and some of its related toys were later imported to the United States, though their impact there was slight. Other Ban-

dai character products were taken from manga, the serial comic books that were hugely popular in Japan. To keep up with a growing demand for its toys, Bandai built the Toy Town Manufacturing Complex in Mibu, which opened in October of 1965.

In the latter half of the 1960s, the company had hits with Water Motor, Thunderbird, and Naughty Flipper toys, as well as Crazy Foam. In the fall of 1969, Bandai formed a Travel Services unit and acquired an additional factory in Shimizu City, where it would manufacture plastic model toys such as the World Car, Thunderbird 2, and Beetle series.

The firm established Tonka Japan in 1970 in a marketing tie-up with that company, and a year later it added a Models unit and created Popy as a manufacturer of character toys. In 1975 Bandai again changed its logo and trademark designs as part of the launch of a new worldwide marketing effort. Ties were established in October of that year with U.S. modelmaker Monogram, and in 1976 toy giant Mattel began selling Bandai's Mazinger action figures in the United States under the brand name Shogun. Bandai entered the publishing business in the fall of 1976 with the *Moving Picture Book*, later formally establishing Bandai Publishing as a subsidiary.

In November of 1976 the company opened a new factory for Popy toys and in April of 1977 began marketing encapsulated toys in vending machines. During the same year, the firm founded its first overseas manufacturing entity, Bandai (H.K.) Co., Ltd., in Hong Kong. In 1978 Bandai America Inc. was formed to market the company's toys in the United States, and the following year the B-AI Electronics and B-AI Mibu units were formed.

MAKOTO YAMASHINA TAKES CONTROL OF FIRM: 1980

In 1980 Naoharu Yamashina's son took over the job of president from his father, who continued to serve as board chairman. Thirty-five-year old Makoto Yamashina, who had a degree in economics from Keio University, had originally worked at a publishing firm, where he wanted to become an editor. When he was instead assigned to sell encyclopedias, he left to join his father at Bandai.

After taking over as president, the younger Yamashina fired many of his father's senior executives and replaced them with people closer to his own age. This was a shocking move to many in the "lifetime employment" culture of Japan, but Makoto Yamashina was interested in operating his company in a different way, modeled more on the U.S. style. He also began making

KEY DATES

∎

1947: Naoharu Yamashina begins distributing toys in Tokyo for his brother-in-law.

1950: Yamashina takes over the business and renames it Bandai.

1963: The company creates its first toys based on characters from a television program.

1980: Yamashina's son Makoto is named president of the firm.

1984: Gobots toys are launched in United States but are outsold by Transformers.

1993: Power Rangers toys become a huge success in United States and other markets.

1996: Tamagotchi virtual pets are introduced.

2000: Digital content unit is spun off to create Bandai Networks Co. Inc.

2002: Ground is broken for the company's new 15-story headquarters in Tokyo.

2003: Bandai announces its plan to create a holding company structure by 2005.

2005: Merger with Namco.

changes to the traditional distribution pattern for toys, dealing directly with large retail chains rather than selling to them through middlemen.

Shortly after Makoto Yamashina took control of the company, Bandai launched its Gundam toy line, based on a cartoon program about futuristic warriors. The series was popular, and, like Ultraman, Gundam became a long-term moneymaker for the company. In 1981 the firm marketed its first candy products and expanded to Europe, opening French and Italian subsidiaries. These were followed in 1982 by Dutch, British, and Australian branches. The year 1982 also saw Bandai form a department to develop and create original animation and film projects, and a new subsidiary, Emotion, which began to open video shops in Japan. In 1983 the company added an apparel department, founded a division called A.E. Planning (later Bandai Visual), and launched its first original feature film, *Daws*, which came out in the fall.

GOBOTS INVADE AMERICA: 1984

In 1984 Bandai made another attempt at the U.S. market with toys called Gobots, which were Americanized versions of the popular Machine Robo line that had been available in Japan and elsewhere for several years. Gobots were mechanical creatures that could change into vehicles and fight battles against a series of evil

counterparts. Despite the best efforts of Bandai and Tonka, their U.S. distributor, the Gobots were ultimately displaced by the rival Transformers, which were marketed by toy giant Hasbro and based on a line made by a Bandai competitor. Transformers were larger, and their associated television program was perceived as better than one featuring the Gobots, while Tonka also had some problems supplying retailers with the toys when they began to sell. It would be almost a decade before Bandai would again make an impact in the U.S. market.

Meanwhile, the company had begun expanding its operations in Asia, opening a second plant in Hong Kong and forming a Chinese joint venture called the China Fuman Toy Company. Bandai was experiencing a sharp decline in sales at this time, with 1985 revenues of ¥70.7 billion ($495 million) down significantly from the previous year's figure of ¥84.5 billion. The company went public with a listing on the Tokyo Stock Exchange's Second Section in January of 1986, but due to the lingering sales downturn cancelled a secondary offering slated for early 1987. A line of products tied to a hit Japanese cartoon and comic book series, *Dragon Ball*, was one bright spot for the company, as was the Kitty Stick furry toy.

As part of its plan to move all manufacturing abroad, in March of 1987 the company formed a joint venture in Thailand, Bandai and K.C. Co., with Imperial Thai Toy. Bandai also moved the production and marketing staff of its overseas division from the firm's headquarters in Tokyo to its Hong Kong subsidiary. Other ventures aimed at strengthening the bottom line included branching out into non-toy areas such as health equipment and video sales. In the latter category, Bandai reached an agreement with the Walt Disney Company to market up to 150 of its video titles in Japan for a two-year period.

In 1989 the company moved into a new headquarters building in Tokyo, and entered the music business by forming the Emotion label and establishing a relationship with the firm Apollon Music Industry. The year also saw the opening of the Ultraman Shot M78 retail outlet. In 1991 Bandai became 5 percent owner of a $200 million satellite-based video-on-demand start-up called Entertainment Made Convenient, formed a sales subsidiary in Taiwan, and began marketing Chara-Can, its first line of toys packaged with drinks.

POWER RANGERS MAKE U.S. DEBUT: 1993

In 1993 Bandai had its biggest international success to date with toys based on the live-action show *Mighty*

Morphin' Power Rangers (called *Jyu Rangah* in Japan when originally shown there). The series once again featured superheroes that battled the forces of evil. Unlike many such exports, the live-action *Power Rangers* show was partially reshot for North American broadcast, adding some non-Asian characters and increasing the ratio of females to males. Soon after its U.S. debut in August 1993 on the Fox network, the program became a surprise hit. Demand for Power Rangers toys quickly outstripped their availability, leading to frantic scenes in stores as parents tried to secure them for their children.

Working to take advantage of this success, in March 1994 Bandai announced it would build factories in Vietnam and Mexico to increase output as well as to lower costs. The firm was hoping to triple production of Power Rangers toys and also add new items to the line, as a Power Rangers motion picture that was in the works was expected to keep interest in the characters high for the foreseeable future. Bandai was now focusing increasingly on the international marketplace, as the Japanese toy market was shrinking due to a declining birthrate in that country.

Despite the company's success with Power Rangers, it experienced a sizable earnings loss for the year as the result of a February 1993 decision to end an agreement with Nintendo to market that company's video game equipment and software in Europe. Several of Bandai's regional subsidiaries experienced drastic revenue drops, and the firm was forced to write off billions of yen worth of outdated games and players, leading to a loss of $18.6 million for the fiscal year.

In its home country, Bandai's reach now extended beyond toys to such items as candy, clothing, shampoo, personal organizers, and word processors. An estimated 20 percent of toy-store shelf space in Japan was occupied by the firm's products. Bandai continued to sponsor a number of cartoon programs on television, notably *Pretty Soldier Sailor Moon*, in which five young girls used the power of the moon to combat aliens, and *Crayon Shin-Chan*, a program about a mischievous preschooler that was watched by viewers of all ages. The company launched about 60 new characters each year, and when one of them caught on marketing and manufacturing would be ramped up to flood stores with products. Bandai might introduce (and pull from the market) between 8,000 and 10,000 items per year, most of which only appeared in Japan. By this time the firm was manufacturing just a quarter of its own products, down from 45 percent in 1988, with the rest contracted out. Character-based items accounted for more than 80 percent of revenues. Other developments at this time included the purchase of majority ownership in Sunrise, one of Japan's top animation companies, and participa-

tion in a joint venture to build a theme park near Tokyo Disneyland.

In November 1994 Bandai took one of its biggest risks to date when it announced it would develop, with computer maker Apple, a multimedia device that would plug into a television monitor and could be used for game play and Web browsing. To be called Pippin, the product would retail for approximately $500, considerably less than a computer at the time but more than a typical video-game player. It was to use CD-ROM discs that would also be playable on Apple computers. The machine could be upgraded with purchase of a keyboard and other peripherals for use as a word processor. Bandai subsequently formed three new U.S. subsidiaries to increase its presence in that country, including Bandai Digital Entertainment Inc., which would market Pippin.

In March 1996 the Pippin Atmark, as it was now called, was introduced in Japan. Its $620 price tag was almost 25 percent higher than originally projected. Reviews were mixed, with a typical response being that the machine was overpriced as a video-game platform but under-equipped as a computer. Both Bandai and Apple had high hopes for Pippin, as the Power Rangers phenomenon was in decline, and Apple was increasingly losing its market share to Windows-based equipment. Bandai officials admitted that the firm was not making money on Pippin players but expressed confidence that sales of software and subscriptions to a Bandai-owned online service would make it profitable.

TAMAGOTCHI VIRTUAL PETS TAKE JAPAN BY STORM: 1996

In November 1996 a toy designed by former housewife Aki Maita was launched that would become the company's next blockbuster hit. This was the Tamagotchi, an electronic egg-shaped device attached to a keychain. A small screen on the front displayed an image of a chicken-like creature, which would have to be "cared for" by manipulating several buttons. If it was not tended to, the creature would die; by pressing a button, another creature could be hatched. If cared for properly, the character could grow and change, "living" for up to several weeks. The toys quickly became popular in Japan, perhaps in part because they annoyed parents, who had to go to great lengths to secure them, after which they were often faced with babysitting the Tamagotchi when the child had other responsibilities.

By February 1997 Bandai was so far behind in filling orders that it issued a public apology, at the same time launching Tamagotchi version 2. Tamagotchis were so difficult to obtain that some Bandai employees reported being threatened with harm by Japanese Yakuza gangsters if they would not turn over copies of the toys, which were reportedly selling for as much as ¥50,000 on the black market, 25 times their list price. New variations were soon in development, including Tamapitchi, a pair of cellphones that could send an animated character from one device to another, enabling it to mate and create a third creature.

While all this was taking place, Bandai was also laying plans for an October 1997 merger with video game giant Sega, which would create an entertainment conglomerate on par with the Walt Disney Company. Bandai's employees showed strong opposition to the move, however, and industry analysts were not enthusiastic. In late May, Makoto Yamashina abruptly called off the deal, simultaneously tendering his resignation as head of the company. He was replaced by a Bandai veteran, Takashi Mogi, who had earlier helped salvage several troubled subsidiaries.

Along with the turmoil caused by the cancelled merger, Bandai was also suffering from the failure of Pippin, which was discontinued in March after total sales of just 42,000 units worldwide. The misfire would end up costing the company more than $200 million in write-offs.

Tamagotchi sales had now peaked in Japan, but the product's launch in the international market had just begun, and it was proving to be nearly as successful abroad. Tamagotchi spinoff items such as clothes and video games were in the pipeline, as was follow-up Digi-Mon, which could be connected to another toy for battles, the winner gaining some of the loser's strength. By the end of 1997, 40 million Tamagotchis had been sold worldwide. On a sad note, in October 1997 Bandai founder Naoharu Yamashina passed away at the age of 79.

In March 1998 the firm opened its first Ultraman Club, which contained shops and amusement machines. The club, one of a projected chain of 10, would be used in part for researching toy trends. A restructuring also took place in the spring which realigned the company into 10 units that included Toys, Entertainment, Service, Production, and Images and Music. Other new developments of the year included formation of a U.S. home video division, creation of a line of character-based gardening tools, and the introduction of Silent Shout, a lollipop that broadcast music into a consumer's head through vibrations in the candy's battery-powered handle. A popular toy of this period was the hyper yo-yo, which had a special bearing inside that allowed more complex movements than a standard yo-yo.

In the spring of 1999 Bandai introduced another new product, WonderSwan, a handheld electronic game toy which could be used by itself or connected to

another unit or a computer. It had been designed by Gunpei Yokoi, creator of Nintendo's similar Game Boy. Also that spring, the company changed its top leadership, with Takeo Takaso becoming president and Yukimasa Sugiura assuming the dual roles of CEO and chairman. Takashi Mogi had stepped down because of the company's poor recent financial performance, which came as the Tamagotchi craze burned itself out. Makoto Yamashina, who had been serving as chairman since stepping down as CEO, was named honorary chairman.

MATTEL BUYS INTO BANDAI: JULY 1999

In the summer of 1999 Bandai announced it was selling a 5 percent stake in the firm to toy industry leader Mattel Inc. as the first step in a new cooperative marketing agreement. Bandai would have the option of buying 5 percent of Mattel as well. The move gave Bandai its first presence in Latin America, while Mattel would be strengthened in Japan, where its prior efforts had met with little success. Bandai would continue to distribute its own toys in the United States in the short term. Other projected benefits of the union were mutual development of new toys and sales of Bandai products through a Web site Mattel was preparing to launch. Bandai had recently also joined with seven other companies to form a joint venture called e-Shopping Toys Corp. to sell toys on the Internet. Another joint venture was announced a few months later in which Bandai and Japan's other top three toy makers would produce robot toys. The company was now increasingly focusing on technology-based offerings, including robotic pets, video and computer games, and digital content provision.

Bandai's revenues were dropping off at this time, but reorganizing efforts were paying off with an increase in net earnings. For the fiscal year ending in March of 2000, the company reported sales of ¥208.62 billion ($1.91 billion) and net earnings of ¥1.28 billion, up from the previous year's loss of ¥16.4 billion.

In the spring of 2000 Bandai announced it would pay a bonus of ¥1 million for each baby an employee had after their second child. Japan's birth rate was at an all-time low, and Bandai's offer was the most generous to date of many that companies were making in an attempt to reverse this trend.

The fall of 2000 saw Bandai spin off a recently created cell phone and Internet content unit to create the wholly owned subsidiary Bandai Networks Co. Inc. In January 2001 the firm sold a 50 percent stake it owned in Upper Deck Group, the California-based trading card maker. Upper Deck would continue to make cards featuring Bandai characters such as Gundam, which had only recently been introduced in the United States. The company also sold one of its Thai manufacturing plants and consolidated production in Thailand at a single facility near Bangkok, causing the loss of a number of jobs. A Chinese plant had been sold several years earlier.

Bandai's financial picture continued to improve in 2001, with profits jumping to ¥12.9 billion on sales of ¥217 billion. In July a joint venture was formed with two Korean firms to create Bandai GV Co., which would develop online games for the Japanese market. The company also announced it would introduce a higher-priced line of capsuled toys, which included such items as a digital watch priced at ¥300. In the fall, the firm began offering shares of its Bandai Visual unit on the JASDAQ Stock Exchange and formed a joint venture in Korea with several Japanese and Korean firms called Daiwon Digital Broadcasting Co. Ltd. to broadcast animated programs via satellite under the name AniOne TV.

In March 2002 another joint venture, Bandai Channel Co., was launched to provide digital content to computers and video game terminals that would be based on characters such as Gundam. The fiscal year just ended proved to be the firm's best ever, with earnings hitting a record ¥21.99 billion ($170.7 million) on sales of ¥227.93 billion.

In the summer Bandai bought Tsukuda Original Co., a doll, toy, and software maker, to help broaden the firm's offerings. The year 2002 also saw Bandai begin construction of a new ¥4 billion headquarters building in Tokyo. Built on land near the company's existing offices, it would feature a Bandai Museum exhibiting toys from the firm's entire 52-year history. In the fall of 2002, Bandai announced it would revive the Strawberry Shortcake line of toys, which had been popular in the United States during the 1980s. Thirty items were to be released, retailing at between $3 and $20. In January 2003 the recently-purchased Tsukuda Original was sold to Wakui Corporation. Shortly afterwards, Bandai announced that the firm's structure would be shifted to a holding company model over the next several years, with all of its various divisions spun off into wholly owned subsidiaries.

After more than a half century, Bandai Co., Ltd., had grown to become the third largest toy maker in the world. The firm continued to offer a wide range of character-based products as well as an ever-changing lineup of electronic toys, videos, video games, clothing, capsuled items, and food. The multifaceted firm was also increasingly expanding into the digital realm with the offerings of its Bandai Networks Co. unit and a series of joint ventures.

BANDAI AND NAMCO MERGE: 2005

In 2005 Bandai merged with Namco Inc. and hoped to become "the world's most inspiring entertainment group." Each company brought a large segment of the entertainment industry to the new giant. Bandai was mostly known for toy and media publishing, while Namco was a premier software developer for video games. Bandai's marketing capabilities and Namco's cutting edge development proved to be a formidable combination. The combined company was the second largest toy and game company in Japan, behind Sega Sammy Holdings Inc.

The Bandai Namco group restructured with four Strategic Business Units: Toys and Hobby (Bandai), Game Contents (Namco Bandai Games), Visual and Music Content (Bandai Visual) and Amusement Facilities (Namco). Each strategic unit covered a whole segment of the entertainment industry. The strengths of each company were particularly highlighted in their amusement facilities. The Namco Wonder Park Hero's Base, a theme park in Japan, was based on the fantasy of meeting one's dream superhero. The park utilized Namco's strengths in location management for amusement locales and Bandai's character development prowess to create a park that attracted about a million visitors per year.

From 2005 through 2008 the newly merged company undertook a complete corporate restructuring with the aim of taking advantage of each company's strengths. As part of the reorganization, Bandai Visual (owner of the Anime television channel) became a wholly owned subsidiary of Namco Bandai Holdings. The company worked toward a new goal of ¥1 trillion sales, ¥100 billion operating income, and 50 percent of sales overseas.

Moving forward, Namco Bandai focused its attention on "entertainment hubs." Similar to a full-service airport terminal, entertainment hubs offer the combination of a multimedia entertainment experience with all of the merchandise and branding needed to make a new product successful. Namco Bandai also continued to build strategic partnerships that allowed it to work with or acquire the companies that made up the essential components of each entertainment hub. Between late 2007 and early 2008, the company purchased large quantities of stock in several key Japanese companies, bringing more diversity to their gaming portfolio.

In 2009 Namco Bandai sealed its first partnership with an apparel company. In anticipation of the release of Tekken 6, a martial arts-themed video game, Namco Bandai partnered with TapouT, a mixed martial arts apparel and lifestyle brand. In the new edition of Tekken,

TapouT gear was to appear in the game as an option for character customization. The same type of apparel would be available for purchase by Tekken fans.

Namco Bandai remained committed to diversifying its audiences and markets. In mid-2009 the company's European branch released a new brain training program for the Apple iPhone, designed to test and improve different areas of brain functioning. Also in 2009, Namco Bandai released a number of applications for download on Facebook, including such nostalgic video games as Pac Man and Dig Dug for a small fee. Through continual self-reflection and expansion into developing markets and technologies, Namco Bandai remained a strong market force in the worldwide entertainment industry.

Frank Uhle
Updated, Robert Jacobson

PRINCIPAL SUBSIDIARIES

Artpresto Co., Ltd.; Banalex Corp.; Bandai Logipal Inc.; Bandai Networks Co., Ltd.; Bandai Visual Co., Ltd.; Banpresto Co., Ltd.; Bee Co., Ltd.; Happinet Corp.; Megahouse Corp.; Plex Co., Ltd.; Seeds Co., Ltd.; Seika Co., Ltd.; Sunrise Inc.; Yutaka Co., Ltd.; Bandai America Inc. (USA); Bandai Entertainment Inc. (USA); Bandai Espana S.A. (Spain); Bandai (H.K.) Co., Ltd. (Hong Kong); Bandai Industrial Co., Ltd. (Thailand); Bandai Korea Co., Ltd. (Korea); Bandai Logipal (H.K.) Ltd. (Hong Kong); Bandai S.A. (France); Bandai Trading (Shanghai) Co., Ltd. (China); Bandai U.K. Ltd. (UK); Banpresto (H.K.) Ltd. (Hong Kong); Hebei Wanrong Co., Ltd. (China); Namco Bandai Games America Inc. (USA).

PRINCIPAL COMPETITORS

Hasbro Inc.; Mattel Inc.; Nintendo Co., Ltd.; SEGA Corp.; Takara Co., Ltd.; Tomy Co., Ltd.

FURTHER READING

"Bandai, Namco to Form Japan's No. 2 Toy-Game Group in Fall," *AsiaPulse News*, May 2, 2005.

"Bandai to Adopt Holding Company System by FY05," *Nikkei Report*, February 17, 2003.

Cody, Jennifer, "Power Rangers Take on the Whole World," *Wall Street Journal*, March 23, 1994, p. B1.

Dougherty, Philip A., "Gobots Set U.S. Invasion," *New York Times*, January 25, 1984, p. D15.

Eisenstodt, Gale, and Kerry A. Dolan, "Watch Out, Barbie," *Forbes*, January 2, 1995, p. 58.

Friedland, Jonathan, "Kid Stuff: Bandai Stays on Top of Japan's Toy Market," *Far Eastern Economic Review*, June 9, 1994, p. 61.

Hamilton, David P., "Sega, Bandai Cite Cultural Differences in Calling Off Billion-Dollar Merger," *Wall Street Journal*, May 28, 1997, p. B6.

Iwai, Makoto, "Marriage License," *Game Developer*, April 2007, p. 38.

"Japan's Bandai Posts Return to Profit after Reorganizing Its Operations," *Dow Jones Business News*, May 9, 2000.

Johannes, Amy, "Curious George Game Gets Multi-Million Dollar Boost," *Promo*, February 1, 2006.

Kunii, Irene M., "How Long Can Bandai Keep Those Cute Little Pets Alive?" *Business Week*, March 16, 1998, p. 29.

Lynch, Stephen, "Big in Japan (er, America) Japan's Hot Toys and Cartoons Have Caught on Here—And It Only Took 20 Years," *Orange County Register*, February 9, 2001, p. 1.

"Namco Bandai Games America Inc. and TapouT Team up to Deliver Fierce Gear for TEKKEN®," *Women's Health Weekly*, August 6, 2009, p. 138.

"Namco Bandai Networks Europe Rolls Out 'Brain Exercise' for iPhone and iPod Touch," *Entertainment Close-up*, June 12, 2009.

"Namco Bandai Offering Downloadable Games over Facebook," *1UP*, March 18, 2009.

"NW: Bandai Stages Sharp Turnaround," *Nikkei Report*, August 12, 2002.

Ono, Yumiko, "Bandai Shares May Draw Power from Mattel Deal," *Asian Wall Street Journal*, July 26, 1999, p. 11.

Pollack, Andrew, "Is Pippin a Breakthrough or Outmoded on Arrival?" *New York Times*, March 14, 1996, p. D1.

———, "Naoharu Yamashina, Toy Maker, Dies at 79," *New York Times*, October 31, 1997, p. D23.

Sims, Calvin, "Japanese Workers Paid Baby Bonuses," *Globe and Mail*, May 31, 2000, p. A12.

National Council of La Raza

Raul Yzaguirre Building
1126 16th Street NW
Washington, D.C. 20036
U.S.A.
Telephone: (202) 785-1670
Fax: (202) 776-1792
Web site: http://www.nclr.org

Nonprofit Company
Founded: 1968
Employees: 120
Total Assets: $143.26 million (2008)
NAICS: 813319 Community Action Advocacy Organizations

■ ■ ■

The National Council of La Raza (NCLR) is the largest Hispanic civil rights and advocacy organization in the United States and serves as an umbrella association for some 300 local Hispanic organizations. Based in Washington D.C., the NCLR draws from a broad network of local and regional Hispanic organizations to encourage civic participation among Hispanics and to provide decision makers with policy recommendations from an Hispanic point of view. NCLR works to build local capacity with advice on management, governance, and fund raising, as well as providing policy reports on areas of interest to Hispanics. Through its subsidiary Raza Development Fund it provides low-cost loans to Hispanic homeowners and charter schools.

LAUNCHING AN ADVOCACY NETWORK IN THE 1970S

The National Council of La Raza developed during the 1960s, a time of widespread awareness of civil rights issues and social change. Raul Yzaguirre, a native Texan born in 1939, witnessed discrimination against Mexican Americans in the Rio Grande Valley and became inspired by the work of Dr. Hector Garcia, a Mexican-American physician and social activist who served on the U.S. Commission on Civil Rights. Garcia envisioned a national movement defending the civil rights of Hispanics in the United States, and Yzaguirre realized the need for an organization to coordinate and lead the movement.

Yzaguirre sought funding from the Ford Foundation to start a group in the Southwest. While the Foundation turned down Yzaguirre's request, its vice-president was intrigued by the project. He approved a $1 million grant to the University of California at Los Angeles to study the Mexican-American community and searched for respected members of the Hispanic community to travel the country and research the issue. Ultimately, he chose three esteemed Latinos: labor organizer Ernesto Galarza, sociologist Julian Samora, and community organizer Herman Gallegos to survey communities throughout the country and identify specific needs. Together they established the Southwest Council of La Raza in Arizona in 1968. To better reflect its national ambitions, the group changed its name to the National Council of La Raza in 1972 and relocated its headquarters to Washington, D.C., the following year.

COMPANY PERSPECTIVES

■

The term "La Raza" has its origins in early 20th-century Latin American literature and translates into English most closely as "the people," or, according to some scholars, "the Hispanic people of the New World." The term was coined by Mexican scholar José Vasconcelos to reflect the fact that the people of Latin America are a mixture of many of the world's races, cultures, and religions. Some people have mistranslated "La Raza" to mean "The Race," implying that it is a term meant to exclude others. In fact, the full term coined by Vasconcelos, *"La Raza Cósmica,"* meaning the "cosmic people," was developed to reflect not purity but the mixture inherent in the Hispanic people. This is an inclusive concept, meaning that Hispanics share with all other peoples of the world a common heritage and destiny.

Yzaguirre initially worked with La Raza as a consultant before becoming its president in 1974. Throughout his 30-year tenure, the NCLR expanded its reach, ultimately evolving into a national network of community-based organizations working on problems such as education and healthcare. "We started out as an essentially Mexican-American organization in the Southwest," he recalled, "but when I came, I had a different vision of a more pan-Hispanic organization."

In order to strengthen the group's ability to advise public policymakers on issues of particular concern to Hispanics, the NCLR established a Policy Analysis Center in 1980 to collect statistics and information on five key areas: finance, civil rights, education, employment, and healthcare. According to the NCLR, the Center's "unique capacity to provide timely policy analyses, combined with its considerable advocacy expertise, a reputation for political independence, and an identifiable constituency, permits NCLR to play an important role in policy and advocacy efforts."

The NCLR began with a grant of $500,000, and in the early years of its existence, the organization was highly dependent on a variety of grants from its chief benefactor, the Ford Foundation, as well as the federal government and other private-sector donors. By 1981 funding had reached $5 million, and the Council employed a staff of nearly 100. However, federal budget cuts during the administration of President Ronald Reagan targeted many programs on which NCLR depended for funding, and the NCLR was hard hit. "We went from 150 employees to 15 in a matter of six months," Yzaguirre recalled. More diversified funding became a necessity.

ADVOCATING EMPOWERMENT AND CIVIC ENGAGEMENT IN THE 1990S

As the 1980s continued, the NCLR secured funding largely from the private sector, undertook a series of health and education initiatives, and advised the government on such issues as AIDS among the Puerto Rican population. In 1992 the NCLR launched a $20 million pilot program in partnership with the Federal National Mortgage Association (Fannie Mae) to increase Hispanic homeownership. Other programs sought to empower community leaders to help guide policy makers in their local communities and to train young people in leadership and management techniques. In 1994 the NCLR established both the Center for Health Promotion to facilitate work on health issues with its wide network of affiliates and a mentorship initiative known as the Youth Leaders Program. By the mid-1990s the NCLR included more than 150 affiliated community organizations in 37 states, Puerto Rico, and Washington, D.C.

The NCLR also worked on both a national and local level to improve the civic involvement of the U.S. Hispanic population, overcoming such barriers as lack of fundraising and organizational skills. NCLR support services sought to provide training that would help grassroots organizers at the community level and then progress to state and national involvement. "Knowing the right circles and the right places to go to raise money can sometimes be daunting," explained NCLR President Janet Murguia.

MAKING HOMEOWNERSHIP AND HEALTHCARE AFFORDABLE: 1998-2004

In 1998 the organization established the Raza Development Fund, a funding entity that provides low-cost loans to needy borrowers within the Hispanic community. The Development Fund supports affordable housing through predevelopment loans, home loans, construction loans, and home improvement loans. By 2009 the initiative had helped more than 22,000 families purchase their first home.

The Raza Development Fund also finances community facilities, such as health centers, with acquisition, construction, and remodeling loans. Lastly, the Development Fund supports charter schools with financing and refinancing for building purchases, as well

KEY DATES

1968: Southwest Council of La Raza (SWCLR) incorporates in Arizona.
1972: SWCLR changes its name to National Council of La Raza (NCLR) to reflect its national outlook.
1973: NCLR relocates its headquarters to Washington, D.C.
1980: NCLR Policy Analysis Center is established.
1994: NCLR establishes its Center for Health Promotion and launches the Youth Leaders Program.
1998: Raza Development Fund is established.
2000: NCLR launches a $25 million initiative to establish 50 charter schools over five years.
2004: The NCLR Institute for Hispanic Health is launched.
2008: NCLR celebrates its 40th anniversary.

as construction loans, leasehold improvement loans, and lease/loan guarantees. A separate School Building Fund was established in partnership with the community development office of Citibank to oversee a $50 million loan fund for schools. The Fund provided loans of up to $5 million for a term of seven years.

Through its Center for Community Educational Excellence, the NCLR focused on ways to increase literacy, graduation rates, and college preparedness among its core constituency. In 2001 the NCLR launched a five-year, $25 million project to open 50 new Latino charter schools across the United States. NCLR research indicated that charter schools are a particularly effective format in the Hispanic community, as the less regulated curriculum allows for an emphasis on Hispanic culture and unique neighborhood needs. Charter schools also give students and families a sense of ownership in the facility, which increases retention rates. The program expanded to more than 115 charter schools serving 25,000 Latino children by 2009. Parental involvement was considered a key to the success of charter schools. Anthony J. Colon, from NCLR's education division, cited examples of parents doing construction work on charter schools themselves, to reduce costs. "I think that's what we're able to provide with the charter school. A sense of mission. You own it."

In 2003 Janet Murguia was named the executive director and chief operating officer of NCLR, and in 2004 Murguia succeeded Yzaguirre as president and CEO. A lawyer by training, Murguia had worked in the policy community, serving as a legislative counsel to U.S. Representative Jim Slattery and then in the Clinton White House as deputy director of legislative affairs and senior White House liaison to Congress. She also served as deputy campaign manager for Al Gore's 2000 presidential bid.

Also in 2004, in support of improved healthcare among Hispanics, the NCLR established the Institute for Hispanic Health. The Institute focuses on making care more accessible, improving the quality of healthcare, augmenting disease prevention efforts and health education, fostering careers in healthcare, and supporting the public and private healthcare industry. NCLR's healthcare programs served more than 100,000 Latinos each year, through a network of health clinics and programs to train lay health educators to disseminate information and advice on preventative medicine.

A TRULY NATIONAL ORGANIZATION: 2005–09

Through its community and family wealth-building programs the NCLR supported financial services and financial education on such topics as auto and mortgage lending, homeownership, foreclosure proceedings, retirement planning, credit card policies, and credit scoring systems. The organization also sought cultural awareness, calling on the entertainment industry and media outlets to be more aware of racial stereotyping and to include Hispanic perspectives on issues.

By 2009 the NCLR received more than $40 million in grants and contributions, with federal funds amounting to only 11 percent of the total. In addition to hundreds of individual donors, corporate sponsors included the Ford Foundation, Allstate, Bank of America, Chevron, Coca Cola, and Starbucks. With over 40 years of experience and 300 affiliates throughout the country, NCLR had established itself as the premier Hispanic advocacy organization in the United States. However, its influence was unevenly spread across the country, especially in the Deep South and Midwest. "We are not the largest minority in many Midwestern states," Yzaguirre noted. "We have a challenge to create an infrastructure in places where our population is not a majority. That is a milestone that we want to accomplish."

Ann E. Robertson

PRINCIPAL SUBSIDIARIES

Raza Development Fund.

FURTHER READING

Antonio, Sam, "'The Race' to Win America: 'The Race' Presented a Moderate Image at Their Recent Los Angeles Conference, but the Group's Ultimate Goal Is a Radical Reconquest of the Southwestern U.S. for Mexico," *New America*, August 7, 2006, pp. 18-20.

Beirich, Heidi, "What's in a Name? The Defamation of the National Council of La Raza," *Hatewatch*, June 10, 2008.

Martinez, Miriam, "Raul Yzaguirre: President of the National Council of La Raza," *Latino Leaders*, December 2003, pp. 42-43.

McKay, Emily Gantz, *The National Council of La Raza: The First Twenty-Five Years*. National Council of La Raza, 1993.

Rauch, Jonathan, "Charter Schools: A New Hope for America's Latinos," *National Journal*, September 29, 2001, p. 2972.

"Ready to Rumble: Civil Rights Heavyweight Raul Yzaguirre on Life, the Evolution of the NCLR, and Giving Latinos a Fighting Chance," *Latino Leaders*, December 2001, pp. 26-29.

"Ten Questions for Janet Murguia," *Campaigns and Elections*, January 2007, p. 24.

NSTAR

---

800 Boylston Street
Boston, Massachusetts 02199-2599
U.S.A.
Telephone: (617) 424-2000
Fax: (617) 441-8886
Web site: http:// www.nstar.com

Public Company
Incorporated: 1999
Employees: 3,250
Sales: $3.34 billion (2008)
Stock Exchanges: New York
Ticker Symbol: NST
NAICS: 221122 Electric Power Distribution

■ ■ ■

NSTAR is a regulated public utility that provides electricity to the Boston area. Its activities include the generation, purchase, transmission, distribution and sale of electrical power. The company serves about 1.1 million customers in 81 communities with electricity. NSTAR also provides a smaller number of customers with natural gas. The coverage area includes over 1,700 square miles of Massachusetts, including Boston. Utility operations account for roughly 96 percent of NSTAR's sales. The company was created through the 1999 merger of two power companies, Boston Edison Co. Energy and Commonwealth Energy System.

HISTORY OF BOSTON EDISON

The Edison Electric Illuminating Company of Boston, known as Boston Edison, was established in 1886. From the beginning, the company had a reputation for innovation in its industry, which was itself in its infancy. Among the key figures in the formation of Boston Edison were electric industry pioneers Edward H. Johnson and Henry Villard. Financier J. P. Morgan, who had invested in many of the earliest U.S. electric operations, was also involved. The company set up its first station in a two-story building that formerly served as a livery stable and tenement house. Early in 1886 Boston Edison began providing electricity for its first customer, the Bijou Theater, which a few years earlier had become the first electrically lighted theater in the United States, using electricity from an isolated power plant.

By 1887 there was fierce competition for the Boston area's electrical market, with thirteen companies in operation. That year Boston Edison opened a second generating station, installed an underground network to replace its overhead power lines, and hired Charles L. Edgar as a station manager. Edgar eventually became one of the electric industry's most important figures, serving as president of Boston Edison from 1900 to 1932.

During the 1890s Boston Edison vied with another company, Boston Electric Light Co., for dominance in Greater Boston. Negotiations for a merger took place around the turn of the century, but plans for uniting the two companies were shot down by some of Boston Edison's directors, including Edgar. Boston Edison effectively put an end to the territorial battle in 1901 by

COMPANY PERSPECTIVES

The world is embracing a new era in clean energy. Massachusetts is a showcase of fresh ideas, and NSTAR is actively turning new opportunities into viable, real options for our customers. At the same time, we are fully dedicated to our mission of delivering great service to our customers; we're financially strong and disciplined in challenging economic times, and we're optimistic about our future.

purchasing a third rival, Suburban Light and Power Company. Boston Electric Light Co. was finally merged into Boston Edison in 1902, and the company became the area's sole provider of electric power.

The period between the turn of the century and the Depression was one of immense territorial growth, as well as tremendous advances in marketing and engineering, for Boston Edison. In 1903 alone, six neighboring power companies were acquired, including Milton Light & Power Company, Framingham Electric Company, and Somerville Electric Light Company. As the company increased its geographical range, it continued adding generating capacity at its existing plants. Doing so enabled the company to meet the increasing power needs of Bostonians as well as those of its new customers outside the city. Electricity also became less expensive, with the price per kilowatt-hour in Boston dropping by half between 1886 and 1909.

In the early part of the 20th century, Boston Edison launched several successful marketing campaigns to spur the use of electricity, some of which involved demonstrations of electrical appliances. The company also staged exhibits around the area, such as the "Farm of Edison Light and Power" and the "Colonial House of Edison Light." In 1911 Boston Edison became active in the development of electric vehicles. Although electric cars eventually lost the battle against the internal combustion engine, the company's efforts were not entirely wasted. Before World War I many private fleets of electric vehicles, mostly used for delivery, were in operation around Boston.

In 1912 Boston Edison invested heavily in its employees, establishing an Employee Loan Fund, an Accident Prevention Committee, and a Medical Department. In addition, the company built a large recreational and technical complex containing a library, dining room, tennis courts, auditorium, pool tables, and many other amenities. The onset of World War I placed

an entirely new set of demands on the nation's utility companies. Although restrictions were placed on lighting and other uses of electricity in order to conserve fuel, the needs of military manufacturing increased the overall demand for electrical power, improving Boston Edison's balance sheet.

With the continued increase in the use of electrical appliances and the growth of manufacturing in the 1920s, the demand for electrical power expanded precipitously. In 1923 Boston Edison launched its own radio station, WTAT, which it operated out of the back of an REO Speedwagon. WTAT was the first station to be operated by an electric utility company and may have been the first portable radio station in the United States. The following year, the company added WEEI, a more powerful station that stayed in one place. WEEI became a fixture on New England's radio dials, providing a full range of music, sports, and news programming.

Meanwhile, the company continued to expand its generating capacity. A major expansion of its L Street Station, acquired in the Boston Electric merger, was completed in 1920. In 1925 operations began at the company's new Edgar Station in Weymouth. This facility was the first "high-pressure" central station in the world. The following year the company received the Charles A. Coffin award, one of the industry's most prestigious, in recognition of its many technological and marketing innovations.

The onset of the Depression in 1929 brought about a reduction in the use of industrial energy, which was reflected in a reduction in Boston Edison's revenues over the next several years. Offsetting the decline, however, was a rise in residential use of electricity, as more and more electrical devices made their way into American homes. The company continued to devise creative marketing and promotional ideas through the 1930s, including the "Friendly Kitchen," an ongoing demonstration of electric cooking techniques. The further expansion of the WEEI radio station provided still more promotional opportunities.

In 1932 Edgar died, and Walter C. Baylies took his place as company president. By the middle of the 1930s, the Depression had caused even residential use of electricity to level off. During this period the company was unable to begin any major construction projects, and some employees were forced to take wage cuts. In 1937 the company's name was officially changed from Edison Electric Illuminating Company of Boston to the less cumbersome Boston Edison Company. The following year Edison's workers joined the wave of unionization sweeping the country. The United Brotherhood of Edison Workers was made the official collective bargaining representative of company employees.

KEY DATES

∎

1886: The Edison Electric Illuminating Company of Boston is established.

1925: Operations begin at Edgar Station in Weymouth, the first high-pressure central station in the world.

1926: New England Gas and Electric Company is founded.

1971: Commonwealth Gas Co. (COM/Gas) is formed by the merger of the Cambridge and Worcester gas companies.

1999: Boston Edison Co. (BEC) Energy and Commonwealth Energy System merge.

2007: Wind power is added.

2009: Company receives approval of a transmission line for hydropower from Quebec, Canada.

In the early 1940s mobilization for World War II began to increase the demand for power. Around this time, Edison president Frank D. Comerford, who had succeeded Baylies in 1935, announced plans for a large new generating station to be built on the Mystic River in Everett, Massachusetts. The first of Mystic Station's three units went into service in 1943. When Comerford died suddenly in 1941, James V. Toner was chosen as his successor. By the end of the war Boston Edison's geographic expansion had ended, but growth continued as a result of rising consumption among its customers. The company's power plants were generating more than two billion kilowatt-hours of electricity per year. That total was double the amount generated ten years earlier, despite the fact that the company's service area and population had remained relatively stable during that period.

The boom years that followed World War II created a bigger demand than ever for electricity, with the proliferation of washing machines, refrigerators, vacuum cleaners, and other household appliances. Boston Edison sold and actively promoted the use of electrical appliances, selling 861 electric ranges in 1950 alone. The widespread introduction of television also increased company revenues, accounting for an estimated $1.5 million in sales for 1950. During this period Boston Edison met increased demand by adding capacity to its existing facilities. Many of the company's technological advances at this time were in the areas of transmission and distribution. New cable technology allowed more power to reach customers more efficiently.

In 1952 the company reorganized its corporate structure. Two new operating organizations were formed: the Engineering and Construction Organization, headed by John T. Ward, and the Steam and Electric Operations Organization, led by Hugo Wellington. By the mid-1950s demand in the suburbs of Boston had increased so much that six new substations had to be built in 1955 alone. A wave of new industrial and commercial development, particularly along Route 128, made Greater Boston a leading center of high-technology manufacturing in the late 1950s, and Boston Edison prospered. Its largest customer, and the area's biggest employer, was Raytheon Corporation. Other major users of Boston Edison power located along that corridor were Singer Sewing Machine Co. and Union Carbide.

The development of computer technology in the 1950s and 1960s enabled Boston Edison to run its operations at new levels of efficiency. In 1954 the company installed its first computer, an IBM machine used for accounting. In 1959 Boston Edison became the first utility company in New England to install a mainframe (a Univac II), and over the next few years computers became an integral part of every major phase of the company's operations. As its customer base in the outlying areas grew in the late 1950s and early 1960s, the company began establishing service centers to provide technical support in those areas.

In November 1965 a huge blackout struck the entire Northeast; in its wake, most utilities changed the way they operated. Boston Edison installed special jet engine backup generators and changed its switching and communications systems to reduce the likelihood of system failure. The blackout also prompted greater coordination between the various utility networks in the region. Boston Edison joined several inter-utility organizations over the next several years, including the Eastern Massachusetts and Vermont Energy Control in 1967; the Rhode Island-Eastern Massachusetts-Vermont Energy Control in 1969; and the New England Power Pool in 1971. Each of these networks served to centralize, to various degrees, the dispatching and transmission of electricity, thereby maximizing efficiency over a larger area.

In late 1967 Boston Edison began construction on the Pilgrim Station, a nuclear generating facility in Plymouth, Massachusetts. By 1969 company revenues had passed the $200 million mark. Commercial and residential electricity sales each made up about one-third of that total, while industrial sales, sales to other utilities, sales of steam, and street lighting made up the rest. The company's customer base of 583,000 was not much bigger than it had been a decade earlier, but those customers were using more than twice as much power as their 1958 counterparts. As the 1970s began, Boston Edison benefited from a rush of commercial development around the Boston area. Among the construction projects that added significantly to the area's power demands were the Marriott Motor Hotel, an office complex of the First Church of Christ, Scientist, and the John Hancock Building.

The 1970s were turbulent years for the entire energy industry, including Boston Edison. The longest strike in company history, lasting nearly three months, took place in 1971. In December 1972 the Pilgrim Station went into operation. The following year the OPEC oil embargo caused huge increases in fuel prices, with devastating effects on companies such as Boston Edison that used large amounts of oil. In response the company ended its tradition of actively promoting the use of electricity, and by 1974 it had closed the last of its appliance stores. Rising energy prices, combined with a growing public awareness of environmental issues, resulted in decreased energy use by the middle of the decade, and plans for another nuclear facility were dropped. Nevertheless, new, more efficient technology enabled the company to thrive financially despite these pressures. The Edgar generating facility was retired in 1977, placing most of the burden on the new Pilgrim plant.

During the 1980s Boston Edison was plagued by regulatory problems, primarily concerning the Pilgrim plant. In 1982 the Nuclear Regulatory Commission (NRC) hit the company with the largest fine it had ever imposed, $550,000, for a litany of management and physical problems at the facility. Boston Edison spent $300 million on upgrades at the plant, but malfunctions continued to plague Pilgrim, which was the source of 40 percent of the company's power by this time. In 1986 the NRC called Pilgrim one of the six worst-managed nuclear plants in the United States, and Boston Edison was forced to shut the plant down to make wholesale improvements. Leadership of the company changed, with Bernard Reznicek replacing Stephen Sweeney as president. Reznicek received permission to restart Pilgrim in 1989 under a plan whereby the company would be rewarded or punished financially based on the plant's performance.

Meanwhile Boston Edison sought to gear itself for the future. In December 1982 the company launched its IMPACT 2000 initiative, which sought to coordinate the company's conservation, environmental, technological, public relations, and load management goals into a single, coherent package. Among the program's results were the conversion of both the Mystic and New Boston stations to dual fuel capability (the ability to burn both

oil and gas), and the installation of scrubbers on the company's generating stations.

In 1991 Boston Edison experienced further problems with the NRC, when the Yankee Rowe nuclear reactor in Rowe, Massachusetts, which was 10 percent owned by Boston Edison, was forced to close for safety reasons. Nevertheless, the company's financial performance was strong during the early 1990s. With Pilgrim back in operation, Boston Edison was able to improve its position as the second highest–cost electricity producer in Massachusetts in 1987 to the status of second lowest–cost producer in 1992. Its financial performance improved accordingly, from a $16 million deficit in 1989 to a profit of $107 million in 1992. As the 1990s progressed, Boston Edison continued to seek savings through improved technology. Among its breakthroughs were the 1993 development of "smart" meters capable of communicating information directly to the company, eliminating the need for meter readers, and the automation of over-the-counter bill payment. Reznicek resigned as chairman and CEO of Boston Edison in 1994 to become dean of the Creighton University School of Business Administration. He was succeeded by Thomas May, the company's president.

HISTORY OF COMMONWEALTH ELECTRIC

Commonwealth Energy System was the name adopted in 1981 for what had been formerly the New England Gas & Electric Association. New England Gas & Electric was founded on the last day of 1926 as an unincorporated trust to control various gas and electric companies. The oldest of these was the Worcester Gas Light Co., formed in 1849 after winning a contract to provide gas street lighting along Main Street in Worcester, Massachusetts. Another early member of the future system, New Bedford Gas Co., was incorporated in 1850. It absorbed New Bedford Electric Light Co. in 1888 and Edison Electric Illuminating Co. of New Bedford in 1890. This consolidated utility became New Bedford Gas & Edison Light Co. in 1891. Another early unit was Cambridge Electric Light Co., organized in 1886 as one of the first electric utilities in the United States.

At the time of its founding New England Gas & Electric was affiliated with the Associated Gas & Electric system through ownership and control of its common shares by important stockholders and officials of Associated Gas & Electric Co. Associated was one of the eight great systems that, with only a few exceptions, controlled all private gas and electric companies in Massachusetts. In 1928 Associated served 50 cities and towns in the state with an aggregate population of

788,000. By the use of the holding-company device, a relatively small investment could result in control of properties many times greater in value. Associated's capital structure was characterized as early as 1927 as "a financial nightmare," and the company was placed in bankruptcy by the federal Securities and Exchange Commission in 1940.

Before federal legislation enacted in 1935 broke up a number of far-flung combines, New England Gas & Electric owned public electric utilities in New Hampshire, Maine, and the maritime provinces of Canada as well as Massachusetts. In 1930 the system owned and operated nine steam, internal-combustion, and hydroelectric generating stations in Massachusetts, New Hampshire, Nova Scotia, and Prince Edward Island. Its gas plants, which at that time provided manufactured rather than natural gas, served Worcester, Cambridge, New Bedford, and a number of smaller Massachusetts communities. In 1929 New England Gas & Electric served 115,204 electric and 141,343 gas customers. Gross earnings came to $14.5 million that year and gross income to $2.2 million.

Service to Canada ended when New England Gas & Electric divested itself of four utility subsidiaries during 1935 and 1936. By 1940 the New Bedford Gas & Edison Light Co. subsidiary was accounting for more than half of the system's electricity sales, followed by Cambridge Electric Light Co. New Hampshire Gas & Electric Co., serving chiefly Portsmouth, was third in sales of electricity, followed closely by Plymouth County Electric Co. and Cape and Vineyard Electric Co., the latter serving the island of Martha's Vineyard and most of Cape Cod. The system's gas sales were chiefly by its Worcester, Cambridge, and New Bedford subsidiaries. Steam for heating was being sold to Cambridge customers by Cambridge Steam Co. Gross income came to $2.8 million in 1939 and net income to $298,424.

Except for the divestiture of electric service to Calais, Maine, the scope of New England Gas & Electric's operations remained the same in the 1940s. In 1950 it was providing electric service to about 151,000 customers in 77 communities and gas service to about 169,000 customers in 39 communities. There was no direct competition in kind from any privately or municipally owned public utility. New England Gas & Electric had taken a 36 percent stake in Algonquin Gas Transmission Co., a company formed in 1949 for the purpose of building natural-gas pipeline. The system's total operating revenues rose from $19.4 million in 1944 to $31.2 million in 1950. Net income rose from $520,864 to more than $2.3 million over the same period.

In 1954 New England Gas & Electric sold its New Hampshire Electric Co. subsidiary and New Hampshire's subsidiary, Kittery Electric Light Co., to Public Service Co. of New Hampshire, thereby restricting its operations to Massachusetts. Due to consolidation, by 1960 only seven operating subsidiaries remained in the system: Cambridge Electric Light Co., Cambridge Gas Co., Cambridge Steam Corp., Cape and Vineyard Electric Co., New Bedford Gas & Edison Light Co., Plymouth County Electric Co., and Worcester Gas Light Co. Electric and gas service now was being provided to 41 communities each. Operating revenues increased from $34 million in 1951 to $52 million in 1959, while net income rose from $2.4 million to $3.8 million during the same period.

New England Gas & Electric fully entered the atomic age in 1968, when the Yankee nuclear power plant began operations in Rowe, Massachusetts. The system took a combined interest, through a consortium, of 15.5 percent in four such plants. The others were Connecticut Yankee of Haddam, Connecticut; Maine Yankee of Wiscasset, Maine; and Vermont Yankee of Vernon, Vermont, all of which became operational in 1972. The Rowe facility was closed in 1992.

In 1966 New England Gas & Electric's operating revenues reached $75 million, and net income was $7.2 million. One of the system's assets was the rise in the year-round population of Cape Cod from 37,000 in 1940 to an estimated 85,000 in 1965. A new subsidiary, Canal Electric Co., formed in 1966, was completing a 560-megawatt oil-fired electric generating station in Sandwich, Massachusetts, at the eastern end of Cape Cod Canal. This facility soon was providing 70 percent of the system's electrical capacity, three-fourths of which was being sold to other utilities. In Cambridge, an influx of diverse industries and research institutes was increasing sales volume. A new superhighway promised to attract industry to Worcester.

The system's electric service was in 1967 reaching about 200,000 customers in 41 communities, while natural gas was being distributed to 177,000 customers in 44 communities, 10 of which were also being served by the system's electricity. Natural gas was being supplied to companies under long-term contracts with Tennessee Gas Transmission Co. as well as by Algonquin Gas Transmission Co. Among the 40-odd Cambridge Steam customers, the best known were Harvard University and Massachusetts Institute of Technology.

In 1971 preliminary agreement was reached for the purchase of a still-uncompleted liquefied natural-gas facility at Hopkinton, Massachusetts, in a joint venture with Air Products and Chemicals, Inc. This facility, which became operational in 1972, gave the system a gas surplus during periods of extreme weather that was also available for sale to other gas companies. COM/

Energy bought out its partner in 1985, but Air Products and Chemicals continued to operate and maintain the facility under contract.

Commonwealth Gas Co. (COM/Gas) was formed in 1971 by the merger of the Cambridge and Worcester gas companies. In the same year Cape and Vineyard was merged into New Bedford Gas & Edison Light. This subsidiary was renamed Commonwealth Electric Co. (COM/Electric) in 1981. Meanwhile, Canal Electric was constructing another large oil-fired generating plant in Sandwich in partnership with Montaup Electric Co. It became operational in 1976.

New England Gas & Electric's record income of $9.6 million in 1967 was not matched until 1971 because of a combination of factors, including higher interest expenses and increased local taxes. By 1981, when New England Gas & Electric Association was renamed Commonwealth Energy System, operating revenues had reached $512.5 million and net income $26.9 million. The number of customers receiving electric service in the system's 41 communities had reached about 267,900. The number of communities receiving gas had reached 47 (of which 12 also received electricity from the system), and the number of customers had reached about 194,600. Also in that year, COM/Gas purchased the gas business and assets of New Bedford Gas & Edison Light, subsequently Commonwealth Electric Co. (COM/Electric).

COM/Energy weathered better than most public utilities the petroleum shortages and price hikes of the 1970s and early 1980s and the waning of nuclear power as an alternative generating fuel. Between 1984 and 1988 it had the third-best annual average return on equity among 24 Northeast utilities, with 17 percent. It had the second-lowest percentage of debt to equity among the 24 in this period, at 75.5 percent.

In the early 1990s, however, COM/Electric came under fire from the Massachusetts Department of Public Utilities for its rates, which were second-highest in the state and among the highest in the country. An audit commissioned by the department in 1991 recommended 62 changes, including stricter budgeting and control processes, more competitive bidding and monitoring of outside service vendors, and major improvements in customer service. In 1993 the state's Division of Energy Resources responded to a Cambridge Electric request for a 10 percent rate hike by asking it and COM/Electric to explore mergers with two competing utilities. State officials were said to feel that Massachusetts's eight electric companies were too many and that high electric rates were a factor in the high cost of doing business there.

The typical COM/Electric residential customer was using about 500 kilowatt-hours of electricity a month in early 1993 and paying $70 per month. The average cost of 14 cents per kilowatt-hour compared with a typical charge of 11 cents per kilowatt-hour by other state electric utilities. In April 1993 COM/Electric announced that it was laying off between 150 and 175 employees in all departments to cut costs. The COM/Energy system also, in 1995, curtailed power purchases from a costly cogeneration plant in Lowell, Massachusetts, and bought out a contract to purchase power supplies from a plant in Pepperell, Massachusetts.

COM/Electric announced a four-year, $10.8 million rate cut in April 1995, which it attributed to its "aggressive cost-cutting" efforts. However, an official in the state attorney general's office said some of the reduction was owed to customers because of "power outages due to management mistakes" and attributed some of the rest to accounting matters that had nothing to do with cost-cutting. As part of the deal with the attorney general's office, COM/Electric agreed to refund to customers half of any earnings above 9.5 percent of revenues through 1998.

COM/Energy's operating revenues rose from $835.8 million in 1990 to $978.6 million in 1994. Of the 1994 total 65 percent came from electricity, 33 percent from gas, and 2 percent from steam. Net income grew from $22.6 million to almost $49 million in this period. Consolidated long-term debt was $418.3 million at the end of 1994.

The system had 356,697 electricity customers at the end of 1994, of which residential customers numbered 311,153. Of its 8.4 million megawatt-hours of electricity sales in 1994, residential sales made up 21 percent; commercial sales, 24 percent; industrial sales, 5 percent; other sales, 5 percent; and wholesale sales to other systems, 45 percent. Of 231,609 natural gas customers at the end of 1994, 211,075 were residential. Of 47.4 billion BTUs of gas sales in 1994, residential sales accounted for 45 percent; commercial sales, 23 percent; industrial sales, 9 percent; other sales, 4 percent; and interruptible and other sales, 19 percent.

COM/Energy system companies owned electric-power generating facilities with capability of 1,046.5 megawatts at the end of 1994. Cambridge Electric Co. had two steam electric-generating stations in Cambridge with a capability of 76.5 megawatts. Canal Electric Co., which did not serve retail customers, owned and operated the 560-megawatt oil-fired steam-generating unit (Unit No. 1) at Sandwich and operated and owned half of the similar 584-megawatt unit (Unit No. 2) at Sandwich. Three-fourths of Unit No. 1's capacity was being sold to neighboring utilities under long-term contract. Canal Electric also had a minor ownership interest in the Seabrook (New Hampshire) 1 nuclear power plant, from which it received 40.5 megawatt capability, and COM/Electric had a minor interest in Central Maine Power Company's oil-fired Wyman Unit 4, from which it received 8.8 megawatt capability. COM/Electric's 60 megawatt New Bedford steam electric-generating plant closed in 1993.

Through equity ownership in Hydro-Quebec Phase II, a Canadian waterpower project, Canal had an entitlement of 67.9 megawatts of electricity. From four nuclear units, an additional 140.7 megawatts were available to the COM/Energy system, which had an equity interest in the Connecticut Yankee, Maine Yankee, and Vermont Yankee units, but not in the fourth, the Pilgrim nuclear power plant in Plymouth, Massachusetts. COM/Energy and its units also purchased and exchanged power with other companies in order to reduce its reliance on oil. Of COM/Energy's retail energy generation in 1994, 38 percent was fueled by natural gas, 25 percent by nuclear power, 24 percent from oil, 2 percent from hydro (waterpower), and 11 percent from waste-to-energy and other sources.

In 1986 COM/Energy sold its interest in Algonquin Gas Transmission Co. to Texas Eastern Corp. for $56.3 million. Prior to a federal order that became effective in 1993, COM/Gas purchased most of its natural gas from either Algonquin or Tennessee Gas Pipeline Co. Following the order, which required interstate pipelines to unbundle existing gas sales contracts into separate components, it turned to third-party vendors for gas while continuing to purchase transportation, storage, and balancing services from Tennessee, Algonquin, and other companies. Hopkinton LNG Corp., another COM/Energy subsidiary, had a liquefaction plant and three above-ground storage tanks in Hopkinton, Massachusetts, and a satellite vaporization plant in Acushnet, Massachusetts, with additional storage capacity. The system's gas properties included 2,761 miles of gas distribution lines at the end of 1994.

COM/Energy Steam Co. was purchasing steam produced by Cambridge Electric in connection with the latter's generation of electricity and was also producing steam itself. In 1994 it distributed steam to 20 customers in Cambridge and to Massachusetts General Hospital in Boston, but in 1995 MIT, its largest customer, turned to cogeneration. During 1994 the company sold a record 1.5 billion pounds of steam. COM/Energy Services Co. provided essential services to the system and its subsidiaries, including executive and financial management, accounting, data processing, and legal and other services.

1999–2009: MERGER AND THE NEW COMPANY—NSTAR

NSTAR was created in 1999 through the merger of Boston Electric Co. Energy and Commonwealth Energy System. As the energy industry began to go through deregulation, Massachusetts was one of the first states to embrace competition in the energy market. Boston Electric began selling off some of its assets and reduced customer rates by 15 percent in anticipation of the merger.

Boston Electric saw that the energy field was going to be dominated by a small number of large companies and set out to acquire the necessary competencies to become one of the companies left standing after deregulation. One of the first tasks was to increase its customer base. By merging with Commonwealth Energy, the new NSTAR had an immediate customer base of 1.1 million, where Boston Electric had roughly half that.

Not everything went smoothly in the transition. There were significant problems with blackouts due to heat in the first summer after the merger. There were complaints that the company was too big and that it took too long to get power restored. One restaurant in Brookline, Massachusetts, complained that because power outages were happening during the middle of the day, four outages of roughly four hours each cost the restaurant $40,000 in lost revenue.

NSTAR also received some bad press early on for raising its rates. The state attorney general testified at a Department of Telecommunications and Energy hearing that NSTAR had not done enough to try to accomplish efficiencies in other areas before raising rates. NSTAR officials argued that the rate increases were directly related to the higher cost of oil. They also pointed to over $1 billion of savings already reaped by customers due to previous efficiency efforts.

By 2007 much of the controversy surrounding NSTAR had passed. NSTAR continued to lower gas prices to residential customers, which helped their public perception. In 2007 NSTAR announced its intention to allow residential and business customers to buy their electricity from wind farms. This environmentally responsible option would cost more for the customers who chose it, but NSTAR was hoping customers would happily pay a little more for the opportunity to benefit the environment.

In 2009 NSTAR made another green-friendly business move. Along with another large New England energy supplier, Northeast Utilities, NSTAR received approval for a high-voltage transmission line to bring hydropower from Quebec, Canada. The project was expected to have a tremendous positive environmental impact, reducing greenhouse gas emissions by four to six million tons per year in New England. NSTAR also began offering a free home energy assessment and added solar power to its portfolio of green energy options.

Robert Jacobson

PRINCIPAL SUBSIDIARIES

Boston Edison Co.; Commonwealth Electric; Cambridge Electric; NSTAR Gas.

PRINCIPAL COMPETITORS

Energy East Corporation; Northeast Utilities; National Grid USA.

FURTHER READING

"Boston Edison Automates Over-the-Counter Payments," *Electrical World*, July 1993, p. 13.

"Boston Edison Reorganizes," *Electrical World*, March 17, 1952, p. 29.

Burr, Michael T, "NSTAR Forges New Model as Wires and Pipes Utility," *Electric Light & Power*, March 2000, p. 16.

Campanella, Frank W., "Big Commercial Demand Sparks Boston Edison," *Barron's*, September 14, 1970, p. 28.

Cavanaugh, H. A., "Having 'Created the Future' at Boston Edison, Reznicek Returns to Omaha," *Electrical World*, August 1994, pp. 9–10.

"Earnings Growth Plus Good Yield," *Financial World*, January 12, 1972, p. 7.

"FERC Approves Funding Plan for Major International Transmission Project," *Transmission & Distribution World*, May 26, 2009.

"From NStar, an Offer in the Wind," *Boston Globe*, July 25, 2007.

"It Electrified the Proper Bostonians," *Electrical World*, June 25, 1951, pp. 11–12.

Kripalani, Manjeet, "Who Needs Meter Readers?" *Forbes*, August 30, 1993, pp. 46–48.

"Low-Cost Facilities Help Fuel Boston Edison Gains," *Barron's*, June 30, 1969, pp. 29–30.

"Northeast Utilities and NSTAR Jointly Pursue Quebec Solutions to New England's Energy Needs," *Transmission & Distribution World*, December 22, 2008, p. 1360.

Qualters, Sheri, "NSTAR Service Generates Complaints from the Suburbs," *Boston Business Journal*, July 27, 2001, p. 6.

Sicilia, David B., *Boston Edison Centennial 1886-1986: History of the Boston Edison Company*, Boston: Boston Edison Company, 1986.

Smith, William D., "Construction Plans for Nuclear Plants Canceled by Utility," *New York Times*, June 29, 1974, p. 1.

Therrien, Lois, "Boston Edison Gets the Work: Fix the Nuke or Fold It," *Business Week*, June 30, 1986, pp. 39–40.

Wald, Matthew L., "A-Plant to Close over Safety Issue," *New York Times*, October 2, 1991, p. Al.

OLYMPUS®

Olympus Corporation

Monolith, 3-1 Nishi-Shinjuku 2-chome,
Shinjuku-ku Tokyo, 163-0914
Japan
Telephone: (+81 813) 3340-2111
Fax: (+81 813) 3340-2062
Web site: http://www.olympus.co.jp/en/

Public Company
Founded: 1919
Employees: 36,772
Sales: $10.75 billion (2008)
Stock Exchanges: Tokyo
Ticker Symbol: OCPNY
NAICS: 333314 Optical Instrument and Lens Manufacturing; 333315 Photographic and Photocopying Equipment Manufacturing; 334310 Audio and Video Equipment Manufacturing; 334510 Electromedical and Electrotherapeutic Apparatus Manufacturing; 335999 All Other Miscellaneous Electrical Equipment and Component Manufacturing

■ ■ ■

The Olympus Corporation is a leading manufacturer of precision optical lenses and equipment. Since its early years as a maker of thermometers and microscopes in Japan during the 1920s, the company has expanded its core product line to include cameras, audio-visual equipment, medical imaging instruments, multimedia devices, and more. Over the course of its history, the company has grown into a formidable global presence, establishing operations throughout North and South America, Europe, and Asia. With annual revenues of close to ¥1 trillion and a staff of more than 35,000 employees, Olympus has consistently ranked among the elite companies in its field, both in Japan and abroad.

THE MICROSCOPE MANUFACTURER'S EARLY YEARS: 1919–35

The original incarnation of Olympus was founded by Takeshi Yamashita, a former lawyer and businessman who had enjoyed considerable success as a sugar trader. After earning substantial profits for his employer, the trading company Tokiwa Shokai, Yamashita began to explore the possibility of creating a new business. To help launch the venture, he recruited an old friend, Shintaro Terada, who made his living building thermometers and microscopes. Terada had established a reputation throughout Japan for his innovative microscope designs; he played a key role in developing the M&KATERA brand of microscopes for the medical equipment manufacturer Iwashiya, and one of his instruments won a bronze medal at the 1914 Taisho Expo. At Yamashita's urging, Terada agreed to join the new company as chief engineer. Officially formed in 1919, the company was called Takachiho Seisakusho, after Mount Takachiho; according to legend, the mountain's peak, Takamagahara, was the mythical dwelling place of eight million Japanese deities.

Takachiho Seisakusho unveiled its debut microscope, the Asahi, in March 1920. Six additional new models followed that same year, including the

COMPANY PERSPECTIVES

■

At Olympus, we believe that the key to making dreams of the future come true lies in opening the mind to possibilities. Thus, we see our purpose lying in people's dreams and ideas as we work to create new value for future generations.

Our overriding passion is to help people around the world have healthier and more fulfilling lives.

This purpose and passion drive us in each of our business areas—such as Medical, Imaging and Life Science—where we are constantly striving to hone the human resources and technologies essential to the creation of new value.

Homare, one of the first industrial microscopes made of brass, and the Fuji. The company's microscopes were aimed primarily at the medical and textile industries, although the Homare was also marketed for use in schools. At the time there was considerable demand for Takachiho's products in the sericulture (or silk farming) trade, as microscopes proved particularly valuable in detecting diseases in silkworms. Because Yamashita's former employer had invested substantial resources in Takachiho Seisakusho, while also taking responsibility for marketing and promoting its products, the company's first line of microscopes was launched under the Tokiwa Shokai name. In 1921, however, the company began marketing its microscopes under the brand Olympus, choosing the name as a way of signifying the exceptional quality of its products.

Over the next few years Takachiho continued to develop new applications for its microscopes, while also manufacturing a line of clinical thermometers. It quickly became clear that Takachiho's microscopes were the key to its future, however, and in 1923 the company sold its thermometer division in order to focus on its core business. Throughout the remainder of the decade, the company made considerable advances in its microscope technology, gearing many of its new products toward scientific research. Notable among these was the Showa GK biological microscope. Launched in collaboration with Iwasaki Microscopes Co. Ltd. in 1927, the Showa GK employed an innovative oil immersion objective lens, which enabled researchers to achieve a magnification of 1000—or roughly 40 percent greater than the company's first Asahi model.

In spite of this improvement, the Showa GK was still considered inferior to more advanced microscopes being imported from Europe at the time. While Takachiho's microscopes were less expensive than their European counterparts, founder Yamashita recognized that establishing a reputation for technical excellence would be essential to the company's long-term success. Intent on capturing a distinctive niche for the company, Yamashita became determined to create high-quality microscopes that were also affordable. Later in 1927 the company released its most advanced microscope to date, the Seika GE. With a magnification power of 1400 times, the Seika GE was considered one of the most advanced microscopes on the market. The instrument went on to receive one of the highest honors at the 1928 Tokyo Exhibition for the Promotion of Domestically Made Products and was later presented as a gift to the Emperor Hirohito, whose intellectual pursuits included research in the field of marine biology.

In the early 1930s with the onset of the Great Depression, as many corporations across the globe were struggling, Takachiho was beginning to thrive. In 1929 the company received an order for 600 microscopes from the Dental and Medical Technical College in Osaka; that year it unveiled its first shared viewing microscope, designed especially for use in university and medical school laboratories. Two new models designed for general use, the Fuji OCE and the Kokka OCD, were launched in 1931. In 1932 Takachiho garnered the top award at the fourth Hatsumei Hakurankai Expo. In 1935 the company produced the Mizuho LCE, with a magnification of 2000 times. Hailed for its clarity and accuracy, as well as for the simplicity of its design, the Mizuho LCE was considered one of the Takachiho's most important achievements of the decade.

NEW BUSINESS OPPORTUNITIES: 1935–50

By the mid-1930s Takachiho Seisakusho had emerged as one of the leading microscope manufacturers in Japan. As its product line expanded and its capitalization increased, it began to devote additional resources to developing a wider variety of applications for its lenses. One critical area of research was initiated in 1934, when the company decided to explore the possibility of manufacturing cameras. The company had worked with photographic technology as early as the mid-1920s, when it developed the Olympus Microphotograph Apparatus PMA and PMB and the Olympus Microphoto for use with its microscopes. With this foundation of research already in place, the leap to manufacturing cameras for consumer use was a relatively simple one.

KEY DATES

1919: Takeshi Yamashita founds Takachiho Sei-sakusho, a manufacturer of thermometers and microscopes.

1920: Company unveils debut microscope, the Asahi 600x, along with its first clinical thermometer.

1921: First "Olympus" trademark is registered.

1936: Company opens Shibuya Plant; debut camera, the Semi-Olympus I, is launched.

1942: Takachiho Seisakusho is renamed Takachiho Optical Co. Ltd.

1944: Company opens Ina Plant.

1949: Company is renamed Olympus Optical Co. Ltd.

1950: Olympus creates the prototype for its first gastrocamera.

1963: Olympus founds the Hachioji Technology Research Institute in Tokyo.

1964: Company's first overseas subsidiary, Olympus Optical Co. (Europa) GmbH (OE), opens in Hamburg, West Germany.

1968: Olympus Corporation of America is formed.

1971: Olympus begins marketing the ACA-III chemistry analyzer.

1979: Company launches the Olympus XA, the first camera to feature a sliding lens barrier.

1987: Olympus acquires KeyMed Ltd. (UK).

1996: Company launches Camedia C-820L digital camera.

2003: Olympus Optical Co. Ltd. is renamed Olympus Corporation.

2009: Olympus sells chemistry analysis business to Beckman Coulter Inc.

In order to launch the new division, the company hired a student from the University of Tokyo Research Institute, Eiichi Sakurai, who was known for his expertise in the field. A year after joining the company, Sakurai completed work on his first camera lens, the Zuiko. The company mounted the lens on a body manufactured by Proud, a Japanese camera maker, and in 1936 began marketing its preliminary camera under the name Semi-Olympus I. The Semi-Olympus I was immediately recognized for its exceptional quality, as well as its high price; at ¥105 yen, it cost roughly 50 percent more than the average Japanese worker's monthly salary.

In 1936 the company relocated its headquarters to a new facility in the Shibuya district of Tokyo. Over the next couple of years the company expanded its line of camera components. The first camera manufactured exclusively with Takachiho parts, the Semi-Olympus II, was released in 1938. At the same time, the company began to integrate its photographic technology into its microscopes. The first Takachiho microscope with built-in photographing capability, the Super Photo, appeared in 1938. Meanwhile, the company's third camera, the Olympus Six, debuted in 1940. The Olympus Six featured a maximum shutter speed of 1/200 of a second and would serve as the basic model for some of the company's best-selling cameras well into the 1950s.

Takachiho suspended its manufacturing operations for the duration of World War II. In 1942 the company was renamed the Takachiho Optical Co. Ltd.; two years later Takachiho opened a new plant in the city of Ina. The company emerged from the war years with the unveiling of its latest microscope, a retooled version of the Showa GK in 1946. Another new offering, the GC, appeared the following year. In 1948 the company resumed its camera production operations with the launch of two major new products: the Olympus 35I, the first 35-millimeter camera made in Japan, and the Olympus Chrome Six I. The Chrome Six proved especially popular among consumers; the camera arrived at a time when amateur photography was rapidly becoming a fashionable hobby in Japan, and reports of customers lined up outside camera stores to purchase it were common during this time.

In 1949 Takachiho changed its name again, becoming Olympus Optical Co. Ltd. That year, a faculty member at the University of Tokyo Medical Center asked the company to build a camera device with the ability to take pictures of the inside of the human stomach. The task posed unique challenges to the company, as the new camera would need particularly small lenses; its developers would also need to address issues of lighting and waterproofing. Within a year, a prototype of the company's first gastrocamera was unveiled at the 1950 Japan Surgery Conference. Although the instrument was not quite ready for practical use, it would soon become the foundation of an important new business line for Olympus.

RAPID EXPANSION: 1950–80

Olympus entered the 1950s as one of the leading camera manufacturers in Japan. In 1951 the company released the Olympus Chrome Six IIIA. The camera featured a unique film stabilizer function, which helped establish unprecedented clarity in picture quality. The Olympus Flex I, the company's first camera to feature a dual lens, debuted in 1952. Although praised for its exceptional quality and multiple features, the camera's price tag was particularly steep; at a cost of ¥47,000, the Flex I was well out of range for the majority of Japanese consumers.

In 1953 the company relocated its headquarters to the Hatagaya district of Tokyo. Two years later the company unveiled a complete line of new cameras, among them the Olympus Chrome Six RIIA and the Olympus 35 S-3.5; 1955 also saw the release of the popular Olympus Wide, the company's first camera to feature a wide-angle lens. More significantly, in 1959 the company announced the release of the first Olympus Pen, variations of which would dominate the company's camera line for much of the 1960s. Throughout this period Olympus also continued to make advances in the production of high-precision microscopes. The company's DF Biological Microscope, which featured an exterior light source and improved focusing capabilities, appeared in 1957. A year later the company unveiled its new E microscope body, which quickly earned a reputation as one of the most precise microscopic instruments on the market. The F microscope body, an improved version of the E series, debuted in 1960, while the SZ Stereo Microscope, the first microscope to feature a zoom function, was released in 1961.

In the 1960s, after decades of steady growth in the domestic market, Olympus began to explore new business opportunities abroad. The company's first international subsidiary, Olympus Optical Co. (Europa) GmbH, opened in 1964 in Hamburg, Germany. In 1968 the company founded the Olympus Corporation of America, with the aim of selling its scientific and medical optical products directly within the United States. Throughout the decade, the company continued to be one of Japan's leading innovators in the field of microscope design and manufacturing. One of its most significant new models was the Photomax (LB) Premier Universal Microscope. Released in 1966, the Photomax enabled users to take color photographs, and it became the foundation for the company's microscopy research for the next several years. In 1969 the company signaled its entrance into the audiovisual market with the release of the Zuiko Pearlcorder, the first microcassette recorder aimed at the consumer market.

At the onset of the 1970s Olympus continued to diversify its product line. One area where the company identified future opportunity was in the field of diagnostic analysis. First developed in 1969 and released into the marketplace two years later, the ACA-III was the company's first high-volume chemistry analyzer. Although the machine's processing capacity was relatively slow, its fully automated analysis system was considered a breakthrough in the field of pathology, and interest in the new analyzers grew quickly within the Japanese scientific and medical communities. To meet demand, the company launched several new diagnostic machines over the next several years, notably the ACA-201, which quickly became the model for the company's future high-speed analysis systems.

Throughout the 1970s the company continued to make advances in its core product line. The release of the Olympus FTL camera in 1971 signified the company's first attempt to market a camera aimed at overseas customers; the camera was replaced by the lightweight OM-1 in 1973. By the end of the decade the company had pioneered the construction of lightweight, high-quality cameras, culminating with the 1979 release of the Olympus XA. Built with the world's first sliding lens protector, the XA eliminated the need for a case, making it among the most portable and convenient cameras on the market. The Olympus XA2, a simplified version of the XA geared for beginner photographers, appeared a year later.

NEW TECHNOLOGIES, NEW PRODUCTS: 1980–2009

Entering the 1980s, Olympus continued to keep abreast of the latest improvements in camera technology. In 1981 the company introduced its Olympus C-AF, its first camera built with an automatic focus feature. Throughout the first half of the decade, Olympus also made significant advances in its other product lines. Its EU-M1 ultrasound endoscope appeared in 1982, and its PK7000 blood analysis system was released in 1983. A year later the company launched its SZH, the company's debut series of stereo microscopes.

By the middle of the decade, however, the company had fallen into a minor slump, caused primarily by poor camera sales. The problem could largely be traced to the MUXXUM 7000, an auto-focus camera manufactured by rival Minolta Camera Co. The widespread popularity of the MUXXUM 7000, particularly in the United States, led to a precipitous decline in consumer demand for similar Olympus cameras, and overall sales for the division had fallen roughly 10 percent by the fall of 1985. To help combat this decline in revenues, Olympus unveiled a series of cameras with a range of new features; notable among these was the company's first compact waterproof camera, the Olympus AF-1 Quartz Date, which hit the market in 1986. More impressive was the 1991 release of the Olympus Stylus, which quickly earned acclaim for its sleek design and variety of functions. In ensuing years the company continued to add new features to the Stylus line, and it soon became one of the best-selling cameras in the world.

By the second half of the decade, digital technology had become a major part of the camera industry. Olympus introduced its first digital still camera aimed at consumers, the Camedia C-820L, in July 1996. With a pixel resolution of 810,000, the camera boasted a picture quality far superior than that offered by its competitors. An upgraded version of the camera, the Camedia C-1400L, was released in 1997. The new model featured a resolution of 1.41 megapixels and was hailed by analysts as one of the most innovative digital cameras on the market. Indeed, the company's digital cameras garnered roughly 25 industry awards in the second half of 1997 alone. With total sales of digital cameras reaching 3.6 million units worldwide in 1998, the company's lead position with the new technology promised to pay dividends into the 21st century.

In late 2000 the company established Olympus Korea. Shortly after launching operations on the peninsula, Olympus had seized a 4 percent share of the country's digital camera market; in less than a year this number skyrocketed to 25 percent. In 2002 the company established a presence in the Philippines, opening a manufacturing facility in the nation's Mactan Economic Zone. That year the company launched the Evis Lucera, the world's first high-definition endoscopic video imaging system. In 2003 the company officially became known as the Olympus Corporation.

By 2004 Olympus was third only to Canon and Sony in the global digital camera market. As demand for digital cameras began to decline mid-decade, however, the company found itself struggling to remain profitable. While the company enjoyed profits of ¥33.6 billion in 2003, it suffered losses of ¥11.8 billion a year later. To address the issue of declining earnings, the company embarked on a major restructuring, cutting close to 4,000 employees worldwide. In early 2006 the company decided to focus on manufacturing high-end digital cameras, in the hope of seizing a dominant share of this small but lucrative market. The move proved to be a shrewd one, as company earnings rose by 57.9 percent for the year, largely through sales of its cameras and endoscopes.

In late 2007 Olympus acquired British medical technology firm Gyrus for ¥210 billion. Many analysts viewed the purchase as a precautionary measure designed to stabilize the company's bottom line in an era of increasing instability for the digital camera industry. In March 2009, as camera sales continued to slump, the company was forced to sell its lucrative diagnostic analysis division as a way of streamlining its operations. Under the terms of the deal, Olympus sold the profitable unit to the American company Beckman Coulter Inc. for ¥77.5 billion. As the first decade of the new century drew to a close, it remained to be seen what other changes the company might be forced to implement in order to remain strong in its core businesses.

Stephen Meyer

PRINCIPAL SUBSIDIARIES

Olympus Imaging Corp.; Olympus Medical Systems Corp.; ITX Corporation; Olympus Corporation of the Americas (USA); Olympus Europa Holding GmbH (Germany); KeyMed (Medical & Industrial Equipment) Ltd. (UK); Olympus (China) Co. Ltd.

PRINCIPAL COMPETITORS

Boston Scientific Corporation (U.S.); Canon Inc.; Carl-Zeiss-Stiftung (Germany); Casio Computer Co. Ltd.; Covidien PLC (Ireland); Fujifilm Holding Corporation; Hoya Corporation; Leica Camera AG (Germany); Nikon Corporation; Panasonic Corporation; Sony Corporation.

FURTHER READING

Bolger, Joe, "Slower Camera Sales a Worry for Olympus," *Times* (London), May 10, 2005, p. 41.

Hoshi, Masamichi, "Hard Times Forcing Olympus to Shed Diagnostic Systems Business," *Nikkei Weekly* (Japan), March 16, 2009.

Inai, Soichi, "Olympus Thriving in Volatile Digicam Market," *Nikkei Weekly* (Japan), May 21, 2007.

———, "Olympus to Acquire Gyrus in Hopes of Stabilizing Earnings," *Nikkei Weekly* (Japan), November 26, 2007.

Kirk, Don, "Olympus Focuses on Digital Cameras," *International Herald Tribune*, November 11, 1999, p. 6.

Kunii, Irene M., "How Olympus Is Scaling the Heights," *Business Week*, July 14, 2003, p. 38.

Layne, Nathan, "Olympus Hit Hard by Digital Era," *Business Day* (South Africa), November 9, 2004, p. 17.

Lim, Roland, "Olympus Banks on Higher-end Digicams," *Business Times Singapore*, February 20, 2006.

Long, Don, "Olympus Gets into Digital Imaging Game," *Toronto Star*, January 15, 1998, p. J5.

Pereira, Geoffrey, "Power or Convenience? New Models from Olympus and Panasonic Illustrate How Some Digital Cameras Are Made to Be Lifestyle Items while Others Are Built to Perform," *Business Times Singapore*, April 25, 2005.

Soto, Carlos A., "Olympus Digital Earns Top Grade," *Washington Post*, November 21, 2002, p. E9.

Sung-jin, Yang, "Digital Camera Market Expanding Rapidly," *Korea Herald*, December 29, 2003.

Oplink Communications, Inc.

46335 Landing Parkway
Fremont, California 94538-6407
U.S.A.
Telephone: (510) 933-7200
Fax: (510) 933-7300
Web site: http://www.oplink.com

Public Company
Founded: 1995
Incorporated: 1995
Employees: 2,828
Sales: $176.25 million (2009 est.)
Stock Exchanges: NASDAQ
Ticker Symbol: OPLK
NAICS: 334210 Telephone Apparatus Manufacturing; 333314 Optical Instrument and Lens Manufacturing; 237130 Power and Communication System Construction

■ ■ ■

Oplink Communications, Inc., is a manufacturer of fiber optic components that are essential in building modern communications networks. Since its founding in 1995, the company has branched out from making components for fiber optics systems to designing complete subsystems that serve the specific needs of its customers. These products include components that expand and improve the capacity of fiber optic networks by dividing, amplifying, and managing the light waves that carry signals across networks, making the most of the higher bandwidth that fiber optic filaments can

handle. With a strong research and development department and the ability to integrate mechanical and software solutions into their products, Oplink has positioned itself to adapt to the continually growing needs of 21st century communications providers.

COMPANY ORIGINS

Oplink was founded in 1995 in Fremont, California. Its principal founder, Joseph Y. Liu, had an extensive background in semiconductors. He spent 10 years serving as chairman and CEO of Techlink Semiconductor and Equipment Corp., a company with offices in California and China. Liu had been educated in both countries, receiving his bachelor's from Chinese Cultural University in Taiwan and his master's from California State University at Chico. During his years at Techlink he realized that combining high-tech U.S. innovations with cost-effective Chinese manufacturing techniques resulted in quality products that cost less and could be marketed to a wider range of clients. Oplink was founded to bring the same approach to manufacturing products for the fiber optics market.

Oplink introduced its first products in 1996 and by 2000 had a wide range of merchandise designed to improve the amount of bandwidth communications providers could get out of their systems. These products included couplers and splitters, which join and split light signals; multiplexers, which transmit multiple signals at different wavelengths of light on the same fiber; and switches, which move optical signals to selected outputs. Whether their customers were providing connections over long distances or to individual

COMPANY PERSPECTIVES

Oplink is emerging as an optical partner with the management depth, resources and expertise of a larger company and the flexibility and agility of a smaller firm. Our Photonic Foundry gives us a cost advantage by allowing us to do full design and manufacturing overseas, enabling us to supply low cost, cutting edge products. This makes it easier for our customers to innovate, compete and continue to drive down the cost of photonic communications hardware worldwide. With ample cash reserves and a healthy balance sheet, Oplink is reliable, stable and here for the long haul. We have a clear vision, a strong management team, and the ability to execute in an ever-changing industry.

homes and businesses within a single city, Oplink's products, many of which were patented, were ready to help provide more bandwidth at lower costs.

Oplink acquired a number of prominent customers in their first five years. Their three biggest customers for fiscal year 2000 were Lucent Technologies, the telecom equipment manufacturer that was once part of Bell Labs and later became part of the giant Alcatel-Lucent; Sycamore Networks, Inc., a Massachusetts-based communications network firm; and JDS Uniphase Corp., another optical communications firm that was also a competitor. Another major customer was Cisco Systems, a huge multinational corporation that sold both networking hardware and software. In August 2000 Cisco Systems invested $50 million in Oplink in return for 3.5 percent of the company's shares when it went public.

GOING PUBLIC

In 2000 communications networks were booming as increasing numbers of people were using the Internet for sharing data. Because fiber optics can move more data at faster speeds than old-fashioned copper wire, analysts estimated that the market for fiber optic components would more than triple between 1999 and 2003. It was in this climate that Oplink announced they would become a publicly traded company. Their initial public offering (IPO) was highly anticipated, and they had to revise their earliest share price estimates from between $10 and $12 to $18 per share. At the end of October 4, 2000, their first day of trading on the NASDAQ,

Oplink stock closed at over $33 a share, raising almost $250 million for the company. Oplink management said they would use the funds to expand their capacity for manufacturing and distribution, invest in research and development, and increase their marketing efforts.

Despite early enthusiasm from investors, Oplink was affected when the dot-com bubble burst between late 2000 and 2001. Speculators had run up the value of many technology stocks, some of which were not good investments, then dumped them when the economy soured in 2001. As a result the NASDAQ, the technology-oriented stock index on which Oplink was listed, lost more than half its value. Many NASDAQ companies were Oplink's customers, and Oplink's own stock plunged to a low of $3.25 per share as its profits declined. Clients were postponing orders according to then-company president and CEO Fred Fromm, who explained to *123 Jump* reporter Adam Peeler, "Since our last [earnings] announcement, we have experienced additional unanticipated delays in orders from many of our customers, who continue to see reduced or deferred capital spending, and are still working through inventory issues."

To deal with declining profits, Oplink management accelerated a plan to cut costs and maximize earnings already in place. Most of the company's manufacturing capacity was moved to China, particularly their factory in Zhuhai, a coastal city five miles north of Macau and less than 40 miles west of Hong Kong. In addition, they laid off one-third of their California staff, which reduced the number of employees from 600 to 400.

SURVIVING THE TECHNOLOGY BUBBLE

After the dot-com bubble burst, several companies in the fiber optics industry began consolidating. In March of 2002, Oplink announced that they would merge with Avanex Corporation, a company that made photonic processors. Avanex was to pay $246 million in stock to purchase Oplink and hoped to save $15 million the first year by combining operations. Although Oplink was a smaller company and had a less complex product line than Avanex, low production costs made them an attractive partner.

However, the merger never was completed. In August 2002 Oplink investors rejected the deal as too risky. The Avanex shares that were to be used in buying the company lost half of their value; the Avanex CEO, who was a major patent-holder, had left the firm; and a supplier had filed a lawsuit against the company. "The points against merging were the risks in not being able to integrate or execute, and general market risks," CEO

KEY DATES

1995: Oplink Communications, Inc., is founded in California.
2000: Company makes initial public offering on the NASDAQ.
2002: Shareholders block merger with Avanex.
2003: Oplink acquires RedClover Networks, Inc., a privately held manufacturer of universal transponders.
2004: Company acquires Accumux Technologies, Inc., and EZconn Corp.; introduces "Green Platform," a line of products that complies with environmental initiatives by eliminating or limiting the use of potentially harmful elements.
2007: Acquires Optical Communication Products, Inc.

Fromm told Sarah Cohen of the *Daily Deal.* Fromm continued, "If Avanex had been the same company it was in March, I think the merger might have gone through." Instead, Oplink management was left to keep the company operating independently in a tightening market.

In fall of 2002 Oplink announced further restructuring. They closed a plant in Shanghai, China, and began moving much of their research and development (R&D) operations from the United States to China. Oplink planned to invest the cost savings in software development that would allow the company to improve the integration of its components into customer communications systems. Soon after this announcement, Oplink co-founder Joseph Y. Liu returned to the company as president and CEO, replacing Fred Fromm. Liu announced an additional reduction of 50 percent to the company's worldwide workforce. The cost savings, along with the announcement of such new products as a wavelength division multiplexer (WDM) for long-haul, undersea networks, satisfied investors enough that the company was able to maintain its listing on the NASDAQ.

EXPANSION THROUGH ACQUISITIONS

As Oplink's management continued to look for ways to offer more optical manufacturing solutions to their customers, acquisitions became an important strategy to broaden their product line. In late 2003 they bought

RedClover Networks, Inc., a privately held manufacturer of universal transponders, which reduce the power requirements and cost of transporting data on communications networks. "The addition of transmission technology will significantly broaden Oplink's comprehensive capabilities to better serve our customers...," president and CEO Liu said in a press release. "We expect that RedClover's technology will give us access to new, high-growth market segments as well as enhance our existing business."

Oplink quickly followed the RedClover acquisition with the purchase of the startup Accumux in early 2004. Accumux was a provider of tunable dispersion compensation modules (TDCM), which help prevent the distortion of signals that travel very long distances at very fast speeds, such as those that move across undersea networks. Company management considered the acquisition to be another move towards making the company a photonic foundry that could provide not only components, but also entire subsystems that could improve the performance of customer communications networks.

Oplink made a second acquisition in late 2004, buying the privately held, Taiwan-based EZconn Corp., a profitable supplier of broadband and fiber-to-the-home (FTTH) components to cable and optical companies, particularly in Asia. The deal was worth $30 million in cash and Oplink stock and offered benefits to both sides, allowing Oplink to diversify both its product line and client base, while EZconn gained the international recognition of the Oplink name.

DIVERSIFICATION INTO SERVICES

The company's acquisition of complementary photonics producers was part of an overall change in strategy. Rather than just supply parts and subsystems, Oplink launched an Optical Manufacturing Services (OMS) strategy, focusing on the design of entire communications subsystems. The company sold some components to its customers, but it also outsourced many other components. According to the company's annual report, by the end of fiscal year 2004 more than 65 percent of Oplink's revenue was coming from "design-in and manufacturing services."

However, Oplink made advances in product development as well. In 2004 the company launched a "Green Platform" line of products designed to comply with certain environmental initiatives by eliminating lead and limiting the use of other potentially harmful elements, including cadmium, mercury, and hexavalent chromium. Later that year Oplink began marketing

NET-Ready, a "plug-and-play" subsystem designed to work with several different network applications to optimize signal transmission and monitoring. The company also made advances in laser light sources and optical switches, among other products.

By fiscal year 2006 Oplink's strategy had led to a 60 percent increase in revenues and regular, if small, profits for their shareholders. The company's list of customers was expanding and included some of the world's biggest telecommunications companies, including Nortel Networks Corp., an international equipment and network supplier; Alcatel-Lucent, an international firm with billions in annual revenues; and Huawei, China's largest supplier of telecommunications and networking equipment. Huawei named Oplink their most valuable supplier for 2005.

STAYING COMPETITIVE IN A TOUGH MARKET

In 2007 Oplink made their biggest acquisition to that time, paying nearly $100 million in cash and stock for a majority stake in Optical Communications Products Inc. (OCP), a manufacturer of transceivers (combination transmitter/receivers). The OCP's reputation for high quality and customer service made it a good fit, as Oplink CEO Liu told Mark R. Madler of the *San Fernando Valley Business Journal*. "That is the reason why we made the effort. Our belief is the team they have had has a good track record. The combination of the two companies can be a strong one." Although there was a slight delay in the acquisition while OCP's management tried to prevent the sale, by the end of 2007 Oplink had completed the purchase of all of OCP's stock, making the transceiver firm a subsidiary of Oplink.

Oplink management quickly took advantage of opportunities for consolidation and cost savings made possible by their purchase of OCP. They closed an OCP plant in California, which had been one of the few telecom production facilities left in the United States, as well as an OCP supplier in Taiwan. Moving all of OCP's production to China meant not only saved costs through consolidation, but also brought their products closer to the growing Asian market. The OCP acquisition also helped Oplink broaden its various optical management offerings. Oplink had a strong background in passive optical components, which were used to split optical signals without the use of powered splitters. OCP had a good track record in the production of active optical components, which use powered switches, routers, or multiplexers to split optical signals. The combination of Oplink and OCP provided the

company the flexibility to supply customers using both kinds of networks.

The acquisition of OCP proved to be an astute move by Oplink management. Revenues almost doubled between fiscal years 2006 and 2007, increasing from $54.8 million to $107.5 million. Nonetheless, share prices began to drop in 2008 due to the economic downturn and a feeling that the optical components industry was due for more consolidation. "I'm very pessimistic," Oplink president and CEO Joseph Liu told Craig Matsumoto of LightReading.com in February 2008. "I myself have been struggling for seven or eight years now. I'm not seeing any fundamental change in the market." Although revenues jumped again in fiscal 2008, rising to $176 million, the company reported a net loss for the year, mainly due to a two-fold increase in the money invested in research and development.

As the company looked to the future, R&D was an important component of Oplink's strategy. At the end of fiscal year 2008, Oplink held 183 patents with an additional 11 patents pending. The emphasis on developing new products and a sound fiscal policy enabled Oplink's management to remain confident that the company had the stability to remain successful in a rapidly changing industry.

Diane E. Telgen

PRINCIPAL SUBSIDIARIES

Optical Communications Products Inc.

PRINCIPAL COMPETITORS

JDS Uniphase Corp.; Finisar Corp.; NeoPhotonics Corp.; Oclaro Inc.; MRV Communications; Chorum Technologies, Inc.; Oz Optics.

FURTHER READING

"Avanex to Buy a Competitor, Oplink Communications," *New York Times*, March 20, 2002, p. C4.

Aversa, Jeannine, "Oplink, Furukawa Enter $84 Million OCP Acquisition Agreement," *America's Intelligence Wire*, April 23, 2007.

Cohen, Sarah, "Oplink, Avanex Scuttle Merger," *Daily Deal*, August 16, 2002.

Dignan, Larry, "The Day Ahead: Oplink IPO Set to Soar, but Watch Lucent Relationship," CNET News, October 12, 2000, http://news.cnet.com/THE-DAY-AHEAD-Oplink-IPO-set-to-soar,-but-watch-Lucent-relationship/2100-12_3-261363.html.

Madler, Mark R., "OCP Building Sold, 124 Jobs Cut in March," *San Fernando Valley Business Journal*, February 18, 2008, p.1.

————, Oplink Files Suit over OCP Buyout Delay Tactics," *San Fernando Valley Business Journal*, May 14, 2007, p. 10.

Matsumoto, Craig, "Oplink Migrates East," LightReading.com, March 12, 2004.

————, "Oplink Nabs Accumux," LightReading.com, February 20, 2004.

————, "Troubles Linger for Optical Components," LightReading.com, February 26, 2008.

"Oplink Comm Acquires Taiwanese Opto-Comm Supplier EZ-conn," *Asia Africa Intelligence Wire*, November 9, 2004.

"Oplink Communications Signs Definitive Agreement to Acquire RedClover Networks" (press release), Fremont, CA: Oplink Communications, Inc., October 22, 2003.

Peeler, Adam, "Fiber Optics Slowdown Hits Small Caps," *123Jump*, April 27, 2001, p. 1008092g9981.

Reeves, Scott, "IPO Outlook: Sector, Underwriter Will Make Oplink a Strong Deal," *Futures World News*, October 2, 2000, p. 1008273r1102.

Otto Group

Wandsbeker Strasse, 3-7
Hamburg, D-22172
Germany
Telephone: (+49-40) 64-61-0
Fax: (+49-40) 64-61-8571
Web site: http://www.ottogroup.com

Private Company
Incorporated: 1949
Employees: 49,539
Sales: €10.11 billion (2008-09)
NAICS: 423430 Computer and Computer Peripheral Equipment and Software Merchant Wholesalers; 452910 Warehouse Clubs and Supercenters; 454111 Electronic Shopping; 492110 Couriers and Express Delivery Services Couriers; 522110 Commercial Banking; 561510 Travel Agencies

■ ■ ■

The Otto Group is one of the largest mail-order companies in the world, with subsidiaries and affiliates in Europe, Asia, and the United States. In spite of its global reach, Otto remains very much a family concern, being majority-owned and operated by the Otto family. Based in Hamburg, the Otto Group offers its customers a variety of ordering methods, including print and on-line catalogs, and includes such business services as travel booking, banking, and delivery. The company owns several holdings in England, notably Freemans PLC and Grattan PLC; in the United States, Otto holds a majority stake in Crate & Barrel Holdings Inc., the prominent chain of home furnishings stores.

COMPANY LAUNCHED IN POSTWAR WEST GERMANY

Otto Versand GmbH & Co. was founded by Werner Otto in 1949 in Hamburg, Federal Republic of Germany (West Germany). A refugee from Communist East Germany, Otto was one of a generation of successful German entrepreneurs after World War II that included such famous names as Max Grundig, Heinz Nixdorf, and Axel Springer. These men rose to prominence after the currency reforms of June 1948 that restored confidence to consumers in the U.S., British, and French zones of occupied Germany. After three years of severe shortages, Germans had little faith in the money issued by the occupation powers. Cigarettes were a more popular parallel currency, and the black market was thriving.

Nevertheless, Ludwig Erhard, director of the economic council for the joint Anglo-U.S. occupation zone, persuaded the Western Allies to accept his currency reform plan, which required the population to exchange a limited amount of the old currency for the new deutsche mark. Goods suddenly appeared as if by magic, and Germans went on a buying spree, first for food, then household goods, and finally clothes, which were to become the mainstay of the Otto Versand mail-order empire. In this new market, Otto's formula was to offer low-cost fashion garments and cheap credit. For the first time, German customers were invoiced, rather than required to pay upon delivery. Later, in 1969, Otto

COMPANY PERSPECTIVES

The common goal is to achieve success through passionate dedication. Despite the variety of market segments, business ideas and distribution channels of our business, not to mention its regional diversity, Otto Group sees itself as a community built on shared values. Our Group's passion for the success is based on four levels of performance, which together represent the true strength of our Group: passion for our customers, passion for innovation, passion for sustainability and passion for integrated networking. Each one of these performance levels is an integral element of the guiding principle and self-image.

Versand acquired the Hanseatic Bank and began offering three-, six-, and nine-month payment plans.

In retrospect, the mail-order market was ripe for development when 300 hand-bound copies of Otto's first, 14-page shoe catalog were distributed in 1950. In West Germany retail distribution was still badly dislocated by World War II. Rationing and shortages meant that many goods had been unavailable for years in local shops, and the range of choice was poor. City commercial centers had been heavily bombed, and the absence of Jewish merchants left a noticeable gap in retail distribution, as in many other fields where Jewish businesses had been successful and innovative before the rise of the Nazis. By 1950, however, West Germany had restored most of its postal and telephone systems, which were a relatively low-cost way to facilitate the distribution of goods in a country in which many store locations were still in ruins. German shop hours were restrictive, giving working people little opportunity to shop. All shops closed at 6:30 PM on weekdays. Retailers closed at 2:00 *pm* on Saturday afternoons, except on the first Saturday of the month, and were closed all day on Sundays. These hours were zealously protected by the shopworkers' union. In fact, the only way Otto Versand was later able to offer 24-hour ordering was to establish its telephone bank in Denmark and hire German-speaking operators.

In 1949 Erhard became economics minister of the new Federal Republic of Germany and pushed through further reforms that, along with Marshall Plan aid, helped create the famous Wirtschaftswunder, or German economic miracle. Rationing and price controls were ended, duties on imports were lowered, and tax on overtime work was abolished. Erhard encouraged production of consumer goods to stimulate employment and economic revival. The boom lasted into the early 1990s, and the wealth spread downward to lower-paid workers. By 1953 living standards were higher than in 1938, and by 1961 Germany was one of the world's largest industrial powers. German incomes tripled between 1950 and 1965. In this rising tide of prosperity, mail order bridged gaps between supply and demand. At the turn of the millennium, Germany remained by far Europe's largest annual per capita spender on mail order with annual sales of DM 43.5 billion. Seventy percent of all German households received at least one catalog, and mail order accounted for 4.6 percent of all retail sales, surpassing the 3.3 percent figure in the United States.

By 1951 Otto's sales had reached DM 1 million, generated by 1,500 catalogs of 20 pages each. In 1952 Werner Otto's next major innovation was to introduce a system whereby customers ordered through agents or representatives who forwarded the orders to the company's main office in Hamburg. Werner Otto believed that his company owed its early success to this form of personal contact. It also enabled the company to keep costs and prices low through lower catalog numbers. By 1953 Otto Versand had more than 100 employees, and the company's catalog had grown to 82 pages. A total of 37,000 copies were distributed, and sales reached DM 5 million.

REFINING MARKETING EFFORTS IN THE 1950S AND 1960S

Unlike Otto's archrival, Quelle, whose market strategy included a safety net of retail stores as well as a mail-order empire, Werner Otto concentrated on mail-order catalogs and representatives throughout the 1950s. From the 1960s onward telephone ordering to Otto's regional centers began to replace representatives.

In the United States, the United Kingdom, and several other countries, mail order had in the past appealed only to low-income bargain hunters or people living in remote rural areas, far from centers of population. By the mid-1950s, however, German consumers began to demand higher quality goods, and Otto Versand discovered that all kinds of potential customer groups could be targeted. The company became most successful by going against the grain of conventional mail-order wisdom. Otto Versand developed a methodical, computerized approach and gained knowledge of preferred customers in highly concentrated urban areas. Catalogs such as Otto Heimwerker targeted specific groups such as home enthusiasts, while Post Shop offered the latest styles to fashion-oriented youth. When the company later began

KEY DATES

1949: Company is founded by Werner Otto.
1950: The first catalog, featuring 14 pages of shoes, is distributed.
1963: Telephone ordering service is introduced.
1969: The Hanseatic Bank is acquired.
1972: Hermes Paketschnelldienst, a proprietary delivery service, is launched.
1981: Michael Otto succeeds his father as chairman.
1982: U.S. mail-order giant Spiegel is acquired.
1987: Otto Versand becomes the world's largest mail-order group.
1990: Otto Versand becomes the first mail-order company to open an order center in the former East Germany.
1995: Company launches e-commerce site www.otto.de.
1998: A majority stake in Crate & Barrel is acquired.
2002: Otto Versand becomes known simply as Otto; eventually adopts the name the Otto Group.
2006: Otto enters the Russian market by founding Direct Catalogue Service in Moscow.

its overseas expansion, areas such as Scandinavia, with its widely dispersed population, were ignored in favor of more urbanized, densely populated countries such as Holland and Belgium.

By the end of Otto's first decade in business, the company had more than 1,000 employees and sales of DM 150 million. In the early 1960s Otto Versand became one of the first German companies to install integrated data-processing equipment. Otto Versand used this equipment to become, in 1963, the first mail-order company to offer telephone ordering.

The 1966 Otto Versand catalog had 828 pages and was now the largest in Germany. It had moved upmarket, featuring designers such as Pierre Balmain, Jean Patou, Nina Ricci, and Christian Dior. In 1972 Otto Versand launched Hermes Paketschnelldienst, a proprietary delivery service named for the mythic Greek messenger. *Stores* magazine called this operation "a significant competitive edge, since it can offer domestic deliveries within 24 hours and free pickup of returned items." By the end of 1972, only 50 percent of all Otto Versand shipments were being handled by the German Federal Post Office.

MID-1970S: INTERNATIONAL EXPANSION

By 1974, the year of the company's 25th anniversary, Otto Versand considered itself strong enough to begin a period of international expansion, which intensified during the 1980s. The company's first move was into France, where it acquired, in 1974, 50 percent of 3 Suisses, the second largest mail-order firm in France. In 1979 Otto Versand founded Otto B.V., which grew to become one of the largest mail-order companies in the Netherlands. Otto Versand formed partnerships with Venca, the largest Spanish mail-order company, and Austria's 3 Pagen. In 1974 Otto Versand acquired an interest in Heinrich Heine, a German company specializing in luxury clothing and household goods. At the same time Otto Versand continued to expand within Germany, acquiring Schwab in 1976, Alba Moda in 1982, the linen and home textiles company Witt Weiden in 1987, and a holding in Sport-Scheck in 1988.

Michael Otto succeeded his father as chairman in 1981. Having set up his own financial and real estate business, the second-generation leader had joined his father's company in 1981, advancing from textile purchasing through the corporate ranks. Michael Otto pushed his family's company to undertake its riskiest venture to date when it seized an opportunity to buy the Spiegel catalog sales company in the United States in 1982. Although Spiegel was still a U.S. household name, its fortunes had been declining for years. Like the early Otto Versand company, it had concentrated on low-cost women's fashions. Otto Versand realized that the U.S. mail-order market had changed and gambled by taking the entire operation upmarket. The image makeover was accompanied by a thorough fiscal reorganization and productivity enhancements.

Spiegel's sales quadrupled within its first two years under its new management, and it had become the largest U.S. mail-order company by the end of the decade. In the meantime, however, the ownership of Spiegel was restructured. In 1984 all of the capital stock was transferred from Otto Versand to members of the Otto family, resulting in common ownership for Otto Versand and Spiegel but no direct financial or legal link between the two. What the family called the Otto Versand Combined Group included both Otto Versand and the so-called Spiegel Group. The latter name was adopted to reflect Spiegel's acquisitions of outdoor clothing specialist Eddie Bauer in 1988 and of Newport News, a catalog offering women's apparel and home furnishings, in 1993.

MOVING INTO EAST GERMANY, EUROPE, AND BEYOND: 1990–93

Otto Versand entered the 1990s as the world's largest mail-order firm, a position it had gained in 1987. German reunification took center stage in the early 1990s, and Otto Versand did not want to be outdone by its rivals in the former East Germany. By March 1990, three months before formal economic unification, Otto Versand had opened mail-order centers in Leipzig, Dresden, and the former East Berlin, becoming the first mail-order company to open an order center in the former East Germany. By July of that year, Otto Versand was the only mail-order house to boast a comprehensive distribution network in all five of the new federal states, the result of an earlier agreement with an East German association of consumer cooperatives. Sales in these new states exceeded DM 1.1 billion, more than double the company's original forecast.

Initially, the company was less interested in the other former communist countries in Eastern Europe, but moves by Quelle and other competitors rapidly changed Otto's outlook. With the formation of Otto-Epoka mbH, Warsaw, a joint venture, Otto Versand entered the Polish market in May 1990. Order centers were established in Czechoslovakia, Hungary, and the Soviet Union. At the same time, Otto Versand worked to strengthen its presence in Western Europe in anticipation of the unified European market. In 1988 Otto Versand acquired a 75 percent stake in Euronova S.R.L., the third largest Italian mail-order house. Five years later, Otto Versand acquired the largest Italian mail-order company, Postalmarket. Meanwhile, the company continued to bolster its customer service: in 1990, introducing 24-hour express delivery service, and in 1991, making telephone sales available 24 hours per day, seven days a week.

Otto Versand had wanted to expand into the United Kingdom for many years before its well publicized £165 million bid for a majority stake in Grattan, the mail-order arm of the troubled Next retailer, finally succeeded in March 1991. In 1986 it had been outbid by Next, which paid £300 million, but in 1991 it was prepared to pay a premium of £15 million above a rival £150 million bid by Sears PLC, which controlled the Freemans mail-order house, to secure this U.K. base. Grattan, the fourth largest U.K. mail-order firm, had a computerized warehouse system, a huge customer base, and 13 percent of the U.K. mail-order market, but it had been devastated by the recession of the early 1990s and a postal strike. Its parent company, Next, desperately needed to refinance a convertible bond issue. Otto Versand had begun to enter the U.K. market in a joint venture with Fine Art Developments Ltd., a greeting card company. In December 1988 Otto Versand launched Rainbow Home Shopping Ltd., a Bradford mail-order firm, and announced that Rainbow would join forces with Grattan, also Bradford-based.

Otto Versand also made significant inroads into largely untapped Asia, forming a joint venture with Sumitomo Corporation, Otto-Sumisho Inc., in 1986. The German company hoped to develop this market, which boasted many of the characteristics of markets in which it had been successful elsewhere, namely urban concentrations of the newly affluent and fashion-conscious. In 1993 Otto Versand, through the Otto-Sumisho joint venture, and Eddie Bauer formed a joint venture to sell the Eddie Bauer line through retail stores and catalogs in Japan. From its Japanese base, Otto Versand developed similar markets on the Pacific Rim, including a 1994 strategic alliance with Burlingtons' in India known as Otto-Burlingtons Mail Order Pvt. Ltd. Initial results were encouraging.

INTEGRATING NEW TECHONLOGIES: MID-1990S

The company did not shy away from new technology or new business opportunities during the early 1990s, becoming the first mail-order firm to offer an interactive CD-ROM catalog in 1994, for example. Having dabbled in the travel industry since the early 1980s, Otto Versand stepped up its efforts in this segment with the 1993 acquisition of a controlling interest in Reisland GmbH's 60 travel agencies. The company also partnered with Rewe in a 1990-created joint venture, Fegro/ Selgros GmbH & Co., which established a cash-and-carry chain offering more than 50,000 food and nonfood items. Otto Versand bought two British collection agencies in 1994.

Retail industry analysts remained divided about the impact of the single European market on the prospects for mail-order firms. Companies such as Otto Versand were expected to achieve economies of scale with pan-European operations, and the development of satellite networks increased opportunities for home shopping, but mail-order firms still had to cope with problems of distance and national distribution networks. Proposed European Community directives also threatened the use of mailing lists. With 25 percent of the European Community market, Otto Versand was also concerned not to breach competition laws. In recognition of this situation, Otto Versand announced that it would continue its policy of operating through national subsidiaries and allowing a degree of freedom to local subsidiaries familiar with local customs and markets.

In his 14 years at Otto Versand's helm, Michael Otto built his father's company into an international retail colossus and garnered high praise from analysts and competitors alike in the process. His "green" side was evinced by environment-friendly business policies such as reducing energy consumption and selecting environmentally sensitive products. He was named Environment Manager of the Year in 1991 and created the Michael Otto Foundation for the Environment in 1993. In 1988 Otto Versand introduced employee equity ownership through participation rights. By 1990 participation rights capital increased by DM 4 million to DM 10 million, and one-third of employees were participating in the profit-sharing scheme. Michael Otto's combination of business sense and social awareness helped win him 1995's National Retail Federation International Award.

These progressive strategies did not preclude growth or profitability. Annual sales increased 17.2 percent from DM 16.42 billion in 1992 to DM 19.25 billion in 1994, and net income increased 32 percent from DM 369.83 million to DM 488.07 million during the same period. By the mid-1990s Otto Versand was represented by 36 mail-order firms on three continents and in a total of 16 countries.

LEADING WITH INTERNET SALES: LATE 1990S

Probably the most significant development during the late 1990s for the entire global mail-order industry was the emergence of the Internet as a new selling channel. Otto Versand was quick to set up a Web site in 1995 from which it began selling the flagship Otto line as well as specialty catalog lines. Two years later the company set up a second Web site, a "virtual mall" featuring a much wider range of products and services from Otto Versand's various companies and joint ventures, including fashion items, furniture, books, CDs, posters, travel services, insurance, and a parcel service (from Hermes). Also featured were computers and other high-tech goods stemming from the company's 1995 investment in Actebis, Germany's second largest distributor of computers. By 1997 sales through the CD-ROM and Internet channels had reached DM 435 million ($247 million).

Otto Versand also continued its aggressive late 20th century expansion through its usual assortment of joint ventures and acquisitions. The company's partnership with Eddie Bauer, which had begun in Japan in 1993, broadened via additional joint ventures, first to Germany in 1995, then to the United Kingdom in 1996. In Asia, Otto Versand partnered with local firms to set up joint-venture catalog and Internet shopping endeavors in Shanghai, China, in 1996, and in both Taiwan and South Korea in 1997. The late 1990s financial difficulties in the region provided these ventures with a difficult launch environment. Italy was also having economic troubles during this period, which particularly affected that country's mail-order sector, leading Otto Versand to sell its Postalmarket stake in 1998 and to concentrate on the Euronova business.

In April 1998 Otto Versand made another bold move into the U.S. market when it acquired a majority stake in Crate & Barrel, which primarily sold through its chain of more than 60 home furnishings stores but which also sold via catalog. Crate & Barrel, whose legal name was actually Euromarket Designs Inc., agreed to the deal in order to tap into the deep pockets of its new parent for expansion; it also hoped that Otto Versand's mail-order expertise could bolster its catalog operation. For Otto Versand, the addition of Crate & Barrel further widened its product range.

Also serving to diversify Otto Versand's activities were several other late 1990s developments. In 1997 that company launched a new mail-order company in Germany called Otto Büro & Technik, which offered a wide range of office products, including furnishings and electronics and telecommunications goods. The following year the travel services unit was bolstered through the purchase of 25 travel offices from American Express Germany. In early 1999 Actebis, the computer distributor, was enlarged through the purchase of a competing firm, Peacock AG.

In April 1999 Otto Versand paid about £150 million to acquire the Freemans U.K. mail-order business from Sears PLC. The acquisition increased Otto Versand's share of the U.K. catalog market from 8 percent to 15 percent, making it the number three player, trailing only Great Universal Stores PLC and Littlewoods Organisation.

This was the last major acquisition of the 20th century for a company that was clearly on the rise heading into the new millennium. Sales had more than doubled during the 1990s, and net income was on the increase as well. During 1999 Otto Versand celebrated its 50th anniversary and could also celebrate its position as the preeminent company in the global mail-order market.

CONTINUED GROWTH IN THE INFORMATION AGE: 2000-09

As Otto Versand entered the new millennium, it continued to explore new opportunities in the rapidly expanding online marketplace. Otto's strategy was embodied in the shrewd and unassuming character of its CEO, Michael Otto, who viewed e-commerce as the core of the company's long-term success. In the year 2000, as part of its efforts to develop a stronger Internet presence, the company established several key Web sites designed to increase its business-to-consumer sales capacity. Most significant among Otto's new online ventures was discount24.de, an online shopping site offering a range of home furnishings, electronics, and other consumer goods at significant markdowns. Other important Internet ventures included the creation of a new Web presence for the subsidiary Otto Office, as well as the purchase of a majority stake in the online retailer myToys.de. That same year, Otto combined the shipping networks of two of its British subsidiaries, Freemans and Grattan, to create Parcelnet Limited, an extensive delivery company serving the United Kingdom. In fiscal year 2000, the company boasted earnings of more than €1.1 billion in Internet revenues, making it second only to Amazon.com in the burgeoning e-commerce sector.

Otto's focus on online sales also helped expand its international reach. By late 2001, more than 50 percent of the company's earnings were generated by business outside of Germany. For the year, Internet revenues topped €1.7 billion, an increase of more than 50 percent over the company's 2000 totals. In spite of these promising trends, the company still saw its overall performance suffer during the economic downturn of late 2001; total annual sales for the fiscal year ending February 2002 fell to €22.1 billion, down 3.1 percent from the previous year. Most of the decline came from the company's U.K. operations, where revenues fell 7.4 percent, and from its U.S. holdings, where sales numbers for Spiegel alone dropped 13.4 percent. Spiegel's poor performance eventually forced the unit to seek bankruptcy protection, and Otto was compelled to sell both Spiegel and Eddie Bauer in order to clear its books of the bad debt. One bright spot in the United States was the company's Crate & Barrel subsidiary, which by 2004 was enjoying annual sales in excess of $1 billion, roughly 25 percent of which came from Internet commerce.

In 2002 the company officially dropped the word "Versand" (German for "shipping") from its name, adopting the simpler, more direct name "Otto" as a way of reflecting its continued emergence as an increasingly global corporation. As the decade progressed, the company became more commonly known as the Otto Group. Over this period, Internet commerce continued to serve as the main engine of growth for the company. By fiscal year 2005, online sales had reached €3 billion, an increase of roughly 30 percent from the year before. At the same time, Otto remained dedicated to expand-

ing into new foreign markets. One notable area of growth was in Russia, where the company established a new retail ordering center, Direct Catalogue Service, in 2006. Headquartered in Moscow, Direct Catalogue Service offered a range of Otto, Bonprix, and Witt Weiden products to Russian consumers, focusing on the country's two largest markets, Moscow and St. Petersburg. In order to facilitate prompt and efficient shipments to its new customers, Otto also created Business Service, a logistics and warehouse division located in the nearby city of Tver.

The Otto Group experienced steady growth in its core businesses through the end of the decade. The company was particularly pleased with the continued expansion of its online sales presence. Internet revenues exceeded €5 billion in 2007, with an annual growth rate of more than 25 percent. International sales also continued to perform strongly, exceeding €6 billion for the same period.

The economic downturn of 2008 forced the company to seek ways to shed businesses and divisions that were underperforming. In 2008 Otto undertook an in-depth evaluation of two of its prominent U.K. holdings, Freemans and Grattan, which had posted steady losses since the middle of the decade. By January 2009 Otto determined to streamline the operations, creating the single entity Freemans Grattan Holdings. At the same time, the Otto Group remained alert to new opportunities overseas, most significantly in Turkey, where it purchased the discount shopping Web site Limango in May 2009. Some analysts cautioned against high expectations for the new venture, insisting that Internet commerce was considerably underdeveloped in Turkey. The company remained undeterred, however, believing that the preponderance of young people in the country, where roughly 57 percent of the population was between the ages of 15 and 34, provided ample reason to be optimistic about long-term growth in the region.

Clark Siewert
Updated, April Dougal Gasbarre;
David E. Salamie; Stephen Meyer

PRINCIPAL SUBSIDIARIES

3 Suisses International S.A. (France; 51%); Alba Moda GmbH; Apart International GmbH; Baumarkt Direkt GmbH & Co KG (50.1%); Baur Versand GmbH & Co KG (49%); Bon Prix Handelsgesellschaft mbH; Business Service (Russia; 70%); Cofidis S.A. (France; 41.2%); Crate & Barrel Holdings Inc. (U.S.A.; 96%); Direct Catalogue Service (Russia; 70%); Discount24 GmbH & Co. KG (50%); Frankonia Handels GmbH & Co. KG; Freemans PLC (UK); Grattan PLC (UK); Hanseatic

Bank GmbH & Co KG (25%); Hanseatic Versicherungsdienst GmbH Versicherungsvermittlung; Heinrich Heine GmbH; HERMES Logistik GmbH & Co. KG; Hermes Warehousing Solutions GmbH; Josef Witt GmbH; Kommanditgesellschaft EOS Holding GmbH & Co.; Küche & Co GmbH; Manufactum GmbH & Co. KG; Mondial Relay SAS (France; 51%); myToys.de GmbH (74.8%); Otto Freizeit und Touristik GmbH; Otto GmbH & Co KG; Otto International GmbH; Otto Japan Inc. (Japan); Otto Office GmbH & Co KG (75.1%); Otto Korea Limited (South Korea; 93%); Parcelnet Limited (UK); Schwab Versand GmbH; SportScheck GmbH.

PRINCIPAL COMPETITORS

Amazon.com Inc.; Arcandor AG (Germany); Costco Wholesale Corporation; eBay Inc.; Kingfisher PLC (UK); Lands' End Inc.; METRO AG (Germany); Staples Inc.; The TJX Companies Inc.

FURTHER READING

Berner, Robert, "Crate & Barrel Sells a Majority Stake to German Mail-Order Firm Versand," *Wall Street Journal*, February 13, 1998, p. B20.

Berwin, Lisa, "Otto's Entry into Turkey Won't Bring Quick Wins," *Retail Week*, May 1, 2009.

Dowling, Melissa, "Translating from the German," *Catalog Age*, February 1995, pp. 53–55.

Ewing, Jack, "Otto the Modest; The German Retailer Is a Powerhouse in Worldwide Online Sales, but It's not Blowing Any Flugelhorns," *Business Week*, June 5, 2006, p. 42.

Hollinger, Peggy, "Green Starts to Unbundle Sears," *Financial Times*, April 8, 1999, p. 29.

Krienke, Mary, "Michael Otto," *Stores*, January 1995, p. 150.

"Marketinglektionene aug dem Versandweg" ("Marketing Lessons the Mail-order Way"), *Absatzwirtschaft* (Düsseldorf), October 1982, pp. 24 +.

Miller, Karen L., "Otto the Great Rules in Germany," *Business Week*, January 31, 1994, p. 70J.

Miller, Paul, "Following Otto's Lead," *Catalog Age*, March 15, 1999, p. 10.

Otto, Werner, *Die Otto-Gruppe: Der Weg zum Grossunternehman*, Düsseldorf: Econ, 1982, 319 p.

Paine, Mandi, and Suzanne Bidlake, "Catalogues Face a New Order," *Marketing*, January 31, 1991, p. 2.

Ryan, John, "World-Class Retailer — Otto Versand — New Directions," *Retail Week*, November 2, 2001, p. 16.

Tyson, Laura, "German Mail-Order Group in Asia Push," *Financial Times*, September 17, 1997, p. 21.

People's United Financial Inc.

850 Main Street
Bridgeport, Connecticut 06604
U.S.A.
Telephone: (203) 338-7171
Toll Free: (800) 894-0300
Fax: (203) 338-2545
Web site: www.peoples.com

Public Company
Founded: 1842
Incorporated: 2007
Employees: 4,500
Total Assetts: $20.17 billion (2008)
Stock Exchanges: NASDAQ
Ticker Symbol: PBCT
NAICS: 522110 Commercial Banking; 522120 Savings
    Institutions

■ ■ ■

People's United Financial Inc. is the parent company of People's United Bank, a prominent savings bank headquartered in Bridgeport, Connecticut. People's United Bank, with its origins in the early 19th century, serves business and individual consumers through about 300 branches in six states and has assets valued at around $20 billion. It also operates under the names Chittenden Bank, Flagship Bank, Maine Bank & Trust, Merrill Bank, Ocean Bank, and Bank of Western Massachusetts. Through numerous mergers and a long-standing reputation for customer service, along with early adoption of technological innovations, the company has become the largest banking organization based in New England.

1842: EARLY SUCCESS

The Bridgeport Savings Bank was chartered in 1842. During the 19th and early 20th centuries, the bank grew and prospered along with its home city as it became one of the United States's leading industrial centers. One of its clients was Bridgeport's most renowned citizen, P. T. Barnum, who received a $10,000 loan to help him construct a prototype residential district in the city. (Fittingly, more than a century later, the bank would lend to redevelopers who were rehabilitating some of these houses.) By 1904 its assets amounted to almost $4 million. In 1917 the bank established an innovative at-work banking program for employees of Remington Arms, one of the nation's leading munitions companies.

In 1927 Bridgeport Savings Bank merged with the People's Savings Bank and adopted that name. During the Depression years of the 1930s, the bank advanced a total of $1 million to help its mortgage borrowers pay overdue taxes on their homes, all of which was paid back. The bank began to expand out of Bridgeport by starting a branch in Stratford in 1953. Two years later the bank merged with Southport Savings Bank and was renamed People's Savings Bank–Bridgeport.

NEW LINES OF BUSINESS LEAD TO RENEWED GROWTH

In the 1970s People's Savings Bank–Bridgeport, already one of the largest mutual savings banks in the country,

COMPANY PERSPECTIVES

The continued strength of our capital, along with our liquidity, asset quality and earnings as well as the fact that our balance sheet continues to be funded almost entirely by deposits and stockholders' equity are attributes that set us apart from most in the industry. Another distinguishing feature ... [is] our long term commitment to customer satisfaction. Our continued core business growth in these challenging times is of course the most tangible indication of our customers' satisfaction. Our conservative underwriting standards coupled with a strong monitoring resolution and loss control practices act as a back stop to our credit discipline (Philip R. Sherringham, as quoted on Seeking Alpha).

began moving into new fields and developing innovations in customer service. In 1976, for example, the bank introduced telephone banking, permitting depositors to check their balances and pay bills from home. The bank also expanded into the brokerage industry by creating People's Securities Inc. in 1983.

In the early 1980s the bank acquired several Connecticut-based savings banks, shortening its name to People's Bank in 1983 after the last set of mergers. At the end of 1982 the bank had $2.2 billion worth of deposits; by 1988 that figure would rise to more than $6 billion. In the 1980s many states passed laws opening up competition to banks from other states. In New England several states adopted regional banking laws, allowing banks based in New England to combine and compete within this region but excluding outside banks. Intense pressure, however, was exerted to liberalize these laws, and some of People's Bank's chief competitors became units of large regional banks.

Fearing that it would be a ripe takeover target if and when regional banking laws were loosened, People's Bank lobbied the Connecticut legislature to pass a distinctive law in 1985 allowing a bank to take the form of a mutual holding company. Such a company could offer a minority of its stock to the public to raise capital but maintain firm control and protect itself against takeovers. People's Bank announced such a conversion in 1987, but it had to delay this plan after the stock market plunged in October. The bank went ahead the following year and created a holding company, People's Mutual Holdings, which offered 20 percent of its stock

in July 1988 at a share price of $8.50, raising $65 million. The promise of high dividends attracted buyers, although many institutional investors scorned this deal on the grounds that stockholders would have no control over the company's direction. The bank became the first of dozens of mutual banks to float stock in this way, as several other states soon passed legislation similar to Connecticut's.

CREDIT CARDS BOOST BANK'S PROFILE

People's Bank began issuing Visa and MasterCard credit cards in 1985, as banks across the country aggressively marketed credit cards to millions of new customers. Its credit card division soon became one of the linchpins of its growth. The bank enjoyed unexpected national publicity in 1987 when consumers' organizations cited its MasterCard for having one of the lowest interest rates in the country at a time of widespread complaints about excessively high credit card rates. People's Bank hence developed, partly by accident, a curious strategy of promoting its credit cards nationwide (and later, abroad) while otherwise remaining tightly focused on community banking in Connecticut.

In 1989 People's Bank was one of the first issuers to introduce a MasterCard that simultaneously served as an ATM card and telephone calling card. The bank processed the first cross-country debit card transaction in August 1992 as it began marketing debit cards widely and launched advertising campaigns targeted at Hispanics, gays and lesbians, and other specialized market niches. Like many of its competitors, it also started offering secured credit cards to persons with credit problems or no credit history. The bank was wary of the industry-wide trend toward co-branding and affiliation cards, finding most such deals too expensive, but it gradually introduced such cards starting in the late 1990s.

1995-2002: NEW SERVICES FOSTER STEADY EXPANSION

People's Bank continued expanding its customer services in its home market in Connecticut, opening dozens of new branches and launching a series of mini-branches in Stop & Shop convenience stores and supermarkets. The company launched Internet banking in 1996; within a year, 25,000 customers were using this service. The following year People's Securities Inc. began supporting online trading.

In the mid-1990s People's Bank branched out into correspondent banking services, helping community banks and local governments by handling tasks such as processing checks, providing currency, and buying and

KEY DATES

■

1842: The Bridgeport Savings Bank is chartered.

1927: The bank merges with People's Savings Bank and adopts the latter's name.

1976: People's Savings Bank becomes the first bank in the United States to introduce telephone banking.

1983: The bank changes its name to People's Bank.

1985: The bank begins issuing credit cards.

1988: People's Bank converts to a mutual holding company and makes an initial public offering on NASDAQ.

1995: People's Bank begins Internet banking and enters a collaboration with the Stop & Shop retail chain.

2004: People's Bank sells its credit card division to the Royal Bank of Scotland Group.

2007: The company converts from a mutual holding company into a full public-stock savings and loan holding company; People's Bank changes its name to People's United Bank; People's Financial Inc., becomes People's United Financial Inc.

2008: The company acquires Chittenden Corp., of Burlington, Vermont.

selling federal funds. The bank also offered asset management through Olson Mobeck & Associates Inc. and leasing through People's Capital & Leasing Corp.

People's Bank's expansion continued in 1998 and 1999 with the purchase of Norwich Financial Corp. and the R. C. Knox and Beardsley and Brown & Bassett Inc. insurance companies. The bank believed that its long experience offering savings bank life insurance equipped it to succeed in this field. Nevertheless, it moved cautiously, preparing its staff carefully before introducing a wide range of insurance products in the following few years.

By 1996 People's Bank had entered the credit card market in the United Kingdom, intending to take advantage of consumer dissatisfaction with limited offerings in an arena dominated by a few issuers. This venture was quite successful—almost too successful for the bank to handle. Bank management decided that maintaining the growth of this unit would demand too much additional investment and sold the U.K. operation to Citibank in 2001. The bank's domestic credit card operations were also suffering amidst the economic

decline that followed the collapse of the high-tech stock boom. Although the bank maintained large reserves and continued to earn profits, the credit card division was dragging its overall performance down.

Over the years, People's Bank had become the corporate flagship of a deeply depressed city, which had lost much of its wealth and population as its once-flourishing industries declined and closed. The bank had signaled its commitment to Bridgeport by erecting a new, 16-story downtown headquarters building, which opened in 1989. The company became active in promoting local economic development, lending to local businesses, and encouraging volunteerism by its employees. For example, the bank started a mentoring program in 2002, setting aside paid time for employees to spend with their mentees.

2003–08: ANOTHER CONVERSION

The bank's management made ambitious plans for growth, not deterred by its small size compared with the industry giants. It spent the next few years boosting the company's earnings and balance sheet in preparation for a conversion to a fully public company in order to raise capital. One important step was to sell the bank's struggling credit card division in 2004 for $360 million to the Royal Bank of Scotland Group, which promised to keep the unit in Bridgeport. In May 2006 People's Bank became a federally chartered savings bank, declaring its intention to open branches in affluent Westchester County, New York. Investors seemed to approve of the company's performance, as its stock value rose from less than $5 in 2000 to more than $20 by the summer of 2006. That September, the company at last announced that it would undertake a second-step conversion from a mutual holding company to a public-stock savings and loan holding company, to be named People's United Financial Inc. The banking subsidiary then changed its name to People's United Bank to differentiate itself from the numerous institutions named People's Bank.

Having raised $3.4 billion from this stock offering, the renamed company was widely expected to purchase one or more competitors to strengthen its position in a rapidly consolidating banking sector. However, when People's United Financial announced in June 2007 that it would purchase the Burlington, Vermont-based Chittenden Corp. for $1.9 billion, many investors were skeptical, regarding the deal as overpriced and questioning why the company had not seized the opportunity to expand deeper into the mid-Atlantic region. Management stated that this merger followed a strategy of strengthening the company's base in New England before venturing elsewhere. In any case, this deal, which was completed on January 1, 2008, gave People's United Bank a major market share in northern as well as southern New England, with more than $20 billion in total assets.

A few months after the merger was announced, John A. Klein, the company's president and CEO since 1999, went on a leave of absence due to treatment for the cancer that he had been struggling with for several years. He would die in January 2008 at the age of 58. Leadership of the company passed to Philip R. Sherringham.

RENEWED OPPORTUNITY AMID FINANCIAL GLOOM

As the financial crisis deepened in late 2008 and early 2009, industry analysts pointed to People's United Financial as one of the few strong performers in a suffering industry. In addition to earning a J. D. Power and Associates award for customer satisfaction, the company retained over $2 billion in capital and had not been involved in sub-prime mortgage lending, and it continued to report profits through the first quarter of 2009.

Even though its share prices had fallen since its conversion, the decline was much slower than that suffered by most competing regional banks. The company felt confident enough to decline funds from the Troubled Asset Relief Program instituted by the U.S. Treasury in the fall of 2008 to bolster tottering banks. Remarkably, by May 2009 People's United Bank had become the 11th-largest bank in the United States by market capitalization, a rise of 24 positions in one year, not so much through internal growth as through the collapse or decline of many larger banks. The company intended to use its spare cash to make further acquisitions in the Northeast and possibly elsewhere to boost its earnings potential, but by the summer of 2009 it had still not announced any deals.

Stephen V. Beitel

PRINCIPAL SUBSIDIARIES

People's United Bank; People's Securities Inc.; People's Capital and Leasing Corp.; People's Mortgage Investment Company; Chittenden Commercial Finance Inc.; Chittenden Insurance Group; R. C. Knox & Company Inc.

PRINCIPAL COMPETITORS

Bank of America Corp.; Citizens Financial Group Inc.; PSB Holdings Inc.; Rockville Financial Inc.; TD Banknorth Inc.; Bancorp Inc.

FURTHER READING

Bielski, Lauren, "Diary of a Website Relaunch: People's Goes Transactional," *ABA Banking Journal*, October 2000, p. 55.

Block, Valerie, "In a Crowded Market, Issuers Seek Niche," *American Banker*, July 11, 1994, p. 12.

Chuvala, Bob, "John Kline Is Passionate about Mentoring," *Westchester County Business Journal*, May 27, 2002.

Fickensher, Lisa, "People's Bank Does Fine by Keeping Card Simple," *American Banker*, December 14, 1995, p. 15.

Gjertsen, Lee Ann, "People's of Conn. Sets Its Insurance Bar High," *American Banker*, July 20, 2001, p. 7.

Gordon, Jennifer, " People's Plans Deeper Cost Cuts Than Promised," *American Banker*, April 4, 2008, p. 20.

Gosselin, Kenneth R., "Chief of People's United Financial Dies at Age 58," *Hartford Courant* (Hartford, CT), January 25, 2008.

————, "Taking a Step to Stand Out: People's Bank Adds 'United' to Its Name as It Prepares to Expand Outside State," *Hartford Courant* (Hartford, CT), June 8, 2007.

Hamilton, Robert A., "Connecticut Bank's 11.5% Rate Brings Flood of Card Requests," *American Banker*, February 24, 1987.

Henriques, Diana, "Conversion with Fingers Crossed—A Mutual Thrift Goes Public, Kind Of," *Barron's*, July 25, 1988.

Johnson, Hilary, "Street Less Than Wowed by People's, Chittenden: Questions on Price, Growth Prospects, and Dilution Greet Deal," *American Banker*, June 28, 2007, p. 1.

King, Resa W., "The Shape of Thrifts to Come?—All Eyes Are on a 'Mutual Holding Company' in Connecticut," *BusinessWeek*, September 18, 1989, p. 102.

Kuehner-Heber, Katie, "CEO: People's United Will Mull Deals in Southeast," *American Banker*, November 26, 2008, p. 20.

Kulikowski, Laurie, "People's of Conn. Takes Second Step," *American Banker*, September 21, 2006, p. 1.

Lee, W. A., " People's: U.K. Unit, Now Citi's, Got Too Big," *American Banker*, April 9, 2001, p. 1.

Norton, Leslie P., "The People's Choice," *Barron's*, August 25, 2008.

"People's Bank Agrees to Sell Credit Card Business to The Royal Bank of Scotland Group to Focus on Profitable Core Banking Franchise; RBS to Maintain Credit Card Employee Base in Bridgeport," *PR Newswire*, February 3, 2004.

"People's United Financial Inc. Q2 2009 Earnings Call Transcript," July 17, 2009, http://seekingalpha.com/article/149558-peoples-united-financial-inc-q2-2009-earnings-call-transcript?page=1.

Pesek, William Jr., "People's Bank of Connecticut Beats the Drum for Debit Cards," *American Banker*, February 16, 1993, p. 4A.

Rieker, Matthias, "People's Goal: Put Extra Capital to Work via Deals," *American Banker*, June 16, 2008, p. 1.

Troxell, Tom, "Reach Out and Charge Someone: A Connecticut Bank Offers a MasterCard That Can Be Used to Pay for Phone Calls," *American Banker*, September 18, 1989.

Varnon, Ron, "People's United Ready to Pounce," *America's Intelligence Wire*, May 8, 2009.

PERRY ELLIS INTERNATIONAL

Perry Ellis International Inc.

•

3000 NW 107th Avenue
Miami, Florida 33172
U.S.A.
Telephone: (305) 592-2830
Fax: (305) 594-2307
Web site: http://www.pery.com/

Public Company
Incorporated: 1967 as Supreme International Corporation
Employees: 1,958
Sales: $864 million (2008)
Stock Exchanges: NASDAQ
Ticker Symbol: PERY
NAICS: 315211 Men's and Boys' Cut and Sew Apparel Contractors; 315224 Men's and Boys' Cut and Sew Trouser, Slack, and Jean Manufacturing

■ ■ ■

Originally founded by the acclaimed fashion designer Perry Ellis to manage the licensing of his name, Perry Ellis International Inc. was purchased in 1999 by Supreme International, a licensing and marketing group run by George Feldenkreis. Supreme International's assumption of the Perry Ellis name and switch to the PERY stock symbol elevated it from the middle ranks of apparel makers to a major worldwide brand status. The company designs, distributes, and licenses men's and women's apparel and accessories. Besides a number of Perry Ellis trademark lines, the company owns or licenses Jantzen, Laundry by Shelli Segal, C&C

California, Original Penguin by Munsingwear, Cubavera, Savane, Farah, Gotcha, Nike Swim, and several other brands.

ORIGINS AS A FASHION MERCHANDISER IN THE 1960S

Perry Ellis never intended to become a designer. He was born in 1940 to a wealthy family in Portsmouth, Virginia, and after majoring in business at the College of William and Mary he earned a master's degree at New York University's School of Retailing. In 1963 he became a management trainee at the upscale Richmond, Virginia, department store of Miller & Rhodes, where he quickly proved to be a brilliant fashion merchandiser. Ellis eventually became one of the top customers of John Meyer of Norwich, Connecticut, a women's sportswear company, which hired him in 1967. For Meyer it was a chance to revitalize a slipping line; for Ellis it was a chance to work in the fashion industry of New York. At John Meyer, Ellis learned about the production and manufacture of clothes, as well as the publicity and marketing side of the business. Even though he did not design, he became involved in the styling of the John Meyer lines. When the owner John Meyer, who had been diagnosed with cancer, was forced to sell the company, Ellis went to work for the Vera Companies in 1974 as vice president and merchandise manager of its sportswear division.

As he had done with John Meyer, Ellis provided a great deal of input on fabrics, colors, and styles at Vera Sportswear. When Frank Rockman took over the division, it became apparent to him that Ellis was providing

COMPANY PERSPECTIVES

Mission Statement: To be the apparel industry leader in all aspects of business operations to increase revenue and Shareholder profitability.

more ideas than the designer, who, in any case, was about to retire. Rockman asked Ellis if he would design the line. Ellis refused at first, but he finally accepted the position, taking over in January 1975. Within a year, Rockman was approaching the executives at Vera's parent corporation, Manhattan Industries, pressing them to allow him to start a contemporary fashion line of women's clothing designed by Ellis. The result was the Portfolio collection in the fall of 1976 and Ellis's quick ascent as a premier fashion designer. He lacked the technical skills to be considered a designer in the traditional sense, but he supplied the ideas that his assistants were then able to render as a sketch or construct into a prototype from which a pattern could be made.

Negotiations with Manhattan Industries for a contract began in 1977 and lasted until August 1978, when Ellis became president and designer of Perry Ellis Sportswear Inc., with a salary of $150,000 a year. As part of the agreement, Ellis retained control over his own name and would be able to license it to other companies in any category of apparel outside of women's sportswear that did not directly compete with Manhattan Industries. Perry Ellis International was subsequently created to manage these license deals, the first of which was with Alixandre, a fur company. Ellis was 38 years old.

As he became a celebrity designer, Ellis ran Perry Ellis International in an offhand manner, albeit with the help of his assistants. In 1981 he asked his companion, Laughlin Barker, to take over as president and legal counsel. After resigning from the New York law firm of Patterson, Belknap, Webb, and Tyler, Barker assumed his new role in June 1982. At this point Perry Ellis had nine licensees that generated some $60 million at wholesale prices and paid a 7.5 percent designer fee. Manhattan Industries received 25 percent of the company's net earnings. In 1982 Perry Ellis signed another seven licensing deals. Among other products that Barker would license were Perry Ellis fragrances and cosmetics, Japanese menswear, and a footwear line. All of the apparel was designed in Ellis's Manhattan studio.

PERRY ELLIS DIES IN 1986

Perry Ellis was at the peak of his career when the acquired immunodeficiency syndrome (AIDS) had a tragic effect on Perry Ellis International in particular and on the fashion industry in general. In January 1986 Barker died of an unspecified illness, then on May 30 Ellis died, reportedly from viral encephalitis, commonly known as sleeping sickness. Even though no one would confirm that either man died from complications caused by AIDS, some newspaper accounts reported rumors that Ellis had contracted AIDS, and others were written in a manner that suggested that Ellis was a victim of the disease. At the time, the fashion industry was engaged in a complex form of denial. A large number of single men between the ages of 25 and 45 who worked on Seventh Avenue were dying from an assortment of ailments that were either rare or not generally considered life threatening, yet any suggestion that AIDS might be involved was expressed only in whispers or innuendo. The issue was further complicated by the public's general fear and misunderstanding about the nature of the disease. The *Daily News Record*, a menswear trade publication, reported that talk of Ellis's AIDS diagnosis had hurt sales because some consumers were afraid they might contract the disease by simply touching Perry Ellis clothing.

Perry Ellis left Perry Ellis International to his heirs, primarily a daughter, Tyler Alexandra Gallagher Ellis, and her mother Barbara Gallagher. Ellis and Gallagher, a screenwriter and producer, had been friends for a number of years. By 1984 he was probably aware of his precarious health, while she was nearing 40 and feared that she would soon be beyond childbearing years. Both expressed a desire to have children and, according to friends, they agreed at a dinner party to conceive a child. When Ellis died, Tyler was 18 months old. Ellis had previously asked another former companion, Robert McDonald, to serve as the executor and trustee of his estate and to take over as president of Perry Ellis International.

Even though McDonald was a former film producer with no background in the fashion industry, he agreed to Ellis's request and kept the company functioning despite the pall cast over the studio by the untimely death of its founder. Licensees in 1986 would generate more than $300 million wholesale, resulting in approximately $22.5 million for Perry Ellis International. In terms of retail volume, the company was generating some $750 million a year. The clear challenge was to keep Perry Ellis International alive despite the loss of Perry Ellis himself. In many respects a fashion designer's name had simply become a brand that actually represented the efforts of many: from design and

KEY DATES

1967: George Feldenkreis founds Supreme International.
1978: Perry Ellis International is founded.
1986: Perry Ellis dies.
1989: Supreme International establishes Natural Issue label.
1993: Supreme International goes public.
1999: Supreme International acquires Perry Ellis and assumes the Perry Ellis International name.

marketing teams to the licensees themselves. Quoted by Lisa Belkin of the *New York Times* shortly after Ellis's death, Jack Hyde, the chairman of the Menswear Department at the Fashion Institute of Technology, said, "Let's face it, Christian Dior has been dead for a number of years, Chanel is dead, Anne Klein is dead. Business can go on. ... There are people who think that Christian Dior is still alive because they see his label."

Longtime Ellis assistants took over the design responsibilities for the mens- and womenswear lines, but business soon began to taper. To complicate matters, Manhattan Industries had been bought out by the more profit-conscious Salant Corporation. A young designer named Marc Jacobs was then hired to oversee womenswear, and another designer, Roger Forsythe, was hired to oversee menswear. In addition, in 1988 McDonald hired Claudia Thomas, another longtime friend of Perry Ellis, who had experience as a marketer of home furnishings. Shortly thereafter, he began to groom her to take over the company, because in March 1990 he, too, died from an AIDS-related illness, and she became president. The company was further diminished in October 1991, when Forsythe died from human immunodeficiency virus–related causes (at the time of death his immune system was not depressed enough to be diagnosed as AIDS). The designer had gone public about his illness in a way that stood as a stark departure from the shame and secrecy that surrounded the subject of AIDS in the fashion industry of the mid-1980s. He wrote an open letter to the Perry Ellis staff and granted a candid interview with the *Daily News Record* to discuss his health.

To many in the fashion industry, Perry Ellis International lacked focus at this stage. Even after Forsythe's death, the mass-market, high-volume menswear business was doing well, but the company's signature womenswear collection, normally regarded as a loss leader, failed to provide synergy with the more mundane

licensed products, where the major profits were actually realized. Even though Jacobs garnered a certain amount of critical acclaim for his extreme fashion, in particular a notorious "grunge" collection, Thomas decided to discontinue manufacturing a womenswear line in 1993. In reality, she was answering to the trustees of the estate of Tyler Ellis. Her mandate was to retain value rather than bankroll an idiosyncratic artistic vision. In effect, Perry Ellis became just a design and licensing operation, leaving others to assume the manufacturing and distribution risks.

Thomas decided to leave Perry Ellis when her contract expired in 1994. She was replaced by Max J. Garelick, who had been the chief executive officer of a North American subsidiary of Rodier Paris. Perry Ellis did fairly well under Garelick, ranking number four among menswear brands, trailing only Polo, Tommy Hilfiger, and Nautica. Its only business in womenswear was a coat license. The company expanded into licensing items such as watches, luggage, and home fashions. By the end of 1998 Perry Ellis brands generated an estimated $900 million a year in retail sales across 39 categories in 60 countries, but Salant, the holder of one of its most important licenses, was forced to file for Chapter 11 bankruptcy protection. In January 1999 the trustees of the Perry Ellis estate decided to sell the company to Supreme International for $75 million in an all-cash transaction. For the trustees, given the situation with Salant, it was simply their fiduciary responsibility to protect the value of the estate by realizing $75 million, which could then be invested in a diversified portfolio for the heir of Perry Ellis. For Supreme International it was a deal that George Feldenkreis hoped would elevate his company to a new level.

SUPREME INTERNATIONAL STARTS UP

Feldenkreis's family were Russian Jews who had fled to Cuba after World War II to escape communism. While his father made a living by importing electric equipment into Cuba, George Feldenkreis became a lawyer. After Fidel Castro assumed power in 1959 and Cuba became a communist country, Feldenkreis fled to Miami, Florida, in 1961 with his pregnant wife, one-year-old son, Oscar, and only $700. Unable to practice law in his new country, Feldenkreis used his father's overseas contacts to start importing diverse products such as automotive parts from Asia and window glass for doors from Portugal. He also began to import guayaberas, the popular Caribbean straight-bottom men's shirt with four pockets. In 1967 he created Supreme International for his burgeoning clothing business. Besides importing on a commission basis, Feldenkreis wanted to manufacture his own goods.

Supreme International was still quite small in 1980, with sales of $5 million and profits around $50,000, when Oscar turned 20, joined the company, and set about establishing Supreme's own brands. For several years he had limited success, but he learned valuable lessons about merchandising. In 1989 he and his designers coined the Natural Issue brand. It was a simple but powerful concept that captured a prevailing desire to use environmentally friendly materials for casual clothing.

Natural Issue proved so successful for Supreme International that the company made an initial public offering of stock in May 1993, raising almost $14 million to fund expansion. It invested $500,000 in computer design equipment to quickly produce new styles. By August 1993 Supreme International acquired two companies: Alexander Martin for $460,000 and Publix Brands for $425,000. Martin brought with it the King Size Catalog, Eagelson, and the Daube clothing lines, and Publix added Albert Nipón, Adolfo, Monte Carlo, Career Club, C.C. Sport, and the Cotton Mill labels. After assimilating the new brands into its operations, Supreme International saw its annual sales reach $50 million in 1994.

Supreme International was now involved in a full range of apparel activities. It still imported guayaberas, but it also designed and manufactured clothing and licensed its labels to others. In 1996 the company cast its net wider when for $3.7 million it purchased Jolem and its labels, including Tipo's, Cross Gear, Monte Fino, and New Step. Later in the year Supreme International made its most important acquisition to that point when it purchased Munsingwear and related brands for $18 million. A year later the company added the sweater manufacturer Crossings. Sales reached $90.6 million in 1995, $121.1 million in 1996, $155.7 million in 1997, and $190.7 million in 1998.

SUPREME INTERNATIONAL ASSUMES THE PERRY ELLIS NAME

The 1999 acquisition of Perry Ellis International for $75 million was a major move for Supreme International. It elevated the Miami company to major status in the international fashion industry. (At the same time, Supreme International also bought the Manhattan and John Henry clothing lines for $35 million from the troubled Salant.) To take full advantage of the Perry Ellis deal, Supreme International decided to change its name to Perry Ellis International. The company's stock would trade under the new name, but the Supreme International name was retained for the operating division. The Perry Ellis International Division would handle the licensing and marketing for all of the corporation's labels.

George and Oscar Feldenkreis then set about raising the profile of Perry Ellis that, although still alive in the minds of many consumers, had clearly slipped in the 15 years since the death of the designer. The company returned to womenswear, signing a licensing agreement with Kellwood to produce a high-end line. Overall, the goal was to make Perry Ellis into a lifestyle brand to compete with the likes of Ralph Lauren and Calvin Klein, from producing children's clothing to housewares. Perry Ellis took a page from Calvin Klein in early 2000 when, as a part of a $10 million marketing plan, it launched a controversial outdoor advertising campaign that featured images of nude and seminude models. When one outdoor company decided the ads were not appropriate for posting in Times Square, Perry Ellis received a bonanza of free advertising—and the kind of cachet coveted by a clothing line trying to establish itself as trendy.

The aggressive pattern of acquisitions continued under the Perry Ellis name. In July 2000 it paid $1.3 million for the Pro-Player, Artex, Fun Gear, and Salem Sportswear labels. In November 2000 it paid $1.8 million for the Mondo trademarks. Sales approached $230 million in 2000 and exceeded $287 million in 2001.

PERRY ELLIS EXPANDS BRAND LINEUP

The 2002 acquisition of Jantzen marked Perry Ellis International's entrance into swimwear. Besides designing and marketing Jantzen and Southpoint women's brands, the company began marketing Nike brand swimwear and related products. A merger with Salant in 2003 gave the company more control of the Perry Ellis brand and added other brands. In 2004 the PGA Tour and Champions Tour selected Perry Ellis International as the licensee to distribute their golf wear.

Perry Ellis International celebrated its 25th anniversary in 2005 by bringing out merchandise created from updated past designs. With the purchase of Tropical Sportswear in 2005, and its Savane and Farah brands, Perry Ellis International became a top-three producer of men's bottoms. The company also began distributing Gotcha, GirlStar, and MCD surfwear on five continents after acquiring the trademarks. It owned 20 brands including Perry Ellis. The Perry Ellis brand alone garnered $1 billion in retail sales in 2004; more than half of these sales were for clothes made by the company and the rest were for licensed goods.

Between 2002 and 2006 sales had tripled as the company focused on retail operations, brand building, and steering toward higher-end markets. Perry Ellis also extended its international reach by licensing deals with companies in South Korea, Japan, and Vietnam to distribute Perry Ellis and Manhattan lines. In 2006 the *Daily News Record* named Perry Ellis International the best-performing apparel company stock, even though company sales were beginning to fall.

PERRY ELLIS RESPONDS TO BUSINESS STRESSES

In the second quarter of 2007 the company reported it had tripled operating income and reduced debt, reversing a loss from the previous year. However, by the fourth quarter income was down $20 million, in part because the company was no longer producing men's pants for Wal-Mart and other mass-market retailers. For the year Perry Ellis International manufactured 72 million garments, some made from organic cotton and other eco-friendly materials. Macy's and Kohl's accounted for 25 percent of the company's sales.

By 2008 analysts were concerned that Perry Ellis International relied too heavily on Chinese suppliers and that it was vulnerable to retailer bankruptcies. However, the company's slant was positive. It announced in its annual report that in 2007 it had $864 million in revenues and experienced a 14 percent growth in earnings. In 2008 the company entered a new market segment when it bought Laundry by Shelli Segal and C&C California for $23 million. The women's contemporary brands sold in upscale stores and were expected to improve revenues because they sold at higher margins.

Despite growth in many areas, the company experienced a 9.7 percent decrease in revenue for the first quarter of 2009. Contributing to this poor performance were the bankruptcies of several customers, including Mervyn's and Goody's. TheStreet.com rating service noted in August 2009 that Perry Ellis's stock was down 57.3 percent over the previous year and did not perform as well as the S&P 500 or even the overall industry.

Perry Ellis expressed confidence that it could capitalize on retail trends in 2009 because of its diversified business. The company owned 23 brands and licensed 7 brands to third parties. Apparel and nonapparel products produced by third parties were found in more than 50 countries and brought in over $500 million. Perry Ellis International customers included the retailers Macy's, Nordstrom, Saks Fifth Avenue, Kohl's, Wal-Mart, and J.C. Penney. Additionally, consumers could buy Perry Ellis International merchandise at company-owned stores and Web sites. The company operated 46 Perry Ellis and 6 Original Penguin stores in mid-2009, with plans to open more of each by year end.

Ed Dinger
Updated, Doris Maxfield

PRINCIPAL OPERATING UNITS

Perry Ellis; Munsingwear; Andrew Fezza; Ping Collection; John Henry; Crossings; Romani; Pro Player; Penguin Sport; Natural Issue; Havana Shirt Co.; Grand Slam; Manhattan; Cubavera.

PRINCIPAL COMPETITORS

Liz Claiborne Inc.; Nautica Enterprises Inc.; Polo Ralph Lauren Corporation; Tommy Hilfiger Corporation.

FURTHER READING

Batts, Battinto, Jr., "The Common Thread of Perry Ellis," *Virginian-Pilot* (Norfolk, VA), December 18, 2005.

Belkin, Lisa, "Will Ellis Company Go On?" *New York Times*, June 24, 1986, p. C8.

Berman, Phyllis, "Grunge Is Out, Licensing Is In," *Forbes*, May 23, 1994, p. 45.

Brown, Heidi, "Testing a Makeover," *Forbes*, June 4, 2007, p. 86.

Burrows, Kate, "'Fashion with a Twist': Perry Ellis International Has Long Been Recognized as a Leader in Classic American Apparel and Cutting-edge Fashion, It Says," *US Business Review*, June 2007, p. 124.

Cardona, Mercedes M., "Perry Ellis Strives to Refashion Itself under New Owner," *Advertising Age*, October 11, 1999, p. 24.

DesMarteau, Kathleen, "The Perry Ellis Growth Strategy: Perry Ellis International Has Integrated More Than a Dozen Brands and Businesses into Its Fold in the Past Decade," *Apparel*, January 2006, p. 14.

Deutsch, Claudia H., "Green and Fashionable," *New York Times*, August 25, 2007, p. C3.

Faber, J. P., "By Design: Miami-Based Perry Ellis International Has Just Had a Record Quarter, Surpassing $100 Million in Sales," *South Florida CEO*, July 2003, p. 20.

Gibbons, William, and Peter Fressola, "The Remaking of Perry Ellis," *Daily News Record*, January 16, 1989, p. 16.

Larson, Kristin, "PEI: 10 Years in the Public Eye," *WWD*, May 21, 2003, p. 8.

———, "Perry Ellis Back in Sportswear," *WWD*, March 1, 2002, p. 2.

Lipke, David, "Pure Perry; Perry Ellis's Rise to Stardom Was Meteoric and Tragically Brief," *Daily News Record*, January 31, 2005, p. 32.

Lohrer, Robert, "Supreme to Acquire Perry Ellis," *WWD*, January 29, 1999, p. 2.

———, "The Supreme Example of Building On," *Daily News Record*, March 16, 1998, p. 1.

Lubanko, Matthew, "Supreme International: Fashionable Growth," *Equities*, April 1994, p. 16.

Mayer, Barbara, "Perry Ellis: His Design Legacy Remains," *Houston Chronicle*, June 11, 1986, p. 2.

Moor, Jonathan, *Perry Ellis*, New York: St. Martin's Press, 1988.

Nguyen, Hang, "Gotcha Seeks to Regain Former Glory," *Orange County Register* (Santa Ana, CA), March 23, 2007.

"Perry Ellis International Inc," TheStreet.com, August 20, 2009, http://www.thestreet.com/quote/PERY.html.

Peterson, Eric, "Perry Ellis International Bullish on Corporate Market," *Wearables Business*, March 1, 2005.

Sasso, Michael, "Behind the Label," *Tampa Tribune*, March 20, 2005.

Seemuth, Mike, "Perry Ellis Duo Cash in Quadrupled Stock," *Palm Beach Daily Business Review*, April 23, 2008.

Shaw, Dan, "Fashion's 'Comeback Kid' Moves on," *San Francisco Chronicle*, March 5, 1993, p. B3.

"US: Perry Ellis Completes Liz Claiborne Acquisitions," *Just-Style.com*, February 5, 2008.

"US: Perry Ellis Posts 36% Q1 Profit Decline," *Just-Style.com*, May 31, 2009.

"US: Perry Ellis Signs Three New Licensing Deals in Asia," *Just-Style.com*, August 30, 2007.

Walsh, Matt, "Winning Team," *Forbes*, March 27, 1995, p. 66.

"Well Dressed: Through Its Multiple Distribution Channels and Strong Portfolio of Brands, Perry Ellis International Is Moving Fashion Forward," *US Business Review*, December 2006, p. 68.

Wilson, Eric, and Antonia Sardone, "After One Season, Perry Ellis Yanks Women's Sportswear Line," *WWD*, April 6, 2001, p. 1.

Zaczkiewicz, Arthur, "PEI Back in Black in Second Quarter," *Daily News Record*, August 27, 2007.

Peter Pan
Bus Lines
Connecting People & Places

Peter Pan Bus Lines Inc.

P.O. Box 1776
Springfield, Massachusetts 01102
U.S.A.
Telephone: (413) 781-2900
Toll Free: (800) 343-9999
Fax: (413) 746-8671
Web site: http://www.peterpanbus.com

Private Company
Founded: 1933
Employees: 1,500
Revenues: $106 million (2007)
NAICS: 485210—Interurban and Rural Bus Lines; 485510—Charter Bus Industry

■ ■ ■

Peter Pan Bus Lines Inc. is the largest independent bus company operating regular route service in the United States. Founded in 1933 in Springfield, Massachusetts, by Peter C. Picknelly, an Italian immigrant, Peter Pan has remained a family-run business for more than 75 years. It has grown from a local transport company operating two Buicks, one Packard, and one Pierce Arrow into a company that runs 300 buses over 25 million miles per year to more than 100 destinations throughout the Northeast.

THE FAMILY BUSINESS

The Peter Pan story is a classic American tale of hard-working immigrants, entrepreneurship, and family ties.

Carmine Picariello, living in Picarelli, a small town in southern Italy, was drafted into the military in 1885. After learning road construction in the Italian army, Picariello immigrated to the United States, where he found employment with the Department of Public Works in East Orange, New Jersey. His wife and two sons came over in 1899, at which time the family changed its last name to Picknelly to appear more American. When Carmine died in 1907, son Peter C. Picknelly, then 15 years old, assumed responsibility for his mother and four siblings, pursuing employment in the transportation arena perhaps because of his father's experience.

Picknelly first worked as a chauffeur and then operated a local New Jersey bus route from East Orange to Newark. In 1925 he and three other Italian-born bus drivers moved to Springfield to open a new company, Interstate Busses Corp., which existed for six years with Picknelly acting as president until he sold his share to open his own company. He bought a local limousine service called Yellow Cab Air Line for $4,500, promptly changing its name: Peter Pan Bus Lines was born in 1933, at the height of the Great Depression.

Named for the boy who refused to grow up, Peter Pan had a fleet that initially comprised four seven-passenger limousines: two 1930 Buicks, one 1929 Packard, and one 1929 Pierce Arrow. As passenger demand grew, the company purchased several small Beck buses. During World War II the availability of new buses was limited, so the company bought any type of vehicle it could. One type of vehicle the company operated during the war was a Chevrolet expanded by the Fitzjohn company to accommodate 11 riders; these vehicles were

COMPANY PERSPECTIVES

We connect our customers with the people, places, and services that enhance the quality and enjoyment of their lives by providing equipment, technology, professional knowledge, and experience required to manage and operate safe, comfortable, and cost efficient ground transportation systems.

At Peter Pan we are customer-driven. Your safety and satisfaction are our #1 priority. Our original motto from the 1930's... still rings true today: "On time if possible with safety ... late if necessary for safety's sake."

more economical to run than standard passenger limos. The company also bought Yellow Coaches, Aerocoaches, and a Ford Transit, and it acquired its first diesel-powered vehicle in 1944, bringing its total number of vehicles to 13. This wide variety of equipment resulted in the company being dubbed "Pots and Pans" by competitors such as Greyhound and Trailways. At the end of World War II Peter Pan began to buy General Motors (GM) buses and continued to purchase vehicles solely from GM for the next 30 years.

In 1948 Bill Picknelly, Peter C. Picknelly's brother, who served as Peter Pan's operations manager, died suddenly. Peter L. Picknelly, Peter C. Picknelly's son, left his first year at Northeastern University to take over the job, becoming the first second-generation Picknelly to hold a management position at the company. Another second-generation family member to join the company was Carmen Picknelly, Bill's son, who in 1946 started a bus maintenance business for Peter Pan, Coach Builders, which he continued to run for the next four decades. For many of those years this was the only bus maintenance facility on the Northeastern seaboard.

POST-WAR GROWTH

Ridership continued to rise throughout the postwar years, and in 1957 Peter Pan was granted access to the Massachusetts Turnpike, over the protests of street rail companies. This shaved commuters' transit time from Springfield and Boston down to two hours and won more customers over to Peter Pan service. The company began equipping its coaches at this time with white wall tires, which were unusual enough to make the buses stand out and earned Peter Pan a new nickname, "The Company with the White Wall Tire Fleet." In 1958

Peter Pan celebrated its 25th anniversary by buying two new Flxible Starliner coaches, increasing the fleet to 27 buses. The 1964 World's Fair in New York also marked a milestone for the company, which that year saw a total of $1 million in sales.

In 1964 Peter C. Picknelly died at age 72, and his son Peter L. Picknelly, then 33, took over. Peter L.'s mother, Jennie Picknelly, also took on a greater role in the company's management, serving for 18 years as vice president and office supervisor. During the 1960s the fleet continued to grow at the rate of three to five new coaches each year. The buses also continued to increase in size, and Peter Pan bought its first 40-foot model in 1968.

Peter Pan has grown in non-vehicular dimensions as well. Following the company's one and only strike, on the Wednesday before Thanksgiving, 1971, Peter L. Picknelly, then in charge, began to think about diversification. Peter Pan owned an 1897 trolley barn that the company had used both as a bus garage and its corporate headquarters. After the 1971 strike the company renovated it into a facility for the rebuilding and refurbishing of buses. Peter Pan, through its affiliate, Coach Builders, would go on to operate eight such facilities throughout the Northeast.

Several other significant developments occurred in the 1970s. In 1974 the company switched over from GM buses to those made by Motor Coach Industries (MCI), as did many of its competitors. Peter Pan would purchase vehicles solely from MCI from then on. In the late 1970s Peter Pan began covering the exterior of its buses with painted graphics, so-called "billlboard buses" that advertised route destinations and areas of the country or depicted characters from the story of Peter Pan. In 1978 the company also rolled out its first wheelchair-assisted bus, a 1975 MCI model that was fitted with a special lift designed by the Peter Pan staff. In 1979 Peter L. Picknelly brought his own son, Peter A. Picknelly, into the business at the age of 21, naming him vice president; four years later Peter A. Picknelly became president.

In 1985 the company merged with Trailways New England, thus doubling in size and bringing Peter Pan service into New York City, which by 2009 would remain its biggest market. In 1992 Peter Pan purchased American Coach Lines, which allowed it to bring service into Washington, D.C.

The company has also invested in real estate, most notably its 1993 acquisition of Monarch Place, a 25-story office building and hotel that transformed the face of downtown Springfield. Monarch Place is, coincidentally, situated exactly where the original Springfield bus terminal stood when Peter C. Picknelly

KEY DATES

1933: Peter Pan is founded by Peter C. Picknelly as a local service with four passenger cars.

1940: The company is licensed to operate intercity service to Boston along Route 20.

1957: Peter Pan wins right to use the Massachusetts Turnpike, cutting time between Springfield and Boston to less than two hours.

1964: Peter C. Picknelly dies; son, Peter L., takes over.

1969: Springfield Bus Terminal opens; Peter Pan has grown to 38 coaches and 70 employees.

1981: Peter Pan opens Coach Builders, the Northeast's only bus body shop, in a renovated trolley barn in Springfield.

1985: Company merges with Trailways New England, doubles in size, and brings Peter Pan to New York City.

1992: Peter Pan enters into the Washington, D.C., market with the purchase of American Coach Lines.

2003: Acquisition of Arrow Lines, Bonanza Bus Lines, Coach USA Boston, Maine Line, and Pawtuxet Valley Lines doubles Peter Pan's size again.

2006: Company operates service to more than 100 cities and runs 8 bus body shops.

2008: Peter Pan celebrates its 75th anniversary with new tagline, "Connecting People and Places."

started Peter Pan. Under the name the Peter Pan Group, the company would go on to own two hotels in Massachusetts: the Hilton Garden Inn in Springfield and the Country Inn & Suites in Holyoke.

GROWING PAINS

Third generation Peter Pan President Peter A. Picknelly had two siblings, Mary Jean and Paul, and disagreements amongst them were a source of tension in the next generation of Peter Pan management. The three were not close growing up, and working in the same office as adults proved impossible. Peter and Paul in particular had different management styles, with Paul maintaining tight control over regional managers under his jurisdiction. Peter A. felt that not letting the managers take initiative and make certain decisions was stagnating to the company's growth. Mary Jean acted as an unwilling mediator between her brothers. Employees

throughout the company were well aware of the problems between the siblings. In a survey of company issues, employees named family squabbles as the major problem they faced. These squabbles also took a financial toll; the company's stock rose just 7 percent per year from 1990 to 1993.

Peter L. Picknelly, eliminated the siblings' problems in 1995 with a series of legal actions and a large sum of money. Using $6 million of company money and borrowing $19 million more, Peter L. Picknelly diversified the company dramatically. He bought a business complex in downtown Springfield with a 25-story office building and a Sheraton hotel. Peter L. Picknelly then put Mary Jean and Paul in charge of the new real estate venture, while Peter A. remained at the helm of the bus company. Peter L. Picknelly also divided ownership of the newly diversified Peter Pan Group to avoid future turf battles or later fights over inheritance issues. Mary Jean and Paul would each own 45 percent of the real estate interests, while Peter A. would own 9 percent; Peter L. Picknelly kept 1 percent for himself. Peter A. Picknelly would own 55 percent of Peter Pan Bus Lines, while his father would keep 30 percent and let Mary Jean and Paul split the remaining 15 percent.

Conflicts aside, the Picknelly family has been closely involved in the development of its hometown of Springfield for more than 50 years, serving on boards of many local civic groups and donating money to local causes. The company has also sponsored and provided buses for the Stuff a Bus Thanksgiving Food Drive, which collects and distributes food for the poor during the month of November.

GROWING SAFELY, GROWING GREEN

Peter Pan acquired several other bus lines throughout its seven-decade history, including the 2003 acquisitions of Arrow Lines, Bonanza Bus Lines, Coach USA Boston, Maine Line, and Pawtuxet Valley Lines that doubled Peter Pan's size again. By 2006 the company had expanded from its origins of three passenger limos circumnavigating Springfield to running 300 buses to 100 cities and operating eight bus maintenance facilities.

Throughout the years Peter Pan has been extremely proud of its long record of passenger safety. As of 2006 the company employed 81 One-Million-Mile Drivers and 19 Two-Million-Mile Drivers, all of whom had driven accident free for at least 12 consecutive years, more than any other bus company. The company was even prouder to employ two 3-Million-Mile Drivers, who had both driven 3 million miles accident free.

The company has been also justifiably proud of the measures it has taken to limit pollution. As of 2006

Peter Pan buses used ultra-low sulfur diesel and/or biodiesel for fuel, and the company's newest vehicles boasted up-to-date technology intended to cut emissions by 90 percent. The newest Peter Pan buses were also equipped with GPS systems that tracked not only the vehicle's location but its idle and brake patterns, information that can lead to a further savings in fuel economy and in tire wear. The company's bus maintenance shops also limit their environmental impact by using low-mercury fluorescent lightbulbs that can be recycled.

Peter Pan boasts the following "green" statistics on their Web site: As of 2009 their buses had twice the fuel efficiency of Amtrak and other train services, three times the fuel efficiency of cars, and four times the fuel efficiency of commercial planes. Each Peter Pan bus can displace approximately 55 cars from a highway. Additionally, Peter Pan's buses emit the smallest percentage of carbon dioxide per passenger of any vehicle on the road; CO_2 emissions are reduced by an average of 85 percent for every individual who chooses to ride a Peter Pan bus instead of driving alone. Buses in general now displace as many as 425 million cars per year from U.S. roads.

The company also likes to underscore the tremendous differences between Peter Pan and the country's major provider of high speed rail transport, Amtrak. According to Peter Pan, more passengers are transported by buses every two weeks than Amtrak carries in an entire year, Amtrak has absorbed over $25 billion in federal subsidies during its 30-year existence, and Amtrak regularly loses money on almost all of its 47 routes.

Peter Pan has grown up, despite its namesake, into a company earning in excess of $100 million per year. By 2009 Peter Pan coaches traversed over 25 million miles per year—the equivalent, as the company points out, of nearly 100 trips to the moon or of one bus circling the globe three times each day. Peter Pan has always prided itself on both its record of safety and the loyalty of its drivers. Peter Pan Bus Lines consistently receives the highest safety ratings from the U.S. Department of Transportation and the Department of Defense.

FUTURE GROWTH

The future for Peter Pan Bus Lines looked bright for the 21st century. With ever-rising gas prices, the demand for bus service increases every year. According to Peter A. Picknelly, in an interview with *National Bus Trader* magazine, "Since July 2005 we have seen a dramatic spike in business on our regular route service systemwide. Every route has shown an increase in double digits. It is obvious that higher fuel prices are putting people on buses.... Assuming that higher fuel prices are here to stay, more and more people will seek bus transportation for their travel needs."

"My major negative concern," continued Peter L. Picknelly for *National Bus Trader*, "is over home heating oil.... A substantial increase in the cost of home heating oil ... could impact family budgets and reduce travel." He also pointed out to Donald Sadler in *American Executive* that the bus industry has long had to contend with negative stereotypes: "The common perception is that a bus isn't a desirable way to travel. But today's point-to-point buses are nice, clean, and modern. The cost of a Peter Pan bus today is $433,000."

The bulk of Peter Pan's clientele were either under 25 years of age (students) or over 45 (senior citizens). "We make no bones about it—the more affluent individual is not our core customer," Peter L. Picknelly told *American Executive*. "I have always felt that bus passengers are people with more time than money while airline passengers are people who have more money than time."

In 2008 Peter Pan celebrated its 75th anniversary with a new tagline, "Connecting People and Places." In addition to connecting people across the country, Peter Pan remained a very connected family. The company is filled with family members, with many husband-and-wife and father-and-son teams, including Peter A. Picknelly and his wife, Melissa, who was the executive director of tours. Their son, Peter, who celebrated his ninth birthday in 2009, may well carry on the family tradition.

Melanie Bush

PRINCIPAL SUBSIDIARIES

Coach Builders.

PRINCIPAL COMPETITORS

Coach USA; Greyhound Lines, Inc.; Amtrak.

FURTHER READING

Bayot, Jennifer, "Peter Picknelly, 73, Chairman of Peter Pan Bus Lines," *New York Times*, October 15, 2004, p. C8.

Bryant, Adam, "Spoils of a Fare War: $5 Bus Rides to Washington," *New York Times*, August 8, 1992, p. 24.

Davis, Leslie, "Seven Most Innovative U.S. Motorcoach Operators," *Metro*, January 2001, p. 24.

Freeman, Stan, "Peter Pan Bus Lines Driver Suspended after Passenger Posts Video of Him on Cell Phone While Driving," *Republican Newsroom*, May 19, 2009.

Deena Maniscalchi, "Driving Vision: The Story of Peter Pan Bus Lines," Springfield, MA: Peter Pan Bus Lines, 2001.

Plachno, Larry, "Peter Pan Bus Lines Yesterday, Today and Tomorrow: From 'Pots and Pans' to 'The People Profession-als,'" *National Bus Trader*, February 2006.

Sadler, Don, "Peter Pan Bus Lines," *American Executive*, May 31, 2004.

Samuelson, James, "Solomonic Solution," *Forbes*, March 11, 1996, p. 80.

The Phillies

———■———

One Citizens Bank Way
Philadelphia, Pennsylvania 19148-5205
U.S.A.
Telephone: (215) 463-6000
Fax: (215) 389-3050
Web site: http://philadelphia.phillies.mlb.com

Private Company
Founded: 1883 as the Philadelphia Quakers
Employees: Not available
Sales: $216 million (2008)
NAICS: 711211 Sports Teams and Clubs

■ ■ ■

Founded in 1883 as the Philadelphia Quakers baseball team, The Phillies, as the team was renamed in 1890, is one of Major League Baseball's oldest franchises. Although the team has enjoyed brief periods of success over the years, the club is known primarily for its long tradition of losing. Indeed, with more than 10,000 defeats and counting, the team holds the record for losses by an American sports team. In spite of this history of futility, the Phillies organization has been home to some of the greatest players ever to wear a baseball uniform, including such Hall of Famers as Steve Carlton, Mike Schmidt, Jim Bunning, Richie Ashburn, Robin Roberts, and Chuck Klein. Since the 1970s, the Phillies have been perennial contenders in the National League East, and in 1980 the team celebrated its first World Series victory in franchise history. A second world championship came in 2008, making The Phillies one of the elite Major League Baseball teams of the early 21st century. During this era the club's accomplishments on the field were matched by comparable financial success, and by 2009 the Phillies organization was worth close to $500 million, making it the seventh-most-valuable franchise in the majors.

THE EARLY YEARS OF A BALL CLUB: 1883–1920

The opportunity to form a new professional baseball team in Philadelphia came after the 1882 National League season, when the Worcester Ruby Legs franchise decided to fold after only three years. League president A. G. Mills asked Al Reach, a former player who owned a successful sporting goods store in Philadelphia, to take over the struggling club. In the eyes of many Philadelphians, Reach was one of the game's most illustrious elder statesmen; he had played on the city's original franchise, the Athletics, from 1871 to 1875, helping the 1871 squad win the first pennant in professional baseball history. Along with local attorney John Rogers, Reach created the new franchise in 1883. Originally dubbed the Philadelphia Quakers, the team played its debut game on May 1, 1883, at Recreation Park, losing to the Providence Grays 4-3. The loss established a persistent theme for the new franchise, as the Quakers dropped 81 out of 98 games in their inaugural season. Starting pitcher John Coleman was credited with 48 of those losses, a major league record that would remain unbroken well into the 21st century.

In 1884 Harry Wright was hired as the team's new manager. Under Wright's leadership, the team gradually

KEY DATES

1883: The Philadelphia Quakers baseball team is formed by Al Reach and John Rogers.

1890: Team officially adopts the name Philadelphia Phillies.

1903: Reach and Rogers sell the team.

1915: Team competes in its first World Series, losing to the Boston Red Sox four games to one.

1928: Phillies sign future Hall of Famer Chuck Klein for $5,000.

1950: The legendary Whiz Kids lead the team to its first pennant in 35 years.

1971: Veterans Stadium is opened.

1980: Phillies win first World Series in franchise history.

2004: Team moves to Citizens Bank Park.

2008: Team wins its second World Series, defeating Tampa Bay Rays.

2009: By May the Phillies sell more than 750,000 tickets, an increase of more than 10 percent over the same period in the previous year.

achieved respectability, consistently finishing in the first division (in other words, among the top four teams) during his decade-long tenure. The Quakers gradually amassed a following of loyal fans, and in 1887 the franchise built a new stadium, dubbed the Huntingdon Street Grounds. At a cost of $101,000, the new park was among the most expensive and luxurious in the league. In 1890 the team officially became known as the Philadelphia Phillies, and the club has retained the name and home city since that year, the longest continuous span in the history of professional athletics. In 1894 a fire devastated large portions of the Phillies ballpark, forcing the team to play its home games at the University of Pennsylvania during the restoration. Reopened the following year as Philadelphia Park, the renovated stadium was constructed of brick and steel, boasted modern roof decks, and seated close to 19,000 fans. The team's play suffered significantly after Wright's departure, and the Phillies failed to place better than second place for the remainder of the decade.

At the beginning of the 20th century, the Phillies seemed poised to reverse their losing ways. The club's roster included several of the most talented players in the sport, including star infielders Nap Lajoie and "Big Ed" Delahanty, as well as the fleet-footed outfielder

Elmer Flick, all of whom were later inducted into the Baseball Hall of Fame. With the formation of the rival American League in 1901, however, the team's new sense of promise quickly evaporated, as a host of new teams began raiding the National League for talent. In 1902 Lajoie and Flick signed with the Cleveland Bronchos (later the Naps), while Delahanty joined the Washington Senators. In addition the team lost several other players to the American League's Philadelphia franchise, the Athletics. While the foundling club had no connection to the Athletics of the 19th century, which had disbanded years earlier, it clearly presented new competition to the Phillies, both for their fan base and players. The Athletics soon became one of the elite squads in the American League, while the Phillies continued to flounder.

In 1903 a roof collapsed during a game at Philadelphia Park, killing 12 spectators and injuring 232 others. In the wake of the disaster, Reach and Rogers put the team up for sale. The Phillies hit a low point a year later, losing 100 games for the first time in their history. For the next decade the club's management was in constant turmoil, with six men serving as team president in a span of 10 years. The organization finally achieved some stability in 1913, when William Baker, who had previously served as police commissioner of New York City, was named president. After rechristening Philadelphia Park the Baker Bowl, the new president set out to create a winning team. The Phillies reached the pinnacle of the sport in 1915 when they won the National League pennant and a showdown against the American League champion Boston Red Sox in the World Series. Although the Phillies took the first game of the best-of-seven series, they lost the next four, dashing their championship hopes. It would be the team's last World Series appearance for the next 35 years.

DECADES OF FUTILITY: 1920–50

The 1920s and 1930s were arguably the most frustrating years in the history of the Phillies franchise. From 1917 to 1932 the team failed to have a single winning season; over the course of the 1920s, the team finished last in the National League six times. In spite of its abysmal record, the team boasted some of the league's most elite hitters during these years. Among them was Chuck Klein, who hit .356 with 43 home runs in 1929, his first year with the club. Indeed, Phillies sluggers were continually among the league leaders in the 1920s and 1930s. One of the team's most impressive offensive seasons came in 1930: five of the team's starters hit over .300, while the club's combined average was .316, the third-best mark in National League history.

Unfortunately, the club's hitting prowess was checked by its comparably dismal pitching staff, which gave up a major league record 1,199 runs over the course of the season. In the end, the free-swinging Phillies lost 102 games that year.

William Baker died in 1930; two years later, the club's business manager, Gerald Nugent, was elected team president. Although Nugent was widely regarded as having a keen eye for baseball talent, his management skills were questionable, and the combination of the Great Depression and Nugent's financial misjudgments proved disastrous to the franchise. In order to keep the team solvent during these years, Nugent was forced to sell or trade a number of its marquee players, among them Chuck Klein, who was sold to the Chicago Cubs for $65,000 following the 1933 season. In 1938 the team abandoned the Baker Bowl, which had deteriorated to such a degree that legendary sportswriter Red Smith compared it to the "city dump," and began sharing Shibe Park with the rival Athletics. Over the remainder of the decade, the Phillies failed to finish higher than seventh place; between 1938 and 1942, the club lost more than 100 games each season.

By this time the Phillies's financial situation had become so dire that Nugent was forced to borrow large sums of money, often from the National League itself, in order to keep the franchise alive. In spite of this assistance, the team was deeply in debt in 1942. That year league president Ford Frick forced Nugent to sell the team to the league for $50,000. After a bidding war erupted among several prospective buyers, the league sold the team to William C. Cox, a prosperous lumber magnate. At 33 years of age, Cox became the youngest team owner and president in the league. His tenure proved to be brief and disastrous. In May 1943 Cox fired popular manager Bucky Harris, inciting a near-revolt among the players, and the team agreed to continue playing only at Harris's urging. A short time later Harris revealed to the press that Cox had placed bets on Phillies games, one of the most serious offenses in the game. Commissioner Kenesaw Mountain Landis launched an inquiry, and Cox was banned from baseball after spending less than a year as owner of the Phillies. In late 1943 new owner R. R. M. Carpenter Sr. acquired the Phillies for $400,000 and promptly named his son, Robert "Ruly" Carpenter Jr., the new team president. The Carpenters brought some much-needed stability to the team and remained as owners until the early 1980s.

Throughout this turmoil, the team attempted to establish a new identity in order to attract a broader fan base. In 1943 after inviting fans to suggest new nicknames for the struggling ball club, the Phillies became known as the "Blue Jays." The team finished the season in seventh place, with a record of 64-90. A year later, the club's record fell to 61-92, as it dropped to last place in the National League, 43 and a half games out of first. By the start of the 1945 season, the team was once again known as the Phillies. The club's struggles continued throughout the rest of the decade, culminating in 1948, when the Phillies finished with a losing record for the seventeenth consecutive season.

BRIGHT SPOTS IN A DIM ERA: 1950–70

By 1949, however, the Phillies had finally begun to assemble a strong team. The improvement was due in large part to the organization's new farm system, which emphasized the development of young, affordable talent as a means of fielding a competitive ball club. The 1949 team finished with a winning record, and Ruly Carpenter was named Major League Baseball Executive of the Year. A year later the "Whiz Kids," a squad led by young stars such as outfielder Richie Ashburn and pitcher Robin Roberts, fought their way to the team's first pennant since 1915. Clinging to a one-game lead in the standings, the Phillies defeated the Brooklyn Dodgers 4-1 in the final game of the season to clinch a spot in the World Series. Although the Phillies were ultimately swept in the series by the more powerful New York Yankees, the season played a key role in resuscitating fan interest in the team, and the Phillies became the most popular baseball team in the city.

The Whiz Kids phenomenon proved ephemeral, however: The Phillies suffered a losing record in 1951, and over the next six seasons they placed no higher than third. By 1958 the team was once again in the National League cellar, where they would remain for the next four years. The team's play became so bad that manager Eddie Sawyer quit just one game into the 1960 season, famously declaring, "I'm 49, and I want to live to be 50." Sawyer was eventually replaced by Gene Mauch, who would manage the team for most of the 1960s. Mauch's first full season as Phillies manager proved less than auspicious, as the 1961 club won only 47 games while setting a modern baseball record with 23 straight losses. By 1964, however, the Phillies had become one of the dominant teams in the league. The club was led by emerging slugger Richie Allen, who earned Rookie of the Year honors for the season, and pitching ace Jim Bunning, who threw a rare perfect game in a June outing against the Mets. Unfortunately, the team's championship ambitions were derailed down the stretch run, when ten straight losses in late September dropped the Phillies to second place in the standings. The team's breakdown would achieve notoriety as one of the most epic late-season collapses in baseball history.

After the failure of the 1964 season, the Phillies once again slipped into mediocrity. Gene Mauch was fired as manager in 1968, and the team would have four managers over the next five years. After a lackluster 1969 season, the Phillies made a fateful transaction, trading Richie Allen to the St. Louis Cardinals for a group of players that included African-American outfielder Curtis Flood. In a move that shocked the entire league, Flood refused to report to the Phillies, accusing both the team and the city of being racist. More significantly, Flood objected to Major League Baseball's reserve clause—a stipulation that allowed teams to control a player's rights in perpetuity, regardless of the player's actual contract status—equating it to a form of slavery. Flood sued the league in a lawsuit that eventually came before the Supreme Court. Although Flood lost his case, his actions emboldened the Major League Players Association, and in 1975 the reserve clause was eliminated.

A TASTE OF GLORY: THE 1970S AND 1980S

In 1971 the Phillies moved into a new park, Veterans Stadium, marking the transition by finishing last in the division. Within a few years, however, the team had once again become a contender. Led by future Hall of Famers Mike Schmidt and Steve Carlton, the Phillies won the National League East division in 1976, eventually falling to the Cincinnati Reds in the playoffs. The team repeated as division winners in 1977 and 1978 but still failed to reach the World Series, falling to the Los Angeles Dodgers in the National League playoffs both years. After missing the playoffs in 1979, the Phillies were back on top a year later, narrowly edging out the Montreal Expos to win the National League East. The team went on to defeat the Houston Astros in a dramatic five-game playoff before beating the American League Champion Kansas City Royals in the World Series, four games to two. After almost a century, the team could finally claim bragging rights over the entire league.

Shortly after the World Series victory, long-time owner Ruly Carpenter announced his decision to sell the team. The team's executive vice president, Bill Giles, had always dreamed of owning a baseball club, and after bringing together a diverse group of investors he bought the Phillies for $30 million. Giles took a 10 percent stake in the team and assumed the role of president. In the strike-shortened season of 1981, the Phillies were well positioned to repeat as division champions after finishing the first half of the season in first place, but the team ultimately lost an unorthodox playoff series against the Montreal Expos, three games to two. After

failing to make the playoffs in 1982, the team once again returned to the World Series a year later. The 1983 team was largely built around the free-agent signings of Pete Rose, Tony Perez, and Joe Morgan, who had been key players for the Cincinnati Reds championship teams of the mid-1970s. Nicknamed the "Wheeze Kids" by sportswriters, the Phillies defeated the heavily favored Dodgers to win the National League pennant before falling to the Baltimore Orioles in the World Series.

After the 1983 World Series defeat, the character of the team changed dramatically, as management released a number of veterans from the 1980 championship team in order to promote some of its younger players. The team failed to regain its competitive form, however, and by the late 1980s the Phillies were once again consistently finishing last.

MACHO ROW: STRUGGLING TO COMPETE IN THE 1990S

The Phillies achieved a brief resurgence of success in 1993. Led by such players as John Kruk, Lenny Dykstra, and Darren Daulton—a group dubbed "Macho Row" because of their uncouth, raucous behavior and slovenly appearance—the team led the division for almost the entire season, while the organization broke its own attendance record by selling more than three million tickets. Philadelphia fans embraced the team's scrappy spirit, and local sportswriters romanticized the team's gruff, blue-collar personality. Even Bill Giles poked fun at the team's coarse character during a late-season television appearance, cautioning fans not to allow their daughters to marry any of the clubs players.

Although the Phillies were widely considered to be underdogs in their World Series battle against the Blue Jays, the team managed to take the series to six games, thanks largely to the pitching performance of ace Curt Schilling. The team lost the series, however, after reliever Mitch Williams gave up a series-clinching homerun to Toronto's Joe Carter in the bottom of the ninth. After suffering a number of key injuries in the strike-shortened 1994 season, the Phillies went into a tailspin, failing to achieve a winning record for the rest of the decade.

A NEW MILLENNIUM AND A NEW BALLPARK

By the year 2000 the Phillies franchise was worth $150 million. Revenues more than doubled during the first half of the decade, rising from $68 million in 2000 to $167 million in 2005. This dramatic increase in earnings enabled the team to finance the construction of an elite new ballpark, and the club opened the 2004 season in Citizens Bank Park. Built for $346 million, the new stadium seated more than 43,000, with the average ticket price at nearly $30. The team still struggled to make the playoffs, finishing the 2004 season in second place. After firing manager Larry Bowa, the team hired Charlie Manuel. Although the Phillies would battle injuries to key players over the next several years, it still managed to field competitive teams. The club fell only two games short of making the playoffs in 2005, and three games shy in 2006.

Prior to the start of the 2007 season, star shortstop Jimmy Rollins declared the Phillies the best team in the East. In spite of this confidence, the team struggled for much of the first half of the season, and by July it still could not maintain a winning record. The club achieved an even more dubious milestone on July 15, 2007, when the Phillies lost to the St. Louis Cardinals, 10-2. With the defeat the Phillies became the first professional franchise in the history of American sports to lose 10,000 games. Still, by the end of the season, the Phillies had made good on their shortstop's boast, clinching the division on the last day of the season. After an early exit in the 2007 playoffs, the team came back stronger in 2008, eventually winning the club's second World Series title by beating the Tampa Bay Rays, four games to one.

By 2009 the team was worth $496 million, an increase of 3 percent compared to 2008 figures, and more than three times the club's value in 2000. This dramatic rise in the organization's financial fortunes saw a commensurate rise in the overall cost of player salaries, as team payroll ballooned to $128 million by 2008. Indeed, following the World Series victory, the team acted aggressively to sign some of its young stars to new contracts. World Series MVP Cole Hamels signed a three-year contract worth more than $20 million, while power-hitting first baseman Ryan Howard agreed to a three-year deal valued at $54 million. On opening day in 2009 the team's payroll was $132 million. The World Series victory also brought the Phillies a sizable increase in revenues. By May 12, 2009, the Phillies had sold more than 725,000 tickets, an increase of 10.2 percent over the same period in 2008. Clearly, winning had its financial advantages as well. On September 30, The Phillies clinced their third consecutive National League East Championship. The team was looking forward to an exciting playoff season with the chance to become the first back-to-back National League champion since 1976.

Stephen Meyer

PRINCIPAL COMPETITORS

Atlanta National League Baseball Club Inc.; The Florida Marlins, LP; Pittsburgh Baseball Club; Sterling Mets LP; Washington Nationals Baseball Club, LLC.

FURTHER READING

Bucci, Steve, *Steve Bucci's Total Phillies Trivia*, Philadelphia: Camino Books, 2009, p. 160.

Fitzpatrick, Frank, "Phillies Icon Harry Kalas Dies," *Philadelphia Inquirer*, April 14, 2009, p. A1.

Graham, Bryan Arman, "100 Seasons ... 100 Heartbreaks," SI.com http://sportsillustrated.cnn.com/2008/more/05/14/ philadelphia.drought/index.html.

Green, Ron, *101 Reasons to Love the Phillies*, New York: Stewart, Tabori & Chang, 2009, p. 119.

Holtzman, Jerome, "Turn Back the Clock ... 1943: Owner William Cox, the Last Man Banned before Pete Rose," *Baseball Digest*, August 2004, pp. 74–76.

Honig, Donald, *The Philadelphia Phillies: An Illustrated History*, New York: Simon & Schuster, 1992.

Jordan, David, *Occasional Glory: A History of the Philadelphia Phillies*, Jefferson, NC: McFarland, 2002.

Kashatus, William C., *Almost a Dynasty: The Rise and Fall of the 1980 Phillies*, Philadelphia: University of Pennsylvania Press, 2008.

Lidz, Franz, "The Beautiful Losers: An Oral History of the Philadelphia Phillies," *Sports Illustrated*, July 2, 2007, pp. 46–50.

Lieb, Frederick George, and Stan Baumgartner, *The Philadelphia Phillies*, New York: Putnam, 1953.

Nemec, David, *The Great Encyclopedia of 19th-Century Major League Baseball*, New York: Donald I. Fine Books, 1997.

Nightengale, Bob, "Phillies, Rays, Brewers Defy 2009 Trend in Stands with Help of '08 Success on Field," *USA Today*, May 12, 2009, p. 5C.

Rader, Benjamin, *Baseball: A History of America's Game*, 3rd ed., Urbana: University of Illinois Press, 2008.

Rossi, John, *The 1964 Phillies: The Story of Baseball's Most Memorable Collapse*, Jefferson, NC: McFarland, 2005.

———, "The Nugent Era: Phillies Phlounder in Phutility," *National Pastime*, January 2005, pp. 15–18.

Russakoff, Dale, "They're Phoul, but They're Our Phillies," *Washington Post*, October 15, 1993, p. D1.

Rys, Richard, "The Phantom Five," *Philadelphia Magazine*, June 2008.

Stark, Jayson, *Worth the Wait: Tales of the 2008 Phillies*, Chicago: Triumph Books, 2009.

Wulf, Steve, "In Philadelphia, They're the Wheeze Kids," *Sports Illustrated*, March 14, 1983, p. 26.

———, "The Orioles All Pitched in (to Win World Series)," *Sports Illustrated*, October 24, 1983.

Piedmont Investment Advisors, LLC

411 West Chapel Hill Street, Suite 1100
Durham, North Carolina 27701
U.S.A.
Telephone: (919) 688-8600
Web site: http://www.piedmontinvestment.com/

Private Company
Founded: 2000
Employees: 23
Total Assets: $133 million (2008 est.)
NAICS: 523120 Securities Brokerage

■ ■ ■

Piedmont Investment Advisors, LLC, has made its name by consistently outperforming bigger money management firms by following a moderate investment strategy designed to produce a good return over a long period of time. Piedmont relies on selecting the top performing stocks in many categories. Within a decade of its founding in 2000, the firm had more than $2 billion under management with a long list of institutional clients. In 2009 the U.S. Treasury selected Piedmont from a pool of over 200 interested firms to help manage $218 billion, a portfolio used to provide capital to banks and financial institutions.

ORIGINS: 2000

When Isaac Green had enough of conforming to company policy as a funds manager at investment firm Loomis Sayles' Detroit office in 2000, he cashed in

$500,000 in stock options, completed industry research, and developed a business plan for a new investment firm, Piedmont Investment Associates, LLC. Two colleagues from Loomis Sayles, Dawn Alston Paige and Sumali Sanyal, soon joined him, becoming senior vice presidents at the new company. All three wanted to break with the prevailing view that an investment firm should invest only in value stocks (stocks valued below the market averages) or growth stocks (stocks valued above the market averages). Instead, they wanted to be part of a firm that invests in the entire market, picking a diverse blend of value stocks and growth stocks, and representing small and large companies and a diverse group of industries.

"The idea that got us started," Green told Nicole Marie Richardson of *Black Enterprise*, "was that you really had to emphasize diversification in portfolios so that the volatility of your returns would be acceptable." Diversification was the key to the trio. After a decade of "niche-oriented investment styles," Green, Paige, and Sanyal believed strongly that the large institutions, such as pension funds, insurance companies, savings plans, and endowments—wanted to branch out. "Clients don't want to be boxed in any more," Green told Chris Serres in the *News & Observer* in Raleigh. "After 10 years of style management, they want diversification." Green and his cofounders set out to provide just that.

Green, Paige, and Sanyal were Piedmont's first clients, eventually investing another $750,000 in the company. Meanwhile they searched for a new home and found it in North Carolina, Green's home state. The partners struck a deal with North Carolina Mutual Life

COMPANY PERSPECTIVES

Our mission is to provide solutions to our client's problems. Our clients are fiduciaries who have money to invest and need to achieve competitive returns. Their problem is that they do not know who they can rely on to work as co-fiduciaries and generate those returns. We are in business to offer an attractive solution for that problem through our products and service.

Insurance Company, the country's largest black-owned life insurance company, which bought a 25 percent interest in Piedmont in return for Piedmont investing the life insurance company's portfolio of reserve funds. A deal was also made with Durham-based Mutual Community Savings Bank, which bought a 12.5 percent stake in Piedmont and then placed its corporate asset portfolio with the investment firm. North Carolina Mutual and Mutual Community together invested more than $150 million with Piedmont, enabling Green to meet his first-year goal of having $100 million under management by the end of 2001.

The investment firm moved into the historic North Carolina Mutual building on West Parish Street in Durham, once known as the nation's "Black Wall Street." Green, an African American, was conscious of his position within the community. He told Anne Fawcett in the *Herald-Sun* in Durham, "We'll offer products and services to a community that's never been served from within before. It's important and special that we are part of the historic Durham financial community."

EMERGING MANAGERS: 2001–07

Shortly after Piedmont was formed, the country entered a recession after the September 11, 2001, terrorist attacks against the United States. Nevertheless, Piedmont outperformed the Standard & Poor's 500 index—an index of 500 stocks commonly used as a benchmark for the overall U.S. stock market—by an average of 300 basis points a year for the first three years of its existence. Charles Keenan of Institutional Investor pointed out that small money managers, which, like Piedmont, often outperform bigger investment firms, had several advantages. Small investment firms could buy and sell stocks more easily than big players could and could provide additional personal client service. In addition, small investment firm managers usually have

equity stakes in the firm, as Piedmont's founders did, giving them an added incentive to pick stocks that provide strong returns. In the first decade of the 21st century several large pension funds recognized the often stellar performance of small money managers and invested portions of their assets with small firms as part of "emerging managers" programs. Piedmont quickly benefited from this trend.

In 2002 Philadelphia-based FIS Funds Management had invested its funds in Piedmont, and shortly thereafter the investment firm added $52 billion of assets from North Carolina's retirement system to its list of big clients. Once North Carolina hired Piedmont, other clients began signing on, including the Detroit General Retirement System, Howard University, and Progress Investment Management Company.

By 2006 Piedmont celebrated the milestone of having $1 billion under management. Green told Nicole Maries Richardson of *Black Enterprise*, "Such an accomplishment opens the door for other sponsors who did not have interest before or the flexibility." The $1 billion mark, as well as the firm's good performance record, had resulted in national interest in the firm. In 2007 the Illinois Teacher's Retirement System terminated seven money managers for poor performance and hired new ones, including Piedmont, which was hired to manage $25 million as part of an emerging manager program. Also in 2007 the California Public Employees Retirement System (CALpers), which was the largest pension fund in the nation, placed its first investment, of $100 million, with Piedmont's Manager Development Program. CALpers also purchased a minority stake in Piedmont in a show of confidence in the firm's success. The CALpers investments pushed the amount of money Piedmont managed to $1.5 billion.

REWARDS FOR STRONG RECORD: 2007-09

Investment from the large state public retirement systems led to increased recognition for Piedmont. In 2007 Institutional Investor's *Money Management Letter*, an asset management industry publication, named Piedmont "Emerging Manager of the Year" in recognition of its excellent record of returns as well as "diligent client service." Also in 2007 Piedmont was profiled on *Pensions & Investments* list of the 500 Largest Money Managers, coming in at number 495. In addition, the company debuted on the *Black Enterprise* Asset Managers List at number 12.

By 2008 Piedmont had $2 billion under management, but the company felt the impact of the global recession of 2008-09. In 2009 the U.S. Department of

KEY DATES

2000: Isaac Green founds Piedmont Investment Advisors, LLC.

2001: Piedmont moves from Detroit, Michigan, to Durham, North Carolina; FIS Funds Management becomes a Piedmont client.

2006: Piedmont has $1 billion under management.

2007: Piedmont is hired by Illinois Teachers' Retirement System to manage $25 million and by California Public Employees Retirement system to manage $100 million as part of the states' emerging managers programs.

2008: Piedmont has $2 billion under management.

2009: The U.S. Department of Treasury selects Piedmont as one of three firms to manage a $218 billion portfolio.

Treasury selected Piedmont, which at the time had $1.8 billion in assets under management, and two other firms to manage a securities portfolio of about $218 billion that was used to provide capital to hundreds of banks and financial institutions. Orim Graves of the National Association of Securities Professionals told *Black Enterprise*, "This is the first time to my knowledge that the federal government has hired a minority firm to manage assets of this magnitude in its history."

That display of confidence could prove to be a pivotal moment in the investment firm's development, as the selection could be used as a selling point to attract clients in the future. At the same time, Piedmont had a wide variety of other institutional clients, including CALpers, the Commonwealth of Pennsylvania, the Chicago Public School Teachers Retirement System, the Freddie Mac Foundation, the Illinois Municipal Retirement Fund, the New York City Employees' Retirement System, the Ohio Public Employees' Retirement System, and the Virginia College Savings Plan, as well as dozens of other institutional clients. The firm's successful track record, combined with its common-sense investment strategy of selecting top performing stocks in many categories and the U.S. Treasury Department's confidence in the firm, was expected to continue to attract high profile clients. Piedmont Investment Advisors surely seems to have a very bright future, indeed.

Melissa J. Doak

PRINCIPAL COMPETITORS

New Amsterdam Partners, LLC; Keeley Asset Management, Corp.; Prima Capital.

FURTHER READING

Anderson, James A., "Keep Large and Small in the Mix: Money Manager Dawn Alston Paige Says Diversification Makes Sense Now," *Black Enterprise*, September 1, 2003.

"B.E. Asset Managers," *Black Enterprise*, June 2009, p. 135.

"California Public Employees' Retirement System Expands Investment Options for Manager Development Program II—Also Develops Asset Rebalancing Plan," *US Fed News*, May 14, 2007.

Fawcett, Anne, "Portfolio Manager Caters to Durham, N.C., African-American Market," *Herald-Sun* (Durham, NC), October 11, 2001.

"Illinois Teacher's Can Seven Managers," *Money Management Letter*, May 18, 2007.

Keenan, Charles, "Bantam Boosters," *Institutional Investor—Americas*, January 15, 2004.

McKinney, Jeffrey, "Digging In: Black Financial Services Firms Entrench Themselves Amid a Rocky Market," *Black Enterprise*, June 1, 2008.

———, "Piedmont to Manage Piece of TARP Pie," *Black Enterprise*, May 15, 2009.

"Piedmont Investment Advisors Named 'Emerging Manager of the Year' by Institutional Investor's *Money Management* Letter" (press release), Durham, NC: Piedmont Investment Advisors, LLC, March 18, 2008.

"Profiles of the 500 Largest Money Managers," *Pensions & Investments*, May 28, 2007.

Ranii, David, "Piedmont Has Big Client," *News & Observer*, March 9, 2007, p. D3.

Reynolds, Rhonda, "Diversification Pays," *Black Enterprise*, September 1, 2004, p. 40.

Richardson, Nicole Marie, "Piedmont Advisors Reaches $1 Billion in Assets: Company Philosophy Stresses Diversification and Trustworthiness," *Black Enterprise*, October 1, 2006.

———, "Risk and Reward: Newest CEOs to Join the BE 100s Each Answered the Call to Entrepreneurship," *Black Enterprise*, June 1, 2007.

Serres, Chris, "Looking for Bright Spots in a Brighter Market," *News & Observer* (Raleigh, NC), December 2, 2001, p. E1.

———, "Owner of Durham, N.C.-based Money Management Firm Enjoys Job," *News & Observer* (Raleigh, NC), October 18, 2001.

Talbert, Marcia Wade, "A Golden State Opportunity: Piedmont Investment Advisors Snags Investment from Country's Largest Pension Fund," *Black Enterprise*, June 1, 2007.

Weisbecker, Lee, "Back Home to Durham Roots," *Business Journal*, October 12, 2001, p. 3.

Williamson, Christine, "Illinois Teachers Puts $1.6 Billion in Alternatives," *Pensions & Investments*, May 28, 2007.

Zimmer, Jeff, "Durham, N.C., Investment Firm Lands Nation's Largest Pension Fund," *Herald-Sun* (Durham, NC), March 7, 2008.

———, "Mutual Community Savings Continues to Lose Money, but Foundations Stay Solid," *Herald-Sun* (Durham, NC), February 27, 2008.

Plantronics, Inc.

345 Encinal Street
Santa Cruz, California 95060-2146
U.S.A.
Telephone: (831) 426-5858
Toll Free: (800) 544-4660
Fax: (831) 426-6098
Web site: http://www.plantronics.com

Public Company
Founded: 1961
Incorporated: 1961
Employees: 4,100
Sales: $856.27 million (2009 est.)
Stock Exchanges: New York
Ticker Symbol: PLT
NAICS: 334210 Communications Headgear, Telephone, Manufacturing; 334310 Home Theater Audio and Video Equipment Manufacturing; 423620 Audio Equipment, Household-Type, Merchant Wholesalers

■ ■ ■

Since the early 1960s, Plantronics, Inc., has been one of the leading manufacturers of communications headsets in the United States. A pioneer in the development of lightweight, high-quality telephone headgear, Plantronics has produced award-winning products for a wide range of clients, including NASA, the airline industry, and numerous other corporate customers. Almost since its inception the company has set the industry standard, and the Plantronics headset remains legendary for its role in maintaining communication during the Apollo 11 moon landing in 1969. During five decades of innovation and growth, Plantronics has expanded its core business to include audio devices, telephone products for the hearing impaired, and wireless headsets using Bluetooth technology. By the early years of the 21st century, Plantronics had established offices in 20 countries worldwide, while making a concerted effort to establish a strong presence in the rapidly -expanding consumer market for headset technology.

FROM COMMERCIAL AIRLINERS TO THE MOON: 1961–69

Plantronics traces its origins to the U.S. aviation industry in the late 1950s when demand for lightweight communications headgear first began to emerge. Until this time, pilots had relied on oversized, unwieldy headsets, which became uncomfortable to wear during long flights. In 1961 commercial airline carrier United Airlines issued an industry-wide challenge to develop better equipment. A United Airlines pilot, Courtney Graham, ultimately found the solution. Working with a friend, Keith Larkin, Graham designed a lightweight alternative to traditional aviation headsets. Their prototype was modeled after a pair of Japanese sunglasses with a transistor radio built into the frames that Larkin had first seen in his work with the importer Plane-Aids.

Initially, Graham and Larkin embedded their communication device into a pair of glasses and submitted the design to United. The airline balked at the design, however, suggesting that the glasses were impractical.

COMPANY PERSPECTIVES

In 1969, a Plantronics headset carried the historic first words from the moon: "That's one small step for man, one giant leap for mankind." Since then, Plantronics has become the headset of choice for mission-critical applications such as air traffic control, 911 dispatch and the New York Stock Exchange. Today, this history of innovation is the basis for every audio product we build for the office, contact center, personal mobile, entertainment and residential markets."

Graham and Larkin subsequently created a headband containing two miniature transducers. United approved the second prototype and encouraged the inventors to work on producing a version suitable for commercial use. In order to spearhead the manufacturing process, Graham and Larkin founded their own company, Pacific Plantronics, Inc. Based in Santa Cruz, California, the company derived its name from a combination of the words "plane" and "electronics." In 1962 Plantronics completed its debut headset, the MS-50, and immediately began marketing it to commercial airline carriers. United Airlines was among the company's first clients.

Within a year Plantronics had begun selling the MS-50 to other communications device manufacturers, notably Indiana-based ITT labs, which integrated the headset into a complex radio system, the Kellorad unit, for use by the National Aeronautics and Space Administration (NASA). The headset component soon caught the attention of astronaut Wally Schirra, who immediately saw other potential uses for the lightweight device. A year earlier, astronaut Virgil "Gus" Grissom had nearly suffered a fatal mishap during the Liberty Bell 7 Mercury mission when his inability to make timely contact with a rescue crew after prematurely blowing open the hatch of the spacecraft resulted in the capsule's sinking shortly after splashdown. Schirra recognized that the capsule might have been salvaged if Grissom had been equipped with a radio headset inside his helmet.

Schirra approached Plantronics with the idea of creating a lightweight headset for use by NASA. To begin their research, Plantronics created a new division, Space Environmental Communications (SPENCOM), which was devoted to developing a headset for use in space. Working in collaboration with Schirra, other

NASA astronauts, and engineers, the company developed an innovative helmet headset, featuring a noise-canceling microphone. In October of that year, Schirra became the first astronaut to use the MS-50 during his mission to orbit the earth. Although the original version of the helmet headset had some minor design flaws, Graham and Larkin quickly addressed the issues, and the MS-50 soon became the standard headset for subsequent NASA missions.

Around this time, Plantronics also was exploring general applications for its headset technology. One area where the company recognized a potential niche was in the field of telephone switchboard operations. There was high demand for lighter weight headgear among operators, many of whom suffered from chronic neck and shoulder pain related to the heavy equipment that was common in the industry. In 1963 Pacific Bell placed an order for the MS-50 headsets, becoming Plantronics's first corporate client outside of the space program. A year later, Plantronics landed a contract with the Federal Aviation Administration (FAA) to become the sole headset provider to the nation's air traffic controllers.

Throughout the 1960s, however, NASA remained the company's most important customer, and Plantronics headsets were integral to the Mercury, Gemini, and Apollo programs. By 1967 the company's earnings figures had climbed to $5.4 million, based on sales of roughly 100,000 headsets. When the Apollo 11 lunar capsule touched down on the moon on July 20, 1969, Neil Armstrong's famous message to earth, "That's one small step for man, one giant leap for mankind," was delivered through the company's signature headset. As NASA celebrated the achievement of its decade-long ambition, Plantronics was able to claim a small share of the glory.

GROWTH AND DIVERSIFICATION: 1970S–80S

After making a vital contribution to the Apollo 11 moon mission, Plantronics was ready to focus on expanding its business, both at home and abroad. In 1970 the company introduced the Starset headset, which featured a unique curved earpiece. Two years later, Plantronics opened Plamex, a manufacturing plant in Tijuana, Mexico. The new facility marked the Plantronic's first step in establishing an international presence. In 1975 the company introduced the Quick Disconnect, a feature that allowed users to become more mobile without losing connections to their calls.

At the beginning of the 1980s Plantronics was one of the premiere telephone headset makers in the United States. As a testament to the popularity of the

KEY DATES

∎

1961: Plantronics is founded in Santa Cruz, California.

1962: Astronaut Walter "Wally" Schirra uses Plantronics MS-50 headset during orbit around the earth.

1963: Pacific Bell orders headsets for switchboard operators.

1964: Plantronics begins manufacturing headsets for the Federal Aviation Administration.

1969: Plantronics headset transmits astronaut Neil Armstrong's famous words, "That's one small step for man, one giant leap for mankind," from the moon during the Apollo 11 lunar landing.

1994: Plantronics introduces the Starset headset, featuring a unique curved earpiece.

1972: Company opens its first overseas manufacturing facility in Tijuana, Mexico.

1984: Plantronics provides the official headsets of the Olympic Games in Los Angeles.

1986: Plantronics opens an office in England.

1994: Plantronics goes public on the New York Stock Exchange.

2004: Plantronics introduces its first Bluetooth headset, the M3500.

2005: Company acquires audio system manufacturer Altec Lansing.

2006: Plantronics opens manufacturing plant in Suzhou, China.

company's products, in 1984 Plantronics served as the official headset of the Los Angeles Summer Olympics. That year, the company unveiled the StarSet Supra, a streamlined version of its StarSet model that was designed specifically for use in high-volume call centers. Another notable innovation from the mid-1980s was the QuietStar noise-canceling telephone headset, which was geared to use by air traffic controllers. Throughout the 1980s Plantronics headsets continued to be used by the U.S. space program in its space shuttle missions.

Plantronics made its first entry into the European marketplace in 1986, when it opened a regional headquarters office in England. The company quickly expanded, establishing a center of operations in the Netherlands and several sales offices throughout Europe and the Middle East. Domestically, Plantronics made a significant acquisition in 1986 when it purchased hear-

ing aid maker Walker Equipment Corporation. The company would eventually integrate Walker's technology into a line of products aimed at the hearing impaired. The company changed the Walker brand name to Clarity in 2004.

SMALLER, LEANER, MORE VERSATILE: 1990-2000

In 1994 Plantronics made an initial public offering on the New York Stock Exchange. A year later, the company introduced the FreeHand, a headset designed to rest in the user's ear for maximum portability. The company unveiled two new headset designs for its corporate customers, the TriStar and the Encore, in 1996. By 1999 Plantronics was able to offer business executives the CS10 line of headgear, which featured a connection radius of 150 feet. Toward the end of the decade, the company also began to focus on the development of headsets for wireless phones. Plantronics' M130 line proved particularly popular and was soon one of the best selling wireless headsets on the market.

In the late 1990s Plantronics made a strategic entry into the emerging market for PC-compatible headsets. One of its more notable offerings in this line was the DSP-500, which was introduced in 2000. The model was equipped with a digital signal processor (DSP), which digitized analog sound for easier computer processing. The headset came with a range of gaming and music accessories, including voice mail software and a digital jukebox program. A review of the DSP-500 by Mark Kellner in the *Washington Times* on October 2, 2000, hailed the model's "radically improved speech recognition," as well as its "incredible audio reproduction." Kellner subsequently admitted that he was actually dictating his review into the headset. He also praised the unit's streamlined size, estimating that it weighed approximately half as much as its predecessor.

A NEW CENTURY, MORE PRODUCTS

At the beginning of the 21st century Plantronics continued to capitalize on rapidly evolving consumer demand for new telephone products. In 2001 the company introduced the DuoPro convertible headset, which was aimed at the call center market and was designed to alleviate pressure on the caller's ear. The M205 earbud was also introduced that year and was the company's latest headset designed for cell phone use. A year later, the company launched the MX100 series. The line featured Plantronic's patented FlexGrip design, which represented a significant advance in the area of earbud comfort and stability, as well as markedly improved audio quality. In recognition of the company's run of successes, it was named one of the country's best small companies by *Forbes Magazine*.

Another source of significant growth during the early years of the new century arose out of government efforts to regulate cell phone use in automobiles. As cities and states began to introduce legislation that prohibited drivers from talking on their cell phones, demand for telephone headsets rose dramatically. The first cell phone ban was implemented in New York in the summer of 2001. Within two days of the law's passage, shares of Plantronics had risen 26 percent. Over the next several years, the trend toward strict regulation continued. In 2004 New Jersey became the second state to impose a cell phone ban, after which sales of Plantronics headsets rose 34 percent.

Another major turning point occurred in 2004, when the company introduced its first Bluetooth headset. Bluetooth technology, which enabled the transfer of various forms of data via a wireless device, represented a new and potentially lucrative area for the headset pioneer. In the early part of the decade, Bluetooth devices had struggled to become popular within the broad marketplace, primarily due to widespread concerns about security breaches, as well as to several significant lapses in overall quality. By the middle of the first decade of the 2000s, however, the Bluetooth was clearly establishing itself as the technology of choice among consumers, particularly in Europe. According to market research conducted by the Plantronics U.K. office, Bluetooth-enabled phones had captured roughly 1 million customers in 2002. The company projected that number would increase 500 percent by 2003 and would reach approximately 50 million by 2007 when Plantronics estimated that roughly 70 percent of all cell phones in Europe would employ Bluetooth technology.

The company's first Bluetooth device, the M3500, featured improved digital audio processing, resulting in the best sound quality offered in a Plantronic's headset. Widespread popularity of the device inspired further innovation, and by 2005 Bluetooth headsets had become the company's signature product, sold under the Pulsar, Discovery, Explorer, and Voyager lines. Within a year, Plantronics had established itself as an industry leader in the emerging technology and was considered to offer the widest range of Bluetooth products on the market.

While Plantronics always had placed a premium on the technological quality of its products, it also had recognized the importance of comfort and style to non-business customers. The core of the company's revenue stream came increasingly from ordinary consumers. At the beginning of the decade, only 4.5 percent of the company's earnings came from consumer sales, but by 2005 this figure had climbed to 22.5 percent. In order to capitalize on increasing demand for Bluetooth technology among European consumers, the company launched a major advertising campaign in the summer of 2005. The highlight of the marketing effort came in Milan, where the company exhibited its full range of Bluetooth products during a runway fashion show.

During this period of vigorous innovation and growth, the company remained committed to broadening the scope of its core business. In August 2005 Plantronics acquired Altec Lansing, an industry leader in the field of audio entertainment products, for $165 million. A year later, the company opened its first manufacturing facility in Suzhou, China.

In the second half of the first decade of the 2000s, the company's annual revenues more than doubled, increasing from $417 million in 2004 to $856 million in 2008. By the summer of 2008, when cell phone use was banned while driving in California and Washington, it was clear that increased consumer demand for headset products would continue to drive the company's long-term profitability. Although the company's performance faltered during the economic recession of the late 2000s, with sales dropping to $765 million, Plantronics remained poised to capitalize on continued future growth. The company continued its commitment to overseas expansion, opening an office in Kuala Lumpur in 2009 to manufacture and market headsets to regional call centers in that country. On July 20, 2009, the company celebrated the milestone fortieth anniversary of the fateful moment when Neil Armstrong sent his message from the moon back to earth on a Plantronics headset. With its reputation as an innovator firmly in place, Plantronics could expect to remain an industry leader for years to come.

Stephen Meyer

PRINCIPAL SUBSIDIARIES

Clarity; Altec Lansing Technologies.

PRINCIPAL COMPETITORS

GN Netcom (Denmark); Logitech International S.A. (Switzerland); Motorola, Inc.

FURTHER READING

Barker, Robert, "Lend an Ear to Plantronics," *Business Week*, November 7, 2005, p. 26.

"Crystal-Clear Communication a Sweet-Sounding Success," *Spinoff*, 2005.

Harmanci, Reyhan, "Now Ear This! Talking the Talk, Walking the Walk, with Wireless Headsets," *San Francisco Chronicle*, August 14, 2005, p. M1.

Hughlett, Mike, "Chicago Cell Phone Law Spurs Sales of Headsets," *Chicago Tribune*, July 5, 2005, p. 1.

Kellner, Mark, "Plantronics' Audio Treats Make Computing Fun," *Washington Times*, October 2, 2000, p. D8.

Kim, Ryan, "New Law a Boon to Headset Makers," *San Francisco Chronicle*, March 24, 2008, p. D1.

Lillington, Karlin, "Buyers over the Moon about Headsets," *Irish Times*, June 13, 2003, p. 55.

"N.Y. Cellphone Driving Ban Spurs Headset Demand: Plantronics up 26%," *National Post* (Canada), June 28, 2001, p. C3.

Plum Creek Timber Company, Inc.

999 Third Avenue, Suite 2300
Seattle, Washington 98104-4096
U.S.A.
Telephone: (206) 467-3600
Toll Free: (800) 858-5347
Fax: (206) 467-3795
Web site: http://www.plumcreek.com

Public Company
Incorporated: 1999
Employees: 1,740
Sales: $1.61 billion (2008)
Stock Exchanges: New York
Ticker Symbol: PCL
NAICS: 113310 Logging; 113110 Timber Tract Operations; 321113 Sawmills; 321211 Hardwood Veneer and Plywood Manufacturing; 321212 Softwood Veneer and Plywood Manufacturing; 321219 Reconstituted Wood Product Manufacturing; 322110 Pulp Mills; 525930 Real Estate Investment Trusts; 551112 Offices of Other Holding Companies

■ ■ ■

Plum Creek Timber Company, Inc., is the largest owner of private timberlands in the United States, with holdings totaling more than seven million acres of land. The company also controls several wood-product conversion facilities and produces a range of wood-fiber products, including medium-density fiberboard and plywood. Plum Creek Timber products are sold through the company's extensive network of warehouses, which are located in several states throughout the country. The company is based in Seattle, Washington, and operates two primary business segments, Northern Resources and Southern Resources, in addition to its manufacturing operations and its real estate development.

FROM RAILROADS TO TIMBER

During the 1800s an act of Congress gave land to railroad corporations as an incentive to build railroads from the Great Lakes region to Puget Sound and the West Coast. Congress intended the land to be sold to settlers. While some of the land was sold and settled, much of it remained in control of the railroads and some was sold to timber companies, such as Weyerhaeuser and Boise Cascade.

In 1989 Burlington Resources, Inc., whose roots were in the railroad industry, spun off Plum Creek Timber, L.P., which took its name from the Minnesota stream where the first U.S. lumber mill was built. Plum Creek Timber was established as a master limited partnership to take advantage of the elimination of double taxation in the tax code. The company started with more than a million acres of forested land in Washington, Idaho, and Montana.

The late 1980s and early 1990s were a tough time for the timber industry. In early 1990 the spotted owl controversy erupted. The owls' habitat is in forests with trees that are hundreds of years old and 200 feet high or more. These trees make the most valuable timber. Environmentalists sued the U.S. Forest Service to

COMPANY PERSPECTIVES

Our Mission is to establish Plum Creek as the premier land and timber company by demonstrating leadership and innovation through: identifying opportunities for value growth from our assets; practicing environmentally responsible resource stewardship; achieving superior returns for our owners; engaging with our communities on matters of common interest; consistently providing quality products and services to our customers; selecting business partners that share common values and beliefs; fostering an ethical business culture that encourages ideas and initiative and rewards accomplishments.

protect the spotted owl, and in 1991 a federal judge issued an injunction against logging in the owls' habitat.

Besides the spotted owl problems, Plum Creek was faced with criticism for its practice of clear-cutting forests quickly and expansively. Forest conservationists were unhappy with Plum Creek's practice of clearing several square miles at a time, what the conservationists referred to as "checkerboarding." Some groups felt Plum Creek over-logged its land. U.S. Representative Rod Chandler, a Republican from Washington, called Plum Creek the "Darth Vader of the state of Washington" in a *Wall Street Journal* article in 1990. Subsequently, Plum Creek set out to clean up its reputation and establish a plan of action that would mollify environmentalists, preserve wildlife, and increase value for its business.

1990S: ENVIRONMENTAL FORESTRY AND EXPANSION

Plum Creek matched the U.S. Forest Service's shift in focus from harvesting to multiuse forest management. The company set three goals: to keep live trees at each site, preserve wildlife as much as possible, and retain dead trees (called snags), which help maintain the habitat and contribute nutrients to the forest. An example of its efforts was a 10-mile strip of forest that was left at Plum Creek's Cougar Ramp site in Washington in 1993. Although hardly a forest, the remaining trees contributed to the overall habitat in terms of shade, seed, and visual appeal.

In 1993 Jerry Franklin, a University of Washington professor and ecosystem analyst, presented ideas on "kinder, gentler forestry" to President Bill Clinton at a timber summit in Portland, Oregon. Shortly thereafter,

Plum Creek hired Franklin as an adviser, and his team developed a program they called "environmental forestry." This involved selective logging, protection of streams and their habitats, and taking into account the aesthetic values of avoiding clear-cuts. Plum Creek reduced clear-cutting to 15 percent in the Northwest and to 10 percent in the Rocky Mountains.

In 1996 Plum Creek acquired 538,000 acres of softwood timberland and three wood products production plants in Louisiana and Arkansas from Riverwood International Corp. The deal increased Plum Creek's timber ownership by 25 percent and diversified its land holdings. As part of the agreement, Plum Creek continued sending pulpwood to Riverwood's Louisiana board mill.

In 1998 Plum Creek purchased 905,000 acres of forests in Maine from South African Pulp and Paper (Sappi) for $180 million. This boosted Plum Creek's acreage to more than 3.3 million acres. The company agreed to supply Sappi's paper facility with fiber from these lands. Environmentalist groups, most notably the Natural Resources Council of Maine, opposed this move. The council speculated that Plum Creek would sell off recreational lands, but Plum Creek vowed that was not their plan.

I-90 LAND SWAP IN WASHINGTON STATE

When the government granted lands to the railroads in the 19th century, it granted only every other square mile. When timber companies logged these land parcels, they often left clear-cut areas starkly next to untouched areas. To help remedy this checkerboard effect and to make better use of its land, Plum Creek participated in a land swap with the U.S. Forest Service in Washington State. Ten years in the making, the swap was coined "The I-90 Land Swap." In the deal, Plum Creek traded 42,000 acres of land that paralleled Interstate 90 east of Seattle for 11,500 acres of federal lands in the Cascades plus $4.3 million.

Supporters of the deal argued that the swap moved private lands to areas where forestry made more sense and created public lands better suited for recreation. As part of the deal, Plum Creek also donated 838 acres to the government and held some lands for possible purchase in the future. Some environmentalists nonetheless protested the deal, claiming the swap violated the National Environmental Policy Act, the Endangered Species act, and other laws.

Further complicating the matter was the discovery of the protected marbled murrelets on the government's land, which meant that Plum Creek could not harvest

KEY DATES

■

1989: Plum Creek Timber Company, L.P., is created when it is spun off from Burlington Resources.

1993: Plum Creek puts in place environmental forestry plans and policies.

1994: The Sustainable Forestry Initiative guidelines are established.

1996: Plum Creek buys 538,000 acres of timberland in Arkansas and Louisiana from Riverwood International Corp.

1997: The company builds a sawmill in Louisiana.

1998: The company purchases close to one million acres of forest in northern Maine for $1.8 million.

1999: Plum Creek becomes a publicly traded real estate investment trust (REIT).

2000: The Washington State I-90 Land Swap is completed.

2001: The company sells 44,500 acres of timberlands to Pope Resources; a merger with Georgia-Pacific's Timber Company is finalized.

2005: Plum Creek negotiates agreement with state of Wisconsin to protect more than 18,000 acres of public land from future development.

2008: Plum Creek receives approval to launch massive real estate development project in Northern Woods region of Maine.

1,000 acres of the land it was to receive. However, Plum Creek surprised many in the timber industry with a new tactic: It sued the environmentalists for the right to log. The U.S. Forest Service and five environmental groups were named as defendants in the lawsuit. With the lawsuits pending and protestors staked out in the trees, the swap was in danger. Finally, however, after a settlement had been reached wherein Plum Creek received about a third less land in exchange for more cash, the deal would be finalized in January 2000.

EMPHASIS ON THE ENVIRONMENT

In 1994 the American Forest and Paper Association had established the Sustainable Forestry Initiative (SFI) to address environmental issues within the forestry industry. Developed by foresters, conservationists, and scientists, the program asked companies to use environmentally sound practices, address the needs of the future, adhere to environmentally responsible guidelines, consider the qualities unique to each area, and continuously improve forest management techniques.

Although Plum Creek had conducted third-party audits of its practices in the past, in 1999 it added the SFI guidelines to its policies and completed audits of all its land holdings in compliance with SFI. The audits concluded that Plum Creek protected water quality, improved wood use, used chemicals prudently, and protected special sites.

Some environmental groups questioned the validity of Plum Creek's audits, but the company strived for a good image. It set guidelines based on SFI that addressed the impact of roads through Plum Creek lands. In June 1997 Plum Creek developed a habitat conservation plan for the bull trout and worked with the National Marine Fisheries Service to create a Native Fish Habitat Conservation plan. The company set up riparian management practices, one of which was maintaining streams with woody debris. Plum Creek also set up land use, range management, and restoration planning. It created policies at its timber mills and wood plants in an attempt to address wood-fiber recovery, safe workplaces, waste disposal, and air quality.

TURN OF THE CENTURY: RESTRUCTURING AND A MAJOR ACQUISITION

In July 1999 Plum Creek reclassified itself from a master limited partnership to a real estate investment trust (REIT). For many timber companies, a move like this would not only have tax and financing advantages, it would also separate timberlands from pulp and paper operations. Because pulp and paper operations had been performing poorly during this time, those areas brought down the stock of an entire timber company. Many timber companies converted these parts of their businesses to REITs in order to preserve their overall stock price and bolster their financials.

Plum Creek, however, did not own any paper operations and instead converted the entire company to a REIT, a move not done before by any other company. The goal was to make it easier to raise capital, broaden the company's appeal to investors, and create REIT stocks, which were much more liquid than partnership shares because REIT shares could be made available to individual investors, who were unable to buy in to a limited partnership. After the REIT conversion, Plum Creek's previous controlling partner, SPO Partners, decreased its ownership to 27 percent.

In September 2000 Plum Creek signed an agreement to merge with the Timber Company, an operating group of the Georgia-Pacific Corporation. In October 2001 the merger was completed. The transaction was valued at about $4 billion and added 4.7 million acres to Plum Creek's holdings of U.S. private timberlands; the company now owned more than 7.9 million acres in 19 states. As part of the deal, Plum Creek assumed $1 billion of the Timber Company's debt and agreed to honor a 10-year wood supply agreement between Georgia-Pacific and the Timber Company.

FROM TIMBER TO REAL ESTATE

Toward the late 1990s, a dramatic shift began to occur in the timber industry, and in many respects Plum Creek was leading the way. As real estate prices continued to rise nationwide, the company began to see tremendous potential for profits in the land development business. Plum Creek was particularly well suited for such a transition. Its status as an REIT exempted it from paying income taxes, enabling it to outbid most other corporations for prime land, while also making it an attractive partner for investors. More significantly, its existing land holdings could deliver much higher returns as real estate property than as working forest.

The immediate financial advantages of such a transition quickly became evident. For example, in 1998 Plum Creek purchased close to a million acres in the North Woods region of Maine, at a cost of approximately $1.8 million, or roughly $180 per acre. The purchase included more than 400,000 acres surrounding Moosehead Lake, a popular spot for outdoor recreation. By 2005 the company was positioned to sell individual lake-front lots on the same land for $70,000 apiece. Other projected uses of the land, including the creation of RV parks and resort property, offered the company additional opportunities to capitalize on its original investment. Writing about the company's emerging strategy in the *Boston Globe* on April 5, 2005, Beth Daley described Plum Creek as "a new type of manager in the timber industry, one that is a hybrid of timber management and real estate development."

The company's increased focus on real estate development provoked a groundswell of concern, particularly among conservationists and public land advocates. Private citizens also had their misgivings. Residents of the Moosehead Lake area, accustomed to unrestricted hunting and fishing access on the timber company's expansive forest lands, began to voice their opposition to the company's proposed transformation of the region. Some observers also objected to the Plum Creek subdivision because they believed it would drive up local real estate prices, making it difficult for many long-time residents to continue living in the area. Plum Creek's real estate activities had elicited similar concerns in other parts of the country. In Cle Ellum, Washington, the company's former land holdings were in the process of being transformed into prime resort property; in 2005 Plum Creek's extensive holdings in Wisconsin had prompted the state government to negotiate a deal to designate nearly 20,000 acres of the company's land to be preserved for public use.

In the face of the public outcry surrounding its proposed Moosehead Lake subdivision, Plum Creek devised an alternate plan. It designated more than 50 secluded ponds for conservation purposes, and it allocated an additional 417,000 acres for continued timber development. According to the company's revised proposal, this land would be protected from additional real estate development for several decades. The company's concessions did little to ease concerns, and local activists mobilized to fight the Plum Creek proposal. By late 2008, however, the company's plan had received the approval of the state's Land Use Regulation Commission, and it was suddenly poised to embark on the biggest residential development project in Maine's history. The commission's ruling soon caught the attention of other areas of the country where Plum Creek controlled substantial acreage. One notable area was Whitefish, Montana, where the company had launched a strategy for developing large sections of waterfront property along Whitefish Lake. As the first decade of the new century came to a close, it remained uncertain how ambitious Plum Creek's development vision would ultimately become.

Kerri DeVault
Updated, Stephen Meyer

PRINCIPAL DIVISIONS

Northern Resources; Southern Resources; Township 110 Land Company.

PRINCIPAL COMPETITORS

Boise Cascade Holdings LLC.; Deltic Timber Corporation; Georgia-Pacific LLC; International Forest Products Limited (Canada); International Paper Company; Longview Fibre Company; Potlatch Corporation; Sierra Pacific Industries; Western Forest Products Inc. (Canada); Weyerhaeuser Company.

FURTHER READING

Berman, David, "Interest Grows in Timber Assets; Forest Lands Provide Valuable Hedge against Market Fluctuations,"

National Post's Financial Post & FP Investing (Canada), June 13, 2007, p. FP10.

Blackman, Ted, "Plum Creek Updates Panel, Lumber Plants in Montana (Parts I & II)," *Wood Technology*, January 1995, p. 30.

Bond, Jeff, "Timber's Good Guys," *Washington CEO*, June 2000.

Carlton, Jim, "Plum Creek Timber to Purchase Land in the Northeast," *Wall Street Journal*, October 7, 1998, p. B2.

Daley, Beth, "Houses, Resorts Planned for North Woods," *Boston Globe*, April 5, 2005, p. A1.

DeSilver, Drew, "More Timber for Plum Creek," *Seattle Times*, July 19, 2000, p. CI.

Devlin, Sherry, "Plum Creek Says Forests Come First," *Missoulian*, January 9, 2000.

Didisheim, Pete, and Judy Berk, "Statement from the Natural Resources Council of Maine," October 6, 1998.

Draffan, George, "Facts about Plum Creek Timber," *Railroads and Clearcuts*, September 1999.

Ervin, Keith, "Plum Creek Sues Activists over Land Swap," *Seattle Times*, October 17, 1999, p. B1.

Fisher, Frank, "Chunk of Maine Forest to Be Sold," Associated Press, October 6, 1998.

———, "Sappi Announces Deal to Sell 905,000 Acres of Maine Woods," *Boston Globe*, October 6, 1998.

"Forests: The Biggest Tree Sale of All," *Economist*, November 6, 1999.

"The I-90 Land Exchange Is Completed," *Seattle Post-Intelligencer*, January 6, 2000.

Johnson, Kirk, "As Logging Fades, Rich Carve Up Land," *New York Times*, October 13, 2007, p. 1.

Knickerbocker, Brad, "'New Forestry': A Kinder, Gentler Approach to Logging," *Christian Science Monitor*, June 20, 1995, p. 10.

Ludwick, Jim, "Corporate Shift Will Open Plum Creek to All Investors," *Missoulian*, June 9, 1998.

Mapes, Lynda V., "Activists, Company Agree on Land Swap," *Seattle Times*, November 3, 1999, p. C1.

———, "Big Timber Swap Hits Snag," *Seattle Times*, July 21, 1999, p. A1.

———, "Land Swap Delights Environmentalists," *Seattle Times*, November 4, 1999, p. B2.

McClure, Robert, "Bird Foils Big Timberland Swap," *Seattle Post-Intelligencer*, July 22, 1999, p. B1.

———, "Partial Buyout Seen as Way around Problem of Endangered Bird," *Seattle Post-Intelligencer*, September 10, 1999, p. A1.

McCoy, Charles, "Plum Creek Timber Aiming to Convert into a REIT, Boosting Acquisition Plans," *Wall Street Journal*, June 8, 1998.

Miller, Sara, "Big Stir over Big Plan for Maine Forest," *Christian Science Monitor*, September 26, 2005, p. 2.

"$180 Million Sale of Maine Woodlands Troubles Environmentalists," *Washington Post*, October 7, 1998, p. A22.

Otanez, Andrea, "Plum Creek Timber, Interior to Sign Pact on Habitat Protection," *Seattle Times*, November 28, 2000.

"Plum Creek Completes Acquisition of Central Maine Forestlands," *Business Wire*, November 12, 1998.

"Plum Creek Plans Audits to Verify Forest Management Practices," *Wood Technology*, March 1999.

"Plum Creek Timber Company to Merge with Georgia-Pacific Subsidiary," *Forestry Source*, September 2000.

"Plum Creek to Buy Products Unit," *Pulp & Paper*, October 1996 pp. 23–25.

"Public's 'Green' Attitudes Force Forest-Sector Changes," *Wood Technology*, September 1995.

Raeburn, Paul, "Can This Man Save Our Forests?" *Popular Science*, June 1, 1994, pp. 81–88.

"Timber Co. Finances Purchase with Private Loan," *Corporate Financing Week*, October 12, 1998.

Thomas, Tom E., "Plum Creek's Chainsaw Massacre," *Business and Society Review*, Fall 1990.

Thompson, Steve, "Seeing the Forest for the Trees," *Missoula Independent*, May 10, 2001.

Turcotte, Deborah, "Plum Creek Timber Firm Seeks to Shed 'Evil' Image," *Bangor Daily News*, October 8, 1998.

"Unkindest Cut," *Wall Street Journal*, June 18, 1990.

Virgin, Bill, "Timber Deal Is Struck: Plum Creek to Buy Spinoff Unit of GP," *Seattle Post-Intelligencer*, July 19, 2000, p. D1.

Quest Diagnostics Inc.

———•———

3 Giralda Farms
Madison, New Jersey 07940
U.S.A.
Telephone: (973) 520-2700
Toll Free: (800) 222-0446
Web site: http://www.questdiagnostics.com

Public company
Incorporated: 1967 as MetPath Inc.
Employees: 43,000
Sales: $7.2 billion (2008)
Stock Exchanges: New York
Ticker Symbol: DGX
NAISC: 621511 Medical Laboratories

■ ■ ■

Quest Diagnostics Inc. is the world's largest provider of diagnostic testing for health care. Through its vast network of laboratories and patient service centers, the company offers a broad range of routine and esoteric services used by the medical profession in the diagnosis, monitoring, and treatment of disease and other medical conditions. On a typical workday, Quest performs testing for more than a half million patients. Its labs operate 24 hours a day, 365 days a year, offering physicians a menu of more than 3,000 tests.

CORNING MEDICAL PRODUCTS AND METPATH TO 1982

The origins of Quest Diagnostics were in the laboratory glassware of Corning Glass Works. Its Pyrex glassware—which spawned a lucrative cookware line—put the company in the laboratory business as far back as World War I. When instrumentation began to replace test tube, flask, and beaker chemistry in the 1960s, Corning added a high powered pH-measuring instrument designed to find how well a critically ill patient's lungs were exchanging oxygen and carbon dioxide to the primitive meter it was already making. The new blood-gas apparatus could not be produced fast enough to keep up with demand in 1977.

By 1975 Corning had also begun marketing white blood cell analyzers to automate one of the last blood tests still being performed manually in clinical laboratories. In 1976 the company had a medical products division making electrodes, pH meters, electrometers, biomedical instruments and systems, photometers, electrophoresis equipment, and densitometers in Medford, Massachusetts, and in Palo Alto, California. In 1977 Corning's health and sciences activities were consolidated into a single operating division with sales amounting to $221 million and a net income at 12 percent of the parent company's total. In 1981 these figures were $374 million and 32 percent, respectively.

Corning's clinical laboratory testing did not begin, however, until it acquired MetPath Inc. in 1982. Paul A. Brown, a pathologist who later said he was "amazed at the sky-high test prices charged by hospitals and clinics," founded what was originally Metropolitan Pathological Laboratory in 1967 with $500 and initially ran it out of his Manhattan apartment. Two years later he invested in a $55,000 device that automatically performed 12 common blood tests, charging $5.50,

COMPANY PERSPECTIVES

■

Quest Diagnostics is People. Dedicated people who understand that behind every specimen and result there is a human life. Our employees play a critical role in healthcare delivery and enable better healthcare choices by providing unsurpassed diagnostic insights to our customers.

compared to more than $40 charged by hospitals and medical laboratories. In 1972 Brown spent over $1 million on two AutoChemist units, which raised the number of blood tests MetPath could perform automatically to 25 and saved significantly on costly chemical reagents needed for analysis. The company began turning a profit in 1971. Two years later, in 1973, Corning Glass Works bought 10 percent of its stock.

By 1975 MetPath had one of the best equipped and largest medical laboratories in the world and was the largest U.S. company devoted entirely to clinical laboratory services. It offered more than 600 laboratory tests to physicians, hospitals, and institutions and performed more than 2 million lab tests a month from specimens of more than 150,000 patients. The tests were being processed at a highly automated central laboratory in Hackensack, New Jersey, with 80 percent of the results delivered to the client within 24 hours after collection of the specimen. Overall, MetPath's average billing per patient transaction was only $9.

By 1979 MetPath was challenging Damon Corp. for first place in the clinical laboratory testing field, which had grown into a $12 billion-a-year business. The company had a net income of $3.8 million in 1978 on revenues of $53.4 million. A $25 million laboratory capable of analyzing up to 30,000 samples a day was completed in Teterboro, New Jersey, in 1978. Fifty local offices made daily collections at doctors' offices and clinics, shipping them via same-day air freight to the laboratory. The results were transmitted to telecommunications terminals at each of the company's local offices. For a package of 29 common tests, MetPath was charging only $20.

MetPath was tops in the clinical laboratory testing field by 1982. The Teterboro laboratory's four IBM mainframe computers were sending results to terminals in 70 branches and 550 doctor's and hospital offices. MetPath had acquired small testing laboratories throughout the country to establish collection points for samples and had built a second clinical laboratory near

O'Hare International Airport in Chicago, Illinois. However, this expansion raised the company's debt so precipitously that it was sold in 1982 to Corning Glass Works for stock worth about $145 million.

METPATH AND OTHER UNITS: 1982–95

MetPath remained autonomous and its revenue kept growing fueled by Medicare funding, a new emphasis on preventive medicine, and a wave of medical malpractice suits, which encouraged doctors to order more tests. However, the company found itself overwhelmed by freight costs. It also had lost business to smaller labs as testing equipment became smaller and more affordable. MetPath's operating profit margin fell from 10 percent in 1981 to 4 percent in 1985, when it wrote off the Chicago area lab and closed some local offices. In response to the loss of business, it decided to transform its testing facilities into a network of regional laboratories close to the physicians being served and capable of quicker response to customer needs. By 1988 MetPath was again solidly in the black, although Smith-Kline Beckman Laboratories was doing twice as much annual business in the clinical testing field as MetPath's $350 million.

Corning regrouped its products and services in 1989 into four industry segments. The science and optical products units were moved from the former Health and Science segment to Specialty Materials, with the remaining businesses forming the Laboratory Services segment. Laboratory Services had net sales of $580.8 million in 1989 and a gross income of $99.2 million. At the end of 1990 the Laboratory Services segment was placed into a subsidiary named Corning Lab Services Inc.

MetPath, able to handle more than 1,400 different clinical tests, remained the major unit. It strengthened its regional network in 1991 with the addition of smaller labs, including Clinical Pathology Facility Inc. in Pittsburgh, Pennsylvania, and Continental Bio-Clinical Laboratories in Grand Rapids, Michigan. Corning Lab Services acquired Southgate Medical Laboratory System, a Cleveland-based operator of clinical testing laboratories in Ohio, Indiana, and Pennsylvania, in 1992, and clinical laboratories in Denver, Colorado; Dallas, Texas; and Phoenix, Arizona, from Unilab Corp. in 1993. Another Corning Lab Services operation was Metropolitan Reference Laboratories Inc. in St. Louis, Missouri. Founded in 1987, it was testing medical samples from 10 midwestern and southern states by 1993.

Also in 1993 Corning acquired, for its Laboratory Services subsidiary, Damon Corp., the nation's fifth

KEY DATES

1967: Paul A. Brown incorporates Metropolitan Pathological Laboratory (MetPath).

1973: MetPath sells 10 percent of its stock to Corning Glass Works.

1978: MetPath builds a clinical laboratory in Teterboro, New Jersey.

1982: MetPath builds a second clinical laboratory in Chicago, Illinois; the company is purchased by Corning Glass Works.

1995: MetPath is renamed Corning Clinical Laboratories.

1996: Corning Clinical Laboratories becomes Quest Diagnostics Inc. when Corning spins off its laboratory testing business to shareholders.

1999: Quest acquires SmithKline Beecham Clinical Laboratories, making it the largest provider of diagnostic testing and related services in the United States.

2001: Quest acquires MedPlus Inc.

2002: Quest acquires American Medical Laboratories.

2003: Quest acquires Unilab Corporation.

2005: Quest acquires LabOne.

2006: Quest acquires Focus Diagnostics Inc.

2007: Quest acquires AmeriPath and the Swedish-based company HemoCue.

2009: Company introduces the first commercial lab test for identifying the H1N1 (swine flu) virus; Quest Diagnostics is named one of the "World's Most Admired Companies" by *Fortune* for the second year in a row.

largest owner of clinical testing laboratories, with 14 in the United States and 1 in Mexico and about 220 satellite labs in remote U.S. locations. This made Corning Lab Services the nation's second largest laboratory testing company.

In 1994 the parent company had been renamed Corning Life Sciences Inc. and had acquired Maryland Medical Laboratory Inc., one of the largest diagnostic and testing operations in Baltimore, Maryland, with annual sales of nearly $100 million, for about $140 million worth of stock. Maryland Medical was conducting regional testing for the acquired immunodeficiency syndrome, immunogenetics, virology, veterinary diagnostics, molecular biology, and computer sciences.

Also in 1994 Corning acquired Nichols Institute, another clinical laboratory testing operation, for about $325 million. Both acquisitions became part of MetPath, which in 1994 accounted for $1.7 billion of the parent company's $4.8 billion in sales and was the nation's largest clinical laboratory company. In 1995 MetPath was renamed Corning Clinical Laboratories.

The business climate for Corning Clinical Laboratories was far from ideal, however, as public demand intensified for cost containment in health care. MetPath and Metwest, a California-based spin-off from MetPath, agreed in 1993 to pay the federal government $39.8 million to settle charges that they had submitted Medicare claims for unnecessary blood tests. In 1995 Corning Clinical Laboratories agreed to pay the federal government $8.6 million for tests that doctors never ordered, and in 1998 Quest Diagnostics, the successor of Corning Clinical Laboratories, agreed to pay $6.8 million to settle a similar case.

The fines, the tougher regulatory climate, the growth of managed care networks limiting the ability of Corning Clinical Laboratories to increase prices, and the difficulty of processing bills by the diverse companies it had acquired put the unit in the red in 1995. Despite net revenues of $1.63 billion in 1995, Corning Clinical Laboratories lost $52.1 million, after the parent company took a charge of $62 million to increase accounts receivable because of the billings problems. Moreover, Corning Clinical Laboratories' long-term debt reached almost $1.2 billion.

QUEST DIAGNOSTICS: 1996–97

In 1996 Corning decided to spin off its laboratory testing and pharmaceutical services businesses to shareholders, creating two independent public companies. The laboratory testing business became Quest Diagnostics Inc. On the last day of 1996, Corning distributed all outstanding shares of common stock of the new company to Corning stockholders, with one share distributed for each eight shares of Corning. Revenues for 1996 came to $1.62 billion, with a loss of $626 million after taking into account special charges of $668.5 million, including a $445 million write-down of intangible assets. However, long-term debt declined to $515 million because Corning assumed more than $700 million of Quest's debt when it spun off the company. In 1997 Quest had a net loss of $22.3 million on revenues of $1.53 billion. The loss reflected special charges totaling $55.5 million in connection with eliminating and consolidating company facilities to reduce excess capacity.

In 1997 Quest had a network of 15 regional laboratories located in major metropolitan areas across the United States and an esoteric testing laboratory and research and development facilities (Nichols Institute) in San Juan Capistrano, California. In addition, Quest had several smaller branch laboratories, including one in Mexico; approximately 150 local laboratories; and about 800 patient service centers. The company was processing about 54 million requisitions for testing each year.

Routine testing services and operations, which were performed at the regional laboratories, included procedures in the areas of blood chemistry, hematology, urine chemistry, virology, tissue pathology, and cytology. This accounted for about 89 percent of Quest's net laboratory revenues in 1997. Esoteric testing by Nichols Institute was being performed in cases where the information provided by routine tests was not specific enough or was inconclusive as to the existence or absence of disease. This generated about 9 percent of the company's net laboratory revenues in 1997.

The balance of Quest's net revenues in 1997 were derived from the manufacture and sale of clinical laboratory test kits by Nichols Institute and from clinical trials and informatics businesses. Quest Informatics was collecting and analyzing laboratory, pharmaceutical, and other data to help large health care customers identify and monitor patients at risk for certain diseases.

QUEST IN THE NEW CENTURY

In 1999 Quest Diagnostics acquired SmithKline Beecham Clinical Laboratories. This acquisition made Quest the nation's leading provider of diagnostic testing and related services. From there, the company continued to expand through both growth and further acquisitions. In 2001 Quest acquired MedPlus Inc. This made the company a major player in point-of-care access to essential online patient information for physicians and hospitals. The following year, Quest added an East Coast outpost of its Nichols Institute operation with the acquisition of American Medical Laboratories and its Chantilly, Virginia, laboratory.

More expansion followed over the next few years, as Quest became the nation's largest owner of private labs. In 2003 it purchased Unilab Corporation, and in 2005 the company expanded into the business of drug abuse testing by acquiring LabOne, with outposts in Kansas and Ohio. This acquisition also allowed Quest to begin offering testing services to life insurance companies. A year later, Quest acquired Focus Diagnostics Inc., a world leader in testing for infectious and immunologic diseases, including the first tests for SARS and West Nile Virus to hit the market.

The 2007 acquisition of the Swedish-based company HemoCue helped solidify Quest's position in the growing field of point-of-care testing. HemoCue made, among other things, handheld systems used to test blood for hemoglobin, glucose, and other substances. Quest also acquired the cancer diagnostics company AmeriPath that year, which along with Quest's existing capabilities made the company the world leader in cancer diagnostics services. By 2008 Quest labs in most major metropolitan areas in the United States, Mexico, the United Kingdom, and India, one of the fastest growing markets in the world.

Quest hit a bump in the road in early 2009, when it was forced to pay a $302 million settlement to resolve criminal and civil claims that it had knowingly sold faulty, misbranded test kits between 2000 and 2006. Another blow—albeit a less expensive one—came around the same time when Quest was forced to acknowledge that it had provided possibly erroneous results to thousands of people who had their vitamin D levels checked over the previous two years.

Despite these hiccups, the news was not all bad for Quest. In May 2009 it introduced the first commercial lab test for identifying the H1N1 (swine flu) virus. This breakthrough came just two months after Quest was named to *Fortune* magazine's list of the "World's Most Admired Companies" for the second straight year. With a testing empire serving about half of the doctors and hospitals in the United States and performing tests for more than half a million patients a day, Quest appeared poised to maintain its dominant position in the diagnostics business for years to come.

Robert Halasz
Updated, Bob Jacobson

PRINCIPAL SUBSIDIARIES

HemoCue; MedPlus; Nichols Institute Diagnostics; Quest Diagnostics India.

PRINCIPAL COMPETITORS

Bio-Reference Laboratories Inc.; Spectrum Laboratory Network.

FURTHER READING

"The Biotech Beat," *BusinessWeek Online*, April 4, 2002.

Blanton, Kimberly, "Needham Lab Fined $119 Million for Fraud," *Boston Globe*, October 10, 1996, pp. Al, A24.

Chilthelen, Ignatius, "Clinical Case," *Forbes*, March 20, 1989, pp. 178, 180.

"Damon Corp.," *Boston Globe*, June 8, 1993, p. 38.

Gross, Daniel, "Corning's Experiment," *Grain's New York Business*, January 22, 1996, p. 26.

Gross, Shera, "Rapid Growth Spurs Metropolitan Lab Move," *St. Louis Business Journal*, November 16, 1992, p. 13.

Holusha, John, "Corning to Spin Off Labs and Drug Units," *New York Times*, May 15, 1996, p. D4.

Kindel, Stephen, "It Takes a Lot of Patience," *Forbes*, September 13, 1982, pp. 82–84.

———, "Management, Know Thyself," *Forbes*, August 16, 1982, pp. 69–71.

"Lab Test Provider Generates Results," *Crain's New York Business*, January 20, 2003, p. 20.

"Machines to Analyze White Blood Cells Are Put on Market," *Wall Street Journal*, January 27, 1975, p. 8.

Magnet, Myron, "Corning Glass Shapes Up," *Fortune*, December 13, 1982, pp. 96, 100.

McConnell, Bill, "Corning Inc. Buys Maryland Medical Laboratories for $149 Million," *Warfield's Business Record*, May 6, 1994, p. 12.

"MetPath: Price-Cutting with a Super-Lab Creates New Growth," *BusinessWeek*, February 26, 1979, pp. 126, 132.

Mullaney, Christine, "MetPath Approach in Budding Industry Pays Off," *Investment Dealers' Digest*, October 7, 1975, pp. 29–30.

Pollack, Andrew, "Quest Acknowledges Errors in Vitamin D Tests," *New York Times*, January 7, 2009.

"Quest Diagnostics Again Named to Fortune Magazine's 'World's Most Admired Companies' List," *Biotech Week*, March 18, 2009.

"Quest Diagnostics Introduces First Commercial Laboratory Test for Identifying the H1N1 Swine Flu Virus," *PR Newswire*, May 11, 2009.

"Quest Diagnostics to Pay U.S. $302 Million to Resolve Allegations That a Subsidiary Sold Misbranded Test Kits" (press release), Washington, DC: U.S. Department of Justice, April 15, 2009, http://www.usdoj.gov/opa/pr/2009/April/09-civ-350.html.

Serwer, Andy, "Last Year's Best Bet? A Company Called Quest," *Fortune*, May 28, 2001, p. 183.

Sims, Calvin, "Blood Labs Agree to Pay $39.8 Million," *New York Times*, September 14, 1993, pp. DI, D5.

Random House Inc.

■

1745 Broadway
New York, New York 10019-4305
U.S.A.
Telephone: (212) 782-9000
Fax: (212) 302-7985
Web site: http://www.randomhouse.com

Wholly Owned Subsidiary of Bertelsmann AG
Founded: 1925
Incorporated: 1925
Employees: 5,764
Sales: €1.72 billion ($2.53 billion; 2008)
NAICS: 511130 Book Publishers

■ ■ ■

Random House Inc. was already the largest general trade book publisher in the English-speaking world when it was acquired by German entertainment and publishing conglomerate Bertelsmann AG in 1998 and merged with Bantam Doubleday Dell (BDD), which Bertelsmann also owned. The new publishing entity continued with the name of its senior partner, Random House Inc., and continued growing through acquisitions and expansions worldwide. By 2008 Random House was reporting revenues of €1.72 billion (about $2.53 billion), with almost half coming from sales outside the United States.

MODERN LIBRARY PROVIDES A SOLID FOUNDATION: 1925–30

When Bennett A. Cerf and Donald S. Klopfer decided to rename their joint publishing venture Random House Inc. (RH) in 1927, its pedigree was well established. The 27-year-old Cerf and his 23-year-old partner had purchased the 109-volume Modern Library line in 1925 for $215,000 from the Boni & Liveright publishing firm in New York. Since 1923, Cerf had worked at Boni & Liveright as a vice-president (replacing Richard L. Simon, who left to form a joint venture with M. Lincoln Schuster), and he had become increasingly aware of the value and potential of the series. When Horace Liveright's financial problems grew untenable and forced him to sell the seven-year-old Modern Library, Cerf and Klopfer jumped at the opportunity.

Inspired by Everyman's Library, founded in 1905 by Londoners Joseph Malaby Dent and Ernest Rhys, Modern Library was considered a classic in its time. Cerf and Klopfer replaced the company's logo with a leaping torch-bearer designed by Lucian Bernhard, bound the books in cloth instead of the original navy lambskin, and recouped their initial investment within two years. The partners soon changed the company's name to "Random House" to reflect their intention of publishing a wide array of fiction and nonfiction without limitations, literally "at random."

EXTRAVAGANCES CUT DURING DEPRESSION: THE 1930S

In 1931 Cerf and Klopfer created the Modern Library Giants, "a collection of the most significant and thought-provoking books in modern literature," as a

COMPANY PERSPECTIVES

■

Random House is a creative enterprise but it is run as a business. While the heart and soul of the company are our authors and books, the backbone is our results-oriented corporate structure. We believe that our publishing divisions have a higher degree of editorial and artistic independence than any other publishing company. At the same time, the divisions share a common corporate infrastructure that provides services such as sales, operations, and finance, and also leads investments in new technologies. In this way, Random House leverages business efficiency and know-how to support the creative work of book publishing. Our infrastructure is unparalleled among book publishers and makes our company comparable to other international leaders in consumer products.

Publishing is no longer the sleepy industry it once was. Advances in technology have radically altered the landscape and Random House is the leader in introducing new technology to book publishing-both in the way we make books and in the way we run our business. We were the first in the industry to adopt integrated enterprise systems, a digital content archive, and a digital printing operation for producing print-on-demand books in our distribution center. An emphasis on innovative technology runs throughout every aspect of our business and isn't sequestered in a "new media" function.

Random House benefits from relationships with other companies that are also owned by our parent organization, Bertelsmann, including book printers and book component manufacturers. While we work closely together, we are independent from one another, ensuring the highest level of efficiency and lowest cost for services.

From this solid platform, Random House continues to grow-through further expansion in trade publishing, growth into new countries, and entry into emerging formats.

sibling to their series of longer classics like Leo Tolstoy's *War and Peace* and Victor Hugo's *Les Miserables*. The partners also produced a few "deluxe" editions like the Rockwell Kent-illustrated version of Voltaire's *Candide* and a lavish version of Mark Twain's *Adventures of Tom*

Sawyer. These indulgences were discontinued when the Depression took a firm hold of the economy in the 1930s.

Moving into less expensive trade books, Cerf immediately set out to sign up the day's literati, including the playwright Eugene O'Neill and the poet Robinson Jeffers. Cerf also flew overseas to secure U.S. publishing rights to James Joyce's *Ulysses*. When his unexpurgated copy of the book was seized by customs as "obscene" material upon his return, Cerf and attorney Morris Ernst gained international acclaim by taking the case to court. On December 6, 1933, Judge John Woolsey issued a decision with historic implications by upholding Cerf's right not only to possess the book, but also to publish an uncensored version of *Ulysses* in the United States. Cerf's precedent-setting crusade made Random House a household word, and the Modern Library's *Ulysses* was published in 1934.

In 1936 Random House purchased Robinson Smith & Robert Haas Inc. and netted several prominent authors in the process, including Isak Dinesen, William Faulkner, Edgar Snow, and Jean de Brunhoff. The acquisition of de Brunhoff, creator of the popular Babar series, proved both timely and prescient, as RH expanded into children's books.

DOMESTIC AND INTERNATIONAL EXPANSION: 1940-70

After World War II ended, Random House sought both domestic and international expansion, beginning with the establishment of Random House Canada and the development of a college books division in 1944. In 1947, after years of research and at a cost of more than $500,000, RH published the *American College Dictionary*, the first of its many reference books. Continuing in this vein but directing its efforts toward children, the publisher initiated a series of Landmark Books about legendary Americans in 1950. Written by such famous authors as Pearl S. Buck, C. S. Forester, and John Gunther, the line was expanded in 1953 to cover historic world events and leaders.

The Random House children's division published a picture book in 1957 called *The Cat in the Hat* by Dr. Seuss (the pen name of Theodor Geisel). Simple and silly, the book was so successful that it was reprinted in 1958 as the first of a new line christened "Beginner Books." The series enjoyed huge success, becoming an enduring favorite for new readers and remaining a staple of libraries and bookstores to this day. The same year, RH hired Saxe Commins as its editor-in-chief. "With Mr. Commins's counsel and Mr. Cerf's instincts," Alden

KEY DATES

1925: Bennett Cerf and Donald Klopfer acquire Modern Library.

1927: Company is renamed Random House Inc.

1934: Random House publishes James Joyce's *Ulysses*.

1944: Company establishes Random House Canada and college books division.

1947: Company publishes *American College Dictionary*, the firm's first reference book.

1950: Landmark Books series for children is introduced.

1957: First Dr. Seuss book, *The Cat in the Hat*, is published.

1959: Random House goes public.

1960: Company acquires Alfred A. Knopf.

1965: Random House is acquired by Radio Corporation of America (RCA).

1966: *Random House Dictionary of the English Language* is published.

1973: Random House acquires Ballantine Books.

1980: Company is acquired by Advance Publications and becomes part of the Newhouse family's media empire.

1986: Fodor's Travel Guides is acquired.

1988: Crown Publishing Group is acquired.

1989: Alberto Vitale becomes president, chairman, and CEO of Random House; Random House UK is established.

1996: Company settles pricing lawsuit with the American Booksellers Association.

1998: Random House is acquired by German conglomerate Bertelsmann AG.

1999: Bertelsmann regroups its trade book publishing operations under the Random House name and appoints Peter Olson chairman and CEO of the new unit.

2000: Random House partners with Audible Inc. to establish RH Audible and sell digitized audio books via the Internet.

2001: Random House sues Rosetta Books to stop publication of electronic versions of books to which it holds the copyrights; Spanish-language joint venture creates Grupo Editorial Random House Mondadori.

2002: An appeals court finds in favor of Rosetta Books, and Random House agrees to license electronic rights in an out-of-court settlement.

2003: Bertelsmann sells the Bertelsmann Tower in Times Square; merges its Random and Ballantine divisions.

2004: Joint venture creates Random House Joong-Ang (later renamed Random House Korea).

2005: Random House begins direct sales of books on company Web site; partners with Focus Features to launch Random House Films.

2008: Bertelsmann appoints Markus Dohle as CEO of Random House.

Whitman observed in the *New York Times*, "Random House began to grow into one of the giants of the books business."

In 1959 Random House went public with an offering of more than 220,000 shares at $11.25 each, with Cerf selling about a third of his stock (he kept 200,000 shares). Much of the proceeds went into rapid expansion, beginning with the 1960 acquisition of Alfred A. Knopf for about $3 million. In Knopf, RH gained one of the nation's most distinguished and respected publishers. Cerf assured the new subsidiary complete editorial independence, and he and Knopf forged a close alliance, both professionally and personally, that endured for decades. The company's second major acquisition was textbook producer L.W. Singer, which

was followed by Helen and Kurt Wolff's brainchild, the 19-year-old Pantheon Books, in 1961. Andre Schiffrin was named editor-in-chief of Pantheon in 1963 at the age of 28.

CHANGES IN OWNERSHIP, EDITORIAL LEADERSHIP: 1965–73

In 1965 the first of several significant events affecting the future of Random House occurred. In a curious role reversal, the acquisitive RH was purchased by Radio Corporation of America (RCA). Cerf became chairman of the board following the sale, and he relinquished the presidency to protégé Robert L. Bernstein the next year. Although the buyout was one "of mingled sadness and joy" for Cerf, he was pleased with his company's record earnings and happy to end the its independence "in a blaze of glory." In 1966 one of the company's crowning achievements came to fruition: the unabridged, 2,059-page *Random House Dictionary of the English Language*, which took more than 10 years to research and compile at an estimated cost of $3 million, was published. It sold significantly more than 500,000 copies within the next five years.

The changing of the guard was nearly complete in 1969, when Random House moved from the old Villard House on Madison Avenue, a historic landmark located behind St. Patrick's Cathedral, to a location at 201 East 50th Street. Cerf stepped down as chairman the following year, with his longtime friend and colleague Donald Klopfer taking over. Cerf remained at RH as a senior editor until his death in 1971 at age 73. Called "a glorious amalgam of pragmatist and leprechaun" by John Daly, former host of *What's My Line?*, a television game show on which Cerf had been a panelist for 16 years, the Random House founder was a popular man whose funeral was a veritable who's who of the publishing and show business worlds. "I wonder," Eudora Welty mused, "if anyone else of such manifold achievements in the publishing world could ever have so many friends."

With Bernstein and Klopfer running the ship, Random House continued to flourish. In 1971 the Modern Library exceeded 400 titles and sold 50 million books. The 1973 acquisition of mass marketer Ballantine Books added considerably to RH's paperback audience.

DECADE OF EXTRAORDINARY GROWTH: THE 1980S

In 1980 RH was the object of a takeover by Advance Publications Inc., part of the Newhouse family's vast holdings, which purchased the publisher from RCA for $70 million. The next decade was one of extraordinary growth, marked by the 1982 purchase of Fawcett Books, the 1983 founding of Villard Books, and the 1984 acquisition of Times Books from the New York Times Company. In 1985 RH launched its AudioBooks division, drawing on the company's extensive backlist to create abridged and unabridged cassette recordings.

Random House continued to expand its reach with the 1986 purchase of Fodor's Travel Guides and the 1987 acquisition of Chatto, Virago, Bodley Head & Jonathan Cape, Ltd., a prestigious British publishing group. "With companies like Bantam and Simon & Schuster becoming more involved overseas, we had a feeling we should do something ourselves," Bernstein told *Publishers Weekly*. As with previous mergers, the companies remained autonomous but also stood to benefit immensely from the alliance for subsidiary rights and other negotiations. Also in 1987, RH's renowned Pantheon Books and the newly acquired Schocken Books were merged editorially.

The following year, Random House again expanded its holdings by acquiring the large, respected Crown Publishing Group, which comprised Crown Books, Clarkson N. Potter Inc., Harmony Books, and the Outlet Book Company. In 1989 the company experienced its second changing of the guard when Bernstein departed RH after 23 years. His replacement as president, chairman, and CEO was Alberto Vitale, former head of rival Bantam Doubleday Dell (BDD).

Among Vitale's immediate concerns at Random House were trimming the fat and overhauling operations. In addition, Vitale focused RH on the 21st century by diversifying into the burgeoning field of electronic and multimedia products. This year also saw further expansion in the United Kingdom with the acquisition of Century Hutchinson, Ltd., which along with the Chatto, Virago, Bodley Head and Cape group became Random House UK with subsidiaries in Australia, New Zealand, and South Africa.

CONTINUING ACQUISITIONS AND CONSOLIDATION: THE EARLY 1990S

In his continuing efforts to streamline the company, Vitale set his sights on the ailing Pantheon Books. Since Bernstein, one of Pantheon's most ardent supporters, was gone, the industry was rife with rumors of the imprint's imminent dissolution. Andre Schiffrin, Pantheon's directional force for 28 years, resigned in 1990 after refusing to go along with Vitale's cost-cutting measures. His departure stirred up a storm of controversy, as Studs Terkel (Pantheon's best-selling author), E. L. Doctorow, Barbara Ehrenreich, Kurt Vonnegut, and 350 others staged a demonstration in front of RH's offices, while another 300 writers signed a letter of protest on Pantheon's behalf. In response, Vitale told *Publishers Weekly*, "I want to most emphatically reaffirm Random House's commitment to maintaining Pantheon's position as one of our most prestigious imprints and to insuring its continuity and success in the future." Vitale soon hired Erroll McDonald, who had criticized the demonstrators in an op-ed piece for the *New York Times*, as the new executive editor of Pantheon, and the imprint continued with a smaller staff and fewer projected titles.

In 1992 Vitale raided his former employer's ranks to hire William Wright, who became his right-hand man as executive vice-president and chief operating officer of Random House. During this year RH also founded the One World imprint under the Ballantine group's umbrella to produce culturally diverse originals and reprints in hardcover and trade paperback. The biggest news of the year, however, was the renaissance of the Modern Library, with the reintroduction of 27 volumes, complete with new bindings and reset pages, to celebrate the 75th anniversary of the series. Simultaneously, those at Knopf put the finishing touches on the revival of Everyman's Library, the long-dormant hardcover classics once published by Dutton that were the original model for RH's Modern Library series. Although there was some concern about competition, Jane Friedman, president of RH Audio, posited, "Would we have been any happier if some other publisher had brought out Everyman's?"

Once again solidifying assets and looking for more, Vitale engineered the purchase of BDD's Bantam Electronic Publishing in 1993. The move was intended to beef up RH's own electronic division, or as Vitale told *Publishers Weekly*, "to create more critical mass in a field that, while evolving, is here to stay." As proof of his commitment, Vitale formed RH's New Media Division to "identify and pursue multimedia opportunities" and installed Randi Benton as its president. In addition, RH formed several joint ventures in 1993, including one to distribute the National Geographic Society's books; a second with Broderbund to create and market story-based multimedia software for children; and another between RH's Electronic Publishing division and Prentice Hall to produce and market a line of computer-oriented books under the newly established imprint of HewlettPackard Press.

With ownership of electronic rights becoming a contentious issue between authors and publishers, RH discovered in 1993 that it did not own the electronic rights to Theodor Geisel's Dr. Seuss books. RH was able to negotiate with representatives from Geisel's estate and acquire the multimedia rights to Dr. Seuss. More significantly, it changed the wording in its author contracts and added tough clauses regarding electronic and other rights not yet defined. The William Morris Agency, angry over the new contract language, refused to do business with RH for about a year before softening its stance. Julia Child, a longtime Knopf author, parted ways with Knopf in a dispute over electronic rights.

Random House continued its trend of acquisition and reorganization in 1994 and 1995. Its investment in Worldview Systems Corporation, a San Francisco-based provider of electronic destination information, enabled RH's Fodor's subsidiary to launch Fodor's Worldview Travel Update, a service that provided buyers of Fodor's

travel guides with updated information sent electronically or via fax or mail. That year RH also entered into an agreement with Kiplinger Washington Editors to publish books on personal finance and other business topics under a new imprint, Times Business Books. RH also acquired a 20 percent interest in the *Princeton Review*. The investment enabled the *Princeton Review* to double its output of book titles from 60 to 120 by the end of 1997. RH was publishing the *Princeton Review's* books and distributing its software to the book market.

CHALLENGES AND CHANGES: THE LATE 1990S

In 1996 Random House withdrew from the annual American Booksellers Association (ABA) convention after the ABA filed a lawsuit against RH charging the company with illegally providing selective discounts to the larger chain bookstores at the expense of smaller independent booksellers. After a federal judge refused to dismiss the ABA's lawsuit, RH and the ABA reached an out-of-court settlement in November 1996. Under the agreement RH admitted no wrongdoing and would not reimburse the ABA's legal fees. Random House agreed to abide by a 10-year consent decree that required the firm to abide by its principles on pricing and promotional allowances. Any changes would be made available to all customers.

Random House also received negative publicity in 1996 when it unsuccessfully attempted to reclaim a $1.3 million advance paid to author Joan Collins. Her contract contained a clause saying the publisher would accept the manuscript regardless of its quality, and the decision to sue Collins was attributed to RH's feisty chairman and CEO, 62-year-old Alberto Vitale. Vitale also was feuding with the ABA over its lawsuit and with several top literary agencies over RH's insistence on purchasing all electronic rights to its books.

Philip Pfeffer became the new president and COO of Random House in 1996, replacing William Wright and reporting to Vitale. Pfeffer was formerly chairman and CEO of the Ingram Distribution Group. In 1997 RH established a new division, RH Client Services, to expand its sales and distribution systems. Gilbert Perlman was named president of the division. RH was distributing books for about 30 other publishers and sought to expand its distribution business. Distribution was seen as an area with significant growth potential.

The RH Information Group, with Walter Weintz as group president, was formed within the company's trade publishing group in 1997. It contained three nonfiction publishing units: Times Books, Princeton Review, and Reference and Information Publishing. That year

Random House UK also acquired the adult trade division of Reed Books, making it England's leading fiction publisher. The acquisition included the lists of William Heinemann, Methuen, and Seeker & Warburg.

In spring 1997, Ann Godoff was promoted to editor-in-chief and executive vice-president of the RH Trade Group (known as "Little Random," to distinguish it from the main company). She had joined RH in 1991 and had become vice-president and associate editorial director in 1994, and editorial director in 1995. At the end of 1997 Harold Evans, head of RH's trade publishing group, left and was replaced by Ann Godoff, who retained her titles of editor-in-chief, executive vice-president, and her membership on the executive committee.

BERTELSMANN PURCHASE AND INTEGRATION: 1998–99

In 1998 RH was acquired by the privately held German publishing and entertainment conglomerate Bertelsmann AG for an estimated $1.2 to $2 billion. Bertelsmann already owned the U.S. publisher BDD. Bertelsmann was known for its marketing savvy, and RH for the quality of its publications. Bertelsmann ran the largest book club business in the world and had acquired publishers in Germany, France, England, Spain, and the United States. Random House and BDD were expected to dominate the best seller lists in the United States. For 1997 the two publishers had a combined total of 69 hardcover and 69 paperback titles on *Publishers Weekly*'s best seller lists, or about a third of all hardcover best sellers and half of the best selling paperbacks. After the merger RH would have 20 percent to 23 percent of the trade publishing market, but only about 7 percent of total U.S. book sales.

An announcement on March 23, 1998, took the U.S. trade publishing industry by surprise. Merger talks had been held over several months in secret between Thomas Middelhoff, Bertelsmann's next CEO, and Si Newhouse, head of RH's parent company Advance Publications. Since both Bertelsmann and Advance were private companies, no financial details concerning the merger were given. *Publishers Weekly*, the book industry trade publication, estimated Bertelsmann would pay about $1.4 billion for RH. Following the merger, BDD and RH would operate under the name of the senior partner, Random House Inc., with estimated annual sales of $1.8 billion, almost double its nearest rivals, Penguin Putnam and Simon & Schuster. The head of the combined U.S. publishers would be Peter Olson, chairman and CEO of Bertelsmann's North American operations. Alberto Vitale became chairman of a newly created supervisory board that would serve as an

advisory board but would have no operating responsibilities for RH.

In April 1998 the U.S. Department of Justice filed suit to block the acquisition. Authors and agents, represented by the Authors Guild and the Association of Authors' Representatives, sent a complaint about the merger to the U.S. Federal Trade Commission (FTC). The complaint claimed that the new Random House would control more than 36 percent of the U.S. adult trade book market, not including textbooks and professional books. Agents and authors were concerned about access to publishers for new and established authors. Bertelsmann pegged the new RH market share at 10.9 percent, including mass market paperbacks and book club sales.

In June the FTC approved the acquisition, and the transaction was completed by July 1, 1998, the start of Bertelsmann's fiscal year. Olson named Erik Engstrom, former head of BDD North America, as president and chief operating officer of the new Random House. Addressing concerns over whether the many RH imprints would continue to bid independently for books (something that BDD imprints were not allowed to do under Bertelsmann), Olson circulated a statement to the company's employees worldwide indicating that Bertelsmann would support "continuity of editorial autonomy of each of the publishing divisions and imprints of BDD and Random House."

With new ownership the Random House organizational structure began to change. In October three new publishing groups were formed. RH Children's Media Group would consist of all the book publishing imprints, video publishing, multimedia activities, outside joint ventures, and third-party distribution arrangements of the previous BDD Books for Young Readers and the RH Children's Publishing divisions; RH Audio Publishing Group; and RH Diversified Publishing Group, which included RH Value Publishing and RH Large Print.

In March 1999 the RH sales force was reorganized into three sales groups, with the Ballantine sales group eliminated. One of the new sales divisions included Ballantine, Bantam, Broadway, Dell, and Doubleday imprints. The children's sales division was expanded significantly to sell titles from all of the company's children's publishing divisions. The RH trade sales division was largely left unchanged, representing books from Crown, Knopf, RH trade publishing, RH information, and Fodor's adult books, as well as audios and large-print titles.

The realignment of RH's adult publishing began in May 1999 with the formation of four new publishing groups. The most significant were the formation of the

Doubleday Broadway Publishing Group and the Bantam Dell Publishing Group, the latter uniting two paperback giants under one roof. Carole Baron, president and publisher of Dell for 18 years, left the company effective June 30. In addition, Anchor Books joined Vintage in the Knopf Publishing Group to form a new trade paperback unit. A new Doubleday Religious Publishing division also was established, which would include RH's WaterBrook religious imprint. All affected imprints were to retain their distinct editorial identities.

Bertelsmann began with a decentralized approach to managing its U.S. publishing property. It gave editors freedom to sign authors and publishers the freedom to run their own publishing programs. Centralization was limited to support services and back-office functions. Random House management was given wide latitude in running the company, and Bertelsmann executives were more interested in long-term results than results for a single year. A year after the merger, RH was receiving the same number of submissions from agents as in the past, and different imprints continued to compete for the same titles. Olson also noted that he had increased the amount an editor could offer to an author before seeking corporate approval.

EXPANSION, CONSOLIDATION, AND TURNOVER: 2000–2002

One strategy of the new Random House was to increase revenues through acquisitions and new technologies, and enhance profits with cost savings realized through consolidations. In July 1999 RH acquired Listening Library Inc., a pioneer in creating unabridged audio titles for children, and made them into the children's audio imprint of the RH Audio Publishing Group. In 2000 RH signed an agreement with Audible Inc. to create RH Audible, to sell digitized audio books online. The company also bought Books on Tape, another large publisher of unabridged audio books, in late 2001.

In 2000 Random House also announced plans for a new digital imprint, AtRandom, to produce original material for e-books and print-on-demand. The initial plan was to release e-books prior to hard copy versions and include shorter works of 50 to 100 pages. "This is the brave new world we want to see," Little Random president and publisher Godoff told David D. Kirkpatrick of the *New York Times*. "No printing, no paper and binding, no need for a sales conference or printed catalogue—we don't know the size of the market, but it could be potentially very profitable for us." After less than a year, however, RH "fine-tuned" its digital list, taking away e-book premieres and eliminating shorter book lengths. The imprint was cancelled less than 18 months later. "I think we did a great job of putting together a program that would have made good e-books available had people been buying e-books in any real numbers," a company spokesman told Kirkpatrick.

Although the company had cancelled its digital imprint, it did not lose interest in producing e-books. The firm offered short e-books as part of RH Children's Books, beginning in early 2002, and launched an online children's comic book in 2007. When start-up Rosetta Books announced plans to develop digital versions of previously published books, RH sued them in 2001. Although Rosetta had negotiated electronic rights deals with such Random House authors as William Styron and Kurt Vonnegut, RH claimed any electronic rights not specified in original book contracts were automatically held by publishers, not authors. A U.S. District Court rejected the Random House argument in July 2001. After an appellate court upheld the ruling, RH settled with Rosetta out of court in late 2002. The settlement gave Rosetta exclusive rights to publish certain e-books, with RH receiving a share of royalties as a licensee.

In the meantime, RH began a course of global expansion. In 2001 the company announced a joint venture with Italian publisher Mondadori to combine their Spanish-language efforts. The new company, called Grupo Editorial Random House Mondadori, was expected to produce almost $100 million in revenue immediately, making it one of the world's biggest Spanish-language publishers. Later that year RH moved its president, Y. S. Chi, to take over the newly created Random House Asia. In 2003 Chi orchestrated a partnership with Japanese publisher Kodansha to create a new Japanese-language publisher. Soon after, RH purchased the Ullstein Heyne paperback list from German media group Axel Springer, giving the company about 28 percent of the German paperback market.

Random House also acquired a number of smaller specialty publishers, adding them to its growing list of imprints. To get into computer game strategy guides, RH acquired Prima Communications in 2001; the publisher later sold Prima's computer book imprint and consolidated sales and management staff, cutting about 60 jobs. In summer 2001 RH formed a partnership with Classic Media to acquire the assets of bankrupt Golden Books Family Entertainment, paying $84 million and assuming the company's debts. Classic Media gained Golden's home video catalog, while RH added Golden's backlist of children's books, including such classics as *Pat the Bunny* and *The Poky Little Puppy*. Random House bought out executive contracts and soon integrated operations into its children's group.

Random House instituted additional restructuring in 2001, combining its sales group with its distribution and inventory efforts. The firm also created a publishing development group by combining its children's group with information, audio, and diversified publishing efforts. That same year, Random House UK combined children's imprints into one division. The biggest news came at the end of the year, however, when RH hired former Penguin Putnam publisher Phyllis Grann, known for developing such authors as Tom Clancy, Patricia Cornwell, Dick Francis, and Nora Roberts into repeat best-sellers. Grann's newly created position of vice-chairman was billed as an advisory one, and insiders hoped she might bring some of her star authors with her to RH. Less than seven months later, however, Grann left the company, claiming boredom with a position in RH's decentralized publishing structure that left her no clear role in the company.

After the terrorist attacks against the United States on September 11, 2001, there was an economic downturn that translated into an operating loss for the last half of the year, the first for Bertelsmann's book division in at least four years. The company announced staff layoffs in late 2001, with further cuts after a complete reorganization of the sales force into three regional groups instead of four. The following summer Bertelsmann CEO Thomas Middelhoff, the executive who had engineered the Germany conglomerate's purchase of RH, was ousted from his position. Reportedly, Middelhoff's emphasis on acquisitions and plans to take the Bertelsmann public did not find favor with the company's directors. RH staffers were uncertain whether new CEO Gunther Thielen would institute changes at RH, one of Bertelsmann's few profitable divisions.

Industry insiders were shocked in early 2003 when RH chief Peter Olson announced that the Little Random and Ballantine groups would be combined into a new division. Former Ballantine publisher Gina Centrello was named its head, leaving RH Trade publisher Godoff out of a job. Centrello was known for her commercial instincts, while Godoff had spent freely to maintain RH's literary reputation. In the end, Godoff went to competitor Penguin Group to establish her own imprint, taking several RH authors with her. Because new Random editor-in-chief Daniel Menaker brought several well-known authors with him from Harper-Collins, this was seen as part of the regular publishing merry-go-round. Eventually the RH/Ballantine merger led to more editorial layoffs, as well as to a further round of job losses when the two sales forces finished merging in 2004.

DEALING WITH TOUGH MARKETS: 2003 AND BEYOND

Declining revenues led to further changes in the way Random House approached its business. In 2003 Bertelsmann sold its eponymous tower in Times Square for $290 million. Although a second tower to house RH offices had been a pet project of former Bertelsmann CEO Middelhoff, it never got off the ground. Instead RH retained its offices at Bertelsmann Tower after the sale, arranging a 15-year lease with the new owners. Retrench-ment was also seen in Bertelsmann's nixing of a deal for RH to purchase AOL Time Warner's book division, home to Little, Brown and at the time the fifth largest publisher in the United States. As Olson told the *New York Times Magazine*, "It's not uncommon for a business deal to fall apart. I'd like to hit a home run every time, but that would be unusual. I would have loved to do this deal. But it wasn't exactly the right timing or the right price. It doesn't change my relationship with the board." Random House was facing many challenges. A combination of slowing sales and a weak dollar meant a one-quarter decline in revenue for the first half of 2003. To cut costs, the company sold its stake in BarnesandNoble.com, laid off technical and sales staff in the United States, and combined literary and commercial divisions at Random House UK.

Although Random House had divested itself of most of its distribution business in 1999, save for a long-term relationship with Boston-based Shambhala Publications, new management saw distribution services as an opportunity for growth. In 2003 the company created Random House Distribution Services to provide warehousing and fulfillment operations for smaller publishers. In 2004 the firm added sales services and signed Steerforth Press, Rizzoli International Publications, and children's publisher Candlewick Press to distribution agreements. A year later RH added Wizards of the Coast to its client list. By 2006 the distribution business had 15 clients and about $100 million in yearly billings.

As the decade progressed, Random House continued looking for ways outside of traditional publishing to increase its revenues. Late in 2004, RH announced it would consider direct sales efforts, via its Web site, and by 2005 the company had made its entire catalog available online. In 2005 the publisher acquired a minority stake in mobile phone content provider Vocel, licensing both foreign language-study and game strategy lines for use on cell phones. Soon afterward RH also purchased a small interest in American Reading Company, a program designed to improve reading skills. In 2005 Random House agreed to test out the Google Print program (later renamed Google Books), which would allow scanning and searching of some of the company's product list. The firm also formed an exploratory venture with Amazon.com for pay-per-page viewing of books. Hoping to keep control of content and potential profits in 2007, Random House began offering its own text search service called Insight. In 2007 the company also debuted the first motion picture produced by Random House Films, a joint venture with Focus Features to create movies based on RH properties.

The company also continued expanding publishing efforts abroad. In 2004 Random House announced a Korean joint venture to be known as Random House JoongAng, and assumed full ownership of the renamed RH Korea two years later. In 2005 the publisher acquired a 50 percent stake in Scotland's Mainstream Publishing and founded Random House India to publish original works in English for the Indian market. That year the company also purchased book lines from German media publisher Frankfurter Allgemeine Zeitung, adding an estimated €20 million in sales. In 2007 Random House opened a flagship store in Shanghai, China, with a capacity of more than 3,000 books.

Random House also continued to expand through purchases of smaller English-language firms, such as Multnomah Press, Triumph Books, and a portion of BBC Books in 2006. In 2008 the company partnered with educational company Sylvan Learning to produce books for the student market. That year RH also purchased Monacelli Press, a visual arts publisher, and Watson-Guptill, a craft and photography publishers. Nevertheless, sales and profits at Random House were dropping in a down economy, and in May 2008 CEO Olson stepped down, reportedly pressured by the Bertelsmann board. Bertelsmann appointed Markus Dohle, an executive in its printing service, as the new CEO of Random House, claiming the company needed management with a fresh perspective. "Markus is a proven entrepreneur within the organization," Bertelsmann chief Harmut Ostrowski told Mark Landler and Motoko Rich in the *New York Times*, one who "has shown he has been able to turn a mature business into a growing business."

Observers expected big changes with new leadership at RH, and at the end of 2008 there was a major restructuring from five divisions to three, with Little Random adding the Bantam and Dell imprints, and the Knopf and Crown groups splitting the lines from Doubleday. Two executives were laid off, and the combination of imprints meant less chance of bidding up prices for manuscripts, as imprints in the same division would not be allowed to compete against each other. "That's the beauty of having [similar imprints] under one roof," a RH spokesperson told Matthew

Flamm in *Crain's New York Business*. "Priorities will be set by a single division, not by two divisions competing with each other."

Although management hoped these changes would reduce costs, global expansion appeared to be the new way for Random House to increase profits. In 2001 North America accounted for 70.6 percent of RH's sales. By 2008, this figure had dropped to 50.8 percent. In 2008 RH was still the largest trade publisher in the United States, with €1.72 billion ($2.53 billion) in sales, but this figure was down from 2007's €1.84 billion. In a climate of declining sales and changing technologies, the future challenge for Random House, CEO Dohle told Jim Milliot in *Publishers Weekly*, is "to stay on a growth path in Europe and to grow our U.S. business again."

Taryn Benbow-Pfalzgraf
Updated, David P. Bianco; Diane E. Telgen

PRINCIPAL DIVISIONS

Crown Publishing Group; Knopf Doubleday Publishing Group; The Monacelli Press; Random House Asia (includes Random House India, Random House Kodansha [Japan], and Random House Korea); Random House Audio Publishing Group; Random House Children's Books; Random House Information Group; Random House International (includes Random House UK and Random House Mondadori); Random House Large Print; Random House Publishing Group.

PRINCIPAL COMPETITORS

Hachette Book Group USA; HarperCollins Publishers; Penguin Group USA; Simon & Schuster Inc.

FURTHER READING

Albanese, Andrew, "Publishers Debut Search Engines," *Library Journal*, April 1, 2007, p. 19.

Alter, Jonathan, "The Rumble at Random House," *Newsweek*, October 26, 1987, p. 62.

Alterman, Eric, "Random Violence," *The Nation*, April 13, 1998, p. 5.

Bagli, Charles V., "Bertelsmann Is Yielding Ground in Manhattan," *New York Times*, June 23, 2003, p. B3.

Baker, John F., "BDD/Random Merger Gets Extra Scrutiny in Washington," *Publishers Weekly*, May 11, 1998, p. 13.

———, "Bertelsmann's Buy of Random Completed," *Publishers Weekly*, July 6, 1998, p. 12.

Baker, John F., and Nora Rawlinson, "BDD Culture Won't Necessarily Prevail at Random," *Publishers Weekly*, April 6,

1998, p. 12.

Benoit, Bertrand, "Random House to Buy Ullstein," *Financial Times*, February 12, 2003, p. 16.

Cerf, Bennett, *At Random: The Reminisces of Bennett Cerf.* New York: Random House, 1977.

Deahl, Rachel, "What's Ahead for Random House?" *Publishers Weekly*, December 8, 2008, p. 4.

Flamm, Matthew, "Literati Read Random House Tea Leaves, and Worries Mount," *Crain's New York Business*, January 19, 2009, p. 4.

Giles, Jeff, and Ray Sawhill, "A Brand-New Chapter," *Newsweek*, April 6, 1998, p. 39.

Hirschberg, Lynn, "Nothing Random," *New York Times Magazine*, July 20, 2003, p. 28.

Kirkpatrick, David D., "After a Gloomy Prognosis, a Loss at Random House," *New York Times*, June 17, 2002, p. C7.

——, "Random House Begins Layoffs as Executives Fear Long Sales Slump," *New York Times*, December 19, 2001, p. C1.

——, "Random House Executive Will Step Down," *New York Times*, July 1, 2002, p. C7.

——, "Random House Is Dropping E-Book Imprint, but Not E-Books," *New York Times*, November 9, 2001, p. C14.

——, "Random House Sues over Rights to Publishing E-Books," *New York Times*, February 28, 2001, p. C5.

——, "Star Publisher Lands a Second Act, Causing Many to Wonder about the New Script," *New York Times*, November 27, 2001, p. C2.

——, "Two Companies Pay $84 Million for Golden Books," *New York Times*, August 16, 2001, p. C5.

Landler, Mark, "Bertelsmann's Chief Is Fired after Clash with the Ownership," *New York Times*, July 29, 2002, p. A1.

Landler, Mark, and Motoko Rich, "Bertelsmann Picks a Publishing Industry Outsider to Head Random House," *New York Times*, May 21, 2008, p. C8.

——, "Chief of Random House Said to Be Stepping Down," *New York Times*, May 6, 2008, p. C1.

Maughan, Shannon, "Random House Acquires Listening Library," *Publishers Weekly*, July 12, 1999, p. 11.

Milliot, Jim, "Chi Named Random House President," *Publishers Weekly*, April 23, 2001, p. 9.

——, "Court Denies RH Move to Dismiss ABA Lawsuit," *Publishers Weekly*, August 19, 1996, p. 11.

——, "A Down Year for Random House," *Publishers Weekly*, March 30, 2009, p. 4.

——, "Pfuhl Appointed President of Random House Inc.," *Publishers Weekly*, November 12, 2001, p. 9.

——, "Publishers Take the Direct Route," *Publishers Weekly*, September 26, 2005, p. 4.

——, "Random Cuts 60 Prima Jobs," *Publishers Weekly*, June 11, 2001, p. 25.

——, "Random House and ABA Settle Antitrust Lawsuit," *Publishers Weekly*, November 25, 1996, p. 10.

——, "Random House Creates Three New Publishing Groups," *Publishers Weekly*, October 12, 1998, p. 11.

——, "Random House Forms New Adult Publishing Groups," *Publishers Weekly*, May 31, 1999, p. 18.

——, "Random House in Korean Joint Venture," *Publishers Weekly*, January 12, 2004, p. 8.

——, "Random House Revamps Its Sales Force," *Publishers Weekly*, January 21, 2002, p.12.

——, "Random House to Reenter Distribution Business," *Publishers Weekly*, May 26, 2003, p. 10.

——, "Random House Trade Merging with Ballantine," *Publishers Weekly*, January 20, 2003, p. 11.

——, "Random Moves Golden Integration Forward," *Publishers Weekly*, October 1, 2001, p. 11.

——, "Random U.S. Even in 2005," *Publishers Weekly*, April 17, 2006, p. 8.

——, "RH Has Widespread Gains in Transition Year," *Publishers Weekly*, August 9, 1999, p. 198.

——, "Six-Month Sales, Earnings Fall at Random House," *Publishers Weekly*, September 8, 2003, p. 9.

Milliot, Jim, and Herbert R. Lottman, "Olson Says Random Expects Difficult Year," *Publishers Weekly*, December 24, 2001, p. 9.

——, "U.S. Is Now No. 1 Market for Bertelsmann," *Publishers Weekly*, September 28, 1998, p. 10.

Milliot, Jim, and John F. Baker, "A Problem with Market Share and Antitrust?" *Publishers Weekly*, March 30, 1998, p. 12.

Model, F. Peter, "A Volvo, Not a Caddy: The Modern Library's Second Coming," *Wilson Library Bulletin*, December 1992, pp. 66–68.

"Panic over Random's Act," *New York Post*, May 21, 2008, p. 38.

"Publishers Join to Offer Books in Spanish," *New York Times*, March 26, 2001, p. C2.

"Random and Prentice Hall Sign Joint Deal with Hewlett-Packard," *Publishers Weekly*, March 15, 1993, p. 9.

"Random, CTW Form New Imprint," *Publishers Weekly*, March 2, 1998, p. 16.

"Random Thoughts: Who Wants to Be in Book Publishing? Bertelsmann, Because of a Revolution in the Business That It Is Bringing About," *Economist*, March 28, 1998, p. 58.

"Random, Wiley in Business Book Deals," *Publishers Weekly*, April 10, 1995, p. 9.

Raymont, Henry, "Cerf Rites Draw Friends of 'Two Worlds,'" *New York Times*, September 1, 1971, p. 40.

Reilly, Patrick M., "Godoff Named Editorial Chief at Random House," *Wall Street Journal*, January 13, 1995, p. B2.

Reuter, Madalynne, "After the UnRandom Showdown," *Publishers Weekly*, October 30, 1987, p. 11.

"RH Buys Stake in Princeton Review," *Publishers Weekly*, July 17, 1995, p. 121.

Richardson, Jean, "Reed Buy Makes Random House U.K. a Formidable Fiction House," *Publishers Weekly*, February 10, 1997, p. 14.

Rosen, Judith, "Random to Distribute Rizzoli," *Publishers Weekly*, July 19, 2004, p. 9.

Sanchanta, Mariko, "Japanese Deal for Random," *Financial Times*, January 24, 2003, p. 31.

"Setting the Stage: Random, Amazon, AOL Plan for Online Opportunities," *Publishers Weekly*, November 7, 2005, p. 16.

Shapiro, Laura, "Publisher at the Barricades," *Newsweek*, March 19, 1990, p. 71.

Turner, Richard, "Wild about Harry: Buzzing about Evans," *Newsweek*, December 8, 1997, p. 76.

Wexler, Diane Patrick, "Random House Tries Online Bookselling," *Publishers Weekly*, May 12, 1997, p. 18.

Wyatt, Edward, "As Sales Flag, Publisher Eyes Retailers' Turf,"

New York Times, December 20, 2004, p. C1.

————, "Publisher Aims at Cellphones," *New York Times*, February 18, 2005, p. C2.

Zeitchik, Steven, "AtRandom's New Direction," *Publishers Weekly*, June 18, 2001, p. 24.

————, "Penguin Authors Weighing Options," *Publishers Weekly*, December 3, 2001, p. 10.

————, "Rosetta, Random House Settle E-Book Lawsuit," *Publishers Weekly*, December 9, 2002, p.9.

————, "Scores of Random Authors Headed to Penguin," *Publishers Weekly*, April 7, 2003, p. 10.

Raycom Media, Inc.

RSA Tower,
201 Monroe Street, 20th Floor
Montgomery, Alabama 36104
U.S.A.
Telephone: (334) 206-1400
Fax: (334) 206-1555
Web site: http://www.raycommedia.com

Private Company
Founded: 1996
Employees: 3,500
Sales: $400.9 million (2008)
NAICS: 515120 Television Broadcasting; 515112 Radio Stations; 517910 Other Telecommunications; 541990 All Other Professional, Scientific and Technical Services; 551112 Offices of Other Holding Companies; 711320 Promoters of Performing Arts, Sports, and Similar Events without Facilities

■ ■ ■

Raycom Media, Inc., an employee-owned company officially formed in 1996, is a television broadcaster that maintains more than 45 stations serving markets throughout some 18 states and reaching 12.6 percent of the U.S. television viewing audience. The company has stations affiliated with all four major networks—ABC, NBC, CBS, and FOX—as well as MyNetworkTV and the CW Television Network. In addition to its TV stations, Raycom is involved in sports programming and promotion through its Charlotte, North Caroline-based Raycom Sports subsidiary, which holds the broadcasting rights to Atlantic Coast Conference (ACC) college basketball games, as well as syndication rights to ACC football games. Raycom Sports also owns the Meineke Car Care Bowl in Charlotte and the LPGA Longs Drugs Challenge, which takes place in San Francisco, California. Raycom Media also maintains post production and advertising sales operations through its other subsidiaries: California-based Raycom Post Production; Broadview Media of Alabama; and CableVantage in South Carolina.

ORIGINS OF RAYCOM DATE TO 1979

Raycom originated with Rick Ray and Dee Birke in 1979 when they established a nationwide syndication company, teaming up with Jefferson-Pilot Sports to promote ACC basketball games. Ray and Birke married in 1981, the same year they launched their new business, Raycom (short for Ray Communications), which would become known as Raycom Sports. Their initial employee was Ann Kent, Birke's sister. She was followed by Ken Haines, who left his job as executive to the president at Virginia Tech. In 1983 Don McGuire came from NBC Sports, and a year later Wayne Spransy joined the mix, bringing his expertise as a certified public accountant. With the company staffed, Rick Ray spent his time acquiring new products and Dee Ray sold advertising. Meanwhile, McGuire produced games, Spransey took care of the financial aspects, and Haines's responsibilities included scheduling games and making sure everything ran smoothly.

In 1988 Raycom hired Ray Warren, who once worked as the vice-president of sales at ABC. Warren

COMPANY PERSPECTIVES

With a strong belief in community, Raycom Media television stations take editorial positions on key community issues. It is the vision of the company that it be involved in the communities its broadcast properties serve. By editorializing on local issues and seeking out divergent points of view, Raycom Media television stations create an atmosphere of community dialog.

was successful in generating Raycom's revenue to about $60 million annually. McGuire left Raycom to pursue the position as head of sports production at Turner Broadcasting, and Peter Rolfe, formerly with NBC, succeeded McGuire. The company was thriving, and in less than a decade they were producing more than 500 events each year, as well as serving as the major regional TV sports network for both college basketball and college football. Within a six-year period Raycom went from 5 employees to more than 80. The company expanded its operations, opening offices in New York City, Dallas, Chicago, Los Angeles, and Ft. Lauderdale.

In 1992 Raycom formed an exclusive partnership with Jefferson-Pilot Sports and would become the rights holder of ACC men's basketball and syndicated football telecasts. The company would eventually own and operate events around the country including LPGA tournaments in Mobile, Alabama, and Sacramento, California. Other successes traceable to the early origins of Raycom and its telecasts include a number of Raycom employees and sports reporters who went on to become recognizable names; among them, according to the company's Web site, are Dan Bonner, James Brown, Dave Barnett, Jimmy Dykes, Larry Farmer, Ron Franklin, Terry Gannon, Mike Gminski, Merle Harmon, Bud Wilkinson, Craig James, Billy Packer, Bill Raftery, Dave Rowe, Roger Twibell, Dick Vermeil, Dick Vitale, Bill Walton, Jim Valvano, Jay Bilas, and Mike Patrick.

RAYCOM MEDIA, INC., FORMED IN 1996

Coinciding with the time the Rays retired, Raycom Sports was sold to Ellis Communications in 1994. Two years later it was officially formed as Raycom Media, Inc., by a group of investors consolidating Ellis Communications, Inc., and another enterprise that included the AFLAC Broadcast Division. The latter was under the umbrella of AFLAC, Inc., which, while an insurance company, had a stake in seven television stations affili-

ated with ABC, CBS, and NBC. At that time, John Edward Hayes was placed at the helm as president of Raycom.

At the foundation of the consolidation that eventually yielded Raycom Media, Inc., was Bert Ellis, who had formed Ellis Communications in 1992. Ellis acquired the exclusive rights of 13 television stations and two radio broadcasting stations before buying Raycom Sports in 1994. Two years later a media group funded by the Retirement Systems of Alabama—who had just completed the purchase of the broadcast division of American Family Life Assurance Company (AFLAC)—acquired Ellis. That followed with the merging of the two groups, and, ultimately, Raycom Media was formed.

A large part of Raycom's early success was the direct result of hiring and placing Hayes in charge. Hayes came to Raycom following his departure as vice-president of television at the Providence Journal Company when the company was sold to A. H. Belo Corp. in 1996. Hayes's vast experience in television began in the late 1960s when he worked as a reporter for WTVJ-TV in Miami, Florida. From there he went to work for the Florida Department of Consumer Services in Tallahassee as a lobbyist in the state government. He returned to television in 1971 as an assistant news director in Tallahassee, a position he held until 1977. For nearly the next two decades before joining Raycom, Hayes would serve as news director or general manager of stations in Birmingham, Alabama; San Jose, California; Las Vegas, Nevada; Buffalo, New York; and Charlotte.

Another significant selection was the hiring in February 1997 of Paul McTear, who had also come from the Providence Journal Company, serving as vice-president of finance and corporate development for about 20 years. Under his leadership at Providence Journal, he played a major role in the debut of two cable programming networks, the Television Food Network and America's Health Network, on top of his other duties in the area of acquisitions and financial planning. Both Hayes and McTear would be the two forces to expand and develop Raycom through the ups and downs of the next decade and beyond.

COMPETITION HEATS UP

Competitive pressures from some rising big players, specifically ESPN and Fox Sports, prompted growing pains for Raycom. Raycom knew it needed to diversify in order to compete. Fox Sports was able to deter the advertising sales rights for Pac-10 and Big-12 college football from Raycom. "The sports business is like a lot of other industries right now: It's going through

KEY DATES

■

1994: Ellis Communications acquires Raycom Sports.

1996: Ellis Communications sells Raycom Sports to a media group, and Raycom Media, Inc., was formed.

1998: Raycom Media purchases Malrite Communications Group.

1999: Raycom Sports and Jefferson-Pilot Sports extend their contract with the Atlantic Coast Conference for all basketball television and marketing rights through the 2010–11 season.

2006: Raycom Media's acquisition of Liberty Corporation's station group for $987 million is completed.

2007: Raycom announces a definitive agreement to acquire the TV broadcasting properties of Lincoln Financial Group and Lincoln Financial Sports for $583 million.

2008: Lincoln Financial Sports merges into Raycom.

tremendous consolidation," McTear was quoted as saying by Erik Spanberg in the *Charlotte Business Journal* in August 1997. "We need to invest in some sports companies or merge or acquire them to be a better competitor. And we have to look at different areas of sports to remain viable."

Raycom announced its intention to acquire Cleveland-based Malrite Communications Group, a deal that was expected to become official before the end of 1998. When the acquisition was realized, Raycom's market presence branched out into such highly populated cities as Cleveland, Toledo, and Cincinnati in Ohio, West Palm Beach in Florida, and Puerto Rico, reaching some 10 million households. Hayes told the *Cincinnati Enquirer* in April 1998: "This purchase allows us to implement our strategy of expanding into major markets." At the time of the announcement, Raycom owned 25 television stations and 2 radio broadcasting stations, and with the acquisition of WXIX-TV that came with the purchase of Malrite, the company was on target to reach an estimated 10 percent of the television viewing audience across the United States.

To entice and retain top Raycom managers, Hayes began offering them part ownership of the company in 1999. Other perks included the option of advancement by relocating to another city. At this time, the company had grown to include 30 broadcast stations serving 24

markets, making it the 22nd-largest nationwide television broadcasting group. Despite strong competition, Raycom Sports shined with many exclusives, from offering color billboards with every television broadcast to being the first to deliver games via satellite and the first to apply "virtual signage" technology in college basketball and professional golf. The company also produced the first broadcast of a college basketball game in high definition TV (HDTV) on December 2, 1999.

Television specials that Raycom produced and broadcast over the years included the *Dove Entertainment Awards; Elvis' Graceland Special; Emmy Awards for Sports; The Making of It's A Wonderful Life; The Naismith Awards; Off the Record with Pat Summerall; Ford Supermodel of the World; Holidays at Home; The Making of the SI Swimsuit Issue; New Year's Eve Coast to Coast; Racing Home; NASCAR Think Fast!; BASS Masters Classic; Golf 2000 with Peter Jacobsen,* and the *Ladies First Celebrity Classic.*

Raycom and its affiliates also received countless awards, including consecutive Medium Market Station of the Year awards, as well as GABBY awards from the Georgia Association of Broadcasters for Station of the Year and Community Service Station of the Year. Raycom's WFIE station in Evansville, Indiana, earned a Best News Operation award in 2006, and the WLOX broadcasting station in Biloxi, Mississippi, received the National Edward R. Murrow Award for its Hurricane Katrina coverage. Among the many other honors received by Raycom's affiliated stations were the First Amendment Leadership Award from the Radio-Television News Directors Association and the National Peabody Award for Broadcast Excellence.

Unlike the late 1990s and early 2000s when the economy was booming and the total number of stations being bought and sold was on the upturn, Raycom sales began to stall. The year 2005 marked an upswing, however, when $3.2 billion changed hands compared with $1.2 billion in 2004. In February 2006 Raycom's $987 million acquisition of South Carolina-based Liberty Corporation's group of stations was finalized. In the wake of the purchase, Raycom planned to shed about 12 stations, some of which they just acquired from Liberty, because of conflicting markets. Allison Romano explained in an April 2006 article for *Broadcasting & Cable,* "Broadcasters still face restrictions on cross-ownership of newspapers and TV stations, limits on the number of stations they can own in a market, and the station-ownership cap." Raycom managed to sell 12 stations to Barrington Broadcasting for $262 million and was searching for a buyer for their KASA station in

Albuquerque, New Mexico. McTear admitted he was still in the market to acquire additional smaller stations, particularly in the Midwest, Southeast, and Texas.

With the 2008 acquisition of the television stations of Lincoln Financial Group, Raycom not only expanded its holdings but picked up premium TV stations, such as NBC affiliate WWBT, in Virginia, and CBS affiliates WBTV in North Carolina and WCSC in South Carolina. "These are excellent television stations that fit our strategy of growing our presence in thriving southern cities, state capitals and university towns," McTear was quoted as saying in a press release on *Business Wire* in April 2008. McTear selected Nick Simonette to head the WBTV station as both vice-president and general manager. Simonette had more than 30 years experience within the industry, including the previous 7 years serving as general manager of Raycom' WAFB-TV in Louisiana. The acquisition also resulted in Lincoln Financial Sports merging into Raycom.

McTear's work at Raycom was rewarded when he was honored with the broadcaster of the year award by the Alabama Broadcasters Association in July 2008. This award is presented to recipients who have demonstrated outstanding community service and who have made a positive difference within the broadcasting industry. By 2009, under McTear's direction, Raycom either owned or operated 42 TV stations throughout 18 states and was responsible for 12.6 percent of the U.S. viewing audience, making it one of the largest privately owned TV broadcast companies in the country. In addition, Raycom stations were the news leaders in the majority of the markets that they served.

Continuing its commitment to uphold the highest standards in news and journalism, Raycom was among more than 70 participants in a media coalition supporting the "Free Flow of Information Act of 2009" (H.R. 985), which was passed in the House of Representatives in April 2009. The Newspaper Association of America quoted U.S. Representative Rick Boucher: "The passage of the Free Flow of Information Act is a major victory for the public's right to know and for the ability of reporters to bring important information to light. The assurance of confidentiality that reporters give to sources is fundamental to their ability to deliver news on highly contentious matters of broad public interest such as corruption in government or misdeeds in corporations. Without the promise of confidentiality, many inside sources would not reveal the information, and opportunity to take corrective action to address the harms would not arise." With its growing share of broadcast news outlets around the country, Raycom seemed determined to both increase its presence in the broadcasting market and continue its delivery of quality news and sports into the 21st century.

Brenda Kubiac

PRINCIPAL SUBSIDIARIES

Broadview Media; CableVantage; Raycom Post Production; Raycom Sports.

PRINCIPAL COMPETITORS

Hearst Television, Inc.; Media General, Inc.; Sinclair Broadcast Group, Inc.

FURTHER READING

"AFLAC Incorporated to Sell Broadcast Division to Raycom Media, Inc.," PRNewswire, August 13, 1996.

Albiniak, Paige, "Taking Stock Spurs Success," *Broadcasting & Cable*, April 19, 1999. p. 131.

"Media Groups Applaud Passage of Federal Shield Bill by the House," Newspaper Association of America, April 1, 2009, http://www.naa.org/PressCenter/SearchPressReleases/2009/MEDIA-GROUPS-APPLAUD-PASSAGE-OF-FEDERAL-SHIELD-BILL-BY-THE-HOUSE.aspx.

Murphy, H. Lee, "Local Broadcast Firm to Buy 12 Stations; Barrington Acquiring Properties for $262 Mil," *Crain's Chicago Business*, April 24, 2006, p. 21.

Neman, Daniel, "Owner of Richmond's WTVR Will Trade Station," *Richmond Times-Dispatch*, January 8, 2009.

"ONA Joins Other Media Groups in Applauding Passage of Federal Shield Bill by the House," Online News Association, April 1, 2009, http://journalists.org/news/24518/ONA-joins-other-media-groups-in-applauding-passage-of-federal-shield-bill-by-the-House.htm.

"Raycom CEO Receives Prestigious Award," WTOC, July 20, 2008, http://www.wtoc.com/global/story.asp?s=8704827.

"Raycom Completes Lincoln Financial Group Television Properties Acquisition," Business Wire, April 1, 2008, http://www.businesswire.com/portal/site/google/?ndmViewId=news_view&newsId=20080401006171&newsLang=en.

Romano, Allison, "Station Market Still Sizzling," *Broadcasting & Cable*, April 3, 2006. p. 16.

Romano, Allison, and Jim Benson, "This Time, They Like What They See," *Broadcasting & Cable*, January 22, 2006.

Spanberg, Erik, "Raycom Drawing A New Game Plan," *Charlotte Business Journal*, August 4, 1997.

———, "Revamped Raycom Makes Charlotte Its Sales Center," *Charlotte Business Journal*, November 22, 2002.

"WXIX Parent Sells to Raycom Media," *Cincinnati Enquirer*, April 7, 1998.

Regions Financial Corporation

■

1900 Fifth Avenue North
Birmingham, Alabama 35203
U.S.A.
Telephone: (205) 944-1300
Toll Free: (800) 734-4667
Fax: (901) 580-3915
Web site: http://www.regions.com

Public Company
Founded: 1971 as First Alabama BancShares Inc.
Incorporated: 2004
Employees: 32,927
Total Assets: $143 billion (2009)
Stock Exchanges: New York
Ticker Symbol: RF
NAICS: 551111 Offices of Bank Holding Companies; 522110 Commercial Banking; 522120 Savings Institutions

■ ■ ■

Birmingham, Alabama-based Regions Financial Corporation is a holding company for banks located primarily in the southeastern United States. One of the country's top 10 banking groups, Regions Financial offers investment banking services, asset management, consumer-based banking, all phases of mortgage lending and management, insurance brokerage, and credit life insurance. The firm has branch offices in Alabama, Arkansas, Florida, Georgia, Illinois, Indiana, Iowa, Kentucky, Louisiana, Mississippi, Missouri, North Carolina, South Carolina, Tennessee, Texas, and Virginia.

DEEP SOUTHERN ROOTS

In 1971 First Alabama Bancshares was formed in Birmingham from the merger of three Alabama banks, the First National Bank of Huntsville, the First Bank of Montgomery, and the Exchange Security Bank of Birmingham. The oldest of them, First National Bank, dated back to pre–Civil War 1856, when Huntsville was a hub for cotton merchants. During the Civil War, the building was pressed into service as a hospital. The First Bank of Montgomery opened for business in 1871. The Exchange Security Bank was established in 1928, marking its place in Birmingham history in 1947 when it moved to a new building that was modern enough to include two firsts: a drive-up window and a parking lot.

The combined resources of these three banks in 1971 provided First Alabama Bancshares with $543 million in assets and 40 new locations, all within three major business centers of the state. By the end of 1974 the bank's assets had doubled, reaching $1.2 billion.

In the early 1980s changes in banking laws had increased the range of financial services for customers. The new regulations permitted holding companies with several banks to merge them into one statewide institution. The holding companies were then able to streamline their operating procedures for their subsidiary banks, although each continued to function independently to fill the needs of local customers. Each bank could offer their customers certificates of deposit, which had been introduced in Alabama in 1978. Begin-

COMPANY PERSPECTIVES

Regions' five core values guide everything we do: do what is right, put people first, reach higher, focus on your customer, enjoy life.

ning in 1981 they could also provide the convenience of automated teller machines (ATMs). Individual retirement accounts were introduced in 1982, while telephone access to account information, which became available in 1987, made First Alabama Bancshares the first bank in the state to offer this convenience to their customers.

ACQUIRING OUT-OF-STATE BANKS: 1980S AND 1990S

In 1986 additional regulatory changes allowed Alabama financial institutions to buy out-of-state banks. First Alabama Bancshares had already purchased several smaller in-state institutions, including the Merchants National Bank of Mobile in 1983. First Alabama Bancshares welcomed the new out-of-state expansion possibilities and was quick to make its first purchase, Santa Rosa State Bank in Milton, Florida. The range of service locations was further expanded because Santa Rosa had a branch in Pensacola. The list of Florida locations multiplied again with the 1988 addition of the Fort Walton Beach-based Sunshine Bank. All Florida operations of First Alabama Bancshares were merged into Sunshine Bank the same year. Further mergers into this bank came in 1991, when First Alabama Bancshares bought five offices from Great Western Bank. First Federal Savings Bank of DeFuniak Springs, Florida, was acquired next, joining the Sunshine Bank group in late 1993. The acquisition resulted in eight new offices and $190 million in assets for First Alabama Bancshares.

In 1990 J. Stanley Mackin became chief executive officer (CEO) of First Alabama Bancshares. A pragmatic businessman with a strategic growth plan based on acquisition, he led First Alabama Bancshares as it acquired 11 banks by 1993, with four additional transactions pending by late 1994. The largest of these was the Secor Bank, a failed thrift in New Orleans, Louisiana, whose assets totaled $1.9 billion. Following the acquisition of Secor, First Alabama Bancshares replaced all of its outdated software for consumer loans a year ahead of schedule, spending $250,000.

With banks in both Florida and Louisiana, the bank turned its expansion efforts to Georgia. Its first

purchase was First Alabama Bank of Columbus, which included the banking offices of three lesser institutions that brought with them deposits of $107 million. Additional acquisitions gave First Alabama Bancshares several locations in Tennessee. One of the Tennessee acquisitions was Franklin County Bank of Winchester, adding four offices and $68 million in assets in June 1993.

In 1993, with 15 subsidiary banks and assets that had grown from $6.3 billion to $10.5 billion, First Alabama Bancshares changed its name to Regions Financial Corporation. The company considered this to be an important step that would give their subsidiaries a common identity throughout the six southern states in which they operated. Regions Financial Corporation was destined to become extremely well-recognized in the future.

ACQUISITIONS AND SUBSIDIARIES IN THE 21ST CENTURY

A major acquisition for Regions Financial came in December 2000 with the purchase of Morgan Keegan & Co., a Memphis, Tennessee-based firm that offered investment banking, wealth and asset management, and securities brokerage. Morgan Keegan had a distinguished 30-year history. Established in 1969, it had quickly become one of the largest investment companies in the South, employing about 900 financial advisers in 142 offices in 25 states by the end of 2002.

Two other subsidiaries, Regions Mortgage, Inc. (RMI), and Equifirst Corporation (which would be sold in 2007 for $76 million) were focused on mortgage banking. RMI's focus was the origination and servicing of mortgage loans for long-term investors, while Equifirst's focus was selling mortgage loans to third-party investors. Like most other Regions operations, RMI and Equifirst had offices throughout the South.

Rebsamen Insurance, Inc., which was acquired in 2001, focused on insurance products such as commercial property insurance. Another subsidiary, Regions Agency, Inc., provided credit life, accident, and health insurance, while Regions Life Insurance Company acted as a reinsurer of credit life, accident, and health insurance.

In January 2004 Regions Financial acquired Union Planters Corporation, a bank in Memphis, which had been formed in 1869. The acquisition of Union Planters cost $5.9 billion and brought $31.9 billion in assets to Regions Financial. With branches in several of the states already familiar to Regions Financial, Union Planters also had operations in Illinois, Indiana, Iowa, Kentucky, Mississippi, and Missouri. Union Planters significantly

KEY DATES

1971: First Alabama Bancshares Inc. is formed.
1993: Secor Bank is acquired.
1994: Name is changed to Regions Financial Corporation.
2000: Morgan Keegan & Co. of Memphis is purchased.
2004: Union Planters Corporation is acquired.
2006: Regions Financial merges with AmSouth Bank.
2007: Company sells Equifirst.
2008: Regions Financial participates in the federal Troubled Asset Relief Program.

expanded Regions Financial's service area, increasing the number of branches to 1,400 and the number of customers to more than five million. The transaction brought the total number of Regions Financial acquisitions to 103 by the end of 2004, for about $28.4 billion in assets.

CONSOLIDATION, IDENTITY THEFT, AND HURRICANE KATRINA: 2005

In May 2005 Regions sold 112 buildings to American Financial Realty Trust, a real estate investment trust, under a leaseback agreement for about $114 million. Some were buildings used by small banks or were branches that became vacant following the merger between Regions Financial and Union Planters.

Later in 2005 Regions instituted an antifraud campaign after a bank executive learned that there had been two million identity theft cases nationwide within the prior year. In addition, a market research survey run by Synovate showed that of 43 percent of U.S. shoppers who had received communications from criminals posing as legitimate business owners, only 5 percent understood how to handle them. In an effort to combat identity theft, Regions Financial formed a partnership with First Data Corporation's Star network, using radio and television clips and ads to promote awareness.

In late August, Hurricane Katrina devastated parts of Louisiana and other southern states. Regions was forced to close 190 of its 1,400 branches for at least a few days. Personnel from these branches were quickly placed in other offices where they could help customers most, and the company waived all late fees assessed as a result of branch closings. Within a week all but 30 of the 190 closed branches had been reopened.

MERGER WITH AMSOUTH BANK: 2006

In 2006 Regions Financial merged with AmSouth Bank in a $10.2 billion transaction. AmSouth Bank had a long and distinguished history in Birmingham, beginning in 1872 as the National Bank of Birmingham in a city that was just one year old. As proof of the South's post–Civil War industrialization, Birmingham's economy was soundly based on iron ore and other minerals. The city was conveniently situated at the junction of two intersecting railroads and attracted workers who needed banks for savings, wages, and mortgages.

Initially, AmSouth was a private bank belonging to Charles Linn, a town merchant. Under his stewardship, it grew and prospered as a single bank until 1884 when it merged with the City Bank of Birmingham, creating the First National Bank of Birmingham. The new bank absorbed several smaller banks, growing steadily within Alabama, but by 1968 First National Bank was ready to expand beyond the state. The trustees cautiously waited for regulatory changes that would allow multistate expansion, forming a holding company called Alabama Bancorporation.

In 1981 the holding company changed its name from Alabama Bancorporation to AmSouth Bank. All of the subsidiary banks were consolidated into the holding company, making AmSouth Alabama the number one bank by the end of 1983, with more than 100 offices. It was also the first Alabama bank listed on the New York Stock Exchange.

AmSouth Bank and Regions benefited from the seamless merger that was completed in 2006. The banks, which were based in the same region, had similar business models, providing customers of each bank with uninterrupted service. Their combined assets were reported to be $140 billion, and they had a total of about 2,000 branches in 16 states with 2,800 ATMs. To resolve some service overlap, however, Regions sold superfluous branches throughout the South, including 39 AmSouth branches in Mobile, Huntsville, Montgomery, Tuscaloosa, Selma, and Decatur, to Royal Bank of Canada's Centura Bank. Terms of this deal were not disclosed, but Royal Bank of Canada reportedly gained $2 billion in deposits and $1.5 billion in loans from these transactions. The merger also provided AmSouth with the investment services of Morgan Keegan, which had been described as "the Cadillac of meeting needs" by banker Jason Epstein, a consumer banking executive for the 12-county north-central Alabama region.

Dowd Ritter, who since 1969 had moved up through the ranks of AmSouth to become CEO, succeeded Jackson Moore as CEO of Regions Financial. Moore was named executive chairman of Regions Financial. If Moore retired or resigned within three years of the merger, Ritter would become executive chairman as well as being CEO. Following the merger, Regions Financial was criticized by analysts who had learned through disclosure that Ritter had earned almost $6 million in 2005, while Moore earned $2.5 million.

TROUBLED TIMES: 2008–09

In 2008 Regions Financial demonstrated corporate social responsibility by partnering with the United Negro College Fund to offer two $7,500 scholarships per year. The bank also established financial literacy centers on the campuses of historically black universities, almost all of which were in the states with Regions's operations. Course subjects included first-time home buying and credit counseling. The program was planned to run for five years.

The downturn in the global economy that began in 2007 had resulted in millions of layoffs, which led to severe losses in the mortgage and construction industries when home owners were unable to make their mortgage payments. Banks began to feel the pinch, particularly in loans initiated between 2001 and 2006, a period in which a housing boom had led to relaxed eligibility standards for borrowers. In an effort to ease the resulting flood of foreclosures, in 2008 the Obama administration instituted the Troubled Asset Relief Program (TARP), under which the government invested in banks' assets. As expected, TARP investments came with conditions. Restrictions were placed on borrowing practices, on the salaries of bank executives, and on hiring practices. In addition, the government investments were to be paid back with interest.

Although the conditions made Regions a bit reluctant to participate in the program, the bank accepted $3.5 billion in TARP money. Speaking at a shareholders' meeting in June 2009, CEO Ritter noted that the government-held preferred shares were costing the company $175 million per year in interest payments. Nevertheless, the company hoped to be allowed to buy back the preferred shares by the end of 2009.

Regions Financial was able to capitalize on the situation when other banks were not in the same position. In August 2008 the bank took over $1.1 billion in assets of the Integrity Bank in Alpharetta, Georgia, which had been closed by the Georgia Department of Banking and Finance. In February 2009 the $337 million in assets of First Bank Financial Services of McDonough, Georgia, suffered the same fate as Integrity Bank and also became part of Regions Financial. In spite of foreclosures and the TARP, by the end of 2008 Regions Financial reported total assets of $146.2 billion.

Gillian Wolf

PRINCIPAL SUBSIDIARIES

Morgan Keegan & Company, Inc.; Regions Bank; Regions Insurance Group, Inc.

PRINCIPAL COMPETITORS

HSBC Holdings PLC; JPMorgan Chase & Co.; Bank of America Corporation; Wells Fargo & Co.; Banco Santander SA; Bnp Paribas; Mitsubishi UFJ Financial Group, Inc.; Barclays PLC; Royal Bank of Canada.

FURTHER READING

"Bank Failure: Integrity Bank, Alpharetta, Georgia," *Calculated-Risk*, August 29, 2008.

Bills, Steve, "Regions Exec: Be Frank about Fraud," *American Banker*, May 20, 2005, p. 12.

———, "Regions to Expand Its Online Offerings," *American Banker*, February 23, 2005, p. 9.

Boraks, David, "Regions Splits Corporate Banking, Credit," *American Banker*, February 19, 2003, p. 19.

Davis, Paul, "RBC Centura Eyes Birmingham as Second Alabama Step," *American Banker*, November 7, 2006, p. 1.

———, "Regions Selling 112 Buildings to REIT," *American Banker*, June 1, 2005, p. 20.

Federal Deposit Insurance Corporation, "Regions Bank Acquires All the Deposits of Integrity Bank, Alpharetta, Georgia" (press release), August 29, 2008.

———, "Regions Bank, Birmingham, AL Acquires All the Deposits of FirstBank Financial Services, McDonough, GA" (press release), February 6, 2009.

Finkelstein, Brad, "Regions, AmSouth Create Big Servicer," *Mortgage Servicing News*, July 2006.

Gilpin, Francis X., "CEO Compensation Gets Washington's Attention," *Montgomery Advertiser*, November 16, 2006.

Green, Lee J.,"Bigger Means Better for AmSouth, Regions Customers Following Merger," *Deep South Jewish Voice*, November 2006, p. 35.

Hubbard, Russell, "Regions Financial Corporation," *Birmingham News*, June 10, 2009.

Jarvis, Crystal, "Regions to Make $43.7M TARP Payment," *Birmingham Business Journal*, July 16, 2009.

Kulikowski, Laurie, "Regions Expecting $50M of Hurricane Credit Losses," *American Banker*, September 14, 2005, p. 20.

Morris, Natalie, "Two Bank Mergers Approved: Bank One, Union Planters Bought," *Springfield (IL) State Journal-Register*, January 4, 2005, p. 17.

"Regions Partners with UNCF for Business Scholarships," *Indianapolis (IN) Recorder*, April 4, 2008, p. C3.

Republic Engineered Products Inc.

2633 Eighth Street
Canton, Ohio 44704-2311
U.S.A.
Telephone: (330) 438-5336
Toll Free: (800) 232-7157
Fax: (330) 438-5814
Web site: http://www.republicengineercd.com

Wholly Owned Subsidiary of Industrias CH SA de CV
Founded: 1886 as Berger Manufacturing Company
Incorporated: 2003
Employees: 2,300
Sales: $1.50 billion (2008)
NAICS: 331513 Steel Foundries (except Investment); 331111 Iron and Steel Mills

■ ■ ■

Republic Engineered Products Inc. is a leading supplier of special bar quality (SBQ) steel. As of 2009 the company operated eight plants in Ohio, Indiana, New York, and Canada. Republic primarily serves the automotive, appliance, energy, industrial, and equipment markets with hot-rolled and cold-finished steel products. Having weathered several industry downturns, bankruptcies, and changes of ownership, the company was revitalized after 2005 under the guidance of its new owners Industrias CH SA de CV of Mexico and generated sales of $1.5 billion in 2008.

COMPANY ORIGINS IN THE 19TH CENTURY

Republic Engineered Products Inc. traces its history to the establishment of the Berger Manufacturing Company in Canton, Ohio, in 1886. Berger was subsumed by United Alloy Steel Company, which was formed in 1916. Over the next 40 years several companies were founded that would later merge to form Republic Steel. Union Drawn Steel was established in Beaver Falls, Pennsylvania, in 1889 and built a new plant in Gary, Indiana, in 1917. Another precursor to Republic Engineered Products, the Central Steel Corporation, which built the world's first electrified steel plant, was founded in Massillon, Ohio, in the early 1900s. Central Steel grew rapidly, particularly during World War I when demand for steel skyrocketed. In 1926 Central Steel merged with Union Drawn and United Alloy to form the Central Alloy Steel Corporation.

In 1930 Cyrus Eaton, a Cleveland industrialist, formed Republic Steel Corporation from a merger between Central Alloy Steel Corporation and the Interstate Iron and Steel Company, a Chicago-based company that had been founded in 1905. With the merger, Republic Steel became the third largest steel producer in the country, competing with United States Steel Corporation and the Bethlehem Steel Corporation. Republic Steel's research staff and skilled workforce, as well as its concentration of electric furnaces suitable for making stainless steel, provided certain commercial advantages over its larger rivals.

COMPANY PERSPECTIVES

Republic Engineered Products is committed to providing our customers with hot rolled & cold finished steel bars and cast products for demanding applications that are delivered on time, meet their quality expectations and provide real value. We accomplish this by fostering a corporate culture that truly listens to its workers and practices continuous improvement as a way of life. "Customer satisfaction is my job" is every employee's focus.

Republic Steel's fortunes were affected by the conditions that influenced the development of all domestic steel producers in the years that followed: the economic constraints of the Great Depression and the growing movement to organize steelworker labor. The steel industry suffered greatly during the Great Depression, with production dropping to pre-1900 levels. Rail production, for example, fell by 1933 to its lowest level since 1865. Full-time employment industrywide fell from 158,000 to 18,000 in 1932, and wages bottomed out at 33 cents an hour for steelworkers. Conditions were ripe for labor organization.

Several steelworker strikes were stymied between 1932 and 1935 for various reasons, but the passage of the National Labor Relations Act in 1935 gave labor organizers renewed confidence. In June 1936, the Steel Workers Organizing Committee (SWOC) was formed and, with $500,000 from the supporting miners union, began recruiting members among the workers at the largest steel mills in the United States, including Republic Steel. Industrialists opposed union formation, and threats and violence against union sympathizers were not uncommon. By 1937, however, the SWOC had organized the nation's largest steel company, United States Steel Corporation, and was representing workers at the bargaining table with U.S. Steel management. Republic Steel and the management at several other steel companies did not recognize the SWOC, who had not achieved as great a membership among their workers as at U.S. Steel. In May and June 1937, the SWOC called for a strike at these "Little Steel" companies. On Memorial Day 1937, steelworkers demonstrating at Republic Steel's mill in South Chicago were confronted by police. In what was later called the Memorial Day Massacre, 10 workers died and approximately 100 were injured, mostly from bullet wounds in the back, yet the SWOC continued to gain momentum. By the time the SWOC

had ratified its constitution and changed its name to the United Steel Workers Union in 1942, it had established a collective bargaining agreement with Republic Steel.

PROSPERITY IN THE MID-20TH CENTURY

World War II brought sudden prosperity to Republic Steel. To meet demands for steel in Europe and in anticipation of the United States entering the war, production had risen dramatically in 1940 and 1941. With steel needed for everything from bullets to tanks to aircraft carriers, Republic's steel works were soon running nonstop, and the company employed a record number of people.

Republic Steel saw a slight drop in production immediately after the war ended, but pent-up demand for consumer goods made with steel, such as cars and appliances, soon had the steelworks booming. Steelworks in Japan, Germany, and England had mostly been destroyed during the war, which left the United States as the world's only significant producer of steel. Republic Steel faced no competition from imports and was able to increase exports to countries struggling with postwar reconstruction. The 1950s and 1960s were years of unparalleled prosperity for Republic Steel.

In 1972 and 1973 Republic Steel, along with the nation's other two steel giants (Bethlehem Steel and U.S. Steel), forged an agreement with the United Steel Workers Union that would have far-reaching effects for the steel industry. The "experimental negotiating agreement" prohibited strikes and lockouts and guaranteed steelworkers a minimum 3 percent raise plus cost-of-living increases every year. Although management was pleased with having eliminated the threat of strikes, it did not anticipate the rampant inflation of the 1970s and the subsequent skyrocketing of employee wages.

Republic Steel, like the rest of the industry, began to show the first signs of trouble during the 1970s. The unprecedented prosperity of the previous decades had encouraged complacency in the steel industry. Payrolls were bloated, graft was rampant, and little investment had been made in technological advances. When finally faced with competition from imported steel and steel products in the 1970s, the steel industry was in no condition to respond decisively. Republic was forced to begin laying off employees and closing steelmaking facilities.

In an effort to compete more effectively with the threats that imported steel products were presenting, Republic Steel was acquired by the LTV Corporation in 1984 and merged with Jones & Laughlin to form LTV

KEY DATES

1886: Berger Manufacturing Company established in Canton, Ohio.

1889: Union Drawn Steel established in Beaver Falls, Pennsylvania.

1917: Union Drawn Steel builds a new plant in Gary, Indiana.

1930: Cyrus Eaton forms Republic Steel Corporation.

1936: Steel Workers Organizing Committee is formed.

1984: Republic Steel is acquired by LTV Corporation and merged with Jones & Laughlin to form LTV Steel Co.

1989: Management and employees buy the bar division from LTV, naming it Republic Engineered Steels Inc.

1993: Republic Engineered Steels purchases Western Steel Group.

1994: Republic Engineered Steels acquires the principal assets of Baltimore Specialty Steels Corporation.

1998: Republic acquired by an investor group led by the Blackstone Group and Veritas Capital, merged with Bar Technologies Inc., and named Republic Technologies International (RTI).

2002: RTI bought by KPS Special Situations Fund LP and Hunt Investment Group LP; re-established as Republic Engineered Products LLC.

2003: Perry Strategic Capital Inc. purchases Republic Engineered Products LLC, establishing Republic Engineered Products Inc.

2005: Industrias CH SA de CV acquires Republic Engineered Products Inc.

2009: Republic Engineered Products relocates its corporate headquarters to its manufacturing operation in Canton, Ohio

Steel Co. However, the merger did not resolve the company's problems, and LTV declared bankruptcy in July 1986. When the company was still in bankruptcy in October 1988, LTV management decided to concentrate on the flat rolled steel business. The other major area of business, the bar division, was offered for sale.

EMPLOYEE BUYOUT IN 1989

Management and employees of the bar division, concerned that a highly leveraged buyer would be more likely to liquidate the division's assets than invest the capital needed to operate it as a going concern, tendered a formal bid to buy the bar division through an Employee Stock Ownership Plan (ESOP). LTV accepted the bid in May 1989, and the purchase was formally signed effective November 28, 1989. Russell W. Maier, who had been president of the bar division, became president and chief executive officer of the new Republic Engineered Steels Inc.

Maier had been with Republic Steel since before the merger that formed LTV Steel. Starting in 1960 as an industrial engineer, Maier was promoted to a series of positions with increasing responsibility. In 1983 he was named chief operating officer and after the merger, he served as executive vice-president of LTV until becoming president and general manager of the bar division in 1985. According to the *New York Times*, Maier initially fought the idea of employee ownership, but came to believe that a combination of employee ownership and full employee participation in decision-making resulted in employee suggestions that led to significant cost savings.

The original initiative for the buyout was said to have come from the steelworkers union, the United Steelworkers of America (USWA). The complex ESOP was designed by New York investment firm Lazard Frères, and the purchase price was set at $280 million. The bar division's 5,000 employees, union and management, contributed an average of $4,000 each for a total of $20 million. Another $190 million was borrowed from the Bank of Boston and Security Pacific Bank, and the remaining $70 million was borrowed from LTV. The transaction left the new Republic in a highly leveraged position, but committed to its own operating future. Federal tax policies advantageous to the ESOP-owned Republic permitted greater use of cash generated from operations. Significant cash obligations for the young company included its debt service, contributions to its ESOP, and a postretirement health benefit fund. In the years that followed, Republic made a major reduction in its debt.

In conjunction with the purchase, a new labor agreement was reached between the USWA and Republic management. Appendix H-l to the agreement acknowledged the need for the involvement of all employees in the success of the business. A committee consisting of union representatives, salaried employees, and management, and known as the H-l committee, determined to develop a new corporate culture conducive to respect and trust between the groups, and oriented toward the profitability of Republic.

The H-l committee established a company-wide education program to enable the new employee-owners to understand the ESOP structure, to make sense of the financial statements, and to grasp the basic elements and goals of Republic's business plan. Republic provided most of the multimillion-dollar cost of the program, which involved an hour of business instruction each month for each employee-owner for 30 months.

REORGANIZATION AND COST-CUTTING IN THE EARLY 1990S

Republic's sales for its first partial year, through June 1990, were approximately $379 million. The next six months, from July 1990 through December 1990, saw a sharp drop to $310 million. Republic blamed the general economic environment and responded by reorganizing into four separate business centers, each with profit accountability: Steel Division, Rolling Division, Cold Finished Division, and Specialty Steel Group.

In addition, in June 1991 Republic announced a goal of $80 million in cost reductions. Employee suggestions on operations were actively sought as alternatives to job cuts. By February 1992, more than 1,000 suggestions had been submitted, valued by Republic at $60 million in savings. One suggestion that made dramatic savings, approximately $3.6 million, was a new plan for the separation of different types of scrap steel for more efficient and reliable use in recycling.

By including "Engineered" in its new corporate name, Republic signified its intent to meet demanding specifications from its customers, more than 50 percent of whom were in the automotive industry. The products of Republic's Rolling Division and Cold Finished Division could be produced in a wide variety of sizes, grades, shapes, and finishes. The Specialty Steel group produced precision bar steel that met critical requirements for aerospace, energy, and defense applications.

Republic's principal competitors in these markets included the U.S. Steel/Kobe joint venture, the Timken Co., MacSteel Co., Bethlehem Steel's bar division, Inland Steel's bar division, and North Star. Low cost minimills like Koppel Steel and Nucor were an increasing threat to Republic as well.

As a privately held company, Republic was not required to release its results of operations to the public. It did, however, disclose financial information on a quarterly basis—including operating income, which was positive for all but one quarter in the first year after its

formation. In any event, within its first 13 months, Republic was able to build a cash reserve of approximately $90 million, out of which it paid down $37 million of its debt.

Republic made only one stock dividend payment, shortly after the ESOP was formed. Since the stock was not publicly traded, employee-owners could only sell their stock back to the company, and then only upon retirement. A minimal gain of a few hundred dollars might be recognized by the individual. However, to most of the employee-owners in the early days, job security was more critical than capital gains. Although Republic was not the first steel company in the United States to respond to financial troubles with employee ownership, its experiment was conducted on a much broader scale than that of Weirton Steel, for instance, which preceded it. As CEO Maier looked to the future in the early 1990s, he was "cautiously optimistic." Maier recognized that the future of Republic was tightly bound with that of the automotive industry that it served and the U.S. economy as a whole.

RENEWED EXPANSION IN THE MID- TO LATE-1990S

Although the steel industry remained slow in the early 1990s in the United States, Republic managed to generate a healthy cash flow. Because of the complex federal tax structure for companies with ESOPs, Republic reported losses of $42 million over its first three years. To allocate common stock placed in ESOP trust at the company's formation, Republic was required to take quarterly noncash charges of $8 million. Although this requirement led to a red bottom line, it left Republic with cash to make capital improvements and to reduce its debt. Within a few years, the company had paid off all of the $260 million of short-term debt used to finance the leveraged buyout, partly through a long-term bond issue in 1993. In addition, the company invested in much-needed modernization of its plants.

The ample cash flow also helped Republic expand through acquisitions. In 1993 the company purchased Western Steel Group, a maker of cold finished bar. The following year, Republic expanded its stainless tool steel and forged products business by acquiring the principal assets of Baltimore Specialty Steels Corporation. The deal with parent company Armco Inc. was made for an undisclosed sum. Republic transformed operations at the plants acquired from both of the troubled acquisitions. By creating flexible, self-directed teams, Republic was able to eliminate 40 percent of the workforce while maintaining the same level of production.

In 1995 Republic floated an initial public offering (IPO) of eight million shares of common stock. With the $64 million it gained from the IPO, Republic repurchased the employees' preferred stock, thus freeing itself from the guaranteed dividends of 16.5 percent instituted with the creation of the ESOP. Although the initial public offering introduced outside influence, the employees still owned 58 percent of the common stock, thus retaining control of the company.

Also in 1995 Republic began construction of a CAST-ROLL facility in Canton, Ohio. The only plant of its kind in North America, the facility cost approximately $165 million. The state-of-the-art plant reduced the time needed to create billets of different sizes and metallurgical grades. By closely linking such processes as ladle refining and rolling operations, the new facility could ready molten steel for shipping in one-sixth the time needed using traditional methods.

In 1997 the ESOP stock was fully allocated and Republic no longer had to take quarterly charges toward it, leaving the company with a much improved bottom line. Republic split its businesses into three independent divisions: Hot Rolled Bar Division, Cold Finished Bar Division, and Stainless and Specialty Steels Division. The same year, Republic signed a four-year technology exchange agreement with the Japanese company Sanyo Special Steel. Sanyo agreed to provide technical assistance to Republic in its steel melting practices and in fine-tuning the operation of its CAST-ROLL facility.

In 1998 Republic agreed to be acquired by an investor group led by the Blackstone Group and Veritas Capital. Blackstone and Veritas bought 19.3 million of Republic's 19.7 million shares, and merged Bar Technologies Inc. (BarTech), which the investors also owned, with Republic to form Republic Technologies International (RTI). Shortly after the new company was formed, BarTech's cold-finished plant in Medina, Ohio, and Republic's ingot production operation in Canton, Ohio, were closed. By mid-August 1999, RTI merged with the USS/Kobe Steel Co., a special-bar-quality (SBQ) producer, making the company the largest North American SBQ producer, but resulting in further job losses at USS/Kobe's plant in Lorain, Ohio. According to an article in *American Metal Market*, RTI's CEO, Thomas N. Tyrrell, thought that this merger had the potential to make RTI a single SBQ source for large customers, such as automobile manufacturers, but added that "the key to financial success is cutting redundancies and focusing on the strengths of the three operations."

EMERGENCE OF REPUBLIC ENGINEERED PRODUCTS INC.: 2000–04

By February 2000, Tyrrell resigned as RTI's CEO, and was replaced by Joseph F. Lapinsky, the company's

president and chief operating officer and a 26-year veteran of the steel industry. Although RTI was now North America's largest SBQ producer and supplier, it was still not the most profitable. By April 2000, RTI was producing 2.5 million tons of the 8 million tons of hot-rolled bar required by the domestic market, 70 percent of which was used in automotive production. The remaining 30 percent ended up as stock in service centers. In order to improve its bottom line, the company had to consider further consolidation of its other operations. It also had to focus on expanding its original equipment manufacturer (OEM) customer-base, while reducing its reliance on the distributor and service center markets.

In 2001 a number of economic conditions including plummeting steel prices, soaring energy prices, and an influx of low cost imports, contributed to a severe downturn in the U.S. steel business. Many domestic companies were facing bankruptcy, and RTI was no exception. In an effort to avoid additional layoffs and quell the threat of filing for Chapter 11 protection, the company temporarily idled some of its operations at the Canton and Lorain facilities; sold some of its equipment and properties, including its former Republic Steel headquarters in Masillon, Ohio; and began plans to upgrade the Canton and Lorain plants. However, in April 2001 the company filed for bankruptcy and secured $420 million in debtor-in-possession (DIP) financing in order to continue operating and complete its reorganization plan, which was due on November 20.

Over the next few months, the company would intermittently idle its facilities in Ohio, Pennsylvania, Indiana, Illinois, and Ontario, and lay-off an additional 700 employees, reducing its workforce by 19 percent. In November, with a few issues still unresolved, RTI was granted a four-month extension. In December, as part of the reorganization plan, the remaining employees agreed to a 15 percent pay cut. On March 28, 2002, RTI was granted a third extension with a deadline of June 28, 2002. In July 2002 RTI was bought by KPS Special Situations Fund LP and Hunt Investment Group LP for $463 million and was re-established as Republic Engineered Products LLC. The buyout also included the sale of many of its operations, resulting in a reduction of its workforce from 4,000 to 2,500. The following month, the U.S. Bankruptcy Court approved approximately $3 million in bonuses to retain the company's top 30 executives.

The company was looking forward to a fresh start, but its first year of operation proved to be testing times. In October 2002 a malfunction at its Canton plant sent 100,000 pounds of molten steel to the floor. There were no injuries, but the damages were extensive, and the plant was disabled for a number of days. Less than three weeks later, 10 workers were injured in an explosion at the Lorain plant. Between January and August of 2003, mechanical and electrical problems surfaced at both the Canton and Lorain plants, and in August 2003 a major power outage caused severe damage to an idle furnace, resulting in a one-month closure and an estimated loss of $10 million. Sharp increases in the costs of natural gas and steel scrap contributed further to the company's losses. With production hampered, shipments delayed, and costs rising, the company was finding it difficult to pay its property tax bill, and by September 2003 Republic Engineered Products found itself re-examining its cost structure. In a memorandum, a company spokesman said "management has been intensely reviewing and taking actions on all means to reduce expenses and control costs. Negotiations on matters of insurance and corporate finance have continued." The spokesman went on to say that the continuity of the business required some "undesired decisions," such as delayed payments and temporary lay-offs.

Once more, on October 6, 2003, Republic Engineered Products LLC filed for Chapter 11 bankruptcy and sought another DIP agreement. "Under the circumstances, this filing was the only way for Republic to restore operations and preserve business," said Lapinsky. In December 2003 a federal bankruptcy judge approved the sale of the company to Perry Strategic Capital Inc. for $277.5 million, and Republic Engineered Products Inc. was established. By May 2004 the company had completed its restructuring and reported first- and second-quarter profits. Business continued to improve, and by March 2005 Republic Engineered Products began work on a $50-million expansion of its Canton facility. The new caster equipment would not only allow for more flexibility in the production schedule, but would also create 170 new jobs.

REVITALIZED UNDER NEW OWNERSHIP: 2005–09

Republic Engineered Products' profitability began to attract the attention of both domestic and foreign investors, and in July 2005 Industrias CH SA de CV (ICH), a Mexican steel producer, acquired the company for $229 million. Republic remained a stand-alone company, but became a subsidiary of the ICH majority-owned company, Grupo Simec SA de CV of Guadalajara. By April of the following year, Grupo Simec had settled Republic's outstanding debt of $166 million. In June 2006, with the company in a healthy financial condition, Joseph Lapinsky resigned the position of president and CEO, and Jaime Vigil, the son of ICH's chairman, took over the reins.

The next 12 months continued to be profitable and in August 2007 Republic employees were considering strike action unless their contract, which was accepted while the company was in bankruptcy, was re-negotiated. Now that the company was successful, the union was demanding increased pension payments, profit sharing, and additional investments in facility upgrades. By August 28, the workers had approved a five-year deal that included substantial pay increases, improved profit sharing, enhanced job security, and better retirement benefits. In addition, within the first two quarters of 2008, the company created a new cold-finished bar products division and invested $20 million in upgrading its Lackawanna bar mill.

In March 2009, in a strategic move, Republic Engineered Products relocated its corporate headquarters from Fairlawn, Ohio, to its manufacturing operation in Canton, Ohio. "We believe being close to our plants gets us more in touch with operations and makes decision-making a more efficient process, resulting in better customer satisfaction and less waste," Vigil said. In June of that same year, American Metal Market LLC (AAM) filed a motion against Republic alleging that the company failed to fulfill the requirements of a four-year supply contract by demanding volume commitments and price increases that were not part of the original contract. On June 25, 2009, in a decision that satisfied both parties, a judge ruled in favor of AAM, ordering Republic to continue to supply the steel products, but with the stipulation that AAM accelerate its payment schedule and post security with the court. By the second half of 2009, with the recession taking its toll on the automotive industry, Republic Engineered Products set its sights on expanding its product line to the energy and construction markets. As their ad said, "Steel-crazy after all these years."

Marcia McDermott
Updated, Susan Windisch Brown; Marie O'Sullivan

PRINCIPAL DIVISIONS

Cold-Finished Bars; Hot-Rolled Bars.

PRINCIPAL COMPETITORS

AK Steel Holding Corporation; Quanex Building Products; The Timken Company.

FURTHER READING

Brennan, Terry, "Republic Bankruptcy Fees Cause Outrage," *The Daily Deal*, May 2, 2001.

Drown, Stuart, "Republic Attempts Recasting," *Beacon Journal*, August 26, 1991.

Ethridge, Mary, and John Russell, "Fairlawn, Ohio Steel Company Adjusts to Difficult Times in Industry," *Akron Beacon Journal*, January 13, 2001.

Kilborn, Peter T., "New Paths in Business When Workers Own," *New York Times*, November 22, 1991.

Kusic, Sam, "Jaime Vigil Named to Take Republic Engineered Helm," *American Metal Market*, June 30, 2006, p. 1.

Leonard, Jim, "Mexico's ICH Takes Its 1st US Step with Republic Buy," *American Metal Market*, July 26, 2005, p. 1.

Petry, Corinna, "AAM Claims Supply Pact Breach in Republic Suit," *American Metal Market*, June 16, 2009, p. 1.

———, "Can Republic Win the Battle of the Bars?" *Metal Center News*, April 2000, p. 36.

———, "Republic, AAM Satisfied by Court Ruling on Shipments," *American Metal Market*, June 26, 2009, p. 6.

———, "Republic Eyeing Growth beyond the Auto Market," *American Metal Market*, June 18, 2009, p. 1.

Prizinsky, David, "New Owners Trying to Right Republic Engineered Ship," *Crain's Cleveland Business*, April 19, 2004, p. 6.

———, "Steelmaker Toughs Out First Year," *Crain's Cleveland Business*, July 28, 2003, p. 3.

"Republic Engineered Steel Company Earnings," *New York Times*, August 25, 1998, p. C8.

Rosen, Robert, *Leading People: Transforming Business from the Inside Out*. New York: Viking Penguin, 1996.

Sacco, John E., "Bankruptcy Judge OKs Perry's Bid for Republic," *American Metal Market*, December 18, 2003, p. 4.

———, "Chess Match in Ohio Court to Determine Republic's Fate," *American Metal Market*, December 4, 2003, p. 1.

———, "New Republic Owners 'Misinterpret' Pact: USW," *American Metal Market*, September 16, 2002, p. 2.

———, "Perry Ups Bid, Named Republic 'Stalking Horse,'" *American Metal Market*, November 6, 2003, p. 4.

———, "Republic Back in Court for Another Ch. 11 Bout," *American Metal Market*, October 7, 2003, p. 1.

———, "Republic Idles Plants as Cash Runs Out; Sales Eyed," *American Metal Market*, October 6, 2003, p. 1.

———, "Republic Still Feels Power Outage 'Aftershock.'" *American Metal Market*, September 12, 2003, p. 3.

———, "Republic Woes Grow as Ohio Tax Bills Mount," *American Metal Market*, September 29, 2003, p. 1.

Serrin, William, *Homestead: The Glory and Tragedy of an American Steel Town*. New York: Random House, 1992.

Sheridan, John H., "Counting on Cash," *Industry Week*, September 2, 1996, pp. 10-15.

Research in Motion Limited

———■———

295 Phillip Street
Waterloo, Ontario N2L 3W8
Canada
Telephone: (519) 888-7465
Fax: (519) 888-7884
Web site: http://www.rim.net

Public Company
Incorporated: 1984
Employees: 8,387 (2009)
Sales: $11.07 billion (2009)
Stock Exchanges: NASDAQ Toronto
Ticker Symbol: RIMM (NASDAQ); RIM (Toronto)
NAICS: 334119 Other Computer Peripheral Equipment Manufacturing; 334210 Telephone Apparatus Manufacturing; 334220 Radio and Television Broadcasting and Wireless Communications Equipment Manufacturing; 334290 Other Communication Equipment Manufacturing; 511210 Software Publishers

■ ■ ■

Research in Motion Ltd. (RIM) is a mobile phone maker and provider of e-mail services. Through its Blackberry brand of wireless devices, RIM pioneered the market for so-called "smart phones"—mobile devices that provide connections to data networks and e-mail as well as voice telephone service. The company survived extensive litigation over the patents to its technologies to remain a leader in the smart phone market. Initially marketed to corporations and business people, the Blackberry brand has expanded into the burgeoning consumer smart phone market, competing with Apple, Samsung, Nokia, and HTC.

EARLY HISTORY: 1984-90

Research in Motion Ltd. was founded by Mike Lazardis in 1984 in Waterloo, Ontario. Lazardis, the son of Greeks who immigrated to Canada from Turkey in 1967, was 23 at the time. He had recently dropped out of the University of Waterloo, where he had been studying electrical engineering. Backed by loans from friends and family, Lazardis and two friends started RIM. The company's first contract came from General Motors of Canada Ltd. for industrial automation. For several years the company survived by moving from contract to contract. By the late 1980s RIM had about $1 million in sales and about a dozen employees.

DEVELOPING DIGITAL WIRELESS SYSTEMS: 1990S

RIM became interested in the long-term potential of digital wireless devices after it received a contract in 1987 from Rogers Cantel Mobile Communications, a paging and cellular telephone operator that was a subsidiary of Rogers Communications. The contract required RIM to investigate the potential of newer wireless digital network systems being developed by Sweden's LM Ericsson. RIM was soon manufacturing tiny wireless radio modems. By the mid-1990s these modems were being used by original equipment manufacturers (OEMs) in products ranging from computers to vending machines.

COMPANY PERSPECTIVES

∎

Research in Motion is a leading designer, manufacturer and marketer of innovative wireless solutions for the worldwide mobile communications market. Through the development of integrated hardware, software and services that support multiple wireless network standards, RIM provides platforms and solutions for seamless access to time-sensitive information including e-mail, phone, SMS messaging, Internet and intranet-based applications. RIM technology also enables a broad array of third party developers and manufacturers to enhance their products and services with wireless connectivity to data. RIM's portfolio of award-winning products, services and embedded technologies are used by thousands of organizations around the world and include the BlackBerry wireless platform, the RIM Wireless Handheld product line, software development tools, radio-modems and software/hardware licensing agreements.

By 1991 RIM was developing software to support a complete wireless e-mail system. The company was part of a three-way partnership with Ericsson GE Mobile Data and Anterior Technology that was formed to develop the system. In January 1992 Ericsson introduced its first portable radio modem, which was designed for Hewlett-Packard Co.'s palmtop computer. Anterior Technology was to provide a gateway to major e-mail systems, and RIM provided the application programming interface (API). RIM's API, called MobiLab-Plus, would be used to develop e-mail packages with Anterior Technology. RIM noted that by using radio packet technology instead of cellular networks, the network could determine the optimum time to send an e-mail message. The system, which was still being developed, featured uninterrupted connectivity.

Realizing that he was better at engineering than corporate finance, Lazaridis hired James Balsillie in 1992 to handle the company's finances and business development. Balsillie, a chartered accountant with an M.B.A. from Harvard University, had previously held executive positions with Ernst & Young in Toronto and with Sutherland-Shultz Ltd. Balsillie subsequently became RIM's chairman and co-CEO with Lazaridis.

In the early 1990s RIM also produced a software developer's kit (SDK) for adding wireless connectivity to

Windows 3.x applications. In 1995 RIM released version 2.5 of the SDK, which was called RAD I/O Connectivity Tools. The core of the SDK was a protocol that acted as an interface to the RAM Mobile Data network, which was a two-way wireless data-packet network compatible with radio modems produced by IBM, Ericsson GE Mobile Communications, and Motorola. The SDK's protocol handled all communications setups between Windows applications and Mobitex, the name of RIM's networking software. In 1996 RIM released a PCMIA plug-in card for computers that enabled wireless e-mail.

By 1996 manufacturers were beginning to focus on developing smart pagers that would utilize packet-based networks to provide wireless Internet access. RIM initially announced it had two such pagers in development for commercial release in 1997, one for the RAM Mobile Data wireless network and another that was compatible with Ardis Co.'s wireless network. RIM's pocket-sized smart pages would let users exchange pages, e-mail, and Internet messages via either network. Other companies developing similar smart pagers included NEC America and Motorola.

When RIM introduced its Inter@ctive pager in September 1996 at the PCS '96 trade show in San Francisco, the pager was able to use both the Ardis and RAM wireless networks. An innovative two-way messaging device, the Inter@ctive pager featured a QWERTY keyboard and a small, text-only display screen that showed four lines of text. It was developed jointly with Intel Corporation and included a 16-bit operating system along with built-in contact manager, scheduler, and forms-based messaging applications. With service provided by Ardis Co. and RAM Mobile Data USA L.P., the Inter@ctive pager could send and receive messages and had its own Internet address. The handheld device could also store 100KB of data and had a variety of pre-programmed response messages, such as "I'll be late." The list price for the Interi@ctive pager was about $675, not including service fees.

Released commercially in 1997, the Inter@ctive pager quickly became RIM's best-known product. By early 1998 the company had signed a contract to supply IBM with Inter@ctive pagers for use by its field service representatives across North America. Other customers included Panasonic Corp., Mobile Integrated Technologies, and Telxon Corp.

RIM completed its initial public offering during fiscal 1998. The company's stock was traded on the Toronto Stock Exchange. That year RIM reported revenue of $21 million and net income of $400,000. In a strong financial position, it had CAD100 million worth of backlogged orders and CAD109 million of cash

KEY DATES

1984: Research in Motion Ltd. (RIM) is founded by Mike Lazardis.
1988: RIM begins working on wireless data-only applications.
1996: RIM develops a PCMIA plug-in card for computer-enabled wireless e-mail.
1997: RIM goes public and is listed on the Toronto Stock Exchange.
1999: RIM introduces the BlackBerry personal digital assistant (PDA); Lazardis and a RIM coworker receive an Academy Award for technical achievement.
2000: The popular BlackBerry is named Product of the Year by *InfoWorld*; RIM launches its Wireless Handheld product line.
2002: RIM introduces the BlackBerry 5810, which incorporates cell phone service.
2003: Oprah Winfrey endorses the BlackBerry on her popular television show, declaring, "I love this so much. I cannot live without this. It's with me everywhere I go."
2006: RIM pays NTP $612.5 million to settle patent-infringement suit.
2008: RIM unveils the Blackberry Storm, the first BlackBerry product to utilize touch screen technology.

and short-term investments. It planned to use about half of its cash on new equipment, sales and marketing, research and development, and as working capital. The company planned to invest 10 to 15 percent of its sales revenue in research and development.

Near the end of 1998 RIM introduced an upgraded version of its Inter@ctive pager. The 950 model was smaller, less costly, and had a longer battery life than its predecessor, the 900 model. The 950 could send and receive e-mail, pages, and peer-to-peer messages as well as send faxes and text-to-voice messages. The Inter@ctive pager 950 was priced at $249, with service from Bell South Wireless Data L.P. available for $25 per month. At the PCS '98 trade show in Orlando, Florida, RIM and Bell South Wireless Data announced they were working together with Sybase to develop a mobile enterprise solution that extended critical business applications to a two-way pager. The solution included the RIM Inter@ctive pager 950 and Sybase's Ultra-Lite, a smaller version of its Adaptive Server Anywhere mobile

database. The solution enabled corporate users to download and upload data on demand from their pagers.

POPULARITY OF RIM'S BLACKBERRY: 1999

Sensing that the time was right for corporate e-mail appliances, RIM introduced the BlackBerry mobile e-mail solution in February 1999. The BlackBerry included a wearable wireless handheld device with service initially provided by BellSouth's wireless network in the United States and Cantel AT&T wireless data network in Canada. A unique aspect of the BlackBerry was that it featured a push system for e-mail delivery, whereby e-mail messages were relayed from the user's personal computer or corporate server to the BlackBerry without having to dial in. The BlackBerry was an always-on, always-connected product that never had to be turned off. At its introduction a BlackBerry subscription package was priced at $399 with a monthly service charge of $40. Around this time RIM introduced the BlackBerry Enterprise Server, an optional add-on server that allowed e-mail to be redirected from the server rather than from the desktop.

Reviews that compared the BlackBerry with 3Com's just-released Palm VII PDA noted two key differences in addition to the fact that the Palm VII cost $599 compared to $399 for the BlackBerry. The BlackBerry had to be left on at all times, as did the user's personal computer or corporate server, while the Palm had an antenna that had to be raised to work. Another key difference was that the BlackBerry notified users of new messages, while the Palm VII did not. Both products included address book, calendar, task list, and alarm clock features.

In 1999 RIM's revenue more than doubled to $47.5 million. Net income was $6.8 million. During the second half of 1999 RIM announced that several operators were offering RIM messaging solutions. In the United States RGN Corp. became the first Internet service provider (ISP) to offer the BlackBerry wireless e-mail solution to subscribers. GoAmerica Communications Corp. announced its support of e-mail access for the Inter@ctive 950 pager and BlackBerry service. Internationally, Venezuela-based Telcel Cellular became the first Mobitex operator in Latin America to offer a messaging solution using RIM's Inter@ctive 950e pager, which was the Spanish-language version of the Inter@ctive 950.

RIM also faced challenges in 1999. In August, competitor Glenayre Technologies filed a patent infringement suit against RIM regarding a patented process involving power generation from a dual battery source. Glenayre claimed that RIM's Inter@ctive pager line used this patented process. In another development BellSouth delayed contract renewal negotiations with RIM. As a result RIM had to report lower-than-expected quarterly earnings. RIM's Inter@ctive pagers were contributing about 70 percent of the company's revenue, and BellSouth was the largest customer for those devices. However, new customers were being signed up, including American Mobile Satellite Corp. and Paging Network. In addition, RIM signed a distribution agreement with Dell Computer whereby Dell account executives would sell BlackBerry devices to large corporate accounts. News of the distribution agreement helped boost RIM's stock price to more than CAD80 per share by the end of 1999, up from CAD46.20 on November 1.

NEW COMPETITORS, LEADING TO UPGRADES: 2000

RIM's BlackBerry enjoyed good reviews and was named Product of the Year by *InfoWorld*, which said, "The BlackBerry wins hands down when it comes to easy and timely access to e-mail messages." In January 2000 RIM and Canadian telecommunications giant Nortel entered into a joint marketing and product development agreement, which included a $25 million investment in RIM by Nortel. It was expected that the joint agreement would lead to making RIM's Inter@ctive pagers and BlackBerry service available in Europe. RIM also signed another agreement with Compaq Computer, which agreed to distribute RIM's BlackBerry service to its corporate clients.

In 2000 RIM reported revenue of $85 million and net income of $10.2 million. In April 2000 the company received a CAD34 million investment from the Canadian government under its Technology Partnerships Canada (TPC) program. Around this time RIM introduced the first of its Wireless Handheld products, the BlackBerry 957, priced at $149. It featured a larger screen than the BlackBerry 950, a 32-bit Intel 386 processor, five megabytes (MB) of Intel flash memory, keyboard, embedded wireless modem, integrated organizer, and full support for the BlackBerry wireless e-mail solution. RIM also upgraded the BlackBerry 950, giving it four MB of memory, and introduced version 2.0 of its BlackBerry software to support both the 950 and the 957.

By mid-2000 RIM's BlackBerry service was hosted by numerous internet service providers (ISPs). The company had just signed a partnership agreement with America Online (AOL) to provide AOL Mail and AOL Instant Messenger service through RIM handheld

devices. While Palm's line of PDAs held the largest market share, RIM was doing well serving the niche market of professionals who required mobile access to business-related e-mail. RIM had about 200,000 BlackBerry units in use, with about 50,000 of them at corporations. Other competitors included Motorola and OmniSky, and in the second half of 2000 Handspring, a new company formed by Palm founder Jeff Hawkins.

By the end of 2000 RIM had released the AOL Mobile Communicator as part of its agreement with AOL. The device, part of AOL's new "AOL Anywhere" strategy, was a two-way pager that let users access AOL e-mail and instant messaging services. In other developments, the company teamed with Certicom to provide secure transactions over its handheld devices, and it reached a new agreement with BellSouth Wireless Data to supply the company with 150,000 wireless handheld devices. BellSouth also agreed to offer the BlackBerry wireless e-mail solution to its corporate clients. In another development, RIM licensed CDMA (code division multiple access) technology and patents from Qualcomm, which allowed the company to expand its customer base to include wireless users on CDMA cellular and PCS networks.

In November 2000 Lazardis committed CAD100 million to fund the Perimeter Institute for Theoretical Physics in Waterloo, Ontario, starting with a CAD20 million donation. It was the largest philanthropic gift in Canadian history.

EXPANSION OF BLACKBERRY SERVICE: 2001

In 2001 BlackBerry wireless e-mail service became more widely available in Europe. In April the British wireless service, BT Cellnet, committed to purchasing 175,000 wireless handheld devices and related software from RIM. Other agreements were signed with Esat Digifone in Ireland and Telfort Mobiel in the Netherlands to offer BlackBerry service.

RIM also expanded in the United States through agreements with companies such as IBM, which agreed to issue about 6,500 BlackBerry devices to its field-support staff and market the service to its customers. Vaultus, a wireless solution provider, agreed to supply at least 50,000 BlackBerry devices to its Global 1000 corporate customers over the next two years. RIM also took steps to target the U.S. military market. It reached an agreement with Kasten Chase to develop secure wireless access to the U.S. government's Defense Messaging System, which had 300,000 users globally. The overall military market included more than two million defense personnel.

Throughout 2001 RIM added enhancements to its products. In January it introduced the BlackBerry Enterprise Edition server for Lotus Notes and Domino. Previously, the BlackBerry system worked only with Microsoft Exchange servers, which had about 58 million users. Lotus Notes and Domino servers had about 65 million users.

In March RIM introduced the BlackBerry Enterprise Server 2.1 at the CTIA Wireless 2001 trade show in Las Vegas. The new version enabled Internet access for BlackBerrys for the first time and also allowed users to send updated calendar information to and from their central system. At the same time the company announced an alliance with GoAmerica Communications Corp. that allowed wireless downloads. These enhancements moved RIM's BlackBerry service significantly beyond wireless e-mail.

In 2001 RIM's revenue more than doubled to $221.3 million. However, increased operating expenses resulted in a net operating loss of $4.7 million. The company's overall net loss was $7.6 million. In May 2001 RIM filed a patent and trademark infringement complaint against competitor Glenayre Technologies, claiming that Glenayre blatantly imitated BlackBerry technology and marketing. Around this time RIM also obtained a U.S. patent called the BlackBerry Single Mailbox Integration patent, which covered technology that gave users the ability to have a single e-mail address on both wireless and desktop systems. The patent applied to the system and method that RIM pioneered for redirecting information between a host computer system and a mobile communications device. Later in 2001 Glenayre's 1999 patent suit against RIM was dismissed. In early 2002 RIM and Glenayre agreed to drop their lawsuits and work together to develop a wireless e-mail device that would incorporate Glenayre's messaging software.

In other developments, RIM expanded its presence in the consumer market by supplying Earthlink with BlackBerry service for its mobile messaging platform. Cingular Interactive, a wireless service provider, was also selling RIM devices to the general public. AOL, meanwhile, dropped the price of its Mobile Communicator from $320 to $99.95. In the enterprise market, RIM signed an agreement with software developer SAP AG to provide wireless access to its enterprise resource planning (ERP) applications. In October PeopleSoft became the first enterprise applications vendor to offer a secure wireless e-mail solution using BlackBerry in the European market. Following the terrorist attacks against the United States on September 11, 2001, BlackBerrys were handed out to all 435 members of the U.S. House of Representatives as a

security measure. BlackBerrys were also cited as providing much needed communications during the crisis, and in January 2002 it was reported that police officers at Boston's Logan Airport had been equipped with BlackBerrys. By the beginning of 2002 RIM could boast that it had 250,000 BlackBerry subscribers among more than 12,000 companies.

EXPANDING OPTIONS, ENTERING NEW MARKETS: 2002-03

At the beginning of 2002 RIM announced that it was developing a wireless device capable of handling both voice and data communications. The new BlackBerry device was being developed in association with Nextel Communications and Motorola. An agreement with VoiceStream Wireless Corp. also laid the groundwork for the new generation of voice-enabled BlackBerry devices, which would run on VoiceStream's GSM/GPRS (Global System for Mobile Communications/General Packet Radio Service), instead of on RIM's less advanced pager network. RIM also teamed with AT&T Wireless to offer AT&T Wireless's corporate customers a BlackBerry that could place telephone calls over AT&T Wireless's GSM/GPRS network. In Canada a similar agreement was reached with Rogers AT&T Wireless, which was developing its own GSM/GPRS network to reach more than 90 percent of all Canadians.

RIM's new BlackBerry with phone service and always-on e-mail connectivity was introduced in March 2002. The BlackBerry 5810 could be purchased through network carriers, including AT&T Wireless, Voice Stream, and Cingular Wireless in the United States and Rogers Wireless and Microcell Telecommunications in Canada. Pricing was determined by the carriers, with VoiceStream offering the 5810 for $499 plus a monthly fee of $39.99 for the data package, which included one MB of Internet downloads. Voice service required a separate account. A similar device, the BlackBerry 5820, was being shipped to the European market. Around this time competitor Handspring launched its all-in-one communication device, the Treo.

With competitors releasing their PDA designs to manufacturers, RIM announced in April 2002 that it would make its BlackBerry designs available to OEMs and original device manufacturers (ODMs). RIM said it would provide consulting, interoperability testing and certification, and hardware and software blueprints. In addition, Analog Devices, which supplied processors for RIM's devices, agreed to provide participating manufacturers with integrated processors that supported both GSM/GPRS wireless communications and Java applications.

RIM's expansion into European markets proceeded in 2002. In April the U.K. mobile operator Vodafone agreed to market BlackBerry wireless devices that operated over its GPRS network in the United Kingdom. In mid-2002 BlackBerry service was launched to corporate customers in Germany through an agreement with Deutsche Telekom, which had recently acquired U.S. wireless operator VoiceStream. Around this time Black-Berry service was also launched in France through an agreement with Vivendi Universal's mobile subsidiary SFR, which operated a GPRS network, and in Italy through Telecom Italia Mobile. In January 2003 Black-Berry service was introduced in Spain through an agreement with Telefonica Móviles S.A. and in Switzerland through an agreement with Swisscom Mobile.

In July 2002 *InfoWorld* magazine announced the results of its Readers' Choice Awards. RIM's BlackBerry won four separate awards, including Product of the Year and Best Handheld for the BlackBerry 957 and Gadget of the Year and Best Wireless Product for the BlackBerry 5810. *PC Magazine* gave the BlackBerry 957 its Editor's Choice Award for 2002. In another development RIM obtained a contract with the National Security Agency to provide it with customized BlackBerry devices that met the stringent security standards of governmental organizations.

RIM continued to add new product features, introduce new models, and partner with technology providers throughout 2002 and 2003. An agreement with BEA Systems called for the development of a framework to build Web-based applications and services for BlackBerry devices. New software developed by Onset Technology enabled BlackBerry users to go to a specific Web page or search the internet without launching a browser. The software, called MetaMessage 4.0, also added network printing capabilities to the fax printing capabilities of earlier versions. Applications from providers such as Arizan Corp., Good Technology, and Onset Technology enabled BlackBerry users to view e-mail attachments. An enterprise solution that made it easy to print from BlackBerry devices was developed in conjunction with Hewlett-Packard and Adobe Systems.

New BlackBerry models introduced in 2002 and 2003 included the 6710 and the 6720, which were Java-based and included an integrated speaker/microphone and delivered e-mail, phone, SMS, browser, and organizer applications. The BlackBerry 6510, which functioned as a walkie-talkie, was introduced by Nextel at the end of 2002, and Nokia announced it was developing a BlackBerry 6800 that functioned as a cell phone. In February 2003 RIM introduced a new, low-

cost 6200 BlackBerry series that was designed to sell for about CAD200. Comparable models, the 6210 and 6220, were launched for the European market. They were smaller than earlier BlackBerry versions but had more memory.

RIM continued to be involved in patent infringement suits in 2002. Good Technology, which developed and sold e-mail software that ran on BlackBerry devices, filed a defensive lawsuit against RIM in anticipation of being sued by RIM. RIM subsequently filed complaints against Good Technology as well as against competitor Handspring. In November RIM agreed to dismiss its suit against Handspring and license some of its keyboard patents to Handspring. In another case, RIM lost a patent suit brought against it by Chicago-based NTP, which held a patent that the court said was used to power BlackBerry devices. In early 2003 the U.S. Patent and Trademark Office announced it would review the decision in *NTP vs. Research in Motion* and re-examine five RIM patents.

Financially, 2002 was a difficult year for RIM. For the fiscal year ending March 2, RIM reported revenue of $294.1 million, a 33 percent increase over the previous year. However, the company reported its second consecutive operating loss, which increased from $4.7 million to $58.7 million. At the beginning of fiscal 2003 RIM reduced its earnings estimates for the coming year, citing delays in carriers rolling out GPRS launches of their BlackBerry services. In November 2002 the company announced it would lay off about 10 percent of its workforce. Nevertheless, RIM CEO Jim Balsillie foresaw rising demand for wireless devices, and the company continued to announce new and enhanced wireless devices and services.

LITIGATION, INNOVATION, AND CONSUMER DEMAND: 2003-09

In order to navigate the rapidly evolving market for its products, RIM began to explore new ways of expanding its business. In 2002 and 2003 it entered into a series of strategic software licensing deals, notably with Finnish mobile phone giant Nokia, which at the time controlled roughly 40 percent of the world's smart phone market. Perhaps more significantly, in early 2003 RIM launched the Blackberry 6210, a smaller, more affordable hand-held device geared toward small business owners and everyday consumers. Dubbed the BlueBerry because of its blue casing, this streamlined version of the Black-Berry represented the company's first entry into the consumer market for wireless data devices.

RIM received a surprise marketing boost on December 15, 2003, when Oprah Winfrey praised the

Blackberry on the *Oprah Winfrey Show*. Praising the product's ease of use and portable e-mail capability, the talk show host called the device her "new favorite thing," and proceeded to give a new BlackBerry to everyone in her audience. Although industry analysts didn't necessarily view Oprah's endorsement as critical to RIM's success, her rave review of the product was certainly a boon. By mid-2004, sales of the Blackberry were skyrocketing. In an article appearing in the *Globe and Mail* on June 30, 2004, Simon Avery reported that "hundreds of thousands of new subscribers, from fire-fighters to real estate agents," were becoming Blackberry customers. Sales of the device increased 158 percent in the quarter ending May 29, 2004. To further capitalize on growing demand, RIM released another consumer-friendly model, the Blackberry 7100t, in the fall of that year. The new device was priced at $200, roughly half the cost of the company's traditional corporate model.

Just when RIM appeared poised to make critical inroads into the broader consumer marketplace, however, the company's long-standing lawsuit with NTP threatened to unravel its success. In March 2005 RIM agreed to a settlement with NTP worth USD 450 million. The deal was struck in order to stave off a court-ordered injunction, which would have prohibited the company from selling BlackBerry products in the United States. In June, however, talks between the companies broke down after NTP decided that the payment plan proposed by RIM was unacceptable. The dispute was thrust back into the U.S. courts, and by late 2005, RIM was confronting the real possibility that they would find themselves shut out of the lucrative U.S. market indefinitely. Even an innovative "workaround" technology, which would have allowed RIM to continue operating in the United States without infringing upon NTP's patents, would have been too costly to implement.

As U.S. circuit court judges repeatedly denied RIM's request for a stay of the injunction, the pressure to reach a settlement with NTP mounted. The companies finally struck a new agreement in March 2006 when RIM agreed to pay NTP $612.5 million. In spite of the steep price, the agreement was vital to RIM's continued growth in the North American market. Fears concerning the company's future had taken a toll on sales. While the company had originally forecast an increase of between 700,000 and 750,000 customers in the first three months of the year, the actual total fell below 630,000. Despite these disappointing figures, at the time of settlement RIM controlled roughly 70 percent of the wireless e-mail market in the United States with approximately 3.2 million subscribers.

With the protracted NTP lawsuit behind it, RIM set out to increase business for its wireless products and services in the U.S. consumer market. In September 2006 the company launched the Pearl, a less expensive smart phone designed for non-business users. Another phone aimed at everyday consumers, the Curve, was unveiled in May 2007. The addition of fresh features, notably Internet browsers and MP3 players, also helped lure new customers to the Blackberry. As RIM thrived, its competitors began to seek ways to seize their own share of the growing wireless market. One of the most substantial threats to RIM's North American dominance emerged in June 2007 when Apple launched the iPhone. A formidable rival to the Blackberry, the iPhone featured an MP3 player and camera, as well as an easy-to-use touch screen interface. To keep abreast of the iPhone's innovative technology and design, RIM created the BlackBerry Bold, which included camera and video capabilities, as well as faster Internet and processor speeds.

Like most corporations, RIM saw its stock value drop during the recession of 2008 as decreased consumer spending affected sales. Despite the widespread economic uncertainty, RIM continued to forge ahead with its efforts to seize a larger share of the consumer market. In October 2008 it launched the Blackberry Storm, the first Blackberry device to feature a touch screen keyboard. Within months, RIM's bold strategy was paying substantial dividends. The Storm sold more than a million units within three months of its unveiling as the company's earnings increased 26 percent in the period between December 2008 and February 2009. Brisk sales led to an expansion of the company's work force and by early 2009 RIM had nearly 9,000 employees, up from 2,000 at the beginning of the decade. By spring of that year, RIM could boast a subscriber base of more than 25 million customers worldwide. Clearly, RIM's early foray into the broader consumer wireless market was off to a promising start.

David P. Bianco
Updated, Stephen Meyer

PRINCIPAL SUBSIDIARIES

Chalk Media Corp.; SlipStream Data Inc.; Research In Motion Corporation (USA); Research In Motion UK Limited; RIM Finance, LLC.

PRINCIPAL COMPETITORS

Alltel Corporation; Apple Inc.; Microsoft Corporation; Motorola, Inc.; Nokia Corporation; QUALCOMM Incorporated.

FURTHER READING

Austen, Ian, "Flavor of the Minute," *Canadian Business*, February 12, 1999, p. 58.

———"Plugged In," *Canadian Business*, December 31, 1999, p. 143.

Beaumont, Claudine, "BlackBerry Mixes It with Apple: The All-Conquering Business Mobile Now has Designs on the Rest of Your Life," *Daily Telegraph*, May 17, 2008, p. 19.

"BlackBerry—or Black Eye?," *Forbes*, November 27, 2000, p. 265.

"BlackBerry Ripens," *T&D*, February 2002, p. 23.

Harvey, Ian, "Who Wants to Squash the Blackberry?," *Globe and Mail*, November 27, 2007, p. 32.

Ingram, Mathew, "Research in Motion at a Crossroads," *Globe and Mail*, March 15, 2003, p. C2.

"It's a Phone! It's a Pager! It's a BlackBerry!," *ExtremeTech.com*, March 4, 2002.

Jenish, D'Arcy, "Pushing the Limits," *Maclean's*, November 6, 2000, p. 55.

Libin, Kevin, "Pop Goes BlackBerry," *Canadian Business*, June 11, 2001, p. 47.

McCall, Margo, "BlackBerry Proving Sweet for RIM," *Wireless Week*, April 16, 2001, p. 8.

O'Hara, Jane, "Mike Lazardis: 'Our Timing Was Perfect. We Couldn't Believe It,'"*Maclean's*, December 18, 2000, p. 70.

"Pushing into BlackBerry's Sweet Spot," *Business Week Online*, April 4, 2002.

Reguly, Eric, "With a Little Adult Supervision, the RIM Bunch Will Be All Right," *Globe and Mail*, March 6, 2007, p. B2.

"RIM Sues Handspring, Good," *Wireless Week*, September 23, 2002, p. 12.

Shafer, Scott Tyler, "Top Ten Technology Innovators: Mike Lazardis," *InfoWorld*, March 4, 2002, p. 46.

Silcoff, Sean, "High Tech, Low Returns," *Canadian Business*, May 1, 2000, p. 128.

"Vodafone to Sell BlackBerry," *EuropeMedia*, April 16, 2002.

Yokomizo, Sean, "RIM Wrangles CDMA Deal," *TechWeb*, December 21, 2000.

Rockwell Collins

400 Collins Road N.E.
Cedar Rapids, Iowa 52498
U.S.A.
Telephone: (319) 295-1000
Toll Free: (888) 265-5467
Fax: (319) 295-9374
Web site: http://www.rockwellcollins.com/

Public Company
Founded: 1931
Incorporated: 2001
Employees: 20,300
Sales: $4,770 million (for most companies)
Stock Exchanges: NYSE
Ticker Symbol: COL
NAICS: 336413 Other Aircraft Part and Auxiliary Equipment Manufacturing; 334220 Radio and Television Broadcasting and Wireless Communications Equipment Manufacturing; 334290 Other Communication Equipment Manufacturing; 334511 Search, Detection, Navigation, Guidance, Aeronautical, and Nautical System and Instrument Manufacturing; 335314 Relay and Industrial Control Manufacturing

■ ■ ■

Rockwell Collins is a leading provider of communication and aviation electronics for commercial and government customers worldwide. With approximately 20,300 employees and a service network spanning 27 countries, the company specializes in flight-deck avionics, airplane cabin electronics, space mission communications, information management, and simulation and training for its services. Rockwell Collins provides design, production, and support of communications and aviation electronics for commercial and military customers, while also offering products and systems for ground and shipboard applications. With two business segments—commercial systems and government systems—Rockwell Collins also provides equipment repair and overhaul, service parts, field service engineering, training, technical information services, and aftermarket used equipment sales. In 2008 the company acquired Athena Technologies, which develops and provides flight control and navigation solutions. The acquisition provided Rockwell Collins with new growth opportunities on both manned and unmanned platforms across both military and commercial market areas.

THE BEGINNINGS OF RADIO

Rockwell Collins has its roots in the Collins Radio Company, founded by Arthur Andrew Collins in 1931. Arthur Collins was born in Kingfisher, Oklahoma, on September 9, 1909. Shortly thereafter he moved to Cedar Rapids, Iowa, with his father, Merle (M. H.) Collins. M. H. Collins, founder of Collins Farm Company, was a visionary in his own right who transformed the farming industry by applying advances in science and engineering to the fields of agriculture and animal husbandry. His ingenuity and inventiveness were an inspiration to his son but, to his father's dismay, Arthur showed little interest in the farming business. Arthur did, however, possess a rare genius that he demonstrated through his favorite hobby, radio.

COMPANY PERSPECTIVES

Working together creating the most trusted source of communication and aviation electronic solutions. The Rockwell Collins Vision Roadmap includes five core values: Teamwork—We know that the best ideas and results are created when we work together. Therefore we embrace diversity; we support each other; and we take ownership for the performance of our team and ourselves; Innovation—We understand that the best source of growth is the creativity of our people. We support that creativity through investment, process efficiencies, professional development and knowledge management; Integrity—We will always be ethical and honest with our stakeholders and each other and never compromise the trust placed in us. This includes complying with all laws governing our corporation, our stewardship of the environment and being good citizens in the communities where we live and work; Customer Focus—Our reason for being is to create customer and shareowner value. We achieve this value by helping our customers be successful and always doing what we say we are going to do; and, Integrity—We take personal responsibility for making our company successful. Each of us has multiple opportunities to please a customer, reward a shareowner, help a colleague and do our job better. We must take full advantage of these opportunities.

The radio craze of the early 20th century was akin to the computer boom of the 1980s, and radio hobbyists, otherwise known as ham operators, were instrumental in the development of radio technology. Initially, the senior Collins was not impressed with his son's preoccupation. His attitude changed, however, when at the age of nine Arthur and his friend, Merrill Lund, made their first crystal receivers using tubes from Lund's father's workplace, the Quaker Oats Company. From that point forward Arthur's father supported him in his endeavors, helping him by purchasing materials and arranging meetings with more experienced radio "hams." One such amateur operator was a police officer named Henry Nemec who, upon meeting the young Arthur, commented, "But there wasn't much that he didn't already know," as quoted on the company Web site. By the age of 14, Arthur took the Federal Radio Commission test and obtained his license. The following year, he completed the construction of an amateur radio station from purchased components and make-shift materials, and he was communicating with amateur operators in the United States and abroad.

During 1924 and 1925 Collins began to carry out experiments with John Reinartz, a prominent radio enthusiast who had developed a new receiver circuit and who had written many articles on the subject. In 1925 Reinartz's radio accomplishments earned him a place as the radio operator on the MacMillan expedition, which set sail from the coast of Maine on the ships *Bowdoin* and *Perry* with Navy Lt. Cdr. Richard E. Byrd as one of the explorers. The *Bowdoin* had planned to relay daily reports to the U.S. Naval radio station in Washington, D.C., but atmospheric conditions were causing interference. The news soon spread that, although the U.S. Navy was unable to accomplish the task, a boy from Cedar Rapids had been making daily contact with Reinartz in Etah, Greenland, from a small room on the third floor of his parent's home using a ham radio that he had built himself. After each night's broadcast, Collins forwarded the messages to Washington, D.C., via the local telegraph office, earning the 15-year-old boy nationwide acclaim as a "radio wizard." As quoted on the company's Web site, an article in the August 4, 1925, *Cedar Rapids Gazette* said, "The mysterious forces of air leaped the boundary of thousands of miles to bring Cedar Rapids in touch with the celebrated MacMillan scientific expedition." At the age of 16, Collins revealed his radio ambitions when he wrote in a technical article for *Radio Age*, "The real thrill in amateur work comes not from talking to stations in distant lands ... but from knowing that by careful and painstaking work and by diligent and systematic study you have been able to accomplish some feat, or establish some fact that is a new step toward more perfect communication."

Collins furthered his electronics studies at Amherst College in Massachusetts, Coe College in Cedar Rapids, and the University of Iowa in Iowa City before embarking on a mini-expedition for the U.S. Naval Observatory in Washington, D.C. In 1927, along with Paul Engle and Winfield Salisbury, Collins set off on a road trip to the southwest states in a truck outfitted with shortwave transmitting and receiving equipment, while a fourth member of the team, Leo Hruska, stayed behind to man the base station in Cedar Rapids. Over the next few years Collins gained national recognition as a leader in the field of radio, and in 1931 Collins Radio Company was opened in the basement of his home with one employee. The main business of the company was producing transmitters to order, making the product the first transmitting device available for purchase as a fully

KEY DATES

■

1931: Arthur Andrew Collins founds the Collins Radio Company; Collins designs and produces the first single unit transmitters made to order.

1934: Collins Radio Company is commissioned to build most of the communications equipment for the Byrd Antarctic expedition.

1938: Collins Radio Company invents the Autotune.

1940: The "Main Plant" is built at 855 35th Street in Cedar Rapids, Iowa.

1945: Collins Radio Company builds the first commercially produced cyclotron, or "atom smasher," at Brookhaven Laboratory on Long Island.

1953: Collins completes construction of a state-of-the-art engineering building in the Midwest.

1969: Collins Radio equipment relays Neil Armstrong's words from the moon.

1972: Arthur Collins leaves the Collins Radio Company to form Arthur A. Collins Consulting, Inc.

1973: Rockwell International acquires the Collins Radio Company and is renamed Rockwell International Corp. Avionics Group.

1974: Rockwell International Corp. Avionics Group is one of four companies selected to develop the Navstar Global Positioning System.

1997: The company enters the in-flight entertainment business with the acquisition of Hughes-Avicom.

2001: Rockwell Collins, Inc., is spun-off from Rockwell International, with Clayton (Clay) M. Jones as president and chief executive officer.

2002: Clay Jones is appointed chairman of the board.

2009: Rockwell Collins is named one of the "Top 25 Noteworthy Companies for Diversity" by *DiversityInc.*

personally designed, produced, tested, packaged, and shipped, eliminated the clutter in a single, stable apparatus.

With the onset of the Great Depression, the Collins Farm Company fell on hard times, and M. H. Collins decided to sell. His son's business, however, was continuing to grow, and Arthur added personnel, including former employees from his father's company. In 1933 the Collins Radio Company moved into leased space at 2920 First Avenue in Cedar Rapids, and in September the company was incorporated under the laws of Delaware. In 1934 the Collins Radio Company, which now consisted of eight employees, received a huge boost when it was commissioned to build most of the communications equipment for the Byrd Antarctic expedition. Word of the Collins shortwave broadcasting station aboard the Byrd ship spread around the world, and orders began to pour in from Africa, Asia, Central and South America, and Europe.

EXPANSION IN THE COMMUNICATIONS FIELD

Arthur Collins also had a keen interest in aviation, and he began to commit some of his resources to the research and development of equipment for this industry, including flight control instruments and radio communications equipment. By 1938 an automatic radio tuning device called the Autotune had been invented, which was incorporated into the ART 13 transmitter, standard equipment on all World War II military aircraft. As the company went from strength to strength, new factory space was needed. In 1940, on what were once corn fields and pastures, the first section of the factory was built. The building, at 855 35th Street, became known as the "Main Plant." There were 150 employees, and with a business office well established in New York City, the company began to receive orders from the armed services in preparation for the entry of United States into World War II. The number of Collins personnel increased significantly to several thousand after the attacks on Pearl Harbor, and there were few families in Cedar Rapids who were not connected to the company in some way. Collins Radio Company consisted of more than 20 separate sections over a 13-mile square area connected by an intricate private telephone network and a system of mail cars. When the Cedar Rapids municipal airport was opened in 1944, Collins leased an area of the grounds and built a hanger, to house the company's DC-3, two twin-engine Beechcrafts, and private planes. a control tower, and associated offices.

Collins entered the field of atomic energy in 1945 and built the world's first commercially produced

assembled working unit. Up to this point there was no standardization between components, and the components were difficult to obtain. Systems consisted of an unsightly array of tubes and wires that was functional but inefficient. Collins's neat units, which he

cyclotron (a device that accelerates charged particles to high energies) at Brookhaven Laboratory, Long Island; a similar installation was built at Argon near Chicago in 1951. The U.S. government had a policy of spreading out strategic plants, and Collins began to move into other geographic areas. In 1946 Collins built a production plant in Burbank, California, which moved to Newport Beach in 1961. This was followed in 1950 with a facility in Dallas, Texas, selected for its year-round flying conditions. By late 1953 Collins completed construction on a state-of-the-art engineering building in the Midwest. This was followed with a sales office in Toronto, Ontario, Canada, to serve the Canadian and British business communities. Over the next few decades, Collins continued to expand its work into all areas of telecommunications, including satellite voice transmissions and communications equipment for the U.S. space program. The Apollo, Mercury, Gemini, and U.S. Skylab programs all used Collins communications equipment, and it was Collins Radio equipment that relayed Neil Armstrong's words from the moon in 1969.

Robert C. Wilson was named president and chief executive officer of Collins Radio in 1972, the same time Arthur Collins left the company to form Arthur A. Collins Consulting, Inc. A year later, with Collins Radio floundering financially, Collins Radio was acquired by Rockwell International and renamed the Rockwell International Corp. Avionics Group. In 1974 the company was one of four contractors selected by the U.S. Air Force to develop the Navstar Global Positioning System and on July 18, 1977, was the first company to receive, track, and decode a GPS satellite signal. Over the next 28 years, the company continued to prove itself as a world leader in aviation electronics, and through a series of alliances and acquisitions, Rockwell Collins expanded its relationships with its customers. In 1997 the company entered the in-flight business with the acquisition of Hughes-Avicom. Other high profile acquisitions included Intertrade, Ltd., and Flight Dynamics in 1999; K Systems, Inc., parent company of Kaiser Aerospace and Electronics, in 2000; and Communication Solutions, Inc., and Airshow, Inc., in 2002.

A NEW ERA FOR ROCKWELL COLLINS

On June 29, 2001, Rockwell Collins, Inc., was spun-off from Rockwell International and began trading on the New York Stock Exchange (NYSE) under the symbol "COL." Clayton (Clay) M. Jones, president and chief executive officer of Rockwell Collins since 2001, was appointed chairman of the board in 2002. Under the direction of Jones, Rockwell Collins remained commit-

ted to sustainable activities, products, and services in all of its business dealings and in 2002 received the Environmental Protection Agency (EPA) Award. This was followed by top honors at the 2008 EPA Region 7 Conference in Wichita, Kansas, where the Rockwell Collins Coralville, Iowa, facility was recognized for making, according to company materials, the "Most Significant Environmental Impact for All Projects over a Three-Year Period." The company was also recognized by the U.S. Green Building Council (USGBC) for its green building initiatives and for its "Leadership in Energy and Environmental Design (LEED)."

One way that Rockwell Collins sought to better serve its customers was by building an empowered and productive workforce, in addition to hiring a diverse group of employees. In recognition of these initiatives, the company has received numerous awards and accolades, including being named one of the "Top 25 Noteworthy Companies for Diversity" by *DiversityInc* in 2008 and 2009. The company's Commercial Systems business unit continued to excel in delivering solutions that enhance the flight experience for both airline personnel and passengers. With its 160 GB hard drive for storing movies and MP3 files, Rockwell Collins's Digital Programmable Audio and Visual Entertainment System (dPAVES), which incorporated the company's multimedia Airshow 4200 Moving Map system, transformed in-flight entertainment. In addition, Rockwell Collins's achievements in its government business unit earned it global recognition, and its advanced products, systems, and services for airborne and surface platforms have been acquired by government agencies, defense contractors, and ministries of defense throughout the world. With more than 60 locations in 27 countries and expanding sales, Rockwell Collins was well-positioned to continue its global growth.

Marie O'Sullivan

PRINCIPAL SUBSIDIARIES

Collins Radio Company; Collins Aviation Maintenance Services (China); Ensambladores Electronicos de Mexico (Mexico); Intertrade Limited; K Systems, Inc.; Kaiser Optical Systems, Inc.; Kaiser Optical Systems SARL (France); Maine Electronics, Inc.; NLX Holding Corporation; RICOMP Claims Management Corp.; Rockwell Collins Aerospace and Electronics, Inc.; Rockwell Collins Australia Pty Limited (Australia); Rockwell Collins Business Services, Inc.; Rockwell Collins Canada, Inc. (Canada); Rockwell Collins Charitable Corporation; Rockwell Collins Control Technologies,

Inc.; Rockwell Collins Danmark ApS (Denmark); Rockwell Collins do Brasil Ltda. (Brazil); Rockwell Collins Deutschland GmbH (Germany); Rockwell Collins Deutschland Holdings GmbH (Germany); Rockwell Collins Deutschland Services GmbH (Germany); Rockwell Collins ElectroMechanical Systems, Inc.; Rockwell Collins European Holdings S.à.r.l. (Luxembourg); Rockwell Collins France S.A.S. (France); Rockwell Collins Government Systems, Inc. (Canada); Rockwell Collins Enterprises Private Limited (India); Rockwell Collins In-Flight Network Company; Rockwell Collins International Holdings Limited (Bermuda); Rockwell Collins International, Inc.; Rockwell Collins Simulation and Training Solutions LLC; Rockwell Collins Systems International, Inc.; Rockwell Collins Network Enabling Software, Inc.; Rockwell Collins Optronics, Inc.; Rockwell Collins Prescription Center, Inc.; Rockwell Collins Sales and Services, Inc.; Rockwell Collins Services Company; Rockwell Collins Southeast Asia Pte. Ltd. (Singapore); Rockwell Collins Support Company; Rockwell Collins Technologies LLC; Rockwell Collins UK Limited (UK); Rockwell Collins Vision Systems, Inc.; Rockwell Collins, Inc.; ZAO Rockwell Collins (Russia).

PRINCIPAL COMPETITORS

BAE Systems plc; Boeing Company; CAE; General Dynamics Corporation; Harris Corporation; Honeywell International, Inc.; L3 Communications Corporation; Northrop Grumman Corporation; Panasonic; Raytheon Company; Thales S.A.

FURTHER READING

Avery, Susan, "Lean but Not Mean," *Purchasing*, September 1, 2005, p. 26.

———, "Rockwell Collins Builds on Success," *Purchasing*, October 19, 2006, p. 38.

Bailey, John, "Rockwell Tipped for 777's Paperless Cockpit," *Flight International*, June 25, 1991, p. 4.

Croft, John, "Rockwell Collins Greases the UAV Public Acceptance Skids," *Flight Daily News*, June 16, 2009.

Farley, Michael G., and Mark D. Chapman, "Monocular SLAM: Alternative Navigation for GPS-Denied Areas," *GPS World*, September 2008, p. 42.

Gale, Sarah Fister, "Training Trouble Sparks Call to Action," *CleanRooms*, March 2004, p. 1.

Kharif, Olga, and Jane Black, "Giving Pilots a New Eye in the Sky," *Business Week Online*, June 19, 2002.

Palmeri, Christopher, "Swords to Plowshares—and Back Again: How the CEO of Rockwell Collins Has Turned a Pretty Profit by Juggling Military and Civilian Work," *Business Week*, February 11, 2008, p. 66.

Pettit, Jeff, "Team Communication: It's in the Cards," *Training & Development*, January 1997, p. 12.

Purington, Cliff, Chris Butler, and Sarah Fister Gale, "Built to Learn: The Inside Story of How Rockwell Collins Became a True Learning Organization," *AMACOM*, 2003.

Siekman, Philip, "A Big Maker of Tiny Batches: Rockwell Collins Thrives on a Thick Catalog of Avionics Products and Up-and-Down Orders," *Fortune*, May 27, 2002, p. 152.

Smith, Frank, "High Tech Tree," *Daily Business Journal*, March 19, 1990, p. 4B.

Tatge, Mark, "Top Gun," *Forbes*, January 9, 2006, p. 98.

Teague, Paul, "Anatomy of a Winner," *Purchasing*, September 1, 2005, p 13.

Trahant, Bill, "Competing for Talent in the Federal Government—Part II," *The Public Manager*, Summer 2006, p. 52.

Wald, Matthew L., "In an Aircraft Safety Effort, New Technology Tests Its Wings," *New York Times*, March 20, 2002, p. A18.

Walker, Karen, "Rockwell Collins Pushes Acceptance of Unmanned Future," *DefenseNews*, June 15, 2009.

Rosneft

26/1 Soviyskaya Embankment 1
Moscow, GSP-8 117997
Russia
Telephone: (+7-495) 777-44-22
Fax: (+7-495) 777-44-44
Web site: http://www.rosneft.com

Joint Stock Company
Founded: 1993
Incorporated: 1995
Employees: 161,912
Sales: $68.99 billion (2008)
Stock Exchanges: Moscow London
Ticker Symbol: ROSN
NAICS: 211111 Crude Petroleum and Natural Gas Extraction; 324110 Petroleum Refineries

∎ ∎ ∎

Rosneft is Russia's largest oil producer, with 784 billion cubic meters of proved gas reserves and 22.3 billion barrels of oil equivalent. As of 2009 the government-owned Rosneftegaz held 75.16 percent of the firm, with the remaining equity divided largely among institutional investors. Rosneft's profits fueled Russian spending during the 2000s, but as oil prices began to collapse in 2008, it had to ramp up production to meet costs. Its refineries processed 360 million barrels of oil in 2008. At that time, Rosneft operated four marine terminals (Tuapse, De-Kastri, Nakhodka, Arkhangelsk) and had 1,700 gas stations.

ORIGINS IN STATE-OWNED INDUSTRY: EARLY 1990S

Under the Soviet system, all economic enterprises were owned by the state. With its vast resources, the USSR was second only to Saudi Arabia in terms of oil exports in the late 20th century, and the sector was controlled by a centralized Ministry of Oil and Gas. Following the collapse of the Soviet Union in 1991, Russia began to privatize state-owned enterprises, offering vouchers to citizens that could be used to bid in auctions. However, many of the enterprises were sold in closed deals, and individuals with business and political ties were able to buy lucrative assets at deep discounts.

The Ministry was converted into Rosneftegaz (Russian Oil and Gas) at independence, and in 1993 the government created the oil company Rosneft. The new company received assets from 176 enterprises, including extensive untapped fields, three refineries, and distribution systems. Rosneft was also designated as the government agent in production-sharing agreements with foreign companies. Moscow initially announced that the firm would be privatized by July 1, 1995. The sale was put on hold, however, when rival oil firm Sidanco challenged Rosneft's ownership of a key production unit worth at least $800 million. That claim was resolved in Rosneft's favor, and the auction was rescheduled for May 1998.

In the meantime, Rosneft was struggling with the demands of capitalism. Many assets were poorly governed, and by 1998 Rosneft's production slipped to only one-third of its capacity. Scheduled against a downturn in the Russian economy, the sale of Rosneft

COMPANY PERSPECTIVES

In executing our strategy, Rosneft is focused not only on creating value for our shareholders, but also on adhering to the highest standards of corporate governance. Indeed, we are convinced that these issues are not distinct and that a commitment to transparent and responsible management of the business is essential to maintaining the trust of the investment community and maximizing the returns we generate for all our shareholders over the long-term.

was important to the Russian government as a source of much-needed income. Special terms were offered to potential bidders, such as lifting the cap on the allowable level of foreign ownership, lowering the minimum bid of $2.1 billion, and reducing a requirement to invest at least $400 million in the company. However, no one bid in May 1998, and a planned second auction in July was postponed when it also failed to draw buyers. Then in August 1998 Russia defaulted on loan repayments to international financial institutions, and many banks closed their doors and refused to pay depositors. As part of an overall strategy to regulate the economy, Moscow replaced the management at many enterprises, including Rosneft. Sergei Bogdanchikov became the president of Rosneft in October 1998.

Under its new management, the company embarked on a strategy of cost reduction, production improvement, and structural upgrades. A major expansion and renovation of the Komsomolsk refinery in Komsomolsk-on-Amur was begun in 1998 and was projected to be completed in 2013. Producing motor and jet fuels, the site was a key supplier of Rosneft products to Asia. In 1999 the company improved its communication network by installing satellite equipment throughout its remote locations.

As the economy stabilized, Rosneft began to post annual production increases of about 11 percent. The company had several options to expand its revenue, including improved technology, exploration, and partnership deals, and President Boris Yeltsin encouraged Western energy companies to partner with Russian firms to help defray research and development costs. A partnership with BP was formed in 2002 to search for oil in a promising area of the Sakhlin shelf in the Sea of Okhotsk.

GROWTH THROUGH ACQUISITIONS: 2003–04

With its close ties to the Russian government, Rosneft became embroiled in a political controversy centering on the rival energy company Yukos in 2003. Yukos was owned by Mikhail Khodorkovsky, a former communist youth leader who had launched Menatep bank in 1987 and began making a series of bargain acquisitions that became Yukos. In total, Khodorkovsky purchased 78 percent of the assets of Yukos (valued at $5 billion) for $310 million. Like many early investors in post-Soviet Russia, Khodorkovsky stripped assets rather than investing in his new acquisitions. In its May 2004 Russian edition, *Forbes* ranked Khodorkovsky as the richest entrepreneur in Russia with a net worth estimated at $15 billion.

Khodorkovsky's brash behavior grated on the Kremlin. During a February 2003 meeting, Khodorkovsky took issue with a recent deal that he claimed allowed Rosneft to purchase the oil producer Severnaya Neft at a discounted price. "Khodorkovsky's denunciation of Rosneft was an open challenge to [President Vladimir] Putin," Marshall Goldman wrote in *Foreign Affairs*. Khodorkovsky ran afoul of Putin ahead of the 2004 presidential election, reportedly offering two opposition parties $100 million to mount a challenge to Putin. He also hinted he might run for the presidency in 2008.

As Khodorkovsky investigated a merger with Sibneft and deals with Exxon-Mobil and Chevron-Texaco, the government announced that Yuganskneftgaz, a subsidiary of Yukos, owed $3.4 billion in back taxes. When Yukos did not pay, Khodorkovsky was arrested, and the Kremlin seized many of his assets.

In December 2004 the government auctioned off Yuganskneftegaz, the core of Yukos. The *Financial Times* and *Washington Post* both described the sale as a curious event. Only two bidders showed up: Baikal Finance Group and Gazpromneft, the oil arm of the state-owned Gazprom, one of the largest natural gas producers in the world. No one had ever heard of Baikal Finance, and its given address was a mobile phone and grocery store in Tver. The auctioneer outlined the rules, including that "participants were not allowed to use mobile phones, move around, or leave and re-enter the room." Baikal started the bidding at $9.3 billion. When the auctioneer asked for Gazpromneft's offer, "Gazpromneft's representative asked to make a call and left the room in clear violation of the rules. After a couple of minutes he silently re-entered the room and sat down. This prompted Baikal to repeat its bid ... but Gazpromneft remained silent. The auctioneer called the price three times, then brought the hammer down." One

KEY DATES

1993: Rosneft is established as state enterprise.
1998: Administrative changes stabilize the company during Russian economic crisis.
2003: Rosneft acquires Severnaya Neft, a natural gas producer.
2004: Rosneft assumes ownership of Yuganskneftegaz.
2006: Initial public offering raises $10.4 billion.
2008: Rosneft secures $15 billion loan from China and begins construction of a petrochemicals plant in Asia.

week later Rosneft reported that it had purchased Baikal Finance. The acquisition of Yuganskneftegaz tripled its oil output. Within four years, the value of those assets had jumped to $40 billion.

In an article published on June 27, 2006, economist Anders Aslund told the *Washington Post* that "Rosneft instigated the Yukos affair. Bogdanchikov and [Putin associate and chairman of Rosneft, Igor] Sechin attacked Khodorkovsky because they wanted his assets.... They want to make an IPO [initial public offering] so they can recycle the money and take over more private companies." The following month Rosneft conducted an initial public offering in London, the fourth largest IPO in history, raising $10.4 billion in return for 13 percent of its stock. Buyers included BP, Patrons, and the China National Petroleum Company. The funds were used to repay a $7.5 billion loan used to purchase Yuganskneftgaz.

EXPANSION 2006–08

Rosneft holdings spanned the Russian Federation, with primary production operations located in Western Siberia. The Priobskoye field, the company's largest, is located there and by 2008 accounted for 30 percent of the company's proved reserves. In 2008 Rosneft and TNK-BP opened the Verkhnechonskoye field in Eastern Siberia, and the Vankor field, which was projected to be the largest petroleum venture in Russia since independence. Rosneft also represented the Russian government in production-sharing agreements around Sakhalin Island in the Sea of Okhotsk. The firm also undertook a series of oil exploration projects, examining Eastern Siberia and the subsurface of the Black Sea, Caspian Sea, and Sea of Azov. The Sakhalin and East Siberia projects offered potential pipeline routes to Asia,

while the sub-sea projects could be shipped through pipelines destined for Europe.

Despite this great potential, however, Russia was unable to pump enough oil to meet rising domestic demand, much less increase its reserves. Untapped oil and gas fields in Russia tended to be located in difficult environments, such as under frozen land in Siberia or under the Caspian or Arctic Seas. After foreign firms helped open some areas, President Putin moved to push them out and reclaim natural assets for Russia. For example, BP, which had worked with Russian-owned TNP on a joint venture, was informed that it owed $1.4 billion in back taxes, while Royal Dutch Shell was forced to abandon exploration at the Sakhalin 2 site in the Sea of Okhotsk when it was accused of causing environmental damage. Rosneft sought to meet energy demands by increasing production from 776 million barrels of oil in 2008 to 1.3 billion barrels per year by 2030. As of 2008 Rosneft had only developed about 22 percent of its proved gas reserves, from which it drew an annual natural gas output of 12 billion cubic meters.

CHALLENGED BY FALLING OIL PRICES: 2008–09

Between 2000 and 2008 the Russian economy expanded due to rising global energy prices, with annual income growing by 8 percent to 10 percent. However, money was quickly spent rather than invested. In addition, although the income was derived from non-renewable natural resources, little effort was made to find alternate sources of income. As the global energy market began to contract in 2008, Rosneft's revenues decreased correspondingly. Net profit fell 64 percent in the fourth quarter of 2008, making it "the most challenging [quarter] in the Russian oil industry's history, due to the sharp decline in prices coupled with unprecedented high tax rates," company president Bogdanchikov remarked.

In the first quarter of 2009, the benchmark price of Urals crude fell from an average of $90 a barrel to $43.70 per barrel. Revenue dropped by 50 percent over the same period, down to $8.26 billion. Rosneft would have suffered even greater losses if the Russian government had not stepped in and slashed export duties by 64 percent. Rosneft turned to China for help. In early 2009 the oil company arranged a 20-year, $15 billion loan from the China Development Bank to help pay its debts and to build a pipeline to China. Under the terms of the deal Rosneft was required to ship 9 million metric tons of oil to China each year.

After a first quarter in which income decreased by 20 percent, Rosneft began to see some improvement in the second quarter of 2009. Among favorable signs, production increased as Rosneft's Vankor facility began operating in 2009, and net debt decreased due to improved cash flow. Revenue increased by 32.5 percent from the first quarter to the second quarter, largely a result of increased domestic demand. Late in the year Rosneft planned to start construction on a $14 billion petrochemicals plant in Primorsky krai. It also announced modernization of its refineries, which "increases the value-added of products and ensures that fuel outputs meet the latest environmental standards." Projecting continued improvement through the remainder of 2009, Bogdanchikov declared in August, "We are on track to have a strong 2009 thanks to our focus on cost control, prudent planning, and solid execution."

Ann E. Robertson

PRINCIPAL SUBSIDIARIES

Komsomolsk NPZ-Rosneft; Komsomolsk Oil Refinery LLC; OJSC Kuibyshev Oil Refinery; OJSC Novokuibyshev Oil Refinery; OJSC Samaraneftegaz; OJSC Tomskneft VNK; OJSC Udmurtneft; Purneftegaz LLC; Rosneft-Groznefteegaz; Rosneft Stavropolneftegaz; Sakhalinmorneftegaz LLC; Severnaya Neft LLC; Tuapse Oil Refinery LLC; Yuganskneftegaz LLC.

PRINCIPAL COMPETITORS

BP PLC; Gazprom; Lukoil Oil Company; TNK-BP Ltd.

FURTHER READING

Aron, Leon, "Russia's Woes Spell Trouble for the U.S.," *Wall Street Journal*, December 31, 2008, p. A9.

Banerjee, Neela, "Russia Giving Birth to Instant Oil Giant," *Wall Street Journal*, April 26, 1995, p. A10.

Brzezinski, Matthew, "Russia's Rosneft Gets Green Light for Privatization," *Wall Street Journal*, October 9, 1997, p. 1.

Clark, Torrey, "Rosneft Net Income Falls 20% after Oil Prices Tumble," *Bloomberg*, May 28, 2009.

Finn, Peter, "A Surprise Bidder Buys Yukos Unit," *Washington Post*, December 20, 2004, p. A17.

Foroohar, Rana, "Energy Strategy: The Coming Oil Shock," *Newsweek*, December 8, 2008.

Glasser, Susan B., and Peter Baker, "Two Visions for Russia and One Battle of Wills," *Washington Post*, November 5, 2003, p. A1.

Goldman, Marshall, "Putin and the Oligarchs," *Foreign Affairs*, November/December 2004.

Gordon, Michael R., "Again Russia Delays Sale of Oil Giant," *New York Times*, July 10, 1998, p. D2.

———, "Sale of Russian Oil Company Gets No Bidders," *New York Times*, May 27, 1998, p. A3.

Gronholt-Pedersen, Jacob, "Earnings: Rosneft Net Drop 64% as Oil Price Tumbles," *Wall Street Journal*, March 5, 2008, p. B6.

Matthews, Owen, "Chaos in the Kremlin," *Newsweek*, March 17, 2008.

———, "Russia's Big Energy Secret," *Newsweek*, December 31, 2007.

———, "Russia: The Wild-Card Country," *Newsweek*, December 4, 2006.

Mufson, Steven, "Russian IPO Is a Hazy Mix of Oil and Politics," *Washington Post*, June 27, 2006, p. D1.

Ostrovsky, Arkady, "Curtain Falls on Final Act of Yukos Farce," *Financial Times*, December 19, 2004.

———, "Rosneft Takes Control of Yukos Unit in Russian Oil Renationalization Move," *Financial Times*, December 23, 2004.

Sestanovich, Stephen, "Russia's Comeuppance," *Newsweek*, November 26, 2008.

Stepek, John, "Is Rosneft Too Risky to Invest In—Or Just Too Expensive?" *Money Week*, October 7, 2007.

Whalen, Jeanne, "Pumping Up—New Force in Energy Markets," *Wall Street Journal*, May 16, 2003, p. A1.

A Wholly Owned Subsidiary of WC Holding, Inc.

SENTEL Corporation

1101 King Street, Suite 550
Alexandria, Virginia 22314
U.S.A.
Telephone: (703) 739-0084
Fax: (703) 739-6028
Web site: http://www.sentel.com

Wholly Owned Subsidiary of WC Holding, Inc.
Founded: 1987
Incorporated: 1987
Employees: 390
Sales: $57 million (2008)
NAICS : 541330 Engineering Services

■ ■ ■

SENTEL Corporation is an engineering services company located within the greater Washington, D.C., area that built its reputation on providing communications systems free of interference and chemical and biological weapons detection systems to the U.S. government and military. While the U.S. Department of Defense is one of the company's largest clients, the company also has handled contracts from NASA, the Federal Aviation Administration, and others. The company began with one Navy contract worth $33,000 and 3 employees, but based on its niche market it grew to nearly 300 employees and $33 million in annual revenues within 10 years of its founding, making it one of the fastest-growing technology companies in the United States. It developed several areas of expertise, including electromagnetic "spectrum management," the testing and evaluation of new military equipment, and

the development of sensors to detect chemical and biological weapons. Although SENTEL remained a small defense contractor in 2009, by developing areas of expertise and designing many of its products to government specifications, SENTEL continued to land profitable government contracts for its products and services.

CHEMICAL AND BIOLOGICAL WEAPONS DETECTION

SENTEL Corporation was founded in 1987 when James F. Garrett decided to leave the Navy early and open a defense technology company in Alexandria, Virginia. He and his partners, Robert Hardie and Merri Sutor, decided to focus on two areas: communications problems caused by electromagnetic interference, and detecting airborne chemical and biological weapons. Garrett believed that to be a successful small defense contractor, his company needed to be niche-oriented rather than diversified. He told *Purchasing,* "That means do whatever you do better than everyone else, or have an expert ability that the competition doesn't have."

The 1991 Persian Gulf War was a boon to SENTEL. During the war the company developed a software system that allowed the allied forces to communicate with one another continuously without interference, avoiding situations like one Garrett later recounted to Michelle Singletary in the *Washington Post,* when Army personnel had to use a pay phone to call for backup air support in Grenada.

In 1993 the firm landed a huge three-year, $33 million Navy contract to help the Navy train personnel in electronic warfare, radar tracking, and target towing.

COMPANY PERSPECTIVES

We provide our customers with the absolute best engineering products, technological solutions, and services worldwide, to help them protect lives and fulfill their missions, and to maintain a company with high integrity and skill where team members can be proud of their organization and their own professional accomplishments.

KEY DATES

1987: SENTEL is founded by James F. Garrett.
1993: SENTEL lands Navy contract to help train Navy personnel.
2001: Development of Remote Data Relay begins.
2004: SENTEL is bought by Dimensions International.
2007: SENTEL is bought from Dimensions by WC Holdings, Inc., and becomes its subsidiary; Darrell L. Crapps succeeds James F. Garrett as CEO.
2009: SENTEL acquires 24/7 Solutions.

CEO James Garrett told the *Washington Post* that the contract would double the company's revenue that year. SENTEL also developed integrated, wearable, hands-free computers for NASA during the 1990s.

After the Persian Gulf War SENTEL benefited from fears that Iraq's Saddam Hussein possessed chemical and biological weapons. During the Iran-Iraq war in the 1980s, Iraq had used chemical weapons against not only Iranians but also its own Kurdish population, and some worried during and after the Persian Gulf War that chemical weapons had been used against allied troops. In 2001 SENTEL made a cooperative research and development agreement with the Joint Program Office for Biological Defense (JPO-BD), established after the Persian Gulf War, to develop technology to network biological and chemical weapons sensors to allow a user to read and control up to 400 sensors from monitoring equipment in a single location. Under the cooperative agreement, SENTEL retained ownership of the product, called Remote Data Relay, a sensor networking system, but built it to the specification of the Department of Defense, which became its main buyer. After the September 11, 2001, terrorist attacks against the United States, SENTEL's Remote Data Relay system was used in chemical-biological agent defense, both in the United States and in Iraq. The company also collaborated with the military on a ground surveillance radar system and on technology that could defuse bombs remotely.

DIMENSIONS INTERNATIONAL AND BEYOND

Nearing retirement, Wright began looking in 2003 for a buyer for SENTEL. He told Alan Hughes in *Black Enterprise*, "I was looking to sell the company and merge with another company. I wanted a culture that fit in with SENTEL's and would allow SENTEL to continue to operate as it always has." In 2004 Dimensions International, another high-tech engineering company based in Alexandria, bought SENTEL

Corporation; Garrett became the president of the SENTEL Division of Dimensions International. Dimensions and SENTEL had been similar-sized companies whose major client had been the U.S. government; Garrett and Russell Wright, CEO of Dimensions, thought that together the companies could compete with the largest defense contractors. SENTEL prospered under the merger, and by 2007, the company had three Defense Department contracts worth $1.71 million. Dimensions also profited, successfully competing for larger and more lucrative defense contracts.

The Dimensions/SENTEL partnership, however, did not last long. In 2007 Dimensions and SENTEL split. Dimensions was bought by Honeywell International, and SENTEL was bought by WC Holding, Inc. SENTEL, now a wholly owned subsidiary of WC Holding, became a 50-50 partnership between the former CEO of Dimensions, Russell Wright, and former executive vice-president and general counsel of Dimensions, Darrell L. Crapps. Crapps took over as president and CEO of SENTEL at that time, replacing Garrett, who retired.

SENTEL continued to thrive despite the split with Dimensions. In 2007 SENTEL appeared on the *Black Enterprise* Industrial/Service List at number 90. In June 2008 SENTEL won a five-year Sensor Technology Engineering Support contract for the U.S. Army worth a maximum of $487 million, one of the largest contracts the company had ever been awarded. SENTEL announced later that year that it had also won a four-year, $21.7 million contract to support the Federal Air Administration's Air Traffic Safety Management System.

All signs pointed to continued prosperity for SENTEL. The War on Terror was far from over in 2009, although the battlefields began shifting from Iraq to Afghanistan under the administration of Barack Obama. In April 2009 SENTEL announced that it had acquired 24/7 Solutions, provider of services to the U.S. intelligence community. Based in McLean, Virginia, the company would become a wholly owned subsidiary of SENTEL. 24/7 provided information technology, intelligence analysis, and counterterrorism operations support to the U.S. intelligence community. CEO Crapps told *Black Enterprise*, "We see this as an opportunity to play in spaces that typically companies like us and our size and our demographics don't necessarily typically play in. So it broadens our footprint into some areas that we feel that we can leverage and grow."

Melissa J. Doak

PRINCIPAL SUBSIDIARIES

24/7 Solutions.

PRINCIPAL COMPETITORS

Lockheed Martin Information Systems; SMF Systems; Stanley, Inc.

FURTHER READING

Bachelor, Blane, "Sense of Duty: For This Government Contractor, Success in the Tumultuous Global Climate Means Maintaining a Strong Foundation," *American Executive*, February 2005, pp. 110–12.

Bollfrass, Alex, "Iran-Iraq Chemical Warfare Aftershocks Persist," *Arms Control Today*, July–August 2007.

Brown, Carolyn M., and Alan Hughes, "Building New Foundations," *Black Enterprise*, June 2008.

"Dimensions International Acquires SENTEL to Build Powerhouse in Information Technology and Engineering Innovation—Two of the Most Successful Black-Owned Companies in U.S. Join Forces," *PR Newswire*, June 16, 2004.

French, Liz, "Partners over Customers: Russ Wright, General Johnnie Wilson, James Garrett, and Jim Kelly Tell Liz French How Their Family of Companies Is Helping Create a Safer World," *American Executive*, March 2006, pp. 126–28.

———, "VIP Employees: James Garrett Stood His Company's Structure on Its Head and Achieved Strong Results," *American Executive*, November 2005, pp. 142–44.

Gair, Cristina, "Soft Landing," *Black Enterprise*, September 2003, p. 51.

Hocker, Cliff, "Powerhouse Tech Companies Merge," *Black Enterprise*, November 2004, p. 28.

Hoffman, Michael P., and Veronica Deschambault, "Sensor Webs Supports Tactical Teamwork," *Signal*, September 1, 2001.

Hughes, Alan, "Critical Mass: When Dimensions International Acquired Fellow BE 100s Firm SENTEL Corp., It Created a New Force in the Homeland Security Sector," *Black Enterprise*, June 2005, pp. 122–29.

———, "Dimensions International Acquired: CEO Says Honeywell Will Take the Company Where He Could Not," *Black Enterprise*, August 2007, p. 27.

———, "SENTEL Acquires Service Provider to U.S. Intelligence Agencies," *Black Enterprise Online*, May 15, 2009, http://www.blackenterprise.com/be-100s/be100s-news/2009/05/15/sentel-acquires-service-provider-to-us-intelligence-agencies.

Jones, Dasha, "Tech Talk Profits," *Black Enterprise*, July 1992, p. 29.

Kaplan, Peter, "Former Navy Engineer Heads Million-Dollar Alexandria, Va.-Based Business," *Washington Times*, December 22, 1997, p. D6.

"Large-Scale Production Contracts for Chemical and Biological Warfare Agent Detectors Intensifies Competition, Reports Frost & Sullivan," *Business Wire*, June 12, 2000.

Lucas, Fred, "SENTEL's CEO Prevails after Humble Start," *Washington Times*, August 2, 1999, p. D3.

Milloy, Courtland, "Hard Knocks Now Paying Big Dividends," *Washington Post*, June 15, 2003, p. C1.

"Minority Firms Must Pursue Partnerships and Niches," *Purchasing*, August 14, 1997, p. 27.

Muhammad, Tariq K., "Tech Boom in the Beltway," *Black Enterprise*, June 1999, pp. 243–48.

"Pentagon Spending 2007: Defense Department Money Spent or Designated to Be Spent on Logistics/Support Services (As of 8/17/07)," *Aerospace Daily & Defense Report*, August 31, 2007.

"Pentagon's Top 500 RTD&E Contractors," *Aerospace Daily*, June 29, 1995, p. 503.

"SENTEL Corporation Acquires 24/7 Solutions," *PR Newswire*, April 16, 2009.

"SENTEL Corporation Wins U.S. Army Contract for Night Vision and Electronic Sensor Technology," *PR Newswire*, June 24, 2008.

"SENTEL Wins Contract to Support FAA Safety Management System," *PR Newswire*, September 8, 2008.

Singletary, Michelle, "Alexandria Contractor Builds on Defense; Firm Sees Opportunity in Still-Huge Budget," *Washington Post*, February 7, 1994, p. F11.

Spruell, Sakina P., "Finding the Right Formula for Growth: From Joint Ventures to Divestitures, the BE Industrial/Service 100 Used a Mix of Strategies to Beat the Competition," *Black Enterprise*, June 2005, pp. 103–10.

Townes, Glenn, "SENTEL Lands $487 Million Deal," *Black Enterprise*, September 2008, p. 32.

"WC Holding, Inc. Acquires SENTEL Corporation from Dimensions International, Inc.," *PR Newswire*, May 23, 2007.

Southern Sun Hotel Interest (Pty) Ltd.

Palazzo Towers East,
Montecasino Boulevard Fourways
Johannesburg, Gauteng 2055
South Africa
Telephone: (+27 011) 510-7500
Fax: (+27 011) 510-7255
Web site: http://www.southernsun.com

Wholly Owned Subsidiary of Tsogo Sun Holdings
Founded: 1969
Employees: 4,220
Sales: $9.39 billion (2008 est.)
NAICS: 721110 Hotels (except Casino Hotels); 721120
    Casino Hotels

■ ■ ■

Southern Sun Hotel Interest (Pty) Ltd., a wholly owned subsidiary of Tsogo Sun Holdings, is one of the largest travel-industry groups in South Africa. Through its Southern Sun Hotels and Resorts line, more than 60 hotels in its lineup serve a wide variety of travelers, including budget-conscious vacationers, midlevel business travelers, and luxury-seeking guests who expect world-class service. Representing several different brands, Southern Sun hotels can be found all over South Africa, as well as in the Seychelles, Tanzania, Zambia, Nigeria, and Dubai. Along with the five casinos in the Tsogo Sun Gaming group, the Southern Sun enterprises are under the umbrella of Tsogo Investment Holding Company, a majority owner of Tsogo Sun Holdings.

QUIET BEGINNINGS

The Southern Sun international hotel chain had its beginnings in a quiet little seaside village called Umhlanga Rocks, just outside Durban, South Africa. In the early 1960s Umhlanga was popular with residents of retirement age and also with younger people who liked a quiet life and an empty beach and who were willing to walk through a tangle of undergrowth to get there. By the end of the decade, though, Sol Kerzner had changed Umhlanga Rocks forever.

Kerzner raised ZAR 1 million, bought the Beverley Hills Hotel, and made it into the most glamorous destination in the country. When completed, the hotel had a sweeping staircase in the foyer, world-class restaurants, access to nearby golf courses and scenic tours, and, a first in South Africa, nightly entertainment. The Beverley Hills Hotel opened in December 1964, and within a year, just as Kerzner had hoped, prominent and well-off clientele had been there and loved it.

KERZNER'S FIRST VENTURES

This was not the first time Kerzner's business instinct led him to see the potential in South Africa. Born in 1935, Kerzner spent several years as a teen helping his parents run their little kosher hotel in Durban. Even in those days he was aware that visitors came to town to be entertained by its beaches, its outdoor markets, and its colorful Zulu crafts. Nevertheless, Kerzner felt there was even more untapped potential for entertainment and that it lay in the dockland area surrounding Durban's harbor, one of Africa's busiest. Busy and rather unsafe during the day, the waterfront warehouses and cranes

COMPANY PERSPECTIVES

Southern Sun's portfolio of hotels provide world-class accommodations across all markets, and offer the widest distribution of hotels in South Africa in major urban centers and key leisure destinations. They are designed to meet the needs of all guests, whether they are travelling for business or leisure.

stood silent at night. Seeing the potential, Kerzner persuaded his parents to buy the Palace Hotel, a dockside sailors' home-away-from-home, whose great advantage was its liquor license. He then leased it from his parents, closed its dining room, and turned the space into a swinging pub for seamen. In 1981 Kerzner told Joseph Lelyveld in the *New York Times*, "It was full of seamen, a bit of a wild place, but we turned the business around and it gave me a taste of the game."

Running the Palace Hotel was hard work, but young Kerzner also thrived at his day job, accounting. He was so good at it that he became a junior partner in a prominent firm at the age of only 25. The position was too boring to keep him at his desk for long, but it added an essential ingredient to his talent. It was Kerzner's accountancy training that made sure there was always a doctor on call for each hotel, that the housekeeping was meticulous, and that the jewel-toned tropical fruits in the Sunday buffet were the freshest to be found—in short, that all was right with the details, which are never dwelled on if they are correct but which cause serious problems when they go wrong.

Kerzner's success at the Palace Hotel and at the Beverley Hills encouraged him to venture into Durban itself, where he built the Elangeni, a 450-room hotel facing the sea. Pleasant and well run, the Elangeni was the hotel of value for a guest who wanted good food and service, and it was a safe distance from the cheap nightclub atmosphere of the town's South Beach.

PARTNERSHIP WITH SOUTH AFRICAN BREWERIES

Financing for the Elangeni came from South African Breweries, with whom Kerzner formed a partnership in 1969. By that time, Kerzner was managing director of the Southern Sun Hotel Corporation, which had six South African hotels: three in the Durban area, two near the famed Kruger National Park, and one in Johannesburg. "South African Breweries wanted to get out of the beer business and into the hotel business," Kerzner told *Hotels* magazine while receiving an award in 2004, "and said they'd finance a pretty huge expansion." Actually, South African Breweries had also decided to merge its nine-hotel Transito chain into Southern Sun, bringing their lineup to 24 by 1973.

By 1975 Kerzner was ready to expand his operations to overseas destinations, and he built and opened Le Saint Géran on the island of Mauritius. As always, he picked his location carefully, provided top-quality service, and made sure that the entertainment, mainly water-based, was the best available. The hotel also included a first for Kerzner—a casino, which would become a mainstay of his hotel operations thereafter. This site soon became a trendy honeymoon getaway for well-heeled South Africans.

Political turmoil, however, was developing in South Africa at this time. Noting that serious opposition to apartheid was increasing in the mid-1970s, the South African government created a series of Bantustans, or homelands, to forcibly remove black South Africans from the cities on the basis of their tribal origins.

APARTHEID ENDS: A HOMELAND GETS A NEW START

Bophuthatswana was one of these Bantustans. Supposedly the home of the Tswana people, it was granted independence on December 18, 1977, in a move acknowledged by no country except South Africa. The downside of the new country was its seven unconnected areas of scrub brush and its scant supply of arable land for supporting the subsistence economy of its 2.5 million inhabitants; the upside was the collection of precious minerals that would one day support the economy with mining, if it were developed. In the meantime, however, there were few ways for the homeland-dwellers to earn a living.

Kerzner saw the potential in the area's blue-green Magaliesberg Mountains, a region where hominids have lived for at least two million years. In addition to its beauty, the location had the advantage of accessibility because Bophuthatswana is only a two-hour drive from Johannesburg, an easy journey for visitors.

Just before the 1977 independence was declared, Kerzner went to see the soon-to-be ruler, Chief Lucas Mangope. Kerzner explained his idea to Mangope, which was to build a luxury hotel complex and casino in Bophuthatswana. The complex, to be called Sun City, would give the new homeland a 50 percent stake. Seeing the possibility of jobs for his poverty-stricken people, Mangope agreed.

With this deal settled, Kerzner erected four buildings, an 18-hole golf course, and the biggest casino

KEY DATES

1964: Beverley Hills Hotel opens in Umhlanga Rocks, just outside Durban, South Africa.

1969: Southern Sun Hotels is founded by Sol Kerzner and South African Breweries.

1975: Le Saint Géran in Mauritius opens, offering the group's first casino.

1979: Sun City in Bophuthatswana opens.

1983: Southern Sun splits; Southern Sun Hotels belongs to South African Breweries and Southern Sun International to Kerzner.

1992: Southern Sun divides its 58 hotels into five divisions.

1998: Southern Sun outsources property management and central reservations to IBM.

2002: SABMIller PLC (formerly South African Breweries) and Tsogo Investment transfer their interests into a new company, Tsogo Sun Holdings.

2004: Southern Sun's collection of super-luxury boutique hotels is created.

within easy reach of South Africans, gambling being strictly forbidden within South Africa itself. The complex cost $175 million and took two years to complete. The investment, however, proved sound. In its first year of operation, the first hotel brought a profit of about $11 million, giving impoverished Bophuthatswana about half of this figure. By the time building number two had its grand opening, the place was so popular that Kerzner was able to pay Frank Sinatra a fee of $1.6 million to entertain the enthusiastic audience.

The location offered various forms of entertainment. Nature lovers found many attractions, the most notable of which was the adjoining Pilanesberg Game Reserve, recently restored and safely fenced, and set inside the bowl of an extinct volcano. Here, guests could view—from a hot air balloon if they chose—the "big five" many people come to Africa to see: elephant, lion, Cape buffalo, leopard, and rhino.

Although the people of Bophuthatswana were both patronizing and working in the hotel and the casino, there was a volley of complaints from all sides. Antiapartheid activists felt Kerzner was helping to perpetuate apartheid by placing his resort in the artificially created homeland. Conservatives felt the place was "wicked" and should be closed down because it was immoral.

Kerzner, however, had another view. He had created 3,000 jobs for impoverished people, he argued. Furthermore, Kerzner maintained, he was giving people a taste of multiracial existence because blacks, whites, Chinese people, and anyone else who was able would come there on weekends—either to stay or to gamble— and enjoy themselves. At the resort the black South Africans who were complaining existed right alongside the right-wing farmers. Also, Kerzner reminded people, he had given a 50 percent stake to the local government, a sum that was helping Bophuthatswana's infrastructure considerably.

The complaints nonetheless swelled, even after major shareholder South African Breweries released its annual reports. In 1977 after-tax profits from Southern Sun reached ZAR 4.8 million. By 1982, with the Sun City complex fully operational, annual revenue was ZAR 188 million, with after-tax profits yielding ZAR 37.3 million. A year later turnover for the hotels reached ZAR 209 million, reflecting a rise of 12 percent and yielding an after-tax profit of ZAR 38.23 million.

This healthy bottom line was not enough to counter the world's determined effort to stamp out South Africa's apartheid. Facing economic sanctions and protests from various groups, in 1983 Kerzner opened and then had to sell the Chobe Game Lodge in Botswana. Several other problematic incidents occurred during this time, all of which prompted Kerzner to leave South Africa.

KERZNER ENDS PARTNERSHIP WITH SOUTH AFRICAN BREWERIES AND HOTELS

An agreement between Kerzner and South African Breweries was reached in 1983, and Southern Sun was split into two entities: Southern Sun Hotels, giving South African Breweries all the South African hotels, and Sun International, Kerzner's company. Kerzner kept all the casinos, though South African Breweries kept a 20 percent stake. This huge transaction involved the transfer of 5.5 million shares from Kerzner's ownership in Southern Sun to South African Breweries in exchange for $34.65 million.

By the end of the 1980s, apartheid was eroding, but South African Breweries' Southern Sun hotel business was floundering to such an extent that the company was delisted from the Johannesburg Stock Exchange in 1990. During the downturn, the catalyst providing the push to improvement was newly appointed Southern Sun leader Ron Stringfellow, previously the managing director of the Zimbabwe Sun Hotels.

A NEW BEGINNING

Stringfellow got off to a brisk start in improving the hotels of Southern Sun. Anticipating an enormous change in the political climate, he knew that the country's beautiful tourist destinations would soon be back in demand and that there would be many more market niches than there had been. He instituted what he called a "jumbo jet" strategy, naming his plan after the many seating options available on a large aircraft. Stringfellow rebranded his long list of hotels with Southern Sun to suit different market segments, awarding each chain one to five stars, depending on service level. For example, the InterContinental chain catered to the luxury-conscious guest, while Holiday Inns, a midlevel chain of 12 hotels acquired in 1985 from the Rennies Group, became the purview of the midlevel traveler. The truly budget-conscious end of the market was served by the Formule 1 chain.

In another move, Stringfellow acknowledged that Southern Sun needed to create casinos in order to generate enough profitability to match their 20 percent stake in Sun International. Noting that after the new government took office in 1994 and that the homelands had been reincorporated into South Africa with each having an extremely profitable casino, Stringfellow decided to split the company into Southern Sun Hotels and Southern Sun Gaming and recruited Jabu Mabuza, a CEO experienced in the gaming world, to create a casino division under the Southern Sun Gaming title.

A third important innovation came to fruition in 1998 when Southern Sun Hotels became the first hotel chain to outsource their reservations and property management. Spread over five years, the $6 million deal routed these services to IBM, which managed them with software from MAI Systems, Inc., a California company. This new technology made it much easier for Southern Sun to run its expanding lineup, consisting of 41 South African hotels, plus 13 others in Kenya, Zambia, and Zimbabwe. The check-ins and check-outs connected with their 9,000 rooms could be recorded within two minutes from anywhere in the world.

By the end of 2000 Southern Sun had 77 hotels, offering almost 12,800 rooms nationwide, plus a new ZAR 375 million convention center at the Sandton Sun in Johannesburg that was large enough outside to provide parking for 11,000 cars. Its pavilion could seat 4,500 people, and its spacious banquet hall could seat 2,000 guests comfortably. The conveniently located convention center soon had a profitable agreement for all events based in the Johannesburg suburb of Gauteng with Reed Exhibitions South Africa, the country's largest events planner. This was a lucrative alliance because shows such as the Computer Faire, just one of many annual events, regularly attracted 500,000 visitors.

In 2003 the South African government introduced Broad Based Black Economic Empowerment. This program was designed to ensure that black South Africans, making up 90 percent of the country's population, had the chance to own and manage large businesses, a right routinely denied them under apartheid. Fully agreeing that entrepreneurial opportunities should be open to all South Africans, South African Breweries turned to a black-owned company, Tsogo, that had been their associate since the mid-1990s. Tsogo had managed to secure five casino licenses around South Africa, enabling South African Breweries' Southern Sun Hotels to sell its formerly profitable 20 percent stake in Kerzner's Southern Sun International and use the ZAR 4 billion it received for its own casino expansion program, in which Tsogo and South African Breweries each held a 50 percent stake. Within a short time there were five casinos, one each in Gauteng, Nelspruit, Witbank, East London, and Durban.

ENTER TSOGO INVESTMENT

In 2003, in order to meet the government's requirements for gaming, South African Breweries sold its 51 percent interest in the hotels and casinos of Southern Sun for ZAR 1.9 billion to the Tsogo Investment subsidiary Tsogo Sun Holdings, retaining 49 percent of Tsogo Sun Holdings and ZAR 400 million of Tsogo Sun Holdings redeemable preference shares. Tsogo Sun Holdings, in turn, owned 100 percent of Tsogo Sun Gaming and Southern Sun Hotels. Each of these subsidiaries was run by a separate management team already in place. Another notable change concerned Stringfellow, who became the CEO of Tsogo Sun Holdings.

In 2004 Southern Sun opened the Southern Sun Collection hotels, representing the absolute top of the line in the industry, offering both spas and golf. The flagship hotel, the Beverley Hills Sun, moved to this collection, undergoing a $3.6 million renovation in the process. Another Southern Sun Collection hotel opened in Knysna, on the Cape's famed Garden Route, and a third, the Paradise Sun, in the Seychelles Islands also joined the lineup.

By the end of the 2008 financial year, there were Southern Sun hotels in Kenya, Mozambique, Tanzania, Seychelles, and Zambia, with a new hotel planned for 2010 in Dubai. All of these enterprises, plus existing ones, brought a handsome reward: in 2008 Southern Sun sales reached an estimated $9.39 billion.

Gillian Wolf

PRINCIPAL SUBSIDIARIES

Southern Sun Hotels and Resorts; SunSquare; Garden Court; StayEasy by Southern Sun; Southern Sun Timeshare Resorts; InterContinental Hotels; Holiday Inn; Formule 1.

PRINCIPAL COMPETITORS

Protea Hospitality Corporation; Global Resorts SA; Kerzner International Ltd.

FURTHER READING

Baumann, Julius, "Court Clears Way for HCI to Lift Stake in Tsogo Sun," *Africa News Service*, September 10, 2008.

Gilmour, Christopher, "Accommodating Taste and Budget," *Financial Mail*, November 14, 2003.

———, "Economic Climate Favours Increased Revenue for the Group," *Financial Mail*, November 14, 2003.

Klein, Marcia, "The Sun King Gets a Licence to Gild His Empire," *Sunday Times Business Times*, November 26, 2007.

Lelyveld, Joseph, "Bringing a Bit of Vegas to South Africa's 'Homelands,'" *New York Times*, July 19, 1981.

Marlow, David, "Crowning Glory: South Africa's Sun City Strikes Gold with Palace," *Chicago Tribune*, March 6, 1994.

"Sol Kerzner Profile," CNN.com, January 11, 2008, http://edition.cnn.com/2008/BUSINESS/01/08/sol.kerzner/index.html.

"Sol the Builder," *Travel Agent*, December 8, 1997.

"South Africa Facility Secures Exclusive Deal with Reed," *Tradeshow Week*, September 30, 2002.

"Southern Sun Hotels in South Africa Now Using Hotel Information Systems PMS and Central Reservation Software," Hotel Online Special Report, October 15, 1998, http://www.hotel-online.com/News/PressReleases1998_4th/Oct98_MAIHIS.html.

Strauss, Karyn, "Southern Sun Shines with New Deluxe Collection," *Hotels*, October 2004.

———, "2004 Corporate Hotelier of the World: Sol Kerzner," *Hotels*, November 1, 2004.

Weinstein, Jeff, and Karyn Strauss, "Hoteliers of the World," *Hotels*, November 2004.

Sport Supply Group, Inc.

1901 Diplomat Drive
Dallas, Texas 75234-8914
U.S.A.
Telephone: (972) 484-9484
Web site: http://www.sportsupplygroup.com

Public Company
Founded: Early 1970s as BSN Corp.
Incorporated: 1991 as Sport Supply
Employees: 340
Sales: $76.1 million (2009 est.)
Stock Exchanges: NASDAQ
Ticker Symbol: RBI
NAICS: 454113 Mail-Order Houses; 454111 Electronic Shopping; 339920 Sporting Goods Manufacturing; 423910 Sporting Goods and Supplies Merchant Wholesalers

■ ■ ■

Sport Supply Group, Inc. (SSG), is the nation's leading marketer, manufacturer, and distributor of sporting goods equipment and physical education, recreational, and leisure products. The company serves institutional and team sports markets, with a customer base that includes public and private schools, state and local governments, dealers, youth sports leagues and programs, YMCAs, YWCAs, athletic clubs and teams, park and recreational organizations, schools, colleges, and churches throughout the United States. SSG manufactures a variety of sports equipment that includes bleachers, backstops, and goal posts and distributes a wide range of popular sports brands. The company marketing efforts are shared by a Catalog Division and a Dealer Division. The Catalog Division's mailings, which consist of more than three million catalogs and other direct mail pieces, are facilitated by a team of 40 telemarketers. With more than 150 road sales professionals, the Dealer Division offers personalized service that is supported by sales events and the company's Web sites. SSG's multifaceted approach that targets consumers as well as businesses serves more than 200,000 customers nationwide.

When Sport Supply emerged in 1991, its presence signaled the return of Michael Blumenfeld, a one-time professional athlete who already had tried two times to establish a successful sporting goods distributorship. The history of Blumenfeld's two companies charts a prodigious rise in the sporting goods industry, beginning with a business born in the back of a pickup truck that evolved into the largest direct mail marketer of sporting goods equipment in the United States. During this nearly three-decade-long period, Blumenfeld took a roller coaster ride in the business world, experiencing the pitfalls and the rewards of operating in a hotly contested industry. His journey began in the early 1970s, shortly after he took off his baseball cleats for the last time. His first attempt was named Blumenfeld Sports Net Co., which became BSN Corp. BSN was highly successful during the 1980s but quickly floundered, prompting Blumenfeld to regroup and try again. His second effort was Sport Supply, which was intertwined with the defunct BSN.

COMPANY PERSPECTIVES

One team of valued employees committed to providing unparalleled service to customers and delivering superior returns to shareholders.

ORIGINS AS BSN CORP.

As a high school student, Blumenfeld demonstrated considerable athletic promise. He was signed by the St. Louis Cardinals out of high school and entered the club's farm system where he spent two years playing in the outfield in the minor leagues. In 1966, Blumenfeld's baseball career was cut short by nagging knee problems. He was forced to look for a job outside baseball, but he did not exit the realm of sports entirely. By the early 1970s, he was struggling to make a living driving around Memphis, Tennessee, trying to sell tennis nets to the region's tennis and country clubs from the back of his truck. It was a modest start, but the absence of conventional business trappings did not discourage Blumenfeld and his wife from nurturing their fledgling entrepreneurial creation. After each sale, Blumenfeld and his wife mailed the customer a hand-drawn brochure describing the merchandise they had for sale. Over time, customers began to ask for items not included within the brochure, so Blumenfeld would find a supplier and add the new merchandise to his brochure.

Before long, the hand-drawn brochures developed into genuine catalogs that were filled with page after page of sporting goods merchandise. As the size of the catalog increased, so did the size of BSN, growing from a start-up business into a legitimate, money-making company. By the end of the 1970s, Blumenfeld was running a robustly growing mail-order operation that was generating millions of dollars in sales each year. Those in the sporting goods industry who had not noticed BSN soon would. In 1980, when annual sales reached $3 million, Blumenfeld made an initial public offering (IPO).

REJECTED BY SUPPLIERS

The money raised from the IPO would be needed as Blumenfeld led his company into the 1980s. He was facing a potentially damaging problem caused by the enviable success of his sporting goods distributorship. BSN had achieved remarkable success in its short existence, emerging from nowhere to compete as a recognizable and fast-growing competitor in an industry populated by companies with considerably more

experience. Blumenfeld believed that the more established retail operators in the country considered BSN's solid growth to be a threat to their own existence. The competition was losing business to the upstart company, which had to be stopped. Blumenfeld considered the reaction against his company to be conspiratorial. He claimed that merchants had threatened him with baseball bats at trade shows. When threats failed to stop BSN's growth, merchants voiced their complaints to their suppliers, the same businesses that supplied Blumenfeld with merchandise. According to reports, the suppliers sided with their more established retail customers and cut Blumenfeld off from some of the merchandise he included in his catalogs. Blumenfeld, who felt he was being pushed aside by the industry's heavyweights, responded with a new strategy that would dramatically change the face of BSN.

With some of his suppliers refusing to do business with him, Blumenfeld decided that he could either fade away or fight back. He opted for the latter and devised a solution that had the company integrating backwards, acquiring sporting goods manufacturers and greatly reducing his dependence on outside suppliers. BSN would thus become a manufacturer as well as a distributor. In 1981, the first manufacturer Blumenfeld acquired was Rol-Dri, Inc., a tennis and golf equipment manufacturer. Blumenfeld was determined to acquire enough sporting goods manufacturers to produce 75 percent of all the products BSN sold through its catalogs. By 1985, Blumenfeld had purchased 13 small manufacturers that together encompassed a broad range of athletic and leisure equipment, apparel, and accessories. Blumenfeld acquired such companies as Hammatt & Sons, a producer of table games; Champion Barbell, which produced weightlifting equipment; and Nelson Knitting Co., a manufacturer of athletic hosiery. With the addition of these companies and others, roughly half of BSN's $30 million in sales during the mid-1980s was amassed from products it manufactured. By this time, the company was offering more than 3,000 products at discounts of up to 30 percent over retail, selling everything from tennis balls to baseball backstops through more than three million catalogs mailed each year. Over the course of four years, Blumenfeld had become not only a strong distributor, but also a rising manufacturer. However, success was never easy for Blumenfeld, and the evolution to manufacturer mirrored that of his growth as a distributor.

Poised as a rising contender in the manufacturing segment of the sporting goods industry, Blumenfeld found himself butting heads with such large manufacturers as Wilson, MacGregor, Rawlings, and Spalding. BSN was much smaller than these rivals,

KEY DATES

1970s: After Michael Blumenfeld begins Blumenfeld Sports Net Co., which became BSN Corp.

1980: Company makes initial public offering.

1981: Blumenfeld acquires tennis and golf equipment manufacturer Rol-Dri, Inc.

1987: Company is manufacturing 75 percent of the merchandise sold in its catalogs.

1991: Sport Supply Group, Inc. (SSG), makes an initial public offering.

1995: SSG acquires the Nitro Golf division from Prince Golf International, Ltd.; company is designated Official Factory Direct Equipment Supplier of Little League Baseball.

1998: SSG's sales reach nearly $100 million.

1999: SSG acquires Conlin Bros. Sporting Goods, Larry Black Sporting Goods Inc., and Flag A Tag, Inc.; company launches esportsonline.com.

2001: SSG secures agreements with the United States Flag and Touch Football League (USFTL) and Fast Action Sports.

2003: SSG sells its Athletic Training Equipment Co. (ATEC) to Amer Group PLC (Finland).

2005: Collegiate Pacific, Inc., acquires 53.2 percent of SSG; Michael Blumenfeld returns to a leadership role.

2006: Collegiate Pacific purchases remaining SSG shares and merges the two companies.

2007: Company is renamed Sport Supply Group, Inc.

2009: SSG acquires Webster's Team Sports.

however, and needed a large acquisition to narrow the gap separating it from its rivals. Blumenfeld tried several times during the mid-1980s to acquire Riddell Sports, the largest maker of football helmets in the country, which would make BSN a major player overnight. Blumenfeld's offers of $7 million in cash and stock were rebuffed. He also tried to buy Wilson Sporting Goods, offering $151 million in BSN stock, but this offer was brushed aside. When Blumenfeld attempted to buy Bike Athletics, the second largest football helmet manufacturer in the United States, no one would listen to his proposal. The idea of conspiracy that had settled into Blumenfeld's mind when suppliers had cut him off years earlier returned. "We're considered the renegade of the world," Blumenfeld remarked to a *Forbes* reporter.

"People fear that BSN is doing so well by itself, for God's sake don't give them something they can sink their teeth into."

Although the competition may have been threatened by BSN's success, their outright rejection of Blumenfeld's offers to purchase their companies was caused primarily by the inclusion of BSN stock as part of the payment. BSN stock was not performing well following the acquisitions of the 1980s. Despite falling earnings, Blumenfeld moved forward with his determination to expand BSN through acquisitions, strengthened by the cold shoulder he had received from the sporting goods community. By 1987, Blumenfeld had achieved his goal of manufacturing 75 percent of the merchandise sold in his catalogs. The company reported sales topping $70 million and was ranked as the nation's leading reconditioner of football equipment, the largest manufacturer of cheerleader's uniforms and supplies and the largest direct distributor of sports equipment to the institutional marketplace. Again, however, success had its price.

THE END OF BSN AND THE BEGINNING OF SPORT SUPPLY

Before Blumenfeld's decade-long acquisition binge was over, he had purchased 48 companies, including dozens of small distributors, manufacturers, and retailers. Some of the acquisitions did not readily fit into BSN's corporate structure, while others had been losing money prior to their acquisition, and still others were in bankruptcy proceedings. The result was an externally strong company, leading the field in several lucrative markets, but with profound internal problems. BSN had become a money loser. Blumenfeld could not contend with the losses of more than $15 million that had been posted between 1989 and 1991. He decided to build from the ashes of BSN and sold much of what he had purchased to gain the financial resources that would enable another attempt in the sporting goods industry. As he reached his mid-40s, Blumenfeld made plans for a future in which the newly-formed Sport Supply would overcome the issues that had caused the demise of BSN.

A complex series of refinancing transactions gave led to the creation of Sport Supply Group, Inc., and gave Blumenfeld another chance to create a successful sporting goods distributor. SSG made an IPO in April 1991 and began the rebuilding process. On the heels of the IPO, SSG's customer base was expanded to include such retailers as J.C. Penney, Sears, Roebuck and Co., and Wal-Mart, while Blumenfeld sought acquisition targets. Blumenfeld promised that he had learned his lesson during the 1980s and would buy only profitable distributors and a few small manufacturers that fit the company's distribution channels.

SPORT SUPPLY GROUP, INC.: 1990–2000

Between 1991 and 1994, SSG acquired 12 sporting goods distributors and signed several important licensing agreements, including the rights to manufacture, market, and distribute merchandise under the MacGregor trade name, which was obtained in 1992. Blumenfeld also gained an exclusive license agreement with AMF Bowling, Inc., to use the AMF name, which had been acquired in 1993, to promote and sell gymnastics equipment in the United States and Canada. During this three-year period, annual sales had increased from $47 million to $67 million. In addition, the company's stock price had more than doubled.

The mid-1990s were years of expansion and divestment for SSG as the company strengthened its position as a distributor of sporting goods and leisure merchandise to the institutional market. In June 1995 the company acquired the Nitro Golf division of Prince Golf International, Ltd., a manufacturer and distributor of new golf balls. A strategic decision implemented a short time later made Nitro Golf only a short-term component of SSG's business. However, the three-year agreement signed with Little League Baseball, Incorporated, in December 1995 had a lasting effect on the company's business. That agreement designated SSG as the "Official Factory Direct Equipment Supplier of Little League Baseball." The deal opened the doors to the estimated three million participants of Little League Baseball, adding measurably to SSG's revenues. In August 1997, the agreement with Little League Baseball was extended through 2001.

While the two agreements with Little League Baseball were made between the end of 1995 and 1997, SSG made the strategic decision to dispose of its golf operations to focus on its core institutional business. In May 1996, SSG sold virtually all the assets of its Gold Eagle Professional Products Division, which sold golf accessory products to the retail market. In December 1996, Emerson Radio Corp. acquired a controlling interest in SSG and replaced Blumenfeld with Geoffrey P. Jurick. Blumenfeld surprised observers when he then resigned from SSG. In March 1997, SSG sold Nitro Leisure Products, Inc.

At the end of the 1990s, SSG had completed the rebuilding process that began when the company was organized from the ruins of BSN. Sales for the 11-month period ending September 1997 was close to $80 million, and the company's net earnings were reported

to be a respectable $2.6 million. SSG ranked as the largest direct mail marketer of sports-related equipment to the institutional market in the United States. The majority of sales were made to schools, universities, athletic clubs, youth sport leagues, government agencies, recreational organizations, and military facilities. SSG offered these customers some 8,000 products, 3,000 of which were manufactured at the four SSG plants in Alabama, California, and Texas. SSG maintained a strong position based on the diversity of its products.

FURTHER DIVERSIFICATION AND ACQUISITIONS

By the end of the 1998 fiscal year, SSG's sales had reached nearly $100 million, and the company was exploring other ways to expand. In January 1999, the company announced plans to launch esportsonline.com, a Web site offering more than 7,500 of its products, by mid-1999. E-commerce was a nice fit for a mail order company, and SSG considered it to be a long-term investment with the potential to reach millions of new customers.

SSG diversified further by entering the $1 billion playground equipment niche market, signing an agreement with JungleBug Play.Works™. In January 1999, SSG began offering 10 playground units through its catalog and direct sales operations, with a price range between $5,000 and $12,000. In its initial mailing, the company distributed more than 125,000 JungleBug catalogs to school districts and municipal parks and planned to add the product line to its esportsonline.com Web site by mid-year.

The acquisition of Conlin Bros. Sporting Goods followed in early 1999. Conlin Bros. was one of California's oldest and largest catalog marketers and distributors, and the purchase would increase SSG's sales in the state more than 50 percent.

SSG's expansion strategy to acquire regional distributors continued, and in February 1999 the company acquired Larry Black Sporting Goods, Inc., the largest school and team dealer of sports equipment in the Kansas/Oklahoma region. The following month, to help SSG meet its growth goals through acquisitions and esportsonline.com, the company received a $40 million credit line from Comerica Bank. John P. Walker, who had been SSG president and chief operating officer since 1997, said in an interview for PR Newswire Association in March 1999 that the financing was "further endorsement by the investment community and commercial banking sector of our demonstrated financial discipline and successful sales growth management."

The acquisition of Flag A Tag, Inc., followed in April 1999, which was expected to help reduce seasonal financial fluctuations. Flag A Tag, a provider of football accessories, would potentially drive sales in SSG's historically weakest fiscal first and fourth quarters. In May 1999, in an effort to encourage customers to use its new Web site, SSG signed an agreement with American Airlines to offer free American AAdvantage Miles to users of esportsonline.com and on June 8, 1999, the Web site was launched.

ADJUSTING SSG'S VISION

In July 1999, MacMark Corporation and Equilink Licensing Corp. announced the termination of SSG's licensing rights to the MacGregor trademark. SSG responded by filing a lawsuit to maintain the license. According to PR Newswire in July 1999, SSG President and COO Walker said that the company had paid Mac-Mark $1 million in 1992 for a royalty-free license to use the MacGregor trademark, and "now that SSG has built up the value of this trademark…MacMark is questioning the wisdom of its prior sale." The trademark litigation was eventually settled on favorable terms, but not before incurring $1.2 million in legal fees and consuming valuable time and resources. SSG did not allow the issue to distract it from its mission, however. Over the next few months the company continued to expand operations and forge new partnerships, including opening a Mid-West Sports Hub in Chicago. In addition, SSG obtained the rights to market and sell Reebok team uniforms and boasted eight marketing Web sites by August 1999.

However, SSG's rapid expansion came with a price. By December 1999 SSG had retained the services of PaineWebber to explore ways to boost its shareholder value, including the potential sale of the company. By the end of the year the company's revenues had risen from $25.3 million to $30.4 million, but its net income had dropped a staggering 68 percent from $1.3 million to $404,000. In a company statement, the decline was blamed on the poor timing of the implementation of the Web sites, which did not allow the company to integrate recent acquisitions in the planned timeframe. By April 2000, SSG was posting losses of $1.1 million, citing increased spending on company Web sites and on the expansion of the company's field sales team.

SSG was determined not to allow these losses to detract from its vision and continued to diversify its portfolio. In May 2000, SSG entered a strategic alliance with Kawama.com to develop and market learning-based physical education materials for the early childhood marketplace through the latter's U.S. Games Division. The partnership would expand the company's customer base to include not only buyers, but also administrators, teachers, students, and parents. The alli-

ance was followed by the announcement that SSG had signed an agreement with The Antigua Group, Inc., to be the exclusive distributor of its product line, which included golf apparel for LPGA and PGA professionals and NBA, NFL, NHL and Major League baseball uniforms, as well as casual sportswear. On December 22, 2000, Emerson Radio Corp., SSG's largest shareholder, offered to purchase 1,629,629 shares at $1.35 per share, for a total of $2.2 million. On the strength of Emerson Radio's commitment, the company amended its original financing arrangement with Comerica Bank. As part of the amendment, SSG agreed to pay $250,000 to Comerica if the refinancing was not completed by March 30, 2001. On March 28, 2001, SSG reported that it had completed a new and more favorable three-year $25 million credit agreement. Within two months of this announcement, Emerson Radio increased its ownership in SSG to 50.1 percent, with SSG changing its fiscal year-end to March 31 to coincide with Emerson's.

CONTINUED ACQUISITIONS IN THE EARLY 21ST CENTURY

The company had become well-positioned to continue its expansion through acquisitions and alliances. New business included management of the Plano (Texas) Sports Authority (PSA) and the New Mexico Police Athletic League (PAL) online sporting goods stores; sponsoring and supplying equipment to the Cal Ripken Baseball Camps; and an agreement to be the exclusive supplier to YouthsportsUSA.com. By November 1, 2001, SSG had secured agreements with the United States Flag and Touch Football League (USFTL) and Fast Action Sports to manage and supply products for USFTL.com and fasports.com, respectively. The company was well on its way to recouping the $8.8 million it had spent since 1998 to upgrade its information technology systems. By June 2002, SSG had entered into agreements with more than 130 organizations and institutions to market and supply company products through associated Web sites.

By the fall of 2003, SSG was once again facing financial difficulties and sold two of its outlets while closing a third. In October 2003 Emerson Radio owned 54 percent of SSG, and when Geoffrey P. Jurick was named chairman, CEO, and president of Emerson Radio, Walker resigned as president and director of SSG, and chairman, CEO and president of Emerson Radio. On November 6, SSG not only amended its loan agreement again, but also sold its Athletic Training Equipment Co. (ATEC) to Amer Group plc (Finland). In an effort to bring the company's expenses in line with revenues, SSG filed Form 15 with the Securities and Exchange Commission (SEC), relieving it of its responsibility to submit periodic reports. Jurick believed that de-registering the company would save substantially on accounting, legal, and administrative costs, money that would be better utilized to enhance the company's bottom line.

Collegiate Pacific, Inc., one of the fastest growing manufacturers in the United States and supplier of sports equipment for institutional and team markets, acquired 53.2 percent of SSG on July 5, 2005. Terrence Babilla retained his position as chief operating officer (COO) of SSG and replaced Jurick as president. Collegiate Pacific' chairman and CEO was Michael Blumenfeld, who returned to his former company in those same positions. In November 2005 Collegiate Pacific purchased an additional 1.66 million of SSG's shares, giving it a 72 percent interest in the company. One year later, Collegiate Pacific purchased the remaining SSG shares for $24 million, and the merger of the nation's two leading sporting goods suppliers was complete. Adam Blumenfeld, Michael's son, held the positions of chairman, CEO, and president, and in July 2007 the newly merged company was renamed Sport Supply Group, Inc. Near the end of the first decade of the 21st century, net income had more than doubled in one year in spite of a difficult economic climate. By June 2009, SSG had acquired Webster's Team Sports, Florida's leading team sports distributor. This was followed by the announcement that the company planned to purchase certain assets of Har-Bell Athletic Goods of Missouri. In the midst of a major global recession, Adam Blumenfeld saw only a challenge that "creates opportunities for those with strong balance sheets and best-of-breed operating platforms."

Jeffrey L. Covell
Updated, Marie O'Sullivan

PRINCIPAL SUBSIDIARIES

Kesslers Team Sports, Inc.; Dixie Sporting Goods Co., Inc.

PRINCIPAL DIVISIONS

Catalog Division; Dealer Division.

PRINCIPAL COMPETITORS

adidas AG (Germany); Amazon.com, Inc.; Amer Sports Corporation (Finland); eBay, Inc.; Nike, Inc.

FURTHER READING

Blumenfeld, Mike, "A Different Take on Internet Selling," *Sporting Goods Dealer*, May–June 2003, p. 12.

———— "Thanks, Uncle Sam," *Catalog Age*, November 1, 2003, p. 12.

Cawley, Rusty, "Sport Supply Nets $40 Million on Loan for Growth," *Dallas Business Journal*, May 7, 1999, p. 1.

"Collegiate Pacific Acquires Majority Interest in Sport Supply Group, Inc.," *Business Wire*, July 5, 2005.

"Emerson Diversifies," *Television Digest*, December 16, 1996, p. 16.

Harris, Kellee "Sparky," "B2B Sports Sites Are Attracting Industry Attention and Venture Funding," *Sporting Goods Business*, June 5, 2000, p. 17.

Heller, Matthew, "Eight Simple Rules for Selling Sporting Goods to Our Daughters," *Sporting Goods Dealer*, March–April 2003, p. 20.

————, "The Largest Team Dealers in America," *Sporting Goods Dealer*, November–December 2002, p. 13.

————, "The Renegade Man," *Forbes*, November 18, 1985, p. 66.

Lampman, Dean, "BSN Seeks Consistent Growth after Sharp Decline in Profits," *Dallas-Fort Worth Business Journal*, September 14, 1987, p. 1.

O'Hara, Kristy J., "Michael Blumenfeld," *Smart Business Dallas*, September 2006.

"Riddell Sports Buys Maxpro, All-American," *Sporting Goods Business*, October 1991, p. 7.

"Sports Supply Changes the Rules of the Game," *Catalog Age*, December 2001, p. 16.

"Sport Supply Group Acquires Conlin Bros. Sporting Goods," PR Newswire, February 22, 1999, p. 9176.

"Sport Supply Group Acquires Leading Oklahoma/Kansas Sporting Goods Dealer," PR Newswire, January 29, 1999, p. 4322.

"Sport Supply Group Acquires the Assets of Flag a Tag, Inc.," PR Newswire, April 12, 1999, p. 8501.

"Sport Supply Group Enters $1 Billion Playground Equipment, Market with 'Junglebug Play.Works™'," PR Newswire, January 12, 1999, p. 2371.

"Sport Supply Group, Inc. and Collegiate Pacific Terminate Merger Agreement," *Business Wire*, November 22, 2005.

"Sport Supply Group, Inc. Announces Arrangement with American Airlines to Drive On-Line Ordering," PR Newswire, May 11, 1999, p. 7636.

"Sport Supply Group, Inc. Announces New $40 Million Credit Facility," PR Newswire, March 23, 1999, p. 1986.

"Sports Supply Group Inc Enters into New Long Term Marketing Ventures," *Market News Publishing*, August 8, 2001, p. 1008220u4697.

"Sport Supply Group Prepares to Launch 'esportsonline.com,'" PR Newswire, January 8, 1999, p. 0622.

"Sports Supply Group Settles MacGregor Litigation and Reports Results of Operations for the Year Ended September 29, 2000," *Business Wire*, December 29, 2000, p. 0106.

Sullivan, R. Lee, "Your Management Team Is Not a Bashful Bunch of Wimps," *Forbes*, September 12, 1994, p. 84.

Starent Networks Corp.

———■———

30 International Place
Tewksbury, Massachusetts 01876-1144
U.S.A.
Telephone: (978) 851-1100
Fax: (978) 640-6825
Web site: http://www.starentnetworks.com

Public Company
Founded: 2000
Incorporated: 2000
Employees: 774
Sales: $254.08 million (2008)
Stock Exchanges: NASDAQ
Ticker Symbol: STAR
NAICS: 334220 Radio and Television Broadcasting and Wireless Communications Equipment Manufacturing

■ ■ ■

Starent Networks Corp., based in Tewksbury, Massachusetts, provides equipment and services that help wireless service operators handle large volumes of transmissions and supply multimedia content. Starent's customers include many of the world's leading mobile operators, such as China Unicom, Cox Communications, Cricket, KDDI, Rural Cellular Corporation, SK Telecom, Sprint Nextel, Tata Teleservices Limited, U.S. Cellular Corporation, Verizon Wireless, Virgin Mobile, and Vodafone. Starent operates in 35 countries and maintains offices in Brazil, Canada, China, Japan, South Korea, and the United Kingdom, along with a research center in Bangalore, India. The company's networks serve nearly 500 million mobile phone customers worldwide. The company has thrived and remained independent by serving a vital niche within the booming mobile wireless communications industry.

STARENT NETWORKS FOUNDED: 2000

Beginning in the early 1980s, Starent founder Ashraf Dahod founded and led a series of telecom companies: Applitek Corp. (renamed LANCity), which developed the first cable modem; Sigma Network Systems; and NetCore Systems. After the last of these companies was sold in 1999 to Tellabs for $575 million, Dahod joined with some of his former colleagues and other respected industry veterans to start another company, incorporated as Starent Networks Corp. in August 2000. Dahod and his partners sought to supply technology that would help mobile phone operators handle the surging growth in wireless traffic and provide advanced data and multimedia applications to their customers. One key to Starent's appeal was that, while many of its competitors aimed to simply adapt wireline telephony technologies for use in wireless networks, Starent would be building its applications from scratch directly for the wireless market.

Starent management believed that rapid innovation and specialized expertise could entice major wireless carriers to select its solutions and help it compete against major telecom equipment suppliers such as Nortel Networks, Nokia, Cisco Systems, Motorola, and Ericsson. "The benefit to being a start-up is we were

COMPANY PERSPECTIVES

Starent Networks' strength is in its leadership. We have a strong team of experienced professionals, who bring together a variety of key strengths and expertise in the mobile wireless communications market. All of Starent's people know how to create innovative solutions and make them a reality.

able to start with a clean sheet of paper and find a solution that is not encumbered by legacy," Dahod said to *Wireless Review*. The new company attracted support from three Massachusetts-based venture capital funds—Matrix Partners, Highland Capital Partners, and North Bridge Venture Partners—which provided $10 million in initial financing and another $22 million the following year. The hopes of the company's founders and investors began to be realized in November 2001, when the Korean electronics giant Samsung Electronics Corp. forged an alliance with Starent to use its technology to expand its CDMA network infrastructure in South Korea. The deal not only provided Starent with a high-profile partner, but also with a customer base on which to test and improve its products.

A GATEWAY TO INDUSTRY SUCCESS

The company's most important product was a wireless packet platform, named the Starent ST16 Intelligent Mobile Gateway. A gateway collects voice and data signals and channels them to their proper destinations, combining the functions of a router and a server. The ST16 gateway seamlessly linked operators' radio networks with wireless IP networks, which allowed for reliable, rapid, high-volume data transmission and expanded wireless Internet applications. This technology converted mobile phone signals into digital packets that could be easily transferred between different wireless networks, reducing the probability of disruptions. Customers could roam much more widely without disrupting their wireless IP connections. Operators could monitor network activity in great detail, which permitted them to offer services to individual customers based on their calling patterns and bill them at particular rates for specific services. Recognizing that many mobile phone users would likely be keeping their old handsets for years to come, Starent designed its technology to be compatible with existing voice-based cellular networks, using the industry standard second-

generation (or 2G) digital technology, as well as with the emerging data-based wireless Internet networks, known as third-generation (or 3G). The S16 gateway was very successful and was eventually repackaged and sold worldwide by Samsung as the Samsung Mobile Access Gateway 400 (or SMAG 400).

Starent initially sought customers in the booming Asian telecom market, especially in China, anticipating that successful deployment of its products there would help it win contracts elsewhere in the world. In 2001 the company became one of the few vendors of gateway equipment approved to operate in China. Chinese telecom companies were seeking partnerships with foreign firms to help them become more internationally competitive as the country adopted WTO protocols mandating trade deregulation and tariff reduction. Starent reached agreements with the Chinese manufacturer Eastern Communications (or Eastcom) to distribute its products and with the two leading Chinese telecom companies, China Unicom and the China Putian Institute of Technology, to integrate the ST16 Mobile Gateway into their mobile wireless infrastructure. Starent started research centers in China with Eastcom and China Putian.

Although the competing GSM[DJ1] network standard dominated many of the world's largest cellular markets (particularly in Europe), Starent quickly established a valuable niche as a coveted vendor for CDMA mobile carriers. It expanded into South America through a contract signed in May 2003 with the Spanish-Portuguese joint venture VIVO, the leading mobile operator in Brazil. Later that year the company gained its first customers in the United States: U.S. Cellular, then the country's eighth largest wireless carrier and Rural Cellular Corporation, a major rural wireless carrier. Also in that year, Samsung chose Starent to help it develop next-generation W-CDMA infrastructure, which SK Telecom, South Korea's leading wireless carrier, adopted for its planned W-CDMA network.

A RAPID RISE CONTINUES IN A BURGEONING INDUSTRY

Starent's early successes helped it attract more investment capital. In early 2003 the company raised an additional $23 million, with Samsung participating as well. The following year it raised another $25 million, with Itochu Technology Inc. of Japan joining as a new investor. In January 2006 the T-Mobile Venture Fund (a unit of Deutsche Telekom) became an investor in Starent.

Starent researchers developed a series of new forms of wireless service and extensions to its gateway

KEY DATES

2000: Starent Networks is founded.
2001: Company obtains its first contract, with Samsung Electronics Co.
2002: Company introduces the Starent ST16 Intelligent Mobile Gateway.
2007: Company introduces the ST40 multimedia core platform and launches an IPO on the NASDAQ.

technology. In 2003 the company began promoting what it called voice instant messaging (VIM), an IP-based service that promised to provide instant, interactive voice and data applications for group as well as individual calls, compatible with both 2G and 3G devices. Researchers also worked on "push to video" applications that could send and receive simultaneous synchronized video and voice with as many as seven participants, using special mobile phones with cameras pointed toward the user as well as away from the user.

Starent's technological innovation, however, did not come without controversy. A 2004 lawsuit in California charged that the company was stealing intellectual property. UTStarcom, a major competitor in the wireless equipment market, asserted that Starent lured away former employees of CommWorks, a company UTStarcom had purchased, and was using their knowledge to infringe patents and steal trade secrets. The court granted summary judgment in Starent's favor in that suit in December 2005, ruling that UTStarcom was inappropriately trying to extend its patent rights. However, another lawsuit UTStarcom filed based on the same charges in Illinois was still unresolved as of the spring of 2009.

In 2004 and 2005 Starent continued to acquire new clients, including Virgin Mobile USA, Japan's KDDI, leading Venezuelan mobile carrier Movilnet, and, most important of all, Verizon Wireless. Starent sold to Verizon a set of mobile gateway switches and other equipment valued at tens of millions of dollars for its BroadbandAccess network, which supported IP wireless services for laptop computers and cell phones, including music, video, and computer games. The still-private company asserted that it was now earning a profit, supplying dozens of networks with a total base of 170 million subscribers as of March 2005.

EMERGING IN THE PUBLICLY TRADED LIMELIGHT

After several years of rapid growth, Starent launched an IPO in June 2007, in which it offered 10.5 million common shares on the NASDAQ at an opening price of $12. The company took advantage of its rising share prices by making another stock offering that November of 8 million shares at $24 per share. However, the company's stock then declined, falling below $10 by November 2008 even as Starent's remarkable growth continued. Between 2005 and 2008 the company's revenue surged from $59.66 million to $254.10 million, and its net income from $904,000 to $60.50 million.

The company's strategy of seeking business from a handful of leading wireless telecoms helped it prosper, but also left it vulnerable. For example, the company had reached an agreement with Nortel Networks to resell its products, which had accounted for 40 percent of Starent's revenue, but this collaboration ended in March 2006. By late 2008 it still relied on five customers for 93 percent of its revenue, with Verizon Wireless making up 60 percent.

NEW PRODUCTS FOR NEW TECHNOLOGIES

As mobile data transmission technologies proliferated, Starent introduced a variety of products aimed at these various technologies, striving to expand its business beyond CDMA carriers. Starent actively participated in numerous telecom industry associations, such as the Global Multi-Service Forum, the 3rd Generation Partnership Project, the IMS Forum, the Mobile WiMAX Forum, and the Femto Forum, where it could help develop and promote industry standards.

In 2006 and early 2007 as industry buzz centered on the upcoming deployment of the IMS (IP multimedia subsystem) standard, Starent sought to be one of the first vendors to provide IMS-compliant equipment. At the Global Multi-Service Interoperability test in October 2006, the company successfully demonstrated its Session Control Manager, which updated the ST16 to support IMS features. The company engaged in a series of "plugfests" sponsored by the IMS Forum in 2007 and 2008, in which vendors and suppliers tested the interoperability of each other's equipment. In April 2007 Starent launched the ST40 multimedia core platform, designed to comply with IMS and to operate on both 3G networks and the even more advanced 4G networks that were just beginning to emerge. This platform would enable mobile carriers to provide services such as streaming video, Voice over Internet Protocol (VoIP) telephone service, mobile TV, photo sharing, and interactive gaming.

In 2006 the company started producing platforms for the dominant GSM networks. Starent made a breakthrough in the GSM sphere in March 2008 with a contract with Vodafone to supply equipment for its German network and become a preferred worldwide vendor for the company. At almost the same time, it scored a major success in the WiMAX market when Sprint agreed to use its equipment in setting up its long-anticipated Xohm network. In early 2008 Starent introduced the Femtocell Gateway, anticipating the emergence of femtocells, low-power wireless base stations that utilize broadband cable or DSL connections to link mobile devices to carriers' networks. Mobile carriers could use femtocells to provide services indoors and in other difficult situations. The company rolled out the Starent XT30 Service Convergence Platform in 2009, which supported femtocells among other cutting-edge applications.

OPTIMISM FOR THE FUTURE

The wireless telecom industry continued to prosper in late 2008 and 2009, defying the worldwide economic recession as the use of so-called smart phones and other portable media devices equipped with e-mail and Internet access continued to spread. The escalating demand for bandwidth drove telecom companies to turn to suppliers, such as Starent, for assistance. The company was still securing new clients. In June 2009, leading U.S. cable provider Cox Communications announced that it would use Starent technology to build its network as it entered the mobile wireless market. Not surprisingly the company's stock values surged from a low of $7.30 in November 2008 to more than $23 by June 2009, reaching a total market capitalization of about $1.8 billion as analysts predicted a bright future.

Stephen V. Beitel

PRINCIPAL SUBSIDIARIES

Starent Network Securities Corp.; Starent International, Corp.; Starent Networks Japan, K.K.; Starent do Brasil Ltda; Starent Networks (India) Pvt. Ltd.; Starent Networks Beijing Co., Ltd.; Starent Networks (UK) Ltd.; Starent Networks Spain, S.L.

PRINCIPAL COMPETITORS

Cisco Systems, Inc.; Huawei Technologies Co., Ltd.; Nokia Oyj; Siemens AG; Telefonaktiebolaget L. M. Ericsson; UTStarcom, Inc.

FURTHER READING

Carroll, Kelly, "Voice Is the Next Generation," *Wireless Review*, July 1, 2002.

"China's Eastcom to Deploy Starent Networks Next Generation Infrastructure; Companies to Jointly Pursue China's Rapidly Growing Mobile Market," *Business Wire*, December 10, 2001, p. 2282.

"Court Grants Starent Networks' Motion for Summary Judgment of Noninfringement of UTStarcom Patent," *Business Wire*, December 12, 2005.

Fitchard, Kevin, "CTIA: Starent Makes Jump to GGSN," *Telephony*, March 31, 2008.

———, "Starent Preparing for 3G 'Tidal Wave.' (Starent Networks Introduces Traffic Control Equipment)," *Telephony*, May 19, 2009.

Harlin, Kevin, "STARENT NETWORKS CORP. Tewksbury, Massachusetts Gear Maker's Hardware Speeds Data along Cellular Networks," *Investor's Business Daily*, February 11, 2009, p. A6.

Hoover, Ken, "Starent Rides Demand for Mobile Internet," *Investor's Business Daily*, May 13, 2009, p. B3.

Howe, Peter J., "Telecom Start-up Gains VC Funding," *Boston Globe*, November 11, 2001.

———, "Tewksbury Firm Cashes in as Internet Calling Grows," *Boston Globe*, March 7, 2005.

———, "Tewksbury, Mass., Wireless Start-up Picks up $25 Million in New Investments," *Boston Globe*, April 6, 2004.

Johnsson, Julie, "The Future of Your Addiction Is Now; Crain's Intrepid Tech Writer Checks out What's New on the Scene," *Crain's Chicago Business*, February 27, 2006, p. 22.

Omatseye, Sam, "Chinese Vendors Partner to Play in WTO Wireless Arena," *RCR Wireless News*, April 22, 2002, p. 1.

———, "Smart Antennas Valuable in Network Enhancement," *RCR Wireless News*, September 30, 2002, p. 8.

———, "Starent Voice Instant Messaging Solution May Challenge PTT Services," *RCR Wireless News*, May 19, 2003, p. 17.

Reeves, Amy, "Firm Thrives in Age of Supercharged Cell Phones," *Investor's Business Daily*, May 29, 2007, p. A4.

"Samsung Selects Starent Networks' Platform for Global Deployments; Solution to Provide New High-Speed Services to CDMA2000 Wireless Networks," *Business Wire*, November 12, 2001, p. 2222.

"SK Telecom to Build 3G System with Starent Networks' Gateway," *Business Wire*, September 2, 2003, p. 5041.

"Starent Networks Chosen for China Unicom Network Expansion; Deal to Include New VPN and Billing Service Capabilities," *Business Wire*, June 14, 2004, p. 5082.

"Starent Networks Offers Femtocell Solution," *Business Wire*, February 11, 2008.

"Starent Networks Ships Gateway Offering Unique Services Through Voice and Data Integration; Starent ST16 Intelligent Mobile Gateway Signals New Breed of Wireless Access," *Business Wire*, June 24, 2002, p. 2214.

"Starent Networks Signs New Customer: CHINA PUTIAN, China's Number One Telecommunications Enterprise; Companies to Jointly Pursue the World's Largest Mobile Market," *Business Wire*, February 25, 2002, p. 2203.

"Starent Networks Unveils Platform for High-Demand Mobile Multimedia Networks," *Business Wire*, April 16, 2007.

"Starent to Offer Network Mobility Solution for Sprint Xohm WiMAX Service," *Wireless News*, April 7, 2008.

"Starent to Support Cox Communications' Wireless Network," *Wireless News*, June 3, 2009.

"Unicom Using Starent; RealNetworks Takes Open Approach," *Wireless Data News*, November 6, 2002.

"VIVO Selects Starent Networks for Its Mobile Wireless Network; Company Cites Innovation and Service Flexibility as Winning Criteria," *Business Wire*, May 19, 2003, p. 5225.

Sterling Financial Corporation

111 North Wall Street
Spokane, Washington 99201-0609
U.S.A.
Telephone: (509) 458-3711
Toll Free: (800) 650-7141
Fax: (509) 458-2391
Web site: http://www.sterlingfinancialcorporation-spokane.com/

Public Company
Founded: 1981 as Sterling Savings Association
Incorporated: 1992
Employees: 2,571
Total Assets: $12.69 billion (2009 est.)
Stock Exchanges: NASDAQ
Ticker Symbol: STSA
NAICS: 522120 Savings Institutions; 522110 Commercial Banking; 523930 Investment Advice; 551111 Offices of Bank Holding Companies

■■■

Sterling Financial Corporation, with headquarters in Spokane, Washington, is the largest banking institution based in Washington. It is the parent company of Sterling Savings Bank, which has nearly 200 branches in Washington, Oregon, California, Idaho, and Montana. Over 250,000 individual depositors and 20,000 businesses use the bank's full-service banking services. The bank is involved in mortgage lending and commercial real estate and construction lending and offers mutual funds and other investment instruments. A long series of carefully selected acquisitions, cultivation of a "Hometown Helpful" bank image, and a conservative investment strategy have helped Sterling Financial Corporation's progress toward its goal of becoming the preeminent community bank in its region.

FOUNDING AND EARLY YEARS

Harold Gilkey and William Zuppe founded the Sterling Savings Association in Spokane, Washington, in October 1981 and began conducting business in April 1983. Even before the new bank opened its doors, state regulators had encouraged it to take over another Washington bank, Lewis and Clark Savings and Loan, giving Sterling Savings Association assets of more than $50 million almost right from the start. It seemed to be an auspicious time to form a savings-and-loan institution. Capital requirements were much lower for starting a thrift than for starting a commercial bank. A series of laws and relaxed federal regulations had expanded the kinds of business savings and loans were allowed to conduct, fostering increased profitability. Many thrift institutions had grown very rapidly, with some investing their profits in high-risk investments in other areas. By the mid-1980s these ambitious and overextended savings and loans were beginning to fail.

Sterling Savings Association soon was highly regarded for skillful management, unlike many of its industry peers. As a result, in 1985 when the Federal Savings and Loan Insurance Corporation (FSLIC) was scrambling to stave off the collapse of additional faltering savings and loan institutions (S&Ls), Sterling was one of the relatively strong S&L banks that received

COMPANY PERSPECTIVES

Sterling is dedicated to providing a high level of quality financial services to its customers. Sterling is committed to managing a safe and sound financial institution, which builds value for its shareholders and opportunity for its employees.

Sterling's long-range goals include the following: Maximize shareholder value; Be a community bank; Remain entrepreneurial to benefit shareholders; Provide leadership in local communities.

funds to help it purchase an insolvent bank. The FSLIC assured Sterling and the other purchasers that capital could include the difference between the purchase price and the book value of the assets of the banks they purchased, also known as "supervisory goodwill." The S&Ls were also allowed to write off the costs on generous depreciation schedules.

In 1987 Sterling was listed on the NASDAQ over-the-counter exchange as well as on the Spokane Stock Exchange. Sterling continued to acquire competing banks and opened more branches. By 1988 Sterling reported $700 million in assets and was of the top 10 S&Ls in the state. That year, Sterling acquired two more failing thrifts with FSLIC assistance.

STANDING UP TO GOVERNMENT PRESSURE

In 1989 the U.S. Congress approved legislation known as the Financial Institutions Reform, Recovery, and Enforcement Act of 1989 (FIRREA) to rescue the savings-and-loan industry. The U.S. Office of Thrift Supervision (OTS) also was established with the objective of tightening control on S&L activities. FIRREA rescinded the goodwill allowances these banks had been granted and made them responsible for the full liabilities of the institutions they had acquired. As a result, even though Sterling Savings Association continued to report profits, its balance sheet had begun to show signs of trouble. The bank seemed to be caught in a no-win situation. Sterling was unwilling to issue preferred stock to raise the required additional capital required by the OTS to remain independent because the regulators refused to allow the bank to offer dividends on that stock, citing insufficient capital.

Dissatisfied with the bank's recovery plans, OTS regulators threatened to force the bank to put itself up

for sale and solicit bids from potential buyers. Sterling resisted this pressure and won a restraining order in May 1990 in U.S. District Court that prevented the OTS from taking control and shutting it. The bank also filed a lawsuit against the OTS for breach of the contracts it had made with FSLIC to rescue the three banks Sterling had purchased.

Sterling's breach of contract litigation against the OTS would be stalled in the courts. The U.S. Supreme Court ruled in 1996 that FIRREA was responsible for breaking the contracts of Sterling and other banks that had purchased insolvent thrifts under FSLIC sanctions. However, determination of damages remained unresolved for Sterling, and it would have to wait in line behind dozens of other banks to have its case heard. The plaintiffs in these cases sought not only to recover the value of the supervisory goodwill, but also the potential profits that had been lost as a result of the restrictions for making loans and issuing stock. In Sterling's case, that figure was estimated to be as high as $90 million. Unlike most of the other banks, Sterling had grown rapidly and consistently beginning in the 1990s, which actually made its lawsuit more difficult to settle, especially since the U.S. Justice Department argued that Sterling's growth proved that government actions had not materially harmed the bank.

RECOVERY AND RENEWED EXPANSION

After Sterling Savings Association had freed itself from OTS pressure, management turned with relief to renewing the bank's growth. It was able to issue 2.5 million shares of common stock in November 1991 at an opening price of about $8. In 1994 Sterling Savings Association offered one million shares of preferred stock at $25 per share. The common share price continued its general upward trend during the 1990s.

In 1992 Sterling Savings Association became a wholly owned subsidiary of the newly created Sterling Financial Corporation holding company. During the next few years the bank grew steadily, opening numerous branches throughout Washington and purchasing branches from other banks. It also acquired one bank completely, American Liberty Corp. of Oakland, California, in 1994. Sterling Financial Corporation had become the largest Spokane-based bank, and although it conducted most of its business in western Washington, bank management insisted on staying in Spokane, citing lower costs and a higher quality of employees. The bank demonstrated its commitment to its hometown by erecting an architecturally distinctive headquarters building in downtown Spokane that opened in 1994.

KEY DATES

1983: Sterling Savings Association opens for business in Spokane, Washington.

1988: Sterling purchases insolvent savings and loans, Key Bank and Big Sky Corp., with the aid of federal funds.

1990: Sterling obtains a court injunction against threats of federal regulators to shut down the bank for insufficient capital.

1992: Sterling Financial Corp. is created as a holding company for Sterling Savings Association.

1998: Sterling Savings Association changes its name to Sterling Savings Bank.

2005: Sterling obtains a commercial bank charter.

2008: U.S. government appeals $1 million judgment in Sterling's lawsuit against U.S. banking regulators.

In spite of the bank's rapid growth, Sterling management chafed under the restrictive savings and loan regulations that had been tightened again after a crisis in the late 1980s. For example, S&Ls had to devote at least 65 percent of their assets to home mortgages. Co-founder Harold Gilkey expressed concern that the S&L industry remained in danger of collapse because its insurance fund was so small that the collapse of one thrift might bankrupt it. At the same time thrifts were paying high premiums to support the fund, which made it harder for them to compete against commercial banks.

In the mid-1990s Sterling's efforts were concentrated on a proposed conversion of the remaining S&Ls into commercial banks and combine their insurance funds. However, when this plan was stopped Sterling Financial Corporation resolved to meet the requirements for a commercial bank charter the long way. It continued to shift its portfolio from residential to commercial, strengthened the quality of its professional staff, opened centers to serve corporate clients, and built up its capital and assets by issuing securities and acquiring competitors. In early 1998 the bank acquired 33 branches from KeyBank National Association in Oregon, Idaho, and Washington and expanded into Montana when it purchased Big Sky Bancorp. In conjunction with these purchases, Sterling Savings Association changed its name to Sterling Savings Bank in June 1988. Acquisitions continued in the first decade of the twenty-first century as the bank acquired Source

Financial Corp. in 2001. Sterling announced the takeover of Klamath First Bancorp in Oregon in July 2003, which brought $1.5 billion and pushed Sterling's total assets to more than $5 billion.

AMBITIOUS PLANS AND PARTIAL VICTORIES

Sterling reached a milestone in its plans for growth when it received a commercial bank charter in Washington in July 2005. No longer encumbered with restrictions, the bank began another series of acquisitions, reorganizing and reconfiguring its business lines to further emphasize commercial loans. In February 2006 it acquired Lynwood Financial Group Inc., which served as the holding company for Golf Savings Bank, a leading mortgage lender in Washington. Sterling made Golf Savings Bank a subsidiary specializing in single-family residential mortgage lending, while Sterling Savings Bank would specialize in commercial lending. That June, Sterling purchased FirstBank NW Corp. of Clarkston, Washington, which was followed by the July acquisition of Mason-McDuffie Financial Corp. of Oakland and the September purchase of Northern Empire Bancshares of Santa Rosa, California. The bank also had opened mortgage offices in such far-flung locations as Reno, Denver, and Phoenix, hinting that they were potential areas of expansion. By 2007 Sterling's lending portfolio included approximately 60 percent of commercial and construction loans.

The stock market seemed to support Sterling's ambitions and successes as the bank's stock generally rose after 2000, remaining consistently high from 2004 through the first half of 2007. The stock reached an all-time high in December 2006 (taking into account stock splits). However, in mid-2007 Sterling shares began a steady decline that increased as the effects of the subprime lending crisis in the United States began to ripple through the banking industry and the global economy.

Sterling continued searching for takeover targets. Co-founder Gilkey announced in June 2007 to *American Banker* that the bank planned to double its total assets to more than $20 billion over the next three to five years to reach its goal of becoming a leading middle-tier community bank. However, the bank's ambitious expansion strategy hit some snags. A planned takeover of North Valley Bancorp of Redding, California, in April 2007 was delayed, in part because the Federal Deposit Insurance Corporation (FDIC), which had assumed responsibility for regulating the S&Ls, suspected that the bank was expanding too rapidly after completing three acquisitions the previous year. North Valley was frustrated by repeated delays during which they were not informed about the negotiations between Sterling and the FDIC, so it withdrew from the agreed merger in December. By this time Sterling management had resolved to avoid further mergers until the subprime mortgage lending crisis had passed.

Meanwhile, Sterling's lawsuit against the U.S. Office of Thrift Supervision was resolved in the summer of 2007 when a U.S. Court of Federal Claims judge traveled to Spokane to take testimony. In February 2008 the judge ruled in favor of Sterling but awarded only $1 million in damages, but the figure was much lower than the legal fees the bank had spent. When the U.S. Department of Justice appealed the decision, the judge agreed with the government's reasoning that the bank's skillful financial management and rapid recovery after the threatened federal shutdown in 1989–90 justified denial of the full damages sought.

WEATHERING THE ECONOMIC STORM

Sterling was unable to escape the effects of the banking downturn and ensuring economic recession in the summer and fall of 2008 with real estate values plummeting around the United States and new housing construction starts shrinking. Although the bank had not offered subprime loans, much of its loan portfolio had been placed in construction and commercial real estate during the subprime boom of the preceding years, and it suffered from the decline of residential construction. As some of these loan clients began to default, the bank was forced to write off increasing quantities of nonperforming loans.

However, Sterling suffered somewhat less than many of its peers. For example, the bank had not invested equity in Fannie Mae and Freddie Mac, the U.S. government-supported mortgage consolidators that were on the verge of collapse. Sterling reported an overall loss in 2008 for the first time since 1996, with losses swelling to $356.3 million in the fourth quarter of that year. In addition, its stock value plummeted from as high as $15 in October 2008 to less than $2 by February 2009 before it recovered slightly later in that year. Nonetheless, Sterling managed to retain most of its asset value through the first half of 2009. In December 2008 the bank decided to accept $303 million in funds from the U.S. Treasury's Capital Purchase Program that had been intended to support lending to stimulate the faltering economy. The bank continued to look optimistically toward the future and moved ahead with the remodeling and expansion of its headquarters building in Spokane in spring 2009.

More than two decades after founding Sterling Savings Association, and guiding the institution's growth beyond their original ambitions, co-founders Gilkey and Zuppe remained at the bank's helm. However, they prepared carefully to hand over responsibility to a new set of managers. Zuppe retired from the company at the end of 2007 and was replaced by Heidi Stanley as president and chief executive officer of Sterling Savings Bank. In 2009 Stanley replaced Zuppe as chairman of the board of directors of the bank as well. In mid-2009 Harold Gilkey retained his positions as CEO and chairman of the board of Sterling Financial Corp.

Stephen V. Beitel

PRINCIPAL SUBSIDIARIES

Action Mortgage Company; The Dime Service Corporation; Golf Savings Bank; Harbor Financial Services, Inc.; Intervest-Mortgage Investment Company; Sterling Savings Bank.

PRINCIPAL COMPETITORS

Bank of America; U.S. Bancorp; Wells Fargo.

FURTHER READING

Caldwell, Bert, "Court Opens Door for Sterling Decision, Allows Thrift to Seek $90 Million Damage Claim," *Spokesman-Review* (Spokane, WA), July 2, 1996, p. A6.

———, "Justice Department to Appeal Sterling Ruling," *Spokesman-Review* (Spokane, WA), April 23, 2008.

———, "New Sterling Building Completed: Downtown Boasts Its Latest Improvement," *Spokesman-Review* (Spokane, WA), September 30, 1994, p. A16.

———, "Rescue Plan Robs Thrifts of Identity: Gilkey Expects S&Ls Will Become Commercial Banks," *Spokesman-Review* (Spokane, WA), August 3, 1995, p. A10.

———, "Sterling, Feds Are Getting Reacquainted," *Spokesman-Review* (Spokane, WA), July 8, 2007.

———, "Sterling Financial Corp. to Acquire Branches in Idaho, Oregon, Washington," *Spokesman Review* (Spokane, WA), February 9, 1998.

———, "Sterling Is Fighting for Principal—and Principle," *Spokesman-Review* (Spokane, WA), March 27, 2007.

———, "Sterling Paves Way for Change," *Spokesman Review* (Spokane, WA), October 25, 1995, p. A12.

———, "Sterling's Earnings Hit by Home-Loan Woes," *Spokesman-Review* (Spokane, WA), April 11, 2008.

———, "Sterling Wins Bank Charter, Bright Future," *Spokesman-Review* (Spokane, WA), July 26, 2005.

———, "Sterling Wins Suit against Feds: Judge Sides with Financial Firm, but Limits Damages to $1 Million," *Spokesman-Review* (Spokane, WA), February 23, 2008.

Caldwell, Bert, and Tom Sowa, "Sterling Closes Food Court Area for Remodeling of Headquarters," *Spokesman-Review* (Spokane, WA), May 8, 2009.

Cole, Jim, "For Washington's Sterling, Midtier Is the Endgame," *American Banker*, June 14, 2007, p. 1.

Dobbs, Kevin, "North Valley Cancels Deal with Sterling of Spokane," *American Banker*, December 4, 2007, p. 2.

Harrell, Lisa, "Sterling Remaking Itself into a Bank," *Journal of Business-Spokane*, May 8, 1997, p. B1.

Jackson, Ben, "Wash.'s Sterling Says Deal Furthers Its Transformation," *American Banker*, February 14, 2006, p. 1.

Kuehner-Hebert, Katie, "Nixing Offer Leads to Far Better One," *American Banker*, June 6, 2006, p. 1.

———, "Sterling Advances Its Bid to Be Force in Northwest," *American Banker*, July 16, 2003, p. 1.

Little, Melodie, "Community Assets: Sterling Savings Grows while Keeping Its Regional Focus," *Spokesman-Review* (Spokane, WA), July 9, 2006.

———, "Sterling Expands Operations in California," *Spokesman-Review* (Spokane, WA), September 19, 2006.

———, "Sterling Job: Zuppe to Relinquish Day-to-Day Control of Bank," *Spokesman-Review* (Spokane, WA), October 23, 2007.

Reosti, John, "Wash. Thrift Sterling to Buy Realty Lender," *American Banker*, July 2, 2001, p. 6.

Ripley, Richard, "Sterling Sees Wildfire Growth," *Journal of Business-Spokane*, June 23, 1994, p. 1.

"Sterling Financial Corporation of Spokane, Washington, Has No Exposure to Fannie Mae or Freddie Mac Equity Investments," *Business Wire*, September 12, 2008.

"Sterling Financial Corporation to Participate in U.S. Treasury Capital Purchase Program," *Business Wire*, November 24, 2008.

Virgin, Bill, "Lynnwood Financial Being Bought by Spokane's Sterling," *Seattle Post-Intelligencer*, February 14, 2006, p. C3.

———, "Win Some, Lose Some: Banks' Tale of 2 Funds," *Seattle Post-Intelligencer*, October 20, 1995, p. D1.

Whiteman, Louis, "Wash. Bank Unveils Montana Thrift Deal," *American Banker*, May 4, 1998, p. 7.

Tecmo Koei Holdings Company Ltd.

1-18-12 Minowa
Kouhoku
Yokohama, 223-8503
Japan
Telephone: (+81 45) 562-8111
Web site: http://tecmokoei.co.uk
http://www.koeitecmo.co.jp

Public Company
Founded: 2009
Employees: 1,700
Sales: ¥42 billion ($454.36 million) (2009 est.)
Stock Exchanges: Tokyo
Ticker Symbol: 9650
NAICS: 511210 Software Publishers

■ ■ ■

Tecmo Koei Holdings Company Ltd. was established in April 2009 following the merger of Tecmo Ltd. and Koei Corporation. Koei was the eighth-largest video game publisher in Japan, whereas Tecmo was not even in the top 10. By merging, Tecmo and Koei became the sixth-largest gaming studio in Japan, and its company executives hoped to use the relative strengths of the former companies to reach action gamers in Western markets. With foreign markets making up 70 percent of its sales, Tecmo is better known overseas, whereas Koei and its many games are better known in Asia. The merger thus married a company that has strong distribution networks with a smaller firm that has popular software that can be sold in new markets. In 2009 the

company planned to market the eagerly anticipated *Ninja Gaiden Sigma 2* and *Trinity: Souls of Zill O'll* and develop several new titles. It also hinted that players may see crossover characters in future versions of its most popular games.

TECMO: FIERCE AND FAST

Originally named Teikoku Kanzai, Tecmo began as a cleaning supply company when it was established in 1967 by Yoshihito Kakihara. Three years later it entered the arcade game market. The company changed its name to Tehkan (an abbreviation of Teikoku Kanzai) in 1981 and then to Tecmo Ltd. in 1986. Tecmo's most popular action games were the *Dead or Alive* and *Ninja Gaiden* series, *Undead Knight*, and *Quantum Theory*. In 2007 it reported sales of ¥12 billion and an operating profit of ¥1.9 billion.

First released in 2004, *Ninja Gaiden* was famous for its degree of difficulty and dynamic high-speed action. "I'm not a controller thrower," one user told *Electronic Gaming Monthly* in June 2004, "but my [Xbox pad] hit the wall a few times and the television once … really hard." Players followed the adventures of super-ninja Ryu Hayabusa, who had to defeat a series of 100 powerful opponents to reclaim a magical sword and avenge his clan's defeat at the hands of the Vigor Empire. The game's creator Tomonobu Itagaki explained, "I'm hoping that everyone can clear Ninja Gaiden in the normal mode, 50 percent in hard mode, and less than 10 percent in very hard mode."

The *Dead or Alive* (DOA) game series began in video arcades and graduated from action game to action

COMPANY PERSPECTIVES

In April 2009, KOEI CO., LTD., and TECMO, LTD., merged to form TECMO KOEI HOLDINGS CO., LTD. The combined organization seeks to be the top entertainment content creation group in the world, through expanding its game lineup, developing new content, promoting entertainment properties in new markets, creating a worldwide brand through region-specific strategies, and promoting the fusion of eastern and western cultures through globalization of human resources and management.

movie in 2007. Moby Games summed up the plot as "a series of fighting games [that] feature a heavy focus on counterattacks and interactive environments, but are best known for their improbably-proportioned female characters." In fact, the company had problems with hackers who discovered how to remove the characters' cyber swimsuits. According to the BBC, in April 2003 the company posted a stern warning on its Web site: "Please do not post anything about nude patches and other hacked information or you will be punished to the fullest extent of the law. So far we're tracking one suspect, anybody care to be the second?"

In 2002 Tecmo inked a deal with Mindfire Entertainment to produce a live-action movie based on the series. The Web site Yahoo! Games noted in March 2002 that the president of Mindfire, Mark Altman, declared, "DOA has set the standard for fighting games on every next-generation gaming console and has a loyal fan base throughout the world that is eagerly anticipating the release of a feature film based on this extraordinary video game series." Released in 2007, the movie *Dead or Alive* was widely panned, with reviews playing off the name. The plot, which the movie review Web site Rotten Tomatoes warned required "checking one's brain at the door," involved a group of men and bikini-clad women engaging in martial arts contests on a tropical island. The film earned $260,713.

DEPARTURES OF TOP PROGRAMMER AND PRESIDENT

Tecmo encountered two major personnel crises in 2008. First, it lost Tomonobu Itagaki, one of the top programmers in the Japanese sector, in June. Known as the head ninja character in *Ninja Gaiden*, Itagaki sued Tecmo, claiming that he had been cheated out of several bonus

offers. Spong.com reported in June 2008 that Tecmo criticized Itagaki in a formal statement, saying, "The reasons for making this lawsuit public are self-centered. … This employee is filing this suit for himself and making it seem like he alone is responsible for the development of the game titles the rest of the Team Ninja staff had poured its heart into." Analysts, such as Jay Defibaugh of Credit Suisse, saw Itagaki's departure as a blow to marketing Tecmo products because he had a loyal following and cultivated a rock-star image by always wearing sunglasses and leather clothing. Defibaugh told Kenji Hall of *Business Week*, "Selling games is as much about building buzz as it is about coming up with a great game."

The second crisis was in August, when Yoshimi Yasuda, the president of Tecmo, resigned. Even though he insisted that any bonus deal for Itagaki had been made by the former president and not approved by the Tecmo board, audiotapes played during the trial contradicted Yasuda's claim and humiliated him. He was also involved in a second lawsuit about questionable overtime practices. Yasuharu Kakihara, Yoshihito Kakihara's son and chairman of the board of directors, was named president.

KOEI: HISTORY OVER FLASH

In 1978 Yoichi Erikawa and his wife, Keiko Erikawa, founded Koei as an extension of their computer retail store. Keiko served as president and chairman, while Yoichi focused on programming. Their products quickly became well known because they were available on multiple platforms and because of their decidedly adult orientation. The first title, *Night Life*, released in 1983, featured a sex diary among other features. The second game was *Tempting Housewife in the Building*, with an equally adult content.

The Erikawas used the profits from these early releases to develop a new genre: strategy games. Rusel DeMaria and Johnny L. Wilson noted that these elaborate games "mixed economic decision making, human resource management, military tactics, and diplomatic skill into exciting historical simulations." Koei eventually developed a library of historical strategy games, including *Nobunaga's Ambition*, *Romance of the Three Kingdoms*, *Genghis Khan*, and *Bandit Kings of Ancient China*.

Koei claimed a significant portion of the Japanese gaming market in the early 1980s with an innovative programming code that would work on the multiple

KEY DATES

1967: Teikoku Kanzai is founded by Yoshihito Kakihara.

1970: Teikoku Kanzai begins selling arcade games in Japan.

1978: Koei Corporation is founded by Yoichi Erikawa and Keiko Erikawa.

1981: Teikoku Kanzai changes its name to Tehkan.

1986: Tehkan changes its name to Tecmo Ltd.

2006: Tecmo founder Kakihara dies.

2009: Tecmo and Koei join forces to create Tecmo Koei Holdings Company Ltd.

platforms that were then competing for dominance. "KOEI DOS" worked on NEC, Mitsubishi, and Sony machines. The Erikawas hired U.S. programmer Bill Swartz in the late 1980s to streamline *Nobunaga's Ambition* and *Romance of the Three Kingdoms* and revise the game's program manuals. *Nobunaga's Ambition* debuted in the United States in 1990.

More recently, Koei had success with its *Dynasty Warriors* series, which drew on characters and storylines from Japanese and Chinese history. Another popular offering was *Gitaroo-Man*, a music game. In 2007 Koei's sales topped ¥29.1 billion, and its operating profit was ¥6.6 billion.

In spite of Koei's success in Asia, it failed to make headway in Western markets. This was mostly because the characters in the games were based on historical figures from Chinese and Japanese history, with which many Western gamers were unfamiliar. Also, Western gamers preferred fast-action play over the slower, strategy-based play of games such as *Dynasty Warriors*.

MERGER PROPOSALS

In September 2008 Square Enix Company Ltd. approached Tecmo with a tender offer of $206 million. The proposal seemed ideal. Square Enix had a large global distribution system, and Tecmo had an impressive software library. Yoichi Wada, the president of Square Enix, explained to Kenji Hall, "These days, you need a certain amount of scale" to be profitable.

Tecmo, however, rejected the proposal and immediately began merger talks with Koei. Even though Square Enix had pledged to retain the Tecmo brand and offered a 30 percent premium on stock, Hall surmised that the smaller firm's owners may have been reluctant

to join such a large firm: "Rather than getting swallowed up, Tecmo may have wanted something closer to a marriage of equals." With Koei, Tecmo would be on a more equal footing rather than a junior partner. Announcing the deal, Tecmo and Koei declared, "Through a merger, we hope to grow by respecting each other's identities and creating an environment that will let employees fully show off their skills."

Many shareholders were not enthusiastic about the proposed merger. In particular, the Singapore-based Effissimo Capital Management, which held a 17.6 percent stake in Tecmo, opposed the merger. Effissimo was the company's second-largest shareholder. *1Up* reported in December 2008 that Takashi Kosaka, the director of Effissimo, noted in a protest filed with the Japanese Ministry of Finance, "We have not had sufficient information from the company to make a judgment on the merger, such as the feasibility of their plan to raise shareholder value."

In spite of Effissimo's protest, the shareholders of both Koei and Tecmo approved the merger in January 2009. Under the terms of the deal, Koei acquired Tecmo for a ¥20 billion stock agreement, nearly double the amount proposed by Square Enix. Tecmo's shareholders received 0.9 shares of the new holding company for each share they held, and Koei's investors received shares in the merged company on a one-to-one ratio.

Koei's president, Kenji Matsubara, was named president of Tecmo Koei Holdings Company Ltd., and Yasuharu Kakihara became the chairman. The Erikawas were named members of the new holding company's board of directors. In explaining the logic behind the merger, Matsubara told Edge Online in October 2008 that the Erikawas had been "close long-time friends" of Yoshihito Kakihara, and he suggested that the change would reassure investors who had been concerned by the recent personnel issues at Tecmo.

EXPANSION STRATEGY

In July 2009 Matsubara outlined a corporate strategy based on expanding products, markets, and platforms. Before the merger, there was little demand in Japan for PlayStation 3 and Xbox, the action-gaming platforms. Matsubara explained to Kat Bailey of *1Up*, "The reason is that [casual Japanese] gamers are waiting for the right time to buy one. They're waiting for a good title made especially for either platform. But this is a publisher and developer problem—we haven't yet provided such a title to satisfy such users." Because demand was high in Western markets, Matsubara noted that "we're hiring developers not only within Japan but overseas too, like in Singapore and Toronto."

To meet market demand, Tecmo Koei decided to focus on all gaming platforms. Following the success of *Tecmo Bowl* for the Nintendo DS, for example, the company planned to launch *Family Fun Football* and *Samurai Warriors 3* for the Nintendo Wii in the fall of 2009, along with *Ninja Gaiden Sigma 2* for PlayStation 3. According to Steve Watts of *1Up*, in July 2009 Matsubara also called on Sony to reduce the cost of the PlayStation 3 to encourage buyers.

In 2009 the new company had combined annual sales of $370 million in 2009, which was still only a fraction of the gaming industry's $48 billion per year.

Ann E. Robertson

PRINCIPAL SUBSIDIARIES

Tecmo Koei Europe Ltd.; Koei Company Ltd.; Tecmo Ltd.

PRINCIPAL COMPETITORS

Konami Corporation; Namco Bandai Games America Inc.; Sega Corporation; Square Enix Company Ltd.; Capcom Entertainment Inc.

FURTHER READING

Alpeyev, Pavel, and Kiyotaka Matsuda, "Koei Plan to Form Holding Company with Tecmo in 2009 (Update 2)," Bloomberg.com, October 1, 2008, http://www.bloomberg.com/apps/news?pid=20601101&sid=aU.bumqOUFnQ&refer=japan.

Ashcraft, Brian, "Troubled Tecmo President Resigns!" Kotaku.com, August 20, 2008, http://kotaku.com/5039243/troubled-tecmo-president-resigns.

Bailey, Kat, "Tecmo Koei Outlines Strategy for Western Market," *1Up*, July 7, 2009.

"Dead or Alive Movie in the Works," Yahoo! Games, March 12, 2002, http://videogames.yahoo.com/news-1109197.

"Dead or Alive Series: Group Description," Moby Games, 2009, http://www.mobygames.com/game-group/dead-or-alive-series.

DeMaria, Rusel, and Johnny L. Wilson, *High Score!: The Illustrated History of Electronic Games*, 2nd ed., Emeryville, CA: McGraw Hill/Osborne, 2004.

"DOA: Dead or Alive (2007)," Rotten Tomatoes, 2007, http://www.rottentomatoes.com/m/doa_dead_or_alive.

Doree, Adam, "Interview: Tecmo Koei CEO, Kenji Matsubara," Kikizo.com, July 3, 2009, http://games.kikizo.com/features/interview-tecmo-koei-president-kenji-matsubara-p1.asp.

"Game Software Makers Koei, Tecmo to Integrate Biz," *Jiji*, November 18, 2008.

Gantayat, Anoop, "Tecmo Koei Holdings Opens Shop," Andriasang.com, April 1, 2009, http://www.andriasang.com/e/blog/2009/04/01/tecmo_koei_holdings.

Hall, Kenji, "The Tug-of-War among Japanese Video Game Makers," *BusinessWeek*, September 5, 2008.

"Investment Fund Opposes Tecmo-Koei Merger," *Jiji*, December 25, 2008.

"Kenji Matsubara Interview," Edge Online, October 15, 2008, http://www.edge-online.com/features/kenji-matsubara-interview.

"Koei and Tecmo Merger Takes Shape," *Screen Digest*, December 2008, p. 376.

"Koei, Tecmo Receive OK from Shareholders for April Merger," *AsiaPulse News*, January 27, 2009.

"Major Tecmo Shareholder Hesitant about Koei Merger," *1Up*, December 27, 2008.

"Ninja Gaiden," *Electronic Gaming Monthly*, October 1, 2003.

"Ninja Gaiden," *Electronic Gaming Monthly*, June 1, 2004.

"Nude Volleyball Angers Game Makers," BBC News, April 1, 2003.

Pereira, Chris, "Tecmo-Koei Merger Gets the Go-Ahead," *1Up*, January 26, 2009.

Quillen, Dustin, "Editorial: Why We're Not So Keen on the Tecmo/Koei Merger," *1Up*, September 4, 2008.

"Tecmo Koei Interview," ComputerAndVideoGames.com, July 6, 2009.

"Tecmo Ready to Turn Fighting Game into Movie," *Japan Toy and Game Software Journal*, June 25, 2002.

"Tecmo: Tomonobu Itagaki Distorted Facts," Spong.com, June 4, 2008, http://news.spong.com/article/15508/Tecmo-Tomonobu-Itagaki-Distorted-Facts.

Watts, Steve, "Tecmo Koei Asks Sony to 'Please Cut [PS3] Price'," *1Up*, July 3, 2009.

Telkom S.A. Ltd.

24th Floor
Telkom Towers North
152 Proes Street
Pretoria, 0002
South Africa
Telephone: (+27 12) 311-3536
Fax: (+27 12) 311-5721
Web site: http://www.telkom.co.za

Public Company
Founded: 1991
Employees: 23,520
Sales: ZAR 6.4 billion ($815.65 million) (2009)
Stock Exchanges: Johannesburg New York
Ticker Symbol: TKG
NAICS: 517110 Wired Telecommunications Carriers; 517212 Cellular and Other Wireless Telecommunications; 517310 Telecommunications Resellers

■ ■ ■

As the largest communications company in South Africa, Telkom S.A. Ltd. provides integrated communications services to both business and residential customers. The company offers landline and cell phone and Internet services throughout the country. In addition, it has taken a major part in constructing and maintaining the undersea cable that now connects several African countries with countries in Europe and Asia.

ARRIVAL OF PRIVATIZATION

Communications service greatly improved after the new South African government came to power in 1994. Before 1994, when the apartheid era officially ended, Telkom was a subsidiary of the government's Department of Posts and Telegraphs and was run as a parastatal (a corporation belonging to the government). The new regime, however, soon realized that this outdated service could not be modernized or made profitable without privatization. The regime also saw it as a way to get rid of the apartheid-era discrimination that had barred almost all black South Africans from having telephone service. As a result, the government decided that rural and urban black communities would henceforth have the phone services they needed and that hospitals, schools, workplaces, and government departments would enjoy more efficient telephone networks. Customer service was also to be completely renovated on all fronts. Furthermore, all of this was to be accomplished as soon as possible with streamlined, world-class technology that could keep pace with the most sophisticated competitors.

The government knew this would not be easy. In fact, it understood that these goals could be reached only by using three interconnected strategic criteria: money, legislative backing, and the expertise of a partner experienced in creating and managing a competitive infrastructure.

The South African government first decided to sell a 30 percent stake in Telkom to a buyer who could meet the first and third criteria. To meet the second criterion, it passed the Telecommunications Act of 1996, which

COMPANY PERSPECTIVES

Our core strategy is to defend and grow profitable revenue, while managing costs. We will seek to defend profitable revenue by providing superior, customized solutions that meet the needs of consumer, business and wholesale customers. We will pursue growth of profitable revenue through fixed-wireless and mobile data services, broadband services and converged services both in South Africa and internationally. We will seek to grow both organically as well as through partnerships and acquisitions, while managing costs.

guaranteed South Africans that they would receive national telephone service. Jay Naidoo, the minister of posts, telecommunications, and broadcasting, outlined the main points of the act in February 1997. He noted that Telkom was to receive a license, valid for 25 years, for public switched telecommunications services (PSTS). The terms of this license obligated Telkom to set up universal telephone service in both urban townships and remote rural villages that did not have an exchange line. Roll-out targets were clearly mandated: 160,000 lines were to be laid out between 1995 and 1996 and another 250,000 were to be laid out between 1996 and 1997, so that the overall goal of 1.8 million lines would be operative within five years.

FIVE-YEAR MONOPOLY

To prepare Telkom for future competition, the act gave the company a five-year monopoly for its PSTS license. It also gave Telkom a value-added network services (VANS) license, which allowed it to broaden its product line with e-mail and Internet offerings. Unlike the PSTS license, the VANS license was also available to other Internet operators. This would eventually cause a great deal of turmoil, because all the other operators would have to buy access to the Internet from Telkom before they could offer Web-based services to their own customers. Mindful of future competition, the act restricted Telkom's five-year monopoly by authorizing its service for both long-distance and local calling, public telephone facilities, Internet access, and even facilities for fixed-lines for mobile telephone services.

These licenses were issued to Telkom in 1997, the same year that SBC Communications Inc. of Texas and Telekom Malaysia agreed to purchase a 30 percent share of Telkom, of which 18 percent would be owned by SBC (later renamed AT&T) and the remaining 12

percent would be owned by Telekom Malaysia. The two companies acquired this share in a venture named Thintana Communications.

Thintana Communications got off to a brisk start by paying ZAR 5.58 billion for its stake and sending a team of experts to South Africa to help install and manage the new infrastructure. A productive year ended well for Telkom, with an attributable 1996–97 profit of ZAR 1.95 billion.

CONTROVERSY OVER INTERNET ACCESS

Despite the presence of Telkom's expert partners, the transformation did not sit well with South Africa's communications community. Complaints from the Internet Service Providers' Association (ISPA), a nonprofit organization representing all Internet providers, were submitted to the South African Telecommunications Regulatory Authority (SATRA), which had been established by the 1996 act to oversee Telkom and to make sure that it followed the act's provisions. These complaints alleged that Telkom was indulging in a conflict of interest because it was selling bandwidth to its customers via Intekom and to other Internet access providers who had no alternative but to buy it. Timothy Wood noted in August 1997 that SATRA tried to improve the situation for these providers by declaring that "the Internet [was] a value-added network service, rather than a public switched telecommunications service, which Telkom only can provide." Wood added that VANS licenses were necessary only for companies providing connectivity services.

Displeased by this declaration, Telkom executives asserted that Internet access service was part of Telkom's PSTS license, not its VANS license. As such, they argued, the company had a monopoly over Internet access service until at least 2002. Nevertheless, as Wood indicated in October 1997, SATRA declared that "the Internet protocol ... was a routing rather than a switching service" and that "access providers can continue routing Internet traffic, and buy bandwidth from Telkom if they have value-added network service licences."

GROWING CHALLENGES

Even though repairs and customer service were improving steadily, Telkom was facing a growing challenge. As international copper prices increased, thieves were becoming increasingly attracted to the copper wire that the company used in its landlines. Copper wire theft was particularly prevalent in remote rural areas, so those

KEY DATES

1991: The Department of Posts and Telecommunications is divided into three entities, one of them being Telkom S.A. Ltd.

1996: The South African government puts a 30 percent stake of Telkom up for sale.

1997: SBC Communications Inc. and Telekom Malaysia agree to buy a 30 percent stake of Telkom, which leads to the creation of the Thintana Communications partnership.

2002: Telkom's period of monopoly comes to an end.

2003: Company is listed on the Johannesburg Stock Exchange and the New York Stock Exchange.

2007: Telkom acquires Africa Online and purchases a 75 percent stake in Multi-links Telecommunications Ltd.

2009: Telkom buys the remaining 25 percent stake in Multi-links.

customers shared the problem of erratic service. This was a constant uphill battle for Telkom, whose technicians often had to travel great distances over unpaved roads.

In spite of this difficulty, Telkom was making progress. The *Economist* indicated in June 2000 that by the end of 1999, 1.6 million new lines had been laid, 86,000 pay phones had been installed, and more than 2,000 villages had been equipped with telephones.

Besides meeting the demand for more landline and Internet service, Telkom was forced to increase its services for cell phones, which were becoming more popular with its customers. The number of cell phones in South Africa had risen from a mere 12,500 in 1993 to 1.6 million by May 1998. By the end of 1999 cell phones were to be found not only in the manicured hangouts of the wealthy but also in the middle-class preserves of status-seekers and even in the urban areas inhabited by the poor. Cell phones had taken on a culturally unique life of their own. In Soweto, near Johannesburg, there were "phone shops" where users could rent time on a cell phone if they did not own one. The wireless service, as one store owner explained to the *Economist* in October 1999, was far more reliable than the landline service, because the latter was dependent on the often-stolen copper wire.

Another challenge that Telkom faced concerned the itemized billing that was stipulated by the government

in the 1996 act. The lives of Telkom's rural customers made this kind of billing difficult—the long distances necessary to pay the bills, the separate printings that had be done for 11 different languages, and the question of how customers living in a subsistence economy could afford such bills were just three of the thorny problems that Telkom had to address. It eventually solved the payment problem by introducing prepaid cards and making them widely available for sale in supermarkets, gas stations, and convenience stores. All this attention to detail brought its reward: Telkom's profits for 1999 reached ZAR 2.3 billion.

NEW FOCUS AND DEVELOPMENTS

By 2000, with the lines installed, Telkom turned its attention to other matters. First, the company trained the spotlight on its service, which, according to its customers, was still not as swift as it should have been. Its target was to repair all telephone glitches, both residential and business, within 48 hours of the complaint. By the end of the year, according to the company's 2000 annual report, residential repairs had improved 15.4 percent and business service had improved 14.4 percent. The company boasted that it had over 5.5 million telephone lines, compared to 5.1 million in 1999. It also had 173,000 pay phones, compared to 153,000 in the previous year. These improvements showed in its year-end revenues, which were ZAR 26.72 billion.

Two more developments in 2000 were the building of the National Network Operations Center (NNOC) and the Data Center. The NNOC featured a 120-meter-wide video wall that provided up-to-the-minute readings on the state of the network anywhere in the country. The state-of-the-art Data Center was designed to continue functioning for four days after any disaster that disrupted electric power.

Another important accomplishment of the year rose out of analysts' predictions that international traffic between Africa and the rest of the world would grow by nearly 60 times by the end of 2005. Joining with telecommunications companies from 35 other countries in 2000, Telkom took part in building a new fiber-optic undersea cable called SAT-3/WASC/SAFE, which covered 28,000 kilometers and linked the African continent with Europe and Asia. The $650 million cable system became operational in 2002.

By May 2002, when Telkom's period of monopoly ended, there were 2,700 villages enjoying their first taste of telephone service. The fixed-line network upgrade meant that 99.8 percent had been digitized, giving customers access to caller identification, voice mail, and call forwarding—all improvements that would cost ZAR 47 billion by year's end. Still, profits rose and 2002 showed revenue growth of 8 percent to ZAR 34.2 billion.

LISTING ON STOCK EXCHANGES

In March 2003 Telkom listed its shares on both the Johannesburg Stock Exchange and the New York Stock Exchange. An unusual ancillary accompanied its initial public offering on the Johannesburg Stock Exchange. Called the Khulisa offer, it made purchases available to all historically disadvantaged individuals (victims of apartheid) at a 20 percent discount. Furthermore, if these people held on to their shares for two years or more, they would receive one extra Telkom share for every five shares they owned. Charges of discrimination by other buyers against this offering began almost immediately, but were deflected by the South African government. Eugene Mokeyane, the government spokesperson, explained in a Department of Public Enterprises press release that this offer had been structured to make sure that the less affluent also had a chance to own shares. The Khulisa purchases had a ceiling of ZAR 5,000, and they could not be sold for three months after being purchased. According to Gordon Platt of *Global Finance*, Telkom's shares were initially listed at $13.98, dipped briefly to $13.90, but finished the first week at $14.90.

By 2007 Telkom was steadily eyeing other potential markets. In February it announced the acquisition of Africa Online, the largest Internet service provider in Africa. Operating throughout most of the African continent, Africa Online gave Telkom access to Ghana, the Ivory Coast, Kenya, Namibia, Swaziland, Tanzania, Uganda, Zambia, and Zimbabwe. In May 2007 the company acquired 75 percent of Multi-links Telecommunications Ltd., a Nigerian-based company, for $285 million. It purchased the remaining 25 percent in January 2009 for $130 million.

Closer to home, South Africa offered a wealth of opportunities. The most notable was a ZAR 1.7 billion five-year contract with Absa Group Ltd., one of the country's biggest banks, to provide an integrated network that would connect Absa's 2,500 sites to each other. This deal helped Telkom end 2008 with an operating profit of ZAR 6.39 billion. The company had come a long way.

Gillian Wolf

PRINCIPAL SUBSIDIARIES

Trudon Pty. Ltd.; Swiftnet; Multi-links Telecommunications Ltd.; Africa Online.

PRINCIPAL COMPETITORS

Millicom International Cellular S.A.; MTN Group; Virgin Mobile Telecoms Ltd.

FURTHER READING

"At the Back of Beyond," *Economist*, October 7, 1999.

Chalmers, Robyn, and Lesley Stones, "2002: End of the Telkom Odyssey?" *Business Day* (South Africa), March 9, 2000.

Currie, Willie, and Robert B. Horwitz, "Another Instance Where Privatization Trumped Liberalization: The Politics of Telecommunications Reform in South Africa—a Ten-Year Retrospective," *Telecommunications Policy*, September–October 2007.

Department of Public Enterprises, "Telkom Share Offer Is Not Discriminatory," press release, May 30, 2006, http://www.dpe.gov.za/home.asp?id=138.

Evans, Garry, "South Africans Back in Business," *Euromoney*, September 1991, p. D63.

Janisch, Hudson N., and Danny M. Kotlowitz, "African Renaissance: Market Romance: Post-apartheid Privatisation and Liberalisation in South African Broadcasting and Telecommunications," paper presented at a symposium by the Columbia Institute of Tele-Information, Columbia University, June 12, 1998.

Lunsche, Sven, "How the Telkom Privatization Corpse Was Brought to Life," *Sunday Times: Business Times*, April 6, 1997.

————, "Telkom Lobs R13bn off Expansion Costs," *Sunday Times: Business Times*, July 6, 1997.

Naidoo, Jay, "Speech by Mr. J Naidoo, Minister of Posts, Telecommunications and Broadcasting, on the Draft Telkom Licenses Encourage Wider and Better Customer Service, International Competitiveness," South African Government Information, February 7, 1997, http://www.search.gov.za/info.

Platt, Gordon, "Corporate Finance: Long-Delayed Telkom IPO Finally Makes It to Market," *Global Finance*, April 1, 2003.

South African Government Information, "Telkom Share Offer Is Not Discriminatory," March 11, 2003, http://www.info.gov.za/speeches/2003/03011311461004.htm.

"South African Telecoms—Wiring the Wilderness," *Economist*, June 10, 2000, p. 67.

"South Africa Privatizes Telkom," Reuters, March 27, 1997.

"South Africa's Telkom Ready for Sell-Off," *BBC News*, July 1, 2002.

Telkom, "SAT-3/WASC/SAFE Submarine Cable System Is Officially Inaugurated," press release, May 27, 2002, http://www.telkom.co.za/common/aboutus/mediacentre/pressrelease/articles/article_461.html.

"Telkom Profits Slide in 2008," *Telegeography's CommsUpdate*, June 23, 2009.

"10 Years of Achievement," *Business Day* (South Africa), February 19, 2004.

Vecchiatto, Paul, "Cable Theft Costs Telkom R100m," ITWeb, April 4, 2007, http://www.itweb.co.za/sections/telecoms/2007/0704041050.
asp?S=Legal%20View&A=LEG&O=google.

"Veldcom," *Economist*, May 16, 1998, p. 64.

Watkins, Thayer, "Privatization in South Africa," February 28, 2007, http://www.applet-magic.com/southafrica.htm.

Wood, Timothy, "Angry Telkom Crackling over Failed Internet Monopoly Bid," *Sunday Times: Business Times*, October 19, 1997.

———, "Telkom, Internet Must Bridge a Yawning Chasm," *Sunday Times: Business Times*, August 24, 1997.

3Com Corporation

350 Campus Drive
Marlborough, Massachusetts 01752-3064
U.S.A.
Telephone: (508) 323-5000
Toll Free: (800) 638-3266
Fax: (508) 323-1111
Web site: http://www.3com.com

Public Company
Incorporated: 1979
Employees: 6,103
Sales: $1.29 billion (2008)
Stock Exchanges: NASDAQ
Ticker Symbol: COMS
NAICS: 334119 Other Computer Peripheral Equipment Manufacturing; 334210 Telephone Apparatus Manufacturing; 334290 Other Communications Equipment Manufacturing; 335931 Current-Carrying Wiring Device Manufacturing; 511210 Software Publishers; 541512 Computer Systems Design Services

■ ■ ■

3Com Corporation is the world's number two provider of computer networking products, systems, and services, trailing only Cisco Systems Inc. A pioneering networking company, particularly in the development of Ethernet network adapters, 3Com offers products and services for local area networks (LANs), wide area networks (WANs), and the Internet. In the 21st century, the company has also aggressively targeted emerging areas for future growth, including home networks, wireless products, broadband cable, digital subscriber line (DSL) services, and Internet telephony. Some of its key products include switches, network hubs (central switching devices for network communication lines), Internetworking routers (devices that automatically select the most effective routes for data being transmitted between networks), remote access systems, network management software, network interface cards, and firewall security products. Launching a major restructuring plan in 2000, the company cut its workforce nearly in half, from just under 12,000 employees to 6,100 in 2008. By 2009 roughly three-quarters of the company's personnel were based in Asia.

ETHERNET ORIGINS

3Com Corporation was founded in 1979 by Robert M. Metcalfe as a consulting firm for computer network technology. The name 3Com was derived from its focus on computers, communication, and compatibility. Bob Metcalfe, an M.I.T.-educated engineer, originally established the firm as a consultancy because the market for computer network products had not yet emerged. Six years earlier at Xerox's Palo Alto Research Center, Metcalfe had led a team that invented Ethernet, one of the first LAN systems for linking computers and peripherals (printers, scanners, modems, etc.) within a building. In 1979, after attending an M.I.T. alumni seminar on starting a business, the 32-year-old Metcalfe quit Xerox to start his own consulting firm. Later that year he incorporated 3Com, with the participation of college friend Howard Charney, an engineer turned patent attorney, and two others as cofounders.

COMPANY PERSPECTIVES

3Com has a long heritage of being a company that promotes and lives by strong values; values that are defined and promoted throughout the company. These include putting customers first, competing aggressively but fairly, forming mutually beneficial partnerships, and of particular note, acting with complete integrity in everything we do. Our 3Com Values and Code of Conduct underscore our commitment to manage our business effectively and win in the marketplace while maintaining high ethical standards.

In 1980 the group of four decided the time was ripe to convert their company into a LAN equipment manufacturing business using the Ethernet technology. It was at this time, with Metcalfe's encouragement, that Xerox had decided to share its Ethernet patent with minicomputer manufacturer Digital Equipment Corporation and microprocessor manufacturer Intel Corporation to establish Ethernet as a LAN industry standard. As a manufacturer, 3Com was a little ahead of its time. Although there were very few enterprises that had multiple computers, most having only one mainframe or at most a handful of mini-computers, Metcalfe foresaw that personal computers would someday become commonplace.

The group began approaching California venture capital firms in October 1980 for financing to begin developing products. 3Com's business plan emphasized a strategy of letting market demand determine its rate of growth, taking the risk that the market might run away, and focusing on long-term growth, rather than short-term market share. Despite the initial slow growth predictions, three venture capitalists contributed a total of $1.1 million in the first round of financing, in large part on the strength of its founders' reputations.

FINDING PROFITABILITY IN PC MARKET GROWTH OF THE 1980S

In March 1981 Metcalfe recruited L. William Krause, the general manager of Hewlett-Packard's General Systems Division, to become 3Com's president. Metcalfe retained the positions of chief executive officer and chairperson and assumed the additional title of vice-president of engineering. Bill Krause also was given a 9 percent share in the company, second in size only to

Metcalfe's 21 percent. At the time 3Com had only nine employees, but Krause had visions of a much larger company. Krause soon hired a vice-president of sales and a vice-president of marketing, and, a few months later, he hired someone else to assume Metcalfe's position of vice-president of engineering.

Krause had a conservative, risk-averse management style. 3Com had begun shipping its first hardware product, an Ethernet transceiver and adapter, in March 1981. When sales were not as high as expected by the following summer, a cash flow problem loomed, and Krause initiated a survival plan that involved a hiring freeze, a pay cut for all employees and officers, and a specific list of objectives. A second round of financing totaling $2.1 million came in January 1982. Sales were $1.8 million for the fiscal year ending May 31, 1982. At the June 1982 board meeting, the board compelled Metcalfe to relinquish his title of CEO to Krause, who had really been in charge since he came to 3Com. Metcalfe then took on a new, more active role in the position of vice-president of sales and marketing.

3Com's sales took off in the summer months of 1982, not long after IBM introduced its 16-bit personal computer. The young company became profitable in 1983, and, in March 1984, 3Com went public, raising $10 million. By then it was expanding by approximately 300 percent annually, having grown from $4.7 million to $16.7 million in sales for the fiscal year ending May 1984. Earnings that year were $2.3 million, and the company had a 15 percent operating profit. Two years later, for the fiscal year ending May 31, 1986, revenues reached $64 million.

The company was doing well selling adapter cards to value-added resellers and to original equipment manufacturers, which were large computer manufacturing companies. The market was rapidly maturing, however, as computer manufacturers, including IBM and Digital Equipment, were beginning to integrate their own networking functions into their computers. In 1986, 3Com held 8 percent of the LAN market, while computer manufacturer IBM had captured 28 percent of the market by including LAN hardware and software within its computers.

PROVIDING COMPUTER NETWORK SYSTEMS IN THE 1980S

In response to the trend, 3Com decided to move in the direction of providing more complete computer network systems. In 1984 Metcalfe had started a new software division to develop advanced network software, and the company shipped its first network operating system

KEY DATES

1979: 3Com Corporation is founded by Robert M. Metcalfe as a consulting firm for computer network technology.

1981: Company ships its first hardware product, an Ethernet transceiver and adapter.

1984: 3Com goes public, raising $10 million, and introduces its first network operating system.

1987: Bridge Communications Inc. is acquired for $151 million.

1990: Restructuring begins in an effort to refocus the company away from client-server networking; Eric Benhamou is named president and COO.

1994: Company acquires Synernetics Inc., Centrum Communications Inc., and NiceCom Ltd.

1995: 3Com acquires Chipcom Corporation, a manufacturer of high-speed switches, for $775 million.

1997: 3Com acquires U.S. Robotics Corporation, a maker of modems, remote access devices, and handheld computing products.

2000: Spinoff of Palm Inc. begins with an $874 million IPO, which includes about 5 percent of Palm stock.

2003: 3Com forms Huawei-3Com, a joint venture with Chinese firm Huawei Technologies.

2004: Company moves headquarters from Santa Clara, California, to Marlborough, Massachusetts.

2007: 3Com acquires Huawei's remaining 49 percent stake in Huawei-3Com.

2008: Bain Capital LLC, a Boston-based investment firm, and Huawei Technologies terminate proposed $2.2 billion acquisition of 3Com in face of U.S. government concerns about national security.

software, 3 +, two years later. Also during this time, 3Com began marketing its own computer called the 3 Server to function as a network server, a computer on a network whose data is accessed by multiple desktop computers in a configuration known as client-server. By the spring of 1986, servers accounted for 32 percent of 3Com's sales. To complete the system, 3Com also wanted to offer computers that functioned as clients. Therefore, in early 1986 it pursued a merger with

Convergent Technologies Inc., which manufactured UNIX-based workstations. Two days before the scheduled shareholder approval in March 1986, however, 3Com's investment banker advised against being acquired by Convergent. On its own, 3Com then began selling systems that included modified personal computers, referred to as network stations, which operated only within its networks.

In 1987, 3Com began marketing itself more as a workgroups computing company that made and marketed PC-network systems. As such, it emphasized products that improved the productivity of workgroups. Several product introductions were made that year, including network servers, software, and industry-standard network adapter cards. With this market strategy, however, 3Com was running into competition with Novell Inc., which offered similar products. One important difference, however, was that 3Com targeted niche markets of more sophisticated users.

In September 1987, 3Com made a significant acquisition by purchasing Bridge Communications Inc. for $151 million. Bridge was a provider of Internetwork gateways and multiple-protocol bridges, devices that link different networks together on a corporate level. Thus Bridge's products complemented 3Com's, and the largest independent networking manufacturer at that time was formed.

Integration of the two companies, however, was not without difficulties. Bridge was completely merged into 3Com by March 1988, but it was not until the end of 1989 that its new internetworking products were introduced. Bridge cofounder William Carrico was appointed president of 3Com, with Krause remaining as CEO, but differences in management styles and corporate cultures prompted Carrico to resign in May 1988, and Krause regained the presidency. At the same time, Bridge Communications Division General Manager Judy Estrin, another cofounder of Bridge, resigned.

GROWING PAINS AND MARKET CHANGES END THE 1980S

The integration of the sales forces also caused problems since 3Com had focused on value-added resellers, whereas Bridge was more involved in direct sales. Therefore, a cooperative selling program was launched whereby sales representatives earned commissions on sales to value-added resellers just as they did for direct sales. The buildup of a direct sales force, however, angered some of 3Com's traditional dealers, and sales of LAN Manager suffered.

Also in 1987, 3Com had entered into a joint effort with Microsoft Corporation to develop and market

LAN Manager network software for the OS-2 operating system. 3Com sold LAN Manager under a license agreement with Microsoft and, beginning in 1988, it also marketed 3 + Open, its own version of LAN Manager. LAN Manager, however, was a direct competitor of Novell's product, NetWare, and OS-2 eventually proved less popular an operating system than expected.

3Com's sales for the year ending May 31, 1988, were $252 million, up from $156 million the previous year, and earnings had risen from $16.2 million to $22.5 million. By 1988, 3Com was the leading company specializing in computer networks. As a provider of networks, it was second only to Digital Equipment and was ahead of IBM.

Then in the summer of 1989 revenue growth began to slow seriously for the first time, in part due to the poor sales of LAN Manager. 3Com had its first annual drop in earnings for the year ending May 1990. The company also was losing in its battle against rival Novell's NetWare, which by 1990 had 65 percent of the network operating system market share. In 1989, 3Com shipped 14,000 copies of its 3 + and 3 + Open software, whereas Novell shipped 181,000 copies of NetWare. Meanwhile, internetworking products, the specialty of the acquired Bridge Communications, were being neglected.

FOCUSING ON NETWORKS IN THE 1990S

Krause responded by implementing a New Renaissance Plan beginning in January 1990 to reorganize and refocus the company. 3Com began marketing itself as a network integrator and a network systems supplier, and as a single source for network hardware and applications software compatible with multiple vendors' systems. Client/server networking was de-emphasized, and the focus shifted to comprehensive networking and internetwork connections. 3Com thus gave up going head-to-head against Novell, and 3Com's hardware henceforth supported both LAN Manager and its former competitor, NetWare. The marketing of LAN Manager, meanwhile, was left to Microsoft.

Krause also centralized the company by reducing the number of divisions from five to three: product development, internal operations, and sales. New executive vice-presidents were named to head each division, replacing the authority of Metcalfe's vice-presidency. Krause then removed himself from daily operations and began looking for someone else to replace him as CEO.

In April 1990, 3Com appointed Eric Benhamou, who had been the executive vice-president of product development, as president and chief operating officer.

Benhamou had been one of the cofounders of the acquired Bridge Communications company. A month later, founder Metcalfe resigned from his posts as vice-president of marketing and board member, after being passed over for the position of president. In August 1990 Krause himself resigned as CEO of 3Com, and Benhamou assumed that post as well. Krause remained as chairman of the board, stepping out of management having accomplished his goal of building 3Com into a significant company of 2,000 employees.

Benhamou continued the process of refocusing the company along the lines of Krause's Renaissance plan. 3Com began investing more in technically innovative products such as network adapters, software, network management, and internetworking. Increasing emphasis was put on the cohesiveness of its products. To that end, in November 1990 two new divisions were created to replace four previous product-oriented groups. A Network Adapter Division was created to sell the company's Ethernet cards, replacing the former Transmission Systems Division. A Network Systems Division, headed directly by Benhamou, assumed the responsibilities of the former Enterprise Systems Division, Distributed Systems Division, and the Management, Messaging and Connectivity Division. Some mid-level managers were removed in the process.

RESTRUCTURING TO REDEFINE OBJECTIVES IN THE EARLY 1990S

In January 1991, 3Com further redefined its business objectives. The company completely gave up the network operating system software business, which had been providing the software packages LAN Manager, 3 +, and 3 + Open, since the LAN Manager royalty contract with Microsoft had become a financial burden. Under the contract, 3Com had to pay Microsoft royalties even if the computer servers it sold did not include LAN Manager but 3Com's 3 + Open instead. Moreover, when LAN Manager was sold independently, not bundled with 3Com hardware, 3Com still had to pay the expense of customer support for LAN Manager, and was losing money. 3Com's exit from the network operating system business freed the company from its royalty contract with Microsoft, and all marketing and support of LAN Manager was turned over to Microsoft. 3Com's LAN operating system, which had been losing market share to Novell's NetWare for the past three years, held only 14 percent of the market when the company dropped out.

The restructuring also meant steering away from providing client and server computers in order to focus on the networks themselves. Benhamou's redirection and reorganization of the company also involved putting two businesses up for sale. Communications Solutions Inc., a manufacturer of connectivity products beyond LANs that had been acquired in 1988, was sold to Attachmate Corporation. The workgroup business, which sold servers and workstations, could not find a buyer and was gradually eliminated. Whereas workgroup-related hardware and software had contributed $113 million, almost one-quarter of 3Com's revenues, in 1990, this figure had dropped to 11 percent in 1991. The reorganization also involved laying off 234 employees, or 12 percent of the workforce, and a $67 million restructuring charge.

Thereafter, the company refocused on its successful LAN adapter line and internetworking products, such as bridges, hubs, adapters, and routers. 3Com had begun to depend increasingly on sales from the internetworking business acquired from Bridge Communications after neglecting it for three years. 3Com had seen its market share in bridges and routers fall from 29 percent in 1988 to 19 percent in 1990, although it was still the third-ranking company in the field, following Cisco Systems Inc. and Vitalink Communications Corporation. Network adapters, meanwhile, came to account for 72 percent of sales in the second half of 1991. 3Com further concentrated on improving its core adapter product line with the development of adapters for wireless notebook computers and adapters for higher speed network systems.

The initial results of the restructuring included lower revenues due to fewer product lines. For calendar year 1991, sales declined 15 percent to $370 million, and the company suffered a loss of $33 million, compared with profits of $24 million the previous year. Lower profits also were caused in part by the more competitive nature of the LAN adapter market that had emerged in the early 1990s. By the end of 1991, 14 percent of the company's workforce had been laid off, leaving a total of 1,676 employees. By 1992, however, the company was back on track, with sales rebounding to $423.8 million for the fiscal year ending May 31, 1992, and earnings becoming positive at $7.96 million.

GROWTH THROUGH ACQUISITION IN THE 1990S

For its other LAN components, 3Com came to rely increasingly on licensing or acquiring third-party technology. The company bolstered its hub business by acquiring the Data Networks business of BICC PLC, one of Europe's largest hub manufacturers, in January 1992. This gave 3Com the LinkBuilder ECS, an Ethernet chassis hub. In September 1992, 3Com introduced LinkBuilder 3GH, a high-end switching hub licensed from Syncrnetics Inc., a manufacturer of LAN switches.

In a move to expand beyond Ethernet LAN structures, in 1993 3Com acquired Star-Tek Inc., which produced hubs for the Token-Ring network architecture. 3Com introduced a multifunction hub, LinkBuilder MSH, which could support both Ethernet and Token-Ring LANs in the spring of 1993. In December of that year, 3Com purchased wireless communications technology from Pacific Monolothics Inc. Early in 1994, 3Com acquired Synernetics, a manufacturer of LAN switches, and Centrum Communications Inc., which provided products for remote network access. In September 1994, 3Com purchased ATM innovator NiceCom Ltd., a subsidiary of Nice Systems based in Tel Aviv, Israel. 3Com rounded out its acquisitions spree in late 1995 with the $775 million purchase of Chipcom Corporation, a maker of multifunction high-speed switches for large computer networks. This acquisition not only gave 3Com its first presence in the large corporate systems segment, it also propelled 3Com into second place among the world's networking companies, behind only Cisco Systems. 3Com's product strategy and acquisitions under Benhamou helped the company reach $2.33 billion in sales for the fiscal year ending in May 1996, nearly six times that of four years prior. Reflecting its rising stature, while at the same time representing an attempt to make the company better known to the general public, 3Com paid $3.9 million to the city of San Francisco to change the name of Candlestick Park, where the Giants played major league baseball, to 3Com Park, a move that angered many baseball fans.

Despite its diversification efforts, 3Com remained primarily a maker of network adapters in the mid-1990s, a period in which the emergence of the Internet heightened demand for networking products of all sorts. While market leader Cisco Systems concentrated mainly on the devices that formed the backbone of the Internet, 3Com focused on the Internet edge with its products that connected personal computers to LANs, WANs, and to the Internet, and those that welded together local area networks. 3Com's key acquisition in its emerging Internet strategy was that of U.S. Robotics Corporation, which was completed in June 1997. Dallas-based U.S. Robotics was the leading maker of low-cost modems, which were used to connect personal computers to the Internet and to other remote networks. The company also had a leading presence on the other end of the modem, that is, in the remote access devices that were the entry points into Internet service providers and corporate networks for users dialing in to the network. U.S. Robotics was particularly strong in the area of corporate remote access devices. In 1995 the company also had acquired Palm Computing, a pioneer in the field of handheld computing devices.

Following the acquisition of U.S. Robotics, 3Com derived more than half of its revenues from the low end of the networking segment, which included network adapters and modems. Overall revenues reached $5.42 billion for the 1998 fiscal year, but the company was barely profitable due to merger-related and other charges totaling $253.7 million. Integrating U.S. Robotics into 3Com proved more difficult than anticipated, in part because of the geographic and cultural divide between Silicon Valley and Texas oil country. An inventory backlog also developed for U.S. Robotics modems for a time while an industry standard was being adopted for another increase in analog modem speed to 56 kilobits per second. In fact, with faster alternative access technologies, including cable modems and digital subscriber lines (DSL) being developed, many analysts were predicting the demise of the analog modem and questioned the wisdom of the U.S. Robotics acquisition. Although the analog modem proved longer lasting than anticipated, and new access technologies were slow to be adopted, 3Com was forced to contend with a number of shareholder lawsuits stemming from the U.S. Robotics purchase and the company's plummeting market value.

For the 1999 fiscal year, 3Com posted net income of $403.9 million on sales of $5.77 billion, representing a vast improvement in profitability but only a slight revenue gain. The company was suffering from intense competition and sagging prices, particularly in its core network adapters and modems segment, where revenues were actually on the decline. The brightest spot was Palm Computers, which had captured 70 percent of the handheld computer market. By late 1999, however, 3Com management had concluded that Palm had become a distraction from the company's networking core. 3Com, therefore, announced that it would spin off Palm during 2000. In early March of that year 3Com sold about 5 percent of the common stock of the newly named Palm Inc. in an initial public offering that raised $874 million in the midst of a technology stock frenzy on Wall Street. 3Com next planned to distribute the remaining Palm stake to 3Com shareholders later in 2000.

As the 21st century began, speculation continued that 3Com would itself become an acquisition target or would be broken up through further spin-offs. Benhamou insisted that the company would remain independent and had the right mix of networking products. 3Com was counting on being a key player in such emerging areas as home networks, wireless products, broadband cable, DSL services, and Internet telephony. To facilitate this, the company was forging alliances with such partners as Microsoft to develop home networking products. In addition, 3Com continued to make strategic acquisitions, including the March 1999

$87.8 million purchase of NBX Corporation, a company specializing in Internet telephony systems that integrated voice and data communications over small business LANs and WANs.

"RADICAL SIMPLICITY": A STREAMLINED BUSINESS MODEL FOR THE 21ST CENTURY

From a financial perspective, 3Com received a major boost from its divesture of Palm, at least in the short term. The company's stock price rose from a lackluster $23 per share in September 1999 to $104 per share at the time of the initial public offering, a gain of more than 350 percent. These proved to be temporary, however, and by September 2000 the company's value had dropped to under $20 a share. That same month, Benhamou resigned as CEO, while retaining his position as company chairman. He was replaced by Bruce Claflin, formerly COO of the company.

In spite of this volatility, 3Com remained confident about its long-term prospects. After selling its remaining stake in Palm, the company announced a major restructuring plan. 3Com's new goal was to target a broader range of consumers and small businesses with lower-end, more affordable products. In particular, 3Com hoped to become a leader in the development of wireless technology, with the aim of enabling reliable, high-speed Internet connections across a variety of platforms. The company was gambling on the idea that as a wider range of portable and computer-based products became available, consumers would begin seeking more affordable and versatile forms of wireless networking capability. With many industry analysts predicting that consumer demand for broadband and other forms of high-speed connectivity would double by 2005, 3Com's strategy seemed sound.

In effect, 3Com's shift in focus seemed to represent a major capitulation to its main rival, Cisco, in the battle to win larger corporate clients. Cisco had come to dominate the high-end marketplace in recent years, making the decision seem like a matter of 3Com's long-term survival. As part of the restructuring, the company decided to discontinue a number of products aimed at its larger customers, notably its CoreBuilder network switches, as well as its line of analog modems. By unloading these products, the company was able to trim its research and development expenses by close to 2 percent, while at the same dedicating most of the remaining budget to creating new products. One area of particular interest to 3Com was the burgeoning field of Internet security, where it hoped to become a leading designer and manufacturer of firewall products for business networks.

Some analysts saw risk in the company's new strategy. For one, while 3Com had earned a high reputation in the business world, it had little brand-name recognition among the general public. At the same time, the decision to discontinue several of its high-end products also alienated many of the company's existing corporate clients that had invested substantial resources in the technology. In order to overcome these concerns, 3Com launched a $100 million re-branding campaign designed to promote the advantages of more integrated forms of connectivity. In press releases and interviews, 3Com described its new strategy in terms of "radical simplicity," extolling the reliability and functionality of its core products. New advertisements also highlighted the company's streamlined approach. One notable television spot depicted two office workers struggling to make sense of a bundle of wires beneath a desk; the ad concluded with the line, "Simple sets you free."

3Com's restructuring plan hit a major snag with the burst of the dot-com bubble in 2000. In February 2001, in the face of mounting financial losses, the company was forced to reduce its personnel by 1,200 employees. The company cut an additional 2,250 jobs, or more than a quarter of its total workforce, in May of that year. At the same time, 3Com's sales dropped 40 percent, while its stock value dropped to under $7 a share. By fall 2001, the company had cut nearly 6,000 jobs. To help create greater efficiency and reduce costs, the company established three principal business segments, each with a unique focus: ISP network-building; networking applications for consumers and small businesses; and switches and other products for corporations. Through this reorganization, the company hoped to increase efficiency, with the aim of cutting expenses by $1 billion per year.

VENTURING INTO ASIA: 2003–09

At the same time, 3Com also began to increase its presence in Asia. In 2003 it entered into a joint venture with Chinese firm Huawei Technologies to create Huawei-3Com, or H3Com. The new subsidiary soon became the primary manufacturing wing of the company, as 3Com shifted the bulk of its global production operations to China. The next several years saw other major changes at the company. In 2004, 3Com shifted its U.S. headquarters from Santa Clara, California, to an existing branch office in Marlborough, Massachusetts. A year later, it acquired TippingPoint, a Texas-based manufacturer of Internet security products. In 2007, 3Com purchased Huawei's remaining 49 percent stake in H3Com. By this time, nearly 5,000 of the company's total workforce of 6,200 were based in Asia. At the same time, the company aimed to create a

powerful market for its products in the region, anticipating that the area would soon account for more than 50 percent of its total sales.

In early 2008 3Com entered into acquisition talks with Huawei Technologies and a Boston-based venture capital firm, Bain Capital LLC. Under the terms of the deal, 3Com would be sold to the two companies for $2.2 billion. Bain Capital ultimately pulled out of the proposed merger, however, when the U.S. Congress expressed concern about chronic Internet security violations in China. Shortly after the failed buyout, 3Com named Robert Mao, formerly executive vice-president of corporate development at the company, as its new CEO. Mao would be based at the company's Hong Kong operations, further signaling the company's intention to continue building up its Asian presence.

In spite of an economic recession in 2008 and 2009, 3Com found itself well positioned to compete for a larger share of the global marketplace. Its line of affordable networking hardware, manufactured primarily at the company's H3Com subsidiary in China, was attracting a wider range of corporations and other organizations seeking to cut costs during the economic downturn. The company's H3C switch, for example, was priced at $10,000, roughly half of the cost of a comparable switch offered by Cisco. Notable new clients included the Massachusetts Institute of Technology, which purchased 100 H3C switches in 2009. Although some businesses remained wary of 3Com's surprising return to the corporate market, it was clear that other large firms were willing to offer the newly streamlined company a second chance.

Heather Behn Hedden
Updated, David E. Salamie; Stephen Meyer

PRINCIPAL SUBSIDIARIES

H3C Technologies Co., Limited (China); TippingPoint.

PRINCIPAL COMPETITORS

Casio Computer Co., Ltd.; Cisco Systems Inc.; Conexant Systems Inc.; General Electric Company; Hewlett-Packard Company; Intel Corporation; Koninklijke Philips Electronics N.V.; Microsoft Corporation; Motorola Inc.; Nortel Networks Corporation; Psion PLC; Sharp Corporation; Siemens Aktiengesellschaft; Sony Corporation; Telecom Italia S.p.A.

FURTHER READING

Alpert, Bill, "The Future Is 3Com," *Barron's*, December 1, 1997, pp. 15-16.

Barney, Cliff, "Sales and Profit Gains Ease the Pain of the 3Com/Bridge Merger," *Electronic Business*, November, 15, 1988, pp. 54-56.

Bransten, Lisa, and Scott Thurm, "For Palm Computers, an IPO and a Flashy Rival," *Wall Street Journal*, September 14, 1999, p. B1.

Bray, Hiawatha, "Once Mighty 3Com Readies Comeback; Networking Firm Sees Boost in Voice, Security Products," *Boston Globe*, April 19, 2007, p. D1.

Burke, Steven, "3Com Recharts Networking Course," *PC Week*, January 14, 1991, pp. 1, 8.

Burrows, Peter, "3Com Is Showing a Lot of Hustle," *Business Week*, October 2, 1995, pp. 130, 132.

Doler, Kathleen, "Eric Benhamou, Chairman and CEO of 3Com Corp.," *Upside*, May 1999, pp. 106-12, 114, 116 +.

Duffy, Jim, "3Com Captain Remains Calm Despite Stormy Forecasts," *Network World*, July 5, 1999, pp. 1, 57.

Epstein, Joseph, "Showtime: 3Com Has Finally Made It into the Big Leagues," *Financial World*, October 24, 1995, p. 29.

Flynn, Laurie, "As Networks of Computers Grow, 3Com Stock Surges," *New York Times*, August 31, 1994, pp. C1, C4.

Franson, Paul, "Challenging Perceptions," *Electronic Business*, June 1999, pp. 74-80 +.

Goldstein, Mark L., "Bill Krause Changes Course," *Industry Week*, June 1, 1987, p. 55.

Gomes, Lee, and Evan Ramstad, "3Com Agrees to Acquire U.S. Robotics," *Wall Street Journal*, February 27, 1997, p. A3.

Hamilton, Tyler, "3Com Refocusing on 'Radical Simplicity,'" *Toronto Globe and Mail* , March 22, 2000, p. B2.

Hill, G. Christian, and William M. Bulkeley, "3Com to Buy Chipcom for $775 Million," *Wall Street Journal*, July 28, 1995, p. A3.

Lewis, Jamie, "3Com's Pulse Strong after Years of Change," *PC Week*, January 25, 1993, p. 64.

Moad, Jeff, "On the Road Again," *Datamation*, May 1, 1986, pp.31-37.

Ould, Andrew, "3Com Reorganizes Divisions; Key Executive Departs," *PC Week*, November 5, 1990, p. 181.

Reinhardt, Andy, "Palmy Days for 3Com?" *Business Week*, March 16, 1998, p. 104.

———, "Why 3Com Is Handing Off Palm," *Business Week*, September 27, 1999, p. 48.

Richman, Tom, "Growing Steady," *Inc.*, September 1984, pp. 69-81.

———, "Who's in Charge Here?" *Inc.*, June 1989, pp. 36-46.

Roth, Daniel, "3Com Tries to Solve Its Palm Problem," *Fortune*, October 11, 1999, pp. 167-68.

Schonfeld, Erick, "The Avis of Networking," *Fortune*, May 11, 1998, pp. 164, 168.

Solomon, Deborah, "3Com Plan: Divide, Conquer; Uphill Battle Coming after Palm Spinoff," *USA Today*, March 2, 2000, p. 3B.

Strom, David, "3Com—Can New Products Save This Company?" *VarBusiness*, December 2, 2002, p. 32.

Thurm, Scott, "3Com Faces Challenges in Developing New Lines," *Wall Street Journal*, March 25, 1999, p. B6.

———, "3Com Tops Expectations but Warns on Growth," *Wall Street Journal*, December 22, 1999, p. B6.

Young, Jeffrey, "Underdog Strategy," *Forbes*, November 3, 1997, pp.364 +.

Trustmark Corporation

248 East Capitol Street
Jackson, Mississippi 39201
U.S.A.
Telephone: (601) 961-6000
Toll Free: (800) 844-2000
Web site: http://www.trustmark.com

Public Company
Incorporated: 1968
Employees: 2,600
Total Assets: $9.79 billion (2008)
Stock Exchanges: NASDAQ
Ticker Symbol: TRMK
NAICS: 551111 Offices of Bank Holding Companies;
    522110 Commercial Banking

■ ■ ■

Established in 1985, Trustmark Corporation is the holding company of Trustmark National Bank. Through its subsidiaries, Trustmark National Bank operates as a financial services organization that offers banking and financial products to corporate, institutional, and individual customers. By 2008 the company comprised more than 2,600 employees working in 150 locations primarily in Mississippi, but also in Tennessee, Texas, and Florida. Trustmark National Bank accounts for substantially all of the assets and revenues of Trustmark Corporation. As of December 31, 2008, Trustmark's as-sets totaled $9.79 billion, with deposits of $6.82 billion and loans of $6.96 billion. In addition to banking activities, Trustmark National Bank provides investment and insurance products and services to its customers through its subsidiaries Trustmark Securities Inc., Trustmark Investment Advisors Inc., the Bottrell Insurance Agency Inc., and Fisher-Brown Inc.

FORMED THROUGH MERGERS IN MISSISSIPPI BANKING

The oldest financial institution in Jackson, Mississippi, Trustmark had its origins in the founding of the Jackson Bank in 1889. Over the next nine decades, the original bank acquired and merged with other financial institutions in the area, operating under the names State National Bank, Jackson-State National Bank, and First National Bank, prior to becoming known as Trustmark in 1985. In the early to mid-1990s, Trustmark completed five acquisitions in Mississippi that totaled $144.6 million.

Trustmark grew its assets to $4.4 billion and controlled 15.6 percent of deposits in Mississippi, making it the largest bank in the state by August 1994. Shortly thereafter, Trustmark's share of deposits within the state grew to 16.8 percent following its merger with the First National Bank in Vicksburg, Mississippi. The Federal Reserve Board approved the merger after an investigation found First National had violated both the Fair Housing Act and the Equal Credit Opportunity Act by charging higher interest rates and stricter terms to black customers than to whites.

COMPANY PERSPECTIVES

We believe building strong customer relationships is the result of knowing our customers, understanding their businesses and needs and providing appropriate financial solutions. We realize the inherent trust you place in your financial institution, and we look forward to the opportunity to prove to you the value behind our name. Trustmark is "People you Trust. Advice that Works."

FACING LEGAL TROUBLES IN THE MID-1990S

In 1994 charges were brought against Trustmark for allegedly overcharging for collateral protection on auto insurance policies. Customer Ken Smith and his loan cosigner, Jesse Holmes, argued that the bank charged an exorbitant amount to their auto loan when Smith failed to renew his auto insurance policy, and the bank purchased one for him and added the related charges to his loan account. Known as "forced-placed insurance," the policy was purchased without Smith's foreknowledge and added about $9,500 to his original $9,200 loan.

The following year, Trustmark lost in a jury trial and was ordered to pay $38.5 million in punitive damages and an additional $500,000 in what was considered actual damages, making it one of the largest awards in the state's history. Following the news, the company's stock fell 8 percent from $16.25 per share to $15.375 per share on the day of the jury's decision, as reported by Terrence O'Hara in *American Banker*. However, after the company announced it would appeal the decision, its stock began trending upward in less than a week.

Trustmark pursued an appeal and in September 1996 settled out of court with Smith and Holmes for an estimated $5 million. However, roughly 5,000 other customers came forward in a similar class-action law suit against Trustmark. Rather than enter a series of protracted legal battles, Trustmark reached an $8.8 million settlement to end the class-action suit. As reported by Gary Wiggers in *American Banker*, the company hoped "to avoid the enormous costs of litigation and diversion of energy required to defend against a series of continuous lawsuits."

The case prompted the Mississippi Bankers Association to investigate the practice of forced-placed insurance. "We want to avoid the situation where a lender makes good efforts but then ends up getting sued," Mac Deaver, executive director of the association noted in *American Banker* in January 1995, adding that "We want to make sure that the rules are specified so that, if they are followed, the banks won't be open to liability from the borrower." Joseph H. Neely, state bank commissioner, told *American Banker*, "Nothing has changed with the statutes or regulations, but that product is effectively dead in Mississippi."

SALES GROWTH UNDER NEW LEADERSHIP: 1997–99

In the first quarter of 1997, Trustmark successfully completed a merger with First Corinth Corp. and its subsidiary National Bank of Commerce. The merger pushed Trustmark's assets up to $5.3 billion by June 1997 compared to $5.2 billion in June 1996. Trustmark completed another acquisition in September, when it paid $9.4 million for Perry County Bank of Mississippi.

In 1997 Frank Day stepped down from his position as chief executive officer of Trustmark after he was diagnosed with Anyotrophic Lateral Scleerosis (Lou Gehrig's disease). He was succeeded by Richard Hickson as chief executive but stayed on as chairman. Assets grew some 14.6 percent, loans increased 24.1 percent under Hickson's leadership, and the company entered a period of increased momentum. "Analysts and observers are adding several new adjectives to describe the longtime Southern bank: proactive, opportunistic and sales-oriented," reported Karen Kahler Holliday in the *Mississippi Business Journal*. Furthermore, Trustmark ranked among the top 20 banks in the nation in 1998 in a survey by *US Banker* and Keefe, Bruyette & Woods.

It soon became apparent that Hickson was ready to move the company in a new direction, especially when it came to sales techniques. Whether it was adding additional sales associates, investing in the latest technology, or enticing business customers away from rival banks, the company was on a mission. For example, board members undertook a program of "adopting" prospects in order to lure potential business away from Trustmark's chief competitors.

Training by Cohen Brown Management Group was implemented throughout the company in 1997 to stimulate aggressive growth from the sales force. Loans climbed 31.7 percent, and a marketing promotion geared at new checking accounts produced 14,500 new accounts for 6,200 new families brought onboard in 1998. With assets that totaled $6.5 billion, Trustmark was the largest bank in Mississippi. At the time it had 108 full-service branches and 32 additional sites offering limited services throughout the state.

Company incentives also helped promote employee performance, according to Karen Holliday in *US Banker*

KEY DATES

1889: Trustmark has its origins in Mississippi with the founding of the Jackson Bank.

1985: Trustmark Corporation is formed as the holding company of Trustmark National Bank.

1995: Trustmark settles the Smith-Holmes auto insurance case for $5 million.

2000: Trustmark expands into Tennessee with the purchase of Barret Bancorp Inc. in Memphis.

2003: Trustmark purchases seven banking centers from the Banc Corp. to expand operations into Florida.

2004: Trustmark operates in Texas through the purchase of Allied Houston Bank.

2006: Trustmark expands presence in Houston through a merger with Republic Bancshares of Texas Inc.

in 1999. The bank paid $160,000 in incentives to teller and customer service associates in 1997. By 1999 the company was averaging $130,000 to $140,000 per month in bonuses to top sellers.

Despite increasingly competitive market conditions, Trustmark was able to secure more than $1 billion in mortgage loans. Trustmark's acquisition strategy targeted financial institutions that provided banking, investment, or insurance products within 300 miles of their corporate headquarters. The acquisition of Taylorsville-based Bottrell Agency in the spring of 1999 fit Trustmark's long-range goal of becoming a "truly diversified financial services corporation," Hickson told Holliday in *US Banker.*

GROWTH AND EXPANSION IN THE EARLY 2000S

Trustmark continued to expand its reach. It extended into neighboring Tennessee in 2001 with the purchase of Barret Bancorp ($503 million in assets), and in 2002 with the acquisition of Nashoba Bancshares Inc. ($172 million in assets). Hickson told the *Mississippi Business Journal* in February 2003 that "Trustmark achieved continued success and made significant progress toward its strategic objectives in 2002 despite a challenging economic and volatile financial environment.... We realigned our customer, commercial and investment businesses enhanced our product offerings and refined delivery channels in an effort to better serve our

customers." The results were $7.1 billion in assets and $4.7 billion in customer deposits.

In 2003 the company expanded further into the Southeast with the acquisition in August of seven branches of The Bank in Florida's Emerald Coast region surrounding Destin. A subsidiary of the Banc Corporation located in Birmingham, Alabama, the operations known as the Emerald Coast Division positioned Trustmark in a prime area of continued growth. Trustmark's assets grew to more than $7 billion with deposits of $5 billion and loans of $4.8 billion in 2003.

In an effort to complement its Florida banking operations, in 2004 Trustmark added Fisher-Brown Inc., an insurance company with offices in Milton, Mary Esther, Destin, and Panama City. Because Fisher-Brown's roots dated back some 90 years, Trustmark decided not to rename the company.

In March 2004 Trustmark established a presence in the greater Houston, Texas, area when it acquired Allied Houston Bank, with five branches and an estimated $160 million in deposits. Expanding further into Texas, in 2006 Trustmark completed a merger with Republic Bancshares of Texas Inc. and integrated Republic National Bank's six branches, $474 million in loans, and $543 million in deposits into Trustmark National Bank. These assets gave Trustmark approximately $710 million in loans and $705 million in deposits in the Houston area.

DEFINING THE CORPORATE CULTURE

In order to ensure the high standards of customer service throughout its multistate operations, Trustmark provided extensive training and education to its employees. For example, newly appointed associates underwent rigorous ethics training, and the company operated a corporate university to bolster employees' knowledge and professional skills. Some received training at Canon Trust School, Louisiana State University School of Banking, Mississippi School of Banking, Southeastern School of Commercial Lending, and the Center for Creative Leadership.

In addition, Trustmark fostered a culture of community outreach, including ongoing participation in such programs as Habitat for Humanity. Trustmark was honored in 2004 with the Governor's Initiative for Volunteer Excellence (GIVE) Award presented by the governor of Mississippi, Haley Barbour. In 2006 the company received the prestigious Governor's Award for Civic Leadership in the Arts.

SUCCEEDING THROUGH ECONOMIC DOWNTURN: 2006–09

The mid-2000s brought a severe downturn in the economy that led to a staggering number of outstanding loans for banks to absorb. When the real estate market began a period of rapid decline after 2006, many banks, including Trustmark, began targeting their marketing strategies more pointedly to commercial and industrial customers.

In September 2008 the U.S. government put aside $700 billion for a financial rescue package that allocated $250 billion for financial institutions on a voluntary basis through the U.S. Troubled Asset Relief Program (TARP). Trustmark participated in late November and sold $215 million in stock to the U.S. Treasury Department as part of the government's bank investment strategy.

In essence, Trustmark's involvement allowed it to provide loans to worthy borrowers, thus positioning itself for expansion as the U.S. economy rebounded. The company focused on internal corporate improvements during 2009, including implementing technology upgrades and enhancing customer service and employee productivity. In July 2009 Hickson announced total tangible assets of $9.31 billion for the second quarter of 2009 and reassured investors of Trustmark's security. Declaring a $0.23 quarterly dividend to shareholders, Hickson said, "We look forward to the future as solid core earnings, coupled with the strength of Trustmark's human and financial capital, have positioned us to take advantage of growth opportunities resulting from this challenging financial environment."

Brenda Kubiac

PRINCIPAL SUBSIDIARIES

Bottrell Insurance Agency Inc.; Fisher-Brown Inc.; TRMK Risk Management Inc.; Trustmark Investment Advisors; Trustmark National Bank; Trustmark Securities Inc.

PRINCIPAL COMPETITORS

BancorpSouth; Capital One; Regions Financial Corporation.

FURTHER READING

"Acquisition Complete," *Mississippi Business Journal*, September 11, 2006, p. 11.

Brannigan, Martha, "Trustmark Agrees to Settle Dispute over Car Insurance," *Wall Street Journal*, September 30, 1996.

"Fed Approves Deals in Illinois, Colorado," *American Banker*, August 31, 1994, p. 3.

Gillam, Carey, "CEO Brings Change to Conservative Trustmark," *American Banker*, June 5, 2004, p. 6.

Harmon, Jennifer, "Merger Helps Trustmark," *National Mortgage News*, October 30, 2006.

Jetter, Lynne W., "Trustmark Invests in Ongoing Employee Motivation, Coaching," *Mississippi Business Journal*, March 22, 2004, p. S14.

Holliday, Karen Kahler, "CEO Putting New Look on Familiar Face," *Mississippi Business Journal*, August 10, 1998.

———, "Making a Good Bank Better," *US Banker*, June 1999.

———, "Trustmark Completes Acquisition of Florida Bank Branches," *Mississippi Business Journal*, September 15, 2003, p. A8.

O'Hara, Terrence, "Judge Slashes Damages against Trustmark in Case Involving Forced-Placed Insurance," *American Banker*, August 9, 1995, p. 8.

———, "Miss. Bank Settles Auto Insurance Case," *American Banker*, October 2, 1996, p. 4.

———, "Trustmark Stock off 8 Percent since Jury Verdict," *American Banker*, January 31, 1995, p. 6.

Rhoads, Christopher, "$39M Awarded in Car Loan Case Brings Slew of Similar Claims," *American Banker*, January 31,1995, p. 6.

———, "Trustmark in $8.8M Settlement of Collateral Insurance Suit," *American Banker*, November 27, 1996, p. 6.

Sheffield, Christopher, "Banks Circling Their Wagons," *Memphis Business Journal*, October 3, 2008.

"Trustmark Announces Second Quarter Earnings," *Business Wire*, July 8, 1997.

"Trustmark Completes Buy," *Mississippi Business Journal*, December 20, 2004, p. 10.

"Trustmark Corporation Announces Second Quarter 2009 Financial Results and Declares $0.23 Quarterly Cash Dividend," Reuters, July 28, 2009.

"Trustmark Corporation Completes Sale of $215 Million in Senior Preferred Shares to the U.S. Treasury," *Business Wire*, November 21, 2008.

"Trustmark Sets New Record," *Mississippi Business Journal*, February 3, 2003, p. 10.

"Washington National Announces Sale of Large Group Life and Health Insurance Business to Trustmark Insurance," *Business Wire*, July 8, 1996.

Ubisoft Entertainment S.A.

28 rue Armand Carrel
Montreuil, Cedex 93 108
France
Telephone: (+33 1) 48-18-50-00
Fax: (+33 1) 48-57-07-41
Web site: http://www.ubisoft.com

Public Company
Founded: 1986
Employees: 5,750
Sales: EUR 928.3 million ($1.32 billion) (2008)
Stock Exchanges: Euronext Paris
Ticker Symbol: UBI
NAICS: 511210 Software Publishers

■ ■ ■

Founded in 1986, Ubisoft Entertainment S.A. is a global producer, publisher, and distributor of interactive entertainment products. From humble beginnings, Ubisoft has grown to become the third-largest independent publisher of video games in Europe and the fourth largest in the United States.

MODEST BEGINNINGS

On the coast of Brittany, France, the Guillemot family owned a small farm supply store that catered to local farmers. Shortly after his parents retired, Michel Guillemot, who was one of five sons, came up with the idea of importing video games from England, where he had just vacationed and discovered that they sold for half of what they sold for in France. The family chose Yves, who was the second oldest of the brothers, to operate the new company they named Ubisoft. The name, according to Geoff Keighley, was derived from *ubiquity* and *software*.

Ubisoft released its first video game, *Zombi*, for the popular Atari system in 1990. During the early 1990s the company established distribution subsidiaries in the United States, the United Kingdom, and Germany before opening its first international studio in Bucharest, Romania, in 1992. A year later, an internal studio was formed in Paris, France, and the Montpellier Studio was also opened in France in 1994. In 1995 Ubisoft's headquarter studio created its second video game, *Rayman*, for the Atari Jaguar system.

By opening studios in Bucharest and Shanghai, China, the company was able to keep its costs down. Locating in cities with no competition also brought Ubisoft some badly needed cash. Inside each studio there were roughly 80 to 90 employees, some of whom were managers who worked together to develop video games. The team effort extended throughout all the studios. For example, while the *Sands of Time* game was developed in Montreal, Canada, the core software was created in a studio in France, and the leading programmer was in Shanghai. The successful collaboration between studios resulted in *Sands of Time* being named the "PS2 Game of the Year" by GameZone in 2003.

Unlike its chief competitor, Electronic Arts Inc., which had costly studios in Southern California, Ubisoft focused on setting up less expensive studios. Ubisoft began in an old 175,000-square-foot textile

COMPANY PERSPECTIVES

A leading creator, publisher and distributor of video games, Ubisoft has grown considerably over the past two decades as a result of our strategy centered on the creation of strong brands, in-house development, and a vast global distribution network. This has allowed us to not only produce innovative, high-quality titles but also acquire an in-depth knowledge of our consumers and their expectations.

factory. Ubisoft's 1,000 employees worked in an open space among intertwined wires that sprawled over the wood floor where such games as *Myst* and *Prince of Persia* were launched.

Ubisoft Paris was established in the Parisian suburb of Montreuil. The original in-house studio was responsible for the creation of *Rayman*, the blockbuster game that would eventually sell over 20 million copies worldwide. The game was followed with *Rayman 2: The Great Escape, Rayman 3: Hoodlum Havoc,* and *Red Steel.* The Paris studio laid the groundwork for the introduction of games, such as *Tom Clancy's Splinter Cell Pandora Tomorrow* and *Tom Clancy's Ghost Recon Advanced Warfighter.*

GLOBAL EXPANSION

In 1992 Ubisoft traveled out of France to establish Ubisoft Bucharest in Romania. Two years later it opened a graphics department in Montpellier, France, which was responsible for developing the popular *Beyond Good and Evil* and *Peter Jackson's King Kong: The Official Game of the Movie,* both of which involved the well-known video game creator Michel Ancel. In 1996 it established Ubisoft Annecy, whose group of game designers produced *Rayman 2: The Great Escape* for the PlayStation 2 game system. The team was also responsible for the online marketing versions of Ubisoft's leading games, such as *Tom Clancy's Splinter Cell Chaos Theory, Tom Clancy's Splinter Cell Double Agent,* and *Dark Messiah of Might and Magic Elements.* That same year the company opened another studio in Shanghai, China, and was listed on the Second Market of the Paris Stock Exchange. In the late 1990s Ubisoft opened studios in Canada, Morocco, Spain, and Italy. In addition, business offices were opened in China, Hong Kong, the Netherlands, and Denmark.

In 2000 Ubisoft acquired 20 percent of the capital in the initial public offering of Gameloft, a mobile

telephone game developer. This purchase was followed with the launch of the Ubi.com online video game portal. That same year Ubisoft acquired Red Storm Entertainment of Morrisville, North Carolina. The year ended with Ubisoft's shares being transferred to the First Market of the Paris Stock Exchange.

After 2000 the company opened additional business offices in Switzerland, Finland, and South Korea. Software developers, including Ubisoft, were disappointed when Sega decided in 2001 against launching its Dreamcast game console, for which developers had been working on games. Ubisoft had four games under development that would never hit the store shelves. This merely added to the gaming industry's woes because it was also experiencing the strain of the tough economic conditions that resulted from the contraction of the dot-com industry between 2000 and 2001.

While sales for Ubisoft's *Rayman* franchise surged in France, its U.S. sales lagged. To boost sales in the United States, the company decided to spend $4 million to market *Rayman 3: Hoodlum Havoc* with television spots on, for example, the Cartoon Network, Comedy Central, Fox Sports, and MTV. The momentum continued with the company spending $20 million during the fourth quarter of 2003 for television spots to promote five of its titles, including the new release *Tom Clancy's Rainbow Six 3.* Perhaps the most significant milestone was reached in 2003, when the company sold its 100 millionth video game.

In December 2004 Electronic Arts bought a 19.9 percent interest in Ubisoft. The *New York Times* noted in December 2004 that even though the news boosted Ubisoft's shares, Ubisoft referred to the purchase as "hostile." Regardless, the Guillemot family still held 26.4 percent of Ubisoft's voting rights. *Screen Digest* noted in January 2005 that given "the high profile nature of this acquisition and speculation in the gaming press over Ubisoft's potential business partners, [the industry] could see this drama being played out for some time." The deal cost Electronic Arts somewhere between $85 million and $100 million.

EXPANDING APPEAL

Beginning in 2004 Ubisoft began to expand the focus of its games to appeal to a larger market of game players. It signed licensing deals with several movie studios, including Universal Studios, Sony Pictures, and LucasArts, to develop games that were based on the studios' movie releases. Among the games that resulted from these deals were *Peter Jackson's King Kong: The Official Game of the Movie* and *Star Wars: Episode III Revenge of the Sith.*

KEY DATES

1986: Ubisoft Entertainment S.A. is founded.
1990: Ubisoft develops and releases its first game, *Zombi*.
1992: Company's first international studio is formed in Bucharest, Romania.
1996: Ubisoft is listed on the Second Market of the Paris Stock Exchange.
2000: Company's stock is transferred to First Market of the Paris Stock Exchange.
2003: Ubisoft sells its 100 millionth video game.
2005: Ubisoft Campus is established to promote video game training programs in Canada.
2008: Ubisoft acquires the intellectual property rights to the Tom Clancy name for video games and related products; the company partners with Sigma Technologies to establish a second Ubisoft Campus.

When Microsoft announced that it was exiting the sports video game market in 2005, Ubisoft bought the assets of Microsoft's team sports video games, such as football, basketball, and hockey.

Although some companies used external methods for game development, Ubisoft continued to conduct its business totally internally. For instance, the company further strengthened its strategy of in-house development by opening Ubisoft Campus in Montreal in 2005. The campus was set up to strengthen team effort and collaboration between studios by providing additional training for current employees, as well as for newcomers entering the gaming industry.

Furthering its video game offerings, Ubisoft acquired the well-known *Driver* franchise in 2006. However, Ubisoft's most significant news flash that year, followed the release of *Tom Clancy's Ghost Recon Advanced Warfighter* for the Xbox 360 game system. The company sold more games during the first week than any previous releases and earned the Best Game of the Year at the British Academy of Film and Television Arts Awards ceremony.

The following year the new video game *Assassin's Creed* sold more than 2.5 million copies in less than four weeks, making it the top-selling video game released in the United States and the United Kingdom. In February 2007 Ubisoft Digital Arts was established to create computer-generated images.

In 2007 U.S. sales in the video game industry topped $18.8 billion, and Western Europe video game sales trailed with $17.9 billion. Ubisoft took in a portion of these sales; since the release of *Assassin's Creed* in November 2007, the company sold over six million copies, making it the largest release in video game franchise history in the United States and the United Kingdom.

In 2008 the company acquired Massive Entertainment, a Swedish-based studio. It then bought Hybride Technologies of Montreal, a creator of visual effects for cinema, television, and advertising. Ubisoft opened additional business offices in Poland and Brazil and established a studio in Ukraine. It also partnered with Sigma Technologies, an audiovisual firm, to create another Ubisoft Campus in Casablanca, Morocco. The joint venture was intended to promote video game training programs in Morocco. Perhaps the biggest accomplishment of the year was in March, when the company announced that it had purchased the intellectual property rights to the Tom Clancy name. This acquisition encompassed video games and related products, such as books and movies.

EFFECTS OF ECONOMIC RECESSION

Even though Ubisoft began 2009 on the upside with the announcement that it had acquired Action Pants Inc., a video game developer in Vancouver, Canada, and Southlogic Studios, an independent video game developer in Brazil, its sales figures were on the downturn. By mid-2009 the company was beginning to feel the effects of the economic recession that began in 2007. Between sluggish sales of Nintendo DS games in both the United States and Europe and a lack of new releases, Ubisoft's sales fell 51 percent by the end of June compared to the year before. Adding to the company's woes, its U.S. market share fell from 5.6 percent in 2008 to 4.8 percent by June 2009.

Laurent Detoc, the president of Ubisoft's U.S. operations, told *Forbes* in June 2008, "We just did 'Assassin's' and are sitting on top of the world, but we have to come back to reality very quickly because you're only as good as your last product." For 2009 the company planned to release five new games.

As the year progressed, the release of *Avatar*, which was based on the 2009 James Cameron film; *Assassin's Creed 2*; and *Tom Clancy's Splinter Cell Conviction* were anticipated to make up for slow sales during the first half of 2009. Ubisoft, however, decided not to release some titles, such as *Red Steel 2*, until the economy improved.

Brenda Kubiac

PRINCIPAL SUBSIDIARIES

Ubisoft France S.A.S.; Ubisoft Montreal; Ubisoft GmbH.

PRINCIPAL COMPETITORS

Atari Corporation; Electronic Arts Inc.; Vivendi S.A.; Microsoft Corporation; Activision Blizzard Inc.; THQ, Inc.

FURTHER READING

"EA Buys Share of Rival Games Company," *Screen Digest*, January 2005, p. 24.

"Electronic Arts Buys Stake in a Rival Game Maker in France," *New York Times*, December 21, 2004, p. C9.

Feldman, Curt, "Electronic Arts Buys State in Ubisoft in 'Hostile' Act," GameSpot, December 20, 2004, http://www.gamespot.com/news/6115370.html.

Hein, Kenneth, "Ubisoft Moves to Make Rayman No. 1," *Brandweek*, March 10, 2003, p. 11.

———, "Ubisoft Reloads 'Clancy' TV Support with $20M: Prince of Persia Also Gets Spotlight in Videogamer's Q4 Effort," *Brandweek*, November 3, 2003, p. 10.

Irwin, Mary Jane, "Europe's Top Gamer," *Forbes*, June 18, 2008.

Keighley, Geoff, "Massively Multinational Player: By Spreading the Work among Nine Countries, Yves Guillemot Made Ubisoft's Game Studios the Cheapest—and the Most Creative—in the Industry," *Business 2.0*, September 2005, p. 64.

"Microsoft Pulls Back from Sports Video Game Market," *PC Magazine Online*, March 2, 2005.

Sanders, Adrienne, "Games Explode," *San Francisco Business Times*, November 11, 2005.

Satariano, Adam, "Ubisoft to Slow Hiring after Adding 1,300, CEO Guillemot Says," Bloomberg.com, May 27, 2009.

Temple, James, "Sega Dampens Prospects in Video Game Market," *San Francisco Business Times*, February 16, 2001, p. 9.

"Ubisoft Pushes $10 Mil. King Kong Game in Wake of Movie." *Adweek*, October 31, 2005, p. 4.

Vodacom Group Pty. Ltd.

Vodacom Corporate Park
082 Vodacom Boulevard
Vodavalley
Midrand, 1685
South Africa
Telephone: (+27 11) 653-5000
Fax: (+27 11) 653-5900
Web site: http://www.vodacom.co.za

Public Company
Founded: 1993
Employees: 7,255
Sales: ZAR 187.1 billion ($23.84 billion)
Stock Exchanges: Johannesburg
Ticker Symbol: VODJ
NAICS: 517110 Telecommunications Internet Service Providers; 517210 Telecommunications Carriers, Cellular Telephone; 518210 Data Processing, Hosting, and Other Services; 541513 Computer Facilities Management Services

■ ■ ■

Vodacom Group Pty. Ltd. brings mobile telephone and Internet-related services to customers in South Africa, Tanzania, the Democratic Republic of the Congo, Lesotho, and Mozambique. The company also provides services related to business data storage, management, and security.

ESTABLISHMENT OF JOINT VENTURE AND NEW GOVERNMENT

Vodacom was established in 1993 as a joint venture between the British-based Vodafone, with a 35 percent stake; the South African parastatal (government-owned) Telkom S.A. Ltd., with a 50 percent stake; and VenFin Ltd., with a 15 percent stake. That same year the company received South Africa's first Global Satellite Mobile (GSM) communications license, ushering in the country's new cell phone industry. By March 1994 at least two base stations were being built every day to prepare for the anticipated demand for cell phone service. On June 1, 1994, the official "switch-on" day, 100,000 customers were connected, with a further 50,000 signing up during the following four weeks.

At the same time, the country was in a fever of excitement over the April 1994 elections. The African National Congress won by a landslide, and Nelson Mandela became the new president. From the outset, the new government made it clear that black empowerment would be a major issue in the postapartheid regime, not only to compensate for the evils of the past but also to extend the same opportunities for advancement to all members of its society, regardless of their heritage. In Vodacom's case, the message was clear. The license issued in 1993 would have to be revised to bring access and empowerment to previously disadvantaged black South Africans. Vodacom was not fazed by this requirement. It even offered a 5 percent stake in the company to any trade union that wanted to buy it.

COMPANY PERSPECTIVES

VODACOM believes that it can enhance people's lives and empower them by making it possible for all people in Africa to have access to mobile telecommunications. We have the will and the means to do so, and will strive to do so in a sensible manner. We will democratise telecommunications.

VODACOM will seek out the impossible to do in mobile communications, which have been made possible by the most innovative technology in the world. Technology will continue to develop and make possible things we cannot even dream of today. We will remain the most competent and innovative of all in this Information and Communications Technology, to not only dream the dreams but to make every dream come true.

Alan Knott-Craig, the chief executive officer of Vodacom, told Sarah Hudleston of *Business Day* in 2007, "The funny thing was that it took a long time before any union took up the shares. Eventually Marcel Golding and Johnny Copelyn of HCI—the investment arm of the South African Commercial, Catering and Allied Workers—bought the 5% stake for R50m [ZAR 50 million], selling it many years later for R1,5bn [ZAR 1.5 billion]."

That was not all, however, the company did to show solidarity with the new regime. Determined to help the disadvantaged, Vodacom budgeted ZAR 5 million for an innovative community services program that was designed to promote financial independence. The company believed that franchises were the best way to provide this independence, so it looked for suitable locations in the black urban townships and offered each would-be entrepreneur the chance to own a phone shop for a fee of ZAR 26,000, which bought a complete setup of five phone lines, sometimes with added fax and data capabilities. Vodacom subsidized these services so that customers who could not afford their own cell phones paid reduced rates. Franchising was a financially sound option because the business owner maintained a steady living of about ZAR 9,000 per month and Vodacom gained brand recognition. Each phone shop was set up inside a converted shipping container that was painted in Vodacom's signature green and prominently displayed its logo.

BRANDING AND A NEW HEADQUARTERS

Nevertheless, company executives were conscious that this type of community service depended on a company's ability to provide the money for it and that the necessary profitability would come from middle- and higher-income subscribers who could afford to pay full price for their cell phones. Knott-Craig asked for help from the highly experienced brand manager Leon Crouse, who suggested a widespread television advertising campaign that appealed to adults and a new market niche for cell phones: teenagers. The advertising campaign proved successful. Vodacom's cell phones quickly became a popular choice among teens because the phones offered games, a wide selection of ring tones, wallpapers devoted to sports, and other appealing accessories.

By the mid-1990s Vodacom was eyeing expansion possibilities for its core South African business premises. It settled on a vast tract of land midway between the two Gauteng Province business hubs, Johannesburg and Pretoria, and began to build a new complex that would eventually be the headquarters for its offices.

Phase one began in March 1998. Called Vodaworld, it was the world's first shopping mall completely devoted to cellular phone communications and Internet service. This mall offered a home to a wide array of telecommunications-based tenants, such as Nokia and Samsung, and even to businesses that sold sound systems and communications accessories for cars and trucks. Conventioneers from out of town appreciated its conference center and offices, as well as its recreational facilities, which included fountains, a chip-putt golf course, a movie center, and three cybercafés. Vodaworld phase one cost ZAR 50 million but the company soon earned its purchase price in convention dates.

Another first for Vodacom came the same year when it launched Vodago, a prepaid phone card that was available in packs from ZAR 10 to ZAR 95. This arrived in tandem with Yebo!net, the world's first prepaid access to the Internet. Vodacom expected to earn back its ZAR 300 million investment in only three years.

The following year signaled even greater changes for the company. During the year Vodacom acquired both GSM Cellular Pty. Ltd. and Teljoy Holdings, a large South African cellular provider that was worth about ZAR 870 million. These two cellular service providers joined two other holdings, Vodac Pty. Ltd. and Cellphones Direct Pty. Ltd., all of which were consolidated into a new company called Vodacom Service Provider Company in 2000. To provide more office space for the new company, plus a spacious single setting for Voda-

KEY DATES

1993: Telkom S.A. Ltd. is issued a license for Vodacom.
1994: Vodacom welcomes its first customers.
1996: Vodacom opens Vodacom Lesotho, its first international subsidiary.
1998: Phase one of Vodaworld is completed.
1999: Phase two of Vodaworld is completed.
2000: Vodacom Tanzania opens.
2002: Vodacom Congo opens.
2003: Vodacom Mozambique opens.
2008: Vodacom acquires Gateway Telecommunications S.A. Pty. Ltd.; the Vodacom Business Data Center opens.
2009: Vodacom is listed on the Johannesburg Stock Exchange.

com's head office, Vodaworld began a second phase of construction. This phase was completed by November 1999 at the cost of ZAR 250 million. Immediately, Vodacom set about the construction of phase three, which eventually supplied a second call center for customer service, a gigantic warehouse for cell phone accessory stocks, and stunning landscaping specifically designed and constructed to have no detrimental effect on the existing environment.

EXPANSION BEYOND THE BORDERS

While all this was in progress, Vodacom had been eyeing possibilities for expansion beyond South Africa's borders. Its first venture had taken place in 1995, when it was awarded a GSM license in Lesotho. Vodacom Lesotho started operating in 1996, with the government of Lesotho as an equal partner. Living in a mountainous country where face-to-face visiting is not always easy, Lesotho citizens took to the cell phone with great eagerness. By March 2003 the country had 77,474 subscribers, all enjoying their first taste of prepaid phone cards.

Lesotho's success prompted Vodacom to try a second enterprise. Its next expansion effort took it to Tanzania, where in 1999 the company obtained a license to activate service. Pausing only to put the necessary infrastructure in place, the company had Vodacom Tanzania up and running by August 2000. Already familiar with corporate strategy, the new subsidiary soon had 98.4 percent of customers paying their bills by means of prepaid phone cards and enjoying midrange prices on most handsets. Tanzanians were so enthusiastic about all of Vodacom's services that their numbers reached a total of 447,438 customers by March 2003.

Vodacom service became available in the Democratic Republic of the Congo as well. Launched in May 2002, Vodacom Congo's subscriber level had reached 247,909 by March 2003. In August of the same year, Vodacom acquired a license in Mozambique, where it was one of only two mobile communications providers. Despite this advantage, the lack of infrastructure, which was a bitter legacy of the country's civil war, delayed its actual launch until December 2003.

The delay in Mozambique notwithstanding, the bottom line for 2003 showed improvement. Vodacom's customer base had increased by 26 percent over the year before, to reach a total of 8.6 million subscribers, contributing to a satisfying overall 2003 revenue of ZAR 19.8 billion for all operations.

The success of Vodacom's international operations clearly showed in its annual report for 2005. Revenue for all operations was ZAR 27.3 billion, with ZAR 183 million contributed by Vodacom Tanzania, ZAR 50 million by Vodacom Congo, and ZAR 25 million by Vodacom Lesotho. The only loss came from Vodacom Mozambique, where the company lost ZAR 454 million despite the country's 265,000 customers. Furthermore, the company's customer base continued to expand. By the end of its financial year for 2005, there were 1.2 million subscribers in Tanzania, a million in the Democratic Republic of the Congo, and 147,000 in Lesotho. In South Africa the number of Vodacom customers had reached 12.8 million.

3G AND VODAFONE

This growth was partly due to third-generation (3G) technology, which had been introduced in December 2003. Providing up-to-the-minute technology, 3G offered greater speed and connectivity for subscribers located anywhere in the world that the service was available. In April 2004 Vodacom made 3G more desirable when Smartphone SP, a subsidiary, acquired 85.7 percent of Smartcom, a designer of software for universal connectivity to the Internet, for ZAR 77.2 billion.

In early 2005 these two innovations came together to enhance an extremely important alliance with one of Vodacom's major shareholders: the British-based Vodafone, the largest international mobile phone operator in the world. Vodacom found two main advantages in this partnership. First, courtesy of Vodafone, it was able to offer customers global news and entertainment, e-mail service, and video calls at the same rate as voice calls. Second, it was able to divide all international service areas into five zones, so that any Vodacom user traveling in one of them could immediately see what his or her roaming charges would be for calling.

In 2006 Vodacom's prepaid customer base reached 16.8 million, partly as a result of a Vodafone share increase from 35 percent to 50 percent. This was achieved in a two-stage deal whereby Vodafone bought VenFin's 35 percent share of Vodacom for ZAR 21 billion, then sold all of VenFin's other assets to a new company for ZAR 5 billion. In another move, the company spent ZAR 25 billion on infrastructure in South Africa, so that it could offer faster High-Speed Downlink Packet Access technology to its customers. Subscribers clearly appreciated the new technology, because the company's profits for 2006 soared to ZAR 8.9 billion, and its customer list rose to 23.5 million.

GRADUATE PROGRAMME FOR FEMALES IN TECHNOLOGY

Besides having to constantly improve its infrastructure, Vodacom had another concern that needed to be addressed. Since 2004 the company had noted that it had a shortage of qualified black women employed in the technology-focused areas of operations—a shortfall that produced an unacceptable drop in its Broad-Based Black Economic Empowerment (BBBEE) standards, a government act that had been passed to address inequality among South African citizens. Vowing to correct this, in 2006 Vodacom allocated ZAR 15 million to open a Graduate Programme for Females in Technology. The three-year course, which was offered at the Midrand headquarters, focused on engineering in the telecommunications industry, business and leadership skills, and the corporate culture of both Vodacom and the telecommunications industry. The program also included a fixed one-year contract, plus hands-on experience in one of the company's international facilities. Permanent employment within the company was a strong possibility.

A NEW DIRECTION

Beginning in 2008 the company started on a new track. Its first step came in February, when the Vodacom Business Data Center was launched to reposition Vodacom as a provider of telecommunications infrastructure and of mobile communications. Later in the year, Vodacom announced a $675 million acquisition of Gateway Telecommunications S.A. Pty. Ltd., a satellite and carrier

services company. Owning Gateway pointed the way toward the next step: the ZAR 100 million Johannesburg-based data center, which opened for business in November 2008. With the capability of handling up to 20,000 client servers at any given moment, the data center offered backup, management, and security services for business clients who preferred to outsource these services.

That same year the shareholders of Vodacom, principally Telkom and Vodafone, agreed to set aside a 6 percent share, totaling ZAR 7.5 billion, to satisfy the equity requirements of BBBEE. Of this amount, 45 percent was to be shared between Royal Bafokeng Holdings, an investment group acting on behalf of the Bafokeng people of the North West Province, and Thebe Investment Corporation, a company that was owned by the Batho Batho Trust, an organization specifically set up to help disadvantaged black South Africans. Twenty-five percent was to be made available for black South African staff members working both within South Africa and beyond its borders, and the remaining 30 percent was to be made available to YeboYethu, a Vodacom-owned company that was created for low-income black South African investors. According to Moneyweb.co.za, the share offer raised ZAR 946 million, and 49 percent of the applicants for the sold-out YeboYethu shares were black women. Of the total, excluding the shares bought by the two preferred companies, 60 percent were for the minimum amount of 100 shares, which could be purchased for ZAR 2,500. The share offer also increased the total number of Vodacom's customers for 2008 to 34 million. Furthermore, the company reported revenues of ZAR 48.2 billion and a net profit of ZAR 7.9 billion.

VODACOM GOES PUBLIC

Vodacom witnessed two major developments in 2009. The first was the purchase of a 51 percent share in Storage Technology Services Pty. Ltd., a black empowerment company that stored, secured, and managed the data systems of businesses that outsourced these functions for greater efficiency.

Then, on May 18, 2009, Vodacom was listed on the Johannesburg Stock Exchange for the first time. The story behind this lay with Telkom and Vodafone, each of which had held a 50 percent share of the Vodacom Group. In 2008 Telkom sold a 15 percent stake to Vodafone, in a deal totaling ZAR 22.5 billion. According to industry analysts, Telkom was expected to unbundle the remaining 35 percent of Vodacom sometime in the future.

When the 2008 fiscal year ended on March 31, 2009, Vodacom reported revenues of ZAR 55.2 billion, a net profit of ZAR 6.2 billion, and 39.6 million subscribers. As for the Vodacom Business Data Center, the first really comprehensive diversification, it offered 28 new products in data management, storage, and security services, and contributed ZAR 4.7 billion after just one full year of operation. The road ahead for Vodacom looked bright with promise.

Gillian Wolf

PRINCIPAL SUBSIDIARIES

Vodacom International Pty. Ltd.; Vodacom Lesotho Pty. Ltd.; Vodacom Congo RDC; Vodacom Mozambique; Vodacom Tanzania Ltd.

PRINCIPAL COMPETITORS

Orange Telecom; Telefónica Europe; T-Mobile International; MTN Group Ltd.

FURTHER READING

Bridges, Sherilee, "Yebo!net Go-Going for a JSE Listing," *Sunday Times: Business Times*, October 25, 1998.

"Cell Giant Grows Investment in Women in Telecoms Programme," *iweek*, February 16, 2009.

"Development without Destruction," *Vodaworld Magazine*, 2001.

Hudleston, Sarah, "Father of SA's Mobile Industry," *Business Day*, August 4, 2007.

Kaye, Alex, "Vodacom Opens R100 Million Data Centre," *IT-Web*, November 14, 2008.

Klein, Marcia, "Rutstein Makes a Splash in Telecoms," *Sunday Times: Business Times*, March 29, 1998.

"Machel's Group Gets Vodacom Stake," Fin24.com, May 12, 2008, http://www.fin24.com/articles/default/display_article.aspx?ArticleId=1518-24_2320878.

Middleton, James, "Vodacom Snaps Up Gateway," Telecoms.com, August 29, 2008, http://www.telecoms.com/5749/vodacom-snaps-up-gateway.

Mochiko, Thabiso, "VenFin Holders Stand to Gain R16bn," *Business Report*, November 4, 2005.

Reck, Jennifer, and Brad Wood, "What Works: Case Study: Vodacom's Community Phone Shops," *World Resources Institute*, August, 2003, http://www.digitaldividend.org/pdf/vodacom.pdf.

Telkom S.A. Ltd., *Report of Foreign Private Issuer*, May 2003, https://secure1.telkom.co.za/apps_static/ir/pdf/financial/pdf/6-K-030703.pdf.

"TKG—Telkom—Results of the YeboYethu Limited Public Offer," Moneyweb.co.za, October 8, 2008, http://moneyweb.profile.co.za/moneyweb/sharedata/scripts/sens.asp?id=127562.

"Vodacom Consolidates Service Providers and Streamlines Operations," *Vodacom News*, 2009, http://www.vodaworld.co.za/showarticle.asp?id=328.

"Vodacom Makes Cash Offer to Acquire Teljoy," Dispatch Online, October 19, 1999, http://www.dispatch.co.za/1999/10/19/business/BUS1.HTM.

"Vodafone to Pay ZAR 22.5 Billion for Acquiring 15 Percent Stake in Vodacom," *Iraq Telecom*, November 2008, p. 16.

Webster Financial Corporation

Webster Plaza
145 Bank Street
Waterbury, Connecticut 06702-2211
U.S.A.
Telephone: (203) 465-4364
Toll Free: (800) 325-2424
Fax: (203) 573-8688
Web site: http://www.websteronline.com

Public Company
Founded: 1935 as First Federal Savings of Waterbury, Connecticut
Incorporated: 1986 as Webster Financial Corporation
Employees: 2,935
Total Assets: $17.6 billion (2008)
Stock Exchanges: New York
Ticker Symbol: WBS
NAICS: 551111 Offices of Bank Holding Companies

■ ■ ■

Webster Financial Corporation is the holding company for Webster Bank, which owns and operates the lending company Webster Business Credit Corporation, the insurance finance company Budget Installment Corporation, Center Capital Corporation, and HSA Bank, a division of Webster Bank that offers health savings account and trustee and administrative services. Headquartered in Waterbury, Connecticut, Webster Financial Corporation is the nation's 29th-largest financial services holding company for federally and state-chartered savings banks and the largest commercial bank in Connecticut.

Webster Bank offers commercial, consumer, and small business products and services, including business and consumer banking, mortgage, financial planning, trust, and investment services through its 181 banking offices, 492 automated teller machines, phone banking, and the Internet. For commercial banking, it provides financial services geared toward businesses with revenues of more than $10 million, including asset-based lending, commercial real estate, organization lending, and international banking. On the consumer and small business banking side, Webster provides traditional products and services, including savings and investments with $10 million or less in revenues. In the area of consumer finance, Webster provides mortgage, equity, and other consumer lending products and services.

EARLY HISTORY

Harold Webster Smith founded First Federal Savings of Waterbury, Connecticut, in 1935, when other banks were failing during the Great Depression. Having borrowed $25,000 from his family and friends to open the savings and loan, the young banking entrepreneur returned the favor by offering low-interest loans to his neighbors. By 1938 the thrift institution had more than $1 million in assets and, according to Annie Sullivan of *American Banker*, was "the first in the state to offer GI loans and the first in the Waterbury area to make FHA [Federal Housing Authority] loans."

In 1986 First Federal became a publicly traded company and established Webster Financial Corporation as its holding company. The following year Smith retired after being the chief executive officer (CEO) for

COMPANY PERSPECTIVES

Webster's culture is firmly rooted in the values it established when it was founded in 1935. These values—what the company today calls "The Webster Way"—were memorialized in 1995 when the company changed its name in honor of its founder, Harold Webster Smith.

The Webster Way

• We take personal responsibility for meeting our customers' needs.

• We respect the dignity of every individual.

• We earn trust through ethical behavior.

• We give of ourselves in the communities we serve.

• We work together to achieve outstanding results.

Webster's "We Find a Way" brand reflects our core beliefs, company culture and the long-standing positive attitude Webster employees bring to serving customers.

52 years and was replaced by his son, James C. Smith. In 1998 Webster merged with Eagle Financial Corporation, making it the 46th largest bank in the United States, with $16 billion in combined assets. A clear milestone was reached in mid-1997, when Webster Financial Corporation was added to the Russell 2000 index of leading U.S. small capitalization stocks. By 1990 one of every four banks in Connecticut was in some capacity part of Webster.

EXPANSION IN THE EARLY TO MID-NINETIES

Smith knew that if Webster was to remain competitive, it had to expand its market presence. Therefore, throughout the 1990s the company announced one acquisition after another. Webster's initial acquisition was in October 1991, with the purchase of Suffield Bank. It acquired First Constitution Bank and Bristol Savings Bank in 1993 and Bristol Mortgage Company in 1994. This trend continued into the following year, with the acquisitions of Shoreline Bank & Trust and Shelton Savings Bank. In November 1995 Smith explained to *PR Newswire* that this growth required reorganization. "Webster Financial Corporation merged

its subsidiary banks and renamed them Webster Bank to present a unified image in all the markets it serves and to achieve operating efficiencies associated with maintaining one bank rather than several institutions," he said. "In renaming the banks Webster Bank, we honor our founder, Harold Webster Smith, who formed the bank 60 years ago."

Following the acquisition of 20 Shawmut National Corporation bank branches in 1996, Webster's assets totaled an estimated $4 billion, and it served the Connecticut counties of New Haven, Fairfield, Hartford, and Litchfield. In 1997 Webster added Darby Savings Bank, People's Savings & Trust, and Sachem Trust. The company continued on its path of expansion by merging with Eagle Financial Corporation in 1998, which increased Webster's total number of branch locations to over 100. That same year it acquired Damman Insurance Associates and Access National Mortgage, an Internet-based mortgage lender. In 1999 Webster began offering mortgages via the Internet through its newly formed subsidiary, Access National Mortgage, LLC. Webster rounded out 1999 by acquiring Maritime Bank & Trust, Village Bank, and New England Bancorp.

NEW DIRECTION

Acquisition activity showed no sign of waning in 2000, when Webster bought Mechanics Savings Bank, six branch locations from Chase Manhattan Bank, and four branch locations from BankBoston. Webster turned its focus to niche markets that would capitalize and drive growth in the financial products and services sector with the acquisitions of Musante Reihl Associates Insurance Agency, Center Capital Corporation, and Wolff-Zackin & Associates Inc. Additionally, Webster continued adding more products and services, such as the launch in June 2000 of Webster Financial Advisors to serve nonprofit organizations and business clients with investments of a minimum of $400,000. In November 2000 it purchased a majority ownership in Duff and Phelps, LLC, to guide investors and assist in handling mergers and acquisitions.

In 2002 Webster was the leading bank in Connecticut, with $12 billion in assets, followed by People's Mutual Holdings in Bridgeport, with $11.8 billion in assets. Even though Webster had over 100 branch offices located throughout Connecticut, plans were under way for 20 additional branches in Fairfield County over the next two years. By June 2003 Webster controlled 11.43 percent of Connecticut's assets, compared to 5.7 percent in 1996, based on figures provided by the Federal Deposit Insurance Corporation. Webster's closest rival, People's Mutual Holdings, had 12.63 percent in deposits for 2003, compared to 9.2 percent in 1996.

KEY DATES

■

1935: Harold Webster Smith founds First Federal Savings of Waterbury, Connecticut.

1938: First Federal's assets grow to more than $1 million.

1986: First Federal becomes a publicly traded company and establishes Webster Financial Corporation as its holding company.

1987: James C. Smith becomes the company's second chief executive officer, succeeding his father, Harold Webster Smith.

1995: Webster Financial Corporation combines its subsidiary banks and renames them as Webster Bank.

1998: Webster's merger with Eagle Financial Corporation brings the total number of branch offices to over 100; Webster purchases Damman Insurance Associates and Access National Mortgage.

2004: Webster becomes a commercial bank; it acquires FirstFed America Bancorp Inc.

2005: Webster acquires HSA Bank and becomes the leading bank administrator and trustee of health savings accounts in the United States.

In 2004 Webster filed the necessary forms with the Office of the Comptroller of the Currency to legally alter its charter from a federal savings bank, or thrift, to a commercial bank. The bank also filed with the Federal Reserve System to become a financial holding company. That May the media took note, as did CEOs from other banking institutions, when Webster acquired FirstFed America Bancorp Inc. of Swansea, Massachusetts, for $465 million. This was the largest purchase based on assets for Webster and the first time the bank ventured outside of Connecticut. In March 2005 Webster expanded its portfolio even further by acquiring HSA Bank, which made it the leading bank-owned administrator and trustee of health savings accounts in the United States.

Competition surrounding health savings accounts began to surface in 2006 as other financial institutions, specifically Mellon Financial Corporation, wanted a piece of the action. HSA Bank, a division of Webster, had more than 150,000 accounts, or about 29 percent of the national total, and wrote up an average of 5,000 accounts per month. The media and marketing company Information Strategies Inc. told Steve Garm-

hausen of the *American Banker* that "the new industry is growing fast. In 2005, the number of financial institutions offering health savings accounts soared from 100 to 600." To retain its dominant market share, Webster would continue building on relationships and partnerships.

VOLATILE MARKET CONDITIONS IN THE 21ST CENTURY

During 2007 volatile market conditions caused a wave of mortgage-related write-downs not only for Webster but also for the banking industry, as home values plummeted, unemployment soared, and foreclosures climbed. In response to these conditions, Webster's focus turned to capturing commercial accounts. It also closed its Peoples Mortgage unit, ended its mezzanine lending business through Webster Growth Capital, and put an end to residential lending outside its primary New England market. Volatile market conditions persisted through 2008, so Webster sold the Webster Insurance subsidiary to USI Holdings and Webster Risk Services, a third-party workers' compensation claims administrator, to PMA Capital. Faced with unprecedented losses, the company was forced to layoff roughly 240 people and close some of its branches in 2008.

These actions did little to offset its declining stock prices, which fell from a high of $44.64 per share during the fourth quarter of 2007 to $26.88 per share in the fourth quarter of 2008. Webster reported a net loss of $321.8 million for 2008, compared to a net income of $96.8 million for 2007. On December 31, 2008, Webster handled consumer and commercial deposits throughout 181 banking offices located in Connecticut, Massachusetts, Rhode Island, and New York.

In response to the financial crisis that affected many financial institutions, Congress passed the Emergency Economic Stabilization Act (EESA) in October 2008. Under the EESA, financial institutions could apply for funding to offset their losses. Even though Webster did not participate in subprime lending, which laid the groundwork for the initial financial meltdown, the bank participated in the Troubled Asset Relief Program (TARP) by receiving $400 million in TARP funds in February 2009. Webster planned to use these funds for community lending and for future acquisitions.

Despite the U.S. government's efforts to stabilize and stimulate the economy, difficult market conditions persisted into 2009. Between the staggering number of foreclosures that translated into bank write-offs and the high level of unemployment, banks were forced to tighten their belts. Whether it was a default on a mortgage or business loan, Webster, too, experienced its share of difficult market conditions. The financial industry was expected to remain volatile until the global economy improved and consumers and businesses felt more confident.

Brenda Kubiac

PRINCIPAL SUBSIDIARIES

Fab Funding Corp.; Firstfed Insurance Agency, LLC; Retirement Planning Associates Inc.; Webster Bank, N.A.; Webster Capital Trust I; Webster Capital Trust II; Webster D and P Holdings Inc.

PRINCIPAL COMPETITORS

Citizens Financial Group; People's United Financial; TD Bank USA; Mellon Financial Corp.

FURTHER READING

Agosta, Veronica, "Webster Appointee's Job: Find Acquisition Targets," *American Banker*, August 7, 2002, p. 1.

Costanzo, Chris, "Getting Serious about Health Savings Accounts," *Bank Director*, 2006.

Garmhausen, Steve, "Webster Fights to Defend Its No. 1 Spot in HSAs," *American Banker*, May 15, 2006, p. 6.

Hammer, David, "Connecticut Bank Tried to Find Niche as Medium-Sized Company," *Waterbury (CT) Republican-American*, November 20, 2000.

Howard, Lee, "Most Banks in Region Say 'No Thanks' to Federal Help," *New London (CT) Day*, February 11, 2009.

Kline, Alan, "Webster Charts Course to Go It Alone," *American Banker*, May 7, 2004, p. 1.

Kulikowski, Laurie, "Webster Seeking Further New England Retail Growth," *American Banker*, May 3, 2005, p. 1.

Smith, David A., "Waterbury, Conn.-Based Banking Firm Opens Financial Services Business," *Waterbury (CT) Republican-American*, August 21, 2001.

Srinivasan, Sujata, "Banking on Expansion," *CT Business*, October 2006, p. 20.

Sullivan, Annie, "Harold Smith Dead at 86; Founded Conn. Bank," *American Banker*, October 28, 1997, p. 8.

Torsiello, John, "Players Profile: Jim Smith," *CT Business*, January–February 2001.

"Webster Financial Merges Subsidiary Banks, Renames New Bank Webster Bank and Introduces New Logo," *PR Newswire*, November 1, 1995.

Whiteman, Louis, "Webster, a Connecticut Thrift, Buying Bank for $220 Million," *American Banker*, July 1, 1999, p. 7.

Westwood One Inc.

40 West 57th Street, 5th Floor
New York, New York 10019
U.S.A.
Telephone: (212) 641-2000
Fax: (212) 641-2185
Web site: http://www.westwoodone.com

Public Company
Founded: 1974
Incorporated: 1975
Employees: 1,671
Sales: $404.4 million (2008)
Stock Exchanges: OTC
Ticker Symbol: WWOZ
NAICS: 711320 Promoters of Performing Arts, Sports, and Similar Events without Facilities

■ ■ ■

Among the largest providers of network radio and television programming and traffic information in the United States, Westwood One Inc. generates revenue by delivering programs to local radio and television stations in exchange for airtime the company sells to national advertisers. As of July 2009, Westwood supplied music, news, entertainment, sports, weather, and traffic programming to more than 5,000 radio and television stations. It also provided digital and cross-platform content delivered through Web sites and map and automotive navigation systems.

ORIGINS IN THE 1970S

In 1974 Norman J. Pattiz was an out-of-work account executive looking for his next paycheck. He had been fired from his job as a television station sales manager in Los Angeles, but instead of landing a job at another station, Pattiz looked at the media industry and discovered what he thought was a good business opportunity. Pattiz noticed a scarcity of national programming networks for local radio stations and decided to start his own. Pattiz planned to provide radio stations with programs and, in return, the radio stations would give Pattiz airtime he could sell to national advertisers. The concept was not a new idea by any means, but Pattiz observed that there were few programming networks in operation during the mid-1970s and that the limited number of program distributors in operation was providing unattractive programs. At the time Pattiz was taking all this in, radio advertising sales in the United States amounted to a $1.8 billion business. A little more than a decade later, annual advertising revenues towered above the $7 billion mark. It was a decade of prodigious growth, and one of the chief benefactors of such growth was Pattiz and his entrepreneurial creation, Westwood One Inc.

Pattiz, the unemployed television sales manager, did not start his entrepreneurial career with a lot of money. He had $10,000 to put into his venture, which represented a modest sum to begin business in the radio programming sector. Successful programming networks boasted hundreds of radio station affiliates, one of the yardsticks by which national advertisers measured a program distributor's stature. The greater the number of affiliates a programming network counted within its fold, the greater its power to attract the advertising

COMPANY PERSPECTIVES

■

Our business strategy is to provide our radio and television affiliates with programs and services that they may not be able to produce on their own on a cost effective basis. We offer local traffic, news, sports and weather information, as well as a wide selection of regularly scheduled and special event syndicated programming. The information and programs are produced by us and, therefore, our affiliates typically have virtually no production costs. In addition, our programs contain available commercial airtime that the affiliates may sell to local advertisers. We typically distribute promotional announcements to the affiliates and occasionally place advertisements in trade and consumer publications to further promote the upcoming broadcast of its programs.

Our robust local and national product offering allows advertisers the ability to easily supplement their national purchases with local and regional purchases from us. It also allows us to develop relationships with local and regional advertisers.

revenue of corporate clientele. Given this scenario, Pattiz's greatest asset was not his money, but his strategy, and it was a simple one. His inspiration came from a 52-hour program of Motown music broadcast by a Los Angeles radio station. He convinced the station to syndicate a similar show, signed up advertisers for the show, and lined up 250 radio stations to broadcast the program. This initial project represented a blueprint for the future. Pattiz planned to give radio stations free pop music programs, provided the stations carried his pre-sold national advertisements. Armed with this advertising formula, Pattiz set out on his own, incorporating Westwood in January 1975, and began what would turn out to be a prolific rise as a network programmer for radio stations.

Although the medium of radio in many respects took a back seat to television, the effectiveness of advertising on the radio was not to be underestimated. On average, there were considerably more radios than television sets in each U.S. household and, perhaps more important, there was a much closer link between a consumer and a radio station than with a particular television program or station. Generally, consumers tuned into their favorite radio station in the morning, listened to that same station while commuting to work,

and tuned in at night. The same could not be said of U.S. television viewing habits, which were governed by a pervasive penchant for channel surfing. This difference was important to advertisers, whose scientific approach to selling to the public was based on demographics. Particular radio stations catered to specific, demographically defined groups, whereas television stations tended to attract a grab bag of viewers. "It's the rifle as opposed to the shotgun approach to reaching your target audience," an advertising executive for General Motors noted, contrasting the fundamental difference between advertising on the radio and advertising on television. Pattiz characterized the difference in another way, frequently explaining, "You can tell an awful lot about a person from the radio station he listens to; you can't tell anything about a person from his favorite television station." This would be Pattiz's mantra, and it would be the driving force behind his company's explosive growth during the 1980s.

Given the limited amount of money with which Pattiz started, Westwood did not bolt out of the starting blocks. Concentrating at first on providing local radio stations with pop concert programs, Pattiz relied on rented equipment and contacts within the music industry to get his company up and running. The relationships forged with musicians were important ones and would prove to be valuable years later after Westwood was shaped into an established market leader. Although he was rich in personal contacts, Pattiz had to make do with the resources at hand and conduct his programming activities as inexpensively as possible. In 1979 Westwood offered its first taped concert, using rented equipment to provide rock concert programming to fewer than 100 stations. With this event, the company emerged as a source for concert promotion and programming to radio stations, one of a few network programmers to offer such a service. It was an encouraging beginning, but the company's most rampant growth would occur several years later. The spark that lit the flame was a ruling by the Federal Communications Commission (FCC).

1980'S ACQUISITIONS

In 1981 the FCC permitted radio station license holders to buy programming rather than having to produce most of it themselves. For Pattiz and others involved in radio programming, the FCC's announcement represented a boon to business, as radio stations could turn to a third party for all their programming if they so chose. During the three years following the FCC ruling, Pattiz used his contacts in the country and rock music worlds to his advantage and exploited the programming market by developing a portfolio of attractive pro-

KEY DATES

1974: Norman J. Pattiz develops his idea of providing free syndicated radio programming to stations in return for airtime to run presold national commercials.

1975: Westwood One Inc. is incorporated.

1979: Company offers first taped concert.

1984: Company distributes more than 30 regularly scheduled shows to some 3,000 stations nationwide.

1993: Company is $164 million in debt despite cutting costs and restructuring.

2009: Westwood One reaches terms with creditors and staves off bankruptcy.

gramming. To industry observers, Pattiz's most remarkable trait during this period was his aggressive pursuit of advertisers, to whom he preached the merits of advertising on the radio. Aggressive marketing on Pattiz's part, coupled with programming featuring celebrities in the pop music industry, fueled Westwood's growth as the company steadily increased its roster of affiliates. By 1984 Pattiz presided over a burgeoning empire that he was ready to take public.

Westwood's initial public offering of stock in 1984 raised more than $30 million, giving Pattiz the financial wherewithal to seriously consider acquisitions as a mode of quick expansion. What investors received for their cash was a piece of a company that produced and distributed more than 30 regularly scheduled shows that were broadcast to roughly 3,000 stations stretching from coast to coast. Westwood provided packaged music programs that varied widely, ranging from two-minute interviews with rock stars to two-hour live concerts. At the heart of the operation, however, were the national advertisements from which Pattiz and his growing staff earned their money. By the end of 1984 the revenues collected by Westwood amounted to nearly $13 million, from which the company earned nearly $2 million. The financial progress the company had made from its days as a start-up during the late 1970s was impressive, as was the rapid increase in the number of affiliates to which Pattiz could point when addressing national advertisers. The 1984 public offering of stock, however, precipitated a period of even greater growth, dwarfing the progress made before the company's debut on the NASDAQ. Nearly all of this growth came from acquisitions.

After its inaugural year as a publicly traded company, Westwood ranked as one of the largest producers and distributors of nationally sponsored radio programs in the United States. Pattiz was quick to build on this enviable foundation by scanning the horizon for an acquisition candidate that would increase further his company's capabilities and boost revenues. When his acquisitive eyes leveled on a target in 1985, the entire industry took notice because Pattiz had selected one of the industry's largest and oldest competitors, the Mutual Broadcasting System. Founded in the 1930s, the Mutual Broadcasting System was owned by Amway Corp. when Pattiz grew interested in the company. His interest stemmed in large part from the differences between his operations and those controlled by the Mutual Broadcasting System. A majority of Mutual's affiliates were adult-oriented in their target demographics. Westwood, with its pop music programming, consisted primarily of youth-oriented affiliates. Further, Mutual had news operations. Westwood did not have a news bureau. Aside from these differences, Mutual was enormous. The company comprised 810 affiliates, or about 10 percent of the commercial radio stations in the United States, and measured twice the size of Westwood. It was a deal Pattiz could not resist.

Westwood acquired the Mutual Broadcasting System from Amway in the fall of 1985, gaining control of the Mutual Radio Network, its affiliation contracts, studios, programming services, and talent, as well as management and staff, including the services of the widely popular Larry King. It was the first time in roughly 30 years that an owner of Mutual was a broadcaster, and Pattiz, as that owner, was ecstatic. "It's a perfect fit," he exclaimed, referring to the new operations and the bevy of adult-oriented affiliates gained in the acquisition. "It's a classic case of two plus two equaling five," he added, realizing the potential of a network programmer that could approach advertisers and deliver target demographics that stretched nearly from cradle to grave. There was one downside to the deal, however, and that was the financial health of Mutual. Under Amway's control, the company was a money loser, but in the euphoria surrounding the acquisition, Pattiz's celebratory mood could not be tempered. Roughly a decade after its formation, his company exited the mid-1980s as the second largest network programmer in the nation.

Trailing only the ABC Radio Network in size, Westwood entered the late 1980s as a formidable force in its industry. Two years after completing the Mutual transaction, the company made another bold move by acquiring the oldest broadcasting network in the country, the NBC Radio Network. From the acquisition of NBC Radio, Westwood gained a 20-year news supply and license agreement with NBC News for the NBC network stations, as well as the U.S. radio broadcast rights to the 1988 Summer Olympics in Seoul, South Korea. The acquisition included the traditional NBC Radio Network and several newer facets of NBC's radio business, including The Source, NBC's young adult network; TalkNet, a nighttime program service; and NBC Radio Entertainment, the program distribution arm of the NBC networks. Like Mutual, NBC Radio was also a money loser prior to its acquisition by Westwood, but the acquisition's effect on Westwood's stature in the industry was enormous, nevertheless. After the deal was completed, Westwood held sway as a giant, supplying nationally sponsored music, news, entertainment, and sports programming to more than 6,000 of the country's nearly 10,000 commercial radio stations. It was extensive coverage of market for advertisers, and it was made more attractive by the stable of celebrities included within Westwood's programming. Featured stars included Larry King, Steve Allen, psychologist Dr. Toni Grant, rock interviewer Mary Turner, and Dr. Demento, all of whom helped make Westwood a programmer few national advertisers could resist.

FINANCIAL WOES ENTERING THE 1990S

Following the completion of the NBC deal, Pattiz and his executive staff focused their efforts on curing the financial ills ailing their two large acquisitions. NBC's news operations, in particular, were demonstrating anemic financial performance. As the work dragged on to turn around both Mutual and NBC, this objective consumed nearly all of the company's energy, becoming the focal point during a two-year period leading up to the end of the 1980s. By 1990, when Westwood's debt totaled $215 million, there was not much evidence that any positive changes had been made. The company generated $146 million, far more than the total collected five years earlier, but registered a hefty $18.2 million loss. As time progressed, financial indicators pointed to profound troubles. Annual sales stagnated, then began to drop, while successive years of multimillion-dollar losses set off alarms at the company's headquarters. Following the $18.2 million loss in 1990, Westwood lost $16.8 million in 1991 and a staggering $24.1 million in 1992. To combat the problems, Pattiz began divesting properties, cutting costs wherever he could, and struggled to trim the company's debt. Despite Pattiz's efforts, Westwood was $164 million in debt by 1993.

As part of his ongoing plan to reduce debt and concentrate on his core network programming business, Pattiz sold Westwood's New York country radio station,

WYNY-FM, in 1993 for $50 million. When the sale was announced in February, Pattiz told reporters, "Two years ago Westwood embarked on an aggressive program to lower costs, improve cash flow, and strengthen its capital structure through debt restructuring and the sale of certain non-core assets. The sale of WYNY is a significant step forward in that plan." Although not upbeat, Pattiz's mood at least reflected a modicum of confidence that progress was being achieved. By May the last traces of optimism were gone. "We just haven't been able to make it work," Pattiz lamented in a handwringing interview with *Forbes*. By the end of 1993 the financial figures posted by Westwood showed no signs of improvement. Sales dipped below $100 million for the year and the company's losses stood at $23.9 million.

MID-1990'S RECOVERY

Help arrived in early 1994 in the form of an acquisition and the arrival of new management. In February Westwood acquired the Unistar Radio Networks from Infinity Broadcasting, which, in turn, was owned by CBS Radio. The acquisition gave Westwood radio production operations and 24-hour satellite broadcasting capabilities, which lifted sales to $136 million by the end of 1994. Perhaps more important, the acquisition brought in new management. The chief executive officer of CBS Radio, Mel Karmazin, became the chief executive officer of Westwood, and CBS Radio's chief financial officer, Farid Suleman, became the chief financial officer of Westwood. In the management shuffle, Pattiz held onto his title as chairman of the board of directors. Under this new management team, the first significant progress in cutting financial losses was made. From the $24 million lost in 1993, the company's profitability recovered dramatically, leading to a loss of $2.7 million in 1994. The following year, the company reported its first profit of the 1990s, earning nearly $10 million.

With profitability restored in short order and annual revenue volume back at the company's 1990 level, Karmazin and Pattiz were ready to expand. In 1996 the company acquired New York Shadow Traffic, Chicago Shadow Traffic, Los Angeles Shadow Traffic, and Philadelphia Express Traffic. The purchases of Shadow Broadcast Services expanded Westwood's business scope, moving the company into the production and distribution of local traffic, news, sports, and weather programming in four of the country's largest metropolitan areas. The addition of the Shadow Traffic operations, coupled with the company's exclusive radio rights to the 1996 Summer Olympics in Atlantic, Georgia, lifted sales nearly 20 percent to $171.7 million. The company's net income recorded a greater increase, nearly doubling to $17.5 million.

NEW APPROACHES AT THE TURN OF THE 21ST CENTURY

However, even as the company hoped expansion into traffic reporting would enhance the bottom line, four of Westwood One's six networks lost audience share, as did other radio networks. Shareholder CBS Corp. took over management of Westwood One in April 1997. The company reported record earnings in the second quarter. Also that year the company shut down its Adult Contemporary Network and Country Network. It created the NBC Radio Network, targeting adults aged 25 to 54, and the NeXtnetwork from its Young Adult and Source networks. The company increased its traffic reporting capabilities in 1999 by purchasing Metro Networks for $900 million in Westwood stock.

By 2000 management approaches appeared to be working. In January 1999 shares in the company sold for $27.75; in January 2000 they were up to $65.50. Consequently, Westwood One announced a 2-for-1 stock split. The company also purchased SmartRoute Systems Inc., a developer of nonbroadcast traffic information, for $25 million. In addition, it inked a deal to establish the VH1 Radio Network that would distribute sound bites, news, and other VH1 content, including simulcast events.

Some 17 percent of Westwood One was owned by Infinity Broadcasting but continued to be managed by CBS. (CBS had merged with Viacom, majority owner of Infinity and parent of VH1.) The company began syndicating talk personalities targeted to listeners under 35 years old. Viacom brands provided on Westwood One networks included Comedy Central and MTV; CMT Radio Network and BET Radio Network would be added. In 2002 the company ranked seventh out of 50 on the S&P Index of top mid-cap stocks.

Despite the departure of Fox News Radio from its line-up, the company strengthened its programming with the addition of NBC News Radio and CNBC business reports in 2003. Using HD technology developed by iBiquity Digital, the company made all its programming available in the superior quality format in 2005.

ECONOMIC WOES RESURFACE IN 2006

In 2006 it was apparent that Westwood One was in another downturn. The company's stock prices were falling along with advertising income. While other radio network stocks dipped 21 percent, Westwood One's dropped 53 percent. The company turned over music

sales, programming, and operations to Excelsior Radio Networks.

Looking to generate more revenue by using new technology to distribute products and services, Westwood One made customers' favorite shows accessible via download, audio streaming, and podcasts beginning in 2006. As of 2009, Westwood One's Metro/Traffic and Network divisions used satellite downloads, live video feeds, Internet, and other means to send customized, as well as editable, local traffic reports, news, and information to 2,300 radio and television affiliates, representing 83 of the top 100 metropolitan markets. The company was also experimenting with sending traffic reports directly to mobile and personal navigation devices, including a TomTom product.

However, new technology and the rights to broadcast major sporting and entertainment events did not stem the flow of red ink. When Westwood One could not maintain $25 million in market capitalization, the New York Stock Exchange delisted its common stock in November 2008. After that point the company's stock was traded on the OTC Bulletin Board. Earlier in the year CBS Radio terminated its management agreement with the company, but agreed to broadcast the company's programming. As the year closed, Westwood One acquired TrafficLand and formed TLAC Inc., a wholly owned subsidiary.

Although it had made salary cuts, restructured, and reduced costs, Westwood One struggled against the effects of radio market consolidation and competition, smaller audiences, and diminished advertising revenues. Operating income had declined from $180 million in 2002 to a loss of $438 million in 2008, making the company close to insolvent. The company reported a net loss of $15.2 million for the first quarter of 2009. It defaulted on loans in 2008 and early 2009. Nonetheless, the company looked forward after successfully restructuring financial instruments and signing exclusive network rights agreements for prestigious radio broadcasts. By August the company was optimistic about a turnaround, and while announcing a $9.9 million loss on revenue of $83.7 million for the second quarter of 2009, Westwood One stressed strengths in such programming areas as sports, talk, finance, and entertainment as key components to increasing the company's profitability. In a press release, president and CFO Rod Sherwood noted, "Our number one strategic initiative is to drive revenue across all businesses with branded content that continues to lead the industry in quality and excitement.... Quality content, and supporting marketing programs, will attract the audiences our affiliate partners and advertising clients need to grow their businesses."

Jeffrey L. Covell
Updated, Doris Maxfield

PRINCIPAL SUBSIDIARIES

Metro Networks Communications Inc.; Metro Networks Communications, Limited Partnership; Metro Networks Inc.; Metro Networks Services Inc.; Smart-Route Systems Inc.; TLAC Inc.; Westwood National Radio Corporation; Westwood One Radio Inc.; Westwood One Properties Inc.; Westwood One Radio Networks Inc.; Westwood One Stations—NYC Inc.

PRINCIPAL DIVISIONS

Metro/Traffic Division; Network Division.

PRINCIPAL COMPETITORS

ABC; CBS Radio; Citadel Broadcasting Corp.; Clear Channel Communications.

FURTHER READING

Bachman, Katy, "Fox News Radio Cuts Ties to Westwood, Goes Solo," *Mediaweek*, March 3, 2003, p. 6.

———, "Turning Off the Static: New Westwood One CEO Beusse Fine-tunes Troubled Net," *Mediaweek*, January 14, 2008, p. 8.

———, "Westwood's Olympics Coverage Set for Affils," *Mediaweek*, January 28, 2002, p. 12.

———, "Westwood Ups Its Syndicated Talk Fare," *Mediaweek*, July 30, 2001, p. 12.

Beauchamp, Marc, "Radio Days," *Forbes*, November 30,1987, p. 200.

Borzillo, Carrie, "New Challenges Afoot for Network 'King' Westwood One," *Billboard*, July 8, 1995, p. 80.

Button, Graham, "Broadcast Blues," *Forbes*, May 10, 1993, p. 16.

Cox, Dan, "Westwood One Letting Listeners Download Popular Shows," *Los Angeles Business Journal*, September 18, 2006, p. 32.

Deeken, Aimee, "Westwood One Adds 'Sam' Format, NFL," *Mediaweek*, May 9, 2005, p. 30.

Eldridge, Robin, "Excelsior to Run Westwood Music Nets," *Mediaweek*, June 5, 2006, p. 30.

Goldsmith, Jill, "A Group Including Viacom Cut Its Stake in Westwood One to 15.8% from 20%," *Daily Variety*, April 2, 2002, p. 8.

Hall, Peter, "On the Air with Westwood One," *Financial World*, October 16, 1985, p. 28.

Hampp, Andrew, "It's Miller Time on Old-school Radio; Q&A: Veteran Comedian Launches a Three-hour Show on Westwood One," *Advertising Age*, April 2, 2007.

Heuton, Cheryl, "Watching Westwood One: Buyers Abuzz about Exec Departures; Company Terms Them Routine," *Mediaweek*, June 12, 1995, p. 12.

Lappen, Alyssa A., "Hot No More," *Forbes*, July 25, 1988, p. 10.

"Let's Hear It for Radio," *Broadcasting*, December 15, 1986, p. 79.

"Mutual Gleam in Westwood One's Eye; Amway Agrees to Sell for Price Estimated at $30 Million," *Broadcasting*, September 23, 1985, p. 25.

"Past and Future," *Crain's New York Business*, March 27, 2006, p. 4.

Pcschiutta, Claudia, "Westwood One Riding Out Slump in Media Advertising," *Los Angeles Business Journal*, September 3, 2001, p. 25.

Petrozzello, Donna, "Anatomy of a Simulcast: Behind the Scenes with Westwood One," *Broadcasting & Cable*, October 17, 1994, p. 5.

———, "Network Radio Ratings Fall in Fall," *Broadcasting & Cable*, March 17, 1997, p. 62.

———, "Westwood Redesigns Its Lineup of Networks," *Broadcasting & Cable*, July 7, 1997, p. 65.

Rathbun, Elizabeth A., "Westwood One Sets Record," *Broadcasting & Cable*, August 11, 1997, p. 32.

Russell, Joel, "Traffic Jams Become Westwood On'es Bread and Butter," *Los Angeles Business Journal*, October 23, 2006, p. 5.

Saxe, Frank, "VH1, Westwood One Team on Network," *Billboard*, August 19, 2000, p. 4.

"Since Its Stock Price Has More Than Doubled in the Past Year, Radio Programmer Westwood One Inc. Is Planning a 2-for-1 Stock Split," *Broadcasting & Cable*, January 31, 2000, p. 65.

Snyder, Nick, "Radio Syndicator Cuts Back Staff in Consolidation Step," *Los Angeles Business Journal*, March 12, 2001, p. 6.

Taylor, Chuck, "Westwood Picks Up CBS Radio Division," *Billboard*, April 12, 1997, p. 72.

Tedesco, Richard, "Website Audio," *Broadcasting & Cable*, July 7, 1997, p. 48.

Torpey-Kemph, Anne, "Westwood Launches CC Segments," *Mediaweek*, February 12, 2001, p. 28.

Viles, Peter, "Westwood Sells WYNY-FM for $50 Million; Company Left with Only One Station," *Broadcasting*, February 1, 1993, p. 32.

"Westwood One Acquires NMC Radio for $50 Million," *Broadcasting*, July 27, 1987, p. 35.

"Westwood One and CBS Radio Ink Definitive Agreement," *Wireless News*, October 8, 2007.

"Westwood One Buys Metro Networks," *Billboard*, June 12, 1999, p. 74.

"Westwood One Gets Heat for Citing Arbitron," *Broadcasting & Cable*, April 1, 1996, p. 41.

"Westwood One to Offer Its Radio Lineup in HD Technology," *Wireless News*, April 18, 2005.

"Westwood One Took a 6% Stake in WebRadio.com in Exchange for On-Air Promotion as Part of a Two-Year Pact with the Audiocast Service," *Broadcasting & Cable*, March 27, 2000, p. 93.

"Westwood Signs with Media Monitors," *Mediaweek*, June 27, 2005, p. 3.

"Westwood to Launch CNBC Net," *Mediaweek*, February 17, 2003.

Wintrust Financial Corporation

727 North Bank Lane
Lake Forest, Illinois 60045
U.S.A.
Telephone: (847) 615-4096
Fax: (847) 615-4091
Web site: http://www.wintrust.com

Public Company
Founded: 1991
Incorporated: 1992
Employees: 2,326
Sales: $613.38 million
Total Assetts: $10.66 billion (2008)
Stock Exchanges: NASDAQ
Ticker Symbol: WTFC
NAICS: 522110 Commercial Banking (Primary); 523120 Securities Brokerage; 523930 Investment Advice; 551111 Offices of Bank Holding Companies

■ ■ ■

Wintrust Financial Corporation is a financial services holding company based in Lake Forest, Illinois. Founded in 1991 with the idea of restoring old-fashioned community banking in an era when banking conglomerates were the norm, the company expanded its holdings rapidly while remaining largely in the greater Chicago area. Catering to a well-heeled clientele, the company soon offered services that included wealth management, commercial insurance premium financing, mortgage origination, short-term accounts receivable financing, and select administrative services. All was not smooth sailing, however, as Wintrust weathered such challenges as a leadership shake-up in the late 1990s and the global economic downturn in the early 21st century. Nonetheless, by 2009 the company boasted assets of more than $10 billion and had managed to remain relatively profitable—no small feat at the time. It also owned 15 banks, with 79 branches, as well as several other subsidiaries, including Wayne Hummer Wealth Management. Although still fairly new and, compared with other financial holding companies, rather small, Wintrust appeared to have settled into the banking industry for the long haul.

FOUNDED IN 1991

Wintrust was the brainchild of a group of Chicago-area bankers and businesspeople who saw opportunity in the proliferation of big banking outfits and resulting dearth of hometown banks. In 1991, as Wintrust CEO Edward J. Wehmer later told Melina Kolb in the *Medill Reports*, those professionals gathered around a "card table with a box of cigars and a case of beer" and came up with a plan to install locally controlled, highly personalized banks in affluent Chicago suburbs. The banks were to be *de novo* (started from scratch), and expansion was key, with each bank slated to open a new branch approximately every 18 months. With a business plan firmly in place, Wintrust founded the Lake Forest Bank & Trust Company that year, and the new enterprise was underway.

Fundamental to both Wintrust's creation and success were two extremely dissimilar men, Wehmer and

COMPANY PERSPECTIVES

Our products and services are specifically tailored to meet the needs of area residents. Plus, you'll always receive prompt assistance from an experienced personal banker, along with our full range of competitive products. From Certificates of Deposit to Home Mortgages and Business Loans to select Savings Accounts, we provide you with everything you need to plan a promising financial future.

That's what hometown banking is all about—innovative ideas that truly benefit you, our friends and neighbors. Products and services that can't be matched by our big bank competitors. And you'll always be greeted by a warm smile and the friendliest service you'd ever hope to find.

We're never too busy to sit down with you and talk over a cup of coffee. So stop by and find out how great hometown banking can really be. You'll be glad you did.

Howard D. Adams. Wehmer, who was hired by Adams as Lake Forest Bank's president upon its inception, was a certified public accountant who had previously been president of Chicago's River Forest Bancorp Inc. (now known as Corus Bankshares Inc.). A bluff and hearty outdoorsman with a fondness for the late U.S. General George S. Patton, he was the antithesis of the slightly built Adams, known for his avid gardening skills. Despite his more decorous style, Adams was a formidable force on his own. He had begun his career implementing acquisitions of rural telephone companies before moving on to become a consultant with Booz Allen Hamilton. He founded his first bank in 1971 (which was later sold to Harris Bankcorp Inc. in 1984) and a finance company in 1979 (which was later absorbed by Wintrust). In short, Adams was long on vision and strategy, while Wehmer excelled at management and operations. For several years they were a winning team.

Adhering to the original business model, Wintrust began establishing other banks in Chicago's tonier suburbs, all named after the communities they served, with branches in the center of town. Hinsdale Bank was founded in 1993, followed by North Shore Bank in 1994, Libertyville Bank in 1995, and Barrington Bank in 1996. In keeping with the hometown bank mandate, each bank had its own name, charter, and board of directors, thus ensuring a large measure of autonomy and customized service. As Wehmer told Melissa Allison in the *Tribune Business News*, "They know better what's going on in their towns than we do. It keeps us from being imperial."

The community banking formula resonated with customers, although Wintrust's rapid asset growth as it expanded was offset by the inherent high expense of creating *de novo* banks, causing it to post earnings losses in 1994 and 1996. Nonetheless, the company's success was such that it was taken public in 1996. With Adams at the helm as chairman and chief executive officer and Wehmer on board as president and chief operating officer (he also remained president of Lake Forest Bank until 1998), Wintrust continued its growth-now, earnings-later strategy. The approach started to pay off with a modest profit in 1997, beginning an annual increase-in-earnings trend that pleased investors and management alike. By 1998 Wintrust had grown to include six banks, having founded Crystal Lake Bank the preceding year, and boasted $1 billion in assets. That year, however, was also a time of dissension and change within the company.

BOARDROOM SHAKE-UP

In 1998 Wintrust had been the fastest-growing bank holding company in the American Midwest during the previous 10 years. The pubic offering had been successful, and the company had been operating in the black for a year. There were apparent internal troubles, however, between the self-avowed "Odd Couple of Chicago Banking" and, more problematically, between Adams and Wintrust's board of directors.

Partially because of his stellar reputation as an amateur gardener and resultant seat on the board of the Chicago Horticultural Society, Adams had long had contacts among socialites and prominent locals with whom he studded Wintrust boards. While he had counted on the Wintrust board to effectively do its job, part of which entailed overseeing Adams's activities, something went amiss with the working relationship between Adams and the board in 1998. The cause of the breakdown was unclear. Reported reasons varied from unhappiness with Adams's general management style, to his allegedly disagreeing with the growth strategy he had originally enacted, to dissatisfaction with his tendency to unilaterally nominate new directors without board input. Whether it was any one of these, or some combination thereof, was immaterial in the end. Adams unexpectedly announced his retirement in May 1998, citing his age (then 65) as normal for such a transition and resolutely denying rumors of either

KEY DATES

1991: Howard D. Adams and Edward J. Wehmer launch their community banking plan with the Lake Forest Bank outside Chicago.

1992: Wintrust Financial is incorporated as a financial holding company.

1996: The company goes public on the NASDAQ.

1998: Adams is ousted as Wintrust's chairman and CEO.

2002: Wintrust enters brokerage business with the acquisition of Wayne Hummer Companies.

2006: A fifteenth bank is added to Wintrust's roster of subsidiaries.

2009: Global economic downturn causes earnings to continue to fall, but Wintrust remains relatively profitable.

internal dissension or outside takeover. At the end of the month the Wintrust board voted 20-3 (Wehmer voting with the majority) to remove him from his position as chairman and chief executive officer. Wehmer replaced his old partner and former boss as CEO, and board member John Lillard became chairman. The move cost Wintrust, which had always implemented higher compensation for fewer employees, $1 million in severance pay and legal expenses.

After the ouster Adams rebounded with all due speed. He founded Baytree National Bank & Trust Company in Lake Forest in 2000. The bank was created on the Wintrust model of banking, although it was never as successful, having had only one profitable year between its inception and 2009, when it came under federal scrutiny for undercapitalization. Adams was spared that final indignity, however, as he had already handed over the bank's leadership to his son, Alan, in November 2008. Wintrust had also long since moved on, but Adams's imprint on the banking industry was indelible.

RECIPE FOR SUCCESS

Despite ongoing speculation around the time of Adams's departure, there was no outside takeover of Wintrust. This was likely due, at least in part, to the company's adopting a "poison pill" in August 1998 that issued rights to additional shares of stocks to existing shareholders if a hostile party accumulated 15 percent, thereby reducing the hostile party's stake by 50 percent. This was designed to give interested acquirers a powerful

incentive to approach Wintrust's board directly, rather than attempt a hostile takeover.

Wintrust continued to thrive under its own auspices. In June 1999 its 6 banks had 22 locations. The company's expansion through *de novo* banks marched on with the opening of Northbrook Bank in 2000, Beverly Bank in 2004, and Old Plank Trail Bank in 2006. In 2003 it veered somewhat from the original business plan by beginning to acquire existing banks, albeit those that fit the profile of those already in its banking portfolio. Advantage Bank was the first of these, acquired in October 2003, and Village Bank joined the roster in December. In September 2004 Wintrust picked up Northview Financial Corporation and its subsidiary, Northview Bank & Trust, renaming the bank Wheaton Bank & Trust in December. In October of that year the company crossed the state line to acquire Town Bank in Wisconsin. In January 2005 State Bank of the Lakes was acquired, and in March the company purchased of First Northwest Bank, which was merged into Village Bank in May. In May 2006 Wintrust added Hinsbrook Bank & Trust to the lineup, which was renamed St. Charles Bank & Trust that November. This flurry of activity enlarged Wintrust's banking franchise considerably, from 3 banks with 5 offices in 1994 to 15 banks with 79 offices at the end of 2008.

However, banking was only a portion of Wintrust's recipe for success. The company also offered an array of niche services through its subsidiaries. First Insurance Funding Corporation (FIFC), founded in 1991, was a commercial insurance premium finance company that had become the fourth-largest firm of its kind in the United States by 2001 and generated $3.2 billion in receivables in 2008. Another subsidiary was Triacom Inc., Wintrust's first acquisition (1999), which provided loans and back-room processing to the temporary staffing industry. Wintrust Mortgage was the company's primary residential home mortgage origination arm. In 2002 Wintrust expanded its wealth management activities by entering the brokerage business via its $28 million acquisition of the Wayne Hummer Companies, which became known as Wayne Hummer Wealth Management. Wayne Hummer was a venerable Chicago firm, founded in 1931, and brought $1.25 billion in assets under management to the table at the time of its acquisition, as well as 35,000 new customers. Given the affluence of Wintrust's clientele base, the potential in offering Wayne Hummer's products was obvious. Other Wintrust services included such specialty lending areas as automobile loans, loan and deposit services for mortgage brokerage companies, and small aircraft lending. In sum, the company positioned itself to supply all of its customers' financial needs from within. As Wehmer explained to Matt Ackermann in *American*

Banker, "Other community banks use third-party products and services, but I don't like giving my customers to anyone."

Somewhat counterintuitively for a company that largely rested its prosperity on a business model of aggressive expansion, Wintrust's management eschewed the prospect of becoming another banking behemoth. None of its banks, for example, was further than an hour-and-a-half drive from its Lake Forest headquarters. "We want to be able to go out and kick the tires if we have to," Wehmer told Katie Burns in the Arlington Heights *Daily Herald*. Furthermore, by concentrating on personal service and the small-town banking concept, the company was able to effectively brand itself as a welcome alternative to the impersonal corporate style of the major players. "One of the biggest things we have to fear is that we start thinking we're big," Wehmer told Steve Watkins in *Investor's Business Daily*. "Then we're the same as our competitors and we lose our edge." In sum, Wintrust based its success on the somewhat unlikely triumvirate of sustained/relentless growth, a full spectrum of services, and old-fashioned hometown banking. The formula worked, but the faltering global economy led to greater challenges ahead.

NEW CHALLENGES

For many years Wintrust grew steadily. Total assets, for instance, rose by approximately $1 billion per year—from $2.3 billion in 2001 to $9.2 billion in 2006. Company income, stock prices, and deposits also increased, with its deposit base being one of Wintrust's particular strengths—from just over $5 billion in 2004 to $7.8 billion in 2006. Much of the growth began to slow in 2006, however, partly by design of the company and partly by operation of the troubled economic times.

The planned component of Wintrust's slowdown was in response to a frenetic mortgage market that was based on the mistaken idea that real estate values would continue to escalate indefinitely. As Wehmer explained to Kolb in the *Medill Reports*, "In March 2005 we said this is crazy. This market is out of control"; he continued, "People have left their reservations as it relates to good underwriting." Reading the writing on the wall, Wintrust management put the brakes on asset growth—slowing it to several hundred million annually—by placing a moratorium on the opening of new banks, lowering interest rates on certificates of deposit, and curbing loan deals. It also maintained its conservative lending practices and raised $50 million in capital in 2008 to help offset the general decline in market liquidity. Such prudence gave the company an edge as the global economy continued to plummet and reces-

sion became a reality, but it did not insulate it completely.

Lowered federal interest rates, nonperforming assets (primarily mortgages), and increasing fraud by desperate borrowers were just a few of the problems posed by the economic turmoil. Wintrust received another capital boost of $250 million from the U.S. Treasury Department's Troubled Asset Relief Program (TARP) in December of 2008, but the year still saw the company's net income fall to a disappointing $20.5 million, down from $55.6 million in 2007 and $66.5 million in 2006. On the other hand, recording a profit at all during that time period was something of an anomaly within the banking industry. Additionally, Wintrust's assets, loans, and deposits ($10.6 billion, $7.6 billion, and $8.3 billion, respectively) had all increased, although not as robustly as in previous years. In short, it appeared that Wintrust's foresight in spotting trouble on the horizon and good sense in planning for it accordingly had resulted in its being well positioned to ride out the tough economic climate and even prosper in the process.

Margaret L. Moser

PRINCIPAL SUBSIDIARIES

Hinsdale Bank & Trust Company; Lake Forest Bank & Trust Company; Libertyville Bank & Trust Company; Northbrook Bank & Trust Company; North Shore Community Bank & Trust Company; St. Charles Bank & Trust; State Bank of the Lakes; Village Bank & Trust; Wheaton Bank & Trust; Town Bank; Advantage National Bank Group; Barrington Bank & Trust Company N.A.; Beverly Bank & Trust Company N.A.; Crystal Lake Bank & Trust Company N.A.; Old Plank Trail Community Bank N.A.; Wayne Hummer Wealth Management; Triacom Inc.; First Insurance Funding Corporation.

PRINCIPAL COMPETITORS

Bank of America; Bank One; Citibank; Corus Bank; JP Morgan Chase; Harris Bank; Midwest Bank & Trust; Catalyst Wealth Management; Chicago Wealth Management.

FURTHER READING

Ackermann, Matt, "Wintrust in Broker Push for Chicago-Area Assets," *American Banker*, May 9, 2003, p. 9.

Allison, Melissa, "Chicago-Area Bank Company Head Leads with Intelligence, Toughness," *Tribune Business News*, August

1, 2000.

Burns, Katie, "Suburban Banking Corporation Manages to Keep Small Town Feel," *Daily Herald* (Arlington Heights, IL), November 10, 2004, p. 1.

Daniels, Steve, "Baytree Bank under Scrutiny from Feds," *Chicago Business*, June 22, 2009.

Gliniewicz, Leah, "How Wintrust Aims to Beat Biggest Banks," *Daily Herald* (Arlington Heights, IL), March 9, 2004, p. 3.

"Illinois Firm Adopts Stock-Dilution Plan," *American Banker*, August 5, 1998, p. 6.

Kolb, Melina, "Wintrust Financial Plays by the Rules as Government Rescues the Reckless," *Medill Reports*, October 16, 2008, http://news.medill.northwestern.edu/chicago/news.aspx?id=101115.

———, "Wintrust Financial Takes a Beating after Sizable Earnings Loss," *Medill Reports*, October 22, 2008, http://news.medill.northwestern.edu/chicago/news.aspx?id=101629.

Kotoky, Anurag, "Wintrust Financial Q4 Profit Surprises, Shares Jump," *Forbes*, January 28, 2009, http://www.forbes.com/feeds/afx/2009/01/28/afx5976594.html.

Much, Marilyn, "Lake Forest, Illinois Tanking Markets Don't Scare Financial Firm," *Investor's Business Daily*, August 8, 2002, p. A08.

Pavlenko-Lutton, Laura, "Founder Ousted as CEO; Directors Say He Opposed Their Growth," *American Banker*, June 3, 1998, p. 9.

Shinkle, Kirk, "Lake Forest, Illinois Bank Looks to Blow Away Windy City Rivals," *Investor's Business Daily*, September 17, 2004, p. A05.

Sinnock, Bonnie, "Wintrust Sees Modest Profit," *National Mortgage News*, February 9, 2009, p. 7.

———, "Wintrust Takes Hits from Servicing, Derivatives," *Mortgage Servicing News*, March 1, 2009, p. 30.

Strahler, Steven R., "Howard's Lend," *Crain's Chicago Business*, November 17, 1997, p. 17(4).

———, "Is Illinois' Wintrust Next to Merge? Sudden Departure of CEO Sets Tongues Wagging about Why," *Investment News*, May 4, 1998, http://www.investmentnews.com/apps/pbcs.dll/article?AID=/19980504/SUB/805040717/1009/TOC&template=printart.

"US Treasury Makes Investment in Wintrust Financial Corporation," *Global Banking News*, January 2, 2009.

Watkins, Steve, "A Bank That Takes the Road Less Traveled," *Investor's Business Daily*, May 7, 2001, p. A10.

"Wintrust Financial Corp. CEO Edward J. Wehmer Talks to the Wall Street Transcript," *Business Wire*, June 15, 1999, p. 0412.

"Wintrust Financial Corporation Hires Bank CEO & St. Charles Lending Team," Reuters, May 22, 2009, http://www.reuters.com/article/pressRelease/idUS184530+22-May-2009+PRN20090522.

Yerak, Becky, "Wintrust Financial Chief Sees Hope for Manufacturing: Wintrust Financial's Edward Wehmer Says Clients 'Starting to See Demand Pick Up a Bit,'" *Chicago Tribune*, April 30, 2009.

Wipro Limited

Doddakannelli Sarjapur Road
Bangalore, Karnataka 560 035
India
Telephone: (+91-80) 844-0011
Fax: (+91-80) 844-0057
Web site: http://www.wiprocorporate.com/

Public Company
Incorporated: 1945
Employees: 90,000
Sales: $4.94 billion (2008)
Stock Exchanges: New York Bombay
Ticker Symbol: WIT (New York), WIPRO (Bombay)
NAICS: 221310 Water Supply and Irrigation Systems; 325630 Toilet Preparations (e.g., Cosmetics, Deodorants, Perfumes) Manufacturing; 333111 Harvesting Machinery and Equipment, Agriculture, Manufacturing; 333120 Construction Machinery Manufacturing; 333995 Hydraulic Cylinders, Fluid Power, Manufacturing; 333996 Hydraulic Pumps, Fluid Power, Manufacturing; 334210 Carrier Equipment (i.e., Analog, Digital), Telephone, Manufacturing; 335110 Bulbs, Electric Light, Complete, Manufacturing; 511210 Software Publishers; 514191 On-Line Information Services; 541512 Information Management Computer Systems Integration Design Services

■ ■ ■

Wipro Limited, based in Bangalore, India, is a global corporation that manufactures and sells a wide range of products and services, from toilet soap and hydraulic cylinders to healthcare instruments and information technology (IT) solutions. Although Wipro's chairman and managing director Azim Hasham Premji is committed to the company's diversified business model, its future clearly lies in its continued successes in software and IT services, which make up roughly 80 percent of the company's sales and have consistently outpaced the growth of Wipro's other businesses. Wipro's world-class technologies division provides a range of high-tech services such as global IT consulting, e-business integration, and legacy systems maintenance to such clients as Cisco Systems, Thomas Cooke, and NEC. Wipro's IT efforts are so reliable that the company became the first in the world to be awarded the Software Engineering Institute's (SEI) coveted Level 5 Certification for quality. After the company's impressive debut on the New York Stock Exchange in 2000, Premji became one of the top billionaires in the world and the richest man in India, with a personal net worth of roughly $6 billion.

HUMBLE BEGINNINGS: MID-1940S TO EARLY-1970S

Western India Vegetable Products Ltd. (Wipro Limited) was founded in 1945 by M. H. Premji. The company sold *vanaspati* solidified sunflower oil to retailers, who sold it in bulk, scooping 50 and 100 grams for customers who brought along their own containers. In 1947, the same year that India gained independence from British rule, 32-year-old Premji laid the foundations of a vegetable oil mill at Amalner in Maharashtra. When Pakistan's prime minister offered him a position as finance minister, Premji turned it down, citing his

COMPANY PERSPECTIVES

At Wipro we aim to

• Have our products and services meet global benchmarks

• Ensure robust processes within the organization

• Consistently meet and exceed customer expectations

• Make Quality a culture within

loyalty to India and his fledgling cooking oil business. Little did either man know that later, in the new millennium, Wipro's value would dwarf Pakistan's gross domestic product. Wipro went public in 1947 for roughly $30,000.

Premji continued his political career along with his business in India. He became the first Indian chairman of the Bombay Electricity Board and a board member of the Reserve Bank of India, the State Bank of India, and the Life Insurance Corporation of India. However, Premji's untimely demise occurred in 1966, due to a heart attack. Soon after, his 21-year-old son Azim left his studies unfinished in engineering at Stanford University in the United States and returned home to India to take over the business. What had formerly been a sleepy business run by various members of the family now became a highly professional one, leaving Azim Premji the only family member working at Wipro, a characteristic that still held true decades later.

Azim Premji planned to professionalize, diversify, and expand his father's business, which was valued at about $3 million. He immediately recruited top-notch managers from the renowned Indian Institute of Management (IIM), where top graduates were courted by blue-chip firms in the West. "We were the pioneers in packaging for the mass market," explains Premji. "We went from bulk packs of vanaspati to [single-use] consumer packs." The packaging innovation took off, and the marketing and distribution network expanded into rural areas. At this point, the company had no plans to go global. By 1971 business nearly doubled from when Azim Premji took over.

GOING HIGH-TECH: MID-1970S TO LATE 1980S

The company's first departure from its main cooking oil business came about in 1975. Drawing on Azim Premji's engineering background, and at the suggestion

of one of the new IIM recruits, M. Seethapathy Rao, Premji launched Wipro Fluid Power, an operation that manufactured hydraulic and pneumatic cylinders. Under the direction of P.S. Pai, Wipro's consumer care division expanded beyond oil in 1979, establishing operations in soaps, toiletries, and baby care products. Along with major expansions in distribution, Wipro's consumer care division gained so much financial strength for the company that the company was able to further diversify into information technology (IT) and healthcare instruments.

Wipro would get into computers almost as soon as India's computer industry began to develop in the mid-1970s. At the time, the Indian government was the largest purchaser of computers sold in India, and was standardized on the Unix-based platform, which helped Indian companies build a solid reputation in Unix-based software development. The growing IT industry in India attracted multinationals, such as IBM, Motorola, and Texas Instruments, who took advantage of India's abundance of low-cost engineering labor. However, in 1977 the Indian government decided to expel U.S. computer giant IBM over a dispute about investment and intellectual property, creating what Premji saw as a golden business opportunity. He quickly set up an electronics unit. Instead of luring ex-IBM employees into his business, Premji hired managers from a truck maker and a refrigeration company.

In 1980 Wipro launched information technology services for the domestic market, setting up in Bangalore a highly skilled team of Research and Development (R&D) and marketing managers, headed by Ashok Narasimhan. Their professionalism, innovation, and insistence on quality were to make Wipro the number one listed IT company in the country within the next 15 years. By 1984 the company had diversified into software, which it would discontinue by 1990, but which led to Wipro's foray into its growth business, software services. Wipro began manufacturing PCs and workstations in 1985, quickly building brand recognition and securing the enviable position of commanding a premium price over competitors' cheap clones. Wipro assembled and redistributed hardware for such U.S. companies as Nortel, Sun Microsystems, and Cisco Systems.

India's $80-million market in medical equipment attracted General Electric Co. (GE), which in 1989 chose Wipro for a joint venture to develop and distribute ultrasound devices and other medical instruments, especially throughout India and South Asia. In addition to creating a new business segment for Wipro, the joint venture instantly secured Wipro's reputation as a software integrator and led to scores of R&D contracts

KEY DATES

1945: Wipro Limited is incorporated.

1947: An oil mill and hydrogenated cooking medium plant is built; Wipro goes public in India, for roughly $30,000.

1968: Founder's son, Azim Hasham Premji assumes leadership of company.

1975: Wipro begins to manufacture hydraulic and pneumatic cylinders.

1985: Wipro begins to manufacture toilet soaps, PCs, and dot-matrix printers.

1989: General Electric and Wipro create a joint venture for medical systems.

1990: Product software business is discontinued; software services begin.

1992: Lighting business is established.

1999: Wipro's software business receives prestigious SEI Level 5 Certification; company restructures to address the Internet market.

2000: Wipro is listed on the New York Stock Exchange.

2002: Wipro establishes offices in Hong Kong.

2007: Wipro acquires IT firm Infocrossing Inc. for $413 million.

with major companies, including Cisco Systems, Hitachi, and Alcatel. Wipro GE came to be the largest exporter of medical systems.

RAPID GROWTH AND EXPANSION IN THE 1990S

India's software industry continued to take off throughout the 1990s, at a compounded annual rate of nearly 60 percent for most of the decade. India quickly became the third-largest supplier of IT labor, and its communications infrastructure rapidly improved. Part of this growth was driven by a growing number of U.S. corporations that began to tap into the low-cost IT labor market in India, often for 40 percent to 60 percent less than the cost of U.S. labor. As a result, Wipro typically contracted out teams of engineers to work at U.S.-based companies. As successful as this business model was, it could not be counted on to last due to mounting competition and Wipro's growing need to offer more sophisticated technology solutions.

Wipro began to shift its IT business away from costly on-site development projects in the United States,

to more profitable offshore development closer to home. To help keep its competitive edge, the company replicated the development labs of some of its major clients, including AT&T, IBM, and Intel Corporation. In addition, while Wipro continued to offer a range of programming services, including hardware design, networking, and communications and operating system support, it continued to diversify into other lines of business. In 1992 the company established a new lighting business, offering a range of lighting solutions for domestic, commercial, industrial, and pharmaceutical lab environments. Wipro discarded its PC brand in 1995 when it formed a joint venture with Acer, a Taiwan-based computer and peripherals manufacturer and distributor.

By 1998 Bangalore had become one of the many IT centers in India, with about 250 high-tech firms in the city and another 100 in the surrounding area. Wipro became the center of this Indian "Silicon Valley," as India's second-largest software exporter. Both software and hardware businesses generated 57 percent of the company's sales and 75 percent of its profits, with software employees numbering over 5,600 of the company's 9,000 total.

Premji saw continued value in keeping Wipro's non-IT businesses, which he was always quick to point out were the best in their niche markets. The company invested about 25 percent of its advertising budget into branding for its consumer care and lighting division. The Santoor brand, for example, grew by 20 percent in 1997. Wipro's power cylinder business grew at a similar rate as its hardware business, and kept the company well poised to benefit from any boom in future infrastructure expenditures. In 1998 Wipro started exporting hydraulic cylinders throughout Southeast Asia. In addition, a number of synergies existed between the medical systems and IT businesses within Wipro. Wipro GE emerged as the largest healthcare systems company in South Asia in 1998, and in that same year became the top exporter of such systems in India.

Wipro proved to be a nimble and formidable competitor throughout the 1990s. From 1991 to 1997, for example, Wipro went through six corporate restructurings, keeping the company ready to adapt to the constantly changing technological landscape. By September of 2000 Wipro's technologies division had completed what may have been the most significant restructuring effort, re-engineering the division's operations toward four major market sectors: content housing platforms (computers and Web servers), content transportation (networking media), content access devices (mobile phones, PCs, etc.), and service providers. It introduced a Six Sigma quality initiative, which aimed to reduce the defect rate to virtually nothing, and led to an eightfold gain over the investments in its first 20 months. Wipro projected that it would apply the Six Sigma concept of allowing a maximum of 3.4 mistakes for every one million opportunities for error to every key process by 2002.

GOING GLOBAL IN THE 21ST CENTURY

Wipro seemed to have survived the effects of the global economic slowdown of 2000, with massive layoffs and profit warnings, and raced ahead in 2001 amid its own soaring growth rates and a huge expansion in its operating margins. Given that 60 percent of India's IT-related services and software exports were tied to the United States, Wipro's unscathed emergence was remarkable. By the end of March 2001, the company's net income hit a record $138 million (up 106 percent from the previous year), and operating margins grew from 18 percent to 24 percent that same year. While revenues from U.S. clients declined to 64 percent from 70 percent, revenues from Europe climbed from 24 percent to 29 percent, and revenues from Japan increased from 5 percent to 6 percent. With a team of 150 Japanese-speaking engineers and some 800 engineers dedicated to Japanese customers, including Fujitsu, NEC, Daiwa, Sony, Toshiba, and NTT DoCoMo, Wipro's Japanese business promised to grow along with other continued investments in a diversified customer base. Wipro decided to set up an Asia-Pacific regional base in Singapore in 2001. By this time, Wipro had a total of 209 active clients, the top five of whom were the fiber-optic network equipment producer Nortel Networks; the British gas transport firm Transco; the U.S. conglomerate GE; the telecom equipment manufacturer Lucent Technologies; and the French telecom equipment maker Alcatel.

Along with diversifying its customer base, Wipro set out to expand and deepen its IT service offerings and become a global tech powerhouse that would directly compete with IT giants IBM Global Consulting, Accenture, and Electronic Data Service. Even though Wipro came out of 2000 quite well, India's IT industry quickly became flanked with growing competition from countries, such as Ireland, China, Vietnam, and the Philippines. Although 60 percent of Indian software exports were absorbed by businesses in the United States in 1999, this number accounted for only 2 percent of the global total.

Wipro decided to go beyond the unglamorous back-office code-writing on contract, and pursue even more high-profile, high-paying projects that involved e-business development, new software products, and end-to-end business/system consulting. Instead of doing small portions of large IT software solutions, Wipro would develop comprehensive, end-to-end solutions that included both software services and hardware and often involved outsourcing the simpler code work to other countries. For example, in August of 2000 Wipro launched a "Portal-in-a-Box" that was a fixed-price, end-to-end solution to help businesses create a sales presence on the Internet. Wipro's new "upstream" strategy would not only help stave off the growing competition, but would enable Wipro to continue its growth and keep its staff immune from the temptation to go West and start up their own software companies. Wipro also continued to aggressively refocus on offshore projects and expand its efforts in the domestic market.

Wipro had come a long way from its simple sunflower oil business. At the start of the new millennium, Wipro continued to prove itself a pioneer in three main businesses—consumer care and lighting, healthcare technology services, and information technology—altogether encompassing a broad range of high-quality products and services. With its solid reputation in these businesses, deep ties with major world companies, and newly opened offices including the United Kingdom, Germany, Paris, Singapore, the Middle East, and the United States, Wipro promised to quickly become a true multinational corporation.

ON THE CUTTING EDGE OF INFORMATION TECHNOLOGY: 2002–09

During the early years of the new century, Wipro remained dedicated to expanding its presence overseas, focusing in particular on the rapidly emerging South Asian marketplace. In late 2001 the company outlined ambitious plans to establish branches throughout the Pacific Rim, notably in the Philippines, Australia, and New Zealand. More significant, in February 2002 Wipro opened an office in Hong Kong. Many analysts viewed the move as a clear sign that the company would soon be exploring more lucrative opportunities in mainland China. Creating a preliminary foothold in Hong Kong was considered strategic on two levels. For one, it would allow the company to familiarize itself with the intricacies of Chinese business law without plunging directly into the bureaucratic complexity of the mainland itself. Perhaps more important, the company's new location would allow it to explore alliances with established Hong Kong businesses, many of which already conducted business on the mainland. Indeed, Wipro's entry into Hong Kong was part of a larger trend that saw a number of Indian technology firms, among them rivals Infosys and Tata, establishing themselves in the territory, as they angled for a strategic advantage in the emerging Chinese market.

At the same time, Wipro continued to become more competitive in the United States. In November 2002 Wipro acquired American Management Systems Inc., a Virginia-based consultancy firm, for $26 million. In 2005 the company announced its intention to begin forming strategic partnerships with U.S. car manufacturers, with the aim of becoming one of the leading purveyors of information technology services to the automobile industry. One of the company's most significant U.S. acquisitions came in July 2007, when it obtained New Jersey-based IT firm Infocrossing Inc. At a cost of $413 million, the deal represented the largest purchase in Wipro's history. While some analysts criticized the merger as overpriced, others saw it as a vital step in the company's efforts to expand its presence in North America. In December 2008, in the midst of the global banking crisis, Wipro acquired Citigroup's IT division for $127 million.

Over the course of the decade, the company's technology business remained the primary engine of its increased profitability. In the early years of the 21st century, sales of software and IT products accounted for approximately two-thirds of Wipro's earnings, with the company's total sales exceeding $900 million in 2002. By 2008 Wipro boasted sales in excess of $4 billion for its information technology software products. Much of this growth stemmed from the increasing number of U.S. and European corporations outsourcing their technology needs to India. Of Wipro's 2008 sales, approximately $2 billion came from the United States, European earnings totaled $1 billion, while another $1 billion in technology revenues came from India. All told, these figures represented more than 80 percent of the company's total revenues. Wipro's growth was not merely reflected on its balance sheet. By 2008 the company had roughly 90,000 employees, compared with 30,000 in 2004.

Throughout this period of unprecedented growth, Wipro CEO Azim Premji began to earn international recognition as one of India's most successful, and famous, entrepreneurs. Journalist Jason Nisse dubbed Premji the "Father of Outsourcing" in a March 6, 2005, interview in the London *Independent*, while American television host Charlie Rose introduced him as "India's Bill Gates" prior to his March 1, 2006, interview with the Wipro chairman. With more Western corporations looking to reduce costs during the economic downturn of 2009, Wipro's prospects of becoming a global leader in the information technology sector seemed more promising than ever.

Heidi Wrightsman
Updated, Stephen Meyer

PRINCIPAL SUBSIDIARIES

Wipro Consumer Care & Lighting; Wipro Infotech; Wipro Infrastructure Engineering; Wipro Technologies.

PRINCIPAL COMPETITORS

Accenture Ltd (Bermuda); Booz Allen Hamilton Inc. (USA); Cognizant Technology Solutions Corporation (USA); Computer Sciences Corporation (USA); Electronic Data Systems, LLC (USA); Hewlett-Packard Company (USA); Infosys Technologies Limited; International Business Machines Corporation (USA); Koninklijke KPN N.V. (Netherlands); Novell Inc. (USA); Perot Systems Corporation (USA); Procter & Gamble Company (USA); Sapient Corporation (USA); Satyam Computer Services Limited; Siemens; Silverline Technologies Ltd.; Tata Consultancy Services Limited; Unilever Group (UK).

FURTHER READING

Beltran, Eamon, "Wipro Launches Operations in Germany," *Business Wire*, May 17, 2001.

Chakravarty, Subrata N., "What's Cooking at Wipro?" *Forbes*, December 14, 1998.

Chanda, Nayan, "How Precarious Is India's Perch?" *Far Eastern Economic Review*, April 12, 2001.

Davidson, Andrew, " Bangalore Bill's Lesson in Giving," *Sunday Times* (London), June 21, 2009.

Dhume, Sadanand, "Who's That Man?" *Far Eastern Economic Review*, August 19, 1999, pp. 48-49.

Einhorn, Bruce, Manjeet Kripalani, and Pete Engardio, "India 3.0," *Business Week*, February 26, 2001, pp. 44-46.

Engardio, Pete, "An Ultrasound Foothold in Asia," *Business Week*, November 8, 1993, p. 68.

Erwin, Jane, and P. C. Douglas, "It's Not Difficult to Change Company Culture," *Supervision*, November 2000.

Fai, Tang Weng, "A Look at Three Indian Examples," *Business Times* (Singapore), March 19, 2001, p. SS2.

Field, Tom, "For a Few Rupees More," *CIO*, December 1, 2000, pp. 168-78.

"From Fringes to Dominance," *DataQuest* (India), July 15, 1997.

Glatzer, Hal, "Software Intrigues India," *Software Magazine*, January, 1989.

Guha, Krishna, "Software Successes Gives Wipro Hard-Core Problem: Diversified Indian Group Must Decide What to Do with Its Other Activities," *Financial Times* (London), January 7, 1999, p.32.

Kleinman, Mark, "How Wipro Boss Is Winning the Race against Himself," *Daily Telegraph* (London), July 27, 2007, p. 5.

James, David, "India Starts Up," *Upside*, April 2000.

Lincoln, Kaye, "Coming Crisis," *Far Eastern Economic Review*, July 10, 1997, pp. 66-68.

Mazumdar, Sudip, "Bangalore, India," *Newsweek*, November 9,1998, p. 52.

Merchant, Khozem, "Defining the Indian Software Brand in a Competitive World: Global Strategies," *Financial Times* (London), February 21, 2001, p. 14.

———, "Survey: IT Indian Sub-Continent," *Financial Times* (London), July 4, 2000, p. 3.

Nisse, Jason, "The Interview: Azim Premji," *The Independent* (London), March 6, 2005, p. 5.

Paradkar, Bageshree, "Second-Richest Man, after You-Know-Who," *Toronto Star*, August 6, 2000.

Popham, Peter, "He Drives an Escort and Hates Luxury: Meet Mr. Premji, The World's Third Richest Man," *The Independent* (London), February 22, 2000, p. 3.

"Profit Soars at Indian Software Tiger Wipro," Reuters, January 19, 2001.

"Richest Man in India Is Mr. Integrity," *Straits Times*, March 5, 2000, p. 16.

Taylor, Paul, "Survey of India," *Financial Times* (London), November 17, 1995, p. 7.

———, "Survey: South Asian Software," *Financial Times* (London), July 1, 1998, p. 1.

"Troubled Citigroup Sells IT Services Arm to India's Wipro," *TechWeb*, December 23, 2008.

Vasuki, S. N., "Not Easy for India's Big Guns," *Business Times* (Singapore), September 27, 1993, p. 2.

Vijayan, Jaikumar, "Look out, Here Comes India," *Computerworld*, February 26, 1996, p. 100.

"Wipro Bucks Trend, Races Ahead," *Computers Today*, May 31, 2001, p. 9.

"Wipro Infotech's E-Com Services," *Hindu Online*, August 30, 2000.

"Wipro Launches B2B Portal for IT Industry," *Hindu Online*, September 20, 2000.

"Wipro Rides High on Software Boom," *The Hindu*, June 1, 1998.

"Wipro to Focus on Offsite Projects," *Hindu Online*, April 25, 2001.

Yee, Amy, "Outsourcing Gaining Speed," *National Post's Financial Post & FP Investing* (Canada), November 24, 2004, p. FP 14.

WWRD Holdings Limited

Wedgwood Drive
Barlaston, Stoke-on-Trent, Staffordshire ST12 9ES
United Kingdom
Telephone: (+44 1782) 204 141
Web site: http://www.waterfordwedgwood.com

Private Company
Founded: 1759
Incorporated: 1947 as Waterford Crystal Limited
Employees: 8,089
Sales: EUR 671.8 million ($983.0 million) (2008)
Stock Exchanges: Irish Stock Exchange (ISEQ)
Ticker Symbol: WTF_U
NAICS: 327112 Vitreous China, Fine Earthenware, and Other Pottery Product Manufacturing; 327215 Glass Product Manufacturing Made of Purchased Glass; 442299 All Other Home Furnishings Stores

■ ■ ■

In March 2009 KPS Capital Partners acquired Waterford Wedgwood, a leading provider of luxury home products, through a newly formed company, WWRD Holdings Limited (WWRD Group). Waterford Crystal, once one of Ireland's most important exports, is the world's leading manufacturer of premium cut-glass crystal. The Waterford factory in Ireland was closed in 2009, but the crystal is still produced at various locations throughout the world. A British producer of bone china and fine ceramics since 1759, Wedgwood is renowned for its distinctive and long-lived patterns. The company's other well-known brands are Royal Doulton, Johnson Brothers, Coalport, Masons, Royal Albert, and Minton, whose products include formal dinnerware, casual tableware, collectable figurines, crystal, and glassware.

WATERFORD CRYSTAL ROOTS AND DEVELOPMENT

The firm's heritage extends back to the 1780s, when a relaxation of trade restrictions on the Irish glass industry ushered in a 40-year period known as the Age of Exuberance. Hopeful entrepreneurs established many new glasshouses during this time, among them the Quaker brothers George and William Penrose. In 1783 the partners invested a then-hefty IRE 10,000 in a crystal factory named for the port county of Waterford in southeast Ireland. They hired more than 50 employees to carry out the extremely labor-intensive crystal-making process.

The operation first involved mixing the batch of heavy flint or crystal glass, which contained 35 percent lead to make the highest grade crystal. This batch of glass was then heated for more than 36 hours to 1400 degrees Celsius, where it reached the consistency necessary for forming. Each piece was hand-blown into a water-soaked wooden mold, forming thick glass walls to accommodate the deep, intricate cuts that came to characterize Waterford crystal. After a period of controlled cooling known as annealing, teams of glass cutters created complex geometric patterns. Waterford employees have used essentially the same tools and techniques throughout the company's history.

COMPANY PERSPECTIVES

Waterford, Wedgwood and Royal Doulton bring excitement into our homes, together with the comfort and the continuity of great traditions. There are few great luxury goods enterprises in the world and we are proud to have our place among them. In our own sphere, however, our offering is clearly unmatched. Together, Waterford, Wedgwood and Royal Doulton form the marvelous synergy that makes us such an exciting company.

The first foreman of the Waterford Glass Works was John Hill, a highly respected craftsman who had brought some of his best craftsmen from England to Ireland to escape excessive glass taxes. Hill was credited with setting up the Waterford factory, but his career there was short-lived. Personal clashes with the wife of owner William Penrose led to Hill's premature exit from the company. Before Hill left, however, he passed on valuable technical information to a clerk, Jonathan Gatchell.

The Penrose family sold its enterprise to Gatchell in 1799. Despite rising taxes and a changing roster of partners, Gatchell was able to pass the Waterford legacy on to his brothers, James and Samuel, and his son-in-law Joseph Walpole. Gatchell died in 1823, and in accordance with his will, these three ceded the works to his son, George, upon his 21st birthday in 1835. Unfortunately, a new excise tax had been enacted just two years after Gatchel's death. George found a partner in George Saunders, a works employee, but Saunders sold out by 1850, as heavy taxation eliminated any profits. Gatchell entered a Waterford piece in the Great Exhibition of 1851 (held in London's Crystal Palace), then closed the business later that year.

Nearly a century elapsed before the Waterford tradition was revived in 1947 by Joseph McGrath and Joseph Griffin. They established their glass company less than two miles from the site of the original Waterford Glass Works and hired talented employees from Czechoslovakia to staff the operation. Following the lead set by their 18th-century antecedents, their chief designer, Miroslav Havel, adopted historical patterns that had been documented by the National Museum of Ireland. McGrath and Griffin focused their sales efforts on the massive and prosperous postwar U.S. market. By the late 1960s, Waterford had captured the largest share of the fine glassware market.

Maintaining dominance of the industry was effortless throughout the 1970s. Waterford did not introduce any new patterns or revise its advertising from 1972 to 1982. In the early 1980s, however, Waterford began to face challengers, and although the market for fine lead crystal tripled from 1979 to 1983, Waterford's sales grew by only about one-fifth and its market share slid five points to 25 percent. The company added new patterns, enlisted a new advertising agency, and, in 1986, acquired Josiah Wedgwood and Sons Ltd. in the hopes of finding retail and distribution synergies.

WEDGWOOD ROOTS AND DEVELOPMENT

The roots of Wedgwood ceramics are most often traced to Josiah Wedgwood, himself the descendant of four generations of potters. Josiah embarked on his life's work at the age of nine when he left school to work under his eldest brother at the family pottery works. An outbreak of smallpox left the youngster physically impaired at the age of 11. (The disease left a lingering infection in his leg, which eventually led to its amputation.) Unable to continue throwing pottery as a result, he turned instead to design and formulation of ceramics and glazes. When Josiah's apprenticeship ended at the age of 19, his brother inexplicably refused to take him on as a partner.

For the next 10 years, the young potter cast about for a business associate; during this period his longest partnership, with Thomas Whieldon, lasted for five years. Wedgwood struck out on his own in 1759. Not content to imitate the generally substandard wares on the market, Wedgwood achieved his first important innovation, No. 7 green glaze, shortly thereafter. The potter used his new glaze to produce rococo-style teapots, plates, compotes, and other practical pieces shaped like fruits, vegetables, and leaves. Wedgwood created demand for his pottery by offering innovative products, including asparagus pans, egg spoons and baskets, sandwich sets, and even special plates for "Dutch fish."

By 1765 word of Wedgwood's elegant yet durable wares had reached Britain's royal family. That year, Queen Charlotte ordered a tea service made of Wedgwood's second important development, a unique cream-colored earthenware. Through this, the first of many "command performances," Wedgwood earned the right to call his ivory-colored pottery Queen's Ware. Needless to say, the endorsement added to the potter's prestige, popularity and sales.

Such successes allowed Wedgwood in 1766 to purchase an estate in Staffordshire, which he named Etruria. A factory on the site was completed three years later, just in time to accommodate an order from Cathe-

KEY DATES

1759: Josiah Wedgwood founds a pottery factory.

1760: Wedgwood begins creating a unique, cream-colored earthenware that becomes known as Queen's Ware.

1769: A factory is completed at Wedgwood's estate, called Etruria.

1774: Wedgwood introduces the innovative and enduring Jasper ware.

1783: George and William Penrose found the Waterford crystal factory in Ireland.

1799: The Penrose family sells Waterford to Jonathan Gatchell.

1810: Josiah Wedgwood II takes full control of the company founded by his father.

1828: Financial difficulties force Wedgwood to close its London showrooms and sell off many of its assets.

1835: George Gatchell, son of Jonathan, takes control of Waterford.

1843: Francis Wedgwood, son of Josiah II, succeeds his father.

1851: Gatchell closes Waterford, which enters a nearly 100-year period of inactivity.

1875: Wedgwood reopens its London showrooms.

1879: Philipe Rosenthal establishes the Rosenthal Company in the Upper Franconian town of Erkersreuth.

1906: The Wedgwood Museum opens; U.S. sales office is established.

1940: A new Wedgwood factory near Barlaston, in Staffordshire, England, begins production.

1947: Joseph McGrath and Joseph Griffin revive the Waterford company.

1950: Wedgwood's Etruria factory is closed.

1963: Sir Arthur Bryan becomes the first non-Wedgwood to serve as managing director.

1966: Josiah Wedgwood and Sons Limited goes public and begins an eight-year acquisition spree.

1986: Waterford acquires Josiah Wedgwood and Sons, forming Waterford Wedgwood plc.

1988: Waterford Wedgwood posts an operating loss for the year, the first of five straight.

1990: Anthony J. F. O'Reilly forms a coalition of investors and purchases about one-third of the company's equity.

1992: The company returns to the black.

1994: O'Reilly is named chairman.

1995: Stuart & Sons, leading U.K. maker of premium crystal, is acquired.

1997: Company gains majority control of Rosenthal AG, a German porcelain maker.

1999: Waterford Wedgwood acquires U.S.-based All-Clad Metalcrafters Inc., a maker of premium cookware; acquires a 15 percent stake in Royal Doulton; designs the Waterford Crystal New Year's Eve Ball used in New York's Times Square to mark the new millennium.

2000: Waterford Wedgwood extends its line of jewelry and executive accessories.

2001: The company acquires W-C Designs.

2002: Royal Doulton moves some of its production to Indonesia.

2003: Waterford Wedgwood moves some of its crystal and china manufacturing to China.

2004: The company sells All-Clad to Groupe SEB and merges Royal Doulton with Wedgwood.

2009: Waterford Wedgwood declares bankruptcy and certain assets are purchased by KPS Capital Partners, LP, forming a new company, WWRD Holdings Limited.

rine the Great of Russia for a 952-piece service for 50. The amazing set featured more than 1,200 hand-painted scenes of the English countryside. Wedgwood named a pattern with maroon flowers after Catherine. That style, as well as the Queen's Ware and Shell Edge styles, exemplified the enduring nature of the founder's designs. All were still in production in the 21st century.

Wedgwood capitalized on the popularity of his wares by expanding his line in the 1770s. With the help of an amicable partner, Thomas Bentley, Wedgwood began producing wall tiles and such ornamental wares as plaques, vases, busts, candlesticks, medallions, and even chess sets. Many early decorative pieces were made of a proprietary ceramic called Black Basalt. Although Wedgwood was sure that Black Basalt would enjoy an enduring popularity, it was his Jasper ware, introduced in 1774, that would symbolize Wedgwood for centuries of consumers and collectors. Jasper, an unglazed, translucent stoneware that assimilated colors well, was produced in green, yellow, maroon, black, white, and the shades of blue that became known as Wedgwood blue. Historian Alison Kelly, author of the *Story of Wedgwood*, asserted, "Connoisseurs of pottery since [Wedgwood's] day have valued [Jasper] both as a technical triumph and as an ornament perfect of its kind."

Wedgwood worked alone for 10 years after Bentley died in 1780. He went into semiretirement in 1790, taking his three sons and a nephew into partnership that year. In addition to his artistic achievements, the founder had invented a pyrometer to measure the heat of his kilns and implemented steam-driven potters' wheels and some principles of mass production. Upon his death in 1795, his second son, also named Josiah, shared management of the works with his cousin, Thomas Byerley. Josiah II assumed full control when Byerley died in 1810.

The Napoleonic Wars, which made trade with continental Europe all but impossible, were followed by an economic slowdown that made the early years of the 19th century difficult for Josiah II. In 1828 financial shortfalls compelled him to close the company's London showrooms and sell the bulk of Wedgwood's stock, molds, and models for £16,000. Still, the Etruria works survived both hardship and Josiah's often-criticized management. His third son, Francis, succeeded him upon his death in 1843. Francis had joined the company in 1827 and would control it for 27 years. He revived the founder's legacies of innovation and modernization, adding machines that mixed and dried the clay, as well as new colored ceramics in the tradition of Jasper. His celadon, a pale gray-green ceramic, a lavender clay, and Parian Ware, which featured marbled effects, appealed to Victorian tastes. By 1875 Francis was able to reopen the London showrooms. He also reinstituted production of bone china, which had been offered briefly in the early 1800s. This line would later form the foundation of Wedgwood's export trade.

WEDGWOOD IN THE 20TH CENTURY

Successive generations of Wedgwoods took the company into the 20th century, which witnessed a revival of interest in the company's classical designs, both among collectors and consumers. The Wedgwood Museum was opened in 1906, the same year that the company established a U.S. sales office. Overseas trade expanded dramatically during the early decades of the 1900s and by 1920, the U.S. office had grown sufficiently to justify a new subsidiary.

Even the Great Depression did not slow Wedgwood's growth. In 1938 the company laid plans to build a modern facility near Barlaston, in Staffordshire. The plant, which featured the first electric pottery kilns used in Britain, began production in 1940 and by 1950, all production had been transferred from Etruria to Barlaston. Since 80 percent of Wedgwood's production was for export, the company was allowed to continue production throughout World War II. At war's end, Wedgwood was poised for expan-sion.

During the late 1940s and early 1950s, the company incorporated Canadian and Australian subsidiaries, expanded its factory, and inaugurated special Wedgwood Rooms in upscale department stores. By the end of the 1950s, the company employed more than 2,000 people at the Barlaston plant.

In 1963 Sir Arthur Bryan became Wedgwood's managing director, marking the first time in the company's history that an individual who was not related to Josiah Wedgwood held that position. Bryan was named chairman five years later.

Wedgwood's first public offering on the London Stock Exchange in 1966 marked the beginning of an eight-year acquisition spree. The company acquired four competitors in 1966 and 1967, including Coalport, manufacturers of high-quality bone china figurines. Wedgwood doubled in size with the acquisition of Johnson Brothers, which included five tableware factories as well as overseas plants. The company entered the glass market with the 1969 purchase of King's Lynn Glass, then began the 1970s with the acquisition of J & G Meakin and Midwinter companies, manufacturers of fine china and earthenware. These purchases gave Wedgwood access to broader markets without compromising the reputation of its premier brand. Additions in the ensuing years helped Wedgwood integrate vertically. They included Precision Studios, a producer of decorative materials for the ceramics industry, and Gered, a retailer and longtime customer of Wedgwood. By 1975 Wedgwood had nearly 9,000 employees in 20 factories.

The company's growth came to an abrupt halt in the early 1980s when recession forced Wedgwood to lay off nearly half of its workforce. As the company struggled, threats of a hostile takeover necessitated Wedgwood's amicable union with Waterford.

WATERFORD WEDGWOOD: POST-MERGER WOES IN THE LATE 1980S AND EARLY 1990S

Waterford and Wedgwood merged in 1986, when the crystal manufacturer executed a "white knight" takeover of the china producer for £252.6 million. A recession in the late 1980s and early 1990s brought the premium crystal market's growth to a halt, as price-conscious consumers traded down. From 1989 to 1992, sales in the premium market in the United States (then the world's largest market) dropped by 25 percent, while sales of second-tier crystal increased by half. At the same time, employment costs for both Waterford and Wedgwood had soared and Waterford's labor expenses, which accounted for more than two-thirds of the company's overhead, grew three times faster than inflation in the late 1980s. From 1987 to 1990, Waterford Crystal alone lost more than £60 million, and total corporate debt had swelled to £150 million.

In 1988 Anthony J. F. "Tony" O'Reilly (chairman, president, and CEO of H. J. Heinz Company, as well as "the wealthiest man in Ireland") offered Waterford Wedgwood chairman Howard Kilroy a buyout. His first attempt was refused, but by early 1990, the struggling company was ready to deal. O'Reilly formed a coalition of investors, including his own Fitzwilton Public Limited Company and New York investment house Morgan Stanley Group Inc. Together, they exchanged an estimated £80 million for about one-third of the tableware firm's equity. Morgan Stanley took 15 percent, 9.4 percent went to Fitzwilton, and O'Reilly personally acquired 5 percent. The deal valued Waterford Wedgwood at £230 million—less than it had paid for Wedgwood alone just three years earlier.

The company's problems were deeper than O'Reilly had surmised. When Waterford Wedgwood lost IEP 1.2 million on IEP 71 million sales in 1991, Don Brennan of Morgan Stanley replaced Kilroy as chairman. The new managers traced their financial woes to expensive labor, especially at Waterford. The company trimmed some of its labor costs and simultaneously countered the contraction of the premium crystal market with the 1991 introduction of the Marquis by Waterford line, which retailed for about 30 percent less than traditional Waterford. This new offering, the company's first new brand of crystal in 200 years, was manufactured in Germany and Slovenia, where wages averaged 10 percent less than in Ireland. Stylistically, Marquis featured designs less elaborately cut than Waterford patterns. Company executives were careful to assert that they were not reaching "down-market," but that the elegant new designs appealed to more modern, youthful, "continental" tastes. The launch was an unquestionable success. From 1992 to 1993, sales of Marquis increased by 24 percent, and the brand captured the number six spot among premium crystal brands sold in the United States.

At the same time, the company was beset by confrontations with its domestic workforce, including strikes and even a shutdown. In 1992, after management threatened to move more of Waterford's produc-

tion to Eastern Europe, the unions agreed to a wage freeze and job cuts. In return, the company pledged to keep its Waterford operations in Ireland as long as it could remain competitive.

Although Waterford Wedgwood's share price sank as low as 12p in 1992, the company recorded its first operating profit (IEP 500,000) since 1987 that year, with sales 4.5 percent higher than in 1991. In 1993 profits increased again, to IEP 10 million, and Waterford Wedgwood's share price grew to 60p. The turnaround was credited to O'Reilly, who had advanced from deputy chairman to chairman in 1994. O'Reilly was confident that his stalwart brands would regain their steady and strong profitability, and he targeted future growth for the mature markets of Japan and the United Kingdom.

MID-1990S AND BEYOND: GROWTH THROUGH ACQUISITIONS

Following up on the success of the lower-priced Marquis by Waterford line, the company in 1995 introduced a new Wedgwood line called Embassy, which was positioned in the mid-priced segment, with a five-piece place setting costing about $80. This was also Wedgwood's first porcelain line. Wedgwood also launched an even less expensive ($50 to $60 per set) and less formal porcelain line dubbed Home. Also in 1995, Wedgwood debuted a new bestselling line called Cornucopia, a fine bone china pattern.

Waterford Wedgwood's improved financial condition set the stage for a new round of acquisitions. The first came in 1995 when Stuart & Sons Ltd. was acquired for about IEP 4.2 million ($6.8 million). Stuart & Sons was a leading U.K. maker of premium crystal and claimed to be the last major U.K. manufacturer making all of its glass in its home country. In early 1997 Waterford Wedgwood spent $1.9 million for a 9.1 percent stake in Rosenthal A.G., a maker of premium porcelain china, tableware, and art, and by the end of 1997 the company had gained majority control of Rosenthal, increasing its stake to 61.5 percent. Based in Selb, Germany, Rosenthal had a long history dating back to its establishment in 1879 by Philipe Rosenthal in the Upper Franconian town of Erkersreuth. Rosenthal had sales of $206 million in 1995, with about 60 percent generated in Germany; the United States and Italy were the company's two largest export markets. In 1998 Waterford Wedgwood increased its stake in Rosenthal to about 85 percent.

In June 1999 Waterford Wedgwood diversified its line of luxury goods through the acquisition of All-Clad

Metalcrafters Inc., a U.S. premium cookware maker, for $110 million (IEP 68 million). Canonsburg, Pennsylvania-based All-Clad was founded in 1973 by John Ulam, a metallurgist who had devised a way to bond sheets of aluminum and stainless steel. The combination resulted in cookware that heated evenly but was easy to clean. Sales for the privately held company were about $52 million in 1998 and were growing rapidly. In fact, high-end cookware was the fastest growing segment of the cookware market, with sales increasing at an annual rate of 18 percent. All-Clad products were sold primarily in upscale department stores, such as Macy's and Bloomingdale's, and in higher-end home furnishings chains, such as Williams Sonoma, Crate & Barrel, and Pottery Barn. Waterford Wedgwood planned to expand the All-Clad brand outside the United States where its overseas sales stood at only 3 percent of the total in 1998. The company also hoped that the addition of All-Clad could help expand the Wedgwood brand into the U.S. home furnishings specialty retail sector, which would represent a new channel.

In addition to pursuing growth through acquisition, Waterford Wedgwood achieved organic growth in the late 1990s through the introduction of new product lines. Particularly successful were cooperative ventures with leading fashion designers, such as Versace, Bulgari, John Rocha, and Jaspar Conran, who helped design ceramics and crystal lines bearing their own names. In 1999 sales in the United States were aided by the employment of Sarah, Duchess of York, as official spokesperson for Waterford Wedgwood in the U.S. market. In November 1999 Waterford Wedgwood purchased a 15 percent stake in British rival Royal Doulton for IEP 11.1 million. Calling the transaction a "strategic investment" and not a prelude to an acquisition, Waterford Wedgwood nevertheless declined to rule out a future bid if a rival takeover company emerged. Capping 1999 in spectacular fashion, Waterford Wedgwood designed the Waterford Crystal New Year's Eve Ball, which was used in New York's Times Square to mark the beginning of the new millennium.

As the 21st century approached, Waterford Wedgwood appeared to be on a clear upward trajectory. Revenues for 1999 increased 20.4 percent over the previous year, nearing the $1 billion mark—almost double the figure of five years earlier. In fact the company had achieved seven straight years of double-digit growth. Meanwhile, operating profits increased by one-third over the one-year period. In the early 21st century, Waterford Wedgwood seemed poised to continue its successful course of organic and purchased growth with the acquisition side leaning toward further diversification along the lines of the All-Clad purchase.

POST-2000 SURVIVAL

In October 2000, after a successful year-long trial in 50 U.S. chains and outlets, the company announced that it would be extending its line of executive accessories and jewelry nationwide through a number of high-profile stores, such as Macy's, Fortunoff's, and Nordstrom. Six months later, Waterford Wedgwood signed an exclusive two-year sponsorship deal with the WeddingChannel. com, the most frequently used wedding registry Web site. Although Waterford Wedgwood plc reported after-tax profits of $58.1 million in the year ending December 31, 2000, industry analysts maintained that the company's debt levels were too great to support further major acquisitions. After the acquisition of W-C Designs, a table and bed linen company, in July 2001, O'Reilly was forced to admit that the company was still perceived by the general public as a tabletop company, rather than a luxury goods provider, and that it would be switching its main focus to organic growth.

In the aftermath of the terrorist attacks against the United States on September 11, 2001, luxury retailers were bracing themselves for a downturn. Although Waterford Wedgwood did manage to achieve more than EUR 1 billion in sales at the close of that year, the company still set out on a worldwide restructuring program to protect the group's profitability. The plan included technological upgrades, warehouse consolidation in the United Kingdom, decentralizing of Wedgwood's sales and administrative offices, and a reduction of its manufacturing capacity in the United Kingdom, Ireland, and Germany. Meanwhile, newly opened boutiques in Cape Town and Taiwan were performing well, prompting the company to open additional outlets in Japan and undertake a refurbishment of all of its existing shops worldwide. Sales were down approximately 4.4 percent but, through its acquisitions of All-Clad and W-C Designs, the company had a presence in specialty and value retailers, such as Williams Sonoma and J.C. Penney, accounting for nearly 20 percent of the total U.S. volume. By September 2002 the company had reduced its debt 12 percent from $460.2 million to $405.2 million.

However, toward the end of 2002, Royal Doulton reported a pre-tax loss of £7.7 million, resulting in job cuts and the relocation of some of its production to Indonesia. This was followed by Waterford Wedgwood moving some of its crystal and china manufacturing to China in June 2003. In that same month, the company announced that it was in the process of negotiating refinancing after a collapse in earnings of its crystal and ceramics products. The moves paid off, and by December 2003 sales matched those of 12 months earlier and operating margins were up 7.7 percent. In

June 2004 Waterford Wedgwood decided to focus its marketing and sales efforts on its master brands and, in an effort to further reduce its debt, sold All-Clad for $250 million to Groupe SEB.

Waterford Wedgwood experienced a bit of a public relations disaster when, in August 2004, the New York attorney general's office fined the company's U.S. arm $500,000 for antitrust violations. The company was alleged to have conspired with Federated Department Stores to keep its products out of Bed, Bath and Beyond. Eager to move forward without admitting liability, the company paid the fine with the agreement that no further action would be taken. In December 2004 O'Reilly merged Royal Doulton with Wedgwood in a deal worth £40 million. O'Reilly saw this move as an opportunity to boost revenues without substantially increasing costs and to restore many jobs by moving Royal Doulton's operations from Asia back to the Wedgwood facility in England.

As a result of the merger, sales had increased nearly 11 percent by September 30, 2005, but the company was still reporting losses, and its share price dropped 14 percent. In May 2006 Waterford Wedgwood, which already held the license for Vera Wang's china and crystal creations, acquired Wang's sterling silver, silverplate, flatware, and gift items license. The company had plans to enter into other high-profile collaborations and predicted that by the end of the first quarter of 2007 it would break even for the first time in three years. Unfortunately all did not go as envisioned, with the company reporting losses of EUR 70.8 million and EUR 241.6 million in 2007 and 2008 respectively. By the end of 2008 Waterford Wedgwood had defaulted on its bank loan, and the company's future was in peril.

By January 2009, with debt approaching EUR 800 million, this iconic company had collapsed, and Sir Anthony O'Reilly resigned from the Board of Directors. Citing poor trading, failed buyout talks, and crippling restructuring costs as the reasons for the company's decline, Waterford Wedgwood was forced to declare bankruptcy. In March 2009 New York-based KPS Capital Partners, LP, acquired certain assets of Waterford Wedgwood plc and formed a new company named WWRD Holdings Limited (WWRD Group). Pierre de Villeméjane, previously chief executive officer of Speedline Technologies, Inc., another company in KPS's portfolio, was appointed CEO of the WWRD Group. Michael Psaros, a managing partner of KPS, said: "As a new company created and owned by KPS, with an accomplished CEO, and a new capital structure, WWRD Holdings is the leading enterprise in the luxury home and lifestyle industry worldwide." In 2009 the WWRD

Group was looking forward to growing the company organically and through acquisitions.

April Dougal Gasbarre
Updated, David E. Salamie; Marie O'Sullivan

PRINCIPAL SUBSIDIARIES

WWRD US, LLC; WWRD United Kingdom Ltd.

PRINCIPAL DIVISIONS

Waterford Crystal/WWRD UK/Ireland Ltd (Ireland); Wedgwood/WWRD United Kingdom Ltd (England); Royal Doulton/WWRD United Kingdom Ltd (England).

PRINCIPAL COMPETITORS

ARC International; Belleek; Corning Incorporated; Fitz and Floyd; Lifetime Brands, Inc.; Noritake Co., Limited; Oneida Ltd.; Tiffany & Co.

FURTHER READING

Aspden, Peter, "Success on a Plate: Wedgwood Museum Wins Award," *Financial Times*, June 19, 2009.

Brown, John Murray, "An Irish Hero Humbled: The Waterford Boss Has Followed the Money One Step Too Far," *Financial Times*, January 10, 2009, p. 7.

———, "Update for Waterford Wedgwood," *Financial Times*, May 1, 1998, p. 25.

———, "Waterford Poised to Break Even," *Financial Times*, November 16, 2006, p. 24.

Brown, John Murray, and Adrienne Roberts, "UK & Ireland: Waterford Wedgwood Ponders Junk Bond as Rights Issue Ruled Out," *Financial Times*, October 4, 2003, p. 2.

Buckley, Christine, "Wedgwood Develops a Pattern for the Future," *Times* (London), September 2, 1995, p. 1.

Carnegy, Hugh, "Waterford, in Search of Added Sparkle," *Financial Times*, October 15, 1986, p. 14.

Cheeseright, Paul, "Waterford Proposes to Reshape Crystal," *Financial Times*, June 1, 1995, p. 12.

Cooke, Kieran, "Crystal Gazing into the Future of a Shattered Empire," *Financial Times*, March 5, 1990, p. 22.

———, "Through a Waterford Crystal Glass Darkly," *Financial Times*, May 15, 1990, p. 31.

Craig, Carole, "Home Truths for Ireland: Mixed Fortunes at Waterford Crystal," *International Management*, May 1993, p. 34.

———, "Waterford Seeks Cash Infusion to Trim Debt," *Wall Street Journal*, January 9, 1990, p. A11.

Dunlevy, Mairead, *Waterford Crystal: The History*, Waterford, Ireland: Waterford Crystal Ltd., 1990.

Dyer, Geoff, "Ambitious Goals in the Crystal Ball," *Financial Times*, April 2, 1996, p. 22.

Fallon, James, "Waterford Wedgwood Scales Back Its Acquisition Strategy," *HFN—The Weekly Newspaper for the Home Furnishing Network*, July 9, 2001, p. 41.

Finn, Edwin A., Jr., and Richard Morais, "Table for Two?" *Forbes*, November 3, 1986, pp. 67.

Freyne, Patrick, "A Year of Living Dangerously," *Europe Intelligence Wire*, December 19, 2008.

Goodhart, David, "Sir Arthur Finds an Irish White Knight," *Financial Times*, October 9, 1986, p. 30.

Hill, Roy, "Why There's a New Gleam at Waterford Glass," *International Management*, May 1985, pp. 70.

Kehoe, Anne-Margaret, "Waterford Stake in Rosenthal," *HFN—The Weekly Newspaper for the Home Furnishing Network*, March 3, 1997, p. 35.

Kelly, Alison, *The Story of Wedgwood*, New York: Viking Press, 1975.

Lohr, Steve, "At Waterford, Honeymoon Is Over," *New York Times*, April 11, 1989, p. D1.

Lynch, Russell, "Waterford Wedgwood Goes into Administration," *Birmingham Post*, January 6, 2009, p. 8.

McKinney, Emma, "US Firm in Deal to Save Waterford Wedgwood," *Birmingham Post* (England), January 12, 2009, p. 6.

Murray, Matt, "Dublin's Waterford to Buy All-Clad for $110 Million," *Wall Street Journal*, May 25, 1999, p. B3.

O'Rourke, Martin, "Casting a Shadow: Brussels Has Been Craving a Strong Euro Ever Since the Single Currency Was Born, But, Now That We Have One, Is It What We Need?" *Office Products International*, July 2001, p. 32.

Penman, Andrew, and Michael Greenwood, "Sorted and the City: Fine for Crystal Makers; Waterford Pays Out Amid Anti-Competition Claims," *Mirror* (London, England), August 12, 2004, p. 42.

"Reviving Waterford Crystal," *Economist*, April 14, 1990, p. 72.

Rigby, Rhymer, "Wedgwood: Journey to Etruria," *Management Today*, December 1998, p. 86.

Salmans, Sandra, "The Worries of Wedgwood," *Management Today*, June 1980, p. 66.

Siklos, Richard, "The Strange Case of O'Reilly and the Retailer," *Sunday Telegraph* (London), January 9, 2005.

Taylor, Marianne, "Breaking Point for Two of the World's Most Luxurious Brands," *Herald*, January 6, 2009.

Toman, Barbara, "Waterford Wedgwood's Chief Resigns as Firm Splits China, Crystal Divisions," *Wall Street Journal*, December 14, 1990, p. A15.

Tomkins, Richard, "White Knight with Slightly Tarnished Armour," *Financial Times*, March 21, 1989, p. 20.

Valante, Judith, "A New Brand Restores Sparkle to Waterford," *Wall Street Journal*, November 10, 1994, p. B1.

Waxler, Caroline, "Wedgwood China, Waterford Crystal Cracked," *Business Insider*, January 5, 2009.

Wheatcroft, Patience, "Plot Thickens at Royal Doulton," *Times* (London), December 14, 2002, p. 59.

Whiteley, Geoffrey, "Why Wedgwood Wobbled," *Management Today*, August 1983, pp. 26.

Wilson, Andrew B., and Amy Dunkin, "Waterford Learns Its Lesson: Snob Appeal Isn't Enough," *Business Week*, December 24, 1984, pp. 63.

Witsil, Frank, "Spenders with Savvy Seek Luxury Bargains," *Tampa Tribune*, December 15, 2001.

Yee, Amy, "Grand Jury Indicts Retired Retailer on Perjury Charge," *Financial Times*, January 5, 2005, p. 28.

Zisko, Allison, "Waterford Acquires Minority Stake in Royal Doulton," *HFN—The Weekly Newspaper for the Home Furnishing Network*, December 13, 1999, p. 48.

Zisko, Allison, and Barbara Thau, "Waterford Buys All-Clad," *HFN—The Weekly Newspaper for the Home Furnishing Network*, June 7, 1999, p. 1.

Cumulative Index to Companies

A

A&E Television Networks, 32 3–7

A&P see The Great Atlantic & Pacific Tea Company, Inc.

A & W Brands, Inc., 25 3–5 see also Cadbury Schweppes PLC.

A-dec, Inc., 53 3–5

A-Mark Financial Corporation, 71 3–6

A. Smith Bowman Distillery, Inc., 104 1–4

A.B. Chance Industries Co., Inc. see Hubbell Inc.

A.B.Dick Company, 28 6–8

A.B. Watley Group Inc., 45 3–5

A.C. Moore Arts & Crafts, Inc., 30 3–5

A.C. Nielsen Company, 13 3–5 see also ACNielsen Corp.

A. Duda & Sons, Inc., 88 1–4

A. F. Blakemore & Son Ltd., 90 1–4

A.G. Edwards, Inc., 8 3–5; 32 17–21 (upd.)

A.H. Belo Corporation, 10 3–5; 30 13–17 (upd.) see also Belo Corp.

A.L. Pharma Inc., 12 3–5 see also Alpharma Inc.

A.M. Castle & Co., 25 6–8

A. Moksel AG, 59 3–6

A. Nelson & Co. Ltd., 75 3–6

A. O. Smith Corporation, 11 3–6; 40 3–8 (upd.); 93 1–9 (upd.)

A.P. Møller - Maersk A/S, 57 3–6

A.S. Watson & Company Ltd., 84 1–4

A.S. Yakovlev Design Bureau, 15 3–6

A. Schulman, Inc., 8 6–8; 49 3–7 (upd.)

A.T. Cross Company, 17 3–5; 49 8–12 (upd.)

A.W. Faber-Castell Unternehmensverwaltung GmbH & Co., 51 3–6

A/S Air Baltic Corporation, 71 35–37

AAF-McQuay Incorporated, 26 3–5

Aalborg Industries A/S, 90 5–8

AAON, Inc., 22 3–6

AAR Corp., 28 3–5

Aardman Animations Ltd., 61 3–5

Aarhus United A/S, 68 3–5

Aaron Brothers Holdings, Inc. see Michaels Stores, Inc.

Aaron Rents, Inc., 14 3–5; 35 3–6 (upd.)

AARP, 27 3–5

Aavid Thermal Technologies, Inc., 29 3–6

AB Volvo, I 209–11; 7 565–68 (upd.); 26 9–12 (upd.); 67 378–83 (upd.)

Abar Corporation see Ipsen International Inc.

ABARTA, Inc., 100 1–4

Abatix Corp., 57 7–9

Abaxis, Inc., 83 1–4

ABB Ltd., II 1–4; 22 7–12 (upd.); 65 3–10 (upd.)

Abbey National plc, 10 6–8; 39 3–6 (upd.)

Abbott Laboratories, I 619–21; 11 7–9 (upd.); 40 9–13 (upd.); 93 10–18 (upd.)

ABC Appliance, Inc., 10 9–11

ABC Carpet & Home Co. Inc., 26 6–8

ABC Family Worldwide, Inc., 52 3–6

ABC, Inc. see Disney/ABC Television Group

ABC Learning Centres Ltd., 93 19–22

ABC Rail Products Corporation, 18 3–5

ABC Stores see MNS, Ltd.

ABC Supply Co., Inc., 22 13–16

Abengoa S.A., 73 3–5

Abercrombie & Fitch Company, 15 7–9; 35 7–10 (upd.); 75 7–11 (upd.)

Abertis Infraestructuras, S.A., 65 11–13

ABF see Associated British Foods plc.

Abigail Adams National Bancorp, Inc., 23 3–5

Abiomed, Inc., 47 3–6

AbitibiBowater Inc., IV 245–47; 25 9–13 (upd.); 99 1–11 (upd.)

ABM Industries Incorporated, 25 14–16 (upd.)

ABN see Algemene Bank Nederland N.V.

ABN AMRO Holding, N.V., 50 3–7

Abrams Industries Inc., 23 6–8 see also Servidyne Inc.

Abraxas Petroleum Corporation, 89 1–5

Abril S.A., 95 1–4

Absa Group Ltd., 106 1–5

Abt Associates Inc., 95 5–9

Abu Dhabi National Oil Company, IV 363–64; **45** 6–9 (upd.)
Academic Press *see* Reed Elsevier plc.
Academy of Television Arts & Sciences, Inc., 55 3–5
Academy Sports & Outdoors, 27 6–8
Acadia Realty Trust, 106 6–10
Acadian Ambulance & Air Med Services, Inc., 39 7–10
Access Business Group *see* Alticor Inc.
ACCION International, 87 1–4
Acciona S.A., 81 1–4
Acclaim Entertainment Inc., 24 3–8
ACCO World Corporation, 7 3–5; **51** 7–10 (upd.)
Accor S.A., 10 12–14; **27** 9–12 (upd.); **69** 3–8 (upd.)
Accredited Home Lenders Holding Co., 91 1–4
Accubuilt, Inc., 74 3–5
Accuray Incorporated, 95 10–13
AccuWeather, Inc., 73 6–8
ACE Cash Express, Inc., 33 3–6
Ace Hardware Corporation, 12 6–8; **35** 11–14 (upd.)
Acer Incorporated, 16 3–6; **73** 9–13 (upd.)
Acergy SA, 97 1–4
Aceros Fortuna S.A. de C.V. *see* Carpenter Technology Corp.
Aceto Corp., 38 3–5
Aché Laboratórios Farmacêuticas S.A., 105 1–4
AchieveGlobal Inc., 90 9–12
Acindar Industria Argentina de Aceros S.A., 87 5–8
Ackerley Communications, Inc., 9 3–5
Ackermans & van Haaren N.V., 97 5–8
ACLU *see* American Civil Liberties Union (ACLU).
Acme-Cleveland Corp., 13 6–8
Acme United Corporation, 70 3–6
ACNielsen Corporation, 38 6–9 (upd.)
Acorn Products, Inc., 55 6–9
Acosta Sales and Marketing Company,Inc., 77 1–4
ACS *see* Affiliated Computer Services, Inc.; Alaska Communications Systems Group, Inc.
Acsys, Inc., 44 3–5
Actavis Group hf., 103 1–5
Actelion Ltd., 83 5–8
Action Performance Companies, Inc., 27 13–15
Activision, Inc., 32 8–11; **89** 6–11 (upd.)
Actuant Corporation, 94 1–8 (upd.)
Acuity Brands, Inc., 90 13–16
Acushnet Company, 64 3–5
Acuson Corporation, 10 15–17; **36** 3–6 (upd.)
Acxiom Corporation, 35 15–18
Adam Opel AG, 7 6–8; **21** 3–7 (upd.); **61** 6–11 (upd.)
Adams Childrenswear Ltd., 95 14–19
The Adams Express Company, 86 1–5
Adams Golf, Inc., 37 3–5

Adams Media Corporation *see* F&W Publications, Inc.
Adani Enterprises Ltd., 97 9–12
Adaptec, Inc., 31 3–6
ADC Telecommunications, Inc., 10 18–21; **30** 6–9 (upd.); **89** 12–17 (upd.)
Adecco S.A., 36 7–11 (upd.)
Adecoagro LLC, 101 1–4
Adelman Travel Group, 105 5–8
Adelphia Communications Corporation, 17 6–8; **52** 7–10 (upd.)
ADESA, Inc., 71 7–10
Adia S.A., 9 9–11 *see also* Adecco S.A.
adidas Group AG, 14 6–9; **33** 7–11 (upd.); **75** 12–17 (upd.)
Aditya Birla Group, 79 1–5
ADM *see* Archer Daniels Midland Co.
Administaff, Inc., 52 11–13
Administración Nacional de Combustibles, Alcohol y Pórtland, 93 23–27
Admiral Co. *see* Maytag Corp.
ADNOC *see* Abu Dhabi National Oil Co.
Adobe Systems Inc., 10 22–24; **33** 12–16 (upd.); **106** 11–17 (upd.)
Adolf Würth GmbH & Co. KG, 49 13–15
Adolfo Dominguez S.A., 72 3–5
Adolor Corporation, 101 5–8
Adolph Coors Company, I 236–38; **13** 9–11 (upd.); **36** 12–16 (upd.) *see also* Molson Coors Brewing Co.
Adolphe Lafont *see* Vivarte SA.
ADP *see* Automatic Data Processing, Inc.
ADT Security Services, Inc., 12 9–11; **44** 6–9 (upd.)
Adtran Inc., 22 17–20
Advance Auto Parts, Inc., 57 10–12
Advance Publications Inc., IV 581–84; **19** 3–7 (upd.); **96** 1–7 (upd.)
Advanced Circuits Inc., 67 3–5
Advanced Fibre Communications, Inc., 63 3–5
Advanced Marketing Services, Inc., 34 3–6
Advanced Medical Optics, Inc., 79 6–9
Advanced Micro Devices, Inc., 6 215–17; **30** 10–12 (upd.); **99** 12–17 (upd.)
Advanced Neuromodulation Systems, Inc., 73 14–17
Advanced Technology Laboratories, Inc., 9 6–8
Advanced Web Technologies *see* Miner Group Int.
Advanstar Communications, Inc., 57 13–17
Advanta Corporation, 8 9–11; **38** 10–14 (upd.)
Advantica Restaurant Group, Inc., 27 16–19 (upd.) *see also* Denny's Corporation
Adventist Health, 53 6–8
The Advertising Council, Inc., 76 3–6
The Advisory Board Company, 80 1–4 *see also* The Corporate Executive Board Co.

Advo, Inc., 6 12–14; **53** 9–13 (upd.)
Advocat Inc., 46 3–5
AECOM Technology Corporation, 79 10–13
AEG A.G., I 409–11
Aegean Marine Petroleum Network Inc., 89 18–21
Aegek S.A., 64 6–8
Aegis Group plc, 6 15–16
AEGON N.V., III 177–79; **50** 8–12 (upd.) *see also* Transamerica–An AEGON Company
AEI Music Network Inc., 35 19–21
AEON Co., Ltd., V 96–99; **68** 6–10 (upd.)
AEP *see* American Electric Power Co.
AEP Industries, Inc., 36 17–19
Aer Lingus Group plc, 34 7–10; **89** 22–27 (upd.)
Aero Mayflower Transit Company *see* Mayflower Group Inc.
Aeroflot - Russian Airlines JSC, 6 57–59; **29** 7–10 (upd.); **89** 28–34 (upd.)
AeroGrow International, Inc., 95 20–23
Aerojet-General Corp., 63 6–9
Aerolíneas Argentinas S.A., 33 17–19; **69** 9–12 (upd.)
Aeronca Inc., 46 6–8
Aéroports de Paris, 33 20–22
Aéropostale, Inc., 89 35–38
Aeroquip Corporation, 16 7–9 *see also* Eaton Corp.
Aerosonic Corporation, 69 13–15
The Aérospatiale Group, 7 9–12; **21** 8–11 (upd.) *see also* European Aeronautic Defence and Space Company EADS N.V.
AeroVironment, Inc., 97 13–16
The AES Corporation, 10 25–27; **13** 12–15 (upd.); **53** 14–18 (upd.)
Aetna, Inc., III 180–82; **21** 12–16 (upd.); **63** 10–16 (upd.)
Aetna Insulated Wire *see* The Marmon Group, Inc.
AFC Enterprises, Inc., 32 12–16 (upd.); **83** 9–15 (upd.)
Affiliated Computer Services, Inc., 61 12–16
Affiliated Foods Inc., 53 19–21
Affiliated Managers Group, Inc., 79 14–17
Affiliated Publications, Inc., 7 13–16
Affinity Group Holding Inc., 56 3–6
Affymetrix Inc., 106 18–24
AFLAC Incorporated, 10 28–30 (upd.); **38** 15–19 (upd.)
African Rainbow Minerals Ltd., 97 17–20
Africare, 59 7–10
After Hours Formalwear Inc., 60 3–5
Aftermarket Technology Corp., 83 16–19
AG Barr plc, 64 9–12
Ag-Chem Equipment Company, Inc., 17 9–11 *see also* AGCO Corp.
Ag Services of America, Inc., 59 11–13
Aga Foodservice Group PLC, 73 18–20

AGCO Corp., 13 16–18; 67 6–10 (upd.)
Agence France-Presse, 34 11–14
Agere Systems Inc., 61 17–19
Agfa Gevaert Group N.V., 59 14–16
Aggregate Industries plc, 36 20–22
Aggreko Plc, 45 10–13
Agilent Technologies Inc., 38 20–23; 93 28–32 (upd.)
Agilysys Inc., 76 7–11 (upd.)
Agnico-Eagle Mines Limited, 71 11–14
Agora S.A. Group, 77 5–8
AGRANA *see* Südzucker AG.
Agri Beef Company, 81 5–9
Agria Corporation, 101 9–13
Agrigenetics, Inc. *see* Mycogen Corp.
Agrium Inc., 73 21–23
AgustaWestland N.V., 75 18–20
Agway, Inc., 7 17–18; 21 17–19 (upd.) *see also* Cargill Inc.
AHL Services, Inc., 27 20–23
Ahlstrom Corporation, 53 22–25
Ahmanson *see* H.F. Ahmanson & Co.
AHMSA *see* Altos Hornos de México, S.A. de C.V.
Ahold *see* Koninklijke Ahold NV.
AHP *see* American Home Products Corp.
AICPA *see* The American Institute of Certified Public Accountants.
AIG *see* American International Group, Inc.
AIMCO *see* Apartment Investment and Management Co.
Ainsworth Lumber Co. Ltd., 99 18–22
Air & Water Technologies Corporation, 6 441–42 *see also* Aqua Alliance Inc.
Air Berlin GmbH & Co. Luftverkehrs KG, 71 15–17
Air Canada, 6 60–62; 23 9–12 (upd.); 59 17–22 (upd.)
Air China, 46 9–11
Air Express International Corporation, 13 19–20
Air France *see* Societe Air France.
Air-India Limited, 6 63–64; 27 24–26 (upd.)
Air Jamaica Limited, 54 3–6
Air Liquide *see* L'Air Liquide SA.
Air Mauritius Ltd., 63 17 19
Air Methods Corporation, 53 26–29
Air Midwest, Inc. *see* Mesa Air Group, Inc.
Air New Zealand Limited, 14 10–12; 38 24–27 (upd.)
Air Pacific Ltd., 70 7–9
Air Partner PLC, 93 33–36
Air Products and Chemicals, Inc., I 297–99; 10 31–33 (upd.); 74 6–9 (upd.)
Air Sahara Limited, 65 14–16
Air T, Inc., 86 6–9
Air Wisconsin Airlines Corporation, 55 10–12
Air Zimbabwe (Private) Limited, 91 5–8
AirAsia Berhad, 93 37–40
Airborne Freight Corporation, 6 345–47; 34 15–18 (upd.) *see also* DHL Worldwide Network S.A./N.V.

Airborne Systems Group, 89 39–42
Airbus Industrie *see* G.I.E. Airbus Industrie.
Airgas, Inc., 54 7–10
Airguard Industries, Inc. *see* CLARCOR Inc.
Airlink Pty Ltd *see* Qantas Airways Ltd.
Airstream *see* Thor Industries, Inc.
AirTouch Communications, 11 10–12 *see also* Vodafone Group PLC.
Airtours Plc, 27 27–29, 90, 92
AirTran Holdings, Inc., 22 21–23
Aisin Seiki Co., Ltd., III 415–16; 48 3–5 (upd.)
Aitchison & Colegrave *see* Bradford & Bingley PLC.
Aiwa Co., Ltd., 30 18–20
Ajegroup S.A, 92 1–4
Ajinomoto Co., Inc., II 463–64; 28 9–11 (upd.)
AK Steel Holding Corporation, 19 8–9; 41 3–6 (upd.)
Akamai Technologies, Inc., 71 18–21
Akbank TAS, 79 18–21
Akeena Solar, Inc., 103 6–10
Akerys S.A., 90 17–20
AKG Acoustics GmbH, 62 3–6
Akin, Gump, Strauss, Hauer & Feld, L.L.P., 33 23–25
Akorn, Inc., 32 22–24
Akro-Mills Inc. *see* Myers Industries, Inc.
Aktiebolaget SKF, III 622–25; 38 28–33 (upd.); 89 401–09 (upd.)
Akzo Nobel N.V., 13 21–23; 41 7–10 (upd.)
Al Habtoor Group L.L.C., 87 9–12
Al-Tawfeek Co. For Investment Funds Ltd. *see* Dallah Albaraka Group.
Alabama Farmers Cooperative, Inc., 63 20–22
Alabama National BanCorporation, 75 21–23
Aladdin Knowledge Systems Ltd., 101 14–17
Alain Afflelou SA, 53 30–32
Alain Manoukian *see* Groupe Alain Manoukian.
Alamo Group Inc., 32 25–28
Alamo Rent A Car, 6 348–50; 24 9–12 (upd.); 84 5–11 (upd.)
ALARIS Medical Systems, Inc., 65 17–20
Alascom, Inc. *see* AT&T Corp.
Alaska Air Group, Inc., 6 65–67; 29 11–14 (upd.)
Alaska Communications Systems Group, Inc., 89 43–46
Alaska Railroad Corporation, 60 6–9
Alba-Waldensian, Inc., 30 21–23 *see also* E.I. du Pont de Nemours and Co.
Albany International Corporation, 8 12–14; 51 11–14 (upd.)
Albany Molecular Research, Inc., 77 9–12
Albaugh, Inc., 105 9–12
Albemarle Corporation, 59 23–25
Alberici Corporation, 76 12–14
The Albert Fisher Group plc, 41 11–13

Albert Heijn NV *see* Koninklijke Ahold N.V. (Royal Ahold).
Alberta Energy Company Ltd., 16 10–12; 43 3–6 (upd.)
Alberto-Culver Company, 8 15–17; 36 23–27 (upd.); 91 9–15 (upd.)
Albert's Organics, Inc. *see* United Natural Foods, Inc.
Albertson's, Inc., II 601–03; 7 19–22 (upd.); 30 24–28 (upd.); 65 21–26 (upd.)
Alcan Aluminium Limited, IV 9–13; 31 7–12 (upd.)
Alcatel S.A., 9 9–11; 36 28–31 (upd.)
Alco Health Services Corporation, III 9–10 *see also* AmeriSource Health Corp.
Alco Standard Corporation, I 412–13
Alcoa Inc., 56 7–11 (upd.)
Alderwoods Group, Inc., 68 11–15 (upd.)
Aldi Einkauf GmbH & Co. OHG, 13 24–26; 86 10–14 (upd.)
Aldila Inc., 46 12–14
Aldus Corporation, 10 34–36 *see also* Adobe Systems Inc.
Alès Groupe, 81 10–13
Alex Lee Inc., 18 6–9; 44 10–14 (upd.)
Alexander & Alexander Services Inc., 10 37–39 *see also* Aon Corp.
Alexander & Baldwin, Inc., 10 40–42; 40 14–19 (upd.)
Alexander's, Inc., 45 14–16
Alexandra plc, 88 5–8
Alexandria Real Estate Equities, Inc., 101 18–22
Alfa Corporation, 60 10–12
Alfa Group, 99 23–26
Alfa-Laval AB, III 417–21; 64 13–18 (upd.)
Alfa Romeo, 13 27–29; 36 32–35 (upd.)
Alfa, S.A. de C.V., 19 10–12
Alfesca hf, 82 1–4
Alfred A. Knopf, Inc. *see* Random House, Inc.
Alfred Dunhill Limited *see* Vendôme Luxury Group plc.
Alfred Kärcher GmbH & Co KG, 94 9–14
Alfred Ritter GmbH & Co. KG, 58 3–7
Alga *see* BRIO AB.
Algar S/A Emprendimentos e Participações, 103 11–14
Algemene Bank Nederland N.V., II 183–84
Algerian Saudi Leasing Holding Co. *see* Dallah Albaraka Group.
Algo Group Inc., 24 13–15
Alico, Inc., 63 23–25
Alienware Corporation, 81 14–17
Align Technology, Inc., 94 15–18
Alimentation Couche-Tard Inc., 77 13–16
Alitalia–Linee Aeree Italiane, S.p.A., 6 68–69; 29 15–17 (upd.); 97 21–27 (upd.)
Aljazeera Satellite Channel, 79 22–25

All American Communications Inc., 20 3–7

The All England Lawn Tennis & Croquet Club, 54 11–13

All Nippon Airways Co., Ltd., 6 70–71; 38 34–37 (upd.); 91 16–20 (upd.)

Allbritton Communications Company, 105 13–16

Alldays plc, 49 16–19

Allders plc, 37 6–8

Alleanza Assicurazioni S.p.A., 65 27–29

Alleghany Corporation, 10 43–45; 60 13–16 (upd.)

Allegheny Energy, Inc., 38 38–41 (upd.)

Allegheny Ludlum Corporation, 8 18–20

Allegheny Power System, Inc., V 543–45 see also Allegheny Energy, Inc.

Allegheny Steel Distributors, Inc. see Reliance Steel & Aluminum Co.

Allegiance Life Insurance Company see Horace Mann Educators Corp.

Allegiant Travel Company, 97 28–31

Allegis Group, Inc., 95 24–27

Allen-Bradley Co. see Rockwell Automation.

Allen Brothers, Inc., 101 23–26

Allen Canning Company, 76 15–17

Allen-Edmonds Shoe Corporation, 61 20–23

Allen Foods, Inc., 60 17–19

Allen Organ Company, 33 26–29

Allen Systems Group, Inc., 59 26–28

Allerderm see Virbac Corp.

Allergan, Inc., 10 46–49; 30 29–33 (upd.); 77 17–24 (upd.)

Allgemeine Elektricitäts-Gesellschaft see AEG A.G.

Allgemeine Handelsgesellschaft der Verbraucher AG see AVA AG.

Allgemeiner Deutscher Automobil-Club e.V., 100 5–10

Alliance and Leicester plc, 88 9–12

Alliance Assurance Company see Royal & Sun Alliance Insurance Group plc.

Alliance Atlantis Communications Inc., 39 11–14

Alliance Boots plc, 83 20–28 (upd.)

Alliance Capital Management Holding L.P., 63 26–28

Alliance Entertainment Corp., 17 12–14 see also Source Interlink Companies, Inc.

Alliance Laundry Holdings LLC, 102 1–5

Alliance Resource Partners, L.P., 81 18–21

Alliance UniChem Plc see Alliance Boots plc.

Alliant Energy Corporation, 106 25–29

Alliant Techsystems Inc., 8 21–23; 30 34–37 (upd.); 77 25–31 (upd.)

Allianz AG, III 183–86; 15 10–14 (upd.); 57 18–24 (upd.)

Allied Corporation see AlliedSignal Inc.

The Allied Defense Group, Inc., 65 30–33

Allied Domecq PLC, 29 18–20

Allied Healthcare Products, Inc., 24 16–19

Allied Irish Banks, plc, 16 13–15; 43 7–10 (upd.); 94 19–24 (upd.)

Allied-Lyons plc, I 215–16 see also Carlsberg A/S.

Allied Plywood Corporation see Ply Gem Industries Inc.

Allied Products Corporation, 21 20–22

Allied-Signal Corp., I 414–16 see also AlliedSignal, Inc.

Allied Signal Engines, 9 12–15

Allied Waste Industries, Inc., 50 13–16

Allied Worldwide, Inc., 49 20–23

AlliedSignal Inc., 22 29–32 (upd.) see also Honeywell Inc.

Allison Gas Turbine Division, 9 16–19

Allmerica Financial Corporation, 63 29–31

Allou Health & Beauty Care, Inc., 28 12–14

Alloy, Inc., 55 13–15

Allscripts-Misys Healthcare Solutions Inc., 104 5–8

The Allstate Corporation, 10 50–52; 27 30–33 (upd.)

ALLTEL Corporation, 6 299–301; 46 15–19 (upd.)

Alltrista Corporation, 30 38–41 see also Jarden Corp.

Allwaste, Inc., 18 10–13

Alma Media Corporation, 98 1–4

Almacenes Exito S.A., 89 47–50

Almaden Vineyards see Canandaigua Brands, Inc.

Almanij NV, 44 15–18 see also Algemeene Maatschappij voor Nijverheidskrediet.

Almay, Inc. see Revlon Inc.

Almost Family, Inc., 93 41–44

Aloha Airlines, Incorporated, 24 20–22

Alon Israel Oil Company Ltd., 104 9–13

Alpargatas S.A.I.C., 87 13–17

Alpha Airports Group PLC, 77 32–35

Alpha Natural Resources Inc., 106 30–33

Alpharma Inc., 35 22–26 (upd.)

Alpine Confections, Inc., 71 22–24

Alpine Electronics, Inc., 13 30–31

Alpine Lace Brands, Inc., 18 14–16 see also Land O'Lakes, Inc.

Alps Electric Co., Ltd., II 5–6; 44 19–21 (upd.)

Alrosa Company Ltd., 62 7–11

Alsco see Steiner Corp.

Alside Inc., 94 25–29

Altadis S.A., 72 6–13 (upd.)

ALTANA AG, 87 18–22

AltaVista Company, 43 11–13

Altera Corporation, 18 17–20; 43 14–18 (upd.)

Alternative Living Services see Alterra Healthcare Corp.

Alternative Tentacles Records, 66 3–6

Alternative Youth Services, Inc. see Res-Care, Inc.

Alterra Healthcare Corporation, 42 3–5

Alticor Inc., 71 25–30 (upd.)

Altiris, Inc., 65 34–36

Altos Hornos de México, S.A. de C.V., 42 6–8

Altran Technologies, 51 15–18

Altron Incorporated, 20 8–10

Aluar Aluminio Argentino S.A.I.C., 74 10–12

Alumalsa see Aluminoy y Aleaciones S.A.

Aluminum Company of America, IV 14–16; 20 11–14 (upd.) see also Alcoa Inc.

Alvin Ailey Dance Foundation, Inc., 52 14–17

Alvis Plc, 47 7–9

ALZA Corporation, 10 53–55; 36 36–39 (upd.)

AMAG Group, 102 6–10

Amalgamated Bank, 60 20–22

AMAX Inc., IV 17–19 see also Cyprus Amex.

Amazon.com, Inc., 25 17–19; 56 12–15 (upd.)

AMB Generali Holding AG, 51 19–23

AMB Property Corporation, 57 25–27

Ambac Financial Group, Inc., 65 37–39

Ambassadors International, Inc., 68 16–18 (upd.)

AmBev see Companhia de Bebidas das Américas.

Amblin Entertainment, 21 23–27

AMC Entertainment Inc., 12 12–14; 35 27–29 (upd.)

AMCC see Applied Micro Circuits Corp.

AMCOL International Corporation, 59 29–33 (upd.)

AMCON Distributing Company, 99 27–30

Amcor Ltd., IV 248–50; 19 13–16 (upd.); 78 1–6 (upd.)

AMCORE Financial Inc., 44 22–26

AMD see Advanced Micro Devices, Inc.

Amdahl Corporation, III 109–11; 14 13–16 (upd.); 40 20–25 (upd.) see also Fujitsu Ltd.

Amdocs Ltd., 47 10–12

Amec Spie S.A., 57 28–31

Amedisys, Inc., 53 33–36; 106 34–37 (upd.)

Amer Group plc, 41 14–16

Amerada Hess Corporation, IV 365–67; 21 28–31 (upd.); 55 16–20 (upd.)

Amerchol Corporation see Union Carbide Corp.

AMERCO, 6 351–52; 67 11–14 (upd.)

Ameren Corporation, 60 23–27 (upd.)

Ameri-Kart Corp. see Myers Industries, Inc.

América Móvil, S.A. de C.V., 80 5–8

America Online, Inc., 10 56–58; 26 16–20 (upd.) see also CompuServe Interactive Services, Inc.; AOL Time Warner Inc.

America West Holdings Corporation, 6 72–74; 34 22–26 (upd.)

American & Efird, Inc., 82 5–9

American Airlines, I 89–91; 6 75–77 (upd.) see also AMR Corp.

American Apparel, Inc., 90 21–24
American Association of Retired Persons *see* AARP.
American Axle & Manufacturing Holdings, Inc., 67 15–17
American Banknote Corporation, 30 42–45
American Bar Association, 35 30–33
American Biltrite Inc., 16 16–18; **43** 19–22 (upd.)
American Brands, Inc., V 395–97 *see also* Fortune Brands, Inc.
American Builders & Contractors Supply Co. *see* ABC Supply Co., Inc.
American Building Maintenance Industries, Inc., 6 17–19 *see also* ABM Industries Inc.
American Business Information, Inc., 18 21–25
American Business Interiors *see* American Furniture Company, Inc.
American Business Products, Inc., 20 15–17
American Campus Communities, Inc., 85 1–5
American Can Co. *see* Primerica Corp.
The American Cancer Society, 24 23–25
American Capital Strategies, Ltd., 91 21–24
American Cast Iron Pipe Company, 50 17–20
American Civil Liberties Union (ACLU), 60 28–31
American Classic Voyages Company, 27 34–37
American Coin Merchandising, Inc., 28 15–17; **74** 13–16 (upd.)
American Colloid Co., 13 32–35 *see* AMCOL International Corp.
American Commercial Lines Inc., 99 31–34
American Cotton Growers Association *see* Plains Cotton Cooperative Association.
American Crystal Sugar Company, 11 13–15; **32** 29–33 (upd.)
American Cyanamid, I 300–02; **8** 24–26 (upd.)
American Eagle Outfitters, Inc., 24 26–28; **55** 21–24 (upd.)
American Ecology Corporation, 77 36–39
American Electric Power Company, V 546–49; **45** 17–21 (upd.)
American Equipment Company, Inc., 104 14–17
American Express Company, II 395–99; **10** 59–64 (upd.); **38** 42–48 (upd.)
American Family Corporation, III 187–89 *see also* AFLAC Inc.
American Financial Group Inc., III 190–92; **48** 6–10 (upd.)
American Foods Group, 43 23–27
American Furniture Company, Inc., 21 32–34
American General Corporation, III 193–94; **10** 65–67 (upd.); **46** 20–23 (upd.)

American General Finance Corp., 11 16–17
American Girl, Inc., 69 16–19 (upd)
American Golf Corporation, 45 22–24
American Gramaphone LLC, 52 18–20
American Greetings Corporation, 7 23–25; **22** 33–36 (upd.); **59** 34–39 (upd.)
American Healthways, Inc., 65 40–42
American Home Mortgage Holdings, Inc., 46 24–26
American Home Products, I 622–24; **10** 68–70 (upd.) *see also* Wyeth.
American Homestar Corporation, 18 26–29; **41** 17–20 (upd.)
American Institute of Certified Public Accountants (AICPA), 44 27–30
American International Group, Inc., III 195–98; **15** 15–19 (upd.); **47** 13–19 (upd.)
American Italian Pasta Company, 27 38–40; **76** 18–21 (upd.)
American Kennel Club, Inc., 74 17–19
American Lawyer Media Holdings, Inc., 32 34–37
American Library Association, 86 15–19
American Licorice Company, 86 20–23
American Locker Group Incorporated, 34 19–21
American Lung Association, 48 11–14
American Machine and Metals *see* AMETEK, Inc.
American Maize-Products Co., 14 17–20
American Management Association, 76 22–25
American Management Systems, Inc., 11 18–20
American Media, Inc., 27 41–44; **82** 10–15 (upd.)
American Medical Alert Corporation, 103 15–18
American Medical Association, 39 15–18
American Medical International, Inc., III 73–75
American Medical Response, Inc., 39 19–22
American Metals Corporation *see* Reliance Steel & Aluminum Co.
American Modern Insurance Group *see* The Midland Co.
American Motors Corp., I 135–37 *see also* DaimlerChrysler AG.
American MSI Corporation *see* Moldflow Corp.
American National Insurance Company, 8 27–29; **27** 45–48 (upd.)
American Nurses Association Inc., 102 11–15
American Olean Tile Company *see* Armstrong Holdings, Inc.
American Oriental Bioengineering Inc., 93 45–48
American Pad & Paper Company, 20 18–21
American Pfauter *see* Gleason Corp.

American Pharmaceutical Partners, Inc., 69 20–22
American Pop Corn Company, 59 40–43
American Power Conversion Corporation, 24 29–31; **67** 18–20 (upd.)
American Premier Underwriters, Inc., 10 71–74
American President Companies Ltd., 6 353–55 *see also* APL Ltd.
American Printing House for the Blind, 26 13–15
American Re Corporation, 10 75–77; **35** 34–37 (upd.)
American Red Cross, 40 26–29
American Reprographics Company, 75 24–26
American Residential Mortgage Corporation, 8 30–31
American Restaurant Partners, L.P., 93 49–52
American Retirement Corporation, 42 9–12 *see also* Brookdale Senior Living.
American Rice, Inc., 33 30–33
American Rug Craftsmen *see* Mohawk Industries, Inc.
American Safety Razor Company, 20 22–24
American Savings Bank *see* Hawaiian Electric Industries, Inc.
American Science & Engineering, Inc., 81 22–25
American Seating Company, 78 7–11
American Skiing Company, 28 18–21
American Society for the Prevention of Cruelty to Animals (ASPCA), 68 19–22
The American Society of Composers, Authors and Publishers (ASCAP), 29 21–24
American Software Inc., 22 214; **25** 20–22
American Standard Companies Inc., III 663–65; **30** 46–50 (upd.)
American States Water Company, 46 27–30
American Steamship Company *see* GATX.
American Stores Company, II 604–06; **22** 37–40 (upd.) *see also* Albertson's, Inc.
American Superconductor Corporation, 97 32–36
American Technical Ceramics Corp., 67 21–23
American Technology Corporation, 103 19–22
American Telephone and Telegraph Company *see* AT&T.
American Tobacco Co. *see* B.A.T. Industries PLC.; Fortune Brands, Inc.
American Tourister, Inc., 16 19–21 *see also* Samsonite Corp.
American Tower Corporation, 33 34–38
American Vanguard Corporation, 47 20–22
American Water Works Company, Inc., 6 443–45; **38** 49–52 (upd.)

American Woodmark Corporation, 31 13–16

American Yearbook Company *see* Jostens, Inc.

AmeriCares Foundation, Inc., 87 23–28

America's Car-Mart, Inc., 64 19–21

America's Favorite Chicken Company, Inc., 7 26–28 *see also* AFC Enterprises, Inc.

Amerigon Incorporated, 97 37–40

AMERIGROUP Corporation, 69 23–26

Amerihost Properties, Inc., 30 51–53

AmeriSource Health Corporation, 37 9–11 (upd.)

AmerisourceBergen Corporation, 64 22–28 (upd.)

Ameristar Casinos, Inc., 33 39–42; 69 27–31 (upd.)

Ameritech Corporation, V 265–68; 18 30–34 (upd.) *see also* AT&T Corp.

Ameritrade Holding Corporation, 34 27–30

Ameriwood Industries International Corp., 17 15–17 *see also* Dorel Industries Inc.

Amerock Corporation, 53 37–40

Ameron International Corporation, 67 24–26

Amersham PLC, 50 21–25

Ames Department Stores, Inc., 9 20–22; 30 54–57 (upd.)

AMETEK, Inc., 9 23–25

N.V. Amev, III 199–202 *see also* Fortis, Inc.

Amey Plc, 47 23–25

AMF Bowling, Inc., 40 30–33

Amfac/JMB Hawaii L.L.C., I 417–18; 24 32–35 (upd.)

Amgen, Inc., 10 78–81; 30 58–61 (upd.); 89 51–57 (upd.)

AMI Metals, Inc. *see* Reliance Steel & Aluminum Co.

AMICAS, Inc., 69 32–34

Amil Participações S.A., 105 17–20

Amkor Technology, Inc., 69 35–37

Ammirati Puris Lintas *see* Interpublic Group of Companies, Inc.

Amnesty International, 50 26–29

Amoco Corporation, IV 368–71; 14 21–25 (upd.) *see also* BP p.l.c.

Amoskeag Company, 8 32–33 *see also* Fieldcrest Cannon, Inc.

AMP, Inc., II 7–8; 14 26–28 (upd.)

Ampacet Corporation, 67 27–29

Ampco-Pittsburgh Corporation, 79 26–29

Ampex Corporation, 17 18–20

Amphenol Corporation, 40 34–37

AMR *see* American Medical Response, Inc.

AMR Corporation, 28 22–26 (upd.); 52 21–26 (upd.)

AMREP Corporation, 21 35–37

AMS *see* Advanced Marketing Services, Inc.

Amscan Holdings, Inc., 61 24–26

AmSouth Bancorporation, 12 15–17; 48 15–18 (upd.)

Amsted Industries Incorporated, 7 29–31

Amsterdam-Rotterdam Bank N.V., II 185–86

Amstrad plc, III 112–14; 48 19–23 (upd.)

AmSurg Corporation, 48 24–27

Amtech *see* American Building Maintenance Industries, Inc.; ABM Industries Inc.

Amtrak *see* The National Railroad Passenger Corp.

Amtran, Inc., 34 31–33

AMVESCAP PLC, 65 43–45

Amway Corporation, III 11–14; 13 36–39 (upd.); 30 62–66 (upd.) *see also* Alticor Inc.

Amylin Pharmaceuticals, Inc., 67 30–32

Amy's Kitchen Inc., 76 26–28

ANA *see* All Nippon Airways Co., Ltd.

Anacomp, Inc., 94 30–34

Anadarko Petroleum Corporation, 10 82–84; 52 27–30 (upd.); 106 38–43 (upd.)

Anadolu Efes Biracilik ve Malt Sanayii A.S., 95 28–31

Anaheim Angels Baseball Club, Inc., 53 41–44

Analex Corporation, 74 20–22

Analog Devices, Inc., 10 85–87

Analogic Corporation, 23 13–16

Analysts International Corporation, 36 40–42

Analytic Sciences Corporation, 10 88–90

Analytical Surveys, Inc., 33 43–45

Anam Group, 23 17–19

Anaren Microwave, Inc., 33 46–48

Anchor Bancorp, Inc., 10 91–93

Anchor BanCorp Wisconsin, Inc., 101 27–30

Anchor Brewing Company, 47 26–28

Anchor Gaming, 24 36–39

Anchor Hocking Glassware, 13 40–42

Andersen, 10 94–95; 29 25–28 (upd.); 68 23–27 (upd.)

The Anderson-DuBose Company, 60 32–34

Anderson Trucking Service, Inc., 75 27–29

The Andersons, Inc., 31 17–21

Andin International, Inc., 100 11–14

Andis Company, Inc., 85 6–9

Andrade Gutierrez S.A., 102 16–19

Andreas Stihl AG & Co. KG, 16 22–24; 59 44–47 (upd.)

Andretti Green Racing, 106 44–48

Andrew Corporation, 10 96–98; 32 38–41 (upd.)

Andrew Peller Ltd., 101 31–34

The Andrews Institute, 99 35–38

Andrews Kurth, LLP, 71 31–34

Andrews McMeel Universal, 40 38–41

Andritz AG, 51 24–26

Andronico's Market, 70 10–13

Andrx Corporation, 55 25–27

Angelica Corporation, 15 20–22; 43 28–31 (upd.)

Angelini SpA, 100 15–18

AngioDynamics, Inc., 81 26–29

Angliss International Group *see* Vestey Group Ltd.

Anglo-Abrasives Ltd. *see* Carbo PLC.

Anglo American PLC, IV 20–23; 16 25–30 (upd.); 50 30–36 (upd.)

Anheuser-Busch InBev, I 217–19; 10 99–101 (upd.); 34 34–37 (upd.); 100 19–25 (upd.)

Anhui Conch Cement Company Limited, 99 39–42

Anixter International Inc., 88 13–16

Anker BV, 53 45–47

Annie's Homegrown, Inc., 59 48–50

Annin & Co., 100 26–30

AnnTaylor Stores Corporation, 13 43–45; 37 12–15 (upd.); 67 33–37 (upd.)

ANR Pipeline Co., 17 21–23

Anritsu Corporation, 68 28–30

The Anschutz Company, 12 18–20; 36 43–47 (upd.); 73 24–30 (upd.)

Ansell Ltd., 60 35–38 (upd.)

Ansoft Corporation, 63 32–34

Anteon Corporation, 57 32–34

Anthem Electronics, Inc., 13 46–47

Anthony & Sylvan Pools Corporation, 56 16–18

Anthracite Industries, Inc. *see* Asbury Carbons, Inc.

Anthropologie, Inc. *see* Urban Outfitters, Inc.

Antinori *see* Marchesi Antinori SRL.

The Antioch Company, 40 42–45

ANTK Tupolev *see* Aviacionny Nauchno-Tehnicheskii Komplex im. A.N. Tupoleva.

Antofagasta plc, 65 46–49

Anton Schlecker, 102 20–24

Antonov Design Bureau, 53 48–51

AO VimpelCom, 48 416–19

AOK-Bundesverband (Federation of the AOK), 78 12–16

AOL Time Warner Inc., 57 35–44 (upd.)

Aon Corporation, III 203–05; 45 25–28 (upd.)

AP *see* The Associated Press.

Apache Corporation, 10 102–04; 32 42–46 (upd.); 89 58–65 (upd.)

Apartment Investment and Management Company, 49 24–26

Apasco S.A. de C.V., 51 27–29

Apax Partners Worldwide LLP, 89 66–69

Apex Digital, Inc., 63 35–37

APH *see* American Printing House for the Blind.

APi Group, Inc., 64 29–32

APL Limited, 61 27–30 (upd.)

APLIX S.A. *see* Velcro Industries N.V.

Apogee Enterprises, Inc., 8 34–36

Apollo Group, Inc., 24 40–42

Applause Inc., 24 43–46 *see also* Russ Berrie and Co., Inc.

Apple & Eve L.L.C., 92 5–8

Apple Bank for Savings, 59 51–53

Apple Computer, Inc., III 115–16; 6 218–20 (upd.); 36 48–51 (upd.); 77 40–45 (upd.)
Apple Corps Ltd., 87 29–34
Applebee's International Inc., 14 29–31; 35 38–41 (upd.)
Appliance Recycling Centers of America, Inc., 42 13–16
Applica Incorporated, 43 32–36 (upd.)
Applied Bioscience International, Inc., 10 105–07
Applied Films Corporation, 48 28–31
Applied Materials, Inc., 10 108–09; 46 31–34 (upd.)
Applied Micro Circuits Corporation, 38 53–55
Applied Power Inc., 9 26–28; 32 47–51 (upd.) *see also* Actuant Corp.
Applied Signal Technology, Inc., 87 35–38
Applied Technology Solutions *see* RWD Technologies, Inc.
Aprilia SpA, 17 24–26
AptarGroup, Inc., 69 38–41
Aqua Alliance Inc., 32 52–54 (upd.)
aQuantive, Inc., 81 30–33
Aquarion Company, 84 12–16
Aquarius Platinum Ltd., 63 38–40
Aquent, 96 8–11
Aquila, Inc., 50 37–40 (upd.)
AR Accessories Group, Inc., 23 20–22
ARA *see* Consorcio ARA, S.A. de C.V.
ARA Services, II 607–08 *see also* Aramark.
Arab Potash Company, 85 10–13
Arabian Gulf Oil Company *see* National Oil Corp.
Aracruz Celulose S.A., 57 45–47
Aral AG, 62 12–15
ARAMARK Corporation, 13 48–50; 41 21–24 (upd.)
Arandell Corporation, 37 16–18
Arapuã *see* Lojas Arapuã S.A.
ARBED S.A., IV 24–27; 22 41–45 (upd.) *see also* Arcelor Gent.
Arbeitsgemeinschaft der öffentlich-rechtlichen Rundfunkanstalten der Bundesrepublick *see* ARD.
The Arbitron Company, 38 56–61
Arbor Drugs Inc., 12 21–23 *see also* CVS Corp.
Arby's Inc., 14 32–34
Arc International, 76 29–31
ARCA *see* Appliance Recycling Centers of America, Inc.
Arcadia Group plc, 28 27–30 (upd.)
Arcadis NV, 26 21–24
Arçelik A.S., 100 31–34
Arcelor Gent, 80 9–12
Arch Chemicals, Inc., 78 17–20
Arch Coal Inc., 98 5–8
Arch Mineral Corporation, 7 32–34
Arch Wireless, Inc., 39 23–26
Archer Daniels Midland Company, I 419–21; 11 21–23 (upd.); 32 55–59 (upd.); 75 30–35 (upd.)

Archie Comics Publications, Inc., 63 41–44
Archon Corporation, 74 23–26 (upd.)
Archstone-Smith Trust, 49 27–30
Archway Cookies, Inc., 29 29–31
ARCO *see* Atlantic Richfield Co.
ARCO Chemical Company, 10 110–11 *see also* Lyondell Chemical Co.
Arcor S.A.I.C., 66 7–9
Arctco, Inc., 16 31–34
Arctic Cat Inc., 40 46–50 (upd.); 96 12–19 (upd.)
Arctic Slope Regional Corporation, 38 62–65
ARD, 41 25–29
Arden Group, Inc., 29 32–35
Áreas S.A., 104 18–21
Arena Leisure Plc, 99 43–46
Arena Resources, Inc., 97 41–44
ARES *see* Groupe Ares S.A.
AREVA NP, 90 25–30 (upd.)
Argentaria Caja Postal y Banco Hipotecario S.A. *see* Banco Bilbao Vizcaya Argentaria S.A.
Argon ST, Inc., 81 34–37
Argos S.A. *see* Cementos Argos S.A.
Argosy Gaming Company, 21 38–41 *see also* Penn National Gaming, Inc.
Argyll Group PLC, II 609–10 *see also* Safeway PLC.
Arianespace S.A., 89 70–73
Ariba, Inc., 57 48–51
Ariens Company, 48 32–34
ARINC Inc., 98 9–14
Aris Industries, Inc., 16 35–38
Aristocrat Leisure Limited, 54 14–16
Aristokraft Inc. *see* MasterBrand Cabinets, Inc.
The Aristotle Corporation, 62 16–18
AriZona Beverages *see* Ferolito, Vultaggio & Sons.
Arjo Wiggins Appleton p.l.c., 34 38–40
Ark Restaurants Corp., 20 25–27
Arkansas Best Corporation, 16 39–41; 94 35–40 (upd.)
Arkema S.A., 100 35–39
Arkla, Inc., V 550–51
Arla Foods amba, 48 35–38
Arlington Tankers Ltd., 101 35–38
Armani *see* Giorgio Armani S.p.A.
Armco Inc., IV 28–30 *see also* AK Steel.
Armor All Products Corp., 16 42–44
Armor Holdings, Inc., 27 49–51
Armour *see* Tommy Armour Golf Co.
Armstrong Air Conditioning Inc. *see* Lennox International Inc.
Armstrong Holdings, Inc., III 422–24; 22 46–50 (upd.); 81 38–44 (upd.)
Army and Air Force Exchange Service, 39 27–29
Arnhold and S. Bleichroeder Advisers, LLC, 97 45–49
Arnold & Porter, 35 42–44
Arnold Clark Automobiles Ltd., 60 39–41
Arnoldo Mondadori Editore S.p.A., IV 585–88; 19 17–21 (upd.); 54 17–23 (upd.)

Arnott's Ltd., 66 10–12
Aro Corp. *see* Ingersoll-Rand Company Ltd.
Arotech Corporation, 93 53–56
ArQule, Inc., 68 31–34
ARRIS Group, Inc., 89 74–77
Arriva PLC, 69 42–44
Arrow Air Holdings Corporation, 55 28–30
Arrow Electronics, Inc., 10 112–14; 50 41–44 (upd.)
Arsenal Holdings PLC, 79 30–33
The Art Institute of Chicago, 29 36–38
Art Van Furniture, Inc., 28 31–33
Artesyn Technologies Inc., 46 35–38 (upd.)
ArthroCare Corporation, 73 31–33
Arthur Andersen & Company, Société Coopérative, 10 115–17 *see also* Andersen.
The Arthur C. Clarke Foundation, 92 9–12
Arthur D. Little, Inc., 35 45–48
Arthur J. Gallagher & Co., 73 34–36
Arthur Lundgren Tecidos S.A., 102 25–28
Arthur Murray International, Inc., 32 60–62
Artisan Confections Company, 103 23–27
Artisan Entertainment Inc., 32 63–66 (upd.)
Arts and Entertainment Network *see* A&E Television Networks.
Art's Way Manufacturing Co., Inc., 101 39–42
Artsana SpA, 92 13–16
Arval *see* PHH Arval.
Arvin Industries, Inc., 8 37–40 *see also* ArvinMeritor, Inc.
ArvinMeritor, Inc., 54 24–28 (upd.)
AS Estonian Air, 71 38–40
Asahi Breweries, Ltd., I 220–21; 20 28–30 (upd.); 52 31–34 (upd.)
Asahi Denka Kogyo KK, 64 33–35
Asahi Glass Company, Ltd., III 666–68; 48 39–42 (upd.)
Asahi Komag Co., Ltd. *see* Komag, Inc.
Asahi National Broadcasting Company, Ltd., 9 29–31
Asahi Shimbun, 9 29–30
Asanté Technologies, Inc., 20 31–33
ASARCO Incorporated, IV 31–34; 40 220–22, 411
Asatsu-DK Inc, 82 16–20
Asbury Automotive Group Inc., 60 42–44
Asbury Carbons, Inc., 68 35–37
ASC, Inc., 55 31–34
ASCAP *see* The American Society of Composers, Authors and Publishers.
Ascend Communications, Inc., 24 47–51 *see also* Lucent Technologies Inc.
Ascendia Brands, Inc., 97 50–53
Ascential Software Corporation, 59 54–57
Ascom AG, 9 32–34

ASDA Group Ltd., II 611–12; 28 34–36 (upd.); 64 36–38 (upd.)

ASEA AB *see* ABB Ltd.

ASG *see* Allen Systems Group, Inc.

Ash Grove Cement Company, 94 41–44

Ashanti Goldfields Company Limited, 43 37–40

Ashdown *see* Repco Corporation Ltd.

Asher's Chocolates, Inc., 103 28–31

Ashland Inc., 19 22–25; 50 45–50 (upd.)

Ashland Oil, Inc., IV 372–74 *see also* Marathon.

Ashley Furniture Industries, Inc., 35 49–51

Ashtead Group plc, 34 41–43

Ashworth, Inc., 26 25–28

Asia Pacific Breweries Limited, 59 58–60

AsiaInfo Holdings, Inc., 43 41–44

Asiana Airlines, Inc., 46 39–42

ASICS Corporation, 57 52–55

ASIX Inc. *see* Manatron, Inc.

ASK Group, Inc., 9 35–37

Ask Jeeves, Inc., 65 50–52

ASML Holding N.V., 50 51–54

ASPCA *see* American Society for the Prevention of Cruelty to Animals (ASPCA).

Aspect Telecommunications Corporation, 22 51–53

Aspen Publishers *see* Wolters Kluwer NV.

Aspen Skiing Company, 15 23–26

Asplundh Tree Expert Co., 20 34–36; 59 61–65 (upd.)

Assicurazioni Generali S.p.A., 103 32–42 (upd.)

Assicurazioni Generali S.p.A., III 206–09; 15 27–31 (upd.); 103 32–42 (upd.)

Assisted Living Concepts, Inc., 43 45–47

Associated British Foods plc, II 465–66; 13 51–53 (upd.); 41 30–33 (upd.)

Associated British Ports Holdings Plc, 45 29–32

Associated Estates Realty Corporation, 25 23–25

Associated Grocers, Incorporated, 9 38–40; 31 22–26 (upd.)

Associated International Insurance Co. *see* Gryphon Holdings, Inc.

Associated Milk Producers, Inc., 11 24–26; 48 43–46 (upd.)

Associated Natural Gas Corporation, 11 27–28

Associated Newspapers Holdings P.L.C. *see* Daily Mail and General Trust plc.

The Associated Press, 13 54–56; 31 27–30 (upd.); 73 37–41 (upd.)

Association des Centres Distributeurs E. Leclerc, 37 19–21

Association of Junior Leagues International Inc., 60 45–47

Assurances Générales de France, 63 45–48

Assured Guaranty Ltd., 93 57–60

AST Research, Inc., 9 41–43

Astec Industries, Inc., 79 34–37

Astellas Pharma Inc., 97 54–58 (upd.)

AstenJohnson Inc., 90 31–34

ASTM SpA *see* Autostrada Torino-Milano S.p.A.

Aston Villa plc, 41 34–36

Astoria Financial Corporation, 44 31–34

Astra *see* PT Astra International Tbk.

AstraZeneca PLC, I 625–26; 20 37–40 (upd.); 50 55–60 (upd.)

Astronics Corporation, 35 52–54

Asur *see* Grupo Aeropuerto del Sureste, S.A. de C.V.

Asurion Corporation, 83 29–32

ASV, Inc., 34 44–47; 66 13–15 (upd.)

AT&T Bell Laboratories, Inc., 13 57–59 *see also* Lucent Technologies Inc.

AT&T Corporation, V 259–64; 29 39–45 (upd.); 61 68 38–45 (upd.)

AT&T Istel Ltd., 14 35–36

AT&T Wireless Services, Inc., 54 29–32 (upd.)

At Home Corporation, 43 48–51

ATA Holdings Corporation, 82 21–25

Atanor S.A., 62 19–22

Atari Corporation, 9 44–47; 23 23–26 (upd.); 66 16–20 (upd.)

ATC Healthcare Inc., 64 39–42

Atchison Casting Corporation, 39 30–32

ATE Investment *see* Atlantic Energy, Inc.

AtheroGenics Inc., 101 43–46

The Athlete's Foot Brands LLC, 84 17–20

The Athletics Investment Group, 62 23–26

ATI Technologies Inc., 79 38–41

Atkins Nutritionals, Inc., 58 8–10

Atkinson Candy Company, 87 39–42

Atlanta Bread Company International, Inc., 70 14–16

Atlanta Gas Light Company, 6 446–48; 23 27–30 (upd.)

Atlanta National League Baseball Club, Inc., 43 52–55

Atlantic & Pacific Tea Company (A&P) *see* The Great Atlantic & Pacific Tea Company, Inc.

Atlantic American Corporation, 44 35–37

Atlantic Coast Airlines Holdings, Inc., 55 35–37

Atlantic Coast Carton Company *see* Caraustar Industries, Inc.

Atlantic Energy, Inc., 6 449–50

The Atlantic Group, 23 31–33

Atlantic Premium Brands, Ltd., 57 56–58

Atlantic Richfield Company, IV 375–77; 31 31–34 (upd.)

Atlantic Southeast Airlines, Inc., 47 29–31

Atlantis Plastics, Inc., 85 14–17

Atlas Air, Inc., 39 33–35

Atlas Bolt & Screw Company *see* The Marmon Group, Inc.

Atlas Copco AB, III 425–27; 28 37–41 (upd.); 85 18–24 (upd.)

Atlas Tag & Label *see* BISSELL, Inc.

Atlas Van Lines Inc., 14 37–39; 106 49–53 (upd.)

Atmel Corporation, 17 32–34

ATMI, Inc., 93 61–64

Atmos Energy Corporation, 43 56–58

Atochem S.A., I 303–04, 676 *see also* Total-Fina-Elf.

Atos Origin S.A., 69 45–47

Atrix Laboratories, Inc. *see* QLT Inc.

Attachmate Corporation, 56 19–21

Attica Enterprises S.A., 64 43–45

Atwood Mobil Products, 53 52–55

Atwood Oceanics, Inc., 100 40–43

Au Bon Pain Co., Inc., 18 35–38

AU Optronics Corporation, 67 38–40

Au Printemps S.A., V 9–11 *see also* Pinault-Printemps-Redoute S.A.

Aubert & Duval Holding *see* Eramet.

Auchan, 37 22–24

The Auchter Company, 78 21–24

Audible Inc., 79 42–45

Audio King Corporation, 24 52–54

Audiovox Corporation, 34 48–50; 90 35–39 (upd.)

August Schell Brewing Company Inc., 59 66–69

August Storck KG, 66 21–23

Ault Incorporated, 34 51–54

Auntie Anne's, Inc., 35 55–57; 102 29–33 (upd.)

Aurea Concesiones de Infraestructuras SA *see* Abertis Infraestructuras, S.A.

Aurora Casket Company, Inc., 56 22–24

Aurora Foods Inc., 32 67–69

Austal Limited, 75 36–39

The Austin Company, 8 41–44; 72 14–18 (upd.)

Austin Nichols *see* Pernod Ricard S.A.

Austin Powder Company, 76 32–35

Australia and New Zealand Banking Group Limited, II 187–90; 52 35–40 (upd.)

Australian Wheat Board *see* AWB Ltd.

Austrian Airlines AG (Österreichische Luftverkehrs AG), 33 49–52

Authentic Fitness Corp., 20 41–43; 51 30–33 (upd.)

Auto Value Associates, Inc., 25 26–28

Autobacs Seven Company Ltd., 76 36–38

Autobytel Inc., 47 32–34

Autocam Corporation, 51 34–36

Autodesk, Inc., 10 118–20; 89 78–82 (upd.)

Autogrill SpA, 49 31–33

Autoliv, Inc., 65 53–55

Autologic Information International, Inc., 20 44–46

Automated Sciences Group, Inc. *see* CACI International Inc.

Automatic Data Processing, Inc., III 117–19; 9 48–51 (upd.); 47 35–39 (upd.)

Automobiles Citroën, 7 35–38

Automobili Lamborghini Holding S.p.A., 13 60–62; 34 55–58 (upd.); 91 25–30 (upd.)
AutoNation, Inc., 50 61–64
Autoridad del Canal de Panamá, 94 45–48
Autoroutes du Sud de la France SA, 55 38–40
Autostrada Torino-Milano S.p.A., 101 47–50
Autotote Corporation, 20 47–49 *see also* Scientific Games Corp.
AutoTrader.com, L.L.C., 91 31–34
AutoZone, Inc., 9 52–54; 31 35–38 (upd.)
Auvil Fruit Company, Inc., 95 32–35
AVA AG (Allgemeine Handelsgesellschaft der Verbraucher AG), 33 53–56
Avado Brands, Inc., 31 39–42
Avalon Correctional Services, Inc., 75 40–43
AvalonBay Communities, Inc., 58 11–13
Avantium Technologies BV, 79 46–49
Avaya Inc., 104 22–25
Avco Financial Services Inc., 13 63–65 *see also* Citigroup Inc.
Avecia Group PLC, 63 49–51
Aveda Corporation, 24 55–57
Avedis Zildjian Co., 38 66–68
Avendt Group, Inc. *see* Marmon Group, Inc.
Aventine Renewable Energy Holdings, Inc., 89 83–86
Avery Dennison Corporation, IV 251–54; 17 27–31 (upd.); 49 34–40 (upd.)
Aviacionny Nauchno-Tehnicheskii Komplek im. A.N. Tupoleva, 24 58–60
Aviacsa *see* Consorcio Aviacsa, S.A. de C.V.
Aviall, Inc., 73 42–45
Avianca Aerovías Nacionales de Colombia SA, 36 52–55
Aviation Sales Company, 41 37–39
Avid Technology Inc., 38 69–73
Avionics Specialties Inc. *see* Aerosonic Corp.
Avions Marcel Dassault-Breguet Aviation, I 44–46 *see also* Groupe Dassault Aviation SA.
Avis Group Holdings, Inc., 6 356–58; 22 54–57 (upd.); 75 44–49 (upd.)
Avista Corporation, 69 48–50 (upd.)
Aviva PLC, 50 65–68 (upd.)
Avnet Inc., 9 55–57
Avocent Corporation, 65 56–58
Avon Products, Inc., III 15–16; 19 26–29 (upd.); 46 43–46 (upd.)
Avondale Industries, Inc., 7 39–41; 41 40–43 (upd.)
AVTOVAZ Joint Stock Company, 65 59–62
AVX Corporation, 67 41–43
AWA *see* America West Holdings Corp.
AWB Ltd., 56 25–27

Awrey Bakeries, Inc., 56 28–30
AXA Colonia Konzern AG, III 210–12; 49 41–45 (upd.)
AXA Equitable Life Insurance Company, 105 21–27 (upd.)
Axcan Pharma Inc., 85 25–28
Axcelis Technologies, Inc., 95 36–39
Axel Johnson Group, I 553–55
Axel Springer Verlag AG, IV 589–91; 20 50–53 (upd.)
Axsys Technologies, Inc., 93 65–68
Aydin Corp., 19 30–32
Aynsley China Ltd. *see* Belleek Pottery Ltd.
Azcon Corporation, 23 34–36
Azelis Group, 100 44–47
Azerbaijan Airlines, 77 46–49
Azienda Generale Italiana Petroli *see* ENI S.p.A.
Aztar Corporation, 13 66–68; 71 41–45 (upd.)
AZZ Incorporated, 93 69–72

B

B&G Foods, Inc., 40 51–54
B&J Music Ltd. *see* Kaman Music Corp.
B&Q plc *see* Kingfisher plc.
B.A.T. Industries PLC, 22 70–73 (upd.) *see also* Brown and Williamson Tobacco Corporation
B. Dalton Bookseller Inc., 25 29–31 *see also* Barnes & Noble, Inc.
B.F. Goodrich Co. *see* The BFGoodrich Co.
B.J. Alan Co., Inc., 67 44–46
The B. Manischewitz Company, LLC, 31 43–46
B.R. Guest Inc., 87 43–46
B.W. Rogers Company, 94 49–52
B/E Aerospace, Inc., 30 72–74
BA *see* British Airways plc.
BAA plc, 10 121–23; 33 57–61 (upd.)
Baan Company, 25 32–34
Babbage's, Inc., 10 124–25 *see also* GameStop Corp.
The Babcock & Wilcox Company, 82 26–30
Babcock International Group PLC, 69 51–54
Babolat VS, S.A., 97 63–66
Baby Lock USA *see* Tacony Corp.
Baby Superstore, Inc., 15 32–34 *see also* Toys 'R Us, Inc.
Bacardi & Company Ltd., 18 39–42; 82 31–36 (upd.)
Baccarat, 24 61–63
Bachman's Inc., 22 58–60
Bachoco *see* Industrias Bachoco, S.A. de C.V.
Back Bay Restaurant Group, Inc., 20 54–56; 102 34–38 (upd.)
Back Yard Burgers, Inc., 45 33–36
Backus y Johnston *see* Unión de Cervecerías Peruanas Backus y Johnston S.A.A.
Bad Boy Worldwide Entertainment Group, 58 14–17
Badger Meter, Inc., 22 61–65

Badger Paper Mills, Inc., 15 35–37
Badger State Ethanol, LLC, 83 33–37
BAE Systems Ship Repair, 73 46–48
Bahamas Air Holdings Ltd., 66 24–26
Bahlsen GmbH & Co. KG, 44 38–41
Baidu.com Inc., 95 40–43
Bailey Nurseries, Inc., 57 59–61
Bain & Company, 55 41–43
Baird & Warner Holding Company, 87 47–50
Bairnco Corporation, 28 42–45
Bajaj Auto Limited, 39 36–38
Baker *see* Michael Baker Corp.
Baker and Botts, L.L.P., 28 46–49
Baker & Daniels LLP, 88 17–20
Baker & Hostetler LLP, 40 55–58
Baker & McKenzie, 10 126–28; 42 17–20 (upd.)
Baker & Taylor Corporation, 16 45–47; 43 59–62 (upd.)
Baker Hughes Incorporated, III 428–29; 22 66–69 (upd.); 57 62–66 (upd.)
Bakkavör Group hf., 91 35–39
Balance Bar Company, 32 70–72
Balchem Corporation, 42 21–23
Baldor Electric Company, 21 42–44; 97 63–67 (upd.)
Baldwin & Lyons, Inc., 51 37–39
Baldwin Piano & Organ Company, 18 43–46 *see also* Gibson Guitar Corp.
Baldwin Richardson Foods Company, 100 48–52
Baldwin Technology Company, Inc., 25 35–39
Balfour Beatty Construction Ltd., 36 56–60 (upd.)
Ball Corporation, I 597–98; 10 129–31 (upd.); 78 25–29 (upd.)
Ball Horticultural Company, 78 30–33
Ballantine Books *see* Random House, Inc.
Ballantyne of Omaha, Inc., 27 56–58
Ballard Medical Products, 21 45–48 *see also* Kimberly-Clark Corp.
Ballard Power Systems Inc., 73 49–52
Ballistic Recovery Systems, Inc., 87 51–54
Bally Manufacturing Corporation, III 430–32
Bally Total Fitness Corporation, 25 40–42; 94 53–57 (upd.)
Balmac International, Inc., 94 58–61
Bâloise-Holding, 40 59–62
Baltek Corporation, 34 59–61
Baltika Brewery Joint Stock Company, 65 63–66
Baltimore & Ohio Railroad *see* CSX Corp.
Baltimore Aircoil Company, Inc., 66 27–29
Baltimore Gas and Electric Company, V 552–54; 25 43–46 (upd.)
Baltimore Orioles L.P., 66 30–33
Baltimore Technologies Plc, 42 24–26
The Bama Companies, Inc., 80 13–16
Banamex *see* Grupo Financiero Banamex S.A.
Banana Republic Inc., 25 47–49 *see also* Gap, Inc.

Banc One Corporation, 10 132–34 *see also* JPMorgan Chase & Co.

Banca Commerciale Italiana SpA, II 191–93

Banca Fideuram SpA, 63 52–54

Banca Intesa SpA, 65 67–70

Banca Monte dei Paschi di Siena SpA, 65 71–73

Banca Nazionale del Lavoro SpA, 72 19–21

Banca Serfin *see* Grupo Financiero Serfin, S.A.

Banco Bilbao Vizcaya Argentaria S.A., II 194–96; 48 47–51 (upd.)

Banco Bradesco S.A., 13 69–71

Banco Central, II 197–98; 56 65 *see also* Banco Santander Central Hispano S.A.

Banco Central del Paraguay, 100 53–56

Banco Comercial Português, SA, 50 69–72

Banco de Chile, 69 55–57

Banco de Comercio, S.A. *see* Grupo Financiero BBVA Bancomer S.A.

Banco de Crédito del Perú, 9273–76

Banco de Crédito e Inversiones *see* Bci.

Banco do Brasil S.A., II 199–200

Banco Espírito Santo e Comercial de Lisboa S.A., 15 38–40 *see also* Espírito Santo Financial Group S.A.

Banco Itaú S.A., 19 33–35

Banco Popular *see* Popular, Inc.

Banco Santander Central Hispano S.A., 36 61–64 (upd.)

Banco Serfin *see* Grupo Financiero Serfin, S.A.

Bancomer S.A. *see* Grupo Financiero BBVA Bancomer S.A.

Bandag, Inc., 19 36–38

Bandai Co., Ltd., 55 44–48 *see also* Namco Bandai Holdings Inc.

Banfi Products Corp., 36 65–67

Banfield, The Pet Hospital *see* Medical Management International, Inc.

Bang & Olufsen Holding A/S, 37 25–28; 86 24–29 (upd.)

Bank Austria AG, 23 37–39; 100 57–60 (upd.)

Bank Brussels Lambert, II 201–03

Bank Hapoalim B.M., II 204–06; 54 33–37 (upd.)

Bank Leumi le-Israel B.M., 60 48–51

Bank of America Corporation, 46 47–54 (upd.); 101 51–64 (upd.)

Bank of Boston Corporation, II 207–09 *see also* FleetBoston Financial Corp.

Bank of China, 63 55–57

Bank of Cyprus Group, 91 40–43

Bank of East Asia Ltd., 63 58–60

Bank of Granite Corporation, 89 87–91

Bank of Hawaii Corporation, 73 53–56

Bank of Ireland, 50 73–76

Bank of Mississippi, Inc., 14 40–41

Bank of Montreal, II 210–12; 46 55–58 (upd.)

Bank of New England Corporation, II 213–15

Bank of New York Company, Inc., II 216–19; 46 59–63 (upd.)

The Bank of Nova Scotia, II 220–23; 59 70–76 (upd.)

The Bank of Scotland *see* The Governor and Company of the Bank of Scotland.

Bank of the Ozarks, Inc., 91 44–47

Bank of the Philippine Islands, 58 18–20

Bank of Tokyo-Mitsubishi Ltd., II 224–25; 15 41–43 (upd.) *see also* Mitsubishi UFJ Financial Group, Inc.

Bank One Corporation, 36 68–75 (upd.) *see also* JPMorgan Chase & Co.

BankAmerica Corporation, II 226–28 *see also* Bank of America.

Bankers Trust New York Corporation, II 229–31

Banknorth Group, Inc., 55 49–53

Bankrate, Inc., 83 38–41

Banner Aerospace, Inc., 14 42–44; 37 29–32 (upd.)

Banner Corporation, 106 54–57

Banorte *see* Grupo Financiero Banorte, S.A. de C.V.

Banque Nationale de Paris S.A., II 232–34 *see also* BNP Paribas Group.

Banta Corporation, 12 24–26; 32 73–77 (upd.); 79 50–56 (upd.)

Banyan Systems Inc., 25 50–52

Baptist Health Care Corporation, 82 37–40

Bar-S Foods Company, 76 39–41

Barbara's Bakery Inc., 88 21–24

Barclay Furniture Co. *see* LADD Furniture, Inc.

Barclays PLC, II 235–37; 20 57–60 (upd.); 64 46–50 (upd.)

BarclaysAmerican Mortgage Corporation, 11 29–30

Barco NV, 44 42–45

Barden Companies, Inc., 76 42–45

Bardwil Industries Inc., 98 15–18

Bare Escentuals, Inc., 91 48–52

Barilla G. e R. Fratelli S.p.A., 17 35–37; 50 77–80 (upd.)

Barings PLC, 14 45–47

Barlow Rand Ltd., I 422–24

Barmag AG, 39 39–42

Barnes & Noble, Inc., 10 135–37; 30 67–71 (upd.); 75 50–55 (upd.)

Barnes Group, Inc., 13 72–74; 69 58–62 (upd.)

Barnett Banks, Inc., 9 58–60 *see also* Bank of America Corp.

Barnett Inc., 28 50–52

Barneys New York Inc., 28 53–55; 104 26–30 (upd.)

Baron de Ley S.A., 74 27–29

Baron Philippe de Rothschild S.A., 39 43–46

Barr *see* AG Barr plc.

Barr Pharmaceuticals, Inc., 26 29–31; 68 46–49 (upd.)

Barratt Developments plc, I 556–57; 56 31–33 (upd.)

Barrett Business Services, Inc., 16 48–50

Barrett-Jackson Auction Company L.L.C., 88 25–28

Barrick Gold Corporation, 34 62–65

Barry Callebaut AG, 29 46–48; 71 46–49 (upd.)

Barry-Wehmiller Companies, Inc., 90 40–43

The Bartell Drug Company, 94 62–65

Barton Malow Company, 51 40–43

Barton Protective Services Inc., 53 56–58

The Baseball Club of Seattle, LP, 50 81–85

BASF Aktiengesellschaft, I 305–08; 18 47–51 (upd.); 50 86–92 (upd.)

Bashas' Inc., 33 62–64; 80 17–21 (upd.)

Basic Earth Science Systems, Inc., 101 65–68

Basin Electric Power Cooperative, 103 43–46

The Basketball Club of Seattle, LLC, 50 93–97

Bass PLC, I 222–24; 15 44–47 (upd.); 38 74–78 (upd.)

Bass Pro Shops, Inc., 42 27–30

Bassett Furniture Industries, Inc., 18 52–55; 95 44–50 (upd.)

BAT Industries plc, I 425–27 *see also* British American Tobacco PLC.

Bata Ltd., 62 27–30

Bates Worldwide, Inc., 14 48–51; 33 65–69 (upd.)

Bath Iron Works Corporation, 12 27–29; 36 76–79 (upd.)

Battelle Memorial Institute, Inc., 10 138–40

Batten Barton Durstine & Osborn *see* Omnicom Group Inc.

Battle Mountain Gold Company, 23 40–42 *see also* Newmont Mining Corp.

Bauer Hockey, Inc., 104 31–34

Bauer Publishing Group, 7 42–43

Bauerly Companies, 61 31–33

Baugur Group hf, 81 45–49

Baumax AG, 75 56–58

Bausch & Lomb Inc., 7 44–47; 25 53–57 (upd.); 96 20–26 (upd.)

Bavaria S.A., 90 44–47

Baxi Group Ltd., 96 27–30

Baxter International Inc., I 627–29; 10 141–43 (upd.)

Baxters Food Group Ltd., 99 47–50

The Bay *see* The Hudson's Bay Co.

Bay State Gas Company, 38 79–82

Bayard SA, 49 46–49

BayBanks, Inc., 12 30–32

Bayer A.G., I 309–11; 13 75–77 (upd.); 41 44–48 (upd.)

Bayerische Hypotheken- und Wechsel-Bank AG, II 238–40 *see also* HVB Group.

Bayerische Motoren Werke A.G., I 138–40; 11 31–33 (upd.); 38 83–87 (upd.)

Bayerische Vereinsbank A.G., II 241–43 *see also* HVB Group.

Bayernwerk AG, V 555–58; 23 43–47 (upd.) *see also* E.On AG.

Bayou Steel Corporation, 31 47–49

BB&T Corporation, 79 57–61

BB Holdings Limited, 77 50–53
BBA *see* Bush Boake Allen Inc.
BBA Aviation plc, 90 48–52
BBAG Osterreichische Brau-Beteiligungs-AG, 38 88–90
BBC *see* British Broadcasting Corp.
BBDO Worldwide *see* Omnicom Group Inc.
BBGI *see* Beasley Broadcast Group, Inc.
BBN Corp., 19 39–42
BBVA *see* Banco Bilbao Vizcaya Argentaria S.A.
BCE, Inc., V 269–71; 44 46–50 (upd.)
Bci, 99 51–54
BDO Seidman LLP, 96 31–34
BE&K, Inc., 73 57–59
BEA *see* Bank of East Asia Ltd.
BEA Systems, Inc., 36 80–83
Beacon Roofing Supply, Inc., 75 59–61
Bear Creek Corporation, 38 91–94
Bear Stearns Companies, Inc., II 400–01; 10 144–45 (upd.); 52 41–44 (upd.)
Bearings, Inc., 13 78–80
Beasley Broadcast Group, Inc., 51 44–46
Beate Uhse AG, 96 35–39
Beatrice Company, II 467–69 *see also* TLC Beatrice International Holdings, Inc.
BeautiControl Cosmetics, Inc., 21 49–52
Beazer Homes USA, Inc., 17 38–41
bebe stores, inc., 31 50–52; 103 47–51 (upd.)
Bechtel Corporation, I 558–59; 24 64–67 (upd.); 99 55–60 (upd.)
Beckett Papers, 23 48–50
Beckman Coulter, Inc., 22 74–77
Beckman Instruments, Inc., 14 52–54
Becton, Dickinson and Company, I 630–31; 11 34–36 (upd.); 36 84–89 (upd.); 101 69–77 (upd.)
Bed Bath & Beyond Inc., 13 81–83; 41 49–52 (upd.)
Beech Aircraft Corporation, 8 49–52 *see also* Raytheon Aircraft Holdings Inc.
Beech-Nut Nutrition Corporation, 21 53–56; 51 47–51 (upd.)
Beef O'Brady's *see* Family Sports Concepts, Inc.
Beer Nuts, Inc., 86 30–33
Beggars Group Ltd., 99 61–65
Behr GmbH & Co. KG, 72 22–25
Behring Diagnostics *see* Dade Behring Holdings Inc.
BEI Technologies, Inc., 65 74–76
Beiersdorf AG, 29 49–53
Bekaert S.A./N.V., 90 53–57
Bekins Company, 15 48–50
Bel *see* Fromageries Bel.
Bel Fuse, Inc., 53 59–62
Bel/Kaukauna USA, 76 46–48
Belco Oil & Gas Corp., 40 63–65
Belden CDT Inc., 19 43–45; 76 49–52 (upd.)
Belgacom, 6 302–04

Belk, Inc., V 12–13; 19 46–48 (upd.); 72 26–29 (upd.)
Bell and Howell Company, 9 61–64; 29 54–58 (upd.)
Bell Atlantic Corporation, V 272–74; 25 58–62 (upd.) *see also* Verizon Communications.
Bell Canada Enterprises Inc. *see* BCE, Inc.
Bell Canada International, Inc., 6 305–08
Bell Helicopter Textron Inc., 46 64–67
Bell Industries, Inc., 47 40–43
Bell Resources *see* TPG NV.
Bell Sports Corporation, 16 51–53; 44 51–54 (upd.)
Bellcore *see* Telcordia Technologies, Inc.
Belleek Pottery Ltd., 71 50–53
Belleville Shoe Manufacturing Company, 92 17–20
Bellisio Foods, Inc., 95 51–54
BellSouth Corporation, V 276–78; 29 59–62 (upd.) *see also* AT&T Corp.
Bellway Plc, 45 37–39
Belo Corporation, 98 19–25 (upd.)
Beloit Corporation, 14 55–57 *see also* Metso Corp.
Belron International Ltd., 76 53–56
Belvedere S.A., 93 77–81
Bemis Company, Inc., 8 53–55; 91 53–60 (upd.)
Ben & Jerry's Homemade, Inc., 10 146–48; 35 58–62 (upd.); 80 22–28 (upd.)
Ben Bridge Jeweler, Inc., 60 52–54
Ben E. Keith Company, 76 57–59
Benchmark Capital, 49 50–52
Benchmark Electronics, Inc., 40 66–69
Benckiser N.V. *see* Reckitt Benckiser plc.
Bendix Corporation, I 141–43
Beneficial Corporation, 8 56–58
Benesse Corporation, 76 60–62
Bénéteau SA, 55 54–56
Benetton Group S.p.A., 10 149–52; 67 47–51 (upd.)
Benfield Greig Group plc, 53 63–65
Benguet Corporation, 58 21–24
Benihana, Inc., 18 56–59; 76 63–66 (upd.)
Benjamin Moore and Co., 13 84–87; 38 95–99 (upd.)
BenQ Corporation, 67 52–54
Benton Oil and Gas Company, 47 44–46
Berean Christian Stores, 96 40–43
Beretta *see* Fabbrica D' Armi Pietro Beretta S.p.A.
Bergdorf Goodman Inc., 52 45–48
Bergen Brunswig Corporation, V 14–16; 13 88–90 (upd.) *see also* AmerisourceBergen Corp.
Berger Bros Company, 62 31–33
Beringer Blass Wine Estates Ltd., 22 78–81; 66 34–37 (upd.)
Berjaya Group Bhd., 67 55–57
Berkeley Farms, Inc., 46 68–70
Berkshire Hathaway Inc., III 213–15; 18 60–63 (upd.); 42 31–36 (upd.); 89 92–99 (upd.)

Berkshire Realty Holdings, L.P., 49 53–55
Berlex Laboratories, Inc., 66 38–40
Berliner Stadtreinigungsbetriebe, 58 25–28
Berliner Verkehrsbetriebe (BVG), 58 29–31
Berlinwasser Holding AG, 90 58–62
Berlitz International, Inc., 13 91–93; 39 47–50 (upd.)
Bernard C. Harris Publishing Company, Inc., 39 51–53
Bernard Chaus, Inc., 27 59–61
Bernard Hodes Group Inc., 86 34–37
Bernard L. Madoff Investment Securities LLC, 106 58–62
Bernard Matthews Ltd., 89 100–04
The Bernick Companies, 75 62–65
Bernina Holding AG, 47 47–50
Bernstein-Rein, 92 21–24
The Berry Company *see* L. M. Berry and Company
Berry Petroleum Company, 47 51–53
Berry Plastics Group Inc., 21 57–59; 98 26–30 (upd.)
Bertelsmann A.G., IV 592–94; 43 63–67 (upd.); 91 61–68 (upd.)
Bertucci's Corporation, 16 54–56; 64 51–54 (upd.)
Berwick Offray, LLC, 70 17–19
Berwind Corporation, 100 61–64
Besix Group S.A./NV, 94 66–69
Besnier SA, 19 49–51 *see also* Groupe Lactalis
Best Buy Co., Inc., 9 65–66; 23 51–53 (upd.); 63 61–66 (upd.)
Best Kosher Foods Corporation, 82 41–44
Bestfoods, 22 82–86 (upd.)
Bestseller A/S, 90 63–66
Bestway Transportation *see* TNT Freightways Corp.
BET Holdings, Inc., 18 64–66
Beth Abraham Family of Health Services, 94 70–74
Beth Israel Medical Center *see* Continuum Health Partners, Inc.
Bethlehem Steel Corporation, IV 35–37; 7 48–51 (upd.); 27 62–66 (upd.)
Betsey Johnson Inc., 100 65–69
Betsy Ann Candies, Inc., 105 28–31
Better Made Snack Foods, Inc., 90 67–69
Bettys & Taylors of Harrogate Ltd., 72 30–32
Betz Laboratories, Inc., I 312–13; 10 153–55 (upd.)
Beverly Enterprises, Inc., III 76–77; 16 57–59 (upd.)
Bewag AG, 39 54–57
BFC Construction Corporation, 25 63–65
The BFGoodrich Company, V 231–33; 19 52–55 (upd.) *see also* Goodrich Corp.
BFI *see* The British Film Institute; Browning-Ferris Industries, Inc.

BFP Holdings Corp. *see* Big Flower Press Holdings, Inc.

BG&E *see* Baltimore Gas and Electric Co.

BG Products Inc., 96 44–47

Bharti Tele-Ventures Limited, 75 66–68

BHC Communications, Inc., 26 32–34

BHP Billiton, 67 58–64 (upd.)

Bhs plc, 17 42–44

Bianchi International (d/b/a Gregory Mountain Products), 76 67–69

Bibliographisches Institut & F.A. Brockhaus AG, 74 30–34

BIC Corporation, 8 59–61; 23 54–57 (upd.)

BICC PLC, III 433–34 *see also* Balfour Beatty plc.

Bicoastal Corporation, II 9–11

Bidvest Group Ltd., 106 63–67

Biffa plc, 92 25–28

Big 5 Sporting Goods Corporation, 55 57–59

Big A Drug Stores Inc., 79 62–65

Big B, Inc., 17 45–47

Big Bear Stores Co., 13 94–96

Big Brothers Big Sisters of America, 85 29–33

Big Dog Holdings, Inc., 45 40–42

Big Flower Press Holdings, Inc., 21 60–62 *see also* Vertis Communications.

The Big Food Group plc, 68 50–53 (upd.)

Big Idea Productions, Inc., 49 56–59

Big Lots, Inc., 50 98–101

Big O Tires, Inc., 20 61–63

Big Rivers Electric Corporation, 11 37–39

Big V Supermarkets, Inc., 25 66–68

Big Y Foods, Inc., 53 66–68

Bigard *see* Groupe Bigard S.A.

BigBen Interactive S.A., 72 33–35

Bilfinger & Berger AG, I 560–61; 55 60–63 (upd.)

Bill & Melinda Gates Foundation, 41 53–55; 100 70–74 (upd.)

Bill Barrett Corporation, 71 54–56

Bill Blass Ltd., 32 78–80

Billabong International Ltd., 44 55–58

Billerud AB, 100 75–79

Billing Concepts, Inc., 26 35–38; 72 36–39 (upd.)

Billing Services Group Ltd., 102 39–43

Bimbo *see* Grupo Industrial Bimbo.

Bindley Western Industries, Inc., 9 67–69 *see also* Cardinal Health, Inc.

The Bing Group, 60 55–58

Bingham Dana LLP, 43 68–71

Binks Sames Corporation, 21 63–66

Binney & Smith Inc., 25 69–72

Bio-Rad Laboratories, Inc., 93 82–86

Biogen Idec Inc., 14 58–60; 36 90–93 (upd.); 71 57–59 (upd.)

Bioindustrias *see* Valores Industriales S.A.

Biokyowa *see* Kyowa Hakko Kogyo Co., Ltd.

Biolase Technology, Inc., 87 55–58

bioMérieux S.A., 75 69–71

Biomet, Inc., 10 156–58; 93 87–94 (upd.)

BioScrip Inc., 98 31–35

Biosite Incorporated, 73 60–62

Biovail Corporation, 47 54–56

BioWare Corporation, 81 50–53

Bird Corporation, 19 56–58

Birds Eye Foods, Inc., 69 66–72 (upd.)

Birkenstock Footprint Sandals, Inc., 12 33–35; 42 37–40 (upd.)

Birmingham Steel Corporation, 13 97–98; 40 70–73 (upd.) *see also* Nucor Corporation

Birse Group PLC, 77 54–58

Birthdays Ltd., 70 20–22

BISSELL, Inc., 9 70–72; 30 75–78 (upd.)

The BISYS Group, Inc., 73 63–65

BIW *see* Bath Iron Works.

BJ Services Company, 25 73–75

BJ's Wholesale Club, Inc., 94 75–78

BKD LLP, 96 48–51

The Black & Decker Corporation, III 435–37; 20 64–68 (upd.); 67 65–70 (upd.)

Black & Veatch LLP, 22 87–90

Black Box Corporation, 20 69–71; 96 52–56 (upd.)

Black Diamond Equipment, Ltd., 62 34–37

Black Entertainment Television *see* BET Holdings, Inc.

Black Hills Corporation, 20 72–74

Blackbaud, Inc., 85 34–37

BlackBerry *see* Research in Motion Ltd.

Blackboard Inc., 89 105–10

Blackfoot Telecommunications Group, 60 59–62

BlackRock, Inc., 79 66–69

Blacks Leisure Group plc, 39 58–60

Blackwater USA, 76 70–73

Blackwell Publishing (Holdings) Ltd., 78 34–37

Blair Corporation, 25 76–78; 31 53–55

Blessings Corp., 19 59–61

Blimpie, 15 55–57; 49 60–64 (upd.); 105 32–38 (upd.)

Blish-Mize Co., 95 55–58

Blizzard Entertainment, 78 38–42

Block Communications, Inc., 81 54–58

Block Drug Company, Inc., 8 62–64; 27 67–70 (upd.) *see also* GlaxoSmithKline plc.

Blockbuster Inc., 9 73–75; 31 56–60 (upd.); 76 74–78 (upd.)

Blodgett Holdings, Inc., 61 34–37 (upd.)

Blokker Holding B.V., 84 21–24

Blom Bank S.A.L., 102 44–47

Blonder Tongue Laboratories, Inc., 48 52–55

Bloomberg L.P., 21 67–71

Bloomingdale's Inc., 12 36–38

Blount International, Inc., 12 39–41; 48 56–60 (upd.)

BLP Group Companies *see* Boron, LePore & Associates, Inc.

Blue Bell Creameries L.P., 30 79–81

Blue Bird Corporation, 35 63–66

Blue Circle Industries PLC, III 669–71 *see also* Lafarge Cement UK.

Blue Coat Systems, Inc., 83 42–45

Blue Cross and Blue Shield Association, 10 159–61

Blue Diamond Growers, 28 56–58

Blue Heron Paper Company, 90 70–73

Blue Martini Software, Inc., 59 77–80

Blue Mountain Arts, Inc., 29 63–66

Blue Nile Inc., 61 38–40

Blue Rhino Corporation, 56 34–37

Blue Ridge Beverage Company Inc., 82 45–48

Blue Square Israel Ltd., 41 56–58

Bluefly, Inc., 60 63–65

Bluegreen Corporation, 80 29–32

BlueLinx Holdings Inc., 97 68–72

Blundstone Pty Ltd., 76 79–81

Blyth, Inc., 18 67–69; 74 35–38 (upd.)

BMC Industries, Inc., 17 48–51; 59 81–86 (upd.)

BMC Software, Inc., 55 64–67

BMG/Music *see* Bertelsmann AG.

BMHC *see* Building Materials Holding Corp.

BMI *see* Broadcast Music Inc.

BMW *see* Bayerische Motoren Werke.

BNA *see* Bureau of National Affairs, Inc.

BNE *see* Bank of New England Corp.

BNL *see* Banca Nazionale del Lavoro S.p.A.

BNP Paribas Group, 36 94–97 (upd.)

Boardwalk Pipeline Partners, LP, 87 59–62

Boart Longyear Company, 26 39–42

Boatmen's Bancshares Inc., 15 58–60 *see also* Bank of America Corp.

Bob Evans Farms, Inc., 9 76–79; 63 67–72 (upd.)

Bob's Discount Furniture LLC, 104 35–3

Bob's Red Mill Natural Foods, Inc., 63 73–75

Bobit Publishing Company, 55 68–70

Bobs Candies, Inc., 70 23–25

BOC Group plc, I 314–16; 25 79–82 (upd.); 78 43–49 (upd.)

Boca Resorts, Inc., 37 33–36

Boddie-Noell Enterprises, Inc., 68 54–56

Bodum Design Group AG, 47 57–59

Body Glove International LLC, 88 29–32

The Body Shop International plc, 11 40–42; 53 69–72 (upd.)

Bodycote International PLC, 63 76–78

Boehringer Ingelheim GmbH *see* C.H. Boehringer Sohn.

The Boeing Company, I 47–49; 10 162–65 (upd.); 32 81–87 (upd.)

Boenning & Scattergood Inc., 102 48–51

Bogen Communications International, Inc., 62 38–41

Bohemia, Inc., 13 99–101

BÖHLER-UDDEHOLM AG, 73 66–69

Boiron S.A., 73 70–72

Boise Cascade Corporation, IV 255–56; 8 65–67 (upd.); 32 88–92 (upd.); 95 59–66 (upd.)
Boizel Chanoine Champagne S.A., 94 79–82
Bojangles Restaurants Inc., 97 73–77
Boliden AB, 80 33–36
Bollinger Shipyards, Inc., 61 41–43
Bols Distilleries NV, 74 39–42
Bolsa Mexicana de Valores, S.A. de C.V., 80 37–40
Bolt Technology Corporation, 99 66–70
Bolton Group B.V., 86 38–41
Bombardier Inc., 42 41–46 (upd.); 87 63–71 (upd.)
The Bombay Company, Inc., 10 166–68; 71 60–64 (upd.)
Bon Appetit Holding AG, 48 61–63
The Bon Marché, Inc., 23 58–60 *see also* Federated Department Stores Inc.
Bon Secours Health System, Inc., 24 68–71
The Bon-Ton Stores, Inc., 16 60–62; 50 106–10 (upd.)
Bond Corporation Holdings Limited, 10 169–71
Bonduelle SA, 51 52–54
Bongard *see* Aga Foodservice Group PLC.
Bongrain S.A., 25 83–85; 102 52–56 (upd.)
Bonhams 1793 Ltd., 72 40–42
Bonneville International Corporation, 29 67–70
Bonneville Power Administration, 50 102–05
Bonnier AB, 52 49–52
Book-of-the-Month Club, Inc., 13 105–07
Booker Cash & Carry Ltd., 68 57–61 (upd.)
Booker plc, 13 102–04; 31 61–64 (upd.)
Books-A-Million, Inc., 14 61–62; 41 59–62 (upd.); 96 57–61 (upd.)
Books Are Fun, Ltd. *see* The Reader's Digest Association, Inc.
Bookspan, 86 42–46
Boole & Babbage, Inc., 25 86–88 *see also* BMC Software, Inc.
Booth Creek Ski Holdings, Inc., 31 65–67
Boots & Coots International Well Control, Inc., 79 70–73
The Boots Company PLC, V 17–19; 24 72–76 (upd.) *see also* Alliance Boots plc.
Booz Allen Hamilton Inc., 10 172–75; 101 78–84 (upd.)
Boral Limited, III 672–74; 43 72–76 (upd.); 103 52–59 (upd.)
Borden, Inc., II 470–73; 22 91–96 (upd.)
Borders Group, Inc., 15 61–62; 43 77–79 (upd.)
Borealis AG, 94 83–86
Borg-Warner Automotive, Inc., 14 63–66; 32 93–97 (upd.)

Borg-Warner Corporation, III 438–41 *see also* Burns International.
BorgWarner Inc., 85 38–44 (upd.)
Borland International, Inc., 9 80–82
Boron, LePore & Associates, Inc., 45 43–45
Bosch *see* Robert Bosch GmbH.
Boscov's Department Store, Inc., 31 68–70
Bose Corporation, 13 108–10; 36 98–101 (upd.)
Boss Holdings, Inc., 97 78–81
Boston Acoustics, Inc., 22 97–99
The Boston Beer Company, Inc., 18 70–73; 50 111–15 (upd.)
Boston Celtics Limited Partnership, 14 67–69
Boston Chicken, Inc., 12 42–44 *see also* Boston Market Corp.
The Boston Consulting Group, 58 32–35
Boston Edison Company, 12 45–47
Boston Globe see Globe Newspaper Company Inc.
Boston Market Corporation, 48 64–67 (upd.)
Boston Pizza International Inc., 88 33–38
Boston Professional Hockey Association Inc., 39 61–63
Boston Properties, Inc., 22 100–02
Boston Scientific Corporation, 37 37–40; 77 58–63 (upd.)
The Boston Symphony Orchestra Inc., 93 95–99
Bou-Matic, 62 42–44
Boulanger S.A., 102 57–60
Bourbon *see* Groupe Bourbon S.A.
Bourbon Corporation, 82 49–52
Bouygues S.A., I 562–64; 24 77–80 (upd.); 97 82–87 (upd.)
Bovis *see* Peninsular and Oriental Steam Navigation Company (Bovis Division)
Bowater PLC, IV 257–59
Bowen Engineering Corporation, 105 39–42
Bowlin Travel Centers, Inc., 99 71–75
Bowman Distillery *see* A. Smith Bowman Distillery, Inc.
Bowne & Co., Inc., 23 61–64; 79 74–80 (upd.)
Bowthorpe plc, 33 70–72
The Boy Scouts of America, 34 66–69
Boyd Bros. Transportation Inc., 39 64–66
Boyd Coffee Company, 53 73–75
Boyd Gaming Corporation, 43 80–82
The Boyds Collection, Ltd., 29 71–73
Boyne USA Resorts, 71 65–68
Boys & Girls Clubs of America, 69 73–75
Bozell Worldwide Inc., 25 89–91
Bozzuto's, Inc., 13 111–12
BP p.l.c., 45 46–56 (upd.); 103 60–74 (upd.)
BPB plc, 83 46–49
Braathens ASA, 47 60–62

Brach's Confections, Inc., 15 63–65; 74 43–46 (upd.)
Bradford & Bingley PLC, 65 77–80
Bradlees Discount Department Store Company, 12 48–50
Bradley Air Services Ltd., 56 38–40
Brady Corporation, 78 50–55 (upd.)
Brake Bros plc, 45 57–59
Bramalea Ltd., 9 83–85
Brambles Industries Limited, 42 47–50
Brammer PLC, 77 64–67
The Branch Group, Inc., 72 43–45
BrandPartners Group, Inc., 58 36–38
Brannock Device Company, 48 68–70
Brascan Corporation, 67 71–73
Brasfield & Gorrie LLC, 87 72–75
Brasil Telecom Participaçoes S.A., 57 67–70
Brass Eagle Inc., 34 70–72
Brauerei Beck & Co., 9 86–87; 33 73–76 (upd.)
Braun GmbH, 51 55–58
Brazil Fast Food Corporation, 74 47–49
Brazos Sportswear, Inc., 23 65–67
Breeze-Eastern Corporation, 95 67–70
Bremer Financial Corporation, 45 60–63; 105 43–49 (upd.)
Brenco, Inc., 104 39–42
Brenntag Holding GmbH & Co. KG, 8 68–69; 23 68–70 (upd.); 101 85–90 (upd.)
Brescia Group *see* Grupo Brescia.
Briazz, Inc., 53 76–79
The Brickman Group, Ltd., 87 76–79
Bricorama S.A., 68 62–64
Bridgeport Machines, Inc., 17 52–54
Bridgestone Corporation, V 234–35; 21 72–75 (upd.); 59 87–92 (upd.)
Bridgford Foods Corporation, 27 71–73
Briggs & Stratton Corporation, 8 70–73; 27 74–78 (upd.)
Brigham Exploration Company, 75 72–74
Brigham's Inc., 72 46–48
Bright Horizons Family Solutions, Inc., 31 71–73
Brightpoint Inc., 18 74–77; 106 68–74 (upd.)
Brillstein-Grey Entertainment, 80 41–45
Brinker International, Inc., 10 176–78; 38 100–03 (upd.); 75 75–79 (upd.)
The Brink's Company, 58 39–43 (upd.)
BRIO AB, 24 81–83; 103 75–79 (upd.)
Brioche Pasquier S.A., 58 44–46
Brioni Roman Style S.p.A., 67 74–76
BRISA Auto-estradas de Portugal S.A., 64 55–58
Bristol Farms, 101 91–95
Bristol Hotel Company, 23 71–73
Bristol-Myers Squibb Company, III 17–19; 9 88–91 (upd.); 37 41–45 (upd.)
Bristow Helicopters Ltd., 70 26–28
Britannia Soft Drinks Ltd. (Britvic), 71 69–71
Britannica.com *see* Encyclopaedia Britannica, Inc.
Brite Voice Systems, Inc., 20 75–78

British Aerospace plc, I 50–53; **24** 84–90 (upd.)

British Airways PLC, I 92–95; **14** 70–74 (upd.); **43** 83–88 (upd.); **105** 50–59 (upd.)

British American Tobacco PLC, 50 116–19 (upd.)

British-Borneo Oil & Gas PLC, 34 73–75

British Broadcasting Corporation Ltd., 7 52–55; **21** 76–79 (upd.); **89** 111–17 (upd.)

British Coal Corporation, IV 38–40

British Columbia Telephone Company, 6 309–11

British Energy Plc, 49 65–68 *see also* British Nuclear Fuels PLC.

The British Film Institute, 80 46–50

British Gas plc, V 559–63 *see also* Centrica plc.

British Land Plc, 54 38–41

British Midland plc, 38 104–06

The British Museum, 71 72–74

British Nuclear Fuels PLC, 6 451–54

British Oxygen Co *see* BOC Group.

The British Petroleum Company plc, IV 378–80; **7** 56–59 (upd.); **21** 80–84 (upd.) *see also* BP p.l.c.

British Railways Board, V 421–24

British Sky Broadcasting Group plc, 20 79–81; **60** 66–69 (upd.)

British Steel plc, IV 41–43; **19** 62–65 (upd.)

British Sugar plc, 84 25–29

British Telecommunications plc, V 279–82; **15** 66–70 (upd.) *see also* BT Group plc.

The British United Provident Association Limited, 79 81–84

British Vita plc, 9 92–93; **33** 77–79 (upd.)

British World Airlines Ltd., 18 78–80

Britvic Soft Drinks Limited *see* Britannia Soft Drinks Ltd. (Britvic)

Broadcast Music Inc., 23 74–77; **90** 74–79 (upd.)

Broadcom Corporation, 34 76–79; **90** 80–85 (upd.)

The Broadmoor Hotel, 30 82–85

Broadwing Corporation, 70 29–32

Broan-NuTone LLC, 104 43–46

Brobeck, Phleger & Harrison, LLP, 31 74–76

Brocade Communications Systems Inc., 106 75–81

Brockhaus *see* Bibliographisches Institut & F.A. Brockhaus AG.

Brodart Company, 84 30–33

Broder Bros. Co., 38 107–09

Broderbund Software, Inc., 13 113–16; **29** 74–78 (upd.)

Broken Hill Proprietary Company Ltd., IV 44–47; **22** 103–08 (upd.) *see also* BHP Billiton.

Bronco Drilling Company, Inc., 89 118–21

Bronco Wine Company, 101 96–99

Bronner Brothers Inc., 92 29–32

Bronner Display & Sign Advertising, Inc., 82 53–57

Brookdale Senior Living, 91 69–73

Brooke Group Ltd., 15 71–73 *see also* Vector Group Ltd.

Brookfield Properties Corporation, 89 122–25

Brooklyn Union Gas, 6 455–57 *see also* KeySpan Energy Co.

Brooks Brothers Inc., 22 109–12

Brooks Sports Inc., 32 98–101

Brookshire Grocery Company, 16 63–66; **74** 50–53 (upd.)

Brookstone, Inc., 18 81–83

Brose Fahrzeugteile GmbH & Company KG, 84 34–38

Brossard S.A., 102 61–64

Brother Industries, Ltd., 14 75–76

Brother's Brother Foundation, 93 100–04

Brothers Gourmet Coffees, Inc., 20 82–85 *see also* The Procter & Gamble Co.

Broughton Foods Co., 17 55–57 *see also* Suiza Foods Corp.

Brouwerijen Alken-Maes N.V., 86 47–51

Brown & Brown, Inc., 41 63–66

Brown & Haley, 23 78–80

Brown & Root, Inc., 13 117–19 *see also* Kellogg Brown & Root Inc.

Brown & Sharpe Manufacturing Co., 23 81–84

Brown and Williamson Tobacco Corporation, 14 77–79; **33** 80–83 (upd.)

Brown Brothers Harriman & Co., 45 64–67

Brown-Forman Corporation, I 225–27; **10** 179–82 (upd.); **38** 110–14 (upd.)

Brown Group, Inc., V 351–53; **20** 86–89 (upd.) *see also* Brown Shoe Company, Inc.

Brown Jordan International Inc., 74 54–57 (upd.)

Brown Printing Company, 26 43–45

Brown Shoe Company, Inc., 68 65–69 (upd.)

Browning-Ferris Industries, Inc., V 749–53; **20** 90–93 (upd.)

Broyhill Furniture Industries, Inc., 10 183–85

Bruce Foods Corporation, 39 67–69

Bruegger's Corporation, 63 79–82

Bruno's Supermarkets, Inc., 7 60–62; **26** 46–48 (upd.); **68** 70–73 (upd.)

Brunschwig & Fils Inc., 96 62–65

Brunswick Corporation, III 442–44; **22** 113–17 (upd.); **77** 68–75 (upd.)

Brush Engineered Materials Inc., 67 77–79

Brush Wellman Inc., 14 80–82

Bruster's Real Ice Cream, Inc., 80 51–54

Bryce Corporation, 100 80–83

BSA *see* The Boy Scouts of America.

BSC *see* Birmingham Steel Corporation

BSH Bosch und Siemens Hausgeräte GmbH, 67 80–84

BSN Groupe S.A., II 474–75 *see also* Groupe Danone

BT Group plc, 49 69–74 (upd.)

BTG, Inc., 45 68–70

BTG Plc, 87 80–83

BTR plc, I 428–30

BTR Siebe plc, 27 79–81 *see also* Invensys PLC.

Buca, Inc., 38 115–17

Buck Consultants, Inc., 55 71–73

Buck Knives Inc., 48 71–74

Buckeye Partners, L.P., 70 33–36

Buckeye Technologies, Inc., 42 51–54

Buckhead Life Restaurant Group, Inc., 100 84–87

The Buckle, Inc., 18 84–86

Bucyrus International, Inc., 17 58–61; **103** 80–87 (upd.)

The Budd Company, 8 74–76 *see also* ThyssenKrupp AG.

Buderus AG, 37 46–49

Budgens Ltd., 59 93–96

Budget Group, Inc., 25 92–94 *see also* Cendant Corp.

Budget Rent a Car Corporation, 9 94–95

Budweiser Budvar, National Corporation, 59 97–100

Buena Vista Home Video *see* The Walt Disney Co.

Bufete Industrial, S.A. de C.V., 34 80–82

Buffalo Grill S.A., 94 87–90

Buffalo Wild Wings, Inc., 56 41–43

Buffets Holdings, Inc., 10 186–87; **32** 102–04 (upd.); **93** 105–09 (upd.)

Bugatti Automobiles S.A.S., 94 91–94

Bugle Boy Industries, Inc., 18 87–88

Buhrmann NV, 41 67–69

Buick Motor Co. *see* General Motors Corp.

Build-A-Bear Workshop Inc., 62 45–48

Building Materials Holding Corporation, 52 53–55

Bulgari S.p.A., 20 94–97; **106** 82–87 (upd.)

Bull *see* Compagnie des Machines Bull S.A.

Bull S.A., 43 89–91 (upd.)

Bulley & Andrews, LLC, 55 74–76

Bulova Corporation, 13 120–22; **41** 70–73 (upd.)

Bumble Bee Seafoods L.L.C., 64 59–61

Bundy Corporation, 17 62–65

Bunge Ltd., 62 49–51

Bunzl plc, IV 260–62; **31** 77–80 (upd.)

Burberry Group plc, 17 66–68; **41** 74–76 (upd.); **92** 33–37 (upd.)

Burda Holding GmbH. & Co., 23 85–89

Burdines, Inc., 60 70–73

The Bureau of National Affairs, Inc., 23 90–93

Bureau Veritas SA, 55 77–79

Burelle S.A., 23 94–96

Burger King Corporation, II 613–15; **17** 69–72 (upd.); **56** 44–48 (upd.)

Burgett, Inc., 97 88–91

Burke, Inc., 88 39–42
Burke Mills, Inc., 66 41–43
Burlington Coat Factory Warehouse Corporation, 10 188–89; 60 74–76 (upd.)
Burlington Industries, Inc., V 354–55; 17 73–76 (upd.)
Burlington Northern Santa Fe Corporation, V 425–28; 27 82–89 (upd.)
Burlington Resources Inc., 10 190–92 *see also* ConocoPhillips.
Burmah Castrol PLC, IV 381–84; 30 86–91 (upd.) *see also* BP p.l.c.
Burns International Security Services, 13 123–25 *see also* Securitas AB.
Burns International Services Corporation, 41 77–80 (upd.)
Burns, Philp & Company Ltd., 63 83–86
Burpee & Co. *see* W. Atlee Burpee & Co.
Burr-Brown Corporation, 19 66–68
Burroughs & Chapin Company, Inc., 86 52–55
The Burton Corporation, V 20–22; 94 95–100 (upd.)
The Burton Group plc, *see also* Arcadia Group plc.
Burton Snowboards Inc., 22 118–20, 460
Burt's Bees, Inc., 58 47–50
Busch Entertainment Corporation, 73 73–75
Bush Boake Allen Inc., 30 92–94 *see also* International Flavors & Fragrances Inc.
Bush Brothers & Company, 45 71–73
Bush Industries, Inc., 20 98–100
Business Men's Assurance Company of America, 14 83–85
Business Objects S.A., 25 95–97
Business Post Group plc, 46 71–73
Butler Manufacturing Company, 12 51–53; 62 52–56 (upd.)
Butterick Co., Inc., 23 97–99
Buttrey Food & Drug Stores Co., 18 89–91
buy.com, Inc., 46 74–77
Buzztime Entertainment, Inc. *see* NTN Buzztime, Inc.
BVR Systems (1998) Ltd., 93 110–13
BWAY Corporation, 24 91–93

C

C&A, 40 74–77 (upd.)
C&A Brenninkmeyer KG, V 23–24
C&G *see* Cheltenham & Gloucester PLC.
C&J Clark International Ltd., 52 56–59
C&K Market, Inc., 81 59–61
C & S Wholesale Grocers, Inc., 55 80–83
C-COR.net Corp., 38 118–21
C-Cube Microsystems, Inc., 37 50–54
C-Tech Industries Inc., 90 90–93
C. Bechstein Pianofortefabrik AG, 96 66–71
C.F. Martin & Co., Inc., 42 55–58
The C.F. Sauer Company, 90 86–89
C.H. Boehringer Sohn, 39 70–73

C.H. Guenther & Son, Inc., 84 39–42
C.H. Heist Corporation, 24 111–13
C.H. Robinson Worldwide, Inc., 11 43–44; 40 78–81 (upd.)
C. Hoare & Co., 77 76–79
C.I. Traders Limited, 61 44–46
C. Itoh & Co., I 431–33 *see also* ITOCHU Corp.
C.R. Bard, Inc., 9 96–98; 65 81–85 (upd.)
C.R. Meyer and Sons Company, 74 58–60
CAA *see* Creative Artists Agency LLC.
Cabela's Inc., 26 49–51; 68 74–77 (upd.)
Cable & Wireless HKT, 30 95–98 (upd.)
Cable and Wireless plc, V 283–86; 25 98–102 (upd.)
Cabletron Systems, Inc., 10 193–94
Cablevision Electronic Instruments, Inc., 32 105–07
Cablevision Systems Corporation, 7 63–65; 30 99–103 (upd.)
Cabot Corporation, 8 77–79; 29 79–82 (upd.); 91 74–80 (upd.)
Cabot Creamery Cooperative, Inc., 102 65–68
Cache Incorporated, 30 104–06
CACI International Inc., 21 85–87; 72 49–53 (upd.)
Cactus Feeders, Inc., 91 81–84
Cactus S.A., 90 94–97
Cadbury plc, 105 60–66 (upd.)
Cadbury Schweppes PLC, II 476–78; 49 75–79 (upd.)
Cadence Design Systems, Inc., 11 45–48; 48 75–79 (upd.)
Cadence Financial Corporation, 106 88–92
Cadmus Communications Corporation, 23 100–03 *see also* Cenveo Inc.
CAE USA Inc., 48 80–82
Caere Corporation, 20 101–03
Caesars World, Inc., 6 199–202
Caffè Nero Group PLC, 63 87–89
Caffyns PLC, 105 67–71
Cagle's, Inc., 20 104–07
Calmers Business Information, 43 92–95
Cains Beer Company PLC, 99 76–80
Caisse des Dépôts et Consignations, 90 98–101
CAL *see* China Airlines.
Cal-Maine Foods, Inc., 69 76–78
CalAmp Corp., 87 84–87
Calavo Growers, Inc., 47 63–66
CalComp Inc., 13 126–29
Calcot Ltd., 33 84–87
Caldor Inc., 12 54–56
Calgon Carbon Corporation, 73 76–79
California Cedar Products Company, 58 51–53
California Pizza Kitchen Inc., 15 74–76; 74 61–63 (upd.)
California Sports, Inc., 56 49–52
California Steel Industries, Inc., 67 85–87

California Water Service Group, 79 85–88
Caliper Life Sciences, Inc., 70 37–40
Callanan Industries, Inc., 60 77–79
Callard and Bowser-Suchard Inc., 84 43–46
Callaway Golf Company, 15 77–79; 45 74–77 (upd.)
Callon Petroleum Company, 47 67–69
Calloway's Nursery, Inc., 51 59–61
CalMat Co., 19 69–72 *see also* Vulcan Materials Co.
Calpine Corporation, 36 102–04
Caltex Petroleum Corporation, 19 73–75 *see also* Chevron Corp.
Calumet Specialty Products Partners, L.P., 106 93–96
Calvin Klein, Inc., 22 121–24; 55 84–88 (upd.)
CAMAC International Corporation, 106 97–99
Camaïeu S.A., 72 54–56
Camargo Corrêa S.A., 93 114–18
CamBar *see* Cameron & Barkley Co.
Cambrex Corporation, 16 67–69; 44 59–62 (upd.)
Cambridge SoundWorks, Inc., 48 83–86
Cambridge Technology Partners, Inc., 36 105–08
Camden Property Trust, 77 80–83
Cameco Corporation, 77 84–87
Camelot Music, Inc., 26 52–54
Cameron & Barkley Company, 28 59–61 *see also* Hagemeyer North America.
Cameron Hughes Wine, 103 88–91
Camp Dresser & McKee Inc., 104 47–50
Campagna-Turano Bakery, Inc., 99 81–84
Campbell-Ewald Advertising, 86 56–60
Campbell-Mithun-Esty, Inc., 16 70–72 *see also* Interpublic Group of Companies, Inc.
Campbell Scientific, Inc., 51 62–65
Campbell Soup Company, II 479–81; 7 66–69 (upd.); 26 55–59 (upd.); 71 75–81 (upd.)
Campeau Corporation, V 25–28
The Campina Group, 78 61–64
Campmor, Inc., 104 51–54
Campo Electronics, Appliances & Computers, Inc., 16 73–75
Campofrío Alimentación S.A, 59 101–03
Canada Bread Company, Limited, 99 85–88
Canada Packers Inc., II 482–85
Canada Trust *see* CT Financial Services Inc.
Canadair, Inc., 16 76–78 *see also* Bombardier Inc.
The Canadian Broadcasting Corporation (CBC), 37 55–58
Canadian Imperial Bank of Commerce, II 244–46; 61 47–51 (upd.)
Canadian National Railway Company, 6 359–62; 71 82–88 (upd.)

Canadian Pacific Railway Limited, V 429–31; 45 78–83 (upd.); 95 71–80 (upd.)

Canadian Solar Inc., 105 72–76

Canadian Tire Corporation, Limited, 71 89–93 (upd.)

Canadian Utilities Limited, 13 130–32; 56 53–56 (upd.)

Canal Plus, 10 195–97; 34 83–86 (upd.)

Canandaigua Brands, Inc., 13 133–35; 34 87–91 (upd.) *see also* Constellation Brands, Inc.

Canary Wharf Group Plc, 30 107–09

Cancer Treatment Centers of America, Inc., 85 45–48

Candela Corporation, 48 87–89

Candie's, Inc., 31 81–84

Candle Corporation, 64 62–65

Candlewood Hotel Company, Inc., 41 81–83

Canfor Corporation, 42 59–61

Canlan Ice Sports Corp., 105 77–81

Cannon Design, 63 90–92

Cannon Express, Inc., 53 80–82

Cannondale Corporation, 21 88–90

Cano Petroleum Inc., 97 92–95

Canon Inc., III 120–21; 18 92–95 (upd.); ; 79 89–95 (upd.)

Canstar Sports Inc., 16 79–81 *see also* NIKE, Inc.

Cantel Medical Corporation, 80 55–58

Canterbury Park Holding Corporation, 42 62–65

Cantine Giorgio Lungarotti S.R.L., 67 88–90

Cantor Fitzgerald, L.P., 92 38–42

CanWest Global Communications Corporation, 35 67–703

Cap Gemini Ernst & Young, 37 59–61

Cap Rock Energy Corporation, 46 78–81

Capario, 104 55–58

Caparo Group Ltd., 90 102–06

Capcom Company Ltd., 83 50–53

Cape Cod Potato Chip Company, 90 107–10

Capel Incorporated, 45 84–86

Capezio/Ballet Makers Inc., 62 57–59

Capita Group PLC, 69 79–81

Capital Cities/ABC Inc., II 129–31 *see also* Disney/ABC Television Group.

Capital City Bank Group, Inc., 105 82–85

Capital Holding Corporation, III 216–19 *see also* Providian Financial Corp.

Capital One Financial Corporation, 52 60–63

Capital Radio plc, 35 71–73

Capital Senior Living Corporation, 75 80–82

Capitalia S.p.A., 65 86–89

Capitol Records, Inc., 90 111–16

CapStar Hotel Company, 21 91–93

Capstone Turbine Corporation, 75 83–85

Captain D's, LLC, 59 104–06

Captaris, Inc., 89 126–29

Car Toys, Inc., 67 91–93

Caradon plc, 20 108–12 (upd.) *see also* Novar plc.

Caraustar Industries, Inc., 19 76–78; 44 63–67 (upd.)

The Carbide/Graphite Group, Inc., 40 82–84

Carbo PLC, 67 94–96 (upd.)

Carbone Lorraine S.A., 33 88–90

Carborundum Company, 15 80–82 *see also* Carbo PLC.

Cardinal Health, Inc., 18 96–98; 50 120–23 (upd.)

Cardo AB, 53 83–85

Cardone Industries Inc., 92 43–47

Cardtronics, Inc., 93 119–23

Career Education Corporation, 45 87–89

CareerBuilder, Inc., 93 124–27

Caremark Rx, Inc., 10 198–200; 54 42–45 (upd.)

Carey International, Inc., 26 60–63

Cargill, Incorporated, II 616–18; 13 136–38 (upd.); 40 85–90 (upd.); 89 130–39 (upd.)

Cargolux Airlines International S.A., 49 80–82

Carhartt, Inc., 30 110–12; 77 88–92 (upd.)

Caribiner International, Inc., 24 94–97

Caribou Coffee Company, Inc., 28 62–65; 97 96–102 (upd.)

Caritas Internationalis, 72 57–59

Carl Allers Etablissement A/S, 72 60–62

Carl Kühne KG (GmbH & Co.), 94 101–05

Carl Zeiss AG, III 445–47; 34 92–97 (upd.); 91 85–92 (upd.)

Carlisle Companies Inc., 8 80–82; 82 58–62 (upd.)

Carl's Jr. *see* CKE Restaurants, Inc.

Carlsberg A/S, 9 99–101; 29 83–85 (upd.); 36–40 (upd.)

Carlson Companies, Inc., 6 363–66; 22 125–29 (upd.); 87 88–95 (upd.)

Carlson Restaurants Worldwide, 69 82–85

Carlson Wagonlit Travel, 55 89–92

Carlton and United Breweries Ltd., I 228–29 *see also* Foster's Group Limited

Carlton Communications plc, 15 83–85; 50 124–27 (upd.) *see also* ITV pcl.

Carma Laboratories, Inc., 60 80–82

CarMax, Inc., 55 93–95

Carmichael Lynch Inc., 28 66–68

Carmike Cinemas, Inc., 14 86–88; 37 62–65 (upd.); 74 64–67 (upd.)

Carnation Company, II 486–89 *see also* Nestlé S.A.

Carnegie Corporation of New York, 35 74–77

The Carnegie Hall Corporation, 101 100–04

Carnival Corporation, 6 367–68; 27 90–92 (upd.); 78 65–69 (upd.)

Carolina First Corporation, 31 85–87

Carolina Freight Corporation, 6 369–72

Carolina Pad and Paper Company *see* CPP International, LLC

Carolina Power & Light Company, V 564–66; 23 104–07 (upd.) *see also* Progress Energy, Inc.

Carolina Telephone and Telegraph Company, 10 201–03

Carpenter Technology Corporation, 13 139–41; 95 81–86 (upd.)

The Carphone Warehouse Group PLC, 83 54–57

CARQUEST Corporation, 29 86–89

Carr-Gottstein Foods Co., 17 77–80

Carrabba's Italian Grill *see* Outback Steakhouse, Inc.

CarrAmerica Realty Corporation, 56 57–59

Carrefour SA, 10 204–06; 27 93–96 (upd.); 64 66–69 (upd.)

Carrere Group S.A., 104 59–63

The Carriage House Companies, Inc., 55 96–98

Carriage Services, Inc., 37 66–68

Carrier Access Corporation, 44 68–73

Carrier Corporation, 7 70–73; 69 86–91 (upd.)

Carrizo Oil & Gas, Inc., 97 103–06

Carroll's Foods, Inc., 46 82–85

Carrols Restaurant Group, Inc., 92 48–51

The Carsey-Werner Company, L.L.C., 37 69–72

Carson, Inc., 31 88–90

Carson Pirie Scott & Company, 15 86–88

CART *see* Championship Auto Racing Teams, Inc.

Carter Hawley Hale Stores, V 29–32

Carter Holt Harvey Ltd., 70 41–44

Carter Lumber Company, 45 90–92

Carter-Wallace, Inc., 8 83–86; 38 122–26 (upd.)

Cartier Monde, 29 90–92

Carus Publishing Company, 93 128–32

Carvel Corporation, 35 78–81

Carver Bancorp, Inc., 94 106–10

Carver Boat Corporation LLC, 88 43–46

Carvin Corp., 89 140–43

Casa Bancária Almeida e Companhia *see* Banco Bradesco S.A.

Casa Cuervo, S.A. de C.V., 31 91–93

Casa Herradura *see* Grupo Industrial Herradura, S.A. de C.V.

Casa Saba *see* Grupo Casa Saba, S.A. de C.V.

Casas Bahia Comercial Ltda., 75 86–89

Cascade Corporation, 65 90–92

Cascade General, Inc., 65 93–95

Cascade Natural Gas Corporation, 9 102–04

Cascades Inc., 71 94–96

Cascal N.V., 103 92–95

Casco Northern Bank, 14 89–91

Casella Waste Systems Inc., 102 69–73

Casey's General Stores, Inc., 19 79–81; 83 58–63 (upd.)

Cash America International, Inc., 20 113–15; 61 52–55 (upd.)

Cash Systems, Inc., 93 133–36

Casino Guichard-Perrachon S.A., 59 107–10 (upd.)

CASIO Computer Co., Ltd., III 448–49; 16 82–84 (upd.); 40 91–95 (upd.)

Cass Information Systems Inc., 100 88–91

Castle & Cooke, Inc., II 490–92; 20 116–19 (upd.) *see also* Dole Food Company, Inc.

Castorama-Dubois Investissements SCA, 104 64–68 (upd.)

Castro Model Ltd., 86 61–64

Casual Corner Group, Inc., 43 96–98

Casual Male Retail Group, Inc., 52 64–66

Caswell-Massey Co. Ltd., 51 66–69

Catalina Lighting, Inc., 43 99–102 (upd.)

Catalina Marketing Corporation, 18 99–102

Catalyst Paper Corporation, 105 86–89

Catalytica Energy Systems, Inc., 44 74–77

Catellus Development Corporation, 24 98–101

Caterpillar Inc., III 450–53; 15 89–93 (upd.); 63 93–99 (upd.)

Cathay Pacific Airways Limited, 6 78–80; 34 98–102 (upd.)

Catherines Stores Corporation, 15 94–97

Catholic Charities USA, 76 82–84

Catholic Health Initiatives, 91 93–98

Catholic Order of Foresters, 24 102–05; 97 107–11 (upd.)

Cato Corporation, 14 92–94

Cattleman's, Inc., 20 120–22

Cattles plc, 58 54–56

Cavco Industries, Inc., 65 96–99

Cazenove Group plc, 72 63–65

CB&I *see* Chicago Bridge & Iron Company N.V.

CB Commercial Real Estate Services Group, Inc., 21 94–98

CB Richard Ellis Group, Inc., 70 45–50 (upd.)

CBI Industries, Inc., 7 74–77 *see also* Chicago Bridge & Iron Company N.V.

CBN *see* The Christian Broadcasting Network, Inc.

CBOT *see* Chicago Board of Trade.

CBP *see* Corporation for Public Broadcasting.

CBRL Group, Inc., 35 82–85 (upd.); 86 65–70 (upd.)

CBS Corporation, II 132–34; 6 157–60 (upd.); 28 69–73 (upd.) *see also* CBS Television Network.

CBS Television Network, 66 44–48 (upd.)

CBSI *see* Complete Business Solutions, Inc.

CCA *see* Corrections Corporation of America.

CCA Industries, Inc., 53 86–89

CCC Information Services Group Inc., 74 68–70

CCG *see* The Clark Construction Group, Inc.

CCH Inc., 14 95–97

CCM Inc. *see* The Hockey Co.

CDC *see* Control Data Corp.

CDC Corporation, 71 97–99

CDI Corporation, 6 139–41; 54 46–49 (upd.)

CDL *see* City Developments Ltd.

CDW Computer Centers, Inc., 16 85–87; 52 67–70 (upd.)

Ce De Candy Inc., 100 92–95

CEC Entertainment, Inc., 31 94–98 (upd.)

CECAB *see* Groupe CECAB S.C.A.

Cedar Fair Entertainment Company, 22 130–32; 98 41–45 (upd.)

CEDC *see* Central European Distribution Corp.

Cegedim S.A., 104 69–73

Celadon Group Inc., 30 113–16

Celanese Corp., I 317–19 *see also* Hoechst Celanese Corp.

Celanese Mexicana, S.A. de C.V., 54 50–52

Celebrate Express, Inc., 70 51–53

Celebrity, Inc., 22 133–35

Celera Genomics, 74 71–74

Celestial Seasonings, Inc., 16 88–91 *see also* The Hain Celestial Group, Inc.

Celestica Inc., 80 59–62

Celgene Corporation, 67 97–100

CellStar Corporation, 83 64–67

Cementos Argos S.A., 91 99–101

CEMEX S.A. de C.V., 20 123–26; 59 111–16 (upd.)

CEMIG *see* Companhia Energética De Minas Gerais S.A.

Cencosud S.A., 69 92–94

Cendant Corporation, 44 78–84 (upd.) *see also* Wyndham Worldwide Corp.

Centel Corporation, 6 312–15 *see also* EMBARQ Corp.

Centennial Communications Corporation, 39 74–76

Centerior Energy Corporation, V 567–68

Centerplate, Inc., 79 96–100

Centex Corporation, 8 87–89; 29 93–96 (upd.); 106 100–04 (upd.)

Centocor Inc., 14 98–100

Central and South West Corporation, V 569–70

Central European Distribution Corporation, 75 90–92

Central European Media Enterprises Ltd., 61 56–59

Central Florida Investments, Inc., 93 137–40

Central Garden & Pet Company, 23 108–10; 58 57–60 (upd.)

Central Hudson Gas And Electricity Corporation, 6 458–60

Central Independent Television, 7 78–80; 23 111–14 (upd.)

Central Japan Railway Company, 43 103–06

Central Maine Power, 6 461–64

Central National-Gottesman Inc., 95 87–90

Central Newspapers, Inc., 10 207–09 *see also* Gannett Company, Inc.

Central Parking System, 18 103–05; 104 74–78 (upd.)

Central Soya Company, Inc., 7 81–83

Central Sprinkler Corporation, 29 97–99

Central Vermont Public Service Corporation, 54 53–56

Centrica plc, 29 100–05 (upd.)

Centuri Corporation, 54 57–59

Century Aluminum Company, 52 71–74

Century Business Services, Inc., 52 75–78

Century Casinos, Inc., 53 90–93

Century Communications Corp., 10 210–12

Century Telephone Enterprises, Inc., 9 105–07; 54 60–63 (upd.)

Century Theatres, Inc., 31 99–101

Cenveo Inc., 71 100–04 (upd.)

CEPCO *see* Chugoku Electric Power Company Inc.

Cephalon, Inc., 45 93–96

Cepheid, 77 93–96

Ceradyne, Inc., 65 100–02

Cerebos Gregg's Ltd., 100 96–99

Cerner Corporation, 16 92–94; 94 111–16 (upd.)

CertainTeed Corporation, 35 86–89

Certegy, Inc., 63 100–03

Cerveceria Polar, I 230–31 *see also* Empresas Polar SA.

Ceské aerolinie, a.s., 66 49–51

Cesky Telecom, a.s., 64 70–73

Cessna Aircraft Company, 8 90–93; 27 97–101 (upd.)

Cetelem S.A., 21 99–102

CeWe Color Holding AG, 76 85–88

ČEZ a. s., 97 112–15

CF Industries Holdings, Inc., 99 89–93

CG&E *see* Cincinnati Gas & Electric Co.

CGM *see* Compagnie Générale Maritime.

CH2M HILL Companies Ltd., 22 136–38; 96 72–77 (upd.)

Chadbourne & Parke, 36 109–12

Chadwick's of Boston, Ltd., 29 106–08

Chalk's Ocean Airways *see* Flying Boat, Inc.

The Chalone Wine Group, Ltd., 36 113–16

Champion Enterprises, Inc., 17 81–84

Champion Industries, Inc., 28 74–76

Champion International Corporation, IV 263–65; 20 127–30 (upd.) *see also* International Paper Co.

Championship Auto Racing Teams, Inc., 37 73–75

Chancellor Beacon Academies, Inc., 53 94–97

Chancellor Media Corporation, 24 106–10

Chanel SA, 12 57–59; 49 83–86 (upd.)
Channel Four Television Corporation, 93 141–44
Chantiers Jeanneau S.A., 96 78–81
Chaoda Modern Agriculture (Holdings) Ltd., 87 96–99
Chaparral Steel Co., 13 142–44
Charal S.A., 90 117–20
Chargeurs International, 6 373–75; 21 103–06 (upd.)
Charisma Brands LLC, 74 75–78
The Charles Machine Works, Inc., 64 74–76
Charles River Laboratories International, Inc., 42 66–69
The Charles Schwab Corporation, 8 94–96; 26 64–67 (upd.); 81 62–68 (upd.)
The Charles Stark Draper Laboratory, Inc., 35 90–92
Charles Vögele Holding AG, 82 63–66
Charlotte Russe Holding, Inc., 35 93–96; 90 121–25 (upd.)
The Charmer Sunbelt Group, 95 91–94
Charming Shoppes, Inc., 8 97–98; 38 127–29 (upd.)
Charoen Pokphand Group, 62 60–63
Chart House Enterprises, Inc., 17 85–88; 96 82–86 (upd.)
Chart Industries, Inc., 21 107–09
Charter Communications, Inc., 33 91–94
Charter Financial Corporation, 103 96–99
Charter Manufacturing Company, Inc., 103 100–03
ChartHouse International Learning Corporation, 49 87–89
Chas. Levy Company LLC, 60 83–85
Chase General Corporation, 91 102–05
The Chase Manhattan Corporation, II 247–49; 13 145–48 (upd.) *see also* JPMorgan Chase & Co.
Chateau Communities, Inc., 37 76–79
Chattanooga Bakery, Inc., 86 75–78
Chattem, Inc., 17 89–92; 88 47–52 (upd.)
Chautauqua Airlines, Inc., 38 130–32
CHC Helicopter Corporation, 67 101–03
Check Into Cash, Inc., 105 90–93
Checker Motors Corp., 89 144–48
Checkers Drive-In Restaurants, Inc., 16 95–98; 74 79–83 (upd.)
CheckFree Corporation, 81 69–72
Checkpoint Systems, Inc., 39 77–80
Chedraui *see* Grupo Comercial Chedraui S.A. de C.V.
The Cheesecake Factory Inc., 17 93–96; 100 100–05 (upd.)
Chef Solutions, Inc., 89 149–52
Chello Zone Ltd., 93 145–48
Chelsea Ltd., 102 74–79
Chelsea Milling Company, 29 109–11
Chelsea Piers Management Inc., 86 79–82
Chelsfield PLC, 67 104–06

Cheltenham & Gloucester PLC, 61 60–62
Chemcentral Corporation, 8 99–101
Chemed Corporation, 13 149–50
Chemfab Corporation, 35 97–101
Chemi-Trol Chemical Co., 16 99–101
Chemical Banking Corporation, II 250–52; 14 101–04 (upd.)
Chemical Waste Management, Inc., 9 108–10
Chemtura Corporation, 91 106–20 (upd.)
CHEP Pty. Ltd., 80 63–66
Cherokee Inc., 18 106–09
Cherry Brothers LLC, 105 94–97
Cherry Lane Music Publishing Company, Inc., 62 64–67
Chesapeake Corporation, 8 102–04; 30 117–20 (upd.); 93 149–55 (upd.)
Chesapeake Utilities Corporation, 56 60–62
Chesebrough-Pond's USA, Inc., 8 105–07
Cheshire Building Society, 74 84–87
Cheung Kong (Holdings) Ltd., IV 693–95; 20 131–34 (upd.); 94 117–24 (upd.)
Chevron Corporation, IV 385–87;19 82–85 (upd.); 47 70–76 (upd.); 103 104–14 (upd.)
Cheyenne Software, Inc., 12 60–62
CHF Industries, Inc., 84 47–50
CHHJ Franchising LLC, 105 98–101
Chi-Chi's Inc., 13 151–53; 51 70–73 (upd.)
Chi Mei Optoelectronics Corporation, 75 93–95
Chiasso Inc., 53 98–100
Chiat/Day Inc. Advertising, 11 49–52 *see also* TBWA/Chiat/Day.
Chibu Electric Power Company, Incorporated, V 571–73
Chic by H.I.S, Inc., 20 135–37 *see also* VF Corp.
Chicago and North Western Holdings Corporation, 6 376–78 *see also* Union Pacific Corp.
Chicago Bears Football Club, Inc., 33 95–97
Chicago Blackhawk Hockey Team, Inc. *see* Wirtz Corp.
Chicago Board of Trade, 41 84–87
Chicago Bridge & Iron Company N.V., 82 67–73 (upd.)
Chicago Mercantile Exchange Holdings Inc., 75 96–99
Chicago National League Ball Club, Inc., 66 52–55
Chicago Pizza & Brewery, Inc., 44 85–88
Chicago Review Press Inc., 84 51–54
Chicago Symphony Orchestra, 106 105–09
Chicago Tribune *see* Tribune Co.
Chick-fil-A Inc., 23 115–18; 90 126–31 (upd.)
Chicken of the Sea International, 24 114–16 (upd.); 106 110–13 (upd.)

Chico's FAS, Inc., 45 97–99
ChildFund International, 106 114–17
ChildrenFirst, Inc., 59 117–20
Children's Comprehensive Services, Inc., 42 70–72
Children's Healthcare of Atlanta Inc., 101 105–09
Children's Hospitals and Clinics, Inc., 54 64–67
The Children's Place Retail Stores, Inc., 37 80–82; 86 83–87 (upd.)
Childtime Learning Centers, Inc., 34 103–06 *see also* Learning Care Group, Inc.
Chiles Offshore Corporation, 9 111–13
China Airlines, 34 107–10
China Automotive Systems Inc., 87 100–103
China Construction Bank Corp., 79 101–04
China Eastern Airlines Co. Ltd., 31 102–04
China FAW Group Corporation, 105 102–07
China Life Insurance Company Limited, 65 103–05
China Merchants International Holdings Co., Ltd., 52 79–82
China National Cereals, Oils and Foodstuffs Import and Export Corporation (COFCO), 76 89–91
China National Petroleum Corporation, 46 86–89
China Nepstar Chain Drugstore Ltd., 97 116–19
China Netcom Group Corporation (Hong Kong) Limited, 73 80–83
China Shenhua Energy Company Limited, 83 68–71
China Southern Airlines Company Ltd., 33 98–100
China Telecom, 50 128–32
Chindex International, Inc., 101 110–13
Chinese Petroleum Corporation, IV 388–90; 31 105–08 (upd.)
Chipotle Mexican Grill, Inc., 67 107–10
CHIPS and Technologies, Inc., 9 114–17
Chiquita Brands International, Inc., 7 84–86; 21 110–13 (upd.); 83 72–79 (upd.)
Chiron Corporation, 10 213–14; 36 117–20 (upd.)
Chisholm-Mingo Group, Inc., 41 88–90
Chittenden & Eastman Company, 58 61–64
Chock Full o'Nuts Corp., 17 97–100
Chocoladefabriken Lindt & Sprüngli AG, 27 102–05
Chocolat Frey AG, 102 80–83
Choice Hotels International, Inc., 14 105–07; 83 80–83 (upd.)
ChoicePoint Inc., 65 106–08
Chongqing Department Store Company Ltd., 105 108–11
Chorus Line Corporation, 30 121–23
Chr. Hansen Group A/S, 70 54–57

Chris-Craft Corporation, 9 118–19; 31 109–12 (upd.); 80 67–71 (upd.)
Christensen Boyles Corporation, 26 68–71
The Christian Broadcasting Network, Inc., 52 83–85
Christian Children's Fund *see* ChildFund International.
Christian Dalloz SA, 40 96–98
Christian Dior S.A., 19 86–88; 49 90–93 (upd.)
Christian Salvesen Plc, 45 100–03
The Christian Science Publishing Society, 55 99–102
Christie Digital Systems, Inc., 103 115–19
Christie's International plc, 15 98–101; 39 81–85 (upd.)
Christofle SA, 40 99–102
Christopher & Banks Corporation, 42 73–75
Chromcraft Revington, Inc., 15 102–05
The Chronicle Publishing Company, Inc., 23 119–22
Chronimed Inc., 26 72–75
Chrysalis Group plc, 40 103–06
Chrysler Corporation, I 144–45; 11 53–55 (upd.) *see also* DaimlerChrysler AG
CHS Inc., 60 86–89
Chubb Corporation, III 220–22; 14 108–10 (upd.); 37 83–87 (upd.)
Chubb, PLC, 50 133–36
Chubu Electric Power Company, Inc., V 571–73; 46 90–93 (upd.)
Chuck E. Cheese *see* CEC Entertainment, Inc.
Chugach Alaska Corporation, 60 90–93
Chugai Pharmaceutical Co., Ltd., 50 137–40
Chugoku Electric Power Company Inc., V 574–76; 53 101–04 (upd.)
Chunghwa Picture Tubes, Ltd., 75 100–02
Chunghwa Telecom Co., Ltd., 101 114–19 (upd.)
Chupa Chups S.A., 38 133–35
Church & Dwight Co., Inc., 29 112–15; 68 78–82 (upd.)
Churchill Downs Incorporated, 29 116–19
Church's Chicken, 66 56–59
Cia Hering, 72 66–68
Cianbro Corporation, 14 111–13
Ciba-Geigy Ltd., I 632–34; 8 108–11 (upd.) *see also* Novartis AG.
CIBC *see* Canadian Imperial Bank of Commerce.
Ciber, Inc., 18 110–12
CiCi Enterprises, L.P., 99 94–99
CIENA Corporation, 54 68–71
Cifra, S.A. de C.V., 12 63–65 *see also* Wal-Mart de Mexico, S.A. de C.V.
CIGNA Corporation, III 223–27; 22 139–44 (upd.); 45 104–10 (upd.)
Cimarex Energy Co., 81 73–76
Cimentos de Portugal SGPS S.A. (Cimpor), 76 92–94

Ciments Français, 40 107–10
Cimpor *see* Cimentos de Portugal SGPS S.A.
Cinar Corporation, 40 111–14
Cincinnati Bell Inc., 6 316–18; 105 112–18 (upd.)
Cincinnati Financial Corporation, 16 102–04; 44 89–92 (upd.)
Cincinnati Gas & Electric Company, 6 465–68 *see also* Duke Energy Corp.
Cincinnati Lamb Inc., 72 69–71
Cincinnati Milacron Inc., 12 66–69 *see also* Milacron, Inc.
Cincom Systems Inc., 15 106–08
Cinemark Holdings, Inc., 95 95–99
Cinemas de la República, S.A. de C.V., 83 84–86
Cinemeccanica S.p.A., 78 70–73
Cineplex Odeon Corporation, 6 161–63; 23 123–26 (upd.)
Cinnabon, Inc., 23 127–29; 90 132–36 (upd.)
Cinram International, Inc., 43 107–10
Cintas Corporation, 21 114–16; 51 74–77 (upd.)
CIPSA *see* Compañia Industrial de Parras, S.A. de C.V. (CIPSA).
CIPSCO Inc., 6 469–72 *see also* Ameren Corp.
The Circle K Company, II 619–20; 20 138–40 (upd.)
Circon Corporation, 21 117–20
Circuit City Stores, Inc., 9 120–22; 29 120–24 (upd.); 65 109–14 (upd.)
Circus Circus Enterprises, Inc., 6 203–05
Cirque du Soleil Inc., 29 125–28; 98 46–51 (upd.)
Cirrus Design Corporation, 44 93–95
Cirrus Logic, Inc., 11 56–57; 48 90–93 (upd.)
Cisco-Linksys LLC, 86 88–91
Cisco Systems, Inc., 11 58–60; 34 111–15 (upd.); 77 97–103 (upd.)
Cisneros Group of Companies, 54 72–75
CIT Group Inc., 76 95–98
Citadel Communications Corporation, 35 102–05
CitFed Bancorp, Inc., 16 105–07 *see also* Fifth Third Bancorp.
CITGO Petroleum Corporation, IV 391–93; 31 113–17 (upd.)
Citi Trends, Inc., 80 72–75
Citibank *see* Citigroup Inc
CITIC Pacific Ltd., 18 113–15
Citicorp, II 253–55; 9 123–26 (upd.) *see also* Citigroup Inc.
Citicorp Diners Club, Inc., 90 137–40
Citigroup Inc., 30 124–28 (upd.); 59 121–27 (upd.)
Citizen Watch Co., Ltd., III 454–56; 21 121–24 (upd.); 81 77–82 (upd.)
Citizens Communications Company, 79 105–08 (upd.)
Citizens Financial Group, Inc., 42 76–80; 87 104–112 (upd.)

Citizens Utilities Company, 7 87–89 *see also* Citizens Communications Company
Citrix Systems, Inc., 44 96–99
Citroën *see* PSA Peugeot Citroen S.A.
City Brewing Company LLC, 73 84–87
City Developments Limited, 89 153–56
City Public Service, 6 473–75
CJ Banks *see* Christopher & Banks Corp.
CJ Corporation, 62 68–70
CJSC Transmash Holding, 93 446–49
CJSC Transmash Holding, 93 446–49
CKE Restaurants, Inc., 19 89–93; 46 94–99 (upd.)
CKX, Inc., 102 84–87
Claire's Stores, Inc., 17 101–03; 94 125–29 (upd.)
CLARCOR Inc., 17 104–07; 61 63–67 (upd.)
Clare Rose Inc., 68 83–85
Clarion Company Ltd., 64 77–79
The Clark Construction Group, Inc., 8 112–13
Clark Equipment Company, 8 114–16
Classic Vacation Group, Inc., 46 100–03
Clayton Homes Incorporated, 13 154–55; 54 76–79 (upd.)
Clayton Williams Energy, Inc., 87 113–116
Clean Harbors, Inc., 73 88–91
Clean Venture, Inc., 104 79–82
Clear Channel Communications, Inc., 23 130–32 *see also* Live Nation, Inc.
Clearly Canadian Beverage Corporation, 48 94–97
Clearwire, Inc., 69 95–97
Cleary, Gottlieb, Steen & Hamilton, 35 106–09
Cleco Corporation, 37 88–91
The Clemens Family Corporation, 93 156–59
Clement Pappas & Company, Inc., 92 52–55
Cleveland-Cliffs Inc., 13 156–58; 62 71–75 (upd.)
Cleveland Indians Baseball Company, Inc., 37 92–94
Click Wine Group, 68 86–88
Clif Bar Inc., 50 141–43
Clifford Chance LLP, 38 136–39
Clinton Cards plc, 39 86–88
Cloetta Fazer AB, 70 58–60
Clopay Corporation, 100 106–10
The Clorox Company, III 20–22; 22 145–48 (upd.); 81 83–90 (upd.)
Close Brothers Group plc, 39 89–92
The Clothestime, Inc., 20 141–44
Clougherty Packing Company, 72 72–74
Club Méditerranée S.A., 6 206–08; 21 125–28 (upd.); 91 121–27 (upd.)
ClubCorp, Inc., 33 101–04
CMC *see* Commercial Metals Co.
CME *see* Campbell-Mithun-Esty, Inc.; Central European Media Enterprises Ltd.; Chicago Mercantile Exchange Inc.
CMG Worldwide, Inc., 89 157–60
CMGI, Inc., 76 99–101

CMIH *see* China Merchants International Holdings Co., Ltd.

CML Group, Inc., 10 215–18

CMO *see* Chi Mei Optoelectronics Corp.

CMP Media Inc., 26 76–80

CMS Energy Corporation, V 577–79; 14 114–16 (**upd.**); 100 111–16 (**upd.**)

CN *see* Canadian National Railway Co.

CNA Financial Corporation, III 228–32; 38 140–46 (**upd.**)

CNET Networks, Inc., 47 77–80

CNG *see* Consolidated Natural Gas Co.

CNH Global N.V., 38 147–56 (**upd.**); 99 100–112 (**upd.**)

CNP *see* Compagnie Nationale à Portefeuille.

CNPC *see* China National Petroleum Corp.

CNS, Inc., 20 145–47 *see also* GlaxoSmithKline plc.

Co-operative Group (CWS) Ltd., 51 86–89

Coach, Inc., 10 219–21; 45 111–15 (**upd.**); 99 113–120 (**upd.**)

Coach USA, Inc., 24 117–19; 55 103–06 (**upd.**)

Coachmen Industries, Inc., 77 104–07

Coal India Ltd., IV 48–50; 44 100–03 (**upd.**)

Coastal Corporation, IV 394–95; 31 118–21 (**upd.**)

Coats plc, V 356–58; 44 104–07 (**upd.**)

COBE Cardiovascular, Inc., 61 68–72

COBE Laboratories, Inc., 13 159–61

Coberco *see* Friesland Coberco Dairy Foods Holding N.V.

Cobham plc, 30 129–32

Coborn's, Inc., 30 133–35

Cobra Electronics Corporation, 14 117–19

Cobra Golf Inc., 16 108–10

Coca-Cola Bottling Co. Consolidated, 10 222–24

The Coca-Cola Company, I 232–35; 10 225–28 (**upd.**); 32 111–16 (**upd.**); 67 111–17 (**upd.**)

Coca-Cola Enterprises, Inc., 13 162–64

Cochlear Ltd., 77 108–11

Cockerill Sambre Group, IV 51–53; 26 81–84 (**upd.**) *see also* Arcelor Gent.

Codelco *see* Corporacion Nacional del Cobre de Chile.

Coeur d'Alene Mines Corporation, 20 148–51

COFCO *see* China National Cereals, Oils and Foodstuffs Import and Export Corp.

The Coffee Beanery, Ltd., 95 100–05

Coffee Holding Co., Inc., 95 106–09

Coflexip S.A., 25 103–05 *see also* Technip.

Cogent Communications Group, Inc., 55 107–10

Cogentrix Energy, Inc., 10 229–31

Cognex Corporation, 76 102–06

Cognizant Technology Solutions Corporation, 59 128–30

Cognos Inc., 44 108–11

Coherent, Inc., 31 122–25

Cohu, Inc., 32 117–19

Coinmach Laundry Corporation, 20 152–54

Coinstar, Inc., 44 112–14

Colas S.A., 31 126–29

Cold Spring Granite Company, 16 111–14; 67 118–22 (**upd.**)

Cold Stone Creamery, 69 98–100

Coldwater Creek Inc., 21 129–31; 74 88–91 (**upd.**)

Coldwell Banker Co. *see* CB Richard Ellis Group, Inc.

Cole National Corporation, 13 165–67; 76 107–10 (**upd.**)

The Coleman Company, Inc., 9 127–29; 30 136–39 (**upd.**)

Coleman Natural Products, Inc., 68 89–91

Coles Express Inc., 15 109–11

Coles Group Limited, V 33–35; 20 155–58 (**upd.**); 85 49–56 (**upd.**)

Cole's Quality Foods, Inc., 68 92–94

Colfax Corporation, 58 65–67

Colgate-Palmolive Company, III 23–26; 14 120–23 (**upd.**); 35 110–15 (**upd.**); 71 105–10 (**upd.**)

Collectors Universe, Inc., 48 98–100

College Hunks Hauling Junk *see* CHHJ Franchising LLC.

Colliers International Property Consultants Inc., 92 56–59

Collins & Aikman Corporation, 13 168–70; 41 91–95 (**upd.**)

The Collins Companies Inc., 102 88–92

Collins Industries, Inc., 33 105–07

Colonial Properties Trust, 65 115–17

Colonial Williamsburg Foundation, 53 105–07

Color Kinetics Incorporated, 85 57–60

Colorado Baseball Management, Inc., 72 75–78

Colorado Boxed Beef Company, 100 117–20

Colorado MEDtech, Inc., 48 101–05

Colt Industries Inc., I 434–36

COLT Telecom Group plc, 41 96–99

Colt's Manufacturing Company, Inc., 12 70–72

Columbia Forest Products Inc., 78 74–77

The Columbia Gas System, Inc., V 580–82; 16 115–18 (**upd.**)

Columbia House Company, 69 101–03

Columbia Sportswear Company, 19 94–96; 41 100–03 (**upd.**)

Columbia TriStar Motion Pictures Companies, II 135–37; 12 73–76 (**upd.**)

Columbia/HCA Healthcare Corporation, 15 112–14

Columbus McKinnon Corporation, 37 95–98

Com Ed *see* Commonwealth Edison.

Comair Holdings Inc., 13 171–73; 34 116–20 (**upd.**)

Combe Inc., 72 79–82

Comcast Corporation, 7 90–92; 24 120–24 (**upd.**)

Comdial Corporation, 21 132–35

Comdisco, Inc., 9 130–32

Comerci *see* Controladora Comercial Mexicana, S.A. de C.V.

Comerica Incorporated, 40 115–17; 101 120–25 (**upd.**)

COMFORCE Corporation, 40 118–20

Comfort Systems USA, Inc., 101 126–29

Cominco Ltd., 37 99–102

Command Security Corporation, 57 71–73

Commerce Clearing House, Inc., 7 93–94 *see also* CCH Inc.

Commercial Credit Company, 8 117–19 *see also* Citigroup Inc.

Commercial Federal Corporation, 12 77–79; 62 76–80 (**upd.**)

Commercial Financial Services, Inc., 26 85–89

Commercial Metals Company, 15 115–17; 42 81–84(**upd.**)

Commercial Union plc, III 233–35 *see also* Aviva PLC.

Commercial Vehicle Group, Inc., 81 91–94

Commerzbank A.G., II 256–58; 47 81–84 (**upd.**)

Commodore International, Ltd., 7 95–97

Commonwealth Edison, V 583–85

Commonwealth Energy System, 14 124–26 *see also* NSTAR.

Commonwealth Telephone Enterprises, Inc., 25 106–08

CommScope, Inc., 77 112–15

Community Coffee Co. L.L.C., 53 108–10

Community Health Systems, Inc., 71 111–13

Community Newspaper Holdings, Inc., 91 128–31

Community Psychiatric Centers, 15 118–20

Compagnia Italiana dei Jolly Hotels S.p.A., 71 114–16

Compagnie de Saint-Gobain, III 675–78; 16 119–23 (**upd.**); 64 80–84 (**upd.**)

Compagnie des Alpes, 48 106–08

Compagnie des Cristalleries de Baccarat *see* Baccarat.

Compagnie des Machines Bull S.A., III 122–23 *see also* Bull S.A.; Groupe Bull.

Compagnie Financière de Paribas, II 259–60 *see also* BNP Paribas Group.

Compagnie Financière Richemont AG, 50 144–47

Compagnie Financière Sucres et Denrées S.A., 60 94–96

Compagnie Générale d'Électricité, II 12–13

Compagnie Générale des Établissements Michelin, V 236–39; 42 85–89 (**upd.**)

Compagnie Générale Maritime et Financière, 6 379–81

Compagnie Maritime Belge S.A., 95 110–13

Compagnie Nationale à Portefeuille, 84 55–58

Companhia Brasileira de Distribuiçao, 76 111–13

Companhia de Bebidas das Américas, 57 74–77

Companhia de Tecidos Norte de Minas - Coteminas, 77 116–19

Companhia Energética de Minas Gerais S.A., 65 118–20

Companhia Siderúrgica Nacional, 76 114–17

Companhia Suzano de Papel e Celulose S.A., 94 130–33

Companhia Vale do Rio Doce, IV 54–57; 43 111–14 (upd.)

Compania Cervecerias Unidas S.A., 70 61–63

Compañia de Minas BuenaventuraS.A.A., 92160–63

Compañia Española de Petróleos S.A. (Cepsa), IV 396–98; 56 63–66 (upd.)

Compañia Industrial de Parras, S.A. de C.V. (CIPSA), 84 59–62

Compañia Sud Americana de Vapores S.A., 100 121–24

Compaq Computer Corporation, III 124–25; 6 221–23 (upd.); 26 90–93 (upd.) *see also* Hewlett-Packard Co.

Compass Bancshares, Inc., 73 92–94

Compass Group PLC, 34 121–24

Compass Minerals International, Inc., 79 109–12

CompDent Corporation, 22 149–51

CompHealth Inc., 25 109–12

Complete Business Solutions, Inc., 31 130–33

Comprehensive Care Corporation, 15 121–23

Comptoirs Modernes S.A., 19 97–99 *see also* Carrefour SA.

Compton Petroleum Corporation, 103 120–23

CompuAdd Computer Corporation, 11 61–63

CompuCom Systems, Inc., 10 232–34

CompuDyne Corporation, 51 78–81

CompUSA, Inc., 10 235–36; 35 116–18 (upd.)

CompuServe Interactive Services, Inc., 10 237–39; 27 106–08 (upd.) *see also* AOL Time Warner Inc.

Computer Associates International, Inc., 6 224–26; 49 94–97 (upd.)

Computer Data Systems, Inc., 14 127–29

Computer Learning Centers, Inc., 26 94–96

Computer Sciences Corporation, 6 227–29

ComputerLand Corp., 13 174–76

Computervision Corporation, 10 240–42

Compuware Corporation, 10 243–45; 30 140–43 (upd.); 66 60–64 (upd.)

Comsat Corporation, 23 133–36 *see also* Lockheed Martin Corp.

Comshare Inc., 23 137–39

Comstock Resources, Inc., 47 85–87

Comtech Telecommunications Corp., 75 103–05

Comverse Technology, Inc., 15 124–26; 43 115–18 (upd.)

Con Ed *see* Consolidated Edison, Inc.

Con-way Inc., 101 130–34

ConAgra Foods, Inc., II 493–95; 12 80–82 (upd.); 42 90–94 (upd.); 85 61–68 (upd.)

Conair Corporation, 17 108–10; 69 104–08 (upd.)

Conaprole *see* Cooperativa Nacional de Productores de Leche S.A. (Conaprole).

Concentra Inc., 71 117–19

Concepts Direct, Inc., 39 93–96

Concha y Toro *see* Viña Concha y Toro S.A.

Concord Camera Corporation, 41 104–07

Concord EFS, Inc., 52 86–88

Concord Fabrics, Inc., 16 124–26

Concur Technologies, Inc., 106 118–22

Concurrent Computer Corporation, 75 106–08

Condé Nast Publications, Inc., 13 177–81; 59 131–34 (upd.)

Cone Mills LLC, 8 120–22; 67 123–27 (upd.)

Conexant Systems Inc., 36 121–25; 106 123–28 (upd.)

Confluence Holdings Corporation, 76 118–20

Congoleum Corporation, 18 116–19; 98 52–57 (upd.)

CONMED Corporation, 87 117–120

Conn-Selmer, Inc., 55 111–14

Connecticut Light and Power Co., 13 182–84

Connecticut Mutual Life Insurance Company, III 236–38

The Connell Company, 29 129–31; 104 83–87 (upd.)

Conner Peripherals, Inc., 6 230–32

Connetics Corporation, 70 64–66

Connors Bros. Income Fund *see* George Weston Ltd.

Conn's, Inc., 67 128–30

ConocoPhillips, IV 399–402; 16 127–32 (upd.); 63 104–15 (upd.)

Conrad Industries, Inc., 58 68–70

Conseco Inc., 10 246–48; 33 108–12 (upd.)

Conso International Corporation, 29 132–34

CONSOL Energy Inc., 59 135–37

Consolidated Delivery & Logistics, Inc., 24 125–28 *see also* Velocity Express Corp.

Consolidated Edison, Inc., V 586–89; 45 116–20 (upd.)

Consolidated Freightways Corporation, V 432–34; 21 136–39 (upd.); 48 109–13 (upd.)

Consolidated Graphics, Inc., 70 67–69

Consolidated Natural Gas Company, V 590–91; 19 100–02 (upd.) *see also* Dominion Resources, Inc.

Consolidated Papers, Inc., 8 123–25; 36 126–30 (upd.)

Consolidated Products, Inc., 14 130–32

Consolidated Rail Corporation, V 435–37

Consorcio ARA, S.A. de C.V., 79 113–16

Consorcio Aviacsa, S.A. de C.V., 85 69–72

Consorcio G Grupo Dina, S.A. de C.V., 36 131–33

Constar International Inc., 64 85–88

Constellation Brands, Inc., 68 95–100 (upd.)

The Consumers Gas Company Ltd., 6 476–79; 43 154 *see also* Enbridge Inc.

Consumers Power Co., 14 133–36

Consumers Union, 26 97–99

Consumers Water Company, 14 137–39

The Container Store, 36 134–36

ContiGroup Companies, Inc., 43 119–22 (upd.)

Continental AG, V 240–43; 56 67–72 (upd.)

Continental Airlines, Inc., I 96–98; 21 140–43 (upd.); 52 89–94 (upd.)

Continental Bank Corporation, II 261–63 *see also* Bank of America.

Continental Cablevision, Inc., 7 98–100

Continental Can Co., Inc., 15 127–30

Continental Corporation, III 239–44

Continental General Tire Corp., 23 140–42

Continental Grain Company, 10 249–51; 13 185–87 (upd.) *see also* ContiGroup Companies, Inc.

Continental Group Co., I 599–600

Continental Medical Systems, Inc., 10 252–54

Continental Resources, Inc., 89 161–65

Continucare Corporation, 101 135–38

Continuum Health Partners, Inc., 60 97–99

Control Data Corporation, III 126–28 *see also* Seagate Technology, Inc.

Control Data Systems, Inc., 10 255–57

Controladora Comercial Mexicana, S.A. de C.V., 36 137–39

Controladora Mabe, S.A. de C.V., 82 74–77

Converse Inc., 9 133–36; 31 134–38 (upd.)

Conzzeta Holding, 80 76–79

Cook Group Inc., 102 93–96

Cooker Restaurant Corporation, 20 159–61; 51 82–85 (upd.)

Cookson Group plc, III 679–82; 44 115–20 (upd.)

CoolBrands International Inc., 35 119–22

CoolSavings, Inc., 77 120–24

Coop Schweiz Genossenschaftsverband, 48 114–16

Coopagri Bretagne, 88 53–56

Cooper Cameron Corporation, 20
162–66 (upd.); 58 71–75 (upd.)
The Cooper Companies, Inc., 39
97–100
Cooper Industries, Inc., II 14–17; 44
121–25 (upd.)
Cooper Tire & Rubber Company, 8
126–28; 23 143–46 (upd.)
Cooperativa Nacional de Productores de
Leche S.A. (Conaprole),92 60–63
Coopers & Lybrand, 9 137–38 *see also*
PricewaterhouseCoopers.
Coors Company *see* Adolph Coors Co.
Copa Holdings, S.A., 93 164–67
Copart Inc., 23 147–49
Copec *see* Empresas Copec S.A.
The Copley Press, Inc., 23 150–52
Coppel, S.A. de C.V., 82 78–81
The Copps Corporation, 32 120–22
Cora S.A./NV, 94 134–37
Corbis Corporation, 31 139–42
Corby Distilleries Limited, 14 140–42
The Corcoran Group, Inc., 58 76–78
Cordis Corporation, 19 103–05; 46
104–07 (upd.)
Cordon Bleu *see* Le Cordon Bleu S.A.
Corel Corporation, 15 131–33; 33
113–16 (upd.); 76 121–24 (upd.)
Corelio S.A./N.V., 96 87–90
CoreStates Financial Corp, 16 111–15
see also Wachovia Corp.
Corinthian Colleges, Inc., 39 101–04;
92 64–69 (upd.)
The Corky McMillin Companies, 98
58–62
Cornelsen Verlagsholding GmbH & Co.,
90 141–46
Corning Inc., III 683–85; 44 126–30
(upd.); 90 147–53 (upd.)
Corporación Geo, S.A. de C.V., 81
95–98
Corporación Interamericana de
Entretenimiento, S.A. de C.V., 83
87–90
Corporación Internacional de Aviación,
S.A. de C.V. (Cintra), 20 167–69
Corporación José R. Lindley S.A., 92
70–73
Corporación Multi-Inversiones, 94
138–42
Corporacion Nacional del Cobre de
Chile, 40 121–23
The Corporate Executive Board
Company, 89 166–69
Corporate Express, Inc., 22 152–55; 47
88–92 (upd.)
Corporate Software Inc., 9 139–41
Corporation for Public Broadcasting, 14
143–45; 89 170–75 (upd.)
Correctional Services Corporation, 30
144–46
Corrections Corporation of America, 23
153–55
Correos y Telegrafos S.A., 80 80–83
Corrpro Companies, Inc., 20 170–73
CORT Business Services Corporation,
26 100–02
Cortefiel S.A., 64 89–91

Corticeira Amorim, Sociedade Gestora
de Participaço es Sociais, S.A., 48
117–20
Corus Bankshares, Inc., 75 109–11
Corus Group plc, 49 98–105 (upd.)
Corvi *see* Grupo Corvi S.A. de C.V.
Cosan Ltd., 102 97–101
Cosi, Inc., 53 111–13
Cosmair Inc., 8 129–32 *see also* L'Oreal.
The Cosmetic Center, Inc., 22 156–58
Cosmo Oil Co., Ltd., IV 403–04; 53
114–16 (upd.)
Cosmolab Inc., 96 91–94
Cost Plus, Inc., 27 109–11
Cost-U-Less, Inc., 51 90–93
CoStar Group, Inc., 73 95–98
Costco Wholesale Corporation, 43
123–25 (upd.); 105 119–23 (upd.)
Coto Centro Integral de
Comercializacion S.A., 66 65–67
Cott Corporation, 52 95–98
Cotter & Company, V 37–38 *see also*
TruServ Corp.
Cotton Incorporated, 46 108–11
Coty, Inc., 36 140–42
Coudert Brothers, 30 147–50
Council on International Educational
Exchange Inc., 81 99–102
Country Kitchen International, Inc., 76
125–27
Countrywide Financial, 16 133–36; 100
125–30 (upd.)
County Seat Stores Inc., 9 142–43
Courier Corporation, 41 108–12
Courtaulds plc, V 359–61; 17 116–19
(upd.) *see also* Akzo Nobel N.V.
Courts Plc, 45 121–24
Cousins Properties Incorporated, 65
121–23
Covance Inc., 30 151–53; 98 63–68
(upd.)
Covanta Energy Corporation, 64 92–95
(upd.)
Coventry Health Care, Inc., 59 138–40
Covidien Ltd., 91 132–35
Covington & Burling, 40 124–27
Cowen Group, Inc., 92 74–77
Cowles Media Company, 23 156–58 *see*
also Primedia Inc.
Cox Enterprises, Inc., IV 595–97; 22
159–63 (upd.); 67 131–35 (upd.)
Cox Radio, Inc., 89 176–80
CP *see* Canadian Pacific Railway Ltd.
CPAC, Inc., 86 92–95
CPC International Inc., II 496–98 *see*
also Bestfoods.
CPI Aerostructures, Inc., 75 112–14
CPI Corp., 38 157–60
CPL *see* Carolina Power & Light Co.
CPP International, LLC, 103 124–27
CPT *see* Chunghwa Picture Tubes, Ltd.
CR England, Inc., 63 116–18
CRA International, Inc., 93 168–71
CRA Limited, IV 58–61 *see also* Rio
Tinto plc.
Cracker Barrel Old Country Store, Inc.,
10 258–59 *see also* CBRL Group, Inc.

Craftmade International, Inc., 44
131–33
Craig Hospital, 99 121–126
craigslist, inc., 89 181–84
Crain Communications, Inc., 12 83–86;
35 123–27 (upd.)
Cram Company *see* The George F. Cram
Company, Inc.
Cramer, Berkowitz & Co., 34 125–27
Cramer-Krasselt Company, 104 88–92
Crane & Co., Inc., 26 103–06; 103
128–34 (upd.)
Crane Co., 8 133–36; 30 154–58
(upd.); 101 139–47 (upd.)
Cranium, Inc., 69 109–11
Cranswick plc, 40 128–30
Crate and Barrel, 9 144–46 *see also*
Euromarket Designs Inc.
Cravath, Swaine & Moore, 43 126–28
Crawford & Company, 87 121–126
Cray Inc., III 129–31; 16 137–40
(upd.); 75 115–21 (upd.)
Creative Artists Agency LLC, 38 161–64
Creative Technology Ltd., 57 78–81
Credence Systems Corporation, 90
154–57
Credit Acceptance Corporation, 18
120–22
Crédit Agricole Group, II 264–66; 84
63–68 (upd.)
Crédit Lyonnais, 9 147–49; 33 117–21
(upd.)
Crédit National S.A., 9 150–52
Crédit Suisse Group, II 267–69; 21
144–47 (upd.); 59 141–47 (upd.) *see*
also Schweizerische Kreditanstalt.
Credito Italiano, II 270–72
Cree Inc., 53 117–20
Cremonini S.p.A., 57 82–84
Creo Inc., 48 121–24
Cresud S.A.C.I.F. y A., 63 119–21
Crete Carrier Corporation, 95 114–17
CRH plc, 64 96–99
Crispin Porter + Bogusky, 83 91–94
Cristalerias de Chile S.A., 67 136–38
Crit *see* Groupe Crit S.A.
Crocs, Inc., 80 84–87
Croda International Plc, 45 125–28
Crompton Corporation, 9 153–55; 36
143–50 (upd.) *see also* Chemtura Corp.
Croscill, Inc., 42 95–97
Crosman Corporation, 62 81–83
Cross Company *see* A.T. Cross Co.
Cross Country Healthcare, Inc., 105
124–27
CROSSMARK, 79 117–20
Crowley Maritime Corporation, 6
382–84; 28 77–80 (upd.)
Crowley, Milner & Company, 19
106–08
Crown Books Corporation, 21 148–50
see also Random House, Inc.
Crown Central Petroleum Corporation,
7 101–03
Crown Crafts, Inc., 16 141–43
Crown Equipment Corporation, 15
134–36; 93 172–76 (upd.)

Crown Holdings, Inc., 83 95–102 (upd.)

Crown Media Holdings, Inc., 45 129–32

Crown Vantage Inc., 29 135–37

Crown, Cork & Seal Company, Inc., I 601–03; 13 188–90 (upd.); 32 123–27 (upd.) *see also* Crown Holdings, Inc.

CRSS Inc., 6 142–44; 23 491

Cruise America Inc., 21 151–53

Crum & Forster Holdings Corporation, 104 93–97

CryoLife, Inc., 46 112–14

CryptoLogic Limited, 106 129–32

Crystal Brands, Inc., 9 156–58

CS First Boston Inc., II 402–04

CSA *see* China Southern Airlines Company Ltd.

CSC *see* Computer Sciences Corp.

CSG Systems International, Inc., 75 122–24

CSK Auto Corporation, 38 165–67

CSM N.V., 65 124–27

CSR Limited, III 686–88; 28 81–84 (upd.); 85 73–80 (upd.)

CSS Industries, Inc., 35 128–31

CSX Corporation, V 438–40; 22 164–68 (upd.); 79 121–27 (upd.)

CT&T *see* Carolina Telephone and Telegraph Co.

CTB International Corporation, 43 129–31 (upd.)

CTG, Inc., 11 64–66

Ctrip.com International Ltd., 97 120–24

CTS Corporation, 39 105–08

Cubic Corporation, 19 109–11; 98 69–74 (upd.)

CUC International Inc., 16 144–46 *see also* Cendant Corp.

Cuisinart Corporation, 24 129–32

Cuisine Solutions Inc., 84 69–72

Culbro Corporation, 15 137–39 *see also* General Cigar Holdings, Inc.

CulinArt, Inc., 92 78–81

Cullen/Frost Bankers, Inc., 25 113–16

Culligan Water Technologies, Inc., 12 87–88; 38 168–70 (upd.)

Culp, Inc., 29 138–40

Culver Franchising System, Inc., 58 79–81

Cumberland Farms, Inc., 17 120–22; 84 73–77 (upd.)

Cumberland Packing Corporation, 26 107–09

Cummins Engine Co., Inc., I 146–48; 12 89–92 (upd.); 40 131–35 (upd.)

Cumulus Media Inc., 37 103–05

CUNA Mutual Group, 62 84–87

Cunard Line Ltd., 23 159–62

CUNO Incorporated, 57 85–89

Current, Inc., 37 106–09

Curtice-Burns Foods, Inc., 7 104–06; 21 154–57 (upd.) *see also* Birds Eye Foods, Inc.

Curtiss-Wright Corporation, 10 260–63; 35 132–37 (upd.)

Curves International, Inc., 54 80–82

Cushman & Wakefield, Inc., 86 96–100

Custom Chrome, Inc., 16 147–49; 74 92–95 (upd.)

Cutera, Inc., 84 78–81

Cutter & Buck Inc., 27 112–14

CVPS *see* Central Vermont Public Service Corp.

CVRD *see* Companhia Vale do Rio Doce Ltd.

CVS Corporation, 45 133–38 (upd.)

CWM *see* Chemical Waste Management, Inc.

Cyan Worlds Inc., 101 148–51

Cybermedia, Inc., 25 117–19

Cyberonics, Inc., 79 128–31

Cybex International, Inc., 49 106–09

Cydsa *see* Grupo Cydsa, S.A. de C.V.

Cygne Designs, Inc., 25 120–23

Cygnus Business Media, Inc., 56 73–77

Cymer, Inc., 77 125–28

Cypress Semiconductor Corporation, 20 174–76; 48 125–29 (upd.)

Cyprus Airways Public Limited, 81 103–06

Cyprus Amax Minerals Company, 21 158–61

Cyprus Minerals Company, 7 107–09

Cyrk Inc., 19 112–14

Cystic Fibrosis Foundation, 93 177–80

Cytec Industries Inc., 27 115–17

Cytyc Corporation, 69 112–14

Czarnikow-Rionda Company, Inc., 32 128–30

D

D&B *see* Dun & Bradstreet Corp.

D&H Distributing Co., 95 118–21

D&K Wholesale Drug, Inc., 14 146–48

D-Link Corporation, 83 103–106

D.A. Davidson & Company, 106 133–37

D. Carnegie & Co. AB, 98 79–83

D.F. Stauffer Biscuit Company, 82 82–85

D.G. Yuengling & Son, Inc., 38 171–73

D.R. Horton, Inc., 58 82–84

Dachser GmbH & Co. KG, 88 57–61

D'Addario & Company, Inc. *see* J. D'Addario & Company, Inc.

Dade Behring Holdings Inc., 71 120–22

Daesang Corporation, 84 82–85

Daewoo Group, III 457–59; 18 123–27 (upd.); 57 90–94 (upd.)

Daffy's Inc., 26 110–12

D'Agostino Supermarkets Inc., 19 115–17

DAH *see* DeCrane Aircraft Holdings Inc.

Dai-Ichi Kangyo Bank Ltd., II 273–75

Dai Nippon *see also* listings under Dainippon.

Dai Nippon Printing Co., Ltd., IV 598–600; 57 95–99 (upd.)

Daido Steel Co., Ltd., IV 62–63

The Daiei, Inc., V 39–40; 17 123–25 (upd.); 41 113–16 (upd.)

Daihatsu Motor Company, Ltd., 7 110–12; 21 162–64 (upd.)

Daiichikosho Company Ltd., 86 101–04

Daikin Industries, Ltd., III 460–61

Daiko Advertising Inc., 79 132–35

Daily Journal Corporation, 101 152–55

Daily Mail and General Trust plc, 19 118–20

The Daimaru, Inc., V 41–42; 42 98–100 (upd.)

Daimler-Benz Aerospace AG, 16 150–52

Daimler-Benz AG, I 149–51; 15 140–44 (upd.)

DaimlerChrysler AG, 34 128–37 (upd.); 64 100–07 (upd.)

Dain Rauscher Corporation, 35 138–41 (upd.)

Daio Paper Corporation, IV 266–67; 84 86–89 (upd.)

Dairy Crest Group plc, 32 131–33

Dairy Farm International Holdings Ltd., 97 125–28

Dairy Farmers of America, Inc., 94 143–46

Dairy Mart Convenience Stores, Inc., 7 113–15; 25 124–27 (upd.) *see also* Alimentation Couche-Tard Inc.

Dairy Queen *see* International Dairy Queen, Inc.

Dairyland Healthcare Solutions, 73 99–101

Daishowa Paper Manufacturing Co., Ltd., IV 268–70; 57 100–03 (upd.)

Daisy Outdoor Products Inc., 58 85–88

Daisytek International Corporation, 18 128–30

Daiwa Bank, Ltd., II 276–77; 39 109–11 (upd.)

Daiwa Securities Company, Limited, II 405–06

Daiwa Securities Group Inc., 55 115–18 (upd.)

Daktronics, Inc., 32 134–37

Dal-Tile International Inc., 22 169–71

Dale and Thomas Popcorn LLC, 100 131–34

Dale Carnegie & Associates Inc., 28 85–87; 78 78–82 (upd.)

Dalgety PLC, II 499–500 *see also* PIC International Group PLC

Dalhoff Larsen & Horneman A/S, 96 95–99

Dalian Shide Group, 91 136–39

Dalkia Holding, 66 68–70

Dallah Albaraka Group, 72 83–86

Dallas Cowboys Football Club, Ltd., 33 122–25

Dallas Semiconductor Corporation, 13 191–93; 31 143–46 (upd.)

Dalli-Werke GmbH & Co. KG, 86 105–10

Dallis Coffee, Inc., 86 111–14

Damark International, Inc., 18 131–34 *see also* Provell Inc.

Damartex S.A., 98 84–87

Dames & Moore, Inc., 25 128–31 *see also* URS Corp.

Dan River Inc., 35 142–46; 86 115–20 (upd.)

Dana Holding Corporation, I 152–53; 10 264–66 (upd.); 99 127–134 (upd.)

Danaher Corporation, 7 116–17; 77 129–33 (upd.)

Danaos Corporation, 91 140–43

Daniel Measurement and Control, Inc., 16 153–55; 74 96–99 (upd.)

Daniel Thwaites Plc, 95 122–25

Danisco A/S, 44 134–37

Dannon Company, Inc., 14 149–51; 106 138–42 (upd.)

Danone Group *see* Groupe Danone.

Danske Bank Aktieselskab, 50 148–51

Danskin, Inc., 12 93–95; 62 88–92 (upd.)

Danzas Group, V 441–43; 40 136–39 (upd.)

D'Arcy Masius Benton & Bowles, Inc., 6 20–22; 32 138–43 (upd.)

Darden Restaurants, Inc., 16 156–58; 44 138–42 (upd.)

Dare Foods Limited, 103 135–38

Darigold, Inc., 9 159–61

Darling International Inc., 85 81–84

Dart Group PLC, 16 159–62; 77 134–37 (upd.)

Darty S.A., 27 118–20

DASA *see* Daimler-Benz Aerospace AG.

Dassault-Breguet *see* Avions Marcel Dassault-Breguet Aviation.

Dassault Systèmes S.A., 25 132–34 *see also* Groupe Dassault Aviation SA.

Data Broadcasting Corporation, 31 147–50

Data General Corporation, 8 137–40 *see also* EMC Corp.

Datapoint Corporation, 11 67–70

Datascope Corporation, 39 112–14

Datek Online Holdings Corp., 32 144–46

Dauphin Deposit Corporation, 14 152–54

Dave & Buster's, Inc., 33 126–29; 104 98–103 (upd.)

The Davey Tree Expert Company, 11 71–73

The David and Lucile Packard Foundation, 41 117–19

The David J. Joseph Company, 14 155–56; 76 128–30 (upd.)

David Jones Ltd., 60 100–02

Davide Campari-Milano S.p.A., 57 104–06

David's Bridal, Inc., 33 130–32

Davis Polk & Wardwell, 36 151–54

Davis Service Group PLC, 45 139–41

DaVita Inc., 73 102–05

DAW Technologies, Inc., 25 135–37

Dawn Food Products, Inc., 17 126–28

Dawson Holdings PLC, 43 132–34

Day & Zimmermann Inc., 9 162–64; 31 151–55 (upd.)

Day International, Inc., 84 90–93

Day Runner, Inc., 14 157–58; 41 120–23 (upd.)

Dayton Hudson Corporation, V 43–44; 18 135–37 (upd.) *see also* Target Corp.

DB *see* Deutsche Bundesbahn.

dba Luftfahrtgesellschaft mbH, 76 131–33

DC Comics Inc., 25 138–41; 98 88–94 (upd.)

DC Shoes, Inc., 60 103–05

DCN S.A., 75 125–27

DDB Worldwide Communications, 14 159–61 *see also* Omnicom Group Inc.

DDi Corp., 7 118–20; 97 129–32 (upd.)

De Agostini Editore S.p.A., 103 139–43

De Beers Consolidated Mines Limited / De Beers Centenary AG, IV 64–68; 7 121–26 (upd.); 28 88–94 (upd.)

De Dietrich & Cie., 31 156–59

De La Rue plc, 10 267–69; 34 138–43 (upd.); 46 251

De Rigo S.p.A., 104 104–07

Dean & DeLuca, Inc., 36 155–57

Dean Foods Company, 7 127–29; 21 165–68 (upd.); 73 106–15 (upd.)

Dean Witter, Discover & Co., 12 96–98 *see also* Morgan Stanley Dean Witter & Co.

Dearborn Mid-West Conveyor Company, 56 78–80

Death Row Records, 27 121–23 *see also* Tha Row Records.

Deb Shops, Inc., 16 163–65; 76 134–37 (upd.)

Debeka Krankenversicherungsverein auf Gegenseitigkeit, 72 87–90

Debenhams plc, 28 95–97; 101 156–60 (upd.)

Debevoise & Plimpton, 39 115–17

DEC *see* Digital Equipment Corp.

Deceuninck N.V., 84 94–97

Dechert, 43 135–38

Deckers Outdoor Corporation, 22 172–74; 98 95–98 (upd.)

Decora Industries, Inc., 31 160–62

Decorator Industries Inc., 68 101–04

DeCrane Aircraft Holdings Inc., 36 158–60

DeepTech International Inc., 21 169–71

Deere & Company, III 462–64; 21 172–76 (upd.); 42 101–06 (upd.)

Defiance, Inc., 22 175–78

Degussa-Hüls AG, IV 69–72; 32 147–53 (upd.)

DeKalb Genetics Corporation, 17 129–31 *see also* Monsanto Co.

Del Laboratories, Inc., 28 98–100

Del Monte Foods Company, 7 130–32; 23 163–66 (upd.); 103 144–51 (upd.)

Del Taco, Inc., 58 89–92

Del Webb Corporation, 14 162–64 *see also* Pulte Homes, Inc.

Delachaux S.A., 76 138–40

Delaware North Companies Inc., 7 133–36; 96 100–05 (upd.)

Delco Electronics Corporation *see* GM Hughes Electronics Corp.

Delhaize Group, 44 143–46; 103 152–57 (upd.)

Deli Universal NV, 66 71–74

dELiA*s Inc., 29 141–44

Delicato Vineyards, Inc., 50 152–55

Dell Computer Corporation, 9 165–66; 31 163–66 (upd.); 63 122–26 (upd.)

Deloitte Touche Tohmatsu International, 9 167–69; 29 145–48 (upd.)

De'Longhi S.p.A., 66 75–77

DeLorme Publishing Company, Inc., 53 121–23

Delphax Technologies Inc., 94 147–50

Delphi Automotive Systems Corporation, 45 142–44

Delta Air Lines, Inc., I 99–100; 6 81–83 (upd.); 39 118–21 (upd.); 92 82–87 (upd.)

Delta and Pine Land Company, 33 133–37; 59 148–50

Delta Woodside Industries, Inc., 8 141–43; 30 159–61 (upd.)

Deltec, Inc., 56 81–83

Deltic Timber Corporation, 46 115–17

Deluxe Corporation, 7 137–39; 22 179–82 (upd.); 73 116–20 (upd.)

Deluxe Entertainment Services Group, Inc., 100 135–39

DEMCO, Inc., 60 106–09

DeMoulas / Market Basket Inc., 23 167–69

Den Norske Stats Oljeselskap AS, IV 405–07 *see also* Statoil ASA.

DenAmerica Corporation, 29 149–51

Denbury Resources, Inc., 67 139–41

Denby Group plc, 44 147–50

Dendrite International, Inc., 70 70–73

Denison International plc, 46 118–20

Denner AG, 88 62–65

Dennis Publishing Ltd., 62 93–95

Dennison Manufacturing Company *see* Avery Dennison Corp.

Denny's Corporation, 105 128–34 (upd.)

DENSO Corporation, 46 121–26 (upd.)

Dentsply International Inc., 10 270–72

Dentsu Inc., I 9–11; 16 166–69 (upd.); 40 140–44 (upd.)

Denver Nuggets, 51 94–97

DEP Corporation, 20 177–80

Department 56, Inc., 14 165–67; 34 144–47 (upd.)

DEPFA BANK PLC, 69 115–17

Deposit Guaranty Corporation, 17 132–35

DePuy, Inc., 30 162–65; 37 110–13 (upd.)

Derco Holding Ltd., 98 99–102

Desarrolladora Homex, S.A. de C.V., 87 127–130

Desc, S.A. de C.V., 23 170–72

Deschutes Brewery, Inc., 57 107–09

Deseret Management Corporation, 101 161–65

Designer Holdings Ltd., 20 181–84

Desnoes and Geddes Limited, 79 136–39

Destec Energy, Inc., 12 99–101

Detroit Diesel Corporation, 10 273–75; 74 100–03 (upd.)

The Detroit Edison Company, V 592–95 *see also* DTE Energy Co.

The Detroit Lions, Inc., 55 119–21
Detroit Media Partnership L.P., 102 102–06
The Detroit Pistons Basketball Company, 41 124–27
Detroit Red Wings, 74 104–06
Detroit Tigers Baseball Club, Inc., 46 127–30
Deutsch, Inc., 42 107–10
Deutsche Babcock AG, III 465–66
Deutsche Bahn AG, 46 131–35 (upd.)
Deutsche Bank AG, II 278–80; 40 145–51 (upd.)
Deutsche Börse AG, 59 151–55
Deutsche BP Aktiengesellschaft, 7 140–43
Deutsche Bundepost Telekom, V 287–90 *see also* Deutsche Telekom AG
Deutsche Bundesbahn, V 444–47
Deutsche Fussball Bund e.V., 98 103–07
Deutsche Lufthansa AG, I 110–11; 26 113–16 (upd.); 68 105–09 (upd.)
Deutsche Messe AG, 104 108–12
Deutsche Post AG, 29 152–58
Deutsche Steinzeug Cremer & Breuer Aktiengesellschaft, 91 144–48
Deutsche Telekom AG, 48 130–35 (upd.)
Deutscher Sparkassen- und Giroverband (DSGV), 84 98–102
Deutz AG, 39 122–26
Deveaux S.A., 41 128–30
Developers Diversified Realty Corporation, 69 118–20
DeVito/Verdi, 85 85–88
Devon Energy Corporation, 61 73–75
Devoteam S.A., 94 151–54
Devro plc, 55 122–24
DeVry Inc., 29 159–61; 82 86–90 (upd.)
Devtek Corporation *see* Héroux-Devtek Inc.
Dewberry, 78 83–86
Dewey Ballantine LLP, 48 136–39
Dex Media, Inc., 65 128–30
Dexia NV/SA, 42 111–13; 88 66–69 (upd.)
The Dexter Corporation, I 320–22; 12 102–04 (upd.) *see also* Invitrogen Corp.
DFS Group Ltd., 66 78–80
DH Technology, Inc., 18 138–40
DHB Industries Inc., 85 89–92
DHL Worldwide Network S.A./N.V., 6 385–87; 24 133–36 (upd.); 69 121–25 (upd.)
Di Giorgio Corp., 12 105–07
Diadora SpA, 86 121–24
Diageo plc, 24 137–41 (upd.); 79 140–48 (upd.)
Diagnostic Products Corporation, 73 121–24
Diagnostic Ventures Inc. *see* DVI, Inc.
Dial-A-Mattress Operating Corporation, 46 136–39
The Dial Corporation, 8 144–46; 23 173–75 (upd.)
Dialogic Corporation, 18 141–43

Diamond of California, 64 108–11 (upd.)
Diamond Shamrock Corporation , IV 408–11 *see also* Ultramar Diamond Shamrock Corp.
DiamondCluster International, Inc., 51 98–101
Diana Shipping Inc., 95 126–29
Diavik Diamond Mines Inc., 85 93–96
Dibrell Brothers, Incorporated, 12 108–10
dick clark productions, inc., 16 170–73
Dick Corporation, 64 112–14
Dick's Sporting Goods, Inc., 59 156–59
Dickten Masch Plastics LLC, 90 158–61
Dictaphone Healthcare Solutions, 78 87–92
Diebold, Incorporated, 7 144–46; 22 183–87 (upd.)
Diedrich Coffee, Inc., 40 152–54
Diehl Stiftung & Co. KG, 79 149–53
Dierbergs Markets Inc., 63 127–29
Diesel SpA, 40 155–57
D'Ieteren S.A./NV, 98 75–78
Dietrich & Cie *see* De Dietrich & Cie.
Dietz and Watson, Inc., 92 88–92
Digex, Inc., 46 140–43
Digi International Inc., 9 170–72
Digital Angel Corporation, 106 143–48
Digital Equipment Corporation, III 132–35; 6 233–36 (upd.) *see also* Compaq Computer Corp.
Digital River, Inc., 50 156–59
Digitas Inc., 81 107–10
Dillard Paper Company, 11 74–76 *see also* International Paper Co.
Dillard's Inc., V 45–47; 16 174–77 (upd.); 68 110–14 (upd.)
Dillingham Construction Corporation, 44 151–54 (upd.)
Dillingham Corp., I 565–66
Dillon Companies Inc., 12 111–13
Dime Savings Bank of New York, F.S.B., 9 173–74 *see also* Washington Mutual, Inc.
Dimension Data Holdings PLC, 69 126–28
DIMON Inc., 27 124–27
Dina *see* Consorcio G Grupo Dina, S.A. de C.V.
Diodes Incorporated, 81 111–14
Dionex Corporation, 46 144–46
Dior *see* Christian Dior S.A.
Dippin' Dots, Inc., 56 84–86
Direct Focus, Inc., 47 93–95
Direct Wines Ltd., 84 103–106
Directed Electronics, Inc., 87 131–135
Directorate General of Telecommunications, 7 147–49 *see also* Chunghwa Telecom Co., Ltd.
DIRECTV, Inc., 38 174–77; 75 128–32 (upd.)
Dirk Rossmann GmbH, 94 155–59
Discount Auto Parts, Inc., 18 144–46
Discount Drug Mart, Inc., 14 172–73
Discount Tire Company Inc., 84 107–110

Discovery Communications, Inc., 42 114–17
Discovery Partners International, Inc., 58 93–95
Discreet Logic Inc., 20 185–87 *see also* Autodesk, Inc.
Disney *see* The Walt Disney Co.
Disney/ABC Television Group, 106 149–54 (upd.)
Dispatch Printing Company, 100 140–44
Distillers Co. plc, I 239–41 *see also* Diageo PLC.
Distribución y Servicio D&S S.A., 71 123–26
Distrigaz S.A., 82 91–94
ditech.com, 93 181–84
The Dixie Group, Inc., 20 188–90; 80 88–92 (upd.)
Dixon Industries, Inc., 26 117–19
Dixon Ticonderoga Company, 12 114–16; 69 129–33 (upd.)
Dixons Group plc, V 48–50; 19 121–24 (upd.); 49 110–13 (upd.)
Djarum PT, 62 96–98
DKB *see* Dai-Ichi Kangyo Bank Ltd.
DKNY *see* Donna Karan International Inc.
DLA Piper, 106 155–58
DLJ *see* Donaldson, Lufkin & Jenrette.
DMB&B *see* D'Arcy Masius Benton & Bowles.
DMGT *see* Daily Mail and General Trust.
DMI Furniture, Inc., 46 147–50
Do it Best Corporation, 30 166–70; 104 113–19 (upd.)
Dobrogea Grup S.A., 82 95–98
Dobson Communications Corporation, 63 130–32
Doctor's Associates Inc., 67 142–45 (upd.)
The Doctors' Company, 55 125–28
Doctors Without Borders *see* Médecins Sans Frontières.
Documentum, Inc., 46 151–53
Dofasco Inc., IV 73–74; 24 142–44 (upd.)
Dogan Sirketler Grubu Holding A.S., 83 107–110
Dogi International Fabrics S.A., 52 99–102
Dolan Media Company, 94 160–63
Dolby Laboratories Inc., 20 191–93
Dolce & Gabbana SpA, 62 99–101
Dole Food Company, Inc., 9 175–76; 31 167–70 (upd.); 68 115–19 (upd.)
Dollar General Corporation, 106 159–62
Dollar Thrifty Automotive Group, Inc., 25 142–45
Dollar Tree Stores, Inc., 23 176–78; 62 102–05 (upd.)
Dollywood Corporation *see* Herschend Family Entertainment Corp.
Doman Industries Limited, 59 160–62
Dominick & Dominick LLC, 92 93–96
Dominick's Finer Foods, Inc., 56 87–89
Dominion Homes, Inc., 19 125–27

Dominion Resources, Inc., V 596–99; 54 83–87 (upd.)
Dominion Textile Inc., 12 117–19
Domino Printing Sciences PLC, 87 136–139
Domino Sugar Corporation, 26 120–22
Domino's, Inc., 7 150–53; 21 177–81 (upd.); 63 133–39 (upd.)
Domtar Corporation, IV 271–73; 89 185–91 (upd.)
Don Massey Cadillac, Inc., 37 114–16
Donaldson Company, Inc., 16 178–81; 49 114–18 (upd.)
Donaldson, Lufkin & Jenrette, Inc., 22 188–91
Donatos Pizzeria Corporation, 58 96–98
Dongfeng Motor Corporation, 105 135–40
Donna Karan International Inc., 15 145–47; 56 90–93 (upd.)
Donnelly Corporation, 12 120–22; 35 147–50 (upd.)
Donnkenny, Inc., 17 136–38
Donruss Playoff L.P., 66 81–84
Dooney & Bourke Inc., 84 111–114
Dorel Industries Inc., 59 163–65
Dorian Drake International Inc., 96 106–09
Dorling Kindersley Holdings plc, 20 194–96 *see also* Pearson plc.
Dorsey & Whitney LLP, 47 96–99
Doskocil Companies, Inc., 12 123–25 *see also* Foodbrands America, Inc.
Dot Foods, Inc., 69 134–37
Dot Hill Systems Corp., 93 185–88
Double-Cola Co.-USA, 70 74–76
DoubleClick Inc., 46 154–57
Doubletree Corporation, 21 182–85
Douglas & Lomason Company, 16 182–85
Douglas Emmett, Inc., 105 141–44
Doux S.A., 80 93–96
Dover Corporation, III 467–69; 28 101–05 (upd.); 90 162–67 (upd.)
Dover Downs Entertainment, Inc., 43 139–41
Dover Publications Inc., 34 148–50
The Dow Chemical Company, I 323–25; 8 147–50 (upd.); 50 160–64 (upd.)
Dow Jones & Company, Inc., IV 601–03; 19 128–31 (upd.); 47 100–04 (upd.)
Dow Jones Telerate, Inc., 10 276–78 *see also* Reuters Group PLC.
DP World, 81 115–18
DPL Inc., 6 480–82; 96 110–15 (upd.)
DQE, 6 483–85; 38 40
Dr. August Oetker KG, 51 102–06
Dr Pepper/Seven Up, Inc., 9 177–78; 32 154–57 (upd.)
Dr. Reddy's Laboratories Ltd., 59 166–69
Drackett Professional Products, 12 126–28 *see also* S.C. Johnson & Son, Inc.
Draftfcb, 94 164–68

Dragados y Construcciones *see* Grupo Dragados SA.
Drägerwerk AG, 83 111–114
Drake Beam Morin, Inc., 44 155–57
Draper and Kramer Inc., 96 116–19
Draper Fisher Jurvetson, 91 149–52
Dräxlmaier Group, 90 168–72
Dreams Inc., 97 133–3
DreamWorks Animation SKG, Inc., 106 163–67
DreamWorks SKG, 43 142–46 *see also* DW II Distribution Co. LLC.
The Drees Company, Inc., 41 131–33
Dresdner Bank A.G., II 281–83; 57 110–14 (upd.)
Dresdner Kleinwort Wasserstein, 60 110–13 (upd.)
The Dress Barn, Inc., 24 145–46
Dresser Industries, Inc., III 470–73; 55 129–31 (upd.)
Drew Industries Inc., 28 106–08
Drexel Burnham Lambert Incorporated, II 407–09 *see also* New Street Capital Inc.
Drexel Heritage Furnishings Inc., 12 129–31
Dreyer's Grand Ice Cream, Inc., 17 139–41 *see also* Nestlé S.A.
The Dreyfus Corporation, 70 77–80
DRI *see* Dominion Resources, Inc.
Drie Mollen Holding B.V., 99 135–138
Dril-Quip, Inc., 81 119–21
Drinker, Biddle and Reath L.L.P., 92 97–101
Drinks Americas Holdings, LTD., 105 145–48
DriveTime Automotive Group Inc., 68 120–24 (upd.)
DRS Technologies, Inc., 58 99–101
Drs. Foster & Smith, Inc., 62 106–08
Drug Emporium, Inc., 12 132–34 *see also* Big A Drug Stores Inc.
Drypers Corporation, 18 147–49
DryShips Inc., 95 130–33
DS Smith Plc, 61 76–79
DSC Communications Corporation, 12 135–37 *see also* Alcatel S.A.
DSGV *see* Deutscher Sparkassen- und Giroverband (DSGV).
DSM N.V., I 326–27; 56 94–96 (upd.)
DSW Inc., 73 125–27
DTAG *see* Dollar Thrifty Automotive Group, Inc.
DTE Energy Company, 20 197–201 (upd.); 94 169–76 (upd.)
DTS, Inc., 80 97–101
Du Pareil au Même, 43 147–49
Du Pont *see* E.I. du Pont de Nemours & Co.
Dualstar Entertainment Group LLC, 76 141–43
Duane Reade Holding Corp., 21 186–88
Dubreuil *see* Groupe Dubreuil S.A.
Ducati Motor Holding SpA, 30 171–73; 86 125–29 (upd.)
Duck Head Apparel Company, Inc., 42 118–21

Ducks Unlimited, Inc., 87 140–143
Duckwall-ALCO Stores, Inc., 24 147–49; 105 149–54 (upd.)
Ducommun Incorporated, 30 174–76
Duferco Group, 94 177–80
Duke Energy Corporation, V 600–02; 27 128–31 (upd.)
Duke Realty Corporation, 57 115–17
The Dun & Bradstreet Corporation, IV 604–05; 19 132–34 (upd.); 61 80–84 (upd.)
Dun & Bradstreet Software Services Inc., 11 77–79
Dunavant Enterprises, Inc., 54 88–90
Duncan Aviation, Inc., 94 181–84
Duncan Toys Company, 55 132–35
Dunham's Athleisure Corporation, 98 108–11
Dunn-Edwards Corporation, 56 97–99
Dunn Industries, Inc. *see* JE Dunn Construction Group, Inc.
Dunnes Stores Ltd., 58 102–04
Duplex Products, Inc., 17 142–44
Dupont *see* E.I. du Pont de Nemours & Co.
Duracell International Inc., 9 179–81; 71 127–31 (upd.)
Durametallic, 21 189–91 *see also* Duriron Company Inc.
Duriron Company Inc., 17 145–47 *see also* Flowserve Corp.
Dürkopp Adler AG, 65 131–34
Duron Inc., 72 91–93 *see also* The Sherwin-Williams Co.
Dürr AG, 44 158–61
Duty Free International, Inc., 11 80–82 *see also* World Duty Free Americas, Inc.
Duvernay Oil Corp., 83 115–118
DVI, Inc., 51 107–09
DW II Distribution Co. LLC, 106 168–73 (upd.)
DXP Enterprises, Inc., 101 166–69
Dyax Corp., 89 192–95
Dyckerhoff AG, 35 151–54
Dycom Industries, Inc., 57 118–20
Dyersburg Corporation, 21 192–95
Dylan's Candy Bar, LLC, 99 139–141
Dylex Limited, 29 162–65
Dynaction S.A., 67 146–48
Dynamic Materials Corporation, 81 122–25
Dynatec Corporation, 87 144–147
Dynatech Corporation, 13 194–96
Dynatronics Corporation, 99 142–146
DynCorp, 45 145–47
Dynea, 68 125–27
Dyneff S.A., 98 112–15
Dynegy Inc., 49 119–22 (upd.)
Dyson Group PLC, 71 132–34

E

E! Entertainment Television Inc., 17 148–50
E-Systems, Inc., 9 182–85
E*Trade Financial Corporation, 20 206–08; 60 114–17 (upd.)
E-Z-EM Inc., 89 196–99
E-Z Serve Corporation, 17 169–71

E. & J. Gallo Winery, I 242–44; 7 154–56 (upd.); 28 109–11 (upd.); 104 120–24 (upd.)

E H Booth & Company Ltd., 90 173–76

E.I. du Pont de Nemours and Company, I 328–30; 8 151–54 (upd.); 26 123–27 (upd.); 73 128–33 (upd.)

E.On AG, 50 165–73 (upd.)

E.W. Howell Co., Inc., 72 94–96 *see also* Obayashi Corporation

The E.W. Scripps Company, IV 606–09; 7 157–59 (upd.); 28 122–26 (upd.); 66 85–89 (upd.)

E.piphany, Inc., 49 123–25

EADS N.V. *see* European Aeronautic Defence and Space Company EADS N.V.

EADS SOCATA, 54 91–94

Eagle Hardware & Garden, Inc., 16 186–89 *see also* Lowe's Companies, Inc.

Eagle-Picher Industries, Inc., 8 155–58; 23 179–83 (upd.) *see also* PerkinElmer Inc.

Eagle-Tribune Publishing Co., 91 153–57

Earl Scheib, Inc., 32 158–61

Earle M. Jorgensen Company, 82 99–102

The Earthgrains Company, 36 161–65

EarthLink, Inc., 36 166–68

East Japan Railway Company, V 448–50; 66 90–94 (upd.)

East Penn Manufacturing Co., Inc., 79 154–57

Easter Seals, Inc., 58 105–07

Eastern Airlines, I 101–03

The Eastern Company, 48 140–43

Eastern Enterprises, 6 486–88

EastGroup Properties, Inc., 67 149–51

Eastland Shoe Corporation, 82 103–106

Eastman Chemical Company, 14 174–75; 38 178–81 (upd.)

Eastman Kodak Company, III 474–77; 7 160–64 (upd.); 36 169–76 (upd.); 91 158–69 (upd.)

Easton Sports, Inc., 66 95–97

easyhome Ltd., 105 155 58

easyJet Airline Company Limited, 39 127–29; 52 330

Eateries, Inc., 33 138–40

Eaton Corporation, I 154–55; 10 279–80 (upd.); 67 152–56 (upd.)

Eaton Vance Corporation, 18 150–53

Ebara Corporation, 83 119–122

eBay Inc., 32 162–65; 67 157–61 (upd.)

EBSCO Industries, Inc., 17 151–53; 40 158–61 (upd.)

EBX Investimentos, 104 125–29

ECC Group plc, III 689–91 *see also* English China Clays plc.

ECC International Corp., 42 122–24

Ecco Sko A/S, 62 109–11

Echlin Inc., I 156–57; 11 83–85 (upd.) *see also* Dana Corp.

Echo Bay Mines Ltd., IV 75–77; 38 182–85 (upd.)

The Echo Design Group, Inc., 68 128–30

EchoStar Communications Corporation, 35 155–59

ECI Telecom Ltd., 18 154–56

Eckerd Corporation, 9 186–87 *see also* J.C. Penney Company, Inc.

Eckes AG, 56 100–03

Eclipse Aviation Corporation, 87 148–151

Eclipsys Corporation, 104 130–33

Ecolab Inc., I 331–33; 13 197–200 (upd.); 34 151–56 (upd.); 85 97–105 (upd.)

eCollege.com, 85 106–09

Ecology and Environment, Inc., 39 130–33

The Economist Group Ltd., 67 162–65

Ecopetrol *see* Empresa Colombiana de Petróleos.

ECS S.A, 12 138–40

Ed S.A.S., 88 70–73

Edasa *see* Embotelladoras del Atlántico, S.A.

Eddie Bauer Holdings, Inc., 9 188–90; 36 177–81 (upd.); 87 152–159 (upd.)

Edeka Zentrale A.G., II 621–23; 47 105–07 (upd.)

edel music AG, 44 162–65

Edelbrock Corporation, 37 117–19

Edelman, 62 112–15

EDF *see* Electricité de France.

EDGAR Online, Inc., 91 170–73

Edgars Consolidated Stores Ltd., 66 98–100

Edge Petroleum Corporation, 67 166–68

Edipresse S.A., 82 107–110

Edison Brothers Stores, Inc., 9 191–93

Edison International, 56 104–07 (upd.)

Edison Schools Inc., 37 120–23

Éditions Gallimard, 72 97–101

Editis S.A., 78 93–97

Editora Abril S.A *see* Abril S.A.

Editorial Television, S.A. de C.V., 57 121–23

EdK *see* Edeka Zentrale A.G.

Edmark Corporation, 14 176–78; 41 134–37 (upd.)

EDO Corporation, 46 158–61

EDP Group *see* Electricidade de Portugal, S.A.

The Edrington Group Ltd., 88 74–78

EDS *see* Electronic Data Systems Corp.

Educate Inc., 86 130–35 (upd.)

Education Management Corporation, 35 160–63

Educational Broadcasting Corporation, 48 144–47

Educational Testing Service, 12 141–43; 62 116–20 (upd.)

Edw. C. Levy Co., 42 125–27

Edward D. Jones & Company L.P., 30 177–79; 66 101–04 (upd.)

Edward Hines Lumber Company, 68 131–33

Edward J. DeBartolo Corporation, 8 159–62

Edwards and Kelcey, 70 81–83

Edwards Brothers, Inc., 92 102–06

Edwards Theatres Circuit, Inc., 31 171–73

EFJ, Inc., 81 126–29

EG&G Incorporated, 8 163–65; 29 166–69 (upd.)

Egan Companies, Inc., 94 185–88

EGAT *see* Electricity Generating Authority of Thailand (EGAT).

Egghead.com, Inc., 9 194–95; 31 174–77 (upd.)

Egis Gyogyszergyar Nyrt, 104 134–37

EGL, Inc., 59 170–73

Egmont Group, 93 189–93

EgyptAir, 6 84–86; 27 132–35 (upd.)

Egyptian General Petroleum Corporation, IV 412–14; 51 110–14 (upd.)

eHarmony.com Inc., 71 135–38

Eiffage, 27 136–38

8x8, Inc., 94 189–92

800-JR Cigar, Inc., 27 139–41

84 Lumber Company, 9 196–97; 39 134–36 (upd.)

EIH Ltd., 103 158–62

Eileen Fisher Inc., 61 85–87

Einstein/Noah Bagel Corporation, 29 170–73

eircom plc, 31 178–81 (upd.)

Eisai Co., Ltd., 101 170–73

Eka Chemicals AB, 92 107–10

Ekco Group, Inc., 16 190–93

El Al Israel Airlines Ltd., 23 184–87

El Camino Resources International, Inc., 11 86–88

El Chico Restaurants, Inc., 19 135–38; 36 162–63

El Corte Inglés Group, 26 128–31 (upd.)

El Corte Inglés, S.A., V 51–53; 26 128–31 (upd.)

El Paso Corporation, 66 105–08 (upd.)

El Paso Electric Company, 21 196–98

El Paso Natural Gas Company, 12 144–46 *see also* El Paso Corp.

El Pollo Loco, Inc., 69 138–40

El Puerto de Liverpool, S.A.B. de C.V., 97 137–40

Elamex, S.A. de C.V., 51 115–17

Elan Corporation PLC, 63 140–43

Elano Corporation, 14 179–81

The Elder-Beerman Stores Corp., 10 281–83; 63 144–48 (upd.)

Elders IXL Ltd., I 437–39

Electrabel N.V., 67 169–71

Electric Boat Corporation, 86 136–39

Electric Lightwave, Inc., 37 124–27

Electricidade de Portugal, S.A., 47 108–11

Electricité de France, V 603–05; 41 138–41 (upd.)

Electricity Generating Authority of Thailand (EGAT), 56 108–10

Electro Rent Corporation, 58 108–10

Electrocomponents PLC, 50 174–77

Electrolux AB, 22 24–28 (upd.); 53 124–29 (upd.)

Electrolux Group, III 478–81
Electromagnetic Sciences Inc., 21 199–201
Electronic Arts Inc., 10 284–86; 85 110–15 (upd.)
Electronic Data Systems Corporation, III 136–38; 28 112–16 (upd.) *see also* Perot Systems Corp.
Electronics Boutique Holdings Corporation, 72 102–05
Electronics for Imaging, Inc., 15 148–50; 43 150–53 (upd.)
Elektra *see* Grupo Elektra, S.A. de C.V.
Elektra Entertainment Group, 64 115–18
Elektrowatt AG, 6 489–91 *see also* Siemens AG.
Element K Corporation, 94 193–96
Elementis plc, 40 162–68 (upd.)
Elephant Pharmacy, Inc., 83 123–126
Elf Aquitaine SA, 21 202–06 (upd.) *see also* Société Nationale Elf Aquitaine.
Eli Lilly and Company, I 645–47; 11 89–91 (upd.); 47 112–16 (upd.)
Elior SA, 49 126–28
Elite World S.A., 94 197–201
Elizabeth Arden, Inc., 8 166–68; 40 169–72 (upd.)
Eljer Industries, Inc., 24 150–52
Elkay Manufacturing Company, 73 134–36
ElkCorp, 52 103–05
Ellen Tracy, Inc., 55 136–38
Ellerbe Becket, 41 142–45
Ellett Brothers, Inc., 17 154–56
Elliott-Lewis Corporation, 100 145–48
Elma Electronic AG, 83 127–130
Elmer Candy Corporation, 88 79–82
Elmer's Restaurants, Inc., 42 128–30
Elpida Memory, Inc., 83 131–134
ElringKlinger AG, 100 149–55
Elscint Ltd., 20 202–05
Elsevier NV, IV 610–11 *see also* Reed Elsevier.
Elsinore Corporation, 48 148–51
Elvis Presley Enterprises, Inc., 61 88–90
EMAK Worldwide, Inc., 105 159–62
EMAP plc, 35 164–66
EMBARQ Corporation, 83 135–138
Embers America Restaurants, 30 180–82
Embotelladora Andina S.A., 71 139–41
Embraer *see* Empresa Brasileira de Aeronáutica S.A.
Embrex, Inc., 72 106–08
EMC Corporation, 12 147–49; 46 162–66 (upd.)
EMCO Enterprises, Inc., 102 107–10
EMCOR Group Inc., 60 118–21
EMCORE Corporation, 97 141–44
Emerson, 46 167–71 (upd.)
Emerson Electric Co., II 18–21
Emerson Radio Corp., 30 183–86
Emery Worldwide Airlines, Inc., 6 388–91; 25 146–50 (upd.)
Emge Packing Co., Inc., 11 92–93
EMI Group plc, 22 192–95 (upd.); 81 130–37 (upd.)
Emigrant Savings Bank, 59 174–76

The Emirates Group, 39 137–39; 81 138–42 (upd.)
Emmis Communications Corporation, 47 117–21
Empi, Inc., 27 132–35
Empire Blue Cross and Blue Shield, III 245–46 *see also* WellChoice, Inc.
The Empire District Electric Company, 77 138–41
Empire Resorts, Inc., 72 109–12
Empire Resources, Inc., 81 143–46
Employee Solutions, Inc., 18 157–60
Empresa Brasileira de Aeronáutica S.A. (Embraer), 36 182–84
Empresa Colombiana de Petróleos, IV 415–18
Empresas Almacenes Paris S.A., 71 142–44
Empresas CMPC S.A., 70 84–87
Empresas Copec S.A., 69 141–44
Empresas ICA Sociedad Controladora, S.A. de C.V., 41 146–49
Empresas Polar SA, 55 139–41 (upd.)
Empresas Públicas de Medellín S.A.E.S.P., 91 174–77
Enbridge Inc., 43 154–58
ENCAD, Incorporated, 25 151–53 *see also* Eastman Kodak Co.
Encho Company Ltd., 104 138–41
Encompass Services Corporation, 33 141–44
Encore Acquisition Company, 73 137–39
Encore Computer Corporation, 13 201–02; 74 107–10 (upd.)
Encore Wire Corporation, 81 147–50
Encyclopedia Britannica, Inc., 7 165–68; 39 140–44 (upd.)
Endemol Entertainment Holding NV, 46 172–74; 53 154
ENDESA S.A., V 606–08; 46 175–79 (upd.)
Endo Pharmaceuticals Holdings Inc., 71 145–47
Endress+Hauser Holding AG, 102 111–15
Endurance Specialty Holdings Ltd., 85 116–19
Energen Corporation, 21 207–09; 97 145–49 (upd.)
Energis plc, 44 363; 47 122–25
Energizer Holdings, Inc., 32 171–74
Energy Brands Inc., 88 83–86
Energy Conversion Devices, Inc., 75 133–36
Enersis S.A., 73 140–43
EnerSys Inc., 99 147–151
Enesco Corporation, 11 94–96
Engelhard Corporation, IV 78–80; 21 210–14 (upd.); 72 113–18 (upd.)
Engineered Support Systems, Inc., 59 177–80
Engle Homes, Inc., 46 180–82
English China Clays Ltd., 15 151–54 (upd.); 40 173–77 (upd.)
Engraph, Inc., 12 150–51 *see also* Sonoco Products Co.
ENI S.p.A., 69 145–50 (upd.)

ENMAX Corporation, 83 139–142
Ennis, Inc., 21 215–17; 97 150–54 (upd.)
Enodis plc, 68 134–37
EnPro Industries, Inc., 93 194–98
Enquirer/Star Group, Inc., 10 287–88 *see also* American Media, Inc.
Enrich International, Inc., 33 145–48
Enron Corporation, V 609–10; 19 139–41; 46 183–86 (upd.)
ENSCO International Incorporated, 57 124–26
Enserch Corp., V 611–13 *see also* Texas Utilities.
Enskilda S.A. *see* Skandinaviska Enskilda Banken AB.
Enso-Gutzeit Oy, IV 274–77 *see also* Stora Enso Oyj.
Ente Nazionale Idrocarburi, IV 419–22 *see also* ENI S.p.A.
Ente Nazionale per l'Energia Elettrica, V 614–17
Entercom Communications Corporation, 58 111–12
Entergy Corporation, V 618–20; 45 148–51 (upd.)
Enterprise Inns plc, 59 181–83
Enterprise Oil plc, 11 97–99; 50 178–82 (upd.)
Enterprise Rent-A-Car Company, 6 392–93; 69 151–54 (upd.)
Entertainment Distribution Company, 89 200–03
Entravision Communications Corporation, 41 150–52
Entreprise Nationale Sonatrach, IV 423–25 *see also* Sonatrach.
Envirodyne Industries, Inc., 17 157–60
Environmental Industries, Inc., 31 182–85
Environmental Power Corporation, 68 138–40
Environmental Systems Research Institute Inc. (ESRI), 62 121–24
Enzo Biochem, Inc., 41 153–55
EOG Resources, 106 174–77
Eon Labs, Inc., 67 172–74
EP Henry Corporation, 104 142–45
EPAM Systems Inc., 96 120–23
EPCOR Utilities Inc., 81 151–54
Epic Systems Corporation, 62 125–28
EPIQ Systems, Inc., 56 111–13
Equant N.V., 52 106–08
Equifax, Inc., 6 23–25; 28 117–21 (upd.); 90 177–83 (upd.)
Equistar Chemicals, LP, 71 148–50
Equitable Life Assurance Society of the United States, III 247–49 *see also* AXA Equitable Life Insurance Co.
Equitable Resources, Inc., 6 492–94; 54 95–98 (upd.)
Equity Marketing, Inc., 26 136–38
Equity Office Properties Trust, 54 99–102
Equity Residential, 49 129–32
Equus Computer Systems, Inc., 49 133–35
Eram SA, 51 118–20

Eramet, 73 144–47

Ercros S.A., 80 102–05

ERGO Versicherungsgruppe AG, 44 166–69

Ergon, Inc., 95 134–37

Erickson Retirement Communities, 57 127–30

Ericsson *see* Telefonaktiebolaget LM Ericsson.

Eridania Béghin-Say S.A., 36 185–88

Erie Indemnity Company, 35 167–69

ERLY Industries Inc., 17 161–62

Ermenegildo Zegna SpA, 63 149–52

Ernie Ball, Inc., 56 114–16

Ernst & Young, 9 198–200; 29 174–77 (upd.)

Eroski *see* Grupo Eroski

Erste Bank der Osterreichischen Sparkassen AG, 69 155–57

ESCADA AG, 71 151–53

Escalade, Incorporated, 19 142–44

Eschelon Telecom, Inc., 72 119–22

ESCO Technologies Inc., 87 160–163

Eskimo Pie Corporation, 21 218–20

Espírito Santo Financial Group S.A., 79 158–63 (upd.)

ESPN, Inc., 56 117–22

Esporta plc, 35 170–72

Esprit de Corp., 8 169–72; 29 178–82 (upd.)

ESS Technology, Inc., 22 196–98

Essar Group Ltd., 79 164–67

Essef Corporation, 18 161–63 *see also* Pentair, Inc.

Esselte, 64 119–21

Esselte Leitz GmbH & Co. KG, 48 152–55

Esselte Pendaflex Corporation, 11 100–01

Essence Communications, Inc., 24 153–55

Essex Corporation, 85 120–23

Essie Cosmetics, Ltd., 102 116–19

Essilor International, 21 221–23

The Estée Lauder Companies Inc., 9 201–04; 30 187–91 (upd.); 92 199–207 (upd.)

Esterline Technologies Corp., 15 155–57

Estes Express Lines, Inc., 86 140–43

Etablissements Economiques du Casino Guichard, Perrachon et ie, S.C.A., 12 152–54 *see also* Casino Guichard-Perrachon S.A.

Etablissements Franz Colruyt N.V., 68 141–43

Établissements Jacquot and Cie S.A.S., 92 111–14

Etam Developpement SA, 44 170–72

ETBD *see* Europe Through the Back Door.

Eternal Word Television Network, Inc., 57 131–34

Ethan Allen Interiors, Inc., 12 155–57; 39 145–48 (upd.)

Ethicon, Inc., 23 188–90

Ethiopian Airlines, 81 155–58

Ethyl Corp., I 334–36; 10 289–91 (upd.)

Etienne Aigner AG, 52 109–12

Etihad Airways PJSC, 89 204–07

EToys, Inc., 37 128–30

ETS *see* Educational Testing Service.

Euralis *see* Groupe Euralis.

Eurazeo, 80 106–09

The Eureka Company, 12 158–60 *see also* White Consolidated Industries Inc.

Euro Disney S.C.A., 20 209–12; 58 113–16 (upd.)

Euro RSCG Worldwide S.A., 13 203–05

Eurocopter S.A., 80 110–13

Eurofins Scientific S.A., 70 88–90

Euromarket Designs Inc., 31 186–89 (upd.); 99 152–157 (upd.)

Euronet Worldwide, Inc., 83 143–146

Euronext N.V., 37 131–33; 89 208–11 (upd.)

Europcar Groupe S.A., 104 146–51

Europe Through the Back Door Inc., 65 135–38

European Aeronautic Defence and Space Company EADS N.V., 52 113–16 (upd.)

European Investment Bank, 66 109–11

Eurotunnel Group, 13 206–08; 37 134–38 (upd.)

EVA Airways Corporation, 51 121–23

Evans & Sutherland Computer Corporation, 19 145–49; 78 98–103 (upd.)

Evans, Inc., 30 192–94

Everex Systems, Inc., 16 194–96

Evergreen Energy, Inc., 97 155–59

Evergreen International Aviation, Inc., 53 130–33

Evergreen Marine Corporation (Taiwan) Ltd., 13 209–11; 50 183–89 (upd.)

Evergreen Solar, Inc., 101 174–78

Everlast Worldwide Inc., 47 126–29

Evialis S.A., 100 156–59

Evraz Group S.A., 97 160–63

EWTN *see* Eternal Word Television Network, Inc.

Exabyte Corporation, 12 161–63; 40 178–81 (upd.)

Exacompta Clairefontaine S.A., 102 120–23

Exactech, Inc., 101 179–82

Exar Corp., 14 182–84

EXCEL Communications Inc., 18 164–67

Excel Technology, Inc., 65 139–42

Executive Jet, Inc., 36 189–91 *see also* NetJets Inc.

Executone Information Systems, Inc., 13 212–14; 15 195

Exel plc, 51 124–30 (upd.)

Exelon Corporation, 48 156–63 (upd.); 49 65

Exide Electronics Group, Inc., 20 213–15

Exito *see* Almacenes Exito S.A.

Expand SA, 48 164–66

Expedia, Inc., 58 117–21

Expeditors International of Washington Inc., 17 163–65; 78 104–08 (upd.)

Experian Information Solutions Inc., 45 152–55

Exponent, Inc., 95 138–41

Exportadora Bananera Noboa, S.A., 91 178–81

Express Scripts Inc., 17 166–68; 44 173–76 (upd.)

Extended Stay America, Inc., 41 156–58

Extendicare Health Services, Inc., 6 181–83

Extreme Pizza *see* OOC Inc.

EXX Inc., 65 143–45

Exxaro Resources Ltd., 106 178–81

Exxon Mobil Corporation, IV 426–30; 7 169–73 (upd.); 32 175–82 (upd.); 67 175–86 (upd.)

Eye Care Centers of America, Inc., 69 158–60

Ezaki Glico Company Ltd., 72 123–25

EZchip Semiconductor Ltd., 106 182–85

EZCORP Inc., 43 159–61

F

F&W Publications, Inc., 71 154–56

F.A.O. Schwarz *see* FAO Schwarz

The F. Dohmen Co., 77 142–45

F. Hoffmann-La Roche & Co. A.G., I 642–44; 50 190–93 (upd.)

F. Korbel & Bros. Inc., 68 144–46

F.W. Webb Company, 95 142–45

F5 Networks, Inc., 72 129–31

Fab Industries, Inc., 27 142–44

Fabbrica D' Armi Pietro Beretta S.p.A., 39 149–51

Faber-Castell *see* A.W. Faber-Castell Unternehmensverwaltung GmbH & Co.

Fabri-Centers of America Inc., 16 197–99 *see also* Jo-Ann Stores, Inc.

Facebook, Inc., 90 184–87

Facom S.A., 32 183–85

FactSet Research Systems Inc., 73 148–50

Faegre & Benson LLP, 97 164–67

FAG—Kugelfischer Georg Schäfer AG, 62 129–32

Fair Grounds Corporation, 44 177–80

Fair, Isaac and Company, 18 168–71

Fairchild Dornier GmbH, 9 205–08; 48 167–71 (upd.)

Fairclough Construction Group plc, I 567–68

Fairfax Financial Holdings Limited, 57 135–37

Fairfax Media Ltd., 94 202–08 (upd.)

Fairfield Communities, Inc., 36 192–95

Fairmont Hotels & Resorts Inc., 69 161–63

Faiveley S.A., 39 152–54

Falcon Products, Inc., 33 149–51

Falconbridge Limited, 49 136–39

Fallon Worldwide, 22 199–201; 71 157–61 (upd.)

Family Christian Stores, Inc., 51 131–34

Family Dollar Stores, Inc., 13 215–17; 62 133–36 (upd.)

Family Golf Centers, Inc., 29 183–85

Family Sports Concepts, Inc., 100 160–63

Famous Brands Ltd., 86 144–47

Famous Dave's of America, Inc., 40 182–84

Fannie Mae, 45 156–59 (upd.)

Fannie May Confections Brands, Inc., 80 114–18

Fansteel Inc., 19 150–52

Fanuc Ltd., III 482–83; 17 172–74 (upd.); 75 137–40 (upd.)

FAO Schwarz, 46 187–90

Farah Incorporated, 24 156–58

Faribault Foods, Inc., 89 212–15

Farley Northwest Industries Inc., I 440–41

Farley's & Sathers Candy Company, Inc., 62 137–39

Farm Family Holdings, Inc., 39 155–58

Farm Journal Corporation, 42 131–34

Farmacias Ahumada S.A., 72 126–28

Farmer Bros. Co., 52 117–19

Farmer Jack Supermarkets, 78 109–13

Farmer Mac see Federal Agricultural Mortgage Corp.

Farmers Insurance Group of Companies, 25 154–56

Farmland Foods, Inc., 7 174–75

Farmland Industries, Inc., 48 172–75

FARO Technologies, Inc., 87 164–167

Farouk Systems, Inc., 78 114–17

Farrar, Straus and Giroux Inc., 15 158–60

Fastenal Company, 14 185–87; 42 135–38 (upd.); 99 158–163 (upd.)

FASTWEB S.p.A., 83 147–150

Fat Face Ltd., 68 147–49

Fatburger Corporation, 64 122–24

FATS, Inc. see Firearms Training Systems, Inc.

Faultless Starch/Bon Ami Company, 55 142–45

Faurecia S.A., 70 91–93

FAvS see First Aviation Services Inc.

FAW Group see China FAW Group Corporation.

Faygo Beverages Inc., 55 146–48

Fazoli's Management, Inc., 27 145–47; 76 144–47 (upd.)

Featherlite Inc., 28 127–29

Fedders Corporation, 18 172–75; 43 162–67 (upd.)

Federal Agricultural Mortgage Corporation, 75 141–43

Federal Deposit Insurance Corporation, 93 208–12

Federal Express Corporation, V 451–53 see also FedEx Corp.

Federal Home Loan Mortgage Corp. see Freddie Mac.

Federal-Mogul Corporation, I 158–60; 10 292–94 (upd.); 26 139–43 (upd.)

Federal National Mortgage Association, II 410–11 see also Fannie Mae.

Federal Paper Board Company, Inc., 8 173–75

Federal Prison Industries, Inc., 34 157–60

Federal Signal Corp., 10 295–97

Federated Department Stores Inc., 9 209–12; 31 190–94 (upd.) see also Macy's, Inc.

Fédération Internationale de Football Association, 27 148–51

Federation Nationale d'Achats des Cadres see FNAC.

Federico Paternina S.A., 69 164–66

FedEx Corporation, 18 176–79 (upd.); 42 139–44 (upd.)

Feed The Children, Inc., 68 150–52

FEI Company, 79 168–71

Feld Entertainment, Inc., 32 186–89 (upd.)

Feldmühle Nobel AG, III 692–95 see also Metallgesellschaft.

Fellowes Manufacturing Company, 28 130–32

Fenaco, 86 148–51

Fender Musical Instruments Company, 16 200–02; 43 168–72 (upd.)

Fenwick & West LLP, 34 161–63

Ferolito, Vultaggio & Sons, 27 152–55; 100 164–69 (upd.)

Ferrara Fire Apparatus, Inc., 84 115–118

Ferrara Pan Candy Company, 90 188–91

Ferrari S.p.A., 13 218–20; 36 196–200 (upd.)

Ferrellgas Partners, L.P., 35 173–75

Ferrero SpA, 54 103–05

Ferretti Group SpA, 90 192–96

Ferro Corporation, 8 176–79; 56 123–28 (upd.)

Ferrovial see Grupo Ferrovial

Ferrovie Dello Stato Societa Di Trasporti e Servizi S.p.A., 105 163–67

FHP International Corporation, 6 184–86

Fiat SpA, I 161–63; 11 102–04 (upd.); 50 194–98 (upd.)

FiberMark, Inc., 37 139–42; 53 24

Fibreboard Corporation, 16 203–05 see also Owens Corning Corp.

Ficosa see Grupo Ficosa International.

Fidelity Investments Inc., II 412–13; 14 188–90 (upd.) see also FMR Corp.

Fidelity National Financial Inc., 54 106–08

Fidelity Southern Corporation, 85 124–27

Fieldale Farms Corporation, 23 191–93

Fieldcrest Cannon, Inc., 9 213–17; 31 195–200 (upd.)

Fielmann AG, 31 201–03

Fiesta Mart, Inc., 101 183–87

FIFA see Fédération Internationale de Football Association.

Fifth Third Bancorp, 13 221–23; 31 204–08 (upd.); 103 163–70 (upd.)

Le Figaro see Société du Figaro S.A.

Figgie International Inc., 7 176–78

Fiji Water LLC, 74 111–13

Fila Holding S.p.A., 20 216–18; 52 120–24 (upd.)

FileNet Corporation, 62 140–43

Fili Enterprises, Inc., 70 94–96

Filipacchi Medias S.A. see Hachette Filipacchi Medias S.A.

Film Roman, Inc., 58 122–24

Filtrona plc, 88 87–91

Fimalac S.A., 37 143–45

FINA, Inc., 7 179–81 see also Total Fina Elf S.A.

Finarte Casa d'Aste S.p.A., 93 213–16

Findel plc, 60 122–24

Findorff see J.H. Findorff and Son, Inc.

Fingerhut Companies, Inc., 9 218–20; 36 201–05 (upd.)

Finisar Corporation, 92 115–18

The Finish Line, Inc., 29 186–88; 68 153–56 (upd.)

FinishMaster, Inc., 24 159–61

Finlay Enterprises, Inc., 16 206–08; 76 148–51 (upd.)

Finmeccanica S.p.A., 84 119–123

Finnair Oy, 6 87–89; 25 157–60 (upd.); 61 91–95 (upd.)

Finning International Inc., 69 167–69

Firearms Training Systems, Inc., 27 156–58

Fired Up, Inc., 82 111–14

Fireman's Fund Insurance Company, III 250–52

Firmenich International S.A., 60 125–27

First Albany Companies Inc., 37 146–48

First Alert, Inc., 28 133–35

The First American Corporation, 52 125–27

First Artist Corporation PLC, 105 168–71

First Aviation Services Inc., 49 140–42

First Bank System Inc., 12 164–66 see also U.S. Bancorp

First Brands Corporation, 8 180–82

First Busey Corporation, 105 172–75

First Cash Financial Services, Inc., 57 138–40

First Chicago Corporation, II 284–87 see also Bank One Corp.

First Choice Holidays PLC, 40 185–87

First Colony Coffee & Tea Company, 84 124–126

First Commerce Bancshares, Inc., 15 161–63 see also Wells Fargo & Co.

First Commerce Corporation, 11 105–07 see also JPMorgan Chase & Co.

First Data Corporation, 30 195–98 (upd.)

First Empire State Corporation, 11 108–10

First Executive Corporation, III 253–55

First Fidelity Bank, N.A., New Jersey, 9 221–23

First Financial Management Corporation, 11 111–13

First Hawaiian, Inc., 11 114–16
First Industrial Realty Trust, Inc., 65 146–48
First International Computer, Inc., 56 129–31
First Interstate Bancorp, II 288–90 *see also* Wells Fargo & Co.
The First Marblehead Corporation, 87 168–171
First Mississippi Corporation, 8 183–86 *see also* ChemFirst, Inc.
First Nationwide Bank, 14 191–93 *see also* Citigroup Inc.
First of America Bank Corporation, 8 187–89
First Pacific Company Limited, 18 180–82
First Security Corporation, 11 117–19 *see also* Wells Fargo & Co.
First Solar, Inc., 95 146–50
First Team Sports, Inc., 22 202–04
First Tennessee National Corporation, 11 120–21; 48 176–79 (upd.)
First Union Corporation, 10 298–300 *see also* Wachovia Corp.
First USA, Inc., 11 122–24
First Virginia Banks, Inc., 11 125–26 *see also* BB&T Corp.
The First Years Inc., 46 191–94
Firstar Corporation, 11 127–29; 33 152–55 (upd.)
FirstGroup plc, 89 216–19
FirstMerit Corporation, 105 176–79
Fiserv, Inc., 11 130–32; 33 156–60 (upd.); 106 186–90 (upd.)
Fish & Neave, 54 109–12
Fisher Auto Parts, Inc., 104 152–55
Fisher Communications, Inc., 99 164–168
Fisher Companies, Inc., 15 164–66
Fisher Controls International, LLC, 13 224–26; 61 96–99 (upd.)
Fisher-Price Inc., 12 167–69; 32 190–94 (upd.)
Fisher Scientific International Inc., 24 162–66 *see also* Thermo Fisher Scientific Inc.
Fishman & Tobin Inc., 102 124–27
Fisk Corporation, 72 132–34
Fiskars Corporation, 33 161–64; 105 180–86 (upd.)
Fisons plc, 9 224–27; 23 194–97 (upd.)
5 & Diner Franchise Corporation, 72 135–37
Five Guys Enterprises, LLC, 99 169–172
FKI Plc, 57 141–44
Flagstar Companies, Inc., 10 301–03 *see also* Advantica Restaurant Group, Inc.
Flanders Corporation, 65 149–51
Flanigan's Enterprises, Inc., 60 128–30
Flatiron Construction Corporation, 92 119–22
Fleer Corporation, 15 167–69
FleetBoston Financial Corporation, 9 228–30; 36 206–14 (upd.)
Fleetwood Enterprises, Inc., III 484–85; 22 205–08 (upd.); 81 159–64 (upd.)

Fleming Companies, Inc., II 624–25; 17 178–81 (upd.)
Fletcher Challenge Ltd., IV 278–80; 19 153–57 (upd.)
Fleury Michon S.A., 39 159–61
Flexsteel Industries Inc., 15 170–72; 41 159–62 (upd.)
Flextronics International Ltd., 38 186–89
Flight Options, LLC, 75 144–46
FlightSafety International, Inc., 9 231–33; 29 189–92 (upd.)
Flint Ink Corporation, 13 227–29; 41 163–66 (upd.)
FLIR Systems, Inc., 69 170–73
Flo *see* Groupe Flo S.A.
Floc'h & Marchand, 80 119–21
Florida Crystals Inc., 35 176–78
Florida East Coast Industries, Inc., 59 184–86
Florida Gaming Corporation, 47 130–33
Florida Progress Corp., V 621–22; 23 198–200 (upd.) *see also* Progress Energy, Inc.
Florida Public Utilities Company, 69 174–76
Florida Rock Industries, Inc., 46 195–97 *see also* Patriot Transportation Holding, Inc.
Florida's Natural Growers, 45 160–62
Florists' Transworld Delivery, Inc., 28 136–38 *see also* FTD Group, Inc.
Florsheim Shoe Group Inc., 9 234–36; 31 209–12 (upd.)
Flotek Industries Inc., 93 217–20
Flour City International, Inc., 44 181–83
Flow International Corporation, 56 132–34
Flowers Industries, Inc., 12 170–71; 35 179–82 (upd.) *see also* Keebler Foods Co.
Flowserve Corporation, 33 165–68; 77 146–51 (upd.)
FLSmidth & Co. A/S, 72 138–40
Fluke Corporation, 15 173–75
Fluor Corporation, I 569–71; 8 190–93 (upd.); 34 164–69 (upd.)
Fluxys SA, 101 188–91
FlyBE *see* Jersey European Airways (UK) Ltd.
Flying Boat, Inc. (Chalk's Ocean Airways), 56 135–37
Flying J Inc., 19 158–60
Flying Pigeon Bicycle Co. *see* Tianjin Flying Pigeon Bicycle Co., Ltd.
FMC Corp., I 442–44; 11 133–35 (upd.); 89 220–27 (upd.)
FMR Corp., 8 194–96; 32 195–200 (upd.)
FNAC, 21 224–26
FNMA *see* Federal National Mortgage Association.
Foamex International Inc., 17 182–85
Focus Features, 78 118–22
Fokker *see* N.V. Koninklijke Nederlandse Vliegtuigenfabriek Fokker.

Foley & Lardner, 28 139–42
Follett Corporation, 12 172–74; 39 162–65 (upd.)
Fonterra Co-Operative Group Ltd., 58 125–27
Food Circus Super Markets, Inc., 88 92–96
The Food Emporium, 64 125–27
Food For The Poor, Inc., 77 152–55
Food Lion LLC, II 626–27; 15 176–78 (upd.); 66 112–15 (upd.)
Foodarama Supermarkets, Inc., 28 143–45 *see also* Wakefern Food Corp.
FoodBrands America, Inc., 23 201–04 *see also* Doskocil Companies, Inc.; Tyson Foods, Inc.
Foodmaker, Inc., 14 194–96 *see also* Jack in the Box Inc.
Foot Locker, Inc., 68 157–62 (upd.)
Foot Petals L.L.C., 95 151–54
Foote, Cone & Belding Worldwide, I 12–15; 66 116–20 (upd.)
Footstar, Incorporated, 24 167–69 *see also* Foot Locker, Inc.
Forbes Inc., 30 199–201; 82 115–20 (upd.)
Force Protection Inc., 95 155–58
The Ford Foundation, 34 170–72
Ford Gum & Machine Company, Inc., 102 128–31
Ford Motor Company, I 164–68; 11 136–40 (upd.); 36 215–21 (upd.); 64 128–34 (upd.)
Ford Motor Company, S.A. de C.V., 20 219–21
FORE Systems, Inc., 25 161–63 *see also* Telefonaktiebolaget LM Ericsson.
Foremost Farms USA Cooperative, 98 116–20
FöreningsSparbanken AB, 69 177–80
Forest City Enterprises, Inc., 16 209–11; 52 128–31 (upd.)
Forest Laboratories, Inc., 11 141–43; 52 132–36 (upd.)
Forest Oil Corporation, 19 161–63; 91 182–87 (upd.)
Forever 21, Inc., 84 127–129
Forever Living Products International Inc., 17 186 88
FormFactor, Inc., 85 128–31
Formica Corporation, 13 230–32
Formosa Plastics Corporation, 14 197–99; 58 128–31 (upd.)
Forrester Research, Inc., 54 113–15
Forstmann Little & Co., 38 190–92
Fort Howard Corporation, 8 197–99 *see also* Fort James Corp.
Fort James Corporation, 22 209–12 (upd.) *see also* Georgia-Pacific Corp.
Fortis, Inc., 15 179–82; 47 134–37 (upd.); 50 4–6
Fortum Corporation, 30 202–07 (upd.) *see also* Neste Oil Corp.
Fortune Brands, Inc., 29 193–97 (upd.); 68 163–67 (upd.)
Fortunoff Fine Jewelry and Silverware Inc., 26 144–46
Forward Air Corporation, 75 147–49

Forward Industries, Inc., 86 152–55

The Forzani Group Ltd., 79 172–76

Fossil, Inc., 17 189–91

Foster Poultry Farms, 32 201–04

Foster Wheeler Corporation, 6 145–47; 23 205–08 (upd.); 76 152–56 (upd.)

FosterGrant, Inc., 60 131–34

Foster's Group Limited, 7 182–84; 21 227–30 (upd.); 50 199–203 (upd.)

Foundation Health Corporation, 12 175–77

Fountain Powerboats Industries, Inc., 28 146–48

Four Seasons Hotels Limited, 9 237–38; 29 198–200 (upd.); 106 191–95 (upd.)

Four Winns Boats LLC, 96 124–27

4imprint Group PLC, 105 187–91

4Kids Entertainment Inc., 59 187–89

Fourth Financial Corporation, 11 144–46

Fox Entertainment Group, Inc., 43 173–76

Fox Family Worldwide, Inc., 24 170–72 *see also* ABC Family Worldwide, Inc.

Fox, Inc. *see* Twentieth Century Fox Film Corp.

Foxboro Company, 13 233–35

FoxHollow Technologies, Inc., 85 132–35

FoxMeyer Health Corporation, 16 212–14 *see also* McKesson Corp.

Fox's Pizza Den, Inc., 98 121–24

Foxworth-Galbraith Lumber Company, 91 188–91

FPL Group, Inc., V 623–25; 49 143–46 (upd.)

Framatome SA, 19 164–67 *aee also* Alcatel S.A.; AREVA.

France Telecom S.A., V 291–93; 21 231–34 (upd.); 99 173–179 (upd.)

Francotyp-Postalia Holding AG, 92 123–27

Frank J. Zamboni & Co., Inc., 34 173–76

Frank Russell Company, 46 198–200

Franke Holding AG, 76 157–59

Frankel & Co., 39 166–69

Frankfurter Allgemeine Zeitung GmbH, 66 121–24

Franklin Covey Company, 11 147–49; 37 149–52 (upd.)

Franklin Electric Company, Inc., 43 177–80

Franklin Electronic Publishers, Inc., 23 209–13

The Franklin Mint, 69 181–84

Franklin Resources, Inc., 9 239–40

Frank's Nursery & Crafts, Inc., 12 178–79

Franz Inc., 80 122–25

Fraport AG Frankfurt Airport Services Worldwide, 90 197–202

Fraser & Neave Ltd., 54 116–18

Fred Alger Management, Inc., 97 168–72

Fred Meyer Stores, Inc., V 54–56; 20 222–25 (upd.); 64 135–39 (upd.)

Fred Perry Limited, 105 192–95

Fred Usinger Inc., 54 119–21

The Fred W. Albrecht Grocery Co., 13 236–38

Fred Weber, Inc., 61 100–02

Freddie Mac, 54 122–25

Frederick Atkins Inc., 16 215–17

Frederick's of Hollywood Inc., 16 218–20; 59 190–93 (upd.)

Fred's, Inc., 23 214–16; 62 144–47 (upd.)

Freedom Communications, Inc., 36 222–25

Freeport-McMoRan Copper & Gold, Inc., IV 81–84; 7 185–89 (upd.); 57 145–50 (upd.)

Freescale Semiconductor, Inc., 83 151–154

Freeze.com LLC, 77 156–59

FreightCar America, Inc., 101 192–95

Freixenet S.A., 71 162–64

French Connection Group plc, 41 167–69

French Fragrances, Inc., 22 213–15 *see also* Elizabeth Arden, Inc.

Frequency Electronics, Inc., 61 103–05

Fresenius AG, 56 138–42

Fresh America Corporation, 20 226–28

Fresh Choice, Inc., 20 229–32

Fresh Enterprises, Inc., 66 125–27

Fresh Express Inc., 88 97–100

Fresh Foods, Inc., 29 201–03

FreshDirect, LLC, 84 130–133

Fretter, Inc., 10 304–06

Freudenberg & Co., 41 170–73

Fried, Frank, Harris, Shriver & Jacobson, 35 183–86

Fried. Krupp GmbH, IV 85–89 *see also* ThyssenKrupp AG.

Friedman, Billings, Ramsey Group, Inc., 53 134–37

Friedman's Inc., 29 204–06

Friedrich Grohe AG & Co. KG, 53 138–41

Friendly Ice Cream Corporation, 30 208–10; 72 141–44 (upd.)

Fricsland Coberco Dairy Foods Holding N.V., 59 194–96

Frigidaire Home Products, 22 216–18

Frisch's Restaurants, Inc., 35 187–89; 92 128–32 (upd.)

Frito-Lay North America, 32 205–10; 73 151–58 (upd.)

Fritz Companies, Inc., 12 180–82

Fromageries Bel, 23 217–19; 25 83–84

Frontera Foods, Inc., 100 170–73

Frontier Airlines Holdings Inc., 22 219–21; 84 134–138 (upd.)

Frontier Corp., 16 221–23

Frontier Natural Products Co-Op, 82 121–24

Frontline Ltd., 45 163–65

Frost & Sullivan, Inc., 53 142–44

Frozen Food Express Industries, Inc., 20 233–35; 98 125–30 (upd.)

Frucor Beverages Group Ltd., 96 128–31

Fruehauf Corp., I 169–70

Fruit of the Loom, Inc., 8 200–02; 25 164–67 (upd.)

Fruth Pharmacy, Inc., 66 128–30

Frymaster Corporation, 27 159–62

Fry's Electronics, Inc., 68 168–70

FSI International, Inc., 17 192–94 *see also* FlightSafety International, Inc.

FTD Group, Inc., 99 180–185 (upd.)

FTI Consulting, Inc., 77 160–63

FTP Software, Inc., 20 236–38

Fubu, 29 207–09

Fuchs Petrolub AG, 102 132–37

Fuel Systems Solutions, Inc., 97 173–77

Fuel Tech, Inc., 85 136–40

FuelCell Energy, Inc., 75 150–53

Fugro N.V., 98 131–34

Fuji Bank, Ltd., II 291–93

Fuji Electric Co., Ltd., II 22–23; 48 180–82 (upd.)

Fuji Photo Film Co., Ltd., III 486–89; 18 183–87 (upd.); 79 177–84 (upd.)

Fuji Television Network Inc., 91 192–95

Fujisawa Pharmaceutical Company, Ltd., I 635–36; 58 132–34 (upd.) *see also* Astellas Pharma Inc.

Fujitsu-ICL Systems Inc., 11 150–51

Fujitsu Limited, III 139–41; 16 224–27 (upd.); 42 145–50 (upd.); 103 171–78 (upd.)

Fulbright & Jaworski L.L.P., 47 138–41

Fuller Smith & Turner P.L.C., 38 193–95

Funai Electric Company Ltd., 62 148–50

Funco, Inc., 20 239–41 *see also* GameStop Corp.

Fuqua Enterprises, Inc., 17 195–98

Fuqua Industries Inc., I 445–47

Furmanite Corporation, 92 133–36

Furniture Brands International, Inc., 39 170–75 (upd.)

Furon Company, 28 149–51 *see also* Compagnie de Saint-Gobain.

Furr's Restaurant Group, Inc., 53 145–48

Furr's Supermarkets, Inc., 28 152–54

Furukawa Electric Co., Ltd., III 490–92

Future Now, Inc., 12 183–85

Future Shop Ltd., 62 151–53

Fyffes PLC, 38 196–99; 106 196–201 (upd.)

G

G&K Holding S.A., 95 159–62

G&K Services, Inc., 16 228–30

G-III Apparel Group, Ltd., 22 222–24

G A Pindar & Son Ltd., 88 101–04

G.D. Searle & Co., I 686–89; 12 186–89 (upd.); 34 177–82 (upd.)

G. Heileman Brewing Co., I 253–55 *see also* Stroh Brewery Co.

G.I.E. Airbus Industrie, I 41–43; 12 190–92 (upd.)

G.I. Joe's, Inc., 30 221–23 *see also* Joe's Sports & Outdoor.

G. Leblanc Corporation, 55 149–52

G.S. Blodgett Corporation, 15 183–85 *see also* Blodgett Holdings, Inc.

Gabelli Asset Management Inc., 30 211–14 *see also* Lynch Corp.

Gables Residential Trust, 49 147–49

Gadzooks, Inc., 18 188–90

GAF, I 337–40; 22 225–29 (upd.)

Gage Marketing Group, 26 147–49

Gaiam, Inc., 41 174–77

Gainsco, Inc., 22 230–32

Galardi Group, Inc., 72 145–47

Galaxy Investors, Inc., 97 178–81

Galaxy Nutritional Foods, Inc., 58 135–37

Gale International LLC, 93 221–24

Galenica AG, 84 139–142

Galeries Lafayette S.A., V 57–59; 23 220–23 (upd.)

Galey & Lord, Inc., 20 242–45; 66 131–34 (upd.)

Galiform PLC, 103 179–83

Gallaher Group Plc, 49 150–54 (upd.)

Gallaher Limited, V 398–400; 19 168–71 (upd.)

Gallo Winery *see* E. & J. Gallo Winery.

Gallup, Inc., 37 153–56; 104 156–61 (upd.)

Galoob Toys *see* Lewis Galoob Toys Inc.

Galp Energia SGPS S.A., 98 135–40

Galtronics Ltd., 100 174–77

Galyan's Trading Company, Inc., 47 142–44

The Gambrinus Company, 40 188–90

Gambro AB, 49 155–57

The GAME Group plc, 80 126–29

GameStop Corp., 69 185–89 (upd.)

GAMI *see* Great American Management and Investment, Inc.

Gaming Partners InternationalCorporation, 92 225–28

Gander Mountain Company, 20 246–48; 90 203–08 (upd.)

Gannett Company, Inc., IV 612–13; 7 190–92 (upd.); 30 215–17 (upd.); 66 135–38 (upd.)

Gano Excel Enterprise Sdn. Bhd., 89 228–31

Gantos, Inc., 17 199–201

Ganz, 98 141–44

GAP *see* Grupo Aeroportuario del Pacífico, S.A. de C.V.

The Gap, Inc., V 60–62; 18 191–94 (upd.); 55 153–57 (upd.)

Garan, Inc., 16 231–33; 64 140–43 (upd.)

The Garden Company Ltd., 82 125–28

Garden Fresh Restaurant Corporation, 31 213–15

Garden Ridge Corporation, 27 163–65

Gardenburger, Inc., 33 169–71; 76 160–63 (upd.)

Gardner Denver, Inc., 49 158–60

Garmin Ltd., 60 135–37

Garst Seed Company, Inc., 86 156–59

Gart Sports Company, 24 173–75 *see also* Sports Authority, Inc.

Gartner, Inc., 21 235–37; 94 209–13 (upd.)

Garuda Indonesia, 6 90–91; 58 138–41 (upd.)

Gas Natural SDG S.A., 69 190–93

GASS *see* Grupo Ángeles Servicios de Salud, S.A. de C.V.

Gasunie *see* N.V. Nederlandse Gasunie.

Gate Gourmet International AG, 70 97–100

GateHouse Media, Inc., 91 196–99

The Gates Corporation, 9 241–43

Gateway Corporation Ltd., II 628–30 *see also* Somerfield plc.

Gateway, Inc., 10 307–09; 27 166–69 (upd.); 63 153–58 (upd.)

The Gatorade Company, 82 129–32

Gatti's Pizza, Inc. *see* Mr. Gatti's, LP.

GATX, 6 394–96; 25 168–71 (upd.)

Gaumont S.A., 25 172–75; 91 200–05 (upd.)

Gaylord Bros., Inc., 100 178–81

Gaylord Container Corporation, 8 203–05

Gaylord Entertainment Company, 11 152–54; 36 226–29 (upd.)

Gaz de France, V 626–28; 40 191–95 (upd.)

Gazprom *see* OAO Gazprom.

GBC *see* General Binding Corp.

GC Companies, Inc., 25 176–78 *see also* AMC Entertainment Inc.

GE *see* General Electric Co.

GE Aircraft Engines, 9 244–46

GE Capital Aviation Services, 36 230–33

GEA AG, 27 170–74

GEAC Computer Corporation Ltd., 43 181–85

Geberit AG, 49 161–64

Gecina SA, 42 151–53

Gedney *see* M.A. Gedney Co.

Geek Squad Inc., 102 138–41

Geerlings & Wade, Inc., 45 166–68

Geest Plc, 38 200–02 *see also* Bakkavör Group hf.

Gefco SA, 54 126–28

Geffen Records Inc., 26 150–52

GEHE AG, 27 175–78

Gehl Company, 19 172–74

GEICO Corporation, 10 310–12; 40 196–99 (upd.)

Geiger Bros., 60 138–41

Gelita AG, 74 114–18

GEMA (Gesellschaft für musikalische Aufführungs- und mechanische Vervielfältigungsrechte), 70 101–05

Gemini Sound Products Corporation, 58 142–44

Gemplus International S.A., 64 144–47

Gen-Probe Incorporated, 79 185–88

Gencor Ltd., IV 90–93; 22 233–37 (upd.) *see also* Gold Fields Ltd.

GenCorp Inc., 9 247–49

Genentech, Inc., I 637–38; 8 209–11 (upd.); 32 211–15 (upd.); 75 154–58 (upd.)

General Accident plc, III 256–57 *see also* Aviva PLC.

General Atomics, 57 151–54

General Bearing Corporation, 45 169–71

General Binding Corporation, 10 313–14; 73 159–62 (upd.)

General Cable Corporation, 40 200–03

The General Chemical Group Inc., 37 157–60

General Cigar Holdings, Inc., 66 139–42 (upd.)

General Cinema Corporation, I 245–46 *see also* GC Companies, Inc.

General DataComm Industries, Inc., 14 200–02

General Dynamics Corporation, I 57–60; 10 315–18 (upd.); 40 204–10 (upd.); 88 105–13 (upd.)

General Electric Company, II 27–31; 12 193–97 (upd.); 34 183–90 (upd.); 63 159–68 (upd.)

General Electric Company, PLC, II 24–26 *see also* Marconi plc.

General Employment Enterprises, Inc., 87 172–175

General Growth Properties, Inc., 57 155–57

General Host Corporation, 12 198–200

General Housewares Corporation, 16 234–36

General Instrument Corporation, 10 319–21 *see also* Motorola, Inc.

General Maritime Corporation, 59 197–99

General Mills, Inc., II 501–03; 10 322–24 (upd.); 36 234–39 (upd.); 85 141–49 (upd.)

General Motors Corporation, I 171–73; 10 325–27 (upd.); 36 240–44 (upd.); 64 148–53 (upd.)

General Nutrition Companies, Inc., 11 155–57; 29 210–14 (upd.) *see also* GNC Corp.

General Public Utilities Corporation, V 629–31 *see also* GPU, Inc.

General Re Corporation, III 258–59; 24 176–78 (upd.)

General Sekiyu K.K., IV 431–33 *see also* TonenGeneral Sekiyu K.K.

General Signal Corporation, 9 250–52 *see also* SPX Corp.

General Tire, Inc., 8 212–14

Generale Bank, II 294–95 *see also* Fortis, Inc.

Générale des Eaux Group, V 632–34 *see* Vivendi Universal S.A.

Generali *see* Assicurazioni Generali.

Genesco Inc., 17 202–06; 84 143–149 (upd.)

Genesee & Wyoming Inc., 27 179–81

Genesis Health Ventures, Inc., 18 195–97 *see also* NeighborCare,Inc.

Genesis Microchip Inc., 82 133–37

Genesys Telecommunications Laboratories Inc., 103 184–87

Genetics Institute, Inc., 8 215–18

Geneva Steel, 7 193–95

Genmar Holdings, Inc., 45 172–75

Genovese Drug Stores, Inc., 18 198–200

Genoyer *see* Groupe Genoyer.

GenRad, Inc., 24 179–83

Gentex Corporation, 26 153–57

Genting Bhd., 65 152–55

Gentiva Health Services, Inc., 79 189–92

Genuardi's Family Markets, Inc., 35 190–92

Genuine Parts Company, 9 253–55; 45 176–79 (upd.)

Genzyme Corporation, 13 239–42; 38 203–07 (upd.); 77 164–70 (upd.)

geobra Brandstätter GmbH & Co. KG, 48 183–86

Geodis S.A., 67 187–90

The Geon Company, 11 158–61

GeoResources, Inc., 101 196–99

Georg Fischer AG Schaffhausen, 61 106–09

George A. Hormel and Company, II 504–06 *see also* Hormel Foods Corp.

The George F. Cram Company, Inc., 55 158–60

George P. Johnson Company, 60 142–44

George S. May International Company, 55 161–63

George W. Park Seed Company, Inc., 98 145–48

George Weston Ltd., II 631–32; 36 245–48 (upd.); 88 114–19 (upd.)

George Wimpey plc, 12 201–03; 51 135–38 (upd.)

Georgia Gulf Corporation, 9 256–58; 61 110–13 (upd.)

Georgia-Pacific LLC, IV 281–83; 9 259–62 (upd.); 47 145–51 (upd.); 101 200–09 (upd.)

Geotek Communications Inc., 21 238–40

Gerald Stevens, Inc., 37 161–63

Gerber Products Company, 7 196–98; 21 241–44 (upd)

Gerber Scientific, Inc., 12 204–06; 84 150–154 (upd.)

Gerdau S.A., 59 200–03

Gerhard D. Wempe KG, 88 120–25

Gericom AG, 47 152–54

Gerling-Konzern Versicherungs-Beteiligungs-Aktiengesellschaft, 51 139–43

German American Bancorp, 41 178–80

Gerresheimer Glas AG, 43 186–89

Gerry Weber International AG, 63 169–72

Gertrude Hawk Chocolates Inc., 104 162–65

Gesellschaft für musikalische Aufführungs-und mechanische Vervielfältigungsrechte *see* GEMA.

Getrag Corporate Group, 92 137–42

Getronics NV, 39 176–78

Getty Images, Inc., 31 216–18

Gevaert *see* Agfa Gevaert Group N.V.

Gévelot S.A., 96 132–35

Gevity HR, Inc., 63 173–77

GF Health Products, Inc., 82 138–41

GFI Informatique SA, 49 165–68

GfK Aktiengesellschaft, 49 169–72

GFS *see* Gordon Food Service Inc.

Ghirardelli Chocolate Company, 30 218–20

Gianni Versace S.p.A., 22 238–40; 106 202–07 (upd.)

Giant Cement Holding, Inc., 23 224–26

Giant Eagle, Inc., 86 160–64

Giant Food LLC, II 633–35; 22 241–44 (upd.); 83 155–161 (upd.)

Giant Industries, Inc., 19 175–77; 61 114–18 (upd.)

Giant Manufacturing Company, Ltd., 85 150–54

GIB Group, V 63–66; 26 158–62 (upd.)

Gibbs and Dandy plc, 74 119–21

Gibraltar Steel Corporation, 37 164–67

Gibson Greetings, Inc., 12 207–10 *see also* American Greetings Corp.

Gibson Guitar Corporation, 16 237–40; 100 182–87 (upd.)

Gibson, Dunn & Crutcher LLP, 36 249–52

Giddings & Lewis, Inc., 10 328–30

Giesecke & Devrient GmbH, 83 162–166

GiFi S.A., 74 122–24

Gifts In Kind International, 101 210–13

Gilbane, Inc., 34 191–93

Gildan Activewear, Inc., 81 165–68

Gildemeister AG, 79 193–97

Gilead Sciences, Inc., 54 129–31

Gillett Holdings, Inc., 7 199–201

The Gillette Company, III 27–30; 20 249–53 (upd.); 68 171–76 (upd.)

Gilman & Ciocia, Inc., 72 148–50

Gilmore Entertainment Group L.L.C., 100 188–91

Ginnie Mae *see* Government National Mortgage Association.

Giorgio Armani S.p.A., 45 180–83

Girl Scouts of the USA, 35 193–96

The Gitano Group, Inc., 8 219–21

GIV *see* Granite Industries of Vermont, Inc.

Givaudan SA, 43 190–93

Given Imaging Ltd., 83 167–170

Givenchy *see* Parfums Givenchy S.A.

GKN plc, III 493–96; 38 208–13 (upd.); 89 232–41 (upd.)

Glaces Thiriet S.A., 76 164–66

Glacier Bancorp, Inc., 35 197–200

Glacier Water Services, Inc., 47 155–58

Glamis Gold, Ltd., 54 132–35

Glanbia plc, 59 204–07, 364

Glatfelter Wood Pulp Company *see* P.H. Glatfelter Company

Glaverbel Group, 80 130–33

Glaxo Holdings plc, I 639–41; 9 263–65 (upd.)

GlaxoSmithKline plc, 46 201–08 (upd.)

Glazer's Wholesale Drug Company, Inc., 82 142–45

Gleason Corporation, 24 184–87

Glen Dimplex, 78 123–27

Glico *see* Ezaki Glico Company Ltd.

The Glidden Company, 8 222–24

Global Berry Farms LLC, 62 154–56

Global Crossing Ltd., 32 216–19

Global Hyatt Corporation, 75 159–63 (upd.)

Global Imaging Systems, Inc., 73 163–65

Global Industries, Ltd., 37 168–72

Global Marine Inc., 9 266–67

Global Outdoors, Inc., 49 173–76

Global Payments Inc., 91 206–10

Global Power Equipment Group Inc., 52 137–39

GlobalSantaFe Corporation, 48 187–92 (upd.)

Globe Newspaper Company Inc., 106 208–12

Globex Utilidades S.A., 103 188–91

Globo Comunicação e Participações S.A., 80 134–38

Glock Ges.m.b.H., 42 154–56

Glon *see* Groupe Glon.

Glotel plc, 53 149–51

Glu Mobile Inc., 95 163–66

Glueck Brewing Company, 75 164–66

GM *see* General Motors Corp.

GM Hughes Electronics Corporation, II 32–36 *see also* Hughes Electronics Corp.

GMH Communities Trust, 87 176–178

GN ReSound A/S, 103 192–96

GNC Corporation, 98 149–55 (upd.)

GNMA *see* Government National Mortgage Association.

The Go-Ahead Group Plc, 28 155–57

The Go Daddy Group Inc., 102 142–45

Go Sport *see* Groupe Go Sport S.A.

Go-Video, Inc. *see* Sensory Science Corp.

Godfather's Pizza Incorporated, 25 179–81

Godiva Chocolatier, Inc., 64 154–57

Goetze's Candy Company, Inc., 87 179–182

Gol Linhas Aéreas Inteligentes S.A., 73 166–68

Gold Fields Ltd., IV 94–97; 62 157–64 (upd.)

Gold Kist Inc., 17 207–09; 26 166–68 (upd.) *see also* Pilgrim's Pride Corp.

Goldcorp Inc., 87 183–186

Golden Belt Manufacturing Co., 16 241–43

Golden Books Family Entertainment, Inc., 28 158–61 *see also* Random House, Inc.

Golden Corral Corporation, 10 331–33; 66 143–46 (upd.)

Golden Enterprises, Inc., 26 163–65

Golden Krust Caribbean Bakery, Inc., 68 177–79

Golden Neo-Life Diamite International, Inc., 100 192–95

Golden State Foods Corporation, 32 220–22

Golden State Vintners, Inc., 33 172–74

Golden Telecom, Inc., 59 208–11

Golden West Financial Corporation, 47 159–61

The Goldman Sachs Group Inc., II 414–16; 20 254–57 (upd.); 51 144–48 (upd.)

Gold'n Plump Poultry, 54 136–38
Gold's Gym International, Inc., 71 165–68
Goldstar Co., Ltd., 12 211–13 *see also* LG Corp.
GoldToeMoretz, LLC, 102 146–49
Golin/Harris International, Inc., 88 126–30
Golub Corporation, 26 169–71; 96 136–39 (upd.)
GOME Electrical Appliances Holding Ltd., 87 187–191
Gomez Inc., 104 166–69
Gonnella Baking Company, 102 150–53
Gonnella Baking Company, 40 211–13
The Good Guys!, Inc., 10 334–35; 30 224–27 (upd.)
The Good Humor-Breyers Ice Cream Company, 14 203–05 *see also* Unilever PLC.
Goodby Silverstein & Partners, Inc., 75 167–69
Goodman Fielder Ltd., 52 140–43
Goodman Holding Company, 42 157–60
GoodMark Foods, Inc., 26 172–74
Goodrich Corporation, 46 209–13 (upd.)
GoodTimes Entertainment Ltd., 48 193–95
Goodwill Industries International, Inc., 16 244–46; 66 147–50 (upd.)
Goody Products, Inc., 12 214–16
The Goodyear Tire & Rubber Company, V 244–48; 20 259–64 (upd.); 75 170–78 (upd.)
Goody's Family Clothing, Inc., 20 265–67; 64 158–61 (upd.)
Google, Inc., 50 204–07; 101 214–19 (upd.)
Gordmans, Inc., 74 125–27
Gordon Biersch Brewery Restaurant Group,Inc., 92 229–32
Gordon Food Service Inc., 8 225–27; 39 179–82 (upd.)
The Gorman-Rupp Company, 18 201–03; 57 158–61 (upd.)
Gorton's, 13 243–44
Gosling Brothers Ltd., 82 146–49
Goss Holdings, Inc., 43 194–97
Gottschalks, Inc., 18 204–06; 91 211–15 (upd.)
Gould Electronics, Inc., 14 206–08
Gould Paper Corporation, 82 150–53
Goulds Pumps Inc., 24 188–91
The Governor and Company of the Bank of Scotland, 10 336–38
Goya Foods Inc., 22 245–47; 91 216–21 (upd.)
GP Strategies Corporation, 64 162–66 (upd.)
GPS Industries, Inc., 81 169–72
GPU *see* General Public Utilities Corp.
GPU, Inc., 27 182–85 (upd.)
Grace *see* W.R. Grace & Co.
GraceKennedy Ltd., 92 143–47
Graco Inc., 19 178–80; 67 191–95 (upd.)

Gradall Industries, Inc., 96 140–43
Graeter's Manufacturing Company, 86 165–68
Grafton Group plc, 104 170–74
Graham Corporation, 62 165–67
Graham Packaging Holdings Company, 87 192–196
Grameen Bank, 31 219–22
Grampian Country Food Group, Ltd., 85 155–59
Granada Group PLC, II 138–40; 24 192–95 (upd.) *see also* ITV plc.
Granaria Holdings B.V., 66 151–53
GranCare, Inc., 14 209–11
Grand Casinos, Inc., 20 268–70
Grand Hotel Krasnapolsky N.V., 23 227–29
Grand Metropolitan plc, I 247–49; 14 212–15 (upd.) *see also* Diageo plc.
Grand Piano & Furniture Company, 72 151–53
Grand Traverse Pie Company, 98 156–59
Grand Union Company, 7 202–04; 28 162–65 (upd.)
Grandoe Corporation, 98 160–63
Grands Vins Jean-Claude Boisset S.A., 98 164–67
GrandVision S.A., 43 198–200
Granite Broadcasting Corporation, 42 161–64
Granite City Food & Brewery Ltd., 94 214–17
Granite Construction Incorporated, 61 119–21
Granite Industries of Vermont, Inc., 73 169–72
Granite Rock Company, 26 175–78
Granite State Bankshares, Inc., 37 173–75
Grant Prideco, Inc., 57 162–64
Grant Thornton International, 57 165–67
Graphic Industries Inc., 25 182–84
Graphic Packaging Holding Company, 96 144–50 (upd.)
Gray Communications Systems, Inc., 24 196–200
Graybar Electric Company, Inc., 54 139–42
Great American Management and Investment, Inc., 8 228–31
The Great Atlantic & Pacific Tea Company, Inc., II 636–38; 16 247–50 (upd.); 55 164–69 (upd.)
Great Harvest Bread Company, 44 184–86
Great Lakes Bancorp, 8 232–33
Great Lakes Chemical Corp., I 341–42; 14 216–18 (upd.) *see also* Chemtura Corp.
Great Lakes Dredge & Dock Company, 69 194–97
Great Plains Energy Incorporated, 65 156–60 (upd.)
The Great Universal Stores plc, V 67–69; 19 181–84 (upd.) *see also* GUS plc.

Great-West Lifeco Inc., III 260–61 *see also* Power Corporation of Canada.
Great Western Financial Corporation, 10 339–41 *see also* Washington Mutual, Inc.
Great White Shark Enterprises, Inc., 89 242–45
Great Wolf Resorts, Inc., 91 222–26
Greatbatch, Inc., 72 154–56
Greater Washington Educational Telecommunication Association, 103 197–200
Grede Foundries, Inc., 38 214–17
Greek Organization of Football Prognostics S.A. (OPAP), 97 182–85
The Green Bay Packers, Inc., 32 223–26
Green Dot Public Schools, 99 186–189
Green Mountain Coffee, Inc., 31 227–30
Green Tree Financial Corporation, 11 162–63 *see also* Conseco, Inc.
The Greenalls Group PLC, 21 245–47
Greenberg Traurig, LLP, 65 161–63
The Greenbrier Companies, 19 185–87
Greencore Group plc, 98 168–71
Greene King plc, 31 223–26
Greene, Tweed & Company, 55 170–72
GreenMan Technologies Inc., 99 190–193
Greenpeace International, 74 128–30
GreenPoint Financial Corp., 28 166–68
Greenwood Mills, Inc., 14 219–21
Greg Manning Auctions, Inc., 60 145–46
Greggs PLC, 65 164–66
Greif Inc., 15 186–88; 66 154–56 (upd.)
Grendene S.A., 102 154–57
Grévin & Compagnie SA, 56 143–45
Grey Global Group Inc., 6 26–28; 66 157–61 (upd.)
Grey Wolf, Inc., 43 201–03
Greyhound Lines, Inc., I 448–50; 32 227–31 (upd.)
Greyston Bakery, Inc., 101 220–23
Griffin Industries, Inc., 70 106–09
Griffin Land & Nurseries, Inc., 43 204–06
Griffith Laboratories Inc., 100 196–99
Griffon Corporation, 34 194–96
Grill Concepts, Inc., 74 131–33
Grinnell Corp., 13 245–47
Grist Mill Company, 15 189–91
Gristede's Foods Inc., 68 31 231–33; 180–83 (upd.)
The Grocers Supply Co., Inc., 103 201–04
Grohe *see* Friedrich Grohe AG & Co. KG.
Grolier Inc., 16 251–54; 43 207–11 (upd.)
Grolsch *see* Royal Grolsch NV.
Grossman's Inc., 13 248–50
Ground Round, Inc., 21 248–51
Group 1 Automotive, Inc., 52 144–46
Group 4 Falck A/S, 42 165–68
Group Health Cooperative, 41 181–84
Groupama S.A., 76 167–70

Groupe Air France, 6 92–94 *see also* Societe Air France.

Groupe Alain Manoukian, 55 173–75

Groupe André, 17 210–12 *see also* Vivarte SA.

ARES *see* Groupe Ares S.A.

Groupe Bigard S.A., 96 151–54

Groupe Bolloré, 67 196–99

Groupe Bourbon S.A., 60 147–49

Groupe Bull *see* Compagnie des Machines Bull.

Groupe Caisse d'Epargne, 100 200–04

Groupe Casino *see* Casino Guichard-Perrachon S.A.

Groupe Castorama-Dubois Investissements, 23 230–32 *see also* Castorama-Dubois Investissements SCA

Groupe CECAB S.C.A., 88 131–34

Groupe Crit S.A., 74 134–36

Groupe Danone, 32 232–36 (upd.); 93 233–40 (upd.)

Groupe Dassault Aviation SA, 26 179–82 (upd.)

Groupe de la Cité, IV 614–16

Groupe DMC (Dollfus Mieg & Cie), 27 186–88

Groupe Dubreuil S.A., 102 162–65

Groupe Euralis, 86 169–72

Groupe Flo S.A., 98 172–75

Groupe Fournier SA, 44 187–89

Groupe Genoyer, 96 155–58

Groupe Glon, 84 155–158

Groupe Go Sport S.A., 39 183–85

Groupe Guillin SA, 40 214–16

Groupe Henri Heuliez S.A., 100 205–09

Groupe Herstal S.A., 58 145–48

Groupe Jean-Claude Darmon, 44 190–92

Groupe Lactalis, 78 128–32 (upd.)

Groupe Lapeyre S.A., 33 175–77

Groupe LDC *see* L.D.C. S.A.

Groupe Le Duff S.A., 84 159–162

Groupe Léa Nature, 88 135–38

Groupe Legris Industries, 23 233–35

Groupe Les Echos, 25 283–85

Groupe Limagrain, 74 137–40

Groupe Louis Dreyfus S.A., 60 150–53

Groupe Monnoyeur, 72 157–59

Groupe Open, 74 141–43

Groupe Partouche SA, 48 196–99

Groupe Pinault-Printemps-Redoute *see* Pinault-Printemps-Redoute S.A.

Groupe Promodès S.A., 19 326–28

Groupe Rougier SA, 21 438–40

Groupe SEB, 35 201–03

Groupe Sidel S.A., 21 252–55

Groupe Soufflet SA, 55 176–78

Groupe Vidéotron Ltée., 20 271–73

Groupe Yves Saint Laurent, 23 236–39 *see also* Gucci Group N.V.

Groupe Zannier S.A., 35 204–07

Grow Biz International, Inc., 18 207–10 *see also* Winmark Corp.

Grow Group Inc., 12 217–19

GROWMARK, Inc., 88 139–42

Groz-Beckert Group, 68 184–86

Grubb & Ellis Company, 21 256–58; 98 176–80 (upd.)

Gruma, S.A.B. de C.V., 31 234–36; 103 205–10 (upd.)

Grumman Corp., I 61–63; 11 164–67 (upd.) *see aslo* Northrop Grumman Corp.

Grunau Company Inc., 90 209–12

Grundfos Group, 83 171–174

Grundig AG, 27 189–92

Gruntal & Co., L.L.C., 20 274–76

Grupo Aeroportuario del Centro Norte, S.A.B. de C.V., 97 186–89

Grupo Aeroportuario del Pacífico, S.A. de C.V., 85 160–63

Grupo Aeropuerto del Sureste, S.A. de C.V., 48 200–02

Grupo Algar *see* Algar S/A Emprendimentos e Participações

Grupo Ángeles Servicios de Salud, S.A. de C.V., 84 163–166

Grupo Brescia, 99 194–197

Grupo Bufete *see* Bufete Industrial, S.A. de C.V.

Grupo Carso, S.A. de C.V., 21 259–61

Grupo Casa Saba, S.A. de C.V., 39 186–89

Grupo Clarín S.A., 67 200–03

Grupo Comercial Chedraui S.A. de C.V., 86 173–76

Grupo Corvi S.A. de C.V., 86 177–80

Grupo Cydsa, S.A. de C.V., 39 190–93

Grupo Dina *see* Consorcio G Grupo Dina, S.A. de C.V.

Grupo Dragados SA, 55 179–82

Grupo Elektra, S.A. de C.V., 39 194–97

Grupo Eroski, 64 167 70

Grupo Ferrovial, S.A., 40 217–19

Grupo Ficosa International, 90 213–16

Grupo Financiero Banamex S.A., 54 143–46

Grupo Financiero Banorte, S.A. de C.V., 51 149–51

Grupo Financiero BBVA Bancomer S.A., 54 147–50

Grupo Financiero Galicia S.A., 63 178–81

Grupo Financiero Serfin, S.A., 19 188–90

Grupo Gigante, S.A. de C.V., 34 197–99

Grupo Herdez, S.A. de C.V., 35 208–10

Grupo IMSA, S.A. de C.V., 44 193–96

Grupo Industrial Bimbo, 19 191–93

Grupo Industrial Durango, S.A. de C.V., 37 176–78

Grupo Industrial Herradura, S.A. de C.V., 83 175–178

Grupo Industrial Lala, S.A. de C.V., 82 154–57

Grupo Industrial Saltillo, S.A. de C.V., 54 151–54

Grupo Leche Pascual S.A., 59 212–14

Grupo Lladró S.A., 52 147–49

Grupo Martins, 104 175–78

Grupo Mexico, S.A. de C.V., 40 220–23

Grupo Modelo, S.A. de C.V., 29 218–20

Grupo Omnilife S.A. de C.V., 88 143–46

Grupo Planeta, 94 218–22

Grupo Portucel Soporcel, 60 154–56

Grupo Posadas, S.A. de C.V., 57 168–70

Grupo Positivo, 105 196–99

Grupo TACA, 38 218–20

Grupo Televisa, S.A., 18 211–14; 54 155–58 (upd.)

Grupo TMM, S.A. de C.V., 50 208–11

Grupo Transportación Ferroviaria Mexicana, S.A. de C.V., 47 162–64

Grupo Viz, S.A. de C.V., 84 167–170

Gruppo Coin S.p.A., 41 185–87

Gruppo Riva Fire SpA, 88 147–50

Gryphon Holdings, Inc., 21 262–64

GSC Enterprises, Inc., 86 181–84

GSD&M Advertising, 44 197–200

GSD&M's Idea City, 90 217–21

GSG&T, Inc. *see* Gulf States Utilities Co.

GSI Commerce, Inc., 67 204–06

GSU *see* Gulf States Utilities Co.

GT Bicycles, 26 183–85

GT Interactive Software, 31 237–41 *see also* Infogrames Entertainment S.A.

GT Solar International, Inc., 101 224–28

GTE Corporation, V 294–98; 15 192–97 (upd.) *see also* British Columbia Telephone Company; Verizon Communications.

GTSI Corp., 57 171–73

Guangzhou Pearl River Piano Group Ltd., 49 177–79

Guangzhou R&F Properties Co., Ltd., 95 167–69

Guardian Financial Services, 11 168–70; 64 171–74 (upd.)

Guardian Industries Corp., 87 197–204

Guardian Media Group plc, 53 152–55

Guardsmark, L.L.C., 77 171–74

Gucci Group N.V., 15 198–200; 50 212–16 (upd.)

Gudang Garam *see* PT Gudang Garam Tbk

Guenther *see* C.H. Guenther & Son, Inc.

Guerbet Group, 46 214–16

Guerlain, 23 240–42

Guess, Inc., 15 201–03; 68 187–91 (upd.)

Guest Supply, Inc., 18 215–17

Guida-Seibert Dairy Company, 84 171–174

Guidant Corporation, 58 149–51

Guilbert S.A., 42 169–71

Guilford Mills Inc., 8 234–36; 40 224–27 (upd.)

Guillemot Corporation, 41 188–91, 407, 409

Guillin *see* Groupe Guillin SA

Guinness/UDV, I 250–52; 43 212–16 (upd.) *see also* Diageo plc.

Guinot Paris S.A., 82 158–61

Guitar Center, Inc., 29 221–23; 68 192–95 (upd.)

Guittard Chocolate Company, 55 183–85

Gulf + Western Inc., I 451–53 *see also* Paramount Communications; Viacom Inc.

Gulf Agency Company Ltd., 78 133–36

Gulf Air Company, 56 146–48

Gulf Island Fabrication, Inc., 44 201–03
Gulf States Utilities Company, 6 495–97 *see also* Entergy Corp.
GulfMark Offshore, Inc., 49 180–82
Gulfstream Aerospace Corporation, 7 205–06; 28 169–72 (upd.)
Gund, Inc., 96 159–62
Gunite Corporation, 51 152–55
The Gunlocke Company, 23 243–45
Gunnebo AB, 53 156–58
GUS plc, 47 165–70 (upd.)
Guthy-Renker Corporation, 32 237–40
Guttenplan's Frozen Dough Inc., 88 151–54
Guy Degrenne SA, 44 204–07
Guyenne et Gascogne, 23 246–48
Gwathmey Siegel & Associates Architects LLC, 26 186–88
GWR Group plc, 39 198–200
Gymboree Corporation, 15 204–06; 69 198–201 (upd.)

H

H&M Hennes & Mauritz AB, 98 181–84 (upd.)
H&R Block, Inc., 9 268–70; 29 224–28 (upd.); 82 162–69 (upd.)
H-P *see* Hewlett-Packard Co.
H.B. Fuller Company, 8 237–40; 32 254–58 (upd.); 75 179–84 (upd.)
H. Betti Industries Inc., 88 155–58
H.D. Vest, Inc., 46 217–19
H. E. Butt Grocery Company, 13 251–53; 32 259–62 (upd.); 85 164–70 (upd.)
H.F. Ahmanson & Company, II 181–82; 10 342–44 (upd.) *see also* Washington Mutual, Inc.
H. J. Heinz Company, II 507–09; 11 171–73 (upd.); 36 253–57 (upd.); 99 198–205 (upd.)
H.J. Russell & Company, 66 162–65
H. Lundbeck A/S, 44 208–11
H.M. Payson & Co., 69 202–04
H.O. Penn Machinery Company, Inc., 96 163–66
The H.W. Wilson Company, 66 166–68
Ha-Lo Industries, Inc., 27 193–95
The Haartz Corporation, 94 223–26
Habersham Bancorp, 25 185–87
The Habitat Company LLC, 106 213–17
Habitat for Humanity International, Inc., 36 258–61; 106 218–22 (upd.)
Hach Co., 18 218–21
Hachette Filipacchi Medias S.A., 21 265–67
Hachette S.A., IV 617–19 *see also* Matra-Hachette S.A.
Haci Omer Sabanci Holdings A.S., 55 186–89 *see also* Akbank TAS
Hackman Oyj Adp, 44 212–15
Hadco Corporation, 24 201–03
Haeger Industries Inc., 88 159–62
Haemonetics Corporation, 20 277–79
Haftpflichtverband der Deutschen Industrie Versicherung auf

Gegenseitigkeit V.a.G. *see* HDI (Haftpflichtverband der Deutschen Industrie Versicherung auf Gegenseitigkeit V.a.G.).
Hagemeyer N.V., 39 201–04
Haggar Corporation, 19 194–96; 78 137–41 (upd.)
Haggen Inc., 38 221–23
Hagoromo Foods Corporation, 84 175–178
Hahn Automotive Warehouse, Inc., 24 204–06
Haier Group Corporation, 65 167–70
Haights Cross Communications, Inc., 84 179–182
The Hain Celestial Group, Inc., 27 196–98; 43 217–20 (upd.)
Hair Club For Men Ltd., 90 222–25
Hakuhodo, Inc., 6 29–31; 42 172–75 (upd.)
HAL Inc., 9 271–73 *see also* Hawaiian Airlines, Inc.
Hal Leonard Corporation, 96 167–71
Hale-Halsell Company, 60 157–60
Half Price Books, Records, Magazines Inc., 37 179–82
Hall, Kinion & Associates, Inc., 52 150–52
Halliburton Company, III 497–500; 25 188–92 (upd.); 55 190–95 (upd.)
Hallmark Cards, Inc., IV 620–21; 16 255–57 (upd.); 40 228–32 (upd.); 87 205–212 (upd.)
Halma plc, 104 179–83
Hamilton Beach/Proctor-Silex Inc., 17 213–15
Hammacher Schlemmer & Company Inc., 21 268–70; 72 160–62 (upd.)
Hammerson plc, IV 696–98; 40 233–35 (upd.)
Hammond Manufacturing Company Limited, 83 179–182
Hamon & Cie (International) S.A., 97 190–94
Hamot Health Foundation, 91 227–32
Hampshire Group Ltd., 82 170–73
Hampton Affiliates, Inc., 77 175–79
Hampton Industries, Inc., 20 280–82
Hancock Fabrics, Inc., 18 222–24
Hancock Holding Company, 15 207–09
Handleman Company, 15 210–12; 86 185–89 (upd.)
Handspring Inc., 49 183–86
Handy & Harman, 23 249–52
Hanesbrands Inc., 98 185–88
Hang Lung Group Ltd., 104 184–87
Hang Seng Bank Ltd., 60 161–63
Hanger Orthopedic Group, Inc., 41 192–95
Hanjin Shipping Co., Ltd., 50 217–21
Hankook Tire Company Ltd., 105 200–03
Hankyu Corporation, V 454–56; 23 253–56 (upd.)
Hankyu Department Stores, Inc., V 70–71; 62 168–71 (upd.)
Hanmi Financial Corporation, 66 169–71

Hanna Andersson Corp., 49 187–90
Hanna-Barbera Cartoons Inc., 23 257–59, 387
Hannaford Bros. Co., 12 220–22; 103 211–17 (upd.)
Hanover Compressor Company, 59 215–17
Hanover Direct, Inc., 36 262–65
Hanover Foods Corporation, 35 211–14
Hansen Natural Corporation, 31 242–45; 76 171–74 (upd.)
Hansgrohe AG, 56 149–52
Hanson Building Materials America Inc., 60 164–66
Hanson PLC, III 501–03; 7 207–10 (upd.); 30 228–32 (upd.)
Hanwha Group, 62 172–75
Hapag-Lloyd AG, 6 397–99; 97 195–203 (upd.)
Happy Kids Inc., 30 233–35
Harbert Corporation, 14 222–23
Harbison-Walker Refractories Company, 24 207–09
Harbour Group Industries, Inc., 90 226–29
Harcourt Brace and Co., 12 223–26
Harcourt Brace Jovanovich, Inc., IV 622–24
Harcourt General, Inc., 20 283–87 (upd.)
Hard Rock Café International, Inc., 12 227–29; 32 241–45 (upd.); 105 204–09 (upd.)
Harding Lawson Associates Group, Inc., 16 258–60
Hardinge Inc., 25 193–95
HARIBO GmbH & Co. KG, 44 216–19
Harkins Amusement Enterprises, Inc., 94 227–31
Harland and Wolff Holdings plc, 19 197–200
Harland Clarke Holdings Corporation, 94 232–35 (upd.)
Harlem Globetrotters International, Inc., 61 122–24
Harlequin Enterprises Limited, 52 153–56
Harley-Davidson, Inc., 7 211–14; 25 196–200 (upd.); 106 223–28 (upd.)
Harley Ellis Devereaux Corporation, 101 229–32
Harleysville Group Inc., 37 183–86
Harman International Industries, Incorporated, 15 213–15; 101 233–39 (upd.)
Harmon Industries, Inc., 25 201–04 *see also* General Electric Co.
Harmonic Inc., 43 221–23
Harmony Gold Mining Company Limited, 63 182–85
Harnischfeger Industries, Inc., 8 241–44; 38 224–28 (upd.) *see also* Joy Global Inc.
Harold's Stores, Inc., 22 248–50
Harper Group Inc., 17 216–19
HarperCollins Publishers, 15 216–18
Harpo Inc., 28 173–75; 66 172–75 (upd.)

Harps Food Stores, Inc., 99 206–209

Harrah's Entertainment, Inc., 16 261–63; 43 224–28 (upd.)

Harris Corporation, II 37–39; 20 288–92 (upd.); 78 142–48 (upd.)

Harris Interactive Inc., 41 196–99; 92 148–53 (upd.)

Harris Publishing *see* Bernard C. Harris Publishing Company, Inc.

The Harris Soup Company (Harry's Fresh Foods),92 154–157

Harris Teeter Inc., 23 260–62; 72 163–66 (upd.)

Harrisons & Crosfield plc, III 696–700 *see also* Elementis plc.

Harrods Holdings, 47 171–74

Harry London Candies, Inc., 70 110–12

Harry N. Abrams, Inc., 58 152–55

Harry Winston Inc., 45 184–87; 104 188–93 (upd.)

Harry's Farmers Market Inc., 23 263–66 *see also* Whole Foods Market, Inc.

Harry's Fresh Foods *see* The Harris Soup Company (Harry's Fresh Foods)

Harsco Corporation, 8 245–47; 105 210–15 (upd.)

Harte-Hanks Communications, Inc., 17 220–22; 63 186–89 (upd.)

Hartmann Inc., 96 172–76

Hartmarx Corporation, 8 248–50; 32 246–50 (upd.)

The Hartstone Group plc, 14 224–26

The Hartz Mountain Corporation, 12 230–32; 46 220 23 (upd.)

Harvey Norman Holdings Ltd., 56 153–55

Harveys Casino Resorts, 27 199–201 *see also* Harrah's Entertainment, Inc.

Harza Engineering Company, 14 227–28

Hasbro, Inc., III 504–06; 16 264–68 (upd.); 43 229–34 (upd.)

Haskel International, Inc., 59 218–20

Hastings Entertainment, Inc., 29 229–31; 104 194–99 (upd.)

Hastings Manufacturing Company, 56 156–58

Hauser, Inc., 46 224–27

Havas, SA, 10 345–48; 33 178–82 (upd.) *see also* Vivendi Universal Publishing

Haverty Furniture Companies, Inc., 31 246–49

Hawaiian Airlines Inc., 22 251–53 (upd.) *see also* HAL Inc.

Hawaiian Electric Industries, Inc., 9 274–77

Hawaiian Holdings, Inc., 96 177–81 (upd.)

Hawk Corporation, 59 221–23

Hawker Siddeley Group Public Limited Company, III 507–10

Hawkeye Holdings LLC, 86 246–49

Hawkins Chemical, Inc., 16 269–72

Haworth Inc., 8 251–52; 39 205–08 (upd.)

Hay Group Holdings, Inc., 100 210–14

Hay House, Inc., 93 241–45

Hayel Saeed Anam Group of Cos., 92 158–61

Hayes Corporation, 24 210–14

Hayes Lemmerz International, Inc., 27 202–04

Haynes International, Inc., 88 163–66

Haynes Publishing Group P.L.C., 71 169–71

Hays plc, 27 205–07; 78 149–53 (upd.)

Hazelden Foundation, 28 176–79

Hazlewood Foods plc, 32 251–53

HBO *see* Home Box Office Inc.

HCA—The Healthcare Company, 35 215–18 (upd.)

HCI Direct, Inc., 55 196–98

HDI (Haftpflichtverband der Deutschen Industrie Versicherung auf Gegenseitigkeit V.a.G.), 53 159–63

HDOS Enterprises, 72 167–69

HDR Inc., 48 203–05

Head N.V., 55 199–201

Headlam Group plc, 95 170–73

Headwaters Incorporated, 56 159–62

Headway Corporate Resources, Inc., 40 236–38

Health Care & Retirement Corporation, 22 254–56

Health Communications, Inc., 72 170–73

Health Management Associates, Inc., 56 163–65

Health O Meter Products Inc., 14 229–31

Health Risk Management, Inc., 24 215–17

Health Systems International, Inc., 11 174–76

HealthExtras, Inc., 75 185–87

HealthMarkets, Inc., 88 167–72 (upd.)

HealthSouth Corporation, 14 232–34; 33 183–86 (upd.)

Healthtex, Inc., 17 223–25 *see also* VF Corp.

The Hearst Corporation, IV 625–27; 19 201–04 (upd.); 46 228–32 (upd.)

Heartland Express, Inc., 18 225–27

The Heat Group, 53 164–66

Hechinger Company, 12 233–36

Hecla Mining Company, 20 293–96

Heekin Can Inc., 13 254–56 *see also* Ball Corp.

Heelys, Inc., 87 213–216

Heery International, Inc., 58 156–59

HEICO Corporation, 30 236–38

Heidelberger Druckmaschinen AG, 40 239–41

Heidelberger Zement AG, 31 250–53

Heidrick & Struggles International, Inc., 28 180–82

Heijmans N.V., 66 176–78

Heileman Brewing Co *see* G. Heileman Brewing Co.

Heilig-Meyers Company, 14 235–37; 40 242–46 (upd.)

Heineken N.V., I 256–58; 13 257–59 (upd.); 34 200–04 (upd.); 90 230–36 (upd.)

Heinrich Deichmann-Schuhe GmbH & Co. KG, 88 173–77

Heinz Co *see* H.J. Heinz Co.

Helen of Troy Corporation, 18 228–30

Helene Curtis Industries, Inc., 8 253–54; 28 183–85 (upd.) *see also* Unilever PLC.

Helix Energy Solutions Group, Inc., 81 173–77

Hella KGaA Hueck & Co., 66 179–83

Hellenic Petroleum SA, 64 175–77

Heller, Ehrman, White & McAuliffe, 41 200–02

Helly Hansen ASA, 25 205–07

Helmerich & Payne, Inc., 18 231–33

Helmsley Enterprises, Inc., 9 278–80; 39 209–12 (upd.)

Helzberg Diamonds, 40 247–49

Hemisphere GPS Inc., 99 210–213

Hemlo Gold Mines Inc., 9 281–82 *see also* Newmont Mining Corp.

Henderson Land Development Company Ltd., 70 113–15

Hendrick Motorsports, Inc., 89 250–53

Henkel KGaA, III 31–34; 34 205–10 (upd.); 95 174–83 (upd.)

Henkel Manco Inc., 22 257–59

The Henley Group, Inc., III 511–12

Hennes & Mauritz AB, 29 232–34 *see also* H&M Hennes & Mauritz AB

Henry Boot plc, 76 175–77

Henry Crown and Company, 91 233–36

Henry Dreyfuss Associates LLC, 88 178–82

Henry Ford Health System, 84 183–187

Henry Modell & Company Inc., 32 263–65

Henry Schein, Inc., 31 254–56; 70 116–19 (upd.)

Hensel Phelps Construction Company, 72 174–77

Hensley & Company, 64 178–80

HEPCO *see* Hokkaido Electric Power Company Inc.

Her Majesty's Stationery Office, 7 215–18

Heraeus Holding GmbH, IV 98–100; 54 159–63 (upd.)

Herald Media, Inc., 91 237–41

Herbalife Ltd., 17 226–29; 41 203–06 (upd.); 92 162–67 (upd.)

Hercules Inc., I 343–45; 22 260–63 (upd.); 66 184–88 (upd.)

Hercules Technology Growth Capital, Inc., 87 217–220

Herley Industries, Inc., 33 187–89

Herman Goelitz, Inc., 28 186–88 *see also* Jelly Belly Candy Co.

Herman Goldner Company, Inc., 100 215–18

Herman Miller, Inc., 8 255–57; 77 180–86 (upd.)

Hermès International S.A., 14 238–40; 34 211–14 (upd.)

Hero Group, 100 219–24

Héroux-Devtek Inc., 69 205–07

Herr Foods Inc., 84 188–191

Herradura *see* Grupo Industrial Herradura, S.A. de C.V.
Herschend Family Entertainment Corporation, 73 173–76
Hershey Foods Corporation, II 510–12; 15 219–22 (upd.); 51 156–60 (upd.)
Herstal *see* Groupe Herstal S.A.
Hertie Waren- und Kaufhaus GmbH, V 72–74
The Hertz Corporation, 9 283–85; 33 190–93 (upd.); 101 240–45 (upd.)
Heska Corporation, 39 213–16
Heublein Inc., I 259–61
Heuer *see* TAG Heuer International SA.
Heuliez *see* Groupe Henri Heuliez S.A.
Hewitt Associates, Inc., 77 187–90
Hewlett-Packard Company, III 142–43; 6 237–39 (upd.); 28 189–92 (upd.); 50 222–30 (upd.)
Hexagon AB, 78 154–57
Hexal AG, 69 208–10
Hexcel Corporation, 28 193–95
HFF, Inc., 103 218–21
hhgregg Inc., 98 189–92
HI *see* Houston Industries Inc.
Hibbett Sporting Goods, Inc., 26 189–91; 70 120–23 (upd.)
Hibernia Corporation, 37 187–90
Hickory Farms, Inc., 17 230–32
HickoryTech Corporation, 92 168–71
High Falls Brewing Company LLC, 74 144–47
High Tech Computer Corporation, 81 178–81
Highland Gold Mining Limited, 95 184–87
Highlights for Children, Inc., 95 188–91
Highmark Inc., 27 208–11
Highsmith Inc., 60 167–70
Highveld Steel and Vanadium Corporation Limited, 59 224–27
Hikma Pharmaceuticals Ltd., 102 166–70
Hilb, Rogal & Hobbs Company, 77 191–94
Hildebrandt International, 29 235–38
Hilding Anders AB, 102 171–74
Hill's Pet Nutrition, Inc., 27 212–14
Hillenbrand Industries, Inc., 10 349–51; 75 188–92 (upd.)
Hillerich & Bradsby Company, Inc., 51 161–64
The Hillhaven Corporation, 14 241–43 *see also* Vencor, Inc.
Hills Industries Ltd., 104 200–04
Hills Stores Company, 13 260–61
Hillsdown Holdings, PLC, II 513–14; 24 218–21 (upd.)
Hilmar Cheese Company, Inc., 98 193–96
Hilo Hattie *see* Pomare Ltd.
Hilti AG, 53 167–69
Hilton Group plc, III 91–93; 19 205–08 (upd.); 62 176–79 (upd.); 49 191–95 (upd.)
Hindustan Lever Limited, 79 198–201
Hines Horticulture, Inc., 49 196–98

Hino Motors, Ltd., 7 219–21; 21 271–74 (upd.)
HiPP GmbH & Co. Vertrieb KG, 88 183–88
Hiram Walker Resources Ltd., I 262–64
Hispanic Broadcasting Corporation, 35 219–22
HIT Entertainment PLC, 40 250–52
Hitachi, Ltd., I 454–55; 12 237–39 (upd.); 40 253–57 (upd.)
Hitachi Metals, Ltd., IV 101–02
Hitachi Zosen Corporation, III 513–14; 53 170–73 (upd.)
Hitchiner Manufacturing Co., Inc., 23 267–70
Hite Brewery Company Ltd., 97 204–07
Hittite Microwave Corporation, 106 229–32
HMI Industries, Inc., 17 233–35
HMV Group plc, 59 228–30
HNI Corporation, 74 148–52 (upd.)
Ho-Chunk Inc., 61 125–28
HOB Entertainment, Inc., 37 191–94
Hobby Lobby Stores Inc., 80 139–42
Hobie Cat Company, 94 236–39
Hochtief AG, 33 194–97; 88 189–94 (upd.)
The Hockey Company, 34 215–18; 70 124–26 (upd.)
Hodes *see* Bernard Hodes Group Inc.
Hodgson Mill, Inc., 88 195–98
Hoechst AG, I 346–48; 18 234–37 (upd.)
Hoechst Celanese Corporation, 13 262–65
Hoenig Group Inc., 41 207–09
Hoesch AG, IV 103–06
Hoffman Corporation, 78 158–12
Hoffmann-La Roche & Co *see* F. Hoffmann-La Roche & Co.
Hogan & Hartson L.L.P., 44 220–23
Hogg Robinson Group PLC, 105 216–20
Hohner *see* Matth. Hohner AG.
HOK Group, Inc., 59 231–33
Hokkaido Electric Power Company Inc. (HEPCO), V 635–37; 58 160–63 (upd.)
Hokuriku Electric Power Company, V 638–40
Holberg Industries, Inc., 36 266–69
Holden Ltd., 62 180–83
Holderbank Financière Glaris Ltd., III 701–02 *see also* Holnam Inc
N.V. Holdingmaatschappij De Telegraaf, 23 271–73 *see also* Telegraaf Media Groep N.V.
Holiday Inns, Inc., III 94–95 *see also* Promus Companies, Inc.
Holiday Retirement Corp., 87 221–223
Holiday RV Superstores, Incorporated, 26 192–95
Holidaybreak plc, 96 182–86
Holland & Knight LLP, 60 171–74
Holland Burgerville USA, 44 224–26
The Holland Group, Inc., 82 174–77

Hollander Home Fashions Corp., 67 207–09
Holley Performance Products Inc., 52 157–60
Hollinger International Inc., 24 222–25; 62 184–88 (upd.)
Holly Corporation, 12 240–42
Hollywood Casino Corporation, 21 275–77
Hollywood Entertainment Corporation, 25 208–10
Hollywood Media Corporation, 58 164–68
Hollywood Park, Inc., 20 297–300
Holme Roberts & Owen LLP, 28 196–99
Holmen AB, 52 161–65 (upd.)
Holnam Inc., 8 258–60; 39 217–20 (upd.)
Hologic, Inc., 106 233–36
Holophane Corporation, 19 209–12
Holson Burnes Group, Inc., 14 244–45
Holt and Bugbee Company, 66 189–91
Holt's Cigar Holdings, Inc., 42 176–78
Holtzbrinck *see* Verlagsgruppe Georg von Holtzbrinck.
Homasote Company, 72 178–81
Home Box Office Inc., 7 222–24; 23 274–77 (upd.); 76 178–82 (upd.)
The Home Depot, Inc., V 75–76; 18 238–40 (upd.); 97 208–13 (upd.)
Home Hardware Stores Ltd., 62 189–91
Home Inns & Hotels Management Inc., 95 195–95
Home Insurance Company, III 262–64
Home Interiors & Gifts, Inc., 55 202–04
Home Product Center plc, 104 205–08
Home Products International, Inc., 55 205–07
Home Properties of New York, Inc., 42 179–81
Home Retail Group plc, 91 242–46
Home Shopping Network, Inc., V 77–78; 25 211–15 (upd.) *see also* HSN.
HomeBase, Inc., 33 198–201 (upd.)
Homestake Mining Company, 12 243–45; 38 229–32 (upd.)
Hometown Auto Retailers, Inc., 44 227–29
HomeVestors of America, Inc., 77 195–98
Homex *see* Desarrolladora Homex, S.A. de C.V.
Hon Hai Precision Industry Co., Ltd., 59 234–36
HON Industries Inc., 13 266–69 *see* HNI Corp.
Honda Motor Company Ltd., I 174–76; 10 352–54 (upd.); 29 239–42 (upd.); 96 187–93 (upd.)
Honeywell Inc., II 40–43; 12 246–49 (upd.); 50 231–35 (upd.)
Hong Kong and China Gas Company Ltd., 73 177–79
Hong Kong Dragon Airlines Ltd., 66 192–94

Hong Kong Telecommunications Ltd., 6 319–21 *see also* Cable & Wireless HKT.

Hongkong and Shanghai Banking Corporation Limited, II 296–99 *see also* HSBC Holdings plc.

Hongkong Electric Holdings Ltd., 6 498–500; 23 278–81 (upd.)

Hongkong Land Holdings Ltd., IV 699–701; 47 175–78 (upd.)

Honshu Paper Co., Ltd., IV 284–85 *see also* Oji Paper Co., Ltd.

Hoogovens *see* Koninklijke Nederlandsche Hoogovens en Staalfabricken NV.

Hooker Furniture Corporation, 80 143–46

Hooper Holmes, Inc., 22 264–67

Hooters of America, Inc., 18 241–43; 69 211–14 (upd.)

The Hoover Company, 12 250–52; 40 258–62 (upd.)

HOP, LLC, 80 147–50

Hops Restaurant Bar and Brewery, 46 233–36

Hopson Development Holdings Ltd., 87 224–227

Horace Mann Educators Corporation, 22 268–70; 90 237–40 (upd.)

Horizon Food Group, Inc., 100 225–28

Horizon Lines, Inc., 98 197–200

Horizon Organic Holding Corporation, 37 195–99

Hormel Foods Corporation, 18 244–47 (upd.); 54 164–69 (upd.)

Hornbach Holding AG, 98 201–07

Hornbeck Offshore Services, Inc., 101 246–49

Hornby PLC, 105 221–25

Horsehead Industries, Inc., 51 165–67

Horseshoe Gaming Holding Corporation, 62 192–95

Horton Homes, Inc., 25 216–18

Horween Leather Company, 83 183–186

Hoshino Gakki Co. Ltd., 55 208–11

Hospira, Inc., 71 172–74

Hospital Central Services, Inc., 56 166–68

Hospital Corporation of America, III 78–80 *see also* HCA - The Healthcare Co.

Hospitality Franchise Systems, Inc., 11 177–79 *see also* Cendant Corp.

Hospitality Worldwide Services, Inc., 26 196–98

Hoss's Steak and Sea House Inc., 68 196–98

Host America Corporation, 79 202–06

Hot Dog on a Stick *see* HDOS Enterprises.

Hot Stuff Foods, 85 171–74

Hot Topic Inc., 33 202–04; 86 190–94 (upd.)

Hotel Properties Ltd., 71 175–77

Houchens Industries Inc., 51 168–70

Houghton Mifflin Company, 10 355–57; 36 270–74 (upd.)

House of Fabrics, Inc., 21 278–80 *see also* Jo-Ann Stores, Inc.

House of Fraser PLC, 45 188–91 *see also* Harrods Holdings.

House of Prince A/S, 80 151–54

Household International, Inc., II 417–20; 21 281–86 (upd.) *see also* HSBC Holdings plc.

Houston Industries Incorporated, V 641–44 *see also* Reliant Energy Inc.

Houston Wire & Cable Company, 97 214–17

Hovnanian Enterprises, Inc., 29 243–45; 89 254–59 (upd.)

Howard Hughes Medical Institute, 39 221–24

Howard Johnson International, Inc., 17 236–39; 72 182–86 (upd.)

Howmet Corporation, 12 253–55 *see also* Alcoa Inc.

HP *see* Hewlett-Packard Co.

HSBC Holdings plc, 12 256–58; 26 199–204 (upd.); 80 155–63 (upd.)

HSN, 64 181–85 (upd.)

Huawei Technologies Company Ltd., 87 228–231

Hub Group, Inc., 38 233–35

Hub International Limited, 89 260–64

Hubbard Broadcasting Inc., 24 226–28; 79 207–12 (upd.)

Hubbell Inc., 9 286–87; 31 257–59 (upd.); 76 183–86 (upd.)

Huddle House, Inc., 105 226–29

The Hudson Bay Mining and Smelting Company, Limited, 12 259–61

Hudson Foods Inc., 13 270–72 *see also* Tyson Foods, Inc.

Hudson River Bancorp, Inc., 41 210–13

Hudson's Bay Company, V 79–81; 25 219–22 (upd.); 83 187–194 (upd.)

Huffy Corporation, 7 225–27; 30 239–42 (upd.)

Hughes Electronics Corporation, 25 223–25

Hughes Hubbard & Reed LLP, 44 230–32

Hughes Markets, Inc., 22 271–73 *see also* Kroger Co.

Hughes Supply, Inc., 14 246–47

Hugo Boss AG, 48 206–09

Huhtamäki Oyj, 64 186–88

HUK-Coburg, 58 169–73

Hulman & Company, 44 233–36

Hüls A.G., I 349–50 *see also* Degussa-Hüls AG.

Human Factors International Inc., 100 229–32

Humana Inc., III 81–83; 24 229–32 (upd.); 101 250–56 (upd.)

The Humane Society of the United States, 54 170–73

Hummel International A/S, 68 199–201

Hummer Winblad Venture Partners, 97 218–21

Hungarian Telephone and Cable Corp., 75 193–95

Hungry Howie's Pizza and Subs, Inc., 25 226–28

Hunt Consolidated, Inc., 7 228–30; 27 215–18 (upd.)

Hunt Manufacturing Company, 12 262–64

Hunt-Wesson, Inc., 17 240–42 *see also* ConAgra Foods, Inc.

Hunter Fan Company, 13 273–75; 98 208–12 (upd.)

Hunting plc, 78 163–16

Huntingdon Life Sciences Group plc, 42 182–85

Huntington Bancshares Incorporated, 11 180–82; 87 232–238 (upd.)

Huntington Learning Centers, Inc., 55 212–14

Huntleigh Technology PLC, 77 199–202

Hunton & Williams, 35 223–26

Huntsman Corporation, 8 261–63; 98 213–17 (upd.)

Huron Consulting Group Inc., 87 239–243

Hurricane Hydrocarbons Ltd., 54 174–77

Husky Energy Inc., 47 179–82

Hutchinson Technology Incorporated, 18 248–51; 63 190–94 (upd.)

Hutchison Whampoa Limited, 18 252–55; 49 199–204 (upd.)

Huttig Building Products, Inc., 73 180–83

HVB Group, 59 237–44 (upd.)

Hvide Marine Incorporated, 22 274–76

Hy-Vee, Inc., 36 275–78

Hyatt Corporation, III 96–97; 16 273–75 (upd.) *see* Global Hyatt Corp.

Hyde Athletic Industries, Inc., 17 243–45 *see also* Saucony Inc.

Hyder plc, 34 219–21

Hydril Company, 46 237–39

Hydro-Quebéc, 6 501–03; 32 266–69 (upd.)

Hylsamex, S.A. de C.V., 39 225–27

Hypercom Corporation, 27 219–21

Hyperion Software Corporation, 22 277–79

Hyperion Solutions Corporation, 76 187–91

Hyster Company, 17 246–48

Hyundai Group, III 515–17; 7 231–34 (upd.); 56 169–73 (upd.)

I

I Grandi Viaggi S.p.A., 105 230–33

I.C. Isaacs & Company, 31 260–62

I.M. Pei & Associates *see* Pei Cobb Freed & Partners Architects LLP.

i2 Technologies, Inc., 87 252–257

IAC Group, 96 194–98

Iams Company, 26 205–07

IAWS Group plc, 49 205–08

Iberdrola, S.A., 49 209–12

Iberia Líneas Aéreas De España S.A., 6 95–97; 36 279–83 (upd.); 91 247–54 (upd.)

IBERIABANK Corporation, 37 200–02

IBJ *see* The Industrial Bank of Japan Ltd.

IBM *see* International Business Machines Corp.
IBP, Inc., II 515–17; 21 287–90 (upd.)
Ibstock Brick Ltd., 37 203–06 (upd.)
Ibstock plc, 14 248–50
IC Industries Inc., I 456–58 *see also* Whitman Corp.
ICA AB, II 639–40
ICEE-USA *see* J & J Snack Foods Corp.
Iceland Group plc, 33 205–07 *see also* The Big Food Group plc.
Icelandair, 52 166–69
Icelandic Group hf, 81 182–85
ICF International, Inc., 28 200–04; 94 240–47 (upd.)
ICI *see* Imperial Chemical Industries plc.
ICL plc, 6 240–42
ICN Pharmaceuticals, Inc., 52 170–73
ICON Health & Fitness, Inc., 38 236–39; 102 175–79 (upd.)
ICU Medical, Inc., 106 237–42
Idaho Power Company, 12 265–67
IDB Communications Group, Inc., 11 183–85
IDB Holding Corporation Ltd., 97 222–25
Ideal Mortgage Bankers, Ltd., 105 234–37
Idealab, 105 238–42
Idearc Inc., 90 241–44
Idemitsu Kosan Co., Ltd., IV 434–36; 49 213–16 (upd.)
Identix Inc., 44 237–40
IDEO Inc., 65 171–73
IDEX Corp., 103 222–26
IDEXX Laboratories, Inc., 23 282–84
IDG Books Worldwide, Inc., 27 222–24 *see also* International Data Group, Inc.
IDG Communications, Inc *see* International Data Group, Inc.
IdraPrince, Inc., 76 192–94
IDT Corporation, 34 222–24; 99 214–219 (upd.)
IDX Systems Corporation, 64 189–92
IEC Electronics Corp., 42 186–88
IFF *see* International Flavors & Fragrances Inc.
IG Group Holdings plc, 97 226–29
IGA, Inc., 99 220–224
Igloo Products Corp., 21 291–93; 105 243–47 (upd.)
IGT *see* International Game Technology.
IHC Caland N.V., 71 178–80
IHI *see* Ishikawajima-Harima Heavy Industries Co., Ltd.
IHOP Corporation, 17 249–51; 58 174–77 (upd.)
Ihr Platz GmbH + Company KG, 77 203–06
IHS Inc., 78 167–70
II-VI Incorporated, 69 353–55
IKEA Group, V 82–84; 26 208–11 (upd.); 94 248–53 (upd.)
IKON Office Solutions, Inc., 50 236–39
Ikonics Corporation, 99 225–228
Il Fornaio (America) Corporation, 27 225–28

ILFC *see* International Lease Finance Corp.
Ilitch Holdings Inc., 37 207–210; 86 195–200 (upd.)
Illinois Bell Telephone Company, 14 251–53
Illinois Central Corporation, 11 186–89
Illinois Power Company, 6 504–07 *see also* Ameren Corp.
Illinois Tool Works Inc., III 518–20; 22 280–83 (upd.); 81 186–91 (upd.)
Illumina, Inc., 93 246–49
illycaffè SpA, 50 240–44
ILX Resorts Incorporated, 65 174–76
Image Entertainment, Inc., 94 254–57
Imagine Entertainment, 91 255–58
Imagine Foods, Inc., 50 245–47
Imasco Limited, V 401–02
Imation Corporation, 20 301–04 *see also* 3M Co.
Imatra Steel Oy Ab, 55 215–17
IMAX Corporation, 28 205–08; 78 171–76 (upd.)
IMC Fertilizer Group, Inc., 8 264–66
ImClone Systems Inc., 58 178–81
IMCO Recycling, Incorporated, 32 270–73
Imerys S.A., 40 176, 263–66 (upd.)
Imetal S.A., IV 107–09
IMG, 78 177–80
IMI plc, 9 288–89; 29 364
Immucor, Inc., 81 192–96
Immunex Corporation, 14 254–56; 50 248–53 (upd.)
Imo Industries Inc., 7 235–37; 27 229–32 (upd.)
IMPATH Inc., 45 192–94
Imperial Chemical Industries plc, I 351–53; 50 254–58 (upd.)
Imperial Holly Corporation, 12 268–70 *see also* Imperial Sugar Co.
Imperial Industries, Inc., 81 197–200
Imperial Oil Limited, IV 437–39; 25 229–33 (upd.); 95 196–203 (upd.)
Imperial Parking Corporation, 58 182–84
Imperial Sugar Company, 32 274–78 (upd.)
Imperial Tobacco Group PLC, 50 259–63
IMS Health, Inc., 57 174–78
In Focus Systems, Inc., 22 287–90
In-N-Out Burgers Inc., 19 213–15; 74 153–56 (upd.)
In-Sink-Erator, 66 195–98
InaCom Corporation, 13 276–78
Inamed Corporation, 79 213–16
Inchcape PLC, III 521–24; 16 276–80 (upd.); 50 264–68 (upd.)
Inco Limited, IV 110–12; 45 195–99 (upd.)
Incyte Genomics, Inc., 52 174–77
Indel, Inc., 78 181–84
Independent News & Media PLC, 61 129–31
Indian Airlines Ltd., 46 240–42
Indian Oil Corporation Ltd., IV 440–41; 48 210–13 (upd.)

Indiana Bell Telephone Company, Incorporated, 14 257–61
Indiana Energy, Inc., 27 233–36
Indianapolis Motor Speedway Corporation, 46 243–46
Indigo Books & Music Inc., 58 185–87
Indigo NV, 26 212–14 *see also* Hewlett-Packard Co.
Indosat *see* PT Indosat Tbk.
Indus International Inc., 70 127–30
Industria de Diseño Textil S.A. (Inditex), 64 193–95
Industrial Bank of Japan, Ltd., II 300–01
Industrial Light & Magic *see* Lucasfilm Ltd.
Industrial Services of America, Inc., 46 247–49
Industrias Bachoco, S.A. de C.V., 39 228–31
Industrias Penoles, S.A. de C.V., 22 284–86
Industrie Natuzzi S.p.A., 18 256–58
Industrie Zignago Santa Margherita S.p.A., 67 210–12
Infineon Technologies AG, 50 269–73
Infinity Broadcasting Corporation, 11 190–92; 48 214–17 (upd.)
InFocus Corporation, 92 172–75
Infogrames Entertainment S.A., 35 227–30
Informa Group plc, 58 188–91
Information Access Company, 17 252–55
Information Builders, Inc., 22 291–93
Information Holdings Inc., 47 183–86
Information Resources, Inc., 10 358–60
Informix Corporation, 10 361–64; 30 243–46 (upd.) *see also* International Business Machines Corp.
InfoSonics Corporation, 81 201–04
InfoSpace, Inc., 91 259–62
Infosys Technologies Ltd., 38 240–43
Ing. C. Olivetti & C., S.p.A., III 144–46 *see also* Olivetti S.p.A
Ingalls Shipbuilding, Inc., 12 271–73
Ingenico—Compagnie Industrielle et Financière d'Ingénierie, 46 250 52
Ingersoll-Rand Company, III 525–27; 15 223–26 (upd.); 55 218–22 (upd.)
Ingles Markets, Inc., 20 305–08
Ingram Industries, Inc., 11 193–95; 49 217–20 (upd.)
Ingram Micro Inc., 52 178–81
INI *see* Instituto Nacional de Industria.
Initial Security, 64 196–98
Inktomi Corporation, 45 200–04
Inland Container Corporation, 8 267–69 *see also* Temple-Inland Inc.
Inland Steel Industries, Inc., IV 113–16; 19 216–20 (upd.)
Innovative Solutions & Support, Inc., 85 175–78
Innovo Group Inc., 83 195–199
INPEX Holdings Inc., 97 230–33
Input/Output, Inc., 73 184–87
Inserra Supermarkets, 25 234–36
Insight Enterprises, Inc., 18 259–61

Insilco Corporation, 16 281–83
Insituform Technologies, Inc., 83 200–203
Inso Corporation, 26 215–19
Instinet Corporation, 34 225–27
Instituto Nacional de Industria, I 459–61
Insurance Auto Auctions, Inc., 23 285–87
Integra LifeSciences Holdings Corporation, 87 244–247
Integrated BioPharma, Inc., 83 204–207
Integrated Defense Technologies, Inc., 54 178–80
Integrity Inc., 44 241–43
Integrity Media, Inc., 102 180–83
Intel Corporation, II 44–46; 10 365–67 (upd.); 36 284–88 (upd.); 75 196–201 (upd.)
IntelliCorp, Inc., 45 205–07
Intelligent Electronics, Inc., 6 243–45
Inter Link Foods PLC, 61 132–34
Inter Parfums Inc., 35 235–38; 86 201–06 (upd.)
Inter-Regional Financial Group, Inc., 15 231–33 *see also* Dain Rauscher Corp.
Interactive Intelligence Inc., 106 243–47
Interbond Corporation of America, 101 257–60
Interbrand Corporation, 70 131–33
Interbrew S.A., 17 256–58; 50 274–79 (upd.)
Interceramic *see* Internacional de Ceramica, S.A. de C.V.
Interco Incorporated, III 528–31 *see also* Furniture Brands International, Inc.
IntercontinentalExchange, Inc., 95 204–07
Intercorp Excelle Foods Inc., 64 199–201
InterDigital Communications Corporation, 61 135–37
Interep National Radio Sales Inc., 35 231–34
Interface, Inc., 8 270–72; 29 246–49 (upd.); 76 195–99 (upd.)
Interfax News Agency, 86 207–10
Intergraph Corporation, 6 246–49; 24 233–36 (upd.)
The Interlake Corporation, 8 273–75
Intermec Technologies Corporation, 72 187–91
INTERMET Corporation, 32 279–82; 77 207–12 (upd.)
Intermix Media, Inc., 83 208–211
Intermountain Health Care, Inc., 27 237–40
Internacional de Ceramica, S.A. de C.V., 53 174–76
International Airline Support Group, Inc., 55 223–25
International Brotherhood of Teamsters, 37 211–14
International Business Machines Corporation, III 147–49; 6 250–53 (upd.); 30 247–51 (upd.); 63 195–201 (upd.)

International Controls Corporation, 10 368–70
International Creative Management, Inc., 43 235–37
International Dairy Queen, Inc., 10 371–74; 39 232–36 (upd.); 105 248–54 (upd.)
International Data Group, Inc., 7 238–40; 25 237–40 (upd.)
International Family Entertainment Inc., 13 279–81 *see also* Disney/ABC Television Group
International Flavors & Fragrances Inc., 9 290–92; 38 244–48 (upd.)
International Game Technology, 10 375–76; 41 214–16 (upd.)
International House of Pancakes *see* IHOP Corp.
International Lease Finance Corporation, 48 218–20
International Management Group, 18 262–65 *see also* IMG.
International Multifoods Corporation, 7 241–43; 25 241–44 (upd.) *see also* The J. M. Smucker Co.
International Olympic Committee, 44 244–47
International Paper Company, IV 286–88; 15 227–30 (upd.); 47 187–92 (upd.); 97 234–43 (upd.)
International Power PLC, 50 280–85 (upd.)
International Profit Associates, Inc., 87 248–251
International Rectifier Corporation, 31 263–66; 71 181–84 (upd.)
International Shipbreaking Ltd. L.L.C., 67 213–15
International Shipholding Corporation, Inc., 27 241–44
International Speedway Corporation, 19 221–23; 74 157–60 (upd.)
International Telephone & Telegraph Corporation, I 462–64; 11 196–99 (upd.)
International Total Services, Inc., 37 215–18
Interpool, Inc., 92 176–79
The Interpublic Group of Companies, Inc., I 16–18; 22 294–97 (upd.); 75 202–05 (upd.)
Interscope Music Group, 31 267–69
Intersil Corporation, 93 250–54
Interstate Bakeries Corporation, 12 274–76; 38 249–52 (upd.)
Interstate Hotels & Resorts Inc., 58 192–94
Intertek Group plc, 95 208–11
InterVideo, Inc., 85 179–82
Intevac, Inc., 92 180–83
Intimate Brands, Inc., 24 237–39
Intrado Inc., 63 202–04
Intrawest Corporation, 15 234–36; 84 192–196 (upd.)
Intres B.V., 82 178–81
Intuit Inc., 14 262–64; 33 208–11 (upd.); 73 188–92 (upd.)
Intuitive Surgical, Inc., 79 217–20

Invacare Corporation, 11 200–02; 47 193–98 (upd.)
Invensys PLC, 50 286–90 (upd.)
inVentiv Health, Inc., 81 205–08
The Inventure Group, Inc., 96 199–202 (upd.)
Inverness Medical Innovations, Inc., 63 205–07
Inversiones Nacional de Chocolates S.A., 88 199–202
Investcorp SA, 57 179–82
Investor AB, 63 208–11
Invitrogen Corporation, 52 182–84
Invivo Corporation, 52 185–87
Iogen Corporation, 81 209–13
Iomega Corporation, 21 294–97
IONA Technologies plc, 43 238–41
Ionatron, Inc., 85 183–86
Ionics, Incorporated, 52 188–90
Iowa Beef Processors *see* IBP, Inc.
Iowa Telecommunications Services, Inc., 85 187–90
Ipalco Enterprises, Inc., 6 508–09
IPC Magazines Limited, 7 244–47
Ipiranga S.A., 67 216–18
Ipsen International Inc., 72 192–95
Ipsos SA, 48 221–24
IranAir, 81 214–17
Irex Contracting Group, 90 245–48
IRIS International, Inc., 101 261–64
Irish Distillers Group, 96 203–07
Irish Life & Permanent Plc, 59 245–47
Irkut Corporation, 68 202–04
iRobot Corporation, 83 212–215
Iron Mountain, Inc., 33 212–14; 104 209–12 (upd.)
IRSA Inversiones y Representaciones S.A., 63 212–15
Irvin Feld & Kenneth Feld Productions, Inc., 15 237–39 *see also* Feld Entertainment, Inc.
Irwin Financial Corporation, 77 213–16
Irwin Toy Limited, 14 265–67
Isbank *see* Turkiye Is Bankasi A.S.
Iscor Limited, 57 183–86
Isetan Company Limited, V 85–87; 36 289–93 (upd.)
Ishikawajima-Harima Heavy Industries Company, Ltd., III 532–33; 86 211–15 (upd.)
The Island ECN, Inc., 48 225–29
Isle of Capri Casinos, Inc., 41 217–19
Ispat Inland Inc., 30 252–54; 40 267–72 (upd.)
Israel Aircraft Industries Ltd., 69 215–17
Israel Chemicals Ltd., 55 226–29
ISS A/S, 49 221–23
Istituto per la Ricostruzione Industriale S.p.A., I 465–67; 11 203–06 (upd.)
Isuzu Motors, Ltd., 9 293–95; 23 288–91 (upd.); 57 187–91 (upd.)
Itaú *see* Banco Itaú S.A.
ITC Holdings Corp., 75 206–08
Itel Corporation, 9 296–99
Items International Airwalk Inc., 17 259–61
ITM Entreprises SA, 36 294–97

Ito En Ltd., 101 265–68
Ito-Yokado Co., Ltd., V 88–89; 42 189–92 (upd.)
ITOCHU Corporation, 32 283–87 (upd.)
Itoh *see* C. Itoh & Co.
Itoham Foods Inc., II 518–19; 61 138–40 (upd.)
Itron, Inc., 64 202–05
ITT Educational Services, Inc., 33 215–17; 76 200–03 (upd.)
ITT Sheraton Corporation, III 98–101 *see also* Starwood Hotels & Resorts Worldwide, Inc.
ITV plc, 104 213–20 (upd.)
ITW *see* Illinois Tool Works Inc.
Ivar's, Inc., 86 216–19
IVAX Corporation, 11 207–09; 55 230–33 (upd.)
IVC Industries, Inc., 45 208–11
iVillage Inc., 46 253–56
Iwerks Entertainment, Inc., 34 228–30
IXC Communications, Inc., 29 250–52

J

J & J Snack Foods Corporation, 24 240–42
J&R Electronics Inc., 26 224–26
The J. Paul Getty Trust, 105 255–59
J. & W. Seligman & Co. Inc., 61 141–43
J.A. Jones, Inc., 16 284–86
J. Alexander's Corporation, 65 177–79
J.B. Hunt Transport Services Inc., 12 277–79
J. Baker, Inc., 31 270–73
J C Bamford Excavators Ltd., 83 216–222
J. C. Penney Company, Inc., V 90–92; 18 269–73 (upd.); 43 245–50 (upd.); 91 263–72 (upd.)
J. Crew Group, Inc., 12 280–82; 34 231–34 (upd.); 88 203–08
J.D. Edwards & Company, 14 268–70 *see also* Oracle Corp.
J.D. Power and Associates, 32 297–301
J. D'Addario & Company, Inc., 48 230 33
J.F. Shea Co., Inc., 55 234–36
J.H. Findorff and Son, Inc., 60 175–78
J.I. Case Company, 10 377–81 *see also* CNH Global N.V.
J.J. Darboven GmbH & Co. KG, 96 208–12
J.J. Keller & Associates, Inc., 81 2180–21
The J. Jill Group, Inc., 35 239–41; 90 249–53 (upd.)
J.L. Hammett Company, 72 196–99
J Lauritzen A/S, 90 254–57
J. Lohr Winery Corporation, 99 229–232
The J. M. Smucker Company, 11 210–12; 87 258–265 (upd.)
J.M. Voith AG, 33 222–25
J.P. Morgan Chase & Co., II 329–32; 30 261–65 (upd.); 38 253–59 (upd.)

J.R. Simplot Company, 16 287–89; 60 179–82 (upd.)
J Sainsbury plc, II 657–59; 13 282–84 (upd.); 38 260–65 (upd.); 95 212–20 (upd.)
J. W. Pepper and Son Inc., 86 220–23
J. Walter Thompson Co. *see* JWT Group Inc.
j2 Global Communications, Inc., 75 219–21
Jabil Circuit, Inc., 36 298–301; 88 209–14
Jack B. Kelley, Inc., 102 184–87
Jack Henry and Associates, Inc., 17 262–65; 94 258–63 (upd.)
Jack in the Box Inc., 89 265–71 (upd.)
Jack Morton Worldwide, 88 215–18
Jack Schwartz Shoes, Inc., 18 266–68
Jackpot Enterprises Inc., 21 298–300
Jackson Hewitt, Inc., 48 234–36
Jackson National Life Insurance Company, 8 276–77
Jacmar Companies, 87 266–269
Jaco Electronics, Inc., 30 255–57
Jacob Leinenkugel Brewing Company, 28 209–11
Jacobs Engineering Group Inc., 6 148–50; 26 220–23 (upd.); 106 248–54 (upd.)
Jacobs Suchard (AG), II 520–22 *see also* Kraft Jacobs Suchard AG.
Jacobson Stores Inc., 21 301–03
Jacor Communications, Inc., 23 292–95
Jacques Torres Chocolate *see* Mrchocolate.com LLC.
Jacques Whitford, 92 184–87
Jacquot *see* Établissements Jacquot and Cie S.A.S.
Jacuzzi Brands Inc., 23 296–98; 76 204–07 (upd.)
JAFCO Co. Ltd., 79 221–24
Jaguar Cars, Ltd., 13 285–87
Jaiprakash Associates Limited, 101 269–72
JAKKS Pacific, Inc., 52 191–94
JAL *see* Japan Airlines Company, Ltd.
Jalate Inc., 25 245–47
Jamba Juice Company, 47 199–202
James Avery Craftsman, Inc., 76 208–10
James Beattie plc, 43 242–44
James Hardie Industries N.V., 56 174–76
James Original Coney Island Inc., 84 197–200
James Purdey & Sons Limited, 87 270–275
James River Corporation of Virginia, IV 289–91 *see also* Fort James Corp.
Jani-King International, Inc., 85 191–94
JanSport, Inc., 70 134–36
Janssen Pharmaceutica N.V., 80 164–67
Janus Capital Group Inc., 57 192–94
Japan Airlines Company, Ltd., I 104–06; 32 288–92 (upd.)
Japan Broadcasting Corporation, 7 248–50
Japan Leasing Corporation, 8 278–80

Japan Pulp and Paper Company Limited, IV 292–93
Japan Tobacco Inc., V 403–04; 46 257–60 (upd.)
Jarden Corporation, 93 255–61 (upd.)
Jardine Cycle & Carriage Ltd., 73 193–95
Jardine Matheson Holdings Limited, I 468–71; 20 309–14 (upd.); 93 262–71 (upd.)
Jarvis plc, 39 237–39
Jason Incorporated, 23 299–301
Jay Jacobs, Inc., 15 243–45
Jayco Inc., 13 288–90
Jaypee Group *see* Jaiprakash Associates Ltd.
Jays Foods, Inc., 90 258–61
Jazz Basketball Investors, Inc., 55 237–39
Jazzercise, Inc., 45 212–14
JB Oxford Holdings, Inc., 32 293–96
JBS S.A., 100 233–36
JCDecaux S.A., 76 211–13
JD Wetherspoon plc, 30 258–60
JDA Software Group, Inc., 101 273–76
JDS Uniphase Corporation, 34 235–37
JE Dunn Construction Group, Inc., 85 195–98
The Jean Coutu Group (PJC) Inc., 46 261–65
Jean-Georges Enterprises L.L.C., 75 209–11
Jeanneau *see* Chantiers Jeanneau S.A.
Jefferies Group, Inc., 25 248–51
Jefferson-Pilot Corporation, 11 213–15; 29 253–56 (upd.)
Jefferson Properties, Inc. *see* JPI.
Jefferson Smurfit Group plc, IV 294–96; 19 224–27 (upd.); 49 224–29 (upd.) *see also* Smurfit-Stone Container Corp.
Jel Sert Company, 90 262–65
Jeld-Wen, Inc., 45 215–17
Jelly Belly Candy Company, 76 214–16
Jenkens & Gilchrist, P.C., 65 180–82
Jennie-O Turkey Store, Inc., 76 217–19
Jennifer Convertibles, Inc., 31 274–76
Jenny Craig, Inc., 10 382–84; 29 257–60 (upd.); 92 188–93 (upd.)
Jenoptik AG, 33 218–21
Jeppesen Sanderson, Inc., 92 194–97
Jerónimo Martins SGPS S.A., 96 213–16
Jerry's Famous Deli Inc., 24 243–45
Jersey European Airways (UK) Ltd., 61 144–46
Jersey Mike's Franchise Systems, Inc., 83 223–226
Jervis B. Webb Company, 24 246–49
Jet Airways (India) Private Limited, 65 183–85
JetBlue Airways Corporation, 44 248–50
Jetro Cash & Carry Enterprises Inc., 38 266–68
Jewett-Cameron Trading Company, Ltd., 89 272–76
JFE Shoji Holdings Inc., 88 219–22
JG Industries, Inc., 15 240–42

Jillian's Entertainment Holdings, Inc., 40 273–75

Jim Beam Brands Worldwide, Inc., 14 271–73; 58 194–96 (upd.)

The Jim Henson Company, 23 302–04; 106 255–59 (upd.)

The Jim Pattison Group, 37 219–22

Jimmy Carter Work Project *see* Habitat for Humanity International.

Jimmy John's Enterprises, Inc., 103 227–30

Jitney-Jungle Stores of America, Inc., 27 245–48

JJB Sports plc, 32 302–04

JKH Holding Co. LLC, 105 260–63

JLA Credit *see* Japan Leasing Corp.

JLG Industries, Inc., 52 195–97

JLL *see* Jones Lang LaSalle Inc.

JLM Couture, Inc., 64 206–08

JM Smith Corporation, 100 237–40

JMB Realty Corporation, IV 702–03 *see also* Amfac/JMB Hawaii L.L.C.

Jo-Ann Stores, Inc., 72 200–03 (upd.)

Jockey International, Inc., 12 283–85; 34 238–42 (upd.); 77 217–23 (upd.)

Joe's Sports & Outdoor, 98 218–22 (upd.)

The Joffrey Ballet of Chicago, 52 198–202

Johanna Foods, Inc., 104 221–24

John B. Sanfilippo & Son, Inc., 14 274–76; 101 277–81 (upd.)

John Brown plc, I 572–74

The John D. and Catherine T. MacArthur Foundation, 34 243–46

John D. Brush Company Inc., 94 264–67

The John David Group plc, 90 266–69

John Deere *see* Deere & Co.

John Dewar & Sons, Ltd., 82 182–86

John F. Kennedy Center for the Performing Arts,106 260–63

John Fairfax Holdings Limited, 7 251–54 *see also* Fairfax Media Ltd.

John Frieda Professional Hair Care Inc., 70 137–39

John H. Harland Company, 17 266–69

John Hancock Financial Services, Inc., III 265–68; 42 193–98 (upd.)

John Laing plc, I 575–76; 51 171–73 (upd.) *see also* Laing O'Rourke PLC.

John Lewis Partnership plc, V 93–95; 42 199–203 (upd.); 99 233–240 (upd.)

John Menzies plc, 39 240–43

The John Nuveen Company, 21 304–065

John Paul Mitchell Systems, 24 250–52

John Q. Hammons Hotels, Inc., 24 253–55

John W. Danforth Company, 48 237–39

John Wiley & Sons, Inc., 17 270–72; 65 186–90 (upd.)

Johnny Rockets Group, Inc., 31 277–81; 76 220–24 (upd.)

Johns Manville Corporation, 64 209–14 (upd.)

Johnson *see* Axel Johnson Group.

Johnson & Higgins, 14 277–80 *see also* Marsh & McLennan Companies, Inc.

Johnson & Johnson, III 35–37; 8 281–83 (upd.); 36 302–07 (upd.); 75 212–18 (upd.)

Johnson Controls, Inc., III 534–37; 26 227–32 (upd.); 59 248–54 (upd.)

Johnson Matthey PLC, IV 117–20; 16 290–94 (upd.); 49 230–35 (upd.)

Johnson Outdoors Inc., 84 201–205 (upd.)

Johnson Publishing Company, Inc., 28 212–14; 72 204–07 (upd.)

Johnson Wax *see* S.C. Johnson & Son, Inc.

Johnson Worldwide Associates, Inc., 28 215–17 *see also* Johnson Outdoors Inc.

Johnsonville Sausage L.L.C., 63 216–19

Johnston Industries, Inc., 15 246–48

Johnston Press plc, 35 242–44

Johnstown America Industries, Inc., 23 305–07

Jolly Hotels *see* Compagnia Italiana dei Jolly Hotels S.p.A.

Jones Apparel Group, Inc., 11 216–18; 39 244–47 (upd.)

Jones, Day, Reavis & Pogue, 33 226–29

Jones Intercable, Inc., 21 307–09

Jones Knowledge Group, Inc., 97 244–48

Jones Lang LaSalle Incorporated, 49 236–38

Jones Medical Industries, Inc., 24 256–58

Jones Soda Co., 69 218–21

Jongleurs Comedy Club *see* Regent Inns plc.

Jordache Enterprises, Inc., 23 308–10

The Jordan Company LP, 70 140–42

Jordan Industries, Inc., 36 308–10

Jordan-Kitt Music Inc., 86 224–27

Jordano's, Inc., 102 188–91

Jos. A. Bank Clothiers, Inc., 31 282–85; 104 225–30 (upd.)

José de Mello SGPS S.A., 96 217–20

Joseph T. Ryerson & Son, Inc., 15 249–51 *see also* Ryerson Tull, Inc.

Jostens, Inc., 7 255–57; 25 252–55 (upd.); 73 196–200 (upd.)

Jotun A/S, 80 168–71

JOULÉ Inc., 58 197–200

Journal Communications, Inc., 86 228–32

Journal Register Company, 29 261–63

Joy Global Inc., 104 231–38 (upd.)

JPI, 49 239–41

JPMorgan Chase & Co., 91 273–84 (upd.)

JPS Textile Group, Inc., 28 218–20

JSC MMC Norilsk Nickel, 48 300–02

JSP Corporation, 74 161–64

JTH Tax Inc., 103 231–34

The Judge Group, Inc., 51 174–76

Jugos del Valle, S.A. de C.V., 85 199–202

Juicy Couture, Inc., 80 172–74

Jujo Paper Co., Ltd., IV 297–98

Julius Baer Holding AG, 52 203–05

Julius Blüthner Pianofortefabric GmbH, 78 185–88

Julius Meinl International AG, 53 177–80

Jumbo S.A., 96 221–24

Jumeirah Group, 83 227–230

Jungheinrich AG, 96 225–30

Juniper Networks, Inc., 43 251–55

Juno Lighting, Inc., 30 266–68

Juno Online Services, Inc., 38 269–72 *see also* United Online, Inc.

Jupitermedia Corporation, 75 222–24

Jurys Doyle Hotel Group plc, 64 215–17

JUSCO Co., Ltd., V 96–99 *see also* AEON Co., Ltd.

Just Bagels Manufacturing, Inc., 94 268–71

Just Born, Inc., 32 305–07

Just For Feet, Inc., 19 228–30

Justin Industries, Inc., 19 231–33 *see also* Berkshire Hathaway Inc.

Juventus F.C. S.p.A, 53 181–83

JVC *see* Victor Company of Japan, Ltd.

JWP Inc., 9 300–02 *see also* EMCOR Group Inc.

JWT Group Inc., I 19–21 *see also* WPP Group plc.

Jysk Holding A/S, 100 241–44

K

K-Swiss Inc., 33 243–45; 89 277–81 (upd.)

K-tel International, Inc., 21 325–28

K&B Inc., 12 286–88

K & G Men's Center, Inc., 21 310–12

K.A. Rasmussen AS, 99 241–244

K2 Inc., 16 295–98; 84 206–211 (upd.)

Kadant Inc., 96 231–34 (upd.)

Kaiser Aluminum Corporation, IV 121–23; 84 212–217 (upd.)

Kaiser Foundation Health Plan, Inc., 53 184–86

Kajima Corporation, I 577–78; 51 177–79 (upd.)

Kal Kan Foods, Inc., 22 298–300

Kaman Corporation, 12 289–92; 42 204–08 (upd.)

Kaman Music Corporation, 68 205–07

Kampgrounds of America, Inc., 33 230–33

Kamps AG, 44 251–54

Kana Software, Inc., 51 180–83

Kanebo, Ltd., 53 187–91

Kanematsu Corporation, IV 442–44; 24 259–62 (upd.); 102 192–95 (upd.)

The Kansai Electric Power Company, Inc., V 645–48; 62 196–200 (upd.)

Kansai Paint Company Ltd., 80 175–78

Kansallis-Osake-Pankki, II 302–03

Kansas City Power & Light Company, 6 510–12 *see also* Great Plains Energy Inc.

Kansas City Southern Industries, Inc., 6 400–02; 26 233–36 (upd.)

The Kansas City Southern Railway Company, 92 198–202

Kao Corporation, III 38–39; 20 315–17 (upd.); 79 225–30 (upd.)

Kaplan, Inc., 42 209–12; 90 270–75 (upd.)

Kar Nut Products Company, 86 233–36

Karan Co. *see* Donna Karan Co.

Karl Kani Infinity, Inc., 49 242–45

Karlsberg Brauerei GmbH & Co KG, 41 220–23

Karmann *see* Wilhelm Karmann GmbH.

Karstadt Aktiengesellschaft, V 100–02; 19 234–37 (upd.)

Karstadt Quelle AG, 57 195–201 (upd.)

Karsten Manufacturing Corporation, 51 184–86

Kash n' Karry Food Stores, Inc., 20 318–20 *see also* Sweetbay Supermarket

Kashi Company, 89 282–85

Kasper A.S.L., Ltd., 40 276–79

kate spade LLC, 68 208–11

Katokichi Company Ltd., 82 187–90

Katy Industries Inc., I 472–74; 51 187–90 (upd.)

Katz Communications, Inc., 6 32–34 *see also* Clear Channel Communications, Inc.

Katz Media Group, Inc., 35 245–48

Kaufhof Warenhaus AG, V 103–05; 23 311–14 (upd.)

Kaufman and Broad Home Corporation, 8 284–86 *see also* KB Home.

Kaufring AG, 35 249–52

Kawai Musical Instruments Manufacturing Co.,Ltd., 78 189–92

Kawasaki Heavy Industries, Ltd., III 538–40; 63 220–23 (upd.)

Kawasaki Kisen Kaisha, Ltd., V 457–60; 56 177–81 (upd.)

Kawasaki Steel Corporation, IV 124–25

Kay-Bee Toy Stores, 15 252–53 *see also* KB Toys.

Kaydon Corporation, 18 274–76

KB Home, 45 218–22 (upd.)

KB Toys, Inc., 35 253–55 (upd.); 86 237–42 (upd.)

KBR Inc., 106 264–70 (upd.)

KC *see* Kenneth Cole Productions, Inc.

KCPL *see* Kansas City Power & Light Co

KCSI *see* Kansas City Southern Industries, Inc.

KCSR *see* The Kansas City Southern Railway.

Keane, Inc., 56 182–86

Keebler Foods Company, 36 311–13

Keio Corporation, V 461–62; 96 235–39 (upd.)

The Keith Companies Inc., 54 181–84

Keithley Instruments Inc., 16 299–301

Kelda Group plc, 45 223–26

Keller Group PLC, 95 221–24

Kelley Blue Book Company, Inc., 84 218–221

Kelley Drye & Warren LLP, 40 280–83

Kellogg Brown & Root, Inc., 62 201–05 (upd.) *see also* KBR Inc.

Kellogg Company, II 523–26; 13 291–94 (upd.); 50 291–96 (upd.)

Kellwood Company, 8 287–89; 85 203–08 (upd.)

Kelly-Moore Paint Company, Inc., 56 187–89

Kelly Services, Inc., 6 35–37; 26 237–40 (upd.)

The Kelly-Springfield Tire Company, 8 290–92

Kelsey-Hayes Group of Companies, 7 258–60; 27 249–52 (upd.)

Kemet Corp., 14 281–83

Kemira Oyj, 70 143–46

Kemper Corporation, III 269–71; 15 254–58 (upd.)

Kemps LLC, 103 235–38

Kendall International, Inc., 11 219–21 *see also* Tyco International Ltd.

Kendall-Jackson Winery, Ltd., 28 221–23

Kendle International Inc., 87 276–279

Kenetech Corporation, 11 222–24

Kenexa Corporation, 87 280–284

Kenmore Air Harbor Inc., 65 191–93

Kennametal, Inc., 13 295–97; 68 212–16 (upd.)

Kennecott Corporation, 7 261–64; 27 253–57 (upd.) *see also* Rio Tinto PLC.

Kennedy-Wilson, Inc., 60 183–85

Kenneth Cole Productions, Inc., 25 256–58

Ken's Foods, Inc., 88 223–26

Kensey Nash Corporation, 71 185–87

Kensington Publishing Corporation, 84 222–225

Kent Electronics Corporation, 17 273–76

Kentucky Electric Steel, Inc., 31 286–88

Kentucky Fried Chicken *see* KFC Corp.

Kentucky Utilities Company, 6 513–15

Kenwood Corporation, 31 289–91

Kenya Airways Limited, 89 286–89

Keolis SA, 51 191–93

Kepco *see* Korea Electric Power Corporation; Kyushu Electric Power Company Inc.

Keppel Corporation Ltd., 73 201–03

Keramik Holding AG Laufen, 51 194–96

Kerasotes ShowPlace Theaters LLC, 80 179–83

Kerr Group Inc., 24 263–65

Kerr-McGee Corporation, IV 445–47; 22 301–04 (upd.); 68 217–21 (upd.)

Kerry Group plc, 27 258–60; 87 285–291 (upd.)

Kerry Properties Limited, 22 305–08

Kerzner International Limited, 69 222–24 (upd.)

Kesa Electricals plc, 91 285–90

Kesko Ltd (Kesko Oy), 8 293–94; 27 261–63 (upd.)

Ketchum Communications Inc., 6 38–40

Kettle Foods Inc., 48 240–42

Kewaunee Scientific Corporation, 25 259–62

Kewpie Kabushiki Kaisha, 57 202–05

Key Safety Systems, Inc., 63 224–26

Key Technology Inc., 106 271–75

Key Tronic Corporation, 14 284–86

KeyCorp, 8 295–97; 92 272–81 (upd.)

Keyes Fibre Company, 9 303–05

Keynote Systems Inc., 102 196–99

Keys Fitness Products, LP, 83 231–234

KeySpan Energy Co., 27 264–66

Keystone International, Inc., 11 225–27 *see also* Tyco International Ltd.

KFC Corporation, 7 265–68; 21 313–17 (upd.); 89 290–96 (upd.)

Kforce Inc., 71 188–90

KGHM Polska Miedz S.A., 98 223–26

KHD Konzern, III 541–44

KI, 57 206–09

Kia Motors Corporation, 12 293–95; 29 264–67 (upd.); 56 173

Kiabi Europe, 66 199–201

Kidde plc, I 475–76; 44 255–59 (upd.)

Kiehl's Since 1851, Inc., 52 209–12

Kikkoman Corporation, 14 287–89; 47 203–06 (upd.)

Kimball International, Inc., 12 296–98; 48 243–47 (upd.)

Kimberly-Clark Corporation, III 40–41; 16 302–05 (upd.); 43 256–60 (upd.); 105 264–71 (upd.)

Kimberly-Clark de México, S.A. de C.V., 54 185–87

Kimco Realty Corporation, 11 228–30

Kimpton Hotel & Restaurant Group, Inc., 105 272–75

Kinder Morgan, Inc., 45 227–30

KinderCare Learning Centers, Inc., 13 298–300

Kinetic Concepts, Inc., 20 321–23

King & Spalding, 23 315–18

The King Arthur Flour Company, 31 292–95

King Kullen Grocery Co., Inc., 15 259–61

King Nut Company, 74 165–67

King Pharmaceuticals, Inc., 54 188–90

King Ranch, Inc., 14 290–92; 60 186–89 (upd.)

King World Productions, Inc., 9 306–08; 30 269–72 (upd.)

Kingfisher plc, V 106–09; 24 266–71 (upd.); 83 235–242 (upd.)

King's Hawaiian Bakery West, Inc., 101 282–85

Kingston Technology Corporation, 20 324–26

Kinki Nippon Railway Company Ltd., V 463–65

Kinko's Inc., 16 306–08; 43 261–64 (upd.)

Kinney Shoe Corp., 14 293–95

Kinray Inc., 85 209–12

Kinross Gold Corporation, 36 314–16

Kintera, Inc., 75 225–27

Kirby Corporation, 18 277–79; 66 202–04 (upd.)

Kirin Brewery Company, Limited, I 265–66; 21 318–21 (upd.); 63 227–31 (upd.)

Kirkland & Ellis LLP, 65 194–96

Kirlin's Inc., 98 227–30

Kirshenbaum Bond + Partners, Inc., 57 210–12
Kit Manufacturing Co., 18 280–82
Kitchell Corporation, 14 296–98
KitchenAid, 8 298–99
Kitty Hawk, Inc., 22 309–11
Kiva, 95 225–29
Kiwi International Airlines Inc., 20 327–29
KKR *see* Kohlberg Kravis Roberts & Co.
KLA-Tencor Corporation, 11 231–33; 45 231–34 (upd.)
Klabin S.A., 73 204–06
Klasky Csupo, Inc., 78 193–97
Klaus Steilmann GmbH & Co. KG, 53 192–95
Klein Tools, Inc., 95 230–34
Kleiner, Perkins, Caufield & Byers, 53 196–98
Kleinwort Benson Group PLC, II 421–23; 22 55 *see also* Dresdner Kleinwort Wasserstein.
Klement's Sausage Company, 61 147–49
KLM Royal Dutch Airlines, 104 239–45 (upd.)
Klöckner-Werke AG, IV 126–28; 58 201–05 (upd.)
Kluwer Publishers *see* Wolters Kluwer NV.
Kmart Corporation, V 110–12; 18 283–87 (upd.); 47 207–12 (upd.)
KMG Chemicals, Inc., 101 286–89
KN *see* Kühne & Nagel Group.
Knape & Vogt Manufacturing Company, 17 277–79
Knauf Gips KG, 100 245–50
K'Nex Industries, Inc., 52 206–08
Knight-Ridder, Inc., IV 628–30; 15 262–66 (upd.); 67 219–23 (upd.)
Knight Trading Group, Inc., 70 147–49
Knight Transportation, Inc., 64 218–21
Knoll, Inc., 14 299–301; 80 184–88 (upd.)
Knorr-Bremse AG, 84 226–231
Knorr Co. *see* C.H. Knorr Co.
The Knot, Inc., 74 168–71
Knott's Berry Farm, 18 288–90
Knouse Foods Cooperative Inc., 102 200–03
Knowledge Learning Corporation, 51 197–99; 54 191
Knowledge Universe, Inc., 54 191–94
KnowledgeWare Inc., 9 309–11; 31 296–98 (upd.)
KOA *see* Kampgrounds of America, Inc.
Koala Corporation, 44 260–62
Kobe Steel, Ltd., IV 129–31; 19 238–41 (upd.)
Kobrand Corporation, 82 191–94
Koç Holding A.S., I 478–80; 54 195–98 (upd.)
Koch Enterprises, Inc., 29 215–17
Koch Industries, Inc., IV 448–49; 20 330–32 (upd.); 77 224–30 (upd.)
Kodak *see* Eastman Kodak Co.
Kodansha Ltd., IV 631–33; 38 273–76 (upd.)
Koenig & Bauer AG, 64 222–26

Kohlberg Kravis Roberts & Co., 24 272–74; 56 190–94 (upd.)
Kohler Company, 7 269–71; 32 308–12 (upd.)
Kohl's Corporation, 9 312–13; 30 273–75 (upd.); 77 231–35 (upd.)
Kohn Pedersen Fox Associates P.C., 57 213–16
Kolbenschmidt Pierburg AG, 97 249–53
The Koll Company, 8 300–02
Kollmorgen Corporation, 18 291–94
Kolmar Laboratories Group, 96 240–43
Komag, Inc., 11 234–35
Komatsu Ltd., III 545–46; 16 309–11 (upd.); 52 213–17 (upd.)
Konami Corporation, 96 244–47
KONE Corporation, 27 267–70; 76 225–28 (upd.)
Konica Corporation, III 547–50; 30 276–81 (upd.)
König Brauerei GmbH & Co. KG, 35 256–58 (upd.)
Koninklijke Ahold N.V., II 641–42; 16 312–14 (upd.)
Koninklijke Grolsch BV *see* Royal Grolsch NV.
Koninklijke Houthandel G Wijma & Zonen BV, 96 248–51
Koninklijke KPN N.V. *see* Royal KPN N.V.
Koninklijke Luchtvaart Maatschappij N.V., I 107–09; 28 224–27 (upd.) *see also* KLM Royal Dutch Airlines.
Koninklijke Nederlandsche Hoogovens en Staalfabrieken NV, IV 132–34
N.V. Koninklijke Nederlandse Vliegtuigenfabriek Fokker, I 54–56; 28 327–30 (upd.)
Koninklijke Nedlloyd N.V., 6 403–05; 26 241–44 (upd.)
Koninklijke Numico N.V. *see* Royal Numico N.V.
Koninklijke Philips Electronics N.V., 50 297–302 (upd.)
Koninklijke PTT Nederland NV, V 299–301 *see also* Royal KPN NV.
Koninklijke Reesink N.V., 104 246–50
Koninklijke Vendex KBB N.V. (Royal Vendex KBB N.V.), 62 206–09 (upd.)
Koninklijke Wessanen nv, II 527–29; 54 199–204 (upd.)
Koo Koo Roo, Inc., 25 263–65
Kookmin Bank, 58 206–08
Kooperativa Förbundet, 99 245–248
Koor Industries Ltd., II 47–49; 25 266–68 (upd.); 68 222–25 (upd.)
Kopin Corporation, 80 189–92
Koppers Industries, Inc., I 354–56; 26 245–48 (upd.)
Korbel Champagne Cellers *see* F. Korbel & Bros. Inc.
Körber AG, 60 190–94
Korea Electric Power Corporation (Kepco), 56 195–98
Korean Air Lines Co. Ltd., 6 98–99; 27 271–73 (upd.)
Koret of California, Inc., 62 210–13

Korn/Ferry International, 34 247–49; 102 204–08 (upd.)
Kos Pharmaceuticals, Inc., 63 232–35
Koss Corporation, 38 277–79
Kotobukiya Co., Ltd., V 113–14; 56 199–202 (upd.)
KPMG International, 10 385–87; 33 234–38 (upd.)
KPN *see* Koninklijke PTT Nederland N.V.
Kraft Foods Inc., II 530–34; 7 272–77 (upd.); 45 235–44 (upd.); 91 291–306 (upd.)
Kraft Jacobs Suchard AG, 26 249–52 (upd.)
KraftMaid Cabinetry, Inc., 72 208–10
Kraus-Anderson Companies, Inc., 36 317–20; 83 243–248 (upd.)
Krause Publications, Inc., 35 259–61
Krause's Furniture, Inc., 27 274–77
Kredietbank N.V., II 304–056
Kreditanstalt für Wiederaufbau, 29 268–72
Kreisler Manufacturing Corporation, 97 254–57
Krispy Kreme Doughnut Corporation, 21 322–24; 61 150–54 (upd.)
The Kroger Company, II 643–45; 15 267–70 (upd.); 65 197–202 (upd.)
Kroll Inc., 57 217–20
Krombacher Brauerei Bernhard Schadeberg GmbH & Co. KG, 104 251–56
Kronos, Inc., 18 295–97; 19 468; 100 251–55 (upd.)
Kruger Inc., 17 280–82; 103 239–45 (upd.)
Krung Thai Bank Public Company Ltd., 69 225–27
Krupp AG *see* Fried. Krupp GmbH; ThyssenKrupp AG.
Kruse International, 88 227–30
The Krystal Company, 33 239–42
KSB AG, 62 214–18
KT&G Corporation, 62 219–21
KTM Power Sports AG, 100 256–59
KU Energy Corporation, 11 236–38 *see also* LG&E Energy Corp.
Kubota Corporation, III 551–53
Kudelski Group SA, 44 263–66
Kuehne & Nagel International AG, V 466–69; 53 199–203 (upd.)
Kuhlman Corporation, 20 333–35
Kühne *see* Carl Kühne KG (GmbH & Co.).
Kühne & Nagel International AG, V 466–69
Kulicke and Soffa Industries, Inc., 33 246–48; 76 229–31 (upd.)
Kumagai Gumi Company, Ltd., I 579–80
Kumho Tire Company Ltd., 105 276–79
Kumon Institute of Education Co., Ltd., 72 211–14
Kuoni Travel Holding Ltd., 40 284–86
Kurzweil Technologies, Inc., 51 200–04

The Kushner-Locke Company, 25 269–71
Kuwait Airways Corporation, 68 226–28
Kuwait Flour Mills & Bakeries Company, 84 232–234
Kuwait Petroleum Corporation, IV 450–52; 55 240–43 (upd.)
Kvaerner ASA, 36 321–23
Kwang Yang Motor Company Ltd., 80 193–96
Kwik-Fit Holdings plc, 54 205–07
Kwik Save Group plc, 11 239–41
Kwizda Holding GmbH, 102 209–12
Kymmene Corporation, IV 299–303 *see also* UPM-Kymmene Corp.
Kyocera Corporation, II 50–52; 21 329–32 (upd.); 79 231–36 (upd.)
Kyokuyo Company Ltd., 75 228–30
Kyowa Hakko Kogyo Co., Ltd., III 42–43; 48 248–50 (upd.)
Kyphon Inc., 87 292–295
Kyushu Electric Power Company Inc., V 649–51

L

L-3 Communications Holdings, Inc., 48 251–53
L. and J.G. Stickley, Inc., 50 303–05
L.A. Darling Company, 92 203–06
L.A. Gear, Inc., 8 303–06; 32 313–17 (upd.)
L.A. T Sportswear, Inc., 26 257–59
L.B. Foster Company, 33 255–58
L.D.C. SA, 61 155–57
L. Foppiano Wine Co., 101 290–93
L.L. Bean, Inc., 10 388–90; 38 280–83 (upd.); 91 307–13 (upd.)
The L.L. Knickerbocker Co., Inc., 25 272–75
L. Luria & Son, Inc., 19 242–44
L. M. Berry and Company, 80 197–200
L.S. Starrett Company, 13 301–03; 64 227–30 (upd.)
La Choy Food Products Inc., 25 276–78
La Doria SpA, 101 294–97
La Madeleine French Bakery & Café, 33 249–51
La Poste, V 270–72; 47 213–16 (upd.)
The La Quinta Companies, 11 242–44; 42 213–16 (upd.)
La Reina Inc., 96 252–55
La Seda de Barcelona S.A., 100 260–63
La Senza Corporation, 66 205–07
La Serenísima *see* Mastellone Hermanos S.A.
La-Z-Boy Incorporated, 14 302–04; 50 309–13 (upd.)
LAB *see* Lloyd Aéreo Boliviano S.A
Lab Safety Supply, Inc., 102 213–16
LaBarge Inc., 41 224–26
Labatt Brewing Company Limited, I 267–68; 25 279–82 (upd.)
Labeyrie SAS, 80 201–04
LabOne, Inc., 48 254–57
Labor Ready, Inc., 29 273–75; 88 231–36 (upd.)

Laboratoires Arkopharma S.A., 75 231–34
Laboratoires de Biologie Végétale Yves Rocher, 35 262–65
Laboratoires Pierre Fabre S.A., 100 353–57
Laboratory Corporation of America Holdings, 42 217–20 (upd.)
LaBranche & Co. Inc., 37 223–25
LaCie Group S.A., 76 232–34
Lacks Enterprises Inc., 61 158–60
Laclede Steel Company, 15 271–73
LaCrosse Footwear, Inc., 18 298–301; 61 161–65 (upd.)
Ladbroke Group PLC, II 141–42; 21 333–36 (upd.) *see also* Hilton Group plc.
LADD Furniture, Inc., 12 299–301 *see also* La-Z-Boy Inc.
Ladish Co., Inc., 30 282–84
Lafarge Cement UK, 54 208–11 (upd.)
Lafarge Coppée S.A., III 703–05
Lafarge Corporation, 28 228–31
Lafuma S.A., 39 248–50
Laidlaw International, Inc., 80 205–08
Laing O'Rourke PLC, 93 282–85 (upd.)
L'Air Liquide SA, I 357–59; 47 217–20 (upd.)
Lakeland Industries, Inc., 45 245–48
Lakes Entertainment, Inc., 51 205–07
Lakeside Foods, Inc., 89 297–301
Lala *see* Grupo Industrial Lala, S.A. de C.V.
Lam Research Corporation, 11 245–47; 31 299–302 (upd.)
Lam Son Sugar Joint Stock Corporation (Lasuco), 60 195–97
Lamar Advertising Company, 27 278–80; 70 150–53 (upd.)
The Lamaur Corporation, 41 227–29
Lamb Weston, Inc., 23 319–21
Lambda Legal Defense and Education Fund, Inc., 106 276–80
Lamborghini *see* Automobili Lamborghini S.p.A.
Lamonts Apparel, Inc., 15 274–76
The Lamson & Sessions Co., 13 304–06; 61 166–70 (upd.)
Lan Chile S.A., 31 303–06
Lancair International, Inc., 67 224–26
Lancaster Colony Corporation, 8 307–09; 61 171–74 (upd.)
Lance, Inc., 14 305–07; 41 230–33 (upd.)
Lancer Corporation, 21 337–39
Land and Houses PCL, 104 257–61
Land O'Lakes, Inc., II 535–37; 21 340–43 (upd.); 81 222–27 (upd.)
Land Securities PLC, IV 704–06; 49 246–50 (upd.)
LandAmerica Financial Group, Inc., 85 213–16
Landauer, Inc., 51 208–10
Landec Corporation, 95 235–38
Landmark Communications, Inc., 12 302–05; 55 244–49 (upd.)
Landmark Theatre Corporation, 70 154–56

Landor Associates, 81 228–31
Landry's Restaurants, Inc., 15 277–79; 65 203–07 (upd.)
Lands' End, Inc., 9 314–16; 29 276–79 (upd.); 82 195–200 (upd.)
Landsbanki Islands hf, 81 232–35
Landstar System, Inc., 63 236–38
Lane Bryant, Inc., 64 231–33
The Lane Co., Inc., 12 306–08
Lanier Worldwide, Inc., 75 235–38
Lanoga Corporation, 62 222–24 *see also* Pro-Build Holdings Inc.
Lapeyre S.A. *see* Groupe Lapeyre S.A.
Larry Flynt Publishing Inc., 31 307–10
Larry H. Miller Group of Companies, 29 280–83; 104 262–67 (upd.)
Las Vegas Sands Corp., 50 306–08; 106 281–84 (upd.)
Laserscope, 67 227–29
LaSiDo Inc., 58 209–11
Lason, Inc., 31 311–13
Lassonde Industries Inc., 68 229–31
Lasuco *see* Lam Son Sugar Joint Stock Corp.
Latécoère S.A., 100 264–68
Latham & Watkins, 33 252–54
Latrobe Brewing Company, 54 212–14
Lattice Semiconductor Corp., 16 315–17
Lauda Air Luftfahrt AG, 48 258–60
Laura Ashley Holdings plc, 13 307–09; 37 226–29 (upd.)
The Laurel Pub Company Limited, 59 255–57
Laurent-Perrier SA, 42 221–23
Laurus N.V., 65 208–11
Lavoro Bank AG *see* Banca Nazionale del Lavoro SpA.
Lawson Software, 38 284–88
Lawter International Inc., 14 308–10 *see also* Eastman Chemical Co.
Layne Christensen Company, 19 245–47
Lazard LLC, 38 289–92
Lazare Kaplan International Inc., 21 344–47
Lazio *see* Società Sportiva Lazio SpA.
Lazy Days RV Center, Inc., 69 228–30
LCA-Vision, Inc, 85 217–20
LCC International, Inc., 84 235–238
LCI International, Inc., 16 318–20 *see also* Qwest Communications International, Inc.
LDB Corporation, 53 204–06
LDC, 68 232–34
LDC S.A. *see* L.D.C. S.A.
LDDS-Metro Communications, Inc., 8 310–12 *see also* MCI WorldCom, Inc.
LDI Ltd., LLC, 76 235–37
LDK Solar Co., Ltd., 101 298–302
Le Bon Marché *see* The Bon Marché.
Le Chateau Inc., 63 239–41
Le Cordon Bleu S.A., 67 230–32
Le Duff *see* Groupe Le Duff S.A.
Le Monde S.A., 33 308–10
Léa Nature *see* Groupe Léa Nature.
Leap Wireless International, Inc., 69 231–33

LeapFrog Enterprises, Inc., 54 215–18
Lear Corporation, 16 321–23; 71 191–95 (upd.)
Lear Siegler Inc., I 481–83
Learjet Inc., 8 313–16; 27 281–85 (upd.)
Learning Care Group, Inc., 76 238–41 (upd.)
The Learning Company Inc., 24 275–78
Learning Tree International Inc., 24 279–82
LeaRonal, Inc., 23 322–24 see also Rohm and Haas Co.
Leaseway Transportation Corp., 12 309–11
Leatherman Tool Group, Inc., 51 211–13
Lebhar-Friedman, Inc., 55 250–52
Leblanc Corporation see G. Leblanc Corp.
LeBoeuf, Lamb, Greene & MacRae, L.L.P., 29 284–86
LECG Corporation, 93 286–89
Leche Pascual see Grupo Leche Pascual S.A.
Lechmere Inc., 10 391–93
Lechters, Inc., 11 248–50; 39 251–54 (upd.)
Leclerc see Association des Centres Distributeurs E. Leclerc.
LeCroy Corporation, 41 234–37
Ledcor Industries Limited, 46 266–69
Ledesma Sociedad Anónima Agrícola Industrial, 62 225–27
Lee Apparel Company, Inc., 8 317–19
Lee Enterprises, Incorporated, 11 251–53; 64 234–37 (upd.)
Leeann Chin, Inc., 30 285–88
Lefrak Organization Inc., 26 260–62
Legal & General Group Plc, III 272–73; 24 283–85 (upd.); 101 303–08 (upd.)
The Legal Aid Society, 48 261–64
Legal Sea Foods Inc., 96 256–60
Legent Corporation, 10 394–96 see also Computer Associates International, Inc.
Legg Mason, Inc., 33 259–62
Leggett & Platt, Inc., 11 254–56; 48 265–68 (upd.)
Lego A/S, 13 310–13; 40 287–91 (upd.)
Legrand SA, 21 348–50
Lehigh Portland Cement Company, 23 325–27
Lehman Brothers Holdings Inc., 99 249–253 (upd.)
Leica Camera AG, 35 266–69
Leica Microsystems Holdings GmbH, 35 270–73
Leidy's, Inc., 93 290–92
Leinenkugel Brewing Company see Jacob Leinenkugel Brewing Co.
Leiner Health Products Inc., 34 250–52
Lend America see Ideal Mortgage Bankers, Ltd.
Lend Lease Corporation Limited, IV 707–09; 17 283–86 (upd.); 52 218–23 (upd.)
LendingTree, LLC, 93 293–96
Lennar Corporation, 11 257–59

Lennox International Inc., 8 320–22; 28 232–36 (upd.)
Lenovo Group Ltd., 80 209–12
Lenox, Inc., 12 312–13
LensCrafters Inc., 23 328–30; 76 242–45 (upd.)
L'Entreprise Jean Lefebvre, 23 331–33 see also Vinci.
Leo Burnett Company, Inc., I 22–24; 20 336–39 (upd.)
The Leona Group LLC, 84 239–242
Leoni AG, 98 231–36
Leprino Foods Company, 28 237–39
Leroux S.A.S., 65 212–14
Leroy Merlin SA, 54 219–21
Les Boutiques San Francisco, Inc., 62 228–30
Les Echos see Groupe Les Echos.
Les Schwab Tire Centers, 50 314–16
Lesaffre see Societe Industrielle Lesaffre.
Lesco Inc., 19 248–50
The Leslie Fay Company, Inc., 8 323–25; 39 255–58 (upd.)
Leslie's Poolmart, Inc., 18 302–04
Leucadia National Corporation, 11 260–62; 71 196–200 (upd.)
Leupold & Stevens, Inc., 52 224–26
Level 3 Communications, Inc., 67 233–35
Levenger Company, 63 242–45
Lever Brothers Company, 9 317–19 see also Unilever.
Levi, Ray & Shoup, Inc., 96 261–64
Levi Strauss & Co., V 362–65; 16 324–28 (upd.); 102 217 23 (upd.)
Levitz Furniture Inc., 15 280–82
Levy Restaurants L.P., 26 263–65
The Lewin Group Inc., 104 268–71
Lewis Drug Inc., 94 272–76
Lewis Galoob Toys Inc., 16 329–31
Lewis-Goetz and Company, Inc., 102 224–27
LEXIS-NEXIS Group, 33 263–67
Lexmark International, Inc., 18 305–07; 79 237–42 (upd.)
LG&E Energy Corporation, 6 516–18; 51 214–17 (upd.)
LG Corporation, 94 277–83 (upd.)
Li & Fung Limited, 59 258–61
Libbey Inc., 49 251–54
The Liberty Corporation, 22 312–14
Liberty Livewire Corporation, 42 224–27
Liberty Media Corporation, 50 317–19
Liberty Mutual Holding Company, 59 262–64
Liberty Orchards Co., Inc., 89 302–05
Liberty Property Trust, 57 221–23
Liberty Travel, Inc., 56 203–06
Libyan National Oil Corporation, IV 453–55 see also National Oil Corp.
Liebherr-International AG, 64 238–42
Life Care Centers of America Inc., 76 246–48
Life is good, Inc., 80 213–16
Life Technologies, Inc., 17 287–89
Life Time Fitness, Inc., 66 208–10
LifeCell Corporation, 77 236–39

Lifeline Systems, Inc., 32 374; 53 207–09
LifeLock, Inc., 91 314–17
LifePoint Hospitals, Inc., 69 234–36
Lifetime Brands, Inc., 27 286–89; 73 207–11 (upd.)
Lifetime Entertainment Services, 51 218–22
Lifetouch Inc., 86 243–47
Lifeway Foods, Inc., 65 215–17
LifeWise Health Plan of Oregon, Inc., 90 276–79
Ligand Pharmaceuticals Incorporated, 10 48; 47 221–23
LILCO see Long Island Lighting Co.
Lillian Vernon Corporation, 12 314–15; 35 274–77 (upd.); 92 207–12 (upd.)
Lilly & Co see Eli Lilly & Co.
Lilly Endowment Inc., 70 157–59
Limagrain see Groupe Limagrain.
The Limited, Inc., V 115–16; 20 340–43 (upd.)
LIN Broadcasting Corp., 9 320–22
Linamar Corporation, 18 308–10
Lincare Holdings Inc., 43 265–67
Lincoln Center for the Performing Arts, Inc., 69 237–41
Lincoln Electric Co., 13 314–16
Lincoln National Corporation, III 274–77; 25 286–90 (upd.)
Lincoln Property Company, 8 326–28; 54 222–26 (upd.)
Lincoln Snacks Company, 24 286–88
Lincoln Telephone & Telegraph Company, 14 311–13
Lindal Cedar Homes, Inc., 29 287–89
Linde AG, I 581–83; 67 236–39 (upd.)
Lindley see Corporación José R. Lindley S.A.
Lindsay Manufacturing Co., 20 344–46
Lindt & Sprüngli see Chocoladefabriken Lindt & Sprüngli AG.
Linear Technology Corporation, 16 332–34; 99 254–258 (upd.)
Linens 'n Things, Inc., 24 289–92; 75 239–43 (upd.)
LinkedIn Corporation, 103 246–49
Lintas: Worldwide, 14 314–16
The Lion Brewery, Inc., 86 248–52
Lion Corporation, III 44–45; 51 223–26 (upd.)
Lion Nathan Limited, 54 227–30
Lionel L.L.C., 16 335–38; 99 259–265 (upd.)
Lions Gate Entertainment Corporation, 35 278–81
Lipman Electronic Engineering Ltd., 81 236–39
Lipton see Thomas J. Lipton Co.
Liqui-Box Corporation, 16 339–41
Liquidity Services, Inc., 101 309–13
Liquidnet, Inc., 79 243–46
LIRR see The Long Island Rail Road Co.
Litehouse Inc., 60 198–201
Lithia Motors, Inc., 41 238–40
Littelfuse, Inc., 26 266–69

Little Caesar Enterprises, Inc., 7 278–79; 24 293–96 (upd.) *see also* Ilitch Holdings Inc.
Little Switzerland, Inc., 60 202–04
Little Tikes Company, 13 317–19; 62 231–34 (upd.)
Littleton Coin Company Inc., 82 201–04
Littlewoods plc, V 117–19; 42 228–32 (upd.)
Litton Industries Inc., I 484–86; 11 263–65 (upd.) *see also* Avondale Industries; Northrop Grumman Corp.
LIVE Entertainment Inc., 20 347–49
Live Nation, Inc., 80 217–22 (upd.)
LivePerson, Inc., 91 318–21
The Liverpool Football Club and Athletic Grounds PLC, 105 280–83
Liz Claiborne, Inc., 8 329–31; 25 291–94 (upd.); 102 228–33 (upd.)
LKQ Corporation, 71 201–03
Lloyd Aéreo Boliviano S.A., 95 239–42
Lloyd's, III 278–81; 22 315–19 (upd.); 74 172–76 (upd.)
Lloyds TSB Group plc, II 306–09; 47 224–29 (upd.)
LM Ericsson *see* Telefonaktiebolaget LM Ericsson.
Loblaw Companies Limited, 43 268–72
Lockheed Martin Corporation, I 64–66; 11 266–69 (upd.); 15 283–86 (upd.); 89 306–11 (upd.)
Loctite Corporation, 8 332–34; 30 289–91 (upd.)
Lodge Manufacturing Company, 103 250–53
LodgeNet Interactive Corporation, 28 240–42; 106 285–89 (upd.)
Loehmann's Inc., 24 297–99
Loewe S.A., 104 272–75
Loewe AG, 90 280–85
The Loewen Group, Inc., 16 342–44; 40 292–95 (upd.) *see also* Alderwoods Group Inc.
Loews Corporation, I 487–88; 12 316–18 (upd.); 36 324–28 (upd.); 93 297–304 (upd.)
Loganair Ltd., 68 235–37
Logan's Roadhouse, Inc., 29 290–92
Logica plc, 14 317–19; 37 230–33 (upd.)
Logicon Inc., 20 350–52 *see also* Northrop Grumman Corp.
Logitech International S.A., 28 243–45; 69 242–45 (upd.)
LoJack Corporation, 48 269–73
Lojas Americanas S.A., 77 240–43
Lojas Arapuã S.A., 22 320–22; 61 175–78 (upd.)
Loma Negra C.I.A.S.A., 95 243–46
London Drugs Ltd., 46 270–73
London Fog Industries, Inc., 29 293–96
London Regional Transport, 6 406–08
London Scottish Bank plc, 70 160–62
London Stock Exchange Limited, 34 253–56
Lone Star Steakhouse & Saloon, Inc., 51 227–29

Lonely Planet Publications Pty Ltd., 55 253–55
The Long & Foster Companies, Inc, 85 221–24
Long Island Bancorp, Inc., 16 345–47
Long Island Power Authority, V 652–54; 102 234–39 (upd.)
The Long Island Rail Road Company, 68 238–40
Long John Silver's, 13 320–22; 57 224–29 (upd.)
Long-Term Credit Bank of Japan, Ltd., II 310–11
The Longaberger Company, 12 319–21; 44 267–70 (upd.)
Longs Drug Stores Corporation, V 120; 25 295–97 (upd.); 83 249–253 (upd.)
Longview Fibre Company, 8 335–37; 37 234–37 (upd.)
Lonmin plc, 66 211–16 (upd.)
Lonrho Plc, 21 351–55 *see also* Lonmin plc.
Lonza Group Ltd., 73 212–14
Lookers plc, 71 204–06
Loos & Dilworth, Inc., 100 269–72
Loral Space & Communications Ltd., 8 338–40; 54 231–35 (upd.)
L'Oréal, III 46–49; 8 341–44 (upd.); 46 274–79 (upd.)
Los Angeles Lakers *see* California Sports, Inc.
Los Angeles Turf Club Inc., 102 240–43
Lost Arrow Inc., 22 323–25
LOT Polish Airlines (Polskie Linie Lotnicze S.A.), 33 268–71
LOT$OFF Corporation, 24 300–01
Lotte Confectionery Company Ltd., 76 249–51
Lotus Cars Ltd., 14 320–22
Lotus Development Corporation, 6 254–56; 25 298–302 (upd.)
LOUD Technologies, Inc., 95 247–50 (upd.)
The Louis Berger Group, Inc., 104 276–79
Louis Dreyfus *see* Groupe Louis Dreyfus S.A.
Louis Vuitton, 10 397–99 *see also* LVMH Moët Hennessy Louis Vuitton SA
The Louisiana Land and Exploration Company, 7 280–83
Louisiana-Pacific Corporation, IV 304–05; 31 314–17 (upd.)
Love's Travel Stops & Country Stores, Inc., 71 207–09
Löwenbräu AG, 80 223–27
Lowe's Companies, Inc., V 122–23; 21 356–58 (upd.); 81 240–44 (upd.)
Lowrance Electronics, Inc., 18 311–14
LPA Holding Corporation, 81 245–48
LSB Industries, Inc., 77 244–47
LSI *see* Lear Siegler Inc.
LSI Logic Corporation, 13 323–25; 64 243–47
LTU Group Holding GmbH, 37 238–41
The LTV Corporation, I 489–91; 24 302–06 (upd.)

The Lubrizol Corporation, I 360–62; 30 292–95 (upd.); 83 254–259 (upd.)
Luby's, Inc., 17 290–93; 42 233–38 (upd.); 99 266–273 (upd.)
Lucas Industries Plc, III 554–57
Lucasfilm Ltd., 12 322–24; 50 320–23 (upd.)
Lucent Technologies Inc., 34 257–60
Lucille Farms, Inc., 45 249–51
Lucky-Goldstar, II 53–54 *see also* LG Corp.
Lucky Stores Inc., 27 290–93
Ludendo S.A., 88 237–40
Lufkin Industries, Inc., 78 198–202
Lufthansa *see* Deutsche Lufthansa AG.
Luigino's, Inc., 64 248–50
Lukens Inc., 14 323–25 *see also* Bethlehem Steel Corp.
LUKOIL *see* OAO LUKOIL.
Lululemon Athletica Inc., 105 284–87
Luminar Plc, 40 296–98
Lunar Corporation, 29 297–99
Lunardi's Super Market, Inc., 99 274–277
Lund Food Holdings, Inc., 22 326–28
Lund International Holdings, Inc., 40 299–301
Lush Ltd., 93 305–08
Lutheran Brotherhood, 31 318–21
Luxottica SpA, 17 294–96; 52 227–30 (upd.)
LVMH Moët Hennessy Louis Vuitton SA, 33 272–77 (upd.) *see also* Christian Dior S.A.
Lycos *see* Terra Lycos, Inc.
Lydall, Inc., 64 251–54
Lyfra-S.A./NV, 88 241–43
Lyman-Richey Corporation, 96 265–68
Lynch Corporation, 43 273–76
Lynden Incorporated, 91 322–25
Lyondell Chemical Company, IV 456–57; 45 252–55 (upd.)
Lyonnaise des Eaux-Dumez, V 655–57 *see also* Suez Lyonnaise des Eaux.

M

M&F Worldwide Corp., 38 293–95
M-real Oyj, 56 252–55 (upd.)
M.A. Bruder & Sons, Inc., 56 207–09
M.A. Gedney Co., 51 230–32
M.A. Hanna Company, 8 345–47 *see also* PolyOne Corp.
M. DuMont Schauberg GmbH & Co. KG, 92 213–17
M.E.P.C. Ltd. *see* MEPC plc.
M.H. Meyerson & Co., Inc., 46 280–83
M.R. Beal and Co., 102 244–47
M. Shanken Communications, Inc., 50 324–27
M6 *see* Métropole Télévision S.A..
Maatschappij tot Exploitatie van de Onderneming Krasnapolsky *see* Grand Hotel Krasnapolsky N.V.
Mabe *see* Controladora Mabe, S.A. de C.V.
Mabuchi Motor Co. Ltd., 68 241–43
Mac Frugal's Bargains - Closeouts Inc., 17 297–99 *see also* Big Lots, Inc.

Mac-Gray Corporation, 44 271–73
The Macallan Distillers Ltd., 63 246–48
MacAndrews & Forbes Holdings Inc., 28 246–49; 86 253–59 (upd.)
MacArthur Foundation *see* The John D. and Catherine T. MacArthur Foundation.
Mace Security International, Inc., 57 230–32
The Macerich Company, 57 233–35
MacGregor Golf Company, 68 244–46
Mack-Cali Realty Corporation, 42 239–41
Mack Trucks, Inc., I 177–79; 22 329–32 (upd.); 61 179–83 (upd.)
Mackay Envelope Corporation, 45 256–59
Mackays Stores Group Ltd., 92 218–21
Mackie Designs Inc., 33 278–81 *see also* LOUD Technologies, Inc.
Macklowe Properties, Inc., 95 251–54
Maclean Hunter Publishing Limited, IV 638–40; 26 270–74 (upd.) *see also* Rogers Communications Inc.
MacMillan Bloedel Limited, IV 306–09 *see also* Weyerhaeuser Co.
Macmillan, Inc., 7 284–86
The MacNeal-Schwendler Corporation, 25 303–05
MacNeil/Lehrer Productions, 87 296–299
Macquarie Bank Ltd., 69 246–49
Macromedia, Inc., 50 328–31
Macrovision Solutions Corporation, 101 314–17
Macy's, Inc., 94 284–93 (upd.)
MADD *see* Mothers Against Drunk Driving.
Madden's on Gull Lake, 52 231–34
Madeco S.A., 71 210–12
Madeira Wine Company, S.A., 49 255–57
Madelaine Chocolate Novelties, Inc., 104 280–83
Madge Networks N.V., 26 275–77
Madison Dearborn Partners, LLC, 97 258–61
Madison Gas and Electric Company, 39 259–62
Madison-Kipp Corporation, 58 213–16
Madrange SA, 58 217–19
Mag Instrument, Inc., 67 240–42
Magazine Luiza S.A., 101 318–21
Magellan Aerospace Corporation, 48 274–76
MaggieMoo's International, 89 312–16
Magma Copper Company, 7 287–90 *see also* BHP Billiton.
Magma Design Automation Inc., 78 203–27
Magma Power Company, 11 270–72
Magna International Inc., 102 248–52
MagneTek, Inc., 15 287–89; 41 241–44 (upd.)
Magneti Marelli Holding SpA, 90 286–89
Magyar Telekom Rt, 78 208–11
MAI Systems Corporation, 11 273–76

Maid-Rite Corporation, 62 235–38
Maidenform, Inc., 20 352–55; 59 265–69 (upd.)
Mail Boxes Etc., 18 315–17; 41 245–48 (upd.) *see also* U.S. Office Products Co.
Mail-Well, Inc., 28 250–52 *see also* Cenveo Inc.
MAIN *see* Makhteshim-Agan Industries Ltd.
Maine & Maritimes Corporation, 56 210–13
Maine Central Railroad Company, 16 348–50
Maines Paper & Food Service Inc., 71 213–15
Maison Louis Jadot, 24 307–09
Majesco Entertainment Company, 85 225–29
The Major Automotive Companies, Inc., 45 260–62
Make-A-Wish Foundation of America, 97 262–65
Makhteshim-Agan Industries Ltd., 85 230–34
Makita Corporation, 22 333–35; 59 270–73 (upd.)
Malayan Banking Berhad, 72 215–18
Malaysian Airline System Berhad, 6 100–02; 29 300–03 (upd.); 97 266–71 (upd.)
Malcolm Pirnie, Inc., 42 242–44
Malden Mills Industries, Inc., 16 351–53 *see also* Polartec LLC.
Malév Plc, 24 310–12
Mallinckrodt Group Inc., 19 251–53
Malt-O-Meal Company, 22 336–38; 63 249–53 (upd.)
Mammoet Transport B.V., 26 278–80
Mammoth Mountain Ski Area, 101 322–25
Man Aktiengesellschaft, III 561–63
Man Group PLC, 106 290–94
MAN Roland Druckmaschinen AG, 94 294–98
Management and Training Corporation, 28 253–56
Manatron, Inc., 86 260–63
Manchester United Football Club plc, 30 296–98
Mandalay Resort Group, 32 322–26 (upd.)
Mandom Corporation, 82 205–08
Manhattan Associates, Inc., 67 243–45
Manhattan Group, LLC, 80 228–31
Manheim, 88 244–48
Manila Electric Company (Meralco), 56 214–16
Manischewitz Company *see* B. Manischewitz Co.
Manitoba Telecom Services, Inc., 61 184–87
Manitou BF S.A., 27 294–96
The Manitowoc Company, Inc., 18 318–21; 59 274–79 (upd.)
Mannatech Inc., 33 282–85
Mannesmann AG, III 564–67; 14 326–29 (upd.); 38 296–301 (upd.) *see also* Vodafone Group PLC.

Mannheim Steamroller *see* American Gramophone LLC.
Manning Selvage & Lee (MS&L), 76 252–54
MannKind Corporation, 87 300–303
Manor Care, Inc., 6 187–90; 25 306–10 (upd.)
Manpower Inc., 9 326–27; 30 299–302 (upd.); 73 215–18 (upd.)
ManTech International Corporation, 97 272–75
Manufactured Home Communities, Inc., 22 339–41
Manufacturers Hanover Corporation, II 312–14 *see also* Chemical Bank.
Manulife Financial Corporation, 85 235–38
Manutan International S.A., 72 219–21
Manville Corporation, III 706–09; 7 291–95 (upd.) *see also* Johns Manville Corp.
MAPCO Inc., IV 458–59
MAPICS, Inc., 55 256–58
Maple Grove Farms of Vermont, 88 249–52
Maple Leaf Foods Inc., 41 249–53
Maple Leaf Sports & Entertainment Ltd., 61 188–90
Maples Industries, Inc., 83 260–263
Marble Slab Creamery, Inc., 87 304–307
Marc Ecko Enterprises, Inc., 105 288–91
March of Dimes, 31 322–25
Marchesi Antinori SRL, 42 245–48
Marchex, Inc., 72 222–24
marchFIRST, Inc., 34 261–64
Marco Business Products, Inc., 75 244–46
Marcolin S.p.A., 61 191–94
Marconi plc, 33 286–90 (upd.)
Marcopolo S.A., 79 247–50
Marco's Franchising LLC, 86 264–67
The Marcus Corporation, 21 359–63
Marelli *see* Magneti Marelli Holding SpA.
Marfin Popular Bank plc, 92 222–26
Margarete Steiff GmbH, 23 334–37
Marie Brizard et Roger International S.A.S., 22 342–44; 97 276–80 (upd.)
Marie Callender's Restaurant & Bakery, Inc., 28 257–59
Mariella Burani Fashion Group, 92 227–30
Marine Products Corporation, 75 247–49
MarineMax, Inc., 30 303–05
Mariner Energy, Inc., 101 326–29
Marion Laboratories Inc., I 648–49
Marion Merrell Dow, Inc., 9 328–29 (upd.)
Marionnaud Parfumeries SA, 51 233–35
Marisa Christina, Inc., 15 290–92
Maritz Inc., 38 302–05
Mark IV Industries, Inc., 7 296–98; 28 260–64 (upd.)
Mark T. Wendell Tea Company, 94 299–302

The Mark Travel Corporation, 80 232–35
Märklin Holding GmbH, 70 163–66
Marks and Spencer p.l.c., V 124–26; 24 313–17 (upd.); 85 239–47 (upd.)
Marks Brothers Jewelers, Inc., 24 318–20 *see also* Whitehall Jewellers, Inc.
Marlin Business Services Corp., 89 317–19
The Marmon Group, Inc., IV 135–38; 16 354–57 (upd.); 70 167–72 (upd.)
Marquette Electronics, Inc., 13 326–28
Marriott International, Inc., III 102–03; 21 364–67 (upd.); 83 264–270 (upd.)
Mars, Incorporated, 7 299–301; 40 302–05 (upd.)
Mars Petcare US Inc., 96 269–72
Marsh & McLennan Companies, Inc., III 282–84; 45 263–67 (upd.)
Marsh Supermarkets, Inc., 17 300–02; 76 255–58 (upd.)
Marshall & Ilsley Corporation, 56 217–20
Marshall Amplification plc, 62 239–42
Marshall Field's, 63 254–63 *see also* Target Corp.
Marshalls Incorporated, 13 329–31
Martek Biosciences Corporation, 65 218–20
Martell and Company S.A., 82 213–16
Marten Transport, Ltd., 84 243–246
Martha Stewart Living Omnimedia, Inc., 24 321–23; 73 219–22 (upd.)
Martha White Foods Inc., 104 284–87
Martignetti Companies, 84 247–250
Martin-Baker Aircraft Company Limited, 61 195–97
Martin Franchises, Inc., 80 236–39
Martin Guitar Company *see* C.F. Martin & Co., Inc.
Martin Industries, Inc., 44 274–77
Martin Marietta Corporation, I 67–69 *see also* Lockheed Martin Corp.
Martini & Rossi SpA, 63 264–66
MartinLogan, Ltd., 85 248–51
Martins *see* Grupo Martins.
Martin's Super Markets, Inc., 101 330–33
Martz Group, 56 221–23
Marubeni Corporation, I 492–95; 24 324–27 (upd.); 104 288–93 (upd.)
Maruha Group Inc., 75 250–53 (upd.)
Marui Company Ltd., V 127; 62 243–45 (upd.)
Maruzen Company Ltd., 18 322–24; 104 294–97 (upd.)
Marvel Entertainment, Inc., 10 400–02; 78 212–19 (upd.)
Marvelous Market Inc., 104 298–301
Marvin Lumber & Cedar Company, 22 345–47
Mary Kay Inc., 9 330–32; 30 306–09 (upd.); 84 251–256 (upd.)
Maryland & Virginia Milk Producers Cooperative Association, Inc., 80 240–43
Maryville Data Systems Inc., 96 273–76

Marzotto S.p.A., 20 356–58; 67 246–49 (upd.)
The Maschhoffs, Inc., 82 217–20
Masco Corporation, III 568–71; 20 359–63 (upd.); 39 263–68 (upd.)
Maserati *see* Officine Alfieri Maserati S.p.A.
Mashantucket Pequot Gaming Enterprise Inc., 35 282–85
Masland Corporation, 17 303–05 *see also* Lear Corp.
Masonite International Corporation, 63 267–69
Massachusetts Mutual Life Insurance Company, III 285–87; 53 210–13 (upd.)
Massey Energy Company, 57 236–38
MasTec, Inc., 55 259–63 (upd.)
Mastellone Hermanos S.A., 101 334–37
Master Lock Company, 45 268–71
Master Spas Inc., 105 292–95
MasterBrand Cabinets, Inc., 71 216–18
MasterCard Worldwide, 9 333–35; 96 277–81 (upd.)
MasterCraft Boat Company, Inc., 90 290–93
Matalan PLC, 49 258–60
Match.com, LP, 87 308–311
Material Sciences Corporation, 63 270–73
The MathWorks, Inc., 80 244–47
Matra-Hachette S.A., 15 293–97 (upd.) *see also* European Aeronautic Defence and Space Company EADS N.V.
Matria Healthcare, Inc., 17 306–09
Matrix Essentials Inc., 90 294–97
Matrix Service Company, 65 221–23
Matrixx Initiatives, Inc., 74 177–79
Matsushita Electric Industrial Co., Ltd., II 55–56; 64 255–58 (upd.)
Matsushita Electric Works, Ltd., III 710–11; 7 302–03 (upd.)
Matsuzakaya Company Ltd., V 129–31; 64 259–62 (upd.)
Matt Prentice Restaurant Group, 70 173–76
Mattel, Inc., 7 304–07; 25 311–15 (upd.); 61 198–203 (upd.)
Matth. Hohner AG, 53 214–17
Matthews International Corporation, 29 304–06; 77 248–52 (upd.)
Mattress Giant Corporation, 103 254–57
Matussière et Forest SA, 58 220–22
Maui Land & Pineapple Company, Inc., 29 307–09; 100 273–77 (upd.)
Maui Wowi, Inc., 85 252–55
Mauna Loa Macadamia Nut Corporation, 64 263–65
Maurices Inc., 95 255–58
Maus Frères SA, 48 277–79
Maverick Ranch Association, Inc., 88 253–56
Maverick Tube Corporation, 59 280–83
Maverik, Inc., 103 258–61
Max & Erma's Restaurants Inc., 19 258–60; 100 278–82 (upd.)
Maxco Inc., 17 310–11

Maxicare Health Plans, Inc., III 84–86; 25 316–19 (upd.)
The Maxim Group, 25 320–22
Maxim Integrated Products, Inc., 16 358–60
MAXIMUS, Inc., 43 277–80
Maxtor Corporation, 10 403–05 *see also* Seagate Technology, Inc.
Maxus Energy Corporation, 7 308–10
Maxwell Communication Corporation plc, IV 641–43; 7 311–13 (upd.)
Maxwell Shoe Company, Inc., 30 310–12 *see also* Jones Apparel Group, Inc.
MAXXAM Inc., 8 348–50
Maxxim Medical Inc., 12 325–27
The May Department Stores Company, V 132–35; 19 261–64 (upd.); 46 284–88 (upd.)
May Gurney Integrated Services PLC, 95 259–62
May International *see* George S. May International Co.
Mayer, Brown, Rowe & Maw, 47 230–32
Mayfield Dairy Farms, Inc., 74 180–82
Mayflower Group Inc., 6 409–11
Mayo Foundation, 9 336–39; 34 265–69 (upd.)
Mayor's Jewelers, Inc., 41 254–57
Maytag Corporation, III 572–73; 22 348–51 (upd.); 82 221–25 (upd.)
Mazda Motor Corporation, 9 340–42; 23 338–41 (upd.); 63 274–79 (upd.)
Mazel Stores, Inc., 29 310–12
Mazzio's Corporation, 76 259–61
MBB *see* Messerschmitt-Bölkow-Blohm.
MBC Holding Company, 40 306–09
MBE *see* Mail Boxes Etc.
MBIA Inc., 73 223–26
MBK Industrie S.A., 94 303–06
MBNA Corporation, 12 328–30; 33 291–94 (upd.)
MC Sporting Goods *see* Michigan Sporting Goods Distributors Inc.
MCA Inc., II 143–45 *see also* Universal Studios.
McAfee Inc., 94 307–10
McAlister's Corporation, 66 217–19
McBride plc, 82 226–30
MCC *see* Morris Communications Corp.
McCain Foods Limited, 77 253–56
McCarthy Building Companies, Inc., 48 280–82
McCaw Cellular Communications, Inc., 6 322–24 *see also* AT&T Wireless Services, Inc.
McClain Industries, Inc., 51 236–38
The McClatchy Company, 23 342–44; 92 231–35 (upd.)
McCormick & Company, Incorporated, 7 314–16; 27 297–300 (upd.)
McCormick & Schmick's Seafood Restaurants, Inc., 71 219–21
McCoy Corporation, 58 223–25
McDATA Corporation, 75 254–56
McDermott International, Inc., III 558–60; 37 242–46 (upd.)

McDonald's Corporation, II 646–48; 7 317–19 (upd.); 26 281–85 (upd.); 63 280–86 (upd.)

McDonnell Douglas Corporation, I 70–72; 11 277–80 (upd.) *see also* Boeing Co.

McGrath RentCorp, 91 326–29

The McGraw-Hill Companies, Inc., IV 634–37; 18 325–30 (upd.); 51 239–44 (upd.)

MCI *see* Melamine Chemicals, Inc.

MCI WorldCom, Inc., V 302–04; 27 301–08 (upd.) *see also* Verizon Communications Inc.

McIlhenny Company, 20 364–67

McJunkin Corporation, 63 287–89

McKechnie plc, 34 270–72

McKee Foods Corporation, 7 320–21; 27 309–11 (upd.)

McKesson Corporation, I 496–98; 12 331–33 (upd.); 47 233–37 (upd.)

McKinsey & Company, Inc., 9 343–45

McLanahan Corporation, 104 302–05

McLane Company, Inc., 13 332–34

McLeodUSA Incorporated, 32 327–30

McMenamins Pubs and Breweries, 65 224–26

McMoRan *see* Freeport-McMoRan Copper & Gold, Inc.

McMurry, Inc., 105 296–99

MCN Corporation, 6 519–22

McNaughton Apparel Group, Inc., 92 236–41 (upd.)

McPherson's Ltd., 66 220–22

McQuay International *see* AAF-McQuay Inc.

MCSi, Inc., 41 258–60

McWane Corporation, 55 264–66

MDC Partners Inc., 63 290–92

MDU Resources Group, Inc., 7 322–25; 42 249–53 (upd.)

The Mead Corporation, IV 310–13; 19 265–69 (upd.) *see also* MeadWestvaco Corp.

Mead Data Central, Inc., 10 406–08 *see also* LEXIS-NEXIS Group.

Mead Johnson & Company, 84 257–262

Meade Instruments Corporation, 41 261–64

Meadowcraft, Inc., 29 313–15; 100 283–87 (upd.)

MeadWestvaco Corporation, 76 262–71 (upd.)

Measurement Specialties, Inc., 71 222–25

MEC *see* Mitsubishi Estate Company, Ltd.

Mecalux S.A., 74 183–85

Mechel OAO, 99 278–281

Mecklermedia Corporation, 24 328–30 *see also* Jupitermedia Corp.

Medarex, Inc., 85 256–59

Medco Containment Services Inc., 9 346–48 *see also* Merck & Co., Inc.

Médecins sans Frontières, 85 260–63

MEDecision, Inc., 95 263–67

Media Arts Group, Inc., 42 254–57

Media General, Inc., 7 326–28; 38 306–09 (upd.)

Media Sciences International, Inc., 104 306–09

Mediacom Communications Corporation, 69 250–52

MediaNews Group, Inc., 70 177–80

Mediaset SpA, 50 332–34

Medical Action Industries Inc., 101 338–41

Medical Information Technology Inc., 64 266–69

Medical Management International, Inc., 65 227–29

Medical Staffing Network Holdings, Inc., 89 320–23

Medicine Shoppe International, Inc., 102 253–57

Medicis Pharmaceutical Corporation, 59 284–86

Medifast, Inc., 97 281–85

MedImmune, Inc., 35 286–89

Mediolanum S.p.A., 65 230–32

Medis Technologies Ltd., 77 257–60

Meditrust, 11 281–83

Medline Industries, Inc., 61 204–06

Medtronic, Inc., 8 351–54; 30 313–17 (upd.); 67 250–55 (upd.)

Medusa Corporation, 24 331–33

Mega Bloks, Inc., 61 207–09

Megafoods Stores Inc., 13 335–37

Meggitt PLC, 34 273–76

Meguiar's, Inc., 99 282–285

Meidensha Corporation, 92 242–46

Meier & Frank Co., 23 345–47 *see also* Macy's, Inc.

Meijer, Inc., 7 329–31; 27 312–15 (upd.); 101 342–46 (upd.)

Meiji Dairies Corporation, II 538–39; 82 231–34 (upd.)

Meiji Mutual Life Insurance Company, III 288–89

Meiji Seika Kaisha Ltd., II 540–41; 64 270–72 (upd.)

Mel Farr Automotive Group, 20 368–70

Melaleuca Inc., 31 326–28

Melamine Chemicals, Inc., 27 316–18 *see also* Mississippi Chemical Corp.

Melco Crown Entertainment Limited, 103 262–65

Melitta Unternehmensgruppe Bentz KG, 53 218–21

Mello Smello *see* The Miner Group International.

Mellon Financial Corporation, II 315–17; 44 278–82 (upd.)

Mellon-Stuart Co., I 584–85 *see also* Michael Baker Corp.

The Melting Pot Restaurants, Inc., 74 186–88

Melville Corporation, V 136–38 *see also* CVS Corp.

Melvin Simon and Associates, Inc., 8 355–57 *see also* Simon Property Group, Inc.

MEMC Electronic Materials, Inc., 81 249–52

Memorial Sloan-Kettering Cancer Center, 57 239–41

Memry Corporation, 72 225–27

The Men's Wearhouse, Inc., 17 312–15; 48 283–87 (upd.)

Menard, Inc., 104 310–14 (upd.)

Menasha Corporation, 8 358–61; 59 287–92 (upd.)

Mendocino Brewing Company, Inc., 60 205–07

The Mentholatum Company Inc., 32 331–33

Mentor Corporation, 26 286–88

Mentor Graphics Corporation, 11 284–86

MEPC plc, IV 710–12

Mercantile Bankshares Corp., 11 287–88

Mercantile Stores Company, Inc., V 139; 19 270–73 (upd.) *see also* Dillard's Inc.

Mercer International Inc., 64 273–75

The Merchants Company, 102 258–61

Mercian Corporation, 77 261–64

Merck & Co., Inc., I 650–52; 11 289–91 (upd.); 34 280–85 (upd.); 95 268–78 (upd.)

Mercury Air Group, Inc., 20 371–73

Mercury Communications, Ltd., 7 332–34 *see also* Cable and Wireless plc.

Mercury Drug Corporation, 70 181–83

Mercury General Corporation, 25 323–25

Mercury Interactive Corporation, 59 293–95

Mercury Marine Group, 68 247–51

Meredith Corporation, 11 292–94; 29 316–19 (upd.); 74 189–93 (upd.)

Merge Healthcare, 85 264–68

Merial Ltd., 102 262–66

Meridian Bancorp, Inc., 11 295–97

Meridian Gold, Incorporated, 47 238–40

Merillat Industries, LLC, 13 338–39; 69 253–55 (upd.)

Merisant Worldwide, Inc., 70 184–86

Merisel, Inc., 12 334–36

Merit Medical Systems, Inc., 29 320–22

Meritage Corporation, 26 289–92

MeritCare Health System, 88 257–61

Merix Corporation, 36 329–31; 75 257–60 (upd.)

Merlin Entertainments Group Ltd., 105 300–03

Merriam-Webster Inc., 70 187–91

Merrill Corporation, 18 331–34; 47 241–44 (upd.)

Merrill Lynch & Co., Inc., II 424–26; 13 340–43 (upd.); 40 310–15 (upd.)

Merry-Go-Round Enterprises, Inc., 8 362–64

The Mersey Docks and Harbour Company, 30 318–20

Mervyn's California, 10 409–10; 39 269–71 (upd.) *see also* Target Corp.

Merz Group, 81 253–56

Mesa Air Group, Inc., 11 298–300; 32 334–37 (upd.); 77 265–70 (upd.)

Mesaba Holdings, Inc., 28 265–67
Messerschmitt-Bölkow-Blohm GmbH., I
73–75 *see also* European Aeronautic
Defence and Space Company EADS
N.V.
Mestek, Inc., 10 411–13
Metal Box plc, I 604–06 *see also* Novar
plc.
Metal Management, Inc., 92 247–50
Metaleurop S.A., 21 368–71
Metalico Inc., 97 286–89
Metallgesellschaft AG, IV 139–42; 16
361–66 (upd.)
Metalurgica Mexicana Penoles, S.A. *see*
Industrias Penoles, S.A. de C.V.
Metatec International, Inc., 47 245–48
Metavante Corporation, 100 288–92
Metcash Trading Ltd., 58 226–28
Meteor Industries Inc., 33 295–97
Methanex Corporation, 40 316–19
Methode Electronics, Inc., 13 344–46
MetLife *see* Metropolitan Life Insurance
Co.
Metris Companies Inc., 56 224–27
Metro AG, 50 335–39
Metro-Goldwyn-Mayer Inc., 25 326–30
(upd.); 84 263–270 (upd.)
Métro Inc., 77 271–75
Metro Information Services, Inc., 36
332–34
Metro International S.A., 93 309–12
Metrocall, Inc., 41 265–68
Metromedia Company, 7 335–37; 14
298–300 (upd.); 61 210–14 (upd.)
Métropole Télévision S.A., 76 272–74
(upd.)
Metropolitan Baseball Club Inc., 39
272–75
Metropolitan Financial Corporation, 13
347–49
Metropolitan Life Insurance Company,
III 290–94; 52 235–41 (upd.)
The Metropolitan Museum of Art, 55
267–70
Metropolitan Opera Association, Inc.,
40 320–23
Metropolitan Transportation Authority,
35 290–92
Metsä-Serla Oy, IV 314–16 *see also*
M-real Oyj.
Metso Corporation, 30 321–25 (upd.);
85 269–77 (upd.)
Mettler-Toledo International Inc., 30
326–28
Mexican Restaurants, Inc., 41 269–71
Mexichem, S.A.B. de C.V., 99 286–290
Meyer International Holdings, Ltd., 87
312–315
MFS Communications Company, Inc.,
11 301–03 *see also* MCI WorldCom,
Inc.
MG&E *see* Madison Gas and Electric.
MGA Entertainment, Inc., 95 279–82
MGIC Investment Corp., 52 242–44
MGM MIRAGE, 17 316–19; 98 237–42
(upd.)

MGM/UA Communications Company,
II 146–50 *see also*
Metro-Goldwyn-Mayer Inc.
MGN *see* Mirror Group Newspapers Ltd.
Miami Herald Media Company, 92
251–55
Michael Anthony Jewelers, Inc., 24
334–36
Michael Baker Corporation, 14 333–35;
51 245–48 (upd.)
Michael C. Fina Co., Inc., 52 245–47
Michael Foods, Inc., 25 331–34
Michael Page International plc, 45
272–74
Michaels Stores, Inc., 17 320–22; 71
226–30 (upd.)
Michelin *see* Compagnie Générale des
Établissements Michelin.
Michigan Bell Telephone Co., 14
336–38
Michigan National Corporation, 11
304–06 *see also* ABN AMRO Holding,
N.V.
Michigan Sporting Goods Distributors,
Inc., 72 228–30
Micrel, Incorporated, 77 276–79
Micro Warehouse, Inc., 16 371–73
MicroAge, Inc., 16 367–70
Microdot Inc., 8 365–68
Micron Technology, Inc., 11 307–09; 29
323–26 (upd.)
Micros Systems, Inc., 18 335–38
Microsemi Corporation, 94 311–14
Microsoft Corporation, 6 257–60; 27
319–23 (upd.); 63 293–97 (upd.)
MicroStrategy Incorporated, 87
316–320
Mid-America Apartment Communities,
Inc., 85 278–81
Mid-America Dairymen, Inc., 7 338–40
Midas Inc., 10 414–15; 56 228–31
(upd.)
Middle East Airlines - Air Liban S.A.L.,
79 251–54
The Middleby Corporation, 22 352–55;
104 315–20 (upd.)
Middlesex Water Company, 45 275–78
The Middleton Doll Company, 53
222–25
Midland Bank plc, II 318–20; 17
323–26 (upd.) *see also* HSBC Holdings
plc.
The Midland Company, 65 233–35
Midway Airlines Corporation, 33
301–03
Midway Games, Inc., 25 335–38; 102
267–73 (upd.)
Midwest Air Group, Inc., 35 293–95;
85 282–86 (upd.)
Midwest Grain Products, Inc., 49
261–63
Midwest Resources Inc., 6 523–25
Miele & Cie. KG, 56 232–35
MiG *see* Russian Aircraft Corporation
(MiG).
Migros-Genossenschafts-Bund, 68
252–55
MIH Limited, 31 329–32

Mikasa, Inc., 28 268–70
Mike-Sell's Inc., 15 298–300
Mikohn Gaming Corporation, 39
276–79
Milacron, Inc., 53 226–30 (upd.)
Milan AC S.p.A., 79 255–58
Milbank, Tweed, Hadley & McCloy, 27
324–27
Miles Laboratories, I 653–55 *see also*
Bayer A.G.
Millea Holdings Inc., 64 276–81 (upd.)
Millennium & Copthorne Hotels plc,
71 231–33
Millennium Pharmaceuticals, Inc., 47
249–52
Miller Brewing Company, I 269–70; 12
337–39 (upd.) *see also* SABMiller plc.
Miller Industries, Inc., 26 293–95
Miller Publishing Group, LLC, 57
242–44
Milliken & Co., V 366–68; 17 327–30
(upd.); 82 235–39 (upd.)
Milliman USA, 66 223–26
Millipore Corporation, 25 339–43; 84
271–276 (upd.)
The Mills Corporation, 77 280–83
Milnot Company, 46 289–91
Milton Bradley Company, 21 372–75
Milton CAT, Inc., 86 268–71
Milwaukee Brewers Baseball Club, 37
247–49
Mine Safety Appliances Company, 31
333–35
Minebea Co., Ltd., 90 298–302
The Miner Group International, 22
356–58
Minera Escondida Ltda., 100 293–96
Minerals & Metals Trading Corporation
of India Ltd., IV 143–44
Minerals Technologies Inc., 11 310–12;
52 248–51 (upd.)
Minnesota Mining & Manufacturing
Company, I 499–501; 8 369–71
(upd.); 26 296–99 (upd.) *see also* 3M
Co.
Minnesota Power, Inc., 11 313–16; 34
286–91 (upd.)
Minntech Corporation, 22 359–61
Minolta Co., Ltd., III 574–76; 18
339–42 (upd.); 43 281–85 (upd.)
The Minute Maid Company, 28 271–74
Minuteman International Inc., 46
292–95
Minyard Food Stores, Inc., 33 304–07;
86 272–77 (upd.)
Miquel y Costas Miquel S.A., 68
256–58
Mirage Resorts, Incorporated, 6
209–12; 28 275–79 (upd.) *see also*
MGM MIRAGE.
Miramax Film Corporation, 64 282–85
Mirant Corporation, 98 243–47
Miroglio SpA, 86 278–81
Mirror Group Newspapers plc, 7
341–43; 23 348–51 (upd.)
Misonix, Inc., 80 248–51
Mississippi Chemical Corporation, 39
280–83

Misys PLC, 45 279–81; 46 296–99
Mitchell Energy and Development
 Corporation, 7 344–46 *see also* Devon
 Energy Corp.
Mitchells & Butlers PLC, 59 296–99
Mitel Corporation, 18 343–46
MITRE Corporation, 26 300–02
MITROPA AG, 37 250–53
Mitsubishi Bank, Ltd., II 321–22 *see also*
 Bank of Tokyo-Mitsubishi Ltd.
Mitsubishi Chemical Corporation, I
 363–64; 56 236–38 (upd.)
Mitsubishi Corporation, I 502–04; 12
 340–43 (upd.)
Mitsubishi Electric Corporation, II
 57–59; 44 283–87 (upd.)
Mitsubishi Estate Company, Limited, IV
 713–14; 61 215–18 (upd.)
Mitsubishi Heavy Industries, Ltd., III
 577–79; 7 347–50 (upd.); 40 324–28
 (upd.)
Mitsubishi Materials Corporation, III
 712–13
Mitsubishi Motors Corporation, 9
 349–51; 23 352–55 (upd.); 57
 245–49 (upd.)
Mitsubishi Oil Co., Ltd., IV 460–62 *see
 also* Nippon Mitsubishi Oil Corp.
Mitsubishi Rayon Co. Ltd., V 369–71
Mitsubishi Trust & Banking
 Corporation, II 323–24
Mitsubishi UFJ Financial Group, Inc.,
 99 291–296 (upd.)
Mitsui & Co., Ltd., I 505–08; 28
 280–85 (upd.)
Mitsui Bank, Ltd., II 325–27 *see also*
 Sumitomo Mitsui Banking Corp.
Mitsui Marine and Fire Insurance
 Company, Limited, III 295–96
Mitsui Mining & Smelting Co., Ltd., IV
 145–46; 102 274–78 (upd.)
Mitsui Mining Company, Limited, IV
 147–49
Mitsui Mutual Life Insurance Company,
 III 297–98; 39 284–86 (upd.)
Mitsui O.S.K. Lines Ltd., V 473–76; 96
 282–87 (upd.)
Mitsui Petrochemical Industries, Ltd., 9
 352–54
Mitsui Real Estate Development Co.,
 Ltd., IV 715–16
Mitsui Trust & Banking Company, Ltd.,
 II 328
Mitsukoshi Ltd., V 142–44; 56 239–42
 (upd.)
Mity Enterprises, Inc., 38 310–12
MIVA, Inc., 83 271–275
Mizuho Financial Group Inc., 25
 344–46; 58 229–36 (upd.)
MN Airlines LLC, 104 321–27
MNS, Ltd., 65 236–38
Mo och Domsjö AB, IV 317–19 *see also*
 Holmen AB
Mobil Corporation, IV 463–65; 7
 351–54 (upd.); 21 376–80 (upd.) *see
 also* Exxon Mobil Corp.
Mobile Mini, Inc., 58 237–39

Mobile Telecommunications
 Technologies Corp., 18 347–49
Mobile TeleSystems OJSC, 59 300–03
Mocon, Inc., 76 275–77
Modell's Sporting Goods *see* Henry
 Modell & Company Inc.
Modern Times Group AB, 36 335–38
Modern Woodmen of America, 66
 227–29
Modine Manufacturing Company, 8
 372–75; 56 243–47 (upd.)
MoDo *see* Mo och Domsjö AB.
Modtech Holdings, Inc., 77 284–87
Moen Incorporated, 12 344–45; 106
 295–98 (upd.)
Moe's Southwest Grill *see* MSWG, LLC.
Moët-Hennessy, I 271–72 *see also* LVMH
 Moët Hennessy Louis Vuitton SA.
Mohawk Industries, Inc., 19 274–76; 63
 298–301 (upd.)
Mohegan Tribal Gaming Authority, 37
 254–57
Moksel *see* A. Moksel AG.
MOL *see* Mitsui O.S.K. Lines, Ltd.
MOL Rt, 70 192–95
Moldflow Corporation, 73 227–30
Molex Incorporated, 11 317–19; 14 27;
 54 236–41 (upd.)
Moliflor Loisirs, 80 252–55
Molinos Río de la Plata S.A., 61
 219–21
Molins plc, 51 249–51
The Molson Companies Limited, I
 273–75; 26 303–07 (upd.)
Molson Coors Brewing Company, 77
 288–300 (upd.)
Monaco Coach Corporation, 31 336–38
Monadnock Paper Mills, Inc., 21
 381–84
Monarch Casino & Resort, Inc., 65
 239–41
The Monarch Cement Company, 72
 231–33
Mondadori *see* Arnoldo Mondadori
 Editore S.p.A.
Mondragón Corporación Cooperativa,
 101 347–51
MoneyGram International, Inc., 94
 315–18
Monfort, Inc., 13 350–52
Monnaie de Paris, 62 246–48
Monnoyeur Group *see* Groupe
 Monnoyeur.
Monoprix S.A., 86 282–85
Monro Muffler Brake, Inc., 24 337–40
Monrovia Nursery Company, 70
 196–98
Monsanto Company, I 365–67; 9
 355–57 (upd.); 29 327–31 (upd.); 77
 301–07 (upd.)
Monsoon plc, 39 287–89
Monster Cable Products, Inc., 69
 256–58
Monster Worldwide Inc., 74 194–97
 (upd.)
Montana Coffee Traders, Inc., 60
 208–10

The Montana Power Company, 11
 320–22; 44 288–92 (upd.)
Montblanc International GmbH, 82
 240–44
Montedison S.p.A., I 368–69; 24
 341–44 (upd.)
Monterey Pasta Company, 58 240–43
Montgomery Ward & Co.,
 Incorporated, V 145–48; 20 374–79
 (upd.)
Montres Rolex S.A., 13 353–55; 34
 292–95 (upd.)
Montupet S.A., 63 302–04
Moody's Corporation, 65 242–44
Moog Inc., 13 356–58
Moog Music, Inc., 75 261–64
Mooney Aerospace Group Ltd., 52
 252–55
Moore Corporation Limited, IV 644–46
 see also R.R. Donnelley & Sons Co.
Moore-Handley, Inc., 39 290–92
Moore Medical Corp., 17 331–33
Moran Towing Corporation, Inc., 15
 301–03
The Morgan Crucible Company plc, 82
 245–50
Morgan Grenfell Group PLC, II 427–29
 see also Deutsche Bank AG.
The Morgan Group, Inc., 46 300–02
Morgan, Lewis & Bockius LLP, 29
 332–34
Morgan Motor Company, 105 304–08
Morgan's Foods, Inc., 101 352 |B5–55
Morgan Stanley Dean Witter &
 Company, II 430–32; 16 374–78
 (upd.); 33 311–14 (upd.)
Morgans Hotel Group Company, 80
 256–59
Morguard Corporation, 85 287–90
Morinaga & Co. Ltd., 61 222–25
Morinda Holdings, Inc., 82 251–54
Morningstar Inc., 68 259–62
Morris Communications Corporation,
 36 339–42
Morris Travel Services L.L.C., 26
 308–11
Morrison & Foerster LLP, 78 220–23
Morrison Knudsen Corporation, 7
 355–58; 28 286–90 (upd.) *see also*
 The Washington Companies.
Morrison Restaurants Inc., 11 323–25
Morrow Equipment Co. L.L.C., 87
 325–327
Morse Shoe Inc., 13 359–61
Morton International, Inc., 9 358–59
 (upd.); 80 260–64 (upd.)
Morton Thiokol Inc., I 370–72 *see also*
 Thiokol Corp.
Morton's Restaurant Group, Inc., 30
 329–31; 88 262–66 (upd.)
The Mosaic Company, 91 330–33
Mosinee Paper Corporation, 15 304–06
 see also Wausau-Mosinee Paper Corp.
Moss Bros Group plc, 51 252–54
Mossimo, 27 328–30; 96 288–92 (upd.)
Mota-Engil, SGPS, S.A., 97 290–93
Motel 6, 13 362–64; 56 248–51 (upd.)
 see also Accor SA

Mothercare plc, 17 334–36; 78 224–27 (upd.)
Mothers Against Drunk Driving (MADD), 51 255–58
Mothers Work, Inc., 18 350–52
The Motley Fool, Inc., 40 329–31
Moto Photo, Inc., 45 282–84
Motor Cargo Industries, Inc., 35 296–99
Motorcar Parts & Accessories, Inc., 47 253–55
Motorola, Inc., II 60–62; 11 326–29 (upd.); 34 296–302 (upd.); 93 313–23 (upd.)
Motown Records Company L.P., 26 312–14
Mott's Inc., 57 250–53
Moulinex S.A., 22 362–65 *see also* Groupe SEB.
Mount *see also* Mt.
Mount Washington Hotel *see* MWH Preservation Limited Partnership.
Mountain States Mortgage Centers, Inc., 29 335–37
Mouvement des Caisses Desjardins, 48 288–91
Movado Group, Inc., 28 291–94
Mövenpick Holding, 104 328–32
Movie Gallery, Inc., 31 339–41
Movie Star Inc., 17 337–39
Moy Park Ltd., 78 228–31
Mozilla Foundation, 106 299–303
MPI *see* Michael Page International plc.
MPRG *see* Matt Prentice Restaurant Group.
MPS Group, Inc., 49 264–67
MPW Industrial Services Group, Inc., 53 231–33
Mr. Bricolage S.A., 37 258–60
Mr. Coffee, Inc., 15 307–09
Mr. Gasket Inc., 15 310–12
Mr. Gatti's, LP, 87 321–324
Mrchocolate.com LLC, 105 309–12
Mrs. Baird's Bakeries, 29 338–41
Mrs. Fields' Original Cookies, Inc., 27 331–35; 104 333–39 (upd.)
Mrs. Grossman's Paper Company Inc., 84 277–280
MS&L *see* Manning Selvage & Lee.
MSC *see* Material Sciences Corp.
MSC Industrial Direct Co., Inc., 71 234–36
MSWG, LLC, 105 313–16
Mt. *see also* Mount.
Mt. Olive Pickle Company, Inc., 44 293–95
MTA *see* Metropolitan Transportation Authority.
MTC *see* Management and Training Corp.
MTel *see* Mobile Telecommunications Technologies Corp.
MTG *see* Modern Times Group AB.
MTI Enterprises Inc., 102 279–82
MTN Group Ltd., 106 304–07
MTR Foods Ltd., 55 271–73
MTR Gaming Group, Inc., 75 265–67
MTS *see* Mobile TeleSystems.
MTS Inc., 37 261–64

Mueller Industries, Inc., 7 359–61; 52 256–60 (upd.)
Mueller Sports Medicine, Inc., 102 283–86
Mulberry Group PLC, 71 237–39
Mullen Advertising Inc., 51 259–61
Multi-Color Corporation, 53 234–36
Multimedia Games, Inc., 41 272–76
Multimedia, Inc., 11 330–32
Munich Re (Münchener Rückversicherungs-Gesellschaft Aktiengesellschaft in München), III 299–301; 46 303–07 (upd.)
Munir Sukhtian Group, 104 340–44
Murdock Madaus Schwabe, 26 315–19
Murphy Family Farms Inc., 22 366–68 *see also* Smithfield Foods, Inc.
Murphy Oil Corporation, 7 362–64; 32 338–41 (upd.); 95 283–89 (upd.)
Murphy's Pizza *see* Papa Murphy's International, Inc.
The Musco Family Olive Co., 91 334–37
Musco Lighting, 83 276–279
Museum of Modern Art, 106 308–12
Musgrave Group Plc, 57 254–57
Music Corporation of America *see* MCA Inc.
Musicland Stores Corporation, 9 360–62; 38 313–17 (upd.)
Mutual Benefit Life Insurance Company, III 302–04
Mutual Life Insurance Company of New York, III 305–07
The Mutual of Omaha Companies, 98 248–52
Muzak, Inc., 18 353–56
MWA *see* Modern Woodmen of America.
MWH Preservation Limited Partnership, 65 245–48
MWI Veterinary Supply, Inc., 80 265–68
Mycogen Corporation, 21 385–87 *see also* Dow Chemical Co.
Myers Industries, Inc., 19 277–79; 96 293–97 (upd.)
Mylan Laboratories Inc., I 656–57; 20 380–82 (upd.); 59 304–08 (upd.)
MYOB Ltd., 86 286–90
Myriad Genetics, Inc., 95 290–95
Myriad Restaurant Group, Inc., 87 328–331
MySpace.com *see* Intermix Media, Inc.

N

N.F. Smith & Associates LP, 70 199–202
N M Rothschild & Sons Limited, 39 293–95
N.V. *see under first word of company name*
Naamloze Vennootschap tot Exploitatie van het Café Krasnapolsky *see* Grand Hotel Krasnapolsky N.V.
Nabisco Brands, Inc., II 542–44 *see also* RJR Nabisco.
Nabisco Foods Group, 7 365–68 (upd.) *see also* Kraft Foods Inc.

Nabors Industries Ltd., 9 363–65; 91 338–44 (upd.)
NACCO Industries, Inc., 7 369–71; 78 232–36 (upd.)
Nadro S.A. de C.V., 86 291–94
Naf Naf SA, 44 296–98
Nagasakiya Co., Ltd., V 149–51; 69 259–62 (upd.)
Nagase & Co., Ltd., 8 376–78; 61 226–30 (upd.)
NAI *see* Natural Alternatives International, Inc.; Network Associates, Inc.
Nalco Holding Company, I 373–75; 12 346–48 (upd.); 89 324–30 (upd.)
Nam Tai Electronics, Inc., 61 231–34
Namco Bandai Holdings Inc., 106 313–19 (upd.)
Nantucket Allserve, Inc., 22 369–71
Napster, Inc., 69 263–66
Narodowy Bank Polski, 100 297–300
NAS *see* National Audubon Society.
NASCAR *see* National Association for Stock Car Auto Racing.
NASD, 54 242–46 (upd.)
The NASDAQ Stock Market, Inc., 92 256–60
Nash Finch Company, 8 379–81; 23 356–58 (upd.); 65 249–53 (upd.)
Nashua Corporation, 8 382–84
Naspers Ltd., 66 230–32
Nastech Pharmaceutical Company Inc., 79 259–62
Nathan's Famous, Inc., 29 342–44
National Amusements Inc., 28 295–97
National Aquarium in Baltimore, Inc., 74 198–200
National Association for Stock Car Auto Racing, 32 342–44
National Association of Securities Dealers, Inc., 10 416–18 *see also* NASD.
National Audubon Society, 26 320–23
National Auto Credit, Inc., 16 379–81
National Bank of Canada, 85 291–94
National Bank of Greece, 41 277–79
The National Bank of South Carolina, 76 278–80
National Bank of Ukraine, 102 287–90
National Beverage Corporation, 26 324–26; 88 267–71 (upd.)
National Broadcasting Company, Inc., II 151–53; 6 164–66 (upd.); 28 298–301 (upd.) *see also* General Electric Co.
National Can Corp., I 607–08
National Car Rental System, Inc., 10 419–20 *see also* Republic Industries, Inc.
Nationa CineMedia, Inc., 103 266–70
National City Corporation, 15 313–16; 97 294–302 (upd.)
National Collegiate Athletic Association, 96 298–302
National Convenience Stores Incorporated, 7 372–75
National Council of La Raza, 106 320–23

National Discount Brokers Group, Inc., 28 302–04 *see also* Deutsche Bank A.G.

National Distillers and Chemical Corporation, I 376–78 *see also* Quantum Chemical Corp.

National Educational Music Co. Ltd., 47 256–58

National Enquirer see American Media, Inc.

National Envelope Corporation, 32 345–47

National Equipment Services, Inc., 57 258–60

National Express Group PLC, 50 340–42

National Financial Partners Corp., 65 254–56

National Football League, 29 345–47 *see also* NFL.

National Frozen Foods Corporation, 94 319–22

National Fuel Gas Company, 6 526–28; 95 296–300 (upd.)

National Geographic Society, 9 366–68; 30 332–35 (upd.); 79 263–69 (upd.)

National Grape Co-operative Association, Inc., 20 383–85

National Grid USA, 51 262–66 (upd.)

National Gypsum Company, 10 421–24

National Health Laboratories Incorporated, 11 333–35 *see also* Laboratory Corporation of America Holdings.

National Heritage Academies, Inc., 60 211–13

National Hockey League, 35 300–03

National Home Centers, Inc., 44 299–301

National Instruments Corporation, 22 372–74

National Intergroup, Inc., V 152–53 *see also* FoxMeyer Health Corp.

National Iranian Oil Company, IV 466–68; 61 235–38 (upd.)

National Jewish Health, 101 356–61

National Journal Group Inc., 67 256–58

National Media Corporation, 27 336–40

National Medical Enterprises, Inc., III 87–88 *see also* Tenet Healthcare Corp.

National Medical Health Card Systems, Inc., 79 270–73

National Oil Corporation, 66 233–37 (upd.)

National Oilwell, Inc., 54 247–50

National Organization for Women, Inc., 55 274–76

National Patent Development Corporation, 13 365–68 *see also* GP Strategies Corp.

National Penn Bancshares, Inc., 103 271–75

National Picture & Frame Company, 24 345–47

National Power PLC, 12 349–51 *see also* International Power PLC.

National Presto Industries, Inc., 16 382–85; 43 286–90 (upd.)

National Public Radio, 19 280–82; 47 259–62 (upd.)

National R.V. Holdings, Inc., 32 348–51

National Railroad Passenger Corporation (Amtrak), 22 375–78; 66 238–42 (upd.)

National Record Mart, Inc., 29 348–50

National Research Corporation, 87 332–335

National Rifle Association of America, 37 265–68

National Sanitary Supply Co., 16 386–87

National Sea Products Ltd., 14 339–41

National Semiconductor Corporation, II 63–65; 6 261–63; 26 327–30 (upd.); 69 267–71 (upd.)

National Service Industries, Inc., 11 336–38; 54 251–55 (upd.)

National Standard Co., 13 369–71

National Starch and Chemical Company, 49 268–70

National Steel Corporation, 12 352–54 *see also* FoxMeyer Health Corp.

National TechTeam, Inc., 41 280–83

National Thoroughbred Racing Association, 58 244–47

National Transcommunications Ltd. *see* NTL Inc.

National Weather Service, 91 345–49

National Westminster Bank PLC, II 333–35

National Wildlife Federation, 103 276–80

National Wine & Spirits, Inc., 49 271–74

Nationale-Nederlanden N.V., III 308–11

Nationale Portefeuille Maatschappij (NPM) *see* Compagnie Nationale à Portefeuille.

NationsBank Corporation, 10 425–27 *see also* Bank of America Corporation

Natrol, Inc., 49 275–78

Natura Cosméticos S.A., 75 268–71

Natural Alternatives International, Inc., 49 279–82

Natural Gas Clearinghouse *see* NGC Corp.

Natural Ovens Bakery, Inc., 72 234–36

Natural Selection Foods, 54 256–58

Natural Wonders Inc., 14 342–44

Naturally Fresh, Inc., 88 272–75

The Nature Conservancy, 28 305–07

Nature's Path Foods, Inc., 87 336–340

Nature's Sunshine Products, Inc., 15 317–19; 102 291–96 (upd.)

Natuzzi Group *see* Industrie Natuzzi S.p.A.

NatWest Bank *see* National Westminster Bank PLC.

Naumes, Inc., 81 257–60

Nautica Enterprises, Inc., 18 357–60; 44 302–06 (upd.)

Navarre Corporation, 24 348–51

Navigant International, Inc., 47 263–66; 93 324–27 (upd.)

The Navigators Group, Inc., 92 261–64

Navistar International Corporation, I 180–82; 10 428–30 (upd.) *see also* International Harvester Co.

NAVTEQ Corporation, 69 272–75

Navy Exchange Service Command, 31 342–45

Navy Federal Credit Union, 33 315–17

NBC *see* National Broadcasting Company, Inc.

NBD Bancorp, Inc., 11 339–41 *see also* Bank One Corp.

NBGS International, Inc., 73 231–33

NBSC Corporation *see* National Bank of South Carolina.

NBTY, Inc., 31 346–48

NCAA *see* National Collegiate Athletic Assn.

NCH Corporation, 8 385–87

NCI Building Systems, Inc., 88 276–79

NCL Corporation, 79 274–77

NCNB Corporation, II 336–37 *see also* Bank of America Corp.

NCO Group, Inc., 42 258–60

NCR Corporation, III 150–53; 6 264–68 (upd.); 30 336–41 (upd.); 90 303–12 (upd.)

NDB *see* National Discount Brokers Group, Inc.

Nebraska Book Company, Inc., 65 257–59

Nebraska Furniture Mart, Inc., 94 323–26

Nebraska Public Power District, 29 351–54

NEBS *see* New England Business Services, Inc.

NEC Corporation, II 66–68; 21 388–91 (upd.); 57 261–67 (upd.)

Neckermann.de GmbH, 102 297–301

N.V. Nederlandse Gasunie, V 658–61

Nedlloyd Group *see* Koninklijke Nedlloyd N.V.

Neenah Foundry Company, 68 263–66

Neff Corp., 32 352–53

NeighborCare, Inc., 67 259–63 (upd.)

The Neiman Marcus Group, Inc., 12 355–57; 49 283–87 (upd.); 105 317–22 (upd.)

Nektar Therapeutics, 91 350–53

Nelsons *see* A. Nelson & Co. Ltd.

Neogen Corporation, 94 327–30

Neopost S.A., 53 237–40

Neptune Orient Lines Limited, 47 267–70

NERCO, Inc., 7 376–79 *see also* Rio Tinto PLC.

NES *see* National Equipment Services, Inc.

Neste Oil Corporation, IV 469–71; 85 295–302 (upd.)

Nestlé S.A., II 545–49; 7 380–84 (upd.); 28 308–13 (upd.); 71 240–46 (upd.)

Nestlé Waters, 73 234–37

NetCom Systems AB, 26 331–33

NetCracker Technology Corporation, 98 253–56

Netezza Corporation, 69 276–78

Netflix, Inc., 58 248–51

NETGEAR, Inc., 81 261–64

NetIQ Corporation, 79 278–81

NetJets Inc., 96 303–07 (upd.)

Netscape Communications Corporation, 15 320–22; 35 304–07 (upd.)

Netto International, 103 281–84

Network Appliance, Inc., 58 252–54

Network Associates, Inc., 25 347–49

Network Equipment Technologies Inc., 92 265–68

Neuberger Berman Inc., 57 268–71

NeuStar, Inc., 81 265–68

Neutrogena Corporation, 17 340–44

Nevada Bell Telephone Company, 14 345–47 *see also* AT&T Corp.

Nevada Power Company, 11 342–44

Nevamar Company, 82 255–58

New Balance Athletic Shoe, Inc., 25 350–52; 68 267–70 (upd.)

New Belgium Brewing Company, Inc., 68 271–74

New Brunswick Scientific Co., Inc., 45 285–87

New Chapter Inc., 96 308–11

New Clicks Holdings Ltd., 86 295–98

New Dana Perfumes Company, 37 269–71

New England Business Service, Inc., 18 361–64; 78 237–42 (upd.)

New England Confectionery Co., 15 323–25

New England Electric System, V 662–64 *see also* National Grid USA.

New England Mutual Life Insurance Co., III 312–14 *see also* Metropolitan Life Insurance Co.

New Flyer Industries Inc., 78 243–46

New Holland N.V., 22 379–81 *see also* CNH Global N.V.

New Jersey Devils, 84 281–285

New Jersey Manufacturers Insurance Company, 96 312–16

New Jersey Resources Corporation, 54 259–61

New Line Cinema, Inc., 47 271–74

New Look Group plc, 35 308–10

New Orleans Saints LP, 58 255–57

The New Piper Aircraft, Inc., 44 307–10

New Plan Realty Trust, 11 345–47

The New School, 103 285–89

New Seasons Market, 75 272–74

New Street Capital Inc., 8 388–90 (upd.) *see also* Drexel Burnham Lambert Inc.

New Times, Inc., 45 288–90

New Valley Corporation, 17 345–47

New World Development Company Limited, IV 717–19; 38 318–22 (upd.)

New World Pasta Company, 53 241–44

New World Restaurant Group, Inc., 44 311–14

New York City Health and Hospitals Corporation, 60 214–17

New York City Off-Track Betting Corporation, 51 267–70

New York Community Bancorp, Inc., 78 247–50

New York Daily News, 32 357–60

New York Eye and Ear Infirmary *see* Continuum Health Partners, Inc.

New York Health Care, Inc., 72 237–39

New York Life Insurance Company, III 315–17; 45 291–95 (upd.)

New York Philharmonic *see* Philharmonic-Symphony Society of New York, Inc.

New York Presbyterian Hospital *see* NewYork-Presbyterian Hospital.

New York Restaurant Group, Inc., 32 361–63

New York Shakespeare Festival Management, 92 328–32

New York State Electric and Gas Corporation, 6 534–36

New York Stock Exchange, Inc., 9 369–72; 39 296–300 (upd.)

The New York Times Company, IV 647–49; 19 283–85 (upd.); 61 239–43 (upd.)

New York Yacht Club, Inc., 103 290–93

The Newark Group, Inc., 102 302–05

Neways, Inc., 78 251–54

Newcom Group, 104 345–48

Newcor, Inc., 40 332–35

Newell Rubbermaid Inc., 9 373–76; 52 261–71 (upd.)

Newfield Exploration Company, 65 260–62

Newhall Land and Farming Company, 14 348–50

Newly Weds Foods, Inc., 74 201–03

Newman's Own, Inc., 37 272–75

Newmont Mining Corporation, 7 385–88; 94 331–37 (upd.)

Newpark Resources, Inc., 63 305–07

Newport Corporation, 71 247–49

Newport News Shipbuilding Inc., 13 372–75; 38 323–27 (upd.)

News America Publishing Inc., 12 358–60

News Communications, Inc., 103 294–98

News Corporation Limited, IV 650–53; 7 389–93 (upd.); 46 308–13 (upd.)

Newsday Media Group, 103 299–303

Newsquest plc, 32 354–56

NewYork-Presbyterian Hospital, 59 309–12

Nexans SA, 54 262–64

NEXCOM *see* Navy Exchange Service Command.

Nexen Inc., 79 282–85

Nexity S.A., 66 243–45

Nexstar Broadcasting Group, Inc., 73 238–41

Next Media Ltd., 61 244–47

Next plc, 29 355–57

Nextel Communications, Inc., 10 431–33; 27 341–45 (upd.)

Neyveli Lignite Corporation Ltd., 65 263–65

NFC plc, 6 412–14 *see also* Exel plc.

NFL *see* National Football League Inc.

NFL Films, 75 275–78

NFO Worldwide, Inc., 24 352–55

NGC Corporation, 18 365–67 *see also* Dynegy Inc.

NGK Insulators Ltd., 67 264–66

NH Hoteles S.A., 79 286–89

NHK Spring Co., Ltd., III 580–82

Niagara Corporation, 28 314–16

Niagara Mohawk Holdings Inc., V 665–67; 45 296–99 (upd.)

NICE Systems Ltd., 83 280–283

Nichii Co., Ltd., V 154–55

Nichimen Corporation, IV 150–52; 24 356–59 (upd.) *see also* Sojitz Corp.

Nichirei Corporation, 70 203–05

Nichiro Corporation, 86 299–302

Nichols plc, 44 315–18

Nichols Research Corporation, 18 368–70

Nicklaus Companies, 45 300–03

Nicole Miller, 98 257–60

Nicor Inc., 6 529–31; 86 303–07 (upd.)

Nidec Corporation, 59 313–16

Nielsen Business Media, Inc., 98 261–65

Nigerian National Petroleum Corporation, IV 472–74; 72 240–43 (upd.)

Nihon Keizai Shimbun, Inc., IV 654–56

NII *see* National Intergroup, Inc.

NIKE, Inc., V 372–74; 8 391–94 (upd.); 36 343–48 (upd.); 75 279–85 (upd.)

Nikken Global Inc., 32 364–67

The Nikko Securities Company Limited, II 433–35; 9 377–79 (upd.)

Nikon Corporation, III 583–85; 48 292–95 (upd.)

Niman Ranch, Inc., 67 267–69

Nimbus CD International, Inc., 20 386–90

Nine West Group Inc., 11 348–49; 39 301–03 (upd.)

99¢ Only Stores, 25 353–55; 100 301–05 (upd.)

Nintendo Co., Ltd., III 586–88; 7 394–96 (upd.); 28 317–21 (upd.); 67 270–76 (upd.)

NIOC *see* National Iranian Oil Co.

Nippon Credit Bank, II 338–39

Nippon Electric Glass Co. Ltd., 95 301–05

Nippon Express Company, Ltd., V 477–80; 64 286–90 (upd.)

Nippon Life Insurance Company, III 318–20; 60 218–21 (upd.)

Nippon Light Metal Company, Ltd., IV 153–55

Nippon Meat Packers, Inc., II 550–51; 78 255–57 (upd.)

Nippon Mining Holdings Inc., IV 475–77; 102 306–10 (upd.)

Nippon Oil Corporation, IV 478–79; 63 308–13 (upd.)

Nippon Seiko K.K., III 589–90

Nippon Sheet Glass Company, Limited, III 714–16

Nippon Shinpan Co., Ltd., II 436–37; 61 248–50 (upd.)

Nippon Soda Co., Ltd., 85 303–06

Nippon Steel Corporation, IV 156–58; 17 348–51 (upd.); 96 317–23 (upd.)

Nippon Suisan Kaisha, Limited, II 552–53; 92 269–72 (upd.)

Nippon Telegraph and Telephone Corporation, V 305–07; 51 271–75 (upd.)

Nippon Yusen Kabushiki Kaisha (NYK), V 481–83; 72 244–48 (upd.)

Nippondenso Co., Ltd., III 591–94 *see also* DENSO Corp.

NIPSCO Industries, Inc., 6 532–33

Nissan Motor Company Ltd., I 183–84; 11 350–52 (upd.); 34 303–07 (upd.); 92 273–79 (upd.)

Nisshin Seifun Group Inc., II 554; 66 246–48 (upd.)

Nisshin Steel Co., Ltd., IV 159–60

Nissho Iwai K.K., I 509–11

Nissin Food Products Company Ltd., 75 286–88

Nitches, Inc., 53 245–47

Nixdorf Computer AG, III 154–55 *see also* Wincor Nixdorf Holding GmbH.

NKK Corporation, IV 161–63; 28 322–26 (upd.)

NL Industries, Inc., 10 434–36

Noah Education Holdings Ltd., 97 303–06

Noah's New York Bagels *see* Einstein/Noah Bagel Corp.

Nobel Industries AB, 9 380–82 *see also* Akzo Nobel N.V.

Nobel Learning Communities, Inc., 37 276–79; 76 281–85 (upd.)

Nobia AB, 103 304–07

Noble Affiliates, Inc., 11 353–55

Noble Roman's Inc., 14 351–53; 99 297–302 (upd.)

Nobleza Piccardo SAICF, 64 291–93

Noboa *see also* Exportadora Bananera Noboa, S.A.

Nocibé SA, 54 265–68

NOF Corporation, 72 249–51

Nokia Corporation, II 69–71; 17 352–54 (upd.); 38 328–31 (upd.); 77 308–13 (upd.)

NOL Group *see* Neptune Orient Lines Ltd.

Noland Company, 35 311–14

Nolo.com, Inc., 49 288–91

Nomura Securities Company, Limited, II 438–41; 9 383–86 (upd.)

Noodle Kidoodle, 16 388–91

Noodles & Company, Inc., 55 277–79

Nooter Corporation, 61 251–53

Noranda Inc., IV 164–66; 7 397–99 (upd.); 64 294–98 (upd.)

Norcal Waste Systems, Inc., 60 222–24

Norddeutsche Affinerie AG, 62 249–53

Nordea AB, 40 336–39

Nordex AG, 101 362–65

NordicTrack, 22 382–84 *see also* Icon Health & Fitness, Inc.

Nordisk Film A/S, 80 269–73

Nordson Corporation, 11 356–58; 48 296–99 (upd.)

Nordstrom, Inc., V 156–58; 18 371–74 (upd.); 67 277–81 (upd.)

Norelco Consumer Products Co., 26 334–36

Norfolk Southern Corporation, V 484–86; 29 358–61 (upd.); 75 289–93 (upd.)

Norinchukin Bank, II 340–41

Norm Thompson Outfitters, Inc., 47 275–77

Norrell Corporation, 25 356–59

Norsk Hydro ASA, 10 437–40; 35 315–19 (upd.)

Norske Skogindustrier ASA, 63 314–16

Norstan, Inc., 16 392–94

Nortek, Inc., 34 308–12

Nortel Networks Corporation, 36 349–54 (upd.)

North American Galvanizing & Coatings, Inc., 99 303–306

North Atlantic Trading Company Inc., 65 266–68

North Carolina National Bank Corporation *see* NCNB Corp.

The North Face, Inc., 18 375–77; 78 258–61 (upd.)

North Fork Bancorporation, Inc., 46 314–17

North Pacific Group, Inc., 61 254–57

North Star Steel Company, 18 378–81

The North West Company, Inc., 12 361–63

North West Water Group plc, 11 359–62 *see also* United Utilities PLC.

Northeast Utilities, V 668–69; 48 303–06 (upd.)

Northern and Shell Network plc, 87 341–344

Northern Foods plc, 10 441–43; 61 258–62 (upd.)

Northern Rock plc, 33 318–21

Northern States Power Company, V 670–72; 20 391–95 (upd.) *see also* Xcel Energy Inc.

Northern Telecom Limited, V 308–10 *see also* Nortel Networks Corp.

Northern Trust Corporation, 9 387–89; 101 366–72 (upd.)

Northland Cranberries, Inc., 38 332–34

Northrop Grumman Corporation, I 76–77; 11 363–65 (upd.); 45 304–12 (upd.)

Northwest Airlines Corporation, I 112–14; 6 103–05 (upd.); 26 337–40 (upd.); 74 204–08 (upd.)

Northwest Natural Gas Company, 45 313–15

NorthWestern Corporation, 37 280–83

Northwestern Mutual Life Insurance Company, III 321–24; 45 316–21 (upd.)

Norton Company, 8 395–97

Norton McNaughton, Inc., 27 346–49 *see also* Jones Apparel Group, Inc.

Norwegian Cruise Lines *see* NCL Corporation

Norwich & Peterborough Building Society, 55 280–82

Norwood Promotional Products, Inc., 26 341–43

Nova Corporation of Alberta, V 673–75

NovaCare, Inc., 11 366–68

Novacor Chemicals Ltd., 12 364–66

Novar plc, 49 292–96 (upd.)

Novartis AG, 39 304–10 (upd.); 105 323–35 (upd.)

NovaStar Financial, Inc., 91 354–58

Novell, Inc., 6 269–71; 23 359–62 (upd.)

Novellus Systems, Inc., 18 382–85

Noven Pharmaceuticals, Inc., 55 283–85

Novo Nordisk A/S, I 658–60; 61 263–66 (upd.)

NOW *see* National Organization for Women, Inc.

NPC International, Inc., 40 340–42

The NPD Group, Inc., 68 275–77

NPM (Nationale Portefeuille Maatschappij) *see* Compagnie Nationale à Portefeuille.

NPR *see* National Public Radio, Inc.

NRG Energy, Inc., 79 290–93

NRT Incorporated, 61 267–69

NS *see* Norfolk Southern Corp.

NSF International, 72 252–55

NSK *see* Nippon Seiko K.K.

NSP *see* Northern States Power Co.

NSS Enterprises, Inc., 78 262–65

NSTAR, 106 324–31 (upd.)

NTCL *see* Northern Telecom Ltd.

NTD Architecture, 101 373–76

NTL Inc., 65 269–72

NTN Buzztime, Inc., 86 308–11

NTN Corporation, III 595–96; 47 278–81 (upd.)

NTTPC *see* Nippon Telegraph and Telephone Public Corp.

NU *see* Northeast Utilities.

Nu-kote Holding, Inc., 18 386–89

Nu Skin Enterprises, Inc., 27 350–53; 31 386–89; 76 286–90 (upd.)

Nucor Corporation, 7 400–02; 21 392–95 (upd.); 79 294–300 (upd.)

Nufarm Ltd., 87 345–348

Nuplex Industries Ltd., 92 280–83

Nuqul Group of Companies, 102 311–14

Nutraceutical International Corporation, 37 284–86

NutraSweet Company, 8 398–400

Nutreco Holding N.V., 56 256–59

Nutrexpa S.A., 92 284–87

NutriSystem, Inc., 71 250–53

Nutrition 21 Inc., 97 307–11

Nutrition for Life International Inc., 22 385–88

Nuveen *see* John Nuveen Co.

NV Umicore SA, 47 411–13

NVIDIA Corporation, 54 269–73

NVR Inc., 8 401–03; 70 206–09 (upd.)

NWA, Inc. *see* Northwest Airlines Corp.
NYK *see* Nippon Yusen Kabushiki Kaisha (NYK).
NYMAGIC, Inc., 41 284–86
NYNEX Corporation, V 311–13 *see also* Verizon Communications.
Nypro, Inc., 101 377–82
NYRG *see* New York Restaurant Group, Inc.
NYSE *see* New York Stock Exchange.
NYSEG *see* New York State Electric and Gas Corp.

O

O&Y *see* Olympia & York Developments Ltd.
O.C. Tanner Co., 69 279–81
Oak Harbor Freight Lines, Inc., 53 248–51
Oak Industries Inc., 21 396–98 *see also* Corning Inc.
Oak Technology, Inc., 22 389–93 *see also* Zoran Corp.
Oakhurst Dairy, 60 225–28
Oakleaf Waste Management, LLC, 97 312–15
Oakley, Inc., 18 390–93; 49 297–302 (upd.)
Oaktree Capital Management, LLC, 71 254–56
Oakwood Homes Corporation, 13 155; **15 326–28**
OAO AVTOVAZ *see* AVTOVAZ Joint Stock Co.
OAO Gazprom, 42 261–65
OAO LUKOIL, 40 343–46
OAO NK YUKOS, 47 282–85
OAO Severstal *see* Severstal Joint Stock Co.
OAO Siberian Oil Company (Sibneft), 49 303–06
OAO Surgutneftegaz, 48 375–78
OAO Tatneft, 45 322–26
Obagi Medical Products, Inc., 95 310–13
Obayashi Corporation, 78 266–69 (upd.)
Oberoi Group *see* EIH Ltd.
Oberto Sausage Company, Inc., 92 288–91
Obie Media Corporation, 56 260–62
Obrascon Huarte Lain S.A., 76 291–94
Observer AB, 55 286–89
Occidental Petroleum Corporation, IV 480–82; 25 360–63 (upd.); 71 257–61 (upd.)
Océ N.V., 24 360–63; 91 359–65 (upd.)
Ocean Beauty Seafoods, Inc., 74 209–11
Ocean Bio-Chem, Inc., 103 308–11
Ocean Group plc, 6 415–17 *see also* Exel plc.
Ocean Spray Cranberries, Inc., 7 403–05; 25 364–67 (upd.); 83 284–290
Oceaneering International, Inc., 63 317–19
Ocesa *see* Corporación Interamericana de Entretenimiento, S.A. de C.V.

O'Charley's Inc., 19 286–88; 60 229–32 (upd.)
OCI *see* Orascom Construction Industries S.A.E.
OCLC Online Computer Library Center, Inc., 96 324–28
The O'Connell Companies Inc., 100 306–09
Octel Messaging, 14 354–56; 41 287–90 (upd.)
Ocular Sciences, Inc., 65 273–75
Odakyu Electric Railway Co., Ltd., V 487–89; 68 278–81 (upd.)
Odebrecht S.A., 73 242–44
Odetics Inc., 14 357–59
Odfjell SE, 101 383–87
ODL, Inc., 55 290–92
Odwalla Inc., 31 349–51; 104 349–53 (upd.)
Odyssey Marine Exploration, Inc., 91 366–70
OEC Medical Systems, Inc., 27 354–56
OENEO S.A., 74 212–15 (upd.)
Office Depot, Inc., 8 404–05; 23 363–65 (upd.); 65 276–80 (upd.)
OfficeMax Incorporated, 15 329–31; 43 291–95 (upd.); 101 388–94 (upd.)
OfficeTiger, LLC, 75 294–96
Officine Alfieri Maserati S.p.A., 13 376–78
Offshore Logistics, Inc., 37 287–89
Ogden Corporation, I 512–14; 6 151–53 *see also* Covanta Energy Corp.
Ogilvy Group Inc., I 25–27 *see also* WPP Group.
Oglebay Norton Company, 17 355–58
Oglethorpe Power Corporation, 6 537–38
Ohbayashi Corporation, I 586–87
The Ohio Art Company, 14 360–62; 59 317–20 (upd.)
Ohio Bell Telephone Company, 14 363–65; *see also* Ameritech Corp.
Ohio Casualty Corp., 11 369–70
Ohio Edison Company, V 676–78
Oil and Natural Gas Commission, IV 483–84; 90 313–17 (upd.)
Oil-Dri Corporation of America, 20 396–99; 89 331–36 (upd.)
Oil States International, Inc., 77 314–17
Oil Transporting Joint Stock Company Transneft, 92 450–54
The Oilgear Company, 74 216–18
Oji Paper Co., Ltd., IV 320–22; 57 272–75 (upd.)
OJSC Novolipetsk Steel, 99 311–315
OJSC Wimm-Bill-Dann Foods, 48 436–39
Oki Electric Industry Company, Limited, II 72–74; 15 125; **21** 390
Oklahoma Gas and Electric Company, 6 539–40
Okuma Holdings Inc., 74 219–21
Okura & Co., Ltd., IV 167–68
Olan Mills, Inc., 62 254–56
Old America Stores, Inc., 17 359–61

Old Dominion Freight Line, Inc., 57 276–79
Old Kent Financial Corp., 11 371–72 *see also* Fifth Third Bancorp.
Old Mutual PLC, IV 535; 61 270–72
Old National Bancorp, 15 332–34; 98 266–70 (upd.)
Old Navy, Inc., 70 210–12
Old Orchard Brands, LLC, 73 245–47
Old Republic International Corporation, 11 373–75; 58 258–61 (upd.)
Old Spaghetti Factory International Inc., 24 364–66
Old Town Canoe Company, 74 222–24
Olga's Kitchen, Inc., 80 274–76
Olin Corporation, I 379–81; 13 379–81 (upd.); 78 270–74 (upd.)
Olivetti S.p.A., 34 316–20 (upd.)
Olsten Corporation, 6 41–43; 29 362–65 (upd.) *see also* Adecco S.A.
Olympia & York Developments Ltd., IV 720–21; 9 390–92 (upd.)
Olympus Corporation, 106 332–36
OM Group, Inc., 17 362–64; 78 275–78 (upd.)
OMA *see* Grupo Aeroportuario del Centro Norte, S.A.B. de C.V.
Omaha Steaks International Inc., 62 257–59
Omega Protein Corporation, 99 316–318
O'Melveny & Myers, 37 290–93
Omni Hotels Corp., 12 367–69
Omnicare, Inc., 13 49 307–10
Omnicell, Inc., 89 337–40
Omnicom Group Inc., I 28–32; 22 394–99 (upd.); 77 318–25 (upd.)
Omnilife *see* Grupo Omnilife S.A. de C.V.
OmniSource Corporation, 14 366–67
OMNOVA Solutions Inc., 59 324–26
Omrix Biopharmaceuticals, Inc., 95 314–17
Omron Corporation, 28 331–35 (upd.); 53 46
Omron Tateisi Electronics Company, II 75–77
OMV AG, IV 485–87; 98 271–74 (upd.)
On Assignment, Inc., 20 400–02
1-800-FLOWERS.COM, Inc., 26 344–46; 102 315–20 (upd.)
1-800-GOT-JUNK? LLC, 74 225–27
180s, L.L.C., 64 299–301
One Price Clothing Stores, Inc., 20 403–05
O'Neal Steel, Inc., 95 306–09
Oneida Ltd., 7 406–08; 31 352–55 (upd.); 88 280–85 (upd.)
ONEOK Inc., 7 409–12
Onet S.A., 92 292–95
Onex Corporation, 16 395–97; 65 281–85 (upd.)
Onion, Inc., 69 282–84
Onoda Cement Co., Ltd., III 717–19 *see also* Taiheiyo Cement Corp.
Ontario Hydro Services Company, 6 541–42; 32 368–71 (upd.)

Ontario Teachers' Pension Plan, 61 273–75
Onyx Acceptance Corporation, 59 327–29
Onyx Software Corporation, 53 252–55
OOC Inc., 97 316–19
OPAP S.A. *see* Greek Organization of Football Prognostics S.A. (OPAP)
Opel AG *see* Adam Opel AG.
Open *see* Groupe Open.
Open Text Corporation, 79 301–05
Openwave Systems Inc., 95 318–22
Operadora Mexicana de Aeropuertos *see* Grupo Aeroportuario del Centro Norte, S.A.B. de C.V.
Operation Smile, Inc., 75 297–99
Opinion Research Corporation, 46 318–22
Oplink Communications, Inc., 106 337–41
The Oppenheimer Group, 76 295–98
Oppenheimer Wolff & Donnelly LLP, 71 262–64
Opsware Inc., 49 311–14
OPTEK Technology Inc., 98 275–78
Option Care Inc., 48 307–10
Optische Werke G. Rodenstock, 44 319–23
Opus Corporation, 34 321–23; 101 395–99 (upd.)
Oracle Corporation, 6 272–74; 24 367–71 (upd.); 67 282–87 (upd.)
Orange Glo International, 53 256–59
Orange S.A., 84 286–289
Orange 21 Inc., 103 312–15
Orascom Construction Industries S.A.E., 87 349–352
OraSure Technologies, Inc., 75 300–03
Orbit International Corp., 105 336–39
Orbital Sciences Corporation, 22 400–03
Orbitz, Inc., 61 276–78
Orbotech Ltd., 75 304–06
The Orchard Enterprises, Inc., 103 316–19
Orchard Supply Hardware Stores Corporation, 17 365–67
Ore-Ida Foods Inc., 13 382–83; 78 279–82 (upd.)
Oregon Chai, Inc., 49 315–17
Oregon Dental Service Health Plan, Inc., 51 276–78
Oregon Freeze Dry, Inc., 74 228–30
Oregon Metallurgical Corporation, 20 406–08
Oregon Steel Mills, Inc., 14 368–70
O'Reilly Automotive, Inc., 26 347–49; 78 283–87 (upd.)
O'Reilly Media, Inc., 99 307–310
Organic To Go Food Corporation, 99 319–322
Organic Valley (Coulee Region Organic Produce Pool), 53 260–62
Organización Soriana, S.A. de C.V., 35 320–22
Orgill, Inc., 99 323–326
ORI *see* Old Republic International Corp.
Orion Oyj, 72 256–59

Orion Pictures Corporation, 6 167–70 *see also* Metro-Goldwyn-Mayer Inc.
ORIX Corporation, II 442–43; 44 324–26 (upd.); 104 354–58 (upd.)
Orkin, Inc., 104 359–62
Orkla ASA, 18 394–98; 82 259–64 (upd.)
Orleans Homebuilders, Inc., 62 260–62
Ormat Technologies, Inc., 87 353–358
Ormet Corporation, 82 265–68
Orrick, Herrington and Sutcliffe LLP, 76 299–301
Orszagos Takarekpenztar es Kereskedelmi Bank Rt. (OTP Bank), 78 288–91
Orthodontic Centers of America, Inc., 35 323–26
Orthofix International NV, 72 260–62
The Orvis Company, Inc., 28 336–39
Oryx Energy Company, 7 413–15
Osaka Gas Company, Ltd., V 679–81; 60 233–36 (upd.)
Oscar Mayer Foods Corp., 12 370–72 *see also* Kraft Foods Inc.
Oshawa Group Limited, II 649–50
OshKosh B'Gosh, Inc., 9 393–95; 42 266–70 (upd.)
Oshkosh Corporation, 7 416–18; 98 279–84 (upd.)
Oshman's Sporting Goods, Inc., 17 368–70 *see also* Gart Sports Co.
OSI Restaurant Partners, Inc., 88 286–91 (upd.)
Osmonics, Inc., 18 399–401
Osram GmbH, 86 312–16
Österreichische Bundesbahnen GmbH, 6 418–20
Österreichische Elektrizitätswirtschafts-AG, 85 307–10
Österreichische Post- und Telegraphenverwaltung, V 314–17
O'Sullivan Industries Holdings, Inc., 34 313–15
Otari Inc., 89 341–44
Otis Elevator Company, Inc., 13 384–86; 39 311–15 (upd.)
Otis Spunkmeyer, Inc., 28 340–42
Otor S.A., 77 326–29
OTP Bank *see* Orszagos Takarekpenztar es Kereskedelmi Bank Rt.
OTR Express, Inc., 25 368–70
Ottakar's plc, 64 302–04
Ottaway Newspapers, Inc., 15 335–37
Otter Tail Power Company, 18 402–05
Otto Bremer Foundation *see* Bremer Financial Corp.
Otto Fuchs KG, 100 310–14
Otto Group, 106 342–48 (upd.)
Otto Versand GmbH & Co., V 159–61; 15 338–40 (upd.); 34 324–28 (upd.)
Outback Steakhouse, Inc., 12 373–75; 34 329–32 (upd.) *see also* OSI Restaurant Partners, Inc.
Outboard Marine Corporation, III 597–600; 20 409–12 (upd.) *see also* Bombardier Inc.

Outdoor Research, Incorporated, 67 288–90
Outdoor Systems, Inc., 25 371–73 *see also* Infinity Broadcasting Corp.
Outlook Group Corporation, 37 294–96
Outokumpu Oyj, 38 335–37
Outrigger Enterprises, Inc., 67 291–93
Overhead Door Corporation, 70 213–16
Overhill Corporation, 51 279–81
Overland Storage Inc., 100 315–20
Overnite Corporation, 14 371–73; 58 262–65 (upd.)
Overseas Shipholding Group, Inc., 11 376–77
Overstock.com, Inc., 75 307–09
Owens & Minor, Inc., 16 398–401; 68 282–85 (upd.)
Owens Corning, III 720–23; 20 413–17 (upd.); 98 285–91 (upd.)
Owens-Illinois, Inc., I 609–11; 26 350–53 (upd.); 85 311–18 (upd.)
Owosso Corporation, 29 366–68
Oxfam GB, 87 359–362
Oxford Health Plans, Inc., 16 402–04
Oxford Industries, Inc., 8 406–08; 84 290–296 (upd.)

P

P&C Foods Inc., 8 409–11
P & F Industries, Inc., 45 327–29
P&G *see* Procter & Gamble Co.
P.C. Richard & Son Corp., 23 372–74
P.F. Chang's China Bistro, Inc., 37 297–99; 86 317–21 (upd.)
P.H. Glatfelter Company, 8 412–14; 30 349–52 (upd.); 83 291–297 (upd.)
P.W. Minor and Son, Inc., 100 321–24
PACCAR Inc., I 185–86; 26 354–56 (upd.)
Pacer International, Inc., 54 274–76
Pacer Technology, 40 347–49
Pacific Basin Shipping Ltd., 86 322–26
Pacific Clay Products Inc., 88 292–95
Pacific Coast Building Products, Inc., 94 338–41
Pacific Coast Feather Company, 67 294–96
Pacific Coast Restaurants, Inc., 90 318–21
Pacific Dunlop Limited, 10 444–46 *see also* Ansell Ltd.
Pacific Enterprises, V 682–84 *see also* Sempra Energy.
Pacific Ethanol, Inc., 81 269–72
Pacific Gas and Electric Company, V 685–87 *see also* PG&E Corp.
Pacific Internet Limited, 87 363–366
Pacific Mutual Holding Company, 98 292–96
Pacific Sunwear of California, Inc., 28 343–45; 104 363–67 (upd.)
Pacific Telecom, Inc., 6 325–28
Pacific Telesis Group, V 318–20 *see also* SBC Communications.
PacifiCare Health Systems, Inc., 11 378–80

PacifiCorp, Inc., V 688–90; 26 357–60 (upd.)

Packaging Corporation of America, 12 376–78; 51 282–85 (upd.)

Packard Bell Electronics, Inc., 13 387–89

Packeteer, Inc., 81 273–76

Paddock Publications, Inc., 53 263–65

Paddy Power plc, 98 297–300

PagesJaunes Groupe SA, 79 306–09

Paging Network Inc., 11 381–83

Pagnossin S.p.A., 73 248–50

PaineWebber Group Inc., II 444–46; 22 404–07 (upd.) *see also* UBS AG.

Pakistan International Airlines Corporation, 46 323–26

Pakistan State Oil Company Ltd., 81 277–80

PAL *see* Philippine Airlines, Inc.

Palace Sports & Entertainment, Inc., 97 320–25

Palfinger AG, 100 325–28

PALIC *see* Pan-American Life Insurance Co.

Pall Corporation, 9 396–98; 72 263–66 (upd.)

Palm Harbor Homes, Inc., 39 316–18

Palm, Inc., 36 355–57; 75 310–14 (upd.)

Palm Management Corporation, 71 265–68

Palmer & Cay, Inc., 69 285–87

Palmer Candy Company, 80 277–81

Palmer Co. *see* R. M. Palmer Co.

Paloma Industries Ltd., 71 269–71

Palomar Medical Technologies, Inc., 22 408–10

Pamida Holdings Corporation, 15 341–43

The Pampered Chef Ltd., 18 406–08; 78 292–96 (upd.)

Pamplin Corp. *see* R.B. Pamplin Corp.

Pan-American Life Insurance Company, 48 311–13

Pan American World Airways, Inc., I 115–16; 12 379–81 (upd.)

Panalpina World Transport (Holding) Ltd., 47 286–88

Panamerican Beverages, Inc., 47 289–91; 54 74

PanAmSat Corporation, 46 327–29

Panattoni Development Company, Inc., 99 327–330

Panavision Inc., 24 372–74

Pancho's Mexican Buffet, Inc., 46 330–32

Panda Restaurant Group, Inc., 35 327–29; 97 326–30 (upd.)

Panera Bread Company, 44 327–29

Panhandle Eastern Corporation, V 691–92 *see also* CMS Energy Corp.

Pantone Inc., 53 266–69

The Pantry, Inc., 36 358–60

Panzani, 84 297–300

Papa Gino's Holdings Corporation, Inc., 86 327–30

Papa John's International, Inc., 15 344–46; 71 272–76 (upd.)

Papa Murphy's International, Inc., 54 277–79

Papeteries de Lancey, 23 366–68

Papetti's Hygrade Egg Products, Inc., 39 319–21

Pappas Restaurants, Inc., 76 302–04

Par Pharmaceutical Companies, Inc., 65 286–88

The Paradies Shops, Inc., 88 296–99

Paradise Music & Entertainment, Inc., 42 271–74

Paradores de Turismo de Espana S.A., 73 251–53

Parallel Petroleum Corporation, 101 400–03

Parametric Technology Corp., 16 405–07

Paramount Pictures Corporation, II 154–56; 94 342–47 (upd.)

Paramount Resources Ltd., 87 367–370

PAREXEL International Corporation, 84 301–304

Parfums Givenchy S.A., 100 329–32

Paribas *see* BNP Paribas Group.

Paris Corporation, 22 411–13

Parisian, Inc., 14 374–76 *see also* Belk, Inc.

Park Corp., 22 414–16

Park-Ohio Holdings Corp., 17 371–73; 85 319–23 (upd.)

Parker Drilling Company, 28 346–48

Parker-Hannifin Corporation, III 601–03; 24 375–78 (upd.); 99 331–337 (upd.)

Parlex Corporation, 61 279–81

Parmalat Finanziaria SpA, 50 343–46

Parque Arauco S.A., 72 267–69

Parras *see* Compañia Industrial de Parras, S.A. de C.V. (CIPSA).

Parsons Brinckerhoff Inc., 34 333–36; 104 368–72 (upd.)

The Parsons Corporation, 8 415–17; 56 263–67 (upd.)

PartnerRe Ltd., 83 298–301

Partouche SA *see* Groupe Partouche SA.

Party City Corporation, 54 280–82

Patch Products Inc., 105 340–44

Pathé SA, 29 369–71 *see also* Chargeurs International.

Pathmark Stores, Inc., 23 369–71; 101 404–08 (upd.)

Patina Oil & Gas Corporation, 24 379–81

Patrick Cudahy Inc., 102 321–25

Patrick Industries, Inc., 30 342–45

Patriot Transportation Holding, Inc., 91 371–74

Patterson Dental Co., 19 289–91

Patterson-UTI Energy, Inc., 55 293–95

Patton Boggs LLP, 71 277–79

Paul Harris Stores, Inc., 18 409–12

Paul, Hastings, Janofsky & Walker LLP, 27 357–59

Paul Mueller Company, 65 289–91

Paul Reed Smith Guitar Company, 89 345–48

The Paul Revere Corporation, 12 382–83

Paul-Son Gaming Corporation, 66 249–51

Paul, Weiss, Rifkind, Wharton & Garrison, 47 292–94

Paulaner Brauerei GmbH & Co. KG, 35 330–33

Paxson Communications Corporation, 33 322–26

Pay 'N Pak Stores, Inc., 9 399–401

Paychex, Inc., 15 347–49; 46 333–36 (upd.)

Payless Cashways, Inc., 11 384–86; 44 330–33 (upd.)

Payless ShoeSource, Inc., 18 413–15; 69 288–92 (upd.)

PayPal Inc., 58 266–69

PBL *see* Publishing and Broadcasting Ltd.

PBS *see* Public Broadcasting Stations.

The PBSJ Corporation, 82 269–73

PC Connection, Inc., 37 300–04

PCA *see* Packaging Corporation of America.

PCA International, Inc., 62 263–65

PCC *see* Companhia Suzano de Papel e Celulose S.A.

PCC Natural Markets, 94 348–51

PCL Construction Group Inc., 50 347–49

PCM Uitgevers NV, 53 270–73

PCS *see* Potash Corp. of Saskatchewan Inc.

PDI, Inc., 52 272–75

PDL BioPharma, Inc., 90 322–25

PDO *see* Petroleum Development Oman.

PDQ Food Stores Inc., 79 310–13

PDS Gaming Corporation, 44 334–37

PDVSA *see* Petróleos de Venezuela S.A.

Peabody Energy Corporation, 10 447–49; 45 330–33 (upd.)

Peabody Holding Company, Inc., IV 169–72

Peace Arch Entertainment Group Inc., 51 286–88

The Peak Technologies Group, Inc., 14 377–80

Peapod, Inc., 30 346–48

Pearl Musical Instrument Company, 78 297–300

Pearle Vision, Inc., 13 390–92

Pearson plc, IV 657–59; 46 337–41 (upd.); 103 320–26 (upd.)

Peavey Electronics Corporation, 16 408–10; 94 352–56 (upd.)

Pechiney S.A., IV 173–75; 45 334–37 (upd.)

PECO Energy Company, 11 387–90 *see also* Exelon Corp.

Pediatric Services of America, Inc., 31 356–58

Pediatrix Medical Group, Inc., 61 282–85

Peebles Inc., 16 411–13; 43 296–99 (upd.)

Peek & Cloppenburg KG, 46 342–45

Peet's Coffee & Tea, Inc., 38 338–40; 100 333–37 (upd.)

Peg Perego SpA, 88 300–03

Pegasus Solutions, Inc., 75 315–18

Pei Cobb Freed & Partners Architects LLP, 57 280–82
Pelican Products, Inc., 86 331–34
Pelikan Holding AG, 92 296–300
Pella Corporation, 12 384–86; 39 322–25 (upd.); 89 349–53 (upd.)
Pemco Aviation Group Inc., 54 283–86
PEMEX *see* Petróleos Mexicanos.
Penaflor S.A., 66 252–54
Penauille Polyservices SA, 49 318–21
Pendleton Grain Growers Inc., 64 305–08
Pendleton Woolen Mills, Inc., 42 275–78
Penford Corporation, 55 296–99
Pengrowth Energy Trust, 95 323–26
The Penguin Group, 100 338–42
The Peninsular and Oriental Steam Navigation Company, V 490–93; 38 341–46 (upd.)
Peninsular and Oriental Steam Navigation Company (Bovis Division), I 588–89 *see also* DP World.
Penn Engineering & Manufacturing Corp., 28 349–51
Penn National Gaming, Inc., 33 327–29
Penn Traffic Company, 13 393–95
Penn Virginia Corporation, 85 324–27
Penney's *see* J.C. Penney Company, Inc.
Pennington Seed Inc., 98 301–04
Pennon Group Plc, 45 338–41
Pennsylvania Blue Shield, III 325–27 *see also* Highmark Inc.
Pennsylvania Power & Light Company, V 693–94
Pennwalt Corporation, I 382–84
PennWell Corporation, 55 300–03
Pennzoil-Quaker State Company, IV 488–90; 20 418–22 (upd.); 50 350–55 (upd.)
Penske Corporation, V 494–95; 19 292–94 (upd.); 84 305–309 (upd.)
Pentair, Inc., 7 419–21; 26 361–64 (upd.); 81 281–87 (upd.)
Pentax Corporation, 78 301–05
Pentech International, Inc., 29 372–74
The Pentland Group plc, 20 423–25; 100 343–47 (upd.)
Penton Media, Inc., 27 360–62
Penzeys Spices, Inc., 79 314–16
People Express Airlines Inc., I 117–18
People's United Financial Inc. , 106 349–52
Peoples Energy Corporation, 6 543–44
PeopleSoft Inc., 14 381–83; 33 330–33 (upd.) *see also* Oracle Corp.
The Pep Boys—Manny, Moe & Jack, 11 391–93; 36 361–64 (upd.); 81 288–94 (upd.)
PEPCO *see* Potomac Electric Power Co.
Pepper *see* J. W. Pepper and Son Inc.
Pepper Hamilton LLP, 43 300–03
Pepperidge Farm, Incorporated, 81 295–300
The Pepsi Bottling Group, Inc., 40 350–53
PepsiAmericas, Inc., 67 297–300 (upd.)

PepsiCo, Inc., I 276–79; 10 450–54 (upd.); 38 347–54 (upd.); 93 333–44 (upd.)
Pequiven *see* Petroquímica de Venezuela S.A.
Perdigao SA, 52 276–79
Perdue Farms Inc., 7 422–24; 23 375–78 (upd.)
Perfetti Van Melle S.p.A., 72 270–73
Performance Food Group, 31 359–62; 96 329–34 (upd.)
Perini Corporation, 8 418–21; 82 274–79 (upd.)
PerkinElmer, Inc., 7 425–27; 78 306–10 (upd.)
Perkins Coie LLP, 56 268–70
Perkins Family Restaurants, L.P., 22 417–19
Perkins Foods Holdings Ltd., 87 371–374
Perma-Fix Environmental Services, Inc., 99 338–341
Pernod Ricard S.A., I 280–81; 21 399–401 (upd.); 72 274–77 (upd.)
Perot Systems Corporation, 29 375–78
Perrigo Company, 12 387–89; 59 330–34 (upd.)
Perry Ellis International Inc., 41 291–94; 106 353–58 (upd.)
Perry's Ice Cream Company Inc., 90 326–29
The Perseus Books Group, 91 375–78
Perstorp AB, I 385–87; 51 289–92 (upd.)
Pertamina, IV 491–93; 56 271–74 (upd.)
Perusahaan Otomobil Nasional Bhd., 62 266–68
Pescanova S.A., 81 301–04
Pet Incorporated, 7 428–31
Petco Animal Supplies, Inc., 29 379–81; 74 231–34 (upd.)
Peter Kiewit Sons' Inc., 8 422–24
Peter Pan Bus Lines Inc., 106 359–63
Peter Piper, Inc., 70 217–19
Peterbilt Motors Company, 89 354–57
Petersen Publishing Company, 21 402–04
Peterson American Corporation, 55 304–06
Pete's Brewing Company, 22 420–22
Petit Bateau, 95 327–31
PetMed Express, Inc., 81 305–08
Petrie Stores Corporation, 8 425–27
Petro-Canada, IV 494–96; 99 342–349 (upd.)
Petrobrás *see* Petróleo Brasileiro S.A.
Petrobras Energia Participaciones S.A., 72 278–81
Petroecuador *see* Petróleos del Ecuador.
Petrofac Ltd., 95 332–35
PetroFina S.A., IV 497–500; 26 365–69 (upd.)
Petrogal *see* Petróleos de Portugal.
Petrohawk Energy Corporation, 79 317–20
Petróleo Brasileiro S.A., IV 501–03
Petróleos de Portugal S.A., IV 504–06

Petróleos de Venezuela S.A., IV 507–09; 74 235–39 (upd.)
Petróleos del Ecuador, IV 510–11
Petróleos Mexicanos (PEMEX), IV 512–14; 19 295–98 (upd.); 104 373–78 (upd.)
Petroleum Development Oman LLC, IV 515–16; 98 305–09 (upd.)
Petroleum Helicopters, Inc., 35 334–36
Petroliam Nasional Bhd (Petronas), 56 275–79 (upd.)
Petrolite Corporation, 15 350–52 *see also* Baker Hughes Inc.
Petromex *see* Petróleos de Mexico S.A.
Petron Corporation, 58 270–72
Petronas, IV 517–20 *see also* Petroliam Nasional Bhd.
Petrossian Inc., 54 287–89
Petry Media Corporation, 102 326–29
PETsMART, Inc., 14 384–86; 41 295–98 (upd.)
Peugeot S.A., I 187–88 *see also* PSA Peugeot Citroen S.A.
The Pew Charitable Trusts, 35 337–40
Pez Candy, Inc., 38 355–57
The Pfaltzgraff Co. *see* Susquehanna Pfaltzgraff Co.
Pfizer Inc., I 661–63; 9 402–05 (upd.); 38 358–67 (upd.); 79 321–33 (upd.)
PFSweb, Inc., 73 254–56
PG&E Corporation, 26 370–73 (upd.)
PGA *see* The Professional Golfers' Association.
Phaidon Press Ltd., 98 310–14
Phantom Fireworks *see* B.J. Alan Co., Inc.
Phar-Mor Inc., 12 390–92
Pharmacia & Upjohn Inc., I 664–65; 25 374–78 (upd.) *see also* Pfizer Inc.
Pharmion Corporation, 91 379–82
Phat Fashions LLC, 49 322–24
Phelps Dodge Corporation, IV 176–79; 28 352–57 (upd.); 75 319–25 (upd.)
PHH Arval, V 496–97; 53 274–76 (upd.)
PHI, Inc., 80 282–86 (upd.)
Philadelphia Eagles, 37 305–08
Philadelphia Electric Company, V 695–97 *see also* Exelon Corp.
Philadelphia Gas Works Company, 92 301–05
Philadelphia Media Holdings LLC, 92 306–10
Philadelphia Suburban Corporation, 39 326–29
Philharmonic-Symphony Society of New York, Inc. (New York Philharmonic), 69 293–97
Philip Environmental Inc., 16 414–16
Philip Morris Companies Inc., V 405–07; 18 416–19 (upd.); 44 338–43 (upd.) *see also* Kraft Foods Inc.
Philip Services Corp., 73 257–60
Philipp Holzmann AG, 17 374–77
Philippine Airlines, Inc., 6 106–08; 23 379–82 (upd.)
Philips Electronics N.V., 13 400–03 (upd.) *see also* Koninklijke Philips Electronics N.V.

Philips Electronics North America Corp., 13 396–99

N.V. Philips Gloeilampenfabriken, II 78–80 *see also* Philips Electronics N.V.

The Phillies, 106 364–68

Phillips Foods, Inc., 63 320–22; 90 330–33 (upd.)

Phillips International, Inc., 78 311–14

Phillips Lytle LLP, 102 330–34

Phillips Petroleum Company, IV 521–23; 40 354–59 (upd.) *see also* ConocoPhillips.

Phillips-Van Heusen Corporation, 24 382–85

Phillips, de Pury & Luxembourg, 49 325–27

Phoenix AG, 68 286–89

Phoenix Footwear Group, Inc., 70 220–22

Phoenix Mecano AG, 61 286–88

The Phoenix Media/Communications Group, 91 383–87

Phones 4u Ltd., 85 328–31

Photo-Me International Plc, 83 302–306

PHP Healthcare Corporation, 22 423–25

PhyCor, Inc., 36 365–69

Physician Sales & Service, Inc., 14 387–89

Physio-Control International Corp., 18 420–23

Piaggio & C. S.p.A., 20 426–29; 100 348–52 (upd.)

PianoDisc *see* Burgett, Inc.

PIC International Group PLC, 24 386–88 (upd.)

Picanol N.V., 96 335–38

Picard Surgeles, 76 305–07

Piccadilly Cafeterias, Inc., 19 299–302

Pick 'n Pay Stores Ltd., 82 280–83

PictureTel Corp., 10 455–57; 27 363–66 (upd.)

Piedmont Investment Advisors, LLC, 106 369–72

Piedmont Natural Gas Company, Inc., 27 367–69

Pier 1 Imports, Inc., 12 393–95; 34 337–41 (upd.); 95 336–43 (upd.)

Pierce Leahy Corporation, 24 389–92 *see also* Iron Mountain Inc.

Piercing Pagoda, Inc., 29 382–84

Pierre & Vacances SA, 48 314–16

Pierre Fabre *see* Laboratoires Pierre Fabre S.A.

Piggly Wiggly Southern, Inc., 13 404–06

Pilgrim's Pride Corporation, 7 432–33; 23 383–85 (upd.); 90 334–38 (upd.)

Pilkington Group Limited, II 724–27; 34 342–47 (upd.); 87 375–383 (upd.)

Pillowtex Corporation, 19 303–05; 41 299–302 (upd.)

Pillsbury Company, II 555–57; 13 407–09 (upd.); 62 269–73 (upd.)

Pillsbury Madison & Sutro LLP, 29 385–88

Pilot Air Freight Corp., 67 301–03

Pilot Corporation, 49 328–30

Pilot Pen Corporation of America, 82 284–87

Pinault-Printemps-Redoute S.A., 19 306–09 (upd.) *see also* PPR S.A.

Pindar *see* G A Pindar & Son Ltd.

Pinguely-Haulotte SA, 51 293–95

Pinkerton's Inc., 9 406–09 *see also* Securitas AB.

Pinnacle Airlines Corp., 73 261–63

Pinnacle West Capital Corporation, 6 545–47; 54 290–94 (upd.)

Pioneer Electronic Corporation, III 604–06; 28 358–61 (upd.) *see also* Agilysis Inc.

Pioneer Hi-Bred International, Inc., 9 410–12; 41 303–06 (upd.)

Pioneer International Limited, III 728–30

Pioneer Natural Resources Company, 59 335–39

Pioneer-Standard Electronics Inc., 19 310–14 *see also* Agilysis Inc.

Piper Jaffray Companies Inc., 22 426–30 *see also* U.S. Bancorp.

Pirelli & C. S.p.A., V 249–51; 15 353–56 (upd.); 75 326–31 (upd.)

Piscines Desjoyaux S.A., 84 310–313

Pitman Company, 58 273–75

Pitney Bowes, Inc., III 156–58, 159; 19 315–18 (upd.); 47 295–99 (upd.)

Pittsburgh Brewing Company, 76 308–11

Pittsburgh Plate Glass Co. *see* PPG Industries, Inc.

Pittsburgh Steelers Sports, Inc., 66 255–57

The Pittston Company, IV 180–82; 19 319–22 (upd.) *see also* The Brink's Co.

Pittway Corporation, 9 413–15; 33 334–37 (upd.)

Pixar Animation Studios, 34 348–51

Pixelworks, Inc., 69 298–300

Pizza Hut Inc., 7 434–35; 21 405–07 (upd.)

Pizza Inn, Inc., 46 346–49

PKF International, 78 315–18

Placer Dome Inc., 20 430–33; 61 289–93 (upd.)

Plain Dealer Publishing Company, 92 311–14

Plains Cotton Cooperative Association, 57 283–86

Planar Systems, Inc., 61 294–97

Planet Hollywood International, Inc., 18 424–26; 41 307–10 (upd.)

Planeta *see* Grupo Planeta.

Plantation Pipe Line Company, 68 290–92

Plante & Moran, LLP, 71 280–83

Plantronics, Inc., 106 373–77

Platinum Entertainment, Inc., 35 341–44

PLATINUM Technology, Inc., 14 390–92 *see also* Computer Associates International, Inc.

Plato Learning, Inc., 44 344–47

Play by Play Toys & Novelties, Inc., 26 374–76

Playboy Enterprises, Inc., 18 427–30

PlayCore, Inc., 27 370–72

Players International, Inc., 22 431–33

Playmates Toys, 23 386–88

Playskool, Inc., 25 379–81 *see also* Hasbro, Inc.

Playtex Products, Inc., 15 357–60

Pleasant Company, 27 373–75 *see also* American Girl, Inc.

Pleasant Holidays LLC, 62 274–76

Plessey Company, PLC, II 81–82 *see also* Marconi plc.

Plexus Corporation, 35 345–47; 80 287–91 (upd.)

Pliant Corporation, 98 315–18

PLIVA d.d., 70 223–25

Plow & Hearth, Inc., 104 379–82

Plum Creek Timber Company, Inc., 43 304–06; 106 378–82 (upd.)

Pluma, Inc., 27 376–78

Ply Gem Industries Inc., 12 396–98

The PMI Group, Inc., 49 331–33

PMP Ltd., 72 282–84

PMT Services, Inc., 24 393–95

The PNC Financial Services Group Inc., II 342–43; 13 410–12 (upd.); 46 350–53 (upd.)

PNM Resources Inc., 51 296–300 (upd.)

Pochet SA, 55 307–09

PODS Enterprises Inc., 103 327–29

Pogo Producing Company, 39 330–32

Pohang Iron and Steel Company Ltd., IV 183–85 *see also* POSCO.

Polar Air Cargo Inc., 60 237–39

Polaris Industries Inc., 12 399–402; 35 348–53 (upd.); 77 330–37 (upd.)

Polaroid Corporation, III 607–09; 7 436–39 (upd.); 28 362–66 (upd.); 93 345–53 (upd.)

Polartec LLC, 98 319–23 (upd.)

Policy Management Systems Corporation, 11 394–95

Policy Studies, Inc., 62 277–80

Poliet S.A., 33 338–40

Polk Audio, Inc., 34 352–54

Polo/Ralph Lauren Corporation, 12 403–05; 62 281–85 (upd.)

Polski Koncern Naftowy ORLEN S.A., 77 338–41

PolyGram N.V., 23 389–92

PolyMedica Corporation, 77 342–45

PolyOne Corporation, 87 384–395 (upd.)

Pomare Ltd., 88 304–07

Pomeroy Computer Resources, Inc., 33 341–44

Ponderosa Steakhouse, 15 361–64

Poof-Slinky, Inc., 61 298–300

Poore Brothers, Inc., 44 348–50 *see also* The Inventure Group, Inc.

Pop Warner Little Scholars, Inc., 86 335–38

Pope & Talbot, Inc., 12 406–08; 61 301–05 (upd.)

Pope Cable and Wire B.V. *see* Belden CDT Inc.
Pope Resources LP, 74 240–43
Popular, Inc., 41 311–13
The Porcelain and Fine China Companies Ltd., 69 301–03
Porsche AG, 13 413–15; 31 363–66 (upd.)
The Port Authority of New York and New Jersey, 48 317–20
Port Imperial Ferry Corporation, 70 226–29
Portal Software, Inc., 47 300–03
Portillo's Restaurant Group, Inc., 71 284–86
Portland General Corporation, 6 548–51
Portland Trail Blazers, 50 356–60
Portmeirion Group plc, 88 308–11
Portucel *see* Grupo Portucel Soporcel.
Portugal Telecom SGPS S.A., 69 304–07
Posadas *see* Grupo Posadas, S.A. de C.V.
POSCO, 57 287–91 (upd.)
Positivo Informatica S.A. *see* Grupo Positivo.
Post Office Group, V 498–501
Post Properties, Inc., 26 377–79
La Poste, V 470–72
Posterscope Worldwide, 70 230–32
Posti- Ja Telelaitos, 6 329–31
Potash Corporation of Saskatchewan Inc., 18 431–33; 101 409–15 (upd.)
Potbelly Sandwich Works, Inc., 83 307–310
Potlatch Corporation, 8 428–30; 34 355–59 (upd.); 87 396–403 (upd.)
Potomac Electric Power Company, 6 552–54
Potter & Brumfield Inc., 11 396–98
Pou Chen Corporation, 81 309–12
Powell Duffryn plc, 31 367–70
Powell's Books, Inc., 40 360–63
Power Corporation of Canada, 36 370–74 (upd.); 85 332–39 (upd.)
Power-One, Inc., 79 334–37
PowerBar Inc., 44 351–53
Powergen PLC, 11 399–401; 50 361–64 (upd.)
Powerhouse Technologies, Inc., 27 379–81
POZEN Inc., 81 313–16
PP&L *see* Pennsylvania Power & Light Co.
PPB Group Berhad, 57 292–95
PPG Industries, Inc., III 731–33; 22 434–37 (upd.); 81 317–23 (upd.)
PPL Corporation, 41 314–17 (upd.)
PPR S.A., 74 244–48 (upd.)
PR Newswire, 35 354–56
Prada Holding B.V., 45 342–45
Prairie Farms Dairy, Inc., 47 304–07
Praktiker Bau- und Heimwerkermärkte AG, 103 330–34
Pranda Jewelry plc, 70 233–35
Pratt & Whitney, 9 416–18
Praxair, Inc., 11 402–04; 48 321–24 (upd.)

Praxis Bookstore Group LLC, 90 339–42
Pre-Paid Legal Services, Inc., 20 434–37
Precision Castparts Corp., 15 365–67
Preferred Hotel Group, 103 335–38
Premark International, Inc., III 610–12 *see also* Illinois Tool Works Inc.
Premcor Inc., 37 309–11
Premier Industrial Corporation, 9 419–21
Premier Parks, Inc., 27 382–84 *see also* Six Flags, Inc.
Premiere Radio Networks, Inc., 102 335–38
Premium Standard Farms, Inc., 30 353–55
PremiumWear, Inc., 30 356–59
Preserver Group, Inc., 44 354–56
President Casinos, Inc., 22 438–40
Pressman Toy Corporation, 56 280–82
Presstek, Inc., 33 345–48
Preston Corporation, 6 421–23
Preussag AG, 17 378–82; 42 279–83 (upd.)
PreussenElektra Aktiengesellschaft, V 698–700 *see also* E.On AG.
PRG-Schultz International, Inc., 73 264–67
Price Communications Corporation, 42 284–86
The Price Company, V 162–64 *see also* Costco Wholesale Corp.
Price Pfister, Inc., 70 236–39
Price Waterhouse LLP, 9 422–24 *see also* PricewaterhouseCoopers
PriceCostco, Inc., 14 393–95 *see also* Costco Wholesale Corp.
Priceline.com Incorporated, 57 296–99
PriceSmart, Inc., 71 287–90
PricewaterhouseCoopers, 29 389–94 (upd.)
PRIDE Enterprises *see* Prison Rehabilitative Industries and Diversified Enterprises, Inc.
Pride International, Inc., 78 319–23
Primark Corp., 13 416–18 *see also* Thomson Corp.
Prime Hospitality Corporation, 52 280–83
Primedex Health Systems, Inc., 25 382–85
Primedia Inc., 22 441–43
Primerica Corporation, I 612–14
Prince Sports Group, Inc., 15 368–70
Princes Ltd., 76 312–14
Princess Cruise Lines, 22 444–46
The Princeton Review, Inc., 42 287–90
Principal Mutual Life Insurance Company, III 328–30
Printpack, Inc., 68 293–96
Printrak, A Motorola Company, 44 357–59
Printronix, Inc., 18 434–36
Prison Rehabilitative Industries and Diversified Enterprises, Inc. (PRIDE), 53 277–79
Pro-Build Holdings Inc., 95 344–48 (upd.)

The Procter & Gamble Company, III 50–53; 8 431–35 (upd.); 26 380–85 (upd.); 67 304–11 (upd.)
Prodigy Communications Corporation, 34 360–62
Prodware S.A., 102 339–42
Proeza S.A. de C.V., 82 288–91
Professional Bull Riders Inc., 55 310–12
The Professional Golfers' Association of America, 41 318–21
Proffitt's, Inc., 19 323–25 *see also* Belk, Inc.
Programmer's Paradise, Inc., 81 324–27
Progress Energy, Inc., 74 249–52
Progress Software Corporation, 15 371–74
Progressive Corporation, 11 405–07; 29 395–98 (upd.)
Progressive Enterprises Ltd., 96 339–42
ProLogis, 57 300–02
Promus Companies, Inc., 9 425–27 *see also* Hilton Hotels Corp.
ProSiebenSat.1 Media AG, 54 295–98
Proskauer Rose LLP, 47 308–10
Protection One, Inc., 32 372–75
Provell Inc., 58 276–79 (upd.)
Providence Health System, 90 343–47
The Providence Journal Company, 28 367–69; 30 15
The Providence Service Corporation, 64 309–12
Provident Bankshares Corporation, 85 340–43
Provident Life and Accident Insurance Company of America, III 331–33 *see also* UnumProvident Corp.
Providian Financial Corporation, 52 284–90 (upd.)
Provigo Inc., II 651–53; 51 301–04 (upd.)
Provimi S.A., 80 292–95
PRS *see* Paul Reed Smith Guitar Co.
Prudential Financial Inc., III 337–41; 30 360–64 (upd.); 82 292–98 (upd.)
Prudential plc, III 334–36; 48 325–29 (upd.)
PSA Peugeot Citroen S.A., 28 370–74 (upd.); 54 126
PSF *see* Premium Standard Farms, Inc.
PSI Resources, 6 555–57
Psion PLC, 45 346–49
Psychemedics Corporation, 89 358–61
Psychiatric Solutions, Inc., 68 297–300
PT Astra International Tbk, 56 283–86
PT Bank Buana Indonesia Tbk, 60 240–42
PT Gudang Garam Tbk, 103 339–42
PT Indosat Tbk, 93 354–57
PT Semen Gresik Tbk, 103 343–46
PTT Public Company Ltd., 56 287–90
Pubco Corporation, 17 383–85
Public Service Company of Colorado, 6 558–60
Public Service Company of New Hampshire, 21 408–12; 55 313–18 (upd.)

Public Service Company of New Mexico, 6 561–64 *see also* PNM Resources Inc.

Public Service Enterprise Group Inc., V 701–03; 44 360–63 (upd.)

Public Storage, Inc., 21 52 291–93

Publicis Groupe, 19 329–32; 77 346–50 (upd.)

Publishers Clearing House, 23 393–95; 64 313–16 (upd.)

Publishers Group, Inc., 35 357–59

Publishing and Broadcasting Limited, 54 299–302

Publix Super Markets, Inc., 7 440–42; 31 371–74 (upd.); 105 345–51 (upd.)

Puck Lazaroff Inc. *see* The Wolfgang Puck Food Company, Inc.

Pueblo Xtra International, Inc., 47 311–13

Puerto Rico Electric Power Authority, 47 314–16

Puget Sound Energy Inc., 6 565–67; 50 365–68 (upd.)

Puig Beauty and Fashion Group S.L., 60 243–46

Pulaski Furniture Corporation, 33 349–52; 80 296–99 (upd.)

Pulitzer Inc., 15 375–77; 58 280–83 (upd.)

Pulsar Internacional S.A., 21 413–15

Pulte Homes, Inc., 8 436–38; 42 291–94 (upd.)

Puma AG Rudolf Dassler Sport, 35 360–63

Pumpkin Masters, Inc., 48 330–32

Punch International N.V., 66 258–60

Punch Taverns plc, 70 240–42

Puratos S.A./NV, 92 315–18

Pure World, Inc., 72 285–87

Purina Mills, Inc., 32 376–79

Puritan-Bennett Corporation, 13 419–21

Purolator Products Company, 21 416–18; 74 253–56 (upd.)

Putt-Putt Golf Courses of America, Inc., 23 396–98

PVC Container Corporation, 67 312–14

PW Eagle, Inc., 48 333–36

PWA Group, IV 323–25 *see also* Svenska Cellulosa.

Pyramid Breweries Inc., 33 353–55; 102 343–47 (upd.)

Pyramid Companies, 54 303–05

PZ Cussons plc, 72 288–90

Q

Q.E.P. Co., Inc., 65 292–94

Qantas Airways Ltd., 6 109–13; 24 396–401 (upd.); 68 301–07 (upd.)

Qatar Airways Company Q.C.S.C., 87 404–407

Qatar National Bank SAQ, 87 408–411

Qatar Petroleum, IV 524–26; 98 324–28 (upd.)

Qatar Telecom QSA, 87 412–415

Qdoba Restaurant Corporation, 93 358–62

Qiagen N.V., 39 333–35

QLT Inc., 71 291–94

QRS Music Technologies, Inc., 95 349–53

QSC Audio Products, Inc., 56 291–93

QSS Group, Inc., 100 358–61

Quad/Graphics, Inc., 19 333–36

Quaker Chemical Corp., 91 388–91

Quaker Fabric Corp., 19 337–39

Quaker Foods North America, II 558–60; 12 409–12 (upd.); 34 363–67 (upd.); 73 268–73 (upd.)

Quaker State Corporation, 7 443–45; 21 419–22 (upd.) *see also* Pennzoil-Quaker State Co.

QUALCOMM Incorporated, 20 438–41; 47 317–21 (upd.)

Quality Chekd Dairies, Inc., 48 337–39

Quality Dining, Inc., 18 437–40

Quality Food Centers, Inc., 17 386–88 *see also* Kroger Co.

Quality Systems, Inc., 81 328–31

Quanex Corporation, 13 422–24; 62 286–89 (upd.)

Quanta Computer Inc., 47 322–24

Quanta Services, Inc., 79 338–41

Quantum Chemical Corporation, 8 439–41

Quantum Corporation, 10 458–59; 62 290–93 (upd.)

Quark, Inc., 36 375–79

Quebéc Hydro-Electric Commission *see* Hydro-Quebéc.

Quebecor Inc., 12 412–14; 47 325–28 (upd.)

Quelle Group, V 165–67 *see also* Karstadt Quelle AG.

Quest Diagnostics Inc., 26 390–92; 106 383–87 (upd.)

Questar Corporation, 6 568–70; 26 386–89 (upd.)

The Quick & Reilly Group, Inc., 20 442–44

Quick Restaurants S.A., 94 357–60

Quicken Loans, Inc., 93 363–67

Quidel Corporation, 80 300–03

The Quigley Corporation, 62 294–97

Quiksilver, Inc., 18 441–43; 79 342–47 (upd.)

QuikTrip Corporation, 36 380–83

Quill Corporation, 28 375–77

Quilmes Industrial (QUINSA) S.A., 67 315–17

Quinn Emanuel Urquhart Oliver & Hedges, LLP, 99 350–353

Quintiles Transnational Corporation, 21 423–25; 68 308–12 (upd.)

Quixote Corporation, 15 378–80

The Quizno's Corporation, 42 295–98

Quovadx Inc., 70 243–46

QVC Inc., 9 428–29; 58 284–87 (upd.)

Qwest Communications International, Inc., 37 312–17

R

R&B, Inc., 51 305–07

R.B. Pamplin Corp., 45 350–52

R.C. Bigelow, Inc., 49 334–36

R.C. Willey Home Furnishings, 72 291–93

R.G. Barry Corp., 17 389–91; 44 364–67 (upd.)

R. Griggs Group Limited, 23 399–402; 31 413–14

R.H. Macy & Co., Inc., V 168–70; 8 442–45 (upd.); 30 379–83 (upd.) *see also* Macy's, Inc.

R.J. Reynolds Tobacco Holdings, Inc., 30 384–87 (upd.)

R. M. Palmer Co., 89 362–64

R.P. Scherer Corporation, I 678–80 *see also* Cardinal Health, Inc.

R.R. Bowker LLC, 100 362–66

R.R. Donnelley & Sons Company, IV 660–62; 38 368–71 (upd.)

Rabobank Group, 26 419; 33 356–58

RAC *see* Roy Anderson Corp.

Racal-Datacom Inc., 11 408–10

Racal Electronics PLC, II 83–84 *see also* Thales S.A.

Racing Champions Corporation, 37 318–20

Rack Room Shoes, Inc., 84 314–317

Radeberger Gruppe AG, 75 332–35

Radian Group Inc., 42 299–301 *see also* Onex Corp.

Radiant Systems Inc., 104 383–87

Radiation Therapy Services, Inc., 85 344–47

@radical.media, 103 347–50

Radio Flyer Inc., 34 368–70

Radio One, Inc., 67 318–21

RadioShack Corporation, 36 384–88 (upd.); 101 416–23 (upd.)

Radius Inc., 16 417–19

RAE Systems Inc., 83 311–314

RAG AG, 35 364–67; 60 247–51 (upd.)

Rag Shops, Inc., 30 365–67

Ragdoll Productions Ltd., 51 308–11

Raiffeisen Zentralbank Österreich AG, 85 348–52

RailTex, Inc., 20 445–47

Railtrack Group PLC, 50 369–72

Rain Bird Corporation, 84 318–321

Rainforest Café, Inc., 25 386 88; 88 312–16 (upd.)

Rainier Brewing Company, 23 403–05

Raisio PLC, 99 354–357

Raleigh UK Ltd., 65 295–97

Raley's Inc., 14 396–98; 58 288–91 (upd.)

Rallye SA, 54 306–09

Rally's, 25 389–91; 68 313–16 (upd.)

Ralph Lauren *see* Polo/Ralph Lauren Corportion.

Ralphs Grocery Company, 35 368–70

Ralston Purina Company, II 561–63; 13 425–27 (upd.) *see also* Ralcorp Holdings, Inc.; Nestlé S.A.

Ramsay Youth Services, Inc., 41 322–24

Ramtron International Corporation, 89 365–68

Ranbaxy Laboratories Ltd., 70 247–49

Rand McNally & Company, 28 378–81; 53 122

Randall's Food Markets, Inc., 40 364–67 *see also* Safeway Inc.

Random House Inc., 13 428–30; 31 375–80 (upd.); 106 388–98 (upd.)

Randon S.A. Implementos e Participações, 79 348–52

Randstad Holding n.v., 16 420–22; 43 307–10 (upd.)

Range Resources Corporation, 45 353–55

The Rank Group plc, II 157–59; 14 399–402 (upd.); 64 317–21 (upd.)

Ranks Hovis McDougall Limited, II 564–65; 28 382–85 (upd.)

RAO Unified Energy System of Russia, 45 356–60

Rapala-Normark Group, Ltd., 30 368–71

Rare Hospitality International Inc., 19 340–42

RAS *see* Riunione Adriatica di Sicurtà SpA.

Rascal House *see* Jerry's Famous Deli Inc.

Rasmussen Group *see* K.A. Rasmussen AS.

Rathbone Brothers plc, 70 250–53

RathGibson Inc., 90 348–51

ratiopharm Group, 84 322–326

Ratner Companies, 72 294–96

Rautakirja Oy, 104 388–92

Raven Industries, Inc., 33 359–61

Ravensburger AG, 64 322–26

Raving Brands, Inc., 64 327–29

Rawlings Sporting Goods Co., Inc., 24 402–04

Raychem Corporation, 8 446–47

Raycom Media, Inc., 106 399–402

Raymarine plc, 104 393–96

Raymond James Financial Inc., 69 308–10

Raymond Ltd., 77 351–54

Rayonier Inc., 24 405–07

Rayovac Corporation, 13 431–34; 39 336–40 (upd.)

Raytech Corporation, 61 306–09

Raytheon Aircraft Holdings Inc., 46 354–57

Raytheon Company, II 85–87; 11 411–14 (upd.); 38 372–77 (upd.); 105 352–59 (upd.)

Razorfish, Inc., 37 321–24

RCA Corporation, II 88–90

RCM Technologies, Inc., 34 371–74

RCN Corporation, 70 254–57

RCS MediaGroup S.p.A., 96 343–46

RDO Equipment Company, 33 362–65

RE/MAX International, Inc., 59 344–46

Read-Rite Corp., 10 463–64

The Reader's Digest Association, Inc., IV 663–64; 17 392–95 (upd.); 71 295–99 (upd.)

Reading International Inc., 70 258–60

The Real Good Food Company plc, 99 358–361

Real Madrid C.F., 73 274–76

Real Times, Inc., 66 261–65

Real Turismo, S.A. de C.V., 50 373–75

The Really Useful Group, 26 393–95

RealNetworks, Inc., 53 280–82

Reckitt Benckiser plc, II 566–67; 42 302–06 (upd.); 91 392–99 (upd.)

Reckson Associates Realty Corp., 47 329–31

Recordati Industria Chimica e Farmaceutica S.p.A., 105 360–64

Recording for the Blind & Dyslexic, 51 312–14

Recoton Corp., 15 381–83

Recovery Engineering, Inc., 25 392–94

Recreational Equipment, Inc., 18 444–47; 71 300–03 (upd.)

Recycled Paper Greetings, Inc., 21 426–28

Red Apple Group, Inc., 23 406–08

Red Bull GmbH, 60 252–54

Red Hat, Inc., 45 361–64

Red McCombs Automotive Group, 91 400–03

Red Robin Gourmet Burgers, Inc., 56 294–96

Red Roof Inns, Inc., 18 448–49 *see also* Accor S.A.

Red Spot Paint & Varnish Company, 55 319–22

Red Wing Pottery Sales, Inc., 52 294–96

Red Wing Shoe Company, Inc., 9 433–35; 30 372–75 (upd.); 83 315–321 (upd.)

Redback Networks, Inc., 92 319–22

Redcats S.A., 102 348–52

Reddy Ice Holdings, Inc., 80 304–07

Redhook Ale Brewery, Inc., 31 381–84; 88 317–21 (upd.)

Redken Laboratories Inc., 84 327–330

Redland plc, III 734–36 *see also* Lafarge Cement UK.

Redlon & Johnson, Inc., 97 331–34

RedPeg Marketing, 73 277–79

RedPrairie Corporation, 74 257–60

Redrow Group plc, 31 385–87

Reebok International Ltd., V 375–77; 9 436–38 (upd.); 26 396–400 (upd.)

Reed & Barton Corporation, 67 322–24

Reed Elsevier plc, 31 388–94 (upd.)

Reed International PLC, IV 665–67; 17 396–99 (upd.)

Reed's, Inc., 103 351–54

Reeds Jewelers, Inc., 22 447–49

Reesnik *see* Koninklijke Reesink N.V.

Regal-Beloit Corporation, 18 450–53; 97 335–42 (upd.)

Regal Entertainment Group, 59 340–43

The Regence Group, 74 261–63

Regency Centers Corporation, 71 304–07

Regent Communications, Inc., 87 416–420

Regent Inns plc, 95 354–57

Régie Nationale des Usines Renault, I 189–91 *see also* Renault S.A.

Regions Financial Corporation, 106 403–07

Regis Corporation, 18 454–56; 70 261–65 (upd.)

REI *see* Recreational Equipment, Inc.

Reichhold Chemicals, Inc., 10 465–67

Reiter Dairy, LLC, 94 361–64

Rejuvenation, Inc., 91 404–07

Reliance Electric Company, 9 439–42

Reliance Group Holdings, Inc., III 342–44

Reliance Industries Ltd., 81 332–36

Reliance Steel & Aluminum Company, 19 343–45; 70 266–70 (upd.)

Reliant Energy Inc., 44 368–73 (upd.)

Reliv International, Inc., 58 292–95

Remedy Corporation, 58 296–99

RemedyTemp, Inc., 20 448–50

Remington Arms Company, Inc., 12 415–17; 40 368–71 (upd.)

Remington Products Company, L.L.C., 42 307–10

Remington Rand *see* Unisys Corp.

Rémy Cointreau Group, 20 451–53; 80 308–12 (upd.)

Renaissance Learning, Inc., 39 341–43; 100 367–72 (upd.)

Renal Care Group, Inc., 72 297–99

Renault Argentina S.A., 67 325–27

Renault S.A., 26 401–04 (upd.); 74 264–68 (upd.)

Renfro Corporation, 99 362–365

Rengo Co., Ltd., IV 326

Renishaw plc, 46 358–60

RENK AG, 37 325–28

Renner Herrmann S.A., 79 353–56

Reno Air Inc., 23 409–11

Reno de Medici S.p.A., 41 325–27

Rent-A-Center, Inc., 45 365–67

Rent-Way, Inc., 33 366–68; 75 336–39 (upd.)

Rental Service Corporation, 28 386–88

Rentokil Initial Plc, 47 332–35

Rentrak Corporation, 35 371–74

Repco Corporation Ltd., 74 269–72

REpower Systems AG, 101 424–27

Repsol-YPF S.A., IV 527–29; 16 423–26 (upd.); 40 372–76 (upd.)

Republic Engineered Products Inc., 7 446–47; 26 405–08 (upd.); 106 408–14 (upd.)

Republic Industries, Inc., 26 409–11 *see also* AutoNation, Inc.

Republic New York Corporation, 11 415–19 *see also* HSBC Holdings plc.

The Republic of Tea, Inc., 105 365–68

Republic Services, Inc., 92 323–26

Res-Care, Inc., 29 399–402

Research in Motion Limited, 54 310–14; 106 415–22 (upd.)

Research Triangle Institute, 83 322–325

Réseau Ferré de France, 66 266–68

Reser's Fine Foods, Inc., 81 337–40

Resorts International, Inc., 12 418–20

Resource America, Inc., 42 311–14

Resources Connection, Inc., 81 341–44

Response Oncology, Inc., 27 385–87

Restaurant Associates Corporation, 66 269–72

Restaurants Unlimited, Inc., 13 435–37

Restoration Hardware, Inc., 30 376–78; 96 347–51 (upd.)

Retail Ventures, Inc., 82 299–03 (upd.)

Retractable Technologies, Inc., 99 366–369
Reuters Group PLC, IV 668–70; 22 450–53 (upd.); 63 323–27 (upd.)
Revco D.S., Inc., V 171–73 see also CVS Corp.
Revell-Monogram Inc., 16 427–29
Revere Electric Supply Company, 96 352–55
Revere Ware Corporation, 22 454–56
Revlon Inc., III 54–57; 17 400–04 (upd.); 64 330–35 (upd.)
Rewards Network Inc., 70 271–75 (upd.)
REWE-Zentral AG, 103 355–59
REX Stores Corp., 10 468–69
Rexam PLC, 32 380–85 (upd.); 85 353–61 (upd.)
Rexel, Inc., 15 384–87
Rexnord Corporation, 21 429–32; 76 315–19 (upd.)
The Reynolds and Reynolds Company, 50 376–79
Reynolds Metals Company, IV 186–88; 19 346–48 (upd.) see also Alcoa Inc.
RF Micro Devices, Inc., 43 311–13
RFC Franchising LLC, 68 317–19
RFF see Réseau Ferré de France.
RGI see Rockefeller Group International.
Rheinmetall AG, 9 443–46; 97 343–49 (upd.)
RHI AG, 53 283–86
Rhino Entertainment Company, 18 457–60; 70 276–80 (upd.)
RHM see Ranks Hovis McDougall.
Rhodes Inc., 23 412–14
Rhodia SA, 38 378–80
Rhône-Poulenc S.A., I 388–90; 10 470–72 (upd.)
Rhythm & Hues Studios, Inc., 103 360–63
Rica Foods, Inc., 41 328–30
Ricardo plc, 90 352–56
Rich Products Corporation, 7 448–49; 38 381–84 (upd.); 93 368–74 (upd.)
The Richards Group, Inc., 58 300–02
Richardson Electronics, Ltd., 17 405–07
Richardson Industries, Inc., 62 298–301
Richfood Holdings, Inc., 7 450–51, see also Supervalu Inc.
Richton International Corporation, 39 344–46
Richtree Inc., 63 328–30
Richwood Building Products, Inc. see Ply Gem Industries Inc.
Rickenbacker International Corp., 91 408–12
Ricoh Company, Ltd., III 159–61; 36 389–93 (upd.)
Ricola Ltd., 62 302–04
Riddell Sports Inc., 22 457–59; 23 449
Ride, Inc., 22 460–63
Ridley Corporation Ltd., 62 305–07
Riedel Tiroler Glashuette GmbH, 99 370–373
The Riese Organization, 38 385–88
Rieter Holding AG, 42 315–17
Riggs National Corporation, 13 438–40

Right Management Consultants, Inc., 42 318–21
Riklis Family Corp., 9 447–50
Rimage Corp., 89 369–72
Rinascente S.p.A., 71 308–10
Rinker Group Ltd., 65 298–301
Rio Tinto plc, 19 349–53 (upd.) 50 380–85 (upd.)
Ripley Corp S.A., 102 353–56
Ripley Entertainment, Inc., 74 273–76
Riser Foods, Inc., 9 451–54 see also Giant Eagle, Inc.
Ritchie Bros. Auctioneers Inc., 41 331–34
Rite Aid Corporation, V 174–76; 19 354–57 (upd.); 63 331–37 (upd.)
Ritter Sport see Alfred Ritter GmbH & Co. KG.
Ritter's Frozen Custard see RFC Franchising LLC.
Ritz Camera Centers, 34 375–77
The Ritz-Carlton Hotel Company, L.L.C., 9 455–57; 29 403–06 (upd.); 71 311–16 (upd.)
Ritz-Craft Corporation of Pennsylvania Inc., 94 365–68
Riunione Adriatica di Sicurtà SpA, III 345–48
Riva Fire see Gruppo Riva Fire SpA.
The Rival Company, 19 358–60
River Oaks Furniture, Inc., 43 314–16
River Ranch Fresh Foods LLC, 88 322–25
Riverbed Technology, Inc., 101 428–31
Riverwood International Corporation, 11 420–23; 48 340–44 (upd.) see also Graphic Packaging Holding Co.
Riviana Foods, 27 388–91
Riviera Holdings Corporation, 75 340–43
Riviera Tool Company, 89 373–76
RJR Nabisco Holdings Corp., V 408–10 see also R.J Reynolds Tobacco Holdings Inc., Nabisco Brands, Inc.; R.J. Reynolds Industries, Inc.
RM Auctions, Inc., 88 326–29
RMC Group p.l.c., III 737–40; 34 378–83 (upd.)
RMH Teleservices, Inc., 42 322–24
Roadhouse Grill, Inc., 22 464–66
Roadmaster Industries, Inc., 16 430–33
Roadway Express, Inc., V 502–03; 25 395–98 (upd.)
Roanoke Electric Steel Corporation, 45 368–70
Robbins & Myers Inc., 15 388–90
Roberds Inc., 19 361–63
Robert Bosch GmbH, I 392–93; 16 434–37 (upd.); 43 317–21 (upd.)
Robert Half International Inc., 18 461–63; 70 281–84 (upd.)
Robert Mondavi Corporation, 15 391–94; 50 386–90 (upd.)
Robert Talbott Inc., 88 330–33
Robert W. Baird & Co. Incorporated, 67 328–30
Robert Wood Johnson Foundation, 35 375–78

Robertet SA, 39 347–49
Roberts Dairy Company, 103 364–67
Roberts Pharmaceutical Corporation, 16 438–40
Robertson-Ceco Corporation, 19 364–66
Robins, Kaplan, Miller & Ciresi L.L.P., 89 377–81
Robinson Helicopter Company, 51 315–17
ROC see Royal Olympic Cruise Lines Inc.
Rocawear Apparel LLC, 77 355–58
Roche Biomedical Laboratories, Inc., 11 424–26 see also Laboratory Corporation of America Holdings.
Roche Bioscience, 14 403–06 (upd.)
Rochester Gas And Electric Corporation, 6 571–73
Rochester Telephone Corporation, 6 332–34
Röchling Gruppe, 94 369–74
Rock Bottom Restaurants, Inc., 25 399–401; 68 320–23 (upd.)
Rock-It Cargo USA, Inc., 86 339–42
Rock of Ages Corporation, 37 329–32
Rock-Tenn Company, 13 441–43; 59 347–51 (upd.)
The Rockefeller Foundation, 34 384–87
Rockefeller Group International Inc., 58 303–06
Rockford Corporation, 43 322–25
Rockford Products Corporation, 55 323–25
RockShox, Inc., 26 412–14
Rockwell Automation, Inc., 43 326–31 (upd.); 103 368–76 (upd.)
Rockwell Collins, 106 423–27
Rockwell International Corporation, I 78–80; 11 427–30 (upd.)
Rockwell Medical Technologies, Inc., 88 334–37
Rocky Brands, Inc., 26 415–18; 102 357–62 (upd.)
Rocky Mountain Chocolate Factory, Inc., 73 280–82
Rodale, Inc., 23 415–17; 47 336–39 (upd.)
Rodamco N.V., 26 419–21
Rodda Paint Company, 98 329–32
Rodriguez Group S.A., 90 357–60
ROFIN-SINAR Technologies Inc, 81 345–48
Rogers Communications Inc., 30 388–92 (upd.) see also Maclean Hunter Publishing Ltd.
Rogers Corporation, 61 310–13; 80 313–17 (upd.)
Rohde & Schwarz GmbH & Co. KG, 39 350–53
Röhm and Haas Company, I 391–93; 26 422–26 (upd.); 77 359–66 (upd.)
ROHN Industries, Inc., 22 467–69
Rohr Incorporated, 9 458–60 see also Goodrich Corp.
Roland Berger & Partner GmbH, 37 333–36
Roland Corporation, 38 389–91
Roland Murten A.G., 7 452–53

Rolex *see* Montres Rolex S.A.
Roll International Corporation, 37 337–39
Rollerblade, Inc., 15 395–98; **34** 388–92 (upd.)
Rollins, Inc., 11 431–34; **104** 397–403 (upd.)
Rolls-Royce Allison, 29 407–09 (upd.)
Rolls-Royce Group PLC, 67 331–36 (upd.)
Rolls-Royce Motors Ltd., I 194–96
Rolls-Royce plc, I 81–83; **7** 454–57 (upd.); **21** 433–37 (upd.)
Rolta India Ltd., 90 361–64
Roly Poly Franchise Systems LLC, 83 326–328
Romacorp, Inc., 58 307–11
Roman Meal Company, 84 331–334
Ron Tonkin Chevrolet Company, 55 326–28
RONA, Inc., 73 283–86
Ronco Corporation, 15 399–401; **80** 318–23 (upd.)
Ronson PLC, 49 337–39
Rooms To Go Inc., 28 389–92
Rooney Brothers Co., 25 402–04
Roosevelt Hospital *see* Continuum Health Partners, Inc.
Roots Canada Ltd., 42 325–27
Roper Industries, Inc., 15 402–04; **50** 391–95 (upd.)
Ropes & Gray, 40 377–80
Rorer Group, I 666–68
Rosauers Supermarkets, Inc., 90 365–68
Rose Acre Farms, Inc., 60 255–57
Rose Art Industries, 58 312–14
Roseburg Forest Products Company, 58 315–17
Rosemount Inc., 15 405–08 *see also* Emerson.
Rosenbluth International Inc., 14 407–09 *see also* American Express Co.
Rose's Stores, Inc., 13 444–46
Rosetta Stone Inc., 93 375–79
Rosneft, 106 428–31
Ross Stores, Inc., 17 408–10; **43** 332–35 (upd.); **101** 432–37 (upd.)
Rossignol Ski Company, Inc. *see* Skis Rossignol S.A.
Rossmann *see* Dirk Rossmann GmbH.
Rostelecom Joint Stock Co., 99 374–377
Rostvertol plc, 62 308–10
Rosy Blue N.V., 84 335–338
Rotary International, 31 395–97
Rothmans UK Holdings Limited, V 411–13; **19** 367–70 (upd.)
Roto-Rooter, Inc., 15 409–11; **61** 314–19 (upd.)
Rotork plc, 46 361–64
The Rottlund Company, Inc., 28 393–95
Rouge Steel Company, 8 448–50
Rougier *see* Groupe Rougier, SA.
Roularta Media Group NV, 48 345–47
Rounder Records Corporation, 79 357–61

Roundy's Inc., 14 410–12; **58** 318–21 (upd.)
The Rouse Company, 15 412–15; **63** 338–41 (upd.)
Roussel Uclaf, I 669–70; **8** 451–53 (upd.)
Rover Group Ltd., 7 458–60; **21** 441–44 (upd.)
Rowan Companies, Inc., 43 336–39
Rowntree Mackintosh PLC, II 568–70 *see also* Nestlé S.A.
The Rowohlt Verlag GmbH, 96 356–61
Roy Anderson Corporation, 75 344–46
Roy F. Weston, Inc., 33 369–72
Royal & Sun Alliance Insurance Group plc, 55 329–39 (upd.)
Royal Ahold N.V. *see* Koninklijke Ahold N.V.
Royal Appliance Manufacturing Company, 15 416–18
The Royal Bank of Canada, II 344–46; **21** 445–48 (upd.); **81** 349–55 (upd.)
The Royal Bank of Scotland Group plc, 12 421–23; **38** 392–99 (upd.)
Royal Brunei Airlines Sdn Bhd, 99 378–381
Royal Canin S.A., 39 354–57
Royal Caribbean Cruises Ltd., 22 470–73; **74** 277–81 (upd.)
Royal Crown Company, Inc., 23 418–20 *see also* Cott Corp.
Royal Doulton plc, 14 413–15; **38** 400–04 (upd.) *see also* WWRD Holdings Ltd.
Royal Dutch Petroleum Company, IV 530–32 *see also* Shell Transport and Trading Company p.l.c.
Royal Dutch/Shell Group, 49 340–44 (upd.)
Royal Grolsch NV, 54 315–18
Royal Group Technologies Limited, 73 287–89
Royal Insurance Holdings plc, III 349–51 *see also* Royal & Sun Alliance Insurance Group plc .
Royal KPN N.V., 30 393–95
Royal Nepal Airline Corporation, 41 335–38
Royal Numico N.V., 37 340–42
Royal Olympic Cruise Lines Inc., 52 297–99
Royal Packaging Industries Van Leer N.V., 30 396–98
Royal Ten Cate N.V., 68 324–26
Royal Vendex KBB N.V. *see* Koninklijke Vendex KBB N.V. (Royal Vendex KBB N.V.).
Royal Vopak NV, 41 339–41
RPC Group PLC, 81 356–59
RPC, Inc., 91 413–16
RPM International Inc., 8 454–57; **36** 394–98 (upd.); **91** 417–25 (upd.)
RSA Security Inc., 46 365–68
RSC *see* Rental Service Corp.
RSM McGladrey Business Services Inc., 98 333–36
RTI Biologics, Inc., 96 362–65
RTL Group SA, 44 374–78

RTM Restaurant Group, 58 322–24
RTZ Corporation PLC, IV 189–92 *see also* Rio Tinto plc.
Rubbermaid Incorporated, III 613–15; **20** 454–57 (upd.) *see also* Newell Rubbermaid Inc.
Rubio's Restaurants, Inc., 35 379–81
Ruby Tuesday, Inc., 18 464–66; **71** 317–20 (upd.)
Rudolph Technologies Inc., 94 375–78
The Rugby Group plc, 31 398–400
Ruger Corporation *see* Sturm, Ruger & Co., Inc.
Ruhrgas AG, V 704–06; **38** 405–09 (upd.)
Ruhrkohle AG, IV 193–95 *see also* RAG AG.
Ruiz Food Products, Inc., 53 287–89
Rural Cellular Corporation, 43 340–42
Rural Press Ltd., 74 282–85
Rural/Metro Corporation, 28 396–98
Rush Communications, 33 373–75 *see also* Phat Fashions LLC.
Rush Enterprises, Inc., 64 336–38
Russ Berrie and Company, Inc., 12 424–26; **82** 304–08 (upd.)
Russell Corporation, 8 458–59; **30** 399–401 (upd.); **82** 309–13 (upd.)
Russell Reynolds Associates Inc., 38 410–12
Russell Stover Candies Inc., 12 427–29; **91** 426–32 (upd.)
Russian Aircraft Corporation (MiG), 86 343–46
Russian Railways Joint Stock Co., 93 380–83
Rust International Inc., 11 435–36
Rusty, Inc., 95 358–61
Ruth's Chris Steak House, 28 399–401; **88** 338–42 (upd.)
RWD Technologies, Inc., 76 320–22
RWE Group, V 707–10; **50** 396–400 (upd.)
Ryan Beck & Co., Inc., 66 273–75
Ryan Companies US, Inc., 99 382–385
Ryanair Holdings plc, 35 382–85
Ryan's Restaurant Group, Inc., 15 419–21; **68** 327–30 (upd.)
Ryder System, Inc., V 504–06; **24** 408–11 (upd.)
Ryerson Tull, Inc., 40 381–84 (upd.)
Ryko Corporation, 83 329–333
The Ryland Group, Inc., 8 460–61; **37** 343–45 (upd.)
Ryoshoku Ltd., 72 300–02
RZB *see* Raiffeisen Zentralbank Österreich AG.
RZD *see* Russian Railways Joint Stock Co.

S

S&C Electric Company, 15 422–24
S&D Coffee, Inc., 84 339–341
S&K Famous Brands, Inc., 23 421–23
S&P *see* Standard & Poor's Corp.
S-K-I Limited, 15 457–59
S.A.C.I. Falabella, 69 311–13
S.A. Cockerill Sambre *see* Cockerill Sambre Group.

s.a. GB-Inno-BM *see* GIB Group.
S.C. Johnson & Son, Inc., III 58–59; 28 409–12 (upd.); 89 382–89 (upd.)
SAA (Pty) Ltd., 28 402–04
Saab Automobile AB, 32 386–89 (upd.); 83 334–339 (upd.)
Saab-Scania A.B., I 197–98; 11 437–39 (upd.)
Saarberg-Konzern, IV 196–99 *see also* RAG AG.
Saatchi & Saatchi plc, I 33–35; 33 328–31 (upd.)
SAB *see* South African Breweries Ltd.
Sabanci Holdings *see* Haci Omer Sabanci Holdings A.S.
Sabaté Diosos SA, 48 348–50 *see also* OENEO S.A.
Sabena S.A./N.V., 33 376–79
SABIC *see* Saudi Basic Industries Corp.
SABMiller plc, 59 352–58 (upd.)
Sabratek Corporation, 29 410–12
Sabre Holdings Corporation, 26 427–30; 74 286–90 (upd.)
Sadia S.A., 59 359–62
Safe Flight Instrument Corporation, 71 321–23
SAFECO Corporation, III 352–54
Safeguard Scientifics, Inc., 10 473–75
Safelite Glass Corp., 19 371–73
SafeNet Inc., 101 438–42
Safeskin Corporation, 18 467–70 *see also* Kimberly-Clark Corp.
Safety 1st, Inc., 24 412–15
Safety Components International, Inc., 63 342–44
Safety-Kleen Systems Inc., 8 462–65; 82 314–20 (upd.)
Safeway Inc., II 654–56; 24 416–19 (upd.); 85 362–69 (upd.)
Safeway PLC, 50 401–06 (upd.)
Saffery Champness, 80 324–27
Safilo SpA, 40 155–56; 54 319–21
SAFRAN, 102 363–71 (upd.)
Saga Communications, Inc., 27 392–94
The Sage Group, 43 343–46
Sage Products Inc., 105 369–72
SAGEM S.A., 37 346–48 *see also* SAFRAN.
Sagicor Life Inc., 98 337–40
Saia, Inc., 98 341–44
SAIC *see* Science Applications International Corp.
Sainsbury's *see* J Sainsbury PLC.
Saint-Gobain *see* Compagnie de Saint Gobain S.A.
Saks Inc., 24 420–23; 41 342–45 (upd.)
Salant Corporation, 12 430–32; 51 318–21 (upd.)
Salem Communications Corporation, 97 359–63
salesforce.com, Inc., 79 370–73
Salick Health Care, Inc., 53 290–92
Salix Pharmaceuticals, Ltd., 93 384–87
Sallie Mae *see* SLM Holding Corp.
Sally Beauty Company, Inc., 60 258–60
Sally Industries, Inc., 103 377–81
Salomon Inc., II 447–49; 13 447–50 (upd.) *see also* Citigroup Inc.

Salomon Worldwide, 20 458–60 *see also* adidas-Salomon AG.
Salt River Project, 19 374–76
Salton, Inc., 30 402–04; 88 343–48 (upd.)
The Salvation Army USA, 32 390–93
Salvatore Ferragamo Italia S.p.A., 62 311–13
Salzgitter AG, IV 200–01; 101 443–49 (upd.)
Sam Ash Music Corporation, 30 405–07
Sam Levin Inc., 80 328–31
Samick Musical Instruments Co., Ltd., 56 297–300
Sam's Club, 40 385–87
Sam's Wine & Spirits, 96 366–69
Samsonite Corporation, 13 451–53; 43 353–57 (upd.)
Samsung Electronics Co., Ltd., 14 416–18; 41 346–49 (upd.)
Samsung Group, I 515–17
Samuel Cabot Inc., 53 293–95
Samuels Jewelers Incorporated, 30 408–10
San Diego Gas & Electric Company, V 711–14 *see also* Sempra Energy.
San Diego Padres Baseball Club L.P., 78 324–27
San Francisco Baseball Associates, L.P., 55 340–43
San Miguel Corporation, 15 428–30; 57 303–08 (upd.)
Sanborn Hermanos, S.A., 20 461–63
Sanborn Map Company Inc., 82 321–24
SanCor Cooperativas Unidas Ltda., 101 450–53
The Sanctuary Group PLC, 69 314–17
Sandals Resorts International, 65 302–05
Sanders Morris Harris Group Inc., 70 285–87
Sanders\Wingo, 99 386–389
Sanderson Farms, Inc., 15 425–27
Sandia National Laboratories, 49 345–48
Sandoz Ltd., I 671–73 *see also* Novartis AG.
Sandvik AB, IV 202–04; 32 394–98 (upd.); 77 367–73 (upd.)
Sanford L.P., 82 325–29
Sanitec Corporation, 51 322–24
Sankyo Company, Ltd., I 674–75; 56 301–04 (upd.)
Sanlam Ltd., 68 331–34
SANLUIS Corporación, S.A.B. de C.V., 95 362–65
The Sanofi-Synthélabo Group, I 676–77; 49 349–51 (upd.)
SanomaWSOY Corporation, 51 325–28
Sanpaolo IMI S.p.A., 50 407–11
Sanrio Company, Ltd., 38 413–15; 104 404–07 (upd.)
Santa Barbara Restaurant Group, Inc., 37 349–52
The Santa Cruz Operation, Inc., 38 416–21

Santa Fe Gaming Corporation, 19 377–79 *see also* Archon Corp.
Santa Fe International Corporation, 38 422–24
Santa Fe Pacific Corporation, V 507–09 *see also* Burlington Northern Santa Fe Corp.
Santa Margherita S.p.A. *see* Industrie Zignago Santa Margherita S.p.A.
Santarus, Inc., 105 373–77
Santos Ltd., 81 360–63
Sanwa Bank, Ltd., II 347–48; 15 431–33 (upd.)
SANYO Electric Co., Ltd., II 91–92; 36 399–403 (upd.); 95 366–73 (upd.)
Sanyo-Kokusaku Pulp Co., Ltd., IV 327–28
Sao Paulo Alpargatas S.A., 75 347–49
SAP AG, 16 441–44; 43 358–63 (upd.)
Sapa AB, 84 342–345
Sapp Bros Travel Centers, Inc., 105 378–81
Sappi Limited, 49 352–55
Sapporo Holdings Limited, I 282–83; 13 454–56 (upd.); 36 404–07 (upd.); 97 364–69 (upd.)
Saputo Inc., 59 363–65
Sara Lee Corporation, II 571–73; 15 434–37 (upd.); 54 322–27 (upd.); 99 390–398 (upd.)
Sarnoff Corporation, 57 309–12
Sarris Candies Inc., 86 347–50
The SAS Group, 34 396–99 (upd.)
SAS Institute Inc., 10 476–78; 78 328–32 (upd.)
Sasol Limited, IV 533–35; 47 340–44 (upd.)
Saturn Corporation, 7 461–64; 21 449–53 (upd.); 80 332–38 (upd.)
Satyam Computer Services Ltd., 85 370–73
Saucony Inc., 35 386–89; 86 351–56 (upd.)
Sauder Woodworking Co., 12 433–34; 35 390–93 (upd.)
Saudi Arabian Airlines, 6 114–16; 27 395–98 (upd.)
Saudi Arabian Oil Company, IV 536–39; 17 411–15 (upd.); 50 412–17 (upd.)
Saudi Basic Industries Corporation (SABIC), 58 325–28
Sauer-Danfoss Inc., 61 320–22
Saul Ewing LLP, 74 291–94
Saur S.A.S., 92 327–30
Savannah Foods & Industries, Inc., 7 465–67 *see also* Imperial Sugar Co.
Savers, Inc., 99 399–403 (upd.)
Sawtek Inc., 43 364–66 (upd.)
Saxton Pierce Restaurant Corporation, 100 373–76
Sbarro, Inc., 16 445–47; 64 339–42 (upd.)
SBC Communications Inc., 32 399–403 (upd.)
SBC Warburg, 14 419–21 *see also* UBS AG.
Sberbank, 62 314–17

SBI *see* State Bank of India.
SBS Technologies, Inc., 25 405–07
SCA *see* Svenska Cellulosa AB.
SCANA Corporation, 6 574–76; **56** 305–08 (upd.)
Scandinavian Airlines System, I 119–20 *see also* The SAS Group.
ScanSource, Inc., 29 413–15; **74** 295–98 (upd.)
Scarborough Public Utilities Commission, 9 461–62
SCB Computer Technology, Inc., 29 416–18
SCEcorp, V 715–17 *see also* Edison International.
Schawk, Inc., 24 424–26
Scheels All Sports Inc., 63 348–50
Scheid Vineyards Inc., 66 276–78
Schell Brewing *see* August Schell Brewing Company Inc.
Schenck Business Solutions, 88 349–53
Schenker-Rhenus Ag, 6 424–26
Scherer *see* R.P. Scherer.
Scherer Brothers Lumber Company, 94 379–83
Schering A.G., I 681–82; **50** 418–22 (upd.)
Schering-Plough Corporation, I 683–85; **14** 422–25 (upd.); **49** 356–62 (upd.); **99** 404–414 (upd.)
Schibsted ASA, 31 401–05
Schieffelin & Somerset Co., 61 323–25
Schincariol Participaçöces e Representações S.A., 102 372–75
Schindler Holding AG, 29 419–22
Schlage Lock Company, 82 330–34
Schlecker *see* Anton Schlecker.
Schlotzsky's, Inc., 36 408–10
Schlumberger Limited, III 616–18; **17** 416–19 (upd.); **59** 366–71 (upd.)
Schmitt Music Company, 40 388–90
Schmolz + Bickenbach AG, 104 408–13
Schneider National, Inc., 36 411–13; **77** 374–78 (upd.)
Schneider S.A., II 93–94; **18** 471–74 (upd.)
Schneiderman's Furniture Inc., 28 405–08
Schneidersöhne Deutschland GmbH & Co. KG, 100 377–81
Schnitzer Steel Industries, Inc., 19 380–82
Scholastic Corporation, 10 479–81; **29** 423–27 (upd.)
Scholle Corporation, 96 370–73
School Specialty, Inc., 68 335–37
School-Tech, Inc., 62 318–20
Schott Brothers, Inc., 67 337–39
Schott Corporation, 53 296–98
Schottenstein Stores Corp., 14 426–28 *see also* Retail Ventures, Inc.
Schouw & Company A/S, 94 384–87
Schreiber Foods, Inc., 72 303–06
Schroders plc, 42 332–35
Schuff Steel Company, 26 431–34
Schultz Sav-O Stores, Inc., 21 454–56; **31** 406–08 (upd.)

Schurz Communications, Inc., 98 345–49
The Schwan Food Company, 7 468–70; **26** 435–38 (upd.); **83** 340–346 (upd.)
The Schwarz Group, 100 382–87
Schwebel Baking Company, 72 307–09
Schweitzer-Mauduit International, Inc., 52 300–02
Schweizerische Post-, Telefon- und Telegrafen-Betriebe, V 321–24
Schweppes Ltd. *see* Cadbury Schweppes PLC.
Schwinn Cycle and Fitness L.P., 19 383–85 *see also* Huffy Corp.
SCI *see* Service Corporation International.
SCI Systems, Inc., 9 463–64
Science Applications International Corporation, 15 438–40
Scientific-Atlanta, Inc., 6 335–37; **45** 371–75 (upd.)
Scientific Games Corporation, 64 343–46 (upd.)
Scientific Learning Corporation, 95 374–77
Scitex Corporation Ltd., 24 427–32
SCO *see* Santa Cruz Operation, Inc.
The SCO Group Inc., 78 333–37
Scolari's Food and Drug Company, 102 376–79
Scope Products, Inc., 94 388–91
SCOR S.A., 20 464–66
The Score Board, Inc., 19 386–88
Scotiabank *see* The Bank of Nova Scotia.
Scotsman Industries, Inc., 20 467–69
Scott Fetzer Company, 12 435–37; **80** 339–43 (upd.)
Scott Paper Company, IV 329–31; **31** 409–12 (upd.)
Scottish & Newcastle plc, 15 441–44; **35** 394–97 (upd.)
Scottish and Southern Energy plc, 13 457–59; **66** 279–84 (upd.)
Scottish Media Group plc, 32 404–06; **41** 350–52
Scottish Power plc, 49 363–66 (upd.)
Scottish Radio Holding plc, 41 350–52
ScottishPower plc, 19 389–91
Scottrade, Inc., 85 374–77
The Scotts Company, 22 474–76
Scotty's, Inc., 22 477–80
The Scoular Company, 77 379–82
Scovill Fasteners Inc., 24 433–36
SCP Pool Corporation, 39 358–60
Screen Actors Guild, 72 310–13
The Scripps Research Institute, 76 323–25
SDGE *see* San Diego Gas & Electric Co.
SDL PLC, 67 340–42
Sea Containers Ltd., 29 428–31
Seaboard Corporation, 36 414–16; **85** 378–82 (upd.)
SeaChange International, Inc., 79 374–78
SEACOR Holdings Inc., 83 347–350
Seagate Technology, 8 466–68; **34** 400–04 (upd.); **105** 382–90 (upd.)
The Seagram Company Ltd., I 284–86; **25** 408–12 (upd.)

Seagull Energy Corporation, 11 440–42
Sealaska Corporation, 60 261–64
Sealed Air Corporation, 14 429–31; **57** 313–17 (upd.)
Sealed Power Corporation, I 199–200 *see also* SPX Corp.
Sealright Co., Inc., 17 420–23
Sealy Inc., 12 438–40
Seaman Furniture Company, Inc., 32 407–09
Sean John Clothing, Inc., 70 288–90
SeaRay Boats Inc., 96 374–77
Sears plc, V 177–79
Sears Roebuck de México, S.A. de C.V., 20 470–72
Sears, Roebuck and Co., V 180–83; **18** 475–79 (upd.); **56** 309–14 (upd.)
Seat Pagine Gialle S.p.A., 47 345–47
Seattle City Light, 50 423–26
Seattle FilmWorks, Inc., 20 473–75
Seattle First National Bank Inc., 8 469–71 *see also* Bank of America Corp.
Seattle Lighting Fixture Company, 92 331–34
Seattle Pacific Industries, Inc., 92 335–38
Seattle Seahawks, Inc., 92 339–43
Seattle Times Company, 15 445–47
Seaway Food Town, Inc., 15 448–50 *see also* Spartan Stores Inc.
SEB Group *see* Skandinaviska Enskilda Banken AB.
SEB S.A. *see* Groupe SEB.
Sebastiani Vineyards, Inc., 28 413–15
The Second City, Inc., 88 354–58
Second Harvest, 29 432–34
Securicor Plc, 45 376–79
Securitas AB, 42 336–39
Security Capital Corporation, 17 424–27
Security Pacific Corporation, II 349–50
SED International Holdings, Inc., 43 367–69
La Seda de Barcelona S.A., 100 260–63
Seddon Group Ltd., 67 343–45
SEGA Corporation, 73 290–93
Sega of America, Inc., 10 482–85
Segway LLC, 48 355–57
SEI Investments Company, 96 378–82
Seibu Department Stores, Ltd., V 184–86; **42** 340–43 (upd.)
Seibu Railway Company Ltd., V 510–11; **74** 299–301 (upd.)
Seigle's Home and Building Centers, Inc., 41 353–55
Seiko Corporation, III 619–21; **17** 428–31 (upd.); **72** 314–18 (upd.)
Seino Transportation Company, Ltd., 6 427–29
Seita, 23 424–27 *see also* Altadis S.A.
Seitel, Inc., 47 348–50
The Seiyu, Ltd., V 187–89; **36** 417–21 (upd.)
Sekisui Chemical Co., Ltd., III 741–43; **72** 319–22 (upd.)
Select Comfort Corporation, 34 405–08
Select Medical Corporation, 65 306–08
Selecta AG, 97 370–73

Selectour SA, 53 299–301
Selee Corporation, 88 359–62
Selfridges Plc, 34 409–11
The Selmer Company, Inc., 19 392–94
SEMCO Energy, Inc., 44 379–82
Semen Gresik *see* PT Semen Gresik Tbk
Seminis, Inc., 29 435–37
Semitool, Inc., 18 480–82; 79 379–82 (upd.)
Sempra Energy, 25 413–16 (upd.)
Semtech Corporation, 32 410–13
Seneca Foods Corporation, 17 432–34; 60 265–68 (upd.)
Sennheiser Electronic GmbH & Co. KG, 66 285–89
Senomyx, Inc., 83 351–354
Sensient Technologies Corporation, 52 303–08 (upd.)
Sensormatic Electronics Corp., 11 443–45
Sensory Science Corporation, 37 353–56
SENTEL Corporation, 106 432–34
La Senza Corporation, 66 205–07
Sephora Holdings S.A., 82 335–39
Sepracor Inc., 45 380–83
Sequa Corporation, 13 460–63; 54 328–32 (upd.)
Sequana Capital, 78 338–42 (upd.)
Serco Group plc, 47 351–53
Serologicals Corporation, 63 351–53
Serono S.A., 47 354–57
Serta, Inc., 28 416–18
Servco Pacific Inc., 96 383–86
Service America Corp., 7 471–73
Service Corporation International, 6 293–95; 51 329–33 (upd.)
Service Merchandise Company, Inc., V 190–92; 19 395–99 (upd.)
The ServiceMaster Company, 6 44–46; 23 428–31 (upd.); 68 338–42 (upd.)
Servidyne Inc., 100 388–92 (upd.)
Servpro Industries, Inc., 85 383–86
7-Eleven, Inc., 32 414–18 (upd.)
Sevenson Environmental Services, Inc., 42 344–46
Seventh Generation, Inc., 73 294–96
Severn Trent PLC, 12 441–43; 38 425–29 (upd.)
Severstal Joint Stock Company, 65 309–12
Seyfarth Shaw LLP, 93 388–91
SFI Group plc, 51 334–36
SFX Entertainment, Inc., 36 422–25
SGI, 29 438–41 (upd.)
Shakespeare Company, 22 481–84
Shaklee Corporation, 12 444–46; 39 361–64 (upd.)
Shamrock Foods Company, 105 391–96
Shanghai Baosteel Group Corporation, 71 327–30
Shanghai Petrochemical Co., Ltd., 18 483–85
Shangri-La Asia Ltd., 71 331–33
Shanks Group plc, 45 384–87
Shannon Aerospace Ltd., 36 426–28
Shared Medical Systems Corporation, 14 432–34 *see also* Siemens AG.

Sharp Corporation, II 95–96; 12 447–49 (upd.); 40 391–95 (upd.)
The Sharper Image Corporation, 10 486–88; 62 321–24 (upd.)
The Shaw Group, Inc., 50 427–30
Shaw Industries, Inc., 9 465–67; 40 396–99 (upd.)
Shaw's Supermarkets, Inc., 56 315–18
Shea Homes *see* J.F. Shea Co., Inc.
Sheaffer Pen Corporation, 82 340–43
Shearer's Foods, Inc., 72 323–25
Shearman & Sterling, 32 419–22
Shearson Lehman Brothers Holdings Inc., II 450–52; 9 468–70 (upd.) *see also* Lehman Brothers Holdings Inc.
Shed Media plc, 104 414–17
Shedd Aquarium Society, 73 297–99
Sheetz, Inc., 85 387–90
Shelby Williams Industries, Inc., 14 435–37
Sheldahl Inc., 23 432–35
Shell Oil Company, IV 540–41; 14 438–40 (upd.); 41 356–60 (upd.) *see also* Royal Dutch/Shell Group.
Shell Transport and Trading Company p.l.c., IV 530–32 *see also* Royal Dutch Petroleum Company; Royal Dutch/Shell.
Shell Vacations LLC, 102 380–83
Sheller-Globe Corporation, I 201–02 *see also* Lear Corp.
Shells Seafood Restaurants, Inc., 43 370–72
Shenandoah Telecommunications Company, 89 390–93
Shenhua Group *see* China Shenhua Energy Company Limited
Shepherd Neame Limited, 30 414–16
Sheplers, Inc., 96 387–90
The Sheridan Group, Inc., 86 357–60
Shermag, Inc., 93 392–97
The Sherwin-Williams Company, III 744–46; 13 469–71 (upd.); 89 394–400 (upd.)
Sherwood Brands, Inc., 53 302–04
Shikoku Electric Power Company, Inc., V 718–20; 60 269–72 (upd.)
Shimano Inc., 64 347–49
Shionogi & Co., Ltd., III 60–61; 17 435–37 (upd.); 98 350–54 (upd.)
Shiseido Company, Limited, III 62–64; 22 485–88 (upd.); 81 364–70 (upd.)
Shochiku Company Ltd., 74 302–04
Shoe Carnival Inc., 14 441–43; 72 326–29 (upd.)
Shoe Pavilion, Inc., 84 346–349
Shoney's North America Corp., 7 474–76; 23 436–39 (upd.); 105 397–403 (upd.)
ShopKo Stores Inc., 21 457–59; 58 329–32 (upd.)
Shoppers Drug Mart Corporation, 49 367–70
Shoppers Food Warehouse Corporation, 66 290–92
Shorewood Packaging Corporation, 28 419–21

Showa Shell Sekiyu K.K., IV 542–43; 59 372–75 (upd.)
ShowBiz Pizza Time, Inc., 13 472–74 *see also* CEC Entertainment, Inc.
Showboat, Inc., 19 400–02 *see also* Harrah's Entertainment, Inc.
Showtime Networks, Inc., 78 343–47
Shred-It Canada Corporation, 56 319–21
Shriners Hospitals for Children, 69 318–20
Shubert Organization Inc., 24 437–39
Shuffle Master Inc., 51 337–40
Shure Inc., 60 273–76
Shurgard Storage Centers, Inc., 52 309–11
Shutterfly, Inc., 98 355–58
SHV Holdings N.V., 55 344–47
The Siam Cement Public Company Limited, 56 322–25
Sideco Americana S.A., 67 346–48
Sidel *see* Groupe Sidel S.A.
Siderar S.A.I.C., 66 293–95
Sidley Austin Brown & Wood, 40 400–03
Sidney Frank Importing Co., Inc., 69 321–23
Siebe plc *see* BTR Siebe plc.
Siebel Systems, Inc., 38 430–34
Siebert Financial Corp., 32 423–25
Siegel & Gale, 64 350–52
Siemens AG, II 97–100; 14 444–47 (upd.); 57 318–23 (upd.)
The Sierra Club, 28 422–24
Sierra Health Services, Inc., 15 451–53
Sierra Nevada Brewing Company, 70 291–93
Sierra On-Line, Inc., 15 454–56; 41 361–64 (upd.)
Sierra Pacific Industries, 22 489–91; 90 369–73 (upd.)
SIFCO Industries, Inc., 41
SIG plc, 71 334–36
Sigma-Aldrich Corporation, I 690–91; 36 429–32 (upd.); 93 398–404 (upd.)
Signet Banking Corporation, 11 446–48 *see also* Wachovia Corp.
Signet Group PLC, 61 326–28
Sikorsky Aircraft Corporation, 24 440–43; 104 418–23 (upd.)
Silhouette Brands, Inc., 55 348–50
Silicon Graphics Inc., 9 471–73 *see also* SGI.
Siliconware Precision Industries Ltd., 73 300–02
Siltronic AG, 90 374–77
Silver Lake Cookie Company Inc., 95 378–81
Silver Wheaton Corp., 95 382–85
SilverPlatter Information Inc., 23 440–43
Silverstar Holdings, Ltd., 99 415–418
Silverstein Properties, Inc., 47 358–60
Simba Dickie Group KG, 105 404–07
Simco S.A., 37 357–59
Sime Darby Berhad, 14 448–50; 36 433–36 (upd.)
Simmons Company, 47 361–64

Simon & Schuster Inc., IV 671–72; 19 403–05 (upd.); 100 393–97 (upd.)

Simon Property Group Inc., 27 399–402; 84 350–355 (upd.)

Simon Transportation Services Inc., 27 403–06

Simplex Technologies Inc., 21 460–63

Simplicity Manufacturing, Inc., 64 353–56

Simpson Investment Company, 17 438–41

Simpson Thacher & Bartlett, 39 365–68

Simula, Inc., 41 368–70

SINA Corporation, 69 324–27

Sinclair Broadcast Group, Inc., 25 417–19

Sine Qua Non, 99 419–422

Singapore Airlines Limited, 6 117–18; 27 407–09 (upd.); 83 355–359 (upd.)

Singapore Press Holdings Limited, 85 391–95

Singer & Friedlander Group plc, 41 371–73

The Singer Company N.V., 30 417–20 (upd.)

The Singing Machine Company, Inc., 60 277–80

Sir Speedy, Inc., 16 448–50

Sirius Satellite Radio, Inc., 69 328–31

Sirti S.p.A., 76 326–28

Siskin Steel & Supply Company, 70 294–96

Sistema JSFC, 73 303–05

Sisters of Charity of Leavenworth Health System, 105 408–12

Six Flags, Inc., 17 442–44; 54 333–40 (upd.)

Sixt AG, 39 369–72

SJM Holdings Ltd., 105 413–17

SJW Corporation, 70 297–99

SK Group, 88 363–67

Skadden, Arps, Slate, Meagher & Flom, 18 486–88

Skalli Group, 67 349–51

Skandia Insurance Company, Ltd., 50 431–34

Skandinaviska Enskilda Banken AB, II 351–53; 56 326–29 (upd.)

Skanska AB, 38 435–38

Skechers U.S.A. Inc., 31 413–15; 88 368–72 (upd.)

Skeeter Products Inc., 96 391–94

SKF see Aktiebolaget SKF.

Skidmore, Owings & Merrill LLP, 13 475–76; 69 332–35 (upd.)

SkillSoft Public Limited Company, 81 371–74

skinnyCorp, LLC, 97 374–77

Skipton Building Society, 80 344–47

Skis Rossignol S.A., 15 460–62; 43 373–76 (upd.)

Skoda Auto a.s., 39 373–75

Skyline Chili, Inc., 62 325–28

Skyline Corporation, 30 421–23

SkyMall, Inc., 26 439–41

SkyWest, Inc., 25 420–24

Skyy Spirits LLC, 78 348–51

SL Green Realty Corporation, 44 383–85

SL Industries, Inc., 77 383–86

Sleeman Breweries Ltd., 74 305–08

Sleepy's Inc., 32 426–28

SLI, Inc., 48 358–61

Slim-Fast Foods Company, 18 489–91; 66 296–98 (upd.)

Slinky, Inc. see Poof-Slinky, Inc.

SLM Holding Corp., 25 425–28 (upd.)

Slough Estates PLC, IV 722–25; 50 435–40 (upd.)

Small Planet Foods, Inc., 89 410–14

Smart & Final LLC, 16 451–53; 94 392–96 (upd.)

Smart Balance, Inc., 100 398–401

SMART Modular Technologies, Inc., 86 361–64

SmartForce PLC, 43 377–80

Smarties see Ce De Candy Inc.

SMBC see Sumitomo Mitsui Banking Corp.

Smead Manufacturing Co., 17 445–48

SMG see Scottish Media Group.

SMH see Sanders Morris Harris Group Inc.; The Swatch Group SA.

Smith & Hawken, Ltd., 68 343–45

Smith & Nephew plc, 17 449–52; 41 374–78 (upd.)

Smith & Wesson Corp., 30 424–27; 73 306–11 (upd.)

The Smith & Wollensky Restaurant Group, Inc., 105 418–22

Smith Barney Inc., 15 463–65 see also Citigroup Inc.

Smith Corona Corp., 13 477–80

Smith International, Inc., 15 466–68; 59 376–80 (upd.)

Smith-Midland Corporation, 56 330–32

Smithfield Foods, Inc., 7 477–78; 43 381–84 (upd.)

SmithKline Beckman Corporation, I 692–94 see also GlaxoSmithKline plc.

SmithKline Beecham plc, III 65–67; 32 429–34 (upd.) see also GlaxoSmithKline plc.

Smith's Food & Drug Centers, Inc., 8 472–74; 57 324–27 (upd.)

Smiths Industries PLC, 25 429–31

Smithsonian Institution, 27 410–13

Smithway Motor Xpress Corporation, 39 376–79

Smoby International SA, 56 333–35

Smorgon Steel Group Ltd., 62 329–32

Smucker's see The J.M. Smucker Co.

Smurfit-Stone Container Corporation, 26 442–46 (upd.) ; 83 360–368 (upd.)

Snap-On, Incorporated, 7 479–80; 27 414–16 (upd.); 105 423–28 (upd.)

Snapfish, 83 369–372

Snapple Beverage Corporation, 11 449–51

SNC-Lavalin Group Inc., 72 330–33

SNCF see Société Nationale des Chemins de Fer Français.

SNEA see Société Nationale Elf Aquitaine.

Snecma Group, 46 369–72 see also SAFRAN.

Snell & Wilmer L.L.P., 28 425–28

SNET see Southern New England Telecommunications Corp.

Snow Brand Milk Products Company, Ltd., II 574–75; 48 362–65 (upd.)

Soap Opera Magazine see American Media, Inc.

Sobeys Inc., 80 348–51

Socata see EADS SOCATA.

Sociedad Química y Minera de Chile S.A.,103 382–85

Sociedade de Jogos de Macau, S.A.see SJM Holdings Ltd.

Società Finanziaria Telefonica per Azioni, V 325–27

Società Sportiva Lazio SpA, 44 386–88

Société Air France, 27 417–20 (upd.).

Société BIC S.A., 73 312–15

Societe des Produits Marnier-Lapostolle S.A., 88 373–76

Société d'Exploitation AOM Air Liberté SA (AirLib), 53 305–07

Société du Figaro S.A., 60 281–84

Société du Louvre, 27 421–23

Société Générale, II 354–56; 42 347–51 (upd.)

Société Industrielle Lesaffre, 84 356–359

Société Luxembourgeoise de Navigation Aérienne S.A., 64 357–59

Société Nationale des Chemins de Fer Français, V 512–15; 57 328–32 (upd.)

Société Nationale Elf Aquitaine, IV 544–47; 7 481–85 (upd.)

Société Norbert Dentressangle S.A., 67 352–54

Société Tunisienne de l'Air-Tunisair, 49 371–73

Society Corporation, 9 474–77

Sodexho SA, 29 442–44; 91 433–36 (upd.)

Sodiaal S.A., 19 50; 36 437–39 (upd.)

SODIMA, II 576–77 see also Sodiaal S.A.

Soft Sheen Products, Inc., 31 416–18

Softbank Corporation, 13 481–83; 38 439–44 (upd.); 77 387–95 (upd.)

Sojitz Corporation, 96 395–403 (upd.)

Sol Meliá S.A., 71 337–39

Sola International Inc., 71 340–42

Solar Turbines Inc., 100 402–06

Solarfun Power Holdings Co., Ltd., 105 429–33

Sole Technology Inc., 93 405–09

Solectron Corporation, 12 450–52; 48 366–70 (upd.)

Solo Cup Company, 104 424–27

Solo Serve Corporation, 28 429–31

Solutia Inc., 52 312–15

Solvay & Cie S.A., I 394–96; 21 464–67 (upd.)

Solvay S.A., 61 329–34 (upd.)

Somerfield plc, 47 365–69 (upd.)

Sommer-Allibert S.A., 19 406–09 see also Tarkett Sommer AG.

Sompo Japan Insurance, Inc., 98 359–63 (upd.)
Sonae SGPS, S.A., 97 378–81
Sonat, Inc., 6 577–78 *see also* El Paso Corp.
Sonatrach, 65 313–17 (upd.)
Sonera Corporation, 50 441–44 *see also* TeliaSonera AB.
Sonesta International Hotels Corporation, 44 389–91
Sonic Automotive, Inc., 77 396–99
Sonic Corp., 14 451–53; 37 360–63 (upd.); 103 386–91 (upd.)
Sonic Innovations Inc., 56 336–38
Sonic Solutions, Inc., 81 375–79
SonicWALL, Inc., 87 421–424
Sonnenschein Nath and Rosenthal LLP, 102 384–87
Sonoco Products Company, 8 475–77; 89 415–22 (upd.)
SonoSite, Inc., 56 339–41
Sony Corporation, II 101–03; 12 453–56 (upd.); 40 404–10 (upd.)
Sophus Berendsen A/S, 49 374–77
Sorbee International Ltd., 74 309–11
Soriana *see* Organización Soriana, S.A. de C.V.
Soros Fund Management LLC, 28 432–34
Sorrento, Inc., 19 51; 24 444–46
SOS Staffing Services, 25 432–35
Sotheby's Holdings, Inc., 11 452–54; 29 445–48 (upd.); 84 360–365 (upd.)
Soufflet SA *see* Groupe Soufflet SA.
Sound Advice, Inc., 41 379–82
Souper Salad, Inc., 98 364–67
The Source Enterprises, Inc., 65 318–21
Source Interlink Companies, Inc., 75 350–53
The South African Breweries Limited, I 287–89; 24 447–51 (upd.) *see also* SABMiller plc.
South Beach Beverage Company, Inc., 73 316–19
South Dakota Wheat Growers Association, 94 397–401
South Jersey Industries, Inc., 42 352–55
Southam Inc., 7 486–89 *see also* CanWest Global Communications Corp.
Southcorp Limited, 54 341–44
Southdown, Inc., 14 454–56 *see also* CEMEX S.A. de C.V.
Southeast Frozen Foods Company, L.P., 99 423–426
The Southern Company, V 721–23; 38 445–49 (upd.)
Southern Connecticut Gas Company, 84 366–370
Southern Electric PLC, 13 484–86 *see also* Scottish and Southern Energy plc.
Southern Financial Bancorp, Inc., 56 342–44
Southern Indiana Gas and Electric Company, 13 487–89 *see also* Vectren Corp.

Southern New England Telecommunications Corporation, 6 338–40
Southern Pacific Transportation Company, V 516–18 *see also* Union Pacific Corp.
Southern Peru Copper Corporation, 40 411–13
Southern Poverty Law Center, Inc., 74 312–15
Southern Progress Corporation, 102 388–92
Southern States Cooperative Incorporated, 36 440–42
Southern Sun Hotel Interest (Pty) Ltd., 106 435–39
Southern Union Company, 27 424–26
Southern Wine and Spirits of America, Inc., 84 371–375
The Southland Corporation, II 660–61; 7 490–92 (upd.) *see also* 7–Eleven, Inc.
Southtrust Corporation, 11 455–57 *see also* Wachovia Corp.
Southwest Airlines Co., 6 119–21; 24 452–55 (upd.); 71 343–47 (upd.)
Southwest Gas Corporation, 19 410–12
Southwest Water Company, 47 370–73
Southwestern Bell Corporation, V 328–30 *see also* SBC Communications Inc.
Southwestern Electric Power Co., 21 468–70
Southwestern Public Service Company, 6 579–81
Southwire Company, Inc., 8 478–80; 23 444–47 (upd.)
Souza Cruz S.A., 65 322–24
Sovereign Bancorp, Inc., 103 392–95
Sovran Self Storage, Inc., 66 299–301
SP Alpargatas *see* Sao Paulo Alpargatas S.A.
Spacehab, Inc., 37 364–66
Spacelabs Medical, Inc., 71 348–50
Spaghetti Warehouse, Inc., 25 436–38
Spago *see* The Wolfgang Puck Food Company, Inc.
Spangler Candy Company, 44 392–95
Spanish Broadcasting System, Inc., 41 383–86
Spansion Inc., 80 352–55
Spanx, Inc., 89 423–27
Spar Aerospace Limited, 32 435–37
Spar Handelsgesellschaft mbH, 35 398–401; 103 396–400 (upd.)
Spark Networks, Inc., 91 437–40
Spartan Motors Inc., 14 457–59
Spartan Stores Inc., 8 481–82; 66 302–05 (upd.)
Spartech Corporation, 19 413–15; 76 329–32 (upd.)
Sparton Corporation, 18 492–95
Spear & Jackson, Inc., 73 320–23
Spear, Leeds & Kellogg, 66 306–09
Spec's Music, Inc., 19 416–18 *see also* Camelot Music, Inc.
Special Olympics, Inc., 93 410–14
Specialist Computer Holdings Ltd., 80 356–59

Specialized Bicycle Components Inc., 50 445–48
Specialty Coatings Inc., 8 483–84
Specialty Equipment Companies, Inc., 25 439–42
Specialty Products & Insulation Co., 59 381–83
Specsavers Optical Group Ltd., 104 428–31
Spector Photo Group N.V., 82 344–47
Spectrum Control, Inc., 67 355–57
Spectrum Organic Products, Inc., 68 346–49
Spee-Dee Delivery Service, Inc., 93 415–18
SpeeDee Oil Change and Tune-Up, 25 443–47
Speedway Motorsports, Inc., 32 438–41
Speedy Hire plc, 84 376–379
Speidel Inc., 96 404–07
Speizman Industries, Inc., 44 396–98
Spelling Entertainment, 14 460–62; 35 402–04 (upd.)
Spencer Stuart and Associates, Inc., 14 463–65 *see also* SSI (U.S.), Inc.
Sperian Protection S.A., 104 432–36
Spherion Corporation, 52 316–18
Spicy Pickle Franchising, Inc., 105 434–37
Spie *see* Amec Spie S.A.
Spiegel, Inc., 10 489–91; 27 427–31 (upd.)
SPIEGEL-Verlag Rudolf Augstein GmbH & Co. KG, 44 399–402
Spin Master, Ltd., 61 335–38
Spinnaker Exploration Company, 72 334–36
Spirax-Sarco Engineering plc, 59 384–86
Spirit Airlines, Inc., 31 419–21
Sport Chalet, Inc., 16 454–56; 94 402–06 (upd.)
Sport Supply Group, Inc., 23 448–50; 106 440–45 (upd.)
Sportmart, Inc., 15 469–71 *see also* Gart Sports Co.
Sports & Recreation, Inc., 17 453–55
The Sports Authority, Inc., 16 457–59; 43 385–88 (upd.)
The Sports Club Company, 25 448–51
The Sportsman's Guide, Inc., 36 443–46
Springs Global US, Inc., V 378–79; 19 419–22 (upd.); 90 378–83 (upd.)
Sprint Communications Company, L.P., 9 478–80 *see also* Sprint Corporation; US Sprint Communications.
Sprint Corporation, 46 373–76 (upd.)
SPS Technologies, Inc., 30 428–30
SPSS Inc., 64 360–63
SPX Corporation, 10 492–95; 47 374–79 (upd.); 103 401–09 (upd.)
Spyglass Entertainment Group, LLC, 91 441–44
SQM *see* Sociedad Química y Minera de Chile S.A.
Square D, 90 384–89

Square Enix Holdings Co., Ltd., 101 454–57

Squibb Corporation, I 695–97 *see also* Bristol-Myers Squibb Co.

SR Teleperformance S.A., 86 365–68

SRA International, Inc., 77 400–03

SRAM Corporation, 65 325–27

SRC Holdings Corporation, 67 358–60

SRI International, Inc., 57 333–36

SSA *see* Stevedoring Services of America Inc.

SSAB Svenskt Stål AB, 89 428–31

Ssangyong Cement Industrial Co., Ltd., III 747–50; 61 339–43 (upd.)

SSI (U.S.), Inc., 103 410–14 (upd.)

SSL International plc, 49 378–81

SSOE Inc., 76 333–35

St Ives plc, 34 393–95

St. *see under* Saint

St. James's Place Capital, plc, 71 324–26

The St. Joe Company, 31 422–25; 98 368–73 (upd.)

St. Joe Paper Company, 8 485–88

St. John Knits, Inc., 14 466–68

St. Jude Medical, Inc., 11 458–61; 43 347–52 (upd.); 97 350–58 (upd.)

St. Louis Music, Inc., 48 351–54

St. Luke's-Roosevelt Hospital Center *see* Continuum Health Partners, Inc.

St. Mary Land & Exploration Company, 63 345–47

St. Paul Bank for Cooperatives, 8 489–90

The St. Paul Travelers Companies, Inc., III 355–57; 22 492–95 (upd.); 79 362–69 (upd.)

STAAR Surgical Company, 57 337–39

The Stabler Companies Inc., 78 352–55

Stage Stores, Inc., 24 456–59; 82 348–52 (upd.)

Stagecoach Group plc, 30 431–33; 104 437–41 (upd.)

Stanadyne Automotive Corporation, 37 367–70

StanCorp Financial Group, Inc., 56 345–48

Standard Candy Company Inc., 86 369–72

Standard Chartered plc, II 357–59; 48 371–74 (upd.)

Standard Commercial Corporation, 13 490–92; 62 333–37 (upd.)

Standard Federal Bank, 9 481–83

Standard Life Assurance Company, III 358–61

Standard Microsystems Corporation, 11 462–64

Standard Motor Products, Inc., 40 414–17

Standard Pacific Corporation, 52 319–22

The Standard Register Company, 15 472–74; 93 419–25 (upd.)

Standex International Corporation, 17 456–59; 44 403–06 (upd.)

Stanhome Inc., 15 475–78

Stanley Furniture Company, Inc., 34 412–14

Stanley Leisure plc, 66 310–12

The Stanley Works, III 626–29; 20 476–80 (upd.); 79 383–91 (upd.)

Staple Cotton Cooperative Association (Staplcotn), 86 373–77

Staples, Inc., 10 496–98; 55 351–56 (upd.)

Star Banc Corporation, 11 465–67 *see also* Firstar Corp.

Star of the West Milling Co., 95 386–89

Starbucks Corporation, 13 493–94; 34 415–19 (upd.); 77 404–10 (upd.)

Starcraft Corporation, 30 434–36; 66 313–16 (upd.)

Starent Networks Corp., 106 446–50

StarHub Ltd., 77 411–14

Starkey Laboratories, Inc., 52 323–25

Starrett *see* L.S. Starrett Co.

Starrett Corporation, 21 471–74

StarTek, Inc., 79 392–95

Starter Corp., 12 457–458

Starwood Hotels & Resorts Worldwide, Inc., 54 345–48

Starz LLC, 91 445–50

The Stash Tea Company, 50 449–52

State Auto Financial Corporation, 77 415–19

State Bank of India, 63 354–57

State Farm Mutual Automobile Insurance Company, III 362–64; 51 341–45 (upd.)

State Financial Services Corporation, 51 346–48

State Street Corporation, 8 491–93; 57 340–44 (upd.)

Staten Island Bancorp, Inc., 39 380–82

Stater Bros. Holdings Inc., 64 364–67

Station Casinos, Inc., 25 452–54; 90 390–95 (upd.)

Statoil ASA, 61 344–48 (upd.)

The Staubach Company, 62 338–41

STC PLC, III 162–64 *see also* Nortel Networks Corp.

Ste. Michelle Wine Estates Ltd., 96 408–11

The Steak n Shake Company, 41 387–90; 96 412–17 (upd.)

Steamships Trading Company Ltd., 82 353–56

Stearns, Inc., 43 389–91

Steel Authority of India Ltd., IV 205–07; 66 317–21 (upd.)

Steel Dynamics, Inc., 52 326–28

Steel Technologies Inc., 63 358–60

Steelcase Inc., 7 493–95; 27 432–35 (upd.)

Stefanel SpA, 63 361–63

Steiff *see* Margarete Steiff GmbH.

Steilmann Group *see* Klaus Steilmann GmbH & Co. KG.

Stein Mart Inc., 19 423–25; 72 337–39 (upd.)

Steinberg Incorporated, II 662–65

Steiner Corporation (Alsco), 53 308–11

Steinway Musical Properties, Inc., 19 426–29

Stelco Inc., IV 208–10; 51 349–52 (upd.)

Stelmar Shipping Ltd., 52 329–31

Stemilt Growers Inc., 94 407–10

Stepan Company, 30 437–39; 105 438–42 (upd.)

The Stephan Company, 60 285–88

Stephens Inc., 92 344–48

Stephens Media, LLC, 91 451–54

Steria SA, 49 382–85

Stericycle, Inc., 33 380–82; 74 316–18 (upd.)

Sterilite Corporation, 97 382–85

STERIS Corporation, 29 449–52

Sterling Chemicals, Inc., 16 460–63; 78 356–61 (upd.)

Sterling Drug Inc., I 698–700

Sterling Electronics Corp., 18 496–98

Sterling European Airlines A/S, 70 300–02

Sterling Financial Corporation, 106 451–55

Sterling Software, Inc., 11 468–70 *see also* Computer Associates International, Inc.

STET *see* Società Finanziaria Telefonica per Azioni.

Steuben Glass *see* Corning Inc.

Steve & Barry's LLC, 88 377–80

Stevedoring Services of America Inc., 28 435–37

Steven Madden, Ltd., 37 371–73

Stew Leonard's, 56 349–51

Stewart & Stevenson Services Inc., 11 471–73

Stewart Enterprises, Inc., 20 481–83

Stewart Information Services Corporation, 78 362–65

Stewart's Beverages, 39 383–86

Stewart's Shops Corporation, 80 360–63

Stickley *see* L. and J.G. Stickley, Inc.

Stiefel Laboratories, Inc., 90 396–99

Stihl *see* Andreas Stihl AG & Co. KG.

Stillwater Mining Company, 47 380–82

Stimson Lumber Company Inc., 78 366–69

Stinnes AG, 8 494–97; 23 451–54 (upd.); 59 387–92 (upd.)

Stirling Group plc, 62 342–44

STMicroelectronics NV, 52 332–35

Stock Yards Packing Co., Inc., 37 374–76

Stoddard International plc, 72 340–43

Stoll-Moss Theatres Ltd., 34 420–22

Stollwerck AG, 53 312–15

Stolt-Nielsen S.A., 42 356–59; 54 349–50

Stolt Sea Farm Holdings PLC, 54 349–51

Stone & Webster, Inc., 13 495–98; 64 368–72 (upd.)

Stone Container Corporation, IV 332–34 *see also* Smurfit-Stone Container Corp.

Stone Manufacturing Company, 14 469–71; 43 392–96 (upd.)

Stonyfield Farm, Inc., 55 357–60

The Stop & Shop Supermarket Company, II 666–67; 24 460–62 (upd.); 68 350–53 (upd.)

Stora Enso Oyj, IV 335–37; 36 447–55 (upd.); 85 396–408 (upd.)

Storage Technology Corporation, 6 275–77

Storage USA, Inc., 21 475–77

Storehouse PLC, 16 464–66 *see also* Mothercare plc.

Stouffer Corp., 8 498–501 *see also* Nestlé S.A.

StrataCom, Inc., 16 467–69

Stratagene Corporation, 70 303–06

Stratasys, Inc., 67 361–63

Strattec Security Corporation, 73 324–27

Stratus Computer, Inc., 10 499–501

Straumann Holding AG, 79 396–99

Strauss Discount Auto, 56 352–54

Strauss-Elite Group, 68 354–57

Strayer Education, Inc., 53 316–19

Stride Rite Corporation, 8 502–04; 37 377–80 (upd.); 86 378–84 (upd.)

Strine Printing Company Inc., 88 381–84

Strix Ltd., 51 353–55

The Strober Organization, Inc., 82 357–60 *see also* Pro-Build Holdings Inc.

The Stroh Brewery Company, I 290–92; 18 499–502 (upd.)

Strombecker Corporation, 60 289–91

Stroock & Stroock & Lavan LLP, 40 418–21

Strouds, Inc., 33 383–86

The Structure Tone Organization, 99 427–430

Stryker Corporation, 11 474–76; 29 453–55 (upd.); 79 400–05 (upd.)

Stuart C. Irby Company, 58 333–35

Stuart Entertainment Inc., 16 470–72

Student Loan Marketing Association, II 453–55 *see also* SLM Holding Corp.

Stuller Settings, Inc., 35 405–07

Sturm, Ruger & Company, Inc., 19 430–32

Stussy, Inc., 55 361–63

Sub Pop Ltd., 97 386–89

Sub-Zero Freezer Co., Inc., 31 426–28

Suburban Propane Partners, L.P., 30 440–42

Subway, 32 442–44 *see also* Doctor's Associates Inc.

Successories, Inc., 30 443–45

Sucden *see* Compagnie Financière Sucres et Denrées.

Suchard Co. *see* Jacobs Suchard.

Sudbury Inc., 16 473–75

Südzucker AG, 27 436–39

Suez Lyonnaise des Eaux, 36 456–59 (upd.)

SUEZ-TRACTEBEL S.A., 97 390–94 (upd.)

Suiza Foods Corporation, 26 447–50 *see also* Dean Foods Co.

Sukhoi Design Bureau Aviation Scientific-Industrial Complex, 24 463–65

Sullivan & Cromwell, 26 451–53

Sulzer Ltd., III 630–33; 68 358–62 (upd.)

Sumitomo Bank, Limited, II 360–62; 26 454–57 (upd.)

Sumitomo Chemical Company Ltd., I 397–98; 98 374–78 (upd.)

Sumitomo Corporation, I 518–20; 11 477–80 (upd.); 102 393–98 (upd.)

Sumitomo Electric Industries, II 104–05

Sumitomo Heavy Industries, Ltd., III 634–35; 42 360–62 (upd.)

Sumitomo Life Insurance Company, III 365–66; 60 292–94 (upd.)

Sumitomo Metal Industries Ltd., IV 211–13; 82 361–66 (upd.)

Sumitomo Metal Mining Co., Ltd., IV 214–16

Sumitomo Mitsui Banking Corporation, 51 356–62 (upd.)

Sumitomo Realty & Development Co., Ltd., IV 726–27

Sumitomo Rubber Industries, Ltd., V 252–53

The Sumitomo Trust & Banking Company, Ltd., II 363–64; 53 320–22 (upd.)

The Summit Bancorporation, 14 472–74 *see also* FleetBoston Financial Corp.

Summit Family Restaurants Inc., 19 433–36

Sun Alliance Group PLC, III 369–74 *see also* Royal & Sun Alliance Insurance Group plc.

Sun Communities Inc., 46 377–79

Sun Company, Inc., IV 548–50 *see also* Sunoco, Inc.

Sun Country Airlines, I 30 446–49 *see also* MN Airlines LLC.

Sun-Diamond Growers of California, 7 496–97 *see also* Diamond of California.

Sun Distributors L.P., 12 459–461

Sun Healthcare Group Inc., 25 455–58

Sun Hydraulics Corporation, 74 319–22

Sun International Hotels Limited, 26 462–65 *see also* Kerzner International Ltd.

Sun Life Financial Inc., 85 409–12

Sun-Maid Growers of California, 82 367–71

Sun Microsystems, Inc., 7 498–501; 30 450–54 (upd.); 91 455–62 (upd.)

Sun Pharmaceutical Industries Ltd., 57 345–47

Sun-Rype Products Ltd., 76 336–38

Sun Sportswear, Inc., 17 460–63

Sun Television & Appliances Inc., 10 502–03

Sun World International, LLC, 93 426–29

SunAmerica Inc., 11 481–83 *see also* American International Group, Inc.

Sunbeam-Oster Co., Inc., 9 484–86

Sunburst Hospitality Corporation, 26 458–61

Sunburst Shutters Corporation, 78 370–72

Suncor Energy Inc., 54 352–54

Suncorp-Metway Ltd., 91 463–66

Sundstrand Corporation, 7 502–04; 21 478–81 (upd.)

Sundt Corp., 24 466–69

SunGard Data Systems Inc., 11 484–85

Sunglass Hut International, Inc., 21 482–84; 74 323–26 (upd.)

Sunkist Growers, Inc., 26 466–69; 102399–404 (upd.)

Sunoco, Inc., 28 438–42 (upd.); 83 373–380 (upd.)

SunOpta Inc., 79 406–10

SunPower Corporation, 91 467–70

The Sunrider Corporation, 26 470–74

Sunrise Greetings, 88 385–88

Sunrise Medical Inc., 11 486–88

Sunrise Senior Living, Inc., 81 380–83

Sunshine Village Corporation, 103 415–18

Sunsweet Growers *see* Diamond of California.

Suntech Power Holdings Company Ltd., 89 432–35

Sunterra Corporation, 75 354–56

Suntory Ltd., 65 328–31

SunTrust Banks Inc., 23 455–58; 101 458–64 (upd.)

Super 8 Motels, Inc., 83 381–385

Super Food Services, Inc., 15 479–81

Supercuts Inc., 26 475–78

Superdrug Stores PLC, 95 390–93

Superior Energy Services, Inc., 65 332–34

Superior Essex Inc., 80 364–68

Superior Industries International, Inc., 8 505–07

Superior Uniform Group, Inc., 30 455–57

Supermarkets General Holdings Corporation, II 672–74 *see also* Pathmark Stores, Inc.

SUPERVALU INC., II 668–71; 18 503–08 (upd.); 50 453–59 (upd.)

Suprema Specialties, Inc., 27 440–42

Supreme International Corporation, 27 443–46

Suramericana de Inversiones S.A., 88 389–92

Surrey Satellite Technology Limited, 83 386–390

The Susan G. Komen Breast CancerFoundation, 78 373–76

Susquehanna Pfaltzgraff Company, 8 508–10

Sutherland Lumber Company, L.P., 99 431–434

Sutter Home Winery Inc., 16 476–78

Suzano *see* Companhia Suzano de Papel e Celulose S.A.

Suzuki Motor Corporation, 9 487–89; 23 459–62 (upd.); 59 393–98 (upd.)

Sveaskog AB, 93 430–33

Svenska Cellulosa Aktiebolaget SCA, IV 338–40; 28 443–46 (upd.); 85 413–20 (upd.)

Svenska Handelsbanken AB, II 365–67; 50 460–63 (upd.)

Sverdrup Corporation, 14 475–78 *see also* Jacobs Engineering Group Inc.

Sveriges Riksbank, 96 418–22

SWA *see* Southwest Airlines.

SWALEC *see* Scottish and Southern Energy plc.

Swales & Associates, Inc., 69 336–38

Swank, Inc., 17 464–66; 84 380–384 (upd.)

Swarovski International Holding AG, 40 422–25

The Swatch Group SA, 26 479–81

Swedish Match AB, 12 462–64; 39 387–90 (upd.); 92 349–55 (upd.)

Swedish Telecom, V 331–33

SwedishAmerican Health System, 51 363–66

Sweet Candy Company, 60 295–97

Sweetbay Supermarket, 103 419–24 (upd.)

Sweetheart Cup Company, Inc., 36 460–64

The Swett & Crawford Group Inc., 84 385–389

SWH Corporation, 70 307–09

Swift & Company, 55 364–67

Swift Energy Company, 63 364–66

Swift Transportation Co., Inc., 42 363–66

Swinerton Inc., 43 397–400

Swire Pacific Ltd., I 521–22; 16 479–81 (upd.); 57 348–53 (upd.)

Swisher International Group Inc., 23 463–65

Swiss Air Transport Company Ltd., I 121–22

Swiss Army Brands, Inc. *see* Victorinox AG.

Swiss Bank Corporation, II 368–70 *see also* UBS AG.

The Swiss Colony, Inc., 97 395–98

Swiss Federal Railways (Schweizerische Bundesbahnen), V 519–22

Swiss International Air Lines Ltd., 48 379–81

Swiss Reinsurance Company (Schweizerische Rückversicherungs-Gesellschaft), III 375–78; 46 380–84 (upd.)

Swiss Valley Farms Company, 90 400–03

Swisscom AG, 58 336–39

Swissport International Ltd., 70 310–12

Sybase, Inc., 10 504–06; 27 447–50 (upd.)

Sybron International Corp., 14 479–81

Sycamore Networks, Inc., 45 388–91

Sykes Enterprises, Inc., 45 392–95

Sylvan, Inc., 22 496–99

Sylvan Learning Systems, Inc., 35 408–11 *see also* Educate Inc.

Symantec Corporation, 10 507–09; 82 372–77 (upd.)

Symbol Technologies, Inc., 15 482–84 *see also* Motorola, Inc.

Symrise GmbH and Company KG, 89 436–40

Syms Corporation, 29 456–58; 74 327–30 (upd.)

Symyx Technologies, Inc., 77 420–23

Synaptics Incorporated, 95 394–98

Synchronoss Technologies, Inc., 95 399–402

Syneron Medical Ltd., 91 471–74

Syngenta International AG, 83 391–394

Syniverse Holdings Inc., 97 399–402

SYNNEX Corporation, 73 328–30

Synopsys, Inc., 11 489–92; 69 339–43 (upd.)

SynOptics Communications, Inc., 10 510–12

Synovus Financial Corp., 12 465–67; 52 336–40 (upd.)

Syntax-Brillian Corporation, 102 405–09

Syntel, Inc., 92 356–60

Syntex Corporation, I 701–03

Synthes, Inc., 93 434–37

Sypris Solutions, Inc., 85 421–25

SyQuest Technology, Inc., 18 509–12

Syratech Corp., 14 482–84

SYSCO Corporation, II 675–76; 24 470–72 (upd.); 75 357–60 (upd.)

System Software Associates, Inc., 10 513–14

Systemax, Inc., 52 341–44

Systems & Computer Technology Corp., 19 437–39

Sytner Group plc, 45 396–98

T

T-Netix, Inc., 46 385–88

T-Online International AG, 61 349–51

T.J. Maxx *see* The TJX Companies, Inc.

T. Marzetti Company, 57 354–56

T. Rowe Price Associates, Inc., 11 493–96; 34 423–27 (upd.)

TA Triumph-Adler AG, 48 382–85

TAB Products Co., 17 467–69

Tabacalera, S.A., V 414–16; 17 470–73 (upd.) *see also* Altadis S.A.

TABCORP Holdings Limited, 44 407–10

TACA *see* Grupo TACA.

Taco Bell Corporation, 7 505–07; 21 485–88 (upd.); 74 331–34 (upd.)

Taco Cabana, Inc., 23 466–68; 72 344–47 (upd.)

Taco John's International Inc., 15 485–87; 63 367–70 (upd.)

Tacony Corporation, 70 313–15

TAG Heuer S.A., 25 459–61; 77 424–28 (upd.)

Tag-It Pacific, Inc., 85 426–29

Taiheiyo Cement Corporation, 60 298–301 (upd.)

Taittinger S.A., 43 401–05

Taiwan Semiconductor Manufacturing Company Ltd., 47 383–87

Taiwan Tobacco & Liquor Corporation, 75 361–63

Taiyo Fishery Company, Limited, II 578–79 *see also* Maruha Group Inc.

Taiyo Kobe Bank, Ltd., II 371–72

Takara Holdings Inc., 62 345–47

Takashimaya Company, Limited, V 193–96; 47 388–92 (upd.)

Take-Two Interactive Software, Inc., 46 389–91

Takeda Chemical Industries, Ltd., I 704–06; 46 392–95 (upd.)

The Talbots, Inc., 11 497–99; 31 429–32 (upd.); 88 393–98 (upd.)

Talisman Energy Inc., 9 490–93; 47 393–98 (upd.); 103 425–34 (upd.)

Talk America Holdings, Inc., 70 316–19

Talley Industries, Inc., 16 482–85

TALX Corporation, 92 361–64

TAM Linhas Aéreas S.A., 68 363–65

Tambrands Inc., 8 511–13 *see also* Procter & Gamble Co.

TAME (Transportes Aéreos Militares Ecuatorianos), 100 407–10

Tamedia AG, 53 323–26

Tamfelt Oyj Abp, 62 348–50

Tamron Company Ltd., 82 378–81

TAMSA *see* Tubos de Acero de Mexico, S.A.

Tandem Computers, Inc., 6 278–80 *see also* Hewlett-Packard Co.

Tandy Corporation, II 106–08; 12 468–70 (upd.) *see also* RadioShack Corp.

Tandycrafts, Inc., 31 433–37

Tanger Factory Outlet Centers, Inc., 49 386–89

Tanimura & Antle Fresh Foods, Inc., 98 379–83

Tanox, Inc., 77 429–32

TAP—Air Portugal Transportes Aéreos Portugueses S.A., 46 396–99 (upd.)

Tapemark Company Inc., 64 373–75

TAQA North Ltd., 95 403–06

Target Corporation, 10 515–17; 27 451–54 (upd.); 61 352–56 (upd.)

Targetti Sankey SpA, 86 385–88

Tarkett Sommer AG, 25 462–64

Tarmac Limited, III 751–54; 28 447–51 (upd.); 95 407–14 (upd.)

Taro Pharmaceutical Industries Ltd., 65 335–37

TAROM S.A., 64 376–78

Tarragon Realty Investors, Inc., 45 399–402

Tarrant Apparel Group, 62 351–53

Taschen GmbH, 101 465–68

Taser International, Inc., 62 354–57

Tastefully Simple Inc., 100 411–14

Tasty Baking Company, 14 485–87; 35 412–16 (upd.)

Tata Iron & Steel Co. Ltd., IV 217–19; 44 411–15 (upd.)

Tata Tea Ltd., 76 339–41

Tate & Lyle PLC, II 580–83; 42 367–72 (upd.); 101 469–77 (upd.)

Tati SA, 25 465–67

Tatneft *see* OAO Tatneft.

Tattered Cover Book Store, 43 406–09

Tatung Co., 23 469–71

Taubman Centers, Inc., 75 364–66

TaurusHolding GmbH & Co. KG, 46 400–03

Taylor & Francis Group plc, 44 416–19

Taylor Corporation, 36 465–67

Taylor Devices, Inc., 97 403–06

Taylor Guitars, 48 386–89

Taylor Made Group Inc., 98 384–87

Taylor Nelson Sofres plc, 34 428–30

Taylor Publishing Company, 12 471–73; 36 468–71 (upd.)

Taylor Woodrow plc, I 590–91; 38 450–53 (upd.)

TaylorMade-adidas Golf, 23 472–74; 96 423–28 (upd.)

TB Wood's Corporation, 56 355–58

TBA Global, LLC, 99 435–438

TBS *see* Turner Broadcasting System, Inc.

TBWA/Chiat/Day, 6 47–49; 43 410–14 (upd.) *see also* Omnicom Group Inc.

TC Advertising *see* Treasure Chest Advertising, Inc.

TCBY Systems LLC, 17 474–76; 98 388–92 (upd.)

TCF Financial Corporation, 47 399–402; 103 435–41 (upd.)

Tchibo GmbH, 82 382–85

TCI *see* Tele-Communications, Inc.

TCO *see* Taubman Centers, Inc.

TD Bank *see* The Toronto-Dominion Bank.

TDC A/S, 63 371–74

TDK Corporation, II 109–11; 17 477–79 (upd.); 49 390–94 (upd.)

TDL Group Ltd., 46 404–06

TDS *see* Telephone and Data Systems, Inc.

TEAC Corporation, 78 377–80

Teachers Insurance and Annuity Association-College Retirement Equities Fund, III 379–82; 45 403–07 (upd.)

Teamsters Union *see* International Brotherhood of Teamsters.

TearDrop Golf Company, 32 445–48

Tech Data Corporation, 10 518–19; 74 335–38 (upd.)

Tech-Sym Corporation, 18 513–15; 44 420–23 (upd.)

TechBooks Inc., 84 390–393

TECHNE Corporation, 52 345–48

Technical Olympic USA, Inc., 75 367–69

Technip, 78 381–84

Technitrol, Inc., 29 459–62

Technology Research Corporation, 94 411–14

Technology Solutions Company, 94 415–19

TechTarget, Inc., 99 439–443

Techtronic Industries Company Ltd., 73 331–34

Teck Corporation, 27 455–58

Tecmo Koei Holdings Company Ltd., 106 456–59

TECO Energy, Inc., 6 582–84

Tecumseh Products Company, 8 514–16; 71 351–55 (upd.)

Ted Baker plc, 86 389–92

Tee Vee Toons, Inc., 57 357–60

Teekay Shipping Corporation, 25 468–71; 82 386–91 (upd.)

Teijin Limited, V 380–82; 61 357–61 (upd.)

Tejon Ranch Company, 35 417–20

Tekelec, 83 395–399

Teknor Apex Company, 97 407–10

Tektronix, Inc., 8 517–21; 78 385–91 (upd.)

Telcordia Technologies, Inc., 59 399–401

Tele-Communications, Inc., II 160–62

Tele Norte Leste Participações S.A., 80 369–72

Telecom Argentina S.A., 63 375–77

Telecom Australia, 6 341–42 *see also* Telstra Corp. Ltd.

Telecom Corporation of New Zealand Limited, 54 355–58

Telecom Eireann, 7 508–10 *see also* eircom plc.

Telecom Italia Mobile S.p.A., 63 378–80

Telecom Italia S.p.A., 43 415–19

Teledyne Technologies Inc., I 523–25; 10 520–22 (upd.); 62 358–62 (upd.)

Telefonaktiebolaget LM Ericsson, V 334–36; 46 407–11 (upd.)

Telefónica de Argentina S.A., 61 362–64

Telefónica de España, S.A., V 337–40

Telefónica S.A., 46 412–17 (upd.)

Telefonos de Mexico S.A. de C.V., 14 488–90; 63 381–84 (upd.)

Telegraaf Media Groep N.V., 98 393–97 (upd.)

Telekom Malaysia Bhd, 76 342–44

Telekomunikacja Polska SA, 50 464–68

Telenor ASA, 69 344–46

Telephone and Data Systems, Inc., 9 494–96

TelePizza S.A., 33 387–89

Television de Mexico, S.A. *see* Grupo Televisa, S.A.

Television Española, S.A., 7 511–12

Télévision Française 1, 23 475–77

TeliaSonera AB, 57 361–65 (upd.)

Telkom S.A. Ltd., 106 460–64

Tellabs, Inc., 11 500–01; 40 426–29 (upd.)

Telsmith Inc., 96 429–33

Telstra Corporation Limited, 50 469–72

Telxon Corporation, 10 523–25

Tembec Inc., 66 322–24

Temple-Inland Inc., IV 341–43; 31 438–42 (upd.); 102 410–16 (upd.)

Tempur-Pedic Inc., 54 359–61

Ten Cate *see* Royal Ten Cate N.V.

Tenaris SA, 63 385–88

Tenedora Nemak, S.A. de C.V., 102 417–20

Tenet Healthcare Corporation, 55 368–71 (upd.)

TenFold Corporation, 35 421–23

Tengasco, Inc., 99 444–447

Tengelmann Group, 27 459–62

Tennant Company, 13 499–501; 33 390–93 (upd.); 95 415–20 (upd.)

Tenneco Inc., I 526–28; 10 526–28 (upd.)

Tennessee Valley Authority, 50 473–77

TenneT B.V., 78 392–95

TEP *see* Tucson Electric Power Co.

TEPPCO Partners, L.P., 73 335–37

Tequila Herradura *see* Grupo Industrial Herradura, S.A. de C.V.

Ter Beke NV, 103 442–45

Teradyne, Inc., 11 502–04; 98 398–403 (upd.)

Terex Corporation, 7 513–15; 40 430–34 (upd.); 91 475–82 (upd.)

Tergal Industries S.A.S., 102 421–25

The Terlato Wine Group, 48 390–92

Terra Industries, Inc., 13 502–04; 94 420–24 (upd.)

Terra Lycos, Inc., 43 420–25

Terremark Worldwide, Inc., 99 448–452

Terrena L'Union CANA CAVAL, 70 320–22

Terumo Corporation, 48 393–95

Tesco plc, II 677–78; 24 473–76 (upd.); 68 366–70 (upd.)

Tesoro Corporation, 7 516–19; 45 408–13 (upd.); 97 411–19 (upd.)

Tessenderlo Group, 76 345–48

The Testor Corporation, 51 367–70

Tetley USA Inc., 88 399–402

Teton Energy Corporation, 97 420–23

Tetra Pak International SA, 53 327–29

Tetra Tech, Inc., 29 463–65

Teva Pharmaceutical Industries Ltd., 22 500–03; 54 362–65 (upd.)

Texaco Inc., IV 551–53; 14 491–94 (upd.); 41 391–96 (upd.) *see also* Chevron Corp.

Texas Air Corporation, I 123–24

Texas Industries, Inc., 8 522–24

Texas Instruments Incorporated, II 112–15; 11 505–08 (upd.); 46 418–23 (upd.)

Texas Pacific Group Inc., 36 472–74

Texas Rangers Baseball, 51 371–74

Texas Roadhouse, Inc., 69 347–49

Texas Utilities Company, V 724–25; 25 472–74 (upd.)

Textron Inc., I 529–30; 34 431–34 (upd.); 88 403–07 (upd.)

Textron Lycoming Turbine Engine, 9 497–99

TF1 *see* Télévision Française 1

TFM *see* Grupo Transportación Ferroviaria Mexicana, S.A. de C.V.

Tha Row Records, 69 350–52 (upd.)

Thai Airways International Public Company Limited, 6 122–24; 27 463–66 (upd.)

Thai Union Frozen Products PCL, 75 370–72

Thales S.A., 42 373–76

Thames Water plc, 11 509–11; 90 404–08 (upd.)

Thane International, Inc., 84 394–397

Thanulux Public Company Limited, 86 393–96

Thermadyne Holding Corporation, 19 440–43

Thermo BioAnalysis Corp., 25 475–78
Thermo Electron Corporation, 7 520–22
Thermo Fibertek, Inc., 24 477–79 *see also* Kadant Inc.
Thermo Fisher Scientific Inc., 105 443–54 (upd.)
Thermo Instrument Systems Inc., 11 512–14
Thermo King Corporation, 13 505–07 *see also* Ingersoll-Rand Company Ltd.
Thermos Company, 16 486–88
Things Remembered, Inc., 84 398–401
Thiokol Corporation, 9 500–02 (upd.); 22 504–07 (upd.)
Thistle Hotels PLC, 54 366–69
Thomas & Betts Corporation, 11 515–17; 54 370–74 (upd.)
Thomas & Howard Company, Inc., 90 409–12
Thomas Cook Travel Inc., 9 503–05; 33 394–96 (upd.)
Thomas Crosbie Holdings Limited, 81 384–87
Thomas H. Lee Co., 24 480–83
Thomas Industries Inc., 29 466–69
Thomas J. Lipton Company, 14 495–97
Thomas Nelson Inc., 14 498–99; 38 454–57 (upd.)
Thomas Publishing Company, 26 482–85
Thomaston Mills, Inc., 27 467–70
Thomasville Furniture Industries, Inc., 12 474–76; 74 339–42 (upd.)
Thomscn Greenhouses and Garden Center, Incorporated, 65 338–40
The Thomson Corporation, 8 525–28; 34 435–40 (upd.); 77 433–39 (upd.)
THOMSON multimedia S.A., II 116–17; 42 377–80 (upd.)
Thor Industries Inc., 39 391–94; 92 365–370 (upd.)
Thorn Apple Valley, Inc., 7 523–25; 22 508–11 (upd.)
Thorn EMI plc, I 531–32 *see also* EMI plc; Thorn plc.
Thorn plc, 24 484–87
Thorntons plc, 46 424–26
ThoughtWorks Inc., 90 413–16
Thousand Trails, Inc., 33 397–99
THQ, Inc., 39 395–97; 92 371–375 (upd.)
Threadless.com *see* skinnyCorp, LLC.
365 Media Group plc, 89 441–44
3Com Corporation, 11 518–21; 34 441–45 (upd.); 106 465–72 (upd.)
The 3DO Company, 43 426–30
3i Group PLC, 73 338–40
3M Company, 61 365–70 (upd.)
Thrifty PayLess, Inc., 12 477–79 *see also* Rite Aid Corp.
Thumann Inc., 104 442–45
ThyssenKrupp AG, IV 221–23; 28 452–60 (upd.); 87 425–438 (upd.)
TI Group plc, 17 480–83
TIAA-CREF *see* Teachers Insurance and Annuity Association-College Retirement Equities Fund.

Tianjin Flying Pigeon Bicycle Co., Ltd., 95 421–24
Tibbett & Britten Group plc, 32 449–52
TIBCO Software Inc., 79 411–14
TIC Holdings Inc., 92 376–379
Ticketmaster, 13 508–10; 37 381–84 (upd.); 76 349–53 (upd.)
Tidewater Inc., 11 522–24; 37 385–88 (upd.)
Tiffany & Co., 14 500–03; 78 396–401 (upd.)
TIG Holdings, Inc., 26 486–88
Tiger Aspect Productions Ltd., 72 348–50
Tigre S.A. Tubos e Conexões, 104 446–49
Tilcon-Connecticut Inc., 80 373–76
Tilia Inc., 62 363–65
Tilley Endurables, Inc., 67 364–66
Tillotson Corp., 15 488–90
TIM *see* Telecom Italia Mobile S.p.A.
Timber Lodge Steakhouse, Inc., 73 341–43
The Timberland Company, 13 511–14; 54 375–79 (upd.)
Timberline Software Corporation, 15 491–93
Time Out Group Ltd., 68 371–73
Time Warner Inc., IV 673–76; 7 526–30 (upd.) *see also* AOL Time Warner Inc.
The Times Mirror Company, IV 677–78; 17 484–86 (upd.) *see also* Tribune Co.
TIMET *see* Titanium Metals Corp.
Timex Corporation, 7 531–33; 25 479–82 (upd.)
The Timken Company, 8 529–31; 42 381–85 (upd.)
Tiscali SpA, 48 396–99
TISCO *see* Tata Iron & Steel Company Ltd.
Tishman Speyer Properties, L.P., 47 403–06
Tissue Technologies, Inc. *see* Palomar Medical Technologies, Inc.
Titan Cement Company S.A., 64 379–81
The Titan Corporation, 36 475–78
Titan International, Inc., 89 445–49
Titan Machinery Inc., 103 446–49
Titanium Metals Corporation, 21 489–92
TiVo Inc., 75 373–75
TJ International, Inc., 19 444–47
The TJX Companies, Inc., V 197–98; 19 448–50 (upd.); 57 366–69 (upd.)
TLC Beatrice International Holdings, Inc., 22 512–15
TMP Worldwide Inc., 30 458–60 *see also* Monster Worldwide Inc.
TNT Freightways Corporation, 14 504–06
TNT Limited, V 523–25
TNT Post Group N.V., 27 471–76 (upd.); 30 461–63 (upd.) *see also* TPG N.V.

Tobu Railway Company Ltd., 6 430–32; 98 404–08 (upd.)
Today's Man, Inc., 20 484–87
TODCO, 87 439–442
The Todd-AO Corporation, 33 400–04 *see also* Liberty Livewire Corp.
Todd Shipyards Corporation, 14 507–09
Todhunter International, Inc., 27 477–79
Tofutti Brands, Inc., 64 382–84
Tohan Corporation, 84 402–405
Toho Co., Ltd., 28 461–63
Tohuku Electric Power Company, Inc., V 726–28
The Tokai Bank, Limited, II 373–74; 15 494–96 (upd.)
Tokheim Corporation, 21 493–95
Tokio Marine and Fire Insurance Co., Ltd., III 383–86 *see also* Millea Holdings Inc.
Tokyo Electric Power Company, V 729–33; 74 343–48 (upd.)
Tokyo Gas Co., Ltd., V 734–36; 55 372–75 (upd.)
TOKYOPOP Inc., 79 415–18
Tokyu Corporation, V 526–28; 47 407–10 (upd.)
Tokyu Department Store Co., Ltd., V 199–202; 32 453–57 (upd.)
Tokyu Land Corporation, IV 728–29
Toll Brothers Inc., 15 497–99; 70 323–26 (upd.)
Tollgrade Communications, Inc., 44 424–27
Tom Brown, Inc., 37 389–91
Tom Doherty Associates Inc., 25 483–86
Tombstone Pizza Corporation, 13 515–17 *see also* Kraft Foods Inc.
Tomen Corporation, IV 224–25; 24 488–91 (upd.)
Tomkins plc, 11 525–27; 44 428–31 (upd.)
Tommy Hilfiger Corporation, 20 488–90; 53 330–33 (upd.)
Tomra Systems ASA, 103 450–54
Tom's Foods Inc., 66 325–27
Tom's of Maine, Inc., 45 414–16
TomTom N.V., 81 388–91
Tomy Company Ltd., 65 341–44
Tone Brothers, Inc., 21 496–98; 74 349–52 (upd.)
Tonen Corporation, IV 554–56; 16 489–92 (upd.)
TonenGeneral Sekiyu K.K., 54 380–86 (upd.)
Tong Yang Cement Corporation, 62 366–68
Tonka Corporation, 25 487–89
Too, Inc., 61 371–73
Toolex International N.V., 26 489–91
Tootsie Roll Industries, Inc., 12 480–82; 82 392–96 (upd.)
The Topaz Group, Inc., 62 369–71
Topco Associates LLC, 60 302–04
Topcon Corporation, 84 406–409

Toppan Printing Co., Ltd., IV 679–81; 58 340–44 (upd.)
The Topps Company, Inc., 13 518–20; 34 446–49 (upd.); 83 400–406 (upd.)
Tops Appliance City, Inc., 17 487–89
Tops Markets LLC, 60 305–07
Toray Industries, Inc., V 383–86; 51 375–79 (upd.)
Torchmark Corporation, 9 506–08; 33 405–08 (upd.)
Toresco Enterprises, Inc., 84 410–413
The Toro Company, 7 534–36; 26 492–95 (upd.); 77 440–45 (upd.)
Toromont Industries, Ltd., 21 499–501
The Toronto-Dominion Bank, II 375–77; 49 395–99 (upd.)
Toronto Maple Leafs *see* Maple Leaf Sports & Entertainment Ltd.
Toronto Raptors *see* Maple Leaf Sports & Entertainment Ltd.
The Torrington Company, 13 521–24 *see also* Timken Co.
Torstar Corporation, 29 470–73 *see also* Harlequin Enterprises Ltd.
Tosco Corporation, 7 537–39 *see also* ConocoPhillips.
Toshiba Corporation, I 533–35; 12 483–86 (upd.); 40 435–40 (upd.); 99 453–461 (upd.)
Tosoh Corporation, 70 327–30
Total Compagnie Française des Pétroles S.A., IV 557–61 *see also* Total Fina Elf S.A.
Total Entertainment Restaurant Corporation, 46 427–29
Total Fina Elf S.A., 50 478–86 (upd.)
TOTAL S.A., 24 492–97 (upd.)
Total System Services, Inc., 18 516–18
Totem Resources Corporation, 9 509–11
TOTO LTD., III 755–56; 28 464–66 (upd.)
Tottenham Hotspur PLC, 81 392–95
Touchstone Films *see* The Walt Disney Co.
TouchTunes Music Corporation, 97 424–28
Toupargel-Agrigel S.A., 76 354–56
Touristik Union International GmbH. and Company K.G., II 163–65 *see also* Preussag AG.
TOUSA *see* Technical Olympic USA, Inc.
Touton S.A., 92 380–383
Tower Air, Inc., 28 467–69
Tower Automotive, Inc., 24 498–500
Towers Perrin, 32 458–60
Town & Country Corporation, 19 451–53
Town Sports International, Inc., 46 430–33
Townsends, Inc., 64 385–87
Toy Biz, Inc., 18 519–21 *see also* Marvel Entertainment, Inc.
Toymax International, Inc., 29 474–76
Toyo Sash Co., Ltd., III 757–58
Toyo Seikan Kaisha Ltd., I 615–16
Toyoda Automatic Loom Works, Ltd., III 636–39

Toyota Motor Corporation, I 203–05; 11 528–31 (upd.); 38 458–62 (upd.); 100 415–22 (upd.)
Toys 'R Us, Inc., V 203–06; 18 522–25 (upd.); 57 370–75 (upd.)
TPG N.V., 64 388–91 (upd.)
Tracor Inc., 17 490–92
Tractebel S.A., 20 491–93 *see also* Suez Lyonnaise des Eaux; SUEZ-TRACTEBEL S.A.
Tractor Supply Company, 57 376–78
Trader Classified Media N.V., 57 379–82
Trader Joe's Company, 13 525–27; 50 487–90 (upd.)
TradeStation Group, Inc., 83 407–410
Traffix, Inc., 61 374–76
Trailer Bridge, Inc., 41 397–99
Trammell Crow Company, 8 532–34; 57 383–87 (upd.)
Trane, 78 402–05
Trans-Lux Corporation, 51 380–83
Trans World Airlines, Inc., I 125–27; 12 487–90 (upd.); 35 424–29 (upd.)
Trans World Entertainment Corporation, 24 501–03; 68 374–77 (upd.)
Transaction Systems Architects, Inc., 29 477–79; 82 397–402 (upd.)
TransAlta Utilities Corporation, 6 585–87
Transamerica—An AEGON Company, I 536–38; 13 528–30 (upd.); 41 400–03 (upd.)
Transammonia Group, 95 425–28
Transatlantic Holdings, Inc., 11 532–33
TransBrasil S/A Linhas Aéreas, 31 443–45
TransCanada Corporation, V 737–38; 93 438–45 (upd.)
Transco Energy Company, V 739–40 *see also* The Williams Companies.
Transiciel SA, 48 400–02
Transitions Optical, Inc., 83 411–415
Transmedia Network Inc., 20 494–97 *see also* Rewards Network Inc.
TransMontaigne Inc., 28 470–72
Transneft *see* Oil Transporting Joint Stock Company Transneft
Transnet Ltd., 6 433–35
Transocean Sedco Forex Inc., 45 417–19
Transport Corporation of America, Inc., 49 400–03
Transportes Aéreas Centro-Americanos *see* Grupo TACA.
Transportes Aéreos Militares Ecuatorianos *see* TAME (Transportes Aéreos Militares Ecuatorianos)
Transportes Aereos Portugueses, S.A., 6 125–27 *see also* TAP—Air Portugal Transportes Aéreos Portugueses S.A.
TransPro, Inc., 71 356–59
The Tranzonic Companies, 15 500–02; 37 392–95 (upd.)
Travel Ports of America, Inc., 17 493–95
Travelers Corporation, III 387–90 *see also* Citigroup Inc.

Travelocity.com, Inc., 46 434–37
Travelzoo Inc., 79 419–22
Travis Boats & Motors, Inc., 37 396–98
Travis Perkins plc, 34 450–52
TRC Companies, Inc., 32 461–64
Treadco, Inc., 19 454–56
Treasure Chest Advertising Company, Inc., 32 465–67
Tredegar Corporation, 52 349–51
Tree of Life, Inc., 29 480–82
Tree Top, Inc., 76 357–59
TreeHouse Foods, Inc., 79 423–26
Trek Bicycle Corporation, 16 493–95; 78 406–10 (upd.)
Trelleborg AB, 93 455–64
Trend-Lines, Inc., 22 516–18
Trend Micro Inc., 97 429–32
Trendwest Resorts, Inc., 33 409–11 *see also* Jeld-Wen, Inc.
Trex Company, Inc., 71 360–62
Tri-State Generation and Transmission Association, Inc., 103 455–59
Tri Valley Growers, 32 468–71
Triarc Companies, Inc., 8 535–37; 34 453–57 (upd.)
Tribune Company, IV 682–84; 22 519–23 (upd.); 63 389–95 (upd.)
Trico Marine Services, Inc., 89 450–53
Trico Products Corporation, 15 503–05
Tridel Enterprises Inc., 9 512–13
Trident Seafoods Corporation, 56 359–61
Trigano S.A., 102 426–29
Trigen Energy Corporation, 42 386–89
Trilon Financial Corporation, II 456–57
TriMas Corp., 11 534–36
Trimble Navigation Limited, 40 441–43
Trina Solar Limited, 103 460–64
Třinecké Železárny A.S., 92 384–87
Trinity Industries, Incorporated, 7 540–41
Trinity Mirror plc, 49 404–10 (upd.)
TRINOVA Corporation, III 640–42
TriPath Imaging, Inc., 77 446–49
Triple Five Group Ltd., 49 411–15
Triple P N.V., 26 496–99
Tripwire, Inc., 97 433–36
TriQuint Semiconductor, Inc., 63 396–99
Trisko Jewelry Sculptures, Ltd., 57 388–90
Triton Energy Corporation, 11 537–39
Triumph-Adler *see* TA Triumph-Adler AG.
Triumph Group, Inc., 31 446–48
Triumph Motorcycles Ltd., 53 334–37
Trizec Corporation Ltd., 10 529–32
The TriZetto Group, Inc., 83 416–419
TRM Copy Centers Corporation, 18 526–28
Tropicana Products, Inc., 28 473–77; 73 344–49 (upd.)
Troutman Sanders L.L.P., 79 427–30
True North Communications Inc., 23 478–80 *see also* Foote, Cone & Belding Worldwide.
True Religion Apparel, Inc., 79 431–34
True Temper Sports, Inc., 95 429–32
True Value Company, 74 353–57 (upd.)

Trump Organization, 23 481–84; 64 392–97 (upd.)
TRUMPF GmbH + Co. KG, 86 397–02
TruServ Corporation, 24 504–07 *see* True Value Co.
Trusthouse Forte PLC, III 104–06
Trustmark Corporation, 106 473–76
TRW Automotive Holdings Corp., I 539–41; 11 540–42 (upd.); 14 510–13 (upd.); 75 376–82 (upd.)
TSA *see* Transaction Systems Architects, Inc.
Tsakos Energy Navigation Ltd., 91 483–86
TSB Group plc, 12 491–93
TSC *see* Tractor Supply Co.
Tsingtao Brewery Group, 49 416–20
TSMC *see* Taiwan Semiconductor Manufacturing Company Ltd.
TSYS *see* Total System Services, Inc.
TTL *see* Taiwan Tobacco & Liquor Corp.
TTX Company, 6 436–37; 66 328–30 (upd.)
Tubby's, Inc., 53 338–40
Tubos de Acero de Mexico, S.A. (TAMSA), 41 404–06
Tucows Inc., 78 411–14
Tucson Electric Power Company, 6 588–91
Tuesday Morning Corporation, 18 529–31; 70 331–33 (upd.)
TUF *see* Thai Union Frozen Products PCL.
TUI *see* Touristik Union International GmbH. and Company K.G.
TUI Group GmbH, 42 283; 44 432–35
Tulip Ltd., 89 454–57
Tullow Oil plc, 83 420–423
Tully's Coffee Corporation, 51 384–86
Tultex Corporation, 13 531–33
Tumaro's Gourmet Tortillas, 85 430–33
Tumbleweed, Inc., 33 412–14; 80 377–81 (upd.)
Tunisair *see* Société Tunisienne de l'Air-Tunisair.
Tupolev Aviation and Scientific Technical Complex, 24 58–60
Tupperware Brands Corporation, 28 478–81; 78 415–20 (upd.)
TurboChef Technologies, Inc., 83 424–427
Turbomeca S.A., 102 430–34
Turkish Airlines Inc. (Türk Hava Yollari A.O.), 72 351–53
Turkiye Is Bankasi A.S., 61 377–80
Türkiye Petrolleri Anonim Ortakliği, IV 562–64
Turner Broadcasting System, Inc., II 166–68; 6 171–73 (upd.); 66 331–34 (upd.)
Turner Construction Company, 66 335–38
The Turner Corporation, 8 538–40; 23 485–88 (upd.)
Turtle Wax, Inc., 15 506–09; 93 465–70 (upd.)
Tuscarora Inc., 29 483–85

The Tussauds Group, 55 376–78
Tutogen Medical, Inc., 68 378–80
Tuttle Publishing, 86 403–06
TV Azteca, S.A. de C.V., 39 398–401
TV Guide, Inc., 43 431–34 (upd.)
TVA *see* Tennessee Valley Authority.
TVE *see* Television Española, S.A.
TVI, Inc., 15 510–12; 99 462–465 *see also* Savers, Inc.
TW Services, Inc., II 679–80
TWA *see* Trans World Airlines.
TWC *see* The Weather Channel Cos.
Tweeter Home Entertainment Group, Inc., 30 464–66
Twentieth Century Fox Film Corporation, II 169–71; 25 490–94 (upd.)
24 Hour Fitness Worldwide, Inc., 71 363–65
24/7 Real Media, Inc., 49 421–24
Twin Disc, Inc., 21 502–04
Twinlab Corporation, 34 458–61
Ty Inc., 33 415–17; 86 407–11 (upd.)
Tyco International Ltd., III 643–46; 28 482–87 (upd.); 63 400–06 (upd.)
Tyco Toys, Inc., 12 494–97 *see also* Mattel, Inc.
Tyler Corporation, 23 489–91
Tyndale House Publishers, Inc., 57 391–94
Tyson Foods, Inc., II 584–85; 14 514–16 (upd.); 50 491–95 (upd.)

U
U.S. *see also* US.
U.S. Aggregates, Inc., 42 390–92
U.S. Army Corps of Engineers, 91 491–95
U.S. Bancorp, 14 527–29; 36 489–95 (upd.); 103 465–75 (upd.)
U.S. Borax, Inc., 42 393–96
U.S. Can Corporation, 30 474–76
U.S. Cellular Corporation, 31 449–52 (upd.); 88 408–13 (upd.)
U.S. Delivery Systems, Inc., 22 531–33 *see also* Velocity Express Corp.
U.S. Foodservice, 26 503–06
U.S. Healthcare, Inc., 6 194–96
U.S. Home Corporation, 8 541–43; 78 421–26 (upd.)
U.S. News & World Report Inc., 30 477–80; 89 458–63 (upd.)
U.S. Office Products Company, 25 500–02
U.S. Physical Therapy, Inc., 65 345–48
U.S. Premium Beef LLC, 91 487–90
U.S. Robotics Corporation, 9 514–15; 66 339–41 (upd.)
U.S. Satellite Broadcasting Company, Inc., 20 505–07 *see also* DIRECTV, Inc.
U.S. Silica Company, 104 455–58
U.S. Steel Corp *see* United States Steel Corp.
U.S. Timberlands Company, L.P., 42 397–400
U.S. Trust Corp., 17 496–98
U.S. Vision, Inc., 66 342–45

U S West, Inc., V 341–43; 25 495–99 (upd.)
UAL Corporation, 34 462–65 (upd.)
UAP *see* Union des Assurances de Paris.
UAW (International Union, United Automobile, Aerospace and Agricultural Implement Workers of America), 72 354–57
Ube Industries, Ltd., III 759–61; 38 463–67 (upd.)
Ubisoft Entertainment S.A., 41 407–09; 106 477–80 (upd.)
UBS AG, 52 352–59 (upd.)
UCB Pharma SA, 98 409–12
UFA TV & Film Produktion GmbH, 80 382–87
UGI Corporation, 12 498–500
Ugine S.A., 20 498–500
Ugly Duckling Corporation, 22 524–27 *see also* DriveTime Automotive Group Inc.
UICI, 33 418–21 *see also* HealthMarkets, Inc.
Ukrop's Super Markets Inc., 39 402–04; 101 478–82 (upd.)
UL *see* Underwriters Laboratories, Inc.
Ulster Television PLC, 71 366–68
Ulta Salon, Cosmetics & Fragrance, Inc., 92471–73
Ultimate Electronics, Inc., 18 532–34; 69 356–59 (upd.)
Ultimate Leisure Group PLC, 75 383–85
Ultra Pac, Inc., 24 512–14
Ultra Petroleum Corporation, 71 369–71
Ultrak Inc., 24 508–11
Ultralife Batteries, Inc., 58 345–48
Ultramar Diamond Shamrock Corporation, IV 565–68; 31 453–57 (upd.)
ULVAC, Inc., 80 388–91
Umbro plc, 88 414–17
Umpqua Holdings Corporation, 87 443–446
Uncle Ben's Inc., 22 528–30
Uncle Ray's LLC, 90 417–19
Under Armour Performance Apparel, 61 381–83
Underberg AG, 92 388–393
Underwriters Laboratories, Inc., 30 467–70
UNG *see* United National Group, Ltd.
Uni-Marts, Inc., 17 499–502
Uni-President Enterprises Corporation, 104 450–54
Unibail SA, 40 444–46
Unibanco Holdings S.A., 73 350–53
Unica Corporation, 77 450–54
UNICEF *see* United Nations International Children's Emergency Fund (UNICEF).
Unicharm Corporation, 84 414–417
Unicom Corporation, 29 486–90 (upd.) *see also* Exelon Corp.
Uniden Corporation, 98 413–16
Unifi, Inc., 12 501–03; 62 372–76 (upd.)

Unified Grocers, Inc., 93 474–77
UniFirst Corporation, 21 505–07
Unigate PLC, II 586–87; 28 488–91 (upd.) *see also* Uniq Plc.
Unilever, II 588–91; 7 542–45 (upd.); 32 472–78 (upd.); 89 464–74 (upd.)
Unilog SA, 42 401–03
Union Bank of California, 16 496–98 *see also* UnionBanCal Corp.
Union Bank of Switzerland, II 378–79 *see also* UBS AG.
Union Camp Corporation, IV 344–46
Union Carbide Corporation, I 399–401; 9 516–20 (upd.); 74 358–63 (upd.)
Unión de Cervecerias Peruanas Backus y Johnston S.A.A., 92 394–397
Union des Assurances de Paris, III 391–94
Union Electric Company, V 741–43 *see also* Ameren Corp.
Unión Fenosa, S.A., 51 387–90
Union Financière de France Banque SA, 52 360–62
Union Pacific Corporation, V 529–32; 28 492–500 (upd.); 79 435–46 (upd.)
Union Planters Corporation, 54 387–90
Union Texas Petroleum Holdings, Inc., 9 521–23
UnionBanCal Corporation, 50 496–99 (upd.)
Uniq plc, 83 428–433 (upd.)
Unique Casual Restaurants, Inc., 27 480–82
Unison HealthCare Corporation, 25 503–05
Unisys Corporation, III 165–67; 6 281–83 (upd.); 36 479–84 (upd.)
Unit Corporation, 63 407–09
United Airlines, I 128–30; 6 128–30 (upd.) *see also* UAL Corp.
United Auto Group, Inc., 26 500–02; 68 381–84 (upd.)
United Biscuits (Holdings) plc, II 592–94; 42 404–09 (upd.)
United Brands Company, II 595–97
United Business Media plc, 52 363–68 (upd.)
United Community Banks, Inc., 98 417–20
United Dairy Farmers, Inc., 74 364–66
United Defense Industries, Inc., 30 471–73; 66 346–49 (upd.)
United Dominion Industries Limited, 8 544–46; 16 499–502 (upd.)
United Dominion Realty Trust, Inc., 52 369–71
United Farm Workers of America, 88 418–22
United Foods, Inc., 21 508–11
United HealthCare Corporation, 9 524–26 *see also* Humana Inc.
The United Illuminating Company, 21 512–14
United Industrial Corporation, 37 399–402
United Industries Corporation, 68 385–87
United Internet AG, 99 466–469

United Jewish Communities, 33 422–25
United Merchants & Manufacturers, Inc., 13 534–37
United Microelectronics Corporation, 98 421–24
United National Group, Ltd., 63 410–13
United Nations International Children's Emergency Fund (UNICEF), 58 349–52
United Natural Foods, Inc., 32 479–82; 76 360–63 (upd.)
United Negro College Fund, Inc., 79 447–50
United News & Media plc, 28 501–05 (upd.) *see also* United Business Media plc.
United Newspapers plc, IV 685–87 *see also* United Business Media plc.
United Online, Inc., 71 372–77 (upd.)
United Overseas Bank Ltd., 56 362–64
United Pan-Europe Communications NV, 47 414–17
United Paper Mills Ltd., IV 347–50 *see also* UPM-Kymmene Corp.
United Parcel Service, Inc., V 533–35; 17 503–06 (upd.); 63 414–19; 94 425–30 (upd.)
United Press International, Inc., 25 506–09; 73 354–57 (upd.)
United Rentals, Inc., 34 466–69
United Retail Group Inc., 33 426–28
United Road Services, Inc., 69 360–62
United Service Organizations, 60 308–11
United States Cellular Corporation, 9 527–29 *see also* U.S. Cellular Corp.
United States Filter Corporation, 20 501–04 *see also* Siemens AG.
United States Health Care Systems, Inc. *see* U.S. Healthcare, Inc.
United States Pipe and Foundry Company, 62 377–80
United States Playing Card Company, 62 381–84
United States Postal Service, 14 517–20; 34 470–75 (upd.)
United States Shoe Corporation, V 207–08
United States Steel Corporation, 50 500–04 (upd.)
United States Surgical Corporation, 10 533–35; 34 476–80 (upd.)
United Stationers Inc., 14 521–23
United Talent Agency, Inc., 80 392–96
United Technologies Automotive Inc., 15 513–15
United Technologies Corporation, I 84–86; 10 536–38 (upd.); 34 481–85 (upd.); 105 455–61 (upd.)
United Telecommunications, Inc., V 344–47 *see also* Sprint Corp.
United Utilities PLC, 52 372–75 (upd.)
United Video Satellite Group, 18 535–37 *see also* TV Guide, Inc.
United Water Resources, Inc., 40 447–50; 45 277
United Way of America, 36 485–88

UnitedHealth Group Incorporated, 103 476–84 (upd.)
Unitika Ltd., V 387–89; 53 341–44 (upd.)
Unitil Corporation, 37 403–06
Unitog Co., 19 457–60 *see also* Cintas Corp.
Unitrin Inc., 16 503–05; 78 427–31 (upd.)
Univar Corporation, 9 530–32
Universal Compression, Inc., 59 402–04
Universal Corporation, V 417–18; 48 403–06 (upd.)
Universal Electronics Inc., 39 405–08
Universal Foods Corporation, 7 546–48 *see also* Sensient Technologies Corp.
Universal Forest Products, Inc., 10 539–40; 59 405–09 (upd.)
Universal Health Services, Inc., 6 191–93
Universal International, Inc., 25 510–11
Universal Manufacturing Company, 88 423–26
Universal Security Instruments, Inc., 96 434–37
Universal Stainless & Alloy Products, Inc., 75 386–88
Universal Studios, Inc., 33 429–33; 100 423–29 (upd.)
Universal Technical Institute, Inc., 81 396–99
The University of Chicago Press, 79 451–55
University of Phoenix *see* Apollo Group, Inc.
Univision Communications Inc., 24 515–18; 83 434–439 (upd.)
UNM *see* United News & Media plc.
Uno Restaurant Holdings Corporation, 18 538–40; 70 334–37 (upd.)
Unocal Corporation, IV 569–71; 24 519–23 (upd.); 71 378–84 (upd.)
UNUM Corp., 13 538–40
UnumProvident Corporation, 52 376–83 (upd.)
Uny Co., Ltd., V 209–10; 49 425–28 (upd.)
UOB *see* United Overseas Bank Ltd.
UPC *see* United Pan-Europe Communications NV.
UPI *see* United Press International.
Upjohn Company, I 707–09; 8 547–49 (upd.) *see also* Pharmacia & Upjohn Inc.; Pfizer Inc.
UPM-Kymmene Corporation, 19 461–65; 50 505–11 (upd.)
The Upper Deck Company, LLC, 105 462–66
UPS *see* United Parcel Service, Inc.
Uralita S.A., 96 438–41
Urban Engineers, Inc., 102 435–38
Urban Outfitters, Inc., 14 524–26; 74 367–70 (upd.)
Urbi Desarrollos Urbanos, S.A. de C.V., 81 400–03
Urbium PLC, 75 389–91
URS Corporation, 45 420–23; 80 397–400 (upd.)

URSI *see* United Road Services, Inc.
US *see also* U.S.
US Airways Group, Inc., I 131–32; 6
   131–32 (upd.); 28 506–09 (upd.); 52
   384–88 (upd.)
US 1 Industries, Inc., 89 475–78
USA Interactive, Inc., 47 418–22 (upd.)
USA Mobility Inc., 97 437–40 (upd.)
USA Truck, Inc., 42 410–13
USAA, 10 541–43; 62 385–88 (upd.)
USANA, Inc., 29 491–93
USCC *see* United States Cellular Corp.
USF&G Corporation, III 395–98 *see also*
   The St. Paul Companies.
USG Corporation, III 762–64; 26
   507–10 (upd.); 81 404–10 (upd.)
Ushio Inc., 91 496–99
Usinas Siderúrgicas de Minas Gerais
   S.A., 77 454–57
Usinger's Famous Sausage *see* Fred Usinger
   Inc.
Usinor SA, IV 226–28; 42 414–17
   (upd.)
USO *see* United Service Organizations.
USPS *see* United States Postal Service.
USSC *see* United States Surgical Corp.
UST Inc., 9 533–35; 50 512–17 (upd.)
USX Corporation, IV 572–74; 7 549–52
   (upd.) *see also* United States Steel Corp.
Utah Medical Products, Inc., 36 496–99
Utah Power and Light Company, 27
   483–86 *see also* PacifiCorp.
UTG Inc., 100 430–33
Utilicorp United Inc., 6 592–94 *see also*
   Aquilla, Inc.
UTStarcom, Inc., 77 458–61
UTV *see* Ulster Television PLC.
Utz Quality Foods, Inc., 72 358–60
UUNET, 38 468–72
Uwajimaya, Inc., 60 312–14
Uzbekistan Airways National Air
   Company, 99 470–473

V

V&S Vin & Sprit AB, 91 504–11 (upd.)
VA TECH ELIN EBG GmbH, 49
   429–31
Vail Resorts, Inc., 11 543–46; 43
   435–39 (upd.)
Vaillant GmbH, 44 436–39
Vaisala Oyj, 104 459–63
Valassis Communications, Inc., 8
   550–51; 37 407–10 (upd.); 76
   364–67 (upd.)
Valeo, 23 492–94; 66 350–53 (upd.)
Valero Energy Corporation, 7 553–55;
   71 385–90 (upd.)
Valhi, Inc., 19 466–68; 94 431–35
   (upd.)
Vallen Corporation, 45 424–26
Valley Media Inc., 35 430–33
Valley National Gases, Inc., 85 434–37
Valley Proteins, Inc., 91 500–03
ValleyCrest Companies, 81 411–14
   (upd.)
Vallourec SA, 54 391–94
Valmet Oy, III 647–49 *see also* Metso
   Corp.

Valmont Industries, Inc., 19 469–72
Valora Holding AG, 98 425–28
Valorem S.A., 88 427–30
Valores Industriales S.A., 19 473–75
The Valspar Corporation, 8 552–54; 32
   483–86 (upd.); 77 462–68 (upd.)
Value City Department Stores, Inc., 38
   473–75 *see also* Retail Ventures, Inc.
Value Line, Inc., 16 506–08; 73 358–61
   (upd.)
Value Merchants Inc., 13 541–43
ValueClick, Inc., 49 432–34
ValueVision International, Inc., 22
   534–36
Valve Corporation, 101 483–86
Van Camp Seafood Company, Inc., 7
   556–57 *see also* Chicken of the Sea
   International.
Van de Velde S.A./NV, 102 439–43
Van Hool S.A./NV, 96 442–45
Van Houtte Inc., 39 409–11
Van Lanschot NV, 79 456–59
Van Leer N.V. *see* Royal Packaging
   Industries Van Leer N.V.; Greif Inc.
Vance Publishing Corporation, 64
   398–401
Vanderbilt University Medical Center,
   99 474–477
The Vanguard Group, Inc., 14 530–32;
   34 486–89 (upd.)
Vanguard Health Systems Inc., 70
   338–40
Vann's Inc., 105 467–70
Van's Aircraft, Inc., 65 349–51
Vans, Inc., 16 509–11; 47 423–26
   (upd.)
Vapores *see* Compañia Sud Americana de
   Vapores S.A.
Varco International, Inc., 42 418–20
Vari-Lite International, Inc., 35 434–36
Varian Associates Inc., 12 504–06
Varian, Inc., 48 407–11 (upd.)
Variety Wholesalers, Inc., 73 362–64
Variflex, Inc., 51 391–93
VARIG S.A. (Viação Aérea
   Rio-Grandense), 6 133–35; 29
   494–97 (upd.)
Varity Corporation, III 650–52 *see also*
   AGCO Corp.
Varlen Corporation, 16 512–14
Varsity Brands, Inc., 15 516–18; 94
   436–40 (upd.)
Varta AG, 23 495–99
VASCO Data Security International,
   Inc., 79 460–63
Vastar Resources, Inc., 24 524–26
Vattenfall AB, 57 395–98
Vaughan Foods, Inc., 105 471–74
Vauxhall Motors Limited, 73 365–69
VBA - Bloemenveiling Aalsmeer, 88
   431–34
VCA Antech, Inc., 58 353–55
Veba A.G., I 542–43; 15 519–21 (upd.)
   see also E.On AG.
Vebego International BV, 49 435–37
VECO International, Inc., 7 558–59 *see*
   also CH2M Hill Ltd.

Vector Aerospace Corporation, 97
   441–44
Vector Group Ltd., 35 437–40 (upd.)
Vectren Corporation, 98 429–36 (upd.)
Vedior NV, 35 441–43
Veeco Instruments Inc., 32 487–90
Veidekke ASA, 98 437–40
Veit Companies, 43 440–42; 92
   398–402 (upd.)
Velcro Industries N.V., 19 476–78; 72
   361–64 (upd.)
Velocity Express Corporation, 49
   438–41; 94 441–46 (upd.)
Velux A/S, 86 412–15
Venator Group Inc., 35 444–49 (upd.)
   see also Foot Locker Inc.
Vencor, Inc., 16 515–17
Vendex International N.V., 13 544–46
   see also Koninklijke Vendex KBB N.V.
   (Royal Vendex KBB N.V.).
Vendôme Luxury Group plc, 27 487–89
Venetian Casino Resort, LLC, 47
   427–29
Ventana Medical Systems, Inc., 75
   392–94
Ventura Foods LLC, 90 420–23
Venture Stores Inc., 12 507–09
VeraSun Energy Corporation, 87
   447–450
Verbatim Corporation, 14 533–35; 74
   371–74 (upd.)
Vereinigte Elektrizitätswerke Westfalen
   AG, IV V 744–47
Veridian Corporation, 54 395–97
VeriFone, Inc., 18 541–44; 76 368–71
   (upd.)
Verint Systems Inc., 73 370–72
VeriSign, Inc., 47 430–34
Veritas Software Corporation, 45
   427–31
Verity Inc., 68 388–91
Verizon Communications Inc., 43
   443–49 (upd.); 78 432–40 (upd.)
Verlagsgruppe Georg von Holtzbrinck
   GmbH, 35 450–53
Verlagsgruppe Weltbild GmbH, 98
   441–46
Vermeer Manufacturing Company, 17
   507–10
The Vermont Country Store, 93 478–82
Vermont Pure Holdings, Ltd., 51
   394–96
The Vermont Teddy Bear Co., Inc., 36
   500–02
Versace *see* Gianni Versace SpA.
Vertex Pharmaceuticals Incorporated, 83
   440–443
Vertis Communications, 84 418–421
Vertrue Inc., 77 469–72
Vestas Wind Systems A/S, 73 373–75
Vestey Group Ltd., 95 433–37
Veuve Clicquot Ponsardin SCS, 98
   447–51
VEW AG, 39 412–15
VF Corporation, V 390–92; 17 511–14
   (upd.); 54 398–404 (upd.)
VHA Inc., 53 345–47

Viacom Inc., 7 560–62; 23 500–03 (upd.); 67 367–71 (upd.) *see also* Paramount Pictures Corp.
Viad Corp., 73 376–78
Viag AG, IV 229–32 *see also* E.On AG.
ViaSat, Inc., 54 405–08
Viasoft Inc., 27 490–93; 59 27
VIASYS Healthcare, Inc., 52 389–91
Viasystems Group, Inc., 67 372–74
Viatech Continental Can Company, Inc., 25 512–15 (upd.)
Vicat S.A., 70 341–43
Vickers plc, 27 494–97
Vicon Industries, Inc., 44 440–42
VICORP Restaurants, Inc., 12 510–12; 48 412–15 (upd.)
Victor Company of Japan, Limited, II 118–19; 26 511–13 (upd.); 83 444–449 (upd.)
Victoria Coach Station Ltd.*see* London Regional Transport.
Victoria Group, III 399–401; 44 443–46 (upd.)
Victorinox AG, 21 515–17; 74 375–78 (upd.)
Victory Refrigeration, Inc., 82 403–06
Vicunha Têxtil S.A., 78 441–44
Videojet Technologies, Inc., 90 424–27
Vidrala S.A., 67 375–77
Viel & Cie, 76 372–74
Vienna Sausage Manufacturing Co., 14 536–37
Viessmann Werke GmbH & Co., 37 411–14
Viewpoint International, Inc., 66 354–56
ViewSonic Corporation, 72 365–67
Viking Office Products, Inc., 10 544–46 *see also* Office Depot, Inc.
Viking Range Corporation, 66 357–59
Viking Yacht Company, 96 446–49
Village Roadshow Ltd., 58 356–59
Village Super Market, Inc., 7 563–64
Village Voice Media, Inc., 38 476–79
Villeroy & Boch AG, 37 415–18
Vilmorin Clause et Cie, 70 344–46
Vilter Manufacturing, LLC, 105 475–79
Vin & Spirit AB, 31 458–61 *see also* V&S Vin & Sprit AB
Viña Concha y Toro S.A., 45 432–34
Vinci, 27 54; 43 450–52; 49 44
Vincor International Inc., 50 518–21
Vinmonopolet A/S, 100 434–37
Vinson & Elkins L.L.P., 30 481–83
Vintage Petroleum, Inc., 42 421–23
Vinton Studios, 63 420–22
Vion Food Group NV, 85 438–41
Virbac Corporation, 74 379–81
Virco Manufacturing Corporation, 17 515–17
Virgin Group Ltd., 12 513–15; 32 491–96 (upd.); 89 479–86 (upd.)
Virginia Dare Extract Company, Inc., 94 447–50
Viridian Group plc, 64 402–04
Visa Inc., 9 536–38; 26 514–17 (upd.); 104 464–69 (upd.)
Viscofan S.A., 70 347–49

Vishay Intertechnology, Inc., 21 518–21; 80 401–06 (upd.)
Vision Service Plan Inc., 77 473–76
Viskase Companies, Inc., 55 379–81
Vista Bakery, Inc., 56 365–68
Vista Chemical Company, I 402–03
Vistana, Inc., 22 537–39
VistaPrint Limited, 87 451–454
VISX, Incorporated, 30 484–86
Vita Food Products Inc., 99 478–481
Vita Plus Corporation, 60 315–17
Vital Images, Inc., 85 442–45
Vitalink Pharmacy Services, Inc., 15 522–24
Vitamin Shoppe Industries, Inc., 60 318–20
Vitasoy International Holdings Ltd., 94 451–54
Viterra Inc., 105 480–83
Vitesse Semiconductor Corporation, 32 497–500
Vitro Corp., 10 547–48
Vitro Corporativo S.A. de C.V., 34 490–92
Vivarte SA, 54 409–12 (upd.)
Vivartia S.A., 82 407–10
Vivendi Universal S.A., 46 438–41 (upd.)
Vivra, Inc., 18 545–47 *see also* Gambro AB.
Vizio, Inc., 100 438–41
Vlasic Foods International Inc., 25 516–19
VLSI Technology, Inc., 16 518–20
VMware, Inc., 90 428–31
VNU N.V., 27 498–501
VNUS Medical Technologies, Inc., 103 485–88
Vocento, 94 455–58
Vodacom Group Pty. Ltd., 106 481–85
Vodafone Group Plc, 11 547–48; 36 503–06 (upd.); 75 395–99 (upd.)
voestalpine AG, IV 233–35; 57 399–403 (upd.)
Voith Sulzer Papiermaschinen GmbH *see* J.M. Voith AG.
Volcan Compañia Minera S.A.A., 92 403–06
Volcom, Inc., 77 477–80
Volga-Dnepr Group, 82 411–14
Volkert and Associates, Inc., 98 452–55
Volkswagen Aktiengesellschaft, I 206–08; 11 549–51 (upd.); 32 501–05 (upd.)
Volt Information Sciences Inc., 26 518–21
Volunteers of America, Inc., 66 360–62
Von Maur Inc., 64 405–08
Vonage Holdings Corp., 81 415–18
The Vons Companies, Inc., 7 569–71; 28 510–13 (upd.); 103 489–95 (upd.)
Vontobel Holding AG, 96 450–53
Voortman Cookies Limited, 103 496–99
Vornado Realty Trust, 20 508–10
Vorwerk & Co., 27 502–04
Vosper Thornycroft Holding plc, 41 410–12
Vossloh AG, 53 348–52

Votorantim Participaçoes S.A., 76 375–78
Vought Aircraft Industries, Inc., 49 442–45
VSM *see* Village Super Market, Inc.
VTech Holdings Ltd., 77 481–84
Vueling Airlines S.A., 97 445–48
Vulcabras S.A., 103 500–04
Vulcan Materials Company, 7 572–75; 52 392–96 (upd.)

W

W + K *see* Wieden + Kennedy.
W.A. Whitney Company, 53 353–56
W. Atlee Burpee & Co., 27 505–08
W.B Doner & Co., 56 369–72
W.B. Mason Company, 98 456–59
W.C. Bradley Co., 69 363–65
W.H. Brady Co., 16 518–21 *see also* Brady Corp.
W. H. Braum, Inc., 80 407–10
W H Smith Group PLC, V 211–13
W Jordan (Cereals) Ltd., 74 382–84
W.L. Gore & Associates, Inc., 14 538–40; 60 321–24 (upd.)
W.P. Carey & Co. LLC, 49 446–48
W.R. Berkley Corporation, 15 525–27; 74 385–88 (upd.)
W.R. Grace & Company, I 547–50; 50 522–29 (upd.)
W.W. Grainger, Inc., V 214–15; 26 537–39 (upd.); 68 392–95 (upd.)
W.W. Norton & Company, Inc., 28 518–20
Waban Inc., 13 547–49 *see also* HomeBase, Inc.
Wabash National Corp., 13 550–52
Wabtec Corporation, 40 451–54
Wachovia Bank of Georgia, N.A., 16 521–23
Wachovia Bank of South Carolina, N.A., 16 524–26
Wachovia Corporation, 12 516–20; 46 442–49 (upd.)
Wachtell, Lipton, Rosen & Katz, 47 435–38
The Wackenhut Corporation, 14 541–43; 63 423–26 (upd.)
Wacker-Chemie GmbH, 35 454–58
Wacker Construction Equipment AG, 95 438–41
Wacoal Corp., 25 520–24
Waddell & Reed, Inc., 22 540–43
Waffle House Inc., 14 544–45; 60 325–27 (upd.)
Wagers Inc. (Idaho Candy Company), 86 416–19
Waggener Edstrom, 42 424–26
Wagon plc, 92 407–10
Wah Chang, 82 415–18
Wahl Clipper Corporation, 86 420–23
Wahoo's Fish Taco, 96 454–57
Wakefern Food Corporation, 33 434–37
Wal-Mart de Mexico, S.A. de C.V., 35 459–61 (upd.)
Wal-Mart Stores, Inc., V 216–17; 8 555–57 (upd.); 26 522–26 (upd.); 63 427–32 (upd.)

Walbridge Aldinger Co., 38 480–82
Walbro Corporation, 13 553–55
Waldbaum, Inc., 19 479–81
Waldenbooks, 17 522–24; 86 424–28 (upd.)
Walgreen Co., V 218–20; 20 511–13 (upd.); 65 352–56 (upd.)
Walker Manufacturing Company, 19 482–84
Walkers Shortbread Ltd., 79 464–67
Walkers Snack Foods Ltd., 70 350–52
Wall Drug Store, Inc., 40 455–57
Wall Street Deli, Inc., 33 438–41
Wallace Computer Services, Inc., 36 507–10
Walsworth Publishing Company, Inc., 78 445–48
The Walt Disney Company, II 172–74; 6 174–77 (upd.); 30 487–91 (upd.); 63 433–38 (upd.)
Walter E. Smithe Furniture, Inc., 105 484–87
Walter Industries, Inc., III 765–67; 22 544–47 (upd.); 72 368–73 (upd.)
Walton Monroe Mills, Inc., 8 558–60 *see also* Avondale Industries.
WaMu *see* Washington Mutual, Inc.
Wanadoo S.A., 75 400–02
Wang Laboratories, Inc., III 168–70; 6 284–87 (upd.) *see also* Getronics NV.
Warburtons Ltd., 89 487–90
WARF *see* Wisconsin Alumni Research Foundation.
The Warnaco Group Inc., 12 521–23; 46 450–54 (upd.) *see also* Authentic Fitness Corp.
Warner Chilcott Limited, 85 446–49
Warner Communications Inc., II 175–77 *see also* AOL Time Warner Inc.
Warner-Lambert Co., I 710–12; 10 549–52 (upd.) *see also* Pfizer Inc.
Warner Music Group Corporation, 90 432–37 (upd.)
Warners' Stellian Inc., 67 384–87
Warrantech Corporation, 53 357–59
Warrell Corporation, 68 396–98
Wärtsilä Corporation, 100 442–46
Warwick Valley Telephone Company, 55 382–84
Wascana Energy Inc., 13 556–58
The Washington Companies, 33 442–45
Washington Federal, Inc., 17 525–27
Washington Football, Inc., 35 462–65
Washington Gas Light Company, 19 485–88
Washington Mutual, Inc., 17 528–31; 93 483–89 (upd.)
Washington National Corporation, 12 524–26
Washington Natural Gas Company, 9 539–41 *see also* Puget Sound Energy Inc.
The Washington Post Company, IV 688–90; 20 515–18 (upd.)
Washington Scientific Industries, Inc., 17 532–34
Washington Water Power Company, 6 595–98 *see also* Avista Corp.

Wassall Plc, 18 548–50
Waste Connections, Inc., 46 455–57
Waste Holdings, Inc., 41 413–15
Waste Management, Inc., V 752–54
Water Pik Technologies, Inc., 34 498–501; 83 450–453 (upd.)
Waterford Wedgwood plc, 12 527–29; 34 493–97 (upd.) *see also* WWRD Holdings Ltd.
Waterhouse Investor Services, Inc., 18 551–53
Waters Corporation, 43 453–57
Watkins-Johnson Company, 15 528–30
Watsco Inc., 52 397–400
Watson Pharmaceuticals Inc., 16 527–29; 56 373–76 (upd.)
Watson Wyatt Worldwide, 42 427–30
Wattie's Ltd., 7 576–78
Watts Industries, Inc., 19 489–91
Watts of Lydney Group Ltd., 71 391–93
Wausau-Mosinee Paper Corporation, 60 328–31 (upd.)
Waverly, Inc., 16 530–32
Wawa Inc., 17 535–37; 78 449–52 (upd.)
The Wawanesa Mutual Insurance Company, 68 399–401
WAXIE Sanitary Supply, 100 447–51
Waxman Industries, Inc., 9 542–44
WAZ Media Group, 82 419–24
WB *see* Warner Communications Inc.
WD-40 Company, 18 554–57; 87 455–460 (upd.)
We-No-Nah Canoe, Inc., 98 460–63
Weather Central Inc., 100 452–55
The Weather Channel Companies, 52 401–04 *see also* Landmark Communications, Inc.
Weather Shield Manufacturing, Inc., 102 444–47
Weatherford International, Inc., 39 416–18
Weaver Popcorn Company, Inc., 89 491–93
Webasto Roof Systems Inc., 97 449–52
Webber Oil Company, 61 384–86
Weber et Broutin France, 66 363–65
Weber-Stephen Products Co., 40 458–60
WebEx Communications, Inc., 81 419–23
WebMD Corporation, 65 357–60
Webster Financial Corporation, 106 486–89
Weeres Industries Corporation, 52 405–07
Weetabix Limited, 61 387–89
Weg S.A., 78 453–56
Wegener NV, 53 360–62
Wegmans Food Markets, Inc., 9 545–46; 41 416–18 (upd.); 105 488–92 (upd.)
Weider Nutrition International, Inc., 29 498–501
Weight Watchers International Inc., 12 530–32; 33 446–49 (upd.); 73 379–83 (upd.)

Weil, Gotshal & Manges LLP, 55 385–87
Weiner's Stores, Inc., 33 450–53
Weingarten Realty Investors, 95 442–45
The Weir Group PLC, 85 450–53
Weirton Steel Corporation, IV 236–38; 26 527–30 (upd.)
Weis Markets, Inc., 15 531–33; 84 422–426 (upd.)
The Weitz Company, Inc., 42 431–34
Welbilt Corp., 19 492–94; *see also* Enodis plc.
Welch Foods Inc., 104 470–73
Welcome Wagon International Inc., 82 425–28
Weleda AG, 78 457–61
The Welk Group, Inc., 78 462–66
Wella AG, III 68–70; 48 420–23 (upd.)
WellCare Health Plans, Inc., 101 487–90
WellChoice, Inc., 67 388–91 (upd.)
Wellco Enterprises, Inc., 84 427–430
Wellcome Foundation Ltd., I 713–15 *see also* GlaxoSmithKline plc.
Wellman, Inc., 8 561–62; 52 408–11 (upd.)
WellPoint, Inc., 25 525–29; 103 505–14 (upd.)
Wells' Dairy, Inc., 36 511–13
Wells Fargo & Company, II 380–84; 12 533–37 (upd.); 38 483–92 (upd.); 97 453–67
Wells-Gardner Electronics Corporation, 43 458–61
Wells Rich Greene BDDP, 6 50–52
Wendell *see* Mark T. Wendell Tea Co.
Wendy's International, Inc., 8 563–65; 23 504–07 (upd.); 47 439–44 (upd.)
Wenner Bread Products Inc., 80 411–15
Wenner Media, Inc., 32 506–09
Werhahn *see* Wilh. Werhahn KG.
Werner Enterprises, Inc., 26 531–33
Weru Aktiengesellschaft, 18 558–61
Wessanen *see* Koninklijke Wessanen nv.
West Bend Co., 14 546–48
West Coast Entertainment Corporation, 29 502–04
West Corporation, 42 435–37
West Fraser Timber Co. Ltd., 17 538–40; 91 512–18 (upd.)
West Group, 34 502–06 (upd.)
West Linn Paper Company, 91 519–22
West Marine, Inc., 17 541–43; 90 438–42 (upd.)
West One Bancorp, 11 552–55 *see also* U.S. Bancorp.
West Pharmaceutical Services, Inc., 42 438–41
West Point-Pepperell, Inc., 8 566–69 *see also* WestPoint Stevens Inc.; JPS Textile Group, Inc.
West Publishing Co., 7 579–81
Westaff Inc., 33 454–57
Westamerica Bancorporation, 17 544–47
Westar Energy, Inc., 57 404–07 (upd.)
WestCoast Hospitality Corporation, 59 410–13

Westcon Group, Inc., 67 392–94

Westdeutsche Landesbank Girozentrale, II 385–87; 46 458–61 (upd.)

Westell Technologies, Inc., 57 408–10

Western Atlas Inc., 12 538–40

Western Beef, Inc., 22 548–50

Western Company of North America, 15 534–36

Western Digital Corporation, 25 530–32; 92 411–15 (upd.)

Western Gas Resources, Inc., 45 435–37

Western Oil Sands Inc., 85 454–57

Western Publishing Group, Inc., 13 559–61 see also Thomson Corp.

Western Resources, Inc., 12 541–43

The WesterN SizzliN Corporation, 60 335–37

Western Union Financial Services, Inc., 54 413–16

Western Wireless Corporation, 36 514–16

Westfield Group, 69 366–69

Westin Hotels and Resorts Worldwide, 9 547–49; 29 505–08 (upd.)

Westinghouse Electric Corporation, II 120–22; 12 544–47 (upd.) see also CBS Radio Group.

WestJet Airlines Ltd., 38 493–95

Westmoreland Coal Company, 7 582–85

Weston Foods Inc. see George Weston Ltd.

Westpac Banking Corporation, II 388–90; 48 424–27 (upd.)

WestPoint Stevens Inc., 16 533–36 see also JPS Textile Group, Inc.

Westport Resources Corporation, 63 439–41

Westvaco Corporation, IV 351–54; 19 495–99 (upd.) see also MeadWestvaco Corp.

Westwood One Inc., 23 508–11; 106 490–96 (upd.)

The Wet Seal, Inc., 18 562–64; 70 353–57 (upd.)

Wetterau Incorporated, II 681–82 see also Supervalu Inc.

Weyco Group, Incorporated, 32 510–13

Weyerhaeuser Company, IV 355–56; 9 550–52 (upd.); 28 514–17 (upd.); 83 454–461 (upd.)

WFS Financial Inc., 70 358–60

WFSC see World Fuel Services Corp.

WGBH Educational Foundation, 66 366–68

WH Smith PLC, 42 442–47 (upd.)

Wham-O, Inc., 61 390–93

Whataburger Restaurants LP, 105 493–97

Whatman plc, 46 462–65

Wheaton Industries, 8 570–73

Wheaton Science Products, 60 338–42 (upd.)

Wheelabrator Technologies, Inc., 6 599–600; 60 343–45 (upd.)

Wheeling-Pittsburgh Corporation, 7 586–88; 58 360–64 (upd.)

Wheels Inc., 96 458–61

Wherehouse Entertainment Incorporated, 11 556–58

Whirlpool Corporation, III 653–55; 12 548–50 (upd.); 59 414–19 (upd.)

Whitbread PLC, I 293–94; 20 519–22 (upd.); 52 412–17 (upd.); 97 468–76 (upd.)

White & Case LLP, 35 466–69

White Castle Management Company, 12 551–53; 36 517–20 (upd.); 85 458–64 (upd.)

White Consolidated Industries Inc., 13 562–64 see also Electrolux.

The White House, Inc., 60 346–48

White Lily Foods Company, 88 435–38

White Mountains Insurance Group, Ltd., 48 428–31

White Rose, Inc., 24 527–29

White Wave, 43 462–64

Whitehall Jewellers, Inc., 82 429–34 (upd.)

Whiting Petroleum Corporation, 81 424–27

Whiting-Turner Contracting Company, 95 446–49

Whitman Corporation, 10 553–55 (upd.) see also PepsiAmericas, Inc.

Whitman Education Group, Inc., 41 419–21

Whitney Holding Corporation, 21 522–24

Whittaker Corporation, I 544–46; 48 432–35 (upd.)

Whittard of Chelsea Plc, 61 394–97

Whole Foods Market, Inc., 20 523–27; 50 530–34 (upd.)

WHX Corporation, 98 464–67

Wickes Inc., V 221–23; 25 533–36 (upd.)

Widmer Brothers Brewing Company, 76 379–82

Wieden + Kennedy, 75 403–05

Wienerberger AG, 70 361–63

Wikimedia Foundation, Inc., 91 523–26

Wilbert, Inc., 56 377–80

Wilbur Chocolate Company, 66 369–71

Wilco Farm Stores, 93 490–93

Wild Oats Markets, Inc., 19 500–02; 41 422–25 (upd.)

Wildlife Conservation Society, 31 462–64

Wilh. Werhahn KG, 101 491–94

Wilh. Wilhelmsen ASA, 94 459–62

Wilhelm Karmann GmbH, 94 463–68

Wilkinson Hardware Stores Ltd., 80 416–18

Wilkinson Sword Ltd., 60 349–52

Willamette Industries, Inc., IV 357–59; 31 465–68 (upd.) see also Weyerhaeuser Co.

Willamette Valley Vineyards, Inc., 85 465–69

Willbros Group, Inc., 56 381–83

William Grant & Sons Ltd., 60 353–55

William Hill Organization Limited, 49 449–52

William Jackson & Son Ltd., 101 495–99

William L. Bonnell Company, Inc., 66 372–74

William Lyon Homes, 59 420–22

William Morris Agency, Inc., 23 512–14; 102 448–52 (upd.)

William Reed Publishing Ltd., 78 467–70

William Zinsser & Company, Inc., 58 365–67

Williams & Connolly LLP, 47 445–48

Williams Communications Group, Inc., 34 507–10

The Williams Companies, Inc., IV 575–76; 31 469–72 (upd.)

Williams Scotsman, Inc., 65 361–64

Williams-Sonoma, Inc., 17 548–50; 44 447–50 (upd.); 103 515–20 (upd.)

Williamson-Dickie Manufacturing Company, 14 549–50; 45 438–41 (upd.)

Willis Group Holdings Ltd., 25 537–39; 100 456–60 (upd.)

Willkie Farr & Gallagher LLPLP, 95 450–53

Willow Run Foods, Inc., 100 461–64

Wilmington Trust Corporation, 25 540–43

Wilson Bowden Plc, 45 442–44

Wilson Sonsini Goodrich & Rosati, 34 511–13

Wilson Sporting Goods Company, 24 530–32; 84 431–436 (upd.)

Wilsons The Leather Experts Inc., 21 525–27; 58 368–71 (upd.)

Wilton Products, Inc., 97 477–80

Winbond Electronics Corporation, 74 389–91

Wincanton plc, 52 418–20

Winchell's Donut Houses Operating Company, L.P., 60 356–59

WinCo Foods Inc., 60 360–63

Wincor Nixdorf Holding GmbH, 69 370–73 (upd.)

Wind River Systems, Inc., 37 419–22

Windmere Corporation, 16 537–39 see also Applica Inc.

Windstream Corporation, 83 462–465

Windswept Environmental Group, Inc., 62 389–92

The Wine Group, Inc., 39 419–21

Winegard Company, 56 384–87

Winmark Corporation, 74 392–95

Winn-Dixie Stores, Inc., II 683–84; 21 528–30 (upd.); 59 423–27 (upd.)

Winnebago Industries, Inc., 7 589–91; 27 509–12 (upd.); 96 462–67 (upd.)

WinsLoew Furniture, Inc., 21 531–33 see also Brown Jordan International Inc.

Winston & Strawn, 35 470–73

Winterthur Group, III 402–04; 68 402–05 (upd.)

Wintrust Financial Corporation, 106 497–501

Wipro Limited, 43 465–68; 106 502–07 (upd.)

The Wiremold Company, 81 428–34

Wirtz Corporation, 72 374–76

Wisconsin Alumni Research Foundation, 65 365–68

Wisconsin Bell, Inc., 14 551–53 *see also* AT&T Corp.

Wisconsin Central Transportation Corporation, 24 533–36

Wisconsin Dairies, 7 592–93

Wisconsin Energy Corporation, 6 601–03; 54 417–21 (upd.)

Wisconsin Public Service Corporation, 9 553–54 *see also* WPS Resources Corp.

Wise Foods, Inc., 79 468–71

Witco Corporation, I 404–06; 16 540–43 (upd.) *see also* Chemtura Corp.

Witness Systems, Inc., 87 461–465

Wizards of the Coast Inc., 24 537–40

WLR Foods, Inc., 21 534–36

Wm. B. Reily & Company Inc., 58 372–74

Wm. Morrison Supermarkets PLC, 38 496–98

Wm. Wrigley Jr.company, 7 594–97; 58 375–79 (upd.)

WMC, Limited, 43 469–72

WMF *see* Württembergische Metallwarenfabrik AG (WMF).

WMS Industries, Inc., 15 537–39; 53 363–66 (upd.)

WMX Technologies Inc., 17 551–54

Wolfgang Puck Worldwide, Inc., 26 534–36; 70 364–67 (upd.)

Wolohan Lumber Co., 19 503–05 *see also* Lanoga Corp.

Wolseley plc, 64 409–12

Wolters Kluwer NV, 14 554–56; 33 458–61 (upd.)

The Wolverhampton & Dudley Breweries, PLC, 57 411–14

Wolverine Tube Inc., 23 515–17

Wolverine World Wide, Inc., 16 544–47; 59 428–33 (upd.)

Womble Carlyle Sandridge & Rice, PLLC, 52 421–24

WonderWorks, Inc., 103 521–24

Wood Hall Trust plc, I 592–93

Wood-Mode, Inc., 23 518–20

Woodbridge Holdings Corporation, 99 482–485

Woodcraft Industries Inc., 61 398–400

Woodward Governor Company, 13 565–68; 49 453–57 (upd.); 105 498–505 (upd.)

Woolrich Inc., 62 393–96

The Woolwich plc, 30 492–95

Woolworth Corporation, V 224–27; 20 528–32 (upd.) *see also* Kingfisher plc; Venator Group Inc.

Woolworths Group plc, 83 466–473

WordPerfect Corporation, 10 556–59 *see also* Corel Corp.

Workflow Management, Inc., 65 369–72

Working Assets Funding Service, 43 473–76

Working Title Films Ltd., 105 506–09

Workman Publishing Company, Inc., 70 368–71

World Acceptance Corporation, 57 415–18

World Bank Group, 33 462–65

World Book, Inc., 12 554–56

World Color Press Inc., 12 557–59 *see also* Quebecor Inc.

World Duty Free Americas, Inc., 29 509–12 (upd.)

World Fuel Services Corporation, 47 449–51

World Kitchen, LLC, 104 474–77

World Publications, LLC, 65 373–75

World Vision International, Inc., 93 494–97

World Wide Technology, Inc., 94 469–72

World Wrestling Federation Entertainment, Inc., 32 514–17

WorldCorp, Inc., 10 560–62

World's Finest Chocolate Inc., 39 422–24

Worldwide Pants Inc., 97 481–84

Worldwide Restaurant Concepts, Inc., 47 452–55

Worms et Cie, 27 513–15 *see also* Sequana Capital.

Worthington Foods, Inc., 14 557–59 *see also* Kellogg Co.

Worthington Industries, Inc., 7 598–600; 21 537–40 (upd.)

WPL Holdings, 6 604–06

WPP Group plc, 6 53–54; 48 440–42 (upd.) *see also* Ogilvy Group Inc.

WPS Resources Corporation, 53 367–70 (upd.)

Wray & Nephew Group Ltd., 98 468–71

WRG *see* Wells Rich Greene BDDP.

Wright Express Corporation, 80 419–22

Wright Medical Group, Inc., 61 401–05

Writers Guild of America, West, Inc., 92 416–20

WS Atkins Plc, 45 445–47

WSI Corporation, 102 453–56

WTD Industries, Inc., 20 533–36

Wunderman, 86 429–32

Württembergische Metallwarenfabrik AG (WMF), 60 364–69

WuXi AppTec Company Ltd., 103 525–28

WVT Communications *see* Warwick Valley Telephone Co.

WWRD Holdings Limited, 106 508–15 (upd.)

Wyant Corporation, 30 496–98

Wyeth, 50 535–39 (upd.)

Wyle Electronics, 14 560–62 *see also* Arrow Electronics, Inc.

Wyman-Gordon Company, 14 563–65

Wyndham Worldwide Corporation, 99 486–493 (upd.)

Wynn's International, Inc., 33 466–70

Wyse Technology, Inc., 15 540–42

X

X-Rite, Inc., 48 443–46

Xantrex Technology Inc., 97 485–88

Xcel Energy Inc., 73 384–89 (upd.)

Xeikon NV, 26 540–42

Xerium Technologies, Inc., 94 473–76

Xerox Corporation, III 171–73; 6 288–90 (upd.); 26 543–47 (upd.); 69 374–80 (upd.)

Xilinx, Inc., 16 548–50; 82 435–39 (upd.)

XM Satellite Radio Holdings, Inc., 69 381–84

Xstrata PLC, 73 390–93

XTO Energy Inc., 52 425–27

Y

Yageo Corporation, 16 551–53; 98 472–75 (upd.)

Yahoo! Inc., 27 516–19; 70 372–75 (upd.)

Yamada Denki Co., Ltd., 85 470–73

Yamaha Corporation, III 656–59; 16 554–58 (upd.); 40 461–66 (upd.); 99 494–501 (upd.)

Yamaichi Securities Company, Limited, II 458–59

Yamato Transport Co. Ltd., V 536–38; 49 458–61 (upd.)

Yamazaki Baking Co., Ltd., 58 380–82

The Yankee Candle Company, Inc., 37 423–26; 38 192

YankeeNets LLC, 35 474–77

Yara International ASA, 94 477–81

Yarnell Ice Cream Company, Inc., 92 421–24

Yasuda Fire and Marine Insurance Company, Limited, III 405–07 *see also* Sompo Japan Insurance, Inc.

Yasuda Mutual Life Insurance Company, III 408–09; 39 425–28 (upd.)

The Yasuda Trust and Banking Company, Limited, II 391–92; 17 555–57 (upd.)

The Yates Companies, Inc., 62 397–99

Yell Group PLC, 79 472–75

Yellow Corporation, 14 566–68; 45 448–51 (upd.) *see also* YRC Worldwide Inc.

Yellow Freight System, Inc. of Deleware, V 539–41

Yeo Hiap Seng Malaysia Bhd., 75 406–09

YES! Entertainment Corporation, 26 548–50

Yingli Green Energy Holding Company Limited, 103 529–33

YMCA of the USA, 31 473–76

YOCREAM International, Inc., 47 456–58

Yokado Co. Ltd *see* Ito-Yokado Co. Ltd.

The Yokohama Rubber Company, Limited, V 254–56; 19 506–09 (upd.); 91 527–33 (upd.)

The York Group, Inc., 50 540–43

York International Corp., 13 569–71; *see also* Johnson Controls, Inc.

York Research Corporation, 35 478–80

Yoshinoya D & C Company Ltd., 88 439–42

Youbet.com, Inc., 77 485–88

Young & Co.'s Brewery, P.L.C., 38 499–502
Young & Rubicam, Inc., I 36–38; 22 551–54 (upd.); 66 375–78 (upd.)
Young Broadcasting Inc., 40 467–69
Young Innovations, Inc., 44 451–53
Young's Bluecrest Seafood Holdings Ltd., 81 435–39
Young's Market Company, LLC, 32 518–20
Younkers, 76 19 510–12; 383–86 (upd.)
Youth Services International, Inc., 21 541–43; 30 146
YouTube, Inc., 90 443–46
YPF Sociedad Anónima, IV 577–78 *see also* Repsol-YPF S.A.
YRC Worldwide Inc., 90 447–55 (upd.)
The Yucaipa Cos., 17 558–62
YUKOS *see* OAO NK YUKOS.
Yule Catto & Company plc, 54 422–25
Yum! Brands Inc., 58 383–85
Yves Rocher *see* Laboratoires de Biologie Végétale Yves Rocher.
YWCA of the U.S.A., 45 452–54

Z

Zachry Group, Inc., 95 454–57
Zacky Farms LLC, 74 396–98
Zain, 102 457–61
Zakłady Azotowe Puławy S.A., 100 465–68
Zale Corporation, 16 559–61; 40 470–74 (upd.); 91 534–41 (upd.)
Zambia Industrial and Mining Corporation Ltd., IV 239–41

Zamboni *see* Frank J. Zamboni & Co., Inc.
Zanett, Inc., 92 425–28
Zany Brainy, Inc., 31 477–79
Zapata Corporation, 25 544–46
Zapf Creation AG, 95 458–61
Zappos.com, Inc., 73 394–96
Zara International, Inc., 83 474–477
Zatarain's, Inc., 64 413–15
ZCMI *see* Zion's Cooperative Mercantile Institution.
Zebra Technologies Corporation, 14 569–71; 53 371–74 (upd.)
Zed Group, 93 498–501
Zeneca Group PLC, 21 544–46 *see also* AstraZeneca PLC.
Zenith Data Systems, Inc., 10 563–65
Zenith Electronics Corporation, II 123–25; 13 572–75 (upd.); 34 514–19 (upd.); 89 494–502 (upd.)
Zentiva N.V./Zentiva, a.s., 99 502–506
ZERO Corporation, 17 563–65; 88 443–47 (upd.)
ZF Friedrichshafen AG, 48 447–51
Ziebart International Corporation, 30 499–501; 66 379–82 (upd.)
The Ziegler Companies, Inc., 24 541–45; 63 442–48 (upd.)
Ziff Davis Media Inc., 12 560–63; 36 521–26 (upd.); 73 397–403 (upd.)
Zila, Inc., 46 466–69
Zildjian *see* Avedis Zildjian Co.
ZiLOG, Inc., 15 543–45; 72 377–80 (upd.)
Ziment Group Inc., 102 462–66

Zimmer Holdings, Inc., 45 455–57
Zindart Ltd., 60 370–72
Zingerman's Community of Businesses, 68 406–08
Zinifex Ltd., 85 474–77
Zinsser *see* William Zinsser & Company, Inc.
Zions Bancorporation, 12 564–66; 53 375–78 (upd.)
Zion's Cooperative Mercantile Institution, 33 471–74
Zipcar, Inc., 92 429–32
Zippo Manufacturing Company, 18 565–68; 71 394–99 (upd.)
Zodiac S.A., 36 527–30
Zogby International, Inc., 99 507–510
Zoltek Companies, Inc., 37 427–30
Zomba Records Ltd., 52 428–31
Zondervan Corporation, 24 546–49; 71 400–04 (upd.)
Zones, Inc., 67 395–97
Zoom Technologies, Inc., 18 569–71; 53 379–82 (upd.)
Zoran Corporation, 77 489–92
Zpizza International Inc., 105 510–13
The Zubair Corporation L.L.C., 96 468–72
Zuffa L.L.C., 89 503–07
Zumiez, Inc., 77 493–96
Zumtobel AG, 50 544–48
Zurich Financial Services, III 410–12; 42 448–53 (upd.); 93 502–10 (upd.)
Zygo Corporation, 42 454–57
Zytec Corporation, 19 513–15 *see also* Artesyn Technologies Inc.

Index to Industries

Accounting

American Institute of Certified Public Accountants (AICPA), 44
Andersen, 29 (upd.); 68 (upd.)
Automatic Data Processing, Inc., III; 9 (upd.); 47 (upd.)
BDO Seidman LLP, 96
BKD LLP, 96
CROSSMARK, 79
Deloitte Touche Tohmatsu International, 9; 29 (upd.)
Ernst & Young, 9; 29 (upd.)
FTI Consulting, Inc., 77
Grant Thornton International, 57
Huron Consulting Group Inc., 87
JKH Holding Co. LLC, 105
KPMG International, 33 (upd.)
L.S. Starrett Co., 13
McLane Company, Inc., 13
NCO Group, Inc., 42
Paychex, Inc., 15; 46 (upd.)
PKF International 78
Plante & Moran, LLP, 71
PRG-Schultz International, Inc., 73
PricewaterhouseCoopers, 9; 29 (upd.)
Resources Connection, Inc., 81
Robert Wood Johnson Foundation, 35
RSM McGladrey Business Services Inc., 98
Saffery Champness, 80
Sanders\Wingo, 99
Schenck Business Solutions, 88
StarTek, Inc., 79
Travelzoo Inc., 79
Univision Communications Inc., 24; 83 (upd.)

Advertising & Other Business Services

ABM Industries Incorporated, 25 (upd.)
Abt Associates Inc., 95
AchieveGlobal Inc., 90
Ackerley Communications, Inc., 9
ACNielsen Corporation, 13; 38 (upd.)
Acosta Sales and Marketing Company, Inc., 77
Acsys, Inc., 44
Adecco S.A., 36 (upd.)
Adelman Travel Group, 105
Adia S.A., 6
Administaff, Inc., 52
The Advertising Council, Inc., 76
The Advisory Board Company, 80
Advo, Inc., 6; 53 (upd.)
Aegis Group plc, 6
Affiliated Computer Services, Inc., 61
AHL Services, Inc., 27
Allegis Group, Inc., 95
Alloy, Inc., 55
Amdocs Ltd., 47
American Building Maintenance Industries, Inc., 6
American Library Association, 86
The American Society of Composers, Authors and Publishers (ASCAP), 29
Amey Plc, 47
Analysts International Corporation, 36
aQuantive, Inc., 81
The Arbitron Company, 38
Ariba, Inc., 57
Armor Holdings, Inc., 27
Asatsu-DK Inc., 82
Ashtead Group plc, 34
The Associated Press, 13
Avalon Correctional Services, Inc., 75

Bain & Company, 55
Barrett Business Services, Inc., 16
Barton Protective Services Inc., 53
Bates Worldwide, Inc., 14; 33 (upd.)
Bearings, Inc., 13
Berlitz International, Inc., 13; 39 (upd.)
Bernard Hodes Group Inc., 86
Bernstein-Rein, 92
Big Flower Press Holdings, Inc., 21
Billing Concepts, Inc., 26; 72 (upd.)
Billing Services Group Ltd., 102
The BISYS Group, Inc., 73
Booz Allen Hamilton Inc., 10; 101 (upd.)
Boron, LePore & Associates, Inc., 45
The Boston Consulting Group, 58
Bozell Worldwide Inc., 25
BrandPartners Group, Inc., 58
Bright Horizons Family Solutions, Inc., 31
Broadcast Music Inc., 23; 90 (upd.)
Buck Consultants, Inc., 55
Bureau Veritas SA, 55
Burke, Inc., 88
Burns International Services Corporation, 13; 41 (upd.)
Cambridge Technology Partners, Inc., 36
Campbell-Ewald Advertising, 86
Campbell-Mithun-Esty, Inc., 16
Cannon Design, 63
Capario, 104
Capita Group PLC, 69
Cardtronics, Inc., 93
Career Education Corporation, 45
Carmichael Lynch Inc., 28
Cash Systems, Inc., 93
Cazenove Group plc, 72
CCC Information Services Group Inc., 74
CDI Corporation, 6; 54 (upd.)
Cegedim S.A., 104
Central Parking System, 18; 104 (upd.)

Century Business Services, Inc., 52
Chancellor Beacon Academies, Inc., 53
ChartHouse International Learning
    Corporation, 49
Chiat/Day Inc. Advertising, 11
Chicago Board of Trade, 41
Chisholm-Mingo Group, Inc., 41
Christie's International plc, 15; 39 (upd.)
Cintas Corporation, 21
CMG Worldwide, Inc., 89
COMFORCE Corporation, 40
Command Security Corporation, 57
Computer Learning Centers, Inc., 26
Concentra Inc., 71
Corporate Express, Inc., 47 (upd.)
CoolSavings, Inc., 77
The Corporate Executive Board Company,
    89
CORT Business Services Corporation, 26
Cox Enterprises, Inc., IV; 22 (upd.); 67
    (upd.)
CRA International, Inc., 93
craigslist, inc., 89
Creative Artists Agency LLC, 38
Crispin Porter + Bogusky, 83
CSG Systems International, Inc., 75
Cyrk Inc., 19
Daiko Advertising Inc., 79
Dale Carnegie & Associates Inc. 28; 78
    (upd.)
D'Arcy Masius Benton & Bowles, Inc., 6;
    32 (upd.)
Dawson Holdings PLC, 43
DDB Needham Worldwide, 14
Deluxe Corporation, 22 (upd.); 73 (upd.)
Dentsu Inc., I; 16 (upd.); 40 (upd.)
Deutsch, Inc., 42
Deutsche Messe AG, 104
Deutsche Post AG, 29
DeVito/Verdi, 85
Dewberry 78
DHL Worldwide Network S.A./N.V., 69
    (upd.)
Digitas Inc., 81
DoubleClick Inc., 46
Draftfcb, 94
Drake Beam Morin, Inc., 44
The Dun & Bradstreet Corporation, 61
    (upd.)
Earl Scheib, Inc., 32
eBay Inc., 67 (upd.)
EBSCO Industries, Inc., 17
Ecolab Inc., I; 13 (upd.); 34 (upd.); 85
    (upd.)
Ecology and Environment, Inc., 39
Edelman, 62
Edison Schools Inc., 37
Educate Inc., 86 (upd.)
Education Management Corporation, 35
Electro Rent Corporation, 58
EMAK Worldwide, Inc., 105
Employee Solutions, Inc., 18
Ennis, Inc., 21; 97 (upd.)
Equifax Inc., 6; 28 (upd.); 90 (upd.)
Equity Marketing, Inc., 26
ERLY Industries Inc., 17
Euro RSCG Worldwide S.A., 13
Expedia, Inc., 58

Fallon Worldwide, 22; 71 (upd.)
FileNet Corporation, 62
Finarte Casa d'Aste S.p.A., 93
Fiserv, Inc., 11; 33 (upd.); 106 (upd.)
FlightSafety International, Inc., 29 (upd.)
Florists' Transworld Delivery, Inc., 28
Foote, Cone & Belding Worldwide, I; 66
    (upd.)
Forrester Research, Inc., 54
4imprint Group PLC, 105
Frankel & Co., 39
Franklin Covey Company, 37 (upd.)
Freeze.com LLC, 77
Frost & Sullivan, Inc., 53
FTI Consulting, Inc., 77
Gage Marketing Group, 26
Gallup, Inc., 37; 104 (upd.)
Gartner, Inc., 21; 94 (upd.)
GEMA (Gesellschaft für musikalische
    Aufführungs- und mechanische
    Vervielfältigungsrechte), 70
General Employment Enterprises, Inc., 87
George P. Johnson Company, 60
George S. May International Company,
    55
Gevity HR, Inc., 63
GfK Aktiengesellschaft, 49
Glotel plc, 53
Golin/Harris International, Inc., 88
Goodby Silverstein & Partners, Inc., 75
Grey Global Group Inc., 6; 66 (upd.)
Group 4 Falck A/S, 42
Groupe Crit S.A., 74
Groupe Jean-Claude Darmon, 44
GSD&M Advertising, 44
GSD&M's Idea City, 90
GSI Commerce, Inc., 67
Guardsmark, L.L.C., 77
Gwathmey Siegel & Associates Architects
    LLC, 26
Ha-Lo Industries, Inc., 27
Hakuhodo, Inc., 6; 42 (upd.)
Hall, Kinion & Associates, Inc., 52
Handleman Company, 15; 86 (upd.)
Harris Interactive Inc., 41; 92 (upd.)
Harte-Hanks, Inc., 63 (upd.)
Havas SA, 33 (upd.)
Hay Group Holdings, Inc., 100
Hays plc, 27; 78 (upd.)
Headway Corporate Resources, Inc., 40
Heidrick & Struggles International, Inc.,
    28
Henry Dreyfuss Associates LLC, 88
The Hertz Corporation, 9; 33 (upd.); 101
    (upd.)
Hewitt Associates, Inc., 77
Hildebrandt International, 29
Hogg Robinson Group PLC, 105
Idearc Inc., 90
IKON Office Solutions, Inc., 50
IMS Health, Inc., 57
Interbrand Corporation, 70
Interep National Radio Sales Inc., 35
International Brotherhood of Teamsters,
    37
International Management Group, 18
International Profit Associates, Inc., 87
International Total Services, Inc., 37

The Interpublic Group of Companies,
    Inc., I; 22 (upd.); 75 (upd.)
Intertek Group plc, 95
inVentiv Health, Inc., 81
Ipsos SA, 48
Iron Mountain, Inc., 33; 104 (upd.)
ITT Educational Services, Inc., 39; 76
    (upd.)
J.D. Power and Associates, 32
Jack Morton Worldwide, 88
Jackson Hewitt, Inc., 48
Jani-King International, Inc., 85
Japan Leasing Corporation, 8
JCDecaux S.A., 76
Jostens, Inc., 25 (upd.)
JOULÉ Inc., 58
JTH Tax Inc., 103
JWT Group Inc., I
Katz Communications, Inc., 6
Katz Media Group, Inc., 35
Keane, Inc., 56
Kelly Services Inc., 6; 26 (upd.)
Ketchum Communications Inc., 6
Kforce Inc., 71
Kinko's Inc., 16; 43 (upd.)
Kirshenbaum Bond + Partners, Inc., 57
Kohn Pedersen Fox Associates P.C., 57
Korn/Ferry International, 34; 102 (upd.)
Kroll Inc., 57
L. M. Berry and Company, 80
Labor Ready, Inc., 29; 88 (upd.)
Lamar Advertising Company, 27; 70
    (upd.)
Landor Associates, 81
Le Cordon Bleu S.A., 67
Learning Care Group, Inc., 76 (upd.)
Learning Tree International Inc., 24
LECG Corporation, 93
Leo Burnett Company Inc., I; 20 (upd.)
The Leona Group LLC, 84
The Lewin Group Inc., 104
LinkedIn Corporation, 103
Lintas: Worldwide, 14
LivePerson, Inc., 91
Mail Boxes Etc., 18; 41 (upd.)
Manhattan Associates, Inc., 67
Manning Selvage & Lee (MS&L), 76
Manpower Inc., 30 (upd.); 73 (upd.)
Marchex, Inc., 72
marchFIRST, Inc., 34
Marco Business Products, Inc., 75
Maritz Inc., 38
Marlin Business Services Corp., 89
MAXIMUS, Inc., 43
McMurry, Inc., 105
MDC Partners Inc., 63
Mediaset SpA, 50
Milliman USA, 66
MIVA, Inc., 83
Monster Worldwide Inc., 74 (upd.)
Moody's Corporation, 65
MPS Group, Inc., 49
Mullen Advertising Inc., 51
Napster, Inc., 69
National CineMedia, Inc., 103
National Equipment Services, Inc., 57
National Media Corporation, 27
Navigant Consulting, Inc., 93

NAVTEQ Corporation, 69
Neopost S.A., 53
New England Business Services Inc., 18; 78 (upd.)
New Valley Corporation, 17
NFO Worldwide, Inc., 24
Nobel Learning Communities, Inc., 37; 76 (upd.)
Norrell Corporation, 25
Norwood Promotional Products, Inc., 26
The NPD Group, Inc., 68
O.C. Tanner Co., 69
Oakleaf Waste Management, LLC, 97
Obie Media Corporation, 56
Observer AB, 55
OfficeTiger, LLC, 75
The Ogilvy Group, Inc., I
Olsten Corporation, 6; 29 (upd.)
Omnicom Group, I; 22 (upd.); 77 (upd.)
On Assignment, Inc., 20
1-800-FLOWERS.COM, Inc., 26; 102 (upd.)
Opinion Research Corporation, 46
Oracle Corporation, 67 (upd.)
Orbitz, Inc., 61
The Orchard Enterprises, Inc., 103
Outdoor Systems, Inc., 25
Paris Corporation, 22
Paychex, Inc., 15; 46 (upd.)
PDI, Inc., 52
Pegasus Solutions, Inc., 75
Pei Cobb Freed & Partners Architects LLP, 57
Penauille Polyservices SA, 49
PFSweb, Inc., 73
Philip Services Corp., 73
Phillips, de Pury & Luxembourg, 49
Pierce Leahy Corporation, 24
Pinkerton's Inc., 9
Plante & Moran, LLP, 71
PMT Services, Inc., 24
Posterscope Worldwide, 70
Priceline.com Incorporated, 57
Publicis Groupe, 19; 77 (upd.)
Publishers Clearing House, 23; 64 (upd.)
Quintiles Transnational Corporation, 68 (upd.)
Quovadx Inc., 70
@radical.media, 103
Randstad Holding n.v., 16; 43 (upd.)
RedPeg Marketing, 73
RedPrairie Corporation, 74
RemedyTemp, Inc., 20
Rental Service Corporation, 28
Rentokil Initial Plc, 47
Research Triangle Institute, 83
Resources Connection, Inc., 81
Rewards Network Inc., 70 (upd.)
The Richards Group, Inc., 58
Right Management Consultants, Inc., 42
Ritchie Bros. Auctioneers Inc., 41
Robert Half International Inc., 18
Roland Berger & Partner GmbH, 37
Ronco Corporation, 15; 80 (upd.)
Russell Reynolds Associates Inc., 38
Saatchi & Saatchi, I; 42 (upd.)
Sanders\Wingo, 99
Schenck Business Solutions, 88

Securitas AB, 42
ServiceMaster Limited Partnership, 6
Servpro Industries, Inc., 85
Shared Medical Systems Corporation, 14
Sir Speedy, Inc., 16
Skidmore, Owings & Merrill LLP, 13; 69 (upd.)
SmartForce PLC, 43
SOS Staffing Services, 25
Sotheby's Holdings, Inc., 11; 29 (upd.); 84 (upd.)
Source Interlink Companies, Inc., 75
Spencer Stuart and Associates, Inc., 14
Spherion Corporation, 52
SSI (U.S.) Inc., 103 (upd.)
Steiner Corporation (Alsco), 53
Strayer Education, Inc., 53
Superior Uniform Group, Inc., 30
Sykes Enterprises, Inc., 45
Sylvan Learning Systems, Inc., 35
Synchronoss Technologies, Inc., 95
TA Triumph-Adler AG, 48
Taylor Nelson Sofres plc, 34
TBA Global, LLC, 99
TBWA/Chiat/Day, 6; 43 (upd.)
Thomas Cook Travel Inc., 33 (upd.)
Ticketmaster, 76 (upd.)
Ticketmaster Group, Inc., 13; 37 (upd.)
TMP Worldwide Inc., 30
TNT Post Group N.V., 30
Towers Perrin, 32
Trader Classified Media N.V., 57
Traffix, Inc., 61
Transmedia Network Inc., 20
Treasure Chest Advertising Company, Inc., 32
TRM Copy Centers Corporation, 18
True North Communications Inc., 23
24/7 Real Media, Inc., 49
Tyler Corporation, 23
U.S. Office Products Company, 25
Unica Corporation, 77
UniFirst Corporation, 21
United Business Media plc, 52 (upd.)
United News & Media plc, 28 (upd.)
Unitog Co., 19
Valassis Communications, Inc., 37 (upd.); 76 (upd.)
ValleyCrest Companies, 81 (upd.)
ValueClick, Inc., 49
Vebego International BV, 49
Vedior NV, 35
Vertis Communications, 84
Vertrue Inc., 77
Viad Corp., 73
W.B Doner & Co., 56
The Wackenhut Corporation, 14; 63 (upd.)
Waggener Edstrom, 42
Warrantech Corporation, 53
WebEx Communications, Inc., 81
Welcome Wagon International Inc., 82
Wells Rich Greene BDDP, 6
Westaff Inc., 33
Whitman Education Group, Inc., 41
Wieden + Kennedy, 75
William Morris Agency, Inc., 23; 102 (upd.)

Williams Scotsman, Inc., 65
Workflow Management, Inc., 65
WPP Group plc, 6; 48 (upd.)
Wunderman, 86
Xerox Corporation, III; 6 (upd.); 26 (upd.); 69 (upd.)
Young & Rubicam, Inc., I; 22 (upd.); 66 (upd.)
Ziment Group Inc., 102
Zogby International, Inc., 99

Aerospace

A.S. Yakovlev Design Bureau, 15
Aerojet-General Corp., 63
Aeronca Inc., 46
Aerosonic Corporation, 69
The Aerospatiale Group, 7; 21 (upd.)
AeroVironment, Inc., 97
AgustaWestland N.V., 75
Airborne Systems Group, 89
Alliant Techsystems Inc., 30 (upd.)
Antonov Design Bureau, 53
Arianespace S.A., 89
Aviacionny Nauchno-Tehnicheskii Komplex im. A.N. Tupoleva, 24
Aviall, Inc., 73
Avions Marcel Dassault-Breguet Aviation, I
B/E Aerospace, Inc., 30
Ballistic Recovery Systems, Inc., 87
Banner Aerospace, Inc., 14
BBA Aviation plc, 90
Beech Aircraft Corporation, 8
Bell Helicopter Textron Inc., 46
The Boeing Company, I; 10 (upd.); 32 (upd.)
Bombardier Inc., 42 (upd.); 87 (upd.)
British Aerospace plc, I; 24 (upd.)
CAE USA Inc., 48
Canadair, Inc., 16
Cessna Aircraft Company, 8
Cirrus Design Corporation, 44
Cobham plc, 30
CPI Aerostructures, Inc., 75
Daimler-Benz Aerospace AG, 16
DeCrane Aircraft Holdings Inc., 36
Derco Holding Ltd., 98
Diehl Stiftung & Co. KG, 79
Ducommun Incorporated, 30
Duncan Aviation, Inc., 94
EADS SOCATA, 54
Eclipse Aviation Corporation, 87
EGL, Inc., 59
Empresa Brasileira de Aeronáutica S.A. (Embraer), 36
European Aeronautic Defence and Space Company EADS N.V., 52 (upd.)
Fairchild Aircraft, Inc., 9
Fairchild Dornier GmbH, 48 (upd.)
Finmeccanica S.p.A., 84
First Aviation Services Inc., 49
G.I.E. Airbus Industrie, I; 12 (upd.)
General Dynamics Corporation, I; 10 (upd.); 40 (upd.); 88 (upd.
GKN plc, III; 38 (upd.); 89 (upd.)
Goodrich Corporation, 46 (upd.)
Groupe Dassault Aviation SA, 26 (upd.)
Grumman Corporation, I; 11 (upd.)

Grupo Aeropuerto del Sureste, S.A. de C.V., 48
Gulfstream Aerospace Corporation, 7; 28 (upd.)
HEICO Corporation, 30
International Lease Finance Corporation, 48
Irkut Corporation, 68
Israel Aircraft Industries Ltd., 69
Kolbenschmidt Pierburg AG, 97
N.V. Koninklijke Nederlandse Vliegtuigenfabriek Fokker, I; 28 (upd.)
Kreisler Manufacturing Corporation, 97
Lancair International, Inc., 67
Learjet Inc., 8; 27 (upd.)
Lockheed Martin Corporation, I; 11 (upd.); 15 (upd.); 89 (upd.)
Loral Space & Communications Ltd., 54 (upd.)
Magellan Aerospace Corporation, 48
Martin Marietta Corporation, I
Martin-Baker Aircraft Company Limited, 61
McDonnell Douglas Corporation, I; 11 (upd.)
Meggitt PLC, 34
Messerschmitt-Bölkow-Blohm GmbH., I
Moog Inc., 13
Mooney Aerospace Group Ltd., 52
The New Piper Aircraft, Inc., 44
Northrop Grumman Corporation, I; 11 (upd.); 45 (upd.)
Orbital Sciences Corporation, 22
Pemco Aviation Group Inc., 54
Pratt & Whitney, 9
Raytheon Aircraft Holdings Inc., 46
Raytheon Company, II; 11 (upd.); 38 (upd.); 105 (upd.)
Robinson Helicopter Company, 51
Rockwell Collins, 106
Rockwell International Corporation, I; 11 (upd.)
Rolls-Royce Allison, 29 (upd.)
Rolls-Royce plc, I; 7 (upd.); 21 (upd.)
Rostvertol plc, 62
Russian Aircraft Corporation (MiG), 86
Safe Flight Instrument Corporation, 71
Sequa Corp., 13
Shannon Aerospace Ltd., 36
Sikorsky Aircraft Corporation, 24; 104 (upd.)
Smiths Industries PLC, 25
Snecma Group, 46
Société Air France, 27 (upd.)
Spacehab, Inc., 37
Spar Aerospace Limited, 32
Sukhoi Design Bureau Aviation Scientific-Industrial Complex, 24
Sundstrand Corporation, 7; 21 (upd.)
Surrey Satellite Technology Limited, 83
Swales & Associates, Inc., 69
Teledyne Technologies Inc., 62 (upd.)
Textron Lycoming Turbine Engine, 9
Thales S.A., 42
Thiokol Corporation, 9; 22 (upd.)
United Technologies Corporation, I; 10 (upd.); 34 (upd.); 105 (upd.)
Van's Aircraft, Inc., 65

Vector Aerospace Corporation, 97
Vought Aircraft Industries, Inc., 49
Whittaker Corporation, 48 (upd.)
Woodward Governor Company, 13; 49 (upd.); 105 (upd.)
Zodiac S.A., 36

Airlines

Aer Lingus Group plc, 34; 89 (upd.)
Aeroflot - Russian Airlines JSC, 6; 29 (upd.); 89 (upd.)
Aerolíneas Argentinas S.A., 33; 69 (upd.)
Air Berlin GmbH & Co. Luftverkehrs KG, 71
Air Canada, 6; 23 (upd.); 59 (upd.)
Air China, 46
Air Jamaica Limited, 54
Air Mauritius Ltd., 63
Air New Zealand Limited, 14; 38 (upd.)
Air Pacific Ltd., 70
Air Partner PLC, 93
Air Sahara Limited, 65
Air Wisconsin Airlines Corporation, 55
Air Zimbabwe (Private) Limited, 91
Air-India Limited, 6; 27 (upd.)
AirAsia Berhad, 93
AirTran Holdings, Inc., 22
Alaska Air Group, Inc., 6; 29 (upd.)
Alitalia-Linee Aeree Italiana, S.p.A., 6; 29 (upd.); 97 (upd.)
All Nippon Airways Co., Ltd., 6; 38 (upd.); 91 (upd.)
Allegiant Travel Company, 97
Aloha Airlines, Incorporated, 24
America West Holdings Corporation, 6; 34 (upd.)
American Airlines, I; 6 (upd.)
AMR Corporation, 28 (upd.); 52 (upd.)
Amtran, Inc., 34
Arrow Air Holdings Corporation, 55
A/S Air Baltic Corporation, 71
AS Estonian Air, 71
Asiana Airlines, Inc., 46
ATA Holdings Corporation, 82
Atlantic Coast Airlines Holdings, Inc., 55
Atlantic Southeast Airlines, Inc., 47
Atlas Air, Inc., 39
Austrian Airlines AG (Österreichische Luftverkehrs AG), 33
Aviacionny Nauchno-Tehnicheskii Komplex im. A.N. Tupoleva, 24
Avianca Aerovías Nacionales de Colombia SA, 36
Azerbaijan Airlines, 77
Bahamas Air Holdings Ltd., 66
Banner Aerospace, Inc., 37 (upd.)
Braathens ASA, 47
Bradley Air Services Ltd., 56
Bristow Helicopters Ltd., 70
British Airways PLC, I; 14 (upd.); 43 (upd.); 105 (upd.)
British Midland plc, 38
British World Airlines Ltd., 18
Cargolux Airlines International S.A., 49
Cathay Pacific Airways Limited, 6; 34 (upd.)
Ceské aerolinie, a.s., 66
Chautauqua Airlines, Inc., 38

China Airlines, 34
China Eastern Airlines Co. Ltd., 31
China Southern Airlines Company Ltd., 33
Comair Holdings Inc., 13; 34 (upd.)
Consorcio Aviacsa, S.A. de C.V., 85
Continental Airlines, Inc., I; 21 (upd.); 52 (upd.)
Copa Holdings, S.A., 93
Corporación Internacional de Aviación, S.A. de C.V. (Cintra), 20
Cyprus Airways Public Limited, 81
dba Luftfahrtgesellschaft mbH, 76
Delta Air Lines, Inc., I; 6 (upd.); 39 (upd.); 92 (upd.)
Deutsche Lufthansa AG, I; 26 (upd.); 68 (upd.)
Eastern Airlines, I
easyJet Airline Company Limited, 39
EgyptAir, 6; 27 (upd.)
El Al Israel Airlines Ltd., 23
The Emirates Group, 39; 81 (upd.)
Ethiopian Airlines, 81
Etihad Airways PJSC, 89
Eurocopter S.A., 80
EVA Airways Corporation, 51
Finnair Oyj, 6; 25 (upd.); 61 (upd.)
Flight Options, LLC, 75
Flying Boat, Inc. (Chalk's Ocean Airways), 56
Frontier Airlines Holdings Inc., 22; 84 (upd.)
Garuda Indonesia, 6
Gol Linhas Aéreas Inteligentes S.A., 73
Groupe Air France, 6
Grupo Aeroportuario del Pacífico, S.A. de C.V., 85
Grupo TACA, 38
Gulf Air Company, 56
Hawaiian Holdings, Inc., 9; 22 (upd.); 96 (upd.)
Hong Kong Dragon Airlines Ltd., 66
Iberia Líneas Aéreas de España S.A., 6; 36 (upd.); 91 (upd.)
Icelandair, 52
Indian Airlines Ltd., 46
IranAir, 81
Japan Air Lines Company Ltd., I; 32 (upd.)
Jersey European Airways (UK) Ltd., 61
Jet Airways (India) Private Limited, 65
JetBlue Airways Corporation, 44
Kenmore Air Harbor Inc., 65
Kenya Airways Limited, 89
Kitty Hawk, Inc., 22
Kiwi International Airlines Inc., 20
KLM Royal Dutch Airlines, 104 (upd.)
Koninklijke Luchtvaart Maatschappij, N.V. (KLM Royal Dutch Airlines), I; 28 (upd.)
Korean Air Lines Co., Ltd., 6; 27 (upd.)
Kuwait Airways Corporation, 68
Lan Chile S.A., 31
Lauda Air Luftfahrt AG, 48
Lloyd Aéreo Boliviano S.A., 95
Loganair Ltd., 68
LOT Polish Airlines (Polskie Linie Lotnicze S.A.), 33

LTU Group Holding GmbH, 37
Malév Plc, 24
Malaysian Airlines System Berhad, 6; 29 (upd.); 97 (upd.)
Mesa Air Group, Inc., 11; 32 (upd.); 77 (upd.)
Mesaba Holdings, Inc., 28
Middle East Airlines - Air Liban S.A.L., 79
Midway Airlines Corporation, 33
Midwest Air Group, Inc., 35; 85 (upd.)
MN Airlines LLC, 104
NetJets Inc., 96 (upd.)
Northwest Airlines Corporation, I; 6 (upd.); 26 (upd.); 74 (upd.)
Offshore Logistics, Inc., 37
Pakistan International Airlines Corporation, 46
Pan American World Airways, Inc., I; 12 (upd.)
Panalpina World Transport (Holding) Ltd., 47
People Express Airlines, Inc., I
Petroleum Helicopters, Inc., 35
PHI, Inc., 80 (upd.)
Philippine Airlines, Inc., 6; 23 (upd.)
Pinnacle Airlines Corp., 73
Preussag AG, 42 (upd.)
Qantas Airways Ltd., 6; 24 (upd.); 68 (upd.)
Qatar Airways Company Q.C.S.C., 87
Reno Air Inc., 23
Royal Brunei Airlines Sdn Bhd, 99
Royal Nepal Airline Corporation, 41
Ryanair Holdings plc, 35
SAA (Pty) Ltd., 28
Sabena S.A./N.V., 33
The SAS Group, 34 (upd.)
Saudi Arabian Airlines, 6; 27 (upd.)
Scandinavian Airlines System, I
Sikorsky Aircraft Corporation, 24; 104 (upd.)
Singapore Airlines Limited, 6; 27 (upd.); 83 (upd.)
SkyWest, Inc., 25
Société d'Exploitation AOM Air Liberté SA (AirLib), 53
Société Luxembourgeoise de Navigation Aérienne S.A., 64
Société Tunisienne de l'Air-Tunisair, 49
Southwest Airlines Co., 6; 24 (upd.); 71 (upd.)
Spirit Airlines, Inc., 31
Sterling European Airlines A/S, 70
Sun Country Airlines, 30
Swiss Air Transport Company, Ltd., I
Swiss International Air Lines Ltd., 48
TAM Linhas Aéreas S.A., 68
TAME (Transportes Aéreos Militares Ecuatorianos), 100
TAP—Air Portugal Transportes Aéreos Portugueses S.A., 46
TAROM S.A., 64
Texas Air Corporation, I
Thai Airways International Public Company Limited, 6; 27 (upd.)
Tower Air, Inc., 28

Trans World Airlines, Inc., I; 12 (upd.); 35 (upd.)
TransBrasil S/A Linhas Aéreas, 31
Transportes Aereos Portugueses, S.A., 6
Turkish Airlines Inc. (Türk Hava Yollari A.O.), 72
TV Guide, Inc., 43 (upd.)
UAL Corporation, 34 (upd.)
United Airlines, I; 6 (upd.)
US Airways Group, Inc., I; 6 (upd.); 28 (upd.); 52 (upd.)
VARIG S.A. (Viação Aérea Rio-Grandense), 6; 29 (upd.)
Virgin Group Ltd., 12; 32 (upd.); 89 (upd.)
Volga-Dnepr Group, 82
Vueling Airlines S.A., 97
WestJet Airlines Ltd., 38
Uzbekistan Airways National Air Company, 99

Automotive

AB Volvo, I; 7 (upd.); 26 (upd.); 67 (upd.)
Accubuilt, Inc., 74
Adam Opel AG, 7; 21 (upd.); 61 (upd.)
ADESA, Inc., 71
Advance Auto Parts, Inc., 57
Aftermarket Technology Corp., 83
Aisin Seiki Co., Ltd., 48 (upd.)
Alamo Rent A Car, Inc., 6; 24 (upd.); 84 (upd.)
Alfa Romeo, 13; 36 (upd.)
Alvis Plc, 47
America's Car-Mart, Inc., 64
American Motors Corporation, I
Amerigon Incorporated, 97
Andretti Green Racing, 106
Applied Power Inc., 32 (upd.)
Arnold Clark Automobiles Ltd., 60
ArvinMeritor, Inc., 8; 54 (upd.)
Asbury Automotive Group Inc., 60
ASC, Inc., 55
Autobacs Seven Company Ltd., 76
Autocam Corporation, 51
Autoliv, Inc., 65
Automobiles Citroen, 7
Automobili Lamborghini Holding S.p.A., 13; 34 (upd.); 91 (upd.)
AutoNation, Inc., 50
AutoTrader.com, L.L.C., 91
AVTOVAZ Joint Stock Company, 65
Bajaj Auto Limited, 39
Bayerische Motoren Werke AG, I; 11 (upd.); 38 (upd.)
Belron International Ltd., 76
Bendix Corporation, I
Blue Bird Corporation, 35
Bombardier Inc., 42 (upd.)
BorgWarner Inc., 14; 32 (upd.); 85 (upd.)
The Budd Company, 8
Bugatti Automobiles S.A.S., 94
Caffyns PLC, 105
Canadian Tire Corporation, Limited, 71 (upd.)
CarMax, Inc., 55
CARQUEST Corporation, 29
Caterpillar Inc., 63 (upd.)

Checker Motors Corp., 89
China Automotive Systems Inc., 87
China FAW Group Corporation, 105
Chrysler Corporation, I; 11 (upd.)
Commercial Vehicle Group, Inc., 81
CNH Global N.V., 38 (upd.); 99 (upd.)
Consorcio G Grupo Dina, S.A. de C.V., 36
Crown Equipment Corporation, 15; 93 (upd.)
CSK Auto Corporation, 38
Cummins Engine Company, Inc., I; 12 (upd.); 40 (upd.)
Custom Chrome, Inc., 16
Daihatsu Motor Company, Ltd., 7; 21 (upd.)
Daimler-Benz A.G., I; 15 (upd.)
DaimlerChrysler AG, 34 (upd.); 64 (upd.)
Dana Holding Corporation, I; 10 (upd.); 99 (upd.)
Danaher Corporation, 77 (upd.)
Deere & Company, 42 (upd.)
Delphi Automotive Systems Corporation, 45
D'Ieteren S.A./NV, 98
Directed Electronics, Inc., 87
Discount Tire Company Inc., 84
Don Massey Cadillac, Inc., 37
Donaldson Company, Inc., 49 (upd.)
Dongfeng Motor Corporation, 105
Douglas & Lomason Company, 16
Dräxlmaier Group, 90
DriveTime Automotive Group Inc., 68 (upd.)
Ducati Motor Holding SpA, 30; 86 (upd.)
Eaton Corporation, I; 10 (upd.); 67 (upd.)
Echlin Inc., I; 11 (upd.)
Edelbrock Corporation, 37
Europcar Groupe S.A., 104
Faurecia S.A., 70
Federal-Mogul Corporation, I; 10 (upd.); 26 (upd.)
Ferrara Fire Apparatus, Inc., 84
Ferrari S.p.A., 13; 36 (upd.)
Fiat SpA, I; 11 (upd.); 50 (upd.)
FinishMaster, Inc., 24
Force Protection Inc., 95
Ford Motor Company, I; 11 (upd.); 36 (upd.); 64 (upd.)
Ford Motor Company, S.A. de C.V., 20
Fruehauf Corporation, I
General Motors Corporation, I; 10 (upd.); 36 (upd.); 64 (upd.)
Gentex Corporation, 26
Genuine Parts Company, 9; 45 (upd.)
GKN plc, III; 38 (upd.); 89 (upd.)
Group 1 Automotive, Inc., 52
Groupe Henri Heuliez S.A., 100
Grupo Ficosa International, 90
Guardian Industries Corp., 87
Harley-Davidson Inc., 7; 25 (upd.); 106 (upd.)
Hastings Manufacturing Company, 56
Hayes Lemmerz International, Inc., 27
Hendrick Motorsports, Inc., 89
The Hertz Corporation, 9; 33 (upd.); 101 (upd.)

Hino Motors, Ltd., 7; 21 (upd.)
Holden Ltd., 62
Holley Performance Products Inc., 52
Hometown Auto Retailers, Inc., 44
Honda Motor Company Limited (Honda Giken Kogyo Kabushiki Kaisha), I; 10 (upd.); 29 (upd.); 96 (upd.)
Hyundai Group, III; 7 (upd.); 56 (upd.)
Insurance Auto Auctions, Inc., 23
Isuzu Motors, Ltd., 9; 23 (upd.); 57 (upd.)
INTERMET Corporation, 77 (upd.)
Jardine Cycle & Carriage Ltd., 73
Kawasaki Heavy Industries, Ltd., 63 (upd.)
Kelsey-Hayes Group of Companies, 7; 27 (upd.)
Key Safety Systems, Inc., 63
Kia Motors Corporation, 12; 29 (upd.)
Kolbenschmidt Pierburg AG, 97
Kwik-Fit Holdings plc, 54
Lazy Days RV Center, Inc., 69
Lear Corporation, 71 (upd.)
Lear Seating Corporation, 16
Les Schwab Tire Centers, 50
Lithia Motors, Inc., 41
LKQ Corporation, 71
Lookers plc, 71
Lotus Cars Ltd., 14
Lund International Holdings, Inc., 40
Mack Trucks, Inc., I; 22 (upd.); 61 (upd.)
The Major Automotive Companies, Inc., 45
Marcopolo S.A., 79
Masland Corporation, 17
Mazda Motor Corporation, 9; 23 (upd.); 63 (upd.)
Mel Farr Automotive Group, 20
Metso Corporation, 30 (upd.)
Midas Inc., 10; 56 (upd.)
Mitsubishi Motors Corporation, 9; 23 (upd.); 57 (upd.)
Monaco Coach Corporation, 31
Monro Muffler Brake, Inc., 24
Montupet S.A., 63
Morgan Motor Company, 105
National R.V. Holdings, Inc., 32
Navistar International Corporation, I; 10 (upd.)
New Flyer Industries Inc. 78
Nissan Motor Company Ltd., I; 11 (upd.); 34 (upd.); 92 (upd.)
O'Reilly Automotive, Inc., 26; 78 (upd.)
Officine Alfieri Maserati S.p.A., 13
Oshkosh Corporation, 7; 98 (upd.)
Paccar Inc., I
PACCAR Inc., 26 (upd.)
Park-Ohio Holdings Corp., 17; 85 (upd.)
Parker-Hannifin Corporation, III; 24 (upd.); 99 (upd.)
Pennzoil-Quaker State Company, IV; 20 (upd.); 50 (upd.)
Penske Corporation, V; 19 (upd.); 84 (upd.)
The Pep Boys—Manny, Moe & Jack, 11; 36 (upd.); 81 (upd.)
Perusahaan Otomobil Nasional Bhd., 62
Peterbilt Motors Company, 89

Peugeot S.A., I
Piaggio & C. S.p.A., 20;100 (upd.)
Pirelli & C. S.p.A., 75 (upd.)
Porsche AG, 13; 31 (upd.)
PSA Peugeot Citroen S.A., 28 (upd.)
R&B, Inc., 51
Randon S.A., 79
Red McCombs Automotive Group, 91
Regal-Beloit Corporation, 18; 97 (upd.)
Regie Nationale des Usines Renault, I
Renault Argentina S.A., 67
Renault S.A., 26 (upd.); 74 (upd.)
Repco Corporation Ltd., 74
Republic Industries, Inc., 26
The Reynolds and Reynolds Company, 50
Rheinmetall AG, 9; 97 (upd.)
Riviera Tool Company, 89
Robert Bosch GmbH., I; 16 (upd.); 43 (upd.)
RockShox, Inc., 26
Rockwell Automation, I; 11 (upd.); 43 (upd.)
Rolls-Royce plc, I; 21 (upd.)
Ron Tonkin Chevrolet Company, 55
Rover Group Ltd., 7; 21 (upd.)
Saab Automobile AB, I; 11 (upd.); 32 (upd.); 83 (upd.)
Safelite Glass Corp., 19
Safety Components International, Inc., 63
SANLUIS Corporación, S.A.B. de C.V., 95
Saturn Corporation, 7; 21 (upd.); 80 (upd.)
Sealed Power Corporation, I
Servco Pacific Inc., 96
Sheller-Globe Corporation, I
Sixt AG, 39
Skoda Auto a.s., 39
Sonic Automotive, Inc., 77
Spartan Motors Inc., 14
SpeeDee Oil Change and Tune-Up, 25
SPX Corporation, 10; 47 (upd.)
Standard Motor Products, Inc., 40
Strattec Security Corporation, 73
Superior Industries International, Inc., 8
Suzuki Motor Corporation, 9; 23 (upd.); 59 (upd.)
Sytner Group plc, 45
Titan International, Inc., 89
Toresco Enterprises, Inc., 84
Tower Automotive, Inc., 24
Toyota Motor Corporation, I; 11 (upd.); 38 (upd.); 100 (upd.)
CJSC Transmash Holding, 93
TransPro, Inc., 71
Triumph Motorcycles Ltd., 53
TRW Automotive Holdings Corp., 75 (upd.)
TRW Inc., 14 (upd.)
Ugly Duckling Corporation, 22
United Auto Group, Inc., 26; 68 (upd.)
United Technologies Automotive Inc., 15
Universal Technical Institute, Inc., 81
Valeo, 23; 66 (upd.)
Van Hool S.A./NV, 96
Vauxhall Motors Limited, 73
Volkswagen Aktiengesellschaft, I; 11 (upd.); 32 (upd.)

Wagon plc, 92
Walker Manufacturing Company, 19
Webasto Roof Systems Inc., 97
Wilhelm Karmann GmbH, 94
Winnebago Industries, Inc., 7; 27 (upd.); 96 (upd.)
Woodward Governor Company, 13; 49 (upd.); 105 (upd.)
The Yokohama Rubber Company, Limited, V; 19 (upd.); 91 (upd.)
ZF Friedrichshafen AG, 48
Ziebart International Corporation, 30; 66 (upd.)

Beverages

A & W Brands, Inc., 25
A. Smith Bowman Distillery, Inc., 104
Adolph Coors Company, I; 13 (upd.); 36 (upd.)
AG Barr plc, 64
Ajegroup S.A., 92
Allied Domecq PLC, 29
Allied-Lyons PLC, I
Anadolu Efes Biracilik ve Malt Sanayii A.S., 95
Anchor Brewing Company, 47
Andrew Peller Ltd., 101
Anheuser-Busch InBev, I; 10 (upd.); 34 (upd.); 100 (upd.)
Apple & Eve L.L.C., 92
Asahi Breweries, Ltd., I; 20 (upd.); 52 (upd.)
Asia Pacific Breweries Limited, 59
August Schell Brewing Company Inc., 59
Bacardi & Company Ltd., 18; 82 (upd.)
Baltika Brewery Joint Stock Company, 65
Banfi Products Corp., 36
Baron de Ley S.A., 74
Baron Philippe de Rothschild S.A., 39
Bass PLC, I; 15 (upd.); 38 (upd.)
Bavaria S.A., 90
BBAG Osterreichische Brau-Beteiligungs-AG, 38
Belvedere S.A., 93
Beringer Blass Wine Estates Ltd., 22; 66 (upd.)
The Bernick Companies, 75
Blue Ridge Beverage Company Inc., 82
Boizel Chanoine Champagne S.A., 94
Bols Distilleries NV, 74
The Boston Beer Company, Inc., 18; 50 (upd.)
Brauerei Beck & Co., 9; 33 (upd.)
Britannia Soft Drinks Ltd. (Britvic), 71
Bronco Wine Company, 101
Brown-Forman Corporation, I; 10 (upd.); 38 (upd.)
Brouwerijen Alken-Maes N.V., 86
Budweiser Budvar, National Corporation, 59
Cadbury Schweppes PLC, 49 (upd.)
Cains Beer Company PLC, 99
Cameron Hughes Wine, 103
Canandaigua Brands, Inc., 13; 34 (upd.)
Cantine Giorgio Lungarotti S.R.L., 67
Caribou Coffee Company, Inc., 28; 97 (upd.)
Carlsberg A/S, 9; 29 (upd.); 98 (upd.)

Carlton and United Breweries Ltd., I
Casa Cuervo, S.A. de C.V., 31
Central European Distribution
    Corporation, 75
Cerveceria Polar, I
The Chalone Wine Group, Ltd., 36
The Charmer Sunbelt Group, 95
City Brewing Company LLC, 73
Clearly Canadian Beverage Corporation,
    48
Clement Pappas & Company, Inc., 92
Click Wine Group, 68
Coca Cola Bottling Co. Consolidated, 10
The Coca-Cola Company, I; 10 (upd.);
    32 (upd.); 67 (upd.)
Coffee Holding Co., Inc., 95
Companhia de Bebidas das Américas, 57
Compania Cervecerias Unidas S.A., 70
Constellation Brands, Inc., 68 (upd.)
Corby Distilleries Limited, 14
Cott Corporation, 52
D.G. Yuengling & Son, Inc., 38
Dallis Coffee, Inc., 86
Daniel Thwaites Plc, 95
Davide Campari-Milano S.p.A., 57
Dean Foods Company, 21 (upd.)
Delicato Vineyards, Inc., 50
Deschutes Brewery, Inc., 57
Desnoes and Geddes Limited, 79
Diageo plc, 79 (upd.)
Direct Wines Ltd., 84
Distillers Company PLC, I
Double-Cola Co.-USA, 70
Dr Pepper/Seven Up, Inc., 9; 32 (upd.)
Drie Mollen Holding B.V., 99
Drinks Americas Holdings, LTD., 105
E. & J. Gallo Winery, I; 7 (upd.); 28
    (upd.); 104 (upd.)
Eckes AG, 56
The Edrington Group Ltd., 88
Embotelladora Andina S.A., 71
Empresas Polar SA, 55 (upd.)
Energy Brands Inc., 88
F. Korbel & Bros. Inc., 68
Faygo Beverages Inc., 55
Federico Paternina S.A., 69
Ferolito, Vultaggio & Sons, 27; 100
    (upd.)
Fiji Water LLC, 74
Florida's Natural Growers, 45
Foster's Group Limited, 7; 21 (upd.); 50
    (upd.)
Freixenet S.A., 71
Frucor Beverages Group Ltd., 96
Fuller Smith & Turner P.L.C., 38
G. Heileman Brewing Company Inc., I
The Gambrinus Company, 40
Gano Excel Enterprise Sdn. Bhd., 89
The Gatorade Company, 82
Geerlings & Wade, Inc., 45
General Cinema Corporation, I
Glazer's Wholesale Drug Company, Inc.,
    82
Gluck Brewing Company, 75
Golden State Vintners, Inc., 33
Gosling Brothers Ltd., 82
Grand Metropolitan PLC, I
Green Mountain Coffee, Inc., 31

The Greenalls Group PLC, 21
Greene King plc, 31
Grands Vins Jean-Claude Boisset S.A., 98
Groupe Danone, 32 (upd.); 93 (upd.)
Grupo Industrial Herradura, S.A. de C.V.,
    83
Grupo Modelo, S.A. de C.V., 29
Guinness/UDV, I; 43 (upd.)
The Hain Celestial Group, Inc., 43 (upd.)
Hansen Natural Corporation, 31; 76
    (upd.)
Heineken N.V, I; 13 (upd.); 34 (upd.); 90
    (upd.)
Heublein, Inc., I
High Falls Brewing Company LLC, 74
Hiram Walker Resources, Ltd., I
Hite Brewery Company Ltd., 97
illycaffè SpA, 50
Imagine Foods, Inc., 50
Interbrew S.A., 17; 50 (upd.)
Irish Distillers Group, 96
Ito En Ltd., 101
J.J. Darboven GmbH & Co. KG, 96
J. Lohr Winery Corporation, 99
Jacob Leinenkugel Brewing Company, 28
JD Wetherspoon plc, 30
Jim Beam Brands Worldwide, Inc., 58
    (upd.)
John Dewar & Sons, Ltd., 82
Jones Soda Co., 69
Jugos del Valle, S.A. de C.V., 85
Karlsberg Brauerei GmbH & Co KG, 41
Kemps LLC, 103
Kendall-Jackson Winery, Ltd., 28
Kikkoman Corporation, 14
Kirin Brewery Company, Limited, I; 21
    (upd.); 63 (upd.)
Kobrand Corporation, 82
König Brauerei GmbH & Co. KG, 35
    (upd.)
Krombacher Brauerei Bernhard
    Schadeberg GmbH & Co. KG, 104
L. Foppiano Wine Co., 101
Labatt Brewing Company Limited, I; 25
    (upd.)
Latrobe Brewing Company, 54
Laurent-Perrier SA, 42
The Lion Brewery, Inc., 86
Lion Nathan Limited, 54
Löwenbräu AG, 80
The Macallan Distillers Ltd., 63
Madeira Wine Company, S.A., 49
Maison Louis Jadot, 24
Marchesi Antinori SRL, 42
Marie Brizard et Roger International
    S.A.S., 22; 97 (upd.)
Mark T. Wendell Tea Company, 94
Martell and Company S.A., 82
Martignetti Companies, 84
Martini & Rossi SpA, 63
Maui Wowi, Inc., 85
MBC Holding Company, 40
Mendocino Brewing Company, Inc., 60
Mercian Corporation, 77
Miller Brewing Company, I; 12 (upd.)
The Minute Maid Company, 28
Mitchells & Butlers PLC, 59
Moët-Hennessy, I

Molson Coors Brewing Company, I; 26
    (upd.); 77 (upd.)
Montana Coffee Traders, Inc., 60
Mott's Inc., 57
National Beverage Corporation, 26; 88
    (upd.)
National Grape Cooperative Association,
    Inc., 20
National Wine & Spirits, Inc., 49
Nestlé Waters, 73
New Belgium Brewing Company, Inc., 68
Nichols plc, 44
Ocean Spray Cranberries, Inc., 7; 25
    (upd.); 83 (upd.)
Odwalla Inc., 31; 104 (upd.)
OENEO S.A., 74 (upd.)
Old Orchard Brands, LLC, 73
Oregon Chai, Inc., 49
Panamerican Beverages, Inc., 47
Parmalat Finanziaria SpA, 50
Paulaner Brauerei GmbH & Co. KG, 35
Peet's Coffee & Tea, Inc., 38; 100 (upd.)
Penaflor S.A., 66
The Pepsi Bottling Group, Inc., 40
PepsiAmericas, Inc., 67 (upd.)
PepsiCo, Inc., I; 10 (upd.); 38 (upd.); 93
    (upd.)
Pernod Ricard S.A., I; 21 (upd.); 72
    (upd.)
Pete's Brewing Company, 22
Philip Morris Companies Inc., 18 (upd.)
Pittsburgh Brewing Company, 76
Pyramid Breweries Inc., 33; 102 (upd.)
Quilmes Industrial (QUINSA) S.A., 67
R.C. Bigelow, Inc., 49
Radeberger Gruppe AG, 75
Rainier Brewing Company, 23
Red Bull GmbH, 60
Redhook Ale Brewery, Inc., 31; 88 (upd.)
Reed's, Inc., 103
Rémy Cointreau Group, 20; 80 (upd.)
The Republic of Tea, Inc., 105
Robert Mondavi Corporation, 15; 50
    (upd.)
Roberts Dairy Company, 103
Royal Crown Company, Inc., 23
Royal Grolsch NV, 54
S&D Coffee, Inc., 84
SABMiller plc, 59 (upd.)
Sam's Wine & Spirits, 96
San Miguel Corporation, 57 (upd.)
Sapporo Holdings Limited, I; 13 (upd.);
    36 (upd.); 97 (upd.)
Scheid Vineyards Inc., 66
Schieffelin & Somerset Co., 61
Schincariol Participaçoces e Representações
    S.A., 102
Scottish & Newcastle plc, 15; 35 (upd.)
The Seagram Company Ltd., I; 25 (upd.)
Sebastiani Vineyards, Inc., 28
Shepherd Neame Limited, 30
Sidney Frank Importing Co., Inc., 69
Sierra Nevada Brewing Company, 70
Sine Qua Non, 99
Skalli Group, 67
Skyy Spirits LLC 78
Sleeman Breweries Ltd., 74
Snapple Beverage Corporation, 11

Societe des Produits Marnier-Lapostolle S.A., 88
The South African Breweries Limited, I; 24 (upd.)
South Beach Beverage Company, Inc., 73
Southcorp Limited, 54
Southern Wine and Spirits of America, Inc., 84
Starbucks Corporation, 13; 34 (upd.); 77 (upd.)
The Stash Tea Company, 50
Ste. Michelle Wine Estates Ltd., 96
Stewart's Beverages, 39
The Stroh Brewery Company, I; 18 (upd.)
Suntory Ltd., 65
Sutter Home Winery Inc., 16
Taittinger S.A., 43
Taiwan Tobacco & Liquor Corporation, 75
Takara Holdings Inc., 62
Tata Tea Ltd., 76
The Terlato Wine Group, 48
Tetley USA Inc., 88
Todhunter International, Inc., 27
Triarc Companies, Inc., 34 (upd.)
Tropicana Products, Inc., 73 (upd.)
Tsingtao Brewery Group, 49
Tully's Coffee Corporation, 51
Underberg AG, 92
Unilever, II; 7 (upd.); 32 (upd.); 89 (upd.)
Unión de Cervecerias Peruanas Backus y Johnston S.A.A., 92
V&S Vin & Sprit AB, 91 (upd.)
Van Houtte Inc., 39
Vermont Pure Holdings, Ltd., 51
Veuve Clicquot Ponsardin SCS, 98
Vin & Spirit AB, 31
Viña Concha y Toro S.A., 45
Vincor International Inc., 50
Vinmonopolet A/S, 100
Whitbread PLC, I; 20 (upd.); 52 (upd.); 97 (upd.)
Widmer Brothers Brewing Company, 76
Willamette Valley Vineyards, Inc., 85
William Grant & Sons Ltd., 60
The Wine Group, Inc., 39
The Wolverhampton & Dudley Breweries, PLC, 57
Wray & Nephew Group Ltd., 98
Young & Co.'s Brewery, P.L.C., 38

Bio-Technology

Actelion Ltd., 83
Affymetrix Inc., 106
Agria Corporation, 101
Amersham PLC, 50
Amgen, Inc., 10; 30 (upd.)
ArQule, Inc., 68
Becton, Dickinson and Company, I; 11 (upd.); 36 (upd.); 101 (upd.)
Bio-Rad Laboratories, Inc., 93
Biogen Idec Inc., 71 (upd.)
Biogen Inc., 14; 36 (upd.)
bioMérieux S.A., 75
BTG Plc, 87
Caliper Life Sciences, Inc., 70
Cambrex Corporation, 44 (upd.)

Celera Genomics, 74
Centocor Inc., 14
Charles River Laboratories International, Inc., 42
Chiron Corporation, 10; 36 (upd.)
Covance Inc., 30; 98 (upd.)
CryoLife, Inc., 46
Cytyc Corporation, 69
Delta and Pine Land Company, 33
Dionex Corporation, 46
Dyax Corp., 89
Embrex, Inc., 72
Enzo Biochem, Inc., 41
Eurofins Scientific S.A., 70
Gen-Probe Incorporated, 79
Genentech, Inc., 32 (upd.)
Genzyme Corporation, 38 (upd.)
Gilead Sciences, Inc., 54
Howard Hughes Medical Institute, 39
Huntingdon Life Sciences Group plc, 42
IDEXX Laboratories, Inc., 23
ImClone Systems Inc., 58
Immunex Corporation, 14; 50 (upd.)
IMPATH Inc., 45
Incyte Genomics, Inc., 52
Inverness Medical Innovations, Inc., 63
Invitrogen Corporation, 52
The Judge Group, Inc., 51
Kendle International Inc., 87
Landec Corporation, 95
Life Technologies, Inc., 17
LifeCell Corporation, 77
Lonza Group Ltd., 73
Martek Biosciences Corporation, 65
Medarex, Inc., 85
Medtronic, Inc., 30 (upd.)
Millipore Corporation, 25; 84 (upd.)
Minntech Corporation, 22
Mycogen Corporation, 21
Nektar Therapeutics, 91
New Brunswick Scientific Co., Inc., 45
Omrix Biopharmaceuticals, Inc., 95
Pacific Ethanol, Inc., 81
Pharmion Corporation, 91
Qiagen N.V., 39
Quintiles Transnational Corporation, 21
Seminis, Inc., 29
Senomyx, Inc., 83
Serologicals Corporation, 63
Sigma-Aldrich Corporation, I; 36 (upd.); 93 (upd.)
Starkey Laboratories, Inc., 52
STERIS Corporation, 29
Stratagene Corporation, 70
Tanox, Inc., 77
TECHNE Corporation, 52
TriPath Imaging, Inc., 77
Viterra Inc., 105
Waters Corporation, 43
Whatman plc, 46
Wisconsin Alumni Research Foundation, 65
Wyeth, 50 (upd.)

Chemicals

A. Schulman, Inc., 8
Aceto Corp., 38

Air Products and Chemicals, Inc., I; 10 (upd.); 74 (upd.)
Airgas, Inc., 54
Akzo Nobel N.V., 13; 41 (upd.)
Albaugh, Inc., 105
Albemarle Corporation, 59
AlliedSignal Inc., 22 (upd.)
ALTANA AG, 87
American Cyanamid, I; 8 (upd.)
American Vanguard Corporation, 47
Arab Potash Company, 85
Arch Chemicals Inc. 78
ARCO Chemical Company, 10
Arkema S.A., 100
Asahi Denka Kogyo KK, 64
Atanor S.A., 62
Atochem S.A., I
Avantium Technologies BV, 79
Avecia Group PLC, 63
Azelis Group, 100
Baker Hughes Incorporated, 22 (upd.); 57 (upd.)
Balchem Corporation, 42
BASF Aktiengesellschaft, I; 18 (upd.); 50 (upd.)
Bayer A.G., I; 13 (upd.); 41 (upd.)
Betz Laboratories, Inc., I; 10 (upd.)
The BFGoodrich Company, 19 (upd.)
BOC Group plc, I; 25 (upd.); 78 (upd.)
Brenntag Holding GmbH & Co. KG, 8; 23 (upd.); 101 (upd.)
Burmah Castrol PLC, 30 (upd.)
Cabot Corporation, 8; 29 (upd.); 91 (upd.)
Calgon Carbon Corporation, 73
Caliper Life Sciences, Inc., 70
Calumet Specialty Products Partners, L.P., 106
Cambrex Corporation, 16
Catalytica Energy Systems, Inc., 44
Celanese Corporation, I
Celanese Mexicana, S.A. de C.V., 54
CF Industries Holdings, Inc., 99
Chemcentral Corporation, 8
Chemi-Trol Chemical Co., 16
Chemtura Corporation, 91 (upd.)
Church & Dwight Co., Inc., 29
Ciba-Geigy Ltd., I; 8 (upd.)
The Clorox Company, III; 22 (upd.); 81 (upd.)
Croda International Plc, 45
Crompton Corporation, 9; 36 (upd.)
Cytec Industries Inc., 27
Degussa-Hüls AG, 32 (upd.)
DeKalb Genetics Corporation, 17
The Dexter Corporation, I; 12 (upd.)
Dionex Corporation, 46
The Dow Chemical Company, I; 8 (upd.); 50 (upd.)
DSM N.V., I; 56 (upd.)
Dynaction S.A., 67
E.I. du Pont de Nemours & Company, I; 8 (upd.); 26 (upd.)
Eastman Chemical Company, 14; 38 (upd.)
Ecolab Inc., I; 13 (upd.); 34 (upd.); 85 (upd.)
Eka Chemicals AB, 92

612

Elementis plc, 40 (upd.)
Engelhard Corporation, 72 (upd.)
English China Clays Ltd., 15 (upd.); 40 (upd.)
Enterprise Rent-A-Car Company, 69 (upd.)
Equistar Chemicals, LP, 71
Ercros S.A., 80
ERLY Industries Inc., 17
Ethyl Corporation, I; 10 (upd.)
Ferro Corporation, 8; 56 (upd.)
Firmenich International S.A., 60
First Mississippi Corporation, 8
FMC Corporation, 89 (upd.)
Formosa Plastics Corporation, 14; 58 (upd.)
Fort James Corporation, 22 (upd.)
Fuchs Petrolub AG, 102
G.A.F., I
The General Chemical Group Inc., 37
Georgia Gulf Corporation, 9; 61 (upd.)
Givaudan SA, 43
Great Lakes Chemical Corporation, I; 14 (upd.)
GROWMARK, Inc., 88
Guerbet Group, 46
H.B. Fuller Company, 32 (upd.); 75 (upd.)
Hauser, Inc., 46
Hawkins Chemical, Inc., 16
Henkel KGaA, III; 34 (upd.); 95 (upd.)
Hercules Inc., I; 22 (upd.); 66 (upd.)
Hoechst A.G., I; 18 (upd.)
Hoechst Celanese Corporation, 13
Huls A.G., I
Huntsman Corporation, 8; 98 (upd.)
IMC Fertilizer Group, Inc., 8
Imperial Chemical Industries PLC, I; 50 (upd.)
International Flavors & Fragrances Inc., 9; 38 (upd.)
Israel Chemicals Ltd., 55
KBR Inc., 106 (upd.)
Kemira Oyj, 70
KMG Chemicals, Inc., 101
Koppers Industries, Inc., I; 26 (upd.)
Kwizda Holding GmbH, 102 (upd.)
I.'Air Liquide SA, I; 47 (upd.)
Lawter International Inc., 14
LeaRonal, Inc., 23
Loctite Corporation, 30 (upd.)
Loos & Dilworth, Inc., 100
Lonza Group Ltd., 73
The Lubrizol Corporation, I; 30 (upd.); 83 (upd.)
Lyondell Chemical Company, 45 (upd.)
M.A. Hanna Company, 8
MacDermid Incorporated, 32
Makhteshim-Agan Industries Ltd., 85
Mallinckrodt Group Inc., 19
MBC Holding Company, 40
Melamine Chemicals, Inc., 27
Methanex Corporation, 40
Mexichem, S.A.B. de C.V., 99
Minerals Technologies Inc., 52 (upd.)
Mississippi Chemical Corporation, 39
Mitsubishi Chemical Corporation, I; 56 (upd.)

Mitsui Petrochemical Industries, Ltd., 9
Monsanto Company, I; 9 (upd.); 29 (upd.)
Montedison SpA, I
Morton International Inc., I; 9 (upd.); 80 (upd.)
The Mosaic Company, 91
Nagase & Company, Ltd., 8
Nalco Holding Company, I; 12 (upd.); 89 (upd.)
National Distillers and Chemical Corporation, I
National Sanitary Supply Co., 16
National Starch and Chemical Company, 49
NCH Corporation, 8
Nippon Soda Co., Ltd., 85
Nisshin Seifun Group Inc., 66 (upd.)
NL Industries, Inc., 10
Nobel Industries AB, 9
NOF Corporation, 72
Norsk Hydro ASA, 35 (upd.)
North American Galvanizing & Coatings, Inc., 99
Novacor Chemicals Ltd., 12
Nufarm Ltd., 87
NutraSweet Company, 8
Occidental Petroleum Corporation, 71 (upd.)
Olin Corporation, I; 13 (upd.); 78 (upd.)
OM Group, Inc., 17; 78 (upd.)
OMNOVA Solutions Inc., 59
Penford Corporation, 55
Pennwalt Corporation, I
Perstorp AB, I; 51 (upd.)
Petrolite Corporation, 15
Pfizer Inc., 79 (upd.)
Pioneer Hi-Bred International, Inc., 41 (upd.)
PolyOne Corporation, 87 (upd.)
Praxair, Inc., 11
Quaker Chemical Corp., 91
Quantum Chemical Corporation, 8
Reichhold Chemicals, Inc., 10
Renner Herrmann S.A., 79
Rhodia SA, 38
Rhône-Poulenc S.A., I; 10 (upd.)
Robertet SA, 39
Rohm and Haas Company, I; 26 (upd.); 77 (upd.)
Roussel Uclaf, I; 8 (upd.)
RPM International Inc., 8; 36 (upd.); 91 (upd.)
RWE AG, 50 (upd.)
S.C. Johnson & Son, Inc., III; 28 (upd.); 89 (upd.)
The Scotts Company, 22
SCP Pool Corporation, 39
Sequa Corp., 13
Shanghai Petrochemical Co., Ltd., 18
Sigma-Aldrich Corporation, I; 36 (upd.); 93 (upd.)
Sociedad Química y Minera de Chile S.A., 103
Solutia Inc., 52
Solvay S.A., I; 21 (upd.); 61 (upd.)
Stepan Company, 30; 105 (upd.)
Sterling Chemicals, Inc., 16; 78 (upd.)

Sumitomo Chemical Company Ltd., I; 98 (upd.)
Takeda Chemical Industries, Ltd., 46 (upd.)
Teknor Apex Company, 97
Terra Industries, Inc., 13
Tessenderlo Group, 76
Teva Pharmaceutical Industries Ltd., 22
Tosoh Corporation, 70
Total Fina Elf S.A., 24 (upd.); 50 (upd.)
Transammonia Group, 95
Ube Industries, Ltd., 38 (upd.)
Union Carbide Corporation, I; 9 (upd.); 74 (upd.)
United Industries Corporation, 68
Univar Corporation, 9
The Valspar Corporation, 32 (upd.); 77 (upd.)
VeraSun Energy Corporation, 87
Vista Chemical Company, I
Witco Corporation, I; 16 (upd.)
Yule Catto & Company plc, 54
WD-40 Company, 87 (upd.)
Zakłady Azotowe Puławy S.A., 100
Zeneca Group PLC, 21

Conglomerates

A.P. Møller - Maersk A/S, 57
ABARTA, Inc., 100
Abengoa S.A., 73
Acciona S.A., 81
Accor SA, 10; 27 (upd.)
Ackermans & van Haaren N.V., 97
Adani Enterprises Ltd., 97
Aditya Birla Group, 79
Administración Nacional de Combustibles, Alcohol y Pórtland, 93
AEG A.G., I
Al Habtoor Group L.L.C., 87
Alcatel Alsthom Compagnie Générale d'Electricité, 9
Alco Standard Corporation, I
Alexander & Baldwin, Inc., 10, 40 (upd.)
Alfa, S.A. de C.V., 19
Alfa Group, 99
Algar S/A Emprendimentos e Participações, 103
Alleghany Corporation, 60 (upd.)
Allied Domecq PLC, 29
Allied-Signal Inc., I
AMFAC Inc., I
Andrade Gutierrez S.A., 102
The Anschutz Company, 73 (upd.)
The Anschutz Corporation, 36 (upd.)
Antofagasta plc, 65
Apax Partners Worldwide LLP, 89
APi Group, Inc., 64
Aramark Corporation, 13
ARAMARK Corporation, 41
Archer Daniels Midland Company, I; 11 (upd.); 75 (upd.)
Arkansas Best Corporation, 16
Associated British Ports Holdings Plc, 45
BAA plc, 33 (upd.)
Barlow Rand Ltd., I
Barratt Developments plc, 56 (upd.)
Bat Industries PLC, I
Baugur Group hf, 81

BB Holdings Limited, 77
Berjaya Group Bhd., 67
Berkshire Hathaway Inc., III; 18 (upd.); 42 (upd.); 89 (upd.)
Block Communications, Inc., 81
Bond Corporation Holdings Limited, 10
Brascan Corporation, 67
BTR PLC, I
Bunzl plc, 31 (upd.)
Burlington Northern Santa Fe Corporation, 27 (upd.)
Business Post Group plc, 46
C. Itoh & Company Ltd., I
C.I. Traders Limited, 61
Camargo Corrêa S.A., 93
Cargill, Incorporated, II; 13 (upd.); 40 (upd.); 89 (upd.)
CBI Industries, Inc., 7
Charoen Pokphand Group, 62
Chemed Corporation, 13
Chesebrough-Pond's USA, Inc., 8
China Merchants International Holdings Co., Ltd., 52
Cisneros Group of Companies, 54
CITIC Pacific Ltd., 18
CJ Corporation, 62
Colgate-Palmolive Company, 71 (upd.)
Colt Industries Inc., I
Compagnie Financiere Richemont AG, 50
The Connell Company, 29; 104 (upd.)
Conzzeta Holding, 80
Cox Enterprises, Inc., IV; 22 (upd.); 67 (upd.)
Cramer-Krasselt Company, 104
Cristalerias de Chile S.A., 67
CSR Limited, III; 28 (upd.); 85 (upd.)
Daewoo Group, 18 (upd.); 57 (upd.)
Dallah Albaraka Group, 72
De Dietrich & Cie., 31
Deere & Company, 21 (upd.)
Delaware North Companies Inc., 7; 96 (upd.)
Desc, S.A. de C.V., 23
Deseret Management Corporation, 101
The Dial Corp., 8
Dogan Sirketler Grubu Holding A.S., 83
Dr. August Oetker KG, 51
E.I. du Pont de Nemours and Company, 73 (upd.)
EBSCO Industries, Inc., 40 (upd.)
EBX Investimentos, 104
El Corte Inglés Group, 26 (upd.)
Elders IXL Ltd., I
Empresas Copec S.A., 69
Engelhard Corporation, 21 (upd.); 72 (upd.)
Essar Group Ltd., 79
Farley Northwest Industries, Inc., I
Fimalac S.A., 37
First Pacific Company Limited, 18
Fisher Companies, Inc., 15
Fletcher Challenge Ltd., 19 (upd.)
Florida East Coast Industries, Inc., 59
FMC Corporation, I; 11 (upd.)
Fortune Brands, Inc., 29 (upd.); 68 (upd.)
Fraser & Neave Ltd., 54
Fuqua Industries, Inc., I

General Electric Company, 34 (upd.); 63 (upd.)
Genting Bhd., 65
GIB Group, 26 (upd.)
Gillett Holdings, Inc., 7
The Gillette Company, 68 (upd.)
Granaria Holdings B.V., 66
Grand Metropolitan PLC, 14 (upd.)
Great American Management and Investment, Inc., 8
Greyhound Corporation, I
Groupe Bolloré, 67
Groupe Dubreuil S.A., 102
Groupe Louis Dreyfus S.A., 60
Grupo Brescia, 99
Grupo Carso, S.A. de C.V., 21
Grupo Clarín S.A., 67
Grupo Industrial Bimbo, 19
Grupo Industrial Saltillo, S.A. de C.V., 54
Gulf & Western Inc., I
Haci Omer Sabanci Holdings A.S., 55
Hagemeyer N.V., 39
Hankyu Corporation, 23 (upd.)
Hanson PLC, III; 7 (upd.)
Hanwha Group, 62
Harbour Group Industries, Inc., 90
Hawk Corporation, 59
Henry Crown and Company, 91
Hitachi Zosen Corporation, 53 (upd.)
Hitachi, Ltd., I; 12 (upd.); 40 (upd.)
Ho-Chunk Inc., 61
Hutchison Whampoa Limited, 18; 49 (upd.)
Hyundai Group, III; 7 (upd.); 56 (upd.)
IC Industries, Inc., I
IDB Holding Corporation Ltd., 97
Idealab, 105
Ilitch Holdings Inc., 37; 86 (upd.)
Inchcape PLC, 16 (upd.); 50 (upd.)
Industria de Diseño Textil S.A. (Inditex), 64
Industrie Zignago Santa Margherita S.p.A., 67
Ingram Industries, Inc., 11; 49 (upd.)
Instituto Nacional de Industria, I
International Controls Corporation, 10
International Telephone & Telegraph Corporation, I; 11 (upd.)
Investor AB, 63
Ishikawajima-Harima Heavy Industries Company, Ltd., III; 86 (upd.)
Istituto per la Ricostruzione Industriale, I
ITOCHU Corporation, 32 (upd.)
J.R. Simplot Company, 60 (upd.)
Jardine Matheson Holdings Limited, I; 20 (upd.); 93 (upd.)
Jason Incorporated, 23
Jefferson Smurfit Group plc, 19 (upd.)
The Jim Pattison Group, 37
Jordan Industries, Inc., 36
José de Mello SGPS S.A., 96
Justin Industries, Inc., 19
Kanematsu Corporation, IV; 24 (upd.); 102 (upd.)
Kao Corporation, 20 (upd.)
Katy Industries, Inc., I
Keppel Corporation Ltd., 73
Kesko Ltd. (Kesko Oy), 8; 27 (upd.)

Kidde plc, I; 44 (upd.)
King Ranch, Inc., 60 (upd.)
Knowledge Universe, Inc., 54
Koç Holding A.S., I; 54 (upd.)
Koch Industries, Inc., 77 (upd.)
Koninklijke Nedlloyd N.V., 26 (upd.)
Koor Industries Ltd., 25 (upd.); 68 (upd.)
Körber AG, 60
K2 Inc., 16; 84 (upd.)
The L.L. Knickerbocker Co., Inc., 25
Lancaster Colony Corporation, 8; 61 (upd.)
Larry H. Miller Group of Companies, 29; 104 (upd.)
LDI Ltd., LLC, 76
Lear Siegler, Inc., I
Lefrak Organization Inc., 26
Leucadia National Corporation, 11; 71 (upd.)
Linde AG, 67 (upd.)
Litton Industries, Inc., I; 11 (upd.)
Loews Corporation, I; 12 (upd.); 36 (upd.); 93 (upd.)
Loral Corporation, 8
LTV Corporation, I; 24 (upd.)
LVMH Moët Hennessy Louis Vuitton SA, 33 (upd.)
The Marmon Group, Inc., 70 (upd.)
Marubeni Corporation, I; 24 (upd.); 104 (upd.)
MAXXAM Inc., 8
McKesson Corporation, I
McPherson's Ltd., 66
Melitta Unternehmensgruppe Bentz KG, 53
Menasha Corporation, 8
Metallgesellschaft AG, 16 (upd.)
Metromedia Company, 7; 61 (upd.)
Minnesota Mining & Manufacturing Company (3M), I; 8 (upd.); 26 (upd.)
Mitsubishi Corporation, I; 12 (upd.)
Mitsubishi Heavy Industries, Ltd., 40 (upd.)
Mitsui & Co., Ltd., I; 28 (upd.)
The Molson Companies Limited, I; 26 (upd.)
Mondragón Corporación Cooperativa, 101
Montedison S.p.A., 24 (upd.)
Munir Sukhtian Group, 104
NACCO Industries, Inc., 7; 78 (upd.)
Nagase & Co., Ltd., 61 (upd.)
National Service Industries, Inc., 11; 54 (upd.)
New Clicks Holdings Ltd., 86
New World Development Company Limited, 38 (upd.)
Nichimen Corporation, 24 (upd.)
Nichirei Corporation, 70
Nissho Iwai K.K., I
Norsk Hydro A.S., 10
Novar plc, 49 (upd.)
Ogden Corporation, I
Onex Corporation, 16; 65 (upd.)
Orkla ASA, 18; 82 (upd.)
Park-Ohio Holdings Corp., 17; 85 (upd.)
Pentair, Inc., 7; 26 (upd.); 81 (upd.)
Petrobras Energia Participaciones S.A., 72

Philip Morris Companies Inc., 44 (upd.)
Poliet S.A., 33
Powell Duffryn plc, 31
Power Corporation of Canada, 36 (upd.); 85 (upd.)
PPB Group Berhad, 57
Preussag AG, 17
The Procter & Gamble Company, III; 8 (upd.); 26 (upd.); 67 (upd.)
Proeza S.A. de C.V., 82
PT Astra International Tbk, 56
Pubco Corporation, 17
Pulsar Internacional S.A., 21
R.B. Pamplin Corp., 45
The Rank Organisation Plc, 14 (upd.)
Raymond Ltd., 77
Red Apple Group, Inc., 23
Roll International Corporation, 37
Rubbermaid Incorporated, 20 (upd.)
Samsung Group, I
San Miguel Corporation, 15
Sara Lee Corporation, II; 15 (upd.); 54 (upd.); 99 (upd.)
S.C. Johnson & Son, Inc., III; 28 (upd.); 89 (upd.)
Schindler Holding AG, 29
Scott Fetzer Company, 12; 80 (upd.)
Sea Containers Ltd., 29
Seaboard Corporation, 36; 85 (upd.)
Sealaska Corporation, 60
Sequa Corporation, 54 (upd.)
Sequana Capital, 78 (upd.)
ServiceMaster Inc., 23 (upd.)
SHV Holdings N.V., 55
Sideco Americana S.A., 67
Sime Darby Berhad, 14; 36 (upd.)
Sistema JSFC, 73
SK Group, 88
Société du Louvre, 27
Sojitz Corporation, 96 (upd.)
Sonae SGPS, S.A., 97
Standex International Corporation, 17; 44 (upd.)
Steamships Trading Company Ltd., 82
Stinnes AG, 23 (upd.)
Sudbury Inc., 16
Sumitomo Corporation, I; 11 (upd.); 102 (upd.)
Swire Pacific Limited, I; 16 (upd.); 57 (upd.)
Talley Industries, Inc., 16
Tandycrafts, Inc., 31
TaurusHolding GmbH & Co. KG, 46
Teijin Limited, 61 (upd.)
Teledyne, Inc., I; 10 (upd.)
Tenneco Inc., I; 10 (upd.)
Textron Inc., I; 34 (upd.); 88 (upd.)
Thomas H. Lee Co., 24
Thorn Emi PLC, I
Thorn plc, 24
TI Group plc, 17
Time Warner Inc., IV; 7 (upd.)
Tokyu Corporation, 47 (upd.)
Tomen Corporation, 24 (upd.)
Tomkins plc, 11; 44 (upd.)
Toshiba Corporation, I; 12 (upd.); 40 (upd.); 99 (upd.)
Tractebel S.A., 20

Transamerica–An AEGON Company, I; 13 (upd.); 41 (upd.)
The Tranzonic Cos., 15
Triarc Companies, Inc., 8
Triple Five Group Ltd., 49
TRW Inc., I; 11 (upd.)
Tyco International Ltd., 63 (upd.)
Unilever, II; 7 (upd.); 32 (upd.); 89 (upd.)
Unión Fenosa, S.A., 51
United Technologies Corporation, I; 10 (upd.); 34 (upd.); 105 (upd.)
Universal Studios, Inc., 33; 100 (upd.)
Valhi, Inc., 19
Valorem S.A., 88
Valores Industriales S.A., 19
Veba A.G., I; 15 (upd.)
Vendôme Luxury Group plc, 27
Viacom Inc., 23 (upd.); 67 (upd.)
Virgin Group Ltd., 12; 32 (upd.); 89 (upd.)
Vivartia S.A., 82
Votorantim Participaçoes S.A., 76
W.R. Grace & Company, I; 50
Walter Industries, Inc., 72 (upd.)
The Washington Companies, 33
Watsco Inc., 52
Wheaton Industries, 8
Whitbread PLC, I; 20 (upd.); 52 (upd.); 97 (upd.)
Whitman Corporation, 10 (upd.)
Whittaker Corporation, I
Wilh. Werhahn KG, 101
Wirtz Corporation, 72
WorldCorp, Inc., 10
Worms et Cie, 27
Yamaha Corporation, III; 16 (upd.); 40 (upd.); 99 (upd.)

Construction

A. Johnson & Company H.B., I
ABC Supply Co., Inc., 22
Abertis Infraestructuras, S.A., 65
Abrams Industries Inc., 23
Acergy SA, 97
Aegek S.A., 64
Alberici Corporation, 76
Amec Spie S.A., 57
AMREP Corporation, 21
Anthony & Sylvan Pools Corporation, 56
Asplundh Tree Expert Co., 59 (upd.)
Astec Industries, Inc., 79
ASV, Inc., 34; 66 (upd.)
The Auchter Company, 78
The Austin Company, 8
Autoroutes du Sud de la France SA, 55
Autostrada Torino-Milano S.p.A., 101
Balfour Beatty plc, 36 (upd.)
Baratt Developments PLC, I
Barton Malow Company, 51
Bauerly Companies, 61
BE&K, Inc., 73
Beazer Homes USA, Inc., 17
Bechtel Corporation, I; 24 (upd.); 99 (upd.)
Bellway Plc, 45
BFC Construction Corporation, 25
Bilfinger & Berger AG, I; 55 (upd.)

Bird Corporation, 19
Birse Group PLC, 77
Black & Veatch LLP, 22
Boral Limited, III; 43 (upd.); 103 (upd.)
Bouygues S.A., I; 24 (upd.); 97 (upd.)
Bowen Engineering Corporation, 105
The Branch Group, Inc., 72
Brasfield & Gorrie LLC, 87
BRISA Auto-estradas de Portugal S.A., 64
Brown & Root, Inc., 13
Bufete Industrial, S.A. de C.V., 34
Building Materials Holding Corporation, 52
Bulley & Andrews, LLC, 55
C.R. Meyer and Sons Company, 74
CalMat Co., 19
Cavco Industries, Inc., 65
Centex Corporation, 8; 29 (upd.); 106 (upd.)
Chugach Alaska Corporation, 60
Cianbro Corporation, 14
The Clark Construction Group, Inc., 8
Colas S.A., 31
Comfort Systems USA, Inc., 101
Consorcio ARA, S.A. de C.V., 79
Corporación Geo, S.A. de C.V., 81
D.R. Horton, Inc., 58
Day & Zimmermann, Inc., 31 (upd.)
Desarrolladora Homex, S.A. de C.V., 87
Dick Corporation, 64
Dillingham Construction Corporation, I; 44 (upd.)
Dominion Homes, Inc., 19
The Drees Company, Inc., 41
Dycom Industries, Inc., 57
E.W. Howell Co., Inc., 72
Edw. C. Levy Co., 42
Eiffage, 27
Ellerbe Becket, 41
EMCOR Group Inc., 60
Empresas ICA Sociedad Controladora, S.A. de C.V., 41
Encompass Services Corporation, 33
Engle Homes, Inc., 46
Environmental Industries, Inc., 31
Eurotunnel PLC, 13
Fairclough Construction Group PLC, I
Flatiron Construction Corporation, 92
Fleetwood Enterprises, Inc., III: 22 (upd.); 81 (upd.)
Fluor Corporation, I; 8 (upd.); 34 (upd.)
Forest City Enterprises, Inc., 52 (upd.)
Fred Weber, Inc., 61
Furmanite Corporation, 92
George Wimpey plc, 12; 51 (upd.)
Gilbane, Inc., 34
Granite Construction Incorporated, 61
Granite Rock Company, 26
Great Lakes Dredge & Dock Company, 69
Grupo Dragados SA, 55
Grupo Ferrovial, S.A., 40
H.J. Russell & Company, 66
The Habitat Company LLC, 106
Habitat for Humanity International, Inc., 36; 106 (upd.)
Heery International, Inc., 58
Heijmans N.V., 66

Henry Boot plc, 76
Hensel Phelps Construction Company, 72
Hillsdown Holdings plc, 24 (upd.)
Hochtief AG, 33; 88 (upd.)
Hoffman Corporation 78
Horton Homes, Inc., 25
Hospitality Worldwide Services, Inc., 26
Hovnanian Enterprises, Inc., 29; 89 (upd.)
IHC Caland N.V., 71
Irex Contracting Group, 90
J.A. Jones, Inc., 16
J C Bamford Excavators Ltd., 83
J.F. Shea Co., Inc., 55
J.H. Findorff and Son, Inc., 60
Jaiprakash Associates Limited, 101
Jarvis plc, 39
JE Dunn Construction Group, Inc., 85
JLG Industries, Inc., 52
John Brown PLC, I
John Laing plc, I; 51 (upd.)
John W. Danforth Company, 48
Kajima Corporation, I; 51 (upd.)
Kaufman and Broad Home Corporation, 8
KB Home, 45 (upd.)
KBR Inc., 106 (upd.)
Kellogg Brown & Root, Inc., 62 (upd.)
Kitchell Corporation, 14
The Koll Company, 8
Komatsu Ltd., 16 (upd.)
Kraus-Anderson Companies, Inc., 36; 83 (upd.)
Kumagai Gumi Company, Ltd., I
L'Entreprise Jean Lefebvre, 23
Laing O'Rourke PLC, 93 (upd.)
Land and Houses PCL, 104
Ledcor Industries Limited, 46
Lennar Corporation, 11
Lincoln Property Company, 8
Lindal Cedar Homes, Inc., 29
Linde A.G., I
MasTec, Inc., 55
Matrix Service Company, 65
May Gurney Integrated Services PLC, 95
McCarthy Building Companies, Inc., 48
Mellon-Stuart Company, I
Michael Baker Corp., 14
Modtech Holdings, Inc., 77
Mota-Engil, SGPS, S.A., 97
Morrison Knudsen Corporation, 7; 28 (upd.)
Morrow Equipment Co. L.L.C., 87
New Holland N.V., 22
Newpark Resources, Inc., 63
NVR Inc., 70 (upd.)
NVR L.P., 8
Obayashi Corporation 78
Obrascon Huarte Lain S.A., 76
The O'Connell Companies Inc., 100
Ohbayashi Corporation, I
Opus Corporation, 34; 101 (upd.)
Orascom Construction Industries S.A.E., 87
Orleans Homebuilders, Inc., 62
Panattoni Development Company, Inc., 99
Parsons Brinckerhoff Inc., 34; 104 (upd.)
The Parsons Corporation, 8; 56 (upd.)

PCL Construction Group Inc., 50
The Peninsular & Oriental Steam Navigation Company (Bovis Division), I
Perini Corporation, 8; 82 (upd.)
Peter Kiewit Sons' Inc., 8
Philipp Holzmann AG, 17
Post Properties, Inc., 26
Pulte Homes, Inc., 8; 42 (upd.)
Pyramid Companies, 54
Redrow Group plc, 31
Rinker Group Ltd., 65
RMC Group p.l.c., 34 (upd.)
Rooney Brothers Co., 25
The Rottlund Company, Inc., 28
Roy Anderson Corporation, 75
Ryan Companies US, Inc., 99
The Ryland Group, Inc., 8; 37 (upd.)
Sandvik AB, 32 (upd.)
Schuff Steel Company, 26
Seddon Group Ltd., 67
Servidyne Inc., 100 (upd.)
Shorewood Packaging Corporation, 28
Simon Property Group Inc., 27; 84 (upd.)
Skanska AB, 38
Skidmore, Owings & Merrill LLP, 69 (upd.)
SNC-Lavalin Group Inc., 72
Speedy Hire plc, 84
Stabler Companies Inc. 78
Standard Pacific Corporation, 52
The Structure Tone Organization, 99
Stone & Webster, Inc., 64 (upd.)
Sundt Corp., 24
Swinerton Inc., 43
Tarmac Limited, III, 28 (upd.); 95 (upd.)
Taylor Woodrow plc, I; 38 (upd.)
Technical Olympic USA, Inc., 75
Terex Corporation, 7; 40 (upd.); 91 (upd.)
ThyssenKrupp AG, IV; 28 (upd.); 87 (upd.)
TIC Holdings Inc., 92
Toll Brothers Inc., 15; 70 (upd.)
Trammell Crow Company, 8
Tridel Enterprises Inc., 9
Turner Construction Company, 66
The Turner Corporation, 8; 23 (upd.)
Urban Engineers, Inc., 102
Urbi Desarrollos Urbanos, S.A. de C.V., 81
U.S. Aggregates, Inc., 42
U.S. Home Corporation, 8; 78 (upd.)
VA TECH ELIN EBG GmbH, 49
Veidekke ASA, 98
Veit Companies, 43; 92 (upd.)
Wacker Construction Equipment AG, 95
Walbridge Aldinger Co., 38
Walter Industries, Inc., 22 (upd.)
The Weitz Company, Inc., 42
Whiting-Turner Contracting Company, 95
Willbros Group, Inc., 56
William Lyon Homes, 59
Wilson Bowden Plc, 45
Wood Hall Trust PLC, I
The Yates Companies, Inc., 62
Zachry Group, Inc., 95

Containers

Ball Corporation, I; 10 (upd.); 78 (upd.)
BWAY Corporation, 24
Chesapeake Corporation, 8; 30 (upd.); 93 (upd.)
Clarcor Inc., 17
Continental Can Co., Inc., 15
Continental Group Company, I
Crown Cork & Seal Company, Inc., I; 13 (upd.); 32 (upd.)
Crown Holdings, Inc., 83 (upd.)
Gaylord Container Corporation, 8
Golden Belt Manufacturing Co., 16
Graham Packaging Holdings Company, 87
Greif Inc., 15; 66 (upd.)
Grupo Industrial Durango, S.A. de C.V., 37
Hanjin Shipping Co., Ltd., 50
Inland Container Corporation, 8
Interpool, Inc., 92
Kerr Group Inc., 24
Keyes Fibre Company, 9
Libbey Inc., 49
Liqui-Box Corporation, 16
The Longaberger Company, 12
Longview Fibre Company, 8
The Mead Corporation, 19 (upd.)
Metal Box PLC, I
Molins plc, 51
National Can Corporation, I
Owens-Illinois, Inc., I; 26 (upd.); 85 (upd.)
Packaging Corporation of America, 51 (upd.)
Primerica Corporation, I
PVC Container Corporation, 67
Rexam PLC, 32 (upd.); 85 (upd.)
Reynolds Metals Company, 19 (upd.)
Royal Packaging Industries Van Leer N.V., 30
RPC Group PLC, 81
Sealright Co., Inc., 17
Shurgard Storage Centers, Inc., 52
Smurfit-Stone Container Corporation, 26 (upd.); 83 (upd.)
Sonoco Products Company, 8; 89 (upd.)
Thermos Company, 16
Toyo Seikan Kaisha, Ltd., I
U.S. Can Corporation, 30
Ultra Pac, Inc., 24
Viatech Continental Can Company, Inc., 25 (upd.)
Vidrala S.A., 67
Vitro Corporativo S.A. de C.V., 34

Drugs & Pharmaceuticals

A. Nelson & Co. Ltd., 75
A.L. Pharma Inc., 12
Abbott Laboratories, I; 11 (upd.); 40 (upd.); 93 (upd.)
Aché Laboratórios Farmacéuticas S.A., 105
Actavis Group hf., 103
Actelion Ltd., 83
Adolor Corporation, 101
Akorn, Inc., 32
Albany Molecular Research, Inc., 77
Allergan, Inc., 77 (upd.)

Alpharma Inc., 35 (upd.)
ALZA Corporation, 10; 36 (upd.)
American Home Products, I; 10 (upd.)
American Oriental Bioengineering Inc., 93
American Pharmaceutical Partners, Inc., 69
AmerisourceBergen Corporation, 64 (upd.)
Amersham PLC, 50
Amgen, Inc., 10; 89 (upd.)
Amylin Pharmaceuticals, Inc., 67
Andrx Corporation, 55
Angelini SpA, 100
Astellas Pharma Inc., 97 (upd.)
AstraZeneca PLC, I; 20 (upd.); 50 (upd.)
AtheroGenics Inc., 101
Axcan Pharma Inc., 85
Barr Pharmaceuticals, Inc., 26; 68 (upd.)
Bayer A.G., I; 13 (upd.)
Berlex Laboratories, Inc., 66
Biovail Corporation, 47
Block Drug Company, Inc., 8
Boiron S.A., 73
Bristol-Myers Squibb Company, III; 9 (upd.); 37 (upd.)
BTG Plc, 87
C.H. Boehringer Sohn, 39
Caremark Rx, Inc., 10; 54 (upd.)
Carter-Wallace, Inc., 8; 38 (upd.)
Celgene Corporation, 67
Cephalon, Inc., 45
Chiron Corporation, 10
Chugai Pharmaceutical Co., Ltd., 50
Ciba-Geigy Ltd., I; 8 (upd.)
D&K Wholesale Drug, Inc., 14
Discovery Partners International, Inc., 58
Dr. Reddy's Laboratories Ltd., 59
Egis Gyogyszergyar Nyrt, 104
Eisai Co., Ltd., 101
Elan Corporation PLC, 63
Eli Lilly and Company, I; 11 (upd.); 47 (upd.)
Endo Pharmaceuticals Holdings Inc., 71
Eon Labs, Inc., 67
Express Scripts Inc., 44 (upd.)
F. Hoffmann-La Roche Ltd., I; 50 (upd.)
Fisons plc, 9; 23 (upd.)
Forest Laboratories, Inc., 52 (upd.)
FoxMeyer Health Corporation, 16
Fujisawa Pharmaceutical Company Ltd., I
G.D. Searle & Co., I; 12 (upd.); 34 (upd.)
Galenica AG, 84
GEHE AG, 27
Genentech, Inc., I; 8 (upd.); 75 (upd.)
Genetics Institute, Inc., 8
Genzyme Corporation, 13, 77 (upd.)
Glaxo Holdings PLC, I; 9 (upd.)
GlaxoSmithKline plc, 46 (upd.)
Groupe Fournier SA, 44
Groupe Léa Nature, 88
H. Lundbeck A/S, 44
Hauser, Inc., 46
Heska Corporation, 39
Hexal AG, 69
Hikma Pharmaceuticals Ltd., 102
Hospira, Inc., 71
Huntingdon Life Sciences Group plc, 42

ICN Pharmaceuticals, Inc., 52
ICU Medical, Inc., 106
Immucor, Inc., 81
Integrated BioPharma, Inc., 83
IVAX Corporation, 55 (upd.)
Janssen Pharmaceutica N.V., 80
Johnson & Johnson, III; 8 (upd.)
Jones Medical Industries, Inc., 24
The Judge Group, Inc., 51
King Pharmaceuticals, Inc., 54
Kinray Inc., 85
Kos Pharmaceuticals, Inc., 63
Kyowa Hakko Kogyo Co., Ltd., 48 (upd.)
Laboratoires Arkopharma S.A., 75
Laboratoires Pierre Fabre S.A., 100
Leiner Health Products Inc., 34
Ligand Pharmaceuticals Incorporated, 47
MannKind Corporation, 87
Marion Merrell Dow, Inc., I; 9 (upd.)
Matrixx Initiatives, Inc., 74
McKesson Corporation, 12; 47 (upd.)
Medicis Pharmaceutical Corporation, 59
MedImmune, Inc., 35
Merck & Co., Inc., I; 11 (upd.); 34 (upd.); 95 (upd.)
Merial Ltd., 102
Merz Group, 81
Miles Laboratories, I
Millennium Pharmaceuticals, Inc., 47
Monsanto Company, 29 (upd.), 77 (upd.)
Moore Medical Corp., 17
Murdock Madaus Schwabe, 26
Mylan Laboratories Inc., I; 20 (upd.); 59 (upd.)
Myriad Genetics, Inc., 95
Nadro S.A. de C.V., 86
Nastech Pharmaceutical Company Inc., 79
National Patent Development Corporation, 13
Natrol, Inc., 49
Natural Alternatives International, Inc., 49
Nektar Therapeutics, 91
Novartis AG, 39 (upd.); 105 (upd.)
Noven Pharmaceuticals, Inc., 55
Novo Nordisk A/S, I; 61 (upd.)
Obagi Medical Products, Inc., 95
Omnicare, Inc., 49
Omrix Biopharmaccuticals, Inc., 95
Par Pharmaceutical Companies, Inc., 65
PDL BioPharma, Inc., 90
Perrigo Company, 59 (upd.)
Pfizer Inc., I; 9 (upd.); 38 (upd.); 79 (upd.)
Pharmacia & Upjohn Inc., I; 25 (upd.)
Pharmion Corporation, 91
PLIVA d.d., 70
PolyMedica Corporation, 77
POZEN Inc., 81
QLT Inc., 71
The Quigley Corporation, 62
Quintiles Transnational Corporation, 21
R.P. Scherer, I
Ranbaxy Laboratories Ltd., 70
ratiopharm Group, 84
Reckitt Benckiser plc, II; 42 (upd.); 91 (upd.)
Recordati Industria Chimica e Farmaceutica S.p.A., 105

Roberts Pharmaceutical Corporation, 16
Roche Bioscience, 14 (upd.)
Rorer Group, I
Roussel Uclaf, I; 8 (upd.)
Salix Pharmaceuticals, Ltd., 93
Sandoz Ltd., I
Sankyo Company, Ltd., I; 56 (upd.)
The Sanofi-Synthélabo Group, I; 49 (upd.)
Santarus, Inc., 105
Schering AG, I; 50 (upd.)
Schering-Plough Corporation, I; 14 (upd.); 49 (upd.); 99 (upd.)
Sepracor Inc., 45
Serono S.A., 47
Shionogi & Co., Ltd., III; 17 (upd.); 98 (upd.)
Sigma-Aldrich Corporation, I; 36 (upd.); 93 (upd.)
SmithKline Beecham plc, I; 32 (upd.)
Solvay S.A., 61 (upd.)
Squibb Corporation, I
Sterling Drug, Inc., I
Stiefel Laboratories, Inc., 90
Sun Pharmaceutical Industries Ltd., 57
The Sunrider Corporation, 26
Syntex Corporation, I
Takeda Chemical Industries, Ltd., I
Taro Pharmaceutical Industries Ltd., 65
Teva Pharmaceutical Industries Ltd., 22; 54 (upd.)
UCB Pharma SA, 98
The Upjohn Company, I; 8 (upd.)
Vertex Pharmaceuticals Incorporated, 83
Virbac Corporation, 74
Vitalink Pharmacy Services, Inc., 15
Warner Chilcott Limited, 85
Warner-Lambert Co., I; 10 (upd.)
Watson Pharmaceuticals Inc., 16; 56 (upd.)
The Wellcome Foundation Ltd., I
WonderWorks, Inc., 103
Zentiva N.V./Zentiva, a.s., 99
Zila, Inc., 46

Electrical & Electronics

ABB ASEA Brown Boveri Ltd., II; 22 (upd.)
ABB Ltd., 65 (upd.)
Acer Incorporated, 16; 73 (upd.)
Acuson Corporation, 10; 36 (upd.)
ADC Telecommunications, Inc., 30 (upd.)
Adtran Inc., 22
Advanced Micro Devices, Inc., 6; 30 (upd.); 99 (upd.)
Advanced Technology Laboratories, Inc., 9
Agere Systems Inc., 61
Agilent Technologies Inc., 38; 93 (upd.)
Agilysys Inc., 76 (upd.)
Aiwa Co., Ltd., 30
AKG Acoustics GmbH, 62
Akzo Nobel N.V., 13; 41 (upd.)
Alienware Corporation, 81
Alliant Techsystems Inc., 30 (upd.); 77 (upd.)
AlliedSignal Inc., 22 (upd.)
Alpine Electronics, Inc., 13
Alps Electric Co., Ltd., II

Altera Corporation, 18; 43 (upd.)
Altron Incorporated, 20
Amdahl Corporation, 40 (upd.)
American Power Conversion Corporation, 24; 67 (upd.)
American Superconductor Corporation, 97
American Technical Ceramics Corp., 67
American Technology Corporation, 103
Amerigon Incorporated, 97
Amkor Technology, Inc., 69
AMP Incorporated, II; 14 (upd.)
Amphenol Corporation, 40
Amstrad plc, 48 (upd.)
Analog Devices, Inc., 10
Analogic Corporation, 23
Anam Group, 23
Anaren Microwave, Inc., 33
Andrew Corporation, 10; 32 (upd.)
Anixter International Inc., 88
Anritsu Corporation, 68
Apex Digital, Inc., 63
Apple Computer, Inc., 36 (upd.); 77 (upd.)
Applied Power Inc., 32 (upd.)
Applied Signal Technology, Inc., 87
Argon ST, Inc., 81
Arotech Corporation, 93
ARRIS Group, Inc., 89
Arrow Electronics, Inc., 10; 50 (upd.)
Ascend Communications, Inc., 24
Astronics Corporation, 35
Atari Corporation, 9; 23 (upd.); 66 (upd.)
ATI Technologies Inc., 79
Atmel Corporation, 17
ATMI, Inc., 93
AU Optronics Corporation, 67
Audiovox Corporation, 34; 90 (upd.)
Ault Incorporated, 34
Autodesk, Inc., 10; 89 (upd.)
Avnet Inc., 9
AVX Corporation, 67
Axcelis Technologies, Inc., 95
Axsys Technologies, Inc., 93
Ballard Power Systems Inc., 73
Bang & Olufsen Holding A/S, 37; 86 (upd.)
Barco NV, 44
Bell Microproducts Inc., 69
Benchmark Electronics, Inc., 40
Bicoastal Corporation, II
Black Box Corporation, 20; 96 (upd.)
Blonder Tongue Laboratories, Inc., 48
Blue Coat Systems, Inc., 83
BMC Industries, Inc., 59 (upd.)
Bogen Communications International, Inc., 62
Bose Corporation, 13; 36 (upd.)
Boston Acoustics, Inc., 22
Bowthorpe plc, 33
Braun GmbH, 51
Brightpoint Inc., 18; 106 (upd.)
Broadcom Corporation, 34; 90 (upd.)
Bull S.A., 43 (upd.)
Burr-Brown Corporation, 19
BVR Systems (1998) Ltd., 93
C-COR.net Corp., 38
Cabletron Systems, Inc., 10

Cadence Design Systems, Inc., 48 (upd.)
Cambridge SoundWorks, Inc., 48
Canadian Solar Inc., 105
Canon Inc., 18 (upd.); 79 (upd.)
Carbone Lorraine S.A., 33
Cardtronics, Inc., 93
Carl Zeiss AG, III; 34 (upd.); 91 (upd.)
Cash Systems, Inc., 93
CASIO Computer Co., Ltd., 16 (upd.); 40 (upd.)
CDW Computer Centers, Inc., 52 (upd.)
Celestica Inc., 80
Checkpoint Systems, Inc., 39
Chi Mei Optoelectronics Corporation, 75
Christie Digital Systems, Inc., 103
Chubb, PLC, 50
Chunghwa Picture Tubes, Ltd., 75
Cirrus Logic, Inc., 48 (upd.)
Cisco Systems, Inc., 34 (upd.); 77 (upd.)
Citizen Watch Co., Ltd., III; 21 (upd.); 81 (upd.)
Clarion Company Ltd., 64
Cobham plc, 30
Cobra Electronics Corporation, 14
Coherent, Inc., 31
Cohu, Inc., 32
Color Kinetics Incorporated, 85
Comfort Systems USA, Inc., 101
Compagnie Générale d'Électricité, II
Concurrent Computer Corporation, 75
Conexant Systems Inc., 36; 106 (upd.)
Cooper Industries, Inc., II
Cray Inc., 75 (upd.)
Cray Research, Inc., 16 (upd.)
Cree Inc., 53
CTS Corporation, 39
Cubic Corporation, 19; 98 (upd.)
Cypress Semiconductor Corporation, 20; 48 (upd.)
D&H Distributing Co., 95
D-Link Corporation, 83
Dai Nippon Printing Co., Ltd., 57 (upd.)
Daiichikosho Company Ltd., 86
Daktronics, Inc., 32
Dallas Semiconductor Corporation, 13; 31 (upd.)
DDi Corp., 97
De La Rue plc, 34 (upd.)
Dell Computer Corporation, 31 (upd.)
DH Technology, Inc., 18
Dictaphone Healthcare Solutions 78
Diehl Stiftung & Co. KG, 79
Digi International Inc., 9
Diodes Incorporated, 81
Directed Electronics, Inc., 87
Discreet Logic Inc., 20
Dixons Group plc, 19 (upd.)
Dolby Laboratories Inc., 20
Dot Hill Systems Corp., 93
DRS Technologies, Inc., 58
DXP Enterprises, Inc., 101
Dynatech Corporation, 13
E-Systems, Inc., 9
Electronics for Imaging, Inc., 15; 43 (upd.)
Elma Electronic AG, 83
Elpida Memory, Inc., 83
EMCORE Corporation, 97

Emerson, II; 46 (upd.)
Emerson Radio Corp., 30
ENCAD, Incorporated, 25
Equant N.V., 52
Equus Computer Systems, Inc., 49
ESS Technology, Inc., 22
Essex Corporation, 85
Everex Systems, Inc., 16
Evergreen Solar, Inc., 101
Exabyte Corporation, 40 (upd.)
Exar Corp., 14
Exide Electronics Group, Inc., 20
Finisar Corporation, 92
First Solar, Inc., 95
Fisk Corporation, 72
Flextronics International Ltd., 38
Fluke Corporation, 15
FormFactor, Inc., 85
Foxboro Company, 13
Freescale Semiconductor, Inc., 83
Frequency Electronics, Inc., 61
FuelCell Energy, Inc., 75
Fuji Electric Co., Ltd., II; 48 (upd.)
Fuji Photo Film Co., Ltd., 79 (upd.)
Fujitsu Limited, III; 16 (upd.); 42 (upd.); 103 (upd.)
Funai Electric Company Ltd., 62
Galtronics Ltd., 100
Gateway, Inc., 63 (upd.)
General Atomics, 57
General Dynamics Corporation, I; 10 (upd.); 40 (upd.); 88 (upd.
General Electric Company, II; 12 (upd.)
General Electric Company, PLC, II
General Instrument Corporation, 10
General Signal Corporation, 9
Genesis Microchip Inc., 82
GenRad, Inc., 24
GM Hughes Electronics Corporation, II
Goldstar Co., Ltd., 12
Gould Electronics, Inc., 14
GPS Industries, Inc., 81
Grundig AG, 27
Guillemot Corporation, 41
Hadco Corporation, 24
Hamilton Beach/Proctor-Silex Inc., 17
Harman International Industries, Incorporated, 15; 101 (upd.)
Harris Corporation, II; 20 (upd.); 78 (upd.)
Hayes Corporation, 24
Hemisphere GPS Inc., 99
Herley Industries, Inc., 33
Hewlett-Packard Company, 28 (upd.); 50 (upd.)
Hittite Microwave Corporation, 106
Holophane Corporation, 19
Hon Hai Precision Industry Co., Ltd., 59
Honeywell Inc., II; 12 (upd.); 50 (upd.)
Hubbell Incorporated, 9; 31 (upd.)
Hughes Supply, Inc., 14
Hutchinson Technology Incorporated, 18; 63 (upd.)
Hypercom Corporation, 27
IDEO Inc., 65
IEC Electronics Corp., 42
Illumina, Inc., 93
Imax Corporation, 28

In Focus Systems, Inc., 22
Indigo NV, 26
InFocus Corporation, 92
Ingram Micro Inc., 52
Innovative Solutions & Support, Inc., 85
Integrated Defense Technologies, Inc., 54
Intel Corporation, II; 10 (upd.); 75 (upd.)
Intermec Technologies Corporation, 72
International Business Machines
    Corporation, III; 6 (upd.); 30 (upd.);
    63 (upd.)
International Rectifier Corporation, 31; 71
    (upd.)
Intersil Corporation, 93
Ionatron, Inc., 85
Itel Corporation, 9
Jabil Circuit, Inc., 36; 88 (upd.)
Jaco Electronics, Inc., 30
JDS Uniphase Corporation, 34
Johnson Controls, Inc., 59 (upd.)
Juno Lighting, Inc., 30
Katy Industries, Inc., 51 (upd.)
Keithley Instruments Inc., 16
Kemet Corp., 14
Kent Electronics Corporation, 17
Kenwood Corporation, 31
Kesa Electricals plc, 91
Kimball International, Inc., 48 (upd.)
Kingston Technology Corporation, 20
KitchenAid, 8
KLA-Tencor Corporation, 45 (upd.)
KnowledgeWare Inc., 9
Kollmorgen Corporation, 18
Konami Corporation, 96
Konica Corporation, III; 30 (upd.)
Koninklijke Philips Electronics N.V., 50
    (upd.)
Koor Industries Ltd., II
Kopin Corporation, 80
Koss Corporation, 38
Kudelski Group SA, 44
Kulicke and Soffa Industries, Inc., 33; 76
    (upd.)
Kyocera Corporation, II; 79 (upd.)
LaBarge Inc., 41
The Lamson & Sessions Co., 61 (upd.)
Lattice Semiconductor Corp., 16
LDK Solar Co., Ltd., 101
LeCroy Corporation, 41
Legrand SA, 21
Lenovo Group Ltd., 80
Leoni AG, 98
Lexmark International, Inc., 79 (upd.)
Linear Technology Corporation, 16; 99
    (upd.)
Littelfuse, Inc., 26
Loewe AG, 90
Loral Corporation, 9
LOUD Technologies, Inc., 95 (upd.)
Lowrance Electronics, Inc., 18
LSI Logic Corporation, 13; 64
Lucent Technologies Inc., 34
Lucky-Goldstar, II
Lunar Corporation, 29
Mackie Designs Inc., 33
MagneTek, Inc., 15; 41 (upd.)
Magneti Marelli Holding SpA, 90
Marconi plc, 33 (upd.)

Marquette Electronics, Inc., 13
Matsushita Electric Industrial Co., Ltd., II
Maxim Integrated Products, Inc., 16
McDATA Corporation, 75
Measurement Specialties, Inc., 71
Medis Technologies Ltd., 77
Merix Corporation, 36; 75 (upd.)
Methode Electronics, Inc., 13
Midway Games, Inc., 25; 102 (upd.)
Mitel Corporation, 18
MITRE Corporation, 26
Mitsubishi Electric Corporation, II; 44
    (upd.)
Molex Incorporated, 54 (upd.)
Monster Cable Products, Inc., 69
Motorola, Inc., II; 11 (upd.); 34 (upd.);
    93 (upd.)
N.F. Smith & Associates LP, 70
Nam Tai Electronics, Inc., 61
National Instruments Corporation, 22
National Presto Industries, Inc., 16; 43
    (upd.)
National Semiconductor Corporation, II;
    26 (upd.); 69 (upd.)
NEC Corporation, II; 21 (upd.); 57
    (upd.)
Network Equipment Technologies Inc., 92
Nexans SA, 54
Nintendo Co., Ltd., 28 (upd.)
Nokia Corporation, II; 17 (upd.); 38
    (upd.); 77 (upd.)
Nortel Networks Corporation, 36 (upd.)
Northrop Grumman Corporation, 45
    (upd.)
Oak Technology, Inc., 22
Océ N.V., 24; 91 (upd.)
Oki Electric Industry Company, Limited,
    II
Omnicell, Inc., 89
Omron Corporation, II; 28 (upd.)
Oplink Communications, Inc., 106
OPTEK Technology Inc., 98
Orbit International Corp., 105
Orbotech Ltd., 75
Otari Inc., 89
Otter Tail Power Company, 18
Palm, Inc., 36; 75 (upd.)
Palomar Medical Technologics, Inc., 22
Parlex Corporation, 61
The Peak Technologies Group, Inc., 14
Peavey Electronics Corporation, 16
Philips Electronics N.V., II; 13 (upd.)
Philips Electronics North America Corp.,
    13
Pioneer Electronic Corporation, 28 (upd.)
Pioneer-Standard Electronics Inc., 19
Pitney Bowes Inc., 47 (upd.)
Pittway Corporation, 9
Pixelworks, Inc., 69
Planar Systems, Inc., 61
Plantronics, Inc., 106
The Plessey Company, PLC, II
Plexus Corporation, 35; 80 (upd.)
Polk Audio, Inc., 34
Polaroid Corporation, III; 7 (upd.); 28
    (upd.); 93 (upd.)
Potter & Brumfield Inc., 11
Premier Industrial Corporation, 9

Protection One, Inc., 32
Quanta Computer Inc., 47; 79 (upd.)
Racal Electronics PLC, II
RadioShack Corporation, 36 (upd.); 101
    (upd.)
Radius Inc., 16
RAE Systems Inc., 83
Ramtron International Corporation, 89
Raychem Corporation, 8
Rayovac Corporation, 13
Raytheon Company, II; 11 (upd.); 38
    (upd.); 105 (upd.)
RCA Corporation, II
Read-Rite Corp., 10
Redback Networks, Inc., 92
Reliance Electric Company, 9
Research in Motion Ltd., 54
Rexel, Inc., 15
Richardson Electronics, Ltd., 17
Ricoh Company, Ltd., 36 (upd.)
Rimage Corp., 89
The Rival Company, 19
Rockford Corporation, 43
Rogers Corporation, 61
S&C Electric Company, 15
SAGEM S.A., 37
St. Louis Music, Inc., 48
Sam Ash Music Corporation, 30
Samsung Electronics Co., Ltd., 14; 41
    (upd.)
SANYO Electric Co., Ltd., II; 36 (upd.);
    95 (upd.)
Sarnoff Corporation, 57
ScanSource, Inc., 29; 74 (upd.)
Schneider S.A., II; 18 (upd.)
SCI Systems, Inc., 9
Scientific-Atlanta, Inc., 45 (upd.)
Scitex Corporation Ltd., 24
Seagate Technology, 8; 34 (upd.); 105
    (upd.)
SEGA Corporation, 73
Semitool, Inc., 79 (upd.)
Semtech Corporation, 32
Sennheiser Electronic GmbH & Co. KG,
    66
Sensormatic Electronics Corp., 11
Sensory Science Corporation, 37
SGI, 29 (upd.)
Sharp Corporation, II; 12 (upd.); 40
    (upd.)
Sheldahl Inc., 23
Shure Inc., 60
Siemens AG, II; 14 (upd.); 57 (upd.)
Silicon Graphics Incorporated, 9
Siltronic AG, 90
SL Industries, Inc., 77
SMART Modular Technologies, Inc., 86
Smiths Industries PLC, 25
Solectron Corporation, 12; 48 (upd.)
Sony Corporation, II; 12 (upd.); 40
    (upd.)
Spansion Inc., 80
Spectrum Control, Inc., 67
SPX Corporation, 47 (upd.); 103 (upd.)
Square D, 90
Sterling Electronics Corp., 18
STMicroelectronics NV, 52
Strix Ltd., 51

Stuart C. Irby Company, 58
Sumitomo Electric Industries, Ltd., II
Sun Microsystems, Inc., 7; 30 (upd.); 91 (upd.)
Sunbeam-Oster Co., Inc., 9
SunPower Corporation, 91
Suntech Power Holdings Company Ltd., 89
Synaptics Incorporated, 95
Syneron Medical Ltd., 91
SYNNEX Corporation, 73
Synopsys, Inc., 11; 69 (upd.)
Syntax-Brillian Corporation, 102
Sypris Solutions, Inc., 85
SyQuest Technology, Inc., 18
Tandy Corporation, II; 12 (upd.)
Tatung Co., 23
TDK Corporation, II; 17 (upd.); 49 (upd.)
TEAC Corporation 78
Tech-Sym Corporation, 18
Technitrol, Inc., 29
Tektronix, Inc., 8
Teledyne Technologies Inc., 62 (upd.)
Telxon Corporation, 10
Teradyne, Inc., 11; 98 (upd.)
Texas Instruments Inc., II; 11 (upd.); 46 (upd.)
Thales S.A., 42
Thomas & Betts Corporation, 11; 54 (upd.)
THOMSON multimedia S.A., II; 42 (upd.)
THQ, Inc., 92 (upd.)
The Titan Corporation, 36
TomTom N.V., 81
Tops Appliance City, Inc., 17
Toromont Industries, Ltd., 21
Trans-Lux Corporation, 51
Trimble Navigation Limited, 40
TriQuint Semiconductor, Inc., 63
Tweeter Home Entertainment Group, Inc., 30
Ultimate Electronics, Inc., 69 (upd.)
Ultrak Inc., 24
Uniden Corporation, 98
United Microelectronics Corporation, 98
Universal Electronics Inc., 39
Universal Security Instruments, Inc., 96
Varian Associates Inc., 12
Veeco Instruments Inc., 32
VIASYS Healthcare, Inc., 52
Viasystems Group, Inc., 67
Vicon Industries, Inc., 44
Victor Company of Japan, Limited, II; 26 (upd.); 83 (upd.)
Vishay Intertechnology, Inc., 21; 80 (upd.)
Vitesse Semiconductor Corporation, 32
Vitro Corp., 10
Vizio, Inc., 100
VLSI Technology, Inc., 16
VTech Holdings Ltd., 77
Wells-Gardner Electronics Corporation, 43
Westinghouse Electric Corporation, II; 12 (upd.)
Winbond Electronics Corporation, 74

Wincor Nixdorf Holding GmbH, 69 (upd.)
WuXi AppTec Company Ltd., 103
Wyle Electronics, 14
Xantrex Technology Inc., 97
Xerox Corporation, III; 6 (upd.); 26 (upd.); 69 (upd.)
Yageo Corporation, 16; 98 (upd.)
York Research Corporation, 35
Zenith Data Systems, Inc., 10
Zenith Electronics Corporation, II; 13 (upd.); 34 (upd.); 89 (upd.)
Zoom Telephonics, Inc., 18
Zoran Corporation, 77
Zumtobel AG, 50
Zytec Corporation, 19

Engineering & Management Services

AAON, Inc., 22
Aavid Thermal Technologies, Inc., 29
Acergy SA, 97
AECOM Technology Corporation, 79
Alliant Techsystems Inc., 30 (upd.)
Altran Technologies, 51
Amey Plc, 47
American Science & Engineering, Inc., 81
Analytic Sciences Corporation, 10
Arcadis NV, 26
Arthur D. Little, Inc., 35
The Austin Company, 8; 72 (upd.)
Autostrada Torino-Milano S.p.A., 101
Babcock International Group PLC, 69
Balfour Beatty plc, 36 (upd.)
BE&K, Inc., 73
Bechtel Corporation, I; 24 (upd.); 99 (upd.)
Birse Group PLC, 77
Bowen Engineering Corporation, 105
Brown & Root, Inc., 13
Bufete Industrial, S.A. de C.V., 34
C.H. Heist Corporation, 24
Camp Dresser & McKee Inc., 104
CDI Corporation, 6; 54 (upd.)
CH2M HILL Companies Ltd., 22; 96 (upd.)
The Charles Stark Draper Laboratory, Inc., 35
Coflexip S.A., 25
Corrections Corporation of America, 23
CRSS Inc., 6
Dames & Moore, Inc., 25
DAW Technologies, Inc., 25
Day & Zimmermann Inc., 9; 31 (upd.)
Donaldson Co. Inc., 16
Dycom Industries, Inc., 57
Edwards and Kelcey, 70
EG&G Incorporated, 8; 29 (upd.)
Eiffage, 27
Essef Corporation, 18
Exponent, Inc., 95
FKI Plc, 57
Fluor Corporation, 34 (upd.)
Forest City Enterprises, Inc., 52 (upd.)
Foster Wheeler Corporation, 6; 23 (upd.)
Foster Wheeler Ltd., 76 (upd.)
Framatome SA, 19

Fraport AG Frankfurt Airport Services Worldwide, 90
Fugro N.V., 98
Gale International Llc, 93
Georg Fischer AG Schaffhausen, 61
Gilbane, Inc., 34
Great Lakes Dredge & Dock Company, 69
Grupo Dragados SA, 55
Halliburton Company, III; 25 (upd.); 55 (upd.)
Halma plc, 104
Harding Lawson Associates Group, Inc., 16
Harley Ellis Devereaux Corporation, 101
Harza Engineering Company, 14
HDR Inc., 48
Hittite Microwave Corporation, 106
HOK Group, Inc., 59
ICF Kaiser International, Inc., 28
IHC Caland N.V., 71
Jacobs Engineering Group Inc., 6; 26 (upd.); 106 (upd.)
Jacques Whitford, 92
Jaiprakash Associates Limited, 101
The Judge Group, Inc., 51
JWP Inc., 9
KBR Inc., 106 (upd.)
The Keith Companies Inc., 54
Keller Group PLC, 95
Klöckner-Werke AG, 58 (upd.)
Kvaerner ASA, 36
Layne Christensen Company, 19
The Louis Berger Group, Inc., 104
The MacNeal-Schwendler Corporation, 25
Malcolm Pirnie, Inc., 42
McDermott International, Inc., 37 (upd.)
McKinsey & Company, Inc., 9
Michael Baker Corporation, 51 (upd.)
Mota-Engil, SGPS, S.A., 97
Nooter Corporation, 61
NTD Architecture, 101
Oceaneering International, Inc., 63
Odebrecht S.A., 73
Ogden Corporation, 6
Opus Corporation, 34; 101 (upd.)
PAREXEL International Corporation, 84
Parsons Brinckerhoff Inc., 34; 104 (upd.)
The Parsons Corporation, 8; 56 (upd.)
The PBSJ Corporation, 82
Petrofac Ltd., 95
Quanta Services, Inc., 79
RCM Technologies, Inc., 34
Renishaw plc, 46
Ricardo plc, 90
Rosemount Inc., 15
Roy F. Weston, Inc., 33
Royal Vopak NV, 41
Rust International Inc., 11
Sandia National Laboratories, 49
Sandvik AB, 32 (upd.)
Sarnoff Corporation, 57
Science Applications International Corporation, 15
SENTEL Corporation, 106
Serco Group plc, 47
Siegel & Gale, 64
Siemens AG, 57 (upd.)

SRI International, Inc., 57
SSOE Inc., 76
Stone & Webster, Inc., 13; 64 (upd.)
Sulzer Ltd., 68 (upd.)
Susquehanna Pfaltzgraff Company, 8
Sverdrup Corporation, 14
Tech-Sym Corporation, 44 (upd.)
Technip 78
Tetra Tech, Inc., 29
ThyssenKrupp AG, IV; 28 (upd.); 87 (upd.)
Towers Perrin, 32
Tracor Inc., 17
TRC Companies, Inc., 32
Underwriters Laboratories, Inc., 30
United Dominion Industries Limited, 8; 16 (upd.)
URS Corporation, 45; 80 (upd.)
U.S. Army Corps of Engineers, 91
VA TECH ELIN EBG GmbH, 49
VECO International, Inc., 7
Vinci, 43
Volkert and Associates, Inc., 98
The Weir Group PLC, 85
Willbros Group, Inc., 56
WS Atkins Plc, 45

Entertainment & Leisure

A&E Television Networks, 32
Aardman Animations Ltd., 61
ABC Family Worldwide, Inc., 52
Academy of Television Arts & Sciences, Inc., 55
Acclaim Entertainment Inc., 24
Activision, Inc., 32; 89 (upd.)
Adelman Travel Group, 105
AEI Music Network Inc., 35
Affinity Group Holding Inc., 56
Airtours Plc, 27
Alaska Railroad Corporation, 60
All American Communications Inc., 20
The All England Lawn Tennis & Croquet Club, 54
Allgemeiner Deutscher Automobil-Club e.V., 100
Alliance Entertainment Corp., 17
Alternative Tentacles Records, 66
Alvin Ailey Dance Foundation, Inc., 52
Amblin Entertainment, 21
AMC Entertainment Inc., 12; 35 (upd.)
American Golf Corporation, 45
American Gramaphone LLC, 52
American Kennel Club, Inc., 74
American Skiing Company, 28
Ameristar Casinos, Inc., 33; 69 (upd.)
AMF Bowling, Inc., 40
Anaheim Angels Baseball Club, Inc., 53
Anchor Gaming, 24
AOL Time Warner Inc., 57 (upd.)
Applause Inc., 24
Apple Corps Ltd., 87
Aprilia SpA, 17
Arena Leisure Plc, 99
Argosy Gaming Company, 21
Aristocrat Leisure Limited, 54
Arsenal Holdings PLC, 79
The Art Institute of Chicago, 29
The Arthur C. Clarke Foundation, 92

Artisan Entertainment Inc., 32 (upd.)
Asahi National Broadcasting Company, Ltd., 9
Aspen Skiing Company, 15
Aston Villa plc, 41
The Athletics Investment Group, 62
Atlanta National League Baseball Club, Inc., 43
The Atlantic Group, 23
Autotote Corporation, 20
Aztar Corporation, 13
Bad Boy Worldwide Entertainment Group, 58
Baker & Taylor Corporation, 16; 43 (upd.)
Bally Total Fitness Holding Corp., 25
Baltimore Orioles L.P., 66
Barden Companies, Inc., 76
The Baseball Club of Seattle, LP, 50
The Basketball Club of Seattle, LLC, 50
Beggars Group Ltd., 99
Bertelsmann A.G., IV; 15 (upd.); 43 (upd.); 91 (upd.)
Bertucci's Inc., 16
Big Idea Productions, Inc., 49
BigBen Interactive S.A., 72
BioWare Corporation, 81
Blockbuster Inc., 9; 31 (upd.); 76 (upd.)
Boca Resorts, Inc., 37
Bonneville International Corporation, 29
Booth Creek Ski Holdings, Inc., 31
Boston Celtics Limited Partnership, 14
Boston Professional Hockey Association Inc., 39
The Boston Symphony Orchestra Inc., 93
The Boy Scouts of America, 34
Boyne USA Resorts, 71
Brillstein-Grey Entertainment, 80
British Broadcasting Corporation Ltd., 7; 21 (upd.); 89 (upd.)
The British Film Institute, 80
The British Museum, 71
British Sky Broadcasting Group plc, 20; 60 (upd.)
Brunswick Corporation, III; 22 (upd.); 77 (upd.)
Busch Entertainment Corporation, 73
Cablevision Systems Corporation, 7
California Sports, Inc., 56
Callaway Golf Company, 45 (upd.)
Canlan Ice Sports Corp., 105
Canterbury Park Holding Corporation, 42
Capcom Company Ltd., 83
Capital Cities/ABC Inc., II
Capitol Records, Inc., 90
Carlson Companies, Inc., 6; 22 (upd.); 87 (upd.)
Carlson Wagonlit Travel, 55
Carmike Cinemas, Inc., 14; 37 (upd.); 74 (upd.)
The Carnegie Hall Corporation, 101
Carnival Corporation, 6; 27 (upd.); 78 (upd.)
Carrere Group S.A., 104
The Carsey-Werner Company, L.L.C., 37
CBS Inc., II; 6 (upd.)
Cedar Fair Entertainment Company, 22; 98 (upd.)

Central European Media Enterprises Ltd., 61
Central Independent Television, 7; 23 (upd.)
Century Casinos, Inc., 53
Century Theatres, Inc., 31
Championship Auto Racing Teams, Inc., 37
Channel Four Television Corporation, 93
Chello Zone Ltd., 93
Chelsea Ltd., 102
Chelsea Piers Management Inc., 86
Chicago Bears Football Club, Inc., 33
Chicago National League Ball Club, Inc., 66
Chicago Symphony Orchestra, 106
Chris-Craft Corporation, 9, 31 (upd.); 80 (upd.)
Chrysalis Group plc, 40
Churchill Downs Incorporated, 29
Cinar Corporation, 40
Cinemark Holdings, Inc., 95
Cinemas de la República, S.A. de C.V., 83
Cineplex Odeon Corporation, 6; 23 (upd.)
Cinram International, Inc., 43
Cirque du Soleil Inc., 29; 98 (upd.)
CKX, Inc., 102
Classic Vacation Group, Inc., 46
Cleveland Indians Baseball Company, Inc., 37
Club Méditerranée S.A., 6; 21 (upd.); 91 (upd.)
ClubCorp, Inc., 33
CMG Worldwide, Inc., 89
Colonial Williamsburg Foundation, 53
Colorado Baseball Management, Inc., 72
Columbia Pictures Entertainment, Inc., II
Columbia TriStar Motion Pictures Companies, 12 (upd.)
Comcast Corporation, 7
Compagnie des Alpes, 48
Confluence Holdings Corporation, 76
Continental Cablevision, Inc., 7
Corporación Interamericana de Entretenimiento, S.A. de C.V., 83
Corporation for Public Broadcasting, 14; 89 (upd.)
Cox Enterprises, Inc., IV; 22 (upd.); 67 (upd.)
Cranium, Inc., 69
Crown Media Holdings, Inc., 45
Cruise America Inc., 21
CryptoLogic Limited, 106
Cunard Line Ltd., 23
Cyan Worlds Inc., 101
Dallas Cowboys Football Club, Ltd., 33
Dave & Buster's, Inc., 33; 104 (upd.)
Death Row Records, 27
Deluxe Entertainment Services Group, Inc., 100
Denver Nuggets, 51
The Detroit Lions, Inc., 55
The Detroit Pistons Basketball Company, 41
Detroit Red Wings, 74
Detroit Tigers Baseball Club, Inc., 46
Deutsche Fussball Bund e.V., 98

dick clark productions, inc., 16
DIRECTV, Inc., 38; 75 (upd.)
Disney/ABC Television Group, 106
Dover Downs Entertainment, Inc., 43
DreamWorks Animation SKG, Inc., 43; 106 (upd.)
Dualstar Entertainment Group LLC, 76
DW II Distribution Co. LLC, 106
E! Entertainment Television Inc., 17
edel music AG, 44
Educational Broadcasting Corporation, 48
Edwards Theatres Circuit, Inc., 31
Egmont Group, 93
Electronic Arts Inc., 10; 85 (upd.)
Elektra Entertainment Group, 64
Elsinore Corporation, 48
Elvis Presley Enterprises, Inc., 61
Empire Resorts, Inc., 72
Endemol Entertainment Holding NV, 46
Entertainment Distribution Company, 89
Equity Marketing, Inc., 26
ESPN, Inc., 56
Esporta plc, 35
Euro Disney S.C.A., 20; 58 (upd.)
Europe Through the Back Door Inc., 65
Fair Grounds Corporation, 44
Family Golf Centers, Inc., 29
FAO Schwarz, 46
Fédération Internationale de Football Association, 27
Feld Entertainment, Inc., 32 (upd.)
Film Roman, Inc., 58
First Artist Corporation PLC, 105
First Choice Holidays PLC, 40
First Team Sports, Inc., 22
Fisher-Price Inc., 32 (upd.)
Florida Gaming Corporation, 47
Focus Features 78
4Kids Entertainment Inc., 59
Fox Entertainment Group, Inc., 43
Fox Family Worldwide, Inc., 24
Fuji Television Network Inc., 91
The GAME Group plc, 80
GameStop Corp., 69 (upd.)
Gaumont SA, 25; 91 (upd.)
Gaylord Entertainment Company, 11; 36 (upd.)
GC Companies, Inc., 25
Geffen Records Inc., 26
Gibson Guitar Corporation, 16; 100 (upd.)
Gilmore Entertainment Group L.L.C., 100
Girl Scouts of the USA, 35
Global Outdoors, Inc., 49
Glu Mobile Inc., 95
GoodTimes Entertainment Ltd., 48
Granada Group PLC, II; 24 (upd.)
Grand Casinos, Inc., 20
Great Wolf Resorts, Inc., 91
Greater Washington Educational Telecommunication Association, 103
Greek Organization of Football Prognostics S.A. (OPAP), 97
The Green Bay Packers, Inc., 32
Grévin & Compagnie SA, 56
Groupe Partouche SA, 48
Grupo Televisa, S.A., 54 (upd.)

H. Betti Industries Inc., 88
Hallmark Cards, Inc., IV; 16 (upd.); 40 (upd.); 87 (upd.)
Hanna-Barbera Cartoons Inc., 23
Hard Rock Café International, Inc., 12; 32 (upd.); 105 (upd.)
Harlem Globetrotters International, Inc., 61
Harpo Inc., 28; 66 (upd.)
Harrah's Entertainment, Inc., 16; 43 (upd.)
Harveys Casino Resorts, 27
Hasbro, Inc., III; 16 (upd.); 43 (upd.)
Hastings Entertainment, Inc., 29; 104 (upd.)
The Hearst Corporation, 46 (upd.)
The Heat Group, 53
Hendrick Motorsports, Inc., 89
Herschend Family Entertainment Corporation, 73
Hilton Group plc, III; 19 (upd.); 49 (upd.)
HIT Entertainment PLC, 40
HOB Entertainment, Inc., 37
Holidaybreak plc, 96
Hollywood Casino Corporation, 21
Hollywood Entertainment Corporation, 25
Hollywood Media Corporation, 58
Hollywood Park, Inc., 20
Home Box Office Inc., 7; 23 (upd.); 76 (upd.)
Horseshoe Gaming Holding Corporation, 62
I Grandi Viaggi S.p.A., 105
IG Group Holdings plc, 97
Imagine Entertainment, 91
IMAX Corporation 28; 78 (upd.)
IMG 78
Indianapolis Motor Speedway Corporation, 46
Infinity Broadcasting Corporation, 48 (upd.)
Infogrames Entertainment S.A., 35
Integrity Inc., 44
International Creative Management, Inc., 43
International Family Entertainment Inc., 13
International Game Technology, 41 (upd.)
International Olympic Committee, 44
International Speedway Corporation, 19; 74 (upd.)
Interscope Music Group, 31
Intrawest Corporation, 15; 84 (upd.)
Irvin Feld & Kenneth Feld Productions, Inc., 15
Isle of Capri Casinos, Inc., 41
iVillage, 46
Iwerks Entertainment, Inc., 34
Jackpot Enterprises Inc., 21
Japan Broadcasting Corporation, 7
Jazz Basketball Investors, Inc., 55
Jazzercise, Inc., 45
Jillian's Entertainment Holdings, Inc., 40
The Jim Henson Company, 23; 106 (upd.)
The Joffrey Ballet of Chicago, 52

John F. Kennedy Center for the Performing Arts, 106
Jurys Doyle Hotel Group plc, 64
Juventus F.C. S.p.A, 53
K'Nex Industries, Inc., 52
Kampgrounds of America, Inc. (KOA), 33
Kerasotes ShowPlace Theaters LLC, 80
Kerzner International Limited, 69 (upd.)
King World Productions, Inc., 9; 30 (upd.)
Klasky Csupo Inc. 78
Knott's Berry Farm, 18
Kuoni Travel Holding Ltd., 40
The Kushner-Locke Company, 25
Ladbroke Group PLC, II; 21 (upd.)
Lakes Entertainment, Inc., 51
Landmark Theatre Corporation, 70
Las Vegas Sands, Inc., 50
Lego A/S, 13; 40 (upd.)
Liberty Livewire Corporation, 42
Liberty Media Corporation, 50
Liberty Travel, Inc., 56
Life Time Fitness, Inc., 66
Lifetime Entertainment Services, 51
Lincoln Center for the Performing Arts, Inc., 69
Lionel L.L.C., 16; 99 (upd.)
Lions Gate Entertainment Corporation, 35
LIVE Entertainment Inc., 20
Live Nation, Inc., 80 (upd.)
The Liverpool Football Club and Athletic Grounds PLC, 105
LodgeNet Interactive Corporation, 28; 106 (upd.)
Los Angeles Turf Club Inc., 102
Lucasfilm Ltd., 12; 50 (upd.)
Luminar Plc, 40
Majesco Entertainment Company, 85
Mammoth Mountain Ski Area, 101
Manchester United Football Club plc, 30
Mandalay Resort Group, 32 (upd.)
Maple Leaf Sports & Entertainment Ltd., 61
Marc Ecko Enterprises, Inc., 105
The Marcus Corporation, 21
The Mark Travel Corporation, 80
Märklin Holding GmbH, 70
Martha Stewart Living Omnimedia, Inc., 73 (upd.)
Mashantucket Pequot Gaming Enterprise Inc., 35
MCA Inc., II
McMenamins Pubs and Breweries, 65
Media General, Inc., 7
Mediaset SpA, 50
Mega Bloks, Inc., 61
Melco Crown Entertainment Limited, 103
Merlin Entertainments Group Ltd., 105
Metro-Goldwyn-Mayer Inc., 25 (upd.); 84 (upd.)
Metromedia Companies, 14
Métropole Télévision, 33
Métropole Télévision S.A., 76 (upd.)
Metropolitan Baseball Club Inc., 39
The Metropolitan Museum of Art, 55
Metropolitan Opera Association, Inc., 40
MGM Grand Inc., 17

MGM/UA Communications Company, II
Midway Games, Inc., 25; 102 (upd.)
Mikohn Gaming Corporation, 39
Milan AC, S.p.A., 79
Milwaukee Brewers Baseball Club, 37
Miramax Film Corporation, 64
Mizuno Corporation, 25
Mohegan Tribal Gaming Authority, 37
Moliflor Loisirs, 80
Monarch Casino & Resort, Inc., 65
Motown Records Company L.P., 26
Movie Gallery, Inc., 31
Mr. Gatti's, LP, 87
MTR Gaming Group, Inc., 75
Multimedia Games, Inc., 41
Museum of Modern Art, 106
Muzak, Inc., 18
Namco Bandai Holdings Inc., 106 (upd.)
National Amusements Inc., 28
National Aquarium in Baltimore, Inc., 74
National Association for Stock Car Auto
    Racing, 32
National Broadcasting Company, Inc., II;
    6 (upd.)
National CineMedia, Inc., 103
National Collegiate Athletic Association,
    96
National Football League, 29
National Hockey League, 35
National Public Radio, Inc., 19; 47 (upd.)
National Rifle Association of America, 37
National Thoroughbred Racing
    Association, 58
Navarre Corporation, 24
Navigant International, Inc., 47
NBGS International, Inc., 73
NCL Corporation, 79
New Jersey Devils, 84
New Line Cinema, Inc., 47
New Orleans Saints LP, 58
New York City Off-Track Betting
    Corporation, 51
New York Shakespeare Festival
    Management, 93
New York Yacht Club, Inc., 103
News Corporation Limited, 46 (upd.)
NFL Films, 75
Nicklaus Companies, 45
Nintendo Company, Ltd., 28 (upd.); 67
    (upd.)
Nordisk Film A/S, 80
O'Charley's Inc., 19
The Orchard Enterprises, Inc., 103
Orion Pictures Corporation, 6
Outrigger Enterprises, Inc., 67
Palace Sports & Entertainment, Inc., 97
Paradise Music & Entertainment, Inc., 42
Paramount Pictures Corporation, II
Patch Products Inc., 105
Pathé SA, 29
Paul Reed Smith Guitar Company, 89
Paul-Son Gaming Corporation, 66
PDS Gaming Corporation, 44
Peace Arch Entertainment Group Inc., 51
Penn National Gaming, Inc., 33
Philadelphia Eagles, 37

Philharmonic-Symphony Society of New
    York, Inc. (New York Philharmonic),
    69
The Phillies, 106
Pierre & Vacances SA, 48
Pittsburgh Steelers Sports, Inc., 66
Pixar Animation Studios, 34
Platinum Entertainment, Inc., 35
Play by Play Toys & Novelties, Inc., 26
Players International, Inc., 22
Pleasant Holidays LLC, 62
PolyGram N.V., 23
Poof-Slinky, Inc., 61
Pop Warner Little Scholars, Inc., 86
Portland Trail Blazers, 50
Powerhouse Technologies, Inc., 27
Premier Parks, Inc., 27
President Casinos, Inc., 22
Preussag AG, 42 (upd.)
Princess Cruise Lines, 22
Professional Bull Riders Inc., 55
The Professional Golfers' Association of
    America, 41
Promus Companies, Inc., 9
ProSiebenSat.1 Media AG, 54
Publishing and Broadcasting Limited, 54
Putt-Putt Golf Courses of America, Inc.,
    23
@radical.media, 103
Radio One, Inc., 67
Ragdoll Productions Ltd., 51
Rainforest Café, Inc., 25; 88 (upd.)
The Rank Group plc, II; 64 (upd.)
Rawlings Sporting Goods Co., Inc., 24
Real Madrid C.F., 73
The Really Useful Group, 26
Regal Entertainment Group, 59
Rentrak Corporation, 35
Rhino Entertainment Company, 18; 70
    (upd.)
Rhythm & Hues Studios, Inc., 103
Ride, Inc., 22
Ripley Entertainment, Inc., 74
Riviera Holdings Corporation, 75
Rollerblade, Inc., 34 (upd.)
Roularta Media Group NV, 48
Rounder Records Corporation, 79
Royal Caribbean Cruises Ltd., 22; 74
    (upd.)
Royal Olympic Cruise Lines Inc., 52
RTL Group SA, 44
Rush Communications, 33
Ryko Corporation, 83
S-K-I Limited, 15
Sabre Holdings Corporation, 74 (upd.)
Sally Industries, Inc., 103
Salomon Worldwide, 20
San Diego Padres Baseball Club LP 78
San Francisco Baseball Associates, L.P., 55
The Sanctuary Group PLC, 69
Santa Fe Gaming Corporation, 19
Schwinn Cycle and Fitness L.P., 19
Scientific Games Corporation, 64 (upd.)
Scottish Radio Holding plc, 41
Seattle FilmWorks, Inc., 20
Seattle Seahawks, Inc., 92
The Second City, Inc., 88
SEGA Corporation, 73

Sega of America, Inc., 10
Selectour SA, 53
SFX Entertainment, Inc., 36
Shed Media plc, 104
Shedd Aquarium Society, 73
Shell Vacations LLC, 102
Shochiku Company Ltd., 74
Showboat, Inc., 19
Showtime Networks Inc. 78
Shubert Organization Inc., 24
Shuffle Master Inc., 51
Silverstar Holdings, Ltd., 99
The Singing Machine Company, Inc., 60
Sirius Satellite Radio, Inc., 69
Six Flags, Inc., 17; 54 (upd.)
SJM Holdings Ltd., 105
Smithsonian Institution, 27
Società Sportiva Lazio SpA, 44
Sony Corporation, II; 12 (upd.); 40
    (upd.)
Southern Sun Hotel Interest (Pty) Ltd.,
    106
Speedway Motorsports, Inc., 32
Spelling Entertainment Group, Inc., 14
Spin Master, Ltd., 61
The Sports Club Company, 25
Spyglass Entertainment Group, LLC, 91
Square Enix Holdings Co., Ltd., 101
Stanley Leisure plc, 66
Starz LLC, 91
Station Casinos, Inc., 25; 90 (upd.)
Stoll-Moss Theatres Ltd., 34
Stuart Entertainment Inc., 16
Sub Pop Ltd., 97
Sunshine Village Corporation, 103
TABCORP Holdings Limited, 44
Take-Two Interactive Software, Inc., 46
TaylorMade-adidas Golf, 23; 96 (upd.)
Tecmo Koei Holdings Company Ltd., 106
Tee Vee Toons, Inc., 57
Tele-Communications, Inc., II
Television Española, S.A., 7
Texas Rangers Baseball, 51
Tha Row Records, 69 (upd.)
Thomas Cook Travel Inc., 9
The Thomson Corporation, 8
Thousand Trails, Inc., 33
THQ, Inc., 39
365 Media Group plc, 89
Ticketmaster Corp., 13
Tiger Aspect Productions Ltd., 72
The Todd-AO Corporation, 33
Toho Co., Ltd., 28
TOKYOPOP Inc., 79
Tomy Company Ltd., 65
The Topps Company, Inc., 13, 34 (upd.);
    83 (upd.)
Tottenham Hotspur PLC, 81
Touristik Union International GmbH. and
    Company K.G., II
Town Sports International, Inc., 46
Toy Biz, Inc., 18
Trans World Entertainment Corporation,
    24
Travelocity.com, Inc., 46
Tribune Company, 63 (upd.)
TUI Group GmbH, 44

Turner Broadcasting System, Inc., II; 6 (upd.); 66 (upd.)
The Tussauds Group, 55
Twentieth Century Fox Film Corporation, II; 25 (upd.)
24 Hour Fitness Worldwide, Inc., 71
Ubisoft Entertainment S.A., 41; 106 (upd.)
Ulster Television PLC, 71
Ultimate Leisure Group PLC, 75
United Pan-Europe Communications NV, 47
United States Playing Card Company, 62
United Talent Agency, Inc., 80
Universal Studios, Inc., 33; 100 (upd.)
Univision Communications Inc., 24; 83 (upd.)
Urbium PLC, 75
USA Interactive, Inc., 47 (upd.)
Vail Resorts, Inc., 11; 43 (upd.)
Valve Corporation, 101
Venetian Casino Resort, LLC, 47
Viacom Inc., 7; 23 (upd.)
Village Roadshow Ltd., 58
Vinton Studios, 63
Vivendi Universal S.A., 46 (upd.)
Vulcabras S.A., 103
The Walt Disney Company, II; 6 (upd.); 30 (upd.); 63 (upd.)
Warner Communications Inc., II
Warner Music Group Corporation, 90 (upd.)
Washington Football, Inc., 35
The Welk Group Inc., 78
West Coast Entertainment Corporation, 29
WGBH Educational Foundation, 66
Wham-O, Inc., 61
Wherehouse Entertainment Incorporated, 11
Whitbread PLC, I; 20 (upd.); 52 (upd.); 97 (upd.)
Wildlife Conservation Society, 31
William Hill Organization Limited, 49
William Morris Agency, Inc., 23; 102 (upd.)
Williams-Sonoma, Inc., 17; 44 (upd.); 103 (upd.)
Wilson Sporting Goods Company, 24; 84 (upd.)
Wizards of the Coast Inc., 24
WMS Industries, Inc., 53 (upd.)
World Wrestling Federation Entertainment, Inc., 32
Worldwide Pants Inc., 97
Writers Guild of America, West, Inc., 92
XM Satellite Radio Holdings, Inc., 69
YankeeNets LLC, 35
YES! Entertainment Corporation, 26
YMCA of the USA, 31
Working Title Films Ltd., 105
Youbet.com, Inc., 77
Young Broadcasting Inc., 40
Zomba Records Ltd., 52
Zuffa L.L.C., 89

Financial Services: Banks

Abbey National plc, 10; 39 (upd.)
Abigail Adams National Bancorp, Inc., 23
ABN AMRO Holding, N.V., 50
Absa Group Ltd., 106
Affiliated Managers Group, Inc., 79
Akbank TAS, 79
Alabama National BanCorporation, 75
Algemene Bank Nederland N.V., II
Alliance and Leicester plc, 88
Allianz AG, 57 (upd.)
Allied Irish Banks, plc, 16; 43 (upd.)
Almanij NV, 44
Amalgamated Bank, 60
AMCORE Financial Inc., 44
American Residential Mortgage Corporation, 8
AmSouth Bancorporation,12; 48 (upd.)
Amsterdam-Rotterdam Bank N.V., II
Anchor Bancorp, Inc., 10
Anchor BanCorp Wisconsin, Inc., 101
Apple Bank for Savings, 59
Astoria Financial Corporation, 44
Australia and New Zealand Banking Group Limited, II; 52 (upd.)
Banca Commerciale Italiana SpA, II
Banca Fideuram SpA, 63
Banca Intesa SpA, 65
Banca Monte dei Paschi di Siena SpA, 65
Banca Nazionale del Lavoro SpA, 72
Banco Bilbao Vizcaya Argentaria S.A., II; 48 (upd.)
Banco Bradesco S.A., 13
Banco Central, II
Banco Central del Paraguay, 100
Banco Comercial Português, SA, 50
Banco de Chile, 69
Banco de Crédito del Perú, 93
Banco do Brasil S.A., II
Banco Espírito Santo e Comercial de Lisboa S.A., 15
Banco Itaú S.A., 19
Banco Santander Central Hispano S.A., 36 (upd.)
Bank Austria AG, 23; 100 (upd.)
Bank Brussels Lambert, II
Bank Hapoalim B.M., II; 54 (upd.)
Bank Leumi le-Israel B.M., 60
Bank of America Corporation, 46 (upd.); 101 (upd.)
Bank of Boston Corporation, II
Bank of China, 63
Bank of Cyprus Group, 91
Bank of East Asia Ltd., 63
Bank of Granite Corporation, 89
Bank of Hawaii Corporation, 73
Bank of Ireland, 50
Bank of Mississippi, Inc., 14
Bank of Montreal, II; 46 (upd.)
Bank of New England Corporation, II
The Bank of New York Company, Inc., II; 46 (upd.)
The Bank of Nova Scotia, II; 59 (upd.)
Bank of the Ozarks, Inc., 91
Bank of the Philippine Islands, 58
Bank of Tokyo-Mitsubishi Ltd., II; 15 (upd.)
Bank One Corporation, 10; 36 (upd.)

BankAmerica Corporation, II; 8 (upd.)
Bankers Trust New York Corporation, II
Banknorth Group, Inc., 55
Banner Corporation, 106
Banque Nationale de Paris S.A., II
Barclays plc, II; 20 (upd.); 64 (upd.)
BarclaysAmerican Mortgage Corporation, 11
Barings PLC, 14
Barnett Banks, Inc., 9
BayBanks, Inc., 12
Bayerische Hypotheken- und Wechsel-Bank AG, II
Bayerische Vereinsbank A.G., II
BB&T Corporation, 79
Bci, 99
Beneficial Corporation, 8
Blom Bank S.A.L., 102
BNP Paribas Group, 36 (upd.)
Boatmen's Bancshares Inc., 15
Bremer Financial Corporation, 45; 105 (upd.)
Brown Brothers Harriman & Co., 45
C. Hoare & Co., 77
Cadence Financial Corporation, 106
Caisse des Dépôts et Consignations, 90
Canadian Imperial Bank of Commerce, II; 61 (upd.)
Capital City Bank Group, Inc., 105
Capitalia S.p.A., 65
Carolina First Corporation, 31
Casco Northern Bank, 14
Charter Financial Corporation, 103
The Chase Manhattan Corporation, II; 13 (upd.)
Cheltenham & Gloucester PLC, 61
Chemical Banking Corporation, II; 14 (upd.)
China Construction Bank Corp., 79
Citicorp, II; 9 (upd.)
Citigroup Inc., 30 (upd.); 59 (upd.)
Citizens Financial Group, Inc., 42; 87 (upd.)
Close Brothers Group plc, 39
Comerica Incorporated, 40; 101 (upd.)
Commercial Credit Company, 8
Commercial Federal Corporation, 12; 62 (upd.)
Commerzbank A.G., II; 47 (upd.)
Compagnie Financiere de Paribas, II
Compass Bancshares, Inc., 73
Continental Bank Corporation, II
CoreStates Financial Corp, 17
Corus Bankshares, Inc., 75
Countrywide Financial, 16; 100 (upd.)
Crédit Agricole Group, II; 84 (upd.)
Crédit Lyonnais, 9; 33 (upd.)
Crédit National S.A., 9
Credit Suisse Group, II; 21 (upd.); 59 (upd.)
Credito Italiano, II
Cullen/Frost Bankers, Inc., 25
CUNA Mutual Group, 62
The Dai-Ichi Kangyo Bank Ltd., II
The Daiwa Bank, Ltd., II; 39 (upd.)
Danske Bank Aktieselskab, 50
Dauphin Deposit Corporation, 14
DEPFA BANK PLC, 69

Deposit Guaranty Corporation, 17
Deutsche Bank AG, II; 14 (upd.); 40 (upd.)
Deutscher Sparkassen- und Giroverband (DSGV), 84
Dexia NV/SA, 42; 88 (upd.)
Dime Savings Bank of New York, F.S.B., 9
Donaldson, Lufkin & Jenrette, Inc., 22
Dresdner Bank A.G., II; 57 (upd.)
Emigrant Savings Bank, 59
Erste Bank der Osterreichischen Sparkassen AG, 69
Espèrito Santo Financial Group S.A., 79 (upd.)
European Investment Bank, 66
Fidelity Southern Corporation, 85
Fifth Third Bancorp, 13; 31 (upd.); 103 (upd.)
First Bank System Inc., 12
First Busey Corporation, 105
First Chicago Corporation, II
First Commerce Bancshares, Inc., 15
First Commerce Corporation, 11
First Empire State Corporation, 11
First Fidelity Bank, N.A., New Jersey, 9
First Hawaiian, Inc., 11
First Interstate Bancorp, II
First Nationwide Bank, 14
First of America Bank Corporation, 8
First Security Corporation, 11
First Tennessee National Corporation, 11; 48 (upd.)
First Union Corporation, 10
First Virginia Banks, Inc., 11
Firstar Corporation, 11; 33 (upd.)
FirstMerit Corporation, 105
Fleet Financial Group, Inc., 9
FleetBoston Financial Corporation, 36 (upd.)
FöreningsSparbanken AB, 69
Fourth Financial Corporation, 11
The Fuji Bank, Ltd., II
Generale Bank, II
German American Bancorp, 41
Glacier Bancorp, Inc., 35
Golden West Financial Corporation, 47
The Governor and Company of the Bank of Scotland, 10
Grameen Bank, 31
Granite State Bankshares, Inc., 37
Great Lakes Bancorp, 8
Great Western Financial Corporation, 10
GreenPoint Financial Corp., 28
Groupe Caisse d'Epargne, 100
Grupo Financiero Banamex S.A., 54
Grupo Financiero Banorte, S.A. de C.V., 51
Grupo Financiero BBVA Bancomer S.A., 54
Grupo Financiero Galicia S.A., 63
Grupo Financiero Serfin, S.A., 19
H.F. Ahmanson & Company, II; 10 (upd.)
Habersham Bancorp, 25
Hancock Holding Company, 15
Hang Seng Bank Ltd., 60
Hanmi Financial Corporation, 66

Hibernia Corporation, 37
Hogg Robinson Group PLC, 105
The Hongkong and Shanghai Banking Corporation Limited, II
HSBC Holdings plc, 12; 26 (upd.); 80 (upd.)
Hudson River Bancorp, Inc., 41
Huntington Bancshares Incorporated, 11; 87 (upd.)
HVB Group, 59 (upd.)
IBERIABANK Corporation, 37
The Industrial Bank of Japan, Ltd., II
Irish Life & Permanent Plc, 59
Irwin Financial Corporation, 77
J Sainsbury plc, II; 13 (upd.); 38 (upd.); 95 (upd.)
J.P. Morgan & Co. Incorporated, II; 30 (upd.)
J.P. Morgan Chase & Co., 38 (upd.)
Japan Leasing Corporation, 8
JPMorgan Chase & Co., 91 (upd.)
Julius Baer Holding AG, 52
Kansallis-Osake-Pankki, II
KeyCorp, 8; 93 (upd.)
Kookmin Bank, 58
Kredietbank N.V., II
Kreditanstalt für Wiederaufbau, 29
Krung Thai Bank Public Company Ltd., 69
Landsbanki Islands hf, 81
Lloyds Bank PLC, II
Lloyds TSB Group plc, 47 (upd.)
Long Island Bancorp, Inc., 16
Long-Term Credit Bank of Japan, Ltd., II
Macquarie Bank Ltd., 69
Malayan Banking Berhad, 72
Manufacturers Hanover Corporation, II
Manulife Financial Corporation, 85
Marfin Popular Bank plc, 92
Marshall & Ilsley Corporation, 56
MBNA Corporation, 12
Mediolanum S.p.A., 65
Mellon Bank Corporation, II
Mellon Financial Corporation, 44 (upd.)
Mercantile Bankshares Corp., 11
Meridian Bancorp, Inc., 11
Metropolitan Financial Corporation, 13
Michigan National Corporation, 11
Midland Bank PLC, II; 17 (upd.)
The Mitsubishi Bank, Ltd., II
The Mitsubishi Trust & Banking Corporation, II
Mitsubishi UFJ Financial Group, Inc., 99 (upd.)
The Mitsui Bank, Ltd., II
The Mitsui Trust & Banking Company, Ltd., II
Mizuho Financial Group Inc., 58 (upd.)
Mouvement des Caisses Desjardins, 48
N M Rothschild & Sons Limited, 39
Narodowy Bank Polski, 100
National Bank of Greece, 41
National Bank of Canada, 85
The National Bank of South Carolina, 76
National Bank of Ukraine, 102
National City Corporation, 15; 97 (upd.)
National Penn Bancshares, Inc., 103
National Westminster Bank PLC, II

NationsBank Corporation, 10
NBD Bancorp, Inc., 11
NCNB Corporation, II
New York Community Bancorp Inc. 78
Nippon Credit Bank, II
Nordea AB, 40
Norinchukin Bank, II
North Fork Bancorporation, Inc., 46
Northern Rock plc, 33
Northern Trust Corporation, 9; 101 (upd.)
NVR L.P., 8
Old Kent Financial Corp., 11
Old National Bancorp, 15; 98 (upd.)
Orszagos Takarekpenztar es Kereskedelmi Bank Rt. (OTP Bank) 78
People's United Financial Inc., 106
The PNC Financial Services Group Inc., II; 13 (upd.); 46 (upd.)
Popular, Inc., 41
Provident Bankshares Corporation, 85
PT Bank Buana Indonesia Tbk, 60
Pulte Corporation, 8
Qatar National Bank SAQ, 87
Rabobank Group, 33
Raiffeisen Zentralbank Österreich AG, 85
Regions Financial Corporation, 106
Republic New York Corporation, 11
Riggs National Corporation, 13
Royal Bank of Canada, II; 21 (upd.); 81 (upd.)
The Royal Bank of Scotland Group plc, 12; 38 (upd.)
The Ryland Group, Inc., 8
St. Paul Bank for Cooperatives, 8
Sanpaolo IMI S.p.A., 50
The Sanwa Bank, Ltd., II; 15 (upd.)
SBC Warburg, 14
Sberbank, 62
Seattle First National Bank Inc., 8
Security Capital Corporation, 17
Security Pacific Corporation, II
Shawmut National Corporation, 13
Signet Banking Corporation, 11
Singer & Friedlander Group plc, 41
Skandinaviska Enskilda Banken AB, II; 56 (upd.)
Société Générale, II; 42 (upd.)
Society Corporation, 9
Southern Financial Bancorp, Inc., 56
Southtrust Corporation, 11
Sovereign Bancorp, Inc., 103
Standard Chartered plc, II; 48 (upd.)
Standard Federal Bank, 9
Star Banc Corporation, 11
State Bank of India, 63
State Financial Services Corporation, 51
State Street Corporation, 8; 57 (upd.)
Staten Island Bancorp, Inc., 39
Sterling Financial Corporation, 106
The Sumitomo Bank, Limited, II; 26 (upd.)
Sumitomo Mitsui Banking Corporation, 51 (upd.)
The Sumitomo Trust & Banking Company, Ltd., II; 53 (upd.)
The Summit Bancorporation, 14
Suncorp-Metway Ltd., 91

SunTrust Banks Inc., 23; 101 (upd.)
Svenska Handelsbanken AB, II; 50 (upd.)
Sveriges Riksbank, 96
Swiss Bank Corporation, II
Synovus Financial Corp., 12; 52 (upd.)
The Taiyo Kobe Bank, Ltd., II
TCF Financial Corporation, 47; 103 (upd.)
The Tokai Bank, Limited, II; 15 (upd.)
The Toronto-Dominion Bank, II; 49 (upd.)
Trustmark Corporation, 106
TSB Group plc, 12
Turkiye Is Bankasi A.S., 61
U.S. Bancorp, 14; 36 (upd.); 103 (upd.)
U.S. Trust Corp., 17
UBS AG, 52 (upd.)
Umpqua Holdings Corporation, 87
Unibanco Holdings S.A., 73
Union Bank of California, 16
Union Bank of Switzerland, II
Union Financière de France Banque SA, 52
Union Planters Corporation, 54
UnionBanCal Corporation, 50 (upd.)
United Community Banks, Inc., 98
United Overseas Bank Ltd., 56
USAA, 62 (upd.)
Van Lanschot NV, 79
Vontobel Holding AG, 96
Wachovia Bank of Georgia, N.A., 16
Wachovia Bank of South Carolina, N.A., 16
Washington Mutual, Inc., 17; 93 (upd.)
Webster Financial Corporation, 106
Wells Fargo & Company, II; 12 (upd.); 38 (upd.); 97 (upd.)
West One Bancorp, 11
Westamerica Bancorporation, 17
Westdeutsche Landesbank Girozentrale, II; 46 (upd.)
Westpac Banking Corporation, II; 48 (upd.)
Whitney Holding Corporation, 21
Wilmington Trust Corporation, 25
Wintrust Financial Corporation, 106
The Woolwich plc, 30
World Bank Group, 33
The Yasuda Trust and Banking Company, Ltd., II; 17 (upd.)
Zions Bancorporation, 12; 53 (upd.)

Financial Services: Excluding Banks

A.B. Watley Group Inc., 45
A.G. Edwards, Inc., 8; 32 (upd.)
ACCION International, 87
Accredited Home Lenders Holding Co., 91
ACE Cash Express, Inc., 33
Advanta Corporation, 8; 38 (upd.)
Ag Services of America, Inc., 59
Alliance Capital Management Holding L.P., 63
Allmerica Financial Corporation, 63
Ambac Financial Group, Inc., 65
America's Car-Mart, Inc., 64
American Capital Strategies, Ltd., 91

American Express Company, II; 10 (upd.); 38 (upd.)
American General Finance Corp., 11
American Home Mortgage Holdings, Inc., 46
Ameritrade Holding Corporation, 34
AMVESCAP PLC, 65
Apax Partners Worldwide LLP, 89
Arnhold and S. Bleichroeder Advisers, LLC, 97
Arthur Andersen & Company, Société Coopérative, 10
Avco Financial Services Inc., 13
Aviva PLC, 50 (upd.)
AXA Equitable Life Insurance Company, 105 (upd.)
Bankrate, Inc., 83
Bear Stearns Companies, Inc., II; 10 (upd.); 52 (upd.)
Benchmark Capital, 49
Bernard L. Madoff Investment Securities LLC, 106
Berwind Corporation, 100
Bill & Melinda Gates Foundation, 41; 100 (upd.
BlackRock, Inc., 79
Boenning & Scattergood Inc., 102
Bolsa Mexicana de Valores, S.A. de C.V., 80
Bozzuto's, Inc., 13
Bradford & Bingley PLC, 65
Cantor Fitzgerald, L.P., 92
Capital One Financial Corporation, 52
Cardtronics, Inc., 93
Carnegie Corporation of New York, 35
Cash America International, Inc., 20; 61 (upd.)
Cash Systems, Inc., 93
Catholic Order of Foresters, 24; 97 (upd.)
Cattles plc, 58
Cendant Corporation, 44 (upd.)
Certegy, Inc., 63
Cetelem S.A., 21
The Charles Schwab Corporation, 8; 26 (upd.); 81 (upd.)
Check Into Cash, Inc., 105
CheckFree Corporation, 81
Cheshire Building Society, 74
Chicago Mercantile Exchange Holdings Inc., 75
CIT Group Inc., 76
Citfed Bancorp, Inc., 16
Citicorp Diners Club, Inc., 90
Coinstar, Inc., 44
Comerica Incorporated, 40; 101 (upd.)
Commercial Financial Services, Inc., 26
Compagnie Nationale à Portefeuille, 84
Concord EFS, Inc., 52
Coopers & Lybrand, 9
Countrywide Financial, 16; 100 (upd.)
Cowen Group, Inc., 92
Cramer, Berkowitz & Co., 34
Credit Acceptance Corporation, 18
Cresud S.A.C.I.F. y A., 63
CS First Boston Inc., II
D. Carnegie & Co. AB, 98
D.A. Davidson & Company, 106
Dain Rauscher Corporation, 35 (upd.)

Daiwa Securities Group Inc., II; 55 (upd.)
Datek Online Holdings Corp., 32
The David and Lucile Packard Foundation, 41
Dean Witter, Discover & Co., 12
Deutsche Börse AG, 59
ditech.com, 93
Dominick & Dominick LLC, 92
Dow Jones Telerate, Inc., 10
Draper Fisher Jurvetson, 91
Dresdner Kleinwort Wasserstein, 60 (upd.)
Drexel Burnham Lambert Incorporated, II
The Dreyfus Corporation, 70
DVI, Inc., 51
E*Trade Financial Corporation, 20; 60 (upd.)
Eaton Vance Corporation, 18
Edward D. Jones & Company L.P., 66 (upd.)
Edward Jones, 30
Eurazeo, 80
Euronet Worldwide, Inc., 83
Euronext N.V., 37; 89 (upd.)
Experian Information Solutions Inc., 45
Fair, Isaac and Company, 18
Fannie Mae, 45 (upd.)
Federal Agricultural Mortgage Corporation, 75
Federal Deposit Insurance Corporation, 93
Federal National Mortgage Association, II
Fidelity Investments Inc., II; 14 (upd.)
First Albany Companies Inc., 37
First Data Corporation, 30 (upd.)
The First Marblehead Corporation, 87
First USA, Inc., 11
FMR Corp., 8; 32 (upd.)
Forstmann Little & Co., 38
Fortis, Inc., 15
Frank Russell Company, 46
Franklin Resources, Inc., 9
Fred Alger Management, Inc., 97
Freddie Mac, 54
Friedman, Billings, Ramsey Group, Inc., 53
Gabelli Asset Management Inc., 30
Gilman & Ciocia, Inc., 72
Global Payments Inc., 91
The Goldman Sachs Group Inc., II; 20 (upd.); 51 (upd.)
Grede Foundries, Inc., 38
Green Tree Financial Corporation, 11
Gruntal & Co., L.L.C., 20
Grupo Financiero Galicia S.A., 63
H&R Block, Inc., 9; 29 (upd.); 82 (upd.)
H.D. Vest, Inc., 46
H.M. Payson & Co., 69
Hercules Technology Growth Capital, Inc., 87
HFF, Inc., 103
Hoenig Group Inc., 41
Household International, Inc., II; 21 (upd.)
Hummer Winblad Venture Partners, 97
Huron Consulting Group Inc., 87
IDB Holding Corporation Ltd., 97
Ideal Mortgage Bankers, Ltd., 105
Idealab, 105

Ingenico—Compagnie Industrielle et Financière d'Ingénierie, 46
Instinet Corporation, 34
Inter-Regional Financial Group, Inc., 15
IntercontinentalExchange, Inc., 95
Investcorp SA, 57
The Island ECN, Inc., 48
Istituto per la Ricostruzione Industriale S.p.A., 11
J. & W. Seligman & Co. Inc., 61
JAFCO Co. Ltd., 79
Janus Capital Group Inc., 57
JB Oxford Holdings, Inc., 32
Jefferies Group, Inc., 25
John Hancock Financial Services, Inc., 42 (upd.)
The John Nuveen Company, 21
Jones Lang LaSalle Incorporated, 49
The Jordan Company LP, 70
JTH Tax Inc., 103
Kansas City Southern Industries, Inc., 26 (upd.)
Kleiner, Perkins, Caufield & Byers, 53
Kleinwort Benson Group PLC, II
Knight Trading Group, Inc., 70
Kohlberg Kravis Roberts & Co., 24; 56 (upd.)
KPMG Worldwide, 10
La Poste, 47 (upd.)
LaBranche & Co. Inc., 37
Lazard LLC, 38
Legal & General Group Plc, III; 24 (upd.); 101 (upd.)
Legg Mason, Inc., 33
Lehman Brothers Holdings Inc. (updates Shearson Lehman), 99 (upd.)
LendingTree, LLC, 93
LifeLock, Inc., 91
Lilly Endowment Inc., 70
Liquidnet, Inc., 79
London Scottish Bank plc, 70
London Stock Exchange Limited, 34
M.H. Meyerson & Co., Inc., 46
M.R. Beal and Co., 102
MacAndrews & Forbes Holdings Inc., 28; 86 (upd.)
Madison Dearborn Partners, LLC, 97
Man Group PLC, 106
MasterCard Worldwide, 9; 96 (upd.)
MBNA Corporation, 33 (upd.)
Merrill Lynch & Co., Inc., II; 13 (upd.); 40 (upd.)
Metris Companies Inc., 56
Morgan Grenfell Group PLC, II
Morgan Stanley Dean Witter & Company, II; 16 (upd.); 33 (upd.)
Mountain States Mortgage Centers, Inc., 29
NASD, 54 (upd.)
The NASDAQ Stock Market, Inc., 92
National Association of Securities Dealers, Inc., 10
National Auto Credit, Inc., 16
National Discount Brokers Group, Inc., 28
National Financial Partners Corp., 65
Navy Federal Credit Union, 33
Neuberger Berman Inc., 57

New Street Capital Inc., 8
New York Stock Exchange, Inc., 9; 39 (upd.)
The Nikko Securities Company Limited, II; 9 (upd.)
Nippon Shinpan Co., Ltd., II; 61 (upd.)
Nomura Securities Company, Limited, II; 9 (upd.)
Norwich & Peterborough Building Society, 55
NovaStar Financial, Inc., 91
Oaktree Capital Management, LLC, 71
Old Mutual PLC, 61
Ontario Teachers' Pension Plan, 61
Onyx Acceptance Corporation, 59
ORIX Corporation, II; 44 (upd.); 104 (upd.)
PaineWebber Group Inc., II; 22 (upd.)
PayPal Inc., 58
The Pew Charitable Trusts, 35
Piedmont Investment Advisors, LLC, 106
Piper Jaffray Companies Inc., 22
Pitney Bowes Inc., 47 (upd.)
Providian Financial Corporation, 52 (upd.)
Prudential Financial Inc., III; 30 (upd.); 82 (upd.)
The Quick & Reilly Group, Inc., 20
Quicken Loans, Inc., 93
Rathbone Brothers plc, 70
Raymond James Financial Inc., 69
Resource America, Inc., 42
Robert W. Baird & Co. Incorporated, 67
Ryan Beck & Co., Inc., 66
Safeguard Scientifics, Inc., 10
St. James's Place Capital, plc, 71
Salomon Inc., II; 13 (upd.)
Sanders Morris Harris Group Inc., 70
Sanlam Ltd., 68
SBC Warburg, 14
Schroders plc, 42
Scottrade, Inc., 85
SEI Investments Company, 96
Shearson Lehman Brothers Holdings Inc., II; 9 (upd.)
Siebert Financial Corp., 32
Skipton Building Society, 80
SLM Holding Corp., 25 (upd.)
Smith Barney Inc., 15
Soros Fund Management LLC, 28
Spear, Leeds & Kellogg, 66
State Street Boston Corporation, 8
Stephens Inc., 92
Student Loan Marketing Association, II
Sun Life Financial Inc., 85
T. Rowe Price Associates, Inc., 11; 34 (upd.)
Teachers Insurance and Annuity Association-College Retirement Equities Fund, 45 (upd.)
Texas Pacific Group Inc., 36
3i Group PLC, 73
Total System Services, Inc., 18
TradeStation Group, Inc., 83
Trilon Financial Corporation, II
United Jewish Communities, 33
The Vanguard Group, Inc., 14; 34 (upd.)
VeriFone Holdings, Inc., 18; 76 (upd.)

Viel & Cie, 76
Visa Inc., 9; 26 (upd.); 104 (upd.)
Wachovia Corporation, 12; 46 (upd.)
Waddell & Reed, Inc., 22
Washington Federal, Inc., 17
Waterhouse Investor Services, Inc., 18
Watson Wyatt Worldwide, 42
Western Union Financial Services, Inc., 54
WFS Financial Inc., 70
Working Assets Funding Service, 43
World Acceptance Corporation, 57
Yamaichi Securities Company, Limited, II
The Ziegler Companies, Inc., 24; 63 (upd.)
Zurich Financial Services, 42 (upd.); 93 (upd.)

Food Products

A. Duda & Sons, Inc., 88
A. Moksel AG, 59
Adecoagro LLC, 101
Agri Beef Company, 81
Agway, Inc., 7
Ajinomoto Co., Inc., II; 28 (upd.)
Alabama Farmers Cooperative, Inc., 63
The Albert Fisher Group plc, 41
Alberto-Culver Company, 8; 36 (upd.); 91 (upd.)
Alfred Ritter GmbH & Co. KG, 58
Alfesca hf, 82
Allen Brothers, Inc., 101
Allen Canning Company, 76
Alpine Confections, Inc., 71
Alpine Lace Brands, Inc., 18
American Crystal Sugar Company, 11; 32 (upd.)
American Foods Group, 43
American Italian Pasta Company, 27; 76 (upd.)
American Licorice Company, 86
American Maize-Products Co., 14
American Pop Corn Company, 59
American Rice, Inc., 33
Amfac/JMB Hawaii L.L.C., 24 (upd.)
Amy's Kitchen Inc., 76
Annie's Homegrown, Inc., 59
Archer-Daniels-Midland Company, 32 (upd.)
Archway Cookies, Inc., 29
Arcor S.A.I.C., 66
Arla Foods amba, 48
Arnott's Ltd., 66
Artisan Confections Company, 103
Asher's Chocolates, Inc., 103
Associated British Foods plc, II; 13 (upd.); 41 (upd.)
Associated Milk Producers, Inc., 11; 48 (upd.)
Atkinson Candy Company, 87
Atlantic Premium Brands, Ltd., 57
August Storck KG, 66
Aurora Foods Inc., 32
Auvil Fruit Company, Inc., 95
Awrey Bakeries, Inc., 56
B&G Foods, Inc., 40
The B. Manischewitz Company, LLC, 31
Bahlsen GmbH & Co. KG, 44
Bakkavör Group hf, 91

Balance Bar Company, 32
Baldwin Richardson Foods Company, 100
Baltek Corporation, 34
The Bama Companies, Inc., 80
Bar-S Foods Company, 76
Barbara's Bakery Inc., 88
Barilla G. e R. Fratelli S.p.A., 17; 50 (upd.)
Barry Callebaut AG, 71 (upd.)
Baxters Food Group Ltd., 99
Bear Creek Corporation, 38
Beatrice Company, II
Beech-Nut Nutrition Corporation, 21; 51 (upd.)
Beer Nuts, Inc., 86
Bel/Kaukauna USA, 76
Bellisio Foods, Inc., 95
Ben & Jerry's Homemade, Inc., 10; 35 (upd.); 80 (upd.)
Berkeley Farms, Inc., 46
Bernard Matthews Ltd., 89
Besnier SA, 19
Best Kosher Foods Corporation, 82
Bestfoods, 22 (upd.)
Betsy Ann Candies, Inc., 105
Better Made Snack Foods, Inc., 90
Bettys & Taylors of Harrogate Ltd., 72
Birds Eye Foods, Inc., 69 (upd.)
Blue Bell Creameries L.P., 30
Blue Diamond Growers, 28
Bob's Red Mill Natural Foods, Inc., 63
Bobs Candies, Inc., 70
Bolton Group B.V., 86
Bonduelle SA, 51
Bongrain S.A., 25; 102 (upd.)
Booker PLC, 13; 31 (upd.)
Borden, Inc., II; 22 (upd.)
Boyd Coffee Company, 53
Brach and Brock Confections, Inc., 15
Brake Bros plc, 45
Bridgford Foods Corporation, 27
Brigham's Inc., 72
Brioche Pasquier S.A., 58
British Sugar plc, 84
Brossard S.A., 102
Brothers Gourmet Coffees, Inc., 20
Broughton Foods Co., 17
Brown & Haley, 23
Bruce Foods Corporation, 39
Bruegger's Corporation, 63
Bruster's Real Ice Cream, Inc., 80
BSN Groupe S.A., II
Bumble Bee Seafoods L.L.C., 64
Bunge Brasil S.A. 78
Bunge Ltd., 62
Bourbon Corporation, 82
Burns, Philp & Company Ltd., 63
Bush Boake Allen Inc., 30
Bush Brothers & Company, 45
The C.F. Sauer Company, 90
C.H. Robinson Worldwide, Inc., 40 (upd.)
C.H. Guenther & Son, Inc., 84
Cabot Creamery Cooperative, Inc., 102
Cactus Feeders, Inc., 91
Cadbury plc, 105 (upd.)
Cadbury Schweppes PLC, II; 49 (upd.)
Cagle's, Inc., 20

Cal-Maine Foods, Inc., 69
Calavo Growers, Inc., 47
Calcot Ltd., 33
Callard and Bowser-Suchard Inc., 84
Campagna-Turano Bakery, Inc., 99
Campbell Soup Company, II; 7 (upd.); 26 (upd.); 71 (upd.)
The Campina Group, 78
Campofrío Alimentación S.A, 59
Canada Bread Company, Limited, 99
Canada Packers Inc., II
Cape Cod Potato Chip Company, 90
Cargill, Incorporated, II; 13 (upd.); 40 (upd.); 89 (upd.)
Carnation Company, II
The Carriage House Companies, Inc., 55
Carroll's Foods, Inc., 46
Carvel Corporation, 35
Castle & Cooke, Inc., II; 20 (upd.)
Cattleman's, Inc., 20
Ce De Candy Inc., 100
Celestial Seasonings, Inc., 16
Cemoi S.A., 86
Central Soya Company, Inc., 7
Cerebos Gregg's Ltd., 100
Chaoda Modern Agriculture (Holdings) Ltd., 87
Charal S.A., 90
Chase General Corporation, 91
Chattanooga Bakery, Inc., 86
Chef Solutions, Inc., 89
Chelsea Milling Company, 29
Cherry Brothers LLC, 105
Chicken of the Sea International, 24 (upd.); 106 (upd.)
China National Cereals, Oils and Foodstuffs Import and Export Corporation (COFCO), 76
Chiquita Brands International, Inc., 7; 21 (upd.); 83 (upd.)
Chock Full o'Nuts Corp., 17
Chocoladefabriken Lindt & Sprüngli AG, 27
Chocolat Frey AG, 102
Chr. Hansen Group A/S, 70
CHS Inc., 60
Chupa Chups S.A., 38
The Clemens Family Corporation, 93
Clif Bar Inc., 50
Cloetta Fazer AB, 70
The Clorox Company, III; 22 (upd.); 81 (upd.)
Clougherty Packing Company, 72
Coca-Cola Enterprises, Inc., 13
Coffee Holding Co., Inc., 95
Cold Stone Creamery, 69
Coleman Natural Products, Inc., 68
Colorado Boxed Beef Company, 100
Community Coffee Co. L.L.C., 53
ConAgra Foods, Inc., II; 12 (upd.); 42 (upd.); 85 (upd.)
The Connell Company, 29; 104 (upd.)
ContiGroup Companies, Inc., 43 (upd.)
Continental Grain Company, 10; 13 (upd.)
CoolBrands International Inc., 35
Coopagri Bretagne, 88

Cooperativa Nacional de Productores de Leche S.A. (Conaprole), 92
Corporación José R. Lindley S.A., 92
Cosan Ltd., 102
CPC International Inc., II
Cranswick plc, 40
CSM N.V., 65
Cuisine Solutions Inc., 84
Cumberland Packing Corporation, 26
Curtice-Burns Foods, Inc., 7; 21 (upd.)
Czarnikow-Rionda Company, Inc., 32
D.F. Stauffer Biscuit Company, 82
Daesang Corporation, 84
Dairy Crest Group plc, 32
Dale and Thomas Popcorn LLC, 100
Dalgery, PLC, II
Danisco A/S, 44
Dannon Company, Inc., 14; 106 (upd.)
Dare Foods Limited, 103
Darigold, Inc., 9
Dawn Food Products, Inc., 17
Dean Foods Company, 7; 21 (upd.); 73 (upd.)
DeKalb Genetics Corporation, 17
Del Monte Foods Company, 7; 23 (upd.); 103 (upd.)
Di Giorgio Corp., 12
Diageo plc, 24 (upd.)
Diamond of California, 64 (upd.)
Dietz and Watson, Inc., 92
Dippin' Dots, Inc., 56
Dobrogea Grup S.A., 82
Dole Food Company, Inc., 9; 31 (upd.); 68 (upd.)
Domino Sugar Corporation, 26
Doskocil Companies, Inc., 12
Dot Foods, Inc., 69
Doux S.A., 80
Dreyer's Grand Ice Cream, Inc., 17
The Earthgrains Company, 36
Elmer Candy Corporation, 88
Emge Packing Co., Inc., 11
Empresas Polar SA, 55 (upd.)
Eridania Béghin-Say S.A., 36
ERLY Industries Inc., 17
Eskimo Pie Corporation, 21
Établissements Jacquot and Cie S.A.S., 92
Evialis S.A., 100
Exportadora Bananera Noboa, S.A., 91
Ezaki Glico Company Ltd., 72
Faribault Foods, Inc., 89
Farley's & Sathers Candy Company, Inc., 62
Farmland Foods, Inc., 7
Farmland Industries, Inc., 48
Ferrara Pan Candy Company, 90
Ferrero SpA, 54
Fieldale Farms Corporation, 23
First Colony Coffee & Tea Company, 84
Fleer Corporation, 15
Fleury Michon S.A., 39
Floc'h & Marchand, 80
Florida Crystals Inc., 35
Flowers Industries, Inc., 12; 35 (upd.)
Fonterra Co-Operative Group Ltd., 58
FoodBrands America, Inc., 23
Ford Gum & Machine Company, Inc., 102

Foremost Farms USA Cooperative, 98
Foster Poultry Farms, 32
Fred Usinger Inc., 54
Fresh America Corporation, 20
Fresh Express Inc., 88
Fresh Foods, Inc., 29
FreshDirect, LLC, 84
Friesland Coberco Dairy Foods Holding N.V., 59
Frito-Lay Company, 32
Frito-Lay North America, 73 (upd.)
Fromageries Bel, 23
Frontera Foods, Inc., 100
Frontier Natural Products Co-Op, 82
Frozen Food Express Industries, Inc., 20; 98 (upd.)
Fyffes Plc, 38; 106 (upd.)
Galaxy Nutritional Foods, Inc., 58
Gano Excel Enterprise Sdn. Bhd., 89
The Garden Company Ltd., 82
Gardenburger, Inc., 33; 76 (upd.)
Geest Plc, 38
General Mills, Inc., II; 10 (upd.); 36 (upd.); 85 (upd.)
George A. Hormel and Company, II
George Weston Ltd., II; 36 (upd.); 88 (upd.)
Gerber Products Company, 7; 21 (upd.)
Gertrude Hawk Chocolates Inc., 104
Ghirardelli Chocolate Company, 30
Givaudan SA, 43
Glaces Thiriet S.A., 76
Glanbia plc, 59
Global Berry Farms LLC, 62
Godiva Chocolatier, Inc., 64
Goetze's Candy Company, Inc., 87
Gold Kist Inc., 17; 26 (upd.)
Gold'n Plump Poultry, 54
Golden Enterprises, Inc., 26
Gonnella Baking Company, 40; 102 (upd.)
Good Humor-Breyers Ice Cream Company, 14
Goodman Fielder Ltd., 52
GoodMark Foods, Inc., 26
Gorton's, 13
Goya Foods Inc., 22; 91 (upd.)
Graeter's Manufacturing Company, 86
Grampian Country Food Group, Ltd., 85
Great Harvest Bread Company, 44
Greencore Group plc, 98
Greyston Bakery, Inc., 101
Griffith Laboratories Inc., 100
Grist Mill Company, 15
Groupe Bigard S.A., 96
Groupe CECAB S.C.A., 88
Groupe Danone, 32 (upd.); 93 (upd.)
Groupe Euralis, 86
Groupe Glon, 84
Groupe Lactalis, 78 (upd.)
Groupe Limagrain, 74
Groupe Soufflet SA, 55
Gruma, S.A.B. de C.V., 31; 103 (upd.)
Grupo Comercial Chedraui S.A. de C.V., 86
Grupo Herdez, S.A. de C.V., 35
Grupo Industrial Lala, S.A. de C.V., 82
Grupo Leche Pascual S.A., 59

Grupo Viz, S.A. de C.V., 84
Guida-Seibert Dairy Company, 84
Guittard Chocolate Company, 55
Guttenplan's Frozen Dough Inc., 88
H.J. Heinz Company, II; 11 (upd.); 36 (upd.); 99 (upd.)
Hagoromo Foods Corporation, 84
The Hain Celestial Group, Inc., 27; 43 (upd.)
Hanover Foods Corporation, 35
HARIBO GmbH & Co. KG, 44
The Harris Soup Company (Harry's Fresh Foods), 92
Harry London Candies, Inc., 70
The Hartz Mountain Corporation, 12
Hayel Saeed Anam Group of Cos., 92
Hazlewood Foods plc, 32
Herman Goelitz, Inc., 28
Hero Group, 100
Herr Foods Inc., 84
Hershey Foods Corporation, II; 15 (upd.); 51 (upd.)
Hill's Pet Nutrition, Inc., 27
Hillsdown Holdings plc, II; 24 (upd.)
Hilmar Cheese Company, Inc., 98
HiPP GmbH & Co. Vertrieb KG, 88
Hodgson Mill, Inc., 88
Horizon Food Group, Inc., 100
Horizon Organic Holding Corporation, 37
Hormel Foods Corporation, 18 (upd.); 54 (upd.)
Hot Stuff Foods, 85
Hudson Foods Inc., 13
Hulman & Company, 44
Hunt-Wesson, Inc., 17
Iams Company, 26
IAWS Group plc, 49
IBP, Inc., II; 21 (upd.)
Iceland Group plc, 33
Icelandic Group hf, 81
Imagine Foods, Inc., 50
Imperial Holly Corporation, 12
Imperial Sugar Company, 32 (upd.)
Industrias Bachoco, S.A. de C.V., 39
Intercorp Excelle Foods Inc., 64
International Multifoods Corporation, 7; 25 (upd.)
Interstate Bakeries Corporation, 12; 38 (upd.)
The Inventure Group, Inc., 96 (upd.)
Inversiones Nacional de Chocolates S.A., 88
Itoham Foods Inc., II; 61 (upd.)
J & J Snack Foods Corporation, 24
The J. M. Smucker Company, 11; 87 (upd.)
J.R. Simplot Company, 16
Jacobs Suchard A.G., II
Jays Foods, Inc., 90
JBS S.A., 100
Jel Sert Company, 90
Jelly Belly Candy Company, 76
Jennie-O Turkey Store, Inc., 76
Jim Beam Brands Co., 14
Johanna Foods, Inc., 104
John B. Sanfilippo & Son, Inc., 14; 101 (upd.)

John Lewis Partnership plc, V; 42 (upd.); 99 (upd.)
Johnsonville Sausage L.L.C., 63
Julius Meinl International AG, 53
Just Born, Inc., 32
Kal Kan Foods, Inc., 22
Kamps AG, 44
Kar Nut Products Company, 86
Kashi Company, 89
Katokichi Company Ltd., 82
Keebler Foods Company, 36
Kellogg Company, II; 13 (upd.); 50 (upd.)
Kemps LLC, 103
Ken's Foods, Inc., 88
Kerry Group plc, 27; 87 (upd.)
Kettle Foods Inc., 48
Kewpie Kabushiki Kaisha, 57
Kikkoman Corporation, 14; 47 (upd.)
The King Arthur Flour Company, 31
King Nut Company, 74
King Ranch, Inc., 14
King's Hawaiian Bakery West, Inc., 101
Klement's Sausage Company, 61
Knouse Foods Cooperative Inc., 102
Koninklijke Wessanen nv, II; 54 (upd.)
Kraft Foods Inc., II; 7 (upd.); 45 (upd.); 91 (upd.)
Kraft Jacobs Suchard AG, 26 (upd.)
Krispy Kreme Doughnuts, Inc., 21; 61 (upd.)
Kuwait Flour Mills & Bakeries Company, 84
Kyokuyo Company Ltd., 75
L.D.C. SA, 61
La Choy Food Products Inc., 25
La Doria SpA, 101
La Reina Inc., 96
Labeyrie SAS, 80
Lakeside Foods, Inc., 89
Lam Son Sugar Joint Stock Corporation (Lasuco), 60
Lamb Weston, Inc., 23
Lance, Inc., 14; 41 (upd.)
Land O'Lakes, Inc., II; 21 (upd.); 81 (upd.)
Lassonde Industries Inc., 68
LDC, 68
Ledesma Sociedad Anónima Agrícola Industrial, 62
Legal Sea Foods Inc., 96
Leidy's, Inc., 93
Leprino Foods Company, 28
Leroux S.A.S., 65
Lifeway Foods, Inc., 65
Liberty Orchards Co., Inc., 89
Lincoln Snacks Company, 24
Litehouse Inc., 60
Lotte Confectionery Company Ltd., 76
Lucille Farms, Inc., 45
Luigino's, Inc., 64
M.A. Gedney Co., 51
Madelaine Chocolate Novelties, Inc., 104
Madrange SA, 58
Malt-O-Meal Company, 22; 63 (upd.)
Maple Grove Farms of Vermont, 88
Maple Leaf Foods Inc., 41
Marble Slab Creamery, Inc., 87

Mars, Incorporated, 7; 40 (upd.)
Mars Petcare US Inc., 96
Maruha Group Inc., 75 (upd.)
Martha White Foods Inc., 104
Maryland & Virginia Milk Producers Cooperative Association, Inc., 80
The Maschhoffs, Inc., 82
Mastellone Hermanos S.A., 101
Maui Land & Pineapple Company, Inc., 29; 100 (upd.)
Mauna Loa Macadamia Nut Corporation, 64
Maverick Ranch Association, Inc., 88
McCain Foods Limited, 77
McCormick & Company, Incorporated, 7; 27 (upd.)
McIlhenny Company, 20
McKee Foods Corporation, 7; 27 (upd.)
Mead Johnson & Company, 84
Medifast, Inc., 97
Meiji Dairies Corporation, II; 82 (upd.)
Meiji Seika Kaisha, Ltd., II
Merisant Worldwide, Inc., 70
Michael Foods, Inc., 25
Mid-America Dairymen, Inc., 7
Midwest Grain Products, Inc., 49
Mike-Sell's Inc., 15
Milnot Company, 46
Molinos Río de la Plata S.A., 61
Monfort, Inc., 13
Morinda Holdings, Inc., 82
Morinaga & Co. Ltd., 61
Moy Park Ltd. 78
Mrchocolate.com LLC, 105
Mrs. Baird's Bakeries, 29
Mrs. Fields' Original Cookies, Inc., 27; 104 (upd.)
Mt. Olive Pickle Company, Inc., 44
MTR Foods Ltd., 55
Murphy Family Farms Inc., 22
The Musco Family Olive Co., 91
Nabisco Foods Group, II; 7 (upd.)
Nantucket Allserve, Inc., 22
Nathan's Famous, Inc., 29
National Presto Industries, Inc., 43 (upd.)
National Sea Products Ltd., 14
Natural Ovens Bakery, Inc., 72
Natural Selection Foods, 54
Naturally Fresh, Inc., 88
Nature's Path Foods, Inc., 87
Nature's Sunshine Products, Inc., 15; 102 (upd.)
Naumes, Inc., 81
Nestlé S.A., II; 7 (upd.); 28 (upd.); 71 (upd.)
New England Confectionery Co., 15
New World Pasta Company, 53
Newhall Land and Farming Company, 14
Newly Weds Foods, Inc., 74
Newman's Own, Inc., 37
Nichiro Corporation, 86
Niman Ranch, Inc., 67
Nippon Meat Packers, Inc., II; 78 (upd.)
Nippon Suisan Kaisha, Ltd., II; 92 (upd.)
Nisshin Seifun Group Inc., II; 66 (upd.)
Nissin Food Products Company Ltd., 75
Northern Foods plc, 10; 61 (upd.)
Northland Cranberries, Inc., 38

Nutraceutical International Corporation, 37
NutraSweet Company, 8
Nutreco Holding N.V., 56
Nutrexpa S.A., 92
NutriSystem, Inc., 71
Oakhurst Dairy, 60
Oberto Sausage Company, Inc., 92
Ocean Beauty Seafoods, Inc., 74
Ocean Spray Cranberries, Inc., 7; 25 (upd.); 83 (upd.)
Odwalla Inc., 31; 104 (upd.)
OJSC Wimm-Bill-Dann Foods, 48
Olga's Kitchen, Inc., 80
Omaha Steaks International Inc., 62
Omega Protein Corporation, 99
Ore-Ida Foods Inc., 13; 78 (upd.)
Oregon Freeze Dry, Inc., 74
Organic To Go Food Corporation, 99
Organic Valley (Coulee Region Organic Produce Pool), 53
Orkla ASA, 18; 82 (upd.)
Oscar Mayer Foods Corp., 12
Otis Spunkmeyer, Inc., 28
Overhill Corporation, 51
Palmer Candy Company, 80
Panzani, 84
Papetti's Hygrade Egg Products, Inc., 39
Parmalat Finanziaria SpA, 50
Patrick Cudahy Inc., 102
Pendleton Grain Growers Inc., 64
Penford Corporation, 55
Penzeys Spices, Inc., 79
Pepperidge Farm, Incorporated, 81
PepsiCo, Inc., I; 10 (upd.); 38 (upd.); 93 (upd.)
Perdigao SA, 52
Perdue Farms Inc., 7; 23 (upd.)
Perfetti Van Melle S.p.A., 72
Performance Food Group, 96 (upd.)
Perkins Foods Holdings Ltd., 87
Perry's Ice Cream Company Inc., 90
Pescanova S.A., 81
Pet Incorporated, 7
Petrossian Inc., 54
Pez Candy, Inc., 38
Philip Morris Companies Inc., 18 (upd.)
Phillips Foods, Inc., 63
PIC International Group PLC, 24 (upd.)
Phillips Foods, Inc., 90 (upd.)
Pilgrim's Pride Corporation, 7; 23 (upd.); 90 (upd.)
The Pillsbury Company, II; 13 (upd.); 62 (upd.)
Pioneer Hi-Bred International, Inc., 9
Pizza Inn, Inc., 46
Poore Brothers, Inc., 44
PowerBar Inc., 44
Prairie Farms Dairy, Inc., 47
Premium Standard Farms, Inc., 30
Princes Ltd., 76
The Procter & Gamble Company, III; 8 (upd.); 26 (upd.); 67 (upd.)
Provimi S.A., 80
Punch Taverns plc, 70
Puratos S.A./NV, 92
Purina Mills, Inc., 32
Quaker Foods North America, 73 (upd.)

Quaker Oats Company, II; 12 (upd.); 34 (upd.)
Quality Chekd Dairies, Inc., 48
R. M. Palmer Co., 89
Raisio PLC, 99
Ralston Purina Company, II; 13 (upd.)
Ranks Hovis McDougall Limited, II; 28 (upd.)
The Real Good Food Company plc, 99
Reckitt Benckiser plc, II; 42 (upd.); 91 (upd.)
Reddy Ice Holdings, Inc., 80
Reser's Fine Foods, Inc., 81
Rica Foods, Inc., 41
Rich Products Corporation, 7; 38 (upd.); 93 (upd.)
Richtree Inc., 63
Ricola Ltd., 62
Ridley Corporation Ltd., 62
River Ranch Fresh Foods LLC, 88
Riviana Foods Inc., 27
Roberts Dairy Company, 103
Rocky Mountain Chocolate Factory, Inc., 73
Roland Murten A.G., 7
Roman Meal Company, 84
Rose Acre Farms, Inc., 60
Rowntree Mackintosh, II
Royal Numico N.V., 37
Ruiz Food Products, Inc., 53
Russell Stover Candies Inc., 12; 91 (upd.)
Sadia S.A., 59
SanCor Cooperativas Unidas Ltda., 101
Sanderson Farms, Inc., 15
Saputo Inc., 59
Sara Lee Corporation, II; 15 (upd.); 54 (upd.); 99 (upd.)
Sarris Candies Inc., 86
Savannah Foods & Industries, Inc., 7
Schlotzsky's, Inc., 36
Schreiber Foods, Inc., 72
The Schwan Food Company, 7; 26 (upd.); 83 (upd.)
Schwebel Baking Company, 72
Seaboard Corporation, 36; 85 (upd.)
See's Candies, Inc., 30
Seminis, Inc., 29
Seneca Foods Corporation, 60 (upd.)
Sensient Technologies Corporation, 52 (upd.)
Shamrock Foods Company, 105
Shearer's Foods, Inc., 72
Silhouette Brands, Inc., 55
Silver Lake Cookie Company Inc., 95
Skalli Group, 67
Slim-Fast Foods Company, 18; 66 (upd.)
Small Planet Foods, Inc., 89
Smart Balance, Inc., 100
Smithfield Foods, Inc., 7; 43 (upd.)
Snow Brand Milk Products Company, Ltd., II; 48 (upd.)
Société Industrielle Lesaffre, 84
Sodiaal S.A., 36 (upd.)
SODIMA, II
Sorbee International Ltd., 74
Sorrento, Inc., 24
Southeast Frozen Foods Company, L.P., 99

Spangler Candy Company, 44
Spectrum Organic Products, Inc., 68
Standard Candy Company Inc., 86
Star of the West Milling Co., 95
Starbucks Corporation, 13; 34 (upd.); 77 (upd.)
Stock Yards Packing Co., Inc., 37
Stollwerck AG, 53
Stolt Sea Farm Holdings PLC, 54
Stolt-Nielsen S.A., 42
Stonyfield Farm, Inc., 55
Stouffer Corp., 8
Strauss-Elite Group, 68
Südzucker AG, 27
Suiza Foods Corporation, 26
Sun-Diamond Growers of California, 7
Sun-Maid Growers of California, 82
Sun-Rype Products Ltd., 76
Sun World International, LLC, 93
Sunkist Growers, Inc., 26; 102 (upd.)
SunOpta Inc., 79
Supervalu Inc., 18 (upd.); 50 (upd.)
Suprema Specialties, Inc., 27
Sweet Candy Company, 60
Swift & Company, 55
The Swiss Colony, Inc., 97
Swiss Valley Farms Company, 90
Sylvan, Inc., 22
Symrise GmbH and Company KG, 89
Syngenta International AG, 83
T. Marzetti Company, 57
Taiyo Fishery Company, Limited, II
Tanimura & Antle Fresh Foods, Inc., 98
Tastefully Simple Inc., 100
Tasty Baking Company, 14; 35 (upd.)
Tate & Lyle PLC, II; 42 (upd.); 101 (upd.)
Taylor Made Group Inc., 98
TCBY Systems LLC, 17; 98 (upd.)
TDL Group Ltd., 46
Ter Beke NV, 103
Terrena L'Union CANA CAVAL, 70
Thai Union Frozen Products PCL, 75
Thomas J. Lipton Company, 14
Thorn Apple Valley, Inc., 7; 22 (upd.)
Thorntons plc, 46
Thumann Inc., 104
TLC Beatrice International Holdings, Inc., 22
Tofutti Brands, Inc., 64
Tom's Foods Inc., 66
Tombstone Pizza Corporation, 13
Tone Brothers, Inc., 21; 74 (upd.)
Tootsie Roll Industries, Inc., 12; 82 (upd.)
Touton S.A., 92
Townsends, Inc., 64
Tree Top, Inc., 76
TreeHouse Foods, Inc., 79
Tri Valley Growers, 32
Trident Seafoods Corporation, 56
Tropicana Products, Inc., 28
Tulip Ltd., 89
Tumaro's Gourmet Tortillas, 85
Tyson Foods, Inc., II; 14 (upd.); 50 (upd.)
U.S. Foodservice, 26
U.S. Premium Beef LLC, 91
Uncle Ben's Inc., 22

Uncle Ray's LLC, 90
Uni-President Enterprises Corporation, 104
Unigate PLC, II; 28 (upd.)
Unilever, II; 7 (upd.); 32 (upd.); 89 (upd.)
Uniq plc, 83 (upd.)
United Biscuits (Holdings) plc, II; 42 (upd.)
United Brands Company, II
United Farm Workers of America, 88
United Foods, Inc., 21
Universal Foods Corporation, 7
Utz Quality Foods, Inc., 72
Vaughan Foods, Inc., 105
Van Camp Seafood Company, Inc., 7
Ventura Foods LLC, 90
Vestey Group Ltd., 95
Vienna Sausage Manufacturing Co., 14
Vilmorin Clause et Cie, 70
Vion Food Group NV, 85
Vista Bakery, Inc., 56
Vita Food Products Inc., 99
Vlasic Foods International Inc., 25
Voortman Cookies Limited, 103
W Jordan (Cereals) Ltd., 74
Wagers Inc. (Idaho Candy Company), 86
Walkers Shortbread Ltd., 79
Walkers Snack Foods Ltd., 70
Warburtons Ltd., 89
Warrell Corporation, 68
Wattie's Ltd., 7
Weaver Popcorn Company, Inc., 89
Weetabix Limited, 61
Weis Markets, Inc., 84 (upd.)
Welch Foods Inc., 104
Wells' Dairy, Inc., 36
Wenner Bread Products Inc., 80
White Lily Foods Company, 88
White Wave, 43
Wilbur Chocolate Company, 66
William Jackson & Son Ltd., 101
Wimm-Bill-Dann Foods, 48
Wisconsin Dairies, 7
Wise Foods, Inc., 79
WLR Foods, Inc., 21
Wm. B. Reily & Company Inc., 58
Wm. Wrigley Jr. Company, 7; 58 (upd.)
World's Finest Chocolate Company, 39
Worthington Foods, Inc., 14
Yamazaki Baking Co., Ltd., 58
Yarnell Ice Cream Company, Inc., 92
Yeo Hiap Seng Malaysia Bhd., 75
YOCREAM International, Inc., 47
Young's Bluecrest Seafood Holdings Ltd., 81
Zacky Farms LLC, 74
Zatarain's, Inc., 64

Food Services & Retailers

A. F. Blakemore & Son Ltd., 90
Advantica Restaurant Group, Inc., 27 (upd.)
AFC Enterprises, Inc., 32 (upd.); 83 (upd.)
Affiliated Foods Inc., 53
Albertson's, Inc., II; 7 (upd.); 30 (upd.); 65 (upd.)

Aldi Einkauf GmbH & Co. OHG, 13; 86 (upd.)
Alex Lee Inc., 18; 44 (upd.)
Allen Foods, Inc., 60
Almacenes Exito S.A., 89
Alpha Airports Group PLC, 77
America's Favorite Chicken Company, Inc., 7
American Restaurant Partners, L.P., 93
American Stores Company, II
Andronico's Market, 70
Applebee's International, Inc., 14; 35 (upd.)
ARA Services, II
Arby's Inc., 14
Arden Group, Inc., 29
Áreas S.A., 104
Arena Leisure Plc, 99
Argyll Group PLC, II
Ark Restaurants Corp., 20
Arthur Lundgren Tecidos S.A., 102
Asahi Breweries, Ltd., 20 (upd.)
ASDA Group Ltd., II; 28 (upd.); 64 (upd.)
Associated Grocers, Incorporated, 9; 31 (upd.)
Association des Centres Distributeurs E. Leclerc, 37
Atlanta Bread Company International, Inc., 70
Au Bon Pain Co., Inc., 18
Auchan, 37
Auntie Anne's, Inc., 35; 102 (upd.)
Autogrill SpA, 49
Avado Brands, Inc., 31
B.R. Guest Inc., 87
Back Bay Restaurant Group, Inc., 20; 102 (upd.)
Back Yard Burgers, Inc., 45
Bashas' Inc., 33; 80 (upd.)
Bear Creek Corporation, 38
Ben E. Keith Company, 76
Benihana, Inc., 18; 76 (upd.)
Bertucci's Corporation, 64 (upd.)
Bettys & Taylors of Harrogate Ltd., 72
Big Bear Stores Co., 13
The Big Food Group plc, 68 (upd.)
Big V Supermarkets, Inc., 25
Big Y Foods, Inc., 53
Blimpie, 15; 49 (upd.); 105 (upd.)
Bob Evans Farms, Inc., 9; 63 (upd.)
Bob's Red Mill Natural Foods, Inc., 63
Boddie-Noell Enterprises, Inc., 68
Bojangles Restaurants Inc., 97
Bon Appetit Holding AG, 48
Boston Market Corporation, 12; 48 (upd.)
Boston Pizza International Inc., 88
Brazil Fast Food Corporation, 74
Briazz, Inc., 53
Brinker International, Inc., 10; 38 (upd.); 75 (upd.)
Bristol Farms, 101
Brookshire Grocery Company, 16; 74 (upd.)
Bruegger's Corporation, 63
Bruno's Supermarkets, Inc., 7; 26 (upd.); 68 (upd.)

631

Buca, Inc., 38
Buckhead Life Restaurant Group, Inc., 100
Budgens Ltd., 59
Buffalo Wild Wings, Inc., 56
Buffets Holdings, Inc., 10; 32 (upd.); 93 (upd.)
Burger King Corporation, II; 17 (upd.); 56 (upd.)
Busch Entertainment Corporation, 73
C&K Market, Inc., 81
C & S Wholesale Grocers, Inc., 55
C.H. Robinson, Inc., 11
Caffè Nero Group PLC, 63
Cains Beer Company PLC, 99
California Pizza Kitchen Inc., 15; 74 (upd.)
Captain D's, LLC, 59
Cargill, Incorporated, II; 13 (upd.); 40 (upd.); 89 (upd.)
Caribou Coffee Company, Inc., 28; 97 (upd.)
Carlson Companies, Inc., 6; 22 (upd.); 87 (upd.)
Carlson Restaurants Worldwide, 69
Carr-Gottstein Foods Co., 17
Carrols Restaurant Group, Inc., 92
Casey's General Stores, Inc., 19; 83 (upd.)
Casino Guichard-Perrachon S.A., 59 (upd.)
CBRL Group, Inc., 35 (upd.); 86 (upd.)
CEC Entertainment, Inc., 31 (upd.)
Centerplate, Inc., 79
Chart House Enterprises, Inc., 17
Checkers Drive-In Restaurants, Inc., 16; 74 (upd.)
The Cheesecake Factory Inc., 17; 100 (upd.)
Chi-Chi's Inc., 13; 51 (upd.)
Chicago Pizza & Brewery, Inc., 44
Chick-fil-A Inc., 23; 90 (upd.)
Chipotle Mexican Grill, Inc., 67
Church's Chicken, 66
CiCi Enterprises, L.P., 99
Cinnabon Inc., 23; 90 (upd.)
The Circle K Corporation, II
CKE Restaurants, Inc., 19; 46 (upd.)
Coborn's, Inc., 30
The Coffee Beanery, Ltd., 95
Coffee Holding Co., Inc., 95
Cold Stone Creamery, 69
Coles Group Limited, V; 20 (upd.); 85 (upd.)
Compass Group PLC, 34
Comptoirs Modernes S.A., 19
Consolidated Products Inc., 14
Controladora Comercial Mexicana, S.A. de C.V., 36
Cooker Restaurant Corporation, 20; 51 (upd.)
The Copps Corporation, 32
Cosi, Inc., 53
Cost-U-Less, Inc., 51
Coto Centro Integral de Comercializacion S.A., 66
Country Kitchen International, Inc., 76
Cracker Barrel Old Country Store, Inc., 10

Cremonini S.p.A., 57
CulinArt, Inc., 92
Culver Franchising System, Inc., 58
D'Agostino Supermarkets Inc., 19
Dairy Mart Convenience Stores, Inc., 7; 25 (upd.)
Daniel Thwaites Plc, 95
Darden Restaurants, Inc., 16; 44 (upd.)
Dave & Buster's, Inc., 33; 104 (upd.)
Dean & DeLuca, Inc., 36
Del Taco, Inc., 58
Delhaize Group, 44; 103 (upd.)
DeMoulas / Market Basket Inc., 23
DenAmerica Corporation, 29
Denner AG, 88
Denny's Corporation, 105 (upd.)
Deschutes Brewery, Inc., 57
Diedrich Coffee, Inc., 40
Dierbergs Markets Inc., 63
Distribución y Servicio D&S S.A., 71
Doctor's Associates Inc., 67 (upd.)
Dominick's Finer Foods, Inc., 56
Domino's, Inc., 7; 21 (upd.); 63 (upd.)
Donatos Pizzeria Corporation, 58
E H Booth & Company Ltd., 90
Eateries, Inc., 33
Ed S.A.S., 88
Edeka Zentrale A.G., II; 47 (upd.)
EIH Ltd., 103
Einstein/Noah Bagel Corporation, 29
El Chico Restaurants, Inc., 19
El Pollo Loco, Inc., 69
Elior SA, 49
Elmer's Restaurants, Inc., 42
Embers America Restaurants, 30
Etablissements Economiques du Casino Guichard, Perrachon et Cie, S.C.A., 12
Family Sports Concepts, Inc., 100
Famous Brands Ltd., 86
Famous Dave's of America, Inc., 40
Farmer Jack Supermarkets 78
Fatburger Corporation, 64
Fazoli's Management, Inc., 27; 76 (upd.)
Fiesta Mart, Inc., 101
Fili Enterprises, Inc., 70
Fired Up, Inc., 82
5 & Diner Franchise Corporation, 72
Five Guys Enterprises, LLC, 99
Flagstar Companies, Inc., 10
Flanigan's Enterprises, Inc., 60
Fleming Companies, Inc., II
Food Circus Super Markets, Inc., 88
The Food Emporium, 64
Food Lion LLC, II; 15 (upd.); 66 (upd.)
Foodarama Supermarkets, Inc., 28
Foodmaker, Inc., 14
Fox's Pizza Den, Inc., 98
The Fred W. Albrecht Grocery Co., 13
Fresh Choice, Inc., 20
Fresh Enterprises, Inc., 66
Fresh Foods, Inc., 29
Friendly Ice Cream Corporation, 30; 72 (upd.)
Frisch's Restaurants, Inc., 35; 92 (upd.)
Fuller Smith & Turner P.L.C., 38
Furr's Restaurant Group, Inc., 53
Furr's Supermarkets, Inc., 28
Galardi Group, Inc., 72

Galaxy Investors, Inc., 97
Garden Fresh Restaurant Corporation, 31
Gate Gourmet International AG, 70
The Gateway Corporation Ltd., II
Genuardi's Family Markets, Inc., 35
George Weston Ltd., II; 36 (upd.); 88 (upd.)
Ghirardelli Chocolate Company, 30
Giant Eagle, Inc., 86
Giant Food LLC, II; 22 (upd.); 83 (upd.)
Godfather's Pizza Incorporated, 25
Golden Corral Corporation, 10; 66 (upd.)
Golden Krust Caribbean Bakery, Inc., 68
Golden State Foods Corporation, 32
The Golub Corporation, 26; 96 (upd.)
Gordon Biersch Brewery Restaurant Group, Inc., 93
Gordon Food Service Inc., 8; 39 (upd.)
Grand Traverse Pie Company, 98
The Grand Union Company, 7; 28 (upd.)
The Great Atlantic & Pacific Tea Company, Inc., II; 16 (upd.); 55 (upd.)
Greggs PLC, 65
Grill Concepts, Inc., 74
Gristede's Foods Inc., 31; 68 (upd.)
The Grocers Supply Co., Inc., 103
Ground Round, Inc., 21
Groupe Flo S.A., 98
Groupe Le Duff S.A., 84
Groupe Promodès S.A., 19
Grupo Corvi S.A. de C.V., 86
Guyenne et Gascogne, 23
H.E. Butt Grocery Company, 13; 32 (upd.); 85 (upd.)
Haggen Inc., 38
Hannaford Bros. Co., 12; 103 (upd.)
Hard Rock Café International, Inc., 12; 32 (upd.); 105 (upd.)
Harps Food Stores, Inc., 99
Harris Teeter Inc., 23; 72 (upd.)
Harry's Farmers Market Inc., 23
HDOS Enterprises, 72
Hickory Farms, Inc., 17
Holberg Industries, Inc., 36
Holland Burgerville USA, 44
Hooters of America, Inc., 18; 69 (upd.)
Hops Restaurant Bar and Brewery, 46
Hoss's Steak and Sea House Inc., 68
Host America Corporation, 79
Hotel Properties Ltd., 71
Houchens Industries Inc., 51
Huddle House, Inc., 105
Hughes Markets, Inc., 22
Hungry Howie's Pizza and Subs, Inc., 25
Hy-Vee, Inc., 36
ICA AB, II
Iceland Group plc, 33
IGA, Inc., 99
IHOP Corporation, 17; 58 (upd.)
Il Fornaio (America) Corporation, 27
In-N-Out Burgers Inc., 19; 74 (upd.)
Ingles Markets, Inc., 20
Inserra Supermarkets, 25
Inter Link Foods PLC, 61
International Dairy Queen, Inc., 10; 39 (upd.); 105 (upd.)
ITM Entreprises SA, 36
Ito-Yokado Co., Ltd., 42 (upd.)

Ivar's, Inc., 86
J Sainsbury plc, II; 13 (upd.); 38 (upd.); 95 (upd.)
J. Alexander's Corporation, 65
Jack in the Box Inc., 89 (upd.)
Jacmar Companies, 87
Jamba Juice Company, 47
James Original Coney Island Inc., 84
JD Wetherspoon plc, 30
Jean-Georges Enterprises L.L.C., 75
Jerónimo Martins SGPS S.A., 96
Jerry's Famous Deli Inc., 24
Jersey Mike's Franchise Systems, Inc., 83
Jimmy John's Enterprises, Inc., 103
Jitney-Jungle Stores of America, Inc., 27
John Lewis Partnership plc, V; 42 (upd.); 99 (upd.)
Johnny Rockets Group, Inc., 31; 76 (upd.)
KFC Corporation, 7; 21 (upd.); 89 (upd.)
King Kullen Grocery Co., Inc., 15
King's Hawaiian Bakery West, Inc., 101
Koninklijke Ahold N.V. (Royal Ahold), II; 16 (upd.)
Koo Koo Roo, Inc., 25
Kooperativa Förbundet, 99
The Kroger Co., II; 15 (upd.); 65 (upd.)
The Krystal Company, 33
Kwik Save Group plc, 11
La Madeleine French Bakery & Café, 33
Landry's Restaurants, Inc., 15; 65 (upd.)
The Laurel Pub Company Limited, 59
Laurus N.V., 65
LDB Corporation, 53
Leeann Chin, Inc., 30
Levy Restaurants L.P., 26
Little Caesar Enterprises, Inc., 7; 24 (upd.)
Loblaw Companies Limited, 43
Logan's Roadhouse, Inc., 29
Lone Star Steakhouse & Saloon, Inc., 51
Long John Silver's, 13; 57 (upd.)
Luby's, Inc., 17; 42 (upd.); 99 (upd.)
Lucky Stores, Inc., 27
Lund Food Holdings, Inc., 22
Lunardi's Super Market, Inc., 99
Madden's on Gull Lake, 52
MaggieMoo's International, 89
Maid-Rite Corporation, 62
Maines Paper & Food Service Inc., 71
Marble Slab Creamery, Inc., 87
Marco's Franchising LLC, 86
Marie Callender's Restaurant & Bakery, Inc., 28
Marsh Supermarkets, Inc., 17; 76 (upd.)
Martin's Super Markets, Inc., 101
Marvelous Market Inc., 104
Matt Prentice Restaurant Group, 70
Maui Wowi, Inc., 85
Max & Erma's Restaurants Inc., 19; 100 (upd.)
Mayfield Dairy Farms, Inc., 74
Mazzio's Corporation, 76
McAlister's Corporation, 66
McCormick & Schmick's Seafood Restaurants, Inc., 71
McDonald's Corporation, II; 7 (upd.); 26 (upd.); 63 (upd.)

Megafoods Stores Inc., 13
Meijer, Inc., 7; 27 (upd.); 101 (upd.)
The Melting Pot Restaurants, Inc., 74
The Merchants Company, 102
Metcash Trading Ltd., 58
Métro Inc., 77
Metromedia Companies, 14
Mexican Restaurants, Inc., 41
The Middleby Corporation, 22; 104 (upd.)
Minyard Food Stores, Inc., 33; 86 (upd.)
MITROPA AG, 37
Monterey Pasta Company, 58
Morgan's Foods, Inc., 101
Morrison Restaurants Inc., 11
Morton's Restaurant Group, Inc., 30; 88 (upd.)
Mr. Gatti's, LP, 87
Mrs. Fields' Original Cookies, Inc., 27; 104 (upd.)
MSWG, LLC, 105
Musgrave Group Plc, 57
Myriad Restaurant Group, Inc., 87
Nash Finch Company, 8; 23 (upd.); 65 (upd.)
Nathan's Famous, Inc., 29
National Convenience Stores Incorporated, 7
Netto International, 103
New Seasons Market, 75
New World Restaurant Group, Inc., 44
New York Restaurant Group, Inc., 32
Noble Roman's, Inc., 14; 99 (upd.)
Noodles & Company, Inc., 55
NPC International, Inc., 40
O'Charley's Inc., 19; 60 (upd.)
Old Spaghetti Factory International Inc., 24
Organic To Go Food Corporation, 99
OOC Inc., 97
The Oshawa Group Limited, II
OSI Restaurant Partners, Inc., 88 (upd.)
Outback Steakhouse, Inc., 12; 34 (upd.)
P&C Foods Inc., 8
P.F. Chang's China Bistro, Inc., 37; 86 (upd.)
Pacific Coast Restaurants, Inc., 90
Palm Management Corporation, 71
Pancho's Mexican Buffet, Inc., 46
Panda Restaurant Group, Inc., 35; 97 (upd.)
Panera Bread Company, 44
Papa Gino's Holdings Corporation, Inc., 86
Papa John's International, Inc., 15; 71 (upd.)
Papa Murphy's International, Inc., 54
Pappas Restaurants, Inc., 76
Pathmark Stores, Inc., 23; 101 (upd.)
Peapod, Inc., 30
Penn Traffic Company, 13
Performance Food Group Company, 31
Perkins Family Restaurants, L.P., 22
Peter Piper, Inc., 70
Petrossian Inc., 54
Phillips Foods, Inc., 63
Picard Surgeles, 76
Piccadilly Cafeterias, Inc., 19

Piggly Wiggly Southern, Inc., 13
Pizza Hut Inc., 7; 21 (upd.)
Planet Hollywood International, Inc., 18; 41 (upd.)
Players International, Inc., 22
Ponderosa Steakhouse, 15
Portillo's Restaurant Group, Inc., 71
Potbelly Sandwich Works, Inc., 83
Progressive Enterprises Ltd., 96
Provigo Inc., II; 51 (upd.)
Publix Super Markets, Inc., 7; 31 (upd.); 105 (upd.)
Pueblo Xtra International, Inc., 47
Qdoba Restaurant Corporation, 93
Quality Dining, Inc., 18
Quality Food Centers, Inc., 17
The Quizno's Corporation, 42
Rainforest Café, Inc., 25; 88 (upd.)
Rally's, 25; 68 (upd.)
Ralphs Grocery Company, 35
Randall's Food Markets, Inc., 40
Rare Hospitality International Inc., 19
Raving Brands, Inc., 64
Red Robin Gourmet Burgers, Inc., 56
Regent Inns plc, 95
Restaurant Associates Corporation, 66
Restaurants Unlimited, Inc., 13
REWE-Zentral AG, 103
RFC Franchising LLC, 68
Richfood Holdings, Inc., 7
Richtree Inc., 63
The Riese Organization, 38
Riser Foods, Inc., 9
Roadhouse Grill, Inc., 22
Rock Bottom Restaurants, Inc., 25; 68 (upd.)
Roly Poly Franchise Systems LLC, 83
Romacorp, Inc., 58
Rosauers Supermarkets, Inc., 90
Roundy's Inc., 58 (upd.)
RTM Restaurant Group, 58
Rubio's Restaurants, Inc., 35
Ruby Tuesday, Inc., 18; 71 (upd.)
Ruth's Chris Steak House, 28; 88 (upd.)
Ryan's Restaurant Group, Inc., 15; 68 (upd.)
Safeway Inc., II; 24 (upd.); 50 (upd.); 85 (upd.)
Santa Barbara Restaurant Group, Inc., 37
Sapporo Holdings Limited, I; 13 (upd.); 36 (upd.); 97 (upd.)
Saxton Pierce Restaurant Corporation, 100
Sbarro, Inc., 16; 64 (upd.)
Schlotzsky's, Inc., 36
Schultz Sav-O Stores, Inc., 21
The Schwan Food Company, 7; 26 (upd.); 83 (upd.)
The Schwarz Group, 100
Seaway Food Town, Inc., 15
Second Harvest, 29
See's Candies, Inc., 30
Selecta AG, 97
Seneca Foods Corporation, 17
Service America Corp., 7
SFI Group plc, 51
Shaw's Supermarkets, Inc., 56
Shells Seafood Restaurants, Inc., 43

Shoney's North America Corp., 7; 23 (upd.); 105 (upd.)
ShowBiz Pizza Time, Inc., 13
Skyline Chili, Inc., 62
Smart & Final, Inc., 16
The Smith & Wollensky Restaurant Group, Inc., 105
Smith's Food & Drug Centers, Inc., 8; 57 (upd.)
Sobeys Inc., 80
Sodexho SA, 29; 91 (upd.)
Somerfield plc, 47 (upd.)
Sonic Corp., 14; 37 (upd.); 103 (upd.)
Souper Salad, Inc., 98
Southeast Frozen Foods Company, L.P., 99
The Southland Corporation, II; 7 (upd.)
Spaghetti Warehouse, Inc., 25
Spar Handelsgesellschaft mbH, 35; 103 (upd.)
Spartan Stores Inc., 8
Spicy Pickle Franchising, Inc., 105
Starbucks Corporation, 13; 34 (upd.); 77 (upd.)
Stater Bros. Holdings Inc., 64
The Steak n Shake Company, 41; 96 (upd.)
Steinberg Incorporated, II
Stew Leonard's, 56
The Stop & Shop Supermarket Company, II; 68 (upd.)
Subway, 32
Super Food Services, Inc., 15
Supermarkets General Holdings Corporation, II
Supervalu Inc., II; 18 (upd.); 50 (upd.)
Sweetbay Supermarket, 103 (upd.)
SWH Corporation, 70
SYSCO Corporation, II; 24 (upd.); 75 (upd.)
Taco Bell Corporation, 7; 21 (upd.); 74 (upd.)
Taco Cabana, Inc., 23; 72 (upd.)
Taco John's International, Inc., 15; 63 (upd.)
TCBY Systems LLC, 17; 98 (upd.)
Tchibo GmbH, 82
TelePizza S.A., 33
Tesco PLC, II
Texas Roadhouse, Inc., 69
Thomas & Howard Company, Inc., 90
Timber Lodge Steakhouse, Inc., 73
Tops Markets LLC, 60
Total Entertainment Restaurant Corporation, 46
Toupargel-Agrigel S.A., 76
Trader Joe's Company, 13; 50 (upd.)
Travel Ports of America, Inc., 17
Tree of Life, Inc., 29
Triarc Companies, Inc., 34 (upd.)
Tubby's, Inc., 53
Tully's Coffee Corporation, 51
Tumbleweed, Inc., 33; 80 (upd.)
TW Services, Inc., II
Ukrop's Super Markets Inc., 39; 101 (upd.)
Unified Grocers, Inc., 93
Unique Casual Restaurants, Inc., 27

United Dairy Farmers, Inc., 74
United Natural Foods, Inc., 32; 76 (upd.)
Uno Restaurant Holdings Corporation, 18; 70 (upd.)
Uwajimaya, Inc., 60
Vail Resorts, Inc., 43 (upd.)
Valora Holding AG, 98
VICORP Restaurants, Inc., 12; 48 (upd.)
Victory Refrigeration, Inc., 82
Village Super Market, Inc., 7
The Vons Companies, Inc., 7; 28 (upd.); 103 (upd.)
W. H. Braum, Inc., 80
Waffle House Inc., 14; 60 (upd.)
Wahoo's Fish Taco, 96
Wakefern Food Corporation, 33
Waldbaum, Inc., 19
Wall Street Deli, Inc., 33
Wawa Inc., 17; 78 (upd.)
Wegmans Food Markets, Inc., 9; 41 (upd.); 105 (upd.)
Weis Markets, Inc., 15
Wendy's International, Inc., 8; 23 (upd.); 47 (upd.)
The WesterN SizzliN Corporation, 60
Wetterau Incorporated, II
Whataburger Restaurants LP, 105
Whitbread PLC, I; 20 (upd.); 52 (upd.); 97 (upd.)
White Castle Management Company, 12; 36 (upd.); 85 (upd.)
White Rose, Inc., 24
Whittard of Chelsea Plc, 61
Whole Foods Market, Inc., 50 (upd.)
Wild Oats Markets, Inc., 19; 41 (upd.)
Willow Run Foods, Inc., 100
Winchell's Donut Houses Operating Company, L.P., 60
WinCo Foods Inc., 60
Winn-Dixie Stores, Inc., II; 21 (upd.); 59 (upd.)
Wm. Morrison Supermarkets PLC, 38
Wolfgang Puck Worldwide, Inc., 26, 70 (upd.)
Worldwide Restaurant Concepts, Inc., 47
Yoshinoya D & C Company Ltd., 88
Young & Co.'s Brewery, P.L.C., 38
Yucaipa Cos., 17
Yum! Brands Inc., 58
Zingerman's Community of Businesses, 68
Zpizza International Inc., 105

Health & Personal Care Products

Abaxis, Inc., 83
Abbott Laboratories, I; 11 (upd.); 40 (upd.); 93 (upd.)
Accuray Incorporated, 95
Advanced Medical Optics, Inc., 79
Advanced Neuromodulation Systems, Inc., 73
Akorn, Inc., 32
ALARIS Medical Systems, Inc., 65
Alberto-Culver Company, 8; 36 (upd.); 91 (upd.)
Alco Health Services Corporation, III
Alès Groupe, 81

Allergan, Inc., 10; 30 (upd.); 77 (upd.)
American Medical Alert Corporation, 103
American Oriental Bioengineering Inc., 93
American Safety Razor Company, 20
American Stores Company, 22 (upd.)
Amway Corporation, III; 13 (upd.)
AngioDynamics, Inc., 81
ArthroCare Corporation, 73
Artsana SpA, 92
Ascendia Brands, Inc., 97
Atkins Nutritionals, Inc., 58
Aveda Corporation, 24
Avon Products, Inc., III; 19 (upd.); 46 (upd.)
Bally Total Fitness Holding Corp., 25
Bare Escentuals, Inc., 91
Bausch & Lomb Inc., 7; 25 (upd.); 96 (upd.)
Baxter International Inc., I; 10 (upd.)
BeautiControl Cosmetics, Inc., 21
Becton, Dickinson and Company, I; 11 (upd.); 36 (upd.); 101 (upd.)
Beiersdorf AG, 29
Big B, Inc., 17
Bindley Western Industries, Inc., 9
Biolase Technology, Inc., 87
Biomet, Inc., 10; 93 (upd.)
BioScrip Inc., 98
Biosite Incorporated, 73
Block Drug Company, Inc., 8; 27 (upd.)
The Body Shop International plc, 53 (upd.)
Boiron S.A., 73
Bolton Group B.V., 86
The Boots Company PLC, 24 (upd.)
Boston Scientific Corporation, 77 (upd.)
Bristol-Myers Squibb Company, III; 9 (upd.)
Bronner Brothers Inc., 92
C.R. Bard Inc., 9
Candela Corporation, 48
Cantel Medical Corporation, 80
Cardinal Health, Inc., 18; 50 (upd.)
Carl Zeiss AG, III; 34 (upd.); 91 (upd.)
Carson, Inc., 31
Carter-Wallace, Inc., 8
Caswell-Massey Co. Ltd., 51
CCA Industries, Inc., 53
Chattem, Inc., 17; 88 (upd.)
Chesebrough-Pond's USA, Inc., 8
Chindex International, Inc., 101
Chronimed Inc., 26
Church & Dwight Co., Inc., 68 (upd.)
Cintas Corporation, 51 (upd.)
The Clorox Company, III; 22 (upd.); 81 (upd.)
CNS, Inc., 20
Colgate-Palmolive Company, III; 14 (upd.); 35 (upd.)
Combe Inc., 72
Conair Corp., 17
CONMED Corporation, 87
Connetics Corporation, 70
Cordis Corp., 19
Cosmair, Inc., 8
Cosmolab Inc., 96
Coty, Inc., 36
Covidien Ltd., 91

Cybex International, Inc., 49
Cytyc Corporation, 69
Dade Behring Holdings Inc., 71
Dalli-Werke GmbH & Co. KG, 86
Datascope Corporation, 39
Del Laboratories, Inc., 28
Deltec, Inc., 56
Dentsply International Inc., 10
DEP Corporation, 20
DePuy, Inc., 30
DHB Industries Inc., 85
Diagnostic Products Corporation, 73
The Dial Corp., 23 (upd.)
Direct Focus, Inc., 47
Drackett Professional Products, 12
Drägerwerk AG, 83
Dynatronics Corporation, 99
E-Z-EM Inc., 89
Elizabeth Arden, Inc., 8; 40 (upd.)
Empi, Inc., 26
Enrich International, Inc., 33
Essie Cosmetics, Ltd., 102
The Estée Lauder Companies Inc., 9; 30
    (upd.); 93 (upd.)
Ethicon, Inc., 23
Exactech, Inc., 101
Farouk Systems Inc. 78
Forest Laboratories, Inc., 11
Forever Living Products International Inc.,
    17
FoxHollow Technologies, Inc., 85
French Fragrances, Inc., 22
G&K Holding S.A., 95
Gambro AB, 49
General Nutrition Companies, Inc., 11;
    29 (upd.)
Genzyme Corporation, 13; 77 (upd.)
GF Health Products, Inc., 82
The Gillette Company, III; 20 (upd.)
Given Imaging Ltd., 83
GN ReSound A/S, 103
GNC Corporation, 98 (upd.)
Golden Neo-Life Diamite International,
    Inc., 100
Groupe Yves Saint Laurent, 23
Grupo Omnilife S.A. de C.V., 88
Guerlain, 23
Guest Supply, Inc., 18
Guidant Corporation, 58
Guinot Paris S.A., 82
Hanger Orthopedic Group, Inc., 41
Helen of Troy Corporation, 18
Helene Curtis Industries, Inc., 8; 28
    (upd.)
Henkel KGaA, III; 34 (upd.); 95 (upd.)
Henry Schein, Inc., 31; 70 (upd.)
Herbalife Ltd., 17; 41 (upd.); 92 (upd.)
Huntleigh Technology PLC, 77
ICON Health & Fitness, Inc., 38; 102
    (upd.)
Immucor, Inc., 81
Inamed Corporation, 79
Integra LifeSciences Holdings
    Corporation, 87
Integrated BioPharma, Inc., 83
Inter Parfums Inc., 35; 86 (upd.)
Intuitive Surgical, Inc., 79
Invacare Corporation, 11

IRIS International, Inc., 101
IVAX Corporation, 11
IVC Industries, Inc., 45
The Jean Coutu Group (PJC) Inc., 46
John Paul Mitchell Systems, 24
Johnson & Johnson, III; 8 (upd.); 36
    (upd.); 75 (upd.)
Kanebo, Ltd., 53
Kao Corporation, III; 79 (upd.)
Kendall International, Inc., 11
Kensey Nash Corporation, 71
Keys Fitness Products, LP, 83
Kimberly-Clark Corporation, III; 16
    (upd.); 43 (upd.); 105 (upd.)
Kolmar Laboratories Group, 96
Kyowa Hakko Kogyo Co., Ltd., III
Kyphon Inc., 87
L'Oréal SA, III; 8 (upd.); 46 (upd.)
Laboratoires de Biologie Végétale Yves
    Rocher, 35
The Lamaur Corporation, 41
Lever Brothers Company, 9
Lion Corporation, III; 51 (upd.)
Lush Ltd., 93
Luxottica SpA, 17; 52 (upd.)
Mandom Corporation, 82
Mannatech Inc., 33
Mary Kay Inc., 9; 30 (upd.); 84 (upd.)
Matrix Essentials Inc., 90
Maxxim Medical Inc., 12
Medco Containment Services Inc., 9
MEDecision, Inc., 95
Medical Action Industries Inc., 101
Medicine Shoppe International, Inc., 102
Medifast, Inc., 97
Medline Industries, Inc., 61
Medtronic, Inc., 8; 67 (upd.)
Melaleuca Inc., 31
The Mentholatum Company Inc., 32
Mentor Corporation, 26
Merck & Co., Inc., I; 11 (upd.); 34
    (upd.); 95 (upd.)
Merit Medical Systems, Inc., 29
Merz Group, 81
Mueller Sports Medicine, Inc., 102
Natura Cosméticos S.A., 75
Nature's Sunshine Products, Inc., 15; 102
    (upd.)
NBTY, Inc., 31
NeighborCare, Inc., 67 (upd.)
Neutrogena Corporation, 17
New Dana Perfumes Company, 37
Neways Inc. 78
Nikken Global Inc., 32
NutriSystem, Inc., 71
Nutrition for Life International Inc., 22
Nutrition 21 Inc., 97
Ocular Sciences, Inc., 65
OEC Medical Systems, Inc., 27
Obagi Medical Products, Inc., 95
OraSure Technologies, Inc., 75
Orion Oyj, 72
Parfums Givenchy S.A., 100
Patterson Dental Co., 19
Perrigo Company, 12
Pfizer Inc., 79 (upd.)
Physician Sales & Service, Inc., 14
Playtex Products, Inc., 15

PolyMedica Corporation, 77
The Procter & Gamble Company, III; 8
    (upd.); 26 (upd.); 67 (upd.)
PZ Cussons plc, 72
Quest Diagnostics Inc., 26; 106 (upd.)
Quidel Corporation, 80
Reckitt Benckiser plc, II; 42 (upd.); 91
    (upd.)
Redken Laboratories Inc., 84
Reliv International, Inc., 58
Retractable Technologies, Inc., 99
Revlon Inc., III; 17 (upd.)
Roche Biomedical Laboratories, Inc., 11
S.C. Johnson & Son, Inc., III; 28 (upd.);
    89 (upd.)
Safety 1st, Inc., 24
Sage Products Inc., 105
St. Jude Medical, Inc., 11; 43 (upd.); 97
    (upd.)
Schering-Plough Corporation, I; 14
    (upd.); 49 (upd.); 99 (upd.)
Sephora Holdings S.A., 82
Shaklee Corporation, 39 (upd.)
Shionogi & Co., Ltd., III; 17 (upd.); 98
    (upd.)
Shiseido Company, Limited, III; 22
    (upd.); 81 (upd.)
Slim-Fast Foods Company, 18; 66 (upd.)
Smith & Nephew plc, 17
SmithKline Beecham PLC, III
Soft Sheen Products, Inc., 31
Sola International Inc., 71
Spacelabs Medical, Inc., 71
STAAR Surgical Company, 57
Straumann Holding AG, 79
Stryker Corporation, 79 (upd.)
Sunrise Medical Inc., 11
Syneron Medical Ltd., 91
Synthes, Inc., 93
Tambrands Inc., 8
Thermo Fisher Scientific Inc., 105 (upd.)
Terumo Corporation, 48
Thane International, Inc., 84
Tom's of Maine, Inc., 45
Transitions Optical, Inc., 83
The Tranzonic Companies, 37
Turtle Wax, Inc., 15; 93 (upd.)
Tutogen Medical, Inc., 68
Unicharm Corporation, 84
United States Surgical Corporation, 10;
    34 (upd.)
USANA, Inc., 29
Utah Medical Products, Inc., 36
Ventana Medical Systems, Inc., 75
VHA Inc., 53
VIASYS Healthcare, Inc., 52
Vion Food Group NV, 85
VISX, Incorporated, 30
Vitamin Shoppe Industries, Inc., 60
VNUS Medical Technologies, Inc., 103
Water Pik Technologies, Inc., 34; 83
    (upd.)
Weider Nutrition International, Inc., 29
Weleda AG 78
Wella AG, III; 48 (upd.)
West Pharmaceutical Services, Inc., 42
Wright Medical Group, Inc., 61
Wyeth, 50 (upd.)

Zila, Inc., 46
Zimmer Holdings, Inc., 45

Health Care Services

Acadian Ambulance & Air Med Services, Inc., 39
Adventist Health, 53
Advocat Inc., 46
Almost Family, Inc., 93
Alterra Healthcare Corporation, 42
Amedisys, Inc., 53; 106 (upd.)
The American Cancer Society, 24
American Healthways, Inc., 65
American Lung Association, 48
American Medical Alert Corporation, 103
American Medical Association, 39
American Medical International, Inc., III
American Medical Response, Inc., 39
American Nurses Association Inc., 102
American Red Cross, 40
AMERIGROUP Corporation, 69
AmeriSource Health Corporation, 37 (upd.)
Amil Participações S.A., 105
AmSurg Corporation, 48
The Andrews Institute, 99
Applied Bioscience International, Inc., 10
Assisted Living Concepts, Inc., 43
ATC Healthcare Inc., 64
Baptist Health Care Corporation, 82
Beverly Enterprises, Inc., III; 16 (upd.)
Bon Secours Health System, Inc., 24
Brookdale Senior Living, 91
C.R. Bard, Inc., 65 (upd.)
Cancer Treatment Centers of America, Inc., 85
Capital Senior Living Corporation, 75
Caremark Rx, Inc., 10; 54 (upd.)
Catholic Health Initiatives, 91
ChildFund International, 106
Children's Comprehensive Services, Inc., 42
Children's Healthcare of Atlanta Inc., 101
Children's Hospitals and Clinics, Inc., 54
Chindex International, Inc., 101
Chronimed Inc., 26
COBE Laboratories, Inc., 13
Columbia/HCA Healthcare Corporation, 15
Community Health Systems, Inc., 71
Community Psychiatric Centers, 15
CompDent Corporation, 22
CompHealth Inc., 25
Comprehensive Care Corporation, 15
Continental Medical Systems, Inc., 10
Continucare Corporation, 101
Continuum Health Partners, Inc., 60
Coventry Health Care, Inc., 59
Craig Hospital, 99
Cross Country Healthcare, Inc., 105
Cystic Fibrosis Foundation, 93
DaVita Inc., 73
Easter Seals, Inc., 58
Erickson Retirement Communities, 57
Express Scripts Incorporated, 17
Extendicare Health Services, Inc., 6
Eye Care Centers of America, Inc., 69
FHP International Corporation, 6

Fresenius AG, 56
Genesis Health Ventures, Inc., 18
Gentiva Health Services, Inc., 79
GranCare, Inc., 14
Group Health Cooperative, 41
Grupo Ángeles Servicios de Salud, S.A. de C.V., 84
Hamot Health Foundation, 91
Hazelden Foundation, 28
HCA - The Healthcare Company, 35 (upd.)
Health Care & Retirement Corporation, 22
Health Management Associates, Inc., 56
Health Risk Management, Inc., 24
Health Systems International, Inc., 11
HealthSouth Corporation, 14; 33 (upd.)
Henry Ford Health System, 84
Highmark Inc., 27
The Hillhaven Corporation, 14
Holiday Retirement Corp., 87
Hologic, Inc., 106
Hooper Holmes, Inc., 22
Hospital Central Services, Inc., 56
Hospital Corporation of America, III
Howard Hughes Medical Institute, 39
Humana Inc., III; 24 (upd.); 101 (upd.)
Intermountain Health Care, Inc., 27
Jenny Craig, Inc., 10; 29 (upd.); 92 (upd.)
Kinetic Concepts, Inc. (KCI), 20
LabOne, Inc., 48
Laboratory Corporation of America Holdings, 42 (upd.)
LCA-Vision, Inc., 85
Life Care Centers of America Inc., 76
Lifeline Systems, Inc., 53
LifePoint Hospitals, Inc., 69
Lincare Holdings Inc., 43
Manor Care, Inc., 6; 25 (upd.)
March of Dimes, 31
Marshfield Clinic Inc., 82
Matria Healthcare, Inc., 17
Maxicare Health Plans, Inc., III; 25 (upd.)
Mayo Foundation, 9; 34 (upd.)
McBride plc, 82
Médecins sans Frontières, 85
Medical Management International, Inc., 65
Medical Staffing Network Holdings, Inc., 89
Memorial Sloan-Kettering Cancer Center, 57
Merge Healthcare, 85
Merit Medical Systems, Inc., 29
MeritCare Health System, 88
Myriad Genetics, Inc., 95
National Health Laboratories Incorporated, 11
National Jewish Health, 101
National Medical Enterprises, Inc., III
National Research Corporation, 87
New York City Health and Hospitals Corporation, 60
New York Health Care, Inc., 72
NewYork-Presbyterian Hospital, 59
NovaCare, Inc., 11
NSF International, 72

Operation Smile, Inc., 75
Option Care Inc., 48
Orthodontic Centers of America, Inc., 35
Oxford Health Plans, Inc., 16
PacifiCare Health Systems, Inc., 11
Palomar Medical Technologies, Inc., 22
Pediatric Services of America, Inc., 31
Pediatrix Medical Group, Inc., 61
PHP Healthcare Corporation, 22
PhyCor, Inc., 36
PolyMedica Corporation, 77
Primedex Health Systems, Inc., 25
Providence Health System, 90
The Providence Service Corporation, 64
Psychemedics Corporation, 89
Psychiatric Solutions, Inc., 68
Quest Diagnostics Inc., 26; 106 (upd.)
Radiation Therapy Services, Inc., 85
Ramsay Youth Services, Inc., 41
Renal Care Group, Inc., 72
Res-Care, Inc., 29
Response Oncology, Inc., 27
Rural/Metro Corporation, 28
Sabratek Corporation, 29
St. Jude Medical, Inc., 11; 43 (upd.); 97 (upd.)
Salick Health Care, Inc., 53
The Scripps Research Institute, 76
Select Medical Corporation, 65
Shriners Hospitals for Children, 69
Sierra Health Services, Inc., 15
Sisters of Charity of Leavenworth Health System, 105
Smith & Nephew plc, 41 (upd.)
Special Olympics, Inc., 93
The Sports Club Company, 25
SSL International plc, 49
Stericycle Inc., 33
Sun Healthcare Group Inc., 25
Sunrise Senior Living, Inc., 81
Susan G. Komen Breast Cancer Foundation 78
SwedishAmerican Health System, 51
Tenet Healthcare Corporation, 55 (upd.)
Twinlab Corporation, 34
U.S. Healthcare, Inc., 6
U.S. Physical Therapy, Inc., 65
Unison HealthCare Corporation, 25
United HealthCare Corporation, 9
United Nations International Children's Emergency Fund (UNICEF), 58
United Way of America, 36
UnitedHealth Group Incorporated, 9; 103 (upd.)
Universal Health Services, Inc., 6
Vanderbilt University Medical Center, 99
Vanguard Health Systems Inc., 70
VCA Antech, Inc., 58
Vencor, Inc., 16
VISX, Incorporated, 30
Vivra, Inc., 18
Volunteers of America, Inc., 66
WellPoint, Inc., 25; 103 (upd.)
World Vision International, Inc., 93
YWCA of the U.S.A., 45

Hotels

Accor S.A., 69 (upd.)
Amerihost Properties, Inc., 30
Ameristar Casinos, Inc., 69 (upd.)
Archon Corporation, 74 (upd.)
Arena Leisure Plc, 99
Aztar Corporation, 13; 71 (upd.)
Bass PLC, 38 (upd.)
Boca Resorts, Inc., 37
Boyd Gaming Corporation, 43
Boyne USA Resorts, 71
Bristol Hotel Company, 23
The Broadmoor Hotel, 30
Caesars World, Inc., 6
Candlewood Hotel Company, Inc., 41
Carlson Companies, Inc., 6; 22 (upd.); 87 (upd.)
Castle & Cooke, Inc., 20 (upd.)
Cedar Fair Entertainment Company, 22; 98 (upd.)
Cendant Corporation, 44 (upd.)
Choice Hotels International, Inc., 14; 83 (upd.)
Circus Circus Enterprises, Inc., 6
City Developments Limited, 89
Club Mediterranée S.A., 6; 21 (upd.); 91 (upd.)
Compagnia Italiana dei Jolly Hotels S.p.A., 71
Daniel Thwaites Plc, 95
Doubletree Corporation, 21
EIH Ltd., 103
Extended Stay America, Inc., 41
Fairmont Hotels & Resorts Inc., 69
Fibreboard Corporation, 16
Four Seasons Hotels Limited, 9; 29 (upd.); 106 (upd.)
Fuller Smith & Turner P.L.C., 38
Gables Residential Trust, 49
Gaylord Entertainment Company, 11; 36 (upd.)
Gianni Versace S.p.A., 22; 106 (upd.)
Global Hyatt Corporation, 75 (upd.)
Granada Group PLC, 24 (upd.)
Grand Casinos, Inc., 20
Grand Hotel Krasnapolsky N.V., 23
Great Wolf Resorts, Inc., 91
Grupo Posadas, S.A. de C.V., 57
Helmsley Enterprises, Inc., 9
Hilton Hotels Corporation, III; 19 (upd.); 49 (upd.); 62 (upd.)
Holiday Inns, Inc., III
Home Inns & Hotels Management Inc., 95
Hospitality Franchise Systems, Inc., 11
Hotel Properties Ltd., 71
Howard Johnson International, Inc., 17; 72 (upd.)
Hyatt Corporation, III; 16 (upd.)
ILX Resorts Incorporated, 65
Interstate Hotels & Resorts Inc., 58
ITT Sheraton Corporation, III
JD Wetherspoon plc, 30
John Q. Hammons Hotels, Inc., 24
Jumeirah Group, 83
Kerzner International Limited, 69 (upd.)
Kimpton Hotel & Restaurant Group, Inc., 105

The La Quinta Companies, 11; 42 (upd.)
Ladbroke Group PLC, 21 (upd.)
Landry's Restaurants, Inc., 65 (upd.)
Las Vegas Sands Corp., 50; 106 (upd.)
Madden's on Gull Lake, 52
Mammoth Mountain Ski Area, 101
Mandalay Resort Group, 32 (upd.)
Manor Care, Inc., 25 (upd.)
The Marcus Corporation, 21
Marriott International, Inc., III; 21 (upd.); 83 (upd.)
McMenamins Pubs and Breweries, 65
Melco Crown Entertainment Limited, 103
MGM MIRAGE, 98 (upd.)
Millennium & Copthorne Hotels plc, 71
Mirage Resorts, Incorporated, 6; 28 (upd.)
Monarch Casino & Resort, Inc., 65
Morgans Hotel Group Company, 80
Motel 6, 13; 56 (upd.)
Mövenpick Holding, 104
MTR Gaming Group, Inc., 75
MWH Preservation Limited Partnership, 65
NH Hoteles S.A., 79
Omni Hotels Corp., 12
Paradores de Turismo de Espana S.A., 73
Park Corp., 22
Players International, Inc., 22
Preferred Hotel Group, 103
Preussag AG, 42 (upd.)
Prime Hospitality Corporation, 52
Promus Companies, Inc., 9
Real Turismo, S.A. de C.V., 50
Red Roof Inns, Inc., 18
Regent Inns plc, 95
Resorts International, Inc., 12
The Ritz-Carlton Hotel Company, L.L.C., 9; 29 (upd.); 71 (upd.)
Riviera Holdings Corporation, 75
Sandals Resorts International, 65
Santa Fe Gaming Corporation, 19
The SAS Group, 34 (upd.)
SFI Group plc, 51
Shangri-La Asia Ltd., 71
Showboat, Inc., 19
Sol Meliá S.A., 71
Sonesta International Hotels Corporation, 44
Southern Sun Hotel Interest (Pty) Ltd., 106
Starwood Hotels & Resorts Worldwide, Inc., 54
Sun International Hotels Limited, 26
Sunburst Hospitality Corporation, 26
Sunshine Village Corporation, 103
Super 8 Motels, Inc., 83
Thistle Hotels PLC, 54
Trusthouse Forte PLC, III
Vail Resorts, Inc., 43 (upd.)
WestCoast Hospitality Corporation, 59
Westin Hotels and Resorts Worldwide, 9; 29 (upd.)
Whitbread PLC, I; 20 (upd.); 52 (upd.); 97 (upd.)
Wyndham Worldwide Corporation (updates Cendant Corporation), 99 (upd.)
Young & Co.'s Brewery, P.L.C., 38

Information Technology

A.B. Watley Group Inc., 45
AccuWeather, Inc., 73
Acxiom Corporation, 35
Adaptec, Inc., 31
Adobe Systems Inc., 10; 33 (upd.); 106 (upd.
Advanced Micro Devices, Inc., 6; 30 (upd.); 99 (upd.)
Agence France-Presse, 34
Agilent Technologies Inc., 38; 93 (upd.)
Akamai Technologies, Inc., 71
Aladdin Knowledge Systems Ltd., 101
Aldus Corporation, 10
Allen Systems Group, Inc., 59
Allscripts-Misys Healthcare Solutions Inc., 104
AltaVista Company, 43
Altiris, Inc., 65
Amdahl Corporation, III; 14 (upd.); 40 (upd.)
Amdocs Ltd., 47
America Online, Inc., 10; 26 (upd.)
American Business Information, Inc., 18
American Management Systems, Inc., 11
American Software Inc., 25
AMICAS, Inc., 69
Amstrad PLC, III
Analex Corporation, 74
Analytic Sciences Corporation, 10
Analytical Surveys, Inc., 33
Anker BV, 53
Ansoft Corporation, 63
Anteon Corporation, 57
AOL Time Warner Inc., 57 (upd.)
Apollo Group, Inc., 24
Apple Computer, Inc., III; 6 (upd.); 77 (upd.)
aQuantive, Inc., 81
The Arbitron Company, 38
Ariba, Inc., 57
Asanté Technologies, Inc., 20
Ascential Software Corporation, 59
AsiaInfo Holdings, Inc., 43
ASK Group, Inc., 9
Ask Jeeves, Inc., 65
ASML Holding N.V., 50
The Associated Press, 73 (upd.)
AST Research Inc., 9
At Home Corporation, 43
AT&T Bell Laboratories, Inc., 13
AT&T Corporation, 29 (upd.)
AT&T Istel Ltd., 14
Atos Origin S.A., 69
Attachmate Corporation, 56
Autodesk, Inc., 10; 89 (upd.)
Autologic Information International, Inc., 20
Automatic Data Processing, Inc., III; 9 (upd.); 47 (upd.)
Autotote Corporation, 20
Avantium Technologies BV, 79
Avid Technology Inc., 38
Avocent Corporation, 65
Aydin Corp., 19
Baan Company, 25
Baidu.com Inc., 95
Baltimore Technologies Plc, 42

Bankrate, Inc., 83
Banyan Systems Inc., 25
Battelle Memorial Institute, Inc., 10
BBN Corp., 19
BEA Systems, Inc., 36
Bell and Howell Company, 9; 29 (upd.)
Bell Industries, Inc., 47
Billing Concepts, Inc., 26; 72 (upd.)
Blackbaud, Inc., 85
Blackboard Inc., 89
Blizzard Entertainment 78
Bloomberg L.P., 21
Blue Martini Software, Inc., 59
BMC Software, Inc., 55
Boole & Babbage, Inc., 25
Booz Allen Hamilton, Inc., 10; 101 (upd.)
Borland International, Inc., 9
Bowne & Co., Inc., 23
Brite Voice Systems, Inc., 20
Brocade Communications Systems Inc., 106
Broderbund Software, 13; 29 (upd.)
BTG, Inc., 45
Bull S.A., 43 (upd.)
Business Objects S.A., 25
C-Cube Microsystems, Inc., 37
CACI International Inc., 21; 72 (upd.)
Cadence Design Systems, Inc., 11
Caere Corporation, 20
Cahners Business Information, 43
CalComp Inc., 13
Cambridge Technology Partners, Inc., 36
Candle Corporation, 64
Canon Inc., III
Cap Gemini Ernst & Young, 37
Captaris, Inc., 89
CareerBuilder, Inc., 93
Caribiner International, Inc., 24
Cass Information Systems Inc., 100
Catalina Marketing Corporation, 18
CDC Corporation, 71
CDW Computer Centers, Inc., 16
Cerner Corporation, 16
CheckFree Corporation, 81
Cheyenne Software, Inc., 12
CHIPS and Technologies, Inc., 9
Ciber, Inc., 18
Cincom Systems Inc., 15
Cirrus Logic, Incorporated, 11
Cisco-Linksys LLC, 86
Cisco Systems, Inc., 11; 77 (upd.)
Citizen Watch Co., Ltd., III; 21 (upd.); 81 (upd.)
Citrix Systems, Inc., 44
CMGI, Inc., 76
CNET Networks, Inc., 47
Cogent Communications Group, Inc., 55
Cognizant Technology Solutions Corporation, 59
Cognos Inc., 44
Commodore International Ltd., 7
Compagnie des Machines Bull S.A., III
Compaq Computer Corporation, III; 6 (upd.); 26 (upd.)
Complete Business Solutions, Inc., 31
CompuAdd Computer Corporation, 11
CompuCom Systems, Inc., 10
CompUSA, Inc., 35 (upd.)

CompuServe Interactive Services, Inc., 10; 27 (upd.)
Computer Associates International, Inc., 6; 49 (upd.)
Computer Data Systems, Inc., 14
Computer Sciences Corporation, 6
Computervision Corporation, 10
Compuware Corporation, 10; 30 (upd.); 66 (upd.)
Comshare Inc., 23
Concur Technologies, Inc., 106
Conner Peripherals, Inc., 6
Control Data Corporation, III
Control Data Systems, Inc., 10
Corbis Corporation, 31
Corel Corporation, 15; 33 (upd.); 76 (upd.)
Corporate Software Inc., 9
CoStar Group, Inc., 73
craigslist, inc., 89
Cray Research, Inc., III
Credence Systems Corporation, 90
CSX Corporation, 79 (upd.)
CTG, Inc., 11
Ctrip.com International Ltd., 97
Cybermedia, Inc., 25
Dairyland Healthcare Solutions, 73
Dassault Systèmes S.A., 25
Data Broadcasting Corporation, 31
Data General Corporation, 8
Datapoint Corporation, 11
Dell Computer Corp., 9
Dendrite International, Inc., 70
Deutsche Börse AG, 59
Dialogic Corporation, 18
DiamondCluster International, Inc., 51
Digex, Inc., 46
Digital Angel Corporation, 106
Digital Equipment Corporation, III; 6 (upd.)
Digital River, Inc., 50
Digitas Inc., 81
Dimension Data Holdings PLC, 69
ditech.com, 93
Documentum, Inc., 46
The Dun & Bradstreet Corporation, IV; 19 (upd.)
Dun & Bradstreet Software Services Inc., 11
DynCorp, 45
E.piphany, Inc., 49
EarthLink, Inc., 36
Eclipsys Corporation, 104
eCollege.com, 85
ECS S.A, 12
EDGAR Online, Inc., 91
Edmark Corporation, 14; 41 (upd.)
Egghead Inc., 9
El Camino Resources International, Inc., 11
Electronic Arts Inc., 10; 85 (upd.)
Electronic Data Systems Corporation, III; 28 (upd.)
Electronics for Imaging, Inc., 43 (upd.)
EMC Corporation, 12; 46 (upd.)
Encore Computer Corporation, 13; 74 (upd.)

Environmental Systems Research Institute Inc. (ESRI), 62
EPAM Systems Inc., 96
Epic Systems Corporation, 62
EPIQ Systems, Inc., 56
Evans and Sutherland Computer Company 19, 78 (upd.)
Exabyte Corporation, 12
Experian Information Solutions Inc., 45
EZchip Semiconductor Ltd., 106
Facebook, Inc., 90
FactSet Research Systems Inc., 73
FASTWEB S.p.A., 83
F5 Networks, Inc., 72
First Financial Management Corporation, 11
Fiserv, Inc., 11; 33 (upd.); 106 (upd.)
FlightSafety International, Inc., 9
FORE Systems, Inc., 25
Franklin Electronic Publishers, Inc., 23
Franz Inc., 80
FTP Software, Inc., 20
Fujitsu Limited, III; 16 (upd.); 42 (upd.); 103 (upd.)
Fujitsu-ICL Systems Inc., 11
Future Now, Inc., 12
Gartner, Inc., 21; 94 (upd.)
Gateway, Inc., 10; 27 (upd.)
GEAC Computer Corporation Ltd., 43
Geek Squad Inc., 102
Genesys Telecommunications Laboratories Inc., 103
Gericom AG, 47
Getronics NV, 39
GFI Informatique SA, 49
Global Imaging Systems, Inc., 73
The Go Daddy Group Inc., 102
Gomez Inc., 104
Google, Inc., 50; 101 (upd.)
Groupe Ares S.A., 102
Groupe Open, 74
Grupo Positivo, 105
GSI Commerce, Inc., 67
GT Interactive Software, 31
Guthy-Renker Corporation, 32
Handspring Inc., 49
Hewlett-Packard Company, III; 6 (upd.)
Human Factors International Inc., 100
Hyperion Software Corporation, 22
Hyperion Solutions Corporation, 76
ICL plc, 6
Identix Inc., 44
IDX Systems Corporation, 64
IKON Office Solutions, Inc., 50
Imation Corporation, 20
Indus International Inc., 70
Infineon Technologies AG, 50
Information Access Company, 17
Information Builders, Inc., 22
Information Resources, Inc., 10
Informix Corporation, 10; 30 (upd.)
InfoSpace, Inc., 91
Infosys Technologies Ltd., 38
Ing. C. Olivetti & C., S.p.a., III
Inktomi Corporation, 45
Input/Output, Inc., 73
Inso Corporation, 26
Integrity Media, Inc., 102

Interactive Intelligence Inc., 106
Intel Corporation, 36 (upd.)
IntelliCorp, Inc., 45
Intelligent Electronics, Inc., 6
Interfax News Agency, 86
Intergraph Corporation, 6; 24 (upd.)
Intermix Media, Inc., 83
International Business Machines
   Corporation, III; 6 (upd.); 30 (upd.);
   63 (upd.)
InterVideo, Inc., 85
Intrado Inc., 63
Intuit Inc., 14; 33 (upd.); 73 (upd.)
Iomega Corporation, 21
IONA Technologies plc, 43
i2 Technologies, Inc., 87
J.D. Edwards & Company, 14
Jack Henry and Associates, Inc., 17
Janus Capital Group Inc., 57
JDA Software Group, Inc., 101
Jones Knowledge Group, Inc., 97
The Judge Group, Inc., 51
Juniper Networks, Inc., 43
Juno Online Services, Inc., 38
Jupitermedia Corporation, 75
Kana Software, Inc., 51
Keane, Inc., 56
Kenexa Corporation, 87
Keynote Systems Inc., 102
Kintera, Inc., 75
KLA Instruments Corporation, 11
Knight Ridder, Inc., 67 (upd.)
KnowledgeWare Inc., 31 (upd.)
Komag, Inc., 11
Kronos, Inc., 18; 100 (upd.)
Kurzweil Technologies, Inc., 51
LaCie Group S.A., 76
Lam Research Corporation, 11
Landauer, Inc., 51
Lason, Inc., 31
Lawson Software, 38
The Learning Company Inc., 24
Learning Tree International Inc., 24
Legent Corporation, 10
LendingTree, LLC, 93
Levi, Ray & Shoup, Inc., 96
LEXIS-NEXIS Group, 33
LifeLock, Inc., 91
LinkedIn Corporation, 103
Logica plc, 14; 37 (upd.)
Logicon Inc., 20
Logitech International S.A., 28; 69 (upd.)
LoJack Corporation, 48
Lotus Development Corporation, 6; 25
   (upd.)
The MacNeal-Schwendler Corporation, 25
Macromedia, Inc., 50
Macrovision Solutions Corporation, 101
Madge Networks N.V., 26
Magma Design Automation Inc. 78
MAI Systems Corporation, 11
Manatron, Inc., 86
ManTech International Corporation, 97
MAPICS, Inc., 55
Maryville Data Systems Inc., 96
Match.com, LP, 87
The MathWorks, Inc., 80
Maxtor Corporation, 10

Mead Data Central, Inc., 10
Mecklermedia Corporation, 24
MEDecision, Inc., 95
Media Sciences International, Inc., 104
Medical Information Technology Inc., 64
Mentor Graphics Corporation, 11
Mercury Interactive Corporation, 59
Merge Healthcare, 85
Merisel, Inc., 12
Metatec International, Inc., 47
Metavante Corporation, 100
Metro Information Services, Inc., 36
Micro Warehouse, Inc., 16
Micron Technology, Inc., 11; 29 (upd.)
Micros Systems, Inc., 18
Microsoft Corporation, 6; 27 (upd.); 63
   (upd.)
MicroStrategy Incorporated, 87
Misys plc, 45; 46
MITRE Corporation, 26
MIVA, Inc., 83
Moldflow Corporation, 73
Morningstar Inc., 68
The Motley Fool, Inc., 40
Mozilla Foundation, 106
National Research Corporation, 87
National Semiconductor Corporation, 6
National TechTeam, Inc., 41
National Weather Service, 91
Navarre Corporation, 24
NAVTEQ Corporation, 69
NCR Corporation, III; 6 (upd.); 30
   (upd.); 90 (upd.)
NetCracker Technology Corporation, 98
Netezza Corporation, 69
NetIQ Corporation, 79
Netscape Communications Corporation,
   15; 35 (upd.)
Network Appliance, Inc., 58
Network Associates, Inc., 25
Nextel Communications, Inc., 10
NFO Worldwide, Inc., 24
NICE Systems Ltd., 83
Nichols Research Corporation, 18
Nimbus CD International, Inc., 20
Nixdorf Computer AG, III
Noah Education Holdings Ltd., 97
Novell, Inc., 6; 23 (upd.)
NVIDIA Corporation, 54
Océ N.V., 24; 91 (upd.)
OCLC Online Computer Library Center,
   Inc., 96
Odetics Inc., 14
Onyx Software Corporation, 53
Open Text Corporation, 79
Openwave Systems Inc., 95
Opsware Inc., 49
Oracle Corporation, 6; 24 (upd.); 67
   (upd.)
Orbitz, Inc., 61
Overland Storage Inc., 100
Packard Bell Electronics, Inc., 13
Packeteer, Inc., 81
Parametric Technology Corp., 16
PC Connection, Inc., 37
Pegasus Solutions, Inc., 75
PeopleSoft Inc., 14; 33 (upd.)
Perot Systems Corporation, 29

Phillips International Inc. 78
Pitney Bowes Inc., III
PLATINUM Technology, Inc., 14
Policy Management Systems Corporation,
   11
Policy Studies, Inc., 62
Portal Software, Inc., 47
Primark Corp., 13
The Princeton Review, Inc., 42
Printrak, A Motorola Company, 44
Printronix, Inc., 18
Prodigy Communications Corporation, 34
Prodware S.A., 102
Programmer's Paradise, Inc., 81
Progress Software Corporation, 15
Psion PLC, 45
QSS Group, Inc., 100
Quality Systems, Inc., 81
Quantum Corporation, 10; 62 (upd.)
Quark, Inc., 36
Quicken Loans, Inc., 93
Racal-Datacom Inc., 11
Radiant Systems Inc., 104
Razorfish, Inc., 37
RCM Technologies, Inc., 34
RealNetworks, Inc., 53
Red Hat, Inc., 45
Remedy Corporation, 58
Renaissance Learning, Inc., 39; 100 (upd.)
The Reynolds and Reynolds Company, 50
Ricoh Company, Ltd., III
Riverbed Technology, Inc., 101
Rocky Mountain Chocolate Factory, Inc.,
   73
Rolta India Ltd., 90
RSA Security Inc., 46
RWD Technologies, Inc., 76
SABRE Group Holdings, Inc., 26
SafeNet Inc., 101
The Sage Group, 43
salesforce.com, Inc., 79
The Santa Cruz Operation, Inc., 38
SAP AG, 16; 43 (upd.)
SAS Institute Inc., 10; 78 (upd.)
Satyam Computer Services Ltd., 85
SBS Technologies, Inc., 25
SCB Computer Technology, Inc., 29
Schawk, Inc., 24
Scientific Learning Corporation, 95
The SCO Group Inc., 78
SDL PLC, 67
Seagate Technology, 8; 34 (upd.); 105
   (upd.)
Siebel Systems, Inc., 38
Sierra On-Line, Inc., 15; 41 (upd.)
SilverPlatter Information Inc., 23
SINA Corporation, 69
SkillSoft Public Limited Company, 81
SmartForce PLC, 43
Softbank Corp., 13; 38 (upd.); 77 (upd.)
Sonic Solutions, Inc., 81
SonicWALL, Inc., 87
Spark Networks, Inc., 91
Specialist Computer Holdings Ltd., 80
SPSS Inc., 64
Square Enix Holdings Co., Ltd., 101
SRA International, Inc., 77
Standard Microsystems Corporation, 11

STC PLC, III
Steria SA, 49
Sterling Software, Inc., 11
Storage Technology Corporation, 6
Stratus Computer, Inc., 10
Sun Microsystems, Inc., 7; 30 (upd.); 91 (upd.)
SunGard Data Systems Inc., 11
Sybase, Inc., 10; 27 (upd.)
Sykes Enterprises, Inc., 45
Symantec Corporation, 10; 82 (upd.)
Symbol Technologies, Inc., 15
Synchronoss Technologies, Inc., 95
SYNNEX Corporation, 73
Synopsys, Inc., 11; 69 (upd.)
Syntel, Inc., 92
System Software Associates, Inc., 10
Systems & Computer Technology Corp., 19
T-Online International AG, 61
TALX Corporation, 92
Tandem Computers, Inc., 6
TechTarget, Inc., 99
TenFold Corporation, 35
Terra Lycos, Inc., 43
Terremark Worldwide, Inc., 99
The Thomson Corporation, 34 (upd.); 77 (upd.)
ThoughtWorks Inc., 90
3Com Corporation, 11; 34 (upd.); 106 (upd.)
The 3DO Company, 43
TIBCO Software Inc., 79
Timberline Software Corporation, 15
TomTom N.V., 81
TradeStation Group, Inc., 83
Traffix, Inc., 61
Transaction Systems Architects, Inc., 29; 82 (upd.)
Transiciel SA, 48
Trend Micro Inc., 97
Triple P N.V., 26
Tripwire, Inc., 97
The TriZetto Group, Inc., 83
Tucows Inc. 78
Ubisoft Entertainment S.A., 41; 106 (upd.)
Unica Corporation, 77
Unilog SA, 42
Unisys Corporation, III; 6 (upd.); 36 (upd.)
United Business Media plc, 52 (upd.)
United Internet AG, 99
United Online, Inc., 71 (upd.)
United Press International, Inc., 73 (upd.)
UUNET, 38
VASCO Data Security International, Inc., 79
Verbatim Corporation, 14
Veridian Corporation, 54
VeriFone Holdings, Inc., 18; 76 (upd.)
Verint Systems Inc., 73
VeriSign, Inc., 47
Veritas Software Corporation, 45
Verity Inc., 68
Viasoft Inc., 27
Vital Images, Inc., 85
VMware, Inc., 90

Volt Information Sciences Inc., 26
Wanadoo S.A., 75
Wang Laboratories, Inc., III; 6 (upd.)
Weather Central Inc., 100
WebMD Corporation, 65
WebEx Communications, Inc., 81
West Group, 34 (upd.)
Westcon Group, Inc., 67
Western Digital Corporation, 25; 92 (upd.)
Wikimedia Foundation, Inc., 91
Wind River Systems, Inc., 37
Wipro Limited, 43; 106 (upd.)
Witness Systems, Inc., 87
Wolters Kluwer NV, 33 (upd.)
WordPerfect Corporation, 10
WSI Corporation, 102
Wyse Technology, Inc., 15
Xerox Corporation, III; 6 (upd.); 26 (upd.); 69 (upd.)
Xilinx, Inc., 16; 82 (upd.)
Yahoo! Inc., 27; 70 (upd.)
YouTube, Inc., 90
Zanett, Inc., 92
Zapata Corporation, 25
Ziff Davis Media Inc., 36 (upd.)
Zilog, Inc., 15

Insurance

AEGON N.V., III; 50 (upd.)
Aetna Inc., III; 21 (upd.); 63 (upd.)
AFLAC Incorporated, 10 (upd.); 38 (upd.)
Alexander & Alexander Services Inc., 10
Alfa Corporation, 60
Alleanza Assicurazioni S.p.A., 65
Alleghany Corporation, 10
Allianz AG, III; 15 (upd.); 57 (upd.)
Allmerica Financial Corporation, 63
The Allstate Corporation, 10; 27 (upd.)
AMB Generali Holding AG, 51
American Family Corporation, III
American Financial Group Inc., III; 48 (upd.)
American General Corporation, III; 10 (upd.); 46 (upd.)
American International Group, Inc., III; 15 (upd.); 47 (upd.)
American National Insurance Company, 8; 27 (upd.)
American Premier Underwriters, Inc., 10
American Re Corporation, 10; 35 (upd.)
N.V. AMEV, III
AOK-Bundesverband (Federation of the AOK) 78
Aon Corporation, III; 45 (upd.)
Arthur J. Gallagher & Co., 73
Assicurazioni Generali S.p.A., III; 15 (upd.); 103 (upd.)
Assurances Générales de France, 63
Assured Guaranty Ltd., 93
Atlantic American Corporation, 44
Aviva PLC, 50 (upd.)
AXA Colonia Konzern AG, 27; 49 (upd.)
AXA Equitable Life Insurance Company, III; 105 (upd.)
B.A.T. Industries PLC, 22 (upd.)
Baldwin & Lyons, Inc., 51

Bâloise-Holding, 40
Benfield Greig Group plc, 53
Berkshire Hathaway Inc., III; 18 (upd.); 42 (upd.); 89 (upd.)
Blue Cross and Blue Shield Association, 10
British United Provident Association Limited (BUPAL), 79
Brown & Brown, Inc., 41
Business Men's Assurance Company of America, 14
Capital Holding Corporation, III
Catholic Order of Foresters, 24; 97 (upd.)
China Life Insurance Company Limited, 65
ChoicePoint Inc., 65
The Chubb Corporation, III; 14 (upd.); 37 (upd.)
CIGNA Corporation, III; 22 (upd.); 45 (upd.)
Cincinnati Financial Corporation, 16; 44 (upd.)
CNA Financial Corporation, III; 38 (upd.)
Commercial Union PLC, III
Connecticut Mutual Life Insurance Company, III
Conseco Inc., 10; 33 (upd.)
The Continental Corporation, III
Crawford & Company, 87
Crum & Forster Holdings Corporation, 104
Debeka Krankenversicherungsverein auf Gegenseitigkeit, 72
The Doctors' Company, 55
Empire Blue Cross and Blue Shield, III
Enbridge Inc., 43
Endurance Specialty Holdings Ltd., 85
Engle Homes, Inc., 46
The Equitable Life Assurance Society of the United States Fireman's Fund Insurance Company, III
ERGO Versicherungsgruppe AG, 44
Erie Indemnity Company, 35
Fairfax Financial Holdings Limited, 57
Farm Family Holdings, Inc., 39
Farmers Insurance Group of Companies, 25
Federal Deposit Insurance Corporation, 93
Fidelity National Financial Inc., 54
The First American Corporation, 52
First Executive Corporation, III
Foundation Health Corporation, 12
Gainsco, Inc., 22
GEICO Corporation, 10; 40 (upd.)
General Accident PLC, III
General Re Corporation, III; 24 (upd.)
Gerling-Konzern Versicherungs-Beteiligungs-Aktiengesellschaft, 51
GraceKennedy Ltd., 92
Great-West Lifeco Inc., III
Groupama S.A., 76
Gryphon Holdings, Inc., 21
Guardian Financial Services, 64 (upd.)
Guardian Royal Exchange Plc, 11
Harleysville Group Inc., 37

HDI (Haftpflichtverband der Deutschen Industrie Versicherung auf Gegenseitigkeit V.a.G.), 53
HealthExtras, Inc., 75
HealthMarkets, Inc., 88 (upd.)
Hilb, Rogal & Hobbs Company, 77
The Home Insurance Company, III
Horace Mann Educators Corporation, 22; 90 (upd.)
Household International, Inc., 21 (upd.)
Hub International Limited, 89
HUK-Coburg, 58
Humana Inc., III; 24 (upd.); 101 (upd.)
Irish Life & Permanent Plc, 59
Jackson National Life Insurance Company, 8
Jefferson-Pilot Corporation, 11; 29 (upd.)
John Hancock Financial Services, Inc., III; 42 (upd.)
Johnson & Higgins, 14
Kaiser Foundation Health Plan, Inc., 53
Kemper Corporation, III; 15 (upd.)
LandAmerica Financial Group, Inc., 85
Legal & General Group Plc, III; 24 (upd.); 101 (upd.)
The Liberty Corporation, 22
Liberty Mutual Holding Company, 59
LifeWise Health Plan of Oregon, Inc., 90
Lincoln National Corporation, III; 25 (upd.)
Lloyd's, 74 (upd.)
Lloyd's of London, III; 22 (upd.)
The Loewen Group Inc., 40 (upd.)
Lutheran Brotherhood, 31
Manulife Financial Corporation, 85
Marsh & McLennan Companies, Inc., III; 45 (upd.)
Massachusetts Mutual Life Insurance Company, III; 53 (upd.)
MBIA Inc., 73
The Meiji Mutual Life Insurance Company, III
Mercury General Corporation, 25
Metropolitan Life Insurance Company, III; 52 (upd.)
MGIC Investment Corp., 52
The Midland Company, 65
Millea Holdings Inc., 64 (upd.)
Mitsui Marine and Fire Insurance Company, Limited, III
Mitsui Mutual Life Insurance Company, III; 39 (upd.)
Modern Woodmen of America, 66
Munich Re (Münchener Rückversicherungs-Gesellschaft Aktiengesellschaft in München), III; 46 (upd.)
The Mutual Benefit Life Insurance Company, III
The Mutual Life Insurance Company of New York, III
The Mutual of Omaha Companies, 98
National Medical Health Card Systems, Inc., 79
Nationale-Nederlanden N.V., III
The Navigators Group, Inc., 92
New England Mutual Life Insurance Company, III

New Jersey Manufacturers Insurance Company, 96
New York Life Insurance Company, III; 45 (upd.)
Nippon Life Insurance Company, III; 60 (upd.)
Northwestern Mutual Life Insurance Company, III; 45 (upd.)
NYMAGIC, Inc., 41
Ohio Casualty Corp., 11
Old Republic International Corporation, 11; 58 (upd.)
Oregon Dental Service Health Plan, Inc., 51
Pacific Mutual Holding Company, 98
Palmer & Cay, Inc., 69
Pan-American Life Insurance Company, 48
PartnerRe Ltd., 83
The Paul Revere Corporation, 12
Pennsylvania Blue Shield, III
The PMI Group, Inc., 49
Preserver Group, Inc., 44
Principal Mutual Life Insurance Company, III
The Progressive Corporation, 11; 29 (upd.)
Provident Life and Accident Insurance Company of America, III
Prudential Financial Inc., III; 30 (upd.); 82 (upd.)
Prudential plc, III; 48 (upd.)
Radian Group Inc., 42
The Regence Group, 74
Reliance Group Holdings, Inc., III
Riunione Adriatica di Sicurtà SpA, III
Royal & Sun Alliance Insurance Group plc, 55 (upd.)
Royal Insurance Holdings PLC, III
SAFECO Corporaton, III
Sagicor Life Inc., 98
The St. Paul Travelers Companies, Inc. III; 22 (upd.); 79 (upd.)
SCOR S.A., 20
Skandia Insurance Company, Ltd., 50
Sompo Japan Insurance, Inc., 98 (upd.)
StanCorp Financial Group, Inc., 56
The Standard Life Assurance Company, III
State Auto Financial Corporation, 77
State Farm Mutual Automobile Insurance Company, III; 51 (upd.)
State Financial Services Corporation, 51
Stewart Information Services Corporation 78
Sumitomo Life Insurance Company, III; 60 (upd.)
The Sumitomo Marine and Fire Insurance Company, Limited, III
Sun Alliance Group PLC, III
Sun Life Financial Inc., 85
SunAmerica Inc., 11
Suncorp-Metway Ltd., 91
Suramericana de Inversiones S.A., 88
Svenska Handelsbanken AB, 50 (upd.)
The Swett & Crawford Group Inc., 84
Swiss Reinsurance Company

(Schweizerische Rückversicherungs-Gesellschaft), III; 46 (upd.)
Teachers Insurance and Annuity Association-College Retirement Equities Fund, III; 45 (upd.)
Texas Industries, Inc., 8
TIG Holdings, Inc., 26
The Tokio Marine and Fire Insurance Co., Ltd., III
Torchmark Corporation, 9; 33 (upd.)
Transatlantic Holdings, Inc., 11
The Travelers Corporation, III
UICI, 33
Union des Assurances de Pans, III
United National Group, Ltd., 63
Unitrin Inc., 16; 78 (upd.)
UNUM Corp., 13
UnumProvident Corporation, 52 (upd.)
USAA, 10
USF&G Corporation, III
UTG Inc., 100
Victoria Group, 44 (upd.)
VICTORIA Holding AG, III
Vision Service Plan Inc., 77
W.R. Berkley Corporation, 15; 74 (upd.)
Washington National Corporation, 12
The Wawanesa Mutual Insurance Company, 68
WellCare Health Plans, Inc., 101
WellChoice, Inc., 67 (upd.)
WellPoint, Inc., 25; 103 (upd.)
Westfield Group, 69
White Mountains Insurance Group, Ltd., 48
Willis Group Holdings Ltd., 25; 100 (upd.)
Winterthur Group, III; 68 (upd.)
The Yasuda Fire and Marine Insurance Company, Limited, III
The Yasuda Mutual Life Insurance Company, III; 39 (upd.)
Zurich Financial Services, 42 (upd.); 93 (upd.)
Zürich Versicherungs-Gesellschaft, III

Legal Services

Akin, Gump, Strauss, Hauer & Feld, L.L.P., 33
American Bar Association, 35
American Lawyer Media Holdings, Inc., 32
Amnesty International, 50
Andrews Kurth, LLP, 71
Arnold & Porter, 35
Baker & Daniels LLP, 88
Baker & Hostetler LLP, 40
Baker & McKenzie, 10; 42 (upd.)
Baker and Botts, L.L.P., 28
Bingham Dana LLP, 43
Brobeck, Phleger & Harrison, LLP, 31
Cadwalader, Wickersham & Taft, 32
Chadbourne & Parke, 36
Cleary, Gottlieb, Steen & Hamilton, 35
Clifford Chance LLP, 38
Coudert Brothers, 30
Covington & Burling, 40
CRA International, Inc., 93

Cravath, Swaine & Moore, 43
Davis Polk & Wardwell, 36
Debevoise & Plimpton, 39
Dechert, 43
Dewey Ballantine LLP, 48
DLA Piper, 106
Dorsey & Whitney LLP, 47
Drinker, Biddle and Reath L.L.P., 92
Faegre & Benson LLP, 97
Fenwick & West LLP, 34
Fish & Neave, 54
Foley & Lardner, 28
Fried, Frank, Harris, Shriver & Jacobson, 35
Fulbright & Jaworski L.L.P., 47
Gibson, Dunn & Crutcher LLP, 36
Greenberg Traurig, LLP, 65
Heller, Ehrman, White & McAuliffe, 41
Hildebrandt International, 29
Hogan & Hartson L.L.P., 44
Holland & Knight LLP, 60
Holme Roberts & Owen LLP, 28
Hughes Hubbard & Reed LLP, 44
Hunton & Williams, 35
Jenkens & Gilchrist, P.C., 65
Jones, Day, Reavis & Pogue, 33
Kelley Drye & Warren LLP, 40
King & Spalding, 23
Kirkland & Ellis LLP, 65
Lambda Legal Defense and Education Fund, Inc., 106
Latham & Watkins, 33
LeBoeuf, Lamb, Greene & MacRae, L.L.P., 29
LECG Corporation, 93
The Legal Aid Society, 48
Mayer, Brown, Rowe & Maw, 47
Milbank, Tweed, Hadley & McCloy, 27
Morgan, Lewis & Bockius LLP, 29
Morrison & Foerster LLP 78
O'Melveny & Myers, 37
Oppenheimer Wolff & Donnelly LLP, 71
Orrick, Herrington and Sutcliffe LLP, 76
Patton Boggs LLP, 71
Paul, Hastings, Janofsky & Walker LLP, 27
Paul, Weiss, Rifkind, Wharton & Garrison, 47
Pepper Hamilton LLP, 43
Perkins Coie LLP, 56
Phillips Lytle LLP, 102
Pillsbury Madison & Sutro LLP, 29
Pre-Paid Legal Services, Inc., 20
Proskauer Rose LLP, 47
Quinn Emanuel Urquhart Oliver & Hedges, LLP, 99
Robins, Kaplan, Miller & Ciresi L.L.P., 89
Ropes & Gray, 40
Saul Ewing LLP, 74
Seyfarth Shaw LLP, 93
Shearman & Sterling, 32
Sidley Austin Brown & Wood, 40
Simpson Thacher & Bartlett, 39
Skadden, Arps, Slate, Meagher & Flom, 18
Snell & Wilmer L.L.P., 28
Sonnenschein Nath and Rosenthal LLP, 102

Southern Poverty Law Center, Inc., 74
Stroock & Stroock & Lavan LLP, 40
Sullivan & Cromwell, 26
Troutman Sanders L.L.P., 79
Vinson & Elkins L.L.P., 30
Wachtell, Lipton, Rosen & Katz, 47
Weil, Gotshal & Manges LLP, 55
White & Case LLP, 35
Williams & Connolly LLP, 47
Willkie Farr & Gallagher LLP, 95
Wilson Sonsini Goodrich & Rosati, 34
Winston & Strawn, 35
Womble Carlyle Sandridge & Rice, PLLC, 52

Manufacturing

A-dec, Inc., 53
A. Schulman, Inc., 49 (upd.)
A.B.Dick Company, 28
A.O. Smith Corporation, 11; 40 (upd.); 93 (upd.)
A.T. Cross Company, 17; 49 (upd.)
A.W. Faber-Castell Unternehmensverwaltung GmbH & Co., 51
AAF-McQuay Incorporated, 26
Aalborg Industries A/S, 90
AAON, Inc., 22
AAR Corp., 28
Aarhus United A/S, 68
ABB Ltd., 65 (upd.)
ABC Rail Products Corporation, 18
Abiomed, Inc., 47
ACCO World Corporation, 7; 51 (upd.)
Accubuilt, Inc., 74
Acindar Industria Argentina de Aceros S.A., 87
Acme United Corporation, 70
Acme-Cleveland Corp., 13
Acorn Products, Inc., 55
Acuity Brands, Inc., 90
Acushnet Company, 64
Acuson Corporation, 36 (upd.)
Adams Golf, Inc., 37
Adolf Würth GmbH & Co. KG, 49
Advanced Circuits Inc., 67
Advanced Neuromodulation Systems, Inc., 73
AEP Industries, Inc., 36
AeroGrow International, Inc., 95
Aftermarket Technology Corp., 83
Ag-Chem Equipment Company, Inc., 17
Aga Foodservice Group PLC, 73
AGCO Corporation, 13; 67 (upd.)
Agfa Gevaert Group N.V., 59
Agrium Inc., 73
Ahlstrom Corporation, 53
Ainsworth Lumber Co. Ltd., 99
Airgas, Inc., 54
Aisin Seiki Co., Ltd., III
AK Steel Holding Corporation, 41 (upd.)
Akeena Solar, Inc., 103
AKG Acoustics GmbH, 62
Aktiebolaget Electrolux, 22 (upd.)
Aktiebolaget SKF, III; 38 (upd.); 89 (upd.)
Alamo Group Inc., 32
ALARIS Medical Systems, Inc., 65

Alberto-Culver Company, 8; 36 (upd.); 91 (upd.)
Aldila Inc., 46
Alfa Laval AB, III; 64 (upd.)
Allen Organ Company, 33
Allen-Edmonds Shoe Corporation, 61
Alliance Laundry Holdings LLC, 102
Alliant Techsystems Inc., 8; 30 (upd.); 77 (upd.)
The Allied Defense Group, Inc., 65
Allied Healthcare Products, Inc., 24
Allied Products Corporation, 21
Allied Signal Engines, 9
AlliedSignal Inc., 22 (upd.)
Allison Gas Turbine Division, 9
Alltrista Corporation, 30
Alps Electric Co., Ltd., 44 (upd.)
Alticor Inc., 71 (upd.)
Aluar Aluminio Argentino S.A.I.C., 74
Alvis Plc, 47
Amer Group plc, 41
American Axle & Manufacturing Holdings, Inc., 67
American Biltrite Inc., 43 (upd.)
American Business Products, Inc., 20
American Cast Iron Pipe Company, 50
American Equipment Company, Inc., 104
American Greetings Corporation, 59 (upd.)
American Homestar Corporation, 18; 41 (upd.)
American Locker Group Incorporated, 34
American Power Conversion Corporation, 67 (upd.)
American Seating Company 78
American Standard Companies Inc., 30 (upd.)
American Technical Ceramics Corp., 67
American Technology Corporation, 103
American Tourister, Inc., 16
American Woodmark Corporation, 31
Ameriwood Industries International Corp., 17
Amerock Corporation, 53
Ameron International Corporation, 67
AMETEK, Inc., 9
AMF Bowling, Inc., 40
Ampacet Corporation, 67
Ampco-Pittsburgh Corporation, 79
Ampex Corporation, 17
Amway Corporation, 30 (upd.)
Analogic Corporation, 23
Anchor Hocking Glassware, 13
Andersen Corporation, 10
The Andersons, Inc., 31
Andis Company, Inc., 85
Andreas Stihl AG & Co. KG, 16; 59 (upd.)
Andritz AG, 51
Ansell Ltd., 60 (upd.)
Anthem Electronics, Inc., 13
Apasco S.A. de C.V., 51
Apex Digital, Inc., 63
Applica Incorporated, 43 (upd.)
Applied Films Corporation, 48
Applied Materials, Inc., 10; 46 (upd.)
Applied Micro Circuits Corporation, 38
Applied Power Inc., 9; 32 (upd.)

AptarGroup, Inc., 69
ARBED S.A., 22 (upd.)
Arc International, 76
Arçelik A.S., 100
Arctco, Inc., 16
Arctic Cat Inc., 40 (upd.); 96 (upd.)
AREVA NP, 90 (upd.)
Ariens Company, 48
The Aristotle Corporation, 62
Armor All Products Corp., 16
Armstrong Holdings, Inc., III; 22 (upd.); 81 (upd.)
Arotech Corporation, 93
Art's Way Manufacturing Co., Inc., 101
Artesyn Technologies Inc., 46 (upd.)
ArthroCare Corporation, 73
ArvinMeritor, Inc., 54 (upd.)
Asahi Glass Company, Ltd., 48 (upd.)
Ashley Furniture Industries, Inc., 35
ASICS Corporation, 57
ASML Holding N.V., 50
Astec Industries, Inc., 79
Astronics Corporation, 35
ASV, Inc., 34; 66 (upd.)
Atlantis Plastics, Inc., 85
Atlas Copco AB, III; 28 (upd.); 85 (upd.)
ATMI, Inc., 93
Atwood Mobil Products, 53
AU Optronics Corporation, 67
Aurora Casket Company, Inc., 56
Austal Limited, 75
Austin Powder Company, 76
Avedis Zildjian Co., 38
Avery Dennison Corporation, 17 (upd.); 49 (upd.)
Avocent Corporation, 65
Avondale Industries, 7; 41 (upd.)
AVX Corporation, 67
AZZ Incorporated, 93
B.J. Alan Co., Inc., 67
The Babcock & Wilcox Company, 82
Badger Meter, Inc., 22
BAE Systems Ship Repair, 73
Baker Hughes Incorporated, III
Babolat VS, S.A., 97
Baldor Electric Company, 21; 97 (upd.)
Baldwin Piano & Organ Company, 18
Baldwin Technology Company, Inc., 25
Balfour Beatty plc, 36 (upd.)
Ballantyne of Omaha, Inc., 27
Ballard Medical Products, 21
Ballard Power Systems Inc., 73
Bally Manufacturing Corporation, III
Baltek Corporation, 34
Baltimore Aircoil Company, Inc., 66
Bandai Co., Ltd., 55
Barmag AG, 39
Barnes Group Inc., 13; 69 (upd.)
Barry Callebaut AG, 29
Barry-Wehmiller Companies, Inc., 90
Bassett Furniture Industries, Inc., 18; 95 (upd.)
Bath Iron Works, 12; 36 (upd.)
Baxi Group Ltd., 96
Beckman Coulter, Inc., 22
Beckman Instruments, Inc., 14
Becton, Dickinson and Company, I; 11 (upd.); 36 (upd.); 101 (upd.)

Behr GmbH & Co. KG, 72
BEI Technologies, Inc., 65
Beiersdorf AG, 29
Bekaert S.A./N.V., 90
Bel Fuse, Inc., 53
Belden CDT Inc., 76 (upd.)
Belden Inc., 19
Bell Sports Corporation, 16; 44 (upd.)
Belleek Pottery Ltd., 71
Belleville Shoe Manufacturing Company, 92
Beloit Corporation, 14
Bemis Company, Inc., 8; 91 (upd.)
Bénéteau SA, 55
Benjamin Moore & Co., 13; 38 (upd.)
BenQ Corporation, 67
Berger Bros Company, 62
Bernina Holding AG, 47
Berry Plastics Group Inc., 21; 98 (upd.)
Berwick Offray, LLC, 70
Bianchi International (d/b/a Gregory Mountain Products), 76
BIC Corporation, 8; 23 (upd.)
BICC PLC, III
Bidvest Group Ltd., 106
Billabong International Ltd., 44
The Bing Group, 60
Binks Sames Corporation, 21
Binney & Smith Inc., 25
bioMérieux S.A., 75
Biomet, Inc., 10; 93 (upd.)
Biosite Incorporated, 73
BISSELL Inc., 9; 30 (upd.)
The Black & Decker Corporation, III; 20 (upd.); 67 (upd.)
Black Diamond Equipment, Ltd., 62
Blodgett Holdings, Inc., 61 (upd.)
Blount International, Inc., 12; 48 (upd.)
Blue Nile Inc., 61
Blundstone Pty Ltd., 76
Blyth Industries, Inc., 18
Blyth, Inc., 74 (upd.)
BMC Industries, Inc., 17; 59 (upd.)
Bob's Discount Furniture LLC, 104
Bodum Design Group AG, 47
BÖHLER-UDDEHOLM AG, 73
Boise Cascade Holdings, L.L.C., IV; 8 (upd.); 32 (upd.); 95 (upd.)
Bolt Technology Corporation, 99
Bombardier Inc., 42 (upd.); 87 (upd.)
Boral Limited, III; 43 (upd.); 103 (upd.)
Borden, Inc., 22 (upd.)
Borg-Warner Corporation, III
BorgWarner Inc., 14; 32 (upd.); 85 (upd.)
Boston Scientific Corporation, 37; 77 (upd.)
Bou-Matic, 62
The Boyds Collection, Ltd., 29
BPB plc, 83
Brach's Confections, Inc., 74 (upd.)
Brady Corporation 78 (upd.)
Brammer PLC, 77
Brannock Device Company, 48
Brass Eagle Inc., 34
Breeze-Eastern Corporation, 95
Brenco, Inc., 104
Bridgeport Machines, Inc., 17

Briggs & Stratton Corporation, 8; 27 (upd.)
BRIO AB, 24; 103 (upd.)
British Vita plc, 9; 33 (upd.)
Broan-NuTone LLC, 104
Brose Fahrzeugteile GmbH & Company KG, 84
Brother Industries, Ltd., 14
Brown & Sharpe Manufacturing Co., 23
Brown Jordan International Inc., 74 (upd.)
Brown-Forman Corporation, 38 (upd.)
Broyhill Furniture Industries, Inc., 10
Brunswick Corporation, III; 22 (upd.); 77 (upd.)
BSH Bosch und Siemens Hausgeräte GmbH, 67
BTR Siebe plc, 27
Buck Knives Inc., 48
Buckeye Technologies, Inc., 42
Bucyrus International, Inc., 17; 103 (upd.)
Bugle Boy Industries, Inc., 18
Building Materials Holding Corporation, 52
Bulgari S.p.A., 20; 106 (upd.)
Bulova Corporation, 13; 41 (upd.)
Bundy Corporation, 17
Burelle S.A., 23
Burgett, Inc., 97
Burton Snowboards Inc., 22
Bush Boake Allen Inc., 30
Bush Industries, Inc., 20
Butler Manufacturing Company, 12; 62 (upd.)
C&J Clark International Ltd., 52
C. Bechstein Pianofortefabrik AG, 96
C.F. Martin & Co., Inc., 42
C.R. Bard, Inc., 65 (upd.)
C-Tech Industries Inc., 90
California Cedar Products Company, 58
California Steel Industries, Inc., 67
Callaway Golf Company, 15; 45 (upd.)
Campbell Scientific, Inc., 51
Canadian Solar Inc., 105
Cannondale Corporation, 21
Canon Inc., 79 (upd.)
Capstone Turbine Corporation, 75
Caradon plc, 20 (upd.)
The Carbide/Graphite Group, Inc., 40
Carbo PLC, 67 (upd.)
Carbone Lorraine S.A., 33
Cardo AB, 53
Cardone Industries Inc., 92
Carhartt, Inc., 77 (upd.)
Carl Zeiss AG, III; 34 (upd.); 91 (upd.)
Carma Laboratories, Inc., 60
Carpenter Technology Corporation, 13; 95 (upd.)
Carrier Corporation, 7; 69 (upd.)
Carter Holt Harvey Ltd., 70
Carver Boat Corporation LLC, 88
Carvin Corp., 89
Cascade Corporation, 65
Cascade General, Inc., 65
CASIO Computer Co., Ltd., III; 40 (upd.)
Catalina Lighting, Inc., 43 (upd.)

Caterpillar Inc., III; 15 (upd.); 63 (upd.)
Cavco Industries, Inc., 65
Cementos Argos S.A., 91
CEMEX S.A. de C.V., 59 (upd.)
Central Garden & Pet Company, 58 (upd.)
Central Sprinkler Corporation, 29
Centuri Corporation, 54
Century Aluminum Company, 52
Cenveo Inc., 71 (upd.)
Cepheid, 77
Ceradyne, Inc., 65
Cessna Aircraft Company, 27 (upd.)
Champion Enterprises, Inc., 17
Chanel SA, 12; 49 (upd.)
Chantiers Jeanneau S.A., 96
Charisma Brands LLC, 74
The Charles Machine Works, Inc., 64
Chart Industries, Inc., 21; 96 (upd.)
Charter Manufacturing Company, Inc., 103
Chicago Bridge & Iron Company N.V., 82 (upd.)
Chittenden & Eastman Company, 58
Chris-Craft Corporation, 9, 31 (upd.); 80 (upd.)
Christian Dalloz SA, 40
Christie Digital Systems, Inc., 103
Christofle SA, 40
Chromcraft Revington, Inc., 15
Cinemeccanica SpA 78
Ciments Français, 40
Cincinnati Lamb Inc., 72
Cincinnati Milacron Inc., 12
Cinram International, Inc., 43
Circon Corporation, 21
Cirrus Design Corporation, 44
Citizen Watch Co., Ltd., III; 21 (upd.); 81 (upd.)
CLARCOR Inc., 17; 61 (upd.)
Clark Equipment Company, 8
Clayton Homes Incorporated, 13; 54 (upd.)
Clopay Corporation, 100
The Clorox Company, III; 22 (upd.); 81 (upd.)
CNH Global N.V., 38 (upd.); 99 (upd.)
Coach, Inc., 45 (upd.); 99 (upd.)
Coachmen Industries, Inc., 77
COBE Cardiovascular, Inc., 61
Cobra Golf Inc., 16
Cochlear Ltd., 77
Cockerill Sambre Group, 26 (upd.)
Cognex Corporation, 76
Cohu, Inc., 32
Colas S.A., 31
The Coleman Company, Inc., 30 (upd.)
Colfax Corporation, 58
Collins & Aikman Corporation, 41 (upd.)
Collins Industries, Inc., 33
Color Kinetics Incorporated, 85
Colorado MEDtech, Inc., 48
Colt's Manufacturing Company, Inc., 12
Columbia Sportswear Company, 19
Columbus McKinnon Corporation, 37
CommScope, Inc., 77
Compagnie de Saint-Gobain, 64 (upd.)
Compass Minerals International, Inc., 79

CompuDyne Corporation, 51
Conair Corporation, 69 (upd.)
Concord Camera Corporation, 41
Congoleum Corporation, 18; 98 (upd.)
Conn-Selmer, Inc., 55
Conrad Industries, Inc., 58
Conso International Corporation, 29
Consorcio G Grupo Dina, S.A. de C.V., 36
Constar International Inc., 64
Controladora Mabe, S.A. de C.V., 82
Converse Inc., 9
Cook Group Inc., 102
Cooper Cameron Corporation, 58 (upd.)
The Cooper Companies, Inc., 39
Cooper Industries, Inc., 44 (upd.)
Cordis Corporation, 46 (upd.)
Corning, Inc., III; 44 (upd.); 90 (upd.)
Corrpro Companies, Inc., 20
Corticeira Amorim, Sociedade Gestora de Participaço es Sociais, S.A., 48
CPAC, Inc., 86
CPP International, LLC, 103
Crane Co., 8; 30 (upd.); 101 (upd.)
Cranium, Inc., 69
Creative Technology Ltd., 57
Creo Inc., 48
CRH plc, 64
Crosman Corporation, 62
Crown Equipment Corporation, 15; 93 (upd.)
CTB International Corporation, 43 (upd.)
Cubic Corporation, 19; 98 (upd.)
Cuisinart Corporation, 24
Culligan Water Technologies, Inc., 12; 38 (upd.)
Cummins Engine Company, Inc., 40 (upd.)
CUNO Incorporated, 57
Curtiss-Wright Corporation, 10; 35 (upd.)
Custom Chrome, Inc., 74 (upd.)
Cutera, Inc., 84
Cutter & Buck Inc., 27
Cyberonics, Inc., 79
Cybex International, Inc., 49
Cymer, Inc., 77
Dade Behring Holdings Inc., 71
Daewoo Group, III
Daikin Industries, Ltd., III
Daisy Outdoor Products Inc., 58
Dalhoff Larsen & Horneman A/S, 96
Dalian Shide Group, 91
Danaher Corporation, 7; 77 (upd.)
Daniel Industries, Inc., 16
Daniel Measurement and Control, Inc., 74 (upd.)
Danisco A/S, 44
Day Runner, Inc., 41 (upd.)
DC Shoes, Inc., 60
DCN S.A., 75
De'Longhi S.p.A., 66
De Rigo S.p.A., 104
Dearborn Mid-West Conveyor Company, 56
Deceuninck N.V., 84
Deckers Outdoor Corporation, 22; 98 (upd.)
Decora Industries, Inc., 31

Decorator Industries Inc., 68
DeCrane Aircraft Holdings Inc., 36
Deere & Company, III; 42 (upd.)
Defiance, Inc., 22
Delachaux S.A., 76
Dell Inc., 63 (upd.)
Deluxe Corporation, 73 (upd.)
DEMCO, Inc., 60
Denby Group plc, 44
Denison International plc, 46
DENSO Corporation, 46 (upd.)
Department 56, Inc., 14
DePuy Inc., 37 (upd.)
Detroit Diesel Corporation, 10; 74 (upd.)
Deutsche Babcock A.G., III
Deutsche Steinzeug Cremer & Breuer Aktiengesellschaft, 91
Deutz AG, 39
Devro plc, 55
DHB Industries Inc., 85
Dial-A-Mattress Operating Corporation, 46
Diadora SpA, 86
Diebold, Incorporated, 7; 22 (upd.)
Diehl Stiftung & Co. KG, 79
Diesel SpA, 40
Dixon Industries, Inc., 26
Dixon Ticonderoga Company, 12; 69 (upd.)
Djarum PT, 62
DMI Furniture, Inc., 46
Domino Printing Sciences PLC, 87
Donaldson Company, Inc., 49 (upd.)
Donnelly Corporation, 12; 35 (upd.)
Dorel Industries Inc., 59
Dot Hill Systems Corp., 93
Douglas & Lomason Company, 16
Dover Corporation, III; 28 (upd.); 90 (upd.)
Dresser Industries, Inc., III
Drew Industries Inc., 28
Drexel Heritage Furnishings Inc., 12
Dril-Quip, Inc., 81
Drypers Corporation, 18
DTS, Inc., 80
Ducommun Incorporated, 30
Duncan Toys Company, 55
Dunn-Edwards Corporation, 56
Duracell International Inc., 9; 71 (upd.)
Durametallic, 21
Duriron Company Inc., 17
Dürkopp Adler AG, 65
Duron Inc., 72
Dürr AG, 44
DXP Enterprises, Inc., 101
Dynatronics Corporation, 99
Dynea, 68
Dyson Group PLC, 71
E-Z-EM Inc., 89
EADS SOCATA, 54
Eagle-Picher Industries, Inc., 8; 23 (upd.)
East Penn Manufacturing Co., Inc., 79
The Eastern Company, 48
Eastman Kodak Company, III; 7 (upd.); 36 (upd.); 91 (upd.)
Easton Sports, Inc., 66
Eaton Corporation, I; 10 (upd.); 67 (upd.)

Ebara Corporation, 83
ECC International Corp., 42
Ecolab Inc., I; 13 (upd.); 34 (upd.); 85
  (upd.)
Eddie Bauer Holdings, Inc., 9; 36 (upd.);
  87 (upd.)
EDO Corporation, 46
EG&G Incorporated, 29 (upd.)
Ekco Group, Inc., 16
Elamex, S.A. de C.V., 51
Elano Corporation, 14
Electric Boat Corporation, 86
Electrolux AB, III; 53 (upd.)
Eljer Industries, Inc., 24
Elkay Manufacturing Company, 73
ElringKlinger AG, 100
Elscint Ltd., 20
EMCO Enterprises, Inc., 102
Empire Resources, Inc., 81
Encompass Services Corporation, 33
Encore Computer Corporation, 13; 74
  (upd.)
Encore Wire Corporation, 81
Endress+Hauser Holding AG, 102
Energizer Holdings, Inc., 32
Energy Conversion Devices, Inc., 75
EnerSys Inc., 99
Enesco Corporation, 11
Engineered Support Systems, Inc., 59
English China Clays Ltd., 40 (upd.)
Ennis, Inc., 21; 97 (upd.)
Enodis plc, 68
EnPro Industries, Inc., 93
Entertainment Distribution Company, 89
Ernie Ball, Inc., 56
Escalade, Incorporated, 19
ESCO Technologies Inc., 87
Esselte, 64
Esselte Leitz GmbH & Co. KG, 48
Essilor International, 21
Esterline Technologies Corp., 15
Ethan Allen Interiors, Inc., 12; 39 (upd.)
The Eureka Company, 12
Evergreen Solar, Inc., 101
Everlast Worldwide Inc., 47
Excel Technology, Inc., 65
EXX Inc., 65
Fabbrica D' Armi Pietro Beretta S.p.A., 39
Facom S.A., 32
FAG—Kugelfischer Georg Schäfer AG, 62
Faiveley S.A., 39
Falcon Products, Inc., 33
Fannie May Confections Brands, Inc., 80
Fanuc Ltd., III; 17 (upd.); 75 (upd.)
Farah Incorporated, 24
Farmer Bros. Co., 52
FARO Technologies, Inc., 87
Fastenal Company, 14; 42 (upd.); 99
  (upd.)
Faultless Starch/Bon Ami Company, 55
Featherlite Inc., 28
Fedders Corporation, 18; 43 (upd.)
Federal Prison Industries, Inc., 34
Federal Signal Corp., 10
FEI Company, 79
Fellowes Manufacturing Company, 28
Fender Musical Instruments Company, 16;
  43 (upd.)

Ferretti Group SpA, 90
Ferro Corporation, 56 (upd.)
Figgie International Inc., 7
Firearms Training Systems, Inc., 27
First Alert, Inc., 28
First Brands Corporation, 8
First International Computer, Inc., 56
First Solar, Inc., 95
The First Years Inc., 46
Fisher Controls International, LLC, 13;
  61 (upd.)
Fisher Scientific International Inc., 24
Fisher-Price Inc., 12; 32 (upd.)
Fiskars Corporation, 33; 105 (upd.)
Fisons plc, 9
Flanders Corporation, 65
Fleetwood Enterprises, Inc., III; 22 (upd.);
  81 (upd.)
Flexsteel Industries Inc., 15; 41 (upd.)
Flextronics International Ltd., 38
Flint Ink Corporation, 41 (upd.)
FLIR Systems, Inc., 69
Florsheim Shoe Company, 9
Flour City International, Inc., 44
Flow International Corporation, 56
Flowserve Corporation, 33; 77 (upd.)
FLSmidth & Co. A/S, 72
Force Protection Inc., 95
Fort James Corporation, 22 (upd.)
Forward Industries, Inc., 86
FosterGrant, Inc., 60
Fountain Powerboats Industries, Inc., 28
Four Winns Boats LLC, 96
Foxboro Company, 13
Framatome SA, 19
Francotyp-Postalia Holding AG, 92
Frank J. Zamboni & Co., Inc., 34
Franke Holding AG, 76
Franklin Electric Company, Inc., 43
The Franklin Mint, 69
FreightCar America, Inc., 101
Freudenberg & Co., 41
Friedrich Grohe AG & Co. KG, 53
Frigidaire Home Products, 22
Frymaster Corporation, 27
FSI International, Inc., 17
Fuel Systems Solutions, Inc., 97
Fuel Tech, Inc., 85
Fuji Photo Film Co., Ltd., III; 18 (upd.);
  79 (upd.)
Fujisawa Pharmaceutical Company, Ltd.,
  58 (upd.)
Fuqua Enterprises, Inc., 17
Furniture Brands International, Inc., 39
  (upd.)
Furon Company, 28
The Furukawa Electric Co., Ltd., III
G. Leblanc Corporation, 55
G.S. Blodgett Corporation, 15
Gaming Partners International
  Corporation, 93
Ganz, 98
Gardner Denver, Inc., 49
The Gates Corporation, 9
Gaylord Bros., Inc., 100
GE Aircraft Engines, 9
GEA AG, 27
Geberit AG, 49

Gehl Company, 19
Gelita AG, 74
Gemini Sound Products Corporation, 58
Gemplus International S.A., 64
Gen-Probe Incorporated, 79
GenCorp Inc., 8; 9 (upd.)
General Atomics, 57
General Bearing Corporation, 45
General Binding Corporation, 73 (upd.)
General Cable Corporation, 40
General Dynamics Corporation, I; 10
  (upd.); 40 (upd.); 88 (upd.
General Housewares Corporation, 16
Genmar Holdings, Inc., 45
geobra Brandstätter GmbH & Co. KG,
  48
Georg Fischer AG Schaffhausen, 61
The George F. Cram Company, Inc., 55
George W. Park Seed Company, Inc., 98
Georgia Gulf Corporation, 61 (upd.)
Gerber Scientific, Inc., 12; 84 (upd.)
Gerresheimer Glas AG, 43
Getrag Corporate Group, 92
Gévelot S.A., 96
Giant Manufacturing Company, Ltd., 85
Giddings & Lewis, Inc., 10
Gildemeister AG, 79
The Gillette Company, 20 (upd.)
GKN plc, III; 38 (upd.); 89 (upd.)
Glaverbel Group, 80
Gleason Corporation, 24
Glen Dimplex 78
The Glidden Company, 8
Global Power Equipment Group Inc., 52
Glock Ges.m.b.H., 42
Goodman Holding Company, 42
Goodrich Corporation, 46 (upd.)
Goody Products, Inc., 12
The Gorman-Rupp Company, 18; 57
  (upd.)
Goss Holdings, Inc., 43
Goulds Pumps Inc., 24
Graco Inc., 19; 67 (upd.)
Gradall Industries, Inc., 96
Graham Corporation, 62
Granite Industries of Vermont, Inc., 73
Grant Prideco, Inc., 57
Greatbatch Inc., 72
Greene, Tweed & Company, 55
Greif Inc., 66 (upd.)
GreenMan Technologies Inc., 99
Griffin Industries, Inc., 70
Griffon Corporation, 34
Grinnell Corp., 13
Groupe André, 17
Groupe Genoyer, 96
Groupe Guillin SA, 40
Groupe Herstal S.A., 58
Groupe Legis Industries, 23
Groupe SEB, 35
Grow Group Inc., 12
Groz-Beckert Group, 68
Grunau Company Inc., 90
Grundfos Group, 83
Grupo Cydsa, S.A. de C.V., 39
Grupo IMSA, S.A. de C.V., 44
Grupo Industrial Saltillo, S.A. de C.V., 54
Grupo Lladró S.A., 52

GT Solar International, Inc., 101
Guangzhou Pearl River Piano Group Ltd., 49
Guardian Industries Corp., 87
Gulf Island Fabrication, Inc., 44
Gund, Inc., 96
Gunite Corporation, 51
The Gunlocke Company, 23
Guy Degrenne SA, 44
H.B. Fuller Company, 8; 32 (upd.); 75 (upd.)
H.O. Penn Machinery Company, Inc., 96
Hach Co., 18
Hackman Oyj Adp, 44
Haeger Industries Inc., 88
Haemonetics Corporation, 20
Haier Group Corporation, 65
Halliburton Company, III; 25 (upd.); 55 (upd.)
Hallmark Cards, Inc., IV; 16 (upd.); 40 (upd.); 87 (upd.)
Hammond Manufacturing Company Limited, 83
Hamon & Cie (International) S.A., 97
Hansgrohe AG, 56
Hanson PLC, 30 (upd.)
Hardinge Inc., 25
Harland and Wolff Holdings plc, 19
Harman International Industries, Incorporated, 15; 101 (upd.)
Harmon Industries, Inc., 25
Harnischfeger Industries, Inc., 8; 38 (upd.)
Harsco Corporation, 8; 105 (upd.)
Hartmann Inc., 96
Hartmarx Corporation, 32 (upd.)
The Hartz Mountain Corporation, 46 (upd.)
Hasbro, Inc., III; 16 (upd.); 43 (upd.)
Haskel International, Inc., 59
Hastings Manufacturing Company, 56
Hawker Siddeley Group Public Limited Company, III
Haworth Inc., 8; 39 (upd.)
Head N.V., 55
Headwaters Incorporated, 56
Health O Meter Products Inc., 14
Heekin Can Inc., 13
HEICO Corporation, 30
Heidelberger Druckmaschinen AG, 40
Hella KGaA Hueck & Co., 66
Hemisphere GPS Inc., 99
Henkel Manco Inc., 22
The Henley Group, Inc., III
Heraeus Holding GmbH, 54 (upd.)
Herman Goldner Company, Inc., 100
Herman Miller, Inc., 8; 77 (upd.)
Hermès International S.A., 34 (upd.)
Héroux-Devtek Inc., 69
Hexagon AB 78
High Tech Computer Corporation, 81
Hilding Anders AB, 102
Hillenbrand Industries, Inc., 10; 75 (upd.)
Hillerich & Bradsby Company, Inc., 51
Hills Industries Ltd., 104
Hillsdown Holdings plc, 24 (upd.)
Hilti AG, 53
Hindustan Lever Limited, 79

Hitachi Zosen Corporation, III
Hitchiner Manufacturing Co., Inc., 23
HMI Industries, Inc., 17
HNI Corporation, 74 (upd.)
The Hockey Company, 70
The Holland Group, Inc., 82
Hollander Home Fashions Corp., 67
Holnam Inc., 8
Hologic, Inc., 106
Holson Burnes Group, Inc., 14
Home Products International, Inc., 55
HON INDUSTRIES Inc., 13
Hooker Furniture Corporation, 80
The Hoover Company, 12; 40 (upd.)
Hornby PLC, 105
Horween Leather Company, 83
Hoshino Gakki Co. Ltd., 55
Host America Corporation, 79
Hubbell Inc., 76 (upd.)
Huffy Corporation, 7; 30 (upd.)
Huhtamäki Oyj, 64
Hummel International A/S, 68
Hunt Manufacturing Company, 12
Hunter Fan Company, 13; 98 (upd.)
Huntleigh Technology PLC, 77
Hydril Company, 46
Hyster Company, 17
Hyundai Group, III; 7 (upd.); 56 (upd.)
IAC Group, 96
ICON Health & Fitness, Inc., 38; 102 (upd.)
IDEO Inc., 65
IDEX Corp., 103
IdraPrince, Inc., 76
Igloo Products Corp., 21; 105 (upd.)
Ikonics Corporation, 99
Illinois Tool Works Inc., III; 22 (upd.); 81 (upd.)
Illumina, Inc., 93
Imatra Steel Oy Ab, 55
IMI plc, 9
Imo Industries Inc., 7; 27 (upd.)
In-Sink-Erator, 66
Inchcape PLC, III; 16 (upd.); 50 (upd.)
Indel Inc. 78
Industrie Natuzzi S.p.A., 18
Infineon Technologies AG, 50
Ingalls Shipbuilding, Inc., 12
Ingersoll-Rand Company Ltd., III; 15 (upd.); 55 (upd.)
Insilco Corporation, 16
Insituform Technologies, Inc., 83
Interco Incorporated, III
Interface, Inc., 8
The Interlake Corporation, 8
INTERMET Corporation, 77 (upd.)
Internacional de Ceramica, S.A. de C.V., 53
International Controls Corporation, 10
International Flavors & Fragrances Inc., 38 (upd.)
International Game Technology, 10
Intevac, Inc., 92
Intuitive Surgical, Inc., 79
Invacare Corporation, 47 (upd.)
Invensys PLC, 50 (upd.)
Invivo Corporation, 52
Ionatron, Inc., 85

Ionics, Incorporated, 52
Ipsen International Inc., 72
IRIS International, Inc., 101
iRobot Corporation, 83
Irwin Toy Limited, 14
Ishikawajima-Harima Heavy Industries Co., Ltd., III; 86 (upd.)
Itron, Inc., 64
J C Bamford Excavators Ltd., 83
J. D'Addario & Company, Inc., 48
J.I. Case Company, 10
J.M. Voith AG, 33
Jabil Circuit, Inc., 36; 88 (upd.)
Jacuzzi Brands Inc., 76 (upd.)
Jacuzzi Inc., 23
JAKKS Pacific, Inc., 52
James Avery Craftsman, Inc., 76
James Hardie Industries N.V., 56
James Purdey & Sons Limited, 87
JanSport, Inc., 70
Japan Tobacco Inc., 46 (upd.)
Jarden Corporation, 93 (upd.)
Jayco Inc., 13
Jeld-Wen, Inc., 45
Jenoptik AG, 33
Jervis B. Webb Company, 24
JLG Industries, Inc., 52
John Frieda Professional Hair Care Inc., 70
Johns Manville Corporation, 64 (upd.)
Johnson Controls, Inc., III; 26 (upd.); 59 (upd.)
Johnson Matthey PLC, 49 (upd.)
Johnson Outdoors Inc., 28; 84 (upd.)
Johnstown America Industries, Inc., 23
Jones Apparel Group, Inc., 11
Jostens, Inc., 7; 25 (upd.); 73 (upd.)
Jotun A/S, 80
Joy Global Inc., 104 (upd.)
JSP Corporation, 74
Julius Blüthner Pianofortefabrik GmbH 78
Jungheinrich AG, 96
K'Nex Industries, Inc., 52
K.A. Rasmussen AS, 99
Kaman Corporation, 12; 42 (upd.)
Kaman Music Corporation, 68
Kansai Paint Company Ltd., 80
Karsten Manufacturing Corporation, 51
Kasper A.S.L., Ltd., 40
Katy Industries, Inc., 51 (upd.)
Kawai Musical Instruments Mfg Co. Ltd. 78
Kawasaki Heavy Industries, Ltd., III; 63 (upd.)
Kaydon Corporation, 18
KB Toys, Inc., 35 (upd.); 86 (upd.)
Kelly-Moore Paint Company, Inc., 56
Kenmore Air Harbor Inc., 65
Kennametal Inc., 68 (upd.)
Keramik Holding AG Laufen, 51
Kerr Group Inc., 24
Kewaunee Scientific Corporation, 25
Key Safety Systems, Inc., 63
Key Technology Inc., 106
Key Tronic Corporation, 14
Keystone International, Inc., 11
KGHM Polska Miedz S.A., 98

KHD Konzern, III
KI, 57
Kimball International, Inc., 12; 48 (upd.)
Kit Manufacturing Co., 18
Klein Tools, Inc., 95
Knape & Vogt Manufacturing Company, 17
Knoll Group Inc., 14; 80 (upd.)
Knorr-Bremse AG, 84
Koala Corporation, 44
Kobe Steel, Ltd., IV; 19 (upd.)
Koch Enterprises, Inc., 29
Koenig & Bauer AG, 64
Kohler Company, 7; 32 (upd.)
Komatsu Ltd., III; 16 (upd.); 52 (upd.)
KONE Corporation, 27; 76 (upd.)
Konica Corporation, III; 30 (upd.)
Kyocera Corporation, 79 (upd.)
KraftMaid Cabinetry, Inc., 72
Kreisler Manufacturing Corporation, 97
KSB AG, 62
KTM Power Sports AG, 100
Kubota Corporation, III; 26 (upd.)
Kuhlman Corporation, 20
Kwang Yang Motor Company Ltd., 80
Kyocera Corporation, 21 (upd.)
L-3 Communications Holdings, Inc., 48
L. and J.G. Stickley, Inc., 50
L.A. Darling Company, 92
L.B. Foster Company, 33
L.S. Starrett Company, 64 (upd.)
La-Z-Boy Incorporated, 14; 50 (upd.)
LaCie Group S.A., 76
Lacks Enterprises Inc., 61
LADD Furniture, Inc., 12
Ladish Co., Inc., 30
Lafarge Cement UK, 28; 54 (upd.)
Lafuma S.A., 39
Lakeland Industries, Inc., 45
Lam Research Corporation, 31 (upd.)
The Lamson & Sessions Co., 13; 61 (upd.)
Lancer Corporation, 21
The Lane Co., Inc., 12
Laserscope, 67
LaSiDo Inc., 58
Latécoère S.A., 100
LDK Solar Co., Ltd., 101
LeapFrog Enterprises, Inc., 54
Lear Corporation, 71 (upd.)
Leatherman Tool Group, Inc., 51
Leggett & Platt, Inc., 11; 48 (upd.)
Leica Camera AG, 35
Leica Microsystems Holdings GmbH, 35
Lennox International Inc., 8; 28 (upd.)
Lenox, Inc., 12
Leupold & Stevens, Inc., 52
Lexmark International, Inc., 18; 79 (upd.)
Liebherr-International AG, 64
Lifetime Brands, Inc., 73 (upd.)
Linamar Corporation, 18
Lincoln Electric Co., 13
Lindal Cedar Homes, Inc., 29
Lindsay Manufacturing Co., 20
Lionel L.L.C., 16; 99 (upd.)
Lipman Electronic Engineering Ltd., 81
Little Tikes Company, 13; 62 (upd.)
Loctite Corporation, 8

Lodge Manufacturing Company, 103
Logitech International S.A., 28; 69 (upd.)
The Longaberger Company, 12; 44 (upd.)
LOUD Technologies, Inc., 95 (upd.)
Louis Vuitton, 10
LSB Industries, Inc., 77
Lucas Industries PLC, III
Lufkin Industries Inc. 78
Luxottica SpA, 17; 52 (upd.)
Lydall, Inc., 64
Lynch Corporation, 43
M&F Worldwide Corp., 38
M.A. Bruder & Sons, Inc., 56
Mabuchi Motor Co. Ltd., 68
MacAndrews & Forbes Holdings Inc., 28; 86 (upd.)
Mace Security International, Inc., 57
MacGregor Golf Company, 68
Mackay Envelope Corporation, 45
Madeco S.A., 71
Madison-Kipp Corporation, 58
Mag Instrument, Inc., 67
Magna International Inc., 102
Maidenform, Inc., 20; 59 (upd.)
Mail-Well, Inc., 28
Makita Corporation, 22; 59 (upd.)
MAN Aktiengesellschaft, III
Manhattan Group, LLC, 80
Manitou BF S.A., 27
The Manitowoc Company, Inc., 18; 59 (upd.)
Mannesmann AG, III; 14 (upd.)
Marcolin S.p.A., 61
Margarete Steiff GmbH, 23
Marine Products Corporation, 75
Marisa Christina, Inc., 15
Mark IV Industries, Inc., 7; 28 (upd.)
Märklin Holding GmbH, 70
The Marmon Group, 16 (upd.)
Marshall Amplification plc, 62
Martin-Baker Aircraft Company Limited, 61
Martin Industries, Inc., 44
MartinLogan, Ltd., 85
Marvin Lumber & Cedar Company, 22
Mary Kay Inc., 9; 30 (upd.); 84 (upd.)
Masco Corporation, III; 20 (upd.); 39 (upd.)
Masonite International Corporation, 63
Master Lock Company, 45
MasterBrand Cabinets, Inc., 71
MasterCraft Boat Company, Inc., 90
Master Spas Inc., 105
Material Sciences Corporation, 63
Matsushita Electric Industrial Co., Ltd., 64 (upd.)
Mattel, Inc., 7; 25 (upd.); 61 (upd.)
Matth. Hohner AG, 53
Matthews International Corporation, 29; 77 (upd.)
Maverick Tube Corporation, 59
Maxco Inc., 17
Maxwell Shoe Company, Inc., 30
Maytag Corporation, III; 22 (upd.); 82 (upd.)
McClain Industries, Inc., 51
McDermott International, Inc., III
McKechnie plc, 34

McWane Corporation, 55
Meade Instruments Corporation, 41
Meadowcraft, Inc., 29; 100 (upd.)
Measurement Specialties, Inc., 71
Mecalux S.A., 74
Medtronic, Inc., 67 (upd.)
Meggitt PLC, 34
Meguiar's, Inc., 99
Meidensha Corporation, 92
Meiji Seika Kaisha Ltd., 64 (upd.)
MEMC Electronic Materials, Inc., 81
Memry Corporation, 72
Menasha Corporation, 59 (upd.)
Merck & Co., Inc., I; 11 (upd.); 34 (upd.); 95 (upd.)
Mercury Marine Group, 68
Merillat Industries, LLC, 13; 69 (upd.)
Mestek, Inc., 10
Metso Corporation, 30 (upd.); 85 (upd.)
Mettler-Toledo International Inc., 30
Meyer International Holdings, Ltd., 87
MGA Entertainment, Inc., 95
Michael Anthony Jewelers, Inc., 24
Micrel, Incorporated, 77
Microdot Inc., 8
The Middleby Corporation, 22; 104 (upd.)
The Middleton Doll Company, 53
Midwest Grain Products, Inc., 49
Miele & Cie. KG, 56
Mikasa, Inc., 28
Mikohn Gaming Corporation, 39
Milacron, Inc., 53 (upd.)
Miller Industries, Inc., 26
Millipore Corporation, 25; 84 (upd.)
Milton Bradley Company, 21
Mine Safety Appliances Company, 31
Minebea Co., Ltd., 90
Minolta Co., Ltd., III; 18 (upd.); 43 (upd.)
Minuteman International Inc., 46
Misonix, Inc., 80
Mitsubishi Heavy Industries, Ltd., III; 7 (upd.)
Mity Enterprises, Inc., 38
Mobile Mini, Inc., 58
Mocon, Inc., 76
Modine Manufacturing Company, 8; 56 (upd.)
Modtech Holdings, Inc., 77
Moen Inc., 12; 106 (upd.)
Mohawk Industries, Inc., 19; 63 (upd.)
Molex Incorporated, 11
The Monarch Cement Company, 72
Monnaie de Paris, 62
Monster Cable Products, Inc., 69
Montblanc International GmbH, 82
Montres Rolex S.A., 13; 34 (upd.)
Montupet S.A., 63
Moog Music, Inc., 75
The Morgan Crucible Company plc, 82
Morrow Equipment Co. L.L.C., 87
Motorcar Parts & Accessories, Inc., 47
Moulinex S.A., 22
Movado Group, Inc., 28
Mr. Coffee, Inc., 15
Mr. Gasket Inc., 15
Mueller Industries, Inc., 7; 52 (upd.)

Multi-Color Corporation, 53
Musco Lighting, 83
Nashua Corporation, 8
National Envelope Corporation, 32
National Gypsum Company, 10
National Oilwell, Inc., 54
National Picture & Frame Company, 24
National Semiconductor Corporation, 69
  (upd.)
National Standard Co., 13
National Starch and Chemical Company,
  49
Natrol, Inc., 49
Natural Alternatives International, Inc., 49
NCI Building Systems, Inc., 88
NCR Corporation, III; 6 (upd.); 30
  (upd.); 90 (upd.)
Neenah Foundry Company, 68
Neopost S.A., 53
NETGEAR, Inc., 81
New Balance Athletic Shoe, Inc., 25
New Holland N.V., 22
Newcor, Inc., 40
Newell Rubbermaid Inc., 9; 52 (upd.)
Newport Corporation, 71
Newport News Shipbuilding Inc., 13; 38
  (upd.)
Nexans SA, 54
NGK Insulators Ltd., 67
NHK Spring Co., Ltd., III
Nidec Corporation, 59
NIKE, Inc., 36 (upd.)
Nikon Corporation, III; 48 (upd.)
Nintendo Company, Ltd., III; 7 (upd.);
  67 (upd.)
Nippon Electric Glass Co. Ltd., 95
Nippon Seiko K.K., III
Nippondenso Co., Ltd., III
NKK Corporation, 28 (upd.)
Nobia AB, 103
NOF Corporation, 72
Nordex AG, 101
NordicTrack, 22
Nordson Corporation, 11; 48 (upd.)
Nortek, Inc., 34
Norton Company, 8
Norton McNaughton, Inc., 27
Novellus Systems, Inc., 18
NSS Enterprises Inc. 78
NTN Corporation, III; 47 (upd.)
Nu-kote Holding, Inc., 18
Nypro, Inc., 101
O'Sullivan Industries Holdings, Inc., 34
Oak Industries Inc., 21
Oakley, Inc., 49 (upd.)
Oakwood Homes Corporation, 15
Ocean Bio-Chem, Inc., 103
ODL, Inc., 55
The Ohio Art Company,14; 59 (upd.)
Oil-Dri Corporation of America, 20; 89
  (upd.)
The Oilgear Company, 74
Okuma Holdings Inc., 74
Old Town Canoe Company, 74
Olympus Corporation, 106
180s, L.L.C., 64
Oneida Ltd., 7; 31 (upd.); 88 (upd.)
Oplink Communications, Inc., 106

Optische Werke G. Rodenstock, 44
Orange Glo International, 53
Orbotech Ltd., 75
O'Reilly Media, Inc., 99
Orthofix International NV, 72
Osmonics, Inc., 18
Osram GmbH, 86
Overhead Door Corporation, 70
Otis Elevator Company, Inc., 13; 39
  (upd.)
Otor S.A., 77
Otto Fuchs KG, 100
Outboard Marine Corporation, III; 20
  (upd.)
Outdoor Research, Incorporated, 67
Owens Corning, 20 (upd.); 98 (upd.)
Owosso Corporation, 29
P & F Industries, Inc., 45
Pacer Technology, 40
Pacific Coast Feather Company, 67
Pacific Dunlop Limited, 10
Pagnossin S.p.A., 73
Palfinger AG, 100
Pall Corporation, 9; 72 (upd.)
Palm Harbor Homes, Inc., 39
Paloma Industries Ltd., 71
Panavision Inc., 24
Park Corp., 22
Park-Ohio Holdings Corp., 17; 85 (upd.)
Parker-Hannifin Corporation, III; 24
  (upd.); 99 (upd.)
Parlex Corporation, 61
Patch Products Inc., 105
Patrick Industries, Inc., 30
Paul Mueller Company, 65
Pearl Corporation 78
Pechiney SA, IV; 45 (upd.)
Peg Perego SpA, 88
Pelican Products, Inc., 86
Pelikan Holding AG, 92
Pella Corporation, 12; 39 (upd.); 89
  (upd.)
Penn Engineering & Manufacturing
  Corp., 28
Pennington Seed Inc., 98
Pentair, Inc., 7; 26 (upd.); 81 (upd.)
Pentax Corporation 78
Pentech International, Inc., 29
PerkinElmer Inc. 7; 78 (upd.)
Peterson American Corporation, 55
Phillips-Van Heusen Corporation, 24
Phoenix AG, 68
Phoenix Mecano AG, 61
Photo-Me International Plc, 83
Physio-Control International Corp., 18
Picanol N.V., 96
Pilkington Group Limited, III; 34 (upd.);
  87 (upd.)
Pilot Pen Corporation of America, 82
Pinguely-Haulotte SA, 51
Pioneer Electronic Corporation, III
Pirelli & C. S.p.A., 75 (upd.)
Piscines Desjoyaux S.A., 84
Pitney Bowes, Inc., 19
Pittway Corporation, 33 (upd.)
Planar Systems, Inc., 61
PlayCore, Inc., 27
Playmates Toys, 23

Playskool, Inc., 25
Pleasant Company, 27
Pliant Corporation, 98
Ply Gem Industries Inc., 12
Pochet SA, 55
Polaris Industries Inc., 12; 35 (upd.); 77
  (upd.)
Polaroid Corporation, III; 7 (upd.); 28
  (upd.); 93 (upd.)
The Porcelain and Fine China Companies
  Ltd., 69
Portmeirion Group plc, 88
Pou Chen Corporation, 81
PPG Industries, Inc., III; 22 (upd.); 81
  (upd.)
Prada Holding B.V., 45
Pranda Jewelry plc, 70
Praxair, Inc., 48 (upd.)
Precision Castparts Corp., 15
Premark International, Inc., III
Pressman Toy Corporation, 56
Presstek, Inc., 33
Price Pfister, Inc., 70
Prince Sports Group, Inc., 15
Printpack, Inc., 68
Printronix, Inc., 18
Puig Beauty and Fashion Group S.L., 60
Pulaski Furniture Corporation, 33; 80
  (upd.)
Pumpkin Masters, Inc., 48
Punch International N.V., 66
Pure World, Inc., 72
Puritan-Bennett Corporation, 13
Purolator Products Company, 21; 74
  (upd.)
PVC Container Corporation, 67
PW Eagle, Inc., 48
Q.E.P. Co., Inc., 65
QRS Music Technologies, Inc., 95
QSC Audio Products, Inc., 56
Quixote Corporation, 15
R. Griggs Group Limited, 23
Racing Champions Corporation, 37
Radio Flyer Inc., 34
Rain Bird Corporation, 84
Raleigh UK Ltd., 65
Rapala Normark Group, Ltd., 30
RathGibson Inc., 90
Raven Industries, Inc., 33
Raychem Corporation, 8
Raymarine plc, 104
Rayovac Corporation, 39 (upd.)
Raytech Corporation, 61
Raytheon Company, II; 11 (upd.); 38
  (upd.); 105 (upd.)
Recovery Engineering, Inc., 25
Red Spot Paint & Varnish Company, 55
Red Wing Pottery Sales, Inc., 52
Red Wing Shoe Company, Inc., 9; 30
  (upd.); 83 (upd.)
Reed & Barton Corporation, 67
Regal-Beloit Corporation, 18; 97 (upd.)
Reichhold Chemicals, Inc., 10
Remington Arms Company, Inc., 12; 40
  (upd.)
Remington Products Company, L.L.C., 42
RENK AG, 37
Renner Herrmann S.A., 79

REpower Systems AG, 101
Revell-Monogram Inc., 16
Revere Ware Corporation, 22
Revlon Inc., 64 (upd.)
Rexam PLC, 32 (upd.); 85 (upd.)
Rexnord Corporation, 21; 76 (upd.)
RF Micro Devices, Inc., 43
Rheinmetall AG, 9; 97 (upd.)
RHI AG, 53
Richardson Industries, Inc., 62
Rickenbacker International Corp., 91
Riddell Sports Inc., 22
Riedel Tiroler Glashuette GmbH, 99
Rieter Holding AG, 42
River Oaks Furniture, Inc., 43
Riviera Tool Company, 89
RMC Group p.l.c., 34 (upd.)
Roadmaster Industries, Inc., 16
Robbins & Myers Inc., 15
Robertson-Ceco Corporation, 19
Rock-Tenn Company, 59 (upd.)
Rockford Products Corporation, 55
RockShox, Inc., 26
Rockwell Automation, Inc., I; 11 (upd.);
    43 (upd.); 103 (upd.)
Rockwell Medical Technologies, Inc., 88
Rodda Paint Company, 98
Rodriguez Group S.A., 90
ROFIN-SINAR Technologies Inc., 81
Rogers Corporation, 61
Rohde & Schwarz GmbH & Co. KG, 39
Rohm and Haas Company, 77 (upd.)
ROHN Industries, Inc., 22
Rohr Incorporated, 9
Roland Corporation, 38
Rollerblade, Inc., 15; 34 (upd.)
Rolls-Royce Group PLC, 67 (upd.)
Ronson PLC, 49
Roper Industries, Inc., 15; 50 (upd.)
Rose Art Industries, 58
Roseburg Forest Products Company, 58
Rotork plc, 46
Royal Appliance Manufacturing Company,
    15
Royal Canin S.A., 39
Royal Doulton plc, 14; 38 (upd.)
Royal Group Technologies Limited, 73
RPC Group PLC, 81
RPM International Inc., 8; 36 (upd.); 91
    (upd.)
RTI Biologics, Inc., 96
Rubbermaid Incorporated, III
Russ Berrie and Company, Inc., 12; 82
    (upd.)
Rusty, Inc., 95
S.C. Johnson & Son, Inc., III; 28 (upd.);
    89 (upd.)
Sabaté Diosos SA, 48
Safe Flight Instrument Corporation, 71
Safeskin Corporation, 18
Safety Components International, Inc., 63
Safilo SpA, 54
SAFRAN, 102 (upd.)
St. Jude Medical, Inc., 11; 43 (upd.); 97
    (upd.)
Salant Corporation, 12; 51 (upd.)
Sally Industries, Inc., 103
Salton, Inc., 30; 88 (upd.)

Salzgitter AG, IV; 101 (upd.)
Samick Musical Instruments Co., Ltd., 56
Samsonite Corporation, 13; 43 (upd.)
Samuel Cabot Inc., 53
Sandvik AB, 32 (upd.); 77 (upd.)
Sanford L.P., 82
Sanitec Corporation, 51
SANLUIS Corporación, S.A.B. de C.V.,
    95
Sanrio Company, Ltd., 38; 104 (upd.)
SANYO Electric Co., Ltd., II; 36 (upd.);
    95 (upd.)
Sapa AB, 84
Sara Lee Corporation, II; 15 (upd.); 54
    (upd.); 99 (upd.)
Sauder Woodworking Company, 12; 35
    (upd.)
Sauer-Danfoss Inc., 61
Sawtek Inc., 43 (upd.)
Schindler Holding AG, 29
Schlage Lock Company, 82
Schlumberger Limited, III
School-Tech, Inc., 62
Schott Corporation, 53
Scotsman Industries, Inc., 20
Scott Fetzer Company, 12; 80 (upd.)
The Scotts Company, 22
Scovill Fasteners Inc., 24
Sea Ray Boats Inc., 96
SeaChange International, Inc., 79
Sealed Air Corporation, 14; 57 (upd.)
Sealy Inc., 12
Seattle Lighting Fixture Company, 92
Segway LLC, 48
Seiko Corporation, III; 17 (upd.); 72
    (upd.)
Select Comfort Corporation, 34
Selee Corporation, 88
The Selmer Company, Inc., 19
Semitool, Inc., 18
Sequa Corp., 13
Serta, Inc., 28
Severstal Joint Stock Company, 65
Shakespeare Company, 22
Shanghai Baosteel Group Corporation, 71
The Shaw Group, Inc., 50
Sheaffer Pen Corporation, 82
Shelby Williams Industries, Inc., 14
Shermag, Inc., 93
The Sherwin-Williams Company, III; 13
    (upd.); 89 (upd.)
Sherwood Brands, Inc., 53
Shimano Inc., 64
Shorewood Packaging Corporation, 28
Shuffle Master Inc., 51
Shurgard Storage Centers, Inc., 52
SIFCO Industries, Inc., 41
Siliconware Precision Industries Ltd., 73
Simmons Company, 47
Simba Dickie Group KG, 105
Simplicity Manufacturing, Inc., 64
Simula, Inc., 41
The Singer Company N.V., 30 (upd.)
The Singing Machine Company, Inc., 60
Skeeter Products Inc., 96
Skis Rossignol S.A., 15; 43 (upd.)
Skyline Corporation, 30
SL Industries, Inc., 77

SLI, Inc., 48
Smead Manufacturing Co., 17
Smith & Wesson Corp., 30; 73 (upd.)
Smith Corona Corp., 13
Smith International, Inc., 15
Smith-Midland Corporation, 56
Smiths Industries PLC, 25
Smoby International SA, 56
Snap-on Incorporated, 7; 27 (upd.); 105
    (upd.)
Société BIC S.A., 73
Sola International Inc., 71
Solar Turbines Inc., 100
Solarfun Power Holdings Co., Ltd., 105
Solo Cup Company, 104
Sonic Innovations Inc., 56
Sonoco Products Company, 8; 89 (upd.)
SonoSite, Inc., 56
Spacelabs Medical, Inc., 71
Sparton Corporation, 18
Spear & Jackson, Inc., 73
Specialized Bicycle Components Inc., 50
Specialty Equipment Companies, Inc., 25
Specialty Products & Insulation Co., 59
Spectrum Control, Inc., 67
Speidel Inc., 96
Speizman Industries, Inc., 44
Sperian Protection S.A., 104
Spin Master, Ltd., 61
Spirax-Sarco Engineering plc, 59
Sport Supply Group, Inc., 23; 106 (upd.)
SPS Technologies, Inc., 30
SPX Corporation, 47 (upd.); 103 (upd.)
SRAM Corporation, 65
SRC Holdings Corporation, 67
Stanadyne Automotive Corporation, 37
The Standard Register Company, 15; 93
    (upd.)
Standex International Corporation, 17
Stanley Furniture Company, Inc., 34
The Stanley Works, III; 20 (upd.); 79
    (upd.)
Starcraft Corporation, 66 (upd.)
Stearns, Inc., 43
Steel Authority of India Ltd., 66 (upd.)
Steel Dynamics, Inc., 52
Steel Technologies Inc., 63
Steelcase, Inc., 7; 27 (upd.)
Steinway Musical Properties, Inc., 19
Stelco Inc., 51 (upd.)
The Stephan Company, 60
Sterilite Corporation, 97
Stewart & Stevenson Services Inc., 11
STMicroelectronics NV, 52
Stratasys, Inc., 67
Strattec Security Corporation, 73
Straumann Holding AG, 79
Strombecker Corporation, 60
Stryker Corporation, 11; 29 (upd.); 79
    (upd.)
Sturm, Ruger & Company, Inc., 19
Sub-Zero Freezer Co., Inc., 31
Sudbury Inc., 16
Sulzer Brothers Limited (Gebruder Sulzer
    Aktiengesellschaft), III
Sumitomo Heavy Industries, Ltd., III; 42
    (upd.)
Sun Hydraulics Corporation, 74

Sunburst Shutter Corporation 78
Superior Essex Inc., 80
Susquehanna Pfaltzgraff Company, 8
Swank, Inc., 17; 84 (upd.)
Swarovski International Holding AG, 40
The Swatch Group SA, 26
Swedish Match AB, 12; 39 (upd.); 92 (upd.)
Sweetheart Cup Company, Inc., 36
Sybron International Corp., 14
Synthes, Inc., 93
Syratech Corp., 14
Systemax, Inc., 52
TAB Products Co., 17
Tacony Corporation, 70
TAG Heuer International SA, 25; 77 (upd.)
Tag-It Pacific, Inc., 85
Taiheiyo Cement Corporation, 60 (upd.)
Taiwan Semiconductor Manufacturing Company Ltd., 47
Tamron Company Ltd., 82
Targetti Sankey SpA, 86
Tarkett Sommer AG, 25
Taser International, Inc., 62
Taylor Devices, Inc., 97
Taylor Guitars, 48
TaylorMade-adidas Golf, 23; 96 (upd.)
TB Wood's Corporation, 56
TDK Corporation, 49 (upd.)
TearDrop Golf Company, 32
Techtronic Industries Company Ltd., 73
Tecumseh Products Company, 8; 71 (upd.)
Tektronix Inc., 8; 78 (upd.)
Telsmith Inc., 96
Tempur-Pedic Inc., 54
Tenaris SA, 63
Tenedora Nemak, S.A. de C.V., 102
Tennant Company, 13; 33 (upd.); 95 (upd.)
Terex Corporation, 7; 40 (upd.); 91 (upd.)
The Testor Corporation, 51
Tetra Pak International SA, 53
Thales S.A., 42
Thermadyne Holding Corporation, 19
Thermo BioAnalysis Corp., 25
Thermo Electron Corporation, 7
Thermo Fibertek, Inc., 24
Thermo Fisher Scientific Inc., 105 (upd.)
Thermo Instrument Systems Inc., 11
Thermo King Corporation, 13
Thiokol Corporation, 22 (upd.)
Thomas & Betts Corp., 11; 54 (upd.)
Thomas Industries Inc., 29
Thomasville Furniture Industries, Inc., 12; 74 (upd.)
Thor Industries Inc., 39; 92 (upd.)
3M Company, 61 (upd.)
ThyssenKrupp AG, IV; 28 (upd.); 87 (upd.)
Tianjin Flying Pigeon Bicycle Co., Ltd., 95
Tigre S.A. Tubos e Conexões, 104
Tilia Inc., 62
Timex Corporation, 7; 25 (upd.)
The Timken Company, 8; 42 (upd.)

Titan Cement Company S.A., 64
Titan International, Inc., 89
TiVo Inc., 75
TJ International, Inc., 19
Todd Shipyards Corporation, 14
Tokheim Corporation, 21
Tomra Systems ASA, 103
Tomy Company Ltd., 65
Tong Yang Cement Corporation, 62
Tonka Corporation, 25
Toolex International N.V., 26
The Topaz Group, Inc., 62
Topcon Corporation, 84
Topps Company, Inc., 13; 34 (upd.)
Toray Industries, Inc., 51 (upd.)
The Toro Company, 7; 26 (upd.); 77 (upd.)
The Torrington Company, 13
TOTO LTD., 28 (upd.)
TouchTunes Music Corporation, 97
Town & Country Corporation, 19
Toymax International, Inc., 29
Toyoda Automatic Loom Works, Ltd., III
Trane 78
CJSC Transmash Holding, 93
TransPro, Inc., 71
Tredegar Corporation, 52
Trek Bicycle Corporation, 16; 78 (upd.)
Trelleborg AB, 93
Trex Company, Inc., 71
Trico Products Corporation, 15
Trigano S.A., 102
TriMas Corp., 11
Trina Solar Limited, 103
Trinity Industries, Incorporated, 7
TRINOVA Corporation, III
TriPath Imaging, Inc., 77
TriQuint Semiconductor, Inc., 63
Trisko Jewelry Sculptures, Ltd., 57
Triumph Group, Inc., 31
True Temper Sports, Inc., 95
TRUMPF GmbH + Co. KG, 86
TRW Automotive Holdings Corp., 75 (upd.)
Tubos de Acero de Mexico, S.A. (TAMSA), 41
Tultex Corporation, 13
Tupperware Corporation, 28
TurboChef Technologies, Inc., 83
Turbomeca S.A., 102
Turtle Wax, Inc., 15; 93 (upd.)
TVI Corporation, 99
Twin Disc, Inc., 21
II-VI Incorporated, 69
Ty Inc., 33; 86 (upd.)
Tyco International Ltd., III; 28 (upd.)
Tyco Toys, Inc., 12
U.S. Robotics Corporation, 9; 66 (upd.)
Ube Industries, Ltd., 38 (upd.)
Ultralife Batteries, Inc., 58
ULVAC, Inc., 80
United Defense Industries, Inc., 30; 66 (upd.)
United Dominion Industries Limited, 8; 16 (upd.)
United Industrial Corporation, 37
United States Filter Corporation, 20

United States Pipe and Foundry Company, 62
Unitika Ltd., 53 (upd.)
Unitog Co., 19
Universal Manufacturing Company, 88
Ushio Inc., 91
Usinas Siderúrgicas de Minas Gerais S.A., 77
Utah Medical Products, Inc., 36
UTStarcom, Inc., 77
VA TECH ELIN EBG GmbH, 49
Vaillant GmbH, 44
Vaisala Oyj, 104
Valley National Gases, Inc., 85
Vallourec SA, 54
Valmet Corporation (Valmet Oy), III
Valmont Industries, Inc., 19
The Valspar Corporation, 8
Vari-Lite International, Inc., 35
Varian, Inc., 48 (upd.)
Variflex, Inc., 51
Varity Corporation, III
Varlen Corporation, 16
Varta AG, 23
Velcro Industries N.V., 19; 72 (upd.)
Velux A/S, 86
Ventana Medical Systems, Inc., 75
Verbatim Corporation, 74 (upd.)
Vermeer Manufacturing Company, 17
Vestas Wind Systems A/S, 73
Viasystems Group, Inc., 67
Vickers plc, 27
Victor Company of Japan, Limited, II; 26 (upd.); 83 (upd.)
Victorinox AG, 21; 74 (upd.)
Videojet Technologies, Inc., 90
Vidrala S.A., 67
Viessmann Werke GmbH & Co., 37
ViewSonic Corporation, 72
Viking Range Corporation, 66
Viking Yacht Company, 96
Villeroy & Boch AG, 37
Vilter Manufacturing, LLC, 105
Virco Manufacturing Corporation, 17
Viscofan S.A., 70
Viskase Companies, Inc., 55
Vita Plus Corporation, 60
Vitro Corporativo S.A. de C.V., 34
voestalpine AG, 57 (upd.)
Vorwerk & Co., 27
Vosper Thornycroft Holding plc, 41
Vossloh AG, 53
VTech Holdings Ltd., 77
W.A. Whitney Company, 53
W.C. Bradley Co., 69
W.H. Brady Co., 17
W.L. Gore & Associates, Inc., 14; 60 (upd.)
W.W. Grainger, Inc., 26 (upd.); 68 (upd.)
Wabash National Corp., 13
Wabtec Corporation, 40
Wacker Construction Equipment AG, 95
Wahl Clipper Corporation, 86
Walbro Corporation, 13
Walter Industries, Inc., 72 (upd.)
Wärtsilä Corporation, 100
Washington Scientific Industries, Inc., 17
Wassall Plc, 18

Waterford Wedgwood plc, 12; 34 (upd.)
Water Pik Technologies, Inc., 34; 83 (upd.)
Waters Corporation, 43
Watts Industries, Inc., 19
Watts of Lydney Group Ltd., 71
WD-40 Company, 18
We-No-Nah Canoe, Inc., 98
Weather Shield Manufacturing, Inc., 102
Webasto Roof Systems Inc., 97
Weber-Stephen Products Co., 40
Weeres Industries Corporation, 52
Weg S.A. 78
The Weir Group PLC, 85
Welbilt Corp., 19
Wellman, Inc., 8; 52 (upd.)
Weru Aktiengesellschaft, 18
West Bend Co., 14
Westell Technologies, Inc., 57
Westerbeke Corporation, 60
Western Digital Corporation, 25; 92 (upd.)
Wheaton Science Products, 60 (upd.)
Wheeling-Pittsburgh Corporation, 58 (upd.)
Whirlpool Corporation, III; 12 (upd.); 59 (upd.)
White Consolidated Industries Inc., 13
Wilbert, Inc., 56
Wilkinson Sword Ltd., 60
William L. Bonnell Company, Inc., 66
William Zinsser & Company, Inc., 58
Williamson-Dickie Manufacturing Company, 45 (upd.)
Wilson Sporting Goods Company, 24; 84 (upd.)
Wilton Products, Inc., 97
Wincor Nixdorf Holding GmbH, 69 (upd.)
Windmere Corporation, 16
Winegard Company, 56
Winnebago Industries, Inc., 7; 27 (upd.); 96 (upd.)
WinsLoew Furniture, Inc., 21
The Wiremold Company, 81
WMS Industries, Inc., 15; 53 (upd.)
Wolverine Tube Inc., 23
Wood-Mode, Inc., 23
Woodcraft Industries Inc., 61
Woodward Governor Company, 13; 49 (upd.); 105 (upd.)
World Kitchen, LLC, 104
Wright Medical Group, Inc., 61
Württembergische Metallwarenfabrik AG (WMF), 60
WuXi AppTec Company Ltd., 103
WWRD Holdings Limited, 106 (upd.)
Wyant Corporation, 30
Wyman-Gordon Company, 14
Wynn's International, Inc., 33
X-Rite, Inc., 48
Xerox Corporation, III; 6 (upd.); 26 (upd.); 69 (upd.)
Yamaha Corporation, III; 16 (upd.); 40 (upd.); 99 (upd.)
The Yokohama Rubber Company, Limited, V; 19 (upd.); 91 (upd.)
The York Group, Inc., 50

York International Corp., 13
Young Innovations, Inc., 44
Zapf Creation AG, 95
Zebra Technologies Corporation, 53 (upd.)
ZERO Corporation, 17; 88 (upd.)
ZiLOG, Inc., 72 (upd.)
Zindart Ltd., 60
Zippo Manufacturing Company, 18; 71 (upd.)
Zodiac S.A., 36
Zygo Corporation, 42

Materials

AK Steel Holding Corporation, 19
American Biltrite Inc., 16
American Colloid Co., 13
American Standard Inc., III
Ameriwood Industries International Corp., 17
Anhui Conch Cement Company Limited, 99
Apasco S.A. de C.V., 51
Apogee Enterprises, Inc., 8
Asahi Glass Company, Limited, III
Asbury Carbons, Inc., 68
Bairnco Corporation, 28
Bayou Steel Corporation, 31
Berry Plastics Group Inc., 21; 98 (upd.)
Blessings Corp., 19
Blue Circle Industries PLC, III
Bodycote International PLC, 63
Boral Limited, III; 43 (upd.); 103 (upd.)
British Vita plc, 9; 33 (upd.)
Brush Engineered Materials Inc., 67
Bryce Corporation, 100
California Steel Industries, Inc., 67
Callanan Industries, Inc., 60
Cameron & Barkley Company, 28
Carborundum Company, 15
Carl Zeiss AG, III; 34 (upd.); 91 (upd.)
Carlisle Companies Inc., 8; 82 (upd.)
Carter Holt Harvey Ltd., 70
Cementos Argos S.A., 91
Cemex SA de CV, 20
Century Aluminum Company, 52
CertainTeed Corporation, 35
Chargeurs International, 6; 21 (upd.)
Chemfab Corporation, 35
Cimentos de Portugal SGPS S.A. (Cimpor), 76
Cold Spring Granite Company Inc., 16; 67 (upd.)
Columbia Forest Products Inc. 78
Compagnie de Saint-Gobain S.A., III; 16 (upd.)
Cookson Group plc, III; 44 (upd.)
Corning Inc., III; 44 (upd.); 90 (upd.)
CSR Limited, III; 28 (upd.); 85 (upd.)
Dal-Tile International Inc., 22
The David J. Joseph Company, 14; 76 (upd.)
The Dexter Corporation, 12 (upd.)
Dickten Masch Plastics LLC, 90
Dyckerhoff AG, 35
Dynamic Materials Corporation, 81
Dyson Group PLC, 71
ECC Group plc, III

Edw. C. Levy Co., 42
84 Lumber Company, 9; 39 (upd.)
ElkCorp, 52
Empire Resources, Inc., 81
English China Clays Ltd., 15 (upd.); 40 (upd.)
Envirodyne Industries, Inc., 17
EP Henry Corporation, 104
Feldmuhle Nobel A.G., III
Fibreboard Corporation, 16
Filtrona plc, 88
Florida Rock Industries, Inc., 46
Foamex International Inc., 17
Formica Corporation, 13
GAF Corporation, 22 (upd.)
The Geon Company, 11
Giant Cement Holding, Inc., 23
Gibraltar Steel Corporation, 37
Granite Rock Company, 26
GreenMan Technologies Inc., 99
Groupe Sidel S.A., 21
Harbison-Walker Refractories Company, 24
Harrisons & Crosfield plc, III
Heidelberger Zement AG, 31
Hexcel Corporation, 28
Holderbank Financière Glaris Ltd., III
Holnam Inc., 39 (upd.)
Holt and Bugbee Company, 66
Homasote Company, 72
Howmet Corp., 12
Huttig Building Products, Inc., 73
Ibstock Brick Ltd., 14; 37 (upd.)
Imerys S.A., 40 (upd.)
Imperial Industries, Inc., 81
Internacional de Ceramica, S.A. de C.V., 53
International Shipbreaking Ltd. L.L.C., 67
Jaiprakash Associates Limited, 101
Joseph T. Ryerson & Son, Inc., 15
Knauf Gips KG, 100
La Seda de Barcelona S.A., 100
Lafarge Coppée S.A., III
Lafarge Corporation, 28
Lehigh Portland Cement Company, 23
Loma Negra C.I.A.S.A., 95
Lyman-Richey Corporation, 96
Manville Corporation, III; 7 (upd.)
Material Sciences Corporation, 63
Matsushita Electric Works, Ltd., III; 7 (upd.)
McJunkin Corporation, 63
Medusa Corporation, 24
Mitsubishi Materials Corporation, III
Nevamar Company, 82
Nippon Sheet Glass Company, Limited, III
North Pacific Group, Inc., 61
Nuplex Industries Ltd., 92
OmniSource Corporation, 14
Onoda Cement Co., Ltd., III
Otor S.A., 77
Owens-Corning Fiberglass Corporation, III
Pacific Clay Products Inc., 88
Pilkington Group Limited, III; 34 (upd.); 87 (upd.)
Pioneer International Limited, III

PolyOne Corporation, 87 (upd.)
PPG Industries, Inc., III; 22 (upd.); 81 (upd.)
PT Semen Gresik Tbk, 103
Redland plc, III
Rinker Group Ltd., 65
RMC Group p.l.c., III
Rock of Ages Corporation, 37
Rogers Corporation, 80 (upd.)
Royal Group Technologies Limited, 73
The Rugby Group plc, 31
Scholle Corporation, 96
Schuff Steel Company, 26
Sekisui Chemical Co., Ltd., III; 72 (upd.)
Severstal Joint Stock Company, 65
Shaw Industries, 9
The Sherwin-Williams Company, III; 13 (upd.); 89 (upd.)
The Siam Cement Public Company Limited, 56
SIG plc, 71
Simplex Technologies Inc., 21
Siskin Steel & Supply Company, 70
Solutia Inc., 52
Sommer-Allibert S.A., 19
Southdown, Inc., 14
Spartech Corporation, 19; 76 (upd.)
Ssangyong Cement Industrial Co., Ltd., III; 61 (upd.)
Steel Technologies Inc., 63
Sun Distributors L.P., 12
Symyx Technologies, Inc., 77
Tarmac Limited, III, 28 (upd.); 95 (upd.)
Tergal Industries S.A.S., 102
Tilcon-Connecticut Inc., 80
TOTO LTD., III; 28 (upd.)
Toyo Sash Co., Ltd., III
Tuscarora Inc., 29
U.S. Aggregates, Inc., 42
Ube Industries, Ltd., III
United States Steel Corporation, 50 (upd.)
USG Corporation, III; 26 (upd.); 81 (upd.)
Usinas Siderúrgicas de Minas Gerais S.A., 77
Vicat S.A., 70
voestalpine AG, 57 (upd.)
Vulcan Materials Company, 7; 52 (upd.)
Wacker-Chemie GmbH, 35
Walter Industries, Inc., III
Waxman Industries, Inc., 9
Weber et Broutin France, 66
Wienerberger AG, 70
Wolseley plc, 64
ZERO Corporation, 17; 88 (upd.)
Zoltek Companies, Inc., 37

Mining & Metals

A.M. Castle & Co., 25
Acindar Industria Argentina de Aceros S.A., 87
African Rainbow Minerals Ltd., 97
Aggregate Industries plc, 36
Agnico-Eagle Mines Limited, 71
Aktiebolaget SKF, III; 38 (upd.); 89 (upd.)
Alcan Aluminium Limited, IV; 31 (upd.)
Alcoa Inc., 56 (upd.)

Alleghany Corporation, 10
Allegheny Ludlum Corporation, 8
Alliance Resource Partners, L.P., 81
Alrosa Company Ltd., 62
Altos Hornos de México, S.A. de C.V., 42
Aluminum Company of America, IV; 20 (upd.)
AMAX Inc., IV
AMCOL International Corporation, 59 (upd.)
Amsted Industries Incorporated, 7
Anglo American Corporation of South Africa Limited, IV; 16 (upd.)
Anglo American PLC, 50 (upd.)
Aquarius Platinum Ltd., 63
ARBED S.A., IV, 22 (upd.)
Arcelor Gent, 80
Arch Coal Inc., 98
Arch Mineral Corporation, 7
Armco Inc., IV
ASARCO Incorporated, IV
Ashanti Goldfields Company Limited, 43
Atchison Casting Corporation, 39
Barrick Gold Corporation, 34
Battle Mountain Gold Company, 23
Benguet Corporation, 58
Bethlehem Steel Corporation, IV; 7 (upd.); 27 (upd.)
BHP Billiton, 67 (upd.)
Birmingham Steel Corporation, 13; 40 (upd.)
Boart Longyear Company, 26
Bodycote International PLC, 63
Boliden AB, 80
Boral Limited, III; 43 (upd.); 103 (upd.)
British Coal Corporation, IV
British Steel plc, IV; 19 (upd.)
Broken Hill Proprietary Company Ltd., IV, 22 (upd.)
Brush Engineered Materials Inc., 67
Brush Wellman Inc., 14
Bucyrus International, Inc., 17; 103 (upd.)
Buderus AG, 37
Cameco Corporation, 77
Caparo Group Ltd., 90
Carpenter Technology Corporation, 13; 95 (upd.)
Chaparral Steel Co., 13
Charter Manufacturing Company, Inc., 103
China Shenhua Energy Company Limited, 83
Christensen Boyles Corporation, 26
Cleveland-Cliffs Inc., 13; 62 (upd.)
Coal India Ltd., IV; 44 (upd.)
Cockerill Sambre Group, IV; 26 (upd.)
Coeur d'Alene Mines Corporation, 20
Cold Spring Granite Company Inc., 16; 67 (upd.)
Cominco Ltd., 37
Commercial Metals Company, 15; 42 (upd.)
Companhia Siderúrgica Nacional, 76
Companhia Vale do Rio Doce, IV; 43 (upd.)
Compañia de Minas Buenaventura S.A.A., 93

CONSOL Energy Inc., 59
Corporacion Nacional del Cobre de Chile, 40
Corus Group plc, 49 (upd.)
CRA Limited, IV
Cyprus Amax Minerals Company, 21
Cyprus Minerals Company, 7
Daido Steel Co., Ltd., IV
De Beers Consolidated Mines Limited/De Beers Centenary AG, IV; 7 (upd.); 28 (upd.)
Degussa Group, IV
Diavik Diamond Mines Inc., 85
Dofasco Inc., IV; 24 (upd.)
Dynatec Corporation, 87
Earle M. Jorgensen Company, 82
Echo Bay Mines Ltd., IV; 38 (upd.)
Engelhard Corporation, IV
Eramet, 73
Evergreen Energy, Inc., 97
Evraz Group S.A., 97
Falconbridge Limited, 49
Fansteel Inc., 19
Fluor Corporation, 34 (upd.)
Freeport-McMoRan Copper & Gold, Inc., IV; 7 (upd.); 57 (upd.)
Fried. Krupp GmbH, IV
Gencor Ltd., IV, 22 (upd.)
Geneva Steel, 7
Gerdau S.A., 59
Glamis Gold, Ltd., 54
Gold Fields Ltd., IV; 62 (upd.)
Goldcorp Inc., 87
Grupo Mexico, S.A. de C.V., 40
Gruppo Riva Fire SpA, 88
Handy & Harman, 23
Hanson Building Materials America Inc., 60
Hanson PLC, 30 (upd.)
Harmony Gold Mining Company Limited, 63
Harsco Corporation, 8; 105 (upd.)
Haynes International, Inc., 88
Hecla Mining Company, 20
Hemlo Gold Mines Inc., 9
Heraeus Holding GmbH, IV
Highland Gold Mining Limited, 95
Highveld Steel and Vanadium Corporation Limited, 59
Hitachi Metals, Ltd., IV
Hoesch AG, IV
Homestake Mining Company, 12; 38 (upd.)
Horsehead Industries, Inc., 51
The Hudson Bay Mining and Smelting Company, Limited, 12
Hylsamex, S.A. de C.V., 39
IMCO Recycling, Incorporated, 32
Imerys S.A., 40 (upd.)
Imetal S.A., IV
Inco Limited, IV; 45 (upd.)
Industrias Penoles, S.A. de C.V., 22
Inland Steel Industries, Inc., IV; 19 (upd.)
Intermet Corporation, 32
Iscor Limited, 57
Ispat Inland Inc., 30; 40 (upd.)
JFE Shoji Holdings Inc., 88
Johnson Matthey PLC, IV; 16 (upd.)

JSC MMC Norilsk Nickel, 48
K.A. Rasmussen AS, 99
Kaiser Aluminum Corporation, IV; 84 (upd.)
Kawasaki Heavy Industries, Ltd., 63 (upd.)
Kawasaki Steel Corporation, IV
Kennecott Corporation, 7; 27 (upd.)
Kentucky Electric Steel, Inc., 31
Kerr-McGee Corporation, 22 (upd.)
Kinross Gold Corporation, 36
Klockner-Werke AG, IV
Kobe Steel, Ltd., IV; 19 (upd.)
Koninklijke Nederlandsche Hoogovens en Staalfabrieken NV, IV
Laclede Steel Company, 15
Layne Christensen Company, 19
Lonmin plc, 66 (upd.)
Lonrho Plc, 21
The LTV Corporation, I; 24 (upd.)
Lukens Inc., 14
Magma Copper Company, 7
The Marmon Group, IV; 16 (upd.)
Massey Energy Company, 57
MAXXAM Inc., 8
McLanahan Corporation, 104
Mechel OAO, 99
Meridian Gold, Incorporated, 47
Metaleurop S.A., 21
Metalico Inc., 97
Metallgesellschaft AG, IV
Minera Escondida Ltda., 100
Minerals and Metals Trading Corporation of India Ltd., IV
Minerals Technologies Inc., 11; 52 (upd.)
Mitsui Mining & Smelting Company, Ltd., IV; 102 (upd.)
Mueller Industries, Inc., 52 (upd.)
National Steel Corporation, 12
NERCO, Inc., 7
Newmont Mining Corporation, 7
Neyveli Lignite Corporation Ltd., 65
Niagara Corporation, 28
Nichimen Corporation, IV
Nippon Light Metal Company, Ltd., IV
Nippon Mining Holdings Inc., 102 (upd.)
Nippon Steel Corporation, IV; 17 (upd.); 96 (upd.)
Nisshin Steel Co., Ltd., IV
NKK Corporation, IV; 28 (upd.)
Noranda Inc., IV; 7 (upd.); 64 (upd.)
Norddeutsche Affinerie AG, 62
North Star Steel Company, 18
Nucor Corporation, 7; 21 (upd.); 79 (upd.)
Oglebay Norton Company, 17
OJSC Novolipetsk Steel, 99
Okura & Co., Ltd., IV
O'Neal Steel, Inc., 95
Oregon Metallurgical Corporation, 20
Oregon Steel Mills, Inc., 14
Ormet Corporation, 82
Outokumpu Oyj, 38
Park Corp., 22
Peabody Coal Company, 10
Peabody Energy Corporation, 45 (upd.)
Peabody Holding Company, Inc., IV
Pechiney SA, IV; 45 (upd.)

Peter Kiewit Sons' Inc., 8
Phelps Dodge Corporation, IV; 28 (upd.); 75 (upd.)
The Pittston Company, IV; 19 (upd.)
Placer Dome Inc., 20; 61 (upd.)
Pohang Iron and Steel Company Ltd., IV
POSCO, 57 (upd.)
Potash Corporation of Saskatchewan Inc., 18; 101 (upd.)
Quanex Corporation, 13; 62 (upd.)
RAG AG, 35; 60 (upd.)
Reliance Steel & Aluminum Co., 19
Republic Engineered Steels, Inc., 7; 26 (upd.)
Reynolds Metals Company, IV
Rio Tinto PLC, 19 (upd.); 50 (upd.)
RMC Group p.l.c., 34 (upd.)
Roanoke Electric Steel Corporation, 45
Rouge Steel Company, 8
The RTZ Corporation PLC, IV
Ruhrkohle AG, IV
Ryerson Tull, Inc., 40 (upd.)
Saarberg-Konzern, IV
Salzgitter AG, IV; 101 (upd.)
Sandvik AB, IV
Saudi Basic Industries Corporation (SABIC), 58
Schmolz + Bickenbach AG, 104
Schnitzer Steel Industries, Inc., 19
Severstal Joint Stock Company, 65
Shanghai Baosteel Group Corporation, 71
Siderar S.A.I.C., 66
Silver Wheaton Corp., 95
Smorgon Steel Group Ltd., 62
Southern Peru Copper Corporation, 40
Southwire Company, Inc., 8; 23 (upd.)
SSAB Svenskt Stål AB, 89
Steel Authority of India Ltd., IV
Stelco Inc., IV
Stillwater Mining Company, 47
Sumitomo Corporation, I; 11 (upd.); 102 (upd.)
Sumitomo Metal Industries Ltd., IV; 82 (upd.)
Sumitomo Metal Mining Co., Ltd., IV
Tata Iron & Steel Co. Ltd., IV; 44 (upd.)
Teck Corporation, 27
Tenaris SA, 63
Texas Industries, Inc., 8
ThyssenKrupp AG, IV; 28 (upd.); 87 (upd.)
The Timken Company, 8; 42 (upd.)
Titanium Metals Corporation, 21
Tomen Corporation, IV
Total Fina Elf S.A., 50 (upd.)
Tinecké Železárny A.S., 92
U.S. Borax, Inc., 42
U.S. Silica Company, 104
Ugine S.A., 20
NV Umicore SA, 47
Universal Stainless & Alloy Products, Inc., 75
Uralita S.A., 96
Usinor SA, IV; 42 (upd.)
Usinor Sacilor, IV
VIAG Aktiengesellschaft, IV
Voest-Alpine Stahl AG, IV
Volcan Compañia Minera S.A.A., 92

Vulcan Materials Company, 52 (upd.)
Wah Chang, 82
Walter Industries, Inc., 22 (upd.)
Weirton Steel Corporation, IV; 26 (upd.)
Westmoreland Coal Company, 7
Wheeling-Pittsburgh Corp., 7
WHX Corporation, 98
WMC, Limited, 43
Worthington Industries, Inc., 7; 21 (upd.)
Xstrata PLC, 73
Zambia Industrial and Mining Corporation Ltd., IV
Zinifex Ltd., 85

Paper & Forestry
AbitibiBowater Inc., IV; 25 (upd.); 99 (upd.)
Albany International Corporation, 51 (upd.)
Amcor Ltd, IV; 19 (upd.); 78 (upd.)
American Greetings Corporation, 59 (upd.)
American Pad & Paper Company, 20
Aracruz Celulose S.A., 57
Arjo Wiggins Appleton p.l.c., 34
Asplundh Tree Expert Co.,20; 59 (upd.)
Avery Dennison Corporation, IV
Badger Paper Mills, Inc., 15
Beckett Papers, 23
Bemis Company, Inc., 8; 91 (upd.)
Billerud AB, 100
Blue Heron Paper Company, 90
Bohemia, Inc., 13
Boise Cascade Holdings, L.L.C.,, IV; 8 (upd.); 32 (upd.); 95 (upd.)
Bowater PLC, IV
Bunzl plc, IV
Canfor Corporation, 42
Caraustar Industries, Inc., 19; 44 (upd.)
Carter Lumber Company, 45
Cascades Inc., 71
Catalyst Paper Corporation, 105
Central National-Gottesman Inc., 95
Champion International Corporation, IV; 20 (upd.)
Chesapeake Corporation, 8; 30 (upd.); 93 (upd.)
The Collins Companies Inc., 102
Consolidated Papers, Inc., 8; 36 (upd.)
Crane & Co., Inc., 26; 103 (upd.)
Crown Vantage Inc., 29
CSS Industries, Inc., 35
Daio Paper Corporation, IV; 84 (upd.)
Daishowa Paper Manufacturing Co., Ltd., IV; 57 (upd.)
Deltic Timber Corporation, 46
Dillard Paper Company, 11
Doman Industries Limited, 59
Domtar Corporation, IV; 89 (upd.)
DS Smith Plc, 61
Empresas CMPC S.A., 70
Enso-Gutzeit Oy, IV
Esselte Pendaflex Corporation, 11
Exacompta Clairefontaine S.A., 102
Federal Paper Board Company, Inc., 8
FiberMark, Inc., 37
Fletcher Challenge Ltd., IV
Fort Howard Corporation, 8

Fort James Corporation, 22 (upd.)
Georgia-Pacific LLC, IV; 9 (upd.); 47 (upd.); 101 (upd.)
Gould Paper Corporation, 82
Graphic Packaging Holding Company, 96 (upd.)
Groupe Rougier SA, 21
Grupo Portucel Soporcel, 60
Guilbert S.A., 42
Hampton Affiliates, Inc., 77
Holmen AB, 52 (upd.)
Honshu Paper Co., Ltd., IV
International Paper Company, IV; 15 (upd.); 47 (upd.); 97 (upd.)
James River Corporation of Virginia, IV
Japan Pulp and Paper Company Limited, IV
Jefferson Smurfit Group plc, IV; 49 (upd.)
Jujo Paper Co., Ltd., IV
Kadant Inc., 96 (upd.)
Kimberly-Clark Corporation, III; 16 (upd.); 43 (upd.); 105 (upd.)
Kimberly-Clark de México, S.A. de C.V., 54
Klabin S.A., 73
Koninklijke Houthandel G Wijma & Zonen BV, 96
Kruger Inc., 17; 103 (upd.)
Kymmene Corporation, IV
Longview Fibre Company, 8; 37 (upd.)
Louisiana-Pacific Corporation, IV; 31 (upd.)
M-real Oyj, 56 (upd.)
MacMillan Bloedel Limited, IV
Matussière et Forest SA, 58
The Mead Corporation, IV; 19 (upd.)
MeadWestvaco Corporation, 76 (upd.)
Mercer International Inc., 64
Metsa-Serla Oy, IV
Metso Corporation, 30 (upd.); 85 (upd.)
Miquel y Costas Miquel S.A., 68
Mo och Domsjö AB, IV
Monadnock Paper Mills, Inc., 21
Mosinee Paper Corporation, 15
Nashua Corporation, 8
National Envelope Corporation, 32
NCH Corporation, 8
The Newark Group, Inc., 102
Norske Skogindustrier ASA, 63
Nuqul Group of Companies, 102
Oji Paper Co., Ltd., IV
P.H. Glatfelter Company, 8; 30 (upd.); 83 (upd.)
Packaging Corporation of America, 12
Papeteries de Lancey, 23
Plum Creek Timber Company, Inc., 43; 106 (upd.)
Pope & Talbot, Inc., 12; 61 (upd.)
Pope Resources LP, 74
Potlatch Corporation, 8; 34 (upd.); 87 (upd.)
PWA Group, IV
Rayonier Inc., 24
Rengo Co., Ltd., IV
Reno de Medici S.p.A., 41
Rexam PLC, 32 (upd.); 85 (upd.)
Riverwood International Corporation, 11; 48 (upd.)

Rock-Tenn Company, 13; 59 (upd.)
Rogers Corporation, 61
The St. Joe Company, 8; 98 (upd.)
Sanyo-Kokusaku Pulp Co., Ltd., IV
Sappi Limited, 49
Schneidersöhne Deutschland GmbH & Co. KG, 100
Schweitzer-Mauduit International, Inc., 52
Scott Paper Company, IV; 31 (upd.)
Sealed Air Corporation, 14
Sierra Pacific Industries, 22; 90 (upd.)
Simpson Investment Company, 17
Smurfit-Stone Container Corporation, 83 (upd.)
Sonoco Products Company, 8; 89 (upd.)
Specialty Coatings Inc., 8
Stimson Lumber Company 78
Stone Container Corporation, IV
Stora Enso Oyj, IV; 36 (upd.); 85 (upd.)
Svenska Cellulosa Aktiebolaget SCA, IV; 28 (upd.); 85 (upd.)
Sveaskog AB, 93
Tapemark Company Inc., 64
Tembec Inc., 66
Temple-Inland Inc., IV; 31 (upd.); 102 (upd.)
Thomsen Greenhouses and Garden Center, Incorporated, 65
TJ International, Inc., 19
U.S. Timberlands Company, L.P., 42
Union Camp Corporation, IV
United Paper Mills Ltd. (Yhtyneet Paperitehtaat Oy), IV
Universal Forest Products, Inc., 10; 59 (upd.)
UPM-Kymmene Corporation, 19; 50 (upd.)
Wausau-Mosinee Paper Corporation, 60 (upd.)
West Fraser Timber Co. Ltd., 17; 91 (upd.)
West Linn Paper Company, 91
Westvaco Corporation, IV; 19 (upd.)
Weyerhaeuser Company, IV; 9 (upd.); 28 (upd.); 83 (upd.)
Wickes Inc., 25 (upd.)
Willamette Industries, Inc., IV; 31 (upd.)
WTD Industries, Inc., 20

Personal Services

AARP, 27
ABC Learning Centres Ltd., 93
Adelman Travel Group, 105
ADT Security Services, Inc., 12; 44 (upd.)
Africare, 59
Alderwoods Group, Inc., 68 (upd.)
Ambassadors International, Inc., 68 (upd.)
American Civil Liberties Union (ACLU), 60
American Management Association, 76
American Retirement Corporation, 42
American Society for the Prevention of Cruelty to Animals (ASPCA), 68
AmeriCares Foundation, Inc., 87
Aquent, 96
Arthur Murray International, Inc., 32
Association of Junior Leagues International Inc., 60

Benesse Corporation, 76
Berlitz International, Inc., 13; 39 (upd.)
Bidvest Group Ltd., 106
Big Brothers Big Sisters of America, 85
Bill & Melinda Gates Foundation, 41; 100 (upd.)
Blackwater USA, 76
Bonhams 1793 Ltd., 72
Boys & Girls Clubs of America, 69
The Brickman Group, Ltd., 87
The Brink's Company, 58 (upd.)
Brother's Brother Foundation, 93
CareerBuilder, Inc., 93
Caritas Internationalis, 72
Carriage Services, Inc., 37
Catholic Charities USA, 76
CDI Corporation, 6; 54 (upd.)
Central Parking System, 18; 104 (upd.)
CeWe Color Holding AG, 76
ChildrenFirst, Inc., 59
Childtime Learning Centers, Inc., 34
Chubb, PLC, 50
Corinthian Colleges, Inc., 39; 92 (upd.)
Correctional Services Corporation, 30
Correos y Telegrafos S.A., 80
Council on International Educational Exchange Inc., 81
CUC International Inc., 16
Curves International, Inc., 54
Cystic Fibrosis Foundation, 93
Davis Service Group PLC, 45
DeVry Inc., 29; 82 (upd.)
Educational Testing Service, 12; 62 (upd.)
eHarmony.com Inc., 71
Elliott-Lewis Corporation, 100
Feed The Children, Inc., 68
First Artist Corporation PLC, 105
Food For The Poor, Inc., 77
The Ford Foundation, 34
Franklin Quest Co., 11
Gifts In Kind International, 101
Gold's Gym International, Inc., 71
Goodwill Industries International, Inc., 16; 66 (upd.)
GP Strategies Corporation, 64 (upd.)
Green Dot Public Schools, 99
Greenpeace International, 74
Greg Manning Auctions, Inc., 60
Grupo Positivo, 105
Gunnebo AB, 53
Hair Club For Men Ltd., 90
Herbalife Ltd., 17; 41 (upd.); 92 (upd.)
The Humane Society of the United States, 54
Huntington Learning Centers, Inc., 55
I Grandi Viaggi S.p.A., 105
Imperial Parking Corporation, 58
Initial Security, 64
Iron Mountain, Inc., 33; 104 (upd.)
The J. Paul Getty Trust, 105
Jazzercise, Inc., 45
The John D. and Catherine T. MacArthur Foundation, 34
Jones Knowledge Group, Inc., 97
Kaplan, Inc., 42; 90 (upd.)
KinderCare Learning Centers, Inc., 13
Kiva, 95
Knowledge Learning Corporation, 51

Kumon Institute of Education Co., Ltd., 72
Labor Ready, Inc., 29; 88 (upd.)
Learning Care Group, Inc., 76 (upd.)
Lifetouch Inc., 86
The Loewen Group Inc., 16; 40 (upd.)
LPA Holding Corporation, 81
Mace Security International, Inc., 57
Make-A-Wish Foundation of America, 97
Management and Training Corporation, 28
Manpower, Inc., 9
Martin Franchises, Inc., 80
Match.com, LP, 87
Michael Page International plc, 45
Mothers Against Drunk Driving (MADD), 51
National Council of La Raza, 106
National Heritage Academies, Inc., 60
National Organization for Women, Inc., 55
National Wildlife Federation, 103
The New School, 103
Noah Education Holdings Ltd., 97
Nobel Learning Communities, Inc., 37; 76 (upd.)
Orkin, Inc., 104
Oxfam GB, 87
PODS Enterprises Inc., 103
Prison Rehabilitative Industries and Diversified Enterprises, Inc. (PRIDE), 53
Recording for the Blind & Dyslexic, 51
Regis Corporation, 18; 70 (upd.)
Robert Half International Inc., 70 (upd.)
The Rockefeller Foundation, 34
Rollins, Inc., 11; 104 (upd.)
Rosenbluth International Inc., 14
Rosetta Stone Inc., 93
Rotary International, 31
The Salvation Army USA, 32
Scientific Learning Corporation, 95
Screen Actors Guild, 72
Service Corporation International, 6; 51 (upd.)
The ServiceMaster Company, 68 (upd.)
Shutterfly, Inc., 98
SOS Staffing Services, 25
Spark Networks, Inc., 91
Special Olympics, Inc., 93
SR Teleperformance S.A., 86
Stewart Enterprises, Inc., 20
Supercuts Inc., 26
24 Hour Fitness Worldwide, Inc., 71
UAW (International Union, United Automobile, Aerospace and Agricultural Implement Workers of America), 72
United Negro College Fund, Inc., 79
United Service Organizations, 60
Weight Watchers International Inc., 12; 33 (upd.); 73 (upd.)
The York Group, Inc., 50
Youth Services International, Inc., 21
YWCA of the U.S.A., 45
World Vision International, Inc., 93

Petroleum

Abraxas Petroleum Corporation, 89

Abu Dhabi National Oil Company, IV; 45 (upd.)
Adani Enterprises Ltd., 97
Aegean Marine Petroleum Network Inc., 89
Agway, Inc., 21 (upd.)
Alberta Energy Company Ltd., 16; 43 (upd.)
Alon Israel Oil Company Ltd., 104
Amerada Hess Corporation, IV; 21 (upd.); 55 (upd.)
Amoco Corporation, IV; 14 (upd.)
Anadarko Petroleum Corporation, 10; 52 (upd.); 106 (upd.)
ANR Pipeline Co., 17
Anschutz Corp., 12
Apache Corporation, 10; 32 (upd.); 89 (upd.)
Aral AG, 62
Arctic Slope Regional Corporation, 38
Arena Resources, Inc., 97
Ashland Inc., 19; 50 (upd.)
Ashland Oil, Inc., IV
Atlantic Richfield Company, IV; 31 (upd.)
Atwood Oceanics, Inc., 100
Aventine Renewable Energy Holdings, Inc., 89
Badger State Ethanol, LLC, 83
Baker Hughes Incorporated, 22 (upd.); 57 (upd.)
Basic Earth Science Systems, Inc., 101
Belco Oil & Gas Corp., 40
Benton Oil and Gas Company, 47
Berry Petroleum Company, 47
BG Products Inc., 96
BHP Billiton, 67 (upd.)
Bill Barrett Corporation, 71
BJ Services Company, 25
Blue Rhino Corporation, 56
Boardwalk Pipeline Partners, LP, 87
Boots & Coots International Well Control, Inc., 79
BP p.l.c., 45 (upd.); 103 (upd.)
Brigham Exploration Company, 75
The British Petroleum Company plc, IV; 7 (upd.); 21 (upd.)
British-Borneo Oil & Gas PLC, 34
Broken Hill Proprietary Company Ltd., 22 (upd.)
Bronco Drilling Company, Inc., 89
Burlington Resources Inc., 10
Burmah Castrol PLC, IV; 30 (upd.)
Callon Petroleum Company, 47
Caltex Petroleum Corporation, 19
Calumet Specialty Products Partners, L.P., 106
CAMAC International Corporation, 106
Cano Petroleum Inc., 97
Carrizo Oil & Gas, Inc., 97
Chevron Corporation, IV; 19 (upd.); 47 (upd.); 103 (upd.)
Chiles Offshore Corporation, 9
Cimarex Energy Co., 81
China National Petroleum Corporation, 46
Chinese Petroleum Corporation, IV; 31 (upd.)

CITGO Petroleum Corporation, IV; 31 (upd.)
Clayton Williams Energy, Inc., 87
The Coastal Corporation, IV; 31 (upd.)
Compañia Española de Petróleos S.A. (Cepsa), IV; 56 (upd.)
Compton Petroleum Corporation, 103
Comstock Resources, Inc., 47
Conoco Inc., IV; 16 (upd.)
ConocoPhillips, 63 (upd.)
CONSOL Energy Inc., 59
Continental Resources, Inc., 89
Cooper Cameron Corporation, 20 (upd.)
Cosmo Oil Co., Ltd., IV; 53 (upd.)
Crown Central Petroleum Corporation, 7
DeepTech International Inc., 21
Den Norse Stats Oljeselskap AS, IV
Denbury Resources, Inc., 67
Deutsche BP Aktiengesellschaft, 7
Devon Energy Corporation, 61
Diamond Shamrock, Inc., IV
Distrigaz S.A., 82
Dril-Quip, Inc., 81
Duvernay Oil Corp., 83
Dyneff S.A., 98
Dynegy Inc., 49 (upd.)
E.On AG, 50 (upd.)
Edge Petroleum Corporation, 67
Egyptian General Petroleum Corporation, IV; 51 (upd.)
El Paso Corporation, 66 (upd.)
Elf Aquitaine SA, 21 (upd.)
Empresa Colombiana de Petróleos, IV
Enbridge Inc., 43
Encore Acquisition Company, 73
Energen Corporation, 21; 97 (upd.)
ENI S.p.A., 69 (upd.)
Enron Corporation, 19
ENSCO International Incorporated, 57
Ente Nazionale Idrocarburi, IV
Enterprise Oil PLC, 11; 50 (upd.)
Entreprise Nationale Sonatrach, IV
EOG Resources, 106
Equitable Resources, Inc., 54 (upd.)
Ergon, Inc., 95
Exxon Mobil Corporation, IV; 7 (upd.); 32 (upd.); 67 (upd.)
Ferrellgas Partners, L.P., 35
FINA, Inc., 7
Fluxys SA, 101
Flying J Inc., 19
Flotek Industries Inc., 93
Forest Oil Corporation, 19; 91 (upd.)
Galp Energia SGPS S.A., 98
OAO Gazprom, 42
General Sekiyu K.K., IV
GeoResources, Inc., 101
Giant Industries, Inc., 19; 61 (upd.)
Global Industries, Ltd., 37
Global Marine Inc., 9
GlobalSantaFe Corporation, 48 (upd.)
Grey Wolf, Inc., 43
Halliburton Company, III; 25 (upd.); 55 (upd.)
Hanover Compressor Company, 59
Hawkeye Holdings LLC, 89
Helix Energy Solutions Group, Inc., 81
Hellenic Petroleum SA, 64

Helmerich & Payne, Inc., 18
Holly Corporation, 12
Hunt Consolidated, Inc., 7; 27 (upd.)
Hunting plc 78
Hurricane Hydrocarbons Ltd., 54
Husky Energy Inc., 47
Idemitsu Kosan Co., Ltd., 49 (upd.)
Idemitsu Kosan K.K., IV
Imperial Oil Limited, IV; 25 (upd.)
Indian Oil Corporation Ltd., IV; 48 (upd.); 95 (upd.)
INPEX Holdings Inc., 97
Input/Output, Inc., 73
Iogen Corporation, 81
Ipiranga S.A., 67
KBR Inc., 106 (upd.)
Kanematsu Corporation, IV; 24 (upd.); 102 (upd.)
Kerr-McGee Corporation, IV; 22 (upd.); 68 (upd.)
Kinder Morgan, Inc., 45
King Ranch, Inc., 14
Koch Industries, Inc., IV; 20 (upd.), 77 (upd.)
Koppers Industries, Inc., 26 (upd.)
Kuwait Petroleum Corporation, IV; 55 (upd.)
Libyan National Oil Corporation, IV
The Louisiana Land and Exploration Company, 7
OAO LUKOIL, 40
Lyondell Petrochemical Company, IV
MAPCO Inc., IV
Mariner Energy, Inc., 101
Maxus Energy Corporation, 7
McDermott International, Inc., 37 (upd.)
Meteor Industries Inc., 33
Mexichem, S.A.B. de C.V., 99
Mitchell Energy and Development Corporation, 7
Mitsubishi Oil Co., Ltd., IV
Mobil Corporation, IV; 7 (upd.); 21 (upd.)
MOL Rt, 70
Murphy Oil Corporation, 7; 32 (upd.); 95 (upd.)
Nabors Industries Ltd., 9; 91 (upd.)
National Fuel Gas Company, 6; 95 (upd.)
National Iranian Oil Company, IV; 61 (upd.)
National Oil Corporation, 66 (upd.)
Neste Oil Corporation, IV; 85 (upd.)
Newfield Exploration Company, 65
Nexen Inc., 79
NGC Corporation, 18
Nigerian National Petroleum Corporation, IV; 72 (upd.)
Nippon Oil Corporation, IV; 63 (upd.)
OAO NK YUKOS, 47
Noble Affiliates, Inc., 11
Occidental Petroleum Corporation, IV; 25 (upd.); 71 (upd.)
Odebrecht S.A., 73
Oil and Natural Gas Corporation Ltd., IV; 90 (upd.)
Oil States International, Inc., 77
OMV AG, IV; 98 (upd.)
Oryx Energy Company, 7

Pacific Ethanol, Inc., 81
Pakistan State Oil Company Ltd., 81
Parallel Petroleum Corporation, 101
Paramount Resources Ltd., 87
Parker Drilling Company, 28
Patina Oil & Gas Corporation, 24
Patterson-UTI Energy, Inc., 55
Pengrowth Energy Trust, 95
Penn Virginia Corporation, 85
Pennzoil-Quaker State Company, IV; 20 (upd.); 50 (upd.)
Pertamina, IV; 56 (upd.)
Petro-Canada, IV; 99 (upd.)
Petrobras Energia Participaciones S.A., 72
Petrofac Ltd., 95
PetroFina S.A., IV; 26 (upd.)
Petrohawk Energy Corporation, 79
Petróleo Brasileiro S.A., IV
Petróleos de Portugal S.A., IV
Petróleos de Venezuela S.A., IV; 74 (upd.)
Petróleos del Ecuador, IV
Petróleos Mexicanos (PEMEX), IV; 19 (upd.); 104 (upd.)
Petroleum Development Oman LLC, IV; 98 (upd.)
Petroliam Nasional Bhd (Petronas), IV; 56 (upd.)
Petron Corporation, 58
Phillips Petroleum Company, IV; 40 (upd.)
Pioneer Natural Resources Company, 59
Pogo Producing Company, 39
Polski Koncern Naftowy ORLEN S.A., 77
Premcor Inc., 37
Pride International Inc. 78
PTT Public Company Ltd., 56
Qatar Petroleum, IV; 98 (upd.)
Quaker State Corporation, 7; 21 (upd.)
Range Resources Corporation, 45
Reliance Industries Ltd., 81
Repsol-YPF S.A., IV; 16 (upd.); 40 (upd.)
Resource America, Inc., 42
Rosneft, 106
Rowan Companies, Inc., 43
Royal Dutch/Shell Group, IV; 49 (upd.)
RPC, Inc., 91
RWE AG, 50 (upd.)
St. Mary Land & Exploration Company, 63
Santa Fe International Corporation, 38
Santos Ltd., 81
Sapp Bros Travel Centers, Inc., 105
Sasol Limited, IV; 47 (upd.)
Saudi Arabian Oil Company, IV; 17 (upd.); 50 (upd.)
Schlumberger Limited, 17 (upd.); 59 (upd.)
Seagull Energy Corporation, 11
Seitel, Inc., 47
Shanghai Petrochemical Co., Ltd., 18
Shell Oil Company, IV; 14 (upd.); 41 (upd.)
Showa Shell Sekiyu K.K., IV; 59 (upd.)
OAO Siberian Oil Company (Sibneft), 49
Smith International, Inc., 59 (upd.)
Société Nationale Elf Aquitaine, IV; 7 (upd.)
Sonatrach, 65 (upd.)

Spinnaker Exploration Company, 72
Statoil ASA, 61 (upd.)
Suburban Propane Partners, L.P., 30
SUEZ-TRACTEBEL S.A., 97 (upd.)
Sun Company, Inc., IV
Suncor Energy Inc., 54
Sunoco, Inc., 28 (upd.); 83 (upd.)
Superior Energy Services, Inc., 65
OAO Surgutneftegaz, 48
Swift Energy Company, 63
Talisman Energy Inc., 9; 47 (upd.); 103 (upd.)
TAQA North Ltd., 95
OAO Tatneft, 45
Tengasco, Inc., 99
TEPPCO Partners, L.P., 73
Tesoro Corporation, 7; 45 (upd.); 97 (upd.)
Teton Energy Corporation, 97
Texaco Inc., IV; 14 (upd.); 41 (upd.)
Tidewater Inc., 37 (upd.)
TODCO, 87
Tom Brown, Inc., 37
Tonen Corporation, IV; 16 (upd.)
TonenGeneral Sekiyu K.K., 54 (upd.)
Tosco Corporation, 7
TOTAL S.A., IV; 24 (upd.)
Transammonia Group, 95
TransCanada Corporation, 93 (upd.)
TransMontaigne Inc., 28
Oil Transporting Joint Stock Company Transneft, 93
Transocean Sedco Forex Inc., 45
Travel Ports of America, Inc., 17
Triton Energy Corporation, 11
Tullow Oil plc, 83
Türkiye Petrolleri Anonim Ortakliği, IV
Ultra Petroleum Corporation, 71
Ultramar Diamond Shamrock Corporation, IV; 31 (upd.)
Union Texas Petroleum Holdings, Inc., 9
Unit Corporation, 63
Universal Compression, Inc., 59
Unocal Corporation, IV; 24 (upd.); 71 (upd.)
USX Corporation, IV; 7 (upd.)
Valero Energy Corporation, 7; 71 (upd.)
Valley National Gases, Inc., 85
Varco International, Inc., 42
Vastar Resources, Inc., 24
VeraSun Energy Corporation, 87
Vintage Petroleum, Inc., 42
Wascana Energy Inc., 13
Weatherford International, Inc., 39
Webber Oil Company, 61
Western Atlas Inc., 12
Western Company of North America, 15
Western Gas Resources, Inc., 45
Western Oil Sands Inc., 85
Westport Resources Corporation, 63
Whiting Petroleum Corporation, 81
The Williams Companies, Inc., IV; 31 (upd.)
World Fuel Services Corporation, 47
XTO Energy Inc., 52
YPF Sociedad Anonima, IV
The Zubair Corporation L.L.C., 96

Publishing & Printing

A.B.Dick Company, 28
A.H. Belo Corporation, 10; 30 (upd.)
AbitibiBowater Inc., IV; 25 (upd.); 99 (upd.)
Abril S.A., 95
AccuWeather, Inc., 73
Advance Publications Inc., IV; 19 (upd.); 96 (upd.)
Advanced Marketing Services, Inc., 34
Advanstar Communications, Inc., 57
Affiliated Publications, Inc., 7
Agence France-Presse, 34
Agora S.A. Group, 77
Aljazeera Satellite Channel, 79
Allbritton Communications Company, 105
Alma Media Corporation, 98
American Banknote Corporation, 30
American Girl, Inc., 69
American Greetings Corporation, 7, 22 (upd.)
American Media, Inc., 27; 82 (upd.)
American Printing House for the Blind, 26
American Reprographics Company, 75
Andrews McMeel Universal, 40
The Antioch Company, 40
AOL Time Warner Inc., 57 (upd.)
Arandell Corporation, 37
Archie Comics Publications, Inc., 63
Arnoldo Mondadori Editore S.p.A., IV; 19 (upd.); 54 (upd.)
The Associated Press, 31 (upd.); 73 (upd.)
The Atlantic Group, 23
Audible Inc., 79
Axel Springer Verlag AG, IV; 20 (upd.)
Banta Corporation, 12; 32 (upd.); 79 (upd.)
Bauer Publishing Group, 7
Bayard SA, 49
Berlitz International, Inc., 13; 39 (upd.)
Bernard C. Harris Publishing Company, Inc., 39
Bertelsmann A.G., IV; 15 (upd.); 43 (upd.); 91 (upd.)
Bibliographisches Institut & F.A. Brockhaus AG, 74
Big Flower Press Holdings, Inc., 21
Blackwell Publishing Ltd. 78
Blue Mountain Arts, Inc., 29
Bobit Publishing Company, 55
Bonnier AB, 52
Book-of-the-Month Club, Inc., 13
Bowne & Co., Inc., 23; 79 (upd.)
Broderbund Software, 13; 29 (upd.)
Brown Printing Company, 26
Burda Holding GmbH. & Co., 23
The Bureau of National Affairs, Inc., 23
Butterick Co., Inc., 23
Cadmus Communications Corporation, 23
Cahners Business Information, 43
Carl Allers Etablissement A/S, 72
Carus Publishing Company, 93
CCH Inc., 14
Central Newspapers, Inc., 10
Champion Industries, Inc., 28

Cherry Lane Music Publishing Company, Inc., 62
Chicago Review Press Inc., 84
ChoicePoint Inc., 65
The Christian Science Publishing Society, 55
The Chronicle Publishing Company, Inc., 23
Chrysalis Group plc, 40
CMP Media Inc., 26
Commerce Clearing House, Inc., 7
Community Newspaper Holdings, Inc., 91
Concepts Direct, Inc., 39
Condé Nast Publications, Inc., 13; 59 (upd.)
Consolidated Graphics, Inc., 70
Consumers Union, 26
The Copley Press, Inc., 23
Corelio S.A./N.V., 96
Cornelsen Verlagsholding GmbH & Co., 90
Courier Corporation, 41
Cowles Media Company, 23
Cox Enterprises, Inc., IV; 22 (upd.); 67 (upd.)
Crain Communications, Inc., 12; 35 (upd.)
Crane & Co., Inc., 26; 103 (upd.)
Current, Inc., 37
Cygnus Business Media, Inc., 56
Dai Nippon Printing Co., Ltd., IV; 57 (upd.)
Daily Journal Corporation, 101
Daily Mail and General Trust plc, 19
Dawson Holdings PLC, 43
Day Runner, Inc., 14
DC Comics Inc., 25; 98 (upd.)
De Agostini Editore S.p.A., 103
De La Rue plc, 10; 34 (upd.)
DeLorme Publishing Company, Inc., 53
Deluxe Corporation, 7; 22 (upd.); 73 (upd.)
Dennis Publishing Ltd., 62
Detroit Media Partnership L.P., 102
Dex Media, Inc., 65
Dispatch Printing Company, 100
Donruss Playoff L.P., 66
Dorling Kindersley Holdings plc, 20
Dover Publications Inc., 34
Dow Jones & Company, Inc., IV; 19 (upd.); 47 (upd.)
The Dun & Bradstreet Corporation, IV; 19 (upd.)
Duplex Products Inc., 17
The E.W. Scripps Company, IV; 7 (upd.); 28 (upd.); 66 (upd.)
Eagle-Tribune Publishing Co., 91
The Economist Group Ltd., 67
Edipresse S.A., 82
Éditions Gallimard, 72
Editis S.A. 78
Edmark Corporation, 14
Edwards Brothers, Inc., 92
Egmont Group, 93
Electronics for Imaging, Inc., 43 (upd.)
Elsevier N.V., IV
EMAP plc, 35

EMI Group plc, 22 (upd.); 81 (upd.)
Encyclopaedia Britannica, Inc., 7; 39 (upd.)
Engraph, Inc., 12
Enquirer/Star Group, Inc., 10
Entravision Communications Corporation, 41
Essence Communications, Inc., 24
F&W Publications, Inc., 71
Farm Journal Corporation, 42
Farrar, Straus and Giroux Inc., 15
Flint Ink Corporation, 13
Follett Corporation, 12; 39 (upd.)
Forbes Inc., 30; 82 (upd.)
Frankfurter Allgemeine Zeitung GmbH, 66
Franklin Electronic Publishers, Inc., 23
Freedom Communications, Inc., 36
G A Pindar & Son Ltd., 88
Gannett Company, Inc., IV; 7 (upd.); 30 (upd.); 66 (upd.)
GateHouse Media, Inc., 91
Geiger Bros., 60
Gibson Greetings, Inc., 12
Giesecke & Devrient GmbH, 83
Globe Newspaper Company Inc., 106
Golden Books Family Entertainment, Inc., 28
Goss Holdings, Inc., 43
Graphic Industries Inc., 25
Gray Communications Systems, Inc., 24
Grolier Incorporated, 16; 43 (upd.)
Groupe de la Cite, IV
Groupe Les Echos, 25
Grupo Clarín S.A., 67
Grupo Positivo, 105
Grupo Televisa, S.A., 54 (upd.)
Guardian Media Group plc, 53
The H.W. Wilson Company, 66
Hachette, IV
Hachette Filipacchi Medias S.A., 21
Haights Cross Communications, Inc., 84
Hal Leonard Corporation, 96
Hallmark Cards, Inc., IV; 16 (upd.); 40 (upd.); 87 (upd.)
Harcourt Brace and Co., 12
Harcourt Brace Jovanovich, Inc., IV
Harcourt General, Inc., 20 (upd.)
Harlequin Enterprises Limited, 52
HarperCollins Publishers, 15
Harris Interactive Inc., 41; 92 (upd.)
Harry N. Abrams, Inc., 58
Harte-Hanks Communications, Inc., 17
Havas SA, 10; 33 (upd.)
Hay House, Inc., 93
Haynes Publishing Group P.L.C., 71
Hazelden Foundation, 28
Health Communications, Inc., 72
The Hearst Corporation, IV; 19 (upd.); 46 (upd.)
Her Majesty's Stationery Office, 7
Herald Media, Inc., 91
Highlights for Children, Inc., 95
N.V. Holdingmaatschappij De Telegraaf, 23
Hollinger International Inc., 24; 62 (upd.)
HOP, LLC, 80

Houghton Mifflin Company, 10; 36 (upd.)
IDG Books Worldwide, Inc., 27
IHS Inc. 78
Independent News & Media PLC, 61
Informa Group plc, 58
Information Holdings Inc., 47
International Data Group, Inc., 7; 25 (upd.)
IPC Magazines Limited, 7
J.J. Keller & Associates, Inc., 81
Jeppesen Sanderson, Inc., 92
John Fairfax Holdings Limited, 7
John H. Harland Company, 17
John Wiley & Sons, Inc., 17; 65 (upd.)
Johnson Publishing Company, Inc., 28; 72 (upd.)
Johnston Press plc, 35
Jostens, Inc., 25 (upd.); 73 (upd.)
Journal Communications, Inc., 86
Journal Register Company, 29
Jupitermedia Corporation, 75
Kaplan, Inc., 42
Kelley Blue Book Company, Inc., 84
Kensington Publishing Corporation, 84
Kinko's, Inc., 43 (upd.)
Knight Ridder, Inc., 67 (upd.)
Knight-Ridder, Inc., IV; 15 (upd.)
The Knot, Inc., 74
Kodansha Ltd., IV; 38 (upd.)
Krause Publications, Inc., 35
Landmark Communications, Inc., 12; 55 (upd.)
Larry Flynt Publishing Inc., 31
Le Monde S.A., 33
Lebhar-Friedman, Inc., 55
Lee Enterprises Inc., 11; 64 (upd.)
LEXIS-NEXIS Group, 33
Lonely Planet Publications Pty Ltd., 55
M. DuMont Schauberg GmbH & Co. KG, 92
M. Shanken Communications, Inc., 50
Maclean Hunter Publishing Limited, IV; 26 (upd.)
Macmillan, Inc., 7
Martha Stewart Living Omnimedia, Inc., 24; 73 (upd.)
Marvel Entertainment Inc., 10; 78 (upd.)
Matra-Hachette S.A., 15 (upd.)
Maxwell Communication Corporation plc, IV; 7 (upd.)
The McClatchy Company, 23; 92 (upd.)
The McGraw-Hill Companies, Inc., IV; 18 (upd.); 51 (upd.)
McMurry, Inc., 105
Mecklermedia Corporation, 24
Media General, Inc., 38 (upd.)
MediaNews Group, Inc., 70
Menasha Corporation, 59 (upd.)
Meredith Corporation, 11; 29 (upd.); 74 (upd.)
Merriam-Webster Inc., 70
Merrill Corporation, 18; 47 (upd.)
Metro International S.A., 93
Miami Herald Media Company, 92
Miller Publishing Group, LLC, 57
The Miner Group International, 22

Mirror Group Newspapers plc, 7; 23 (upd.)
Moore Corporation Limited, IV
Morris Communications Corporation, 36
Mrs. Grossman's Paper Company Inc., 84
MTI Enterprises Inc., 102
Multimedia, Inc., 11
MYOB Ltd., 86
Naspers Ltd., 66
National Audubon Society, 26
National Geographic Society, 9; 30 (upd.); 79 (upd.)
National Journal Group Inc., 67
National Wildlife Federation, 103
New Chapter Inc., 96
New Times, Inc., 45
New York Daily News, 32
The New York Times Company, IV; 19 (upd.); 61 (upd.)
News America Publishing Inc., 12
News Communications, Inc., 103
News Corporation Limited, IV; 7 (upd.)
Newsday Media Group, 103
Newsquest plc, 32
Next Media Ltd., 61
Nielsen Business Media, Inc., 98
Nihon Keizai Shimbun, Inc., IV
Nolo.com, Inc., 49
Northern and Shell Network plc, 87
Oji Paper Co., Ltd., 57 (upd.)
Onion, Inc., 69
Ottaway Newspapers, Inc., 15
Outlook Group Corporation, 37
PagesJaunes Groupe SA, 79
Pantone Inc., 53
PCM Uitgevers NV, 53
Pearson plc, IV; 46 (upd.); 103 (upd.)
The Penguin Group, 100
PennWell Corporation, 55
Penton Media, Inc., 27
The Perseus Books Group, 91
Petersen Publishing Company, 21
Phaidon Press Ltd., 98
Philadelphia Media Holdings LLC, 92
The Phoenix Media/Communications Group, 91
Plain Dealer Publishing Company, 92
Plato Learning, Inc., 44
Playboy Enterprises, Inc., 18
Pleasant Company, 27
PMP Ltd., 72
PR Newswire, 35
Primedia Inc., 22
The Providence Journal Company, 28
Publishers Group, Inc., 35
Publishing and Broadcasting Limited, 54
Pulitzer Inc., 15; 58 (upd.)
Quad/Graphics, Inc., 19
Quebecor Inc., 12; 47 (upd.)
R.L. Polk & Co., 10
R.R. Bowker LLC, 100
R.R. Donnelley & Sons Company, IV; 9 (upd.); 38 (upd.)
Rand McNally & Company, 28
Random House Inc., 13; 31 (upd.); 106 (upd.)
Ravensburger AG, 64
RCS MediaGroup S.p.A., 96

The Reader's Digest Association, Inc., IV; 17 (upd.); 71 (upd.)
Real Times, Inc., 66
Recycled Paper Greetings, Inc., 21
Reed Elsevier plc, IV; 17 (upd.); 31 (upd.)
Reuters Group PLC, IV; 22 (upd.); 63 (upd.)
Rodale, Inc., 23; 47 (upd.)
Rogers Communications Inc., 30 (upd.)
The Rowohlt Verlag GmbH, 96
Rural Press Ltd., 74
St Ives plc, 34
Salem Communications Corporation, 97
Sanborn Map Company Inc., 82
SanomaWSOY Corporation, 51
Schawk, Inc., 24
Schibsted ASA, 31
Scholastic Corporation, 10; 29 (upd.)
Schurz Communications, Inc., 98
Scott Fetzer Company, 12; 80 (upd.)
Scottish Media Group plc, 32
Seat Pagine Gialle S.p.A., 47
Seattle Times Company, 15
The Sheridan Group, Inc., 86
The Sierra Club, 28
Simon & Schuster Inc., IV; 19 (upd.); 100 (upd.)
Singapore Press Holdings Limited, 85
Sir Speedy, Inc., 16
SkyMall, Inc., 26
Société du Figaro S.A., 60
Softbank Corp., 13
The Source Enterprises, Inc., 65
Southam Inc., 7
Southern Progress Corporation, 102
SPIEGEL-Verlag Rudolf Augstein GmbH & Co. KG, 44
The Standard Register Company, 15; 93 (upd.)
Stephens Media, LLC, 91
Strine Printing Company Inc., 88
Sunrise Greetings, 88
Tamedia AG, 53
Taschen GmbH, 101
Taylor & Francis Group plc, 44
Taylor Corporation, 36
Taylor Publishing Company, 12; 36 (upd.)
TechBooks Inc., 84
TechTarget, Inc., 99
Telegraaf Media Groep N.V., 98 (upd.)
Thomas Crosbie Holdings Limited, 81
Thomas Nelson, Inc., 14; 38 (upd.)
Thomas Publishing Company, 26
The Thomson Corporation, 8; 34 (upd.); 77 (upd.)
Time Out Group Ltd., 68
The Times Mirror Company, IV; 17 (upd.)
Tohan Corporation, 84
TOKYOPOP Inc., 79
Tom Doherty Associates Inc., 25
Toppan Printing Co., Ltd., IV; 58 (upd.)
The Topps Company, Inc., 13; 34 (upd.); 83 (upd.)
Torstar Corporation, 29
Trader Classified Media N.V., 57
Tribune Company, IV, 22 (upd.); 63 (upd.)

Trinity Mirror plc, 49 (upd.)
Tuttle Publishing, 86
Tyndale House Publishers, Inc., 57
U.S. News & World Report Inc., 30; 89 (upd.)
United Business Media plc, 52 (upd.)
United News & Media plc, IV; 28 (upd.)
United Press International, Inc., 25; 73 (upd.)
The University of Chicago Press, 79
Valassis Communications, Inc., 8
Value Line, Inc., 16; 73 (upd.)
Vance Publishing Corporation, 64
Verlagsgruppe Georg von Holtzbrinck GmbH, 35
Verlagsgruppe Weltbild GmbH, 98
Village Voice Media, Inc., 38
VistaPrint Limited, 87
VNU N.V., 27
Volt Information Sciences Inc., 26
W.W. Norton & Company, Inc., 28
Wallace Computer Services, Inc., 36
Walsworth Publishing Co. 78
The Washington Post Company, IV; 20 (upd.)
Waverly, Inc., 16
WAZ Media Group, 82
Wegener NV, 53
Wenner Media, Inc., 32
West Group, 7; 34 (upd.)
Western Publishing Group, Inc., 13
WH Smith PLC, V; 42 (upd.)
William Reed Publishing Ltd. 78
Wolters Kluwer NV, 14; 33 (upd.)
Workman Publishing Company, Inc., 70
World Book, Inc., 12
World Color Press Inc., 12
World Publications, LLC, 65
Xeikon NV, 26
Yell Group PLC, 79
Zebra Technologies Corporation, 14
Ziff Davis Media Inc., 12; 36 (upd.); 73 (upd.)
Zondervan Corporation, 24; 71 (upd.)

Real Estate

Acadia Realty Trust, 106
Akerys S.A., 90
Alexander's, Inc., 45
Alexandria Real Estate Equities, Inc., 101
Alico, Inc., 63
AMB Property Corporation, 57
American Campus Communities, Inc., 85
Amfac/JMB Hawaii L.L.C., 24 (upd.)
Apartment Investment and Management Company, 49
Archstone-Smith Trust, 49
Associated Estates Realty Corporation, 25
AvalonBay Communities, Inc., 58
Baird & Warner Holding Company, 87
Berkshire Realty Holdings, L.P., 49
Bluegreen Corporation, 80
Boston Properties, Inc., 22
Bouygues S.A., I; 24 (upd.); 97 (upd.)
Bramalea Ltd., 9
British Land Plc, 54
Brookfield Properties Corporation, 89
Burroughs & Chapin Company, Inc., 86

Camden Property Trust, 77
Canary Wharf Group Plc, 30
CapStar Hotel Company, 21
CarrAmerica Realty Corporation, 56
Castle & Cooke, Inc., 20 (upd.)
Catellus Development Corporation, 24
CB Commercial Real Estate Services Group, Inc., 21
CB Richard Ellis Group, Inc., 70 (upd.)
Central Florida Investments, Inc., 93
Chateau Communities, Inc., 37
Chelsfield PLC, 67
Cheung Kong (Holdings) Limited, IV; 20 (upd.)
City Developments Limited, 89
Clayton Homes Incorporated, 54 (upd.)
Colliers International Property Consultants Inc., 92
Colonial Properties Trust, 65
The Corcoran Group, Inc., 58
The Corky McMillin Companies, 98
CoStar Group, Inc., 73
Cousins Properties Incorporated, 65
CSX Corporation 79 (upd.)
Cushman & Wakefield, Inc., 86
Del Webb Corporation, 14
Desarrolladora Homex, S.A. de C.V., 87
Developers Diversified Realty Corporation, 69
Douglas Emmett, Inc., 105
Draper and Kramer Inc., 96
Duke Realty Corporation, 57
Ducks Unlimited, Inc., 87
EastGroup Properties, Inc., 67
The Edward J. DeBartolo Corporation, 8
Enterprise Inns plc, 59
Equity Office Properties Trust, 54
Equity Residential, 49
Erickson Retirement Communities, 57
Fairfield Communities, Inc., 36
First Industrial Realty Trust, Inc., 65
Forest City Enterprises, Inc., 16; 52 (upd.)
Gale International Llc, 93
Gecina SA, 42
General Growth Properties, Inc., 57
GMH Communities Trust, 87
Great White Shark Enterprises, Inc., 89
Griffin Land & Nurseries, Inc., 43
Grubb & Ellis Company, 21; 98 (upd.)
Guangzhou R&F Properties Co., Ltd., 95
The Habitat Company LLC, 106
The Haminerson Property Investment and Development Corporation plc, IV
Hammerson plc, 40
Hang Lung Group Ltd., 104
Harbert Corporation, 14
Helmsley Enterprises, Inc., 39 (upd.)
Henderson Land Development Company Ltd., 70
Home Properties of New York, Inc., 42
HomeVestors of America, Inc., 77
Hongkong Land Holdings Limited, IV; 47 (upd.)
Holiday Retirement Corp., 87
Hopson Development Holdings Ltd., 87
Hovnanian Enterprises, Inc., 29; 89 (upd.)
Hyatt Corporation, 16 (upd.)

ILX Resorts Incorporated, 65
IRSA Inversiones y Representaciones S.A., 63
J.F. Shea Co., Inc., 55
Jardine Cycle & Carriage Ltd., 73
JMB Realty Corporation, IV
Jones Lang LaSalle Incorporated, 49
JPI, 49
Kaufman and Broad Home Corporation, 8
Kennedy-Wilson, Inc., 60
Kerry Properties Limited, 22
Kimco Realty Corporation, 11
The Koll Company, 8
Land Securities PLC, IV; 49 (upd.)
Lefrak Organization Inc., 26
Lend Lease Corporation Limited, IV; 17 (upd.); 52 (upd.)
Liberty Property Trust, 57
Lincoln Property Company, 8; 54 (upd.)
The Loewen Group Inc., 40 (upd.)
The Long & Foster Companies, Inc., 85
The Macerich Company, 57
Mack-Cali Realty Corporation, 42
Macklowe Properties, Inc., 95
Manufactured Home Communities, Inc., 22
Maui Land & Pineapple Company, Inc., 29; 100 (upd.)
Maxco Inc., 17
Meditrust, 11
Melvin Simon and Associates, Inc., 8
MEPC plc, IV
Meritage Corporation, 26
Mid-America Apartment Communities, Inc., 85
The Middleton Doll Company, 53
The Mills Corporation, 77
Mitsubishi Estate Company, Limited, IV; 61 (upd.)
Mitsui Real Estate Development Co., Ltd., IV
Morguard Corporation, 85
The Nature Conservancy, 28
New Plan Realty Trust, 11
New World Development Company Ltd., IV
Newhall Land and Farming Company, 14
Nexity S.A., 66
NRT Incorporated, 61
Olympia & York Developments Ltd., IV; 9 (upd.)
Panattoni Development Company, Inc., 99
Park Corp., 22
Parque Arauco S.A., 72
Perini Corporation, 8
Plum Creek Timber Company, Inc., 43; 106 (upd.)
Pope Resources LP, 74
Post Properties, Inc., 26
Potlatch Corporation, 8; 34 (upd.); 87 (upd.)
ProLogis, 57
Public Storage, Inc., 52
Railtrack Group PLC, 50
RE/MAX International, Inc., 59
Reading International Inc., 70

Reckson Associates Realty Corp., 47
Regency Centers Corporation, 71
Rockefeller Group International Inc., 58
Rodamco N.V., 26
The Rouse Company, 15; 63 (upd.)
The St. Joe Company, 8; 98 (upd.)
Sapporo Holdings Limited, I; 13 (upd.);
    36 (upd.); 97 (upd.)
Shubert Organization Inc., 24
The Sierra Club, 28
Silverstein Properties, Inc., 47
Simco S.A., 37
SL Green Realty Corporation, 44
Slough Estates PLC, IV; 50 (upd.)
Sovran Self Storage, Inc., 66
Starrett Corporation, 21
The Staubach Company, 62
Storage USA, Inc., 21
Sumitomo Realty & Development Co.,
    Ltd., IV
Sun Communities Inc., 46
Sunterra Corporation, 75
Tanger Factory Outlet Centers, Inc., 49
Tarragon Realty Investors, Inc., 45
Taubman Centers, Inc., 75
Taylor Woodrow plc, 38 (upd.)
Technical Olympic USA, Inc., 75
Tejon Ranch Company, 35
Tishman Speyer Properties, L.P., 47
Tokyu Land Corporation, IV
Trammell Crow Company, 8; 57 (upd.)
Trendwest Resorts, Inc., 33
Tridel Enterprises Inc., 9
Trizec Corporation Ltd., 10
The Trump Organization, 23; 64 (upd.)
Unibail SA, 40
United Dominion Realty Trust, Inc., 52
Vistana, Inc., 22
Vornado Realty Trust, 20
W.P. Carey & Co. LLC, 49
Weingarten Realty Investors, 95
William Lyon Homes, 59
Woodbridge Holdings Corporation, 99

Retail & Wholesale

A-Mark Financial Corporation, 71
A.C. Moore Arts & Crafts, Inc., 30
A.S. Watson & Company Ltd., 84
A.T. Cross Company, 49 (upd.)
Aaron Rents, Inc., 14; 35 (upd.)
Abatix Corp., 57
ABC Appliance, Inc., 10
ABC Carpet & Home Co. Inc., 26
Abercrombie & Fitch Company, 15; 75
    (upd.)
Academy Sports & Outdoors, 27
Ace Hardware Corporation, 12; 35 (upd.)
Action Performance Companies, Inc., 27
Adams Childrenswear Ltd., 95
ADESA, Inc., 71
Adolfo Dominguez S.A., 72
AEON Co., Ltd., 68 (upd.)
Aéropostale, Inc., 89
After Hours Formalwear Inc., 60
Alabama Farmers Cooperative, Inc., 63
Alain Afflelou SA, 53
Alba-Waldensian, Inc., 30

Alberto-Culver Company, 8; 36 (upd.); 91
    (upd.)
Albertson's, Inc., 65 (upd.)
Alimentation Couche-Tard Inc., 77
Alldays plc, 49
Allders plc, 37
Alliance Boots plc (updates Boots Group
    PLC), 83 (upd.)
Allou Health & Beauty Care, Inc., 28
Almacenes Exito S.A., 89
Alpha Airports Group PLC, 77
Alrosa Company Ltd., 62
Alticor Inc., 71 (upd.)
AMAG Group, 102
Amazon.com, Inc., 25; 56 (upd.)
AMCON Distributing Company, 99
AMERCO, 67 (upd.)
American Coin Merchandising, Inc., 28;
    74 (upd.)
American Eagle Outfitters, Inc., 24; 55
    (upd.)
American Furniture Company, Inc., 21
American Girl, Inc., 69 (upd.)
American Stores Company, 22 (upd.)
AmeriSource Health Corporation, 37
    (upd.)
Ames Department Stores, Inc., 9; 30
    (upd.)
Amscan Holdings, Inc., 61
Amway Corporation, 13; 30 (upd.)
The Anderson-DuBose Company, 60
The Andersons, Inc., 31
AnnTaylor Stores Corporation, 13; 37
    (upd.); 67 (upd.)
Anton Schlecker, 102
Appliance Recycling Centers of America,
    Inc., 42
Arbor Drugs Inc., 12
Arcadia Group plc, 28 (upd.)
Army and Air Force Exchange Service, 39
Art Van Furniture, Inc., 28
ASDA Group plc, 28 (upd.)
Ashworth, Inc., 26
Au Printemps S.A., V
Audio King Corporation, 24
Authentic Fitness Corporation, 20; 51
    (upd.)
Auto Value Associates, Inc., 25
Autobytel Inc., 47
AutoNation, Inc., 50
AutoTrader.com, L.L.C., 91
AutoZone, Inc., 9; 31 (upd.)
AVA AG (Allgemeine Handelsgesellschaft
    der Verbraucher AG), 33
Aveda Corporation, 24
Aviall, Inc., 73
Aviation Sales Company, 41
AWB Ltd., 56
B. Dalton Bookseller Inc., 25
Babbage's, Inc., 10
Baby Superstore, Inc., 15
Baccarat, 24
Bachman's Inc., 22
Bailey Nurseries, Inc., 57
Ball Horticultural Company 78
Banana Republic Inc., 25
Bare Escentuals, Inc., 91

Barnes & Noble, Inc., 10; 30 (upd.); 75
    (upd.)
Barnett Inc., 28
Barneys New York Inc., 28; 104 (upd.)
Barrett-Jackson Auction Company L.L.C.,
    88
Bass Pro Shops, Inc., 42
Baumax AG, 75
Beacon Roofing Supply, Inc., 75
Bear Creek Corporation, 38
Bearings, Inc., 13
Beate Uhse AG, 96
bebe stores, inc., 31; 103 (upd.)
Bed Bath & Beyond Inc., 13; 41 (upd.)
Belk Stores Services, Inc., V; 19 (upd.)
Belk, Inc., 72 (upd.)
Ben Bridge Jeweler, Inc., 60
Benetton Group S.p.A., 10; 67 (upd.)
Berean Christian Stores, 96
Bergdorf Goodman Inc., 52
Bergen Brunswig Corporation, V; 13
    (upd.)
Bernard Chaus, Inc., 27
Best Buy Co., Inc., 9; 23 (upd.); 63
    (upd.)
Bestseller A/S, 90
Betsy Ann Candies, Inc., 105
Bhs plc, 17
Bidvest Group Ltd., 106
Big A Drug Stores Inc., 79
Big Dog Holdings, Inc., 45
Big 5 Sporting Goods Corporation, 55
The Big Food Group plc, 68 (upd.)
Big Lots, Inc., 50
Big O Tires, Inc., 20
Birkenstock Footprint Sandals, Inc., 42
    (upd.)
Birthdays Ltd., 70
Black Box Corporation, 20; 96 (upd.)
Blacks Leisure Group plc, 39
Blair Corporation, 25; 31 (upd.)
Blish-Mize Co., 95
Blokker Holding B.V., 84
Bloomingdale's Inc., 12
Blue Nile Inc., 61
Blue Square Israel Ltd., 41
Bluefly, Inc., 60
BlueLinx Holdings Inc., 97
Blyth Industries, Inc., 18
The Body Shop International PLC, 11
The Bombay Company, Inc., 10; 71
    (upd.)
The Bon Marché, Inc., 23
The Bon-Ton Stores, Inc., 16; 50 (upd.)
Booker Cash & Carry Ltd., 68 (upd.)
Books-A-Million, Inc., 14; 41 (upd.); 96
    (upd.)
Bookspan, 86
The Boots Company PLC, V; 24 (upd.)
Borders Group, Inc., 15; 43 (upd.)
Boscov's Department Store, Inc., 31
Boss Holdings, Inc., 97
Boulanger S.A., 102
Bowlin Travel Centers, Inc., 99
Bozzuto's, Inc., 13
Bradlees Discount Department Store
    Company, 12
Brambles Industries Limited, 42

Bricorama S.A., 68
Brioni Roman Style S.p.A., 67
Brodart Company, 84
Broder Bros. Co., 38
Bronner Display & Sign Advertising, Inc., 82
Brooks Brothers Inc., 22
Brookstone, Inc., 18
Brown Shoe Company, Inc., 68 (upd.)
Brunswick Corporation, 77 (upd.)
The Buckle, Inc., 18
Buhrmann NV, 41
Build-A-Bear Workshop Inc., 62
Building Materials Holding Corporation, 52
Burdines, Inc., 60
Burlington Coat Factory Warehouse Corporation, 10; 60 (upd.)
Burt's Bees, Inc., 58
The Burton Group plc, V
Buttrey Food & Drug Stores Co., 18
buy.com, Inc., 46
C&A, V; 40 (upd.)
C&J Clark International Ltd., 52
Cabela's Inc., 26; 68 (upd.)
Cablevision Electronic Instruments, Inc., 32
Cache Incorporated, 30
Cactus S.A., 90
Caffyns PLC, 105
Caldor Inc., 12
Calloway's Nursery, Inc., 51
Camaïeu S.A., 72
Camelot Music, Inc., 26
Campeau Corporation, V
Campmor, Inc., 104
Campo Electronics, Appliances & Computers, Inc., 16
Car Toys, Inc., 67
The Carphone Warehouse Group PLC, 83
Carrefour SA, 10; 27 (upd.); 64 (upd.)
Carson Pirie Scott & Company, 15
Carter Hawley Hale Stores, Inc., V
Carter Lumber Company, 45
Cartier Monde, 29
Casas Bahia Comercial Ltda., 75
Casey's General Stores, Inc., 19; 83 (upd.)
Castorama-Dubois Investissements SCA, 104 (upd.)
Castro Model Ltd., 86
Casual Corner Group, Inc., 43
Casual Male Retail Group, Inc., 52
Catherines Stores Corporation, 15
Cato Corporation, 14
CDW Computer Centers, Inc., 16
Celebrate Express, Inc., 70
Celebrity, Inc., 22
CellStar Corporation, 83
Cencosud S.A., 69
Central European Distribution Corporation, 75
Central Garden & Pet Company, 23
Cenveo Inc., 71 (upd.)
Chadwick's of Boston, Ltd., 29
Charlotte Russe Holding, Inc., 35; 90 (upd.)
Charming Shoppes, Inc., 38
Chas. Levy Company LLC, 60

Cherry Brothers LLC, 105
ChevronTexaco Corporation, 47 (upd.)
Chiasso Inc., 53
The Children's Place Retail Stores, Inc., 37; 86 (upd.)
China Nepstar Chain Drugstore Ltd., 97
Chongqing Department Store Company Ltd., 105
Christian Dior S.A., 49 (upd.)
Christopher & Banks Corporation, 42
Cifra, S.A. de C.V., 12
The Circle K Company, 20 (upd.)
Circuit City Stores, Inc., 9; 29 (upd.); 65 (upd.)
Clare Rose Inc., 68
Clinton Cards plc, 39
The Clothestime, Inc., 20
CML Group, Inc., 10
Co-operative Group (CWS) Ltd., 51
Coach, Inc., 45 (upd.); 99 (upd.)
Coborn's, Inc., 30
Coinmach Laundry Corporation, 20
Coldwater Creek Inc., 21; 74 (upd.)
Cole National Corporation, 13; 76 (upd.)
Cole's Quality Foods, Inc., 68
Coles Group Limited, V; 20 (upd.); 85 (upd.)
Collectors Universe, Inc., 48
Columbia House Company, 69
Comdisco, Inc., 9
Compagnie Financière Sucres et Denrées S.A., 60
Companhia Brasileira de Distribuiçao, 76
CompUSA, Inc., 10
Computerland Corp., 13
Concepts Direct, Inc., 39
Conn's, Inc., 67
The Container Store, 36
Controladora Comercial Mexicana, S.A. de C.V., 36
CoolSavings, Inc., 77
Coop Schweiz Genossenschaftsverband, 48
Coppel, S.A. de C.V., 82
Corby Distilleries Limited, 14
Corporate Express, Inc., 22; 47 (upd.)
Cortefiel S.A., 64
The Cosmetic Center, Inc., 22
Cost Plus, Inc., 27
Costco Wholesale Corporation, V; 43 (upd.); 105 (upd.)
Cotter & Company, V
County Seat Stores Inc., 9
Courts Plc, 45
CPI Corp., 38
Crate and Barrel, 9
Croscill, Inc., 42
CROSSMARK, 79
Crowley, Milner & Company, 19
Crown Books Corporation, 21
Cumberland Farms, Inc., 17; 84 (upd.)
CVS Corporation, 45 (upd.)
D&H Distributing Co., 95
Daffy's Inc., 26
The Daiei, Inc., V; 17 (upd.); 41 (upd.)
The Daimaru, Inc., V; 42 (upd.)
Dairy Farm International Holdings Ltd., 97

Dairy Mart Convenience Stores, Inc., 25 (upd.)
Daisytek International Corporation, 18
Damark International, Inc., 18
Dart Group Corporation, 16
Darty S.A., 27
David Jones Ltd., 60
David's Bridal, Inc., 33
Dayton Hudson Corporation, V; 18 (upd.)
Deb Shops, Inc., 16; 76 (upd.)
Debenhams Plc, 28; 101 (upd.)
Deli Universal NV, 66
dELiA*s Inc., 29
Department 56, Inc., 34 (upd.)
Designer Holdings Ltd., 20
Deveaux S.A., 41
DFS Group Ltd., 66
Dick's Sporting Goods, Inc., 59
Diesel SpA, 40
Digital River, Inc., 50
Dillard Department Stores, Inc., V; 16 (upd.)
Dillard's Inc., 68 (upd.)
Dillon Companies Inc., 12
Discount Auto Parts, Inc., 18
Discount Drug Mart, Inc., 14
Dixons Group plc, V; 19 (upd.); 49 (upd.)
Do it Best Corporation, 30; 104 (upd.)
Dollar General Corporation, 106
Dollar Tree Stores, Inc., 23; 62 (upd.)
Donna Karan International Inc., 56 (upd.)
Dorian Drake International Inc., 96
Dreams Inc., 97
The Dress Barn, Inc., 24; 55 (upd.)
Drs. Foster & Smith, Inc., 62
Drug Emporium, Inc., 12
DSW Inc., 73
Du Pareil au Même, 43
Duane Reade Holding Corp., 21
Duckwall-ALCO Stores, Inc., 24; 105 (upd.)
Dunham's Athleisure Corporation, 98
Dunnes Stores Ltd., 58
Duron Inc., 72
Duty Free International, Inc., 11
Dylan's Candy Bar, LLC, 99
Dylex Limited, 29
E-Z Serve Corporation, 17
Eagle Hardware & Garden, Inc., 16
Eastman Kodak Company, III; 7 (upd.); 36 (upd.); 91 (upd.)
easyhome Ltd., 105
eBay Inc., 32
Eckerd Corporation, 9; 32 (upd.)
Eddie Bauer Holdings, Inc., 9; 36 (upd.); 87 (upd.)
Edgars Consolidated Stores Ltd., 66
Edward Hines Lumber Company, 68
Egghead.com, Inc., 31 (upd.)
Eileen Fisher Inc., 61
El Corte Inglés Group, V
El Puerto de Liverpool, S.A.B. de C.V., 97
The Elder-Beerman Stores Corp., 10; 63 (upd.)
Electrocomponents PLC, 50

Electronics Boutique Holdings Corporation, 72
Elephant Pharmacy, Inc., 83
Ellett Brothers, Inc., 17
EMI Group plc, 22 (upd.); 81 (upd.)
Empresas Almacenes Paris S.A., 71
Encho Company Ltd., 104
Ermenegildo Zegna SpA, 63
ESCADA AG, 71
The Estée Lauder Companies Inc., 9; 30 (upd.); 93 (upd.)
Etablissements Franz Colruyt N.V., 68
Ethan Allen Interiors, Inc., 39 (upd.)
EToys, Inc., 37
Euromarket Designs Inc., 31 (upd.); 99 (upd.)
Evans, Inc., 30
Eye Care Centers of America, Inc., 69
EZCORP Inc., 43
F.W. Webb Company, 95
The F. Dohmen Co., 77
Family Christian Stores, Inc., 51
Family Dollar Stores, Inc., 13; 62 (upd.)
Fannie May Confections Brands, Inc., 80
Farmacias Ahumada S.A., 72
Fastenal Company, 14; 42 (upd.); 99 (upd.)
Faultless Starch/Bon Ami Company, 55
Fay's Inc., 17
Federated Department Stores, Inc., 9; 31 (upd.)
Fenaco, 86
Fielmann AG, 31
Fila Holding S.p.A., 20; 52 (upd.)
Finarte Casa d'Aste S.p.A., 93
Findel plc, 60
Fingerhut Companies, Inc., 9; 36 (upd.)
The Finish Line, Inc., 29; 68 (upd.)
Finlay Enterprises, Inc., 16; 76 (upd.)
Finning International Inc., 69
First Cash Financial Services, Inc., 57
Fisher Auto Parts, Inc., 104
Fleming Companies, Inc., 17 (upd.)
Florsheim Shoe Group Inc., 9; 31 (upd.)
FNAC, 21
Follett Corporation, 12
Foot Locker, Inc., 68 (upd.)
Footstar, Incorporated, 24
Forever 21, Inc., 84
Fortunoff Fine Jewelry and Silverware Inc., 26
The Forzani Group Ltd., 79
Foxworth-Galbraith Lumber Company, 91
Frank's Nursery & Crafts, Inc., 12
Fred Meyer Stores, Inc., V; 20 (upd.); 64 (upd.)
Fred's, Inc., 23; 62 (upd.)
Frederick Atkins Inc., 16
Frederick's of Hollywood, Inc., 59 (upd.)
Freeze.com LLC, 77
Fretter, Inc., 10
Friedman's Inc., 29
Fruth Pharmacy, Inc., 66
Fry's Electronics, Inc., 68
FTD Group, Inc., 99 (upd.)
Funco, Inc., 20
Future Shop Ltd., 62
G&K Holding S.A., 95

G.I. Joe's, Inc., 30
Gadzooks, Inc., 18
Gaiam, Inc., 41
Galeries Lafayette S.A., V; 23 (upd.)
Galiform PLC, 103
Galyan's Trading Company, Inc., 47
GameStop Corp., 69 (upd.)
Gander Mountain, Inc., 20; 90 (upd.)
Gantos, Inc., 17
The Gap, Inc., V; 18 (upd.); 55 (upd.)
Garden Ridge Corporation, 27
Garst Seed Company, Inc., 86
Gart Sports Company, 24
GEHE AG, 27
General Binding Corporation, 10
General Host Corporation, 12
Genesco Inc., 17; 84 (upd.)
Genovese Drug Stores, Inc., 18
Genuine Parts Company, 45 (upd.)
Gerald Stevens, Inc., 37
Gerhard D. Wempe KG, 88
Giant Food Inc., 22 (upd.)
GIB Group, V; 26 (upd.)
Gibbs and Dandy plc, 74
GiFi S.A., 74
Glacier Water Services, Inc., 47
Global Imaging Systems, Inc., 73
Globex Utilidades S.A., 103
GOME Electrical Appliances Holding Ltd., 87
The Good Guys, Inc., 10; 30 (upd.)
Goodwill Industries International, Inc., 16
Goody's Family Clothing, Inc., 20; 64 (upd.)
Gordmans, Inc., 74
Gottschalks, Inc., 18; 91 (upd.)
Grafton Group plc, 104
Grand Piano & Furniture Company, 72
GrandVision S.A., 43
Graybar Electric Company, Inc., 54
The Great Universal Stores plc, V; 19 (upd.)
Griffin Land & Nurseries, Inc., 43
Grossman's Inc., 13
Groupe Alain Manoukian, 55
Groupe Castorama-Dubois Investissements, 23
Groupe DMC (Dollfus Mieg & Cie), 27
Groupe Go Sport S.A., 39
Groupe Lapeyre S.A., 33
Groupe Monnoyeur, 72
Groupe Zannier S.A., 35
Grow Biz International, Inc., 18
Grupo Casa Saba, S.A. de C.V., 39
Grupo Elektra, S.A. de C.V., 39
Grupo Eroski, 64
Grupo Gigante, S.A. de C.V., 34
Grupo Martins, 104
Gruppo Coin S.p.A., 41
GSC Enterprises, Inc., 86
GT Bicycles, 26
GTSI Corp., 57
Gucci Group N.V., 15; 50 (upd.)
Guilbert S.A., 42
Guitar Center, Inc., 29; 68 (upd.)
GUS plc, 47 (upd.)
Gymboree Corporation, 69 (upd.)

H&M Hennes & Mauritz AB, 29; 98 (upd.)
Hahn Automotive Warehouse, Inc., 24
Hale-Halsell Company, 60
Half Price Books, Records, Magazines Inc., 37
Hallmark Cards, Inc., IV; 16 (upd.); 40 (upd.); 87 (upd.)
Hammacher Schlemmer & Company Inc., 21; 72 (upd.)
Hancock Fabrics, Inc., 18
Hankyu Department Stores, Inc., V; 62 (upd.)
Hanna Andersson Corp., 49
Hanover Compressor Company, 59
Hanover Direct, Inc., 36
Harold's Stores, Inc., 22
Harrods Holdings, 47
Harry Winston Inc., 45; 104 (upd.)
Harsco Corporation, 8; 105 (upd.)
Harvey Norman Holdings Ltd., 56
Hasbro, Inc., III; 16 (upd.); 43 (upd.)
Hastings Entertainment, Inc., 29; 104 (upd.)
Haverty Furniture Companies, Inc., 31
Headlam Group plc, 95
Hechinger Company, 12
Heilig-Meyers Company, 14; 40 (upd.)
Heinrich Deichmann-Schuhe GmbH & Co. KG, 88
Helzberg Diamonds, 40
H&M Hennes & Mauritz AB, 29; 98 (upd.)
Henry Modell & Company Inc., 32
Hensley & Company, 64
Hertie Waren- und Kaufhaus GmbH, V
hhgregg Inc., 98
Hibbett Sporting Goods, Inc., 26; 70 (upd.)
Highsmith Inc., 60
Hills Stores Company, 13
Hines Horticulture, Inc., 49
HMV Group plc, 59
Hobby Lobby Stores Inc., 80
The Hockey Company, 34
Holiday RV Superstores, Incorporated, 26
Holt's Cigar Holdings, Inc., 42
The Home Depot, Inc., V; 18 (upd.); 97 (upd.)
Home Hardware Stores Ltd., 62
Home Interiors & Gifts, Inc., 55
Home Product Center plc, 104
Home Retail Group plc, 91
Home Shopping Network, Inc., V; 25 (upd.)
HomeBase, Inc., 33 (upd.)
Hornbach Holding AG, 98
Hot Topic Inc., 33; 86 (upd.)
House of Fabrics, Inc., 21
House of Fraser PLC, 45
Houston Wire & Cable Company, 97
HSN, 64 (upd.)
Hudson's Bay Company, V; 25 (upd.); 83 (upd.)
Huttig Building Products, Inc., 73
Ihr Platz GmbH + Company KG, 77
IKEA International A/S, V; 26 (upd.)
InaCom Corporation, 13

Indigo Books & Music Inc., 58
Insight Enterprises, Inc., 18
Interbond Corporation of America, 101
Intermix Media, Inc., 83
International Airline Support Group, Inc., 55
Intimate Brands, Inc., 24
Intres B.V., 82
Isetan Company Limited, V; 36 (upd.)
Ito-Yokado Co., Ltd., V; 42 (upd.)
J&R Electronics Inc., 26
J. Baker, Inc., 31
The J. Jill Group Inc., 35; 90 (upd.)
J. C. Penney Company, Inc., V; 18 (upd.); 43 (upd.); 91 (upd.)
J.L. Hammett Company, 72
J. W. Pepper and Son Inc., 86
Jack Schwartz Shoes, Inc., 18
Jacobson Stores Inc., 21
Jalate Inc., 25
James Beattie plc, 43
Jay Jacobs, Inc., 15
Jennifer Convertibles, Inc., 31
Jetro Cash & Carry Enterprises Inc., 38
Jewett-Cameron Trading Company, Ltd., 89
JG Industries, Inc., 15
JJB Sports plc, 32
JM Smith Corporation, 100
Jo-Ann Stores, Inc., 72 (upd.)
Joe's Sports & Outdoor, 98 (upd.)
John Lewis Partnership plc, V; 42 (upd.); 99 (upd.)
Jordan-Kitt Music Inc., 86
Jordano's, Inc., 102
Jumbo S.A., 96
JUSCO Co., Ltd., V
Just For Feet, Inc., 19
Jysk Holding A/S, 100
K & B Inc., 12
K & G Men's Center, Inc., 21
K-tel International, Inc., 21
Karstadt Aktiengesellschaft, V; 19 (upd.)
Kash n' Karry Food Stores, Inc., 20
Kasper A.S.L., Ltd., 40
kate spade LLC, 68
Kaufhof Warenhaus AG, V; 23 (upd.)
Kaufring AG, 35
Kay-Bee Toy Stores, 15
Keys Fitness Products, LP, 83
Kiabi Europe, 66
Kiehl's Since 1851, Inc., 52
Kingfisher plc, V; 24 (upd.); 83 (upd.)
Kinney Shoe Corp., 14
Kirlin's Inc., 98
Kmart Corporation, V; 18 (upd.); 47 (upd.)
Knoll Group Inc., 14
Kohl's Corporation, 9; 30 (upd.); 77 (upd.)
Koninklijke Reesink N.V., 104
Koninklijke Vendex KBB N.V. (Royal Vendex KBB N.V.), 62 (upd.)
Kotobukiya Co., Ltd., V; 56 (upd.)
Krause's Furniture, Inc., 27
Krispy Kreme Doughnuts, Inc., 21; 61 (upd.)
Kruse International, 88

L. and J.G. Stickley, Inc., 50
L. Luria & Son, Inc., 19
L.A. T Sportswear, Inc., 26
L.L. Bean, Inc., 10; 38 (upd.); 91 (upd.)
La Senza Corporation, 66
La-Z-Boy Incorporated, 14; 50 (upd.)
Lab Safety Supply, Inc., 102
Lamonts Apparel, Inc., 15
Lands' End, Inc., 9; 29 (upd.); 82 (upd.)
Lane Bryant, Inc., 64
Lanier Worldwide, Inc., 75
Lanoga Corporation, 62
Laura Ashley Holdings plc, 37 (upd.)
Lazare Kaplan International Inc., 21
Le Chateau Inc., 63
Lechmere Inc., 10
Lechters, Inc., 11; 39 (upd.)
LensCrafters Inc., 23; 76 (upd.)
Leroy Merlin SA, 54
Les Boutiques San Francisco, Inc., 62
Lesco Inc., 19
Leslie's Poolmart, Inc., 18
Leupold & Stevens, Inc., 52
Levenger Company, 63
Levitz Furniture Inc., 15
Lewis Galoob Toys Inc., 16
Lewis-Goetz and Company, Inc., 102
Li & Fung Limited, 59
Liberty Orchards Co., Inc., 89
Life is Good, Inc., 80
Lifetime Brands, Inc., 27; 73 (upd.)
Lillian Vernon Corporation, 12; 35 (upd.); 92 (upd.)
The Limited, Inc., V; 20 (upd.)
Linens 'n Things, Inc., 24; 75 (upd.)
Liquidity Services, Inc., 101
Little Switzerland, Inc., 60
Littleton Coin Company Inc., 82
Littlewoods plc, V; 42 (upd.)
LivePerson, Inc., 91
Liz Claiborne Inc., 8; 25 (upd.); 102 (upd.)
LKQ Corporation, 71
Loehmann's Inc., 24
Lojas Americanas S.A., 77
Lojas Arapuã S.A., 22; 61 (upd.)
London Drugs Ltd., 46
Longs Drug Stores Corporation, V; 25 (upd.); 83 (upd.)
Lookers plc, 71
Lost Arrow Inc., 22
LOT$OFF Corporation, 24
Love's Travel Stops & Country Stores, Inc., 71
Lowe's Companies, Inc., V; 21 (upd.); 81 (upd.)
Ludendo S.A., 88
Lululemon Athletica Inc., 105
Luxottica SpA, 17; 52 (upd.)
Lyfra-S.A./NV, 88
Mac Frugal's Bargains - Closeouts Inc., 17
Mac-Gray Corporation, 44
Mackays Stores Group Ltd., 92
Magazine Luiza S.A., 101
Manheim, 88
Manutan International S.A., 72
Maples Industries, Inc., 83
Marc Ecko Enterprises, Inc., 105

MarineMax, Inc., 30
Marionnaud Parfumeries SA, 51
Marks and Spencer Group p.l.c., V; 24 (upd.); 85 (upd.)
Marks Brothers Jewelers, Inc., 24
Marlin Business Services Corp., 89
Marshall Field's, 63
Marshalls Incorporated, 13
Marui Company Ltd., V; 62 (upd.)
Maruzen Company Ltd., 18; 104 (upd.)
Mary Kay Inc., 9; 30 (upd.); 84 (upd.)
Matalan PLC, 49
Matsuzakaya Company Ltd., V; 64 (upd.)
Mattress Giant Corporation, 103
Maurices Inc., 95
Maus Frères SA, 48
Maverik, Inc., 103
The Maxim Group, 25
The May Department Stores Company, V; 19 (upd.); 46 (upd.)
Mayor's Jewelers, Inc., 41
Mazel Stores, Inc., 29
McCoy Corporation, 58
McGrath RentCorp, 91
McJunkin Corporation, 63
McKesson Corporation, 47 (upd.)
McLane Company, Inc., 13
McNaughton Apparel Group, Inc., 92 (upd.)
MCSi, Inc., 41
Media Arts Group, Inc., 42
Meier & Frank Co., 23
Meijer, Inc., 7; 27 (upd.); 101 (upd.)
Melville Corporation, V
The Men's Wearhouse, Inc., 17; 48 (upd.)
Menard, Inc., 34; 104 (upd.)
Mercantile Stores Company, Inc., V; 19 (upd.)
Mercury Drug Corporation, 70
Merry-Go-Round Enterprises, Inc., 8
Mervyn's California, 10; 39 (upd.)
Metal Management, Inc., 92
Metro AG, 50
Michael C. Fina Co., Inc., 52
Michaels Stores, Inc., 17; 71 (upd.)
Michigan Sporting Goods Distributors, Inc., 72
Micro Warehouse, Inc., 16
MicroAge, Inc., 16
Migros-Genossenschafts-Bund, 68
Milton CAT, Inc., 86
Mitsukoshi Ltd., V; 56 (upd.)
MNS, Ltd., 65
Monoprix S.A., 86
Monrovia Nursery Company, 70
Monsoon plc, 39
Montgomery Ward & Co., Incorporated, V; 20 (upd.)
Moore-Handley, Inc., 39
Morrow Equipment Co. L.L.C., 87
Morse Shoe Inc., 13
Moss Bros Group plc, 51
Mothercare plc, 78 (upd.)
Mothers Work, Inc., 18
Moto Photo, Inc., 45
Mr. Bricolage S.A., 37
MSC Industrial Direct Co., Inc., 71
MTS Inc., 37

Mulberry Group PLC, 71
Musicland Stores Corporation, 9; 38 (upd.)
MWI Veterinary Supply, Inc., 80
Nagasakiya Co., Ltd., V; 69 (upd.)
Nash Finch Company, 65 (upd.)
National Educational Music Co. Ltd., 47
National Home Centers, Inc., 44
National Intergroup, Inc., V
National Record Mart, Inc., 29
National Wine & Spirits, Inc., 49
Natura Cosméticos S.A., 75
Natural Wonders Inc., 14
Navy Exchange Service Command, 31
Nebraska Book Company, Inc., 65
Neckermann.de GmbH, 102
Neff Corp., 32
NeighborCare, Inc., 67 (upd.)
The Neiman Marcus Group, Inc., 12; 49 (upd.); 105 (upd.)
Netflix, Inc., 58
New Look Group plc, 35
Next plc, 29
Nichii Co., Ltd., V
NIKE, Inc., 36 (upd.)
Nine West Group Inc., 11
99¢ Only Stores, 25; 100 (upd.)
Nocibé SA, 54
Noland Company, 35
Noodle Kidoodle, 16
Nordstrom, Inc., V; 18 (upd.); 67 (upd.)
Norelco Consumer Products Co., 26
Norm Thompson Outfitters, Inc., 47
North Pacific Group, Inc., 61
The North West Company, Inc., 12
Norton McNaughton, Inc., 27
Nu Skin Enterprises, Inc., 27; 76 (upd.)
Oakley, Inc., 49 (upd.)
Office Depot, Inc., 8; 23 (upd.); 65 (upd.)
OfficeMax Incorporated, 15; 43 (upd.); 101 (upd.)
Olan Mills, Inc., 62
Old America Stores, Inc., 17
Old Navy, Inc., 70
1-800-FLOWERS.COM, Inc., 26; 102 (upd.)
One Price Clothing Stores, Inc., 20
O'Neal Steel, Inc., 95
The Oppenheimer Group, 76
Orchard Supply Hardware Stores Corporation, 17
Organización Soriana, S.A. de C.V., 35
Orgill, Inc., 99
The Orvis Company, Inc., 28
OshKosh B'Gosh, Inc., 42 (upd.)
Oshman's Sporting Goods, Inc., 17
Ottakar's plc, 64
Otto Group, 106
Otto Versand (GmbH & Co.), V; 15 (upd.); 34 (upd.)
Overstock.com, Inc., 75
Owens & Minor, Inc., 16; 68 (upd.)
P.C. Richard & Son Corp., 23
P.W. Minor and Son, Inc., 100
Pamida Holdings Corporation, 15
The Pampered Chef, Ltd., 18; 78 (upd.)
The Pantry, Inc., 36

The Paradies Shops, Inc., 88
Parisian, Inc., 14
Party City Corporation, 54
Paul Harris Stores, Inc., 18
Pay 'N Pak Stores, Inc., 9
Payless Cashways, Inc., 11; 44 (upd.)
Payless ShoeSource, Inc., 18; 69 (upd.)
PCA International, Inc., 62
PDQ Food Stores, Inc., 79
Pearle Vision, Inc., 13
Peebles Inc., 16; 43 (upd.)
Peet's Coffee & Tea, Inc., 38; 100 (upd.)
Penzeys Spices, Inc., 79
The Pep Boys—Manny, Moe & Jack, 11; 36 (upd.); 81 (upd.)
Petco Animal Supplies, Inc., 29; 74 (upd.)
Petit Bateau, 95
PetMed Express, Inc., 81
Petrie Stores Corporation, 8
PETsMART, Inc., 14; 41 (upd.)
PFSweb, Inc., 73
Phar-Mor Inc., 12
Phones 4u Ltd., 85
Photo-Me International Plc, 83
Pick 'n Pay Stores Ltd., 82
Pier 1 Imports, Inc., 12; 34 (upd.); 95 (upd.)
Piercing Pagoda, Inc., 29
Pilot Corporation, 49
Pinault-Printemps Redoute S.A., 19 (upd.)
Pitman Company, 58
Plow & Hearth, Inc., 104
Polartec LLC, 98 (upd.)
Pomeroy Computer Resources, Inc., 33
Powell's Books, Inc., 40
PPR S.A., 74 (upd.)
Praktiker Bau- und Heimwerkermärkte AG, 103
Praxis Bookstore Group LLC, 90
The Price Company, V
PriceCostco, Inc., 14
PriceSmart, Inc., 71
Pro-Build Holdings Inc., 95 (upd.)
Proffitt's, Inc., 19
Provell Inc., 58 (upd.)
Provigo Inc., 51 (upd.)
Publishers Clearing House, 64 (upd.)
Puig Beauty and Fashion Group S.L., 60
Purina Mills, Inc., 32
Quelle Group, V
QuikTrip Corporation, 36
Quiksilver, Inc., 79 (upd.)
Quill Corporation, 28
QVC Inc., 58 (upd.)
R.C. Willey Home Furnishings, 72
R.H. Macy & Co., Inc., V; 8 (upd.); 30 (upd.)
RadioShack Corporation, 36 (upd.); 101 (upd.)
Rag Shops, Inc., 30
Raley's Inc., 14; 58 (upd.)
Rallye SA, 54
Rapala-Normark Group, Ltd., 30
Ratner Companies, 72
Rautakirja Oy, 104
RDO Equipment Company, 33
Reckitt Benckiser plc, II; 42 (upd.); 91 (upd.)

Recoton Corp., 15
Recreational Equipment, Inc., 18; 71 (upd.)
Red McCombs Automotive Group, 91
Red Wing Shoe Company, Inc., 9; 30 (upd.); 83 (upd.)
Redcats S.A., 102
Redlon & Johnson, Inc., 97
Reeds Jewelers, Inc., 22
Rejuvenation, Inc., 91
Reliance Steel & Aluminum Company, 70 (upd.)
Rent-A-Center, Inc., 45
Rent-Way, Inc., 33; 75 (upd.)
The Republic of Tea, Inc., 105
Restoration Hardware, Inc., 30; 96 (upd.)
Retail Ventures, Inc., 82 (upd.)
Revco D.S., Inc., V
REWE-Zentral AG, 103
REX Stores Corp., 10
Rhodes Inc., 23
Richton International Corporation, 39
Riklis Family Corp., 9
Rinascente S.p.A., 71
Ripley Corp S.A., 102
Rite Aid Corporation, V; 19 (upd.); 63 (upd.)
Ritz Camera Centers, 34
RM Auctions, Inc., 88
Roberds Inc., 19
Rocky Shoes & Boots, Inc., 26
Rogers Communications Inc., 30 (upd.)
RONA, Inc., 73
Ronco Corporation, 15; 80 (upd.)
Rooms To Go Inc., 28
Roots Canada Ltd., 42
Rose's Stores, Inc., 13
Ross Stores, Inc., 17; 43 (upd.); 101 (upd.)
Rosy Blue N.V., 84
Roundy's Inc., 14
Rush Enterprises, Inc., 64
Ryoshoku Ltd., 72
S&K Famous Brands, Inc., 23
S.A.C.I. Falabella, 69
Saks Inc., 24; 41 (upd.)
Sally Beauty Company, Inc., 60
Sam Ash Music Corporation, 30
Sam Levin Inc., 80
Sam's Club, 40
Samuels Jewelers Incorporated, 30
Sanborn Hermanos, S.A., 20
SanomaWSOY Corporation, 51
Sapp Bros Travel Centers, Inc., 105
Savers, Inc., 99 (upd.)
Scheels All Sports Inc., 63
Schmitt Music Company, 40
Schneiderman's Furniture Inc., 28
School Specialty, Inc., 68
Schottenstein Stores Corp., 14
Schultz Sav-O Stores, Inc., 31
Scolari's Food and Drug Company, 102
The Score Board, Inc., 19
Scotty's, Inc., 22
The Scoular Company, 77
SCP Pool Corporation, 39
Seaman Furniture Company, Inc., 32
Sean John Clothing, Inc., 70

Sears plc, V
Sears Roebuck de México, S.A. de C.V.,
  20
Sears, Roebuck and Co., V; 18 (upd.); 56
  (upd.)
SED International Holdings, Inc., 43
Seibu Department Stores, Ltd., V; 42
  (upd.)
Seigle's Home and Building Centers, Inc.,
  41
The Seiyu, Ltd., V; 36 (upd.)
Selfridges Plc, 34
Service Merchandise Company, Inc., V; 19
  (upd.)
7-Eleven, Inc., 32 (upd.)
Seventh Generation, Inc., 73
Shaklee Corporation, 12
The Sharper Image Corporation, 10; 62
  (upd.)
Sheetz, Inc., 85
Sheplers, Inc., 96
The Sherwin-Williams Company, 89
  (upd.)
Shoe Carnival Inc., 14; 72 (upd.)
ShopKo Stores Inc., 21; 58 (upd.)
Shoppers Drug Mart Corporation, 49
Shoppers Food Warehouse Corporation,
  66
SIG plc, 71
Signet Group PLC, 61
skinnyCorp, LLC, 97
SkyMall, Inc., 26
Sleepy's Inc., 32
Smith & Hawken, Ltd., 68
Snapfish, 83
Solo Serve Corporation, 28
Sophus Berendsen A/S, 49
Sound Advice, Inc., 41
Source Interlink Companies, Inc., 75
Southern States Cooperative Incorporated,
  36
Spar Handelsgesellschaft mbH, 35; 103
  (upd.)
Spartan Stores Inc., 66 (upd.)
Spec's Music, Inc., 19
Specsavers Optical Group Ltd., 104
Spector Photo Group N.V., 82
Spiegel, Inc., 10; 27 (upd.)
Sport Chalet, Inc., 16
Sport Supply Group, Inc., 23; 106 (upd.)
Sportmart, Inc., 15
Sports & Recreation, Inc., 17
The Sports Authority, Inc., 16; 43 (upd.)
The Sportsman's Guide, Inc., 36
Stage Stores, Inc., 24; 82 (upd.)
Stanhome Inc., 15
Staple Cotton Cooperative Association
  (Staplcotn), 86
Staples, Inc., 10; 55 (upd.)
Starbucks Corporation, 13; 34 (upd.); 77
  (upd.)
Starcraft Corporation, 30
Stefanel SpA, 63
Stein Mart Inc., 19; 72 (upd.)
Steve & Barry's LLC, 88
Stewart's Shops Corporation, 80
Stinnes AG, 8

The Stop & Shop Companies, Inc., 24
  (upd.)
Storehouse PLC, 16
Strauss Discount Auto, 56
Stride Rite Corporation, 8
The Strober Organization, Inc., 82
Strouds, Inc., 33
Stuller Settings, Inc., 35
Successories, Inc., 30
Sun Television & Appliances Inc., 10
Sunglass Hut International, Inc., 21; 74
  (upd.)
Superdrug Stores PLC, 95
Supreme International Corporation, 27
Sutherland Lumber Company, L.P., 99
Swarovski International Holding AG, 40
The Swiss Colony, Inc., 97
Syms Corporation, 29; 74 (upd.)
Systemax, Inc., 52
Takashimaya Company, Limited, V; 47
  (upd.)
The Talbots, Inc., 11; 31 (upd.); 88
  (upd.)
Target Corporation, 61 (upd.)
Target Stores, 10; 27 (upd.)
Tati SA, 25
Tattered Cover Book Store, 43
Tech Data Corporation, 10; 74 (upd.)
Tengelmann Group, 27
Tesco plc, 24 (upd.); 68 (upd.)
Things Remembered, Inc., 84
Thomsen Greenhouses and Garden
  Center, Incorporated, 65
Thrifty PayLess, Inc., 12
Tiffany & Co., 14; 78 (upd.)
The Timberland Company, 13; 54 (upd.)
Titan Machinery Inc., 103
The TJX Companies, Inc., V; 19 (upd.);
  57 (upd.)
Today's Man, Inc., 20
Tokyu Department Store Co., Ltd., V; 32
  (upd.)
Too, Inc., 61
Topco Associates LLC, 60
Tops Appliance City, Inc., 17
Total Fina Elf S.A., 50 (upd.)
Toys 'R' Us, Inc., V; 18 (upd.); 57 (upd.)
Tractor Supply Company, 57
Trans World Entertainment Corporation,
  68 (upd.)
Travis Boats & Motors, Inc., 37
Travis Perkins plc, 34
Trend-Lines, Inc., 22
True Value Company, 74 (upd.)
TruServ Corporation, 24
Tuesday Morning Corporation, 18; 70
  (upd.)
Tupperware Corporation, 28; 78 (upd.)
TVI, Inc., 15
Tweeter Home Entertainment Group,
  Inc., 30
U.S. Vision, Inc., 66
Ulta Salon, Cosmetics & Fragrance, Inc.,
  93
Ultimate Electronics, Inc., 18; 69 (upd.)
Ultramar Diamond Shamrock
  Corporation, 31 (upd.)
Uni-Marts, Inc., 17

United Rentals, Inc., 34
The United States Shoe Corporation, V
United Stationers Inc., 14
Universal International, Inc., 25
Uny Co., Ltd., V; 49 (upd.)
The Upper Deck Company, LLC, 105
Urban Outfitters, Inc., 14; 74 (upd.)
Uwajimaya, Inc., 60
Vallen Corporation, 45
Valley Media Inc., 35
Value City Department Stores, Inc., 38
Value Merchants Inc., 13
ValueVision International, Inc., 22
Vann's Inc., 105
Vans, Inc., 47 (upd.)
Variety Wholesalers, Inc., 73
VBA - Bloemenveiling Aalsmeer, 88
Venator Group Inc., 35 (upd.)
Vendex International N.V., 13
Venture Stores Inc., 12
The Vermont Country Store, 93
The Vermont Teddy Bear Co., Inc., 36
VF Corporation, 54 (upd.)
Viewpoint International, Inc., 66
Viking Office Products, Inc., 10
Viterra Inc., 105
Vivarte SA, 54 (upd.)
Volcom, Inc., 77
Von Maur, Inc., 64
The Vons Companies, Inc., 7; 28 (upd.);
  103 (upd.)
Vorwerk & Co., 27
W. Atlee Burpee & Co., 27
W.B. Mason Company, 98
W.W. Grainger, Inc., V
Waban Inc., 13
Wacoal Corp., 25
Wal-Mart de Mexico, S.A. de C.V., 35
  (upd.)
Wal-Mart Stores, Inc., V; 8 (upd.); 26
  (upd.); 63 (upd.)
Waldenbooks, 17; 86 (upd.)
Walgreen Co., V; 20 (upd.); 65 (upd.)
Wall Drug Store, Inc., 40
Walter E. Smithe Furniture, Inc., 105
Warners' Stellian Inc., 67
WAXIE Sanitary Supply, 100
Weiner's Stores, Inc., 33
West Marine, Inc., 17; 90 (upd.)
Western Beef, Inc., 22
The Wet Seal, Inc., 18; 70 (upd.)
Weyco Group, Incorporated, 32
WH Smith PLC, V; 42 (upd.)
The White House, Inc., 60
Whitehall Jewellers, Inc., 82 (upd.)
Whole Foods Market, Inc., 20
Wickes Inc., V; 25 (upd.)
Wilco Farm Stores, 93
Wilkinson Hardware Stores Ltd., 80
Williams Scotsman, Inc., 65
Williams-Sonoma, Inc., 17; 44 (upd.);
  103 (upd.)
Wilsons The Leather Experts Inc., 21; 58
  (upd.)
Wilton Products, Inc., 97
Windstream Corporation, 83
Winmark Corporation, 74
Wolohan Lumber Co., 19

Wolverine World Wide, Inc., 59 (upd.)
Woolworth Corporation, V; 20 (upd.)
Woolworths Group plc, 83
World Duty Free Americas, Inc., 29 (upd.)
Yamada Denki Co., Ltd., 85
The Yankee Candle Company, Inc., 37
Yingli Green Energy Holding Company Limited, 103
Young's Market Company, LLC, 32
Younkers, 76 (upd.)
Younkers, Inc., 19
Zale Corporation, 16; 40 (upd.); 91 (upd.)
Zany Brainy, Inc., 31
Zappos.com, Inc., 73
Zara International, Inc., 83
Ziebart International Corporation, 30
Zion's Cooperative Mercantile Institution, 33
Zipcar, Inc., 92
Zones, Inc., 67
Zumiez, Inc., 77

Rubber & Tires

Aeroquip Corporation, 16
Bandag, Inc., 19
The BFGoodrich Company, V
Bridgestone Corporation, V; 21 (upd.); 59 (upd.)
Canadian Tire Corporation, Limited, 71 (upd.)
Carlisle Companies Incorporated, 8
Compagnie Générale des Établissements Michelin, V; 42 (upd.)
Continental AG, V; 56 (upd.)
Continental General Tire Corp., 23
Cooper Tire & Rubber Company, 8; 23 (upd.)
Day International, Inc., 84
Elementis plc, 40 (upd.)
General Tire, Inc., 8
The Goodyear Tire & Rubber Company, V; 20 (upd.); 75 (upd.)
Hankook Tire Company Ltd., 105
The Kelly-Springfield Tire Company, 8
Kumho Tire Company Ltd., 105
Les Schwab Tire Centers, 50
Myers Industries, Inc., 19; 96 (upd.)
Pirelli S.p.A., V; 15 (upd.)
Safeskin Corporation, 18
Sumitomo Rubber Industries, Ltd., V
Trelleborg AB, 93
Tillotson Corp., 15
Treadco, Inc., 19
Ube Industries, Ltd., 38 (upd.)
The Yokohama Rubber Company, Limited, V; 19 (upd.); 91 (upd.)

Telecommunications

A.H. Belo Corporation, 30 (upd.)
Abertis Infraestructuras, S.A., 65
Abril S.A., 95
Acme-Cleveland Corp., 13
ADC Telecommunications, Inc., 10; 89 (upd.)
Adelphia Communications Corporation, 17; 52 (upd.)
Adtran Inc., 22
Advanced Fibre Communications, Inc., 63
AEI Music Network Inc., 35
AirTouch Communications, 11
Alaska Communications Systems Group, Inc., 89
Alcatel S.A., 36 (upd.)
Allbritton Communications Company, 105
Alliance Atlantis Communications Inc., 39
ALLTEL Corporation, 6; 46 (upd.)
América Móvil, S.A. de C.V., 80
American Tower Corporation, 33
Ameritech Corporation, V; 18 (upd.)
Amstrad plc, 48 (upd.)
AO VimpelCom, 48
AOL Time Warner Inc., 57 (upd.)
Arch Wireless, Inc., 39
ARD, 41
ARINC Inc., 98
ARRIS Group, Inc., 89
Ascom AG, 9
Aspect Telecommunications Corporation, 22
Asurion Corporation, 83
AT&T Bell Laboratories, Inc., 13
AT&T Corporation, V; 29 (upd.); 68 (upd.)
AT&T Wireless Services, Inc., 54 (upd.)
Avaya Inc., 104
Basin Electric Power Cooperative, 103
BCE Inc., V; 44 (upd.)
Beasley Broadcast Group, Inc., 51
Belgacom, 6
Bell Atlantic Corporation, V; 25 (upd.)
Bell Canada, 6
BellSouth Corporation, V; 29 (upd.)
Belo Corporation, 98 (upd.)
Bertelsmann A.G., IV; 15 (upd.); 43 (upd.); 91 (upd.)
BET Holdings, Inc., 18
Bharti Tele-Ventures Limited, 75
BHC Communications, Inc., 26
Blackfoot Telecommunications Group, 60
Bonneville International Corporation, 29
Bouygues S.A., I; 24 (upd.); 97 (upd.)
Brasil Telecom Participaçoes S.A., 57
Brightpoint Inc., 18; 106 (upd.)
Brite Voice Systems, Inc., 20
British Broadcasting Corporation Ltd., 7; 21 (upd.); 89 (upd.)
British Columbia Telephone Company, 6
British Telecommunications plc, V; 15 (upd.)
Broadwing Corporation, 70
BT Group plc, 49 (upd.)
C-COR.net Corp., 38
Cable & Wireless HKT, 30 (upd.)
Cable and Wireless plc, V; 25 (upd.)
Cablevision Systems Corporation, 30 (upd.)
CalAmp Corp., 87
The Canadian Broadcasting Corporation (CBC), 37
Canal Plus, 10; 34 (upd.)
CanWest Global Communications Corporation, 35
Capital Radio plc, 35
Carlton Communications PLC, 15; 50 (upd.)
Carolina Telephone and Telegraph Company, 10
The Carphone Warehouse Group PLC, 83
Carrier Access Corporation, 44
CBS Corporation, 28 (upd.)
CBS Television Network, 66 (upd.)
Centel Corporation, 6
Centennial Communications Corporation, 39
Central European Media Enterprises Ltd., 61
Century Communications Corp., 10
Century Telephone Enterprises, Inc., 9; 54 (upd.)
Cesky Telecom, a.s., 64
Chancellor Media Corporation, 24
Channel Four Television Corporation, 93
Charter Communications, Inc., 33
Chello Zone Ltd., 93
China Netcom Group Corporation (Hong Kong) Limited, 73
China Telecom, 50
Chris-Craft Corporation, 9, 31 (upd.); 80 (upd.)
The Christian Broadcasting Network, Inc., 52
Chrysalis Group plc, 40
Chugach Alaska Corporation, 60
Chunghwa Telecom Co., Ltd., 101 (upd.)
CIENA Corporation, 54
Cincinnati Bell, Inc., 6; 105 (upd.)
Citadel Communications Corporation, 35
Citizens Communications Company, 79 (upd.)
Clear Channel Communications, Inc., 23
Clearwire, Inc., 69
Cogent Communications Group, Inc., 55
COLT Telecom Group plc, 41
Comcast Corporation, 24 (upd.)
Comdial Corporation, 21
Commonwealth Telephone Enterprises, Inc., 25
CommScope, Inc., 77
Comsat Corporation, 23
Comtech Telecommunications Corp., 75
Comverse Technology, Inc., 15; 43 (upd.)
Corning Inc., III; 44 (upd.); 90 (upd.)
Corporation for Public Broadcasting, 14; 89 (upd.)
Cox Radio, Inc., 89
Craftmade International, Inc., 44
Cumulus Media Inc., 37
DDI Corporation, 7
Deutsche Telekom AG, V; 48 (upd.)
Dialogic Corporation, 18
Digital Angel Corporation, 106
Directorate General of Telecommunications, 7
DIRECTV, Inc., 38; 75 (upd.)
Discovery Communications, Inc., 42
Dobson Communications Corporation, 63
DSC Communications Corporation, 12
EchoStar Communications Corporation, 35
ECI Telecom Ltd., 18
Egmont Group, 93

eircom plc, 31 (upd.)
Electric Lightwave, Inc., 37
Electromagnetic Sciences Inc., 21
EMBARQ Corporation, 83
Emmis Communications Corporation, 47
Empresas Públicas de Medellín S.A.E.S.P., 91
Energis plc, 47
Entercom Communications Corporation, 58
Entravision Communications Corporation, 41
Equant N.V., 52
Eschelon Telecom, Inc., 72
ESPN, Inc., 56
Eternal Word Television Network, Inc., 57
EXCEL Communications Inc., 18
Executone Information Systems, Inc., 13
Expand SA, 48
Facebook, Inc., 90
FASTWEB S.p.A., 83
Fisher Communications, Inc., 99
4Kids Entertainment Inc., 59
Fox Family Worldwide, Inc., 24
France Telecom S.A., V; 21 (upd.); 99 (upd.)
Frontier Corp., 16
Fuji Television Network Inc., 91
Gannett Co., Inc., 30 (upd.)
Garmin Ltd., 60
General DataComm Industries, Inc., 14
Geotek Communications Inc., 21
Getty Images, Inc., 31
Global Crossing Ltd., 32
Globo Comunicação e Participações S.A., 80
Glu Mobile Inc., 95
Golden Telecom, Inc., 59
Granite Broadcasting Corporation, 42
Gray Communications Systems, Inc., 24
Greater Washington Educational Telecommunication Association, 103
Groupe Vidéotron Ltée., 20
Grupo Televisa, S.A., 18; 54 (upd.)
GTE Corporation, V; 15 (upd.)
Guthy-Renker Corporation, 32
GWR Group plc, 39
Harmonic Inc., 43
Havas, SA, 10
HickoryTech Corporation, 92
Hispanic Broadcasting Corporation, 35
Hong Kong Telecommunications Ltd., 6
Huawei Technologies Company Ltd., 87
Hubbard Broadcasting Inc., 24; 79 (upd.)
Hughes Electronics Corporation, 25
Hungarian Telephone and Cable Corp., 75
IDB Communications Group, Inc., 11
IDT Corporation, 34; 99 (upd.)
Illinois Bell Telephone Company, 14
Indiana Bell Telephone Company, Incorporated, 14
PT Indosat Tbk, 93
Infineon Technologies AG, 50
Infinity Broadcasting Corporation, 11
InfoSonics Corporation, 81
Interactive Intelligence Inc., 106

InterDigital Communications Corporation, 61
Iowa Telecommunications Services, Inc., 85
ITV plc, 104 (upd.)
IXC Communications, Inc., 29
Jacor Communications, Inc., 23
Jones Intercable, Inc., 21
j2 Global Communications, Inc., 75
Koninklijke PTT Nederland NV, V
Landmark Communications, Inc., 55 (upd.)
LCC International, Inc., 84
LCI International, Inc., 16
LDDS-Metro Communications, Inc., 8
Leap Wireless International, Inc., 69
Level 3 Communications, Inc., 67
LIN Broadcasting Corp., 9
Lincoln Telephone & Telegraph Company, 14
LodgeNet Interactive Corporation, 28; 106 (upd.)
Loral Space & Communications Ltd., 54 (upd.)
MacNeil/Lehrer Productions, 87
Magyar Telekom Rt. 78
Manitoba Telecom Services, Inc., 61
Mannesmann AG, 38
MasTec, Inc., 19; 55 (upd.)
McCaw Cellular Communications, Inc., 6
MCI WorldCom, Inc., V; 27 (upd.)
McLeodUSA Incorporated, 32
Mediacom Communications Corporation, 69
Mercury Communications, Ltd., 7
Metrocall, Inc., 41
Metromedia Companies, 14
Métropole Télévision, 33
Métropole Télévision S.A., 76 (upd.)
MFS Communications Company, Inc., 11
Michigan Bell Telephone Co., 14
MIH Limited, 31
MITRE Corporation, 26
Mobile Telecommunications Technologies Corp., 18
Mobile TeleSystems OJSC, 59
Modern Times Group AB, 36
The Montana Power Company, 44 (upd.)
Motorola, Inc., II; 11 (upd.); 34 (upd.); 93 (upd.)
MTN Group Ltd., 106
Multimedia, Inc., 11
National Broadcasting Company, Inc., 28 (upd.)
National Grid USA, 51 (upd.)
National Weather Service, 91
NCR Corporation, III; 6 (upd.); 30 (upd.); 90 (upd.)
NetCom Systems AB, 26
NeuStar, Inc., 81
Nevada Bell Telephone Company, 14
New Valley Corporation, 17
Newcom Group, 104
Nexans SA, 54
Nexstar Broadcasting Group, Inc., 73
Nextel Communications, Inc., 27 (upd.)
Nippon Telegraph and Telephone Corporation, V; 51 (upd.)

Nokia Corporation, 77 (upd.)
Norstan, Inc., 16
Nortel Networks Corporation, 36 (upd.)
Northern Telecom Limited, V
NTL Inc., 65
NTN Buzztime, Inc., 86
NYNEX Corporation, V
Octel Messaging, 14; 41 (upd.)
Ohio Bell Telephone Company, 14
Olivetti S.p.A., 34 (upd.)
Orange S.A., 84
Österreichische Post- und Telegraphenverwaltung, V
Pacific Internet Limited, 87
Pacific Telecom, Inc., 6
Pacific Telesis Group, V
Paging Network Inc., 11
PanAmSat Corporation, 46
Paxson Communications Corporation, 33
Petry Media Corporation, 102
The Phoenix Media/Communications Group, 91
PictureTel Corp., 10; 27 (upd.)
Portugal Telecom SGPS S.A., 69
Posti- ja Telelaitos, 6
Premiere Radio Networks, Inc., 102
Price Communications Corporation, 42
ProSiebenSat.1 Media AG, 54
Publishing and Broadcasting Limited, 54
Qatar Telecom QSA, 87
QUALCOMM Incorporated, 20; 47 (upd.)
QVC Network Inc., 9
Qwest Communications International, Inc., 37
Raycom Media, Inc., 106
RCN Corporation, 70
Regent Communications, Inc., 87
Research in Motion Limited, 54; 106 (upd.)
RMH Teleservices, Inc., 42
Rochester Telephone Corporation, 6
Rockwell Collins, 106
Rogers Communications Inc., 30 (upd.)
Rostelecom Joint Stock Co., 99
Royal KPN N.V., 30
Rural Cellular Corporation, 43
Saga Communications, Inc., 27
Salem Communications Corporation, 97
Sawtek Inc., 43 (upd.)
SBC Communications Inc., 32 (upd.)
Schweizerische Post-, Telefon- und Telegrafen-Betriebe, V
Scientific-Atlanta, Inc., 6; 45 (upd.)
Seat Pagine Gialle S.p.A., 47
Securicor Plc, 45
Shenandoah Telecommunications Company, 89
Sinclair Broadcast Group, Inc., 25
Sirius Satellite Radio, Inc., 69
Sirti S.p.A., 76
Società Finanziaria Telefonica per Azioni, V
Softbank Corporation, 77 (upd.)
Sonera Corporation, 50
Southern New England Telecommunications Corporation, 6
Southwestern Bell Corporation, V

Spanish Broadcasting System, Inc., 41
Spelling Entertainment, 35 (upd.)
Sprint Corporation, 9; 46 (upd.)
Starent Networks Corp., 106
StarHub Ltd., 77
StrataCom, Inc., 16
Swedish Telecom, V
Swisscom AG, 58
Sycamore Networks, Inc., 45
Syniverse Holdings Inc., 97
SynOptics Communications, Inc., 10
T-Netix, Inc., 46
Talk America Holdings, Inc., 70
TDC A/S, 63
Tekelec, 83
Telcordia Technologies, Inc., 59
Tele Norte Leste Participações S.A., 80
Telecom Argentina S.A., 63
Telecom Australia, 6
Telecom Corporation of New Zealand Limited, 54
Telecom Eireann, 7
Telecom Italia Mobile S.p.A., 63
Telecom Italia S.p.A., 43
Telefonaktiebolaget LM Ericsson, V; 46 (upd.)
Telefónica de Argentina S.A., 61
Telefónica S.A., V; 46 (upd.)
Telefonos de Mexico S.A. de C.V., 14; 63 (upd.)
Telekom Malaysia Bhd, 76
Telekomunikacja Polska SA, 50
Telenor ASA, 69
Telephone and Data Systems, Inc., 9
Télévision Française 1, 23
TeliaSonera AB, 57 (upd.)
Tellabs, Inc., 11; 40 (upd.)
Telkom S.A. Ltd., 106
Telstra Corporation Limited, 50
Terremark Worldwide, Inc., 99
Thomas Crosbie Holdings Limited, 81
Tiscali SpA, 48
The Titan Corporation, 36
Tollgrade Communications, Inc., 44
TV Azteca, S.A. de C.V., 39
U.S. Satellite Broadcasting Company, Inc., 20
U S West, Inc., V; 25 (upd.)
U.S. Cellular Corporation, 9; 31 (upd.); 88 (upd.)
UFA TV & Film Produktion GmbH, 80
United Pan-Europe Communications NV, 47
United Telecommunications, Inc., V
United Video Satellite Group, 18
Univision Communications Inc., 24; 83 (upd.)
USA Interactive, Inc., 47 (upd.)
USA Mobility Inc., 97 (upd.)
UTStarcom, Inc., 77
Verizon Communications Inc. 43 (upd.); 78 (upd.)
ViaSat, Inc., 54
Vivendi Universal S.A., 46 (upd.)
Vodacom Group Pty. Ltd., 106
Vodafone Group Plc, 11; 36 (upd.); 75 (upd.)
Vonage Holdings Corp., 81

The Walt Disney Company, II; 6 (upd.); 30 (upd.); 63 (upd.)
Wanadoo S.A., 75
Watkins-Johnson Company, 15
The Weather Channel Companies, 52
West Corporation, 42
Western Union Financial Services, Inc., 54
Western Wireless Corporation, 36
Westwood One Inc., 23; 106 (upd.)
Williams Communications Group, Inc., 34
The Williams Companies, Inc., 31 (upd.)
Wipro Limited, 43; 106 (upd.)
Wisconsin Bell, Inc., 14
Working Assets Funding Service, 43
Worldwide Pants Inc., 97
XM Satellite Radio Holdings, Inc., 69
Young Broadcasting Inc., 40
Zain, 102
Zed Group, 93
Zoom Technologies, Inc., 53 (upd.)

Textiles & Apparel

Abercrombie & Fitch Company, 35 (upd.); 75 (upd.)
Adams Childrenswear Ltd., 95
adidas Group AG, 14; 33 (upd.); 75 (upd.)
Adolfo Dominguez S.A., 72
Aéropostale, Inc., 89
Alba-Waldensian, Inc., 30
Albany International Corp., 8
Alexandra plc, 88
Algo Group Inc., 24
Alpargatas S.A.I.C., 87
American & Efird, Inc., 82
American Apparel, Inc., 90
American Safety Razor Company, 20
Amoskeag Company, 8
Andin International, Inc., 100
Angelica Corporation, 15; 43 (upd.)
Annin & Co., 100
AR Accessories Group, Inc., 23
Aris Industries, Inc., 16
ASICS Corporation, 57
AstenJohnson Inc., 90
The Athlete's Foot Brands LLC, 84
Authentic Fitness Corporation, 20; 51 (upd.)
Babolat VS, S.A., 97
Banana Republic Inc., 25
Bardwil Industries Inc., 98
Bata Ltd., 62
Bauer Hockey, Inc., 104
bebe stores, inc., 31; 103 (upd.)
Benetton Group S.p.A., 10; 67 (upd.)
Betsey Johnson Inc., 100
Bill Blass Ltd., 32
Birkenstock Footprint Sandals, Inc., 12
Blair Corporation, 25
Body Glove International LLC, 88
Boss Holdings, Inc., 97
Brazos Sportswear, Inc., 23
Brioni Roman Style S.p.A., 67
Brooks Brothers Inc., 22
Brooks Sports Inc., 32
Brown Group, Inc., V; 20 (upd.)
Brunschwig & Fils Inc., 96

Bugle Boy Industries, Inc., 18
Burberry Group plc, 17; 41 (upd.); 92 (upd.)
Burke Mills, Inc., 66
Burlington Industries, Inc., V; 17 (upd.)
Calcot Ltd., 33
Calvin Klein, Inc., 22; 55 (upd.)
Candie's, Inc., 31
Canstar Sports Inc., 16
Capel Incorporated, 45
Capezio/Ballet Makers Inc., 62
Carhartt, Inc., 30, 77 (upd.)
Cato Corporation, 14
Chargeurs International, 6; 21 (upd.)
Charles Vögele Holding AG, 82
Charming Shoppes, Inc., 8
Cherokee Inc., 18
CHF Industries, Inc., 84
Chic by H.I.S, Inc., 20
Chico's FAS, Inc., 45
Chorus Line Corporation, 30
Christian Dior S.A., 19; 49 (upd.)
Christopher & Banks Corporation, 42
Cia Hering, 72
Cintas Corporation, 51 (upd.)
Citi Trends, Inc., 80
Claire's Stores, Inc., 17
Coach Leatherware, 10
Coats plc, V; 44 (upd.)
Collins & Aikman Corporation, 13
Columbia Sportswear Company, 19; 41 (upd.)
Companhia de Tecidos Norte de Minas - Coteminas, 77
Compañia Industrial de Parras, S.A. de C.V. (CIPSA), 84
Concord Fabrics, Inc., 16
Cone Mills LLC, 8; 67 (upd.)
Converse Inc., 31 (upd.)
Cotton Incorporated, 46
Courtaulds plc, V; 17 (upd.)
Crocs, Inc., 80
Croscill, Inc., 42
Crown Crafts, Inc., 16
Crystal Brands, Inc., 9
Culp, Inc., 29
Cygne Designs, Inc., 25
Damartex S.A., 98
Dan River Inc., 35; 86 (upd.)
Danskin, Inc., 12; 62 (upd.)
Deckers Outdoor Corporation, 22; 98 (upd.)
Delta and Pine Land Company, 59
Delta Woodside Industries, Inc., 8; 30 (upd.)
Designer Holdings Ltd., 20
The Dixie Group, Inc., 20; 80 (upd.)
Dogi International Fabrics S.A., 52
Dolce & Gabbana SpA, 62
Dominion Textile Inc., 12
Donna Karan International Inc., 15; 56 (upd.)
Donnkenny, Inc., 17
Dooney & Bourke Inc., 84
Duck Head Apparel Company, Inc., 42
Dunavant Enterprises, Inc., 54
Dyersburg Corporation, 21
Eastland Shoe Corporation, 82

Ecco Sko A/S, 62
The Echo Design Group, Inc., 68
Edison Brothers Stores, Inc., 9
Eileen Fisher Inc., 61
Ellen Tracy, Inc., 55
Ennis, Inc., 21; 97 (upd.)
Eram SA, 51
Ermenegildo Zegna SpA, 63
ESCADA AG, 71
Esprit de Corp., 8; 29 (upd.)
Etam Developpement SA, 44
Etienne Aigner AG, 52
Evans, Inc., 30
Fab Industries, Inc., 27
Fabri-Centers of America Inc., 16
Fat Face Ltd., 68
Fieldcrest Cannon, Inc., 9; 31 (upd.)
Fila Holding S.p.A., 20
Fishman & Tobin Inc., 102
Florsheim Shoe Group Inc., 31 (upd.)
Foot Petals L.L.C., 95
Fossil, Inc., 17
Fred Perry Limited, 105
Frederick's of Hollywood Inc., 16
French Connection Group plc, 41
Fruit of the Loom, Inc., 8; 25 (upd.)
Fubu, 29
G&K Services, Inc., 16
G-III Apparel Group, Ltd., 22
Galey & Lord, Inc., 20; 66 (upd.)
Garan, Inc., 16; 64 (upd.)
Gerry Weber International AG, 63
Gianni Versace S.p.A., 22; 106 (upd.)
Gildan Activewear, Inc., 81
Giorgio Armani S.p.A., 45
The Gitano Group, Inc. 8
GoldToeMoretz, LLC, 102
Gottschalks, Inc., 18; 91 (upd.)
Grandoe Corporation, 98
Great White Shark Enterprises, Inc., 89
Greenwood Mills, Inc., 14
Grendene S.A., 102
Groupe DMC (Dollfus Mieg & Cie), 27
Groupe Yves Saint Laurent, 23
Gucci Group N.V., 15; 50 (upd.)
Guess, Inc., 15; 68 (upd.)
Guilford Mills Inc., 8; 40 (upd.)
Gymboree Corporation, 15; 69 (upd.)
Haggar Corporation, 19; 78 (upd.)
Hampshire Group Ltd., 82
Hampton Industries, Inc., 20
Hanesbrands Inc., 98
Happy Kids Inc., 30
Hartmarx Corporation, 8
The Hartstone Group plc, 14
HCI Direct, Inc., 55
Healthtex, Inc., 17
Heelys, Inc., 87
Helly Hansen ASA, 25
Hermès S.A., 14
The Hockey Company, 34
Horween Leather Company, 83
Hugo Boss AG, 48
Hummel International A/S, 68
Hyde Athletic Industries, Inc., 17
I.C. Isaacs & Company, 31
Industria de Diseño Textil S.A., 64
Innovo Group Inc., 83

Interface, Inc., 8; 29 (upd.); 76 (upd.)
Irwin Toy Limited, 14
Items International Airwalk Inc., 17
J. Crew Group, Inc., 12; 34 (upd.); 88 (upd.)
JLM Couture, Inc., 64
Jockey International, Inc., 12; 34 (upd.); 77 (upd.)
The John David Group plc, 90
John Lewis Partnership plc, V; 42 (upd.); 99 (upd.)
Johnston Industries, Inc., 15
Jones Apparel Group, Inc., 39 (upd.)
Jordache Enterprises, Inc., 23
Jos. A. Bank Clothiers, Inc., 31; 104 (upd.)
JPS Textile Group, Inc., 28
Juicy Couture, Inc., 80
K-Swiss, Inc., 33; 89 (upd.)
Karl Kani Infinity, Inc., 49
Kellwood Company, 8; 85 (upd.)
Kenneth Cole Productions, Inc., 25
Kinney Shoe Corp., 14
Klaus Steilmann GmbH & Co. KG, 53
Koret of California, Inc., 62
L.A. Gear, Inc., 8; 32 (upd.)
L.L. Bean, Inc., 10; 38 (upd.); 91 (upd.)
LaCrosse Footwear, Inc., 18; 61 (upd.)
Laura Ashley Holdings plc, 13
Lee Apparel Company, Inc., 8
The Leslie Fay Company, Inc., 8; 39 (upd.)
Levi Strauss & Co., V; 16 (upd.); 102 (upd.)
Liz Claiborne Inc., 8; 25 (upd.); 102 (upd.)
Loewe S.A., 104
London Fog Industries, Inc., 29
Lost Arrow Inc., 22
Lululemon Athletica Inc., 105
Maidenform, Inc., 20; 59 (upd.)
Malden Mills Industries, Inc., 16
Maples Industries, Inc., 83
Marc Ecko Enterprises, Inc., 105
Mariella Burani Fashion Group, 92
Marzotto S.p.A., 20; 67 (upd.)
Maurices Inc., 95
Milliken & Co., V; 17 (upd.); 82 (upd.)
Miroglio SpA, 86
Mitsubishi Rayon Co., Ltd., V
Mossimo, Inc., 27; 96 (upd.)
Mothercare plc, 17; 78 (upd.)
Movie Star Inc., 17
Mulberry Group PLC, 71
Naf Naf SA, 44
Nautica Enterprises, Inc., 18; 44 (upd.)
New Balance Athletic Shoe, Inc., 25; 68 (upd.)
Nicole Miller, 98
NIKE, Inc., V; 8 (upd.); 75 (upd.)
Nine West Group, Inc., 39 (upd.)
Nitches, Inc., 53
The North Face Inc., 18; 78 (upd.)
Oakley, Inc., 18
Orange 21 Inc., 103
Ormat Technologies, Inc., 87
OshKosh B'Gosh, Inc., 9; 42 (upd.)
Oxford Industries, Inc., 8; 84 (upd.)

Pacific Sunwear of California, Inc., 28; 104 (upd.)
Peek & Cloppenburg KG, 46
Pendleton Woolen Mills, Inc., 42
The Pentland Group plc, 20; 100 (upd.)
Perry Ellis International Inc., 41; 106 (upd.)
Petit Bateau, 95
Phat Fashions LLC, 49
Phoenix Footwear Group, Inc., 70
Pillowtex Corporation, 19; 41 (upd.)
Plains Cotton Cooperative Association, 57
Pluma, Inc., 27
Polo/Ralph Lauren Corporation, 12; 62 (upd.)
Pomare Ltd., 88
Prada Holding B.V., 45
PremiumWear, Inc., 30
Puma AG Rudolf Dassler Sport, 35
Quaker Fabric Corp., 19
Quiksilver, Inc., 18; 79 (upd.)
R.G. Barry Corporation, 17; 44 (upd.)
Rack Room Shoes, Inc., 84
Raymond Ltd., 77
Recreational Equipment, Inc., 18
Red Wing Shoe Company, Inc., 9; 30 (upd.); 83 (upd.)
Reebok International Ltd., V; 9 (upd.); 26 (upd.)
Reliance Industries Ltd., 81
Renfro Corporation, 99
Rieter Holding AG, 42
Robert Talbott Inc., 88
Rocawear Apparel LLC, 77
Rocky Brands, Inc., 102 (upd.)
Rollerblade, Inc., 15
Royal Ten Cate N.V., 68
Russell Corporation, 8; 30 (upd.); 82 (upd.)
Rusty, Inc., 95
St. John Knits, Inc., 14
Salant Corporation, 51 (upd.)
Salvatore Ferragamo Italia S.p.A., 62
Sao Paulo Alpargatas S.A., 75
Saucony Inc., 35; 86 (upd.)
Schott Brothers, Inc., 67
Seattle Pacific Industries, Inc., 92
Shaw Industries, Inc., 40 (upd.)
Shelby Williams Industries, Inc., 14
Shoe Pavilion, Inc., 84
Skechers U.S.A. Inc., 31; 88 (upd.)
skinnyCorp, LLC, 97
Sole Technology Inc., 93
Sophus Berendsen A/S, 49
Spanx, Inc., 89
Springs Global US, Inc., V; 19 (upd.); 90 (upd.)
Starter Corp., 12
Stefanel SpA, 63
Steiner Corporation (Alsco), 53
Steven Madden, Ltd., 37
Stirling Group plc, 62
Stoddard International plc, 72
Stone Manufacturing Company, 14; 43 (upd.)
Stride Rite Corporation, 8; 37 (upd.); 86 (upd.)
Stussy, Inc., 55

Sun Sportswear, Inc., 17
Superior Uniform Group, Inc., 30
Tag-It Pacific, Inc., 85
The Talbots, Inc., 11; 31 (upd.); 88
    (upd.)
Tamfelt Oyj Abp, 62
Tarrant Apparel Group, 62
Ted Baker plc, 86
Teijin Limited, V
Thanulux Public Company Limited, 86
Thomaston Mills, Inc., 27
Tillcy Endurables, Inc., 67
The Timberland Company, 13; 54 (upd.)
Tommy Hilfiger Corporation, 20; 53
    (upd.)
Too, Inc., 61
Toray Industries, Inc., V
True Religion Apparel, Inc., 79
Tultex Corporation, 13
Under Armour Performance Apparel, 61
Unifi, Inc., 12; 62 (upd.)
United Merchants & Manufacturers, Inc.,
    13
United Retail Group Inc., 33
Unitika Ltd., V
Umbro plc, 88
Van de Velde S.A./NV, 102
Vans, Inc., 16; 47 (upd.)
Varsity Spirit Corp., 15
VF Corporation, V; 17 (upd.); 54 (upd.)
Vicunha Têxtil S.A. 78
Volcom, Inc., 77
Vulcabras S.A., 103
Walton Monroe Mills, Inc., 8
The Warnaco Group Inc., 12; 46 (upd.)
Wellco Enterprises, Inc., 84
Wellman, Inc., 8; 52 (upd.)
West Point-Pepperell, Inc., 8
WestPoint Stevens Inc., 16
Weyco Group, Incorporated, 32
Williamson-Dickie Manufacturing
    Company, 14
Wolverine World Wide, Inc., 16; 59
    (upd.)
Woolrich Inc., 62
Zara International, Inc., 83

Tobacco

Altadis S.A., 72 (upd.)
American Brands, Inc., V
B.A.T. Industries PLC, 22 (upd.)
British American Tobacco PLC, 50 (upd.)
Brooke Group Ltd., 15
Brown & Williamson Tobacco
    Corporation, 14; 33 (upd.)
Culbro Corporation, 15
Dibrell Brothers, Incorporated, 12
DIMON Inc., 27
800-JR Cigar, Inc., 27
Gallaher Group Plc, V; 19 (upd.); 49
    (upd.)
General Cigar Holdings, Inc., 66 (upd.)
Holt's Cigar Holdings, Inc., 42
House of Prince A/S, 80
Imasco Limited, V
Imperial Tobacco Group PLC, 50
Japan Tobacco Incorporated, V
KT&G Corporation, 62

Nobleza Piccardo SAICF, 64
North Atlantic Trading Company Inc., 65
Philip Morris Companies Inc., V; 18
    (upd.)
PT Gudang Garam Tbk, 103
R.J. Reynolds Tobacco Holdings, Inc., 30
    (upd.)
RJR Nabisco Holdings Corp., V
Rothmans UK Holdings Limited, V; 19
    (upd.)
Seita, 23
Souza Cruz S.A., 65
Standard Commercial Corporation, 13; 62
    (upd.)
Swedish Match AB, 12; 39 (upd.); 92
    (upd.)
Swisher International Group Inc., 23
Tabacalera, S.A., V; 17 (upd.)
Taiwan Tobacco & Liquor Corporation,
    75
Universal Corporation, V; 48 (upd.)
UST Inc., 9; 50 (upd.)
Vector Group Ltd., 35 (upd.)

Transport Services

Abertis Infraestructuras, S.A., 65
The Adams Express Company, 86
Aegean Marine Petroleum Network Inc.,
    89
Aéroports de Paris, 33
Air Express International Corporation, 13
Air Partner PLC, 93
Air T, Inc., 86
Airborne Freight Corporation, 6; 34
    (upd.)
Alamo Rent A Car, Inc., 6; 24 (upd.); 84
    (upd.)
Alaska Railroad Corporation, 60
Alexander & Baldwin, Inc., 10, 40 (upd.)
Allied Worldwide, Inc., 49
AMCOL International Corporation, 59
    (upd.)
Amerco, 6
AMERCO, 67 (upd.)
American Classic Voyages Company, 27
American Commercial Lines Inc., 99
American President Companies Ltd., 6
Anderson Trucking Service, Inc., 75
Anschutz Corp., 12
APL Limited, 61 (upd.)
Aqua Alliance Inc., 32 (upd.)
Arlington Tankers Ltd., 101
Arriva PLC, 69
Atlas Van Lines Inc., 14; 106 (upd.)
Attica Enterprises S.A., 64
Avis Group Holdings, Inc., 75 (upd.)
Avis Rent A Car, Inc., 6; 22 (upd.)
BAA plc, 10
Bekins Company, 15
Berliner Verkehrsbetriebe (BVG), 58
Bollinger Shipyards, Inc., 61
Boyd Bros. Transportation Inc., 39
Brambles Industries Limited, 42
The Brink's Company, 58 (upd.)
British Railways Board, V
Broken Hill Proprietary Company Ltd.,
    22 (upd.)
Buckeye Partners, L.P., 70

Budget Group, Inc., 25
Budget Rent a Car Corporation, 9
Burlington Northern Santa Fe
    Corporation, V; 27 (upd.)
C.H. Robinson Worldwide, Inc., 40
    (upd.)
Canadian National Railway Company, 71
    (upd.)
Canadian National Railway System, 6
Canadian Pacific Railway Limited, V; 45
    (upd.); 95 (upd.)
Cannon Express, Inc., 53
Carey International, Inc., 26
Carlson Companies, Inc., 6; 22 (upd.); 87
    (upd.)
Carolina Freight Corporation, 6
Celadon Group Inc., 30
Central Japan Railway Company, 43
Chargeurs International, 6; 21 (upd.)
CHC Helicopter Corporation, 67
CHEP Pty. Ltd., 80
Chicago and North Western Holdings
    Corporation, 6
Christian Salvesen Plc, 45
Coach USA, Inc., 24; 55 (upd.)
Coles Express Inc., 15
Compagnie Générale Maritime et
    Financière, 6
Compagnie Maritime Belge S.A., 95
Compañia Sud Americana de Vapores
    S.A., 100
Con-way Inc., 101
Consolidated Delivery & Logistics, Inc.,
    24
Consolidated Freightways Corporation, V;
    21 (upd.); 48 (upd.)
Consolidated Rail Corporation, V
CR England, Inc., 63
Crete Carrier Corporation, 95
Crowley Maritime Corporation, 6; 28
    (upd.)
CSX Corporation, V; 22 (upd.); 79 (upd.)
Ctrip.com International Ltd., 97
Dachser GmbH & Co. KG, 88
Danaos Corporation, 91
Danzas Group, V; 40 (upd.)
Dart Group PLC, 77
Deutsche Bahn AG, V; 46 (upd.)
DHL Worldwide Network S.A./N.V., 6;
    24 (upd.); 69 (upd.)
Diana Shipping Inc., 95
Dollar Thrifty Automotive Group, Inc.,
    25
Dot Foods, Inc., 69
DP World, 81
DryShips Inc., 95
East Japan Railway Company, V; 66
    (upd.)
EGL, Inc., 59
Emery Air Freight Corporation, 6
Emery Worldwide Airlines, Inc., 25 (upd.)
Enterprise Rent-A-Car Company, 6
Estes Express Lines, Inc., 86
Eurotunnel Group, 37 (upd.)
EVA Airways Corporation, 51
Evergreen International Aviation, Inc., 53
Evergreen Marine Corporation (Taiwan)
    Ltd., 13; 50 (upd.)

Executive Jet, Inc., 36
Exel plc, 51 (upd.)
Expeditors International of Washington
  Inc., 17; 78 (upd.)
Federal Express Corporation, V
FedEx Corporation, 18 (upd.); 42 (upd.)
Ferrovie Dello Stato Societa Di Trasporti e
  Servizi S.p.A., 105
FirstGroup plc, 89
Forward Air Corporation, 75
Fritz Companies, Inc., 12
Frontline Ltd., 45
Frozen Food Express Industries, Inc., 20;
  98 (upd.)
Garuda Indonesia, 58 (upd.)
GATX Corporation, 6; 25 (upd.)
GE Capital Aviation Services, 36
Gefco SA, 54
General Maritime Corporation, 59
Genesee & Wyoming Inc., 27
Geodis S.A., 67
The Go-Ahead Group Plc, 28
The Greenbrier Companies, 19
Greyhound Lines, Inc., 32 (upd.)
Groupe Bourbon S.A., 60
Grupo Aeroportuario del Centro Norte,
  S.A.B. de C.V., 97
Grupo Aeroportuario del Pacífico, S.A. de
  C.V., 85
Grupo TMM, S.A. de C.V., 50
Grupo Transportación Ferroviaria
  Mexicana, S.A. de C.V., 47
Gulf Agency Company Ltd. 78
GulfMark Offshore, Inc., 49
Hanjin Shipping Co., Ltd., 50
Hankyu Corporation, V; 23 (upd.)
Hapag-Lloyd AG, 6; 97 (upd.)
Harland and Wolff Holdings plc, 19
Harper Group Inc., 17
Heartland Express, Inc., 18
The Hertz Corporation, 9; 33 (upd.); 101
  (upd.)
Holberg Industries, Inc., 36
Horizon Lines, Inc., 98
Hornbeck Offshore Services, Inc., 101
Hospitality Worldwide Services, Inc., 26
Hub Group, Inc., 38
Hvide Marine Incorporated, 22
Illinois Central Corporation, 11
International Shipholding Corporation,
  Inc., 27
J.B. Hunt Transport Services Inc., 12
J Lauritzen A/S, 90
Jack B. Kelley, Inc., 102
John Menzies plc, 39
Kansas City Southern Industries, Inc., 6;
  26 (upd.)
The Kansas City Southern Railway
  Company, 92
Kawasaki Kisen Kaisha, Ltd., V; 56 (upd.)
Keio Corporation, V; 96 (upd.)
Keolis SA, 51
Kinki Nippon Railway Company Ltd., V
Kirby Corporation, 18; 66 (upd.)
Knight Transportation, Inc., 64
Koninklijke Nedlloyd Groep N.V., 6
Kuehne & Nagel International AG, V; 53
  (upd.)

La Poste, V; 47 (upd.)
Laidlaw International, Inc., 80
Landstar System, Inc., 63
Leaseway Transportation Corp., 12
Loma Negra C.I.A.S.A., 95
London Regional Transport, 6
The Long Island Rail Road Company, 68
Lynden Incorporated, 91
Maine Central Railroad Company, 16
Mammoet Transport B.V., 26
Marten Transport, Ltd., 84
Martz Group, 56
Mayflower Group Inc., 6
Mercury Air Group, Inc., 20
The Mersey Docks and Harbour
  Company, 30
Metropolitan Transportation Authority, 35
Miller Industries, Inc., 26
Mitsui O.S.K. Lines Ltd., V; 96 (upd.)
Moran Towing Corporation, Inc., 15
The Morgan Group, Inc., 46
Morris Travel Services L.L.C., 26
Motor Cargo Industries, Inc., 35
National Car Rental System, Inc., 10
National Express Group PLC, 50
National Railroad Passenger Corporation
  (Amtrak), 22; 66 (upd.)
Neptune Orient Lines Limited, 47
NFC plc, 6
Nippon Express Company, Ltd., V; 64
  (upd.)
Nippon Yusen Kabushiki Kaisha (NYK),
  V; 72 (upd.)
Norfolk Southern Corporation, V; 29
  (upd.); 75 (upd.)
Oak Harbor Freight Lines, Inc., 53
Ocean Group plc, 6
Odakyu Electric Railway Co., Ltd., V; 68
  (upd.)
Odfjell SE, 101
Odyssey Marine Exploration, Inc., 91
Oglebay Norton Company, 17
Old Dominion Freight Line, Inc., 57
OMI Corporation, 59
The Oppenheimer Group, 76
Oshkosh Corporation, 7; 98 (upd.)
Österreichische Bundesbahnen GmbH, 6
OTR Express, Inc., 25
Overnite Corporation, 14; 58 (upd.)
Overseas Shipholding Group, Inc., 11
Pacer International, Inc., 54
Pacific Basin Shipping Ltd., 86
Patriot Transportation Holding, Inc., 91
The Peninsular and Oriental Steam
  Navigation Company, V; 38 (upd.)
Penske Corporation, V; 19 (upd.); 84
  (upd.)
Peter Pan Bus Lines Inc., 106
PHH Arval, V; 53 (upd.)
Pilot Air Freight Corp., 67
Plantation Pipe Line Company, 68
PODS Enterprises Inc., 103
Polar Air Cargo Inc., 60
The Port Authority of New York and New
  Jersey, 48
Port Imperial Ferry Corporation, 70
Post Office Group, V
Preston Corporation, 6

RailTex, Inc., 20
Railtrack Group PLC, 50
REpower Systems AG, 101
Réseau Ferré de France, 66
Roadway Express, Inc., V; 25 (upd.)
Rock-It Cargo USA, Inc., 86
Royal Olympic Cruise Lines Inc., 52
Royal Vopak NV, 41
Russian Railways Joint Stock Co., 93
Ryder System, Inc., V; 24 (upd.)
Saia, Inc., 98
Santa Fe Pacific Corporation, V
Schenker-Rhenus AG, 6
Schneider National, Inc., 36; 77 (upd.)
Seaboard Corporation, 36; 85 (upd.)
SEACOR Holdings Inc., 83
Securicor Plc, 45
Seibu Railway Company Ltd., V; 74
  (upd.)
Seino Transportation Company, Ltd., 6
Simon Transportation Services Inc., 27
Smithway Motor Xpress Corporation, 39
Société Nationale des Chemins de Fer
  Français, V; 57 (upd.)
Société Norbert Dentressangle S.A., 67
Southern Pacific Transportation Company,
  V
Spee-Dee Delivery Service, Inc., 93
Stagecoach Group plc, 30; 104 (upd.)
Stelmar Shipping Ltd., 52
Stevedoring Services of America Inc., 28
Stinnes AG, 8; 59 (upd.)
Stolt-Nielsen S.A., 42
Sunoco, Inc., 28 (upd.); 83 (upd.)
Swift Transportation Co., Inc., 42
The Swiss Federal Railways
  (Schweizerische Bundesbahnen), V
Swissport International Ltd., 70
Teekay Shipping Corporation, 25; 82
  (upd.)
Tibbett & Britten Group plc, 32
Tidewater Inc., 11; 37 (upd.)
TNT Freightways Corporation, 14
TNT Post Group N.V., V; 27 (upd.); 30
  (upd.)
Tobu Railway Company Ltd., 6; 98
  (upd.)
Tokyu Corporation, V
Totem Resources Corporation, 9
TPG N.V., 64 (upd.)
Trailer Bridge, Inc., 41
Transnet Ltd., 6
Transport Corporation of America, Inc.,
  49
Trico Marine Services, Inc., 89
Tsakos Energy Navigation Ltd., 91
TTX Company, 6; 66 (upd.)
U.S. Delivery Systems, Inc., 22
Union Pacific Corporation, V; 28 (upd.);
  79 (upd.)
United Parcel Service of America Inc., V;
  17 (upd.)
United Parcel Service, Inc., 63
United Road Services, Inc., 69
United States Postal Service, 14; 34 (upd.)
US 1 Industries, Inc., 89
USA Truck, Inc., 42
Velocity Express Corporation, 49

Werner Enterprises, Inc., 26
Wheels Inc., 96
Wincanton plc, 52
Wisconsin Central Transportation
    Corporation, 24
Wright Express Corporation, 80
Yamato Transport Co. Ltd., V; 49 (upd.)
Yellow Corporation, 14; 45 (upd.)
Yellow Freight System, Inc. of Delaware,
    V
YRC Worldwide Inc., 90 (upd.)

Utilities

AES Corporation, 10; 13 (upd.); 53
    (upd.)
Aggreko Plc, 45
Air & Water Technologies Corporation, 6
Alberta Energy Company Ltd., 16; 43
    (upd.)
Allegheny Energy, Inc., V; 38 (upd.)
Alliant Energy Corporation, 106
Ameren Corporation, 60 (upd.)
American Electric Power Company, Inc.,
    V; 45 (upd.)
American States Water Company, 46
American Water Works Company, Inc., 6;
    38 (upd.)
Aquarion Company, 84
Aquila, Inc., 50 (upd.)
Arkla, Inc., V
Associated Natural Gas Corporation, 11
Atlanta Gas Light Company, 6; 23 (upd.)
Atlantic Energy, Inc., 6
Atmos Energy Corporation, 43
Avista Corporation, 69 (upd.)
Baltimore Gas and Electric Company, V;
    25 (upd.)
Basin Electric Power Cooperative, 103
Bay State Gas Company, 38
Bayernwerk AG, V; 23 (upd.)
Berlinwasser Holding AG, 90
Bewag AG, 39
Big Rivers Electric Corporation, 11
Black Hills Corporation, 20
Bonneville Power Administration, 50
Boston Edison Company, 12
Bouygues S.A., I; 24 (upd.); 97 (upd.)
British Energy Plc, 49
British Gas plc, V
British Nuclear Fuels plc, 6
Brooklyn Union Gas, 6
California Water Service Group, 79
Calpine Corporation, 36
Canadian Utilities Limited, 13; 56 (upd.)
Cap Rock Energy Corporation, 46
Carolina Power & Light Company, V; 23
    (upd.)
Cascade Natural Gas Corporation, 9
Cascal N.V., 103
Centerior Energy Corporation, V
Central and South West Corporation, V
Central Hudson Gas and Electricity
    Corporation, 6
Central Maine Power, 6
Central Vermont Public Service
    Corporation, 54
Centrica plc, 29 (upd.)
ČEZ a. s., 97

Chesapeake Utilities Corporation, 56
China Shenhua Energy Company
    Limited, 83
Chubu Electric Power Company, Inc., V;
    46 (upd.)
Chugoku Electric Power Company Inc.,
    V; 53 (upd.)
Cincinnati Gas & Electric Company, 6
CIPSCO Inc., 6
Citizens Utilities Company, 7
City Public Service, 6
Cleco Corporation, 37
CMS Energy Corporation, V, 14 (upd.);
    100 (upd.)
The Coastal Corporation, 31 (upd.)
Cogentrix Energy, Inc., 10
The Coleman Company, Inc., 9
The Columbia Gas System, Inc., V; 16
    (upd.)
Commonwealth Edison Company, V
Commonwealth Energy System, 14
Companhia Energética de Minas Gerais
    S.A. CEMIG, 65
Compañia de Minas Buenaventura S.A.A.,
    93
Connecticut Light and Power Co., 13
Consolidated Edison, Inc., V; 45 (upd.)
Consolidated Natural Gas Company, V;
    19 (upd.)
Consumers Power Co., 14
Consumers Water Company, 14
Consumers' Gas Company Ltd., 6
Covanta Energy Corporation, 64 (upd.)
Dalkia Holding, 66
Destec Energy, Inc., 12
The Detroit Edison Company, V
Dominion Resources, Inc., V; 54 (upd.)
DPL Inc., 6; 96 (upd.)
DQE, Inc., 6
DTE Energy Company, 20 (upd.)
Duke Energy Corporation, V; 27 (upd.)
E.On AG, 50 (upd.)
Eastern Enterprises, 6
Edison International, 56 (upd.)
El Paso Electric Company, 21
El Paso Natural Gas Company, 12
Electrabel N.V., 67
Electricidade de Portugal, S.A., 47
Electricité de France, V; 41 (upd.)
Electricity Generating Authority of
    Thailand (EGAT), 56
Elektrowatt AG, 6
The Empire District Electric Company,
    77
Empresas Públicas de Medellín S.A.E.S.P.,
    91
Enbridge Inc., 43
ENDESA S.A., V; 46 (upd.)
Enersis S.A., 73
ENMAX Corporation, 83
Enron Corporation, V; 46 (upd.)
Enserch Corporation, V
Ente Nazionale per L'Energia Elettrica, V
Entergy Corporation, V; 45 (upd.)
Environmental Power Corporation, 68
EPCOR Utilities Inc., 81
Equitable Resources, Inc., 6; 54 (upd.)
Exelon Corporation, 48 (upd.)

Florida Progress Corporation, V; 23 (upd.)
Florida Public Utilities Company, 69
Fortis, Inc., 15; 47 (upd.)
Fortum Corporation, 30 (upd.)
FPL Group, Inc., V; 49 (upd.)
Gas Natural SDG S.A., 69
Gaz de France, V; 40 (upd.)
General Public Utilities Corporation, V
Générale des Eaux Group, V
GPU, Inc., 27 (upd.)
Great Plains Energy Incorporated, 65
    (upd.)
Gulf States Utilities Company, 6
Hawaiian Electric Industries, Inc., 9
Hokkaido Electric Power Company Inc.
    (HEPCO), V; 58 (upd.)
Hokuriku Electric Power Company, V
Hong Kong and China Gas Company
    Ltd., 73
Hongkong Electric Holdings Ltd., 6; 23
    (upd.)
Houston Industries Incorporated, V
Hyder plc, 34
Hydro-Québec, 6; 32 (upd.)
Iberdrola, S.A., 49
Idaho Power Company, 12
Illinois Bell Telephone Company, 14
Illinois Power Company, 6
Indiana Energy, Inc., 27
International Power PLC, 50 (upd.)
IPALCO Enterprises, Inc., 6
ITC Holdings Corp., 75
The Kansai Electric Power Company, Inc.,
    V; 62 (upd.)
Kansas City Power & Light Company, 6
Kelda Group plc, 45
Kenetech Corporation, 11
Kentucky Utilities Company, 6
KeySpan Energy Co., 27
Korea Electric Power Corporation
    (Kepco), 56
KU Energy Corporation, 11
Kyushu Electric Power Company Inc., V
LG&E Energy Corporation, 6; 51 (upd.)
Long Island Power Authority, V; 102
    (upd.)
Lyonnaise des Eaux-Dumez, V
Madison Gas and Electric Company, 39
Magma Power Company, 11
Maine & Maritimes Corporation, 56
Manila Electric Company (Meralco), 56
MCN Corporation, 6
MDU Resources Group, Inc., 7; 42 (upd.)
Middlesex Water Company, 45
Midwest Resources Inc., 6
Minnesota Power, Inc., 11; 34 (upd.)
Mirant Corporation, 98
The Montana Power Company, 11; 44
    (upd.)
National Fuel Gas Company, 6; 95 (upd.)
National Grid USA, 51 (upd.)
National Power PLC, 12
Nebraska Public Power District, 29
N.V. Nederlandse Gasunie, V
Nevada Power Company, 11
New England Electric System, V
New Jersey Resources Corporation, 54
New York State Electric and Gas, 6

Neyveli Lignite Corporation Ltd., 65
Niagara Mohawk Holdings Inc., V; 45 (upd.)
Nicor Inc., 6; 86 (upd.)
NIPSCO Industries, Inc., 6
North West Water Group plc, 11
Northeast Utilities, V; 48 (upd.)
Northern States Power Company, V; 20 (upd.)
Northwest Natural Gas Company, 45
NorthWestern Corporation, 37
Nova Corporation of Alberta, V
NRG Energy, Inc., 79
NSTAR, 106 (upd.)
Oglethorpe Power Corporation, 6
Ohio Edison Company, V
Oklahoma Gas and Electric Company, 6
ONEOK Inc., 7
Ontario Hydro Services Company, 6; 32 (upd.)
Osaka Gas Company, Ltd., V; 60 (upd.)
Österreichische Elektrizitätswirtschafts-AG, 85
Otter Tail Power Company, 18
Pacific Enterprises, V
Pacific Gas and Electric Company, V
PacifiCorp, V; 26 (upd.)
Panhandle Eastern Corporation, V
Paddy Power plc, 98
PECO Energy Company, 11
Pennon Group Plc, 45
Pennsylvania Power & Light Company, V
Peoples Energy Corporation, 6
PG&E Corporation, 26 (upd.)
Philadelphia Electric Company, V
Philadelphia Gas Works Company, 92
Philadelphia Suburban Corporation, 39
Piedmont Natural Gas Company, Inc., 27
Pinnacle West Capital Corporation, 6; 54 (upd.)
PNM Resources Inc., 51 (upd.)
Portland General Corporation, 6
Potomac Electric Power Company, 6
Power-One, Inc., 79
Powergen PLC, 11; 50 (upd.)
PPL Corporation, 41 (upd.)
PreussenElektra Aktiengesellschaft, V
Progress Energy, Inc., 74
PSI Resources, 6
Public Service Company of Colorado, 6
Public Service Company of New Hampshire, 21; 55 (upd.)
Public Service Company of New Mexico, 6
Public Service Enterprise Group Inc., V; 44 (upd.)
Puerto Rico Electric Power Authority, 47
Puget Sound Energy Inc., 6; 50 (upd.)
Questar Corporation, 6; 26 (upd.)
RAO Unified Energy System of Russia, 45
Reliant Energy Inc., 44 (upd.)
Revere Electric Supply Company, 96
Rochester Gas and Electric Corporation, 6
Ruhrgas AG, V; 38 (upd.)
RWE AG, V; 50 (upd.)
Salt River Project, 19
San Diego Gas & Electric Company, V
SCANA Corporation, 6; 56 (upd.)

Scarborough Public Utilities Commission, 9
SCEcorp, V
Scottish and Southern Energy plc, 66 (upd.)
Scottish Hydro-Electric PLC, 13
Scottish Power plc, 19; 49 (upd.)
Seattle City Light, 50
SEMCO Energy, Inc., 44
Sempra Energy, 25 (upd.)
Severn Trent PLC, 12; 38 (upd.)
Shikoku Electric Power Company, Inc., V; 60 (upd.)
SJW Corporation, 70
Sonat, Inc., 6
South Jersey Industries, Inc., 42
The Southern Company, V; 38 (upd.)
Southern Connecticut Gas Company, 84
Southern Electric PLC, 13
Southern Indiana Gas and Electric Company, 13
Southern Union Company, 27
Southwest Gas Corporation, 19
Southwest Water Company, 47
Southwestern Electric Power Co., 21
Southwestern Public Service Company, 6
Suez Lyonnaise des Eaux, 36 (upd.)
SUEZ-TRACTEBEL S.A., 97 (upd.)
TECO Energy, Inc., 6
Tennessee Valley Authority, 50
Tennet BV 78
Texas Utilities Company, V; 25 (upd.)
Thames Water plc, 11; 90 (upd.)
Tohoku Electric Power Company, Inc., V
The Tokyo Electric Power Company, 74 (upd.)
The Tokyo Electric Power Company, Incorporated, V
Tokyo Gas Co., Ltd., V; 55 (upd.)
TransAlta Utilities Corporation, 6
TransCanada PipeLines Limited, V
Transco Energy Company, V
Tri-State Generation and Transmission Association, Inc., 103
Trigen Energy Corporation, 42
Tucson Electric Power Company, 6
UGI Corporation, 12
Unicom Corporation, 29 (upd.)
Union Electric Company, V
The United Illuminating Company, 21
United Utilities PLC, 52 (upd.)
United Water Resources, Inc., 40
Unitil Corporation, 37
Utah Power and Light Company, 27
UtiliCorp United Inc., 6
Vattenfall AB, 57
Vectren Corporation, 98 (upd.)
Vereinigte Elektrizitätswerke Westfalen AG, V
VEW AG, 39
Viridian Group plc, 64
Warwick Valley Telephone Company, 55
Washington Gas Light Company, 19
Washington Natural Gas Company, 9
Washington Water Power Company, 6
Westar Energy, Inc., 57 (upd.)
Western Resources, Inc., 12
Wheelabrator Technologies, Inc., 6

Wisconsin Energy Corporation, 6; 54 (upd.)
Wisconsin Public Service Corporation, 9
WPL Holdings, Inc., 6
WPS Resources Corporation, 53 (upd.)
Xcel Energy Inc., 73 (upd.)

Waste Services

Allied Waste Industries, Inc., 50
Allwaste, Inc., 18
American Ecology Corporation, 77
Appliance Recycling Centers of America, Inc., 42
Azcon Corporation, 23
Berliner Stadtreinigungsbetriebe, 58
Biffa plc, 92
Brambles Industries Limited, 42
Browning-Ferris Industries, Inc., V; 20 (upd.)
Casella Waste Systems Inc., 102
Chemical Waste Management, Inc., 9
CHHJ Franchising LLC, 105
Clean Harbors, Inc., 73
Clean Venture, Inc., 104
Copart Inc., 23
Darling International Inc., 85
E.On AG, 50 (upd.)
Ecolab Inc., I; 13 (upd.); 34 (upd.); 85 (upd.)
Ecology and Environment, Inc., 39
Empresas Públicas de Medellín S.A.E.S.P., 91
Fuel Tech, Inc., 85
Industrial Services of America, Inc., 46
Ionics, Incorporated, 52
ISS A/S, 49
Jani-King International, Inc., 85
Kelda Group plc, 45
MPW Industrial Services Group, Inc., 53
Newpark Resources, Inc., 63
Norcal Waste Systems, Inc., 60
Oakleaf Waste Management, LLC, 97
1-800-GOT-JUNK? LLC, 74
Onet S.A., 92
Pennon Group Plc, 45
Perma-Fix Environmental Services, Inc., 99
Philip Environmental Inc., 16
Philip Services Corp., 73
Republic Services, Inc., 92
Roto-Rooter, Inc., 15; 61 (upd.)
Safety-Kleen Systems Inc., 8; 82 (upd.)
Saur S.A.S., 92
Sevenson Environmental Services, Inc., 42
Severn Trent PLC, 38 (upd.)
Servpro Industries, Inc., 85
Shanks Group plc, 45
Shred-It Canada Corporation, 56
Stericycle, Inc., 33; 74 (upd.)
TRC Companies, Inc., 32
Valley Proteins, Inc., 91
Veit Companies, 43; 92 (upd.)
Waste Connections, Inc., 46
Waste Holdings, Inc., 41
Waste Management, Inc., V
Wheelabrator Technologies, Inc., 60 (upd.)

Windswept Environmental Group, Inc., 62

WMX Technologies Inc., 17

Geographic Index

Algeria
Sonatrach, IV; 65 (upd.)

Argentina
Acindar Industria Argentina de Aceros
    S.A., 87
Adecoagro LLC, 101
Aerolíneas Argentinas S.A., 33; 69 (upd.)
Alpargatas S.A.I.C., 87
Aluar Aluminio Argentino S.A.I.C., 74
Arcor S.A.I.C., 66
Atanor S.A., 62
Coto Centro Integral de Comercializacion
    S.A., 66
Cresud S.A.C.I.F. y A., 63
Grupo Clarín S.A., 67
Grupo Financiero Galicia S.A., 63
IRSA Inversiones y Representaciones S.A.,
    63
Ledesma Sociedad Anónima Agrícola
    Industrial, 62
Loma Negra C.I.A.S.A., 95
Mastellone Hermanos S.A., 101
Molinos Río de la Plata S.A., 61
Nobleza Piccardo SAICF, 64
Penaflor S.A., 66
Petrobras Energia Participaciones S.A., 72
Quilmes Industrial (QUINSA) S.A., 67
Renault Argentina S.A., 67
SanCor Cooperativas Unidas Ltda., 101
Sideco Americana S.A., 67
Siderar S.A.I.C., 66
Telecom Argentina S.A., 63
Telefónica de Argentina S.A., 61
YPF Sociedad Anonima, IV

Australia
ABC Learning Centres Ltd., 93
Amcor Limited, IV; 19 (upd.), 78 (upd.)

Ansell Ltd., 60 (upd.)
Aquarius Platinum Ltd., 63
Aristocrat Leisure Limited, 54
Arnott's Ltd., 66
Austal Limited, 75
Australia and New Zealand Banking
    Group Limited, II; 52 (upd.)
AWB Ltd., 56
BHP Billiton, 67 (upd.)
Billabong International Ltd., 44
Blundstone Pty Ltd., 76
Bond Corporation Holdings Limited, 10
Boral Limited, III; 43 (upd.); 103 (upd.)
Brambles Industries Limited, 42
Broken Hill Proprietary Company Ltd.,
    IV; 22 (upd.)
Burns, Philp & Company Ltd., 63
Carlton and United Breweries Ltd., I
Coles Group Limited, V; 20 (upd.); 85
    (upd.)
Cochlear Ltd., 77
CRA Limited, IV; 85 (upd.)
CSR Limited, III; 28 (upd.)
David Jones Ltd., 60
Elders IXL Ltd., I
Fairfax Media Ltd., 94 (upd.)
Foster's Group Limited, 7; 21 (upd.); 50
    (upd.)
Goodman Fielder Ltd., 52
Harvey Norman Holdings Ltd., 56
Hills Industries Ltd., 104
Holden Ltd., 62
James Hardie Industries N.V., 56
John Fairfax Holdings Limited, 7
Lend Lease Corporation Limited, IV; 17
    (upd.); 52 (upd.)
Lion Nathan Limited, 54
Lonely Planet Publications Pty Ltd., 55
Macquarie Bank Ltd., 69

McPherson's Ltd., 66
Metcash Trading Ltd., 58
MYOB Ltd., 86
News Corporation Limited, IV; 7 (upd.);
    46 (upd.)
Nufarm Ltd., 87
Pacific Dunlop Limited, 10
Pioneer International Limited, III
PMP Ltd., 72
Publishing and Broadcasting Limited, 54
Qantas Airways Ltd., 6; 24 (upd.); 68
    (upd.)
Repco Corporation Ltd., 74
Ridley Corporation Ltd., 62
Rinker Group Ltd., 65
Rural Press Ltd., 74
Santos Ltd., 81
Smorgon Steel Group Ltd., 62
Southcorp Limited, 54
Suncorp-Metway Ltd., 91
TABCORP Holdings Limited, 44
Telecom Australia, 6
Telstra Corporation Limited, 50
Village Roadshow Ltd., 58
Westpac Banking Corporation, II; 48
    (upd.)
WMC, Limited, 43
Zinifex Ltd., 85

Austria
AKG Acoustics GmbH, 62
Andritz AG, 51
Austrian Airlines AG (Österreichische
    Luftverkehrs AG), 33
Bank Austria AG, 23; 100 (upd.)
Baumax AG, 75
BBAG Osterreichische
    Brau-Beteiligungs-AG, 38
BÖHLER-UDDEHOLM AG, 73

Borealis AG, 94
Erste Bank der Osterreichischen
  Sparkassen AG, 69
Gericom AG, 47
Glock Ges.m.b.H., 42
Julius Meinl International AG, 53
Kwizda Holding GmbH, 102 (upd.)
KTM Power Sports AG, 100
Lauda Air Luftfahrt AG, 48
OMV AG, IV; 98 (upd.)
Österreichische Bundesbahnen GmbH, 6
Österreichische Elektrizitätswirtschafts-AG,
  85
Österreichische Post- und
  Telegraphenverwaltung, V
Palfinger AG, 100
Raiffeisen Zentralbank Österreich AG, 85
Red Bull GmbH, 60
RHI AG, 53
Riedel Tiroler Glashuette GmbH, 99
VA TECH ELIN EBG GmbH, 49
voestalpine AG, IV; 57 (upd.)
Wienerberger AG, 70
Zumtobel AG, 50

Azerbaijan
Azerbaijan Airlines, 77

Bahamas
Bahamas Air Holdings Ltd., 66
Kerzner International Limited, 69 (upd.)
Sun International Hotels Limited, 26
Teekay Shipping Corporation, 25; 82
  (upd.)

Bahrain
Gulf Air Company, 56
Investcorp SA, 57

Bangladesh
Grameen Bank, 31

Barbados
Sagicor Life Inc., 98

Belgium
Ackermans & van Haaren N.V., 97
Agfa Gevaert Group N.V., 59
Almanij NV, 44
Arcelor Gent, 80
Bank Brussels Lambert, II
Barco NV, 44
Bekaert S.A./N.V., 90
Belgacom, 6
Besix Group S.A./NV, 94
Brouwerijen Alken-Maes N.V., 86
C&A, 40 (upd.)
Cockerill Sambre Group, IV; 26 (upd.)
Compagnie Maritime Belge S.A., 95
Compagnie Nationale à Portefeuille, 84
Cora S.A./NV, 94
Corelio S.A./N.V., 96
Deceuninck N.V., 84
Delhaize Group, 44; 103 (upd.)
Dexia NV/SA, 88 (upd.)
DHL Worldwide Network S.A./N.V., 69
  (upd.)

D'Ieteren S.A./NV, 98
Distrigaz S.A., 82
Electrabel N.V., 67
Etablissements Franz Colruyt N.V., 68
Fluxys SA, 101
Generale Bank, II
GIB Group, V; 26 (upd.)
Glaverbel Group, 80
Groupe Herstal S.A., 58
Hamon & Cie (International) S.A., 97
Interbrew S.A., 17; 50 (upd.)
Janssen Pharmaceutica N.V., 80
Kredietbank N.V., II
Lyfra-S.A./NV, 88
PetroFina S.A., IV; 26 (upd.)
Picanol N.V., 96
Punch International N.V., 66
Puratos S.A./NV, 92
Quick Restaurants S.A., 94
Rosy Blue N.V., 84
Roularta Media Group NV, 48
Sabena S.A./N.V., 33
Solvay S.A., I; 21 (upd.); 61 (upd.)
Spector Photo Group N.V., 82
SUEZ-TRACTEBEL S.A., 97 (upd.)
Ter Beke NV, 103
Tessenderlo Group, 76
Tractebel S.A., 20
UCB Pharma SA, 98
NV Umicore SA, 47
Van de Velde S.A./NV, 102
Van Hool S.A./NV, 96
Xeikon NV, 26

Belize
BB Holdings Limited, 77

Bermuda
Arlington Tankers Ltd., 101
Assured Guaranty Ltd., 93
Bacardi & Company Ltd., 18; 82 (upd.)
Central European Media Enterprises Ltd.,
  61
Covidien Ltd., 91
Endurance Specialty Holdings Ltd., 85
Frontline Ltd., 45
Gosling Brothers Ltd., 82
Jardine Matheson Holdings Limited, I; 20
  (upd.); 93 (upd.)
Nabors Industries Ltd., 91 (upd.)
PartnerRe Ltd., 83
Sea Containers Ltd., 29
Tyco International Ltd., III; 28 (upd.); 63
  (upd.)
VistaPrint Limited, 87
Warner Chilcott Limited, 85
White Mountains Insurance Group, Ltd.,
  48

Bolivia
Lloyd Aéreo Boliviano S.A., 95

Brazil
Abril S.A., 95
Aché Laboratórios Farmacéuticas S.A., 105
Algar S/A Emprendimentos e
  Participações, 103
Amil Participações S.A., 105

Andrade Gutierrez S.A., 102
Aracruz Celulose S.A., 57
Arthur Lundgren Tecidos S.A., 102
Banco Bradesco S.A., 13
Banco Itaú S.A., 19
Brasil Telecom Participaçoes S.A., 57
Brazil Fast Food Corporation, 74
Bunge Brasil S.A. 78
Camargo Corrêa S.A., 93
Casas Bahia Comercial Ltda., 75
Cia Hering, 72
Companhia Brasileira de Distribuiçao, 76
Companhia de Bebidas das Américas, 57
Companhia de Tecidos Norte de Minas -
  Coteminas, 77
Companhia Energética de Minas Gerais
  S.A. CEMIG, 65
Companhia Siderúrgica Nacional, 76
Companhia Suzano de Papel e Celulose
  S.A., 94
Companhia Vale do Rio Doce, IV; 43
  (upd.)
Cosan Ltd., 102
EBX Investimentos, 104
Empresa Brasileira de Aeronáutica S.A.
  (Embraer), 36
G&K Holding S.A., 95
Gerdau S.A., 59
Globex Utilidades S.A., 103
Globo Comunicação e Participações S.A.,
  80
Gol Linhas Aéreas Inteligentes S.A., 73
Grendene S.A., 102
Grupo Martins, 104
Grupo Positivo, 105
Ipiranga S.A., 67
JBS S.A., 100
Klabin S.A., 73
Lojas Americanas S.A., 77
Lojas Arapua S.A., 22; 61 (upd.)
Magazine Luiza S.A., 101
Marcopolo S.A. 79
Natura Cosméticos S.A., 75
Odebrecht S.A., 73
Perdigao SA, 52
Petróleo Brasileiro S.A., IV
Randon S.A. 79
Renner Herrmann S.A. 79
Sadia S.A., 59
Sao Paulo Alpargatas S.A., 75
Schincariol Participaçôces e Representações
  S.A., 102
Souza Cruz S.A., 65
TAM Linhas Aéreas S.A., 68
Tele Norte Leste Participações S.A., 80
Tigre S.A. Tubos e Conexões, 104
TransBrasil S/A Linhas Aéreas, 31
Unibanco Holdings S.A., 73
Usinas Siderúrgicas de Minas Gerais S.A.,
  77
VARIG S.A. (Viaçâo Aérea
  Rio-Grandense), 6; 29 (upd.)
Vicunha Têxtil S.A. 78
Votorantim Participaçoes S.A., 76
Vulcabras S.A., 103
Weg S.A. 78

INTERNATIONAL DIRECTORY OF COMPANY HISTORIES, VOLUME 106

Brunei

Royal Brunei Airlines Sdn Bhd, 99

Canada

AbitibiBowater Inc., V; 25 (upd.); 99 (upd.)
Abitibi-Price Inc., IV
Agnico-Eagle Mines Limited, 71
Agrium Inc., 73
Ainsworth Lumber Co. Ltd., 99
Air Canada, 6; 23 (upd.); 59 (upd.)
Alberta Energy Company Ltd., 16; 43 (upd.)
Alcan Aluminium Limited, IV; 31 (upd.)
Alderwoods Group, Inc., 68 (upd.)
Algo Group Inc., 24
Alimentation Couche-Tard Inc., 77
Alliance Atlantis Communications Inc., 39
Andrew Peller Ltd., 101
ATI Technologies Inc. 79
Axcan Pharma Inc., 85
Ballard Power Systems Inc., 73
Bank of Montreal, II; 46 (upd.)
The Bank of Nova Scotia, II; 59 (upd.)
Barrick Gold Corporation, 34
Bata Ltd., 62
BCE Inc., V; 44 (upd.)
Bell Canada, 6
BFC Construction Corporation, 25
BioWare Corporation, 81
Biovail Corporation, 47
Bombardier Inc., 42 (upd.); 87 (upd.)
Boston Pizza International Inc., 88
Bradley Air Services Ltd., 56
Bramalea Ltd., 9
Brascan Corporation, 67
British Columbia Telephone Company, 6
Brookfield Properties Corporation, 89
Cameco Corporation, 77
Campeau Corporation, V
Canada Bread Company, Limited, 99
Canada Packers Inc., II
Canadair, Inc., 16
The Canadian Broadcasting Corporation (CBC), 37
Canadian Imperial Bank of Commerce, II; 61 (upd.)
Canadian National Railway Company, 6; 71 (upd.)
Canadian Pacific Railway Limited, V; 45 (upd.); 95 (upd.)
Canadian Solar Inc., 105
Canadian Tire Corporation, Limited, 71 (upd.)
Canadian Utilities Limited, 13; 56 (upd.)
Canfor Corporation, 42
Canlan Ice Sports Corp., 105
Canstar Sports Inc., 16
CanWest Global Communications Corporation, 35
Cascades Inc., 71
Catalyst Paper Corporation, 105
Celestica Inc., 80
CHC Helicopter Corporation, 67
Cinar Corporation, 40
Cineplex Odeon Corporation, 6; 23 (upd.)
Cinram International, Inc., 43

Cirque du Soleil Inc., 29; 98 (upd.)
Clearly Canadian Beverage Corporation, 48
Cognos Inc., 44
Cominco Ltd., 37
Compton Petroleum Corporation, 103
Consumers' Gas Company Ltd., 6
CoolBrands International Inc., 35
Corby Distilleries Limited, 14
Corel Corporation, 15; 33 (upd.); 76 (upd.)
Cott Corporation, 52
Creo Inc., 48
Dare Foods Limited, 103
Diavik Diamond Mines Inc., 85
Discreet Logic Inc., 20
Dofasco Inc., IV; 24 (upd.)
Doman Industries Limited, 59
Dominion Textile Inc., 12
Domtar Corporation, IV; 89 (upd.)
Dorel Industries Inc., 59
Duvernay Oil Corp., 83
Dynatec Corporation, 87
Dylex Limited, 29
easyhome Ltd., 105
Echo Bay Mines Ltd., IV; 38 (upd.)
Enbridge Inc., 43
ENMAX Corporation, 83
EPCOR Utilities Inc., 81
Extendicare Health Services, Inc., 6
Fairfax Financial Holdings Limited, 57
Fairmont Hotels & Resorts Inc., 69
Falconbridge Limited, 49
Finning International Inc., 69
Fortis, Inc., 15; 47 (upd.)
The Forzani Group Ltd. 79
Four Seasons Hotels Limited, 9; 29 (upd.); 106 (upd.)
Future Shop Ltd., 62
Ganz, 98
GEAC Computer Corporation Ltd., 43
George Weston Ltd, II; 36 (upd.); 88 (upd.)
Gildan Activewear, Inc., 81
Goldcorp Inc., 87
GPS Industries, Inc., 81
Great-West Lifeco Inc., III
Groupe Vidéotron Ltée., 20
Hammond Manufacturing Company Limited, 83
Harlequin Enterprises Limited, 52
Hemisphere GPS Inc., 99
Hemlo Gold Mines Inc., 9
Héroux-Devtek Inc., 69
Hiram Walker Resources, Ltd., I
The Hockey Company, 34; 70
Hollinger International Inc., 62 (upd.)
Home Hardware Stores Ltd., 62
The Hudson Bay Mining and Smelting Company, Limited, 12
Hudson's Bay Company, V; 25 (upd.); 83 (upd.)
Hurricane Hydrocarbons Ltd., 54
Husky Energy Inc., 47
Hydro-Québec, 6; 32 (upd.)
Imasco Limited, V
IMAX Corporation 28, 78 (upd.)

Imperial Oil Limited, IV; 25 (upd.); 95 (upd.)
Imperial Parking Corporation, 58
Inco Limited, IV; 45 (upd.)
Indigo Books & Music Inc., 58
Intercorp Excelle Foods Inc., 64
Intrawest Corporation, 15; 84 (upd.)
Iogen Corporation, 81
Irwin Toy Limited, 14
Jacques Whitford, 92
The Jean Coutu Group (PJC) Inc., 46
The Jim Pattison Group, 37
Kinross Gold Corporation, 36
Kruger Inc., 17; 103 (upd.)
La Senza Corporation, 66
Labatt Brewing Company Limited, I; 25 (upd.)
LaSiDo Inc., 58
Lassonde Industries Inc., 68
Le Chateau Inc., 63
Ledcor Industries Limited, 46
Les Boutiques San Francisco, Inc., 62
Linamar Corporation, 18
Lions Gate Entertainment Corporation, 35
Loblaw Companies Limited, 43
The Loewen Group, Inc., 16; 40 (upd.)
London Drugs Ltd., 46
Lululemon Athletica Inc., 105
Maclean Hunter Publishing Limited, IV; 26 (upd.)
MacMillan Bloedel Limited, IV
Magellan Aerospace Corporation, 48
Magna International Inc., 102
Manitoba Telecom Services, Inc., 61
Manulife Financial Corporation, 85
Maple Leaf Foods Inc., 41
Maple Leaf Sports & Entertainment Ltd., 61
Masonite International Corporation, 63
McCain Foods Limited, 77
MDC Partners Inc., 63
Mega Bloks, Inc., 61
Methanex Corporation, 40
Métro Inc., 77
Mitel Corporation, 18
The Molson Companies Limited, I; 26 (upd.)
Moore Corporation Limited, IV
Morguard Corporation, 85
Mouvement des Caisses Desjardins, 48
National Bank of Canada, 85
National Sea Products Ltd., 14
Nature's Path Foods, Inc., 87
New Flyer Industries Inc. 78
Nexen Inc. 79
Noranda Inc., IV; 7 (upd.); 64 (upd.)
Nortel Networks Corporation, 36 (upd.)
The North West Company, Inc., 12
Northern Telecom Limited, V
Nova Corporation of Alberta, V
Novacor Chemicals Ltd., 12
Olympia & York Developments Ltd., IV; 9 (upd.)
1-800-GOT-JUNK? LLC, 74
Onex Corporation, 16; 65 (upd.)
Ontario Hydro Services Company, 6; 32 (upd.)

Ontario Teachers' Pension Plan, 61
Open Text Corporation 79
The Oppenheimer Group, 76
The Oshawa Group Limited, II
Paramount Resources Ltd., 87
PCL Construction Group Inc., 50
Peace Arch Entertainment Group Inc., 51
Pengrowth Energy Trust, 95
Petro-Canada, IV; 99 (upd.)
Philip Environmental Inc., 16
Placer Dome Inc., 20; 61 (upd.)
Potash Corporation of Saskatchewan Inc.,
    18; 101 (upd.)
Power Corporation of Canada, 36 (upd.);
    85 (upd.)
Provigo Inc., II; 51 (upd.)
QLT Inc., 71
Quebecor Inc., 12; 47 (upd.)
Research in Motion Limited, 54; 106
    (upd.)
Richtree Inc., 63
Ritchie Bros. Auctioneers Inc., 41
RM Auctions, Inc., 88
Rogers Communications Inc., 30 (upd.)
RONA, Inc., 73
Roots Canada Ltd., 42
Royal Bank of Canada, II; 21 (upd.), 81
    (upd.)
Royal Group Technologies Limited, 73
Saputo Inc., 59
Scarborough Public Utilities Commission,
    9
The Seagram Company Ltd., I; 25 (upd.)
Shermag, Inc., 93
Shoppers Drug Mart Corporation, 49
Shred-It Canada Corporation, 56
Silver Wheaton Corp., 95
Sleeman Breweries Ltd., 74
SNC-Lavalin Group Inc., 72
Sobeys Inc., 80
Southam Inc., 7
Spar Aerospace Limited, 32
Spin Master, Ltd., 61
Steinberg Incorporated, II
Stelco Inc., IV; 51 (upd.)
Sun Life Financial Inc., 85
Sun-Rype Products Ltd., 76
Suncor Energy Inc., 54
SunOpta Inc. 79
Sunshine Village Corporation, 103
Talisman Energy Inc., 9; 47 (upd.); 103
    (upd.)
TAQA North Ltd., 95
TDL Group Ltd., 46
Teck Corporation, 27
Tembec Inc., 66
The Thomson Corporation, 8; 34 (upd.);
    77 (upd.)
Tilley Endurables, Inc., 67
Toromont Industries, Ltd., 21
The Toronto-Dominion Bank, II; 49
    (upd.)
Torstar Corporation, 29
TransAlta Utilities Corporation, 6
TransCanada Corporation, V; 93 (upd.)
Tridel Enterprises Inc., 9
Trilon Financial Corporation, II
Triple Five Group Ltd., 49

Trizec Corporation Ltd., 10
Tucows Inc. 78
Van Houtte Inc., 39
Varity Corporation, III
Vector Aerospace Corporation, 97
Vincor International Inc., 50
Viterra Inc., 105
Voortman Cookies Limited, 103
Wascana Energy Inc., 13
The Wawanesa Mutual Insurance
    Company, 68
West Fraser Timber Co. Ltd., 17; 91
    (upd.)
Western Oil Sands Inc., 85
WestJet Airlines Ltd., 38
Xantrex Technology Inc., 97

Cayman Islands
Garmin Ltd., 60
Herbalife Ltd., 92 (upd.)
Seagate Technology, 105 (upd.)
United National Group, Ltd., 63

Chile
Banco de Chile, 69
BCI, 99
Cencosud S.A., 69
Compania Cervecerias Unidas S.A., 70
Compañia Sud Americana de Vapores
    S.A., 100
Corporacion Nacional del Cobre de Chile,
    40
Cristalerias de Chile S.A., 67
Distribución y Servicio D&S S.A., 71
Embotelladora Andina S.A., 71
Empresas Almacenes Paris S.A., 71
Empresas CMPC S.A., 70
Empresas Copec S.A., 69
Enersis S.A., 73
Farmacias Ahumada S.A., 72
Lan Chile S.A., 31
Madeco S.A., 71
Minera Escondida Ltda., 100
Parque Arauco S.A., 72
Ripley Corp S.A., 102
S.A.C.I. Falabella, 69
Sociedad Química y Minera de Chile
    S.A., 103
Viña Concha y Toro S.A., 45

China
Agria Corporation, 101
Air China, 46
American Oriental Bioengineering Inc., 93
Anhui Conch Cement Company Limited,
    99
Asia Info Holdings, Inc., 43
Baidu.com Inc., 95
Bank of China, 63
Canadian Solar Inc., 105
China Automotive Systems Inc., 87
China Construction Bank Corp. 79
China Eastern Airlines Co. Ltd., 31
China FAW Group Corporation, 105
China Life Insurance Company Limited,
    65
China National Cereals, Oils and
    Foodstuffs Import and Export
    Corporation (COFCO), 76

China National Petroleum Corporation,
    46
China Nepstar Chain Drugstore Ltd., 97
China Netcom Group Corporation (Hong
    Kong) Limited, 73
China Shenhua Energy Company
    Limited, 83
China Southern Airlines Company Ltd.,
    33
China Telecom, 50
Chinese Petroleum Corporation, IV; 31
    (upd.)
Chongqing Department Store Company
    Ltd., 105
Ctrip.com International Ltd., 97
Dalian Shide Group, 91
Dongfeng Motor Corporation, 105
Egmont Group, 93
Guangzhou Pearl River Piano Group Ltd.,
    49
Haier Group Corporation, 65
Home Inns & Hotels Management Inc.,
    95
Huawei Technologies Company Ltd., 87
LDK Solar Co., Ltd., 101
Li & Fung Limited, 59
Noah Education Holdings Ltd., 97
Shanghai Baosteel Group Corporation, 71
Shanghai Petrochemical Co., Ltd., 18
SINA Corporation, 69
Solarfun Power Holdings Co., Ltd., 105
Suntech Power Holdings Company Ltd.,
    89
Tianjin Flying Pigeon Bicycle Co., Ltd.,
    95
Trina Solar Limited, 103
Tsingtao Brewery Group, 49
WonderWorks, Inc., 103
WuXi AppTec Company Ltd., 103
Zindart Ltd., 60

Colombia
Almacenes Exito S.A., 89
Avianca Aerovías Nacionales de Colombia
    SA, 36
Bavaria S.A., 90
Cementos Argos S.A., 91
Empresa Colombiana de Petróleos, IV
Empresas Públicas de Medellín S.A.E.S.P.,
    91
Inversiones Nacional de Chocolates S.A.,
    88
Suramericana de Inversiones S.A., 88
Valorem S.A., 88

Croatia
PLIVA d.d., 70

Cyprus
Bank of Cyprus Group, 91
Cyprus Airways Public Limited, 81
Marfin Popular Bank plc, 92

Czech Republic
Budweiser Budvar, National Corporation,
    59
Ceské aerolinie, a.s., 66
Cesky Telecom, a.s., 64

ČEZ a. s., 97
Skoda Auto a.s., 39
Třinecké Železárny A.S., 92
Zentiva N.V./Zentiva, a.s., 99

Denmark
A.P. Møller - Maersk A/S, 57
Aalborg Industries A/S, 90
Aarhus United A/S, 68
Arla Foods amba, 48
Bang & Olufsen Holding A/S, 37; 86 (upd.)
Bestseller A/S, 90
Carl Allers Etablissement A/S, 72
Carlsberg A/S, 9; 29 (upd.); 98 (upd.)
Chr. Hansen Group A/S, 70
Dalhoff Larsen & Horneman A/S, 96
Danisco A/S, 44
Danske Bank Aktieselskab, 50
Ecco Sko A/S, 62
FLSmidth & Co. A/S, 72
GN ReSound A/S, 103
Group 4 Falck A/S, 42
Grundfos Group, 83
H. Lundbeck A/S, 44
House of Prince A/S, 80
Hummel International A/S, 68
IKEA International A/S, V; 26 (upd.)
ISS A/S, 49
J Lauritzen A/S, 90
Jysk Holding A/S, 100
Lego A/S, 13; 40 (upd.)
Netto International, 103
Nordisk Film A/S, 80
Novo Nordisk A/S, I; 61 (upd.)
Schouw & Company A/S, 94
Sophus Berendsen A/S, 49
Sterling European Airlines A/S, 70
TDC A/S, 63
Velux A/S, 86
Vestas Wind Systems A/S, 73

Ecuador
Exportadora Bananera Noboa, S.A., 91
Petróleos del Ecuador, IV
TAME (Transportes Aéreos Militares Ecuatorianos), 100

Egypt
EgyptAir, 6; 27 (upd.)
Egyptian General Petroleum Corporation, IV; 51 (upd.)
Orascom Construction Industries S.A.E., 87

El Salvador
Grupo TACA, 38

Estonia
AS Estonian Air, 71

Ethiopia
Ethiopian Airlines, 81

Fiji
Air Pacific Ltd., 70

Finland
Ahlstrom Corporation, 53
Alma Media Corporation, 98

Amer Group plc, 41
Dynea, 68
Enso-Gutzeit Oy, IV
Finnair Oyj, 6; 25 (upd.); 61 (upd.)
Fiskars Corporation, 33; 105 (upd.)
Fortum Corporation, 30 (upd.)
Hackman Oyj Adp, 44
Huhtamäki Oyj, 64
Imatra Steel Oy Ab, 55
Kansallis-Osake-Pankki, II
Kemira Oyj, 70
Kesko Ltd. (Kesko Oy), 8; 27 (upd.)
KONE Corporation, 27; 76 (upd.)
Kymmene Corporation, IV
M-real Oyj, 56 (upd.)
Metsa-Serla Oy, IV
Metso Corporation, 30 (upd.); 85 (upd.)
Neste Oil Corporation, IV; 85 (upd.)
Nokia Corporation, II; 17 (upd.); 38 (upd.); 77 (upd.)
Orion Oyj, 72
Outokumpu Oyj, 38
Posti- ja Telelaitos, 6
Raisio PLC, 99
Rautakirja Oy, 104
Sanitec Corporation, 51
SanomaWSOY Corporation, 51
Sonera Corporation, 50
Stora Enso Oyj, 36 (upd.); 85 (upd.)
Tamfelt Oyj Abp, 62
United Paper Mills Ltd. (Yhtyneet Paperitehtaat Oy), IV
UPM-Kymmene Corporation, 19; 50 (upd.)
Vaisala Oyj, 104
Valmet Corporation (Valmet Oy), III
Wärtsilä Corporation, 100

France
Accor S.A., 10; 27 (upd.); 69 (upd.)
Aéroports de Paris, 33
The Aerospatiale Group, 7; 21 (upd.)
Agence France-Presse, 34
Akerys S.A., 90
Alain Afflelou SA, 53
Alcatel S.A., 9; 36 (upd.)
Alès Groupe, 81
Altran Technologies, 51
Amec Spie S.A., 57
Arc International, 76
AREVA NP, 90 (upd.)
Arianespace S.A., 89
Arkema S.A., 100
Association des Centres Distributeurs E. Leclerc, 37
Assurances Générales de France, 63
Atochem S.A., I
Atos Origin S.A., 69
Au Printemps S.A., V
Auchan, 37
Automobiles Citroen, 7
Autoroutes du Sud de la France SA, 55
Avions Marcel Dassault-Breguet Aviation, I
Axa, III
Babolat VS, S.A., 97
Baccarat, 24
Banque Nationale de Paris S.A., II

Baron Philippe de Rothschild S.A., 39
Bayard SA, 49
Belvedere S.A., 93
Bénéteau SA, 55
Besnier SA, 19
BigBen Interactive S.A., 72
bioMérieux S.A., 75
BNP Paribas Group, 36 (upd.)
Boiron S.A., 73
Boizel Chanoine Champagne S.A., 94
Bonduelle SA, 51
Bongrain S.A., 25; 102 (upd.)
Boulanger S.A., 102
Bouygues S.A., I; 24 (upd.); 97 (upd.)
Bricorama S.A., 68
Brioche Pasquier S.A., 58
Brossard S.A., 102
BSN Groupe S.A., II
Buffalo Grill S.A., 94
Bugatti Automobiles S.A.S., 94
Bull S.A., 43 (upd.)
Bureau Veritas SA, 55
Burelle S.A., 23
Business Objects S.A., 25
Camaïeu S.A., 72
Caisse des Dépôts et Consignations, 90
Canal Plus, 10; 34 (upd.)
Cap Gemini Ernst & Young, 37
Carbone Lorraine S.A., 33
Carrefour SA, 10; 27 (upd.); 64 (upd.)
Carrere Group S.A., 104
Casino Guichard-Perrachon S.A., 59 (upd.)
Castorama-Dubois Investissements SCA, 104 (upd.)
Cegedim S.A., 104
Cemoi S.A., 86
Cetelem S.A., 21
Chanel SA, 12; 49 (upd.)
Chantiers Jeanneau S.A., 96
Charal S.A., 90
Chargeurs International, 6; 21 (upd.)
Christian Dalloz SA, 40
Christian Dior S.A., 19; 49 (upd.)
Christofle SA, 40
Ciments Français, 40
Club Mediterranée S.A., 6; 21 (upd.); 91 (upd.)
Coflexip S.A., 25
Colas S.A., 31
Compagnie de Saint-Gobain, III; 16 (upd.); 64 (upd.)
Compagnie des Alpes, 48
Compagnie des Machines Bull S.A., III
Compagnie Financiere de Paribas, II
Compagnie Financière Sucres et Denrées S.A., 60
Compagnie Générale d'Électricité, II
Compagnie Générale des Établissements Michelin, V; 42 (upd.)
Compagnie Générale Maritime et Financière, 6
Comptoirs Modernes S.A., 19
Coopagri Bretagne, 88
Crédit Agricole Group, II; 84 (upd.)
Crédit Lyonnais, 9; 33 (upd.)
Crédit National S.A., 9
Dalkia Holding, 66

Damartex S.A., 98
Darty S.A., 27
Dassault Systèmes S.A., 25
DCN S.A., 75
De Dietrich & Cie., 31
Delachaux S.A., 76
Deveaux S.A., 41
Devoteam S.A., 94
Dexia Group, 42
Doux S.A., 80
Du Pareil au Même, 43
Dynaction S.A., 67
Dyneff S.A., 98
EADS SOCATA, 54
ECS S.A, 12
Ed S.A.S., 88
Éditions Gallimard, 72
Editis S.A. 78
Eiffage, 27
Electricité de France, V; 41 (upd.)
Elf Aquitaine SA, 21 (upd.)
Elior SA, 49
Eram SA, 51
Eramet, 73
Eridania Béghin-Say S.A., 36
Essilor International, 21
Etablissements Economiques du Casino
    Guichard, Perrachon et Cie, S.C.A., 12
Établissements Jacquot and Cie S.A.S., 92
Etam Developpement SA, 44
Eurazeo, 80
Euro Disney S.C.A., 20; 58 (upd.)
Euro RSCG Worldwide S.A., 13
Eurocopter S.A., 80
Eurofins Scientific S.A., 70
Euronext Paris S.A., 37
Europcar Groupe S.A., 104
Evialis S.A., 100
Exacompta Clairefontaine S.A., 102
Expand SA, 48
Facom S.A., 32
Faiveley S.A., 39
Faurecia S.A., 70
Fimalac S.A., 37
Fleury Michon S.A., 39
Floc'h & Marchand, 80
FNAC, 21
Framatome SA, 19
France Telecom S.A., V; 21 (upd.); 99
    (upd.)
Fromageries Bel, 23
G.I.E. Airbus Industrie, I; 12 (upd.)
Galeries Lafayette S.A., V; 23 (upd.)
Gaumont S.A., 25; 91 (upd.)
Gaz de France, V; 40 (upd.)
Gecina SA, 42
Gefco SA, 54
Générale des Eaux Group, V
Geodis S.A., 67
Gévelot S.A., 96
GFI Informatique SA, 49
GiFi S.A., 74
Glaces Thiriet S.A., 76
Grands Vins Jean-Claude Boisset S.A., 98
GrandVision S.A., 43
Grévin & Compagnie SA, 56
Groupama S.A., 76
Groupe Air France, 6

Groupe Alain Manoukian, 55
Groupe André, 17
Groupe Ares S.A., 102
Groupe Bigard S.A., 96
Groupe Bolloré, 67
Groupe Bourbon S.A., 60
Groupe Caisse d'Epargne, 100
Groupe Castorama-Dubois
    Investissements, 23
Groupe CECAB S.C.A., 88
Groupe Crit S.A., 74
Groupe Danone, 32 (upd.); 93 (upd.)
Groupe Dassault Aviation SA, 26 (upd.)
Groupe de la Cite, IV
Groupe DMC (Dollfus Mieg & Cie), 27
Groupe Dubreuil S.A., 102
Groupe Euralis, 86
Groupe Flo S.A., 98
Groupe Fournier SA, 44
Groupe Genoyer, 96
Groupe Glon, 84
Groupe Go Sport S.A., 39
Groupe Guillin SA, 40
Groupe Henri Heuliez S.A., 100
Groupe Jean-Claude Darmon, 44
Groupe Lactalis 78 (upd.)
Groupe Lapeyre S.A., 33
Groupe Le Duff S.A., 84
Groupe Léa Nature, 88
Groupe Legris Industries, 23
Groupe Les Echos, 25
Groupe Limagrain, 74
Groupe Louis Dreyfus S.A., 60
Groupe Monnoyeur, 72
Groupe Monoprix S.A., 86
Groupe Open, 74
Groupe Partouche SA, 48
Groupe Promodès S.A., 19
Groupe Rougier SA, 21
Groupe SEB, 35
Groupe Sequana Capital 78 (upd.)
Groupe Sidel S.A., 21
Groupe Soufflet SA, 55
Groupe Yves Saint Laurent, 23
Groupe Zannier S.A., 35
Guerbet Group, 46
Guerlain, 23
Guilbert S.A., 42
Guillemot Corporation, 41
Guinot Paris S.A., 82
Guy Degrenne SA, 44
Guyenne et Gascogne, 23
Hachette, IV
Hachette Filipacchi Medias S.A., 21
Havas, SA, 10; 33 (upd.)
Hermès International S.A., 14; 34 (upd.)
Imerys S.A., 40 (upd.)
Imetal S.A., IV
Infogrames Entertainment S.A., 35
Ingenico—Compagnie Industrielle et
    Financière d'Ingénierie, 46
ITM Entreprises SA, 36
JCDecaux S.A., 76
Keolis SA, 51
Kiabi Europe, 66
L'Air Liquide SA, I; 47 (upd.)
L'Entreprise Jean Lefebvre, 23
L'Oréal SA, III; 8 (upd.); 46 (upd.)

L.D.C. SA, 61
La Poste, V; 47 (upd.)
Labeyrie SAS, 80
Laboratoires Arkopharma S.A., 75
Laboratoires de Biologie Végétale Yves
    Rocher, 35
Laboratoires Pierre Fabre S.A., 100
LaCie Group S.A., 76
Lafarge Coppée S.A., III
Lafuma S.A., 39
Latécoère S.A., 100
Laurent-Perrier SA, 42
Lazard LLC, 38
LDC, 68
Le Cordon Bleu S.A., 67
Le Monde S.A., 33
Legrand SA, 21
Leroux S.A.S., 65
Leroy Merlin SA, 54
Ludendo S.A., 88
LVMH Möet Hennessy Louis Vuitton SA,
    I; 10; 33 (upd.)
Lyonnaise des Eaux-Dumez, V
Madrange SA, 58
Maison Louis Jadot, 24
Manitou BF S.A., 27
Manutan International S.A., 72
Marie Brizard & Roger International
    S.A.S., 22; 97 (upd.)
Marionnaud Parfumeries SA, 51
Martell and Company S.A., 82
Matra-Hachette S.A., 15 (upd.)
Matussière et Forest SA, 58
MBK Industrie S.A., 94
Metaleurop S.A., 21
Métropole Télévision, 33
Métropole Télévision S.A., 76 (upd.)
Moliflor Loisirs, 80
Monnaie de Paris, 62
Montupet S.A., 63
Moulinex S.A., 22
Mr. Bricolage S.A., 37
Naf Naf SA, 44
Neopost S.A., 53
Nestlé Waters, 73
Nexans SA, 54
Nexity S.A., 66
Nocibé SA, 54
OENEO S.A., 74 (upd.)
Onet S.A., 92
Otor S.A., 77
PagesJaunes Groupe SA 79
Panzani, 84
Papeteries de Lancey, 23
Parfums Givenchy S.A., 100
Pathé SA, 29
Pechiney SA, IV; 45 (upd.)
Penauille Polyservices SA, 49
Pernod Ricard S.A., I; 21 (upd.); 72
    (upd.)
Petit Bateau, 95
Peugeot S.A., I
Picard Surgeles, 76
Pierre & Vacances SA, 48
Pinault-Printemps Redoute S.A., 19 (upd.)
Pinguely-Haulotte SA, 51
Piscines Desjoyaux S.A., 84
Pochet SA, 55

Poliet S.A., 33
Prodware S.A., 102
PPR S.A., 74 (upd.)
Provimi S.A., 80
PSA Peugeot Citroen S.A., 28 (upd.)
Publicis S.A., 19; 77 (upd.)
Rallye SA, 54
Redcats S.A., 102
Regie Nationale des Usines Renault, I
Rémy Cointreau Group, 20, 80 (upd.)
Renault S.A., 26 (upd.); 74 (upd.)
Réseau Ferré de France, 66
Rhodia SA, 38
Rhône-Poulenc S.A., I; 10 (upd.)
Robertet SA, 39
Rodriguez Group S.A., 90
Roussel Uclaf, I; 8 (upd.)
Royal Canin S.A., 39
Sabaté Diosos SA, 48
SAFRAN, 102 (upd.)
SAGEM S.A., 37
Salomon Worldwide, 20
The Sanofi-Synthélabo Group, I; 49 (upd.)
Saur S.A.S., 92
Schneider S.A., II; 18 (upd.)
SCOR S.A., 20
Seita, 23
Selectour SA, 53
Sephora Holdings S.A., 82
Simco S.A., 37
Skalli Group, 67
Skis Rossignol S.A., 15; 43 (upd.)
Smoby International SA, 56
Snecma Group, 46
Société Air France, 27 (upd.)
Société BIC S.A., 73
Société d'Exploitation AOM Air Liberté SA (AirLib), 53
Societe des Produits Marnier-Lapostolle S.A., 88
Société du Figaro S.A., 60
Société du Louvre, 27
Société Générale, II; 42 (upd.)
Société Industrielle Lesaffre, 84
Société Nationale des Chemins de Fer Français, V; 57 (upd.)
Société Nationale Elf Aquitaine, IV; 7 (upd.)
Société Norbert Dentressangle S.A., 67
Sodexho SA, 29; 91 (upd.)
Sodiaal S.A., 36 (upd.)
SODIMA, II
Sommer-Allibert S.A., 19
Sperian Protection S.A., 104
SR Teleperformance S.A., 86
Steria SA, 49
Suez Lyonnaise des Eaux, 36 (upd.)
Taittinger S.A., 43
Tati SA, 25
Technip 78
Télévision Française 1, 23
Tergal Industries S.A.S., 102
Terrena L'Union CANA CAVAL, 70
Thales S.A., 42
THOMSON multimedia S.A., II; 42 (upd.)

Total Fina Elf S.A., IV; 24 (upd.); 50 (upd.)
Toupargel-Agrigel S.A., 76
Touton S.A., 92
Transiciel SA, 48
Trigano S.A., 102
Turbomeca S.A., 102
Ubisoft Entertainment S.A., 41; 106 (upd.)
Ugine S.A., 20
Unibail SA, 40
Unilog SA, 42
Union des Assurances de Pans, III
Union Financière de France Banque SA, 52
Usinor SA, IV; 42 (upd.)
Valeo, 23; 66 (upd.)
Vallourec SA, 54
Veuve Clicquot Ponsardin SCS, 98
Vicat S.A., 70
Viel & Cie, 76
Vilmorin Clause et Cie, 70
Vinci, 43
Vivarte SA, 54 (upd.)
Vivendi Universal S.A., 46 (upd.)
Wanadoo S.A., 75
Weber et Broutin France, 66
Worms et Cie, 27
Zodiac S.A., 36

Germany

A. Moksel AG, 59
A.W. Faber-Castell Unternehmensverwaltung GmbH & Co., 51
Adam Opel AG, 7; 21 (upd.); 61 (upd.)
adidas Group AG, 14; 33 (upd.); 75 (upd.)
Adolf Würth GmbH & Co. KG, 49
AEG A.G., I
Air Berlin GmbH & Co. Luftverkehrs KG, 71
Aldi Einkauf GmbH & Co. OHG 13; 86 (upd.)
Alfred Kärcher GmbH & Co KG, 94
Alfred Ritter GmbH & Co. KG, 58
Allgemeiner Deutscher Automobil-Club e.V., 100
Allianz AG, III; 15 (upd.); 57 (upd.)
ALTANA AG, 87
AMB Generali Holding AG, 51
Andreas Stihl AG & Co. KG, 16; 59 (upd.)
Anton Schlecker, 102
AOK-Bundesverband (Federation of the AOK) 78
Aral AG, 62
ARD, 41
August Storck KG, 66
AVA AG (Allgemeine Handelsgesellschaft der Verbraucher AG), 33
AXA Colonia Konzern AG, 27; 49 (upd.)
Axel Springer Verlag AG, IV; 20 (upd.)
Bahlsen GmbH & Co. KG, 44
Barmag AG, 39
BASF Aktiengesellschaft, I; 18 (upd.); 50 (upd.)
Bauer Publishing Group, 7

Bayer A.G., I; 13 (upd.); 41 (upd.)
Bayerische Hypotheken- und Wechsel-Bank AG, II
Bayerische Motoren Werke AG, I; 11 (upd.); 38 (upd.)
Bayerische Vereinsbank A.G., II
Bayernwerk AG, V; 23 (upd.)
Beate Uhse AG, 96
Behr GmbH & Co. KG, 72
Beiersdorf AG, 29
Berliner Stadtreinigungsbetriebe, 58
Berliner Verkehrsbetriebe (BVG), 58
Berlinwasser Holding AG, 90
Bertelsmann A.G., IV; 15 (upd.); 43 (upd.); 91 (upd.)
Bewag AG, 39
Bibliographisches Institut & F.A. Brockhaus AG, 74
Bilfinger & Berger AG, I; 55 (upd.)
Brauerei Beck & Co., 9; 33 (upd.)
Braun GmbH, 51
Brenntag Holding GmbH & Co. KG, 8; 23 (upd.); 101 (upd.)
Brose Fahrzeugteile GmbH & Company KG, 84
BSH Bosch und Siemens Hausgeräte GmbH, 67
Buderus AG, 37
Burda Holding GmbH. & Co., 23
C&A Brenninkmeyer KG, V
C. Bechstein Pianofortefabrik AG, 96
C.H. Boehringer Sohn, 39
Carl Kühne KG (GmbH & Co.), 94
Carl Zeiss AG, III; 34 (upd.); 91 (upd.)
CeWe Color Holding AG, 76
Commerzbank A.G., II; 47 (upd.)
Continental AG, V; 56 (upd.)
Cornelsen Verlagsholding GmbH & Co., 90
Dachser GmbH & Co. KG, 88
Daimler-Benz Aerospace AG, 16
DaimlerChrysler AG, I; 15 (upd.); 34 (upd.); 64 (upd.)
Dalli-Werke GmbH & Co. KG, 86
dba Luftfahrtgesellschaft mbH, 76
Debeka Krankenversicherungsverein auf Gegenseitigkeit, 72
Degussa Group, IV
Degussa-Huls AG, 32 (upd.)
Deutsche Babcock A.G., III
Deutsche Bahn AG, 46 (upd.)
Deutsche Bank AG, II; 14 (upd.); 40 (upd.)
Deutsche BP Aktiengesellschaft, 7
Deutsche Bundesbahn, V
Deutsche Bundespost TELEKOM, V
Deutsche Börse AG, 59
Deutsche Fussball Bund e.V., 98
Deutsche Lufthansa AG, I; 26 (upd.); 68 (upd.)
Deutsche Messe AG, 104
Deutsche Post AG, 29
Deutsche Steinzeug Cremer & Breuer Aktiengesellschaft, 91
Deutsche Telekom AG, 48 (upd.)
Deutscher Sparkassen- und Giroverband (DSGV), 84
Deutz AG, 39

Diehl Stiftung & Co. KG 79
Dirk Rossmann GmbH, 94
Dr. August Oetker KG, 51
Drägerwerk AG, 83
Dräxlmaier Group, 90
Dresdner Bank A.G., II; 57 (upd.)
Dürkopp Adler AG, 65
Dürr AG, 44
Dyckerhoff AG, 35
E.On AG, 50 (upd.)
Eckes AG, 56
Edeka Zentrale A.G., II; 47 (upd.)
edel music AG, 44
ElringKlinger AG, 100
ERGO Versicherungsgruppe AG, 44
ESCADA AG, 71
Esselte Leitz GmbH & Co. KG, 48
Etienne Aigner AG, 52
FAG—Kugelfischer Georg Schäfer AG, 62
Fairchild Dornier GmbH, 48 (upd.)
Feldmuhle Nobel A.G., III
Fielmann AG, 31
Francotyp-Postalia Holding AG, 92
Frankfurter Allgemeine Zeitung GmbH, 66
Fraport AG Frankfurt Airport Services Worldwide, 90
Fresenius AG, 56
Freudenberg & Co., 41
Fried. Krupp GmbH, IV
Friedrich Grohe AG & Co. KG, 53
Fuchs Petrolub AG, 102
GEA AG, 27
GEHE AG, 27
Gelita AG, 74
GEMA (Gesellschaft für musikalische Aufführungs- und mechanische Vervielfältigungsrechte), 70
geobra Brandstätter GmbH & Co. KG, 48
Gerhard D. Wempe KG, 88
Gerling-Konzern Versicherungs-Beteiligungs-Aktiengesellschaft, 51
Gerresheimer Glas AG, 43
Gerry Weber International AG, 63
Getrag Corporate Group, 92
GfK Aktiengesellschaft, 49
Giesecke & Devrient GmbH, 83
Gildemeister AG 79
Groz-Beckert Group, 68
Grundig AG, 27
Hansgrohe AG, 56
Hapag-Lloyd AG, 6; 97 (upd.)
HARIBO GmbH & Co. KG, 44
HDI (Haftpflichtverband der Deutschen Industrie Versicherung auf Gegenseitigkeit V.a.G.), 53
Heidelberger Druckmaschinen AG, 40
Heidelberger Zement AG, 31
Heinrich Deichmann-Schuhe GmbH & Co. KG, 88
Hella KGaA Hueck & Co., 66
Henkel KGaA, III; 34 (upd.); 95 (upd.)
Heraeus Holding GmbH, IV; 54 (upd.)
Hertie Waren- und Kaufhaus GmbH, V
Hexal AG, 69
HiPP GmbH & Co. Vertrieb KG, 88
Hochtief AG, 33; 88 (upd.)

Hoechst A.G., I; 18 (upd.)
Hoesch AG, IV
Hornbach Holding AG, 98
Hugo Boss AG, 48
HUK-Coburg, 58
Huls A.G., I
HVB Group, 59 (upd.)
Ihr Platz GmbH + Company KG, 77
Infineon Technologies AG, 50
J.J. Darboven GmbH & Co. KG, 96
J.M. Voith AG, 33
Jenoptik AG, 33
Julius Blüthner Pianofortefabrik GmbH 78
Jungheinrich AG, 96
Kamps AG, 44
Karlsberg Brauerei GmbH & Co KG, 41
Karstadt Quelle AG, V; 19 (upd.); 57 (upd.)
Kaufhof Warenhaus AG, V; 23 (upd.)
Kaufring AG, 35
KHD Konzern, III
Klaus Steilmann GmbH & Co. KG, 53
Klöckner-Werke AG, IV; 58 (upd.)
Knauf Gips KG, 100
Knorr-Bremse AG, 84
Koenig & Bauer AG, 64
Kolbenschmidt Pierburg AG, 97
König Brauerei GmbH & Co. KG, 35 (upd.)
Körber AG, 60
Kreditanstalt für Wiederaufbau, 29
Krombacher Brauerei Bernhard Schadeberg GmbH & Co. KG, 104
KSB AG, 62
Leica Camera AG, 35
Leica Microsystems Holdings GmbH, 35
Leoni AG, 98
Linde AG, I; 67 (upd.)
Loewe AG, 90
Löwenbräu AG, 80
LTU Group Holding GmbH, 37
M. DuMont Schauberg GmbH & Co. KG, 92
MAN Aktiengesellschaft, III
MAN Roland Druckmaschinen AG, 94
Manncsmann AG, III; 14 (upd.); 38 (upd.)
Margarete Steiff GmbH, 23
Märklin Holding GmbH, 70
Matth. Hohner AG, 53
Melitta Unternehmensgruppe Bentz KG, 53
Merz Group, 81
Messerschmitt-Bölkow-Blohm GmbH., I
Metallgesellschaft AG, IV; 16 (upd.)
Metro AG, 50
Miele & Cie. KG, 56
MITROPA AG, 37
Montblanc International GmbH, 82
Munich Re (Münchener Rückversicherungs-Gesellschaft Aktiengesellschaft in München), III; 46 (upd.)
Neckermann.de GmbH, 102
Nixdorf Computer AG, III
Norddeutsche Affinerie AG, 62
Nordex AG, 101

Optische Werke G. Rodenstock, 44
Osram GmbH, 86
Otto Fuchs KG, 100
Otto Group, 106
Otto Versand GmbH & Co., V; 15 (upd.); 34 (upd.)
Paulaner Brauerei GmbH & Co. KG, 35
Peek & Cloppenburg KG, 46
Philipp Holzmann AG, 17
Phoenix AG, 68
Porsche AG, 13; 31 (upd.)
Praktiker Bau- und Heimwerkermärkte AG, 103
Preussag AG, 17; 42 (upd.)
PreussenElektra Aktiengesellschaft, V
ProSiebenSat.1 Media AG, 54
Puma AG Rudolf Dassler Sport, 35
PWA Group, IV
Qiagen N.V., 39
Quelle Group, V
Radeberger Gruppe AG, 75
RAG AG, 35; 60 (upd.)
ratiopharm Group, 84
Ravensburger AG, 64
RENK AG, 37
REpower Systems AG, 101
REWE-Zentral AG, 103
Rheinmetall AG, 9; 97 (upd.)
Robert Bosch GmbH, I; 16 (upd.); 43 (upd.)
Röchling Gruppe, 94
Rohde & Schwarz GmbH & Co. KG, 39
Roland Berger & Partner GmbH, 37
The Rowohlt Verlag GmbH, 96
Ruhrgas AG, V; 38 (upd.)
Ruhrkohle AG, IV
RWE AG, V; 50 (upd.)
Saarberg-Konzern, IV
Salzgitter AG, IV; 101 (upd.)
SAP AG, 16; 43 (upd.)
Schneidersöhne Deutschland GmbH & Co. KG, 100
Schenker-Rhenus AG, 6
Schering AG, I; 50 (upd.)
The Schwarz Group, 100
Sennheiser Electronic GmbH & Co. KG, 66
Siemens AG, II; 14 (upd.); 57 (upd.)
Siltronic AG, 90
Simba Dickie Group KG, 105
Sixt AG, 39
Spar Handelsgesellschaft mbH, 35; 103 (upd.)
SPIEGEL-Verlag Rudolf Augstein GmbH & Co. KG, 44
Stinnes AG, 8; 23 (upd.); 59 (upd.)
Stollwerck AG, 53
Südzucker AG, 27
Symrise GmbH and Company KG, 89
T-Online International AG, 61
TA Triumph-Adler AG, 48
Tarkett Sommer AG, 25
Taschen GmbH, 101
TaurusHolding GmbH & Co. KG, 46
Tchibo GmbH, 82
Tengelmann Group, 27
ThyssenKrupp AG, IV; 28 (upd.); 87 (upd.)

Touristik Union International GmbH. and Company K.G., II
TRUMPF GmbH + Co. KG, 86
TUI Group GmbH, 44
UFA TV & Film Produktion GmbH, 80
United Internet AG, 99
Vaillant GmbH, 44
Varta AG, 23
Veba A.G., I; 15 (upd.)
Vereinigte Elektrizitätswerke Westfalen AG, V
Verlagsgruppe Georg von Holtzbrinck GmbH, 35
Verlagsgruppe Weltbild GmbH, 98
VEW AG, 39
VIAG Aktiengesellschaft, IV
Victoria Group, III; 44 (upd.)
Viessmann Werke GmbH & Co., 37
Wilh. Werhahn KG, 101
Wilhelm Karmann GmbH, 94
Villeroy & Boch AG, 37
Volkswagen Aktiengesellschaft, I; 11 (upd.); 32 (upd.)
Vorwerk & Co., 27
Vossloh AG, 53
Wacker-Chemie GmbH, 35
Wacker Construction Equipment AG, 95
WAZ Media Group, 82
Wella AG, III; 48 (upd.)
Weru Aktiengesellschaft, 18
Westdeutsche Landesbank Girozentrale, II; 46 (upd.)
Wincor Nixdorf Holding GmbH, 69 (upd.)
Württembergische Metallwarenfabrik AG (WMF), 60
Zapf Creation AG, 95
ZF Friedrichshafen AG, 48

Ghana
Ashanti Goldfields Company Limited, 43

Greece
Aegean Marine Petroleum Network Inc., 89
Aegek S.A., 64
Attica Enterprises S.A., 64
Danaos Corporation, 91
Diana Shipping Inc., 95
DryShips Inc., 95
Greek Organization of Football Prognostics S.A. (OPAP), 97
Hellenic Petroleum SA, 64
Jumbo S.A., 96
National Bank of Greece, 41
Royal Olympic Cruise Lines Inc., 52
Stelmar Shipping Ltd., 52
Titan Cement Company S.A., 64
Tsakos Energy Navigation Ltd., 91
Vivartia S.A., 82

Guatemala
Corporación Multi-Inversiones, 94

Hong Kong
A.S. Watson & Company Ltd., 84
Bank of East Asia Ltd., 63
Cable & Wireless HKT, 30 (upd.)

Cathay Pacific Airways Limited, 6; 34 (upd.)
CDC Corporation, 71
Chaoda Modern Agriculture (Holdings) Ltd., 87
Cheung Kong (Holdings) Ltd., IV; 20 (upd.); 94 (upd.)
China Merchants International Holdings Co., Ltd., 52
CITIC Pacific Ltd., 18
Dairy Farm International Holdings Ltd., 97
First Pacific Company Limited, 18
The Garden Company Ltd., 82
GOME Electrical Appliances Holding Ltd., 87
Guangzhou R&F Properties Co., Ltd., 95
Hang Lung Group Ltd., 104
Hang Seng Bank Ltd., 60
Henderson Land Development Company Ltd., 70
Hong Kong and China Gas Company Ltd., 73
Hong Kong Dragon Airlines Ltd., 66
Hong Kong Telecommunications Ltd., 6
The Hongkong and Shanghai Banking Corporation Limited, II
Hongkong Electric Holdings Ltd., 6; 23 (upd.)
Hongkong Land Holdings Limited, IV; 47 (upd.)
Hopson Development Holdings Ltd., 87
Hutchison Whampoa Limited, 18; 49 (upd.)
Kerry Properties Limited, 22
Melco Crown Entertainment Limited, 103
Meyer International Holdings, Ltd., 87
Nam Tai Electronics, Inc., 61
New World Development Company Limited, IV; 38 (upd.)
Next Media Ltd., 61
Pacific Basin Shipping Ltd., 86
Playmates Toys, 23
Shangri-La Asia Ltd., 71
The Singer Company N.V., 30 (upd.)
SJM Holdings Ltd., 105
Swire Pacific Limited, I; 16 (upd.); 57 (upd.)
Techtronic Industries Company Ltd., 73
Tommy Hilfiger Corporation, 20; 53 (upd.)
Vitasoy International Holdings Ltd., 94
VTech Holdings Ltd., 77

Hungary
Egis Gyogyszergyar Nyrt, 104
Magyar Telekom Rt. 78
Malév Plc, 24
MOL Rt, 70
Orszagos Takarekpenztar es Kereskedelmi Bank Rt. (OTP Bank) 78

Iceland
Actavis Group hf., 103
Alfesca hf, 82
Bakkavör Group hf., 91
Baugur Group hf, 81
Icelandair, 52

Icelandic Group hf, 81
Landsbanki Islands hf, 81

India
Adani Enterprises Ltd., 97
Aditya Birla Group 79
Air Sahara Limited, 65
Air-India Limited, 6; 27 (upd.)
Bajaj Auto Limited, 39
Bharti Tele-Ventures Limited, 75
Coal India Limited, IV; 44 (upd.)
Dr. Reddy's Laboratories Ltd., 59
EIH Ltd., 103
Essar Group Ltd. 79
Hindustan Lever Limited 79
Indian Airlines Ltd., 46
Indian Oil Corporation Ltd., IV; 48 (upd.)
Infosys Technologies Ltd., 38
Jaiprakash Associates Limited, 101
Jet Airways (India) Private Limited, 65
Minerals and Metals Trading Corporation of India Ltd., IV
MTR Foods Ltd., 55
Neyveli Lignite Corporation Ltd., 65
Oil and Natural Gas Corporation Ltd., IV; 90 (upd.)
Ranbaxy Laboratories Ltd., 70
Raymond Ltd., 77
Reliance Industries Ltd., 81
Rolta India Ltd., 90
Satyam Computer Services Ltd., 85
State Bank of India, 63
Steel Authority of India Ltd., IV; 66 (upd.)
Sun Pharmaceutical Industries Ltd., 57
Tata Iron & Steel Co. Ltd., IV; 44 (upd.)
Tata Tea Ltd., 76
Wipro Limited, 43; 106 (upd.)

Indonesia
Djarum PT, 62
Garuda Indonesia, 6; 58 (upd.)
PERTAMINA, IV
Pertamina, 56 (upd.)
PT Astra International Tbk, 56
PT Bank Buana Indonesia Tbk, 60
PT Gudang Garam Tbk, 103
PT Indosat Tbk, 93
PT Semen Gresik Tbk, 103

Iran
IranAir, 81
National Iranian Oil Company, IV; 61 (upd.)

Ireland
Aer Lingus Group plc, 34; 89 (upd.)
Allied Irish Banks, plc, 16; 43 (upd.); 94 (upd.)
Baltimore Technologies Plc, 42
Bank of Ireland, 50
CRH plc, 64
CryptoLogic Limited, 106
DEPFA BANK PLC, 69
Dunnes Stores Ltd., 58
eircom plc, 31 (upd.)

Elan Corporation PLC, 63
Fyffes PLC, 38; 106 (upd.)
Glanbia plc, 59
Glen Dimplex 78
Grafton Group plc, 104
Greencore Group plc, 98
Harland and Wolff Holdings plc, 19
IAWS Group plc, 49
Independent News & Media PLC, 61
IONA Technologies plc, 43
Irish Distillers Group, 96
Irish Life & Permanent Plc, 59
Jefferson Smurfit Group plc, IV; 19 (upd.); 49 (upd.)
Jurys Doyle Hotel Group plc, 64
Kerry Group plc, 27; 87 (upd.)
Musgrave Group Plc, 57
Paddy Power plc, 98
Ryanair Holdings plc, 35
Shannon Aerospace Ltd., 36
SkillSoft Public Limited Company, 81
Telecom Eireann, 7
Thomas Crosbie Holdings Limited, 81
Waterford Wedgwood plc, 34 (upd.)

Israel

Aladdin Knowledge Systems Ltd., 101
Alon Israel Oil Company Ltd., 104
Amdocs Ltd., 47
Bank Hapoalim B.M., II; 54 (upd.)
Bank Leumi le-Israel B.M., 60
Blue Square Israel Ltd., 41
BVR Systems (1998) Ltd., 93
Castro Model Ltd., 86
ECI Telecom Ltd., 18
El Al Israel Airlines Ltd., 23
Elscint Ltd., 20
EZchip Semiconductor Ltd., 106
Galtronics Ltd., 100
Given Imaging Ltd., 83
IDB Holding Corporation Ltd., 97
Israel Aircraft Industries Ltd., 69
Israel Chemicals Ltd., 55
Koor Industries Ltd., II; 25 (upd.); 68 (upd.)
Lipman Electronic Engineering Ltd., 81
Makhteshim-Agan Industries Ltd., 85
NICE Systems Ltd., 83
Orbotech Ltd., 75
Scitex Corporation Ltd., 24
Strauss-Elite Group, 68
Syneron Medical Ltd., 91
Taro Pharmaceutical Industries Ltd., 65
Teva Pharmaceutical Industries Ltd., 22; 54 (upd.)

Italy

AgustaWestland N.V., 75
Alfa Romeo, 13; 36 (upd.)
Alitalia—Linee Aeree Italiana, S.p.A., 6; 29 (upd.); 97 (upd.)
Alleanza Assicurazioni S.p.A., 65
Angelini SpA, 100
Aprilia SpA, 17
Arnoldo Mondadori Editore S.p.A., IV; 19 (upd.); 54 (upd.)
Artsana SpA, 92
Assicurazioni Generali S.p.A., III; 15 (upd.); 103 (upd.)

Autogrill SpA, 49
Automobili Lamborghini Holding S.p.A., 13; 34 (upd.); 91 (upd.)
Autostrada Torino-Milano S.p.A., 101
Azelis Group, 100
Banca Commerciale Italiana SpA, II
Banca Fideuram SpA, 63
Banca Intesa SpA, 65
Banca Monte dei Paschi di Siena SpA, 65
Banca Nazionale del Lavoro SpA, 72
Barilla G. e R. Fratelli S.p.A., 17; 50 (upd.)
Benetton Group S.p.A., 10; 67 (upd.)
Brioni Roman Style S.p.A., 67
Bulgari S.p.A., 20; 106 (upd.)
Cantine Giorgio Lungarotti S.R.L., 67
Capitalia S.p.A., 65
Cinemeccanica SpA 78
Compagnia Italiana dei Jolly Hotels S.p.A., 71
Credito Italiano, II
Cremonini S.p.A., 57
Davide Campari-Milano S.p.A., 57
De Agostini Editore S.p.A., 103
De Rigo S.p.A., 104
De'Longhi S.p.A., 66
Diadora SpA, 86
Diesel SpA, 40
Dolce & Gabbana SpA, 62
Ducati Motor Holding SpA, 30; 86 (upd.)
ENI S.p.A., 69 (upd.)
Ente Nazionale Idrocarburi, IV
Ente Nazionale per L'Energia Elettrica, V
Ermenegildo Zegna SpA, 63
Fabbrica D' Armi Pietro Beretta S.p.A., 39
FASTWEB S.p.A., 83
Ferrari S.p.A., 13; 36 (upd.)
Ferrero SpA, 54
Ferretti Group SpA, 90
Ferrovie Dello Stato Societa Di Trasporti e Servizi S.p.A., 105
Fiat SpA, I; 11 (upd.); 50 (upd.)
Fila Holding S.p.A., 20; 52 (upd.)
Finarte Casa d'Aste S.p.A., 93
Finmeccanica S.p.A., 84
Gianni Versace S.p.A., 22; 106 (upd.)
Giorgio Armani S.p.A., 45
Gruppo Coin S.p.A., 41
Gruppo Riva Fire SpA, 88
Guccio Gucci, S.p.A., 15
I Grandi Viaggi S.p.A., 105
illycaffè SpA, 50
Industrie Natuzzi S.p.A., 18
Industrie Zignago Santa Margherita S.p.A., 67
Ing. C. Olivetti & C., S.p.a., III
Istituto per la Ricostruzione Industriale S.p.A., I; 11
Juventus F.C. S.p.A, 53
La Doria SpA, 101
Luxottica SpA, 17; 52 (upd.)
Magneti Marelli Holding SpA, 90
Marchesi Antinori SRL, 42
Marcolin S.p.A., 61
Mariella Burani Fashion Group, 92
Martini & Rossi SpA, 63
Marzotto S.p.A., 20; 67 (upd.)
Mediaset SpA, 50

Mediolanum S.p.A., 65
Milan AC, S.p.A. 79
Miroglio SpA, 86
Montedison SpA, I; 24 (upd.)
Officine Alfieri Maserati S.p.A., 13
Olivetti S.p.A., 34 (upd.)
Pagnossin S.p.A., 73
Parmalat Finanziaria SpA, 50
Peg Perego SpA, 88
Perfetti Van Melle S.p.A., 72
Piaggio & C. S.p.A., 20; 100 (upd.)
Pirelli & C. S.p.A., 75 (upd.)
Pirelli S.p.A., V; 15 (upd.)
RCS MediaGroup S.p.A., 96
Recordati Industria Chimica e Farmaceutica S.p.A., 105
Reno de Medici S.p.A., 41
Rinascente S.p.A., 71
Riunione Adriatica di Sicurtè SpA, III
Safilo SpA, 54
Salvatore Ferragamo Italia S.p.A., 62
Sanpaolo IMI S.p.A., 50
Seat Pagine Gialle S.p.A., 47
Sirti S.p.A., 76
Società Finanziaria Telefonica per Azioni, V
Società Sportiva Lazio SpA, 44
Stefanel SpA, 63
Targetti Sankey SpA, 86
Telecom Italia Mobile S.p.A., 63
Telecom Italia S.p.A., 43
Tiscali SpA, 48

Jamaica

Air Jamaica Limited, 54
Desnoes and Geddes Limited 79
GraceKennedy Ltd., 92
Wray & Nephew Group Ltd., 98

Japan

AEON Co., Ltd., 68 (upd.)
Aisin Seiki Co., Ltd., III; 48 (upd.)
Aiwa Co., Ltd., 30
Ajinomoto Co., Inc., II; 28 (upd.)
All Nippon Airways Co., Ltd., 6; 38 (upd.); 91 (upd.)
Alpine Electronics, Inc., 13
Alps Electric Co., Ltd., II; 44 (upd.)
Anritsu Corporation, 68
Asahi Breweries, Ltd., I; 20 (upd.); 52 (upd.)
Asahi Denka Kogyo KK, 64
Asahi Glass Company, Ltd., III; 48 (upd.)
Asahi National Broadcasting Company, Ltd., 9
Asatsu-DK Inc., 82
ASICS Corporation, 57
Astellas Pharma Inc., 97 (upd.)
Autobacs Seven Company Ltd., 76
Bandai Co., Ltd., 55
Bank of Tokyo-Mitsubishi Ltd., II; 15 (upd.)
Benesse Corporation, 76
Bourbon Corporation, 82
Bridgestone Corporation, V; 21 (upd.); 59 (upd.)
Brother Industries, Ltd., 14

C. Itoh & Company Ltd., I
Canon Inc., III; 18 (upd.); 79 (upd.)
Capcom Company Ltd., 83
CASIO Computer Co., Ltd., III; 16 (upd.); 40 (upd.)
Central Japan Railway Company, 43
Chubu Electric Power Company, Inc., V; 46 (upd.)
Chugai Pharmaceutical Co., Ltd., 50
Chugoku Electric Power Company Inc., V; 53 (upd.)
Citizen Watch Co., Ltd., III; 21 (upd.); 81 (upd.)
Clarion Company Ltd., 64
Cosmo Oil Co., Ltd., IV; 53 (upd.)
Dai Nippon Printing Co., Ltd., IV; 57 (upd.)
The Dai-Ichi Kangyo Bank Ltd., II
Daido Steel Co., Ltd., IV
The Daiei, Inc., V; 17 (upd.); 41 (upd.)
Daihatsu Motor Company, Ltd., 7; 21 (upd.)
Daiichikosho Company Ltd., 86
Daikin Industries, Ltd., III
Daiko Advertising Inc. 79
The Daimaru, Inc., V; 42 (upd.)
Daio Paper Corporation, IV, 84 (upd.)
Daishowa Paper Manufacturing Co., Ltd., IV; 57 (upd.)
The Daiwa Bank, Ltd., II; 39 (upd.)
Daiwa Securities Group Inc., II; 55 (upd.)
DDI Corporation, 7
DENSO Corporation, 46 (upd.)
Dentsu Inc., I; 16 (upd.); 40 (upd.)
East Japan Railway Company, V; 66 (upd.)
Ebara Corporation, 83
Eisai Co., Ltd., 101
Elpida Memory, Inc., 83
Encho Company Ltd., 104
Ezaki Glico Company Ltd., 72
Fanuc Ltd., III; 17 (upd.); 75 (upd.)
The Fuji Bank, Ltd., II
Fuji Electric Co., Ltd., II; 48 (upd.)
Fuji Photo Film Co., Ltd., III; 18 (upd.); 79 (upd.)
Fuji Television Network Inc., 91
Fujisawa Pharmaceutical Company, Ltd., I; 58 (upd.)
Fujitsu Limited, III; 16 (upd.); 42 (upd.); 103 (upd.)
Funai Electric Company Ltd., 62
The Furukawa Electric Co., Ltd., III
General Sekiyu K.K., IV
Hakuhodo, Inc., 6; 42 (upd.)
Hankyu Department Stores, Inc., V; 23 (upd.); 62 (upd.)
Hagoromo Foods Corporation, 84
Hino Motors, Ltd., 7; 21 (upd.)
Hitachi, Ltd., I; 12 (upd.); 40 (upd.)
Hitachi Metals, Ltd., IV
Hitachi Zosen Corporation, III; 53 (upd.)
Hokkaido Electric Power Company Inc. (HEPCO), V; 58 (upd.)
Hokuriku Electric Power Company, V
Honda Motor Company Ltd., I; 10 (upd.); 29 (upd.); 96 (upd.)
Honshu Paper Co., Ltd., IV

Hoshino Gakki Co. Ltd., 55
Idemitsu Kosan Co., Ltd., IV; 49 (upd.)
The Industrial Bank of Japan, Ltd., II
INPEX Holdings Inc., 97
Isetan Company Limited, V; 36 (upd.)
Ishikawajima-Harima Heavy Industries Company, Ltd., III; 86 (upd.)
Isuzu Motors, Ltd., 9; 23 (upd.); 57 (upd.)
Ito En Ltd., 101
Ito-Yokado Co., Ltd., V; 42 (upd.)
ITOCHU Corporation, 32 (upd.)
Itoham Foods Inc., II; 61 (upd.)
Japan Airlines Company, Ltd., I; 32 (upd.)
JAFCO Co. Ltd. 79
Japan Broadcasting Corporation, 7
Japan Leasing Corporation, 8
Japan Pulp and Paper Company Limited, IV
Japan Tobacco Inc., V; 46 (upd.)
JFE Shoji Holdings Inc., 88
JSP Corporation, 74
Jujo Paper Co., Ltd., IV
JUSCO Co., Ltd., V
Kajima Corporation, I; 51 (upd.)
Kanebo, Ltd., 53
Kanematsu Corporation, IV; 24 (upd.); 102 (upd.)
The Kansai Electric Power Company, Inc., V; 62 (upd.)
Kansai Paint Company Ltd., 80
Kao Corporation, III; 20 (upd.); 79 (upd.)
Katokichi Company Ltd., 82
Kawai Musical Instruments Mfg Co. Ltd. 78
Kawasaki Heavy Industries, Ltd., III; 63 (upd.)
Kawasaki Kisen Kaisha, Ltd., V; 56 (upd.)
Kawasaki Steel Corporation, IV
Keio Corporation, V; 96 (upd.)
Kenwood Corporation, 31
Kewpie Kabushiki Kaisha, 57
Kikkoman Corporation, 14; 47 (upd.)
Kinki Nippon Railway Company Ltd., V
Kirin Brewery Company, Limited, I; 21 (upd.); 63 (upd.)
Kobe Steel, Ltd., IV; 19 (upd.)
Kodansha Ltd., IV; 38 (upd.)
Komatsu Ltd., III; 16 (upd.); 52 (upd.)
Konami Corporation, 96
Konica Corporation, III; 30 (upd.)
Kotobukiya Co., Ltd., V; 56 (upd.)
Kubota Corporation, III; 26 (upd.)
Kumagai Gumi Company, Ltd., I
Kumon Institute of Education Co., Ltd., 72
Kyocera Corporation, II; 21 (upd.); 79 (upd.)
Kyokuyo Company Ltd., 75
Kyowa Hakko Kogyo Co., Ltd., III; 48 (upd.)
Kyushu Electric Power Company Inc., V
Lion Corporation, III; 51 (upd.)
Long-Term Credit Bank of Japan, Ltd., II
Mabuchi Motor Co. Ltd., 68
Makita Corporation, 22; 59 (upd.)

Mandom Corporation, 82
Marubeni Corporation, I; 24 (upd.); 104 (upd.)
Maruha Group Inc., 75 (upd.)
Marui Company Ltd., V; 62 (upd.)
Maruzen Company Ltd., 18; 104 (upd.)
Matsushita Electric Industrial Co., Ltd., II; 64 (upd.)
Matsushita Electric Works, Ltd., III; 7 (upd.)
Matsuzakaya Company Ltd., V; 64 (upd.)
Mazda Motor Corporation, 9; 23 (upd.); 63 (upd.)
Meidensha Corporation, 92
Meiji Dairies Corporation, II; 82 (upd.)
The Meiji Mutual Life Insurance Company, III
Meiji Seika Kaisha Ltd., II; 64 (upd.)
Mercian Corporation, 77
Millea Holdings Inc., 64 (upd.)
Minebea Co., Ltd., 90
Minolta Co., Ltd., III; 18 (upd.); 43 (upd.)
The Mitsubishi Bank, Ltd., II
Mitsubishi Chemical Corporation, I; 56 (upd.)
Mitsubishi Corporation, I; 12 (upd.)
Mitsubishi Electric Corporation, II; 44 (upd.)
Mitsubishi Estate Company, Limited, IV; 61 (upd.)
Mitsubishi Heavy Industries, Ltd., III; 7 (upd.); 40 (upd.)
Mitsubishi Materials Corporation, III
Mitsubishi Motors Corporation, 9; 23 (upd.); 57 (upd.)
Mitsubishi Oil Co., Ltd., IV
Mitsubishi Rayon Co., Ltd., V
The Mitsubishi Trust & Banking Corporation, II
Mitsubishi UFJ Financial Group, Inc., 99 (upd.)
Mitsui & Co., Ltd., 28 (upd.)
The Mitsui Bank, Ltd., II
Mitsui Bussan K.K., I
Mitsui Marine and Fire Insurance Company, Limited, III
Mitsui Mining & Smelting Company, Ltd., IV; 102 (upd.)
Mitsui Mining Company, Limited, IV
Mitsui Mutual Life Insurance Company, III; 39 (upd.)
Mitsui O.S.K. Lines, Ltd., V; 96 (upd.)
Mitsui Petrochemical Industries, Ltd., 9
Mitsui Real Estate Development Co., Ltd., IV
The Mitsui Trust & Banking Company, Ltd., II
Mitsukoshi Ltd., V; 56 (upd.)
Mizuho Financial Group Inc., 58 (upd.)
Mizuno Corporation, 25
Morinaga & Co. Ltd., 61
Nagasakiya Co., Ltd., V; 69 (upd.)
Nagase & Co., Ltd., 8; 61 (upd.)
Namco Bandai Holdings Inc., 106 (upd.)
NEC Corporation, II; 21 (upd.); 57 (upd.)
NGK Insulators Ltd., 67

NHK Spring Co., Ltd., III
Nichii Co., Ltd., V
Nichimen Corporation, IV; 24 (upd.)
Nichirei Corporation, 70
Nichiro Corporation, 86
Nidec Corporation, 59
Nihon Keizai Shimbun, Inc., IV
The Nikko Securities Company Limited, II; 9 (upd.)
Nikon Corporation, III; 48 (upd.)
Nintendo Co., Ltd., III; 7 (upd.); 28 (upd.); 67 (upd.)
Nippon Credit Bank, II
Nippon Electric Glass Co. Ltd., 95
Nippon Express Company, Ltd., V; 64 (upd.)
Nippon Life Insurance Company, III; 60 (upd.)
Nippon Light Metal Company, Ltd., IV
Nippon Meat Packers Inc., II, 78 (upd.)
Nippon Mining Holdings Inc., 102 (upd.)
Nippon Oil Corporation, IV; 63 (upd.)
Nippon Seiko K.K., III
Nippon Sheet Glass Company, Limited, III
Nippon Shinpan Co., Ltd., II; 61 (upd.)
Nippon Soda Co., Ltd., 85
Nippon Steel Corporation, IV; 17 (upd.); 96 (upd.)
Nippon Suisan Kaisha, Ltd., II; 92 (upd.)
Nippon Telegraph and Telephone Corporation, V; 51 (upd.)
Nippon Yusen Kabushiki Kaisha (NYK), V; 72 (upd.)
Nippondenso Co., Ltd., III
Nissan Motor Company Ltd., I; 11 (upd.); 34 (upd.); 92 (upd.)
Nisshin Seifun Group Inc., II; 66 (upd.)
Nisshin Steel Co., Ltd., IV
Nissho Iwai K.K., I
Nissin Food Products Company Ltd., 75
NKK Corporation, IV; 28 (upd.)
NOF Corporation, 72
Nomura Securities Company, Limited, II; 9 (upd.)
Norinchukin Bank, II
NTN Corporation, III; 47 (upd.)
Obayashi Corporation 78
Odakyu Electric Railway Co., Ltd., V; 68 (upd.)
Ohbayashi Corporation, I
Oji Paper Co., Ltd., IV; 57 (upd.)
Oki Electric Industry Company, Limited, II
Okuma Holdings Inc., 74
Okura & Co., Ltd., IV
Olympus Corporation, 106
Omron Corporation, II; 28 (upd.)
Onoda Cement Co., Ltd., III
ORIX Corporation, II; 44 (upd.); 104 (upd.)
Osaka Gas Company, Ltd., V; 60 (upd.)
Otari Inc., 89
Paloma Industries Ltd., 71
Pearl Corporation 78
Pentax Corporation 78
Pioneer Electronic Corporation, III; 28 (upd.)

Rengo Co., Ltd., IV
Ricoh Company, Ltd., III; 36 (upd.)
Roland Corporation, 38
Ryoshoku Ltd., 72
Sankyo Company, Ltd., I; 56 (upd.)
Sanrio Company, Ltd., 38; 104 (upd.)
The Sanwa Bank, Ltd., II; 15 (upd.)
SANYO Electric Co., Ltd., II; 36 (upd.); 95 (upd.)
Sanyo-Kokusaku Pulp Co., Ltd., IV
Sapporo Holdings Limited, I; 13 (upd.); 36 (upd.); 97 (upd.)
SEGA Corporation, 73
Seibu Department Stores, Ltd., V; 42 (upd.)
Seibu Railway Company Ltd., V; 74 (upd.)
Seiko Corporation, III; 17 (upd.); 72 (upd.)
Seino Transportation Company, Ltd., 6
The Seiyu, Ltd., V; 36 (upd.)
Sekisui Chemical Co., Ltd., III; 72 (upd.)
Sharp Corporation, II; 12 (upd.); 40 (upd.)
Shikoku Electric Power Company, Inc., V; 60 (upd.)
Shimano Inc., 64
Shionogi & Co., Ltd., III; 17 (upd.); 98 (upd.)
Shiseido Company, Limited, III; 22 (upd.), 81 (upd.)
Shochiku Company Ltd., 74
Sompo Japan Insurance, Inc., 98 (upd.)
Showa Shell Sekiyu K.K., IV; 59 (upd.)
Snow Brand Milk Products Company, Ltd., II; 48 (upd.)
Softbank Corp., 13; 38 (upd.)
Sojitz Corporation, 96 (upd.)
Sony Corporation, II; 12 (upd.); 40 (upd.)
Square Enix Holdings Co., Ltd., 101
The Sumitomo Bank, Limited, II; 26 (upd.)
Sumitomo Chemical Company Ltd., I; 98 (upd.)
Sumitomo Corporation, I; 11 (upd.); 102 (upd.)
Sumitomo Electric Industries, Ltd., II
Sumitomo Heavy Industries, Ltd., III; 42 (upd.)
Sumitomo Life Insurance Company, III; 60 (upd.)
The Sumitomo Marine and Fire Insurance Company, Limited, III
Sumitomo Metal Industries Ltd., IV; 82 (upd.)
Sumitomo Metal Mining Co., Ltd., IV
Sumitomo Mitsui Banking Corporation, 51 (upd.)
Sumitomo Realty & Development Co., Ltd., IV
Sumitomo Rubber Industries, Ltd., V
The Sumitomo Trust & Banking Company, Ltd., II; 53 (upd.)
Suntory Ltd., 65
Suzuki Motor Corporation, 9; 23 (upd.); 59 (upd.)
Taiheiyo Cement Corporation, 60 (upd.)

Taiyo Fishery Company, Limited, II
The Taiyo Kobe Bank, Ltd., II
Takara Holdings Inc., 62
Takashimaya Company, Limited, V; 47 (upd.)
Takeda Chemical Industries, Ltd., I; 46 (upd.)
Tamron Company Ltd., 82
TDK Corporation, II; 17 (upd.); 49 (upd.)
TEAC Corporation 78
Tecmo Koei Holdings Company Ltd., 106
Teijin Limited, V; 61 (upd.)
Terumo Corporation, 48
Tobu Railway Company Ltd., 6; 98 (upd.)
Tohan Corporation, 84
Toho Co., Ltd., 28
Tohoku Electric Power Company, Inc., V
The Tokai Bank, Limited, II; 15 (upd.)
The Tokio Marine and Fire Insurance Co., Ltd., III
The Tokyo Electric Power Company, 74 (upd.)
The Tokyo Electric Power Company, Incorporated, V
Tokyo Gas Co., Ltd., V; 55 (upd.)
Tokyu Corporation, V; 47 (upd.)
Tokyu Department Store Co., Ltd., V; 32 (upd.)
Tokyu Land Corporation, IV
Tomen Corporation, IV; 24 (upd.)
Tomy Company Ltd., 65
TonenGeneral Sekiyu K.K., IV; 16 (upd.); 54 (upd.)
Topcon Corporation, 84
Toppan Printing Co., Ltd., IV; 58 (upd.)
Toray Industries, Inc., V; 51 (upd.)
Toshiba Corporation, I; 12 (upd.); 40 (upd.); 99 (upd.)
Tosoh Corporation, 70
TOTO LTD., III; 28 (upd.)
Toyo Sash Co., Ltd., III
Toyo Seikan Kaisha, Ltd., I
Toyoda Automatic Loom Works, Ltd., III
Toyota Motor Corporation, I; 11 (upd.); 38 (upd.); 100 (upd.)
Trend Micro Inc., 97
Ube Industries, Ltd., III; 38 (upd.)
ULVAC, Inc., 80
Unicharm Corporation, 84
Uniden Corporation, 98
Unitika Ltd., V; 53 (upd.)
Uny Co., Ltd., V; 49 (upd.)
Ushio Inc., 91
Victor Company of Japan, Limited, II; 26 (upd.); 83 (upd.)
Wacoal Corp., 25
Yamada Denki Co., Ltd., 85
Yamaha Corporation, III; 16 (upd.); 40 (upd.); 99 (upd.)
Yamaichi Securities Company, Limited, II
Yamato Transport Co. Ltd., V; 49 (upd.)
Yamazaki Baking Co., Ltd., 58
The Yasuda Fire and Marine Insurance Company, Limited, III
The Yasuda Mutual Life Insurance Company, III; 39 (upd.)

The Yasuda Trust and Banking Company, Ltd., II; 17 (upd.)
The Yokohama Rubber Company, Limited, V; 19 (upd.); 91 (upd.)
Yoshinoya D & C Company Ltd., 88

Jordan
Arab Potash Company, 85
Hikma Pharmaceuticals Ltd., 102
Munir Sukhtian Group, 104
Nuqul Group of Companies, 102

Kenya
Kenya Airways Limited, 89

Kuwait
Kuwait Airways Corporation, 68
Kuwait Flour Mills & Bakeries Company, 84
Kuwait Petroleum Corporation, IV; 55 (upd.)
Zain, 102

Latvia
A/S Air Baltic Corporation, 71

Lebanon
Blom Bank S.A.L., 102
Middle East Airlines - Air Liban S.A.L. 79

Libya
National Oil Corporation, IV; 66 (upd.)

Liechtenstein
Hilti AG, 53

Luxembourg
ARBED S.A., IV; 22 (upd.)
Cactus S.A., 90
Cargolux Airlines International S.A., 49
Elite World S.A., 94
Espèrito Santo Financial Group S.A. 79 (upd.)
Gemplus International S.A., 64
Metro International S.A., 93
RTL Group SA, 44
Société Luxembourgeoise de Navigation Aérienne S.A., 64
Tenaris SA, 63

Malaysia
AirAsia Berhad, 93
Berjaya Group Bhd., 67
Gano Excel Enterprise Sdn. Bhd., 89
Genting Bhd., 65
Malayan Banking Berhad, 72
Malaysian Airlines System Berhad, 6; 29 (upd.); 97 (upd.)
Perusahaan Otomobil Nasional Bhd., 62
Petroliam Nasional Bhd (Petronas), IV; 56 (upd.)
PPB Group Berhad, 57
Sime Darby Berhad, 14; 36 (upd.)
Telekom Malaysia Bhd, 76
Yeo Hiap Seng Malaysia Bhd., 75

Mauritius
Air Mauritius Ltd., 63

Mexico
Alfa, S.A. de C.V., 19
Altos Hornos de México, S.A. de C.V., 42
América Móvil, S.A. de C.V., 80
Apasco S.A. de C.V., 51
Bolsa Mexicana de Valores, S.A. de C.V., 80
Bufete Industrial, S.A. de C.V., 34
Casa Cuervo, S.A. de C.V., 31
Celanese Mexicana, S.A. de C.V., 54
CEMEX S.A. de C.V., 20; 59 (upd.)
Cifra, S.A. de C.V., 12
Cinemas de la República, S.A. de C.V., 83
Compañia Industrial de Parras, S.A. de C.V. (CIPSA), 84
Consorcio ARA, S.A. de C.V. 79
Consorcio Aviacsa, S.A. de C.V., 85
Consorcio G Grupo Dina, S.A. de C.V., 36
Controladora Comercial Mexicana, S.A. de C.V., 36
Controladora Mabe, S.A. de C.V., 82
Coppel, S.A. de C.V., 82
Corporación Geo, S.A. de C.V., 81
Corporación Interamericana de Entretenimiento, S.A. de C.V., 83
Corporación Internacional de Aviación, S.A. de C.V. (Cintra), 20
Desarrolladora Homex, S.A. de C.V., 87
Desc, S.A. de C.V., 23
Editorial Television, S.A. de C.V., 57
Empresas ICA Sociedad Controladora, S.A. de C.V., 41
El Puerto de Liverpool, S.A.B. de C.V., 97
Ford Motor Company, S.A. de C.V., 20
Gruma, S.A.B. de C.V., 31; 103 (upd.)
Grupo Aeroportuario del Centro Norte, S.A.B. de C.V., 97
Grupo Aeroportuario del Pacífico, S.A. de C.V., 85
Grupo Aeropuerto del Sureste, S.A. de C.V., 48
Grupo Ángeles Servicios de Salud, S.A. de C.V., 84
Grupo Carso, S.A. de C.V., 21
Grupo Casa Saba, S.A. de C.V., 39
Grupo Comercial Chedraui S.A. de C.V., 86
Grupo Corvi S.A. de C.V., 86
Grupo Cydsa, S.A. de C.V., 39
Grupo Elektra, S.A. de C.V., 39
Grupo Financiero Banamex S.A., 54
Grupo Financiero Banorte, S.A. de C.V., 51
Grupo Financiero BBVA Bancomer S.A., 54
Grupo Financiero Serfin, S.A., 19
Grupo Gigante, S.A. de C.V., 34
Grupo Herdez, S.A. de C.V., 35
Grupo IMSA, S.A. de C.V., 44
Grupo Industrial Bimbo, 19
Grupo Industrial Durango, S.A. de C.V., 37
Grupo Industrial Herradura, S.A. de C.V., 83
Grupo Industrial Lala, S.A. de C.V., 82
Grupo Industrial Saltillo, S.A. de C.V., 54
Grupo Mexico, S.A. de C.V., 40
Grupo Modelo, S.A. de C.V., 29
Grupo Omnilife S.A. de C.V., 88
Grupo Posadas, S.A. de C.V., 57
Grupo Televisa, S.A., 18; 54 (upd.)
Grupo TMM, S.A. de C.V., 50
Grupo Transportación Ferroviaria Mexicana, S.A. de C.V., 47
Grupo Viz, S.A. de C.V., 84
Hylsamex, S.A. de C.V., 39
Industrias Bachoco, S.A. de C.V., 39
Industrias Penoles, S.A. de C.V., 22
Internacional de Ceramica, S.A. de C.V., 53
Jugos del Valle, S.A. de C.V., 85
Kimberly-Clark de México, S.A. de C.V., 54
Mexichem, S.A.B. de C.V., 99
Nadro S.A. de C.V., 86
Organización Soriana, S.A. de C.V., 35
Petróleos Mexicanos (PEMEX), IV; 19 (upd.); 104 (upd.)
Proeza S.A. de C.V., 82
Pulsar Internacional S.A., 21
Real Turismo, S.A. de C.V., 50
Sanborn Hermanos, S.A., 20
SANLUIS Corporación, S.A.B. de C.V., 95
Sears Roebuck de México, S.A. de C.V., 20
Telefonos de Mexico S.A. de C.V., 14; 63 (upd.)
Tenedora Nemak, S.A. de C.V., 102
Tubos de Acero de Mexico, S.A. (TAMSA), 41
TV Azteca, S.A. de C.V., 39
Urbi Desarrollos Urbanos, S.A. de C.V., 81
Valores Industriales S.A., 19
Vitro Corporativo S.A. de C.V., 34
Wal-Mart de Mexico, S.A. de C.V., 35 (upd.)

Mongolia
Newcom, LLC, 104

Nepal
Royal Nepal Airline Corporation, 41

Netherlands
ABN AMRO Holding, N.V., 50
AEGON N.V., III; 50 (upd.)
Akzo Nobel N.V., 13; 41 (upd.)
Algemene Bank Nederland N.V., II
Amsterdam-Rotterdam Bank N.V., II
Arcadis NV, 26
ASML Holding N.V., 50
Avantium Technologies BV 79
Baan Company, 25
Blokker Holding B.V., 84
Bols Distilleries NV, 74
Bolton Group B.V., 86
Buhrmann NV, 41
The Campina Group, The 78
Chicago Bridge & Iron Company N.V., 82 (upd.)
CNH Global N.V., 38 (upd.); 99 (upd.)
CSM N.V., 65

Deli Universal NV, 66
Drie Mollen Holding B.V., 99
DSM N.V., I; 56 (upd.)
Elsevier N.V., IV
Endemol Entertainment Holding NV, 46
Equant N.V., 52
Euronext N.V., 89 (upd.)
European Aeronautic Defence and Space
   Company EADS N.V., 52 (upd.)
Friesland Coberco Dairy Foods Holding
   N.V., 59
Fugro N.V., 98
Getronics NV, 39
Granaria Holdings B.V., 66
Grand Hotel Krasnapolsky N.V., 23
Greenpeace International, 74
Gucci Group N.V., 50
Hagemeyer N.V., 39
Head N.V., 55
Heijmans N.V., 66
Heineken N.V., I; 13 (upd.); 34 (upd.);
   90 (upd.)
IHC Caland N.V., 71
IKEA Group, 94 (upd.)
Indigo NV, 26
Intres B.V., 82
Ispat International N.V., 30
KLM Royal Dutch Airlines, 104 (upd.)
Koninklijke Ahold N.V. (Royal Ahold), II;
   16 (upd.)
Koninklijke Houthandel G Wijma &
   Zonen BV, 96
Koninklijke Luchtvaart Maatschappij,
   N.V. (KLM Royal Dutch Airlines), I;
   28 (upd.)
Koninklijke Nederlandsche Hoogovens en
   Staalfabrieken NV, IV
Koninklijke Nedlloyd N.V., 6; 26 (upd.)
Koninklijke Philips Electronics N.V., 50
   (upd.)
Koninklijke PTT Nederland NV, V
Koninklijke Reesink N.V., 104
Koninklijke Vendex KBB N.V. (Royal
   Vendex KBB N.V.), 62 (upd.)
Koninklijke Wessanen nv, II; 54 (upd.)
KPMG International, 10; 33 (upd.)
Laurus N.V., 65
Mammoet Transport B.V., 26
MIH Limited, 31
N.V. AMEV, III
N.V. Holdingmaatschappij De Telegraaf,
   23
N.V. Koninklijke Nederlandse
   Vliegtuigenfabriek Fokker, I; 28 (upd.)
N.V. Nederlandse Gasunie, V
Nationale-Nederlanden N.V., III
New Holland N.V., 22
Nutreco Holding N.V., 56
Océ N.V., 24; 91 (upd.)
PCM Uitgevers NV, 53
Philips Electronics N.V., II; 13 (upd.)
PolyGram N.V., 23
Prada Holding B.V., 45
Qiagen N.V., 39
Rabobank Group, 33
Randstad Holding n.v., 16; 43 (upd.)
Rodamco N.V., 26
Royal Dutch/Shell Group, IV; 49 (upd.)

Royal Grolsch NV, 54
Royal KPN N.V., 30
Royal Numico N.V., 37
Royal Packaging Industries Van Leer N.V.,
   30
Royal Ten Cate N.V., 68
Royal Vopak NV, 41
SHV Holdings N.V., 55
Telegraaf Media Groep N.V., 98 (upd.)
Tennet BV 78
TNT Post Group N.V., V; 27 (upd.); 30
   (upd.)
Toolex International N.V., 26
TomTom N.V., 81
TPG N.V., 64 (upd.)
Trader Classified Media N.V., 57
Triple P N.V., 26
Unilever N.V., II; 7 (upd.); 32 (upd.)
United Pan-Europe Communications NV,
   47
Van Lanschot NV 79
VBA - Bloemenveiling Aalsmeer, 88
Vebego International BV, 49
Vedior NV, 35
Velcro Industries N.V., 19
Vendex International N.V., 13
Vion Food Group NV, 85
VNU N.V., 27
Wegener NV, 53
Wolters Kluwer NV, 14; 33 (upd.)
Zentiva N.V./Zentiva, a.s., 99

Netherlands Antilles
Orthofix International NV, 72
Velcro Industries N.V., 72

New Zealand
Air New Zealand Limited, 14; 38 (upd.)
Carter Holt Harvey Ltd., 70
Cerebos Gregg's Ltd., 100
Fletcher Challenge Ltd., IV; 19 (upd.)
Fonterra Co-Operative Group Ltd., 58
Frucor Beverages Group Ltd., 96
Nuplex Industries Ltd., 92
Progressive Enterprises Ltd., 96
Telecom Corporation of New Zealand
   Limited, 54
Wattie's Ltd., 7

Nigeria
Nigerian National Petroleum Corporation,
   IV; 72 (upd.)

Norway
Braathens ASA, 47
Den Norse Stats Oljeselskap AS, IV
Helly Hansen ASA, 25
Jotun A/S, 80
K.A. Rasmussen AS, 99
Kvaerner ASA, 36
Norsk Hydro ASA, 10; 35 (upd.)
Norske Skogindustrier ASA, 63
Odfjell SE, 101
Orkla ASA, 18; 82 (upd.)
Schibsted ASA, 31
Statoil ASA, 61 (upd.)
Stolt Sea Farm Holdings PLC, 54

Telenor ASA, 69
Tomra Systems ASA, 103
Veidekke ASA, 98
Vinmonopolet A/S, 100
Wilh. Wilhelmsen ASA, 94
Yara International ASA, 94

Oman
Petroleum Development Oman LLC, IV;
   98 (upd.)
The Zubair Corporation L.L.C., 96

Pakistan
Pakistan International Airlines
   Corporation, 46
Pakistan State Oil Company Ltd., 81

Panama
Autoridad del Canal de Panamá, 94
Copa Holdings, S.A., 93
Panamerican Beverages, Inc., 47
Willbros Group, Inc., 56

Papua New Guinea
Steamships Trading Company Ltd., 82

Paraguay
Banco Central del Paraguay, 100

Peru
Ajegroup S.A., 92
Banco de Crédito del Perú, 93
Compañia de Minas Buenaventura S.A.A.,
   93
Corporación José R. Lindley S.A., 92
Grupo Brescia, 99
Southern Peru Copper Corporation, 40
Unión de Cervecerias Peruanas Backus y
   Johnston S.A.A., 92
Volcan Compañia Minera S.A.A., 92

Philippines
Bank of the Philippine Islands, 58
Benguet Corporation, 58
Manila Electric Company (Mcralco), 56
Mercury Drug Corporation, 70
Petron Corporation, 58
Philippine Airlines, Inc., 6; 23 (upd.)
San Miguel Corporation, 15; 57 (upd.)

Poland
Agora S.A. Group, 77
LOT Polish Airlines (Polskie Linie
   Lotnicze S.A.), 33
KGHM Polska Miedz S.A., 98
Narodowy Bank Polski, 100
Polski Koncern Naftowy ORLEN S.A., 77
Telekomunikacja Polska SA, 50
Zakłady Azotowe Puławy S.A., 100

Portugal
Banco Comercial Português, SA, 50
Banco Espírito Santo e Comercial de
   Lisboa S.A., 15
BRISA Auto-estradas de Portugal S.A., 64
Cimentos de Portugal SGPS S.A.
   (Cimpor), 76

Corticeira Amorim, Sociedade Gestora de
    Participaço es Sociais, S.A., 48
Electricidade de Portugal, S.A., 47
Galp Energia SGPS S.A., 98
Grupo Portucel Soporcel, 60
Jerónimo Martins SGPS S.A., 96
José de Mello SGPS S.A., 96
Madeira Wine Company, S.A., 49
Mota-Engil, SGPS, S.A., 97
Petróleos de Portugal S.A., IV
Portugal Telecom SGPS S.A., 69
Sonae SGPS, S.A., 97
TAP—Air Portugal Transportes Aéreos
    Portugueses S.A., 46
Transportes Aereos Portugueses, S.A., 6

Puerto Rico
Puerto Rico Electric Power Authority, 47

Qatar
Aljazeera Satellite Channel 79
Qatar Airways Company Q.C.S.C., 87
Qatar General Petroleum Corporation, IV
Qatar National Bank SAQ, 87
Qatar Petroleum, 98
Qatar Telecom QSA, 87

Republic of Yemen
Hayel Saeed Anam Group of Cos., 92

Romania
Dobrogea Grup S.A., 82
TAROM S.A., 64

Russia
A.S. Yakovlev Design Bureau, 15
Aeroflot - Russian Airlines JSC, 6; 29
    (upd.); 89 (upd.)
Alfa Group, 99
Alrosa Company Ltd., 62
AO VimpelCom, 48
Aviacionny Nauchno-Tehnicheskii
    Komplex im. A.N. Tupoleva, 24
AVTOVAZ Joint Stock Company, 65
Baltika Brewery Joint Stock Company, 65
Evraz Group S.A., 97
Golden Telecom, Inc., 59
Interfax News Agency, 86
Irkut Corporation, 68
JSC MMC Norilsk Nickel, 48
Mechel OAO, 99
Mobile TeleSystems OJSC, 59
OAO Gazprom, 42
OAO LUKOIL, 40
OAO NK YUKOS, 47
OAO Siberian Oil Company (Sibneft), 49
OAO Surgutneftegaz, 48
OAO Tatneft, 45
OJSC Novolipetsk Steel, 99
OJSC Wimm-Bill-Dann Foods, 48
RAO Unified Energy System of Russia, 45
Rosneft, 106
Rostelecom Joint Stock Co., 99
Rostvertol plc, 62
Russian Aircraft Corporation (MiG), 86
Russian Railways Joint Stock Co., 93
Sberbank, 62

Severstal Joint Stock Company, 65
Sistema JSFC, 73
Sukhoi Design Bureau Aviation
    Scientific-Industrial Complex, 24
CJSC Transmash Holding, 93
Oil Transporting Joint Stock Company
    Transneft, 93
Volga-Dnepr Group, 82

Saudi Arabia
Dallah Albaraka Group, 72
Saudi Arabian Airlines, 6; 27 (upd.)
Saudi Arabian Oil Company, IV; 17
    (upd.); 50 (upd.)
Saudi Basic Industries Corporation
    (SABIC), 58

Scotland
Arnold Clark Automobiles Ltd., 60
Distillers Company PLC, I
General Accident PLC, III
The Governor and Company of the Bank
    of Scotland, 10
The Royal Bank of Scotland Group plc,
    12
Scottish & Newcastle plc, 15
Scottish Hydro-Electric PLC, 13
Scottish Media Group plc, 32
ScottishPower plc, 19
Stagecoach Holdings plc, 30
The Standard Life Assurance Company,
    III

Singapore
Asia Pacific Breweries Limited, 59
City Developments Limited, 89
Creative Technology Ltd., 57
Flextronics International Ltd., 38
Fraser & Neave Ltd., 54
Hotel Properties Ltd., 71
Jardine Cycle & Carriage Ltd., 73
Keppel Corporation Ltd., 73
Neptune Orient Lines Limited, 47
Pacific Internet Limited, 87
Singapore Airlines Limited, 6; 27 (upd.);
    83 (upd.)
Singapore Press Holdings Limited, 85
StarHub Ltd., 77
United Overseas Bank Ltd., 56

South Africa
Absa Group Ltd., 106
African Rainbow Minerals Ltd., 97
Anglo American Corporation of South
    Africa Limited, IV; 16 (upd.)
Barlow Rand Ltd., I
Bidvest Group Ltd., 106
De Beers Consolidated Mines Limited/De
    Beers Centenary AG, IV; 7 (upd.); 28
    (upd.)
Dimension Data Holdings PLC, 69
Edgars Consolidated Stores Ltd., 66
Exxaro Resources Ltd., 106
Famous Brands Ltd., 86
Gencor Ltd., IV; 22 (upd.)
Gold Fields Ltd., IV; 62 (upd.)
Harmony Gold Mining Company
    Limited, 63

Highveld Steel and Vanadium
    Corporation Limited, 59
Iscor Limited, 57
MTN Group Ltd., 106
Naspers Ltd., 66
New Clicks Holdings Ltd., 86
Pick 'n Pay Stores Ltd., 82
SAA (Pty) Ltd., 28
Sanlam Ltd., 68
Sappi Limited, 49
Sasol Limited, IV; 47 (upd.)
The South African Breweries Limited, I;
    24 (upd.)
Southern Sun Hotel Interest (Pty) Ltd.,
    106
Telkom S.A. Ltd., 106
Transnet Ltd., 6
Vodacom Group Pty. Ltd., 106

South Korea
Anam Group, 23
Asiana Airlines, Inc., 46
CJ Corporation, 62
Daesang Corporation, 84
Daewoo Group, III; 18 (upd.); 57 (upd.)
Electronics Co., Ltd., 14
Goldstar Co., Ltd., 12
Hanjin Shipping Co., Ltd., 50
Hankook Tire Company Ltd., 105
Hanwha Group, 62
Hite Brewery Company Ltd., 97
Hyundai Group, III; 7 (upd.); 56 (upd.)
Kia Motors Corporation, 12; 29 (upd.)
Kookmin Bank, 58
Korea Electric Power Corporation
    (Kepco), 56
Korean Air Lines Co., Ltd., 6; 27 (upd.)
KT&G Corporation, 62
Kumho Tire Company Ltd., 105
LG Corporation, 94 (upd.)
Lotte Confectionery Company Ltd., 76
Lucky-Goldstar, II
Pohang Iron and Steel Company Ltd., IV
POSCO, 57 (upd.)
Samick Musical Instruments Co., Ltd., 56
Samsung Electronics Co., Ltd., I; 41
    (upd.)
SK Group, 88
Ssangyong Cement Industrial Co., Ltd.,
    III; 61 (upd.)
Tong Yang Cement Corporation, 62

Spain
Abengoa S.A., 73
Abertis Infraestructuras, S.A., 65
Acciona S.A., 81
Adolfo Dominguez S.A., 72
Altadis S.A., 72 (upd.)
Áreas S.A., 104
Banco Bilbao Vizcaya Argentaria S.A., II;
    48 (upd.)
Banco Central, II
Banco do Brasil S.A., II
Banco Santander Central Hispano S.A.,
    36 (upd.)
Baron de Ley S.A., 74
Campofrío Alimentación S.A, 59
Chupa Chups S.A., 38

Compañia Española de Petróleos S.A. (Cepsa), IV; 56 (upd.)
Cortefiel S.A., 64
Correos y Telegrafos S.A., 80
Dogi International Fabrics S.A., 52
El Corte Inglés Group, V; 26 (upd.)
ENDESA S.A., V; 46 (upd.)
Ercros S.A., 80
Federico Paternina S.A., 69
Freixenet S.A., 71
Gas Natural SDG S.A., 69
Grupo Dragados SA, 55
Grupo Eroski, 64
Grupo Ferrovial, S.A., 40
Grupo Ficosa International, 90
Grupo Leche Pascual S.A., 59
Grupo Lladró S.A., 52
Grupo Planeta, 94
Iberdrola, S.A., 49
Iberia Líneas Aéreas de España S.A., 6; 36 (upd.); 91 (upd.)
Industria de Diseño Textil S.A., 64
Instituto Nacional de Industria, I
La Seda de Barcelona S.A., 100
Loewe S.A., 104
Mecalux S.A., 74
Miquel y Costas Miquel S.A., 68
Mondragón Corporación Cooperativa, 101
NH Hoteles S.A. 79
Nutrexpa S.A., 92
Obrascon Huarte Lain S.A., 76
Paradores de Turismo de Espana S.A., 73
Pescanova S.A., 81
Puig Beauty and Fashion Group S.L., 60
Real Madrid C.F., 73
Repsol-YPF S.A., IV; 16 (upd.); 40 (upd.)
Sol Meliá S.A., 71
Tabacalera, S.A., V; 17 (upd.)
Telefónica S.A., V; 46 (upd.)
TelePizza S.A., 33
Television Española, S.A., 7
Terra Lycos, Inc., 43
Unión Fenosa, S.A., 51
Uralita S.A., 96
Vidrala S.A., 67
Viscofan S.A., 70
Vocento, 94
Vueling Airlines S.A., 97
Zara International, Inc., 83
Zed Group, 93

Sweden

A. Johnson & Company H.B., I
AB Volvo, I; 7 (upd.); 26 (upd.); 67 (upd.)
Aktiebolaget Electrolux, 22 (upd.)
Aktiebolaget SKF, III; 38 (upd.); 89 (upd.)
Alfa Laval AB, III; 64 (upd.)
Astra AB, I; 20 (upd.)
Atlas Copco AB, III; 28 (upd.); 85 (upd.)
Autoliv, Inc., 65
Billerud AB, 100
Boliden AB, 80
Bonnier AB, 52
BRIO AB, 24; 103 (upd.)
Cardo AB, 53

Cloetta Fazer AB, 70
D. Carnegie & Co. AB, 98
Electrolux AB, III; 53 (upd.)
Eka Chemicals AB, 92
FöreningsSparbanken AB, 69
Gambro AB, 49
Gunnebo AB, 53
H&M Hennes & Mauritz AB, 98 (upd.)
Hennes & Mauritz AB, 29
Hexagon AB 78
Hilding Anders AB, 102
Holmen AB, 52 (upd.)
ICA AB, II
Investor AB, 63
Kooperativa Förbundet, 99
Mo och Domsjö AB, IV
Modern Times Group AB, 36
NetCom Systems AB, 26
Nobel Industries AB, 9
Nobia AB, 103
Nordea AB, 40
Observer AB, 55
Perstorp AB, I; 51 (upd.)
Saab Automobile AB, I; 11 (upd.); 32 (upd.); 83 (upd.)
Sandvik AB, IV; 32 (upd.); 77 (upd.)
Sapa AB, 84
The SAS Group, 34 (upd.)
Scandinavian Airlines System, I
Securitas AB, 42
Skandia Insurance Company, Ltd., 50
Skandinaviska Enskilda Banken AB, II; 56 (upd.)
Skanska AB, 38
SSAB Svenskt Stål AB, 89
Stora Kopparbergs Bergslags AB, IV
Sveaskog AB, 93
Svenska Cellulosa Aktiebolaget SCA, IV; 28 (upd.); 85 (upd.)
Svenska Handelsbanken AB, II; 50 (upd.)
Sveriges Riksbank, 96
Swedish Match AB, 12; 39 (upd.); 92 (upd.)
Swedish Telecom, V
Telefonaktiebolaget LM Ericsson, V; 46 (upd.)
TeliaSonera AB, 57 (upd.)
Trelleborg AB, 93
Vattenfall AB, 57
V&S Vin & Sprit AB, 91 (upd.)
Vin & Spirit AB, 31

Switzerland

ABB ASEA Brown Boveri Ltd., II; 22 (upd.)
ABB Ltd., 65 (upd.)
Actelion Ltd., 83
Adecco S.A., 36 (upd.)
Adia S.A., 6
AMAG Group, 102
Arthur Andersen & Company, Société Coopérative, 10
Ascom AG, 9
Bâloise-Holding, 40
Barry Callebaut AG, 29; 71 (upd.)
Bernina Holding AG, 47
Bodum Design Group AG, 47
Bon Appetit Holding AG, 48

Charles Vögele Holding AG, 82
Chocoladefabriken Lindt & Sprüngli AG, 27
Chocolat Frey AG, 102
Ciba-Geigy Ltd., I; 8 (upd.)
Compagnie Financiere Richemont AG, 50
Conzzeta Holding, 80
Coop Schweiz Genossenschaftsverband, 48
Credit Suisse Group, II; 21 (upd.); 59 (upd.)
Danzas Group, V; 40 (upd.)
De Beers Consolidated Mines Limited/De Beers Centenary AG, IV; 7 (upd.); 28 (upd.)
Denner AG, 88
Duferco Group, 94
Edipresse S.A., 82
Elektrowatt AG, 6
Elma Electronic AG, 83
Endress+Hauser Holding AG, 102
F. Hoffmann-La Roche Ltd., I; 50 (upd.)
Fédération Internationale de Football Association, 27
Fenaco, 86
Firmenich International S.A., 60
Franke Holding AG, 76
Galenica AG, 84
Gate Gourmet International AG, 70
Geberit AG, 49
Georg Fischer AG Schaffhausen, 61
Givaudan SA, 43
Hero Group, 100
Holderbank Financière Glaris Ltd., III
International Olympic Committee, 44
Jacobs Suchard A.G., II
Julius Baer Holding AG, 52
Keramik Holding AG Laufen, 51
Kraft Jacobs Suchard AG, 26 (upd.)
Kudelski Group SA, 44
Kuehne & Nagel International AG, V; 53 (upd.)
Kuoni Travel Holding Ltd., 40
Liebherr-International AG, 64
Logitech International S.A., 28; 69 (upd.)
Lonza Group Ltd., 73
Maus Frères SA, 48
Médecins sans Frontières, 85
Mettler-Toledo International Inc., 30
Migros-Genossenschafts-Bund, 68
Montres Rolex S.A., 13; 34 (upd.)
Mövenpick Holding, 104
Nestlé S.A., II; 7 (upd.); 28 (upd.); 71 (upd.)
Novartis AG, 39 (upd.); 105 (upd.)
Panalpina World Transport (Holding) Ltd., 47
Pelikan Holding AG, 92
Phoenix Mecano AG, 61
Ricola Ltd., 62
Rieter Holding AG, 42
Roland Murten A.G., 7
Sandoz Ltd., I
Schindler Holding AG, 29
Schmolz + Bickenbach AG, 104
Schweizerische Post-, Telefon- und Telegrafen-Betriebe, V
Selecta AG, 97
Serono S.A., 47

STMicroelectronics NV, 52
Straumann Holding AG 79
Sulzer Ltd., III; 68 (upd.)
Swarovski International Holding AG, 40
The Swatch Group SA, 26
Swedish Match S.A., 12
Swiss Air Transport Company, Ltd., I
Swiss Bank Corporation, II
The Swiss Federal Railways
    (Schweizerische Bundesbahnen), V
Swiss International Air Lines Ltd., 48
Swiss Reinsurance Company
    (Schweizerische
    Rückversicherungs-Gesellschaft), III; 46
    (upd.)
Swisscom AG, 58
Swissport International Ltd., 70
Syngenta International AG, 83
Synthes, Inc., 93
TAG Heuer International SA, 25; 77
    (upd.)
Tamedia AG, 53
Tetra Pak International SA, 53
UBS AG, 52 (upd.)
Underberg AG, 92
Union Bank of Switzerland, II
Valora Holding AG, 98
Victorinox AG, 21; 74 (upd.)
Vontobel Holding AG, 96
Weleda AG 78
Winterthur Group, III; 68 (upd.)
Xstrata PLC, 73
Zurich Financial Services, 42 (upd.); 93
    (upd.)
Zürich Versicherungs-Gesellschaft, III

Taiwan
Acer Incorporated, 16; 73 (upd.)
AU Optronics Corporation, 67
BenQ Corporation, 67
Chi Mei Optoelectronics Corporation, 75
China Airlines, 34
Chunghwa Picture Tubes, Ltd., 75
Chunghwa Telecom Co., Ltd., 101 (upd.)
D-Link Corporation, 83
Directorate General of
    Telecommunications, 7
EVA Airways Corporation, 51
Evergreen Marine Corporation (Taiwan)
    Ltd., 13; 50 (upd.)
First International Computer, Inc., 56
Formosa Plastics Corporation, 14; 58
    (upd.)
Giant Manufacturing Company, Ltd., 85
High Tech Computer Corporation, 81
Hon Hai Precision Industry Co., Ltd., 59
Kwang Yang Motor Company Ltd., 80
Pou Chen Corporation, 81
Quanta Computer Inc., 47
Siliconware Precision Industries Ltd., 73
Taiwan Semiconductor Manufacturing
    Company Ltd., 47
Taiwan Tobacco & Liquor Corporation,
    75
Tatung Co., 23
Uni-President Enterprises Corporation,
    104
United Microelectronics Corporation, 98

Winbond Electronics Corporation, 74
Yageo Corporation, 16; 98 (upd.)

Thailand
Charoen Pokphand Group, 62
Electricity Generating Authority of
    Thailand (EGAT), 56
Home Product Center plc, 104
Krung Thai Bank Public Company Ltd.,
    69
Land and Houses PCL, 104
Pranda Jewelry plc, 70
PTT Public Company Ltd., 56
The Siam Cement Public Company
    Limited, 56
Thai Airways International Public
    Company Limited, 6; 27 (upd.)
Thai Union Frozen Products PCL, 75
Thanulux Public Company Limited, 86
The Topaz Group, Inc., 62

Tunisia
Société Tunisienne de l'Air-Tunisair, 49

Turkey
Akbank TAS 79
Anadolu Efes Biracilik ve Malt Sanayii
    A.S., 95
Dogan Sirketler Grubu Holding A.S., 83
Haci Omer Sabanci Holdings A.S., 55
Koç Holding A.S., I; 54 (upd.)
Turkish Airlines Inc. (Türk Hava Yollari
    A.O.), 72
Turkiye Is Bankasi A.S., 61
Türkiye Petrolleri Anonim Ortakliği, IV

Ukraine
Antonov Design Bureau, 53
National Bank of Ukraine, 102

United Arab Emirates
Abu Dhabi National Oil Company, IV;
    45 (upd.)
Al Habtoor Group L.L.C., 87
DP World, 81
The Emirates Group, 39; 81 (upd.)
Etihad Airways PJSC, 89
Gulf Agency Company Ltd. 78
Jumeirah Group, 83

United Kingdom
A. F. Blakemore & Son Ltd., 90
A. Nelson & Co. Ltd., 75
Aardman Animations Ltd., 61
Abbey National plc, 10; 39 (upd.)
Acergy SA, 97
Adams Childrenswear Ltd., 95
Aegis Group plc, 6
AG Barr plc, 64
Aga Foodservice Group PLC, 73
Aggregate Industries plc, 36
Aggreko Plc, 45
AgustaWestland N.V., 75
Air Partner PLC, 93
Airtours Plc, 27
The Albert Fisher Group plc, 41

Alexandra plc, 88
The All England Lawn Tennis & Croquet
    Club, 54
Alldays plc, 49
Allders plc, 37
Alliance and Leicester plc, 88
Alliance Boots plc, 83 (upd.)
Allied Domecq PLC, 29
Allied-Lyons PLC, I
Alpha Airports Group PLC, 77
Alvis Plc, 47
Amersham PLC, 50
Amey Plc, 47
Amnesty International, 50
Amstrad plc, III; 48 (upd.)
AMVESCAP PLC, 65
Anglo American PLC, 50 (upd.)
Anker BV, 53
Antofagasta plc, 65
Apax Partners Worldwide LLP, 89
Apple Corps Ltd., 87
Arcadia Group plc, 28 (upd.)
Arena Leisure Plc, 99
Argyll Group PLC, II
Arjo Wiggins Appleton p.l.c., 34
Arriva PLC, 69
Arsenal Holdings PLC 79
ASDA Group Ltd., II; 28 (upd.); 64
    (upd.)
Ashtead Group plc, 34
Associated British Foods plc, II; 13 (upd.);
    41 (upd.)
Associated British Ports Holdings Plc, 45
Aston Villa plc, 41
AstraZeneca PLC, 50 (upd.)
AT&T Istel Ltd., 14
Avecia Group PLC, 63
Aviva PLC, 50 (upd.)
BAA plc, 10; 33 (upd.)
Babcock International Group PLC, 69
Balfour Beatty plc, 36 (upd.)
Barclays plc, II; 20 (upd.); 64 (upd.)
Barings PLC, 14
Barratt Developments plc, I; 56 (upd.)
Bass PLC, I; 15 (upd.); 38 (upd.)
Bat Industries PLC, I; 20 (upd.)
Baxi Group Ltd., 96
Baxters Food Group Ltd., 99
BBA Aviation plc, 90
Beggars Group Ltd., 99
Belleek Pottery Ltd., 71
Bellway Plc, 45
Belron International Ltd., 76
Benfield Greig Group plc, 53
Bernard Matthews Ltd., 89
Bettys & Taylors of Harrogate Ltd., 72
Bhs plc, 17
BICC PLC, III
Biffa plc, 92
The Big Food Group plc, 68 (upd.)
Birse Group PLC, 77
Birthdays Ltd., 70
Blacks Leisure Group plc, 39
Blackwell Publishing Ltd. 78
Blue Circle Industries PLC, III
BOC Group plc, I; 25 (upd.); 78 (upd.)

The Body Shop International plc, 11; 53 (upd.)
Bodycote International PLC, 63
Bonhams 1793 Ltd., 72
Booker Cash & Carry Ltd., 13; 31 (upd.); 68 (upd.)
The Boots Company PLC, V; 24 (upd.)
Bowater PLC, IV
Bowthorpe plc, 33
BP p.l.c., 45 (upd.); 103 (upd.)
BPB plc, 83
Bradford & Bingley PLC, 65
Brake Bros plc, 45
Brammer PLC, 77
Bristow Helicopters Ltd., 70
Britannia Soft Drinks Ltd. (Britvic), 71
British Aerospace plc, I; 24 (upd.)
British Airways PLC, I; 14 (upd.); 43 (upd.); 105 (upd.)
British American Tobacco PLC, 50 (upd.)
British Broadcasting Corporation Ltd., 7; 21 (upd.); 89 (upd.)
British Coal Corporation, IV
British Energy Plc, 49
The British Film Institute, 80
British Gas plc, V
British Land Plc, 54
British Midland plc, 38
The British Museum, 71
British Nuclear Fuels plc, 6
The British Petroleum Company plc, IV; 7 (upd.); 21 (upd.)
British Railways Board, V
British Sky Broadcasting Group plc, 20; 60 (upd.)
British Steel plc, IV; 19 (upd.)
British Sugar plc, 84
British Telecommunications plc, V; 15 (upd.)
British United Provident Association Limited (BUPA) 79
British Vita plc, 9; 33 (upd.)
British World Airlines Ltd., 18
British-Borneo Oil & Gas PLC, 34
BT Group plc, 49 (upd.)
BTG Plc, 87
BTR PLC, I
BTR Siebe plc, 27
Budgens Ltd., 59
Bunzl plc, IV; 31 (upd.)
Burberry Group plc, 17; 41 (upd.); 92 (upd.)
Burmah Castrol PLC, IV; 30 (upd.)
The Burton Group plc, V
Business Post Group plc, 46
C&J Clark International Ltd., 52
C. Hoare & Co., 77
C.I. Traders Limited, 61
Cable and Wireless plc, V; 25 (upd.)
Cadbury plc, 105 (upd.)
Cadbury Schweppes PLC, II; 49 (upd.)
Caffè Nero Group PLC, 63
Caffyns PLC, 105
Cains Beer Company PLC, 99
Canary Wharf Group Plc, 30
Caparo Group Ltd., 90
Capita Group PLC, 69
Capital Radio plc, 35

Caradon plc, 20 (upd.)
Carbo PLC, 67 (upd.)
Carlton Communications PLC, 15; 50 (upd.)
The Carphone Warehouse Group PLC, 83
Cartier Monde, 29
Cascal N.V., 103
Cattles plc, 58
Cazenove Group plc, 72
Central Independent Television, 7; 23 (upd.)
Centrica plc, 29 (upd.)
Channel Four Television Corporation, 93
Chello Zone Ltd., 93
Chelsea Ltd., 102
Chelsfield PLC, 67
Cheltenham & Gloucester PLC, 61
Cheshire Building Society, 74
Christian Salvesen Plc, 45
Christie's International plc, 15; 39 (upd.)
Chrysalis Group plc, 40
Chubb, PLC, 50
Clifford Chance LLP, 38
Clinton Cards plc, 39
Close Brothers Group plc, 39
Co-operative Group (CWS) Ltd., 51
Coats plc, V; 44 (upd.)
Cobham plc, 30
COLT Telecom Group plc, 41
Commercial Union PLC, III
Compass Group PLC, 34
Cookson Group plc, III; 44 (upd.)
Corus Group plc, 49 (upd.)
Courtaulds plc, V; 17 (upd.)
Courts Plc, 45
Cranswick plc, 40
Croda International Plc, 45
Daily Mail and General Trust plc, 19
Dairy Crest Group plc, 32
Dalgety, PLC, II
Daniel Thwaites Plc, 95
Dart Group PLC, 77
Davis Service Group PLC, 45
Dawson Holdings PLC, 43
De La Rue plc, 10; 34 (upd.)
Debenhams plc, 28; 101 (upd.)
Denby Group plc, 44
Denison International plc, 46
Dennis Publishing Ltd., 62
Devro plc, 55
Diageo plc, 24 (upd.); 79 (upd.)
Direct Wines Ltd., 84
Dixons Group plc, V; 19 (upd.); 49 (upd.)
Domino Printing Sciences PLC, 87
Dorling Kindersley Holdings plc, 20
Dresdner Kleinwort Wasserstein, 60 (upd.)
DS Smith Plc, 61
Dyson Group PLC, 71
E H Booth & Company Ltd., 90
easyJet Airline Company Limited, 39
ECC Group plc, III
The Economist Group Ltd., 67
The Edrington Group Ltd., 88
Electrocomponents PLC, 50
Elementis plc, 40 (upd.)
EMAP plc, 35
EMI Group plc, 22 (upd.); 81 (upd.)

Energis plc, 47
English China Clays Ltd., 15 (upd.); 40 (upd.)
Enodis plc, 68
Enterprise Inns plc, 59
Enterprise Oil PLC, 11; 50 (upd.)
Esporta plc, 35
Eurotunnel Group, 13; 37 (upd.)
Exel plc, 51 (upd.)
Fairclough Construction Group PLC, I
Fat Face Ltd., 68
Filtrona plc, 88
Findel plc, 60
First Artist Corporation PLC, 105
First Choice Holidays PLC, 40
FirstGroup plc, 89
Fisons plc, 9; 23 (upd.)
FKI Plc, 57
4imprint Group PLC, 105
Fred Perry Limited, 105
French Connection Group plc, 41
Fuller Smith & Turner P.L.C., 38
G A Pindar & Son Ltd., 88
Galiform PLC, 103
Gallaher Group Plc, 49 (upd.)
Gallaher Limited, V; 19 (upd.)
The GAME Group plc, 80
The Gateway Corporation Ltd., II
Geest plc, 38
General Electric Company PLC, II
George Wimpey PLC, 12; 51 (upd.)
Gibbs and Dandy plc, 74
GKN plc, III; 38 (upd.); 89 (upd.)
GlaxoSmithKline plc, I; 9 (upd.); 46 (upd.)
Glotel plc, 53
The Go-Ahead Group Plc, 28
Grampian Country Food Group, Ltd., 85
Granada Group PLC, II; 24 (upd.)
Grand Metropolitan PLC, I; 14 (upd.)
The Great Universal Stores plc, V; 19 (upd.)
The Greenalls Group PLC, 21
Greene King plc, 31
Greggs PLC, 65
Guardian Financial Services, 64 (upd.)
Guardian Media Group plc, 53
Guardian Royal Exchange Plc, 11
Guinness/UDV, I; 43 (upd.)
GUS plc, 47 (upd.)
GWR Group plc, 39
Halma plc, 104
Hammerson plc, 40
The Hammerson Property Investment and Development Corporation plc, IV
Hanson PLC, III; 7 (upd.); 30 (upd.)
Harrisons & Crosfield plc, III
Harrods Holdings, 47
The Hartstone Group plc, 14
Hawker Siddeley Group Public Limited Company, III
Haynes Publishing Group P.L.C., 71
Hays Plc, 27; 78 (upd.)
Hazlewood Foods plc, 32
Headlam Group plc, 95
Henry Boot plc, 76
Her Majesty's Stationery Office, 7
Highland Gold Mining Limited, 95

Hillsdown Holdings plc, II; 24 (upd.)
Hilton Group plc, 49 (upd.)
HIT Entertainment PLC, 40
HMV Group plc, 59
Hogg Robinson Group PLC, 105
Holidaybreak plc, 96
Home Retail Group plc, 91
Hornby PLC, 105
House of Fraser PLC, 45
HSBC Holdings plc, 12; 26 (upd.); 80 (upd.)
Hunting plc 78
Huntingdon Life Sciences Group plc, 42
Huntleigh Technology PLC, 77
IAC Group, 96
Ibstock Brick Ltd., 14; 37 (upd.)
ICL plc, 6
IG Group Holdings plc, 97
IMI plc, 9
ITV plc, 104 (upd.)
Imperial Chemical Industries PLC, I; 50 (upd.)
Imperial Tobacco Group PLC, 50
Inchcape PLC, III; 16 (upd.); 50 (upd.)
Informa Group plc, 58
Inter Link Foods PLC, 61
International Power PLC, 50 (upd.)
Intertek Group plc, 95
Invensys PLC, 50 (upd.)
IPC Magazines Limited, 7
J C Bamford Excavators Ltd., 83
J Sainsbury plc, II; 13 (upd.); 38 (upd.); 95 (upd.)
James Beattie plc, 43
James Purdey & Sons Limited, 87
Jarvis plc, 39
JD Wetherspoon plc, 30
Jersey European Airways (UK) Ltd., 61
JJB Sports plc, 32
John Brown PLC, I
The John David Group plc, 90
John Dewar & Sons, Ltd., 82
John Laing plc, I; 51 (upd.)
John Lewis Partnership plc, V; 42 (upd.); 99 (upd.)
John Menzies plc, 39
Johnson Matthey PLC, IV; 16 (upd.); 49 (upd.)
Johnston Press plc, 35
Kelda Group plc, 45
Keller Group PLC, 95
Kennecott Corporation, 7; 27 (upd.)
Kesa Electricals plc, 91
Kidde plc, 44 (upd.)
Kingfisher plc, V; 24 (upd.); 83 (upd.)
Kleinwort Benson Group PLC, II
Kvaerner ASA, 36
Kwik-Fit Holdings plc, 54
Ladbroke Group PLC, II; 21 (upd.)
Lafarge Cement UK, 54 (upd.)
Land Securities PLC, IV; 49 (upd.)
Laing O'Rourke PLC, 93 (upd.)
Laura Ashley Holdings plc, 13; 37 (upd.)
The Laurel Pub Company Limited, 59
Legal & General Group Plc, III; 24 (upd.); 101 (upd.)
Littlewoods plc, V; 42 (upd.)

The Liverpool Football Club and Athletic Grounds PLC, 105
Lloyd's, III; 22 (upd.); 74 (upd.)
Lloyds TSB Group plc, II; 47 (upd.)
Loganair Ltd., 68
Logica plc, 14; 37 (upd.)
London Regional Transport, 6
London Scottish Bank plc, 70
London Stock Exchange Limited, 34
Lonmin plc, 66 (upd.)
Lonrho Plc, 21
Lookers plc, 71
Lotus Cars Ltd., 14
Lucas Industries PLC, III
Luminar Plc, 40
Lush Ltd., 93
The Macallan Distillers Ltd., 63
Mackays Stores Group Ltd., 92
Madge Networks N.V., 26
Man Group PLC, 106
Manchester United Football Club plc, 30
Marconi plc, 33 (upd.)
Marks and Spencer Group p.l.c., V; 24 (upd.); 85 (upd.)
Marshall Amplification plc, 62
Martin-Baker Aircraft Company Limited, 61
Matalan PLC, 49
Maxwell Communication Corporation plc, IV; 7 (upd.)
May Gurney Integrated Services PLC, 95
McBride plc, 82
McKechnie plc, 34
Meggitt PLC, 34
MEPC plc, IV
Mercury Communications, Ltd., 7
Merlin Entertainments Group Ltd., 105
The Mersey Docks and Harbour Company, 30
Metal Box PLC, I
Michael Page International plc, 45
Midland Bank PLC, II; 17 (upd.)
Millennium & Copthorne Hotels plc, 71
Mirror Group Newspapers plc, 7; 23 (upd.)
Misys plc, 45; 46
Mitchells & Butlers PLC, 59
Molins plc, 51
Monsoon plc, 39
The Morgan Crucible Company plc, 82
Morgan Grenfell Group PLC, II
Morgan Motor Company, 105
Moss Bros Group plc, 51
Mothercare plc, 17; 78 (upd.)
Moy Park Ltd. 78
Mulberry Group PLC, 71
N M Rothschild & Sons Limited, 39
National Express Group PLC, 50
National Power PLC, 12
National Westminster Bank PLC, II
New Look Group plc, 35
Newsquest plc, 32
Next plc, 29
NFC plc, 6
Nichols plc, 44
North West Water Group plc, 11
Northern and Shell Network plc, 87
Northern Foods plc, 10; 61 (upd.)

Northern Rock plc, 33
Norwich & Peterborough Building Society, 55
Novar plc, 49 (upd.)
NTL Inc., 65
Ocean Group plc, 6
Old Mutual PLC, 61
Orange S.A., 84
Ottakar's plc, 64
Oxfam GB, 87
Pearson plc, IV; 46 (upd.); 103 (upd.)
The Penguin Group, 100
The Peninsular & Oriental Steam Navigation Company (Bovis Division), I
The Peninsular and Oriental Steam Navigation Company, V; 38 (upd.)
Pennon Group Plc, 45
The Pentland Group plc, 20; 100 (upd.)
Perkins Foods Holdings Ltd., 87
Petrofac Ltd., 95
Phaidon Press Ltd., 98
Phones 4u Ltd., 85
Photo-Me International Plc, 83
PIC International Group PLC, 24 (upd.)
Pilkington Group Limited, III; 34 (upd.); 87 (upd.)
PKF International 78
The Plessey Company, PLC, II
The Porcelain and Fine China Companies Ltd., 69
Portmeirion Group plc, 88
Post Office Group, V
Posterscope Worldwide, 70
Powell Duffryn plc, 31
Powergen PLC, 11; 50 (upd.)
Princes Ltd., 76
Prudential plc, 48 (upd.)
Psion PLC, 45
Punch Taverns plc, 70
PZ Cussons plc, 72
R. Griggs Group Limited, 23
Racal Electronics PLC, II
Ragdoll Productions Ltd., 51
Railtrack Group PLC, 50
Raleigh UK Ltd., 65
The Rank Group plc, II; 14 (upd.); 64 (upd.)
Ranks Hovis McDougall Limited, II; 28 (upd.)
Rathbone Brothers plc, 70
Raymarine plc, 104
The Real Good Food Company plc, 99
The Really Useful Group, 26
Reckitt Benckiser plc, II; 42 (upd.); 91 (upd.)
Redland plc, III
Redrow Group plc, 31
Reed Elsevier plc, IV; 17 (upd.); 31 (upd.)
Regent Inns plc, 95
Renishaw plc, 46
Rentokil Initial Plc, 47
Reuters Group PLC, IV; 22 (upd.); 63 (upd.)
Rexam PLC, 32 (upd.); 85 (upd.)
Ricardo plc, 90
Rio Tinto PLC, 19 (upd.); 50 (upd.)
RMC Group p.l.c., III; 34 (upd.)

Rolls-Royce Group PLC, 67 (upd.)
Rolls-Royce plc, I; 7 (upd.); 21 (upd.)
Ronson PLC, 49
Rothmans UK Holdings Limited, V; 19 (upd.)
Rotork plc, 46
Rover Group Ltd., 7; 21 (upd.)
Rowntree Mackintosh, II
Royal & Sun Alliance Insurance Group plc, 55 (upd.)
The Royal Bank of Scotland Group plc, 38 (upd.)
Royal Doulton plc, 14; 38 (upd.)
Royal Dutch Petroleum Company/ The Shell Transport and Trading Company p.l.c., IV
Royal Insurance Holdings PLC, III
RPC Group PLC, 81
The RTZ Corporation PLC, IV
The Rugby Group plc, 31
Saatchi & Saatchi PLC, I
SABMiller plc, 59 (upd.)
Safeway PLC, 50 (upd.)
Saffery Champness, 80
The Sage Group, 43
St. James's Place Capital, plc, 71
The Sanctuary Group PLC, 69
SBC Warburg, 14
Schroders plc, 42
Scottish & Newcastle plc, 35 (upd.)
Scottish and Southern Energy plc, 66 (upd.)
Scottish Power plc, 49 (upd.)
Scottish Radio Holding plc, 41
SDL PLC, 67
Sea Containers Ltd., 29
Sears plc, V
Securicor Plc, 45
Seddon Group Ltd., 67
Selfridges Plc, 34
Serco Group plc, 47
Severn Trent PLC, 12; 38 (upd.)
SFI Group plc, 51
Shanks Group plc, 45
Shed Media plc, 104
Shepherd Neame Limited, 30
SIG plc, 71
Signet Group PLC, 61
Singer & Friedlander Group plc, 41
Skipton Building Society, 80
Slough Estates PLC, IV; 50 (upd.)
Smith & Nephew plc, 17;41 (upd.)
SmithKline Beecham plc, III; 32 (upd.)
Smiths Industries PLC, 25
Somerfield plc, 47 (upd.)
Southern Electric PLC, 13
Specialist Computer Holdings Ltd., 80
Specsavers Optical Group Ltd., 104
Speedy Hire plc, 84
Spirax-Sarco Engineering plc, 59
SSL International plc, 49
St Ives plc, 34
Stagecoach Group plc, 104
Standard Chartered plc, II; 48 (upd.)
Stanley Leisure plc, 66
STC PLC, III
Stirling Group plc, 62
Stoddard International plc, 72

Stoll-Moss Theatres Ltd., 34
Stolt-Nielsen S.A., 42
Storehouse PLC, 16
Strix Ltd., 51
Superdrug Stores PLC, 95
Surrey Satellite Technology Limited, 83
Sun Alliance Group PLC, III
Sytner Group plc, 45
Tarmac Limited, III; 28 (upd.); 95 (upd.)
Tate & Lyle PLC, II; 42 (upd.); 101 (upd.)
Taylor & Francis Group plc, 44
Taylor Nelson Sofres plc, 34
Taylor Woodrow plc, I; 38 (upd.)
Ted Baker plc, 86
Tesco plc, II; 24 (upd.); 68 (upd.)
Thames Water plc, 11; 90 (upd.)
Thistle Hotels PLC, 54
Thorn Emi PLC, I
Thorn plc, 24
Thorntons plc, 46
3i Group PLC, 73
365 Media Group plc, 89
TI Group plc, 17
Tibbett & Britten Group plc, 32
Tiger Aspect Productions Ltd., 72
Time Out Group Ltd., 68
Tomkins plc, 11; 44 (upd.)
Tottenham Hotspur PLC, 81
Travis Perkins plc, 34
Trinity Mirror plc, 49 (upd.)
Triumph Motorcycles Ltd., 53
Trusthouse Forte PLC, III
TSB Group plc, 12
Tulip Ltd., 89
Tullow Oil plc, 83
The Tussauds Group, 55
Ulster Television PLC, 71
Ultimate Leisure Group PLC, 75
Ultramar PLC, IV
Umbro plc, 88
Unigate PLC, II; 28 (upd.)
Unilever, II; 7 (upd.); 32 (upd.); 89 (upd.)
Uniq plc, 83 (upd.)
United Biscuits (Holdings) plc, II; 42 (upd.)
United Business Media plc, 52 (upd.)
United News & Media plc, IV; 28 (upd.)
United Utilities PLC, 52 (upd.)
Urbium PLC, 75
Vauxhall Motors Limited, 73
Vendôme Luxury Group plc, 27
Vestey Group Ltd., 95
Vickers plc, 27
Virgin Group Ltd., 12; 32 (upd.); 89 (upd.)
Viridian Group plc, 64
Vodafone Group Plc, 11; 36 (upd.); 75 (upd.)
Vosper Thornycroft Holding plc, 41
W Jordan (Cereals) Ltd., 74
Wagon plc, 92
Walkers Shortbread Ltd. 79
Walkers Snack Foods Ltd., 70
Warburtons Ltd., 89
Wassall Plc, 18
Waterford Wedgwood Holdings PLC, 12

Watson Wyatt Worldwide, 42
Watts of Lydney Group Ltd., 71
Weetabix Limited, 61
The Weir Group PLC, 85
The Wellcome Foundation Ltd., I
WH Smith PLC, V, 42 (upd.)
Whatman plc, 46
Whitbread PLC, I; 20 (upd.); 52 (upd.); 97 (upd.)
Whittard of Chelsea Plc, 61
Wilkinson Hardware Stores Ltd., 80
Wilkinson Sword Ltd., 60
William Grant & Sons Ltd., 60
William Hill Organization Limited, 49
William Jackson & Son Ltd., 101
William Reed Publishing Ltd. 78
Willis Group Holdings Ltd., 25; 100 (upd.)
Wilson Bowden Plc, 45
Wincanton plc, 52
Wm. Morrison Supermarkets PLC, 38
Wolseley plc, 64
The Wolverhampton & Dudley Breweries, PLC, 57
Wood Hall Trust PLC, I
The Woolwich plc, 30
Woolworths Group plc, 83
Working Title Films Ltd., 105
WPP Group plc, 6; 48 (upd.)
WS Atkins Plc, 45
WWRD Holdings Limited, 106 (upd.)
Xstrata PLC, 73
Yell Group PLC 79
Young & Co.'s Brewery, P.L.C., 38
Young's Bluecrest Seafood Holdings Ltd., 81
Yule Catto & Company plc, 54
Zeneca Group PLC, 21
Zomba Records Ltd., 52

United States

A & E Television Networks, 32
A & W Brands, Inc., 25
A-dec, Inc., 53
A-Mark Financial Corporation, 71
A.B. Watley Group Inc., 45
A.B.Dick Company, 28
A.C. Moore Arts & Crafts, Inc., 30
A. Duda & Sons, Inc., 88
A.G. Edwards, Inc., 8; 32
A.H. Belo Corporation, 10; 30 (upd.)
A.L. Pharma Inc., 12
A.M. Castle & Co., 25
A.O. Smith Corporation, 11; 40 (upd.); 93 (upd.)
A. Schulman, Inc., 8; 49 (upd.)
A. Smith Bowman Distillery, Inc., 104
A.T. Cross Company, 17; 49 (upd.)
AAF-McQuay Incorporated, 26
AAON, Inc., 22
AAR Corp., 28
Aaron Rents, Inc., 14; 35 (upd.)
AARP, 27
Aavid Thermal Technologies, Inc., 29
ABARTA, Inc., 100
Abatix Corp., 57
Abaxis, Inc., 83

Abbott Laboratories, I; 11 (upd.); 40 (upd.); 93 (upd.)
ABC Appliance, Inc., 10
ABC Carpet & Home Co. Inc., 26
ABC Family Worldwide, Inc., 52
ABC Rail Products Corporation, 18
ABC Supply Co., Inc., 22
Abercrombie & Fitch Company, 15; 35 (upd.); 75 (upd.)
Abigail Adams National Bancorp, Inc., 23
Abiomed, Inc., 47
ABM Industries Incorporated, 25 (upd.)
Abrams Industries Inc., 23
Abraxas Petroleum Corporation, 89
Abt Associates Inc., 95
Academy of Television Arts & Sciences, Inc., 55
Academy Sports & Outdoors, 27
Acadia Realty Trust, 106
Acadian Ambulance & Air Med Services, Inc., 39
ACCION International, 87
Acclaim Entertainment Inc., 24
ACCO World Corporation, 7; 51 (upd.)
Accredited Home Lenders Holding Co., 91
Accubuilt, Inc., 74
Accuray Incorporated, 95
AccuWeather, Inc., 73
ACE Cash Express, Inc., 33
Ace Hardware Corporation, 12; 35 (upd.)
Aceto Corp., 38
AchieveGlobal Inc., 90
Ackerley Communications, Inc., 9
Acme United Corporation, 70
Acme-Cleveland Corp., 13
ACNielsen Corporation, 13; 38 (upd.)
Acorn Products, Inc., 55
Acosta Sales and Marketing Company, Inc., 77
Acsys, Inc., 44
Action Performance Companies, Inc., 27
Activision, Inc., 32; 89 (upd.)
Actuant Corporation, 94 (upd.)
Acuity Brands, Inc., 90
Acushnet Company, 64
Acuson Corporation, 10; 36 (upd.)
Acxiom Corporation, 35
The Adams Express Company, 86
Adams Golf, Inc., 37
Adaptec, Inc., 31
ADC Telecommunications, Inc., 10; 30 (upd.); 89 (upd.)
Adelman Travel Group, 105
Adelphia Communications Corporation, 17; 52 (upd.)
ADESA, Inc., 71
Administaff, Inc., 52
Adobe Systems Inc., 10; 33 (upd.); 106 (upd.)
Adolor Corporation, 101
Adolph Coors Company, I; 13 (upd.); 36 (upd.)
ADT Security Services, Inc., 12; 44 (upd.)
Adtran Inc., 22
Advance Auto Parts, Inc., 57
Advance Publications Inc., IV; 19 (upd.); 96 (upd.)

Advanced Circuits Inc., 67
Advanced Fibre Communications, Inc., 63
Advanced Marketing Services, Inc., 34
Advanced Medical Optics, Inc. 79
Advanced Micro Devices, Inc., 6; 30 (upd.); 99 (upd.)
Advanced Neuromodulation Systems, Inc., 73
Advanced Technology Laboratories, Inc., 9
Advanstar Communications, Inc., 57
Advanta Corporation, 8; 38 (upd.)
Advantica Restaurant Group, Inc., 27 (upd.)
Adventist Health, 53
The Advertising Council, Inc., 76
The Advisory Board Company, 80
Advo, Inc., 6; 53 (upd.)
Advocat Inc., 46
AECOM Technology Corporation 79
AEI Music Network Inc., 35
AEP Industries, Inc., 36
AeroGrow International, Inc., 95
Aerojet-General Corp., 63
Aeronca Inc., 46
Aéropostale, Inc., 89
Aeroquip Corporation, 16
Aerosonic Corporation, 69
AeroVironment, Inc., 97
The AES Corporation, 10; 13 (upd.); 53 (upd.)
Aetna Inc., III; 21 (upd.); 63 (upd.)
AFC Enterprises, Inc., 32; 83 (upd.)
Affiliated Computer Services, Inc., 61
Affiliated Foods Inc., 53
Affiliated Managers Group, Inc. 79
Affiliated Publications, Inc., 7
Affinity Group Holding Inc., 56
Affymetrix Inc., 106
AFLAC Incorporated, 10 (upd.); 38 (upd.)
Africare, 59
After Hours Formalwear Inc., 60
Aftermarket Technology Corp., 83
Ag Services of America, Inc., 59
Ag-Chem Equipment Company, Inc., 17
AGCO Corporation, 13; 67 (upd.)
Agere Systems Inc., 61
Agilent Technologies Inc., 38; 93 (upd.)
Agilysys Inc., 76 (upd.)
Agri Beef Company, 81
Agway, Inc., 7; 21 (upd.)
AHL Services, Inc., 27
Air & Water Technologies Corporation, 6
Air Express International Corporation, 13
Air Methods Corporation, 53
Air Products and Chemicals, Inc., I; 10 (upd.); 74 (upd.)
Air T, Inc., 86
Air Wisconsin Airlines Corporation, 55
Airborne Freight Corporation, 6; 34 (upd.)
Airborne Systems Group, 89
Airgas, Inc., 54
AirTouch Communications, 11
AirTran Holdings, Inc., 22
AK Steel Holding Corporation, 19; 41 (upd.)
Akamai Technologies, Inc., 71

Akeena Solar, Inc., 103
Akin, Gump, Strauss, Hauer & Feld, L.L.P., 33
Akorn, Inc., 32
Alabama Farmers Cooperative, Inc., 63
Alabama National BanCorporation, 75
Alamo Group Inc., 32
Alamo Rent A Car, 6; 24 (upd.); 84 (upd.)
ALARIS Medical Systems, Inc., 65
Alaska Air Group, Inc., 6; 29 (upd.)
Alaska Communications Systems Group, Inc., 89
Alaska Railroad Corporation, 60
Alba-Waldensian, Inc., 30
Albany International Corporation, 8; 51 (upd.)
Albany Molecular Research, Inc., 77
Albaugh, Inc., 105
Albemarle Corporation, 59
Alberici Corporation, 76
Alberto-Culver Company, 8; 36 (upd.); 91 (upd.)
Albertson's, Inc., II; 7 (upd.); 30 (upd.); 65 (upd.)
Alco Health Services Corporation, III
Alco Standard Corporation, I
Alcoa Inc., 56 (upd.)
Aldila Inc., 46
Aldus Corporation, 10
Alex Lee Inc., 18; 44 (upd.)
Alexander & Alexander Services Inc., 10
Alexander & Baldwin, Inc., 10; 40 (upd.)
Alexander's, Inc., 45
Alexandria Real Estate Equities, Inc., 101
Alfa Corporation, 60
Alico, Inc., 63
Alienware Corporation, 81
Align Technology, Inc., 94
All American Communications Inc., 20
Allbritton Communications Company, 105
Alleghany Corporation, 10; 60 (upd.)
Allegheny Energy, Inc., 38 (upd.)
Allegheny Ludlum Corporation, 8
Allegheny Power System, Inc., V
Allegiant Travel Company, 97
Allegis Group, Inc., 95
Allen Brothers, Inc., 101
Allen Canning Company, 76
Allen Foods, Inc., 60
Allen Organ Company, 33
Allen Systems Group, Inc., 59
Allen-Edmonds Shoe Corporation, 61
Allergan, Inc., 10; 30 (upd.); 77 (upd.)
Alliance Capital Management Holding L.P., 63
Alliance Entertainment Corp., 17
Alliance Laundry Holdings LLC, 102
Alliance Resource Partners, L.P., 81
Alliant Energy Corporation, 106
Alliant Techsystems Inc., 8; 30 (upd.); 77 (upd.)
The Allied Defense Group, Inc., 65
Allied Healthcare Products, Inc., 24
Allied Products Corporation, 21
Allied Signal Engines, 9
Allied Waste Industries, Inc., 50

Allied Worldwide, Inc., 49
AlliedSignal Inc., I; 22 (upd.)
Allison Gas Turbine Division, 9
Allmerica Financial Corporation, 63
Allou Health & Beauty Care, Inc., 28
Alloy, Inc., 55
Allscripts-Misys Healthcare Solutions Inc., 104
The Allstate Corporation, 10; 27 (upd.)
ALLTEL Corporation, 6; 46 (upd.)
Alltrista Corporation, 30
Allwaste, Inc., 18
Almost Family, Inc., 93
Aloha Airlines, Incorporated, 24
Alpha Natural Resources Inc., 106
Alpharma Inc., 35 (upd.)
Alpine Confections, Inc., 71
Alpine Lace Brands, Inc., 18
Alside Inc., 94
AltaVista Company, 43
Altera Corporation, 18; 43 (upd.)
Alternative Tentacles Records, 66
Alterra Healthcare Corporation, 42
Alticor Inc., 71 (upd.)
Altiris, Inc., 65
Altron Incorporated, 20
Aluminum Company of America, IV; 20 (upd.)
Alvin Ailey Dance Foundation, Inc., 52
ALZA Corporation, 10; 36 (upd.)
Amalgamated Bank, 60
AMAX Inc., IV
Amazon.com, Inc., 25; 56 (upd.)
AMB Property Corporation, 57
Ambac Financial Group, Inc., 65
Ambassadors International, Inc., 68 (upd.)
Amblin Entertainment, 21
AMC Entertainment Inc., 12; 35 (upd.)
AMCOL International Corporation, 59 (upd.)
AMCON Distributing Company, 99
AMCORE Financial Inc., 44
Amdahl Corporation, III; 14 (upd.); 40 (upd.)
Amdocs Ltd., 47
Amedisys, Inc., 53; 106 (upd.)
Amerada Hess Corporation, IV; 21 (upd.); 55 (upd.)
Amerco, 6
AMERCO, 67 (upd.)
Ameren Corporation, 60 (upd.)
America Online, Inc., 10; 26 (upd.)
America West Holdings Corporation, 6; 34 (upd.)
America's Car-Mart, Inc., 64
America's Favorite Chicken Company, Inc., 7
American & Efird, Inc., 82
American Airlines, I; 6 (upd.)
American Apparel, Inc., 90
American Axle & Manufacturing Holdings, Inc., 67
American Banknote Corporation, 30
American Bar Association, 35
American Biltrite Inc., 16; 43 (upd.)
American Brands, Inc., V
American Building Maintenance Industries, Inc., 6

American Business Information, Inc., 18
American Business Products, Inc., 20
American Campus Communities, Inc., 85
The American Cancer Society, 24
American Capital Strategies, Ltd., 91
American Cast Iron Pipe Company, 50
American Civil Liberties Union (ACLU), 60
American Classic Voyages Company, 27
American Coin Merchandising, Inc., 28; 74 (upd.)
American Colloid Co., 13
American Commercial Lines Inc., 99
American Crystal Sugar Company, 9; 32 (upd.)
American Cyanamid, I; 8 (upd.)
American Eagle Outfitters, Inc., 24; 55 (upd.)
American Ecology Corporation, 77
American Electric Power Company, Inc., V; 45 (upd.)
American Equipment Company, Inc., 104
American Express Company, II; 10 (upd.); 38 (upd.)
American Family Corporation, III
American Financial Group Inc., III; 48 (upd.)
American Foods Group, 43
American Furniture Company, Inc., 21
American General Corporation, III; 10 (upd.); 46 (upd.)
American General Finance Corp., 11
American Girl, Inc., 69 (upd.)
American Golf Corporation, 45
American Gramaphone LLC, 52
American Greetings Corporation, 7; 22 (upd.); 59 (upd.)
American Healthways, Inc., 65
American Home Mortgage Holdings, Inc., 46
American Home Products, I; 10 (upd.)
American Homestar Corporation, 18; 41 (upd.)
American Institute of Certified Public Accountants (AICPA), 44
American International Group, Inc., III; 15 (upd.); 47 (upd.)
American Italian Pasta Company, 27; 76 (upd.)
American Kennel Club, Inc., 74
American Lawyer Media Holdings, Inc., 32
American Library Association, 86
American Licorice Company, 86
American Locker Group Incorporated, 34
American Lung Association, 48
American Maize-Products Co., 14
American Management Association, 76
American Management Systems, Inc., 11
American Media, Inc., 27; 82 (upd.)
American Medical Alert Corporation, 103
American Medical Association, 39
American Medical International, Inc., III
American Medical Response, Inc., 39
American Motors Corporation, I
American National Insurance Company, 8; 27 (upd.)
American Nurses Association Inc., 102

American Pad & Paper Company, 20
American Pharmaceutical Partners, Inc., 69
American Pop Corn Company, 59
American Power Conversion Corporation, 24; 67 (upd.)
American Premier Underwriters, Inc., 10
American President Companies Ltd., 6
American Printing House for the Blind, 26
American Re Corporation, 10; 35 (upd.)
American Red Cross, 40
American Reprographics Company, 75
American Residential Mortgage Corporation, 8
American Restaurant Partners, L.P., 93
American Retirement Corporation, 42
American Rice, Inc., 33
American Safety Razor Company, 20
American Science & Engineering, Inc., 81
American Seating Company 78
American Skiing Company, 28
American Society for the Prevention of Cruelty to Animals (ASPCA), 68
The American Society of Composers, Authors and Publishers (ASCAP), 29
American Software Inc., 25
American Standard Companies Inc., III; 30 (upd.)
American States Water Company, 46
American Stores Company, II; 22 (upd.)
American Superconductor Corporation, 97
American Technical Ceramics Corp., 67
American Technology Corporation, 103
American Tourister, Inc., 16
American Tower Corporation, 33
American Vanguard Corporation, 47
American Water Works Company, Inc., 6; 38 (upd.)
American Woodmark Corporation, 31
AmeriCares Foundation, Inc., 87
Amerigon Incorporated, 97
AMERIGROUP Corporation, 69
Amerihost Properties, Inc., 30
AmeriSource Health Corporation, 37 (upd.)
AmerisourceBergen Corporation, 64 (upd.)
Ameristar Casinos, Inc., 33; 69 (upd.)
Ameritech Corporation, V; 18 (upd.)
Ameritrade Holding Corporation, 34
Ameriwood Industries International Corp., 17
Amerock Corporation, 53
Ameron International Corporation, 67
Ames Department Stores, Inc., 9; 30 (upd.)
AMETEK, Inc., 9
AMF Bowling, Inc., 40
Amfac/JMB Hawaii L.L.C., I; 24 (upd.)
Amgen, Inc., 10; 30 (upd.); 89 (upd.)
AMICAS, Inc., 69
Amkor Technology, Inc., 69
Amoco Corporation, IV; 14 (upd.)
Amoskeag Company, 8
AMP Incorporated, II; 14 (upd.)
Ampacet Corporation, 67

Ampco-Pittsburgh Corporation 79
Ampex Corporation, 17
Amphenol Corporation, 40
AMR Corporation, 28 (upd.); 52 (upd.)
AMREP Corporation, 21
Amscan Holdings, Inc., 61
AmSouth Bancorporation, 12; 48 (upd.)
Amsted Industries Incorporated, 7
AmSurg Corporation, 48
Amtran, Inc., 34
Amway Corporation, III; 13 (upd.); 30 (upd.)
Amy's Kitchen Inc., 76
Amylin Pharmaceuticals, Inc., 67
Anacomp, Inc., 94
Anadarko Petroleum Corporation, 10; 52 (upd.); 106 (upd.)
Anaheim Angels Baseball Club, Inc., 53
Analex Corporation, 74
Analog Devices, Inc., 10
Analogic Corporation, 23
Analysts International Corporation, 36
Analytic Sciences Corporation, 10
Analytical Surveys, Inc., 33
Anaren Microwave, Inc., 33
Anchor Bancorp, Inc., 10
Anchor BanCorp Wisconsin, Inc., 101
Anchor Brewing Company, 47
Anchor Gaming, 24
Anchor Hocking Glassware, 13
Andersen, 10; 29 (upd.); 68 (upd.)
Anderson Trucking Service, Inc., 75
The Anderson-DuBose Company, 60
The Andersons, Inc., 31
Andin International, Inc., 100
Andis Company, Inc., 85
Andretti Green Racing, 106
Andrew Corporation, 10; 32 (upd.)
The Andrews Institute, 99
Andrews Kurth, LLP, 71
Andrews McMeel Universal, 40
Andronico's Market, 70
Andrx Corporation, 55
Angelica Corporation, 15; 43 (upd.)
AngioDynamics, Inc., 81
Anheuser-Busch InBev, I; 10 (upd.); 34 (upd.); 100 (upd.)
Anixter International Inc., 88
Annie's Homegrown, Inc., 59
Annin & Co., 100
AnnTaylor Stores Corporation, 13; 37 (upd.); 67 (upd.)
ANR Pipeline Co., 17
The Anschutz Company, 12; 36 (upd.); 73 (upd.)
Ansoft Corporation, 63
Anteon Corporation, 57
Anthem Electronics, Inc., 13
Anthony & Sylvan Pools Corporation, 56
The Antioch Company, 40
AOL Time Warner Inc., 57 (upd.)
Aon Corporation, III; 45 (upd.)
Apache Corporation, 10; 32 (upd.); 89 (upd.)
Apartment Investment and Management Company, 49
Apex Digital, Inc., 63
APi Group, Inc., 64

APL Limited, 61 (upd.)
Apogee Enterprises, Inc., 8
Apollo Group, Inc., 24
Applause Inc., 24
Apple & Eve L.L.C., 92
Apple Bank for Savings, 59
Apple Computer, Inc., III; 6 (upd.); 36 (upd.); 77 (upd.)
Applebee's International Inc., 14; 35 (upd.)
Appliance Recycling Centers of America, Inc., 42
Applica Incorporated, 43 (upd.)
Applied Bioscience International, Inc., 10
Applied Films Corporation, 48
Applied Materials, Inc., 10; 46 (upd.)
Applied Micro Circuits Corporation, 38
Applied Power, Inc., 9; 32 (upd.)
Applied Signal Technology, Inc., 87
AptarGroup, Inc., 69
Aqua Alliance Inc., 32 (upd.)
aQuantive, Inc., 81
Aquarion Company, 84
Aquent, 96
Aquila, Inc., 50 (upd.)
AR Accessories Group, Inc., 23
ARA Services, II
ARAMARK Corporation, 13; 41 (upd.)
Arandell Corporation, 37
The Arbitron Company, 38
Arbor Drugs Inc., 12
Arby's Inc., 14
Arch Chemicals Inc. 78
Arch Coal Inc., 98
Arch Mineral Corporation, 7
Arch Wireless, Inc., 39
Archer Daniels Midland Company, I; 11 (upd.); 32 (upd.); 75 (upd.)
Archie Comics Publications, Inc., 63
Archon Corporation, 74 (upd.)
Archstone-Smith Trust, 49
Archway Cookies, Inc., 29
ARCO Chemical Company, 10
Arctco, Inc., 16
Arctic Cat Inc., 40 (upd.); 96 (upd.)
Arctic Slope Regional Corporation, 38
Arden Group, Inc., 29
Arena Resources, Inc., 97
Argon ST, Inc., 81
Argosy Gaming Company, 21
Ariba, Inc., 57
Ariens Company, 48
ARINC Inc., 98
Aris Industries, Inc., 16
The Aristotle Corporation, 62
Ark Restaurants Corp., 20
Arkansas Best Corporation, 16; 94 (upd.)
Arkla, Inc., V
Armco Inc., IV
Armor All Products Corp., 16
Armor Holdings, Inc., 27
Armstrong Holdings, Inc., III; 22 (upd.); 81 (upd.)
Army and Air Force Exchange Service, 39
Arnhold and S. Bleichroeder Advisers, LLC, 97
Arnold & Porter, 35
Arotech Corporation, 93

ArQule, Inc., 68
ARRIS Group, Inc., 89
Arrow Air Holdings Corporation, 55
Arrow Electronics, Inc., 10; 50 (upd.)
The Art Institute of Chicago, 29
Art Van Furniture, Inc., 28
Art's Way Manufacturing Co., Inc., 101
Artesyn Technologies Inc., 46 (upd.)
ArthroCare Corporation, 73
The Arthur C. Clarke Foundation, 92
Arthur D. Little, Inc., 35
Arthur J. Gallagher & Co., 73
Arthur Murray International, Inc., 32
Artisan Confections Company, 103
Artisan Entertainment Inc., 32 (upd.)
ArvinMeritor, Inc., 8; 54 (upd.)
Asanté Technologies, Inc., 20
ASARCO Incorporated, IV
Asbury Automotive Group Inc., 60
Asbury Carbons, Inc., 68
ASC, Inc., 55
Ascend Communications, Inc., 24
Ascendia Brands, Inc., 97
Ascential Software Corporation, 59
Ash Grove Cement Company, 94
Asher's Chocolates, Inc., 103
Ashland Inc., 19; 50 (upd.)
Ashland Oil, Inc., IV
Ashley Furniture Industries, Inc., 35
Ashworth, Inc., 26
ASK Group, Inc., 9
Ask Jeeves, Inc., 65
Aspect Telecommunications Corporation, 22
Aspen Skiing Company, 15
Asplundh Tree Expert Co., 20; 59 (upd.)
Assisted Living Concepts, Inc., 43
Associated Estates Realty Corporation, 25
Associated Grocers, Incorporated, 9; 31 (upd.)
Associated Milk Producers, Inc., 11; 48 (upd.)
Associated Natural Gas Corporation, 11
The Associated Press, 13; 31 (upd.); 73 (upd.)
Association of Junior Leagues International Inc., 60
AST Research Inc., 9
Astec Industries, Inc. 79
AstenJohnson Inc., 90
Astoria Financial Corporation, 44
Astronics Corporation, 35
Asurion Corporation, 83
ASV, Inc., 34; 66 (upd.)
At Home Corporation, 43
AT&T Bell Laboratories, Inc., 13
AT&T Corporation, V; 29 (upd.); 68 (upd.)
AT&T Wireless Services, Inc., 54 (upd.)
ATA Holdings Corporation, 82
Atari Corporation, 9; 23 (upd.); 66 (upd.)
ATC Healthcare Inc., 64
Atchison Casting Corporation, 39
AtheroGenics Inc., 101
The Athlete's Foot Brands LLC, 84
The Athletics Investment Group, 62
Atkins Nutritionals, Inc., 58
Atkinson Candy Company, 87

Atlanta Bread Company International, Inc., 70
Atlanta Gas Light Company, 6; 23 (upd.)
Atlanta National League Baseball Club, Inc., 43
Atlantic American Corporation, 44
Atlantic Coast Airlines Holdings, Inc., 55
Atlantic Energy, Inc., 6
The Atlantic Group, 23
Atlantic Premium Brands, Ltd., 57
Atlantic Richfield Company, IV; 31 (upd.)
Atlantic Southeast Airlines, Inc., 47
Atlantis Plastics, Inc., 85
Atlas Air, Inc., 39
Atlas Van Lines Inc., 14; 106 (upd.)
Atmel Corporation, 17
ATMI, Inc., 93
Atmos Energy Corporation, 43
Attachmate Corporation, 56
Atwood Mobil Products, 53
Atwood Oceanics, Inc., 100
Au Bon Pain Co., Inc., 18
The Auchter Company, The 78
Audible Inc. 79
Audio King Corporation, 24
Audiovox Corporation, 34; 90 (upd.)
August Schell Brewing Company Inc., 59
Ault Incorporated, 34
Auntie Anne's, Inc., 35; 102 (upd.)
Aurora Casket Company, Inc., 56
Aurora Foods Inc., 32
The Austin Company, 8; 72 (upd.)
Austin Powder Company, 76
Authentic Fitness Corporation, 20; 51 (upd.)
Auto Value Associates, Inc., 25
Autobytel Inc., 47
Autocam Corporation, 51
Autodesk, Inc., 10; 89 (upd.)
Autologic Information International, Inc., 20
Automatic Data Processing, Inc., III; 9 (upd.); 47 (upd.)
AutoNation, Inc., 50
Autotote Corporation, 20
AutoTrader.com, L.L.C., 91
AutoZone, Inc., 9; 31 (upd.)
Auvil Fruit Company, Inc., 95
Avado Brands, Inc., 31
Avalon Correctional Services, Inc., 75
AvalonBay Communities, Inc., 58
Avaya Inc., 104
Avco Financial Services Inc., 13
Aveda Corporation, 24
Avedis Zildjian Co., 38
Aventine Renewable Energy Holdings, Inc., 89
Avery Dennison Corporation, IV; 17 (upd.); 49 (upd.)
Aviall, Inc., 73
Aviation Sales Company, 41
Avid Technology Inc., 38
Avis Group Holdings, Inc., 75 (upd.)
Avis Rent A Car, Inc., 6; 22 (upd.)
Avista Corporation, 69 (upd.)
Avnet Inc., 9
Avocent Corporation, 65

Avon Products, Inc., III; 19 (upd.); 46 (upd.)
Avondale Industries, 7; 41 (upd.)
AVX Corporation, 67
Awrey Bakeries, Inc., 56
AXA Equitable Life Insurance Company, 105 (upd.)
Axcelis Technologies, Inc., 95
Axsys Technologies, Inc., 93
Aydin Corp., 19
Azcon Corporation, 23
Aztar Corporation, 13; 71 (upd.)
AZZ Incorporated, 93
B&G Foods, Inc., 40
B. Dalton Bookseller Inc., 25
The B. Manischewitz Company, LLC, 31
B/E Aerospace, Inc., 30
B.J. Alan Co., Inc., 67
B.R. Guest Inc., 87
B.W. Rogers Company, 94
Babbage's, Inc., 10
The Babcock & Wilcox Company, 82
Baby Superstore, Inc., 15
Bachman's Inc., 22
Back Bay Restaurant Group, Inc., 20; 102 (upd.)
Back Yard Burgers, Inc., 45
Bad Boy Worldwide Entertainment Group, 58
Badger Meter, Inc., 22
Badger Paper Mills, Inc., 15
Badger State Ethanol, LLC, 83
BAE Systems Ship Repair, 73
Bailey Nurseries, Inc., 57
Bain & Company, 55
Baird & Warner Holding Company, 87
Bairnco Corporation, 28
Baker & Daniels LLP, 88
Baker & Hostetler LLP, 40
Baker & McKenzie, 10; 42 (upd.)
Baker & Taylor Corporation, 16; 43 (upd.)
Baker and Botts, L.L.P., 28
Baker Hughes Incorporated, III; 22 (upd.); 57 (upd.)
Balance Bar Company, 32
Balchem Corporation, 42
Baldor Electric Company, 21; 97 (upd.)
Baldwin & Lyons, Inc., 51
Baldwin Piano & Organ Company, 18
Baldwin Richardson Foods Company, 100
Baldwin Technology Company, Inc., 25
Ball Corporation, I; 10; 78 (upd.)
Ball Horticultural Company 78
Ballantyne of Omaha, Inc., 27
Ballard Medical Products, 21
Ballistic Recovery Systems, Inc., 87
Bally Manufacturing Corporation, III
Bally Total Fitness Corporation, 25; 94 (upd.)
Balmac International, Inc., 94
Baltek Corporation, 34
Baltimore Aircoil Company, Inc., 66
Baltimore Gas and Electric Company, V; 25 (upd.)
Baltimore Orioles L.P., 66
The Bama Companies, Inc., 80
Banana Republic Inc., 25

Bandag, Inc., 19
Banfi Products Corp., 36
Bank of America Corporation, 46 (upd.); 101 (upd.)
Bank of Boston Corporation, II
Bank of Granite Corporation, 89
Bank of Hawaii Corporation, 73
Bank of Mississippi, Inc., 14
Bank of New England Corporation, II
The Bank of New York Company, Inc., II; 46 (upd.)
Bank of the Ozarks, Inc., 91
Bank One Corporation, 10; 36 (upd.)
BankAmerica Corporation, II; 8 (upd.)
Bankers Trust New York Corporation, II
Banknorth Group, Inc., 55
Bankrate, Inc., 83
Banner Aerospace, Inc., 14; 37 (upd.)
Banner Corporation, 106
Banta Corporation, 12; 32 (upd.); 79 (upd.)
Banyan Systems Inc., 25
Baptist Health Care Corporation, 82
Bar-S Foods Company, 76
BarclaysAmerican Mortgage Corporation, 11
Barbara's Bakery Inc., 88
Barden Companies, Inc., 76
Bardwil Industries Inc., 98
Bare Escentuals, Inc., 91
Barnes & Noble, Inc., 10; 30 (upd.); 75 (upd.)
Barnes Group Inc., 13; 69 (upd.)
Barnett Banks, Inc., 9
Barnett Inc., 28
Barneys New York Inc., 28; 104 (upd.)
Barr Pharmaceuticals, Inc., 26; 68 (upd.)
Barrett Business Services, Inc., 16
Barrett-Jackson Auction Company L.L.C., 88
Barry-Wehmiller Companies, Inc., 90
The Bartell Drug Company, 94
Barton Malow Company, 51
Barton Protective Services Inc., 53
The Baseball Club of Seattle, LP, 50
Bashas' Inc., 33; 80 (upd.)
Basic Earth Science Systems, Inc., 101
Basin Electric Power Cooperative, 103
The Basketball Club of Seattle, LLC, 50
Bass Pro Shops, Inc., 42
Bassett Furniture Industries, Inc., 18; 95 (upd.)
Bates Worldwide, Inc., 14; 33 (upd.)
Bath Iron Works, 12; 36 (upd.)
Battelle Memorial Institute, Inc., 10
Battle Mountain Gold Company, 23
Bauer Hockey, Inc., 104
Bauerly Companies, 61
Bausch & Lomb Inc., 7; 25 (upd.); 96 (upd.)
Baxter International Inc., I; 10 (upd.)
Bay State Gas Company, 38
BayBanks, Inc., 12
Bayou Steel Corporation, 31
BB&T Corporation 79
BBN Corp., 19
BDO Seidman LLP, 96
BE&K, Inc., 73

BEA Systems, Inc., 36
Beacon Roofing Supply, Inc., 75
Bear Creek Corporation, 38
Bear Stearns Companies, Inc., II; 10 (upd.); 52 (upd.)
Bearings, Inc., 13
Beasley Broadcast Group, Inc., 51
Beatrice Company, II
BeautiControl Cosmetics, Inc., 21
Beazer Homes USA, Inc., 17
bebe stores, inc., 31; 103 (upd.)
Bechtel Corporation, I; 24 (upd.); 99 (upd.)
Beckett Papers, 23
Beckman Coulter, Inc., 22
Beckman Instruments, Inc., 14
Becton, Dickinson and Company, I; 11 (upd.); 36 (upd.); 101 (upd.)
Bed Bath & Beyond Inc., 13; 41 (upd.)
Beech Aircraft Corporation, 8
Beech-Nut Nutrition Corporation, 21; 51 (upd.)
Beer Nuts, Inc., 86
BEI Technologies, Inc., 65
Bekins Company, 15
Bel Fuse, Inc., 53
Bel/Kaukauna USA, 76
Belco Oil & Gas Corp., 40
Belden CDT Inc., 76 (upd.)
Belden Inc., 19
Belk Stores Services, Inc., V; 19 (upd.)
Belk, Inc., 72 (upd.)
Bell and Howell Company, 9; 29 (upd.)
Bell Atlantic Corporation, V; 25 (upd.)
Bell Helicopter Textron Inc., 46
Bell Industries, Inc., 47
Bell Microproducts Inc., 69
Bell Sports Corporation, 16; 44 (upd.)
Belleville Shoe Manufacturing Company, 92
Bellisio Foods, Inc., 95
BellSouth Corporation, V; 29 (upd.)
Belo Corporation, 98 (upd.)
Beloit Corporation, 14
Bemis Company, Inc., 8; 91 (upd.)
Ben & Jerry's Homemade, Inc., 10; 35 (upd.); 80 (upd.)
Ben Bridge Jeweler, Inc., 60
Ben E. Keith Company, 76
Benchmark Capital, 49
Benchmark Electronics, Inc., 40
Bendix Corporation, I
Beneficial Corporation, 8
Benihana, Inc., 18; 76 (upd.)
Benjamin Moore & Co., 13; 38 (upd.)
Benton Oil and Gas Company, 47
Berean Christian Stores, 96
Bergdorf Goodman Inc., 52
Bergen Brunswig Corporation, V; 13 (upd.)
Berger Bros Company, 62
Beringer Blass Wine Estates Ltd., 66 (upd.)
Beringer Wine Estates Holdings, Inc., 22
Berkeley Farms, Inc., 46
Berkshire Hathaway Inc., III; 18 (upd.); 42 (upd.); 89 (upd.)
Berkshire Realty Holdings, L.P., 49

Berlex Laboratories, Inc., 66
Berlitz International, Inc., 13; 39 (upd.)
Bernard C. Harris Publishing Company, Inc., 39
Bernard Chaus, Inc., 27
Bernard Hodes Group Inc., 86
Bernard L. Madoff Investment Securities LLC, 106
The Bernick Companies, 75
Bernstein-Rein, 92
Berry Plastics Group Inc., 21; 98 (upd.)
Berry Plastics Corporation, 21
Bertucci's Corporation, 16; 64 (upd.)
Berwick Offray, LLC, 70
Berwind Corporation, 100
Best Buy Co., Inc., 9; 23 (upd.); 63 (upd.)
Best Kosher Foods Corporation, 82
Bestfoods, 22 (upd.)
BET Holdings, Inc., 18
Beth Abraham Family of Health Services, 94
Bethlehem Steel Corporation, IV; 7 (upd.); 27 (upd.)
Betsey Johnson Inc., 100
Betsy Ann Candies, Inc., 105
Better Made Snack Foods, Inc., 90
Betz Laboratories, Inc., I; 10 (upd.)
Beverly Enterprises, Inc., III; 16 (upd.)
The BFGoodrich Company, V; 19 (upd.)
BG Products Inc., 96
BHC Communications, Inc., 26
Bianchi International (d/b/a Gregory Mountain Products), 76
BIC Corporation, 8; 23 (upd.)
Bicoastal Corporation, II
Big A Drug Stores Inc. 79
Big B, Inc., 17
Big Bear Stores Co., 13
Big Brothers Big Sisters of America, 85
Big Dog Holdings, Inc., 45
Big 5 Sporting Goods Corporation, 55
Big Flower Press Holdings, Inc., 21
Big Idea Productions, Inc., 49
Big Lots, Inc., 50
Big O Tires, Inc., 20
Big Rivers Electric Corporation, 11
Big V Supermarkets, Inc., 25
Big Y Foods, Inc., 53
Bill & Melinda Gates Foundation, 41; 100 (upd.)
Bill Barrett Corporation, 71
Bill Blass Ltd., 32
Billing Concepts, Inc., 26; 72 (upd.)
Billing Services Group Ltd., 102
Bindley Western Industries, Inc., 9
The Bing Group, 60
Bingham Dana LLP, 43
Binks Sames Corporation, 21
Binney & Smith Inc., 25
Bio-Rad Laboratories, Inc., 93
Biogen Idec Inc., 71 (upd.)
Biogen Inc., 14; 36 (upd.)
Biolase Technology, Inc., 87
Biomet, Inc., 10; 93 (upd.)
BioScrip Inc., 98
Biosite Incorporated, 73
Bird Corporation, 19

Birds Eye Foods, Inc., 69 (upd.)
Birkenstock Footprint Sandals, Inc., 12; 42 (upd.)
Birmingham Steel Corporation, 13; 40 (upd.)
BISSELL Inc., 9; 30 (upd.)
The BISYS Group, Inc., 73
BJ Services Company, 25
BJ's Wholesale Club, Inc., 94
BKD LLP, 96
The Black & Decker Corporation, III; 20 (upd.); 67 (upd.)
Black & Veatch LLP, 22
Black Box Corporation, 20; 96 (upd.)
Black Diamond Equipment, Ltd., 62
Black Hills Corporation, 20
Blackbaud, Inc., 85
Blackboard Inc., 89
Blackfoot Telecommunications Group, 60
BlackRock, Inc. 79
Blackwater USA, 76
Blair Corporation, 25; 31
Blessings Corp., 19
Blimpie, 15; 49 (upd.); 105 (upd.)
Blish-Mize Co., 95
Blizzard Entertainment 78
Block Communications, Inc., 81
Block Drug Company, Inc., 8; 27 (upd.)
Blockbuster Inc., 9; 31 (upd.); 76 (upd.)
Blodgett Holdings, Inc., 61 (upd.)
Blonder Tongue Laboratories, Inc., 48
Bloomberg L.P., 21
Bloomingdale's Inc., 12
Blount International, Inc., 12; 48 (upd.)
Blue Bell Creameries L.P., 30
Blue Bird Corporation, 35
Blue Coat Systems, Inc., 83
Blue Cross and Blue Shield Association, 10
Blue Diamond Growers, 28
Blue Heron Paper Company, 90
Blue Martini Software, Inc., 59
Blue Mountain Arts, Inc., 29
Blue Nile Inc., 61
Blue Rhino Corporation, 56
Blue Ridge Beverage Company Inc., 82
Bluefly, Inc., 60
Bluegreen Corporation, 80
BlueLinx Holdings Inc., 97
Blyth, Inc., 18; 74 (upd.)
BMC Industries, Inc., 17; 59 (upd.)
BMC Software, Inc., 55
Boardwalk Pipeline Partners, LP, 87
Boart Longyear Company, 26
Boatmen's Bancshares Inc., 15
Bob Evans Farms, Inc., 9; 63 (upd.)
Bob's Discount Furniture LLC, 104
Bob's Red Mill Natural Foods, Inc., 63
Bobit Publishing Company, 55
Bobs Candies, Inc., 70
Boca Resorts, Inc., 37
Boddie-Noell Enterprises, Inc., 68
Body Glove International LLC, 88
The Boeing Company, I; 10 (upd.); 32 (upd.)
Boenning & Scattergood Inc., 102
Bogen Communications International, Inc., 62

Bohemia, Inc., 13
Boise Cascade Holdings, L.L.C., IV; 8 (upd.); 32 (upd.); 95 (upd.)
Bojangles Restaurants Inc., 97
Bollinger Shipyards, Inc., 61
Bolt Technology Corporation, 99
The Bombay Company, Inc., 10; 71 (upd.)
The Bon Marché, Inc., 23
Bon Secours Health System, Inc., 24
The Bon-Ton Stores, Inc., 16; 50 (upd.)
Bonneville International Corporation, 29
Bonneville Power Administration, 50
Book-of-the-Month Club, Inc., 13
Books-A-Million, Inc., 14; 41 (upd.); 96 (upd.)
Bookspan, 86
Boole & Babbage, Inc., 25
Booth Creek Ski Holdings, Inc., 31
Boots & Coots International Well Control, Inc. 79
Booz Allen Hamilton Inc., 10; 101 (upd.)
Borden, Inc., II; 22 (upd.)
Borders Group, Inc., 15; 43 (upd.)
Borg-Warner Corporation, III
BorgWarner Inc., 14; 32 (upd.); 85 (upd.)
Borland International, Inc., 9
Boron, LePore & Associates, Inc., 45
Boscov's Department Store, Inc., 31
Bose Corporation, 13; 36 (upd.)
Boss Holdings, Inc., 97
Boston Acoustics, Inc., 22
The Boston Beer Company, Inc., 18; 50 (upd.)
Boston Celtics Limited Partnership, 14
The Boston Consulting Group, 58
Boston Edison Company, 12
Boston Market Corporation, 12; 48 (upd.)
Boston Professional Hockey Association Inc., 39
Boston Properties, Inc., 22
Boston Scientific Corporation, 37; 77 (upd.)
The Boston Symphony Orchestra Inc., 93
Bou-Matic, 62
Bowen Engineering Corporation, 105
Bowlin Travel Centers, Inc., 99
Bowne & Co., Inc., 23; 79 (upd.)
The Boy Scouts of America, 34
Boyd Bros. Transportation Inc., 39
Boyd Coffee Company, 53
Boyd Gaming Corporation, 43
The Boyds Collection, Ltd., 29
Boyne USA Resorts, 71
Boys & Girls Clubs of America, 69
Bozell Worldwide Inc., 25
Bozzuto's, Inc., 13
Brach and Brock Confections, Inc., 15
Brach's Confections, Inc., 74 (upd.)
Bradlees Discount Department Store Company, 12
Brady Corporation 78 (upd.)
The Branch Group, Inc., 72
BrandPartners Group, Inc., 58
Brannock Device Company, 48
Brasfield & Gorrie LLC, 87
Brass Eagle Inc., 34

Brazos Sportswear, Inc., 23
Breeze-Eastern Corporation, 95
Bremer Financial Corporation, 45; 105 (upd.)
Brenco, Inc., 104
Briazz, Inc., 53
The Brickman Group, Ltd., 87
Bridgeport Machines, Inc., 17
Bridgford Foods Corporation, 27
Briggs & Stratton Corporation, 8; 27 (upd.)
Brigham Exploration Company, 75
Brigham's Inc., 72
Bright Horizons Family Solutions, Inc., 31
Brightpoint Inc., 18; 106 (upd.)
Brillstein-Grey Entertainment, 80
The Brink's Company, 58 (upd.)
Brinker International, Inc., 10; 38 (upd.); 75 (upd.)
Bristol Farms, 101
Bristol Hotel Company, 23
Bristol-Myers Squibb Company, III; 9 (upd.); 37 (upd.)
Brite Voice Systems, Inc., 20
Broadcast Music Inc., 23; 90 (upd.)
Broadcom Corporation, 34; 90 (upd.)
The Broadmoor Hotel, 30
Broadwing Corporation, 70
Broan-NuTone LLC, 104
Brobeck, Phleger & Harrison, LLP, 31
Brocade Communications Systems Inc., 106
Brodart Company, 84
Broder Bros. Co., 38
Broderbund Software, Inc., 13; 29 (upd.)
Bronco Drilling Company, Inc., 89
Bronco Wine Company, 101
Bronner Brothers Inc., 92
Bronner Display & Sign Advertising, Inc., 82
Brookdale Senior Living, 91
Brooke Group Ltd., 15
Brooklyn Union Gas, 6
Brooks Brothers Inc., 22
Brooks Sports Inc., 32
Brookshire Grocery Company, 16; 74 (upd.)
Brookstone, Inc., 18
Brother's Brother Foundation, 93
Brothers Gourmet Coffees, Inc., 20
Broughton Foods Co., 17
Brown & Brown, Inc., 41
Brown & Haley, 23
Brown & Root, Inc., 13
Brown & Sharpe Manufacturing Co., 23
Brown & Williamson Tobacco Corporation, 14; 33 (upd.)
Brown Brothers Harriman & Co., 45
Brown Jordan International Inc., 74 (upd.)
Brown Printing Company, 26
Brown Shoe Company, Inc., V; 20 (upd.); 68 (upd.)
Brown-Forman Corporation, I; 10 (upd.); 38 (upd.)
Browning-Ferris Industries, Inc., V; 20 (upd.)
Broyhill Furniture Industries, Inc., 10

Bruce Foods Corporation, 39
Bruegger's Corporation, 63
Bruno's Supermarkets, Inc., 7; 26 (upd.); 68 (upd.)
Brunschwig & Fils Inc., 96
Brunswick Corporation, III; 22 (upd.); 77 (upd.)
Brush Engineered Materials Inc., 67
Brush Wellman Inc., 14
Bruster's Real Ice Cream, Inc., 80
Bryce Corporation, 100
BTG, Inc., 45
Buca, Inc., 38
Buck Consultants, Inc., 55
Buck Knives Inc., 48
Buckeye Partners, L.P., 70
Buckeye Technologies, Inc., 42
Buckhead Life Restaurant Group, Inc., 100
The Buckle, Inc., 18
Bucyrus International, Inc., 17; 103 (upd.)
The Budd Company, 8
Budget Group, Inc., 25
Budget Rent a Car Corporation, 9
Buffalo Wild Wings, Inc., 56
Buffets Holdings, Inc., 10; 32 (upd.); 93 (upd.)
Bugle Boy Industries, Inc., 18
Build-A-Bear Workshop Inc., 62
Building Materials Holding Corporation, 52
Bulley & Andrews, LLC, 55
Bulova Corporation, 13; 41 (upd.)
Bumble Bee Seafoods L.L.C., 64
Bundy Corporation, 17
Bunge Ltd., 62
Burdines, Inc., 60
The Bureau of National Affairs, Inc., 23
Burger King Corporation, II; 17 (upd.); 56 (upd.)
Burgett, Inc., 97
Burke, Inc., 88
Burke Mills, Inc., 66
Burlington Coat Factory Warehouse Corporation, 10; 60 (upd.)
Burlington Industries, Inc., V; 17 (upd.)
Burlington Northern Santa Fe Corporation, V; 27 (upd.)
Burlington Resources Inc., 10
Burns International Services Corporation, 13; 41 (upd.)
Burr-Brown Corporation, 19
Burroughs & Chapin Company, Inc., 86
Burt's Bees, Inc., 58
The Burton Corporation, 22; 94 (upd.)
Busch Entertainment Corporation, 73
Bush Boake Allen Inc., 30
Bush Brothers & Company, 45
Bush Industries, Inc., 20
Business Men's Assurance Company of America, 14
Butler Manufacturing Company, 12; 62 (upd.)
Butterick Co., Inc., 23
Buttrey Food & Drug Stores Co., 18
buy.com, Inc., 46
BWAY Corporation, 24

C&K Market, Inc., 81
C & S Wholesale Grocers, Inc., 55
C-COR.net Corp., 38
C-Cube Microsystems, Inc., 37
C.F. Martin & Co., Inc., 42
The C.F. Sauer Company, 90
C.H. Guenther & Son, Inc., 84
C.H. Heist Corporation, 24
C.H. Robinson Worldwide, Inc., 11; 40
  (upd.)
C.R. Bard, Inc., 9; 65 (upd.)
C.R. Meyer and Sons Company, 74
C-Tech Industries Inc., 90
Cabela's Inc., 26; 68 (upd.)
Cabletron Systems, Inc., 10
Cablevision Electronic Instruments, Inc.,
  32
Cablevision Systems Corporation, 7; 30
  (upd.)
Cabot Corporation, 8; 29 (upd.); 91
  (upd.)
Cabot Creamery Cooperative, Inc., 102
Cache Incorporated, 30
CACI International Inc., 21; 72 (upd.)
Cactus Feeders, Inc., 91
Cadence Design Systems, Inc., 11; 48
  (upd.)
Cadence Financial Corporation, 106
Cadmus Communications Corporation,
  23
Cadwalader, Wickersham & Taft, 32
CAE USA Inc., 48
Caere Corporation, 20
Caesars World, Inc., 6
Cagle's, Inc., 20
Cahners Business Information, 43
Cal-Maine Foods, Inc., 69
CalAmp Corp., 87
Calavo Growers, Inc., 47
CalComp Inc., 13
Calcot Ltd., 33
Caldor Inc., 12
Calgon Carbon Corporation, 73
California Cedar Products Company, 58
California Pizza Kitchen Inc., 15; 74
  (upd.)
California Sports, Inc., 56
California Steel Industries, Inc., 67
California Water Service Group 79
Caliper Life Sciences, Inc., 70
Callanan Industries, Inc., 60
Callard and Bowser-Suchard Inc., 84
Callaway Golf Company, 15; 45 (upd.)
Callon Petroleum Company, 47
Calloway's Nursery, Inc., 51
CalMat Co., 19
Calpine Corporation, 36
Caltex Petroleum Corporation, 19
Calumet Specialty Products Partners, L.P.,
  106
Calvin Klein, Inc., 22; 55 (upd.)
CAMAC International Corporation, 106
Cambrex Corporation, 16; 44 (upd.)
Cambridge SoundWorks, Inc., 48
Cambridge Technology Partners, Inc., 36
Camden Property Trust, 77
Camelot Music, Inc., 26
Cameron & Barkley Company, 28

Cameron Hughes Wine, 103
Camp Dresser & McKee Inc., 104
Campagna-Turano Bakery, Inc., 99
Campbell-Ewald Advertising, 86
Campbell-Mithun-Esty, Inc., 16
Campbell Scientific, Inc., 51
Campbell Soup Company, II; 7 (upd.); 26
  (upd.); 71 (upd.)
Campmor, Inc., 104
Campo Electronics, Appliances &
  Computers, Inc., 16
Canandaigua Brands, Inc., 13; 34 (upd.)
Cancer Treatment Centers of America,
  Inc., 85
Candela Corporation, 48
Candie's, Inc., 31
Candle Corporation, 64
Candlewood Hotel Company, Inc., 41
Cannon Design, 63
Cannon Express, Inc., 53
Cannondale Corporation, 21
Cano Petroleum Inc., 97
Cantel Medical Corporation, 80
Canterbury Park Holding Corporation, 42
Cantor Fitzgerald, L.P., 92
Cap Rock Energy Corporation, 46
Capario, 104
Cape Cod Potato Chip Company, 90
Capel Incorporated, 45
Capezio/Ballet Makers Inc., 62
Capital Cities/ABC Inc., II
Capital City Bank Group, Inc., 105
Capital Holding Corporation, III
Capital One Financial Corporation, 52
Capitol Records, Inc., 90
Capital Senior Living Corporation, 75
CapStar Hotel Company, 21
Capstone Turbine Corporation, 75
Captain D's, LLC, 59
Captaris, Inc., 89
Car Toys, Inc., 67
Caraustar Industries, Inc., 19; 44 (upd.)
The Carbide/Graphite Group, Inc., 40
Carborundum Company, 15
Cardinal Health, Inc., 18; 50 (upd.)
Cardone Industries Inc., 92
Cardtronics, Inc., 93
Career Education Corporation, 45
CareerBuilder, Inc., 93
Caremark Rx, Inc., 10; 54 (upd.)
Carey International, Inc., 26
Cargill, Incorporated, II; 13 (upd.); 40
  (upd.); 89 (upd.)
Carhartt, Inc., 30; 77 (upd.)
Caribiner International, Inc., 24
Caribou Coffee Company, Inc., 28; 97
  (upd.)
Carlisle Companies Inc., 8; 82 (upd.)
Carlson Companies, Inc., 6; 22 (upd.); 87
  (upd.)
Carlson Restaurants Worldwide, 69
Carlson Wagonlit Travel, 55
Carma Laboratories, Inc., 60
CarMax, Inc., 55
Carmichael Lynch Inc., 28
Carmike Cinemas, Inc., 14; 37 (upd.); 74
  (upd.)
Carnation Company, II

Carnegie Corporation of New York, 35
The Carnegie Hall Corporation, 101
Carnival Corporation, 6; 27 (upd.); 78
  (upd.)
Carolina First Corporation, 31
Carolina Freight Corporation, 6
Carolina Power & Light Company, V; 23
  (upd.)
Carolina Telephone and Telegraph
  Company, 10
Carpenter Technology Corporation, 13;
  95 (upd.)
CARQUEST Corporation, 29
Carr-Gottstein Foods Co., 17
CarrAmerica Realty Corporation, 56
The Carriage House Companies, Inc., 55
Carriage Services, Inc., 37
Carrier Access Corporation, 44
Carrier Corporation, 7; 69 (upd.)
Carrizo Oil & Gas, Inc., 97
Carroll's Foods, Inc., 46
Carrols Restaurant Group, Inc., 92
The Carsey-Werner Company, L.L.C., 37
Carson Pirie Scott & Company, 15
Carson, Inc., 31
Carter Hawley Hale Stores, Inc., V
Carter Lumber Company, 45
Carter-Wallace, Inc., 8; 38 (upd.)
Carus Publishing Company, 93
Carvel Corporation, 35
Carver Bancorp, Inc., 94
Carver Boat Corporation LLC, 88
Carvin Corp., 89
Cascade Corporation, 65
Cascade General, Inc., 65
Cascade Natural Gas Corporation, 9
Casco Northern Bank, 14
Casella Waste Systems Inc., 102
Casey's General Stores, Inc., 19; 83 (upd.)
Cash America International, Inc., 20; 61
  (upd.)
Cash Systems, Inc., 93
Cass Information Systems Inc., 100
Castle & Cooke, Inc., II; 20 (upd.)
Casual Corner Group, Inc., 43
Casual Male Retail Group, Inc., 52
Caswell-Massey Co. Ltd., 51
Catalina Lighting, Inc., 43 (upd.)
Catalina Marketing Corporation, 18
Catalytica Energy Systems, Inc., 44
Catellus Development Corporation, 24
Caterpillar Inc., III; 15 (upd.); 63 (upd.)
Catherines Stores Corporation, 15
Catholic Charities USA, 76
Catholic Health Initiatives, 91
Catholic Order of Foresters, 24; 97 (upd.)
Cato Corporation, 14
Cattleman's, Inc., 20
Cavco Industries, Inc., 65
CB Commercial Real Estate Services
  Group, Inc., 21
CB Richard Ellis Group, Inc., 70 (upd.)
CBI Industries, Inc., 7
CBRL Group, Inc., 35 (upd.); 86 (upd.)
CBS Corporation, II; 6 (upd.); 28 (upd.)
CBS Television Network, 66 (upd.)
CCA Industries, Inc., 53
CCC Information Services Group Inc., 74

CCH Inc., 14
CDI Corporation, 6; 54 (upd.)
CDW Computer Centers, Inc., 16; 52 (upd.)
Ce De Candy Inc., 100
CEC Entertainment, Inc., 31 (upd.)
Cedar Fair Entertainment Company, 22; 98 (upd.)
Celadon Group Inc., 30
Celanese Corporation, I
Celebrate Express, Inc., 70
Celebrity, Inc., 22
Celera Genomics, 74
Celestial Seasonings, Inc., 16
Celgene Corporation, 67
CellStar Corporation, 83
Cendant Corporation, 44 (upd.)
Centel Corporation, 6
Centennial Communications Corporation, 39
Centerior Energy Corporation, V
Centerplate, Inc. 79
Centex Corporation, 8; 29 (upd.); 106 (upd.)
Centocor Inc., 14
Central and South West Corporation, V
Central European Distribution Corporation, 75
Central Florida Investments, Inc., 93
Central Garden & Pet Company, 23; 58 (upd.)
Central Hudson Gas and Electricity Corporation, 6
Central Maine Power, 6
Central National-Gottesman Inc., 95
Central Newspapers, Inc., 10
Central Parking System, 18; 104 (upd.)
Central Soya Company, Inc., 7
Central Sprinkler Corporation, 29
Central Vermont Public Service Corporation, 54
Centuri Corporation, 54
Century Aluminum Company, 52
Century Business Services, Inc., 52
Century Casinos, Inc., 53
Century Communications Corp., 10
Century Telephone Enterprises, Inc., 9; 54 (upd.)
Century Theatres, Inc., 31
Cenveo Inc., 71 (upd.)
Cephalon, Inc., 45
Cepheid, 77
Ceradyne, Inc., 65
Cerner Corporation, 16; 94 (upd.)
CertainTeed Corporation, 35
Certegy, Inc., 63
Cessna Aircraft Company, 8; 27 (upd.)
CF Industries Holdings, Inc., 99
Chadbourne & Parke, 36
Chadwick's of Boston, Ltd., 29
The Chalone Wine Group, Ltd., 36
Champion Enterprises, Inc., 17
Champion Industries, Inc., 28
Champion International Corporation, IV; 20 (upd.)
Championship Auto Racing Teams, Inc., 37
Chancellor Beacon Academies, Inc., 53

Chancellor Media Corporation, 24
Chaparral Steel Co., 13
Charisma Brands LLC, 74
The Charles Machine Works, Inc., 64
Charles River Laboratories International, Inc., 42
The Charles Schwab Corporation, 8; 26 (upd.); 81 (upd.)
The Charles Stark Draper Laboratory, Inc., 35
Charlotte Russe Holding, Inc., 35; 90 (upd.)
The Charmer Sunbelt Group, 95
Charming Shoppes, Inc., 8; 38
Chart House Enterprises, Inc., 17
Chart Industries, Inc., 21; 96 (upd.)
Charter Communications, Inc., 33
Charter Financial Corporation, 103
Charter Manufacturing Company, Inc., 103
ChartHouse International Learning Corporation, 49
Chas. Levy Company LLC, 60
Chase General Corporation, 91
The Chase Manhattan Corporation, II; 13 (upd.)
Chateau Communities, Inc., 37
Chattanooga Bakery, Inc., 86
Chattem, Inc., 17; 88 (upd.)
Chautauqua Airlines, Inc., 38
Check Into Cash, Inc., 105
Checker Motors Corp., 89
Checkers Drive-In Restaurants, Inc., 16; 74 (upd.)
CheckFree Corporation, 81
Checkpoint Systems, Inc., 39
The Cheesecake Factory Inc., 17; 100 (upd.)
Chef Solutions, Inc., 89
Chelsea Milling Company, 29
Chelsea Piers Management Inc., 86
Chemcentral Corporation, 8
Chemed Corporation, 13
Chemfab Corporation, 35
Chemi-Trol Chemical Co., 16
Chemical Banking Corporation, II; 14 (upd.)
Chemical Waste Management, Inc., 9
Chemtura Corporation, 91 (upd.)
CHEP Pty. Ltd., 80
Cherokee Inc., 18
Cherry Brothers LLC, 105
Cherry Lane Music Publishing Company, Inc., 62
Chesapeake Corporation, 8; 30 (upd.); 93 (upd.)
Chesapeake Utilities Corporation, 56
Chesebrough-Pond's USA, Inc., 8
Chevron Corporation, 103 (upd.)
ChevronTexaco Corporation, IV; 19 (upd.); 47 (upd.)
Cheyenne Software, Inc., 12
CHF Industries, Inc., 84
CHHJ Franchising LLC, 105
Chi-Chi's Inc., 13; 51 (upd.)
Chiasso Inc., 53
Chiat/Day Inc. Advertising, 11
Chic by H.I.S, Inc., 20

Chicago and North Western Holdings Corporation, 6
Chicago Bears Football Club, Inc., 33
Chicago Board of Trade, 41
Chicago Mercantile Exchange Holdings Inc., 75
Chicago National League Ball Club, Inc., 66
Chicago Review Press Inc., 84
Chicago Symphony Orchestra, 106
Chick-fil-A Inc., 23; 90 (upd.)
Chicken of the Sea International, 24 (upd.); 106 (upd.)
Chico's FAS, Inc., 45
ChildFund International, 106
Children's Comprehensive Services, Inc., 42
Children's Healthcare of Atlanta Inc., 101
Children's Hospitals and Clinics, Inc., 54
The Children's Place Retail Stores, Inc., 37; 86 (upd.)
ChildrenFirst, Inc., 59
Childtime Learning Centers, Inc., 34
Chiles Offshore Corporation, 9
Chindex International, Inc., 101
Chipotle Mexican Grill, Inc., 67
CHIPS and Technologies, Inc., 9
Chiquita Brands International, Inc., 7; 21 (upd.); 83 (upd.)
Chiron Corporation, 10; 36 (upd.)
Chisholm-Mingo Group, Inc., 41
Chittenden & Eastman Company, 58
Chock Full o' Nuts Corp., 17
Choice Hotels International Inc., 14; 83 (upd.)
ChoicePoint Inc., 65
Chorus Line Corporation, 30
Chris-Craft Corporation, 9; 31 (upd.); 80 (upd.)
Christensen Boyles Corporation, 26
The Christian Broadcasting Network, Inc., 52
The Christian Science Publishing Society, 55
Christie Digital Systems, Inc., 103
Christopher & Banks Corporation, 42
Chromcraft Revington, Inc., 15
The Chronicle Publishing Company, Inc., 23
Chronimed Inc., 26
Chrysler Corporation, I; 11 (upd.)
CHS Inc., 60
CH2M HILL Companies Ltd., 22; 96 (upd.)
The Chubb Corporation, III; 14 (upd.); 37 (upd.)
Chugach Alaska Corporation, 60
Church & Dwight Co., Inc., 29; 68 (upd.)
Church's Chicken, 66
Churchill Downs Incorporated, 29
Cianbro Corporation, 14
Ciber, Inc., 18
CiCi Enterprises, L.P., 99
CIENA Corporation, 54
CIGNA Corporation, III; 22 (upd.); 45 (upd.)
Cimarex Energy Co., 81

Cincinnati Bell Inc., 6; 105 (upd.)
Cincinnati Financial Corporation, 16; 44 (upd.)
Cincinnati Gas & Electric Company, 6
Cincinnati Lamb Inc., 72
Cincinnati Milacron Inc., 12
Cincom Systems Inc., 15
Cinemark Holdings, Inc., 95
Cinnabon, Inc., 23; 90 (upd.)
Cintas Corporation, 21; 51 (upd.)
CIPSCO Inc., 6
The Circle K Company, II; 20 (upd.)
Circon Corporation, 21
Circuit City Stores, Inc., 9; 29 (upd.); 65 (upd.)
Circus Circus Enterprises, Inc., 6
Cirrus Design Corporation, 44
Cirrus Logic, Inc., 11; 48 (upd.)
Cisco-Linksys LLC, 86
Cisco Systems, Inc., 11; 34 (upd.); 77 (upd.)
CIT Group Inc., 76
Citadel Communications Corporation, 35
Citfed Bancorp, Inc., 16
CITGO Petroleum Corporation, IV; 31 (upd.)
Citi Trends, Inc., 80
Citicorp Diners Club, Inc., 90
Citigroup Inc., II; 9 (upd.); 30 (upd.); 59 (upd.)
Citizens Communications Company 7; 79 (upd.)
Citizens Financial Group, Inc., 42; 87 (upd.)
Citrix Systems, Inc., 44
City Brewing Company LLC, 73
City Public Service, 6
CKE Restaurants, Inc., 19; 46 (upd.)
CKX, Inc., 102
Claire's Stores, Inc., 17; 94 (upd.)
CLARCOR Inc., 17; 61 (upd.)
Clare Rose Inc., 68
The Clark Construction Group, Inc., 8
Clark Equipment Company, 8
Classic Vacation Group, Inc., 46
Clayton Homes Incorporated, 13; 54 (upd.)
Clayton Williams Energy, Inc., 87
Clean Harbors, Inc., 73
Clean Venture, Inc., 104
Clear Channel Communications, Inc., 23
Clearwire, Inc., 69
Cleary, Gottlieb, Steen & Hamilton, 35
Cleco Corporation, 37
The Clemens Family Corporation, 93
Clement Pappas & Company, Inc., 92
Cleveland Indians Baseball Company, Inc., 37
Cleveland-Cliffs Inc., 13; 62 (upd.)
Click Wine Group, 68
Clif Bar Inc., 50
Clopay Corporation, 100
The Clorox Company, III; 22 (upd.); 81 (upd.)
The Clothestime, Inc., 20
Clougherty Packing Company, 72
ClubCorp, Inc., 33
CMG Worldwide, Inc., 89

CMGI, Inc., 76
CML Group, Inc., 10
CMP Media Inc., 26
CMS Energy Corporation, V; 14 (upd.); 100 (upd.)
CNA Financial Corporation, III; 38 (upd.)
CNET Networks, Inc., 47
CNH Global N.V., 99 (upd.)
CNS, Inc., 20
Coach, Inc., 10; 45 (upd.); 99 (upd.)
Coach USA, Inc., 24; 55 (upd.)
Coachmen Industries, Inc., 77
The Coastal Corporation, IV, 31 (upd.)
COBE Cardiovascular, Inc., 61
COBE Laboratories, Inc., 13
Coborn's, Inc., 30
Cobra Electronics Corporation, 14
Cobra Golf Inc., 16
Coca Cola Bottling Co. Consolidated, 10
The Coca-Cola Company, I; 10 (upd.); 32 (upd.); 67 (upd.)
Coca-Cola Enterprises, Inc., 13
Coeur d'Alene Mines Corporation, 20
The Coffee Beanery, Ltd., 95
Coffee Holding Co., Inc., 95
Cogent Communications Group, Inc., 55
Cogentrix Energy, Inc., 10
Cognex Corporation, 76
Cognizant Technology Solutions Corporation, 59
Coherent, Inc., 31
Cohu, Inc., 32
Coinmach Laundry Corporation, 20
Coinstar, Inc., 44
Cold Spring Granite Company, 16
Cold Spring Granite Company Inc., 67 (upd.)
Cold Stone Creamery, 69
Coldwater Creek Inc., 21; 74 (upd.)
Cole National Corporation, 13; 76 (upd.)
Cole's Quality Foods, Inc., 68
The Coleman Company, Inc., 9; 30 (upd.)
Coleman Natural Products, Inc., 68
Coles Express Inc., 15
Colfax Corporation, 58
Colgate-Palmolive Company, III; 14 (upd.); 35 (upd.); 71 (upd.)
Collectors Universe, Inc., 48
Colliers International Property Consultants Inc., 92
Collins & Aikman Corporation, 13; 41 (upd.)
The Collins Companies Inc., 102
Collins Industries, Inc., 33
Colonial Properties Trust, 65
Colonial Williamsburg Foundation, 53
Color Kinetics Incorporated, 85
Colorado Baseball Management, Inc., 72
Colorado Boxed Beef Company, 100
Colorado MEDtech, Inc., 48
Colt Industries Inc., I
Colt's Manufacturing Company, Inc., 12
Columbia Forest Products Inc., 78
The Columbia Gas System, Inc., V; 16 (upd.)
Columbia House Company, 69

Columbia Sportswear Company, 19; 41 (upd.)
Columbia TriStar Motion Pictures Companies, II; 12 (upd.)
Columbia/HCA Healthcare Corporation, 15
Columbus McKinnon Corporation, 37
Comair Holdings Inc., 13; 34 (upd.)
Combe Inc., 72
Comcast Corporation, 7; 24 (upd.)
Comdial Corporation, 21
Comdisco, Inc., 9
Comerica Incorporated, 40; 101 (upd.)
COMFORCE Corporation, 40
Comfort Systems USA, Inc., 101
Command Security Corporation, 57
Commerce Clearing House, Inc., 7
Commercial Credit Company, 8
Commercial Federal Corporation, 12; 62 (upd.)
Commercial Financial Services, Inc., 26
Commercial Metals Company, 15; 42 (upd.)
Commercial Vehicle Group, Inc., 81
Commodore International Ltd., 7
Commonwealth Edison Company, V
Commonwealth Energy System, 14
Commonwealth Telephone Enterprises, Inc., 25
CommScope, Inc., 77
Community Coffee Co. L.L.C., 53
Community Health Systems, Inc., 71
Community Newspaper Holdings, Inc., 91
Community Psychiatric Centers, 15
Compaq Computer Corporation, III; 6 (upd.); 26 (upd.)
Compass Bancshares, Inc., 73
Compass Minerals International, Inc. 79
CompDent Corporation, 22
CompHealth Inc., 25
Complete Business Solutions, Inc., 31
Comprehensive Care Corporation, 15
CompuAdd Computer Corporation, 11
CompuCom Systems, Inc., 10
CompuDyne Corporation, 51
CompUSA, Inc., 10; 35 (upd.)
CompuServe Interactive Services, Inc., 10; 27 (upd.)
Computer Associates International, Inc., 6; 49 (upd.)
Computer Data Systems, Inc., 14
Computer Learning Centers, Inc., 26
Computer Sciences Corporation, 6
Computerland Corp., 13
Computervision Corporation, 10
Compuware Corporation, 10; 30 (upd.); 66 (upd.)
Comsat Corporation, 23
Comshare Inc., 23
Comstock Resources, Inc., 47
Comtech Telecommunications Corp., 75
Comverse Technology, Inc., 15; 43 (upd.)
Con-way Inc., 101
ConAgra Foods, Inc., II; 12 (upd.); 42 (upd.); 85 (upd.)
Conair Corporation, 17; 69 (upd.)
Concentra Inc., 71

Concepts Direct, Inc., 39
Concord Camera Corporation, 41
Concord EFS, Inc., 52
Concord Fabrics, Inc., 16
Concur Technologies, Inc., 106
Concurrent Computer Corporation, 75
Condé Nast Publications, Inc., 13; 59 (upd.)
Cone Mills LLC, 8; 67 (upd.)
Conexant Systems Inc., 36; 106 (upd.)
Confluence Holdings Corporation, 76
Congoleum Corporation, 18; 98 (upd.)
CONMED Corporation, 87
Conn's, Inc., 67
Conn-Selmer, Inc., 55
Connecticut Light and Power Co., 13
Connecticut Mutual Life Insurance Company, III
The Connell Company, 29; 104 (upd.)
Conner Peripherals, Inc., 6
Connetics Corporation, 70
ConocoPhillips, IV; 16 (upd.); 63 (upd.)
Conrad Industries, Inc., 58
Conseco, Inc., 10; 33 (upd.)
Conso International Corporation, 29
CONSOL Energy Inc., 59
Consolidated Delivery & Logistics, Inc., 24
Consolidated Edison, Inc., V; 45 (upd.)
Consolidated Freightways Corporation, V; 21 (upd.); 48 (upd.)
Consolidated Graphics, Inc., 70
Consolidated Natural Gas Company, V; 19 (upd.)
Consolidated Papers, Inc., 8; 36 (upd.)
Consolidated Products Inc., 14
Consolidated Rail Corporation, V
Constar International Inc., 64
Constellation Brands, Inc., 68 (upd.)
Consumers Power Co., 14
Consumers Union, 26
Consumers Water Company, 14
The Container Store, 36
ContiGroup Companies, Inc., 43 (upd.)
Continental Airlines, Inc., I; 21 (upd.); 52 (upd.)
Continental Bank Corporation, II
Continental Cablevision, Inc., 7
Continental Can Co., Inc., 15
The Continental Corporation, III
Continental General Tire Corp., 23
Continental Grain Company, 10; 13 (upd.)
Continental Group Company, I
Continental Medical Systems, Inc., 10
Continental Resources, Inc., 89
Continucare Corporation, 101
Continuum Health Partners, Inc., 60
Control Data Corporation, III
Control Data Systems, Inc., 10
Converse Inc., 9; 31 (upd.)
Cook Group Inc., 102
Cooker Restaurant Corporation, 20; 51 (upd.)
CoolSavings, Inc., 77
Cooper Cameron Corporation, 20 (upd.); 58 (upd.)
The Cooper Companies, Inc., 39

Cooper Industries, Inc., II; 44 (upd.)
Cooper Tire & Rubber Company, 8; 23 (upd.)
Coopers & Lybrand, 9
Copart Inc., 23
The Copley Press, Inc., 23
The Copps Corporation, 32
Corbis Corporation, 31
The Corcoran Group, Inc., 58
Cordis Corporation, 19; 46 (upd.)
CoreStates Financial Corp, 17
Corinthian Colleges, Inc., 39; 92 (upd.)
The Corky McMillin Companies, 98
Corning Inc., III; 44 (upd.); 90 (upd.)
The Corporate Executive Board Company, 89
Corporate Express, Inc., 22; 47 (upd.)
Corporate Software Inc., 9
Corporation for Public Broadcasting, 14; 89 (upd.)
Correctional Services Corporation, 30
Corrections Corporation of America, 23
Corrpro Companies, Inc., 20
CORT Business Services Corporation, 26
Corus Bankshares, Inc., 75
Cosi, Inc., 53
Cosmair, Inc., 8
The Cosmetic Center, Inc., 22
Cosmolab Inc., 96
Cost Plus, Inc., 27
Cost-U-Less, Inc., 51
CoStar Group, Inc., 73
Costco Wholesale Corporation, V; 43 (upd.); 105 (upd.)
Cotter & Company, V
Cotton Incorporated, 46
Coty, Inc., 36
Coudert Brothers, 30
Council on International Educational Exchange, 81
Country Kitchen International, Inc., 76
Countrywide Financial, 16; 100 (upd.)
County Seat Stores Inc., 9
Courier Corporation, 41
Cousins Properties Incorporated, 65
Covance Inc., 30; 98 (upd.)
Covanta Energy Corporation, 64 (upd.)
Coventry Health Care, Inc., 59
Covington & Burling, 40
Cowen Group, Inc., 92
Cowles Media Company, 23
Cox Enterprises, Inc., IV; 22 (upd.); 67 (upd.)
Cox Radio, Inc., 89
CPAC, Inc., 86
CPC International Inc., II
CPI Aerostructures, Inc., 75
CPI Corp., 38
CPP International, LLC, 103
CR England, Inc., 63
CRA International, Inc., 93
Cracker Barrel Old Country Store, Inc., 10
Craftmade International, Inc., 44
Craig Hospital, 99
craigslist, inc., 89
Crain Communications, Inc., 12; 35 (upd.)

Cramer, Berkowitz & Co., 34
Cramer-Krasselt Company, 104
Crane & Co., Inc., 26; 103 (upd.)
Crane Co., 8; 30 (upd.); 101 (upd.)
Cranium, Inc., 69
Crate and Barrel, 9
Cravath, Swaine & Moore, 43
Crawford & Company, 87
Cray Inc., 75 (upd.)
Cray Research, Inc., III; 16 (upd.)
Creative Artists Agency LLC, 38
Credence Systems Corporation, 90
Credit Acceptance Corporation, 18
Cree Inc., 53
Crete Carrier Corporation, 95
Crispin Porter + Bogusky, 83
Crocs, Inc., 80
Crompton Corporation, 9; 36 (upd.)
Croscill, Inc., 42
Crosman Corporation, 62
Cross Country Healthcare, Inc., 105
CROSSMARK 79
Crowley Maritime Corporation, 6; 28 (upd.)
Crowley, Milner & Company, 19
Crown Books Corporation, 21
Crown Central Petroleum Corporation, 7
Crown Crafts, Inc., 16
Crown Equipment Corporation, 15; 93 (upd.)
Crown Holdings, Inc., 83 (upd.)
Crown Media Holdings, Inc., 45
Crown Vantage Inc., 29
Crown, Cork & Seal Company, Inc., I; 13; 32 (upd.)
CRSS Inc., 6
Cruise America Inc., 21
Crum & Forster Holdings Corporation, 104
CryoLife, Inc., 46
Crystal Brands, Inc., 9
CS First Boston Inc., II
CSG Systems International, Inc., 75
CSK Auto Corporation, 38
CSS Industries, Inc., 35
CSX Corporation, V; 22 (upd.); 79 (upd.)
CTB International Corporation, 43 (upd.)
CTG, Inc., 11
CTS Corporation, 39
Cubic Corporation, 19; 98 (upd.)
CUC International Inc., 16
Cuisinart Corporation, 24
Cuisine Solutions Inc., 84
Culbro Corporation, 15
CulinArt, Inc., 92
Cullen/Frost Bankers, Inc., 25
Culligan Water Technologies, Inc., 12; 38 (upd.)
Culp, Inc., 29
Culver Franchising System, Inc., 58
Cumberland Farms, Inc., 17; 84 (upd.)
Cumberland Packing Corporation, 26
Cummins Engine Company, Inc., I; 12 (upd.); 40 (upd.)
Cumulus Media Inc., 37
CUNA Mutual Group, 62
Cunard Line Ltd., 23
CUNO Incorporated, 57

Current, Inc., 37
Curtice-Burns Foods, Inc., 7; 21 (upd.)
Curtiss-Wright Corporation, 10; 35 (upd.)
Curves International, Inc., 54
Cushman & Wakefield, Inc., 86
Custom Chrome, Inc., 16; 74 (upd.)
Cutera, Inc., 84
Cutter & Buck Inc., 27
CVS Corporation, 45 (upd.)
Cyan Worlds Inc., 101
Cybermedia, Inc., 25
Cyberonics, Inc. 79
Cybex International, Inc., 49
Cygne Designs, Inc., 25
Cygnus Business Media, Inc., 56
Cymer, Inc., 77
Cypress Semiconductor Corporation, 20; 48 (upd.)
Cyprus Amax Minerals Company, 21
Cyprus Minerals Company, 7
Cyrk Inc., 19
Cystic Fibrosis Foundation, 93
Cytec Industries Inc., 27
Cytyc Corporation, 69
Czarnikow-Rionda Company, Inc., 32
D&H Distributing Co., 95
D&K Wholesale Drug, Inc., 14
D.A. Davidson & Company, 106
D'Agostino Supermarkets Inc., 19
D'Arcy Masius Benton & Bowles, Inc., VI; 32 (upd.)
D.F. Stauffer Biscuit Company, 82
D.G. Yuengling & Son, Inc., 38
D.R. Horton, Inc., 58
Dade Behring Holdings Inc., 71
Daffy's Inc., 26
Daily Journal Corporation, 101
Dain Rauscher Corporation, 35 (upd.)
Dairy Farmers of America, Inc., 94
Dairy Mart Convenience Stores, Inc., 7; 25 (upd.)
Dairyland Healthcare Solutions, 73
Daisy Outdoor Products Inc., 58
Daisytek International Corporation, 18
Daktronics, Inc., 32
Dal-Tile International Inc., 22
Dale and Thomas Popcorn LLC, 100
Dale Carnegie & Associates Inc. 28; 78 (upd.)
Dallas Cowboys Football Club, Ltd., 33
Dallas Semiconductor Corporation, 13; 31 (upd.)
Dallis Coffee, Inc., 86
Damark International, Inc., 18
Dames & Moore, Inc., 25
Dan River Inc., 35; 86 (upd.)
Dana Holding Corporation, I; 10 (upd.); 99 (upd.)
Danaher Corporation, 7; 77 (upd.)
Daniel Industries, Inc., 16
Daniel Measurement and Control, Inc., 74 (upd.)
Dannon Company, Inc., 14; 106 (upd.)
Danskin, Inc., 12; 62 (upd.)
Darden Restaurants, Inc., 16; 44 (upd.)
Darigold, Inc., 9
Darling International Inc., 85
Dart Group Corporation, 16

Data Broadcasting Corporation, 31
Data General Corporation, 8
Datapoint Corporation, 11
Datascope Corporation, 39
Datek Online Holdings Corp., 32
Dauphin Deposit Corporation, 14
Dave & Buster's, Inc., 33; 104 (upd.)
The Davey Tree Expert Company, 11
The David and Lucile Packard Foundation, 41
The David J. Joseph Company, 14; 76 (upd.)
David's Bridal, Inc., 33
Davis Polk & Wardwell, 36
DaVita Inc., 73
DAW Technologies, Inc., 25
Dawn Food Products, Inc., 17
Day & Zimmermann Inc., 9; 31 (upd.)
Day International, Inc., 84
Day Runner, Inc., 14; 41 (upd.)
Dayton Hudson Corporation, V; 18 (upd.)
DC Comics Inc., 25; 98 (upd.)
DC Shoes, Inc., 60
DDB Needham Worldwide, 14
DDi Corp., 97
Dean & DeLuca, Inc., 36
Dean Foods Company, 7; 21 (upd.); 73 (upd.)
Dean Witter, Discover & Co., 12
Dearborn Mid-West Conveyor Company, 56
Death Row Records, 27
Deb Shops, Inc., 16; 76 (upd.)
Debevoise & Plimpton, 39
Dechert, 43
Deckers Outdoor Corporation, 22; 98 (upd.)
Decora Industries, Inc., 31
Decorator Industries, Inc., 68
DeCrane Aircraft Holdings Inc., 36
DeepTech International Inc., 21
Deere & Company, III; 21 (upd.); 42 (upd.)
Defiance, Inc., 22
DeKalb Genetics Corporation, 17
Del Laboratories, Inc., 28
Del Monte Foods Company, 7; 23 (upd.); 103 (upd.)
Del Taco, Inc., 58
Del Webb Corporation, 14
Delaware North Companies Inc., 7; 96 (upd.)
dELiA*s Inc., 29
Delicato Vineyards, Inc., 50
Dell Inc., 9; 31 (upd.); 63 (upd.)
Deloitte Touche Tohmatsu International, 9; 29 (upd.)
DeLorme Publishing Company, Inc., 53
Delphax Technologies Inc., 94
Delphi Automotive Systems Corporation, 45
Delta Air Lines, Inc., I; 6 (upd.); 39 (upd.); 92 (upd.)
Delta and Pine Land Company, 33; 59
Delta Woodside Industries, Inc., 8; 30 (upd.)
Deltec, Inc., 56

Deltic Timber Corporation, 46
Deluxe Corporation, 7; 22 (upd.); 73 (upd.)
Deluxe Entertainment Services Group, Inc., 100
DEMCO, Inc., 60
DeMoulas / Market Basket Inc., 23
DenAmerica Corporation, 29
Denbury Resources, Inc., 67
Dendrite International, Inc., 70
Denison International plc, 46
Denny's Corporation, 105 (upd.)
Dentsply International Inc., 10
Denver Nuggets, 51
DEP Corporation, 20
Department 56, Inc., 14; 34 (upd.)
Deposit Guaranty Corporation, 17
DePuy Inc., 30; 37 (upd.)
Derco Holding Ltd., 98
Deschutes Brewery, Inc., 57
Deseret Management Corporation, 101
Designer Holdings Ltd., 20
Destec Energy, Inc., 12
Detroit Diesel Corporation, 10; 74 (upd.)
The Detroit Edison Company, V
The Detroit Lions, Inc., 55
Detroit Media Partnership L.P., 102
The Detroit Pistons Basketball Company, 41
Detroit Red Wings, 74
Detroit Tigers Baseball Club, Inc., 46
Deutsch, Inc., 42
Developers Diversified Realty Corporation, 69
DeVito/Verdi, 85
Devon Energy Corporation, 61
DeVry Inc., 29; 82 (upd.)
Dewberry 78
Dewey Ballantine LLP, 48
Dex Media, Inc., 65
The Dexter Corporation, I; 12 (upd.)
DFS Group Ltd., 66
DH Technology, Inc., 18
DHB Industries Inc., 85
DHL Worldwide Express, 6; 24 (upd.)
Di Giorgio Corp., 12
Diagnostic Products Corporation, 73
The Dial Corp., 8; 23 (upd.)
Dial-A-Mattress Operating Corporation, 46
Dialogic Corporation, 18
Diamond of California, 64 (upd.)
Diamond Shamrock, Inc., IV
DiamondCluster International, Inc., 51
Dibrell Brothers, Incorporated, 12
dick clark productions, inc., 16
Dick Corporation, 64
Dick's Sporting Goods, Inc., 59
Dickten Masch Plastics LLC, 90
Dictaphone Healthcare Solutions 78
Diebold, Incorporated, 7; 22 (upd.)
Diedrich Coffee, Inc., 40
Dierbergs Markets Inc., 63
Dietz and Watson, Inc., 92
Digex, Inc., 46
Digi International Inc., 9
Digital Angel Corporation, 106

Digital Equipment Corporation, III; 6 (upd.)
Digital River, Inc., 50
Digitas Inc., 81
Dillard Paper Company, 11
Dillard's Inc., V; 16 (upd.); 68 (upd.)
Dillingham Construction Corporation, I; 44 (upd.)
Dillon Companies Inc., 12
Dime Savings Bank of New York, F.S.B., 9
DIMON Inc., 27
Diodes Incorporated, 81
Dionex Corporation, 46
Dippin' Dots, Inc., 56
Direct Focus, Inc., 47
Directed Electronics, Inc., 87
DIRECTV, Inc., 38; 75 (upd.)
Discount Auto Parts, Inc., 18
Discount Drug Mart, Inc., 14
Discount Tire Company Inc., 84
Discovery Communications, Inc., 42
Discovery Partners International, Inc., 58
Disney/ABC Television Group, 106
Dispatch Printing Company, 100
ditech.com, 93
The Dixie Group, Inc., 20; 80 (upd.)
Dixon Industries, Inc., 26
Dixon Ticonderoga Company, 12; 69 (upd.)
DLA Piper, 106
DMI Furniture, Inc., 46
Do it Best Corporation, 30; 104 (upd.)
Dobson Communications Corporation, 63
Doctor's Associates Inc., 67 (upd.)
The Doctors' Company, 55
Documentum, Inc., 46
Dolan Media Company, 94
Dolby Laboratories Inc., 20
Dole Food Company, Inc., 9; 31 (upd.); 68 (upd.)
Dollar General Corporation, 106
Dollar Thrifty Automotive Group, Inc., 25
Dollar Tree Stores, Inc., 23; 62 (upd.)
Dominick & Dominick LLC, 92
Dominick's Finer Foods, Inc., 56
Dominion Homes, Inc., 19
Dominion Resources, Inc., V; 54 (upd.)
Domino Sugar Corporation, 26
Domino's Pizza, Inc., 7; 21 (upd.)
Domino's, Inc., 63 (upd.)
Don Massey Cadillac, Inc., 37
Donaldson Company, Inc., 16; 49 (upd.)
Donaldson, Lufkin & Jenrette, Inc., 22
Donatos Pizzeria Corporation, 58
Donna Karan International Inc., 15; 56 (upd.)
Donnelly Corporation, 12; 35 (upd.)
Donnkenny, Inc., 17
Donruss Playoff L.P., 66
Dooney & Bourke Inc., 84
Dorian Drake International Inc., 96
Dorsey & Whitney LLP, 47
Doskocil Companies, Inc., 12
Dot Foods, Inc., 69
Dot Hill Systems Corp., 93
Double-Cola Co.-USA, 70

DoubleClick Inc., 46
Doubletree Corporation, 21
Douglas & Lomason Company, 16
Douglas Emmett, Inc., 105
Dover Corporation, III; 28 (upd.); 90 (upd.)
Dover Downs Entertainment, Inc., 43
Dover Publications Inc., 34
The Dow Chemical Company, I; 8 (upd.); 50 (upd.)
Dow Jones & Company, Inc., IV; 19 (upd.); 47 (upd.)
Dow Jones Telerate, Inc., 10
DPL Inc., 6; 96 (upd.)
DQE, Inc., 6
Dr Pepper/Seven Up, Inc., 9; 32 (upd.)
Drackett Professional Products, 12
Draftfcb, 94
Drake Beam Morin, Inc., 44
Draper and Kramer Inc., 96
Draper Fisher Jurvetson, 91
Dreams Inc., 97
DreamWorks Animation SKG, Inc., 43; 106 (upd.)
The Drees Company, Inc., 41
The Dress Barn, Inc., 24; 55 (upd.)
Dresser Industries, Inc., III
Drew Industries Inc., 28
Drexel Burnham Lambert Incorporated, II
Drexel Heritage Furnishings Inc., 12
Dreyer's Grand Ice Cream, Inc., 17
The Dreyfus Corporation, 70
Dril-Quip, Inc., 81
Drinker, Biddle and Reath L.L.P., 92
Drinks Americas Holdings, LTD., 105
DriveTime Automotive Group Inc., 68 (upd.)
DRS Technologies, Inc., 58
Drs. Foster & Smith, Inc., 62
Drug Emporium, Inc., 12
Drypers Corporation, 18
DSC Communications Corporation, 12
DSW Inc., 73
DTE Energy Company, 20 (upd.); 94 (upd.)
DTS, Inc., 80
Dualstar Entertainment Group LLC, 76
Duane Reade Holding Corp., 21
Duck Head Apparel Company, Inc., 42
Ducks Unlimited, Inc., 87
Duckwall-ALCO Stores, Inc., 24; 105 (upd.)
Ducommun Incorporated, 30
Duke Energy Corporation, V; 27 (upd.)
Duke Realty Corporation, 57
The Dun & Bradstreet Corporation, IV; 19 (upd.); 61 (upd.)
Dun & Bradstreet Software Services Inc., 11
Dunavant Enterprises, Inc., 54
Duncan Aviation, Inc., 94
Duncan Toys Company, 55
Dunham's Athleisure Corporation, 98
Dunn-Edwards Corporation, 56
Duplex Products Inc., 17
Duracell International Inc., 9; 71 (upd.)
Durametallic, 21
Duriron Company Inc., 17

Duron Inc., 72
Duty Free International, Inc., 11
DVI, Inc., 51
DW II Distribution Co. LLC, 106
DXP Enterprises, Inc., 101
Dyax Corp., 89
Dycom Industries, Inc., 57
Dyersburg Corporation, 21
Dylan's Candy Bar, LLC, 99
Dynamic Materials Corporation, 81
Dynatech Corporation, 13
Dynatronics Corporation, 99
DynCorp, 45
Dynegy Inc., 49 (upd.)
E! Entertainment Television Inc., 17
E*Trade Financial Corporation, 20; 60 (upd.)
E. & J. Gallo Winery, I; 7 (upd.); 28 (upd.); 104 (upd.)
E.I. du Pont de Nemours and Company, I; 8 (upd.); 26 (upd.); 73 (upd.)
E.piphany, Inc., 49
E-Systems, Inc., 9
E.W. Howell Co., Inc., 72
The E.W. Scripps Company, IV; 7 (upd.); 28 (upd.); 66 (upd.)
E-Z Serve Corporation, 17
E-Z-EM Inc., 89
Eagle Hardware & Garden, Inc., 16
Eagle-Picher Industries, Inc., 8; 23 (upd.)
Eagle-Tribune Publishing Co., 91
Earl Scheib, Inc., 32
Earle M. Jorgensen Company, 82
The Earthgrains Company, 36
EarthLink, Inc., 36
East Penn Manufacturing Co., Inc. 79
Easter Seals, Inc., 58
Eastern Airlines, I
The Eastern Company, 48
Eastern Enterprises, 6
EastGroup Properties, Inc., 67
Eastland Shoe Corporation, 82
Eastman Chemical Company, 14; 38 (upd.)
Eastman Kodak Company, III; 7 (upd.); 36 (upd.); 91 (upd.)
Easton Sports, Inc., 66
Eateries, Inc., 33
Eaton Corporation, I; 10 (upd.); 67 (upd.)
Eaton Vance Corporation, 18
eBay Inc., 32; 67 (upd.)
EBSCO Industries, Inc., 17; 40 (upd.)
ECC International Corp., 42
Echlin Inc., I; 11 (upd.)
The Echo Design Group, Inc., 68
EchoStar Communications Corporation, 35
Eckerd Corporation, 9; 32 (upd.)
Eclipse Aviation Corporation, 87
Eclipsys Corporation, 104
Ecolab Inc., I; 13 (upd.); 34 (upd.); 85 (upd.)
eCollege.com, 85
Ecology and Environment, Inc., 39
Eddie Bauer, Inc., 9; 36 (upd.); 87 (upd.)
Edelbrock Corporation, 37
Edelman, 62

706

EDGAR Online, Inc., 91
Edge Petroleum Corporation, 67
Edison Brothers Stores, Inc., 9
Edison International, 56 (upd.)
Edison Schools Inc., 37
Edmark Corporation, 14; 41 (upd.)
EDO Corporation, 46
Educate Inc. 86 (upd.)
Education Management Corporation, 35
Educational Broadcasting Corporation, 48
Educational Testing Service, 12; 62 (upd.)
Edw. C. Levy Co., 42
Edward D. Jones & Company L.P., 30; 66 (upd.)
Edward Hines Lumber Company, 68
The Edward J. DeBartolo Corporation, 8
Edwards and Kelcey, 70
Edwards Brothers, Inc., 92
Edwards Theatres Circuit, Inc., 31
EFJ, Inc., 81
EG&G Incorporated, 8; 29 (upd.)
Egan Companies, Inc., 94
Egghead.com, Inc., 9; 31 (upd.)
EGL, Inc., 59
eHarmony.com Inc., 71
8x8, Inc., 94
84 Lumber Company, 9; 39 (upd.)
800-JR Cigar, Inc., 27
Eileen Fisher Inc., 61
Einstein/Noah Bagel Corporation, 29
Ekco Group, Inc., 16
El Camino Resources International, Inc., 11
El Chico Restaurants, Inc., 19
El Paso Corporation, 66 (upd.)
El Paso Electric Company, 21
El Paso Natural Gas Company, 12
El Pollo Loco, Inc., 69
Elamex, S.A. de C.V., 51
Elano Corporation, 14
The Elder-Beerman Stores Corp., 10; 63 (upd.)
Electric Boat Corporation, 86
Electric Lightwave, Inc., 37
Electro Rent Corporation, 58
Electromagnetic Sciences Inc., 21
Electronic Arts Inc., 10; 85 (upd.)
Electronic Data Systems Corporation, III; 28 (upd.)
Electronics Boutique Holdings Corporation, 72
Electronics for Imaging, Inc., 15; 43 (upd.)
Elektra Entertainment Group, 64
Element K Corporation, 94
Elephant Pharmacy, Inc., 83
Eli Lilly and Company, I; 11 (upd.); 47 (upd.)
Elizabeth Arden, Inc., 8; 40 (upd.)
Eljer Industries, Inc., 24
Elkay Manufacturing Company, 73
ElkCorp, 52
Ellen Tracy, Inc., 55
Ellerbe Becket, 41
Ellett Brothers, Inc., 17
Elliott-Lewis Corporation, 100
Elmer Candy Corporation, 88
Elmer's Restaurants, Inc., 42

Elsinore Corporation, 48
Elvis Presley Enterprises, Inc., 61
EMAK Worldwide, Inc., 105
EMBARQ Corporation, 83
Embers America Restaurants, 30
Embrex, Inc., 72
EMC Corporation, 12; 46 (upd.)
EMCO Enterprises, Inc., 102
EMCOR Group Inc., 60
EMCORE Corporation, 97
Emerson, II; 46 (upd.)
Emerson Radio Corp., 30
Emery Worldwide Airlines, Inc., 6; 25 (upd.)
Emge Packing Co., Inc., 11
Emigrant Savings Bank, 59
Emmis Communications Corporation, 47
Empi, Inc., 26
Empire Blue Cross and Blue Shield, III
The Empire District Electric Company, 77
Empire Resorts, Inc., 72
Empire Resources, Inc., 81
Employee Solutions, Inc., 18
ENCAD, Incorporated, 25
Encompass Services Corporation, 33
Encore Acquisition Company, 73
Encore Computer Corporation, 13; 74 (upd.)
Encore Wire Corporation, 81
Encyclopaedia Britannica, Inc., 7; 39 (upd.)
Endo Pharmaceuticals Holdings Inc., 71
Energen Corporation, 21; 97 (upd.)
Energizer Holdings, Inc., 32
Energy Brands Inc., 88
Energy Conversion Devices, Inc., 75
Enesco Corporation, 11
EnerSys Inc., 99
Engelhard Corporation, IV; 21 (upd.); 72 (upd.)
Engineered Support Systems, Inc., 59
Engle Homes, Inc., 46
Engraph, Inc., 12
Ennis, Inc., 21; 97 (upd.)
EnPro Industries, Inc., 93
Enquirer/Star Group, Inc., 10
Enrich International, 33
Enron Corporation, V; 19; 46 (upd.)
ENSCO International Incorporated, 57
Ensearch Corporation, V
Entercom Communications Corporation, 58
Entergy Corporation, V; 45 (upd.)
Enterprise Rent-A-Car Company, 6; 69 (upd.)
Entertainment Distribution Company, 89
Entravision Communications Corporation, 41
Envirodyne Industries, Inc., 17
Environmental Industries, Inc., 31
Environmental Power Corporation, 68
Environmental Systems Research Institute Inc. (ESRI), 62
Enzo Biochem, Inc., 41
EOG Resources, 106
Eon Labs, Inc., 67
EP Henry Corporation, 104

EPAM Systems Inc., 96
Epic Systems Corporation, 62
EPIQ Systems, Inc., 56
Equifax Inc., 6; 28 (upd.); 90 (upd.)
Equistar Chemicals, LP, 71
Equitable Life Assurance Society of the United States, III
Equitable Resources, Inc., 6; 54 (upd.)
Equity Marketing, Inc., 26
Equity Office Properties Trust, 54
Equity Residential, 49
Equus Computer Systems, Inc., 49
Ergon, Inc., 95
Erickson Retirement Communities, 57
Erie Indemnity Company, 35
ERLY Industries Inc., 17
Ernie Ball, Inc., 56
Ernst & Young, 9; 29 (upd.)
Escalade, Incorporated, 19
Eschelon Telecom, Inc., 72
ESCO Technologies Inc., 87
Eskimo Pie Corporation, 21
ESPN, Inc., 56
Esprit de Corp., 8; 29 (upd.)
ESS Technology, Inc., 22
Essef Corporation, 18
Esselte, 64
Esselte Pendaflex Corporation, 11
Essence Communications, Inc., 24
Essex Corporation, 85
Essie Cosmetics, Ltd., 102
The Estée Lauder Companies Inc., 9; 30 (upd.); 93 (upd.)
Esterline Technologies Corp., 15
Estes Express Lines, Inc., 86
Eternal Word Television Network, Inc., 57
Ethan Allen Interiors, Inc., 12; 39 (upd.)
Ethicon, Inc., 23
Ethyl Corporation, I; 10 (upd.)
EToys, Inc., 37
The Eureka Company, 12
Euromarket Designs Inc., 31 (upd.); 99 (upd.)
Euronet Worldwide, Inc., 83
Europe Through the Back Door Inc., 65
Evans and Sutherland Computer Company 19; 78 (upd.)
Evans, Inc., 30
Everex Systems, Inc., 16
Evergreen Energy, Inc., 97
Evergreen International Aviation, Inc., 53
Evergreen Solar, Inc., 101
Everlast Worldwide Inc., 47
Exabyte Corporation, 12; 40 (upd.)
Exactech, Inc., 101
Exar Corp., 14
EXCEL Communications Inc., 18
Excel Technology, Inc., 65
Executive Jet, Inc., 36
Executone Information Systems, Inc., 13
Exelon Corporation, 48 (upd.)
Exide Electronics Group, Inc., 20
Expedia, Inc., 58
Expeditors International of Washington Inc., 17; 78 (upd.)
Experian Information Solutions Inc., 45
Exponent, Inc., 95
Express Scripts Inc., 17; 44 (upd.)

Extended Stay America, Inc., 41
EXX Inc., 65
Exxon Corporation, IV; 7 (upd.); 32 (upd.)
Exxon Mobil Corporation, 67 (upd.)
Eye Care Centers of America, Inc., 69
EZCORP Inc., 43
F&W Publications, Inc., 71
The F. Dohmen Co., 77
F. Korbel & Bros. Inc., 68
F.W. Webb Company, 95
Fab Industries, Inc., 27
Fabri-Centers of America Inc., 16
Facebook, Inc., 90
FactSet Research Systems Inc., 73
Faegre & Benson LLP, 97
Fair Grounds Corporation, 44
Fair, Isaac and Company, 18
Fairchild Aircraft, Inc., 9
Fairfield Communities, Inc., 36
Falcon Products, Inc., 33
Fallon McElligott Inc., 22
Fallon Worldwide, 71 (upd.)
Family Christian Stores, Inc., 51
Family Dollar Stores, Inc., 13; 62 (upd.)
Family Golf Centers, Inc., 29
Family Sports Concepts, Inc., 100
Famous Dave's of America, Inc., 40
Fannie Mae, 45 (upd.)
Fannie May Confections Brands, Inc., 80
Fansteel Inc., 19
FAO Schwarz, 46
Farah Incorporated, 24
Faribault Foods, Inc., 89
Farley Northwest Industries, Inc., I
Farley's & Sathers Candy Company, Inc., 62
Farm Family Holdings, Inc., 39
Farm Journal Corporation, 42
Farmer Bros. Co., 52
Farmer Jack Supermarkets 78
Farmers Insurance Group of Companies, 25
Farmland Foods, Inc., 7
Farmland Industries, Inc., 48
FARO Technologies, Inc., 87
Farouk Systems Inc. 78
Farrar, Straus and Giroux Inc., 15
Fastenal Company, 14; 42 (upd.); 99 (upd.)
Fatburger Corporation, 64
Faultless Starch/Bon Ami Company, 55
Fay's Inc., 17
Faygo Beverages Inc., 55
Fazoli's Management, Inc., 76 (upd.)
Fazoli's Systems, Inc., 27
Featherlite Inc., 28
Fedders Corporation, 18; 43 (upd.)
Federal Agricultural Mortgage Corporation, 75
Federal Deposit Insurance Corporation, 93
Federal Express Corporation, V
Federal National Mortgage Association, II
Federal Paper Board Company, Inc., 8
Federal Prison Industries, Inc., 34
Federal Signal Corp., 10

Federal-Mogul Corporation, I; 10 (upd.); 26 (upd.)
Federated Department Stores Inc., 9; 31 (upd.)
FedEx Corporation, 18 (upd.); 42 (upd.)
Feed The Children, Inc., 68
FEI Company 79
Feld Entertainment, Inc., 32 (upd.)
Fellowes Manufacturing Company, 28
Fender Musical Instruments Company, 16; 43 (upd.)
Fenwick & West LLP, 34
Ferolito, Vultaggio & Sons, 27; 100 (upd.)
Ferrara Fire Apparatus, Inc., 84
Ferrara Pan Candy Company, 90
Ferrellgas Partners, L.P., 35
Ferro Corporation, 8; 56 (upd.)
F5 Networks, Inc., 72
FHP International Corporation, 6
FiberMark, Inc., 37
Fibreboard Corporation, 16
Fidelity Investments Inc., II; 14 (upd.)
Fidelity National Financial Inc., 54
Fidelity Southern Corporation, 85
Fieldale Farms Corporation, 23
Fieldcrest Cannon, Inc., 9; 31 (upd.)
Fiesta Mart, Inc., 101
Fifth Third Bancorp, 13; 31 (upd.); 103 (upd.)
Figgie International Inc., 7
Fiji Water LLC, 74
FileNet Corporation, 62
Fili Enterprises, Inc., 70
Film Roman, Inc., 58
FINA, Inc., 7
Fingerhut Companies, Inc., 9; 36 (upd.)
Finisar Corporation, 92
The Finish Line, Inc., 29; 68 (upd.)
FinishMaster, Inc., 24
Finlay Enterprises, Inc., 16; 76 (upd.)
Firearms Training Systems, Inc., 27
Fired Up, Inc., 82
Fireman's Fund Insurance Company, III
First Albany Companies Inc., 37
First Alert, Inc., 28
The First American Corporation, The 52
First Aviation Services Inc., 49
First Bank System Inc., 12
First Brands Corporation, 8
First Busey Corporation, 105
First Cash Financial Services, Inc., 57
First Chicago Corporation, II
First Colony Coffee & Tea Company, 84
First Commerce Bancshares, Inc., 15
First Commerce Corporation, 11
First Data Corporation, 30 (upd.)
First Empire State Corporation, 11
First Executive Corporation, III
First Fidelity Bank, N.A., New Jersey, 9
First Financial Management Corporation, 11
First Hawaiian, Inc., 11
First Industrial Realty Trust, Inc., 65
First Interstate Bancorp, II
The First Marblehead Corporation, 87
First Mississippi Corporation, 8
First Nationwide Bank, 14

First of America Bank Corporation, 8
First Security Corporation, 11
First Solar, Inc., 95
First Team Sports, Inc., 22
First Tennessee National Corporation, 11; 48 (upd.)
First Union Corporation, 10
First USA, Inc., 11
First Virginia Banks, Inc., 11
The First Years Inc., 46
Firstar Corporation, 11; 33 (upd.)
FirstMerit Corporation, 105
Fiserv, Inc., 11; 33 (upd.); 106 (upd.)
Fish & Neave, 54
Fisher Auto Parts, Inc., 104
Fisher Communications, Inc., 99
Fisher Companies, Inc., 15
Fisher Controls International, LLC, 13; 61 (upd.)
Fisher Scientific International Inc., 24
Fisher-Price Inc., 12; 32 (upd.)
Fishman & Tobin Inc., 102
Fisk Corporation, 72
5 & Diner Franchise Corporation, 72
Five Guys Enterprises, LLC, 99
Flagstar Companies, Inc., 10
Flanders Corporation, 65
Flanigan's Enterprises, Inc., 60
Flatiron Construction Corporation, 92
Fleer Corporation, 15
FleetBoston Financial Corporation, 9; 36 (upd.)
Fleetwood Enterprises, Inc., III; 22 (upd.); 81 (upd.)
Fleming Companies, Inc., II; 17 (upd.)
Flexsteel Industries Inc., 15; 41 (upd.)
Flight Options, LLC, 75
FlightSafety International, Inc., 9; 29 (upd.)
Flint Ink Corporation, 13; 41 (upd.)
FLIR Systems, Inc., 69
Florida Crystals Inc., 35
Florida East Coast Industries, Inc., 59
Florida Gaming Corporation, 47
Florida Progress Corporation, V; 23 (upd.)
Florida Public Utilities Company, 69
Florida Rock Industries, Inc., 46
Florida's Natural Growers, 45
Florists' Transworld Delivery, Inc., 28
Florsheim Shoe Group Inc., 9; 31 (upd.)
Flotek Industries Inc., 93
Flour City International, Inc., 44
Flow International Corporation, 56
Flowers Industries, Inc., 12; 35 (upd.)
Flowserve Corporation, 33; 77 (upd.)
Fluke Corporation, 15
Fluor Corporation, I; 8 (upd.); 34 (upd.)
Flying Boat, Inc. (Chalk's Ocean Airways), 56
Flying J Inc., 19
FMC Corporation, I; 11 (upd.); 89 (upd.)
FMR Corp., 8; 32 (upd.)
Foamex International Inc., 17
Focus Features 78
Foley & Lardner, 28
Follett Corporation, 12; 39 (upd.)
Food Circus Super Markets, Inc., 88
The Food Emporium, 64

Food For The Poor, Inc., 77
Food Lion LLC, II; 15 (upd.); 66 (upd.)
Foodarama Supermarkets, Inc., 28
FoodBrands America, Inc., 23
Foodmaker, Inc., 14
Foot Locker, Inc., 68 (upd.)
Foot Petals L.L.C., 95
Foote, Cone & Belding Worldwide, I; 66 (upd.)
Footstar, Incorporated, 24
Forbes Inc., 30; 82 (upd.)
Force Protection Inc., 95
The Ford Foundation, 34
Ford Gum & Machine Company, Inc., 102
Ford Motor Company, I; 11 (upd.); 36 (upd.); 64 (upd.)
FORE Systems, Inc., 25
Foremost Farms USA Cooperative, 98
Forest City Enterprises, Inc., 16; 52 (upd.)
Forest Laboratories, Inc., 11; 52 (upd.)
Forest Oil Corporation, 19; 91 (upd.)
Forever Living Products International Inc., 17
Forever 21, Inc., 84
FormFactor, Inc., 85
Formica Corporation, 13
Forrester Research, Inc., 54
Forstmann Little & Co., 38
Fort Howard Corporation, 8
Fort James Corporation, 22 (upd.)
Fortune Brands, Inc., 29 (upd.); 68 (upd.)
Fortunoff Fine Jewelry and Silverware Inc., 26
Forward Air Corporation, 75
Forward Industries, Inc., 86
Fossil, Inc., 17
Foster Poultry Farms, 32
Foster Wheeler Corporation, 6; 23 (upd.)
Foster Wheeler Ltd., 76 (upd.)
FosterGrant, Inc., 60
Foundation Health Corporation, 12
Fountain Powerboats Industries, Inc., 28
Four Winns Boats LLC, 96
4Kids Entertainment Inc., 59
Fourth Financial Corporation, 11
Fox Entertainment Group, Inc., 43
Fox Family Worldwide, Inc., 24
Fox's Pizza Den, Inc., 98
Foxboro Company, 13
FoxHollow Technologies, Inc., 85
FoxMeyer Health Corporation, 16
Foxworth-Galbraith Lumber Company, 91
FPL Group, Inc., V; 49 (upd.)
Frank J. Zamboni & Co., Inc., 34
Frank Russell Company, 46
Frank's Nursery & Crafts, Inc., 12
Frankel & Co., 39
Franklin Covey Company, 11; 37 (upd.)
Franklin Electric Company, Inc., 43
Franklin Electronic Publishers, Inc., 23
The Franklin Mint, 69
Franklin Resources, Inc., 9
Franz Inc., 80
Fred Alger Management, Inc., 97
Fred Meyer Stores, Inc., V; 20 (upd.); 64 (upd.)

Fred Usinger Inc., 54
The Fred W. Albrecht Grocery Co., 13
Fred Weber, Inc., 61
Fred's, Inc., 23; 62 (upd.)
Freddie Mac, 54
Frederick Atkins Inc., 16
Frederick's of Hollywood, Inc., 16; 59 (upd.)
Freedom Communications, Inc., 36
Freeport-McMoRan Copper & Gold, Inc., IV; 7 (upd.); 57 (upd.)
Freescale Semiconductor, Inc., 83
Freeze.com LLC, 77
FreightCar America, Inc., 101
French Fragrances, Inc., 22
Frequency Electronics, Inc., 61
Fresh America Corporation, 20
Fresh Choice, Inc., 20
Fresh Enterprises, Inc., 66
Fresh Express Inc., 88
Fresh Foods, Inc., 29
FreshDirect, LLC, 84
Fretter, Inc., 10
Fried, Frank, Harris, Shriver & Jacobson, 35
Friedman's Inc., 29
Friedman, Billings, Ramsey Group, Inc., 53
Friendly Ice Cream Corporation, 30; 72 (upd.)
Frigidaire Home Products, 22
Frisch's Restaurants, Inc., 35; 92 (upd.)
Frito-Lay North America, 32; 73 (upd.)
Fritz Companies, Inc., 12
Frontera Foods, Inc., 100
Frontier Airlines Holdings Inc., 22; 84 (upd.)
Frontier Corp., 16
Frontier Natural Products Co-Op, 82
Frost & Sullivan, Inc., 53
Frozen Food Express Industries, Inc., 20; 98 (upd.)
Fruehauf Corporation, I
Fruit of the Loom, Inc., 8; 25 (upd.)
Fruth Pharmacy, Inc., 66
Fry's Electronics, Inc., 68
Frymaster Corporation, 27
FSI International, Inc., 17
FTD Group, Inc., 99 (upd.)
FTI Consulting, Inc., 77
FTP Software, Inc., 20
Fubu, 29
Fuel Systems Solutions, Inc., 97
Fuel Tech, Inc., 85
FuelCell Energy, Inc., 75
Fujitsu-ICL Systems Inc., 11
Fulbright & Jaworski L.L.P., 47
Funco, Inc., 20
Fuqua Enterprises, Inc., 17
Fuqua Industries, Inc., I
Furmanite Corporation, 92
Furniture Brands International, Inc., 39 (upd.)
Furon Company, 28
Furr's Restaurant Group, Inc., 53
Furr's Supermarkets, Inc., 28
Future Now, Inc., 12
G&K Services, Inc., 16

G-III Apparel Group, Ltd., 22
G. Heileman Brewing Company Inc., I
G. Leblanc Corporation, 55
G.A.F., I
G.D. Searle & Company, I; 12 (upd.); 34 (upd.)
G.I. Joe's, Inc., 30
G.S. Blodgett Corporation, 15
Gabelli Asset Management Inc., 30
Gables Residential Trust, 49
Gadzooks, Inc., 18
GAF Corporation, 22 (upd.)
Gage Marketing Group, 26
Gaiam, Inc., 41
Gainsco, Inc., 22
Galardi Group, Inc., 72
Galaxy Investors, Inc., 97
Galaxy Nutritional Foods, Inc., 58
Gale International Llc, 93
Galey & Lord, Inc., 20; 66 (upd.)
Gallup, Inc., 37; 104 (upd.)
Galyan's Trading Company, Inc., 47
The Gambrinus Company, 40
GameStop Corp., 69 (upd.)
Gaming Partners International Corporation, 93
Gander Mountain Company, 20; 90 (upd.)
Gannett Company, Inc., IV; 7 (upd.); 30 (upd.); 66 (upd.)
Gantos, Inc., 17
The Gap, Inc., V; 18 (upd.); 55 (upd.)
Garan, Inc., 16; 64 (upd.)
Garden Fresh Restaurant Corporation, 31
Garden Ridge Corporation, 27
Gardenburger, Inc., 33; 76 (upd.)
Gardner Denver, Inc., 49
Gart Sports Company, 24
Gartner, Inc., 21; 94 (upd.)
Garst Seed Company, Inc., 86
GateHouse Media, Inc., 91
The Gates Corporation, 9
Gateway, Inc., 10; 27 (upd.); 63 (upd.)
The Gatorade Company, 82
GATX Corporation, 6; 25 (upd.)
Gaylord Bros., Inc., 100
Gaylord Container Corporation, 8
Gaylord Entertainment Company, 11; 36 (upd.)
GC Companies, Inc., 25
GE Aircraft Engines, 9
GE Capital Aviation Services, 36
Geek Squad Inc., 102
Geerlings & Wade, Inc., 45
Geffen Records Inc., 26
Gehl Company, 19
GEICO Corporation, 10; 40 (upd.)
Geiger Bros., 60
Gemini Sound Products Corporation, 58
Gen-Probe Incorporated 79
GenCorp Inc., 8; 9
Genentech, Inc., I; 8 (upd.); 32 (upd.); 75 (upd.)
General Atomics, 57
General Bearing Corporation, 45
General Binding Corporation, 10; 73 (upd.)
General Cable Corporation, 40

The General Chemical Group Inc., 37
General Cigar Holdings, Inc., 66 (upd.)
General Cinema Corporation, I
General DataComm Industries, Inc., 14
General Dynamics Corporation, I; 10
 (upd.); 40 (upd.); 88 (upd.)
General Electric Company, II; 12 (upd.);
 34 (upd.); 63 (upd.)
General Employment Enterprises, Inc., 87
General Growth Properties, Inc., 57
General Host Corporation, 12
General Housewares Corporation, 16
General Instrument Corporation, 10
General Maritime Corporation, 59
General Mills, Inc., II; 10 (upd.); 36
 (upd.); 85 (upd.)
General Motors Corporation, I; 10 (upd.);
 36 (upd.); 64 (upd.)
General Nutrition Companies, Inc., 11;
 29 (upd.)
General Public Utilities Corporation, V
General Re Corporation, III; 24 (upd.)
General Signal Corporation, 9
General Tire, Inc., 8
Genesco Inc., 17; 84 (upd.)
Genesee & Wyoming Inc., 27
Genesis Health Ventures, Inc., 18
Genesis Microchip Inc., 82
Genesys Telecommunications Laboratories
 Inc., 103
Genetics Institute, Inc., 8
Geneva Steel, 7
Genmar Holdings, Inc., 45
Genovese Drug Stores, Inc., 18
GenRad, Inc., 24
Gentex Corporation, 26
Gentiva Health Services, Inc. 79
Genuardi's Family Markets, Inc., 35
Genuine Parts Company, 9; 45 (upd.)
Genzyme Corporation, 13; 38 (upd.); 77
 (upd.)
The Geon Company, 11
GeoResources, Inc., 101
George A. Hormel and Company, II
The George F. Cram Company, Inc., 55
George P. Johnson Company, 60
George S. May International Company,
 55
George W. Park Seed Company, Inc., 98
Georgia Gulf Corporation, 9; 61 (upd.)
Georgia-Pacific LLC, IV; 9 (upd.); 47
 (upd.); 101 (upd.)
Geotek Communications Inc., 21
Gerald Stevens, Inc., 37
Gerber Products Company, 7; 21 (upd.)
Gerber Scientific, Inc., 12; 84 (upd.)
German American Bancorp, 41
Gertrude Hawk Chocolates Inc., 104
Getty Images, Inc., 31
Gevity HR, Inc., 63
GF Health Products, Inc., 82
Ghirardelli Chocolate Company, 30
Giant Cement Holding, Inc., 23
Giant Eagle, Inc., 86
Giant Food LLC, II; 22 (upd.); 83 (upd.)
Giant Industries, Inc., 19; 61 (upd.)
Gibraltar Steel Corporation, 37
Gibson Greetings, Inc., 12

Gibson Guitar Corporation, 16; 100
 (upd.)
Gibson, Dunn & Crutcher LLP, 36
Giddings & Lewis, Inc., 10
Gifts In Kind International, 101
Gilbane, Inc., 34
Gilead Sciences, Inc., 54
Gillett Holdings, Inc., 7
The Gillette Company, III; 20 (upd.); 68
 (upd.)
Gilman & Ciocia, Inc., 72
Gilmore Entertainment Group L.L.C.,
 100
Girl Scouts of the USA, 35
The Gitano Group, Inc., 8
Glacier Bancorp, Inc., 35
Glacier Water Services, Inc., 47
Glamis Gold, Ltd., 54
Glazer's Wholesale Drug Company, Inc.,
 82
Gleason Corporation, 24
The Glidden Company, 8
Global Berry Farms LLC, 62
Global Crossing Ltd., 32
Global Hyatt Corporation, 75 (upd.)
Global Imaging Systems, Inc., 73
Global Industries, Ltd., 37
Global Marine, Inc., 9
Global Outdoors, Inc., 49
Global Payments Inc., 91
Global Power Equipment Group Inc., 52
GlobalSantaFe Corporation, 48 (upd.)
Globe Newspaper Company Inc., 106
Glu Mobile Inc., 95
Gluek Brewing Company, 75
GM Hughes Electronics Corporation, II
GMH Communities Trust, 87
GNC Corporation, 98 (upd.)
The Go Daddy Group Inc., 102
Godfather's Pizza Incorporated, 25
Godiva Chocolatier, Inc., 64
Goetze's Candy Company, Inc., 87
Gold Kist Inc., 17; 26 (upd.)
Gold'n Plump Poultry, 54
Gold's Gym International, Inc., 71
Golden Belt Manufacturing Co., 16
Golden Books Family Entertainment, Inc.,
 28
Golden Corral Corporation, 10; 66 (upd.)
Golden Enterprises, Inc., 26
Golden Krust Caribbean Bakery, Inc., 68
Golden Neo-Life Diamite International,
 Inc., 100
Golden State Foods Corporation, 32
Golden State Vintners, Inc., 33
Golden West Financial Corporation, 47
The Goldman Sachs Group Inc., II; 20
 (upd.); 51 (upd.)
GoldToeMoretz, LLC, 102
Golin/Harris International, Inc., 88
Golub Corporation, 26; 96 (upd.)
Gomez Inc., 104
Gonnella Baking Company, 40; 102
 (upd.)
The Good Guys, Inc., 10; 30 (upd.)
Good Humor-Breyers Ice Cream
 Company, 14
Goodby Silverstein & Partners, Inc., 75

Goodman Holding Company, 42
GoodMark Foods, Inc., 26
Goodrich Corporation, 46 (upd.)
GoodTimes Entertainment Ltd., 48
Goodwill Industries International, Inc.,
 16; 66 (upd.)
Goody Products, Inc., 12
Goody's Family Clothing, Inc., 20; 64
 (upd.)
The Goodyear Tire & Rubber Company,
 V; 20 (upd.); 75 (upd.)
Google, Inc., 50; 101 (upd.)
Gordmans, Inc., 74
Gordon Biersch Brewery Restaurant
 Group, Inc., 93
Gordon Food Service Inc., 8; 39 (upd.)
The Gorman-Rupp Company, 18; 57
 (upd.)
Gorton's, 13
Goss Holdings, Inc., 43
Gottschalks, Inc., 18; 91 (upd.)
Gould Electronics, Inc., 14
Gould Paper Corporation, 82
Goulds Pumps Inc., 24
Goya Foods Inc., 22; 91 (upd.)
GP Strategies Corporation, 64 (upd.)
GPU, Inc., 27 (upd.)
Graco Inc., 19; 67 (upd.)
Gradall Industries, Inc., 96
Graeter's Manufacturing Company, 86
Graham Corporation, 62
Graham Packaging Holdings Company,
 87
GranCare, Inc., 14
Grand Casinos, Inc., 20
Grand Piano & Furniture Company, 72
Grand Traverse Pie Company, 98
The Grand Union Company, 7; 28 (upd.)
Grandoe Corporation, 98
Granite Broadcasting Corporation, 42
Granite City Food & Brewery Ltd., 94
Granite Construction Incorporated, 61
Granite Industries of Vermont, Inc., 73
Granite Rock Company, 26
Granite State Bankshares, Inc., 37
Grant Prideco, Inc., 57
Grant Thornton International, 57
Graphic Industries Inc., 25
Graphic Packaging Holding Company, 96
 (upd.)
Gray Communications Systems, Inc., 24
Graybar Electric Company, Inc., 54
Great American Management and
 Investment, Inc., 8
The Great Atlantic & Pacific Tea
 Company, Inc., II; 16 (upd.); 55 (upd.)
Great Harvest Bread Company, 44
Great Lakes Bancorp, 8
Great Lakes Chemical Corporation, I; 14
 (upd.)
Great Lakes Dredge & Dock Company,
 69
Great Plains Energy Incorporated, 65
 (upd.)
Great Western Financial Corporation, 10
Great White Shark Enterprises, Inc., 89
Great Wolf Resorts, Inc., 91
Greatbatch Inc., 72

Greater Washington Educational Telecommunication Association, 103
Grede Foundries, Inc., 38
The Green Bay Packers, Inc., 32
Green Dot Public Schools, 99
Green Mountain Coffee, Inc., 31
Green Tree Financial Corporation, 11
Greenberg Traurig, LLP, 65
The Greenbrier Companies, 19
GreenMan Technologies Inc., 99
Greene, Tweed & Company, 55
GreenPoint Financial Corp., 28
Greenwood Mills, Inc., 14
Greg Manning Auctions, Inc., 60
Greif Inc., 15; 66 (upd.)
Grey Advertising, Inc., 6
Grey Global Group Inc., 66 (upd.)
Grey Wolf, Inc., 43
Greyhound Lines, Inc., I; 32 (upd.)
Greyston Bakery, Inc., 101
Griffin Industries, Inc., 70
Griffin Land & Nurseries, Inc., 43
Griffith Laboratories Inc., 100
Griffon Corporation, 34
Grill Concepts, Inc., 74
Grinnell Corp., 13
Grist Mill Company, 15
Gristede's Foods Inc., 31; 68 (upd.)
The Grocers Supply Co., Inc., 103
Grolier Incorporated, 16; 43 (upd.)
Grossman's Inc., 13
Ground Round, Inc., 21
Group 1 Automotive, Inc., 52
Group Health Cooperative, 41
Grow Biz International, Inc., 18
Grow Group Inc., 12
GROWMARK, Inc., 88
Grubb & Ellis Company, 21; 98 (upd.)
Grumman Corporation, I; 11 (upd.)
Grunau Company Inc., 90
Gruntal & Co., L.L.C., 20
Gryphon Holdings, Inc., 21
GSC Enterprises, Inc., 86
GSD&M Advertising, 44
GSD&M's Idea City, 90
GSI Commerce, Inc., 67
GT Bicycles, 26
GT Interactive Software, 31
GT Solar International, Inc., 101
GTE Corporation, V; 15 (upd.)
GTSI Corp., 57
Guangzhou Pearl River Piano Group Ltd., 49
Guardian Industries Corp., 87
Guccio Gucci, S.p.A., 15
Guess, Inc., 15; 68 (upd.)
Guest Supply, Inc., 18
Guida-Seibert Dairy Company, 84
Guidant Corporation, 58
Guilford Mills Inc., 8; 40 (upd.)
Guitar Center, Inc., 29; 68 (upd.)
Guittard Chocolate Company, 55
Gulf & Western Inc., I
Gulf Island Fabrication, Inc., 44
Gulf States Utilities Company, 6
GulfMark Offshore, Inc., 49
Gulfstream Aerospace Corporation, 7; 28 (upd.)

Gund, Inc., 96
Gunite Corporation, 51
The Gunlocke Company, 23
Guardsmark, L.L.C., 77
Guthy-Renker Corporation, 32
Guttenplan's Frozen Dough Inc., 88
Gwathmey Siegel & Associates Architects LLC, 26
Gymboree Corporation, 15; 69 (upd.)
H&R Block, Inc., 9; 29 (upd.); 82 (upd.)
H.B. Fuller Company, 8; 32 (upd.); 75 (upd.)
H. Betti Industries Inc., 88
H.D. Vest, Inc., 46
H.E. Butt Grocery Company, 13; 32 (upd.); 85 (upd.)
H.F. Ahmanson & Company, II; 10 (upd.)
H.J. Heinz Company, II; 11 (upd.); 36 (upd.); 99 (upd.)
H.J. Russell & Company, 66
H.M. Payson & Co., 69
H.O. Penn Machinery Company, Inc., 96
The H.W. Wilson Company, 66
Ha-Lo Industries, Inc., 27
The Haartz Corporation, 94
Habersham Bancorp, 25
The Habitat Company LLC, 106
Habitat for Humanity International, Inc., 36; 106 (upd.)
Hach Co., 18
Hadco Corporation, 24
Haeger Industries Inc., 88
Haemonetics Corporation, 20
Haggar Corporation, 19; 78 (upd.)
Haggen Inc., 38
Hahn Automotive Warehouse, Inc., 24
Haights Cross Communications, Inc., 84
The Hain Celestial Group, Inc., 27; 43 (upd.)
Hair Club For Men Ltd., 90
HAL Inc., 9
Hal Leonard Corporation, 96
Hale-Halsell Company, 60
Half Price Books, Records, Magazines Inc., 37
Hall, Kinion & Associates, Inc., 52
Halliburton Company, III; 25 (upd.); 55 (upd.)
Hallmark Cards, Inc., IV; 16 (upd.); 40 (upd.); 87 (upd.)
Hamilton Beach/Proctor-Silex Inc., 17
Hammacher Schlemmer & Company Inc., 21; 72 (upd.)
Hamot Health Foundation, 91
Hampshire Group Ltd., 82
Hampton Affiliates, Inc., 77
Hampton Industries, Inc., 20
Hancock Fabrics, Inc., 18
Hancock Holding Company, 15
Handleman Company, 15; 86 (upd.)
Handspring Inc., 49
Handy & Harman, 23
Hanesbrands Inc., 98
Hanger Orthopedic Group, Inc., 41
Hanmi Financial Corporation, 66
Hanna Andersson Corp., 49
Hanna-Barbera Cartoons Inc., 23

Hannaford Bros. Co., 12; 103 (upd.)
Hanover Compressor Company, 59
Hanover Direct, Inc., 36
Hanover Foods Corporation, 35
Hansen Natural Corporation, 31; 76 (upd.)
Hanson Building Materials America Inc., 60
Happy Kids Inc., 30
Harbert Corporation, 14
Harbison-Walker Refractories Company, 24
Harbour Group Industries, Inc., 90
Harcourt Brace and Co., 12
Harcourt Brace Jovanovich, Inc., IV
Harcourt General, Inc., 20 (upd.)
Hard Rock Café International, Inc., 12; 32 (upd.); 105 (upd.)
Harding Lawson Associates Group, Inc., 16
Hardinge Inc., 25
Harkins Amusement, 94
Harland Clarke Holdings Corporation, 94 (upd.)
Harlem Globetrotters International, Inc., 61
Harley-Davidson, Inc., 7; 25 (upd.); 106 (upd.)
Harman International Industries, Incorporated, 15; 101 (upd.)
Harleysville Group Inc., 37
Harman International Industries Inc., 15
Harmon Industries, Inc., 25
Harmonic Inc., 43
Harnischfeger Industries, Inc., 8; 38 (upd.)
Harold's Stores, Inc., 22
Harper Group Inc., 17
HarperCollins Publishers, 15
Harpo Inc., 28; 66 (upd.)
Harps Food Stores, Inc., 99
Harrah's Entertainment, Inc., 16; 43 (upd.)
Harris Corporation, II; 20 (upd.); 78 (upd.)
Harris Interactive Inc., 41; 92 (upd.)
The Harris Soup Company (Harry's Fresh Foods), 92
Harris Teeter Inc., 23; 72 (upd.)
Harry London Candies, Inc., 70
Harry N. Abrams, Inc., 58
Harry Winston Inc., 45; 104 (upd.)
Harry's Farmers Market Inc., 23
Harsco Corporation, 8; 105 (upd.)
Harte-Hanks, Inc., 17; 63 (upd.)
Hartmann Inc., 96
Hartmarx Corporation, 8; 32 (upd.)
The Hartz Mountain Corporation, 12; 46 (upd.)
Harveys Casino Resorts, 27
Harza Engineering Company, 14
Hasbro, Inc., III; 16 (upd.); 43 (upd.)
Haskel International, Inc., 59
Hastings Entertainment, Inc., 29; 104 (upd.)
Hastings Manufacturing Company, 56
Hauser, Inc., 46
Haverty Furniture Companies, Inc., 31

Hawaiian Electric Industries, Inc., 9
Hawaiian Holdings, Inc., 22 (upd.); 96 (upd.)
Hawk Corporation, 59
Hawkeye Holdings LLC, 89
Hawkins Chemical, Inc., 16
Haworth Inc., 8; 39 (upd.)
Hay Group Holdings, Inc., 100
Hay House, Inc., 93
Hayes Corporation, 24
Hayes Lemmerz International, Inc., 27
Haynes International, Inc., 88
Hazelden Foundation, 28
HCA - The Healthcare Company, 35 (upd.)
HCI Direct, Inc., 55
HDOS Enterprises, 72
HDR Inc., 48
Headwaters Incorporated, 56
Headway Corporate Resources, Inc., 40
Health Care & Retirement Corporation, 22
Health Communications, Inc., 72
Health Management Associates, Inc., 56
Health O Meter Products Inc., 14
Health Risk Management, Inc., 24
Health Systems International, Inc., 11
HealthExtras, Inc., 75
HealthMarkets, Inc., 88 (upd.)
HealthSouth Corporation, 14; 33 (upd.)
Healthtex, Inc., 17
The Hearst Corporation, IV; 19 (upd.); 46 (upd.)
Heartland Express, Inc., 18
The Heat Group, 53
Hechinger Company, 12
Hecla Mining Company, 20
Heekin Can Inc., 13
Heelys, Inc., 87
Heery International, Inc., 58
HEICO Corporation, 30
Heidrick & Struggles International, Inc., 28
Heilig-Meyers Company, 14; 40 (upd.)
Helen of Troy Corporation, 18
Helene Curtis Industries, Inc., 8; 28 (upd.)
Helix Energy Solutions Group, Inc., 81
Heller, Ehrman, White & McAuliffe, 41
Helmerich & Payne, Inc., 18
Helmsley Enterprises, Inc., 9; 39 (upd.)
Helzberg Diamonds, 40
Hendrick Motorsports, Inc., 89
Henkel Manco Inc., 22
The Henley Group, Inc., III
Henry Crown and Company, 91
Henry Dreyfuss Associates LLC, 88
Henry Ford Health System, 84
Henry Modell & Company Inc., 32
Henry Schein, Inc., 31; 70 (upd.)
Hensel Phelps Construction Company, 72
Hensley & Company, 64
Herald Media, Inc., 91
Herbalife International, Inc., 17; 41 (upd.)
Hercules Inc., I; 22 (upd.); 66 (upd.)
Hercules Technology Growth Capital, Inc., 87

Herley Industries, Inc., 33
Herman Goelitz, Inc., 28
Herman Goldner Company, Inc., 100
Herman Miller, Inc., 8; 77 (upd.)
Herr Foods Inc., 84
Herschend Family Entertainment Corporation, 73
Hershey Foods Corporation, II; 15 (upd.); 51 (upd.)
The Hertz Corporation, 9; 33 (upd.); 101 (upd.)
Heska Corporation, 39
Heublein, Inc., I
Hewitt Associates, Inc., 77
Hewlett-Packard Company, III; 6 (upd.); 28 (upd.); 50 (upd.)
Hexcel Corporation, 28
HFF, Inc., 103
hhgregg Inc., 98
Hibbett Sporting Goods, Inc., 26; 70 (upd.)
Hibernia Corporation, 37
Hickory Farms, Inc., 17
HickoryTech Corporation, 92
High Falls Brewing Company LLC, 74
Highlights for Children, Inc., 95
Highmark Inc., 27
Highsmith Inc., 60
Hilb, Rogal & Hobbs Company, 77
Hildebrandt International, 29
Hill's Pet Nutrition, Inc., 27
Hillenbrand Industries, Inc., 10; 75 (upd.)
Hillerich & Bradsby Company, Inc., 51
The Hillhaven Corporation, 14
Hills Stores Company, 13
Hilmar Cheese Company, Inc., 98
Hilton Hotels Corporation, III; 19 (upd.); 62 (upd.)
Hines Horticulture, Inc., 49
Hispanic Broadcasting Corporation, 35
Hitchiner Manufacturing Co., Inc., 23
Hittite Microwave Corporation, 106
HMI Industries, Inc., 17
HNI Corporation, 74 (upd.)
Ho-Chunk Inc., 61
HOB Entertainment, Inc., 37
Hobby Lobby Stores Inc., 80
Hobie Cat Company, 94
Hodgson Mill, Inc., 88
Hoechst Celanese Corporation, 13
Hoenig Group Inc., 41
Hoffman Corporation 78
Hogan & Hartson L.L.P., 44
HOK Group, Inc., 59
Holberg Industries, Inc., 36
Holiday Inns, Inc., III
Holiday Retirement Corp., 87
Holiday RV Superstores, Incorporated, 26
Holland & Knight LLP, 60
Holland Burgerville USA, 44
The Holland Group, Inc., 82
Hollander Home Fashions Corp., 67
Holley Performance Products Inc., 52
Hollinger International Inc., 24
Holly Corporation, 12
Hollywood Casino Corporation, 21
Hollywood Entertainment Corporation, 25

Hollywood Media Corporation, 58
Hollywood Park, Inc., 20
Holme Roberts & Owen LLP, 28
Holnam Inc., 8; 39 (upd.)
Hologic, Inc., 106
Holophane Corporation, 19
Holson Burnes Group, Inc., 14
Holt and Bugbee Company, 66
Holt's Cigar Holdings, Inc., 42
Homasote Company, 72
Home Box Office Inc., 7; 23 (upd.); 76 (upd.)
The Home Depot, Inc., V; 18 (upd.); 97 (upd.)
The Home Insurance Company, III
Home Interiors & Gifts, Inc., 55
Home Products International, Inc., 55
Home Properties of New York, Inc., 42
Home Shopping Network, Inc., V; 25 (upd.)
HomeBase, Inc., 33 (upd.)
Homestake Mining Company, 12; 38 (upd.)
Hometown Auto Retailers, Inc., 44
HomeVestors of America, Inc., 77
HON INDUSTRIES Inc., 13
Honda Motor Company Limited, I; 10 (upd.); 29 (upd.)
Honeywell Inc., II; 12 (upd.); 50 (upd.)
Hooker Furniture Corporation, 80
Hooper Holmes, Inc., 22
Hooters of America, Inc., 18; 69 (upd.)
The Hoover Company, 12; 40 (upd.)
HOP, LLC, 80
Hops Restaurant Bar and Brewery, 46
Horace Mann Educators Corporation, 22; 90 (upd.)
Horizon Lines, Inc., 98
Horizon Organic Holding Corporation, 37
Hormel Foods Corporation, 18 (upd.); 54 (upd.)
Hornbeck Offshore Services, Inc., 101
Horsehead Industries, Inc., 51
Horseshoe Gaming Holding Corporation, 62
Horton Homes, Inc., 25
Horween Leather Company, 83
Hospira, Inc., 71
Hospital Central Services, Inc., 56
Hospital Corporation of America, III
Hospitality Franchise Systems, Inc., 11
Hospitality Worldwide Services, Inc., 26
Hoss's Steak and Sea House Inc., 68
Host America Corporation 79
Hot Stuff Foods, 85
Hot Topic, Inc., 33; 86 (upd.)
Houchens Industries Inc., 51
Houghton Mifflin Company, 10; 36 (upd.)
House of Fabrics, Inc., 21
Household International, Inc., II; 21 (upd.)
Houston Industries Incorporated, V
Houston Wire & Cable Company, 97
Hovnanian Enterprises, Inc., 29; 89 (upd.)
Howard Hughes Medical Institute, 39

Howard Johnson International, Inc., 17; 72 (upd.)
Howmet Corp., 12
HSN, 64 (upd.)
Hub Group, Inc., 38
Hub International Limited, 89
Hubbard Broadcasting Inc., 24; 79 (upd.)
Hubbell Inc., 9; 31 (upd.); 76 (upd.)
Huddle House Inc., 105
Hudson Foods Inc., 13
Hudson River Bancorp, Inc., 41
Huffy Corporation, 7; 30 (upd.)
Hughes Electronics Corporation, 25
Hughes Hubbard & Reed LLP, 44
Hughes Markets, Inc., 22
Hughes Supply, Inc., 14
Hulman & Company, 44
Human Factors International Inc., 100
Humana Inc., III; 24 (upd.); 101 (upd.)
The Humane Society of the United States, 54
Hummer Winblad Venture Partners, 97
Hungarian Telephone and Cable Corp., 75
Hungry Howie's Pizza and Subs, Inc., 25
Hunt Consolidated, Inc., 27 (upd.)
Hunt Manufacturing Company, 12
Hunt Oil Company, 7
Hunt-Wesson, Inc., 17
Hunter Fan Company, 13; 98 (upd.)
Huntington Bancshares Incorporated, 11; 87 (upd.)
Huntington Learning Centers, Inc., 55
Hunton & Williams, 35
Huntsman Corporation, 8; 98 (upd.)
Huron Consulting Group Inc., 87
Hutchinson Technology Incorporated, 18; 63 (upd.)
Huttig Building Products, Inc., 73
Hvide Marine Incorporated, 22
Hy-Vee, Inc., 36
Hyatt Corporation, III; 16 (upd.)
Hyde Athletic Industries, Inc., 17
Hydril Company, 46
Hypercom Corporation, 27
Hyperion Software Corporation, 22
Hyperion Solutions Corporation, 76
Hyster Company, 17
I.C. Isaacs & Company, 31
Iams Company, 26
IBERIABANK Corporation, 37
IBP, Inc., II; 21 (upd.)
IC Industries, Inc., I
ICF International, Inc., 28; 94 (upd.)
ICN Pharmaceuticals, Inc., 52
ICON Health & Fitness, Inc., 38; 102 (upd.)
ICU Medical, Inc., 106
Idaho Power Company, 12
IDB Communications Group, Inc., 11
Ideal Mortgage Bankers, Ltd., 105
Idealab, 105
Idearc Inc., 90
Identix Inc., 44
IDEO Inc., 65
IDEX Corp., 103
IDEXX Laboratories, Inc., 23
IDG Books Worldwide, Inc., 27

IdraPrince, Inc., 76
IDT Corporation, 34; 99 (upd.)
IDX Systems Corporation, 64
IEC Electronics Corp., 42
IGA, Inc., 99
Igloo Products Corp., 21; 105 (upd.)
IHOP Corporation, 17; 58 (upd.)
IHS Inc. 78
IKON Office Solutions, Inc., 50
Il Fornaio (America) Corporation, 27
Ilitch Holdings Inc., 37; 86 (upd.)
Illinois Bell Telephone Company, 14
Illinois Central Corporation, 11
Illinois Power Company, 6
Illinois Tool Works Inc., III; 22 (upd.); 81 (upd.)
Illumina, Inc., 93
Ikonics Corporation, 99
ILX Resorts Incorporated, 65
Image Entertainment, Inc., 94
Imagine Entertainment, 91
Imagine Foods, Inc., 50
Imation Corporation, 20
IMC Fertilizer Group, Inc., 8
ImClone Systems Inc., 58
IMCO Recycling, Incorporated, 32
IMG 78
Immucor, Inc., 81
Immunex Corporation, 14; 50 (upd.)
Imo Industries Inc., 7; 27 (upd.)
IMPATH Inc., 45
Imperial Holly Corporation, 12
Imperial Industries, Inc., 81
Imperial Sugar Company, 32 (upd.)
IMS Health, Inc., 57
In Focus Systems, Inc., 22
In-N-Out Burgers Inc., 19; 74 (upd.)
In-Sink-Erator, 66
InaCom Corporation, 13
Inamed Corporation 79
Incyte Genomics, Inc., 52
Indel Inc. 78
Indiana Bell Telephone Company, Incorporated, 14
Indiana Energy, Inc., 27
Indianapolis Motor Speedway Corporation, 46
Indus International Inc., 70
Industrial Services of America, Inc., 46
Infinity Broadcasting Corporation, 11; 48 (upd.)
InFocus Corporation, 92
Information Access Company, 17
Information Builders, Inc., 22
Information Holdings Inc., 47
Information Resources, Inc., 10
Informix Corporation, 10; 30 (upd.)
InfoSonics Corporation, 81
InfoSpace, Inc., 91
Ingalls Shipbuilding, Inc., 12
Ingersoll-Rand Company Ltd., III; 15 (upd.); 55 (upd.)
Ingles Markets, Inc., 20
Ingram Industries, Inc., 11; 49 (upd.)
Ingram Micro Inc., 52
Initial Security, 64
Inktomi Corporation, 45
Inland Container Corporation, 8

Inland Steel Industries, Inc., IV; 19 (upd.)
Innovative Solutions & Support, Inc., 85
Innovo Group Inc., 83
Input/Output, Inc., 73
Inserra Supermarkets, 25
Insight Enterprises, Inc., 18
Insilco Corporation, 16
Insituform Technologies, Inc., 83
Inso Corporation, 26
Instinet Corporation, 34
Insurance Auto Auctions, Inc., 23
Integra LifeSciences Holdings Corporation, 87
Integrated BioPharma, Inc., 83
Integrated Defense Technologies, Inc., 54
Integrity Inc., 44
Integrity Media, Inc., 102
Intel Corporation, II; 10 (upd.); 36 (upd.); 75 (upd.)
IntelliCorp, Inc., 45
Intelligent Electronics, Inc., 6
Inter Parfums Inc., 35; 86 (upd.)
Inter-Regional Financial Group, Inc., 15
Interactive Intelligence Inc., 106
Interbond Corporation of America, 101
Interbrand Corporation, 70
Interco Incorporated, III
IntercontinentalExchange, Inc., 95
InterDigital Communications Corporation, 61
Interep National Radio Sales Inc., 35
Interface, Inc., 8; 29 (upd.); 76 (upd.)
Intergraph Corporation, 6; 24 (upd.)
The Interlake Corporation, 8
Intermec Technologies Corporation, 72
INTERMET Corporation, 32, 77 (upd.)
Intermix Media, Inc., 83
Intermountain Health Care, Inc., 27
International Airline Support Group, Inc., 55
International Brotherhood of Teamsters, 37
International Business Machines Corporation, III; 6 (upd.); 30 (upd.); 63 (upd.)
International Controls Corporation, 10
International Creative Management, Inc., 43
International Dairy Queen, Inc., 10; 39 (upd.); 105 (upd.)
International Data Group, Inc., 7; 25 (upd.)
International Family Entertainment Inc., 13
International Flavors & Fragrances Inc., 9; 38 (upd.)
International Game Technology, 10; 41 (upd.)
International Lease Finance Corporation, 48
International Management Group, 18
International Multifoods Corporation, 7; 25 (upd.)
International Paper Company, IV; 15 (upd.); 47 (upd.); 97 (upd.)
International Profit Associates, Inc., 87
International Rectifier Corporation, 31; 71 (upd.)
International Shipbreaking Ltd. L.L.C., 67

International Shipholding Corporation, Inc., 27
International Speedway Corporation, 19; 74 (upd.)
International Telephone & Telegraph Corporation, I; 11 (upd.)
International Total Services, Inc., 37
Interpool, Inc., 92
The Interpublic Group of Companies, Inc., I; 22 (upd.); 75 (upd.)
Interscope Music Group, 31
Intersil Corporation, 93
Interstate Bakeries Corporation, 12; 38 (upd.)
Interstate Hotels & Resorts Inc., 58
InterVideo, Inc., 85
Intevac, Inc., 92
Intimate Brands, Inc., 24
Intrado Inc., 63
Intuit Inc., 14; 33 (upd.); 73 (upd.)
Intuitive Surgical, Inc. 79
Invacare Corporation, 11; 47 (upd.)
inVentiv Health, Inc., 81
The Inventure Group, Inc., 96 (upd.)
Inverness Medical Innovations, Inc., 63
Invitrogen Corporation, 52
Invivo Corporation, 52
Iomega Corporation, 21
Ionatron, Inc., 85
Ionics, Incorporated, 52
Iowa Telecommunications Services, Inc., 85
IPALCO Enterprises, Inc., 6
Ipsen International Inc., 72
Irex Contracting Group, 90
IRIS International, Inc., 101
iRobot Corporation, 83
Iron Mountain, Inc., 33; 104 (upd.)
Irvin Feld & Kenneth Feld Productions, Inc., 15
Irwin Financial Corporation, 77
The Island ECN, Inc., 48
Isle of Capri Casinos, Inc., 41
Ispat Inland Inc., 40 (upd.)
ITC Holdings Corp., 75
Itel Corporation, 9
Items International Airwalk Inc., 17
Itron, Inc., 64
ITT Educational Services, Inc., 33; 76 (upd.)
ITT Sheraton Corporation, III
i2 Technologies, Inc., 87
Ivar's, Inc., 86
IVAX Corporation, 11; 55 (upd.)
IVC Industries, Inc., 45
iVillage Inc., 46
Iwerks Entertainment, Inc., 34
IXC Communications, Inc., 29
J & J Snack Foods Corporation, 24
J&R Electronics Inc., 26
J. & W. Seligman & Co. Inc., 61
J. Alexander's Corporation, 65
J. Baker, Inc., 31
J. Crew Group. Inc., 12; 34 (upd.); 88 (upd.)
J. C. Penney Company, Inc., V; 18 (upd.); 43 (upd.); 91 (upd.)
J. D'Addario & Company, Inc., 48

The J. Jill Group, Inc., 35; 90 (upd.)
J.A. Jones, Inc., 16
J.B. Hunt Transport Services Inc., 12
J.D. Edwards & Company, 14
J.D. Power and Associates, 32
J.F. Shea Co., Inc., 55
J.H. Findorff and Son, Inc., 60
J.I. Case Company, 10
J.J. Keller & Associates, Inc., 81
J.L. Hammett Company, 72
J. Lohr Winery Corporation, 99
The J. M. Smucker Company, 11; 87 (upd.)
J.P. Morgan Chase & Co., II; 30 (upd.); 38 (upd.)
The J. Paul Getty Trust, 105
J.R. Simplot Company, 16; 60 (upd.)
J. W. Pepper and Son Inc., 86
Jabil Circuit, Inc., 36; 88 (upd.)
Jack B. Kelley, Inc., 102
Jack Henry and Associates, Inc., 17; 94 (upd.)
Jack in the Box Inc., 89 (upd.)
Jack Morton Worldwide, 88
Jack Schwartz Shoes, Inc., 18
Jackpot Enterprises Inc., 21
Jackson Hewitt, Inc., 48
Jackson National Life Insurance Company, 8
Jacmar Companies, 87
Jaco Electronics, Inc., 30
Jacob Leinenkugel Brewing Company, 28
Jacobs Engineering Group Inc., 6; 26 (upd.); 106 (upd.)
Jacobson Stores Inc., 21
Jacor Communications, Inc., 23
Jacuzzi Brands Inc., 76 (upd.)
Jacuzzi Inc., 23
JAKKS Pacific, Inc., 52
Jalate Inc., 25
Jamba Juice Company, 47
James Avery Craftsman, Inc., 76
James Original Coney Island Inc., 84
James River Corporation of Virginia, IV
Jani-King International, Inc., 85
JanSport, Inc., 70
Janus Capital Group Inc., 57
Jarden Corporation, 93 (upd.)
Jason Incorporated, 23
Jay Jacobs, Inc., 15
Jayco Inc., 13
Jays Foods, Inc., 90
Jazz Basketball Investors, Inc., 55
Jazzercise, Inc., 45
JB Oxford Holdings, Inc., 32
JDA Software Group, Inc., 101
JDS Uniphase Corporation, 34
JE Dunn Construction Group, Inc., 85
Jean-Georges Enterprises L.L.C., 75
Jefferies Group, Inc., 25
Jefferson-Pilot Corporation, 11; 29 (upd.)
Jel Sert Company, 90
Jeld-Wen, Inc., 45
Jelly Belly Candy Company, 76
Jenkens & Gilchrist, P.C., 65
Jennie-O Turkey Store, Inc., 76
Jennifer Convertibles, Inc., 31

Jenny Craig, Inc., 10; 29 (upd.); 92 (upd.)
Jeppesen Sanderson, Inc., 92
Jerry's Famous Deli Inc., 24
Jersey Mike's Franchise Systems, Inc., 83
Jervis B. Webb Company, 24
JetBlue Airways Corporation, 44
Jetro Cash & Carry Enterprises Inc., 38
Jewett-Cameron Trading Company, Ltd., 89
JG Industries, Inc., 15
Jillian's Entertainment Holdings, Inc., 40
Jim Beam Brands Worldwide, Inc., 14; 58 (upd.)
The Jim Henson Company, 23; 106 (upd.)
Jimmy John's Enterprises, Inc., 103
Jitney-Jungle Stores of America, Inc., 27
JKH Holding Co. LLC, 105
JLG Industries, Inc., 52
JLM Couture, Inc., 64
JM Smith Corporation, 100
JMB Realty Corporation, IV
Jo-Ann Stores, Inc., 72 (upd.)
Jockey International, Inc., 12; 34 (upd.); 77 (upd.)
Joe's Sports & Outdoor, 98 (upd.)
The Joffrey Ballet of Chicago 52
Johanna Foods, Inc., 104
John B. Sanfilippo & Son, Inc., 14; 101 (upd.)
The John D. and Catherine T. MacArthur Foundation, 34
John D. Brush Company Inc., 94
John F. Kennedy Center for the Performing Arts, 106
John Frieda Professional Hair Care Inc., 70
John H. Harland Company, 17
John Hancock Financial Services, Inc., III; 42 (upd.)
The John Nuveen Company, 21
John Paul Mitchell Systems, 24
John Q. Hammons Hotels, Inc., 24
John W. Danforth Company, 48
John Wiley & Sons, Inc., 17; 65 (upd.)
Johnny Rockets Group, Inc., 31; 76 (upd.)
Johns Manville Corporation, 64 (upd.)
Johnson & Higgins, 14
Johnson & Johnson, III; 8 (upd.); 36 (upd.); 75 (upd.)
Johnson Controls, Inc., III; 26 (upd.); 59 (upd.)
Johnson Outdoors Inc., 28; 84 (upd.)
Johnson Publishing Company, Inc., 28; 72 (upd.)
Johnsonville Sausage L.L.C., 63
Johnston Industries, Inc., 15
Johnstown America Industries, Inc., 23
Jones Apparel Group, Inc., 11; 39 (upd.)
Jones, Day, Reavis & Pogue, 33
Jones Intercable, Inc., 21
Jones Knowledge Group, Inc., 97
Jones Lang LaSalle Incorporated, 49
Jones Medical Industries, Inc., 24
Jones Soda Co., 69
Jordache Enterprises, Inc., 23

The Jordan Company LP, 70
Jordan Industries, Inc., 36
Jordan-Kitt Music Inc., 86
Jordano's, Inc., 102
Jos. A. Bank Clothiers, Inc., 31; 104 (upd.)
Joseph T. Ryerson & Son, Inc., 15
Jostens, Inc., 7; 25 (upd.); 73 (upd.)
JOULÉ Inc., 58
Journal Communications, Inc., 86
Journal Register Company, 29
Joy Global Inc., 104 (upd.)
JPI, 49
JPMorgan Chase & Co., 91 (upd.)
JPS Textile Group, Inc., 28
JTH Tax Inc., 103
j2 Global Communications, Inc., 75
Juicy Couture, Inc., 80
The Judge Group, Inc., 51
Juniper Networks, Inc., 43
Juno Lighting, Inc., 30
Juno Online Services, Inc., 38
Jupitermedia Corporation, 75
Just Bagels Manufacturing, Inc., 94
Just Born, Inc., 32
Just For Feet, Inc., 19
Justin Industries, Inc., 19
JWP Inc., 9
JWT Group Inc., I
K & B Inc., 12
K & G Men's Center, Inc., 21
K'Nex Industries, Inc., 52
K-Swiss, Inc., 33; 89 (upd.)
K-tel International, Inc., 21
Kadant Inc., 96 (upd.)
Kaiser Aluminum Corporation, IV; 84 (upd.)
Kaiser Foundation Health Plan, Inc., 53
Kal Kan Foods, Inc., 22
Kaman Corporation, 12; 42 (upd.)
Kaman Music Corporation, 68
Kampgrounds of America, Inc. 33
Kana Software, Inc., 51
Kansas City Power & Light Company, 6
Kansas City Southern Industries, Inc., 6; 26 (upd.)
The Kansas City Southern Railway Company, 92
Kaplan, Inc., 42; 90 (upd.)
Kar Nut Products Company, 86
Karl Kani Infinity, Inc., 49
Karsten Manufacturing Corporation, 51
Kash n' Karry Food Stores, Inc., 20
Kashi Company, 89
Kasper A.S.L., Ltd., 40
kate spade LLC, 68
Katy Industries, Inc., I; 51 (upd.)
Katz Communications, Inc., 6
Katz Media Group, Inc., 35
Kaufman and Broad Home Corporation, 8
Kaydon Corporation, 18
KB Home, 45 (upd.)
KB Toys, 15; 35 (upd.); 86 (upd.)
KBR Inc., 106 (upd.)
Keane, Inc., 56
Keebler Foods Company, 36
The Keith Companies Inc., 54

Keithley Instruments Inc., 16
Kelley Blue Book Company, Inc., 84
Kelley Drye & Warren LLP, 40
Kellogg Brown & Root, Inc., 62 (upd.)
Kellogg Company, II; 13 (upd.); 50 (upd.)
Kellwood Company, 8; 85 (upd.)
Kelly Services Inc., 6; 26 (upd.)
Kelly-Moore Paint Company, Inc., 56
The Kelly-Springfield Tire Company, 8
Kelsey-Hayes Group of Companies, 7; 27 (upd.)
Kemet Corp., 14
Kemper Corporation, III; 15 (upd.)
Kemps LLC, 103
Ken's Foods, Inc., 88
Kendall International, Inc., 11
Kendall-Jackson Winery, Ltd., 28
Kendle International Inc., 87
Kenetech Corporation, 11
Kenexa Corporation, 87
Kenmore Air Harbor Inc., 65
Kennametal Inc., 68 (upd.)
Kennedy-Wilson, Inc., 60
Kenneth Cole Productions, Inc., 25
Kensey Nash Corporation, 71
Kensington Publishing Corporation, 84
Kent Electronics Corporation, 17
Kentucky Electric Steel, Inc., 31
Kentucky Utilities Company, 6
Kerasotes ShowPlace Theaters LLC, 80
Kerr Group Inc., 24
Kerr-McGee Corporation, IV; 22 (upd.); 68 (upd.)
Ketchum Communications Inc., 6
Kettle Foods Inc., 48
Kewaunee Scientific Corporation, 25
Key Safety Systems, Inc., 63
Key Tronic Corporation, 14
Key Technology Inc., 106
KeyCorp, 8; 93 (upd.)
Keyes Fibre Company, 9
Keynote Systems Inc., 102
Keys Fitness Products, LP, 83
KeySpan Energy Co., 27
Keystone International, Inc., 11
KFC Corporation, 7; 21 (upd.); 89 (upd.)
Kforce Inc., 71
KI, 57
Kidde, Inc., I
Kiehl's Since 1851, Inc., 52
Kolmar Laboratories Group, 96
Lewis Drug Inc., 94
Lifetouch Inc., 86
LifeWise Health Plan of Oregon, Inc., 90
Kikkoman Corporation, 47 (upd.)
Kimball International, Inc., 12; 48 (upd.)
Kimberly-Clark Corporation, III; 16 (upd.); 43 (upd.); 105 (upd.)
Kimco Realty Corporation, 11
Kimpton Hotel & Restaurant Group, Inc., 105
Kinder Morgan, Inc., 45
KinderCare Learning Centers, Inc., 13
Kinetic Concepts, Inc. (KCI), 20
King & Spalding, 23
The King Arthur Flour Company, 31
King Kullen Grocery Co., Inc., 15

King Nut Company, 74
King Pharmaceuticals, Inc., 54
King Ranch, Inc., 14; 60 (upd.)
King World Productions, Inc., 9; 30 (upd.)
King's Hawaiian Bakery West, Inc., 101
Kingston Technology Corporation, 20
Kinko's, Inc., 16; 43 (upd.)
Kinney Shoe Corp., 14
Kinray Inc., 85
Kintera, Inc., 75
Kirby Corporation, 18; 66 (upd.)
Kirkland & Ellis LLP, 65
Kirlin's Inc., 98
Kirshenbaum Bond + Partners, Inc., 57
Kit Manufacturing Co., 18
Kitchell Corporation, 14
KitchenAid, 8
Kitty Hawk, Inc., 22
Kiva, 95
Kiwi International Airlines Inc., 20
KLA-Tencor Corporation, 11; 45 (upd.)
Klasky Csupo Inc. 78
Klein Tools, Inc., 95
Kleiner, Perkins, Caufield & Byers, 53
Klement's Sausage Company, 61
Kmart Corporation, V; 18 (upd.); 47 (upd.)
KMG Chemicals, Inc., 101
Knape & Vogt Manufacturing Company, 17
Knight Ridder, Inc., 67 (upd.)
Knight Trading Group, Inc., 70
Knight Transportation, Inc., 64
Knight-Ridder, Inc., IV; 15 (upd.)
Knoll, Inc., 14; 80 (upd.)
The Knot, Inc., 74
Knott's Berry Farm, 18
Knouse Foods Cooperative Inc., 102
Knowledge Learning Corporation, 51
Knowledge Universe, Inc., 54
KnowledgeWare Inc., 9; 31 (upd.)
Koala Corporation, 44
Kobrand Corporation, 82
Koch Enterprises, Inc., 29
Koch Industries, Inc., IV; 20 (upd.); 77 (upd.)
Kohl's Corporation, 9; 30 (upd.); 77 (upd.)
Kohlberg Kravis Roberts & Co., 24; 56 (upd.)
Kohler Company, 7; 32 (upd.)
Kohn Pedersen Fox Associates P.C., 57
The Koll Company, 8
Kollmorgen Corporation, 18
Komag, Inc., 11
Koo Koo Roo, Inc., 25
Kopin Corporation, 80
Koppers Industries, Inc., I; 26 (upd.)
Koret of California, Inc., 62
Korn/Ferry International, 34; 102 (upd.)
Kos Pharmaceuticals, Inc., 63
Koss Corporation, 38
Kraft Foods Inc., II; 7 (upd.); 45 (upd.); 91 (upd.)
KraftMaid Cabinetry, Inc., 72
Kraus-Anderson Companies, Inc., 36; 83 (upd.)

Krause Publications, Inc., 35
Krause's Furniture, Inc., 27
Kreisler Manufacturing Corporation, 97
Krispy Kreme Doughnuts, Inc., 21; 61 (upd.)
The Kroger Company, II; 15 (upd.); 65 (upd.)
Kroll Inc., 57
Kronos, Inc., 18; 100 (upd.)
Kruse International, 88
The Krystal Company, 33
K2 Inc., 16; 84 (upd.)
KU Energy Corporation, 11
Kuhlman Corporation, 20
Kulicke and Soffa Industries, Inc., 33; 76 (upd.)
Kurzweil Technologies, Inc., 51
The Kushner-Locke Company, 25
Kyphon Inc., 87
L-3 Communications Holdings, Inc., 48
L. and J.G. Stickley, Inc., 50
L. Foppiano Wine Co., 101
L. Luria & Son, Inc., 19
L.A. Darling Company, 92
L.A. Gear, Inc., 8; 32 (upd.)
L.A. T Sportswear, Inc., 26
L.B. Foster Company, 33
L.L. Bean, Inc., 10; 38 (upd.); 91 (upd.)
The L.L. Knickerbocker Co., Inc., 25
L. M. Berry and Company, 80
L.S. Starrett Company, 13; 64 (upd.)
La Choy Food Products Inc., 25
La Madeleine French Bakery & Café, 33
The La Quinta Companies, 11; 42 (upd.)
La Reina Inc., 96
La-Z-Boy Incorporated, 14; 50 (upd.)
Lab Safety Supply, Inc., 102
LaBarge Inc., 41
LabOne, Inc., 48
Labor Ready, Inc., 29; 88 (upd.)
Laboratory Corporation of America Holdings, 42 (upd.)
LaBranche & Co. Inc., 37
Lacks Enterprises Inc., 61
Laclede Steel Company, 15
LaCrosse Footwear, Inc., 18; 61 (upd.)
LADD Furniture, Inc., 12
Ladish Co., Inc., 30
Lafarge Corporation, 28
Laidlaw International, Inc., 80
Lakeland Industries, Inc., 45
Lakes Entertainment, Inc., 51
Lakeside Foods, Inc., 89
Lam Research Corporation, 11; 31 (upd.)
Lamar Advertising Company, 27; 70 (upd.)
The Lamaur Corporation, 41
Lamb Weston, Inc., 23
Lambda Legal Defense and Education Fund, Inc., 106
Lamonts Apparel, Inc., 15
The Lamson & Sessions Co., 13; 61 (upd.)
Lancair International, Inc., 67
Lancaster Colony Corporation, 8; 61 (upd.)
Lance, Inc., 14; 41 (upd.)
Lancer Corporation, 21

Land O'Lakes, Inc., II; 21 (upd.); 81 (upd.)
LandAmerica Financial Group, Inc., 85
Landauer, Inc., 51
Landec Corporation, 95
Landmark Communications, Inc., 12; 55 (upd.)
Landmark Theatre Corporation, 70
Landor Associates, 81
Landry's Restaurants, Inc., 65 (upd.)
Landry's Seafood Restaurants, Inc., 15
Lands' End, Inc., 9; 29 (upd.); 82 (upd.)
Landstar System, Inc., 63
Lane Bryant, Inc., 64
The Lane Co., Inc., 12
Lanier Worldwide, Inc., 75
Lanoga Corporation, 62
Larry Flynt Publishing Inc., 31
Larry H. Miller Group of Companies, 29; 104 (upd.)
Las Vegas Sands Corp., 50; 106 (upd.)
Laserscope, 67
Lason, Inc., 31
Latham & Watkins, 33
Latrobe Brewing Company, 54
Lattice Semiconductor Corp., 16
Lawson Software, 38
Lawter International Inc., 14
Layne Christensen Company, 19
Lazare Kaplan International Inc., 21
Lazy Days RV Center, Inc., 69
LCA-Vision, 85
LCC International, Inc., 84
LCI International, Inc., 16
LDB Corporation, 53
LDDS-Metro Communications, Inc., 8
LDI Ltd., LLC, 76
Leap Wireless International, Inc., 69
LeapFrog Enterprises, Inc., 54
Lear Corporation, 71 (upd.)
Lear Seating Corporation, 16
Lear Siegler, Inc., I
Learjet Inc., 8; 27 (upd.)
Learning Care Group, Inc., 76 (upd.)
The Learning Company Inc., 24
Learning Tree International Inc., 24
LeaRonal, Inc., 23
Leaseway Transportation Corp., 12
Leatherman Tool Group, Inc., 51
Lebhar-Friedman, Inc., 55
LeBoeuf, Lamb, Greene & MacRae, L.L.P., 29
LECG Corporation, 93
Lechmere Inc., 10
Lechters, Inc., 11; 39 (upd.)
LeCroy Corporation, 41
Lee Apparel Company, Inc., 8
Lee Enterprises Inc., 11; 64 (upd.)
Leeann Chin, Inc., 30
Lefrak Organization Inc., 26
The Legal Aid Society, 48
Legal Sea Foods Inc., 96
Legent Corporation, 10
Legg Mason, Inc., 33
Leggett & Platt, Inc., 11; 48 (upd.)
Lehigh Portland Cement Company, 23
Lehman Brothers Holdings Inc., 99 (upd.)
Leidy's, Inc., 93

Leiner Health Products Inc., 34
LendingTree, LLC, 93
Lennar Corporation, 11
Lennox International Inc., 8; 28 (upd.)
Lenovo Group Ltd., 80
Lenox, Inc., 12
LensCrafters Inc., 23; 76 (upd.)
Leo Burnett Company Inc., I; 20 (upd.)
The Leona Group LLC, 84
Leprino Foods Company, 28
Les Schwab Tire Centers, 50
Lesco Inc., 19
The Leslie Fay Companies, Inc., 8; 39 (upd.)
Leslie's Poolmart, Inc., 18
Leucadia National Corporation, 11; 71 (upd.)
Leupold & Stevens, Inc., 52
Level 3 Communications, Inc., 67
Levenger Company, 63
Lever Brothers Company, 9
Levi, Ray & Shoup, Inc., 96
Levi Strauss & Co., V; 16 (upd.); 102 (upd.)
Levitz Furniture Inc., 15
Levy Restaurants L.P., 26
The Lewin Group Inc., 104
Lewis Galoob Toys Inc., 16
Lewis-Goetz and Company, Inc., 102
LEXIS-NEXIS Group, 33
Lexmark International, Inc., 18; 79 (upd.)
LG&E Energy Corporation, 6; 51 (upd.)
Libbey Inc., 49
The Liberty Corporation, 22
Liberty Livewire Corporation, 42
Liberty Media Corporation, 50
Liberty Mutual Holding Company, 59
Liberty Orchards Co., Inc., 89
Liberty Property Trust, 57
Liberty Travel, Inc., 56
Life Care Centers of America Inc., 76
Life is Good, Inc., 80
Life Technologies, Inc., 17
Life Time Fitness, Inc., 66
LifeCell Corporation, 77
Lifeline Systems, Inc., 53
LifeLock, Inc., 91
LifePoint Hospitals, Inc., 69
Lifetime Brands, Inc., 73 (upd.)
Lifetime Entertainment Services, 51
Lifetime Hoan Corporation, 27
Lifeway Foods, Inc., 65
Ligand Pharmaceuticals Incorporated, 47
Lillian Vernon Corporation, 12; 35 (upd.); 92 (upd.)
Lilly Endowment Inc., 70
The Limited, Inc., V; 20 (upd.)
LIN Broadcasting Corp., 9
Lincare Holdings Inc., 43
Lincoln Center for the Performing Arts, Inc., 69
Lincoln Electric Co., 13
Lincoln National Corporation, III; 25 (upd.)
Lincoln Property Company, 8; 54 (upd.)
Lincoln Snacks Company, 24
Lincoln Telephone & Telegraph Company, 14

Lindal Cedar Homes, Inc., 29
Lindsay Manufacturing Co., 20
Linear Technology Corporation, 16; 99 (upd.)
Linens 'n Things, Inc., 24; 75 (upd.)
LinkedIn Corporation, 103
Lintas: Worldwide, 14
The Lion Brewery, Inc., 86
Lionel L.L.C., 16; 99 (upd.)
Liqui-Box Corporation, 16
Liquidity Services, Inc., 101
Liquidnet, Inc. 79
Litehouse Inc., 60
Lithia Motors, Inc., 41
Littelfuse, Inc., 26
Little Caesar Enterprises, Inc., 7; 24 (upd.)
Little Tikes Company, 13; 62 (upd.)
Littleton Coin Company Inc., 82
Litton Industries, Inc., I; 11 (upd.)
LIVE Entertainment Inc., 20
Live Nation, Inc., 80 (upd.)
LivePerson, Inc., 91
Liz Claiborne Inc., 8; 25 (upd.); 102 (upd.)
LKQ Corporation, 71
Lockheed Martin Corporation, I; 11 (upd.); 15 (upd.); 89 (upd.)
Loctite Corporation, 8; 30 (upd.)
Lodge Manufacturing Company, 103
LodgeNet Interactive Corporation, 28; 106 (upd.)
Loehmann's Inc., 24
Loews Corporation, I; 12 (upd.); 36 (upd.); 93 (upd.)
Logan's Roadhouse, Inc., 29
Logicon Inc., 20
LoJack Corporation, 48
London Fog Industries, Inc., 29
Lone Star Steakhouse & Saloon, Inc., 51
The Long & Foster Companies, Inc., 85
Long Island Bancorp, Inc., 16
Long Island Power Authority, V; 102 (upd.)
The Long Island Rail Road Company, 68
Long John Silver's, 13; 57 (upd.)
The Longaberger Company, 12; 44 (upd.)
Longs Drug Stores Corporation, V; 25 (upd.); 83 (upd.)
Longview Fibre Company, 8; 37 (upd.)
Loos & Dilworth, Inc., 100
Loral Space & Communications Ltd., 8; 9; 54 (upd.)
Los Angeles Turf Club Inc., 102
Lost Arrow Inc., 22
LOT$OFF Corporation, 24
Lotus Development Corporation, 6; 25 (upd.)
LOUD Technologies, Inc., 95 (upd.)
The Louis Berger Group, Inc., 104
The Louisiana Land and Exploration Company, 7
Louisiana-Pacific Corporation, IV; 31 (upd.)
Love's Travel Stops & Country Stores, Inc., 71
Lowe's Companies, Inc., V; 21 (upd.); 81 (upd.)

Lowrance Electronics, Inc., 18
LPA Holding Corporation, 81
LSB Industries, Inc., 77
LSI Logic Corporation, 13; 64
The LTV Corporation, I; 24 (upd.)
The Lubrizol Corporation, I; 30 (upd.); 83 (upd.)
Luby's, Inc., 17; 42 (upd.); 99 (upd.)
Lucasfilm Ltd., 12; 50 (upd.)
Lucent Technologies Inc., 34
Lucille Farms, Inc., 45
Lucky Stores, Inc., 27
Lufkin Industries Inc. 78
Luigino's, Inc., 64
Lukens Inc., 14
Lunar Corporation, 29
Lunardi's Super Market, Inc., 99
Lund Food Holdings, Inc., 22
Lund International Holdings, Inc., 40
Lutheran Brotherhood, 31
Lydall, Inc., 64
Lyman-Richey Corporation, 96
Lynch Corporation, 43
Lynden Incorporated, 91
Lyondell Chemical Company, IV; 45 (upd.)
M&F Worldwide Corp., 38
M. Shanken Communications, Inc., 50
M.A. Bruder & Sons, Inc., 56
M.A. Gedney Co., 51
M.A. Hanna Company, 8
M.H. Meyerson & Co., Inc., 46
M.R. Beal and Co., 102
Mac Frugal's Bargains - Closeouts Inc., 17
Mac-Gray Corporation, 44
MacAndrews & Forbes Holdings Inc., 28; 86 (upd.)
MacDermid Incorporated, 32
Mace Security International, Inc., 57
The Macerich Company, 57
MacGregor Golf Company, 68
Mack Trucks, Inc., I; 22 (upd.); 61 (upd.)
Mack-Cali Realty Corporation, 42
Mackay Envelope Corporation, 45
Mackie Designs Inc., 33
Macklowe Properties, Inc., 95
Macmillan, Inc., 7
MacNeil/Lehrer Productions, 87
The MacNeal-Schwendler Corporation, 25
Macromedia, Inc., 50
Macrovision Solutions Corporation, 101
Macy's, Inc., 94 (upd.)
Madden's on Gull Lake, 52
Madelaine Chocolate Novelties, Inc., 104
Madison Dearborn Partners, LLC, 97
Madison Gas and Electric Company, 39
Madison-Kipp Corporation, 58
Mag Instrument, Inc., 67
MaggieMoo's International, 89
Magma Copper Company, 7
Magma Design Automation Inc. 78
Magma Power Company, 11
MagneTek, Inc., 15; 41 (upd.)
MAI Systems Corporation, 11
Maid-Rite Corporation, 62
Maidenform, Inc., 20; 59 (upd.)
Mail Boxes Etc., 18; 41 (upd.)
Mail-Well, Inc., 28

Make-A-Wish Foundation of America, 97
Maine & Maritimes Corporation, 56
Maine Central Railroad Company, 16
Maines Paper & Food Service Inc., 71
Majesco Entertainment Company, 85
The Major Automotive Companies, Inc., 45
Malcolm Pirnie, Inc., 42
Malden Mills Industries, Inc., 16
Mallinckrodt Group Inc., 19
Malt-O-Meal Company, 22; 63 (upd.)
Mammoth Mountain Ski Area, 101
Management and Training Corporation, 28
Manatron, Inc., 86
Mandalay Resort Group, 32 (upd.)
Manhattan Associates, Inc., 67
Manhattan Group, LLC, 80
Manheim, 88
The Manitowoc Company, Inc., 18; 59 (upd.)
Mannatech Inc., 33
Manning Selvage & Lee (MS&L), 76
MannKind Corporation, 87
Manor Care, Inc., 6; 25 (upd.)
Manpower Inc., 9; 30 (upd.); 73 (upd.)
ManTech International Corporation, 97
Manufactured Home Communities, Inc., 22
Manufacturers Hanover Corporation, II
Manville Corporation, III; 7 (upd.)
MAPCO Inc., IV
MAPICS, Inc., 55
Maple Grove Farms of Vermont, 88
Maples Industries, Inc., 83
Marble Slab Creamery, Inc., 87
Marc Ecko Enterprises, Inc., 105
March of Dimes, 31
Marchex, Inc., 72
marchFIRST, Inc., 34
Marco Business Products, Inc., 75
Marco's Franchising LLC, 86
The Marcus Corporation, 21
Marie Callender's Restaurant & Bakery, Inc., 28
Marine Products Corporation, 75
MarineMax, Inc., 30
Mariner Energy, Inc., 101
Marion Laboratories, Inc., I
Marisa Christina, Inc., 15
Maritz Inc., 38
Mark IV Industries, Inc., 7; 28 (upd.)
Mark T. Wendell Tea Company, 94
The Mark Travel Corporation, 80
Marks Brothers Jewelers, Inc., 24
Marlin Business Services Corp., 89
The Marmon Group, Inc., IV; 16 (upd.); 70 (upd.)
Marquette Electronics, Inc., 13
Marriott International, Inc., III; 21 (upd.); 83 (upd.)
Mars, Incorporated, 7; 40 (upd.)
Mars Petcare US Inc., 96
Marsh & McLennan Companies, Inc., III; 45 (upd.)
Marsh Supermarkets, Inc., 17; 76 (upd.)
Marshall & Ilsley Corporation, 56
Marshall Field's, 63

Marshalls Incorporated, 13
Marshfield Clinic Inc., 82
Martek Biosciences Corporation, 65
Marten Transport, Ltd., 84
Martha Stewart Living Omnimedia, Inc.,
  24; 73 (upd.)
Martha White Foods Inc., 104
Martignetti Companies, 84
Martin Franchises, Inc., 80
Martin Industries, Inc., 44
Martin Marietta Corporation, I
Martin's Super Markets, Inc., 101
MartinLogan, Ltd., 85
Martz Group, 56
Marvel Entertainment Inc., 10; 78 (upd.)
Marvelous Market Inc., 104
Marvin Lumber & Cedar Company, 22
Mary Kay Inc., 9; 30 (upd.); 84 (upd.)
Maryland & Virginia Milk Producers
  Cooperative Association, Inc., 80
Maryville Data Systems Inc., 96
The Maschhoffs, Inc., 82
Masco Corporation, III; 20 (upd.); 39
  (upd.)
Mashantucket Pequot Gaming Enterprise
  Inc., 35
Masland Corporation, 17
Massachusetts Mutual Life Insurance
  Company, III; 53 (upd.)
Massey Energy Company, 57
MasTec, Inc., 19; 55 (upd.)
Master Lock Company, 45
Master Spas Inc., 105
MasterBrand Cabinets, Inc., 71
MasterCard Worldwide, 9; 96 (upd.)
MasterCraft Boat Company, Inc., 90
Match.com, LP, 87
Material Sciences Corporation, 63
The MathWorks, Inc., 80
Matria Healthcare, Inc., 17
Matrix Essentials Inc., 90
Matrix Service Company, 65
Matrixx Initiatives, Inc., 74
Matt Prentice Restaurant Group, 70
Mattel, Inc., 7; 25 (upd.); 61 (upd.)
Matthews International Corporation, 29;
  77 (upd.)
Mattress Giant Corporation, 103
Maui Land & Pineapple Company, Inc.,
  29; 100 (upd.)
Maui Wowi, Inc., 85
Mauna Loa Macadamia Nut Corporation,
  64
Maurices Inc., 95
Maverick Ranch Association, Inc., 88
Maverick Tube Corporation, 59
Maverik, Inc., 103
Max & Erma's Restaurants Inc., 19; 100
  (upd.)
Maxco Inc., 17
Maxicare Health Plans, Inc., III; 25 (upd.)
The Maxim Group, 25
Maxim Integrated Products, Inc., 16
MAXIMUS, Inc., 43
Maxtor Corporation, 10
Maxus Energy Corporation, 7
Maxwell Shoe Company, Inc., 30
MAXXAM Inc., 8

Maxxim Medical Inc., 12
The May Department Stores Company, V;
  19 (upd.); 46 (upd.)
Mayer, Brown, Rowe & Maw, 47
Mayfield Dairy Farms, Inc., 74
Mayflower Group Inc., 6
Mayo Foundation, 9; 34 (upd.)
Mayor's Jewelers, Inc., 41
Maytag Corporation, III; 22 (upd.); 82
  (upd.)
Mazel Stores, Inc., 29
Mazzio's Corporation, 76
MBC Holding Company, 40
MBIA Inc., 73
MBNA Corporation, 12; 33 (upd.)
MCA Inc., II
McAfee Inc., 94
McAlister's Corporation, 66
McCarthy Building Companies, Inc., 48
McCaw Cellular Communications, Inc., 6
McClain Industries, Inc., 51
The McClatchy Company, 33; 92 (upd.)
McCormick & Company, Incorporated, 7;
  27 (upd.)
McCormick & Schmick's Seafood
  Restaurants, Inc., 71
McCoy Corporation, 58
McDATA Corporation, 75
McDermott International, Inc., III; 37
  (upd.)
McDonald's Corporation, II; 7 (upd.); 26
  (upd.); 63 (upd.)
McDonnell Douglas Corporation, I; 11
  (upd.)
McGrath RentCorp, 91
The McGraw-Hill Companies, Inc., IV;
  18 (upd.); 51 (upd.)
MCI WorldCom, Inc., V; 27 (upd.)
McIlhenny Company, 20
McJunkin Corporation, 63
McKee Foods Corporation, 7; 27 (upd.)
McKesson Corporation, I; 12; 47 (upd.)
McKinsey & Company, Inc., 9
McLanahan Corporation, 104
McLane Company, Inc., 13
McLeodUSA Incorporated, 32
McMenamins Pubs and Breweries, 65
McMurry, Inc., 105
McNaughton Apparel Group, Inc., 92
  (upd.)
MCN Corporation, 6
MCSi, Inc., 41
McWane Corporation, 55
MDU Resources Group, Inc., 7; 42 (upd.)
The Mead Corporation, IV; 19 (upd.)
Mead Data Central, Inc., 10
Mead Johnson & Company, 84
Meade Instruments Corporation, 41
Meadowcraft, Inc., 29; 100 (upd.)
MeadWestvaco Corporation, 76 (upd.)
Measurement Specialties, Inc., 71
Mecklermedia Corporation, 24
Medarex, Inc., 85
Medco Containment Services Inc., 9
MEDecision, Inc., 95
Media Arts Group, Inc., 42
Media General, Inc., 7; 38 (upd.)
Media Sciences International, Inc., 104

Mediacom Communications Corporation,
  69
MediaNews Group, Inc., 70
Medicine Shoppe International, Inc., 102
Medical Action Industries Inc., 101
Medical Information Technology Inc., 64
Medical Management International, Inc.,
  65
Medical Staffing Network Holdings, Inc.,
  89
Medicis Pharmaceutical Corporation, 59
Medifast, Inc., 97
MedImmune, Inc., 35
Medis Technologies Ltd., 77
Meditrust, 11
Medline Industries, Inc., 61
Medtronic, Inc., 8; 30 (upd.); 67 (upd.)
Medusa Corporation, 24
Megafoods Stores Inc., 13
Meguiar's, Inc., 99
Meier & Frank Co., 23
Meijer, Inc., 7; 27 (upd.); 101 (upd.)
Mel Farr Automotive Group, 20
Melaleuca Inc., 31
Melamine Chemicals, Inc., 27
Mellon Bank Corporation, II
Mellon Financial Corporation, 44 (upd.)
Mellon-Stuart Company, I
The Melting Pot Restaurants, Inc., 74
Melville Corporation, V
Melvin Simon and Associates, Inc., 8
MEMC Electronic Materials, Inc., 81
Memorial Sloan-Kettering Cancer Center,
  57
Memry Corporation, 72
The Men's Wearhouse, Inc., 17; 48 (upd.)
Menard, Inc., 34; 104 (upd.)
Menasha Corporation, 8; 59 (upd.)
Mendocino Brewing Company, Inc., 60
The Mentholatum Company Inc., 32
Mentor Corporation, 26
Mentor Graphics Corporation, 11
Mercantile Bankshares Corp., 11
Mercantile Stores Company, Inc., V; 19
  (upd.)
Mercer International Inc., 64
The Merchants Company, 102
Merck & Co., Inc., I; 11 (upd.); 34
  (upd.); 95 (upd.)
Mercury Air Group, Inc., 20
Mercury General Corporation, 25
Mercury Interactive Corporation, 59
Mercury Marine Group, 68
Meredith Corporation, 11; 29 (upd.); 74
  (upd.)
Merge Healthcare, 85
Merial Ltd., 102
Meridian Bancorp, Inc., 11
Meridian Gold, Incorporated, 47
Merillat Industries Inc., 13
Merillat Industries, LLC, 69 (upd.)
Merisant Worldwide, Inc., 70
Merisel, Inc., 12
Merit Medical Systems, Inc., 29
MeritCare Health System, 88
Meritage Corporation, 26
Merix Corporation, 36; 75 (upd.)
Merrell Dow, Inc., I; 9 (upd.)

Merriam-Webster Inc., 70
Merrill Corporation, 18; 47 (upd.)
Merrill Lynch & Co., Inc., II; 13 (upd.); 40 (upd.)
Merry-Go-Round Enterprises, Inc., 8
Mervyn's California, 10; 39 (upd.)
Mesa Air Group, Inc., 11; 32 (upd.); 77 (upd.)
Mesaba Holdings, Inc., 28
Mestek Inc., 10
Metal Management, Inc., 92
Metalico Inc., 97
Metatec International, Inc., 47
Metavante Corporation, 100
Meteor Industries Inc., 33
Methode Electronics, Inc., 13
Metris Companies Inc., 56
Metro Information Services, Inc., 36
Metro-Goldwyn-Mayer Inc., 25 (upd.); 84 (upd.)
Metrocall, Inc., 41
Metromedia Company, 7; 14; 61 (upd.)
Metropolitan Baseball Club Inc., 39
Metropolitan Financial Corporation, 13
Metropolitan Life Insurance Company, III; 52 (upd.)
The Metropolitan Museum of Art, 55
Metropolitan Opera Association, Inc., 40
Metropolitan Transportation Authority, 35
Mexican Restaurants, Inc., 41
MFS Communications Company, Inc., 11
MGA Entertainment, Inc., 95
MGIC Investment Corp., 52
MGM MIRAGE, 17; 98 (upd.)
MGM/UA Communications Company, II
Miami Herald Media Company, 92
Michael Anthony Jewelers, Inc., 24
Michael Baker Corporation, 14; 51 (upd.)
Michael C. Fina Co., Inc., 52
Michael Foods, Inc., 25
Michaels Stores, Inc., 17; 71 (upd.)
Michigan Bell Telephone Co., 14
Michigan National Corporation, 11
Michigan Sporting Goods Distributors, Inc., 72
Micrel, Incorporated, 77
Micro Warehouse, Inc., 16
MicroAge, Inc., 16
Microdot Inc., 8
Micron Technology, Inc., 11; 29 (upd.)
Micros Systems, Inc., 18
Microsemi Corporation, 94
Microsoft Corporation, 6; 27 (upd.); 63 (upd.)
MicroStrategy Incorporated, 87
Mid-America Apartment Communities, Inc., 85
Mid-America Dairymen, Inc., 7
Midas Inc., 10; 56 (upd.)
The Middleby Corporation, 22; 104 (upd.)
Middlesex Water Company, 45
The Middleton Doll Company, 53
The Midland Company, 65
Midway Airlines Corporation, 33
Midway Games, Inc., 25; 102 (upd.)
Midwest Air Group, Inc., 35; 85 (upd.)
Midwest Grain Products, Inc., 49

Midwest Resources Inc., 6
Mikasa, Inc., 28
Mike-Sell's Inc., 15
Mikohn Gaming Corporation, 39
Milacron, Inc., 53 (upd.)
Milbank, Tweed, Hadley & McCloy, 27
Miles Laboratories, I
Millennium Pharmaceuticals, Inc., 47
Miller Brewing Company, I; 12 (upd.)
Miller Industries, Inc., 26
Miller Publishing Group, LLC, 57
Milliken & Co., V; 17 (upd.); 82 (upd.)
Milliman USA, 66
Millipore Corporation, 25; 84 (upd.)
The Mills Corporation, 77
Milnot Company, 46
Milton Bradley Company, 21
Milton CAT, Inc., 86
Milwaukee Brewers Baseball Club, 37
Mine Safety Appliances Company, 31
The Miner Group International, 22
Minerals Technologies Inc., 11; 52 (upd.)
Minnesota Mining & Manufacturing Company (3M), I; 8 (upd.); 26 (upd.)
Minnesota Power, Inc., 11; 34 (upd.)
Minntech Corporation, 22
The Minute Maid Company, 28
Minuteman International Inc., 46
Minyard Food Stores, Inc., 33; 86 (upd.)
Mirage Resorts, Incorporated, 6; 28 (upd.)
Miramax Film Corporation, 64
Mirant Corporation, 98
Misonix, Inc., 80
Mississippi Chemical Corporation, 39
Mitchell Energy and Development Corporation, 7
MITRE Corporation, 26
Mity Enterprises, Inc., 38
MIVA, Inc., 83
MN Airlines LLC, 104
MNS, Ltd., 65
Mobil Corporation, IV; 7 (upd.); 21 (upd.)
Mobile Mini, Inc., 58
Mobile Telecommunications Technologies Corp., 18
Mocon, Inc., 76
Modern Woodmen of America, 66
Modine Manufacturing Company, 8; 56 (upd.)
Modtech Holdings, Inc., 77
Moen Inc., 12; 106 (upd.)
Mohawk Industries, Inc., 19; 63 (upd.)
Mohegan Tribal Gaming Authority, 37
Moldflow Corporation, 73
Molex Incorporated, 11; 54 (upd.)
Molson Coors Brewing Company, 77 (upd.)
Monaco Coach Corporation, 31
Monadnock Paper Mills, Inc., 21
Monarch Casino & Resort, Inc., 65
The Monarch Cement Company, 72
MoneyGram International, Inc., 94
Monfort, Inc., 13
Monro Muffler Brake, Inc., 24
Monrovia Nursery Company, 70
The Mosaic Company, 91

Monsanto Company, I; 9 (upd.); 29 (upd.); 77 (upd.)
Monster Cable Products, Inc., 69
Monster Worldwide Inc., 74 (upd.)
Montana Coffee Traders, Inc., 60
The Montana Power Company, 11; 44 (upd.)
Monterey Pasta Company, 58
Montgomery Ward & Co., Incorporated, V; 20 (upd.)
Moody's Corporation, 65
Moog Inc., 13
Moog Music, Inc., 75
Mooney Aerospace Group Ltd., 52
Moore Medical Corp., 17
Moore-Handley, Inc., 39
Moran Towing Corporation, Inc., 15
The Morgan Group, Inc., 46
Morgan, Lewis & Bockius LLP, 29
Morgan Stanley Dean Witter & Company, II; 16 (upd.); 33 (upd.)
Morgan's Foods, Inc., 101
Morgans Hotel Group Company, 80
Morinda Holdings, Inc., 82
Morningstar Inc., 68
Morris Communications Corporation, 36
Morris Travel Services L.L.C., 26
Morrison & Foerster LLP 78
Morrison Knudsen Corporation, 7; 28 (upd.)
Morrison Restaurants Inc., 11
Morrow Equipment Co. L.L.C., 87
Morse Shoe Inc., 13
Morton International Inc., I; 9 (upd.); 80 (upd.)
Morton Thiokol, Inc., I
Morton's Restaurant Group, Inc., 30; 88 (upd.)
Mosinee Paper Corporation, 15
Mossimo, 27; 96 (upd.)
Motel 6, 13; 56 (upd.)
Mothers Against Drunk Driving (MADD), 51
Mothers Work, Inc., 18
The Motley Fool, Inc., 40
Moto Photo, Inc., 45
Motor Cargo Industries, Inc., 35
Motorcar Parts & Accessories, Inc., 47
Motorola, Inc., II; 11 (upd.); 34 (upd.); 93 (upd.)
Motown Records Company L.P., 26
Mott's Inc., 57
Mountain States Mortgage Centers, Inc., 29
Movado Group, Inc., 28
Movie Gallery, Inc., 31
Movie Star Inc., 17
Mozilla Foundation, 106
MPS Group, Inc., 49
MPW Industrial Services Group, Inc., 53
Mr. Coffee, Inc., 15
Mr. Gasket Inc., 15
Mr. Gatti's, LP, 87
Mrchocolate.com LLC, 105
Mrs. Baird's Bakeries, 29
Mrs. Fields' Original Cookies, Inc., 27; 104 (upd.)
Mrs. Grossman's Paper Company Inc., 84

MSC Industrial Direct Co., Inc., 71
MSWG, LLC, 105
Mt. Olive Pickle Company, Inc., 44
MTI Enterprises Inc., 102
MTR Gaming Group, Inc., 75
MTS Inc., 37
Mueller Industries, Inc., 7; 52 (upd.)
Mueller Sports Medicine, Inc., 102
Mullen Advertising Inc., 51
Multi-Color Corporation, 53
Multimedia Games, Inc., 41
Multimedia, Inc., 11
Murdock Madaus Schwabe, 26
Murphy Family Farms Inc., 22
Murphy Oil Corporation, 7; 32 (upd.); 95 (upd.)
The Musco Family Olive Co., 91
Musco Lighting, 83
Museum of Modern Art, 106
Musicland Stores Corporation, 9; 38 (upd.)
The Mutual Benefit Life Insurance Company, III
The Mutual Life Insurance Company of New York, III
The Mutual of Omaha Companies, 98
Muzak, Inc., 18
MWH Preservation Limited Partnership, 65
MWI Veterinary Supply, Inc., 80
Mycogen Corporation, 21
Myers Industries, Inc., 19; 96 (upd.
Mylan Laboratories Inc., I; 20 (upd.); 59 (upd.)
Myriad Restaurant Group, Inc., 87
Myriad Genetics, Inc., 95
N.F. Smith & Associates LP, 70
Nabisco Foods Group, II; 7 (upd.)
Nabors Industries, Inc., 9
NACCO Industries Inc., 7; 78 (upd.)
Nalco Holding Company, I; 12 (upd.); 89 (upd.)
Nantucket Allserve, Inc., 22
Napster, Inc., 69
NASD, 54 (upd.)
The NASDAQ Stock Market, Inc., 92
Nash Finch Company, 8; 23 (upd.); 65 (upd.)
Nashua Corporation, 8
Nastech Pharmaceutical Company Inc. 79
Nathan's Famous, Inc., 29
National Amusements Inc., 28
National Aquarium in Baltimore, Inc., 74
National Association for Stock Car Auto Racing, 32
National Association of Securities Dealers, Inc., 10
National Audubon Society, 26
National Auto Credit, Inc., 16
The National Bank of South Carolina, 76
National Beverage Corporation, 26; 88 (upd.)
National Broadcasting Company, Inc., II; 6 (upd.); 28 (upd.)
National Can Corporation, I
National Car Rental System, Inc., 10
National CineMedia, Inc., 103
National City Corporation, 15; 97 (upd.)

National Collegiate Athletic Association, 96
National Convenience Stores Incorporated, 7
National Council of La Raza, 106
National Discount Brokers Group, Inc., 28
National Distillers and Chemical Corporation, I
National Educational Music Co. Ltd., 47
National Envelope Corporation, 32
National Equipment Services, Inc., 57
National Financial Partners Corp., 65
National Football League, 29
National Frozen Foods Corporation, 94
National Fuel Gas Company, 6; 95 (upd.)
National Geographic Society, 9; 30 (upd.); 79 (upd.)
National Grape Cooperative Association, Inc., 20
National Grid USA, 51 (upd.)
National Gypsum Company, 10
National Health Laboratories Incorporated, 11
National Heritage Academies, Inc., 60
National Hockey League, 35
National Home Centers, Inc., 44
National Instruments Corporation, 22
National Intergroup, Inc., V
National Jewish Health, 101
National Journal Group Inc., 67
National Media Corporation, 27
National Medical Enterprises, Inc., III
National Medical Health Card Systems, Inc. 79
National Oilwell, Inc., 54
National Organization for Women, Inc., 55
National Patent Development Corporation, 13
National Penn Bancshares, Inc., 103
National Picture & Frame Company, 24
National Presto Industries, Inc., 16; 43 (upd.)
National Public Radio, Inc., 19; 47 (upd.)
National R.V. Holdings, Inc., 32
National Railroad Passenger Corporation (Amtrak), 22; 66 (upd.)
National Record Mart, Inc., 29
National Research Corporation, 87
National Rifle Association of America, 37
National Sanitary Supply Co., 16
National Semiconductor Corporation, II; VI, 26 (upd.); 69 (upd.)
National Service Industries, Inc., 11; 54 (upd.)
National Standard Co., 13
National Starch and Chemical Company, 49
National Steel Corporation, 12
National TechTeam, Inc., 41
National Thoroughbred Racing Association, 58
National Weather Service, 91
National Wildlife Federation, 103
National Wine & Spirits, Inc., 49
NationsBank Corporation, 10
Natrol, Inc., 49

Natural Alternatives International, Inc., 49
Natural Ovens Bakery, Inc., 72
Natural Selection Foods, 54
Natural Wonders Inc., 14
Naturally Fresh, Inc., 88
The Nature Conservancy, 28
Nature's Sunshine Products, Inc., 15; 102 (upd.)
Naumes, Inc., 81
Nautica Enterprises, Inc., 18; 44 (upd.)
Navarre Corporation, 24
Navigant Consulting, Inc., 93
Navigant International, Inc., 47
The Navigators Group, Inc., 92
Navistar International Corporation, I; 10 (upd.)
NAVTEQ Corporation, 69
Navy Exchange Service Command, 31
Navy Federal Credit Union, 33
NBD Bancorp, Inc., 11
NBGS International, Inc., 73
NBTY, Inc., 31
NCH Corporation, 8
NCI Building Systems, Inc., 88
NCL Corporation 79
NCNB Corporation, II
NCO Group, Inc., 42
NCR Corporation, III; 6 (upd.); 30 (upd.); 90 (upd.)
Nebraska Book Company, Inc., 65
Nebraska Furniture Mart, Inc., 94
Nebraska Public Power District, 29
Neenah Foundry Company, 68
Neff Corp., 32
NeighborCare, Inc., 67 (upd.)
The Neiman Marcus Group, Inc., 12; 49 (upd.); 105 (upd.)
Nektar Therapeutics, 91
Neogen Corporation, 94
NERCO, Inc., 7
NetCracker Technology Corporation, 98
Netezza Corporation, 69
Netflix, Inc., 58
NETGEAR, Inc., 81
NetIQ Corporation 79
NetJets Inc., 96 (upd.)
Netscape Communications Corporation, 15; 35 (upd.)
Network Appliance, Inc., 58
Network Associates, Inc., 25
Network Equipment Technologies Inc., 92
The Newark Group, Inc., 102
Neuberger Berman Inc., 57
NeuStar, Inc., 81
Neutrogena Corporation, 17
Nevada Bell Telephone Company, 14
Nevada Power Company, 11
Nevamar Company, 82
New Balance Athletic Shoe, Inc., 25; 68 (upd.)
New Belgium Brewing Company, Inc., 68
New Brunswick Scientific Co., Inc., 45
New Chapter Inc., 96
New Dana Perfumes Company, 37
New England Business Service Inc., 18; 78 (upd.)
New England Confectionery Co., 15
New England Electric System, V

New England Mutual Life Insurance Company, III
New Jersey Devils, 84
New Jersey Manufacturers Insurance Company, 96
New Jersey Resources Corporation, 54
New Line Cinema, Inc., 47
New Orleans Saints LP, 58
The New Piper Aircraft, Inc., 44
New Plan Realty Trust, 11
The New School, 103
New Seasons Market, 75
New Street Capital Inc., 8
New Times, Inc., 45
New Valley Corporation, 17
New World Pasta Company, 53
New World Restaurant Group, Inc., 44
New York City Health and Hospitals Corporation, 60
New York City Off-Track Betting Corporation, 51
New York Community Bancorp Inc. 78
New York Daily News, 32
New York Health Care, Inc., 72
New York Life Insurance Company, III; 45 (upd.)
New York Restaurant Group, Inc., 32
New York Shakespeare Festival Management, 93
New York State Electric and Gas, 6
New York Stock Exchange, Inc., 9; 39 (upd.)
The New York Times Company, IV; 19 (upd.); 61 (upd.)
New York Yacht Club, Inc., 103
Neways Inc. 78
Newcor, Inc., 40
Newell Rubbermaid Inc., 9; 52 (upd.)
Newfield Exploration Company, 65
Newhall Land and Farming Company, 14
Newly Weds Foods, Inc., 74
Newman's Own, Inc., 37
Newmont Mining Corporation, 7; 94 (upd.)
Newpark Resources, Inc., 63
Newport Corporation, 71
Newport News Shipbuilding Inc., 13; 38 (upd.)
News America Publishing Inc., 12
News Communications, Inc., 103
Newsday Media Group, 103
NewYork-Presbyterian Hospital, 59
Nexstar Broadcasting Group, Inc., 73
Nextel Communications, Inc., 10; 27 (upd.)
NFL Films, 75
NFO Worldwide, Inc., 24
NGC Corporation, 18
Niagara Corporation, 28
Niagara Mohawk Holdings Inc., V; 45 (upd.)
Nichols Research Corporation, 18
Nicklaus Companies, 45
Nicole Miller, 98
Nicor Inc., 6; 86 (upd.)
Nielsen Business Media, Inc., 98
NIKE, Inc., V; 8 (upd.); 36 (upd.); 75 (upd.)

Nikken Global Inc., 32
Niman Ranch, Inc., 67
Nimbus CD International, Inc., 20
Nine West Group, Inc., 11; 39 (upd.)
99¢ Only Stores, 25; 100 (upd.)
NIPSCO Industries, Inc., 6
Nitches, Inc., 53
NL Industries, Inc., 10
Nobel Learning Communities, Inc., 37; 76 (upd.)
Noble Affiliates, Inc., 11
Noble Roman's Inc., 14; 99 (upd.)
Noland Company, 35
Nolo.com, Inc., 49
Noodle Kidoodle, 16
Noodles & Company, Inc., 55
Nooter Corporation, 61
Norcal Waste Systems, Inc., 60
NordicTrack, 22
Nordson Corporation, 11; 48 (upd.)
Nordstrom, Inc., V; 18 (upd.); 67 (upd.)
Norelco Consumer Products Co., 26
Norfolk Southern Corporation, V; 29 (upd.); 75 (upd.)
Norm Thompson Outfitters, Inc., 47
Norrell Corporation, 25
Norstan, Inc., 16
Nortek, Inc., 34
North American Galvanizing & Coatings, Inc., 99
North Atlantic Trading Company Inc., 65
The North Face, Inc., 18; 78 (upd.)
North Fork Bancorporation, Inc., 46
North Pacific Group, Inc., 61
North Star Steel Company, 18
Northeast Utilities, V; 48 (upd.)
Northern States Power Company, V; 20 (upd.)
Northern Trust Corporation, 9; 101 (upd.)
Northland Cranberries, Inc., 38
Northrop Grumman Corporation, I; 11 (upd.); 45 (upd.)
Northwest Airlines Corporation, I; 6 (upd.); 26 (upd.); 74 (upd.)
Northwest Natural Gas Company, 45
NorthWestern Corporation, 37
Northwestern Mutual Life Insurance Company, III; 45 (upd.)
Norton Company, 8
Norton McNaughton, Inc., 27
Norwood Promotional Products, Inc., 26
NovaCare, Inc., 11
NovaStar Financial, Inc., 91
Novell, Inc., 6; 23 (upd.)
Novellus Systems, Inc., 18
Noven Pharmaceuticals, Inc., 55
NPC International, Inc., 40
The NPD Group, Inc., 68
NRG Energy, Inc. 79
NRT Incorporated, 61
NSF International, 72
NSS Enterprises Inc. 78
NSTAR, 106 (upd.)
NTD Architecture, 101
NTN Buzztime, Inc., 86
Nu Skin Enterprises, Inc., 27; 76 (upd.)
Nu-kote Holding, Inc., 18

Nucor Corporation, 7; 21 (upd.); 79 (upd.)
Nutraceutical International Corporation, 37
NutraSweet Company, 8
Nutrition 21 Inc., 97
NutriSystem, Inc., 71
Nutrition for Life International Inc., 22
NVIDIA Corporation, 54
NVR Inc., 8; 70 (upd.)
NYMAGIC, Inc., 41
NYNEX Corporation, V
Nypro, Inc., 101
O.C. Tanner Co., 69
Oak Harbor Freight Lines, Inc., 53
Oak Industries Inc., 21
Oak Technology, Inc., 22
Oakhurst Dairy, 60
Oakleaf Waste Management, LLC, 97
Oakley, Inc., 18; 49 (upd.)
Oaktree Capital Management, LLC, 71
Oakwood Homes Corporation, 15
Obagi Medical Products, Inc., 95
Oberto Sausage Company, Inc., 92
Obie Media Corporation, 56
Occidental Petroleum Corporation, IV; 25 (upd.); 71 (upd.)
Ocean Beauty Seafoods, Inc., 74
Ocean Bio-Chem, Inc., 103
Ocean Spray Cranberries, Inc., 7; 25 (upd.); 83 (upd.)
Oceaneering International, Inc., 63
O'Charley's Inc., 19; 60 (upd.)
OCLC Online Computer Library Center, Inc., 96
The O'Connell Companies Inc., 100
Octel Messaging, 14; 41 (upd.)
Ocular Sciences, Inc., 65
Odetics Inc., 14
ODL, Inc., 55
Odwalla Inc., 31; 104 (upd.)
Odyssey Marine Exploration, Inc., 91
OEC Medical Systems, Inc., 27
Office Depot, Inc., 8; 23 (upd.); 65 (upd.)
OfficeMax Incorporated, 15; 43 (upd.); 101 (upd.)
OfficeTiger, LLC, 75
Offshore Logistics, Inc., 37
Ogden Corporation, I; 6
The Ogilvy Group, Inc., I
Oglebay Norton Company, 17
Oglethorpe Power Corporation, 6
The Ohio Art Company, 14; 59 (upd.)
Ohio Bell Telephone Company, 14
Ohio Casualty Corp., 11
Ohio Edison Company, V
Oil-Dri Corporation of America, 20; 89 (upd.)
Oil States International, Inc., 77
The Oilgear Company, 74
Oklahoma Gas and Electric Company, 6
Olan Mills, Inc., 62
Old America Stores, Inc., 17
Old Dominion Freight Line, Inc., 57
Old Kent Financial Corp., 11
Old National Bancorp, 15; 98 (upd.)
Old Navy, Inc., 70

Old Orchard Brands, LLC, 73
Old Republic International Corporation, 11; 58 (upd.)
Old Spaghetti Factory International Inc., 24
Old Town Canoe Company, 74
Olga's Kitchen, Inc., 80
Olin Corporation, I; 13 (upd.); 78 (upd.)
Olsten Corporation, 6; 29 (upd.)
OM Group Inc. 17; 78 (upd.)
Omaha Steaks International Inc., 62
Omega Protein Corporation, 99
O'Melveny & Myers, 37
OMI Corporation, 59
Omni Hotels Corp., 12
Omnicare, Inc., 49
Omnicell, Inc., 89
Omnicom Group, Inc., I; 22 (upd.); 77 (upd.)
OmniSource Corporation, 14
OMNOVA Solutions Inc., 59
Omrix Biopharmaceuticals, Inc., 95
On Assignment, Inc., 20
180s, L.L.C., 64
One Price Clothing Stores, Inc., 20
1-800-FLOWERS.COM, Inc., 26; 102 (upd.)
O'Neal Steel, Inc., 95
Oneida Ltd., 7; 31 (upd.); 88 (upd.)
ONEOK Inc., 7
Onion, Inc., 69
Onyx Acceptance Corporation, 59
Onyx Software Corporation, 53
OOC Inc., 97
Openwave Systems Inc., 95
Operation Smile, Inc., 75
Opinion Research Corporation, 46
Oplink Communications, Inc., 106
Oppenheimer Wolff & Donnelly LLP, 71
Opsware Inc., 49
OPTEK Technology Inc., 98
Option Care Inc., 48
Opus Corporation, 34; 101 (upd.)
Oracle Corporation, 6; 24 (upd.); 67 (upd.)
Orange Glo International, 53
Orange 21 Inc., 103
OraSure Technologies, Inc., 75
Orbit International Corp., 105
Orbital Sciences Corporation, 22
Orbitz, Inc., 61
The Orchard Enterprises, Inc., 103
Orchard Supply Hardware Stores Corporation, 17
Ore-Ida Foods Inc., 13; 78 (upd.)
Oregon Chai, Inc., 49
Oregon Dental Service Health Plan, Inc., 51
Oregon Freeze Dry, Inc., 74
Oregon Metallurgical Corporation, 20
Oregon Steel Mills, Inc., 14
O'Reilly Automotive, Inc., 26; 78 (upd.)
O'Reilly Media, Inc., 99
Organic To Go Food Corporation, 99
Organic Valley (Coulee Region Organic Produce Pool), 53
Orgill, Inc., 99
Orion Pictures Corporation, 6

Orkin, Inc., 104
Orleans Homebuilders, Inc., 62
Ormat Technologies, Inc., 87
Ormet Corporation, 82
Orrick, Herrington and Sutcliffe LLP, 76
Orthodontic Centers of America, Inc., 35
The Orvis Company, Inc., 28
Oryx Energy Company, 7
Oscar Mayer Foods Corp., 12
OshKosh B'Gosh, Inc., 9; 42 (upd.)
Oshkosh Corporation, 7; 98 (upd.)
Oshman's Sporting Goods, Inc., 17
OSI Restaurant Partners, Inc., 88 (upd.)
Osmonics, Inc., 18
O'Sullivan Industries Holdings, Inc., 34
Otis Elevator Company, Inc., 13; 39 (upd.)
Otis Spunkmeyer, Inc., 28
OTR Express, Inc., 25
Ottaway Newspapers, Inc., 15
Otter Tail Power Company, 18
Outback Steakhouse, Inc., 12; 34 (upd.)
Outboard Marine Corporation, III; 20 (upd.)
Outdoor Research, Incorporated, 67
Outdoor Systems, Inc., 25
Outlook Group Corporation, 37
Outrigger Enterprises, Inc., 67
Overhead Door Corporation, 70
Overhill Corporation, 51
Overland Storage Inc., 100
Overnite Corporation, 14; 58 (upd.)
Overseas Shipholding Group, Inc., 11
Overstock.com, Inc., 75
Owens & Minor, Inc., 16; 68 (upd.)
Owens Corning, III; 20 (upd.); 98 (upd.)
Owens-Illinois, Inc., I; 26 (upd.); 85 (upd.)
Owosso Corporation, 29
Oxford Health Plans, Inc., 16
Oxford Industries, Inc., 8; 84 (upd.)
P&C Foods Inc., 8
P & F Industries, Inc., 45
P.C. Richard & Son Corp., 23
P.F. Chang's China Bistro, Inc., 37; 86 (upd.)
P.H. Glatfelter Company, 8; 30 (upd.); 83 (upd.)
P.W. Minor and Son, Inc., 100
Paccar Inc., I; 26 (upd.)
Pacer International, Inc., 54
Pacer Technology, 40
Pacific Clay Products Inc., 88
Pacific Coast Building Products, Inc., 94
Pacific Coast Feather Company, 67
Pacific Coast Restaurants, Inc., 90
Pacific Ethanol, Inc., 81
Pacific Enterprises, V
Pacific Gas and Electric Company, V
Pacific Mutual Holding Company, 98
Pacific Sunwear of California, Inc., 28; 104 (upd.)
Pacific Telecom, Inc., 6
Pacific Telesis Group, V
PacifiCare Health Systems, Inc., 11
PacifiCorp, V; 26 (upd.)
Packaging Corporation of America, 12; 51 (upd.)

Packard Bell Electronics, Inc., 13
Packeteer, Inc., 81
Paddock Publications, Inc., 53
Paging Network Inc., 11
PaineWebber Group Inc., II; 22 (upd.)
Palace Sports & Entertainment, Inc., 97
Pall Corporation, 9; 72 (upd.)
Palm Harbor Homes, Inc., 39
Palm Management Corporation, 71
Palm, Inc., 36; 75 (upd.)
Palmer & Cay, Inc., 69
Palmer Candy Company, 80
Palomar Medical Technologies, Inc., 22
Pamida Holdings Corporation, 15
The Pampered Chef, Ltd., 18; 78 (upd.)
Pan American World Airways, Inc., I; 12 (upd.)
Pan-American Life Insurance Company, 48
Panamerican Beverages, Inc., 47
PanAmSat Corporation, 46
Panattoni Development Company, Inc., 99
Panavision Inc., 24
Pancho's Mexican Buffet, Inc., 46
Panda Restaurant Group, Inc., 35; 97 (upd.)
Panera Bread Company, 44
Panhandle Eastern Corporation, V
Pantone Inc., 53
The Pantry, Inc., 36
Papa Gino's Holdings Corporation, Inc., 86
Papa John's International, Inc., 15; 71 (upd.)
Papa Murphy's International, Inc., 54
Papetti's Hygrade Egg Products, Inc., 39
Pappas Restaurants, Inc., 76
Par Pharmaceutical Companies, Inc., 65
The Paradies Shops, Inc., 88
Paradise Music & Entertainment, Inc., 42
Parallel Petroleum Corporation, 101
Parametric Technology Corp., 16
Paramount Pictures Corporation, II; 94 (upd.)
PAREXEL International Corporation, 84
Paris Corporation, 22
Parisian, Inc., 14
Park Corp., 22
Park-Ohio Industries Inc., 17; 85 (upd.)
Parker Drilling Company, 28
Parker-Hannifin Corporation, III; 24 (upd.); 99 (upd.)
Parlex Corporation, 61
Parsons Brinckerhoff, Inc., 34; 104 (upd.)
The Parsons Corporation, 8; 56 (upd.)
Party City Corporation, 54
Patch Products Inc., 105
Pathmark Stores, Inc., 23; 101 (upd.)
Patina Oil & Gas Corporation, 24
Patrick Cudahy Inc., 102
Patrick Industries, Inc., 30
Patriot Transportation Holding, Inc., 91
Patterson Dental Co., 19
Patterson-UTI Energy, Inc., 55
Patton Boggs LLP, 71
Paul Harris Stores, Inc., 18

Paul, Hastings, Janofsky & Walker LLP, 27
Paul Mueller Company, 65
Paul Reed Smith Guitar Company, 89
The Paul Revere Corporation, 12
Paul, Weiss, Rifkind, Wharton & Garrison, 47
Paul-Son Gaming Corporation, 66
Paxson Communications Corporation, 33
Pay 'N Pak Stores, Inc., 9
Paychex, Inc., 15; 46 (upd.)
Payless Cashways, Inc., 11; 44 (upd.)
Payless ShoeSource, Inc., 18; 69 (upd.)
PayPal Inc., 58
The PBSJ Corporation, 82
PC Connection, Inc., 37
PCA International, Inc., 62
PCC Natural Markets, 94
PDI, Inc., 52
PDL BioPharma, Inc., 90
PDQ Food Stores, Inc. 79
PDS Gaming Corporation, 44
Peabody Coal Company, 10
Peabody Energy Corporation, 45 (upd.)
Peabody Holding Company, Inc., IV
The Peak Technologies Group, Inc., 14
Peapod, Inc., 30
Pearle Vision, Inc., 13
Peavey Electronics Corporation, 16; 94 (upd.)
PECO Energy Company, 11
Pediatric Services of America, Inc., 31
Pediatrix Medical Group, Inc., 61
Peebles Inc., 16; 43 (upd.)
Peet's Coffee & Tea, Inc., 38; 100 (upd.)
Pegasus Solutions, Inc., 75
Pei Cobb Freed & Partners Architects LLP, 57
Pelican Products, Inc., 86
Pella Corporation, 12; 39 (upd.); 89 (upd.)
Pemco Aviation Group Inc., 54
Pendleton Grain Growers Inc., 64
Pendleton Woolen Mills, Inc., 42
Penford Corporation, 55
Penn Engineering & Manufacturing Corp., 28
Penn National Gaming, Inc., 33
Penn Traffic Company, 13
Penn Virginia Corporation, 85
Pennington Seed Inc., 98
Pennsylvania Blue Shield, III
Pennsylvania Power & Light Company, V
Pennwalt Corporation, I
PennWell Corporation, 55
Pennzoil-Quaker State Company, IV; 20 (upd.); 50 (upd.)
Penske Corporation, V; 19 (upd.); 84 (upd.)
Pentair, Inc., 7; 26 (upd.); 81 (upd.)
Pentech International, Inc., 29
Penton Media, Inc., 27
Penzeys Spices, Inc. 79
People Express Airlines, Inc., I
People's United Financial Inc., 106
Peoples Energy Corporation, 6
PeopleSoft Inc., 14; 33 (upd.)

The Pep Boys—Manny, Moe & Jack, 11; 36 (upd.); 81 (upd.)
Pepper Hamilton LLP, 43
Pepperidge Farm, Incorporated, 81
The Pepsi Bottling Group, Inc., 40
PepsiAmericas, Inc., 67 (upd.)
PepsiCo, Inc., I; 10 (upd.); 38 (upd.); 93 (upd.)
Perma-Fix Environmental Services, Inc., 99
Perdue Farms Inc., 7; 23 (upd.)
Performance Food Group, 31; 96 (upd.)
Perini Corporation, 8; 82 (upd.)
PerkinElmer Inc. 7; 78 (upd.)
Perkins Coie LLP, 56
Perkins Family Restaurants, L.P., 22
Perot Systems Corporation, 29
Perrigo Company, 12; 59 (upd.)
Perry Ellis International, Inc., 41; 106 (upd.)
Perry's Ice Cream Company Inc., 90
The Perseus Books Group, 91
Pet Incorporated, 7
Petco Animal Supplies, Inc., 29; 74 (upd.)
Pete's Brewing Company, 22
Peter Kiewit Sons' Inc., 8
Peter Pan Bus Lines Inc., 106
Peter Piper, Inc., 70
Peterbilt Motors Company, 89
Petersen Publishing Company, 21
Peterson American Corporation, 55
PetMed Express, Inc., 81
Petrie Stores Corporation, 8
Petrohawk Energy Corporation 79
Petroleum Helicopters, Inc., 35
Petrolite Corporation, 15
Petrossian Inc., 54
Petry Media Corporation, 102
PETsMART, Inc., 14; 41 (upd.)
The Pew Charitable Trusts, 35
Pez Candy, Inc., 38
Pfizer Inc., I; 9 (upd.); 38 (upd.); 79 (upd.)
PFSweb, Inc., 73
PG&E Corporation, 26 (upd.)
Phar-Mor Inc., 12
Pharmacia & Upjohn Inc., I; 25 (upd.)
Pharmion Corporation, 91
Phat Fashions LLC, 49
Phelps Dodge Corporation, IV; 28 (upd.); 75 (upd.)
PHH Arval, V; 53 (upd.)
PHI, Inc., 80 (upd.)
Philadelphia Eagles, 37
Philadelphia Electric Company, V
Philadelphia Gas Works Company, 92
Philadelphia Media Holdings LLC, 92
Philadelphia Suburban Corporation, 39
Philharmonic-Symphony Society of New York, Inc. (New York Philharmonic), 69
Philip Morris Companies Inc., V; 18 (upd.); 44 (upd.)
Philip Services Corp., 73
Philips Electronics North America Corp., 13
The Phillies, 106
Phillips, de Pury & Luxembourg, 49

Phillips Foods, Inc., 63; 90 (upd.)
Phillips International Inc. 78
Phillips Lytle LLP, 102
Phillips Petroleum Company, IV; 40 (upd.)
Phillips-Van Heusen Corporation, 24
Phoenix Footwear Group, Inc., 70
The Phoenix Media/Communications Group, 91
PHP Healthcare Corporation, 22
PhyCor, Inc., 36
Physician Sales & Service, Inc., 14
Physio-Control International Corp., 18
Piccadilly Cafeterias, Inc., 19
PictureTel Corp., 10; 27 (upd.)
Piedmont Investment Advisors, LLC, 106
Piedmont Natural Gas Company, Inc., 27
Pier 1 Imports, Inc., 12; 34 (upd.); 95 (upd.)
Pierce Leahy Corporation, 24
Piercing Pagoda, Inc., 29
Piggly Wiggly Southern, Inc., 13
Pilgrim's Pride Corporation, 7; 23 (upd.); 90 (upd.
Pillowtex Corporation, 19; 41 (upd.)
The Pillsbury Company, II; 13 (upd.); 62 (upd.)
Pillsbury Madison & Sutro LLP, 29
Pilot Air Freight Corp., 67
Pilot Corporation, 49
Pilot Pen Corporation of America, 82
Pinkerton's Inc., 9
Pinnacle Airlines Corp., 73
Pinnacle West Capital Corporation, 6; 54 (upd.)
Pioneer Hi-Bred International, Inc., 9; 41 (upd.)
Pioneer Natural Resources Company, 59
Pioneer-Standard Electronics Inc., 19
Piper Jaffray Companies Inc., 22
Pitman Company, 58
Pitney Bowes Inc., III; 19; 47 (upd.)
Pittsburgh Brewing Company, 76
Pittsburgh Steelers Sports, Inc., 66
The Pittston Company, IV; 19 (upd.)
Pittway Corporation, 9; 33 (upd.)
Pixar Animation Studios, 34
Pixelworks, Inc., 69
Pizza Hut Inc., 7; 21 (upd.)
Pizza Inn, Inc., 46
Plain Dealer Publishing Company, 92
Plains Cotton Cooperative Association, 57
Planar Systems, Inc., 61
Planet Hollywood International, Inc., 18; 41 (upd.)
Plantation Pipe Line Company, 68
Plante & Moran, LLP, 71
Plantronics, Inc., 106
Platinum Entertainment, Inc., 35
PLATINUM Technology, Inc., 14
Plato Learning, Inc., 44
Play by Play Toys & Novelties, Inc., 26
Playboy Enterprises, Inc., 18
PlayCore, Inc., 27
Players International, Inc., 22
Playskool, Inc., 25
Playtex Products, Inc., 15
Pleasant Company, 27

Pleasant Holidays LLC, 62
Plexus Corporation, 35; 80 (upd.)
Pliant Corporation, 98
Plow & Hearth, Inc., 104
Plum Creek Timber Company, Inc., 43; 106 (upd.)
Pluma, Inc., 27
Ply Gem Industries Inc., 12
The PMI Group, Inc., 49
PMT Services, Inc., 24
The PNC Financial Services Group Inc., II; 13 (upd.); 46 (upd.)
PNM Resources Inc., 51 (upd.)
PODS Enterprises Inc., 103
Pogo Producing Company, 39
Polar Air Cargo Inc., 60
Polaris Industries Inc., 12; 35 (upd.); 77 (upd.)
Polaroid Corporation, III; 7 (upd.); 28 (upd.); 93 (upd.)
Polartec LLC, 98 (upd.)
Policy Management Systems Corporation, 11
Policy Studies, Inc., 62
Polk Audio, Inc., 34
Polo/Ralph Lauren Corporation, 12; 62 (upd.)
PolyGram N.V., 23
PolyMedica Corporation, 77
PolyOne Corporation, 87 (upd.)
Pomare Ltd., 88
Pomeroy Computer Resources, Inc., 33
Ponderosa Steakhouse, 15
Poof-Slinky, Inc., 61
Poore Brothers, Inc., 44
Pop Warner Little Scholars, Inc., 86
Pope & Talbot, Inc., 12; 61 (upd.)
Pope Resources LP, 74
Popular, Inc., 41
The Port Authority of New York and New Jersey, 48
Port Imperial Ferry Corporation, 70
Portal Software, Inc., 47
Portillo's Restaurant Group, Inc., 71
Portland General Corporation, 6
Portland Trail Blazers, 50
Post Properties, Inc., 26
Potbelly Sandwich Works, Inc., 83
Potlatch Corporation, 8; 34 (upd.); 87 (upd.)
Potomac Electric Power Company, 6
Potter & Brumfield Inc., 11
Powell's Books, Inc., 40
Power-One, Inc. 79
PowerBar Inc., 44
Powerhouse Technologies, Inc., 27
POZEN Inc., 81
PPG Industries, Inc., III; 22 (upd.); 81 (upd.)
PPL Corporation, 41 (upd.)
PR Newswire, 35
Prairie Farms Dairy, Inc., 47
Pratt & Whitney, 9
Praxair, Inc., 11; 48 (upd.)
Praxis Bookstore Group LLC, 90
Pre-Paid Legal Services, Inc., 20
Precision Castparts Corp., 15
Preferred Hotel Group, 103

Premark International, Inc., III
Premcor Inc., 37
Premier Industrial Corporation, 9
Premier Parks, Inc., 27
Premiere Radio Networks, Inc., 102
Premium Standard Farms, Inc., 30
PremiumWear, Inc., 30
Preserver Group, Inc., 44
President Casinos, Inc., 22
Pressman Toy Corporation, 56
Presstek, Inc., 33
Preston Corporation, 6
PRG-Schultz International, Inc., 73
Price Communications Corporation, 42
The Price Company, V
Price Pfister, Inc., 70
PriceCostco, Inc., 14
Priceline.com Incorporated, 57
PriceSmart, Inc., 71
PricewaterhouseCoopers, 9; 29 (upd.)
Pride International Inc. 78
Primark Corp., 13
Prime Hospitality Corporation, 52
Primedex Health Systems, Inc., 25
Primedia Inc., 22
Primerica Corporation, I
Prince Sports Group, Inc., 15
Princess Cruise Lines, 22
The Princeton Review, Inc., 42
Principal Mutual Life Insurance Company, III
Printpack, Inc., 68
Printrak, A Motorola Company, 44
Printronix, Inc., 18
Prison Rehabilitative Industries and Diversified Enterprises, Inc. (PRIDE), 53
Pro-Build Holdings Inc., 95 (upd.)
The Procter & Gamble Company, III; 8 (upd.); 26 (upd.); 67 (upd.)
Prodigy Communications Corporation, 34
Professional Bull Riders Inc., 55
The Professional Golfers' Association of America, 41
Proffitt's, Inc., 19
Programmer's Paradise, Inc., 81
Progress Energy, Inc., 74
Progress Software Corporation, 15
The Progressive Corporation, 11; 29 (upd.)
ProLogis, 57
Promus Companies, Inc., 9
Proskauer Rose LLP, 47
Protection One, Inc., 32
Provell Inc., 58 (upd.)
Providence Health System, 90
The Providence Journal Company, 28
The Providence Service Corporation, 64
Provident Bankshares Corporation, 85
Provident Life and Accident Insurance Company of America, III
Providian Financial Corporation, 52 (upd.)
Prudential Financial Inc., III; 30 (upd.); 82 (upd.)
PSI Resources, 6
Psychemedics Corporation, 89
Psychiatric Solutions, Inc., 68

Pubco Corporation, 17
Public Service Company of Colorado, 6
Public Service Company of New Hampshire, 21; 55 (upd.)
Public Service Company of New Mexico, 6
Public Service Enterprise Group Inc., V; 44 (upd.)
Public Storage, Inc., 52
Publishers Clearing House, 23; 64 (upd.)
Publishers Group, Inc., 35
Publix Super Markets, Inc., 7; 31 (upd.); 105 (upd.)
Pueblo Xtra International, Inc., 47
Puget Sound Energy Inc., 6; 50 (upd.)
Pulaski Furniture Corporation, 33; 80 (upd.)
Pulitzer Inc., 15; 58 (upd.)
Pulte Corporation, 8
Pulte Homes, Inc., 42 (upd.)
Pumpkin Masters, Inc., 48
Pure World, Inc., 72
Purina Mills, Inc., 32
Puritan-Bennett Corporation, 13
Purolator Products Company, 21; 74 (upd.)
Putt-Putt Golf Courses of America, Inc., 23
PVC Container Corporation, 67
PW Eagle, Inc., 48
Pyramid Breweries Inc., 33; 102 (upd.)
Pyramid Companies, 54
Q.E.P. Co., Inc., 65
Qdoba Restaurant Corporation, 93
QRS Music Technologies, Inc., 95
QSC Audio Products, Inc., 56
QSS Group, Inc., 100
Quad/Graphics, Inc., 19
Quaker Chemical Corp., 91
Quaker Fabric Corp., 19
Quaker Foods North America, 73 (upd.)
The Quaker Oats Company, II; 12 (upd.); 34 (upd.)
Quaker State Corporation, 7; 21 (upd.)
QUALCOMM Incorporated, 20; 47 (upd.)
Quality Chekd Dairies, Inc., 48
Quality Dining, Inc., 18
Quality Food Centers, Inc., 17
Quality Systems, Inc., 81
Quanex Corporation, 13; 62 (upd.)
Quanta Services, Inc. 79
Quantum Chemical Corporation, 8
Quantum Corporation, 10; 62 (upd.)
Quark, Inc., 36
Quest Diagnostics Inc., 26; 106 (upd.)
Questar Corporation, 6; 26 (upd.)
The Quick & Reilly Group, Inc., 20
Quicken Loans, Inc., 93
Quidel Corporation, 80
The Quigley Corporation, 62
Quiksilver, Inc., 18; 79 (upd.)
QuikTrip Corporation, 36
Quill Corporation, 28
Quinn Emanuel Urquhart Oliver & Hedges, LLP, 99
Quintiles Transnational Corporation, 21; 68 (upd.)

Quixote Corporation, 15
The Quizno's Corporation, 42
Quovadx Inc., 70
QVC Inc., 9; 58 (upd.)
Qwest Communications International, Inc., 37
R&B, Inc., 51
R.B. Pamplin Corp., 45
R.C. Bigelow, Inc., 49
R.C. Willey Home Furnishings, 72
R.G. Barry Corporation, 17; 44 (upd.)
R.H. Macy & Co., Inc., V; 8 (upd.); 30 (upd.)
R.J. Reynolds Tobacco Holdings, Inc., 30 (upd.)
R.L. Polk & Co., 10
R. M. Palmer Co., 89
R.P. Scherer, I
R.R. Bowker LLC, 100
R.R. Donnelley & Sons Company, IV; 9 (upd.); 38 (upd.)
Racal-Datacom Inc., 11
Racing Champions Corporation, 37
Rack Room Shoes, Inc., 84
Radian Group Inc., 42
Radiant Systems Inc., 104
Radiation Therapy Services, Inc., 85
@radical.media, 103
Radio Flyer Inc., 34
Radio One, Inc., 67
RadioShack Corporation, 36 (upd.); 101 (upd.)
Radius Inc., 16
RAE Systems Inc., 83
Rag Shops, Inc., 30
RailTex, Inc., 20
Rain Bird Corporation, 84
Rainforest Café, Inc., 25; 88 (upd.)
Rainier Brewing Company, 23
Raley's Inc., 14; 58 (upd.)
Rally's, 25; 68 (upd.)
Ralphs Grocery Company, 35
Ralston Purina Company, II; 13 (upd.)
Ramsay Youth Services, Inc., 41
Ramtron International Corporation, 89
Rand McNally & Company, 28
Randall's Food Markets, Inc., 40
Random House Inc., 13; 31 (upd.); 106 (upd.)
Range Resources Corporation, 45
Rapala-Normark Group, Ltd., 30
Rare Hospitality International Inc., 19
RathGibson Inc., 90
Ratner Companies, 72
Raven Industries, Inc., 33
Raving Brands, Inc., 64
Rawlings Sporting Goods Co., Inc., 24
Raychem Corporation, 8
Raycom Media, Inc., 106
Raymond James Financial Inc., 69
Rayonier Inc., 24
Rayovac Corporation, 13; 39 (upd.)
Raytech Corporation, 61
Raytheon Aircraft Holdings Inc., 46
Raytheon Company, II; 11 (upd.); 38 (upd.); 105 (upd.)
Razorfish, Inc., 37
RCA Corporation, II

RCM Technologies, Inc., 34
RCN Corporation, 70
RDO Equipment Company, 33
RE/MAX International, Inc., 59
Read-Rite Corp., 10
The Reader's Digest Association, Inc., IV; 17 (upd.); 71 (upd.)
Reading International Inc., 70
Real Times, Inc., 66
RealNetworks, Inc., 53
Reckson Associates Realty Corp., 47
Recording for the Blind & Dyslexic, 51
Recoton Corp., 15
Recovery Engineering, Inc., 25
Recreational Equipment, Inc., 18; 71 (upd.)
Recycled Paper Greetings, Inc., 21
Red Apple Group, Inc., 23
Red Hat, Inc., 45
Red McCombs Automotive Group, 91
Red Robin Gourmet Burgers, Inc., 56
Red Roof Inns, Inc., 18
Red Spot Paint & Varnish Company, 55
Red Wing Pottery Sales, Inc., 52
Red Wing Shoe Company, Inc., 9; 30 (upd.); 83 (upd.)
Redback Networks, Inc., 92
Reddy Ice Holdings, Inc., 80
Redhook Ale Brewery, Inc., 31; 88 (upd.)
Redken Laboratories Inc., 84
Redlon & Johnson, Inc., 97
RedPeg Marketing, 73
Reebok International Ltd., V; 9 (upd.); 26 (upd.)
Reed & Barton Corporation, 67
Reed's, Inc., 103
Reeds Jewelers, Inc., 22
Regal Entertainment Group, 59
Regal-Beloit Corporation, 18; 97 (upd.)
The Regence Group, 74
Regency Centers Corporation, 71
Regent Communications, Inc., 87
Regions Financial Corporation, 106
Regis Corporation, 18; 70 (upd.)
Reichhold Chemicals, Inc., 10
Reiter Dairy, LLC, 94
Rejuvenation, Inc., 91
Reliance Electric Company, 9
Reliance Group Holdings, Inc., III
Reliance Steel & Aluminum Company, 19; 70 (upd.)
Reliant Energy Inc., 44 (upd.)
Reliv International, Inc., 58
Remedy Corporation, 58
RemedyTemp, Inc., 20
Remington Arms Company, Inc., 12; 40 (upd.)
Remington Products Company, L.L.C., 42
Renaissance Learning, Inc., 39; 100 (upd.)
Renal Care Group, Inc., 72
Renfro Corporation, 99
Reno Air Inc., 23
Rent-A-Center, Inc., 45
Rent-Way, Inc., 33; 75 (upd.)
Rental Service Corporation, 28
Rentrak Corporation, 35
Republic Engineered Products Inc., 7; 26 (upd.); 106 (upd.)

Republic Industries, Inc., 26
Republic New York Corporation, 11
The Republic of Tea, Inc., 105
Republic Services, Inc., 92
Res-Care, Inc., 29
Research Triangle Institute, 83
Reser's Fine Foods, Inc., 81
Resorts International, Inc., 12
Resource America, Inc., 42
Resources Connection, Inc., 81
Response Oncology, Inc., 27
Restaurant Associates Corporation, 66
Restaurants Unlimited, Inc., 13
Restoration Hardware, Inc., 30; 96 (upd.)
Retail Ventures, Inc., 82 (upd.)
Retractable Technologies, Inc., 99
Revco D.S., Inc., V
Revell-Monogram Inc., 16
Revere Electric Supply Company, 96
Revere Ware Corporation, 22
Revlon Inc., III; 17 (upd.); 64 (upd.)
Rewards Network Inc., 70 (upd.)
REX Stores Corp., 10
Rexel, Inc., 15
Rexnord Corporation, 21; 76 (upd.)
The Reynolds and Reynolds Company, 50
Reynolds Metals Company, IV; 19 (upd.)
RF Micro Devices, Inc., 43
RFC Franchising LLC, 68
Rhino Entertainment Company, 18; 70 (upd.)
Rhodes Inc., 23
Rhythm & Hues Studios, Inc., 103
Rica Foods, Inc., 41
Rich Products Corporation, 7; 38 (upd.); 93 (upd.)
The Richards Group, Inc., 58
Richardson Electronics, Ltd., 17
Richardson Industries, Inc., 62
Richfood Holdings, Inc., 7
Richton International Corporation, 39
Rickenbacker International Corp., 91
Riddell Sports Inc., 22
Ride, Inc., 22
The Riese Organization, 38
Riggs National Corporation, 13
Right Management Consultants, Inc., 42
Riklis Family Corp., 9
Rimage Corp., 89
Ripley Entertainment, Inc., 74
Riser Foods, Inc., 9
Rite Aid Corporation, V; 19 (upd.); 63 (upd.)
Ritz Camera Centers, 34
The Ritz-Carlton Hotel Company, L.L.C., 9; 29 (upd.); 71 (upd.)
Ritz-Craft Corporation of Pennsylvania Inc., 94
The Rival Company, 19
River Oaks Furniture, Inc., 43
River Ranch Fresh Foods LLC, 88
Riverbed Technology, Inc., 101
Riverwood International Corporation, 11; 48 (upd.)
Riviana Foods Inc., 27
Riviera Holdings Corporation, 75
Riviera Tool Company, 89
RJR Nabisco Holdings Corp., V

RMH Teleservices, Inc., 42
Roadhouse Grill, Inc., 22
Roadmaster Industries, Inc., 16
Roadway Express, Inc., V; 25 (upd.)
Roanoke Electric Steel Corporation, 45
Robbins & Myers Inc., 15
Robins, Kaplan, Miller & Ciresi L.L.P., 89
Roberds Inc., 19
Robert Half International Inc., 18; 70 (upd.)
Robert Mondavi Corporation, 15; 50 (upd.)
Robert Talbott Inc., 88
Robert W. Baird & Co. Incorporated, 67
Robert Wood Johnson Foundation, 35
Roberts Dairy Company, 103
Roberts Pharmaceutical Corporation, 16
Robertson-Ceco Corporation, 19
Robinson Helicopter Company, 51
Rocawear Apparel LLC, 77
Roche Bioscience, 11; 14 (upd.)
Rochester Gas and Electric Corporation, 6
Rochester Telephone Corporation, 6
Rock Bottom Restaurants, Inc., 25; 68 (upd.)
Rock-It Cargo USA, Inc., 86
Rock of Ages Corporation, 37
Rock-Tenn Company, 13; 59 (upd.)
The Rockefeller Foundation, 34
Rockefeller Group International Inc., 58
Rockford Corporation, 43
Rockford Products Corporation, 55
RockShox, Inc., 26
Rockwell Automation, Inc., 43 (upd.); 103 (upd.)
Rockwell Collins, 106
Rockwell International Corporation, I; 11 (upd.)
Rockwell Medical Technologies, Inc., 88
Rocky Brands, Inc., 26; 102 (upd.)
Rocky Mountain Chocolate Factory, Inc., 73
Rodale, Inc., 23; 47 (upd.)
Rodda Paint Company, 98
ROFIN-SINAR Technologies Inc., 81
Rogers Corporation, 61; 80 (upd.)
Rohm and Haas Company, I; 26 (upd.); 77 (upd.)
ROHN Industries, Inc., 22
Rohr Incorporated, 9
Roll International Corporation, 37
Rollerblade, Inc., 15; 34 (upd.)
Rollins, Inc., 11; 104 (upd.)
Rolls-Royce Allison, 29 (upd.)
Roly Poly Franchise Systems LLC, 83
Romacorp, Inc., 58
Roman Meal Company, 84
Ron Tonkin Chevrolet Company, 55
Ronco Corporation, 15; 80 (upd.)
Rooms To Go Inc., 28
Rooney Brothers Co., 25
Roper Industries, Inc., 15; 50 (upd.)
Ropes & Gray, 40
Rorer Group, I
Rosauers Supermarkets, Inc., 90
Rose Acre Farms, Inc., 60
Rose Art Industries, 58
Rose's Stores, Inc., 13

Roseburg Forest Products Company, 58
Rosemount Inc., 15
Rosenbluth International Inc., 14
Rosetta Stone Inc., 93
Ross Stores, Inc., 17; 43 (upd.); 101 (upd.)
Rotary International, 31
Roto-Rooter, Inc., 15; 61 (upd.)
The Rottlund Company, Inc., 28
Rouge Steel Company, 8
Rounder Records Corporation 79
Roundy's Inc., 14; 58 (upd.)
The Rouse Company, 15; 63 (upd.)
Rowan Companies, Inc., 43
Roy Anderson Corporation, 75
Roy F. Weston, Inc., 33
Royal Appliance Manufacturing Company, 15
Royal Caribbean Cruises Ltd., 22; 74 (upd.)
Royal Crown Company, Inc., 23
RPC, Inc., 91
RPM International Inc., 8; 36 (upd.); 91 (upd.)
RSA Security Inc., 46
RSM McGladrey Business Services Inc., 98
RTI Biologics, Inc., 96
RTM Restaurant Group, 58
Rubbermaid Incorporated, III; 20 (upd.)
Rubio's Restaurants, Inc., 35
Ruby Tuesday, Inc., 18; 71 (upd.)
Rudolph Technologies Inc., 94
Ruiz Food Products, Inc., 53
Rural Cellular Corporation, 43
Rural/Metro Corporation, 28
Rush Communications, 33
Rush Enterprises, Inc., 64
Russ Berrie and Company, Inc., 12; 82 (upd.)
Russell Corporation, 8; 30 (upd.); 82 (upd.)
Russell Reynolds Associates Inc., 38
Russell Stover Candies Inc., 12; 91 (upd.)
Rust International Inc., 11
Rusty, Inc., 95
Ruth's Chris Steak House, 28; 88 (upd.)
RWD Technologies, Inc., 76
Ryan Beck & Co., Inc., 66
Ryan Companies US, Inc., 99
Ryan's Restaurant Group, Inc., 15; 68 (upd.)
Ryder System, Inc., V; 24 (upd.)
Ryerson Tull, Inc., 40 (upd.)
Ryko Corporation, 83
The Ryland Group, Inc., 8; 37 (upd.)
S&C Electric Company, 15
S&D Coffee, Inc., 84
S&K Famous Brands, Inc., 23
S-K-I Limited, 15
S.C. Johnson & Son, Inc., III; 28 (upd.); 89 (upd.)
Saatchi & Saatchi, 42 (upd.)
Sabratek Corporation, 29
SABRE Group Holdings, Inc., 26
Sabre Holdings Corporation, 74 (upd.)
Safe Flight Instrument Corporation, 71
SAFECO Corporaton, III

Safeguard Scientifics, Inc., 10
Safelite Glass Corp., 19
SafeNet Inc., 101
Safeskin Corporation, 18
Safety Components International, Inc., 63
Safety 1st, Inc., 24
Safety-Kleen Systems Inc., 8; 82 (upd.)
Safeway Inc., II; 24 (upd.); 85 (upd.)
Saga Communications, Inc., 27
Sage Products Inc., 105
Saia, Inc., 98
The St. Joe Company, 31; 98 (upd.)
St. Joe Paper Company, 8
St. John Knits, Inc., 14
St. Jude Medical, Inc., 11; 43 (upd.); 97 (upd.)
St. Louis Music, Inc., 48
St. Mary Land & Exploration Company, 63
St. Paul Bank for Cooperatives, 8
The St. Paul Travelers Companies, Inc. III; 22 (upd.); 79 (upd.)
Ste. Michelle Wine Estates Ltd., 96
Saks Inc., 24; 41 (upd.)
Salant Corporation, 12; 51 (upd.)
Salem Communications Corporation, 97
salesforce.com, Inc. 79
Salick Health Care, Inc., 53
Salix Pharmaceuticals, Ltd., 93
Sally Beauty Company, Inc., 60
Sally Industries, Inc., 103
Salomon Inc., II; 13 (upd.)
Salt River Project, 19
Salton, Inc., 30; 88 (upd.)
The Salvation Army USA, 32
Sam Ash Music Corporation, 30
Sam Levin Inc., 80
Sam's Club, 40
Sam's Wine & Spirits, 96
Samsonite Corporation, 13; 43 (upd.)
Samuel Cabot Inc., 53
Samuels Jewelers Incorporated, 30
San Diego Gas & Electric Company, V
San Diego Padres Baseball Club LP 78
Sanborn Map Company Inc., 82
Sandals Resorts International, 65
Sanders Morris Harris Group Inc., 70
Sanders\Wingo, 99
Sanderson Farms, Inc., 15
Sandia National Laboratories, 49
Sanford L.P., 82
Santa Barbara Restaurant Group, Inc., 37
The Santa Cruz Operation, Inc., 38
Santa Fe Gaming Corporation, 19
Santa Fe International Corporation, 38
Santa Fe Pacific Corporation, V
Santarus, Inc., 105
Sapp Bros Travel Centers, Inc., 105
Sara Lee Corporation, II; 15 (upd.); 54 (upd.); 99 (upd.)
Sarnoff Corporation, 57
Sarris Candies Inc., 86
SAS Institute Inc., 10; 78 (upd.)
Saturn Corporation, 7; 21 (upd.); 80 (upd.)
Saucony Inc., 35; 86 (upd.)
Sauder Woodworking Company, 12; 35 (upd.)

Sauer-Danfoss Inc., 61
Saul Ewing LLP, 74
Savannah Foods & Industries, Inc., 7
Savers, Inc., 99 (upd.)
Sawtek Inc., 43 (upd.)
Saxton Pierce Restaurant Corporation, 100
Sbarro, Inc., 16; 64 (upd.)
SBC Communications Inc., 32 (upd.)
SBS Technologies, Inc., 25
SCANA Corporation, 6; 56 (upd.)
ScanSource, Inc., 29; 74 (upd.)
SCB Computer Technology, Inc., 29
SCEcorp, V
Schawk, Inc., 24
Scheels All Sports Inc., 63
Scheid Vineyards Inc., 66
Scherer Brothers Lumber Company, 94
Schering-Plough Corporation, I; 14 (upd.); 49 (upd.); 99 (upd.)
Schieffelin & Somerset Co., 61
Schlage Lock Company, 82
Schlotzsky's, Inc., 36
Schlumberger Limited, III; 17 (upd.); 59 (upd.)
Schmitt Music Company, 40
Schenck Business Solutions, 88
Schneider National, Inc., 36; 77 (upd.)
Schneiderman's Furniture Inc., 28
Schnitzer Steel Industries, Inc., 19
Scholastic Corporation, 10; 29 (upd.)
Scholle Corporation, 96
School Specialty, Inc., 68
School-Tech, Inc., 62
Schott Brothers, Inc., 67
Schott Corporation, 53
Schottenstein Stores Corp., 14
Schreiber Foods, Inc., 72
Schuff Steel Company, 26
Schultz Sav-O Stores, Inc., 21; 31 (upd.)
Schurz Communications, Inc., 98
The Schwan Food Company, 83 (upd.)
Schwan's Sales Enterprises, Inc., 7; 26 (upd.)
Schwebel Baking Company, 72
Schweitzer-Mauduit International, Inc., 52
Schwinn Cycle and Fitness L.P., 19
SCI Systems, Inc., 9
Science Applications International Corporation, 15
Scientific-Atlanta, Inc., 6; 45 (upd.)
Scientific Games Corporation, 64 (upd.)
Scientific Learning Corporation, 95
The SCO Group Inc. 78
Scolari's Food and Drug Company, 102
Scope Products, Inc., 94
The Score Board, Inc., 19
Scotsman Industries, Inc., 20
Scott Fetzer Company, 12; 80 (upd.)
Scott Paper Company, IV; 31 (upd.)
The Scotts Company, 22
Scottrade, Inc., 85
Scotty's, Inc., 22
The Scoular Company, 77
Scovill Fasteners Inc., 24
SCP Pool Corporation, 39
Screen Actors Guild, 72
The Scripps Research Institute, 76

Sea Ray Boats Inc., 96
Seaboard Corporation, 36; 85 (upd.)
SeaChange International, Inc. 79
SEACOR Holdings Inc., 83
Seagate Technology, Inc., 8; 34 (upd.)
Seagull Energy Corporation, 11
Sealaska Corporation, 60
Sealed Air Corporation, 14; 57 (upd.)
Sealed Power Corporation, I
Sealright Co., Inc., 17
Sealy Inc., 12
Seaman Furniture Company, Inc., 32
Sean John Clothing, Inc., 70
Sears, Roebuck and Co., V; 18 (upd.); 56 (upd.)
Seattle City Light, 50
Seattle FilmWorks, Inc., 20
Seattle First National Bank Inc., 8
Seattle Lighting Fixture Company, 92
Seattle Pacific Industries, Inc., 92
Seattle Seahawks, Inc., 92
Seattle Times Company, 15
Seaway Food Town, Inc., 15
Sebastiani Vineyards, Inc., 28
The Second City, Inc., 88
Second Harvest, 29
Security Capital Corporation, 17
Security Pacific Corporation, II
SED International Holdings, Inc., 43
See's Candies, Inc., 30
Sega of America, Inc., 10
Segway LLC, 48
SEI Investments Company, 96
Seigle's Home and Building Centers, Inc., 41
Seitel, Inc., 47
Select Comfort Corporation, 34
Select Medical Corporation, 65
Selee Corporation, 88
The Selmer Company, Inc., 19
SEMCO Energy, Inc., 44
Seminis, Inc., 29
Semitool, Inc., 18; 79 (upd.)
Sempra Energy, 25 (upd.)
Semtech Corporation, 32
Seneca Foods Corporation, 17; 60 (upd.)
Senomyx, Inc., 83
Sensient Technologies Corporation, 52 (upd.)
Sensormatic Electronics Corp., 11
Sensory Science Corporation, 37
SENTEL Corporation, 106
Sepracor Inc., 45
Sequa Corporation, 13; 54 (upd.)
Serologicals Corporation, 63
Serta, Inc., 28
Servco Pacific Inc., 96
Service America Corp., 7
Service Corporation International, 6; 51 (upd.)
Service Merchandise Company, Inc., V; 19 (upd.)
The ServiceMaster Company, 6; 23 (upd.); 68 (upd.)
Servidyne Inc., 100 (upd.)
Servpro Industries, Inc., 85
7-11, Inc., 32 (upd.)
Sevenson Environmental Services, Inc., 42

Seventh Generation, Inc., 73
Seyfarth Shaw LLP, 93
SFX Entertainment, Inc., 36
SGI, 29 (upd.)
Shakespeare Company, 22
Shaklee Corporation, 12; 39 (upd.)
Shamrock Foods Company, 105
Shared Medical Systems Corporation, 14
The Sharper Image Corporation, 10; 62 (upd.)
The Shaw Group, Inc., 50
Shaw Industries, Inc., 9; 40 (upd.)
Shaw's Supermarkets, Inc., 56
Shawmut National Corporation, 13
Sheaffer Pen Corporation, 82
Shearer's Foods, Inc., 72
Shearman & Sterling, 32
Shearson Lehman Brothers Holdings Inc., II; 9 (upd.)
Shedd Aquarium Society, 73
Sheetz, Inc., 85
Shelby Williams Industries, Inc., 14
Sheldahl Inc., 23
Shell Oil Company, IV; 14 (upd.); 41 (upd.)
Shell Vacations LLC, 102
Sheller-Globe Corporation, I
Shells Seafood Restaurants, Inc., 43
Shenandoah Telecommunications Company, 89
Sheplers, Inc., 96
The Sheridan Group, Inc., 86
The Sherwin-Williams Company, III; 13 (upd.); 89 (upd.)
Sherwood Brands, Inc., 53
Shoe Carnival Inc., 14; 72 (upd.)
Shoe Pavilion, Inc., 84
Shoney's North America Corp., 7; 23 (upd.); 105 (upd.)
ShopKo Stores Inc., 21; 58 (upd.)
Shoppers Food Warehouse Corporation, 66
Shorewood Packaging Corporation, 28
ShowBiz Pizza Time, Inc., 13
Showboat, Inc., 19
Showtime Networks Inc. 78
Shriners Hospitals for Children, 69
Shubert Organization Inc., 24
Shuffle Master Inc., 51
Shure Inc., 60
Shurgard Storage Centers, Inc., 52
Shutterfly, Inc., 98
Sidley Austin Brown & Wood, 40
Sidney Frank Importing Co., Inc., 69
Siebel Systems, Inc., 38
Siebert Financial Corp., 32
Siegel & Gale, 64
The Sierra Club, 28
Sierra Health Services, Inc., 15
Sierra Nevada Brewing Company, 70
Sierra On-Line, Inc., 15; 41 (upd.)
Sierra Pacific Industries, 22; 90 (upd.)
SIFCO Industries, Inc., 41
Sigma-Aldrich Corporation, I; 36 (upd.); 93 (upd.)
Signet Banking Corporation, 11; 104 (upd.)
Sikorsky Aircraft Corporation, 24

Silhouette Brands, Inc., 55
Silicon Graphics Incorporated, 9
Silver Lake Cookie Company Inc., 95
SilverPlatter Information Inc., 23
Silverstar Holdings, Ltd., 99
Silverstein Properties, Inc., 47
Simmons Company, 47
Simon & Schuster Inc., IV; 19 (upd.); 100 (upd.)
Simon Property Group Inc., 27; 84 (upd.)
Simon Transportation Services Inc., 27
Simplex Technologies Inc., 21
Simplicity Manufacturing, Inc., 64
Simpson Investment Company, 17
Simpson Thacher & Bartlett, 39
Simula, Inc., 41
Sinclair Broadcast Group, Inc., 25
Sine Qua Non, 99
The Singing Machine Company, Inc., 60
Sir Speedy, Inc., 16
Sirius Satellite Radio, Inc., 69
Siskin Steel & Supply Company, 70
Sisters of Charity of Leavenworth Health System, 105
Six Flags, Inc., 17; 54 (upd.)
SJW Corporation, 70
Skadden, Arps, Slate, Meagher & Flom, 18
Skechers U.S.A. Inc., 31; 88 (upd.)
Skeeter Products Inc., 96
Skidmore, Owings & Merrill LLP, 13; 69 (upd.)
skinnyCorp, LLC, 97
Skyline Chili, Inc., 62
Skyline Corporation, 30
SkyMall, Inc., 26
SkyWest, Inc., 25
Skyy Spirits LLC 78
SL Green Realty Corporation, 44
SL Industries, Inc., 77
Sleepy's Inc., 32
SLI, Inc., 48
Slim-Fast Foods Company, 18; 66 (upd.)
SLM Holding Corp., 25 (upd.)
Small Planet Foods, Inc., 89
Smart & Final LLC, 16; 94 (upd.)
Smart Balance, Inc., 100
SMART Modular Technologies, Inc., 86
SmartForce PLC, 43
Smead Manufacturing Co., 17
Smith & Hawken, Ltd., 68
Smith & Wesson Corp., 30; 73 (upd.)
Smith Barney Inc., 15
Smith Corona Corp., 13
Smith International, Inc., 15; 59 (upd.)
The Smith & Wollensky Restaurant Group, Inc., 105
Smith's Food & Drug Centers, Inc., 8; 57 (upd.)
Smith-Midland Corporation, 56
Smithfield Foods, Inc., 7; 43 (upd.)
SmithKline Beckman Corporation, I
Smithsonian Institution, 27
Smithway Motor Xpress Corporation, 39
Smurfit-Stone Container Corporation, 26 (upd.); 83 (upd.)
Snap-on Incorporated, 7; 27 (upd.); 105 (upd.)

Snapfish, 83
Snapple Beverage Corporation, 11
Snell & Wilmer L.L.P., 28
Society Corporation, 9
Soft Sheen Products, Inc., 31
Softbank Corporation, 77 (upd.)
Sola International Inc., 71
Solar Turbines Inc., 100
Sole Technology Inc., 93
Solectron Corporation, 12; 48 (upd.)
Solo Cup Company, 104
Solo Serve Corporation, 28
Solutia Inc., 52
Sonat, Inc., 6
Sonesta International Hotels Corporation, 44
Sonic Automotive, Inc., 77
Sonic Corp., 14; 37 (upd.); 103 (upd.)
Sonic Innovations Inc., 56
Sonic Solutions, Inc., 81
SonicWALL, Inc., 87
Sonnenschein Nath and Rosenthal LLP, 102
Sonoco Products Company, 8; 89 (upd.)
SonoSite, Inc., 56
Sorbee International Ltd., 74
Soros Fund Management LLC, 28
Sorrento, Inc., 24
SOS Staffing Services, 25
Sotheby's Holdings, Inc., 11; 29 (upd.); 84 (upd.)
Sound Advice, Inc., 41
Souper Salad, Inc., 98
The Source Enterprises, Inc., 65
Source Interlink Companies, Inc., 75
South Beach Beverage Company, Inc., 73
South Dakota Wheat Growers Association, 94
South Jersey Industries, Inc., 42
Southdown, Inc., 14
Southeast Frozen Foods Company, L.P., 99
The Southern Company, V; 38 (upd.)
Southern Connecticut Gas Company, 84
Southern Financial Bancorp, Inc., 56
Southern Indiana Gas and Electric Company, 13
Southern New England Telecommunications Corporation, 6
Southern Pacific Transportation Company, V
Southern Poverty Law Center, Inc., 74
Southern Progress Corporation, 102
Southern States Cooperative Incorporated, 36
Southern Union Company, 27
Southern Wine and Spirits of America, Inc., 84
The Southland Corporation, II; 7 (upd.)
Southtrust Corporation, 11
Southwest Airlines Co., 6; 24 (upd.); 71 (upd.)
Southwest Gas Corporation, 19
Southwest Water Company, 47
Southwestern Bell Corporation, V
Southwestern Electric Power Co., 21
Southwestern Public Service Company, 6
Southwire Company, Inc., 8; 23 (upd.)

Sovran Self Storage, Inc., 66
Sovereign Bancorp, Inc., 103
Spacehab, Inc., 37
Spacelabs Medical, Inc., 71
Spaghetti Warehouse, Inc., 25
Spangler Candy Company, 44
Spanish Broadcasting System, Inc., 41
Spansion Inc., 80
Spanx, Inc., 89
Spark Networks, Inc., 91
Spartan Motors Inc., 14
Spartan Stores Inc., 8; 66 (upd.)
Spartech Corporation, 19; 76 (upd.)
Sparton Corporation, 18
Spear & Jackson, Inc., 73
Spear, Leeds & Kellogg, 66
Spec's Music, Inc., 19
Special Olympics, Inc., 93
Specialized Bicycle Components Inc., 50
Specialty Coatings Inc., 8
Specialty Equipment Companies, Inc., 25
Specialty Products & Insulation Co., 59
Spectrum Control, Inc., 67
Spectrum Organic Products, Inc., 68
Spee-Dee Delivery Service, Inc., 93
SpeeDee Oil Change and Tune-Up, 25
Speedway Motorsports, Inc., 32
Speidel Inc., 96
Speizman Industries, Inc., 44
Spelling Entertainment, 14; 35 (upd.)
Spencer Stuart and Associates, Inc., 14
Spherion Corporation, 52
Spicy Pickle Franchising, Inc., 105
Spiegel, Inc., 10; 27 (upd.)
Spinnaker Exploration Company, 72
Spirit Airlines, Inc., 31
Sport Chalet, Inc., 16; 94 (upd.)
Sport Supply Group, Inc., 23; 106 (upd.)
Sportmart, Inc., 15
Sports & Recreation, Inc., 17
The Sports Authority, Inc., 16; 43 (upd.)
The Sports Club Company, 25
The Sportsman's Guide, Inc., 36
Springs Global US, Inc., V; 19 (upd.); 90 (upd.)
Sprint Corporation, 9; 46 (upd.)
SPS Technologies, Inc., 30
SPSS Inc., 64
SPX Corporation, 10; 47 (upd.); 103 (upd.)
Spyglass Entertainment Group, LLC, 91
Square D, 90
Squibb Corporation, I
SRA International, Inc., 77
SRAM Corporation, 65
SRC Holdings Corporation, 67
SRI International, Inc., 57
SSI (U.S.), Inc., 103 (upd.)
SSOE Inc., 76
STAAR Surgical Company, 57
Stabler Companies Inc. 78
Stage Stores, Inc., 24; 82 (upd.)
Stanadyne Automotive Corporation, 37
StanCorp Financial Group, Inc., 56
Standard Candy Company Inc., 86
Standard Commercial Corporation, 13; 62 (upd.)
Standard Federal Bank, 9

Standard Microsystems Corporation, 11
Standard Motor Products, Inc., 40
Standard Pacific Corporation, 52
The Standard Register Company, 15, 93 (upd.)
Standex International Corporation, 17; 44 (upd.)
Stanhome Inc., 15
Stanley Furniture Company, Inc., 34
The Stanley Works, III; 20 (upd.); 79 (upd.)
Staple Cotton Cooperative Association (Staplcotn), 86
Staples, Inc., 10; 55 (upd.)
Star Banc Corporation, 11
Star of the West Milling Co., 95
Starbucks Corporation, 13; 34 (upd.); 77 (upd.)
Starcraft Corporation, 30; 66 (upd.)
Starent Networks Corp., 106
Starkey Laboratories, Inc., 52
Starrett Corporation, 21
StarTek, Inc. 79
Starter Corp., 12
Starwood Hotels & Resorts Worldwide, Inc., 54
Starz LLC, 91
The Stash Tea Company, 50
State Auto Financial Corporation, 77
State Farm Mutual Automobile Insurance Company, III; 51 (upd.)
State Financial Services Corporation, 51
State Street Corporation, 8; 57 (upd.)
Staten Island Bancorp, Inc., 39
Stater Bros. Holdings Inc., 64
Station Casinos, Inc., 25; 90 (upd.)
The Staubach Company, 62
The Steak n Shake Company, 41; 96 (upd.)
Stearns, Inc., 43
Steel Dynamics, Inc., 52
Steel Technologies Inc., 63
Steelcase, Inc., 7; 27 (upd.)
Stein Mart Inc., 19; 72 (upd.)
Steiner Corporation (Alsco), 53
Steinway Musical Properties, Inc., 19
Stemilt Growers Inc., 94
Stepan Company, 30; 105 (upd.)
Stephan Company, 60
Stephens Media, LLC, 91
Stephens Inc., 92
Stericycle, Inc., 33; 74 (upd.)
Sterilite Corporation, 97
STERIS Corporation, 29
Sterling Chemicals Inc., 16; 78 (upd.)
Sterling Drug, Inc., I
Sterling Electronics Corp., 18
Sterling Financial Corporation, 106
Sterling Software, Inc., 11
Steve & Barry's LLC, 88
Stevedoring Services of America Inc., 28
Steven Madden, Ltd., 37
Stew Leonard's, 56
Stewart & Stevenson Services Inc., 11
Stewart Enterprises, Inc., 20
Stewart Information Services Corporation 78
Stewart's Beverages, 39

Stewart's Shops Corporation, 80
Stiefel Laboratories, Inc., 90
Stillwater Mining Company, 47
Stimson Lumber Company 78
Stock Yards Packing Co., Inc., 37
Stone & Webster, Inc., 13; 64 (upd.)
Stone Container Corporation, IV
Stone Manufacturing Company, 14; 43 (upd.)
Stonyfield Farm, Inc., 55
The Stop & Shop Supermarket Company, II; 24 (upd.); 68 (upd.)
Storage Technology Corporation, 6
Storage USA, Inc., 21
Stouffer Corp., 8
StrataCom, Inc., 16
Stratagene Corporation, 70
Stratasys, Inc., 67
Strattec Security Corporation, 73
Stratus Computer, Inc., 10
Strauss Discount Auto, 56
Strayer Education, Inc., 53
The Stride Rite Corporation, 8; 37 (upd.); 86 (upd.)
Strine Printing Company Inc., 88
The Strober Organization, Inc., 82
The Stroh Brewery Company, I; 18 (upd.)
Strombecker Corporation, 60
Stroock & Stroock & Lavan LLP, 40
Strouds, Inc., 33
The Structure Tone Organization, 99
Stryker Corporation, 11; 29 (upd.); 79 (upd.)
Stuart C. Irby Company, 58
Stuart Entertainment Inc., 16
Student Loan Marketing Association, II
Stuller Settings, Inc., 35
Sturm, Ruger & Company, Inc., 19
Stussy, Inc., 55
Sub Pop Ltd., 97
Sub-Zero Freezer Co., Inc., 31
Suburban Propane Partners, L.P., 30
Subway, 32
Successories, Inc., 30
Sudbury Inc., 16
Suiza Foods Corporation, 26
Sullivan & Cromwell, 26
The Summit Bancorporation, 14
Summit Family Restaurants, Inc. 19
Sun Communities Inc., 46
Sun Company, Inc., IV
Sun Country Airlines, 30
Sun-Diamond Growers of California, 7
Sun Distributors L.P., 12
Sun Healthcare Group Inc., 25
Sun Hydraulics Corporation, 74
Sun-Maid Growers of California, 82
Sun Microsystems, Inc., 7; 30 (upd.); 91 (upd.)
Sun Sportswear, Inc., 17
Sun Television & Appliances Inc., 10
Sun World International, LLC, 93
SunAmerica Inc., 11
Sunbeam-Oster Co., Inc., 9
Sunburst Hospitality Corporation, 26
Sunburst Shutter Corporation 78
Sundstrand Corporation, 7; 21 (upd.)
Sundt Corp., 24

SunGard Data Systems Inc., 11
Sunglass Hut International, Inc., 21; 74 (upd.)
Sunkist Growers, Inc., 26; 102 (upd.)
Sunoco, Inc., 28 (upd.); 83 (upd.)
SunPower Corporation, 91
The Sunrider Corporation, 26
Sunrise Greetings, 88
Sunrise Medical Inc., 11
Sunrise Senior Living, Inc., 81
Sunterra Corporation, 75
SunTrust Banks Inc., 23; 101 (upd.)
Super 8 Motels, Inc., 83
Super Food Services, Inc., 15
Supercuts Inc., 26
Superior Essex Inc., 80
Superior Energy Services, Inc., 65
Superior Industries International, Inc., 8
Superior Uniform Group, Inc., 30
Supermarkets General Holdings Corporation, II
SUPERVALU Inc., II; 18 (upd.); 50 (upd.)
Suprema Specialties, Inc., 27
Supreme International Corporation, 27
Susan G. Komen Breast Cancer Foundation 78
Susquehanna Pfaltzgraff Company, 8
Sutherland Lumber Company, L.P., 99
Sutter Home Winery Inc., 16
Sverdrup Corporation, 14
Swales & Associates, Inc., 69
Swank, Inc., 17; 84 (upd.)
SwedishAmerican Health System, 51
Sweet Candy Company, 60
Sweetheart Cup Company, Inc., 36
Sweetbay Supermarket, 103 (upd.)
The Swett & Crawford Group Inc., 84
SWH Corporation, 70
Swift & Company, 55
Swift Energy Company, 63
Swift Transportation Co., Inc., 42
Swinerton Inc., 43
Swisher International Group Inc., 23
The Swiss Colony, Inc., 97
Swiss Valley Farms Company, 90
Sybase, Inc., 10; 27 (upd.)
Sybron International Corp., 14
Sycamore Networks, Inc., 45
Sykes Enterprises, Inc., 45
Sylvan Learning Systems, Inc., 35
Sylvan, Inc., 22
Symantec Corporation, 10; 82 (upd.)
Symbol Technologies, Inc., 15
Syms Corporation, 29; 74 (upd.)
Symyx Technologies, Inc., 77
Synaptics Incorporated, 95
Synchronoss Technologies, Inc., 95
Syniverse Holdings Inc., 97
SYNNEX Corporation, 73
Synopsys, Inc., 11; 69 (upd.)
SynOptics Communications, Inc., 10
Synovus Financial Corp., 12; 52 (upd.)
Syntax-Brillian Corporation, 102
Syntel, Inc., 92
Syntex Corporation, I
Sypris Solutions, Inc., 85
SyQuest Technology, Inc., 18

Syratech Corp., 14
SYSCO Corporation, II; 24 (upd.); 75 (upd.)
System Software Associates, Inc., 10
Systemax, Inc., 52
Systems & Computer Technology Corp., 19
T-Netix, Inc., 46
T. Marzetti Company, 57
T. Rowe Price Associates, Inc., 11; 34 (upd.)
TAB Products Co., 17
Taco Bell Corporation, 7; 21 (upd.); 74 (upd.)
Taco Cabana, Inc., 23; 72 (upd.)
Taco John's International, Inc., 15; 63 (upd.)
Tacony Corporation, 70
Tag-It Pacific, Inc., 85
Take-Two Interactive Software, Inc., 46
The Talbots, Inc., 11; 31 (upd.); 88 (upd.)
Talk America Holdings, Inc., 70
Talley Industries, Inc., 16
TALX Corporation, 92
Tambrands Inc., 8
Tandem Computers, Inc., 6
Tandy Corporation, II; 12 (upd.)
Tandycrafts, Inc., 31
Tanger Factory Outlet Centers, Inc., 49
Tanimura & Antle Fresh Foods, Inc., 98
Tanox, Inc., 77
Tapemark Company Inc., 64
Target Corporation, 10; 27 (upd.); 61 (upd.)
Tarragon Realty Investors, Inc., 45
Tarrant Apparel Group, 62
Taser International, Inc., 62
Tastefully Simple Inc., 100
Tasty Baking Company, 14; 35 (upd.)
Tattered Cover Book Store, 43
Taubman Centers, Inc., 75
Taylor Corporation, 36
Taylor Devices, Inc., 97
Taylor Guitars, 48
Taylor Made Group Inc., 98
TaylorMade-adidas Golf, 23; 96 (upd.)
Taylor Publishing Company, 12; 36 (upd.)
TB Wood's Corporation, 56
TBA Global, LLC, 99
TBWA/Chiat/Day, 6; 43 (upd.)
TCBY Systems LLC, 17; 98 (upd.)
TCF Financial Corporation, 47; 103 (upd.)
Teachers Insurance and Annuity Association-College Retirement Equities Fund, III; 45 (upd.)
TearDrop Golf Company, 32
Tech Data Corporation, 10; 74 (upd.)
Tech-Sym Corporation, 18; 44 (upd.)
TechBooks Inc., 84
TECHNE Corporation, 52
Technical Olympic USA, Inc., 75
Technitrol, Inc., 29
Technology Research Corporation, 94
Technology Solutions Company, 94
TechTarget, Inc., 99
TECO Energy, Inc., 6

Tecumseh Products Company, 8; 71 (upd.)
Tee Vee Toons, Inc., 57
Tejon Ranch Company, 35
Tekelec, 83
Teknor Apex Company, 97
Tektronix Inc., 8; 78 (upd.)
Telcordia Technologies, Inc., 59
Tele-Communications, Inc., II
Teledyne Technologies Inc., I; 10 (upd.); 62 (upd.)
Telephone and Data Systems, Inc., 9
Tellabs, Inc., 11; 40 (upd.)
Telsmith Inc., 96
Telxon Corporation, 10
Temple-Inland Inc., IV; 31 (upd.); 102 (upd.)
Tempur-Pedic Inc., 54
Tenet Healthcare Corporation, 55 (upd.)
TenFold Corporation, 35
Tengasco, Inc., 99
Tennant Company, 13; 33 (upd.); 95 (upd.)
Tenneco Inc., I; 10 (upd.)
Tennessee Valley Authority, 50
TEPPCO Partners, L.P., 73
Teradyne, Inc., 11; 98 (upd.)
Terex Corporation, 7; 40 (upd.); 91 (upd.)
The Terlato Wine Group, 48
Terra Industries, Inc., 13; 94 (upd.)
Terremark Worldwide, Inc., 99
Tesoro Corporation, 7; 45 (upd.); 97 (upd.)
The Testor Corporation, 51
Tetley USA Inc., 88
Teton Energy Corporation, 97
Tetra Tech, Inc., 29
Texaco Inc., IV; 14 (upd.); 41 (upd.)
Texas Air Corporation, I
Texas Industries, Inc., 8
Texas Instruments Inc., II; 11 (upd.); 46 (upd.)
Texas Pacific Group Inc., 36
Texas Rangers Baseball, 51
Texas Roadhouse, Inc., 69
Texas Utilities Company, V; 25 (upd.)
Textron Inc., I; 34 (upd.); 88 (upd.)
Textron Lycoming Turbine Engine, 9
Tha Row Records, 69 (upd.)
Thane International, Inc., 84
Thermadyne Holding Corporation, 19
Thermo BioAnalysis Corp., 25
Thermo Electron Corporation, 7
Thermo Fibertek, Inc., 24
Thermo Fisher Scientific Inc., 105 (upd.)
Thermo Instrument Systems Inc., 11
Thermo King Corporation, 13
Thermos Company, 16
Things Remembered, Inc., 84
Thiokol Corporation, 9; 22 (upd.)
Thomas & Betts Corporation, 11; 54 (upd.)
Thomas & Howard Company, Inc., 90
Thomas Cook Travel Inc., 9; 33 (upd.)
Thomas H. Lee Co., 24
Thomas Industries Inc., 29
Thomas J. Lipton Company, 14

Thomas Nelson, Inc., 14; 38 (upd.)
Thomas Publishing Company, 26
Thomaston Mills, Inc., 27
Thomasville Furniture Industries, Inc., 12; 74 (upd.)
Thomsen Greenhouses and Garden Center, Incorporated, 65
Thor Industries Inc., 39; 92 (upd.)
Thorn Apple Valley, Inc., 7; 22 (upd.)
ThoughtWorks Inc., 90
Thousand Trails, Inc., 33
THQ, Inc., 39; 92 (upd.)
3Com Corporation, 11; 34 (upd.); 106 (upd.)
The 3DO Company, 43
3M Company, 61 (upd.)
Thrifty PayLess, Inc., 12
Thumann Inc., 104
TIBCO Software Inc. 79
TIC Holdings Inc., 92
Ticketmaster, 76 (upd.)
Ticketmaster Group, Inc., 13; 37 (upd.)
Tidewater Inc., 11; 37 (upd.)
Tiffany & Co., 14; 78 (upd.)
TIG Holdings, Inc., 26
Tilia Inc., 62
Tillotson Corp., 15
Timber Lodge Steakhouse, Inc., 73
The Timberland Company, 13; 54 (upd.)
Timberline Software Corporation, 15
Time Warner Inc., IV; 7 (upd.)
The Times Mirror Company, IV; 17 (upd.)
Timex Corporation, 7; 25 (upd.)
The Timken Company, 8; 42 (upd.)
Tishman Speyer Properties, L.P., 47
The Titan Corporation, 36
Titan International, Inc., 89
Titan Machinery Inc., 103
Titanium Metals Corporation, 21
TiVo Inc., 75
TJ International, Inc., 19
The TJX Companies, Inc., V; 19 (upd.); 57 (upd.)
TLC Beatrice International Holdings, Inc., 22
TMP Worldwide Inc., 30
TNT Freightways Corporation, 14
Today's Man, Inc., 20
TODCO, 87
Todd Shipyards Corporation, 14
The Todd-AO Corporation, 33
Todhunter International, Inc., 27
Tofutti Brands, Inc., 64
Tokheim Corporation, 21
TOKYOPOP Inc. 79
Toll Brothers Inc., 15; 70 (upd.)
Tollgrade Communications, Inc., 44
Tom Brown, Inc., 37
Tom Doherty Associates Inc., 25
Tom's Foods Inc., 66
Tom's of Maine, Inc., 45
Tombstone Pizza Corporation, 13
Tone Brothers, Inc., 21; 74 (upd.)
Tonka Corporation, 25
Too, Inc., 61
Tootsie Roll Industries, Inc., 12; 82 (upd.)
Topco Associates LLC, 60

INTERNATIONAL DIRECTORY OF COMPANY HISTORIES, VOLUME 106

The Topps Company, Inc., 13; 34 (upd.); 83 (upd.)
Tops Appliance City, Inc., 17
Tops Markets LLC, 60
Torchmark Corporation, 9; 33 (upd.)
Toresco Enterprises, Inc., 84
The Toro Company, 7; 26 (upd.); 77 (upd.)
The Torrington Company, 13
Tosco Corporation, 7
Total Entertainment Restaurant Corporation, 46
Total System Services, Inc., 18
Totem Resources Corporation, 9
TouchTunes Music Corporation, 97
Tower Air, Inc., 28
Tower Automotive, Inc., 24
Towers Perrin, 32
Town & Country Corporation, 19
Town Sports International, Inc., 46
Townsends, Inc., 64
Toy Biz, Inc., 18
Toymax International, Inc., 29
Toys 'R Us, Inc., V; 18 (upd.); 57 (upd.)
Tracor Inc., 17
Tractor Supply Company, 57
Trader Joe's Company, 13; 50 (upd.)
TradeStation Group, Inc., 83
Traffix, Inc., 61
Trailer Bridge, Inc., 41
Trammell Crow Company, 8; 57 (upd.)
Trane 78
Trans World Airlines, Inc., I; 12 (upd.); 35 (upd.)
Trans World Entertainment Corporation, 24; 68 (upd.)
Trans-Lux Corporation, 51
Transaction Systems Architects, Inc., 29; 82 (upd.)
Transamerica–An AEGON Company, I; 13 (upd.); 41 (upd.)
Transammonia Group, 95
Transatlantic Holdings, Inc., 11
Transco Energy Company, V
Transitions Optical, Inc., 83
Transmedia Network Inc., 20
TransMontaigne Inc., 28
Transocean Sedco Forex Inc., 45
Transport Corporation of America, Inc., 49
TransPro, Inc., 71
The Tranzonic Companies, 37
Travel Ports of America, Inc., 17
The Travelers Corporation, III
Travelocity.com, Inc., 46
Travelzoo Inc. 79
Travis Boats & Motors, Inc., 37
TRC Companies, Inc., 32
Treadco, Inc., 19
Treasure Chest Advertising Company, Inc., 32
Tredegar Corporation, 52
Tree of Life, Inc., 29
Tree Top, Inc., 76
TreeHouse Foods, Inc. 79
Trek Bicycle Corporation, 16; 78 (upd.)
Trend-Lines, Inc., 22
Trendwest Resorts, Inc., 33

Trex Company, Inc., 71
Tri-State Generation and Transmission Association, Inc., 103
Tri Valley Growers, 32
Triarc Companies, Inc., 8; 34 (upd.)
Tribune Company, IV; 22 (upd.); 63 (upd.)
Trico Products Corporation, 15
Trico Marine Services, Inc., 89
Tilcon-Connecticut Inc., 80
Trident Seafoods Corporation, 56
Trigen Energy Corporation, 42
TriMas Corp., 11
Trimble Navigation Limited, 40
Trinity Industries, Incorporated, 7
TRINOVA Corporation, III
TriPath Imaging, Inc., 77
Triple Five Group Ltd., 49
TriQuint Semiconductor, Inc., 63
Tripwire, Inc., 97
Trisko Jewelry Sculptures, Ltd., 57
Triton Energy Corporation, 11
Triumph Group, Inc., 31
The TriZetto Group, Inc., 83
TRM Copy Centers Corporation, 18
Tropicana Products, Inc., 28; 73 (upd.)
Troutman Sanders L.L.P. 79
True North Communications Inc., 23
True Religion Apparel, Inc. 79
True Temper Sports, Inc., 95
True Value Company, 74 (upd.)
The Trump Organization, 23; 64 (upd.)
TruServ Corporation, 24
Trustmark Corporation, 106
TRW Automotive Holdings Corp., 75 (upd.)
TRW Inc., I; 11 (upd.); 14 (upd.)
TTX Company, 6; 66 (upd.)
Tubby's, Inc., 53
Tucson Electric Power Company, 6
Tuesday Morning Corporation, 18; 70 (upd.)
Tully's Coffee Corporation, 51
Tultex Corporation, 13
Tumaro's Gourmet Tortillas, 85
Tumbleweed, Inc., 33; 80 (upd.)
Tupperware Corporation, 28; 78 (upd.)
TurboChef Technologies, Inc., 83
Turner Broadcasting System, Inc., II; 6 (upd.); 66 (upd.)
Turner Construction Company, 66
The Turner Corporation, 8; 23 (upd.)
Turtle Wax, Inc., 15; 93 (upd.)
Tuscarora Inc., 29
Tutogen Medical, Inc., 68
Tuttle Publishing, 86
TV Guide, Inc., 43 (upd.)
TVI, Inc., 15
TVI Corporation, 99
TW Services, Inc., II
Tweeter Home Entertainment Group, Inc., 30
Twentieth Century Fox Film Corporation, II; 25 (upd.)
24 Hour Fitness Worldwide, Inc., 71
24/7 Real Media, Inc., 49
Twin Disc, Inc., 21
Twinlab Corporation, 34

II-VI Incorporated, 69
Ty Inc., 33; 86 (upd.)
Tyco Toys, Inc., 12
Tyler Corporation, 23
Tyndale House Publishers, Inc., 57
Tyson Foods, Inc., II; 14 (upd.); 50 (upd.)
U S West, Inc., V; 25 (upd.)
U.S. Aggregates, Inc., 42
U.S. Army Corps of Engineers, 91
U.S. Bancorp, 14; 36 (upd.); 103 (upd.)
U.S. Borax, Inc., 42
U.S. Can Corporation, 30
U.S. Cellular Corporation, 31 (upd.); 88 (upd.)
U.S. Delivery Systems, Inc., 22
U.S. Foodservice, 26
U.S. Healthcare, Inc., 6
U.S. Home Corporation, 8; 78 (upd.)
U.S. News & World Report Inc., 30; 89 (upd.)
U.S. Office Products Company, 25
U.S. Physical Therapy, Inc., 65
U.S. Premium Beef LLC, 91
U.S. Robotics Corporation, 9; 66 (upd.)
U.S. Satellite Broadcasting Company, Inc., 20
U.S. Silica Company, 104
U.S. Timberlands Company, L.P., 42
U.S. Trust Corp., 17
U.S. Vision, Inc., 66
UAL Corporation, 34 (upd.)
UAW (International Union, United Automobile, Aerospace and Agricultural Implement Workers of America), 72
UGI Corporation, 12
Ugly Duckling Corporation, 22
UICI, 33
Ukrop's Super Markets, Inc., 39; 101 (upd.)
Ulta Salon, Cosmetics & Fragrance, Inc., 93
Ultimate Electronics, Inc., 18; 69 (upd.)
Ultra Pac, Inc., 24
Ultra Petroleum Corporation, 71
Ultrak Inc., 24
Ultralife Batteries, Inc., 58
Ultramar Diamond Shamrock Corporation, 31 (upd.)
Umpqua Holdings Corporation, 87
Uncle Ben's Inc., 22
Uncle Ray's LLC, 90
Under Armour Performance Apparel, 61
Underwriters Laboratories, Inc., 30
Uni-Marts, Inc., 17
Unica Corporation, 77
Unicom Corporation, 29 (upd.)
Unifi, Inc., 12; 62 (upd.)
Unified Grocers, Inc., 93
UniFirst Corporation, 21
Union Bank of California, 16
Union Camp Corporation, IV
Union Carbide Corporation, I; 9 (upd.); 74 (upd.)
Union Electric Company, V
Union Pacific Corporation, V; 28 (upd.); 79 (upd.)
Union Planters Corporation, 54

Union Texas Petroleum Holdings, Inc., 9
UnionBanCal Corporation, 50 (upd.)
Unique Casual Restaurants, Inc., 27
Unison HealthCare Corporation, 25
Unisys Corporation, III; 6 (upd.); 36 (upd.)
Unit Corporation, 63
United Airlines, I; 6 (upd.)
United Auto Group, Inc., 26; 68 (upd.)
United Brands Company, II
United Community Banks, Inc., 98
United Dairy Farmers, Inc., 74
United Defense Industries, Inc., 30; 66 (upd.)
United Dominion Industries Limited, 8; 16 (upd.)
United Dominion Realty Trust, Inc., 52
United Farm Workers of America, 88
United Foods, Inc., 21
United HealthCare Corporation, 9
The United Illuminating Company, 21
United Industrial Corporation, 37
United Industries Corporation, 68
United Jewish Communities, 33
United Merchants & Manufacturers, Inc., 13
United National Group, Ltd., 63
United Nations International Children's Emergency Fund (UNICEF), 58
United Natural Foods, Inc., 32; 76 (upd.)
United Negro College Fund, Inc. 79
United Online, Inc., 71 (upd.)
United Parcel Service of America Inc., V; 17 (upd.)
United Parcel Service, Inc., 63; 94 (upd.)
United Press International, Inc., 25; 73 (upd.)
United Rentals, Inc., 34
United Retail Group Inc., 33
United Road Services, Inc., 69
United Service Organizations, 60
United States Cellular Corporation, 9
United States Filter Corporation, 20
United States Pipe and Foundry Company, 62
United States Playing Card Company, 62
United States Postal Service, 14; 34 (upd.)
The United States Shoe Corporation, V
United States Steel Corporation, 50 (upd.)
United States Surgical Corporation, 10; 34 (upd.)
United Stationers Inc., 14
United Talent Agency, Inc., 80
United Technologies Automotive Inc., 15
United Technologies Corporation, I; 10 (upd.); 34 (upd.); 105 (upd.)
United Telecommunications, Inc., V
United Video Satellite Group, 18
United Water Resources, Inc., 40
United Way of America, 36
UnitedHealth Group Incorporated, 103 (upd.)
Unitil Corporation, 37
Unitog Co., 19
Unitrin Inc., 16; V
Univar Corporation, 9
Universal Compression, Inc., 59
Universal Corporation, V; 48 (upd.)

Universal Electronics Inc., 39
Universal Foods Corporation, 7
Universal Forest Products, Inc., 10; 59 (upd.)
Universal Health Services, Inc., 6
Universal International, Inc., 25
Universal Manufacturing Company, 88
Universal Security Instruments, Inc., 96
Universal Stainless & Alloy Products, Inc., 75
Universal Studios, Inc., 33; 100 (upd.)
Universal Technical Institute, Inc., 81
The University of Chicago Press 79
Univision Communications Inc., 24; 83 (upd.)
Uno Restaurant Corporation, 18
Uno Restaurant Holdings Corporation, 70 (upd.)
Unocal Corporation, IV; 24 (upd.); 71 (upd.)
UnumProvident Corporation, 13; 52 (upd.)
The Upjohn Company, I; 8 (upd.)
The Upper Deck Company, LLC, 105
Urban Engineers, Inc., 102
Urban Outfitters, Inc., 14; 74 (upd.)
URS Corporation, 45; 80 (upd.)
US Airways Group, Inc., I; 6 (upd.); 28 (upd.); 52 (upd.)
US 1 Industries, Inc., 89
USA Interactive, Inc., 47 (upd.)
USA Mobility Inc., 97 (upd.)
USA Truck, Inc., 42
USAA, 10; 62 (upd.)
USANA, Inc., 29
USF&G Corporation, III
USG Corporation, III; 26 (upd.); 81 (upd.)
UST Inc., 9; 50 (upd.)
USX Corporation, IV; 7 (upd.)
Utah Medical Products, Inc., 36
Utah Power and Light Company, 27
UTG Inc., 100
UtiliCorp United Inc., 6
UTStarcom, Inc., 77
Utz Quality Foods, Inc., 72
UUNET, 38
Uwajimaya, Inc., 60
Vail Resorts, Inc., 11; 43 (upd.)
Valassis Communications, Inc., 8; 37 (upd.); 76 (upd.)
Valero Energy Corporation, 7; 71 (upd.)
Valhi, Inc., 19; 94 (upd.)
Vallen Corporation, 45
Valley Media Inc., 35
Valley National Gases, Inc., 85
Valley Proteins, Inc., 91
ValleyCrest Companies, 81 (upd.)
Valmont Industries, Inc., 19
The Valspar Corporation, 8; 32 (upd.); 77 (upd.)
Value City Department Stores, Inc., 38
Value Line, Inc., 16; 73 (upd.)
Value Merchants Inc., 13
ValueClick, Inc., 49
ValueVision International, Inc., 22
Valve Corporation, 101
Van Camp Seafood Company, Inc., 7

Van's Aircraft, Inc., 65
Vance Publishing Corporation, 64
Vanderbilt University Medical Center, 99
The Vanguard Group, Inc., 14; 34 (upd.)
Vanguard Health Systems Inc., 70
Vann's Inc., 105
Vans, Inc., 16; 47 (upd.)
Varco International, Inc., 42
Vari-Lite International, Inc., 35
Varian, Inc., 12; 48 (upd.)
Variety Wholesalers, Inc., 73
Variflex, Inc., 51
Varlen Corporation, 16
Varsity Spirit Corp., 15
VASCO Data Security International, Inc. 79
Vastar Resources, Inc., 24
Vaughan Foods, Inc., 105
VCA Antech, Inc., 58
VECO International, Inc., 7
Vector Group Ltd., 35 (upd.)
Vectren Corporation, 98 (upd.)
Veeco Instruments Inc., 32
Veit Companies, 43; 92 (upd.)
Velocity Express Corporation, 49; 94 (upd.)
Venator Group Inc., 35 (upd.)
Vencor, Inc., 16
Venetian Casino Resort, LLC, 47
Ventana Medical Systems, Inc., 75
Ventura Foods LLC, 90
Venture Stores Inc., 12
VeraSun Energy Corporation, 87
Verbatim Corporation, 14; 74 (upd.)
Veridian Corporation, 54
VeriFone Holdings, Inc., 18; 76 (upd.)
Verint Systems Inc., 73
VeriSign, Inc., 47
Veritas Software Corporation, 45
Verity Inc., 68
Verizon Communications, 43 (upd.); 78 (upd.)
Vermeer Manufacturing Company, 17
The Vermont Country Store, 93
Vermont Pure Holdings, Ltd., 51
The Vermont Teddy Bear Co., Inc., 36
Vertex Pharmaceuticals Incorporated, 83
Vertis Communications, 84
Vertrue Inc., 77
VF Corporation, V; 17 (upd.); 54 (upd.)
VHA Inc., 53
Viacom Inc., 7; 23 (upd.); 67 (upd.)
Viad Corp., 73
ViaSat, Inc., 54
Viasoft Inc., 27
VIASYS Healthcare, Inc., 52
Viasystems Group, Inc., 67
Viatech Continental Can Company, Inc., 25 (upd.)
Vicon Industries, Inc., 44
VICORP Restaurants, Inc., 12; 48 (upd.)
Victory Refrigeration, Inc., 82
Videojet Technologies, Inc., 90
Vienna Sausage Manufacturing Co., 14
Viewpoint International, Inc., 66
ViewSonic Corporation, 72
Viking Office Products, Inc., 10
Viking Range Corporation, 66

INTERNATIONAL DIRECTORY OF COMPANY HISTORIES, VOLUME 106

Viking Yacht Company, 96
Village Super Market, Inc., 7
Village Voice Media, Inc., 38
Vilter Manufacturing, LLC, 105
Vinson & Elkins L.L.P., 30
Vintage Petroleum, Inc., 42
Vinton Studios, 63
Virbac Corporation, 74
Virco Manufacturing Corporation, 17
Virginia Dare Extract Company, Inc., 94
Visa Inc., 9; 26 (upd.); 104 (upd.)
Vishay Intertechnology, Inc., 21; 80
 (upd.)
Vision Service Plan Inc., 77
Viskase Companies, Inc., 55
Vista Bakery, Inc., 56
Vista Chemical Company, I
Vistana, Inc., 22
VISX, Incorporated, 30
Vita Food Products Inc., 99
Vita Plus Corporation, 60
Vital Images, Inc., 85
Vitalink Pharmacy Services, Inc., 15
Vitamin Shoppe Industries, Inc., 60
Vitesse Semiconductor Corporation, 32
Vitro Corp., 10
Vivra, Inc., 18
Vizio, Inc., 100
Vlasic Foods International Inc., 25
VLSI Technology, Inc., 16
VMware, Inc., 90
VNUS Medical Technologies, Inc., 103
Volcom, Inc., 77
Volkert and Associates, Inc., 98
Volt Information Sciences Inc., 26
Volunteers of America, Inc., 66
Von Maur Inc., 64
Vonage Holdings Corp., 81
The Vons Companies, Inc., 7; 28 (upd.);
 103 (upd.)
Vornado Realty Trust, 20
Vought Aircraft Industries, Inc., 49
Vulcan Materials Company, 7; 52 (upd.)
W. Atlee Burpee & Co., 27
W.A. Whitney Company, 53
W.B Doner & Co., 56
W.B. Mason Company, 98
W.C. Bradley Co., 69
W. H. Braum, Inc., 80
W.H. Brady Co., 17
W.L. Gore & Associates, Inc., 14; 60
 (upd.)
W.P. Carey & Co. LLC, 49
W.R. Berkley Corporation, 15; 74 (upd.)
W.R. Grace & Company, I; 50 (upd.)
W.W. Grainger, Inc., V; 26 (upd.); 68
 (upd.)
W.W. Norton & Company, Inc., 28
Waban Inc., 13
Wabash National Corp., 13
Wabtec Corporation, 40
Wachovia Bank of Georgia, N.A., 16
Wachovia Bank of South Carolina, N.A.,
 16
Wachovia Corporation, 12; 46 (upd.)
Wachtell, Lipton, Rosen & Katz, 47
The Wackenhut Corporation, 14; 63
 (upd.)

Waddell & Reed, Inc., 22
Waffle House Inc., 14; 60 (upd.)
Wagers Inc. (Idaho Candy Company), 86
Waggener Edstrom, 42
Wah Chang, 82
Wahl Clipper Corporation, 86
Wahoo's Fish Taco, 96
Wakefern Food Corporation, 33
Wal-Mart Stores, Inc., V; 8 (upd.); 26
 (upd.); 63 (upd.)
Walbridge Aldinger Co., 38
Walbro Corporation, 13
Waldbaum, Inc., 19
Waldenbooks, 17; 86 (upd.)
Walgreen Co., V; 20 (upd.); 65 (upd.)
Walker Manufacturing Company, 19
Wall Drug Store, Inc., 40
Wall Street Deli, Inc., 33
Wallace Computer Services, Inc., 36
Walsworth Publishing Co. 78
The Walt Disney Company, II; 6 (upd.);
 30 (upd.); 63 (upd.)
Walter E. Smithe Furniture, Inc., 105
Walter Industries, Inc., II; 22 (upd.); 72
 (upd.)
Walton Monroe Mills, Inc., 8
Wang Laboratories, Inc., III; 6 (upd.)
The Warnaco Group Inc., 12; 46 (upd.)
Warner Communications Inc., II
Warner Music Group Corporation, 90
 (upd.)
Warner-Lambert Co., I; 10 (upd.)
Warners' Stellian Inc., 67
Warrantech Corporation, 53
Warrell Corporation, 68
Warwick Valley Telephone Company, 55
The Washington Companies, 33
Washington Federal, Inc., 17
Washington Football, Inc., 35
Washington Gas Light Company, 19
Washington Mutual, Inc., 17; 93 (upd.)
Washington National Corporation, 12
Washington Natural Gas Company, 9
The Washington Post Company, IV; 20
 (upd.)
Washington Scientific Industries, Inc., 17
Washington Water Power Company, 6
Waste Connections, Inc., 46
Waste Holdings, Inc., 41
Waste Management, Inc., V
Water Pik Technologies, Inc., 34; 83
 (upd.)
Waterhouse Investor Services, Inc., 18
Waters Corporation, 43
Watkins-Johnson Company, 15
Watsco Inc., 52
Watson Pharmaceuticals Inc., 16; 56
 (upd.)
Watson Wyatt Worldwide, 42
Watts Industries, Inc., 19
Wausau-Mosinee Paper Corporation, 60
 (upd.)
Waverly, Inc., 16
Wawa Inc., 17; 78 (upd.)
WAXIE Sanitary Supply, 100
Waxman Industries, Inc., 9
WD-40 Company, 18; 87 (upd.)
We-No-Nah Canoe, Inc., 98

Weather Central Inc., 100
The Weather Channel Companies 52
Weather Shield Manufacturing, Inc., 102
Weatherford International, Inc., 39
Weaver Popcorn Company, Inc., 89
Webasto Roof Systems Inc., 97
Webber Oil Company, 61
Weber-Stephen Products Co., 40
WebEx Communications, Inc., 81
WebMD Corporation, 65
Webster Financial Corporation, 106
Weeres Industries Corporation, 52
Wegmans Food Markets, Inc., 9; 41
 (upd.); 105 (upd.)
Weider Nutrition International, Inc., 29
Weight Watchers International Inc., 12;
 33 (upd.), 73 (upd.)
Weil, Gotshal & Manges LLP, 55
Weiner's Stores, Inc., 33
Weingarten Realty Investors, 95
Weirton Steel Corporation, IV; 26 (upd.)
Weis Markets, Inc., 15; 84 (upd.)
The Weitz Company, Inc., 42
Welbilt Corp., 19
Welch Foods Inc., 104
Welcome Wagon International Inc., 82
The Welk Group Inc. 78
WellCare Health Plans, Inc., 101
WellChoice, Inc., 67 (upd.)
Wellco Enterprises, Inc., 84
Wellman, Inc., 8; 52 (upd.)
WellPoint, Inc., 25; 103 (upd.)
Wells Fargo & Company, II; 12 (upd.);
 38 (upd.); 97 (upd.)
Wells Rich Greene BDDP, 6
Wells' Dairy, Inc., 36
Wells-Gardner Electronics Corporation,
 43
Wendy's International, Inc., 8; 23 (upd.);
 47 (upd.)
Wenner Bread Products Inc., 80
Wenner Media, Inc., 32
Werner Enterprises, Inc., 26
West Bend Co., 14
West Coast Entertainment Corporation,
 29
West Corporation, 42
West Group, 34 (upd.)
West Linn Paper Company, 91
West Marine, Inc., 17; 90 (upd.)
West One Bancorp, 11
West Pharmaceutical Services, Inc., 42
West Point-Pepperell, Inc., 8
West Publishing Co., 7
Westaff Inc., 33
Westamerica Bancorporation, 17
Westar Energy, Inc., 57 (upd.)
WestCoast Hospitality Corporation, 59
Westcon Group, Inc., 67
Westell Technologies, Inc., 57
Westerbeke Corporation, 60
Western Atlas Inc., 12
Western Beef, Inc., 22
Western Company of North America, 15
Western Digital Corporation, 25; 92
 (upd.)
Western Gas Resources, Inc., 45
Western Publishing Group, Inc., 13

Western Resources, Inc., 12
The WesterN SizzliN Corporation, 60
Western Union Financial Services, Inc., 54
Western Wireless Corporation, 36
Westfield Group, 69
Westin Hotels and Resorts Worldwide, 9; 29 (upd.)
Westinghouse Electric Corporation, II; 12 (upd.)
Westmoreland Coal Company, 7
WestPoint Stevens Inc., 16
Westport Resources Corporation, 63
Westvaco Corporation, IV; 19 (upd.)
Westwood One Inc., 23; 106 (upd.)
The Wet Seal, Inc., 18; 70 (upd.)
Wetterau Incorporated, II
Weyco Group, Incorporated, 32
Weyerhaeuser Company, IV; 9 (upd.); 28 (upd.); 83 (upd.)
WFS Financial Inc., 70
WGBH Educational Foundation, 66
Wham-O, Inc., 61
Whataburger Restaurants LP, 105
Wheaton Industries, 8
Wheaton Science Products, 60 (upd.)
Wheelabrator Technologies, Inc., 6; 60 (upd.)
Wheeling-Pittsburgh Corporation, 7; 58 (upd.)
Wheels Inc., 96
Wherehouse Entertainment Incorporated, 11
Whirlpool Corporation, III; 12 (upd.); 59 (upd.)
White & Case LLP, 35
White Castle Management Company, 12; 36 (upd.); 85 (upd.)
White Consolidated Industries Inc., 13
The White House, Inc., 60
White Lily Foods Company, 88
White Rose, Inc., 24
Whitehall Jewellers, Inc., 82 (upd.)
Whiting Petroleum Corporation, 81
Whiting-Turner Contracting Company, 95
Whitman Corporation, 10 (upd.)
Whitman Education Group, Inc., 41
Whitney Holding Corporation, 21
Whittaker Corporation, I; 48 (upd.)
Whole Foods Market, Inc., 20; 50 (upd.)
WHX Corporation, 98
Wickes Inc., V; 25 (upd.)
Widmer Brothers Brewing Company, 76
Wieden + Kennedy, 75
Wilbert, Inc., 56
Wilbur Chocolate Company, 66
Wilco Farm Stores, 93
Wild Oats Markets, Inc., 19; 41 (upd.)
Wildlife Conservation Society, 31
Wikimedia Foundation, Inc., 91
Willamette Industries, Inc., IV; 31 (upd.)
Willamette Valley Vineyards, Inc., 85
William L. Bonnell Company, Inc., 66
William Lyon Homes, 59
William Morris Agency, Inc., 23; 102 (upd.)
William Zinsser & Company, Inc., 58
Williams & Connolly LLP, 47

Williams Communications Group, Inc., 34
The Williams Companies, Inc., IV; 31 (upd.)
Williams Scotsman, Inc., 65
Williams-Sonoma, Inc., 17; 44 (upd.)
Williamson-Dickie Manufacturing Company, 14; 45 (upd.)
Willkie Farr & Gallagher LLP, 95
Willow Run Foods, Inc., 100
Wilmington Trust Corporation, 25
Wilson Sonsini Goodrich & Rosati, 34
Wilson Sporting Goods Company, 24; 84 (upd.)
Wilsons The Leather Experts Inc., 21; 58 (upd.)
Wilton Products, Inc., 97
Winchell's Donut Houses Operating Company, L.P., 60
WinCo Foods Inc., 60
Wind River Systems, Inc., 37
Windmere Corporation, 16
Windstream Corporation, 83
Windswept Environmental Group, Inc., 62
The Wine Group, Inc., 39
Winegard Company, 56
Winmark Corporation, 74
Winn-Dixie Stores, Inc., II; 21 (upd.); 59 (upd.)
Winnebago Industries, Inc., 7; 27 (upd.); 96 (upd.)
WinsLoew Furniture, Inc., 21
Winston & Strawn, 35
Wintrust Financial Corporation, 106
The Wiremold Company, 81
Wirtz Corporation, 72
Wisconsin Alumni Research Foundation, 65
Wisconsin Bell, Inc., 14
Wisconsin Central Transportation Corporation, 24
Wisconsin Dairies, 7
Wisconsin Energy Corporation, 6; 54 (upd.)
Wisconsin Public Service Corporation, 9
Wise Foods, Inc. 79
Witco Corporation, I; 16 (upd.)
Witness Systems, Inc., 87
Wizards of the Coast Inc., 24
WLR Foods, Inc., 21
Wm. B. Reily & Company Inc., 58
Wm. Wrigley Jr. Company, 7; 58 (upd.)
WMS Industries, Inc., 15; 53 (upd.)
WMX Technologies Inc., 17
Wolfgang Puck Worldwide, Inc., 26, 70 (upd.)
Wolohan Lumber Co., 19
Wolverine Tube Inc., 23
Wolverine World Wide, Inc., 16; 59 (upd.)
Womble Carlyle Sandridge & Rice, PLLC, 52
Wood-Mode, Inc., 23
Woodbridge Holdings Corporation, 99
Woodcraft Industries Inc., 61
Woodward Governor Company, 13; 49 (upd.); 105 (upd.)

Woolrich Inc., 62
Woolworth Corporation, V; 20 (upd.)
WordPerfect Corporation, 10
Workflow Management, Inc., 65
Working Assets Funding Service, 43
Workman Publishing Company, Inc., 70
World Acceptance Corporation, 57
World Bank Group, 33
World Book, Inc., 12
World Color Press Inc., 12
World Duty Free Americas, Inc., 29 (upd.)
World Fuel Services Corporation, 47
World Kitchen, LLC, 104
World Publications, LLC, 65
World Vision International, Inc., 93
World Wide Technology, Inc., 94
World Wrestling Federation Entertainment, Inc., 32
World's Finest Chocolate Inc., 39
WorldCorp, Inc., 10
Worldwide Restaurant Concepts, Inc., 47
Worldwide Pants Inc., 97
Worthington Foods, Inc., 14
Worthington Industries, Inc., 7; 21 (upd.)
WPL Holdings, Inc., 6
WPS Resources Corporation, 53 (upd.)
Writers Guild of America, West, Inc., 92
Wright Express Corporation, 80
Wright Medical Group, Inc., 61
WSI Corporation, 102
WTD Industries, Inc., 20
Wunderman, 86
Wyant Corporation, 30
Wyeth, 50 (upd.)
Wyle Electronics, 14
Wyman-Gordon Company, 14
Wyndham Worldwide Corporation, 99 (upd.)
Wynn's International, Inc., 33
Wyse Technology, Inc., 15
X-Rite, Inc., 48
Xcel Energy Inc., 73 (upd.)
Xerium Technologies, Inc., 94
Xerox Corporation, III; 6 (upd.); 26 (upd.); 69 (upd.)
Xilinx, Inc., 16; 82 (upd.)
XM Satellite Radio Holdings, Inc., 69
XTO Energy Inc., 52
Yahoo! Inc., 27; 70 (upd.)
Yarnell Ice Cream Company, Inc., 92
The Yankee Candle Company, Inc., 37
YankeeNets LLC, 35
The Yates Companies, Inc., 62
Yellow Corporation, 14; 45 (upd.)
Yellow Freight System, Inc. of Delaware, V
YES! Entertainment Corporation, 26
YMCA of the USA, 31
YOCREAM International, Inc., 47
The York Group, Inc., 50
York International Corp., 13
York Research Corporation, 35
Youbet.com, Inc., 77
YouTube, Inc., 90
Young & Rubicam, Inc., I; 22 (upd.); 66 (upd.)
Young Broadcasting Inc., 40

Young Innovations, Inc., 44
Young's Market Company, LLC, 32
Younkers, 76 (upd.)
Younkers, Inc., 19
Youth Services International, Inc., 21
YRC Worldwide Inc., 90 (upd.)
Yucaipa Cos., 17
Yum! Brands Inc., 58
YWCA of the United States, 45
Zachry Group, Inc., 95
Zacky Farms LLC, 74
Zale Corporation, 16; 40 (upd.); 91 (upd.)
Zanett, Inc., 92
Zany Brainy, Inc., 31
Zapata Corporation, 25
Zappos.com, Inc., 73
Zatarain's, Inc., 64
Zebra Technologies Corporation, 14; 53 (upd.)
Zenith Data Systems, Inc., 10
Zenith Electronics Corporation, II; 13 (upd.); 34 (upd.); 89 (upd.)
ZERO Corporation, 17; 88 (upd.)
Ziebart International Corporation, 30; 66 (upd.)
The Ziegler Companies, Inc., 24; 63 (upd.)
Ziff Davis Media Inc., 12; 36 (upd.); 73 (upd.)

Zila, Inc., 46
ZiLOG, Inc., 15; 72 (upd.)
Ziment Group Inc., 102
Zimmer Holdings, Inc., 45
Zingerman's Community of Businesses, 68
Zion's Cooperative Mercantile Institution, 33
Zions Bancorporation, 12; 53 (upd.)
Zipcar, Inc., 92
Zippo Manufacturing Company, 18; 71 (upd.)
Zogby International, Inc., 99
Zoltek Companies, Inc., 37
Zondervan Corporation, 24; 71 (upd.)
Zoncs, Inc., 67
Zoom Technologies, Inc., 18; 53 (upd.)
Zoran Corporation, 77
Zpizza International Inc., 105
Zuffa L.L.C., 89
Zumiez, Inc., 77
Zygo Corporation, 42
Zytec Corporation, 19

Uruguay
Administración Nacional de Combustibles, Alcohol y Pórtland, 93
Cooperativa Nacional de Productores de Leche S.A. (Conaprole), 92

Uzbekistan
Uzbekistan Airways National Air Company, 99

Vatican City
Caritas Internationalis, 72

Venezuela
Cerveceria Polar, I
Cisneros Group of Companies, 54
Empresas Polar SA, 55 (upd.)
Petróleos de Venezuela S.A., IV; 74 (upd.)

Vietnam
Lam Son Sugar Joint Stock Corporation (Lasuco), 60

Virgin Islands
Little Switzerland, Inc., 60

Wales
Hyder plc, 34
Iceland Group plc, 33
Kwik Save Group plc, 11

Zambia
Zambia Industrial and Mining Corporation Ltd., IV

Zimbabwe
Air Zimbabwe (Private) Limited, 91

Ref.
338.7409 I61d
v.106
International directory of
company histories

WITHDRAWN